# AIRLINE FLEETS
# 2012

Edited by Lyn Buttifant, Chris Chatfield and Terry Smith

in collaboration withTony Beales, Colin Frost, Rolf Larsson,
Geoff Pyke, Barrie Towey,
Tony Wheeler and John Wilkinson

Published by Air-Britain (Historians) Ltd

Sales Department

41 Penshurst Road, Leigh
Tonbridge, Kent TN11 8HL

Membership Enquiries

1 Rose Cottages, 179 Penn Road
Hazlemere,Bucks HP15 7NE

Further information is available on our website: http://www.air-britain.co.uk

PHOTO CAPTIONS

*Front cover*:  Antonov An-148-100B R-61705 of Rossiya has been operating into London-Gatwick in 2012 (Paul Seymour)

*Rear cover*:  Top: Gulf Air Airbus A340-313X A9C-LI was painted in special Formula 1 Bahrain Grand Prix 2011 titles, although the race itself was cancelled that year (Roger Birchall)
Centre: Embraer ERJ-170LR 5Y-KYH of Kenya Airways (Paul Seymour)
Bottom: VH-UZI Swearingen SA.227AT Expediter freighter of Toll Priority at Tamworth, NSW on 19 March 2010 (Stuart Kedar)

ISBN   978-0-85130-443-4        ISSN  0262-1657

Printed by Bell & Bain Ltd, Glasgow

Air-Britain supports the fight against terrorism and the efforts of the Police and other Authorities in protecting airports and airfields from criminal activity.
If you see anything suspicious do not hesitate to call the
**Anti-Terrorist Hotline  0800 789321**
or alert a Police Officer.

# INTRODUCTION

### Information and Changes for the 2012 Edition

This year sees a new editorial team take over from Pete Webber, the incumbent for the previous three years. A few minor changes have been made to make the book even more user-friendly. For example, alternative names used by some operators have been included both in the main text and the operator index. Enhancements introduced in the last three years have been retained. Please take the time to look at the section at the end of these notes that details the use of abreviations and symbols, Clear understanding of these will help you better to use the book. For example the ♦ symbol is used to highlight the introduction of a new aircraft to a particular fleet, although this notation has not been used in the section devoted to Jet and Turboprop airliners in non-airline use.

Once again this year space has been made available for deliveries expected through the year, although given the fluidity of the market it is doubtful that every potential delivery will have been included; nevertheless the reader should be able to keep the book reasonably updated throughout the year.

Looking at the industry overall, prospects have not diminished significantly.

Airbus, with over 10,000 orders booked, continues to sell its A320 'family' (A318/319/320/321) and the A330 is still attracting orders and benefitting from the delays in A350 and Boeing 787 deliveries. Production of the A330 is also boosted by military tanker orders. The A380 fleet continues to grow, with more carriers acquiring their first aircraft and others placing their first orders.

Boeing has begun deliveries of the 787 and 747-800 deliveries have commenced. The 737 line goes on and on. Established operators continue to expand their fleets and older generation aircraft are finding a good second-hand market in the old Soviet states. Boeing are still addresssing yet another 737 model with new engines.

The 767 line is still continuing slowly with over 1000 delivered, and 777 sales have benefittd from the 787 delays.

Embraer's 170 and 190 family aircraft continue to sell well, with over 800 delivered by the start of 2012. The smaller 145 line is mostly taken up with Legacy corporate aircraft.

In Canada Bombardier continues to deliver its CRJ700, CRJ900 and CRJ1000 models, and de Havilland Canada DHC-8-400s are maintaining their niche market with worldwide deliveries.

The Russian industry continues to find market penetration difficult in the face of Western-built airliners, and most Soviet-era jets have now been taken out of service. The ability of the fledgling Chinese airliner industry to make any immediate headway remains questionable.

### Details included

Details are included for over 2,500 operators in 200 countries – also included in the main text are those airlines whose fleets have been deleted since the last edition, along with the reason.   As a general guideline, the complete fleets of operators with an IATA two- or three-letter code are included, (unless they only operate corporate flights) , together with non-IATA coded operators of regular services where fleets are known.   Many of the world's major helicopter fleets down to Bell 206 size are included, with the large majority of all twin-engined aircraft and many single-engined aircraft down to Piper Cherokee Six that are also operated on passenger or express freight services.

The larger fleets are shown in type and registration order, with a space separating types. For space-saving reasons, smaller fleets and those with a large number of types but only one or two aircraft of each type are listed in registration order. This format is being developed all the time and has hopefully resulted in as clean a presentation of the data as is possible within sensible boundaries.

Civil registered jet and turboprop airliners in non-airline use, i.e. those owned and operated by the manufacturers or used in executive or special purpose roles, are again included in this year's edition. This section **does not** include details of the stored ex-airline aircraft.

The component parts of the US majors have again been grouped together under the airline heading and cross-referenced to the individual feeder carriers although this is becoming increasingly difficult as more and more operators provide feeder services to a range of airlines including, in some cases, regionals owned by one US major operating services for a competitor. As a result some of the feeders are listed separately for at least part of their fleets although they are cross-referenced to the majors as appropriate.

## Credits

We are indebted to the following for contributions, corrections, assistance and the use of information, Tony Beales, Ian Burnett, Colin Frost, Peter Gerhadt, Ken Marshall, Geoff Pyke, Terry Smith, Chris Swan, Barrie Towey, John Wilkinson, all contributors to the Commercial Scene section of Air-Britain News edited by Tony Wheeler; Aviation Letter, and the various Air-Britain publications as well as relevant web-sites.

## Update Information

For readers who are not already members of Air-Britain, this edition can be kept up-to-date by reading Commercial Scene in Air-Britain News and other sections of our regular publications. Details of the many benefits of membership are included at the end of this book.

Where possible, information received up to **31st March 2012** has been incorporated in the main text. Naturally, in a work of this complexity and scope, some errors and omissions will occur, and any reader who can add to, amend or correct the information included in this publication is invited to write to the address below.

Updates and corrections should be sent to the following address:

airlinefleets@air-britain.co.uk

# EXPLANATORY NOTES

### 1 Noise Regulations

With effect from 01Jan85 FAR Part 36 Stage 2 regulations came into force with respect to four-engined aircraft. These prevented any further civil operations of Boeing 707/720 and DC-8 (except -70 series) aircraft to or from US airports unless they were fitted with hushkits so that they conformed to the new noise standards. Similar regulations applied in the UK from 01Jan88. Stage 3 requirements are now implemented with all non-compliant aircraft required to be hush-kitted or re-engined; this applies to 707s, 727s, 737s (srs-100/200s), DC-8/9s, 1-11s, Tu-134/154s and Il-62/76s. Many of these aircraft are being withdrawn from service as the economic situation makes it uneconomic to undertake the costly conversions (indeed some of the planned hush-kitting schemes have been abandoned. In the main text of the book reference is made, where known, to the type of hush-kit fitted to Boeing 707, 727, early 737s and Douglas DC-8s and 9s and whether it is Stage 2 or Stage 3 compliant. (For example, FedEx 3 means a 727 fitted with a Stage 3 compliant FedEx hush-kit). Stage 4 hush-kits are now available for MD-80 series and the first ones are included in this volume.

### 2 Chapter 11

In the US section of this book, reference is sometimes made to 'Chapter 11'. This refers to a section of the US bankruptcy code designed to give a company protection from its creditors while it attempts a financial reorganisation. Plans for such a reorganisation have to be submitted to and approved by the bankruptcy court. A Chapter 11 filing may or may not be accompanied by a cessation of operations. If operations do continue, then it is usually at a very much reduced level. If they are suspended, then it is possible that they may be restarted in some form at a future date. If the reorganisation plan fails, then an application for liquidation under Chapter 7 will be made.

Since a Chapter 11 filing does not automatically result in a permanent cessation of operations, airlines are only deleted from this book if at the time of writing it appears that resumption of operations in the near future is unlikely.

### 3 Boeing 747 Suffixes

An M suffix after Boeing 747-200s indicates that the aircraft is a Combi (Mixed) version fitted with a Side Cargo Door. While not used officially in national registers, the M suffix convention is used in Boeing official literature and is therefore adopted in this publication. Suffixes SCD and EUD indicate converted Side Cargo Door and Extended Upper Deck versions. SF indicates that the aircraft is a 'Special Freighter' conversion and BCF a Boeing Converted Freighter and BDSF is similar but converted by IAI without Boeing support (for 747-400 passenger to freight conversions).

### 4 Boeing 737 Test Registrations and Winglets

Several Boeing 737s complete their first flights from Renton (PAE) to Boeing Field (BFI) with the registration N1786B or other test registration and these are shown when known. In the book the suffix /W indicates that the aircraft is fitted with Aviation Partner Boeing winglets.

### 5 German Spellings

German place names appear in anglicised form for operator bases but in the native German spelling for aircraft names (e.g. in the Lufthansa fleet).

### 6 Description of Entries

Countries are listed in alphabetical order of nationality prefix, with the airlines in each country also in alphabetical order. Fleets are listed in alphabetical order of aircraft manufacturer where five or more of the same type occur, otherwise they are listed in registration order. Aircraft type descriptions generally quote the manufacturer currently considered responsible for producing the aircraft. The immediate previous identity appears after the constructor's number and helps determine the source of newly acquired aircraft.

Each Country is identified in bold and italics and enclosed in a box; followed by airlines in alphabetical order, each again enclosed in a box. The details listed for each airline are its name (and any trading or alternative name where appropriate); airline call-sign; the two letter IATA designator and three-letter ICAO codes in brackets (where allocated and known); and their main operating base(s), again with the recognised three-letter code in brackets (where allocated).

Each individual entry, from the left, lists current registration (or that known to be reserved and likely to be taken up with that operator in brackets), followed by type. The next column lists the construction number, followed, for

Boeing and McDonnell-Douglas types, by the line number separated by a slash (/). There then appears the immediate past identity (where known) followed by any fleet number or name. The final entry indicates any lease arrangements or other comments. Any three-letter designation refers to another airline and these codes will be found indexed later in the book. Aircraft on order (recognized by o/o against their entry) are listed where either delivery is due in the year following the date of publication or where details of the aircraft are known. Otherwise details of aircraft on order for delivery in subsequent years are listed at the bottom of the aircraft type or airline entry; also listed there are any alliances, franchises or ownership details of interest.

Leased (lsd) aircraft will be found in the owner's fleet as well as that of the leasing airline. Where it is known that an aircraft is due to change operator during the currency of this book, it is shown in both fleets with a suitable note. Aircraft that have been withdrawn from service (wfs) are listed unless they are known to have been broken up or are beyond repair. Likewise, aircraft that have been involved in accidents but not confirmed as written off are still included.

## 7 Abbreviations

Abbreviations and symbols used in the text have the following meanings:

| | |
|---|---|
| ♦ | Any entry that is a new delivery, new aircraft in the fleet, addition of winglets, storage or lease. |
| [xxx] | Any 3-letter code in square brackets indicates a storage location |
| < | Leased in from |
| > | Leased out to |
| c/s | Colour Scheme |
| FP | Floatplane |
| Frtr | Freighter |
| o/o | On Order and expected to be delivered before the next edition |
| SPB | Seaplane Base |
| WS | Wheels/Skis |

## AP-        PAKISTAN (Islamic Republic of Pakistan)

### AIRBLUE                                    Pakblue (ED/ABQ)                              Karachi (KHI)

| | | | | | |
|---|---|---|---|---|---|
| ☐ AP-BIE | Airbus A319-112 | 3385 | ex EI-DZY | | |
| ☐ AP-BIF | Airbus A319-112 | 3388 | ex EI-DZZ | | |
| ☐ AP-EDA | Airbus A320-214 | 3974 | ex F-WWIT | | |
| ☐ AP-EDB | Airbus A319-111 | 3364 | ex D-AHIH | | |
| ☐ AP-EDC | Airbus A319-111 | 3403 | ex D-AHII | | |

### BHOJA AIR                                  (BHO)

| | | | | | |
|---|---|---|---|---|---|
| ☐ AP-BKD | Boeing 737-236 | 21793/635 | ex ZS-NNG | | ♦ |
| ☐ AP-BKE | Boeing 737-236 | 21797/653 | ex ZS-NNH | | [KHI]♦ |
| ☐ AP-BKF | Boeing 737-430 | 27004/2344 | ex N418BC | | [KHI]♦ |
| ☐ AP- | Boeing 737-236 | 23163/1058 | ex ZS-OLA | | o/o♦ |

### JS FOCUS AIR                               JS Charters (JSJ)                             Karachi (KHI)

| | | | | |
|---|---|---|---|---|
| ☐ AP-BJC | Beech 1900C-1 | UC-119 | ex N119YV | |
| ☐ AP-BJS | Beech 1900C-1 | UC-145 | ex ZS-PCD | |

### HAWK AIRLINES

| | | | | | |
|---|---|---|---|---|---|
| ☐ AP-BIY | Britten-Norman BN-2B-21 Islander | 2132 | ex G-HEBR | | ♦ |
| ☐ AP-BJJ | Britten-Norman BN-2A-27 Islander | 476 | ex G-BDJV | | ♦ |

### PAKISTAN INTERNATIONAL AIRLINES     Pakistan (PK/PIA)                              Karachi (KHI)

| | | | | | |
|---|---|---|---|---|---|
| ☐ AP-BDZ | Airbus A310-308 | 585 | ex F-WWCH | | |
| ☐ AP-BEB | Airbus A310-308 | 587 | ex F-WWCT | | |
| ☐ AP-BEC | Airbus A310-308 | 590 | ex F-WWCX | Nowshera-Defenders of the Land | |
| ☐ AP-BEG | Airbus A310-308 | 653 | ex F-WWCZ | Gilgit-The Silk Route | |
| ☐ AP-BEQ | Airbus A310-308 | 656 | ex F-WWCB | | |
| ☐ AP-BEU | Airbus A310-308 | 691 | ex F-WWCD | Peshawar- Gateway to the East | |
| ☐ AP-BGN | Airbus A310-324ET | 676 | ex F-WQTG | Taxila-The Exquisite Ghandhara | |
| ☐ AP-BGO | Airbus A310-324ET | 678 | ex F-WQTC | Gwadar-The New Port City | |
| ☐ AP-BGP | Airbus A310-324ET | 682 | ex F-WQTF | Murree-Songs of the Pines | |
| ☐ AP-BGQ | Airbus A310-325ET | 660 | ex F-OGYT | Sialkot-The Diligence of Industry | |
| ☐ AP-BGR | Airbus A310-325ET | 687 | ex F-OGYU | Mohenjodaro-Indus Valley Civilization | |
| ☐ AP-BGS | Airbus A310-325ET | 689 | ex F-OGYV | Ziarat-The City of Flowers | |
| | | | | | |
| ☐ AP-BHH | ATR 42-500 | 0645 | ex F-WWLE | Gwadar-The New Port City | |
| ☐ AP-BHI | ATR 42-500 | 0653 | ex F-WWLK | Ziarat-The City of Flowers | |
| ☐ AP-BHJ | ATR 42-500 | 0657 | ex F-WWLO | Mohenjodaro-IndusValley Civilization | |
| ☐ AP-BHM | ATR 42-500 | 0659 | ex F-WWLQ | Hala-Shades of Ash and Azure | |
| ☐ AP-BHN | ATR 42-500 | 0661 | ex F-WWLS | Chitral-Mysteries of the Kalash | |
| ☐ AP-BHO | ATR 42-500 | 0663 | ex F-WWLU | Hansanabdal-The Gurdwara Glory | |
| ☐ AP-BHP | ATR 42-500 | 0665 | ex F-WWLW | Gilgit-The Silk Route | |
| | | | | | |
| ☐ AP-BCA | Boeing 737-340 | 23294/1114 | | Gilgit-The Silk Route | |
| ☐ AP-BCB | Boeing 737-340 | 23295/1116 | | Multan-City of Saints | |
| ☐ AP-BCD | Boeing 737-340 | 23297/1122 | | Turbat-Romantic Interludes | |
| ☐ AP-BCF | Boeing 737-340 | 23299/1235 | | Sukkur | |
| ☐ AP-BEH | Boeing 737-33A | 25504/2341 | | Chitral-Mysteries of the Kalash | |
| ☐ AP-BFT | Boeing 737-340 | 23298/1123 | ex AP-BCE | Bahawalpur-The Splendour and Majesty | |
| | | | | | |
| ☐ AP-BAK | Boeing 747-240M | 21825/383 | | Thar-Colours of the Desert | |
| ☐ AP-BFU | Boeing 747-367 | 23392/634 | ex B-HIJ | Islamabad-The Margalla Magic | |
| ☐ AP-BFV | Boeing 747-367 | 23534/659 | ex B-HIK | | |
| ☐ AP-BFW | Boeing 747-367 | 23221/615 | ex B-HII | Lahore-Garden of the Mughals | |
| ☐ AP-BFY | Boeing 747-367 | 23920/690 | ex B-HOM | Ziarat-The City of Flowers | |
| ☐ AP-BGG | Boeing 747-367 | 24215/709 | ex B-HON | Kaghan-Mountain Paradise | |
| | | | | | |
| ☐ AP-BGJ | Boeing 777-240ER | 33775/467 | | | |
| ☐ AP-BGK | Boeing 777-240ER | 33776/469 | | | |
| ☐ AP-BGL | Boeing 777-240ER | 33777/473 | | | |
| ☐ AP-BGY | Boeing 777-240LR | 33781/504 | ex N5022E | | |
| ☐ AP-BGZ | Boeing 777-240LR | 33782/519 | ex N6066Z | | |
| ☐ AP-BHV | Boeing 777-340ER | 33778/601 | | Thar-Colours of the Desert | |
| ☐ AP-BHW | Boeing 777-240ER | 33779/611 | | Lahore-Garden of the Mughal | |
| ☐ AP-BHX | Boeing 777-240ER | 35296/613 | | Quetta-Nature's Orchard | |
| ☐ AP-BID | Boeing 777-340ER | 33780/705 | | | |

### RAYYAN AIR                                 (RAB)                                       Islamabad (ISB)

| | | | | | |
|---|---|---|---|---|---|
| ☐ AP-BIB | Boeing 747-21AC | 23652/669 | ex N652AP | | |
| ☐ AP-BIO | Boeing 747-243F | 22545/545 | ex N545SG | | ♦ |
| ☐ AP-BKI | Boeing 747-230F | 21592/347 | ex N592AC | | ♦ |

| **SHAHEEN AIR CARGO** | **Shaheen Cargo (SEE)** | **Islamabad (ISB)** |

Ops freight flights with Boeing 707-320Cs leased from Pakistan AF, and Ilyushin Il-76s leased from other operators, as required.

| **SHAHEEN AIR INTERNATIONAL** | | **Shaheen Air (NL/SAI)** | | **Karachi (KHI)** |
|---|---|---|---|---|
| ☐ AP-BHA | Boeing 737-277 (Nordam 3) | 22645/768 | ex N178AW | |
| ☐ AP-BHB | Boeing 737-277 (Nordam 3) | 22655/872 | ex N188AW | Chundam |
| ☐ AP-BHC | Boeing 737-291 (Nordam 3) | 21509/521 | ex EX-040 | |
| ☐ AP-BIK | Boeing 737-2B7 (Nordam 3) | 23114/997 | ex N281AU | |
| ☐ AP-BIP | Boeing 737-230 (Nordam 3) | 22634/840 | ex ZS-OIV | |
| ☐ AP-BIQ | Boeing 737-258 (Nordam 3) | 22857/919 | ex ZS-OOD | |
| ☐ AP-BIR | Boeing 737-228 | 23006/944 | ex ZS-OVE | |
| ☐ AP-BIS | Boeing 737-228 | 23008/952 | ex ZS-OVF | |
| ☐ AP-BIT | Boeing 737-236 | 21803/677 | ex ZS-OKD | |
| ☐ AP-BIU | Boeing 737-236 | 21807/710 | ex ZS-OKE | |
| ☐ AP-BJN | Boeing 737-4H6 | 26460/2533 | ex N829AR | dam 22Apr12♦ |
| ☐ AP- | Boeing 737-4H6 | 26465/2362 | ex N104HK | ♦ |

| **STAR AIR AVIATION** | | **(6S/URJ)** | | **Karachi (KHI)** |
|---|---|---|---|---|
| ☐ AP-ESC | Douglas DC-9-32 | 48150/1014 | ex A6-ESC | ♦ |
| ☐ AP-URJ | Boeing 727-224F | 20660/985 | ex N895AJ | |

| **VISION AIR INTERNATIONAL** | | **(VIS)** | | **Karachi (KHI)** |
|---|---|---|---|---|
| ☐ AP-BIA | Boeing 737-2H3 | 22625/776 | ex UP-B3705 | |
| ☐ AP-BIV | Boeing 747-246F | 22477/494 | ex N224JT | |

## A2-   BOTSWANA (Republic of Botswana)

| **AIR BOTSWANA** | | **Botswana (BP/BOT)** | | **Gaborone (GBE)** |
|---|---|---|---|---|
| ☐ A2-ABD | British Aerospace 146 Srs.100 | E1101 | ex (G-CBAE) | [GBE] |
| ☐ A2-ABF | British Aerospace 146 Srs.100 | E1160 | ex G-BVLJ | |
| ☐ A2-ABN | ATR 42-500 | 0507 | ex F-WQNG | Chobe |
| ☐ A2-ABO | ATR 42-500 | 0511 | ex F-WQNC | Okavango |
| ☐ A2-ABP | ATR 42-500 | 0512 | ex F-WQNI | Makgadikgadi |
| ☐ A2-ABR | ATR 72-212A | 0786 | ex F-WWEE | |
| ☐ A2-ABS | ATR 72-212A | 0788 | ex F-WWEG | |
| ☐ A2-NAC | Beech 1900D | UE-325 | ex ZS-OYM | <NAC Executive |

| **AIR CHARTER BOTSWANA** | | | |
|---|---|---|---|
| ☐ A2-SPA | Pilatus PC-12 | 788 | ♦ |

| **DELTA AIR** | | | **Maun (MUB)** |
|---|---|---|---|
| ☐ A2-AGR | Cessna U206F Stationair | U20601837 | ex ZS-OCC |
| ☐ A2-AHN | Cessna U206G Stationair 6 II | U20606432 | ex ZS-LKX |
| ☐ A2-AIW | Cessna 210N Centurion II | 21064163 | ex ZS-MYC |
| ☐ A2-AJA | Britten-Norman BN-2A Islander | 271 | ex ZS-LKE |
| ☐ A2-AJJ | Cessna 210L Centurion II | 21061533 | ex ZS-KPV |

| **KALAHARI AIR SERVICES AND CHARTER** | | | **Gaborone (GBE)** |
|---|---|---|---|
| ☐ A2-AFK | Cessna 210N Centurion II | 21064203 | ex N5427Y |
| ☐ A2-AHZ | Beech 200 Super King Air | BB-95 | ex ZS-JPD |
| ☐ A2-DBH | Beech C90 King Air | LJ-988 | ex ZS-LUU |
| ☐ A2-KAB | Beech 1900C-1 | UC-150 | ex ZS-PCE |
| ☐ A2-KAS | Beech 200 Super King Air | BB-614 | ex ZS-LKA |

| **KAVANGO AIR** | | | |
|---|---|---|---|
| ☐ A2-NUV | Cessna 208B Caravan I | 208B0596 | ex ZS-NUV | ♦ |

| **MACK AIR** | | | **Maun (MUB)** |
|---|---|---|---|
| ☐ A2-AIC | Cessna U206G Stationair 6 II | U20606419 | ex N9353Z |
| ☐ A2-AJI | Cessna U206G Stationair 6 II | U20606842 | ex ZS-NSS |
| ☐ A2-AKB | Cessna U206F Stationair | U20601889 | ex A2-ZHJ |
| ☐ A2-FMD | Cessna U206G Stationair 6 II | U20606005 | ex ZS-KSM |
| ☐ A2-ZFF | Cessna U206D Super Skywagon | U206-1263 | ex ZS-FPD |
| ☐ A2-AJZ | Gippsland GA-8 Airvan | GA8-04-059 | ex VH-CRQ |
| ☐ A2-AKI | Cessna 208B Caravan I | 208B0552 | ex 5Y-VIJ |

| ☐ A2-MAC | Cessna 210N Centurion II | 21063337 | ex V5-MRW | |
|---|---|---|---|---|
| ☐ A2-MEG | Cessna 208B Caravan I | 208B0944 | ex N4085S | |
| ☐ A2-NVH | Cessna 208B Caravan I | 208b0473 | ex ZS-NVH | ♦ |

## MAJOR BLUE AIR

| ☐ A2-MBA | Cessna 208B Caravan I | 2136 | ex N6251V | ♦ |
|---|---|---|---|---|
| ☐ A2-MBB | Cessna U206H Stationair II | 20608276 | ex ZS-AAT | ♦ |
| ☐ A2-MBC | Cessna 172S | 172S10112 | ex ZS-OHY | ♦ |

## MOREMI AIR SERVICES         *Maun (MUB)*

| ☐ A2-AEI | Cessna U206F Stationair | U20602470 | ex ZS-LDJ |
|---|---|---|---|
| ☐ A2-AKD | Cessna 208B Caravan I | 208B0582 | ex ZS-JML |
| ☐ A2-TEN | Cessna 210L Centurion II | 21061141 | ex A2-AIY |
| ☐ A2-ZED | Britten-Norman BN-2A-21 Islander | 736 | ex ZS-XGF |

## NAC EXECUTIVE CHARTER         *Gaborone (GBE)*

| ☐ A2-AJO | Beech 58 Baron | TH-614 | ex ZS-OGB | |
|---|---|---|---|---|
| ☐ A2-CDC | Beech C90 King Air | LJ-1947 | | ♦ |
| ☐ A2-MXI | Beech 200T Super King Air | BT-5 | ex N205EC | |
| ☐ A2-NAC | Beech 1900D | UE-325 | ex ZS-OYM | <BOT |

## NORTHERN AIR CHARTER         *Maun (MUB)*

| ☐ A2-ADK | Cessna U206G Stationair 6 II | U20606056 | ex ZS-KUO | |
|---|---|---|---|---|
| ☐ A2-AER | Cessna U206G Stationair 6 II | U20606324 | ex ZS-KXE | |
| ☐ A2-NAB | Cessna U206G Stationair 6 II | U20605439 | ex ZS-KDA | |
| ☐ A2-NAP | Cessna 208B Caravan I | 208B0727 | ex ZS-NAP | ♦ |

## SAFARI AIR         *Maun (MUB)*

| ☐ A2-AIX | Cessna U206F Stationair | U20601944 | ex ZS-MAD |
|---|---|---|---|
| ☐ A2-AJS | Gippsland GA-8 Airvan | GA8-04-047 | ex VH-LED |
| ☐ A2-CEX | Cessna 207 Skywagon | 20700154 | ex ZS-IDG |

## SEFOFANE AIR CHARTER         *Maun (MUB)*

| ☐ A2-AIV | Cessna U206G Stationair 6 II | U20606410 | ex ZS-LUA | | |
|---|---|---|---|---|---|
| ☐ A2-ANT | Cessna U206G Stationair 6 II | U20606237 | ex ZS-ANT | | |
| ☐ A2-BEE | Cessna U206G Stationair 6 II | U20605665 | ex ZS-KUL | | |
| ☐ A2-JET | Cessna 206H Stationair | 20608027 | ex ZS-OIA | | |
| ☐ A2-OWL | Cessna U206G Stationair 6 II | U20606978 | ex ZS-NXR | | |
| ☐ A2-XIG | Cessna U206G Stationair 6 II | U20605528 | ex ZS-NSU | | |
| | | | | | |
| ☐ A2-BUF | Cessna 208B Caravan I | 208B0815 | ex ZS-BUF | Kwatale | |
| ☐ A2-EGL | Cessna 208B Caravan I | 208B1158 | ex ZS-ABR | | |
| ☐ A2-LEO | Cessna 208B Caravan I | 208B0820 | ex N1307A | | |
| ☐ A2-NAS | Cessna 208B Caravan I | 208B0704 | ex ZS-TSW | | |
| ☐ A2-ZEB | Cessna 208B Caravan I | 208B0750 | ex A2-AEB | | |
| ☐ 9J-TAU | Cessna 208B Caravan I | 1262 | ex N1239Y | | ♦ |
| | | | | | |
| ☐ A2-HOP | Bell 206B Jet Ranger | 2551 | ex ZS-HHW | | ♦ |

## XUGANA AIR         *Maun (MUB)*

| ☐ A2-AKH | Cessna 208 Caravan I | 20800288 | ex C-FWTK |
|---|---|---|---|
| ☐ A2-AKK | Cessna 208B Caravan I | 208B0441 | ex ZS-OAR |
| ☐ A2-AKO | Cessna 208B Caravan I | 208B0736 | ex ZS-OWW |

## A3-    TONGA (Kingdom of Tonga)

### AIRLINES TONGA         *Tongatapu-Fua'amotu International (TBU)*

| ☐ DQ-FHC | Harbin Y-12 II | 0056 | | Save our Oceans | Op by FAJ |
|---|---|---|---|---|---|
| ☐ DQ-FHF | Harbin Y-12 II | 0047 | ex B-531L | | Op by FAJ |

### CHATHAMS PACIFIC         *Nukuialofa*

| ☐ A3-LYP | Britten-Norman BN-2A-27 Islander | 821 | ex ZK-LYP | ♦ |
|---|---|---|---|---|

### PEAU VAVA'U AIR     (30/PVU)     *Tongatapu-Fua'amotu International (TBU)*

| ☐ A3-AWP | Douglas DC-3C | 16387/33135 | ex ZK-AWP | Lucille | |
|---|---|---|---|---|---|
| ☐ A3-FEW | Beech 65-80 Queen Air | LC-168 | ex DQ-FEW | | Queenaire 8800 conversion |

## A4O-  OMAN (Sultanate of Oman)

| OMAN AIR | | Khanjar (WY/OMA) | | | Muscat-Seeb Intl (MCT) |
|---|---|---|---|---|---|
| ☐ A4O-DA | Airbus A330-243 | 1038 | ex F-WWYM | | |
| ☐ A4O-DB | Airbus A330-343X | 1044 | ex F-WWKA | | |
| ☐ A4O-DC | Airbus A330-243 | 1049 | ex F-WWKL | | |
| ☐ A4O-DD | Airbus A330-343X | 1063 | ex F-WWYN | | |
| ☐ A4O-DE | Airbus A330-343X | 1093 | ex F-WWYM | | |
| ☐ A4O-DF | Airbus A330-243 | 1120 | ex F-WWYA | | |
| ☐ A4O-DG | Airbus A330-243 | 1227 | ex F-WWYG | | ♦ |
| ☐ A4O-BA | Boeing 737-8BK/W | 29685/2457 | ex N1786B | Fahud | |
| ☐ A4O-BB | Boeing 737-8Q8/W | 30721/2255 | | | |
| ☐ A4O-BC | Boeing 737-81M/W | 35284/2738 | ex N1786B | Ras Al Had | |
| ☐ A4O-BD | Boeing 737-81M/W | 35287/2804 | ex N1786B | | |
| ☐ A4O-BE | Boeing 737-81M/W | 37161/2919 | ex N1786B | | |
| ☐ A4O-BF | Boeing 737-8FZ/W | 29637/3051 | | | |
| ☐ A4O-BG | Boeing 737-8FZ/W | 29664/3060 | ex N1787B | | |
| ☐ A4O-BJ | Boeing 737-81M/W | 34242/1674 | | | |
| ☐ A4O-BM | Boeing 737-8FZ/W | 29682/2853 | | | |
| ☐ A4O-BN | Boeing 737-8Q8/W | 30652/1018 | ex N1795B | Muscat | |
| ☐ A4O-BP | Boeing 737-8Q8/W | 35272/2537 | ex N1786B | | |
| ☐ A4O-BR | Boeing 737-81M/W | 33104/1337 | | | |
| ☐ A4O-BU | Boeing 737-81M/W | 35108/2554 | ex N1786B | | |
| ☐ A4O- | Boeing 737-8 | | | | o/o |
| ☐ A4O- | Boeing 737-8 | | | | o/o |
| ☐ A4O-EA | Embraer ERJ-175LR | 17000323 | ex PT-TBT | | ♦ |
| ☐ A4O-EB | Embraer ERJ-175LR | 17000324 | ex PT-TCJ | | ♦ |
| ☐ A4O- | Embraer ERJ-175LR | | | | o/o♦ |
| ☐ A4O- | Embraer ERJ-175LR | | | | o/o♦ |
| ☐ A4O- | Embraer ERJ-175LR | | | | o/o♦ |
| ☐ A4O-AS | ATR 42-500 | 0574 | ex VT-ADL | | |
| ☐ A4O-AT | ATR 42-500 | 0576 | ex VT-ADN | | |
| ☐ A4O-BO | Boeing 737-71M | 33103/1154 | ex N6066Z | | |
| ☐ A4O-BS | Boeing 737-7Q8 | 30649/1048 | | | |

## A5-  BHUTAN (Kingdom of Bhutan)

| DRUKAIR | | Royal Bhutan (KB/DRK) | | Paro (PBH) |
|---|---|---|---|---|
| ☐ A5-RGF | Airbus A319-115 | 2306 | ex D-AVYA | |
| ☐ A5-RGG | Airbus A319-115 | 2346 | ex D-AVWO | |
| ☐ A5-RGH | ATR42-500 | 0622 | ex F-OITQ | ♦ |

## A6-  UNITED ARAB EMIRATES (Al Imarat al-Arabiya al-Muttahida)

| ABU DHABI AVIATION | | | | Abu Dhabi-Bateen (AZI) |
|---|---|---|---|---|
| ☐ A6-AWA | Agusta AW139 | 31044 | ex I-EASJ | |
| ☐ A6-AWB | Agusta AW139 | 31053 | | |
| ☐ A6-AWC | Agusta AW139 | 31058 | | |
| ☐ A6-AWF | Agusta AW139 | 31118 | | |
| ☐ A6-AWH | Agusta AW139 | 41011 | | |
| ☐ A6-AWK | Agusta AW139 | 31150 | | |
| ☐ A6-AWL | Agusta AW139 | 31153 | | |
| ☐ A6-AWO | Agusta AW139 | 41215 | ex N341SH | ♦ |
| ☐ A6-BAM | Bell 212 | 31165 | ex C-GTHQ | |
| ☐ A6-BBC | Bell 212 | 30777 | | |
| ☐ A6-BBE | Bell 212 | 30783 | ex N9937K | |
| ☐ A6-BBK | Bell 212 | 30802 | | |
| ☐ A6-BBL | Bell 212 | 30822 | | |
| ☐ A6-BBP | Bell 212 | 30917 | | |
| ☐ A6-BBQ | Bell 212 | 30942 | | |
| ☐ A6-BBR | Bell 212 | 30976 | | |
| ☐ A6-BBS | Bell 212 | 30977 | | |
| ☐ A6-BBV | Bell 212 | 31189 | | |
| ☐ A6-BBY | Bell 212 | 32125 | | |
| ☐ A6- | Bell 212 | 30891 | ex C-FRUT | |
| ☐ A6-BAE | Bell 412HP | 36072 | | |
| ☐ A6-BAH | Bell 412HP | 36119 | ex C-GBUP | |
| ☐ A6-BAI | Bell 412HP | 36122 | | |
| ☐ A6-BAL | Bell 412HP | 36150 | | |
| ☐ A6-BAO | Bell 412HP | 36152 | | |

| | | | | |
|---|---|---|---|---|
| ☐ A6-BAP | Bell 412HP | 36189 | ex N52091 | |
| ☐ A6-BAQ | Bell 412EP | 36190 | | |
| ☐ A6-BAS | Bell 412EP | 36215 | | |
| ☐ A6-HBM | Bell 412EP | 36280 | ex C-GJCO | |
| | | | | |
| ☐ A6-ADA | de Havilland DHC-8Q-202 | 471 | ex C-GLOT | |
| ☐ A6-ADB | de Havilland DHC-8Q-315 | 650 | ex C-FLUJ | |
| ☐ A6-ADC | de Havilland DHC-8Q-202 | 473 | ex C-GFRP | |
| ☐ A6-ADD | de Havilland DHC-8Q-315 | 627 | ex V2-LGL | |
| ☐ A6-ADE | de Havilland DHC-8Q-315 | 628 | ex V2-LGM | |
| ☐ A6-ADF | de Havilland DHC-8Q-315 | 610 | ex V2-LGJ | |
| ☐ A6-ADG | de Havilland DHC-8Q-315MSA | 624 | ex V2-LGK | SAR/AEW |
| | | | | |
| ☐ A6-ADK | de Havilland DHC-8-402Q | 4222 | ex C-FTIA | |
| ☐ A6-BCE | Bell 206B JetRanger III | 2185 | | |
| ☐ A6-BCF | Bell 206B JetRanger III | 2423 | | |
| ☐ A6-BCK | Bell 206B JetRanger III | 2426 | | |
| ☐ A6-BCL | Bell 206B JetRanger III | 2720 | | |

## AEROGULF SERVICES — Aerogulf — Dubai (DXB)

| | | | | |
|---|---|---|---|---|
| ☐ A6-ALA | Bell 212 | 30664 | ex N71AL | |
| ☐ A6-ALC | Bell 212 | 30790 | ex N2781A | |
| ☐ A6-ALD | Bell 212 | 30809 | ex N143AL | |
| ☐ A6-ALU | Bell 212 | 30729 | ex C-GBKC | |
| ☐ A6-ALW | Bell 212 | 35065 | ex N62200 | |
| ☐ A6-ALX | Bell 212 | 30888 | ex YV-191CP | |
| | | | | |
| ☐ A6-ALO | Bell 206L-3 LongRanger III | 51435 | ex PT-YBK | |
| ☐ A6-ALP | Bell 206B JetRanger III | 2495 | ex (A6-BCJ) | |

## AIR ARABIA — Arabia (G9/ABY) — Sharjah (SHJ)

| | | | | | |
|---|---|---|---|---|---|
| ☐ A6-ABD | Airbus A320-214 | 2349 | ex F-WWBP | Sharjah | |
| ☐ A6-ABE | Airbus A320-214 | 2712 | ex F-WWBB | Al Heera | |
| ☐ A6-ABG | Airbus A320-214 | 2930 | ex F-WWBU | | |
| ☐ A6-ABH | Airbus A320-214 | 2964 | ex F-WWDA | Al Khan | |
| ☐ A6-ABI | Airbus A320-214 | 3044 | ex F-WWDP | Al Layyeh | |
| ☐ A6-ABJ | Airbus A320-214 | 3218 | ex F-WWBB | Kalba | |
| ☐ A6-ABK | Airbus A320-214 | 3444 | ex F-WWIF | Khor Fakkan | |
| ☐ A6-ABL | Airbus A320-214 | 3476 | ex F-WWDG | | |
| ☐ A6-ABM | Airbus A320-214 | 3246 | ex EC-KJY | | >RBG |
| ☐ A6-ABO | Airbus A320-214 | 3626 | ex F-WWIR | | |
| ☐ A6-ABP | Airbus A320-214 | 3802 | ex F-WWBV | | |
| ☐ A6-ABQ | Airbus A320-214 | 3840 | ex F-WWBM | | |
| ☐ A6-ABR | Airbus A320-214 | 3925 | ex F-WWBP | | |
| ☐ A6-ABS | Airbus A320-214 | 4061 | ex F-WWBE | | |
| ☐ A6-ABT | Airbus A320-214 | 4243 | ex F-WWDO | | |
| ☐ A6-ABU | Airbus A320-214 | 4310 | ex CN-NMD | | ♦ |
| ☐ A6-ANA | Airbus A320-214 | 4468 | ex D-AXAD | | |
| ☐ A6-ANB | Airbus A320-214 | 4524 | ex F-WWDK | | |
| ☐ A6-ANC | Airbus A320-214 | 4539 | ex F-WWIN | | |
| ☐ A6-AND | Airbus A320-214 | 4568 | ex F-WWBH | | ♦ |
| ☐ A6-ANE | Airbus A320-214 | 4806 | ex D-AVVY | | ♦ |
| ☐ A6-ANF | Airbus A320-214 | 4848 | ex F-WWIY | | ♦ |
| ☐ A6-ANG | Airbus A320-214 | 4890 | ex D-AVVF | | ♦ |
| ☐ A6-ANH | Airbus A320-214 | 4958 | ex D-AXAX | | ♦ |
| ☐ A6-ANI | Airbus A320-214 | 5017 | ex F-WWIX | | ♦ |
| ☐ A6-ANJ | Airbus A320-214 | 5143 | ex | | o/o♦ |
| ☐ A6- | Airbus A320-214 | | | | o/o♦ |
| ☐ A6- | Airbus A320-214 | | | | o/o♦ |
| ☐ A6- | Airbus A320-214 | | | | o/o♦ |
| ☐ A6- | Airbus A320-214 | | | | o/o♦ |

## AVE.COM — Phoenix Sharjah (2E/PHW) — Sharjah (SHJ)

| | | | | |
|---|---|---|---|---|
| ☐ A6-PHA | Boeing 737-2T4 | 23444/1154 | ex EX-027 | |
| ☐ A6-PHC | Boeing 737-33A | 23626/1284 | ex EC-JJV | |
| ☐ A6-PHF | Boeing 737-219 | 21645/535 | ex EX-012 | |
| ☐ A6-PHH | Boeing 737-3Q8 | 26314/2707 | ex G-THOF | |

## DOLPHIN AIR — Dolphin (ZD/FDN) — Sharjah (SHJ)

| | | | | |
|---|---|---|---|---|
| ☐ A6-ZYA | Boeing 737-2S2C | 21926/597 | ex N720A | [RKT] |
| ☐ A6-ZYC | Boeing 737-2X2 | 22679/807 | ex N719A | wfs |

## EASTERN SKYJETS — (ESJ) — Dubai (DXB)

| | | | | |
|---|---|---|---|---|
| ☐ A6-ESA | Douglas DC-9-51 (ABS 3) | 48136/993 | ex TG-JII | [JNB] |
| ☐ A6-ESF | Boeing 737-4Y0 | 25177/2176 | ex EI-EMY | |

12

| | | | | |
|---|---|---|---|---|
| ☐ A6-ESK | British Aerospace Jetstream 41 | 41090 | ex G-CEDS | |
| ☐ A6- | Boeing 737-33A | 25119/2069 | ex G-STRJ | o/o♦ |

| **EMIRATES** | | **Emirates (EK/UAE)** | | **Dubai (DXB)** |
|---|---|---|---|---|
| ☐ A6-EAA | Airbus A330-243 | 348 | ex F-WWYK | |
| ☐ A6-EAD | Airbus A330-243 | 382 | ex F-WWYR | |
| ☐ A6-EAE | Airbus A330-243 | 384 | ex F-WWYS | |
| ☐ A6-EAF | Airbus A330-243 | 392 | ex F-WWYX | |
| ☐ A6-EAG | Airbus A330-243 | 396 | ex F-WWKJ | |
| ☐ A6-EAH | Airbus A330-243 | 409 | ex F-WWKT | |
| ☐ A6-EAI | Airbus A330-243 | 437 | ex F-WWYI | |
| ☐ A6-EAJ | Airbus A330-243 | 451 | ex F-WWKE | |
| ☐ A6-EAK | Airbus A330-243 | 452 | ex F-WWKF | |
| ☐ A6-EAL | Airbus A330-243 | 462 | ex F-WWKK | [DXB] |
| ☐ A6-EAM | Airbus A330-243 | 491 | ex F-WWYO | |
| ☐ A6-EAN | Airbus A330-243 | 494 | ex F-WWKJ | |
| ☐ A6-EAO | Airbus A330-243 | 509 | ex F-WWYX | |
| ☐ A6-EAP | Airbus A330-243 | 525 | ex F-WWKV | |
| ☐ A6-EAQ | Airbus A330-243 | 518 | ex F-WWKT | |
| ☐ A6-EAR | Airbus A330-243 | 536 | ex F-WWYF | |
| ☐ A6-EAS | Airbus A330-243 | 455 | ex F-WWKH | |
| ☐ A6-EKQ | Airbus A330-243 | 248 | ex F-WWYX | |
| ☐ A6-EKR | Airbus A330-243 | 251 | ex F-WWKO | |
| ☐ A6-EKS | Airbus A330-243 | 283 | ex F-WWKH | |
| ☐ A6-EKT | Airbus A330-243 | 293 | ex F-WWKR | |
| ☐ A6-EKU | Airbus A330-243 | 295 | ex F-WWYF | |
| ☐ A6-EKV | Airbus A330-243 | 314 | ex F-WWYR | |
| ☐ A6-EKW | Airbus A330-243 | 316 | ex F-WWYS | |
| ☐ A6-EKX | Airbus A330-243 | 326 | ex F-WWYV | |
| ☐ A6-EKY | Airbus A330-243 | 328 | ex F-WWYX | |
| ☐ A6-EKZ | Airbus A330-243 | 345 | ex F-WWYI | |
| ☐ A6-ERM | Airbus A340-313X | 236 | ex D-AIFL | |
| ☐ A6-ERN | Airbus A340-313X | 166 | ex D-ASIC | |
| ☐ A6-ERO | Airbus A340-313X | 163 | ex D-ASIB | |
| ☐ A6-ERP | Airbus A340-313X | 185 | ex D-AGBM | |
| ☐ A6-ERQ | Airbus A340-313X | 190 | ex D-AJGP | |
| ☐ A6-ERR | Airbus A340-313X | 202 | ex D-ASID | |
| ☐ A6-ERS | Airbus A340-313X | 139 | ex D-ASIM | |
| ☐ A6-ERT | Airbus A340-313X | 149 | ex D-ASIN | |
| ☐ A6-ERA | Airbus A340-541 | 457 | ex F-WWTI | |
| ☐ A6-ERB | Airbus A340-541 | 471 | ex F-WWTK | |
| ☐ A6-ERC | Airbus A340-541 | 485 | ex F-WWTL | |
| ☐ A6-ERD | Airbus A340-541 | 520 | ex F-WWTS | |
| ☐ A6-ERE | Airbus A340-541 | 572 | ex F-WWTV | |
| ☐ A6-ERF | Airbus A340-541 | 394 | ex F-WWTE | |
| ☐ A6-ERG | Airbus A340-541 | 608 | ex F-WWTX | |
| ☐ A6-ERH | Airbus A340-541 | 611 | ex F-WWTY | |
| ☐ A6-ERI | Airbus A340-541 | 685 | ex F-WWTP | |
| ☐ A6-ERJ | Airbus A340-541 | 694 | ex F-WWTQ | |
| ☐ A6-EDA | Airbus A380-861 | 011 | ex D-AXXA | |
| ☐ A6-EDB | Airbus A380-861 | 013 | ex D-AXAB | |
| ☐ A6-EDC | Airbus A380-861 | 016 | ex D-AXAC | |
| ☐ A6-EDD | Airbus A380-861 | 020 | ex D-AXAD | |
| ☐ A6-EDE | Airbus A380-861 | 017 | ex D-AXAE | |
| ☐ A6-EDF | Airbus A380-861 | 007 | ex F-WWJB | |
| ☐ A6-EDG | Airbus A380-861 | 023 | ex F-WWST | |
| ☐ A6-EDH | Airbus A380-861 | 025 | ex F-WWSV | |
| ☐ A6-EDI | Airbus A380-861 | 028 | ex F-WWSZ | |
| ☐ A6-EDJ | Airbus A380-861 | 009 | ex F-WWEA | |
| ☐ A6-EDK | Airbus A380-861 | 030 | ex F-WWSD | |
| ☐ A6-EDL | Airbus A380-861 | 046 | ex F-WWAG | |
| ☐ A6-EDM | Airbus A380-861 | 042 | ex F-WWAO | |
| ☐ A6-EDN | Airbus A380-861 | 056 | ex F-WWAR | |
| ☐ A6-EDO | Airbus A380-861 | 057 | ex F-WWAS | |
| ☐ A6-EDP | Airbus A380-861 | 077 | ex F-WWSY | |
| ☐ A6-EDQ | Airbus A380-861 | 080 | ex F-WWSV | |
| ☐ A6-EDR | Airbus A380-861 | 083 | ex F-WWSZ | |
| ☐ A6-EDS | Airbus A380-861 | 086 | ex F-WWSB | |
| ☐ A6-EDT | Airbus A380-861 | 090 | ex F-WWSE | |
| ☐ A6-EDU | Airbus A380-861 | 098 | ex F-WWAB | ♦ |
| ☐ A6-EDV | Airbus A380-861 | 101 | ex F-WWAG | o/o♦ |
| ☐ A6-EDW | Airbus A380-861 | 103 | ex F-WWAL | o/o♦ |
| ☐ A6-EDX | Airbus A380-861 | 105 | ex F-WWAK | o/o♦ |
| ☐ A6-EDY | Airbus A380-861 | 106 | ex F-WWAS | o/o♦ |
| ☐ A6-EDZ | Airbus A380-861 | 107 | ex F-WWSD | o/o♦ |
| ☐ A6-EEA | Airbus A380-861 | 108 | erx F-WWSI | o/o♦ |
| ☐ A6-EEB | Airbus A380-861 | 109 | ex F-WWSN | o/o♦ |
| ☐ A6-EEC | Airbus A380-861 | 110 | ex F-WWAE | o/o♦ |

| | | | | |
|---|---|---|---|---|
| ☐ A6-EED | Airbus A380-861 | 111 | ex F-WWAQ | o/o♦ |
| ☐ A6-EEE | Airbus A380-861 | 112 | ex F-WWAU | o/o♦ |
| | | | | |
| ☐ N408MC | Boeing 747-47UF | 29261/1192 | ex (N495MC) | <GTI |
| ☐ N415MC | Boeing 747-47UF | 32837/1304 | | <GTI |
| ☐ N497MC | Boeing 747-47UF | 29258/1220 | | <GTI |
| ☐ OO-THC | Boeing 747-4HAERF | 35235/1389 | ex N50217 | <TAY |
| ☐ OO-THD | Boeing 747-4HAERF | 35236/1399 | | <TAY |
| | | | | |
| ☐ A6-EMD | Boeing 777-21H | 27247/30 | | |
| ☐ A6-EME | Boeing 777-21H | 27248/33 | | |
| ☐ A6-EMF | Boeing 777-21H | 27249/42 | | |
| ☐ A6-EMG | Boeing 777-21HER | 27252/63 | ex N5020K | |
| ☐ A6-EMH | Boeing 777-21HER | 27251/54 | | |
| ☐ A6-EMI | Boeing 777-21HER | 27250/47 | ex N5028Y | |
| ☐ A6-EMJ | Boeing 777-21HER | 27253/91 | | |
| ☐ A6-EMK | Boeing 777-21HER | 29324/171 | | |
| ☐ A6-EML | Boeing 777-21HER | 29325/176 | | |
| ☐ A6-EWA | Boeing 777-21HLR | 35572/654 | | |
| ☐ A6-EWB | Boeing 777-21HLR | 35573/662 | ex N5573S | |
| ☐ A6-EWC | Boeing 777-21HLR | 35576/677 | | |
| ☐ A6-EWD | Boeing 777-21HLR | 35577/688 | ex N5017V | |
| ☐ A6-EWE | Boeing 777-21HLR | 35582/725 | | |
| ☐ A6-EWF | Boeing 777-21HLR | 35586/739 | ex N5017V | |
| ☐ A6-EWG | Boeing 777-21HLR | 35578/741 | ex N6018N | |
| ☐ A6-EWH | Boeing 777-21HLR | 35587/747 | | |
| ☐ A6-EWI | Boeing 777-21HLR | 35589/757 | ex N5017V | |
| ☐ A6-EWJ | Boeing 777-21HLR | 35590/775 | ex N5017V | |
| | | | | |
| ☐ A6-EBA | Boeing 777-31HER | 32706/506 | | |
| ☐ A6-EBB | Boeing 777-36NER | 32789/508 | | |
| ☐ A6-EBC | Boeing 777-36NER | 32790/512 | | |
| ☐ A6-EBD | Boeing 777-31HER | 33501/516 | ex N5022E | |
| ☐ A6-EBE | Boeing 777-36NER | 32788/532 | | |
| ☐ A6-EBF | Boeing 777-31HER | 32708/536 | | |
| ☐ A6-EBG | Boeing 777-36NER | 33862/535 | | |
| ☐ A6-EBH | Boeing 777-31HER | 32707/539 | | |
| ☐ A6-EBI | Boeing 777-36NER | 32785/540 | | |
| ☐ A6-EBJ | Boeing 777-36NER | 32787/542 | | |
| ☐ A6-EBK | Boeing 777-31HER | 34481/549 | ex N5020K | |
| ☐ A6-EBL | Boeing 777-31HER | 32709/551 | ex N5017V | |
| ☐ A6-EBM | Boeing 777-31HER | 34482/556 | | |
| ☐ A6-EBN | Boeing 777-36NER | 32791/560 | | |
| ☐ A6-EBO | Boeing 777-36NER | 32792/568 | | |
| ☐ A6-EBP | Boeing 777-31HER | 32710/569 | ex N5017V | |
| ☐ A6-EBQ | Boeing 777-36NER | 33863/576 | ex N5017V | |
| ☐ A6-EBR | Boeing 777-31HER | 34483/578 | | |
| ☐ A6-EBS | Boeing 777-31HER | 32715/582 | | |
| ☐ A6-EBT | Boeing 777-31HER | 32730/585 | | |
| ☐ A6-EBU | Boeing 777-31HER | 34484/590 | | |
| ☐ A6-EBV | Boeing 777-31HER | 32728/594 | | |
| ☐ A6-EBW | Boeing 777-36NER | 32793/598 | | |
| ☐ A6-EBX | Boeing 777-31HER | 32729/619 | ex N5017V | |
| ☐ A6-EBY | Boeing 777-36NER | 33864/622 | ex N5017V | |
| ☐ A6-EBZ | Boeing 777-31HER | 32713/628 | | |
| ☐ A6-ECA | Boeing 777-36NER | 32794/632 | ex N5017B | |
| ☐ A6-ECB | Boeing 777-31HER | 32714/641 | ex N5016R | |
| ☐ A6-ECC | Boeing 777-31HER | 33865/664 | ex N5020K | |
| ☐ A6-ECD | Boeing 777-36NER | 32795/669 | ex N5017V | |
| ☐ A6-ECE | Boeing 777-31HER | 35575/681 | | |
| ☐ A6-ECF | Boeing 777-31HER | 35574/690 | | |
| ☐ A6-ECG | Boeing 777-31HER | 35579/709 | | |
| ☐ A6-ECH | Boeing 777-31HER | 35581/714 | | |
| ☐ A6-ECI | Boeing 777-31HER | 35580/728 | ex N1785B | |
| ☐ A6-ECJ | Boeing 777-31HER | 35583/734 | | |
| ☐ A6-ECK | Boeing 777-31HER | 35584/743 | | |
| ☐ A6-ECL | Boeing 777-36NER | 37704/748 | | |
| ☐ A6-ECM | Boeing 777-36NER | 37703/755 | ex N5017V | |
| ☐ A6-ECN | Boeing 777-36NER | 37705/761 | | |
| ☐ A6-ECO | Boeing 777-36NER | 37706/765 | | |
| ☐ A6-ECP | Boeing 777-36NER | 37707/768 | | |
| ☐ A6-ECQ | Boeing 777-31HER | 35588/779 | | |
| ☐ A6-ECR | Boeing 777-31HER | 35592/794 | ex N5017V | |
| ☐ A6-ECS | Boeing 777-31HER | 38980/803 | ex N5017V | |
| ☐ A6-ECT | Boeing 777-31HER | 35591/808 | | |
| ☐ A6-ECU | Boeing 777-31HER | 35593/817 | | |
| ☐ A6-ECV | Boeing 777-31HER | 35594/824 | | |
| ☐ A6-ECW | Boeing 777-31HER | 38981/828 | | |
| ☐ A6-ECX | Boeing 777-31HER | 38982/830 | | |
| ☐ A6-ECY | Boeing 777-31HER | 35595/840 | ex N5017V | |
| ☐ A6-ECZ | Boeing 777-31HER | 38983/847 | | |
| ☐ A6-EGA | Boeing 777-31HER | 38984/861 | ex N5017V | |

| | Reg | Type | MSN | Notes | |
|---|---|---|---|---|---|
| ☐ | A6-EGB | Boeing 777-31HER | 38985/929 | | ♦ |
| ☐ | A6-EGC | Boeing 777-31HER | 35596/945 | | ♦ |
| ☐ | A6-EGD | Boeing 777-31HER | 38988/946 | | ♦ |
| ☐ | A6-EGE | Boeing 777-31HER | 35597/951 | | ♦ |
| ☐ | A6-EGF | Boeing 777-31HER | 38987/961 | | ♦ |
| ☐ | A6-EGG | Boeing 777-31HER | 41070/965 | | |
| ☐ | A6-EGH | Boeing 777-31HER | 35585/969 | | ♦ |
| ☐ | A6-EGI | Boeing 777-31HER | 38986/974 | | o/o♦ |
| ☐ | A6-EGJ | Boeing 777-31HER | 38989/978 | | o/o♦ |
| ☐ | A6-EGK | Boeing 777-31HER | 41071/981 | | o/o♦ |
| ☐ | A6-EGL | Boeing 777-31HER | 41072/985 | | o/o♦ |
| ☐ | A6-EGM | Boeing 777-31HER | 41073/988 | | o/o♦ |
| ☐ | A6-EGN | Boeing 777-31HER | 41074/993 | | ♦ |
| ☐ | A6-EGO | Boeing 777-31HER | 35598/1000 | | ♦ |
| ☐ | A6-EGQ | Boeing 777-31HER | 41076 | | o/o♦ |
| ☐ | A6-EGR | Boeing 777-31HER | 41077 | | o/o♦ |
| ☐ | A6-EGS | Boeing 777-31HER | 41078 | | o/o♦ |
| ☐ | A6-EGT | Boeing 777-31HER | 35600 | | o/o♦ |
| ☐ | A6-EGU | Boeing 777-31HER | 41079 | | o/o♦ |
| ☐ | A6-EGV | Boeing 777-31HER | 38990 | | o/o♦ |
| ☐ | A6-EGW | Boeing 777-31HER | 35601 | | o/o♦ |
| ☐ | A6-EGX | Boeing 777-31HER | 35602 | | o/o♦ |
| ☐ | A6-EGY | Boeing 777-31HER | 41080 | | o/o♦ |
| ☐ | A6-EGZ | Boeing 777-31HER | 41081 | | o/o♦ |
| ☐ | A6-EMM | Boeing 777-31H | 29062/256 | | |
| ☐ | A6-EMN | Boeing 777-31H | 29063/262 | | |
| ☐ | A6-EMO | Boeing 777-31H | 28680/300 | | |
| ☐ | A6-EMP | Boeing 777-31H | 29395/326 | ex N50281 | |
| ☐ | A6-EMQ | Boeing 777-31H | 32697/396 | | |
| ☐ | A6-EMR | Boeing 777-31H | 29396/402 | | |
| ☐ | A6-EMS | Boeing 777-31H | 29067/408 | ex N50281 | |
| ☐ | A6-EMT | Boeing 777-31H | 32699/414 | ex N5014K | |
| ☐ | A6-EMU | Boeing 777-31H | 29064/418 | | |
| ☐ | A6-EMV | Boeing 777-31H | 28687/432 | | |
| ☐ | A6-EMW | Boeing 777-31H | 32700/434 | | |
| ☐ | A6-EMX | Boeing 777-31H | 32702/444 | | |
| ☐ | A6-ENA | Boeing 777-31HER | 41082 | | o/o♦ |
| ☐ | A6-ENB | Boeing 777-31HER | 41075 | | o/o♦ |
| ☐ | A6-ENC | Boeing 777-31HER | 41083 | | o/o♦ |
| ☐ | A6-END | Boeing 777-31HER | 41084 | | o/o♦ |
| ☐ | A6-ENE | Boeing 777-31HER | 35603 | | o/o♦ |
| ☐ | A6-EFD | Boeing 777-F1H | 35606/766 | | |
| ☐ | A6-EFE | Boeing 777-F1H | 35607/788 | ex N5017V | |
| ☐ | A6-EFF | Boeing 777-F1H | 35612/955 | | ♦ |
| ☐ | A6-EFG | Boeing 777-F1H | 35613/996 | | ♦ |
| ☐ | A6-EFH | Boeing 777-F1H | 35608/ | | o/o♦ |
| ☐ | A6-EFI | Boeing 777-F1H | 35609/ | | o/o♦ |
| ☐ | A6-EFJ | Boeing 777-F1H | 35610/ | | o/o♦ |
| ☐ | A6-EIP | Airbus A320-232 | 5095 | ex D-AUBN | ♦ |
| ☐ | A6- | Boeing 747-81HF | 37451 | | o/o |
| ☐ | A6- | Boeing 747-81HF | | | o/o |

## ETIHAD AIRWAYS — Etihad (EY/ETD) — Abu Dhabi (AUH)

| | Reg | Type | MSN | Notes | |
|---|---|---|---|---|---|
| ☐ | A6-EIA | Airbus A320-232 | 1944 | ex PH-MPD | |
| ☐ | A6-EIB | Airbus A320-232 | 1945 | ex PH-MPE | Abu Dhabi Grand Prix colours |
| ☐ | A6-EIC | Airbus A320-232 | 2167 | ex PH-MPF | |
| ☐ | A6-EIF | Airbus A320-232 | 3004 | ex EI-EAO | |
| ☐ | A6-EIG | Airbus A320-232 | 3050 | ex EI-EAN | |
| ☐ | A6-EIH | Airbus A320-232 | 3693 | ex F-WWBH | |
| ☐ | A6-EII | Airbus A320-232 | 3713 | ex F-WWIX | |
| ☐ | A6-EIJ | Airbus A320-232 | 3902 | ex F-WWIA | |
| ☐ | A6-EIK | Airbus A320-232 | 3676 | ex VT-INW | |
| ☐ | A6-EIL | Airbus A320-232 | 4066 | ex F-WWBH | |
| ☐ | A6-EIM | Airbus A320-232 | 4077 | ex F-WWBO | |
| ☐ | A6-EIN | Airbus A320-232 | 4124 | ex F-WWIN | |
| ☐ | A6-EIO | Airbus A320-214 | 4934 | ex F-WWBP | ♦ |
| ☐ | A6-EIZ | Airbus A320-211 | 0350 | ex 9H-AFE | |
| ☐ | A6-DCA | Airbus A330-243F | 1032 | ex F-WWKG | |
| ☐ | A6-DCB | Airbus A330-243F | 1070 | ex F-WWYF | |
| ☐ | A6-EYD | Airbus A330-243 | 658 | ex F-WWYN | |
| ☐ | A6-EYE | Airbus A330-243 | 688 | ex F-WWYJ | |
| ☐ | A6-EYF | Airbus A330-243 | 717 | ex F-WWYN | |
| ☐ | A6-EYG | Airbus A330-243 | 724 | ex F-WWKN | |
| ☐ | A6-EYH | Airbus A330-243 | 729 | ex F-WWKR | |
| ☐ | A6-EYI | Airbus A330-243 | 730 | ex F-WWKS | |
| ☐ | A6-EYJ | Airbus A330-243 | 737 | ex F-WWYB | |
| ☐ | A6-EYK | Airbus A330-243 | 788 | ex F-WWKM | |
| ☐ | A6-EYL | Airbus A330-243 | 809 | ex F-WWYB | |

| | | | | |
|---|---|---|---|---|
| ☐ A6-EYM | Airbus A330-243 | 824 | ex F-WWKD | |
| ☐ A6-EYN | Airbus A330-243 | 832 | ex F-WWKN | |
| ☐ A6-EYO | Airbus A330-243 | 852 | ex F-WWKT | |
| ☐ A6-EYP | Airbus A330-243 | 854 | ex F-WWYY | |
| ☐ A6-EYQ | Airbus A330-243 | 868 | ex F-WWYQ | |
| ☐ A6-EYR | Airbus A330-243 | 975 | ex F-WWKS | |
| ☐ A6-EYS | Airbus A330-243 | 991 | ex F-WWKM | |
| | | | | |
| ☐ A6-AFA | Airbus A330-343X | 1071 | ex F-WWYP | |
| ☐ A6-AFB | Airbus A330-343X | 1081 | ex F-WWYL | |
| ☐ A6-AFC | Airbus A330-343X | 1167 | ex F-WWYR | |
| ☐ A6-AFD | Airbus A330-343X | 1205 | ex F-WWKN | |
| ☐ A6-AFE | Airbus A330-343X | 1226 | ex F-WWKM | ♦ |
| ☐ A6-AFF | Airbus A330-343X | 1245 | ex F-WWKU | ♦ |
| | | | | |
| ☐ A6-EHE | Airbus A340-642HGW | 829 | ex F-WWCG | |
| ☐ A6-EHF | Airbus A340-642HGW | 837 | ex F-WWCB | |
| ☐ A6-EHH | Airbus A340-642HGW | 870 | ex F-WWCK | |
| ☐ A6-EHI | Airbus A340-642HGW | 929 | ex F-WWCB | |
| ☐ A6-EHJ | Airbus A340-642HGW | 933 | ex F-WWCF | |
| ☐ A6-EHK | Airbus A340-642HGW | 1030 | ex F-WWCX | |
| ☐ A6-EHL | Airbus A340-642HGW | 1040 | ex F-WWCH | |
| | | | | |
| ☐ A6-ETA | Boeing 777-3FXER | 34597/538 | ex N6018N | |
| ☐ A6-ETB | Boeing 777-3FXER | 34598/543 | ex N5020K | |
| ☐ A6-ETC | Boeing 777-3FXER | 34599/544 | | |
| ☐ A6-ETD | Boeing 777-3FXER | 34600/547 | | |
| ☐ A6-ETE | Boeing 777-3FXER | 34601/548 | | |
| ☐ A6-ETF | Boeing 777-3FXER | 39700/832 | ex N1794B | |
| ☐ A6-ETG | Boeing 777-3FXER | 39681/932 | | ♦ |
| ☐ A6-ETH | Boeing 777-3FXER | 39683/957 | | ♦ |
| ☐ A6-ETI | Boeing 777-3FXER | 39684/987 | | ♦ |
| ☐ A6-ETJ | Boeing 777-3FXER | 39685/994 | | ♦ |
| ☐ A6-ETK | Boeing 777-3FXER | 39689 | | o/o♦ |
| | | | | |
| ☐ A6-DDA | Boeing 777-FFX | 39682/939 | | ♦ |
| ☐ A6-EID | Airbus A319-132 | 1947 | ex D-APAA | |
| ☐ A6-EIE | Airbus A319-132 | 1955 | ex D-APAB | |
| ☐ A6-EHA | Airbus A340-541 | 748 | ex F-WWTS | |
| ☐ A6-EHB | Airbus A340-541 | 757 | ex F-WWTU | |
| ☐ A6-EHC | Airbus A340-541 | 761 | ex F-WWTV | |
| ☐ A6-EHD | Airbus A340-541 | 783 | ex F-WWTY | |

## FALCON EXPRESS CARGO AIRLINES  (FC/FVS)  Dubai (DXB)

| | | | | |
|---|---|---|---|---|
| ☐ A6-FCA | Beech 1900C-1 | UC-57 | ex OY-GED | |
| ☐ A6-FCB | Beech 1900C-1 | UC-66 | ex OY-GEI | |
| ☐ A6-FCC | Beech 1900C-1 | UC-68 | ex OY-GEJ | |
| ☐ A6-FCD | Beech 1900C-1 | UC-71 | ex OY-GEK | |
| ☐ A6-FCX | Beech 1900C-1 | UC-40 | ex F-GLPJ | ♦ |
| | | | | |
| ☐ A6-FCY | Fokker F.27 Friendship 500 | 10370 | ex HA-FAB | |
| ☐ A6-FCZ | Fokker F.27 Friendship 500 | 10448 | ex HB-ITY | |

## FLYDUBAI  (FZ/FDB)  Dubai (DXB)

| | | | | |
|---|---|---|---|---|
| ☐ A6-FAA | Boeing 737-8KN/W | 40254/ | | o/o♦ |
| ☐ A6-FDC | Boeing 737-8KN/W | 40233/2952 | ex N1786B | |
| ☐ A6-FDD | Boeing 737-8KN/W | 40234/2966 | | |
| ☐ A6-FDE | Boeing 737-8KN/W | 40235/3053 | | |
| ☐ A6-FDF | Boeing 737-8KN/W | 40236/3110 | | |
| ☐ A6-FDG | Boeing 737-8KN/W | 29636/3197 | | |
| ☐ A6-FDH | Boeing 737-8KN/W | 31716/3270 | | |
| ☐ A6-FDI | Boeing 737-8KN/W | 31765/3302 | | |
| ☐ A6-FDJ | Boeing 737-8KN/W | 40237/3356 | ex N6046P | |
| ☐ A6-FDK | Boeing 737-8KN/W | 40238/3391 | | |
| ☐ A6-FDL | Boeing 737-8KN/W | 40239/3460 | | |
| ☐ A6-FDM | Boeing 737-8KN/W | 40240/3485 | | |
| ☐ A6-FDN | Boeing 737-8KN/W | 40241/3517 | | ♦ |
| ☐ A6-FDO | Boeing 737-8KN/W | 40242/3540 | | ♦ |
| ☐ A6-FDP | Boeing 737-8KN/W | 40243/3582 | | ♦ |
| ☐ A6-FDQ | Boeing 737-8KN/W | 40244/3619 | | ♦ |
| ☐ A6-FDR | Boeing 737-8KN/W | 40245/3640 | | ♦ |
| ☐ A6-FDS | Boeing 737-8KN/W | 40246/3659 | | ♦ |
| ☐ A6-FDT | Boeing 737-8KN/W | 40247/3706 | | ♦ |
| ☐ A6-FDU | Boeing 737-8KN/W | 40249/3720 | | ♦ |
| ☐ A6-FDV | Boeing 737-8KN/W | 40248/3768 | | ♦ |
| ☐ A6-FDW | Boeing 737-8KN/W | 40250/3868 | | ♦ |
| ☐ A6-FDX | Boeing 737-8KN/W | 40251/3901 | | ♦ |
| ☐ A6-FDY | Boeing 737-8KN/W | 40252/3923 | | ♦ |
| ☐ A6-FDZ | Boeing 737-8KN/W | 40253/ | | o/o♦ |

## GCS CARGO

| | | | | |
|---|---|---|---|---|
| ☐ EK-30277 | Airbus A300F4-203 | 0277 | ex N277EF | ♦ |

## GLOBAL JET UAE

**(GBG)**      **Dubai (DXB)**

| | | | | |
|---|---|---|---|---|
| ☐ A6-JAK | Boeing 737-406 | 24959/1949 | ex N959PR | ♦ |
| ☐ A6-JMK | Boeing 737-322 | 24674/1928 | ex N399UA | ♦ |
| ☐ A6-JUD | Boeing 737-306 | 23541/1309 | ex PH-CDE | ♦ |

## MAXIMUS AIR CARGO

**Cargo Max (MXU)**      **Abu Dhabi (AUH)**

| | | | | |
|---|---|---|---|---|
| ☐ A6-HAZ | Airbus A300B4-622RF | 837 | ex JA015D | ♦ |
| ☐ A6-MAC | Lockheed L-382G-44K-30 Hercules | 5024 | ex 1215 | <UAE AF |
| ☐ A6-MAX | Lockheed L-382G-44K-30 Hercules | 4895 | ex 1216 | <UAE AF |
| ☐ A6-MXA | Airbus A300B4-622RF | 788 | ex TF-ELA | <ABD |
| ☐ A6-MXB | Airbus A300B4-622RF | 767 | ex TF-ELE | <ABD |
| ☐ A6-NIN | Airbus A300B4-622RF | 797 | ex JA012D | ♦ |
| ☐ A6-QFY | Lockheed L-382G Hercules | 4834 | ex 311` | ♦ |
| ☐ A6-SUL | Airbus A300B4-622RF | 836 | ex JA014D | ♦ |
| ☐ UR-BXQ | Ilyushin Il-76TD | 1023410360 | ex EX-832 | <UKL |
| ☐ UR-BXR | Ilyushin Il-76TD | 1023411384 | ex EX-411 | <UKL |
| ☐ UR-BXS | Ilyushin Il-76TD | 1023411368 | ex EX-436 | <UKL |
| ☐ UR-ZYD | Antonov An-124 Ruslan | 19530502843 | ex UR-CCX | <UAK |

## MIDEX AIRLINES

**(MG/MIX)**      **Al Ain (AAN)**

| | | | | |
|---|---|---|---|---|
| ☐ A6-MDA | Airbus A300B4-203F | 157 | ex N371PC | Midex 1 |
| ☐ A6-MDB | Airbus A300B4-203F | 196 | ex N372PC | Midex 2 |
| ☐ A6-MDC | Airbus A300B4-203F | 218 | ex N373PC | Midex 3 |
| ☐ A6-MDD | Airbus A300B4-203F | 203 | ex N473AS | |
| ☐ A6-MDE | Airbus A300B4-203F | 125 | ex N472AS | |
| ☐ A6-MDF | Airbus A300B4-203F | 134 | ex N370PC | Midex 6 |
| | | | | |
| ☐ A6-MDG | Boeing 747-228F | 25266/878 | ex PH-MCN | |
| ☐ A6-MDH | Boeing 747-228F | 24735/772 | ex F-WCZY | Midex 8 |
| ☐ A6-MDI | Boeing 747-228F | 24879/822 | ex F-WCZY | Midex 9 |

## RAK AIRWAYS

**Rakair (RT/RKM)**      **Ras Al Khaimah (RKT)**

| | | | | | |
|---|---|---|---|---|---|
| ☐ A6-ABA | Airbus A320-214 | 2158 | ex F-WWDF | Al Bdee'a | ♦ |
| ☐ A6-ESE | Boeing 737-46J | 27213/2585 | ex N213TH | | ♦ |
| ☐ A6-RKB | Airbus A320-214 | 3907 | ex EI-ERX | | ♦ |
| ☐ A6-RKC | Airbus A320-214 | 2158 | ex A6-ABA | | ♦ |
| ☐ G-LSAK | Boeing 757-23N | 27973/735 | ex N517AT | | <EXS♦ |

## ROTANA JET

**Abu Dhabi (AUH)**

| | | | | |
|---|---|---|---|---|
| ☐ A6-RRA | Embraer ERJ-145MP | 145398 | ex F-GUBA | ♦ |
| ☐ A6-RRB | Embraer ERJ-145MP | 145419 | ex F-GUBB | ♦ |

## SEAWINGS

| | | | | |
|---|---|---|---|---|
| ☐ A6-SEA | Cessna 208 Caravan I | 20800118 | ex TF-SEA | FP |
| ☐ A6-SEB | Cessna 208 Caravan I | 20800401 | ex N1000X | FP |

## SILVER AIR

| | | | | |
|---|---|---|---|---|
| ☐ A6-JUD | Boeing 737-306 | 23541/1309 | ex (N801GS) | |

## SKA ARABIA

**Dubai (DXB)**

| | | | | |
|---|---|---|---|---|
| ☐ 4L-NAM | Boeing 737-2T5 | 22632/847 | ex E3-NAM | <Georgian Star Intl♦ |

## SKYLINE FZE

| | | | | |
|---|---|---|---|---|
| ☐ 5Y-UAE | Douglas DC-9-34CF | 47707/823 | ex S9-PSR | ♦ |

## SKYLINK ARABIA

**Dubai (DXB)**

| | | | | |
|---|---|---|---|---|
| ☐ ER-AVA | Antonov An-26B-100 | 11409 | | ♦ |
| ☐ ER-AVB | Antonov An-26B-100 | 57303204 | ex UR-26556 | |
| ☐ ER-AZN | Antonov An-24RV | 37308801 | ex | |
| ☐ ER-AZX | Antonov An-24RV | 47309804 | | ♦ |
| ☐ RDPL-34155 | Ilyushin Il-76T | 073411338 | | ♦ |
| ☐ RDPL-34157 | Ilyushin Il-76T | 093418556 | ex ER-IBP | |
| ☐ UP-I7611 | Ilyushin Il-76T | 093418548 | ex UN-76031 | |
| ☐ UP-I7630 | Ilyushin Il-76T | 0023441189 | ex RA-76823 | |
| ☐ UP-AN203 | Antonov An-12BK | 900346508 | ex ER-ADZ | |

| | | | | |
|---|---|---|---|---|
| ☐ UP-AN204 | Antonov An-12BK | 00347408 | ex UN-11021 | [RKT]♦ |
| ☐ ZS-IRE | Boeing 727-2Q9F (FedEx 3) | 21931/1531 | ex N741DH | ♦ |

## A7- QATAR (State of Qatar)

### GULF HELICOPTERS                                    Doha (DOH)

| | | | | |
|---|---|---|---|---|
| ☐ A7-GHA | Agusta AW139 | 31132 | | |
| ☐ A7-GHB | Agusta AW139 | 31140 | | |
| ☐ A7-GHC | Agusta AW139 | 31225 | | |
| ☐ A7-GHD | Agusta AW139 | 31233 | | |
| ☐ A7-GHE | Agusta AW139 | 31235 | | |
| ☐ A7-GHF | Agusta AW139 | 31242 | | |
| ☐ A7-GHG | Agusta AW139 | 41222 | ex N420SM | ♦ |
| ☐ A7-GHH | Agusta AW139 | 41225 | ex N413SM | ♦ |
| ☐ A7-GHK | Agusta AW139 | 41248 | ex N460SM | ♦ |
| ☐ A7-GHI | Agusta AW139 | 41018 | | ♦ |
| ☐ A7-GHJ | Agusta AW139 | 41241 | ex N459SM | |
| ☐ A7-GHL | Agusta AW139 | 31381 | | ♦ |
| ☐ A7-HBT | Agusta AW139 | 31068 | ex I-EASO | |
| ☐ A7-HAV | Bell 412SP | 33205 | ex D-HHNN | |
| ☐ A7-HAW | Bell 412HP | 36046 | ex N9142N | |
| ☐ A7-HAY | Bell 412EP | 36126 | ex N2045S | |
| ☐ A7-HAZ | Bell 412HP | 36041 | ex N92801 | |
| ☐ A7-HBB | Bell 412EP | 36259 | ex N9026K | |
| ☐ A7-HBC | Bell 412EP | 36276 | ex N9154J | |
| ☐ A7-HBD | Bell 412EP | 36088 | ex N4324X | |
| ☐ A7-HBH | Bell 412EP | 36326 | ex N8067Q | |
| ☐ A7-HBI | Bell 412EP | 36270 | ex PP-MBE | |
| ☐ A7-HBJ | Bell 412EP | 36370 | ex N43939 | |
| ☐ A7-HBL | Bell 412SP | 33117 | ex EP-HUC | |
| ☐ A7-HBM | Bell 412EP | 36400 | ex N2116N | |
| ☐ A7-HBP | Bell 412SP | 36016 | ex EP-HUF | |
| ☐ A7-HBQ | Bell 412EP | 36412 | ex N7512Z | |
| ☐ A7-HBR | Bell 412SP | 36017 | ex EP-HUG | |
| ☐ A7-HBS | Bell 412SP | 33116 | ex A7-HBK | |
| ☐ VT-HGF | Bell 412EP | 36206 | ex A7-HBE | >United Helicharters |
| ☐ A7-HAO | Agusta-Bell 206B JetRanger II | 8044 | ex A4O-DC | |
| ☐ A7-HBF | Bell 230 | 23015 | ex N236X | |
| ☐ A7-HBN | Bell 212 | 31130 | ex VT-HGE | |
| ☐ A7-HBO | Bell 212 | 30911 | ex EP-HUE | |
| ☐ A7-HHT | Sikorsky S-92A | 920031 | ex N7113U | |

### QATAR AIRWAYS                    Qatari (QR/QTR)                    Doha (DOH)

| | | | | | |
|---|---|---|---|---|---|
| ☐ A7-ADA | Airbus A320-232 | 1566 | ex F-WWBG | Al Zubara | |
| ☐ A7-ADB | Airbus A320-232 | 1648 | ex F-WWDU | Dukhan | |
| ☐ A7-ADC | Airbus A320-232 | 1773 | ex F-WWDG | Mesaieed | |
| ☐ A7-ADD | Airbus A320-232 | 1895 | ex F-WWBT | Halul | |
| ☐ A7-ADE | Airbus A320-232 | 1957 | ex F-WWIG | Al Gharafa | |
| ☐ A7-ADF | Airbus A320-232 | 2097 | ex F-WWIP | Al Wukeir | |
| ☐ A7-ADG | Airbus A320-232 | 2121 | ex F-WWIT | Al Ghuweriyah | |
| ☐ A7-ADH | Airbus A320-232 | 2138 | ex F-WWBI | Al Jumeilliyah | |
| ☐ A7-ADI | Airbus A320-232 | 2161 | ex F-WWBK | Al Khuraytiyat | |
| ☐ A7-ADJ | Airbus A320-232 | 2288 | ex F-WWBS | Al Samriya | |
| ☐ A7-ADU | Airbus A320-232 | 3071 | ex F-WWIM | | |
| ☐ A7-AHA | Airbus A320-232 | 4110 | ex F-WWDT | | |
| ☐ A7-AHB | Airbus A320-232 | 4130 | ex F-WWIR | | |
| ☐ A7-AHC | Airbus A320-232 | 4183 | ex F-WWIB | | |
| ☐ A7-AHD | Airbus A320-232 | 4436 | ex D-AVVW | | |
| ☐ A7-AHE | Airbus A320-232 | 4479 | ex D-AUBC | | |
| ☐ A7-AHF | Airbus A320-232 | 4496 | ex F-WWIJ | | |
| ☐ A7-AHG | Airbus A320-232 | 4615 | ex D-AXAV | | |
| ☐ A7-AHH | Airbus A320-232 | 4700 | ex F-WWBD | | ♦ |
| ☐ A7-AHI | Airbus A320-232 | 4754 | ex F-WWDA | | ♦ |
| ☐ A7-AHJ | Airbus A320-232 | 4784 | ex F-WWDT | | ♦ |
| ☐ A7-AHL | Airbus A320-232 | 4802 | ex F-WWBC | | ♦ |
| ☐ A7-AHO | Airbus A320-232 | 4810 | ex F-WWDI | | ♦ |
| ☐ A7-AHP | Airbus A320-232 | 4858 | ex F-WWBJ | | ♦ |
| ☐ A7-AHQ | Airbus A320-232 | 4930 | ex F-WWBI | | ♦ |
| ☐ A7-AHR | Airbus A320-232 | 4968 | ex F-WWDV | | ♦ |
| ☐ A7-AHS | Airbus A320-232 | 5010 | ex F-WWDX | | ♦ |
| ☐ A7-AHT | Airbus A320-232 | 5078 | ex F-WW | | ♦ |
| ☐ A7-AHU | Airbus A320-232 | 5127 | ex F-WW | | o/o♦ |
| ☐ A7-AHV | Airbus A320-232 | 5182 | ex F-WW | | o/o♦ |
| ☐ A7-AHW | Airbus A320-232 | 5217 | ex F-WW | | o/o♦ |
| ☐ A7-AHX | Airbus A320-232 | 5361 | ex F-WW | | o/o♦ |
| ☐ A7-AHY | Airbus A320-232 | 5395 | ex F-WW | | o/o♦ |

18

| | | | | | |
|---|---|---|---|---|---|
| ☐ A7-ADK | Airbus A321-231 | 1487 | ex OE-LOS | | |
| ☐ A7-ADS | Airbus A321-231 | 1928 | ex D-AVXA | Al Aaliyah | |
| ☐ A7-ADT | Airbus A321-231 | 2107 | ex D-AVXD | Al Saffiyah | |
| ☐ A7-ADV | Airbus A321-231 | 3274 | ex D-AVZM | | |
| ☐ A7-ADW | Airbus A321-231 | 3369 | ex D-AVZJ | | |
| ☐ A7-ADX | Airbus A321-231 | 3397 | ex D-AVZP | | |
| ☐ A7-ADY | Airbus A321-231 | 3636 | ex D-AVZK | | |
| ☐ A7-ADZ | Airbus A321-231 | 3669 | ex D-AVZY | | |
| ☐ A7-AIA | Airbus A321-231 | 4173 | ex D-AZAB | | |
| ☐ A7-AIB | Airbus A321-231 | 4382 | ex D-AVZY | | |
| ☐ A7-AIC | Airbus A321-231 | 4406 | ex D-AZAD | | |
| ☐ A7-AID | Airbus A321-231 | 4530 | ex D-AVZJ | | ♦ |
| | | | | | |
| ☐ A7-ACA | Airbus A330-202 | 473 | ex F-WWKR | Al Wajbah | |
| ☐ A7-ACB | Airbus A330-202 | 489 | ex F-WWYN | Al Majida | |
| ☐ A7-ACC | Airbus A330-202 | 511 | ex F-WWKR | Al Shahaniya | |
| ☐ A7-ACD | Airbus A330-202 | 521 | ex F-WWKU | Al Wuseil | |
| ☐ A7-ACE | Airbus A330-202 | 571 | ex F-WWKF | Al Dhakira | |
| ☐ A7-ACF | Airbus A330-202 | 638 | ex F-WWYQ | Al Kara'anah | |
| ☐ A7-ACG | Airbus A330-202 | 743 | ex F-WWKV | Al Wabra | |
| ☐ A7-ACH | Airbus A330-202 | 441 | ex F-WWYK | Al Mafjar | |
| ☐ A7-ACI | Airbus A330-202 | 746 | ex F-WWKV | Muathier | |
| ☐ A7-ACJ | Airbus A330-202 | 760 | ex F-WWYO | Zikreet | |
| ☐ A7-ACK | Airbus A330-202 | 792 | ex F-WWKP | | |
| ☐ A7-ACL | Airbus A330-202 | 820 | ex F-WWKA | | |
| ☐ A7-ACM | Airbus A330-202 | 849 | ex F-WWKP | | |
| ☐ A7-AFL | Airbus A330-202 | 612 | ex F-WWKZ | Al Messila | |
| ☐ A7-AFM | Airbus A330-202 | 616 | ex F-WWKT | Al-Udaid | |
| ☐ A7-AFP | Airbus A330-202 | 684 | ex F-WWYG | Al Shamal | |
| | | | | | |
| ☐ A7-AEA | Airbus A330-302 | 623 | ex F-WWYC | Al Muntazah | |
| ☐ A7-AEB | Airbus A330-302 | 637 | ex F-WWYP | Al Sayliyah | |
| ☐ A7-AEC | Airbus A330-302 | 659 | ex F-WWYX | Al Markhiya | |
| ☐ A7-AED | Airbus A330-302 | 680 | ex F-WWYD | Al Nu'uman | |
| ☐ A7-AEE | Airbus A330-302 | 711 | ex F-WWYK | Semaisma | |
| ☐ A7-AEF | Airbus A330-302 | 721 | ex F-WWKJ | Al Rumellah | |
| ☐ A7-AEG | Airbus A330-302 | 734 | ex F-WWYU | Al Duhell | |
| ☐ A7-AEH | Airbus A330-302 | 789 | ex F-WWKN | | |
| ☐ A7-AEI | Airbus A330-302 | 813 | ex F-WWYI | | |
| ☐ A7-AEJ | Airbus A330-302 | 826 | ex F-WWKF | | |
| ☐ A7-AEM | Airbus A330-302 | 893 | ex F-WWYK | | |
| ☐ A7-AEN | Airbus A330-302 | 907 | ex F-WWYE | | |
| ☐ A7-AEO | Airbus A330-302 | 918 | ex F-WWYQ | | |
| | | | | | |
| ☐ A7-BBA | Boeing 777-2DZLR | 36012/753 | ex N1788B | Alhuwaila | |
| ☐ A7-BBB | Boeing 777-2DZLR | 36013/762 | ex N50281 | Gaza | |
| ☐ A7-BBC | Boeing 777-2DZLR | 36015/825 | ex N5023Q | | |
| ☐ A7-BBD | Boeing 777-2DZLR | 36016/831 | ex N5573S | | |
| ☐ A7-BBE | Boeing 777-2DZLR | 36017/837 | | | |
| ☐ A7-BBF | Boeing 777-2DZLR | 36018/842 | | | |
| ☐ A7-BBG | Boeing 777-2DZLR | 36101/883 | | | |
| ☐ A7-BBH | Boeing 777-2DZLR | 36102/885 | | | |
| ☐ A7-BBI | Boeing 777-2DZLR | 41061/962 | | Jaow Alsalam | ♦ |
| | | | | | |
| ☐ A7-BAA | Boeing 777-3DZER | 36009/676 | | | |
| ☐ A7-BAB | Boeing 777-3DZER | 36103/686 | | Um-Alamad | |
| ☐ A7-BAC | Boeing 777-3DZER | 36010/731 | ex N5016R | | |
| ☐ A7-BAE | Boeing 777-3DZER | 36104/769 | | Almas-Habia | |
| ☐ A7-BAF | Boeing 777-3DZER | 37661/815 | | | |
| ☐ A7-BAG | Boeing 777-3DZER | 36014/819 | ex N5017Q | Littoriya | |
| ☐ A7-BAH | Boeing 777-3DZER | 37662/849 | | | |
| ☐ A7-BAI | Boeing 777-3DZER | 36095/742 | ex N5028Y | | |
| ☐ A7-BAJ | Boeing 777-3DZER | 36096/851 | | | |
| ☐ A7-BAK | Boeing 777-3DZER | 36097/859 | | | |
| ☐ A7-BAL | Boeing 777-3DZER | 38244/893 | ex N52081 | | |
| ☐ A7-BAM | Boeing 777-3DZER | 38245/922 | | | |
| ☐ A7-BAN | Boeing 777-3DZER | 38246/925 | | | |
| ☐ A7-BAO | Boeing 777-3DZER | 36011/750 | | | |
| ☐ A7-BAP | Boeing 777-3DZER | 38248/958 | | Al Qattard | |
| ☐ A7-BAQ | Boeing 777-3DZER | 38247/910 | | | |
| ☐ A7-BAS | Boeing 777-3DZER | 41062/997 | | Bu Funtas | ♦ |
| ☐ A7-BAX | Boeing 777-3DZER | 41780 | | | o/o♦ |
| | | | | | |
| ☐ A7-BFA | Boeing 777-FDZ | 36098/865 | | | |
| ☐ A7-BFB | Boeing 777-FDZ | 36100/874 | | | |
| ☐ A7-BFC | Boeing 777-FDZ | 36099/970 | | Lbeshairiya | ♦ |
| ☐ A7-BFD | Boeing 777-FDZ | 41427/1004 | | | ♦ |
| ☐ A7-BFF | Boeing 777-FDZ | 39644 | | | o/o♦ |
| | | | | | |
| ☐ A7-ABX | Airbus A300B4-622RF | 554 | ex HL7537 | Al Dawha | |
| ☐ A7-ABY | Airbus A300B4-622RF | 560 | ex HL7294 | Fuwairit | |
| ☐ A7-AFB | Airbus A300B4-622RF | 614 | ex HL7298 | Al'ArishCargo titles | |

| ☐ A7-AGA | Airbus A340-642HGW | 740 | ex F-WWCP | | |
| ☐ A7-AGB | Airbus A340-642HGW | 715 | ex F-WWCR | Ras Dukhan | |
| ☐ A7-AGC | Airbus A340-642HGW | 766 | ex F-WWCM | Ras Ushainij | |
| ☐ A7-AGD | Airbus A340-642HGW | 798 | ex F-WWCL | | |
| ☐ A7-CJA | Airbus A319-133LR | 1656 | ex D-AVYT | Al Hilal | |
| ☐ A7-CJB | Airbus A319-133LR | 2341 | ex D-AVWK | Al Jasra | |
| ☐ A7- | Boeing 787-8 | | | | o/o |
| ☐ A7- | Boeing 787-8 | | | | o/o |
| ☐ A7- | Boeing 787-8 | | | | o/o |
| ☐ A7- | Boeing 787-8 | | | | o/o |

## A9C-  BAHRAIN (State of Bahrain)

### BAHRAIN AIR                                            (2B/BAB)                                            Bahrain (BAH)

| ☐ A9C-BAO | Airbus A320-214 | 4600 | ex D-AXAQ | ♦ |
| ☐ A9C-BAU | Airbus A320-214 | 4055 | ex F-WWBB | |
| ☐ A9C-BAV | Airbus A320-214 | 3861 | ex F-WWDP | |
| ☐ A9C-BAW | Airbus A319-111 | 2763 | ex N946FR | |
| ☐ A9C-BAX | Airbus A319-111 | 2700 | ex N944FR | |

### DHL INTERNATIONAL AVIATION          Dilmun (ES/DHX)                              Bahrain (BAH)

| ☐ HZ-SNA | Boeing 727-264F (FedEx 3) | 20896/1051 | ex A9C-SNA | all-white | Joint ops with RSE |
| ☐ HZ-SNB | Boeing 727-223F (FedEx 3) | 21084/1199 | ex EC-HAH | all-white | Joint ops with RSE |
| ☐ HZ-SNC | Boeing 727-230F (FedEx 3) | 20905/1091 | ex EC-IVF | | Joint ops with RSE |
| ☐ HZ-SND | Boeing 727-223F (FedEx 3) | 20994/1190 | ex EC-IVE | all-white | Joint ops with RSE |
| ☐ HZ-SNF | Boeing 727-277F (FedEx 3) | 22643/1762 | ex ZS-DPE | | Joint ops with RSE |
| | | | | | |
| ☐ A9C-DHB | Swearingen SA.227AT Merlin IVC | AT-434 | ex HZ-SN8 | SNAS c/s | Frtr |
| ☐ A9C-DHC | Boeing 757-225SF | 22211/74 | ex N314ST | | ♦ |
| ☐ A9C-DHD | Boeing 757-225SF | 22611/75 | ex PP-BIY | | ♦ |

### GULF AIR                                Gulf Air (GF/GFA)                              Bahrain (BAH)

| ☐ A9C-CA | Airbus A321-231 | 5025 | ex D-AZAL | ♦ |
| ☐ A9C-CB | Airbus A321-231 | 5074 | ex D-AVZN | ♦ |
| ☐ A9C-CC | Airbus A321-231 | 5180 | ex D-AVZK | o/o♦ |
| ☐ A9C-CE | Airbus A321-231 | 5321 | ex D-A | o/o♦ |
| ☐ A9C- | Airbus A321-231 | 5025 | ex D-AZAL | o/o♦ |
| | | | | |
| ☐ A9C-AA | Airbus A320-214 | 3706 | ex F-WJKJ | |
| ☐ A9C-AB | Airbus A320-214 | 4030 | ex F-WWIB | |
| ☐ A9C-AC | Airbus A320-214 | 4059 | ex F-WWBD | |
| ☐ A9C-AD | Airbus A320-214 | 4083 | ex F-WWBT | |
| ☐ A9C-AE | Airbus A320-214 | 4146 | ex D-AVVG | |
| ☐ A9C-AF | Airbus A320-214 | 4158 | ex F-WWBQ | |
| ☐ A9C-AG | Airbus A320-214 | 4188 | ex F-WWIG | |
| ☐ A9C-AH | Airbus A320-214 | 4218 | ex F-WWBH | |
| ☐ A9C-AI | Airbus A320-214 | 4255 | ex F-WWIO | |
| ☐ A9C-AJ | Airbus A320-214 | 4502 | ex F-WWIU | |
| ☐ A9C-AK | Airbus A320-214 | 4541 | ex D-AXAM | |
| ☐ A9C-AL | Airbus A320-214 | 4780 | ex F-WWDP | |
| ☐ A9C-AM | Airbus A320-214 | 4827 | ex D-AXAL | ♦ |
| ☐ A9C-AN | Airbus A320-214 | 4865 | ex D-AUBP | ♦ |
| ☐ A9C-AO | Airbus A320-214 | 4860 | ex F-WWDF | ♦ |
| | | | | |
| ☐ A9C-KA | Airbus A330-243 | 276 | ex A4O-KA | 501 | |
| ☐ A9C-KB | Airbus A330-243 | 281 | ex A4O-KB | 502 | |
| ☐ A9C-KC | Airbus A330-243 | 286 | ex A4O-KC | 503 | |
| ☐ A9C-KD | Airbus A330-243 | 287 | ex A4O-KD | 504 | |
| ☐ A9C-KE | Airbus A330-243 | 334 | ex A4O-KE | 505 | |
| ☐ A9C-KF | Airbus A330-243 | 340 | ex A4O-KF | 506 Aldafra | |
| ☐ A9C-KG | Airbus A330-243 | 527 | ex F-OMEA | | |
| ☐ A9C-KH | Airbus A330-243 | 529 | ex F-OMEB | | |
| ☐ A9C-KI | Airbus A330-243 | 532 | ex F-OMEC | | |
| ☐ A9C-KJ | Airbus A330-243 | 992 | ex F-WWKN | | |
| | | | | | |
| ☐ A9C-EU | Airbus A319-112 | 1884 | ex C-GTDT | | |
| ☐ A9C-EV | Airbus A319-112 | 1901 | ex C-GTDS | | |
| ☐ A9C-LG | Airbus A340-313X | 212 | ex A4O-LG | 407 | |
| ☐ A9C-LH | Airbus A340-313X | 215 | ex A4O-LH | 408 | |
| ☐ A9C-LI | Airbus A340-313X | 554 | ex A4O-LI | 409 | |
| ☐ A9C-LJ | Airbus A340-313X | 282 | ex A4O-LL | 410 | |
| ☐ A9C-MA | Embraer ERJ170LR | 17000278 | ex PT-TQE | | |
| ☐ A9C-MB | Embraer ERJ170LR | 17000293 | ex PT-TQT | | |
| ☐ A9C-MC | Embraer ERJ-190AR | 19000372 | ex PT-XNJ | | |
| ☐ A9C-MD | Embraer ERJ-190AR | 19000373 | ex PT-XNK | | |

| | | | | |
|---|---|---|---|---|
| **MENA AEROSPACE CARGO** | | **(MEN)** | | |
| ☐ A9C-JNC | Boeing 737-3G7F | 24710/1825 | ex N308AW | ♦ |
| ☐ A9C-JWC | Boeing 737-3G7F | 24711/1843 | ex A6-HLH | ♦ |

## B- CHINA (People's Republic Of China)

| | | | |
|---|---|---|---|
| **AIR CHINA** | **Air China (CA/CCA)** | | **Beijing-Capital (PEK)** |

Member of Star Alliance

| | | | | | |
|---|---|---|---|---|---|
| ☐ B-2223 | Airbus A319-111 | 1679 | ex D-AVWI | | |
| ☐ B-2225 | Airbus A319-111 | 1654 | ex D-AVYS | | |
| ☐ B-2339 | Airbus A319-111 | 1753 | ex D-AVYJ | | |
| ☐ B-2364 | Airbus A319-115 | 2499 | ex D-AVWB | | |
| ☐ B-2404 | Airbus A319-131 | 2454 | ex D-AVWE | | |
| ☐ B-6004 | Airbus A319-115 | 2508 | ex D-AVWO | | |
| ☐ B-6014 | Airbus A319-115 | 2525 | ex D-AVWE | | |
| ☐ B-6022 | Airbus A319-131 | 2000 | ex D-AVYZ | | |
| ☐ B-6023 | Airbus A319-131 | 2007 | ex D-AVWM | | |
| ☐ B-6024 | Airbus A319-131 | 2015 | ex D-AVWT | | |
| ☐ B-6031 | Airbus A319-131 | 2172 | ex D-AVWW | | |
| ☐ B-6032 | Airbus A319-131 | 2202 | ex D-AVYF | | |
| ☐ B-6033 | Airbus A319-131 | 2205 | ex D-AVYJ | | |
| ☐ B-6034 | Airbus A319-115 | 2237 | ex D-AVWL | | |
| ☐ B-6035 | Airbus A319-115 | 2269 | ex D-AVWX | | |
| ☐ B-6036 | Airbus A319-115 | 2285 | ex D-AVYS | | |
| ☐ B-6037 | Airbus A319-115 | 2293 | ex D-AVYY | | |
| ☐ B-6038 | Airbus A319-115 | 2298 | ex D-AVWF | | |
| ☐ B-6044 | Airbus A319-115 | 2532 | ex D-AVWL | | |
| ☐ B-6046 | Airbus A319-115 | 2545 | ex D-AVWW | | |
| ☐ B-6047 | Airbus A319-115 | 2551 | ex D-AVYJ | | |
| ☐ B-6048 | Airbus A319-131 | 2559 | ex D-AVYU | | |
| ☐ B-6213 | Airbus A319-131 | 2614 | ex D-AVXS | | |
| ☐ B-6216 | Airbus A319-131 | 2643 | ex D-AVWO | | |
| ☐ B-6223 | Airbus A319-115 | 2805 | ex D-AVWV | | |
| ☐ B-6225 | Airbus A319-115 | 2819 | ex D-AVXB | | |
| ☐ B-6226 | Airbus A319-115 | 2839 | ex D-AVYI | | |
| ☐ B-6227 | Airbus A319-115 | 2847 | ex D-AVXG | | |
| ☐ B-6228 | Airbus A319-115 | 2890 | ex D-AVYI | | |
| ☐ B-6235 | Airbus A319-131 | 3195 | ex D-AVWC | | |
| ☐ B-6236 | Airbus A319-131 | 3200 | ex D-AVWG | | |
| ☐ B-6237 | Airbus A319-131 | 3226 | ex D-AVYJ | | |
| ☐ B-6238 | Airbus A319-115 | 3250 | ex D-AVWO | | |
| ☐ B-2210 | Airbus A320-214 | 1296 | ex F-WWBG | | |
| ☐ B-2376 | Airbus A320-214 | 0876 | ex F-WWIF | | |
| ☐ B-2377 | Airbus A320-214 | 0921 | ex F-WWDY | | |
| ☐ B-6606 | Airbus A320-214 | 3337 | ex B-6350 | | |
| ☐ B-6607 | Airbus A320-214 | 3461 | ex B-6390 | | |
| ☐ B-6608 | Airbus A320-214 | 3601 | ex B-6393 | | |
| ☐ B-6609 | Airbus A320-214 | 3215 | ex B-6336 | | |
| ☐ B-6610 | Airbus A320-214 | 3221 | ex B-6337 | | ♦ |
| ☐ B-6611 | Airbus A320-214 | 3506 | ex B-6391 | | ♦ |
| ☐ B-6767 | Airbus A320-214 | 4803 | ex D-AVVW | | ♦ |
| ☐ B-6793 | Airbus A320-214 | 4829 | ex F-WWIM | | ♦ |
| ☐ B-6822 | Airbus A320-214 | 4900 | ex D-AVVI | | ♦ |
| ☐ B-6828 | Airbus A320-214 | 4963 | ex F-WWDP | | ♦ |
| ☐ B-6846 | Airbus A320-214 | 4985 | ex F-WWIL | | ♦ |
| ☐ B-6847 | Airbus A320-214 | 4895 | ex B- | | ♦ |
| ☐ B-6882 | Airbus A320-214 | 4997 | ex B- | o/o♦ | |
| ☐ B-6676 | Airbus A320-232 | 4317 | ex F-WWBR | | |
| ☐ B-6677 | Airbus A320-232 | 4348 | ex F-WWBU | | |
| ☐ B-6731 | Airbus A320-232 | 4473 | ex B- | | ♦ |
| ☐ B-6733 | Airbus A320-232 | 4566 | ex B- | | ♦ |
| ☐ B-6745 | Airbus A320-232 | 4593 | ex B- | | ♦ |
| ☐ B-6773 | Airbus A320-232 | 4775 | ex F-WWDJ | | ♦ |
| ☐ B-6823 | Airbus A320-232 | 4873 | ex D-AVZA | | ♦ |
| ☐ B-6326 | Airbus A321-213 | 3329 | ex D-AVZX | | |
| ☐ B-6327 | Airbus A321-213 | 3307 | ex D-AVZT | | |
| ☐ B-6361 | Airbus A321-213 | 3523 | ex D-AVZX | Beautiful Sichuan c/s | |
| ☐ B-6362 | Airbus A321-213 | 3623 | ex D-AVZG | | |
| ☐ B-6363 | Airbus A321-213 | 3653 | ex D-AVZV | | |
| ☐ B-6365 | Airbus A321-213 | 3655 | ex D-AVZW | | |
| ☐ B-6382 | Airbus A321-213 | 3665 | ex D-AVZX | | |
| ☐ B-6383 | Airbus A321-213 | 3678 | ex D-AZAE | | |
| ☐ B-6385 | Airbus A321-213 | 3722 | ex D-AZAH | | |
| ☐ B-6386 | Airbus A321-213 | 3725 | ex D-AZVS | | |

| | | | | | |
|---|---|---|---|---|---|
| ☐ B-6555 | Airbus A321-213 | 3766 | ex D-AZAO | | |
| ☐ B-6556 | Airbus A321-213 | 3806 | ex D-AVZD | | |
| ☐ B-6593 | Airbus A321-213 | 3973 | ex D-AVZS | | |
| ☐ B-6595 | Airbus A321-213 | 4022 | ex D-AVZG | | |
| ☐ B-6596 | Airbus A321-213 | 4031 | ex D-AVZI | | |
| ☐ B-6597 | Airbus A321-213 | 4062 | ex D-AVZO | | |
| ☐ B-6599 | Airbus A321-213 | 3940 | ex D-AZAI | | |
| ☐ B-6603 | Airbus A321-213 | 4131 | ex D-AZAJ | | |
| ☐ B-6605 | Airbus A321-213 | 4091 | ex D-AVZX | | |
| ☐ B-6631 | Airbus A321-213 | 4180 | ex D-AZAM | | |
| ☐ B-6632 | Airbus A321-213 | 4221 | ex D-AVZJ | | |
| ☐ B-6633 | Airbus A321-213 | 4283 | ex D-AZAQ | | |
| ☐ B-6665 | Airbus A321-213 | 4318 | ex D-AVZW | | ♦ |
| ☐ B-6675 | Airbus A321-213 | 4377 | ex D-AZAA | | ♦ |
| ☐ B-6701 | Airbus A321-213 | 4472 | ex D-AVZE | | |
| ☐ B-6711 | Airbus A321-213 | 4494 | ex D-AVZF | | |
| ☐ B-6712 | Airbus A321-213 | 4494 | ex D-AVZF | | ♦ |
| ☐ B-6741 | Airbus A321-232 | 4617 | ex D-AZAN | | ♦ |
| ☐ B-6742 | Airbus A321-213 | 4719 | ex D-AVZE | | ♦ |
| ☐ B-6791 | Airbus A321-232 | 4771 | ex D-AVZK | | ♦ |
| ☐ B-6792 | Airbus A321-232 | 4834 | ex D-AVZK | | ♦ |
| ☐ B-6823 | Airbus A321-232 | 4873 | ex D-AVZU | | ♦ |
| ☐ B-6825 | Airbus A321-232 | 4949 | ex D-AZAD | | ♦ |
| ☐ B-6848 | Airbus A321-232 | 5054 | ex D-AZAR | | ♦ |
| ☐ B-6883 | Airbus A321-232 | 5124 | ex D-AVZA | | o/o♦ |
| | | | | | |
| ☐ B-6070 | Airbus A330-243 | 750 | ex F-WWKA | | |
| ☐ B-6071 | Airbus A330-243 | 756 | ex F-WWYQ | | |
| ☐ B-6072 | Airbus A330-243 | 759 | ex F-WWYK | | |
| ☐ B-6073 | Airbus A330-243 | 780 | ex F-WWKY | | |
| ☐ B-6075 | Airbus A330-243 | 785 | ex F-WWYY | | |
| ☐ B-6076 | Airbus A330-243 | 797 | ex F-WWKU | | |
| ☐ B-6079 | Airbus A330-243 | 810 | ex F-WWYF | | |
| ☐ B-6080 | Airbus A330-243 | 815 | ex F-WWYL | | |
| ☐ B-6081 | Airbus A330-243 | 839 | ex F-WWYO | | |
| ☐ B-6090 | Airbus A330-243 | 860 | ex F-WWYN | | |
| ☐ B-6091 | Airbus A330-243 | 867 | ex F-WWYP | Star Alliance colours | |
| ☐ B-6092 | Airbus A330-243 | 873 | ex F-WWKV | | |
| ☐ B-6093 | Airbus A330-243 | 884 | ex F-WWKO | Star Alliance colours | |
| ☐ B-6113 | Airbus A330-243 | 890 | ex F-WWYM | | |
| ☐ B-6115 | Airbus A330-243 | 909 | ex F-WWYG | | |
| ☐ B-6117 | Airbus A330-243 | 903 | ex F-WWKR | | |
| ☐ B-6130 | Airbus A330-243 | 930 | ex F-WWKS | | |
| ☐ B-6131 | Airbus A330-243 | 941 | ex F-WWKO | | |
| ☐ B-6132 | Airbus A330-243 | 944 | ex F-WWYT | | |
| ☐ B-6505 | Airbus A330-243 | 957 | ex F-WWYC | | |
| ☐ B-6533 | Airbus A330-243 | 1237 | ex F-WWKG | | ♦ |
| ☐ B-6536 | Airbus A330-243 | 1260 | ex F-WWYY | | ♦ |
| ☐ B-6540 | Airbus A330-243 | 1282 | ex F-WWKS | | ♦ |
| ☐ B-6541 | Airbus A330-243 | 1304 | ex F-WWYT | | o/o♦ |
| | | | | | |
| ☐ B-6511 | Airbus A330-343 | 1110 | ex F-WWYG | | ♦ |
| ☐ B-6512 | Airbus A330-343 | 1087 | ex F-WWKD | | |
| ☐ B-6513 | Airbus A330-343 | 1130 | ex F-WWKN | | |
| ☐ B-6523 | Airbus A330-343 | 1187 | ex F-WWYP | | |
| ☐ B-6525 | Airbus A330-343 | 1199 | ex F-WWYU | | |
| ☐ B-6530 | Airbus A330-343 | 1216 | ex F-WWKP | | |
| | | | | | |
| ☐ B-2385 | Airbus A340-313X | 192 | ex B-HMX | | |
| ☐ B-2386 | Airbus A340-313X | 199 | ex B-HMY | | |
| ☐ B-2387 | Airbus A340-313X | 201 | ex B-HMZ | | |
| ☐ B-2388 | Airbus A340-313X | 242 | ex F-WWJD | | |
| ☐ B-2389 | Airbus A340-313X | 243 | ex F-WWJE | | |
| ☐ B-2390 | Airbus A340-313X | 264 | ex F-WWJY | | |
| | | | | | |
| ☐ B-2530 | Boeing 737-3Z0 | 27046/2252 | | | |
| ☐ B-2533 | Boeing 737-3Z0 | 27138/2436 | | | |
| ☐ B-2535 | Boeing 737-3J6 | 25078/2002 | | | |
| ☐ B-2580 | Boeing 737-3J6 | 25080/2254 | | | |
| ☐ B-2581 | Boeing 737-3J6 | 25081/2263 | | | |
| ☐ B-2584 | Boeing 737-3J6 | 25891/2385 | | | |
| ☐ B-2586 | Boeing 737-3Z0 | 27047/2357 | | | |
| ☐ B-2587 | Boeing 737-3J6 | 25892/2396 | | | |
| ☐ B-2588 | Boeing 737-3J6 | 25893/2489 | | | |
| ☐ B-2590 | Boeing 737-3Z0 | 27126/2370 | | | |
| ☐ B-2597 | Boeing 737-3Z0 | 27176/2495 | | | |
| ☐ B-2599 | Boeing 737-3Z0 | 25896/2558 | | | |
| ☐ B-2627 | Boeing 737-36E | 26315/2706 | ex N141LF | | |
| ☐ B-2630 | Boeing 737-36E | 26317/2719 | ex N151LF | | |
| ☐ B-2947 | Boeing 737-33A | 25511/2599 | | | |
| ☐ B-2948 | Boeing 737-3J6 | 27361/2631 | | | |
| ☐ B-2949 | Boeing 737-3J6 | 27372/2650 | | | [TSN] |

| ☐ B-2953 | Boeing 737-3J6 | 27523/2710 | |
| ☐ B-2954 | Boeing 737-3J6 | 27518/2768 | |
| ☐ B-5035 | Boeing 737-36N | 28672/2976 | ex F-GRFA |
| ☐ B-5036 | Boeing 737-36N | 28673/2995 | ex F-GRFB |
| | | | |
| ☐ B-2612 | Boeing 737-79L | 33411/1538 | |
| ☐ B-2613 | Boeing 737-79L | 33412/1544 | ex N1786B |
| ☐ B-2700 | Boeing 737-79L | 33413/1560 | |
| ☐ B-5043 | Boeing 737-79L | 33408/1331 | |
| ☐ B-5044 | Boeing 737-79L | 33409/1351 | |
| ☐ B-5045 | Boeing 737-79L | 33410/1354 | |
| ☐ B-5201 | Boeing 737-79L/W | 34023/1795 | ex N1786B |
| ☐ B-5202 | Boeing 737-79L/W | 34537/1837 | ex N1786B |
| ☐ B-5203 | Boeing 737-79L/W | 34538/1853 | |
| ☐ B-5211 | Boeing 737-79L | 34019/1749 | |
| ☐ B-5213 | Boeing 737-79L/W | 34020/1769 | ex N1786B |
| ☐ B-5214 | Boeing 737-79L/W | 34021/1774 | |
| ☐ B-5217 | Boeing 737-79L/W | 34022/1786 | |
| ☐ B-5220 | Boeing 737-79L/W | 34539/1856 | ex (B-5204) |
| ☐ B-5226 | Boeing 737-79L/W | 34540/1877 | ex N1787B |
| ☐ B-5227 | Boeing 737-79L/W | 34541/1937 | |
| ☐ B-5228 | Boeing 737-79L/W | 34542/1993 | |
| ☐ B-5229 | Boeing 737-79L/W | 34543/2006 | |
| | | | |
| ☐ B-2161 | Boeing 737-86N | 28655/965 | ex N1786B |
| ☐ B-2509 | Boeing 737-8Z0 | 30072/466 | ex N1787B |
| ☐ B-2510 | Boeing 737-8Z0 | 30071/381 | ex N1786B |
| ☐ B-2511 | Boeing 737-8Z0 | 30073/487 | ex N1786B |
| ☐ B-2641 | Boeing 737-89L | 29876/337 | |
| ☐ B-2642 | Boeing 737-89L | 29877/359 | |
| ☐ B-2643 | Boeing 737-89L | 29878/379 | ex N1786B |
| ☐ B-2645 | Boeing 737-89L | 29879/427 | ex N1786B |
| ☐ B-2648 | Boeing 737-89L | 29880/511 | ex N1786B |
| ☐ B-2649 | Boeing 737-89L | 30159/572 | ex N1784B |
| ☐ B-2650 | Boeing 737-89L | 30160/594 | |
| ☐ B-2657 | Boeing 737-89L | 30517/1224 | |
| ☐ B-2670 | Boeing 737-89L | 30514/1055 | |
| ☐ B-2671 | Boeing 737-89L | 30515/1165 | |
| ☐ B-2672 | Boeing 737-89L | 30516/1168 | |
| ☐ B-2673 | Boeing 737-86N | 29888/1133 | ex N1786B |
| ☐ B-2690 | Boeing 737-86N | 29889/1153 | |
| ☐ B-5167 | Boeing 737-808 | 34701/1887 | ex N1787B |
| ☐ B-5168 | Boeing 737-808 | 34702/1917 | |
| ☐ B-5169 | Boeing 737-808 | 34703/1941 | ex N1795B |
| ☐ B-5170 | Boeing 737-808 | 34705/1998 | |
| ☐ B-5171 | Boeing 737-808 | 34706/2014 | ex N1786B |
| ☐ B-5172 | Boeing 737-8Q8 | 30704/1985 | |
| ☐ B-5173 | Boeing 737-8Q8 | 30705/2001 | |
| ☐ B-5175 | Boeing 737-86N | 35209/2067 | |
| ☐ B-5176 | Boeing 737-86N | 34258/2096 | special c/s |
| ☐ B-5177 | Boeing 737-86N | 35210/2127 | special c/s |
| ☐ B-5178 | Boeing 737-86N | 32682/2117 | ex N1787B  special c/s |
| ☐ B-5179 | Boeing 737-86N | 35211/2146 | |
| ☐ B-5197 | Boeing 737-86N/W | 36811/2777 | |
| ☐ B-5198 | Boeing 737-89L/W | 36491/2759 | |
| ☐ B-5311 | Boeing 737-8Q8 | 29373/2171 | |
| ☐ B-5312 | Boeing 737-8Q8 | 29374/2203 | ex N1786B |
| ☐ B-5313 | Boeing 737-8Q8 | 30716/2210 | ex N1786B |
| ☐ B-5325 | Boeing 737-86N | 32692/2275 | ex N1786B |
| ☐ B-5326 | Boeing 737-86N | 35214/2308 | |
| ☐ B-5327 | Boeing 737-86N | 35219/2371 | ex N1779B |
| ☐ B-5328 | Boeing 737-86N | 35221/2444 | ex N1786B |
| ☐ B-5329 | Boeing 737-86N | 35222/2463 | |
| ☐ B-5341 | Boeing 737-89L/W | 36483/2403 | ex N1786B |
| ☐ B-5342 | Boeing 737-89L/W | 36484/2441 | ex N1786B |
| ☐ B-5343 | Boeing 737-89L/W | 36485/2470 | |
| ☐ B-5387 | Boeing 737-89L/W | 36492/2828 | |
| ☐ B-5390 | Boeing 737-89L/W | 36486/2606 | |
| ☐ B-5391 | Boeing 737-89L/W | 36487/2664 | |
| ☐ B-5392 | Boeing 737-89L/W | 36488/2674 | |
| ☐ B-5397 | Boeing 737-89L/W | 36489/2704 | ex N1787B |
| ☐ B-5398 | Boeing 737-89L/W | 36490/2715 | |
| ☐ B-5422 | Boeing 737-89L/W | 36741/2845 | ex N1787B |
| ☐ B-5423 | Boeing 737-89L/W | 36742/2877 | |
| ☐ B-5425 | Boeing 737-89L/W | 36743/2896 | |
| ☐ B-5426 | Boeing 737-89L/W | 36744/2969 | |
| ☐ B-5431 | Boeing 737-86N | 36812/2918 | ex N1787B |
| ☐ B-5436 | Boeing 737-86N | 36813/2976 | |
| ☐ B-5437 | Boeing 737-86N/W | 36815/3020 | |
| ☐ B-5438 | Boeing 737-86N/W | 36816/3032 | |
| ☐ B-5442 | Boeing 737-86N/W | 36745/3049 | |
| ☐ B-5443 | Boeing 737-86N/W | 36746/3072 | ex N1786B |

| | | | | |
|---|---|---|---|---|
| ☐ B-5447 | Boeing 737-89L/W | 40015/3509 | | |
| ☐ B-5477 | Boeing 737-89L/W | 36755/3387 | | |
| ☐ B-5485 | Boeing 737-89L/W | 36747/3124 | ex N1796B | |
| ☐ B-5486 | Boeing 737-89L/W | 36748/3127 | ex N1786B | |
| ☐ B-5495 | Boeing 737-89L/W | 36749/3145 | | |
| ☐ B-5496 | Boeing 737-89L/W | 36750/3155 | | |
| ☐ B-5497 | Boeing 737-89L/W | 36751/3167 | | |
| ☐ B-5500 | Boeing 737-89L/W | 36752/3188 | ex N1786B | |
| ☐ B-5507 | Boeing 737-89L/W | 36753/3247 | ex N1796B | |
| ☐ B-5508 | Boeing 737-86N/W | 36545/3275 | | |
| ☐ B-5509 | Boeing 737-86N/W | 36547/3300 | | |
| ☐ B-5510 | Boeing 737-86N/W | 36548/3312 | ex N1795B | |
| ☐ B-5518 | Boeing 737-89L/W | 36754/3336 | ex N1786B | |
| ☐ B-5519 | Boeing 737-86N | 36802/3350 | ex N1787B | |
| ☐ B-5525 | Boeing 737-86N | 37886/3436 | | |
| ☐ B-5570 | Boeing 737-89L/W | 40032/3608 | | |
| ☐ B-5572 | Boeing 737-89L/W | 40027/3670 | | ♦ |
| ☐ B-5582 | Boeing 737-89L/W | 40028/3707 | | ♦ |
| ☐ B-5583 | Boeing 737-89L/W | 40016/3749 | | ♦ |
| ☐ B-5585 | Boeing 737-89L/W | 40029/3756 | | ♦ |
| ☐ B-5621 | Boeing 737-89L/W | 40030/3846 | | ♦ |
| ☐ B-5622 | Boeing 737-89L/W | 40031/3859 | | ♦ |
| ☐ B-5639 | Boeing 737-89L/W | 40033/ | | o/o♦ |
| ☐ B-5642 | Boeing 737-89L/W | 40017/ | | o/o♦ |
| | | | | |
| ☐ B-2443 | Boeing 747-4J6 | 25881/957 | | |
| ☐ B-2445 | Boeing 747-4J6 | 25882/1021 | | |
| ☐ B-2447 | Boeing 747-4J6 | 25883/1054 | | |
| ☐ B-2467 | Boeing 747-4J6M | 28754/1119 | | |
| ☐ B-2468 | Boeing 747-4J6M | 28755/1128 | | |
| ☐ B-2469 | Boeing 747-4J6M | 28756/1175 | | |
| ☐ B-2470 | Boeing 747-4J6M | 29070/1181 | | |
| ☐ B-2471 | Boeing 747-4J6M | 29071/1229 | | |
| ☐ B-2472 | Boeing 747-4J6 | 30158/1243 | | |
| | | | | |
| ☐ B-2820 | Boeing 757-2Z0 | 25885/476 | | |
| ☐ B-2821 | Boeing 757-2Z0 | 25886/480 | | |
| ☐ B-2826 | Boeing 757-2Y0 | 26155/495 | | |
| ☐ B-2836 | Boeing 757-2Z0 | 27258/595 | | |
| ☐ B-2840 | Boeing 757-2Z0 | 27270/622 | | |
| ☐ B-2841 | Boeing 757-2Z0 | 27367/624 | | |
| ☐ B-2844 | Boeing 757-2Z0 | 27511/669 | | |
| ☐ B-2845 | Boeing 757-2Z0 | 27512/674 | | |
| ☐ B-2855 | Boeing 757-2Z0 | 29792/822 | | |
| ☐ B-2856 | Boeing 757-2Z0 | 29793/833 | | |
| | | | | |
| ☐ B-2059 | Boeing 777-2J6 | 29153/168 | | |
| ☐ B-2060 | Boeing 777-2J6 | 29154/173 | | |
| ☐ B-2061 | Boeing 777-2J6 | 29155/179 | | |
| ☐ B-2063 | Boeing 777-2J6 | 29156/214 | | |
| ☐ B-2064 | Boeing 777-2J6 | 29157/240 | | |
| ☐ B-2065 | Boeing 777-2J6 | 29744/280 | | |
| ☐ B-2066 | Boeing 777-2J6 | 29745/290 | | |
| ☐ B-2067 | Boeing 777-2J6 | 29746/338 | | |
| ☐ B-2068 | Boeing 777-2J6 | 29747/344 | | |
| ☐ B-2069 | Boeing 777-2J6 | 29748/349 | | |
| | | | | |
| ☐ B-2031 | Boeing 777-39LER | 38670 | | o/o♦ |
| ☐ B-2032 | Boeing 777-39LER | 38671 | | o/o♦ |
| ☐ B-2033 | Boeing 777-39LER | 38673 | | o/o♦ |
| ☐ B-2035 | Boeing 777-39LER | 38674 | | o/o♦ |
| ☐ B-2085 | Boeing 777-39LER | 38666/943 | | |
| ☐ B-2086 | Boeing 777-39LER | 38667/966 | | ♦ |
| ☐ B-2087 | Boeing 777-3LER | 38672/954 | | ♦ |
| ☐ B-2088 | Boeing 777-3LER | 38668/979 | | ♦ |
| ☐ B-2089 | Boeing 777-39LER | 38675/990 | | ♦ |
| ☐ B-2090 | Boeing 777-39LER | 38669 | | o/o♦ |
| | | | | |
| ☐ B-2499 | Boeing 767-332ER | 30597/797 | ex B-4025 | |
| ☐ B-2559 | Boeing 767-3J6 | 25877/530 | | |
| ☐ B-2560 | Boeing 767-3J6 | 25878/569 | | |

| **AIR CHINA CARGO** | **AirChina Freight (CA/CAO)** | | **Beijing-Capital (PEK)** | |
|---|---|---|---|---|
| ☐ B-2409 | Boeing 747-412 (SF) | 26560/1052 | ex 9V-SFC | |
| ☐ B-2453 | Boeing 747-412BCF | 27134/981 | ex B-KAH | <CPA♦ |
| ☐ B-2455 | Boeing 747-412BCF | 27070/1049 | ex B-HKS | |
| ☐ B-2456 | Boeing 747-4J6BCF | 24346/743 | | |
| ☐ B-2458 | Boeing 747-4J6BCF | 24347/775 | | |
| ☐ B-2457 | Boeing 747-412BCF | 27067/953 | ex B-KAG | |
| ☐ B-2458 | Boeing 747-4J6BCF | 24347/775 | | ♦ |
| ☐ B-2460 | Boeing 747-4J6BCF | 24348/792 | | ♦ |

| | | | | |
|---|---|---|---|---|
| ☐ B-2463 | Boeing 747-412BCF | 26547/921 | ex B-KAF | <CPA♦ |
| ☐ B-2475 | Boeing 747-4FTF | 34239/1367 | | |
| ☐ B-2476 | Boeing 747-4FTF | 34240/1373 | | |
| ☐ B-2477 | Boeing 747-433BCF | 24998/840 | ex N998GP | |
| ☐ B-2478 | Boeing 747-433BCF | 25075/868 | ex N575GP | |
| | | | | |
| ☐ B-2871 | Tupolev Tu-204-120SE | 1450743664030 | | |
| ☐ B-2872 | Tupolev Tu-204-120SE | 145074..64031 | | o/o |
| ☐ B-2872 | Tupolev Tu-204-120SE | 145074..64031 | | o/o |
| ☐ B- | Tupolev Tu-204-120SE | | | o/o |
| ☐ B- | Tupolev Tu-204-120SE | | | o/o |
| | | | | |
| ☐ B-2462 | Boeing 747-2J6F | 24960/814 | | |

## BEIJING CAPITAL AIRLINES · (JD/CBJ) · Beijing-Capital (PEK)

| | | | | |
|---|---|---|---|---|
| ☐ B-6156 | Airbus A319-112 | 2849 | ex D-AVXJ | |
| ☐ B-6157 | Airbus A319-112 | 2891 | ex D-AVYS | |
| ☐ B-6169 | Airbus A319-112 | 2985 | ex D-AVXJ | |
| ☐ B-6177 | Airbus A319-112 | 3285 | ex D-AVYY | |
| ☐ B-6178 | Airbus A319-132 | 3548 | ex D-AVWK | |
| ☐ B-6179 | Airbus A319-132 | 3561 | ex D-AVWR | |
| ☐ B-6180 | Airbus A319-132 | 3578 | ex D-AVYA | |
| ☐ B-6181 | Airbus A319-132 | 3580 | ex D-AVYB | |
| ☐ B-6182 | Airbus A319-132 | 3520 | ex D-AVWA | |
| ☐ B-6192 | Airbus A319-132 | 3768 | ex D-AVXG | |
| ☐ B-6193 | Airbus A319-133 | 3849 | ex D-AVYV | |
| ☐ B-6198 | Airbus A319-112 | 2617 | ex D-AVYI | |
| ☐ B-6199 | Airbus A319-112 | 2644 | ex D-AVWP | |
| ☐ B-6210 | Airbus A319-115 | 2557 | ex D-AVYK | ♦ |
| ☐ B-6211 | Airbus A319-115 | 2561 | ex D-AVYO | ♦ |
| ☐ B-6215 | Airbus A319-112 | 2611 | ex D-AVXR | |
| ☐ B-6221 | Airbus A319-112 | 2746 | ex D-AVYL | |
| ☐ B-6222 | Airbus A319-112 | 2733 | ex D-AVXL | |
| ☐ B-6245 | Airbus A319-133 | 3851 | ex D-AVYW | |
| ☐ B-6400 | Airbus A319-132 | 3638 | ex B-502L | |
| ☐ B-6401 | Airbus A319-132 | 3842 | ex B-510L | |
| ☐ B-6402 | Airbus A319-132 | 3914 | ex B-507L | |
| ☐ B-6403 | Airbus A319-132 | 3958 | ex B-509L | |
| ☐ B-6405 | Airbus A319-132 | 3982 | ex B-511L | |
| ☐ B-6415 | Airbus A319-133 | 4410 | ex B-516L | ♦ |
| ☐ B-6416 | Airbus A319-133 | 4529 | ex D-AVYK | ♦ |
| ☐ B-6417 | Airbus A319-133 | 4522 | ex D-AVYJ | |
| | | | | |
| ☐ B-6709 | Airbus A320-232 | 4412 | ex D-AVVH | |
| ☐ B-6710 | Airbus A320-232 | 4440 | ex F-WWDT | |
| ☐ B-6723 | Airbus A320-232 | 4483 | ex D-AUBE | |
| ☐ B-6725 | Airbus A320-232 | 4471 | ex F-WWBZ | ♦ |
| ☐ B-6726 | Airbus A320-232 | 4505 | ex F-WWBC | |
| ☐ B-6727 | Airbus A320-232 | 4513 | ex F-WWBM | ♦ |
| ☐ B-6746 | Airbus A320-232 | 4580 | ex F-WWIH | ♦ |
| ☐ B-6747 | Airbus A320-232 | 4540 | ex B- | ♦ |
| ☐ B-6748 | Airbus A320-232 | 4602 | ex B- | ♦ |
| ☐ B-6795 | Airbus A320-232 | 4677 | ex B- | ♦ |
| | | | | |
| ☐ B-2113 | Boeing 737-36N | 28602/3118 | ex EI-DRY | |
| ☐ B-3000 | Boeing 737-36Q | 29326/3020 | ex N932HA | |

## CHANG AN AIRLINES · Changan (HU/CGN) · Xi'an (SIA)

| | | | | |
|---|---|---|---|---|
| ☐ B-3444 | AVIC I Y7-100C | 09701 | | |
| ☐ B-3445 | AVIC I Y7-100C | 09705 | | |
| ☐ B-3475 | AVIC I Y7-100C | 06703 | | |
| ☐ B-3707 | AVIC I Y7-100C | 12701 | | |
| ☐ B-3708 | AVIC I Y7-100C | 11705 | | |
| | | | | |
| ☐ B-5115 | Boeing 737-8FH/W | 29640/1649 | | |
| ☐ B-5116 | Boeing 737-8FH/W | 29672/1745 | ex N1786B | |
| ☐ B-5180 | Boeing 737-8FH/W | 35089/2042 | | |
| ☐ B-5181 | Boeing 737-8FH/W | 35090/2073 | | |

## CHENGDU AIRLINES · (EU/UEA) · Chengdu (CTU)

| | | | | |
|---|---|---|---|---|
| ☐ B-2340 | Airbus A320-232 | 0540 | ex F-WWDK | ♦ |
| ☐ B-6728 | Airbus A320-214 | 2696 | ex D-ABDE | ♦ |
| ☐ B-6729 | Airbus A320-214 | 2820 | ex D-ABDF | ♦ |
| ☐ B-6730 | Airbus A320-214 | 2835 | ex D-ABDG | ♦ |
| ☐ B-6850 | Airbus A320-214 | 4347 | ex OE-IBB | ♦ |
| ☐ B-6900 | Airbus A320-214 | 2654 | ex D-ABDC | ♦ |
| ☐ B-6907 | Airbus A320-214 | 5003 | ex OE-LEI | ♦ |

| | | | | |
|---|---|---|---|---|
| ☐ B-6155 | Airbus A319-112 | 0949 | ex N707UW | |
| ☐ B-6163 | Airbus A319-112 | 3024 | ex D-AVXR | |
| ☐ B-6229 | Airbus A319-115 | 2762 | ex B-1136L | |
| ☐ B-6230 | Airbus A319-112 | 2774 | ex D-AVYF | |

## CHINA CARGO AIRLINES — Cargo King (CK/CKK) — Shanghai-Pu Dong Intl (PVG)

| | | | | |
|---|---|---|---|---|
| ☐ B-2425 | Boeing 747-40BERF | 35207/1377 | | |
| ☐ B-2426 | Boeing 747-40BERF | 35208/1392 | | |
| ☐ B-2428 | Boeing 747-412F | 28263/1094 | ex 9V-SFE | ♦ |
| ☐ B-2430 | Boeing 747-412BCF | 27137/990 | ex N137GP | ♦ |
| ☐ B-2433 | Boeing 747-412F | 28027/1256 | ex 9V-SFI | ♦ |
| ☐ B-2076 | Boeing 777-F6N | 37711/846 | ex N5573S | |
| ☐ B-2077 | Boeing 777-F6N | 37713/856 | | |
| ☐ B-2078 | Boeing 777-F6N | 37714/869 | | |
| ☐ B-2079 | Boeing 777-F6N | 37715/876 | | |
| ☐ B-2082 | Boeing 777-F6N | 37716/942 | | |
| ☐ B-2083 | Boeing 777-F6N | 37717/949 | | |
| ☐ B-2177 | McDonnell-Douglas MD-11F | 48544/580 | ex N105EV | |
| ☐ B-2178 | McDonnell-Douglas MD-11F | 48543/572 | ex N7821B | |
| ☐ B-2179 | McDonnell-Douglas MD-11F | 48545/587 | ex N106BV | |
| ☐ B-2306 | Airbus A300B4-605RF | 521 | | |
| ☐ B-2307 | Airbus A300B4-605RF | 525 | | |
| ☐ B-2308 | Airbus A300B4-605RF | 532 | ex F-WWAH | |
| ☐ B- | Tupolev Tu-204-120SE | 145074..64041 | | o/o |

## CHINA EASTERN AIRLINES — China Eastern (MU/CES) — Shanghai-Pu Dong Intl (PVG)

| | | | |
|---|---|---|---|
| ☐ B-2317 | Airbus A300B4-605R | 741 | ex F-WWAY |
| ☐ B-2318 | Airbus A300B4-605R | 707 | ex F-WWAU |
| ☐ B-2319 | Airbus A300B4-605R | 732 | ex F-WWAT |
| ☐ B-2324 | Airbus A300B4-622R | 725 | ex F-WWAR |
| ☐ B-2325 | Airbus A300B4-605R | 746 | ex F-WWAA |
| ☐ B-2326 | Airbus A300B4-605R | 754 | ex F-WWAY |
| ☐ B-2330 | Airbus A300B4-605R | 763 | ex F-WWAH |
| ☐ B-2215 | Airbus A319-112 | 1541 | ex D-AVWI |
| ☐ B-2216 | Airbus A319-112 | 1551 | ex D-AVWN |
| ☐ B-2217 | Airbus A319-112 | 1601 | ex D-AVWX |
| ☐ B-2222 | Airbus A319-112 | 1603 | ex D-AVWY |
| ☐ B-2226 | Airbus A319-112 | 1786 | ex D-AVYP |
| ☐ B-2227 | Airbus A319-112 | 1778 | ex D-AVYE |
| ☐ B-2331 | Airbus A319-112 | 1285 | ex D-AVYT |
| ☐ B-2332 | Airbus A319-112 | 1303 | ex D-AVWN |
| ☐ B-2333 | Airbus A319-112 | 1377 | ex D-AVWE |
| ☐ B-2334 | Airbus A319-112 | 1386 | ex D-AVWC |
| ☐ B-6167 | Airbus A319-115 | 3168 | ex D-AVWB |
| ☐ B-6172 | Airbus A319-115 | 3186 | ex D-AVYG |
| ☐ B-6217 | Airbus A319-115 | 2693 | ex D-AVXC |
| ☐ B-6218 | Airbus A319-115 | 2757 | ex D-AVWH |
| ☐ B-6231 | Airbus A319-115 | 2825 | ex D-AVXD |
| ☐ B-6332 | Airbus A319-115 | 3262 | ex D-AVZB |
| ☐ B-2201 | Airbus A320-214 | 0914 | ex F-WWDV |
| ☐ B-2202 | Airbus A320-214 | 0925 | ex F-WWID |
| ☐ B-2203 | Airbus A320-214 | 1005 | ex F-WWDL |
| ☐ B-2205 | Airbus A320-214 | 0984 | ex F-WWDI |
| ☐ B-2206 | Airbus A320-214 | 0986 | ex F-WWDJ |
| ☐ B-2207 | Airbus A320-214 | 1028 | ex F-WWDG |
| ☐ B-2208 | Airbus A320-214 | 1070 | ex F-WWBH |
| ☐ B-2209 | Airbus A320-214 | 1030 | ex F-WWDU |
| ☐ B-2211 | Airbus A320-214 | 1041 | ex F-WWID |
| ☐ B-2212 | Airbus A320-214 | 1316 | ex F-WWDG |
| ☐ B-2213 | Airbus A320-214 | 1345 | ex F-WWDX |
| ☐ B-2219 | Airbus A320-214 | 1532 | ex F-WWIP |
| ☐ B-2220 | Airbus A320-214 | 1542 | ex F-WWIV |
| ☐ B-2221 | Airbus A320-214 | 1639 | ex F-WWDZ |
| ☐ B-2228 | Airbus A320-214 | 1906 | ex F-WWDK |
| ☐ B-2229 | Airbus A320-214 | 1911 | ex F-WWDT |
| ☐ B-2230 | Airbus A320-214 | 1964 | ex F-WWDR |
| ☐ B-2335 | Airbus A320-214 | 1312 | ex F-WWBZ |
| ☐ B-2336 | Airbus A320-214 | 1330 | ex F-WWDV |
| ☐ B-2337 | Airbus A320-214 | 1357 | ex F-WWBF |
| ☐ B-2338 | Airbus A320-214 | 1361 | ex F-WWBU |
| ☐ B-2356 | Airbus A320-214 | 0665 | ex F-WWBB |
| ☐ B-2357 | Airbus A320-214 | 0754 | ex F-WWIY |
| ☐ B-2358 | Airbus A320-214 | 0838 | ex F-WWBB |
| ☐ B-2359 | Airbus A320-214 | 0854 | ex F-WWBK |
| ☐ B-2362 | Airbus A320-214 | 0828 | ex F-WWIM |

| | | | | |
|---|---|---|---|---|
| ☐ B-2363 | Airbus A320-214 | 0883 | ex F-WWDC | |
| ☐ B-2372 | Airbus A320-214 | 0897 | ex F-WWDK | |
| ☐ B-2375 | Airbus A320-214 | 0909 | ex F-WWDS | |
| ☐ B-2378 | Airbus A320-214 | 0939 | ex F-WWIQ | |
| ☐ B-2379 | Airbus A320-214 | 0967 | ex F-WWBN | |
| ☐ B-2398 | Airbus A320-214 | 1108 | ex F-WWDH | |
| ☐ B-2399 | Airbus A320-214 | 1093 | ex F-WWIZ | |
| ☐ B-2400 | Airbus A320-214 | 1072 | ex F-WWBI | |
| ☐ B-2410 | Airbus A320-214 | 2437 | ex F-WWIX | |
| ☐ B-2411 | Airbus A320-214 | 2451 | ex F-WWDF | |
| ☐ B-2412 | Airbus A320-214 | 2478 | ex F-WWDV | |
| ☐ B-2413 | Airbus A320-214 | 2493 | ex F-WWDZ | |
| ☐ B-2415 | Airbus A320-214 | 2498 | ex F-WWIL | |
| ☐ B-6001 | Airbus A320-214 | 1981 | ex F-WWDL | |
| ☐ B-6002 | Airbus A320-214 | 2022 | ex F-WWDG | |
| ☐ B-6003 | Airbus A320-214 | 2034 | ex F-WWIF | |
| ☐ B-6005 | Airbus A320-214 | 2036 | ex F-WWIZ | |
| ☐ B-6006 | Airbus A320-214 | 2068 | ex F-WWIL | |
| ☐ B-6007 | Airbus A320-214 | 2056 | ex F-WWIR | |
| ☐ B-6008 | Airbus A320-214 | 2049 | ex F-WWII | |
| ☐ B-6009 | Airbus A320-214 | 2219 | ex F-WWDN | |
| ☐ B-6010 | Airbus A320-214 | 2221 | ex F-WWIU | |
| ☐ B-6011 | Airbus A320-214 | 2235 | ex F-WWBY | |
| ☐ B-6012 | Airbus A320-214 | 2239 | ex F-WWDP | |
| ☐ B-6013 | Airbus A320-214 | 2244 | ex F-WWIR | |
| ☐ B-6015 | Airbus A320-214 | 2212 | ex F-WWBF | |
| ☐ B-6016 | Airbus A320-214 | 2155 | ex F-WWDU | |
| ☐ B-6017 | Airbus A320-214 | 2274 | ex F-WWIJ | |
| ☐ B-6028 | Airbus A320-214 | 2171 | ex F-WWDG | |
| ☐ B-6029 | Airbus A320-214 | 2182 | ex F-WWIO | |
| ☐ B-6030 | Airbus A320-214 | 2199 | ex F-WWDX | |
| ☐ B-6259 | Airbus A320-214 | 2562 | ex F-WWIZ | |
| ☐ B-6260 | Airbus A320-214 | 2591 | ex F-WWDT | |
| ☐ B-6261 | Airbus A320-214 | 2606 | ex F-WWBR  Young Pioneers c/s | |
| ☐ B-6262 | Airbus A320-214 | 2627 | ex F-WWDV | |
| ☐ B-6333 | Airbus A320-214 | 3170 | ex F-WWIN | |
| ☐ B-6335 | Airbus A320-214 | 3197 | ex F-WWIX | |
| ☐ B-6346 | Airbus A320-232 | 3481 | ex F-WWDL | |
| ☐ B-6370 | Airbus A320-214 | 3559 | ex F-WWBF | |
| ☐ B-6371 | Airbus A320-214 | 3611 | ex D-AVVF | |
| ☐ B-6756 | Airbus A320-214 | 4659 | ex D-AXAD | ♦ |
| ☐ B-6757 | Airbus A320-214 | 4709 | ex  F-WWBH | ♦ |
| ☐ B-6758 | Airbus A320-214 | 4718 | ex F-WWBX | ♦ |
| ☐ B-6759 | Airbus A320-214 | 4723 | ex F-WWDG | ♦ |
| ☐ B-6760 | Airbus A320-214 | 4627 | ex B- | ♦ |
| ☐ B-6796 | Airbus A320-214 | 4765 | ex F-WWBV | ♦ |
| ☐ B-6797 | Airbus A320-214 | 4685 | ex B-519L | ♦ |
| ☐ B-6798 | Airbus A320-214 | 4702 | ex B-520L | ♦ |
| ☐ B-6799 | Airbus A320-214 | 4711 | ex B-501L | ♦ |
| ☐ B-6801 | Airbus A320-214 | 4722 | ex B-502L | ♦ |
| ☐ B-6802 | Airbus A320-214 | 4729 | ex B- | ♦ |
| ☐ B-6803 | Airbus A320-214 | 4748 | ex B-505L | ♦ |
| ☐ B-6805 | Airbus A320-214 | 4877 | ex F-WWDZ | ♦ |
| ☐ B-6829 | Airbus A320-214 | 4769 | ex B-507L | ♦ |
| ☐ B-6830 | Airbus A320-214 | 4776 | ex B-508L | ♦ |
| ☐ B-6831 | Airbus A320-214 | 4799 | ex B-509L | ♦ |
| ☐ B-6832 | Airbus A320-214 | 4831 | ex B-512L | ♦ |
| ☐ B-6870 | Airbus A320-214 | 4844 | ex B-515L | ♦ |
| ☐ B-6871 | Airbus A320-214 | 4857 | ex B-516L | ♦ |
| ☐ B-6872 | Airbus A320-214 | 4886 | ex B-519L | ♦ |
| ☐ B-6873 | Airbus A320-214 | 4903 | ex B-501L | ♦ |
| ☐ B-6875 | Airbus A320-214 | 5053 | ex F-WWBO | ♦ |
| ☐ B-6876 | Airbus A320-214 | 5135 | ex | o/o♦ |
| ☐ B-6877 | Airbus A320-214 | 5144 | ex | o/o♦ |
| ☐ B-6890 | Airbus A320-214 | 5048 | ex D-AXAO | ♦ |
| ☐ B-6891 | Airbus A320-214 | 5047 | ex F-WWDQ | ♦ |
| ☐ B-6892 | Airbus A320-214 | 5063 | ex F-WWBT | ♦ |
| ☐ B-6893 | Airbus A320-214 | 5136 | ex | o/o♦ |
| | | | | |
| ☐ B-6372 | Airbus A320-232 | 3613 | ex F-WWIH | |
| ☐ B-6373 | Airbus A320-232 | 3650 | ex F-WWDP | |
| ☐ B-6375 | Airbus A320-232 | 3677 | ex F-WWBC | |
| ☐ B-6376 | Airbus A320-232 | 3692 | ex F-WWBF | |
| ☐ B-6399 | Airbus A320-232 | 3716 | ex F-WWBJ | |
| ☐ B-6558 | Airbus A320-232 | 3793 | ex F-WWBH | |
| ☐ B-6559 | Airbus A320-232 | 3904 | ex F-WWIB | |
| ☐ B-6560 | Airbus A320-232 | 3937 | ex F-WWDQ | |
| ☐ B-6585 | Airbus A320-232 | 3965 | ex F-WWIE | |
| ☐ B-6586 | Airbus A320-232 | 3775 | ex B-504L | |
| ☐ B-6587 | Airbus A320-232 | 3797 | ex B-505L | |
| ☐ B-6600 | Airbus A320-232 | 3870 | ex B-506L | |
| ☐ B-6601 | Airbus A320-232 | 4037 | ex F-WWIL | |

| | | | | |
|---|---|---|---|---|
| ☐ B-6616 | Airbus A320-232 | 3929 | ex B-508L | |
| ☐ B-6617 | Airbus A320-232 | 4144 | ex D-AVVC | |
| ☐ B-6635 | Airbus A320-232 | 4027 | ex B-513L | |
| ☐ B-6636 | Airbus A320-232 | 4043 | ex B-514L | |
| ☐ B-6637 | Airbus A320-232 | 4111 | ex B-517L | ♦ |
| ☐ B-6638 | Airbus A320-232 | 4240 | ex F-WWDI | ♦ |
| ☐ B-6639 | Airbus A320-232 | 4252 | ex F-WWIN | |
| ☐ B-6671 | Airbus A320-232 | 4186 | ex B-520L | |
| ☐ B-6672 | Airbus A320-232 | 4220 | ex B-502L | o/o |
| ☐ B-6673 | Airbus A320-232 | 4340 | ex F-WWBF | |
| ☐ B-6693 | Airbus A320-232 | 4239 | ex B-504L | ♦ |
| ☐ B-6695 | Airbus A320-232 | 4297 | ex B-508L | |
| ☐ B-6696 | Airbus A320-232 | 4309 | ex B-509L | ♦ |
| ☐ B-6713 | Airbus A320-232 | 4342 | ex B-511L | ♦ |
| ☐ B-6715 | Airbus A320-232 | 4355 | ex B-512L | |
| ☐ B-6716 | Airbus A320-232 | 4423 | ex B- | ♦ |
| ☐ B-6755 | Airbus A320-231 | 4746 | ex D-AVZG | ♦ |
| | | | | |
| ☐ B-2289 | Airbus A321-211 | 2309 | ex D-AVZD | |
| ☐ B-2290 | Airbus A321-211 | 2315 | ex D-AVZM | |
| ☐ B-2291 | Airbus A321-211 | 2543 | ex D-AVZF | |
| ☐ B-2292 | Airbus A321-211 | 2549 | ex D-AVZI | |
| ☐ B-2419 | Airbus A321-211 | 2882 | ex D-AVZJ | |
| ☐ B-2420 | Airbus A321-211 | 2895 | ex D-AVZA | |
| ☐ B-6329 | Airbus A321-211 | 3233 | ex D-AVZH | |
| ☐ B-6330 | Airbus A321-211 | 3247 | ex D-AVZK | |
| ☐ B-6331 | Airbus A321-211 | 3249 | ex D-AVZO | |
| ☐ B-6332 | Airbus A321-211 | 3262 | ex D-AVZB | |
| ☐ B-6345 | Airbus A321-211 | 3471 | ex D-AVZV | |
| ☐ B-6366 | Airbus A321-211 | 3593 | ex D-AZAB | |
| ☐ B-6367 | Airbus A321-211 | 3612 | ex D-AZAD | |
| ☐ B-6368 | Airbus A321-211 | 3639 | ex D-AVZT | |
| ☐ B-6369 | Airbus A321-211 | 3682 | ex D-AVZB | |
| | | | | |
| ☐ B-6591 | Airbus A321-231 | 3969 | ex D-AVVA | ♦ |
| ☐ B-6592 | Airbus A321-231 | 4045 | ex D-AVZL | ♦ |
| ☐ B-6642 | Airbus A321-231 | 4198 | ex D-AVZE | ♦ |
| ☐ B-6643 | Airbus A321-231 | 4209 | ex D-AVZF | ♦ |
| ☐ B-6668 | Airbus A321-232 | 4374 | ex D-AVZX | ♦ |
| ☐ B-6753 | Airbus A321-231 | 4638 | ex D-AZAT | ♦ |
| ☐ B-6755 | Airbus A321-231 | 4746 | ex D-AVZG | ♦ |
| | | | | |
| ☐ B-6082 | Airbus A330-243 | 821 | ex F-WWKB | |
| ☐ B-6099 | Airbus A330-243 | 916 | ex F-WWYP | |
| ☐ B-6121 | Airbus A330-243 | 728 | ex F-WWKQ | |
| ☐ B-6122 | Airbus A330-243 | 732 | ex F-WWKT | |
| ☐ B-6123 | Airbus A330-243 | 735 | ex F-WWYA | |
| ☐ B-6537 | Airbus A330-243 | 1262 | ex F-WWKT | ♦ |
| ☐ B-6538 | Airbus A330-243 | 1267 | ex F-WWKH | ♦ |
| ☐ B-6543 | Airbus A330-243 | 1280 | ex F-WWKM | ♦ |
| ☐ B-6545 | Airbus A330-243 | 1291 | ex F-WWYB | ♦ |
| ☐ B-6546 | Airbus A330-243 | 1303 | ex F-WWYS | o/o♦ |
| | | | | |
| ☐ B-6083 | Airbus A330-343E | 830 | ex F-WWKK | |
| ☐ B-6085 | Airbus A330-343E | 836 | ex F-WWYK | |
| ☐ B-6095 | Airbus A330-343E | 851 | ex F-WWKR | |
| ☐ B-6096 | Airbus A330-343E | 862 | ex F-WWYG | |
| ☐ B-6097 | Airbus A330-343E | 866 | ex F-WWYL | |
| ☐ B-6100 | Airbus A330-343E | 928 | ex F-WWKJ | |
| ☐ B-6119 | Airbus A330-343 | 713 | ex F-WWYT | |
| ☐ B-6120 | Airbus A330-343 | 720 | ex F-WWYZ | |
| ☐ B-6125 | Airbus A330-343 | 773 | ex F-WWKF | |
| ☐ B-6126 | Airbus A330-343 | 777 | ex F-WWKK | |
| ☐ B-6127 | Airbus A330-343 | 781 | ex F-WWYT | |
| ☐ B-6128 | Airbus A330-343 | 782 | ex F-WWYV | |
| ☐ B-6129 | Airbus A330-343 | 791 | ex F-WWKO | |
| ☐ B-6506 | Airbus A330-343E | 936 | ex F-WWKG | |
| ☐ B-6507 | Airbus A330-343E | 942 | ex F-WWYK | |
| ☐ B- | Airbus A330-343E | 1303 | ex F-WWYS | o/o |
| ☐ B- | Airbus A330-343E | | ex | o/o |
| ☐ B- | Airbus A330-343E | | ex | o/o |
| | | | | |
| ☐ B-2380 | Airbus A340-313X | 129 | ex F-WWJQ | |
| ☐ B-2381 | Airbus A340-313X | 131 | ex F-WWJO | |
| ☐ B-2382 | Airbus A340-313X | 141 | ex F-WWJC | |
| ☐ B-2383 | Airbus A340-313X | 161 | ex F-WWJQ | |
| ☐ B-2384 | Airbus A340-313X | 182 | ex F-WWJM | |
| | | | | |
| ☐ B-6050 | Airbus A340-642 | 468 | ex F-WWCP | |
| ☐ B-6051 | Airbus A340-642 | 488 | ex F-WWCT | |
| ☐ B-6052 | Airbus A340-642 | 514 | ex F-WWCU | |
| ☐ B-6053 | Airbus A340-642 | 577 | ex F-WWCM | |

| | | | | |
|---|---|---|---|---|
| ☐ B-6055 | Airbus A340-642 | 586 | ex F-WWCR Expo 2010 c/s | |
| | | | | |
| ☐ B-2571 | Boeing 737-39P | 29410/3053 | | |
| ☐ B-2572 | Boeing 737-39P | 29411/3071 | | |
| ☐ B-2573 | Boeing 737-39P | 29412/3080 | ex N1786B | |
| ☐ B-2969 | Boeing 737-36R | 30102/3108 | ex N1787B | |
| ☐ B-2988 | Boeing 737-36R | 29087/2970 | | |
| | | | | |
| ☐ B-2680 | Boeing 737-76Q | 30282/1143 | ex N706BA | |
| ☐ B-2681 | Boeing 737-79P | 33037/1198 | | |
| ☐ B-2682 | Boeing 737-79P | 33038/1219 | | |
| ☐ B-2683 | Boeing 737-79P | 28253/1247 | | |
| ☐ B-2684 | Boeing 737-79P | 33039/1227 | | |
| ☐ B-2685 | Boeing 737-79P | 33040/1244 | | |
| ☐ B-5030 | Boeing 737-79P | 30651/1267 | | |
| ☐ B-5031 | Boeing 737-79P | 28255/1284 | | |
| ☐ B-5032 | Boeing 737-79P | 30035/1288 | | |
| ☐ B-5033 | Boeing 737-79P | 30657/1319 | | |
| ☐ B-5034 | Boeing 737-79P | 30036/1336 | | |
| ☐ B-5208 | Boeing 737-79P/W | 33041/1902 | ex N1787B | |
| ☐ B-5209 | Boeing 737-79P/W | 33042/1947 | ex N1779B | |
| ☐ B-5210 | Boeing 737-79P/W | 33043/1976 | | |
| ☐ B-5223 | Boeing 737-79P/W | 33044/1987 | | |
| ☐ B-5243 | Boeing 737-79P/W | 36270/2398 | | |
| ☐ B-5257 | Boeing 737-79P/W | 33759/2968 | ex N1786B | |
| ☐ B-5258 | Boeing 737-79P/W | 36760/3009 | | |
| ☐ B-5262 | Boeing 737-79P/W | 36764/3067 | ex N1787B | |
| ☐ B-5276 | Boeing 737-79P/W | 39719/3741 | | ♦ |
| ☐ B-5282 | Boeing 737-79P/W | 39720/3840 | ex N1786B | ♦ |
| | | | | |
| ☐ B-2665 | Boeing 737-86R | 30495/876 | | |
| ☐ B-5085 | Boeing 737-89P/W | 30691/1702 | | |
| ☐ B-5086 | Boeing 737-89P/W | 32800/1681 | | |
| ☐ B-5087 | Boeing 737-89P/W | 32802/1725 | | |
| ☐ B-5100 | Boeing 737-89P/W | 30681/1645 | ex N1786B | |
| ☐ B-5101 | Boeing 737-89P/W | 30682/1673 | | |
| ☐ B-5199 | Boeing 737-89P/W | 36272/2753 | | |
| ☐ B-5376 | Boeing 737-86N/W | 35226/2641 | | |
| ☐ B-5472 | Boeing 737-89P/W | 36761/3001 | ex N1779B | |
| ☐ B-5473 | Boeing 737-89P/W | 36763/3036 | ex N1786B | |
| ☐ B-5475 | Boeing 737-89P/W | 36765/3065 | | |
| ☐ B-5492 | Boeing 737-89P/W | 29661/3083 | ex N1787B | |
| ☐ B-5493 | Boeing 737-89P/W | 29652/3121 | | |
| ☐ B-5501 | Boeing 737-89P/W | 39388/3204 | | |
| ☐ B-5515 | Boeing 737-89P/W | 36769/3311 | | |
| ☐ B-5516 | Boeing 737-89P/W | 39389/3304 | ex N1787B | |
| ☐ B-5517 | Boeing 737-89P/W | 29653/3294 | ex N1786B | |
| ☐ B-5530 | Boeing 737-89P/W | 29655/3351 | ex N1786B | |
| ☐ B-5647 | Boeing 737-8HX/W | 38105/3959 | | ♦ |
| ☐ B-5665 | Boeing 737-8HX/W | 38106/3976 | | ♦ |
| | | | | |
| ☐ B-3049 | Embraer ERJ-145LI | 14500839 | ex PT-SOA | |
| ☐ B-3050 | Embraer ERJ-145LI | 14500848 | ex PT-SOB | |
| ☐ B-3051 | Embraer ERJ-145LI | 14500898 | ex PT-SOD | |
| ☐ B-3052 | Embraer ERJ-145LI | 14500905 | ex PT-SOE | |
| ☐ B-3053 | Embraer ERJ-145LI | 14500882 | ex PT-SOC | |
| ☐ B-3055 | Embraer ERJ-145LI | 14500921 | | |
| ☐ B-3056 | Embraer ERJ-145LI | 14500928 | | |
| ☐ B-3057 | Embraer ERJ-145LI | 14500932 | | |
| ☐ B-3058 | Embraer ERJ-145LI | 14500958 | | |
| ☐ B-3059 | Embraer ERJ-145LI | 14500949 | | |
| | | | | |
| ☐ B-5001 | Boeing 767-3W0ER | 28264/644 | | wfs |

## CHINA EASTERN YUNNAN AIRLINES

| | | | | |
|---|---|---|---|---|
| ☐ B-2538 | Boeing 737-3W0 | 25090/2040 | | ♦ |
| ☐ B-2589 | Boeing 737-3W0 | 27127/2377 | | ♦ |
| ☐ B-2594 | Boeing 737-341 | 26853/2275 | ex (PP-VPB) | ♦ |
| ☐ B-2955 | Boeing 737-33A | 27453/2687 | | ♦ |
| ☐ B-2956 | Boeing 737-33A | 27907/2690 | | ♦ |
| ☐ B-2958 | Boeing 737-3W0 | 27522/2727 | | ♦ |
| ☐ B-2966 | Boeing 737-33A | 27462/2765 | | ♦ |
| ☐ B-2981 | Boeing 737-3W0 | 28972/2919 | | ♦ |
| ☐ B-2983 | Boeing 737-3W0 | 28973/2941 | | ♦ |
| ☐ B-2985 | Boeing 737-3W0 | 29068/2945 | | ♦ |
| ☐ B-2986 | Boeing 737-3W0 | 29069/2951 | | ♦ |
| | | | | |
| ☐ B-2502 | Boeing 737-7W0 | 30075/311 | | ♦ |
| ☐ B-2503 | Boeing 737-7W0 | 30074/292 | ex N1786B | ♦ |
| ☐ B-2639 | Boeing 737-7W0 | 29912/140 | ex N1787B | ♦ |
| ☐ B-2640 | Boeing 737-7W0 | 29913/148 | ex N1800B | ♦ |

| | | | | |
|---|---|---|---|---|
| ☐ B-5054 | Boeing 737-79P | 29365/1841 | ex N1784B | ♦ |
| ☐ B-5074 | Boeing 737-79P | 33008/1718 | ex N1786B | ♦ |
| ☐ B-5084 | Boeing 737-79P | 33009/1728 | ex N1786B | ♦ |
| ☐ B-5093 | Boeing 737-79P/W | 29357/1630 | | ♦ |
| ☐ B-5094 | Boeing 737-79P/W | 29358/1651 | | ♦ |
| ☐ B-5095 | Boeing 737-79P/W | 29361/1694 | | ♦ |
| ☐ B-5096 | Boeing 737-79P/W | 29362/1713 | | ♦ |
| ☐ B-5097 | Boeing 737-79P | 29364/1823 | ex N6067E | ♦ |
| ☐ B-5225 | Boeing 737-79P/W | 33045/1999 | | ♦ |
| ☐ B-5231 | Boeing 737-79P/W | 33046/2034 | | ♦ |
| ☐ B-5242 | Boeing 737-79P/W | 36269/2357 | | ♦ |
| ☐ B-5245 | Boeing 737-79P/W | 36271/2697 | | ♦ |
| ☐ B-5255 | Boeing 737-79P/W | 36757/2902 | ex N1786B | ♦ |
| ☐ B-5256 | Boeing 737-79P/W | 36758/2949 | | ♦ |
| ☐ B-5259 | Boeing 737-79P/W | 36762/3046 | | |
| ☐ B-5263 | Boeing 737-79P/W | 36766/3086 | ex N1796B | ♦ |
| ☐ B-5265 | Boeing 737-79P/W | 36767/3239 | ex N1786B | ♦ |
| ☐ B-5267 | Boeing 737-79P/W | 36768/3269 | | ♦ |
| ☐ B-5270 | Boeing 737-79P/W | 36770/3330 | | ♦ |
| ☐ B-5271 | Boeing 737-79P/W | 36772/3444 | ex N1787B | ♦ |
| | | | | |
| ☐ B-3013 | Canadair CRJ-200LR | 7571 | ex C-FVAZ | ♦ |
| ☐ B-3019 | Canadair CRJ-200LR | 7581 | ex C-FMMX | ♦ |
| ☐ B-3021 | Canadair CRJ-200LR | 7596 | ex C-FMNW | ♦ |
| ☐ B-3070 | Canadair CRJ-200LR | 7647 | ex C-FMLB | ♦ |
| ☐ B-3071 | Canadair CRJ-200LR | 7684 | ex C-FMMT | ♦ |
| | | | | |
| ☐ B-5515 | Boeing 737-89P/W | 36769/3311 | | ♦ |
| ☐ B-5527 | Boeing 737-89P/W | 36771/3343 | | ♦ |

## CHINA EXPRESS AIRLINES — China Express (G5/HXA) — Guiyang (KWE)

| | | | | |
|---|---|---|---|---|
| ☐ B-3001 | Canadair CRJ-200LR | 7565 | ex B-KBJ | |
| ☐ B-3012 | Canadair CRJ-200LR | 7557 | ex C-FMLB | |
| ☐ B-3016 | Canadair CRJ-200LR | 7614 | ex C-FMKV | |
| ☐ B-7700 | Canadair CRJ-200LR | 7704 | ex N387DF | |

## CHINA FLYING DRAGON AVIATION CO — Feilong (CFA) — Harbin - Ping Fang

| | | | | |
|---|---|---|---|---|
| ☐ B-7420 | Aérospatiale AS350B2 Ecureuil | 2522 | ex F-WYMH | |
| ☐ B-7421 | Aérospatiale AS350B2 Ecureuil | 2523 | ex F-WYMG | |
| ☐ B-7422 | Aérospatiale AS350B2 Ecureuil | 2534 | ex F-WYMB | |
| ☐ B-7423 | Aérospatiale AS350B2 Ecureuil | 2538 | ex F-WYMF | |
| ☐ B-7424 | Aérospatiale AS350B2 Ecureuil | 2547 | ex F-WYME | |
| ☐ B-7425 | Aérospatiale AS350B2 Ecureuil | 2554 | ex F-WYMF | |
| ☐ B-7427 | Aérospatiale AS350B2 Ecureuil | 2566 | | |
| | | | | |
| ☐ B-3201 | AVIC II Y-11B | 003 | | prototype, status? |
| ☐ B-3862 | AVIC II Y-11 | (11)0407 | | |
| ☐ B-3863 | AVIC II Y-11 | (11)0408 | | |
| ☐ B-3864 | AVIC II Y-11 | (11)0409 | | |
| ☐ B-3874 | AVIC II Y-11 | (11)0102 | | |
| ☐ B-3875 | AVIC II Y-11 | (11)0105 | | |
| ☐ B-3876 | AVIC II Y-11 | (11)0106 | | |
| ☐ B-3877 | AVIC II Y-11 | (11)0107 | | |
| ☐ B-3878 | AVIC II Y-11 | (11)0110 | | |
| ☐ B-3879 | AVIC II Y-11 | (11)0201 | | |
| ☐ B-3880 | AVIC II Y-11 | (11)0202 | | |
| ☐ B-3881 | AVIC II Y-11 | (11)0203 | | |
| ☐ B-3882 | AVIC II Y-11 | (11)0204 | | |
| ☐ B-3883 | AVIC II Y-11 | (11)0205 | | |
| ☐ B-3884 | AVIC II Y-11 | (11)0210 | | |
| | | | | |
| ☐ B-3801 | Harbin Y-12 II | 0006 | | Frtr |
| ☐ B-3803 | Harbin Y-12 II | 0003 | | Surveyor |
| ☐ B-3804 | Harbin Y-12 II | 0011 | | Surveyor |
| ☐ B-3805 | Harbin Y-12 II | 0005 | | Surveyor |
| ☐ B-3806 | Harbin Y-12 II | 0008 | | Frtr |
| ☐ B-3807 | Harbin Y-12 II | 0016 | | Op for Maritime Service |
| ☐ B-3808 | Harbin Y-12 II | 0017 | | Op for Maritime Service |
| ☐ B-3819 | Harbin Y-12 II | 0004 | | Frtr |
| ☐ B-3825 | Harbin Y-12 IV | 007 | | ♦ |
| ☐ B-3830 | Harbin Y-12 II | 003 | | ♦ |
| ☐ B-3831 | Harbin Y-12E | 004 | | ♦ |
| ☐ B-3835 | Harbin Y-12 | 009 | | ♦ |
| ☐ B-3837 | Harbin Y-12 | 012 | | ♦ |
| ☐ B-3842 | Harbin Y-12 IV | 0062 | ex 9N-AHQ | ♦ |
| ☐ B-3846 | Harbin Y-12 IV | 013 | ex DQ-AFR | ♦ |
| ☐ B-3852 | Harbin Y-12 IV | 036 | | ♦ |
| ☐ B-3855 | Harbin Y-12 IV | 047 | | ♦ |
| ☐ B-3858 | Harbin Y-12 IV | 039 | | ♦ |

| | | | |
|---|---|---|---|
| ☐ B-3659 | Beriev Be-103 | 3503 | ◆ |
| ☐ B-3660 | Beriev Be-103 | 3504 | ◆ |
| ☐ B-7109 | AVIC II Z-9A Haitun (SA365N) | 045 | Op for Ministry of Forestry |
| ☐ B-7110 | AVIC II Z-9A Haitun (SA365N) | 047 | Op for Ministry of Forestry |
| ☐ B-7112 | AVIC II Z-9A Haitun (SA365N) | | |
| ☐ B-7802 | M.IM-25TC | 34001212169 | ◆ |

| **CHINA POSTAL AIRLINES** | *China Post (8Y/CYZ)* | | **Nanjing-Lukou (NKG)** |
|---|---|---|---|

| | | | |
|---|---|---|---|
| ☐ B-3101 | AVIC II Y-8F-100 | 10(08)01 | |
| ☐ B-3102 | AVIC II Y-8F-100 | 10(08)02 | |
| ☐ B-3103 | AVIC II Y-8F-100 | 10(08)05 | |
| ☐ B-3109 | AVIC II Y-8F-100 | 13(08)03 | |
| ☐ B-3110 | AVIC II Y-8F-100 | 13(08)04 | c/n not confirmed |
| | | | |
| ☐ B-2135 | Boeing 737-45R(SF) | 29035/3046 | ex N202BK |
| ☐ B-2513 | Boeing 737-45R (SF) | 29034/3015 | ex N653AC |
| ☐ B-2526 | Boeing 737-3Y0 (SF) | 25172/2089 | |
| ☐ B-2527 | Boeing 737-3Y0 (SF) | 25173/2097 | |
| ☐ B-2528 | Boeing 737-3Y0 (SF) | 25174/2168 | |
| ☐ B-2655 | Boeing 737-3Q8 (SF) | 26288/2480 | ex N339LF ◆ |
| ☐ B-2656 | Boeing 737-3Q8 (SF) | 26292/2519 | ex N141LF |
| ☐ B-2661 | Boeing 737-3Q8 (SF) | 26284/2418 | ex N379BC |
| ☐ B-2662 | Boeing 737-3Q8 (SF) | 24988/2466 | ex N441LF |
| ☐ B-2881 | Boeing 737-45R (SF) | 29032/2943 | ex N651AC |
| ☐ B-2882 | Boeing 737-45R (SF) | 29033/2963 | ex N652AC |
| ☐ B-2891 | Boeing 737-46J (SF) | 28334/2802 | ex N212BF |
| ☐ B-2892 | Boeing 737-46J (SF) | 28271/2801 | ex N211BF |
| ☐ B-5071 | Boeing 737-341 (QC) | 24277/1658 | ex N277HE |
| ☐ B-5072 | Boeing 737-341 (QC) | 24279/1673 | ex N279HE |

| **CHINA SOUTHERN AIRLINES** | *China Southern (CZ/CSN)* | | **Guangzhou (CAN)** |
|---|---|---|---|

Member of Skyteam

| | | | |
|---|---|---|---|
| ☐ B-2294 | Airbus A319-132 | 2371 | ex D-AVWL |
| ☐ B-2295 | Airbus A319-132 | 2408 | ex D-AVWB |
| ☐ B-2296 | Airbus A319-132 | 2426 | ex D-AVYZ |
| ☐ B-2297 | Airbus A319-132 | 2435 | ex D-AVYH |
| ☐ B-6018 | Airbus A319-132 | 1971 | ex D-AVYC |
| ☐ B-6019 | Airbus A319-132 | 1986 | ex D-AVYJ |
| ☐ B-6020 | Airbus A319-133 | 2004 | ex D-AVWB |
| ☐ B-6021 | Airbus A319-133 | 2008 | ex D-AVWN |
| ☐ B-6039 | Airbus A319-132 | 2200 | ex D-AVYE |
| ☐ B-6040 | Airbus A319-132 | 2203 | ex D-AVYG |
| ☐ B-6041 | Airbus A319-132 | 2232 | ex D-AVWI |
| ☐ B-6042 | Airbus A319-132 | 2273 | ex D-AVWZ |
| ☐ B-6158 | Airbus A319-132 | 2901 | ex D-AVWP |
| ☐ B-6160 | Airbus A319-132 | 2940 | ex D-AVWW |
| ☐ B-6161 | Airbus A319-132 | 2948 | ex D-AVXB |
| ☐ B-6162 | Airbus A319-132 | 2969 | ex D-AVYT |
| ☐ B-6168 | Airbus A319-132 | 3020 | ex D-AVXN |
| ☐ B-6183 | Airbus A319-115 | 3828 | ex D-AVYK |
| ☐ B-6187 | Airbus A319-115 | 3903 | ex D-AVWQ |
| ☐ B-6190 | Airbus A319-132 | 3860 | ex D-AVWC |
| ☐ B-6191 | Airbus A319-132 | 3890 | ex D-AVWJ |
| ☐ B-6195 | Airbus A319-112 | 3983 | ex D-AVYF |
| ☐ B-6200 | Airbus A319-115 | 2519 | ex D-AVYX |
| ☐ B-6201 | Airbus A319-115 | 2541 | ex D-AVWV |
| ☐ B-6202 | Airbus A319-115 | 2546 | ex D-AVWX |
| ☐ B-6203 | Airbus A319-112 | 2554 | ex D-AVYS |
| ☐ B-6205 | Airbus A319-132 | 2505 | ex D-AVWG |
| ☐ B-6206 | Airbus A319-132 | 2574 | ex D-AVXD |
| ☐ B-6207 | Airbus A319-132 | 2579 | ex D-AVXF |
| ☐ B-6208 | Airbus A319-112 | 2555 | ex D-AVWU |
| ☐ B-6209 | Airbus A319-112 | 2558 | ex D-AVYP |
| ☐ B-6219 | Airbus A319-132 | 2667 | ex D-AVYG |
| ☐ B-6220 | Airbus A319-132 | 2815 | ex D-AVWX |
| ☐ B-6239 | Airbus A319-132 | 3144 | ex D-AVXT |
| ☐ B-6240 | Airbus A319-132 | 3258 | ex D-AVXM |
| ☐ B-6241 | Airbus A319-132 | 3269 | ex D-AVYA |
| ☐ B-6242 | Airbus A319-132 | 3311 | ex D-AVYR |
| ☐ B-6243 | Airbus A319-132 | 3342 | ex D-AVYJ |
| ☐ B-6407 | Airbus A319-132 | 4036 | ex D-AVYK |
| ☐ B-6408 | Airbus A319-112 | 4038 | ex D-AVYL |
| ☐ B-6409 | Airbus A319-112 | 4071 | ex D-AVYU |
| | | | |
| ☐ B-2406 | Airbus A320-214 | 2354 | ex F-WWIP |
| ☐ B-2408 | Airbus A320-214 | 2361 | ex F-WWBM |
| ☐ B-2459 | Airbus A320-214 | 0709 | ex F-OHCX |
| ☐ B-6251 | Airbus A320-214 | 2484 | ex F-WWIO |

| | Registration | Type | MSN | History | Notes |
|---|---|---|---|---|---|
| ☐ | B-6252 | Airbus A320-214 | 2506 | ex F-WWBP | |
| ☐ | B-6253 | Airbus A320-214 | 2511 | ex F-WWIT | |
| ☐ | B-6255 | Airbus A320-214 | 2637 | ex F-WWBX | |
| ☐ | B-6263 | Airbus A320-214 | 2708 | ex F-WWIU | |
| ☐ | B-6272 | Airbus A320-214 | 2770 | ex F-WWDM | |
| ☐ | B-6281 | Airbus A320-214 | 2796 | ex F-WWIC | |
| ☐ | B-6282 | Airbus A320-214 | 2824 | ex F-WWDF | |
| ☐ | B-6283 | Airbus A320-214 | 2834 | ex F-WWBP | |
| ☐ | B-6287 | Airbus A320-214 | 2899 | ex F-WWDB | |
| ☐ | B-6288 | Airbus A320-214 | 2855 | ex F-WWIS | |
| ☐ | B-6289 | Airbus A320-214 | 2861 | ex F-WWIY | |
| ☐ | B-6290 | Airbus A320-214 | 2877 | ex F-WWBK | |
| ☐ | B-6291 | Airbus A320-214 | 2915 | ex F-WWDM | |
| ☐ | B-6292 | Airbus A320-214 | 2960 | ex F-WWBN | |
| ☐ | B-6293 | Airbus A320-214 | 2986 | ex F-WWIG | |
| ☐ | B-6303 | Airbus A320-214 | 2950 | ex F-WWIL | |
| ☐ | B-6620 | Airbus A320-214 | 4172 | ex F-WWDM | |
| ☐ | B-6623 | Airbus A320-214 | 4205 | ex D-AVVZ | |
| ☐ | B-6656 | Airbus A320-214 | 4322 | ex D-AXAN | |
| ☐ | B-6681 | Airbus A320-214 | 4365 | ex F-WWDQ | |
| ☐ | B-6682 | Airbus A320-214 | 4325 | ex B-510L | |
| ☐ | B-6702 | Airbus A320-214 | 4362 | ex B- | ♦ |
| ☐ | B-6703 | Airbus A320-214 | 4396 | ex B-515L | ♦ |
| ☐ | B-6737 | Airbus A320-214 | 4456 | ex B- | ♦ |
| ☐ | B-6738 | Airbus A320-214 | 4507 | ex B- | ♦ |
| ☐ | B-6739 | Airbus A320-214 | 4550 | ex B- | ♦ |
| ☐ | B-6775 | Airbus A320-214 | 4613 | ex D-AXAU | ♦ |
| ☐ | B-6776 | Airbus A320-214 | 4671 | ex D-ABFR | ♦ |
| ☐ | B-6782 | Airbus A320-214 | 4794 | ex D-ABFV | ♦ |
| ☐ | B-6783 | Airbus A320-214 | 4808 | ex D-ABFW | ♦ |
| ☐ | B-6785 | Airbus A320-214 | 4854 | ex D-AUBN | ♦ |
| ☐ | B-6815 | Airbus A320-214 | 4928 | ex D-AXAC | ♦ |
| ☐ | B-6817 | Airbus A320-214 | 4880 | ex D-AVVA | ♦ |
| ☐ | B-6827 | Airbus A320-214 | 4982 | ex D-AVVQ | ♦ |
| | | | | | |
| ☐ | B-2350 | Airbus A320-232 | 0712 | ex F-WWDI | |
| ☐ | B-2351 | Airbus A320-233 | 0718 | ex F-WWBI | |
| ☐ | B-2352 | Airbus A320-232 | 0720 | ex F-WWBU | |
| ☐ | B-2353 | Airbus A320-232 | 0722 | ex F-WWBM | |
| ☐ | B-2365 | Airbus A320-232 | 0849 | ex F-WWBI | |
| ☐ | B-2366 | Airbus A320-232 | 0859 | ex F-WWBO | |
| ☐ | B-2367 | Airbus A320-232 | 0881 | ex F-WWDB | |
| ☐ | B-2368 | Airbus A320-232 | 0895 | ex F-WWDJ | |
| ☐ | B-2369 | Airbus A320-232 | 0900 | ex F-WWDM | |
| ☐ | B-2391 | Airbus A320-232 | 0950 | ex F-WWIZ | |
| ☐ | B-2392 | Airbus A320-232 | 0966 | ex F-WWBK | |
| ☐ | B-2393 | Airbus A320-232 | 1035 | ex F-WWDX | |
| ☐ | B-2395 | Airbus A320-232 | 1039 | ex F-WWDZ | |
| ☐ | B-2396 | Airbus A320-232 | 1057 | ex F-WWIO | |
| ☐ | B-6269 | Airbus A320-232 | 2743 | ex F-WWBK | |
| ☐ | B-6275 | Airbus A320-232 | 2680 | ex F-WWIY | |
| ☐ | B-6276 | Airbus A320-232 | 2689 | ex F-WWIG | |
| ☐ | B-6277 | Airbus A320-232 | 2701 | ex F-WWIR | |
| ☐ | B-6278 | Airbus A320-232 | 2714 | ex F-WWBD | |
| ☐ | B-6279 | Airbus A320-232 | 2772 | ex F-WWDR | |
| ☐ | B-6575 | Airbus A320-232 | 3910 | ex F-WWIS | |
| ☐ | B-6577 | Airbus A320-232 | 3959 | ex F-WWDJ | |
| ☐ | B-6582 | Airbus A320-232 | 3999 | ex F-WWDK | |
| ☐ | B-6583 | Airbus A320-232 | 4003 | ex F-WWDP | |
| ☐ | B-6588 | Airbus A320-232 | 4017 | ex F-WWBX | |
| ☐ | B-6627 | Airbus A320-232 | 4225 | ex F-WWBO | |
| ☐ | B-6641 | Airbus A320-232 | 4140 | ex B-518L | |
| ☐ | B-6651 | Airbus A320-232 | 4260 | ex F-WWBC | |
| ☐ | B-6652 | Airbus A320-232 | 4290 | ex F-WWIX | |
| ☐ | B-6653 | Airbus A320-232 | 4232 | ex B-503L | ♦ |
| ☐ | B-6655 | Airbus A320-232 | 4350 | ex D-AXAU | |
| ☐ | B-6678 | Airbus A320-232 | 4248 | ex B-505L | ♦ |
| ☐ | B-6679 | Airbus A320-232 | 4370 | ex F-WWBJ | ♦ |
| ☐ | B-6680 | Airbus A320-232 | 4279 | ex B-507L | ♦ |
| ☐ | B-6761 | Airbus A320-232 | 4696 | ex F-WWDM | ♦ |
| ☐ | B-6762 | Airbus A320-232 | 4751 | ex D-AVVM | ♦ |
| ☐ | B-6786 | Airbus A320-232 | 4782 | ex F-WWDS | ♦ |
| ☐ | B-6812 | Airbus A320-232 | 4883 | ex D-AVVD | ♦ |
| ☐ | B-6813 | Airbus A320-232 | 4864 | ex F-WWDG | ♦ |
| ☐ | B-6816 | Airbus A320-232 | 4912 | ex F-WWBQ | ♦ |
| ☐ | B-6826 | Airbus A320-232 | 4836 | ex B-513L | ♦ |
| ☐ | B- | Airbus A320-232 | 4919 | ex B-503L | o/o♦ |
| | | | | | |
| ☐ | B-2280 | Airbus A321-231 | 1596 | ex D-AVZL | |
| ☐ | B-2281 | Airbus A321-231 | 1614 | ex D-AVZA | |
| ☐ | B-2282 | Airbus A321-231 | 1776 | ex D-AVZC | |
| ☐ | B-2283 | Airbus A321-231 | 1788 | ex D-AVZE | |

| | | | | |
|---|---|---|---|---|
| ☐ B-2284 | Airbus A321-231 | 1974 | ex D-AVZN | |
| ☐ B-2285 | Airbus A321-231 | 1995 | ex D-AVZZ | |
| ☐ B-2287 | Airbus A321-231 | 2080 | ex D-AVZW | |
| ☐ B-2288 | Airbus A321-231 | 2067 | ex D-AVZP | |
| ☐ B-2417 | Airbus A321-231 | 2521 | ex D-AVZC | |
| ☐ B-2418 | Airbus A321-231 | 2530 | ex D-AVZD | |
| ☐ B-6265 | Airbus A321-231 | 2713 | ex D-AVZI | |
| ☐ B-6267 | Airbus A321-231 | 2741 | ex D-AVZK | |
| ☐ B-6270 | Airbus A321-231 | 2759 | ex D-AVZL | |
| ☐ B-6271 | Airbus A321-231 | 2767 | ex D-AVZM | |
| ☐ B-6273 | Airbus A321-231 | 2809 | ex D-AVZC | |
| ☐ B-6302 | Airbus A321-231 | 2936 | ex D-AVZT | |
| ☐ B-6305 | Airbus A321-231 | 2971 | ex D-AVZM | |
| ☐ B-6306 | Airbus A321-231 | 3067 | ex D-AVZJ | |
| ☐ B-6307 | Airbus A321-231 | 3075 | ex D-AVZB | |
| ☐ B-6308 | Airbus A321-231 | 3112 | ex D-AVZE | |
| ☐ B-6317 | Airbus A321-231 | 3217 | ex D-AVZD | |
| ☐ B-6318 | Airbus A321-231 | 3251 | ex D-AVZP | |
| ☐ B-6319 | Airbus A321-231 | 3241 | ex D-AVZJ | |
| ☐ B-6339 | Airbus A321-231 | 3507 | ex D-AVZJ | |
| ☐ B-6342 | Airbus A321-231 | 3459 | ex D-AVZT | |
| ☐ B-6343 | Airbus A321-231 | 3493 | ex D-AVZF | |
| ☐ B-6353 | Airbus A321-231 | 3552 | ex D-AVZP | |
| ☐ B-6355 | Airbus A321-231 | 3566 | ex D-AVZS | |
| ☐ B-6356 | Airbus A321-231 | 3587 | ex D-AVZR | |
| ☐ B-6378 | Airbus A321-231 | 3645 | ex D-AVZU | |
| ☐ B-6379 | Airbus A321-231 | 3681 | ex D-AZAF | |
| ☐ B-6389 | Airbus A321-231 | 3764 | ex D-AZAN | |
| ☐ B-6397 | Airbus A321-231 | 3784 | ex D-AZAQ | |
| ☐ B-6398 | Airbus A321-231 | 3847 | ex D-AVZH | |
| ☐ B-6552 | Airbus A321-231 | 3867 | ex D-AVZL | |
| ☐ B-6553 | Airbus A321-231 | 3920 | ex D-AVZY | |
| ☐ B-6578 | Airbus A321-231 | 3934 | ex D-AZAE | |
| ☐ B-6579 | Airbus A321-231 | 3938 | ex D-AZAH | |
| ☐ B-6580 | Airbus A321-231 | 3951 | ex D-AZAT | |
| ☐ B-6581 | Airbus A321-231 | 3981 | ex D-AZAM | |
| ☐ B-6622 | Airbus A321-211 | 4194 | ex D-AVZD | |
| ☐ B-6625 | Airbus A321-231 | 4184 | ex D-AZAN | |
| ☐ B-6626 | Airbus A321-231 | 4189 | ex D-AVZB | |
| ☐ B-6628 | Airbus A321-231 | 4217 | ex D-AVZI | |
| ☐ B-6629 | Airbus A321-231 | 4224 | ex D-AVZL | |
| ☐ B-6630 | Airbus A321-231 | 4230 | ex D-AVZQ | |
| ☐ B-6657 | Airbus A321-231 | 4266 | ex D-AVZH | |
| ☐ B-6658 | Airbus A321-231 | 4271 | ex D-AVZR | ♦ |
| ☐ B-6659 | Airbus A321-231 | 4292 | ex D-AZAV | |
| ☐ B-6660 | Airbus A321-231 | 4299 | ex D-AZAX | |
| ☐ B-6661 | Airbus A321-231 | 4341 | ex D-AZAS | |
| ☐ B-6662 | Airbus A321-211 | 4274 | ex D-AVZT | ♦ |
| ☐ B-6663 | Airbus A321-221 | 4338 | ex D-AZAR | |
| ☐ B-6683 | Airbus A321-231 | 4369 | ex D-AVZS | |
| ☐ B-6685 | Airbus A321-231 | 4416 | ex D-AZAE | |
| ☐ B-6686 | Airbus A321-231 | 4387 | ex D-AZAC | |
| ☐ B-6687 | Airbus A321-231 | 4430 | ex D-AZAI | |
| | | | | |
| ☐ B-6056 | Airbus A330-243 | 649 | ex F-WWKI | |
| ☐ B-6057 | Airbus A330-243 | 652 | ex F-WWKL | |
| ☐ B-6058 | Airbus A330-243 | 656 | ex F-WWYV | |
| ☐ B-6059 | Airbus A330-243 | 664 | ex F-WWKP | |
| ☐ B-6077 | Airbus A330-243 | 818 | ex F-WWYQ | |
| ☐ B-6078 | Airbus A330-243 | 840 | ex F-WWYS | |
| ☐ B-6135 | Airbus A330-243 | 1096 | ex F-WWYT | |
| ☐ B-6515 | Airbus A330-243 | 1116 | ex F-WWKJ | |
| ☐ B-6516 | Airbus A330-243 | 1129 | ex F-WWKE | |
| ☐ B-6526 | Airbus A330-223 | 1220 | ex F-WWKD | ♦ |
| ☐ B-6528 | Airbus A330-223 | 1202 | ex F-WWYB | ♦ |
| ☐ B-6531 | Airbus A330-223 | 1233 | ex F-WWYK | ♦ |
| ☐ B-6532 | Airbus A330-223 | 1244 | ex F-WWYU | ♦ |
| ☐ B-6542 | Airbus A330-223 | 1297 | ex F-WWYZ | ♦ |
| ☐ B- | Airbus A330-233 | 1309 | ex F-WWKI | o/o♦ |
| | | | | |
| ☐ B-6086 | Airbus A330-343E | 879 | ex F-WWKG | |
| ☐ B-6087 | Airbus A330-343E | 889 | ex F-WWKZ | |
| ☐ B-6098 | Airbus A330-343E | 908 | ex F-WWYF | |
| ☐ B-6111 | Airbus A330-343E | 935 | ex F-WWKF | |
| ☐ B-6112 | Airbus A330-343E | 937 | ex F-WWKI | |
| ☐ B-6500 | Airbus A330-343E | 954 | ex F-WWKT | |
| ☐ B-6501 | Airbus A330-343E | 964 | ex F-WWYK | |
| ☐ B-6502 | Airbus A330-343E | 958 | ex F-WWYD | |
| ☐ B- | Airbus A330-343E | | ex F-WW | o/o |
| | | | | |
| ☐ B-6136 | Airbus A380-841 | 031 | ex F-WWSF | |
| ☐ B-6137 | Airbus A380-841 | 036 | ex F-WWAM | ♦ |

| | | | | | |
|---|---|---|---|---|---|
| ☐ | B-6138 | Airbus A380-841 | 054 | ex F-WWAX | ♦ |
| ☐ | B-6139 | Airbus A380-841 | 088 | ex F-WWAR | o/o♦ |
| ☐ | B-6140 | Airbus A380-841 | 120 | ex F-WW | o/o♦ |
| | | | | | |
| ☐ | B-2539 | Boeing 737-3Y0 | 26068/2306 | | |
| ☐ | B-2574 | Boeing 737-37K | 29407/3100 | ex N1786B | |
| ☐ | B-2575 | Boeing 737-37K | 29408/3104 | ex N1800B | |
| ☐ | B-2582 | Boeing 737-31B | 25895/2499 | | |
| ☐ | B-2583 | Boeing 737-31B | 25897/2554 | | |
| ☐ | B-2596 | Boeing 737-31B | 27151/2437 | | |
| ☐ | B-2909 | Boeing 737-3Y0 | 26082/2456 | | |
| ☐ | B-2910 | Boeing 737-3Y0 | 26083/2459 | | |
| ☐ | B-2911 | Boeing 737-3Y0 | 26084/2460 | | |
| ☐ | B-2920 | Boeing 737-3Q8 | 27271/2523 | | |
| ☐ | B-2921 | Boeing 737-3Q8 | 27286/2528 | | |
| ☐ | B-2922 | Boeing 737-31B | 27272/2555 | | |
| ☐ | B-2923 | Boeing 737-31B | 27275/2565 | | |
| ☐ | B-2924 | Boeing 737-31B | 27287/2575 | | |
| ☐ | B-2926 | Boeing 737-31B | 27289/2593 | | |
| ☐ | B-2927 | Boeing 737-31B | 27290/2595 | | |
| ☐ | B-2929 | Boeing 737-31B | 27343/2619 | | |
| ☐ | B-2930 | Boeing 737-31L | 27273/2556 | | |
| ☐ | B-2931 | Boeing 737-31L | 27276/2567 | | |
| ☐ | B-2935 | Boeing 737-37K | 27283/2547 | | |
| ☐ | B-2936 | Boeing 737-37K | 27335/2609 | | |
| ☐ | B-2941 | Boeing 737-31B | 27344/2622 | | |
| ☐ | B-2946 | Boeing 737-37K | 27375/2655 | | |
| ☐ | B-2952 | Boeing 737-31B | 27519/2678 | | |
| ☐ | B-2959 | Boeing 737-31B | 27520/2775 | | |
| | | | | | |
| ☐ | B-2162 | Boeing 737-7K9 | 30041/909 | ex N1786B | |
| ☐ | B-2163 | Boeing 737-7K9 | 30042/931 | ex N1786B | |
| ☐ | B-2169 | Boeing 737-71B | 32936/1531 | | |
| ☐ | B-2620 | Boeing 737-71B | 32937/1569 | | |
| ☐ | B-2622 | Boeing 737-71B | 32938/1603 | | |
| ☐ | B-2698 | Boeing 737-76N | 32583/994 | ex N583SF | |
| ☐ | B-2699 | Boeing 737-76N | 32596/1028 | ex N1786B | |
| ☐ | B-2916 | Boeing 737-71B | 32939/1607 | | |
| ☐ | B-2917 | Boeing 737-71B | 32940/1624 | | |
| ☐ | B-5068 | Boeing 737-71B | 32933/1430 | | |
| ☐ | B-5069 | Boeing 737-71B | 32934/1465 | | |
| ☐ | B-5070 | Boeing 737-71B | 32935/1507 | | |
| ☐ | B-5107 | Boeing 737-7K9 | 34320/1763 | | |
| ☐ | B-5108 | Boeing 737-7K9 | 34321/1802 | ex N1786B | |
| ☐ | B-5232 | Boeing 737-71B | 35360/2051 | | |
| ☐ | B-5233 | Boeing 737-71B | 35361/2077 | | |
| ☐ | B-5235 | Boeing 737-71B | 29370/2137 | | |
| ☐ | B-5236 | Boeing 737-71B | 35362/2102 | | |
| ☐ | B-5237 | Boeing 737-71B | 29372/2131 | ex N1786B | |
| ☐ | B-5238 | Boeing 737-71B | 35363/2066 | | |
| ☐ | B-5239 | Boeing 737-71B | 35364/2156 | | |
| ☐ | B-5240 | Boeing 737-71B | 35368/2264 | | |
| ☐ | B-5241 | Boeing 737-71B | 35372/2291 | | |
| ☐ | B-5247 | Boeing 737-71B | 35377/2980 | ex N1786B | |
| ☐ | B-5250 | Boeing 737-71B | 35378/2346 | | |
| ☐ | B-5251 | Boeing 737-71B | 35384/2446 | | |
| ☐ | B-5252 | Boeing 737-71B | 35382/3034 | ex N1786B | |
| ☐ | B-5253 | Boeing 737-71B | 35383/3005 | | |
| ☐ | B-5275 | Boeing 737-71B/W | 38912/3730 | | ♦ |
| ☐ | B-5281 | Boeing 737-71B/W | 38914/3864 | | ♦ |
| ☐ | B-5283 | Boeing 737-71B/W | 38919 | | o/o♦ |
| ☐ | B-5285 | Boeing 737-71B/W | 38917/3922 | | ♦ |
| ☐ | B- | Boeing 737-71B | | | o/o |
| ☐ | B- | Boeing 737-71B | | | o/o |
| | | | | | |
| ☐ | B-2693 | Boeing 737-81B | 32921/1187 | ex N6065Y | |
| ☐ | B-2694 | Boeing 737-81B | 32922/1199 | | |
| ☐ | B-2695 | Boeing 737-81B | 32923/1213 | | |
| ☐ | B-2696 | Boeing 737-81B | 32924/1230 | | |
| ☐ | B-2697 | Boeing 737-81B | 32925/1250 | | |
| ☐ | B-5020 | Boeing 737-81B | 32926/1268 | | |
| ☐ | B-5021 | Boeing 737-81B | 32927/1290 | | |
| ☐ | B-5022 | Boeing 737-81B | 32928/1323 | | |
| ☐ | B-5040 | Boeing 737-81B | 32929/1348 | | |
| ☐ | B-5041 | Boeing 737-81B | 32930/1355 | | |
| ☐ | B-5042 | Boeing 737-81B | 32931/1362 | | |
| ☐ | B-5067 | Boeing 737-81B | 32932/1395 | | |
| ☐ | B-5112 | Boeing 737-86N | 34248/1806 | | |
| ☐ | B-5113 | Boeing 737-81B | 34250/1784 | | |
| ☐ | B-5120 | Boeing 737-83N/W | 32580/1024 | ex N313TZ | |
| ☐ | B-5122 | Boeing 737-83N/W | 32610/1110 | ex N320TZ | |
| ☐ | B-5123 | Boeing 737-83N/W | 32611/1135 | ex N322TZ | |

| | | | | | |
|---|---|---|---|---|---|
| ☐ B-5128 | Boeing 737-83N/W | 32882/1163 | ex N324TZ | | |
| ☐ B-5129 | Boeing 737-83N/W | 32884/1181 | ex N325TZ | | |
| ☐ B-5133 | Boeing 737-86N | 34252/1851 | ex N1787B | | |
| ☐ B-5147 | Boeing 737-81B | 30697/1915 | ex N1786B | | |
| ☐ B-5149 | Boeing 737-81B | 30699/1933 | | | |
| ☐ B-5155 | Boeing 737-8K5/W | 30783/804 | ex N307TA | | |
| ☐ B-5156 | Boeing 737-81Q/W | 30786/1138 | ex N786TA | | |
| ☐ B-5157 | Boeing 737-81Q/W | 30787/1234 | ex N787TM | | |
| ☐ B-5163 | Boeing 737-81B | 30708/2087 | | | |
| ☐ B-5165 | Boeing 737-81B | 30709/1961 | | | |
| ☐ B-5166 | Boeing 737-81B | 33006/1983 | | | |
| ☐ B-5189 | Boeing 737-81B | 35365/2191 | | | |
| ☐ B-5190 | Boeing 737-81B | 35366/2223 | | | |
| ☐ B-5191 | Boeing 737-81B | 35367/2237 | ex N1786B | | |
| ☐ B-5192 | Boeing 737-81B | 35369/2272 | | | |
| ☐ B-5193 | Boeing 737-81B | 35370/2299 | | | |
| ☐ B-5195 | Boeing 737-81B | 35371/2302 | | | |
| ☐ B-5300 | Boeing 737-81B | 35375/2314 | | | |
| ☐ B-5310 | Boeing 737-81B | 35376/2329 | | | |
| ☐ B-5339 | Boeing 737-81B | 35380/2372 | ex N1782B | | |
| ☐ B-5340 | Boeing 737-81B | 35381/2402 | | | |
| ☐ B-5356 | Boeing 737-81B | 35385/2486 | ex N1787B | | |
| ☐ B-5419 | Boeing 737-81B | 35379/2957 | ex N1787B | | |
| ☐ B-5420 | Boeing 737-81B | 35374/2940 | | | |
| ☐ B-5421 | Boeing 737-81B | 35373/2881 | | | |
| ☐ B-5445 | Boeing 737-81B | 35388/3154 | | | |
| ☐ B-5446 | Boeing 737-81B | 35389/3144 | | | |
| ☐ B-5468 | Boeing 737-81B | 35386/3068 | ex N1786B | | |
| ☐ B-5469 | Boeing 737-81B | 35387/3041 | | | |
| ☐ B-5586 | Boeing 737-86J/W | 36878/3631 | | | ♦ |
| ☐ B-5587 | Boeing 737-81B/W | 38966/3650 | | | ♦ |
| ☐ B-5596 | Boeing 737-81B/W | 38964/3700 | | | ♦ |
| ☐ B-5597 | Boeing 737-81B/W | 38913/3776 | | | ♦ |
| ☐ B-5598 | Boeing 737-86J/W | 36877/3784 | | | ♦ |
| ☐ B-5609 | Boeing 737-81B/W | 38963/3838 | | | ♦ |
| ☐ B-5640 | Boeing 737-81B/W | 38918/3961 | | | ♦ |
| ☐ B-5641 | Boeing 737-81B/W | 38916/3898 | | | ♦ |
| ☐ B-5643 | Boeing 737-81B/W | 38920 | | | o/o♦ |
| ☐ B-5645 | Boeing 737-81B/W | 38922 | | | o/o♦ |
| ☐ B-5646 | Boeing 737-81B/W | 38932 | | | o/o♦ |
| | | | | | |
| ☐ B-2812 | Boeing 757-28S | 32341/961 | | | |
| ☐ B-2813 | Boeing 757-28S | 32342/966 | | | |
| ☐ B-2818 | Boeing 757-21B | 25259/392 | | | |
| ☐ B-2822 | Boeing 757-21B | 25884/461 | | | |
| ☐ B-2823 | Boeing 757-21B | 25888/575 | | | |
| ☐ B-2824 | Boeing 757-21B | 25889/583 | | | |
| ☐ B-2825 | Boeing 757-21B | 25890/585 | | | |
| ☐ B-2827 | Boeing 757-2Y0 | 26156/503 | | | |
| ☐ B-2830 | Boeing 757-28S | 32343/1015 | ex N60668 | | |
| ☐ B-2831 | Boeing 757-2Y0 | 26153/482 | | | |
| ☐ B-2835 | Boeing 757-236 | 25598/445 | ex N5573P | | |
| ☐ B-2838 | Boeing 757-2Z0 | 27260/613 | | | |
| ☐ B-2851 | Boeing 757-28S | 29215/797 | | | |
| ☐ B-2853 | Boeing 757-28S | 29216/811 | | | |
| ☐ B-2859 | Boeing 757-28S | 29217/868 | | | |
| | | | | | |
| ☐ B-2051 | Boeing 777-21B | 27357/20 | | Toyota Camry c/s | |
| ☐ B-2052 | Boeing 777-21B | 27358/24 | ex N5017V | | |
| ☐ B-2053 | Boeing 777-21B | 27359/46 | | | |
| ☐ B-2054 | Boeing 777-21B | 27360/48 | | | |
| ☐ B-2055 | Boeing 777-21BER | 27524/55 | | | |
| ☐ B-2056 | Boeing 777-21BER | 27525/66 | | | |
| ☐ B-2057 | Boeing 777-21BER | 27604/106 | ex N5022E | Pearl of The South | |
| ☐ B-2058 | Boeing 777-21BER | 27605/110 | ex N5028Y | | |
| ☐ B-2062 | Boeing 777-21BER | 27606/121 | ex N688CZ | | |
| ☐ B-2070 | Boeing 777-21BER | 32703/472 | | | |
| | | | | | |
| ☐ B-2071 | Boeing 777-F1B | 37309/760 | ex N447BA | | |
| ☐ B-2072 | Boeing 777-F1B | 37310/770 | ex N448BA | | |
| ☐ B-2073 | Boeing 777-F1B | 37311/811 | ex N553BA | | |
| ☐ B-2075 | Boeing 777-F1B | 37312/820 | ex N554BA | | |
| ☐ B-2080 | Boeing 777-F1B | 37314/983 | | | ♦ |
| ☐ B-2081 | Boeing 777-F1B | 37313/888 | | | |
| | | | | | |
| ☐ B-3060 | Embraer ERJ-145LI | 145701 | ex PT-SGF | | |
| ☐ B-3061 | Embraer ERJ-145LI | 145755 | ex PT-SNA | | |
| ☐ B-3062 | Embraer ERJ-145LI | 145781 | ex PT-SNB | | |
| ☐ B-3063 | Embraer ERJ-145LI | 14500804 | | | |
| ☐ B-3065 | Embraer ERJ-145LI | 14500815 | | | |
| ☐ B-3066 | Embraer ERJ-145LI | 14500823 | ex PT-SXL | | |

| | | | | | |
|---|---|---|---|---|---|
| ☐ B-3146 | Embraer ERJ-190LR | 19000476 | | | ♦ |
| ☐ B-3147 | Embraer ERJ-190LR | 19000477 | ex PT-TOX | | ♦ |
| ☐ B-3148 | Embraer ERJ-190LR | 19000483 | ex PT-TPI | | ♦ |
| ☐ B-3149 | Embraer ERJ-190LR | 19000488 | ex PT-TPN | | ♦ |
| ☐ B-3197 | Embraer ERJ-190LR | 19000456 | ex PT-TNX | | ♦ |
| ☐ B-3198 | Embraer ERJ-190LR | 19000465 | ex PT-TOI | | ♦ |
| ☐ B-3199 | Embraer ERJ-190LR | 19000469 | ex PT-TOL | | ♦ |
| ☐ B-3136 | Embraer ERJ-190LR | 19000513 | ex PT-TSR | | ♦ |
| ☐ B-3137 | Embraer ERJ-190LR | 19000524 | ex PT-TUL | | ♦ |
| ☐ B-3138 | Embraer ERJ-190LR | 19000529 | ex PT-TUR | | ♦ |
| ☐ B- | Embraer ERJ-190LR | 19000536 | ex PT-TUZ | | o/o♦ |
| ☐ B- | Embraer ERJ-190LR | 19000539 | ex PT- | | o/o♦ |
| | | | | | |
| ☐ B-7118 | Sikorsky S-76C+ | 760819 | ex N819S | | ♦ |
| ☐ B-7303 | Sikorsky S-76A | 760289 | | | |
| ☐ B-7304 | Sikorsky S-76A | 760293 | | | |
| ☐ B-7306 | Sikorsky S-76A | 760106 | ex VH-XHA | | |
| ☐ B-7307 | Sikorsky S-76C+ | 760478 | | | |
| ☐ B-7308 | Sikorsky S-76C+ | 760480 | | | |
| ☐ B-7311 | Sikorsky S-76C+ | 760192 | | | |
| ☐ B-7320 | Sikorsky S-76C+ | 760263 | | | |
| ☐ B-7323 | Sikorsky S-76C+ | 760772 | ex N772L | | ♦ |
| ☐ B-7329 | Sikorsky S-76C++ | 760769 | | | |
| ☐ B-7330 | Sikorsky S-76C++ | 760771 | | | |
| ☐ B-7331 | Sikorsky S-76C++ | 760715 | ex N2557H | | |
| | | | | | |
| ☐ B-2267 | McDonnell-Douglas MD-90-30 | 53533/2258 | [MZJ] | | |
| ☐ B-2461 | Boeing 747-41BF | 32804/1312 | | | |
| ☐ B-2473 | Boeing 747-41BF | 32803/1306 | ex N1788B | | |
| ☐ B-3026 | ATR 72-212A | 0552 | ex F-WWLP | | wfs |
| ☐ B-3027 | ATR 72-212A | 0555 | ex F-WWLL | | wfs |
| ☐ B-7116 | Sikorsky S-92A | 920147 | ex N2208U | | ♦ |
| ☐ B- | Boeing 787-8 | | | | o/o |
| ☐ B- | Boeing 787-8 | | | | o/o |
| ☐ B- | Boeing 787-8 | | | | o/o |

## CHINA UNITED AIRLINES — Lianhang (KN/CUA) — Beijing-Nanyuan (NAY)

| | | | | | |
|---|---|---|---|---|---|
| ☐ B-4008 | Boeing 737-3T0 | 23839/1507 | ex N19357 | | Op for Govt |
| ☐ B-4009 | Boeing 737-3T0 | 23840/1516 | ex N27358 | | Op for Govt |
| ☐ B-4018 | Boeing 737-33A | 25502/2310 | | | Op for Govt |
| ☐ B-4019 | Boeing 737-33A | 25503/2313 | | | Op for Govt |
| ☐ B-4020 | Boeing 737-34N | 28081/2746 | | | Op for Govt |
| ☐ B-4021 | Boeing 737-34N | 28082/2747 | | | Op for Govt |
| ☐ B-4052 | Boeing 737-3Q8 | 24701/1957 | ex PK-GWI | | Op for Govt |
| ☐ B-4053 | Boeing 737-3Q8 | 24702/1994 | ex PK-GWJ | | Op for Govt |
| | | | | | |
| ☐ B-5183 | Boeing 737-8Q8/W | 30711/2159 | ex N1787B | | <CSH |
| ☐ B-5323 | Boeing 737-8Q8/W | 30725/2292 | | | <CSH |
| ☐ B-5353 | Boeing 737-8Q8 | 30728/2386 | | | ♦ |
| ☐ B-5399 | Boeing 737-86N/W | 35224/2617 | | | <CSH |
| ☐ B-5448 | Boeing 737-86N/W | 38021/3679 | | | ♦ |
| ☐ B-5470 | Boeing 737-86D/W | 35774/3010 | ex N1786B | | ♦ |
| ☐ B-5471 | Boeing 737-86D/W | 35775/3098 | ex N1796B | | ♦ |
| ☐ B-5547 | Boeing 737-86N/W | 36806/3448 | | | |
| | | | | | |
| ☐ B-4005 | Canadair CRJ-200LR | 7138 | ex C-FZAT | Op for Govt | |
| ☐ B-4006 | Canadair CRJ-200LR | 7149 | ex C-FZIS | Op for Govt | |
| ☐ B-4007 | Canadair CRJ-200LR | 7180 | ex C-GATM | Op for Govt | |
| ☐ B-4010 | Canadair CRJ-200LR | 7189 | ex C-GATY | Op for Govt | |
| ☐ B-4011 | Canadair CRJ-200LR | 7193 | ex C-GBFR | Op for Govt | |
| ☐ B-4701 | Canadair CRJ-200LR | 7639 | ex C-GKAK | Op for China Maritime Service | |
| ☐ B-4702 | Canadair CRJ-200LR | 7455 | ex C-GHUT | Op for China Maritime Service | |
| | | | | | |
| ☐ B-4072 | Harbin Y-7G | 0204 | | | ♦ |
| ☐ B-4073 | Harbin Y-7G | 0205 | | operator unconfirmed | ♦ |
| ☐ B-4074 | Harbin Y-7G | 0206 | | operator unconfirmed | ♦ |
| ☐ B-4075 | Harbin Y-7G | 0207 | | operator unconfirmed | ♦ |
| ☐ B-4076 | Harbin Y-7G | 0208 | | operator unconfirmed | ♦ |
| ☐ B-4077 | Harbin Y-7G | 0209 | | operator unconfirmed | ♦ |
| | | | | | |
| ☐ B-2663 | Boeing 737-7AD | 28437/72 | ex N701EW | | <CSH |
| ☐ B-2997 | Boeing 737-7Q8 | 28223/272 | | | <CSH |
| ☐ B-4012 | Yakovlev Yak-42D | 4520424914375 | | | Op for Chinese Navy |
| ☐ B-4013 | Yakovlev Yak-42D | 45204249144..? | | | Op for Chinese Navy |
| ☐ B-4016 | Tupolev Tu-154M | 91A872 | | | |
| ☐ B-4017 | Tupolev Tu-154M | 91A873 | | | |
| ☐ B-4025 | Boeing 737-76D | 33470/1334 | ex B-5048 | | Op for Govt |
| ☐ B-4026 | Boeing 737-76D | 33472/1343 | ex B-2689 | | Op for Govt |
| ☐ B-4028 | Tupolev Tu-154M | 93A967 | | | VIP |
| ☐ B-4061 | Canadair CRJ-701ER | 10183 | ex C-FCRA | | Op for Chinese AF |
| ☐ B-4062 | Canadair CRJ-701ER | 10187 | ex C-FCRF | | Op for Chinese AF |

| | | | | |
|---|---|---|---|---|
| ☐ B-4063 | Canadair CRJ-701ER | 10204 | ex C-FEHT | Op for Chinese AF |
| ☐ B-4064 | Canadair CRJ-701ER | 10206 | ex C-FEHU | Op for Chinese AF |
| ☐ B-4071 | Harbin Y-7G | 0201 | | ♦ |
| ☐ B-4090 | Airbus A319-115 | 5023 | ex D-AVYJ | ♦ |
| ☐ B-4091 | Airbus A319-115 | 5088 | ex D-AVYP | ♦ |

| CHINA XINHUA AIRLINES | | Xinhua (HU/CXH) | | Tianjin (TSN) |
|---|---|---|---|---|
| ☐ B-5080 | Boeing 737-86N | 28614/477 | ex N614LS | |
| ☐ B-5081 | Boeing 737-86N | 30231/515 | ex N302LS | |
| ☐ B-5082 | Boeing 737-883 | 30193/587 | ex LN-RCS | |
| ☐ B-5138 | Boeing 737-84P/W | 32607/1832 | | <CHH |
| ☐ B-5139 | Boeing 737-84P/W | 32608/1855 | | <CHH |
| ☐ B-5141 | Boeing 737-84P/W | 34030/1800 | | <CHH |
| ☐ B-5153 | Boeing 737-84P/W | 34029/1921 | | <CHH |
| | | | | |
| ☐ B-2579 | Boeing 737-33A | 25505/2342 | ex N402AW | ♦ |
| ☐ B-2989 | Boeing 737-46Q | 28758/2939 | | |
| ☐ B-2993 | Boeing 737-46Q | 28759/2981 | | |

| CHONGQING AIRLINES | | Chongqing (OQ/CQN) | | Chongqing (CKG) |
|---|---|---|---|---|
| ☐ B-2343 | Airbus A320-233 | 0696 | ex F-WWII | |
| ☐ B-2345 | Airbus A320-233 | 0698 | ex F-WWBT | |
| ☐ B-2346 | Airbus A320-233 | 0704 | ex F-WWDY | |
| ☐ B-2347 | Airbus A320-233 | 0705 | ex F-WWIL | ♦ |
| ☐ B-6576 | Airbus A320-232 | 3941 | ex F-WWDS | ♦ |
| | | | | |
| ☐ B-6246 | Airbus A319-133 | 3836 | ex D-AVYO | |
| ☐ B-6247 | Airbus A319-133 | 3876 | ex D-AVWG | |
| ☐ B-6248 | Airbus A319-133 | 3901 | ex D-AVWP | |

| CITIC OFFSHORE HELICOPTERS | | China Helicopter (CHC) | | Shenzhen Heliport |
|---|---|---|---|---|
| ☐ B-7127 | Eurocopter EC225LP | 2676 | | |
| ☐ B-7128 | Eurocopter EC225LP | 2687 | | |
| ☐ B-7951 | Aérospatiale AS.332L | 2165 | ex F-WYMQ | |
| ☐ B-7956 | Aérospatiale AS.332L1 | 2356 | ex HL9202 | |
| ☐ B-7957 | Aérospatiale AS.332L1 | 9000 | | |
| ☐ B-7958 | Aérospatiale AS.332L1 | 9001 | ex F-WQDT | |
| ☐ B-7959 | Aérospatiale AS.332L1 | 2087 | ex F-WYMR | |
| ☐ B-7961 | Aérospatiale AS.332L1 | 2641 | | |
| ☐ B-7962 | Aérospatiale AS.332L1 | 2644 | | |
| ☐ B-7101 | Aérospatiale AS365N | 6012 | | |
| ☐ B-7102 | Aérospatiale AS365N | 6013 | | |
| ☐ B-7103 | Aérospatiale AS365N | 6041 | | |
| ☐ B-7105 | Aérospatiale AS365N | 6046 | | |
| ☐ B-7106 | Aérospatiale AS365N | 6047 | | |
| ☐ B-7107 | Aérospatiale AS365N | 6027 | | |
| | | | | |
| ☐ B-7005 | Eurocopter EC155B | 6639 | | |
| ☐ B-7006 | Eurocopter EC155B | 6641 | | |
| ☐ B-7007 | Eurocopter EC135T2 | 0246 | | |
| ☐ B-7008 | Eurocopter EC155B | 6623 | | |
| ☐ B-7120 | Eurocopter EC155B1 | 6717 | ex F-WWOU | |
| ☐ B-7132 | Eurocopter EC155B1 | 6904 | | |
| ☐ B-7133 | Eurocopter EC155B1 | 6912 | | |
| ☐ B-7135 | Eurocopter EC115B1 | 6915 | | ♦ |
| ☐ B-7141 | Eurocopter EC155B1 | 6941 | | ♦ |
| | | | | |
| ☐ B-7429 | Aérospatiale AS.350B3 | 4627 | | |
| ☐ B-7772 | Agusta A.109E Power | 11136 | | |
| ☐ B-7776 | Agusta A.109S | 22132 | | ♦ |
| ☐ B-7778 | Agusta A.109S | 22139 | | ♦ |

| DALIAN AIRLINES | | | | |
|---|---|---|---|---|
| ☐ B-5196 | Boeing 737-86N | 36810/2699 | | ♦ |
| ☐ B-5553 | Boeing 737-89L/W | 40026/3576 | | ♦ |

| DONGHAI AIRLINES | | Donghai Air (J5/EPA) | | Shenzhen Bao'an (SZX) |
|---|---|---|---|---|
| ☐ B-2517 | Boeing 737-3W0 (SF) | 23396/1166 | ex N5573K | |
| ☐ B-2518 | Boeing 737-3W0 (SF) | 23397/1193 | ex N1791B | |
| ☐ B-2897 | Boeing 737-3Y0F | 24902/1973 | ex N108KH | |
| ☐ B-2898 | Boeing 737-3Y0F | 24916/2066 | ex N106KH | |
| ☐ B-5046 | Boeing 737-341 (SF) | 24276/1645 | ex N276HE | ♦ |
| ☐ B-5047 | Boeing 737-341 (SF) | 24278/1660 | ex N278HE | ♦ |
| ☐ B-2608 | Boeing 737-36Q | 28662/659 | ex N662AG | ♦ |

## DONGHUA AIRLINES — Jinjiang (JJN)

| | | | |
|---|---|---|---|
| ☐ B-3889 | AVIC II Y-11 | (11)0305 | |

## GRAND CHINA AIRLINES — Grand China (CN/GDC) — Haikou (HAK)

| | | | | |
|---|---|---|---|---|
| ☐ B-2637 | Boeing 737-86N | 28576/103 | ex N576GE | |
| ☐ B-2652 | Boeing 737-84P | 30475/731 | | Jin Sui Piao Xiang special c/s |
| ☐ B-5089 | Boeing 737-883 | 28320/551 | ex OY-KKU | ♦ |

## GRANDSTAR CARGO INTERNATIONAL — (GD/GSC)

| | | | |
|---|---|---|---|
| ☐ B-2427 | Boeing 747-4B5F | 26401/1087 | ex HL7497 |

## GUIZHOU AIRLINES — (CGH)

| | | | | |
|---|---|---|---|---|
| ☐ B-5120 | Boeing 737-83N/W | 32580/1024 | ex N313TZ | ♦ |
| ☐ B-5121 | Boeing 737-83N/W | 32609/1059 | ex N316TZ | ♦ |
| ☐ B-5125 | Boeing 737-83N/W | 32612/1184 | ex N326TZ | ♦ |
| ☐ B-5126 | Boeing 737-83N/W | 32613/1197 | ex N327TZ | ♦ |
| ☐ B-5127 | Boeing 737-83N/W | 32615/1207 | ex N329TZ | ♦ |
| ☐ B-5221 | Boeing 737-71B | 29366/1872 | ex N1795B | ♦ |
| ☐ B-5222 | Boeing 737-71B | 29367/1896 | ex N1784B | ♦ |
| ☐ B-5230 | Boeing 737-71B | 29371/2064 | | ♦ |

## HAINAN AIRLINES — Hainan (HU/CHH) — Haikou (HAK)

| | | | | |
|---|---|---|---|---|
| ☐ B-6858 | Airbus A320-214 | 5008 | ex F-WWDR | ♦ |
| ☐ B-6865 | Airbus A320-214 | 5006 | ex F-WWDM | ♦ |
| ☐ B-6859 | Airbus A320-214 | 5072 | ex F-WWDK | ♦ |
| ☐ B-6903 | Airbus A320-214 | 5117 | ex F-WWBH | o/o♦ |
| ☐ B- | Airbus A320-214 | 5114 | ex F-WWIT | o/o♦ |
| ☐ B- | Airbus A320-232 | | ex | o/o |
| ☐ B- | Airbus A320-232 | | ex | o/o |
| ☐ B- | Airbus A320-232 | | ex | o/o |
| ☐ B- | Airbus A320-232 | | ex | o/o |
| ☐ B- | Airbus A320-232 | | ex | o/o |
| ☐ B-6088 | Airbus A330-243 | 906 | ex F-WWYD | |
| ☐ B-6089 | Airbus A330-243 | 919 | ex F-WWYS | |
| ☐ B-6116 | Airbus A330-243 | 875 | ex F-WWKB | |
| ☐ B-6118 | Airbus A330-243 | 881 | ex F-WWKI | |
| ☐ B-6133 | Airbus A330-243 | 982 | ex F-WWYY | |
| ☐ B-6519 | Airbus A330-243 | 1159 | ex F-WWKF | |
| ☐ B-2501 | Boeing 737-44P | 29914/3067 | ex N1786B | |
| ☐ B-2576 | Boeing 737-44P | 29915/3106 | ex N1786B | flower c/s |
| ☐ B-2960 | Boeing 737-4Q8 | 24332/1866 | ex N191LF | |
| ☐ B-2965 | Boeing 737-4Q8 | 26334/2782 | | [SAW] |
| ☐ B-2967 | Boeing 737-4Q8 | 26335/2793 | | |
| ☐ B-2970 | Boeing 737-4Q8 | 26337/2811 | | |
| ☐ B-2989 | Boeing 737-46Q | 28758/2939 | | >CXH |
| ☐ B-2993 | Boeing 737-46Q | 28759/2981 | | |
| ☐ B-2157 | Boeing 737-84P/W | 32600/1015 | ex N1786B | |
| ☐ B-2158 | Boeing 737-84P/W | 32601/1033 | | |
| ☐ B-2159 | Boeing 737-84P/W | 32599/972 | ex N1787B | |
| ☐ B-2636 | Boeing 737-86N | 28574/67 | ex N574GE | |
| ☐ B-2638 | Boeing 737-8Q8 | 28220/212 | ex N361LF | special palm c/s |
| ☐ B-2646 | Boeing 737-8Q8 | 28056/273 | ex N371LF | special orchid c/s |
| ☐ B-2647 | Boeing 737-84P | 29947/345 | ex N1787B | special Happy Sea Wave c/s |
| ☐ B-2651 | Boeing 737-84P | 30474/607 | ex N1787B | |
| ☐ B-2675 | Boeing 737-86Q/W | 32885/1147 | | |
| ☐ B-2676 | Boeing 737-84P/W | 32602/1170 | | |
| ☐ B-2677 | Boeing 737-84P/W | 32604/1191 | | |
| ☐ B-5083 | Boeing 737-883 | 28319/548 | ex LN-RCO | |
| ☐ B-5090 | Boeing 737-883 | 28321/577 | ex LN-RCR | |
| ☐ B-5136 | Boeing 737-84P/W | 32605/1796 | ex B-KBE | |
| ☐ B-5137 | Boeing 737-84P/W | 32606/1805 | ex B-KBF | |
| ☐ B-5182 | Boeing 737-808/W | 34708/2097 | | |
| ☐ B-5337 | Boeing 737-84P/W | 35747/2433 | | |
| ☐ B-5338 | Boeing 737-84P/W | 35749/2330 | | |
| ☐ B-5346 | Boeing 737-8BK/W | 29673/2373 | ex N1786B | |
| ☐ B-5358 | Boeing 737-84P/W | 35077/2419 | ex N1787B | |
| ☐ B-5359 | Boeing 737-8FH/W | 35101/2459 | ex N1786B | |
| ☐ B-5371 | Boeing 737-84P/W | 35752/2556 | ex N1787B | |
| ☐ B-5372 | Boeing 737-84P/W | 35758/2593 | | |
| ☐ B-5373 | Boeing 737-84P/W | 35754/2618 | ex N1787B | |
| ☐ B-5375 | Boeing 737-84P/W | 35762/2648 | | |

| | | | | |
|---|---|---|---|---|
| ☐ B-5403 | Boeing 737-84P/W | 35756/2691 | | |
| ☐ B-5405 | Boeing 737-84P/W | 35759/2668 | | |
| ☐ B-5406 | Boeing 737-84P/W | 35760/2678 | | |
| ☐ B-5408 | Boeing 737-84P/W | 35764/2778 | ex N1786B | |
| ☐ B-5416 | Boeing 737-84P/W | 34031/2801 | ex N1780B | |
| ☐ B-5417 | Boeing 737-86N/W | 35639/2821 | | |
| ☐ B-5418 | Boeing 737-86N/W | 36541/2769 | ex N1786B | |
| ☐ B-5427 | Boeing 737-8Q8/W | 35285/2772 | ex N1787B | |
| ☐ B-5428 | Boeing 737-86N/W | 36542/2806 | ex N1796B | |
| ☐ B-5429 | Boeing 737-86N/W | 36543/2831 | ex N1796B | |
| ☐ B-5430 | Boeing 737-84P/W | 34032/2827 | ex N1787B | |
| ☐ B-5433 | Boeing 737-86N/W | 36542/2806 | | ♦ |
| ☐ B-5439 | Boeing 737-808/W | 34707/2046 | ex B-KBH | |
| ☐ B-5449 | Boeing 737-808/W | 34971/2400 | ex B-KXH | |
| ☐ B-5462 | Boeing 737-84P/W | 36780/3095 | ex N1796B | |
| ☐ B-5463 | Boeing 737-84P/W | 35755/3339 | | ♦ |
| ☐ B-5465 | Boeing 737-84P/W | 34033/2854 | ex N1787B | |
| ☐ B-5466 | Boeing 737-84P/W | 34034/2912 | | |
| ☐ B-5467 | Boeing 737-84P/W | 36779/2885 | | |
| ☐ B-5478 | Boeing 737-84P/W | 35751/3038 | ex N1786B | |
| ☐ B-5479 | Boeing 737-84P/W | 35753/3066 | ex N1786B | |
| ☐ B-5480 | Boeing 737-86N/W | 35648/2973 | | |
| ☐ B-5481 | Boeing 737-86N/W | 35649/2981 | | |
| ☐ B-5482 | Boeing 737-84P/W | 35748/2938 | ex N1786B | |
| ☐ B-5483 | Boeing 737-84P/W | 35750/3007 | | |
| ☐ B-5502 | Boeing 737-84P/W | 35757/3192 | ex N1786B | |
| ☐ B-5503 | Boeing 737-84P/W | 36782/3186 | | |
| ☐ B-5520 | Boeing 737-84P/W | 35765/3344 | | |
| ☐ B-5521 | Boeing 737-84P/W | 35766/3313 | | |
| ☐ B-5522 | Boeing 737-84P/W | 36781/3278 | ex N1786B | |
| ☐ B-5538 | Boeing 737-84P/W | 36783/3382 | | |
| ☐ B-5539 | Boeing 737-84P/W | 35763/3378 | | |
| ☐ B-5540 | Boeing 737-84P/W | 35761/3392 | | ♦ |
| ☐ B-5579 | Boeing 737-84P/W | 39223/3610 | | ♦ |
| ☐ B-5580 | Boeing 737-84P/W | 39224/3647 | | ♦ |
| ☐ B-5581 | Boeing 737-84P/W | 38143/3713 | | ♦ |
| ☐ B-5611 | Boeing 737-84P/W | 38145/3783 | | ♦ |
| ☐ B-5620 | Boeing 737-84P/W | 38144/3733 | | ♦ |
| ☐ B-5623 | Boeing 737-84P/W | 38148/3865 | | ♦ |
| ☐ B-5625 | Boeing 737-84P/W | 38146/3812 | | ♦ |
| ☐ B-5636 | Boeing 737-84P/W | 38149/3889 | | ♦ |
| ☐ B-5637 | Boeing 737-84P/W | 38150/3937 | | ♦ |
| ☐ B-5638 | Boeing 737-84P/W | 38151/3951 | | ♦ |
| ☐ B-5661 | Boeing 737-84P/W | 38152/ | | o/o♦ |
| ☐ B-5662 | Boeing 737-84P/W | 38153/ | | o/o♦ |
| ☐ B-5663 | Boeing 737-84P/W | 38154/ | | o/o♦ |
| | | | | |
| ☐ B-2112 | Boeing 737-36N | 28599/3115 | ex EI-DRS | |
| ☐ B-2490 | Boeing 767-34PER | 33047/889 | | |
| ☐ B-2491 | Boeing 767-34PER | 33048/891 | | |
| ☐ B-2492 | Boeing 767-34PER | 33049/893 | | |
| ☐ B-5060 | Boeing 737-76N | 28582/154 | ex N582HE | |
| ☐ B-5062 | Boeing 737-76N | 28585/173 | ex N585HE | |
| ☐ B-6420 | Airbus A319-133 | 5105 | ex D-AVYS | o/o♦ |
| ☐ B-6421 | Airbus A319-133 | 4995 | ex D-AVYF | |
| ☐ B-6508 | Airbus A340-642 | 436 | ex B-HQA | |
| ☐ B-6509 | Airbus A340-642 | 453 | ex B-HQB | |
| ☐ B-6510 | Airbus A340-642 | 475 | ex B-HQC | |
| ☐ B-6520 | Airbus A330-343X | 1168 | ex F-WWYJ | |
| ☐ B-6527 | Airbus A330-343X | 1178 | ex F-WWKE | |
| ☐ B-6529 | Airbus A330-343X | 1190 | ex F-WWKG | |
| ☐ B-6539 | Airbus A330-343X | 1255 | ex F-WWYM | |

| *HEBEI AIRLINES* | | *(NS/HBH)* | | *Shenyang* |
|---|---|---|---|---|
| ☐ B-3040 | Embraer ERJ-145LR | 145317 | ex PT-SMI | |
| ☐ B-3041 | Embraer ERJ-145LR | 145349 | ex PT-SNP | |
| ☐ B-3042 | Embraer ERJ-145LR | 145352 | ex PT-SNR | |
| ☐ B-3043 | Embraer ERJ-145LR | 145377 | ex PT-SQB | ♦ |
| ☐ B-3045 | Embraer ERJ-145LR | 145470 | ex PT-SVP | |
| | | | | |
| ☐ B-3187 | Embraer ERJ-190LR | 19000497 | ex PT-TPW | ♦ |
| ☐ B-3188 | Embraer ERJ-190LR | 19000502 | ex PT-TRJ | ♦ |
| ☐ B-5212 | Boeing 737-75C | 34024/1703 | | ♦ |
| ☐ B-5215 | Boeing 737-75C | 34025/1724 | | ♦ |
| ☐ B-6025 | Airbus A320-232 | 0573 | ex B-MAD | ♦ |
| ☐ B-6170 | Airbus A319-132 | 2396 | ex N101LF | |

| *HENAN AIRLINES* | | *(VD/KPA)* | | *Xian (SIA)* |
|---|---|---|---|---|
| ☐ B-3126 | Embraer ERJ-190LR | 19000201 | ex PT-SGJ | |

| ☐ B-3131 | Embraer ERJ-190LR | 19000220 | ex PT-SIB | |
| ☐ B-3132 | Embraer ERJ-190LR | 19000263 | ex PT-TLD | |
| ☐ B-3133 | Embraer ERJ-190LR | 19000264 | ex PT-TLE | |

## JADE CARGO INTERNATIONAL — Jade Cargo (JI/JAE) — Shenzhen (SZX)

| ☐ B-2421 | Boeing 747-4EVERF | 35169/1391 | ex N1794B | |
| ☐ B-2422 | Boeing 747-4EVERF | 35173/1387 | | |
| ☐ B-2423 | Boeing 747-4EVERF | 35174/1398 | | |
| ☐ B-2439 | Boeing 747-4EVERF | 35170/1376 | | |
| ☐ B-2440 | Boeing 747-4EVERF | 35171/1380 | | |
| ☐ B-2441 | Boeing 747-4EVERF | 35172/1383 | | |

Aircraft grounded Dec11

## JIANGNAN UNIVERSAL AVIATION — Changzhou-West Suburbs (CZX)

| ☐ B-3865 | AVIC II Y-11 | (11)0410 | | |
| ☐ B-3866 | AVIC II Y-11 | (11)0104 | | |
| ☐ B-3867 | AVIC II Y-11 | (11)0206 | | |
| ☐ B-3868 | AVIC II Y-11 | (11)0109 | | |
| ☐ B-3821 | Harbin Y-12 II | 0032 | ex JU-1019 | |
| ☐ B-3823 | Harbin Y-12 II | 0068 | ex JU-1021 | |

## JOY AIR / HAPPY AIRLINES — Xian-Yanliang (SIA)

| ☐ B-3430 | AVIC MA60 | 0102 | | ♦ |
| ☐ B-3431 | AVIC MA60 | 0103 | | ♦ |
| ☐ B-3432 | AVIC MA60 | 0105 | | ♦ |
| ☐ B-3433 | AVIC MA60 | 0715 | | ♦ |
| ☐ B-3451 | AVIC MA60 | 0705 | | ♦ |
| ☐ B-3452 | AVIC MA60 | 0706 | | ♦ |
| ☐ B-3453 | AVIC MA60 | 0707 | | ♦ |
| ☐ B-3455 | AVIC MA60 | 0803 | | ♦ |
| ☐ B-3459 | AVIC MA60 | 0804 | | ♦ |
| ☐ B-3476 | AVIC MA60 | 0805 | | ♦ |

## JUNEYAO AIRLINES — Air Juneyao (HO/DKH) — Shanghai-Hongqiao (SHA)

| ☐ B-6298 | Airbus A320-214 | 2975 | ex F-WWDO | |
| ☐ B-6311 | Airbus A320-214 | 3027 | ex F-WWBM | |
| ☐ B-6338 | Airbus A320-214 | 3368 | ex F-WWDE | |
| ☐ B-6340 | Airbus A320-214 | 3234 | ex F-WWBH | |
| ☐ B-6341 | Airbus A320-214 | 3268 | ex F-WWBU | |
| ☐ B-6381 | Airbus A320-214 | 3485 | ex F-WWIG | |
| ☐ B-6395 | Airbus A320-214 | 3596 | ex F-WWDI | |
| ☐ B-6396 | Airbus A320-214 | 3605 | ex F-WWDN | |
| ☐ B-6572 | Airbus A320-214 | 3967 | ex F-WWIF | |
| ☐ B-6602 | Airbus A320-214 | 3984 | ex F-WWBJ | |
| ☐ B-6618 | Airbus A320-214 | 4102 | ex F-WWDO | |
| ☐ B-6619 | Airbus A320-214 | 4154 | ex F-WWBK | |
| ☐ B-6640 | Airbus A320-214 | 4064 | ex B-515L | |
| ☐ B-6670 | Airbus A320-214 | 4276 | ex F-WWDU | |
| ☐ B-6717 | Airbus A320-214 | 4401 | ex F-WWBK | |
| ☐ B-6735 | Airbus A320-214 | 4429 | ex B- | |
| ☐ B-6736 | Airbus A320-214 | 4573 | ex F-WWBT | |
| ☐ B-6768 | Airbus A320-214 | 4833 | ex F-WWIV | ♦ |
| ☐ B-6787 | Airbus A320-214 | 4587 | ex B- | ♦ |
| ☐ B-6788 | Airbus A320-214 | 4652 | ex B- | ♦ |
| ☐ B--6860 | Airbus A320-214 | 4981 | ex D-AVVN | ♦ |
| ☐ B-6861 | Airbus A320-214 | 4840 | ex B-514L | ♦ |
| ☐ B-6901 | Airbus A320-214 | 5070 | ex D-AUBG | ♦ |
| ☐ B- | Airbus A320-214 | | ex | o/o |
| ☐ B- | Airbus A320-214 | | ex | o/o |
| ☐ B-6232 | Airbus A319-112 | 2879 | ex D-AVXN | |
| ☐ B-6233 | Airbus A319-112 | 2913 | ex D-AVWZ | |

## KUNMING AIRLINES — (KY/KNA) — Kunming (KMG)

| ☐ B-2666 | Boeing 737-78S | 30169/631 | | ♦ |
| ☐ B-2668 | Boeing 737-78S | 30171/681 | ex N1786B | |
| ☐ B-2678 | Boeing 737-76N | 32244/895 | ex N315ML | |
| ☐ B-2679 | Boeing 737-76N | 29893/710 | ex N313ML | |
| ☐ B-5025 | Boeing 737-7BX | 30742/864 | ex N366ML | ♦ |

## LUCKY AIRLINES — Lucky Air (8L/LKE) — Dali City (DLU)

| ☐ B-5061 | Boeing 737-76N | 28583/163 | ex N583HE | |
| ☐ B-5091 | Boeing 737-705 | 29091/230 | ex VH-VBW | |
| ☐ B-5092 | Boeing 737-705 | 29092/260 | ex VH-VBX | ♦ |
| ☐ B-5246 | Boeing 737-7Q8/W | 30674/1511 | ex N751AL | |

| | | | | |
|---|---|---|---|---|
| ☐ B-5248 | Boeing 737-790/W | 30626/1273 | ex N629AS | |
| ☐ B-5249 | Boeing 737-790 | 33011/1291 | ex N645AS | |
| ☐ B-5268 | Boeing 737-790/W | 30662/1382 | ex N648AS | |
| ☐ B-5272 | Boeing 737-790/W | 30663/1386 | ex N649AS | |
| | | | | |
| ☐ B-5407 | Boeing 737-808/W | 34967/2239 | ex B-HXF | ♦ |
| ☐ B-5409 | Boeing 737-808/W | 34968/2265 | ex B-KXG | ♦ |
| ☐ B-6198 | Airbus A319-112 | 2617 | ex D-AYVI | ♦ |
| ☐ B-6212 | Airbus A319-115 | 2581 | ex D-AVXG | ♦ |

| **OKAY AIRWAYS** | *Okayjet (BK/OKA)* | | | *Tianjin (TSN)* |
|---|---|---|---|---|
| ☐ B-2863 | Boeing 737-83N/W | 30673/1500 | ex N333TZ | |
| ☐ B-2865 | Boeing 737-83N/W | 30679/1404 | ex N332TZ | |
| ☐ B-5367 | Boeing 737-8Q8/W | 30733/2452 | ex N1786B | |
| ☐ B-5562 | Boeing 737-8HO/W | 37934/3491 | | |
| ☐ B-5571 | Boeing 737-86N/W | 35643/2884 | ex N546MS | |
| ☐ B-5573 | Boeing 737-8HO/W | 37932/3498 | | |
| ☐ B-5575 | Boeing 737-8AS/W | 33554/1418 | ex N598MS | |
| ☐ B-5577 | Boeing 737-8ASW | 33557/1438 | ex N594MS | ♦ |
| ☐ B-5578 | Boeing 737-8AS/W | 33560/1447 | ex N328MS | ♦ |
| ☐ B- | Boeing 737-8HO/W | | | o/o |
| ☐ B- | Boeing 737-8HO/W | | | o/o |
| ☐ B- | Boeing 737-8HO/W | | | o/o |
| ☐ B- | Boeing 737-8HO/W | | | o/o |
| | | | | |
| ☐ B-2117 | Boeing 737-3Q8 (SF) | 24961/2133 | ex N141LF | |
| ☐ B-3433 | AVIC MA60 | 0715 | | ♦ |
| ☐ B-3440 | AVIC MA60 | 0714 | | ♦ |
| ☐ B-3709 | AVIC MA60 | 0509 | | ♦ |
| ☐ B-3710 | AVIC MA60 | 0510 | ex B-895L | ♦ |
| B-4071 | Shaanxi Y-8F-100 | | | ♦ |
| ☐ B-4072 | Shaanxi Y-8F-100 | | | ♦ |

| **RAINBOW JET** | *Cai Hong (RBW)* | | | *Jinan (TNA)* |
|---|---|---|---|---|
| ☐ B-3631 | Cessna 208 Caravan I | 20800333 | ex N1228V | FP |
| ☐ B-3632 | Cessna 208 Caravan I | 20800332 | ex N1284F | FP |
| ☐ B-3636 | Cessna 208 Caravan I | 20800338 | ex N1321L | FP |
| ☐ B-3639 | Cessna 208 Caravan I | 20800354 | ex N5283U | FP |

| **SF AIRLINES** | *(O3)* | | | |
|---|---|---|---|---|
| ☐ B-2828 | Boeing 757-25CPCF | 25899/565 | | ♦ |
| ☐ B-2829 | Boeing 757-25CPCF | 25900/574 | | ♦ |
| ☐ B-2832 | Boeing 757-2Z0PCF | 25887/554 | | ♦ |
| ☐ B-2839 | Boeing 757-2Z0PCF | 27269/615 | | ♦ |
| ☐ B-2899 | Boeing 757-21B(SF) | 24401/232 | ex N401AN | |
| | | | | |
| ☐ B-2598 | Boeing 737-3J6 (SF) | 27128/2493 | | ♦ |
| ☐ B-2951 | Boeing 737-3Z0(SF) | 27373/2658 | | ♦ |

| **SHAN XI AIRLINES** | *Shanxi (CXI)* | | | *Taiyuan-Wusu (TYN)* |
|---|---|---|---|---|
| ☐ B-3701 | AVIC I Y7-100C | 12705 | | [TYN] |
| ☐ B-3702 | AVIC I Y7-100C | 12707 | | [TYN] |
| ☐ B-3703 | AVIC I Y7-100C | 12708 | | [TYN] |
| ☐ B-5135 | Boeing 737-84P/W | 32603/1766 | ex N1786B | ♦ |

| **SHANDONG AIRLINES** | *Shandong (SC/CDG)* | | | *Jinan (TNA)* |
|---|---|---|---|---|
| ☐ B-2111 | Boeing 737-36Q | 29405/3047 | ex N405GT | |
| ☐ B-2877 | Boeing 737-33V | 29331/3062 | ex G-EZYG | |
| ☐ B-2961 | Boeing 737-35N | 28156/2774 | | |
| ☐ B-2962 | Boeing 737-35N | 28157/2778 | | |
| ☐ B-2968 | Boeing 737-35N | 28158/2818 | | |
| ☐ B-2995 | Boeing 737-35N | 29315/3054 | | |
| ☐ B-2996 | Boeing 737-35N | 29316/3065 | | |
| ☐ B-5066 | Boeing 737-36Q | 28761/3011 | ex N286CH | |
| | | | | |
| ☐ B-5111 | Boeing 737-85N/W | 33660/1752 | | |
| ☐ B-5117 | Boeing 737-85N/W | 33661/1770 | | |
| ☐ B-5118 | Boeing 737-85N/W | 33664/1726 | | |
| ☐ B-5119 | Boeing 737-85N/W | 33665/1775 | ex N1781B | |
| ☐ B-5321 | Boeing 737-8AL/W | 35073/2197 | | |
| ☐ B-5331 | Boeing 737-8AL/W | 35075/2287 | | |
| ☐ B-5332 | Boeing 737-8FH/W | 35095/2295 | | |
| ☐ B-5333 | Boeing 737-8FH/W | 35096/2336 | ex N1782B | |
| ☐ B-5335 | Boeing 737-8FH/W | 35097/2345 | ex N1787B | |
| ☐ B-5336 | Boeing 737-8FH/W | 35098/2361 | | |
| ☐ B-5347 | Boeing 737-85N/W | 36190/2429 | | |

| | | | | | |
|---|---|---|---|---|---|
| ☐ B-5348 | Boeing 737-85N/W | 36191/2453 | ex N1786B | | |
| ☐ B-5349 | Boeing 737-85N/W | 36192/2642 | | | |
| ☐ B-5350 | Boeing 737-85N/W | 36193/2669 | ex N1786B | | |
| ☐ B-5351 | Boeing 737-85N/W | 36194/2684 | | | |
| ☐ B-5352 | Boeing 737-85N/W | 36195/2823 | | | |
| ☐ B-5450 | Boeing 737-85N/W | 36773/2874 | ex N1786B | | |
| ☐ B-5451 | Boeing 737-85N/W | 36776/2998 | | | |
| ☐ B-5452 | Boeing 737-85N/W | 36777/3045 | ex N1796B | | |
| ☐ B-5453 | Boeing 737-85N/W | 36778/3277 | | | |
| ☐ B-5490 | Boeing 737-85P/W | 35493/3594 | | | |
| ☐ B-5491 | Boeing 737-85P/W | 36584/3626 | | | ♦ |
| ☐ B-5513 | Boeing 737-86N/W | 36546/3293 | ex N1796B | | ♦ |
| ☐ B-5526 | Boeing 737-8FZ/W | 31717/3237 | ex N1796B | | |
| ☐ B-5531 | Boeing 737-8FZ/W | 29659/3280 | | | ♦ |
| ☐ B-5536 | Boeing 737-8AL/W | 37424/3342 | ex N1786B | | |
| ☐ B-5537 | Boeing 737-8AL/W | 37954/3359 | | | ♦ |
| ☐ B-5541 | Boeing 737-85N/W | 40882/3368 | ex N1789B | | |
| ☐ B-5542 | Boeing 737-85N/W | 40883/3383 | ex N1786B | | |
| ☐ B-5543 | Boeing 737-86N/W | 39392/3447 | ex N1786B | | |
| ☐ B-5560 | Boeing 737-86N/W | 38013/3560 | | | ♦ |
| ☐ B-5561 | Boeing 737-86N/W | 38016/3589 | | | ♦ |
| ☐ B-5590 | Boeing 737-85N/W | 39128/3708 | | | ♦ |
| ☐ B-5591 | Boeing 737-8HX/W | 38098/3711 | | | ♦ |
| ☐ B-5592 | Boeing 737-8HX/W | 38099/3757 | | | ♦ |
| ☐ B-5593 | Boeing 737-85N/W | 39115/3742 | | | ♦ |
| ☐ B-5626 | Boeing 737-8HX/W | 38103/3903 | | | ♦ |
| ☐ B-5627 | Boeing 737-85N/W | 38637/3890 | | | ♦ |
| ☐ B-5628 | Boeing 737-85N/W | 39125/3934 | | | ♦ |
| ☐ B-5629 | Boeing 737-85N/W | 38638/3957 | | | ♦ |
| ☐ B-5648 | Boeing 737-85N/W | 38639/ | | | o/o♦ |
| ☐ B-5649 | Boeing 737-85N/W | 38640/ | | | o/o♦ |
| ☐ B-5650 | Boeing 737-85N/W | 38641/ | | | o/o♦ |
| ☐ B-5651 | Boeing 737-85N/W | 38642/ | | | o/o♦ |
| ☐ B-5652 | Boeing 737-85N/W | 39126/ | | | o/o♦ |
| | | | | | |
| ☐ B-3005 | Canadair CRJ-200LR | 7435 | ex C-FMKW | | |
| ☐ B-3006 | Canadair CRJ-200LR | 7443 | ex C-FMLV | | |
| ☐ B-3007 | Canadair CRJ-200LR | 7498 | ex C-FMLF | | |
| ☐ B-3008 | Canadair CRJ-200LR | 7512 | ex B-604L | | |
| ☐ B-3009 | Canadair CRJ-200LR | 7522 | ex C-FMMY | | |
| | | | | | |
| ☐ B-3079 | Canadair CRJ-701ER | 10118 | | | |
| ☐ B-3080 | Canadair CRJ-701ER | 10120 | | | |
| ☐ B-3630 | Cessna 208B Caravan I | 208B0883 | ex N12285 | | ♦ |
| ☐ B-5205 | Boeing 737-75N/W | 33654/1790 | | | |
| ☐ B-5206 | Boeing 737-75N/W | 33666/1742 | ex N1779B | | |
| ☐ B-5207 | Boeing 737-75N/W | 33663/1838 | ex N1787B | | |

| SHANGHAI AIRLINES | Shanghai Air (FM/CSH) | Shanghai-Hongqiao (SHA) |
|---|---|---|

Member of Star Alliance, merging with China Eastern

| | | | | | |
|---|---|---|---|---|---|
| ☐ B-2577 | Boeing 737-76D | 30168/600 | ex N1786B | | |
| ☐ B-2631 | Boeing 737-7Q8 | 28212/35 | ex N301LF | | |
| ☐ B-2632 | Boeing 737-7Q8 | 28216/122 | ex N1795B | | |
| ☐ B-2913 | Boeing 737-76D | 30167/550 | ex N1786B | | |
| ☐ B-5260 | Boeing 737-76D/W | 35777/3037 | | | |
| ☐ B-5261 | Boeing 737-76D/W | 35778/3064 | ex N1786B | | |
| ☐ B-5269 | Boeing 737-76D/W | 35779/3235 | | | ♦ |
| | | | | | |
| ☐ B-2153 | Boeing 737-8Q8 | 28242/942 | ex N1786B | | |
| ☐ B-2167 | Boeing 737-8Q8 | 30631/1047 | | | |
| ☐ B-2168 | Boeing 737-8Q8 | 30632/1086 | | | |
| ☐ B-2686 | Boeing 737-8Q8 | 28251/1200 | | | |
| ☐ B-2688 | Boeing 737-86D/W | 33471/1192 | ex N60668 | | |
| ☐ B-5076 | Boeing 737-86N | 32739/1434 | | | |
| ☐ B-5077 | Boeing 737-86N | 32742/1464 | | | |
| ☐ B-5088 | Boeing 737-82R | 30666/1460 | ex N171LF | | |
| ☐ B-5130 | Boeing 737-8Q8 | 32801/1666 | | | |
| ☐ B-5131 | Boeing 737-8Q8 | 30686/1704 | ex N1784B | | |
| ☐ B-5132 | Boeing 737-8Q8 | 30685/1789 | | | |
| ☐ B-5140 | Boeing 737-8Q8 | 30698/1911 | | | |
| ☐ B-5142 | Boeing 737-8Q8 | 30700/1942 | ex N1782B | | |
| ☐ B-5143 | Boeing 737-86N/W | 32691/2033 | | | |
| ☐ B-5145 | Boeing 737-8Q8 | 33007/1986 | | | |
| ☐ B-5148 | Boeing 737-86N/W | 34254/1897 | | | |
| ☐ B-5185 | Boeing 737-8Q8/W | 30715/2230 | | | |
| ☐ B-5315 | Boeing 737-86D | 35767/2316 | | | |
| ☐ B-5316 | Boeing 737-86D | 35768/2362 | | | |
| ☐ B-5320 | Boeing 737-8Q8/W | 30718/2251 | ex N1786B | | |
| ☐ B-5330 | Boeing 737-86N/W | 35212/2277 | ex N1786B | | |
| ☐ B-5368 | Boeing 737-8Q8 | 35273/2567 | | | |

| | | | | |
|---|---|---|---|---|
| ☐ B-5369 | Boeing 737-8Q8/W | 35281/2709 | | |
| ☐ B-5370 | Boeing 737-8Q8/W | 35271/2551 | ex N1786B | |
| ☐ B-5393 | Boeing 737-86D/W | 35769/2632 | | |
| ☐ B-5395 | Boeing 737-86D/W | 35770/2698 | ex N1786B | |
| ☐ B-5396 | Boeing 737-86D/W | 35771/2740 | ex N1786B | |
| ☐ B-5460 | Boeing 737-86D/W | 35772/3047 | | |
| ☐ B-5461 | Boeing 737-86D/W | 35773/2939 | ex N1787B | |
| ☐ B-5523 | Boeing 737-86D/W | 35776/3360 | | |
| ☐ B-5545 | Boeing 737-86N/W | 36803/3376 | | |
| ☐ B-5546 | Boeing 737-86N/W | 39391/3431 | ex N1786B | |
| ☐ B-5548 | Boeing 737-86N/W | 36807/3479 | ex N1795B | |
| ☐ B-5549 | Boeing 737-86N/W | 37888/3470 | ex N1796B | |
| ☐ B-5550 | Boeing 737-86N/W | 39393/3483 | | |
| ☐ B-5576 | Boeing 737-86N/W | 38011/3531 | | ♦ |
| ☐ B-5610 | Boeing 737-86N/W | 37906/3744 | ex N1786B | ♦ |
| | | | | |
| ☐ B-2833 | Boeing 757-26D | 27152/560 | | |
| ☐ B-2834 | Boeing 757-26D | 27183/576 | | |
| ☐ B-2842 | Boeing 757-26D | 27342/626 | | |
| ☐ B-2843 | Boeing 757-26D | 27681/684 | | |
| ☐ B-2850 | Boeing 757-231 | 30338/891 | ex N725TW | |
| ☐ B-2857 | Boeing 757-26D | 33959/1044 | | |
| ☐ B-2858 | Boeing 757-26D | 33960/1045 | | |
| ☐ B-2875 | Boeing 757-26D | 33966/1049 | ex N1795B | |
| ☐ B-2876 | Boeing 757-26D | 33967/1050 | | last 757 built |
| ☐ B-2880 | Boeing 757-26D | 33961/1046 | ex N1795B | |
| | | | | |
| ☐ B-2498 | Boeing 767-36D | 27684/849 | | |
| ☐ B-2500 | Boeing 767-36DER | 35155/946 | | |
| ☐ B-2563 | Boeing 767-36D | 27309/546 | | |
| ☐ B-2566 | Boeing 767-36DER | 35156/950 | | |
| ☐ B-2567 | Boeing 767-36D | 27685/686 | | |
| ☐ B-2570 | Boeing 767-36D | 27941/770 | | Star Alliance Colours |
| ☐ B-5018 | Boeing 767-3Q8ER | 28207/695 | ex N635TW | |
| | | | | |
| ☐ B-3011 | Canadair CRJ-200ER | 7556 | ex C-FMKZ | |
| ☐ B-3018 | Canadair CRJ-200ER | 7453 | ex C-FMNQ | [SIA] |
| ☐ B-3020 | Canadair CRJ-200ER | 7459 | ex C-FMMQ | |

## SHANGHAI AIRLINES CARGO (F4/SHQ) Shanghai-Pu Dong Intl (PVG)

| | | | | |
|---|---|---|---|---|
| ☐ B-2808 | Boeing 757-26D (PCF) | 24471/231 | ex N1792B | Frtr |
| ☐ B-2809 | Boeing 757-26D (PCF) | 24472/235 | ex N5573B | Frtr |

## SHENZHEN AIRLINES Shenzhen Air (ZH/CSZ) Shenzhen (SZX)

| | | | | |
|---|---|---|---|---|
| ☐ B-6153 | Airbus A319-115 | 2841 | ex D-AVYM | |
| ☐ B-6159 | Airbus A319-112 | 2905 | ex D-AVWQ | |
| ☐ B-6165 | Airbus A319-115X | 2935 | ex D-AVWM | |
| ☐ B-6196 | Airbus A319-115 | 2672 | ex D-AVYK | |
| ☐ B-6197 | Airbus A319-115 | 2684 | ex D-AVWM | |
| ☐ B- | Airbus A319-115 | | ex D-AV | o/o |
| | | | | |
| ☐ B-6286 | Airbus A320-214 | 2909 | ex F-WWDU | |
| ☐ B-6296 | Airbus A320-214 | 2973 | ex F-WWDN | |
| ☐ B-6297 | Airbus A320-214 | 2980 | ex F-WWBP | |
| ☐ B-6312 | Airbus A320-214 | 3131 | ex F-WWBK | |
| ☐ B-6313 | Airbus A320-214 | 3132 | ex F-WWBP | |
| ☐ B-6315 | Airbus A320-214 | 3153 | ex F-WWBZ | |
| ☐ B-6316 | Airbus A320-214 | 3206 | ex F-WWII | |
| ☐ B-6351 | Airbus A320-214 | 3366 | ex F-WWIU | |
| ☐ B-6352 | Airbus A320-214 | 3383 | ex F-WWDN | |
| ☐ B-6357 | Airbus A320-214 | 3440 | ex F-WWDZ | |
| ☐ B-6358 | Airbus A320-214 | 3435 | ex F-WWDV | |
| ☐ B-6359 | Airbus A320-214 | 3456 | ex D-AVVA | |
| ☐ B-6360 | Airbus A320-214 | 3528 | ex F-WWDV | |
| ☐ B-6377 | Airbus A320-214 | 3599 | ex F-WWDK | |
| ☐ B-6392 | Airbus A320-214 | 3696 | ex D-AVVA | |
| ☐ B-6550 | Airbus A320-214 | 3756 | ex F-WWBX | ♦ |
| ☐ B-6563 | Airbus A320-214 | 3698 | ex B-503L | |
| ☐ B-6565 | Airbus A320-214 | 3971 | ex F-WWIO | |
| ☐ B-6566 | Airbus A320-214 | 3855 | ex F-WWDK | |
| ☐ B-6567 | Airbus A320-214 | 3887 | ex F-WWBS | |
| ☐ B-6568 | Airbus A320-214 | 3898 | ex F-WWDN | |
| ☐ B-6569 | Airbus A320-214 | 3848 | ex F-WWDE | |
| ☐ B-6570 | Airbus A320-214 | 4010 | ex B-512L | |
| ☐ B-6571 | Airbus A320-232 | 3935 | ex F-WWDO | |
| ☐ B-6589 | Airbus A320-214 | 4028 | ex F-WWIA | |
| ☐ B-6613 | Airbus A320-232 | 4176 | ex F-WWDY | |
| ☐ B-6615 | Airbus A320-232 | 4214 | ex F-WWIM | |
| ☐ B-6647 | Airbus A320-214 | 4226 | ex F-WWBT | |

| | | | | | |
|---|---|---|---|---|---|
| ☐ B-6648 | Airbus A320-214 | 4159 | ex B-519L | | |
| ☐ B-6649 | Airbus A320-214 | 4208 | ex B-501L | | |
| ☐ B-6650 | Airbus A320-232 | 4300 | ex F-WWBQ | | ♦ |
| ☐ B-6690 | Airbus A320-232 | 4359 | ex F-WWDL | | |
| ☐ B-6691 | Airbus A320-232 | 4409 | ex D-AVVE | | |
| ☐ B-6692 | Airbus A320-232 | 4407 | ex F-WWDS | | |
| ☐ B-6697 | Airbus A320-232 | 4288 | ex F-WWIS | | ♦ |
| ☐ B-6720 | Airbus A320-232 | 4474 | ex F-WWDC | | ♦ |
| ☐ B-6721 | Airbus A320-232 | 4514 | ex D-AXAF | | |
| ☐ B-6722 | Airbus A320-232 | 4531 | ex F-WWDQ | | |
| ☐ B-6740 | Airbus A320-232 | 4435 | ex D-AVVT | | |
| ☐ B-6749 | Airbus A320-232 | 4633 | ex F-WWDU | | ♦ |
| ☐ B-6750 | Airbus A320-232 | 4666 | ex F-WWBC | | ♦ |
| ☐ B-6780 | Airbus A320-232 | 4729 | ex D-AUBL | | ♦ |
| ☐ B-6781 | Airbus A320-232 | 4620 | ex B- | | ♦ |
| ☐ B-6806 | Airbus A320-232 | 4845 | ex D-AUBF | | ♦ |
| ☐ B-6807 | Airbus A320-232 | 4897 | ex D-AVVH | | ♦ |
| ☐ B-6833 | Airbus A320-232 | 4920 | ex F-WWIB | | ♦ |
| ☐ B-6835 | Airbus A320-232 | 4986 | ex D-AVVS | | ♦ |
| ☐ B-6853 | Airbus A320-223 | 4866 | ex B-517L | | ♦ |
| ☐ B-6855 | Airbus A320-214 | 4876 | ex B-518L | | ♦ |
| ☐ B-6856 | Airbus A320-232 | 4929 | ex | | o/o♦ |
| ☐ B-6957 | Airbus A320-232 | 5002 | ex D-AVVW | | ♦ |
| | | | | | |
| ☐ B-2633 | Boeing 737-79K | 29190/110 | ex N1786B | | |
| ☐ B-2635 | Boeing 737-79K | 29191/127 | ex N1786B | | |
| ☐ B-2666 | Boeing 737-78S | 30169/631 | ex N1786B | | |
| ☐ B-2667 | Boeing 737-78S | 30170/654 | | | |
| ☐ B-2668 | Boeing 737-78S | 30171/681 | ex N1786B | | |
| ☐ B-2669 | Boeing 737-77L | 32722/1023 | ex N1786B | | |
| ☐ B-5026 | Boeing 737-7BX | 30741/823 | ex N367ML | | |
| | | | | | |
| ☐ B-2691 | Boeing 737-8Q8 | 30628/808 | ex N802SY | | |
| ☐ B-2692 | Boeing 737-8Q8 | 28241/841 | ex N803SY | | |
| ☐ B-5049 | Boeing 737-86N | 28639/772 | ex N639SH | | |
| ☐ B-5050 | Boeing 737-86N | 28643/828 | ex N643SH | | |
| ☐ B-5073 | Boeing 737-8Q8/W | 30680/1402 | | | |
| ☐ B-5075 | Boeing 737-8Q8 | 30692/1410 | | | |
| ☐ B-5078 | Boeing 737-8Q8 | 30690/1414 | ex N1779B | | |
| ☐ B-5079 | Boeing 737-8Q8 | 30693/1422 | | | |
| ☐ B-5186 | Boeing 737-8BK | 33020/2103 | | | |
| ☐ B-5187 | Boeing 737-8BK | 33828/2124 | | | |
| ☐ B-5317 | Boeing 737-86N/W | 32686/2175 | ex N1781B | | |
| ☐ B-5322 | Boeing 737-86N/W | 32688/2218 | | | |
| ☐ B-5345 | Boeing 737-86N/W | 35215/2306 | ex N1780B | | |
| ☐ B-5357 | Boeing 737-8AL/W | 35081/2519 | ex N1787B | | |
| ☐ B-5360 | Boeing 737-86J/W | 30062/485 | ex D-ABAW | | <BER |
| ☐ B-5361 | Boeing 737-86J/W | 30063/517 | ex D-ABAX | | <BER |
| ☐ B-5362 | Boeing 737-86J/W | 30499/567 | ex D-ABAY | | <BER |
| ☐ B-5363 | Boeing 737-86J/W | 30500/593 | ex D-ABAZ | | <BER |
| ☐ B-5365 | Boeing 737-86J/W | 30501/619 | ex D-ABAC | | <BER |
| ☐ B-5377 | Boeing 737-8AL/W | 35079/2555 | ex N1786B | | |
| ☐ B-5378 | Boeing 737-8AL/W | 35085/2563 | ex N1787B | | |
| ☐ B-5379 | Boeing 737-8AL/W | 35087/2605 | ex N1786B | | |
| ☐ B-5380 | Boeing 737-87L/W | 35527/2616 | | | |
| ☐ B-5381 | Boeing 737-87L/W | 35528/2631 | | City of Hohhot | |
| ☐ B-5400 | Boeing 737-87L/W | 35529/2677 | | | |
| ☐ B-5401 | Boeing 737-87L/W | 35530/2703 | ex N1786B | | |
| ☐ B-5402 | Boeing 737-87L/W | 35531/2726 | ex N1786B | | |
| ☐ B-5410 | Boeing 737-8AL/W | 35088/2771 | | | |
| ☐ B-5411 | Boeing 737-87L/W | 35532/2851 | | | |
| ☐ B-5412 | Boeing 737-87L/W | 35533/2900 | | | |
| ☐ B-5413 | Boeing 737-87L/W | 35535/2895 | ex N1786B | | |
| ☐ B-5440 | Boeing 737-87L/W | 35534/3003 | | | |
| ☐ B-5441 | Boeing 737-87L/W | 35536/3019 | ex N1786B | | |
| ☐ B-5606 | Boeing 737-87L/W | 39143/3624 | | | ♦ |
| ☐ B-5607 | Boeing 737-87L/W | 39144/3643 | | | ♦ |
| ☐ B-5608 | Boeing 737-87L/W | 39145/3656 | ex N1796B | | ♦ |
| ☐ B-5612 | Boeing 737-87L/W | 39146/3698 | | | ♦ |
| ☐ B-5613 | Boeing 737-87L/W | 39147/3705 | | | ♦ |
| ☐ B-5615 | Boeing 737-87L/W | 39148/3736 | | | ♦ |
| ☐ B-5616 | Boeing 737-87L/W | 39149/3755 | | | ♦ |
| ☐ B-5617 | Boeing 737-87L/W | 39150/3770 | | | ♦ |
| ☐ B-5618 | Boeing 737-87L/W | 39151/3828 | | | ♦ |
| ☐ B-5619 | Boeing 737-87L/W | 39152/3841 | | | ♦ |
| ☐ B-5670 | Boeing 737-87L/W | 39129/ | | | o/o♦ |
| | | | | | |
| ☐ B-5102 | Boeing 737-97L | 33644/1750 | | | ♦ |
| ☐ B-5103 | Boeing 737-97L | 33645/1760 | | | ♦ |
| ☐ B-5105 | Boeing 737-97L | 33646/1764 | ex N1784B | | ♦ |
| ☐ B-5106 | Boeing 737-97L | 33648/1722 | | | ♦ |
| ☐ B-5109 | Boeing 737-97L | 33649/1755 | | | ♦ |

| | | | | |
|---|---|---|---|---|
| ☐ B-2971 | Boeing 737-3Q8 | 25373/2290 | ex N221LF | |
| ☐ B-2972 | Boeing 737-33A | 27463/2831 | | |

## SHENZHEN GRAND SEA AVIATION

| | | | | |
|---|---|---|---|---|
| ☐ B-9426 | Cessna 208B Caravan I | 208B2202 | ex N2052G | ♦ |

## SHUANGYANG AVIATION — Shuangyang (CSY) — Anshun (AOG)

| | | | | |
|---|---|---|---|---|
| ☐ B-3811 | Harbin Y-12 II | 0012 | | Combi |
| ☐ B-3813 | Harbin Y-12 II | 0025 | | Sprayer |
| ☐ B-3814 | Harbin Y-12 II | 0026 | | Sprayer |
| ☐ B-3827 | Harbin Y-12 II | 0063 | ex 9N-ACF | ♦ |
| ☐ B-3828 | Harbin Y-12 II | 0071 | ex 9N-ADB | ♦ |
| | | | | |
| ☐ B-3895 | AVIC II Y-11 | (11)0401 | | |
| ☐ B-3896 | AVIC II Y-11 | (11)0402 | | |
| ☐ B-3897 | AVIC II Y-11 | (11)0403 | | |
| ☐ B-3898 | AVIC II Y-11 | (11)0404 | | |

## SICHUAN AIRLINES — Chuanhang (3U/CSC) — Chengdu (CTU)

| | | | | |
|---|---|---|---|---|
| ☐ B-2298 | Airbus A319-133 | 2534 | ex D-AVYM | |
| ☐ B-2299 | Airbus A319-133 | 2597 | ex D-AVXN | |
| ☐ B-2300 | Airbus A319-133 | 2639 | ex D-AVWK | |
| ☐ B-6043 | Airbus A319-133 | 2313 | ex D-AVYI | |
| ☐ B-6045 | Airbus A319-133 | 2348 | ex D-AVYH | |
| ☐ B-6054 | Airbus A319-133 | 2510 | ex D-AVWC | |
| ☐ B-6170 | Airbus A319-132 | 2396 | ex N101LF | |
| ☐ B-6171 | Airbus A319-132 | 2431 | ex N112CG | |
| ☐ B-6173 | Airbus A319-133 | 3114 | ex D-AYYA | |
| ☐ B-6175 | Airbus A319-133 | 3116 | ex D-AYYB | |
| ☐ B-6176 | Airbus A319-133 | 3124 | ex D-AYYC | |
| ☐ B-6185 | Airbus A319-133 | 3680 | ex D-AVYY | |
| ☐ B-6406 | Airbus A319-133 | 3962 | ex D-AVXP | |
| ☐ B-6410 | Airbus A319-133 | 4018 | ex D-AVYG | |
| ☐ B-6419 | Airbus A319-133 | 4660 | ex B- | ♦ |
| | | | | |
| ☐ B-2341 | Airbus A320-232 | 0551 | ex F-WWBI | |
| ☐ B-2342 | Airbus A320-232 | 0556 | ex F-WWIL | |
| ☐ B-2348 | Airbus A320-233 | 0912 | ex EI-TAA | |
| ☐ B-2373 | Airbus A320-233 | 0919 | ex F-WWIC | |
| ☐ B-2397 | Airbus A320-233 | 1013 | ex F-WWDP | |
| ☐ B-6026 | Airbus A320-232 | 0582 | ex B-MAE | |
| ☐ B-6027 | Airbus A320-233 | 1007 | ex N460TA | |
| ☐ B-6049 | Airbus A320-233 | 0902 | ex (D-ANNI) | |
| ☐ B-6295 | Airbus A320-233 | 1500 | ex N481TA | |
| ☐ B-6321 | Airbus A320-232 | 3210 | ex F-WWIK | |
| ☐ B-6322 | Airbus A320-232 | 3158 | ex F-WWDP | |
| ☐ B-6323 | Airbus A320-232 | 3167 | ex F-WWIM | |
| ☐ B-6325 | Airbus A320-232 | 3196 | ex F-WWIE | |
| ☐ B-6347 | Airbus A320-232 | 3386 | ex F-WWDP | |
| ☐ B-6348 | Airbus A320-232 | 3449 | ex F-WWIY | |
| ☐ B-6388 | Airbus A320-232 | 3591 | ex B-501L | |
| ☐ B-6621 | Airbus A320-232 | 4068 | ex F-WWBI | |
| ☐ B-6697 | Airbus A320-232 | 4288 | ex F-WWIS | |
| ☐ B-6700 | Airbus A320-232 | 4326 | ex F-WWIA | |
| ☐ B-6719 | Airbus A320-232 | 4424 | ex F-WWBD | |
| ☐ B-6732 | Airbus A320-232 | 4378 | ex B- | ♦ |
| ☐ B-6770 | Airbus A320-232 | 4642 | ex F-WWBU | ♦ |
| ☐ B-6771 | Airbus A320-232 | 4619 | ex D-AXAW | ♦ |
| ☐ B-6772 | Airbus A320-232 | 4525 | ex B- | ♦ |
| ☐ B-6778 | Airbus A320-232 | 4707 | ex F-WWBE | ♦ |
| ☐ B-6779 | Airbus A320-232 | 4575 | ex F-WWBE | ♦ |
| ☐ B-6843 | Airbus A320-232 | 4905 | ex D-AVVJ | ♦ |
| ☐ B- | Airbus A320-232 | 4911 | ex B- | o/o♦ |
| ☐ B- | Airbus A320-232 | 5041 | ex B- | o/o♦ |
| | | | | |
| ☐ B-2286 | Airbus A321-131 | 0550 | ex N550BR | |
| ☐ B-2293 | Airbus A321-131 | 0591 | ex N451LF | |
| ☐ B-2370 | Airbus A321-231 | 0878 | ex D-AVZF | |
| ☐ B-2371 | Airbus A321-231 | 0915 | ex D-AVZM | |
| ☐ B-6285 | Airbus A321-231 | 1060 | ex HL7590 | |
| ☐ B-6300 | Airbus A321-231 | 1293 | ex HL7549 | |
| ☐ B-6387 | Airbus A321-231 | 3583 | ex D-AVZE | |
| ☐ B-6551 | Airbus A321-231 | 3730 | ex D-AZAI | |
| ☐ B-6590 | Airbus A321-231 | 3893 | ex D-AVZV | |
| ☐ B-6598 | Airbus A321-231 | 3996 | ex D-AZAQ | |
| ☐ B-6718 | Airbus A321-232 | 4420 | ex D-AZAF | ♦ |
| ☐ B-6810 | Airbus A321-231 | 4731 | ex D-AVZH | ♦ |
| ☐ B-6836 | Airbus A321-231 | 4824 | ex D-AVZK | ♦ |

| | | | | |
|---|---|---|---|---|
| ☐ B-6838 | Airbus A321-231 | 4856 | ex D-AVZZ | ♦ |
| ☐ B-6839 | Airbus A321-231 | 4830 | ex D-AVZT | ♦ |
| ☐ B-6845 | Airbus A321-231 | 4923 | ex D-AVZI | ♦ |
| | | | | |
| ☐ B-6517 | Airbus A330-243 | 1138 | ex F-WWYZ | |
| ☐ B-6518 | Airbus A330-243 | 1082 | ex F-WWYZ | |
| ☐ B-6535 | Airbus A330-243 | 1241 | ex F-WWYB | ♦ |

## SICHUAN AOLIN GENERAL AVIATION — Chengdu (CTU)

| | | | |
|---|---|---|---|
| ☐ B-3637 | Cessna 208B Caravan I | 208B0919 | ex N1294D |
| ☐ B-3640 | Cessna 208B Caravan I | 208B0952 | ex N1132X |
| ☐ B-3641 | Cessna 208B Caravan I | 208B0953 | ex N1133B |

## SOUTH CHINA SEA RESCUE AVIATION

| | | | | |
|---|---|---|---|---|
| ☐ B-7136 | Eurocopter EC225LP | 2781 | ex F-WJXR | ♦ |

## SPRING AIRLINES — Air Spring (9S/CQH) — Shanghai-Hongqiao (SHA)

| | | | | |
|---|---|---|---|---|
| ☐ B-6250 | Airbus A320-214 | 1372 | ex EI-DKS | |
| ☐ B-6280 | Airbus A320-214 | 1286 | ex N120US | |
| ☐ B-6301 | Airbus A320-214 | 2939 | ex F-WWIO | |
| ☐ B-6309 | Airbus A320-214 | 3014 | ex F-WWBO | |
| ☐ B-6310 | Airbus A320-214 | 3023 | ex F-WWBZ | |
| ☐ B-6320 | Airbus A320-214 | 1686 | ex N686RL | |
| ☐ B-6328 | Airbus A320-214 | 0978 | ex N888CQ | |
| ☐ B-6349 | Airbus A320-214 | 1852 | ex I-EEZC | |
| ☐ B-6380 | Airbus A320-214 | 1769 | ex EC-JDK | |
| ☐ B-6561 | Airbus A320-214 | 3819 | ex F-WWIO | |
| ☐ B-6562 | Airbus A320-214 | 3747 | ex F-WWIL | |
| ☐ B-6573 | Airbus A320-214 | 1920 | ex I-EEZD | |
| ☐ B-6612 | Airbus A320-214 | 4072 | ex F-WWBM | |
| ☐ B-6645 | Airbus A320-214 | 4168 | ex D-AVVQ | |
| ☐ B-6646 | Airbus A320-214 | 4093 | ex B-516L | |
| ☐ B-6667 | Airbus A320-214 | 4244 | ex F-WWDP | |
| ☐ B-6705 | Airbus A320-214 | 4331 | ex D-AXAQ | |
| ☐ B-6706 | Airbus A320-214 | 4366 | ex D-AXAX | |
| ☐ B-6707 | Airbus A320-214 | 4373 | ex F-WWBO | |
| ☐ B-6708 | Airbus A320-214 | 4375 | ex D-AVVB | |
| ☐ B-6751 | Airbus A320-214 | 4499 | ex B- | ♦ |
| ☐ B-6752 | Airbus A320-214 | 4586 | ex F-WWIP | ♦ |
| ☐ B-6820 | Airbus A320-214 | 4738 | ex F-WWIP | ♦ |
| ☐ B-6821 | Airbus A320-214 | 4750 | ex F-WWIV | ♦ |
| ☐ B-6840 | Airbus A320-214 | 4760 | ex B-506L | ♦ |
| ☐ B-6841 | Airbus A320-214 | 4816 | ex F-WWDX | ♦ |
| ☐ B-6851 | Airbus A320-214 | 4909 | ex F-WWBG | ♦ |
| ☐ B-6852 | Airbus A320-214 | 4809 | ex B-510L | ♦ |
| ☐ B-6862 | Airbus A320-214 | 4983 | ex F-WWIH | ♦ |
| ☐ B-6863 | Airbus A320-214 | 4978 | ex F-WWIE | ♦ |
| ☐ B-6902 | Airbus A320-214 | 5108 | ex F-WWIV♦ | o/o♦ |

## TIANJIN AIRLINES — (GS/GCR) — Tianjin (TSN)

| | | | | |
|---|---|---|---|---|
| ☐ B-3873 | Dornier 328-310 (328JET) | 3201 | ex D-BDXO | [SIA] |
| ☐ B-3946 | Dornier 328-310 (328JET) | 3208 | ex D-BDXI | [SIA] |
| ☐ B-3947 | Dornier 328-310 (328JET) | 3203 | ex D-BXXX | [SIA] |
| ☐ B-3948 | Dornier 328-310 (328JET) | 3204 | ex D-BDXT | [SIA] |
| ☐ B-3949 | Dornier 328-310 (328JET) | 3198 | ex N328AB | [SIA] |
| ☐ B-3960 | Dornier 328-310 (328JET) | 3123 | ex D-BDXJ | [TSN] |
| ☐ B-3961 | Dornier 328-310 (328JET) | 3128 | ex D-BDXK | [SIA] |
| ☐ B-3962 | Dornier 328-310 (328JET) | 3143 | ex D-BDXX | [SIA] |
| ☐ B-3963 | Dornier 328-310 (328JET) | 3138 | ex D-BDXT | [TSN] |
| ☐ B-3965 | Dornier 328-310 (328JET) | 3140 | ex D-BDXW | [SIA] |
| ☐ B-3966 | Dornier 328-310 (328JET) | 3135 | ex D-BDXQ | [SIA] |
| ☐ B-3967 | Dornier 328-310 (328JET) | 3144 | ex D-BDXB | [SIA] |
| ☐ B-3968 | Dornier 328-310 (328JET) | 3148 | ex D-BDXE | |
| ☐ B-3969 | Dornier 328-310 (328JET) | 3153 | ex D-BDXN | [SIA] |
| ☐ B-3970 | Dornier 328-310 (328JET) | 3154 | ex D-BDXP | [SIA] |
| ☐ B-3971 | Dornier 328-310 (328JET) | 3172 | ex D-BDXJ | [SIA] |
| ☐ B-3972 | Dornier 328-310 (328JET) | 3175 | ex D-BDXK | [SIA] |
| ☐ B-3973 | Dornier 328-310 (328JET) | 3158 | ex D-BDXQ | [SIA] |
| ☐ B-3975 | Dornier 328-310 (328JET) | 3159 | ex D-BDXU | [TSN] |
| ☐ B-3976 | Dornier 328-310 (328JET) | 3177 | ex D-BDXY | [SIA] |
| ☐ B-3977 | Dornier 328-310 (328JET) | 3182 | ex D-BDXD | [SIA] |
| ☐ B-3978 | Dornier 328-310 (328JET) | 3187 | ex D-BDXP | [SIA] |
| ☐ B-3979 | Dornier 328-310 (328JET) | 3191 | ex D-BDXJ | [SIA] |
| ☐ B-3982 | Dornier 328-310 (328JET) | 3195 | ex D-BDXJ | [SIA] |
| ☐ B-3983 | Dornier 328-310 (328JET) | 3211 | ex N328KL | [SIA] |
| ☐ B-3985 | Dornier 328-310 (328JET) | 3215 | ex D-BHUU | [SAI] |
| ☐ B-3986 | Dornier 328-310 (328JET) | 3217 | ex D-BJUU | [SIA] |

| | | | | |
|---|---|---|---|---|
| ☐ B-3987 | Dornier 328-310 (328JET) | 3218 | ex D-BKUU | [SIA] |
| | | | | |
| ☐ B-3030 | Embraer ERJ-145LI | 14501009 | ex PT-SOX | |
| ☐ B-3031 | Embraer ERJ-145LI | 14501013 | ex PT-SOY | |
| ☐ B-3032 | Embraer ERJ-145LI | 14501019 | ex PT-SOZ | |
| ☐ B-3033 | Embraer ERJ-145LI | 14501022 | ex PT-SZJ | |
| ☐ B-3035 | Embraer ERJ-145LI | 14500996 | ex PT-SOU | |
| ☐ B-3036 | Embraer ERJ-145LI | 14501000 | ex PT-S | |
| ☐ B-3037 | Embraer ERJ-145LI | 14501005 | ex PT-S | |
| ☐ B-3038 | Embraer ERJ-145LI | 14501024 | ex PT-SZK | |
| ☐ B-3039 | Embraer ERJ-145LI | 14500992 | ex PT-SOT | |
| ☐ B-3067 | Embraer ERJ-145LI | 14501036 | ex PT-SZR | |
| ☐ B-3068 | Embraer ERJ-145LI | 14501040 | ex PT-SZS | |
| ☐ B-3069 | Embraer ERJ-145LI | 14501043 | ex PT-SZT | |
| ☐ B-3081 | Embraer ERJ-145LI | 14501027 | ex PT-SZN | |
| ☐ B-3082 | Embraer ERJ-145LI | 14501030 | ex PT-SZP | |
| ☐ B-3083 | Embraer ERJ-145LI | 14501033 | ex PT-SZQ | |
| ☐ B-3085 | Embraer ERJ-145LI | 14501047 | ex PT-SZU | |
| ☐ B-3086 | Embraer ERJ-145LI | 14501050 | ex PT-SZV | |
| ☐ B-3087 | Embraer ERJ-145LI | 14501053 | ex PT-SZW | |
| ☐ B-3088 | Embraer ERJ-145LI | 14501056 | ex PT-SZX | |
| ☐ B-3089 | Embraer ERJ-145LI | 14501059 | ex PT-SZY | |
| ☐ B-3090 | Embraer ERJ-145LI | 14501063 | ex PT-TKK | ♦ |
| ☐ B-3091 | Embraer ERJ-145LI | 14501065 | ex PT-TKM | |
| ☐ B-3092 | Embraer ERJ-145LI | 14501068 | ex PT-XUQ | |
| ☐ B-3093 | Embraer ERJ-145LI | 14501070 | ex PT-TBU | ♦ |
| ☐ B-3095 | Embraer ERJ-145LI | 14501073 | ex PT-TBW | ♦ |
| | | | | |
| ☐ B-3120 | Embraer ERJ-190LR | 19000171 | ex PT-SDG | |
| ☐ B-3121 | Embraer ERJ-190LR | 19000181 | ex PT-SDP | |
| ☐ B-3122 | Embraer ERJ-190LR | 19000186 | ex PT-SDU | |
| ☐ B-3123 | Embraer ERJ-190LR | 19000192 | ex PT-SGA | |
| ☐ B-3125 | Embraer ERJ-190LR | 19000194 | ex PT-SGC | |
| ☐ B-3127 | Embraer ERJ-190LR | 19000207 | ex PT-SGQ | |
| ☐ B-3128 | Embraer ERJ-190LR | 19000229 | ex PT-SIA | |
| ☐ B-3129 | Embraer ERJ-190LR | 19000246 | ex PT-SIR | |
| ☐ B-3150 | Embraer ERJ-190LR | 19000253 | ex PT-SIY | |
| ☐ B-3151 | Embraer ERJ-190LR | 19000268 | ex PT-TLI | |
| ☐ B-3152 | Embraer ERJ-190LR | 19000274 | ex PT-TLO | |
| ☐ B-3153 | Embraer ERJ-190LR | 19000284 | ex PT-TLY | |
| ☐ B-3155 | Embraer ERJ-190LR | 19000293 | ex PT-TZH | |
| ☐ B-3156 | Embraer ERJ-190LR | 19000299 | ex PT-TZN | |
| ☐ B-3157 | Embraer ERJ-190LR | 19000306 | ex PT-TZU | |
| ☐ B-3158 | Embraer ERJ-190LR | 19000313 | ex PT-TXB | |
| ☐ B-3159 | Embraer ERJ-190LR | 19000318 | ex PT-TXG | |
| ☐ B-3160 | Embraer ERJ-190LR | 19000323 | ex PT-TXL | |
| ☐ B-3161 | Embraer ERJ-190LR | 19000328 | ex PT-TXQ | |
| ☐ B-3162 | Embraer ERJ-190LR | 19000331 | ex PT-TXR | |
| ☐ B-3163 | Embraer ERJ-190LR | 19000335 | ex PT-TXV | |
| ☐ B-3165 | Embraer ERJ-190LR | 19000340 | ex PT-TXZ | |
| ☐ B-3166 | Embraer ERJ-190LR | 19000348 | ex PT-XQO | |
| ☐ B-3167 | Embraer ERJ-190LR | 19000352 | ex PT-XQS | |
| ☐ B-3168 | Embraer ERJ-190LR | 19000355 | ex PT-XQU | |
| ☐ B-3169 | Embraer ERJ-190LR | 19000369 | ex PT-XNH | |
| ☐ B-3170 | Embraer ERJ-190LR | 19000371 | ex PT-XNI | |
| ☐ B-3171 | Embraer ERJ-190LR | 19000379 | ex PT-XNO | |
| ☐ B-3172 | Embraer ERJ-190LR | 19000385 | ex PT-XNT | |
| ☐ B-3173 | Embraer ERJ-190LR | 19000394 | ex PT-XUA | |
| ☐ B-3175 | Embraer ERJ-190LR | 19000405 | ex PT-TYY | |
| ☐ B-3176 | Embraer ERJ-190LR | 19000406 | ex PT-TYZ | |
| ☐ B-3177 | Embraer ERJ-190LR | 19000410 | ex PT-TBI | ♦ |
| ☐ B-3178 | Embraer ERJ-190LR | 19000417 | ex PT-TBO | ♦ |
| ☐ B-3179 | Embraer ERJ-190LR | 19000426 | ex PT-TCK | ♦ |
| ☐ B-3180 | Embraer ERJ-190LR | 19000442 | ex PT-TIC | ♦ |
| ☐ B-3181 | Embraer ERJ-190LR | 19000454 | ex PT-TJY | ♦ |
| ☐ B-3182 | Embraer ERJ-190LR | 19000459 | ex PT-TNZ | ♦ |
| ☐ B-3183 | Embraer ERJ-190LR | 19000472 | ex PT-TOS | ♦ |
| ☐ B-3185 | Embraer ERJ-190LR | 19000480 | ex PT-TPF | ♦ |
| ☐ B-3186 | Embraer ERJ-190LR | 19000489 | ex PT- | ♦ |
| ☐ B-3189 | Embraer ERJ-190LR | 19000508 | ex PT-TSE | ♦ |
| ☐ B-3190 | Embraer ERJ-190LR | 19000517 | ex PT-TUE | ♦ |
| ☐ B-3191 | Embraer ERJ-190LR | 19000535 | ex PT-TUY | ♦ |
| | | | | |
| ☐ B-6789 | Airbus A320-232 | 4739 | ex B-504L | ♦ |
| ☐ B-6837 | Airbus A320-232 | 4809 | ex B-511L | ♦ |

## TIBET AIRLINES

| | | | | |
|---|---|---|---|---|
| ☐ B-6436 | Airbus A319-115 | 4766 | ex D-AVYH | ♦ |
| ☐ B-6437 | Airbus A319-115 | 4801 | ex D-AVWA | ♦ |
| ☐ B-6438 | Airbus A319-115 | 4846 | ex D-AVWQ | ♦ |

## UNI-TOP AIRLINES                                (UW)

| | | | | |
|---|---|---|---|---|
| ☐ B-2448 | Boeing 747-2J6B (SF) | 23461/628 | ex N60668 | [WUH] |
| ☐ B-2450 | Boeing 747-2J6B (SF) | 23746/670 | ex N6018N | [PEK] |

## UNIVERSAL AIRLINES

| | | | | |
|---|---|---|---|---|
| ☐ B-3101 | Shaanxi Y-8F-100 | 100801 | ex Chinese AF | ♦ |
| ☐ B-9457 | Cessna 208B Caravan I | 208B2224 | ex N60214 | ♦ |
| ☐ B-9458 | Cessna 208B Caravan I | 208B2233 | ex N30439 | ♦ |
| ☐ B-9459 | Cessna 208B Caravan I | 208B2235 | ex N303355 | ♦ |
| ☐ B-9460 | Cessna 208B Caravan I | 208B2237 | ex N6023R | ♦ |

## WEST AIR                                (PN/CHB)                          Chongqing (CKG)

| | | | | |
|---|---|---|---|---|
| ☐ B-6743 | Airbus A320-232 | 4569 | ex D-AVVB | ♦ |
| ☐ B-6763 | Airbus A320-232 | 4482 | ex B- | ♦ |
| ☐ B-6765 | Airbus A320-232 | 4688 | ex D-AUBB | ♦ |
| ☐ B-6790 | Airbus A320-232 | 4686 | ex F-WWIJ | ♦ |
| ☐ B-6811 | Airbus A320-232 | 4644 | ex B- | ♦ |
| | | | | |
| ☐ B-6412 | Airbus A319-132 | 4262 | ex B-506L | |
| ☐ B-6413 | Airbus A319-132 | 4452 | ex D-AVYB | |
| ☐ B-2112 | Boeing 737-36N | 28599/3115 | ex EI-DRS | ♦ |
| ☐ B-2115 | Boeing 737-36N | 28606/3124 | ex EI-DRZ | ♦ |
| ☐ B-2963 | Boeing 737-3Q8 | 26325/2772 | | < |

## XIAMEN AIRLINES                    Xiamen Air (MF/CXA)                    Xiamen (XMN)

| | | | | |
|---|---|---|---|---|
| ☐ B-2658 | Boeing 737-75C | 30512/637 | ex N1786B | |
| ☐ B-2659 | Boeing 737-75C | 30513/676 | | |
| ☐ B-2991 | Boeing 737-75C | 29085/90 | | |
| ☐ B-2992 | Boeing 737-75C | 29086/108 | ex N1786B | |
| ☐ B-2998 | Boeing 737-75C | 29042/73 | ex N1786B | |
| ☐ B-2999 | Boeing 737-75C | 29084/86 | ex N1796B | |
| ☐ B-5028 | Boeing 737-75C | 30034/1275 | | |
| ☐ B-5029 | Boeing 737-75C | 30634/1229 | | |
| ☐ B-5038 | Boeing 737-7Q8 | 30656/1304 | ex N1787B | |
| ☐ B-5039 | Boeing 737-75C | 28258/1315 | | |
| ☐ B-5216 | Boeing 737-75C | 34026/1733 | | |
| ☐ B-5218 | Boeing 737-75C | 34027/1767 | ex N1786B | |
| ☐ B-5219 | Boeing 737-75C | 34028/1771 | | |
| ☐ B-5277 | Boeing 737-75C/W | 38381/3697 | | |
| ☐ B-5278 | Boeing 737-75C/W | 38383/3734 | | ♦ |
| ☐ B-5279 | Boeing 737-75C/W | 38384/3721 | | ♦ |
| ☐ B-5280 | Boeing 737-75C/W | 35385/3752 | | ♦ |
| | | | | |
| ☐ B-5146 | Boeing 737-86N/W | 34253/1866 | | |
| ☐ B-5151 | Boeing 737-86N/W | 34255/1975 | | |
| ☐ B-5152 | Boeing 737-86N/W | 34256/1990 | | |
| ☐ B-5159 | Boeing 737-85C/W | 35044/2018 | ex N1784B | |
| ☐ B-5160 | Boeing 737-85C/W | 35045/2050 | | |
| ☐ B-5161 | Boeing 737-85C/W | 35046/2105 | | |
| ☐ B-5162 | Boeing 737-85C/W | 35047/2130 | ex N1787B | |
| ☐ B-5301 | Boeing 737-85C/W | 35048/2194 | | |
| ☐ B-5302 | Boeing 737-85C/W | 35049/2271 | | |
| ☐ B-5303 | Boeing 737-85C/W | 35050/2305 | ex N1780B | |
| ☐ B-5305 | Boeing 737-85C/W | 35051/2364 | | |
| ☐ B-5306 | Boeing 737-85C/W | 35052/2418 | ex N1786B | |
| ☐ B-5307 | Boeing 737-85C/W | 35053/2447 | | |
| ☐ B-5308 | Boeing 737-86N/W | 32687/2229 | | |
| ☐ B-5309 | Boeing 737-86N/W | 32689/2254 | | |
| ☐ B-5318 | Boeing 737-85C/W | 30723/2283 | | |
| ☐ B-5319 | Boeing 737-8FH/W | 35102/2471 | ex N1796B | |
| ☐ B-5355 | Boeing 737-8FH/W | 35104/2495 | ex N1780B | |
| ☐ B-5382 | Boeing 737-86N/W | 36540/2681 | | |
| ☐ B-5383 | Boeing 737-86N/W | 35631/2693 | | |
| ☐ B-5385 | Boeing 737-86N/W | 35633/2741 | | |
| ☐ B-5386 | Boeing 737-86N/W | 35634/2732 | | |
| ☐ B-5388 | Boeing 737-86N/W | 35635/2764 | | |
| ☐ B-5389 | Boeing 737-86N/W | 35636/2775 | ex N1786B | |
| ☐ B-5432 | Boeing 737-86N/W | 35641/2852 | | |
| ☐ B-5433 | Boeing 737-86N/W | 35642/2855 | ex N1796B | |
| ☐ B-5435 | Boeing 737-86N/W | 35644/2922 | | |
| ☐ B-5456 | Boeing 737-85C/W | 35054/2914 | ex N1786B | |
| ☐ B-5458 | Boeing 737-85C/W | 35055/3016 | ex N1786B | |
| ☐ B-5459 | Boeing 737-85C/W | 35057/2992 | | |
| ☐ B-5476 | Boeing 737-85C/W | 35056/3091 | | |
| ☐ B-5487 | Boeing 737-85C/W | 35058/3150 | | |
| ☐ B-5488 | Boeing 737-85C/W | 37148/3104 | | |
| ☐ B-5489 | Boeing 737-85C/W | 37149/3142 | | |

48

| | | | | |
|---|---|---|---|---|
| ☐ B-5498 | Boeing 737-85C/W | 37574/3160 | | |
| ☐ B-5499 | Boeing 737-85C/W | 37575/3190 | ex N1786B | |
| ☐ B-5511 | Boeing 737-85C/W | 37576/3245 | ex N1787B | |
| ☐ B-5512 | Boeing 737-85C/W | 37577/3255 | | |
| ☐ B-5528 | Boeing 737-85C/W | 37578/3332 | | ♦ |
| ☐ B-5529 | Boeing 737-85C/W | 37150/3386 | | |
| ☐ B-5532 | Boeing 737-85C/W | 37151/3397 | | |
| ☐ B-5533 | Boeing 737-85C/W | 37152/3403 | | ♦ |
| ☐ B-5535 | Boeing 737-85C/W | 37579/3424 | | |
| ☐ B-5551 | Boeing 737-84P/W | 36697/3443 | ex N1786B | |
| ☐ B-5552 | Boeing 737-84P/W | 37425/3408 | | |
| ☐ B-5563 | Boeing 737-86N/W | 38012/3550 | | ♦ |
| ☐ B-5565 | Boeing 737-86N/W | 38015/3566 | | ♦ |
| ☐ B-5566 | Boeing 737-85C/W | 37153/3571 | | ♦ |
| ☐ B-5595 | Boeing 737-86N/W | 38017/3614 | ex N1786B | ♦ |
| ☐ B-5601 | Boeing 737-86N/W | 36823/3712 | | ♦ |
| ☐ B-5602 | Boeing 737-86N/W | 36824/3703 | | ♦ |
| ☐ B-5603 | Boeing 737-86N/W | 38020/3638 | | ♦ |
| ☐ B-5605 | Boeing 737-86N/W | 38022/3672 | | ♦ |
| ☐ B-5630 | Boeing 737-85C/W | 38386/3897 | | ♦ |
| ☐ B-5631 | Boeing 737-85C/W | 38387/3929 | | ♦ |
| ☐ B-5632 | Boeing 737-85C/W | 38388/3973 | | ♦ |
| ☐ B-5633 | Boeing 737-85C/W | 38389/3987 | | ♦ |
| | | | | |
| ☐ B-2848 | Boeing 757-25C | 27513/685 | | |
| ☐ B-2849 | Boeing 757-25C | 27517/698 | | |
| ☐ B-2862 | Boeing 757-25C | 34008/1047 | | |
| ☐ B-2866 | Boeing 757-25C | 34009/1048 | | |
| ☐ B-2868 | Boeing 757-25C | 32941/993 | | |
| ☐ B-2869 | Boeing 757-25C | 32942/1009 | | |

## XINJIANG GENERAL AVIATION — Shihezi

| | | | |
|---|---|---|---|
| ☐ B-3869 | AVIC II Y-11 | (11)0501 | |
| ☐ B-3870 | AVIC II Y-11 | (11)0502 | |
| ☐ B-3885 | AVIC II Y-11 | (11)0301 | |
| ☐ B-3887 | AVIC II Y-11 | (11)0303 | |
| ☐ B-3888 | AVIC II Y-11 | (11)0304 | |
| ☐ B-3890 | AVIC II Y-11 | (11)0306 | |
| ☐ B-3891 | AVIC II Y-11 | (11)0307 | |
| ☐ B-3894 | AVIC II Y-11 | (11)0310 | |
| | | | |
| ☐ B-3815 | Harbin Y-12 II | 0023 | Geological survey |
| ☐ B-3817 | Harbin Y-12 II | 0029 | Photographic survey |
| ☐ B-3818 | Harbin Y-12 II | 0030 | Photographic survey |
| ☐ B-3847 | Harbin Y-12 IV | 045 | ♦ |
| ☐ B-3849 | Harbin Y-12 IV | 036 | ♦ |
| ☐ B-3850 | Harbin Y-12 IV | 007 | ♦ |

## YANGTZE RIVER EXPRESS — Yangtze River (Y8/YZR) — Shanghai-Hongqiao (SHA)

| | | | | | |
|---|---|---|---|---|---|
| ☐ B-2578 | Boeing 737-33A | 25603/2333 | ex N401AW | special flower c/s | ♦ |
| ☐ B-2908 | Boeing 737-341 (SF) | 26854/2303 | ex PP-VPC | | ♦ |
| ☐ B-2942 | Boeing 737-332 (SF) | 25997/2506 | ex N304DE | | ♦ |
| ☐ B-2945 | Boeing 737-39K | 27362/2639 | | | ♦ |
| ☐ B-5053 | Boeing 737-322F | 24378/1704 | ex N357UA | | |
| ☐ B-5055 | Boeing 737-330(QC) | 24283/1677 | ex N283A | | |
| ☐ B-5056 | Boeing 737-330(QC) | 23836/1508 | ex N836Y | | |
| ☐ B-5057 | Boeing 737-330(QC) | 23837/1514 | ex N837Y | | |
| ☐ B-5058 | Boeing 737-330(QC) | 23835/1465 | ex N835A | | |
| ☐ B-5059 | Boeing 737-322F | 24362/1696 | ex N356UA | | |
| | | | | | |
| ☐ B-2431 | Boeing 747-409F | 30761/1254 | ex N703CL | | <CAL |
| ☐ B-2432 | Boeing 747-481(SF) | 28283/1142 | ex N200FQ | | |
| ☐ B-2435 | Boeing 747-481(SF) | 28282/1133 | ex N483YR | | |
| ☐ B-2437 | Boeing 747-481F | 25207/870 | ex N599MS | | ♦ |
| ☐ B-5900 | Airbus A330-243F | 1175 | ex F-WWKT | | o/o♦ |

## ZHONGFEI GENERAL AVIATION — Zhongfei (CFZ) — Xi'an-Yanliang (SIA)

| | | | |
|---|---|---|---|
| ☐ B-3820 | Harbin Y-12 II | 0031 | |
| ☐ B-3829 | Harbin Y-12 II | 0031 | |
| ☐ B-3856 | Harbin Y-12 IV | 040 | ♦ |
| ☐ B-3857 | Harbin Y-12 IV | 049 | ♦ |
| ☐ B-3858 | Harbin Y-12 IV | 039 | ♦ |
| | | | |
| ☐ B-9457 | Cessna 208B Caravan I | 208B2224 | ex N60214 | ♦ |
| ☐ B-9458 | Cessna 208B Caravan I | 208B2233 | ex N30439 | ♦ |
| ☐ B-9459 | Cessna 208B Caravan I | 208B2235 | ex N30355 | ♦ |
| ☐ B-9460 | Cessna 208B Caravan I | 208B2237 | ex N6023P | ♦ |

## YING'AN AIRLINES

| ☐ B-3832 | Harbin Y-12E | 011 | | ♦ |

## ZHONGSHAN EAGLE

| ☐ B-9327 | Cessna 208B Caravan I | 208B2196 | ex N1035Q | ♦ |

## ZHUHAI GENERAL AVIATION

| ☐ B-3812 | Harbin Y-12 II | 0024 | | ♦ |

# B-H/K/L    CHINA - HONG KONG

## AIR HONG KONG | Air Hong Kong (LD/AHK) | Hong Kong (HKG)

| ☐ B-LDA | Airbus A300F4-605R | 855 | ex F-WWAN | | |
| ☐ B-LDB | Airbus A300F4-605R | 856 | ex F-WWAP | | |
| ☐ B-LDC | Airbus A300F4-605R | 857 | ex F-WWAQ | | |
| ☐ B-LDD | Airbus A300F4-605R | 858 | ex F-WWAR | | |
| ☐ B-LDE | Airbus A300F4-605R | 859 | ex F-WWAS | | |
| ☐ B-LDF | Airbus A300F4-605R | 860 | ex F-WWAT | | |
| ☐ B-LDG | Airbus A300F4-605R | 870 | ex F-WWAJ | | |
| ☐ B-LDH | Airbus A300F4-605R | 871 | ex F-WWAK | | |
| ☐ TC-AGK | Airbus A300B4-203F | 117 | ex G-CEXH | Siirt 5 | <KZU |
| ☐ B-HOU | Boeing 747-467BCF | 24925/834 | ex VR-HOU | | ♦ |
| ☐ B-HUR | Boeing 747-444BCF | 24976/827 | ex ZS-SAV | | ♦ |
| ☐ B-HUS | Boeing 747-444BCF | 25152/861 | ex ZS-SAW | | ♦ |

## CATHAY PACIFIC AIRWAYS | Cathay (CX/CPA) | Hong Kong (HKG)

Member of Oneworld

| ☐ B-HLA | Airbus A330-342 | 071 | ex VR-HLA | | |
| ☐ B-HLD | Airbus A330-342 | 102 | ex VR-HLD | | |
| ☐ B-HLF | Airbus A330-342 | 113 | ex VR-HLF | | |
| ☐ B-HLG | Airbus A330-342 | 118 | ex VR-HLG | | |
| ☐ B-HLH | Airbus A330-342 | 121 | ex VR-HLH | | |
| ☐ B-HLI | Airbus A330-342 | 155 | ex VR-HLI | | |
| ☐ B-HLJ | Airbus A330-342 | 012 | ex VR-HLJ | | |
| ☐ B-HLK | Airbus A330-342 | 017 | ex VR-HLK | | |
| ☐ B-HLL | Airbus A330-342 | 244 | ex F-WWKG | | |
| ☐ B-HLM | Airbus A330-343X | 386 | ex F-WWYT | | |
| ☐ B-HLN | Airbus A330-343X | 389 | ex F-WWYV | | |
| ☐ B-HLO | Airbus A330-343X | 393 | ex F-WWYY | | |
| ☐ B-HLP | Airbus A330-343X | 418 | ex F-WWKV | | |
| ☐ B-HLQ | Airbus A330-343X | 420 | ex F-WWYB | | |
| ☐ B-HLR | Airbus A330-343X | 421 | ex F-WWYC | | |
| ☐ B-HLS | Airbus A330-343X | 423 | ex F-WWYD | | |
| ☐ B-HLT | Airbus A330-343X | 439 | ex F-WWYJ | | |
| ☐ B-HLU | Airbus A330-343X | 539 | ex F-WWYG | | |
| ☐ B-HLV | Airbus A330-343X | 548 | ex F-WWYI | | |
| ☐ B-HLW | Airbus A330-343X | 565 | ex F-WWYR | | |
| ☐ B-LAA | Airbus A330-342E | 669 | ex F-WWKS | Asia's World City titles | |
| ☐ B-LAB | Airbus A330-342E | 673 | ex F-WWKZ | Asia's World City titles | |
| ☐ B-LAC | Airbus A330-342E | 679 | ex F-WWYC | | |
| ☐ B-LAD | Airbus A330-342E | 776 | ex F-WWKI | Progress Hong Kong c/s | |
| ☐ B-LAE | Airbus A330-342E | 850 | ex F-WWKQ | | |
| ☐ B-LAF | Airbus A330-342E | 855 | ex F-WWYC | | |
| ☐ B-LAG | Airbus A330-342E | 895 | ex F-WWYV | | |
| ☐ B-LAH | Airbus A330-342E | 915 | ex F-WWYN | | |
| ☐ B-LAI | Airbus A330-342E | 959 | ex F-WWYE | | |
| ☐ B-LAJ | Airbus A330-343X | 1163 | ex F-WWKR | | |
| ☐ B-LAK | Airbus A330-343X | 1196 | ex F-WWYD | | |
| ☐ B-LAL | Airbus A330-343X | 1222 | ex F-WWYC | | ♦ |
| ☐ B-LAM | Airbus A330-343X | 1239 | ex F-WWKL | | ♦ |
| ☐ B-LAN | Airbus A330-343X | 1285 | ex F-WWYE | | ♦ |
| ☐ B-HXA | Airbus A340-313X | 136 | ex VR-HXA | | |
| ☐ B-HXB | Airbus A340-313X | 137 | ex VR-HXB | | |
| ☐ B-HXC | Airbus A340-313X | 142 | ex VR-HXC | | |
| ☐ B-HXD | Airbus A340-313X | 147 | ex VR-HXD | | |
| ☐ B-HXE | Airbus A340-313X | 157 | ex VR-HXE | | |
| ☐ B-HXF | Airbus A340-313X | 160 | ex VR-HXF | | |
| ☐ B-HXG | Airbus A340-313X | 208 | ex F-WWJC | | |
| ☐ B-HXH | Airbus A340-313X | 218 | ex F-WWJT | | |
| ☐ B-HXI | Airbus A340-313X | 220 | ex F-WWJO | | |
| ☐ B-HXJ | Airbus A340-313X | 227 | ex F-WWJL | | |

| | | | | |
|---|---|---|---|---|
| ☐ B-HXK | Airbus A340-313X | 228 | ex F-WWJI | |
| ☐ B-HXM | Airbus A340-313X | 123 | ex 9V-SJA | [XMN] |
| | | | | |
| ☐ B-HKE | Boeing 747-412 | 25127/859 | ex N127LC | |
| ☐ B-HKF | Boeing 747-412 | 25128/860 | ex 9V-SML | |
| ☐ B-HKH | Boeing 747-412BCF | 24227/831 | ex 9V-SMH | |
| ☐ B-HKJ | Boeing 747-412BCF | 27133/962 | ex 9V-SMR | |
| ☐ B-HKT | Boeing 747-412 | 27132/955 | ex 4X-ELS | |
| ☐ B-HKU | Boeing 747-412 | 27069/1010 | ex 9V-SMV | |
| ☐ B-HKV | Boeing 747-412 | 26552/1056 | ex 9V-SPD | |
| ☐ B-HKX | Boeing 747-412BCF | 26557/1101 | ex 9V-SPL | |
| ☐ B-HOP | Boeing 747-467 | 23815/728 | ex VR-HOP | |
| ☐ B-HOR | Boeing 747-467 | 24631/771 | ex VR-HOR | |
| ☐ B-HOS | Boeing 747-467 | 24850/788 | ex VR-HOS | |
| ☐ B-HOT | Boeing 747-467 | 24851/813 | ex VR-HOT | |
| ☐ B-HOV | Boeing 747-467 | 25082/849 | ex VR-HOV | |
| ☐ B-HOW | Boeing 747-467 | 25211/873 | ex VR-HOW | |
| ☐ B-HOX | Boeing 747-467 | 24955/877 | ex VR-HOX | |
| ☐ B-HOY | Boeing 747-467 | 25351/887 | ex VR-HOY | Asia's World City c/s |
| ☐ B-HOZ | Boeing 747-467BCF | 25871/925 | ex VR-HOZ | |
| ☐ B-HUA | Boeing 747-467 | 25872/930 | ex VR-HUA | |
| ☐ B-HUB | Boeing 747-467 | 25873/937 | ex VR-HUB | |
| ☐ B-HUD | Boeing 747-467 | 25874/949 | ex VR-HUD | |
| ☐ B-HUE | Boeing 747-467 | 27117/970 | ex VR-HUE | |
| ☐ B-HUF | Boeing 747-467 | 25869/993 | ex VR-HUF | |
| ☐ B-HUG | Boeing 747-467 | 25870/1007 | ex VR-HUG | |
| ☐ B-HUH | Boeing 747-467F | 27175/1020 | ex VR-HUH | |
| ☐ B-HUI | Boeing 747-467 | 27230/1033 | ex VR-HUI | |
| ☐ B-HUJ | Boeing 747-467 | 27595/1061 | ex VR-HUJ | |
| ☐ B-HUK | Boeing 747-467F | 27503/1065 | ex VR-HUK | |
| ☐ B-HUL | Boeing 747-467F | 30804/1255 | | |
| ☐ B-HUO | Boeing 747-467F | 32571/1271 | ex B-HUM | |
| ☐ B-HUP | Boeing 747-467F | 30805/1282 | ex (B-HUN) | |
| ☐ B-HUQ | Boeing 747-467F | 34150/1356 | | |
| ☐ B-KAE | Boeing 747-412BCF | 25068/852 | ex 9V-SMJ | [VCV] |
| ☐ B-KAF | Boeing 747-412BCF | 26547/921 | ex 9V-SMM | >CAO |
| ☐ B-KAH | Boeing 747-412BCF | 27134/981 | ex 9V-SMS | >CAO |
| ☐ B-KAI | Boeing 747-412BCF | 27217/1023 | ex 9V-SMY | |
| ☐ B-LIA | Boeing 747-467ERF | 37299/1404 | | |
| ☐ B-LIB | Boeing 747-467ERF | 36867/1409 | ex N5014K | |
| ☐ B-LIC | Boeing 747-467ERF | 36868/1413 | ex N5014K | |
| ☐ B-LID | Boeing 747-467ERF | 36869/1414 | | |
| ☐ B-LIE | Boeing 747-467ERF | 36870/1415 | ex N5022E | |
| ☐ B-LIF | Boeing 747-467ERF | 36871/1417 | | |
| | | | | |
| ☐ B-LJA | Boeing 747-867F | 39238/1427 | | |
| ☐ B-LJB | Boeing 747-867F | 39239/1428 | | |
| ☐ B-LJC | Boeing 747-867F | 39240/1433 | | o/o |
| ☐ B-LJD | Boeing 747-867F | 39241 | | o/o♦ |
| ☐ B-LJE | Boeing 747-867F | 39242/1441 | | ♦ |
| ☐ B-LJF | Boeing 747-867F | 39243/1447 | | ♦ |
| ☐ B-LJG | Boeing 747-867F | 39244/1450 | | ♦ |
| ☐ B-LJH | Boeing 747-867F | 39245 | | o/o♦ |
| ☐ B-LJI | Boeing 747-867F | 39247 | | o/o♦ |
| ☐ B-LJJ | Boeing 747-867F | 39246 | | o/o♦ |
| | | | | |
| ☐ B-HNA | Boeing 777-267 | 27265/14 | ex VR-HNA | |
| ☐ B-HNB | Boeing 777-267 | 27266/18 | ex VR-HNB | |
| ☐ B-HNC | Boeing 777-267 | 27263/28 | ex VR-HNC | |
| ☐ B-HND | Boeing 777-267 | 27264/31 | ex VR-HND | |
| ☐ B-HNL | Boeing 777-267 | 27116/1 | ex N7771 | ♦ |
| | | | | |
| ☐ B-HNE | Boeing 777-367 | 27507/94 | ex N5014K | |
| ☐ B-HNF | Boeing 777-367 | 27506/102 | ex N5016R | |
| ☐ B-HNG | Boeing 777-367 | 27505/118 | ex N5017V | |
| ☐ B-HNH | Boeing 777-367 | 27504/136 | | |
| ☐ B-HNI | Boeing 777-367 | 27508/204 | | |
| ☐ B-HNJ | Boeing 777-367 | 27509/224 | | |
| ☐ B-HNK | Boeing 777-367 | 27510/248 | | |
| ☐ B-HNM | Boeing 777-367 | 33702/456 | | |
| ☐ B-HNN | Boeing 777-367 | 33703/462 | | |
| ☐ B-HNO | Boeing 777-367 | 33704/470 | | |
| ☐ B-HNP | Boeing 777-367 | 34243/513 | | |
| ☐ B-HNQ | Boeing 777-367 | 34244/567 | ex N6009F | |
| ☐ B-KPA | Boeing 777-367ER | 36154/661 | ex N1788B | |
| ☐ B-KPB | Boeing 777-367ER | 35299/670 | | |
| ☐ B-KPC | Boeing 777-367ER | 34432/674 | | |
| ☐ B-KPD | Boeing 777-367ER | 36155/680 | | |
| ☐ B-KPE | Boeing 777-367ER | 36156/685 | | |
| ☐ B-KPF | Boeing 777-367ER | 36832/692 | | Asia's World City c/s |
| ☐ B-KPG | Boeing 777-367ER | 35300/700 | | |
| ☐ B-KPH | Boeing 777-367ER | 35301/720 | ex N50281 | |

| ☐ B-KPI | Boeing 777-367ER | 36833/746 | | | |
| ☐ B-KPJ | Boeing 777-367ER | 36157/754 | ex N5016R | | |
| ☐ B-KPK | Boeing 777-367ER | 36158/783 | ex N5023Q | | |
| ☐ B-KPL | Boeing 777-367ER | 36161/818 | | | |
| ☐ B-KPM | Boeing 777-367ER | 36159/835 | | | |
| ☐ B-KPN | Boeing 777-367ER | 36165/839 | | | |
| ☐ B-KPO | Boeing 777-367ER | 36160/843 | | | |
| ☐ B-KPP | Boeing 777-367ER | 36164/845 | ex N1785B | | |
| ☐ B-KPQ | Boeing 777-367ER | 36162/860 | ex N5016R | | |
| ☐ B-KPR | Boeing 777-367ER | 36163/877 | | | |
| ☐ B-KPS | Boeing 777-367ER | 39232/920 | | | ♦ |
| ☐ B-KPT | Boeing 777-367ER | 37896/927 | | | ♦ |
| ☐ B-KPU | Boeing 777-367ER | 39233/934 | | | ♦ |
| ☐ B-KPV | Boeing 777-367ER | 37901/941 | | | ♦ |
| ☐ B-KPW | Boeing 777-367ER | 39234/950 | | | ♦ |
| ☐ B-KPX | Boeing 777-367ER | 37897/956 | | | ♦ |
| ☐ B-KPY | Boeing 777-367ER | 37899/991 | | | ♦ |
| ☐ B-KPZ | Boeing 777-367ER | 37900/1003 | | | ♦ |
| ☐ B-KQA | Boeing 777-367ER | 37898 | | | o/o♦ |
| ☐ B-KQB | Boeing 777-367ER | 39235 | | | o/o♦ |
| ☐ B-KQC | Boeing 777-367ER | 39236 | | | o/o♦ |
| | | | | | |
| ☐ B-HMD | Boeing 747-2L5B(SF) | 22105/435 | ex VR-HMD | | [VCV] |
| ☐ B-HME | Boeing 747-2L5B(SF) | 22106/443 | ex VR-HME | | [VCV] |
| ☐ B-HVX | Boeing 747-267F | 24568/776 | ex VR-HVX | | [VCV] |
| ☐ B-HVZ | Boeing 747-267F | 23864/687 | ex VR-HVZ | | [VCV] |

## DRAGONAIR — Dragon (KA/HDA) — Hong Kong (HKG)

| ☐ B-HSD | Airbus A320-232 | 0756 | ex F-WWBC | | |
| ☐ B-HSE | Airbus A320-232 | 0784 | ex F-WWDL | | |
| ☐ B-HSG | Airbus A320-232 | 0812 | ex B-22315 | | |
| ☐ B-HSI | Airbus A320-232 | 0930 | ex F-WWIE | | |
| ☐ B-HSJ | Airbus A320-232 | 1253 | ex F-WWIU | | |
| ☐ B-HSK | Airbus A320-232 | 1721 | ex F-WWDF | | |
| ☐ B-HSL | Airbus A320-232 | 2229 | ex F-WWIE | | |
| ☐ B-HSM | Airbus A320-232 | 2238 | ex F-WWDG | | |
| ☐ B-HSN | Airbus A320-232 | 2428 | ex F-WWBI | | |
| ☐ B-HSO | Airbus A320-232 | 4023 | ex F-WWDN | | |
| ☐ B-HSP | Airbus A320-232 | 4247 | ex F-WWDV | | |
| ☐ B-HSQ | Airbus A320-232 | 5024 | ex F-WWBD | | |
| ☐ B-HSR | Airbus A320-232 | 5030 | ex D-AXAK | | ♦ |
| | | | | | |
| ☐ B-HTD | Airbus A321-231 | 0993 | ex D-AVZF | | ♦ |
| ☐ B-HTE | Airbus A321-231 | 1024 | ex D-AVZD | | |
| ☐ B-HTF | Airbus A321-231 | 0633 | ex G-OZBC | | |
| ☐ B-HTG | Airbus A321-231 | 1695 | ex D-AVZA | | |
| ☐ B-HTH | Airbus A321-231 | 1984 | ex D-AVZX | | |
| ☐ B-HTI | Airbus A321-231 | 2021 | ex D-AVXJ | | |
| | | | | | |
| ☐ B-HLB | Airbus A330-342 | 083 | ex VR-HLB | | ♦ |
| ☐ B-HLC | Airbus A330-342 | 099 | ex VR-HLC | | ♦ |
| ☐ B-HLE | Airbus A330-342 | 109 | ex VR-HLE | | ♦ |
| ☐ B-HWF | Airbus A330-343 | 654 | ex F-WWYM | | |
| ☐ B-HWG | Airbus A330-343 | 662 | ex F-WWYZ | The Way of the Dragon | |
| ☐ B-HWH | Airbus A330-343 | 692 | ex F-WWYO | | |
| ☐ B-HWI | Airbus A330-343 | 716 | ex F-WWYX | | |
| ☐ B-HWJ | Airbus A330-343 | 741 | ex F-WWYE | | |
| ☐ B-HWK | Airbus A330-343 | 786 | ex F-WWYZ | | |
| ☐ B-HYB | Airbus A330-342 | 106 | ex VR-HYB | | |
| ☐ B-HYF | Airbus A330-342 | 234 | ex F-WWKF | | |
| ☐ B-HYG | Airbus A330-343 | 405 | ex F-WWKQ | | |
| ☐ B-HYI | Airbus A330-343 | 479 | ex F-WWKU | | |
| ☐ B-HYJ | Airbus A330-343 | 512 | ex F-WWYR | | |
| ☐ B-HYQ | Airbus A330-343 | 581 | ex F-WWKK | | |

## HONG KONG AIRLINES — Bauhina (HX/CRK) — Hong Kong (HKG)

| ☐ B-LNC | Airbus A330-223 | 1031 | ex F-WWKF | | |
| ☐ B-LND | Airbus A330-223 | 1042 | ex F-WWKK | | |
| ☐ B-LNE | Airbus A330-223 | 1039 | ex F-WWYO | | |
| ☐ B-LNF | Airbus A330-223 | 1059 | ex F-WWKV | | |
| ☐ B-LNG | Airbus A330-223 | 1054 | ex F-WWYC | | |
| ☐ B-LNI | Airbus A330-223 | 1034 | ex B-6521 | | ♦ |
| ☐ B-LNJ | Airbus A330-243 | 1277 | ex F-WWYJ | | ♦ |
| ☐ B-LNK | Airbus A330-243 | 1286 | ex F-WWYH | | ♦ |
| ☐ B-LNX | Airbus A330-243F | 1115 | ex WWKO | | ♦ |
| ☐ B-LNY | Airbus A330-243F | 1062 | ex F-WWKD | | |
| ☐ B-LNZ | Airbus A330-243F | 1051 | ex F-WWKU | | |
| ☐ B- | Airbus A330-243F | 1175 | ex F-WW | | o/o♦ |
| ☐ B- | Airbus A330-243 | 1322 | ex F-WW | | o/o♦ |

| | | | | | |
|---|---|---|---|---|---|
| ☐ B-KBI | Boeing 737-808/W | 34709/2121 | ex N1787B | | |
| ☐ B-KBU | Boeing 737-84P/W | 37953/3299 | | | <CHH |
| ☐ B-LHN | Boeing 737-39K (SF) | 27274/2559 | | ex B-2934 | ♦ |
| ☐ B-LHO | Boeing 737-332 (SF) | 25998/2510 | ex B-2943 | | ♦ |
| ☐ B-LPB | Airbus A320-214 | 4970 | ex F-WWID | | ♦ |

### HONG KONG EXPRESS AIRWAYS — Hong Kong Shuttle (UO/HKE) — Hong Kong (HKG)

| | | | | |
|---|---|---|---|---|
| ☐ B-KBK | Boeing 737-84P/W | 35072/2155 | ex N1786B | ♦ |
| ☐ B-KBM | Boeing 737-84P/W | 35076/2380 | | |
| ☐ B-KBQ | Boeing 737-84P/W | 35274/2570 | | |
| ☐ B-KBR | Boeing 737-84P/W | 35276/2611 | | |
| ☐ B-KBT | Boeing 737-84P/W | 37422/3241 | | ♦ |
| ☐ B-KXE | Boeing 737-808/W | 34710/2144 | | <CHH |
| | | | | |
| ☐ N599MS | Boeing 747-481F | 25207/870 | ex JA8098 | >YZR♦ |

### SKY SHUTTLE HELICOPTERS — Heli Hong Kong (UO/HHK) — HK / Macau Heliport

| | | |
|---|---|---|
| ☐ B-KHM | Agusta AW139 | 31238 |
| ☐ B-KHN | Agusta AW139 | 31243 |
| ☐ B-MHI | Agusta AW139 | 31220 |
| ☐ B-MHK | Agusta AW139 | 31229 |
| ☐ B-MHL | Agusta AW139 | 31230 |
| | | |
| ☐ B-HJR | Sikorsky S-76C+ | 760497 |

## B-M   CHINA - MACAU

### AIR MACAU — Air Macau (NX/AMU) — Macau (MFM)

| | | | | |
|---|---|---|---|---|
| ☐ B-MAK | Airbus A319-132 | 1758 | ex D-AVYF | Rio Yangtze |
| ☐ B-MAL | Airbus A319-132 | 1790 | ex D-AVYR | Rio Amarelo |
| ☐ B-MAM | Airbus A319-112 | 1893 | ex D-AVYJ | Lago Sul Lua |
| ☐ B-MAN | Airbus A319-132 | 1912 | ex D-AVWZ | Rio Huang Pu |
| ☐ B-MAO | Airbus A319-132 | 1962 | ex D-AVWU | Rio Yaluzangbu |
| | | | | |
| ☐ B-MAB | Airbus A321-131 | 0557 | ex VN-A341 | Lotus |
| ☐ B-MAF | Airbus A321-131 | 0620 | ex CS-MAF | Acores |
| ☐ B-MAG | Airbus A321-131 | 0631 | ex CS-MAG | Ilha de Coloane |
| ☐ B-MAJ | Airbus A321-231 | 0908 | ex CS-MAJ | Farol da Guia |
| ☐ B-MAP | Airbus A321-231 | 1850 | ex D-AVZX | Rio das Perolas |
| ☐ B-MAQ | Airbus A321-231 | 1926 | ex D-AVZS | Lago Tai |
| ☐ B-MAR | Airbus A321-131 | 0597 | ex VN-A346 | Hao Jiang |
| | | | | |
| ☐ B-MAS | Airbus A300B4-622RF | 743 | ex N221LF | Cargo titles |
| ☐ B-MAH | Airbus A320-232 | 0805 | ex CS-MAH | Ilha da Madeira |
| ☐ B-MAX | Airbus A320-232 | 0928 | ex N928MD | |
| ☐ B-MBJ | Airbus A300B4-622RF | 677 | ex TC-OAY | wfs |

## B-   CHINA- TAIWAN (Republic of China)

### CHINA AIRLINES — China Airlines/Dynasty (CI/CAL) — Taipei-Chiang Kai Shek/Sung Shan (TPE/TSA)

| | | | | | |
|---|---|---|---|---|---|
| ☐ B-18301 | Airbus A330-302 | 602 | ex F-WWYM | | |
| ☐ B-18302 | Airbus A330-302 | 607 | ex F-WWYY | | |
| ☐ B-18303 | Airbus A330-302 | 641 | ex F-WWYS | | |
| ☐ B-18305 | Airbus A330-302 | 671 | ex F-WWKN | orchid c/s | |
| ☐ B-18306 | Airbus A330-302 | 675 | ex F-WWYU | | |
| ☐ B-18307 | Airbus A330-302 | 691 | ex F-WWYL | | |
| ☐ B-18308 | Airbus A330-302 | 699 | ex F-WWKA | | |
| ☐ B-18309 | Airbus A330-302 | 707 | ex F-WWKI | | |
| ☐ B-18310 | Airbus A330-302 | 714 | ex F-WWYV | | |
| ☐ B-18311 | Airbus A330-302 | 752 | ex F-WWKZ | Taiwanese Fruits c/s | |
| ☐ B-18312 | Airbus A330-302 | 769 | ex F-WWYS | | |
| ☐ B-18315 | Airbus A330-302 | 823 | ex F-WWKS | | |
| ☐ B-18316 | Airbus A330-302 | 838 | ex F-WWYM | | |
| ☐ B-18317 | Airbus A330-302 | 861 | ex F-WWYA | | |
| ☐ B-18351 | Airbus A330-302 | 725 | ex F-WWKO | | |
| ☐ B-18352 | Airbus A330-302 | 805 | ex F-WWYG | | |
| ☐ B-18353 | Airbus A330-302 | 920 | ex F-WWYU | | |
| ☐ B-18355 | Airbus A330-302 | 1177 | ex F-WWYI | | |
| ☐ B-18356 | Airbus A330-302 | 1272 | ex F-WWKD | | ♦ |
| ☐ B-18357 | Airbus A330-302 | 1278 | ex F-WWYK | | ♦ |
| ☐ B-18391 | Airbus A330-343X | 1206 | ex (G-VLUV) | | <VIR♦ |
| ☐ B-18392 | Airbus A330-343X | 1215 | ex (G-VGEM) | | <VIR♦ |
| | | | | | |
| ☐ B-18801 | Airbus A340-313X | 402 | ex F-WWJC | | |
| ☐ B-18802 | Airbus A340-313X | 406 | ex F-WWJK | | |

| Reg | Type | MSN/Line | Notes | |
|---|---|---|---|---|
| ☐ B-18803 | Airbus A340-313X | 411 | ex F-WWJL | |
| ☐ B-18805 | Airbus A340-313X | 415 | ex F-WWJO | |
| ☐ B-18806 | Airbus A340-313X | 433 | ex F-WWJS | |
| ☐ B-18807 | Airbus A340-313X | 541 | ex F-WWJK | |
| ☐ B-18601 | Boeing 737-809/W | 28402/113 | ex N1787B | |
| ☐ B-18605 | Boeing 737-809/W | 28404/130 | ex N1784B | |
| ☐ B-18606 | Boeing 737-809/W | 28405/132 | | |
| ☐ B-18607 | Boeing 737-809/W | 29104/139 | | |
| ☐ B-18608 | Boeing 737-809/W | 28406/141 | | |
| ☐ B-18609 | Boeing 737-809/W | 28407/161 | | |
| ☐ B-18610 | Boeing 737-809/W | 29105/295 | | |
| ☐ B-18612 | Boeing 737-809/W | 30173/695 | ex N1785B | |
| ☐ B-18615 | Boeing 737-809/W | 30174/1175 | ex N6067E | |
| ☐ B-16817 | Boeing 737-809/W | 29106/302 | ex B-18611 | |
| ☐ B-18201 | Boeing 747-409 | 28709/1114 | | |
| ☐ B-18202 | Boeing 747-409 | 28710/1132 | | |
| ☐ B-18203 | Boeing 747-409 | 28711/1136 | | |
| ☐ B-18205 | Boeing 747-409 | 28712/1137 | | |
| ☐ B-18206 | Boeing 747-409 | 29030/1145 | | |
| ☐ B-18207 | Boeing 747-409 | 29219/1176 | | |
| ☐ B-18208 | Boeing 747-409 | 29031/1186 | | |
| ☐ B-18210 | Boeing 747-409 | 33734/1353 | Dreamliner c/s | |
| ☐ B-18211 | Boeing 747-409 | 33735/1354 | | |
| ☐ B-18212 | Boeing 747-409 | 33736/1357 | | |
| ☐ B-18215 | Boeing 747-409 | 33737/1358 | | |
| ☐ B-18251 | Boeing 747-409 | 27965/1063 | ex B-16801 | |
| ☐ B-18701 | Boeing 747-409F | 30759/1249 | | |
| ☐ B-18702 | Boeing 747-409F | 30760/1252 | | [VCV] |
| ☐ B-18705 | Boeing 747-409F | 30762/1263 | ex B-2436 | [VCV] |
| ☐ B-18706 | Boeing 747-409F | 30763/1267 | | |
| ☐ B-18707 | Boeing 747-409F | 30764/1269 | | |
| ☐ B-18708 | Boeing 747-409F | 30765/1288 | | |
| ☐ B-18709 | Boeing 747-409F | 30766/1294 | | |
| ☐ B-18710 | Boeing 747-409F | 30767/1300 | | |
| ☐ B-18711 | Boeing 747-409F | 30768/1314 | | |
| ☐ B-18712 | Boeing 747-409F | 33729/1332 | | |
| ☐ B-18715 | Boeing 747-409F | 33731/1334 | | |
| ☐ B-18716 | Boeing 747-409F | 33732/1339 | | |
| ☐ B-18717 | Boeing 747-409F | 30769/1346 | | |
| ☐ B-18718 | Boeing 747-409F | 30770/1348 | | |
| ☐ B-18719 | Boeing 747-409F | 33739/1355 | | |
| ☐ B-18720 | Boeing 747-409F | 33733/1359 | | |
| ☐ B-18721 | Boeing 747-409F | 33738/1362 | | |
| ☐ B-18722 | Boeing 747-409F | 34265/1372 | all-white | |
| ☐ B-18723 | Boeing 747-409F | 34266/1379 | | |
| ☐ B-18725 | Boeing 747-409F | 30771/1385 | | |
| ☐ N168CL | Boeing 747-409 | 29906/1219 | ex B-18209 | |

## DAILY AIR — Taipei-Sung Shan (TSA)

| Reg | Type | MSN | Notes |
|---|---|---|---|
| ☐ B-55561 | Dornier 228-212 | 8215 | ex B-12253 |
| ☐ B-55563 | Dornier 228-212 | 8224 | ex B-12259 |
| ☐ B-55565 | Dornier 228-212 | 8234 | ex B-11152 |
| ☐ B-55567 | Dornier 228-212 | 8235 | ex B-11156 |

## EVA AIRWAYS — Eva (BR/EVA) — Taipei-Chiang Kai Shek (TPE)

| Reg | Type | MSN/Line | Notes |
|---|---|---|---|
| ☐ B-16301 | Airbus A330-203 | 530 | ex F-WWYA |
| ☐ B-16302 | Airbus A330-203 | 535 | ex F-WWYE |
| ☐ B-16303 | Airbus A330-203 | 555 | ex F-WWYL |
| ☐ B-16305 | Airbus A330-203 | 573 | ex F-WWYP |
| ☐ B-16306 | Airbus A330-203 | 587 | ex F-WWKL |
| ☐ B-16307 | Airbus A330-203 | 634 | ex F-WWYJ |
| ☐ B-16308 | Airbus A330-203 | 655 | ex F-WWYT |
| ☐ B-16309 | Airbus A330-203 | 661 | ex F-WWYY |
| ☐ B-16310 | Airbus A330-203 | 678 | ex F-WWYB |
| ☐ B-16311 | Airbus A330-203 | 693 | ex F-WWYP |
| ☐ B-16312 | Airbus A330-203 | 755 | ex F-WWYP |
| ☐ B-16401 | Boeing 747-45E | 27062/942 | |
| ☐ B-16402 | Boeing 747-45EBDSF | 27063/947 | |
| ☐ B-16403 | Boeing 747-45EM | 27141/976 | ex N403EV |
| ☐ B-16405 | Boeing 747-45EM | 27142/982 | ex N405EV |
| ☐ B-16406 | Boeing 747-45EMBDSF | 27898/1051 | ex N406EV |
| ☐ B-16407 | Boeing 747-45EMSF | 27899/1053 | ex N407EV |
| ☐ B-16408 | Boeing 747-45EM | 28092/1076 | ex N408EV |
| ☐ B-16409 | Boeing 747-45EM | 28093/1077 | ex N409EV |
| ☐ B-16410 | Boeing 747-45E | 29061/1140 | |
| ☐ B-16411 | Boeing 747-45E | 29111/1151 | |

| | | | | |
|---|---|---|---|---|
| ☐ B-16412 | Boeing 747-45E | 29112/1159 | | |
| ☐ B-16462 | Boeing 747-45EMBDSF | 27173/998 | | |
| ☐ B-16463 | Boeing 747-45EMBDSF | 27174/1004 | | |
| ☐ B-16481 | Boeing 747-45EF | 30607/1251 | | |
| ☐ B-16482 | Boeing 747-45EF | 30608/1279 | | |
| ☐ B-16483 | Boeing 747-45EF | 30609/1309 | | |
| | | | | |
| ☐ B-16701 | Boeing 777-35EER | 32639/524 | | |
| ☐ B-16702 | Boeing 777-35EER | 32640/531 | | |
| ☐ B-16703 | Boeing 777-35EER | 32643/572 | | |
| ☐ B-16705 | Boeing 777-35EER | 32645/597 | ex N6009F | |
| ☐ B-16706 | Boeing 777-35EER | 33750/612 | | |
| ☐ B-16707 | Boeing 777-35EER | 33751/634 | | |
| ☐ B-16708 | Boeing 777-35EER | 33752/658 | | |
| ☐ B-16709 | Boeing 777-35EER | 33753/683 | | |
| ☐ B-16710 | Boeing 777-35EER | 32641/707 | | |
| ☐ B-16711 | Boeing 777-35EER | 33754/721 | ex N5028Y | |
| ☐ B-16712 | Boeing 777-35EER | 33755/735 | | |
| ☐ B-16713 | Boeing 777-35EER | 33756/758 | | |
| ☐ B-16715 | Boeing 777-35EER | 33757/810 | | |
| ☐ B-16716 | Boeing 777-35EER | 32642/822 | | |
| ☐ B-16717 | Boeing 777-35EER | 32644/863 | ex N559BA | |
| | | | | |
| ☐ B-16101 | McDonnell-Douglas MD-11F | 48542/570 | | |
| ☐ B-16107 | McDonnell-Douglas MD-11F | 48546/589 | | |
| ☐ B-16108 | McDonnell-Douglas MD-11F | 48778/619 | | |
| ☐ B-16109 | McDonnell-Douglas MD-11F | 48779/620 | | |
| ☐ B-16110 | McDonnell-Douglas MD-11F | 48786/630 | | |
| ☐ B-16111 | McDonnell-Douglas MD-11F | 48787/631 | | |
| ☐ B-16112 | McDonnell-Douglas MD-11F | 48789/633 | ex N90178 | |
| ☐ B-16113 | McDonnell-Douglas MD-11F | 48790/634 | ex N9030Q | |
| | | | | |
| ☐ B-16331 | Airbus A330-302 | 1254 | ex F-WWYF | ♦ |
| ☐ B-16332 | Airbus A330-302 | 1268 | ex F-WWKN | ♦ |
| ☐ B-16333 | Airbus A330-302 | 1274 | ex F-WWKE | ♦ |
| ☐ B-17917 | McDonnell-Douglas MD-90-30ER | 53572/2217 | | <UIA |
| ☐ B-17925 | McDonnell-Douglas MD-90-30ER | 53568/2171 | ex B-16902 | <UIA |
| ☐ B-17926 | McDonnell-Douglas MD-90-30ER | 53567/2169 | ex B-15301 | <UIA |

## FAR EASTERN AIR TRANSPORT — Far Eastern (FE/FEA) — Taipei-Sung Shan (TSA)

| | | | | |
|---|---|---|---|---|
| ☐ B-28007 | McDonnell-Douglas MD-83 | 49807/1829 | | [TPE]♦ |
| ☐ B-28011 | McDonnell-Douglas MD-83 | 53118/1954 | | [TPE]♦ |
| ☐ B-28017 | McDonnell-Douglas MD-83 | 53166/2052 | | [TPE]♦ |
| ☐ B-28021 | McDonnell-Douglas MD-83 | 53167/2056 | | [TPE]♦ |
| ☐ B-28025 | McDonnell-Douglas MD-83 | 53602/2214 | | ♦ |
| ☐ B-28027 | McDonnell-Douglas MD-83 | 53603/2218 | | ♦ |
| ☐ B-28035 | McDonnell-Douglas MD-82 | 53480/2127 | | ♦ |
| ☐ B-28037 | McDonnell-Douglas MD-82 | 53479/2124 | | ♦ |
| | | | | |
| ☐ B-27013 | Boeing 757-27AEM | 29608/835 | | [TPE]♦ |
| ☐ B-27015 | Boeing 757-27AEM | 29609/876 | | [TPE]♦ |

## GREAT WING AIRLINES — Taichung

| | | | |
|---|---|---|---|
| ☐ B-69832 | Britten-Norman BN-2A-26 Islander | 2039 | ex B-12232 |

## MANDARIN AIRLINES — Mandarin Air (AE/MDA) — Taipei-Sung Shan (TSA)

| | | | |
|---|---|---|---|
| ☐ B-16821 | Embraer ERJ-190AR | 19000087 | ex PT-SNF |
| ☐ B-16822 | Embraer ERJ-190AR | 19000091 | ex PT-SNK |
| ☐ B-16823 | Embraer ERJ-190AR | 19000099 | ex PT-SNT |
| ☐ B-16825 | Embraer ERJ-190AR | 19000167 | ex PT-SAZ |
| ☐ B-16826 | Embraer ERJ-190AR | 19000175 | ex PT-SDK |
| ☐ B-16827 | Embraer ERJ-190AR | 19000182 | ex PT-SDQ |
| ☐ B-16828 | Embraer ERJ-190AR | 19000190 | ex PT-SDY |
| ☐ B-16829 | Embraer ERJ-190AR | 19000302 | ex PT-TZQ |

## ROC AVIATION — Taipei-Sung Shan (TSA)

| | | | |
|---|---|---|---|
| ☐ B-68801 | Britten-Norman BN-2B-26 Islander | 2255 | ex G-BTVI |
| ☐ B-68802 | Britten-Norman BN-2B-20 Islander | 2241 | ex G-BSPU |

## TRANSASIA AIRWAYS — Transasia (GE/TNA) — Taipei-Sung Shan (TSA)

| | | | |
|---|---|---|---|
| ☐ B-22601 | Airbus A321-131 | 0538 | ex F-WGYZ |
| ☐ B-22602 | Airbus A321-131 | 0555 | ex F-WFYZ |
| ☐ B-22605 | Airbus A321-131 | 0606 | ex F-WGYY |
| ☐ B-22606 | Airbus A321-131 | 0731 | ex F-WQGL |
| ☐ B-22607 | Airbus A321-131 | 0746 | ex F-WQGM |

| | | | | |
|---|---|---|---|---|
| ☐ B-22801 | ATR 72-212A | 0517 | ex F-WWLK | |
| ☐ B-22802 | ATR 72-212A | 0525 | ex F-WWLB | |
| ☐ B-22803 | ATR 72-212A | 0527 | ex F-WWLC | |
| ☐ B-22805 | ATR 72-212A | 0558 | ex F-WQIU | |
| ☐ B-22806 | ATR 72-212A | 0560 | ex F-WQIY | |
| ☐ B-22807 | ATR 72-212A | 0567 | ex F-WQIZ | |
| ☐ B-22810 | ATR 72-212A | 0642 | ex F-WQMF | |
| ☐ B-22811 | ATR 72-212A | 0749 | ex F-WQNC | |
| ☐ B-22812 | ATR 72-212A | 0774 | ex F-WWEM | |
| | | | | |
| ☐ B-22310 | Airbus A320-232 | 0791 | ex F-WWDR | |
| ☐ B-22311 | Airbus A320-232 | 0822 | ex F-WWBY | |
| ☐ B-22312 | Airbus A320-232 | 2914 | ex 4R-ABH | |
| ☐ B-22316 | Airbus A320-232 | 5055 | ex F-WWBS | ♦ |
| | | | | ♦ |

## UNI AIR        Glory (B7/UIA)        Taipei-Sung Shan (TSA)

| | | | | |
|---|---|---|---|---|
| ☐ B-15217 | de Havilland DHC-8-311A | 379 | ex C-GEOA | |
| ☐ B-15219 | de Havilland DHC-8-311A | 381 | ex C-FDHD | |
| ☐ B-15225 | de Havilland DHC-8-311B | 405 | ex C-GFHZ | |
| ☐ B-15231 | de Havilland DHC-8-311B | 414 | ex C-GFBW | |
| ☐ B-15233 | de Havilland DHC-8-311B | 402 | ex C-GDFT | |
| ☐ B-15235 | de Havilland DHC-8Q-311B | 443 | ex C-FWBB | |
| ☐ B-15237 | de Havilland DHC-8Q-311B | 467 | ex C-GELN | |
| ☐ B-15239 | de Havilland DHC-8Q-311B | 571 | ex C-GEWI | |
| | | | | |
| ☐ B-17911 | McDonnell-Douglas MD-90-30 | 53535/2158 | | |
| ☐ B-17913 | McDonnell-Douglas MD-90-30 | 53537/2162 | | |
| ☐ B-17917 | McDonnell-Douglas MD-90-30ER | 53572/2217 | | >EVA |
| ☐ B-17918 | McDonnell-Douglas MD-90-30ER | 53571/2193 | ex B-16903 | |
| ☐ B-17919 | McDonnell-Douglas MD-90-30 | 53569/2173 | ex N6206F | |
| ☐ B-17920 | McDonnell-Douglas MD-90-30 | 53574/2186 | | |
| ☐ B-17921 | McDonnell-Douglas MD-90-30 | 53554/2166 | ex SU-BNN | |
| ☐ B-17922 | McDonnell-Douglas MD-90-30 | 53601/2243 | ex SU-BMT | |
| ☐ B-17923 | McDonnell-Douglas MD-90-30ER | 53534/2153 | ex B-16901 | >EVA |
| ☐ B-17925 | McDonnell-Douglas MD-90-30ER | 53568/2171 | ex B-16902 | >EVA |
| ☐ B-17926 | McDonnell-Douglas MD-90-30ER | 53567/2169 | ex B-15301 | >EVA |

# C-    CANADA

## ABITIBI HELICOPTERS      La Sarre, QC/Calgary-Springbank, AB (SSQ/-)

| | | | |
|---|---|---|---|
| ☐ C-FHAJ | Aérospatiale AS.350BA+ AStar | 1493 | ex N511WW |
| ☐ C-FHAK | Aérospatiale AS.350AS350BA+ AStar | 1545 | ex N517WW |
| ☐ C-FHAP | Aérospatiale AS.350AS350B2 AStar | 3292 | |
| ☐ C-FHAU | Aérospatiale AS.350AS350A AStar | 2778 | |
| ☐ C-FXAH | Aérospatiale AS.350AS350BA AStar | 2509 | ex N905BK |
| ☐ C-FXBP | Aérospatiale AS.350AS350BA AStar | 1553 | ex I-VBIT |
| ☐ C-FXDM | Aérospatiale AS.350AS350BA AStar | 1548 | ex N798JH |
| ☐ C-FXED | Aérospatiale AS.350AS350BA AStar | 3087 | |
| ☐ C-FXEJ | Aérospatiale AS.350AS350BA AStar | 1031 | |
| ☐ C-FXHP | Aérospatiale AS.350AS350BA AStar | 3100 | |
| ☐ C-GHSM | Aérospatiale AS.350AS350BA+ AStar | 1468 | ex N700WW |

## AC JETZ      Montreal-Mirabel/Montreal-Trudeau, QC (YMX/YUL)

Specialist sports charter and VIP division of Air Canada.

## ADLAIR AVIATION      Cambridge Bay, NT/Yellowknife, NT (YCB/YZF)

| | | | | | |
|---|---|---|---|---|---|
| ☐ C-FGYN | de Havilland DHC-2 Beaver | 134 | ex CF-GYN | | FP/WS |
| ☐ C-GBFP | Learjet 25B | 25B-167 | ex N664CL | Ernie Lyall | EMS |
| ☐ C-GBYN | Beech B200 Super King Air | BB-1232 | ex N209CM | | EMS |
| ☐ C-GCYN | Beech 200 Super King Air | BB-710 | ex C-GXHW | | |
| ☐ C-GFYN | de Havilland DHC-6 Twin Otter 200 | 209 | ex N915SA | FP/WS | |

## ADVENTURE AIR      Lac du Bonnet, MB (YAX)

| | | | | |
|---|---|---|---|---|
| ☐ CF-JFA | de Havilland DHC-2 Beaver | 1581 | ex N5563 | FP |
| ☐ C-FKLR | Cessna 208 Caravan I | 20800223 | ex N899A | eFP |
| ☐ C-FXPC | de Havilland DHC-2 Beaver | 1196 | ex CF-XPC | FP |
| ☐ C-GAAX | Cessna 208B Caravan I | 208B0348 | ex N32JA | |
| ☐ C-GGRJ | Cessna A185F Skywagon | 18502745 | ex (N1090F) | FP |
| ☐ C-GRRJ | de Havilland DHC-3 Otter | 296 | ex C-FXZD | FP♦ |
| ☐ C-GUEH | Piper PA-31 Turbo Navajo C | 31-7712057 | ex N27255 | |
| ☐ C-GWQE | Cessna 337F Super Skymaster II | 33701459 | ex N1859M | |

## AIR BRAVO
*Thunder Bay, ON (YQT)*

| | | | | |
|---|---|---|---|---|
| ☐ C-FAJV | Pilatus PC-12/45 | 234 | ex HB-FRE | |
| ☐ C-FCLB | Pilatus PC-12/47 | 834 | ex N695QF | ♦ |
| ☐ C-FKPA | Pilatus PC-12/45 | 275 | ex N275PC | |
| ☐ C-FKSL | Pilatus PC-12/45 | 324 | ex N324PC | |
| ☐ C-FKVL | Pilatus PC-12/45 | 307 | ex N307PB | ♦ |
| ☐ C-FPCI | Pilatus PC-12/45 | 399 | ex N399PB | |
| ☐ C-FPCN | Pilatus PC-12/45 | 258 | ex N258WC | |
| ☐ C-FTAB | Pilatus PC-12/45 | 229 | ex C-FMPO | |
| ☐ C-FXAB | Pilatus PC-12/45 | 239 | | ♦ |
| ☐ C-GFIL | Pilatus PC-12/45 | 268 | ex N268PC | |
| ☐ C-GVKC | Pilatus PC-12/45 | 207 | ex ZS-OEV | |
| | | | | |
| ☐ C-GBCM | Rockwell Commander 700 | 70027 | ex N700DL | |
| ☐ C-GVWX | Rockwell Commander 700 | 70005 | ex N9905S | |

## AIR BELLEVUE

| | | | | |
|---|---|---|---|---|
| ☐ C-GABM | Cessna 208 Caravan I | 20800308 | ex N12712 | ♦ |

## AIR CAB
*Vancouver-Coal Harbour, BC (CXH)*

| | | | | |
|---|---|---|---|---|
| ☐ C-FBMO | Cessna A185E Skywagon | 18501627 | ex N1934U | FP |
| ☐ C-FQGZ | Cessna A185E Skywagon | 18501691 | ex N1967U | FP |
| ☐ C-FRJG | de Havilland DHC-2 Beaver | 1550 | ex CF-RJG | FP |
| ☐ C-GAXE | de Havilland DHC-2 Beaver | 841 | ex 54-1698 | FP |
| ☐ C-GJGC | de Havilland DHC-2 Beaver | 88 | ex CF-GQM | FP |
| ☐ C-GJZE | de Havilland DHC-2 Beaver | 1276 | ex N87780 | FP |

## AIR CANADA
*Air Canada (AC/ACA)*   *Montreal-Mirabel/Montreal-Trudeau, QC (YMX/YUL)*

Member of Star Alliance

| | | | | | |
|---|---|---|---|---|---|
| ☐ C-FBLJ | Airbus A319-112 | 1630 | ex XA-MXG | | [YMX] |
| ☐ C-FYIY | Airbus A319-114 | 0634 | ex D-AVYP | 252 | |
| ☐ C-FYJE | Airbus A319-114 | 0656 | ex D-AVYZ | 255 | |
| ☐ C-FYJG | Airbus A319-114 | 0670 | ex D-AVYE | 256 | |
| ☐ C-FYJH | Airbus A319-114 | 0672 | ex D-AVYF | 257 | |
| ☐ C-FYJI | Airbus A319-114 | 0682 | ex D-AVYH | 258 | |
| ☐ C-FYJP | Airbus A319-114 | 0688 | ex D-AVYJ | 259 | |
| ☐ C-FYKC | Airbus A319-114 | 0691 | ex D-AVYP | 260 | |
| ☐ C-FYKR | Airbus A319-114 | 0693 | ex D-AVYQ | 261 | |
| ☐ C-FYKW | Airbus A319-114 | 0695 | ex D-AVYS | 262 | |
| ☐ C-FYNS | Airbus A319-114 | 0572 | ex D-AVYK | 251 | |
| ☐ C-FZUG | Airbus A319-114 | 0697 | ex D-AVYT | 263 | |
| ☐ C-FZUH | Airbus A319-114 | 0711 | ex D-AVYV | 264 TCA retro c/s | |
| ☐ C-FZUJ | Airbus A319-114 | 0719 | ex D-AVYW | 265 | |
| ☐ C-FZUL | Airbus A319-114 | 0721 | ex D-AVYY | 266 | |
| ☐ C-GAPY | Airbus A319-114 | 0728 | ex D-AVYE | 267 | |
| ☐ C-GAQL | Airbus A319-114 | 0732 | ex D-AVYX | 268 | |
| ☐ C-GAQX | Airbus A319-114 | 0736 | ex D-AVYG | 269 | |
| ☐ C-GAQZ | Airbus A319-114 | 0740 | ex D-AVYH | 270 | |
| ☐ C-GARG | Airbus A319-114 | 0742 | ex D-AVYM | 271 | |
| ☐ C-GARJ | Airbus A319-114 | 0752 | ex D-AVYP | 272 | |
| ☐ C-GARO | Airbus A319-114 | 0757 | ex D-AVYQ | 273 | |
| ☐ C-GBHM | Airbus A319-114 | 0769 | ex D-AVYB | 274 | |
| ☐ C-GBHN | Airbus A319-114 | 0773 | ex D-AVYK | 275 | |
| ☐ C-GBHO | Airbus A319-114 | 0779 | ex D-AVYT | 276 | |
| ☐ C-GBHR | Airbus A319-114 | 0785 | ex D-AVYU | 277 | |
| ☐ C-GBHY | Airbus A319-114 | 0800 | ex D-AVYE | 278 | |
| ☐ C-GBHZ | Airbus A319-114 | 0813 | ex D-AVYG | 279 | |
| ☐ C-GBIA | Airbus A319-114 | 0817 | ex D-AVYM | 280 | |
| ☐ C-GBIJ | Airbus A319-114 | 0829 | ex D-AVYH | 281 | |
| ☐ C-GBIK | Airbus A319-114 | 0831 | ex D-AVYI | 282 | |
| ☐ C-GBIM | Airbus A319-114 | 0840 | ex D-AVYQ | 283 | |
| ☐ C-GBIN | Airbus A319-114 | 0845 | ex D-AVYA | 284 | |
| ☐ C-GBIP | Airbus A319-114 | 0546 | ex D-AVYV | 285 | |
| ☐ C-GITP | Airbus A319-112 | 1562 | ex D-AVYR | 286 | |
| ☐ C-GITR | Airbus A319-112 | 1577 | ex D-AVWR | 287 | |
| ☐ C-GJVY | Airbus A319-112 | 1742 | ex XA-MXI | 292 | ♦ |
| ☐ C-GKNW | Airbus A319-112 | 1805 | ex XA-MXJ | | [YMX] |
| ☐ C-GKOB | Airbus A319-112 | 1853 | ex N571SX | 296 | |
| ☐ C-GSJB | Airbus A319-112 | 1673 | ex XA-MXH | 290 | ♦ |
| | | | | | |
| ☐ C-FDCA | Airbus A320-211 | 0232 | ex F-WWIY | 405 | |
| ☐ C-FDQQ | Airbus A320-211 | 0059 | ex F-WWDI | 201 | |
| ☐ C-FDQV | Airbus A320-211 | 0068 | ex F-WWDO | 202 | |
| ☐ C-FDRH | Airbus A320-211 | 0073 | ex F-WWDC | 203 | |
| ☐ C-FDRK | Airbus A320-211 | 0084 | ex F-WWDP | 204 | |
| ☐ C-FDRP | Airbus A320-211 | 0122 | ex F-WWIP | 205 | |

| | | | | | | |
|---|---|---|---|---|---|---|
| ☐ C-FDSN | Airbus A320-211 | 0126 | ex F-WWIU | 206 | | |
| ☐ C-FDST | Airbus A320-211 | 0127 | ex F-WWIV | 207 | | |
| ☐ C-FDSU | Airbus A320-211 | 0141 | ex F-WWDH | 208 | | |
| ☐ C-FFWI | Airbus A320-211 | 0149 | ex F-WWDP | 209 | | |
| ☐ C-FFWJ | Airbus A320-211 | 0150 | ex F-WWDQ | 210 | | |
| ☐ C-FFWM | Airbus A320-211 | 0154 | ex F-WWDY | 211 | | |
| ☐ C-FFWN | Airbus A320-211 | 0159 | ex F-WWIG | 212 | | |
| ☐ C-FGYL | Airbus A320-211 | 0254 | ex F-WWBF | 218 | | |
| ☐ C-FGYS | Airbus A320-211 | 0255 | ex F-WWBG | 219 | | |
| ☐ C-FKCK | Airbus A320-211 | 0265 | ex 'G-FKCK' | 220 | | |
| ☐ C-FKCO | Airbus A320-211 | 0277 | ex F-WWDX | 221 | | |
| ☐ C-FKCR | Airbus A320-211 | 0290 | ex F-WWBY | 222 | | |
| ☐ C-FKOJ | Airbus A320-211 | 0330 | ex F-WWIB | 226 | | |
| ☐ C-FKPT | Airbus A320-211 | 0324 | ex F-WWDC | 225 | | |
| ☐ C-FLSS | Airbus A320-211 | 0284 | ex F-WWBU | 408 | | |
| ☐ C-FLSU | Airbus A320-211 | 0309 | ex F-WWIJ | 411 | | |
| ☐ C-FMSX | Airbus A320-211 | 0378 | ex 'C-FMSK' | 232 | | |
| ☐ C-FNVU | Airbus A320-211 | 0403 | ex F-WWBO | 415 | | |
| ☐ C-FNVV | Airbus A320-211 | 0404 | ex F-WWDF | 416 | | |
| ☐ C-FPDN | Airbus A320-211 | 0341 | ex F-WWBR | 228 | | |
| ☐ C-FPWD | Airbus A320-211 | 0231 | ex F-WWDV | 404 | | |
| ☐ C-FPWE | Airbus A320-211 | 0175 | ex F-WWIN | 402 | | |
| ☐ C-FTJO | Airbus A320-211 | 0183 | ex F-WWIX | 213 | | |
| ☐ C-FTJP | Airbus A320-211 | 0233 | ex F-WWIQ | 214 | | |
| ☐ C-FTJQ | Airbus A320-211 | 0242 | ex F-WWDJ | 215 | | |
| ☐ C-FTJR | Airbus A320-211 | 0248 | ex F-WWDT | 216 | | |
| ☐ C-FTJS | Airbus A320-211 | 0253 | ex F-WWBE | 217 | | |
| ☐ C-FXCD | Airbus A320-214 | 2018 | ex F-WWBV | 239 | | |
| ☐ C-FZQS | Airbus A320-214 | 2145 | ex F-WWDI | 240 | | |
| ☐ C-FZUB | Airbus A320-214 | 1940 | ex F-WWIP | 238 | | |
| ☐ C-GJVT | Airbus A320-214 | 1719 | ex F-WWBC | 235 | | |
| ☐ C-GKOD | Airbus A320-214 | 1864 | ex F-WWIE | 236 | | |
| ☐ C-GKOE | Airbus A320-214 | 1874 | ex F-WWBN | 237 | | |
| ☐ C-GPWG | Airbus A320-211 | 0174 | ex F-WWIM | 401 | | |
| ☐ C-GQCA | Airbus A320-211 | 0210 | ex F-WWIC | 403 | | |
| | | | | | | |
| ☐ C-GITU | Airbus A321-211 | 1602 | ex D-AMTA | 451 | | |
| ☐ C-GITY | Airbus A321-211 | 1611 | ex D-AVAV | 452 | | |
| ☐ C-GIUB | Airbus A321-211 | 1623 | ex D-AMTB | 453 | | |
| ☐ C-GIUE | Airbus A321-211 | 1632 | ex D-AMTC | 454 | | |
| ☐ C-GIUF | Airbus A321-211 | 1638 | ex D-AMTD | 455 | | |
| ☐ C-GJVX | Airbus A321-211 | 1726 | ex D-AVXC | 456 | | |
| ☐ C-GJWD | Airbus A321-211 | 1748 | ex D-AVXE | 457 | | |
| ☐ C-GJWI | Airbus A321-211 | 1772 | ex D-AVZA | 458 | | |
| ☐ C-GJWN | Airbus A321-211 | 1783 | ex D-AVZD | 459 | | |
| ☐ C-GJWO | Airbus A321-211 | 1811 | ex D-AVZI | 460 | | |
| | | | | | | |
| ☐ C-GFAF | Airbus A330-343X | 277 | ex F-WWKO | 931 | | |
| ☐ C-GFAH | Airbus A330-343X | 279 | ex F-WWYB | 932 | | |
| ☐ C-GFAJ | Airbus A330-343X | 284 | ex F-WWYA | 933 | | |
| ☐ C-GFUR | Airbus A330-343X | 344 | ex F-WWYC | 934 | | |
| ☐ C-GHKR | Airbus A330-343X | 400 | ex F-WWKM | 935 | | |
| ☐ C-GHKW | Airbus A330-343X | 408 | ex F-WWKS | 936 | | |
| ☐ C-GHKX | Airbus A330-343X | 412 | ex F-WWKU | 937 | | |
| ☐ C-GHLM | Airbus A330-343X | 419 | ex F-WWYA | 938 Star Alliance c/s | | |
| | | | | | | |
| ☐ C-FBEF | Boeing 767-233ER | 24323/250 | ex N6009F | 617 | | [ROW] |
| ☐ C-FBEG | Boeing 767-233ER | 24324/252 | ex N6009F | 618 | | [ROW] |
| ☐ C-FBEM | Boeing 767-233ER | 24325/254 | ex N6038E | 619 | | [ROW] |
| ☐ C-FVNM | Boeing 767-209ER | 22681/18 | ex ZK-NBF | 621 | | [ROW] |
| ☐ C-GAVC | Boeing 767-233ER | 22527/102 | ex N1783B | 611 | | [ROW] |
| ☐ C-GDSP | Boeing 767-233ER | 24142/229 | ex N6009F | 613 all-silver fuselage | | [ROW] |
| ☐ C-GDSU | Boeing 767-233ER | 24144/234 | ex N6018N | 615 | | [ROW] |
| ☐ C-GDSY | Boeing 767-233ER | 24145/236 | ex N6005C | 616 | | [ROW] |
| | | | | | | |
| ☐ C-FCAB | Boeing 767-375ER | 24082/213 | ex N6055X | 681 | | |
| ☐ C-FCAE | Boeing 767-375ER | 24083/215 | ex N6046P | 682 | | |
| ☐ C-FCAF | Boeing 767-375ER | 24084/219 | ex N6038E | 683 | | |
| ☐ C-FCAG | Boeing 767-375ER | 24085/220 | ex N6009F | 684 | | |
| ☐ C-FMWP | Boeing 767-333ER | 25583/508 | | 631 | | |
| ☐ C-FMWQ | Boeing 767-333ER | 25584/596 | | 632 | | |
| ☐ C-FMWU | Boeing 767-333ER | 25585/597 | | 633 | | |
| ☐ C-FMWV | Boeing 767-333ER | 25586/599 | | 634 | | |
| ☐ C-FMWY | Boeing 767-333ER | 25587/604 | | 635 10 Year Star Alliance c/s | | |
| ☐ C-FMXC | Boeing 767-333ER | 25588/606 | | 636 | | |
| ☐ C-FOCA | Boeing 767-375ER | 24575/311 | | 640 | | |
| ☐ C-FPCA | Boeing 767-375ER | 24306/258 | | 637 | | |
| ☐ C-FTCA | Boeing 767-375ER | 24307/259 | | 638 | | |
| ☐ C-FXCA | Boeing 767-375ER | 24574/302 | | 639 | | |
| ☐ C-GBZR | Boeing 767-38EER | 25404/411 | ex HL7267 | 645 Free Spirit c/s | | |
| ☐ C-GDUZ | Boeing 767-38EER | 25347/399 | ex HL7266 | 646 | | |
| ☐ C-GEOQ | Boeing 767-375ER | 30112/765 | | 647 | | |

| | | | | |
|---|---|---|---|---|
| ☐ C-GEOU | Boeing 767-375ER | 30108/771 | | 648 |
| ☐ C-GHLA | Boeing 767-35HER | 26387/445 | ex VH-BZL | 656 |
| ☐ C-GHLK | Boeing 767-35HER | 26388/456 | ex VH-BZM | 657 |
| ☐ C-GHLQ | Boeing 767-333ER | 30846/832 | ex N6009F | 658 |
| ☐ C-GHLT | Boeing 767-333ER | 30850/835 | ex N6018N | 659 |
| ☐ C-GHLU | Boeing 767-333ER | 30851/836 | ex N6046P | 660 |
| ☐ C-GHLV | Boeing 767-333ER | 30852/843 | ex N6055X | 661 |
| ☐ C-GHOZ | Boeing 767-375ER | 24087/249 | ex N487CT | 685 |
| ☐ C-GHPD | Boeing 767-3Y0ER | 24999/354 | ex N25034 | 687 |
| ☐ C-GHPE | Boeing 767-33AER | 33423/897 | ex N591HA | |
| ☐ C-GHPN | Boeing 767-33AER | 33424/901 | ex N593HA | |
| ☐ C-GLCA | Boeing 767-375ER | 25120/361 | | 641 |
| ☐ C-GSCA | Boeing 767-375ER | 25121/372 | ex B-2564 | 642 |
| | | | | |
| ☐ C-FIUA | Boeing 777-233LR | 35239/640 | | 701 |
| ☐ C-FIUF | Boeing 777-233LR | 35243/651 | ex N1788B | 702 |
| ☐ C-FIUJ | Boeing 777-233LR | 35244/679 | | 703 |
| ☐ C-FIVK | Boeing 777-233LR | 35245/689 | | 704 |
| ☐ C-FNND | Boeing 777-233LR | 35246/695 | | 705 |
| ☐ C-FNNH | Boeing 777-233LR | 35247/699 | | 706 |
| | | | | |
| ☐ C-FITL | Boeing 777-333ER | 35256/620 | | 731 |
| ☐ C-FITU | Boeing 777-333ER | 35254/626 | | 732 |
| ☐ C-FITW | Boeing 777-333ER | 35298/638 | | 733 |
| ☐ C-FIUL | Boeing 777-333ER | 35255/642 | | 734 |
| ☐ C-FIUR | Boeing 777-333ER | 35242/649 | | 735 |
| ☐ C-FIUV | Boeing 777-333ER | 35248/702 | | 736 |
| ☐ C-FIUW | Boeing 777-333ER | 35249/712 | | 737 |
| ☐ C-FIVM | Boeing 777-333ER | 35251/717 | | 738 |
| ☐ C-FIVQ | Boeing 777-333ER | 35240/749 | | 740 |
| ☐ C-FIVR | Boeing 777-333ER | 35241/763 | | 741 |
| ☐ C-FIVS | Boeing 777-333ER | 35784/797 | | 742 |
| ☐ C-FRAM | Boeing 777-333ER | 35250/726 | | 739 |
| | | | | |
| ☐ C-FEIQ | Embraer ERJ-175SU | 17000083 | ex PT-SZI | 371 |
| ☐ C-FEIX | Embraer ERJ-175SU | 17000085 | ex PT-SZK | 372 |
| ☐ C-FEJB | Embraer ERJ-175SU | 17000086 | ex PT-SZL | 373 |
| ☐ C-FEJC | Embraer ERJ-175SU | 17000089 | ex PT-SZP | 374 |
| ☐ C-FEJD | Embraer ERJ-175SU | 17000090 | ex PT-SZQ | 375 |
| ☐ C-FEJF | Embraer ERJ-175SU | 17000091 | ex PT-SZR | 376 |
| ☐ C-FEJL | Embraer ERJ-175SU | 17000095 | ex PT-SZV | 377 |
| ☐ C-FEJP | Embraer ERJ-175SU | 17000096 | ex PT-SZW | 378 |
| ☐ C-FEJY | Embraer ERJ-175SU | 17000097 | ex PT-SZX | 379 |
| ☐ C-FEKD | Embraer ERJ-175SU | 17000101 | ex PT-SAC | 380 |
| ☐ C-FEKH | Embraer ERJ-175SU | 17000102 | ex PT-SAH | 381 |
| ☐ C-FEKI | Embraer ERJ-175SU | 17000103 | ex PT-SAI | 382 |
| ☐ C-FEKJ | Embraer ERJ-175SU | 17000109 | ex PT-SAR | 383 |
| ☐ C-FEKS | Embraer ERJ-175SU | 17000110 | ex PT-SAS | 384 |
| ☐ C-FFYG | Embraer ERJ-175SU | 17000116 | ex PT-SDD | 385 |
| | | | | |
| ☐ C-FFYJ | Embraer ERJ-190AR | 19000013 | ex PT-STM | 302 |
| ☐ C-FFYM | Embraer ERJ-190AR | 19000015 | ex PT-STP | 303 |
| ☐ C-FFYT | Embraer ERJ-190AR | 19000018 | ex PT-STS | 304 |
| ☐ C-FGLW | Embraer ERJ-190AR | 19000022 | ex PT-STW | 306 |
| ☐ C-FGLX | Embraer ERJ-190AR | 19000024 | ex PT-STY | 307 |
| ☐ C-FGLY | Embraer ERJ-190AR | 19000028 | ex PT-SGC | 308 |
| ☐ C-FGMF | Embraer ERJ-190AR | 19000019 | ex PT-STT | 305 |
| ☐ C-FHIQ | Embraer ERJ-190AR | 19000031 | ex PT-SGF | 309 |
| ☐ C-FHIS | Embraer ERJ-190AR | 19000036 | ex PT-SGK | 310 |
| ☐ C-FHIU | Embraer ERJ-190AR | 19000037 | ex PT-SGL | 311 |
| ☐ C-FHJJ | Embraer ERJ-190AR | 19000041 | ex PT-SGQ | 312 |
| ☐ C-FHJT | Embraer ERJ-190AR | 19000043 | ex PT-SGS | 313 |
| ☐ C-FHJU | Embraer ERJ-190AR | 19000044 | ex PT-SGT | 314 |
| ☐ C-FHKA | Embraer ERJ-190AR | 19000046 | ex PT-SGV | 315 |
| ☐ C-FHKE | Embraer ERJ-190AR | 19000048 | ex PT-SGX | 316 |
| ☐ C-FHKI | Embraer ERJ-190AR | 19000052 | ex PT-SIB | 317 |
| ☐ C-FHKP | Embraer ERJ-190AR | 19000055 | ex PT-SIE | 318 |
| ☐ C-FHKS | Embraer ERJ-190AR | 19000064 | ex PT-SJC | 319 |
| ☐ C-FHLH | Embraer ERJ-190AR | 19000068 | ex PT-SJH | 320 |
| ☐ C-FHNL | Embraer ERJ-190AR | 19000070 | ex PT-SJJ | 321 |
| ☐ C-FHNP | Embraer ERJ-190AR | 19000071 | ex PT-SJK | 322 |
| ☐ C-FHNV | Embraer ERJ-190AR | 19000075 | ex PT-SJP | 323 |
| ☐ C-FHNW | Embraer ERJ-190AR | 19000077 | ex PT-SJS | 324 |
| ☐ C-FHNX | Embraer ERJ-190AR | 19000083 | ex PT-SNA | 325 |
| ☐ C-FHNY | Embraer ERJ-190AR | 19000085 | ex PT-SND | 326 |
| ☐ C-FHON | Embraer ERJ-190AR | 19000097 | ex PT-SNR | 330 |
| ☐ C-FHOS | Embraer ERJ-190AR | 19000101 | ex PT-SNV | 331 |
| ☐ C-FHOY | Embraer ERJ-190AR | 19000105 | ex PT-SNZ | 332 |
| ☐ C-FLWE | Embraer ERJ-190AR | 19000092 | ex PT-SNL | 327 |
| ☐ C-FLWH | Embraer ERJ-190AR | 19000094 | ex PT-SNO | 328 |
| ☐ C-FLWK | Embraer ERJ-190AR | 19000096 | ex PT-SNQ | 329 |
| ☐ C-FMYV | Embraer ERJ-190AR | 19000108 | ex PT-SQC | 333 |

| | | | | | |
|---|---|---|---|---|---|
| ☐ C-FMZB | Embraer ERJ-190AR | 19000111 | ex PT-SQF | 334 | |
| ☐ C-FMZD | Embraer ERJ-190AR | 19000115 | ex PT-SQJ | 335 | |
| ☐ C-FMZR | Embraer ERJ-190AR | 19000116 | ex PT-SQK | 336 | |
| ☐ C-FMZU | Embraer ERJ-190AR | 19000118 | ex PT-SQM | 337 | |
| ☐ C-FMZW | Embraer ERJ-190AR | 19000124 | ex PT-SQT | 338 | |
| ☐ C-FNAI | Embraer ERJ-190AR | 19000132 | ex PT-SYK | 339 | |
| ☐ C-FNAJ | Embraer ERJ-190AR | 19000134 | ex PT-SYM | 340 | |
| ☐ C-FNAN | Embraer ERJ-190AR | 19000136 | ex PT-SYO | 341 | |
| ☐ C-FNAP | Embraer ERJ-190AR | 19000142 | ex PT-SYU | 342 | |
| ☐ C-FNAQ | Embraer ERJ-190AR | 19000146 | ex PT-SYY | 343 | |
| ☐ C-FNAW | Embraer ERJ-190AR | 19000149 | ex PT-SAC | 344 | |
| ☐ C-FNAX | Embraer ERJ-190AR | 19000151 | ex PT-SAG | 345 | |
| ☐ C-GWEN | Embraer ERJ-190AR | 19000010 | ex PT-STJ | 301 | |
| | | | | | |
| ☐ CF-TCC | Lockheed L-10A | 1116 | ex N3749 | Trans Canada Airlines c/s | |
| ☐ C-GKOL | Airbus A340-541 | 445 | ex PT-MSN | | >TAM♦ |

---

## AIR CANADA EXPRESS          Jazz (QK/JZA)

### Halifax, NS/Calgary, AB/London, ON/Vancouver, BC (YHZ/YYC/YXU/YVR)

Note: Fleet is being repainted into mainline Air Canada c/s, colours will be replaced.....

| | | | | |
|---|---|---|---|---|
| ☐ C-FRIA | Canadair CRJ-100ER | 7045 | ex C-FMLQ | 101 red |
| ☐ C-FRIB | Canadair CRJ-100ER | 7047 | ex C-FMLT | 102 green |
| ☐ C-FRID | Canadair CRJ-100ER | 7049 | ex C-FMLV | 103 yellow |
| ☐ C-FSJF | Canadair CRJ-100ER | 7054 | ex C-FMMT | 105 orange |
| ☐ C-FSJJ | Canadair CRJ-100ER | 7058 | ex C-FMNB | 106 orange |
| ☐ C-FSJU | Canadair CRJ-100ER | 7060 | ex C-FMNH | 107 orange |
| ☐ C-FSKE | Canadair CRJ-100ER | 7065 | ex C-FMOI | 108 red |
| ☐ C-FSKM | Canadair CRJ-100ER | 7071 | ex C-FMKZ | 110 orange |
| ☐ C-FVKM | Canadair CRJ-100ER | 7074 | ex C-FMLI | 111 green |
| ☐ C-FVKN | Canadair CRJ-100ER | 7078 | ex C-FMLU | 112 orange |
| ☐ C-FVKR | Canadair CRJ-100ER | 7083 | ex C-FMNQ | 114 green |
| ☐ C-FVMD | Canadair CRJ-100ER | 7082 | | 113 orange |
| ☐ C-FWJB | Canadair CRJ-100ER | 7087 | | 115 green |
| ☐ C-FWJF | Canadair CRJ-100ER | 7095 | | 116 orange |
| ☐ C-FWJI | Canadair CRJ-100ER | 7096 | | 117 red |
| ☐ C-FWJS | Canadair CRJ-100ER | 7097 | | 118 red |
| ☐ C-FWJT | Canadair CRJ-100ER | 7098 | | 119 green |
| ☐ C-FWRR | Canadair CRJ-100ER | 7107 | | 120 red |
| ☐ C-FWRS | Canadair CRJ-100ER | 7112 | | 121 red |
| ☐ C-FWRT | Canadair CRJ-100ER | 7118 | | 122 red |
| ☐ C-FWSC | Canadair CRJ-100ER | 7120 | | 123 green |
| ☐ C-FXMY | Canadair CRJ-100ER | 7124 | | 124 yellow |
| | | | | |
| ☐ C-FDJA | Canadair CRJ-200ER | 7979 | ex C-FMLI | 162 green♦ |
| ☐ C-FEJA | Canadair CRJ-200ER | 7983 | ex C-FMLV | 163 yellow♦ |
| ☐ C-FFJA | Canadair CRJ-200ER | 7985 | ex C-FMNH | 164 orange♦ |
| ☐ C-FIJA | Canadair CRJ-200ER | 7987 | ex C-FMNX | 165 red♦ |
| ☐ C-FZJA | Canadair CRJ-200ER | 7988 | ex C-FMNY | 166 green |
| ☐ C-GGJA | Canadair CRJ-200ER | 8002 | ex C-FMMY | 167 yellow |
| ☐ C-GJZJ | Canadair CRJ-200ER | 7553 | ex N706BR | 157 orange |
| ☐ C-GJZZ | Canadair CRJ-200ER | 7978 | ex C-FMLF | 161 red |
| ☐ C-GKEJ | Canadair CRJ-200ER | 7269 | ex N577ML | 180 red |
| ☐ C-GKEK | Canadair CRJ-200ER | 7270 | ex N578ML | 181 green |
| ☐ C-GKEM | Canadair CRJ-200ER | 7277 | ex N579ML | 182 yellow |
| ☐ C-GKEP | Canadair CRJ-200ER | 7303 | ex N581ML | 183 orange |
| ☐ C-GKER | Canadair CRJ-200ER | 7368 | ex N588ML | 184 red |
| ☐ C-GKEU | Canadair CRJ-200ER | 7376 | ex N589ML | 185 green |
| ☐ C-GKEW | Canadair CRJ-200ER | 7385 | ex N590ML | 186 yellow |
| ☐ C-GKEZ | Canadair CRJ-200ER | 7327 | ex N583ML | 187 orange |
| ☐ C-GKFR | Canadair CRJ-200ER | 7330 | ex N584ML | 188 red |
| ☐ C-GKGC | Canadair CRJ-200ER | 7334 | ex N585ML | 189 green |
| ☐ C-GMJA | Canadair CRJ-200ER | 8003 | ex C-FMNB | 168 orange |
| ☐ C-GNJA | Canadair CRJ-200ER | 8004 | ex C-FMKV | 169 red |
| ☐ C-GOJA | Canadair CRJ-200ER | 8009 | ex C-FMLI | 170 yellow |
| ☐ C-GQJA | Canadair CRJ-200ER | 7963 | ex C-FCGX | 171 Star Alliance c/s |
| ☐ C-GTJA | Canadair CRJ-200ER | 7966 | ex C-FCLV | 172 green |
| ☐ C-GUJA | Canadair CRJ-200ER | 8011 | ex C-FMLS | 173 orange |
| ☐ C-GXJA | Canadair CRJ-200ER | 8017 | ex C-FMNX | 174 yellow |
| ☐ C-GZJA | Canadair CRJ-200ER | 8018 | ex C-FMNY | 175 orange |
| | | | | |
| ☐ C-FBJZ | Canadair CRJ-705ER | 15037 | | 702 green |
| ☐ C-FCJZ | Canadair CRJ-705ER | 15040 | | 703 orange |
| ☐ C-FDJZ | Canadair CRJ-705ER | 15041 | | 704 yellow |
| ☐ C-FJJZ | Canadair CRJ-705ER | 15043 | | 705 red |
| ☐ C-FKJZ | Canadair CRJ-705ER | 15044 | | 706 green |
| ☐ C-FLJZ | Canadair CRJ-705ER | 15045 | | 707 yellow |
| ☐ C-FNJZ | Canadair CRJ-705ER | 15046 | | 708 orange |
| ☐ C-FTJZ | Canadair CRJ-705ER | 15047 | | 709 red |

| | | | | |
|---|---|---|---|---|
| ☐ C-FUJZ | Canadair CRJ-705ER | 15048 | | 710 Star Alliance c/s |
| ☐ C-GDJZ | Canadair CRJ-705ER | 15049 | | 711 green |
| ☐ C-GFJZ | Canadair CRJ-705ER | 15050 | | 712 yellow |
| ☐ C-GJAZ | Canadair CRJ-705ER | 15036 | | 701 red |
| ☐ C-GLJZ | Canadair CRJ-705ER | 15051 | | 713 orange |
| ☐ C-GNJZ | Canadair CRJ-705ER | 15052 | | 714 red |
| ☐ C-GOJZ | Canadair CRJ-705ER | 15053 | | 715 green |
| ☐ C-GPJZ | Canadair CRJ-705ER | 15055 | ex C-FGND | 716 red |
| | | | | |
| ☐ C-FABA | de Havilland DHC-8-102 | 092 | | 805 orange |
| ☐ C-FABN | de Havilland DHC-8-102 | 044 | | 803 red |
| ☐ C-FABT | de Havilland DHC-8-102 | 049 | | 848 green |
| ☐ C-FABW | de Havilland DHC-8-102 | 097 | | 806 green |
| ☐ C-FACD | de Havilland DHC-8-102 | 150 | | 808 yellow |
| ☐ C-FGQK | de Havilland DHC-8-102 | 193 | | 819 yellow |
| ☐ C-FGRC | de Havilland DHC-8-102 | 195 | | 821 green |
| ☐ C-FGRM | de Havilland DHC-8-102 | 199 | | 820 red |
| ☐ C-FGRP | de Havilland DHC-8-102 | 207 | | 822 green |
| ☐ C-FGRY | de Havilland DHC-8-102 | 212 | | 844 red |
| ☐ C-FJMG | de Havilland DHC-8-102A | 255 | | 824 orange |
| ☐ C-FPON | de Havilland DHC-8-102 | 171 | | 836 orange |
| ☐ C-GABF | de Havilland DHC-8-102 | 025 | | 816 green |
| ☐ C-GANF | de Havilland DHC-8-102 | 042 | | 802 orange |
| ☐ C-GANI | de Havilland DHC-8-102 | 064 | | 830 green |
| ☐ C-GANK | de Havilland DHC-8-102 | 087 | | 831 yellow |
| ☐ C-GANQ | de Havilland DHC-8-102 | 096 | | 833 yellow |
| ☐ C-GANS | de Havilland DHC-8-102 | 057 | | 828 green |
| ☐ C-GCTC | de Havilland DHC-8-102 | 065 | ex V2-LEE | 846 orange |
| ☐ C-GION | de Havilland DHC-8-102 | 127 | | 832 yellow |
| ☐ C-GJIG | de Havilland DHC-8-102 | 068 | | 826 orange |
| ☐ C-GJMI | de Havilland DHC-8-102 | 077 | | 825 yellow |
| ☐ C-GJMO | de Havilland DHC-8-102 | 079 | | 834 yellow |
| ☐ C-GJSV | de Havilland DHC-8-102 | 085 | | 814 green |
| ☐ C-GJSX | de Havilland DHC-8-102 | 088 | | 835 red |
| ☐ C-GKON | de Havilland DHC-8-102 | 130 | | 815 red |
| ☐ C-GOND | de Havilland DHC-8-102 | 090 | | 840 red |
| ☐ C-GONJ | de Havilland DHC-8-102 | 095 | | 839 orange |
| ☐ C-GONN | de Havilland DHC-8-102 | 101 | | 898 yellow |
| ☐ C-GONO | de Havilland DHC-8-102 | 102 | | 807 orange |
| ☐ C-GONR | de Havilland DHC-8-102 | 109 | | 841 green |
| ☐ C-GONW | de Havilland DHC-8-102 | 112 | | 843 green |
| ☐ C-GONX | de Havilland DHC-8-102 | 118 | | 829 red |
| ☐ C-GONY | de Havilland DHC-8-102 | 115 | | 827 yellow |
| ☐ C-GTAI | de Havilland DHC-8-102 | 078 | | 853 yellow |
| ☐ C-GTBP | de Havilland DHC-8-102 | 066 | | 855 green |
| | | | | |
| ☐ C-FACF | de Havilland DHC-8-311A | 259 | | 308 yellow |
| ☐ C-FACT | de Havilland DHC-8-311A | 262 | | 309 green |
| ☐ C-FACV | de Havilland DHC-8-311A | 278 | | 311 red |
| ☐ C-FADF | de Havilland DHC-8-311A | 272 | ex C-FACU | 310 red |
| ☐ C-FJFM | de Havilland DHC-8-311A | 240 | | 324 yellow |
| ☐ C-FJVV | de Havilland DHC-8-311A | 271 | | 306 red |
| ☐ C-FJXZ | de Havilland DHC-8-311A | 264 | ex C-FTAQ | 326 red |
| ☐ C-FMDW | de Havilland DHC-8-311A | 269 | | 305 green |
| ☐ C-FRUZ | de Havilland DHC-8-311 | 293 | ex N2492B | 327 red |
| ☐ C-FSOU | de Havilland DHC-8-311A | 342 | ex LN-WFA | 328 green |
| ☐ C-FTAK | de Havilland DHC-8-311A | 246 | | 323 red |
| ☐ C-GABO | de Havilland DHC-8-311A | 248 | | 312 green |
| ☐ C-GABP | de Havilland DHC-8-311A | 257 | | 307 green |
| ☐ C-GETA | de Havilland DHC-8-301 | 186 | | 321 red |
| ☐ C-GEWQ | de Havilland DHC-8-311A | 202 | | 325 red |
| ☐ C-GHTA | de Havilland DHC-8-301 | 198 | | 316 orange |
| ☐ C-GKTA | de Havilland DHC-8-301 | 124 | | 317 green |
| ☐ C-GLTA | de Havilland DHC-8-301 | 154 | | 318 green |
| ☐ C-GMON | de Havilland DHC-8-301 | 131 | | 301 orange |
| ☐ C-GMTA | de Havilland DHC-8-301 | 174 | | 319 yellow |
| ☐ C-GNON | de Havilland DHC-8-301 | 137 | | 302 green |
| ☐ C-GSTA | de Havilland DHC-8-301 | 182 | | 320 yellow |
| ☐ C-GTAG | de Havilland DHC-8-301 | 200 | | 315 orange |
| ☐ C-GTAQ | de Havilland DHC-8-301 | 180 | ex C-FGVK | 313 red |
| ☐ C-GTAT | de Havilland DHC-8-301 | 188 | ex C-FGVT | 314 red |
| ☐ C-GUON | de Havilland DHC-8-301 | 143 | | 303 green |
| ☐ C-GVON | de Havilland DHC-8-301 | 149 | | 304 orange |
| ☐ C-GVTA | de Havilland DHC-8-301 | 190 | | 322 red |
| | | | | |
| ☐ C-GGMN | de Havilland DHC-8-402Q | 4405 | | o/o♦ |
| ☐ C-GGMQ | de Havilland DHC-8-402Q | 4403 | | o/o♦ |
| ☐ C-GGMU | de Havilland DHC-8-402Q | 4397 | | 411♦ |
| ☐ C-GGMZ | de Havilland DHC-8-402Q | 4399 | | 407♦ |
| ☐ C-GGND | de Havilland DHC-8-402Q | 4394 | | 410♦ |
| ☐ C-GGNF | de Havilland DHC-8-402Q | 4393 | | 409♦ |
| ☐ C-GGNW | de Havilland DHC-8-402Q | 4388 | | 408♦ |

| | | | | | |
|---|---|---|---|---|---|
| ☐ C-GGNY | de Havilland DHC-8-402Q | 4386 | | | 407♦ |
| ☐ C-GGNZ | de Havilland DHC-8-402Q | 4384 | | | 406♦ |
| ☐ C-GGOF | de Havilland DHC-8-402Q | 4383 | | | 405♦ |
| ☐ C-GGOI | de Havilland DHC-8-402Q | 4381 | | | 404♦ |
| ☐ C-GGOK | de Havilland DHC-8-402Q | 4372 | | | 403♦ |
| ☐ C-GGOY | de Havilland DHC-8-402Q | 4365 | | | 401♦ |
| ☐ C-GKUK | de Havilland DHC-8-402Q | 4369 | | | 402♦ |
| | | | | | |
| ☐ C-GJZB | Boeing 757-28AER | 28203/802 | ex G-TCBA | | <TCX |
| ☐ C-GJZD | Boeing 757-2G5 | 26278/671 | ex G-JMCG | | <TCX♦ |
| ☐ C-GJZH | Boeing 757-25F | 30758/932 | ex G-JMCE | | <TCX |
| ☐ C-GJZX | Boeing 757-25F | 28718/752 | exG-FCLD | | <TCX♦ |

| **AIR CREEBEC** | | *Cree (YN/CRQ)* | | *Val d'Or, QC / Timmins, ON (YVO/YTS)* | |
|---|---|---|---|---|---|
| ☐ C-FCJD | de Havilland DHC-8-102 | 158 | | | ♦ |
| ☐ C-FCLS | de Havilland DHC-8-102 | 249 | ex N841EX | | |
| ☐ C-FCSK | de Havilland DHC-8-102 | 122 | | | |
| ☐ C-FDWO | de Havilland DHC-8-106 | 277 | ex N880CC | | |
| ☐ C-GAIS | de Havilland DHC-8-102 | 138 | ex C-FCIZ | | |
| ☐ C-GJOP | de Havilland DHC-8-102 | 121 | ex N381BC | | |
| ☐ C-GTCO | de Havilland DHC-8-102 | 119 | | | |
| ☐ C-GYWX | de Havilland DHC-8-102 | 175 | ex N283BC | | |
| ☐ C-GZEW | de Havilland DHC-8-314 | 393 | ex N801SA | | |
| | | | | | |
| ☐ C-FHGG | Beech A100 King Air | B-207 | ex N727LE | | |
| ☐ C-FLIY | Hawker Siddeley HS.748 Srs.2A/244 | 1723 | ex SE-LEG | | Frtr |
| ☐ C-FPCU | Embraer EMB.110P1 Bandeirante | 110445 | ex LN-TDA | | |
| ☐ C-FPJR | Hawker Siddeley HS.748 Srs.2A/244 | 1725 | ex SE-LEK | | Frtr |
| ☐ C-FTQR | Beech 1900D | UE-129 | | | |
| ☐ C-FYRH | Embraer EMB.110P1 Bandeirante | 110259 | ex N91PB | | |
| ☐ C-GIZX | Beech A100 King Air | B-172 | ex N753DB | | |

| **AIR-DALE FLYING SERVICE** | | | *Ranger Lake SPB, ON/Wawa Hawk Junction SPB, ON* | |
|---|---|---|---|---|
| ☐ C-FGYT | de Havilland DHC-2 Beaver | 182 | ex CF-GYT | FP |
| ☐ CF-ODE | de Havilland DHC-2 Beaver | 131 | | FP |
| ☐ C-GELP | de Havilland DHC-2 Beaver | 780 | ex N5318G | FP |
| ☐ C-GQXI | de Havilland DHC-2 Beaver | 427 | ex N1059 | FP |

| **AIR GEORGIAN / AIR ALLIANCE** | | *Georgian (ZX/GGN)* | | *Toronto-Pearson Intl, ON (YYZ)* | |
|---|---|---|---|---|---|
| ☐ C-GAAR | Beech 1900D | UE-207 | ex N10625 | 964 Baie-Saint Laurent | |
| ☐ C-GAAS | Beech 1900D | UE-209 | ex N10659 | 965 Iles de la Madelaine | |
| ☐ C-GAAU | Beech 1900D | UE-232 | ex N10705 | 904 Baie Comeau | |
| ☐ C-GAAV | Beech 1900D | UE-235 | ex N10708 | 967 | |
| ☐ C-GGGA | Beech 1900D | UE-291 | ex N20704 | 951 | |
| ☐ C-GHGA | Beech 1900D | UE-293 | ex N21063 | 953 | |
| ☐ C-GMGA | Beech 1900D | UE-315 | ex N22890 | 956 Baie Comeau | |
| ☐ C-GORA | Beech 1900D | UE-326 | ex N23164 | 957 | |
| ☐ C-GORC | Beech 1900D | UE-320 | ex N22976 | 959 | |
| ☐ C-GORF | Beech 1900D | UE-330 | ex N23222 | 958 | |
| ☐ C-GORI | Beech 1900D | UE-47 | ex(N147MJ) | 970 | |
| ☐ C-GORN | Beech 1900D | UE-403 | ex N330DH | | ♦ |
| ☐ C-GORZ | Beech 1900D | UE-134 | ex N860CA | 973 | |
| ☐ C-GVGA | Beech 1900D | UE-292 | ex N20707 | 952 | |
| ☐ C-GWGA | Beech 1900D | UE-309 | ex N22874 | 955 | |
| ☐ C-GZGA | Beech 1900D | UE-306 | ex N22700 | 954 | |
| | | | | | |
| ☐ C-FDKL | Hawker 800XP | 258337 | ex N733TA | | ♦ |

| **AIR INUIT** | | *Air Inuit (3H/AIE)* | | *Kuujjuaq, QC (YVP)* | |
|---|---|---|---|---|---|
| ☐ C-FAIY | de Havilland DHC-6 Twin Otter 300 | 362 | ex C-FASS | | FP/WS |
| ☐ C-FJFR | de Havilland DHC-6 Twin Otter 300 | 784 | ex HK-2762 | | |
| ☐ C-FTJJ | de Havilland DHC-6 Twin Otter 300 | 325 | ex 8Q-MAJ | | N93NC res |
| ☐ C-GMDC | de Havilland DHC-6 Twin Otter 300 | 763 | | | |
| ☐ C-GNDO | de Havilland DHC-6 Twin Otter 300 | 430 | | | |
| ☐ C-GTYX | de Havilland DHC-6 Twin Otter 300 | 631 | | | |
| | | | | | |
| ☐ C-FAID | de Havilland DHC-8Q-314 | 400 | ex OE-LTD | | ♦ |
| ☐ C-FEAI | de Havilland DHC-8Q-311 | 334 | ex G-WOWB | | o/o♦ |
| ☐ C-FIAI | de Havilland DHC-8Q-314 | 485 | ex OE-LTL | | ♦ |
| ☐ C-FOAI | de Havilland DHC-8Q-314 | 466 | ex OE-LTI | | ♦ |
| ☐ C-GRAI | de Havilland DHC-8Q-314 | 483 | ex OE-LTK | | |
| ☐ C-GUAI | de Havilland DHC-8Q-314 | 423 | ex OE-LTF | | |
| ☐ C-GXAI | de Havilland DHC-8Q-314 | 481 | ex OE-LTJ | | ♦ |
| | | | | | |
| ☐ C-FAIO | Beech A100 King Air | B-132 | ex C-GXHP | | |
| ☐ C-FAIP | Beech A100 King Air | B-193 | ex F-GXAB | | |

| | | | | |
|---|---|---|---|---|
| ☐ C-FAIV | de Havilland DHC-8-102 | 235 | ex N828EX | |
| ☐ C-FDAO | de Havilland DHC-8-102 | 123 | | |
| ☐ C-FDOX | Hawker Siddeley HS.748 Srs.2A/310LFD | 1749 | ex TJ-CCD | |
| ☐ C-GAIG | Boeing 737-2S2C | 21928/603 | ex A6-ZYB | |
| ☐ C-GAII | de Havilland DHC-8-102 | 160 | ex N831EX | |
| ☐ C-GAIK | Beech A100 King Air | B-104 | ex C-GCFD | |
| ☐ C-GAIW | de Havilland DHC-8-102 | 155 | ex N830EX | |
| ☐ C-GEGJ | Hawker Siddeley HS.748 Srs.2A/244 | 1711 | ex TF-GMB | |
| ☐ C-GAIG | Boeing 737-2S2C | 21928/603 | ex A6-ZYB | |
| ☐ C-GMAI | Boeing 737-2Q2C | 21467/515 | ex TN-AHW | |

## AIR IVANHOE                                                                         Foleyet-Ivanhoe Lake, ON

| | | | | |
|---|---|---|---|---|
| ☐ C-GERE | de Havilland DHC-2 Beaver | 352 | ex N62784 | FP |
| ☐ C-GPUS | de Havilland DHC-2 Beaver | 624 | ex 53-2824 | FP |

## AIR LABRADOR / LABRADOR AIRWAYS     Lab Air (WJ/LAL)                 Goose Bay, NL (YYR)

| | | | | |
|---|---|---|---|---|
| ☐ C-FGON | de Havilland DHC-6 Twin Otter 300 | 369 | ex CF-GON | FP/WS |
| ☐ C-FOPN | de Havilland DHC-6 Twin Otter 300 | 291 | | FP/WS♦ |
| ☐ C-GKSN | de Havilland DHC-6 Twin Otter 300 | 493 | ex N148DE | ♦ |
| ☐ C-GLAI | de Havilland DHC-6 Twin Otter 300 | 296 | ex N5377G | FP/WS |
| ☐ C-GNQY | de Havilland DHC-6 Twin Otter 300 | 450 | ex N965HA | FP/WS |
| ☐ C-GKSN | de Havilland DHC-6 Twin Otter 300 | 493 | ex N148DE | |
| | | | | |
| ☐ C-FXON | de Havilland DHC-8-102 | 183 | ex V2-LDZ | |
| ☐ C-GLON | de Havilland DHC-8-102 | 133 | | |
| ☐ C-GTMB | Beech 1900D | UE-345 | ex N23388 | |
| ☐ C-GUYR | Cessna 208 Caravan I | 20800031 | ex N604MA | |
| ☐ C-GZUZ | Beech A100 King Air | B-143 | | ♦ |

## AIR MELANCON                                                                          St Anne-du-Lac, QC

| | | | | |
|---|---|---|---|---|
| ☐ C-FQQD | de Havilland DHC-2 Beaver | 1580 | ex FAP 64-374 | FP/WS |
| ☐ C-FZVP | de Havilland DHC-2 Beaver | 1033 | ex N564 | FP/WS |
| ☐ C-GQXH | de Havilland DHC-2 Beaver | 536 | ex N1579 | FP/WS |

## AIR MIKISEW                                       Air Mikisew (V8)              Fort McMurray, AB (YMM)

Ceased ops

## AIR MONT-LAURIER                                                                      Ste-Veronique, QC

| | | | | |
|---|---|---|---|---|
| ☐ C-FQQC | de Havilland DHC-2 Beaver | 56 | ex CF-QQC | FP |
| ☐ C-FSUB | de Havilland DHC-3 Otter | 8 | ex RCAF 3662 | FP |
| ☐ C-FTUR | de Havilland DHC-2 Beaver | 1529 | ex CF-TUR | FP |
| ☐ C-GGSC | de Havilland DHC-3 Otter | 366 | ex N5072F | FP |
| ☐ C-GMGP | Cessna A185F Skywagon | 18502077 | ex N9054F | FP |
| ☐ C-GUML | de Havilland DHC-2 Beaver | 307 | ex N1402Z | FP |
| ☐ C-GVLK | Cessna U206G Stationair 6 II | U20604329 | ex N756SW | FP |

## AIR MONTMAGNY / MONTMAGNY AIR SERVICE                                          Montmagny, QC

| | | | | |
|---|---|---|---|---|
| ☐ C-GBFU | Britten-Norman BN-2A-27 Islander | 535 | ex N70JA | |
| ☐ C-GCTM | Cessna U206G Stationair | U20603794 | ex N8920G | |
| ☐ C-GGJG | Britten-Norman BN-2B-26 Islander | 2219 | ex F-ODUP | |
| ☐ C-GOSJ | Partenavia P.68 Observer | 241-02 | | ♦ |
| ☐ C-GTMQ | Cessna 206H Stationair | 20608038 | ex N7255B | |

## AIR NORTH                                         Air North (4N/ANT)              Whitehorse, YT (YXY)

| | | | | |
|---|---|---|---|---|
| ☐ C-FANB | Boeing 737-48E | 25764/2314 | ex N764TA | |
| ☐ C-FJLB | Boeing 737-201 (Nordam 3) | 22273/680 | ex N233US | |
| ☐ C-GANH | Boeing 737-505/W | 27153/2516 | ex VP-BOQ | |
| ☐ C-GANV | Boeing 737-2X6C | 23122/1036 | ex N816AL | |
| ☐ C-GNAU | Boeing 737-201 (Nordam 3) | 21817/602 | ex N228US | |
| | | | | |
| ☐ C-FAGI | Hawker Siddeley HS.748 Srs.2A/276 | 1699 | ex G-11-6 | |
| ☐ C-FCSE | Hawker Siddeley HS.748 Srs 2A/269 | 1679 | ex G-AYFL | |
| ☐ C-FYDU | Hawker Siddeley HS.748 Srs.2A/273 | 1694 | ex ZK-MCP | |
| ☐ C-FYDY | Hawker Siddeley HS.748 Srs.2A/233 | 1661 | ex ZK-MCJ | Frtr |
| ☐ C-GLIZ | Cessna 206 Super Skywagon | 206-0156 | ex N5156U | |

## AIR NUNAVUT                                       Air Baffin (BFF)                 Iqaluit, NT (YFB)

| | | | | |
|---|---|---|---|---|
| ☐ C-FCGW | Beech 200 Super King Air | BB-207 | ex N111WH | CatPass 200 conversion |
| ☐ C-FZNQ | Beech 200 Super King Air | BB-264 | ex N465CJ | CatPass 200 conversion |
| ☐ C-GZYO | Beech 200 Super King Air | BB-383 | ex N384DB | |

## AIR ROBERVAL                                                                    Robertval, PQ (YRJ)

| | | | | | |
|---|---|---|---|---|---|
| ☐ | C-FDGW | Cessna 208 Caravan I | 20800272 | ex C-FCPW | |
| ☐ | C-FNFI | de Havilland DHC-3 Otter | 379 | | FP/WS |
| ☐ | C-FNME | Cessna 208 Caravan I | 20800318 | ex N208JL | ♦ |
| ☐ | C-FVVY | de Havilland DHC-3 Turbo Otter | 410 | ex RCAF 9427 | FP/WS |
| ☐ | C-GLIE | Cessna 208B Caravan I | 208B0703 | ex N903DP | ♦ |
| ☐ | C-GLPM | de havilland DHC-3 Turbo Otter | 147 | ex C-FJFJ | ♦ |

## AIR SAGUENAY                                                                Lac St-Sebastien, QC

| | | | | | |
|---|---|---|---|---|---|
| ☐ | C-FIUS | de Havilland DHC-2 Beaver | 901 | ex CF-IUS | FP/WS |
| ☐ | C-FJAC | de Havilland DHC-2 Beaver | 937 | ex CF-JAC | FP/WS |
| ☐ | C-FJGV | de Havilland DHC-2 Beaver | 977 | ex CF-JGV | FP/WS♦ |
| ☐ | C-FJKI | de Havilland DHC-2 Beaver | 992 | ex CF-JKI | FP/WS |
| ☐ | C-FKRJ | de Havilland DHC-2 Beaver | 1210 | ex CF-KRJ | FP/WS |
| ☐ | C-FOCU | de Havilland DHC-2 Beaver | 73 | ex CF-OCU | FP/WS♦ |
| ☐ | C-FPQC | de Havilland DHC-2 Beaver | 873 | ex CF-IKQ | FP/WS♦ |
| ☐ | C-FUWJ | de Havilland DHC-2 Beaver | 453 | ex N7691 | FP/WS♦ |
| ☐ | C-FYYT | de Havilland DHC-2 Beaver | 1569 | ex VH-IDZ | FP/WS♦ |
| ☐ | C-GAEF | de Havilland DHC-2 Beaver | 372 | ex 51-16830 | FP/WS |
| ☐ | C-GPUO | de Havilland DHC-2 Beaver | 810 | ex 54-1677 | FP/WS |
| ☐ | C-GUJI | de Havilland DHC-2 Beaver | 1141 | ex N68013 | FP/WS |
| ☐ | C-GUJU | de Havilland DHC-2 Beaver | 1639 | | FP/WS♦ |
| ☐ | C-GWAE | de Havilland DHC-2 Beaver | 1094 | ex N93434 | FP/WS♦ |
| ☐ | C-FAZW | de Havilland DHC-3 Otter | 451 | ex JW-9101 | FP/WS♦ |
| ☐ | C-FDAK | de Havilland DHC-3 Otter | 157 | ex CF-DAK | FP/WS |
| ☐ | C-FJZN | de Havilland DHC-3 Otter | 205 | ex CF-JZN | FP/WS♦ |
| ☐ | C-FODT | de Havilland DHC-3 Turbo Otter | 218 | ex CF-ODT | FP/WS |
| ☐ | C-GLCO | de Havilland DHC-3 Turbo Otter | 420 | | FP/WS♦ |
| ☐ | C-GLJI | de Havilland DHC-3 Otter | 150 | ex 55-3297 | FP/WS♦ |
| ☐ | C-GLFL | de Havilland DHC-3 Turbo Otter | 329 | ex 58-1712 | FP/WS |
| ☐ | C-GLMT | de Havilland DHC-3 Turbo Otter | 216 | ex IM-1716 | FP/WS |
| ☐ | C-GQDU | de Havilland DHC-3 Turbo Otter | 43 | ex N94472 | FP/WS |
| ☐ | C-GUTQ | de Havilland DHC-3 Otter | 402 | ex HK-3049X | FP/WS |
| ☐ | C-GVNX | de Havilland DHC-3 Otter | 353 | ex N5335G | FP/WS♦ |
| ☐ | C-FYAO | Cessna A185E Skywagon | 18501472 | ex (N2722J) | FP/WS |
| ☐ | C-FYVT | Cessna A185E Skywagon | 1851561 | | ♦ |
| ☐ | C-GAYC | Cessna A185F Skywagon | 18503999 | | ♦ |
| ☐ | C-GTBY | Cessna 208 Caravan I | 20800261 | ex C-GFLN | FP/WS |
| ☐ | C-GUBN | Cessna U206F Stationair II | U20602860 | ex (N1185Q) | FP/WS♦ |

## AIR-SPRAY                          Air Spray (ASB)        Edmonton-Municipal/Red Deer, AB (YEG/YQF)

| | | | | | |
|---|---|---|---|---|---|
| ☐ | CF-CBK | Douglas B-26C Invader | 28940 | ex N9996Z | 11 |
| ☐ | CF-CUI | Douglas B-26C Invader | 28803 | ex N9401Z | 12 |
| ☐ | C-FKBM | Douglas A-26B Invader | 27415 | ex N8017E | 20 |
| ☐ | C-FOVC | Douglas B-26C Invader | 28776 | ex N3426G | 56 |
| ☐ | C-FPGF | Douglas A-26B Invader | 29154 | ex 44-35875 | 1 |
| ☐ | CF-ZTC | Douglas B-26C Invader | 29136 | ex N9300R | 13 Lucky Jack |
| ☐ | C-GHZM | Douglas A-26B Invader | 27400 | ex N4805E | 5 Fire Eater |
| ☐ | C-FLJO | Lockheed L-188C Electra | 1103 | ex N429NA | 82 |
| ☐ | C-FLXT | Lockheed L-188C Electra | 1130 | ex N308D | |
| ☐ | C-FVFH | Lockheed L-188A Electra | 1006 | ex PK-RLF | 89 |
| ☐ | C-FVFI | Lockheed L-188C Electra | 1082 | ex PK-RLD | [YQF] |
| ☐ | C-FZCS | Lockheed L-188C Electra | 1060 | ex HR-SHN | 87 |
| ☐ | C-GHZI | Lockheed L-188C Electra | 2007 | ex N1968R | 84 |
| ☐ | C-GJTZ | Lockheed L-188C Electra | 1133 | ex N290F | |
| ☐ | C-GKIL | Lockheed L-188A Electra | 1038 | ex N344HA | ♦ |
| ☐ | C-GNPB | Lockheed L-188A Electra | 1028 | ex Honduras 555 | ♦ |
| ☐ | C-GOIZ | Lockheed L-188AF Electra | 1053 | ex N343HA | ♦ |
| ☐ | C-GYVI | Lockheed L-188CF Electra | 1112 | ex N360Q | 83 [YQI] |
| ☐ | C-GZCF | Lockheed L-188CF Electra | 1091 | ex G-CEXS | 90 |
| ☐ | C-GZVM | Lockheed L-188A Electra | 1036 | ex N351Q | 85 |
| ☐ | C-GZYH | Lockheed L-188A Electra | 1124 | ex HR-AMM | [YQF] |
| ☐ | C-FAKP | Rockwell 690 Turbo Commander | 11040 | ex N690DC | 56 |
| ☐ | C-FIIL | Rockwell 690A Turbo Commander | 11167 | ex N85AB | |
| ☐ | C-FMCX | Rockwell 690B Turbo Commander | 11446 | ex N137BW | |
| ☐ | C-FZRQ | Rockwell 690 Turbo Commander | 11025 | ex N100LS | 51 |
| ☐ | C-GFPP | Rockwell 690 Turbo Commander | 11032 | ex N349AC | 52 |
| ☐ | C-GJFO | Rockwell 690 Turbo Commander | 11035 | ex N15VZ | 53 |
| ☐ | C-GKDZ | Rockwell 690 Turbo Commander | 11016 | ex N428SJ | 54 |
| ☐ | C-GZON | Rockwell 690 Turbo Commander | 11020 | ex N14CV | 55 |
| ☐ | C-FEHK | Ted Smith Aerostar 600A | 60-0400-140 | ex N17LH | 307 |
| ☐ | C-FGWE | Cessna 310Q II | 310Q0920 | ex (N69686) | 302 for sale |
| ☐ | C-FJCF | Ted Smith Aerostar 600A | 60-0153-067 | ex N37HA | 308 |

| | | | | | |
|---|---|---|---|---|---|
| ☐ C-GXJP | Cessna 310P | 310P0073 | ex N101QC | 305 | for sale |
| ☐ C-GXXN | Cessna T310P | 310P0002 | ex N5702M | 306 | for sale |

## AIR TINDI

**Air Tindi (8T)**  **Yellowknife, NT (YZF)**

| | | | | | |
|---|---|---|---|---|---|
| ☐ C-FATA | Beech 200 Super King Air | BB-283 | ex N283JP | | |
| ☐ C-FCGU | Beech 200B Super King Air | BB-301 | ex N611SW | | CatPass 200 conversion |
| ☐ C-FYKN | Beech B300 Super King Air | FL-36 | ex N96KA | | ♦ |
| ☐ C-GDPB | Beech 200C Super King Air | BL-44 | ex N18379 | | EMS |
| ☐ C-GTUC | Beech 200 Super King Air | BB-268 | ex N565RA | | |
| ☐ C-GXHF | Beech 200 Super King Air | BB-1343 | ex 5Y-ECO | | Beech 1300 conversion |
| | | | | | |
| ☐ C-FATM | de Havilland DHC-6 Twin Otter 300 | 265 | ex PJ-ATL | | FP/WS |
| ☐ C-FATN | de Havilland DHC-6 Twin Otter 200 | 226 | ex N153BU | | FP/WS |
| ☐ C-FATO | de Havilland DHC-6 Twin Otter 310 | 674 | ex A6-MRM | | FP/WS |
| ☐ C-FATW | de Havilland DHC-6 Twin Otter 300 | 525 | ex PK-BRA | | FP/WS |
| ☐ C-GMAS | de Havilland DHC-6 Twin Otter 300 | 438 | ex N546N | | FP/WS |
| ☐ C-GNPS | de Havilland DHC-6 Twin Otter 300 | 558 | | | FP/WS |
| | | | | | |
| ☐ C-FKAY | Cessna 208B Caravan I | 208B0470 | ex N1294N | | |
| ☐ C-FWZV | de Havilland DHC-7-103 | 081 | ex P2-ANP | | |
| ☐ C-FXUY | de Havilland DHC-3 Turbo Otter | 142 | ex N214L | | FP/WS |
| ☐ C-FYKN | Beech B300 Super King Air | FL-36 | ex N96KA | | ♦ |
| ☐ C-GATH | Cessna 208B Caravan I | 208B1244 | ex N5225K | | |
| ☐ C-GATY | Cessna 208 Caravan I | 20800305 | ex N52627 | | FP/WS |
| ☐ C-GCEV | de Havilland DHC-7-102 | 063 | ex HB-IVY | | |
| ☐ C-GCPY | de Havilland DHC-7-102 | 101 | ex OY-CTC | | ♦ |
| ☐ C-GFFL | de Havilland DHC-7-102 | 074 | ex HB-IVY | | |
| ☐ C-GHUE | Beech 1900D | UE-52 | ex N152MJ | | |
| ☐ C-GPHO | Cessna A185F Skywagon | 18503099 | ex (N80151) | | FP/WS |
| ☐ C-GWXI | Cessna A185F Skywagon | 18502818 | ex (N1298F) | | FP/WS |
| ☐ C-GXCB | Learjet 35A | 35A-417 | ex LX-ONE | | ♦ |

## AIR TRANSAT

**Transat (TS/TSC)**  **Montreal-Trudeau, QC (YUL)**

| | | | | |
|---|---|---|---|---|
| ☐ C-FDAT | Airbus A310-308 | 658 | ex A6-EKK | 305 |
| ☐ C-GFAT | Airbus A310-304 | 545 | ex A6-EKG | 301 |
| ☐ C-GLAT | Airbus A310-308 | 588 | ex A6-EKI | 302 |
| ☐ C-GPAT | Airbus A310-308 | 597 | ex A6-EKJ | 303 |
| ☐ C-GSAT | Airbus A310-308 | 600 | ex 5Y-KQM | 304 |
| ☐ C-GTSF | Airbus A310-304 | 472 | ex CS-TEZ | 345 |
| ☐ C-GTSH | Airbus A310-308 | 599 | ex D-AIDN | 343 |
| ☐ C-GTSK | Airbus A310-304 | 541 | ex CS-TEW | 347 |
| ☐ C-GTSW | Airbus A310-304 | 483 | ex CS-TEH | 483 |
| ☐ C-GTSX | Airbus A310-304 | 527 | ex D-AIDH | 346 |
| ☐ C-GTSY | Airbus A310-304 | 447 | ex N447DN | 344 |

| | | | | | |
|---|---|---|---|---|---|
| ☐ C-GCTS | Airbus A330-342 | 177 | ex B-HYE | 002 | |
| ☐ C-GGTS | Airbus A330-243 | 250 | ex F-WWKK | 101 | |
| ☐ C-GITS | Airbus A330-243 | 271 | ex F-WWKY | 102 | |
| ☐ C-GKTS | Airbus A330-342 | 111 | ex B-HYC | 100 | |
| ☐ C-GPTS | Airbus A330-243 | 480 | ex F-WWKV | 103 | |
| ☐ C-GTSD | Airbus A330-343 | 407 | ex TC-SGJ | 004 | |
| ☐ C-GTSI | Airbus A330-243 | 427 | ex G-OJMB | 105 | ♦ |
| ☐ C-GTSJ | Airbus A330-243 | 795 | ex G-TCXA | 203 | ♦ |
| ☐ C-GTSN | Airbus A330-243 | 369 | ex HB-IQZ | 104 | ♦ |
| ☐ C-GTSO | Airbus A330-342 | 132 | ex B-HYD | 003 | ♦ |
| ☐ C-GTSR | Airbus A330-243 | 966 | ex XA-MSP | 201 | ♦ |
| ☐ C-GTSZ | Airbus A330-243 | 971 | ex XA-MSQ | 202 | ♦ |

## AIR TUNILIK

**Schefferville-Squaw Lake, QC (YKL)**

| | | | | |
|---|---|---|---|---|
| ☐ C-FLLX | de Havilland DHC-2 Beaver | 1293 | ex CF-LLX | FP/WS |
| ☐ C-GNKR | de Havilland DHC-2 Beaver | 331 | ex N5698 | |

## AIR WEMINDJI

| | | | |
|---|---|---|---|
| ☐ C-FKLC | de Havilland DHC-3 Otter | 255 | |
| ☐ C-FSVP | de Havilland DHC-3 Turbo Otter | 28 | ex N252KA |

## AIRCO AIRCRAFT CHARTERS

**Edmonton-Municipal, AB (YXD)**

| | | | |
|---|---|---|---|
| ☐ C-FTOW | Beech 1900D | UE-130 | |
| ☐ C-FWPG | Beech 100 King Air | B-67 | ex N26KW |
| ☐ C-FWYF | Beech 100 King Air | B-89 | ex N169RA |
| ☐ C-FWYN | Beech 100 King Air | B-47 | ex C-GNAX |
| ☐ C-FWYO | Beech 100 King Air | B-28 | ex N27JJ |
| ☐ C-GBMI | Piper PA-31-350 Chieftain | 31-8352007 | ex N23NP |
| ☐ C-GZNB | Piper PA-31-350 Navajo Chieftain | 31-7752079 | ex N6654B |

## AIREXPRESS ONTARIO                                                                 Oshawa, ON (YOO)

| | | | | |
|---|---|---|---|---|
| ☐ C-FSKX | Beech 200 Super King Air | BB-1126 | ex N650JW | |
| ☐ C-GBBS | Beech 200 Super King Air | BB-757 | ex N948MB | |

## ALBERTA CENTRAL AIRWAYS                                                        Lac la Biche, AB (YLB)

| | | | | |
|---|---|---|---|---|
| ☐ C-FNED | Beech 65-C90 King Air | LJ-680 | ex N928RD | |
| ☐ C-FSUG | Beech B200 Super King Air | BB-1699 | | ♦ |
| ☐ C-FTMU | DHC-6 Twin Otter 300 | 782 | | ♦ |
| ☐ C-FTSU | de Havilland DHC-6 Twin Otter 300 | 451 | ex C-FINM | |
| ☐ C-FTMU | de Havilland DHC-6 Twin Otter 300 | 782 | ex C-FZPQ | ♦ |
| ☐ C-FTWU | de Havilland DHC-6 Twin Otter 300 | 372 | ex N17GL | |
| ☐ C-GACA | Beech 200 Super King Air | BB-1309 | ex N4277C | Beech 1300 conversion |
| ☐ C-GACN | Beech 200 Super King Air | BB-1384 | ex N575T | Beech 1300 conversion |
| ☐ C-GYUW | Cessna U206G Stationair 6 | U20603738 | | |

## ALKAN AIR                                 Alkan Air (AKN)                        Whitehorse, YT (YXY)

| | | | | |
|---|---|---|---|---|
| ☐ C-FAKN | Beech 200 Super King Air | BB-216 | ex LN-VIU | |
| ☐ C-FAKW | Beech 300LW Super King Air | FA-183 | ex N19NC | |
| ☐ C-FAKZ | Cessna 208B Caravan I | 208B0666 | ex N939JL | |
| ☐ C-FCPV | de Havilland DHC-6 Twin Otter 300 | 371 | ex N371SS | |
| ☐ C-FCSW | de Havilland DHC-6 Twin Otter 300 | 355 | ex CF-CSW | ♦ |
| ☐ C-FLPC | Beech 300 Super King Air | FL-127 | ex N300LS | ♦ |
| ☐ C-FSKF | Cessna 208B Caravan I | 208B0673 | ex N5268M | |
| ☐ C-GLCS | de Havilland DHC-3 Turbo Otter | 428 | ex N17685 | |
| ☐ C-GMOC | Beech 200 Super King Air | BB-513 | ex N513SA | |
| ☐ C-GSDT | Piper PA-31-350 Chieftain | 31-8152102 | ex N120FL | |
| ☐ C-GYTB | Cessna U206G Stationair | U20603685 | ex (N7579N) | |

## ALLEN AIRWAYS                                                                  Sioux Lookout, ON (YXL)

| | | | | |
|---|---|---|---|---|
| ☐ C-FERZ | Cessna 180K | 18053071 | ex N2799K | FP |
| ☐ C-FYCK | Cessna A185E Skywagon | 185-1478 | ex CF-YCK | FP/WS |
| ☐ C-GQDO | Cessna A185F Skywagon | 18503745 | ex (N8585Q) | FP/WS |

## ALPINE AVIATION                                                                 Whitehorse, YT (YXY)

| | | | | |
|---|---|---|---|---|
| ☐ C-FGSI | Cessna U206F Stationair | U20602165 | ex CF-GSI | FP |
| ☐ C-GLFW | Cessna 180J Skywagon | 18052625 | | FP♦ |
| ☐ C-GMGD | de Havilland DHC-2 Beaver | 519 | ex N67091 | FP |

## ALPINE HELICOPTERS                                                               Kelowna, BC (YLW)

| | | | | |
|---|---|---|---|---|
| ☐ C-FJCH | Bell 206L-1 LongRanger | 45737 | ex N144JD | |
| ☐ C-GALH | Bell 206L-3 LongRanger III | 51297 | ex N753HL | |
| ☐ C-GALJ | Bell 206L-3 LongRanger III | 51010 | ex N22654 | |
| ☐ C-GALL | Bell 206L-3 LongRanger III | 51015 | ex N22660 | |
| ☐ C-GRLK | Bell 206L-3 LongRanger III | 51028 | ex N42814 | |
| | | | | |
| ☐ C-FAHB | Bell 212 | 30794 | ex A6-BBH | |
| ☐ C-FAHC | Bell 212 | 31246 | ex N212HT | |
| ☐ C-FAHG | Bell 212 | 30940 | ex N8530F | |
| ☐ C-FAHK | Bell 212 | 30852 | ex XA-SSE | |
| ☐ C-FAHL | Bell 212 | 30588 | ex XA-SSJ | |
| ☐ C-FAHP | Bell 212 | 30933 | ex D-HELL | |
| ☐ C-FAHR | Bell 212 | 30789 | ex A6-BBI | |
| ☐ C-FAHZ | Bell 212 | 30562 | ex XA-SSI | |
| ☐ C-FALK | Bell 212 | 30982 | ex N212EL | |
| ☐ C-FALV | Bell 212 | 30816 | ex N74AL | |
| ☐ C-GAHO | Bell 212 | 30937 | | |
| ☐ C-GAHV | Bell 212 | 30699 | ex N90221 | |
| ☐ C-GALI | Bell 212 | 30525 | ex JA9510 | |
| ☐ C-GIRZ | Bell 212 | 30622 | ex RP-C1677 | |
| ☐ C-GRNR | Bell 212 | 30999 | | |
| | | | | |
| ☐ C-FAHI | Bell 407 | 53016 | ex N409KA | |
| ☐ C-FALA | Bell 407 | 53115 | | |
| ☐ C-FALC | Bell 407 | 53056 | | ♦ |
| ☐ C-FALF | Bell 407 | 53271 | ex CC-CWS | |
| ☐ C-FALM | Bell 407 | 53018 | ex N409KA | |
| ☐ C-FNOB | Bell 407 | 53070 | ex N57416 | |
| ☐ C-GALG | Bell 407 | 53059 | ex N409PH | |
| ☐ C-GYAA | Bell 407 | 53152 | ex N407RH | |
| | | | | |
| ☐ C-FALU | Bell 206B JetRanger III | 1072 | | |
| ☐ C-GALR | Bell 206B JetRanger III | 1892 | ex N100YB | |
| ☐ C-GALX | Bell 206B JetRanger | 1046 | ex N58096 | |

## ALPINE LAKES AIR

| | | | | |
|---|---|---|---|---|
| ☐ C-FSKR | Bell 206L-1 LongRanger | 45607 | ex N171KA | ♦ |
| ☐ C-GFTZ | de Havilland  DHC-3 Turbo Otter | 174 | ex N90574 | ♦ |

## ALTA FLIGHTS

**Alta Flights (ALZ)**

**Edmonton-Intl/Calgary-Intl/Fort McMurray, AB (YEG/YYC/YMM)**

| | | | | |
|---|---|---|---|---|
| ☐ C-FAFG | Cessna 208B Caravan I | 208B0724 | ex N997Q | ♦ |
| ☐ C-FAFK | Cessna 208B Caravan I | 208B0663 | ex N1229A | ♦ |
| ☐ C-FTNY | Piper PA-31-350 Chieftain | 31-7952245 | ex N2169X | |
| ☐ C-FVVS | Piper PA-31-350 Chieftain | 31-7952199 | ex N35347 | |
| ☐ C-GAAF | Swearingen SA.227DC Metro 23 | DC-891B | ex B-3956 | |
| ☐ C-GSAF | Swearingen SA.227DC Metro 23 | DC-866B | ex B-3951 | |

## ARCTIC SUNWEST CHARTERS

**Yellowknife, NT (YZF)**

| | | | | |
|---|---|---|---|---|
| ☐ C-FASC | de Havilland DHC-8-102 | 038 | ex C-GJUZ | |
| ☐ C-FASN | Beech B100 King Air | BE-17 | ex N178NC | |
| ☐ C-FASQ | de Havilland DHC-6 Twin Otter 100 | 78 | ex C-FAKM | FP/WS |
| ☐ C-FASV | de Havilland DHC-5A Buffalo | 95A | ex 5Y-GBA | |
| ☐ C-FASY | de Havilland DHC-5A Buffalo | 107A | ex 5Y-GAA | |
| ☐ C-FKCL | Piper PA-31-350 Navajo Chieftain | 31-7752134 | ex C-GJET | |
| ☐ C-FOEV | de Havilland DHC-2 Turbo Beaver III | 1680/TB48 | ex CF-OEV | FP/WS |
| ☐ C-FOPE | de Havilland DHC-2 Turbo Beaver III | 1691/TB59 | ex CF-OPE | FP/WS |
| ☐ C-FSWN | Piper PA-31-350 Chieftain | 31-7952182 | ex C-GREP | |
| ☐ C-FTFX | de Havilland DHC-6 Twin Otter 300 | 340 | ex CF-TFX | FP/WS |
| ☐ C-FTXQ | de Havilland DHC-6 Twin Otter 300 | 308 | ex N776A | <FAB |
| ☐ C-GASB | de Havilland DHC-8-102 | 013 | ex N802MX | |
| ☐ C-GASW | Beech 99A | U-39 | ex N99LP | |
| ☐ C-GSDJ | Cessna A185F Skywagon | 18504212 | ex N31079 | FP/WS |

## ATIKOKAN AERO SERVICE

**Atikokan-Municipal, ON (YIB)**

| | | | | |
|---|---|---|---|---|
| ☐ CF-IPL | de Havilland DHC-2 Beaver | 132 | | FP/WS |
| ☐ C-GDZH | de Havilland DHC-2 Beaver | 356 | ex 51-16555 | FP/WS |

## ATLEO RIVER AIR SERVICE

**Tofino, BC (YTP)**

| | | | | |
|---|---|---|---|---|
| ☐ C-GIYQ | Cessna A185F Skywagon II | 18503618 | ex (N7582Q) | FP/WS |
| ☐ C-GYJX | Cessna A185F Skywagon | 18503187 | ex (N93161) | FP |

## ATLIN AIR CHARTERS

**Atlin, BC**

| | | | | |
|---|---|---|---|---|
| ☐ C-GGEK | Cessna 207A Stationair 8 II | 20700731 | ex N63AK | |
| ☐ C-GOZR | de Havilland DHC-2 Beaver | 800 | ex 54-1670 | |

## AVIATION MAURICIE

**Lac à la Tortue/Lac Sept-Iles, QC**

| | | | | |
|---|---|---|---|---|
| ☐ C-FASO | Cessna U206F Stationair | U20602081 | ex N70558 | FP/WS |
| ☐ C-FIDG | de Havilland DHC-2 Beaver | 718 | ex N99872 | FP/WS |
| ☐ C-FVDG | Cessna U206B Super Skywagon | U206-0666 | ex CF-VDG | FP/WS |
| ☐ C-GOER | de Havilland DHC-2 Beaver | 514 | ex N99830 | FP/WS |
| ☐ C-GYXE | Cessna U206F Stationair | U20603801 | | FP/WS |

## BAMAJI AIR

**Sioux Lookout, ON (YXL)**

| | | | | |
|---|---|---|---|---|
| ☐ C-FHEP | de Havilland DHC-2 Beaver | 69 | ex C-FIOB | FP/WS |
| ☐ C-FKAC | Found FBA-2C1 Bush Hawk XP | 42 | | FP/WS |
| ☐ C-GBKA | Cessna A185F Skywagon | 18502375 | ex N53099 | FP/WS |
| ☐ C-GFDS | de Havilland DHC-2 Beaver | 1269 | ex 31343 | FP/WS |
| ☐ C-GIPR | Cessna 208 Caravan I | 20800343 | | FP/WS |

## BAR XH AIR dba Integra Air (qv)

**Palliser (BXH)**

**Medicine Hat, AB (YXH)**

| | | | | | |
|---|---|---|---|---|---|
| ☐ C-FCGB | Beech 200 Super King Air | BB-24 | ex N183MC | 035 | CatPass 200 conversion EMS |
| ☐ C-GXHD | Beech 200 Super King Air | BB-1338 | ex N915YW | | Beech 1300 conversion |
| ☐ C-GXHG | Beech 200 Super King Air | BB-1383 | ex N913YW | | Beech 1300 conversion |
| ☐ C-GXHN | Beech 200 Super King Air | BB-693 | ex N245JS | | |
| ☐ C-GXHR | Beech 200 Super King Air | BB-1305 | ex 5Y-EOB | | Beech 1300 conversion |
| ☐ C-GXHS | Beech 200 Super King Air | BB-1302 | ex PP-WYY | | Beech 1300 conversion |
| | | | | | |
| ☐ C-GMDF | Piper PA-31T Cheyenne | 31T-7620019 | ex N82000 | | |

## BAYVIEW AIR SERVICE

| | | | | |
|---|---|---|---|---|
| ☐ C-GWYD | Beech 99A | | ex N295R | ♦ |

## BEARSKIN AIRLINES /BEARSKIN LAKE AIR SERVICE
### Bearskin (JV/BLS)          Sioux Lookout, ON (YXL)

| | | | | | |
|---|---|---|---|---|---|
| ☐ C-FAMC | Swearingen SA.227AC Metro III | AC-719B | ex N436MA | | |
| ☐ C-FFZN | Swearingen SA.227AC Metro III | AC-785B | ex N30019 | Spirit of Service | |
| ☐ C-FYAG | Swearingen SA.227AC Metro III | AC-670B | ex N670VG | Spirit of Fort Frances | |
| ☐ C-FYWG | Swearingen SA.227AC Metro III | AC-782B | ex N3000S | Spirit of Winnipeg | |
| ☐ C-GYHD | Swearingen SA.227AC Metro III | AC-739B | ex N227JH | Spirit of Dryden | |
| ☐ C-GYQT | Swearingen SA.227AC Metro III | AC-644B | ex N644VG | Spirit of Thunder Bay | |
| ☐ C-GYRL | Swearingen SA.227AC Metro III | AC-706B | ex G-BUKA | | |
| ☐ C-GYXL | Swearingen SA.227AC Metro III | AC-725B | ex N227FA | | |
| | | | | | |
| ☐ C-FXUS | Swearingen SA.227CC Metro 23 | CC-841B | ex N456LA | | |
| ☐ C-GAFQ | Swearingen SA.227DC Metro 23 | DC-890B | ex N211SA | | |
| ☐ C-GJVB | Swearingen SA.227DC Metro 23 | DC-902B | ex N902WB | | |
| ☐ C-GJVC | Swearingen SA.227DC Metro 23 | DC-885B | ex N885ML | | |
| ☐ C-GJVH | Swearingen SA.227DC Metro 23 | DC-898B | ex N898ML | | |
| ☐ C-GJVO | Swearingen SA.227AC Metro 23 | DC-846B | ex VH-KEU | | |
| ☐ C-GYTL | Swearingen SA.227CC Metro 23 | CC-829B | ex N30154 | Spirit of Big Trout Lake | |
| | | | | | |
| ☐ C-GEHY | Piper PA-23-250 Aztec C | 27-3843 | ex N6548Y | | |
| ☐ C-GFVY | Cessna A185F Skywagon | 18503056 | ex (N21379) | | FP/WS |
| ☐ C-GKAJ | Beech A100 King Air | B-232 | ex N9192S | | ♦ |

## BEAVER AIR SERVICES          The Pas, MN (YQD)

| | | | | | |
|---|---|---|---|---|---|
| ☐ C-GKHI | Beech B200 Super King Air | BB-1265 | ex N544P | | ♦ |

## BLACK SHEEP AVIATION          Whitehorse, YT (YXY)

| | | | | | |
|---|---|---|---|---|---|
| ☐ C-GDJW | de Havilland DHC-3 Otter | 10 | ex C-FGTL | | FP/WS |
| ☐ C-GMCW | de Havilland DHC-3 Otter | 108 | ex N5339G | | FP/WS |
| ☐ C-GZTQ | Cessna A185F Skywagon II | 18503491 | ex (N1824Q) | | FP/WS |

## BLUE WATER AVIATION SERVICES          Silver Falls, MB

| | | | | | |
|---|---|---|---|---|---|
| ☐ C-FCUW | Cessna 337 Super Skymaster | 337-0009 | ex N2109X | | |
| ☐ C-FKOA | de Havilland DHC-3 Turbo Otter | 130 | ex CF-KOA | | FP/WS♦ |
| ☐ C-GBTU | de Havilland DHC-3 Turbo Otter | 209 | ex IM1711 | | FP/WS |
| ☐ C-GDCJ | de Havilland DHC-2 Beaver | 1056 | ex N44AAF | | FP/WS♦ |
| ☐ C-GFVZ | Cessna A185F Skywagon | 18503058 | ex (N21451) | | FP/WS |
| ☐ C-GGGD | Cessna TU206G Stationair 8 | U20605664 | ex (N5348X) | | FP/WS |
| ☐ C-GHYB | de Havilland DHC-3 Otter | 386 | ex UB656 | | FP/WS |
| ☐ C-GSMG | de Havilland Turbo Otter | 363 | ex RCAF 9405 | | FP/WS♦ |

## BUFFALO AIRWAYS          Buffalo (J4/BFL)          Hay River, NT/Yellowknife (YHY/YZF)

| | | | | | |
|---|---|---|---|---|---|
| ☐ C-FAYN | Canadair CL215 | 1105 | | 282 | ♦ |
| ☐ C-GBPD | Canadair CL215 | 1084 | | 291 | Op for NWT Govt |
| ☐ C-GBYU | Canadair CL215 | 1083 | ex C-GKEA | 290 | Op for NWT Govt |
| ☐ C-GCSX | Canadair CL215 | 1088 | ex c-GKEA | 295 | Op for NWT Govt |
| ☐ C-GDHN | Canadair CL215 | 1089 | ex C-GKEE | 296 | Op for NWT Govt |
| ☐ C-GDKW | Canadair CL215 | 1095 | | 280 | ♦ |
| ☐ C-GNCS | Canadair CL215 | 1008 | ex N215NC | | Op for NWT Govt♦ |
| | | | | | |
| ☐ C-FBAE | Douglas DC-3 | 12591 | ex C-FDTH | | ♦ |
| ☐ C-FCUE | Douglas DC-3 | 12983 | ex NC41407 | | |
| ☐ C-FDTB | Douglas DC-3 | 12597 | ex CF-TEC | | [YQF] |
| ☐ C-FFAY | Douglas DC-3 | 4785 | ex CF-FAY | | [YQF] |
| ☐ C-FLFR | Douglas DC-3 | 13155 | ex CF-LFR | | |
| ☐ C-FROD | Douglas DC-3 | 13028 | ex C-GPNW | | |
| ☐ CF-FTR | Douglas DC-3 | 16095 | | | ♦ |
| ☐ C-GJKM | Douglas DC-3 | 13580 | ex CAF 12946 | | |
| ☐ C-GPNR | Douglas DC-3 | 13333 | ex CAF 12932 | | |
| ☐ C-GWIR | Douglas DC-3 | 9371 | ex N18262 | | |
| ☐ C-GWZS | Douglas DC-3 | 12327 | ex CAF 12913 | | |
| | | | | | |
| ☐ C-FBAA | Douglas C-54D-DC | 10653 | ex N4994H | 12 Arctic Expeditor | [YZF] |
| ☐ C-FBAJ | Douglas C-54A-DC | 3088 | ex N11712 | 02 | [YHY] |
| ☐ C-FBAK | Douglas C-54D-DC | 10613 | ex N62342 | | [YHY] |
| ☐ C-FBAM | Douglas C-54G-DC | 36009 | ex N4958M | | [YHY] |
| ☐ C-FBAP | Douglas C-54A-DC | 36089 | ex N2742G | 15 | [YHY] |
| ☐ C-FIQM | Douglas C-54G-DC | 36088 | ex N4218S | 57 Arctic Trader | Tanker |
| ☐ C-GBAJ | Douglas C-54A-DC | 27328 | ex N62297 | | Tanker |
| ☐ C-GBNV | Douglas C-54G-DC | 35988 | ex N3303F | 56 | Tanker |
| ☐ C-GBSK | Douglas C-54G-DC | 36049 | ex N4989N | | |
| ☐ C-GCTF | Douglas C-54E-DC | 27281 | ex N51819 | 58 | Tanker |
| ☐ C-GPSH | Douglas C-54A-DC | 7458 | ex N7171H | 1 Arctic Distributor | |

| | | | | | | |
|---|---|---|---|---|---|---|
| ☐ C-GQIC | Douglas C-54E-DC | 27343 | | | | ♦ |
| ☐ C-GXKN | Douglas C-54G-DC | 13028 | | | | ♦ |
| | | | | | | |
| ☐ C-FAVO | Curtiss C-46D Commando | 33242 | ex N9891Z | Arctic Thunder | | |
| ☐ C-FBAQ | Lockheed L-188AF Electra | 1039 | ex OE-ILB | | | |
| ☐ C-FCGE | Beech 65-A90 King Air | LJ-118 | ex CF-CGE | Birddog 1 | | |
| ☐ C-FCGH | Beech 65-A90 King Air | LJ-203 | ex CF-CGH | Birddog 4 | | |
| ☐ C-FCGI | Beech 65-A90 King Air | LJ-220 | | | | ♦ |
| ☐ C-FIJV | Lockheed L-188C Electra | 1140 | ex N4HG | | | ♦ |
| ☐ C-FIJX | Lockheed L-188CF Electra | 2010 | ex N2RK | | | |
| ☐ C-FPQM | Consolidated PBY-5A Catalina | CV-425 | ex CF-GMS | 714 | | |
| ☐ CF-SAN | Noorduyn Norseman V | N29-29 | ex CF-SAN | | | FP |
| ☐ C-FULX | Beech 95-C55 Baron | TE-147 | ex CF-ULX | Birddog 3 | | |
| ☐ C-FUPT | Cessna A185E Skywagon | 185-1075 | ex (N4568F) | 141 | | |
| ☐ C-GBAU | Beech 95-D55 Baron | TE-701 | ex N7907R | 3 | | |
| ☐ C-GIWJ | Beech 95 Travel Air | TD-32 | ex N2707Y | | | |
| ☐ C-GLBA | Lockheed L-188AF Electra | 1145 | ex OE-ILA | | | |
| | | | | | | |
| ☐ C-GTFC | Consolidated Vultee | 279 | ex N152PA | | | |
| ☐ C-GTPO | Curtiss C-46 Commando | 22556 | | | | ♦ |
| ☐ C-GTXW | Curtiss C-46A Commando | 30386 | ex 5Y-TXW | | | [YZF] |
| ☐ C-GWCB | Beech B95 Travel Air | TD-369 | ex N9914R | 140 | | |
| ☐ C-GYFM | Beech 95 Travel Air | TD-202 | ex N654Q | | | |

## CALM AIR · Calm Air (MO/CAV) · Thompson, MB (YTH)

| | | | | | | |
|---|---|---|---|---|---|---|
| ☐ C-FCIJ | ATR 42-300 | 0139 | ex ZS-OSN | | | |
| ☐ C-FECI | ATR 42-320 | 0203 | ex F-WNUG | | | |
| ☐ C-FJYV | ATR 42-300 | 0216 | ex N216AT | 421 | | |
| ☐ C-FJYW | ATR 42-300 | 0235 | ex N233RM | 422 | | |
| ☐ C-FMAK | ATR 42-300 | 0142 | ex N142GP | | | |
| | | | | | | |
| ☐ C-FSPB | SAAB SF.340B | 340B-351 | ex B-3656 | 345 | | |
| ☐ C-FTJV | SAAB SF.340B | 340B-366 | ex SE-C66 | 341 | | Combi |
| ☐ C-FTJW | SAAB SF.340B | 340B-377 | ex SE-C77 | 342 | | Combi |
| ☐ C-FTLW | SAAB SF.340B | 340B-336 | ex SE-C36 | 346 | | |
| ☐ C-GMNM | SAAB SF.340B | 340B-364 | ex SE-LHO | 344 | | |
| ☐ C-GTJY | SAAB SF.340B | 340B-166 | ex N587MA | 343 | | |
| | | | | | | |
| ☐ C-FAMO | Hawker Siddeley HS.748 Srs.2A/258LFD | 1669 | ex CF-AMO | 746 | | |
| ☐ C-FCRZ | ATR 72-202 | 0357 | ex F-WDHA | | | |
| ☐ C-FSKS | Cessna 208B Caravan I | 208B0722 | ex N5268M | | | |
| ☐ C-FULE | ATR 72-212 | 0215 | ex F-WNUE | | | |
| ☐ C-GEPB | Hawker Siddeley HS.748 Srs.2A/254 | 1686 | ex 9G-ABX | 743 | | [YTH] |
| ☐ C-GHSC | Hawker Siddeley HS.748 Srs.2B/LFD | 1790 | ex G-BJTL | 745 | | |

## CAMERON AIR SERVICE · Toronto-City Centre, ON (YTZ)

| | | | | |
|---|---|---|---|---|
| ☐ C-FKCA | Cessna 208 Caravan I | 20800211 | ex N211PA | |
| ☐ C-FXWH | Cessna U206C Super Skywagon | U206-1170 | ex CF-XWH | |
| ☐ C-GCGA | Cessna 208 Caravan I | 20800242 | ex (A6-CGA) | |
| ☐ C-GGSG | Cessna TU206G Stationair 6 | U20605852 | ex (N6281X) | |

## CANADIAN HELICOPTERS · Canadian (CDN) · Montreal-Les Cedres, QC /Edmonton, AB

| | | | |
|---|---|---|---|
| ☐ C-FCCA | Aérospatiale AS350BA AStar | 2900 | |
| ☐ C-FCHN | Aérospatiale AS350BA AStar | 2921 | |
| ☐ C-FETA | Aérospatiale AS350D AStar | 1085 | ex N137BH |
| ☐ C-FFBU | Aérospatiale AS350BA AStar | 1215 | ex N3605B |
| ☐ C-FHVH | Aérospatiale AS350BA AStar | 1256 | ex N36075 |
| ☐ C-FPBA | Aérospatiale AS350B2 AStar | 2492 | ex JA6091 |
| ☐ C-FPER | Aérospatiale AS350BA AStar | 2552 | ex F-WYMK |
| ☐ C-FPLJ | Aérospatiale AS350D AStar | 1060 | ex C-FQNS |
| ☐ C-FQNS | Aérospatiale AS350B2 AStar | 1423 | ex N5783Y |
| ☐ C-FSHV | Aérospatiale AS350B AStar | 1287 | ex N5143R |
| ☐ C-FSLB | Aérospatiale AS350B AStar | 2142 | ex JA9786 |
| ☐ C-FVVH | Aérospatiale AS350BA AStar | 2612 | |
| ☐ C-FYCO | Aérospatiale AS350BA AStar | 2899 | |
| ☐ C-GAHH | Aérospatiale AS350B AStar | 1036 | ex XA-... |
| ☐ C-GAHI | Aérospatiale AS350BA AStar | 1086 | |
| ☐ C-GALD | Aérospatiale AS350BA AStar | 1146 | |
| ☐ C-GALE | Aérospatiale AS350B AStar | 1350 | |
| ☐ C-GATX | Aérospatiale AS350BA AStar | 1221 | |
| ☐ C-GAYX | Aérospatiale AS350BA AStar | 1179 | |
| ☐ C-GBCZ | Aérospatiale AS350B2 AStar | 1159 | ex N3600W |
| ☐ C-GBPS | Aérospatiale AS350BA AStar | 1277 | ex N3610R |
| ☐ C-GCEC | Aérospatiale AS350B AStar | 1431 | ex N666JK |
| ☐ C-GCHH | Aérospatiale AS350B-2 AStar | 2461 | ex ZK-HND |
| ☐ C-GCKP | Aérospatiale AS350D AStar | 1138 | ex N140BH |

| | | | | |
|---|---|---|---|---|
| ☐ C-GCWD | Aérospatiale AS350BA AStar | 2047 | ex N844BP | |
| ☐ C-GCWW | Aérospatiale AS350B2 AStar | 1435 | ex N340DF | |
| ☐ C-GDKD | Aérospatiale AS350BA AStar | 1432 | ex N5785H | |
| ☐ C-GDSX | Aérospatiale AS350BA AStar | 1134 | ex N35972 | |
| ☐ C-GDUF | Aérospatiale AS350BA AStar | 1309 | | |
| ☐ C-GELC | Aérospatiale AS350B AStar | 1162 | | ♦ |
| ☐ C-GEPH | Aérospatiale AS350BA AStar | 1193 | ex ZK-HET | |
| ☐ C-GEVH | Aérospatiale AS350BA AStar | 2620 | ex F-WYMN | |
| ☐ C-GFHS | Aérospatiale AS350B AStar | 1401 | | |
| ☐ C-GGIE | Aérospatiale AS350B2 AStar | 3280 | | |
| ☐ C-GHVD | Aérospatiale AS350B2 AStar | 1236 | | ♦ |
| ☐ C-GLNE | Aérospatiale AS350BA AStar | 1128 | ex N3599N | |
| ☐ C-GLNK | Aérospatiale AS350D AStar | 1261 | ex N3608C | |
| ☐ C-GLNM | Aérospatiale AS350B2 AStar | 1262 | ex N3608D | |
| ☐ C-GLNO | Aérospatiale AS350D AStar | 1264 | ex N3608N | |
| ☐ C-GMEY | Aérospatiale AS350B AStar | 1004 | ex N350AS | |
| ☐ C-GMIZ | Aérospatiale AS350B2 AStar | 1170 | | |
| ☐ C-GNMN | Aérospatiale AS350BA AStar | 1315 | ex XA-SNA | |
| ☐ C-GRBT | Aérospatiale AS350B2 AStar | 1246 | ex N877JM | |
| ☐ C-GRGJ | Aérospatiale AS350B AStar | 1171 | ex N3600G | |
| ☐ C-GRGU | Aérospatiale AS350BA AStar | 1213 | ex N7172H | |
| ☐ C-GSLF | Aérospatiale AS350D AStar | 1310 | | |
| ☐ C-GTPF | Aérospatiale AS350BA AStar | 2932 | | |
| ☐ C-GTVH | Aérospatiale AS350BA AStar | 2611 | ex N600CH | |
| | | | | |
| ☐ C-GYNF | Agusta AW139 | 41226 | | EMS♦ |
| ☐ C-GYNG | Agusta AW139 | 41227 | | EMS♦ |
| ☐ C-GYNH | Agusta AW139 | 41230 | | EMS♦ |
| ☐ C-GYNJ | Agusta AW139 | 41232 | | EMS♦ |
| ☐ C-GYNK | Agusta AW139 | 41236 | | EMS♦ |
| ☐ C-GYNL | Agusta AW139 | 41238 | | EMS♦ |
| ☐ C-GYNM | Agusta AW139 | 41245 | | EMS♦ |
| ☐ C-GYNN | Agusta AW139 | 41247 | | EMS♦ |
| ☐ C-GYNO | Agusta AW139 | 41250 | | EMS♦ |
| ☐ C-GYNP | Agusta AW139 | 41257 | ex N478SM | ♦ |
| | | | | |
| ☐ C-FAHW | Bell 206B JetRanger II | 785 | ex CF-AHW | |
| ☐ C-FBQH | Bell 206B JetRanger II | 745 | ex CF-BQH | |
| ☐ C-FHTP | Bell 206B JetRanger II | 1024 | ex CF-HTP | |
| ☐ C-FHTS | Bell 206B JetRanger II | 1037 | ex CF-HTS | |
| ☐ C-FKNX | Bell 206B JetRanger III | 2440 | ex N5003X | |
| ☐ C-FOAN | Bell 206B JetRanger II | 791 | ex CF-OAN | |
| ☐ C-GAHC | Bell 206B JetRanger II | 468 | ex N2959W | |
| ☐ C-GBHE | Bell 206B JetRanger II | 1335 | | |
| ☐ C-GBHI | Bell 206B JetRanger III | 1758 | ex N49584 | |
| ☐ C-GCIR | Bell 206B JetRanger III | 3029 | | |
| ☐ C-GDBA | Bell 206B JetRanger III | 2232 | ex N16821 | |
| ☐ C-GETF | Bell 206B JetRanger III | 3036 | | |
| ☐ C-GFQH | Bell 206B JetRanger II | 1090 | ex N100JG | |
| ☐ C-GIFY | Bell 206B JetRanger II | 2008 | | |
| ☐ C-GIXS | Bell 206B JetRanger III | 2304 | ex N272RM | |
| ☐ C-GMKT | Bell 206B JetRanger II | 774 | ex N101PN | |
| ☐ C-GNLD | Bell 206B JetRanger III | 2357 | ex N57PH | |
| ☐ C-GNLE | Bell 206B JetRanger III | 2358 | ex N56PH | |
| ☐ C-GNLG | Bell 206B JetRanger III | 2360 | | |
| ☐ C-GNPH | Bell 206B JetRanger III | 2352 | ex N58148 | |
| ☐ C-GOKE | Bell 206B JetRanger III | 1830 | ex N49655 | |
| ☐ C-GRGN | Bell 206B JetRanger III | 1824 | ex N333WW | |
| ☐ C-GSHP | Bell 206B JetRanger II | 1259 | ex N259CH | |
| ☐ C-GXHC | Bell 206B JetRanger II | 395 | ex N28956 | |
| ☐ C-GYQH | Bell 206B JetRanger III | 1394 | ex N111BH | |
| | | | | |
| ☐ C-FNYQ | Bell 206L LongRanger | 45047 | ex N20LT | |
| ☐ C-GGZQ | Bell 206L LongRanger | 45006 | ex N49637 | |
| ☐ C-GLMV | Bell 206L-1 LongRanger II | 45430 | ex N454CH | |
| ☐ C-GLQY | Bell 206L LongRanger | 45146 | | |
| ☐ C-GMHS | Bell 206L LongRanger | 45120 | | ♦ |
| ☐ C-GMHT | Bell 206L LongRanger | 45127 | ex N16847 | |
| ☐ C-GMHY | Bell 206L LongRanger | 45145 | ex N16924 | |
| ☐ C-GNLC | Bell 206L LongRanger | 45055 | ex N9978K | |
| ☐ C-GNMC | Bell 206L LongRanger | 45067 | | |
| ☐ C-GNZR | Bell 206L LongRanger | 45118 | ex N16809 | |
| ☐ C-GQEZ | Bell 206L LongRanger | 45038 | ex N9942K | |
| ☐ C-GTLB | Bell 206L LongRanger | 45031 | ex N9927K | |
| ☐ C-GTOM | Bell 206L LongRanger | 45010 | | |
| ☐ C-GVHX | Bell 206L LongRanger | 45138 | ex N90AC | |
| | | | | |
| ☐ C-FBHF | Bell 212 | 30509 | ex N7072J | |
| ☐ C-FNJJ | Bell 212 | 30944 | ex N2093S | |
| ☐ C-FOKV | Bell 212 | 30819 | ex N16787 | |
| ☐ C-GAHD | Bell 212 | 30570 | ex N7034J | |
| ☐ C-GFQP | Bell 212 | 30578 | ex N58120 | |

| ☐ | C-GHVH | Bell 212 | 30877 | ex N8555V | | |
| ☐ | C-GICH | Bell 212 | 30950 | ex N507EH | | |
| ☐ | C-GKCH | Bell 212 | 31213 | ex N360EH | | |
| ☐ | C-GOKG | Bell 212 | 30843 | | | |
| ☐ | C-GOKL | Bell 212 | 30597 | ex N2990W | | |
| ☐ | C-GOKX | Bell 212 | 30680 | ex VH-LHX | | |
| ☐ | C-GOKY | Bell 212 | 30698 | ex (5H-  ) | | |
| | | | | | | |
| ☐ | C-FDCH | Sikorsky S-61N | 61773 | ex ZS-PWR | | |
| ☐ | C-FMAY | Sikorsky S-61N | 61363 | | | ♦ |
| ☐ | C-FXEC | Sikorsky S-61N | 61821 | | | ♦ |
| ☐ | C-GJQG | Sikorsky S-61N | 61722 | ex HS-HTC | | ♦ |
| ☐ | C-GJQN | Sikorsky S-61N | 61815 | ex HS-HTA | | ♦ |
| | | | | | | |
| ☐ | C-FABH | Sikorsky S-76A | 760271 | | | EMS♦ |
| ☐ | C-FSBH | Sikorsky S-76A | 760168 | | | EMS♦ |
| ☐ | C-GFFJ | Sikorsky S-76A | 760138 | | | EMS♦ |
| ☐ | C-GIMA | Sikorsky S-76A | 760018 | | | EMS♦ |
| ☐ | C-GIMB | Sikorsky S-76A | 760111 | | | EMS♦ |
| ☐ | C-GIMM | Sikorsky S-76A | 760044 | | | EMS♦ |
| ☐ | C-GIMN | Sikorsky S-76A | 760110 | ex G-BIAV | | EMS |
| ☐ | C-GIMR | Sikorsky S-76A | 760079 | ex G-BHYB | | |
| ☐ | C-GIMT | Sikorsky S-76A | 760130 | | | EMS♦ |
| ☐ | C-GIMV | Sikorsky S-76A | 760005 | ex VH-WXE | | EMS♦ |
| ☐ | C-GIMW | Sikorsky S-76A | 760226 | ex N76FB | | EMS♦ |
| ☐ | C-GIMY | Sikorsky S-76A | 760055 | ex N376LL | | EMS♦ |
| ☐ | C-GIMZ | Sikorsky S-76A | 760169 | ex N399PK | | EMS♦ |
| ☐ | C-GLFO | Sikorsky S-76A | 760149 | ex N76LA | | |
| | | | | | | |
| ☐ | C-FAVI | Bell 407 | 53315 | | | ♦ |
| ☐ | C-FBCH | Eurocopter EC120B | 1467 | | | ♦ |
| ☐ | C-FFAB | Eurocopter EC120B | 1486 | | | |
| ☐ | C-FLCN | Eurocopter EC120B | 1055 | | | |
| ☐ | C-FOCH | Eurocopter EC120B | 1547 | | | |
| ☐ | C-FXIH | Aérospatiale AS355N Twin Star | 5740 | | | ♦ |
| ☐ | C-GHCB | Bell 412 | 33066 | ex ZK-HDA | | ♦ |
| ☐ | C-GHCD | Aérospatiale AS355N Twin Star | 5702 | ex N441L | | ♦ |
| ☐ | C-GHCY | Bell 412SP | 33204 | ex ZK-HNI | | ♦ |
| ☐ | C-GVHC | Aérospatiale AS355F2 Twin Star | 5195 | ex N5801T | | |
| ☐ | C-GVHK | Aérospatiale AS355F1 Twin Star | 5098 | ex N60031 | | |

## CANADIAN NORTH — Norterra (5T/ANX) — Yellowknife, NT (YZF)

| ☐ | C-GCNS | Boeing 737-275 | 23283/1109 | ex C9-BAN | | |
| ☐ | C-GCNV | Boeing 737-232 | 23074/993 | ex N302DL | 586 | |
| ☐ | C-GDPA | Boeing 737-2T2C (AvAero 3) | 22056/655 | | 584 Spirit of Yellowknife | |
| ☐ | C-GFPW | Boeing 737-275C (AvAero 3) | 21294/481 | | 552 | |
| ☐ | C-GKCP | Boeing 737-217 (AvAero 3) | 22729/915 | | 523 | |
| ☐ | C-GNDU | Boeing 737-242C (AvAero 3) | 22877/880 | | 562 | |
| ☐ | C-GOPW | Boeing 737-275C (AvAero 3) | 22160/688 | ex N8288V | 582 Spirit of Nunavut | |
| ☐ | C-GSPW | Boeing 737-275C (AvAero 3) | 22618/813 | | 583 | |
| | | | | | | |
| ☐ | C-GCNU | Boeing 737-36Q/W | 29140/3013 | ex N291AG | 592 | ♦ |
| ☐ | C-GCNW | Boeing 737-36Q | 28760/2989 | ex VP-CAK | | ♦ |
| ☐ | C-GCNZ | Boeing 737-36Q | 28664/2940 | ex N664AG | | ♦ |
| ☐ | C-GECN | de Havilland DHC-8-106 | 324 | ex C-FSQY | | |
| ☐ | C-GRGI | de Havilland DHC-8-106 | 304 | ex N829PH | | |
| ☐ | C-GRGO | de Havilland DHC-8-106 | 258 | ex N735AG | | |
| ☐ | C-GXCN | de Havilland DHC-8-106 | 345 | ex RA-67255 | | |
| ☐ | C- | Boeing 737-36Q | 29189/3057 | ex N892AG | | o/o♦ |

## CANJET — Canjet (C6/CJA) — Halifax-Intl, NS (YHZ)

| ☐ | C-FTCX | Boeing 737-8AS/W | 29921/560 | ex EI-CSF | 801 | |
| ☐ | C-FTCZ | Boeing 737-8AS/W | 29923/576 | ex EI-CSH | 802 | |
| ☐ | C-FXGG | Boeing 737-81Q/W | 29051/479 | ex N290AN | | |
| ☐ | C-FYQN | Boeing 737-8AS/W | 29933/1038 | ex EI-CST | | |
| ☐ | C-FYQO | Boeing 737-8AS/W | 29934/1050 | ex EI-CSV | | |
| ☐ | C-GDGQ | Boeing 737-8FH/W | 35093/2176 | ex D-AXLD | | <GLX♦ |
| ☐ | C-GDGT | Boeing 737-8Q8/W | 30724/2286 | ex D-AXLE | | <GXL♦ |
| ☐ | C-GDGY | Boeing 737-8Q8/W | 28218/160 | ex D-AXLF | | <GXL |
| ☐ | C-GRWZ | Boeing 737-8K5/W | 39094/3641 | ex D-ATUK | | <TUI♦ |
| ☐ | F-GZHB | Boeing 737-8GJ/W | 34902/2309 | ex (VT-SPO) | | <TVF♦ |
| ☐ | OO-JAQ | Boeing 737-8K5/W | 35148/2790 | ex N1786B | | <JAF♦ |

## CAN-WEST CORPORATE AIR CHARTER — Slave Lake, AB (YZH)

| ☐ | C-FBCW | Cessna 560 Citation | 560-0191 | | | ♦ |
| ☐ | C-FCWW | Piper PA-31-350 Chieftain | 31-8152192 | ex N4097L | | |
| ☐ | C-FKCW | Beech 200 Super King Air | BB-973 | ex C-FEVC | | |
| ☐ | C-FOOS | Cessna U206E Stationair | U20601698 | ex (N9498G) | | |

| | | | | |
|---|---|---|---|---|
| ☐ C-FSAO | Beech 200 Super King Air | BB-1610 | ex N713TA | |
| ☐ C-FSAT | Beech 200 Super King Air | BB-1526 | ex N417MC | |
| ☐ C-GAYZ | Cessna A185F Skywagon | 18504040 | ex (N6416E) | |
| ☐ C-GJMZ | Partenavia P.68 Observer | 369270B | | |
| ☐ C-GKOX | Beech 200 Super King Air | BB-389 | ex C-GKOS | |
| ☐ C-GLGD | Cessna U206G Stationair 6 | U20606261 | ex (N6388Z) | |
| ☐ C-GNCW | Beech Baron 58 | TH-1313 | ex N6138C | |
| ☐ C-GSAZ | Piper PA-31 Navajo C | 31-8112063 | ex N4094Y | |
| ☐ C-GXNL | Cessna 210L Centurion II | 21060909 | ex N5327V | |
| ☐ C-GYDD | Cessna A185F Skywagon | 18503124 | ex (N80516) | |

## CARGOJET AIRWAYS — Cargojet (W8/CJT)

### Winnipeg-Intl, MB/Toronto-Pearson Intl, QC (YWG/YYZ)

| | | | | |
|---|---|---|---|---|
| ☐ C-FCJF | Boeing 727-223F (FedEx 3) | 22011/1653 | ex C-GACG | |
| ☐ C-FCJI | Boeing 727-225F (FedEx 3) | 22435/1674 | ex N804MA | [YHM] |
| ☐ C-FCJP | Boeing 727-223F (FedEx 3) | 22012/1655 | ex C-FUAC | |
| ☐ C-FCJU | Boeing 727-260F (FedEx 3) | 22759/1789 | ex C-FACM | |
| ☐ C-GCJB | Boeing 727-225F (FedEx 3) | 21855/1535 | ex N886MA | <Flagship Intl |
| ☐ C-GCJD | Boeing 727-231F (FedEx 3) | 21988/1586 | ex N808MA | <Flagship Intl |
| ☐ C-GCJN | Boeing 727-225F (FedEx 3) | 21451/1310 | ex N610PA | |
| ☐ C-GCJQ | Boeing 727-225F (FedEx 3) | 22437/1682 | ex N806MA | <Flagship Intl |
| ☐ C-GCJZ | Boeing 727-225F (FedEx 3) | 21854/1532 | ex N889MA | |
| ☐ C-GUJC | Boeing 727-260F (FedEx 3) | 21979/1534 | ex C-FACJ | |
| | | | | |
| ☐ C-FGAJ | Boeing 767-223F | 22319/112 | ex N317AA | |
| ☐ C-FKCJ | Boeing 757-236F | 24792/279 | ex SE-DUO | |
| ☐ C-FMCJ | Boeing 767-223F | 22316/95 | ex N313AA | |
| ☐ N340AQ | SAAB SF.340AF | 340A-019 | ex C-GYQM | >PEN |

## CARSON AIR — Kelowna, BC (YLW)

| | | | | |
|---|---|---|---|---|
| ☐ C-FBWQ | Swearingen SA.226TC Metro II | TC-379 | ex N1011U | |
| ☐ C-FKKR | Swearingen SA.226TC Metro II | TC-308 | ex N300GL | |
| ☐ C-GCAU | Swearingen SA.226TC Metro II | TC-331E | ex N255AM | Frtr |
| ☐ C-GCAW | Swearingen SA.226TC Metro II | TC-358 | ex N1009R | no titles |
| ☐ C-GDLK | Swearingen SA.226TC Metro II | TC-302 | ex N151SA | |
| ☐ C-GKKC | Swearingen SA.226TC Metro II | TC-370 | ex N125AV | |
| ☐ C-GKLJ | Swearingen SA.226TC Metro II | TC-380 | ex C-GMET | |
| ☐ C-GKLN | Swearingen SA.226TC Metro II | TC-253 | ex N328BA | |
| ☐ C-GLSC | Swearingen SA.226TC Metro II | TC-325 | ex N162SW | |
| ☐ C-GSKC | Swearingen SA.226TC Metro II | TC-235 | ex N235BA | |
| | | | | |
| ☐ C-FAFR | Swearingen SA.227AC Metro III | AC-684B | ex N585MA | |
| ☐ C-FJKK | Swearingen SA.227AC Metro III | AC-713B | ex N2719H | |
| ☐ C-FTSK | Swearingen SA.227AC Metro III | AC-674B | ex C-FAFM | Frtr |
| ☐ C-GAMI | Swearingen SA.227AC Metro III | AC-587 | ex N3115T | |
| ☐ C-GKLK | Swearingen SA.227AC Metro III | AC-741B | ex N41NE | |
| | | | | |
| ☐ C-FAFF | Beech B300 Super King Air | FL-112 | ex N405J | |
| ☐ C-FCAV | Piper PA-42 Cheyenne III | 42-8001006 | ex N131RC | |
| ☐ C-FCAW | Swearingen SA.26AT Merlin IIB | T26-172E | ex N135SR | |
| ☐ C-FRLD | Beech B300 Super King Air | FL-33 | ex N15WS | |
| ☐ C-FVKC | Beech B300 Super King Air | FL-273 | ex OY-JVL | |
| ☐ C-FWPR | Beech B300 Super King Air | FL-125 | ex N32KC | |
| ☐ C-GJLK | Beech B300 Super King Air | FL-13 | ex C-FWXR | EMS, for BC Ambulance Service |

## CENTRAL MOUNTAIN AIR / NORTHERN THUNDERBIRD AIR (NTA)

### Glacier (9M/GLR) — Smithers, BC (YYD)

| | | | | | |
|---|---|---|---|---|---|
| ☐ C-FCMB | Beech 1900D | UE-278 | | 916 | (NTA) |
| ☐ C-FCME | Beech 1900D | UE-277 | | 915 | |
| ☐ C-FCMN | Beech 1900D | UE-276 | | 914 | (NTA) |
| ☐ C-FCMO | Beech 1900D | UE-281 | | 917 | (NTA) |
| ☐ C-FCMP | Beech 1900D | UE-271 | ex N11037 | 912 | (NTA) |
| ☐ C-FCMR | Beech 1900D | UE-283 | ex N21872 | 918 | |
| ☐ C-FCMU | Beech 1900D | UE-285 | | 919 | |
| ☐ C-FCMV | Beech 1900D | UE-272 | ex N11079 | 913 | |
| ☐ C-FDTR | Beech 1900D | UE-76 | ex N76ZV | | (NTA) |
| ☐ C-GCMA | Beech 1900D | UE-289 | | 920 | |
| ☐ C-GCML | Beech 1900D | UE-243 | ex N10879 | 925 | |
| ☐ C-GCMY | Beech 1900D | UE-287 | | 921 | (NTA) |
| ☐ C-GFSV | Beech 1900D | UE-346 | ex N23424 | 922 | |
| ☐ C-GGBY | Beech 1900D | UE-351 | ex YV-654C | 923 | |
| ☐ C-GGCA | Beech 1900D | UE-359 | ex N31559 | 924 | |
| | | | | | |
| ☐ C-FGQN | de Havilland DHC-2 Beaver | 96 | | | |
| ☐ C-FHVX | Dornier 328-110 | 3094 | ex D-CMTM | | |
| ☐ C-FJFW | de Havilland DHC-8-311 | 315 | ex N315SN | | |
| ☐ C-GWRN | Piper PA-31 Navajo Chieftain | 31-7852062 | | | |

## CHC HELICOPTERS INTERNATIONAL — Vancouver-International, BC (YVR)

| | | | | | |
|---|---|---|---|---|---|
| ☐ | C-FCPM | Aérospatiale AS.332L Puma | 2069 | ex G-BUZD | ♦ |
| ☐ | C-FYPO | Aérospatiale AS.332L Puma | 2077 | ex LN-OMK | |
| ☐ | C-FYZD | Aérospatiale AS.332L Puma | 2007 | ex OY-HEO | |
| ☐ | C-GGKY | Aérospatiale AS.332LI Puma | 2381 | | ♦ |
| ☐ | C-GJEB | Aérospatiale AS.332L Puma | 2075 | ex G-PUMB | ♦ |
| ☐ | C-GHYO | Aérospatiale AS.332L Puma | 2038 | ex G-PUMA | ♦ |
| ☐ | C-GLGB | Aérospatiale AS.332L Puma | 2107 | ex VH-LHK | ♦ |
| ☐ | C-GLNW | Aérospatiale AS.332L Puma | 2015 | ex PR-CHZ | ♦ |
| ☐ | C-GOSE | Aérospatiale AS.332L Puma | 2048 | ex C-GTCH | ♦ |
| ☐ | C-GOSI | Aérospatiale AS.332L Puma | 2074 | ex C-GVCH | |
| | | | | | |
| ☐ | C-FGDO | Sikorsky S-76C+ | 760602 | ex 5N-BIV | |
| ☐ | C-FRHM | Sikorsky S-76C++ | 760689 | ex N25042 | |
| ☐ | C-FUVS | Sikorsky S-76C+ | 760547 | ex ZS-RRX | |
| ☐ | C-FUVU | Sikorsky S-76C+ | 760548 | ex ZS-RRY | |
| ☐ | C-FZUT | Sikorsky S-76C++ | 760764 | ex N764L | |
| ☐ | C-FZUY | Sikorsky S-76C++ | 760765 | ex N765L | |
| ☐ | C-GARC | Sikorsky S-76C+ | 760596 | ex XA-GFT | ♦ |
| ☐ | C-GBVZ | Sikorsky S-76A+ | 760183 | ex G-BVCX | |
| ☐ | C-GBWC | Sikorsky S-76A+ | 760201 | ex G-DRNT | |
| ☐ | C-GHRE | Sikorsky S-76C+ | 760575 | ex N7100C | |
| ☐ | C-GHRJ | Sikorsky S-76C | 760574 | ex 5N-BHP | ♦ |
| ☐ | C-GHRU | Sikorsky S-76C | 760593 | ex 5N-BIJ | ♦ |
| ☐ | C-GIHO | Sikorsky S-76A++ | 760015 | ex HS-HTO | |
| ☐ | C-GIMJ | Sikorsky S-76A++ | 760009 | ex D2-EXZ | |
| ☐ | C-GIMQ | Sikorsky S-76A++ | 760102 | ex HS-HTQ | |
| ☐ | C-GIMX | Sikorsky S-76A+ | 760213 | ex PR-MCH | |
| ☐ | C-GIRD | Sikorsky S-76C+ | 760581 | ex XA-MJV | ♦ |
| ☐ | C-GIRN | Sikorsky S-76C+ | 760582 | ex XA-RYT | ♦ |
| ☐ | C-GKWS | Sikorsky S-76A++ | 760297 | ex EP-HCS | |
| ☐ | C-GKWT | Sikorsky S-76A++ | 760295 | ex B-HZD | based Yangon |
| ☐ | C-GLAY | Sikorsky S-76C+ | 760466 | ex 5N-BCX | ♦ |
| ☐ | C-GMNB | Sikorsky S-76C+ | 760490 | ex VT-HGH | |
| ☐ | C-GOLH | Sikorsky S-76C+ | 760598 | ex XA-RSY | ♦ |
| ☐ | C-GHRJ | Sikorsky S-76C | 760574 | | ♦ |
| ☐ | C-GHRU | Sikorsky S-76C | 760593 | | ♦ |
| ☐ | C-GHRW | Sikorsky S-76C+ | 760570 | ex 5N-BHF | ♦ |
| ☐ | C-GHRX | Sikorsky S-76C+ | 760589 | ex 5N-BIE | ♦ |
| ☐ | PR-BGI | Sikorsky S-76C+ | 760537 | ex C-GETL | ♦ |
| ☐ | PR-BGJ | Sikorsky S-76C+ | 760570 | ex C-GHRW | ♦ |
| ☐ | C- | Sikorsky S-76A++ | 760032 | ex HS-HTR | |
| ☐ | C- | Sikorsky S-76A++ | 760148 | ex HS-HTI | |
| | | | | | |
| ☐ | C-FBOA | de Havilland DHC-8Q-315 | 608 | ex 5N-BIA | [MST]♦ |
| ☐ | C-FLGJ | de Havilland DHC-8Q-315 | 609 | ex 5N-BIB | [MST]♦ |
| ☐ | C-FRWF | Bell 212 | 30894 | ex ZS-RXB | |
| ☐ | C-FYQC | Aérospatiale SA.365N Dauphin 2 | 6419 | ex 5N-BJF | |
| ☐ | C-GDVO | Aérospatiale AS.365N2 Dauphin 2 | 6424 | ex G-BTUX | |
| ☐ | C-GGVW | Aérospatiale AS.365N3 Dauphin 2 | 6593 | ex 5N-BGF | |
| ☐ | C-GIHK | Bell 412 | 36050 | ex VT-HGG | ♦ |
| ☐ | C-GJMY | Sikorsky S-92A | 920141 | ex N1004C | ♦ |
| ☐ | C-GLGO | Bell 412EP | 36399 | ex XA-VVD | ♦ |
| ☐ | C-GLGP | Bell 412EP | 36402 | ex XA-VVG | ♦ |
| ☐ | C-GLIS | Eurocopter EC225LP | 2798 | | ♦ |
| ☐ | C-GMJI | Eurocopter EC225LP | 2801 | ex F-WWOK | ♦ |
| ☐ | C-GMOH | de Havilland DHC-8-311 | 276 | ex PH-SDT | ♦ |
| ☐ | C-GNCU | Agusta AW139 | 31070 | ex 5N-BJC | ♦ |
| ☐ | C-GNDG | Agusta AW139 | 31072 | ex PH-EUA | ♦ |
| ☐ | C-GNUA | Sikorsky S-92A | 920153 | ex N153SF | ♦ |
| ☐ | C-GSAB | Aérospatiale AS.365N3 Dauphin 2 | 4738 | ex 5N-BIY | ♦ |
| ☐ | PR-MEX | Sikorsky S-61N | 61753 | ex PH-NZG | |

## CHIMO AIR SERVICE — Red Lake SPB, ON (YRL)

| | | | | | |
|---|---|---|---|---|---|
| ☐ | CF-HZA | Beech D-18S | A-111 | | FP |
| ☐ | CF-JIN | Noorduyn Norseman V | CCF-55 | ex CF-LFR | FP |
| ☐ | CF-KAO | Noorduyn Norseman VI | 636 | ex 44-70371 | FP |

## CLEARWATER AIRWAYS — Burditt Lake SPB, ON

| | | | | | |
|---|---|---|---|---|---|
| ☐ | C-FGUE | Beech C-18S | 8107 | ex N480DB | FP |
| ☐ | C-GESW | Beech C-18S | 7911 | ex N4858V | FP |

## COCHRANE AIR SERVICES — Cochrane-Lillabelle Lake, ON (YCN)

| | | | | | |
|---|---|---|---|---|---|
| ☐ | C-FEYQ | de Havilland DHC-2 Beaver | 465 | ex CF-EYQ | FP |
| ☐ | C-FGBF | de Havilland DHC-2 Beaver | 168 | ex CF-GBF | FP |

## CONAIR AVIATION — Conair Canada (CRC) — Abbotsford, BC (YXX)

| | | | | | | |
|---|---|---|---|---|---|---|
| ☐ | C-FEFK | Conair Firecat | G-360/014 | ex F-ZBEH | 574 | |
| ☐ | C-FEFX | Conair Firecat | G-527/031 | ex N425DF | 575 | |
| ☐ | C-FJOH | Conair Firecat | G-254/034 | ex N424DF | 576 | |
| ☐ | C-FOPU | Conair Firecat | DHC-38/007 | ex RCN1539 | 564 | |
| ☐ | C-FOPV | Conair Firecat | DHC-34/006 | ex RCN1535 | 566 | |
| ☐ | C-FOPY | Conair Firecat | DHC-24/019 | ex CF-IOF | 569 | |
| ☐ | C-GABC | Conair Firecat | DHC-90/011 | ex RCAF12191 | | 567 |
| ☐ | C-GHDY | Conair Firecat | G-374/029 | ex Bu136465 | 573 | |
| ☐ | C-GHPJ | Conair Firecat | G-509/022 | ex Bu136600 | 571 | |
| ☐ | C-GWHK | Conair Firecat | DHC-37/016 | ex CAF12138 | 2 | Tanker |
| ☐ | C-GWUO | Conair Firecat | DHC-39/003 | ex N99261 | 563 | |
| ☐ | C-GWUP | Conair Firecat | DHC-19/012 | ex RCN12120 | 568 | |
| ☐ | C-FEKF | Convair 580F | 80 | ex C-GEVB | 445 | Tanker 45 |
| ☐ | C-FFKF | Convair 580 | 179 | ex C-GEVC | 444 | Tanker 44 |
| ☐ | C-FHKF | Convair 580 | 374 | ex C-GEUZ | 455 | Tanker 55 |
| ☐ | C-FJVD | Convair 580 | 478 | ex N8099S | | [YYX] |
| ☐ | C-FKFA | Convair 580 | 100 | ex C-FLVY | 452 | Tanker 52 |
| ☐ | C-FKFB | Convair 580 | 57 | ex N568JA | 447 | Tanker 47 |
| ☐ | C-FKFL | Convair 580 | 465 | ex C-FZQS | 449 | Tanker 49 |
| ☐ | C-FKFM | Convair 580F | 70 | ex N73133 | 454 | Tanker 54 |
| ☐ | C-GKFO | Convair 580F | 78 | ex N5815 | 453 | Tanker 53 |
| ☐ | C-GYXC | Convair 580 | 507 | ex VH-PDV | | |
| ☐ | C-GYXS | Convair 580 | 501 | ex VH-PAL` | | |
| ☐ | C-GLVG | Piper PA-60 Aerostar 600A | 60-0695-7961217 | ex N6072U | 111 | |
| ☐ | C-GMGZ | Piper PA-60 Aerostar 600A | 60-0708-7961220 | ex N6075C | 112 | |
| ☐ | C-GOSX | Piper PA-60 Aerostar 600A | 60-0863-8161246 | ex N3647B | 110 | |
| ☐ | C-GUHK | Piper PA-60 Aerostar 600A | 60-0761-8061230 | ex N8EA | 119 | |
| ☐ | C-GUSZ | Piper PA-60 Aerostar 600A | 60-0894-8161253 | ex N6893Q | 118 | |
| ☐ | C-FCZZ | Rockwell 690A Turbo Commander | 11106 | ex N57106 | 135 | |
| ☐ | C-GAAL | Rockwell 690A Turbo Commander | 11104 | ex N690AZ | 131 | |
| ☐ | C-GBQD | Rockwell 690A Turbo Commander | 11237 | | | ♦ |
| ☐ | C-GDCL | Rockwell 690A Turbo Commander | 11192 | ex N57192 | 134 | |
| ☐ | C-GHWF | Rockwell 690A Turbo Commander | 11134 | ex N45VT | 132 | |
| ☐ | C-GWEW | Rockwell 690 Turbo Commander | 11057 | ex N376TC | 133 | |
| ☐ | C-FDON | Cessna 208B Caravan I | 208B2015 | ex N5067U | | ♦ |
| ☐ | C-FYYJ | Lockheed L-188AC Electra | 1143 | ex G-LOFD | | |
| ☐ | C-GFHY | Bell 206B JetRanger | 367 | | | ♦ |
| ☐ | C-GFSK | Canadair CL215 | 1085 | ex C-GKDN | 201 | |
| ☐ | C-GFSL | Canadair CL215T | 1086 | ex C-GKDP | 202 | |
| ☐ | C-GFSM | Canadair CL215 | 1098 | | 203 | |
| ☐ | C-GFSN | Canadair CL215 | 1099 | | 204 | |
| ☐ | C-GHLY | Douglas DC-6B | 45501/953 | ex OO-VGE | 446 | Tanker |
| ☐ | C-GIBS | Douglas DC-6A/C | 45531/1015 | ex HB-IBS | 451 | Tanker |
| ☐ | C-GKUG | Douglas DC-6A/B | 45177/859 | ex N863TA | 450 | Tanker |
| ☐ | C-GSDG | Cessna 208B Caravan I | 208B0376 | ex N1118P | 127 | |
| ☐ | C-GXGA | Bell 206B JetRanger | 2009 | | | ♦ |
| ☐ | C-GYCG | Lockheed L-188PF Electra | 1138 | ex C-FIJR | | |
| ☐ | C- | Lockheed L-188CF Electra | 2014 | ex G-FIZU | | ♦ |

## CORILAIR CHARTERS — Campbell River, BC

| | | | | | |
|---|---|---|---|---|---|
| ☐ | C-FEWP | Cessna U206D Skylane | U206-1344 | ex CF-EWP | |
| ☐ | C-FJPB | de Havilland DHC-2 Beaver | 1319 | ex N1019T | FP |
| ☐ | C-GACK | de Havilland DHC-2 Beaver | 711 | ex 53-7903 | FP |
| ☐ | C-GTNE | Cessna A185E Skywagon | 18501889 | ex CF-QLN | FP |

## CORPORATE EXPRESS AIRLINE — Penta (CPB) — Calgary-Intl, AB (YYC)

| | | | | | |
|---|---|---|---|---|---|
| ☐ | C-GXPS | SAAB SF.340A | 340A-075 | ex N75UW | [YYC] |

Ceased ops

## COUGAR HELICOPTERS — Cougar (CHI) — Halifax-Waterfront Heliport, NS (YWF)

| | | | | | |
|---|---|---|---|---|---|
| ☐ | C-GDKN | Sikorsky S-92A | 920111 | ex N21278 | |
| ☐ | C-GEKN | Sikorsky S-92A | 920114 | exN21222 | |
| ☐ | C-GIKN | Sikorsky S-92A | 920126 | ex N2183N | |
| ☐ | C-GKKN | Sikorsky S-92A | 920124 | ex N2195Z | |
| ☐ | C-GKNR | Sikorsky S-92A | 920054 | ex ZS-RSH | ♦ |
| ☐ | C-GMCH | Sikorsky S-92A | 920023 | ex N8016B | |
| ☐ | C-GQCH | Sikorsky S-92A | 920074 | ex N2581T | |
| ☐ | C-GSCH | Sikorsky S-92A | 920010 | ex N7108J | |
| ☐ | C-GVCH | Sikorsky S-92A | 920080 | ex N25837 | |
| ☐ | N920VH | Sikorsky S-92A | 920061 | ex C-GTCH | |
| ☐ | C-FHCH | Sikorsky S-61N | 61761 | ex N613RM | |

| | | | | | |
|---|---|---|---|---|---|
| ☐ C-FNCH | Sikorsky S-61N | 61757 | ex N461AL | | |
| ☐ C-GIHS | Sikorsky S-76A++ | 760150 | ex HS-HTS | | |
| ☐ C-GVIY | Bell 222U | 47562 | | | ♦ |

## COULSON AIRCRANE                                        Port Alberni, BC (YPB)

| | | | | | |
|---|---|---|---|---|---|
| ☐ C-FBSF | Sikorsky S-61N | 61222 | | | ♦ |
| ☐ C-FCLM | Sikorsky S-61N | 61492 | ex N265F | | |
| ☐ C-FIRX | Sikorsky S-61N | 61257 | ex N562EH | | ♦ |
| ☐ C-FMAY | Sikorsky S-61N | 61363 | ex N306V | | |
| ☐ C-FTNK | Sikorsky S-61N | 61473 | ex ZS-HSZ | | ♦ |
| ☐ C-FXEC | Sikorsky S-61N | 61821 | ex N264F | | ♦ |
| ☐ C-GJQE | Sikorsky S-61N | 61703 | ex N9119S | | ♦ |
| | | | | | |
| ☐ C-FDYK | Bell 206B JetRanger II | 972 | ex CF-DYK | | |
| ☐ C-FIRW | Sikorsky S-76B | 760355 | | | ♦ |
| ☐ C-FLYK | Martin JRM-3 Mars | 76820 | ex Bu76820 | Philippine Mars | Tanker |
| ☐ C-FLYL | Martin JRM-3 Mars | 76823 | ex Bu76823 | Hawaii Mars | Tanker |
| ☐ C-GXOH | Bell 206B JetRanger II | 865 | ex N14844 | | |

## COURTESY AIR                                        Buffalo Narrows, SK (YVT)

| | | | | | |
|---|---|---|---|---|---|
| ☐ C-FCAK | Beech A100 King Air | B-96 | ex N116RJ | dam 12Dec10 | |
| ☐ C-FCAZ | Beech 100 King Air | B-44 | | | ♦ |
| ☐ C-FCBZ | Beech A100 King Air | B-116 | | | ♦ |
| ☐ C-FJDF | Beech 1900C | UB-68 | ex N68GH | | |
| ☐ C-FJKY | Beech A100 King Air | B-202 | | | ♦ |
| ☐ C-FJMF | Beech C99 | U-180 | ex OY-PAG | | |
| ☐ C-FJTF | Beech 1900C | UB-39 | ex N888MX | | ♦ |
| ☐ C-FLMF | Beech C99 | U-189 | ex N189AV | | |
| ☐ C-FNMF | Beech C99 | U-167 | ex N167EE | | |
| ☐ C-GDVD | Beech 58 Baron | TH-668 | ex N4557S | | |
| ☐ C-GFFH | Beech B60 Duke | P-310 | | | ♦ |
| ☐ C-GKLO | Piper PA-31-350 Chieftain | 31-8152118 | ex N4505N | | |
| ☐ C-GKNL | Piper PA-31-350 Chieftain | 31-7852083 | ex N27607 | | |
| ☐ C-GMFV | Cessna U206G Stationair 6 II | U20604714 | ex N732RY | | |
| ☐ C-GMJN | Cessna 550 Citation II | 550-0433 | ex N7ZU | | ♦ |
| ☐ C-GNRM | Piper PA-31-350 Navajo Chieftain | 31-7752145 | ex N27315 | | |

## CUSTOM HELICOPTERS                                Winnipeg-St Andrews, MB (YAV)

| | | | | | |
|---|---|---|---|---|---|
| ☐ C-FCHJ | Aérospatiale AS350B2 AStar | 2603 | ex XC-JAK | | |
| ☐ C-GAVQ | Aérospatiale AS350B2 AStar | 2781 | ex N350PD | | ♦ |
| ☐ C-GCHX | Aérospatiale AS350BA AStar | 2517 | ex CP-2335 | | |
| ☐ C-GOGJ | Aérospatiale AS350B2 AStar | 2749 | | | ♦ |
| ☐ C-GOGQ | Aérospatiale AS350B3 AStar | 3196 | | | ♦ |
| | | | | | |
| ☐ C-FJMH | Bell 206B JetRanger II | 1331 | ex N70711 | | |
| ☐ C-FKBV | Bell 206B JetRanger II | 364 | ex N465CC | | |
| ☐ C-FSVG | Bell 206B JetRanger III | 2865 | ex N1074G | | |
| ☐ C-FZSJ | Bell 206B JetRanger II | 648 | ex CF-ZSJ | | |
| ☐ C-GAQS | Bell 206B JetRanger II | 2382 | | | ♦ |
| ☐ C-GBWN | Bell 206B JetRanger II | 2204 | | | |
| ☐ C-GFIV | Bell 206B JetRanger II | 424 | ex N1481W | | |
| ☐ C-GGZS | Bell 206B JetRanger II | 1885 | | | |
| ☐ C-GKBU | Bell 206B JetRanger II | 386 | ex N1448W | | |
| ☐ C-GQQO | Bell 206B JetRanger II | 1096 | ex N83182 | | |
| ☐ C-GQQT | Bell 206B JetRanger II | 1657 | ex N90218 | | |
| ☐ C-GSHJ | Bell 206B JetRanger II | 114 | ex N125GW | | |
| | | | | | |
| ☐ C-FYHN | Bell 206L LongRanger | 45050 | ex N600FB | | |
| ☐ C-GAVH | Bell 206L-1 LongRanger III | 45740 | ex N385FP | | |
| ☐ C-GCHG | Bell 206L-1 LongRanger II | 51508 | ex N8592X | | |
| ☐ C-GCHI | Bell 206L-1 LongRanger II | 45516 | ex N141VG | | |
| ☐ C-GCHZ | Bell 206L-1 LongRanger III | 45314 | ex N210AH | | |
| ☐ C-GIPG | Bell 206L-1 LongRanger II | 45592 | ex N3895K | | |
| ☐ C-GOFH | Bell 206L-1 LongRanger III | 45359 | | | ♦ |
| ☐ C-GOFI | Bell 206L-1 LongRanger III | 45342 | | | ♦ |
| | | | | | |
| ☐ C-FCHD | Bell 205A-1 | 30014 | ex N5598M | | |
| ☐ C-FCHE | Bell 205A-1 | 30167 | ex XA-SSR | | |
| ☐ C-FCHJ | Aérospatiale AS350B2 AStar | 2603 | ex XC-JAK | | |
| ☐ C-GCHX | Aérospatiale AS350BA AStar | 2517 | ex CP-2335 | | |
| ☐ C-GRWK | Bell 205A-1 | 30005 | ex N3764U | | |

## EAGLE COPTERS                                        Calgary, AB (YYC)

| | | | | | |
|---|---|---|---|---|---|
| ☐ C-FDEF | Bell 205A | 30038 | ex CS-HET | | |
| ☐ C-GAMH | Bell 205A-1 | 30215 | | | ♦ |
| ☐ C-GCZG | Bell 205A-1 | 30136 | ex N58126 | | |
| ☐ C-GEAG | Bell 205A-1 | 30262 | ex XC-CIC | | |

| | | | | |
|---|---|---|---|---|
| ☐ C-GEAK | Bell 205A-1 | 30096 | | ♦ |
| ☐ C-GHUM | Bell 205A-1 | 30252 | | ♦ |
| ☐ C-GQLG | Bell 205A-1 | 30008 | | ♦ |
| | | | | |
| ☐ C-FBHY | Bell 212 | 31194 | | |
| ☐ C-FBUA | Bell 212 | 30826 | | |
| ☐ C-FNOS | Bell 212 | 30866 | | |
| ☐ C-FNOU | Bell 212 | 30787 | ex 5N-AXX | |
| ☐ C-FXXU | Bell 212 | 30803 | | |
| ☐ C-GAZF | Bell 212 | 30640 | ex HK-4518X | |
| ☐ C-GBBP | Bell 212 | 30934 | ex OB-1847P | |
| ☐ C-GBHH | Bell 212 | 30962 | ex C-GLYK | ♦ |
| ☐ C-GLYO | Bell 212 | 31161 | ex B-7709 | ♦ |
| ☐ C-GNYI | Bell 212 | 30569 | ex N29AL | ♦ |
| | | | | |
| ☐ C-FDDI | Bell 412 | 36065 | ex VT-AZL | ♦ |
| ☐ C-GFPV | Bell 412EP | 36547 | | ♦ |
| ☐ C-GLOQ | Bell 412EP | 36322 | ex ZS-HAU | ♦ |
| ☐ C-GMVN | Bell 412EP | 36253 | ex XA-AAB | ♦ |
| ☐ C-GMVX | Bell 412EP | 36254 | ex XA-AAN | ♦ |
| ☐ C-GMVY | Bell 412EP | 36255 | ex XA-AAR | ♦ |
| ☐ C-GNTH | Bell 412 | 33046 | ex 5N-BDD | ♦ |
| ☐ C-GKVV | Bell 412 | 36233 | ex N514PD | |
| ☐ N142EC | Bell 412 | 36142 | ex N512PD | |
| | | | | |
| ☐ C-FHED | Bell 407 | 53597 | | ♦ |
| ☐ C-FTIW | Sikorsky S-76A+ | 760186 | | |
| ☐ C-FWZI | Bell 206L-1 LongRanger II | 45447 | ex N202EC | |
| ☐ C-FZXH | Bell 206B JetRanger II | 622 | | |
| ☐ C-GAHN | Bell 204B | 2044 | ex N120BX | |
| ☐ C-GBHF | Bell 206B JetRanger II | 1028 | | |
| ☐ C-GIYO | Aérospatiale AS350BA AStar | 2274 | | |
| ☐ C-GJDQ | Eurocopter EC130B4 | 3841 | ex N995PT | ♦ |
| ☐ C-GLAE | Eurocopter EC130B4 | 3755 | ex N998PT | ♦ |
| ☐ C-GNMP | Aérospatiale AS.350B Astar | 1040 | | ♦ |
| ☐ C-GQKU | Bell 206B JetRanger II | 2173 | | |
| ☐ C-GXXH | Bell 407 | 53197 | ex N782FS | |

## ELBOW RIVER HELICOPTERS | Calgary-Springbank, AB (YBW)

| | | | | |
|---|---|---|---|---|
| ☐ C-GERB | Bell 206L-3 LongRanger III | 51008 | | |
| ☐ C-GERW | Bell 212 | 30814 | ex C-FRWM | |
| ☐ C-GKCA | Bell 206L-3 LongRanger III | 51341 | | |
| ☐ C-GTKE | Bell 212 | 30704 | | ♦ |
| ☐ C-GZAV | Bell 407 | 53002 | | |

## EXPLOITS VALLEY AIR SERVICES | Gander, NL (YQX)

| | | | | |
|---|---|---|---|---|
| ☐ C-FEVA | Beech 1900D | UE-126 | ex N126YV | |
| ☐ C-GAAT | Beech 1900D | UE-217 | ex N1564J 963 | |
| ☐ C-GERI | Beech 1900D | UE-162 | ex N162ZV | |
| ☐ C-GLHO | Beech 1900D | UE-266 | ex N10950 | ♦ |
| ☐ C-GLXV | Beech 1900D | UE-242 | ex N242YV | ♦ |
| | | | | |
| ☐ C-GZUZ | Beech A100 King Air | B-143 | ex C-GNVB | |

## EXPRESS AIR | Expressair (WEW) | Ottawa, ON (YOW)

| | | | | |
|---|---|---|---|---|
| ☐ C-FKAZ | Cessna 208 Caravan I | 20800236 | | FP |
| ☐ C-GAWP | Pilatus PC-12/45 | 187 | ex N187PC | |

## FAST AIR | Winnipeg-Intl, MB (YWG)

| | | | | |
|---|---|---|---|---|
| ☐ C-FDEB | Beech 200 Super King Air | BB-55 | ex N200BC | |
| ☐ C-FFAP | Beech 200 Super King Air | BB-257 | | ♦ |
| ☐ C-FFAR | Beech 200 Super King Air | BB-864 | ex N847TS | |
| ☐ C-GDHF | Beech B200 Super King Air | BB-1129 | ex CS-DDF | CatPass 250 conversion |
| ☐ C-GFAD | Beech B200 Super King Air | BB-1428 | ex N660MW | |
| ☐ C-GFAV | Beech 200 Super King Air | BB-492 | ex N64DC | ♦ |
| ☐ C-GFSB | Beech 200 Super King Air | BB-84 | | |
| ☐ C-GWGI | Beech B200 Super King Air | BB-1022 | ex C-FDGP | |
| | | | | |
| ☐ C-FJAL | Piper PA-31-350 Navajo Chieftain | 31-7752160 | ex N19LA | |
| ☐ C-FJOJ | IAI 112A Jet Commander | 271 | | ♦ |
| ☐ C-FREE | IAI Gulfstream 150 | 296 | | ♦ |
| ☐ C-GCGS | British Aerospace 125 Srs.800A | 258123 | ex N353WG | ♦ |
| ☐ C-GDSR | IAI 112A Jet Commander | 313 | ex N611WV | ♦ |
| ☐ C-GNDI | Piper PA-31T Cheyenne | 31T-7620036 | ex N73TB | |
| ☐ C-GPNP | Piper PA-31T Cheyenne | 31T-7520024 | ex N431AC | |
| ☐ C-GWPK | IAI Gulfstream 150 | 288 | ex N208GA | ♦ |

## FIRST AIR / BRADLEY AIR SERVICES — Firstair (7F/FAB)

Carp, ON/Iqaluit, NT/Yellowknife, NT (YRP/YFB/YZF)

| | | | | | |
|---|---|---|---|---|---|
| ☐ C-FIQR | ATR 42-300 (QC) | 0133 | ex F-WWEE | | |
| ☐ C-FIQU | ATR 42-300 (QC) | 0138 | ex F-WWEK | | |
| ☐ C-FTCP | ATR 42-300 (QC) | 0143 | ex F-WWEO | | |
| ☐ C-FTJB | ATR 42-300 (QC) | 0119 | ex N423TE | | |
| ☐ C-GHCP | ATR 42-300 (QC) | 0123 | ex F-WWET | | |
| ☐ C-GKLB | ATR 42-310 | 0331 | ex G-CDFF | | |
| ☐ C-GSRR | ATR 42-300 (QC) | 0125 | ex OY-MUH | | |
| ☐ C-GULU | ATR 42-310 | 0155 | ex 5R-MJD | | |
| ☐ C-GUNO | ATR 42-310 | 0132 | ex 5R-MJC | | |
| | | | | | |
| ☐ C-FACP | Boeing 737-2L9 (AvAero 3) | 22072/623 | ex C2-RN9 | | |
| ☐ C-FNVK | Boeing 737-2R4C | 23130/1040 | ex JY-JAF | | Frtr |
| ☐ C-FNVT | Boeing 737-248C (AvAero 3) | 21011/411 | ex F-GKTK | Snowy Owl c/s | |
| ☐ C-GCPT | Boeing 737-217 (AvAero 3) | 22258/770 | | Inukshuk tail logo | |
| ☐ C-GNDC | Boeing 737-242C (AvAero 3) | 21728/580 | | | |
| ☐ C-GNDE | Boeing 737-247 | 23521/1342 | ex N352CC | | ♦ |
| ☐ C-GNDF | Boeing 737-25A | 23790/1422 | ex C-GCNO | | ♦ |
| | | | | | |
| ☐ C-FUFA | Boeing 727-233F (FedEx 3) | 20941/1128 | ex N727LS | | |
| ☐ C-GHPW | Lockheed L-382G-42C Hercules | 4799 | | Capt Harry Sorenson | |
| ☐ C-GKLY | Boeing 767-223 (SCD) | 22314/73 | ex N714AX | | |
| ☐ C-GLHR | ATR 72-212 | 0423 | ex EI-CLB | | ♦ |
| ☐ C-GRMZ | ATR 72-212 | 0432 | ex EI-CLD | | ♦ |
| ☐ C-GUSI | Lockheed L-328G-31C Hercules | 4600 | ex ZS-RSI | EARL titles | |
| ☐ C-GXFA | Boeing 727-233F (Raisbeck 3) | 20938/1105 | ex C-GAAG | | |

## FLAIR AIRLINES — Flair (FLE) — Kelowna, BC (YLW)

| | | | | |
|---|---|---|---|---|
| ☐ C-FLEJ | Boeing 737-4B3 | 24751/2107 | ex CN-RPB | <KFA |
| ☐ C-FLEN | Boeing 737-4K5 | 24769/1839 | ex OK-VGZ | |
| ☐ C-FLER | Boeing 737-46B | 24573/1844 | ex N41XA | <KFA |
| ☐ C-GJRH | Cessna 340 | 340-0058 | ex N340BD | ♦ |

## FORT FRANCES SPORTSMEN AIRWAYS — Fort Frances, ON (YAG)

| | | | | |
|---|---|---|---|---|
| ☐ C-GBQC | de Havilland DHC-3 Otter | 401 | ex RCAF 9420 | FP/WS |
| ☐ C-GMDG | de Havilland DHC-3 Turbo Otter | 302 | ex N90575 | FP/WS |
| ☐ C-GUTL | de Havilland DHC-3 Turbo Otter | 365 | ex HK-3048X | FP/WS♦ |

## FUGRO AVIATION CANADA — Ottawa-Rockcliffe, ON (YRO)

| | | | | |
|---|---|---|---|---|
| ☐ C-FYAU | Cessna 404 Titan II | 404-0431 | ex N408EX | Tail magnetometer |
| ☐ C-FZLK | Cessna 208B Caravan I | 208B0569 | ex N1210N | Tail magnetometer |
| ☐ C-GDPP | CASA 212-200 | CC50-3-265 | ex N430CA | Nose & tail magnetometer |
| ☐ C-GGRD | Cessna 208B Caravan I | 208B1150 | ex N208ML | |
| ☐ C-GJPI | de Havilland DHC-7-102 | 036 | | ♦ |
| ☐ C-GNCA | Cessna 208B Caravan I | 208B0764 | ex N208KC | Tail magnetometer |

## GILLAM AIR SERVICES — Gillam, MB (YGX)

| | | | | |
|---|---|---|---|---|
| ☐ C-GBZS | de Havilland DHC-2 Beaver | 1595 | | ♦ |
| ☐ C-GPPP | Britten-Norman BN-2A-27 Islander | 423 | ex (N93JA) | |
| ☐ C-GSAD | Britten-Norman BN-2A-26 Islander | 7 | ex N32JC | |
| ☐ C-GXQV | Cessna A185F Skywagon | 18503375 | | |

## GOGAL AIR SERVICES — Snow Lake, MB

| | | | | |
|---|---|---|---|---|
| ☐ CF-ECG | Noorduyn Norseman V | N29-43 | | FP/WS |
| ☐ CF-GLI | Noorduyn Norseman VI | 365 | ex N88719 | FP/WS |
| ☐ CF-JFA | de Havilland DHC-2 Beaver | 1581 | ex N5563 | FP/WS♦ |
| ☐ C-GAGP | Cessna 208B Caravan I | 208B1213 | ex N208EE | ♦ |
| ☐ C-GBAO | Piper PA-31-350 Navajo Chieftain | 31-7405234 | ex N54309 | |
| ☐ C-GCWO | Cessna A185F Skywagon | 18503207 | ex N93275 | FP/WS |
| ☐ C-GLDZ | Piper PA-31T Cheyenne | 31T-8166062 | | ♦ |

## GOLDAK AIRBORNE SURVEYS — Saskatoon, SK (YXE)

| | | | | |
|---|---|---|---|---|
| ☐ C-GJBA | Piper PA-31 Turbo Navajo | 31-159 | ex N9119Y | Surveyor, tail magnetometer |
| ☐ C-GJBB | Piper PA-31 Turbo Navajo | 31-519 | ex N310DS | Surveyor |
| ☐ C-GJBG | Piper PA-31 Navajo C | 31-7612003 | ex N59718 | Surveyor |
| ☐ C-GLDX | Cessna 208 Caravan I | 20800366 | ex C-FFCL | |

## GOVERNMENT OF QUEBEC — Quebec (QUE) — Quebec, QC (YQB)

| | | | | |
|---|---|---|---|---|
| ☐ C-FASE | Canadair CL215T | 1114 | ex Greece 1114 238 | |
| ☐ C-FAWQ | Canadair CL215T | 1115 | ex Greece 1115 239 | |

| | | | | | |
|---|---|---|---|---|---|
| ☐ C-FTXG | Canadair CL215 | 1014 | ex CF-TXG | 228 | |
| ☐ C-FTXJ | Canadair CL215 | 1017 | ex CF-TXJ | 230 | |
| ☐ C-FTXK | Canadair CL215 | 1018 | ex CF-TXK | 231 | |
| ☐ C-GDKY | Canadair CL215 | 1096 | | | |
| ☐ C-GFQB | Canadair CL215 | 1092 | ex C-GKDP | 237 | ♦ |
| | | | | | |
| ☐ C-GOGY | Canadair CL415 | 2040 | | 177 | ♦ |
| ☐ C-GQBA | Canadair CL415 | 2005 | ex C-GKDN | 240 | |
| ☐ C-GQBC | Canadair CL415 | 2012 | ex C-GKET | 241 | |
| ☐ C-GQBD | Canadair CL415 | 2016 | ex C-GBPU | 242 | |
| ☐ C-GQBE | Canadair CL415 | 2017 | ex C-GKEA | 243 | |
| ☐ C-GQBF | Canadair CL415 | 2019 | ex C-FVKV | 244 | |
| ☐ C-GQBG | Canadair CL415 | 2022 | ex C-FVLW | 245 | |
| ☐ C-GQBI | Canadair CL415 | 2023 | ex C-FVLI | 246 | |
| ☐ C-GQBK | Canadair CL415 | 2026 | ex C-FVLY | 247 | |
| | | | | | |
| ☐ C-GBPQ | Bell 206B JetRanger III | 2897 | ex YU-HLL | | |
| ☐ C-GQBQ | Canadair Challenger 604 | 5051 | ex N300KC | | EMS |
| ☐ C-GQBT | de Havilland DHC-8Q-202 | 470 | ex P2-ANL | | EMS/VIP |
| ☐ C-GSQA | Bell 206LT TwinRanger | 52060 | | | Police |
| ☐ C-GSQL | Bell 412EP | 36262 | ex N6077U | | |

## GREEN AIRWAYS                                                 Red Lake, ON (YRL)

| | | | | | |
|---|---|---|---|---|---|
| ☐ C-FLEA | de Havilland DHC-3 Otter | 286 | ex CF-LEA | | FP/WS |
| ☐ C-FLNC | Cessna 180 Skywagon | 18032497 | | | ♦ |
| ☐ C-FOBE | Noorduyn UC-64A Norseman | 480 | ex 43-35406 | | FP/WS |
| ☐ C-FODJ | de Havilland DHC-3 Otter | 14 | ex CF-ODJ | | FP/WS |
| ☐ C-FVIA | de Havilland DHC-2 Beaver | 714 | ex N9047U | | FP/WS |
| ☐ C-GEZU | de Havilland DHC-2 Beaver | 647 | ex 53-8159 | | FP/WS |
| ☐ C-GYUY | Cessna A185F Skywagon II | 18503731 | ex (N8550Q) | | FP/WS |

## GRONDAIR / GRONDIN TRANSPORT                          St Frederic du Beauce, QC

| | | | | | |
|---|---|---|---|---|---|
| ☐ C-FNNM | Cessna TR182RG Skylane | R18200946 | ex N738NR | | |
| ☐ C-FQTA | Cessna R182RG Skylane | R18200324 | ex N4107C | | |
| ☐ C-FQTC | Cessna R182RG Skylane | R18201717 | ex N4608T | | |
| ☐ C-FRGN | Cessna R182RG Skylane | R18200394 | ex N9083C | | |
| ☐ C-FRYF | Cessna R182RG Skylane | R18201001 | ex N65ET | | |
| ☐ C-FRYP | Cessna R182RG Skylane | R18200479 | ex N9879C | | |
| ☐ C-FRZE | Cessna R182RG Skylane | R18200197 | ex N2657C | | |
| ☐ C-GCJA | Cessna R182RG Skylane | R18201219 | ex (N757DM) | | |
| ☐ C-GHVC | Cessna R182RG Skylane | R18201886 | ex N5532T | | |
| ☐ C-GRUA | Cessna R182RG Skylane | R18200077 | ex N7325X | | |
| ☐ C-GSCF | Cessna R182RG Skylane | R18201257 | ex N757QM | | |
| ☐ C-GVCV | Cessna R182RG Skylane | R18200030 | ex N7343T | | |
| | | | | | |
| ☐ C-FINP | Cessna 337G Super Skymaster II | 33701523 | | | ♦ |
| ☐ C-FONY | Beech A100 King Air | B-154 | ex N46JK | | |
| ☐ C-GAST | Cessna 310R | 310R0730 | ex N5009J | | |
| ☐ C-GBRC | Cessna 310R | 310R1284 | ex N6116X | | |
| ☐ C-GIGB | Cessna 337G Super Skymaster II | 33701599 | ex N72478 | | |
| ☐ C-GJGW | Cessna 310R | 310R0960 | ex N37200 | | |
| ☐ C-GRIR | Beech A100 King Air | B-144 | | | ♦ |
| ☐ C-GSRW | Piper PA-31 Turbo Navajo | 31-262 | ex N707FR | | |
| ☐ C-GUMQ | Piper PA-31 Turbo Navajo | 31-84 | ex N777GS | | |

## HARBOUR AIR SEAPLANES            Harbour Air (H3)         Vancouver-Coal Harbour, BC (CXH)

| | | | | | |
|---|---|---|---|---|---|
| ☐ C-FAXI | de Havilland DHC-2 Beaver | 1514 | ex N6535D | 205 | FP |
| ☐ C-FFHQ | de Havilland DHC-2 Beaver | 42 | ex CF-FHQ | 203 | FP |
| ☐ C-FJFQ | de Havilland DHC-2 Beaver | 963 | ex CF-JFQ | 206 | FP |
| ☐ C-FMXS | de Havilland DHC-2 Beaver | 1010 | ex N43882 | 202 | FP |
| ☐ C-FOCJ | de Havilland DHC-2 Beaver | 39 | ex CF-OCJ | | FP |
| ☐ C-FOCY | de Havilland DHC-2 Beaver | 79 | ex CF-OCY | 204 | FP |
| ☐ C-FOSP | de Havilland DHC-2 Beaver | 1501 | ex N2961 | 207 | FP |
| ☐ C-GCYM | de Havilland DHC-2 Beaver | 354 | ex N63PS | | FP |
| ☐ C-GTBQ | de Havilland DHC-2 Beaver | 1316 | | | ♦ |
| | | | | | |
| ☐ C-FHAA | de Havilland DHC-3 Turbo Otter | 357 | ex C-GIWT | 309 | FP |
| ☐ C-FHAD | de Havilland DHC-3 Turbo Otter | 119 | ex N81FW | 315 | FP |
| ☐ C-FHAS | de Havilland DHC-3 Turbo Otter | 382 | ex N382BH | | FP♦ |
| ☐ C-FHAX | de Havilland DHC-3 Turbo Otter | 339 | ex N41755 | 313 | FP |
| ☐ C-FITF | de Havilland DHC-3 Turbo Otter | 89 | ex CF-ITF | 303 | FP |
| ☐ C-FIUZ | de Havilland DHC-3 Turbo Otter | 135 | ex F-OAKK | 306 | FP |
| ☐ C-FJHA | de Havilland DHC-3 Turbo Otter | 393 | ex 4R-ARB | | FP |
| ☐ C-FLAP | de havilland DHC-3 Otter | 289 | | | FP♦ |
| ☐ C-FODH | de Havilland DHC-3 Turbo Otter | 3 | ex CF-ODH | 307 | FP |
| ☐ C-FRNO | de Havilland DHC-3 Turbo Otter | 21 | ex N128F | 301 | FP |
| ☐ C-GHAG | de Havilland DHC-3 Turbo Otter | 214 | ex 4R-ARA | | FP♦ |
| ☐ C-GHAQ | de Havilland DHC-3 Turbo Otter | 288 | ex DQ-GLL | | FP♦ |

| | | | | | |
|---|---|---|---|---|---|
| ☐ C-GHAR | de Havilland DHC-3 Turbo Otter | 42 | ex N234KA | 308 | FP |
| ☐ C-GHAS | de Havilland DHC-3 Turbo Otter | 284 | ex N84SF | 310 | FP |
| ☐ C-GHAZ | de Havilland DHC-3 Turbo Otter | 19 | ex C-FEYY | | FP |
| ☐ C-GLCP | de Havilland DHC-3 Turbo Otter | 422 | ex N17682 | | FP |
| ☐ C-GOPP | de Havilland DHC-3 Turbo Otter | 355 | ex N53KA | 305 | FP |
| ☐ C-GUTW | de Havilland DHC-3 Turbo Otter | 405 | ex RCAF 9423 | 302 | FP |
| ☐ C-GVNL | de Havilland DHC-3 Turbo Otter | 105 | ex N5341G | 304 | FP |
| | | | | | |
| ☐ C-GCRE | Cessna A185F Skywagon | 18502522 | ex (N1807R) | | FP |
| ☐ C-GZSH | Cessna A185F Skywagon | 18503482 | ex (N1463Q) | | FP |

## HAUTS-MONTS  Quebec, QC / Jackson, MS (YQB/JAN)

| | | | | |
|---|---|---|---|---|
| ☐ C-GPSP | Cessna 441 Conquest II | 441-0058 | ex OY-BHM | Photo/survey |
| ☐ C-GPSQ | Cessna 441 Conquest II | 441-0076 | ex N441RC | Photo/survey |
| ☐ C-GPSR | Cessna 441 Conquest II | 441-0143 | ex N26PK | Photo/survey |
| ☐ N454EA | Cessna 441 Conquest II | 441-0054 | ex C-GRSL | Photo/survey |
| ☐ N8970N | Cessna 441 Conquest II | 441-0092 | | Photo/survey |
| | | | | |
| ☐ C-GHMN | Piper PA-23-250 Aztec C | 27-3893 | ex N6590Y | Photo/survey |
| ☐ C-GNZQ | Piper PA-23-250 Aztec E | 27-7554067 | ex N54755 | Photo/survey |
| ☐ C-GPSZ | Cessna 421C Golden Eagle II | 421C0148 | ex N303HC | Photo/survey |

## HAWK AIR  Wawa-Hawk Junction, ON (YXZ)

| | | | | |
|---|---|---|---|---|
| ☐ C-FBBG | de Havilland DHC-2 Beaver | 358-173 | ex N2848D | FP |
| ☐ C-FOUZ | Cessna 180F Skywagon | 18051238 | | FP♦ |
| ☐ C-FQMN | de Havilland DHC-3 Otter | 184 | ex N2959W | FP |

## HAWKAIR AVIATION SERVICE  Hawkair (BH)  Terrace, BC (YXT)

| | | | |
|---|---|---|---|
| ☐ C-FCJE | de Havilland DHC-8-102 | 165 | |
| ☐ C-FDNG | de Havilland DHC-8-102 | 166 | |
| ☐ C-FIDL | de Havilland DHC-8-311 | 305 | ex V2-LFW |

## HEARST AIR SERVICE  Hearst, ON (YHF)

| | | | | |
|---|---|---|---|---|
| ☐ C-FBTU | de Havilland DHC-2 Beaver | 1564 | ex CF-BTU | FP/WS |
| ☐ C-FDDX | de Havilland DHC-3 Turbo Otter | 165 | ex CF-DDX | FP/WS |
| ☐ C-FKAE | Cessna 208 Caravan I | 20800316 | ex C-FKAL | ♦ |
| ☐ C-FOEK | de Havilland DHC-2 Turbo Beaver | 1650/TB28 | ex CF-OEK | FP/WS♦ |

## HELI-EXPRESS  Quebec, QC (YQB)

| | | | | |
|---|---|---|---|---|
| ☐ C-FCCI | Aérospatiale AS350BA AStar | 1303 | ex N5768Y | |
| ☐ C-GDEH | Aérospatiale AS350BA AStar | 1348 | ex N905DB | |
| ☐ C-GHEX | Aérospatiale AS350B2 AStar | 2867 | ex CP-2392 | |
| ☐ C-GIMG | Aérospatiale AS350D AStar | 1382 | ex ZK-HZZ | |
| ☐ C-GJPC | Aérospatiale AS350BA AStar | 1398 | ex N269JM | |
| ☐ C-GRDI | Aérospatiale AS350B2 AStar | 2866 | ex C-FWAU | |
| ☐ C-GSRQ | Aérospatiale AS350BA AStar | 1081 | | ♦ |
| ☐ C-GVEM | Aérospatiale AS350BA AStar | 2510 | ex N752BH | |
| | | | | |
| ☐ C-GADA | Bell 205A-1 | 30031 | ex PK-UHJ | |

## HELI-LIFT INTERNATIONAL  Yorkton, SK (YQV)

| | | | | |
|---|---|---|---|---|
| ☐ C-GHLE | Bell 205A-1 | 30195 | ex HL9150 | |
| ☐ C-GHLJ | Bell 206L-3 LongRanger III | 51280 | ex N60992 | |
| ☐ C-GHLX | Aérospatiale AS350B AStar | 1589 | ex N85PB | |
| ☐ C-GIYN | Aérospatiale AS350BA AStar | 1776 | ex JA9368 | |
| ☐ C-GMOR | Bell 205A-1 | 30159 | ex LX-HOR | |
| ☐ C-GQCW | Aérospatiale AS350BA AStar | 1255 | ex N3607T | |
| ☐ C-GSHK | Bell 204B | 2067 | ex Thai 920 | |

## HELIFOR INDUSTRIES  Campbell River, BC (YBL)

| | | | | |
|---|---|---|---|---|
| ☐ C-FHCN | Boeing Vertol 107 II | 404 | ex N194CH | |
| ☐ C-FHFB | Boeing Vertol 234UT Chinook | MJ-005 | ex N238CH | <WCO |
| ☐ C-FHFV | Boeing Vertol 107-II | 4 | ex N6674D | <WCO |
| ☐ C-GHFF | Boeing Vertol 107 II | 406 | ex N195CH | <WCO |

## HELIJET INTERNATIONAL  Helijet (JB/JBA)  Vancouver-Intl, BC (YVR)

| | | | | |
|---|---|---|---|---|
| ☐ C-GCHJ | Sikorsky S-76C | 760496 | ex N397U | ♦ |
| ☐ C-GHHJ | Sikorsky S-76C | 760500 | ex N88CP | ♦ |
| ☐ C-GHJG | Sikorsky S-76A | 760186 | | ♦ |
| ☐ C-GHJL | Sikorsky S-76A II | 760214 | ex N101PB | EMS |
| ☐ C-GHJP | Sikorsky S-76A II | 760065 | ex (C-GHJT) | |

| | | | | | |
|---|---|---|---|---|---|
| ☐ C-GHJT | Sikorsky S-76A | 760052 | ex VH-XHZ | | |
| ☐ C-GHJV | Sikorsky S-76A | 760167 | ex N5426U | | |
| ☐ C-GHJW | Sikorsky S-76A II | 760074 | ex N586C | | |
| ☐ C-GIHJ | Sikorsky S-76C | 760438 | ex N986AH | | ♦ |
| ☐ C-GNYO | Sikorsky S-76C1 | 760499 | ex N76LQ | | ♦ |
| | | | | | |
| ☐ C-GFHA | Bell 205A-1 | 30086 | | | ♦ |
| ☐ C-GHJJ | Learjet 31A | 102 | ex N681AF | | EMS |
| ☐ C-GHJU | Learjet 31A | 120 | ex N200TJ | | EMS |
| ☐ C-GVIQ | Bell 206L-1 LongRanger III | 45492 | ex N83MT | | ♦ |
| ☐ C-GVIZ | Bell 206L-1 LongRanger III | 45346 | ex N26SH | | ♦ |
| ☐ C-GXHJ | Bell 206L-1 LongRanger | 45741 | ex N3174P | | |

## HIGHLAND HELICOPTERS · Vancouver-Intl, BC (YVR)

| | | | | |
|---|---|---|---|---|
| ☐ C-FHHC | Aérospatiale AS350B2 AStar | 2569 | ex N2PW | |
| ☐ C-FHHU | Aérospatiale AS350B2 AStar | 2790 | ex C-FSQY | |
| ☐ C-FHHY | Aérospatiale AS350BA AStar | 1650 | ex C-GSKI | |
| ☐ C-FJHH | Aérospatiale AS350B2 AStar | 3279 | | |
| ☐ C-FKHH | Aérospatiale AS350B2 AStar | 2736 | | |
| ☐ C-FYYA | Aérospatiale AS350BA AStar | 2295 | ex ZK-HOU | |
| ☐ C-GDHH | Aérospatiale AS350B2 AStar | 4103 | | |
| ☐ C-GGTO | Aérospatiale AS350B2 AStar | 4393 | | |
| ☐ C-GHHH | Aérospatiale AS350B2 AStar | 3270 | | |
| ☐ C-GHHV | Aérospatiale AS350B2 AStar | 2918 | ex N4034Q | |
| ☐ C-GHHW | Aérospatiale AS350B2 AStar | 3039 | | |
| ☐ C-GHHZ | Aérospatiale AS350B2 AStar | 3054 | | |
| ☐ C-GNHH | Aérospatiale AS350B2 AStar | 2737 | ex N9446H | |
| ☐ C-GRHH | Aérospatiale AS350B2 AStar | 3315 | ex N37PT | |
| ☐ C-GRJO | Aérospatiale AS350B2 AStar | 4277 | | |
| ☐ C-GTIA | Aérospatiale AS350B2 AStar | 4328 | ex F-WWPZ | |
| ☐ C-GXHH | Aérospatiale AS350B2 AStar | 4058 | ex F-WQDF | |
| | | | | |
| ☐ C-FCDL | Bell 206B JetRanger III | 3852 | ex N93AJ | |
| ☐ C-FCOY | Bell 206B JetRanger III | 3280 | ex N7023J | |
| ☐ C-FETC | Bell 206B JetRanger III | 3515 | ex C-GTIA | |
| ☐ C-FHHB | Bell 206B JetRanger | 519 | ex CF-HHB | |
| ☐ C-FHHI | Bell 206B JetRanger III | 2310 | ex N101CD | |
| ☐ C-GHHD | Bell 206B JetRanger | 1566 | ex N90003 | |
| ☐ C-GHHG | Bell 206B JetRanger | 1396 | ex N918TR | |
| ☐ C-GHHM | Bell 206B JetRanger III | 2712 | | |
| ☐ C-GHHO | Bell 206B JetRanger | 1690 | | |
| ☐ C-GHHR | Bell 206B JetRanger II | 1963 | | |
| ☐ C-GHHX | Bell 206B JetRanger III | 2714 | | |
| ☐ C-GHXJ | Bell 206B JetRanger | 1832 | | |
| ☐ C-GIZO | Bell 206B JetRanger III | 2715 | | |
| ☐ C-GJJA | Bell 206B JetRanger II | 2032 | ex N9958K | |
| ☐ C-GJMJ | Bell 206B JetRanger | 620 | ex N7112J | |
| ☐ C-GKDG | Bell 206B JetRanger III | 2969 | | |
| ☐ C-GKGI | Bell 206B JetRanger | 1790 | ex N49629 | |
| ☐ C-GKJL | Bell 206B JetRanger III | 3005 | | |
| ☐ C-GMDX | Bell 206B JetRanger III | 3032 | | |
| ☐ C-GMZH | Bell 206B JetRanger III | 3203 | | |
| ☐ C-GNLT | Bell 206B JetRanger III | 2973 | | |
| ☐ C-GNSQ | Bell 206B JetRanger III | 3274 | | |
| ☐ C-GOPF | Bell 206B JetRanger III | 3227 | | |
| ☐ C-GOPK | Bell 206B JetRanger III | 3247 | | |
| | | | | |
| ☐ C-GAXW | Bell 206L-3 LongRanger III | 51395 | ex N6501S | |
| ☐ C-GFHH | Bell 206L-3 LongRanger III | 51362 | ex C-FPCL | |

## HORNE AIR · Hornepayne, ON (YHN)

| | | | | |
|---|---|---|---|---|
| ☐ C-FFHP | de Havilland DHC-2 Beaver | 57 | ex CF-FHP | FP |
| ☐ C-FIDM | de Havilland DHC-2 Beaver | 1323 | ex N99871 | FP |
| ☐ C-GEWG | de Havilland DHC-2 Beaver | 842 | ex N87572 | FP |

## HURON AIR AND OUTFITTERS · Armstrong, ON (YYW)

| | | | | |
|---|---|---|---|---|
| ☐ C-FDPW | de Havilland DHC-2 Beaver | 1339 | ex 58-2011 | FP/WS |
| ☐ C-FGSR | Noorduyn Norseman V | N29-47 | ex CF-GSR | FP |
| ☐ C-FIOF | de Havilland DHC-3 Otter | 24 | ex LN-SUV | FP/WS |

## HYDRO-QUEBEC (SERVICE TRANSPORT AERIEN)
### Hydro (HYD) · Montreal-Trudeau, QC (YUL)

| | | | | |
|---|---|---|---|---|
| ☐ C-GHQL | de Havilland DHC-8-402Q | 4115 | | Op by AIE |
| ☐ C-GHQP | de Havilland DHC-8-402Q | 4004 | ex C-GIHK | Op by AIE |
| ☐ C-GJNL | de Havilland DHC-8-311 | 422 | ex G-BXPZ | Op by AIE |

## ICARUS FLYING SERVICE — Ile de la Madelaine, QC (YGR)

| | | | | |
|---|---|---|---|---|
| ☐ C-GFBF | Britten-Norman BN-2B-27 Islander | 2125 | ex VP-FBF | |

## IGNACE AIRWAYS — Ignace/Thunder Bay, ON (ZUC/YQT)

| | | | | |
|---|---|---|---|---|
| ☐ C-FAPR | de Havilland DHC-3 Otter | 31 | ex LN-LMM | FP |
| ☐ C-FMAM | Noorduyn Norseman V | N29-26 | | FP♦ |
| ☐ CF-TTL | Cessna U206C Super Skywagon | U206-1062 | ex N29088 | FP |
| ☐ C-GZBR | de Havilland DHC-2 Beaver | 1272 | ex N434GR | FP |

## INFINITY FLIGHT SERVICES — Edmonton-Municipal, AB (YXD)

| | | | | |
|---|---|---|---|---|
| ☐ C-GNGI | British Aerospace Jetstream 3112 | 739 | ex N855JS | ♦ |
| ☐ C-GNGV | Cessna 560 Citation V | 560-0053 | ex C-FACC | ♦ |
| ☐ C-GSWF | Beech B100 King Air | BE-129 | ex LV-VCU | |

## INLAND AIR CHARTERS — Prince Rupert, BC (YPR)

| | | | | |
|---|---|---|---|---|
| ☐ C-FGQC | de Havilland DHC-2 Beaver | 75 | ex CF-GQC | FP |
| ☐ C-FIAX | de Havilland DHC-2 Beaver | 140 | ex VH-AAD | FP |
| ☐ C-FJOM | de Havilland DHC-2 Beaver | 1024 | ex CF-JOM | FP |
| ☐ C-FJPX | de Havilland DHC-2 Beaver | 1076 | ex CF-JPX | FP |

## INTEGRA AIR — Lethbridge, AB (YQL)

| | | | | |
|---|---|---|---|---|
| ☐ C-FFIA | British Aerospace Jetstream 31 | 779 | ex C-FSAS | |
| ☐ C-GGIA | British Aerospace Jetstream 31 | 778 | ex C-FMIP | |
| ☐ C-GZOS | British Aerospace Jetstream 31 | 796 | ex N424UE | ♦ |
| Assoc with Bar XH Air (qv) | | | | |

## ISLAND VALLEY AIRWAYS — Vancouver, BC (YVR)

| | | | | |
|---|---|---|---|---|
| ☐ C-FWBK | Pilatus PC-12/45 | 503 | ex N503WS | ♦ |

## JACKSON AIR SERVICES — Jackson (JCK) — Flin Flon, MB (YFO)

| | | | | |
|---|---|---|---|---|
| ☐ C-FMAJ | de Havilland DHC-3 Otter | 383 | ex 4655 | FP/WS |
| ☐ C-FODW | de Havilland DHC-3 Turbo Otter | 403 | ex CF-ODW | FP/WS♦ |
| ☐ C-GDYR | Cessna A185F Skywagon | 18503018 | | FP/WS |
| ☐ C-GISX | Cessna A185F Skywagon II | 18503836 | ex N4669E | FP/WS |
| ☐ C-GJMZ | Partenavia P.68B Observer | 369-27/OB | | |
| ☐ C-GVOQ | Cessna A185F Skywagon | 18503790 | | ♦ |

## JOHNNY MAY'S AIR CHARTERS — Kuujjuaq, QC (YVP)

| | | | | | |
|---|---|---|---|---|---|
| ☐ C-FCEE | de Havilland DHC-3 Otter | 282 | ex 57-6134 | | FP/WS |
| ☐ C-GMAY | de Havilland DHC-2 Beaver | 1123 | ex 56-0393 | Pengo Palee | FP/WS |

## KABEELO AIRWAYS — Confederation Lake, ON (YMY)

| | | | | |
|---|---|---|---|---|
| ☐ C-GDYT | de Havilland DHC-2 Beaver | 1109 | ex 56-4403 | FP |
| ☐ C-GLSA | de Havilland DHC-2 Beaver | 1389 | ex N94471 | FP |

## KASBA AIR SERVICE — Kasba Lake, NT (YDU)

| | | | | |
|---|---|---|---|---|
| ☐ CF-MAS | de Havilland DHC-2 Beaver | 38 | ex C-FMAS | FP |

## KAYAIR — Ear Falls, ON (YMY)

| | | | | |
|---|---|---|---|---|
| ☐ CF-TBH | Beech 3T | 6226 | 43-35671 | FP |

## K.D. AIR — Kay Dee (XC/KDC) — Port Alberni, BC (YPB)

| | | | | |
|---|---|---|---|---|
| ☐ C-GPCA | Piper PA-31 Turbo Navajo | 31-42 | ex N333DG | |
| ☐ C-GXEY | Piper PA-31-350 Navajo Chieftain | 31-7305044 | ex N74910 | |

## KEEWATIN AIR — (FK) — Churchill, MB/Rankin Inlet, NU (YYQ /YRT)

| | | | | |
|---|---|---|---|---|
| ☐ C-FCGT | Beech 200 Super King Air | BB-159 | ex N47FH | EMS |
| ☐ C-FRMV | Beech B200 Super King Air | BB-979 | ex N22TP | |
| ☐ C-FSKN | Beech B200 Super King Air | BB-1109 | ex F-GLLH | |
| ☐ C-FSKO | Beech B200 Super King Air | BB-1007 | ex N514MA | EMS |
| ☐ C-FZPW | Beech B200 Super King Air | BB-940 | ex N519SA | EMS |
| ☐ C-GYGT | Beech B200 Super King Air | BB-1323 | | ♦ |
| | | | | |
| ☐ C-FJXL | Beech 1900C-1 | UC-102 | ex N15479 | ♦ |
| ☐ C-FJXO | Beech 1900C | UC-124 | ex N124CU | |
| ☐ C-FZPQ | de Havilland DHC-6 Twin Otter 300 | 782 | ex | ♦ |
| ☐ C-GFLA | Pilatus PC-12/45 | 293 | | ♦ |

## KELOWNA FLIGHTCRAFT AIR CHARTER *Flightcraft (KW/KFA)*      Kelowna, BC (YLW)

| | | | | | | |
|---|---|---|---|---|---|---|
| ☐ C-GGKF | Boeing 727-223F (FedEx 3) | 21523/1467 | ex C-FMKF | 718 | Op for Purolator Courier | |
| ☐ C-GIKF | Boeing 727-227F (FedEx 3) | 20772/982 | ex N99763 | 721 | Op for Purolator Courier | |
| ☐ C-GJKF | Boeing 727-227F (FedEx 3) | 21042/1106 | ex N10756 | 722 | Op for Purolator Courier | |
| ☐ C-GKFJ | Boeing 727-281F (Raisbeck 3) | 21455/1316 | ex C-FLHJ | 715 | Op for Purolator Courier | |
| ☐ C-GKKF | Boeing 727-227F (FedEx 3) | 21043/1113 | ex N16758 | 723 | Op for Purolator Courier | |
| ☐ C-GLKF | Boeing 727-227F (FedEx 3) | 21118/1167 | ex N14760 | 724 | Op for Purolator Courier | |
| ☐ C-GMKF | Boeing 727-227F (FedEx 3) | 21119/1175 | ex N16761 | 725 | Op for Purolator Courier | |
| ☐ C-GNKF | Boeing 727-227F (FedEx 3) | 20839/1031 | ex N88770 | 726 | Op for Purolator Courier | |
| ☐ C-GQKF | Boeing 727-243F (FedEx 3) | 21265/1226 | ex N17402 | 720 | Op for Purolator Courier | |
| ☐ C-GTKF | Boeing 727-225F (FedEx 3) | 21580/1435 | ex N8883Z | 728 | Op for Purolator Courier | |
| ☐ C-GWKF | Boeing 727-243F/W (Duganair 3) | 21270/1231 | ex N17407 | 719 | Op for Purolator Courier | |
| ☐ C-GXKF | Boeing 727-243F/W (Duganair 3) | 21663/1438 | ex N17410 | 716 | Op for Purolator Courier | |
| | | | | | | |
| ☐ C-FIWM | Convair 580 | 128 | ex XA-FOU | | | ♦ |
| ☐ C-FKFS | Convair 580F | 279 | | | | |
| ☐ C-FKFZ | Convair 580F | 151 | ex N11151 | 510 | | |
| ☐ C-GKFF | Convair 580F | 160 | ex N9067R | 511 | Op for Purolator Courier | |
| ☐ C-GKFG | Convair 580F | 22 | ex N32KA | 516 | [YLW] | |
| ☐ C-GKFS | Convair 5800 | 279 | ex N5824N | | | ♦ |
| ☐ C-GKFU | Convair 580F | 82 | ex N90857 | 501 | Op for Purolator Courier | |
| ☐ C-GKFY | Convair 580F | 91 | | | | ♦ |
| ☐ C-GLWF | Convair 580 | | ex C-FNCL | | | ♦ |
| ☐ C-GNDK | Convair 580 | 117 | ex C-GNCM | | | ♦ |
| ☐ N538JA | Convair 580F | 38 | ex N73120 | | [YLW]♦ | |
| ☐ N569JA | Convair 580F | 58 | ex N73132 | | [YLW]♦ | |
| | | | | | | |
| ☐ C-FDAX | IAI 1125 Astra | 058 | ex N1125E | | | |
| ☐ C-FLEJ | Boeing 737-4B3 | 24751/2107 | ex CN-RPB | | >FLE♦ | |
| ☐ C-FLER | Boeing 737-46B | 24573/1844 | ex N41XA | | >FLE♦ | |
| ☐ C-GKFA | Douglas DC-10-30F | 46921/214 | ex N811SL | 101 | | |
| ☐ C-GKFB | Douglas DC-10-30F | 46949/179 | ex N949PL | 102 | [YHM] | |
| ☐ C-GKFD | Douglas DC-10-30F | 47928/192 | ex N304WL | 103 | | |
| ☐ C-GJRH | Cessna 340 | 340-0058 | ex N340BD | | | |
| ☐ C-GKFX | Beech A60 Duke | P-235 | ex N60GF | | | |
| ☐ C- | Douglas DC-10-30F | 46917/211 | ex N303WL | | [YHM] | |

## KENN BOREK AIR      *Borek Air (4K/KBA)*
### Calgary-Intl, AB/Edmonton-Intl, AB/ Iqaluit, NT/Resolute Bay, NT (YYC/YEG/YFB/YRB)

| | | | | | | |
|---|---|---|---|---|---|---|
| ☐ C-FMKB | Basler BT-67 | 47/19560 | ex N57NA | Frtr; dam Dec07 | | |
| ☐ C-GAWI | Basler BT-67 | 50/19227 | ex N79017 | Lidia | >Alfred Wegener Institute | |
| ☐ C-GEAI | Basler BT-67 | 1-16305/33053 | ex N200AN | | | |
| ☐ C-GEAJ | Basler B7-67 | 35/14615/26120 | ex N40386 | | | ♦ |
| ☐ C-GHGF | Basler BT-67 | 14519/25964 | ex N9923S | | | ♦ |
| ☐ C-GJKB | Basler BT-67 | 28/13383 | ex N167BT | | | |
| ☐ C-GVKB | Basler BT-67 | 54/12300 | ex N907Z | | | |
| | | | | | | |
| ☐ C-FMWM | Beech A100 King Air | B-59 | ex N702JL | | | |
| ☐ C-FRKB | Beech 100 King Air | B-72 | ex C-GTLF | | | |
| ☐ C-GKBQ | Beech 100 King Air | B-62 | ex LN-NLB | | | |
| ☐ C-GKBZ | Beech 100 King Air | B-85 | ex LN-PAJ | | | |
| ☐ C-GWWA | Beech 100 King Air | B-27 | ex G-BOFN | | | |
| | | | | | | |
| ☐ C-FAKB | de Havilland DHC-6 Twin Otter 300 | 533 | ex N533SW | | | ♦ |
| ☐ C-FASG | de Havilland DHC-6 Twin Otter 300 | 373 | ex CF-ASG | | | ♦ |
| ☐ C-FBBV | de Havilland DHC-6 Twin Otter 300 | 311 | ex C-FMPC | | | |
| ☐ C-FBBW | de Havilland DHC-6 Twin Otter 300 | 588 | ex 8Q-KBA | | | |
| ☐ C-FBKB | de Havilland DHC-6 Twin Otter 310 | 611 | ex 8Q-MAQ | FP♦ | | |
| ☐ C-FDHB | de Havilland DHC-6 Twin Otter 300 | 338 | ex CF-DHB | | | |
| ☐ C-FHKB | de Havilland DHC-6 Twin Otter 300 | 402 | ex N204SA | | | |
| ☐ C-GBPE | de Havilland DHC-6 Twin Otter 100 | 21 | ex 8Q-QHC | | | |
| ☐ C-GCKB | de Havilland DHC-6 Twin Otter 300 | 312 | ex C-FMPF | | | |
| ☐ C-GDHC | de Havilland DHC-6 Twin Otter 300 | 494 | | | | |
| ☐ C-GIKB | de Havilland DHC-6 Twin Otter 100 | 64 | ex 8Q-CSL | | [YYC] | |
| ☐ C-GKBC | de Havilland DHC-6 Twin Otter 300 | 650 | ex N55921 | | | |
| ☐ C-GKBG | de Havilland DHC-6 Twin Otter 300 | 733 | | | | |
| ☐ C-GKBH | de Havilland DHC-6 Twin Otter 300 | 732 | ex 8Q-MAV | | | |
| ☐ C-GKBO | de Havilland DHC-6 Twin Otter 300 | 725 | ex HP-1273APP | | | |
| ☐ C-GKBR | de Havilland DHC-6 Twin Otter 300 | 617 | ex 8Q-MAU | | | |
| ☐ C-GKCS | de Havilland DHC-6 Twin Otter 300 | 693 | ex 8Q-MAA | | | ♦ |
| ☐ C-GKBV | de Havilland DHC-6 Twin Otter 300 | 287 | ex 8Q-MAB | | [YYC]♦ | |
| ☐ C-GLKB | de Havilland DHC-6 Twin Otter 300 | 321 | ex 8Q-MAL | | | ♦ |
| ☐ C-GOKB | de Havilland DHC-6 Twin Otter 300 | 339 | ex 8Q-MAM | | | ♦ |
| ☐ C-GOPQ | de Havilland DHC-6 Twin Otter 300 | 464 | ex 8Q-MAE | | | ♦ |
| ☐ C-GQBE | de Havilland DHC-6 Twin Otter 300 | 693 | ex 8Q-MAA | | | ♦ |
| ☐ C-GTKB | de Havilland DHC-6 Twin Otter 100 | 60 | ex 8Q-MAC | | | |
| ☐ C-GXXB | de Havilland DHC-6 Twin Otter 300 | 426 | ex 8Q-MAN | | | |
| | | | | | | |
| ☐ C-FLKB | Embraer EMB.110P1 Bandeirante | 110397 | ex N903LE | | | |

| | | | | |
|---|---|---|---|---|
| ☐ C-FBCN | Beech 200 Super King Air | BB-7 | | |
| ☐ C-FEKB | Beech 200 Super King Air | BB-468 | ex N9UT | Beech 1300 conversion |
| ☐ C-GANR | Embraer EMB.110P1 Bandeirante | 110373 | ex HP-931APP | wfs |
| ☐ C-GBBR | Embraer EMB.110P1 Bandeirante | 110444 | ex HP-1177AP | wfs |
| ☐ C-GFKB | Embraer EMB.110P1 Bandeirante | 110400 | ex 9N-AFF | wfs |
| ☐ C-GKBA | Beech B99 | U-164 | ex SE-GRB | |
| ☐ C-GKBB | Beech 65-C90 King Air | LJ-607 | ex N48DA | |
| ☐ C-GKBN | Beech 200 Super King Air | BB-404 | ex N315MS | |
| ☐ C-GKBP | Beech 200 Super King Air | BB-505 | ex HP-1083P | |
| ☐ C-GKKB | Beech B99 | U-149 | ex HP-1230APP | w/o hangar fire 04Nov10?♦ |

## KENORA AIR SERVICE                                        Kenora SPB, ON (YQK)

| | | | | |
|---|---|---|---|---|
| ☐ CF-CBA | de Havilland DHC-3 Otter | 230 | ex C-FCBA | FP |
| ☐ CF-JEI | de Havilland DHC-2 Beaver | 1020 | | FP |
| ☐ C-FNOT | de Havilland DHC-2 Beaver | 1067 | ex N4193A | FP |
| ☐ CF-TBX | Beech D18S | A-479 | ex N841B | FP |
| ☐ C-FWDB | Cessna A185E Skywagon | 185-1250 | ex (N4783Q) | FP |
| ☐ C-FWMM | Cessna A185F Skywagon | 18502238 | ex N4361Q | FP |
| ☐ C-GAQJ | de Havilland DHC-2 Beaver | 1130 | ex 56-4411 | FP |
| ☐ C-GEHX | Beech 3NM | CA-112 | ex CF-ZNF | FP |
| ☐ C-GOTD | Cessna A185F Skywagon | 18502445 | ex (N1724R) | FP |
| ☐ C-GPVC | de Havilland DHC-2 Beaver | 290 | ex N9257Z | FP |
| ☐ C-GYJY | Cessna A185F Skywagon | 18502468 | ex N1748R | FP |
| ☐ C-GYXY | Cessna A185F Skywagon | 18503370 | | FP♦ |

## KEYSTONE AIR SERVICE          Keystone (BZ/KEE)          Swan River, MB (YSE)

| | | | | |
|---|---|---|---|---|
| ☐ C-FAFT | Beech 200 Super King Air | BB-57 | ex N121DA | |
| ☐ C-FPCD | Beech B99 | U-151 | ex C-FBRO | |
| ☐ C-FSPN | Beech 200 Super King Air | BB-745 | ex N428P | |
| ☐ C-FXLO | Piper PA-31-350 Chieftain | 31-8052022 | ex N3547N | |
| ☐ C-GBDN | Piper PA-31-350 Navajo Chieftain | 31-7652035 | ex N59763 | |
| ☐ C-GCJH | Piper PA-31-350 Chieftain | 31-7952109 | ex N42FL | |
| ☐ C-GFOL | Beech 200 Super King Air | BB-27 | ex N120DP | |
| ☐ C-GGQU | Piper PA-31 Turbo Navajo | 31-155 | ex N9116Y | |
| ☐ C-GNHM | Beech 200 Super King Air | BB-188 | | ♦ |
| ☐ C-GOSU | Piper PA-31-350 Navajo Chieftain | 31-7752148 | ex N27327 | |

## KISSISSING AIR / KISSISSING LAKE LODGE          Kississing Lake/Pine Falls, MB

| | | | | |
|---|---|---|---|---|
| ☐ C-FENB | Noorduyn UC-64A Norseman | 324 | ex 43-5384 | FP |
| ☐ C-FIKP | de Havilland DHC-2 Beaver | 890 | ex CF-IKP | FP |
| ☐ C-FKIX | Cessna 185A Skywagon | 18503794 | ex N9866Q | FP |
| ☐ C-FOBR | Noorduyn Norseman V | N29-35 | ex CF-OBR | FP |
| ☐ C-FRHW | de havilland DHC-3 Turbo Otter | 455 | | FP♦ |
| ☐ C-FVQD | de Havilland DHC-3 Turbo Otter | 466 | ex CF-VQD | FP♦ |
| ☐ C-FVQD | de Havilland DHC-3 Turbo Otter | 466 | EX cc-vqd | |
| ☐ C-FYMV | de Havilland DHC-2 Beaver | 1589 | ex CF-YMV | FP |
| ☐ C-GADE | de Havilland DHC-2 Beaver | 730 | ex 53-7919 | FP |
| ☐ C-GDLO | Cessna TU206B Super Skywagon | U206-0690 | ex N4990F | FP |
| ☐ C-GMGV | de Havilland DHC-2 Beaver | 432 | ex N62278 | PF♦ |

## KIVALLIQ AIR          Kivalliq(FK)   Winnipeg-Intl, MB/Rankin Inlet, NU (YWG/YRT)

| | | | | |
|---|---|---|---|---|
| ☐ C-FJXL | Beech 1900C | UC-102 | ex N15479 | |

## KLUANE AIRWAYS                                        Whitehorse, YT (YXY)

| | | | | |
|---|---|---|---|---|
| ☐ C-FMPS | de Havilland DHC-2 Beaver | 1114 | ex CF-MPS | FP |

## L AND A AVIATION                                        Hay River, NT (YHY)

| | | | | |
|---|---|---|---|---|
| ☐ CF-ZEB | Cessna 337F Super Skymaster | 33701428 | ex N1828M | |
| ☐ C-GHYT | Beech A100 King Air | B-98 | ex N998RC | |

## LABRADOR AIR SAFARI                                        Baie Comeau, QC (YBC)

| | | | | |
|---|---|---|---|---|
| ☐ C-FPQC | de Havilland DHC-2 Beaver | 873 | ex CF-IKQ | FP/WS |
| ☐ C-GIZF | de Havilland DHC-6 Twin Otter 300 | 549 | ex N61UT | FP/WS♦ |

## LAC LA CROIX QUETICO AIR SERVICE          Lac la Croix, ON/Crane Lake, MB

| | | | | |
|---|---|---|---|---|
| ☐ C-FHAN | de Havilland DHC-2 Beaver | 316 | ex N11255 | FP |
| ☐ C-FVSF | Cessna A185E Skywagon | 185-1223 | ex CF-VSF | FP |
| ☐ C-GDZD | de Havilland DHC-2 Beaver | 496 | ex 52-6116 | FP |
| ☐ C-GUEC | Cessna A185F Skywagon | 18503986 | ex N5513E | FP |

## LAC SEUL AIRWAYS
Ear Falls, ON (YMY)

| | | | | |
|---|---|---|---|---|
| ☐ CF-HXY | de Havilland DHC-3 Otter | 67 | | FP |
| ☐ C-GLLO | Cessna U206F Stationair II | U20602913 | ex N1602Q | FP |

## LAKELAND AIRWAYS
Temagami, ON

| | | | |
|---|---|---|---|
| ☐ C-FJKT | de Havilland DHC-2 Beaver | 1023 | ex CF-JKT |
| ☐ C-GUFH | Cessna A185F Skywagon | 18502857 | ex (N1488F) |

## LAKELSE AIR
Terrace, BC (YXT)

| | | | | |
|---|---|---|---|---|
| ☐ C-FHQT | Bell 204B | 2024 | ex C-GEAV | |
| ☐ C-FMGM | Kaman K-1200 K-MAX | A94-0013 | ex N163KA | |
| ☐ C-FNBR | Aérospatiale AS350B2 AStar | 2565 | ex N60618 | |
| ☐ C-FXPM | Aérospatiale AS350BA AStar | 1428 | ex C-FBHX | ♦ |
| ☐ C-GALU | Bell 206B JetRanger III | 2511 | ex N50071 | |
| ☐ C-GBCN | Aérospatiale AS350B2 AStar | 2609 | ex F-GLHP | |
| ☐ C-GHQW | Bell 206B JetRanger III | 1708 | | |
| ☐ C-GHWO | Bell 206L LongRanger | 45013 | ex N3GH | |
| ☐ C-GMNI | Aérospatiale AS350B2 AStar | 2986 | | ♦ |
| ☐ C-GPTC | Aérospatiale AS350B2 AStar | 2092 | ex OY-HDY | |
| ☐ C-GWHO | Bell 206L LongRanger | 45013 | ex N3GH | |

## LAKES DISTRICT AIR SERVICES
Burns Lake, BC (YPZ)

| | | | | |
|---|---|---|---|---|
| ☐ C-FBPB | de Havilland DHC-2 Beaver | 1434 | ex VH-IDF | FP/WS♦ |
| ☐ C-FFHS | de Havilland DHC-2 Beaver | 51 | ex CF-HHS | FP/WS |
| ☐ C-FVXQ | Cessna A185E Skywagon | 185-1198 | ex CF-XVQ | FP/WS |

## LAUZON AVIATION
Elliot Lake, ON (YEL)

| | | | | |
|---|---|---|---|---|
| ☐ C-FRUY | de Havilland DHC-2 Beaver | 687 | ex N74157 | FP |
| ☐ C-FSDY | de Havilland DHC-2 Beaver | 897 | | FP♦ |
| ☐ C-FUET | Cessna 180H | 18051673 | | FP♦ |

## LEUENBERGER AIR SERVICE
Nakina SPB, ON (YQN)

| | | | | | |
|---|---|---|---|---|---|
| ☐ C-FSOX | de Havilland DHC-3 Turbo Otter | 437 | ex CF-SOX | FP | |
| ☐ C-GLCW | de Havilland DHC-3 Turbo Otter | 172 | ex 55-3310 | | FP |
| ☐ C-GYLX | Cessna A185F Skywagon | 18503354 | | | FP♦ |

## LITTLE RED AIR SERVICE
Little Red (LRA)
Fort Vermilion, AB

| | | | | |
|---|---|---|---|---|
| ☐ C-FGWR | Beech B200 Super King Air | BB-1599 | ex C-FGWD | |
| ☐ C-FLRD | Beech A100 King Air | B-243 | ex PT-OFZ | |
| ☐ C-FPQQ | Beech B200 Super King Air | BB-1304 | ex N3173K | |
| ☐ C-GGUH | Cessna 208B Caravan I | 208B0827 | ex N51478 | |
| ☐ C-GHJF | Beech B200 Super King Air | BB-1493 | | ♦ |
| ☐ C-GICJ | Cessna U206F Stationair | U20603044 | ex N4318Q | |
| ☐ C-GWVT | Cessna U206F Stationair | U20602918 | ex (N1721Q) | |

## MANITOBA GOVERNMENT AIR SERVICES
Winnipeg-Intl/Thompson, MB (YWG/YTH)

| | | | | | |
|---|---|---|---|---|---|
| ☐ C-FTUV | Canadair CL215 | 1020 | ex CF-TUV | 256 | |
| ☐ C-FTXI | Canadair CL215 | 1016 | ex CF-TXI | 255 | |
| ☐ C-GBOW | Canadair CL215 | 1087 | ex C-GKDY | 253 | |
| ☐ C-GMAF | Canadair CL215 | 1044 | ex C-GUMW | 250 | |
| ☐ C-GMAK | Canadair CL215 | 1107 | | 254 | |
| ☐ C-GUMW | Canadair CL215 | 1065 | | 251 | |
| ☐ C-GYJB | Canadair CL215 | 1068 | | 252 | |
| | | | | | |
| ☐ C-FWAH | de Havilland DHC-6 Twin Otter 300 | 240 | ex CF-WAH | | |
| ☐ C-GBNE | Cessna 560 Citation V | 560-0244 | ex N701NB | | ♦ |
| ☐ C-GBNX | Cessna 560 Citation V | 0074 | ex N593MD | | EMS |
| ☐ C-GDAT | Cessna 310R | 310R1883 | ex N315U | | |
| ☐ C-GMFW | Canadair CL415 | 2082 | | | ♦ |
| ☐ C-GMFX | Canadair CL415 | 2083 | | | ♦ |
| ☐ C-GMFY | Canadair CL415 | 2078 | | | ♦ |
| ☐ C-GMLN | Cessna 310R | 310R1884 | ex N316U | | |
| ☐ C-GRNE | Piper PA-31-350 Chieftain | 31-7952224 | ex N91834 | | |
| ☐ C-GYNE | Cessna 310R | 310R1367 | ex N4086C | | |

## MARITIME AIR CHARTER
Halifax, NS (YHZ)

| | | | | |
|---|---|---|---|---|
| ☐ C-FCAI | Piper PA-31 Turbo Navajo | 31-475 | ex N22DC | |
| ☐ C-FDOR | Beech A100 King Air | B-103 | ex CF-DOR | |
| ☐ C-FYKQ | Piper PA-31 Turbo Navajo | 31-399 | ex CF-YKQ | |
| ☐ C-GILS | Britten-Norman BN-2A-21 Islander | 0416 | ex N92JA | |
| ☐ C-GUND | Beech 200 Super King Air | BB-139 | ex N810JB | ♦ |
| ☐ C-GXUG | Piper PA-31 Turbo Navajo | 31-665 | ex N1GY | |

## MARTINI AVIATION — Fort Langley, BC

| | | | | |
|---|---|---|---|---|
| ☐ C-GMLZ | Agusta A109C | 7655 | | ♦ |
| ☐ C-GPLT | Pilatus PC-12/45 | 566 | ex HB-FPX | |
| ☐ C-GTMW | de Havilland DHC-3 Otter | 427 | ex C-FODX | ♦ |
| ☐ C-GUWF | de Havilland DHC-2 Beaver | 287 | ex N91364 | |

## MAX AVIATION — Max Aviation (MAX) — Montreal-St Hubert, QC (YHU)

| | | | | |
|---|---|---|---|---|
| ☐ C-FJDQ | Beech B100 King Air | BE-16 | | ♦ |
| ☐ C-FOGP | Beech B100 King Air | BE-134 | ex N363EA | |
| ☐ C-FSIK | Beech B100 King Air | BE-39 | | ♦ |
| ☐ C-GCVS | Beech B200C Super King Air | BL-13 | | ♦ |
| ☐ C-GMNL | Beech B100 King Air | BE-48 | ex N2830S | ♦ |
| ☐ C-GPJL | Beech B100 King Air | BE-107 | ex N3699B | |
| ☐ C-GPRU | Beech B100 King Air | BE-26 | ex N36WH | |
| ☐ C-GSWG | Beech B100 King Air | BE-131 | ex N6354H | |
| ☐ C-GVIK | Beech A100 King Air | BE-7 | ex N57HT | |

## McMURRAY AVIATION — Fort McMurray, AB (YMM)

| | | | | |
|---|---|---|---|---|
| ☐ C-FKEY | Cessna 208 Caravan I | 20800307 | ex N526KA | ♦ |
| ☐ C-GHLI | Cessna 208B Caravan I | 208B0565 | ex N5858J | |
| ☐ C-GKOM | Cessna 208 Caravan I | 20800365 | ex N675TF | |
| ☐ C-GWKO | Cessna 208B Caravan I | 208B1245 | ex N52591 | |
| ☐ C-GWRK | Cessna 208B Caravan I | 208B1229 | ex N208LC | ♦ |
| | | | | |
| ☐ C-GHGT | Cessna U206G Stationair | U20605874 | | |
| ☐ C-GHJB | Cessna U206E Stationair | U20601677 | ex N9477G | |
| ☐ C-GRKO | Cessna U206G Stationair | U20606617 | ex N9707Z | |
| ☐ C-GZZD | Cessna U206F Stationair | U20601957 | ex N50946 | |

## MELAIRE — Fort Frances, ON (YAG)

| | | | | |
|---|---|---|---|---|
| ☐ C-FOMJ | de Havilland DHC-2 Turbo Beaver | 1683/TB51 | ex CF-OMJ | FP/WS |

## MINIPI AVIATION — Goose Bay, NL (YYR)

| | | | | |
|---|---|---|---|---|
| ☐ C-FCOO | de Havilland DHC-2 Beaver | 314 | ex N377JW | FP |

## MISSINIPPI AIRWAYS / BEAVER AIR SERVICES — The Pas, MB/Pukatawagan. MB (YQD/XPK)

| | | | | |
|---|---|---|---|---|
| ☐ C-FJKM | Piper PA-31-350 Chieftain | 31-7952089 | ex N764A | |
| ☐ C-GADW | Piper PA-31-350 Navajo Chieftain | 31-7752078 | ex N27191 | |
| ☐ C-GHQF | Piper PA-31-350 Chieftain | 31-8052050 | ex N633WA | |
| ☐ C-GMKO | Piper PA-31-350 Chieftain | 31-7952063 | ex N932LA | |
| ☐ C-GWHW | Piper PA-31-350 Chieftain | 31-8052060 | ex N223CH | |
| ☐ C-GYQD | Piper PA-31-350 Chieftain | 31-8152039 | ex N4075T | |
| | | | | |
| ☐ C-FTYO | Beech 200 Super King Air | BB-1222 | ex N126KA | |
| ☐ C-FWXI | Beech 200 Super King Air | BB-1224 | ex C-GTLA | EMS |
| ☐ C-GGGT | Cessna TU206G Stationair | U20604170 | ex N756LF | |
| ☐ C-GKHI | Beech B200 Super King Air | BB-1265 | | ♦ |
| ☐ C-GOCN | Cessna 208B Caravan I | 208B0780 | ex N308KC | |
| ☐ C-GOGT | Beech B200 Super King Air | BB-535 | | |
| Ops suspended Oct11 | | | | |

## MOLSON AIR — Wabowden, MB

| | | | | |
|---|---|---|---|---|
| ☐ C-FBQY | de Havilland DHC-2 Beaver | 1496 | ex N147Q | FP/WS |
| ☐ C-GYBQ | Cessna A185F Skywagon | 18503568 | ex N4014Q | FP/WS |

## MORNINGSTAR AIR EXPRESS — Morningstar (MAL) — Edmonton-Intl, AB (YEG)

| | | | | | |
|---|---|---|---|---|---|
| ☐ C-FEXB | Cessna 208B Caravan I | 208B0539 | ex N758FX | | Lsd fr/op for FDX |
| ☐ C-FEXE | Cessna 208B Caravan I | 208B0244 | ex N750FE | | Lsd fr/op for FDX |
| ☐ C-FEXF | Cessna 208B Caravan I | 208B0508 | ex N749FX | | Lsd fr/op for FDX |
| ☐ C-FEXO | Cessna 208B Caravan I | 208B0535 | ex N757FX | | Lsd fr/op for FDX♦ |
| ☐ C-FEXV | Cessna 208B Caravan I | 208B0482 | ex N738FX | | Lsd fr/op for FDX |
| ☐ C-FEXX | Cessna 208B Caravan I | 208B0209 | ex (N877FE) | | Lsd fr/op for FDX |
| ☐ C-FEXY | Cessna 208B Caravan I | 208B0226 | ex N896FE | | Lsd fr/op for FDX |
| | | | | | |
| ☐ C-FMAI | Boeing 757-2B7SF | 27199/586 | ex N908FD | | Lsd fr/op for FDX |
| ☐ C-FMEP | Boeing 757-2B7SF | 27144/544 | ex N904FD | | Lsd fr/op for FDX |
| ☐ C-FMES | Boeing 727-225F (FedEx 3) | 22548/1734 | ex N461FE | Carolina | Lsd fr/op for FDX |
| ☐ C-FMEY | Boeing 727-247F (FedEx 3) | 21328/1251 | ex N234FE | | Lsd fr/op for FDX |
| ☐ C-FMFG | Boeing 757-2B7 | 27198/584 | ex N904FD | | Lsd fr/op for FDX |
| ☐ C-GATK | ATR 42-310F | 0135 | ex N923FX | | Lsd fr/op for FDX |

## MUSTANG HELICOPTERS — Red Deer, AB (YQF)

| Reg | Type | Serial | Ex | |
|---|---|---|---|---|
| ☐ C-FAOV | Aérospatiale AS350B2 AStar | 9066 | | |
| ☐ C-FAOX | Aérospatiale AS350B2 AStar | 9067 | | |
| ☐ C-FAOZ | Aérospatiale AS350B2 AStar | 9068 | ex N68CQ | |
| ☐ C-FHVV | Aérospatiale AS350BA AStar | 1225 | | |
| ☐ C-FIFL | Aérospatiale AS350BA AStar | 1453 | | ♦ |
| ☐ C-FJYL | Aérospatiale AS350BA AStar | 2959 | | ♦ |
| ☐ C-FLIZ | Aérospatiale AS350A AStar | 2484 | | ♦ |
| ☐ C-FLOD | Aérospatiale AS350A AStar | 2739 | | |
| ☐ C-FMGB | Aérospatiale AS350BA+ AStar | 1292 | ex N350SS | ♦ |
| ☐ C-FMHI | Aérospatiale AS350B2 AStar | 9037 | ex EI-MYO | ♦ |
| ☐ C-FMNE | Aérospatiale AS350B2 AStar | 9082 | | |
| ☐ C-FMOZ | Aérospatiale AS350BA AStar | 1374 | ex F-GHFR | ♦ |
| ☐ C-FNWE | Aérospatiale AS350B2 AStar | 9086 | | |
| ☐ C-FNYE | Aérospatiale AS350B2 AStar | 9091 | | |
| ☐ C-FNYF | Aérospatiale AS350B2 AStar | 9092 | | |
| ☐ C-FNYG | Aérospatiale AS350B2 AStar | 9093 | | ♦ |
| ☐ C-FNYK | Aérospatiale AS350B2 AStar | 9088 | | |
| ☐ C-FONZ | Aérospatiale AS350BA AStar | 1400 | ex HR-ANU | ♦ |
| ☐ C-FPHK | Aérospatiale AS350B3 AStar | 4635 | ex CC-AEF | ♦ |
| ☐ C-FPHY | Aérospatiale AS350A AStar | 1496 | | ♦ |
| ☐ C-FZXY | Aérospatiale AS350BA AStar | 2082 | ex N6102E | ♦ |
| ☐ C-GAKF | Aérospatiale AS350B3 AStar | 4995 | | ♦ |
| ☐ C-GAKZ | Aérospatiale AS350B3 AStar | 7130 | | ♦ |
| ☐ C-GAWV | Aérospatiale AS350B2 AStar | 2998 | | ♦ |
| ☐ C-GGHA | Aérospatiale AS350BA AStar | 2624 | ex F-GHYK | ♦ |
| ☐ C-GGIS | Aérospatiale AS350BA AStar | 1110 | ex N40445 | ♦ |
| ☐ C-GJHC | Aérospatiale AS350BA AStar | 3412 | | ♦ |
| ☐ C-GJPA | Aérospatiale AS350BA AStar | 1075 | ex C-FHAH | ♦ |
| ☐ C-GMAN | Aérospatiale AS350B2 AStar | 3073 | | ♦ |
| ☐ C-GMIM | Aérospatiale AS350B2 AStar | 1257 | | ♦ |
| ☐ C-GMQM | Aérospatiale AS350D AStar | 1380 | ex N108SH | ♦ |
| ☐ C-GMYG | Aérospatiale AS350D AStar | 1201 | ex N3604X | ♦ |
| ☐ C-GPHN | Aérospatiale AS350BA AStar | 1251 | | ♦ |
| ☐ C-GXTH | Aérospatiale AS350B2 AStar | 9049 | | ♦ |
| ☐ C-GXTO | Aérospatiale AS350B2 AStar | 9061 | ex N681CC | ♦ |
| ☐ C-GZGM | Aérospatiale AS350B2 AStar | 9056 | | ♦ |
| ☐ C-GZGN | Aérospatiale AS350B2 AStar | 9062 | ex N680CC | |
| ☐ C-FCNV | Bell 205A-1 | 30288 | | ♦ |
| ☐ C-FFHB | Bell 205A-1 | 30294 | ex VH-HHW | |
| ☐ C-FSMI | Bell 205A-1 | 30263 | ex (N205HT) | ♦ |
| ☐ C-GFHW | Bell 205A-1 | 30115 | | ♦ |
| ☐ C-GFRE | Bell 205A-1 | 30185 | ex EC-FYX | |
| ☐ C-GHUF | Bell 205A-1 | 30106 | ex N687CC | |
| ☐ C-GVHP | Bell 205A-1 | 30119 | ex N688CC | |
| ☐ C-GVHQ | Bell 205A-1 | 30110 | ex N689CC | ♦ |
| ☐ C-FGDT | Bell 206B JetRanger III | 2993 | | ♦ |
| ☐ C-GARE | Bell 206B JetRanger II | 1852 | | ♦ |
| ☐ C-GIVV | Bell 206B JetRanger III | 2823 | ex N2757C | |
| ☐ C-GOLT | Bell 206B JetRanger III | 3553 | | |
| ☐ C-FUMN | Piper PA-31 Navajo C | 31-8112076 | ex N4095F | |
| ☐ C-FXHA | Aérospatiale AS3552 Twin Star | 5426 | | ♦ |
| ☐ C-FXHE | Aéerospatiale AS3552 Twin Star | 5074 | | ♦ |
| ☐ C-FXKL | Aérospatiale AS355F2 Twin Star | 5148 | | ♦ |
| ☐ C-GFIT | Bell 214B-1 | 28040 | | ♦ |
| ☐ C-GHNQ | Bell 206L LongRanger | 45014 | ex N259MH | ♦ |
| ☐ C-GKHX | Bell 206L LongRanger | 46612 | | ♦ |
| ☐ C-GYHZ | Bell 206L LongRanger | 45126 | | ♦ |
| ☐ C-GZAS | Cessna 402B | 402B0626 | | ♦ |
| ☐ C-GZNF | Bell 212 | 30580 | | ♦ |

## NADEAU AIR SERVICE — Trois Rivières, QC

| Reg | Type | Serial | Ex | |
|---|---|---|---|---|
| ☐ C-GMNQ | Piper PA-31-350 Navajo Chieftain | 31-7405455 | ex N331MB | ♦ |

## NAKINA OUTPOST CAMPS AND AIR SERVICE (T2) — Nakina, ON (YQN)

| Reg | Type | Serial | Ex | Notes |
|---|---|---|---|---|
| ☐ C-FDGV | de Havilland DHC-6 Twin Otter 200 | 154 | ex TF-JMD | |
| ☐ CF-MIQ | de Havilland DHC-3 Turbo Otter | 336 | | FP/WS |
| ☐ C-FMPY | de Havilland DHC-3 Turbo Otter | 324 | ex CF-MPY | FP/WS |
| ☐ C-FNQB | Cessna 208 Caravan I | 20800387 | ex N5184N | |
| ☐ C-FTIN | Cessna A185F Skywagon | 18503362 | ex N7325H | FP/WS |
| ☐ C-FUYC | Cessna 208B Caravan I | 208B1204 | ex N208DD | |
| ☐ C-FZRJ | Cessna 208B Caravan I | 208B0597 | ex N52609 | |
| ☐ C-GEOW | Pilatus PC-12/45 | 244 | ex HB-FRO | |
| ☐ C-GKAY | Pilatus PC-12/45 | 178 | | ♦ |
| ☐ C-GMVB | Cessna 208B Caravan I | 208B0317 | | |
| ☐ C-GNQZ | Pilatus PC-12/47E | 1309 | ex N309NG | ♦ |

## NATIONAL HELICOPTERS                                        Toronto, ON

| | | | | |
|---|---|---|---|---|
| ☐ C-FFUJ | Bell 206B JetRanger III | 2982 | ex N525W | |
| ☐ C-FLYC | Bell 206L-1 LongRanger II | 45478 | ex XA-SPN | |
| ☐ C-FNHE | MBB Bo105S | S-349 | | ♦ |
| ☐ C-FNHG | Bell 206L-1 LongRanger II | 45784 | ex N220HC | |
| ☐ C-GFTE | Bell 206L-4 LongRanger IV | 52301 | | ♦ |
| ☐ C-GIGS | Bell 206B JetRanger | 1434 | ex N59474 | |
| ☐ C-GSZZ | Bell 206B JetRanger III | 2319 | ex XA-TCU | |

## NESTOR FALLS FLY-IN OUTPOSTS                          Nestor Falls SPB, ON

| | | | | |
|---|---|---|---|---|
| ☐ C-FMDB | de Havilland DHC-2 Beaver | 268 | ex N2104X | FP |
| ☐ C-FODK | de Havilland DHC-3 Otter | 13 | ex CF-ODK | FP |
| ☐ C-FSOR | de Havilland DHC-3 Otter | 239 | ex IM 1725 | FP |
| ☐ C-GDWB | Cessna U206G Stationair | U20604460 | ex N756YJ | FP |
| ☐ C-GYGL | Cessna A185F Skywagon | 18503298 | ex (N94269) | FP |

## NEWFOUNDLAND & LABRADOR AIR SERVICES               St John's, NL (YYT)

| | | | | | |
|---|---|---|---|---|---|
| ☐ C-FGFS | de Havilland DHC-2 Turbo Beaver | 1634/TB19 | ex CF-GFS | | ♦ |
| ☐ C-FIZU | Canadair CL415 | 2076 | ex C-GDMI | 286 | |
| ☐ C-FOFI | Canadair CL415 | 2081 | | 288♦ | |
| ☐ C-FNJC | Canadair CL415 | 2077 | | 287 | |
| ☐ C-FTXA | Canadair CL215 | 1006 | ex CF-TXA | 284 | |
| ☐ C-FYWP | Canadair CL215 | 1002 | ex CF-YWP | 285 | |
| ☐ C-GDKY | Canadair CL215 | 1096 | | 281 | |
| ☐ C-GLFY | Cessna 337G Super Skymaster | 33701700 | ex (N53557) | | |
| ☐ C-GMFY | Canadair CL415 | 2078 | | | |
| ☐ C-GNLA | Beech B300 Super King Air | FL-26 | ex N59TF | | |
| ☐ C-GNLF | Beech B300 Super King Air | FL-591 | | | ♦ |
| ☐ C-GNLO | Beech C300 Super King Air | FM-46 | ex N81454 | | ♦ |

## NOLINOR AVIATION                    Nolinor (NRL)        Montreal-Trudeau, QC (YUL)

| | | | | |
|---|---|---|---|---|
| ☐ C-FAWV | Convair 580F | 154 | ex C-FMGB | Frtr |
| ☐ C-FHNM | Convair 580F | 454 | ex N583P | >GV |
| ☐ C-FTAP | Convair 580 | 334 | ex N580N | |
| ☐ C-GKFP | Convair 580 | 446 | ex N589PL | poss w/o 13Aug11 |
| ☐ C-GQHB | Convair 580 | 376 | ex ZS-KRX | |
| ☐ C-GRLQ | Convair 580 | 347 | ex N580TA | |
| | | | | |
| ☐ C-GNLN | Boeing 737-2B6C (Nordam 3) | 23050/975 | ex CN-RMN | Frtr |
| ☐ C-GNRD | Boeing 737-229C (Nordam 3) | 21738/576 | ex XA-TWP | ♦ |
| ☐ C-GTUK | Boeing 737-2B6C (Nordam 3) | 23049/951 | ex CN-RMM | Frtr |

## NORDPLUS                                       Schefferville-Squaw Lake, QC (YKL)

| | | | | |
|---|---|---|---|---|
| ☐ C-FODG | de Havilland DHC-2 Beaver | 205 | | FP |
| ☐ C-GFUT | de Havilland DHC-3 Otter | 404 | ex CAF9422 | FP |

## NORTH CARIBOO AIR / FLYING SERVICE
##                          North Caribou (NCB)        Fort St John, BC (YXJ)

| | | | | |
|---|---|---|---|---|
| ☐ C-FMXY | Beech 100 King Air | B-40 | ex N923K | |
| ☐ C-FSKA | Beech A100 King Air | B-239 | ex N154TC | |
| ☐ C-GNCV | Beech 100 King Air | B-23 | ex N701RJ | |
| ☐ C-GPCB | Beech A100 King Air | B-45 | ex N704S | |
| ☐ C-GTLS | Beech 100 King Air | B-35 | ex N178WM | |
| | | | | |
| ☐ C-FCGC | Beech 200 Super King Air | BB-236 | ex N46KA | CatPass 200 conversion |
| ☐ C-FCGM | Beech 200 Super King Air | BB-217 | ex N200CD | CatPass 200 conversion |
| ☐ C-GDFN | Beech 200 Super King Air | BB-359 | ex N351MA | |
| ☐ C-GDFT | Beech 200 Super King Air | BB-354 | ex N221BG | |
| ☐ C-GZRX | Beech 200 Super King Air | BB-574 | ex N75WL | |
| | | | | |
| ☐ C-FCWP | de Havilland DHC-8-102 | 111 | ex N925CA | |
| ☐ C-FLSX | de Havilland DHC-8-102 | 285 | ex N834EX | |
| ☐ C-FNSA | de Havilland DHC-8-315 | 354 | ex ZS-NLZ | ♦ |
| ☐ C-FODL | de Havilland DHC-8-102 | 294 | ex N881CC | |
| ☐ C-GAQN | de Havilland DHC-8-311 | 548 | ex 5N-BHW | |
| ☐ C-GLWN | de Havilland DHC-8-311A | 311 | ex G-WOWC | ♦ |
| ☐ C-GNCF | de Havilland DHC-8-311A | 244 | ex PH-ABQ | |
| | | | | |
| ☐ C-FMCN | Beech 1900D | UE-20 | ex N220CJ | ♦ |
| ☐ C-FMKD | Beech 65-B90 King Air | LJ-376 | ex N300RV | |
| ☐ C-FMPC | de Havilland DHC-2 Turbo Beaver | 1300 | ex S2-ACE | ♦ |
| ☐ C-FNCL | Beech 1900D | UE-11 | ex C-FSKT | |
| ☐ C-FNCP | Beech 1900D | UE-58 | ex C-GSKY | |
| ☐ C-FNCT | Cessna 550 Citation II | 550-0155 | | ♦ |

| | | | | |
|---|---|---|---|---|
| ☐ CF-QSX | Cessna A185F Skywagon | 18502116 | ex (N70334) | |
| ☐ C-GCFM | Beech 65-C90 King Air | LJ-886 | ex N15SL | |
| ☐ C-GLAC | Beech 58 Baron | TH-339 | ex N6YC | |
| ☐ C-GMWO | Piper PA-31 Navajo C | 31-8112042 | ex N4086Y | |
| ☐ C-GRNT | British Aerospace 146-200 | E2140 | | ♦ |

## NORTH PACIFIC SEAPLANES  Prince Rupert, BC (YPR)

| | | | | |
|---|---|---|---|---|
| ☐ C-FIFQ | de Havilland DHC-2 Beaver | 825 | ex CF-IFQ | FP |
| ☐ C-FJOS | de Havilland DHC-2 Beaver | 1030 | ex CF-JOS | FP |
| ☐ C-FKDC | de Havilland DHC-2 Beaver | 1080 | ex CF-KDC | FP |
| ☐ C-FOCZ | de Havilland DHC-2 Beaver | 100 | ex N254BD | FP |

## NORTH STAR AIR  Pickle Lake, ON (YPL)

| | | | | |
|---|---|---|---|---|
| ☐ C-FIXS | Cessna 208B Caravan I | 208B1209 | | ♦ |
| ☐ C-FLNB | Cessna 208B Caravan I | 208B0799 | ex N799B | |
| ☐ C-FVPC | Pilatus PC-12/45 | 358 | ex N358PC | |
| ☐ C-GCQA | de Havilland DHC-3 Otter | 77 | ex N129JH | FP/WS |
| ☐ C-GHRK | Britten-Norman BN-2A-9 Islander | 333 | | ♦ |
| ☐ C-GJAS | Cessna 208 Caravan I | 20800322 | ex N51869 | FP/WS |

## NORTH-WRIGHT AIRWAYS  Northwright (HW/NWL)
Norman Wells/Good Hope/Deline, NT (YVQ/YGH/YWJ)

| | | | | |
|---|---|---|---|---|
| ☐ C-FBAX | Cessna 207 Skywagon | 20700355 | ex N1755U | |
| ☐ C-FKHD | Beech 99 | U-11 | ex F-BRUN | |
| ☐ C-FNWH | Beech 1900D | UE-112 | ex N112ZV | ♦ |
| ☐ C-FNWL | de Havilland DHC-6 Twin Otter 300 | 596 | ex N16NG | |
| ☐ C-FVCE | Beech 99A | U-118 | ex N918BB | FP |
| ☐ C-GAAP | Pilatus PC-6/B1-H2 Turbo Porter | 569 | ex N2851T | FP |
| ☐ C-GALF | Cessna 207A Stationair 8 II | 20700674 | ex N9118M | |
| ☐ C-GDBI | Cessna 207 Skywagon | 20700039 | ex N91052 | |
| ☐ C-GDLC | Cessna 208B Caravan I | 208B0767 | ex N5151D | |
| ☐ C-GFCV | Cessna U206C Super Skywagon | U206-1213 | ex N4345E | |
| ☐ C-GHDT | Helio 295 Super Courier | 1401 | ex N6327V | |
| ☐ C-GHXR | Cessna U206F Stationair | U20603064 | | FP♦ |
| ☐ C-GJGZ | Cessna A185F Skywagon II | 18503856 | ex (N4750E) | |
| ☐ C-GMOK | Cessna 207A Stationair 8 II | 20700673 | ex N6373D | |
| ☐ C-GNWA | Cessna A185F Skywagon II | 18503345 | ex C-GFJC | |
| ☐ C-GRDD | de Havilland DHC-6 Twin Otter 100 | 54 | ex N8081N | FP/WS |
| ☐ C-GZGO | Britten-Norman BN-2A-26 Islander | 2017 | ex N59360 | |
| ☐ C-GZIZ | Cessna 208B Caravan I | 208B0546 | ex N5262W | |
| ☐ C-GZVX | Cessna U206G Stationair 6 | U20604110 | ex (N756HT) | |

## NORTHERN AIR CHARTER  Peace River, AB (YPE)

| | | | | |
|---|---|---|---|---|
| ☐ C-GIRG | Cessna A185F Skywagon II | 18504181 | ex (N61424) | |
| ☐ C-GNAC | Piper PA-31 Navajo C | 31-7812106 | ex N27707 | |
| ☐ C-GNAG | Beech B200 Super King Air | BB-1239 | | ♦ |
| ☐ C-GNAJ | Beech A100 King Air | B-107 | ex LN-AAH | |
| ☐ C-GNAK | Beech B200 Super King Air | BB-1376 | ex HK-3990X | Catpass 200 conversion |
| ☐ C-GNAM | Beech B200 Super King Air | BB-1339 | ex N252AF | EMS, Beech 1300 conversion |
| ☐ C-GNAP | Piper PA-23-250 Aztec F | 27-8054002 | ex C-GTGS | |
| ☐ C-GNAR | Beech 1900D | UE-252 | ex JA017A | |
| ☐ C-GNAX | Beech B200 Super King Air | BB-1419 | ex N146SB | |

## NORTHERN AIR SOLUTIONS  Bracebridge, ON

| | | | | |
|---|---|---|---|---|
| ☐ C-GBJV | Pilatus PC-12/45 | 237 | | ♦ |
| ☐ C-GHGV | Pilatus PC-12/45 | 342 | ex N372GT | ♦ |

## NORTHERN THUNDERBIRD AIR  Prince George, BC (YXS)

See NT Air

## NORTHWARD AIR  Dawson Creek, BC (YDQ)

| | | | | |
|---|---|---|---|---|
| ☐ C-FOMF | Cessna A185A Skywagon | 185-0423 | ex (N1623Z) | |
| ☐ CF-SLV | Cessna U206 Super Skywagon | U206-0412 | ex N8012Z | |
| ☐ C-GGKB | Piper PA-23 Aztec 250 | 27-3694 | | ♦ |
| ☐ C-GLKM | Helio H-391B Courier | 034 | | FP♦ |

## NORTHWAY AVIATION  Northway (NAL)  St Andrews, MB

| | | | | |
|---|---|---|---|---|
| ☐ C-FHDL | Cessna 180 | 18030430 | ex N1730G | |
| ☐ C-GNWD | Cessna 208B Caravan I | 208B1188 | ex N471MC | ♦ |
| ☐ C-GNWG | Cessna 208 Caravan I | 20800412 | ex N52136 | |
| ☐ C-GNWI | Cessna 208 Caravan I | 20800391 | ex N85EE | ♦ |
| ☐ C-GNWV | Cessna 208B Caravan I | 208B1115 | ex N5093D | |

## NORTHWEST FLYING
**Nestor Falls SPB, ON**

| | | | | |
|---|---|---|---|---|
| ☐ CF-NKL | Beech C-45H | AF-378 | ex N9864Z | FP |
| ☐ C-GEBL | de Havilland DHC-2 Beaver | 1068 | ex N33466 | FP |
| ☐ C-GIUN | Cessna 180K | 18052803 | | FP♦ |
| ☐ C-GYYS | de Havilland DHC-3 Otter | 276 | ex N1UW | FP |

## NORTHWESTERN AIR
**Polaris (J3/PLR)**  **Fort Smith, NT (YSM)**

| | | | | | |
|---|---|---|---|---|---|
| ☐ C-FCPE | British Aerospace Jetstream 31 | 825 | ex G-31-825 | | |
| ☐ C-FNAE | British Aerospace Jetstream 31 | 881 | ex N431AM | | |
| ☐ C-FNAF | British Aerospace Jetstream 31 | 789 | ex N411UE | | |
| ☐ C-FNAM | British Aerospace Jetstream 31 | 767 | ex N767JX | | |
| ☐ C-FNAZ | British Aerospace Jetstream 32 | 843 | ex C-GEAZ | | |
| ☐ C-GNAQ | British Aerospace Jetstream 32EP | 837 | ex C-FZYB | | |
| ☐ C-FLLL | de Havilland DHC-3 Turbo Otter | 292 | | | ♦ |
| ☐ C-GAIX | Cessna A185F Skymaster | 18503890 | | | ♦ |
| ☐ C-GIJL | Cessna 210L Centurion | 21061226 | | | ♦ |
| ☐ C-GNAH | Beech 99 | U-107 | ex N207BH | | |
| ☐ C-GNAL | Beech 99 | U-57 | ex TF-ELD | | |
| ☐ C-GTOI | de Havilland DHC-2 Beaver | 712 | | | ♦ |
| ☐ C-GTPU | Cessna U206G Stationair | U20604749 | | | ♦ |
| ☐ C-GWQW | Cessna U206E Stationair | U20601573 | | | ♦ |

## NT AIR / NORTHERN THUNDERBIRD AIR
**Thunderbird (NTA)**  **Prince George/Smithers, BC (YXS/YYD)**

| | | | | | |
|---|---|---|---|---|---|
| ☐ C-FEYT | Beech A100 King Air | B-210 | ex N75GR | | |
| ☐ C-GCMT | Beech 1900C-1 | UC-120 | ex N15683 | | |
| ☐ C-GCMZ | Beech 1900C-1 | UC-61 | ex N1568L | 929 | |
| ☐ C-GBCE | Beech 300 Super King Air | FL-502 | | | ♦ |
| ☐ C-GDOX | Cessna 208B Caravan I | 208B0541 | ex N621BB | | |
| ☐ C-GEFA | Beech 1900C-1 | UC-94 | ex N80346 | 927 | |
| ☐ C-GJSU | Beech 100 King Air | B-88 | | | ♦ |
| ☐ C-GXRX | Beech 100 King Air | B-36 | | | ♦ |

## NUELTIN LAKE AIR SERVICE
**Nueltin Lake, MB**

| | | | | |
|---|---|---|---|---|
| ☐ C-FDCL | Cessna U206G Stationair | U20603542 | ex N8790Q | FP |
| ☐ C-FSAP | Noorduyn Norseman VI | 231 | ex 43-5240 | FP |

## OCEAN PACIFIC AIR SERVICES
**Prince Rupert, BC**

| | | | | |
|---|---|---|---|---|
| ☐ C-FTCW | de Havilland DHC-2 Beaver | 646 | ex VH-SMH | FP♦ |
| ☐ C-FWOP | Cessna 180 Skywagon | 18032463 | | FP♦ |
| ☐ C-FWZE | de Havilland DHC-2 Beaver | 1214 | | FP♦ |

## ONTARIO MINISTRY OF NATURAL RESOURCES AVIATION SERVICES
**Trillium (TRI)**  **Sault Ste Marie, ON (YAM)**

| | | | | | |
|---|---|---|---|---|---|
| ☐ C-GOGD | Canadair CL415 | 2028 | ex C-GAOI | 270 | |
| ☐ C-GOGE | Canadair CL415 | 2031 | ex C-GAUR | 271 | |
| ☐ C-GOGF | Canadair CL415 | 2032 | ex C-GBGE | 272 | |
| ☐ C-GOGG | Canadair CL415 | 2033 | ex C-GBFY | 273 | |
| ☐ C-GOGH | Canadair CL415 | 2034 | ex C-GCNO | 274 | |
| ☐ C-GOGW | Canadair CL415 | 2037 | ex C-GBPM | 275 | |
| ☐ C-GOGX | Canadair CL415 | 2038 | ex C-GBPU | 276 | |
| ☐ C-GOGY | Canadair CL415 | 2040 | | 277 | |
| ☐ C-GOGZ | Canadair CL415 | 2043 | | 278 | |
| ☐ C-FOEH | de Havilland DHC-2 Turbo Beaver | 1644/TB24 | ex CF-OEH | | FP/WS |
| ☐ C-FOER | de Havilland DHC-2 Turbo Beaver | 1671/TB41 | ex CF-OER | | FP/WS |
| ☐ C-FOEU | de Havilland DHC-2 Turbo Beaver | 1678/TB46 | ex CF-OEU | | FP/WS |
| ☐ C-FOEW | de Havilland DHC-2 Turbo Beaver | 1682/TB50 | ex CF-OEW | | FP/WS |
| ☐ C-FOPA | de Havilland DHC-2 Turbo Beaver | 1688/TB56 | ex CF-OPA | | FP/WS |
| ☐ C-FOPG | de Havilland DHC-6 Twin Otter 300 | 232 | ex CF-OPG | | FP/WS |
| ☐ C-FOPI | de Havilland DHC-6 Twin Otter 300 | 243 | ex CF-OPI | | FP/WS |
| ☐ C-FOPJ | de Havilland DHC-6 Twin Otter 300 | 344 | ex CF-OPJ | | FP/WS |
| ☐ C-GOGA | de Havilland DHC-6 Twin Otter 300 | 739 | | | FP/WS |
| ☐ C-GOGB | de Havilland DHC-6 Twin Otter 300 | 761 | | | FP/WS |
| ☐ C-GOGC | de Havilland DHC-6 Twin Otter 300 | 750 | | | FP/WS |
| ☐ C-FATR | Eurocopter EC130B4 | 3759 | | | |
| ☐ C-FMNR | Eurocopter EC130B4 | 4391 | | | |
| ☐ C-FONA | Eurocopter EC130B4 | 4945 | | | ♦ |
| ☐ C-FONC | Eurocopter EC130B4 | 4702 | | | ♦ |
| ☐ C-FONM | Eurocopter EC130B4 | 4566 | | | ♦ |
| ☐ C-GONB | Eurocopter EC130B4 | 4885 | | | ♦ |
| ☐ C-GONT | Eurocopter EC130B4 | 4423 | | | |

| | | | | | |
|---|---|---|---|---|---|
| ☐ C-FOPD | Pilatus PC12/45 | 1182 | | | ♦ |
| ☐ C-FOPP | Eurocopter EC135P2+ | 0948 | | | ♦ |
| ☐ C-FOPS | Eurocopter EC135P2+ | 0959 | | | ♦ |
| ☐ C-GOGL | Aérospatiale AS350B2 AStar | 2738 | | | |
| ☐ C-GOGS | Beech B300 Super King Air | FL-269 | ex N3169N | | |
| ☐ C-GOIC | Beech B300 Super King Air | FL-272 | ex N3172N | | |
| ☐ C-GOXY | Cessna T206H Stationair | T20608804 | | | ♦ |

## ORCA AIR                                                   Richmond, BC (YVR)

| | | | | | |
|---|---|---|---|---|---|
| ☐ C-FFFH | Piper PA-31-350 Navajo Chieftain | 31-7552130 | | | ♦ |
| ☐ C-FLRA | Piper PA-31-350 Navajo Chieftain | 31-7752091 | ex N52MS | | |
| ☐ C-FTUP | Piper PA-31-350 Navajo Chieftain | 31-7682101 | | | |
| ☐ C-GGQM | Piper PA-31-350 Navajo Chieftain | 31-7952033 | ex TF-EGU | | ♦ |
| ☐ C-GHXK | Piper PA-31-350 Navajo Chieftain | 31-7752108 | ex N115SC | | |
| ☐ C-GIKA | Piper PA-31-350 Chieftain | 31-7952161 | | | |
| ☐ C-GNAE | Piper PA-31-350 Chieftain | 31-7952157 | | | |
| ☐ C-GNAZ | Piper PA-31-350 Navajo Chieftain | 31-7752162 | | | |
| ☐ C-GPAK | Piper PA-31-350 Chieftain | 31-8052070 | ex N3558S | | |
| ☐ C-GPMP | Piper PA-31-350 Chieftain | 31-7852024 | ex C-GWTT | | |
| ☐ C-GPQP | Piper PA-31-350 Navajo | 31-7405143 | ex N31CS | | ♦ |
| ☐ C-GPWP | Piper PA-31-350 Chieftain | 31-7952090 | ex N35164 | | |
| ☐ C-GWXL | Piper PA-31-350 Chieftain | 31-7952036 | ex C-GLYG | | |
| ☐ C-GZBO | Piper PA-31-350 Chieftain | 31-8252048 | ex N430S | | |
| ☐ C-GYYK | Piper PA-31-350 Navajo Chieftain | 31-7752029 | | | ♦ |
| | | | | | |
| ☐ C-FAXD | Beech B200 Super King Air | BB-1827 | | | ♦ |
| ☐ C-FAXE | Beech 100 King Air | B-41 | | | ♦ |

## ORNGE AIR

| | | | | |
|---|---|---|---|---|
| ☐ C-GRXA | Pilatus PC-12/47E | 1083 | ex N983NG | EMS |
| ☐ C-GRXB | Pilatus PC-12/47E | 1094 | ex N994NG | EMS |
| ☐ C-GRXD | Pilatus PC-12/47E | 1106 | ex N106PC | EMS |
| ☐ C-GRXE | Pilatus PC-12/47E | 1117 | ex N117PZ | EMS |
| ☐ C-GRXH | Pilatus PC-12/47E | 1163 | ex N163NP | EMS |
| ☐ C-GRXM | Pilatus PC-12/47E | 1169 | ex N169NP | EMS |
| ☐ C-GRXN | Pilatus PC-12/47E | 1224 | ex N224NG | EMS |
| ☐ C-GRXO | Pilatus PC-12/47E | 1225 | ex N225NG | EMS |
| ☐ C-GRXP | Pilatus PC-12/47E | 1249 | ex N249NG | EMS |
| ☐ C-GRXR | Pilatus PC-12/47E | 1255 | ex N255NG | EMS |

## OSNABURGH AIRWAYS                                          Pickle Lake, ON (YPL)

| | | | | |
|---|---|---|---|---|
| ☐ C-FCZO | de Havilland DHC-3 Otter | 71 | ex CF-CZO | FP/WS |
| ☐ C-FFQX | Noorduyn Norseman VI | 625 | ex N51131 | FP/WS |
| ☐ C-GMAU | de Havilland DHC-2 Beaver | 1134 | ex N775E | FP/WS |

## OSPREY WINGS                                               La Ronge, SK (YVC)

| | | | | |
|---|---|---|---|---|
| ☐ C-FASZ | de Havilland DHC-3 Turbo Otter | 463 | ex IM672 | FP/WS |
| ☐ C-FBPK | Beech 1900D | UE-128 | ex N128EU | ♦ |
| ☐ CF-DIZ | de Havilland DHC-3 Turbo Otter | 460 | ex JW-9107 | FP/WS |
| ☐ C-FLXP | de Havilland DHC-6 Twin Otter 200 | 217 | ex N201EH | FP/WS |
| ☐ C-FTCT | de Havilland DHC-2 Beaver | 962 | ex FAP-0205 | FP/WS |
| ☐ C-FVEG | de Havilland DHC-6 Twin Otter 300 | 260 | ex OH-SLK | FP/WS |
| ☐ C-FXRI | de Havilland DHC-3 Turbo Otter | 258 | ex VH-SBT | FP/WS |
| ☐ C-GAIJ | de Havilland DHC-2 Beaver | 1373 | ex N5334G | FP/WS |
| ☐ C-GCIM | Cessna A185F Skywagon II | 18503953 | ex (N5308E) | FP/WS |
| ☐ C-GIGK | de Havilland DHC-6 Twin Otter 300 | 492 | ex N300BC | ♦ |
| ☐ C-GJUM | Piper PA-31T Cheyenne | 31T-7520021 | | ♦ |
| ☐ C-GKJR | Cessna A185F Skywagon | 18504232 | | FP/WS♦ |
| ☐ C-GPHD | de Havilland DHC-3 Turbo Otter | 113 | ex 55-3267 | FP/WS |
| ☐ C-GQKS | de Havilland DHC-2 Beaver | 1096 | ex N690 | FP/WS |
| ☐ C-GQOQ | de Havilland DHC-6 Twin Otter 200 | 155 | ex EC-BPE | FP/WS |
| ☐ C-GTGP | Beech B200 Super King Air | BB-1292 | ex N333TP | ♦ |
| ☐ C-GUWL | de Havilland DHC-2 Beaver | 1223 | ex 67-6140 | FP/WS |

## PACIFIC COASTAL AIRLINES            Pasco (8P/PCO)            Port Hardy, BC (YZT)

| | | | | |
|---|---|---|---|---|
| ☐ C-FPCO | Beech 1900C | UB-52 | ex C-GKHB | |
| ☐ C-FPCV | Beech 1900C | UB-9 | ex N189GA | 302 |
| ☐ C-FPCX | Beech 1900C | UB-66 | ex OY-JRF | |
| ☐ C-GBPC | Beech 1900C | UB-43 | ex N565M | |
| ☐ C-GCPZ | Beech 1900C | UB-71 | ex C-GNPG | |
| ☐ C-GIPC | Beech 1900C-1 | UC-110 | ex N210CU | Special colours |
| ☐ C-GPCY | Beech 1900C | UB-45 | ex C-FYZD | 301 |
| | | | | |
| ☐ C-GCPU | SAAB SF.340A | 340A-140 | ex N140CQ | |
| ☐ C-GPCE | SAAB SF.340A | 340A-004 | ex N340SZ | Trawler c/s |
| ☐ C-GPCG | SAAB SF.340A | 340A-094 | ex N107EA | |

| | | | | | | |
|---|---|---|---|---|---|---|
| ☐ C-GPCJ | SAAB SF.340A | | 340A-006 | ex N360SZ | Sailing boat c/s | wfs |
| ☐ C-GPCN | SAAB SF.340A | | 340A-027 | ex N27XJ | | o/o♦ |
| ☐ C-GPCQ | SAAB SF.340A | | 340A-043 | ex N43SZ | | |
| | | | | | | |
| ☐ C-FDSG | de Havilland DHC-2 Beaver | | 892 | ex 54-1737 | | FP |
| ☐ C-FHUZ | Grumman G-21A Goose | | B-83 | ex BuA37830 | | |
| ☐ C-FIOL | Grumman G-21A Goose | | B-107 | ex RCN 397 | | |
| ☐ C-FMAZ | de Havilland DHC-2 Beaver | | 1413 | ex CF-MAZ | | FP |
| ☐ C-FUAZ | Grumman G-21A Goose | | 1077 | ex N95400 | | |
| ☐ C-FUVQ | de Havilland DHC-2 Beaver | | 696 | | | FP♦ |
| ☐ C-GASF | de Havilland DHC-2 Beaver | | 1202 | ex 57-2561 | | FP |
| ☐ C-GDDJ | Grumman G-21A Goose | | 1184 | ex N1257A | | |
| ☐ C-GPCF | Short SD.3-60 | | SH3620 | ex (N366AC) | 706 | |
| ☐ C-GPCP | Beech 200 Super King Air | | BB-140 | | 302 | Catpass 200 conversion |
| ☐ C-GPCW | Short SD.3-60 | | SH3622 | ex 8Q-OCA | 703 | |

## PASCAN AVIATION — Pascan (PSC) — Quebec, QC (YQB)

| | | | | | |
|---|---|---|---|---|---|
| ☐ C-FHQA | British Aerospace Jetstream 32 | | 876 | ex N876CP | |
| ☐ C-FIBA | British Aerospace Jetstream 32 | | 863 | ex N3126 | |
| ☐ C-FKQA | British Aerospace Jetstream 32 | | 877 | ex N877CP | ♦ |
| ☐ C-FPSC | British Aerospace Jetstream 32EP | | 930 | ex N930AE | ♦ |
| ☐ C-FPSI | British Aerospace Jetstream 32EP | | 963 | ex N963AE | ♦ |
| ☐ C-FPSJ | British Aerospace Jetstream 32EP | | 957 | ex N957AE | ♦ |
| ☐ C-FZVY | British Aerospace Jetstream 32 | | 833 | ex ZP-CNP | ♦ |
| ☐ C-GPPS | British Aerospace Jetstream 32EP | | 961 | ex N961AE | ♦ |
| ☐ C-GPSK | British Aerospace Jetstream 32EP | | 958 | ex N958AE | ♦ |
| ☐ C-GQJT | British Aerospace Jetstream 32EP | | 886 | ex N886CP | ♦ |
| ☐ C-GUSC | British Aerospace Jetstream 32 | | 902 | ex N242BM | |
| | | | | | |
| ☐ C-FAXY | Pilatus PC-12/45 | | 274 | | ♦ |
| ☐ C-FHSC | Beech B100 King Air | | BE-105 | ex N87XX | |
| ☐ C-FIDC | Beech B100 King Air | | BE-27 | ex N87JE | |
| ☐ C-FLKS | Beech B100 King Air | | BE-123 | ex N827RM | ♦ |
| ☐ C-FODC | Beech B100 King Air | | BE-59 | ex N777DQ | |
| ☐ C-FYUT | Pilatus PC-12/45 | | 254 | ex N254PC | |
| ☐ C-GBTL | Pilatus PC-12/45 | | 159 | ex N159PB | |
| ☐ C-GNSC | Beech B100 King Air | | BE-102 | ex N57TJ | |
| ☐ C-GPEA | ATR 42-300 (QC) | | 0158 | ex D-BCRP | ♦ |
| ☐ C-GRDC | Pilatus PC-12/45 | | 214 | ex PT-XTG | |
| ☐ C-GVDQ | Piper PA-31-350 Chieftain | | 31-8152119 | ex N40869 | ♦ |

## PELICAN NARROWS AIR SERVICES — Pelican Narrows, SK

| | | | | | |
|---|---|---|---|---|---|
| ☐ C-GFZA | Cessna A185F Skywagon | | 18503084 | | FP/WS |
| ☐ C-GTBC | de Havilland DHC-2 Beaver | | 1364 | ex 58-2032 | FP/WS |

## PERIMETER AVIATION — Perimeter (4B/PAG) — Winnipeg-Intl, MB (YWG)

| | | | | | |
|---|---|---|---|---|---|
| ☐ C-FBTL | Swearingen SA.226TC Metro II | | TC-385 | ex XA-TGG | |
| ☐ C-FFDB | Swearingen SA.226TC Metro II | | TC-249 | ex N327BA | |
| ☐ C-FIHB | Swearingen SA.226TC Metro II | | TC-361 | ex N166SW | |
| ☐ C-FIHE | Swearingen SA.226TC Metro II | | TC-373 | ex N1010Z | |
| ☐ C-FIIA | Swearingen SA.226TC Metro II | | TC-329 | ex N236AM | |
| ☐ C-FJNW | Swearingen SA.226TC Metro IIA | | TC-352 | ex N167MA | |
| ☐ C-FSLZ | Swearingen SA.226TC Metro II | | TC-222EE | ex N104GS | |
| ☐ C-FSWT | Swearingen SA.226TC Metro II | | TC-382 | ex N1011N | |
| ☐ C-FUZY | Swearingen SA.226TC Metro II | | TC-343 | ex VH-UZY | |
| ☐ C-GIQF | Swearingen SA.226TC Metro II | | TC-279 | ex F-GFGE | |
| ☐ C-GIQG | Swearingen SA.226TC Metro II | | TC-285 | ex F-GFGD | |
| ☐ C-GIQK | Swearingen SA.226TC Metro II | | TC-288 | ex F-GFGF | |
| ☐ C-GQAJ | Swearingen SA.226TC Metro II | | TC-295 | ex C-FUIF | Aeromed titles | EMS |
| ☐ C-GQAP | Swearingen SA.226TC Metro II | | TC-263 | ex N103UR | |
| ☐ C-GYRD | Swearingen SA.226TC Metro II | | TC-278 | ex N5493M | Jt ops with Dene Cree Air |
| | | | | | |
| ☐ C-FFJM | Swearingen SA.227AC Metro III | | AC-700 | ex N459AM | |
| ☐ C-FJLO | Swearingen SA.227AC Metro III | | AC-678B | ex (N941BC) | ♦ |
| ☐ C-FLRY | Swearingen SA.227AC Metro III | | AC-756 | ex ZS-SDM | ♦ |
| ☐ C-FJTS | Swearingen SA.227AC Metro III | | AC-696B | ex N227LD | ♦ |
| ☐ C-FMAV | Swearingen SA.227AC Metro III | | AC-616 | ex VH-UUF | |
| ☐ C-GFWX | Swearingen SA.227AC Metro III | | AC-650B | ex N26863 | |
| ☐ C-GWVH | Swearingen SA.227AC Metro IIIA | | AC-714 | ex VH-UUQ | |
| | | | | | |
| ☐ C-FAMF | Swearingen SA.226T Merlin IIIA | | T-274 | ex I-SWAA | |
| ☐ C-FDMX | Beech D95A Travel Air | | TD-587 | ex N5663K | |
| ☐ C-FEQK | Beech 95-B55 Baron | | TC-1374 | ex CF-EQK | |
| ☐ C-FLPN | Beech 95-A55 Baron | | TC-1251 | | ♦ |
| ☐ C-FKMZ | Beech E95 Travel Air | | TD-708 | ex N6223V | |
| ☐ C-FOFR | de Havilland DHC-8-106 | | 317 | ex N288DH | |
| ☐ C-FPPW | de Havilland DHC-8-102A | | 390 | ex N827EX | |
| ☐ C-FRQI | Beech 99A | | U-124 | ex TF-ELB | |

| □ C-GFQC | Beech B99 | U-120 | ex N47156 | |
| □ C-GMWW | Swearingden SA.227DC Metro 23 | DC-852B | ex N453LA | |
| □ C-GPCL | Swearingen SA.226AT Merlin IV | AT-017 | ex N511M | ♦ |
| □ C-GQQC | Beech D95A Travel Air | TD-676 | ex N7874L | Frtr |
| □ C-GWPS | de Havilland DHC-8-102 | 120 | ex N928HA | |

## POINTS NORTH AIR    La Ronge, SK (YVC)

| □ C-FASD | Cessna 402B | 402B1354 | | ♦ |

## PORTER AIRLINES (PD/POE)   Toronto-City Centre, ON (YTZ)

| □ C-FLQY | de Havilland DHC-8-402Q | 4306 | 819 | |
| □ C-GKQA | de Havilland DHC-8-402Q | 4357 | 821 | |
| □ C-GKQB | de Havilland DHC-8-402Q | 4359 | 822 | ♦ |
| □ C-GKQC | de Havilland DHC-8-402Q | 4360 | 823 | ♦ |
| □ C-GKQD | de Havilland DHC-8-402Q | 4361 | 824 | ♦ |
| □ C-GKQE | de Havilland DHC-8-402Q | 4390 | 825 | ♦ |
| □ C-GKQF | de Havilland DHC-8-402Q | 4391 | 826 | ♦ |
| □ C-GLQB | de Havilland DHC-8-402Q | 4130 | 801 | |
| □ C-GLQC | de Havilland DHC-8-402Q | 4134 | 802 | |
| □ C-GLQD | de Havilland DHC-8-402Q | 4138 | 803 | |
| □ C-GLQE | de Havilland DHC-8-402Q | 4140 | 804 | |
| □ C-GLQF | de Havilland DHC-8-402Q | 4193 | 805 | |
| □ C-GLQG | de Havilland DHC-8-402Q | 4194 | 806 | |
| □ C-GLQH | de Havilland DHC-8-402Q | 4225 | 807 | |
| □ C-GLQJ | de Havilland DHC-8-402Q | 4228 | 808 | |
| □ C-GLQK | de Havilland DHC-8-402Q | 4247 | 809 | |
| □ C-GLQL | de Havilland DHC-8-402Q | 4249 | 810 | |
| □ C-GLQM | de Havilland DHC-8-402Q | 4252 | 811 | |
| □ C-GLQN | de Havilland DHC-8-402Q | 4254 | 812 | |
| □ C-GLQO | de Havilland DHC-8-402Q | 4270 | 813 | |
| □ C-GLQP | de Havilland DHC-8-402Q | 4271 | 814 | |
| □ C-GLQQ | de Havilland DHC-8-402Q | 4272 | 815 | |
| □ C-GLQR | de Havilland DHC-8-402Q | 4278 | 816 | |
| □ C-GLQV | de Havilland DHC-8-402Q | 4279 | 817 | |
| □ C-GLQX | de Havilland DHC-8-402Q | 4282 | 818 | |
| □ C-GLQZ | de Havilland DHC-8-402Q | 4308 | 820 | |
| □ C- | de Havilland DHC-8-402Q | | | o/o |
| □ C- | de Havilland DHC-8-402Q | | | o/o |

## PROPAIR Propair (PRO)   Rouyn-Noranda, QC (YUY)

| □ C-FDJX | Beech A100 King Air | B-165 | ex N811CU | |
| □ C-FDOU | Beech A100 King Air | B-112 | ex CF-DOU | |
| □ C-FPAJ | Beech A100 King Air | B-151 | ex N324B | |
| □ C-FWRM | Beech A100 King Air | B-125 | ex N89JM | |
| □ C-GDPI | Beech A100 King Air | B-156 | | ♦ |
| □ C-GJBV | Beech A100 King Air | B-100 | | ♦ |
| □ C-GJJF | Beech A100 King Air | B-123 | ex N741EB | ♦ |
| □ C-GJLJ | Beech A100 King Air | B-235 | ex N23517 | |
| □ C-GJLP | Beech A100 King Air | B-148 | ex N67V | |
| | | | | |
| □ C-FAWE | Grumman G.159 Gulfstream 1 | 188 | ex HB-LDT | |
| □ C-FOGY | Beech 200 Super King Air | BB-168 | ex N10VW | |
| □ C-GLPJ | Beech 1900C-1 | UC-139 | ex N253RM | |
| □ C-GQAB | Cessna A185F Skywagon | 18502766 | ex (N1203F) | FP/WS |

## PROVINCE OF ALBERTA AIR TRANSPORTATION SERVICES
## Alberta (GOA)   Edmonton-Municipal, AB (YXD)

| □ C-FIAE | Douglas DC-3 | 4563 | | ♦ |
| □ C-GFSA | Beech B300 Super King Air | FL-174 | | |
| □ C-GFSD | Beech B200 Super King Air | BB-1962 | ex N7162V | |
| □ C-GFSE | Beech B200 Super King Air | BB-1963 | ex N7063F | |
| □ C-GFSJ | de Havilland DHC-8-103 | 017 | | |

## PROVINCIAL AIRLINES (PB/SPR)   St Johns, NL (YYT)

| □ C-FGFZ | Beech 200 Super King Air | BB-403 | ex N147K | |
| □ C-FMGP | Beech B300 Super King Air | PL-783 | ex N8043D | |
| □ C-FMUN | Beech B300 Super King Air | FL-658 | | ♦ |
| □ C-GEHS | Beech 200 Super King Air | BB-227 | | ♦ |
| □ C-GGAO | Beech 200 Super King Air | BB-659 | ex N77QX | |
| □ C-GGJF | Beech B200 Super King Air | BB-939 | ex N125KW | |
| □ C-GMRS | Beech 200 Super King Air | BB-187 | ex N630DB | Maritime Patrol |
| □ C-GMWR | Beech 200 Super King Air | BB-68 | ex N844N | Maritime Patrol |
| □ C-GRJZ | Beech B300 Super King Air | FL-285 | | ♦ |
| □ C-GTJZ | Beech 200 Super King Air | BB-499 | ex N499TT | |

| | | | | | |
|---|---|---|---|---|---|
| ☐ | C-FUMY | de Havilland DHC-6 Twin Otter 300 | 675 | ex PJ-TOD | |
| ☐ | C-FWLG | de Havilland DHC-6 Twin Otter 300 | 731 | ex N915MA | |
| ☐ | C-GIED | de Havilland DHC-6 Twin Otter 300 | 600 | ex N604NA | |
| ☐ | C-GIMK | de Havilland DHC-6 Twin Otter 300 | 352 | ex N300EH | ♦ |
| ☐ | C-GJDE | de Havilland DHC-6 Twin Otter 300 | 471 | ex C-GMPK | FP/WS |
| ☐ | C-FHRC | de Havilland DHC-8-102 | 209 | ex TR-LGL | |
| ☐ | C-GPAB | de Havilland DHC-8-106MPA | 275 | ex N827PH | |
| ☐ | C-FPAE | de Havilland DHC-8-315 | 562 | ex EC-ICA | ♦ |
| ☐ | C-FYDH | de Havilland DHC-8-102 | 083 | ex N809LR | >TSH♦ |
| ☐ | C-GPAL | de Havilland DHC-8-102 | 157 | ex N824PH | |
| ☐ | C-GPAR | de Havilland DHC-8-311 | 519 | ex HP-1625PST | ♦ |
| ☐ | C-GPAU | de Havilland DHC-8-106 | 282 | ex N833EX | |
| ☐ | C-GRNN | de Havilland DHC-8-106MPA | 314 | ex N830PH | |
| ☐ | C-FABF | Cessna S550 Citation II | S550-0101 | | ♦ |
| ☐ | C-FGGJ | Piper PA-34-200 Seneca | 34-7350240 | | ♦ |
| ☐ | C-FMPV | de Havilland DHC-2 Beaver | 1304 | ex CF-MPV | FP |
| ☐ | C-FPAG | SAAB SF.340A | 340A-028 | ex N336BE | |
| ☐ | C-FPAI | SAAB SF.340A | 340A-047 | ex N337BE | |
| ☐ | C-FPKA | Piper PA-23-250 Aztec | 27-2404 | | ♦ |
| ☐ | C-GMEW | Swearingen SA.227AC Metro III | AC-668B | ex N668JS | |

## QUANTUM HELICOPTERS — Terrace, BC (YXT)

| | | | | | |
|---|---|---|---|---|---|
| ☐ | C-FFHK | Bell 206B JetRanger | 1065 | ex CF-FHK | |
| ☐ | C-FHKJ | Bell 206L LongRanger | 45116 | ex N222CD | |
| ☐ | C-FHQH | Bell 206B JetRanger | 1344 | | ♦ |
| ☐ | C-FRCL | Bell 206LR+ LongRanger | 45019 | ex SE-HUD | |
| ☐ | C-GMQHF | Bell 206L LongRanger | 45103 | ex PH-HXH | |
| ☐ | C-GQNS | Bell 206LR+ LongRanger | 45134 | | |
| ☐ | C-GSLV | Bell 206B JetRanger III | 4199 | ex N3202G | |
| ☐ | C-GTVL | Bell 206B JetRanger II | 2166 | | |
| ☐ | C-FETK | Bell 205A-1 | 30299 | ex OE-XEH | |
| ☐ | C-FNTR | Bell 205B | 30297 | ex OE-XBT | |
| ☐ | C-FSOZ | Aérospatiale AS350B2 AStar | 2129 | ex N141MB | ♦ |
| ☐ | C-GTUP | Aéospatiale AS350B AStar | 2155 | ex JA9793 | ♦ |

## RAINBOW AIRWAYS — Dunchurch, ON

| | | | | | |
|---|---|---|---|---|---|
| ☐ | C-FOCB | de Havilland DHC-2 Beaver | 21 | | FP♦ |

## RCMP - GRC AIR SERVICES (ROYAL CANADIAN MOUNTED POLICE) — Ottawa, ON

| | | | | | |
|---|---|---|---|---|---|
| ☐ | C-FGSB | Aérospatiale AS350B3 AStar | 3796 | | |
| ☐ | C-FMPG | Aérospatiale AS350B3 AStar | 3082 | | |
| ☐ | C-FMPH | Aérospatiale AS350B3 AStar | 3683 | | |
| ☐ | C-FMPP | Aérospatiale AS350B3 AStar | 4124 | | |
| ☐ | C-FRPQ | Aérospatiale AS350B3 AStar | 3636 | ex F-WQDZ | |
| ☐ | C-GMPF | Aérospatiale AS350B3 AStar | 4229 | | |
| ☐ | C-GMPK | Aérospatiale AS350B3 AStar | 3923 | | |
| ☐ | C-GMPN | Aérospatiale AS350B3 AStar | 3072 | | |
| ☐ | C-FMPA | Pilatus PC-12/47E | 1216 | ex N216NX | |
| ☐ | C-FMPB | Pilatus PC-12/45 | 283 | ex N283PC | |
| ☐ | C-FMPE | Pilatus PC-12/45 | 314 | ex HB-FQZ | |
| ☐ | C-FMPF | Pilatus PC-12/45 | 768 | ex HB-FSY | |
| ☐ | C-FMPK | Pilatus PC-12/47E | 1092 | | |
| ☐ | C-GMPA | Pilatus PC-12/47E | 1262 | ex N262NX | ♦ |
| ☐ | C-GMPE | Pilatus PC-12/47E | 1073 | | |
| ☐ | C-GMPM | Pilatus PC-12/47E | 1011 | ex N911NG | |
| ☐ | C-GMPO | Pilatus PC-12/47E | 1197 | ex N197PE | |
| ☐ | C-GMPP | Pilatus PC-12/45 | 374 | ex N374PC | |
| ☐ | C-GMPV | Pilatus PC-12/47E | 1181 | ex N181PE | |
| ☐ | C-GMPX | Pilatus PC-12/47E | 1017 | | |
| ☐ | C-GMPY | Pilatus PC-12/45 | 311 | ex N311PB | |
| ☐ | C-GMPZ | Pilatus PC-12/45 | 272 | ex N272PC | |
| ☐ | C-FHGY | Cessna T206H Stationair | T20608583 | | ♦ |
| ☐ | C-FHVP | Cessna 210R Centurion | 21064920 | | ♦ |
| ☐ | C-FMOM | Cessna 210B Centurion | 21064924 | | ♦ |
| ☐ | C-FMPL | de Havilland DHC-6 Twin Otter 300 | 320 | ex CF-MPL | |
| ☐ | C-FMPQ | Eurocopter EC120B Colibri | 1533 | | |
| ☐ | C-FRPH | Cessna 208B Caravan I | 208B0377 | ex N1118B | |
| ☐ | C-FSUJ | Cessna 208B Caravan I | 208B0373 | ex N973CC | |
| ☐ | C-FSWC | Cessna T206H Stationair | T20608438 | | |
| ☐ | C-GFOX | Piaggio P.180 Avanti | 1065 | ex N126PA | |
| ☐ | C-GMPI | Quest Kodiak 100 | 100-0047 | ex N496KQ | ♦ |
| ☐ | C-GMPJ | de Havilland DHC-6 Twin Otter 300 | 534 | | |
| ☐ | C-GMPR | Cessna 208 Caravan I | 20800253 | ex N208CF | |

| | | | | |
|---|---|---|---|---|
| ☐ C-GMPT | Eurocopter EC120B Colibri | 1355 | | |
| ☐ C-GNMK | Cessna 210R Centurion | 21064938 | | |
| ☐ C-GNSE | Cessna T206H Stationair | T20608847 | | ♦ |
| ☐ C-GTJN | Cessna T206H Stationair | T20608443 | | ♦ |
| ☐ C-GTCT | Cessna 210R Centurion | 21064949 | | ♦ |

## RED SUCKER LAKE AIR SERVICES — Red Sucker Lake, MB

| | | | | |
|---|---|---|---|---|
| ☐ C-FODO | de Havilland DHC-2 Beaver | 822 | | FP/WS |
| ☐ C-FTHE | Piper PA-31 Navajo C | 31-7512005 | ex N121L | |
| ☐ C-GMAM | de Havilland DHC-2 Beaver | 1558 | ex G-AZLU | FP/WS |

## REGIONAL 1 AIRLINES — Transcanada (TSH) — Calgary-Intl, AB (YYC)

| | | | | |
|---|---|---|---|---|
| ☐ C-FDND | de Havilland DHC-8-102 | 129 | | ♦ |
| ☐ C-FYDH | de Havilland DHC-8-102 | 083 | ex N809LR | <SPR♦ |
| ☐ C-GOSW | de Havilland DHC-8-201 | 428 | ex HK-44332 | ♦ |
| ☐ C-GRGF | de Havilland DHC-8-301 | 184 | ex N184AV | ♦ |
| ☐ C-GRGK | de Havilland DHC-8Q-202 | 522 | ex B-17201 | |
| ☐ N192PF | de Havilland DHC-8-301 | 192 | ex N355AT | wfs♦ |
| | | | | |
| ☐ C-GRGD | Canadair CRJ-200ER | 7572 | ex N549MS | ♦ |
| ☐ C-GRIA | Canadair CRJ-200ER | 7561 | ex N127MN | ♦ |

## RIVER AIR — Kenora/Menaki, ON (YQK/-)

| | | | | |
|---|---|---|---|---|
| ☐ C-FAYM | Cessna U206E Skywagon | U20601541 | ex (N9141M) | FP |
| ☐ C-FFYC | Cessna 208 Caravan I | 20800111 | ex N9647F | FP |
| ☐ C-FMAQ | de Havilland DHC-2 Beaver | 14 | ex CF-MAQ | FP/WS |
| ☐ C-FRSW | Beech 3NM | CA-105 | ex CF-RSW | |
| ☐ C-GHOJ | Cessna 180K Skywagon | 18053042 | | FP♦ |
| ☐ C-GIAT | Cessna A185F Skywagon | 18502619 | ex N4851C | FP |
| ☐ C-GPDS | de Havilland DHC-2 Beaver | 1349 | ex N62352 | FP |
| ☐ C-GYKO | de Havilland DHC-3 Otter | 287 | ex N22UT | FP |

## ROSS AIR — Clearwater Lake SPB, ON

| | | | | |
|---|---|---|---|---|
| ☐ CF-PFC | Beech C-45H | AF-199 | ex N9942Z | |
| ☐ C-GCIZ | Cessna A185F Skywagon | 18503316 | ex N1614H | FP |
| ☐ C-GDCN | de Havilland DHC-2 Turbo Beaver | 1661/TB35 | ex N8PE | FP |

## ROSS AIR SERVICE — Sandy Bay, SK

| | | | | |
|---|---|---|---|---|
| ☐ C-FWXV | Cessna A185E Skywagon | 185-1355 | ex CF-WXV | FP/WS |

## RUSTY MYERS FLYING SERVICE — Fort Frances, ON (YAG)

| | | | | |
|---|---|---|---|---|
| ☐ C-FERM | Beech 3N | CA-62 | ex CAF 1487 | FP |
| ☐ C-FKSJ | Cessna 208 Caravan I | 20800035 | ex N9382F | FP |
| ☐ C-FOBT | de Havilland DHC-2 Beaver | 3 | ex CF-OBT | FP |
| ☐ C-FOBY | de Havilland DHC-2 Beaver | 13 | ex CF-OBY | FP |
| ☐ C-FRPL | Beech 3NM | CA-225 | ex CAF 2346 | FP |
| ☐ C-FRVL | Beech 3T | 7835 | ex CAF 1396 | FP |
| ☐ CF-ZRI | Beech D18S | A-940 | ex N164U | FP |
| ☐ C-GAGK | Cessna 208 Caravan I | 20800342 | ex N51744 | FP |

## SABOURIN LAKE LODGE — Sabourin Lake, MB

| | | | | |
|---|---|---|---|---|
| ☐ C-FSJX | de Havilland DHC-2 Beaver | 1592 | ex CF-SJX | FP |
| ☐ C-GYER | Cessna U206F Stationair | U20603503 | ex N8750Q | FP |

## SALTSPRING ISLAND AIR — Saltspring Island, BC

| | | | | |
|---|---|---|---|---|
| ☐ C-FAOP | de Havilland DHC-2 Beaver | 1249 | ex CF-AOP | FP |
| ☐ C-FJFL | de Havilland DHC-2 Beaver | 898 | ex CF-JFL | FP |
| ☐ CF-ZZJ | de Havilland DHC-2 Beaver | 1019 | ex 5H-TCP | FP |
| ☐ C-GHMC | de Havilland DHC-2 Beaver | 1215 | | FP♦ |

## SALTWATER WEST ENTERPRISES — Smithers, BC (YYD)

| | | | | |
|---|---|---|---|---|
| ☐ CF-TWO | Cessna A185E Skywagon | 18501700 | | FP♦ |
| ☐ C-GFTZ | de Havilland DHC-3 Otter | 174 | ex N90574 | FP |

## SANDY LAKE SEAPLANE SERVICE — Sandy Lake, ON (ZSI)

| | | | | |
|---|---|---|---|---|
| ☐ C-FBHP | Cessna 207A Skywagon | 20700647 | | FP/WS♦ |
| ☐ C-GBBZ | Cessna U206G Stationair | U20605712 | ex (N5396X) | FP/WS |
| ☐ C-GBGJ | Cessna U206G Stationair | U20605249 | ex N5368U | FP/WS |
| ☐ C-GEBZ | Cessna 207 Skywagon | 20700303 | ex N1703U | FP/WS |
| ☐ C-GFIQ | de Havilland DHC-2 Beaver | 632 | | FP/WS♦ |

| | | | | |
|---|---|---|---|---|
| ☐ C-GHKB | Cessna 207 Skywagon | 20700228 | | FP/WS♦ |
| ☐ C-GTCC | Cessna U206F Stationair | U20602167 | ex N7303Q | FP/WS |

## SAPAWE AIR · Eva Lake, QC

| | | | | |
|---|---|---|---|---|
| ☐ C-FEYR | de Havilland DHC-2 Beaver | 497 | ex CF-EYR | FP |
| ☐ C-FOCC | de Havilland DHC-2 Beaver | 23 | ex CF-OOC | FP |
| ☐ C-GKBW | de Havilland DHC-2 Beaver | 310 | ex N1441Z | FP |

## SASKATCHEWAN GOVERNMENT NORTHERN AIR OPERATIONS
### Saskatchewan (SGS) · La Ronge/Saskatoon, SK (YVC/YXE)

| | | | | | |
|---|---|---|---|---|---|
| ☐ C-GLLS | Beech B200 Super King Air | BB-1601 | ex N2303F | | |
| ☐ C-GSAE | Beech B200 Super King Air | BB-1748 | ex N50848 | | EMS |
| ☐ C-GSAH | Beech B200 Super King Air | BB-1972 | ex N7022F | | EMS |
| ☐ C-GSAU | Beech B200 Super King Air | BB-1974 | ex N7074N | | EMS |
| ☐ C-GSAV | Beech B200 Super King Air | BB-1790 | ex N4470T | | EMS |
| ☐ C-FAFN | Canadair CL215 | 1093 | ex C-GKDY | 216 | |
| ☐ C-FAFO | Canadair CL215 | 1094 | ex C-GKBO | 217 | |
| ☐ C-FAFP | Canadair CL215 | 1100 | ex C-GKEA | 218 | |
| ☐ C-FAFQ | Canadair CL215 | 1101 | ex C-GKEE | 219 | |
| ☐ C-FYWO | Canadair CL215 | 1003 | ex CF-YWO | 214 | |
| ☐ C-FYXG | Canadair CL215 | 1009 | ex CF-YXG | 215 | |
| ☐ C-GEHP | Grumman CS2F-2 Tracker | DHC-97 | ex CAF12198 1 | | Tanker |
| ☐ C-GEHR | Grumman CS2F-2 Tracker | DHC-51 | ex CAF12185 3 | | Tanker |
| ☐ C-GEQC | Grumman CS2F-2 Tracker | DHC-53 | ex CAF12187 4 | | Tanker |
| ☐ C-GEQD | Grumman CS2F-2 Tracker | DHC-98 | ex CAF12199 5 | | Tanker |
| ☐ C-GEQE | Grumman CS2F-2 Tracker | DHC-92 | ex CAF12193 6 | | Tanker |
| ☐ C-FMFP | Rockwell 690A Turbo Commander | 11307 | ex N690TD | | |
| ☐ C-FNAO | Gulfstream Commander 690C | 11731 | ex N815BC | | |
| ☐ C-FSPM | Gulfstream Commander 690D | 15002 | ex N721ML | | |
| ☐ C-GEAS | Beech 350 Super King Air | FL-17 | ex N56872 | | |
| ☐ C-GOVT | Gulfstream Commander 695A | 15020 | ex N600CM | | |
| ☐ C-GSAO | Beech 95-B55 Baron | TC-2149 | ex N4974M | | |
| ☐ C-GSKQ | Convair 580 | 217 | ex N723ES | | Tanker |
| ☐ C-GSKR | Convair 580 | 509 | ex N57RD | 471 | Tanker |
| ☐ C-GSPG | Beech 95-B55 Baron | TC-2213 | ex N2064A | | |
| ☐ C-GVSE | Beech 95-B55 Baron | TC-2270 | ex N717BC | | |
| ☐ C-GVSK | Convair 580 | 238 | ex N43938 | | Tanker |
| ☐ C-GYSK | Convair 580 | 234 | ex N131SF | | Tanker |

## SEAIR SEAPLANES · Vancouver-International SPB, BC

| | | | | |
|---|---|---|---|---|
| ☐ C-FJOE | Cessna 208 Caravan I | 20800390 | ex N5254Y | FP |
| ☐ C-FLAC | Cessna 208 Caravan I | 20800357 | ex N5267J | FP |
| ☐ C-GMOW | Cessna 208 Caravan I | 20800528 | ex N5036Q | ♦ |
| ☐ C-GSAS | Cessna 208 Caravan I | 20800341 | ex N5154J | FP |
| ☐ C-GURL | Cessna 208 Caravan I | 20800501 | ex N52475 | FP |
| ☐ C-FDHC | de Havilland DHC-2 Turbo Beaver | 1677/TB45 | ex N164WC | FP |
| ☐ C-FPCG | de Havilland DHC-2 Beaver | 1000 | ex N188JM | FP |
| ☐ C-FPMA | de Havilland DHC-2 Turbo Beaver | 1625/TB15 | ex N1454T | FP |
| ☐ C-GOBC | de Havilland DHC-2 Beaver | 1560 | ex N159M | FP |
| ☐ C-GTMC | de Havilland DHC-2 Beaver | 1171 | ex N100HF | FP♦ |
| ☐ C-GYIX | Cessna A185F Skywagon | 18503162 | ex (N93021) | FP |

## SELKIRK AIR / ENTERPRISE AIR SERVICES · Selkirk, MB

| | | | | |
|---|---|---|---|---|
| ☐ C-FIQC | Cessna 180 | 18032280 | | FP/WS♦ |
| ☐ C-FSFH | Beech 3T | | ex 43-35481 | FP/WS♦ |
| ☐ C-FYNW | Cessna U206D Stationair | U2061370 | | FP/WS♦ |
| ☐ C-GCKZ | Cessna A185F Skywagon | 18502665 | ex (N4949C) | FP/WS |
| ☐ C-GPHI | de Havilland DHC-2 Beaver | 838 | ex N67687 | FP/WS |

## SHARP WINGS · Williams Lake, BC

| | | | | |
|---|---|---|---|---|
| ☐ C-FMQG | Cessna TU206G Turbo Skywagon | U206-1101 | ex CF-MQG | FP/WS |
| ☐ C-GHNH | Cessna A185F Skywagon | 18502705 | ex (N1048F) | FP/WS♦ |
| ☐ C-GKMN | de Havilland DHC-2 Beaver | 348 | ex N9755Z | FP/WS |

## SHOWALTER'S FLY-IN SERVICE · Ear Falls SPB, ON (YMY)

| | | | | |
|---|---|---|---|---|
| ☐ C-FAIH | Cessna 180 Skywagon | 18051690 | | FP♦ |
| ☐ C-FXUO | Beech D18S | CA-208 | ex RCAF 2329 | FP |
| ☐ C-FZNG | Beech D18S | CA-182 | ex RCAF 2309 | FP |
| ☐ C-FZYE | de Havilland DHC-2 Beaver | 192 | ex CF-ZYE | FP |

## SIFTON AIR YUKON
**Haines Junction, YK (YHT)**

| | | | | |
|---|---|---|---|---|
| ☐ C-FRKA | Cessna 206 Super Skywagon | 206-0200 | ex N5200U | FP |
| ☐ C-GEXT | Cessna U206F Stationair | U20603249 | ex (N8338Q) | FP |
| ☐ C-GFER | Cessna U206B Stationair | U2040837 | | FP♦ |
| ☐ C-GVKJ | Cessna 205 (210-5) | 205-0092 | ex N1892Z | FP |

## SIMPSON AIR
**Commuter Canada (NCS)**          **Fort Simpson, NT (YFS)**

| | | | | |
|---|---|---|---|---|
| ☐ CF-FHZ | de Havilland DHC-2 Beaver | 66 | ex C-FFHZ | FP |
| ☐ C-FNEQ | Cessna U206G Stationair | U20605036 | | FP♦ |
| ☐ C-FNML | Piper PA-23-250 Aztec | 27-7554075 | ex N8VV | |
| ☐ C-GGHU | Cessna U206G Stationair 6 II | U20605723 | ex (N5407X) | FP |
| ☐ C-GPMS | Cessna U206G Stationair 6 II | U20604207 | ex (N756MU) | FP |

## SIOUX NARROWS AIRWAYS
**Great Bear Lake, NT (DAS)**

| | | | | |
|---|---|---|---|---|
| ☐ CF-GTP | Noorduyn UC-64A Norseman | 423 | 43-35349 | FP |
| ☐ CF-QHY | Douglas DC-3 | 26005 | | ♦ |
| ☐ C-GBDW | de Havilland DHC-2 Beaver | 954 | ex C9-AGS | FP |
| ☐ C-GMXS | de Havilland DHC-2 Beaver | 1213 | ex N5382G | FP |
| ☐ C-GUJY | de Havilland DHC-2 Beaver | 393 | ex C-GVMH | FP |

## SKYLINK EXPRESS
**Comet (CME)**          **Charlottetown, PE (YYG)**

| | | | | |
|---|---|---|---|---|
| ☐ C-FKAX | Beech 1900C | UB-67 | ex N3067X | Frtr |
| ☐ C-GKGA | Beech 1900C-1 | UC-117 | ex N117ZR | Frtr |
| ☐ C-GSKA | Beech 1900C | UB-32 | ex N317BH | |
| ☐ C-GSKG | Beech 1900C-1 | UC-22 | ex N19016 | |
| ☐ C-GSKM | Beech 1900C | UB-21 | ex N61MK | |
| ☐ C-GSKN | Beech 1900C-1 | UC-54 | ex N31729 | |
| ☐ C-GSKU | Beech 1900C | UB-35 | ex N735GL | |
| ☐ C-GSKW | Beech 1900C | UB-33 | ex N318BH | |
| ☐ C-GTGA | Beech 1900C-1 | UC-62 | ex N62YV | Frtr |

| | | | | |
|---|---|---|---|---|
| ☐ C-FFGA | Cessna 208B Caravan I | 208B0662 | ex N5264E | 026 |
| ☐ C-FHGA | Cessna 208B Caravan I | 208B0047 | ex C-FESH | 024 |
| ☐ C-GEGA | Cessna 208B Caravan I | 208B0379 | ex N1119A | |
| ☐ C-GLGA | Cessna 208B Caravan I | 208B0350 | ex N64AP | |
| ☐ C-GSKS | Cessna 208B Caravan I | 208B0762 | ex N52623 | |
| ☐ C-GSKT | Cessna 208B Caravan I | 208B0759 | ex N5262W | |
| ☐ C-GSKV | Cessna 208B Caravan I | 208B0847 | | ♦ |

| | | | | |
|---|---|---|---|---|
| ☐ C-FFFH | Piper PA-31-350 Navajo Chieftain | 31-7552130 | ex N54CG | |
| ☐ C-GGQM | Piper PA-31-350 Navajo Chieftain | 31-7952033 | ex TF-EGU | |
| ☐ C-GIIZ | Piper PA-31-350 Navajo Chieftain | 31-7552099 | ex N29TW | |
| ☐ C-GYVJ | Piper PA-31-350 Navajo Chieftain | 31-7652086 | ex N59833 | |

## SKYNORTH AIR
**Winnipeg International, MB (YWG)**

| | | | | |
|---|---|---|---|---|
| ☐ C-FSDA | Piper PA-31-350 Navajo Chieftain | 31-7752167 | ex N27413 | |
| ☐ C-GAVI | Beech A100 King Air | B-201 | ex G-BBVM | ♦ |
| ☐ C-GBTI | Beech 65-E90 King Air | LW-111 | | ♦ |
| ☐ C-GKBB | Beech 65-C90 King Air | LW-607 | | ♦ |
| ☐ C-GNAA | Beech 100 King Air | B-24 | | ♦ |
| ☐ C-GRTG | Piper PA-31-350 Navajo Chieftain | 31-7652004 | ex N180RM | |
| ☐ C-GSNM | Beech 65-E90 King Air | LW-194 | | ♦ |
| ☐ C-GTZK | Piper PA-31 Turbo Navajo | 31-381 | ex N9SG | |

## SKY REGIONAL AIRLINES
**(SKV)**          **Toronto-Island (YTZ)**

| | | | | |
|---|---|---|---|---|
| ☐ C-FSRJ | de Havilland DHC-8-402Q | 4165 | ex N501LX | |
| ☐ C-FSRN | de Havilland DHC-8-402Q | 4170 | ex N503LX | |
| ☐ C-FSRW | de Havilland DHC-8-402Q | 4172 | ex N504LX | |
| ☐ C-FRSY | de Havilland DHC-8-402Q | 4174 | ex N505LX | |
| ☐ C-FSRZ | de Havilland DHC-8-402Q | 4176 | ex N506LX | ♦ |

## SLATE FALLS AIRWAYS
**(SYJ)**          **Sioux Lookout, ON (YXL)**

| | | | | |
|---|---|---|---|---|
| ☐ CF-DIN | de Havilland DHC-2 Beaver | 68 | | FP/WS |
| ☐ C-FCZP | de Havilland DHC-3 Turbo Otter | 69 | ex CF-CZP | FP/WS |
| ☐ C-FNWX | de Havilland DHC-3 Turbo Otter | 412 | ex CF-NWX | FP/WS |
| ☐ C-GGHW | Cessna TU206G Stationair | U20605726 | | FP/WS♦ |
| ☐ C-GGPW | Cessna U206G Stationair | U20605029 | | FP/WS♦ |
| ☐ C-GGRW | Cessna U206G Stationair 6 II | U20605689 | ex N5373X | FP/WS |
| ☐ C-GQZE | Piper PA-31-350 Navajo Chieftain | 31-7912068 | | ♦ |

## SOUTH NAHANNI AIRWAYS

| | | | | |
|---|---|---|---|---|
| ☐ C-GGLE | de Havilland DHC-6 Twin Otter 100 | 71 | ex C-GSOL | ♦ |

## SONTAIR — Sontair (STI) — Chatham, ON (XCM)

| | | | | |
|---|---|---|---|---|
| ☐ C-GSKT | Cessna 208B Caravan I | 208B0759 | ex N5262W | |

## STARLINK AVIATION — Avionair (ANU) — Montreal-Trudeau, QC (YUL)

| | | | | | |
|---|---|---|---|---|---|
| ☐ C-GCCN | British Aerospace Jetstream 31 | 704 | ex N333PX | | |
| ☐ C-GCCZ | British Aerospace Jetstream 31 | 712 | ex N335PX | | |
| ☐ C-GDFW | British Aerospace Jetstream 31 | 720 | ex G-HDGS | | |
| ☐ C-GEMQ | British Aerospace Jetstream 31 | 747 | ex N103XV | | |
| ☐ C-GOAD | Embraer EMB.120ER Brasilia | 120086 | ex N19704 | GoAir Citylink colours | [YUL] |
| ☐ C-GOHI | Pilatus PC-12/47E | 1297 | ex HF-F.. | | ♦ |

## STRAIT AIR — L'Anse au Clair, NL

| | | | | |
|---|---|---|---|---|
| ☐ C-FVTQ | Piper PA-31-350 Chieftain | 31-7853034 | ex N300DT | |
| ☐ C-GFAL | Piper PA-31-350 Navajo Chieftain | 31-7405161 | | ♦ |
| ☐ C-GPXW | Piper PA-31-350 Navajo Chieftain | 31-7652134 | | ♦ |
| ☐ C-GQAM | Piper PA-31 Navajo | 31-7912093 | | ♦ |
| ☐ C-GQZE | Piper PA-31-350 Chieftain | 31-7912605 | | ♦ |
| ☐ C-GRRJ | Piper PA-31 Navajo | 31-7812031 | | ♦ |
| ☐ C-GRYE | Piper PA-31-350 Navajo Chieftain | 31-7852155 | | ♦ |
| ☐ C-FPLG | Beech A100 King Air | B-224 | | ♦ |
| ☐ C-GJBQ | Beech A100 King Air | B-191 | | ♦ |
| ☐ C-GJXF | Beech A100 King Air | B-159 | | ♦ |

## SUDBURY AVIATION — Whitewater Lake, ON

| | | | | |
|---|---|---|---|---|
| ☐ C-FHVT | de Havilland DHC-2 Beaver I | 284 | ex VP-PAT | FP/WS |
| ☐ C-FIUU | de Havilland DHC-2 Beaver I | 945 | ex CF-IUU | FP/WS |
| ☐ C-GQVG | Cessna A185F Skywagon | 18503818 | ex N4619E | FP/WS |

## SUMMIT AIR CHARTERS — Yellowknife, NT/Atlin, BC/Whitehorse, YT (YZF/YSQ/YXY)

| | | | | |
|---|---|---|---|---|
| ☐ C-FEQV | Dornier 228-202 | 8126 | ex P2-MBR | [OBF] |
| ☐ C-FEQW | Dornier 228-202 | 8103 | ex P2-MBQ | ♦ |
| ☐ C-FEQX | Dornier 228-202 | 8101 | ex P2-MBP | |
| ☐ C-FPSA | Dornier 228-202 | 8122 | ex D-CLUU | [OBF] |
| ☐ C-FPSH | Dornier 228-202 | 8071 | ex N253MC | |
| ☐ C-FUCN | Dornier 228-202 | 8109 | ex N276MC | op for UNHAS |
| ☐ C-GJPY | Dornier 228-202 | 8088 | ex 6Y-JQM | |
| ☐ C-GSAX | Dornier 228-202 | 8153 | ex P2-MBV | |
| ☐ C-FYSQ | Short SC.7 Skyvan | SH1968 | ex N491AS | Frtr |
| ☐ C-GIWO | Learjet 35A | 35A-407 | | ♦ |
| ☐ C-GJGS | Short SC.7 Skyvan | SH1909 | ex N56NS | Frtr |
| ☐ C-GKOA | Short SC.7 Skyvan | SH1905 | ex N52NS | Frtr |

## SUNWEST AVIATION — Chinook (CNK) — Calgary-Intl, AB (YYC)

| | | | | | |
|---|---|---|---|---|---|
| ☐ C-GSLX | Beech 1900D | UE-264 | ex C-GSLB | | |
| ☐ C-GSWB | Beech 1900D | UE-386 | ex N847CA | | |
| ☐ C-GSWV | Beech 1900D | UE-141 | ex N17354 | all-white | |
| ☐ C-GSWX | Beech 1900D | UE-63 | ex N166K | | |
| ☐ C-GSWZ | Beech 1900D | UE-337 | ex N23159 | | |
| ☐ C-FAFJ | Cessna 208B Caravan I | 208B0641 | ex N52655 | | |
| ☐ C-FBOM | Beech 200 Super King Air | BB-693 | ex C-GXHN | | |
| ☐ C-FDOI | Piper PA-31-350 Chieftain | 31-8152150 | ex N40901 | | |
| ☐ C-FGEW | Swearingen SA.226TC Metro II | TC-347 | ex N330BA | | |
| ☐ C-FLFI | Cessna 680 | 680-0238 | ex N28WE | | ♦ |
| ☐ C-FMIX | Hawker 800XP | 258392 | ex F-HBOM | | ♦ |
| ☐ C-FNOC | Cessna 208 Caravan I | 20800090 | ex N9536F | | |
| ☐ C-FPCP | Beech B300 Super King Air | FL-317 | ex N3217V | | |
| ☐ C-GAPC | Cessna 560 Citation V | 560-0033 | | | ♦ |
| ☐ C-GCIL | Learjet 55 | 55-089 | | | ♦ |
| ☐ C-GDLR | Cessna 550 Citation II | 550-0062 | | | ♦ |
| ☐ C-GGWH | Canadair Challenger | 5371 | | | ♦ |
| ☐ C-GHOP | Beech 200 Super King Air | BB-120 | ex N6773S | | |
| ☐ C-GIWO | Learjet 35A | 35A-407 | | | ♦ |
| ☐ C-GJFY | Beech 200 Super King Air | BB-812 | ex C-GYUI | | |
| ☐ C-GMOZ | Piper PA-31-350 Chieftain | 31-8052067 | ex N3556B | | |
| ☐ C-GMTR | British Aerospace 125-800A | NA0435 | | | ♦ |
| ☐ C-GOAG | Dassault Falcon 900EX | 15 | | | ♦ |
| ☐ C-GOHO | Piper PA-31-350 Chieftain | 31-8152167 | ex N38SL | | |
| ☐ C-GPDB | Learjet 45 | 45-041 | | | ♦ |
| ☐ C-GPDQ | Gulfstream 150 | 282 | | | ♦ |
| ☐ C-GPGF | Beech B300 Super King Air | FL-572 | ex N902CE | | ♦ |
| ☐ C-GRWN | Piper PA-31-350 Chieftain | 31-8152044 | ex N4076J | | |

| | | | | | | |
|---|---|---|---|---|---|---|
| ☐ C-GSBC | Beech B200 Super King Air | BB-1780 | ex N46TF | | | |
| ☐ C-GSHV | Swearingen SA.227DC Metro 23 | DC-900B | ex D-CJKO | | | |
| ☐ C-GSHY | Swearingen SA.227DC Metro 23 | DC-897B | ex N3051Q | | | |
| ☐ C-GSHZ | Swearingen SA.227DC Metro 23 | DC-887B | ex N3007C | | | |
| ☐ C-GSOC | Cessna 680 Citation | 680-0195 | | | | ♦ |
| ☐ C-GSOE | Cessna 680 Citation | 680-0223 | | | | ♦ |
| ☐ C-GSWK | Swearingen SA.226TC Metro II | TC-368 | ex F-GEBU | The Spirit of Medicine Hat | | |
| ☐ C-GSWO | Cessna 208 Caravan I | 20800153 | ex N1016M | | | |
| ☐ C-GSWP | Learjet 55 | 55-019 | | | | ♦ |
| ☐ C-GSWQ | Learjet 45 | 45-022 | | | | ♦ |
| ☐ C-GTJL | Learjet 35A | 35A-124 | | | | ♦ |
| ☐ C-GVVZ | Learjet 45 | 45-020 | | | | ♦ |

## SUNWING AIRLINES — Sunwing (WG/SWG) — Toronto-Pearson Intl, ON (YYZ)

| | | | | | |
|---|---|---|---|---|---|
| ☐ C-FEAK | Boeing 737-86Q/W | 30292/1451 | ex N292AG | | |
| ☐ C-FGVK | Boeing 737-86N/W | 32740/1444 | ex OK-TVK | | <TVS♦ |
| ☐ C-FLSW | Boeing 737-8HX/W | 36552/2658 | | | |
| ☐ C-FLZR | Boeing 737-8K5/W | 35145/2849 | ex G-FDZR | | ♦ |
| ☐ C-FTAH | Boeing 737-8Q8/W | 29351/1471 | ex OK-TVJ | | |
| ☐ C-FTDW | Boeing 737-808/W | 34704/1958 | ex N1786B | Joan Maria | |
| ☐ C-FTJH | Boeing 737-8BK | 29642/2247 | ex N1786B | | |
| ☐ C-FTLK | Boeing 737-8K5/W | 35143/2763 | ex D-AHLK | | <TUI♦ |
| ☐ C-FTOH | Boeing 737-8HX/W | 29647/2865 | | | |
| ☐ C-FUAA | Boeing 737-8BK/W | 29660/2355 | ex OO-JAA | | ♦ |
| ☐ C-FYLC | Boeing 737-8BK/W | 33029/1945 | ex G-OXLC | | |
| ☐ C-FYUH | Boeing 737-8K5/W | 34689/1935 | ex D-ATUH | | <TUI♦ |
| ☐ C-GOFW | Boeing 737-8BK/W | 33018/1488 | ex LN-NOS | | ♦ |
| ☐ C-GRKB | Boeing 737-86Q/W | 30294/1469 | ex HA-LKB | | <TVL♦ |
| ☐ C-GTVF | Boeing 737-8FH/W | 29669/1692 | ex OK-TVF | | <TVS♦ |
| ☐ C-GTVG | Boeing 737-8Q8/W | 30719/2257 | ex OK-TVG | | <TVS♦ |
| ☐ C-GVVH | Boeing 737-8Q8/W | 35275/2604 | ex OK-TVH | | <TVS♦ |
| ☐ G-FDZA | Boeing 737-8K5/W | 35134/2152 | | | <TOM♦ |
| ☐ G-FDZF | Boeing 737-8K5/W | 35138/2499 | ex N1786B | | <TOM♦ |
| ☐ OK-TVT | Boeing 737-86N/W | 39394/3899 | | | <TVS♦ |

## SUSTUT AIR — Smithers, BC (YYD)

| | | | | | |
|---|---|---|---|---|---|
| ☐ C-FAFV | Cessna 208B Caravan I | 208B0528 | ex N9510W | | |
| ☐ C-FWCR | Aérospatiale AS350B2 AStar | 2204 | | | ♦ |
| ☐ C-GGSY | Aérospatiale AS350B2 AStar | 1591 | | | ♦ |

## SWANBERG AIR — Grande Prairie, AB (YQU)

| | | | | | |
|---|---|---|---|---|---|
| ☐ C-GCTH | Piper PA-31-350 Navajo Chieftain | 31-7752063 | ex N37620 | | |
| ☐ C-GPSB | Piper PA-42 Cheyenne III | 42-8001030 | ex N855GA | | |
| ☐ C-GPSI | Canadair Challenger | 3027 | | | ♦ |
| ☐ C-GPSN | British Aerospace Jetstream 31 | 783 | ex C-GHGI | | |
| ☐ C-GPSO | British Aerospace Jetstream 31 | 756 | ex C-GJPX | | |
| ☐ C-GPSV | British Aerospace Jetstream 31 | 816 | ex C-FBII | | |
| ☐ C-GPSW | British Aerospace Jetstream 31 | 735 | ex N854JS | | |
| ☐ C-GPSX | Piper PA-31P Pressurised Navajo | 31P-7300113 | ex N100MC | | |

## THUNDER AIRLINES — Air Thunder (THU) — Thunder Bay, ON (YQT)

| | | | | | |
|---|---|---|---|---|---|
| ☐ C-FFFG | Mitsubishi MU-2L | 662 | ex N5191B | | |
| ☐ C-FFSS | Mitsubishi MU-2B | 783SA | | | ♦ |
| ☐ C-FRWK | Mitsubishi MU-2L | 1521SA | ex N437MA | | |
| ☐ C-GAMC | Mitsubishi MU-2L | 785SA | ex N273MA | | |
| ☐ C-GGDC | Mitsubishi MU-2B | 796SA | | | ♦ |
| ☐ C-GZNS | Mitsubishi MU-2L | 1550SA | ex N64WB | | |
| | | | | | |
| ☐ C-FASB | Beech A100 King Air | B-163 | ex SE-ING | | |
| ☐ C-FWVR | Cessna 208B Caravan I | 208B0483 | ex N51426 | | |
| ☐ C-GASI | Beech A100 King Air | B-126 | ex N23BW | | |
| ☐ C-GNEX | Beech A100 King Air | B-211 | ex N9194F | | |
| ☐ C-GUPP | Beech A100 King Air | B-157 | ex N123CS | | |
| ☐ C-GYQK | Beech A100 King Air | B-153 | ex N120AS | | ♦ |

## THUNDERBIRD AVIATION — Stony Rapids, SK (YSF)

| | | | | | |
|---|---|---|---|---|---|
| ☐ CF-PEM | de Havilland DHC-3 Otter | 438 | | | FP |

## TOFINO AIR LINES — Tofino, BC (YTP)

| | | | | | |
|---|---|---|---|---|---|
| ☐ C-FGCY | de Havilland DHC-2 Beaver | 216 | ex CF-GCY | | FP |
| ☐ C-FGQZ | de Havilland DHC-2 Beaver | 118 | | | FP♦ |
| ☐ C-FHRT | de Havilland DHC-2 Beaver | 1203 | ex N64390 | | FP |
| ☐ C-FICK | de Havilland DHC-2 Beaver | 796 | | | FP♦ |
| ☐ C-FJIM | de Havilland DHC-2 Beaver | 461 | ex N66035 | | FP |
| ☐ C-FMXR | de Havilland DHC-2 Beaver | 374 | | | FP♦ |

| | | | | |
|---|---|---|---|---|
| ☐ C-FOCL | de Havilland DHC-2 Beaver | 41 | | FP♦ |
| ☐ C-GFLT | de Havilland DHC-2 Beaver | 279 | ex N5149G | FP |
| | | | | |
| ☐ C-FITS | de Havilland DHC-3 Otter | 90 | ex CF-ITS | FP |
| ☐ C-GHBX | Cessna 180J | 18052449 | ex (N52029) | FP |
| ☐ C-GHZR | Cessna 180J | 18052667 | ex (N7542K) | FP |
| ☐ C-GIDX | Cessna 180J | 18052709 | ex (N7716K) | FP |
| ☐ C-GYFO | Cessna 180J | 18052759 | ex (N7825K) | FP |

## TRANS CAPITAL AIR　　　　　　　　　　　　　　　Toronto-City Centre, ON (YTZ)

| | | | | |
|---|---|---|---|---|
| ☐ C-FJHQ | de Havilland DHC-7-103 | 011 | ex PK-TVS | Op for UN |
| ☐ C-FPBJ | de Havilland DHC-7-103 | 009 | ex OY-GRD | wfs♦ |
| ☐ C-FWYU | de Havilland DHC-7-103 | 012 | ex N678MA | Op for UN as UN-234 |
| ☐ C-GCPP | de Havilland DHC-7-102 | 087 | ex HK-3111W | [YTZ] |
| ☐ C-GGXS | de Havilland DHC-7-102 | 064 | ex 4X-AHB | |
| ☐ C-GNUY | de Havilland DHC-7-102 | 033 | ex N330KK | ♦ |
| ☐ C-GVPP | de Havilland DHC-7-102 | 072 | ex N272EP | Op for UN |
| ☐ C-GVWD | de Havilland DHC-7-102 | 108 | ex HK-3340W | Op for UN as UN-311 |
| ☐ C-GYTZ | de Havilland DHC-7-102 | 077 | ex N770DD | ♦ |

## TRANSPORT CANADA　　　　　　　　　　　　　　　　　　　　　　Various

| | | | |
|---|---|---|---|
| ☐ C-FGXE | Beech 65-C90A King Air | LJ-1179 | ex N179RC |
| ☐ C-FGXG | Beech 65-C90A King Air | LJ-1139 | ex N212RL |
| ☐ C-FGXH | Beech 65-C90A King Air | LJ-1162 | ex N477JA |
| ☐ C-FGXJ | Beech 65-C90A King Air | LJ-1178 | ex N357CY |
| ☐ C-FGXL | Beech 65-C90A King Air | LJ-1189 | ex N200SL |
| ☐ C-FGXO | Beech 65-C90A King Air | LJ-1200 | ex N68TW |
| ☐ C-FGXQ | Beech 65-C90A King Air | LJ-1192 | ex N616SC |
| ☐ C-FGXS | Beech 65-C90A King Air | LJ-1207 | ex N207RC |
| ☐ C-FGXT | Beech 65-C90A King Air | LJ-1230 | ex N1564P |
| ☐ C-FGXU | Beech 65-C90A King Air | LJ-1140 | ex N8841 |
| ☐ C-FGXX | Beech 65-C90A King Air | LJ-1151 | ex N126RL |
| ☐ C-FGXZ | Beech 65-C90A King Air | LJ-1177 | ex N479JA |
| ☐ C-GCFB | Beech 65-C90A King Air | LJ-929 | ex N81DD |
| | | | |
| ☐ C-FCGK | Bell 206B JetRanger | 24 | |
| ☐ C-FCGO | Bell 206B JetRanger | 140 | |
| ☐ C-FCGQ | Bell 206B JetRanger | 182 | |
| ☐ C-FCGR | Bell 206B JetRanger | 189 | |
| ☐ C-FDOC | Bell 206B JetRanger | 349 | |
| ☐ C-FDOD | Bell 206B JetRanger | 379 | |
| ☐ C-FDOE | Bell 206B JetRanger | 381 | |
| | | | |
| ☐ C-FDOF | Bell 212 | 30536 | |
| ☐ C-FDOP | Bell 212 | 30567 | |
| ☐ C-GCGB | Bell 212 | 30930 | ex N241LG |
| ☐ C-GCHF | Bell 212 | 30617 | |
| ☐ C-GCHT | Bell 212 | 30910 | |
| | | | |
| ☐ C-FJCZ | Cessna C550 Citation II | 550-0700 | |
| ☐ C-FJWZ | Cessna C550 Citation II | 550-0685 | |
| ☐ C-FJXN | Cessna C550 Citation II | 550-0684 | ex N6778L |
| ☐ C-FKCE | Cessna C550 Citation II | 550-0686 | |
| ☐ C-FKDX | Cessna C550 Citation II | 550-0687 | ex N6778Y |
| ☐ C-FKEB | Cessna C550 Citation II | 550-0688 | |
| ☐ C-FKLB | Cessna C550 Citation II | 550-0699 | |
| ☐ C-FLZA | Cessna C550 Citation II | 550-0701 | |
| ☐ C-FMFM | Cessna C550 Citation II | 550-0702 | |
| | | | |
| ☐ C-GCFN | MBB 105CBS-4 | S-682 | |
| ☐ C-GCFO | MBB 105CBS-4 | S-715 | |
| ☐ C-GCFQ | MBB 105CBS-4 | S-716 | |
| ☐ C-GCFS | MBB 105CBS-4 | S-725 | |
| ☐ C-GCFT | MBB 105CBS-4 | S-726 | |
| ☐ C-GCFU | MBB 105CBS-4 | S-727 | |
| ☐ C-GCFV | MBB 105CBS-4 | S-728 | |
| ☐ C-GCFX | MBB 105CBS-4 | S-730 | |
| ☐ C-GCFY | MBB 105CBS-4 | S-733 | |
| ☐ C-GCHU | MBB 105CBS-4 | S-696 | |
| ☐ C-GCHV | MBB 105CBS-4 | S-641 | |
| ☐ C-GCHW | MBB 105CBS-4 | S-681 | ♦ |
| ☐ C-GCHY | MBB 105CBS-4 | S-729 | |
| ☐ C-GGGM | MBB 105CBS-4 | S-618 | |
| | | | |
| ☐ C-FMOT | Bell 407 | 53664 | ♦ |
| ☐ C-GCFR | de Havilland DHC-7-102 | 102 | |
| ☐ C-GCFJ | de Havilland DHC-8-100 | 020 | |
| ☐ C-GCHM | Bell 206L LongRanger | 45083 | ♦ |
| ☐ C-GCHR | Bell 206L-1 LongRanger | 45220 | ♦ |

| | | | | |
|---|---|---|---|---|
| ☐ C-GCHS | Bell 206L-1 LongRanger | 45221 | | ♦ |
| ☐ C-GDOT | Bell 407 | 53672 | | ♦ |
| ☐ C-GSUR | de Havilland DHC-8-102 | 046 | ex C-GJVB | ♦ |

### TRANSWEST AIR                Athabaska(9T/ABS)    La Ronge/Stony Rapids, SK (YVC/YSF)

| | | | | |
|---|---|---|---|---|
| ☐ C-FGHY | de Havilland DHC-2 Beaver | 1344 | ex 58-2015 | FP/WS |
| ☐ C-FGQD | de Havilland DHC-2 Beaver | 76 | ex CF-QGD | FP/WS |
| ☐ C-FIFJ | de Havilland DHC-2 Beaver | 831 | ex CF-IFJ | FP/WS |
| ☐ C-FOED | de Havilland DHC-2 Turbo Beaver | 1591/TB9 | ex CF-OED | FP/WS |
| ☐ C-FORC | de Havilland DHC-2 Beaver | 1499 | | FP/WS♦ |
| ☐ C-GAEB | de Havilland DHC-2 Beaver | 703 | ex 53-7895 | FP/WS |
| ☐ C-GMAQ | de Havilland DHC-2 Beaver | 234 | ex 51-16784 | FP/WS |
| | | | | |
| ☐ C-FCCE | de Havilland DHC-6 Twin Otter 100 | 8 | ex CF-CCE | FP/WS |
| ☐ C-FGLF | de Havilland DHC-6 Twin Otter 200 | 138 | ex LV-APT | FP/WS |
| ☐ C-FPGE | de Havilland DHC-6 Twin Otter 200 | 197 | ex CF-PGE | FP/WS |
| ☐ C-FSCA | de Havilland DHC-6 Twin Otter 100 | 17 | ex CF-SCA | FP/WS |
| ☐ C-FVOG | de Havilland DHC-6 Twin Otter 100 | 35 | ex CF-VOG | FP/WS |
| | | | | |
| ☐ C-FAAF | Piper PA-31-350 Navajo Chieftain | 31-7752096 | ex N27229 | |
| ☐ C-FNVH | Piper PA-31-350 Navajo Chieftain | 31-7305098 | ex N98BJ | |
| ☐ C-FZPJ | Piper PA-31-350 Navajo Chieftain | 31-7752185 | ex N27359 | |
| ☐ C-GAYY | Piper PA-31 Navajo C | 31-8012006 | | |
| ☐ C-GGIQ | Piper PA-31-350 Navajo Chieftain | 31-7552082 | ex N59989 | |
| ☐ C-GQHV | Piper PA-31-350 Navajo Chieftain | 31-7405230 | ex N54293 | |
| ☐ C-GUNP | Piper PA-31-350 Chieftain | 31-8052048 | ex N3554D | |
| ☐ C-GWUM | Piper PA-31-350 Navajo Chieftain | 31-7405404 | ex N66878 | |
| | | | | |
| ☐ C-FEYP | Beech A100 King Air | B-206 | ex N86BM | |
| ☐ C-FHPE | de Havilland DHC-3 Turbo Otter | 273 | ex Burma 4651 | FP/WS |
| ☐ C-FJTG | Bell 205A-1 | 30104 | ex N8138J | |
| ☐ C-FOHG | Bell 407 | 53187 | ex N478WN | |
| ☐ C-FOKD | Bell 407 | 53193 | ex N407NR | |
| ☐ C-FRRQ | Beech 200 Super King Air | BB-560 | | ♦ |
| ☐ C-FSGD | de Havilland DHC-3 Turbo Otter | 316 | ex N521BK | FP/WS |
| ☐ C-FTMC | Bell 206L-4 LongRanger IV | 52223 | ex XC-CJS | |
| ☐ C-GAON | Cessna 310R II | 310R1627 | ex N2632Y | |
| ☐ C-GALM | Cessna A185F Skywagon | 18503711 | ex N783A | FP/WS |
| ☐ C-GCJM | Cessna A185F Skywagon | 18503955 | ex (N5330E) | FP/WS |
| ☐ C-GXZA | Cessna A185F Skywagon | 18503019 | ex N5211R | FP/WS |
| ☐ C-GZVF | Cessna A185F Skywagon | 18503202 | ex N93256 | FP/WS |
| ☐ C-GCNC | Bell 206B JetRanger II | 1142 | ex N58152 | |
| ☐ C-GELT | Bell 206B JetRanger III | 2994 | ex N5744V | |
| ☐ C-GFSG | Beech 200 Super King Air | BB-671 | | |
| ☐ C-GJHW | Beech A100 King Air | B-175 | ex N92DL | |
| ☐ C-GKCY | SAAB SF.340A | 340A-133 | ex SE-ISM | |
| ☐ C-GPNO | Beech 95-B55 Baron | TC-734 | ex N174E | |
| ☐ C-GTJX | SAAB SF.340B | 340B-165 | ex N586MA | |
| ☐ C-GTWG | Beech 1900D | UE-79 | ex N79SK | |
| ☐ C-GTWK | SAAB SF.340B | 340B-190 | ex XA-TUQ | |
| ☐ C-GYHY | Bell 206B JetRanger III | 2317 | ex N16825 | |

### TRIUMPH AIRWAYS                                                    Oshawa, ON (YOO)

| | | | | |
|---|---|---|---|---|
| ☐ C-FOOW | Douglas DC-3 | 13342 | ex 8P-OOW | painted as CF-OOW |

### TSAYTA AVIATION                                              Fort St James, BC (YXJ)

| | | | | |
|---|---|---|---|---|
| ☐ C-GCXF | Britten-Norman BN-2A Islander | 84 | | ♦ |
| ☐ C-GDER | Cessna TU206G Stationair | U20605730 | | FP♦ |
| ☐ C-GKAW | Britten-Norman BN-2A-8 Islander | 128 | ex N158MA | |
| ☐ C-GMZP | Britten-Norman BN-2A-21 Islander | 874 | ex N341CC | |
| ☐ C-GWDW | de Havilland DHC-2 Beaver | 306 | ex N311N | FP♦ |
| ☐ C-GWKX | Cessna A185E Skywagon | 18502032 | ex N70167 | FP/WS |

### TUDHOPE AIRWAYS                                                        Hudson, ON

| | | | | |
|---|---|---|---|---|
| ☐ C-FOCP | de Havilland DHC-2 Beaver | 49 | ex CF-OCP | FP/WS |
| ☐ C-FSDC | Found FBA-2C | 17 | ex CF-SDC | FP/WS |

### TWEEDSMUIR AIR SERVICES                                        Nimpo Lake, BC

| | | | | |
|---|---|---|---|---|
| ☐ C-FFHT | de Havilland DHC-2 Beaver | 55 | ex CF-FHT | FP |
| ☐ C-GFRJ | Cessna A185F Skywagon II | 18504011 | | FP |

### TYAX AIR SERVICE                                                Gold Bridge, BC

| | | | | |
|---|---|---|---|---|
| ☐ C-GIYV | de Havilland DHC-2 Beaver | 1488 | ex XP823 | FP/WS |

## UNIVERSAL HELICOPTERS                                    Goose Bay, NL (YYR)

| | | | | |
|---|---|---|---|---|
| ☐ C-FCNG | Bell 206L LongRanger | 45149 | ex C-GMPT | |
| ☐ C-FCWR | Bell 206L LongRanger | 45086 | ex C-GMPM | |
| ☐ C-FLIA | Bell 206L-4 LongRanger IV | 52149 | ex N9221U | |
| ☐ C-FPHO | Bell 206L LongRanger | 45147 | ex N3247K | |
| ☐ C-GAHS | Bell 206LR+ LongRanger | 45048 | ex D-HMHS | |
| ☐ C-GDCA | Bell 206LR+ LongRanger | 45021 | ex N31DM | |
| ☐ C-GIZY | Bell 206LR+ LongRanger | 45027 | ex N176KH | |
| ☐ C-GLSH | Bell 206LR+ LongRanger | 45018 | | |
| ☐ C-GQIX | Bell 206L LongRanger | 45008 | ex N8EL | |
| ☐ C-GVYO | Bell 206LR+ LongRanger | 46609 | ex N16950 | |
| | | | | |
| ☐ C-FEPR | Bell 407 | 53888 | | ♦ |
| ☐ C-FTJU | Bell 407 | 53331 | ex G-CEOA | |
| ☐ C-FXYF | Bell 407 | 53022 | | |
| ☐ C-GEPA | Bell 407 | 53739 | ex C-FLPA | |
| ☐ C-GOFL | Bell 407 | 53130 | | |
| | | | | |
| ☐ C-FHHH | Aérospatiale AS350BA AStar | 1421 | ex N5782X | |
| ☐ C-FXAL | Aérospatiale AS350B AStar | 1816 | ex SE-HNP | |
| ☐ C-GNAI | Aérospatiale AS350B AStar | 1685 | ex N380NA | |
| ☐ C-GVYM | Bell 206L LongRanger | 45143 | | ♦ |

## VANCOUVER ISLAND AIR                              Campbell River, BC (YBL)

| | | | | |
|---|---|---|---|---|
| ☐ C-FCSN | Beech D18S | CA-16 | ex RCAF1441 | FP |
| ☐ CF-GNR | Beech 3NM | CA-191 | ex (CF-SIK) | FP |
| ☐ C-FIZB | Cessna 180J | 18052409 | ex N46262 | FP |
| ☐ C-FWCA | de Havilland DHC-2 Beaver | 1285 | ex C-GUDB | FP |
| ☐ C-GAIV | Beech TC-45G | AF-80 | ex N711KP | FP |
| ☐ C-GVIX | de Havilland DHC-3 Turbo Otter | 97 | ex C-GGOR | FP♦ |

## VIH HELICOPTERS                                            Victoria, BC (YYJ)

| | | | | |
|---|---|---|---|---|
| ☐ C-FDUB | Aérospatiale AS350BA AStar | 3041 | ex N4073S | |
| ☐ C-FVIG | Aérospatiale AS350B2 AStar | 2893 | ex N333AS | |
| ☐ C-FVIT | Aérospatiale AS350B2 AStar | 2890 | ex N544AS | |
| ☐ C-FXHS | Aérospatiale AS350B1 AStar | 2248 | | |
| ☐ C-GNME | Aérospatiale AS350B2 AStar | 2826 | ex N351WW | |
| ☐ C-GNMJ | Aérospatiale AS350BA AStar | 2829 | | |
| ☐ C-GOLV | Aérospatiale AS350BA AStar | 1108 | ex N3595N | |
| ☐ C-GPHM | Aérospatiale AS350B2 AStar | 2488 | | |
| ☐ C-GPHQ | Aérospatiale AS350B1 AStar | 2017 | ex N855NM | |
| ☐ C-GPHR | Aérospatiale AS350B1 AStar | 2268 | | |
| ☐ C-GPTL | Aérospatiale AS350B2 AStar | 2103 | ex OY-HEH | |
| ☐ C-GPWO | Aérospatiale AS350B2 AStar | 2236 | ex N2BQ | |
| ☐ C-GVIA | Aérospatiale AS350B1 AStar | 2297 | ex N442BV | |
| | | | | |
| ☐ C-FVIH | Bell 205A-1 | 30164 | ex N205WW | |
| ☐ C-GAYB | Bell 205A-1 | 30295 | | |
| ☐ C-GKVI | Bell 205A-1 | 30182 | ex C-GOLE | |
| ☐ C-GLVI | Bell 205A-1 | 30209 | ex C-GPET | |
| ☐ C-GVIE | Bell 205B | 30188 | ex JA9854 | |
| ☐ C-GVIJ | Bell 205A-1 | 30105 | ex C-FOAR | |
| | | | | |
| ☐ C-FBER | Bell 206B JetRanger III | 2648 | ex N5018L | |
| ☐ C-FHSO | Bell 206B JetRanger | 165 | ex CF-HSO | |
| ☐ C-GCXT | Bell 206B JetRanger II | 1551 | ex N4432V | |
| ☐ C-GNMT | Bell 206B JetRanger III | 2295 | ex N722CH | |
| ☐ C-GORO | Bell 206B JetRanger II | 2086 | ex N15558 | |
| ☐ C-GWGS | Bell 206B JetRanger | 447 | ex N2230W | |
| | | | | |
| ☐ C-FIBN | Sikorsky S-61N | 61811 | | ♦ |
| ☐ C-FNMD | Bell 212 | 30730 | ex PT-HRK | |
| ☐ C-FNSA | Bell 212 | 30524 | ex N144WA | |
| ☐ C-FPZR | Sikorsky S-61L | 61362 | ex N305V | |
| ☐ C-FQNG | Sikorsky S-61N | 61032 | ex N301Y | |
| ☐ C-FTVI | Sikorsky S-61N | 61818 | ex N4240S | |
| ☐ C-FWDV | Bell 212 | 30973 | ex N2768N | |
| ☐ C-FXBC | Aérospatiale AS355F2 Twin Star | 5274 | | ♦ |
| ☐ C-GCVI | Bell 407 | 53854 | | |
| ☐ C-GGSM | Bell 212 | 30741 | | ♦ |
| ☐ C-GGSO | Bell 212 | 30696 | ex N90220 | |
| ☐ C-GGVI | Bell 407 | 53834 | | |
| ☐ C-GHTN | Sikorsky S-61N | 61755 | ex N219AC | ♦ |
| ☐ C-GKHL | Kamov Ka-32-IIBC | (31594)8801/03 | ex RA-31594 | |
| ☐ C-GVIB | Bell 407 | 53826 | ex C-FTLZ | |
| ☐ C-GVIU | Bell 407 | 53789 | ex C-FPNX | |

## VILLERS AIR SERVICES
**Fort Nelson, BC (YYE)**

| | | | | |
|---|---|---|---|---|
| ☐ C-FGAQ | Britten-Norman BN-2A-27 Islander | 212 | ex G-51-212 | |
| ☐ C-FJBD | Beech 58 Baron | TH-260 | ex N518SW | |
| ☐ C-FTVP | Cessna 208B Caravan I | 208B1264 | ex N5090Y | |
| ☐ C-GEBH | Cessna U206E Stationair | U20601697 | ex N8232Q | |
| ☐ C-GPMV | Piper PA-31 Navajo C | 31-7712081 | ex N273PE | |

## VOYAGE AIR
**Fort McMurray, AB (ZFM)**

| | | | | |
|---|---|---|---|---|
| ☐ C-GBNA | de Havilland DHC-3 Otter | 125 | ex N5368G | FP/WS |
| ☐ C-GDOB | de Havilland DHC-2 Beaver | 774 | ex C-GEZR | FP/WS |
| ☐ C-GOLB | Cessna A185F Skywagon | 18503188 | ex N93173 | FP/WS |
| ☐ C-GOZP | Cessna A185F Skywagon | 18503258 | ex (N93874) | FP/WS |
| ☐ C-GQQJ | de Havilland DHC-2 Beaver | 719 | ex N202PS | FP/WS |
| ☐ C-GUJW | de Havilland DHC-2 Beaver | 1657 | ex 305 | FP/WS |
| ☐ C-GZSI | de Havilland DHC-2 Beaver | 1003 | ex N5327 | FP/WS |

## VOYAGEUR AIRWAYS
**Voyageur (VC/VAL)**　　　**Sudbury/North Bay, ON (YSB/YYB)**

| | | | | |
|---|---|---|---|---|
| ☐ C-FEXZ | de Havilland DHC-8-314 | 319 | ex G-BRYJ | |
| ☐ C-FEYG | de Havilland DHC-8-311 | 320 | ex N320BC | |
| ☐ C-FEZD | de Havilland DHC-8-314 | 385 | ex LN-WFR | op for UN |
| ☐ C-FIQT | de Havilland DHC-8-314 | 395 | ex N342EN | |
| ☐ C-FNCU | de Havilland DHC-8-314 | 517 | ex G-NVSB | op for UN? |
| ☐ C-GHQZ | de Havilland DHC-8-314 | 370 | ex OE-LLY | op for UN |
| | | | | |
| ☐ C-FMCY | Canadair CRJ-200 | 7064 | ex D-ACLP | |
| ☐ C-FMUV | Canadair CRJ-200 | 7073 | ex D-ACLQ | op for UN |
| ☐ C-FTYS | Canadair CRJ-200LR | 7039 | ex N653ML | [YYB] |
| ☐ C-FWWU | Canadair CRJ-200LR | 7299 | ex N299BS | |
| ☐ C-FXHC | Canadair CRJ-200ER | 7329 | ex N329BS | op for UN |
| ☐ C-FXLH | Canadair CRJ-200LR | 7283 | ex G-MKSA | |
| ☐ C-GIXR | Canadair CRJ-200LR | 7434 | ex VT-SAS | ♦ |
| ☐ C-GMKG | Canadair CRJ-200LR | 7191 | ex N27191 | ♦ |
| | | | | |
| ☐ C-FAPP | Beech A100 King Air | B-169 | ex N305TZ | |
| ☐ C-FBGS | Beech A100 King Air | B-204 | ex N108JL | |
| ☐ C-FZKM | de Havilland DHC-7-102 | 061 | ex N903HA | op for UN |
| ☐ C-FZVW | Beech 200 Super King Air | BB-787 | ex N26G | |
| ☐ C-FZVX | Beech 200 Super King Air | BB-231 | ex N200FH | |
| ☐ C-GFOF | de Havilland DHC-7-102 | 037 | ex N67RM | op for UN |
| ☐ C-GGUL | de Havilland DHC-7-102 | 070 | ex N905HA | |
| ☐ C-GJJT | Beech 200 Super King Air | BB-828 | ex N62GA | |
| ☐ C-GLOL | de Havilland DHC-7-102 | 039 | ex HB-IVW | op for UN |

## WAASHESHKUN AIRWAYS
**Baie du Poste (Mistassini Lake), ON**

| | | | | |
|---|---|---|---|---|
| ☐ C-FDIO | de Havilland DHC-3 Otter | 452 | ex TAF 9102 | FP/WS |

## WABAKIMI AIR
**Armstrong, ON (YYW)**

| | | | | |
|---|---|---|---|---|
| ☐ CF-BJY | de Havilland DHC-2 Beaver | 173 | ex N4792C | FP/WS |
| ☐ C-FBPC | de Havilland DHC-2 Beaver | 144 | ex VH-AAS | FP/WS |
| ☐ C-FYLZ | de Havilland DHC-3 Otter | 247 | ex VH-SBR | FP/WS |

## WAHKASH CONTRACTING
**Campbell River, BC (YBL)**

| | | | | |
|---|---|---|---|---|
| ☐ C-FIGF | de Havilland DHC-2 Beaver | 834 | ex CF-IGF | FP |
| ☐ C-GVHT | de Havilland DHC-2 Beaver | 257 | ex 51-16797 | FP |

## WAMAIR SERVICE & OUTFITTING
**Matheson Island, MB**

| | | | | |
|---|---|---|---|---|
| ☐ C-FLXY | Cessna 208 Caravan I | 20800297 | ex N208LA | |
| ☐ C-GEIF | Cessna U206F Stationair 6 | U20602938 | | FP/WS |
| ☐ C-GJPX | Cessna 208 Caravan I | 20800302 | ex N1284N | FP/WS |
| ☐ C-GKCK | Cessna U206E Super Skywagon | U20601487 | ex N1487M | FP/WS |
| ☐ C-GYWQ | Cessna U206G Stationair | U20604439 | | FP/WS♦ |

## WASAYA AIRWAYS
**Wasaya (WT/WSG)**　　　**Thunder Bay, ON (YQT)**

| | | | | |
|---|---|---|---|---|
| ☐ C-FQWA | Beech 1900D | UE-75 | ex N175MH | |
| ☐ C-FWAU | Beech 1900D | UE-164 | ex N861CA | |
| ☐ C-FWAX | Beech 1900D | UE-297 | ex N21679 | |
| ☐ C-FWZK | Beech 1900D | UE-8 | ex D-CBSF | |
| ☐ C-GSWA | Beech 1900D | UE-34 | ex N83801 | |
| ☐ C-GZVJ | Beech 1900D | UE-223 | ex N1123J | |
| | | | | |
| ☐ C-FKPI | Pilatus PC-12/45 | 250 | ex N250PB | |
| ☐ C-FKRB | Pilatus PC-12/45 | 233 | ex HB-FRD | |

| | | | | | |
|---|---|---|---|---|---|
| ☐ C-FPCL | Pilatus PC-12/45 | 276 | ex N276CN | | |
| ☐ C-FWAV | Pilatus PC-12/45 | 280 | ex N280PC | | |
| ☐ C-FYZS | Pilatus PC-12/45 | 227 | ex N227PC | | |
| ☐ C-GBJV | Pilatus PC-12/45 | 237 | ex HB-FRH | | |
| ☐ C-GBXW | Pilatus PC-12/45 | 170 | ex N170PD | | |
| ☐ C-GKAY | Pilatus PC-12/45 | 178 | ex N178PC | | |
| ☐ C-GPAI | Pilatus PC-12/45 | 491 | ex N491VA | | |
| | | | | | |
| ☐ C-FHWA | Cessna 208B Caravan I | 208B0967 | ex N428FC | | ♦ |
| ☐ C-FKAD | Cessna 208B Caravan I | 208B0327 | | | |
| ☐ C-FKDL | Cessna 208B Caravan I | 208B0240 | ex (N5127B) | | |
| ☐ C-FPCC | Cessna 208B Caravan I | 208B0840 | ex N52623 | | |
| ☐ C-FWAW | Cessna 208B Caravan I | 208B0895 | ex N5265B | | |
| | | | | | |
| ☐ C-FFFS | Hawker Siddeley HS.748 Srs.2A/209LFD | 1663 | ex G-BHCJ | 806 | |
| ☐ C-FTTW | Hawker Siddeley HS.748 Srs.2A/264 | 1681 | ex G-AYIR | 805 | Frtr |
| ☐ C-GLTC | Hawker Siddeley HS.748 Srs.2A/244LFD | 1656 | ex N57910 | 801 | Super Tanker |
| ☐ C-GMAA | Hawker Siddeley HS.748 Srs.2A/214LFD | 1576 | ex TR-LQY | 807 | |
| ☐ C-GMWT | de Havilland DHC-8Q-314 | 442 | ex OE-LTH | | ♦ |

## WATSON'S SKYWAYS                                                       Wawa-Hawk Junction, ON (YXZ)

| | | | | | |
|---|---|---|---|---|---|
| ☐ C-FAZQ | Cessna U206 Super Skywagon | U206-0337 | ex CF-AZQ | | FP/WS |
| ☐ C-GIKP | Cessna 208 Caravan I | 20800141 | ex C-GHGV | | FP |
| ☐ C-GOFB | de Havilland DHC-3 Turbo Otter | 39 | | | FP♦ |

## WAWEIG AIR

| | | | | | |
|---|---|---|---|---|---|
| ☐ C-FQND | de Havilland DHC-3 Turbo Otter | 233 | | | FP♦ |
| ☐ C-FYCX | de Havilland DHC-3 Turbo Otter | 44 | ex N10704 | | FP♦ |
| ☐ C-GLAB | de Havilland DHC-3 Turbo Otter | 348 | ex 55-2210 | | ♦ |

## WEAGAMOW AIR                                                           Weagamow-Round Lake, ON (ZRJ)

| | | | | | |
|---|---|---|---|---|---|
| ☐ C-GNNO | Cessna A185F Skywagon | 18502685 | ex (N1016F) | | FP |

## WEST CARIBOU AIR SERVICE                                               Thunder Bay, ON (YQT)

| | | | | | |
|---|---|---|---|---|---|
| ☐ C-FBWP | Cessna 185A Skywagon | 1850430 | | | FP♦ |
| ☐ CF-FOX | Noorduyn Norseman VI | 340 | | | FP♦ |
| ☐ C-FKAS | Noorduyn Norseman | UC-64A | ex 43-5376 | | FP♦ |
| ☐ C-GKYG | de Havilland DHC-3 Turbo Otter | 261 | ex N2750 | | FP♦ |
| ☐ C-GSUV | de Havilland DHC-3 Turbo Otter | 376 | ex N445FD | | FP♦ |

## WEST COAST AIR                            (8O)             Vancouver-Coal Harbor, BC (CXH)

| | | | | | |
|---|---|---|---|---|---|
| ☐ C-FAWA | de Havilland DHC-2 Beaver | 1430 | ex VH-IDR | | FP |
| ☐ C-FEBE | de Havilland DHC-2 Beaver | 792 | ex N9983B | | FP |
| ☐ C-FJBP | de Havilland DHC-2 Beaver | 942 | ex CF-JBP | | FP |
| ☐ C-FWAC | de Havilland DHC-2 Beaver | 1356 | ex N68089 | | FP |
| ☐ C-GEZS | de Havilland DHC-2 Beaver | 1277 | ex 57-6170 | | FP |
| ☐ C-GFDI | de Havilland DHC-2 Beaver | 606 | ex 53-2810 | | FP |
| ☐ C-GMKP | de Havilland DHC-2 Beaver | 1374 | ex N87775 | | FP |
| ☐ C-GOLC | de Havilland DHC-2 Beaver | 1392 | ex N62354 | | FP |
| | | | | | |
| ☐ C-FGQE | de Havilland DHC-6 Twin Otter 100 | 40 | ex CF-GQE | 609 | FP |
| ☐ C-FGQH | de Havilland DHC-6 Twin Otter 100 | 106 | ex 8Q-MAF | 604 | FP |
| ☐ C-FMHR | de Havilland DHC-6 Twin Otter 100 | 51 | ex CF-MHR | 605 | FP |
| ☐ C-FWTE | de Havilland DHC-6 Twin Otter 100 | 96 | ex CF-WTE | 603 | FP |
| ☐ C-GQKN | de Havilland DHC-6 Twin Otter 100 | 94 | ex PZ-TAV | 606 | FP |

## WEST WIND AVIATION / PRONTO AIRWAYS
##                               Westwind (WEW)                        Regina, SK (YQR)

| | | | | | |
|---|---|---|---|---|---|
| ☐ C-FWWF | Beech 200 Super King Air | BB-374 | ex N111UR | | |
| ☐ C-FWWQ | Beech 200 Super King Air | BB-667 | ex N667NA | | |
| ☐ C-GWWN | Beech 200 Super King Air | BB-14 | ex N418CS | | |
| ☐ C-GWWV | Beech 200 Super King Air | BB-287 | ex N498AC | | |
| ☐ C-GYDQ | Beech 200 Super King Air | | | | ♦ |
| | | | | | |
| ☐ C-FCPD | British Aerospace Jetstream 31 | 822 | ex G-31-822 | | |
| ☐ C-FZJE | Cessna 401B | 401B0032 | ex (N7931Q) | | |
| ☐ C-GAXR | Cessna 401B | 401B0050 | ex N1250C | | |
| ☐ C-GDCG | Beech 1900D | UE-368 | ex C-GWEA | | ♦ |
| ☐ C-GEUY | Cessna 414 II | 414-0821 | | | |

| Reg | Type | c/n | ex | Notes |
|---|---|---|---|---|
| C-GHGK | British Aerospace Jetstream 31 | 786 | ex N786SC | |
| C-GGPX | Cessna 402C II | 402C0280 | ex C-GGSN | |
| C-GPRT | Beech 1900C-1 | UC-140 | ex N140YV | Pronto A/w colours |
| C-GPRZ | Beech 1900C-1 | UC-76 | ex ZS-PJM | |
| C-GRSY | Cessna 401 | 401-0248 | ex N8400F | |
| C-GWEA | Beech 1900D | UE-368 | ex N368DC | ◆ |
| C-GWWB | Cessna 414 | 414-0514 | ex N414DM | |
| C-GWWC | ATR 42-300 | 0209 | ex N209AT | |
| C-GWWD | ATR 42-300 | 0211 | ex N213AT | |
| C-GWWK | Beech 1900D | UE-395 | ex VH-RUI | ◆ |
| C-GWWR | ATR 42-300 | 0238 | ex G-RHUM | |
| C-GWWU | Cessna 560 Citation | 560-0304 | bb-455 | ◆ |
| C-GWWX | Beech 1900C-1 | UC-44 | ex OY-JRI | |
| C-GWWY | Beech 1900C-1 | UC-63 | ex ZS-PDI | |

## WESTJET — Westjet (WS/WJA) — Calgary-Intl, AB (YYC)

| Reg | Type | c/n | ex | Fleet |
|---|---|---|---|---|
| C-GBWS | Boeing 737-6CT | 34288/1931 | | 608 |
| C-GEWJ | Boeing 737-6CT | 35571/2045 | | 615 |
| C-GPWS | Boeing 737-6CT | 34284/1759 | | 601 |
| C-GWCQ | Boeing 737-6CT | 35111/2004 | | 610 |
| C-GWCT | Boeing 737-6CT | 35112/2016 | | 611 |
| C-GWCY | Boeing 737-6CT | 35113/2022 | | 612 |
| C-GWJU | Boeing 737-6CT | 34289/1956 | | 609 |
| C-GWSB | Boeing 737-6CT | 34285/1797 | | 602 |
| C-GWSI | Boeing 737-6CT | 34286/1816 | | 603 |
| C-GWSJ | Boeing 737-6CT | 34621/1862 | | 605 |
| C-GWSK | Boeing 737-6CT | 34287/1912 | ex N1787B | 607 |
| C-GWSL | Boeing 737-6CT | 34633/1884 | | 606 |
| C-GXWJ | Boeing 737-6CT | 35570/2032 | | 613 |
| C-FBWJ | Boeing 737-7CT/W | 32767/1629 | ex (C-GWSA) | 230 |
| C-FBWS | Boeing 737-7CT/W | 37088/3080 | ex N1786B | 255 |
| C-FCWJ | Boeing 737-7CT/W | 35086/2613 | | 250 |
| C-FEWJ | Boeing 737-7CT/W | 32769/1665 | | 232 |
| C-FGWJ | Boeing 737-7CT/W | 32764/1553 | | 226 |
| C-FIBW | Boeing 737-7CT/W | 37956/3649 | | 266 ◆ |
| C-FIWJ | Boeing 737-7CT/W | 30712/2185 | | 240 |
| C-FIWS | Boeing 737-76N/W | 32404/851 | | 001 |
| C-FJWS | Boeing 737-76N/W | 28651/872 | | 002 |
| C-FKIW | Boeing 737-7CT/W | 37955/3616 | ex N1796B | 265 |
| C-FKWS | Boeing 737-76N/W | 30134/905 | ex N1787B | 003 ◆ |
| C-FLWJ | Boeing 737-7CT/W | 38096/3520 | | 262 |
| C-FMWJ | Boeing 737-7CT/W | 32771/1754 | | 233 |
| C-FTWJ | Boeing 737-7CT/W | 30713/2220 | ex N1786B | 241 |
| C-FUWS | Boeing 737-7CT/W | 32765/1574 | | 228 |
| C-FWAD | Boeing 737-7CT/W | 32753/1222 | | 201 |
| C-FWAF | Boeing 737-7CT/W | 32747/1239 | | 202 |
| C-FWAI | Boeing 737-7CT/W | 33656/1246 | | 203 |
| C-FWAO | Boeing 737-7CT/W | 33657/1254 | | 205 |
| C-FWAQ | Boeing 737-7CT/W | 32748/1266 | | 206 |
| C-FWBG | Boeing 737-7CT/W | 32749/1281 | | 207 |
| C-FWBL | Boeing 737-7CT/W | 32750/1286 | | 208 |
| C-FWBW | Boeing 737-7CT/W | 33697/1303 | | 209 |
| C-FWBX | Boeing 737-7CT/W | 32751/1333 | | 210 |
| C-FWCC | Boeing 737-7CT/W | 32752/1339 | | 211 |
| C-FWCN | Boeing 737-7CT/W | 33698/1346 | | 212 |
| C-FWSF | Boeing 737-7CT/W | 32758/1431 | | 218 |
| C-FWSI | Boeing 737-7CT/W | 36691/2983 | | 253 |
| C-FWSK | Boeing 737-7CT/W | 36420/2671 | | 251 |
| C-FWSO | Boeing 737-7CT/W | 32759/1445 | | 219 |
| C-FWSV | Boeing 737-7CT/W | 32760/1472 | | 220 |
| C-FWSX | Boeing 737-7CT/W | 32761/1493 | | 221 |
| C-FWSY | Boeing 737-7CT/W | 32762/1501 | | 222 |
| C-FXWJ | Boeing 737-7CT/W | 32768/1648 | ex (C-GZWS) | 231 |
| C-FZWS | Boeing 737-76N/W | 32731/1044 | | 006 |
| C-GCWJ | Boeing 737-7CT/W | 33970/1556 | | 227 |
| C-GGWJ | Boeing 737-7CT/W | 35503/2334 | | 242 |
| C-GLWS | Boeing 737-76N/W | 32581/1009 | ex N1787B | 005 |
| C-GMWJ | Boeing 737-7CT/W | 35985/2135 | ex N1779B | 239 |
| C-GQWJ | Boeing 737-7CT/W | 35505/2436 | ex N1786B | 246 |
| C-GRWS | Boeing 737-76N/W | 32881/1155 | | 007 |
| C-GSWJ | Boeing 737-7CT/W | 37423/3357 | | 261 |
| C-GTWS | Boeing 737-76N/W | 32883/1179 | | 008 |
| C-GUWJ | Boeing 737-7CT/W | 36422/2497 | ex N1786B | 248 |
| C-GUWS | Boeing 737-76N/W | 33378/1206 | | 009 |
| C-GVWJ | Boeing 737-7CT/W | 36421/2484 | ex N1786B | 247 |
| C-GWAZ | Boeing 737-7CT/W | 32763/1522 | | 223 |
| C-GWBF | Boeing 737-7CT/W | 32757/1370 | | 213 |
| C-GWBJ | Boeing 737-7CT/W | 32754/1385 | ex N1787B | 215 |
| C-GWBN | Boeing 737-7CT/W | 34155/1772 | | 235 |
| C-GWBT | Boeing 737-7CT/W | 32755/1396 | | 216 |

| | | | | | |
|---|---|---|---|---|---|
| ☐ C-GWBX | Boeing 737-7CT/W | 34156/1793 | | 236 | |
| ☐ C-GWCM | Boeing 737-7CT/W | 32756/1413 | | 217 | |
| ☐ C-GWCN | Boeing 737-7CT/W | 34157/1818 | ex N1784B | 237 | |
| ☐ C-GWJE | Boeing 737-7CT/W | 35078/2431 | | 245 | |
| ☐ C-GWJF | Boeing 737-7CT/W | 32766/1599 | | 229 | |
| ☐ C-GWJG | Boeing 737-7CT/W | 35504/2366 | ex N1786B | 243 | |
| ☐ C-GWJK | Boeing 737-7CT/W | 35084/2564 | ex N1786B | 249 | |
| ☐ C-GWJO | Boeing 737-7CT/W | 33969/1527 | | 225 | |
| | | | | | |
| ☐ C-GWSE | Boeing 737-76N/W | 33379/1216 | | 010 | |
| ☐ C-GWSH | Boeing 737-76N/W | 29886/1258 | | 011 | |
| ☐ C-GWSN | Boeing 737-7CT/W | 37089/3090 | ex N1796B | 256 | |
| ☐ C-GWSO | Boeing 737-7CT/W | 37090/3092 | ex N1796B | 257 | |
| ☐ C-GWSP | Boeing 737-7CT/W | 36693/3108 | | 258 | |
| ☐ C-GWSQ | Boeing 737-7CT/W | 37091/3134 | | 259 | |
| ☐ C-GWSU | Boeing 737-7CT/W | 36689/2860 | ex N1787B | 252 | |
| ☐ C-GWSY | Boeing 737-7CT/W | 37421/3184 | ex N1786B | 260 | ♦ |
| ☐ C-GWSZ | Boeing 737-8CT/W | 37092/3164 | ex N1787B | 812 | |
| ☐ C-GWTJ | Boeing 737-7CT/W | 40338/3529 | | 263 | ♦ |
| ☐ C-GYWJ | Boeing 737-7CT/W | 32772/1879 | | 238 | |
| ☐ C- | Boeing 737- | | | | o/o |
| ☐ C- | Boeing 737- | | | | o/o |
| | | | | | |
| ☐ C-FAWJ | Boeing 737-8CT/W | 35502/2323 | | 807 | |
| ☐ C-FCNW | Boeing 737-8CT/W | 39092/3580 | | 816 | |
| ☐ C-FKWJ | Boeing 737-8CT/W | 36435/3469 | | 815 | |
| ☐ C-FWIJ | Boeing 737-8CT/W | 39072/ | | | o/o♦ |
| ☐ C-FWSE | Boeing 737-8CT/W | 36690/2987 | | 811 | |
| ☐ C-FWVJ | Boeing 737-8CT/W | 37962/3863 | | 817 | ♦ |
| ☐ C-GJWS | Boeing 737-8CT/W | 34152/1714 | | 802 | |
| ☐ C-GKWJ | Boeing 737-8CT/W | 34151/1684 | | 801 | |
| ☐ C-GWBL | Boeing 737-8CT/W | 34154/1734 | | 806 | |
| ☐ C-GWRG | Boeing 737-8CT/W | 390713931 | | 818 | ♦ |
| ☐ C-GWSA | Boeing 737-8CT/W | 34153/1731 | | 805 | |
| ☐ C-GWSR | Boeing 737-8CT/W | 35288/2802 | | 809 | |
| ☐ C-GWSV | Boeing 737-8CT/W | 37158/2841 | | 810 | |
| ☐ C-GWSX | Boeing 737-8CT/W | 36696/3314 | | 813 | |
| ☐ C-GWSZ | Boeing 737-8CT/W | 37092/3164 | | 812 | |
| ☐ C-GWWJ | Boeing 737-8CT/W | 35080/2524 | ex N1786B | 808 | |
| ☐ C-GZWS | Boeing 737-8CT/W | 32770/1719 | | 803 | |
| | | | | | |
| ☐ G-WJAN | Boeing 757-21K | 28674/746 | ex C-FFAN | | <TCX♦ |

## WHISTLER AIR SERVICES — Whistler, BC (YWS)

| | | | | |
|---|---|---|---|---|
| ☐ C-FSKZ | de Havilland DHC-2 Beaver | 1594 | ex CF-SKZ | FP |
| ☐ C-GEND | de Havilland DHC-3 Turbo Otter | 371 | ex N83U | FP |
| ☐ C-GSFA | Cessna 208 Caravan | 20800212 | ex 8Q-MAT | FP |

## WHITE RIVER AIR — White River, ON (YWR)

| | | | | |
|---|---|---|---|---|
| ☐ CF-FHR | de Havilland DHC-2 Beaver | 46 | | FP |
| ☐ C-FWRA | de Havilland DHC-3 Otter | 213 | ex India IM1714 | FP |

## WILDERNESS AIR — Vermilion Bay, ON (YVG)

| | | | | |
|---|---|---|---|---|
| ☐ C-FGMK | de Havilland DHC-2 Beaver | 1329 | ex 58-2003 | FP |
| ☐ C-FJOF | de Havilland DHC-2 Beaver | 1053 | ex CF-JOF | FP♦ |
| ☐ C-FODV | de Havilland DHC-3 Otter | 411 | ex CF-ODV | FP |
| ☐ C-FWTK | Bell 412SP | 36001 | ex N2148K | ♦ |
| ☐ C-FWTQ | Bell 412SP | 36002 | ex N2149S | ♦ |
| ☐ C-FWTY | Bell 412SP | 36004 | ex N33008 | ♦ |
| ☐ C-GFZF | Cessna A185E Skywagon | 18502002 | ex N70118 | FP |
| ☐ C-GWDJ | Bell 212 | 30817 | | ♦ |
| ☐ C-GNFN | Cessna 208 Caravan I | 20800502 | | |

## WINGS OVER KISSISSING

| | | | | |
|---|---|---|---|---|
| ☐ C-FFVZ | de Havilland DHC-3 Turbo Otter | 145 | ex N80944 | FP/WS |
| ☐ C-FKIE | Cessna 180A Skywagon | 18050180 | | FP/WS♦ |
| ☐ C-FPSM | de Havilland DHC-2 Turbo Beaver | 1543/TB2 | ex ET-AKI | FP/WS♦ |
| ☐ C-FRHW | de Havilland DHC-3 Otter | 445 | | FP/WS♦ |
| ☐ C-FWEJ | de Havilland DHC-3 Turbo Otter | 208 | ex IM1710 | FP/WS |
| ☐ C-GBWP | Bell 206B JetRanger | 1537 | | ♦ |
| ☐ C-GEWP | de Havilland DHC-2 Turbo Beaver | 1543/TB2 | ex ET-AKI | FP/WS |
| ☐ C-GHGN | de Havilland DHC-2 Beaver | 80 | | FP/WS♦ |
| ☐ C-GMLL | Cessna 337 Skymaster | 33700004 | | ♦ |

## WOLVERINE AIR — Fort Simpson, NT (YFS)

| | | | | |
|---|---|---|---|---|
| ☐ C-FTOE | Piper PA-31 Navajo | 31-7401213 | | ♦ |

| | | | | |
|---|---|---|---|---|
| ☐ C-FTQB | Cessna A185F Skywagon | 18501655 | ex (N1948U) | |
| ☐ C-GIHF | Britten-Norman BN-2A-26 Islander | 475 | ex G-BDJU | |
| ☐ C-GQOA | Cessna U206G Stationair 6 | U20604993 | ex (N4600U) | |

## CC- CHILE (Republic of Chile)

### AEROCARDAL (CDA) Santiago-Benitez Intl (SCL)

| | | | | |
|---|---|---|---|---|
| ☐ CC-AAQ | Dornier 228-202 | 8119 | ex CS-TGO | |
| ☐ CC-ACG | Dornier 328-110 | 3063 | ex OE-LKE | |
| ☐ CC-ACK | Agusta A.109S | 22170 | | |
| ☐ CC-ACK | Agusta A109S | 22170 | | ◆ |
| ☐ CC-AEY | Dornier 328-110 | 3072 | ex OE-LKD | ◆ |
| ☐ CC-AEX | Eurocopter EC135T2 | 0316 | | ◆ |
| ☐ CC-CWA | MBB 105LSA-3 | 2006 | ex N96LB | ◆ |
| ☐ CC-CWB | Piper PA-31-325 Navajo C/R | 31-8312017 | ex N500SM | ◆ |
| ☐ CC-CWC | Dornier 228-202K | 8162 | ex D-CLUE | ◆ |
| ☐ CC-CWD | Piper PA-31T1 Cheyenne 1 | 31T-8104071 | ex CC-CRU | ◆ |
| ☐ CC-CWE | Cessna 421C | 421C0614 | ex CC-PJB | ◆ |
| ☐ CC-CWI | MBB 105CB-2 | S-193 | ex C-11 | ◆ |
| ☐ CC-CWK | IAI Gulfstream G150 | 219 | ex N219GA | ◆ |
| ☐ CC-CWW | Cessna S550 Citation II | S550-0002 | ex N211VP | ◆ |
| ☐ CC-CWX | Dornier 228-101 | 7027 | ex CC-CSA | |
| ☐ CC-CWZ | Cessna S550 Citation S/II | S550-0143 | ex N458PE | ◆ |

### AEROSERVICIO Santiago-Tobalaba (SCTB)

| | | | | |
|---|---|---|---|---|
| ☐ CC-CDR | Cessna 208B | 208B1202 | ex N13194 | ◆ |
| ☐ CC-CEI | Cessna 421C Golden Eagle III | 421C0655 | ex CC-PFM | |

### AEROVIAS DAP (ATLANTIC AIRWAYS) Dap (DAP) Punta Arenas (PUQ)

| | | | | |
|---|---|---|---|---|
| ☐ CC-ACO | British Aerospace 146 Srs.200 | E2094 | ex OY-RCB | |
| ☐ CC-ACQ | Beech 300 Super King Air | FA-205 | ex N205FA | ◆ |
| ☐ CC-AEH | Cessna 404 | 404-0440 | ex CC-ETC | ◆ |
| ☐ CC-CHV | de Havilland DHC-6 Twin Otter 300 | 709 | ex G-BHUY | |
| ☐ CC-CLT | CASA C.212-100 | A10-1-103 | ex E-210 | [PUQ] |
| ☐ CC-CLV | Cessna 402C | 402C0073 | ex CC-CDU | |
| ☐ CC-CLY | Beech 100 King Air | B-79 | ex CC-PIE | |
| ☐ CC-COV | Cessna 402C | 402C0282 | ex CC-CDS | |
| ☐ CC-CZP | British Aerospace 146 Srs.200 | E2042 | ex G-FLTD | |
| ☐ CC- | British Aerospace 146 Srs.200 | E2115 | ex OY-RCW | ◆ |

### DAP HELICOPTEROS HeliDap (DHE) Punta Arenas (PUQ)

| | | | | |
|---|---|---|---|---|
| ☐ CC-ACM | MBB Bo 105CB-4 | S-414 | ex EC-HNT | ◆ |
| ☐ CC-ACN | MBB Bo 105CBS-4 | S-672 | ex EC-HPB | ◆ |
| ☐ CC-AEI | MBB Bo 105CBS-4 | S-615 | ex EC-IKT | ◆ |
| ☐ CC-AEJ | MBB Bo 105CBS-4 | S-661 | ex EC-IKO | ◆ |
| ☐ CC-CHK | MBB Bo 105CB-4-2 | S-687 | ex H-62 | EMS |
| ☐ CC-CHM | MBB Bo 105CB-4-2 | S-688 | ex H-63 | EMS |
| ☐ CC-CHN | MBB Bo 105CB-4-2 | S-689 | ex H-64 | EMS |
| ☐ CC-CHQ | MBB Bo 105CB-4-2 | S-708 | ex H-65 | EMS |
| ☐ CC-CHR | MBB Bo 105CB-4-2 | S-710 | ex H-66 | EMS |
| ☐ CC-AEK | Aérospatiale AS.350B3 Ecureuil | 4092 | ex EC-JTM | ◆ |
| ☐ CC-CCA | Eurocopter EC135T1 | 0122 | ex N214TD | |
| ☐ CC-CIB | Aérospatiale AS355F2 Twin Star | 5371 | ex XA-MDE | |
| ☐ CC-CIK | Aérospatiale AS355F2 Twin Star | 5413 | ex N710KM | |
| ☐ CC-CIN | Aérospatiale AS355F1 Twin Star | 5147 | ex N22TS | >INAER |

### EMPRESSA AERO - SERVICIOS PARRAGUE Aspar (PRG) Santiago

| | | | | |
|---|---|---|---|---|
| ☐ CC-CDT | Canadian Vickers PBY-5A Catalina | CV-332 | ex F-YCHB | 32 |
| ☐ CC-CNP | Consolidated PBY-6A Catalina | 2029 | ex EC-FXN | 35 |

### HELIDUERO

| | | | |
|---|---|---|---|
| ☐ CC-ACT | Agusta AW.119 MkII | 14754 | ◆ |
| ☐ CC-ACU | Agusta AW.119 MkII | 14749 | ◆ |

### HELIWORKS Heliworks (HLW) Concepcion (CCP)

| | | | | |
|---|---|---|---|---|
| ☐ CC-AQD | Mitsubishi MU-2B-36A | 7075A | ex LV- | ◆ |
| ☐ CC-CHU | Lockheed P2V-7S Neptune | 726-7217 | ex N703AU | 03 |
| ☐ CC-CRE | Piper PA-34-200T Seneca II | 34-7770432 | ex CC-PTP | ◆ |
| ☐ CC-PRI | Piper PA-34-200T Seneca II | 34-8070034 | ex CC-CCI | ◆ |

## INAER HELICOPTER CHILE — Santiago-Benitez Intl (SCL)

| | | | | | |
|---|---|---|---|---|---|
| ☐ CC-ACL | Bell 212 | 31123 | ex PT-HQG | | ♦ |
| ☐ CC-ACW | Aérospatiale AS355N Ecureuil 2 | 5598 | ex EC-KUC | | ♦ |
| ☐ CC-ACX | Eurocopter AS350B-3 | 4934 | ex EC-LGO | | ♦ |
| ☐ CC-AEB | Beech B300 | FL-128 | ex EC-GSQ | | ♦ |
| ☐ CC-AEO | Agusta A109E | 11119 | ex I-REMV | | ♦ |
| ☐ CC-CIS | Bell 212 | 30932 | ex CS-HFY | | |
| ☐ CC-CIU | Bell 407 | 53727 | ex C-FLFC | | |
| ☐ CC-CIX | Eurocopter AS350B-3 | 4288 | ex F-WWPK | | ♦ |
| ☐ CC-CIY | Bell 212 | 30685 | ex CS-HFW | | |
| ☐ CC-CRA | Bell 407 | 53795 | ex C-FPUU | | ♦ |
| ☐ CC-CRB | Bell 212 | 30558 | ex EC-FBL | | ♦ |

## LAN AIRLINES — LAN (LA/LAN) — Santiago-Benitez Intl (SCL)

Member of Oneworld

| | | | | | |
|---|---|---|---|---|---|
| ☐ CC-CVP | Airbus A318-121 | 3371 | ex D-AUAC | | |
| ☐ CC-CVR | Airbus A318-121 | 3390 | ex D-AUAH | | |
| ☐ CC-CVS | Airbus A318-121 | 3438 | ex D-AUAA | | |
| ☐ CC-CVU | Airbus A318-121 | 3469 | ex D-AUAD | | |
| ☐ CC-CVV | Airbus A318-121 | 3509 | ex D-AUAE | | |
| ☐ CC-CZJ | Airbus A318-121 | 3585 | ex D-AUAB | | |
| ☐ CC-CZN | Airbus A318-121 | 3602 | ex D-AUAF | | |
| ☐ CC-CZQ | Airbus A318-121 | 3606 | ex D-AUAG | | |
| ☐ CC-CZR | Airbus A318-121 | 3635 | ex D-AUAI | | |
| ☐ CC-CZS | Airbus A318-121 | 3642 | ex D-AUAJ | | |
| ☐ CC-BCA | Airbus A319-132 | 4563 | ex D-AVWB | | |
| ☐ CC-BCB | Airbus A319-132 | 4598 | ex D-AVWG | | |
| ☐ CC-BCC | Airbus A319-132 | 4605 | ex D-AVWH | | |
| ☐ CC-BCD | Airbus A319-132 | 4871 | ex D-AVYA | | ♦ |
| ☐ CC-BCE | Airbus A319-112 | 5005 | ex D-AVYH | | ♦ |
| ☐ CC-BCF | Airbus A319-112 | 5097 | ex D-AVYQ | | ♦ |
| ☐ CC-COX | Airbus A319-132 | 2096 | ex D-AVYN | | |
| ☐ CC-COY | Airbus A319-132 | 2295 | ex D-AVWA | | |
| ☐ CC-COZ | Airbus A319-132 | 2304 | ex D-AVWN | | |
| ☐ CC-CPJ | Airbus A319-132 | 2845 | ex D-AVYX | | |
| ☐ CC-CPL | Airbus A319-132 | 2858 | ex D-AVYB | | |
| ☐ CC-CYE | Airbus A319-132 | 3663 | ex D-AVYV | | |
| ☐ CC-CYF | Airbus A319-132 | 3671 | ex D-AVYW | | |
| ☐ CC-CYI | Airbus A319-132 | 3770 | ex D-AVXE | | |
| ☐ CC-CYJ | Airbus A319-132 | 3772 | ex D-AVXH | | |
| ☐ CC-CYL | Airbus A319-132 | 3779 | ex D-AVXJ | | |
| ☐ CC-BAF | Airbus A320-233 | 4516 | ex D-AXAG | | |
| ☐ CC-BAG | Airbus A320-233 | 4546 | ex D-AXAO | | |
| ☐ CC-BAH | Airbus A320-233 | 4549 | ex D-AUBQ | | |
| ☐ CC-BAI | Airbus A320-233 | 4543 | ex F-WWIS | | |
| ☐ CC-BAJ | Airbus A320-232 | 4576 | ex F-WWBX | | |
| ☐ CC-BAK | Airbus A320-232 | 4597 | ex D-AVVH | | |
| ☐ CC-BAL | Airbus A320-232 | 4657 | ex D-AXAC | | |
| ☐ CC-BAM | Airbus A320-232 | 4697 | ex D-AUBD | | ♦ |
| ☐ CC-BAN | Airbus A320-214 | 4758 | ex F-WWBP | | ♦ |
| ☐ CC-BAO | Airbus A320-214 | 4767 | ex F-WWBZ | | ♦ |
| ☐ CC-BAP | Airbus A320-214 | 4815 | ex D-AXAJ | | ♦ |
| ☐ CC-BAQ | Airbus A320-214 | 4839 | ex D-AXAD | | ♦ |
| ☐ CC-BAR | Airbus A320-214 | 4892 | ex D-AVVG | | ♦ |
| ☐ CC-BAS | Airbus A320-214 | 4896 | ex F-WWBO | | ♦ |
| ☐ CC-BAT | Airbus A320-214 | 4921 | ex D-AXAA | | ♦ |
| ☐ CC-BAU | Airbus A320-214 | 4943 | ex D-AXAQ | | ♦ |
| ☐ CC-BAV | Airbus A320-214 | 4972 | ex D-AVVC | | ♦ |
| ☐ CC-BAW | Airbus A320-214 | 5125 | ex D-AVVD | o/o♦ | |
| ☐ CC-BJB | Airbus A320-232 | 3264 | ex HK-4740 | | ♦ |
| ☐ CC-BJC | Airbus A320-232 | 3330 | ex HK-4738 | | ♦ |
| ☐ CC-COF | Airbus A320-233 | 1355 | ex F-WWBE | | |
| ☐ CC-COM | Airbus A320-233 | 1626 | ex F-WWDL | | |
| ☐ CC-CQP | Airbus A320-233 | 3556 | ex F-WWBC | | |
| ☐ CC-CQA | Airbus A340-313X | 359 | ex F-WWJY | | |
| ☐ CC-CQC | Airbus A340-313X | 363 | ex F-WWJZ | | |
| ☐ CC-CQE | Airbus A340-313X | 429 | ex F-WWJQ | | |
| ☐ CC-CQF | Airbus A340-313X | 442 | ex F-WWJY | | |
| ☐ CC-CQG | Airbus A340-313X | 167 | ex C-FYLC | | |
| ☐ CC-BDA | Boeing 767-316ER/W | 40798/1011 | | | ♦ |
| ☐ CC-BDB | Boeing 767-316ER/W | 40590/1014 | | | ♦ |
| ☐ CC-BDC | Boeing 767-316ER | 40591/1016 | | | ♦ |
| ☐ CC-BDD | Boeing 767-316ER | 40799 | | o/o♦ | |
| ☐ CC-BDE | Boeing 767-316ER | 40592 | | o/o♦ | |

| | | | | |
|---|---|---|---|---|
| ☐ CC-BDF | Boeing 767-316ER | 41746 | | o/o♦ |
| ☐ CC-BDG | Boeing 767-316ER | 41747 | | o/o♦ |
| ☐ CC-BDH | Boeing 767-316ER | 41748 | | o/o♦ |
| ☐ CC-BDI | Boeing 767-316ER | 40593 | | o/o♦ |
| ☐ CC-BJA | Boeing 767-316ER/W | 26329/641 | ex LV-BMR | |
| ☐ CC-CBJ | Boeing 767-316ER | 27613/652 | | |
| ☐ CC-CDM | Boeing 767-352ER | 26261/575 | ex VN-A763 | |
| ☐ CC-CDP | Boeing 767-316ER/W | 27597/602 | | |
| ☐ CC-CEB | Boeing 767-316ER/W | 26327/621 | | |
| ☐ CC-CML | Boeing 767-3Q8ER/W | 28206/694 | ex HC-CGZ | ♦ |
| ☐ CC-CRG | Boeing 767-375ER/W | 25865/430 | ex LV-BTE | |
| ☐ CC-CRH | Boeing 767-375ER | 25864/426 | ex B-2562 | |
| ☐ CC-CRV | Boeing 767-316ER/W | 27615/681 | ex LV-BFU | |
| ☐ CC-CWF | Boeing 767-316ER/W | 34626/940 | | |
| ☐ CC-CWG | Boeing 767-316ER/W | 34629/944 | | |
| ☐ CC-CWV | Boeing 767-316ER/W | 35230/955 | | |
| ☐ CC-CWY | Boeing 767-316ER/W | 35231/961 | | |
| ☐ CC-CXC | Boeing 767-316ER/W | 36710/962 | | |
| ☐ CC-CXF | Boeing 767-316ER/W | 36711/970 | ex HC-CIZ | ♦ |
| ☐ CC-CXG | Boeing 767-316ER/W | 36712/972 | ex N5020K | |
| ☐ CC-CXH | Boeing 767-316ER/W | 35698/973 | ex HC-CJA | ♦ |
| ☐ CC-CXI | Boeing 767-316ER/W | 37800/984 | | |
| ☐ CC-CXJ | Boeing 767-316ER/W | 37801/985 | | |
| ☐ CC-CXK | Boeing 767-316ER/W | 37802/987 | | |
| ☐ CC-CXL | Boeing 767-31BER | 26265/570 | ex LV-BFD | |
| ☐ CC-CZT | Boeing 767-316ER/W | 29228/699 | | |
| ☐ CC-CZU | Boeing 767-316ER/W | 29229/729 | | |
| ☐ CC-CZW | Boeing 767-316ER/W | 29227/698 | | |
| | | | | |
| ☐ CC- | Boeing 787-816 | 38464/10 | | o/o |
| ☐ CC- | Boeing 787-816 | 38475/16 | | o/o |

## LAN CARGO        LAN Cargo (UC/LCO)        Santiago-Benitez Intl (SCL)

| | | | | |
|---|---|---|---|---|
| ☐ CC-CZZ | Boeing 767-316F/W | 25756/712 | | |
| ☐ N312LA | Boeing 767-316F | 32572/846 | | |
| ☐ N314LA | Boeing 767-316F/W | 32573/848 | | >MAA |
| ☐ N316LA | Boeing 767-316F/W | 30842/860 | | op by FWL |
| ☐ N420LA | Boeing 767-316F/W | 34627/948 | | >MAA |
| ☐ N524LA | Boeing 767-346F | 35816/956 | ex JA631J | |
| ☐ PR-ABD | Boeing 767-316F/W | 34245/935 | | >TUS |
| | | | | |
| ☐ N772LA | Boeing 777-F6N | 37708/774 | | |
| ☐ N774LA | Boeing 777-F6N | 37710/782 | | |
| ☐ N776LA | Boeing 777-F16 | 38091 | | o/o♦ |
| ☐ N778LA | Boeing 777-F16 | 41518 | | o/o♦ |

## LAN EXPRESS        LANExpres (LU/LXP)        Santiago-Benitez Intl (SCL)

99.4% owned subsidiary of LAN Airlines and operates aircraft leased from the parent.

## LASSA - LINEAS DE AEROSERVICIOS        (LSE)        Santiago-Tobalaba (SCTB)

| | | | | |
|---|---|---|---|---|
| ☐ CC-AEV | Piper PA-31 Cheyenne | 31T-7920031 | ex N26SL | ♦ |
| ☐ CC-CIZ | Bell UH-1B | 1124 | ex EC-EOH | |
| ☐ CC-CPR | Piper PA-31T2 Cheyenne | 31T-8166070 | ex CC-PTA | ♦ |

## LINEA AEREA COSTA NORTE        Costa Norte (NOT)        Iquique (IQQ)

| | | | | |
|---|---|---|---|---|
| ☐ CC-CAJ | Cessna 337H Super Skymaster II | 33701860 | ex N1368L | |
| ☐ CC-CFU | Rockwell 500S Shrike Commander | 3320 | ex N348TT | |
| ☐ CC-CFW | Rockwell 500S Shrike Commander | 3230 | ex N567PT | |
| ☐ CC-CGB | Cessna 337H Super Skymaster II | 33701941 | ex N123YM | |
| ☐ CC-CGK | Cessna 337H Super Skymaster II | 33701818 | ex N1326L | |
| ☐ CC-CGX | Rockwell 500S Shrike Commander | 3306 | ex N10PP | <S/A Aeropecsa |
| ☐ CC-CHG | Rockwell 500S Shrike Commander | 3293 | ex N916AC | <S/A Aeropecsa |

## PAL AIRLINES        (5P/PCP)        Santiago-Benitez Intl (SCL)

| | | | | |
|---|---|---|---|---|
| ☐ CC-ACD | Boeing 737-2K9 | 23404/1176 | ex C9-BAK | |
| ☐ CC-ACE | Boeing 737-322 | 24669/1907 | ex N394UA | |
| ☐ CC-ADZ | Boeing 737-3G7 | 24634/1823 | ex N307AW | ♦ |
| ☐ CC-CRP | Boeing 737-230 | 22134/777 | ex N234AG | ♦ |
| ☐ CC-CZK | Boeing 737-236 | 21804/686 | ex G-BGDP | |

## PATAGONIA AIRLINES        Puerto Montt (PMC)

| | | | | |
|---|---|---|---|---|
| ☐ CC-CTS | Cessna 208B Caravan I | 208B1316 | ex N21424 | |

## SKY AIRLINE — Aerosky (H2/SKU) — Santiago-Benitez Intl (SCL)

| | | | | |
|---|---|---|---|---|
| ☐ CC-ABV | Airbus A320-233 | 1400 | ex N470TA | ♦ |
| ☐ CC-ABW | Airbus A320-233 | 1523 | ex N484TA | |
| ☐ CC-ADO | Airbus A320-231 | 0447 | ex N447AG | ♦ |
| ☐ CC-ADP | Airbus A320-231 | 0406 | ex N406PR | |
| ☐ CC-ADQ | Airbus A320-231 | 179 | ex N971GT | ♦ |
| | | | | |
| ☐ CC-AAG | Boeing 737-247 | 23608/1399 | ex LV-BIF | |
| ☐ CC-ABD | Boeing 737-2Q3 | 22736/896 | ex N763BA | ♦ |
| ☐ CC-CAP | Boeing 737-236 | 22027/654 | ex CC-CZM | |
| ☐ CC-CDB | Boeing 737-230 (Nordam 3) | 22120/715 | ex N122NJ | |
| ☐ CC-CRQ | Boeing 737-230 | 22135 | ex CX-PUF | ♦ |
| ☐ CC-CTB | Boeing 737-2Q3 | 23481/1241 | ex N381AC | |
| ☐ CC-CTD | Boeing 737-2Q3 | 23117/1033 | ex N380AC | |
| ☐ CC-CTF | Boeing 737-230 (Nordam 3) | 22122/721 | ex LV-BCD | |
| ☐ CC-CTH | Boeing 737-230 (Nordam 3) | 22636/808 | ex N271LR | |
| ☐ CC-CTK | Boeing 737-230 (Nordam 3) | 22402/744 | ex N261LR | |
| ☐ CC-CTM | Boeing 737-230 | 22139/791 | ex LV-BBO | |
| ☐ CC-CTO | Boeing 737-230 | 22114/657 | ex LV-BBI | |
| ☐ CC-CTX | Boeing 737-2T4 (AvAero 3) | 22698/823 | ex N722WN | |
| ☐ CC-CVI | Boeing 737-2Q3 | 22367/706 | ex N763AA | ♦ |
| | | | | |
| ☐ CC-AFX | Airbus A319-111 | 2263 | ex G-EZEU | ♦ |
| ☐ CC-AFY | Airbus A319-111 | 2442 | ex G-EZID | o/o♦ |
| ☐ CC-AFZ | Airbus A319-111 | 2446 | ex G-EZIE | o/o♦ |

## TRANSPORTES AEREOS CORPORATIVOS — Santiago-Tobalaba

| | | | | |
|---|---|---|---|---|
| ☐ CC-AAI | Dornier 228-202K | 8156 | ex LN-MOL | ♦ |

## TRANSPORTES SAN FRANCISCO

| | | | | |
|---|---|---|---|---|
| ☐ CC-ACH | de Havilland DHC-6-300 Twin Otter | 613 | ex C-GGPM | ♦ |
| ☐ CC-ADX | de Havilland DHC-8-202 | 536 | ex C-GBGC | ♦ |

## CN-    MOROCCO (Kingdom of Morocco)

### AIR ARABIA MAROC — (3O/MAC)

| | | | | |
|---|---|---|---|---|
| ☐ CN-NMA | Airbus A320-214 | 3809 | ex F-WWDV | |
| ☐ CN-NMB | Airbus A320-214 | 3833 | ex D-ABDV | |
| ☐ CN-NME | Airbus A320-214 | 2166 | ex A6-ABB | ♦ |

### JET4YOU — Argan( 8J/JFU) — Casablanca-Mohamed V (CMN)

| | | | | |
|---|---|---|---|---|
| ☐ CN-RPE | Boeing 737-8K5/W | 27990/246 | ex D-AHFJ | [BRU] |

### MED AIRLINES

| | | | | |
|---|---|---|---|---|
| ☐ CN-MMA | Fokker F.27 Friendship 500 | 10550 | ex TC-MBH | ♦ |

### REGIONAL AIR LINES — Maroc Regional (FN/RGL) — Casablanca-Anfa (CAS)

| | | | | |
|---|---|---|---|---|
| ☐ CN-RLA | Beech 1900D | UE-259 | ex N10863 | |
| ☐ CN-RLG | ATR 42-320 | 0366 | ex F-WQNM | |

### ROYAL AIR MAROC — Royalair Maroc (AT/RAM) — Casablanca-Mohamed V (CMN)

| | | | | |
|---|---|---|---|---|
| ☐ CN-COA | ATR 72-201 | 441 | ex F-WKVB | |
| ☐ CN-COB | ATR 72-202 | 444 | ex F-WKVD | |
| ☐ CN-COC | ATR 72-201 | 470 | ex F-WKVI | |
| ☐ CN-COE | ATR 72-600 | 0960 | ex F-WWLP | Royal Air Maroc Express |
| ☐ CN-COF | ATR 72-600 | 0958 | ex F-WWLO | Royal Air Maroc Express |
| | | | | |
| ☐ CN-RMV | Boeing 737-5B6 | 25317/2157 | | |
| ☐ CN-RMW | Boeing 737-5B6 | 25364/2166 | | [GSO] |
| ☐ CN-RMY | Boeing 737-5B6 | 26525/2209 | | |
| ☐ CN-RNB | Boeing 737-5B6 | 26527/2472 | | |
| ☐ CN-RNG | Boeing 737-5B6 | 27679/2734 | ex (CN-RNF) | |
| ☐ CN-RNH | Boeing 737-5B6 | 27680/2855 | | |
| | | | | |
| ☐ CN-RNL | Boeing 737-7B6/W | 28982/236 | ex N1786B | |
| ☐ CN-RNM | Boeing 737-7B6/W | 28984/294 | ex N1786B | |
| ☐ CN-RNQ | Boeing 737-7B6/W | 28985/501 | ex N1786B | |
| ☐ CN-RNR | Boeing 737-7B6/W | 28986/519 | ex N1787B | |
| ☐ CN-RNV | Boeing 737-7B6/W | 28988/1261 | | |
| ☐ CN-ROD | Boeing 737-7B6/W | 33062/1883 | | ♦ |

| | | | | |
|---|---|---|---|---|
| ☐ CN-RGE | Boeing 737-86N/W | 36822/3746 | | ♦ |
| ☐ CN-RGF | Boeing 737-86N/W | 36826/3773 | | ♦ |
| ☐ CN-RGG | Boeing 737-86N/W | 36829/3815 | | ♦ |
| ☐ CN-RGH | Boeing 737-86N/W | 36828/3850 | | ♦ |
| ☐ CN-RGI | Boeing 737-86N/W | 36831/3858 | | ♦ |
| ☐ CN-RGJ | Boeing 737-8B6/W | 33072/3949 | | ♦ |
| ☐ CN-RGK | Boeing 737-8B6/W | 33073/3970 | | ♦ |
| ☐ CN-RNJ | Boeing 737-8B6/W | 28980/55 | | |
| ☐ CN-RNK | Boeing 737-8B6/W | 28981/60 | | |
| ☐ CN-RNP | Boeing 737-8B6/W | 28983/492 | ex N1786B | |
| ☐ CN-RNU | Boeing 737-8B6/W | 28987/1095 | | |
| ☐ CN-RNW | Boeing 737-8B6/W | 33057/1347 | ex N1787B | |
| ☐ CN-RNZ | Boeing 737-8B6/W | 33058/1432 | | |
| ☐ CN-ROA | Boeing 737-8B6/W | 33059/1457 | | |
| ☐ CN-ROB | Boeing 737-8B6/W | 33060/1646 | | |
| ☐ CN-ROC | Boeing 737-8B6/W | 33061/1661 | | |
| ☐ CN-ROE | Boeing 737-8B6/W | 33063/1913 | ex N1781B | |
| ☐ CN-ROH | Boeing 737-85P | 33978/1957 | | |
| ☐ CN-ROJ | Boeing 737-85P | 33979/1963 | | |
| ☐ CN-ROK | Boeing 737-8B6/W | 33064/2180 | ex N1786B | |
| ☐ CN-ROL | Boeing 737-8B6/W | 33065/2206 | ex N1787B | |
| ☐ CN-ROP | Boeing 737-8B6/W | 33066/2506 | ex N1782B | |
| ☐ CN-ROR | Boeing 737-8B6/W | 33067/2527 | ex N1786B | |
| ☐ CN-ROS | Boeing 737-8B6/W | 37718/2773 | | |
| ☐ CN-ROT | Boeing 737-8B6/W | 33068/2883 | | |
| ☐ CN-ROU | Boeing 737-8B6/W | 33069/2911 | | |
| ☐ CN-ROY | Boeing 737-8B6/W | 33070/3233 | | |
| ☐ CN-ROZ | Boeing 737-8B6/W | 33071/3258 | ex N1786B | |
| ☐ CN- | Boeing 737-8B6/W | | | o/o |
| ☐ CN- | Boeing 737-8B6/W | | | o/o |
| | | | | |
| ☐ CN-CDF | Beech 200 Super King Air | BB-577 | | Trainer |
| ☐ CN-CDN | Beech 200 Super King Air | BB-713 | ex N36741 | Trainer |
| ☐ CN-CDU | ATR 42-300 | 0134 | ex F-WWEF | [NTE] |
| ☐ CN-CDV | ATR 42-300 | 0137 | ex F-WWEI | [SBK] |
| ☐ CN-RGA | Boeing 747-428 | 25629/956 | ex F-OGTG | |
| ☐ CN-RMF | Boeing 737-4B6 | 24807/1880 | | wfs |
| ☐ CN-RMG | Boeing 737-4B6 | 24808/1888 | | |
| ☐ CN-RMT | Boeing 757-2B6 | 23686/103 | ex N32831 | |
| ☐ CN-RMZ | Boeing 757-2B6 | 23687/106 | | |
| ☐ CN-RNC | Boeing 737-4B6 | 26529/2584 | | |
| ☐ CN-RND | Boeing 737-4B6 | 26530/2588 | | |
| ☐ CN-RNS | Boeing 767-36NER | 30115/863 | | |
| ☐ CN-RNT | Boeing 767-36NER | 30843/867 | | |
| ☐ CN-RNX | Airbus A321-211 | 2064 | ex D-AVZO | |
| ☐ CN-RNY | Airbus A321-211 | 2076 | ex D-AVZS | |
| ☐ CN-ROF | Airbus A321-211 | 2726 | ex D-AVZO | |
| ☐ CN-ROM | Airbus A321-211 | 3070 | ex D-AVZA | all-white |
| ☐ CN-ROV | Boeing 767-3Q8ER | 27686/793 | ex N201LF | |
| ☐ CN-ROW | Boeing 767-343ER | 30008/743 | ex N768MT | |
| ☐ CN-ROX | Boeing 737-3M8F | 24020/1614 | ex N240MT | |
| ☐ CN- | Boeing 787-8 | 35507/17 | | o/o |
| ☐ CN- | Boeing 787-8 | 35508/19 | | o/o |

## CP-    BOLIVIA (Republic of Bolivia)

### AEROCON                           Aerocon (AEK)                          Trinidad (TDD)

| | | | | |
|---|---|---|---|---|
| ☐ CP-2477 | Swearingen SA.227DC Metro 23 | DC-830B | ex N1119K | |
| ☐ CP-2485 | Swearingen SA.227DC Metro 23 | DC-817B | ex VH-UUD | |
| ☐ CP-2527 | Swearingen SA.227DC Metro 23 | DC-824B | ex N471Z | |
| ☐ CP-2563 | Swearingen SA.227BC Metro 23 | BC-783B | ex N783ML | |
| ☐ CP-2590 | Swearingen SA.227BC Metro 23 | BC-773B | ex N773US | |
| ☐ CP-2602 | Swearingen SA.227BC Metro 23 | BC-780B | ex N780A | dam 01Dec09 |
| ☐ CP-2655 | Swearingen SA.227DC Metro 23 | DC-819B | | ♦ |
| ☐ CP- | Swearingen SA.227BC Metro 23 | BC-781B | ex N781ML | |
| | | | | |
| ☐ CP-2176 | Dornier Do.228-202K | 8163 | ex D-CIKI | |
| ☐ CP-2393 | LET L-410UVP-E3 | 872020 | ex Soviet AF 2020 | ♦ |
| ☐ CP-2500 | Swearingen SA.227AC Metro III | AC-733B | ex N160MC | |

### AEROESTE                         Aeroeste (ROE)            Santa Cruz-El Trompillo (SRZ)

| | | | | |
|---|---|---|---|---|
| ☐ CP-2266 | Rockwell 690B Turbo Commander | 11395 | ex N816PC | |
| ☐ CP-2328 | LET L-410UVP-E20 | 912536 | ex S9-TAY | |
| ☐ CP-2349 | LET L-410UVP-E20 | 912530 | ex S9-TBM | |
| ☐ CP-2382 | LET L-410UVP-E9 | 861727 | ex S9-TBH | |
| ☐ CP-2673 | Beech 1900D | UE-343 | ex YV-1371 | ♦ |

## AEROSUR — Aerosur (5L/RSU) — Santa Cruz-Viru Viru (VVI)

| | | | | | |
|---|---|---|---|---|---|
| ☐ CP-2595 | Boeing 737-33A | 24790/1955 | ex N790AW | | |
| ☐ CP-2640 | Boeing 737-382 | 24366/1699 | ex N934PG | | ♦ |
| ☐ CP-2656 | Boeing 737-36N | 28554/2835 | ex N541MS | | ♦ |
| ☐ CP-2691 | Boeing 737-3M8 | 25071/2039 | ex N250AG | | ♦ |
| ☐ CP-2699 | Boeing 737-3Q8 | 26296/2581 | ex N296AG | | ♦ |
| | | | | | |
| ☐ CP-2244 | LET L-410UVP-E | 912534 | ex OK-WDD | | ♦ |
| ☐ CP-2245 | LET L-410UVP-E | 912535 | ex OK-WDE | | ♦ |
| ☐ CP-2253 | Swearingen SA.227DC Metro 23 | DC-825B | ex N3021A | | ♦ |
| ☐ CP-2438 | Boeing 737-201 (Nordam 3) | 21815/589 | ex C-FNAX | | |
| ☐ CP-2462 | Boeing 727-264 (FedEx 3) | 22158/1642 | ex XA-MEF | | |
| ☐ CP-2498 | Boeing 727-223 (FedEx 3) | 22463/1755 | ex CP-2463 | | |
| ☐ CP-2515 | Boeing 727-222 | 21904/1528 | ex N346PA | | |
| ☐ CP-2561 | Boeing 737-2P6 | 21613/530 | ex N835AL | | ♦ |
| ☐ CP-2653 | Boeing 737-497 | 25663/2382 | ex PK-GZA | | ♦ |
| ☐ CP-2659 | Boeing 767-284ER | 24742/303 | ex N988AN | | |

Ceased ops 31Mar12

## AMAZONAS TRANSPORTES AEREOS — Amazonas (Z8) — La Paz (LPB)

| | | | | | |
|---|---|---|---|---|---|
| ☐ CP-2459 | Swearingen SA.227DC Metro 23 | DC-847B | ex N847LS | | ♦ |
| ☐ CP-2473 | Swearingen SA.227DC Metro 23 | DC-842B | ex N510FS | | |

## BOLIVIANA DE AVIACION — (OB/BOV) — La Paz (LPB)

| | | | | | |
|---|---|---|---|---|---|
| ☐ CP-2550 | Boeing 737-33A | 25118/2065 | ex N401LF | | |
| ☐ CP-2551 | Boeing 737-382 | 24449/1857 | ex N449AN | | |
| ☐ CP-2552 | Boeing 737-3M8 | 25041/2024 | ex D-ADIJ | | |
| ☐ CP-2553 | Boeing 737-382 | 24450/1873 | ex N460XS | | |
| ☐ CP-2555 | Boeing 737-3Q8 | 26303/2635 | ex EI-ELS | | ♦ |
| ☐ CP-2684 | Boeing 737-33A | 27455/2709 | ex N455AN | | ♦ |

## ECO EXPRESS — La Paz (LPB)

| | | | | |
|---|---|---|---|---|
| ☐ CP-2026 | Convair 340-70 | 249 | ex 53-7797 | |

## LINEAS AEREAS CANEDO — (LCN) — Cochabamba (CBB)

| | | | | |
|---|---|---|---|---|
| ☐ CP-744 | Aero Commander 680 | 680341-34 | ex OB-M-573 | Juan Salvador Gaviota |
| ☐ CP-896 | Aero Commander 680 | 680-548-216 | ex N316E | Jose Fernando Gaviota |
| ☐ CP-973 | Curtiss C-46C Commando | 32941 | ex N32227 | |
| ☐ CP-1080 | Curtiss C-46A Commando | 26771 | ex TAM61 | [LPB] |
| ☐ CP-1093 | Aero Commander 680F | 680F-1035-51 | ex N6197X | |
| ☐ CP-1128 | Douglas DC-3D | 1998 | ex N15M | on rebuild [CBB] |
| ☐ CP-1960 | Douglas DC-3C | 18993 | ex PT-KVN | [TDD] |
| ☐ CP-2421 | Douglas C-117D | 12979/43365 | ex N545CT | >RSU |

## TAB CARGO / TRANSPORTES AEREOS BOLIVIANOS — Bol (BOL) — La Paz (LPB)

| | | | | |
|---|---|---|---|---|
| ☐ CP-1376 | Lockheed 382C-72D Hercules | 4759 | ex TAM-91 | |
| ☐ CP-2184 | Lockheed 182A-2A Hercules | 3228 | ex TAM-69 | |
| ☐ CP-2489 | Douglas DC-10-10F | 46903/43 | ex N68044 | wfs |
| ☐ CP-2555 | Douglas DC-10-30F | 46937/152 | ex N833LA | |

## TAM - TRANSPORTES AEREO MILITAR — La Paz (LPB)

| | | | | | |
|---|---|---|---|---|---|
| ☐ FAB-61 | Lockheed 282-1B Hercules | 3549 | ex 58-0750 | | |
| ☐ FAB-65 | Lockheed 282-1B Hercules | 3588 | ex 59-1536 | | |
| ☐ FAB-66 | Lockheed 282-1B Hercules | 3560 | ex TAM-66 | | |
| ☐ FAB-86 | CASA C212-100 | AV2-2-70 | ex T.12C-44 | | ♦ |
| ☐ FAB-87 | CASA C212-100 | AA1-13-110 | ex T.12B-57 | | ♦ |
| ☐ FAB-90 | Fokker F.27M Troopship 400M | 10578 | ex TAM-90 | | |
| ☐ FAB-93 | Fokker F.27M Troopship 400M | 10599 | ex TAM-93 | | |
| ☐ FAB-97 | CAIC MA60 | 0412 | ex B-858L | | |
| ☐ TAM-85 | CASA C212-100 | A7-3-90 | ex Nicaragua 221 | | ♦ |

## TAM BOLIVIA — La Paz (LPB)

| | | | | | |
|---|---|---|---|---|---|
| ☐ FAB-100 | British Aerospace 146 Srs.200 | E2080 | ex N290UE | | ♦ |
| ☐ FAB-101 | British Aerospace 146 Srs.200 | E2041 | ex OY-RCZ | | ♦ |
| ☐ FAB-102 | British Aerospace 146 Srs.200 | E2023 | ex G-CLHD | | ♦ |
| ☐ FAB-103 | British Aerospace 146 Srs.200 | E2040 | ex EI-DJJ | | ♦ |
| ☐ CP-1367 | Boeing 727-2K3/W (Duganair 3) | 21495/1403 | | | ♦ |
| ☐ CP-2499 | Boeing 727-224 (FedEx 3) | 22449/1756 | ex N296SC | | ♦ |

## CS-    PORTUGAL (Republic of Portugal)

### AEROVIP                                                                                    Cascais-Tires

| ☐ CS-AYT | Dornier 228-200 | 8084 | ex VP-FBK | |
| ☐ CS-TGG | Dornier 228-202K | 8160 | ex D-CORA | |
| ☐ CS-TLJ | Short SD.3-60 | SH3692 | ex OY-MUD | wfs |

### AGROAR                                        (GRR)

| ☐ CS-TQR | Boeing 737-301F | 23258/1126 | ex OE-IAU | o/o♦ |

### AIRLINAIR PORTUGAL                            (RLP)

| ☐ CS-DTO | ATR 42-320 | 0095 | ex F-GKYN | ♦ |

### EURO ATLANTIC AIRWAYS          EuroAtlantic (MM/MMZ)                          Lisbon (LIS)

| ☐ CS-TFM | Boeing 777-212ER | 28513/144 | ex 9V-SRA | |
| ☐ CS-TFS | Boeing 767-3Y0ER | 25411/408 | ex S9-DBW | |
| ☐ CS-TFT | Boeing 767-3Y0ER | 26208/505 | ex S9-DBY | |
| ☐ CS-TLO | Boeing 767-383ER | 24318/257 | ex N318SR | |
| ☐ CS-TLZ | Boeing 767-375ERF | 24086/248 | ex N240LD | |
| ☐ CS-TQU | Boeing 737-8K2/W | 30646/1122 | ex PH-HZY | ♦ |

### HELIPORTUGAL                     Heliportugal (HPL)                           Cascais-Tires

| ☐ CS-HFI | Aérospatiale AS350B2 Ecureuil | 1216 | ex PT-YJC | |
| ☐ CS-HFO | Aérospatiale AS350B2 Ecureuil | 1824 | ex F-GFDL | |
| ☐ CS-HFX | Aérospatiale AS350B2 Ecureuil | 4081 | ex F-WWXD | |
| ☐ CS-HGG | Aérospatiale AS350B2 Ecureuil | 9085 | | |
| ☐ CS-HGO | Aérospatiale AS350B3 Ecureuil | 4521 | | ♦ |
| ☐ CS-HHO | Aérospatiale AS350B3 Ecureuil | 4888 | | ♦ |
| ☐ CS-HFV | Aérospatiale SA365N Dauphin 2 | 6338 | ex N661ME | |
| ☐ CS-HGA | Aérospatiale SA365N Dauphin 2 | 6336 | ex JA9978 | |
| ☐ CS-HGV | Aérospatiale SA365N Dauphin 2 | 6829 | | |
| ☐ CS-HGW | Aérospatiale SA365N Dauphin 2 | 6830 | | |
| ☐ CS-HGX | Aérospatiale SA365N Dauphin 3 | 6138 | ex 5N-BIK | ♦ |
| ☐ CS-HHF | Aérospatiale SA365N Dauphin 3 | 6128 | | ♦ |
| ☐ CS-HHI | Aérospatiale SA365N1 Dauphin 3 | 6089 | ex F-OIBJ | ♦ |
| ☐ CS-HHR | Aérospatiale AS365N3 Dauphin 2 | 6841 | ex F-OJTU | ♦ |
| ☐ CS-HEX | Eurocopter EC120B Colibri | 1183 | ex F-WQDV | |
| ☐ CS-HFP | Eurocopter EC130B4 | 4033 | ex F-WQDB | |
| ☐ CS-HGH | Agusta AW139 | 31135 | | ♦ |
| ☐ CS-HGQ | Agusta AW139 | 31057 | ex N915DH | |
| ☐ CS-HGU | Agusta AW139 | 31143 | | |

### HI FLY                             Sky Flyer (5K/HFY)                         Lisbon (LIS)

| ☐ CS-TEI | Airbus A310-304 | 495 | ex F-WWCO all white c/s | |
| ☐ CS-TEX | Airbus A310-304 | 565 | ex F-WWCC | |
| ☐ CS-TFW | Airbus A340-541 | 910 | ex F-WJKH | <ARA♦ |
| ☐ CS-TFX | Airbus A340-541 | 912 | ex F-WWTL | <ARA♦ |
| ☐ CS-TFZ | Airbus A330-243 | 1008 | ex F-WW | |
| ☐ CS-TMT | Airbus A330-322 | 096 | ex F-WQSA | Op for Belgium AF |
| ☐ CS-TQL | Airbus A340-312 | 133 | ex M-YRGQ | ♦ |
| ☐ CS-TQM | Airbus A340-313X | 117 | ex A6-EYC | |
| ☐ CS-TQP | Airbus A330-202 | 211 | ex N272LF | ♦ |
| ☐ EI-ETI | Airbus A330-322 | 171 | ex D-AERS | o/o♦ |

### OMNI - AVIACAO E TECNOLOGIA       Omni (OC/OAV)                             Cascais-Tires

| ☐ CS-HCO | Agusta-Bell 206B JetRanger III | 8678 | ex I-BDPL | | |
| ☐ CS-HDS | Bell 222 | 47028 | ex G-META | EMS | |
| ☐ CS-TLU | Airbus A319-133CJ | 1256 | ex F-GSVU | | >WHT |
| ☐ CS-TMU | Beech 1900D | UE-335 | ex N23269 | Castor | Op for LIS |
| ☐ CS-TMV | Beech 1900D | UE-341 | ex N23309 | Esquilio | Op for LIS |

### ORBEST                             Orbest (OBS)                              Lisbon (LIS)

| ☐ CS-TRH | Airbus A330-343 | 833 | ex EC-KCP | <IWD♦ |

### PGA EXPRESS                        Lisbon (LIS)

| ☐ CS-TMU | Beech 1900D | UE-335 | ex N23269 | Castor | Op by OAV |
| ☐ CS-TMV | Beech 1900D | UE-341 | ex N23309 | Esquilio | Op by OAV |

## PORTUGALIA AIRLINES — Portugalia (NI/PGA) — Lisbon (LIS)

| | | | | | |
|---|---|---|---|---|---|
| ☐ CS-TPG | Embraer ERJ-145EP | 145014 | ex PT-SYK | Melro | |
| ☐ CS-TPH | Embraer ERJ-145EP | 145017 | ex PT-SYN | Pardal | |
| ☐ CS-TPI | Embraer ERJ-145EP | 145031 | ex PT-SYZ | Cuco | |
| ☐ CS-TPJ | Embraer ERJ-145EP | 145036 | ex PT-SZC | Chapim | |
| ☐ CS-TPK | Embraer ERJ-145EP | 145041 | ex PT-SZG | Gaio | |
| ☐ CS-TPL | Embraer ERJ-145EP | 145051 | ex PT-SZQ | Pisco | |
| ☐ CS-TPM | Embraer ERJ-145EP | 145095 | ex PT-SBR | Rola | |
| ☐ CS-TPN | Embraer ERJ-145EP | 145099 | ex PT-SBV | Brigao | |
| | | | | | |
| ☐ CS-TPA | Fokker 100 | 11257 | ex PH-LMF | Albatroz | |
| ☐ CS-TPB | Fokker 100 | 11262 | ex PH-EZE | Pelicano | |
| ☐ CS-TPC | Fokker 100 | 11287 | ex PH-LML | Flamingo | |
| ☐ CS-TPD | Fokker 100 | 11317 | ex EP-IDK | Condor | |
| ☐ CS-TPE | Fokker 100 | 11342 | ex PH-LNJ | Gaviao | |
| ☐ CS-TPF | Fokker 100 | 11258 | ex PH-EZD | Grifo | |

## SATA AIR ACORES — SATA (SP/SAT) — Ponta Delgada (PDL)

| | | | | | |
|---|---|---|---|---|---|
| ☐ CS-TRB | de Havilland DHC-8Q-202 | 476 | ex C-FXBX | Graciosa | |
| ☐ CS-TRC | de Havilland DHC-8Q-202 | 480 | ex C-FXBZ | Faial | |
| ☐ CS-TRD | de Havilland DHC-8-402Q | 4291 | ex C-GAUA | | |
| ☐ CS-TRE | de Havilland DHC-8-402Q | 4295 | ex C-GBIY | | |
| ☐ CS-TRF | de Havilland DHC-8-402Q | 4297 | ex C-GBJE | | |
| ☐ CS-TRG | de Havilland DHC-8-402Q | 4298 | ex C-GBJF | | |
| | | | | | |
| ☐ CS-TGX | British Aerospace ATP | 2025 | ex G-BRLY | | [SEN] |

## SATA INTERNACIONAL — Air Azores (S4/RZO) — Ponta Delgada (PDL)

| | | | | | |
|---|---|---|---|---|---|
| ☐ CS-TGU | Airbus A310-304 | 571 | ex F-GJKQ | Terceira | |
| ☐ CS-TGV | Airbus A310-304 | 651 | ex F-WQKR | Sao Miguel | |
| ☐ CS-TKJ | Airbus A320-212 | 0795 | ex C-FTDA | Pico | |
| ☐ CS-TKK | Airbus A320-214 | 2390 | ex F-WWII | Corvo | |
| ☐ CS-TKL | Airbus A320-214 | 2425 | ex F-WWBH | Sao Jorge | |
| ☐ CS-TKM | Airbus A310-304 | 661 | ex JY-AGL | Autonomia | |
| ☐ CS-TKN | Airbus A310-325ET | 624 | ex TF-ELR | Macaronesia | |
| ☐ CS-TKO | Airbus A320-214 | 3891 | ex F-WWDC | Diaspora | |

## TAP AIR PORTUGAL — Air Portugal (TP/TAP) — Lisbon (LIS)

Member of Star Alliance

| | | | | | |
|---|---|---|---|---|---|
| ☐ CS-TTA | Airbus A319-111 | 0750 | ex D-AVYO | Vieira da Silva | |
| ☐ CS-TTB | Airbus A319-111 | 0755 | ex D-AVYJ | Gago Coutinho | |
| ☐ CS-TTC | Airbus A319-111 | 0763 | ex D-AVYS | Fernando Pessoa | |
| ☐ CS-TTD | Airbus A319-111 | 0790 | ex D-AVYC | Amadeo de Souza-Cardoso | |
| ☐ CS-TTE | Airbus A319-111 | 0821 | ex D-AVYN | Francisco d'Ollanda | |
| ☐ CS-TTF | Airbus A319-111 | 0837 | ex D-AVYL | Calouste Gulbenkian | |
| ☐ CS-TTG | Airbus A319-111 | 0906 | ex D-AVYN | Humberto Delgado | |
| ☐ CS-TTH | Airbus A319-111 | 0917 | ex D-AVYJ | Antonio Sergio | |
| ☐ CS-TTI | Airbus A319-111 | 0933 | ex D-AVYP | Eça de Queirós | |
| ☐ CS-TTJ | Airbus A319-111 | 0979 | ex D-AVYM | Eusébio | |
| ☐ CS-TTK | Airbus A319-111 | 1034 | ex D-AVYL | Miguel Torga | |
| ☐ CS-TTL | Airbus A319-111 | 1100 | ex D-AVYX | Almeida Garrett | |
| ☐ CS-TTM | Airbus A319-111 | 1106 | ex D-AVWR | Alexandre Herculano | |
| ☐ CS-TTN | Airbus A319-111 | 1120 | ex D-AVYI | Camilo Castelo Branco | |
| ☐ CS-TTO | Airbus A319-111 | 1127 | ex D-AVYH | Antero de Quental | |
| ☐ CS-TTP | Airbus A319-111 | 1165 | ex D-AVWV | Josefa d'Obidos | |
| ☐ CS-TTQ | Airbus A319-112 | 0629 | ex SU-LBF | Agostinho da Silva | |
| ☐ CS-TTR | Airbus A319-112 | 1756 | ex C-GJWE | Soares dos Reis | |
| ☐ CS-TTS | Airbus A319-112 | 1765 | ex C-GJWF | Guilhermina Suggia | |
| | | | | | |
| ☐ CS-TMW | Airbus A320-214 | 1667 | ex F-WWII | Luisa Todi | |
| ☐ CS-TNG | Airbus A320-214 | 0945 | ex F-WWIX | Mouzinho de Silveira | |
| ☐ CS-TNH | Airbus A320-214 | 0960 | ex F-WWBH | Almada Negreiros | |
| ☐ CS-TNI | Airbus A320-214 | 0982 | ex F-WWDF | Aquilino Ribeiro | |
| ☐ CS-TNJ | Airbus A320-214 | 1181 | ex F-WWDS | Florbela Espanca | |
| ☐ CS-TNK | Airbus A320-214 | 1206 | ex F-WWIL | Teofilo Braga | |
| ☐ CS-TNL | Airbus A320-214 | 1231 | ex F-WWIJ | Vitorino Nemésio | |
| ☐ CS-TNM | Airbus A320-214 | 1799 | ex F-WWIF | Natalia Correia | |
| ☐ CS-TNN | Airbus A320-214 | 1816 | ex F-WWID | Gil Vicente | |
| ☐ CS-TNP | Airbus A320-214 | 2178 | ex 9H-AER | Alexandre O'Neill Star Alliance c/s | |
| ☐ CS-TNQ | Airbus A320-214 | 3769 | ex F-WWDQ | Jose Regio | |
| ☐ CS-TNR | Airbus A320-214 | 3883 | ex F-WWIU | Luis De Freitas Branco | |
| ☐ CS-TNS | Airbus A320-214 | 4021 | ex F-WWDM | D Afonso Henriques | |
| ☐ CS-TNT | Airbus A320-214 | 4095 | ex F-WWDI | Rafael Bordalo Pinheiro | |
| ☐ CS-TNU | Airbus A320-214 | 4106 | ex F-WWDR | Columbano Bordalo Pinheiro | |
| ☐ CS-TNV | Airbus A320-214 | 4145 | ex F-WWIY | Grao Vasco | |
| ☐ CS-TQD | Airbus A320-214 | 0870 | ex HB-IJT | Eugénio de Andrade | |

| | | | | |
|---|---|---|---|---|
| ☐ CS-TOE | Airbus A330-223 | 305 | ex D-AXEL | Pedro Alvares Cabral |
| ☐ CS-TOF | Airbus A330-223 | 308 | ex D-ARND | Infante D Henrique |
| ☐ CS-TOG | Airbus A330-223 | 312 | ex D-ARNO | Bartolomeu de Gusmão |
| ☐ CS-TOH | Airbus A330-223 | 181 | ex OE-LAO | Nuno GonçalvesStar Alliance c/s |
| ☐ CS-TOI | Airbus A330-223 | 195 | ex OE-LAN | Damião de Góis |
| ☐ CS-TOJ | Airbus A330-223 | 223 | ex OE-LAM | D João II 'O Príncipe Perfeito' |
| ☐ CS-TOK | Airbus A330-223 | 317 | ex OE-LAP | Padre António Vieira |
| ☐ CS-TOL | Airbus A330-223 | 877 | ex F-WWKF | Joao Goncalves Zarco |
| ☐ CS-TOM | Airbus A330-202 | 899 | ex F-WWKN | Vasco da Gama |
| ☐ CS-TON | Airbus A330-202 | 904 | ex F-WWKT | Joao XXI |
| ☐ CS-TOO | Airbus A330-202 | 914 | ex F-WWYL | Fernao de Magalhaes |
| ☐ CS-TOP | Airbus A330-202 | 934 | ex F-WWKZ | Pedro Nunes |
| ☐ CS-TJE | Airbus A321-211 | 1307 | ex D-AVZM | Pero Vaz de Caminha |
| ☐ CS-TJF | Airbus A321-211 | 1399 | ex D-AVZI | Luis Vaz de Camões |
| ☐ CS-TJG | Airbus A321-211 | 1713 | ex D-AVZS | Amalia Rodrigues |
| ☐ CS-TOA | Airbus A340-312 | 041 | ex F-WWJB | Fernao Mendes Pinto |
| ☐ CS-TOB | Airbus A340-312 | 044 | ex F-WWJN | D. Joao de Castro |
| ☐ CS-TOC | Airbus A340-312 | 079 | ex F-WWJS | Wenceslau de Moraes |
| ☐ CS-TOD | Airbus A340-312 | 091 | ex F-WWJA | D. Francisco de Almeida |

**WHITE**     *Young Sky (WHT)*     *Lisbon (LIS)*

| | | | | | |
|---|---|---|---|---|---|
| ☐ CS-TDI | Airbus A310-308 | 573 | ex JY-AGK | | |
| ☐ CS-TKI | Airbus A310-304 | 448 | ex C-GRYA | | |
| ☐ CS-TQS | Airbus A320-211 | 0384 | ex YL-LCB | Flygrey | ♦ |
| ☐ PR-WTA | Airbus A310-304 | 494 | ex CS-TEJ | | wfs |

## CU- CUBA (Republic of Cuba)

### AEROCARIBBEAN     *AeroCaribbean (7L/CRN)*     *Havana (HAV)*

| | | | | |
|---|---|---|---|---|
| ☐ CU-T1506 | Antonov An-26 | 87306710 | ex CU-T110 | |
| ☐ CU-T1509 | ATR 42-300 | 0009 | ex CU-T1296 | |
| ☐ CU-T1512 | ATR 42-300 | 0136 | ex CU-T1298 | |
| ☐ CU-C1515 | Ilyushin Il-18GrM | 188010805 | ex CU-C132 | Frtr |
| ☐ CU-T1537 | Yakovlev Yak-40 | 9021360 | ex CU-T1450 | |
| ☐ CU-T1538 | Yakovlev Yak-40 | 9021260 | ex CU-T1449 | |
| ☐ CU-T1540 | Embraer EMB.110C Bandeirante | 110091 | ex CU-T1108 | ♦ |
| ☐ CU-T1544 | ATR 72-212 | 0472 | ex F-WQNG | |
| ☐ CU-T1545 | ATR 72-212 | 0473 | ex F-WQNI | |
| ☐ CU-T1547 | ATR 72-212 | 0485 | ex F-WQNB | |
| ☐ CU-T1548 | ATR 72-212 | 0453 | ex F-WQNQ | ♦ |
| ☐ CU-T1550 | ATR 42-300 | 0014 | ex PP-PTE | |
| ☐ CU-T1551 | Embraer EMB.110P1 Bandeirante | 110132 | ex PT-GKV | |

### AEROGAVIOTA     *Gaviota (KG/GTV)*     *Havana (HAV)*

| | | | | |
|---|---|---|---|---|
| ☐ CU-T1228 | Antonov An-26 | 12604 | | ♦ |
| ☐ CU-T1238 | Antonov An-26 | 7803 | | ♦ |
| ☐ CU-T1239 | Antonov An-26 | 7907 | | ♦ |
| ☐ CU-T1240 | Antonov An-26 | 11210 | | ♦ |
| ☐ CU-T1241 | Antonov An-26 | 11301 | | ♦ |
| ☐ CU-T1402 | Antonov An-26B | 12605 | ex 14-02 | |
| ☐ CU-T1403 | Antonov An-26B | 12905 | ex 14-03 | |
| ☐ CU-T1406 | Antonov An-26B | 13502 | ex 14-06 | |
| ☐ CU-T1408 | Antonov An-26 | 6903 | ex 14-28 | |
| ☐ CU-T1417 | Antonov An-26 | | | |
| ☐ CU-T1420 | Antonov An-26 | 87306607 | ex 14-20 | |
| ☐ CU-T1421 | Antonov An-26 | 6610 | ex 14-21 | status uncertain |
| ☐ CU-T1423 | Antonov An-26 | 3806 | | ♦ |
| ☐ CU-T1425 | Antonov An-26 | 6904 | ex 14-25 | |
| ☐ CU-T1426 | Antonov An-26 | 5603 | ex 14-26 | |
| ☐ CU-T1428 | Antonov An-26B | 11303 | ex 14-28 | |
| ☐ CU-T1429 | Antonov An-26 | 7006 | ex 14-29 | |
| ☐ CU-T1432 | Antonov An-26 | 7306 | ex 14-32 | status uncertain |
| ☐ CU-T1433 | Antonov An-26 | 7309 | ex 14-33 | status uncertain |
| ☐ CU-T1434 | Antonov An-26 | 7701 | ex 14-34 | |
| ☐ CU-T1435 | Antonov An-26 | 7702 | ex 14-35 | |
| ☐ CU-H1423 | Mil Mi-8T | | | |
| ☐ CU-H1424 | Mil Mi-8P | | | |
| ☐ CU-H1427 | Mil Mi-8PS | | | |
| ☐ CU-H1431 | Mil Mi-8P | | | |
| ☐ CU-H1436 | Mil Mi-8T | | | |
| ☐ CU-T1232 | Yakovlev Yak-40 | 9011060 | | ♦ |
| ☐ CU-T1240 | ATR 42-500 | 0617 | ex F-WWLB | VIP lsd to/op in CUB c/s |
| ☐ CU-H1429 | Mil Mi-17 (Mi-8MTV-1) | | | |
| ☐ CU-H1430 | Mil Mi-17 (Mi-8MTV-1) | | | |

| | | | | |
|---|---|---|---|---|
| ☐ CU-T1454 | ATR 42-500 | 0616 | ex F-WWLA | |
| ☐ CU-T1455 | ATR 42-500 | 0618 | ex F-WWLC | |
| ☐ CU-T1456 | ATR 42-500 | 0619 | ex F-WWLD | |

## AEROTAXI | Seraer *(CNI)* | Havana *(HAV)*

| | | | | |
|---|---|---|---|---|
| ☐ CU-T1195 | LET L-410UVP-E | | | ♦ |
| ☐ CU-T1196 | LET L-410UVP-E | | | ♦ |
| ☐ CU-T1541 | Embraer EMB.110C Bandeirante | 110116 | ex CU-T1109 | |
| ☐ CU-T1542 | Embraer EMB.110C Bandeirante | 110136 | ex PT-GKY | |

## CUBANA DE AVIACION | Cubana *(CU/CUB)* | Havana *(HAV)*

| | | | | |
|---|---|---|---|---|
| ☐ CU-C1257 | Antonov An-24RV | 37309104 | ex CU-T1536 | Cubana Cargo titles |
| ☐ CU-T1214 | Antonov An-24RV | 47309404 | ex CU-T923 | |
| ☐ CU-T1223 | Antonov An-24RV | 47309405 | ex CU-T924 | |
| ☐ CU-T1237 | Antonov An-24RV | 37308909 | | ♦ |
| ☐ CU-T1244 | Antonov An-24RV | 57310301 | ex JU-1011 | |
| ☐ CU-T1257 | Antonov An-24RV | 37309104 | | ♦ |
| ☐ CU-T1260 | Antonov An-24RV | 57310307 | ex CCCP-47307 | La Pinta |
| ☐ CU-T1263 | Antonov An-24RV | 47309610 | ex RA-46678 | |
| ☐ CU-T1706 | Antonov An-24RV | 67310701 | | ♦ |
| ☐ CU-T1255 | Yakovlev Yak-42D | 4520424116664 | ex RA-42443 | |
| ☐ CU-T1279 | Yakovlev Yak-42D | 452044814057 | | ♦ |
| ☐ CU-T1707 | Yakovlev Yak-42D | 4520423016269 | ex UR-CFA | |
| ☐ CU-T1708 | Yakovlev Yak-42D | 4520423606235 | ex UR-CFH | |
| ☐ CU-T1709 | Yakovlev Yak-42D | 4520424811442 | ex RA-42364 | |
| ☐ CU-T1230 | Antonov An-26 | 14306 | | ♦ |
| ☐ CU-T1240 | ATR 42-500 | 0617 | ex F-WWLB | VIP Lsd fr/op by GTV |
| ☐ CU-T1250 | Ilyushin Il-96-300 | 74393202015 | | |
| ☐ CU-T1251 | Ilyushin Il-96-300 | 74393202016 | | |
| ☐ CU-T1254 | Ilyushin Il-96-300 | 74393202017 | | |
| ☐ CU-T1280 | Ilyushin Il-62M | 3749648 | 15 de Febrero | stored? |
| ☐ CU-T1282 | Ilyushin Il-62M | 2052456 | | [HAV] |
| ☐ CU-C1700 | Tupolev Tu-204-100SE | 1450744664036 | ex RA-64035 | |
| ☐ CU-T1701 | Tupolev Tu-204-100E | 1450743164035 | ex RA-64036 | |
| ☐ CU-T1702 | Tupolev Tu-204-100E | 1450743164042 | ex RA-64042 | |
| ☐ CU-C1703 | Tupolev Tu-204-100SE | 1450744664037 | | |
| ☐ LY-VEZ | Airbus A320-212 | 0299 | ex PH-AAZ | .<NVD♦ |

# CX-    URUGUAY (Republic of Uruguay)

## AEROMAS | Aeromas Express *(MSM)* | Montevideo-Carrasco *(MVD)*

| | | | | |
|---|---|---|---|---|
| ☐ CX-BDI | Piper PA-23-250 Aztec B | 27-2265 | ex N5217Y | |
| ☐ CX-BRM | Beech A80 Queen Air | LD-200 | ex N326JB | Excalibur Queenaire conv [MVD] |
| ☐ CX-MAS | Embraer EMB.110P1 Bandeirante | 110393 | ex N91DA | |
| ☐ CX-MAX | Cessna 208A Caravan I | 208A00042 | ex ZP-TYT | |

## AIR CLASS /AERO VIP | Acla *(QD/QCL)* | Montevideo-Carrasco *(MVD)*

| | | | | |
|---|---|---|---|---|
| ☐ CX-CAR | Boeing 727-214F (FedEx 3) | 21958/1533 | ex N788AT | ♦ |
| ☐ CX-CLA | Swearingen SA.227AC Metro III | AC-736 | ex N339LC | Op for DHL |
| ☐ CX-CLS | Swearingen SA.227AC Metro III | AC-755B | ex N27465 | |
| ☐ CX-CSS | Swearingen SA.227AC Metro III | AC-642 | ex N821BC | |
| ☐ CX-LAS | Swearingen SA.227AC Metro III | AC-482 | ex N784C | |

## BQB LINEAS AÉREAS | | Montevideo-Carrasco *(MVD)*

| | | | | |
|---|---|---|---|---|
| ☐ CX-JCL | ATR 72-212A | 0805 | ex F-WWEQ | Jean Mermoz |
| ☐ CX-JPL | ATR 72-212A | 0816 | ex F-WWEF | Antoine de Saint-Exupery |

## DELBITUR

| | | | | |
|---|---|---|---|---|
| ☐ CX-CAF | British Aerospace Jetstream 41 | 41101 | ex N333UE | |

## PLUNA LINEAS AÉREAS URUGUAYAS | Pluna *(PU/PUA)* | Montevideo-Carrasco *(MVD)*

| | | | | |
|---|---|---|---|---|
| ☐ CX-CRA | Canadair CRJ-900 | 15165 | ex C-FTMF | Blue c/s |
| ☐ CX-CRB | Canadair CRJ-900 | 15169 | | Turquoise c/s |
| ☐ CX-CRC | Canadair CRJ-900 | 15175 | | Red c/s |
| ☐ CX-CRD | Canadair CRJ-900 | 15180 | | Purple c/s |
| ☐ CX-CRE | Canadair CRJ-900 | 15185 | | Red c/s |
| ☐ CX-CRF | Canadair CRJ-900 | 15204 | | Blue c/s |
| ☐ CX-CRG | Canadair CRJ-900 | 15209 | | ♦ |
| ☐ CX-CRH | Canadair CRJ-900 | 15233 | | |
| ☐ CX-CRI | Canadair CRJ-900 | 15234 | | Purple c/s |

| | | | | |
|---|---|---|---|---|
| ☐ CX-CRK | Canadair CRJ-900 | 15239 | | |
| ☐ CX-CRL | Canadair CRJ-900 | 15273 | ex C-GZQL | ✦ |
| ☐ CX-CRM | Canadair CRJ-900 | 15274 | ex C-GZQC | ✦ |
| ☐ CX-CRN | Canadair CRJ-900 | 15275 | ex C- | ✦ |
| ☐ CX-PUF | Boeing 737-230 | 22135/781 | ex LV-BBM | |

## C2- NAURU (Republic of Nauru)

### OUR AIRLINE — Air Nauru (ON/RON) — Brisbane, QLD (BNE)

| | | | | |
|---|---|---|---|---|
| ☐ VH-INU | Boeing 737-3Y0 | 23684/1353 | ex N323AW | |
| ☐ VH-JWL | Boeing 737-406SF | 24529/1770 | ex N529PR | [BNE]✦ |
| ☐ VH-NLK | Boeing 737-33A | 23635/1436 | ex N635AN | ✦ |

## C3- ANDORRA (Principality of Andorra)

### HELIAND — La Massana Heliport

| | | | | |
|---|---|---|---|---|
| ☐ F-GYDJ | Aérospatiale AS350B3 Ecureuil | 3719 | ex N5219F | Lsd to/op by SHP |

### HELITRANS — Grau Roig Heliport

Leases Aérospatiale Ecureuil helicopters from Heliswiss Iberica when required

## C5- GAMBIA (Republic of The Gambia)

### SLOK AIR INTERNATIONAL — Slok Gambia (S0/OKS) — Banjul (BJL)

| | | | | | |
|---|---|---|---|---|---|
| ☐ C5-EUN | Boeing 737-201 (Nordam 3) | 22798/924 | ex 5N-EUN | Ibrahim Babangida | |
| ☐ C5-IFY | Boeing 737-201 (Nordam 3) | 22797/916 | ex 5N-IFY | Olusegun Obasanjo | |
| ☐ C5-NYA | Boeing 737-201 (Nordam 3) | 22799/932 | ex 5N-NYA | John Kuffour | [PGF] |
| ☐ C5-OBJ | Boeing 737-201 (Nordam 3) | 22795/912 | ex N253AU | Atiku Abubakar | |
| ☐ C5-OUK | Boeing 737-201 (Nordam 3) | 22796/914 | ex N254AU | Yahya Jammeh | |
| ☐ C5-ZNA | Boeing 737-201 (Nordam 3) | 22806/938 | ex 5N-ZNA | Ahmadu Bello | |
| Ceased ops | | | | | |

## C6- BAHAMAS (Commonwealth of the Bahamas)

### ABACO AIR — Marsh Harbour (MHH)

| | | | | |
|---|---|---|---|---|
| ☐ C6-BAA | Britten-Norman BN-2A-21 Islander | 214 | ex N214TL | |
| ☐ C6-BFQ | Britten-Norman BN-2A-8 Islander | 347 | ex N69HA | |
| ☐ C6-BFR | Aero Commander 500 | 825 | ex N846VK | |
| ☐ C6-BFS | Aero Commander 500 | 685 | ex N6285B | |
| ☐ C6-BHH | Britten-Norman BN-2B-26 Islander | 2021 | ex N599MS | |
| ☐ C6-BHY | Aero Commander 500 | 834 | ex N521SQ | |

### BAHAMASAIR — Bahamas (UP/BHS) — Nassau (NAS)

| | | | | |
|---|---|---|---|---|
| ☐ C6-BFG | de Havilland DHC-8-311A | 288 | ex C-GESR | |
| ☐ C6-BFH | de Havilland DHC-8-311A | 291 | ex C-GFOD | |
| ☐ C6-BFJ | de Havilland DHC-8Q-311 | 323 | ex N583DS | |
| ☐ C6-BFO | de Havilland DHC-8-301 | 164 | ex N802XV | |
| ☐ C6-BFP | de Havilland DHC-8Q-311 | 309 | ex N994DC | |
| ☐ C6-BFE | Boeing 737-528 | 26450/2503 | ex LV-BAR | ✦ |
| ☐ C6-BFM | Boeing 737-2K5 (Nordam 3) | 22596/763 | ex N231TA | |
| ☐ C6-BFW | Boeing 737-2K5 (Nordam 3) | 22601/833 | ex N233TA | |

### CAT ISLAND AIR — Nassau (NAS)

| | | | | |
|---|---|---|---|---|
| ☐ C6-CAA | SAAB SF.340A | 340A-122 | ex N379KB | |
| ☐ C6-CAH | Embraer EMB.110P1 Bandeirante | 110249 | ex C6-BHA | [NAS] |
| ☐ C6-CAP | Embraer EMB.110P1 Bandeirante | 110304 | ex J8-VAZ | |
| ☐ C6-CAT | Piper PA-23-250 Aztec E | 27-7554083 | ex N54779 | |

### CHEROKEE AIR — Marsh Harbour (MHH)

| | | | | |
|---|---|---|---|---|
| ☐ C6-BGS | Piper PA-23-250 Aztec F | 27-7854067 | ex N17MR | |
| ☐ C6-SBH | Cessna 208B Caravan I | 208B0822 | ex N822SA | |

### LEAIR CHARTER SERVICES — Nassau (NAS)

| | | | | |
|---|---|---|---|---|
| ☐ C6-BGJ | Cessna 402C II | 402C0106 | ex VQ-THC | |

| | | | | |
|---|---|---|---|---|
| ☐ C6-CAB | Embraer EMB.110P1 Bandeirante | 110198 | ex G-ONEW | |
| ☐ C6-LEE | Piper PA-23-250 Aztec F | 27-7654049 | ex N62568 | |

### MAJOR'S AIR SERVICES — Freeport (FPO)

| | | | | |
|---|---|---|---|---|
| ☐ C6-RRM | Beech C99 | U-231 | ex N141RM | |

### PINEAPPLE AIR — Pineapple (PNP) — Nassau (NAS)

| | | | | |
|---|---|---|---|---|
| ☐ N60MJ | Beech 1900D | UE-60 | ex N85445 | |
| ☐ N157PA | Beech 1900C | UB-56 | ex N505RH | |
| ☐ N381CR | Beech 1900C | UB-69 | ex N331CR | |
| ☐ C6-HAN | Beech C99 | U-165 | ex N42517 | |

### REGIONAL AIR — Nassau (NAS)

| | | | | |
|---|---|---|---|---|
| ☐ C6-RAL | Cessna 208B Caravan I | 208B0841 | ex N1295G | |
| ☐ C6-RAS | Cessna 208B Caravan I | 208B0693 | ex N90HE | |

### SALAMIS AVIATION — Nassau (NAS)

| | | | | |
|---|---|---|---|---|
| ☐ N75X | Swearingen SA.227TT Merlin IIIC | TT-421 | ex N90BJ | |
| ☐ N81WS | Swearingen SA.227TT Merlin IIIC | TT-480 | ex N500DB | |

### SEAIR AIRWAYS — Seair (DYL) — Nassau (NAS)

| | | | | |
|---|---|---|---|---|
| ☐ C6-BGT | Piper PA-23-250 Aztec E | 27-7305051 | ex N89BB | |
| ☐ C6-BUS | Britten-Norman BN-2A-26 Islander | 2040 | ex N23US | |

### SKY BAHAMAS — Sky Bahamas (SBM) — Nassau (NAS)

| | | | | |
|---|---|---|---|---|
| ☐ C6-SBB | SAAB SF.340A | 340A-149 | ex N779SB | |
| ☐ C6-SBD | SAAB SF.340A | 340A-021 | ex N776SB | |
| ☐ C6-SBG | SAAB SF.340A | 340A-110 | ex N110XJ | |
| ☐ C6-SBJ | SAAB SF.340B | 340B-316 | ex N676PA | ♦ |
| ☐ C6-SFB | Beech 1900D | UE-2 | ex N2YV | ♦ |

### SOUTHERN AIR CHARTER — Southern (PL/SOA) — Nassau (NAS)

| | | | | |
|---|---|---|---|---|
| ☐ C6-BGY | Piper PA-23-250 Aztec E | 27-7554044 | ex N166PG | |
| ☐ N70JL | Beech 100 King Air | B-87 | ex N125DB | |
| ☐ N376SA | Beech 1900C | UB-72 | ex N504RH | |
| ☐ N378SA | Beech 1900C | UB-31 | ex N196GA | |

### VISION AIR — Freeport (FPO)

| | | | | |
|---|---|---|---|---|
| ☐ N800MX | Beech 1900C | UB-48 | ex N896FM | ♦ |

### WESTERN AIR — (WST) — Freeport (FPO)

| | | | | |
|---|---|---|---|---|
| ☐ C6-ASD | Swearingen SA.227AC Metro III | AC-749B | ex 86-0457 | ♦ |
| ☐ C6-FPO | Swearingen SA.227AC Metro III | AC-652 | ex N26877 | |
| ☐ C6-HBW | SAAB SF.340A | 340A-067 | ex N712MG | |
| ☐ C6-JAY | SAAB SF.340A | 340A-120 | ex N418MW | |
| ☐ C6-JER | Swearingen SA.227AC Metro III | AC-588 | ex N892MA | |
| ☐ C6-RMW | SAAB SF.340A | 340A-121 | ex N121CQ | |
| ☐ C6-SAR | Swearingen SA.227AC Metro III | AC-598 | ex N3116Z | |
| ☐ C6-VIP | SAAB SF.340A | 340A-098 | ex N98XJ | |
| ☐ C6-WAL | Piper PA-31-350 Navajo Chieftain | 31-7652129 | ex N70FS | |

## C9-  MOZAMBIQUE (Republic of Mozambique)

### KAYA AIRLINES — (TWM) — Maputo/Beira (MPM/BEW)

| | | | | | |
|---|---|---|---|---|---|
| ☐ C9-AUQ | Embraer EMB.120ER Brasilia | 120139 | ex 3D-BCI | | ♦ |
| ☐ C9- | Embraer EMB.120RT Brasilia | 120200 | ex ZS-OEN | | ♦ |
| ☐ 3D-BEE | Beech 1900C-1 | UC-148 | ex N148YV | | ♦ |
| ☐ 3D-NVA | LET L-410UVP-E3 | 882035 | ex 3D-ZZM | | ♦ |
| ☐ 3D-NVC | LET L-410UVP | 831033 | ex 5Y-BLC | Sluffy | ♦ |

### LAM - LINHAS AEREAS DE MOCAMBIQUE — Mozambique (TM/LAM) — Maputo (MPM)

| | | | | | |
|---|---|---|---|---|---|
| ☐ C9-AUY | de Havilland DHC-8-402Q | 4021 | ex G-ECOW | | ♦ |
| ☐ C9-BAJ | Boeing 737-205 | 23464/1223 | ex N464BA | Pemba | |
| ☐ C9-BAO | Boeing 737-205 (Nordam 3) | 23467/1245 | ex XA-ABC | Quirimbas | |
| ☐ C9-EMA | Embraer ERJ-190AR | 19000301 | ex PT-TZP | Cobue | |
| ☐ C9-EMB | Embraer ERJ-190AR | 19000309 | ex PT-TZX | Chiloane | |

## MOCAMBIQUE EXPRESSO — Mozambique Express (MXE) — Maputo / Beira (MPM/BEW)

| | | | | |
|---|---|---|---|---|
| ☐ C9-AUK | British Aerospace Jetstream 41 | 41044 | ex ZS-NUO | |
| ☐ C9-AUL | de Havilland DHC-8-402Q | 4019 | ex LN-RDC | |
| ☐ C9-AUM | de Havilland DHC-8-402Q | 4020 | ex LN-RDE | ♦ |
| ☐ ZS-AAB | Embraer EMB.120RT Brasilia | 120228 | ex N248CA | ♦ |

## STA - SOCIEDADE DE TRANSPORTS AÉREOS — Maputo (MPM)

Ops services with Islanders leased from sister company TTA and other aircraft as required

## TTA – SOCIEDADE DE TRANSPORTE E TRABALHO AEREO
### Kanimanbo (TTA) — Maputo (MPM)

| | | | | |
|---|---|---|---|---|
| ☐ C9-AMH | Piper PA-32-300 Cherokee Six C | 32-40682 | ex ZS-IGO | [MPM] |
| ☐ C9-AOV | Britten-Norman BN-2A-3 Islander | 624 | ex G-AYJF | |
| ☐ C9-APD | Britten-Norman BN-2A-9 Islander | 683 | ex G-AZXO | |

# D-    GERMANY (Federal Republic of Germany)

## ADVANCED AVIATION — Bad Saulgau / Bangui (-/BGF)

| | | | | |
|---|---|---|---|---|
| ☐ D-CAAL | Dornier 228-202K | 8152 | ex CS-TGH | op by Minair |
| ☐ D-FLIP | Cessna 208B Caravan I | 208B0331 | ex N3331 | |
| ☐ D4-CBK | Dornier 228-212 | 8222 | ex 7Q-YKS | Op for Guardia Costiera |

## AEROLINE — Sylt-Air (7E/AWU) — Westerland (GWT)

| | | | |
|---|---|---|---|
| ☐ D-GFPG | Partenavia P.68B | 170 | |
| ☐ D-IOLB | Cessna 404 Titan II | 404-0691 | ex SE-IVG |

## AEROLOGIC — (BOX) — Leipzig-Halle (LEJ)

| | | | |
|---|---|---|---|
| ☐ D-AALA | Boeing 777-FZN | 36001/780 | |
| ☐ D-AALB | Boeing 777-FZN | 36002/799 | ex N5017Q |
| ☐ D-AALC | Boeing 777-FZN | 36003/836 | |
| ☐ D-AALD | Boeing 777-FZN | 36004/838 | |
| ☐ D-AALE | Boeing 777-FZN | 36198/872 | |
| ☐ D-AALF | Boeing 777-FZN | 36201/881 | |
| ☐ D-AALG | Boeing 777-FZN | 36199/894 | |
| ☐ D-AALH | Boeing 777-FZN | 36200/904 | |

## AIR ALLIANCE

| | | | | |
|---|---|---|---|---|
| ☐ D-FAAA | Cessna 208B Caravan I | 208B1279 | ex (ES-MAA) | ♦ |
| ☐ D-FAAE | Cessna 208B Caravan I | 208B1139 | ex EC-JKU | ♦ |
| ☐ D-FAAF | Cessna 208B Caravan I | 208B1125 | ex EC-JHI | ♦ |
| ☐ D-FAAI | Cessna 208B Caravan I | 208B2039 | ex N2077F | ♦ |
| ☐ D-FAAJ | Cessna 208B Caravan I | 208B2003 | ex N208AE | ♦ |
| ☐ D-FAAL | Cessna 208B Caravan I | 208B2128 | ex N61882 | ♦ |
| ☐ D-FROB | Cessna 208B Caravan I | 208B2066 | ex N5130J | ♦ |

## AIR CARGO GERMANY — (6U/ACX) — Frankfurt Hahn (HHN)

| | | | | |
|---|---|---|---|---|
| ☐ D-ACGA | Boeing 747-409(BDSF) | 24311/869 | ex N481AT | |
| ☐ D-ACGB | Boeing 747-409(BDSF) | 24312/954 | ex N482AT | |
| ☐ D-ACGC | Boeing 747-412BCF | 24975/838 | ex PH-MPQ | |
| ☐ D-ACGD | Boeing 747-412BCF | 24061/717 | ex PH-MPP | ♦ |

## AIR HAMBURG — Uetersen (QSM)

| | | | | |
|---|---|---|---|---|
| ☐ D-IAEB | Britten-Norman BN-2A-6 Islander | 218 | ex OH-BNB | |
| ☐ D-ISKY | Beech B200 Super King Air | BB-2014 | | ♦ |

## AIR PACK EXPRESS

| | | | | |
|---|---|---|---|---|
| ☐ D-FAAC | Cessna 208B Caravan I | 208B1141 | ex EC-JLS | ♦ |
| ☐ D- | Cessna 208B Caravan I | 208B1142 | ex EC-JLT | ♦ |

## AIR SERVICE BERLIN — Berlin-Schonefeld (SXF)

| | | | | |
|---|---|---|---|---|
| ☐ D-CXXX | Douglas DC-3 | 16124/32872 | ex G-AMPZ | Jack Bennett |

## AIR SERVICE WILDGRUBER — Friedrichshafen-Loewental (FDH)

| | | | |
|---|---|---|---|
| ☐ D-IEXE | Beech 99 | U-46 | ex (N99LM) |

| **AIRBERLIN** | | **AirBerlin (AB/BER)** | | **Berlin-Tegel (TXL)** |
|---|---|---|---|---|
| ☐ D-ABGC | Airbus A319-132 | 2468 | ex N815BR | >AEE |
| ☐ D-ABGH | Airbus A319-112 | 3245 | ex D-AVWE | >BHP |
| ☐ D-ABGJ | Airbus A319-112 | 3415 | ex D-AVYI | |
| ☐ D-ABGK | Airbus A319-112 | 3447 | ex D-AVYS | |
| ☐ D-ABGN | Airbus A319-112 | 3661 | ex D-AVYU | |
| ☐ D-ABGO | Airbus A319-112 | 3689 | ex D-AVWF | |
| ☐ D-ABGP | Airbus A319-112 | 3728 | ex D-AVWF | |
| ☐ D-ABGQ | Airbus A319-112 | 3700 | ex D-AVWM | |
| ☐ D-ABGR | Airbus A319-112 | 3704 | ex D-AVWJ | |
| ☐ D-ABGS | Airbus A319-112 | 3865 | ex D-AVWD | |
| ☐ D-ABCC | Airbus A320-214 | 4334 | ex D-AZAK | ♦ |
| ☐ D-ABDB | Airbus A320-214 | 2619 | ex F-WWDK | |
| ☐ D-ABDP | Airbus A320-214 | 3093 | ex F-WWIT | |
| ☐ D-ABDQ | Airbus A320-214 | 3121 | ex F-WWBD | |
| ☐ D-ABDR | Airbus A320-214 | 3242 | ex F-WWBP | |
| ☐ D-ABDS | Airbus A320-214 | 3289 | ex F-WWDS | |
| ☐ D-ABDU | Airbus A320-214 | 3516 | ex D-AVVC | |
| ☐ D-ABDW | Airbus A320-214 | 3945 | ex F-WWDX | |
| ☐ D-ABDX | Airbus A320-214 | 3995 | ex F-WWDG | |
| ☐ D-ABDY | Airbus A320-214 | 4013 | ex F-WWIG | |
| ☐ D-ABFA | Airbus A320-214 | 4101 | ex D-AVVK | |
| ☐ D-ABFB | Airbus A320-214 | 4128 | ex F-WWIQ | |
| ☐ D-ABFC | Airbus A320-214 | 4161 | ex D-AVVP | |
| ☐ D-ABFE | Airbus A320-214 | 4269 | ex D-AXAE | |
| ☐ D-ABFF | Airbus A320-214 | 4329 | ex D-AXAP | |
| ☐ D-ABFG | Airbus A320-214 | 4291 | ex D-AXAG | |
| ☐ D-ABFK | Airbus A320-214 | 4433 | ex D-AVVQ | |
| ☐ D-ABFL | Airbus A320-214 | 4463 | ex D-AXAC | |
| ☐ D-ABFN | Airbus A320-214 | 4510 | ex F-WWBK | |
| ☐ D-ABFO | Airbus A320-214 | 4565 | ex D-AVVA | |
| ☐ D-ABFP | Airbus A320-214 | 4606 | ex D-AXAS | |
| ☐ D-ABFT | Airbus A320-214 | 4674 | ex D-AXAF | ♦ |
| ☐ D-ABFU | Airbus A320-214 | 4743 | ex D-AVVJ | ♦ |
| ☐ D-ABFZ | Airbus A320-214 | 4988 | ex D-AVVT | ♦ |
| ☐ D-ALTE | Airbus A320-214 | 1504 | ex OE-LTU | |
| ☐ D-ALTF | Airbus A320-214 | 1553 | ex OE-LTV | |
| ☐ D-ALTK | Airbus A320-214 | 1931 | ex F-WWIH | |
| ☐ D-ALTL | Airbus A320-214 | 2009 | ex F-WWBO | |
| ☐ D-ABCA | Airbus A321-211 | 3708 | ex D-AVZO | |
| ☐ D-ABCB | Airbus A321-211 | 3749 | ex D-AVZC | |
| ☐ D-ABCC | Airbus A321-211 | 4334 | ex D-AZAK | ♦ |
| ☐ D-ABCF | Airbus A321-211 | 1966 | ex N221LF | |
| ☐ D-ABCG | Airbus A321-211 | 1988 | ex N341LF | |
| ☐ D-ABCH | Airbus A321-211 | 4728 | ex D-AVZF | ♦ |
| ☐ D-ABCI | Airbus A321-211 | 5038 | ex D-AZAO | ♦ |
| ☐ D-ABCJ | Airbus A321-211 | 5126 | ex | o/o♦ |
| ☐ D-ABCK | Airbus A321-211 | 5133 | ex | o/o♦ |
| ☐ D-ABGP | Airbus A321-212 | 3728 | ex D-AVWF | ♦ |
| ☐ D-ALSA | Airbus A321-211 | 1629 | ex D-AVZC | |
| ☐ D-ALSB | Airbus A321-211 | 1994 | ex D-AVZR | |
| ☐ D-ALSC | Airbus A321-211 | 2005 | ex D-AVXI | |
| ☐ D-ALSD | Airbus A321-211 | 1607 | ex I-PEKN | |
| ☐ D-ABXA | Airbus A330-223 | 288 | ex HB-IQH | ♦ |
| ☐ D-ABXB | Airbus A330-223 | 322 | ex HB-IQQ | ♦ |
| ☐ D-ALPA | Airbus A330-223 | 403 | ex F-WWKO | |
| ☐ D-ALPB | Airbus A330-223 | 432 | ex F-WWYG | |
| ☐ D-ALPC | Airbus A330-223 | 444 | ex F-WWKD | |
| ☐ D-ALPD | Airbus A330-223 | 454 | ex F-WWKG | |
| ☐ D-ALPE | Airbus A330-223 | 469 | ex F-WWKO | |
| ☐ D-ALPF | Airbus A330-223 | 476 | ex F-WWKT | |
| ☐ D-ALPG | Airbus A330-223 | 493 | ex F-WWKI | |
| ☐ D-ALPH | Airbus A330-223 | 739 | ex F-WWYD | |
| ☐ D-ALPI | Airbus A330-223 | 828 | ex F-WWKI | |
| ☐ D-ALPJ | Airbus A330-223 | 911 | ex F-WWYA | |
| ☐ D-ABBS | Boeing 737-76N/W | 28654/986 | ex N743AL | |
| ☐ D-ABBT | Boeing 737-76N/W | 32582/1013 | ex N744AL | |
| ☐ D-ABBV | Boeing 737-7Q8 | 30629/1011 | ex P4-CAS | |
| ☐ D-ABBW | Boeing 737-7Q8 | 30642/1097 | ex P4-DAS | |
| ☐ D-ABLA | Boeing 737-76J/W | 36114/2421 | ex N1786B | |
| ☐ D-ABLB | Boeing 737-76J/W | 36115/2692 | | |
| ☐ D-ABLC | Boeing 737-76J/W | 36116/2730 | | |
| ☐ D-ABLD | Boeing 737-76J/W | 36117/2776 | ex N1787B | |
| ☐ D-ABLE | Boeing 737-76J/W | 36873/3496 | ex N1786B | |
| ☐ D-ABLF | Boeing 737-76J/W | 36874/3488 | | o/o |
| ☐ D-AGEC | Boeing 737-76J/W | 36118/2832 | ex D-ABLE | |

| | | | | |
|---|---|---|---|---|
| ☐ D- | Boeing 737-76J/W | | | o/o |
| ☐ D- | Boeing 737-76J/W | | | o/o |
| ☐ D- | Boeing 737-76J/W | | | o/o |
| ☐ D- | Boeing 737-76J/W | | | o/o |
| ☐ D- | Boeing 737-76J/W | | | o/o |
| ☐ D-ABAF | Boeing 737-86J/W | 30878/844 | ex N1787B | |
| ☐ D-ABAG | Boeing 737-86J/W | 30879/871 | ex N1786B | |
| ☐ D-ABAP | Boeing 737-86J/W | 28070/106 | | |
| ☐ D-ABAQ | Boeing 737-86J/W | 28071/133 | | |
| ☐ D-ABAR | Boeing 737-86J/W | 28072/147 | ex N1786B | |
| ☐ D-ABAS | Boeing 737-86J/W | 28073/200 | ex N1795B | |
| ☐ D-ABBB | Boeing 737-86J/W | 32624/961 | ex N1798B | |
| ☐ D-ABBC | Boeing 737-86J/W | 32625/995 | ex N1786B | |
| ☐ D-ABBD | Boeing 737-86J/W | 30880/1043 | | >IZM |
| ☐ D-ABBE | Boeing 737-86J/W | 30881/1067 | | |
| ☐ D-ABBF | Boeing 737-86J/W | 32917/1210 | | |
| ☐ D-ABBG | Boeing 737-86J/W | 32918/1255 | | |
| ☐ D-ABBJ | Boeing 737-86Q/W | 30286/1280 | ex N1787B | |
| ☐ D-ABBK | Boeing 737-8BK/W | 33013/1317 | | |
| ☐ D-ABBX | Boeing 737-808 | 34969/2293 | | |
| ☐ D-ABBY | Boeing 737-808 | 34970/2379 | ex N1787B | |
| ☐ D-ABKA | Boeing 737-82R | 29329/224 | ex TC-APG | |
| ☐ D-ABKB | Boeing 737-86J/W | 37740/2638 | ex YR-BGP | ♦ |
| ☐ D-ABKC | Boeing 737-86J/W | 37741/2686 | ex YR-BGR | ♦ |
| ☐ D-ABKD | Boeing 737-86J/W | 37742/2796 | | |
| ☐ D-ABKE | Boeing 737-86J/W | 37743/2834 | ex N1787B | >IZM |
| ☐ D-ABKF | Boeing 737-86J/W | 37745/3044 | ex N1787B | >IZM |
| ☐ D-ABKG | Boeing 737-86J/W | 37746/3109 | ex N1786B | >PGT |
| ☐ D-ABKI | Boeing 737-86J/W | 37748/3157 | | |
| ☐ D-ABKJ | Boeing 737-86J/W | 37749/3176 | ex N1786B | |
| ☐ D-ABKK | Boeing 737-86J/W | 37753/3261 | ex N1787B | |
| ☐ D-ABKM | Boeing 737-86J/W | 37755/3349 | ex N1769B | |
| ☐ D-ABKN | Boeing 737-86J/W | 37756/3371 | | |
| ☐ D-ABKO | Boeing 737-86J/W | 37757/3377 | ex N1786B | |
| ☐ D-ABKP | Boeing 737-86J/W | 37758/3439 | ex N1787B | |
| ☐ D-ABKQ | Boeing 737-86J/W | 37760/3545 | | ♦ |
| ☐ D-ABKS | Boeing 737-86J/W | 36880/3685 | | ♦ |
| ☐ D-ABKT | Boeing 737-86J/W | 36881/3671 | | ♦ |
| ☐ D-ABKU | Boeing 737-86J/W | 37744/3694 | | ♦ |
| ☐ D-ABKW | Boeing 737-86J/W | 36884/3732 | | ♦ |
| ☐ D-ABKY | Boeing 737-86J/W | 36886/3777 | | ♦ |
| ☐ D-ABMB | Boeing 737-86J/W | 36121/3853 | | ♦ |
| ☐ D-ABMC | Boeing 737-86J/W | 37752/3835 | ex N1787B | ♦ |
| ☐ D-ABMD | Boeing 737-86J/W | 37761/3887 | | ♦ |
| ☐ D-ABME | Boeing 737-86J/W | 37766/ | | o/o♦ |
| ☐ D-ABMF | Boeing 737-86J/W | 37767/ | | o/o♦ |
| ☐ D-ABMG | Boeing 737-86J/W | 37768/ | | o/o♦ |
| ☐ D-ABQA | de Havilland DHC-8-402Q | 4223 | ex C-FTID | >LGW |
| ☐ D-ABQB | de Havilland DHC-8-402Q | 4226 | ex C-FTUM | >LGW |
| ☐ D-ABQC | de Havilland DHC-8-402Q | 4231 | ex C-FUCI | >LGW |
| ☐ D-ABQD | de Havilland DHC-8-402Q | 4234 | ex C-FUCS | >LGW |
| ☐ D-ABQE | de Havilland DHC-8-402Q | 4239 | ex C-FURQ | >LGW |
| ☐ D-ABQF | de Havilland DHC-8-402Q | 4245 | ex C-FVGV | >LGW |
| ☐ D-ABQG | de Havilland DHC-8-402Q | 4250 | ex C-FVUN | >LGW |
| ☐ D-ABQH | de Havilland DHC-8-402Q | 4256 | ex C-FWGO | >LGW |
| ☐ D-ABQI | de Havilland DHC-8-402Q | 4264 | ex C-FXIW | >LGW |
| ☐ D-ABQJ | de Havilland DHC-8-402Q | 4274 | ex C-FYGN | >LGW |
| ☐ D-AERK | Airbus A330-322 | 120 | ex F-WWKN | |
| ☐ D-AERQ | Airbus A330-322 | 127 | ex F-WWKO | |

## ARCUS AIR | Arcus Air (ZE/AZE) | Mannheim (MHG)

| | | | | |
|---|---|---|---|---|
| ☐ D-CAAM | Dornier 228-212 | 8205 | ex D-CBDH | |
| ☐ D-CAAR | Dornier 228-212 | 8211 | ex 57+02 | |
| ☐ D-CAAZ | Dornier 228-212 | 8212 | ex 57+03 | |
| ☐ D-CUTT | Dornier 228-212 | 8200 | ex D-CBDC | |

## AUGSBURG AIRWAYS | Augsburg Air (IQ/AUB) | Munich (MUC)

| | | | | |
|---|---|---|---|---|
| ☐ D-ADHA | de Havilland DHC-8-402Q | 4028 | ex C-GFBW | |
| ☐ D-ADHB | de Havilland DHC-8-402Q | 4029 | ex C-GFCA | |
| ☐ D-ADHC | de Havilland DHC-8-402Q | 4045 | ex C-GDIW | |
| ☐ D-ADHD | de Havilland DHC-8-402Q | 4056 | ex C-GFYI | >BEL |
| ☐ D-ADHE | de Havilland DHC-8-402Q | 4066 | ex C-GEOA | |
| ☐ D-ADHP | de Havilland DHC-8-402Q | 4003 | ex C-FHUP | |
| ☐ D-ADHQ | de Havilland DHC-8-402Q | 4016 | ex C-FSPV | |
| ☐ D-ADHR | de Havilland DHC-8-402Q | 4041 | ex C-FRGT | |

| | | | | |
|---|---|---|---|---|
| ☐ D-ADHS | de Havilland DHC-8-402Q | 4044 | ex C-FRBO | |
| ☐ D-ADHT | de Havilland DHC-8-402Q | 4281 | ex C-FYMQ | |
| | | | | |
| ☐ D-AEMA | Embraer ERJ-190LR | 19000290 | ex PT-TZE | |
| ☐ D-AEMB | Embraer ERJ-190LR | 19000297 | ex PT-TZL | |
| ☐ D-AEMC | Embraer ERJ-190LR | 19000300 | ex PT-TZO | |
| ☐ D-AEMD | Embraer ERJ-190LR | 19000305 | ex PT-TZT | |
| ☐ D-AEME | Embraer ERJ-190LR | 19000308 | ex PT-TXH | |
| ☐ D-AEMF | Embraer ERJ-190LR | 19000310 | ex PT-TZY | |
| ☐ D-AEMG | Embraer ERJ-190LR | 19000404 | ex PT-TYX | >DLA |

## AVANTI AIR — Euroexpress (ATV) — Frankfurt (FRA)

| | | | | |
|---|---|---|---|---|
| ☐ D-ANFC | ATR 72-202 | 0237 | ex F-WWEG | |
| ☐ D-BCRN | ATR 42-300 | 0329 | ex G-WLSH | |
| ☐ D-BSSS | ATR 42-500 | 0602 | ex F-WWLA | >ELO♦ |
| ☐ D-BTTT | ATR 42-500 | 0603 | ex F-WWLD | >ELO♦ |

## BINAIR AERO SERVICE — Binair (BID) — Munich (MUC)

| | | | | |
|---|---|---|---|---|
| ☐ D-CBIN | Swearingen SA.226AT Expediter IV | AT-440B | ex I-FSAD | |
| ☐ D-CAVA | Swearingen SA.227AC Metro III | AC-754B | ex F-GPSN | ♦ |
| ☐ D-CCCC | Swearingen SA.227AT Merlin IVC | AT-511 | ex N600N | |
| ☐ D-CKPP | Swearingen SA.227DC Metro 23 | DC-805B | ex N715MQ | |
| ☐ D-CNAF | Swearingen SA.227AC Metro III | AC-505B | ex TF-BBG | ♦ |
| ☐ D-CNAY | Swearingen SA.227AT Merlin IVC | AT-493 | | ♦ |
| ☐ D-CSAL | Swearingen SA.227AC Metro III | AC-601 | ex I-FSAH | ♦ |
| ☐ D-CPSW | Swearingen SA.227AC Metro III | AC-757B | ex F-GJPN | |

## BUSINESSWINGS / AEROTRANS FLUGCHARTER — Kassel-Calden (KSF)

| | | | | |
|---|---|---|---|---|
| ☐ D-CULT | Dornier 228-212 | 8192 | ex LN-BER | |
| ☐ D-FALK | Cessna 208 Caravan I | 20800023 | ex N9354F | |
| ☐ D-FAST | Cessna 208 Caravan I | 20800207 | ex N208MC | |
| ☐ D-IROL | Dornier 228-100 | 7003 | ex SE-KHL | |
| ☐ D-IVER | de Havilland DHC-6 Twin Otter 300 | 411 | ex SE-IYP | |

## CIRRUS AIRLINES — Cirrus (C9/RUS) — Saarbrücken-Ensheim (SCN)

| | | | | |
|---|---|---|---|---|
| ☐ D-BGAE | Dornier 328-300 (328JET) | 3146 | ex D-BDXC | |
| ☐ D-BGAL | Dornier 328-300 (328JET) | 3131 | ex D-BDXN | |
| ☐ D-BGAQ | Dornier 328-300 (328JET) | 3130 | ex D-BDXL | |
| ☐ D-BGAS | Dornier 328-300 (328JET) | 3139 | ex D-BDXZ | ♦ |
| ☐ D-CCIR | Dornier 328-130 | 3100 | ex D-CDXA | |
| ☐ D-CIRB | Dornier 328-110 | 3017 | ex HB-AEF | |
| ☐ D-CIRC | Dornier 328-110 | 3041 | ex HB-AEI | |
| ☐ D-CIRD | Dornier 328-110 | 3011 | ex HB-AEG | |
| ☐ D-CIRI | Dornier 328-110 | 3005 | ex TF-CSC | |
| ☐ D-CIRJ | Dornier 328-120 | 3035 | ex N335LS | |
| ☐ D-CIRK | Dornier 328-120 | 3050 | ex N350AD | |
| ☐ D-CIRP | Dornier 328-120 | 3006 | ex TF-CSD | |
| ☐ D-COSA | Dornier 328-110 | 3085 | ex D-CDXR [SCN] | |
| ☐ D-CPRW | Dornier 328-110 | 3097 | ex D-CDXY | |
| | | | | |
| ☐ D-ALIA | Embraer ERJ-170LR | 17000006 | ex PT-SVD | |
| ☐ D-ALIE | Embraer ERJ-170LR | 17000059 | ex PT-SVI | [MUC] |
| ☐ S5-AAE | Canadair CRJ-200LR | 7170 | ex C-GAIK | <ADR |

Ceased ops 20Jan12

## CONDOR — Condor (DE/CFG) — Frankfurt (FRA)

| | | | | |
|---|---|---|---|---|
| ☐ D-ABOA | Boeing 757-330/W | 29016/804 | ex N757X | |
| ☐ D-ABOB | Boeing 757-330/W | 29017/810 | ex N6067B | |
| ☐ D-ABOC | Boeing 757-330/W | 29015/818 | ex N6069B | |
| ☐ D-ABOE | Boeing 757-330/W | 29012/839 | ex N1012N | |
| ☐ D-ABOF | Boeing 757-330/W | 29013/846 | | |
| ☐ D-ABOG | Boeing 757-330/W | 29014/849 | | |
| ☐ D-ABOH | Boeing 757-330/W | 30030/855 | ex N1787B | |
| ☐ D-ABOI | Boeing 757-330/W | 29018/909 | ex N1002R | |
| ☐ D-ABOJ | Boeing 757-330/W | 29019/915 | | |
| ☐ D-ABOK | Boeing 757-330/W | 29020/918 | ex N1795B | |
| ☐ D-ABOL | Boeing 757-330/W | 29021/923 | | |
| ☐ D-ABOM | Boeing 757-330/W | 29022/926 | | |
| ☐ D-ABON | Boeing 757-330/W | 29023/929 | ex N1003M | |
| | | | | |
| ☐ D-ABUA | Boeing 767-330ER/W | 26991/455 | | |
| ☐ D-ABUB | Boeing 767-330ER/W | 26987/466 | | |
| ☐ D-ABUC | Boeing 767-330ER/W | 26992/470 | | |
| ☐ D-ABUD | Boeing 767-330ER/W | 26983/471 | | |
| ☐ D-ABUE | Boeing 767-330ER/W | 26984/518 | ex N1788B | |

| | | | | | |
|---|---|---|---|---|---|
| ☐ D-ABUF | Boeing 767-330ER/W | 26985/537 | | | |
| ☐ D-ABUH | Boeing 767-330ER/W | 26986/553 | ex N6046P | | |
| ☐ D-ABUI | Boeing 767-330ER/W | 26988/562 | | | |
| ☐ D-ABUK | Boeing 767-343/W | 30009/746 | ex EI-CRM | | ♦ |
| ☐ D-ABUZ | Boeing 767-330ER/W | 25209/382 | ex (N634TW) | | |
| ☐ D-ABUL | Boeing 767-31BER | 26259/534 | ex EI-CRD | [AUH]♦ | |
| ☐ G-DAJC | Boeing 767-31KER/W | 27206/533 | ex C-GJJC | <TCX♦ | |

### CONDOR BERLIN — Condor Berlin (CIB) — Berlin-Schönefeld (SXF)

| | | | | |
|---|---|---|---|---|
| ☐ D-AICA | Airbus A320-212 | 0774 | ex F-WWDN | Hans |
| ☐ D-AICC | Airbus A320-212 | 0809 | ex F-WWIE | |
| ☐ D-AICD | Airbus A320-212 | 0884 | ex F-WWDE | |
| ☐ D-AICE | Airbus A320-212 | 0894 | ex F-WWDI | |
| ☐ D-AICF | Airbus A320-212 | 0905 | ex F-WWDP | |
| ☐ D-AICG | Airbus A320-212 | 0957 | ex F-WWBE | |
| ☐ D-AICH | Airbus A320-212 | 0971 | ex F-WWBY | |
| ☐ D-AICI | Airbus A320-212 | 1381 | ex F-WWIP | |
| ☐ D-AICJ | Airbus A320-212 | 1402 | ex F-WWDB | |
| ☐ D-AICK | Airbus A320-212 | 1416 | ex F-WWDZ | |
| ☐ D-AICL | Airbus A320-212 | 1437 | ex F-WWBG | |
| ☐ D-AICN | Airbus A320-214 | 1968 | ex G-TCKE | |

### CONTACT AIR — Contactair (KIS) — Stuttgart (STR)

| | | | |
|---|---|---|---|
| ☐ D-AFKA | Fokker 100 | 11517 | ex B-12293 |
| ☐ D-AFKB | Fokker 100 | 11527 | ex PH-MJL |
| ☐ D-AFKC | Fokker 100 | 11496 | ex PH-MJQ |
| ☐ D-AFKD | Fokker 100 | 11500 | ex PH-MJR |
| ☐ D-AFKE | Fokker 100 | 11505 | ex PH-MJP |
| ☐ D-AFKF | Fokker 100 | 11470 | ex PH-MJK |
| ☐ D-AGPH | Fokker 100 | 11308 | ex PH-CXH |
| ☐ D-AGPK | Fokker 100 | 11313 | ex PH-CXK |

### EAT LEIPZIG — (QY/BCS) — Leipzig-Halle (LEJ)

| | | | | |
|---|---|---|---|---|
| ☐ D-AEAC | Airbus A300B4-622RF | 602 | ex N4602 | o/o♦ |
| ☐ D-AEAD | Airbus A300B4-622RF | 617 | ex N2617 | o/o♦ |
| ☐ D-AEAE | Airbus A300B4-622RF | 753 | ex N4753 | o/o♦ |
| ☐ D-AEAF | Airbus A300B4-622RF | 770 | ex N770E | o/o♦ |
| ☐ D-AEAG | Airbus A300B4-622RF | 621 | ex N2621 | ♦ |
| ☐ D-AEAH | Airbus A300B4-622RF | 783 | ex N5783 | o/o♦ |
| ☐ D-AEAL | Airbus A300B4-622RF | 679 | ex N4679 | ♦ |
| ☐ D-AEAO | Airbus A300B4-622RF | 711 | ex N7151 | ♦ |
| ☐ D-AEAP | Airbus A300B4-622RF | 724 | ex N1724 | ♦ |
| ☐ D-AEAQ | Airbus A300B4-622RF | 729 | ex N3729 | o/o♦ |
| ☐ D-AEAR | Airbus A300B4-622RF | 730 | ex N4730 | o/o♦ |
| ☐ D-AEAT | Airbus A300B4-622RF | 740 | ex N3637 | o/o♦ |
| | | | | |
| ☐ D-ALEA | Boeing 757-236 (SF) | 22172/9 | ex OO-DLN | |
| ☐ D-ALEB | Boeing 757-236 (SF) | 22173/10 | ex OO-DPF | |
| ☐ D-ALEC | Boeing 757-236 (SF) | 22175/13 | ex OO-DLQ | |
| ☐ D-ALED | Boeing 757-236 (SF) | 22179/24 | ex OO-DLP | |
| ☐ D-ALEE | Boeing 757-236 (SF) | 22183/32 | ex OO-DPB | |
| ☐ D-ALEF | Boeing 757-236 (SF) | 22189/58 | ex OO-DPM | |
| ☐ D-ALEG | Boeing 757-236 (SF) | 23398/77 | ex OO-DPO | |
| ☐ D-ALEH | Boeing 757-236 (SF) | 23492/89 | ex OO-DPK | |
| ☐ D-ALEI | Boeing 757-236 (SF) | 23493/90 | ex OO-DPJ | |
| ☐ D-ALEJ | Boeing 757-23APF | 24971/340 | ex OO-DLJ | |
| ☐ D-ALEK | Boeing 757-236 (SF) | 23533/93 | ex OO-DPN | |
| ☐ G-CSVS | Boeing 757-236PCF | 25620/449 | ex N701AX | ♦ |

### EUROWINGS — Eurowings (EW/EWG) — Dortmund/Nuremberg (DTM/NUE)

| | | | | |
|---|---|---|---|---|
| ☐ D-ACNA | Canadair CRJ-900NG | 15229 | ex C-GZQA | Amberg |
| ☐ D-ACNB | Canadair CRJ-900NG | 15230 | ex C-GZQM | Wermelskirchen |
| ☐ D-ACNC | Canadair CRJ-900NG | 15236 | ex C-GIBO | |
| ☐ D-ACND | Canadair CRJ-900NG | 15238 | ex C-GIBT | |
| ☐ D-ACNE | Canadair CRJ-900NG | 15241 | ex C-GICL | |
| ☐ D-ACNF | Canadair CRJ-900NG | 15243 | ex C-GIAU | |
| ☐ D-ACNG | Canadair CRJ-900NG | 15245 | ex C-GZQF | |
| ☐ D-ACNH | Canadair CRJ-900NG | 15247 | ex C-GZQK | |
| ☐ D-ACNI | Canadair CRJ-900NG | 15248 | | |
| ☐ D-ACNJ | Canadair CRJ-900NG | 15249 | ex C-GZQX | Bad Segeberg |
| ☐ D-ACNK | Canadair CRJ-900NG | 15251 | ex C-GIBL | |
| ☐ D-ACNL | Canadair CRJ-900NG | 15252 | ex C-GZQA | |
| ☐ D-ACNM | Canadair CRJ-900NG | 15253 | ex C-GHZZ | |
| ☐ D-ACNN | Canadair CRJ-900NG | 15254 | ex C-GIAH | |
| ☐ D-ACNO | Canadair CRJ-900NG | 15255 | ex C-GIBN | |
| ☐ D-ACNP | Canadair CRJ-900NG | 15259 | ex C-GZQV | |
| ☐ D-ACNQ | Canadair CRJ-900NG | 15260 | ex C-GIBG | |

| | | | | | |
|---|---|---|---|---|---|
| ☐ D-ACNR | Canadair CRJ-900NG | 15263 | | | ♦ |
| ☐ D-ACNT | Canadair CRJ-900NG | 15264 | | | ♦ |
| ☐ D-ACNU | Canadair CRJ-900NG | 15267 | | | ♦ |
| ☐ D-ACNV | Canadair CRJ-900NG | 15268 | | | ♦ |
| ☐ D-ACNW | Canadair CRJ-900NG | 15269 | | | ♦ |
| ☐ D-ACNX | Canadair CRJ-900NG | 15270 | | | ♦ |
| | | | | | |
| ☐ D-ACRG | Canadair CRJ-200LR | 7630 | ex C-FMOW | | [EXT] |
| ☐ D-ACRH | Canadair CRJ-200LR | 7738 | ex C-FMLF | Herzogenaurach | [SVQ] |
| ☐ D-ACRJ | Canadair CRJ-200LR | 7864 | ex C-GZOZ | | [DUS] |
| ☐ D-ACRO | Canadair CRJ-200LR | 7494 | ex I-ADJC | | [DUS] |

## EXCELLENT AIR
**Excellent Air (GZA)** — **Münster-Osnabrück**

| | | | | |
|---|---|---|---|---|
| ☐ D-IICE | Beech 200 Super King Air | BB-269 | ex N269D | EMS |

## FLM AVIATION
**FLM (FKI)** — **Hamburg/ Kiel/ Parchim (HAM/KEL/-)**

| | | | | |
|---|---|---|---|---|
| ☐ D-CMNX | Dornier 228-202K | 8065 | ex TF-CSG | >MX |
| ☐ D-CNAG | Swearingen SA.227DC Metro 23 | DC-893B | ex N3032A | op for Manx2 |
| ☐ D-GBRD | Partenavia P.68B | 14 | ex OY-DZR | |
| ☐ D-IFFB | Beech 300LW Super King Air | FA-224 | ex N56449 | Frtr |
| ☐ D-IFLM | Dornier 228-201 | 8046 | ex TF-CSF | >MX |
| ☐ D-ILKA | Dornier 228-100 | 7005 | ex LN-HTB | wfs |

## FLY EXPRESS

| | | | | |
|---|---|---|---|---|
| ☐ D-FLYE | Cessna 208B Caravan I | 208B2148 | ex N52114 | ♦ |

## FRISIA LUFTVERKEHR
**Norden-Norddeich (NOE)**

| | | | | |
|---|---|---|---|---|
| ☐ D-IFKU | Britten-Norman BN-2B-20 Islander | 2290 | ex G-BVXY | Norderney |
| ☐ D-IFTI | Britten-Norman BN-2B-20 Islander | 2299 | ex G-BWYY | Norddeich |

## GERMANIA
**Germania (ST/GMI)** — **Cologne (CGN)**

| | | | | | |
|---|---|---|---|---|---|
| ☐ D-AHIL | Airbus A319-112 | 3589 | ex (D-AHIM) | | ♦ |
| ☐ D-AHIM | Airbus A319-112 | 3818 | ex (D-AHIN) | | ♦ |
| ☐ D-ASTA | Airbus A319-112 | 4663 | ex D-AVYF | Dr Heinrich Bischoff | ♦ |
| ☐ D-ASTB | Airbus A319-112 | 4691 | ex D-AVYO | | ♦ |
| ☐ D-ASTC | Airbus A319-112 | 5085 | ex D-AVYO | | ♦ |
| ☐ D-ASTX | Airbus A319-112 | 3202 | ex HB-IOY | | ♦ |
| ☐ D-ASTY | Airbus A319-112 | 3407 | ex OE-LED | | ♦ |
| ☐ D-ASTZ | Airbus A319-112 | 3019 | ex OE-LEK | | ♦ |
| | | | | | |
| ☐ D-AGEL | Boeing 737-75B | 28110/5 | ex N1791B | | |
| ☐ D-AGEN | Boeing 737-75B | 28100/16 | ex N1789B | | |
| ☐ D-AGEP | Boeing 737-75B | 28102/18 | ex N5573B | | |
| ☐ D-AGEQ | Boeing 737-75B | 28103/23 | ex N1787B | | |
| ☐ D-AGER | Boeing 737-75B | 28107/27 | ex N1002R | | |
| ☐ D-AGES | Boeing 737-75B | 28108/28 | | | |
| ☐ D-AGET | Boeing 737-75B | 28109/31 | | | |
| ☐ D-AGEU | Boeing 737-75B | 28104/39 | | | |

## GERMANWINGS
**German Wings (4U/GWI)** — **Cologne (CGN)**

| | | | | |
|---|---|---|---|---|
| ☐ D-AGWA | Airbus A319-132 | 2813 | ex D-AVWM | |
| ☐ D-AGWB | Airbus A319-132 | 2833 | ex D-AVXI | |
| ☐ D-AGWC | Airbus A319-132 | 2976 | ex D-AVYX | |
| ☐ D-AGWD | Airbus A319-132 | 3011 | ex D-AVWB | |
| ☐ D-AGWE | Airbus A319-132 | 3128 | ex D-AVXB | |
| ☐ D-AGWF | Airbus A319-132 | 3172 | ex D-AVXG | |
| ☐ D-AGWG | Airbus A319-132 | 3193 | ex D-AVYS | |
| ☐ D-AGWH | Airbus A319-132 | 3352 | ex D-AVYX | |
| ☐ D-AGWI | Airbus A319-132 | 3358 | ex D-AVYZ | |
| ☐ D-AGWJ | Airbus A319-132 | 3375 | ex D-AVWB | |
| ☐ D-AGWK | Airbus A319-132 | 3500 | ex D-AVYW | |
| ☐ D-AGWL | Airbus A319-132 | 3534 | ex D-AVWB | |
| ☐ D-AGWM | Airbus A319-132 | 3839 | ex D-AVYQ | |
| ☐ D-AGWN | Airbus A319-132 | 3841 | ex D-AVYS | |
| ☐ D-AGWO | Airbus A319-132 | 4166 | ex D-AVWH | |
| ☐ D-AGWP | Airbus A319-132 | 4227 | ex D-AVYK | |
| ☐ D-AGWQ | Airbus A319-132 | 4256 | ex D-AVYP | |
| ☐ D-AGWR | Airbus A319-132 | 4285 | ex D-AVWS | |
| ☐ D-AGWS | Airbus A319-132 | 4998 | ex D- | |
| ☐ D-AGWT | Airbus A319-132 | 5066 | ex D-AVYL | ♦ |
| ☐ D-AKNK | Airbus A319-112 | 1077 | ex N718UW | |
| ☐ D-AKNL | Airbus A319-112 | 1084 | ex N719US | |
| ☐ D-AKNM | Airbus A319-112 | 1089 | ex N720US | |
| ☐ D-AKNN | Airbus A319-112 | 1136 | ex N726US | |
| ☐ D-AKNO | Airbus A319-112 | 1147 | ex N727UW | |

| | | | | |
|---|---|---|---|---|
| ☐ D-AKNP | Airbus A319-112 | 1155 | ex N728UW | |
| ☐ D-AKNQ | Airbus A319-112 | 1170 | ex N729US | |
| ☐ D-AKNR | Airbus A319-112 | 1209 | ex N736US | |
| ☐ D-AKNS | Airbus A319-112 | 1277 | ex N743UW | |
| ☐ D-AKNT | Airbus A319-112 | 2607 | ex D-AVXQ | |
| ☐ D-AKNU | Airbus A319-112 | 2628 | ex D-AVWB | |
| ☐ D-AKNV | Airbus A319-112 | 2632 | ex D-AVWE | |

## GERMAN SKY AIRLINES  (GHY)  Dusseldorf (DUS)

| | | | | |
|---|---|---|---|---|
| ☐ D-AGSA | Boeing 737-883 | 28323/625 | ex OY-CJS | |
| ☐ D-AGSB | Boeing 737-883 | 30194/666 | ex TC-SKU | ♦ |

## HAMBURG AIRWAYS  Hamburg Jet (HK/HAY)  Hamburg (HAM)

| | | | | |
|---|---|---|---|---|
| ☐ D-AHHA | Airbus A319-111 | 3533 | ex D-AHIJ | ♦ |
| ☐ D-AHHB | Airbus A319-112 | 3560 | ex D-AHIK | ♦ |
| ☐ D-AHHC | Airbus A320-214 | 2745 | ex EI-ERR | ♦ |

## HELOG LUFTTRANSPORT  Ainring / Salzburg

| | | | | |
|---|---|---|---|---|
| ☐ D-HAXH | Aérospatiale SA.330J Puma | 1410 | | Op for UN |
| ☐ D-HAXK | Aérospatiale SA.330J Puma | 1442 | | Op for UN |
| ☐ D-HAXP | Aérospatiale SA.330J Puma | 1545 | | Op for UN♦ |
| ☐ D-HAXR | Aérospatiale SA.330J Puma | 1553 | | Op for UN |

## JETISFACTION  M☐nster-Osnabruck (FMO)

| | | | | |
|---|---|---|---|---|
| ☐ PH-RNG | Beeech 1900D | UE-70 | ex ZS-PZH | ♦ |

## LGW - LUFTFAHRTGESELLSCHAFT WALTER Walter (HE/LGW)  Dortmund (DTM)

| | | | | |
|---|---|---|---|---|
| ☐ D-ABQA | de Havilland DHC-8-402Q | 4223 | ex C-FTID | <BER |
| ☐ D-ABQB | de Havilland DHC-8-402Q | 4226 | ex C-FTUM | <BER |
| ☐ D-ABQC | de Havilland DHC-8-402Q | 4231 | ex C-FUCI | <BER |
| ☐ D-ABQD | de Havilland DHC-8-402Q | 4234 | ex C-FUCS | <BER |
| ☐ D-ABQE | de Havilland DHC-8-402Q | 4239 | ex C-FURQ | <BER |
| ☐ D-ABQF | de Havilland DHC-8-402Q | 4245 | ex C-FVGV | <BER |
| ☐ D-ABQG | de Havilland DHC-8-402Q | 4250 | ex C-FVUN | <BER |
| ☐ D-ABQH | de Havilland DHC-8-402Q | 4256 | ex C-FWGO | <BER |
| ☐ D-ABQI | de Havilland DHC-8-402Q | 4264 | ex C-FXIW | <BER |
| ☐ D-ABQJ | de Havilland DHC-8-402Q | 4274 | ex C-FYGN | <BER |
| ☐ D-IKBA | Dornier 228-201 | 8066 | ex D-CBDR | |
| ☐ D-ILWB | Dornier 228-200 | 8035 | ex D-CDIZ | |
| ☐ D-ILWS | Dornier 228-200 | 8002 | ex D-CBDU | |

## LUFTHANSA  Lufthansa (LH/DLH)  Frankfurt (FRA)

Member of Star Alliance

| | | | | | |
|---|---|---|---|---|---|
| ☐ D-AIBA | Airbus A319-112 | 4141 | ex D-AVWG | | |
| ☐ D-AIBB | Airbus A319-112 | 4182 | ex D-AVWK | Aalen | |
| ☐ D-AIBC | Airbus A319-112 | 4332 | ex D-AVXF | | |
| ☐ D-AIBD | Airbus A319-112 | 4455 | ex D-AVYC | Pirmasens | |
| ☐ D-AIBE | Airbus A319-112 | 4511 | ex D-AVYH | Schönefeld | |
| ☐ D-AIBF | Airbus A319-112 | 4976 | ex D-AVYZ | Sinsheim | ♦ |
| ☐ D-AIBG | Airbus A319-112 | 4841 | ex D-AVWF | | ♦ |
| ☐ D-AILA | Airbus A319-114 | 0609 | ex D-AVYF | Frankfurt an der Oder | |
| ☐ D-AILB | Airbus A319-114 | 0610 | ex D-AVYG | Lutherstadt Wittenberg | |
| ☐ D-AILC | Airbus A319-114 | 0616 | ex D-AVYI | Rüsselsheim | |
| ☐ D-AILD | Airbus A319-114 | 0623 | ex D-AVYL | Dinkelsbühl | |
| ☐ D-AILE | Airbus A319-114 | 0627 | ex D-AVYO | Kelsterbach | |
| ☐ D-AILF | Airbus A319-114 | 0636 | ex D-AVYS | Trier | |
| ☐ D-AILH | Airbus A319-114 | 0641 | ex D-AVYV | Norderstedt | |
| ☐ D-AILI | Airbus A319-114 | 0651 | ex D-AVYY | Ingolstadt | |
| ☐ D-AILK | Airbus A319-114 | 0679 | ex D-AVYG | Aschaffenburg | |
| ☐ D-AILL | Airbus A319-114 | 0689 | ex D-AVYL | Marburg | |
| ☐ D-AILM | Airbus A319-114 | 0694 | ex D-AVYR | Friedrichshafen | |
| ☐ D-AILN | Airbus A319-114 | 0700 | ex D-AVYU | Idar-Oberstein | |
| ☐ D-AILP | Airbus A319-114 | 0717 | ex D-AVYA | Tübingen | |
| ☐ D-AILR | Airbus A319-114 | 0723 | ex D-AVYD | Tegernsee | |
| ☐ D-AILS | Airbus A319-114 | 0729 | ex D-AVYF | Heide | |
| ☐ D-AILT | Airbus A319-114 | 0738 | ex D-AVYN | Straubing | |
| ☐ D-AILU | Airbus A319-114 | 0744 | ex D-AVYI | Verden | |
| ☐ D-AILW | Airbus A319-114 | 0853 | ex D-AVYO | Donaueschingen | |
| ☐ D-AILX | Airbus A319-114 | 0860 | ex D-AVYS | Fellbach | |
| ☐ D-AILY | Airbus A319-114 | 0875 | ex D-AVYC | Schweinfurt | |
| ☐ D-AKNF | Airbus A319-112 | 0646 | ex D-AVYB | | [SOF]♦ |
| ☐ D-AKNG | Airbus A319-112 | 0654 | ex D-AVYX | | [SOF]♦ |
| ☐ D-AKNH | Airbus A319-112 | 0794 | ex D-AVYD | | wfs♦ |

| | | | | | |
|---|---|---|---|---|---|
| ☐ | D-AKNI | Airbus A319-112 | 1016 | ex D-AVYK | wfs♦ |
| ☐ | D-AKNJ | Airbus A319-112 | 1172 | ex D-AVWF | [BUD]♦ |
| | | | | | |
| ☐ | D-AIPA | Airbus A320-211 | 0069 | ex F-WWII | Buxtehude |
| ☐ | D-AIPB | Airbus A320-211 | 0070 | ex F-WWIJ | Heidelberg |
| ☐ | D-AIPC | Airbus A320-211 | 0071 | ex F-WWIO | Braunschweig |
| ☐ | D-AIPD | Airbus A320-211 | 0072 | ex F-WWIP | Freiburg |
| ☐ | D-AIPE | Airbus A320-211 | 0078 | ex F-WWIU | Kassel |
| ☐ | D-AIPF | Airbus A320-211 | 0083 | ex F-WWDE | Deggendorf |
| ☐ | D-AIPH | Airbus A320-211 | 0086 | ex F-WWDJ | Münster |
| ☐ | D-AIPK | Airbus A320-211 | 0093 | ex F-WWDQ | Wiesbaden |
| ☐ | D-AIPL | Airbus A320-211 | 0094 | ex 7T-VKO | Ludwigshafen am Rhein |
| ☐ | D-AIPM | Airbus A320-211 | 0104 | ex F-WWIG | Troisdorf |
| ☐ | D-AIPP | Airbus A320-211 | 0110 | ex F-WWID | Starnberg |
| ☐ | D-AIPR | Airbus A320-211 | 0111 | ex F-WWIE | Kaufbeuren |
| ☐ | D-AIPS | Airbus A320-211 | 0116 | ex F-WWIK | Augsburg |
| ☐ | D-AIPT | Airbus A320-211 | 0117 | ex F-WWIL | Cottbus |
| ☐ | D-AIPU | Airbus A320-211 | 0135 | ex F-WWDB | |
| ☐ | D-AIPW | Airbus A320-211 | 0137 | ex F-WWDD | Schwerin |
| ☐ | D-AIPX | Airbus A320-211 | 0147 | ex F-WWDN | Mannheim |
| ☐ | D-AIPY | Airbus A320-211 | 0161 | ex F-WWIA | Magdeburg |
| ☐ | D-AIPZ | Airbus A320-211 | 0162 | ex F-WWDS | |
| ☐ | D-AIQA | Airbus A320-211 | 0172 | ex F-WWIK | |
| ☐ | D-AIQB | Airbus A320-211 | 0200 | ex F-WWDJ | Bielefeld |
| ☐ | D-AIQC | Airbus A320-211 | 0201 | ex F-WWDL | Zwickau |
| ☐ | D-AIQD | Airbus A320-211 | 0202 | ex F-WWDM | Jena |
| ☐ | D-AIQE | Airbus A320-211 | 0209 | ex F-WWDY | Gera |
| ☐ | D-AIQF | Airbus A320-211 | 0216 | ex F-WWDR | Halle a.d.Saale |
| ☐ | D-AIQH | Airbus A320-211 | 0217 | ex F-WWDS | Dessau |
| ☐ | D-AIQK | Airbus A320-211 | 0218 | ex F-WWDX | Rostock |
| ☐ | D-AIQL | Airbus A320-211 | 0267 | ex F-WWDY | Stralsund |
| ☐ | D-AIQM | Airbus A320-211 | 0268 | ex F-WWIB | Nordenham |
| ☐ | D-AIQN | Airbus A320-211 | 0269 | ex F-WWIC | Laupheim |
| ☐ | D-AIQP | Airbus A320-211 | 0346 | ex F-WWDX | Suhl |
| ☐ | D-AIQR | Airbus A320-211 | 0382 | ex F-WWIZ | Lahr/Schwarzwald |
| ☐ | D-AIQS | Airbus A320-211 | 0401 | ex F-WWBD | Eisenach |
| ☐ | D-AIQT | Airbus A320-211 | 1337 | ex F-WWDO | Gotha |
| ☐ | D-AIQU | Airbus A320-211 | 1365 | ex F-WWIG | Backnang |
| ☐ | D-AIQW | Airbus A320-211 | 1367 | ex F-WWIH | Kleve |
| ☐ | D-AIZA | Airbus A320-214 | 4097 | ex D-AVVF | |
| ☐ | D-AIZB | Airbus A320-214 | 4120 | ex D-AVVV | |
| ☐ | D-AIZC | Airbus A320-214 | 4153 | ex D-AVVL | Budingen |
| ☐ | D-AIZD | Airbus A320-214 | 4191 | ex D-AVVD | |
| ☐ | D-AIZE | Airbus A320-214 | 4261 | ex D-AXAC | |
| ☐ | D-AIZF | Airbus A320-214 | 4289 | ex D-AXAF | |
| ☐ | D-AIZG | Airbus A320-214 | 4324 | ex D-AXAO | |
| ☐ | D-AIZH | Airbus A320-214 | 4363 | ex D-AXAW | Ahlen |
| ☐ | D-AIZI | Airbus A320-214 | 4398 | ex D-AVVL | |
| ☐ | D-AIZJ | Airbus A320-214 | 4449 | ex D-AVVM | |
| ☐ | D-AIZK | Airbus A320-214 | 5122 | ex D- | o/o♦ |
| | | | | | |
| ☐ | D-AIRA | Airbus A321-131 | 0458 | ex F-WWIQ | Finkenwerder |
| ☐ | D-AIRB | Airbus A321-131 | 0468 | ex F-WWIS | Baden-Baden |
| ☐ | D-AIRC | Airbus A321-131 | 0473 | ex D-AVZC | Erlangen |
| ☐ | D-AIRD | Airbus A321-131 | 0474 | ex D-AVZD | Coburg |
| ☐ | D-AIRE | Airbus A321-131 | 0484 | ex D-AVZF | Osnabrück |
| ☐ | D-AIRF | Airbus A321-131 | 0493 | ex D-AVZH | Kempten |
| ☐ | D-AIRH | Airbus A321-131 | 0412 | ex D-AVZA | Garmisch-Partenkirchen |
| ☐ | D-AIRK | Airbus A321-131 | 0502 | ex D-AVZL | Freudenstadt/Schwarzwald |
| ☐ | D-AIRL | Airbus A321-131 | 0505 | ex D-AVZM | Kulmbach |
| ☐ | D-AIRM | Airbus A321-131 | 0518 | ex D-AVZT | Darmstadt |
| ☐ | D-AIRN | Airbus A321-131 | 0560 | ex D-AVZK | Kaiserslautern |
| ☐ | D-AIRO | Airbus A321-131 | 0563 | ex D-AVZN | Konstanz |
| ☐ | D-AIRP | Airbus A321-131 | 0564 | ex D-AVZL | Lunenburg |
| ☐ | D-AIRR | Airbus A321-131 | 0567 | ex D-AVZM | Wismar |
| ☐ | D-AIRS | Airbus A321-131 | 0595 | ex D-AVZX | Husum |
| ☐ | D-AIRT | Airbus A321-131 | 0652 | ex D-AVZI | Regensburg |
| ☐ | D-AIRU | Airbus A321-131 | 0692 | ex D-AVZT | Würzburg |
| ☐ | D-AIRW | Airbus A321-131 | 0699 | ex D-AVZY | Heilbronn |
| ☐ | D-AIRX | Airbus A321-131 | 0887 | ex D-AVZI | Weimar | retro c/s |
| ☐ | D-AIRY | Airbus A321-131 | 0901 | ex D-AVZK | Flensburg |
| | | | | | |
| ☐ | D-AIDA | Airbus A321-231 | 4360 | ex D-AVZM | |
| ☐ | D-AIDB | Airbus A321-231 | 4545 | ex D-AVZZ | |
| ☐ | D-AIDC | Airbus A321-231 | 4560 | ex D-AZAB | |
| ☐ | D-AIDD | Airbus A321-231 | 4585 | ex D-AVZC | |
| ☐ | D-AIDE | Airbus A321-231 | 4607 | ex D-AIDE | |
| ☐ | D-AIDF | Airbus A321-231 | 4626 | ex D-AZAO | |
| ☐ | D-AIDG | Airbus A321-231 | 4672 | ex D-AVWF | |
| ☐ | D-AIDH | Airbus A321-231 | 4710 | ex D-AZAF | |
| ☐ | D-AIDI | Airbus A321-231 | 4753 | ex D-AVZI | ♦ |
| ☐ | D-AIDJ | Airbus A321-231 | 4792 | ex D-AIDJ | ♦ |

| | | | | | |
|---|---|---|---|---|---|
| ☐ D-AIDK | Airbus A321-231 | 4819 | ex D-AVZQ | | ♦ |
| ☐ D-AIDL | Airbus A321-231 | 4881 | ex D-AVZC | | ♦ |
| ☐ D-AIDM | Airbus A321-231 | 4916 | ex D-AVZH | | ♦ |
| ☐ D-AIDN | Airbus A321-231 | 4976 | ex D-AZAI | | ♦ |
| ☐ D-AIDO | Airbus A321-231 | 4994 | ex D-AZAJ | | ♦ |
| ☐ D-AIDP | Airbus A321-231 | 5049 | ex D-AZAQ | | ♦ |
| ☐ D-AIDQ | Airbus A321-231 | 5028 | ex D-AZAM | | ♦ |
| ☐ D-AIDT | Airbus A321-231 | 5087 | ex D-AZAU | | ♦ |
| ☐ D-AISB | Airbus A321-231 | 1080 | ex D-AVZP | Hameln | |
| ☐ D-AISC | Airbus A321-231 | 1161 | ex D-AVZG | Speyer | |
| ☐ D-AISD | Airbus A321-231 | 1188 | ex F-WWDD | Chemnitz | |
| ☐ D-AISE | Airbus A321-231 | 1214 | ex D-AVZS | Neudstadt an der Weinstrasse | |
| ☐ D-AISF | Airbus A321-231 | 1260 | ex D-AVZI | Lippstadt | |
| ☐ D-AISG | Airbus A321-231 | 1273 | ex D-AVZU | Dormagen | |
| ☐ D-AISH | Airbus A321-231 | 3265 | ex D-AVZL | | |
| ☐ D-AISI | Airbus A321-231 | 3339 | ex D-AVZD | Bergheim | |
| ☐ D-AISJ | Airbus A321-231 | 3360 | ex D-AVZF | Gutersloh | |
| ☐ D-AISK | Airbus A321-231 | 3387 | ex D-AVZO | Emden | |
| ☐ D-AISL | Airbus A321-231 | 3434 | ex D-AVZD | Arnsberg | |
| ☐ D-AISN | Airbus A321-231 | 3592 | ex D-AZAA | Goppingen | |
| ☐ D-AISO | Airbus A321-231 | 3625 | ex D-AVZH | Bocholt | |
| ☐ D-AISP | Airbus A321-231 | 3864 | ex D-AVZK | Rosenheim | |
| ☐ D-AISQ | Airbus A321-231 | 3936 | ex D-AZAF | Lindau | |
| ☐ D-AISR | Airbus A321-231 | 3987 | ex D-AZAN | Donauworth | |
| ☐ D-AIST | Airbus A321-231 | 4005 | ex D-AVZD | Erbach | |
| ☐ D-AISU | Airbus A321-231 | 4016 | ex D-AVZF | Nordlingen | |
| ☐ D-AISV | Airbus A321-231 | 4047 | ex D-AZAG | Bingen | |
| ☐ D-AISW | Airbus A321-231 | 4054 | ex D-AZAR | Stade | |
| ☐ D-AISX | Airbus A321-231 | 4073 | ex D-AVZR | | |
| ☐ D-AISZ | Airbus A321-231 | 4085 | ex D-AVZW | | |
| | | | | | |
| ☐ D-AIKA | Airbus A330-343X | 570 | ex F-WWYV | Minden | |
| ☐ D-AIKB | Airbus A330-343X | 576 | ex F-WWKN | Cuxhaven | |
| ☐ D-AIKC | Airbus A330-343X | 579 | ex F-WWKG | Hamm | |
| ☐ D-AIKD | Airbus A330-343X | 629 | ex F-WWYF | Siegen | |
| ☐ D-AIKE | Airbus A330-343X | 636 | ex F-WWYL | Landshut | |
| ☐ D-AIKF | Airbus A330-343X | 642 | ex F-WWKV | Witten | |
| ☐ D-AIKG | Airbus A330-343X | 645 | ex F-WWKE | Ludwigsburg | |
| ☐ D-AIKH | Airbus A330-343X | 648 | ex F-WWKG | | |
| ☐ D-AIKI | Airbus A330-343X | 687 | ex F-WWYI | | |
| ☐ D-AIKJ | Airbus A330-343X | 701 | ex F-WWKD | Bottrop | |
| ☐ D-AIKK | Airbus A330-343X | 896 | ex F-WWYX | Furth | |
| ☐ D-AIKL | Airbus A330-343X | 905 | ex F-WWYC | Ingolstadt | |
| ☐ D-AIKM | Airbus A330-343X | 913 | ex F-WWYJ | | |
| ☐ D-AIKN | Airbus A330-343X | 922 | ex F-WWYY | | |
| ☐ D-AIKO | Airbus A330-343X | 989 | ex F-WWKJ | | |
| ☐ D-AIKP | Airbus A330-343X | 1292 | ex F-WWYQ | | |
| ☐ D-AIKQ | Airbus A330-343X | 1305 | ex F-WWYV | | o/o♦ |
| ☐ D-AIKR | Airbus A330-343X | 1314 | ex F-WW | | o/o♦ |
| | | | | | |
| ☐ D-AIFA | Airbus A340-313X | 352 | ex F-WWJU | Dorsten | |
| ☐ D-AIFC | Airbus A340-313X | 379 | ex F-WWJJ | Gander & Halifax | |
| ☐ D-AIFD | Airbus A340-313X | 390 | ex F-WWJE | Giessen | |
| ☐ D-AIFE | Airbus A340-313X | 434 | ex F-WWJT | Passau | |
| ☐ D-AIFF | Airbus A340-313X | 447 | ex F-WWJB | Delmenhorst | |
| ☐ D-AIGA | Airbus A340-311 | 020 | ex F-WWJK | Oldenburg | |
| ☐ D-AIGB | Airbus A340-311 | 024 | ex F-WWJO | Recklinghausen | |
| ☐ D-AIGC | Airbus A340-311 | 027 | ex F-WWJR | Wilhelmshaven | Star Alliance c/s |
| ☐ D-AIGD | Airbus A340-311 | 028 | ex F-WWJS | Remscheid | |
| ☐ D-AIGF | Airbus A340-311 | 035 | ex F-WWJV | Göttingen | |
| ☐ D-AIGH | Airbus A340-311 | 052 | ex F-WWJQ | Koblenz | |
| ☐ D-AIGI | Airbus A340-311 | 053 | ex F-WWJJ | Worms | |
| ☐ D-AIGK | Airbus A340-311 | 056 | ex F-WWJK | Bayreuth | |
| ☐ D-AIGL | Airbus A340-313X | 135 | ex F-WWJS | Herne | |
| ☐ D-AIGM | Airbus A340-313X | 158 | ex F-WWJN | Görlitz | |
| ☐ D-AIGN | Airbus A340-313X | 213 | ex F-WWJM | Solingen | |
| ☐ D-AIGO | Airbus A340-313X | 233 | ex F-WWJJ | Offenbach | |
| ☐ D-AIGP | Airbus A340-313X | 252 | ex F-WWJM | Paderborn | |
| ☐ D-AIGS | Airbus A340-313X | 297 | ex F-WWJK | Bergisch-Gladbach | |
| ☐ D-AIGT | Airbus A340-313X | 304 | ex F-WWJY | Viersen | |
| ☐ D-AIGU | Airbus A340-313X | 321 | ex F-WWJM | Castrop-Rauxel | |
| ☐ D-AIGV | Airbus A340-313X | 325 | ex F-WWJN | Dinslaken | |
| ☐ D-AIGW | Airbus A340-313X | 327 | ex F-WWJO | Gladbeck | |
| ☐ D-AIGX | Airbus A340-313X | 354 | ex F-WWJV | Düren | |
| ☐ D-AIGY | Airbus A340-313X | 335 | ex F-WWJS | Lünen | |
| ☐ D-AIGZ | Airbus A340-313X | 347 | ex F-WWJT | Villingen-Schwenningen | |
| | | | | | |
| ☐ D-AIHA | Airbus A340-642 | 482 | ex F-WWCS | Nürnberg | Star Alliance c/s |
| ☐ D-AIHB | Airbus A340-642 | 517 | ex F-WWCR | Bremerhaven | |
| ☐ D-AIHC | Airbus A340-642 | 523 | ex F-WWCV | Essen | |
| ☐ D-AIHD | Airbus A340-642 | 537 | ex F-WWCZ | Stuttgart | |
| ☐ D-AIHE | Airbus A340-642 | 540 | ex F-WWCF | Leverkusen | |

| | | | | | |
|---|---|---|---|---|---|
| ☐ D-AIHF | Airbus A340-642 | 543 | ex F-WWCE | Lübeck | |
| ☐ D-AIHH | Airbus A340-642 | 566 | ex F-WWCJ | Wiesbaden | |
| ☐ D-AIHI | Airbus A340-642 | 569 | ex F-WWCB | Monchengladbach | |
| ☐ D-AIHK | Airbus A340-642 | 580 | ex F-WWCN | Mainz | |
| ☐ D-AIHL | Airbus A340-642 | 583 | ex F-WWCQ | | |
| ☐ D-AIHM | Airbus A340-642 | 762 | ex F-WWCI | Wuppertal | |
| ☐ D-AIHN | Airbus A340-642 | 763 | ex F-WWCJ | | |
| ☐ D-AIHO | Airbus A340-642 | 767 | ex F-WWCN | | |
| ☐ D-AIHP | Airbus A340-642 | 771 | ex F-WWCQ | | |
| ☐ D-AIHQ | Airbus A340-642 | 790 | ex F-WWCE | | |
| ☐ D-AIHR | Airbus A340-642 | 794 | ex F-WWCF | | |
| ☐ D-AIHS | Airbus A340-642 | 812 | ex F-WWCX | | |
| ☐ D-AIHT | Airbus A340-642 | 846 | ex F-WWCH | | |
| ☐ D-AIHU | Airbus A340-642 | 848 | ex F-WWCI | | |
| ☐ D-AIHV | Airbus A340-642 | 897 | ex F-WWTI | | |
| ☐ D-AIHW | Airbus A340-642 | 972 | ex F-WWCL | | |
| ☐ D-AIHX | Airbus A340-642 | 981 | ex F-WWCN | | |
| ☐ D-AIHY | Airbus A340-642 | 987 | ex F-WWCQ | | |
| ☐ D-AIHZ | Airbus A340-642 | 1005 | ex F-WWCR | | |
| | | | | | |
| ☐ D-AIMA | Airbus A380-841 | 038 | ex F-WWSH | Frankfurt am Main | |
| ☐ D-AIMB | Airbus A380-841 | 041 | ex F-WWAF | Munchen | |
| ☐ D-AIMC | Airbus A380-841 | 044 | ex F-WWAJ | Peking | |
| ☐ D-AIMD | Airbus A380-841 | 048 | ex F-WWAK | Tokio | |
| ☐ D-AIME | Airbus A380-841 | 061 | | | |
| ☐ D-AIMF | Airbus A380-841 | 066 | ex F-WWSN | | |
| ☐ D-AIMG | Airbbus A380-841 | 069 | ex F-WWSO | | |
| ☐ D-AIMH | Airbus A380-841 | 070 | ex F-WWSG | | |
| ☐ D-AIMI | Airbus A380-841 | 072 | ex F-WWSR | | o/o♦ |
| ☐ D-AIMJ | Airbus A380-841 | 073 | ex F-WWSP | | o/o♦ |
| ☐ D-AIMK | Airbus A380-841 | 118 | ex F-WW | | o/o♦ |
| | | | | | |
| ☐ D-ABEA | Boeing 737-330 | 24565/1818 | | Saarbrucken | |
| ☐ D-ABEB | Boeing 737-330 | 25148/2077 | | Xanten | |
| ☐ D-ABEC | Boeing 737-330 | 25149/2081 | | Karlsruhe | |
| ☐ D-ABED | Boeing 737-330 | 25215/2082 | | Hagen | |
| ☐ D-ABEE | Boeing 737-330 | 25216/2084 | | Ulm | |
| ☐ D-ABEF | Boeing 737-330 | 25217/2094 | | Weiden i.d.Opf | |
| ☐ D-ABEH | Boeing 737-330 | 25242/2102 | | Bad Kissingen | |
| ☐ D-ABEI | Boeing 737-330 | 25359/2158 | ex (D-ABJK) | Bamberg | |
| ☐ D-ABEK | Boeing 737-330 | 25414/2164 | ex (D-ABJL) | | |
| ☐ D-ABEL | Boeing 737-330 | 25415/2175 | ex (D-ABJM) | Pforzheim | |
| ☐ D-ABEM | Boeing 737-330 | 25416/2182 | ex (D-ABJN) | Eberswalde-Finow | |
| ☐ D-ABEN | Boeing 737-330 | 26428/2196 | ex (D-ABJP) | Neubrandenburg | |
| ☐ D-ABEO | Boeing 737-330 | 26429/2207 | ex (D-ABJR) | Plauen | |
| ☐ D-ABEP | Boeing 737-330 | 26430/2216 | ex (D-ABJS) | Naumburg/Saale | |
| ☐ D-ABER | Boeing 737-330 | 26431/2242 | ex TC-SUK | Merseburg | |
| ☐ D-ABES | Boeing 737-330 | 26432/2247 | ex (D-ABJU) | Köthen/Anhalt | |
| ☐ D-ABET | Boeing 737-330 | 27903/2682 | | Gelsenkirchen | |
| ☐ D-ABEU | Boeing 737-330 | 27904/2691 | | Goslar | |
| ☐ D-ABEW | Boeing 737-330 | 27905/2705 | | Detmold | |
| ☐ D-ABWH | Boeing 737-330 (QC) | 24284/1685 | | Rothenburg o.d. Tauber | |
| ☐ D-ABXL | Boeing 737-330 | 23531/1307 | | Neuss | |
| ☐ D-ABXM | Boeing 737-330 | 23871/1433 | | Herford | |
| ☐ D-ABXN | Boeing 737-330 | 23872/1447 | | Böblingen | |
| ☐ D-ABXO | Boeing 737-330 | 23873/1489 | | Schwäbisch Gmünd | |
| ☐ D-ABXP | Boeing 737-330 | 23874/1495 | | Fulda | |
| ☐ D-ABXR | Boeing 737-330 | 23875/1500 | | Celle | |
| ☐ D-ABXS | Boeing 737-330 | 24280/1656 | | Sindelfingen | |
| ☐ D-ABXT | Boeing 737-330 | 24281/1664 | | Reutlingen | |
| ☐ D-ABXU | Boeing 737-330 | 24282/1671 | | Seeheim-Jugenheim | |
| ☐ D-ABXW | Boeing 737-330 | 24561/1785 | | Hanau | |
| ☐ D-ABXX | Boeing 737-330 | 24562/1787 | | Bad Homburg v d Höhe | |
| ☐ D-ABXY | Boeing 737-330 | 24563/1801 | | Hof | |
| ☐ D-ABXZ | Boeing 737-330 | 24564/1807 | | Bad Mergentheim | |
| | | | | | |
| ☐ D-ABIA | Boeing 737-530 | 24815/1933 | ex OK-SWY | Greifswald | |
| ☐ D-ABIB | Boeing 737-530 | 24816/1958 | ex OK-SWZ | Esslingen | |
| ☐ D-ABIC | Boeing 737-530 | 24817/1967 | | Krefeld | |
| ☐ D-ABID | Boeing 737-530 | 24818/1974 | | Aachen | |
| ☐ D-ABIE | Boeing 737-530 | 24819/1979 | | Hildesheim | |
| ☐ D-ABIF | Boeing 737-530 | 24820/1985 | | Landau | |
| ☐ D-ABIH | Boeing 737-530 | 24821/1993 | | Bruchsal | |
| ☐ D-ABII | Boeing 737-530 | 24822/1997 | | Lörrach | |
| ☐ D-ABIK | Boeing 737-530 | 24823/2000 | | Rastatt | |
| ☐ D-ABIL | Boeing 737-530 | 24824/2006 | | Memmingen | |
| ☐ D-ABIM | Boeing 737-530 | 24937/2011 | | Salzgitter | |
| ☐ D-ABIN | Boeing 737-530 | 24938/2023 | | Langenhagen | |
| ☐ D-ABIO | Boeing 737-530 | 24939/2031 | | Wesel | |
| ☐ D-ABIP | Boeing 737-530 | 24940/2034 | | Oberhausen | |
| ☐ D-ABIR | Boeing 737-530 | 24941/2042 | | Anklam | |
| ☐ D-ABIS | Boeing 737-530 | 24942/2048 | | Rendsburg | |

| | | | | | |
|---|---|---|---|---|---|
| ☐ D-ABIT | Boeing 737-530 | 24943/2049 | | Neumünster | |
| ☐ D-ABIU | Boeing 737-530 | 24944/2051 | | Limburg | |
| ☐ D-ABIW | Boeing 737-530 | 24945/2063 | | Bad Nauheim | |
| ☐ D-ABIX | Boeing 737-530 | 24946/2070 | | Iserlohn | |
| ☐ D-ABIY | Boeing 737-530 | 25243/2086 | | Lingen | |
| ☐ D-ABJB | Boeing 737-530 | 25271/2117 | | Rheine | |
| ☐ D-ABJI | Boeing 737-530 | 25358/2151 | | Siegburg | [FRA] |
| | | | | | |
| ☐ D-ABTA | Boeing 747-430M | 24285/747 | | Sachsen | |
| ☐ D-ABTB | Boeing 747-430M | 24286/749 | | Brandenburg | |
| ☐ D-ABTC | Boeing 747-430M | 24287/754 | | Mecklenburg-Vorpommern | |
| ☐ D-ABTD | Boeing 747-430M | 24715/785 | | Hamburg | |
| ☐ D-ABTE | Boeing 747-430M | 24966/846 | ex N6046P | Sachsen-Anhalt | |
| ☐ D-ABTF | Boeing 747-430M | 24967/848 | | Thüringen | |
| ☐ D-ABTH | Boeing 747-430M | 25047/856 | | Duisburg | |
| ☐ D-ABTK | Boeing 747-430 | 29871/1293 | ex (D-ABVI) | Kiel | |
| ☐ D-ABTL | Boeing 747-430 | 29872/1299 | ex (D-ABVG) | Dresden | |
| ☐ D-ABVC | Boeing 747-430 | 24288/757 | | Baden-Württemberg | |
| ☐ D-ABVD | Boeing 747-430 | 24740/786 | ex N60668 | Bochum | |
| ☐ D-ABVE | Boeing 747-430 | 24741/787 | | Potsdam | |
| ☐ D-ABVF | Boeing 747-430 | 24761/796 | ex N6018N | Frankfurt am Main | |
| ☐ D-ABVH | Boeing 747-430 | 25045/845 | ex N6018N | Düsseldorf | |
| ☐ D-ABVK | Boeing 747-430 | 25046/847 | ex N6009F | Hannover | |
| ☐ D-ABVL | Boeing 747-430 | 26425/898 | ex N60659 | München | |
| ☐ D-ABVM | Boeing 747-430 | 29101/1143 | ex (V8-AC2) | Hessen | |
| ☐ D-ABVN | Boeing 747-430 | 26427/915 | | Dortmund | |
| ☐ D-ABVO | Boeing 747-430 | 28086/1080 | | Mülheim an der Ruhr | |
| ☐ D-ABVP | Boeing 747-430 | 28284/1103 | | Bremen | |
| ☐ D-ABVR | Boeing 747-430 | 28285/1106 | | Köln | |
| ☐ D-ABVS | Boeing 747-430 | 28286/1109 | | Saarland | |
| ☐ D-ABVT | Boeing 747-430 | 28287/1110 | | Rheinland-Pfalz | |
| ☐ D-ABVU | Boeing 747-430 | 29492/1191 | | Bayern | |
| ☐ D-ABVW | Boeing 747-430 | 29493/1205 | | Wolfsburg | |
| ☐ D-ABVX | Boeing 747-430 | 29868/1237 | | Schleswig-Holstein | |
| ☐ D-ABVY | Boeing 747-430 | 29869/1261 | | Nordrhein-Westfalen | |
| ☐ D-ABVZ | Boeing 747-430 | 29870/1264 | | Niedersachsen | |
| | | | | | |
| ☐ D-ABYA | Boeing 747-830 | 37827/1443 | ex N5018R | | o/o♦ |
| ☐ D-ABYC | Boeing 747-830 | 37828 | | | o/o♦ |
| ☐ D-ABYD | Boeing 747-830 | 37829 | | | o/o♦ |
| ☐ D-ABYE | Boeing 747-830 | 37826 | ex N6067U | | o/o♦ |
| ☐ D-ABYF | Boeing 747-830 | 37830 | | | o/o♦ |
| ☐ D-ABYG | Boeing 747-830 | 37831 | | | o/o♦ |
| ☐ D-ABYH | Boeing 747-830 | 37832 | | | o/o♦ |
| ☐ D-ABYI | Boeing 747-830 | 37833 | | | o/o♦ |
| ☐ D-ABYJ | Boeing 747-830 | 37834 | | | o/o♦ |
| ☐ D-ABYK | Boeing 747-830 | 37835 | | | o/o♦ |
| ☐ D-ABYL | Boeing 747-830 | 37836 | | | o/o♦ |
| ☐ D-ABYM | Boeing 747-830 | 37837 | | | o/o♦ |
| ☐ D-ABYN | Boeing 747-830 | 37838 | | | o/o♦ |
| ☐ D-ABYO | Boeing 747-830 | 37839 | | | o/o♦ |
| ☐ D-ABYP | Boeing 747-830 | 37840 | | | o/o♦ |
| ☐ D-ABYQ | Boeing 747-830 | 37841 | | | o/o♦ |
| ☐ D-ABYR | Boeing 747-830 | 37842 | | | o/o♦ |
| ☐ D-ABYS | Boeing 747-830 | 37843 | | | o/o♦ |
| ☐ D-ABYT | Boeing 747-830 | 37844 | | | o/o♦ |
| ☐ D-ABYU | Boeing 747-830 | 37845 | | | o/o♦ |
| | | | | | |
| ☐ D-CDLH | Junkers Ju52/3m g8e | 130714 | ex N52JU | Tempelhof | Painted as D-AQUI |

## LUFTHANSA CARGO — Lufthansa Cargo (LH/GEC) — Frankfurt (FRA)

| | | | | | |
|---|---|---|---|---|---|
| ☐ D-ALCA | McDonnell-Douglas MD-11F | 48781/625 | ex N9020Q | Wilhelm Althen | |
| ☐ D-ALCB | McDonnell-Douglas MD-11F | 48782/626 | ex N9166N | | |
| ☐ D-ALCC | McDonnell-Douglas MD-11F | 48783/627 | | Karl-Ulrich Garnadt | |
| ☐ D-ALCD | McDonnell-Douglas MD-11F | 48784/628 | | | |
| ☐ D-ALCE | McDonnell-Douglas MD-11F | 48785/629 | | | |
| ☐ D-ALCF | McDonnell-Douglas MD-11F | 48798/637 | | | |
| ☐ D-ALCG | McDonnell-Douglas MD-11F | 48799/639 | | | |
| ☐ D-ALCH | McDonnell-Douglas MD-11F | 48801/640 | | | |
| ☐ D-ALCI | McDonnell-Douglas MD-11F | 48800/641 | | | |
| ☐ D-ALCJ | McDonnell-Douglas MD-11F | 48802/642 | | | |
| ☐ D-ALCK | McDonnell-Douglas MD-11F | 48803/643 | ex N9166N | | |
| ☐ D-ALCL | McDonnell-Douglas MD-11F | 48804/644 | | | |
| ☐ D-ALCM | McDonnell-Douglas MD-11F | 48805/645 | ex N6069R | | |
| ☐ D-ALCN | McDonnell-Douglas MD-11F | 48806/646 | | | |
| ☐ D-ALCO | McDonnell-Douglas MD-11F | 48413/488 | ex N413LT | light green | |
| ☐ D-ALCP | McDonnell-Douglas MD-11F | 48414/491 | ex N414LT | purple | |
| ☐ D-ALCR | McDonnell-Douglas MD-11F | 48581/565 | ex N581LT | dark blue | |
| ☐ D-ALCS | McDonnell-Douglas MD-11F | 48630/567 | ex N630LT | orange | |

## LUFTHANSA CITYLINE      Hansaline (CL/CLH)      Frankfurt/Cologne (FRA/CGN)

| | | | | | |
|---|---|---|---|---|---|
| ☐ D-AVRA | Avro 146-RJ85 | E2256 | ex G-6-256 | | |
| ☐ D-AVRJ | Avro 146-RJ85 | E2277 | ex G-BWKY | | |
| ☐ D-AVRK | Avro 146-RJ85 | E2278 | ex G-6-278 | | [CGN] |
| ☐ D-AVRP | Avro 146-RJ85 | E2303 | ex G-6-303 | | |
| ☐ D-AVRQ | Avro 146-RJ85 | E2304 | ex G-6-304 | | |
| ☐ D-AVRR | Avro 146-RJ85 | E2317 | ex G-6-317 | | |
| | | | | | |
| ☐ D-ACPA | Canadair CRJ-701ER | 10012 | ex C-GHZV | Westerland/Sylt | |
| ☐ D-ACPB | Canadair CRJ-701ER | 10013 | ex C-GHZY | Rüdesheim am Rhein | |
| ☐ D-ACPC | Canadair CRJ-701ER | 10014 | ex C-GISW | Espelkamp | |
| ☐ D-ACPD | Canadair CRJ-701ER | 10015 | ex C-GISZ | Vilshofen an der Donau | |
| ☐ D-ACPE | Canadair CRJ-701ER | 10027 | ex C-GIAZ | Belzig | |
| ☐ D-ACPF | Canadair CRJ-701ER | 10030 | ex C-GIBI | Uhingen | |
| ☐ D-ACPG | Canadair CRJ-701ER | 10034 | ex C-GIBO | Leinfelden-Echterdingen | |
| ☐ D-ACPH | Canadair CRJ-701ER | 10043 | ex C-GHZY | Eschwege | |
| ☐ D-ACPI | Canadair CRJ-701ER | 10046 | ex C-GIAE | Viernheim | |
| ☐ D-ACPJ | Canadair CRJ-701ER | 10040 | ex C-GKCO | Neumarkt in der Oberpfalz | |
| ☐ D-ACPK | Canadair CRJ-701ER | 10063 | ex C-GIBN | Besigheim | |
| ☐ D-ACPL | Canadair CRJ-701ER | 10076 | ex C-GIAE | Halberstadt | |
| ☐ D-ACPM | Canadair CRJ-701ER | 10080 | ex C-GIAO | Heidenheim an der Brenz | |
| ☐ D-ACPN | Canadair CRJ-701ER | 10083 | ex C-GIAU | Quedlinburg | |
| ☐ D-ACPO | Canadair CRJ-701ER | 10085 | ex C-FZYS | Spaichingen | |
| ☐ D-ACPP | Canadair CRJ-701ER | 10086 | ex C-GIGJ | Torgau | |
| ☐ D-ACPQ | Canadair CRJ-701ER | 10091 | ex C-GZJA | Lubbecke | Star Alliance c/s |
| ☐ D-ACPR | Canadair CRJ-701ER | 10098 | | Weinheim an der Bergstrasse | |
| ☐ D-ACPS | Canadair CRJ-701ER | 10100 | | Berchtesgaden | Star Alliance c/s |
| ☐ D-ACPT | Canadair CRJ-701ER | 10103 | ex C-GJLZ | Altötting | Star Alliance c/s |
| | | | | | |
| ☐ D-ACKA | Canadair CRJ-900LR | 15072 | | Pfaffenhofen a.d.Ilm | |
| ☐ D-ACKB | Canadair CRJ-900LR | 15073 | ex C-FJVT | Schliersee | |
| ☐ D-ACKC | Canadair CRJ-900LR | 15078 | | Mettman | |
| ☐ D-ACKD | Canadair CRJ-900LR | 15080 | | Wittlich | |
| ☐ D-ACKE | Canadair CRJ-900LR | 15081 | | Wernigerode | |
| ☐ D-ACKF | Canadair CRJ-900LR | 15083 | ex C-FJVR | Prenzlau | |
| ☐ D-ACKG | Canadair CRJ-900LR | 15084 | ex C-GIAO | Glücksburg | |
| ☐ D-ACKH | Canadair CRJ-900LR | 15085 | ex C-GICL | Radebeul | |
| ☐ D-ACKI | Canadair CRJ-900LR | 15088 | ex C-GIAP | Tuttlingen | |
| ☐ D-ACKJ | Canadair CRJ-900LR | 15089 | | Ilmenau | |
| ☐ D-ACKK | Canadair CRJ-900LR | 15094 | | Fürstenwalde | |
| ☐ D-ACKL | Canadair CRJ-900LR | 15095 | | Bad Bergzabern | |
| ☐ D- | Canadair CRJ-900LR | | ex C- | | o/o |
| ☐ D- | Canadair CRJ-900LR | | ex C- | | o/o |
| ☐ D- | Canadair CRJ-900LR | | ex C- | | o/o |
| ☐ D- | Canadair CRJ-900LR | | ex C- | | o/o |
| | | | | | |
| ☐ D-AECA | Embraer ERJ-190LR | 19000327 | ex PT-TXP | | |
| ☐ D-AECB | Embraer ERJ-190LR | 19000332 | ex PT-TXS | | |
| ☐ D-AECC | Embraer ERJ-190LR | 19000333 | ex PT-TXT | | |
| ☐ D-AECD | Embraer ERJ-190LR | 19000337 | ex PT-TXW | | |
| ☐ D-AECE | Embraer ERJ-190LR | 19000341 | ex PT-XQI | | |
| ☐ D-AECF | Embraer ERJ-190LR | 19000359 | ex PT-XNA | Kronberg/Taunus | |
| ☐ D-AECG | Embraer ERJ-190LR | 19000368 | ex PT-XNG | | |
| ☐ D-AECH | Embraer ERJ-190LR | 19000376 | ex PT-XNM | Alzey | |
| ☐ D-AECI | Embraer ERJ-190LR | 19000381 | ex PT-XNQ | | |
| | | | | | |
| ☐ D-AEBA | Embraer ERJ-195LR | 19000314 | ex PT-TXC | | |
| ☐ D-AEBB | Embraer ERJ-195LR | 19000316 | ex PT-TXE | | |
| ☐ D-AEBC | Embraer ERJ-195LR | 19000320 | ex PT-TXI | | |
| ☐ D-AEBD | Embraer ERJ-195LR | 19000324 | ex PT-TXM | | |
| ☐ D-AEBE | Embraer ERJ-195LR | 19000350 | ex PT-XQQ | | |
| ☐ D-AEBF | Embraer ERJ-195LR | 19000411 | ex PT- | | ♦ |
| ☐ D-AEBG | Embraer ERJ-195LR | 19000423 | ex PT-TBZ | | ♦ |
| ☐ D-AEBH | Embraer ERJ-195LR | 19000447 | ex PT-TBJ | Freising | ♦ |
| ☐ D-AEBI | Embraer ERJ-195LR | 19000464 | ex PT-TOH | Erding | ♦ |
| ☐ D-AEBJ | Embraer ERJ-195LR | 19000486 | ex PT-TPK | | ♦ |
| ☐ D-AEBK | Embraer ERJ-195LR | 19000500 | ex PT-TRF | | ♦ |
| ☐ D-AEBL | Embraer ERJ-195LR | 19000507 | ex PT-TSD | | ♦ |
| ☐ D-AEBM | Embraer ERJ-195LR | 19000523 | ex PT-TUK | | ♦ |
| ☐ D-AEBN | Embraer ERJ-195LR | 19000532 | ex PT-TUV | | o/o♦ |
| ☐ D-AEBO | Embraer ERJ-195LR | 19000542 | ex PT- | | o/o♦ |

## LUFTVERKEHR FRIESLAND HARLE           Harle

| | | | | | |
|---|---|---|---|---|---|
| ☐ D-ILFA | Britten-Norman BN-2B-26 Islander | 2243 | ex G-BSWO | | |
| ☐ D-ILFD | Britten-Norman BN-2B-20 Islander | 2296 | ex JA02TY | | |
| ☐ D-ILFH | Britten-Norman BN-2B-26 Islander | 2212 | ex G-BPXS | | |
| ☐ D-IORF | Britten-Norman BN-2A-26 Islander | 2020 | ex N100DA | | <Ostseeflug |
| ☐ D-IQST | Britten-Norman BN-2B-26 Islander | 2253 | | | ♦ |

| | | | |
|---|---|---|---|
| ☐ D-IADE | Cessna 340A | 340A0607 | ex OE-FSK |

## NIGHTEXPRESS — Executive (EXT) — Frankfurt (FRA)

| | | | |
|---|---|---|---|
| ☐ D-CCAS | Short SD.3-60 | SH3737 | ex G-OLBA |
| ☐ D-CRAS | Short SD.3-60 | SH3744 | ex N825BE |
| ☐ D-IEXB | Beech 99 | U-70 | ex G-NUIT |

## OLT - OSTFRIESISCHE LUFTTRANSPORT — Oltra (OL/OLT) — Emden/Bremen (EME/BRE)

| | | | | | |
|---|---|---|---|---|---|
| ☐ D-AOLB | SAAB 2000 | 2000-005 | ex SE-005 | | |
| ☐ D-AOLC | SAAB 2000 | 2000-016 | ex SE-016 | | |
| ☐ D-AOLG | Fokker 100 | 11452 | ex PH-RRN | Toulouse | |
| ☐ D-AOLH | Fokker 100 | 11265 | ex PH-SEM | | |
| ☐ D-AOLT | SAAB 2000 | 2000-037 | ex HB-IZU | Emden | |
| ☐ D-COLB | Swearingen SA.227AC Metro III | AC-754B | ex N54NE | | [BRE] |
| ☐ D-COLE | SAAB SF.340A | 340A-144 | ex LV-WTF | Bremen | |
| ☐ D-EOLF | Gippsland GA-8 Airvan | GA8-05-080 | ex VH-IMI | Borkum | |
| ☐ D-FOLE | Cessna 208B Caravan I | 208B0523 | ex N5197A | | |
| ☐ D-IFBN | Britten-Norman BN-2B-26 Islander | 2185 | ex G-BLNF | Juist | |
| ☐ D-IOLK | Britten-Norman BN-2B-26 Islander | 2306 | ex G-CEUB | | |

## OSTSEEFLUG — Rostock-Laage (RLG)

| | | | | |
|---|---|---|---|---|
| ☐ D-IORF | Britten-Norman BN-2A-26 Islander | 2020 | ex N100DA | >L Friesland Harle |

## PRIVATAIR — PrivatJet (PTG) — Düsseldorf (DUS)

| | | | |
|---|---|---|---|
| ☐ D-APBB | Boeing 737-8Q8/W | 35278/2625 | ex N812SY |
| ☐ D-APBC | Boeing 737-8BK/W | 33016/1588 | ex N807SY |
| ☐ D-APBD | Boeing 737-8BK/W | 33021/1667 | ex N808SY |

## PRIVATE WINGS — Private Wings (8W/PWF) — Berlin-Schönefeld (SXF)

| | | | | |
|---|---|---|---|---|
| ☐ D-BIRD | Dornier 328-300 (328JET) | 3180 | ex N422FJ | |
| ☐ D-BJET | Dornier 328-300 (328JET) | 3207 | exD-BDXE | |
| ☐ D-CATZ | Dornier 328-110 | 3090 | ex N404SS | |
| ☐ D-CDAX | Dornier 328-110 | 3087 | ex N463PS | |
| ☐ D-CPWF | Dornier 328-110 | 3112 | ex D-CFWF | ♦ |
| ☐ D-CREW | Dornier 328-110 | 3113 | ex D-CGAO | |
| ☐ D-CSUE | Dornier 328-110 | 3019 | ex N328DC | ♦ |
| ☐ OE-LKC | Dornier 328-110 | 3119 | ex D-CDXK | ♦ |
| ☐ D-COCA | Beech 1900D | UE-224 | ex N224YV | |

## PTL LUFTFAHRTUNTERNEHMEN — King Star (KST) — Landshut (QLG)

| | | |
|---|---|---|
| ☐ D-IBAD | Beech B200 Super King Air | BB-1229 |

## REGIO-AIR — German Link (RAG) — Trollenhagen

| | | | | |
|---|---|---|---|---|
| ☐ D-IBIJ | Cessna 402B | 402B0327 | ex YU-BIJ | <Goller |
| ☐ D-IESS | Swearingen SA.226TC Metro II | TC-338 | ex N90141 | |

## SUNEXPRESS GERMANY — (XG/SXD)

| | | | | |
|---|---|---|---|---|
| ☐ D-ASXD | Boeing 737-8AS/W | 33562/1466 | ex EI-DCD | |
| ☐ D-ASXE | Boeing 737-8CX/W | 32365/1209 | ex TC-SUG | <SXS |
| ☐ D-ASXF | Boeing 737-8AS/W | 33558/1441 | ex EI-DAY | |
| ☐ D-ASXG | Boeing 737-8CX/W | 32366/1235 | ex TC-SUH | <SXS |
| ☐ D-ASXH | Boeing 737-8CX/W | 32368/1289 | ex TC-SUJ | <SXS |
| ☐ D-ASXS | Boeing 737-8AS/W | 33563/1473 | ex EI-DCE | |

## TUIFLY — Tuifly (X3/TUI) — Hanover (HAJ)

| | | | | |
|---|---|---|---|---|
| ☐ D-AHIA | Boeing 737-73S | 29082/229 | ex D-ASKH | |
| ☐ D-AHXA | Boeing 737-7K5/W | 30714/2202 | ex N1786B | |
| ☐ D-AHXB | Boeing 737-7K5/W | 30717/2228 | | Robinson Club Granada |
| ☐ D-AHXC | Boeing 737-7K5/W | 34693/2260 | | Robinson Club Alpffwang |
| ☐ D-AHXD | Boeing 737-7K5/W | 30726/2298 | | |
| ☐ D-AHXE | Boeing 737-7K5/W | 35135/2451 | | Robinson Club Piz Buin |
| ☐ D-AHXF | Boeing 737-7K5/W | 35136/2465 | | Robinson Club Arosa |
| ☐ D-AHXG | Boeing 737-7K5/W | 35140/2575 | | |
| ☐ D-AHXH | Boeing 737-7K5/W | 35282/2585 | | |
| ☐ D-AHXJ | Boeing 737-7K5/W | 35277/2609 | | |
| ☐ D-AHFA | Boeing 737-8K5/W | 27981/7 | ex C-GCQS | Robinson Club Pamfilya |
| ☐ D-AHFH | Boeing 737-8K5/W | 27983/218 | ex N1786B | Robinson Club Fleesensee |

| | | | | | |
|---|---|---|---|---|---|
| ☐ D-AHFI | Boeing 737-8K5/W | 27984/220 | ex N1787B | | |
| ☐ D-AHFK | Boeing 737-8K5/W | 27991/248 | ex HA-LKC | | |
| ☐ D-AHFL | Boeing 737-8K5/W | 27985/470 | ex HA-LKD | | |
| ☐ D-AHFM | Boeing 737-8K5/W | 27986/474 | | Goldbair | |
| ☐ D-AHFO | Boeing 737-8K5/W | 27987/499 | | | |
| ☐ D-AHFP | Boeing 737-8K5/W | 27988/508 | ex N1786B | | |
| ☐ D-AHFR | Boeing 737-8K5/W | 30593/528 | ex N1787B | Robinson Club Agadir | |
| ☐ D-AHFS | Boeing 737-8K5/W | 28623/556 | | | |
| ☐ D-AHFT | Boeing 737-8K5/W | 30413/636 | ex N1015B | | |
| ☐ D-AHFV | Boeing 737-8K5/W | 30415/719 | ex N1786B | | |
| ☐ D-AHFW | Boeing 737-8K5/W | 30882/760 | ex N1786B | | |
| ☐ D-AHFX | Boeing 737-8K5/W | 30416/778 | ex N1786B | | |
| ☐ D-AHFY | Boeing 737-8K5/W | 30417/781 | ex N1787B | | |
| ☐ D-AHFZ | Boeing 737-8K5/W | 30883/783 | ex N1786B | Robinson Club Cala Serena | |
| ☐ D-AHLK | Boeing 737-8K5/W | 35143/2763 | ex C-FTLK | | >SWG |
| ☐ D-ATUA | Boeing 737-8K5/W | 37245/3486 | | | |
| ☐ D-ATUB | Boeing 737-8K5/W | 37247/3497 | ex N1786B | | |
| ☐ D-ATUC | Boeing 737-8K5/W | 34684/1870 | ex N1786B | | |
| ☐ D-ATUD | Boeing 737-8K5/W | 34685/1901 | | | |
| ☐ D-ATUE | Boeing 737-8K5/W | 34686/1903 | | | |
| ☐ D-ATUF | Boeing 737-8K5/W | 34687/1907 | ex N1786B | | Retro c/s |
| ☐ D-ATUG | Boeing 737-8K5/W | 34688/1909 | | | |
| ☐ D-ATUH | Boeing 737-8K5/W | 34689/1935 | | | >SWG |
| ☐ D-ATUI | Boeing 737-8K5/W | 37252/3554 | | | ♦ |
| ☐ D-ATUK | Boeing 737-8K5/W | 39094/3641 | ex N1786B | | >CJT♦ |
| ☐ D-ATUL | Boeing 737-8K5/W | 38820/3653 | | | ♦ |
| ☐ D- | Boeing 737-8K5/W | | | | o/o |

## WDL AVIATION — WDL (WE/WDL) — Cologne (CGN)

| | | | | | |
|---|---|---|---|---|---|
| ☐ D-ALIN | British Aerospace 146 Srs.300 | E3142 | ex EI-DEW | | [CGN] |
| ☐ D-AMAJ | British Aerospace 146 Srs.200 | E2028 | ex G-BZBA | | |
| ☐ D-AMAX | British Aerospace 146 Srs.300 | E3157 | ex EI-DEX | | [CGN] |
| ☐ D-AMGL | British Aerospace 146 Srs.200 | E2055 | ex G-CBFL | all-white | |
| ☐ D-AWBA | British Aerospace 146 Srs.300A | E3134 | ex ZK-NZF | | |
| ☐ D-AWDL | British Aerospace 146 Srs.100 | E1011 | ex G-UKJF | | [CGN]♦ |
| ☐ D-AWUE | British Aerospace 146 Srs.200 | E2050 | ex PK-PJP | | |
| ☐ D-ADEP | Fokker F.27 Friendship 600 | 10318 | ex OY-CCK | | |
| ☐ D-AELJ | Fokker F.27 Friendship 600 | 10342 | ex F-BYAB | Flying Dutchman | [CGN] |
| ☐ D-AELK | Fokker F.27 Friendship 600 | 10361 | ex F-GCJV | Petra | |

## XL AIRWAYS GERMANY — (GV/GXL) — Frankfurt (FRA)

| | | | | | |
|---|---|---|---|---|---|
| ☐ D-ABBI | Boeing 737-86J/W | 32920/1293 | | | >LGL♦ |
| ☐ D-AXLD | Boeing 737-8FH/W | 35093/2176 | ex C-FYLD | | >CJT |
| ☐ D-AXLE | Boeing 737-8Q8/W | 30724/2286 | ex C-GDGT | | >CJT |
| ☐ D-AXLF | Boeing 737-8Q8/W | 28218/160 | ex C-GDGY | >CJT | |
| ☐ D-AXLG | Boeing 737-8Q8 | 28226/77 | ex G-XLAA | | |

## DQ- FIJI (Republic of Fiji)

### AIR FIJI — Fijiair (PC/FAJ) — Suva-Nausori (SUV)

| | | | | | |
|---|---|---|---|---|---|
| ☐ DQ-FHC | Harbin Y-12 II | 0056 | | | [SUV] |
| ☐ DQ-FHF | Harbin Y-12 II | 0047 | ex B-531L | | [SUV] |
| ☐ DQ-FET | Britten-Norman BN-2A-21 Islander | 661 | ex ZK-NNE | | [SUV] |
| ☐ DQ-FIC | Britten-Norman BN-2A-21 Islander | 511 | ex ZK-KHB | Island Shuttle titles | |

Ceased ops 04May09

### AIR KAIBU

| | | | | |
|---|---|---|---|---|
| ☐ DQ-KVV | de Havilland DHC-6 Twin Otter 300 | 838 | ex C-GIAZ | ♦ |

### AIR PACIFIC — Pacific (FJ/FJI) — Nadi (NAN)

| | | | | | |
|---|---|---|---|---|---|
| ☐ DQ-FJF | Boeing 737-7X2/W | 28878/96 | ex N1786B | Island of Koro | |
| ☐ DQ-FJG | Boeing 737-8X2/W | 29968/275 | ex N1786B | Island of Kadavu | |
| ☐ DQ-FJH | Boeing 737-8X2/W | 29969/339 | ex N1786B | Island of Gau | |
| ☐ DQ-FJK | Boeing 747-412 | 24064/755 | ex 9V-SMD | Island of Vanua Levu | <SIA |
| ☐ DQ-FJL | Boeing 747-412 | 24062/722 | ex 9V-SMB | Island of Viti Levu | <SIA |
| ☐ DQ-FJM | Boeing 737-86J/W | 37754/3306 | ex D-ABKL | Mamamuca Islands | ♦ |

### AIR WAKAYA — Suva-Nausori (SUV)

| | | | | |
|---|---|---|---|---|
| ☐ DQ-DHG | Cessna 208B Caravan I | 208B1120 | ex N1274X | |
| ☐ DQ-FHG | Britten-Norman BN-2B-26 Islander | 2230 | ex G-BSAC | |

## ISLAND HOPPERS — Nadi (NAN)

| | | | | | |
|---|---|---|---|---|---|
| ☐ DQ-KBD | Pacific Aerospace 750XL | 169 | ex ZK-KBD | | ♦ |
| ☐ DQ-KBP | Pacific Aerospace 750XL | 178 | ex ZK-KBP | | ♦ |

## NORTHERN AIR CHARTER SERVICES — Suva-Nausori (SUV)

| | | | | | |
|---|---|---|---|---|---|
| ☐ DQ-JJS | Britten-Norman BN-2A-26 Islander | 856 | ex VH-IFA | | |
| ☐ DQ-SSS | Britten-Norman BN-2A-21 Islander | 811 | ex DQ-FIC | | ♦ |

## PACIFIC ISLAND AIR — Nadi (NAN)

| | | | | | |
|---|---|---|---|---|---|
| ☐ DQ-GEE | de Havilland DHC-2 Beaver | 1358 | ex C-GSKY | | FP |
| ☐ DQ-SLM | Britten-Norman BN-2A-26 Islander | 605 | ex VH-XFI | | |
| ☐ DQ-YIR | Britten-Norman BN-2A-26 Islander | 845 | ex VH-FCO | | |
| ☐ DQ- | Rockwell Aero Commander 5008 | 1116-66 | ex N620DR | | ♦ |

## PACIFIC SUN — Sunflower (PI/SUF) — Nadi (NAN)

| | | | | | |
|---|---|---|---|---|---|
| ☐ DQ-FEY | de Havilland DHC-6 Twin Otter 100 | 87 | ex N64NB | Spirit of the North | |
| ☐ DQ-FEZ | de Havilland DHC-6 Twin Otter 100 | 09 | ex F-OCFJ | Spirit of the West | |
| ☐ DQ-FIE | de Havilland DHC-6 Twin Otter 300 | 660 | ex N933CL | Spirit of Nadi | |
| ☐ DQ-PSD | de Havilland DHC-6 Twin Otter 310 | 414 | ex N38535 | | |
| ☐ DQ- | de Havilland DHC-6 Twin Otter 300 | 410 | ex N974SW | | ♦ |
| | | | | | |
| ☐ DQ-FCX | Britten-Norman BN-2A-27 Islander | 833 | ex G-BEMJ | Adi Yasawa | |
| ☐ DQ-FDV | Britten-Norman BN-2A-26 Islander | 41 | ex 9M-MDA | Bui Nigone | [NAN] |
| ☐ DQ-FDW | Britten-Norman BN-2A-26 Islander | 602 | ex 9M-MDC | Adi Makutu | |
| ☐ DQ-FIN | Britten-Norman BN-2A-26 Islander | 159 | ex VH-ISA | | |
| ☐ DQ-PSA | ATR 42-500 | 554 | ex 3B-NBB | | |
| ☐ DQ-PSB | ATR 42-500 | 534 | ex 3B-NBA | | |
| ☐ DQ-PSC | Britten-Norman BN-2B-21 Islander | 2177 | ex YJ007 | | ♦ |

## TURTLE AIRWAYS — Turtle (TLT) — Nadi-Newtown Beach

| | | | | | |
|---|---|---|---|---|---|
| ☐ DQ-FEX | Cessna U206G Stationair 6 II | U20605706 | ex ZK-FHE | | FP |
| ☐ DQ-TAL | de Havilland DHC-2 Beaver | 1255 | ex C-GLED | | FP |
| ☐ DQ-TAM | de Havilland DHC-2 Beaver | 1433 | ex VH-IME | | FP |
| ☐ DQ-TAN | Cessna U206G Stationair 6 II | U20605574 | ex VH-HBX | | FP |

# D2-    ANGOLA (Republic of Angola)

## AIR 26 — Air 26 (DCD) — Luanda (LAD)

| | | | | | |
|---|---|---|---|---|---|
| ☐ D2-EYN | Embraer EMB.120ER Brasilia | 120165 | ex N264AS | Nova Erce | |
| ☐ D2-EYO | Embraer EMB.120RT Brasilia | 120210 | ex N269AS | | |
| ☐ D2-EYP | Embraer EMB.120RT Brasilia | 120146 | ex N262AS | | |
| ☐ D2-EYV | Embraer EMB.120ER Brasilia | 120145 | ex N284UE | | [HLA] |
| ☐ D2-EYQ | Embraer EMB.120ER Brasilia | 120062 | ex F-GFEO | | |
| ☐ D2-EZC | Embraer EMB.120ER Brasilia | 120199 | ex N652CT | | |
| ☐ D2-EZZ | Embraer EMB.120FC Brasilia | 120102 | ex N126AM | | Frtr |
| | | | | | |
| ☐ D2-EBC | Embraer EMB-145LR | 145003 | ex N850HK | | <SEAA♦ |

## AIR GEMINI — Twins (GLL) — Luanda (LAD)

| | | | | | |
|---|---|---|---|---|---|
| ☐ D2-ERJ | Douglas DC-9-32 (ABS 3) | 47765/900 | ex N924LG | | wfs |
| ☐ D2-ERL | Douglas DC-9-32 (ABS 3) | 47788/901 | ex N925LG | | [JNB] |
| ☐ D2-ERN | Boeing 727-25C (FedEx 3) | 19358/367 | ex S9-BAU | | wfs |
| ☐ D2-ERS | Douglas DC-9-32 | 47110/167 | ex N923LG | | wfs |
| ☐ S9-BAR | Boeing 727-22C | 19098/318 | ex N832RV | | [LAD] |
| ☐ S9-BOE | Boeing 727-22C (FedEx 3) | 19192/388 | ex N706DH | | [PTG] |
| Ceased ops Dec09 | | | | | |

## AIRJET ANGOLA — Mabeco (MBC) — Luanda (LAD)

| | | | | | |
|---|---|---|---|---|---|
| ☐ D2-EDE | Embraer EMB.120RT Brasilia | 120037 | ex N187SW | | ♦ |
| ☐ D2-EDF | Embraer EMB.120ER Brasilia | 120039 | ex N188SW | | |
| ☐ D2-FDK | Embraer EMB.120ER Brasilia | 120281 | ex N215SW | | |
| ☐ D2-FDO | Embraer EMB.120RT Brasilia | 120082 | ex N102SK | | ♦ |
| ☐ D2-FDT | Embraer EMB.120RT Brasilia | 120081 | ex N103SK | | ♦ |
| ☐ D2-FET | Embraer EMB.120ER Brasilia | 120175 | ex OM-SKY | | [MST] |
| | | | | | |
| ☐ D2-FER | Yakovlev Yak-40 | 9541844 | ex RA-87994 | | |

## ALADA — Air Alada (RAD) — Luanda (LAD)

| | | | | |
|---|---|---|---|---|
| ☐ D2-FAM | Ilyushin Il-18V | 184007401 | | ♦ |
| ☐ D2-FAP | Antonov An-32B | 2903 | | ♦ |
| ☐ D2-FAX | Antonov An-32A | 1510 | ex RA-48115  Kimoka | |
| ☐ D2-FFR | Ilyushin Il-18D | 0393607150 | ex UR-75896 | converted Il-22 |
| ☐ D2-FRB | Antonov An-32 | 2208 | ex Hungary 208 | |

## ANGOLA AIR CHARTER — Angola Charter (AGO) — Luanda (LAD)

| | | | |
|---|---|---|---|
| ☐ D2-FCO | Ilyushin Il-76MD | 0043454615 | ex ER-IBE |
| ☐ D2-MBV | Antonov An-12BP | 5343208 | ex ER-AXH |

Ceased ops

## ANGOLA AIR SERVICES — Luanda (LAD)

| | | | | |
|---|---|---|---|---|
| ☐ ZS-NYK | British Aerospace Jetstream 4121 | 41095 | G-4-095 | |
| ☐ ZS-PCA | Beech 1900C-1 | UC-138 | ex N138GA | |
| ☐ D2-ERU | Boeing 727-2S7 | 22020/1592 | ex N681CA | ♦ |
| ☐ D2-FHE | British Aerospace Jetstream 4101 | 41046 | ex N146KM | |
| ☐ D2-FHF | British Aerospace Jetstream 4101 | 41049 | ex N149KM | |

## DIEXIM EXPRESS — Luanda (LAD)

| | | | | |
|---|---|---|---|---|
| ☐ D2-EDE | Embraer EMB.120ER Brasilia | 120037 | ex N187SW | ♦ |
| ☐ D2-FFE | Embraer EMB.120ER Brasilia | 120242 | ex N8078V | |
| ☐ D2-FFP | Embraer EMB.120RT Brasilia | 120235 | ex F-GJTF | |
| ☐ D2-FFU | Embraer EMB.120ER Brasilia | 120244 | ex F-GTBH | |
| ☐ D2-FFY | Embraer EMB.120RT Brasilia | 120171 | ex N221CR | |
| ☐ D2-FFO | Beech B300 Super King Air | FL-10 | ex N350FH | |
| ☐ D2-FFW | Embraer ERJ-145MP | 145360 | ex F-OIJE    Il Aladia | |

## FLY540 ANGOLA

| | | | | |
|---|---|---|---|---|
| ☐ D2-FLA | ATR-72-320 | 0240 | ex 5Y-BUT | [MPL]♦ |
| ☐ D2-FLB | ATR 72-202 | 0470 | ex M-ABEF | ♦ |
| ☐ D2-FLC | ATR 72-202 | 0483 | ex M-ABEG | ♦ |
| ☐ D2-FLY | ATR 72-212A | 0826 | ex F-WWEU | ♦ |

## GIRA GLOBO — Gira Globo (GGL) — Luanda (LAD)

| | | | | |
|---|---|---|---|---|
| ☐ D2-FCN | Ilyushin Il-76TD | 0053462872 | ex UR-76651 | Op for Angolan AF as T-900 |
| ☐ D2-FDG | Antonov An-32B | 2201 | ex RA-48116  Mulanda | |
| ☐ D2-FEM | Ilyushin Il-76TD | 0063469062 | ex UR-76688  Rei-Ekuikui | Op for Angolan AF as T-905 |
| ☐ D2-FEW | Ilyushin Il-76TD | 0073475239 | ex UR-76721 | Op for Angolan AF as T-904 |

## HM AIRWAYS (HELI-MALONGO) — Luanda (LAD)

| | | | |
|---|---|---|---|
| ☐ D2-EYA | Bell 427 | 56037 | ex N51804 |
| ☐ D2-EYB | Bell 427 | 56046 | ex N427MM |
| ☐ D2-EYC | Bell 427 | 56048 | ex N804RM |
| ☐ D2-EYD | Bell 427 | 56049 | ex N88PQ |
| ☐ D2-EYE | Bell 427 | 56050 | ex N918RB |
| ☐ D2-EYF | Bell 427 | 56051 | ex N96EA |
| ☐ D2-EYG | Bell 427 | 56052 | ex N97EA |
| ☐ D2-EYH | Bell 427 | 56053 | ex N97TZ |
| ☐ D2-EUO | de Havilland DHC-8-402NG | 4312 | ex C-GDCQ |
| ☐ D2-EUP | de Havilland DHC-8-402NG | 4315 | ex C-GDFF |
| ☐ D2-EUQ | de Havilland DHC-8-402NG | 4322 | ex C-GEVB |
| ☐ D2-EUR | de Havilland DHC-8-402NG | 4325 | ex C-GEZN |
| ☐ D2-EYI | Bell 430 | 49102 | ex N41786 |
| ☐ D2-EYJ | Bell 430 | 49108 | ex N767MM |
| ☐ D2-EYK | Bell 430 | 49109 | ex N825GB |
| ☐ D2-EYU | de Havilland DHC-8-315 | 645 | ex C-FLKI |

## SAL - SOCIEDADE DE AVIACAO LIGEIRA — Luanda (LAD)

| | | | | |
|---|---|---|---|---|
| ☐ D2-ECN | Cessna F406 Caravan II | F406-0002 | ex PH-MNS | |
| ☐ D2-ECO | Cessna F406 Caravan II | F406-0011 | ex D-IDAA | |
| ☐ D2-ECP | Cessna F406 Caravan II | F406-0016 | ex PH-LAS | |
| ☐ D2-ECQ | Cessna F406 Caravan II | F406-0019 | ex G-CVAN | |
| ☐ D2-ECW | Beech B300 Super King Air | FL-102 | ex S9-TAP | |
| ☐ D2-ECX | Beech B200 Super King Air | BB-1362 | ex N1565F | |
| ☐ D2-ECY | Beech B200C Super King Air | BL-135 | ex S9-NAP | |
| ☐ D2-EDA | Cessna 208B Caravan I | 208B0568 | ex N1215K | |
| ☐ D2-EDB | Cessna 208B Caravan I | 208B0665 | ex N1256G | |
| ☐ D2-EOD | Short SC.7 Skyvan 3 | SH1938 | ex CR-LOD | [LAD] |

## SEAA — Luanda (LAD)

| | | | | | |
|---|---|---|---|---|---|
| ☐ D2-EBC | Embraer ERJ-145LR | 145003 | ex N850HK | | >DCD♦ |
| ☐ D2-SRA | Embraer ERJ-145EP | 145155 | ex EI-DKH | | ♦ |

## SERVIS AIR — Luanda (LAD)

| | | | | | |
|---|---|---|---|---|---|
| ☐ D2-ACY | McDonnell-Douglas MD-82 | 53059/1942 | ex I-DACY | | [LAD]♦ |
| ☐ D2-ATU | McDonnell-Douglas MD-82 | 53220/2073 | ex I-DATU | | [LAD] |
| ☐ D2-EVD | Boeing 727-29C | 19403/435 | ex CB-02 | | wfs♦ |
| ☐ D2-MFI | McDonnell-Douglas MD-82 | 53059/1942 | ex I-DACY | | [LAD]♦ |

## SONAIR — Sonair (SOR) — Luanda (LAD)

| | | | | | |
|---|---|---|---|---|---|
| ☐ D2-EQD | Aérospatiale SA365N2 Dauphin 2 | 6521 | ex F-GJIA | | |
| ☐ D2-EQE | Aérospatiale SA365N2 Dauphin 2 | 6531 | ex F-WQSR | | |
| ☐ D2-EUO | Aérospatiale SA365N Dauphin 2 | 9000 | | | |
| ☐ D2-EVE | Aérospatiale SA365N2 Dauphin 2 | 6418 | ex F-WQSR | | |
| ☐ D2-EVF | Aérospatiale SA365N2 Dauphin 2 | 6410 | ex F-GHRX | | |
| ☐ D2-EXX | Aérospatiale SA365N2 Dauphin 2 | 6439 | ex F-WQSR | | |
| | | | | | |
| ☐ D2-EFN | Beech 1900D | UE-329 | ex N23183 | | ♦ |
| ☐ D2-ERQ | Beech 1900D | UE-274 | ex N11015 | | |
| ☐ D2-EVJ | Beech 1900D | UE-111 | ex N3119U | | |
| ☐ D2-EVK | Beech 1900D | UE-121 | ex N3221A | | |
| ☐ D2-EVN | Beech 1900D | UE-370 | ex N30539 | | |
| ☐ D2-EVR | Beech 1900D | UE-280 | ex N11284 | | |
| ☐ D2-EVX | Beech 1900D | UE-340 | ex(F-GSVC) | | |
| ☐ D2-EVY | Beech 1900D | UE-249 | ex N249GL | | |
| ☐ D2-EWR | Beech 1900D | UE-193 | ex N69548 | | ♦ |
| ☐ D2-EWW | Beech 1900D | UE-399 | ex N854CA | | |
| ☐ D2-EWX | Beech 1900D | UE-405 | ex N856CA | | |
| ☐ D2-EWY | Beech 1900D | UE-401 | ex N840CA | | |
| ☐ D2-FFJ | Beech 1900D | UE-412 | ex N44828 | | |
| | | | | | |
| ☐ D2-EVA | de Havilland DHC-6 Twin Otter 310 | 728 | ex V2-LDD | | |
| ☐ D2-EVB | de Havilland DHC-6 Twin Otter 310 | 810 | ex V2-LDH | | |
| ☐ D2-EVC | de Havilland DHC-6 Twin Otter 310 | 809 | ex V2-LDG | | |
| ☐ D2-EVH | de Havilland DHC-6 Twin Otter 300 | 511 | ex HB-LOM | | |
| ☐ D2-FVM | de Havilland DHC-6 Twin Otter 310 | 794 | ex HB-LRF | | |
| ☐ D2-FVN | de Havilland DHC-6 Twin Otter 310 | 817 | ex N817L | | |
| ☐ D2-FVO | de Havilland DHC-6 Twin Otter 310 | 821 | ex N821L | | |
| ☐ D2-FVP | de Havilland DHC-6 Twin Otter 310 | 743 | ex 5Y-TMF | | |
| ☐ D2-FVQ | de Havilland DHC-6 Twin Otter 310 | 704 | ex 5N-ASP | | |
| | | | | | |
| ☐ D2-EVS | Sikorsky S-76C | 760603 | ex C-GHRI | | <CHC Helicopters Intl |
| ☐ D2-EXG | Sikorsky S-76A | 760042 | ex ZS-RKE | | <Heli-Union |
| ☐ D2-EXH | Sikorsky S-76A | 760268 | ex ZS-RBE | | <CHC Helicopter (Africa) |
| ☐ D2-EXK | Sikorsky S-76C | 760525 | ex N9017U | | |
| ☐ D2-EXL | Sikorsky S-76C | 760526 | ex N9007U | | |
| ☐ D2-EXP | Sikorsky S-76C | 760544 | ex N2048K | | |
| | | | | | |
| ☐ D2-EQH | Eurocopter EC.225LP | 2743 | | | |
| ☐ D2-EQI | Eurocopter EC.225LP | 2746 | | | |
| ☐ D2-EQL | Eurocopter EC.225LP | ex F-WWOX | | | ♦ |
| ☐ D2-ESN | Fokker F.27 Friendship 500 | 10610 | ex PH-FTY | Kwanda | |
| ☐ D2-ESU | Boeing 727-23F | 19431/372 | ex N516FE | | |
| ☐ D2-ESW | Fokker 50 | 20241 | ex PH-RRM | | <Golfo Intl |
| ☐ D2-ESZ | Aérospatiale AS.332L2 II | 2503 | ex F-WQPA | | |
| ☐ D2-EVG | Boeing 727-29C | 19402/415 | ex N70PA | | |
| ☐ D2-EVP | Aérospatiale AS.332L2 II | 2398 | ex F-WQEA | | <CHC Helicopter (Africa) |
| ☐ D2-EVT | Eurocopter EC.225LP | ex F-WQDI | | | |
| ☐ D2-EVW | Boeing 737-7HB | 35954/2310 | | | |
| ☐ D2-EWK | Beech B300 Super King Air | FL-294 | ex S9-CAN | | <Golfo Intl |
| ☐ D2-EWL | Beech B300 Super King Air | FL-163 | ex S9-CAM | | <Golfo Intl |
| ☐ D2-EWS | Boeing 737-7HBC/W | 35956/2536 | | | |
| ☐ D2-EXN | Aérospatiale AS.332L2 II | 2590 | | | |
| ☐ D2-FSA | Boeing 727-29C | 19987/634 | ex HZ-HE4 | | Frtr |
| ☐ N263SG | Boeing 747-481 | 29263/1204 | ex B-LFC | | >GTI |
| ☐ N322SG | Boeing 747-481 | 30322/1250 | ex B-LFD | | >GTI |

## TAAG ANGOLA AIRLINES — DTA (DT/DTA) — Luanda (LAD)

| | | | | | |
|---|---|---|---|---|---|
| ☐ D2-TBF | Boeing 737-7M2/W | 34559/2013 | ex N6067U | | |
| ☐ D2-TBG | Boeing 737-7M2/W | 34560/2036 | | | |
| ☐ D2-TBH | Boeing 737-7M2/W | 34561/2043 | | | |
| ☐ D2-TBJ | Boeing 737-7M2/W | 34562/2149 | | | |
| ☐ D2-TBK | Boeing 737-7HBC/W | 35955/2531 | ex D2-EVZ | | ♦ |
| | | | | | |
| ☐ D2-TED | Boeing 777-2M2ER | 34565/581 | | | |
| ☐ D2-TEE | Boeing 777-2M2ER | 34566/587 | | Kuitu Kuanavale | |

| | | | | |
|---|---|---|---|---|
| ☐ D2-TEF | Boeing 777-2M2ER | 34567/687 | | |
| ☐ D2-TEG | Boeing 777-3M2ER | 40805/935 | | ◆ |
| ☐ D2-TEH | Boeing 777-3M2ER | 40806/944 | | ◆ |
| | | | | |
| ☐ D2-TBC | Boeing 737-2M2C | 21173/447 | ex D2-TAB | |
| ☐ D2-TBO | Boeing 737-2M2 | 22776/891 | ex N1782B | |
| ☐ D2-TBX | Boeing 737-2M2 | 23351/1117 | | |

### TROPICANA                                                                        Luanda (LAD)

| | | | | |
|---|---|---|---|---|
| ☐ D2-EBF | Beech B200 Super King Air | BB-836 | ex S9-NAQ | |
| ☐ D2-FFL | Beech 200 Super King Air | BB-126 | ex N777XZ | Capembe |
| ☐ D2-FFM | Beech 1900D | UE-108 | ex N118SK | Mavinga |

## D4-    CAPE VERDE ISLANDS (Republic of Cape Verde)

### CABO VERDE EXPRESS                                (CVE)                           Sal (SID)

| | | | | |
|---|---|---|---|---|
| ☐ D4-CBL | LET L-410UVP-E10 | 902511 | ex 9Q-CUM | |
| ☐ D4-CBR | LET L-410UVP-E20 | 912533 | ex D-CLED | |
| ☐ D4-JCA | LET L-410UVP-E20 | 912604 | ex OY-PEY | |

### HALCYON AIR                                       (HCV)                          Praia (RAI)

| | | | | |
|---|---|---|---|---|
| ☐ D4-CBQ | ATR 42-320 | 0296 | ex J5-GZZ | Santa Maria |

### TACV - TRANSPORTES AEREOS DE CABO VERDE / CAPE VERDE AIRLINES
                                    Cabo Verde (VR/TCV)                             Praia (RAI)

| | | | | |
|---|---|---|---|---|
| ☐ D4-CBG | Boeing 757-2Q8 | 27599/696 | | B Leza |
| ☐ D4-CBP | Boeing 757-2Q8 | 30045/957 | ex N301AM | Emigranti |
| ☐ D4-CBT | ATR 72-212A | 0747 | ex F-WWEH | Jorge Barbosa |
| ☐ D4-CBU | ATR 72-212A | 0755 | ex F-WWEP | Baltizar Lopes |
| ☐ D4-CBV | ATR 42-512 | 0669 | ex F-WWLC | |

## D6-    COMOROS (Federal Islamic Republic of the Comores)

### COMORES AIR SERVICE                                                              Moroni (YVA)

| | | | | |
|---|---|---|---|---|
| ☐ D6-CAM | LET L-410UVP | 851336 | ex D6-GDH | |
| ☐ D6-CAN | LET L-410UVP | 841331 | ex 9L-LCZ | |

### COMORES AVIATION                       Comores (KR/KMZ)                          Moroni (YVA)

| | | | | |
|---|---|---|---|---|
| ☐ ZS-AAY | British Aerospace 146 Srs.200 | E2044 | ex TN-AIC | |
| ☐ D6-CAL | LET L-410UVP | 800526 | ex HA-LAB | |

### COMOROS ISLANDS AIRWAYS                        (CIN)                             Moroni (YVA)

| | | | | |
|---|---|---|---|---|
| ☐ D6-CAS | Airbus A320-214 | 3040 | ex EC-KAX | |

### HERITAGE AVIATION                                                               Moroni (YVA)

| | | | |
|---|---|---|---|
| ☐ D6-CAQ | LET L-410UVP | | |

Status uncertain

## EC-    SPAIN (Kingdom of Spain)

### AERONOVA                               Aeronova (OVA)                            Valencia (VLC)

| | | | | |
|---|---|---|---|---|
| ☐ EC-GUS | Swearingen SA.227AC Metro III | AC-648 | ex N2685L | ◆ |
| ☐ EC-GVE | Swearingen SA.227AC Metro III | AC-669B | ex N2702Z | |
| ☐ EC-HCH | Swearingen SA.227AC Metro III | AC-658B | ex N2692P | |
| ☐ EC-HZH | Swearingen SA.227AC Metro III | AC-720 | ex N2724S | |
| ☐ EC-IXL | Swearingen SA.227AC Metro III | AC-689B | ex D-COLC | |
| ☐ EC-JCU | Swearingen SA.227AC Metro III | AC-679B | ex N6UB | |

### AIR EUROPA                             Europa (UX/AEA)                    Palma de Mallorca (PMI)

Associate member of Skyteam

| | | | | |
|---|---|---|---|---|
| ☐ EC-JPF | Airbus A330-202 | 733 | ex F-WWKU | |
| ☐ EC-JQG | Airbus A330-202 | 745 | ex F-WWYG | Estepona-Costa del Sol |
| ☐ EC-JQQ | Airbus A330-202 | 749 | ex F-WWYJ | |
| ☐ EC-JZL | Airbus A330-202 | 814 | ex F-WWYJ | David Bisbal |

| | | | | | | |
|---|---|---|---|---|---|---|
| ☐ EC-KOM | Airbus A330-202 | 931 | ex F-WWKU | | | |
| ☐ EC-KTG | Airbus A330-202 | 950 | ex F-WWKQ | | | |
| ☐ EC-LKE | Airbus A330-243 | 461 | ex CS-TRA | | | |
| ☐ EC-LMN | Airbus A330-243 | 597 | ex EI-EOL | | | ♦ |
| ☐ EC-LNH | Airbus A330-243 | 551 | ex EI-EON | | | ♦ |
| ☐ EC-LQP | Airbus A330-243 | 526 | ex 5B-DBT | | | ♦ |
| | | | | | | |
| ☐ EC-HJP | Boeing 737-85P | 28535/480 | ex N1800B | | | |
| ☐ EC-HJQ | Boeing 737-85P | 28387/522 | ex N1786B | | | |
| ☐ EC-HKQ | Boeing 737-85P/W | 28388/533 | | San Pedro Alcantara | [BUD] | |
| ☐ EC-HKR | Boeing 737-85P/W | 28536/540 | ex N1787B | | | |
| ☐ EC-HZS | Boeing 737-86Q/W | 30276/920 | ex N747BX | | | |
| ☐ EC-IDA | Boeing 737-86Q/W | 32773/1051 | ex N73792 | | | |
| ☐ EC-IDT | Boeing 737-86Q/W | 30281/1076 | ex N73793 | | | |
| ☐ EC-III | Boeing 737-86Q/W | 30284/1233 | | | | |
| ☐ EC-ISE | Boeing 737-86Q/W | 30290/1406 | ex N1786B | | | |
| ☐ EC-ISN | Boeing 737-86Q/W | 30291/1435 | | | | |
| ☐ EC-JAP | Boeing 737-85P/W | 33971/1580 | | | | |
| ☐ EC-JBJ | Boeing 737-85P/W | 33972/1598 | | Salamanca | | |
| ☐ EC-JBK | Boeing 737-85P/W | 33973/1606 | | | | |
| ☐ EC-JBL | Boeing 737-85P/W | 33974/1610 | | | | |
| ☐ EC-JHK | Boeing 737-85P/W | 33975/1716 | ex N1787B | | | |
| ☐ EC-JHL | Boeing 737-85P/W | 33976/1740 | | | | |
| ☐ EC-JNF | Boeing 737-85P/W | 33977/1878 | | Mutua Madrileqa | | |
| ☐ EC-KCG | Boeing 737-85P/W | 33981/2269 | | | | |
| ☐ EC-LPQ | Boeing 737-85P/W | 35496/ | | | o/o♦ | |
| ☐ EC-LPR | Boeing 737-85P/W | 36588/ | | | o/o♦ | |
| | | | | | | |
| ☐ EC-KRJ | Embraer ERJ-195LR | 19000196 | ex PT-SGE | | | |
| ☐ EC-KXD | Embraer ERJ-195LR | 19000244 | ex PT-SIP | | | |
| ☐ EC-KYO | Embraer ERJ-195LR | 19000276 | ex PT-TLQ | | | |
| ☐ EC-KYP | Embraer ERJ-195LR | 19000281 | ex PT-TLV | | | |
| ☐ EC-LCQ | Embraer ERJ-195LR | 19000303 | ex PT-TZR | | | |
| ☐ EC-LEK | Embraer ERJ-195LR | 19000344 | ex PT-XQG | | | |
| ☐ EC-LFZ | Embraer ERJ-195LR | 19000357 | ex PT-XQV | | | |
| ☐ EC-LIN | Embraer ERJ-195LR | 19000401 | ex PT-XUG | | | |
| ☐ EC-LKM | Embraer ERJ-195LR | 19000425 | ex PT-TBV | | | ♦ |
| ☐ EC-LKX | Embraer ERJ-195LR | 19000437 | | | | ♦ |
| ☐ EC-LLR | Embraer ERJ-195LR | 19000452 | ex PT-YCW | | | ♦ |
| | | | | | | |
| ☐ EC-HSV | Boeing 767-3Q8ER | 29387/840 | | | >SDM | |

## AIR NOSTRUM        Nostrum Air (YW/ANE)        Valencia (VLC)

| | | | | | | |
|---|---|---|---|---|---|---|
| ☐ EC-HBY | ATR 72-212A | 0578 | ex F-WWEA | Abeto | | |
| ☐ EC-HCG | ATR 72-212A | 0580 | ex F-WWEC | Castano | dam 21Jan12 | |
| ☐ EC-HEI | ATR 72-212A | 0570 | ex F-WWEG | Eucalipto | | |
| ☐ EC-HEJ | ATR 72-212A | 0565 | ex F-WWEE | Carrasca | | |
| ☐ EC-HJI | ATR 72-212A | 0562 | ex F-WWLZ | Sauce | | |
| ☐ EC- | ATR 72-600 | 995 | ex F-WWLT | | o/o♦ | |
| ☐ EC- | ATR 72-600 | 999 | ex F-WWLX | | o/o♦ | |
| ☐ EC- | ATR 72-600 | 1023 | ex F-WW | | o/o♦ | |
| ☐ EC- | ATR 72-600 | | ex | | o/o | |
| | | | | | | |
| ☐ EC-GYI | Canadair CRJ-200ER | 7249 | ex C-GDDM | Pinazo | | |
| ☐ EC-GZA | Canadair CRJ-200ER | 7252 | ex C-GDDO | Beniliure | | |
| ☐ EC-HEK | Canadair CRJ-200ER | 7320 | ex C-GFCN | Cecilio Pla | | |
| ☐ EC-HHI | Canadair CRJ-200ER | 7343 | ex C-GFKQ | Genaro Lahuerta Lopez | | |
| ☐ EC-HHV | Canadair CRJ-200ER | 7350 | ex C-GFKR | Sorolla | | |
| ☐ EC-HPR | Canadair CRJ-200ER | 7430 | ex C-GHDM | Mompo | | |
| ☐ EC-HSH | Canadair CRJ-200ER | 7466 | ex C-GHWD | J Michavilla | | |
| ☐ EC-HTZ | Canadair CRJ-200ER | 7493 | ex C-GIHJ | Ricardo Verde | | |
| ☐ EC-HXM | Canadair CRJ-200ER | 7514 | ex C-GIQL | Francisco Dominguez | [VLC] | |
| ☐ EC-HYG | Canadair CRJ-200ER | 7529 | ex C-GIXG | E Sales Frances | [VLC] | |
| ☐ EC-IBM | Canadair CRJ-200ER | 7591 | ex C-GJQZ | J Navarro Llorens | | |
| ☐ EC-IDC | Canadair CRJ-200ER | 7622 | ex C-GJYV | Francisco Ribalta | | |
| ☐ EC-IGO | Canadair CRJ-200ER | 7661 | ex C-FVAZ | Juan de Juanes | | |
| ☐ EC-IJE | Canadair CRJ-200ER | 7700 | ex C-GZJZ | Josquin Agrasot | | |
| ☐ EC-IJF | Canadair CRJ-200ER | 7705 | ex C-GZKC | Vicente Magip | | |
| ☐ EC-IJS | Canadair CRJ-200ER | 7706 | ex C-GZKD | Manuel Benedito | | |
| ☐ EC-IKZ | Canadair CRJ-200ER | 7732 | ex C-GZUR | Tomas Yepes | | |
| ☐ EC-ILF | Canadair CRJ-200ER | 7746 | ex C-FZQR | Vincente Lopez | | |
| ☐ EC-INF | Canadair CRJ-200ER | 7785 | ex C-GYVM | Pedro de Valencia | | |
| ☐ EC-IRI | Canadair CRJ-200ER | 7851 | ex C-GZNF | Benjamin Palencia | | |
| ☐ EC-ITU | Canadair CRJ-200ER | 7866 | ex C-GZSQ | Pons Arnau | | |
| ☐ EC-IVH | Canadair CRJ-200ER | 7915 | ex C-FADU | José Mongrell | | |
| ☐ EC-IZP | Canadair CRJ-200ER | 7950 | ex C-FBFI | Enriqe Martinez Cubells | | |
| ☐ EC-JCG | Canadair CRJ-200ER | 7973 | ex C-FCEU | José Vergara | | |
| ☐ EC-JCL | Canadair CRJ-200ER | 7975 | ex C-FCID | | | |
| ☐ EC-JCM | Canadair CRJ-200ER | 7981 | ex C-FCNN | Beato de Liebana | | |
| ☐ EC-JCO | Canadair CRJ-200ER | 7984 | ex C-FCRX | | | |
| ☐ EC-JEE | Canadair CRJ-200ER | 7989 | ex C-FCZD | Juan Ignacio Pombo | | |

| | | | | |
|---|---|---|---|---|
| ☐ EC-JEF | Canadair CRJ-200ER | 8008 | ex C-FDKH | José Monleon |
| ☐ EC-JEN | Canadair CRJ-200ER | 7958 | ex C-FBQO | |
| ☐ EC-JNX | Canadair CRJ-200ER | 8058 | ex C-FGEP | Catedral de Leon |
| ☐ EC-JOD | Canadair CRJ-200ER | 8061 | ex C-FGYE | |
| ☐ EC-JOY | Canadair CRJ-200ER | 8064 | ex C-FHCW | Catedral de Leon |
| | | | | |
| ☐ EC-JNB | Canadair CRJ-900ER | 15057 | | |
| ☐ EC-JTS | Canadair CRJ-900ER | 15071 | ex C-FJTF | |
| ☐ EC-JTT | Canadair CRJ-900ER | 15074 | ex C-FJTJ | |
| ☐ EC-JTU | Canadair CRJ-900ER | 15079 | ex C-FJTE | |
| ☐ EC-JXZ | Canadair CRJ-900ER | 15087 | ex C-FLGI | |
| ☐ EC-JYA | Canadair CRJ-900ER | 15090 | ex C-FLIX | |
| ☐ EC-JYV | Canadair CRJ-900ER | 15106 | ex C-FLMJ | |
| ☐ EC-JZS | Canadair CRJ-900ER | 15111 | ex C-FLMK | |
| ☐ EC-JZT | Canadair CRJ-900ER | 15113 | ex C-FLMN | |
| ☐ EC-JZU | Canadair CRJ-900ER | 15115 | ex C-FLMQ | |
| ☐ EC-JZV | Canadair CRJ-900ER | 15117 | ex C-FLMS | |

| | | | | |
|---|---|---|---|---|
| ☐ EC-LJR | Canadair CRJ-1000ER | 19002 | ex C-GCBN | |
| ☐ EC-LJS | Canadair CRJ-1000ER | 19003 | ex C-GIZJ | |
| ☐ EC-LJT | Canadair CRJ-1000ER | 19005 | ex C-GIBJ | |
| ☐ EC-LJX | Canadair CRJ-1000ER | 19008 | ex C- | ♦ |
| ☐ EC-LKF | Canadair CRJ-1000ER | 19011 | ex C-GHZZ | ♦ |
| ☐ EC-LOJ | Canadair CRJ-1000ER | 19018 | ex C-GIAD | ♦ |
| ☐ EC-LOV | Canadair CRJ-1000ER | 19019 | ex C-GIBT | ♦ |
| ☐ EC-LOX | Canadair CRJ-1000ER | 19020 | ex C | ♦ |
| ☐ EC-LPG | Canadair CRJ-1000ER | 19021 | ex C-GZQW | ♦ |
| ☐ EC-LPN | Canadair CRJ-1000ER | 19022 | ex C-GICB | ♦ |
| ☐ EC- | Canadair CRJ-1000ER | | ex C- | o/o |

## ALBA STAR (LAV)

| | | | | |
|---|---|---|---|---|
| ☐ EC-LAV | Boeing 737-408 | 24352/1705 | ex EC-KTM | |
| ☐ EC-LKB | Boeing 737-4B7 | 24559/1847 | ex EC-KKJ | ♦ |
| ☐ EC-LNC | Boeing 737-4K5 | 24130/1827 | ex N721VX | ♦ |

## AQUALATA AIR

| | | | |
|---|---|---|---|
| ☐ EC-FIP | Britten-Norman BN-2A-26 Islander | 623 | ♦ |

## BINTER CANARIAS (NT/IBB)

### Las Palmas-Gran Canaria/Tenerife-Sur, Reine Sofia (LPA/TFS)

| | | | | |
|---|---|---|---|---|
| ☐ EC-IYC | ATR 72-212A | 0709 | ex F-WWEI | <Canair♦ |
| ☐ EC-JAH | ATR 72-212A | 0712 | ex F-WWEL | |
| ☐ EC-JBI | ATR 72-212A | 0713 | ex F-WWEM | |
| ☐ EC-JEV | ATR 72-212A | 0717 | ex F-WWER | |
| ☐ EC-JQL | ATR 72-212A | 0726 | ex F-WWEG | Teide |

## BKS AIR — Cosmos (CKM) — Bilbao (BIO)

| | | | |
|---|---|---|---|
| ☐ EC-JGB | Beech B200 Super King Air | BB-1478 | ex D-IHAN |

## CALIMA AVIACION (CMV) — Las Palmas (LPA)

| | | | |
|---|---|---|---|
| ☐ EC-LDN | Boeing 737-448 | 24474/1742 | ex N474EA |
| ☐ EC-LKO | Boeing 737-85F | 28821/151 | ex D-ABBL |

## CANAIR

| | | | | |
|---|---|---|---|---|
| ☐ EC-IYC | ATR 72-212A | 0709 | ex F-WWEI | <IBB♦ |
| ☐ EC-IZO | ATR 72-212A | 0711 | ex F-WWEK | ♦ |
| ☐ EC-JEH | ATR 72-212A | 0716 | ex F-WWEP | Villa Cisneros | ♦ |

## CANARIAS AERONAUTICA

| | | | | |
|---|---|---|---|---|
| ☐ EC-IRS | Swearingen SA.227BC Metro III | BC-786B | ex N61AJ | ♦ |
| ☐ EC-LMX | ATR 42-320 | 0115 | ex EI-SLI | <ABR♦ |

## CEGISA — Salamanca-Matacan (SLM)

| | | | | |
|---|---|---|---|---|
| ☐ EC-GBP | Canadair CL-215 | 1031 | ex EC-957 | Tanker op for DGCN |
| ☐ EC-GBQ | Canadair CL-215 | 1033 | ex EC-958 | Tanker op for DGCN |
| ☐ EC-GBR | Canadair CL-215 | 1051 | ex EC-983 | Tanker op for DGCN |
| ☐ EC-GBS | Canadair CL-215 | 1052 | ex EC-984 | Tanker op for DGCN |
| ☐ EC-GBT | Canadair CL-215 | 1054 | ex EC-985 | Tanker op for DGCN |
| ☐ EC-HET | Canadair CL-215 | 1034 | ex I-SISB | Tanker op for Hisporavia |
| ☐ EC-HEU | Canadair CL-215 | 1038 | ex I-SISC | Tanker op for Hisporavia |

| | | | | | |
|---|---|---|---|---|---|
| ☐ EC-IQC | Air Tractor AT-802A | 802A-0155 | ex N8512Q | | Tanker |
| ☐ EC-IUJ | Air Tractor AT-802A | 802A-0154 | ex C-GYZB | | Tanker |

## EURO CONTINENTAL AIR — Euro Continental (ECN) — Barcelona (BCN)

| | | | | | |
|---|---|---|---|---|---|
| ☐ EC-GPS | Swearingen SA.227AC Metro III | AC-722 | ex N439MA | | Frtr Lsd to/op for EAL |
| ☐ EC-JQC | Swearingen SA.226AC Merlin IVA | AT-066 | ex N5FY | | |

## FLIGHTLINE — Flight-Avia (FTL) — Barcelona (BCN)

| | | | | | |
|---|---|---|---|---|---|
| ☐ EC-GFK | Swearingen SA.226AT Merlin IVA | AT-062 | ex EC-125 | | |
| ☐ EC-GXJ | Swearingen SA.226TC Metro II | TC-374 | ex OY-AUO | | ♦ |
| ☐ EC-HBF | Swearingen SA.226AT Merlin IVA | AT-074 | ex EC-GDR | MRW Courier titles | |
| ☐ EC-HHN | Embraer EMB.120RT Brasilia | 120103 | ex N127AM | all-white | |
| ☐ EC-JIP | Swearingen SA.226TC Metro II | TC-301 | ex N5FY | | [BAR]♦ |

## GESTAIR CARGO — (RGN) — Madrid-Barajas (MAD)

| | | | | | |
|---|---|---|---|---|---|
| ☐ EC-FTR | Boeing 757-256 (PCF) | 26239/553 | ex EC-420 | | |
| ☐ EC-KLD | Boeing 757-256 (PCF) | 24121/183 | ex N28AT | | |
| ☐ EC-LKI | Boeing 767-383ER (BDSF) | 26544/412 | ex N767FF | | |
| ☐ EC-LKV | Boeing 767-383ER (BDSF) | 24729/358 | ex N767NF | | |

## HELICSA HELICOPTEROS — Helicsa (HHH) — Albacete-Helicsa Heliport/Madrid

| | | | | | |
|---|---|---|---|---|---|
| ☐ EC-DXM | Aérospatiale SA365C2 Dauphin 2 | 5007 | ex PH-SSL | | |
| ☐ EC-FOX | Aérospatiale SA365C2 Dauphin 2 | 5024 | ex EC-136 | | EMS |
| ☐ EC-GCZ | Aérospatiale SA365C2 Dauphin 2 | 5037 | ex EC-887 | | EMS |
| ☐ EC-GXY | Aérospatiale SA365N1 Dauphin 2 | 6242 | ex N12AE | | EMS |
| ☐ EC-HCL | Aérospatiale AS365N2 Dauphin 2 | 6416 | ex SE-JAE | | SAR |
| ☐ EC-HIM | Aérospatiale AS365N2 Dauphin 2 | 6478 | ex SE-JCE | | SAR |
| ☐ EC-HRL | Aérospatiale AS365C2 Dauphin 2 | 5055 | ex PH-SSY | | EMS |
| ☐ EC-IEL | Aérospatiale SA365C3 Dauphin 2 | 5017 | ex F-GHXF | | EMS |
| ☐ EC-IGM | Aérospatiale SA365N3 Dauphin 2 | 6616 | ex F-WQDA | | Survey |
| ☐ EC-ILN | Aérospatiale SA365N1 Dauphin 2 | 6234 | ex LV-WLU | | EMS |
| ☐ EC-JDQ | Aérospatiale SA365N3 Dauphin 2 | 6679 | ex EC-IZQ | | Survey |
| ☐ EC-JLV | Aérospatiale SA365N1 Dauphin 2 | 6264 | ex LN-OPM | | EMS |
| ☐ EC-JLX | Aérospatiale SA365N1 Dauphin 2 | 6346 | ex LN-OPL | | EMS |
| ☐ EC-JVG | Aérospatiale AS365N3 Dauphin 2 | 6718 | ex F-WWOQ | | |
| | | | | | |
| ☐ EC-EEQ | Bell 212 | 30612 | ex D-HOBB | | EMS |
| ☐ EC-FBM | Bell 212 | 30574 | ex EC-552 | | SAR |
| ☐ EC-GID | Bell 212 | 31150 | ex OY-HCS | | SAR |
| ☐ EC-GLS | Bell 212 | 31155 | ex OY-HCU | | SAR |
| ☐ EC-GVP | Bell 212 | 30572 | ex LN-OQG | | SAR |
| ☐ EC-GXA | Bell 212 | 30812 | ex LN-OQJ | | SAR |
| ☐ EC-HTJ | Bell 212 | 30648 | ex PK-HMC | | SAR |
| ☐ EC-INN | Bell 212 | 31146 | ex SE-JLP | | |
| | | | | | |
| ☐ EC-IKY | Eurocopter EC135T2 | 0255 | ex D-HECO | | EMS |
| ☐ EC-ITJ | Eurocopter EC135T2 | 0306 | | | EMS |
| ☐ EC-IUN | Eurocopter EC135T2 | 0317 | | | EMS |
| ☐ EC-JDG | Eurocopter EC135T2 | 0354 | | | EMS |
| ☐ EC-JHT | Eurocopter EC135T2 | 0396 | | | EMS |
| ☐ EC-JUE | Eurocopter EC135T2 | 0345 | ex EC-067 | | EMS |
| | | | | | |
| ☐ EC-DVK | MBB Bo.105CB | S-630 | ex D-HDSZ | Argos I | |
| ☐ EC-DVL | MBB Bo.105CB | S-631 | ex D-HDTA | Argos II | |
| ☐ EC-ESX | MBB BK-117B-1 | 7176 | ex D-HBHS | | |
| ☐ EC-FFV | MBB Bo.105CBS | S-852 | ex D-HFHJ | | |
| ☐ EC-FMZ | Sikorsky S-61N | 61361 | ex LN-ORH | | Op for SASEMAR |
| ☐ EC-FTB | Sikorsky S-61N | 61741 | ex LN-OSY | | Op for SASEMAR |
| ☐ EC-FVO | Sikorsky S-61N | 61756 | ex EC-575 | | Op for SASEMAR |
| ☐ EC-FZJ | Sikorsky S-61N | 61758 | ex EC-717 | | Op for SASEMAR |
| ☐ EC-GHY | Aérospatiale AS355F1 Ecureuil 2 | 5089 | ex EC-293 | | EMS |
| ☐ EC-GSK | Bell 412 | 33092 | ex SE-HVL | | |
| ☐ EC-HEE | Aérospatiale AS355N Ecureuil 2 | 5645 | ex F-OHVD | | |
| ☐ EC-HXZ | Bell 412 | 33106 | ex PK-HMT | | EMS |
| ☐ EC-JTO | Aérospatiale AS350B3 Ecureuil | 3091 | ex LN-OPK | | |
| ☐ EC-JTP | Aérospatiale AS350B3 Ecureuil | 3445 | ex SE-JHK | | |
| ☐ EC-JYE | Aérospatiale SA.330J Puma | 1241 | ex D-HAXC | | |
| ☐ EC-KDO | Aérospatiale AS350B3 Ecureuil | 3667 | ex LN-OMA | | |
| ☐ EC-LCH | Agusta AW139 | 31257 | | | |

## HELISURESTE — Helisureste (UV/HSE) — Alicante-San Vincente Heliport

| | | | | | |
|---|---|---|---|---|---|
| ☐ EC-DZT | Agusta A.109A | 7159 | ex HB-XIU | | EMS |
| ☐ EC-FUY | Agusta A.109C | 7670 | ex EC-453 | | Fishery Patrol |
| ☐ EC-GCQ | Agusta A.109C | 7665 | ex EC-895 | | Fishery Patrol |
| ☐ EC-HBQ | Agusta A.109A II | 7399 | ex I-SOCC | | EMS |

| | | | | | | |
|---|---|---|---|---|---|---|
| ☐ EC-HHQ | Agusta A.109E Power | 11058 | | | | EMS |
| ☐ EC-IJR | Agusta A.109E Power | 11137 | | | | EMS |
| ☐ EC-ILA | Agusta A.109E Power | 11028 | ex F-GSMP | | | |
| ☐ EC-IRQ | Agusta A.109E Power | 11205 | | | | |
| ☐ EC-IUS | Agusta A.109E Power | 11229 | | | | |
| ☐ EC-JGC | Agusta A.109E Power | 11622 | | | | |
| ☐ EC-JKP | Agusta A.109E Power | 11637 | | | | >EDO |
| ☐ EC-JUS | Agusta A.109E Power | 11675 | | | | |
| ☐ EC-KJU | Agusta A.109S Grand | 11709 | | | | |
| ☐ I-REMS | Agusta A.109S Grand | 22024 | | | | |
| | | | | | | |
| ☐ EC-JOU | Agusta AW139 | 31034 | ex I-RAII | | | |
| ☐ EC-KHV | Agusta AW139 | 31089 | | | | |
| ☐ EC-KJT | Agusta AW139 | 31104 | ex I-EASK | | | |
| ☐ EC-KLM | Agusta AW139 | 31201 | ex I-EASB | 201 | o/o Op for SASEMAR | |
| ☐ EC-KLN | Agusta AW139 | 31202 | | 202 | Op for SASEMAR | |
| ☐ EC-LBM | Agusta AW139 | 31226 | | | | |
| | | | | | | |
| ☐ EC-FEL | Agusta-Bell 412SP | 25576 | ex EC-607 | | | |
| ☐ EC-GOP | Bell 412HP | 36031 | ex N4603T | | | |
| ☐ EC-GPA | Bell 412HP | 36071 | ex N7238Y | | | |
| ☐ EC-HXX | Bell 412 | 33062 | ex N4014U | | | |
| ☐ EC-HZD | Bell 412 | 33056 | ex N4031F | | | |
| ☐ EC-IPM | Bell 412 | 33050 | ex C-GJKT | | | |
| ☐ EC-JJE | Bell 412EP | 33004 | ex N164EH | | | |
| ☐ EC-JJQ | Bell 412EP | 36376 | ex N46372 | | | |
| ☐ EC-JXQ | Bell 412EP | 36091 | ex N5087V | | | |
| ☐ EC-KBB | Bell 412EP | 36426 | ex N94479 | | | |
| ☐ EC-KBT | Bell 412EP | 36423 | ex C-FLOX | | | |
| ☐ EC-KGZ | Bell 412EP | 36434 | ex C-FMQC | | | |
| ☐ EC-KUV | Agusta-Bell 412 | 25602 | ex I-MAGM | | | |
| ☐ EC-LBL | Agusta-Bell 412SP | 25600 | ex I-CGCL | | | |
| | | | | | | |
| ☐ EC-EUT | Bell 206L-3 LongRanger III | 51337 | ex N8212U | | | |
| ☐ EC-FCO | Bell 206L-3 LongRanger III | 51179 | ex N52CH | | | |
| ☐ EC-JAR | Bell 407 | 53370 | ex N54LM | | | |
| ☐ EC-JBU | Bell 407 | 53241 | ex I-FREC | | | |
| ☐ EC-JBV | Bell 407 | 53613 | ex C-FBXL | | | |
| ☐ EC-JKG | Bell 206L-4 LongRanger IV | 52068 | ex OK-YIP | | | |
| ☐ EC-JSD | Bell 407 | 53687 | ex C-FHYS | | | |
| | | | | | | |
| ☐ EC-DYQ | Agusta-Bell 206B JetRanger III | 8677 | ex HB-XML | | | |
| ☐ EC-FBL | Bell 212 | 30558 | ex EC-553 | | | |
| ☐ EC-IFA | Bell 212 | 30689 | ex N1074C | | | |
| ☐ EC-IYO | Bell 212 | 30946 | ex C-GZMZ | | | |
| ☐ EC-IYP | Bell 212 | 30533 | ex C-FZPX | | | |
| ☐ EC-KIJ | Eurocopter EC135T2i | 0579 | | | | |
| ☐ EC-KJP | Aérospatiale AS355NP Ecureuil 2 | 5752 | | | | |

## HELISWISS IBERICA — Iberswiss (HSW) — Barcelona-Sabadell/Baqueira-Beret

| | | | | |
|---|---|---|---|---|
| ☐ EC-GQH | Bell 206B JetRanger | 578 | ex HB-XDH | |
| ☐ EC-JID | Aérospatiale AS350BA Ecureuil | 1452 | ex F-GKCF | |

## HELITT LINEAS AEREAS — (H9)

| | | | | |
|---|---|---|---|---|
| ☐ EC-LNP | ATR 72-202 | 0285 | ex OK-XFA | ♦ |
| ☐ EC-LNQ | ATR 72-202 | 0303 | ex OK-XFD | ♦ |
| ☐ EC-LNR | ATR 72-212 | 0428 | ex I-ATRQ | ♦ |

## IBERIA EXPRESS — Madrid-Barajas (MAD)

| | | | | |
|---|---|---|---|---|
| ☐ EC-FDB | Airbus A320-211 | 0173 | ex EC-580 | ♦ |
| ☐ EC-FLP | Airbus A320-211 | 0266 | ex EC-881 | ♦ |
| ☐ EC-FNR | Airbus A320-211 | 0323 | ex EC-885 | ♦ |
| ☐ EC-LKH | Airbus A320-214 | 1101 | ex EC-HDP | ♦ |

## IBERIA LINEAS AEREAS DE ESPANA — Iberia (IB/IBE) — Madrid-Barajas (MAD)

Member of Oneworld

| | | | | |
|---|---|---|---|---|
| ☐ EC-HGR | Airbus A319-111 | 1154 | ex D-AVYY | Ribeira Sacra |
| ☐ EC-HGS | Airbus A319-111 | 1180 | ex D-AVWR | Bardenas Reales |
| ☐ EC-HGT | Airbus A319-111 | 1247 | ex D-AVYV | Ignitas de Enciso |
| ☐ EC-HKO | Airbus A319-111 | 1362 | ex D-AVWJ | Gorbea |
| ☐ EC-JAZ | Airbus A319-111 | 2264 | ex D-AVWQ | Las Medulas |
| ☐ EC-JDL | Airbus A319-111 | 2365 | ex D-AVYN | Los Llanos de Aridane |
| ☐ EC-JEI | Airbus A319-111 | 2311 | ex D-AVYG | Xativa |
| ☐ EC-JVE | Airbus A319-111 | 2843 | ex D-AVYT | Puerto de la Cruz |
| ☐ EC-JXV | Airbus A319-111 | 2897 | ex D-AVWH | Concejo de Cabrales |
| ☐ EC-KBJ | Airbus A319-111 | 3054 | ex D-AVYS | Lince Iberico |

| | | | | | |
|---|---|---|---|---|---|
| ☐ EC-KBX | Airbus A319-111 | 3078 | ex D-AVYH | Oso Pardo | |
| ☐ EC-KDI | Airbus A319-111 | 3102 | ex D-AVYA | Cigüeña Negra | |
| ☐ EC-KFT | Airbus A319-111 | 3179 | ex D-AVXK | Nutria | |
| ☐ EC-KHM | Airbus A319-111 | 3209 | ex D-AVWL | Búho Real | |
| ☐ EC-KKS | Airbus A319-111 | 3320 | ex D-AVYF | Halcón Peregrino | retro colours |
| ☐ EC-KMD | Airbus A319-111 | 3380 | ex D-AVWE | | |
| ☐ EC-KOY | Airbus A319-111 | 3443 | ex D-AVYN | | |
| ☐ EC-KUB | Airbus A319-111 | 3651 | ex D-AVKA | | |
| ☐ EC-LEI | Airbus A319-111 | 3744 | ex D-AVWZ | Vison Europeo | |
| | | | | | |
| ☐ EC-FDA | Airbus A320-211 | 0176 | ex EC-581 | Lagunas de Ruidera | |
| ☐ EC-FGR | Airbus A320-211 | 0224 | ex EC-586 | Dehesa de Moncayo | [MAD] |
| ☐ EC-FGV | Airbus A320-211 | 0207 | ex EC-584 | Monfrague | [MAD] |
| ☐ EC-FLQ | Airbus A320-211 | 0274 | ex EC-882 | Dunas de Liencres | [MAD] |
| ☐ EC-HAG | Airbus A320-214 | 1059 | ex F-WWIP | Senorio de Bertiz | |
| ☐ EC-HDK | Airbus A320-214 | 1067 | ex F-WWBF | Mar Ortigola | |
| ☐ EC-HDT | Airbus A320-214 | 1119 | ex F-WWBO | Museo Guggenheim Bilbao | |
| ☐ EC-HGZ | Airbus A320-214 | 1208 | ex F-WWIM | Boi Taull | |
| ☐ EC-HSF | Airbus A320-214 | 1255 | ex EC-HHC | Mar Menor | |
| ☐ EC-HTA | Airbus A320-214 | 1516 | ex F-WWIK | Cadaques | |
| ☐ EC-HTB | Airbus A320-214 | 1530 | ex F-WWIO | Playa de las Americas | |
| ☐ EC-HTC | Airbus A320-214 | 1540 | ex F-WWIU | Alpujarra | |
| ☐ EC-HUJ | Airbus A320-214 | 1292 | ex EC-HKL | Getaria | |
| ☐ EC-HUK | Airbus A320-214 | 1318 | ex EC-HKM | Laguna Negra | |
| ☐ EC-HUL | Airbus A320-214 | 1347 | ex EC-HKN | Monasterio de Rueda | |
| ☐ EC-HYC | Airbus A320-214 | 1262 | ex EC-HKI | Ciudad de Ceuta | |
| ☐ EC-HYD | Airbus A320-214 | 1288 | ex EC-HKX | Maspalomas | |
| ☐ EC-IEF | Airbus A320-214 | 1655 | ex F-WWDY | Castillo de Loarre | |
| ☐ EC-IEG | Airbus A320-214 | 1674 | ex F-WWIL | Costa Brava | |
| ☐ EC-IEI | Airbus A320-214 | 1694 | ex F-WWBT | Monasterio de Valldigna | |
| ☐ EC-ILQ | Airbus A320-214 | 1736 | ex F-WWDJ | La Padrera | |
| ☐ EC-ILR | Airbus A320-214 | 1793 | ex F-WWIM | San Juan de la Pena | |
| ☐ EC-ILS | Airbus A320-214 | 1809 | ex F-WWBC | Sierra de Cameros | |
| ☐ EC-IZH | Airbus A320-214 | 2225 | ex F-WWID | San Pere de Roda | |
| ☐ EC-IZR | Airbus A320-214 | 2242 | ex F-WWDA | Urkiola | |
| ☐ EC-JFN | Airbus A320-214 | 2391 | ex F-WWDB | Sierra de las Nieves | |
| ☐ EC-JSB | Airbus A320-214 | 2776 | ex F-WWDV | Benalmadena | |
| ☐ EC-JSK | Airbus A320-214 | 2807 | ex F-WWIN | Ciudad Encantada | |
| ☐ EC-KHJ | Airbus A320-214 | 2347 | ex XA-UDT | Muralla de Lugo | |
| ☐ EC-KNM | Airbus A320-214 | 1229 | ex XA-MXD | Hoces de Gabriel | |
| ☐ EC-KOH | Airbus A320-214 | 2248 | ex XA-UDU | Fontibre | |
| ☐ EC-LEA | Airbus A320-214 | 1099 | ex EC-HDO | Formentera | |
| ☐ EC-LKG | Airbus A320-214 | 1047 | ex ec-haf | Santiago de Compostela♦ | |
| ☐ EC- | Airbus A320-214 | | ex | | o/o |
| ☐ EC- | Airbus A320-214 | | ex | | o/o |
| ☐ EC- | Airbus A320-214 | | ex | | o/o |
| | | | | | |
| ☐ EC-HUH | Airbus A321-211 | 1021 | ex EC-HAC | Benidorm | |
| ☐ EC-HUI | Airbus A321-211 | 1027 | ex EC-HAE | Comunidad Autonoma de la Rioja | |
| ☐ EC-IGK | Airbus A321-211 | 1572 | ex EC-HTF | Costa Calida | |
| ☐ EC-IIG | Airbus A321-211 | 1554 | ex EC-HTE | Ciudad de Siguenza | |
| ☐ EC-IJN | Airbus A321-211 | 1836 | ex D-AVZN | Merida | |
| ☐ EC-ILO | Airbus A321-211 | 1681 | ex D-AVZW | Cueva de Nerja | |
| ☐ EC-ILP | Airbus A321-211 | 1716 | ex D-AVZT | Peniscola | |
| ☐ EC-ITN | Airbus A321-211 | 2115 | ex D-AVXG | Empuries | |
| ☐ EC-IXD | Airbus A321-211 | 2220 | ex D-AVZR | Valle de Aran | |
| ☐ EC-JDM | Airbus A321-211 | 2357 | ex D-AVZV | Cantabria | |
| ☐ EC-JDR | Airbus A321-211 | 2488 | ex D-AVXD | Sierra Cebollera | |
| ☐ EC-JEJ | Airbus A321-211 | 2381 | ex D-AVZI | Riofrio | |
| ☐ EC-JGS | Airbus A321-211 | 2472 | ex D-AVXA | Guadalupe | |
| ☐ EC-JLI | Airbus A321-211 | 2563 | ex D-AVZB | Delta Del Llobregat | |
| ☐ EC-JMR | Airbus A321-211 | 2599 | ex D-AVZL | Aranjuez | |
| ☐ EC-JNI | Airbus A321-211 | 2270 | ex D-AVZA | Palmeral de Elche | |
| ☐ EC-JQZ | Airbus A321-211 | 2736 | ex D-AVZJ | Generalife | |
| ☐ EC-JRE | Airbus A321-211 | 2756 | ex D-AVZA | Villa de Uncastillo | |
| ☐ EC-JZM | Airbus A321-211 | 2996 | ex D-AVZP | Aquila Imperial | |
| | | | | | |
| ☐ EC-GGS | Airbus A340-313 | 125 | ex EC-154 | Concha Espina | |
| ☐ EC-GHX | Airbus A340-313 | 134 | ex EC-155 | Rosalia de Castro | |
| ☐ EC-GJT | Airbus A340-313 | 145 | ex EC-156 | Rosa Chacel | |
| ☐ EC-GLE | Airbus A340-313 | 146 | ex EC-157 | Concepcion Arenal | |
| ☐ EC-GPB | Airbus A340-313X | 193 | ex F-WWJR | Teresa de Avila | |
| ☐ EC-GUP | Airbus A340-313X | 217 | ex F-WWJG | Agustina de Aragon | |
| ☐ EC-GUQ | Airbus A340-313X | 221 | ex F-WWJA | Beatriz Galindo | |
| ☐ EC-HDQ | Airbus A340-313X | 302 | ex F-WWJU | Sor Juana Ines de la Cruz | |
| ☐ EC-HGU | Airbus A340-313X | 318 | ex F-WWJL | Maria de Molina | |
| ☐ EC-HGV | Airbus A340-313X | 329 | ex F-WWJP | Maria Guerrero | |
| ☐ EC-HGX | Airbus A340-313X | 332 | ex F-WWJR | Maria Pita | |
| ☐ EC-ICF | Airbus A340-313X | 459 | ex F-WWJU | Maria Zambrano | |
| ☐ EC-IDF | Airbus A340-313X | 474 | ex F-WWJG | Mariana Pineda | Op for ADI |
| ☐ EC-IIH | Airbus A340-313X | 483 | ex F-WWJI | Maria Barbara de Braganza | Op for ADI |
| ☐ EC-KCL | Airbus A340-311 | 005 | ex F-GLZA | | Op for ADI |

| | | | | | | |
|---|---|---|---|---|---|---|
| ☐ EC-KOU | Airbus A340-313 | 088 | ex C-FTNQ | | | |
| ☐ EC-KSE | Airbus A340-313X | 170 | ex C-FYLD | | | |
| ☐ EC-LHM | Airbus A340-313X | 387 | ex F-WJKK | | | |
| ☐ EC-LKS | Airbus A340-313X | 414 | ex OE-IAN | Placido Domingo | | ♦ |
| | | | | | | |
| ☐ EC-INO | Airbus A340-642 | 431 | ex F-WWCI | Gaudi | | |
| ☐ EC-IOB | Airbus A340-642 | 440 | ex F-WWCL | Julio Romero de Torres | | |
| ☐ EC-IQR | Airbus A340-642 | 460 | ex F-WWCO | Salvador Dali | | |
| ☐ EC-IZX | Airbus A340-642 | 601 | ex F-WWCS | Mariano Benlliure | | |
| ☐ EC-IZY | Airbus A340-642 | 604 | ex F-WWCH | Ignacio de Zuloaga | | |
| ☐ EC-JBA | Airbus A340-642 | 606 | ex F-WWCV | Joaquin Rodrigo | | |
| ☐ EC-JCY | Airbus A340-642 | 617 | ex F-WWCL | Andres Segovia | | |
| ☐ EC-JCZ | Airbus A340-642 | 619 | ex F-WWCP | Vincente Aleixandre | | |
| ☐ EC-JFX | Airbus A340-642 | 672 | ex F-WWCB | Jacinto Benavente | | |
| ☐ EC-JLE | Airbus A340-642 | 702 | ex F-WWCM | Santiago Ramon y Cajal | | |
| ☐ EC-JNQ | Airbus A340-642 | 727 | ex F-WWCV | Antonio Machado | | |
| ☐ EC-JPU | Airbus A340-642 | 744 | ex F-WWCF | Pio Baroja | | |
| ☐ EC-KZI | Airbus A340-642 | 1017 | ex F-WWCS | | | |
| ☐ EC-LCZ | Airbus A340-642 | 993 | ex F-WWCK | | | |
| ☐ EC-LEU | Airbus A340-642 | 960 | ex F-WWCG | Virgen de Montsserat | | |
| ☐ EC-LEV | Airbus A340-642 | 1079 | ex F-WWCE | | | |
| ☐ EC-LFS | Airbus A340-642 | 1122 | ex F-WWCF | | | |
| | | | | | | |
| ☐ EC-FIG | McDonnell-Douglas MD-88 | 53195/1929 | ex EC-753 | Penon de Ifach | [MAD] | |
| ☐ EC-FJE | McDonnell-Douglas MD-88 | 53197/1940 | ex EC-755 | Gibraltaro | [MAD] | |
| ☐ EC-FLN | McDonnell-Douglas MD-88 | 53303/1974 | ex EC-945 | Puerta de Tierra | wfs | |
| ☐ EC-FND | McDonnell-Douglas MD-88 | 53305/2001 | ex EC-964 | Playa de la Concha | [MAD] | |
| ☐ EC-FOF | McDonnell-Douglas MD-88 | 53307/2015 | ex EC-966 | Puerta de Alcala | [MAD] | |
| ☐ EC-FOG | McDonnell-Douglas MD-88 | 53306/2014 | ex EC-965 | Cesar Manrique Lanzarote | [MAD] | |
| ☐ EC-FOZ | McDonnell-Douglas MD-88 | 53308/2022 | ex EC-987 | Montjuic | wfs | |
| ☐ EC-FPD | McDonnell-Douglas MD-88 | 53309/2023 | ex EC-988 | Lago de Coradonga | ]wfs | |
| ☐ EC-FPJ | McDonnell-Douglas MD-88 | 53310/2024 | ex EC-989 | | [MAD] | |
| | | | | | | |
| ☐ EC-EXG | McDonnell-Douglas MD-87 | 49833/1706 | ex EC-296 | Ciudad de Almeria | | |
| ☐ EC-FFA | McDonnell-Douglas MD-87 | 53209/1867 | ex EC-635 | Ciudad de Avila | [MAD] | |
| ☐ EC-FHK | McDonnell-Douglas MD-87 | 53213/1879 | ex EC-639 | Ciudad de Tarragona | [MAD] | |

## IMD AIRWAYS (IMD)

| | | | | | |
|---|---|---|---|---|---|
| ☐ EC-KSF | McDonnell-Douglas MD-87 | 53207/1862 | ex EC-FEZ | | ♦ |
| ☐ EC-LMY | McDonnell-Douglas MD-83 | 49620/1484 | ex N620MD | | ♦ |

## ISLAS AIRWAYS           Pintadera (IF/ISW)           Tenerife Norte (TNR)

| | | | | | |
|---|---|---|---|---|---|
| ☐ EC-IKQ | ATR 72-202 | 0477 | ex F-WQNM | La Palma | |
| ☐ EC-JCD | ATR 72-202 | 0452 | ex F-WQND | | |
| ☐ EC-KKZ | ATR 72-212 | 0766 | ex F-WWEE | Isla de Fuerteventura | |
| ☐ EC-KNO | ATR 72-212 | 0770 | ex F-WWEI | Isla de la Palma | |
| ☐ EC-KUR | ATR 72-212A | 0808 | ex F-WWES | Isla de Lanzarote | |
| ☐ EC-LKK | ATR 72-212 | 0461 | ex F-GVZF | | |
| ☐ EC- | ATR 72-500 | | ex | | o/o |
| ☐ EC- | ATR 72-500 | | ex | | o/o |
| ☐ EC- | ATR 72-500 | | ex | | o/o |

## LETS FLY (LLY)

| | | | | | |
|---|---|---|---|---|---|
| ☐ EC-GEN | Swearingen SA.227AC Metro III | AC-688 | ex N727C | | ♦ |
| ☐ EC-IDG | ATR 42-320 | 0003 | ex F-OICG | | ♦ |

## MINT AIRWAYS (MIC)

| | | | | |
|---|---|---|---|---|
| ☐ EC-LBC | Boeing 757-28A | 26276/704 | ex G-CEJM | Tato Goya |
| ☐ EC-LHL | Boeing 757-28A | 24544/280 | ex OM-ASG | David Summers |

## NAYSA AEROTAXIS           Naysa (ZN/NAY)           Las Palmas-Gran Canaria (LPA)

| | | | | | |
|---|---|---|---|---|---|
| ☐ EC-GQF | ATR 72-202 | 0489 | ex F-WWLJ | | |
| ☐ EC-GRP | ATR 72-202 | 0488 | ex F-WWLI | | |
| ☐ EC-GRU | ATR 72-202 | 0493 | ex F-WWLN | | |
| ☐ EC-KGI | ATR 72-212A | 0752 | ex F-WWEM | Bentayga | |
| ☐ EC-KGJ | ATR 72-212A | 0753 | ex F-WWEN | Madeira | |
| ☐ EC-KRY | ATR 72-212A | 0795 | ex F-WWEV | Azero | |
| ☐ EC-KSG | ATR 72-212A | 0796 | ex F-WWEW | Malvasia Volcánica | |
| ☐ EC-KYI | ATR 72-212A | 0850 | ex F-WWET | Guarapo | |
| ☐ EC-LAD | ATR 72-212A | 0864 | ex F-WWEJ | Baifo | |
| ☐ EC-LFA | ATR 72-212A | 0902 | ex F-WWER | Rapadura | ♦ |
| ☐ EC-LGF | ATR 72-212A | 0907 | ex F-WWEX | Pejeverde | ♦ |
| | | | | | |
| ☐ EC-IJO | Beech 1900D | UE-300 | ex F-GRPM | Garajonal | |

## ORBEST ORIZONIA AIRLINES — Orbest (IWD) — Palma de Mallorca (PMI)

| | Reg | Type | c/n | ex | Notes |
|---|---|---|---|---|---|
| ☐ | EC-LLX | Airbus A320-214 | 4735 | ex D-AVVD | ♦ |
| ☐ | EC-INZ | Airbus A320-214 | 2011 | ex F-WWBR | ♦ |
| ☐ | EC-KYZ | Airbus A320-214 | 3758 | ex F-WWBZ | ♦ |
| ☐ | EC-KZG | Airbus A320-214 | 3868 | ex F-WWIC | ♦ |
| ☐ | EC-LAJ | Airbus A320-214 | 3889 | ex F-WWBX | ♦ |
| ☐ | EC-LAQ | Airbus A320-214 | 3933 | ex F-WWBU | >GOW♦ |
| ☐ | EC-JHP | Airbus A330-343X | 670 | ex F-WWKU | |
| ☐ | EC-KCP | Airbus A330-343 | 833 | ex F-WWKO | >ORB♦ |
| ☐ | EC-LEQ | Airbus A330-343E | 1097 | ex F-WWKL | ♦ |

## PANAIR LINEAS AEREAS — Skyjet (PV/PNR) — Madrid-Barajas (MAD)

| | Reg | Type | c/n | ex | Notes |
|---|---|---|---|---|---|
| ☐ | EC-ELT | British Aerospace 146 Srs.200QT | E2102 | ex EC-198 | |
| ☐ | EC-FVY | British Aerospace 146 Srs.200QT | E2117 | ex EC-615 | |
| ☐ | EC-FZE | British Aerospace 146 Srs.200QT | E2105 | ex EC-719 | |
| ☐ | EC-GQO | British Aerospace 146 Srs.200QT | E2086 | ex D-ADEI | |
| ☐ | EC-HDH | British Aerospace 146 Srs.200QT | E2056 | ex G-TNTA | |
| ☐ | EC-HJH | British Aerospace 146 Srs.200QT | E2112 | ex G-BOMK | |
| ☐ | EC-LMR | British Aerospace 146 Srs.300QT | E3151 | ex OO-TAA | ♦ |
| ☐ | EC-LOF | British Aerospace 146 Srs.300QT | E3150 | ex OO-TAK | ♦ |

## PIRINAIR EXPRESS — Pirinair Express (PRN) — Zaragoza (ZAZ)

| | Reg | Type | c/n | ex | Notes |
|---|---|---|---|---|---|
| ☐ | EC-FZB | Swearingen SA.226TC Metro II | TC-221 | ex EC-666 | |
| ☐ | EC-JCV | Swearingen SA.226AT Merlin IVA | AT-038 | ex SX-BGT | |

## PRIVILEGE STYLE — (PVG)

| | Reg | Type | c/n | ex | Notes |
|---|---|---|---|---|---|
| ☐ | EC-HDS | Boeing 757-256 | 26252/900 | | Milagros Diaz |
| ☐ | EC-ISY | Boeing 757-256 | 26241/572 | ex N26ND | |

## PULLMANTUR AIR — Pullmantur (PLM) — Madrid-Barajas (MAD)

| | Reg | Type | c/n | ex | Notes |
|---|---|---|---|---|---|
| ☐ | EC-KQC | Boeing 747-412 | 26549/1030 | ex 9V-SMZ | |
| ☐ | EC-KSM | Boeing 747-412 | 27178/1015 | ex 9V-SMW | |
| ☐ | EC-KXN | Boeing 747-4H6 | 25703/1025 | ex N703AC | |
| ☐ | EC-LNA | Boeing 747-446 | 26346/897 | ex N346AS | [MAD]♦ |

## RYJET — Malaga (AGP)

| | Reg | Type | c/n | ex | Notes |
|---|---|---|---|---|---|
| ☐ | EC-JHE | SAAB SF.340A | 340A-018 | ex SE-LMV | |
| ☐ | G-EIGG | BAe Jetstream 31 | 773 | ex SE-LGH | <Links Air♦ |

## SERAIR — Cargopress (SEV) — Las Palmas-Gran Canaria (LPA)

| | Reg | Type | c/n | ex | Notes |
|---|---|---|---|---|---|
| ☐ | EC-GTM | Beech 1900C | UB-30 | ex N7210R | |
| ☐ | EC-GUD | Beech 1900C-1 | UC-156 | ex N156YV | |
| ☐ | EC-GZG | Beech 1900C-1 | UC-161 | ex N55635 | |
| ☐ | EC-JDY | Beech 1900C-1 | UC-91 | ex N91YV | |

## SPANAIR — Spanair (JK/JKK) — Palma de Mallorca (PMI)

Member of Star Alliance

| | Reg | Type | c/n | ex | Name | Notes |
|---|---|---|---|---|---|---|
| ☐ | EC-GCV | McDonnell-Douglas MD-82 | 53165/2042 | ex EC-894 | Sunburst | [MAD] |
| ☐ | EC-GQG | McDonnell-Douglas MD-83 | 49577/1454 | ex EC-FSY | | Star Alliance c/s; wfs |
| ☐ | EC-GVO | McDonnell-Douglas MD-83 | 49642/1421 | ex N462GE | Sunspot | [MAD] |
| ☐ | EC-GXU | McDonnell-Douglas MD-83 | 49622/1498 | ex EC-FTT | | Star Alliance c/s; wfs |
| ☐ | EC-IAZ | Airbus A320-232 | 1631 | ex F-WWDP | | [SNN] |
| ☐ | EC-ICL | Airbus A320-232 | 1682 | ex F-WWBD | | [SNN] |

Ceased ops 27Jan12

## SWIFTAIR — Swift (SWT) — Madrid-Barajas (MAD)

| | Reg | Type | c/n | ex | Notes | |
|---|---|---|---|---|---|---|
| ☐ | EC-ISX | ATR 42-320 | 0242 | ex N242AT | | Frtr; no titles |
| ☐ | EC-IVP | ATR 42-300 | 0231 | ex F-GKND | | Frtr |
| ☐ | EC-JAD | ATR 42-300 | 0321 | ex F-GHPY | | |
| ☐ | EC-JBN | ATR 42-300 (QC) | 0218 | ex F-GHPK | all-white | |
| ☐ | EC-JBX | ATR 42-300 | 0254 | ex N255AE | | Frtr |
| ☐ | EC-KAI | ATR 42-300F | 0141 | ex EI-FXF | | |
| ☐ | EC-INV | ATR 72-201 | 0274 | ex N274AT | | Frtr |
| ☐ | EC-IYH | ATR 72-212 | 0330 | ex F-WQUI | | Frtr |
| ☐ | EC-JDX | ATR 72-201 | 0234 | ex F-GHPV | all-white | Frtr |
| ☐ | EC-JQF | ATR 72-201F | 0147 | ex SE-LVK | | |
| ☐ | EC-JRP | ATR 72-212 | 0446 | ex D-AEWK | | |
| ☐ | EC-JXF | ATR 72-201F | 0150 | ex OY-CIV | | |

| | | | | | | |
|---|---|---|---|---|---|---|
| ☐ EC-KAD | ATR 72-202F | 0171 | ex F-GKPC | | | |
| ☐ EC-KIZ | ATR 72-202F | 0204 | ex F-GPOA | | | <FPO |
| ☐ EC-KJA | ATR 72-202F | 0207 | ex F-GPOB | | | <FPO |
| ☐ EC-KKQ | ATR 72-212A | 0763 | ex F-WWEB | | | |
| ☐ EC-KUL | ATR 72-212A | 0809 | ex F-WWET | | | >BWA |
| ☐ EC-KVI | ATR 72-212A | 0824 | ex F-WWEM | | | |
| ☐ EC-LHV | ATR 72-202 | 0416 | ex F-WNUH | | | ♦ |
| | | | | | | |
| ☐ EC-KLR | Boeing 737-3Q8 (SF) | 23766/1375 | ex N237CP | | | |
| ☐ EC-KRA | Boeing 737-3Y0F | 24679/1897 | ex SX-BGK | | | |
| ☐ EC-KTZ | Boeing 737-375F | 23708/1395 | ex N111KH | | | |
| ☐ EC-KVD | Boeing 737-306F | 23538/1288 | ex N102KH | | | |
| ☐ EC-LAC | Boeing 737-3M8F | 24022/1662 | ex N107KH | | | |
| ☐ EC-LJI | Boeing 737-301 (SF) | 23512/1291 | ex OO-TNI | | | |
| | | | | | | |
| ☐ EC-GQA | Embraer EMB-120ER Brasilia | 120027 | ex EC-GMT | | | Frtr |
| ☐ EC-HAK | Embraer EMB-120ER Brasilia | 120008 | ex N212AS | | | Frtr |
| ☐ EC-HCF | Embraer EMB.120ER Brasilia | 120007 | ex N211AS | | | Frtr |
| ☐ EC-HFK | Embraer EMB-120ER Brasilia | 120063 | ex N7215U | | | Frtr |
| ☐ EC-HMY | Embraer EMB.120ER Brasilia | 120009 | ex N214AS | all-white | | Frtr |
| ☐ EC-HTS | Embraer EMB.120ER Brasilia | 120168 | ex N168CA | | | Frtr |
| ☐ EC-IMX | Embraer EMB.120ER Brasilia | 120158 | ex N312FV | | | Frtr |
| ☐ EC-JBD | Embraer EMB.120ER Brasilia | 120012 | ex D-CAOB | | | Frtr |
| ☐ EC-JBE | Embraer EMB.120ER Brasilia | 120013 | ex D-CAOA | | | Frtr |
| ☐ EC-JKH | Embraer EMB.120ER Brasilia | 120092 | ex OM-SPY | | | |
| | | | | | | |
| ☐ EC-JQV | McDonnell-Douglas MD-83 | 49526/1342 | ex N14879 | Real Madrid c/s | | |
| ☐ EC-JUF | McDonnell-Douglas MD-83 | 53168/2061 | ex N802NK | | | Op for UN |
| ☐ EC-JUG | McDonnell-Douglas MD-83 | 49847/1585 | ex N834NK | | | |
| ☐ EC-KCX | McDonnell-Douglas MD-83 | 49619/1483 | ex N814NK | | | |
| ☐ EC-LEY | McDonnell-Douglas MD-83 | 53182/2068 | ex I-SMED | | | >VOS |
| | | | | | | |
| ☐ A9C-SWA | Boeing 727-230F (FedEx 3) | 21442/1326 | ex EC-JHU | | | ♦ |

## TAS - TRANSPORTES AEREOS DEL SUR

| | | | | | | |
|---|---|---|---|---|---|---|
| ☐ EC-KEK | CASA CN-235-300MPA | C166 | ex EC-235 | 101 | | Op for SASEMA |
| ☐ EC-KEL | CASA CN-235-300MPA | C169 | ex EC-027 | 102 | | Op for SASEMA |
| ☐ EC-KEM | CASA CN-235-300MPA | C171 | ex EC-021 | 103 | | Op for SASEMA |

## TOP-FLY    Topfly (TLY)    Barcelona (BCN)

| | | | | | | |
|---|---|---|---|---|---|---|
| ☐ EC-EYV | Piper PA-34-220T Seneca III | 34-8233109 | ex OE-FYB | | | |
| ☐ EC-HZM | Piper PA-34-200 Seneca | 34-7250169 | ex F-GFJE | | | |
| ☐ EC-JYJ | Aérospatiale AS355F2 Twin Star | 5425 | ex N225NR | | | |
| Ceased ops | | | | | | |

## TRANPORTES AEREOS DEL SUR / TRAGSA    TAS (HSS)    Seville (SVQ)

| | | | | | | |
|---|---|---|---|---|---|---|
| ☐ EC-GHS | Partenavia P.68 Observer | 329-20-OB | ex G-OBSV | | | |
| ☐ EC-HAP | CASA C.212-300MPA | 465 | ex EC-011 | | | |
| ☐ EC-HTU | CASA C.212-300MPA | 470 | | | | Maritime Patrol |
| ☐ EC-IFL | Vulcanair P.68C | 412 | ex N412VR | | | |
| ☐ EC-ILE | Beech B200 Super King Air | BB-1792 | ex N5092K | Muxtamel | | EMS |
| ☐ EC-INX | CASA C.212-300MPA | 472 | | | | Maritime Patrol |
| ☐ EC-IUX | Beech B200 Super King Air | BB-1840 | ex N816LD | | | |

## VOLOTEA AIRLINES    (VOE)    Palma de Mallorca (PMI)

| | | | | | | |
|---|---|---|---|---|---|---|
| ☐ EC-LPM | Boeing 717-2BL | 55185/5145 | ex N923ME | | | ♦ |
| ☐ EC-LQI | Boeing 717-2BL | 55167/5117 | ex N408BC | | | ♦ |
| ☐ EC-LQS | Boeing 717-2BL | 55169/5119 | ex N903ME | | | ♦ |

## VUELING AIRLINES    Vueling (VY/VLG)    Barcelona (BCN)

| | | | | | | |
|---|---|---|---|---|---|---|
| ☐ EC-FCB | Airbus A320-211 | 0158 | ex EC-579 | Montana de Covadonga | | |
| ☐ EC-FQY | Airbus A320-211 | 0356 | ex EC-886 | | | ♦ |
| ☐ EC-GRG | Airbus A320-211 | 0143 | ex EC-FBS | | | |
| ☐ EC-GRH | Airbus A320-211 | 0146 | ex EC-FBR | | | |
| ☐ EC-HHA | Airbus A320-214 | 1221 | ex F-WWBF | | | |
| ☐ EC-HQI | Airbus A320-214 | 1396 | ex F-WWIX | | | |
| ☐ EC-HQJ | Airbus A320-214 | 1430 | ex F-WWBR | | | |
| ☐ EC-HQL | Airbus A320-214 | 1461 | ex F-WWDD | Click on Vueling | | |
| ☐ EC-HTD | Airbus A320-214 | 1550 | ex F-WWDC | Unos vuelan, otros Vueling | | |
| ☐ EC-ICQ | Airbus A320-211 | 0199 | ex EC-FGU | Iker Ochandrena | | |
| ☐ EC-ICR | Airbus A320-211 | 0240 | ex EC-FIA | | | |
| ☐ EC-ICS | Airbus A320-211 | 0241 | ex EC-FIC | | | |
| ☐ EC-ICT | Airbus A320-211 | 0264 | ex EC-FKD | | | |
| ☐ EC-IZD | Airbus A320-214 | 2207 | ex F-WWDS | Barceloning | | |
| ☐ EC-JFF | Airbus A320-214 | 2388 | ex F-WWIH | Vueling the world | | |
| ☐ EC-JFG | Airbus A320-214 | 2143 | ex F-WWBV | Valle de Ricote | | ♦ |

| | | | | | |
|---|---|---|---|---|---|
| ☐ EC-JFH | Airbus A320-214 | 2104 | ex F-WWBE | | ♦ |
| ☐ EC-JGM | Airbus A320-214 | 2407 | ex F-WWDC | The joy of Vueling | |
| ☐ EC-JSY | Airbus A320-214 | 2785 | ex F-WWBU | Connie Baraja | |
| ☐ EC-JTQ | Airbus A320-214 | 2794 | ex F-WWBN | Vueling, que es gerundio | |
| ☐ EC-JTR | Airbus A320-214 | 2798 | ex F-WWIF | no Vueling, no party | |
| ☐ EC-JYX | Airbus A320-214 | 2962 | ex F-WWDJ | Elisenda Masana | |
| ☐ EC-JZI | Airbus A320-214 | 2988 | ex F-WWII | Vueling in love | |
| ☐ EC-JZQ | Airbus A320-214 | 0992 | ex TC-JLE | I Want to Vueling | |
| ☐ EC-KBU | Airbus A320-214 | 1413 | ex TC-JLF | Be Vueling my friend | |
| ☐ EC-KCU | Airbus A320-216 | 3109 | ex F-WWIR | My name is Ling. Vue Ling | |
| ☐ EC-KDG | Airbus A320-214 | 3095 | ex F-WWIY | | |
| ☐ EC-KDH | Airbus A320-214 | 3083 | ex F-WWIX | Ain't no Vueling high enough | |
| ☐ EC-KDT | Airbus A320-216 | 3145 | ex F-WWBM | Ready, steady, Vueling | |
| ☐ EC-KDX | Airbus A320-216 | 3151 | ex F-WWBU | | |
| ☐ EC-KFI | Airbus A320-216 | 3174 | ex F-WWIP | | |
| ☐ EC-KHN | Airbus A320-216 | 3203 | ex F-WWIG | | |
| ☐ EC-KJD | Airbus A320-216 | 3237 | ex F-WWBJ | | |
| ☐ EC-KKT | Airbus A320-214 | 3293 | ex F-WWDU | Vueling Together | |
| ☐ EC-KLB | Airbus A320-214 | 3321 | ex F-WWBY | Vuela y punto | |
| ☐ EC-KLT | Airbus A320-216 | 3376 | ex F-WWDI | | |
| ☐ EC-KMI | Airbus A320-216 | 3400 | ex F-WWBT | How are you? I'm Vueling! | |
| ☐ EC-KRH | Airbus A320-214 | 3529 | ex D-AVVD | | |
| ☐ EC-LAA | Airbus A320-214 | 2678 | ex A6-ABZ | | |
| ☐ EC-LAB | Airbus A320-214 | 2761 | ex OE-LEV | | |
| ☐ EC-LLJ | Airbus A320-216 | 4661 | ex F-WWII | | >ANS♦ |
| ☐ EC-LLM | Airbus A320-214 | 4681 | ex F-WWDX | | ♦ |
| ☐ EC-LML | Airbus A320-214 | 4742 | ex F-WWIR | | ♦ |
| ☐ EC-LOB | Airbus A320-214 | 4849 | ex D-AUBJ | | ♦ |
| ☐ EC-LOC | Airbus A320-214 | 4855 | ex F-WWBF | Vueling on heaven's door | ♦ |
| ☐ EC-LOP | Airbus A320-214 | 4937 | ex D-AXAG | All you need is Vueling | ♦ |
| ☐ EC-LQJ | Airbus A320-232 | 1979 | ex EI-EUK | | ♦ |
| ☐ EC-LQK | Airbus A320-232 | 2589 | ex EI-EUP | | ♦ |
| ☐ EC-LQL | Airbus A320-232 | 1749 | ex EI-EUF | | ♦ |
| ☐ EC-LQM | Airbus A320-232 | 2223 | ex EI-EUN | | ♦ |
| ☐ EC-LQN | Airbus A320-232 | 2168 | ex EI-EUM | | ♦ |
| | | | | | |
| ☐ EC-JXJ | Airbus A319-111 | 2889 | ex D-AVYH | Un Vueling si'il vous plait | ♦ |

| **VUELOS MEDITERRANEO** | **Vuelos Mediterraneo (VMM)** | | | **Valencia (VLC)** |
|---|---|---|---|---|
| ☐ EC-FCC | Cessna 402B II | 402B1013 | ex EC-614 | |
| ☐ EC-HCU | Swearingen SA.226TC Metro II | TC-390 | ex N19WP | wfs |

| **ZOREX** | **Zorex (ORZ)** | | | **Madrid-Barajas (MAD)** |
|---|---|---|---|---|
| ☐ EC-HJC | Swearingen SA.226TC Metro II | TC-318 | ex OY-JEO | |
| ☐ EC-JYC | Swearingen SA.226TC Metro II | TC-303 | ex N117AR | |

## EI-    IRELAND (Eire)

| **AER ARANN REGIONAL AIR** | **Aer Arann (RE/REA)** | | | **Dublin (DUB)** |
|---|---|---|---|---|
| ☐ EI-REH | ATR 72-202 | 0260 | ex OY-RTA | |
| ☐ EI-REI | ATR 72-202 | 0267 | ex OY-RTB | |
| ☐ EI-REL | ATR 72-212A | 0748 | ex F-WWEI | |
| ☐ EI-REM | ATR 72-212A | 0760 | ex F-WWEW | |
| ☐ EI-REO | ATR 72-212A | 0787 | ex F-WWEF | |
| ☐ EI-REP | ATR 72-212A | 0797 | ex F-WWEZ | |
| ☐ EI-RES | ATR 72-212A | | ex F-WW | o/o |
| ☐ EI-RET | ATR 72-212A | | ex F-WW | o/o |
| ☐ EI-REU | ATR 72-212A | | ex F-WW | o/o |
| ☐ EI-REV | ATR 72-212A | | ex F-WW | o/o |
| | | | | |
| ☐ EI-BYO | ATR 42-310 | 0161 | ex OY-CIS | |
| ☐ EI-CBK | ATR 42-310 | 0199 | ex F-WWEM | |
| ☐ EI-CPT | ATR 42-300 | 0191 | ex (SE-KCX) St Fintan/Fionntain | |
| ☐ EI-EHH | ATR 42-300 | 0196 | ex G-SSEA | |

| **AER ARANN ISLANDS** | | | | **Galway (GWY)** |
|---|---|---|---|---|
| ☐ EI-AYN | Britten-Norman BN-2A-8 Islander | 704 | ex G-BBFJ | |
| ☐ EI-BCE | Britten-Norman BN-2A-26 Islander | 519 | ex G-BDUV | |
| ☐ EI-CUW | Britten-Norman BN-2B-26 Islander | 2293 | ex G-BWYW | |

| **AER LINGUS** | **Shamrock (EI/EIN)** | | | **Dublin (DUB)** |
|---|---|---|---|---|
| ☐ EI-CVA | Airbus A320-214 | 1242 | ex F-WWIT | St Schira/Scire | [DUB] |
| ☐ EI-CVB | Airbus A320-214 | 1394 | ex F-WWIV | St Mobhi/Mobhi | |
| ☐ EI-CVC | Airbus A320-214 | 1443 | ex F-WWBS | St Kealin/Caolfhionn | |
| ☐ EI-CVD | Airbus A320-214 | 1467 | ex F-WWDG | St Kevin/Caoimhin | |

| | | | | | |
|---|---|---|---|---|---|
| ☐ EI-DEA | Airbus A320-214 | 2191 | ex F-WWBX | St Fidelma/Fiedeilme | |
| ☐ EI-DEB | Airbus A320-214 | 2206 | ex F-WWBP | St Nathy/Naithi | |
| ☐ EI-DEC | Airbus A320-214 | 2217 | ex F-WWBH | St Fergal/Fearghal | |
| ☐ EI-DEE | Airbus A320-214 | 2250 | ex F-WWBE | St Ultan/Ultan | |
| ☐ EI-DEF | Airbus A320-214 | 2256 | ex F-WWBK | St Declan/Deaglan | |
| ☐ EI-DEG | Airbus A320-214 | 2272 | ex F-WWIB | St Fachtna/Fachtna | |
| ☐ EI-DEH | Airbus A320-214 | 2294 | ex F-WWBX | St Conleth/Connlaodh | |
| ☐ EI-DEI | Airbus A320-214 | 2374 | ex F-WWDU | St Oliver Plunkett/Oilibh Plunceid | |
| ☐ EI-DEJ | Airbus A320-214 | 2364 | ex F-WWDI | St Kilian/Cillian | |
| ☐ EI-DEK | Airbus A320-214 | 2399 | ex F-WWIZ | St Eunan/Eunan | |
| ☐ EI-DEL | Airbus A320-214 | 2409 | ex F-WWDE | St Canice/Cainneach | |
| ☐ EI-DEM | Airbus A320-214 | 2411 | ex F-WWDG | St Ibar/Ibhar | |
| ☐ EI-DEN | Airbus A320-214 | 2432 | ex F-WWBK | St Kieran/Ciaran | |
| ☐ EI-DEO | Airbus A320-214 | 2486 | ex F-WWIV | St Senan/Seanan | |
| ☐ EI-DEP | Airbus A320-214 | 2542 | ex F-WWIU | St Eugene/Eoghan | |
| ☐ EI-DER | Airbus A320-214 | 2583 | ex F-WWDE | St Mel/Mel | |
| ☐ EI-DES | Airbus A320-214 | 2635 | ex F-WWDZ | St Pappin/Paipan | |
| ☐ EI-DET | Airbus A320-214 | 2810 | ex F-WWIP | St Brendan/Breandan | |
| ☐ EI-DVE | Airbus A320-214 | 3129 | ex F-WWBJ | St Aideen/Etaoin | |
| ☐ EI-DVF | Airbus A320-214 | 3136 | ex F-WWDF | St Jarlath/Iarfhlaith | |
| ☐ EI-DVG | Airbus A320-214 | 3318 | ex F-WWIV | St Flannan/Flannan | |
| ☐ EI-DVH | Airbus A320-214 | 3345 | ex F-WWBP | | |
| ☐ EI-DVI | Airbus A320-214 | 3501 | ex F-WWBQ | St Emer/Eimaer | |
| ☐ EI-DVJ | Airbus A320-214 | 3857 | ex F-WWDL | St Macarthan/Macarthain | |
| ☐ EI-DVK | Airbus A320-214 | 4572 | ex D-AUBY | St Brigid/Birghid | |
| ☐ EI-DVL | Airbus A320-214 | 4678 | ex F-WWDR | St Moling/Moling | ♦ |
| ☐ EI-DVM | Airbus A320-214 | 4634 | ex F-WWDV | | ♦ |
| ☐ EI-DVN | Airbus A320-214 | 4715 | ex D-AUBH | | ♦ |
| ☐ EI-EDP | Airbus A320-214 | 3781 | ex F-WWIR | | |
| ☐ EI-EDS | Airbus A320-214 | 3755 | ex F-WWBU | St Malachy/Maolmhaodhog | |
| | | | | | |
| ☐ EI-DAA | Airbus A330-202 | 397 | ex F-WWKK | St Keeva/Caoimhe | |
| ☐ EI-DUO | Airbus A330-202 | 841 | ex F-WWYT | St Columba/Colum | |
| ☐ EI-DUZ | Airbus A330-302 | 847 | ex F-WWKM | St Aoife/Aoife | |
| ☐ EI-EAV | Airbus A330-302 | 985 | ex F-WWKF | Ronan | |
| ☐ EI-EDY | Airbus A330-302 | 1025 | ex F-WWYU | Maincin | |
| ☐ EI-ELA | Airbus A330-302X | 1106 | ex F-WWYH | St Patrick/Padraig | |
| ☐ EI-LAX | Airbus A330-202 | 269 | ex F-WWKV | St Mella/Mella | |
| | | | | | |
| ☐ EI-EPR | Airbus A319-111 | 3169 | ex EC-KEV | St Davnet/Damhnat | ♦ |
| ☐ EI-EPS | Airbus A319-111 | 3377 | ex EC-KME | St Fergus/Feargus | ♦ |
| ☐ EI-CPE | Airbus A321-211 | 0926 | ex D-AVZQ | St Enda/Eanna | |
| ☐ EI-CPG | Airbus A321-211 | 1023 | ex D-AVZR | St Aidan/Aodhan | |
| ☐ EI-CPH | Airbus A321-211 | 1094 | ex F-WWDD | St Dervilla/Dearbhile | |

## AIR CONTRACTORS — Contract / Rapex (AG/ABR) — Dublin (DUB)

| | | | | | |
|---|---|---|---|---|---|
| ☐ EI-DHL | Airbus A300B4-203F | 274 | ex OO-DIB | | |
| ☐ EI-EAB | Airbus A300B4-203F | 199 | ex OO-DLW | | |
| ☐ EI-EAC | Airbus A300B4-203F | 250 | ex OO-DLT | | |
| ☐ EI-EAD | Airbus A300B4-203F | 289 | ex OO-DLU | | |
| ☐ EI-OZB | Airbus A300B4-103F | 184 | ex OO-DIH | | |
| ☐ EI-OZD | Airbus A300B4-203F | 236 | ex OO-DLE | | |
| ☐ EI-OZE | Airbus A300B4-203F | 152 | ex OO-DLC | | |
| ☐ EI-OZF | Airbus A300B4-203F | 259 | ex OO-DLD | | |
| ☐ EI-OZH | Airbus A300B4-203F | 234 | ex OO-DLI | | |
| ☐ EI-OZI | Airbus A300B4-203F | 219 | ex OO-DLZ | | |
| ☐ EI-SAF | Airbus A300B4-203F | 220 | ex OO-DIC | | |
| | | | | | |
| ☐ EI-FXA | ATR 42-320F | 0282 | ex N282AT | Lsd fr/op for FDX | |
| ☐ EI-FXB | ATR 42-320F | 0243 | ex (N924FX) | Lsd fr/op for FDX | |
| ☐ EI-FXC | ATR 42-320F | 0310 | ex (N925FX) | Lsd fr/op for FDX | |
| ☐ EI-FXD | ATR 42-300F | 0273 | ex (N927FX) | Lsd fr/op for FDX | |
| ☐ EI-FXE | ATR 42-300F | 0327 | ex (N926FX) | Lsd fr/op for FDX | |
| ☐ EI-SLA | ATR 42-300F | 0149 | ex SE-LST | >MSA | |
| ☐ EI-SLI | ATR 42-320 | 0115 | ex 5Y-BVD | >Canarias Aeronautica | |
| | | | | | |
| ☐ EI-FXG | ATR 72-202F | 0224 | ex (N814FX) | | |
| ☐ EI-FXH | ATR 72-202F | 0229 | ex N815FX | | |
| ☐ EI-FXI | ATR 72-202F | 0294 | ex N818FX | | |
| ☐ EI-FXJ | ATR 72-202F | 0292 | ex N813FX | | |
| ☐ EI-FXK | ATR 72-202F | 0256 | ex N817FX | Lsd fr/op for FDX | |
| ☐ EI-REJ | ATR 72-202F | 0126 | ex ES-KRA | | |
| ☐ EI-SLF | ATR 72-202F | 0210 | ex OY-RUA | | |
| ☐ EI-SLG | ATR 72-202F | 0183 | ex F-WQNI | | |
| ☐ EI-SLH | ATR 72-202F | 0157 | ex OY-RTG | | |
| ☐ EI-SLJ | ATR 72-201 | 0324 | ex LY-PTK | | |
| ☐ EI-SLK | ATR 72-212 | 0395 | ex N642AS | | |
| ☐ EI-SLL | ATR 72-212 | 0387 | ex N641AS | | |
| ☐ EI-SLN | ATR 72-212 | 0405 | ex N640AS | St Cormac/Cormac | |
| | | | | | |
| ☐ EI-STA | Boeing 737-31S | 29057/2942 | ex G-THOG | | ♦ |

| | | | | |
|---|---|---|---|---|
| ☐ EI-JIV | Lockheed L-382G-35C Hercules | 4673 | ex ZS-JIV | <SFR |

## BOND AIR SERVICES (IRELAND)

| | | | | |
|---|---|---|---|---|
| ☐ EI-KEL | Eurocopter EC135T2 | 0848 | ex G-CGHP | ♦ |

## CHC IRELAND        Dublin (DUB)

| | | | | |
|---|---|---|---|---|
| ☐ EI-CXS | Sikorsky S-61N | 61816 | ex IAC 257 | IMES Rescue based Sligo |
| ☐ EI-CZN | Sikorsky S-61N | 61740 | ex G-CBWC | IMES Rescue standby |
| ☐ EI-GCE | Sikorsky S-61N | 61817 | ex LN-ORC | IMES Rescue based Shannon |
| ☐ EI-MES | Sikorsky S-61N | 61776 | ex G-BXAE | IMES Rescue based Dublin |
| ☐ EI-RCG | Sikorsky S-61N | 61807 | ex G-87-1 | IMES Rescue based Shannon |
| ☐ EI-SAR | Sikorsky S-61N | 61143 | ex G-AYOM | IMES Rescue based Waterford |
| | | | | |
| ☐ EI-ICG | Sikorsky S-72A | 920150 | ex N150AL | ♦ |
| ☐ EI-MIP | Aérospatiale SA365N2 Dauphin 2 | 6119 | ex G-BLEY | |

## CITYJET        City-Ireland (WX/BCY)        Dublin (DUB)

| | | | | | |
|---|---|---|---|---|---|
| ☐ EI-RJA | Avro 146-RJ85 | E2329 | ex G-CDYK | Rathlin Island | |
| ☐ EI-RJB | Avro 146-RJ85 | E2330 | ex G-CEBS | Bere Island | |
| ☐ EI-RJC | Avro 146-RJ85 | E2333 | ex G-CEHA | Achill Island | |
| ☐ EI-RJD | Avro 146-RJ85 | E2334 | ex G-CEFL | Valentia Island | |
| ☐ EI-RJE | Avro 146-RJ85 | E2335 | ex G-CEBU | St MacDara's Island | |
| ☐ EI-RJF | Avro 146-RJ85 | E2337 | ex G-CEFN | Great Blasket Island | |
| ☐ EI-RJG | Avro 146-RJ85 | E2344 | ex G-CEHB | Sherkin Island | |
| ☐ EI-RJH | Avro 146-RJ85 | E2345 | ex G-CEIC | Inishturko/o | |
| ☐ EI-RJI | Avro 146-RJ85 | E2346 | ex (G-CDZP) | Skellig Michael | |
| ☐ EI-RJJ | Avro 146-RJ85 | E2347 | ex G-CEIF | Hare Island | |
| ☐ EI-RJK | Avro 146-RJ85 | E2348 | ex N523XJ | Collanmore Island | [NWI] |
| ☐ EI-RJL | Avro 146-RJ85 | E2349 | ex OH-SAQ | | [NWI] |
| ☐ EI-RJM | Avro 146-RJ85 | E2350 | ex OH-SAR | | [NWI] |
| ☐ EI-RJN | Avro 146-RJ85 | E2351 | ex N526XJ | Lake Isle of Inisheer | CityJet c/s |
| ☐ EI-RJO | Avro 146-RJ85 | E2352 | ex N527XJ | Inis Mor | |
| ☐ EI-RJR | Avro 146-RJ85 | E2364 | ex N530XJ | Tory Island | |
| ☐ EI-RJS | Avro 146-RJ85 | E2365 | ex N531XJ | Dursey Island | CityJet c/s |
| ☐ EI-RJT | Avro 146-RJ85 | E2366 | ex N532XJ | Inishbofin | CityJet c/s |
| ☐ EI-RJU | Avro 146-RJ85 | E2367 | ex N533XJ | Cape Clear | |
| ☐ EI-RJV | Avro 146-RJ85 | E2370 | ex N534XJ | Lambay Island | [NWI] |
| ☐ EI-RJW | Avro 146-RJ85 | E2371 | ex N535XJ | Garinish Island | |
| ☐ EI-RJX | Avro 146-RJ85 | E2372 | ex N536XJ | Scattery Island | |
| ☐ EI-RJY | Avro 146-RJ85 | E2307 | ex N502XJ | Inishcealtra | |
| ☐ EI-RJZ | Avro 146-RJ85 | E2326 | ex N512XJ | | |
| ☐ EI-WXA | Avro 146-RJ85 | E2310 | ex N503XJ | | |
| ☐ EI-WXB | Avro 146-RJ85 | E2311 | ex N504XJ | | [NWI] |

## IRISH HELICOPTERS        Dublin/Cork (DUB/ORK)

| | | | | |
|---|---|---|---|---|
| ☐ EI-BLD | MBB Bo.105DB | S-381 | ex D-HDLQ | |

## RYANAIR        Ryanair (FR/RYR)        Dublin (DUB)

| | | | | |
|---|---|---|---|---|
| ☐ EI-DAC | Boeing 737-8AS/W | 29938/1240 | | |
| ☐ EI-DAD | Boeing 737-8AS/W | 33544/1249 | | |
| ☐ EI-DAE | Boeing 737-8AS/W | 33545/1252 | | |
| ☐ EI-DAF | Boeing 737-8AS/W | 29939/1262 | | |
| ☐ EI-DAG | Boeing 737-8AS/W | 29940/1265 | | |
| ☐ EI-DAH | Boeing 737-8AS/W | 33546/1269 | | |
| ☐ EI-DAI | Boeing 737-8AS/W | 33547/1271 | | |
| ☐ EI-DAJ | Boeing 737-8AS/W | 33548/1274 | | |
| ☐ EI-DAK | Boeing 737-8AS/W | 33717/1310 | | |
| ☐ EI-DAL | Boeing 737-8AS/W | 33718/1311 | | |
| ☐ EI-DAM | Boeing 737-8AS/W | 33719/1312 | | |
| ☐ EI-DAN | Boeing 737-8AS/W | 33549/1361 | | |
| ☐ EI-DAO | Boeing 737-8AS/W | 33550/1366 | ex N1800B | |
| ☐ EI-DAP | Boeing 737-8AS/W | 33551/1368 | ex N6066U | |
| ☐ EI-DAR | Boeing 737-8AS/W | 33552/1371 | ex EI-DAQ | |
| ☐ EI-DAS | Boeing 737-8AS/W | 33553/1372 | ex EI-DAR | |
| ☐ EI-DCF | Boeing 737-8AS/W | 33804/1529 | | |
| ☐ EI-DCG | Boeing 737-8AS/W | 33806/1530 | | |
| ☐ EI-DCH | Boeing 737-8AS/W | 33566/1546 | | |
| ☐ EI-DCI | Boeing 737-8AS/W | 33567/1547 | | |
| ☐ EI-DCJ | Boeing 737-8AS/W | 33564/1562 | | |
| ☐ EI-DCK | Boeing 737-8AS/W | 33565/1563 | | |
| ☐ EI-DCL | Boeing 737-8AS/W | 33806/1576 | ex N1786B | Dreamliner c/s |
| ☐ EI-DCM | Boeing 737-8AS/W | 33807/1578 | | |
| ☐ EI-DCN | Boeing 737-8AS/W | 33808/1590 | ex N60436 | |
| ☐ EI-DCO | Boeing 737-8AS/W | 33809/1592 | | |
| ☐ EI-DCP | Boeing 737-8AS/W | 33810/1595 | | |
| ☐ EI-DCR | Boeing 737-8AS/W | 33811/1613 | | |

| | | | |
|---|---|---|---|
| ☐ EI-DCW | Boeing 737-8AS/W | 33568/1631 | |
| ☐ EI-DCX | Boeing 737-8AS/W | 33569/1635 | |
| ☐ EI-DCY | Boeing 737-8AS/W | 33570/1637 | |
| ☐ EI-DCZ | Boeing 737-8AS/W | 33815/1638 | |
| ☐ EI-DHA | Boeing 737-8AS/W | 33571/1642 | |
| ☐ EI-DHB | Boeing 737-8AS/W | 33572/1652 | |
| ☐ EI-DHC | Boeing 737-8AS/W | 33573/1655 | |
| ☐ EI-DHD | Boeing 737-8AS/W | 33816/1657 | ex N1784B |
| ☐ EI-DHE | Boeing 737-8AS/W | 33574/1658 | ex N1786B |
| ☐ EI-DHF | Boeing 737-8AS/W | 33575/1660 | ex N1782B |
| ☐ EI-DHG | Boeing 737-8AS/W | 33576/1670 | ex N1787B |
| ☐ EI-DHH | Boeing 737-8AS/W | 33817/1677 | |
| ☐ EI-DHI | Boeing 737-8AS/W | 33818/1685 | [PIK] |
| ☐ EI-DHJ | Boeing 737-8AS/W | 33819/1691 | [PIK] |
| ☐ EI-DHK | Boeing 737-8AS/W | 33820/1696 | |
| ☐ EI-DHM | Boeing 737-8AS/W | 33821/1698 | |
| ☐ EI-DHN | Boeing 737-8AS/W | 33577/1782 | |
| ☐ EI-DHO | Boeing 737-8AS/W | 33578/1792 | ex N1786B |
| ☐ EI-DHP | Boeing 737-8AS/W | 33579/1794 | |
| ☐ EI-DHR | Boeing 737-8AS/W | 33822/1798 | |
| ☐ EI-DHS | Boeing 737-8AS/W | 33580/1807 | |
| ☐ EI-DHT | Boeing 737-8AS/W | 33581/1809 | |
| ☐ EI-DHV | Boeing 737-8AS/W | 33582/1811 | |
| ☐ EI-DHW | Boeing 737-8AS/W | 33823/1819 | ex N1786B |
| ☐ EI-DHX | Boeing 737-8AS/W | 33585/1824 | ex N60436 |
| ☐ EI-DHY | Boeing 737-8AS/W | 33824/1826 | ex N1781B |
| ☐ EI-DHZ | Boeing 737-8AS/W | 33583/1834 | |
| ☐ EI-DLB | Boeing 737-8AS/W | 33584/1836 | ex N5573L |
| ☐ EI-DLC | Boeing 737-8AS/W | 33586/1844 | ex N1786B |
| ☐ EI-DLD | Boeing 737-8AS/W | 33825/1847 | |
| ☐ EI-DLE | Boeing 737-8AS/W | 33587/1864 | |
| ☐ EI-DLF | Boeing 737-8AS/W | 33588/1867 | |
| ☐ EI-DLG | Boeing 737-8AS/W | 33589/1869 | ex N1786B |
| ☐ EI-DLH | Boeing 737-8AS/W | 33590/1886 | |
| ☐ EI-DLI | Boeing 737-8AS/W | 33591/1894 | ex N1786B |
| ☐ EI-DLJ | Boeing 737-8AS/W | 34177/1899 | |
| ☐ EI-DLK | Boeing 737-8AS/W | 33592/1904 | ex N1786B |
| ☐ EI-DLL | Boeing 737-8AS/W | 33593/1914 | |
| ☐ EI-DLM | Boeing 737-8AS/W | 33594/1923 | |
| ☐ EI-DLN | Boeing 737-8AS/W | 33595/1926 | |
| ☐ EI-DLO | Boeing 737-8AS/W | 34178/1929 | |
| ☐ EI-DLR | Boeing 737-8AS/W | 33596/2057 | |
| ☐ EI-DLS | Boeing 737-8AS/W | 33621/2058 | |
| ☐ EI-DLT | Boeing 737-8AS/W | 33597/2060 | |
| ☐ EI-DLV | Boeing 737-8AS/W | 33598/2063 | |
| ☐ EI-DLW | Boeing 737-8AS/W | 33599/2078 | |
| ☐ EI-DLX | Boeing 737-8AS/W | 33600/2082 | |
| ☐ EI-DLY | Boeing 737-8AS/W | 33601/2088 | |
| ☐ EI-DLZ | Boeing 737-8AS/W | 33622/2101 | |
| ☐ EI-DPA | Boeing 737-8AS/W | 33602/2109 | |
| ☐ EI-DPB | Boeing 737-8AS/W | 33603/2112 | ex N1787B |
| ☐ EI-DPC | Boeing 737-8AS/W | 33604/2120 | ex N1786B |
| ☐ EI-DPD | Boeing 737-8AS/W | 33623/2123 | ex N1786B |
| ☐ EI-DPE | Boeing 737-8AS/W | 33605/2140 | ex N1787B |
| ☐ EI-DPF | Boeing 737-8AS/W | 33606/2158 | |
| ☐ EI-DPG | Boeing 737-8AS/W | 33607/2163 | |
| ☐ EI-DPH | Boeing 737-8AS/W | 33624/2168 | |
| ☐ EI-DPI | Boeing 737-8AS/W | 33608/2173 | |
| ☐ EI-DPJ | Boeing 737-8AS/W | 33609/2179 | |
| ☐ EI-DPK | Boeing 737-8AS/W | 33610/2183 | |
| ☐ EI-DPL | Boeing 737-8AS/W | 33611/2189 | |
| ☐ EI-DPM | Boeing 737-8AS/W | 33640/2198 | |
| ☐ EI-DPN | Boeing 737-8AS/W | 35549/2200 | ex N1787B |
| ☐ EI-DPO | Boeing 737-8AS/W | 33612/2207 | ex N1786B |
| ☐ EI-DPP | Boeing 737-8AS/W | 33613/2213 | |
| ☐ EI-DPR | Boeing 737-8AS/W | 33614/2219 | ex N1786B |
| ☐ EI-DPS | Boeing 737-8AS/W | 33641/2222 | |
| ☐ EI-DPT | Boeing 737-8AS/W | 35550/2227 | ex N1787B |
| ☐ EI-DPV | Boeing 737-8AS/W | 35551/2236 | ex N1779B |
| ☐ EI-DPW | Boeing 737-8AS/W | 35552/2263 | |
| ☐ EI-DPX | Boeing 737-8AS/W | 35553/2279 | |
| ☐ EI-DPY | Boeing 737-8AS/W | 33615/2375 | ex N1781B |
| ☐ EI-DPZ | Boeing 737-8AS/W | 33616/2376 | |
| ☐ EI-DWA | Boeing 737-8AS/W | 33617/2377 | |
| ☐ EI-DWB | Boeing 737-8AS/W | 36075/2382 | |
| ☐ EI-DWC | Boeing 737-8AS/W | 36076/2384 | |
| ☐ EI-DWD | Boeing 737-8AS/W | 33642/2389 | ex N1781B |
| ☐ EI-DWE | Boeing 737-8AS/W | 36074/2391 | |
| ☐ EI-DWF | Boeing 737-8AS/W | 33619/2396 | |
| ☐ EI-DWG | Boeing 737-8AS/W | 33620/2397 | |
| ☐ EI-DWH | Boeing 737-8AS/W | 33637/2408 | ex N1787B |
| ☐ EI-DWI | Boeing 737-8AS/W | 33643/2410 | |

| | | | |
|---|---|---|---|
| ☐ EI-DWJ | Boeing 737-8AS/W | 36077/2411 | |
| ☐ EI-DWK | Boeing 737-8AS/W | 36078/2415 | ex N1786B |
| ☐ EI-DWL | Boeing 737-8AS/W | 33618/2416 | ex N1787B |
| ☐ EI-DWM | Boeing 737-8AS/W | 36080/2430 | |
| ☐ EI-DWO | Boeing 737-8AS/W | 36079/2440 | |
| ☐ EI-DWP | Boeing 737-8AS/W | 36082/2443 | |
| ☐ EI-DWR | Boeing 737-8AS/W | 36081/2448 | ex N1786B |
| ☐ EI-DWS | Boeing 737-8AS/W | 33625/2472 | ex N1786B |
| ☐ EI-DWT | Boeing 737-8AS/W | 33626/2489 | |
| ☐ EI-DWV | Boeing 737-8AS/W | 33627/2492 | |
| ☐ EI-DWW | Boeing 737-8AS/W | 33629/2507 | ex N1781B |
| ☐ EI-DWX | Boeing 737-8AS/W | 33630/2508 | |
| ☐ EI-DWY | Boeing 737-8AS/W | 33638/2518 | ex N1781B |
| ☐ EI-DWZ | Boeing 737-8AS/W | 33628/2520 | ex N1796B |
| ☐ EI-DYA | Boeing 737-8AS/W | 33631/2529 | ex N1786B |
| ☐ EI-DYB | Boeing 737-8AS/W | 33633/2542 | |
| ☐ EI-DYC | Boeing 737-8AS/W | 36567/2543 | ex N1787B |
| ☐ EI-DYD | Boeing 737-8AS/W | 33632/2544 | ex N1786B |
| ☐ EI-DYE | Boeing 737-8AS/W | 36568/2548 | |
| ☐ EI-DYF | Boeing 737-8AS/W | 36569/2549 | ex N1786B |
| ☐ EI-DYH | Boeing 737-8AS/W | 36570/2573 | |
| ☐ EI-DYI | Boeing 737-8AS/W | 36571/2574 | |
| ☐ EI-DYJ | Boeing 737-8AS/W | 36572/2580 | |
| ☐ EI-DYK | Boeing 737-8AS/W | 36573/2581 | |
| ☐ EI-DYL | Boeing 737-8AS/W | 36574/2635 | |
| ☐ EI-DYM | Boeing 737-8AS/W | 36575/2636 | |
| ☐ EI-DYN | Boeing 737-8AS/W | 36576/2367 | |
| ☐ EI-DYO | Boeing 737-8AS/W | 33636/2728 | |
| ☐ EI-DYP | Boeing 737-8AS/W | 37515/2729 | |
| ☐ EI-DYR | Boeing 737-8AS/W | 37513/2734 | |
| ☐ EI-DYS | Boeing 737-8AS/W | 37514/2735 | |
| ☐ EI-DYT | Boeing 737-8AS/W | 33634/2745 | |
| ☐ EI-DYV | Boeing 737-8AS/W | 37512/2746 | |
| ☐ EI-DYW | Boeing 737-8AS/W | 33635/2747 | |
| ☐ EI-DYX | Boeing 737-8AS/W | 37517/2754 | |
| ☐ EI-DYY | Boeing 737-8AS/W | 37521/2755 | ex N1787B |
| ☐ EI-DYZ | Boeing 737-8AS/W | 37518/2760 | |
| ☐ EI-EBA | Boeing 737-8AS/W | 37516/2761 | |
| ☐ EI-EBB | Boeing 737-8AS/W | 37519/2779 | ex N1787B |
| ☐ EI-EBC | Boeing 737-8AS/W | 37520/2780 | ex N1795B |
| ☐ EI-EBD | Boeing 737-8AS/W | 37522/2781 | ex N1796B |
| ☐ EI-EBE | Boeing 737-8AS/W | 37523/2788 | |
| ☐ EI-EBF | Boeing 737-8AS/W | 37524/2791 | ex N1796B |
| ☐ EI-EBG | Boeing 737-8AS/W | 37525/2792 | |
| ☐ EI-EBH | Boeing 737-8AS/W | 37526/2797 | |
| ☐ EI-EBI | Boeing 737-8AS/W | 37527/2798 | |
| ☐ EI-EBK | Boeing 737-8AS/W | 37528/2807 | |
| ☐ EI-EBL | Boeing 737-8AS/W | 37529/2808 | ex N1796B |
| ☐ EI-EBM | Boeing 737-8AS/W | 35002/2839 | ex N1787B |
| ☐ EI-EBN | Boeing 737-8AS/W | 35003/2840 | |
| ☐ EI-EBO | Boeing 737-8AS/W | 35004/2843 | ex N1796B |
| ☐ EI-EBP | Boeing 737-8AS/W | 37531/2844 | |
| ☐ EI-EBR | Boeing 737-8AS/W | 37530/2856 | ex N1779B |
| ☐ EI-EBS | Boeing 737-8AS/W | 35001/2857 | ex N1786B |
| ☐ EI-EBT | Boeing 737-8AS/W | 35000/2858 | |
| ☐ EI-EBV | Boeing 737-8AS/W | 35009/2872 | |
| ☐ EI-EBW | Boeing 737-8AS/W | 35010/2873 | |
| ☐ EI-EBX | Boeing 737-8AS/W | 35007/2882 | |
| ☐ EI-EBY | Boeing 737-8AS/W | 35006/2886 | |
| ☐ EI-EBZ | Boeing 737-8AS/W | 35008/2887 | |
| ☐ EI-EFA | Boeing 737-8AS/W | 35005/2892 | ex N1786B |
| ☐ EI-EFB | Boeing 737-8AS/W | 37532/2893 | |
| ☐ EI-EFC | Boeing 737-8AS/W | 35015/2901 | |
| ☐ EI-EFD | Boeing 737-8AS/W | 35011/2903 | ex N1787B |
| ☐ EI-EFE | Boeing 737-8AS/W | 37533/2905 | |
| ☐ EI-EFF | Boeing 737-8AS/W | 35016/2917 | ex N1786B |
| ☐ EI-EFG | Boeing 737-8AS/W | 35014/2921 | ex N1786B |
| ☐ EI-EFH | Boeing 737-8AS/W | 35012/2923 | ex N1787B |
| ☐ EI-EFI | Boeing 737-8AS/W | 35013/2924 | ex N1786B |
| ☐ EI-EFJ | Boeing 737-8AS/W | 37536/2936 | ex N1786B |
| ☐ EI-EFK | Boeing 737-8AS/W | 37537/2948 | ex N1786B |
| ☐ EI-EFL | Boeing 737-8AS/W | 37534/2958 | |
| ☐ EI-EFM | Boeing 737-8AS/W | 37535/2960 | ex N1787B |
| ☐ EI-EFN | Boeing 737-8AS/W | 37538/2967 | ex N1787B |
| ☐ EI-EFO | Boeing 737-8AS/W | 37539/2978 | |
| ☐ EI-EFP | Boeing 737-8AS/W | 37540/2979 | |
| ☐ EI-EFR | Boeing 737-8AS/W | 37541/3012 | ex N1786B |
| ☐ EI-EFS | Boeing 737-8AS/W | 37542/3021 | |
| ☐ EI-EFT | Boeing 737-8AS/W | 37543/3023 | ex N1787B |
| ☐ EI-EFV | Boeing 737-8AS/W | 35017/3052 | ex N60659 |
| ☐ EI-EFW | Boeing 737-8AS/W | 35018/3078 | ex N1786B |
| ☐ EI-EFX | Boeing 737-8AS/W | 35019/3079 | ex N1787B |

| | | | |
|---|---|---|---|
| ☐ EI-EFY | Boeing 737-8AS/W | 35020/3084 | ex N1786B |
| ☐ EI-EFZ | Boeing 737-8AS/W | 38489/3089 | ex N1787B |
| ☐ EI-EGA | Boeing 737-8AS/W | 38490/3096 | ex N1787B |
| ☐ EI-EGB | Boeing 737-8AS/W | 38491/3097 | ex N1787B |
| ☐ EI-EGC | Boeing 737-8AS/W | 38492/3099 | ex N1786B |
| ☐ EI-EGD | Boeing 737-8AS/W | 34981/3420 | |
| ☐ EI-EKA | Boeing 737-8AS/W | 35022/3139 | |
| ☐ EI-EKB | Boeing 737-8AS/W | 38494/3141 | |
| ☐ EI-EKC | Boeing 737-8AS/W | 38495/3143 | |
| ☐ EI-EKD | Boeing 737-8AS/W | 35024/3146 | |
| ☐ EI-EKE | Boeing 737-8AS/W | 35023/3148 | |
| ☐ EI-EKF | Boeing 737-8AS/W | 35025/3152 | |
| ☐ EI-EKG | Boeing 737-8AS/W | 35021/3161 | |
| ☐ EI-EKH | Boeing 737-8AS/W | 38493/3162 | |
| ☐ EI-EKI | Boeing 737-8AS/W | 38496/3168 | ex N1786B |
| ☐ EI-EKJ | Boeing 737-8AS/W | 38497/3173 | ex N1796B |
| ☐ EI-EKK | Boeing 737-8AS/W | 38500/3174 | ex N1787B |
| ☐ EI-EKL | Boeing 737-8AS/W | 38498/3179 | ex N1796B |
| ☐ EI-EKM | Boeing 737-8AS/W | 38499/3181 | ex N1786B |
| ☐ EI-EKN | Boeing 737-8AS/W | 35026/3187 | ex N1787B |
| ☐ EI-EKO | Boeing 737-8AS/W | 35027/3198 | ex N1795B |
| ☐ EI-EKP | Boeing 737-8AS/W | 35028/3199 | ex N1786B |
| ☐ EI-EKR | Boeing 737-8AS/W | 38503/3202 | ex N1786B |
| ☐ EI-EKS | Boeing 737-8AS/W | 38504/3203 | ex N1796B |
| ☐ EI-EKT | Boeing 737-8AS/W | 38505/3206 | ex N1786B |
| ☐ EI-EKV | Boeing 737-8AS/W | 38507/3211 | |
| ☐ EI-EKW | Boeing 737-8AS/W | 38506/3221 | ex N1786B |
| ☐ EI-EKX | Boeing 737-8AS/W | 35030/3222 | ex N1787B |
| ☐ EI-EKY | Boeing 737-8AS/W | 35031/3230 | |
| ☐ EI-EKZ | Boeing 737-8AS/W | 38508/3234 | |
| ☐ EI-EMA | Boeing 737-8AS/W | 35032/3240 | |
| ☐ EI-EMB | Boeing 737-8AS/W | 35811/3241 | ex N1796B |
| ☐ EI-EMC | Boeing 737-8AS/W | 38510/3246 | |
| ☐ EI-EMD | Boeing 737-8AS/W | 38509/3248 | ex N1786B |
| ☐ EI-EME | Boeing 737-8AS/W | 35029/3254 | |
| ☐ EI-EMF | Boeing 737-8AS/W | 34978/3256 | ex N1786B |
| ☐ EI-EMH | Boeing 737-8AS/W | 34974/3262 | |
| ☐ EI-EMI | Boeing 737-8AS/W | 34979/3263 | |
| ☐ EI-EMJ | Boeing 737-8AS/W | 34975/3271 | ex N1786B |
| ☐ EI-EMK | Boeing 737-8AS/W | 38512/3272 | ex N1786B |
| ☐ EI-EML | Boeing 737-8AS/W | 38513/3283 | ex N1786B |
| ☐ EI-EMM | Boeing 737-8AS/W | 35814/3284 | ex N1786B |
| ☐ EI-EMN | Boeing 737-8AS/W | 35815/3285 | |
| ☐ EI-EMO | Boeing 737-8AS/W | 40283/3318 | |
| ☐ EI-EMP | Boeing 737-8AS/W | 40285/3322 | ex N1787B |
| ☐ EI-EMR | Boeing 737-8AS/W | 40284/3323 | |
| ☐ EI-ENA | Boeing 737-8AS/W | 34983/3416 | ex N1796B |
| ☐ EI-ENB | Boeing 737-8AS/W | 40289/3418 | |
| ☐ EI-ENC | Boeing 737-8AS/W | 34980/3419 | |
| ☐ EI-ENE | Boeing 737-8AS/W | 34976/3428 | |
| ☐ EI-ENF | Boeing 737-8AS/W | 35034/3451 | |
| ☐ EI-ENG | Boeing 737-8AS/W | 34977/3453 | ex N1787B |
| ☐ EI-ENH | Boeing 737-8AS/W | 35033/3454 | ex N1796B |
| ☐ EI-ENI | Boeing 737-8AS/W | 40300/3514 | |
| ☐ EI-ENJ | Boeing 737-8AS/W | 40301/3514 | ex N1796B |
| ☐ EI-ENK | Boeing 737-8AS/W | 40303/3524 | |
| ☐ EI-ENL | Boeing 737-8AS/W | 35037/3527 | |
| ☐ EI-ENM | Boeing 737-8AS/W | 35038/3528 | |
| ☐ EI-ENN | Boeing 737-8AS/W | 35036/3533 | |
| ☐ EI-ENO | Boeing 737-8AS/W | 40302/3534 | |
| ☐ EI-ENP | Boeing 737-8AS/W | 40304/3535 | |
| ☐ EI-ENR | Boeing 737-8AS/W | 35041/3538 | |
| ☐ EI-ENS | Boeing 737-8AS/W | 40307/3541 | ♦ |
| ☐ EI-ENT | Boeing 737-8AS/W | 35040/3544 | ♦ |
| ☐ EI-ENV | Boeing 737-8AS/W | 35039/3546 | ♦ |
| ☐ EI-ENW | Boeing 737-8AS/W | 40306/3551 | ♦ |
| ☐ EI-ENX | Boeing 737-8AS/W | 40305/3556 | ♦ |
| ☐ EI-ENY | Boeing 737-8AS/W | 35042/3559 | ♦ |
| ☐ EI-ENZ | Boeing 737-8AS/W | 40308/3561 | ♦ |
| ☐ EI-EPA | Boeing 737-8AS/W | 34987/3568 | ♦ |
| ☐ EI-EPB | Boeing 737-8AS/W | 34986/3570 | ♦ |
| ☐ EI-EPC | Boeing 737-8AS/W | 40312/3574 | ♦ |
| ☐ EI-EPD | Boeing 737-8AS/W | 40310/3578 | ♦ |
| ☐ EI-EPE | Boeing 737-8AS/W | 34984/3587 | ♦ |
| ☐ EI-EPF | Boeing 737-8AS/W | 40309/3593 | ♦ |
| ☐ EI-EPG | Boeing 737-8AS/W | 34985/3597 | ♦ |
| ☐ EI-EPH | Boeing 737-8AS/W | 40311/3599 | ♦ |
| ☐ EI-ESL | Boeing 737-8AS/W | 34988/3767 | ex N7235C ♦ |
| ☐ EI-ESM | Boeing 737-8AS/W | 34992/3772 | ex N441BA ♦ |
| ☐ EI-ESN | Boeing 737-8AS/W | 34991/3780 | ex N742BA ♦ |
| ☐ EI-ESO | Boeing 737-8AS/W | 34989/3787 | ex N734BA ♦ |
| ☐ EI-ESP | Boeing 737-8AS/W | 3499/3789 | ex N751BA ♦ |

| | | | | |
|---|---|---|---|---|
| ☐ EI-ESR | Boeing 737-8AS/W | 34995/3795 | ex N759BA | ♦ |
| ☐ EI-ESS | Boeing 737-8AS/W | 35043/3800 | ex N760BA | ♦ |
| ☐ EI-EST | Boeing 737-8AS/W | 34994/3804 | ex N761BA | ♦ |
| ☐ EI-ESV | Boeing 737-8AS/W | 34993/3814 | ex N762BA | ♦ |
| ☐ EI-ESW | Boeing 737-8AS/W | 34997/3821 | | ♦ |
| ☐ EI-ESX | Boeing 737-8AS/W | 34998/3822 | | ♦ |
| ☐ EI-ESY | Boeing 737-8AS/W | 34999/3829 | | ♦ |
| ☐ EI-ESZ | Boeing 737-8AS/W | 34996/3842 | | ♦ |
| ☐ EI-EVA | Boeing 737-8AS/W | 40288/3884 | | ♦ |
| ☐ EI-EVB | Boeing 737-8AS/W | 34982/3886 | | ♦ |
| ☐ EI-EVC | Boeing 737-8AS/W | 40286/3905 | | ♦ |
| ☐ EI-EVD | Boeing 737-8AS/W | 40287/3908 | | ♦ |
| ☐ EI-EVE | Boeing 737-8AS/W | 35035/3920 | | ♦ |
| ☐ EI-EVF | Boeing 737-8AS/W | 402913926 | | ♦ |
| ☐ Ei-EVG | Boeing 737-8AS/W | 40292/3928 | | ♦ |
| ☐ EI-EVH | Boeing 737-8AS/W | 40290/3938 | | ♦ |
| ☐ EI-EVI | Boeing 737-8AS/W | 38502/3945 | | ♦ |
| ☐ EI-EVJ | Boeing 737-8AS/W | 38501/3953 | | ♦ |
| ☐ EI-EVK | Boeing 737-8AS/W | 40298/3958 | | ♦ |
| ☐ EI-EVL | Boeing 737-8AS/W | 40299/3974 | | ♦ |
| ☐ EI-EVM | Boeing 737-8AS/W | 40296/3983 | | ♦ |
| ☐ EI-EVN | Boeing 737-8AS/W | 40294/3992 | | ♦ |
| ☐ EI-EVO | Boeing 737-8AS/W | 40297 | | o/o♦ |
| ☐ EI-EVP | Boeing 737-8AS/W | 40293 | | o/o♦ |

## EK- ARMENIA (Republic of Armenia)

### AIR ARMENIA — Air Armenia (QN/ARR) — Yerevan-Zvartnots (EVN)

| | | | | |
|---|---|---|---|---|
| ☐ D-ABCJ | Airbus A321-211 | 5126 | ex | o/o♦ |

### AIR ARMENIA CARGO

| | | | | |
|---|---|---|---|---|
| ☐ EK-11001 | Antonov An-12BK | 8346107 | ex CCCP-11244 | ♦ |
| ☐ EK-11810 | Antonov An-12BP | 5342908 | ex UR-11810 | |
| ☐ EK-12104 | Antonov An-12BK | 8346104 | ex CCCP-12110 | ♦ |
| ☐ EK-12112 | Antonov An-12TB | 01347907 | | >Airmark Avn♦ |
| ☐ EK-12335 | Antonov An-12BP | 5343305 | | ♦ |
| ☐ EK-32500 | Antonov An-32B | 2009 | ex 9L-LFP | ♦ |
| ☐ EK-65848 | Tupolev Tu-134A | 23136 | | [EVN]♦ |

### AIR HIGHNESSES — (HNS) — Yerevan-Zvartnots (EVN)

| | | | | |
|---|---|---|---|---|
| ☐ EK-11986 | Antonov An-12B | 401901 | | ♦ |
| ☐ EK-12006 | Antonov An-12B | 01348006 | ex UR-CGR | |
| ☐ EK-12335 | Antonov An-12BP | 5343305 | | ♦ |
| ☐ EK-12803 | Antonov An-12B | 1347803 | | ♦ |
| ☐ EK-12908 | Antonov An-12B | 7344908 | ex EK-11029 | |
| ☐ EK-76310 | Ilyushin Il-76T | 1013409310 | ex RDPL-34148 | |

### ARARAT INTERNATIONAL AIRLINES — (RRN) — Yerevan-Zvartnots (EVN)

| | | | | |
|---|---|---|---|---|
| ☐ EK-82221 | McDonnell-Douglas MD-82 | 53221/2079 | ex LZ-LDE | >IRK♦ |
| ☐ EK-82224 | McDonnell-Douglas MD-82 | 53224/2084 | ex LZ-LDB | >IRK |
| ☐ EK-82226 | McDonnell-Douglas MD-82 | 53226/2087 | ex I—DATH | >IRK♦ |
| ☐ EK-82228 | McDonnell-Douglas MD-82 | 53228/2104 | ex LZ-LDM | ♦ |
| ☐ EK-82229 | McDonnell-Douglas MD-82 | 53229/2105 | ex LZ-LDL | >IRK♦ |
| ☐ EK-82524 | McDonnell-Douglas MD-82 | 49524/1746 | ex B-2140 | >TBM♦ |

### ARK AIRWAYS

| | | | | |
|---|---|---|---|---|
| ☐ EK-74739 | Boeing 747-281F | 23139/608 | ex ES- | ♦ |
| ☐ EK-76555 | Ilyushin Il-76TD | 1033416515 | ex UP-I7616 | |

### ARMAVIA — Armavia (U8/RNV) — Yerevan-Zvartnots (EVN)

| | | | | | |
|---|---|---|---|---|---|
| ☐ EK-RA01 | Airbus A319-132 | 0913 | ex HZ-NAS | | Op for Govt |
| ☐ EK-20014 | Canadair CRJ-200LR | 7282 | ex D-ACJI | Sergey Mergelyan | ♦ |
| ☐ EK-20017 | Canadair CRJ-200LR | 7431 | ex D-ACHF | | ♦ |
| ☐ EK-20018 | Canadair CRJ-200LR | 7499 | ex D-ACHK | | ♦ |
| ☐ EK-42362 | Yakovlev Yak-42D | 4520424811431 | ex UR-CDU | | |
| ☐ EK-42470 | Yakovlev Yak-42D | 4520424116677 | ex RA-42444 | | |
| ☐ EK-65072 | Tupolev Tu-134A-3 | 49972 | ex CCCP-65072 | | op for Govt |
| ☐ EK-73771 | Boeing 737-55S | 28471/2885 | ex OK-CGK | | >Slovakian A/L |
| ☐ EK-73772 | Boeing 737-55S | 28472/3004 | ex OK-DGL | | >CSA |
| ☐ EK-73775 | Boeing 737-55S | 28475/3096 | ex OK-EGO | | |
| ☐ EK-86118 | Ilyushin Il-86 | 51483209086 | ex CCCP-86118 | | |

| | | | | | |
|---|---|---|---|---|---|
| ☐ EK-95015 | Sukhoi Superjet 100 | 95007 | | Yuri Gagarin | o/o |
| ☐ EK-95016 | Sukhoi Superjet 100 | 95009 | | | o/o |

## AYK AVIA
**Yerevan-Zvartnots (EVN)**

| | | | | |
|---|---|---|---|---|
| ☐ EK-17104 | Mil Mi-17 | 103M04 | ex Bulgaria 404 | ♦ |
| ☐ EK-17107 | Mil Mi-17 | 103M07 | ex Bulgaria 407 | ♦ |
| ☐ EK-20042 | Beech 200C Super King Air | BL-42 | | ♦ |
| ☐ EK-32410 | Antonov An-32 | 2416 | ex 9L-LFU | |
| ☐ EK-74043 | Antonov An-74-200 | 36547096923 | ex RA-74043 | |
| ☐ EK-76707 | Ilyushin Il-76TD | 0073410292 | | ♦ |

## BLUE SKY
**Blue Armenia (BLM)**     **Yerevan-Zvartnots (EVN)**

| | | | | |
|---|---|---|---|---|
| ☐ EK-74713 | Boeing 747-3B3 (SCD) | 23413/632 | ex F-GETA | >IRM |
| ☐ EP-MNA | Boeing 747-422 | 24383/811 | ex EK-74783 | wfs♦ |
| ☐ EP-MNB | Boeing 747-422 | 24363/740 | ex EK-74763 | wfs♦ |
| ☐ EP-MNC | Boeing 747-422 | 26879/973 | ex EK-74779 | >IRM |
| ☐ EP-MNE | Boeing 747-3B3 | 23480/641 | ex EK-74780 | >IRM♦ |

## CENTRAL AIRWAYS

| | | | | |
|---|---|---|---|---|
| ☐ EK-26443 | Antonov An-26 | 17311705 | ex ER-AFL | |

## NAVIGATOR AIRLINES

| | | | | |
|---|---|---|---|---|
| ☐ EK-26440 | Antonov An-26 | 57303504 | ex RA-26640 | |

## PHOENIX AVIA
**Phoenix Armenia (PHY)**     **Yerevan-Zvartnots (EVN)**

| | | | | |
|---|---|---|---|---|
| ☐ EK-76442 | Ilyushin Il-76TD | 1023414450 | | ♦ |
| ☐ EK-76464 | Ilyushin Il-76TD | 0023437090 | ex RA-76464 | |

## SOUTH AIRLINES
**South (STH)**     **Sharjah (SHJ)**

| | | | | |
|---|---|---|---|---|
| ☐ EK-26407 | Antonov An-26 | 6407 | | ♦ |
| ☐ EK-26878 | Antonov An-26 | 8302 | ex 3X-GFH | ♦ |
| ☐ EK-72101 | Antonov An-72-100 | 36572040548 | ex 4L-VAS | |
| ☐ EK-74045 | Antonov An-74-200 | 36547098966 | ex RA-74060 | |
| ☐ EK-76717 | Ilyushin Il-76TD | 0043450484 | ex UR-76581 | |
| ☐ EK-76727 | Ilyushin Il-76TD | 0063467021 | ex UR-76681 | |
| ☐ EK-76737 | Ilyushin Il-76MD | 0083483502 | ex UR-76778 | |

## TARON AVIA
**(TRV)**

| | | | | |
|---|---|---|---|---|
| ☐ EK-11112 | Antonov An-12BP | 5343307 | | ♦ |
| ☐ EK-12005 | Antonov An-12BP | 5343005 | ex XU-U4C | |
| ☐ EK-12129 | Antonov An-12BP | 5342903 | ex EK-11772 | |
| ☐ EK-76643 | Ilyushin Il-76TD | 0083488643 | ex UR-UCD | |
| ☐ TN-AIT | Boeing 737-2T5 | 22395/729 | ex EK-73777 | ♦ |

## VERTIR
**(VRZ)**

| | | | | |
|---|---|---|---|---|
| ☐ EK-30064 | Airbus A300B4-605R | 464 | ex HS-TAG | [THR]♦ |
| ☐ EK-30098 | Airbus A300B4-610 | 398 | ex HS-TAF | [THR]♦ |
| ☐ EK-31095 | Airbus A310-304 | 595 | ex C-GTSI | >IRM |
| ☐ EK-32303 | Airbus A320-211 | 303 | ex EC-ICU | >IRA♦ |
| ☐ EK-32312 | Airbus A320-211 | 312 | ex EC-ICV | >IRA♦ |
| ☐ EK-74711 | Boeing 747SR-81 | 22711/559 | ex SX-DCB | wfs |

## VETERAN AIRLINE
**Veteran (VPB)**     **Yerevan-Zvartnots (EVN)**

| | | | | | |
|---|---|---|---|---|---|
| ☐ EK-74723 | Boeing 747-281FM | 23813/683 | ex N283RF | | ♦ |
| ☐ EK-74798 | Boeing 747-281BSF | 23698/667 | ex N288RF | | ♦ |
| ☐ EK-74799 | Boeing 747-281BF | 24399/750 | ex N281RF | >SVA | ♦ |
| ☐ EK-76381 | Ilyushin Il-76MD | 1033418596 | ex ST-ATI | | ♦ |
| ☐ EK-76401 | Ilyushin Il-76MD | 1023412399 | | | ♦ |
| ☐ EK-76783 | Ilyushin Il-76MD | 9903498974 | | | ♦ |

# EP-    IRAN (Islamic Republic of Iran)

## ARIA AIR
**Aria (IRX)**     **Lar/Bandar Abbas (LRR/BND)**

| | | | | |
|---|---|---|---|---|
| ☐ EP-EAF | Fokker 50 | 20235 | ex D-AFKP | |
| ☐ EP-EAH | Fokker 50 | 20234 | ex D-AFKO | |

## ATA AIR
**(IE/TBZ)**

| | | | | |
|---|---|---|---|---|
| ☐ UR-CDN | McDonnell-Douglas MD-83 | 53520/2137 | ex TC-OAV | <KHO |

| | | | | | |
|---|---|---|---|---|---|
| ☐ UR-CHM | McDonnell-Douglas MD-83 | 53465/2093 | ex TC-OAS | | <KHO♦ |
| ☐ UR-CHP | McDonnell-Douglas MD-83 | 53466/2101 | ex TC-OAT | | <KHO |
| ☐ UR-CHQ | McDonnell-Douglas MD-83 | 53488/2134 | ex TC-OAU | | <KHO |
| ☐ UR-CJC | McDonnell-Douglas MD-83 | 49986/1842 | ex 9A-CDB | | <KHO♦ |
| | | | | | |
| ☐ UR-CFW | Airbus A320-231 | 0361 | ex N361DA | | <KHO♦ |
| ☐ UR-CJD | Airbus A320-231 | 0362 | ex N362BV | | <KHO♦ |
| ☐ UR-CJF | Airbus A320-231 | 0405 | ex N405MX | | <KHO♦ |

### CASPIAN AIRLINES — Caspian (RV/CPN) — Rasht (RAS)

| | | | | | |
|---|---|---|---|---|---|
| ☐ EP-CPN | Tupolev Tu-154M | 91A898 | ex EP-JAZ | | |
| ☐ EP-CPO | Tupolev Tu-154M | 91A899 | ex EP-ARG | | |
| ☐ EP-CPS | Tupolev Tu-154M | 93A957 | ex UN-85775 | | |
| ☐ EP-CPT | Tupolev Tu-154M | 93A964 | | | ♦ |
| ☐ EP-CPU | McDonnell-Douglas MD-83 | 53149/1817 | ex 4L-YAA | | ♦ |
| ☐ UR-BHJ | McDonnell-Douglas MD-83 | 53184/2088 | ex TC-AKL | | <BKV |
| ☐ UR-CBO | McDonnell-Douglas MD-82 | 49483/1314 | ex RP-C2986 | | <KHO♦ |

### ERAM AIR — Eram Air (YE/IRY) — Tabriz (TBZ)

| | | | | | |
|---|---|---|---|---|---|
| ☐ EP-EKC | Tupolev Tu-154M | 89A799 | ex EP-MCE | | |
| ☐ EP-EKD | Tupolev Tu-154M | 89A800 | | | |
| ☐ EP-EKE | Tupolev Tu-154M | 92A940 | ex EP-MCK | | ♦ |

### FARS AIR — (QFZ) — Qeshm-Dayrestan (GSM)

| | | | | |
|---|---|---|---|---|
| ☐ EP-QFA | Yakovlev Yak-42D | 4520422007018 | ex ER-YCE | |
| ☐ EP-QFB | Yakovlev Yak-42D | 4520422003019 | ex ER-YCF | |

### HELICOPTER SERVICES — Tehran

| | | | | |
|---|---|---|---|---|
| ☐ EP-HEB | Aérospatiale AS350B2 Ecureuil | 3050 | ex F-WQDA | |
| ☐ EP-HEC | Aérospatiale AS350B3 Ecureuil | 3621 | ex F-WQDD | |
| ☐ EP-HED | Aérospatiale AS350B3 Ecureuil | 3629 | ex F-WQDJ | |
| ☐ EP-HEE | Aérospatiale AS350B3 Ecureuil | 3644 | ex F-WQDK | |
| ☐ EP-HEF | Aérospatiale AS350B3 Ecureuil | 3655 | | |
| ☐ EP-HEG | Aérospatiale AS350B3 Ecureuil | 3658 | | |
| ☐ EP-HEH | Aérospatiale AS350B3 Ecureuil | 3668 | | |
| | | | | |
| ☐ EP-HBJ | Bell 212 | 30504 | ex N8112J | |
| ☐ EP-HDV | Aérospatiale AS365N2 Dauphin 2 | 6467 | ex F-GLMZ | |
| ☐ EP-HTN | Bell 212 | 30885 | ex N5009K | |
| ☐ EP-HTO | Bell 205A-1 | 30163 | ex N64743 | |
| ☐ EP-HTQ | Bell 205A-1 | 30189 | ex N90039 | |
| ☐ EP-HUA | Bell 212 | 31176 | ex HB-XPO | |

### IRAN AIR — Iranair (IR/IRA) — Tehran-Mehrabad (THR)

| | | | | | |
|---|---|---|---|---|---|
| ☐ EP-IBA | Airbus A300B4-605R | 723 | ex F-WWAL | | |
| ☐ EP-IBB | Airbus A300B4-605R | 727 | ex F-WWAZ | | |
| ☐ EP-IBC | Airbus A300B4-605R | 632 | ex SX-BEK | | |
| ☐ EP-IBD | Airbus A300B4-605R | 696 | ex SX-BEL | | |
| ☐ EP-IBG | Airbus A300B4-203F | 299 | ex EP-MDA | | |
| ☐ EP-IBH | Airbus A300B4-203F | 302 | ex EP-MDB | | |
| ☐ EP-IBI | Airbus A300B4-2C | 151 | ex TC-FLK | | |
| ☐ EP-IBJ | Airbus A300B4-2C | 256 | ex TC-FLL | | |
| ☐ EP-IBS | Airbus A300B2-203 | 080 | ex F-WZEO | | |
| ☐ EP-IBT | Airbus A300B2-203 | 185 | ex F-WZMB | | |
| ☐ EP-IBV | Airbus A300B2-203 | 187 | ex F-WZMD | | |
| ☐ EP-IBZ | Airbus A300B2-203 | 226 | ex F-WZME | | |
| ☐ EP-ICE | Airbus A300B4-203F | 139 | ex TC-KZT | | |
| ☐ EP-ICF | Airbus A300B4-203 | 173 | ex TC-KZU | | ♦ |
| | | | | | |
| ☐ EP-IEB | Airbus A320-232 | 0575 | ex EP-MHN | | |
| ☐ EP-IEC | Airbus A320-232 | 0857 | ex EP-MHJ | | [THR] |
| ☐ EP-IED | Airbus A320-212 | 0345 | ex VP-CBZ | | |
| ☐ EP-IEE | Airbus A320-211 | 0303 | ex EK-32303 | | <VRZ |
| ☐ EP-IEF | Airbus A320-211 | 0312 | ex EK-32312 | | <VRZ |
| ☐ EP-IEG | Airbus A320-211 | 2054 | ex EK-32054 | | |
| | | | | | |
| ☐ EP-IAA | Boeing 747SP-86 | 20998/275 | | | |
| ☐ EP-IAB | Boeing 747SP-86 | 20999/278 | | Khorasan | |
| ☐ EP-IAC | Boeing 747SP-86 | 21093/307 | | Fars | |
| ☐ EP-IAD | Boeing 747SP-86 | 21758/371 | ex N1800B | Khorasan | |
| ☐ EP-IAG | Boeing 747-286M | 21217/291 | | Azarabadegan | |
| ☐ EP-IAH | Boeing 747-286M | 21218/300 | | Khuzestan | |
| ☐ EP-IAI | Boeing 747-230M | 22670/550 | ex EP-AUA | | |
| ☐ EP-IAM | Boeing 747-186B | 21759/381 | ex N5573P | | |
| ☐ EP-ICD | Boeing 747-21AC | 24134/712 | ex TC-AKZ | | |
| ☐ EP- | Boeing 747-338 | 23408/638 | ex C5-SAM | | [THR]♦ |

| ☐ EP-CFD | Fokker 100 | 11442 | ex PT-MRI | |
| ☐ EP-CFE | Fokker 100 | 11422 | ex F-GRMV | |
| ☐ EP-CFH | Fokker 100 | 11443 | ex F-GSTG | |
| ☐ EP-CFI | Fokker 100 | 11511 | ex PT-MRU | |
| ☐ EP-CFJ | Fokker 100 | 11516 | ex PT-MRV | |
| ☐ EP-CFK | Fokker 100 | 11518 | ex PT-MRW | |
| ☐ EP-CFL | Fokker 100 | 11343 | ex PT-MRY | |
| ☐ EP-CFM | Fokker 100 | 11394 | ex PT-MQL | |
| ☐ EP-CFN | Fokker 100 | 11423 | ex PT-MQO | |
| ☐ EP-CFO | Fokker 100 | 11389 | ex PT-MQE | |
| ☐ EP-CFP | Fokker 100 | 11409 | ex PT-MQN | |
| ☐ EP-CFQ | Fokker 100 | 11429 | ex PT-MQT | |
| ☐ EP-CFR | Fokker 100 | 11383 | ex PT-MQD | ♦ |
| ☐ EP-IDA | Fokker 100 | 11292 | ex PH-LMG | |
| ☐ EP-IDD | Fokker 100 | 11294 | ex PH-LMM | |
| ☐ EP-IDF | Fokker 100 | 11298 | ex PH-LMN | |
| ☐ EP-IDG | Fokker 100 | 11302 | ex PH-LMW | |
| | | | | |
| ☐ EP-IBK | Airbus A310-304 | 671 | ex SU-MWB | |
| ☐ EP-IBL | Airbus A310-304 | 436 | ex A6-EKB | |
| ☐ EP-IBP | Airbus A310-203 | 370 | ex TC-JCR | [THR] |
| ☐ EP-IBQ | Airbus A310-203 | 389 | ex TC-JCS | |
| ☐ EP-IRR | Boeing 727-286 | 20946/1052 | | |
| ☐ EP-IRS | Boeing 727-286 | 20947/1070 | | |
| ☐ EP-IRT | Boeing 727-286 | 21078/1114 | | |

## IRAN AIR TOUR AIRLINE       Iran Air Tour (B9/IRB)    Tehran-Mehrabad/Mashad (THR/MHD)

| ☐ EP-MDD | McDonnell-Douglas MD-82 | 49852/1959 | ex EP-ARB | ♦ |
| ☐ EP-MDE | McDonnell-Douglas MD-82 | 49523/1724 | ex4L-YAB | >TBN♦ |
| ☐ UR-BXL | McDonnell-Douglas MD-82 | 49512/1548 | ex G-CEPG | <BKV |
| ☐ UR-BXM | McDonnell-Douglas MD-82 | 49505/1381 | ex G-CEPD | <BKV |
| ☐ UR-BXO | McDonnell-Douglas MD-83 | 53150/1831 | ex LZ-LDH | <BKV♦ |
| ☐ UR-CHW | McDonnell-Douglas MD-82 | 49510/1514 | ex S5-ACY | <BKV♦ |
| ☐ UR-CHZ | McDonnell-Douglas MD-82 | 53169/2063 | ex G-CEPI | <BKV♦ |
| ☐ UR-CJQ | McDonnell-Douglas MD-82 | 49502/1300 | ex G-CEPC | <BKV♦ |
| | | | | |
| ☐ EP-MBQ | Tupolev Tu-154M | 92A931 | ex RA-85747 | |
| ☐ EP-MBT | Tupolev Tu-154M | 92A930 | ex RA-85749 | |
| ☐ EP-MCL | Tupolev Tu-154M | 91A880 | ex RA-85705 | |
| ☐ EP-MCM | Tupolev Tu-154M | 90A855 | ex RA-85085 | |
| ☐ EP-MCN | Tupolev Tu-154M | 88A792 | ex RA-85847 | |
| ☐ EP-MCO | Tupolev Tu-154M | 88A774 | ex RA-85831 | |
| ☐ EP-MCP | Tupolev Tu-154M | 85A724 | ex RA-85146 | |
| ☐ EP-MCS | Tupolev Tu-154M | 88A795 | ex RA-85653 | |
| ☐ EP-MCT | Tupolev Tu-154M | 90A860 | ex RA-85689 | |
| ☐ EP-MCU | Tupolev Tu-154M | 93A977 | ex RA-85793 | |
| ☐ EP-MCV | Tupolev Tu-154M | 85A706 | ex RA-85037 | |
| ☐ EP-MCX | Tupolev Tu-154M | 85A707 | ex LZ-HMW | |

## IRAN ASEMAN AIRLINES            (EP/IRC)              Tehran-Mehrabad (THR)

| ☐ EP-ATA | ATR 72-212 | 0334 | ex F-WWLQ | |
| ☐ EP-ATH | ATR 72-212 | 0339 | ex F-WWLU | |
| ☐ EP-ATS | ATR 72-212 | 0391 | ex F-WWED | |
| ☐ EP-ATU | ATR 72-212A | 0697 | ex F-OIRA | |
| ☐ EP-ATX | ATR 72-212A | 0573 | ex F-OIRB | |
| ☐ EP-ATZ | ATR 72-212 | 0398 | ex F-WWEK | |
| | | | | |
| ☐ EP-ASG | Fokker 100 | 11438 | ex HL7210 | |
| ☐ EP-ASH | Fokker 100 | 11439 | ex HL7211 | ♦ |
| ☐ EP-ASI | Fokker 100 | 11519 | ex HL7215 | |
| ☐ EP-ASJ | Fokker 100 | 11378 | ex HL7206 | |
| ☐ EP-ASK | Fokker 100 | 11388 | ex HL7208 | |
| ☐ EP-ASM | Fokker 100 | 11433 | ex F-GIOI | |
| ☐ EP-ASO | Fokker 100 | 11454 | ex F-GIOJ | |
| ☐ EP-ASP | Fokker 100 | 11504 | ex HL7213 | |
| ☐ EP-ASQ | Fokker 100 | 11513 | ex HL7214 | |
| ☐ EP-ASR | Fokker 100 | 11522 | ex HL7216 | |
| ☐ EP-AST | Fokker 100 | 11523 | ex HL7217 | |
| ☐ EP-ASU | Fokker 100 | 11430 | ex PT-MQP | |
| ☐ EP-ASX | Fokker 100 | 11431 | ex PT-MQS | |
| ☐ EP-ASZ | Fokker 100 | 11421 | ex PT-MQR | |
| ☐ EP-ATB | Fokker 100 | 11401 | ex PT-MQF | |
| ☐ EP-ATC | Fokker 100 | 11296 | ex F-GPXM | |
| ☐ EP-ATD | Fokker 100 | 11387 | ex F-GPXG | |
| ☐ EP-ATE | Fokker 100 | 11323 | ex F-GPXJ | ♦ |
| ☐ EP-ATF | Fokker 100 | 11476 | ex F-GPXH | |
| ☐ EP-ATG | Fokker 100 | 11329 | ex F-GPXK | |
| | | | | |
| ☐ EP-APA | Airbus A340-311 | 002 | ex M-YRGU | ♦ |

| | | | | |
|---|---|---|---|---|
| ☐ EP-ASA | Boeing 727-228 | 22081/1594 | ex LX-IRA | |
| ☐ EP-ASB | Boeing 727-228 | 22082/1603 | ex LX-IRB | |
| ☐ EP-ASC | Boeing 727-228 | 22084/1638 | ex LX-IRC | |
| ☐ EP-ASD | Boeing 727-228 | 22085/1665 | ex LX-IRD | [THR] |

## KISH AIR      Kishair (Y9/IRK)      Tehran-Mehrabad (THR)

| | | | | |
|---|---|---|---|---|
| ☐ EP-LBV | Fokker 50 | 20158 | ex VP-CSE | |
| ☐ EP-LCB | Fokker 50 | 20274 | ex EC-GKV | |
| ☐ EP-LCC | Fokker 50 | 20275 | ex EC-GKX | |
| ☐ EP-LCE | Fokker 50 | 20265 | ex PH-LXF | |
| ☐ EP-LCF | Fokker 50 | 20263 | ex PH-LXE | |
| ☐ EP-LCG | Fokker 50 | 20236 | ex PH-JXL | |
| ☐ EK-82221 | McDonnell-Douglas MD-82 | 53221/2079 | ex LZ-LDE | >RRN |
| ☐ EP-LCH | McDonnell-Douglas MD-83 | 49572/1468 | ex UR-CHS | [THR]♦ |
| ☐ EP-LCI | McDonnell-Douglas MD-83 | 49844/1579 | ex UR-CHR | <KHO |
| ☐ EP-LCK | McDonnell-Douglas MD-82 | 53224/2084 | ex EK-82224 | ♦ |
| ☐ EP-LCM | McDonnell-Douglas MD-82 | 53226/2087 | ex EK-82226 | <RRN♦ |
| ☐ EP-LCL | McDonnell-Douglas MD-82 | 53229/2105 | ex EK-82229 | >RRN♦ |
| ☐ UR-BXN | McDonnell-Douglas MD-83 | 49569/1405 | ex LZ-LDV | <KHO |
| ☐ UR-CDM | McDonnell-Douglas MD-82 | 49279/1230 | ex SX-BMP | <KHO♦ |

## MAHAN AIR      Mahan Air (W5/IRM)      Kerman (KER)

| | | | | |
|---|---|---|---|---|
| ☐ EP-MHA | Airbus A300B2K-3C | 160 | ex EK-30060 | |
| ☐ EP-MHF | Airbus A300B4-103 | 055 | ex S7-AAZ | |
| ☐ EP-MHG | Airbus A300B4-203 | 204 | ex AP-BFL | |
| ☐ EP-MHL | Airbus A300B4-203 | 175 | ex SU-BMM | |
| ☐ EP-MHM | Airbus A300B2K-3C | 090 | ex TC-SGA | |
| ☐ EP-MHP | Airbus A300B2K-3C | 244 | ex EK-30044 | ♦ |
| ☐ EP-MNG | Airbus A300B4-603 | 401 | ex D-AIAK | |
| ☐ EP-MNH | Airbus A300B4-603 | 405 | ex D-AIAL | ♦ |
| ☐ EP-MNI | Airbus A300B4-603 | 408 | ex D-AIAM | |
| ☐ EP-MNJ | Airbus A300B4-603 | 380 | ex D-AIAH | |
| ☐ EP-MNK | Airbus A300B4-603 | 618 | ex D-AIAT | |
| ☐ EP-MNL | Airbus A300B4-603 | 623 | ex D-AIAU | |
| ☐ EP-MNM | Airbus A300B4-605R | 773 | ex D-AIAX | |
| ☐ EP-MNN | Airbus A300B4-605R | 701 | ex D-AIAZ | |
| ☐ EP-MNQ | Airbus A300B4-603 | 553 | ex EX-35010 | |
| ☐ EP-MNR | Airbus A300B4-603 | 411 | ex EX-35009 | |
| ☐ EP-MNS | Airbus A300B4-603 | 414 | ex EX-35008 | |
| ☐ EP-MNT | Airbus A300B4-603 | 546 | ex EX-35007 [MHD] | |
| ☐ EP-MNU | Airbus A300B4-605R | 608 | ex EX-35006 | |
| ☐ EX-35011 | Airbus A300B4-622R | 838 | ex 5H-VAL | <KTC♦ |
| ☐ EP-MHO | Airbus A310-304 | 488 | ex EK-31088 | <Blue Sky |
| ☐ EP-MNO | Airbus A310-304 | 595 | ex EK-31095 <VRZ♦ | |
| ☐ EP-MNP | Airbus A310-308 | 620 | ex EX-35004 <KTC♦ | |
| ☐ EP-MNV | Airbus A310-304 | 567 | ex EX-35003 <KTC♦ | |
| ☐ EP-MNX | Airbus A310-304 | 564 | ex EX-35005 | |
| ☐ EP-VIP | Airbus A310-304 | 499 | ex 10+22 | VIP♦ |
| ☐ EX-301 | Airbus A310-304 | 524 | ex D-AIDF | <KTC |
| ☐ F-OJHH | Airbus A310-304ER | 586 | ex EP-MHH | |
| ☐ F-OJHI | Airbus A310-304ER | 537 | ex EP-MHI | |
| ☐ EP-MNA | Boeing 747-422 | 24383/811 | ex EK-74783 | wfs |
| ☐ EP-MNB | Boeing 747-422 | 24363/740 | ex EK-74763 | [THR] |
| ☐ EP-MNC | Boeing 747-422 | 26879/973 | ex EK-74779 | wfs |
| ☐ EP-MND | Boeing 747-3B3 (SCD) | 23413/632 | ex EK-74713 | |
| ☐ EP-MNE | Boeing 747-3B3 (SCD) | 23480/641 | ex EK-74780 | |
| ☐ EP-MOA | British Aerospace 146 Srs.300 | E3216 | ex EK-27000 | [THR] |
| ☐ UR-CIL | British Aerospace 146 Srs.300 | E3149 | ex G-BTZN | >Palm Avn♦ |
| ☐ UR-CJJ | British Aerospace 146 Srs.300 | E3165 | ex G-BSNR | <UKM♦ |
| ☐ UR-CJM | British Aerospace 146 Srs.300 | E3129 | ex G-BTXN | <UKM♦ |

## NAFT AIR / IRANIAN AIR TRANSPORT      NAFT (IRG)      Ahwaz (AWZ)

| | | | | |
|---|---|---|---|---|
| ☐ EP-AWZ | Fokker 100 | 11497 | ex PH-AFO | ♦ |
| ☐ EP-GAS | Fokker 50 | 20224 | ex PH-JXA | |
| ☐ EP-IOD | de Havilland DHC-6 Twin Otter 300 | 460 | | Op for NIOC |
| ☐ EP-IOE | de Havilland DHC-6 Twin Otter 300 | 425 | | Op for NIOC |
| ☐ EP-IOP | de Havilland DHC-6 Twin Otter 300 | 577 | | |
| ☐ EP-MIS | Fokker 100 | 11503 | ex F-GPXI | |
| ☐ EP-NFT | Fokker 50 | 20220 | ex PH-RRF | |
| ☐ EP-OIL | Fokker 50 | 20222 | ex PH-LNZ | |
| ☐ EP-OPI | Fokker 100 | 11509 | ex F-GLIR | |
| ☐ EP-PET | Fokker 50 | 20283 | ex PH-MXF | |
| ☐ EP-SUS | Fokker 100 | 11487 | ex F-GPXA | |

## PAYAM INTERNATIONAL AIR — Payamair (2F/IRP) — Karaj-Payam (QKC)

| | | | | | |
|---|---|---|---|---|---|
| ☐ EP-TPH | Embraer EMB.110P1A Bandeirante | 110453 | ex EP-TPM | Tehran | |
| ☐ EP-TPI | Embraer EMB.110P1 Bandeirante | 110438 | ex EP-TPA | Kerrian | |
| ☐ EP-TPJ | Embraer EMB.110P1 Bandeirante | 110442 | ex EP-TPT | Kashan | |
| ☐ EP-TPK | Embraer EMB.110P1 Bandeirante | 110386 | ex EP-TPG | Esfahan | |
| ☐ EP-TPL | Embraer EMB.110P1 Bandeirante | 110423 | ex EP-TPS | Semnan | |
| | | | | | |
| ☐ EP-ATQ | Boeing 727-222F (FedEx 3) | 21917/1616 | ex A6-RCB | | ◆ |
| ☐ EP-ATT | Boeing 727-222F (FedEx 3) | 21920/1634 | ex A6-RCA | | ◆ |
| ☐ EP-TPC | Bell 212 | 30516 | ex 6-9202 | | |
| ☐ EP-TPN | Bell 212 | 30517 | ex 6-9203 | | |
| ☐ EP-TPQ | Shaanxi Y-8F-100 | 110801 | ex EP-BOA | | ◆ |
| ☐ EP-TPX | Shaanxi Y-8F-100 | 110802 | ex EP-BOB | | ◆ |

## SAFAT AIRLINES — (IRV)

| | | | |
|---|---|---|---|
| ☐ EP-SAJ | Antonov An-26 | 57314002 | ex RA-26592 |
| ☐ EP-SAK | Antonov An-26 | 57314001 | ex RA-26591 |

## SAFIRAN AIRLINES — Safiran (SFN) — Tehran-Mehrabad (THR)

| | | | | |
|---|---|---|---|---|
| ☐ EP-SFD | Ir.An-140 | 9001 | ex HESA-01 | |
| ☐ EP-SFE | Ir.An-140 | 9002 | | Op by Police Avn |
| ☐ EP-SFF | Ir.An-140 | 9003 | | Op by Police Avn as HESA 90-03 |

## SAHA AIRLINES — Saha (IRZ) — Tehran-Mehrabad (THR)

| | | | | |
|---|---|---|---|---|
| ☐ EP-SHG | Boeing 707-3J9C | 20830/876 | ex 5-8301 | |
| ☐ EP-SHK | Boeing 707-3J9C | 21128/917 | ex 5-8312 | [AWZ] |
| ☐ EP-SHV | Boeing 707-3J9C | 21125/912 | ex 5-8309 | |
| ☐ EP-SIF | Airbus A300B4-622R | 762 | ex ZS-TSA | |
| ☐ EP-SIG | Airbus A300B4-622R | 750 | ex B-2327 | |

## TABAN AIR — Taban (TBM) — Mashad (MHD)

| | | | | |
|---|---|---|---|---|
| ☐ EP-ARA | McDonnell-Douglas MD-82 | 49524/1746 | ex EK-82524 | <RRN |
| ☐ UR-CIX | McDonnell-Douglas MD-88 | 53546/2167 | ex TC-ONM | <BKV |
| ☐ UR-CIY | McDonnell-Douglas MD-88 | 53547/2176 | ex TC-ONN | <BKV |
| ☐ UR-CIZ | McDonnell-Douglas MD-88 | 53549/2185 | ex TC-ONP | <BKV |
| ☐ UR-CJK | McDonnell-Douglas MD-88 | 53548/2180 | ex TC-ONO | <UKM |
| ☐ UR-CJL | McDonnell-Douglas MD-88 | 53550/2187 | ex TC-ONR | <BKV |
| | | | | |
| ☐ EP-TBA | Tupolev Tu-154M | 97A1008 | ex RA-85819 | |

## TAFTAN AIR

| | | | | |
|---|---|---|---|---|
| ☐ EP-TFN | Fokker 50 | 20302 | ex PH-JCE | [ZAH]◆ |
| ☐ EP-TFT | Fokker 50 | 20298 | ex PH-MXR | [ZAH]◆ |

## YAS AIR — Tehran-Mehrabad (THR)

| | | | |
|---|---|---|---|
| ☐ EP-GOL | Ilyushin Il-76 | 1013409297 | ex EP-PCC |
| ☐ EP-GOM | Ilyushin Il-76TD | 1023409321 | ex EP-PCB |
| ☐ EP-GOQ | Antonov An-74-200 | 365470991021 | ex 15-2250 |

## ZAGROS AIRLINES — (IZG)

| | | | | |
|---|---|---|---|---|
| ☐ EP-ZAB | McDonnell-Douglas MD-83 | 49930/1720 | ex UR-CJB | <KHO |
| ☐ EP-ZAG | McDonnell-Douglas MD-82 | 49372/1252 | ex UR-CDQ | <KHO |

## ER-    MOLDOVA (Republic of Moldova)

## AIR MOLDOVA — Air Moldova (9U/MLD) — Kishinev-Chisinau (KIV)

| | | | | |
|---|---|---|---|---|
| ☐ ER-AXP | Airbus A320-233 | 0741 | ex N452TA | |
| ☐ ER-AXT | Airbus A320-231 | 0249 | ex PR-MAF | ◆ |
| ☐ ER-AXV | Airbus A320-211 | 0622 | ex F-WQSG | |
| ☐ ER-EMA | Embraer EMB.120RT Brasilia | 120223 | ex N246CA | >TDM |
| ☐ ER-ECB | Embraer ERJ-190LR | 19000325 | ex PT-TXN | |
| ☐ ER- | Airbus A320-231 | 0368 | ex N368MX | ◆ |

## PECOTOX AIR

| | | | |
|---|---|---|---|
| ☐ ER-AZB | Antonov An-24RV | 27307507 | ◆ |
| ☐ ER-AZP | Antonov An-24RV | 17307002 | ◆ |
| ☐ ER-AZX | Antonov An-24RV | 47309804 | ◆ |

## VALAN INTERNATIONAL CARGO

| ☐ ER-AUW | Antonov An-26 | 8004 | | ♦ |
| ☐ ER-AVB | Antonov An-26-100 | 3204 | | ♦ |

## ES-    ESTONIA (Republic of Estonia)

### AVIES AIR COMPANY | | Avies (U3/AIA) | | Tallinn-Ylemiste (TLL) |

| ☐ ES-PJG | British Aerospace Jetstream 31 | 701 | ex ES-LJD | Tooru |
| ☐ ES-PJR | British Aerospace Jetstream 32EP | 949 | ex SE-LNU | |
| ☐ ES-PLB | LET L-410UVP | 851413 | ex LY-AVY | |

### ENIMEX | | Enimex (ENI) | | Tallinn-Ylemiste (TLL) |

| ☐ ES-NOB | Antonov An-72-100 | 36572070695 | ex CCCP-72931 | >UN as UNO-215 |
| ☐ ES-NOI | Antonov An-72-100 | 36572096914 | ex 3C-QQO | |

### ESTONIAN AIR | | Estonian (OV/ELL) | | Tallinn-Ylemiste (TLL) |

| ☐ ES-ABJ | Boeing 737-33R | 28873/2975 | ex ZK-NGA | [TLL] |
| ☐ ES-ABL | Boeing 737-5L9 | 28997/3008 | ex OK-DGB | |
| ☐ ES-ACB | Canadair CRJ-900 | 15261 | ex C-GIBH | |
| ☐ ES-ACC | Canadair CRJ-900 | 15262 | ex C-GIBQ | ♦ |
| ☐ ES-ACD | Canadair CRJ-900 | 15276 | ex C-GZQK | ♦ |
| ☐ ES-AEA | Embraer ERJ-170STD | 17000093 | ex OH-LEE | <FIN♦ |
| ☐ ES-AEB | Embraer ERJ-170STD | 17000106 | ex OH-LEF | <FIN♦ |
| ☐ ES-AEC | Embraer ERJ-170STD | 17000107 | ex OH-LEG | <FIN |
| ☐ ES-AED | Embraer ERJ-170STD | 17000112 | ex OH-LEH | <FIN |
| ☐ ES-ASM | SAAB SF.340A | 340A-132 | ex SE-LMT | ♦ |
| ☐ ES-ASN | SAAB SF.340A | 340A-151 | ex SE-KUU | ♦ |
| ☐ ES- | Canadair CRJ-900 | 15277 | ex C-GIAZ | o/o♦ |

### JP AIR CARGO | | | | Tallinn-Ylemiste (TLL) |

| ☐ ES-JFA | Swearingen SA.227AC Metro III | AC-657 | ex SX-BBX | Jussi |

### SMALL PLANET AIRLINES ESTONIA | | (ELC) | | Tallin-Ylemiste (TLL) |

| ☐ LY-AQV | Boeing 737-35B | 25069/2053 | ex ES-LBD | ♦ |

## ET-    ETHIOPIA (Federal Democratic Republic of Ethiopia)

### ABYSSINIAN FLIGHT SERVICES | | | | Addis Ababa (ADD) |

| ☐ ET-ALF | Cessna TU206F Turbo Stationair II | U20602598 | ex N206AM | |
| ☐ ET-AMI | Cessna 208B Caravan I | 208B1260 | ex N10966 | |

### ETHIOPIAN AIRLINES | | Ethiopian (ET/ETH) | | Addis Ababa (ADD) |

| ☐ ET-ALK | Boeing 737-760/W | 33764/1408 | | |
| ☐ ET-ALM | Boeing 737-760/W | 33765/1539 | | |
| ☐ ET-ALN | Boeing 737-760/W | 33766/1757 | | |
| ☐ ET-ALQ | Boeing 737-76N/W | 33420/1459 | | |
| ☐ ET-ALU | Boeing 737-76N/W | 32741/1487 | | |
| ☐ ET-ANG | Boeing 737-7K9/W | 34401/2216 | ex OY-MRP | ♦ |
| ☐ ET-ANH | Boeing 737-7K9/W | 34402/2270 | ex OY-MRR | ♦ |
| ☐ ET-AOK | Boeing 737-790/W | 33012/1306 | ex M-ABDH | ♦ |
| ☐ ET-AMZ | Boeing 737-8BK/W | 29646/2282 | ex G-CEJP | |
| ☐ ET-ANA | Boeing 737-86R/W | 30494/786 | ex B-2660 | |
| ☐ ET-ANZ | Boeing 737-8HO/W | 37933/3437 | | |
| ☐ ET-AOA | Boeing 737-8HO/W | 37936/3459 | ex N1786B | |
| ☐ ET-AOB | Boeing 737-8HO/W | 37937/3467 | ex N1796B | |
| ☐ ET-APF | Boeing 737-860/W | 40961/3827 | | ♦ |
| ☐ ET-APK | Boeing 737-860/W | 40964 | | o/o♦ |
| ☐ ET-APL | Boeing 737-860/W | 40965 | | o/o♦ |
| ☐ ET-AJS | Boeing 757-260PF | 24845/300 | ex N3519L | |
| ☐ ET-AJX | Boeing 757-260 (PCF) | 25014/348 | | |
| ☐ ET-AKC | Boeing 757-260 | 25353/408 | | |
| ☐ ET-AKE | Boeing 757-260ER | 26057/444 | | |
| ☐ ET-AKF | Boeing 757-260ER | 26058/496 | | |
| ☐ ET-ALZ | Boeing 757-231 | 30319/883 | ex N720TW | |
| ☐ ET-AMK | Boeing 757-23N | 32449/974 | ex C-GMYE | |
| ☐ ET-AMT | Boeing 757-23N | 27976/814 | ex N520AT | |
| ☐ ET-AMU | Boeing 757-23N | 27975/779 | ex N519AT | |

| | | | | |
|---|---|---|---|---|
| ☐ ET-ALC | Boeing 767-33AER | 28043/734 | | |
| ☐ ET-ALH | Boeing 767-3BGER | 30565/802 | ex HB-IHW | |
| ☐ ET-ALJ | Boeing 767-360ER | 33767/918 | ex N5020K | |
| ☐ ET-ALL | Boeing 767-3BGER | 30564/798 | ex OO-IHV | |
| ☐ ET-ALO | Boeing 767-360ER | 33768/922 | | |
| ☐ ET-ALP | Boeing 767-360ER | 33769/933 | | |
| ☐ ET-AME | Boeing 767-306ER | 27611/633 | ex PH-BZH | |
| ☐ ET-AMF | Boeing 767-3BGER | 30563/786 | ex B-2561 | |
| ☐ ET-AMG | Boeing 767-3BGER | 30566/817 | ex B-2562 | |
| ☐ ET-AMQ | Boeing 767-33AER | 27909/591 | ex PR-VAA | |
| ☐ ET-ANU | Boeing 767-3Q8ER | 27993/619 | ex N27993 | ♦ |
| | | | | |
| ☐ ET-ANN | Boeing 777-260LR | 40770/900 | The Blue Nile | |
| ☐ ET-ANO | Boeing 777-260LR | 40770/908 | | |
| ☐ ET-ANP | Boeing 777-260LR | 40772/914 | | ♦ |
| ☐ ET-ANQ | Boeing 777-260LR | 40773/930 | The Mount Kilimanjaro | ♦ |
| ☐ ET-ANR | Boeing 777-260LR | 40773/948 | | ♦ |
| | | | | |
| ☐ ET-ANI | de Havilland DHC-8-402Q | 4299 | ex C-GBKC | |
| ☐ ET-ANJ | de Havilland DHC-8-402Q | 4303 | ex C-GCLU | |
| ☐ ET-ANK | de Havilland DHC-8-402Q | 4304 | ex C-GCPF | |
| ☐ ET-ANL | de Havilland DHC-8-402Q | 4307 | ex C-GCPY | |
| ☐ ET-ANV | de Havilland DHC-8-402Q | 4317 | ex C-GEHI | |
| ☐ ET-ANW | de Havilland DHC-8-402Q | 4320 | ex C-GEUN | >SKK |
| ☐ ET-ANX | de Havilland DHC-8-402Q | 4330 | ex C-GSNH | |
| ☐ ET-ANY | de Havilland DHC-8-402Q | 4334 | | |
| | | | | |
| ☐ ET-AIT | de Havilland DHC-6 Twin Otter 310 | 820 | ex C-GDNG | |
| ☐ ET-AIU | de Havilland DHC-6 Twin Otter 300 | 822 | ex C-GDCZ | ♦ |
| ☐ ET-AIX | de Havilland DHC-6 Twin Otter 300 | 835 | ex C-GDFT | |
| ☐ ET-AKG | Lockheed L-382G Hercules | 5306 | | ♦ |
| ☐ ET-AML | McDonnell-Douglas MD-11ERF | 48758/615 | ex N742BC | |
| ☐ ET-AND | McDonnell-Douglas MD-11BCF | 48780/624 | ex N588BC | |
| ☐ ET-AOO | Boeing 787-8 | 34743 | | o/o♦ |
| ☐ ET-AOP | Boeing 787-8 | 34744 | | o/o♦ |
| ☐ ET-APS | Boeing 777-F6N | 41846 | | o/o♦ |
| ☐ ET- | Boeing 787-8 | | | o/o |
| ☐ ET- | Boeing 787-8 | | | o/o |

### FLY AIR ETHIOPIA

| | | | | |
|---|---|---|---|---|
| ☐ ET-AMX | Beech 1900C | UC-107 | ex 5Y-BTY | wfs♦ |

| **TRANS NATION AIRWAYS** | | **Trans Nation (TNW)** | **Addis Ababa/Jeddah (ADD/JED)** | |
|---|---|---|---|---|
| ☐ ET-AKZ | de Havilland DHC-8-202 | 469 | ex C-GLOT | >BBZ |
| ☐ ET-ALX | de Havilland DHC-8-202 | 475 | ex ZK-ECR | |
| ☐ ET-AMR | Bell 222UT | 47554 | ex N111DS | |

## EW-  BELARUS (Republic of Belarus)

| **BELAVIA BELARUSSIAN AIRLINES** | | **Belarus Avia (B2/BRU)** | **Minsk 1 (MHP)** | |
|---|---|---|---|---|
| ☐ EW-250PA | Boeing 737-524 | 26319/2748 | ex N427LF | |
| ☐ EW-251PA | Boeing 737-5Q8 | 27634/2889 | ex PT-SSC | |
| ☐ EW-252PA | Boeing 737-524 | 26340/2777 | ex LY-AGZ | |
| ☐ EW-253PA | Boeing 737-524 | 26339/2771 | ex LY-AGQ | |
| ☐ EW-290PA | Boeing 737-5Q8 | 27629/2834 | ex N381LF | |
| ☐ EW-294PA | Boeing 737-505 | 26338/2822 | ex B-2975 | |
| | | | | |
| ☐ EW-001PA | Boeing 737-8EV/W | 33079/1075 | ex N375BC | Op for Govt BBJ2♦ |
| ☐ EW-100PJ | Canadair CRJ-200LR | 7309 | ex N400MJ | |
| ☐ EW-254PA | Boeing 737-3Q8 | 26294/2550 | ex N201LF | |
| ☐ EW-276PJ | Canadair CRJ-200ER | 7799 | ex N698BR | |
| ☐ EW-277PJ | Canadair CRJ-200ER | 7852 | ex N710BR | |
| ☐ EW-282PA | Boeing 737-3Q8 | 26321/2764 | ex B-5024 | |
| ☐ EW-283PA | Boeing 737-3Q8 | 26333/2786 | ex B-2604 | |
| ☐ EW-303PJ | Canadair CRJ-200ER | 7436 | ex OY-MBI | ♦ |
| ☐ EW-308PA | Boeing 737-3K2 | 24328/1856 | ex LN-KKH | ♦ |
| ☐ EW-26127 | Antonov An-26A | 12701 | | >AIT♦ |
| ☐ EW-85703 | Tupolev Tu-154M | 91A878 | ex CCCP-85703 | |
| ☐ EW-85706 | Tupolev Tu-154M | 91A881 | ex CCCP-85706 | |
| ☐ EW-85741 | Tupolev Tu-154M | 91A896 | ex ES-LTC | |
| ☐ EW-85748 | Tupolev Tu-154M | 92A924 | | |
| ☐ EW-88187 | Yakovlev Yak-40 | 9620748 | ex CCCP-88187 | Op for Govt |

### GENEX

| | | | | |
|---|---|---|---|---|
| ☐ EW-246TG | Antonov An-26B | 67314403 | ex UR-26214 | Op by Airest |
| ☐ EW-259TG | Antonov An-26B | 27312706 | ex UR-26094 | |

☐ EW-278TG   Antonov An-26     13306     ex HA-TCZ

## GOMELAVIA — Gomel (YD/GOM) — Gomel (GME)

| | | | | |
|---|---|---|---|---|
| ☐ EW-245TI | Antonov An-12BP | 6344608 | ex EX-096 | |
| ☐ EW-46250 | Antonov An-24B | 77303208 | ex CCCP-46250 | [GME] |
| ☐ EW-46304 | Antonov An-24B | 97305304 | ex CCCP-46304 | [GME] |
| ☐ EW-46631 | Antonov An-24RV | 37308810 | ex CCCP-46631 | |
| ☐ EW-47697 | Antonov An-24RV | 27307604 | ex CCCP-47697 | |

Ops suspended 22Feb11

## RUBYSTAR — RubyStar (RSB) — Minsk-Machulishchy

| | | | |
|---|---|---|---|
| ☐ EW-275TI | Antonov An-12BK | 00347210 | ex RA--13392 |
| ☐ EW-47808 | Antonov An-24RV | 17306910 | ex CCCP-47808 |

## TRANS AVIA EXPORT CARGO AIRLINES — Transexport (AL/TXC) — Minsk-Machulishchy

| | | | | |
|---|---|---|---|---|
| ☐ EW-76710 | Ilyushin Il-76TD | 0063473182 | ex RA-76710 | |
| ☐ EW-76712 | Ilyushin Il-76TD | 0063473190 | ex CCCP-76712 | [MSQ] |
| ☐ EW-76734 | Ilyushin Il-76TD | 0073476312 | | >DVA♦ |
| ☐ EW-76735 | Ilyushin Il-76TD | 0073476314 | ex CCCP-76735 | [MSQ] |
| ☐ EW-76737 | Ilyushin Il-76TD | 0073477323 | ex CCCP-76737 | [MSQ] |
| ☐ EW-78769 | Ilyushin Il-76MD | 0083487607 | ex CCCP-78769 | [MSQ] |
| ☐ EW-78779 | Ilyushin Il-76TD | 0083489662 | ex CCCP-78779 | [MSQ] |
| ☐ EW-78787 | Ilyushin Il-76MD | 0083490698 | ex CCCP-78787 | [MSQ] |
| ☐ EW-78792 | Ilyushin Il-76TD | 0093490718 | ex EP-CFA | all-white |
| ☐ EW-78799 | Ilyushin Il-76TD | 0093491754 | ex CCCP-78799 | [MSQ] |
| ☐ EW-78801 | Ilyushin Il-76TD | 0093492763 | ex CCCP-78801 | [MSQ] |
| ☐ EW-78808 | Ilyushin Il-76TD | 0093493794 | ex CCCP-78808 | |
| ☐ EW-78819 | Ilyushin Il-76TD | 0093495883 | ex CCCP-78819 | |
| ☐ EW-78827 | Ilyushin Il-76TD | 1003499997 | ex CCCP-78827 | [MSQ] |
| ☐ EW-78839 | Ilyushin Il-76TD | 1003402047 | ex CCCP-78839 | [MSQ] |
| ☐ EW-78843 | Ilyushin Il-76TD | 1003403082 | | >AZS♦ |
| ☐ EW-78848 | Ilyushin Il-76TD | 1003405159 | ex CCCP-78848 | <ESL |
| | | | | |
| ☐ EW-269TI | Antonov An-12BP | 1340106 | ex UN-11018 | |

## EX-  KYRGYZSTAN (Republic of Kyrgyzstan)

## AEROVISTA AIRLINES — Aerovista Group (AAP) — Sharjah (SHJ)

| | | | | |
|---|---|---|---|---|
| ☐ EX-417 | LET L-410UVP | 851416 | ex CCCP67513 | ♦ |
| ☐ EX-37501 | Boeing 737-59D/W | 26419/2186 | ex G-GFFD | >LYN♦ |
| ☐ EX-87250 | Yakovlev Yak-40 | 9310726 | ex CCCP-87250 | <TLR |
| ☐ EX-87664 | Yakovlev Yak-40 | 9240825 | ex CCCP-87664 | >TLR |
| ☐ EX-88207 | Yakovlev Yak-40K | 9631149 | ex EY-87207 | >TLR |
| ☐ EX-88270 | Yakovlev Yak-40 | 9720853 | ex RA-88270 | >TLR |

## AIR BISHKEK

| | | | | |
|---|---|---|---|---|
| ☐ EX-32001 | Airbus A320-212 | 0445 | ex N187AT | <EAA♦ |
| ☐ EX-32002 | Airbus A320-231 | 0386 | ex EY-621 | <EAA♦ |
| ☐ EX-32003 | Airbus A320-212 | 0325 | ex EY-622 | <ETJ♦ |

## AIR MANAS — Air Manas (MBB) — Bishkek-Manas (FRU)

| | | | | |
|---|---|---|---|---|
| ☐ EX-73401 | Boeing 737-484 | 25361/2130 | ex N761AS | ♦ |

## AL SAYEGH AIRLINES

| | | | | |
|---|---|---|---|---|
| ☐ XT-DMA | Boeing 747-338 | 23224/610 | ex A6- | wfs♦ |
| ☐ XT-SAG | Boeing 747-338 | 23823/678 | ex N177SG | [JED]♦ |

## ANIKAY AIR — Anikay (AKF) — Bishkek-Manas/Sharjah (FRU/SHJ)

| | | | | |
|---|---|---|---|---|
| ☐ EX-405 | Ilyushin Il-18D | 184007405 | ex T9-ABB | no titles |
| ☐ EX-601 | Ilyushin Il-18E | 185008601 | ex EL-ALD | National Paints titles |

## AVIA TRAFFIC COMPANY — Atomic (AIF) — Bishkek-Manas (FRU)

| | | | | |
|---|---|---|---|---|
| ☐ EX-008 | Antonov An-24RV | 37308307 | | ♦ |
| ☐ EX-051 | Antonov An-24RV | 57310105 | ex ER-AZG | |
| ☐ EX-150 | Antonov An-24RV | 47309810 | | ♦ |
| ☐ EX-252 | Antonov An-24RV | 27307704 | | ♦ |
| ☐ EX-27002 | British Aerospace 146 Srs.200 | E2172 | ex OO-DJH | |
| ☐ EX-27007 | British Aerospace 146 Srs.200 | E2180 | ex OO-DJG | |
| ☐ EX-37005 | Boeing 737-3Y0 | 24681/1929 | ex N554MS | ♦ |

| **BOTIR-AVIA** | | **Botir-Avia (B8/BTR)** | | **Bishkek-Manas (FRU)** |
|---|---|---|---|---|
| ☐ EX-89616 | Ilyushin Il-76T | 0023438120 | ex UR-86916 | [SHJ] |

| **BRITISH GULF INTERNATIONAL AIRLINES** | | **Gulf Inter (BGK)** | | **Bishkek-Manas/Sharjah (FRU/SHJ)** |
|---|---|---|---|---|
| ☐ S9-SAH | Antonov An-12B | 5343703 | ex EX-164 | Alex |
| ☐ S9-SAV | Antonov An-12AP | 2340602 | ex EX-045 | Igor |

| **CLICK AIRWAYS** | | **Click (4C/CGK)** | | **Sharjah (SHJ)** |
|---|---|---|---|---|
| ☐ EK-11418 | Antonov An-12BP | 7344705 | ex EX-166 | |
| ☐ EK-76400 | Ilyushin Il-76TD | 1023413438 | ex JY-JIB | |
| ☐ EX-033 | Ilyushin Il-76TD | 0033446235 | ex RA-76788 | |
| ☐ EX-035 | Ilyushin Il-76TD | 0093498962 | ex RA-76795 | |
| ☐ EX-036 | Ilyushin Il-76TD | 0093495863 | ex RA-76785 | >Ababeel |

| **ESEN AIR** | | | | **Essen (ESD)** |
|---|---|---|---|---|
| ☐ EX-777 | Boeing 737-268 | 21654/532 | ex HZ-AGS | [ALA] |

| **GARINCO AIRWAYS** | | | | |
|---|---|---|---|---|
| ☐ EX-87820 | Yakovlev Yak-40 | 9231224 | ex RA-87820 | |

| **INTAL AIR** | | **Intal (INL)** | | **Bishkek-Manas/Sharjah (FRU/SHJ)** |
|---|---|---|---|---|
| ☐ EK-73755 | Boeing 737-229C (Nordam 3) | 21139/437 | ex EX-050 | |
| ☐ EX-061 | Boeing 737-2S2C (Nordam 3) | 21927/600 | ex N806AL | |
| ☐ EX-75905 | Ilyushin Il-18Gr | 186008905 | | ♦ |

| **ITEK AIR** | | **Itek Air (GI/IKA)** | | **Bishkek-Manas (FRU)** |
|---|---|---|---|---|
| ☐ EX-73733 | Boeing 737-275 (AvAero 3) | 21819/627 | ex AP-BHU wfs | |
| ☐ E3-NAD | Boeing 737-268 | 21276/468 | ex 4L-EUL | >NAS♦ |

| **KYRGYZ AIRWAYS** | | **(KR/EAA)** | | **Bishkek-Manas (FRU)** |
|---|---|---|---|---|
| ☐ EX-32001 | Airbus A320-212 | 0445 | ex N187AT | >Air Bishkek♦ |
| ☐ EX-32002 | Airbus A320-231 | 0386 | ex EY-621 | >Air Bishkek♦ |
| ☐ EX-37001 | Boeing 737-301 | 23937/1587 | ex E7-BBA | ♦ |
| ☐ EX-42301 | ATR 42-320 | 0213 | ex OY-PCD | o/o |

| **KYRGYZ TRANS AVIA** | | **Dinafra (KTC)** | | **Bishkek-Manas (FRU)** |
|---|---|---|---|---|
| ☐ EX-301 | Airbus A310-304 | 524 | ex D-AIDF | >IRM |
| ☐ EX-35003 | Airbus A310-304 | 567 | ex OK-WAB | >IRM |
| ☐ EX-35004 | Airbus A310-308 | 620 | ex D-AHLC | >IRM |
| ☐ EX-35011 | Airbus A300B4-622R | 838 | ex 5H-VAL | >IRM♦ |

| **KYRGYZSTAN** | | **Altyn Avia (QH/LYN)** | | **Bishkek-Manas (FRU)** |
|---|---|---|---|---|
| ☐ EX-014 | Antonov An-24RV | 77310807 | ex 4R-SEL | |
| ☐ EX-00002 | Tupolev Tu-154M | 91A904 | | ♦ |
| ☐ EX-37501 | Boeing 737-59D/W | 26419/2186 | ex G-GFFD | >AAP♦ |
| ☐ EX-85718 | Tupolev Tu-154M | 91A900 | ex CCCP-85718 | |

| **KYRGYZSTAN AIRLINES** | | **Kyrgyz (R8/KGA)** | | **Bishkek-Manas / Karakol / Osh (FRU/-/OSS)** |
|---|---|---|---|---|
| ☐ EX-87259 | Yakolev Yak-40 | 9311626 | | wfs♦ |
| ☐ EX-87275 | Yakolev Yak-40 | 9311127 | | ♦ |
| ☐ EX-87293 | Yakolev Yak-40 | 9320828 | | wfs♦ |
| ☐ EX-87331 | Yakolev Yak-40 | 9510239 | | ♦ |
| ☐ EX-87442 | Yakolev Yak-40 | 9431935 | | wfs♦ |
| ☐ EX-87445 | Yakolev Yak-40 | 9430236 | | ♦ |
| ☐ EX-87571 | Yakolev Yak-40 | 9221521 | ex CCCP-87571 | |
| ☐ EX-87589 | Yakolev Yak-40 | 9220123 | ex CCCP-87589 | |
| ☐ EX-87631 | Yakolev Yak-40 | 9131219 | | wfs♦ |
| ☐ EX-87632 | Yakolev Yak-40 | 9131319 | | wfs♦ |
| ☐ EX-87664 | Yakolev Yak-40 | 9240825 | | ♦ |
| ☐ EX-87836 | Yakolev Yak-40 | 9240226 | | wfs♦ |
| ☐ EX-65779 | Tupolev Tu-134A-3 | 62602 | | [FRU]♦ |
| ☐ EX-65789 | Tupolev Tu-134A-3 | 62850 | | ♦ |
| ☐ EX-85590 | Tupolev Tu-154B-2 | 84A590 | ex CCCP-85590 | |
| ☐ EX-85762 | Tupolev Tu-154M | 92A945 | ex RA-85762 | |

## TENIR AIRLINES — Tenir Air (TEB) — Sharjah (SHJ)

| | | | | |
|---|---|---|---|---|
| ☐ EX-54000 | Ilyushin Il-76T | 0013428839 | | ♦ |

## TRAST AERO — Trast Aero (S5/TSJ) — Sharjah (SHJ)

| | | | | |
|---|---|---|---|---|
| ☐ S9-GBC | Antonov An-26 | | | ♦ |
| ☐ TN-AGB | Antonov An-26B-100 | 87307210 | | |
| ☐ 3X-GET | Antonov An-26B | 67304104 | ex S9-KAV | |
| ☐ 3X-GFC | Antonov An-26 | | | |
| ☐ 3X-GFH ? | Antonov An-26 | 97308303 | | ♦ |
| ☐ 3X-GFN | Antonov An-26 | | | ♦ |
| ☐ 3X-GGU | Antonov An-26 | 187009904 | | ♦ |
| ☐ 4L-26026(2) | Antonov An-26 | | | ♦ |
| | | | | |
| ☐ ER-AUR | Antonov An-24 | | | ♦ |
| ☐ EX-215 | ROMBAC One-Eleven 510ED | 141 | | ♦ |
| ☐ EX-041(2) | Antonov An-24B | 97304910 | | ♦ |
| ☐ 3X-GES(1) | Antonov An-32A | 1408 ? | | ♦ |

## EY-    TAJIKISTAN (Republic of Tajikistan)

### ASIA AIRWAYS

| | | | | |
|---|---|---|---|---|
| ☐ EY-401 | Antonov An-12BP | 8345607 | | |
| ☐ EY-402 | Antonov An-12B | 8346006 | | ♦ |
| ☐ EY-403 | Antonov An-12BK | 00347107 | | ♦ |
| ☐ EY-604 | Ilyushin Il-76TD | 1023410355 | | ♦ |

### ASIAN EXPRESS AIRLINES

| | | | | |
|---|---|---|---|---|
| ☐ EY- | Avro 146-RJ85 | E2363 | ex EI-RJP | ♦ |

### EAST AIR — (EG/ETJ) — Dushanbe (DYU)

| | | | | |
|---|---|---|---|---|
| ☐ EX-37002 | Boeing 737-3Z0 | 27521/2738 | ex B-2957 | wfs♦ |
| ☐ EY-532 | Boeing 737-25A | 23791/1486 | ex EX-734 | |
| ☐ EY-533 | Boeing 737-247 | 23605/1371 | ex N378DL | ♦ |
| ☐ EY-534 | Boeing 737-247 (Nordam 3) | 23517/1261 | ex EX-736 | ♦ |
| ☐ EY-537 | Boeing 737-4B7 | 24550/1793 | ex N245DT | >JBW♦ |
| ☐ EY-538 | Boeing 737-4Y0 | 23980/1667 | ex N239DT | [IST] |
| ☐ EY-539 | Boeing 737-3B7 | 23700/1461 | ex AP-BIW | ♦ |
| ☐ EY-622 | Airbus A320-212 | 0325 | ex N223AT | >Air Bishkek♦ |
| ☐ EY-623 | Airbus A320-231 | 0428 | ex N428MX | >Sky Bosnia♦ |

### RUS AVIATION — (RLB) — Sharjah (SHJ)

| | | | | | |
|---|---|---|---|---|---|
| ☐ EK-76111 | Ilyushin Il-767D | 0073479367 | | | ♦ |
| ☐ EK-76155 | Ilyushin Il-76 | 0093421637 | | | ♦ |
| ☐ EK-76425 | Ilyushin Il-76TD | 1003405167 | | | ♦ |
| ☐ EK-76485 | Ilyushin Il76TD | 0063470088 | | | ♦ |
| ☐ EK-76808 | Ilyushin Il-76TD | 1013405177 | | | ♦ |
| | | | | | |
| ☐ A6-JIL | Airbus A300B4-605RF | 626 | ex N77080 | Sami | ♦ |
| ☐ A6-JIM | Airbus A300B4-605RF | 643 | ex N7082A | Darina | ♦ |
| ☐ RA-67634 | LET L-410UVP-E | 902427 | | | ♦ |

### SOMON AIR — (4J / SMR) — Dushanbe (DYU)

| | | | | | |
|---|---|---|---|---|---|
| ☐ EY-555 | Boeing 737-3Y5 | 25613/2446 | ex LN-KKV | | ♦ |
| ☐ EY-777 | Boeing 737-8GJ/W | 34960/2765 | ex N960BB | Sadriddin Ayni | |
| ☐ EY-787 | Boeing 737-8GJ/W | 34955/2512 | ex N349FD | Ismoil Somoni | |
| ☐ EY- | Boeing 737-3K2 | 24326/1683 | ex N412BC | | ♦ |
| ☐ P4-SOM | Boeing 737-93YER | 40889/3837 | ex N1786B | Bobojon Ghafurov | ♦ |
| ☐ P4-TAJ | Boeing 737-93YER/W | 40888/3771 | | Shirinsho Shotemur | ♦ |

### TAJIK AIR — Tajikistan (7J/TJK) — Dushanbe/Khudzhand (DYU/LBD)

| | | | | |
|---|---|---|---|---|
| ☐ EY-87214 | Yakovlev Yak-40K | 9640851 | ex HA-LJB | |
| ☐ EY-87217 | Yakovlev Yak-40 | 9510340 | ex EP-EAL | |
| ☐ EY-87434 | Yakovlev Yak-40 | 9431035 | ex EP-TUF | |
| ☐ EY-87446 | Yakovlev Yak-40 | 9430336 | | [DYU]♦ |
| ☐ EY-87922 | Yakovlev Yak-40K | 9731355 | ex EP-EAM | |
| ☐ EY-87963 | Yakovlev Yak-40K | 9831058 | ex EP-EAK | |
| ☐ EY-87967 | Yakovlev Yak-40K | 9831158 | ex EP-CPI | |
| ☐ EY-88267 | Yakovlev Yak-40K | 9720553 | ex CCP-66267 | |
| | | | | |
| ☐ EY-444 | Boeing 737-3L9 | 26441/2550 | ex XA-UNG | ♦ |
| ☐ EY-201 | CAIC MA-60 | | | ♦ |

| | | | | |
|---|---|---|---|---|
| ☐ EY-751 | Boeing 757-2Q8 | 24964/424 | ex N926JS | |
| ☐ EY-26205 | Antonov An-26B | 14107 | ex CCCP-26205 | |
| ☐ EY-26658 | Antonov An-26 | 7904 | ex 26658 | |
| ☐ EY-28736 | WSK-PZL/Antonov An-28 | 1AJ007-24 | ex CCCP-28736 | |
| ☐ EY-28921 | WSK-PZL/Antonov An-28 | 1AJ008-07 | ex CCCP-28921 | |
| ☐ EY-46365 | Antonov An-24B | 07305906 | ex CCCP-46365 | |
| ☐ EY-45595 | Antonov An-24B | 97305105 | ex UR-45595 | |
| ☐ EY-47693 | Antonov An-24RV | 27307510 | ex CCCP-47693 | >DAO |
| ☐ EY-47802 | Antonov An-24RV | 17306901 | ex UN-47802 | |
| ☐ EY-65763 | Tupolev Tu-134A-3 | 62299 | ex CCCP-65763 | |
| ☐ EY-65788 | Tupolev Tu-134A-3 | 62835 | ex CCCP-65788 | |
| ☐ EY-85651 | Tupolev Tu-154M | 88A793 | ex RA-85651 | |
| ☐ EY-85691 | Tupolev Tu-154M | 90A864 | ex EP-EAB | >IRX |
| ☐ EY-85692 | Tupolev Tu-154M | 90A865 | ex EP-TUE | |
| ☐ EY-85717 | Tupolev Tu-154M | 91A897 | ex EP-EAA | |

## EZ-    TURKMENISTAN (Republic of Turkmenistan)

| TURKMENISTAN AIRLINES | | Turkmenistan (T5/TUA) | | Askhabad (ASB) |
|---|---|---|---|---|
| ☐ EZ-A101 | Boeing 717-22K | 55153/5072 | ex N6202S | |
| ☐ EZ-A102 | Boeing 717-22K | 55154/5078 | | |
| ☐ EZ-A103 | Boeing 717-22K | 55155/5086 | | |
| ☐ EZ-A104 | Boeing 717-22K | 55195/5130 | | |
| ☐ EZ-A105 | Boeing 717-22K | 55196/5133 | | |
| ☐ EZ-A106 | Boeing 717-22K | 55186/5146 | | [MZJ] |
| ☐ EZ-A107 | Boeing 717-22K | 55187/5147 | | [MZJ] |
| ☐ EZ-S701 | Sikorsky S-76C+ | 760463 | | op for Govt |
| ☐ EZ-S702 | Sikorsky S-76C+ | 760461 | | |
| ☐ EZ-S703 | Sikorsky S-76A+ | 760294 | ex VH-XHL | |
| ☐ EZ-S704 | Sikorsky S-76A++ | 760056 | ex G-BJFL | ♦ |
| ☐ EZ-S70. | Sikorsky S-76A++ | 760032 | ex G-BHBF | ♦ |
| ☐ EZ-F422 | Ilyushin Il-76TD | 1023410348 | | [ASB]♦ |
| ☐ EZ-F423 | Ilyushin Il-76TD | 1033418608 | | [ASB]♦ |
| ☐ EZ-F424 | Ilyushin Il-76TD | 1033418592 | | [ASB]♦ |
| ☐ EZ-F425 | Ilyushin Il-76TD | 1023410336 | | [ASB]♦ |
| ☐ EZ-F426 | Ilyushin Il-76TD | 1033418609 | | |
| ☐ EZ-F427 | Ilyushin Il-76TD | 1033418620 | | |
| ☐ EZ-F428 | Ilyushin Il-76TD | 1043418624 | | |
| ☐ EZ-A001 | Boeing 737-341 | 26855/2305 | ex EK-A001 | |
| ☐ EZ-A002 | Boeing 737-332 | 25994/2439 | ex N301DE | |
| ☐ EZ-A003 | Boeing 737-332 | 25995/2455 | ex N302DE | |
| ☐ EZ-A004 | Boeing 737-82K/W | 36088/2181 | ex N1795B | |
| ☐ EZ-A005 | Boeing 737-82K/W | 36089/2233 | | |
| ☐ EZ-A006 | Boeing 737-7GL/W | 37236/2986 | ex N1786B | |
| ☐ EZ-A007 | Boeing 737-7GL/W | 37234/2682 | | |
| ☐ EZ-A008 | Boeing 737-7GL/W | 37237/2988 | ex N1787B | |
| ☐ EZ-A009 | Boeing 737-7GL/W | 37235/2993 | ex N3134C | |
| ☐ EZ-A010 | Boeing 757-23A | 25345/412 | ex N58AW | |
| ☐ EZ-A011 | Boeing 757-22K | 28336/725 | | |
| ☐ EZ-A012 | Boeing 757-22K | 28337/726 | | |
| ☐ EZ-A014 | Boeing 757-22K | 30863/952 | | |
| ☐ EZ-A700 | Boeing 767-32KER | 33968/926 | op for Govt | |
| ☐ EZ-A777 | Boeing 777-22KLR | 39548/889 | op for Govt | |
| ☐ EZ-P710 | Aérospatiale AS.332L2 | 2577 | ex F-WQDJ | op for Govt |
| ☐ EZ-P711 | Aérospatiale AS.332L2 | 2578 | ex F-WWOU | op for Govt |
| ☐ EZ-S720 | Sikorsky S-92 | 920017 | ex N7118Z | op for Govt |
| ☐ EZ-S721 | Sikorsky S-92 | 920026 | ex N8103U | op for Govt |

## E3-    ERITREA (State of Eritrea)

| ERITREAN AIRLINES | | Eritrean (B8/ERT) | | Asmara (ASM) |
|---|---|---|---|---|
| ☐ E3-AAQ | Boeing 767-238ER | 23309/129 | ex N771WD | |
| ☐ LZ-BHF | Airbus A320-214 | 1087 | ex EC-HDN | <BGH♦ |

| NAS AIR | | (UE/NAS) | | Asmara (ASM) |
|---|---|---|---|---|
| ☐ E3-NAD | Boeing 737-268 | 21276/468 | ex 4L-EUL | <IKA |
| ☐ ST-ATA | Airbus A300B4-622R | 775 | ex TF-ELC | >SUD♦ |

| RED SEA AIR | | | | |
|---|---|---|---|---|
| ☐ E3-AAI | Harbin Y-12 II | 0059 | | ♦ |

## E5-    COOK ISLANDS

### AIR RAROTONGA | Air Rarotonga (GZ) | Rarotonga (RAR)

| | | | | | |
|---|---|---|---|---|---|
| ☐ E5-EFS | SAAB SF.340A | 340A-049 | ex ZK-EFS | | |
| ☐ E5-TAI | Embraer EMB 110P1 Bandeirante | 110447 | ex VH-MWF | | [RAR]♦ |
| ☐ E5-FTS | Embraer EMB.110P1 Bandeirante | 110239 | ex ZK-FTS | | |
| ☐ E5-TAK | Embraer EMB.110P1 Bandeirante | 110448 | ex ZK-TAK | | |
| ☐ E5- | Embraer EMB.110P1 Bandeirante | 110245 | ex VH-UQA | | o/o♦ |

## E7-    BOSNIA-HERZEGOVINA (Republic of Bosnia-Herzegovina)

### BH AIRLINES | Air Bosna (JA/BON) | Banja Luka

| | | | | | |
|---|---|---|---|---|---|
| ☐ E7-AAD | ATR 72-212 | 464 | ex T9-AAD | Sarajevo | |
| ☐ E7-AAE | ATR 72-212 | 465 | ex T9-AAE | Mostar | |
| ☐ E7-ABA | CAS C.212-200 | A48-1-302 | ex T9-ABA | | ♦ |

### ICAR AIRLINES

| | | | |
|---|---|---|---|
| ☐ E7-AAK | LET L-410UVP-E13 | 892321 | ex T9-AAK |

### SKY BOSNIA

| | | | | |
|---|---|---|---|---|
| ☐ E7-SKA | Airbus A320-231 | 0428 | ex EY-623 | <ETJ♦ |

## F-    FRANCE (French Republic)

### AERO SOTRAVIA | Nangis les Loges

| | | | |
|---|---|---|---|
| ☐ F-GCPO | Piper PA-34-200T Seneca II | 34-8070358 | ex N8266V |
| ☐ F-GDHD | Britten-Norman BN-2A-9 Islander | 591 | ex 9Q-CMJ |
| ☐ F-GMLJ | Cessna 414 | 414-0635 | ex I-CCEE |

### AIGLE AZUR | Aigle Azur (ZI/AAF)   Paris-Orly/Charles de Gaulle (ORY/CDG)

| | | | | | |
|---|---|---|---|---|---|
| ☐ F-GJVF | Airbus A320-211 | 0244 | | | |
| ☐ F-GUAA | Airbus A321-211 | 0808 | ex G-JSJX | | |
| ☐ F-GXAH | Airbus A319-112 | 1846 | ex C-GTDX | | |
| ☐ F-HBAB | Airbus A321-211 | 0823 | ex F-WBAB | | |
| ☐ F-HBAF | Airbus A321-211 | 1006 | ex EC-IXY | | |
| ☐ F-HBAO | Airbus A320-214 | 4589 | ex F-WWIQ | | ♦ |
| ☐ F-HBAL | Airbus A319-111 | 2870 | ex EC-JXA | | ♦ |
| ☐ F-HBAP | Airbus A320-214 | 4675 | ex F-WWDE | | ♦ |
| ☐ F-HBII | Airbus A320-214 | 3852 | ex F-WWDH | | |
| ☐ F-HBMI | Airbus A319-114 | 0639 | ex N573SX | | |
| ☐ F-HCAI | Airbus A321-211 | 1451 | ex TC-KTC | | |
| ☐ F-HCZI | Airbus A319-112 | 4268 | ex D-AVWP | | ♦ |

### AIR CORSICA | Corsica (XK/CCM) | Ajaccio (AJA)

| | | | | | |
|---|---|---|---|---|---|
| ☐ F-GRPI | ATR 72-212A | 0722 | ex F-WWEC | | |
| ☐ F-GRPJ | ATR 72-212A | 0724 | ex F-WWEI | | |
| ☐ F-GRPK | ATR 72-212A | 0727 | ex F-WWEH | | |
| ☐ F-GRPX | ATR 72-212A | 0734 | ex F-WWEO | | |
| ☐ F-GRPY | ATR 72-212A | 0742 | ex F-WWEC | | |
| ☐ F-GRPZ | ATR 72-212A | 0745 | ex F-WWEF | | |
| ☐ F-HAPL | ATR 72-212A | 0654 | ex F-OIJG | | |
| ☐ F-GYFM | Airbus A319-112 | 1068 | ex F-WQRR | | |
| ☐ F-GYJM | Airbus A319-112 | 1145 | ex F-WQRT | | |
| ☐ F-HBEV | Airbus A320-216 | 3952 | ex F-WWBI | Calanche de Piana | |
| ☐ F-HBSA | Airbus A320-216 | 3882 | ex F-WWIP | Scala di Santa Regina | |
| ☐ F-HDGK | Airbus A320-214 | 4478 | ex D-ABFM | U Capi Corsu | ♦ |
| ☐ F-HDMF | Airbus A320-214 | 4463 | ex D-ABFL | | o/o♦ |

### AIR FRANCE | Airfrans (AF/AFR)   Paris Charles de Gaulle/Orly (CDG/ORY)

Member of Skyteam

| | | | |
|---|---|---|---|
| ☐ F-GUGA | Airbus A318-111 | 2035 | ex D-AUAD |
| ☐ F-GUGB | Airbus A318-111 | 2059 | ex D-AUAF |
| ☐ F-GUGC | Airbus A318-111 | 2071 | ex D-AUAG |
| ☐ F-GUGD | Airbus A318-111 | 2081 | ex D-AUAH |
| ☐ F-GUGE | Airbus A318-111 | 2100 | ex D-AUAI |
| ☐ F-GUGF | Airbus A318-111 | 2109 | ex D-AUAJ |
| ☐ F-GUGG | Airbus A318-111 | 2317 | ex D-AUAA |
| ☐ F-GUGH | Airbus A318-111 | 2344 | ex D-AUAF |

| | | | | | |
|---|---|---|---|---|---|
| ☐ F-GUGI | Airbus A318-111 | 2350 | ex D-AUAG | | |
| ☐ F-GUGJ | Airbus A318-111 | 2582 | ex D-AUAE | | |
| ☐ F-GUGK | Airbus A318-111 | 2601 | ex D-AUAF | | |
| ☐ F-GUGL | Airbus A318-111 | 2686 | ex D-AUAA | | |
| ☐ F-GUGM | Airbus A318-111 | 2750 | ex D-AUAB | | |
| ☐ F-GUGN | Airbus A318-111 | 2918 | ex D-AUAB | | |
| ☐ F-GUGO | Airbus A318-111 | 2951 | ex D-AUAD | | |
| ☐ F-GUGP | Airbus A318-111 | 2967 | ex D-AUAF | | |
| ☐ F-GUGQ | Airbus A318-111 | 2972 | ex D-AUAG | | |
| ☐ F-GUGR | Airbus A318-111 | 3009 | ex D-AUAJ | | |
| | | | | | |
| ☐ F-GPMA | Airbus A319-113 | 0598 | ex D-AVYD | | |
| ☐ F-GPMB | Airbus A319-113 | 0600 | ex D-AVYC | | |
| ☐ F-GPMC | Airbus A319-113 | 0608 | ex D-AVYE | | |
| ☐ F-GPMD | Airbus A319-113 | 0618 | ex D-AVYJ | | |
| ☐ F-GPME | Airbus A319-113 | 0625 | ex D-AVYQ | | |
| ☐ F-GPMF | Airbus A319-113 | 0637 | ex D-AVYT | | |
| ☐ F-GRHA | Airbus A319-111 | 0938 | ex D-AVYS | | |
| ☐ F-GRHB | Airbus A319-111 | 0985 | ex D-AVYO | | |
| ☐ F-GRHC | Airbus A319-111 | 0998 | ex D-AVYW | | |
| ☐ F-GRHD | Airbus A319-111 | 1000 | ex D-AVYP | | |
| ☐ F-GRHE | Airbus A319-111 | 1020 | ex D-AVYX | | |
| ☐ F-GRHF | Airbus A319-111 | 1025 | ex D-AVYE | | |
| ☐ F-GRHG | Airbus A319-111 | 1036 | ex D-AVYS | | |
| ☐ F-GRHH | Airbus A319-111 | 1151 | ex D-AVWK | | |
| ☐ F-GRHI | Airbus A319-111 | 1169 | ex D-AVYX | | |
| ☐ F-GRHJ | Airbus A319-111 | 1176 | ex D-AVWN | | |
| ☐ F-GRHK | Airbus A319-111 | 1190 | ex D-AVYQ | | |
| ☐ F-GRHL | Airbus A319-111 | 1201 | ex D-AVWT | | |
| ☐ F-GRHM | Airbus A319-111 | 1216 | ex D-AVYF | | |
| ☐ F-GRHN | Airbus A319-111 | 1267 | ex D-AVWB | | |
| ☐ F-GRHO | Airbus A319-111 | 1271 | ex D-AVWC | | |
| ☐ F-GRHP | Airbus A319-111 | 1344 | ex D-AVYQ | | |
| ☐ F-GRHQ | Airbus A319-111 | 1404 | ex D-AVYB | | |
| ☐ F-GRHR | Airbus A319-111 | 1415 | ex D-AVYF | | |
| ☐ F-GRHS | Airbus A319-111 | 1444 | ex D-AVWA | | |
| ☐ F-GRHT | Airbus A319-111 | 1449 | ex D-AVWD | | |
| ☐ F-GRHU | Airbus A319-111 | 1471 | ex D-AVYR | | |
| ☐ F-GRHV | Airbus A319-111 | 1505 | ex D-AVYF | | |
| ☐ F-GRHX | Airbus A319-111 | 1524 | ex D-AVWC | | |
| ☐ F-GRHY | Airbus A319-111 | 1616 | ex D-AVWG | | |
| ☐ F-GRHZ | Airbus A319-111 | 1622 | ex D-AVYO | | |
| ☐ F-GRXA | Airbus A319-111 | 1640 | ex D-AVYJ | | |
| ☐ F-GRXB | Airbus A319-111 | 1645 | ex D-AVYC | | |
| ☐ F-GRXC | Airbus A319-111 | 1677 | ex D-AVWF | | |
| ☐ F-GRXD | Airbus A319-111 | 1699 | ex D-AVYG | | |
| ☐ F-GRXE | Airbus A319-111 | 1733 | ex D-AVWT | | |
| ☐ F-GRXF | Airbus A319-111 | 1938 | ex D-AVWG | | |
| ☐ F-GRXG | Airbus A319-115LR | 2213 | ex D-AVYM | Dedicate | |
| ☐ F-GRXH | Airbus A319-115LR | 2228 | ex D-AVWC | Dedicate | |
| ☐ F-GRXJ | Airbus A319-115LR | 2456 | ex D-AVYX | Dedicate | |
| ☐ F-GRXK | Airbus A319-115LR | 2716 | ex D-AVYX | Dedicate | |
| ☐ F-GRXL | Airbus A319-111 | 2938 | ex D-AVWV | | |
| ☐ F-GRXM | Airbus A319-111 | 2961 | ex D-AVYI | | |
| ☐ F-GRXN | Airbus A319-115LR | 3065 | ex D-AVWP | Dedicate | |
| | | | | | |
| ☐ F-GFKH | Airbus A320-211 | 0061 | | Ville de Bruxelles | |
| ☐ F-GFKJ | Airbus A320-211 | 0063 | | Ville de Copenhague | Retro c/s |
| ☐ F-GFKM | Airbus A320-211 | 0102 | | Ville de Luxembourg | |
| ☐ F-GFKR | Airbus A320-211 | 0186 | | Ville de Barcelonne | |
| ☐ F-GFKS | Airbus A320-211 | 0187 | | | |
| ☐ F-GFKV | Airbus A320-211 | 0227 | | Ville de Bordeaux | |
| ☐ F-GFKY | Airbus A320-211 | 0285 | | Ville de Toulouse | |
| ☐ F-GFKZ | Airbus A320-211 | 0286 | | Ville de Turin | |
| ☐ F-GHQC | Airbus A320-211 | 0044 | ex F-GGEH | | [OPF] |
| ☐ F-GHQE | Airbus A320-211 | 0115 | | | |
| ☐ F-GHQG | Airbus A320-211 | 0155 | | | |
| ☐ F-GHQJ | Airbus A320-211 | 0214 | | | |
| ☐ F-GHQK | Airbus A320-211 | 0236 | | | |
| ☐ F-GHQL | Airbus A320-211 | 0239 | | | |
| ☐ F-GHQM | Airbus A320-211 | 0237 | | | |
| ☐ F-GHQO | Airbus A320-211 | 0278 | | | |
| ☐ F-GHQP | Airbus A320-211 | 0337 | | | |
| ☐ F-GHQQ | Airbus A320-211 | 0352 | | | |
| ☐ F-GHQR | Airbus A320-211 | 0377 | | | |
| ☐ F-GJVA | Airbus A320-211 | 0144 | ex F-WWDK | | |
| ☐ F-GJVB | Airbus A320-211 | 0145 | ex F-WWDL | | |
| ☐ F-GJVG | Airbus A320-211 | 0270 | | | |
| ☐ F-GJVW | Airbus A320-211 | 0491 | | | |
| ☐ F-GKXA | Airbus A320-211 | 0287 | | Ville de Nantes | |
| ☐ F-GKXC | Airbus A320-214 | 1502 | ex F-WWIG | | |
| ☐ F-GKXD | Airbus A320-214 | 1873 | ex F-WWDV | | |

| | | | | | |
|---|---|---|---|---|---|
| ☐ | F-GKXE | Airbus A320-214 | 1879 | ex F-WWDX | |
| ☐ | F-GKXF | Airbus A320-214 | 1885 | | |
| ☐ | F-GKXG | Airbus A320-214 | 1894 | ex F-WWDV | |
| ☐ | F-GKXH | Airbus A320-214 | 1924 | | |
| ☐ | F-GKXI | Airbus A320-214 | 1949 | | |
| ☐ | F-GKXJ | Airbus A320-214 | 1900 | | |
| ☐ | F-GKXK | Airbus A320-214 | 2140 | ex F-WWBR | |
| ☐ | F-GKXL | Airbus A320-214 | 2705 | | |
| ☐ | F-GKXM | Airbus A320-214 | 2721 | ex F-WWXM | |
| ☐ | F-GKXN | Airbus A320-214 | 3008 | ex F-WWBH | |
| ☐ | F-GKXO | Airbus A320-214 | 3420 | ex F-WWIP | |
| ☐ | F-GKXP | Airbus A320-214 | 3470 | ex F-WWBP | |
| ☐ | F-GKXQ | Airbus A320-214 | 3777 | ex D-AVVH | |
| ☐ | F-GKXR | Airbus A320-214 | 3795 | ex F-WWBM | |
| ☐ | F-GKXS | Airbus A320-214 | 3825 | ex F-WWIV | |
| ☐ | F-GKXT | Airbus A320-214 | 3859 | ex F-WWDM | |
| ☐ | F-GKXU | Airbus A320-214 | 4063 | ex F-WWBF | |
| ☐ | F-GKXV | Airbus A320-214 | 4084 | ex D-AVVA | |
| ☐ | F-GKXY | Airbus A320-214 | 4105 | ex D-AVVR | |
| ☐ | F-GKXZ | Airbus A320-214 | 4137 | ex F-WWIZ | |
| ☐ | F-HBNA | Airbus A320-214 | 4335 | ex F-WWIU | |
| ☐ | F-HBNB | Airbus A320-214 | 4402 | ex F-WWBS | |
| ☐ | F-HBNC | Airbus A320-214 | 4601 | ex F-WWID | ◆ |
| ☐ | F-HBND | Airbus A320-214 | 4604 | ex F-WWIE | ◆ |
| ☐ | F-HBNE | Airbus A320-214 | 4664 | ex F-WWIC | ◆ |
| ☐ | F-HBNF | Airbus A320-214 | 4714 | ex F-WWBS | ◆ |
| ☐ | F-HBNG | Airbus A320-214 | 4747 | ex F-WWIT | ◆ |
| ☐ | F-HBNH | Airbus A320-214 | 4800 | ex F-WWIK | ◆ |
| ☐ | F-HBNI | Airbus A320-214 | 4105 | ex F-WWIC | ◆ |
| ☐ | F-HBNJ | Airbus A320-214 | 4908 | ex F-WWDK | ◆ |
| ☐ | F-HBNK | Airbus A320-214 | 5086 | ex F-WWII | ◆ |
| ☐ | F-HEPA | Airbus A320-214 | 4139 | ex F-WWIX | |
| ☐ | F-HEPB | Airbus A320-214 | 4241 | ex F-WWDK | |
| ☐ | F-HEPC | Airbus A320-214 | 4267 | ex F-WWBM | |
| ☐ | F-HEPD | Airbus A320-214 | 4295 | ex F-WWIZ | |
| ☐ | F-HEPE | Airbus A320-214 | 4298 | ex F-WWIC | |
| | | | | | |
| ☐ | F-GMZA | Airbus A321-111 | 0498 | ex D-AVZK | |
| ☐ | F-GMZB | Airbus A321-111 | 0509 | ex D-AVZN | |
| ☐ | F-GMZC | Airbus A321-111 | 0521 | ex D-AVZW | |
| ☐ | F-GMZD | Airbus A321-111 | 0529 | ex D-AVZA | |
| ☐ | F-GMZE | Airbus A321-111 | 0544 | ex D-AVZF | |
| ☐ | F-GTAD | Airbus A321-212 | 0777 | ex D-AVZI | |
| ☐ | F-GTAE | Airbus A321-212 | 0796 | ex D-AVZN | |
| ☐ | F-GTAH | Airbus A321-212 | 1133 | ex D-AVZD | |
| ☐ | F-GTAI | Airbus A321-212 | 1299 | ex D-AVZP | |
| ☐ | F-GTAJ | Airbus A321-212 | 1476 | ex D-AVZF | |
| ☐ | F-GTAK | Airbus A321-212 | 1658 | ex D-AVZP | |
| ☐ | F-GTAL | Airbus A321-212 | 1691 | ex D-AVZY | |
| ☐ | F-GTAM | Airbus A321-212 | 1859 | ex D-AVZY | |
| ☐ | F-GTAN | Airbus A321-212 | 3051 | ex D-AVZD | |
| ☐ | F-GTAO | Airbus A321-212 | 3098 | ex D-AVZQ | |
| ☐ | F-GTAP | Airbus A321-212 | 3372 | ex D-AVZK | |
| ☐ | F-GTAQ | Airbus A321-212 | 3399 | ex D-AVZQ | |
| ☐ | F-GTAR | Airbus A321-212 | 3401 | ex D-AVZR | |
| ☐ | F-GTAS | Airbus A321-212 | 3419 | ex D-AVZE | |
| ☐ | F-GTAT | Airbus A321-212 | 3441 | ex D-AVZH | |
| ☐ | F-GTAU | Airbus A321-212 | 3814 | ex D-AVZE | |
| ☐ | F-GTAV | Airbus A321-212 | 3884 | ex D-AVZU | |
| ☐ | F-GTAX | Airbus A321-212 | 3930 | ex D-AZAD | |
| ☐ | F-GTAY | Airbus A321-212 | 4251 | ex D-AZAG | |
| ☐ | F-GTAZ | Airbus A321-212 | 4901 | ex D-AVZG | ◆ |
| | | | | | |
| ☐ | F-GZCA | Airbus A330-203 | 422 | | |
| ☐ | F-GZCB | Airbus A330-203 | 443 | | |
| ☐ | F-GZCC | Airbus A330-203 | 448 | | |
| ☐ | F-GZCD | Airbus A330-203 | 458 | ex (F-WWJH) | |
| ☐ | F-GZCE | Airbus A330-203 | 465 | ex F-WWKM | |
| ☐ | F-GZCF | Airbus A330-203 | 481 | | |
| ☐ | F-GZCG | Airbus A330-203 | 498 | ex F-WWKI | |
| ☐ | F-GZCH | Airbus A330-203 | 500 | | |
| ☐ | F-GZCI | Airbus A330-203 | 502 | ex F-WWKJ | |
| ☐ | F-GZCJ | Airbus A330-203 | 503 | | |
| ☐ | F-GZCK | Airbus A330-203 | 516 | | |
| ☐ | F-GZCL | Airbus A330-203 | 519 | | |
| ☐ | F-GZCM | Airbus A330-203 | 567 | ex (F-WWYT) | |
| ☐ | F-GZCN | Airbus A330-203 | 584 | | |
| ☐ | F-GZCO | Airbus A330-203 | 657 | | |
| | | | | | |
| ☐ | F-GLZC | Airbus A340-311 | 029 | | |
| ☐ | F-GLZH | Airbus A340-311 | 078 | | |
| ☐ | F-GLZI | Airbus A340-311 | 084 | | |

| ☐ F-GLZJ | Airbus A340-313X | 186 | | |
| ☐ F-GLZK | Airbus A340-313X | 207 | | |
| ☐ F-GLZL | Airbus A340-313X | 210 | | |
| ☐ F-GLZM | Airbus A340-313X | 237 | | |
| ☐ F-GLZN | Airbus A340-313X | 245 | | |
| ☐ F-GLZO | Airbus A340-313X | 246 | | |
| ☐ F-GLZP | Airbus A340-313X | 260 | | |
| ☐ F-GLZR | Airbus A340-313X | 307 | | |
| ☐ F-GLZS | Airbus A340-313X | 310 | | |
| ☐ F-GLZT | Airbus A340-313X | 319 | | |
| ☐ F-GLZU | Airbus A340-313X | 377 | | |
| ☐ F-GNIG | Airbus A340-313X | 174 | | |
| ☐ F-GNII | Airbus A340-313X | 399 | | |
| | | | | |
| ☐ F-HPJA | Airbus A380-861 | 033 | ex F-WWSB | |
| ☐ F-HPJB | Airbus A380-861 | 040 | ex F-WWSE | |
| ☐ F-HPJC | Airbus A380-861 | 043 | ex F-WWAB | |
| ☐ F-HPJD | Airbus A380-861 | 049 | ex F-WWAL | |
| ☐ F-HPJE | Airbus A380-861 | 052 | ex F-WWAN | |
| ☐ F-HPJF | Airbus A380-861 | 064 | ex F-WWAU | |
| ☐ F-HPJG | Airbus A380-861 | 067 | ex F-WWSQ | o/o |
| ☐ F-HPJH | Airbus A380-861 | 099 | ex F-WWAF | o/o |
| ☐ F-HPII | Airbus A380-861 | 104 | ex F-WW | o/o♦ |
| | | | | |
| ☐ F-GEXA | Boeing 747-4B3 | 24154/741 | | |
| ☐ F-GEXB | Boeing 747-4B3M | 24155/864 | | |
| ☐ F-GISC | Boeing 747-428M | 25599/899 | | [GSO] |
| ☐ F-GISD | Boeing 747-428M | 25628/934 | | |
| ☐ F-GITD | Boeing 747-428 | 25600/901 | | |
| ☐ F-GITE | Boeing 747-428 | 25601/906 | | |
| ☐ F-GITF | Boeing 747-428 | 25602/909 | | |
| ☐ F-GITH | Boeing 747-428 | 32868/1325 | | |
| ☐ F-GITI | Boeing 747-428 | 32869/1327 | | |
| ☐ F-GITJ | Boeing 747-428 | 32871/1343 | | |
| ☐ F-GIUA | Boeing 747-428ERF | 32866/1315 | ex N5017Q | |
| ☐ F-GIUC | Boeing 747-428ERF | 32867/1318 | | |
| ☐ F-GIUD | Boeing 747-428ERF | 32870/1344 | | |
| | | | | |
| ☐ F-GSPA | Boeing 777-228ER | 29002/129 | | |
| ☐ F-GSPB | Boeing 777-228ER | 29003/133 | | |
| ☐ F-GSPC | Boeing 777-228ER | 29004/138 | | |
| ☐ F-GSPD | Boeing 777-228ER | 29005/187 | | |
| ☐ F-GSPE | Boeing 777-228ER | 29006/189 | | |
| ☐ F-GSPF | Boeing 777-228ER | 29007/201 | | |
| ☐ F-GSPG | Boeing 777-228ER | 27609/195 | | |
| ☐ F-GSPH | Boeing 777-228ER | 28675/210 | | |
| ☐ F-GSPI | Boeing 777-228ER | 29008/258 | | |
| ☐ F-GSPJ | Boeing 777-228ER | 29009/263 | | |
| ☐ F-GSPK | Boeing 777-228ER | 29010/267 | | |
| ☐ F-GSPL | Boeing 777-228ER | 30457/284 | ex N50281 | |
| ☐ F-GSPM | Boeing 777-228ER | 30456/307 | | |
| ☐ F-GSPN | Boeing 777-228ER | 29011/314 | | |
| ☐ F-GSPO | Boeing 777-228ER | 30614/320 | | |
| ☐ F-GSPP | Boeing 777-228ER | 30615/327 | | |
| ☐ F-GSPQ | Boeing 777-228ER | 28682/331 | | |
| ☐ F-GSPR | Boeing 777-228ER | 28683/367 | | |
| ☐ F-GSPS | Boeing 777-228ER | 32306/370 | | |
| ☐ F-GSPT | Boeing 777-228ER | 32308/382 | | |
| ☐ F-GSPU | Boeing 777-228ER | 32309/383 | | |
| ☐ F-GSPV | Boeing 777-228ER | 28684/385 | | |
| ☐ F-GSPX | Boeing 777-228ER | 32698/392 | | |
| ☐ F-GSPY | Boeing 777-228ER | 32305/395 | | |
| ☐ F-GSPZ | Boeing 777-228ER | 32310/401 | | |
| | | | | |
| ☐ F-GSQA | Boeing 777-328ER | 32723/466 | ex N5017Q | |
| ☐ F-GSQB | Boeing 777-328ER | 32724/478 | | |
| ☐ F-GSQC | Boeing 777-328ER | 32727/480 | | |
| ☐ F-GSQD | Boeing 777-328ER | 32726/490 | | |
| ☐ F-GSQE | Boeing 777-328ER | 32851/492 | | |
| ☐ F-GSQF | Boeing 777-328ER | 32849/494 | ex N50217 | |
| ☐ F-GSQG | Boeing 777-328ER | 32850/500 | ex N5028Y | |
| ☐ F-GSQH | Boeing 777-328ER | 32711/501 | | |
| ☐ F-GSQI | Boeing 777-328ER | 32725/502 | ex N60697 | |
| ☐ F-GSQJ | Boeing 777-328ER | 32852/510 | | |
| ☐ F-GSQK | Boeing 777-328ER | 32845/530 | ex N5017Q | |
| ☐ F-GSQL | Boeing 777-328ER | 32853/545 | | |
| ☐ F-GSQM | Boeing 777-328ER | 32848/558 | | |
| ☐ F-GSQN | Boeing 777-328ER | 32960/565 | | |
| ☐ F-GSQO | Boeing 777-328ER | 32961/570 | | |
| ☐ F-GSQP | Boeing 777-328ER | 35676/573 | | |
| ☐ F-GSQR | Boeing 777-328ER | 35677/579 | | |
| ☐ F-GSQS | Boeing 777-328ER | 32962/608 | | |

| | | | | |
|---|---|---|---|---|
| ☐ F-GSQT | Boeing 777-328ER | 32846/616 | | |
| ☐ F-GSQU | Boeing 777-328ER | 32847/624 | ex N5022E | |
| ☐ F-GSQV | Boeing 777-328ER | 32854/636 | | |
| ☐ F-GSQX | Boeing 777-328ER | 32963/645 | ex N5014K | |
| ☐ F-GSQY | Boeing 777-328ER | 35678/647 | | |
| ☐ F-GZNA | Boeing 777-328ER | 35297/671 | ex N50217 | |
| ☐ F-GZNB | Boeing 777-328ER | 32964/715 | | |
| ☐ F-GZNC | Boeing 777-328ER | 35542/723 | | Gille Dehove |
| ☐ F-GZND | Boeing 777-328ER | 35543/777 | ex N1785B | |
| ☐ F-GZNE | Boeing 777-328ER | 37432/790 | | |
| ☐ F-GZNF | Boeing 777-328ER | 37433/792 | ex N50281 | |
| ☐ F-GZNG | Boeing 777-328ER | 32968/795 | | |
| ☐ F-GZNH | Boeing 777-328ER | 35544/905 | ex N5017V | |
| ☐ F-GZNI | Boeing 777-328ER | 39973/924 | | ♦ |
| ☐ F-GZNJ | Boeing 777-328ER | 38706/928 | | ♦ |
| ☐ F-GZNK | Boeing 777-328ER | 39971/931 | | ♦ |
| ☐ F-GZNL | Boeing 777-328ER | 40063/1001 | | ♦ |
| ☐ F-GZNN | Boeing 777-328ER | 40376 | | o/o♦ |
| ☐ F-GZNO | Boeing 777-328ER | 38665 | | o/o♦ |
| | | | | |
| ☐ F-GUOB | Boeing 777-F28 | 32965/732 | ex N5023Q | |
| ☐ F-GUOC | Boeing 777-F28 | 32966/752 | | |

## AIR FRANCE REGIONAL                                    *Various*

The majority of services are operated in full Air France colours with titles 'Air France by' the appropriate airline, Airlinair, Brit'Air, CCM Airlines, Regional and Cityjet.

## AIR MEDITERRANÉE                 *Mediterranée (BIE)*                 *Tarbes (LDE)*

| | | | | | |
|---|---|---|---|---|---|
| ☐ F-GYAJ | Airbus A321-211 | 2707 | ex D-AVZF | | |
| ☐ F-GYAN | Airbus A321-111 | 0535 | ex F-WQQU | | |
| ☐ F-GYAO | Airbus A321-111 | 0642 | ex F-WQQV | | >Hermes |
| ☐ F-GYAP | Airbus A321-111 | 0517 | ex HB-IOA | | |
| ☐ F-GYAQ | Airbus A321-211 | 0827 | ex HB-IOI | | |
| ☐ F-GYAR | Airbus A321-211 | 0891 | ex HB-IOJ | FRAM colours | |
| ☐ F-GYAZ | Airbus A321-111 | 0519 | ex D-ANJA | | .>MMA |
| | | | | | |
| ☐ F-GYAI | Airbus A320-211 | 0293 | ex 9H-ABQ | | >Hermes |
| ☐ F-HCOA | Boeing 737-5L9 | 28084/2788 | ex OY-APB | | |
| ☐ SX-BHR | Boeing 737-5L9 | 29234/3068 | ex TC-AAG | | >Hermes♦ |

## AIRBUS TRANSPORT INTERNATIONAL  Super Transport  (4Y/BGA)        *Toulouse-Blagnac (TLS)*

| | | | | |
|---|---|---|---|---|
| ☐ F-GSTA | Airbus A300B4-608ST Beluga | 655/001 | ex F-WAST | Super Transporter 1 |
| ☐ F-GSTB | Airbus A300B4-608ST Beluga | 751/002 | ex F-WSTB | Super Transporter 2 |
| ☐ F-GSTC | Airbus A300B4-608ST Beluga | 765/003 | ex F-WSTC | Super Transporter 3 |
| ☐ F-GSTD | Airbus A300B4-608ST Beluga | 776/004 | ex F-WSTD | Super Transporter 4 |
| ☐ F-GSTF | Airbus A300B4-608ST Beluga | 796/005 | ex F-WSTF | Super Transporter 5 |

## AIRLEC AIR ESPACE                   *AirLec (ARL)*                 *Bordeaux (BOD)*

| | | | | |
|---|---|---|---|---|
| ☐ F-GGVG | Swearingen SA.226T Merlin IIIB | T-293 | ex D-IBBB | |
| ☐ F-GLPT | Swearingen SA.226T Merlin IIIB | T-298 | ex VH-AWU | |
| ☐ F-GRNT | Swearingen SA.226T Merlin IIIB | T-312 | ex N84GA | |

## AIRLINAIR                        *Airlinair (A5/RLA)*              *Paris-Orly (ORY)*

| | | | | | |
|---|---|---|---|---|---|
| ☐ F-GPYA | ATR 42-500 | 0457 | ex F-WWET | | |
| ☐ F-GPYB | ATR 42-500 | 0480 | ex F-WWLZ | | |
| ☐ F-GPYC | ATR 42-500 | 0484 | ex F-WWEB | | |
| ☐ F-GPYD | ATR 42-500 | 0490 | ex F-WWLJ | | |
| ☐ F-GPYF | ATR 42-500 | 0495 | ex F-WWLM | | op for AFR |
| ☐ F-GPYK | ATR 42-500 | 0537 | ex F-WWLC | | op for AFR |
| ☐ F-GPYL | ATR 42-500 | 0542 | ex F-WWLH | | op for AFR |
| ☐ F-GPYM | ATR 42-500 | 0520 | ex F-WWLR | | op for AFR |
| ☐ F-GPYN | ATR 42-500 | 0539 | ex F-WWLO | | op for AFR |
| ☐ F-GPYO | ATR 42-500 | 0544 | ex F-WWLH | | |
| ☐ F-GVZB | ATR 42-500 | 0524 | ex F-OHQL | | |
| ☐ F-GVZC | ATR 42-500 | 0516 | ex F-WNUA | | ♦ |
| ☐ F-GVZD | ATR 42-500 | 0530 | ex F-WNUJ | | ♦ |
| | | | | | |
| ☐ F-GKPD | ATR 72-202 | 0177 | ex F-WWE | all-white | |
| ☐ F-GPOC | ATR 72-202 (QC) | 0311 | ex B-22707 | | op for AFR |
| ☐ F-GPOD | ATR 72-202 (QC) | 0361 | ex B-22711 | | op for AFR |
| ☐ F-GVZG | ATR 72-201 | 0145 | ex G-HERM | | |
| ☐ F-GVZL | ATR 72-212A | 0553 | ex F-OHJO | | |
| ☐ F-GVZM | ATR 72-212A | 0590 | ex F-OHJT | | |
| ☐ F-GVZN | ATR 72-212A | 0563 | ex F-OHJU | | |

| | | | |
|---|---|---|---|
| ☐ F-GVZO | ATR 42-320 | 0080 | ex OY-PCG |
| ☐ F-GVZZ | ATR 42-300 | 0055 | ex F-WVZZ |

## ALSAIR · *Alsair (AL/LSR)* · *Colmar (CMR)*

| | | | |
|---|---|---|---|
| ☐ F-GEOU | Beech 65-C90 King Air | LJ-941 | ex N3804C |

## ATLANTIQUE AIR ASSISTANCE · *Triple A (TLB)* · *Nantes (NTE)*

| | | | |
|---|---|---|---|
| ☐ F-GIZB | Beech 65-C90 King Air | LJ-955 | ex N786SB |
| ☐ F-GNBR | Beech 1900D | UE-327 | ex N23154 |
| ☐ F-GPYY | Beech 1900C-1 | UC-115 | ex N115YV |
| ☐ F-HAAV | ATR 42-320 | 0019 | ex F-WKVB |
| ☐ F-HBSO | ATR 42-320 | 0066 | ex D4-CBS |

## BRIT'AIR · *Brit Air (DB/BZH)* · *Morlaix (MXN)*

| | | | | |
|---|---|---|---|---|
| ☐ F-GRJG | Canadair CRJ-100ER | 7143 | ex C-FMMQ | |
| ☐ F-GRJI | Canadair CRJ-100ER | 7147 | ex C-FZAL | |
| ☐ F-GRJJ | Canadair CRJ-100ER | 7190 | ex C-GBFF | |
| ☐ F-GRJK | Canadair CRJ-100ER | 7219 | ex C-FMMQ | |
| ☐ F-GRJL | Canadair CRJ-100ER | 7221 | ex C-FMNX | |
| ☐ F-GRJM | Canadair CRJ-100ER | 7222 | ex C-FMMY | |
| ☐ F-GRJN | Canadair CRJ-100ER | 7262 | ex C-FMLT | |
| ☐ F-GRJO | Canadair CRJ-100ER | 7296 | ex C-FMNW | |
| ☐ F-GRJP | Canadair CRJ-100ER | 7301 | ex C-FVAZ | |
| ☐ F-GRJQ | Canadair CRJ-100ER | 7321 | ex C-FMLS | |
| ☐ F-GRJR | Canadair CRJ-100ER | 7375 | ex C-FMKW | |
| ☐ F-GRJT | Canadair CRJ-100ER | 7389 | ex C-FMOS | |
| ☐ F-GRJU | Canadair CRJ-100ER | 7162 | ex 5X-UGD | ♦ |
| | | | | |
| ☐ F-GRZA | Canadair CRJ-701 | 10006 | ex C-GHCE | |
| ☐ F-GRZB | Canadair CRJ-701 | 10007 | ex C-GHCF | |
| ☐ F-GRZC | Canadair CRJ-701 | 10008 | ex C-GHCO | |
| ☐ F-GRZD | Canadair CRJ-701 | 10016 | ex C-GJEZ | |
| ☐ F-GRZE | Canadair CRJ-701 | 10032 | ex C-GIBL | |
| ☐ F-GRZF | Canadair CRJ-701 | 10036 | ex C-GIBQ | |
| ☐ F-GRZG | Canadair CRJ-701 | 10037 | ex C-GIBT | |
| ☐ F-GRZH | Canadair CRJ-701 | 10089 | ex C-GIBI | |
| ☐ F-GRZI | Canadair CRJ-701 | 10093 | | |
| ☐ F-GRZJ | Canadair CRJ-701 | 10096 | | |
| ☐ F-GRZK | Canadair CRJ-701 | 10198 | | |
| ☐ F-GRZL | Canadair CRJ-701 | 10245 | | |
| ☐ F-GRZM | Canadair CRJ-701 | 10263 | | |
| ☐ F-GRZN | Canadair CRJ-701 | 10264 | | |
| ☐ F-GRZO | Canadair CRJ-701 | 10265 | | |
| | | | | |
| ☐ F-HMLA | Canadair CRJ-1000 | 19004 | ex C-GELU | |
| ☐ F-HMLC | Canadair CRJ-1000 | 19006 | ex C-GHKA | |
| ☐ F-HMLD | Canadair CRJ-1000 | 19007 | ex C-GIBR | |
| ☐ F-HMLE | Canadair CRJ-1000 | 19009 | ex C-GZQJ | ♦ |
| ☐ F-HMLF | Canadair CRJ-1000 | 19010 | ex C-GZQX | ♦ |
| ☐ F-HMLG | Canadair CRJ-1000 | 19012 | ex C-GZQW | ♦ |
| ☐ F-HMLH | Canadair CRJ-1000 | 19013 | ex C-GIAH | ♦ |
| ☐ F-HMLI | Canadair CRJ-1000 | 19014 | ex C-GIBJ | ♦ |
| ☐ F-HMLJ | Canadair CRJ-1000 | 19015 | ex C-GIAV | ♦ |
| ☐ F-HMLK | Canadair CRJ-1000 | 19016 | ex C-GZQA | ♦ |
| ☐ F-HMLL | Canadair CRJ-1000 | 19017 | ex C-GZQJ | ♦ |
| ☐ F-HMLM | Canadair CRJ-1000 | 19023 | ex C-GICL | ♦ |
| ☐ F-HMLN | Canadair CRJ-1000 | 19024 | ex C-GICP | ♦ |
| | | | | |
| ☐ F-GPXB | Fokker 100 | 11492 | ex PH-EZK | [NWI] |
| ☐ F-GPXE | Fokker 100 | 11495 | ex PH-EZP | [BTS] |

## CHALAIR AVIATION / CATOVAIR · *Chalar (CLG)* · *Caen-Carpiquet (CFR)*

| | | | |
|---|---|---|---|
| ☐ F-GOOB | Beech 1900C-1 | UC-153 | ex N153YV |
| ☐ F-HBCA | Beech 1900D | UE-188 | ex SE-KXV |
| ☐ F-HBCB | Beech 1900D | UE-390 | ex 3B-VTL |
| ☐ F-HBCC | Beech 1900D | UE-350 | ex 3B-VIP |
| ☐ F-HBCE | Beech 1900D | UE-323 | ex OY-CHU |
| | | | |
| ☐ F-BXPY | Beech 65-C90 King Air | LJ-684 | |
| ☐ F-GHVV | Beech 200 Super King Air | BB-676 | ex N1362B |
| ☐ F-GIJB | Beech 200 Super King Air | BB-13 | ex N83MA |

## CORSAIR · *Corsair (SS/CRL)* · *Ajaccio (AJA)*

| | | | | |
|---|---|---|---|---|
| ☐ F-GTUI | Boeing 747-422 | 26875/931 | ex N186UA | |
| ☐ F-HKIS | Boeing 747-422 | 25380/913 | ex F-WKIS | |
| ☐ F-HLOV | Boeing 747-422 | 25379/911 | ex F-WLOV | ♦ |

| ☐ F-HSEA | Boeing 747-422 | 26877/944 | ex F-WSEA |
| ☐ F-HSUN | Boeing 747-422 | 26880/984 | ex F-WSUN |

| ☐ F-HBIL | Airbus A330-243 | 320 | |
| ☐ F-HCAT | Airbus A330-243 | 285 | ex F-WWKB |

## EUROPE AIRPOST — French Post (5O/FPO) — Paris-Charles de Gaulle (CDG)

| ☐ F-GFUF | Boeing 737-3B3 (QC) | 24388/1725 | |
| ☐ F-GIXB | Boeing 737-33A (QC) | 24789/1953 | ex F-OGSD |
| ☐ F-GIXC | Boeing 737-38B (QC) | 25124/2047 | ex F-OGSS | Saint-Louis |
| ☐ F-GIXD | Boeing 737-33A (QC) | 25744/2198 | ex N3213T |
| ☐ F-GIXE | Boeing 737-3B3 (QC) | 26850/2235 | ex N854WT |
| ☐ F-GIXF | Boeing 737-3B3 (QC) | 26851/2267 | ex N4361V |
| ☐ F-GIXH | Boeing 737-3S3 (QC) | 23788/1393 | ex N271LF |
| ☐ F-GIXI | Boeing 737-348 (QC) | 23809/1458 | ex F-OGSY |
| ☐ F-GIXJ | Boeing 737-3Y0 (QC) | 23685/1357 | ex G-MONH |
| ☐ F-GIXL | Boeing 737-348 (QC) | 23810/1474 | ex F-OHCS |
| ☐ F-GIXO | Boeing 737-3Q8 (QC) | 24132/1555 | ex N241LF |
| ☐ F-GIXR | Boeing 737-3H6 (SF) | 27125/2415 | ex 9M-MZA |
| ☐ F-GIXS | Boeing 737-3H6 (SF) | 27347/2615 | ex 9M-MZB |
| ☐ F-GIXT | Boeing 737-39M (QC) | 28898/2906 | ex F-ODZZ |
| ☐ F-GZTA | Boeing 737-33V (QC) | 29333/3084 | ex HA-LKV |
| ☐ F-GZTB | Boeing 737-33VF | 29336/3102 | ex HA-LKU |

| ☐ F-GPOA | ATR 72-202 (QC) | 0204 | ex F-ORAC | >SWT |
| ☐ F-GPOB | ATR 72-202 (QC) | 0207 | ex F-ORAN | >SWT |
| ☐ F-GZTC | Boeing 737-73V | 32414/1214 | ex G-EZJS | |
| ☐ F-GZTD | Boeing 737-73V | 32418/1300 | ex G-EZJW | |

## FINIST'AIR — Finistair (FTR) — Brest (BES)

| ☐ F-GHGZ | Cessna 208A Caravan I | 208A00188 | ex (N9769F) |
| ☐ F-GJFI | Cessna 208B Caravan I | 208B0230 | ex N208GC |

## FLEET MANAGEMENT AIRWAYS

| ☐ F-GUME | Beech 1900D | UE-371 | ex CS-DOC | ♦ |

## HELI-UNION — Heli Union (HLU) Paris-Heliport/Toussus-le-Noble (JDP/TNF)

| ☐ F-GJPZ | Aérospatiale SA365N Dauphin 2 | 6115 | ex LN-OLN | |
| ☐ F-GKCU | Aérospatiale SA365N Dauphin 2 | 6011 | ex PH-SEC | based PNR |
| ☐ F-GMAY | Aérospatiale SA365N Dauphin 2 | 6137 | | |
| ☐ F-GRCF | Aérospatiale AS365N3 Dauphin 2 | 9000 | ex F-WWOR | |
| ☐ F-GVGV | Aérospatiale AS365N3 Dauphin 2 | 6724 | ex F-WWOL | |
| ☐ F-GXVY | Aérospatiale AS.365N Dauphin 2 | 9001 | ex D2-EXT | ♦ |
| ☐ TJ-SAH | Aérospatiale SA365N Dauphin 2 | 6037 | ex F-GMHI | |

| ☐ F-GHOY | Aérospatiale AS.332L1 | 9005 | ex F-WQEB | |
| ☐ F-GJTU | Aérospatiale AS350B3 Ecureuil | 3449 | ex EP-HEU | based Cayenne |
| ☐ F-GTNB | Sikorsky S-76C | 760788 | ex N788Y | ♦ |
| ☐ F-GYSH | Aérospatiale AS.332L1 | 9006 | ex F-WQEE | |
| ☐ F-GYVL | Sikorsky S-76C | 760805 | ex N805N | ♦ |
| ☐ F-GZAT | Sikorsky S-76C | 760786 | ex N20878 | ♦ |
| ☐ F-GZKP | Sikorsky S-76C+ | 760806 | ex N806K | ♦ |
| ☐ F-HUMB | Eurocopter EC225LP | 2821 | | ♦ |
| ☐ F-HUPM | Eurocopter EC225LP | 2815 | ex F-WJXL | ♦ |

## HEX'AIR — Hex Airline (UD/HER) — Le Puy (LPY)

| ☐ F-GUPE | Beech 1900D | UE-248 | ex N10882 | >PEA |

## OPENSKIES — (BOS) — Paris-Orly (ORY)

| ☐ F-GPEK | Boeing 757-236/W | 25808/665 | ex G-BPEK | Lauren |
| ☐ F-HAVI | Boeing 757-26D/W | 24473/301 | ex N473AP | Violetta |
| ☐ F-HAVN | Boeing 757-230/W | 25140/382 | ex D-ABNF | Gloria |

## OYONNAIR

| ☐ F-HETS | Beech 1900D | UE-360 | ex (PH-RNH) | ♦ |

## PAN EUROPÉENNE AIR SERVICE — Pan Euro (PEA) — Chambéry (CMF)

| ☐ F-GOPE | Beech 1900D | UE-103 | ex (F-GMSA) | <HER♦ |
| ☐ F-GUPE | Beech 1900D | UE-248 | ex N10882 | <HER |
| ☐ F-GYPE | Embraer ERJ-135LR | 145492 | ex PT-SXL | |
| ☐ F-GZPE | Piaggio P.180 Avanti | 1064 | | |
| ☐ F-HAPE | Beech 1900D | UE-367 | ex N30515 | |

| | | | | | |
|---|---|---|---|---|---|
| ☐ F-HBPE | Embraer ERJ-145LR | 145106 | ex PH-RXC | | |
| ☐ F-HIPE | Embraer EMB-505 Phenom 300 | 50500016 | ex PT-PVD | | ♦ |

## RÉGIONAL — Régional Europe (YS/RAE) — Nantes (NTE)

| | | | | |
|---|---|---|---|---|
| ☐ F-GOHC | Embraer ERJ-135ER | 145243 | ex PT-SJF | >NMB |
| ☐ F-GOHD | Embraer ERJ-135ER | 145252 | ex PT-SJJ | |
| ☐ F-GOHE | Embraer ERJ-135ER | 145335 | ex PT-SNB | >NBM |
| ☐ F-GOHF | Embraer ERJ-135ER | 145347 | ex PT-SNN | >NMB |
| ☐ F-GRGP | Embraer ERJ-135ER | 145188 | ex PT-SFL | |
| ☐ F-GRGQ | Embraer ERJ-135ER | 145233 | ex PT-SJB | |
| ☐ F-GRGR | Embraer ERJ-135ER | 145236 | ex PT-SJE | |
| | | | | |
| ☐ F-GRGA | Embraer ERJ-145EP | 145008 | ex PT-SYE | |
| ☐ F-GRGB | Embraer ERJ-145EP | 145010 | ex PT-SYG | |
| ☐ F-GRGC | Embraer ERJ-145EP | 145012 | ex PT-SYI | |
| ☐ F-GRGD | Embraer ERJ-145EP | 145043 | ex PT-SZI | |
| ☐ F-GRGE | Embraer ERJ-145EP | 145047 | ex PT-SZM | |
| ☐ F-GRGF | Embraer ERJ-145EP | 145050 | ex PT-SZP | |
| ☐ F-GRGG | Embraer ERJ-145EP | 145118 | ex PT-SCT | |
| ☐ F-GRGH | Embraer ERJ-145EP | 145120 | ex PT-SCW | |
| ☐ F-GRGI | Embraer ERJ-145EP | 145152 | ex PT-SED | |
| ☐ F-GRGJ | Embraer ERJ-145EP | 145297 | ex PT-SKO | |
| ☐ F-GRGK | Embraer ERJ-145EP | 145324 | ex PT-SMQ | |
| ☐ F-GRGL | Embraer ERJ-145EP | 145375 | ex PT-SOZ | |
| ☐ F-GRGM | Embraer ERJ-145EP | 145418 | ex PT-STP | |
| ☐ F-GUAM | Embraer ERJ-145MP | 145266 | ex PT-SIY | |
| ☐ F-GUBC | Embraer ERJ-145MP | 145556 | ex PT-SZR | |
| ☐ F-GUBD | Embraer ERJ-145MP | 145333 | ex PT-SMZ | |
| ☐ F-GUBE | Embraer ERJ-145MP | 145668 | ex PT-SFC | |
| ☐ F-GUBF | Embraer ERJ-145MP | 145669 | ex PT-SFD | |
| ☐ F-GUBG | Embraer ERJ-145MP | 14500890 | ex PT-SYD | |
| ☐ F-GUEA | Embraer ERJ-145MP | 145342 | ex PT-SNI | |
| ☐ F-GUFD | Embraer ERJ-145MP | 145197 | ex PT-SGN | |
| ☐ F-GUMA | Embraer ERJ-145MP | 145405 | ex PT-STC | |
| ☐ F-GUPT | Embraer ERJ-145MP | 145294 | ex PT-SKL | |
| ☐ F-GVHD | Embraer ERJ-145MP | 145178 | ex PT-SEZ | |
| | | | | |
| ☐ F-HBXA | Embraer ERJ-170STD | 17000237 | ex PT-SFN | |
| ☐ F-HBXB | Embraer ERJ-170STD | 17000250 | ex PT-SJB | |
| ☐ F-HBXC | Embraer ERJ-170STD | 17000263 | ex PT-SJR | |
| ☐ F-HBXD | Embraer ERJ-170STD | 17000281 | ex PT-TQH | |
| ☐ F-HBXE | Embraer ERJ-170STD | 17000286 | ex PT-TQM | |
| ☐ F-HBXF | Embraer ERJ-170STD | 17000292 | ex PT-TQS | |
| ☐ F-HBXG | Embraer ERJ-170STD | 17000301 | ex PT-XQA | |
| ☐ F-HBXH | Embraer ERJ-170STD | 17000307 | ex PT-XQH | |
| ☐ F-HBXI | Embraer ERJ-170STD | 17000310 | ex PT-XQX | |
| ☐ F-HBXJ | Embraer ERJ-170STD | 17000312 | ex PT-XQZ | |
| ☐ F-HBXK | Embraer ERJ-170LR | 17000008 | ex EI-DFG | ♦ |
| ☐ F-HBXP | Embraer ERJ-170LR | 17000036 | ex EI-DFL | ♦ |
| ☐ F- | Embraer ERJ-170LR | 17000009 | ex EI-DFH | o/o♦ |
| ☐ F- | Embraer ERJ-170LR | 17000010 | ex EI-DFI | o/o♦ |
| ☐ F- | Embraer ERJ-170LR | 17000011 | ex EI-DFJ | o/o♦ |
| ☐ F- | Embraer ERJ-170LR | 17000032 | ex EI-DFK | o/o♦ |
| | | | | |
| ☐ F-HBLA | Embraer ERJ-190LR | 19000051 | ex PT-SIA | |
| ☐ F-HBLB | Embraer ERJ-190LR | 19000060 | ex PT-SIN | |
| ☐ F-HBLC | Embraer ERJ-190LR | 19000080 | ex PT-SJW | |
| ☐ F-HBLD | Embraer ERJ-190LR | 19000113 | ex PT-SQH | |
| ☐ F-HBLE | Embraer ERJ-190LR | 19000123 | ex PT-SQS | |
| ☐ F-HBLF | Embraer ERJ-190LR | 19000158 | ex PT-SAO | |
| ☐ F-HBLG | Embraer ERJ-190LR | 19000254 | ex PT-SIZ | |
| ☐ F-HBLH | Embraer ERJ-190LR | 19000266 | ex PT-TLG | |
| ☐ F-HBLI | Embraer ERJ-190STD | 19000298 | ex PT-TZM | |
| ☐ F-HBLJ | Embraer ERJ-190STD | 19000311 | ex PT-TZZ | |

## REGOURD AVIATION

| | | | | | |
|---|---|---|---|---|---|
| ☐ F-GVZJ | ATR 42-300 | 0093 | ex F-WQNO | | ♦ |
| ☐ F-HEKF | ATR 42-300 | 0173 | ex F-WEKF | | >EQA |
| ☐ F-HTOP | Embraer ERJ-135LR | 14500886 | ex LX-LGK | | ♦ |

## SÉCURITÉ CIVILE — Marseille (MRS)

| | | | | | |
|---|---|---|---|---|---|
| ☐ F-ZBEG | Canadair CL415 | 2015 | ex C-FXBH | 19 | ♦ |
| ☐ F-ZBEU | Canadair CL415 | 2024 | ex C-FZDE | 42 | |
| ☐ F-ZBFN | Canadair CL415 | 2006 | ex C-FVUK | 33 | |
| ☐ F-ZBFP | Canadair CL415 | 2002 | ex C-FBET | 31 | |
| ☐ F-ZBFS | Canadair CL415 | 2001 | ex C-GSCT | 32 | |
| ☐ F-ZBFV | Canadair CL415 | 2013 | ex C-FWPE | 37 | |
| ☐ F-ZBFW | Canadair CL415 | 2014 | ex C-FWZH | 38 | |
| ☐ F-ZBFX | Canadair CL415 | 2007 | ex C-FVUJ | 34 | |

| | | | | |
|---|---|---|---|---|
| ☐ F-ZBFY | Canadair CL415 | 2010 | ex C-FVDY | 35 |
| ☐ F-ZBME | Canadair CL415 | 2057 | ex C-GILN | 44 |
| ☐ F-ZBMF | Canadair CL415 | 2063 | ex C-FGZT | 45 |
| ☐ F-ZBMG | Canadair CL415 | 2065 | ex C-FLFW | 48 |
| | | | | |
| ☐ F-ZBAA | Conair Turbo Firecat | 456/027 | ex F-WEOL | 22 |
| ☐ F-ZBAP | Conair Turbo Firecat | 567/026 | ex F-ZBDA | 12 |
| ☐ F-ZBAZ | Conair Turbo Firecat | DHC-57/008 | ex F-WEOL | 01 |
| ☐ F-ZBCZ | Conair Turbo Firecat | DHC-94/036 | ex F-ZBCA | 23 |
| ☐ F-ZBEH | Conair Turbo Firecat | 410/035 | ex F-WEOJ | 20 |
| ☐ F-ZBET | Conair Turbo Firecat | 703/028 | ex F-WEOJ | 15 |
| ☐ F-ZBEW | Conair Turbo Firecat | 621/025 | ex F-WEOL | 11 |
| ☐ F-ZBEY | Conair Turbo Firecat | 400/017 | ex F-WEOK | 07 |
| ☐ F-ZBMA | Conair Turbo Firecat | 461/021 | ex C-GFZG | 24 |
| | | | | |
| ☐ F-ZBFJ | Beech B200 Super King Air | BB-1102 | ex D-IWAN | 98 |
| ☐ F-ZBFK | Beech B200 Super King Air | BB-876 | ex F-GHSC | 96 |
| ☐ F-ZBMB | Beech B200 Super King Air | BB-1379 | ex F-GJFD | 97 |
| ☐ F-ZBMC | de Havilland DHC-8-402QMRT | 4040 | ex C-FBAM | 73 |
| ☐ F-ZBMD | de Havilland DHC-8-402QMRT | 4043 | ex C-FBSG | 74 |
| ☐ F-ZBQJ | MBB BK.117C-2 | 9323 | ex D-HMBG | |
| ☐ F-ZBQK | MBB BK.117C-2 | 9372 | ex D-HADC | ♦ |
| ☐ F-ZBQL | MBB BK.117C-2 | 9452 | ex D-HADK | ♦ |

## TRANSAVIA FRANCE — Transavia (TO/TVF) — Paris-Orly (ORY)

| | | | | |
|---|---|---|---|---|
| ☐ F-GZHA | Boeing 737-8GJ/W | 34901/2267 | ex (VT-SPN) | |
| ☐ F-GZHB | Boeing 737-8GJ/W | 34902/2309 | ex (VT-SPO) | >CJT |
| ☐ F-GZHC | Boeing 737-8K2/W | 29651/2534 | | |
| ☐ F-GZHD | Boeing 737-8K2/W | 29650/2583 | | |
| ☐ F-GZHE | Boeing 737-8K2/W | 29678/2615 | ex N1787B | |
| ☐ F-GZHF | Boeing 737-8HX/W | 29677/2946 | ex PH-ZOM | |
| ☐ F-GZHN | Boeing 737-85H/W | 29445/186 | ex OY-SEI | |
| ☐ F-GZHV | Boeing 737-85H/W | 29444/178 | ex OY-SEH | |

## TWIN JET — Twin Jet (T7/TJT) — Marseille (MRS)

| | | | | |
|---|---|---|---|---|
| ☐ F-GLND | Beech 1900D | UE-196 | ex N3234G | |
| ☐ F-GLNE | Beech 1900D | UE-197 | ex N3234U | |
| ☐ F-GLNF | Beech 1900D | UE-69 | ex YR-RLA | |
| ☐ F-GLNH | Beech 1900D | UE-73 | ex YR-RLB | |
| ☐ F-GLNK | Beech 1900D | UE-269 | ex N11017 | |
| ☐ F-GRYL | Beech 1900D | UE-301 | ex N22161 | |
| ☐ F-GTKJ | Beech 1900D | UE-348 | ex N23406 | |
| ☐ F-GTVC | Beech 1900D | UE-349 | ex N23430 | Op for Ministère de l'Interieur |

## XL AIRWAYS FRANCE — Starway (SE/XLF) — Paris-Orly (ORY)

| | | | | |
|---|---|---|---|---|
| ☐ F-GKHK | Airbus A320-212 | 0343 | ex OO-TCK | |
| ☐ F-GRSQ | Airbus A330-243 | 501 | ex F-WWKG | |
| ☐ F-GSEU | Airbus A330-243 | 635 | ex F-WWYO | |
| ☐ F-HAXL | Boeing 737-8Q8/W | 35279 | ex G-XLFR | |
| ☐ F-HJER | Boeing 737-86N/W | 32736/1113 | ex TC-AAP | ♦ |
| ☐ F-HJUL | Boeing 737-8Q8/W | 38819/3519 | | ♦ |

# F-O   PACIFIC TERRITORIES (French Polynesia and New Caledonia)

## AIR ARCHIPELS — Archipels (RHL) — Papeete (PPT)

| | | | | |
|---|---|---|---|---|
| ☐ F-OIQK | Beech B200C Super King Air | BL-149 | ex N36949 | |
| ☐ F-OIQL | Beech B200C Super King Air | BL-148 | ex N36948 | |

## AIR CALÉDONIE INTERNATIONAL — AirCal (TY/TPC) — Nouméa (NOU)

| | | | | |
|---|---|---|---|---|
| ☐ F-OIAQ | de Havilland DHC-6 Twin Otter 300 | 381 | ex VH-RPZ | |
| ☐ F-OIPI | ATR 42-500 | 0647 | ex F-WWLE | |
| ☐ F-OIPN | ATR 72-212A | 0735 | ex F-WWEP | |
| ☐ F-OIPS | ATR 72-212A | 0764 | ex F-WWEC | |

## AIR LOYAUTÉ — Iazur (VZR) — Nouméa (NOU)

| | | | | |
|---|---|---|---|---|
| ☐ F-OIAY | de Havilland DHC-6 Twin Otter 300 | 507 | ex P2-KSR | |
| ☐ F-OIJI | de Havilland DHC-6 Twin Otter 300 | 277 | ex (ZS-OVL) | ♦ |
| ☐ F-ONCA | de Havilland DHC-6 Twin Otter 300 | 840 | ex C-FZYG | ♦ |

## AIR MOOREA — Air Moorea (QE/TAH) — Papeete (PPT)

| | | | | |
|---|---|---|---|---|
| ☐ F-OHJG | de Havilland DHC-6 Twin Otter 300 | 603 | ex Fr AF 603 | |
| ☐ F-OIQF | de Havilland DHC-6 Twin Otter 300 | 815 | ex N45KH | |
| ☐ F-OIQP | de Havilland DHC-6 Twin Otter 300 | 715 | ex 5Y-SKL | |

| **AIR TAHITI** | | *Air Tahiti (VT/VTA)* | | | *Papeete (PPT)* |
|---|---|---|---|---|---|
| ☐ F-OIQB | ATR 42-500 | 0621 | ex F-WWLB | | |
| ☐ F-OIQC | ATR 42-500 | 0627 | ex F-WWLH | | |
| ☐ F-OIQD | ATR 42-500 | 0631 | ex F-WWLL | | |
| ☐ F-O | ATR 42-600 | | ex F-WW | | o/o |
| ☐ F-O | ATR 42-600 | | ex F-WW | | o/o♦ |
| ☐ F-O | ATR 42-600 | | ex F-WW | | o/o♦ |
| ☐ F-OHJS | ATR 72-212A | 0696 | ex F-WWES | | |
| ☐ F-OIQN | ATR 72-212A | 0719 | ex F-WWET | | |
| ☐ F-OIQO | ATR 72-212A | 0731 | ex F-WWEL | | |
| ☐ F-OIQR | ATR 72-212A | 0862 | ex F-WWEJ | | |
| ☐ F-OIQT | ATR 72-212A | 0829 | ex F-WWEW | | ♦ |
| ☐ F-OIQU | ATR 72-212A | 0751 | ex F-WWEL | | |
| ☐ F-OIQV | ATR 72-212A | 0806 | ex F-WWER | | |

| **AIR TAHITI NUI** | | *Tahiti Airlines (TN/THT)* | | | *Papeete (PPT)* |
|---|---|---|---|---|---|
| ☐ F-OJGF | Airbus A340-313X | 385 | ex F-WWJC | Mangareva | |
| ☐ F-OJTN | Airbus A340-313X | 395 | ex C-GZIA | Bora Bora | |
| ☐ F-OLOV | Airbus A340-313E | 668 | ex F-WWJD | Nuku Hiva | |
| ☐ F-OSEA | Airbus A340-313X | 438 | ex F-WWJV | Rangiroa | |
| ☐ F-OSUN | Airbus A340-313X | 446 | ex F-WWJA | Moorea | |

| **AIRCALIN** | | *AirCalin (SB/ACI)* | | *Nouméa (NOU)* |
|---|---|---|---|---|
| ☐ F-OCQZ | de Havilland DHC-6 Twin Otter 300 | 412 | | |
| ☐ F-OHSD | Airbus A330-202 | 507 | ex F-WWYS | |
| ☐ F-OIAQ | de Havilland DHC-6 Twin Otter300 | 381 | ex VH-VHM | ♦ |
| ☐ F-OJSB | Airbus A320-232 | 2152 | | |
| ☐ F-OJSE | Airbus A330-202 | 510 | ex F-WWYT | |

## F-O ATLANTIC / INDIAN OCEAN TERRITORIES (St Pierre & Miquelon and Réunion)

| **AIR AUSTRAL** | | *Réunion (UU/REU)* | | *St Denis-Gilot (RUN)* |
|---|---|---|---|---|
| ☐ F-OLRA | Boeing 777-29MLR | 40955/952 | | Antoine de Bertin | ♦ |
| ☐ F-OLRB | Boeing 777-29MLR | 40993 | | | o/o♦ |
| ☐ F-OMAY | Boeing 777-2Q8ER | 29402/517 | | | |
| ☐ F-ONOU | Boeing 777-3Q8ER | 35783/786 | ex N5573S | Leon Dierx | |
| ☐ F-OREU | Boeing 777-39MER | 37434/912 | | | |
| ☐ F-ORUN | Boeing 777-2Q8ER | 28676/246 | ex EI-CRT | Pierre Legourque | |
| ☐ F-OSYD | Boeing 777-3Q8ER | 35782/778 | ex N5014K | C. Leconte de Lisle | |
| ☐ F-OHSF | ATR 72-212A | 0650 | ex F-WWEC | | |
| ☐ F-OMRU | ATR 72-212A | 0855 | ex F-WWEI | | |
| ☐ F-ONGA | Boeing 737-89M/W | 40910/3484 | | | |
| ☐ F-ONGB | Boeing 737-89M/W | 40911/3504 | ex N1786B | | |
| ☐ F-OZSE | ATR 72-212A | 0813 | ex F-WWEC | | |

| **AIR ST-PIERRE** | | *Saint-Pierre (PJ/SPM)* | | *St-Pierre et Miquelon (FSP)* |
|---|---|---|---|---|
| ☐ F-OFSP | ATR 42-500 | 0801 | ex F-WWLT | |
| ☐ F-OSPJ | Reims Cessna F406 Caravan II | F406-0091 | | |

## F-O FRENCH CARIBBEAN (Guadeloupe & Saint-Barthélemy, Martinique and French Guyana)

| **AIR CARAIBES** | | *French West (TX/FWI)* | | |
|---|---|---|---|---|
| | | *Pointe-à-Pitre/Fort-de-France/St Barthélemy/St Martin (PTP/FDF/SBH/SFG)* | | |
| ☐ F-OIJH | ATR 72-212A | 0682 | ex F-WWEE | |
| ☐ F-OIJK | ATR 72-212A | 0736 | ex F-WWEQ | |
| ☐ F-OIXL | ATR 72-212A | 0888 | ex F-WWES | |
| ☐ F-OSUD | Embraer ERJ-190LR | 19000130 | ex PT-SQZ | |

| **AIR CARAIBES ATLANTIQUE** | | *Car Line (TX/CAJ)* | | | *Pointe-à-Pitre (PTP)* |
|---|---|---|---|---|---|
| ☐ F-GOTO | Airbus A330-323E | 1021 | ex F-WWYN | | |
| ☐ F-HPTP | Airbus A330-323X | 1268 | ex F-WWKZ | | ♦ |
| ☐ F-OFDF | Airbus A330-223 | 253 | ex HB-IQD | | |
| ☐ F-OONE | Airbus A330-323E | 965 | ex F-WWYL | Region Guyane | |
| ☐ F-ORLY | Airbus A330-323X | 758 | ex F-WWYR | | |

## AIR GUYANE EXPRESS — Green Bird (3S/GUY) — Cayenne (CAY)

| | | | | | |
|---|---|---|---|---|---|
| ☐ F-OIJL | de Havilland DHC-6 Twin Otter 300 | 281 | ex HB-LSV | | |
| ☐ F-OIJY | de Havilland DHC-6 Twin Otter 300 | 797 | ex D-IFLY | | |
| ☐ F-OIXD | ATR 42-500 | 0695 | ex F-WWLQ | | ♦ |
| ☐ F-OIXE | ATR 42-500 | 0807 | ex F-WWLX | | ♦ |
| ☐ F-OIXF | LET L-410UVP-E | 092635 | ex OK-2635 | | ♦ |
| ☐ F-OIXG | LET L-410UVP-E20 | 2734 | ex OK-AIS | | ♦ |
| ☐ F-OIXH | ATR 42-500 | 0831 | ex F-WWLD | | ♦ |
| ☐ F-OIXI | LET L-410UVP-E20 | 2807 | | | ♦ |

## AIRAWAK — Fort-de-France (FDF)

| | | | | |
|---|---|---|---|---|
| ☐ F-OGXA | Britten-Norman BN-2A-26 Islander | 788 | ex D-IHUG | |
| ☐ F-OIXB | Cessna 402B II | 402B1220 | ex V2-LEW | |

## ST BARTH COMMUTER — Black Fin (PV/SBU) — St Barthélemy (SBH)

| | | | | |
|---|---|---|---|---|
| ☐ F-OGXB | Britten-Norman BN-2A-2 Islander | 303 | ex D-IHVH | stored |
| ☐ F-OHQX | Britten-Norman BN-2A-26 Islander | 3009 | ex F-OHQW | |
| ☐ F-OHQY | Britten-Norman BN-2B-20 Islander | 2251 | ex V2-LFE | |
| ☐ F-OIJS | Britten-Norman BN-2B-20 Islander | 2294 | ex VH-CSS | |
| ☐ F-OIJU | Britten-Norman BN-2B-20 Islander | 2291 | ex G-BVYD | |
| | | | | |
| ☐ F-OSBC | Cessna 208B Caravan I | 208B2188 | ex N1029J | |
| ☐ F-OSBH | Cessna 208B Caravan I | 208B2117 | ex N6137Y | |

## TAKE AIR LINES — Fort-de-France (FDF)

| | | | | |
|---|---|---|---|---|
| ☐ F-OHQN | Cessna 208B Caravan I | 208B0715 | ex N1258H | ♦ |

## TROPIC AIR LINES — Pointe-à-Pitre (PTP)

| | | | | |
|---|---|---|---|---|
| ☐ F-OHQU | Cessna 208B Caravan I | 208B0725 | ex N12326 | |
| ☐ F-OIJO | Cessna 208B Caravan I | 208B0961 | ex N4109K | |

## WANAIR

| | | | | |
|---|---|---|---|---|
| ☐ F-OHRX | Beech 1900D | UE-282 | ex N11296 | ♦ |

## G- UNITED KINGDOM (United Kingdom of Great Britain and Northern Ireland)

## AIR ATLANTIQUE — Atlantic (7M/AAG) — Coventry (CVT)

| | | | | |
|---|---|---|---|---|
| ☐ G-APSA | Douglas DC-6A | 45497/995 | ex 4W-ABQ | |

## ATLANTIC AIRLINES / WEST ATLANTIC — Neptune (NPT) — Coventry (CVT)

| | | | | |
|---|---|---|---|---|
| ☐ G-BTPA | British Aerospace ATP (LFD) | 2007 | ex EC-HGC | |
| ☐ G-BTPC | British Aerospace ATP (LFD) | 2010 | ex SE-MAI | |
| ☐ G-BTPE | British Aerospace ATP (LFD) | 2012 | ex EC-HGE | |
| ☐ G-BTPF | British Aerospace ATP (LFD) | 2013 | ex EC-HCY | |
| ☐ G-BTPG | British Aerospace ATP (LFD) | 2014 | ex (G-JEMF) | |
| ☐ G-BTPH | British Aerospace ATP (LFD) | 2015 | ex (G-JEMF) | |
| ☐ G-BTTO | British Aerospace ATP (LFD) | 2033 | ex EC-HNA | |
| ☐ G-BUUP | British Aerospace ATP (LFD) | 2008 | ex G-MANU | |
| ☐ G-BUUR | British Aerospace ATP (LFD) | 2024 | ex EC-GUX | |
| ☐ G-MANH | British Aerospace ATP (LFD) | 2017 | ex G-LOGC | |
| ☐ G-MANO | British Aerospace ATP (LFD) | 2006 | ex SE-MAN | ♦ |
| ☐ G-OAAF | British Aerospace ATP | 2029 | ex G-JEMB | |
| ☐ LZ-BPS | British Aerospace ATP (LFD) | 2005 | ex SX-BPS | [CVT]♦ |
| | | | | |
| ☐ G-FIZU | Lockheed L-188CF Electra | 2014 | ex EI-CHY | |
| ☐ G-JMCL | Boeing 737-322F | 23951/1532 | ex D-AGEA | |
| ☐ G-LOFC | Lockheed L-188CF Electra | 1100 | ex N665F | |
| ☐ G-LOFE | Lockheed L-188CF Electra | 1144 | ex EI-CET | |

## ATLANTIC RECONNAISSANCE — Atlantic (AAG) — Coventry (CVT)

| | | | | |
|---|---|---|---|---|
| ☐ G-BCEN | Britten-Norman BN-2A-26 Islander | 403 | ex 4X-AYG | Maritime & Coastguard Agency |
| ☐ G-BWLF | Cessna 404 | 404-0414 | | ♦ |
| ☐ G-EXEX | Cessna 404 Titan | 404-0037 | ex SE-GZF | Maritime & Coastguard Agency |
| ☐ G-FIND | Reims Cessna F406 Caravan II | 0045 | | ♦ |
| ☐ G-LEAF | Reims Cessna F406 Caravan II | 0018 | | ♦ |
| ☐ G-MAPP | Cessna 402B | 402B-0583 | | ♦ |
| ☐ G-MIND | Cessna 404 Titan | 404-0004 | ex G-SKKC | Op for Enviroment Agency |
| ☐ G-NOSE | Cessna 402B | 402B0823 | ex N98AR | Pollution control |

| | | | | |
|---|---|---|---|---|
| ☐ G-SOUL | Cessna 310R II | 310R0140 | ex N5020J | Op for OSRL |
| ☐ G-TASK | Cessna 404 Titan | 404-0829 | ex PH-MPC | Maritime & Coastguard Agency |
| ☐ G-TURF | Reims Cessna F406 Caravan II | F406-0020 | ex PH-FWF | Maritime & Coastguard Agency |

## AURIGNY AIR SERVICES　　　　　Ayline (GR/AUR)　　　　　　　　Guernsey (GCI)

| | | | | |
|---|---|---|---|---|
| ☐ G-BDTO | Britten-Norman BN-2A Mk.III-2 Trislander | 1027 | ex G-RBSI | |
| ☐ G-BEVT | Britten-Norman BN-2A Mk.III-2 Trislander | 1057 | | |
| ☐ G-FTSE | Britten-Norman BN-2A Mk.III-2 Trislander | 1053 | ex G-BEPI | |
| ☐ G-JOEY | Britten-Norman BN-2A Mk.III-2 Trislander | 1016 | ex G-BDGG | Joey |
| ☐ G-RBCI | Britten-Norman BN-2A Mk.III-2 Trislander | 1035 | ex G-BDWV | |
| ☐ G-RLON | Britten-Norman BN-2A Mk.III-2 Trislander | 1008 | ex G-ITEX | Royal London Asset Mgt c/s |
| ☐ G-XTOR | Britten-Norman BN-2A Mk.III-2 Trislander | 359 | ex G-BAXD | |
| ☐ G-BWDB | ATR 72-202 | 0449 | ex F-WQNI | |
| ☐ G-COBO | ATR 72-212A | 0852 | ex F-WWEV | |
| ☐ G-VZON | ATR 72-212A | 0853 | ex F-WWEW | |

## BA CITYFLYER　　　　　　　　　Flyer (CJ/CFE)　　　　　　　　London City (LCY)

| | | | | |
|---|---|---|---|---|
| ☐ G-LCYD | Embraer ERJ-170STD | 17000294 | ex PT-TQU | |
| ☐ G-LCYE | Embraer ERJ-170STD | 17000296 | ex PT-TQW | |
| ☐ G-LCYF | Embraer ERJ-170STD | 17000298 | ex PT-TQR | |
| ☐ G-LCYG | Embraer ERJ-170STD | 17000300 | ex PT-TQZ | |
| ☐ G-LCYH | Embraer ERJ-170STD | 17000302 | ex PT-XQB | |
| ☐ G-LCYI | Embraer ERJ-170STD | 17000305 | ex PT-XQE | |
| ☐ G-LCYJ | Embraer ERJ-190SR | 19000339 | ex PT-TXY | |
| ☐ G-LCYK | Embraer ERJ-190SR | 19000343 | ex PT-XQK | |
| ☐ G-LCYL | Embraer ERJ-190SR | 19000346 | ex PT-XQM | |
| ☐ G-LCYM | Embraer ERJ-190SR | 19000351 | ex PT-XQR | |
| ☐ G-LCYN | Embraer ERJ-190SR | 19000392 | ex PT-XNY | |
| ☐ G-LCYO | Embraer ERJ-190SR | 19000430 | ex PT-TCQ | ♦ |
| ☐ G-LCYP | Embraer ERJ-190SR | 19000443 | ex PT-TJD | ♦ |

## BLUE ISLANDS　　　　　　　　　Blue Island (XA/BCI)　　　　　　Jersey (JER)

| | | | | |
|---|---|---|---|---|
| ☐ G-FARA | British Aerospace Jetstream 31 | 740 | ex LN-FAM | ♦ |
| ☐ G-ISLB | British Aerospace Jetstream 32 | 871 | ex N871JX | |
| ☐ G-ISLC | British Aerospace Jetstream 32 | 873 | ex N873JX | |
| ☐ G-ISLD | British Aerospace Jetstream 32EP | 915 | ex N915AE | |
| ☐ G-JIBO | British Aerospace Jetstream 31 | 711 | ex G-OJSA | ♦ |
| ☐ G-DRFC | ATR 42-320 | 0007 | ex OY-CIB | |
| ☐ G-ISLF | ATR 42-500 | 0546 | ex D-BMMM | ♦ |
| ☐ G-XAXA | Britten-Norman BN-2A-26 Islander | 530 | ex G-LOTO | |

## BMI BRITISH MIDLAND INTERNATIONAL　　Midland (BD/BMA)
## 　　　　　　East Midland-Nottingham/London-Heathrow (EMA/LHR)

Member of Star Alliance

| | | | | |
|---|---|---|---|---|
| ☐ G-DBCA | Airbus A319-131 | 2098 | ex D-AVYV | |
| ☐ G-DBCB | Airbus A319-131 | 2188 | ex D-AVYA | |
| ☐ G-DBCC | Airbus A319-131 | 2194 | ex D-AVYT | |
| ☐ G-DBCD | Airbus A319-131 | 2389 | ex D-AVYJ | |
| ☐ G-DBCE | Airbus A319-131 | 2429 | ex D-AVWG | |
| ☐ G-DBCF | Airbus A319-131 | 2466 | ex D-AVYA | |
| ☐ G-DBCG | Airbus A319-131 | 2694 | ex D-AVXD | |
| ☐ G-DBCH | Airbus A319-131 | 2697 | ex D-AVXE | |
| ☐ G-DBCI | Airbus A319-131 | 2720 | ex D-AVWC | |
| ☐ G-DBCJ | Airbus A319-131 | 2981 | ex D-AVXG | |
| ☐ G-DBCK | Airbus A319-131 | 3049 | ex D-AVYG | |
| ☐ G-MEDH | Airbus A320-232 | 1922 | ex F-WWBX | |
| ☐ G-MEDK | Airbus A320-232 | 2441 | ex F-WWBQ | |
| ☐ G-MIDO | Airbus A320-232 | 1987 | ex F-WWIR | |
| ☐ G-MIDS | Airbus A320-232 | 1424 | ex F-WWBO | |
| ☐ G-MIDT | Airbus A320-232 | 1418 | ex F-WWBI | |
| ☐ G-MIDX | Airbus A320-232 | 1177 | ex F-WWDP | Star Alliance c/s |
| ☐ G-MIDY | Airbus A320-232 | 1014 | ex F-WWDQ | |
| ☐ G-MEDF | Airbus A321-231 | 1690 | ex D-AVZX | |

| | | | | |
|---|---|---|---|---|
| ☐ G-MEDG | Airbus A321-231 | 1711 | ex D-AVZK | |
| ☐ G-MEDJ | Airbus A321-231 | 2190 | ex D-AVZD | |
| ☐ G-MEDL | Airbus A321-231 | 2653 | ex D-AVZC | |
| ☐ G-MEDM | Airbus A321-231 | 2799 | ex D-AVZP | |
| ☐ G-MEDN | Airbus A321-231 | 3512 | ex D-AVZK | |
| ☐ G-MEDU | Airbus A321-231 | 3926 | ex D-AZAB | |
| | | | | |
| ☐ G-WWBD | Airbus A330-243 | 401 | ex F-WWKN | Star Alliance c/s |
| ☐ G-WWBM | Airbus A330-243 | 398 | ex F-WWKL | |

Purchased by International Airlines Group Dec11;  to be merged with British Airways

---

## BMI REGIONAL — Granite (BD/BMR) — Aberdeen/East Midlands-Nottingham (ABZ/EMA)

| | | | | |
|---|---|---|---|---|
| ☐ G-EMBI | Embraer ERJ-145EP | 145126 | ex PT-SDG | |
| ☐ G-EMBJ | Embraer ERJ-145MP | 145134 | ex PT-SDL | |
| ☐ G-EMBN | Embraer ERJ-145EP | 145201 | ex PT-SGQ | |
| ☐ G-EMBP | Embraer ERJ-145EU | 145300 | ex PT-SKR | |
| ☐ G-RJXA | Embraer ERJ-145EP | 145136 | ex PT-SDP | |
| ☐ G-RJXB | Embraer ERJ-145EP | 145142 | ex PT-SDS | |
| ☐ G-RJXC | Embraer ERJ-145EP | 145153 | ex PT-SEE | |
| ☐ G-RJXD | Embraer ERJ-145EP | 145207 | ex PT-SGX | |
| ☐ G-RJXE | Embraer ERJ-145EP | 145245 | ex PT-SIJ | |
| ☐ G-RJXF | Embraer ERJ-145EP | 145280 | ex PT-SJW | |
| ☐ G-RJXG | Embraer ERJ-145EP | 145390 | ex PT-SQO | |
| ☐ G-RJXH | Embraer ERJ-145EP | 145442 | ex PT-SUN | |
| ☐ G-RJXI | Embraer ERJ-145EP | 145454 | ex PT-SUZ | Star Alliance c/s |
| ☐ G-RJXM | Embraer ERJ-145MP | 145216 | ex PH-RXA | |
| ☐ G-RJXP | Embraer ERJ-135ER | 145431 | ex G-CDFS | |
| ☐ G-RJXR | Embraer ERJ-145EP | 145070 | ex G-CCYH | |
| | | | | |
| ☐ G-RJXJ | Embraer ERJ-135ER | 145473 | ex PT-SVS | |
| ☐ G-RJXK | Embraer ERJ-135ER | 145494 | ex PT-SXN | Star Alliance c/s |
| ☐ G-RJXL | Embraer ERJ-135ER | 145376 | ex PT-SQA | |

---

## BMIBABY — Baby (WW/BMI) — East Midlands-Nottingham (EMA)

| | | | | | |
|---|---|---|---|---|---|
| ☐ G-OBMP | Boeing 737-3Q8 | 24963/2193 | | robin hood baby | |
| ☐ G-ODSK | Boeing 737-37Q | 28537/2904 | | baby dragon fly | |
| ☐ G-OGBD | Boeing 737-3L9 | 27833/2688 | ex OY-MAR | olly cat baby | |
| ☐ G-TOYD | Boeing 737-3Q8 | 26307/2664 | ex G-EZYT | | |
| ☐ G-TOYF | Boeing 737-36N | 28557/2862 | ex G-IGOO | Rainbow baby | |
| ☐ G-TOYG | Boeing 737-36N | 28872/3082 | ex G-IGOJ | Butterfly baby | |
| ☐ G-TOYH | Boeing 737-36N | 28570/3010 | ex G-IGOY | Baby of the north | |
| ☐ G-TOYI | Boeing 737-3Q8 | 28054/3016 | ex YJ-AV18 | Geordie baby | |
| ☐ G-TOYJ | Boeing 737-36M | 28332/2809 | ex PK-GGW | | |
| ☐ G-TOYK | Boeing 737-33R | 28870/2899 | ex N870GX | jump in baby | |
| ☐ G-TOYL | Boeing 737-36N | 28594/3107 | ex G-THOL | | ♦ |
| ☐ G-TOYM | Boeing 737-36Q | 29141/3035 | ex VT-SJD | Groovy baby | |
| | | | | | |
| ☐ G-BVKB | Boeing 737-59D | 27268/2592 | ex SE-DNM | foxy baby | |
| ☐ G-BVZE | Boeing 737-59D | 26422/2412 | ex SE-DNL | little costa baby | |

---

## BOND AIR SERVICES — Red Head (RHD) — Gloucestershire (GLO)

| | | | | | |
|---|---|---|---|---|---|
| ☐ G-BZRS | Eurocopter EC135T2 | 0166 | ex D-HECL | back-up | |
| ☐ G-CGPI | Eurocopter EC135T2+ | 0341 | | | ♦ |
| ☐ G-CGXK | Eurocopter EC135T1 | 0044 | ex D-HJAR | | ♦ |
| ☐ G-CGZD | Eurocopter EC135P2 | 0460 | ex G-214007 | | ♦ |
| ☐ G-DAAT | Eurocopter EC135T2 | 0312 | | EMS Devon | |
| ☐ G-DORS | Eurocopter EC135T2+ | 0517 | | EMS Dorset & Somerset | |
| ☐ G-EMAA | Eurocopter EC135T2 | 0448 | | EMS | |
| ☐ G-GOWF | Eurocopter EC135T2+ | 0785 | | | ♦ |
| ☐ G-HBOB | Eurocopter EC135T2+ | 0664 | | Thames Valley Air Ambulance | |
| ☐ G-HWAA | Eurocopter EC135T2 | 0375 | | EMS | |
| ☐ G-KRNW | Eurocopter EC135T2 | 0175 | | EMS Cornwall Air Ambulance | |
| ☐ G-NWAA | Eurocopter EC135T2 | 0427 | | EMS North West Air Ambulance | |
| ☐ G-NWEM | Eurocopter EC135T2 | 0270 | ex G-SSXX | EMS North West Air Ambulance | |
| ☐ G-SASA | Eurocopter EC135T2 | 0147 | | EMS Scottish Ambulance Service | |
| ☐ G-SASB | Eurocopter EC135T2 | 0151 | | EMS Scottish Ambulance Service | |
| ☐ G-SPAO | Eurocopter EC135T2+ | 0546 | | Strathclyde Police | |
| ☐ G-SPHU | Eurocopter EC135T2+ | 0245 | ex D-HKBA | Great Western Air Ambulance | |
| ☐ G-WASN | Eurocopter EC135T2+ | 0746 | | | ♦ |
| ☐ G-WASS | Eurocopter EC135T2+ | 0745 | | | ♦ |
| ☐ G-WMAS | Eurocopter EC135T2 | 0174 | | EMS County Air Ambulance | |
| ☐ G-WONN | Eurocopter EC135T2+ | 0597 | | Strathclyde Police | |
| | | | | | |
| ☐ G-BUXS | MBB Bo.105DBS-4 | S-41/913 | ex G-PASA | Northern Lighthouse | |
| ☐ G-CDBS | MBB Bo.105DBS-4 | S-738 | ex D-HDRZ | EMS | |
| ☐ G-NAAA | MBB Bo.105DBS-4 | S-34/912 | ex G-BUTN | EMS | |
| ☐ G-NDAA | MBB Bo.105DBS-4 | S-135/914 | ex G-WMAA | EMS Devon Air Ambulance | |
| ☐ G-WAAS | MBB Bo.105DBS-4 | S-138/911 | ex G-ESAM | EMS Welsh Air Ambulance | |

## BOND OFFSHORE HELICOPTERS — Bond (BND) — Gloucestershire/Aberdeen (GLO/ABZ)

| | Reg | Type | c/n | ex | Notes | |
|---|---|---|---|---|---|---|
| ☐ | G-PUMR | Eurocopter EC225LP | 2818 | | | ♦ |
| ☐ | G-REDJ | Aérospatiale AS.332L2 II | 2608 | ex F-WWOJ | | |
| ☐ | G-REDK | Aérospatiale AS.332L2 II | 2610 | ex F-WWOM | | |
| ☐ | G-REDM | Aérospatiale AS.332L2 II | 2614 | ex F-WWOF | | |
| ☐ | G-REDN | Aérospatiale AS.332L2 II | 2616 | ex F-WQDH | | |
| ☐ | G-REDO | Aérospatiale AS.332L2 II | 2622 | ex F-WWOH | | |
| ☐ | G-REDP | Aérospatiale AS.332L2 II | 2634 | ex F-WWOB | | |
| ☐ | G-REDR | Eurocopter EC225LP | 2699 | | | |
| ☐ | G-REDT | Eurocopter EC225LP | 2701 | | | |
| ☐ | G-REDV | Eurocopter EC225LP | 2732 | | | |
| ☐ | G-REDW | Eurocopter EC225LP | 2734 | | | |
| ☐ | G-REDG | Aérospatiale AS365N3 Dauphin 3 | 6907 | | | ♦ |
| ☐ | G-REDH | Aérospatiale AS365N3 Dauphin 3 | 6911 | | | ♦ |
| ☐ | G-PERA | Agusta AW139 | 31322 | ex N819JA | | ♦ |
| ☐ | G-PERB | Agusta AW139 | 41261 | ex N389SH | | ♦ |

## BRISTOW HELICOPTERS — Bristow (BHL) — Redhill/Aberdeen (KRH/ABZ)

| | Reg | Type | c/n | ex | Notes | |
|---|---|---|---|---|---|---|
| ☐ | G-BLXR | Aérospatiale AS.332L | 2154 | | Cromarty | |
| ☐ | G-BMCW | Aérospatiale AS.332L | 2161 | ex F-WYMG | Monifieth | |
| ☐ | G-BMCX | Aérospatiale AS.332L | 2164 | | Lossiemouth | |
| ☐ | G-BWWI | Aérospatiale AS.332L | 2040 | ex OY-HMF | Johnshaven | |
| ☐ | G-BWZX | Aérospatiale AS.332L | 2120 | ex F-WQDE | Muchalls | |
| ☐ | G-TIGC | Aérospatiale AS.332L | 2024 | ex (G-BJYH) | Royal Burgh of Montrose | |
| ☐ | G-TIGE | Aérospatiale AS.332L | 2028 | ex (G-BJYJ) | City of Dundee | |
| ☐ | G-TIGF | Aérospatiale AS.332L | 2030 | ex F-WKQJ | Peterhead | |
| ☐ | G-TIGG | Aérospatiale AS.332L | 2032 | ex F-WXFT | Macduff | |
| ☐ | G-TIGJ | Aérospatiale AS.332L | 2042 | ex VH-BHT | Rosehearty | |
| ☐ | G-TIGS | Aérospatiale AS.332L | 2086 | | Findochty | |
| ☐ | G-TIGV | Aérospatiale AS.332L | 2099 | ex LN-ONC | Burghead | |
| ☐ | G-CGUA | Eurocopter EC225LP | 2785 | | | ♦ |
| ☐ | G-CGUB | Eurocopter EC225LP | 2790 | | | ♦ |
| ☐ | G-CGUC | Eurocopter EC225LP | 2792 | | | ♦ |
| ☐ | G-ZZSA | Eurocopter EC225LP | 2603 | ex F-WWOJ | | |
| ☐ | G-ZZSB | Eurocopter EC225LP | 2615 | ex F-WWOG | | |
| ☐ | G-ZZSC | Eurocopter EC225LP | 2654 | ex F-WWOG | | |
| ☐ | G-ZZSD | Eurocopter EC225LP | 2658 | ex F-WWOQ | | |
| ☐ | G-ZZSE | Eurocopter EC225LP | 2660 | ex F-WWOJ | | |
| ☐ | G-ZZSF | Eurocopter EC225LP | 2662 | ex F-WWOR | | |
| ☐ | G-ZZSG | Eurocopter EC225LP | 2714 | | | |
| ☐ | G-ZZSI | Eurocopter EC225LP | 2736 | ex G-CGES | | |
| ☐ | G-BIEJ | Sikorsky S-76A+ | 760097 | | Glen Lossie | |
| ☐ | G-BISZ | Sikorsky S-76A+ | 760156 | | | |
| ☐ | G-BJGX | Sikorsky S-76A+ | 760026 | ex N103BH | Glen Elgin | |
| ☐ | G-CEYZ | Sikorsky S-76C++ | 760669 | ex N4514R | | |
| ☐ | G-CFDV | Sikorsky S-76C++ | 760666 | ex N45140 | | |
| ☐ | G-CFJC | Sikorsky S-76C++ | 760708 | ex N415Y | | |
| ☐ | G-CFPZ | Sikorsky S-76C+ | 760744 | ex N2039J | | |
| ☐ | G-CGIW | Sikorsky S-76C+ | 760773 | ex N773L | | |
| ☐ | G-CGOP | Sikorsky S-76C+ | 760778 | ex N778T | | |
| ☐ | G-CGOU | Sikorsky S-76C+ | 760780 | ex N20868 | | |
| ☐ | G-CGRU | Sikorsky S-76C | 760656 | ex N76TZ | | |
| ☐ | G-CGVW | Sikorsky S-76C++ | 760903 | ex N803K | | ♦ |
| ☐ | G-KAZA | Sikorsky S-76C+ | 760615 | ex N81085 | | |
| ☐ | G-KAZB | Sikorsky S-76C+ | 760614 | ex N8094S | | |
| ☐ | G-CGUX | Sikorsky S-92A | 920088 | ex N920AL | | ♦ |
| ☐ | G-CGYW | Sikorsky S-92A | 920157 | | | ♦ |
| ☐ | G-CGZS | Sikorsky S-92A | 920054 | ex C-GKNR | | ♦ |
| ☐ | G-IACA | Sikorsky S-92A | 920050 | ex N81254 | | |
| ☐ | G-IACB | Sikorsky S-92A | 920062 | ex N4516G | | |
| ☐ | G-IACC | Sikorsky S-92A | 920063 | ex N45158 | | |
| ☐ | G-IACD | Sikorsky S-92A | 920065 | ex N4515G | | |
| ☐ | G-IACE | Sikorsky S-92A | 920066 | ex N45148 | | |
| ☐ | G-IACF | Sikorsky S-92A | 920068 | ex N4509G | | |
| ☐ | G-ISST | Eurocopter EC155 B1 | 6778 | | | |
| ☐ | G-ISSU | Eurocopter EC155 B1 | 6762 | | | |
| ☐ | G-BIMU | Sikorsky S-61N II | 61752 | ex N8511Z | Stac Pollaidh | SAR |
| ☐ | G-BPWB | Sikorsky S-61N II | 61822 | ex EI-BHO | Portland Castle | SAR |
| ☐ | G-ISSV | Eurocopter EC155 B1 | 6757 | | | |
| ☐ | G-ISSW | Eurocopter EC155 B1 | 6755 | | | |

**BRITISH AIRWAYS**          *Speedbird & Shuttle (BA/BAW/SHT)*

*London-Heathrow/Gatwick & Manchester (LHR/LGW/MAN)*

Member of Oneworld

| | | | |
|---|---|---|---|
| ☐ G-EUOA | Airbus A319-131 | 1513 | ex D-AVYE |
| ☐ G-EUOB | Airbus A319-131 | 1529 | ex D-AVWH |
| ☐ G-EUOC | Airbus A319-131 | 1537 | ex D-AVYP |
| ☐ G-EUOD | Airbus A319-131 | 1558 | ex D-AVYJ |
| ☐ G-EUOE | Airbus A319-131 | 1574 | ex D-AVWF |
| ☐ G-EUOF | Airbus A319-131 | 1590 | ex D-AVYW |
| ☐ G-EUOG | Airbus A319-131 | 1594 | ex D-AVVWU |
| ☐ G-EUOH | Airbus A319-131 | 1604 | ex D-AVYM |
| ☐ G-EUOI | Airbus A319-131 | 1606 | ex D-AVYN |
| ☐ G-EUPA | Airbus A319-131 | 1082 | ex D-AVYK |
| ☐ G-EUPB | Airbus A319-131 | 1115 | ex D-AVYT |
| ☐ G-EUPC | Airbus A319-131 | 1118 | ex D-AVYU |
| ☐ G-EUPD | Airbus A319-131 | 1142 | ex D-AVWG |
| ☐ G-EUPE | Airbus A319-131 | 1193 | ex D-AVYT |
| ☐ G-EUPF | Airbus A319-131 | 1197 | ex D-AVWS |
| ☐ G-EUPG | Airbus A319-131 | 1222 | ex D-AVYG |
| ☐ G-EUPH | Airbus A319-131 | 1225 | ex D-AVYK |
| ☐ G-EUPJ | Airbus A319-131 | 1232 | ex D-AVYJ |
| ☐ G-EUPK | Airbus A319-131 | 1236 | ex D-AVYO |
| ☐ G-EUPL | Airbus A319-131 | 1239 | ex D-AVYP |
| ☐ G-EUPM | Airbus A319-131 | 1258 | ex D-AVYR |
| ☐ G-EUPN | Airbus A319-131 | 1261 | ex D-AVWA |
| ☐ G-EUPO | Airbus A319-131 | 1279 | ex D-AVYU |
| ☐ G-EUPP | Airbus A319-131 | 1295 | ex D-AVWU |
| ☐ G-EUPR | Airbus A319-131 | 1329 | ex D-AVYH |
| ☐ G-EUPS | Airbus A319-131 | 1338 | ex D-AVYM |
| ☐ G-EUPT | Airbus A319-131 | 1380 | ex D-AVWH |
| ☐ G-EUPU | Airbus A319-131 | 1384 | ex D-AVWP |
| ☐ G-EUPV | Airbus A319-131 | 1423 | ex D-AVYE |
| ☐ G-EUPW | Airbus A319-131 | 1440 | ex D-AVYP |
| ☐ G-EUPX | Airbus A319-131 | 1445 | ex D-AVWB |
| ☐ G-EUPY | Airbus A319-131 | 1466 | ex D-AVYU |
| ☐ G-EUPZ | Airbus A319-131 | 1510 | ex D-AVYY |
| | | | |
| ☐ G-EUUA | Airbus A320-232 | 1661 | ex F-WWIH |
| ☐ G-EUUB | Airbus A320-232 | 1689 | ex F-WWBE |
| ☐ G-EUUC | Airbus A320-232 | 1696 | ex F-WWIO |
| ☐ G-EUUD | Airbus A320-232 | 1760 | ex F-WWBN |
| ☐ G-EUUE | Airbus A320-232 | 1782 | ex F-WWDO |
| ☐ G-EUUF | Airbus A320-232 | 1814 | ex F-WWIY |
| ☐ G-EUUG | Airbus A320-232 | 1829 | ex F-WWIU |
| ☐ G-EUUH | Airbus A320-232 | 1665 | ex F-WWIG |
| ☐ G-EUUI | Airbus A320-232 | 1871 | ex F-WWBI |
| ☐ G-EUUJ | Airbus A320-232 | 1883 | ex F-WWBQ |
| ☐ G-EUUK | Airbus A320-232 | 1899 | ex F-WWDO |
| ☐ G-EUUL | Airbus A320-232 | 1708 | ex F-WWIV |
| ☐ G-EUUM | Airbus A320-232 | 1907 | ex F-WWDN |
| ☐ G-EUUN | Airbus A320-232 | 1910 | ex F-WWDP |
| ☐ G-EUUO | Airbus A320-232 | 1958 | ex F-WWIT |
| ☐ G-EUUP | Airbus A320-232 | 2038 | ex F-WWDB |
| ☐ G-EUUR | Airbus A320-232 | 2040 | ex F-WWID |
| ☐ G-EUUS | Airbus A320-232 | 3301 | ex F-WWIF |
| ☐ G-EUUT | Airbus A320-232 | 3314 | ex F-WWIT |
| ☐ G-EUUU | Airbus A320-232 | 3351 | ex F-WWID |
| ☐ G-EUUV | Airbus A320-232 | 3468 | ex F-WWBO |
| ☐ G-EUUW | Airbus A320-232 | 3499 | ex F-WWIN |
| ☐ G-EUUX | Airbus A320-232 | 3550 | ex F-WWDM |
| ☐ G-EUUY | Airbus A320-232 | 3607 | ex F-WWIC |
| ☐ G-EUUZ | Airbus A320-232 | 3649 | ex F-WWDO |
| ☐ G-EUYA | Airbus A320-232 | 3697 | ex F-WWBM |
| ☐ G-EUYB | Airbus A320-232 | 3703 | ex F-WWBV |
| ☐ G-EUYC | Airbus A320-232 | 3721 | ex F-WWBY |
| ☐ G-EUYD | Airbus A320-232 | 3726 | ex F-WWDH |
| ☐ G-EUYE | Airbus A320-232 | 3912 | ex F-WWBB |
| ☐ G-EUYF | Airbus A320-232 | 4185 | ex F-WWIC |
| ☐ G-EUYG | Airbus A320-232 | 4238 | ex F-WWDH |
| ☐ G-EUYH | Airbus A320-232 | 4265 | ex F-WWBK |
| ☐ G-EUYI | Airbus A320-232 | 4306 | ex F-WWIC |
| ☐ G-EUYJ | Airbus A320-232 | 4464 | ex F-WWBQ |
| ☐ G-EUYK | Airbus A320-232 | 4551 | ex F-WWBE |
| ☐ G-EUYL | Airbus A320-232 | 4725 | ex F-WWDY |
| ☐ G-EUYM | Airbus A320-232 | 4791 | ex |
| ☐ G-EUYN | Airbus A320-232 | 4975 | ex F-WWDT |
| ☐ G-TTOB | Airbus A320-232 | 1687 | ex F-WWIM |
| ☐ G-TTOE | Airbus A320-232 | 1754 | ex F-WWDH |

| | | | | |
|---|---|---|---|---|
| ☐ G-EUXC | Airbus A321-231 | 2305 | ex D-AVZE | |
| ☐ G-EUXD | Airbus A321-231 | 2320 | ex D-AVZO | |
| ☐ G-EUXE | Airbus A321-231 | 2323 | ex D-AVZP | |
| ☐ G-EUXF | Airbus A321-231 | 2324 | ex D-AVZQ | |
| ☐ G-EUXG | Airbus A321-231 | 2351 | ex D-AVZU | |
| ☐ G-EUXH | Airbus A321-231 | 2363 | ex D-AVZW | |
| ☐ G-EUXI | Airbus A321-231 | 2536 | ex D-AVZE | |
| ☐ G-EUXJ | Airbus A321-231 | 3081 | ex D-AVZL | |
| ☐ G-EUXK | Airbus A321-231 | 3235 | ex D-AVZI | |
| ☐ G-EUXL | Airbus A321-231 | 3254 | ex D-AVZV | |
| ☐ G-EUXM | Airbus A321-231 | 3290 | ex D-AVZC | |
| | | | | |
| ☐ G-DOCA | Boeing 737-436 | 25267/2131 | | |
| ☐ G-DOCB | Boeing 737-436 | 25304/2144 | | |
| ☐ G-DOCE | Boeing 737-436 | 25350/2167 | | |
| ☐ G-DOCF | Boeing 737-436 | 25407/2178 | | |
| ☐ G-DOCG | Boeing 737-436 | 25408/2183 | | |
| ☐ G-DOCH | Boeing 737-436 | 25428/2185 | | |
| ☐ G-DOCL | Boeing 737-436 | 25842/2228 | | |
| ☐ G-DOCN | Boeing 737-436 | 25848/2379 | | |
| ☐ G-DOCO | Boeing 737-436 | 25849/2381 | | |
| ☐ G-DOCS | Boeing 737-436 | 25852/2390 | | |
| ☐ G-DOCT | Boeing 737-436 | 25853/2409 | | |
| ☐ G-DOCU | Boeing 737-436 | 25854/2417 | | |
| ☐ G-DOCV | Boeing 737-436 | 25855/2420 | | |
| ☐ G-DOCW | Boeing 737-436 | 25856/2422 | | |
| ☐ G-DOCX | Boeing 737-436 | 25857/2451 | | |
| ☐ G-DOCY | Boeing 737-436 | 25844/2514 | ex OO-LTQ | |
| ☐ G-DOCZ | Boeing 737-436 | 25858/2522 | ex EC-FXJ | |
| ☐ G-GBTA | Boeing 737-436 | 25859/2532 | ex G-BVHA | |
| ☐ G-GBTB | Boeing 737-436 | 25860/2545 | ex OO-LTS | |
| | | | | |
| ☐ G-BNLA | Boeing 747-436 | 23908/727 | ex N60665 | [VCV] |
| ☐ G-BNLD | Boeing 747-436 | 23911/744 | ex N6018N | [VCV] |
| ☐ G-BNLE | Boeing 747-436 | 24047/753 | | |
| ☐ G-BNLF | Boeing 747-436 | 24048/773 | | |
| ☐ G-BNLG | Boeing 747-436 | 24049/774 | | |
| ☐ G-BNLH | Boeing 747-436 | 24050/779 | ex VH-NLH | [VCV] |
| ☐ G-BNLI | Boeing 747-436 | 24051/784 | | |
| ☐ G-BNLJ | Boeing 747-436 | 24052/789 | ex N60668 | |
| ☐ G-BNLK | Boeing 747-436 | 24053/790 | ex N6009F | |
| ☐ G-BNLL | Boeing 747-436 | 24054/794 | | |
| ☐ G-BNLM | Boeing 747-436 | 24055/795 | ex N6009F | |
| ☐ G-BNLN | Boeing 747-436 | 24056/802 | | |
| ☐ G-BNLO | Boeing 747-436 | 24057/817 | | |
| ☐ G-BNLP | Boeing 747-436 | 24058/828 | | |
| ☐ G-BNLR | Boeing 747-436 | 24447/829 | ex N6005C | |
| ☐ G-BNLS | Boeing 747-436 | 24629/841 | | |
| ☐ G-BNLT | Boeing 747-436 | 24630/842 | | |
| ☐ G-BNLU | Boeing 747-436 | 25406/895 | | |
| ☐ G-BNLV | Boeing 747-436 | 25427/900 | | |
| ☐ G-BNLW | Boeing 747-436 | 25432/903 | | |
| ☐ G-BNLX | Boeing 747-436 | 25435/908 | | |
| ☐ G-BNLY | Boeing 747-436 | 27090/959 | ex N60659 | |
| ☐ G-BNLZ | Boeing 747-436 | 27091/964 | | |
| ☐ G-BYGA | Boeing 747-436 | 28855/1190 | | |
| ☐ G-BYGB | Boeing 747-436 | 28856/1194 | | |
| ☐ G-BYGC | Boeing 747-436 | 25823/1195 | | |
| ☐ G-BYGD | Boeing 747-436 | 28857/1196 | | |
| ☐ G-BYGE | Boeing 747-436 | 28858/1198 | | |
| ☐ G-BYGF | Boeing 747-436 | 25824/1200 | | |
| ☐ G-BYGG | Boeing 747-436 | 28859/1212 | | |
| ☐ G-CIVA | Boeing 747-436 | 27092/967 | | |
| ☐ G-CIVB | Boeing 747-436 | 25811/1018 | | |
| ☐ G-CIVC | Boeing 747-436 | 25812/1022 | | |
| ☐ G-CIVD | Boeing 747-436 | 27349/1048 | | |
| ☐ G-CIVE | Boeing 747-436 | 27350/1050 | | |
| ☐ G-CIVF | Boeing 747-436 | 25434/1058 | ex (G-BNLY) | |
| ☐ G-CIVG | Boeing 747-436 | 25813/1059 | ex N6009F | |
| ☐ G-CIVH | Boeing 747-436 | 25809/1078 | | |
| ☐ G-CIVI | Boeing 747-436 | 25814/1079 | | |
| ☐ G-CIVJ | Boeing 747-436 | 25817/1102 | | |
| ☐ G-CIVK | Boeing 747-436 | 25818/1104 | | |
| ☐ G-CIVL | Boeing 747-436 | 27478/1108 | | |
| ☐ G-CIVM | Boeing 747-436 | 28700/1116 | | |
| ☐ G-CIVN | Boeing 747-436 | 28848/1129 | | |
| ☐ G-CIVO | Boeing 747-436 | 28849/1135 | ex N6046P | |
| ☐ G-CIVP | Boeing 747-436 | 28850/1144 | | |
| ☐ G-CIVR | Boeing 747-436 | 25820/1146 | | |
| ☐ G-CIVS | Boeing 747-436 | 28851/1148 | | |
| ☐ G-CIVT | Boeing 747-436 | 25821/1149 | | |

| | | | |
|---|---|---|---|
| ☐ G-CIVU | Boeing 747-436 | 25810/1154 | |
| ☐ G-CIVV | Boeing 747-436 | 25819/1156 | ex N6009F |
| ☐ G-CIVW | Boeing 747-436 | 25822/1157 | |
| ☐ G-CIVX | Boeing 747-436 | 28852/1172 | |
| ☐ G-CIVY | Boeing 747-436 | 28853/1178 | |
| ☐ G-CIVZ | Boeing 747-436 | 28854/1183 | |
| | | | |
| ☐ G-BNWA | Boeing 767-336ER | 24333/265 | ex N6009F |
| ☐ G-BNWB | Boeing 767-336ER | 24334/281 | ex N6046P |
| ☐ G-BNWC | Boeing 767-336ER | 24335/284 | |
| ☐ G-BNWD | Boeing 767-336ER | 24336/286 | ex N6018N |
| ☐ G-BNWH | Boeing 767-336ER | 24340/335 | ex N6005C |
| ☐ G-BNWI | Boeing 767-336ER | 24341/342 | |
| ☐ G-BNWM | Boeing 767-336ER | 25204/376 | |
| ☐ G-BNWN | Boeing 767-336ER | 25444/398 | |
| ☐ G-BNWO | Boeing 767-336ER | 25442/418 | |
| ☐ G-BNWR | Boeing 767-336ER | 25732/421 | |
| ☐ G-BNWS | Boeing 767-336ER | 25826/473 | ex N6018N |
| ☐ G-BNWT | Boeing 767-336ER | 25828/476 | |
| ☐ G-BNWU | Boeing 767-336ER | 25829/483 | |
| ☐ G-BNWV | Boeing 767-336ER | 27140/490 | |
| ☐ G-BNWW | Boeing 767-336ER | 25831/526 | |
| ☐ G-BNWX | Boeing 767-336ER | 25832/529 | |
| ☐ G-BNWY | Boeing 767-336ER | 25834/608 | ex N5005C |
| ☐ G-BNWZ | Boeing 767-336ER | 25733/648 | |
| ☐ G-BZHA | Boeing 767-336ER | 29230/702 | |
| ☐ G-BZHB | Boeing 767-336ER | 29231/704 | |
| ☐ G-BZHC | Boeing 767-336ER | 29232/708 | |
| | | | |
| ☐ G-RAES | Boeing 777-236ER | 27491/76 | ex (G-ZZZP) |
| ☐ G-VIIA | Boeing 777-236ER | 27483/41 | ex N5022E |
| ☐ G-VIIB | Boeing 777-236ER | 27484/49 | ex (G-ZZZG) |
| ☐ G-VIIC | Boeing 777-236ER | 27485/53 | ex (G-ZZZH) |
| ☐ G-VIID | Boeing 777-236ER | 27486/56 | ex (G-ZZZI) |
| ☐ G-VIIE | Boeing 777-236ER | 27487/58 | ex (G-ZZZJ) |
| ☐ G-VIIF | Boeing 777-236ER | 27488/61 | ex (G-ZZZK) |
| ☐ G-VIIG | Boeing 777-236ER | 27489/65 | ex (G-ZZZL) |
| ☐ G-VIIH | Boeing 777-236ER | 27490/70 | ex (G-ZZZM) |
| ☐ G-VIIJ | Boeing 777-236ER | 27492/111 | ex (G-ZZZN) |
| ☐ G-VIIK | Boeing 777-236ER | 28840/117 | |
| ☐ G-VIIL | Boeing 777-236ER | 27493/127 | |
| ☐ G-VIIM | Boeing 777-236ER | 28841/130 | |
| ☐ G-VIIN | Boeing 777-236ER | 29319/157 | |
| ☐ G-VIIO | Boeing 777-236ER | 29320/182 | |
| ☐ G-VIIP | Boeing 777-236ER | 29321/193 | |
| ☐ G-VIIR | Boeing 777-236ER | 29322/203 | |
| ☐ G-VIIS | Boeing 777-236ER | 29323/206 | |
| ☐ G-VIIT | Boeing 777-236ER | 29962/217 | |
| ☐ G-VIIU | Boeing 777-236ER | 29963/221 | |
| ☐ G-VIIV | Boeing 777-236ER | 29964/228 | |
| ☐ G-VIIW | Boeing 777-236ER | 29965/233 | |
| ☐ G-VIIX | Boeing 777-236ER | 29966/236 | |
| ☐ G-VIIY | Boeing 777-236ER | 29967/251 | |
| ☐ G-YMMA | Boeing 777-236ER | 30302/242 | ex N5017Q |
| ☐ G-YMMB | Boeing 777-236ER | 30303/265 | |
| ☐ G-YMMC | Boeing 777-236ER | 30304/268 | |
| ☐ G-YMMD | Boeing 777-236ER | 30305/269 | |
| ☐ G-YMME | Boeing 777-236ER | 30306/275 | |
| ☐ G-YMMF | Boeing 777-236ER | 30307/281 | |
| ☐ G-YMMG | Boeing 777-236ER | 30308/301 | |
| ☐ G-YMMH | Boeing 777-236ER | 30309/303 | |
| ☐ G-YMMI | Boeing 777-236ER | 30310/308 | |
| ☐ G-YMMJ | Boeing 777-236ER | 30311/311 | |
| ☐ G-YMMK | Boeing 777-236ER | 30312/312 | |
| ☐ G-YMML | Boeing 777-236ER | 30313/334 | |
| ☐ G-YMMN | Boeing 777-236ER | 30316/346 | |
| ☐ G-YMMO | Boeing 777-236ER | 30317/361 | |
| ☐ G-YMMP | Boeing 777-236ER | 30315/369 | |
| ☐ G-YMMR | Boeing 777-236ER | 36516/771 | ex N5014K |
| ☐ G-YMMS | Boeing 777-236ER | 36517/784 | |
| ☐ G-YMMT | Boeing 777-236ER | 36518/791 | |
| ☐ G-YMMU | Boeing 777-236ER | 36519/796 | ex N6009F |
| ☐ G-ZZZA | Boeing 777-236 | 27105/6 | ex N77779 |
| ☐ G-ZZZB | Boeing 777-236 | 27106/10 | ex N77771 |
| ☐ G-ZZZC | Boeing 777-236 | 27107/15 | ex N5014K |
| | | | |
| ☐ G-STBA | Boeing 777-336ER | 40542/879 | |
| ☐ G-STBB | Boeing 777-36NER | 39286/887 | |
| ☐ G-STBC | Boeing 777-36NER | 39287/901 | ex N6018N |
| ☐ G-STBD | Boeing 777-336ER | 38695/968 | |
| ☐ G-STBE | Boeing 777-336ER | 38696/980 | |
| ☐ G-STBF | Boeing 777-336ER | 40543/995 | |

| | | | | |
|---|---|---|---|---|
| ☐ G-ZBJA | Boeing 787-8 | 38609 | | o/o♦ |
| ☐ G-ZBJB | Boeing 787-8 | 38610 | | o/o♦ |
| ☐ G-ZBJC | Boeing 787-8 | 38611 | | o/o♦ |
| ☐ G-JBZD | Boeing 787-8 | 38612 | | o/o♦ |
| ☐ G-ZBJE | Boeing 787-8 | 38613 | | o/o♦ |
| ☐ G-ZBJF | Boeing 787-8 | 38614 | | o/o♦ |
| ☐ G-ZBJG | Boeing 787-8 | 38615 | | o/o♦ |
| ☐ G-ZBJH | Boeing 787-8 | 38619 | | o/o♦ |
| | | | | |
| ☐ G-EUNA | Airbus A318-112 | 4007 | ex D-AUAC | |
| ☐ G-EUNB | Airbus A318-112 | 4039 | ex D-AUAF | |
| ☐ G-GSSD | Boeing 747-87UF | 37561/1442 | | op for BAW <GTI♦ |
| ☐ G-GSSE | Boeing 747-87UF | 37568/1444 | ex (N851GT) | op for BAW <GTI♦ |
| ☐ G-GSSF | Boeing 747-87UF | 37569/1445 | ex (N852GT) | op for BAW <GTI♦ |
| ☐ G-XLEA | Airbus A380-841 | 095 | | o/o♦ |
| ☐ G-XLEB | Airbus A380-841 | 121 | | o/o♦ |
| ☐ G-XLEC | Airbus A380-841 | 144 | | o/o♦ |

## BRITISH INTERNATIONAL — Brintel (BS/VRA) — Cardiff, Penzance & Plymouth (CWL/PZE/PLH)

| | | | | |
|---|---|---|---|---|
| ☐ G-ATBJ | Sikorsky S-61N | 61269 | ex N10043 | |
| ☐ G-ATFM | Sikorsky S-61N | 61270 | ex CF-OKY | based Falklands Is |
| ☐ G-BCEB | Sikorsky S-61N | 61454 | ex N4023S | The Isles of Scilly |
| ☐ G-BFFJ | Sikorsky S-61N | 61777 | ex N6231 | Tresco |
| ☐ G-BFRI | Sikorsky S-61N II | 61809 | | |
| | | | | |
| ☐ G-CHCR | Aérospatiale AS.365N2 Dauphin 2 | 6423 | | ♦ |

## CHC SCOTIA HELICOPTERS — Helibus (SHZ) — Aberdeen (ABZ)

| | | | | |
|---|---|---|---|---|
| ☐ G-BKZE | Aérospatiale AS.332L | 2102 | ex F-WKQE | |
| ☐ G-CHCF | Aérospatiale AS.332L2 | 2567 | | |
| ☐ G-CHCG | Aérospatiale AS.332L2 | 2592 | | |
| ☐ G-CHCH | Aérospatiale AS.332L2 | 2601 | | |
| ☐ G-CHCI | Aérospatiale AS.322L | 2395 | ex LN-OHD | |
| ☐ G-CHCJ | Eurocopter EC225LP | 2745 | | |
| ☐ G-CHCL | Eurocopter EC225LP | 2674 | | |
| ☐ G-CHCM | Eurocopter EC225LP | 2675 | | |
| ☐ G-CHCN | Eurocopter EC225LP | 2679 | | |
| ☐ G-CHCU | Aérospatiale AS.332L2 | 2167 | ex LN-OHL | ♦ |
| ☐ G-CHCX | Eurocopter EC225LP | 2681 | ex LN-OHZ | ♦ |
| ☐ G-JSKN | Eurocopter EC225LP | 2822 | | ♦ |
| ☐ G-PUMN | Aérospatiale AS.332L2 | 2484 | ex LN-OHF | <HKS |
| ☐ G-PUMO | Aérospatiale AS.332L2 | 2467 | | |
| ☐ G-PUMS | Aérospatiale AS.332L2 | 2504 | | |
| | | | | |
| ☐ G-BKXD | Aérospatiale SA365N Dauphin 2 | 6088 | ex F-WMHD | |
| ☐ G-BTEU | Aérospatiale SA365N2 Dauphin 2 | 6392 | | |
| ☐ G-BTNC | Aérospatiale SA365N2 Dauphin 2 | 6409 | | |
| ☐ G-BVME | Aérospatiale AS365N2 Dauphin 2 | 6301 | | ♦ |
| ☐ G-CHCO | Aérospatiale AS365N2 Dauphin 2 | 6358 | ex LN-ODB | |
| ☐ G-CHCR | Aérospatiale AS365N2 Dauphin 2 | 6423 | | ♦ |
| | | | | |
| ☐ G-CGIJ | Agusta AW139 | 31203 | | Op for HM Coastguard |
| ☐ G-CGWB | Agusta AW139 | 31209 | | Op for HM Coastguard |
| ☐ G-CHCP | Agusta AW139 | 31046 | ex PH-IEH | |
| ☐ G-CHCT | Agusta AW139 | 31042 | ex PH-TRH | |
| ☐ G-CHCV | Agusta AW139 | 41005 | ex N106AW | |
| ☐ G-JEZA | Agusta AW139 | 31255 | | |
| ☐ G-SARD | Agusta AW139 | 31208 | | op for HM Coastguard |
| ☐ G-SNSA | Agusta AW139 | 31308 | | |
| ☐ G-SNSB | Agusta AW139 | 31295 | ex PH-EUD | ♦ |
| | | | | |
| ☐ G-CGMU | Sikorsky S-92A | 920034 | ex N8010S | op for HM Coastguard |
| ☐ G-CGOC | Sikorsky S-92A | 920051 | ex N45165 | |
| ☐ G-CHCK | Sikorsky S-92A | 920030 | ex N8001N | |
| ☐ G-CHCS | Sikorsky S-92A | 920125 | | |
| ☐ G-CHCZ | Sikorsky S-92A | 920143 | ex N143SU | ♦ |
| ☐ G-SARB | Sikorsky S-92A | 920045 | ex N80562 | op for HM Coastguard |
| ☐ G-SARC | Sikorsky S-92A | 920052 | ex N45168 | op for HM Coastguard |
| ☐ G-WNSA | Sikorsky S-92A | 920152 | ex N152RM | ♦ |
| | | | | |
| ☐ G-SSSC | Sikorsky S-76C | 760408 | | |
| ☐ G-SSSD | Sikorsky S-76C | 760415 | | |
| ☐ G-SSSE | Sikorsky S-76C | 760417 | | |

## DHL AIR — World Express (D0/DHK) — East Midlands-Nottingham/Brussels (EMA/BRU)

| | | | |
|---|---|---|---|
| ☐ G-BIKC | Boeing 757-236 (SF) | 22174/11 | |
| ☐ G-BIKF | Boeing 757-236 (SF) | 22177/16 | |
| ☐ G-BIKG | Boeing 757-236 (SF) | 22178/23 | |
| ☐ G-BIKI | Boeing 757-236 (SF) | 22180/25 | ex OO-DLO |
| ☐ G-BIKJ | Boeing 757-236 (SF) | 22181/29 | |
| ☐ G-BIKK | Boeing 757-236 (SF) | 22182/30 | |
| ☐ G-BIKM | Boeing 757-236 (SF) | 22184/33 | ex N8293V |
| ☐ G-BIKN | Boeing 757-236 (SF) | 22186/50 | |
| ☐ G-BIKO | Boeing 757-236 (SF) | 22187/52 | |
| ☐ G-BIKP | Boeing 757-236 (SF) | 22188/54 | |
| ☐ G-BIKS | Boeing 757-236 (SF) | 22190/63 | |
| ☐ G-BIKU | Boeing 757-236 (SF) | 23399/78 | |
| ☐ G-BIKV | Boeing 757-236 (SF) | 23400/81 | |
| ☐ G-BIKZ | Boeing 757-236 (SF) | 23532/98 | |
| ☐ G-BMRA | Boeing 757-236 (SF) | 23710/123 | |
| ☐ G-BMRB | Boeing 757-236 (SF) | 23975/145 | |
| ☐ G-BMRC | Boeing 757-236 (SF) | 24072/160 | |
| ☐ G-BMRD | Boeing 757-236 (SF) | 24073/166 | |
| ☐ G-BMRE | Boeing 757-236 (SF) | 24074/168 | |
| ☐ G-BMRF | Boeing 757-236 (SF) | 24101/175 | |
| ☐ G-BMRH | Boeing 757-236 (SF) | 24266/210 | |
| ☐ G-BMRJ | Boeing 757-236 (SF) | 24268/214 | |
| ☐ G-DHLE | Boeing 767-3JHF/W | 37805/980 | |
| ☐ G-DHLF | Boeing 767-3JHF/W | 37806/981 | |
| ☐ G-DHLG | Boeing 767-3JHF/W | 37807/982 | |

## DIRECTFLIGHT — Metman/Watchdog (DCT) — Cranfield/Exeter (-/EXT)

| | | | | |
|---|---|---|---|---|
| ☐ G-LUXE | British Aerospace 146 Srs.301 | E3001 | ex G-5-300 | Atmospheric Research, op for FAAM |
| ☐ G-MAFA | Reims Cessna F406 Caravan II | F406-0036 | ex G-DFLT | Op for DEFRA |
| ☐ G-MAFB | Reims Cessna F406 Caravan II | F406-0080 | ex F-WWSR | Op for DEFRA |
| ☐ G-SICA | Britten-Norman BN-2B-20 Islander | 2304 | ex G-SLAP | Op for Shetland Islands Council |
| ☐ G-SICB | Britten-Norman BN-2B-20 Islander | 2260 | ex G-NESU | Op for Shetland Islands Council |

## EASTERN AIRWAYS — Eastflight (T3/EZE) — Humberside (HUY)

| | | | | |
|---|---|---|---|---|
| ☐ G-CDYI | British Aerospace Jetstream 41 | 41019 | ex N305UE | [HUY] |
| ☐ G-MAJA | British Aerospace Jetstream 41 | 41032 | ex G-4-032 | |
| ☐ G-MAJB | British Aerospace Jetstream 41 | 41018 | ex G-BVKT | |
| ☐ G-MAJC | British Aerospace Jetstream 41 | 41005 | ex G-LOGJ | |
| ☐ G-MAJD | British Aerospace Jetstream 41 | 41006 | ex G-WAWR | |
| ☐ G-MAJE | British Aerospace Jetstream 41 | 41007 | ex G-LOGK | |
| ☐ G-MAJF | British Aerospace Jetstream 41 | 41008 | ex G-WAWL | |
| ☐ G-MAJG | British Aerospace Jetstream 41 | 41009 | ex G-LOGL | |
| ☐ G-MAJH | British Aerospace Jetstream 41 | 41010 | ex G-WAYR | |
| ☐ G-MAJI | British Aerospace Jetstream 41 | 41011 | ex G-WAND | |
| ☐ G-MAJJ | British Aerospace Jetstream 41 | 41024 | ex G-WAFT | |
| ☐ G-MAJK | British Aerospace Jetstream 41 | 41070 | ex SX-SEB | ♦ |
| ☐ G-MAJL | British Aerospace Jetstream 41 | 41087 | ex G-4-087 | |
| ☐ G-MAJU | British Aerospace Jetstream 41 | 41071 | ex N558HK | |
| ☐ G-MAJW | British Aerospace Jetstream 41 | 41015 | ex N303UE | |
| ☐ G-MAJY | British Aerospace Jetstream 41 | 41099 | ex N331UE | |
| ☐ G-MAJZ | British Aerospace Jetstream 41 | 41100 | ex N332UE | |
| ☐ G-CDEA | SAAB 2000 | 2000-009 | ex SE-009 | |
| ☐ G-CDEB | SAAB 2000 | 2000-036 | ex SE-036 | |
| ☐ G-CDKA | SAAB 2000 | 2000-006 | ex SE-006 | |
| ☐ G-CDKB | SAAB 2000 | 2000-032 | ex SE-032 | |
| ☐ G-CERY | SAAB 2000 | 2000-008 | ex D-AOLA | |
| ☐ G-CERZ | SAAB 2000 | 2000-042 | ex SE-LSA | |
| ☐ G-CFLU | SAAB 2000 | 2000-055 | ex SE-LSG | |
| ☐ G-CFLV | SAAB 2000 | 2000-023 | ex SE-023 | |
| ☐ G-CGMB | Embraer ERJ-135ER | 145189 | ex F-GOHA | ♦ |
| ☐ G-CGMC | Embraer ERJ-135ER | 145198 | ex F-GOHB | ♦ |
| ☐ G-CGWV | Embraer ERJ-145MP | 145362 | ex F-GIJG | ♦ |

## EASYJET AIRLINE — Easy (U2/EZY) — London-Luton (LTN)

| | | | |
|---|---|---|---|
| ☐ G-EJAR | Airbus A319-111 | 2412 | ex D-AVWH |
| ☐ G-EJJB | Airbus A319-111 | 2380 | ex D-AVWV |
| ☐ G-EZAA | Airbus A319-111 | 2677 | ex D-AVYU |
| ☐ G-EZAB | Airbus A319-111 | 2681 | ex D-AVYY |
| ☐ G-EZAC | Airbus A319-111 | 2691 | ex D-AVXB |
| ☐ G-EZAD | Airbus A319-111 | 2702 | ex D-AVXI |
| ☐ G-EZAF | Airbus A319-111 | 2715 | ex D-AVYT |

| | | | | |
|---|---|---|---|---|
| ☐ G-EZAG | Airbus A319-111 | 2727 | ex D-AVXG | |
| ☐ G-EZAI | Airbus A319-111 | 2735 | ex D-AVXM | |
| ☐ G-EZAJ | Airbus A319-111 | 2742 | ex D-AVXP | |
| ☐ G-EZAK | Airbus A319-111 | 2744 | ex D-AVXQ | |
| ☐ G-EZAL | Airbus A319-111 | 2754 | ex D-AVWG | |
| ☐ G-EZAM | Airbus A319-111 | 2037 | ex HB-JZA | |
| ☐ G-EZAN | Airbus A319-111 | 2765 | ex D-AVWL | |
| ☐ G-EZAO | Airbus A319-111 | 2769 | ex D-AVWO | |
| ☐ G-EZAP | Airbus A319-111 | 2777 | ex D-AVYG | |
| ☐ G-EZAS | Airbus A319-111 | 2779 | ex D-AVYH | |
| ☐ G-EZAT | Airbus A319-111 | 2782 | ex D-AVYO | |
| ☐ G-EZAU | Airbus A319-111 | 2795 | ex D-AVWQ | |
| ☐ G-EZAV | Airbus A319-111 | 2803 | ex D-AVWV | |
| ☐ G-EZAW | Airbus A319-111 | 2812 | ex D-AVYU | |
| ☐ G-EZAX | Airbus A319-111 | 2818 | ex D-AVXA | |
| ☐ G-EZAY | Airbus A319-111 | 2827 | ex D-AVXE | |
| ☐ G-EZAZ | Airbus A319-111 | 2829 | ex D-AVXF | |
| ☐ G-EZBA | Airbus A319-111 | 2860 | ex D-AVWB | |
| ☐ G-EZBB | Airbus A319-111 | 2854 | ex D-AVXM | |
| ☐ G-EZBC | Airbus A319-111 | 2866 | ex D-AVWD | |
| ☐ G-EZBD | Airbus A319-111 | 2873 | ex D-AVWK | |
| ☐ G-EZBE | Airbus A319-111 | 2884 | ex D-AVXO | |
| ☐ G-EZBF | Airbus A319-111 | 2923 | ex D-AVYK | |
| ☐ G-EZBG | Airbus A319-111 | 2946 | ex D-AVXA | |
| ☐ G-EZBH | Airbus A319-111 | 2959 | ex D-AVXH | |
| ☐ G-EZBI | Airbus A319-111 | 3003 | ex D-AVYB | Madrid |
| ☐ G-EZBJ | Airbus A319-111 | 3036 | ex D-AVWJ | |
| ☐ G-EZBK | Airbus A319-111 | 3041 | ex D-AVWK | |
| ☐ G-EZBL | Airbus A319-111 | 3053 | ex D-AVYJ | |
| ☐ G-EZBM | Airbus A319-111 | 3059 | ex D-AVWE | Edinburgh |
| ☐ G-EZBN | Airbus A319-111 | 3061 | ex D-AVWH | |
| ☐ G-EZBO | Airbus A319-111 | 3082 | ex D-AVYK | |
| ☐ G-EZBR | Airbus A319-111 | 3088 | ex D-AVYY | 100th Airbus titles |
| ☐ G-EZBT | Airbus A319-111 | 3090 | ex D-AVWM | |
| ☐ G-EZBU | Airbus A319-111 | 3118 | ex D-AVWW | |
| ☐ G-EZBV | Airbus A319-111 | 3122 | ex D-AVWX | |
| ☐ G-EZBW | Airbus A319-111 | 3134 | ex D-AVXE | |
| ☐ G-EZBX | Airbus A319-111 | 3137 | ex D-AVXH | |
| ☐ G-EZBY | Airbus A319-111 | 3176 | ex D-AVXJ | |
| ☐ G-EZBZ | Airbus A319-111 | 3184 | ex D-AVYF | |
| ☐ G-EZDA | Airbus A319-111 | 3413 | ex D-AVYH | |
| ☐ G-EZDB | Airbus A319-111 | 3411 | ex D-AVYF | |
| ☐ G-EZDC | Airbus A319-111 | 2043 | ex HB-JZB | |
| ☐ G-EZDD | Airbus A319-111 | 3442 | ex D-AVYL | |
| ☐ G-EZDE | Airbus A319-111 | 3426 | ex D-AVYP | |
| ☐ G-EZDF | Airbus A319-111 | 3432 | ex D-AVYG | |
| ☐ G-EZDH | Airbus A319-111 | 3466 | ex D-AVWM | |
| ☐ G-EZDI | Airbus A319-111 | 3537 | ex D-AVWC | |
| ☐ G-EZDJ | Airbus A319-111 | 3544 | ex D-AVWJ | I Love Malpensa |
| ☐ G-EZDK | Airbus A319-111 | 3555 | ex D-AVWP | |
| ☐ G-EZDL | Airbus A319-111 | 3569 | ex D-AVWT | |
| ☐ G-EZDM | Airbus A319-111 | 3571 | ex D-AVWU | |
| ☐ G-EZDN | Airbus A319-111 | 3608 | ex D-AVYJ | |
| ☐ G-EZDO | Airbus A319-111 | 3634 | ex D-AVYP | |
| ☐ G-EZDP | Airbus A319-111 | 3675 | ex D-AVYX | |
| ☐ G-EZDR | Airbus A319-111 | 3683 | ex D-AVYZ | |
| ☐ G-EZDS | Airbus A319-111 | 3702 | ex D-AVWP | |
| ☐ G-EZDT | Airbus A319-111 | 3720 | ex D-AVWR | |
| ☐ G-EZDU | Airbus A319-111 | 3735 | ex D-AVWX | |
| ☐ G-EZDV | Airbus A319-111 | 3742 | ex D-AVWY | |
| ☐ G-EZDW | Airbus A319-111 | 3746 | ex D-AVXA | |
| ☐ G-EZDX | Airbus A319-111 | 3754 | ex D-AVXB | |
| ☐ G-EZDY | Airbus A319-111 | 3763 | ex D-AVXF | |
| ☐ G-EZDZ | Airbus A319-111 | 3774 | ex D-AVXI | |
| ☐ G-EZEA | Airbus A319-111 | 2119 | ex D-AVWZ | |
| ☐ G-EZEB | Airbus A319-111 | 2120 | ex D-AVYK | |
| ☐ G-EZEC | Airbus A319-111 | 2129 | ex D-AVWR | |
| ☐ G-EZED | Airbus A319-111 | 2170 | ex D-AVWT | |
| ☐ G-EZEF | Airbus A319-111 | 2176 | ex D-AVYS | |
| ☐ G-EZEG | Airbus A319-111 | 2181 | ex D-AVWF | |
| ☐ G-EZEP | Airbus A319-111 | 2251 | ex D-AVYQ | |
| ☐ G-EZET | Airbus A319-111 | 2271 | ex D-AVWY | |
| ☐ G-EZEV | Airbus A319-111 | 2289 | ex D-AVYV | |
| ☐ G-EZEW | Airbus A319-111 | 2300 | ex D-AVWH | |
| ☐ G-EZEZ | Airbus A319-111 | 2360 | ex D-AVWP | |
| ☐ G-EZFA | Airbus A319-111 | 3788 | ex D-AVXK | |
| ☐ G-EZFB | Airbus A319-111 | 3799 | ex D-AVXN | |
| ☐ G-EZFC | Airbus A319-111 | 3808 | ex D-AVYC | |
| ☐ G-EZFD | Airbus A319-111 | 3810 | ex D-AVYF | |
| ☐ G-EZFE | Airbus A319-111 | 3824 | ex D-AVYI | |
| ☐ G-EZFF | Airbus A319-111 | 3844 | ex D-AVYT | |
| ☐ G-EZFG | Airbus A319-111 | 3845 | ex D-AVYU | |

| | | | | | | |
|---|---|---|---|---|---|---|
| ☐ G-EZFH | Airbus A319-111 | 3854 | ex D-AVWA | | | |
| ☐ G-EZFI | Airbus A319-111 | 3888 | ex D-AVWH | | | |
| ☐ G-EZFJ | Airbus A319-111 | 4040 | ex D-AVYM | | | |
| ☐ G-EZFK | Airbus A319-111 | 4048 | ex D-AVYP | | | |
| ☐ G-EZFL | Airbus A319-111 | 4056 | ex D-AVYS | | | |
| ☐ G-EZFM | Airbus A319-111 | 4069 | ex D-AVYT | | | |
| ☐ G-EZFN | Airbus A319-111 | 4076 | ex D-AVYV | | | |
| ☐ G-EZFO | Airbus A319-111 | 4080 | ex D-AVYW | | | |
| ☐ G-EZFP | Airbus A319-111 | 4087 | ex D-AVYX | | | |
| ☐ G-EZFR | Airbus A319-111 | 4125 | ex D-AVWC | | | |
| ☐ G-EZFS | Airbus A319-111 | 4129 | ex D-AVWE | | | |
| ☐ G-EZFT | Airbus A319-111 | 4132 | ex D-AVWF | Sir George White | | |
| ☐ G-EZFU | Airbus A319-111 | 4313 | ex D-AVXC | | | |
| ☐ G-EZFV | Airbus A319-111 | 4327 | ex D-AVXE | | | |
| ☐ G-EZFW | Airbus A319-111 | 4380 | ex D-AVYQ | | | |
| ☐ G-EZFX | Airbus A319-111 | 4385 | ex D-AVYS | | | |
| ☐ G-EZFY | Airbus A319-111 | 4418 | ex D-AVXJ | | | |
| ☐ G-EZFZ | Airbus A319-111 | 4425 | ex D-AVXL | | | |
| ☐ G-EZGA | Airbus A319-111 | 4427 | ex D-AVXM | | | |
| ☐ G-EZGB | Airbus A319-111 | 4437 | ex D-AVXO | | | |
| ☐ G-EZGC | Airbus A319-111 | 4444 | ex D-AVXP | | | |
| ☐ G-EZGD | Airbus A319-111 | 4451 | ex D-AVYA | | | |
| ☐ G-EZGE | Airbus A319-111 | 4624 | ex D-AVWK | | | ♦ |
| ☐ G-EZGF | Airbus A319-111 | 4635 | ex D-AVWO | | | ♦ |
| ☐ G-EZGG | Airbus A319-111 | 4640 | ex D-AVWP | | | ♦ |
| ☐ G-EZGH | Airbus A319-111 | 4667 | ex D-AVYM | | | ♦ |
| ☐ G-EZGI | Airbus A319-111 | 4693 | ex D-AVYP | | | ♦ |
| ☐ G-EZGJ | Airbus A319-111 | 4705 | ex D-AVYR | | | ♦ |
| ☐ G-EZGK | Airbus A319-111 | 4717 | ex D-AVYT | | | ♦ |
| ☐ G-EZGL | Airbus A319-111 | 4744 | ex D-AVYB | | | ♦ |
| ☐ G-EZGM | Airbus A319-111 | 4778 | ex D-AVYU | | | ♦ |
| ☐ G-EZGN | Airbus A319-111 | 4781 | ex D-AVYV | | | ♦ |
| ☐ G-EZGO | Airbus A319-111 | 4787 | ex D-AVYX | | | ♦ |
| ☐ G-EZGP | Airbus A319-111 | 4787 | ex D-AVYX | | | ♦ |
| ☐ G-EZGR | Airbus A319-111 | 4837 | ex D-AVWD | | | ♦ |
| ☐ G-EZIC | Airbus A319-111 | 2436 | ex D-AVWC | | | |
| ☐ G-EZID | Airbus A319-111 | 2442 | ex D-AVWT | '100' titles | | [SEN] |
| ☐ G-EZIE | Airbus A319-111 | 2446 | ex D-AVWQ | | | [SEN] |
| ☐ G-EZIG | Airbus A319-111 | 2460 | ex D-AVYM | | | |
| ☐ G-EZIH | Airbus A319-111 | 2463 | ex D-AVWV | | | |
| ☐ G-EZII | Airbus A319-111 | 2471 | ex D-AVYK | | | |
| ☐ G-EZIJ | Airbus A319-111 | 2477 | ex D-AVYU | | | |
| ☐ G-EZIK | Airbus A319-111 | 2481 | ex D-AVYV | | | |
| ☐ G-EZIL | Airbus A319-111 | 2492 | ex D-AVWM | | | |
| ☐ G-EZIM | Airbus A319-111 | 2495 | ex D-AVYO | | | |
| ☐ G-EZIN | Airbus A319-111 | 2503 | ex D-AVYZ | | | |
| ☐ G-EZIO | Airbus A319-111 | 2512 | ex D-AVWP | | | |
| ☐ G-EZIP | Airbus A319-111 | 2514 | ex D-AVWQ | | | |
| ☐ G-EZIR | Airbus A319-111 | 2527 | ex D-AVWK | | | |
| ☐ G-EZIS | Airbus A319-111 | 2528 | ex D-AVWJ | | | |
| ☐ G-EZIT | Airbus A319-111 | 2538 | ex D-AVYN | | | |
| ☐ G-EZIU | Airbus A319-111 | 2548 | ex D-AVYF | | | |
| ☐ G-EZIV | Airbus A319-111 | 2565 | ex D-AVYY | | | |
| ☐ G-EZIW | Airbus A319-111 | 2578 | ex D-AVXE | | | |
| ☐ G-EZIX | Airbus A319-111 | 2605 | ex D-AVXP | | | |
| ☐ G-EZIY | Airbus A319-111 | 2636 | ex D-AVWH | | | |
| ☐ G-EZIZ | Airbus A319-111 | 2646 | ex D-AVWQ | | | |
| ☐ G-EZMH | Airbus A319-111 | 2053 | ex HB-JZD | | | |
| ☐ G-EZMS | Airbus A319-111 | 2378 | ex D-AVWS | | | |
| ☐ G-EZNC | Airbus A319-111 | 2050 | ex HB-JZC | | | |
| ☐ G-EZPG | Airbus A319-111 | 2385 | ex D-AVYD | | | |
| ☐ G-EZSM | Airbus A319-111 | 2062 | ex HB-JZE | | | |
| | | | | | | |
| ☐ G-EZTA | Airbus A320-214 | 3805 | ex D-AVVD | | | |
| ☐ G-EZTB | Airbus A320-214 | 3843 | ex F-WWBO | | | |
| ☐ G-EZTC | Airbus A320-214 | 3871 | ex F-WWIG | | | |
| ☐ G-EZTD | Airbus A320-214 | 3909 | ex D-AVVB | | | |
| ☐ G-EZTE | Airbus A320-214 | 3913 | ex D-AVVF | | | |
| ☐ G-EZTF | Airbus A320-214 | 3922 | ex D-AVVG | | | |
| ☐ G-EZTG | Airbus A320-214 | 3946 | ex D-AVVJ | | | |
| ☐ G-EZTH | Airbus A320-214 | 3953 | ex D-AVVM | | | |
| ☐ G-EZTI | Airbus A320-214 | 3975 | ex D-AVVN | | | |
| ☐ G-EZTJ | Airbus A320-214 | 3979 | ex D-AVVO | | | |
| ☐ G-EZTK | Airbus A320-214 | 3991 | ex D-AVVP | | | |
| ☐ G-EZTL | Airbus A320-214 | 4012 | ex D-AVVC | | | |
| ☐ G-EZTM | Airbus A320-214 | 4014 | ex D-AVVD | | | |
| ☐ G-EZTN | Airbus A320-214 | 4006 | ex F-WWDY | | | |
| ☐ G-EZTR | Airbus A320-214 | 4179 | ex D-AVVX | | | |
| ☐ G-EZTT | Airbus A320-214 | 4219 | ex D-AVVM | | | |
| ☐ G-EZTV | Airbus A320-214 | 4234 | ex F-WWBZ | | | |
| ☐ G-EZTX | Airbus A320-214 | 4286 | ex F-WWIR | | | |
| ☐ G-EZTY | Airbus A320-214 | 4543 | ex D-AUBS | | | |

| | | | | | |
|---|---|---|---|---|---|
| ☐ | G-EZTZ | Airbus A320-214 | 4556 | ex D-AUBW | |
| ☐ | G-EZUA | Airbus A320-214 | 4588 | ex D-AVVE | |
| ☐ | G-EZUC | Airbus A320-214 | 4591 | ex D-AVVF | |
| ☐ | G-EZUD | Airbus A320-214 | 4636 | ex G-AXAZ | ♦ |
| ☐ | G-EZUE | Airbus A320-214 | 4646 | ex D-AVVP | ♦ |
| ☐ | G-EZUF | Airbus A320-214 | 4676 | ex D-AXAG | ♦ |
| ☐ | G-EZUG | Airbus A320-214 | 4680 | ex D-AXAH | ♦ |
| ☐ | GEZUH | Airbus A320-214 | 4708 | ex D-AUBG | ♦ |
| ☐ | G-EZUI | Airbus A320-214 | 4721 | ex D-AUBI | ♦ |
| ☐ | G-EZUJ | Airbus A320-214 | 4740 | ex D-AVVL | ♦ |
| ☐ | G-EZUK | Airbus A320-214 | 4749 | ex D-AVVL | ♦ |
| ☐ | G-EZUL | Airbus A320-214 | 5019 | ex D-AXAH | ♦ |
| ☐ | G-EZUM | Airbus A320-214 | 5020 | ex D-EZUM | ♦ |
| ☐ | G-EZUN | Airbus A320-214 | 5046 | ex D-AXAN | ♦ |
| ☐ | G-EZUO | Airbus A320-214 | 5052 | ex D-AUBA | ♦ |
| ☐ | G-EZUP | Airbus A320-214 | 5056 | ex D-AUBB | ♦ |
| ☐ | G-EZUR | Airbus A320-214 | 5064 | ex D-AUBD | ♦ |
| ☐ | G-EZUS | Airbus A320-214 | 5104 | ex D-AUBS | ♦ |
| ☐ | G-EZUT | Airbus A320-214 | 5113 | ex D-AUBW | o/o♦ |
| ☐ | G-EZUU | Airbus A320-214 | 5150 | ex | o/o♦ |
| ☐ | G-EZUV | Airbus A320-214 | 5111 | ex | o/o♦ |
| ☐ | G-EZUW | Airbus A320-214 | 5116 | ex | o/o♦ |
| ☐ | G-EZUX | Airbus A320-214 | 5138 | ex | o/o♦ |
| ☐ | G-EZUY | Airbus A320-214 | 5146 | ex | o/o♦ |
| ☐ | G-EZUZ | Airbus A320-214 | 5187 | ex | o/o♦ |
| ☐ | G-EZWA | Airbus A320-214 | 5201 | ex | o/o♦ |
| ☐ | G-EZWB | Airbus A320-214 | 5224 | ex | o/o♦ |
| ☐ | G-EZWC | Airbus A320-214 | 5236 | ex | o/o♦ |
| ☐ | G-EZWD | Airbus A320-214 | 5249 | ex | o/o♦ |
| ☐ | G-EZWE | Airbus A320-214 | 5319 | ex | o/o♦ |

## FLYBE — Jersey (BE/BEE) — Jersey/Exeter (JER/EXT)

| | | | | | |
|---|---|---|---|---|---|
| ☐ | G-ECOA | de Havilland DHC-8-402Q | 4180 | ex C-FMUE | |
| ☐ | G-ECOB | de Havilland DHC-8-402Q | 4185 | ex LN-WDT | |
| ☐ | G-ECOC | de Havilland DHC-8-402Q | 4197 | ex LN-WDU | |
| ☐ | G-ECOD | de Havilland DHC-8-402Q | 4206 | ex C-FPEX | |
| ☐ | G-ECOE | de Havilland DHC-8-402Q | 4212 | ex LN-WDV | |
| ☐ | G-ECOF | de Havilland DHC-8-402Q | 4216 | ex LN-WDW | |
| ☐ | G-ECOG | de Havilland DHC-8-402Q | 4220 | ex C-FSRQ | |
| ☐ | G-ECOH | de Havilland DHC-8-402Q | 4221 | ex C-FSRW | >BEL |
| ☐ | G-ECOI | de Havilland DHC-8-402Q | 4224 | ex C-FTIE | >BEL |
| ☐ | G-ECOJ | de Havilland DHC-8-402Q | 4229 | ex C-FTUS | |
| ☐ | G-ECOK | de Havilland DHC-8-402Q | 4230 | ex C-FTUT | |
| ☐ | G-ECOM | de Havilland DHC-8-402Q | 4233 | ex C-FUCR | |
| ☐ | G-ECOO | de Havilland DHC-8-402Q | 4237 | ex C-FUOH | |
| ☐ | G-ECOP | de Havilland DHC-8-402Q | 4242 | ex C-FUTG | |
| ☐ | G-ECOR | de Havilland DHC-8-402Q | 4248 | ex C-FVUJ | |
| ☐ | G-ECOT | de Havilland DHC-8-402Q | 4251 | ex C-FVUV | |
| ☐ | G-FLBA | de Havilland DHC-8-402Q | 4253 | ex C-FVVB | |
| ☐ | G-FLBB | de Havilland DHC-8-402Q | 4255 | ex C-FWGE | |
| ☐ | G-FLBC | de Havilland DHC-8-402Q | 4257 | ex C-FWGY | |
| ☐ | G-FLBD | de Havilland DHC-8-402Q | 4259 | ex C-FWZN | |
| ☐ | G-FLBE | de Havilland DHC-8-402Q | 4261 | ex C-FXAB | |
| ☐ | G-JECE | de Havilland DHC-8-402Q | 4094 | ex C-FDHU | The Wembley Grecians |
| ☐ | G-JECF | de Havilland DHC-8-402Q | 4095 | ex C-FDHV | |
| ☐ | G-JECG | de Havilland DHC-8-402Q | 4098 | ex C-FAQH | |
| ☐ | G-JECH | de Havilland DHC-8-402Q | 4103 | ex C-FCQC | |
| ☐ | G-JECI | de Havilland DHC-8-402Q | 4105 | ex C-FCQK | |
| ☐ | G-JECJ | de Havilland DHC-8-402Q | 4110 | ex C-FCVN | |
| ☐ | G-JECK | de Havilland DHC-8-402Q | 4113 | ex C-FDRL | |
| ☐ | G-JECL | de Havilland DHC-8-402Q | 4114 | ex C-FDRN | The George Best |
| ☐ | G-JECM | de Havilland DHC-8-402Q | 4118 | ex C-FFCE | |
| ☐ | G-JECN | de Havilland DHC-8-402Q | 4120 | ex C-FFCL | |
| ☐ | G-JECO | de Havilland DHC-8-402Q | 4126 | ex C-FFPT | |
| ☐ | G-JECP | de Havilland DHC-8-402Q | 4136 | ex C-FHEL | |
| ☐ | G-JECR | de Havilland DHC-8-402Q | 4139 | ex C-FHQM | |
| ☐ | G-JECX | de Havilland DHC-8-402Q | 4155 | ex C-FLKO | |
| ☐ | G-JECY | de Havilland DHC-8-402Q | 4157 | ex C-FLKV | |
| ☐ | G-JECZ | de Havilland DHC-8-402Q | 4179 | ex C-FMTY | |
| ☐ | G-JEDK | de Havilland DHC-8-402Q | 4065 | ex C-GEMU | Vignoble de Bergerac |
| ☐ | G-JEDL | de Havilland DHC-8-402Q | 4067 | ex C-GEOZ | |
| ☐ | G-JEDM | de Havilland DHC-8-402Q | 4077 | ex C-FGNP | |
| ☐ | G-JEDN | de Havilland DHC-8-402Q | 4078 | ex C-FNGB | |
| ☐ | G-JEDO | de Havilland DHC-8-402Q | 4079 | ex C-GDFT | |
| ☐ | G-JEDP | de Havilland DHC-8-402Q | 4085 | ex C-FDHO | Special colours |
| ☐ | G-JEDR | de Havilland DHC-8-402Q | 4087 | ex C-FDHI | |
| ☐ | G-JEDT | de Havilland DHC-8-402Q | 4088 | ex C-FDHP | |
| ☐ | G-JEDU | de Havilland DHC-8-402Q | 4089 | ex C-GEMU | Pride of Exeter |
| ☐ | G-JEDV | de Havilland DHC-8-402Q | 4090 | ex C-FDHX | |
| ☐ | G-JEDW | de Havilland DHC-8-402Q | 4093 | ex C-GFBW | |
| ☐ | G-KKEV | de Havilland DHC-8-402Q | 4201 | ex C-FOUU | Kevin Keegan |

| | | | | |
|---|---|---|---|---|
| ☐ G-FBEO | Embraer ERJ-175LR | 17000326 | | ♦ |
| ☐ G-FBJA | Embraer ERJ-175LR | 17000326 | ex PT-TIB | ♦ |
| ☐ G-FBJP | Embraer ERJ-175LR | 17000327 | ex PT-TOB | ♦ |
| ☐ G-FBJC | Embraer ERJ-175LR | 17000328 | ex PT-TOO | ♦ |
| ☐ G-FBJD | Embraer ERJ-175LR | 17000329 | ex PT-TOZ | ♦ |
| ☐ G-FBJE | Embraer ERJ-175LR | 17000336 | ex PT-TUS | ♦ |
| | | | | |
| ☐ G-FBEA | Embraer ERJ-195LR | 19000029 | ex PT-SGD | Wings of the Community |
| ☐ G-FBEB | Embraer ERJ-195LR | 19000057 | ex PT-SII | |
| ☐ G-FBEC | Embraer ERJ-195LR | 19000069 | ex PT-SJI | |
| ☐ G-FBED | Embraer ERJ-195LR | 19000084 | ex PT-SNB | |
| ☐ G-FBEE | Embraer ERJ-195LR | 19000093 | ex PT-SNN | |
| ☐ G-FBEF | Embraer ERJ-195LR | 19000104 | ex PT-SNY | |
| ☐ G-FBEG | Embraer ERJ-195LR | 19000120 | ex PT-SQO | |
| ☐ G-FBEH | Embraer ERJ-195LR | 19000128 | ex PT-SQX | |
| ☐ G-FBEI | Embraer ERJ-195LR | 19000143 | ex PT-SYV | |
| ☐ G-FBEJ | Embraer ERJ-195LR | 19000155 | ex PT-SAK | |
| ☐ G-FBEK | Embraer ERJ-195LR | 19000168 | ex PT-SDC | |
| ☐ G-FBEL | Embraer ERJ-195LR | 19000184 | ex PT-SDS | |
| ☐ G-FBEM | Embraer ERJ-195LR | 19000204 | ex PT-SGN | |
| ☐ G-FBEN | Embraer ERJ-195LR | 19000213 | ex PT-SGW | |

## GLOBAL SUPPLY SYSTEMS — JetLift (GSS) — London-Stansted (STN)

| | | | |
|---|---|---|---|
| ☐ G-GSSD | Boeing 747-87UF | 37561/1429 | op for BAW <GTI |
| ☐ G-GSSE | Boeing 747-87UF | 37568/1432 | op for BAW <GTI <GTI |
| ☐ G-GSSF | Boeing 747-87UF | 37569 | op for BAW <GTI |

## HEBRIDEAN AIR SERVICES — Cumbernauld

| | | | | |
|---|---|---|---|---|
| ☐ G-AYRU | Britten-Norman BN-2A-6 Islander | 181 | | ♦ |
| ☐ G-BPLR | Britten-Norman BN-2B-20 Islander | 2209 | ex TF-VEJ | ♦ |
| ☐ G-HEBI | Britten-Norman BN-2B-20 Islander | 2240 | ex G-BSPT | |
| ☐ G-HEBS | Britten-Norman BN-2B-26 Islander | 2267 | ex G-BUBJ | |

## ISLES OF SCILLY SKYBUS — Scillonia (5Y/IOS) — Lands End-St Just (LEQ)

| | | | |
|---|---|---|---|
| ☐ G-BIHO | de Havilland DHC-6 Twin Otter 310 | 738 | ex A6-ADB |
| ☐ G-BUBN | Britten-Norman BN-2B-26 Islander | 2270 | |
| ☐ G-CBML | de Havilland DHC-6 Twin Otter 310 | 695 | ex C-FZSP |
| ☐ G-CEWM | de Havilland DHC-6 Twin Otter 300 | 656 | ex N70551 |
| ☐ G-SBUS | Britten-Norman BN-2A-26 Islander | 3013 | ex G-BMMH |
| ☐ G-SSKY | Britten-Norman BN-2B-26 Islander | 2247 | ex G-BSWT |

## JET2 — Channex (LS/EXS) — Leeds-Bradford /Manchester (LBA/MAN)

| | | | | | |
|---|---|---|---|---|---|
| ☐ G-CELA | Boeing 737-377 | 23663/1323 | ex VH-CZK | Jet2 Newcastle | |
| ☐ G-CELB | Boeing 737-377 | 23664/1326 | ex VH-CZL | Jet2 Yorkshire | |
| ☐ G-CELC | Boeing 737-33A | 23831/1471 | ex N190FH | Jet2 Tunisia | |
| ☐ G-CELD | Boeing 737-33A | 23832/1473 | ex N191FH | Jet2 Espana | |
| ☐ G-CELE | Boeing 737-33A | 24029/1601 | ex VH-CZX | Jet2 Belfast | |
| ☐ G-CELF | Boeing 737-377 | 24302/1618 | ex S7-ABB | Jet2 Sardinia | |
| ☐ G-CELG | Boeing 737-377 | 24303/1620 | ex S7-ABD | Helen Normington | |
| ☐ G-CELH | Boeing 737-330 (QC) | 23525/1278 | ex D-ABXD | Jet2 Faro | |
| ☐ G-CELI | Boeing 737-330 | 23526/1282 | ex D-ABXE | Jet2 Manchester | |
| ☐ G-CELJ | Boeing 737-330 | 23529/1293 | ex LZ-BOG | Jet2 Italia | |
| ☐ G-CELK | Boeing 737-330 | 23530/1297 | ex LZ-BOH | Jet2 Edinburgh | |
| ☐ G-CELO | Boeing 737-33A (QC) | 24028/1599 | ex TF-ELO | Jet2 Faro | |
| ☐ G-CELP | Boeing 737-330 (QC) | 23522/1246 | ex TF-ELP | Jet2 Private Charter | |
| ☐ G-CELR | Boeing 737-330 (QC) | 23523/1271 | ex TF-ELR | Jet2 Corfu | |
| ☐ G-CELS | Boeing 737-377 | 23660/1294 | ex VH-CZH | Jet2 Leeds-Bradford | |
| ☐ G-CELU | Boeing 737-377 | 23657/1280 | ex VH-CZE | Jet2 Barcelona | |
| ☐ G-CELV | Boeing 737-377 | 23661/1314 | ex VH-CZI | Jet2 Amsterdam | |
| ☐ G-CELW | Boeing 737-377F | 23669/1292 | ex N659DG | | |
| ☐ G-CELX | Boeing 737-377 | 23654/1273 | ex VH-CZB | Jet2 Malaga | |
| ☐ G-CELY | Boeing 737-377F | 23662/1316 | ex N622DG | Jet2 Ireland | |
| ☐ G-CELZ | Boeing 737-377F | 23658/1281 | ex VH-CZF | Jet2 Paris | |
| ☐ G-GDFB | Boeing 737-33A | 25743/2206 | ex SX-BBU | | |
| ☐ G-GDFE | Boeing 737-3Q8 (QC) | 24131/1541 | ex OO-TNF | | |
| ☐ G-GDFG | Boeing 737-36Q | 28658/2865 | ex LN-KKQ | Jet2 Budapest | ♦ |
| ☐ G-GDFH | Boeing 737-3Y5 | 25615/2478 | ex LN-KKC | | [BEG]♦ |
| ☐ G-GDFK | Boeing 737-36N | 28572/3031 | ex N4620F | | [NWI]♦ |
| ☐ G- | Boeing 737-3U3 | 28740/3003 | ex G-THOP | | o/o♦ |
| | | | | | |
| ☐ G-LSAA | Boeing 757-236 | 24122/187 | ex N241CV | Jet2 Tenerife | |
| ☐ G-LSAB | Boeing 757-27B/W | 24136/169 | ex N136CV | Jet2 Menorca | |
| ☐ G-LSAC | Boeing 757-23A/W | 25488/471 | ex N254DG | Jet2 Lanzarote | |
| ☐ G-LSAD | Boeing 757-236 | 24397/221 | ex SX-BLW | | |
| ☐ G-LSAE | Boeing 757-27B/W | 24135/165 | ex OM-SNA | Jet2 Murcia | |
| ☐ G-LSAG | Boeing 757-21B | 24014/144 | ex B-2801 | | |

| | | | | |
|---|---|---|---|---|
| ☐ G-LSAH | Boeing 757-21B | 24015/148 | ex B-2802 | |
| ☐ G-LSAI | Boeing 757-21B | 24016/150 | ex B-2803 | |
| ☐ G-LSAJ | Boeing 757-236 | 24793/292 | ex G-CDUP | Jet2 New York |
| ☐ G-LSAK | Boeing 757-23N | 27973/735 | ex N517AT | >RKM |
| ☐ G-LSAL | Boeing 757-204/W | 26967/522 | ex G-BYAI | ♦ |
| ☐ G-LSAM | Boeing 757-204/W | 26966/520 | ex G-BYAH | ♦ |
| | | | | |
| ☐ G-GDFC | Boeing 737-8K2/W | 28375/85 | ex PH-HZC | ♦ |
| ☐ G-GDFD | Boeing 737-8K5/W | 27982/8 | ex D-AHFB | ♦ |
| ☐ G-GDFF | Boeing 737-85P | 28385/421 | ex EC-HGP | ♦ |
| ☐ G-GDFG | Boeing 737-804 | 28227/452 | ex G-CDZH | [BRU]♦ |

## LINKS AIR (LNQ)

| | | | | |
|---|---|---|---|---|
| ☐ G-CCPW | British Aerospace Jetstream 31 | 785 | ex SE-LDI | [IOM] |
| ☐ G-EIGG | British Aerospace Jetstream 31 | 773 | ex SE-LGH | |

## LOCH LOMOND SEAPLANES — Luss

| | | | | |
|---|---|---|---|---|
| ☐ G-MDJE | Cessna 208 Caravan I | 20800336 | ex N208FM | |

## LOGANAIR — Logan (LOG) — Glasgow (GLA)

| | | | | |
|---|---|---|---|---|
| ☐ G-GNTB | SAAB SF.340A (QC) | 340A-082 | ex HB-AHL | |
| ☐ G-GNTF | SAAB SF.340A (QC) | 340A-113 | ex SE-F13 | all-white |
| ☐ G-LGNA | SAAB SF.340B | 340B-199 | ex N592MA | Flybe c/s |
| ☐ G-LGNB | SAAB SF.340B | 340B-216 | ex N595MA | Flybe c/s |
| ☐ G-LGNC | SAAB SF.340B | 340B-318 | ex SE-KXC | Flybe c/s |
| ☐ G-LGND | SAAB SF.340B | 340B-169 | ex G-GNTH | Flybe c/s |
| ☐ G-LGNE | SAAB SF.340B | 340B-172 | ex G-GNTI | Flybe c/s |
| ☐ G-LGNF | SAAB SF.340B | 340B-192 | ex N192JE | Flybe c/s |
| ☐ G-LGNG | SAAB SF.340B | 340B-327 | ex SE-C27 | Flybe c/s |
| ☐ G-LGNH | SAAB SF.340B | 340B-333 | ex SE-C33 | Flybe c/s |
| ☐ G-LGNI | SAAB SF.340B | 340B-160 | ex SE-F60 | Flybe c/s |
| ☐ G-LGNJ | SAAB SF.340B | 340B-173 | ex SE-F73 | Flybe c/s |
| ☐ G-LGNK | SAAB SF.340B | 340B-185 | ex SE-F85 | Flybe c/s |
| ☐ G-LGNL | SAAB SF.340B | 340B-246 | ex SE-G46 | Flybe c/s |
| ☐ G-LGNM | SAAB SF.340B | 340B-187 | ex SE-F47 | Flybe c/s |
| ☐ G-LGNN | SAAB SF.340B | 340B-197 | ex SE-F97 | |
| | | | | |
| ☐ G-BLDV | Britten-Norman BN-2B-26 Islander | 2179 | ex D-INEY | |
| ☐ G-BPCA | Britten-Norman BN-2B-26 Islander | 2198 | ex G-BLNX | Capt David Barclay MBE |
| ☐ G-BVVK | de Havilland DHC-6 Twin Otter 310 | 666 | ex LN-BEZ | Flybe c/s |
| ☐ G-BZFP | de Havilland DHC-6 Twin Otter 310 | 696 | ex C-GGNF | Flybe c/s |

## MANX2 AIRLINES — Manx2 (MX) — Ronaldsway (IOM)

| | | | | |
|---|---|---|---|---|
| ☐ D-CMNX | Dornier 228-202K | 8065 | ex TF-CSG | <FKI |
| ☐ D-IFLM | Dornier 228-201 | 8046 | ex TF-CSF | <FKI |
| ☐ OK-ASA | LET L-410UVP-E | 902439 | ex SP-KPY | Lsd fr/op by Van Air |
| ☐ OK-TCA | LET L-410UVP-E | 902431 | ex SP-KPZ | Lsd fr/op by Van Air |
| ☐ OK-UBA | LET L-410UVP-E | 892319 | ex SP-TXA | Lsd fr/op by Van Air |

## MONARCH AIRLINES — Monarch (ZB/MON) — London-Luton (LTN)

| | | | | |
|---|---|---|---|---|
| ☐ G-MONX | Airbus A320-212 | 0392 | ex F-WWDR | |
| ☐ G-MPCD | Airbus A320-212 | 0379 | ex C-GZCD | |
| ☐ G-MRJK | Airbus A320-214 | 1081 | ex PH-BMC | |
| ☐ G-OZBB | Airbus A320-212 | 0389 | ex C-GZUM | |
| ☐ G-OZBK | Airbus A320-214 | 1370 | ex PH-BMD | |
| ☐ G-OZBW | Airbus A320-214 | 1571 | ex G-OOPP | ♦ |
| ☐ G-OZBX | Airbus A320-214 | 1637 | ex G-OOPU | ♦ |
| | | | | |
| ☐ G-MARA | Airbus A321-231 | 0983 | ex D-AVZB | |
| ☐ G-OJEG | Airbus A321-231 | 1015 | ex D-AVZN | |
| ☐ G-OZBE | Airbus A321-231 | 1707 | ex D-AVZH | |
| ☐ G-OZBF | Airbus A321-231 | 1763 | ex D-AVZB | |
| ☐ G-OZBG | Airbus A321-231 | 1941 | ex D-AVXC | |
| ☐ G-OZBH | Airbus A321-231 | 2105 | ex D-AVXB | |
| ☐ G-OZBI | Airbus A321-231 | 2234 | ex D-AVZV | |
| ☐ G-OZBL | Airbus A321-231 | 0864 | ex G-MIDE | |
| ☐ G-OZBM | Airbus A321-231 | 1045 | ex G-MIDJ | |
| ☐ G-OZBN | Airbus A321-231 | 1153 | ex G-MIDK | |
| ☐ G-OZBO | Airbus A321-231 | 1207 | ex G-MIDM | |
| ☐ G-OZBP | Airbus A321-231 | 1433 | ex G-TTIB | |
| ☐ G-OZBR | Airbus A321-231 | 1794 | ex N586NK | |
| ☐ G-OZBS | Airbus A321-231 | 1428 | ex G-TTIA | |
| ☐ G-OZBT | Airbus A321-231 | 3546 | ex G-TTIH | |
| ☐ G-OZBU | Airbus A321-231 | 3575 | ex G-TTII | |
| | | | | |
| ☐ G-DAJB | Boeing 757-2T7ER | 23770/125 | | |

| ☐ G-EOMA | Airbus A330-243 | 265 | ex F-WWKU | |
| ☐ G-MAJS | Airbus A300B4-605R | 604 | ex F-WWAX | |
| ☐ G-MONJ | Boeing 757-2T7ER | 24104/170 | | |
| ☐ G-MONK | Boeing 757-2T7ER | 24105/172 | | |
| ☐ G-MONR | Airbus A300B4-605R | 540 | ex VH-YMJ | |
| ☐ G-MONS | Airbus A300B4-605R | 556 | ex VH-YMK | |
| ☐ G-OJMR | Airbus A300B4-605R | 605 | ex F-WWAY | |
| ☐ G-SMAN | Airbus A330-243 | 261 | ex F-WWKR | |

## PDG HELICOPTERS — Osprey (PDG) — Inverness / Glasgow (INV/GLA)

| ☐ G-BXGA | Aérospatiale AS350B2 Ecureuil | 2493 | ex OO-RCH | |
| ☐ G-PDGF | Aérospatiale AS350B2 Ecureuil | 9024 | ex G-FROH | |
| ☐ G-PDGI | Aérospatiale AS350B1 Ecureuil | 1991 | ex EI-FAC | ♦ |
| ☐ G-PDGR | Aérospatiale AS350B2 Ecureuil | 2559 | ex G-RICC | |
| ☐ G-PLMH | Aérospatiale AS350B2 Ecureuil | 2156 | ex F-WQDJ | |
| ☐ G-BPRJ | Aérospatiale AS355F1 Twin Star | 5201 | ex N368E | |
| ☐ G-BVLG | Aérospatiale AS355F1 Twin Star | 5011 | ex N57745 | |
| ☐ G-NETR | Aérospatiale AS355F2 Ecureuil 2 | 5164 | ex G-JARV | op for Network Rail |
| ☐ G-NTWK | Aérospatiale AS355F2 Ecureuil 2 | 5347 | ex G-FTWO | op for Network Rail |
| ☐ G-PDGT | Aérospatiale AS355F2 Twin Star | 5374 | ex N325SC | |
| ☐ G-PDGK | Aérospatiale AS365N Dauphin 2 | 6009 | ex G-HEMS | |
| ☐ G-PDGN | Aérospatiale SA365N Dauphin 2 | 6074 | ex PH-SSU | |
| ☐ G-PLMI | Aérospatiale SA365C1 Dauphin 2 | 5001 | ex F-GFYH | |
| ☐ G-WAAN | MBB Bo.105DB | S-20 | ex G-AZOR | op for Great North Air Ambulance |

## POLICE AVIATION SERVICES — Special (PLC) — Gloucester (GLO)

| ☐ G-CPAS | Eurocopter EC135P2+ | 0920 | | op for Cleveland Police♦ |
| ☐ G-HEOI | Eurocopter EC135 | 0825 | | op for W Mercia & Staffordshire Police♦ |
| ☐ G-NWOI | Eurocopter EC135 | 0887 | | op for N Wales Police♦ |
| ☐ G-TVHB | Eurocopter EC135 | 0874 | | op for Thames Valley Police♦ |
| ☐ G-WCAO | Eurocopter EC135T2 | 0204 | ex D-HECU | op for Western Counties Police |
| ☐ G-WMAO | Eurocopter EC135P2+ | 0501 | | op for West Midlands Police |
| ☐ G-WPDA | Eurocopter EC135P1 | 0109 | ex D-HIPT | |
| ☐ G-WPDB | Eurocopter EC135P1 | 0112 | ex D-HAIT | ♦ |
| ☐ G-BXZK | MD Helicopters MD902 Explorer | 900-00057 | ex N9238T | op for Dorset Police |
| ☐ G-CEMS | MD Helicopters MD902 Explorer | 900-00089 | ex PK-OCR | op for Yorkshire Air Ambulance |
| ☐ G-COTH | MD Helicopters MD902 Explorer | 900-00035 | ex N3ND | ♦ |
| ☐ G-EHAA | MD Helicopters MD902 Explorer | 900-00079 | ex G-GNAA | |
| ☐ G-HAAT | MD Helicopters MD902 Explorer | 900-0081 | ex G-GMPS | ♦ |
| ☐ G-KAAT | MD Helicopters MD902 Explorer | 900-00056 | ex G-PASS | op for Kent Air Ambulance |
| ☐ G-KSSH | MD Helicopters MD902 Explorer | 900-00062 | ex G-WMID | op for Surrey Air Ambulance |
| ☐ G-LNAA | MD Helicopters MD902 Explorer | 900-00074 | ex G-76-074 | op for Lincs & Notts Air Ambulance |
| ☐ G-LNCT | MD Helicopters MD902 Explorer | 900-0134 | | ♦ |
| ☐ G-SASH | MD Helicopters MD902 Explorer | 900-00080 | ex PH-SHF | op for Yorkshire Air Ambulance |
| ☐ G-SUSX | MD Helicopters MD902 Explorer | 900-00065 | ex N3065W | op for South East Air Support |
| ☐ G-WPAS | MD Helicopters MD902 Explorer | 900-00053 | ex N92237 | op for Wiltshire Police |
| ☐ G-YPOL | MD Helicopters MD902 Explorer | 900-00078 | ex N7038S | op for West Yorkshire Police |
| ☐ G-NWPS | Eurocopter EC135T1 | 0063 | | ♦ |
| ☐ G-WCAO | Eurocopter EC135T2 | 0204 | ex D-HECU | op for Avon & Somerset Police |
| ☐ G-WMAS | Eurocopter EC135T2 | 0174 | | op for Midlands Air Ambulance |
| ☐ G-WYPA | MBB Bo.105DBS-4 | S-815 | ex D-HDZY | |

## PREMIAIR AVIATION SERVICES — Premiere (PGL) — Denham

| ☐ G-BURS | Sikorsky S-76A+ | 760040 | ex G-OHTL | |
| ☐ G-URSA | Sikorsky S-76C | 760699 | | ♦ |
| ☐ G-VONA | Sikorsky S-76A | 760086 | ex G-BUXB | |
| ☐ G-VONB | Sikorsky S-76B | 760339 | ex G-POAH | |
| ☐ G-VONC | Sikorsky S-76B | 760354 | ex N966PR | |
| ☐ VP-BIR | Sikorsky S-76B | 760430 | ex N9HM | |
| ☐ G-VOND | Bell 222 | 47041 | ex G-OWCG | |
| ☐ G-VONE | Aérospatiale AS355N Ecureuil 2 | 5572 | ex G-LCON | |
| ☐ G-VONG | Aérospatiale AS355F1 Ecureuil 2 | 5327 | ex G-OILX | |
| ☐ G-VONH | Aérospatiale AS355F1 Ecureuil 2 | 5303 | ex G-BKUL | |

## SCOTAIRWAYS — Suckling (CB/SAY) — Cambridge (CBG)

| ☐ G-BWIR | Dornier 328-110 | 3023 | ex D-CDXF | |
| ☐ G-BWWT | Dornier 328-110 | 3022 | ex D-CDXO | |
| ☐ G-BYHG | Dornier 328-110 | 3098 | ex D-CDAE | |
| ☐ G-BYMK | Dornier 328-110 | 3062 | ex LN-ASK | |
| ☐ G-BZOG | Dornier 328-110 | 3088 | ex D-CDXI | |
| ☐ G-CCGS | Dornier 328-110 | 3101 | ex D-CPRX | |

| SKYSOUTH | | Skydrift (SDL) | | Norwich / Shoreham (NWI/-) |
|---|---|---|---|---|
| ☐ G-OETV | Piper PA-31-350 Chieftain | 31-7852073 | ex N27597 | |
| ☐ G-STHA | Piper PA-31-350 Chieftain | 31-8052077 | ex G-GLUG | |

| THOMAS COOK AIRLINES | | Top Jet (MT/TCX) | | Manchester (MAN) |
|---|---|---|---|---|
| ☐ G-CRPH | Airbus A320-231 | 0424 | ex C-GJUU | |
| ☐ G-DHJZ | Airbus A320-214 | 1965 | ex C-FOJZ | |
| ☐ G-DHRG | Airbus A320-214 | 1942 | ex C-GHRG | |
| ☐ G-KKAZ | Airbus A320-214 | 2003 | ex C-FZAZ | |
| ☐ G-SUEW | Airbus A320-214 | 1961 | ex C-GUEW | |
| ☐ G-TCAD | Airbus A320-214 | 2114 | ex EC-JDO | |
| ☐ G-FCLA | Boeing 757-28A | 27621/738 | ex C-GJZV | |
| ☐ G-FCLB | Boeing 757-28A | 28164/749 | ex N751NA | |
| ☐ G-FCLC | Boeing 757-28A | 28166/756 | | |
| ☐ G-FCLD | Boeing 757-25F | 28718/752 | ex C-FULD | >JZA |
| ☐ G-FCLE | Boeing 757-28A | 28171/805 | | |
| ☐ G-FCLF | Boeing 757-28A | 28835/858 | exC-GJZT | |
| ☐ G-FCLH | Boeing 757-28A | 26274/676 | ex N751LF | |
| ☐ G-FCLI | Boeing 757-28A | 26275/672 | ex N161LF | |
| ☐ G-FCLJ | Boeing 757-2Y0 | 26160/555 | ex N160GE | |
| ☐ G-FCLK | Boeing 757-2Y0 | 26161/557 | ex EI-CJY | |
| ☐ G-JMAA | Boeing 757-3CQ | 32241/960 | ex N5002K | |
| ☐ G-JMAB | Boeing 757-3CQ | 32242/963 | ex N1795B | |
| ☐ G-JMCD | Boeing 757-25F | 30757/928 | ex C-GJZK | |
| ☐ G-JMCE | Boeing 757-25F | 30758/932 | ex C-GJZH | >JZA |
| ☐ G-JMCG | Boeing 757-2G5 | 26278/671 | ex C-JMCG | >JZA |
| ☐ G-TCBA | Boeing 757-28AER | 28203/802 | ex G-OOOY | >JZA |
| ☐ G-TCBB | Boeing 757-236 | 29945/873 | ex N945BB | |
| ☐ G-TCBC | Boeing 757-236 | 29946/877 | ex N9468B | |
| ☐ G-WJAN | Boeing 757-21K | 28674/746 | ex C-FFAN | >WJA |
| ☐ G-DAJC | Boeing 767-31KER/W | 27206/533 | ex C-GJJC | >CFG |
| ☐ G-DHJH | Airbus A321-211 | 1238 | ex D-AVZL | |
| ☐ G-MDBD | Airbus A330-243 | 266 | ex F-WWKG | |
| ☐ G-MLJL | Airbus A330-243 | 254 | ex F-WWKT | |
| ☐ G-NIKO | Airbus A321-211 | 1250 | ex D-AVZF | |
| ☐ G-OJMB | Airbus A330-243 | 427 | ex F-WWYH | |
| ☐ G-OMYJ | Airbus A321-211 | 0677 | ex G-OOAF | |
| ☐ G-OMYT | Airbus A330-243 | 301 | ex G-MOJO | |
| ☐ G-TCDA | Airbus A321-211 | 2060 | ex TC-JMG | |
| ☐ G-TCCA | Boeing 767-31KER/W | 27205/528 | ex G-SJMC | |
| ☐ G-TCCB | Boeing 767-31KER/W | 28865/657 | ex G-DIMB | |

| THOMSONFLY.COM | | Thomson (BY/TOM) | | London-Luton/Coventry (LTN/CVT) |
|---|---|---|---|---|
| ☐ G-CDZH | Boeing 737-804 | 28227/452 | ex SE-DZH | [BRU] |
| ☐ G-CDZL | Boeing 737-804 | 30465/502 | ex D-ATUA | |
| ☐ G-CDZM | Boeing 737-804 | 30466/505 | ex D-ATUB | |
| ☐ G-FDZA | Boeing 737-8K5/W | 35134/2152 | | >SWG |
| ☐ G-FDZB | Boeing 737-8K5/W | 35131/2242 | | |
| ☐ G-FDZD | Boeing 737-8K5/W | 35132/2276 | | |
| ☐ G-FDZE | Boeing 737-8K5/W | 35137/2482 | ex C-GDZE | |
| ☐ G-FDZF | Boeing 737-8K5/W | 35138/2499 | ex N1786B | >SWG |
| ☐ G-FDZG | Boeing 737-8K5/W | 35139/2538 | ex C-FRZG | |
| ☐ G-FDZJ | Boeing 737-8K5/W | 34690/2184 | ex C-FRZJ | |
| ☐ G-FDZS | Boeing 737-8K5/W | 35147/2866 | ex N1786B | |
| ☐ G-FDZT | Boeing 737-8K5/W | 37248/3532 | | |
| ☐ G-FDZU | Boeing 737-8K5/W | 37253/3562 | | |
| ☐ G-FDZW | Boeing 737-8K5/W | 37254/3586 | | |
| ☐ G-FDZX | Boeing 737-8K5/W | 37258/3655 | | |
| ☐ G-FDZY | Boeing 737-8K5/W | 37261/3844 | | |
| ☐ G-FDZZ | Boeing 737-8K5/W | 37262/3876 | | |
| ☐ G-TAWA | Boeing 737-8K5/W | 37264/3907 | | ♦ |
| ☐ G-TAWB | Boeing 737-8K5/W | 37242/3917 | | ♦ |
| ☐ G-TAWC | Boeing 737-8k5/W | 39922/3925 | | ♦ |
| ☐ G-TAWD | Boeing 737-8K5/W | 37265/3939 | | ♦ |
| ☐ G-TAWF | Boeing 737-8K5/W | 37244/3955 | | ♦ |
| ☐ G-TAWG | Boeing 737-8K5/W | 37266/3867 | | ♦ |
| ☐ G-TAWH | Boeing 737-8K5/W | 38107 | | o/o♦ |
| ☐ G-TAWI | Boeing 737-8K5/W | 37267 | | o/o♦ |
| ☐ G-TAWJ | Boeing 737-8K5/W | 38108 | | o/o♦ |
| ☐ G-BYAL | Boeing 757-204 | 25626/549 | | |
| ☐ G-BYAT | Boeing 757-204 | 27208/606 | | Becky Davey |
| ☐ G-BYAU | Boeing 757-204 | 27220/618 | | |
| ☐ G-BYAW | Boeing 757-204 | 27234/663 | | Philip Stanley |
| ☐ G-BYAX | Boeing 757-204/W | 28834/850 | | |
| ☐ G-BYAY | Boeing 757-204/W | 28836/861 | ex N1786B | |

| | | | | | |
|---|---|---|---|---|---|
| ☐ G-CPEU | Boeing 757-236/W | 29941/864 | ex C-FLEU | | |
| ☐ G-CPEV | Boeing 757-236/W | 29943/871 | ex C-GOEV | | |
| ☐ G-OOBA | Boeing 757-28A/W | 32446/950 | ex C-GUBA | | |
| ☐ G-OOBB | Boeing 757-28A/W | 32447/951 | ex C-GTBB | | |
| ☐ G-OOBC | Boeing 757-28A/W | 33098/1026 | | | |
| ☐ G-OOBD | Boeing 757-28A/W | 33099/1028 | | | |
| ☐ G-OOBE | Boeing 757-28A/W | 33100/1029 | | | |
| ☐ G-OOBF | Boeing 757-28A/W | 33101/1041 | | | |
| ☐ G-OOBG | Boeing 757-236/W | 29942/867 | ex C-FUBG | | |
| ☐ G-OOBH | Boeing 757-236/W | 29944/872 | ex C-FOBH | | |
| ☐ G-OOBI | Boeing 757-2B7 | 27146/551 | ex N615AU | | |
| ☐ G-OOBJ | Boeing 757-2B7 | 27147/552 | ex N616AU | | |
| ☐ G-OOBN | Boeing 757-2Q8ER | 29379/919 | ex HB-IHR | | |
| ☐ G-OOBP | Boeing 757-2Q8ER | 30394/922 | ex HB-IHS | | |
| ☐ G-OOBR | Boeing 757-204/W | 27219/596 | ex SE-RFP | | |
| ☐ G-OOOX | Boeing 757-2Y0ER | 26158/526 | ex C-FLOX | | ♦ |
| | | | | | |
| ☐ G-DBLA | Boeing 767-35EER/W | 26063/434 | ex B-16603 | | |
| ☐ G-OBYD | Boeing 767-304ER/W | 28042/649 | ex SE-DZG | Bill Travers | |
| ☐ G-OBYE | Boeing 767-304ER/W | 28979/691 | ex D-AGYE | | >TFL |
| ☐ G-OBYF | Boeing 767-304ER/W | 28208/705 | ex D-AGYF | | |
| ☐ G-OBYG | Boeing 767-304ER/W | 29137/733 | | | |
| ☐ G-OBYH | Boeing 767-304ER/W | 28883/737 | ex SE-DZO | | |
| ☐ G-OOAN | Boeing 767-39HER/W | 26256/484 | ex G-UKLH | Caribbean Star | |
| ☐ G-OOBK | Boeing 767-324ER/W | 27392/568 | ex VN-A762 | | |
| ☐ G-OOBL | Boeing 767-324ER/W | 27393/571 | ex VN-A764 | | |
| ☐ G-OOBM | Boeing 767-324ER/W | 27568/593 | ex VN-A765 | | |
| ☐ G-PJLO | Boeing 767-35EER | 26064/438 | ex B-16605 | | |
| | | | | | |
| ☐ G-THOO | Boeing 737-33V | 29335/3094 | ex HA-LKT | | |
| ☐ G-THOP | Boeing 737-3U3 | 28740/3003 | ex N335AW | | [MAN] |
| ☐ G-OOAR | Airbus A320-214 | 1320 | ex F-WWDT | | |
| ☐ G-OOPE | Airbus A321-211 | 0852 | ex G-OOAE | | |
| ☐ G-OOPH | Airbus A321-211 | 0781 | ex G-OOAH | | |
| ☐ G-OOPT | Airbus A320-214 | 1605 | ex C-GTDH | | [MAN] |

### TITAN AIRWAYS                 Zap (ZT/AWC)                 London-Stansted (STN)

| | | | | | |
|---|---|---|---|---|---|
| ☐ G-POWC | Boeing 737-33A (QC) | 25402/2159 | ex SE-DPB | | |
| ☐ G-POWD | Boeing 767-36NER | 30847/902 | ex N308TL | | |
| ☐ G-POWF | Avro 146-RJ100 | E3373 | ex G-CFAA | | |
| ☐ G-WELY | Agusta A.109E Power | 11710 | | | |
| ☐ G-ZAPK | British Aerospace 146 Srs.200 (QC) | E2148 | ex G-BTIA | | |
| ☐ G-ZAPN | British Aerospace 146 Srs.200 (QC) | E2119 | ex ZK-NZC | | |
| ☐ G-ZAPV | Boeing 737-3Y0 (SF) | 24546/1811 | ex G-IGOC | Royal Mail | |
| ☐ G-ZAPW | Boeing 737-3L9 (QC) | 24219/1600 | ex G-IGOX | Crystal Holidays | |
| ☐ G-ZAPX | Boeing 757-256 | 29309/936 | ex EC-HIS | | |
| ☐ G-ZAPZ | Boeing 737-33A (QC) | 25401/2067 | ex SE-DPA | | |
| ☐ G- | Boeing 757-256 | 29307/924 | ex TC-OGS | | o/o♦ |
| ☐ G- | Boeing 757-256 | 29308/935 | ex TC-OGT | | o/o♦ |

### VIRGIN ATLANTIC AIRWAYS       Virgin (VS/VIR)       London-Gatwick/Heathrow (LGW/LHR)

| | | | | | |
|---|---|---|---|---|---|
| ☐ G-VGEM | Airbus A330-343E | 1215 | ex F-WWKK | | >CAL |
| ☐ G-VINE | Airbus A330-343E | 1231 | ex F-WWYA | | >RYN |
| ☐ G-VKSS | Airbus A330-343E | 1201 | ex F-WWKU | | |
| ☐ G-VLUV | Airbus A330-343E | 1206 | ex F-WWYH | | >CAL |
| ☐ G-VRAY | Airbus A330-343E | 1296 | ex F-WWKF | | ♦ |
| ☐ G-VSXY | Airbus A330-343E | 1195 | ex F-WWKY | | |
| | | | | | |
| ☐ G-VATL | Airbus A340-642 | 376 | ex F-WWCC | Miss Kitty | |
| ☐ G-VBLU | Airbus A340-642 | 723 | ex F-WWCS | Soul Sister | |
| ☐ G-VBUG | Airbus A340-642HGW | 804 | ex F-WWCV | Lady Bird | |
| ☐ G-VEIL | Airbus A340-642 | 575 | ex F-WWCK | Queen of the Skies | |
| ☐ G-VFIT | Airbus A340-642 | 753 | ex F-WWCG | Dancing Queen | |
| ☐ G-VFIZ | Airbus A340-642 | 764 | ex F-WWCB | Bubbles | |
| ☐ G-VFOX | Airbus A340-642 | 449 | ex F-WWCM | Silver Lady | |
| ☐ G-VGAS | Airbus A340-642 | 639 | ex F-WWCI | Varga Girl | |
| ☐ G-VGOA | Airbus A340-642 | 371 | ex F-WWCB | Indian Princess | |
| ☐ G-VMEG | Airbus A340-642 | 391 | ex F-WWCK | Mystic Maiden | |
| ☐ G-VNAP | Airbus A340-642 | 622 | ex F-WWCE | Sleeping Beauty | |
| ☐ G-VOGE | Airbus A340-642 | 416 | ex F-WWCF | Cover Girl | |
| ☐ G-VRED | Airbus A340-642 | 768 | ex F-WWCH | Scarlet Lady | |
| ☐ G-VSHY | Airbus A340-642 | 383 | ex F-WWCD | Madam Butterfly | |
| ☐ G-VSSH | Airbus A340-642 | 615 | ex F-WWCZ | Sweet Dreamer | |
| ☐ G-VWEB | Airbus A340-642 | 787 | ex F-WWCZ | Surfer Girl | |
| ☐ G-VWIN | Airbus A340-642 | 736 | ex F-WWCL | Lady Luck | |
| ☐ G-VWKD | Airbus A340-642 | 706 | ex F-WWCQ | Miss Behavin' | |
| ☐ G-VYOU | Airbus A340-642 | 765 | ex F-WWCK | Emmeline Heansy | |

| | | | | |
|---|---|---|---|---|
| ☐ G-VAST | Boeing 747-41R | 28757/1117 | | Ladybird |
| ☐ G-VBIG | Boeing 747-4Q8 | 26255/1081 | | Tinker Belle |
| ☐ G-VFAB | Boeing 747-4Q8 | 24958/1028 | | Lady Penelope |
| ☐ G-VGAL | Boeing 747-443 | 32337/1272 | ex (EI-CVH) | Jersey Girl |
| ☐ G-VHOT | Boeing 747-4Q8 | 26326/1043 | | Tubular Belle |
| ☐ G-VLIP | Boeing 747-443 | 32338/1274 | ex (EI-CVI) | Hot Lips |
| ☐ G-VROC | Boeing 747-41R | 32746/1336 | | Mustang Sally |
| ☐ G-VROM | Boeing 747-443 | 32339/1275 | ex CP-2603 | ♦ |
| ☐ G-VROS | Boeing 747-443 | 30885/1268 | ex (EI-CVG) | English Rose |
| ☐ G-VROY | Boeing 747-443 | 32340/1277 | ex (EI-CVK) | Pretty Woman |
| ☐ G-VTOP | Boeing 747-4Q8 | 28194/1100 | | Virginia Plain |
| ☐ G-VWOW | Boeing 747-41R | 32745/1287 | | Cosmic Girl |
| ☐ G-VXLG | Boeing 747-41R | 29406/1177 | | Ruby Tuesday |
| | | | | |
| ☐ G-VAIR | Airbus A340-313X | 164 | ex F-WWJA | Maiden Tokyo |
| ☐ G-VELD | Airbus A340-313X | 214 | ex F-WWJY | African Queen |
| ☐ G-VFAR | Airbus A340-313X | 225 | ex F-WWJZ | Diana |
| ☐ G-VSUN | Airbus A340-313 | 114 | ex F-WWJI | Rainbow Lady |

## WOODGATE EXECUTIVE AIR SERVICES — Woodair (CWY) — Belfast-Aldergrove (BFS)

| | | | |
|---|---|---|---|
| ☐ G-JAJK | Piper PA-31-350 Chieftain | 31-8152014 | ex G-OLDB |

## HA- HUNGARY (Hungarian Republic)

### ABC AIR HUNGARY — ABC Hungary (AHU) — Budapest (BUD)

| | | | | |
|---|---|---|---|---|
| ☐ HA-LAZ | LET L-410UVP-E | 902504 | ex SP-KTZ | <BPS |
| ☐ HA-TAE | Saab SF.340A | 340A-007 | ex S5-BAT | ♦ |

### ATLANT HUNGARY — Atlant-Hungary (ATU) — Budapest (BUD)

| | | | |
|---|---|---|---|
| ☐ HA-TCK | Ilyushin IL-76TD | 1023409280 | ex T-902 |

### BUDAPEST AIR SERVICES — Base (BPS) — Budapest (BUD)

| | | | | | |
|---|---|---|---|---|---|
| ☐ HA-FAI | Embraer EMB.120ER Brasilia | 120123 | ex F-GTSI | | |
| ☐ HA-FAL | Embraer EMB.120RT Brasilia | 120176 | ex F-GTSJ | | |
| ☐ HA-FAN | Embraer EMB.120ER Brasilia | 120104 | ex F-GTSH | | |
| ☐ HA-LAZ | LET L-410UVP-E | 902504 | ex SP-KTZ | no titles | [SOF] |
| ☐ HA-TCT | Antonov An-26B | 13505 | ex UR-ELA | | |
| ☐ HA-YFD | LET L-410UVP-E17 | 892324 | | Op for Hungarian Air Ambulance | |

### CITYLINE HUNGARY — Cityhun (ZM/CNB) — Budapest (BUD)

| | | | | |
|---|---|---|---|---|
| ☐ HA-TCM | Antonov An-26 | 14009 | ex UR-ELI | |
| ☐ HA-TCN | Antonov An-26 | 7705 | ex UR-26244 | for sale |
| ☐ HA-TCO | Antonov An-26 | 2208 | ex UR-CEP | <Hegedus |

### FARNAIR HUNGARY — Blue Strip (FAH) — Budapest (BUD)

| | | | | |
|---|---|---|---|---|
| ☐ HA-FAJ | Beech 1900C-1 | UC-79 | ex A6-FCE | |
| ☐ HA-FAM | Beech 1900D | UE-16 | ex N16UE | |
| ☐ HA-FAO | Swearingen SA.227AC | AC-451B | ex SE-LEF | ♦ |
| ☐ HA-LAD | LET L410UVP-E8A | 902516 | | ♦ |

### FLEET AIR INTERNATIONAL

| | | | | |
|---|---|---|---|---|
| ☐ HA-TAB | SAAB SF.340A | 340A-083 | ex EC-IUP | |
| ☐ HA-TAD | SAAB SF.340A | 340A-126 | ex SE-LSP | |
| ☐ HA-TAE | SAAB SF.340AF | 340A-007 | ex S5-BAT | ♦ |

### MALEV – HUNGARIAN AIRLINES — Malev (MA/MAH) — Budapest (BUD)

Member of Oneworld

| | | | | |
|---|---|---|---|---|
| ☐ HA-LHB | Boeing 767-27GER | 27049/482 | ex N60668 | [BUD] |
| ☐ HA-LQB | de Havilland DHC-8-402Q | 4057 | ex OY-KCE | [INN] |

Ceased ops 03Feb12

### TRAVEL SERVICE HUNGARY — Traveller (TVL) — Budapest (BUD)

| | | | | |
|---|---|---|---|---|
| ☐ HA-LKB | Boeing 737-86Q/W | 30294/1469 | ex C-GRKB | >SWG |
| ☐ HA-LKE | Boeing 737-86Q/W | 30278/963 | ex OK-TVC | |

### WIZZ AIR — (W6/WZZ) — Budapest (BUD)

| | | | |
|---|---|---|---|
| ☐ HA-LPD | Airbus A320-233 | 1902 | ex EI-DGB |
| ☐ HA-LPE | Airbus A320-233 | 1892 | ex EI-DFU |

| ☐ HA-LPF | Airbus A320-233 | 1834 | ex EI-DGC | |
| ☐ HA-LPI | Airbus A320-232 | 2752 | ex F-WWDE | |
| ☐ HA-LPJ | Airbus A320-232 | 3127 | ex F-WWBH | |
| ☐ HA-LPK | Airbus A320-232 | 3143 | ex F-WWBI | |
| ☐ HA-LPL | Airbus A320-232 | 3166 | ex F-WWIL | |
| ☐ HA-LPM | Airbus A320-232 | 3177 | ex F-WWDG | |
| ☐ HA-LPN | Airbus A320-232 | 3354 | ex F-WWIG | |
| ☐ HA-LPO | Airbus A320-232 | 3384 | ex F-WWDO | |
| ☐ HA-LPQ | Airbus A320-232 | 3409 | ex F-WWIC | |
| ☐ HA-LPR | Airbus A320-232 | 3430 | ex F-WWBC | |
| ☐ HA-LPS | Airbus A320-232 | 3771 | ex F-WWDS | |
| ☐ HA-LPT | Airbus A320-232 | 3807 | ex F-WWDR | |
| ☐ HA-LPU | Airbus A320-232 | 3877 | ex F-WWIJ | |
| ☐ HA-LPV | Airbus A320-232 | 3927 | ex F-WWBR | |
| ☐ HA-LPW | Airbus A320-232 | 3947 | ex F-WWBD | |
| ☐ HA-LPX | Airbus A320-232 | 3968 | ex F-WWIN | |
| ☐ HA-LPY | Airbus A320-232 | 4109 | ex D-AVVS | |
| ☐ HA-LPZ | Airbus A320-232 | 4174 | ex F-WWDU | |
| ☐ HA-LWA | Airbus A320-232 | 4223 | ex F-WWBI | |
| ☐ HA-LWB | Airbus A320-232 | 4246 | ex F-WWDR | |
| ☐ HA-LWC | Airbus A320-232 | 4323 | ex F-WWDT | |
| ☐ HA-LWD | Airbus A320-232 | 4351 | ex F-WWBZ | |
| ☐ HA-LWE | Airbus A320-232 | 4372 | ex F-WWBM | |
| ☐ HA-LWF | Airbus A320-232 | 3562 | ex F-WWBH | ♦ |
| ☐ HA-LWG | Airbus A320-232 | 4308 | ex LZ-WZC | ♦ |
| ☐ HA-LWH | Airbus A320-232 | 4621 | ex F-WWBV | ♦ |
| ☐ HA-LWI | Airbus A320-232 | 4628 | ex F-WWDH | ♦ |
| ☐ HA-LWJ | Airbus A320-232 | 4683 | ex F-WWIF | ♦ |
| ☐ HA-LWK | Airbus A320-232 | 4716 | ex F-WWBT | ♦ |
| ☐ HA-LWL | Airbus A320-232 | 4736 | ex F-WWIO | ♦ |
| ☐ HA-LWM | Airbus A320-232 | 5021 | ex F-WWIY | ♦ |
| ☐ HA-LWN | Airbus A320-232 | 5075 | ex F-WWIB | ♦ |
| ☐ HA-LWO | Airbus A320-232 | 5123 | ex F-WWBP | o/o♦ |
| ☐ HA-LWP | Airbus A320-232 | 5139 | ex | o/o♦ |

## HB-    SWITZERLAND & LIECHTENSTEIN (Swiss Confederation)

### AIR GLACIERS

**Air Glaciers (7T/AGV)**

**Sion (SIR)**

| ☐ HB-CGW | Cessna U206G Stationair 6 | U20604822 | ex D-ELML | |
| ☐ HB-FCT | Pilatus PC-6/B2-H2 Turbo Porter | 637 | | |
| ☐ HB-FDU | Pilatus PC-6/B1-H2 Turbo Porter | 663 | | |
| ☐ HB-GIL | Beech 200 Super King Air | BB-194 | ex N502EB | |
| ☐ HB-GJI | Beech 200 Super King Air | BB-451 | ex D-IBOW | |
| ☐ HB-GJM | Beech 200 Super King Air | BB-255 | ex N32KD | |
| ☐ HB-ZCZ | Aérospatiale AS350B3 Ecureuil | 3434 | ex F-WQDG | |
| ☐ HB-ZEP | Eurocopter EC120B Colibri | 1336 | ex F-WWPO | |
| ☐ HB-ZFB | Eurocopter EC130B4 | 3536 | ex F-GNLD | |

### AIR ZERMATT

**Air Zermatt (AZF)**

**Zermatt Heliport**

| ☐ HB-XSU | Aérospatiale AS350B2 Ecureuil | 2115 | | |
| ☐ HB-ZCC | Aérospatiale AS350B2 Ecureuil | 2107 | ex I-REGL | |
| ☐ HB-ZCX | Aérospatiale AS350B2 Ecureuil | 3105 | ex I-AOLA | |
| ☐ HB-ZEF | Eurocopter EC135T2 | 0259 | ex D-HECA | |
| ☐ HB-ZPB | Aérospatiale AS350B3 Ecureuil | 7309 | | ♦ |

### BELAIR AIRLINES

**Belair (4T/BHP)**

**Zurich (ZRH)**

| ☐ HB-IOP | Airbus A320-214 | 4187 | ex D-AVVY | |
| ☐ HB-IOQ | Airbus A320-214 | 3422 | ex D-ABDT | |
| ☐ HB-IOR | Airbus A320-214 | 4033 | ex D-ABDZ | |
| ☐ HB-IOS | Airbus A320-214 | 2968 | ex D-ABDK | |
| ☐ HB-IOW | Airbus A320-214 | 3055 | ex D-ABDO | |
| ☐ HB-IOZ | Airbus A320-214 | 4294 | ex D-ABFH | |
| ☐ HB-JOZ | Airbus A320-214 | 4631 | ex (D-ABFR) | ♦ |
| ☐ HB-IOX | Airbus A319-112 | 3604 | ex D-ABGM | |
| ☐ HB-JOY | Airbus A319-112 | 3245 | ex D-ABGH | >BER♦ |

### DARWIN AIRLINE

**Darwin (0D/DWT)**

**Lugano (LUG)**

| ☐ HB-IYD | SAAB 2000 | 2000-059 | ex VP-BPP | |
| ☐ HB-IZG | SAAB 2000 | 2000-010 | ex SE-010 | Insubria |
| ☐ HB-IZH | SAAB 2000 | 2000-011 | ex SE-011 | Ticino |
| ☐ HB-IZJ | SAAB 2000 | 2000-015 | ex (F-GOZJ) | Verbano |
| ☐ HB-IZP | SAAB 2000 | 2000-031 | ex N168GC | |
| ☐ HB-IZZ | SAAB 2000 | 2000-048 | ex SE-048 | Ceresio ♦ |

| | | | | | |
|---|---|---|---|---|---|
| ☐ HB-JQA | de Havilland DHC-8-402Q | 4017 | ex C-FJJG | | ♦ |
| ☐ HB-JQB | de Havilland DHC-8-402Q | 4175 | ex C-FMKK | | ♦ |

## EASYJET SWITZERLAND — Topswiss (DS/EZS) — Geneva (GVA)

| | | | | | |
|---|---|---|---|---|---|
| ☐ HB-JZF | Airbus A319-111 | 2184 | ex G-EZEH | | |
| ☐ HB-JZI | Airbus A319-111 | 2245 | ex G-EZEN | | |
| ☐ HB-JZJ | Airbus A319-111 | 2265 | ex G-EZES | | |
| ☐ HB-JZK | Airbus A319-111 | 2319 | ex G-EZEX | | |
| ☐ HB-JZL | Airbus A319-111 | 2353 | ex G-EZEY | | |
| ☐ HB-JZM | Airbus A319-111 | 2370 | ex G-EZMK | | |
| ☐ HB-JZN | Airbus A319-111 | 2387 | ex G-EZBS | | |
| ☐ HB-JZO | Airbus A319-111 | 2398 | ex G-HMCC | | |
| ☐ HB-JZP | Airbus A319-111 | 2427 | ex G-EZIB | | |
| ☐ HB-JZS | Airbus A319-111 | 3084 | ex G-EZBP | | |
| ☐ HB-JZT | Airbus A319-111 | 2420 | ex G-EZIA | | ♦ |
| ☐ HB-JZU | Airbus A319-111 | 2402 | ex G-EZNM | | |
| ☐ HB-JZV | Airbus A319-111 | 2709 | ex G-EZAE | | |
| ☐ HB-JZW | Airbus A319-111 | 2729 | ex G-EZAH | | |
| | | | | | |
| ☐ HB-JYA | Airbus A320-214 | 4250 | ex G-EZTW | | ♦ |
| ☐ HB-JZR | Airbus A320-214 | 4034 | ex G-EZTO | | ♦ |
| ☐ HB-JZX | Airbus A320-214 | 4157 | ex G-EZTP | | ♦ |
| ☐ HB-JZY | Airbus A320-214 | 4196 | ex G-EZTS | | ♦ |
| ☐ HB-JZZ | Airbus A320-214 | 4233 | ex G-EZTU | | ♦ |

## EDELWEISS AIR — Edelweiss (WK/EDW) — Zurich (ZRH)

| | | | | | |
|---|---|---|---|---|---|
| ☐ HB-IHX | Airbus A320-214 | 0942 | ex F-WWIU | Calvaro | |
| ☐ HB-IHY | Airbus A320-214 | 0947 | ex F-WWIY | Upali | |
| ☐ HB-IHZ | Airbus A320-214 | 1026 | ex F-WWDD | Viktoria | |
| ☐ HB-IQI | Airbus A330-223 | 291 | ex F-WWKS | | ♦ |
| ☐ HB-JHQ | Airbus A330-343E | 1193 | ex F-WWKQ | | <SWR♦ |

## FARNAIR SWITZERLAND — Farner (FAT) — Basle (BSL)

| | | | | | |
|---|---|---|---|---|---|
| ☐ HB-AFG | ATR 72-201F | 0108 | ex F-WQNA | | |
| ☐ HB-AFH | ATR 72-202F | 0313 | ex F-GJKP | | >QuikJet |
| ☐ HB-AFJ | ATR 72-202F | 0154 | ex OY-RTE | | |
| ☐ HB-AFK | ATR 72-202F | 0232 | ex F-GKOB | | |
| ☐ HB-AFL | ATR 72-202F | 0222 | ex F-GKPF | | |
| ☐ HB-AFM | ATR 72-202F | 0364 | ex B-22712 | | |
| ☐ HB-AFN | ATR 72-202F | 0389 | ex B-22716 | | |
| ☐ HB-AFP | ATR 72-201F | 0381 | ex B-22715 | | |
| ☐ HB-AFR | ATR 72-201F | 0195 | ex F-WKVC | | |
| ☐ HB-AFS | ATR 72-201F | 0198 | ex F-WKVJ | | |
| ☐ HB-AFV | ATR 72-202F | 0341 | ex F-WKVJ | | >QuikJet |
| ☐ HB-AFW | ATR 72-202F | 0419 | ex F-WNUD | | >QuikJet |
| | | | | | |
| ☐ HB-AFC | ATR 42-320F | 0087 | ex F-WQLF | | |
| ☐ HB-AFD | ATR 42-320 | 0121 | ex F-WQNA | | |
| ☐ HB-AFF | ATR 42-320 | 0264 | ex F-GOBK | | |

## HELLO — Fly Hello (HW/FHE) — Basle (BSL)

| | | | | | |
|---|---|---|---|---|---|
| ☐ HB-JIW | Airbus A320-214 | 0888 | ex F-HBAC | | ♦ |
| ☐ HB-JIX | Airbus A320-214 | 1210 | ex RP-C3231 | | ♦ |
| ☐ HB-JIY | Airbus A320-214 | 1171 | ex RP-C3230 | | |
| ☐ HB-JIZ | Airbus A320-214 | 0936 | ex RP-C3229 | | |

## HELVETIC AIRWAYS — Helvetic (2L/OAW) — Zurich (ZRH)

| | | | | | |
|---|---|---|---|---|---|
| ☐ HB-JVC | Fokker 100 | 11501 | ex N1468A | | |
| ☐ HB-JVE | Fokker 100 | 11459 | ex N1450A | | |
| ☐ HB-JVF | Fokker 100 | 11466 | ex N1454D | | |
| ☐ HB-JVG | Fokker 100 | 11478 | ex N1458H | | |
| ☐ HB-JVH | Fokker 100 | 11324 | ex F-GPNK | | |
| ☐ HB-JVI | Fokker 100 | 11325 | ex F-GPNL | | |

## PRIVATAIR — PrivatAir (PTI) — Geneva (GVA)

| | | | | | |
|---|---|---|---|---|---|
| ☐ D-APBB | Boeing 737-8Q8/W | 35278/2625 | ex N812SY | | |
| ☐ HB-IEE | Boeing 757-23A/W | 24527/249 | ex HB-IHU | | |
| ☐ HB-IIQ | Boeing 737-7CN/W (BBJ) | 30752/451 | ex N1026G | | [AMM] |
| ☐ HB-IIR | Boeing 737-86Q/W | 30295/1600 | | | |
| ☐ HB-JJA | Boeing 737-7AK/W (BBJ) | 34303/1758 | ex N1780B | | >KLM |
| ☐ HB-JJB | Boeing 737-306 | 27421/2438 | ex PH-BTE | | ♦ |
| ☐ HB-JJC | Boeing 737-306 | 27420/2406 | ex PH-BTD | | ♦ |
| ☐ HB-JJD | Boeing 757-236 | 25807/610 | ex F-GPEJ | | [LHR]♦ |

| ☐ HB-JJG | Boeing 767-306ER | 30393/781 | ex PH-BZO | | [FRA] |
|---|---|---|---|---|---|

## SKYWORK AIRLINES — Skyfox (SRK) — Bern (BRP)

| ☐ HB-AEO | Dornier 328-100 | 3061 | ex OY-NCK | | ♦ |
|---|---|---|---|---|---|
| ☐ HB-AER | Dornier 328-110 | 3066 | ex D-CPRP | | ♦ |
| ☐ HB-AES | Dornier 328-110 | 3021 | ex D-CHIC | | ♦ |
| ☐ HB-AEV | Dornier 320-110 | 3056 | ex I-IRTI | | ♦ |
| ☐ HB-GTX | Beech C90GTI King Air | LJ-2032 | ex N81423 | | ♦ |
| ☐ HB-GTY | Beech B300 Super King Air | FL-774 | ex N81474 | | ♦ |
| ☐ HB-JGA | de Havilland DHC-8-402Q | 4198 | ex C-FOKB | | |
| ☐ HB-JIJ | de Havilland DHC8-402Q | 4184 | ex C-GARX | | |
| ☐ HB-JIK | de Havilland DHC-8-402Q | 4265 | ex N511LX | | ♦ |

## SWISS EUROPEAN AIR LINES — Euroswiss (SWU)
### Basle, Lugano, Geneva, Zurich (BSL/LUG/GVA/ZRH)

| ☐ HB-IXN | Avro 146-RJ100 | E3286 | ex G-6-286 | Balmhorn |
|---|---|---|---|---|
| ☐ HB-IXO | Avro 146-RJ100 | E3284 | ex G-6-284 | Brisen |
| ☐ HB-IXP | Avro 146-RJ100 | E3283 | ex G-6-283 | Chestenberg |
| ☐ HB-IXQ | Avro 146-RJ100 | E3282 | ex G-6-282 | Corno Gries |
| ☐ HB-IXR | Avro 146-RJ100 | E3281 | ex G-6-281 | Hohe Winde |
| ☐ HB-IXS | Avro 146-RJ100 | E3280 | ex G-6-280 | Mont Velan |
| ☐ HB-IXT | Avro 146-RJ100 | E3259 | ex G-BVYS | Ottenberg |
| ☐ HB-IXU | Avro 146-RJ100 | E3276 | ex G-6-276 | Pfannenstiel |
| ☐ HB-IXV | Avro 146-RJ100 | E3274 | ex G-6-274 | Saxer First |
| ☐ HB-IXW | Avro 146-RJ100 | E3272 | ex G-6-272 | Schafarnisch |
| ☐ HB-IXX | Avro 146-RJ100 | E3262 | ex G-6-262 | Siberen |
| ☐ HB-IYQ | Avro 146-RJ100 | E3384 | ex G-CFAH | Piz Bruin |
| ☐ HB-IYR | Avro 146-RJ100 | E3382 | ex G-CFAF | Vrenelisgärtli |
| ☐ HB-IYS | Avro 146-RJ100 | E3381 | ex G-CFAE | Churfirsten special c/s |
| ☐ HB-IYT | Avro 146-RJ100 | E3380 | ex G-CFAD | Bluemlisalp |
| ☐ HB-IYU | Avro 146-RJ100 | E3379 | ex G-CFAC | Rot Turm Star Alliance c/s |
| ☐ HB-IYV | Avro 146-RJ100 | E3377 | ex G-CFAB | Pizzo Barone Star Alliance c/s |
| ☐ HB-IYW | Avro 146-RJ100 | E3359 | ex G-6-359 | Spitzmeilen |
| ☐ HB-IYY | Avro 146-RJ100 | E3339 | ex G-6-339 | Titlis |
| ☐ HB-IYZ | Avro 146-RJ100 | E3338 | ex G-6-338 | Tour d'Ai |

## SWISS INTERNATIONAL AIRLINES — Swiss (LX/SWR) — Zurich (ZRH)

Member of Star Alliance

| ☐ HB-IPR | Airbus A319-112 | 1018 | ex D-AVYQ | Piz Morteratsch | |
|---|---|---|---|---|---|
| ☐ HB-IPS | Airbus A319-112 | 0734 | ex D-AVYZ | Clariden | |
| ☐ HB-IPT | Airbus A319-112 | 0727 | ex D-AVYC | Rotsandnollen | |
| ☐ HB-IPU | Airbus A319-112 | 0713 | ex D-AVYB | Schrattenflue | |
| ☐ HB-IPV | Airbus A319-112 | 0578 | ex D-AVYA | Castelegns | |
| ☐ HB-IPX | Airbus A319-112 | 0612 | ex D-AVYH | Mont Racine | |
| ☐ HB-IPY | Airbus A319-112 | 0621 | ex D-AVYK | Les Ordons | |
| ☐ HB-IJB | Airbus A320-214 | 0545 | ex TC-JLA | | |
| ☐ HB-IJD | Airbus A320-214 | 0553 | ex TC-JLH | | |
| ☐ HB-IJE | Airbus A320-214 | 0559 | ex TC-JLI | Arosa | |
| ☐ HB-IJF | Airbus A320-214 | 0562 | ex TC-JLB | | |
| ☐ HB-IJH | Airbus A320-214 | 0574 | ex TC-JLD | | |
| ☐ HB-IJI | Airbus A320-214 | 0577 | ex F-WWDT | Basodino | |
| ☐ HB-IJJ | Airbus A320-214 | 0585 | ex F-WWIV | Les Diablerets | |
| ☐ HB-IJK | Airbus A320-214 | 0596 | ex F-WWBH | Wissigstock | |
| ☐ HB-IJL | Airbus A320-214 | 0603 | ex F-WWBK | Pizol | |
| ☐ HB-IJM | Airbus A320-214 | 0635 | ex F-WWDD | Schilthorn | |
| ☐ HB-IJN | Airbus A320-214 | 0643 | ex F-WWDI | Vanil Noir | |
| ☐ HB-IJO | Airbus A320-214 | 0673 | ex F-WWBF | Lisengrat | |
| ☐ HB-IJP | Airbus A320-214 | 0681 | ex F-WWBH | Nollen | |
| ☐ HB-IJQ | Airbus A320-214 | 0701 | ex F-WWDL | Locarno | |
| ☐ HB-IJR | Airbus A320-214 | 0703 | ex F-WWDS | Dammastock | |
| ☐ HB-IJS | Airbus A320-214 | 0782 | ex F-WWDS | Creux du Van | |
| ☐ HB-IJU | Airbus A320-214 | 1951 | ex F-WWIQ | Bietschhorn | |
| ☐ HB-IJV | Airbus A320-214 | 2024 | ex F-WWDK | Wildspitz | |
| ☐ HB-IJW | Airbus A320-214 | 2134 | ex F-WWBO | Bachtel | |
| ☐ HB-IJX | Airbus A320-214 | 1762 | ex D-ALTG | Davos | |
| ☐ HB-JLP | Airbus A320-214 | 4618 | ex F-WWBP | | |
| ☐ HB-JLQ | Airbus A320-214 | 4673 | ex F-WWBM | | ♦ |
| ☐ HB-JLR | Airbus A320-214 | 5037 | ex F-WWDF | Bassersdorf | ♦ |
| ☐ HB-JLS | Airbus A320-214 | 5069 | ex F-WWDC | | ♦ |
| ☐ HB-IOC | Airbus A321-111 | 0520 | ex D-AVZV | Eiger | |
| ☐ HB-IOD | Airbus A321-111 | 0522 | ex TC-JMA | | |
| ☐ HB-IOF | Airbus A321-111 | 0541 | ex TC-JMB | | |
| ☐ HB-IOH | Airbus A321-111 | 0664 | ex D-AVZL | Pitz Palu | |
| ☐ HB-IOK | Airbus A321-111 | 0987 | ex D-AVZC | Biefertenstock | |

| | | | | | |
|---|---|---|---|---|---|
| ☐ HB-IOL | Airbus A321-111 | 1144 | ex D-AVZE | Kaiseregg | |
| ☐ HB-IOM | Airbus A321-212 | 4534 | ex D-AVZL | Biel/Bienne | |
| | | | | | |
| ☐ HB-IQA | Airbus A330-223 | 229 | ex F-WWKS | Lauteraarhorn | >BEL |
| ☐ HB-IQC | Airbus A330-223 | 249 | ex F-WWKI | Breithorn | >BEL |
| ☐ HB-IQR | Airbus A330-223 | 324 | ex VH-SSA | | [HNL] |
| ☐ HB-JHA | Airbus A330-343E | 1000 | ex F-WWYX | Schwyz | |
| ☐ HB-JHB | Airbus A330-343E | 1018 | ex F-WWYJ | Sion | |
| ☐ HB-JHC | Airbus A330-343E | 1029 | ex F-WWYY | Bellinzona | |
| ☐ HB-JHD | Airbus A330-343E | 1026 | ex F-WWKE | St. Gallen | |
| ☐ HB-JHE | Airbus A330-343E | 1084 | ex F-WWKE | Fribourg | |
| ☐ HB-JHF | Airbus A330-343E | 1089 | ex F-WWKI | Bern | |
| ☐ HB-JHG | Airbus A330-343E | 1101 | ex F-WWYI | Glarus | |
| ☐ HB-JHH | Airbus A330-343E | 1145 | ex F-WWYD | Neuchatel | |
| ☐ HB-JHI | Airbus A330-343E | 1181 | ex F-WWKM | | |
| ☐ HB-JHJ | Airbus A330-343E | 1188 | ex F-WWYQ | Appenzell | |
| ☐ HB-JHK | Airbus A330-343E | 1276 | ex F-WWYI | Herisau | ◆ |
| ☐ HB-JHL | Airbus A330-343E | 1290 | ex F-WWKU | Sarnen | ◆ |
| ☐ HB-JHQ | Airbus A330-343E | 1193 | ex F-WWKQ | Chamsin | >EDW◆ |
| | | | | | |
| ☐ HB-JMA | Airbus A340-313X | 538 | ex F-WWJJ | Matterhorn | |
| ☐ HB-JMB | Airbus A340-313X | 545 | ex F-WWJL | Zurich | |
| ☐ HB-JMC | Airbus A340-313X | 546 | ex F-WWJM | Basel | |
| ☐ HB-JMD | Airbus A340-313X | 556 | ex F-WWJN | Liestal | |
| ☐ HB-JME | Airbus A340-313X | 559 | ex F-WWJP | Dom | |
| ☐ HB-JMF | Airbus A340-313X | 561 | ex F-WWJQ | Liskamm | |
| ☐ HB-JMG | Airbus A340-313X | 562 | ex F-WWJR | Luzern | |
| ☐ HB-JMH | Airbus A340-313E | 585 | ex F-WWJV | Chur | |
| ☐ HB-JMI | Airbus A340-313E | 598 | ex F-WWJX | Schaffhausen | |
| ☐ HB-JMJ | Airbus A340-313X | 150 | ex C-FYKX | City of Basel | |
| ☐ HB-JMK | Airbus A340-313X | 169 | ex OE-LAK | | |
| ☐ HB-JML | Airbus A340-313X | 263 | ex OE-LAL | Stans | <AUA |
| ☐ HB-JMM | Airbus A340-313X | 154 | ex C-FYKZ | | |
| ☐ HB-JMN | Airbus A340-313X | 175 | ex C-FYLG | Altdorf | |
| ☐ HB-JMO | Airbus A340-313X | 179 | ex C-FYLU | | |
| | | | | | |
| ☐ HB-IIR | Boeing 737-86Q/W | 30295/1600 | | | <PTI |

## ZIMEX AVIATION — Zimex (C4/IMX) — Zurich (ZRH)

| | | | | | |
|---|---|---|---|---|---|
| ☐ HB-LRO | de Havilland DHC-6 Twin Otter 300 | 523 | ex F-GKTO | | |
| ☐ HB-LRR | de Havilland DHC-6 Twin Otter 300 | 505 | ex 5Y-KZT | | |
| ☐ HB-LTG | de Havilland DHC-6 Twin Otter 300 | 628 | ex D-IFLY | | |
| ☐ HB-LTR | de Havilland DHC-6 Twin Otter 300 | 238 | ex C-GHTO | | |
| ☐ HB-LUC | de Havilland DHC-6 Twin Otter 300 | 351 | ex N353PM | | |
| ☐ HB-LUE | de Havilland DHC-6 Twin Otter 300 | 233 | ex PK-LTX | | |
| ☐ HB-LUM | de Havilland DHC-6 Twin Otter 300 | 420 | ex PK-TWG | | |
| ☐ HB-LUX | de Havilland DHC-6 Twin Otter 400 | 845 | ex C-FMJO | | ◆ |
| | | | | | |
| ☐ HB-FLB | Pilatus PC-6/B2-H4 | 906 | ex 5A-FLE | | ◆ |

## HC-    ECUADOR (Republic of Ecuador)

## AEROGAL — Aerogal (2K/GLG) — Shell-Mera/Quito (-/UIO)

| | | | | | |
|---|---|---|---|---|---|
| ☐ HC-CKL | Airbus A319-112 | 1866 | ex N866MX | | |
| ☐ HC-CKM | Airbus A319-112 | 1872 | ex N872MX | | ◆ |
| ☐ HC-CKN | Airbus A319-112 | 1882 | ex N882MX | | ◆ |
| ☐ HC-CKO | Airbus A319-112 | 1925 | ex N925MX | | ◆ |
| ☐ HC-CKP | Airbus A319-112 | 2126 | ex EI-ERK | | ◆ |
| ☐ HC-CLF | Airbus A319-112 | 2078 | ex N778CT | | ◆ |
| | | | | | |
| ☐ HC-CFG | Boeing 737-281 (AvAero 3) | 21770/588 | ex N746AP | | |
| ☐ HC-CFR | Boeing 737-244 | 22581/796 | ex ZS-SIB | | |
| ☐ HC-CHB | Boeing 737-3M8 | 24376/1717 | ex PR-BRD | | ◆ |
| ☐ HC-CIJ | Boeing 767-322ER | 25287/449 | ex N287AV | | [GYE] |
| ☐ HC-CJM | Airbus A320-214 | 4379 | ex F-WWIF | | |
| ☐ HC-CJV | Airbus A320-214 | 4547 | ex D-AUBP | | |
| ☐ HC-CJW | Airbus A320-214 | 4487 | ex D-AUBG | | |

## AEROMASTER AIRWAYS — Quito (UIO)

| | | | | | |
|---|---|---|---|---|---|
| ☐ HC-CBH | Bell 206L-1 LongRanger III | 45354 | ex N213HC | | |
| ☐ HC-CBT | Bell 427 | 56028 | ex N40560 | | |
| ☐ HC-CHG | Sikorsky S-64F Skycrane | 64075 | ex N722HT | | |

### AEROPACSA        Aeropacsa (RPC)        Guayaquil (GYE)

| | | | | |
|---|---|---|---|---|
| ☐ HC-BDV | Cessna TU206F Turbo Stationair II | U20603439 | | |
| ☐ HC-CBD | Dornier 28D-2 Skyservant | 4182 | ex HK-4004 | |
| ☐ HC-CDI | Dornier 28D-2 Skyservant | 4152 | ex 58+77 | |

### AEROVIC

| | | | | |
|---|---|---|---|---|
| ☐ HC-CJH | Cessna 208B Caravan I | 208B0962 | ex N602RL | ♦ |

### EMETEBE TAXI AEREO        Emetebe (EMT)        Puerto Baquerizo Moreno

| | | | | |
|---|---|---|---|---|
| ☐ HC-BDX | Britten-Norman BN-2A-27 Islander | 51 | ex F-OGEB | |
| ☐ HC-BNE | Piper PA-23-250 Aztec D | 27-3959 | ex N6742Y | |
| ☐ HC-BZF | Britten-Norman BN-2A-27 Islander | 200 | ex F-BTGO | |

### ICARO EXPRESS        Icaro (X8/ICD)        Quito (UIO)

| | | | | |
|---|---|---|---|---|
| ☐ HC-CDK | Aérospatiale AS350B Ecureuil | 3001 | ex N444LH | |
| ☐ HC-CEC | Aérospatiale AS350B Ecureuil | 3009 | ex N483AE | |
| ☐ HC-CFL | Boeing 737-236 | 22026/644 | ex ZS-SIU | |
| ☐ HC-CJI | Boeing 737-205 | 22022/616 | ex N771LS | [UIO] |

### LAN ECUADOR        Aerolane (XL/LNE)        Quito (UIO)

| | | | | |
|---|---|---|---|---|
| ☐ HC-CLA | Airbus A320-233 | 4383 | ex CC-BAA | ♦ |
| ☐ HC-CLB | Airbus A320-233 | 4400 | ex CC-BAB | ♦ |
| ☐ HC-CLC | Airbus A320-233 | 4439 | ex CC-BAC | ♦ |
| ☐ HC-CLD | Airbus A320-233 | 4476 | ex CC-BAD | ♦ |
| ☐ HC-CLE | Airbus A320-233 | 4509 | ex CC-BAE | ♦ |
| | | | | |
| ☐ HC-CJX | Boeing 767-316ER/W | 35697/967 | ex CC-CXD | |
| ☐ HC-CKY | Boeing 767-316ER/W | 35696/968 | ex CC-CXE | ♦ |

### SAEREO        Saereo (SRO)        Quito (UIO)

| | | | | |
|---|---|---|---|---|
| ☐ HC-BUD | Gulfstream Commander 690C | 11669 | ex N844MA | |
| ☐ HC-BVN | Beech 1900C | UB-53 | ex N814BE | |
| ☐ HC-BYH | Cessna T207A Stationair 8 II | 20700749 | ex N9905M | |
| ☐ HC-BZO | Bell 407 | 53302 | ex N8226A | |
| ☐ HC-CBC | Beech 1900D | UE-17 | ex N17YV | [UIO] |
| ☐ HC-CEM | Embraer EMB.120ER Brasilia | 120227 | ex N198SW | |

### SERVICIO AEREO REGIONAL

| | | | | |
|---|---|---|---|---|
| ☐ HC-BHC | Britten-Norman BN-2A-20 Islander | 59 | | ♦ |
| ☐ HC-CLI | Cessna 421c | 1106 | ex N6869G | ♦ |

### TAME        Tame (EQ/TAE)        Quito (UIO)

| | | | | |
|---|---|---|---|---|
| ☐ HC-CGJ | Airbus A320-214 | 0657 | ex F-GRSE | |
| ☐ HC-CGT | Airbus A319-132 | 2659 | ex N511NK | |
| ☐ HC-CGW | Airbus A320-233 | 2084 | ex N487TA | Ciudad de Quito |
| ☐ HC-CID | Airbus A320-232 | 0934 | ex N934BV | |
| ☐ HC-CLT | ATR 42-500 | 0844 | ex F-WWLG | ♦ |
| ☐ HC-CMB | ATR 42-500 | 0849 | ex F-WWLH | |
| ☐ HC-CEX | Embraer ERJ-170LR | 17000087 | ex PT-SZM | Francisco de Orellana |
| ☐ HC-CEY | Embraer ERJ-170LR | 17000092 | ex PT-SZS | Puerto Baquerizo Moreno |
| ☐ HC-CGF | Embraer ERJ-190LR | 19000137 | ex PT-SYQ | Ciudad de Loja |
| ☐ HC-CGG | Embraer ERJ-190LR | 19000141 | ex PT-SYT | Ciudad de Manta |
| ☐ HC-CMH | ATR 42-500 | 0854 | ex F-WWIJ | ♦ |

### TRANS AM        Aero Transam (7T/RTM)        Guayaquil (GYE)

| | | | | |
|---|---|---|---|---|
| ☐ HC-CDX | ATR 42-300F | 0081 | ex YV-914C | Op for DHL |

### VIP-VUELOS INTERNOS PRIVADOS        Vipec (V6/VUR)        Quito (UIO)

| | | | | |
|---|---|---|---|---|
| ☐ HC-CFC | Dornier 328-110 | 3018 | ex N422JS | |
| ☐ HC-CFS | Dornier 328-110 | 3039 | ex N427JS | |

## HH-     HAITI (Republic of Haiti)

### CARIBINTAIR / CARIBAIR        Caribintair (CRT)        Port-au-Prince (PAP)

| | | | | |
|---|---|---|---|---|
| ☐ HH-CRT | LET L-410UVP-E | 861721 | ex LY-AZF | |
| ☐ HH-DMX | British Aerospace Jetstream 31 | 753 | ex N842JS | |
| ☐ HH- | British Aerospace Jetstream 32EP | 922 | ex N922CX | ♦ |

### HANAIR

| | | | | |
|---|---|---|---|---|
| ☐ HH- | Britten-Norman BN-2A-26 Islander | 150 | ex 4X-CAH | |

### NATION AIR

| | | | | |
|---|---|---|---|---|
| ☐ HH-NAT | LET L-410UVP | 851439 | ex HI-693CT | |

### SALSA D'HAITI

| | | | | |
|---|---|---|---|---|
| ☐ HH- | British Aerospace Jetstream 31 | 666 | ex N525PA | ♦ |

### SUNRISE AIRWAYS

| | | | | |
|---|---|---|---|---|
| ☐ HH-BET | LET L-410UVP | 851403 | ex 3D-DSI | ♦ |

### TORTUG'AIR                                                    Port-au-Prince (PAP)

| | | | | |
|---|---|---|---|---|
| ☐ HH-AET | LET L-410UVP-E3 | 871816 | ex 3D-CCE | |
| ☐ HH-CRB | LET L-410UVP | 800413 | ex HI-671CT | ♦ |
| ☐ HH-JET | British Aerospace Jetstream 32 | 883 | ex N883CH | |
| ☐ HH-LET | LET L-410UVP-E3 | 871927 | ex PT-XCP | ♦ |
| ☐ HH-LOG | LET L-410UVP-E3 | 871827 | ex S9-DIV | |
| ☐ HH-TOR | LET L-410UVP-E | 871930 | ex S9-BAO | |
| ☐ HH-YET | British Aerospace Jetstream 32 | 914 | ex N914AE | |
| ☐ HH-ZET | British Aerospace Jetstream 32 | 922 | ex N922CX | ♦ |

### TROPICAL AIRWAYS

| | | | | |
|---|---|---|---|---|
| ☐ HH-PRN | LET L-410UVP-E3 | 871906 | ex HR-IBA | ♦ |

### VISION AIR

| | | | | |
|---|---|---|---|---|
| ☐ HH-RPL | Britten-Norman BN-2A Mk.III-2 Trislander | 1040 | ex XA-TYU | |

## HI-    DOMINICAN REPUBLIC (Republica Dominicana)

### ACSA                                                          Santo Domingo-Herrara (HEX)

| | | | | |
|---|---|---|---|---|
| ☐ HI-744CT | Cessna 401B | 401B0214 | ex N7995Q | |
| ☐ HI772 | British Aerospace Jetstream 3101 | 660 | exHI-772CT | |
| ☐ HI816 | British Aerospace Jetstream 31 | 694 | exHI-816 | |
| ☐ HI840 | British Aerospace Jetstream 32EP | 819 | exHI-840 | |

### AERODOMCA                                                     Santo Domingo-Herrara (HEX)

| | | | | |
|---|---|---|---|---|
| ☐ HI761 | LET L-410UVP-E | 3871938 | ex HI-761CT | |

### AEROLINEAS MAS

| | | | | |
|---|---|---|---|---|
| ☐ HI-874 | British Aerospace Jetstream 32 | 810 | ex N494UE | ♦ |
| ☐ HI- | British Aerospace Jetstream 31 | 717 | ex N170PC | ♦ |
| ☐ HI- | SAAB SF.340B | 340B-360 | ex N875PC | [MIA]♦ |

### AIR INTER ISLAND                                              Santo Domingo-Herrara (HEX)

| | | | | |
|---|---|---|---|---|
| ☐ HI-787 | Britten-Norman BN-2A-8 Islander | 5429 | ex HI-787SP | ♦ |

### AIR SANTO DOMINGO        Aero Domingo (EX/SDO)        Santo Domingo-Herrara (HEX)

| | | | | |
|---|---|---|---|---|
| ☐ HI-657CT | Short SD.3-60 | SH3672 | ex 8P-SCD | |
| ☐ HI-679CT | LET L-410UVP-E | 882023 | ex HI-679CA | |
| ☐ HI-688CT | LET L-410UVP-E | 861616 | ex HI-688CA | |
| ☐ HI-760CT | Cessna 208B Caravan I | 208B0802 | ex N1326D | |

### CARIBAIR                       Caribair (CBC)        Santo Domingo-Herrara (HEX)

| | | | | |
|---|---|---|---|---|
| ☐ HI-569CT | Piper PA-31 Turbo Navajo B | 31-700 | ex HI-569CA | |
| ☐ HI-585CA | Piper PA-31 Turbo Navajo B | 31-850 | ex N333GT | |
| ☐ HI-653CA | Britten-Norman BN-2A-26 Islander | 8 | ex N28BN | |
| ☐ HI-666CT | LET L-410UVP | 851517 | ex TG-TJV | |
| ☐ HI-697CT | LET L-410UVP-E9A | 882040 | ex S9-TAV | |
| ☐ HI-698CT | LET L-410UVP-E9A | 882039 | ex S9-TAU | status? |
| ☐ HI-713CT | LET L-410UVP | 851340 | ex HI-713CA | |
| ☐ HI-746CT | British Aerospace Jetstream 3101 | 692 | ex HI-746CA  no titles | |
| ☐ HI-830 | British Aerospace Jetstream 3101 | 780 | ex HI-830CT | |
| ☐ HI-888 | British Aerospace Jetstream 3201 | | | o/o♦ |

## PAN AM DOMINICA — (7Q/PWD) — Santo Domingo-Herrara (HEX)

| | | | | | |
|---|---|---|---|---|---|
| ☐ HI-817CT | British Aerospace Jetstream 31 | 673 | ex N507PA | | [HEX] |
| ☐ HI-841CT | British Aerospace Jetstream 31 | 674 | ex N508PA | | [HEX] |
| ☐ HI869 | Douglas DC-9-32 | 47566/691 | ex N949N | | [HEX] |
| ☐ HI876 | Douglas DC-9-32 | 47046/168 | ex N602NW | | [HEX] |
| ☐ HI-914 | McDonnell-Douglas MD-82 | 49476/1439 | ex N450AA | | [HEX] |
| ☐ N206ZT | Bell 206B JetRanger III | 2906 | ex N330B | | |

Ceased ops

## SAPAIR / SERVICIOS AEREOS PROFESIONALES
### Proservicios (5S/PSV) — Santo Domingo-Herrara (HEX)

| | | | | |
|---|---|---|---|---|
| ☐ HI644 | de Havilland DHC-6 Twin Otter 200 | 46 | ex HI-644 | |
| ☐ HI657 | Short SD.3-60 | SH3672 | ex HI-657CT | ◆ |
| ☐ HI-691CT | LET L-410UVP | 831107 | ex S9-TAW | |
| ☐ HI-720CT | Embraer EMB.120RT Brasilia | 120038 | ex N332JS | |
| ☐ HI819 | British Aerospace Jetstream 31 | 811 | ex HI-819 | |
| ☐ HI851 | British Aerospace Jetstream 32EP | 940 | exHI-851 | |
| ☐ HI856 | British Aerospace Jetstream 32EP | 919 | ex HI-856 | |
| ☐ HI858 | British Aerospace Jetstream 32EP | 938 | exHI-858 | |

## VOL AIR — Santo Domingo-Herrara (HEX)

| | | | | |
|---|---|---|---|---|
| ☐ HI-785CT | Piper PA-31-350 Navajo Chieftain | 31-7305066 | ex N74923 | |
| ☐ HI-789CA | Britten-Norman BN-2A-21 Islander | 849 | ex HI-640CA | |
| ☐ HI862 | British Aerospace Jetstream 31 | 826 | ex N16EX | |
| ☐ HI877 | British Aerospace Jetstream 31 | 743 | ex N16EN | ◆ |

# HK-   COLOMBIA (Republic of Colombia)

## ADA – AEROLINEAS DE ANTIOQUIA — Antioquia (ANQ) — Medellin-Olaya Herrera (MDE)

| | | | | | |
|---|---|---|---|---|---|
| ☐ HK-4364 | British Aerospace Jetstream 32EP | 897 | ex N482UE | | |
| ☐ HK-4381 | British Aerospace Jetstream 32EP | 898 | ex N483UE | | |
| ☐ HK-4398 | British Aerospace Jetstream 32EP | 828 | ex N473UE | | |
| ☐ HK-4515 | British Aerospace Jetstream 32EP | 900 | ex N496UE | | |
| ☐ HK-4548 | British Aerospace Jetstream 32EP | 893 | ex N479UE | | |
| ☐ HK-4792 | British Aerospace Jetstream 32EP | 865 | ex N865CY | | ◆ |
| ☐ HK-2548 | de Havilland DHC-6 Twin Otter 300 | 718 | ex HK-2548X | | |
| ☐ HK-2603 | de Havilland DHC-6 Twin Otter 300 | 749 | | | |
| ☐ HK-2669 | de Havilland DHC-6 Twin Otter 300 | 760 | ex HK-2669X | Arcangel Rafael | |
| ☐ HK-3972 | Dornier 28D-2 Skyservant | 4156 | ex YS-400P | | |
| ☐ HK-4000 | Dornier 28D-2 Skyservant | 4177 | ex YS-404P | | |
| ☐ HK-4042 | Cessna T303 Crusader | T30300155 | ex N6421C | | |
| ☐ HK-4073 | Dornier 28D-2 Skyservant | 4114 | ex N952 | | |
| ☐ HK- | Dornier 328-110 | 3084 | ex HC-CFI | | [MDE]◆ |

## AER CARIBE

| | | | | |
|---|---|---|---|---|
| ☐ HK-4257 | Antonov An-32B | 3203 | ex OB-1699 | |
| ☐ HK-4427 | Antonov An-32 | 1909 | ex HK-4427X | |

## AEROEXPRESSO DE LA FRONTERA

| | | | | |
|---|---|---|---|---|
| ☐ HK-3804P | Cessna 208B Caravan I | 208B0315 | ex HK-3804 | ◆ |
| ☐ HK-3539 | Cessna 208 Caravan I | 20800165 | ex N9741F | ◆ |
| ☐ HK-3916 | Cessna 208B Caravan I | 208B0372 | ex YV1622 | ◆ |

## AEROLINEAS DE LA PAZ — Villavicencio (VVC)

| | | | | |
|---|---|---|---|---|
| ☐ HK-1663 | Cessna U206F Stationair | U20601962 | ex N50961 | |
| ☐ HK-3035 | Cessna T303 Crusader | T30300191 | | |
| ☐ HK-4189 | Douglas DC-3 | 4319 | ex HK-3994 | |
| ☐ HK-4292X | Douglas DC-3 | 17061/34328 | ex OB-1756 | status? |

## AEROLINEAS DEL CARIBE

| | | | | |
|---|---|---|---|---|
| ☐ HK-4728 | Antonov An-26B | 8205 | ex EK-26205 | ◆ |
| ☐ HK-4729 | Antonov An-26B | 12602 | | ◆ |
| ☐ HK-4730 | Antonov An-26B | 07309510 | ex EK-26510 | ◆ |

## AEROSUCRE — Aerosucre (6N/KRE)Barranquilla (BAQ)

| | Reg | Type | Serial | Notes |
|---|---|---|---|---|
| ☐ | HK-727 | Boeing 727-59F | 19127/243 | |
| ☐ | HK-4465 | Boeing 727-222F (FedEx 3) | 19915/681 | ex N7642U |
| ☐ | HK-4504 | Boeing 727-2J0F (FedEx 3) | 21108/1174 | ex N284KH |
| ☐ | HK-4544 | Boeing 727-2J0F (FedEx 3) | 21105/1158 | ex N281KH |
| ☐ | HK-4216 | Boeing 737-230C (Nordam 3) | 20253/223 | ex HP-1408PVI |
| ☐ | HK-4253X | Boeing 737-2H6C (Nordam 3) | 21109/436 | ex HP-1311CMP |
| ☐ | HK-4328 | Boeing 737-2S5C (Nordam 3) | 22148/663 | ex N802AL |

## AEROVANGUARDIA — Villavicencio (VVC)

| | Reg | Type | Serial | Notes | |
|---|---|---|---|---|---|
| ☐ | HK-2820 | Douglas DC-3 | 20171 | | ♦ |
| ☐ | HK-3199 | Douglas DC-3 | 14599/26044 | ex FAC1123  El Viejo | |
| ☐ | HK-3286 | Douglas DC-3 | 6144 | | ♦ |
| ☐ | HK-4292 | Douglas DC-3 | 13177 | | ♦ |

## AERUPIA — Villavicencio (VVC)

| | Reg | Type | Serial | Notes |
|---|---|---|---|---|
| ☐ | HK-2713 | Piper PA-34-220T Seneca III | 34-8133241 | |
| ☐ | HK-2822 | Britten-Norman BN-2B-27 Islander | 2109 | ex N2643X |

## AIR COLOMBIA — Villavicencio (VVC)

| | Reg | Type | Serial | Notes | |
|---|---|---|---|---|---|
| ☐ | HK-1175 | Douglas DC-3 | 20432 | | ♦ |
| ☐ | HK-3292 | Douglas DC-3 | 19661 | ex N9101S | |
| ☐ | HK-3293X | Douglas DC-3 | 9186 | ex N46877 | |

## ALIANSA — Villavicencio (VVC)

| | Reg | Type | Serial | Notes | |
|---|---|---|---|---|---|
| ☐ | HK-122 | Douglas DC-3 | 4414 | ex C-122 | Frtr [VCV] |
| ☐ | HK-1315 | Douglas DC-3 | 4307 | | ♦ |
| ☐ | HK-2006 | Douglas DC-3 | 43086 | | ♦ |

## ARKAS

| | Reg | Type | Serial | Notes |
|---|---|---|---|---|
| ☐ | HK-4492X | ATR 42-300 | 0015 | ex PR-TTA |
| ☐ | HK-4493X | ATR 42-300F | 0018 | ex F-GPIA |

## AVIANCA — Avianca (AV/AVA) — Bogota-Eldorado (BOG)

| | Reg | Type | Serial | Notes | |
|---|---|---|---|---|---|
| ☐ | N589AV | Airbus A318-111 | 2575 | ex N599EL | ♦ |
| ☐ | N590EL | Airbus A318-111 | 2328 | ex XA-UBQ | |
| ☐ | N591EL | Airbus A318-111 | 2333 | ex XA-UBR | |
| ☐ | N592EL | Airbus A318-111 | 2358 | ex XA-UBS | |
| ☐ | N593EL | Airbus A318-111 | 2367 | ex XA-UBT | |
| ☐ | N594EL | Airbus A318-111 | 2377 | ex XA-UBU | |
| ☐ | N595EL | Airbus A318-111 | 2394 | ex XA-UBV | |
| ☐ | N596EL | Airbus A318-111 | 2523 | ex XA-UBW | |
| ☐ | N597EL | Airbus A318-111 | 2544 | ex XA-UBX | |
| ☐ | N598EL | Airbus A318-111 | 2552 | ex XA-UBY | |
| ☐ | N599EL | Airbus A318-111 | 2575 | ex XA-UBZ | |
| ☐ | HK-4552 | Airbus A319-112 | 3518 | ex D-AVYZ | ♦ |
| ☐ | HK-4553 | Airbus A319-112 | 3467 | ex D-AVWN | ♦ |
| ☐ | N266CT | Airbus A319-112 | 2662 | ex XA-UER | ♦ |
| ☐ | N422AV | Airbus A319-115 | 4200 | ex D-AVYC | ♦ |
| ☐ | N519AV | Airbus A319-115 | 5119 | ex | o/o♦ |
| ☐ | N557AV | Airbus A319-115 | 5057 | ex D-AVYM | ♦ |
| ☐ | N612MX | Airbus A319-112 | 1612 | ex D-AVWC | ♦ |
| ☐ | N618MX | Airbus A319-112 | 1618 | ex D-AVWH | ♦ |
| ☐ | N634MX | Airbus A319-112 | 1634 | ex D-AVYH | |
| ☐ | N647AV | Airbus A319-115 | 3647 | ex D-AVYQ | |
| ☐ | N691AV | Airbus A319-115 | 3691 | ex D-AVWG | |
| ☐ | N992TA | Airbus A319-112 | 2066 | ex N602CT | <TAI♦ |
| ☐ | HK-4549 | Airbus A320-214 | 3408 | ex F-WWBZ | |
| ☐ | HK-4659 | Airbus A320-214 | 4100 | ex F-WWDK | |
| ☐ | N281AV | Airbus A320-214 | 4281 | ex F-WWIH | |
| ☐ | N284AV | Airbus A320-214 | 4284 | ex F-WWIP | |
| ☐ | N345AV | Airbus A320-214 | 4345 | ex F-WWBI | |
| ☐ | N398AV | Airbus A320-214 | 3988 | ex F-WWBO | |
| ☐ | N401AV | Airbus A320-214 | 4001 | ex F-WWDL | |
| ☐ | N411AV | Airbus A320-214 | 4011 | ex F-WWIC | |
| ☐ | N416AV | Airbus A320-214 | 4167 | ex F-WWBY | |
| ☐ | N417AV | Airbus A320-214 | 4175 | ex D-AVVT | |
| ☐ | N426AV | Airbus A320-214 | 4026 | ex F-WWDU | |
| ☐ | N446AV | Airbus A320-214 | 4046 | ex D-AVVI | |
| ☐ | N451AV | Airbus A320-214 | 4051 | ex F-WWIP | |
| ☐ | N481AV | Airbus A320-214 | 4381 | ex F-WWBB | |

| | | | | | |
|---|---|---|---|---|---|
| ☐ N567AV | Airbus A320-214 | 4567 | ex F-WWBG | | ♦ |
| ☐ N599 AV | Airbus A320-214 | 4599 | ex F-WWBQ | | ♦ |
| ☐ N664AV | Airbus A320-214 | 3664 | ex F-WWDX | | |
| ☐ N763AV | Airbus A320-214 | 4763 | ex F-WWDX | | ♦ |
| ☐ N789AV | Airbus A320-214 | 4789 | ex F-WWDV | | ♦ |
| ☐ N821AV | Airbus A320-214 | 4821 | ex F-WWIF | | ♦ |
| ☐ N862AV | Airbus A320-214 | 4862 | ex F-WWBR | | ♦ |
| ☐ N961AV | Airbus A320-214 | 3961 | ex F-WWDV | | |
| ☐ N980AV | Airbus A320-214 | 3980 | ex F-WWIZ | | |
| ☐ N939AV | Airbus A320-214 | 4939 | ex F-WWBN | | ♦ |
| ☐ N992AV | Airbus A320-214 | 3992 | ex F-WWDE | | |
| | | | | | |
| ☐ N279AV | Airbus A330-243 | 1279 | ex F-WWYN | | ♦ |
| ☐ N948AC | Airbus A330-243 | 948 | ex F-WWKN | | |
| ☐ N967CG | Airbus A330-243 | 967 | ex F-WWYI | | |
| ☐ N968AV | Airbus A330-243 | 1009 | ex F-WWYE | | |
| ☐ N969AV | Airbus A330-243 | 1016 | ex F-WWYI | | |
| ☐ N973AV | Airbus A330-243 | 1073 | ex F-WWKZ | | |
| ☐ N974AV | Airbus A330-243 | 1208 | ex F-WWYM | | ♦ |
| ☐ N975AV | Airbus A330-243 | 1224 | ex F-WWKJ | | ♦ |
| | | | | | |
| ☐ HK-4467 | Fokker 50 | 20301 | ex PH-MXZ | | |
| ☐ HK-4468X | Fokker 50 | 20300 | ex PH-MXT | | |
| ☐ HK-4469X | Fokker 50 | 20285 | ex PH-AVJ | | |
| ☐ HK-4470 | Fokker 50 | 20297 | ex PH-AVO | | |
| ☐ HK-4487X | Fokker 50 | 20266 | ex PH-LXW | | |
| ☐ HK-4496X | Fokker 50 | 20278 | ex PH-AVG | | |
| ☐ HK-4497X | Fokker 50 | 20288 | ex PH-MXJ | | |
| ☐ HK-4501X | Fokker 50 | 20299 | ex PH-MXS | | |
| ☐ HK-4580 | Fokker 50 | 20281 | ex PR-OAW | | |
| ☐ HK-4581 | Fokker 50 | 20296 | ex PR-OAX | | |
| | | | | | |
| ☐ HK-4419 | Fokker 100 | 11457 | ex N1448A | [WOE]♦ | |
| ☐ HK-4430 | Fokker 100 | 11465 | ex N1453D | [WOE]♦ | |
| ☐ HK-4443 | Fokker 100 | 11479 | ex N1459A | wfs♦ | |
| ☐ HK-4444 | Fokker 100 | 11458 | ex N1449D | [WOE]♦ | |
| ☐ HK-4445 | Fokker 100 | 11449 | ex N1446A | wfs♦ | |
| ☐ HK-4486 | Fokker 100 | 11414 | ex OB-1831-P | wfs♦ | |
| ☐ HK-4488 | Fokker 100 | 11376 | ex OB-1821-P | wfs♦ | |
| ☐ HK-4489 | Fokker 100 | 11377 | ex OB-1816-P | wfs♦ | |
| ☐ HK-4578 | Fokker 100 | 11413 | ex PR-OAH | wfs♦ | |
| ☐ HK-4579 | Fokker 100 | 11419 | ex PR-OAV | wfs♦ | |
| | | | | | |
| ☐ HK- | Boeing 757-2K2/W | 26635/608 | ex HC-CIY | wfs♦ | |
| ☐ N984AN | Boeing 767-383ER | 24357/262 | ex LN-RCB [MIA] | | |

## AVIHECO COLOMBIA

Bogota-Eldorado/Ibague (BOG/IBE)

| | | | | | |
|---|---|---|---|---|---|
| ☐ HK-3039 | Bell 206L-2 LongRanger III | 51052 | | | |
| ☐ HK-4267 | Bell 206L-2 LongRanger III | 51252 | ex N37CA | | |
| ☐ HK-4306 | Bell 206L-2 LongRanger III | 51606 | ex HC-BXA | | |
| ☐ HK-4334 | Convair 580F | 176 | ex N631MB | Used by CIA/DAC | |
| ☐ HK-4735 | Aérospatiale AS.350B2 Ecureuil | 2886 | | | ♦ |
| ☐ HK-4736 | Bell 212 | 30665 | ex N665L | | ♦ |
| ☐ HK-4777 | Aérospatiale AS.350B Ecureuil | 3547 | ex EC-JPM | | ♦ |

## COPA AIRLINES COLOMBIA

*Aerorepublica (P5/RPB)*            Bogota-Eldorado (BOG)

| | | | | | |
|---|---|---|---|---|---|
| ☐ HK-4505X | Embraer ERJ-190LR | 19000114 | ex PT-SQI | | |
| ☐ HK-4506X | Embraer ERJ-190LR | 19000110 | ex PT-SQE | | |
| ☐ HK-4507X | Embraer ERJ-190LR | 19000122 | ex PT-SQQ | | |
| ☐ HK-4508X | Embraer ERJ-190LR | 19000138 | ex PT-SYR | | |
| ☐ HK-4453X | Embraer ERJ-190LR | 19000063 | ex PT-SJB | | |
| ☐ HK-4454X | Embraer ERJ-190LR | 19000061 | ex PT-SIO | | |
| ☐ HK-4456X | Embraer ERJ-190LR | 19000074 | ex PT-SJN | | |
| ☐ HK-4559X | Embraer ERJ-190LR | 19000200 | ex PT-SGI | | |
| ☐ HK-4560X | Embraer ERJ-190LR | 19000208 | ex PT-SGR | | |
| ☐ HK-4599 | Embraer ERJ-190LR | 19000269 | ex PT-TLJ | | |
| ☐ HK-4601 | Embraer ERJ-190LR | 19000251 | ex PT-SIW | | |
| ☐ HP-1562CMP | Embraer ERJ-190AR | 19000095 | ex PT-SNP | <CMP | |
| ☐ HP-1563CMP | Embraer ERJ-190AR | 19000098 | ex PT-SNS | <CMP♦ | |
| ☐ HP-1566CMP | Embraer ERJ-190AR | 19000165 | ex PT-SAX | <CMP♦ | |
| | | | | | |
| ☐ HP-1371CMP | Boeing 737-7V3/W | 30049/388 | | <CMP♦ | |
| ☐ HP-1372CMP | Boeing 737-7V3/W | 28607/399 | | <CMP♦ | |

## COSMOS AIR CARGO

Bogota-Eldorado (BOG)

| | | | | |
|---|---|---|---|---|
| ☐ HK-4386X | Boeing 727-82C/W (FedEx 3) | 19968/660 | ex N709DH | |
| ☐ HK-4407X | Boeing 727-30C/W (Duganair 3) | 19011/387 | ex N701DH | |

## CV CARGO (V9/GSE)

| | | | | |
|---|---|---|---|---|
| ☐ HK-4702 | Boeing 737-290QC | 22577/760 | ex HC-CFY | ♦ |
| ☐ HK-4607 | Boeing 727-259F (FedEx 3) | 22476/1747 | ex N901LF | ♦ |

## EASYFLY (ESY) Bogota-Eldorado (BOG)

| | | | | |
|---|---|---|---|---|
| ☐ HK-4502 | British Aerospace Jetstream 4101 | 41091 | ex N572HK | |
| ☐ HK-4503 | British Aerospace Jetstream 4101 | 41093 | ex N574HK | |
| ☐ HK-4521 | British Aerospace Jetstream 4101 | 41092 | ex N573HK | |
| ☐ HK-4522 | British Aerospace Jetstream 4101 | 41086 | ex N568HK | |
| ☐ HK-4551 | British Aerospace Jetstream 4101 | 41089 | ex N570HK | |
| ☐ HK-4568 | British Aerospace Jetstream 4101 | 41057 | ex N552HK | |
| ☐ HK-4584X | British Aerospace Jetstream 4101 | 41073 | ex N556HK | [BOG] |
| ☐ HK-4585X | British Aerospace Jetstream 4101 | 41067 | ex N554HK | |
| ☐ HK-4596X | British Aerospace Jetstream 4101 | 41079 | ex N563HK | |
| ☐ HK-4765X | British Aerospace Jetstream 41 | 41074 | ex G-MAJV | ♦ |
| ☐ HK-4775X | British Aerospace Jetstream 41 | 41039 | ex G-MAJP | ♦ |
| ☐ HK-4786X | British Aerospace Jetstream 41 | 41098 | ex G-MAJX | ♦ |
| ☐ N569HK | British Aerospace Jetstream 4101 | 41088 | | [MQY]♦ |

## HELICOL Helicol (HEL) Bogota-Eldorado (BOG)

| | | | | |
|---|---|---|---|---|
| ☐ HK-3303X | Bell 212 | 30654 | ex N59608 | |
| ☐ HK-3336X | Bell 212 | 31207 | ex N2180J | |
| ☐ HK-3578G | Bell 412 | 33203 | | |
| ☐ HK-3633X | Bell 206L-1 LongRanger II | 45510 | ex N57497 | |
| ☐ HK-4031X | Bell 212 | 31203 | ex HK-3184X | |
| ☐ HK-4213G | Bell 407 | 53405 | ex (N2382Z) | |
| ☐ HK-4731 | Bell 412EP | 36325 | | ♦ |
| ☐ HK-4744 | Bell 412 | 33009 | ex N412HL | ♦ |
| ☐ HK-4767 | Bell 412 | 33065 | ex N968FM | ♦ |

## HELISTAR COLOMBIA

| | | | | |
|---|---|---|---|---|
| ☐ HK-4722 | MBB BK.117C-2 | 9324 | | ♦ |

## HELITAXI

| | | | | |
|---|---|---|---|---|
| ☐ HK-4208 | Beech 1900C-1 | UC-152 | ex HK-4208X | ♦ |

## INTERANDES

| | | | | |
|---|---|---|---|---|
| ☐ HK-3226 | Cessna 208 Caravan I | 20800002 | ex N9182F | ♦ |

## LAN AIRLINES COLOMBIA Aires (4C/ARE) Bogota-Eldorado (BOG)

| | | | | |
|---|---|---|---|---|
| ☐ EI-EEB | Boeing 737-73S/W | 29081/215 | ex HK-4623 | |
| ☐ EI-EEV | Boeing 737-73S/W | 29080/211 | ex HK-4608 | |
| ☐ HK-4627 | Boeing 737-73S/W | 29078/187 | ex OY-MLW | |
| ☐ HK-4641 | Boeing 737-73V/W | 30244/1148 | ex G-EZJO | |
| ☐ HK-4660X | Boeing 737-752/W | 34296/1783 | ex XA-WAM | |
| ☐ HK-4675X | Boeing 737-73V/W | 32415/1260 | ex G-EZJT | |
| ☐ HK-4694 | Boeing 737-7Q8/W | 30687/2252 | ex N171LF | |
| ☐ HK-4695 | Boeing 737-7Q8/W | 30710/2188 | ex N225LF | |
| ☐ HK-4473 | de Havilland DHC-8Q-201 | 479 | ex N985HA | |
| ☐ HK-4480 | de Havilland DHC-8Q-201 | 509 | ex N998HA | |
| ☐ HK-4491 | de Havilland DHC-8Q-201 | 478 | ex N983HA | |
| ☐ HK-4495 | de Havilland DHC-8Q-201 | 497 | ex N996HA | |
| ☐ HK-4509 | de Havilland DHC-8Q-201 | 507 | ex N997HA | |
| ☐ HK-4513X | de Havilland DHC-8Q-201 | 468 | ex N969HA | |
| ☐ HK-4520 | de Havilland DHC-8Q-201 | 465 | ex N968HA | |
| ☐ HK-4539 | de Havilland DHC-8Q-201 | 452 | ex N966HA | |
| ☐ HK-4554X | de Havilland DHC-8Q-201 | 450 | ex N965HA | |
| ☐ HK-4618 | de Havilland DHC-8-201 | 432 | ex HC-CFK | |
| ☐ CC-CQM | Airbus A320-233 | 3280 | ex F-WWDM | ♦ |
| ☐ CC-CQN | Airbus A320-233 | 3319 | ex F-WWBC | ♦ |
| ☐ CC-CQO | Airbus A320-233 | 3535 | ex F-WWDZ | ♦ |
| ☐ HK-4724X | de Havilland DHC-8-402Q | 4137 | ex HL5255 | |
| ☐ HK-4725X | de Havilland DHC-8-402Q | 4124 | ex HL5252 | |
| ☐ HK-4726 | de Havilland DHC-8-402Q | 4119 | ex HL5251 | |
| ☐ HK-4727X | de Havilland DHC-8-402Q | 4129 | ex HL5254 | |

## LAN CARGO COLOMBIA Bogota-Eldorado (BOG)

| | | | |
|---|---|---|---|
| ☐ N418LA | Boeing 767-316F/W | 34246/936 | |

## LATINA DE AVIACION · Villavicencio (VVC)

| | | | |
|---|---|---|---|
| ☐ HK-4173X | Beech 1900C-1 | UC-14 | ex N38015 |
| ☐ HK-2006 | Douglas DC-3C | 43086 | ex N43A |

## LINEAS AÉREAS SURAMERICANAS COLOMBIA · Suramericano (LAU) · Bogota-Eldorado (BOG)

| | | | | |
|---|---|---|---|---|
| ☐ HK-1271 | Boeing 727-24C (Raisbeck 3) | 19524/428 | ex N1781B | |
| ☐ HK-1273 | Boeing 727-24C (Raisbeck 3) | 19526/442 | ex N8320 | Voyager |
| ☐ HK-4154 | Boeing 727-51F (Raisbeck 3) | 18804/162 | ex N5607 | Orion |
| ☐ HK-4261 | Boeing 727-251F (FedEx 3) | 21156/1170 | ex N296AJ | |
| ☐ HK-4262 | Boeing 727-2F9F/W (Duganair 3) | 21427/1291 | ex N299AJ | |
| ☐ HK-4401 | Boeing 727-2X3F (FedEx 3) | 22609/1731 | ex N797AJ | |
| ☐ HK-4636 | Boeing 727-2S2F (FedEx 3) | 22927/1821 | ex N129FB | |
| ☐ HK-4637 | Boeing 727-2S2F (FedEx 3) | 22928/1822 | ex N131FB | |

## NACIONAL DE AVIACION COLOMBIA

| | | | | |
|---|---|---|---|---|
| ☐ HK-4013 | LET L-410UVP-E | 861601 | ex HK-4013X | ◆ |
| ☐ HK-4151X | LET L-410UVP-E | 861610 | ex N16100 | ◆ |

## PETROLEUM AIR SERVICE

| | | | | |
|---|---|---|---|---|
| ☐ HK-4564 | Beech 1900D | UE-402 | ex N842CA | ◆ |
| ☐ HK-4577 | Beech 1900D | UE-50 | ex HK-4557X | ◆ |
| ☐ HK-4732 | Beech 1900D | UE-160 | ex N877NA | ◆ |

## SADELCA · Sadelca (SDK) · Neiva (NVA)

| | | | | | |
|---|---|---|---|---|---|
| ☐ HK-1149 | Douglas DC-3 | 26593 | | | ◆ |
| ☐ HK-2494 | Douglas DC-3 | 16357/33105 | ex N87611 | | |
| ☐ HK-2664 | Douglas DC-3 | 19433 | ex HK-2665 | Angela Sofia | |
| ☐ HK-4296X | Antonov An-32A | 1704 | | | ◆ |
| ☐ HK-4356 | Antonov An-26-100 | 5109 | | | ◆ |

## SARPA – RENT AIR · Medellin-Olaya Herrara (MDE)

| | | | | |
|---|---|---|---|---|
| ☐ HK-4350 | British Aerospace Jetstream 32EP | 836 | ex G-OEST | |
| ☐ HK-4362 | British Aerospace Jetstream 32EP | 840 | ex G-BYMA | |
| ☐ HK-4394E | British Aerospace Jetstream 32EP | 905 | ex N486UE | EMS |
| ☐ HK-4405E | British Aerospace Jetstream 32EP | 849 | ex N474UE | |
| ☐ HK-4411 | British Aerospace Jetstream 32 | 870 | ex N870CY | ◆ |
| ☐ HK-4540X | British Aerospace Jetstream 32EP | 933 | ex N933CX | |
| ☐ HK-4541 | British Aerospace Jetstream 32EP | 937 | ex N937AE | |
| ☐ HK-4772 | British Aerospace Jetstream 32EP | 950 | ex N341TE | |
| ☐ HK-4791 | British Aerospace Jetstream 32EP | 917 | ex N917AE | ◆ |
| ☐ HK-4803 | British Aerospace Jetstream 32EP | 924 | ex N924AE | ◆ |
| | | | | |
| ☐ HK-4099 | Agusta-Bell 212 | 5630 | | |
| ☐ HK-4100 | Agusta-Bell 212 | 5631 | | |
| ☐ HK-4124 | Bell 212 | 30844 | ex N405RA | |
| ☐ HK-4232 | Bell 212 | 30993 | ex XA-SRZ | |
| ☐ HK-4233 | Bell 212 | 31164 | ex XA-LAM | |

## SATENA · Satena (9N/NSE) · Bogota-Eldorado (BOG)

| | | | | |
|---|---|---|---|---|
| ☐ HK-4531X | Dornier 328-120 | 3079 | ex FAC-1160 El Cafetero | |
| ☐ HK-4523X | Dornier 328-120 | 3080 | ex FAC-1161 La Macarena | |
| ☐ HK-4524X | Dornier 328-120 | 3082 | ex FAC-1162 Bahia Solano | |
| ☐ HK-4532X | Dornier 328-120 | 3081 | ex FAC-1163 El Antioqueño | |
| ☐ HK-4533X | Dornier 328-120 | 3092 | ex FAC-1164 El Casanereno | |
| ☐ HK-4534X | Dornier 328-120 | 3103 | ex FAC-1165 El Guambiano | |
| | | | | |
| ☐ FAC-1171 | Embraer ERJ-145LR | 145774 | ex PT-SME Milenium I | |
| ☐ FAC-1172 | Embraer ERJ-145LR | 145776 | ex PT-SMG Milenium II | |
| ☐ FAC-1103 | LET L-410UVP-E | 902420 | ex HK-4224 | Lsd fr/op by SRC |
| ☐ HK-4528 | Embraer ERJ-170LR | 17000151 | ex FAC-1180 | |
| ☐ HK-4536 | Embraer ERJ-145LR | 14500879 | ex FAC-1173 | [MVP] |
| ☐ HK-4747 | ATR 42-500 | 0526 | ex FAC-1182 | |
| ☐ HK-4748 | ATR 42-500 | 0522 | ex FAC-1183 | |
| ☐ HK-4806 | ATR 42-500 | 0513 | ex N513NA | |
| ☐ HK-4827X | ATR 42-500 | 0532 | ex N532FA | |
| ☐ HK-4828X | ATR 72-500 | 0521 | ex N521NA | |

## SEARCA COLOMBIA · Searca (SRC) · Medellin-Olaya Herrara (MDE)

| | | | |
|---|---|---|---|
| ☐ HK-4266 | Beech 1900C-1 | UC-64 | exHK-4266X |
| ☐ HK-4282 | Beech 1900C-1 | UC-60 | ex N901SC |
| ☐ HK-4476 | Beech 1900D | UE-123 | ex N123YV |
| ☐ HK-4499 | Beech 1900D | UE-110 | ex N110YV |

| | | | | |
|---|---|---|---|---|
| ☐ HK-4512 | Beech 1900D | UE-105 | ex N105YV | |
| ☐ HK-4537 | Beech 1900D | UE-95 | ex N95YV | |
| ☐ HK-4558 | Beech 1900D | UE-156 | ex N156E | |
| ☐ HK-4563 | Beech 1900D | UE-113 | ex N113YV | |
| ☐ HK-4598 | Beech 1900D | UE-183 | ex N48544 | |
| ☐ HK-4600 | Beech 1900D | UE-99 | ex N99YV | |
| ☐ HK-4630 | Beech 1900D | UE-93 | ex N93ZV | |
| ☐ HK-4673 | Beech 1900D | UE-104 | ex N104YV | |
| ☐ HK-4681 | Beech 1900D | UE-213 | ex N3199Q | |
| ☐ HK-4709 | Beech 1900D | UE-140 | ex N140ZV | ♦ |
| | | | | |
| ☐ HK-4038 | LET L-410UVP | 851323 | ex HK-4038X | |
| ☐ HK-4048 | LET L-410UVP-E | 912626 | ex OM-111 | |
| ☐ HK-4150 | LET L-410UVP-E | 861613 | ex N5957N | |
| ☐ HK-4161 | LET L-410UVP-E | 861612 | ex N6968L | |
| ☐ HK-4235 | LET L-410UVP-E | 902423 | ex S9-BAD | |
| ☐ HK-4367 | LET L-410UVP-E | 20B841334 | ex CP-2252 | ♦ |
| ☐ FAC-1103 | LET L-410UVP-E | 902420 | ex HK-4224 | Lsd to/op for NSE |
| | | | | |
| ☐ HK-4108 | Beech 200 Super King Air | BB-60 | ex HK-4108X | |
| ☐ HK-4801 | Beeh 400A | RK-173 | | ♦ |

## SELVA

| | | | | |
|---|---|---|---|---|
| ☐ HK-4052 | Antonov An-32 | 1805 | ex YN-CBU | |
| ☐ HK-4295 | Antonov An-26 | 67304702 | ex LZ-NHA | |
| ☐ HK-4369 | Antonov An-32 | 2510 | ex ER-AWA | wfs |
| ☐ HK-4388 | Antonov An-26B-100 | 27312402 | ex LZ-NHE | |
| ☐ HK-4706 | Antonov An-26B-100 | 27312203 | ex 3X-GFB | |

## TAMPA AIRLINES — Tampa (QT/TPA) — Medellin-Olaya Herrara (MDE)

| | | | | |
|---|---|---|---|---|
| ☐ N767QT | Boeing 767-241ER (SF) | 23804/178 | ex PP-VNQ | |
| ☐ N768QT | Boeing 767-241ER (SF) | 23803/161 | ex N803HE | |
| ☐ N769QT | Boeing 767-241ER (SF) | 23801/170 | ex PP-VNO | |
| ☐ N770QT | Boeing 767-241ER (SF) | 23802/172 | ex PP-VNP | |
| ☐ N771QT | Boeing 767-381F | 33404/885 | ex JA601F | ♦ |

## TAS - TRANSPORTE AEREO DE SANTANDER — Bucaramanga (BGA)

| | | | | |
|---|---|---|---|---|
| ☐ HK-4102 | Dornier 28D-2 Skyservant | 4187 | ex D-IDES | |
| ☐ HK-4104 | Dornier 28D-2 Skyservant | 4193 | ex D-IDRV | |
| ☐ HK-4139 | Dornier 28D-2 Skyservant | 4153 | ex D-IDRF | |
| ☐ HK-4290X | Cessna 402C | 402C0427 | ex N717A | |

## TAXI AÉREA DE CALDAS

| | | | | |
|---|---|---|---|---|
| ☐ HK-4610 | Beech 1900D | UE-82 | ex HK-4610X | ♦ |
| ☐ HK-4634 | Beech 1900D | UE-54 | ex N54YV | ♦ |

## TAXI AÉREO CUSIANA — Bogota-Eldorado (BOG)

| | | | | |
|---|---|---|---|---|
| ☐ HK-2522 | Cessna 402C II | 402C0322 | ex N2522P | |
| ☐ HK-4225 | LET L-410UVP-E3 | 871929 | ex HK-4225X | |
| ☐ HK-4260 | LET L-410UVP-E3 | 871933 | ex HK-4260X | ♦ |

## TAXI AÉREO DE IBAGUE

| | | | | |
|---|---|---|---|---|
| ☐ HK-3743P | Cessna 208 Caravan I | 20800216 | ex HK-3743 | ♦ |

## TRANS ORIENTE — Villavicencio (VVC)

| | | | | |
|---|---|---|---|---|
| ☐ HK-3981 | Dornier 28D-2 Skyservant | 4162 | ex D-IDND | |
| ☐ HK-3982 | Dornier 28D-2 Skyservant | 4169 | ex D-IDNC | |
| ☐ HK-3991X | Dornier 28D-2 Skyservant | 4148 | ex D-IDNF | |
| ☐ HK-3992X | Dornier 28D-2 Skyservant | 4161 | ex D-IDNE | |
| ☐ HK-4053X | Dornier 28D-1 Skyservant | 4105 | ex D-IDNH | |

## TRANSPORTE AEREO DE COLOMBIA

| | | | | |
|---|---|---|---|---|
| ☐ HK-4196 | LET L-410UVP-E | 861617 | ex HK-4196X | ♦ |

## VERTICAL DE AVIACION – AIRFREIGHT AVIATION — Bogota-Guaymaral

| | | | | |
|---|---|---|---|---|
| ☐ HK-3730X | Mil Mi-8TV-1 | 95728 | ex CCCP-25112 | |
| ☐ HK-3731X | Mil Mi-8TV-1 | 95586 | ex CCCP-25447 | |
| ☐ HK-3732X | Mil Mi-8TV-1 | 95729 | ex CCCP-25113 | |
| ☐ HK-3758X | Mil Mi-8TV-1 | 95908 | ex HC-BSG | |
| ☐ HK-3779X | Mil Mi-8TV-1 | 95645 | ex CCCP-25500 | |
| ☐ HK-3780X | Mil Mi-8TV-1 | 95909 | ex RA-27068 | |

| | | | | |
|---|---|---|---|---|
| ☐ HK-3862 | Mil Mi-8TV-1 | 95923 | ex CCCP-27087 | |
| ☐ HK-3863 | Mil Mi-8TV-1 | 95894 | ex CCCP-27060 | |
| ☐ HK-3864 | Mil Mi-8TV-1 | 95893 | ex CCCP-27059 | |
| ☐ HK-3865 | Mil Mi-8TV-1 | 95892 | ex CCCP-27058 | |
| ☐ HK-3882X | Mil Mi-8TV-1 | 96018 | | |
| ☐ HK-3888X | Mil Mi-8TV-1 | 95838 | | |
| ☐ HK-3908X | Mil Mi-8TV-1 | 95823 | | |
| ☐ HK-3910X | Mil Mi-8TV-1 | 96008 | ex RA-27185 | |
| ☐ HK-3911X | Mil Mi-8TV-1 | 96124 | ex RA-25768 | |
| | | | | |
| ☐ HK-3250 | Bell 212 | 31219 | ex HC-BSI | |
| ☐ HK-3723 | Bell 212 | 32122 | ex N1080V | |
| ☐ HK-4796 | Mil Mi-171 | 59489617778 | | ♦ |
| ☐ HK-4797 | Mil Mi-171 | 171P00784073403 | | ♦ |

## VIARCO　　　　　　　　　　　　　　　　　　　　　　　Villavicencio (VVC)

| | | | |
|---|---|---|---|
| ☐ HK-1315 | Douglas DC-3 | 4307 | ex PP-ANG |
| ☐ HK-1842 | Cessna U206F Stationair II | U20603487 | ex (N8734Q) |
| ☐ HK-3349X | Douglas DC-3 | 11825 | ex FAE 92066/HC-AVC |

## VIAS AEREAS NACIONALES

| | | | | |
|---|---|---|---|---|
| ☐ HK-3734 | Cessna 208B Caravan I | 208B0297 | ex N5444B | ♦ |

## VIVA COLOMBIA

| | | | | |
|---|---|---|---|---|
| ☐ HK-4811 | Airbus A320-214 | 1564 | ex N260AV | wfs♦ |
| ☐ HK-4848 | Airbus A320-214 | 1306 | ex N136AG | [MDE]♦ |

## WEST CARIBBEAN AIRLINES

| | | | | |
|---|---|---|---|---|
| ☐ HK-4125 | LET L-410UVP-E | 912605 | ex OK-WDZ | ♦ |
| ☐ HK-4187X | LET L-410UVP-E | 902432 | ex HA-LAT | ♦ |

## HL-　　SOUTH KOREA (Republic of Korea)

## AIR BUSAN　　　　　　　　　　　(BX/ABL)　　　　　　　Busan-Gimhae (PVS)

| | | | | |
|---|---|---|---|---|
| ☐ HL7232 | Boeing 737-58E | 25767/2614 | | |
| ☐ HL7233 | Boeing 737-58E | 25768/2724 | | |
| ☐ HL7250 | Boeing 737-58E | 25769/2737 | | |
| ☐ HL7510 | Boeing 737-48E | 25771/2816 | | |
| ☐ HL7517 | Boeing 737-48E | 25774/2909 | | |
| | | | | |
| ☐ HL8213 | Airbus A321-231 | 1970 | ex EI-LVB | |
| ☐ HL8236 | Airbus A321-231 | 1174 | ex N174AG | ♦ |

## AIR KOREA

| | | | | |
|---|---|---|---|---|
| ☐ HL5107 | Cessna 208 Caravan I | 20800238 | ex N9824F | ♦ |
| ☐ HL5111 | Cessna 208 Caravan I | 20800328 | ex N36964 | ♦ |
| ☐ HL5115 | Cessna 208B Caravan I | 208B2011 | ex N22430 | ♦ |

## ASIANA AIRLINES　　　　　　Asiana (OZ/AAR)　　　Seoul-Incheon/Kimpo (ICN/SEL)

Member of Star Alliance

| | | | |
|---|---|---|---|
| ☐ HL7737 | Airbus A320-232 | 2397 | ex F-WWIU |
| ☐ HL7738 | Airbus A320-232 | 2459 | ex F-WWDM |
| ☐ HL7744 | Airbus A320-232 | 2808 | ex F-WWIO |
| ☐ HL7745 | Airbus A320-232 | 2840 | ex F-WWIE |
| ☐ HL7753 | Airbus A320-232 | 2943 | ex F-WWIM |
| ☐ HL7762 | Airbus A320-232 | 3244 | ex F-WWBQ |
| ☐ HL7769 | Airbus A320-232 | 3437 | ex F-WWDX |
| ☐ HL7772 | Airbus A320-232 | 3483 | ex F-WWDN |
| ☐ HL7773 | Airbus A320-232 | 3496 | ex F-WWIL |
| ☐ HL7776 | Airbus A320-232 | 3641 | ex F-WWBS |
| ☐ HL7788 | Airbus A320-232 | 3873 | ex F-WWIH |
| | | | |
| ☐ HL7594 | Airbus A321-231 | 1356 | ex D-AVZA |
| ☐ HL7703 | Airbus A321-231 | 1511 | ex D-AVZA |
| ☐ HL7711 | Airbus A321-231 | 1636 | ex D-AVZG |
| ☐ HL7712 | Airbus A321-231 | 1670 | ex G-ABDM |
| ☐ HL7713 | Airbus A321-231 | 1734 | ex D-AVXD |
| ☐ HL7722 | Airbus A321-231 | 2041 | ex D-AVZA |
| ☐ HL7723 | Airbus A321-231 | 2045 | ex D-AVZC |
| ☐ HL7729 | Airbus A321-231 | 2110 | ex D-AVXF |
| ☐ HL7730 | Airbus A321-231 | 2226 | ex D-AVZU |

| ☐ HL7731 | Airbus A321-231 | 2247 | ex D-AVZG | |
| ☐ HL7735 | Airbus A321-231 | 2290 | ex D-AVZB | |
| ☐ HL7761 | Airbus A321-231 | 1227 | ex N127AG | |
| ☐ HL7763 | Airbus A321-231 | 3297 | ex D-AVZR | |
| ☐ HL7767 | Airbus A321-231 | 0802 | ex N802BV | |
| ☐ HL7789 | Airbus A321-231 | 4112 | ex D-AZAE | |
| ☐ HL7790 | Airbus A321-231 | 4142 | ex D-AVZM | |
| ☐ HL8255 | Airbus A321-231 | 5035 | ex D-AZAN | ♦ |
| | | | | |
| ☐ HL7736 | Airbus A330-323X | 640 | ex F-WWYR | |
| ☐ HL7740 | Airbus A330-323X | 676 | ex F-WWYA | |
| ☐ HL7741 | Airbus A330-323X | 708 | ex F-WWKL | |
| ☐ HL7746 | Airbus A330-323X | 772 | ex F-WWKE | |
| ☐ HL7747 | Airbus A330-323X | 803 | ex F-WWYE | |
| ☐ HL7754 | Airbus A330-323X | 845 | ex F-WWYZ | |
| ☐ HL7792 | Airbus A330-323X | 1001 | ex F-WWKL | |
| ☐ HL7793 | Airbus A330-323X | 1055 | ex F-WWYD | |
| ☐ HL7794 | Airbus A330-323X | 1151 | ex F-WWYS | |
| ☐ HL7795 | Airbus A330-323X | 1211 | ex F-WWYV | ♦ |
| | | | | |
| ☐ HL7413 | Boeing 747-48EM (SF) | 25405/880 | | |
| ☐ HL7414 | Boeing 747-48EM (SF) | 25452/892 | | |
| ☐ HL7415 | Boeing 747-48EM (SF) | 25777/946 | | |
| ☐ HL7417 | Boeing 747-48EM | 25779/1006 | | |
| ☐ HL7418 | Boeing 747-48E | 25780/1035 | ex N6018N | |
| ☐ HL7419 | Boeing 747-48EF | 25781/1044 | | |
| ☐ HL7420 | Boeing 747-48EF | 25783/1064 | | |
| ☐ HL7421 | Boeing 747-48EM | 25784/1086 | | |
| ☐ HL7423 | Boeing 747-48EM | 25782/1115 | | |
| ☐ HL7428 | Boeing 747-48E | 28552/1160 | ex N6018N | |
| ☐ HL7436 | Boeing 747-48EF | 29170/1305 | ex N1785B | |
| ☐ HL7616 | Boeing 747-446F | 33748/1351 | ex N401AL | ♦ |
| | | | | |
| ☐ HL7247 | Boeing 767-38E | 25757/523 | | |
| ☐ HL7248 | Boeing 767-38E | 25758/582 | | |
| ☐ HL7506 | Boeing 767-38E | 25760/639 | | |
| ☐ HL7507 | Boeing 767-38EF | 25761/616 | ex N6005C | |
| ☐ HL7514 | Boeing 767-38E | 25763/656 | | Tea Changum c/s |
| ☐ HL7515 | Boeing 767-38E | 25762/658 | ex N6055X | |
| ☐ HL7516 | Boeing 767-38E | 25759/668 | | Star Alliance c/s |
| ☐ HL7528 | Boeing 767-38E | 29129/693 | ex N6005C | |
| | | | | |
| ☐ HL7500 | Boeing 777-28EER | 28685/400 | | |
| ☐ HL7596 | Boeing 777-28EER | 28681/322 | | |
| ☐ HL7597 | Boeing 777-28EER | 28686/359 | | |
| ☐ HL7700 | Boeing 777-28EER | 30859/403 | ex N5014K | |
| ☐ HL7732 | Boeing 777-28EER | 29174/481 | | |
| ☐ HL7739 | Boeing 777-28EER | 29175/526 | | |
| ☐ HL7742 | Boeing 777-28EER | 29171/553 | | |
| ☐ HL7755 | Boeing 777-28EER | 30861/646 | | |
| ☐ HL7756 | Boeing 777-28EER | 30860/659 | | |
| ☐ HL7775 | Boeing 777-28EER | 30862/738 | | |
| ☐ HL7791 | Boeing 777-28EER | 35525/853 | | |
| ☐ HL8254 | Boeing 777-28EER | 40198 | | o/o |
| | | | | |
| ☐ HL7508 | Boeing 737-48E | 25772/2791 | | |
| ☐ HL7511 | Boeing 737-48E | 27630/2848 | | |
| ☐ HL7513 | Boeing 737-48E | 25776/2860 | | |

## EAST ASIA AIRLINES

| ☐ HL5237 | Swearingen SA-227DC Metro 23 | DC-822B | ex VH-HAN | ♦ |

## EASTARJET        (ZE/ESR)        Seoul-Gimpo (GMP/SEL)

| ☐ HL7797 | Boeing 737-73V | 30240/974 | ex N240CL | |
| ☐ HL8204 | Boeing 737-73V | 30248/1118 | ex G-EZJM | |
| ☐ HL8205 | Boeing 737-73V | 32412/1151 | ex G-EZJP | |
| ☐ HL8207 | Boeing 737-73V | 32413/1202 | ex G-EZJR | |
| ☐ HL8215 | Boeing 737-73V | 32417/1285 | ex G-EZJV | |
| | | | | |
| ☐ HL7781 | Boeing 737-683 | 28302/243 | ex G-CDKD | |
| ☐ HL8264 | Boeing 737-88J/W | 28088/36 | ex N862AG | ♦ |

## JEJU AIR        (7C/JJA)        Cheju International (CJU)

| ☐ HL7779 | Boeing 737-85F | 28824/180 | ex VT-SPC | |
| ☐ HL7780 | Boeing 737-85F | 28827/467 | ex VT-SPD | |
| ☐ HL7796 | Boeing 737-86N/W | 28628/573 | ex N372LZ | |
| ☐ HL8206 | Boeing 737-86J/W | 30877/782 | ex D-ABAE | |
| ☐ HL8214 | Boeing 737-86N/W | 28608/410 | ex D-ABBQ | |
| ☐ HL8233 | Boeing 737-85P/W | 28383/266 | ex EC-HBN | |

| | | | | | |
|---|---|---|---|---|---|
| ☐ HL8234 | Boeing 737-86Q/W | 30285/1237 | ex OO-VAS | | |
| ☐ HL8239 | Boeing 737-82R | 29344/849 | ex TC-APU | | |
| ☐ HL8260 | Boeing 737-8BK/W | 30622/1108 | ex VH-VOB | | ◆ |
| ☐ HL8262 | Boeing 737-8Q8/W | 28214/78 | ex N225LF | | ◆ |

## JIN AIR

**(LJ/JNA)** · **Seoul-Incheon/Kimpo (ICN/SEL)**

| | | | | | |
|---|---|---|---|---|---|
| ☐ HL7555 | Boeing 737-86N | 30230/460 | ex N1786B | | |
| ☐ HL7556 | Boeing 737-86N | 28615/482 | ex N1787B | | ◆ |
| ☐ HL7558 | Boeing 737-86N | 28625/590 | ex N1786B | | |
| ☐ HL7563 | Boeing 737-86N | 28636/756 | | | ◆ |
| ☐ HL7564 | Boeing 737-86N | 28638/765 | | | |
| ☐ HL7798 | Boeing 737-809/W | 28236/739 | ex B-16802 | | |

## KOREAN AIR

**Koreanair (KE/KAL)** · **Seoul-Incheon/Kimpo (ICN/SEL)**

Member of Skyteam

| | | | | | |
|---|---|---|---|---|---|
| ☐ HL7239 | Airbus A300B4-622R | 627 | ex F-WWAD | | |
| ☐ HL7240 | Airbus A300B4-622R | 631 | ex F-WWAB | | |
| ☐ HL7241 | Airbus A300B4-622R | 662 | ex F-WWAT | | |
| ☐ HL7243 | Airbus A300B4-622R | 692 | ex F-WWAR | | |
| ☐ HL7245 | Airbus A300B4-622R | 731 | ex F-WWAK | | |
| ☐ HL7295 | Airbus A300B4-622R | 582 | ex F-WWAM | | |
| ☐ HL7297 | Airbus A300B4-622R | 609 | ex F-WWAE | | |
| ☐ HL7538 | Airbus A330-223 | 222 | ex F-WWKP | | |
| ☐ HL7539 | Airbus A330-223 | 226 | ex F-WWKR | | |
| ☐ HL7552 | Airbus A330-223 | 258 | ex F-WWKQ | | |
| ☐ HL8211 | Airbus A330-223 | 1133 | ex F-WWKA | | |
| ☐ HL8212 | Airbus A330-223 | 1155 | ex F-WWKI | | ◆ |
| ☐ HL8227 | Airbus A330-223 | 1200 | ex F-WWKI | | ◆ |
| ☐ HL8228 | Airbus A330-223 | 1203 | ex F-WWYE | | ◆ |
| ☐ HL7524 | Airbus A330-322 | 206 | ex HL7552 | | |
| ☐ HL7525 | Airbus A330-322 | 219 | ex F-WWKO | | |
| ☐ HL7540 | Airbus A330-322 | 241 | ex F-WWKF | | |
| ☐ HL7550 | Airbus A330-322 | 162 | ex F-WWKK | | |
| ☐ HL7551 | Airbus A330-322 | 172 | ex F-WWKI | | |
| ☐ HL7553 | Airbus A330-323X | 267 | ex F-WWKZ | | |
| ☐ HL7554 | Airbus A330-323X | 256 | ex F-WWKN | | |
| ☐ HL7584 | Airbus A330-323X | 338 | ex F-WWKP | | |
| ☐ HL7585 | Airbus A330-323X | 350 | ex F-WWYF | | |
| ☐ HL7586 | Airbus A330-323X | 351 | ex F-WWYH | | |
| ☐ HL7587 | Airbus A330-323X | 368 | ex F-WWKF | | |
| ☐ HL7701 | Airbus A330-323 | 425 | ex F-WWYE | | |
| ☐ HL7702 | Airbus A330-323 | 428 | ex F-WWYF | | |
| ☐ HL7709 | Airbus A330-323 | 484 | ex F-WWKD | | |
| ☐ HL7710 | Airbus A330-323 | 490 | ex F-WWKF | | |
| ☐ HL7720 | Airbus A330-323 | 550 | ex F-WWKP | | |
| ☐ HL7611 | Airbus A380-861 | 035 | ex (HL8226) | | |
| ☐ HL7612 | Airbus A380-861 | 039 | ex (HL-8226) | | |
| ☐ HL7613 | Airbus A380-861 | 059 | ex F-WWAY | | ◆ |
| ☐ HL7614 | Airbus A380-861 | 068 | ex F-WWSJ | | ◆ |
| ☐ HL7615 | Airbus A380-861 | 075 | ex F-WWSS | | ◆ |
| ☐ HL | Airbus A380-861 | 096 | ex F-WWAP | | o/o◆ |
| ☐ HL7557 | Boeing 737-86N | 28622/562 | ex N1786B | | |
| ☐ HL7559 | Boeing 737-86N | 28626/611 | | | |
| ☐ HL7560 | Boeing 737-8B5/W | 29981/622 | | | |
| ☐ HL7561 | Boeing 737-8B5/W | 29982/663 | | | |
| ☐ HL7562 | Boeing 737-8B5 | 29983/678 | | | |
| ☐ HL7565 | Boeing 737-8B5/W | 29984/848 | | | |
| ☐ HL7566 | Boeing 737-8B5/W | 29985/852 | | | |
| ☐ HL7567 | Boeing 737-86N | 28647/878 | | | |
| ☐ HL7568 | Boeing 737-8B5/W | 29986/891 | | | |
| ☐ HL7757 | Boeing 737-8GQ/W | 35790/2119 | | | |
| ☐ HL7758 | Boeing 737-8GQ/W | 35791/2150 | | | |
| ☐ HL7785 | Boeing 737-8Q8/W | 37162/2906 | ex N1795B | | |
| ☐ HL7786 | Boeing 737-8Q8/W | 37163/2955 | ex N1786B | | |
| ☐ HL8224 | Boeing 737-8Q8/W | 38822/3704 | | | ◆ |
| ☐ HL8225 | Boeing 737-8Q8/W | 38823/3818 | | | ◆ |
| ☐ HL8240 | Boeing 737-8BK/W | 39447/3794 | | | ◆ |
| ☐ HL8241 | Boeing 737-8BK/W | 38129/3852 | | | ◆ |
| ☐ HL8242 | Boeing 737-8Q8/W | 38824/3895 | | | ◆ |
| ☐ HL8243 | Boeing 737-8Q8/W | 38825/3927 | | | ◆ |
| ☐ HL8244 | Boeing 737-8Q8/W | 38826/3943 | | | ◆ |
| ☐ HL8245 | Boeing 737-8Q8/W | 38827/3980 | | | ◆ |
| ☐ HL8246 | Boeing 737-8HL/W | 41299 | | | o/o◆ |
| ☐ HL | Boeing 737-8 | 41300 | | | o/o◆ |

| | | | |
|---|---|---|---|
| ☐ HL7569 | Boeing 737-9B5 | 29987/999 | ex B-5110 |
| ☐ HL7599 | Boeing 737-9B5 | 29988/1026 | ex N1795B |
| ☐ HL7704 | Boeing 737-9B5 | 29989/1082 | ex N1786B |
| ☐ HL7705 | Boeing 737-9B5 | 29990/1162 | |
| ☐ HL7706 | Boeing 737-9B5 | 29991/1188 | |
| ☐ HL7707 | Boeing 737-9B5 | 29992/1190 | |
| ☐ HL7708 | Boeing 737-9B5 | 29993/1208 | ex N60659 |
| ☐ HL7716 | Boeing 737-9B5 | 29994/1320 | |
| ☐ HL7717 | Boeing 737-9B5 | 29995/1332 | |
| ☐ HL7718 | Boeing 737-9B5 | 29996/1338 | |
| ☐ HL7719 | Boeing 737-9B5 | 29997/1416 | |
| ☐ HL7724 | Boeing 737-9B5 | 29998/1494 | |
| ☐ HL7725 | Boeing 737-9B5 | 29999/1512 | |
| ☐ HL7726 | Boeing 737-9B5 | 30001/1729 | ex N1786B |
| ☐ HL7727 | Boeing 737-9B5 | 30000/1536 | ex N6066U |
| ☐ HL7728 | Boeing 737-9B5 | 30002/1620 | |
| ☐ HL8221 | Boeing 737-9B5 | 37633/3645 | ex N1786B |
| ☐ HL8223 | Boeing 737-9B5 | 37634/3681 | |
| | | | |
| ☐ HL7400 | Boeing 747-4B5F | 26414/1295 | |
| ☐ HL7402 | Boeing 747-4B5 | 26407/1155 | ex N6038E |
| ☐ HL7403 | Boeing 747-4B5F | 26408/1163 | ex N60659 |
| ☐ HL7404 | Boeing 747-4B5 | 26409/1170 | ex N6009F |
| ☐ HL7434 | Boeing 747-4B5F | 32809/1316 | |
| ☐ HL7437 | Boeing 747-4B5F | 32808/1323 | |
| ☐ HL7438 | Boeing 747-4B5ERF | 33515/1329 | ex N6005X |
| ☐ HL7439 | Boeing 747-4B5ERF | 33516/1338 | |
| ☐ HL7448 | Boeing 747-4B5F | 26416/1246 | |
| ☐ HL7449 | Boeing 747-4B5F | 26411/1248 | |
| ☐ HL7460 | Boeing 747-4B5 | 26404/1107 | |
| ☐ HL7461 | Boeing 747-4B5 | 26405/1118 | |
| ☐ HL7462 | Boeing 747-4B5F | 26406/1123 | |
| ☐ HL7465 | Boeing 747-4B5 | 26412/1284 | |
| ☐ HL7466 | Boeing 747-4B5F | 26413/1286 | |
| ☐ HL7467 | Boeing 747-4B5F | 27073/1291 | |
| ☐ HL7472 | Boeing 747-4B5 | 26403/1095 | |
| ☐ HL7473 | Boeing 747-4B5 | 28335/1098 | |
| ☐ HL7482 | Boeing 747-4B5BCF | 25205/853 | |
| ☐ HL7483 | Boeing 747-4B5BCF | 25275/874 | |
| ☐ HL7484 | Boeing 747-4B5 | 26392/893 | |
| ☐ HL7485 | Boeing 747-4B5 | 26395/922 | |
| ☐ HL7486 | Boeing 747-4B5 | 26396/951 | |
| ☐ HL7487 | Boeing 747-4B5 | 26393/958 | |
| ☐ HL7488 | Boeing 747-4B5 | 26394/986 | |
| ☐ HL7489 | Boeing 747-4B5 | 27072/1013 | |
| ☐ HL7490 | Boeing 747-4B5 | 27177/1019 | |
| ☐ HL7491 | Boeing 747-4B5 | 27341/1037 | |
| ☐ HL7492 | Boeing 747-4B5 | 26397/1055 | |
| ☐ HL7493 | Boeing 747-4B5 | 26398/1057 | |
| ☐ HL7494 | Boeing 747-4B5 | 27662/1067 | |
| ☐ HL7495 | Boeing 747-4B5 | 28096/1073 | |
| ☐ HL7498 | Boeing 747-4B5 | 26402/1092 | |
| ☐ HL7499 | Boeing 747-4B5ERF | 33517/1340 | |
| ☐ HL7600 | Boeing 747-4B5ERF | 33945/1347 | |
| ☐ HL7601 | Boeing 747-4B5ERF | 33946/1350 | |
| ☐ HL7602 | Boeing 747-4B5ERF | 34301/1365 | |
| ☐ HL7603 | Boeing 747-4B5ERF | 34302/1368 | |
| ☐ HL7605 | Boeing 747-4B5ERF | 35526/1375 | |
| ☐ HL7606 | Boeing 747-4B5BCF | 24199/739 | ex VT-EVJ |
| ☐ HL7608 | Boeing 747-4B5BCF | 24621/830 | ex VT-AID |
| | | | |
| ☐ HL7526 | Boeing 777-2B5ER | 27947/148 | ex N50217 |
| ☐ HL7530 | Boeing 777-2B5ER | 27945/59 | |
| ☐ HL7531 | Boeing 777-2B5ER | 27946/62 | |
| ☐ HL7574 | Boeing 777-2B5ER | 28444/305 | |
| ☐ HL7575 | Boeing 777-2B5ER | 28445/309 | |
| ☐ HL7598 | Boeing 777-2B5ER | 27949/356 | |
| ☐ HL7714 | Boeing 777-2B5ER | 27951/411 | |
| ☐ HL7715 | Boeing 777-2B5ER | 28372/416 | |
| ☐ HL7721 | Boeing 777-2B5ER | 33727/452 | |
| ☐ HL7733 | Boeing 777-2B5ER | 34206/520 | ex N5023Q |
| ☐ HL7734 | Boeing 777-2B5ER | 34207/528 | |
| ☐ HL7743 | Boeing 777-2B5ER | 34208/584 | |
| ☐ HL7750 | Boeing 777-2B5ER | 34209/633 | |
| ☐ HL7751 | Boeing 777-2B5ER | 34210/657 | ex N6018N |
| ☐ HL7752 | Boeing 777-2B5ER | 34211/682 | |
| ☐ HL7764 | Boeing 777-2B5ER | 34214/684 | ex N50281 |
| ☐ HL7765 | Boeing 777-2B5ER | 34212/711 | |
| ☐ HL7766 | Boeing 777-2B5ER | 34213/730 | |
| | | | |
| ☐ HL7532 | Boeing 777-3B5 | 28371/162 | |
| ☐ HL7533 | Boeing 777-3B5 | 27948/178 | |

| □ HL7534 | Boeing 777-3B5 | 27950/120 | ex N5020K | |
|---|---|---|---|---|
| □ HL7573 | Boeing 777-3B5 | 27952/288 | | |
| □ HL7782 | Boeing 777-3B5ER | 37643/785 | | |
| □ HL7783 | Boeing 777-3B5ER | 37644/806 | ex N5020K | |
| □ HL7784 | Boeing 777-3B5ER | 37136/823 | | |
| □ HL8208 | Boeing 777-3B5ER | 37645/867 | | |
| □ HL8209 | Boeing 777-3B5ER | 37646/875 | | |
| □ HL8210 | Boeing 777-3B5ER | 40377/882 | ex N5016R | |
| □ HL8216 | Boeing 777-3B5ER | 37647/933 | | ♦ |
| □ HL8217 | Boeing 777-3B5ER | 37648/938 | | ♦ |
| □ HL8218 | Boeing 777-3B5ER | 37649/976 | | ♦ |
| | | | | |
| □ HL7609 | Boeing 747-8HTF | 37132/1425 | | o/o |
| □ HL7610 | Boeing 747-8HTF | 37133/1426 | | o/o♦ |
| □ HL8250 | Boeing 777-F85 | 37650 | | ♦ |
| □ HL8251 | Boeing 777-F85 | 37639/989 | | o/o♦ |
| □ HL8252 | Boeing 777-F85 | 37638 | | |

### KOREAN AIR EXPRESS

| □ HL5231 | Beech 1900D | UE-317 | ex N713UE | ♦ |
|---|---|---|---|---|
| □ HL5238 | Beech 1900D | UE-222 | ex N789BL | ♦ |

### T WAY AIR (TW/TWB)

| □ HL8232 | Boeing 737-8K5/W | 27979/44 | ex D-AHFE | ♦ |
|---|---|---|---|---|
| □ HL8235 | Boeing 737-8KG/W | 39448/3362 | | ♦ |
| □ HL8237 | Boeing 737-8Q8/W | 30654/1295 | ex N651LF | ♦ |
| □ HL8253 | Boeing 737-86J/W | 28069/42 | ex N962AG | ♦ |

## HP-    PANAMA (Republic of Panama)

### AEROPERLAS — Aeroperlas (WL/APP) — Panama City-Albrook (BLB)

| □ HP-004APP | ATR 42-300 | 0004 | ex TG-IAX | wfs |
|---|---|---|---|---|
| □ HP-1251APP | Short SD.3-60 | SH3610 | ex N715NC | wfs |
| □ HP-1319APP | Short SD.3-60 | SH3607 | ex N361MQ | wfs |
| □ HP-1320APP | Cessna 208B Caravan I | 208B.... | | ♦ |
| □ HP-1445APP | Canadair CL-66B Cosmopolitan | CL66B-7 | ex N4FY | |
| □ HP-1679APP | ATR 42-300 | 0120 | ex HR-IAY | wfs |
| Status uncertain | | | | |

### AIR PANAMA — Turismo Aereo (PST) — Panama City-Albrook (BLB)

| □ HP-639PS | Britten-Norman BN-2A-8 Islander | 60 | ex HP-639KN | |
|---|---|---|---|---|
| □ HP-1153PS | Britten-Norman BN-2A-26 Islander | 672 | ex HP-1153XI | |
| □ HP-1345PS | Cessna 208B Caravan I | 208B0380 | ex HP-1354AR | |
| □ HP-1494PS | Britten-Norman BN-2A-3 Islander | 673 | ex CN-TCC | |
| □ HP-1507PS | de Havilland DHC-6 Twin Otter 300 | 532 | ex C-GQKZ | |
| □ HP-1509PS | de Havilland DHC-6 Twin Otter 300 | 360 | ex HP-1509APP | |
| □ HP-1542PST | Fokker F.27 Friendship 500F | 10560 | ex HP-1542PS | |
| □ HP-1604PST | Fokker F.27 Friendship 500F | 10471 | ex N716FE | |
| □ HP-1605PST | Fokker 50 | 20178 | ex LN-RND | ♦ |
| □ HP-1606PST | Fokker 50 | 20179 | ex LN-RNE | |
| □ HP-1631PST | Fokker F.27 Friendship 500 | 10658 | ex N725FE | |
| □ HP-1670PST | SAAB SF.340B | 340B-299 | ex N299CJ | |
| □ HP-1671PST | SAAB SF.340B | 340B-294 | ex N294CJ | |
| □ HP-1731PST | Fokker 70 | 11521 | ex N322K | ♦ |
| □ HP-1732PST | Fokker 70 | 11545 | ex N324K | ♦ |
| □ HP-1763PST | Fokker 100 | 11315 | ex PH-DIM | o/o♦ |
| □ HP- | Britten-Norman BN-2A-8 Islander | 626 | ex N9149D | ♦ |
| □ HP- | Fokker 100 | 11364 | ex F-GIOG | o/o♦ |

### COPA AIRLINES — Copa (CM/CMP) — Panama City-Tocumen Intl (PTY)

| □ HP-1369CMP | Boeing 737-71Q/W | 29047/235 | ex N8251R | 669 | |
|---|---|---|---|---|---|
| □ HP-1370CMP | Boeing 737-71Q/W | 29048/288 | ex N82521 | 670 | |
| □ HP-1371CMP | Boeing 737-7V3/W | 30049/388 | ex N1787B | 671 | >RPB |
| □ HP-1372CMP | Boeing 737-7V3/W | 28607/399 | | 672 | >RPB |
| □ HP-1373CMP | Boeing 737-7V3/W | 30458/459 | | 673 | |
| □ HP-1374CMP | Boeing 737-7V3/W | 30459/494 | ex N1787B | 674 | |
| □ HP-1375CMP | Boeing 737-7V3/W | 30460/558 | ex N1787B | 675 | |
| □ HP-1376CMP | Boeing 737-7V3/W | 30497/574 | | 676 | |
| □ HP-1377CMP | Boeing 737-7V3/W | 30462/1161 | | 677 | |
| □ HP-1378CMP | Boeing 737-7V3/W | 30461/1173 | | 678 | |
| □ HP-1379CMP | Boeing 737-7V3/W | 30463/1221 | | 679 | |
| □ HP-1380CMP | Boeing 737-7V3/W | 30464/1241 | | 680 | |
| □ HP-1520CMP | Boeing 737-7V3/W | 33707/1376 | | 681 | |
| □ HP-1521CMP | Boeing 737-7V3/W | 33708/1379 | | 682 | |
| □ HP-1524CMP | Boeing 737-7V3/W | 33705/1505 | | 683 | |

| | | | | | |
|---|---|---|---|---|---|
| ☐ HP-1525CMP | Boeing 737-7V3/W | 33706/1518 | | 684 | |
| ☐ HP-1527CMP | Boeing 737-7V3/W | 30676/1619 | | 685 | |
| ☐ HP-1528CMP | Boeing 737-7V3/W | 29360/1644 | | 686 | |
| ☐ HP-1530CMP | Boeing 737-7V3/W | 34535/1962 | | 687 | |
| ☐ HP-1531CMP | Boeing 737-7V3/W | 34536/1995 | | 688 | |
| | | | | | |
| ☐ HP-1522CMP | Boeing 737-8V3/W | 33709/1387 | | 480 | |
| ☐ HP-1523CMP | Boeing 737-8V3/W | 33710/1397 | | 481 | |
| ☐ HP-1526CMP | Boeing 737-8V3/W | 34006/1585 | ex N1782B | 482 | |
| ☐ HP-1529CMP | Boeing 737-8V3/W | 29670/1711 | | 483 | |
| ☐ HP-1532CMP | Boeing 737-8V3/W | 35068/2343 | | 484 | |
| ☐ HP-1533CMP | Boeing 737-8V3/W | 35067/2423 | | 485 | |
| ☐ HP-1534CMP | Boeing 737-8V3/W | 35125/2624 | | 486 | |
| ☐ HP-1535CMP | Boeing 737-8V3/W | 35126/2805 | ex N1786B | 487 | |
| ☐ HP-1536CMP | Boeing 737-8V3/W | 35127/2963 | | 488 | |
| ☐ HP-1537CMP | Boeing 737-8V3/W | 36550/3114 | | 489 | |
| ☐ HP-1538CMP | Boeing 737-8V3/W | 36554/3130 | | 490 | |
| ☐ HP-1539CMP | Boeing 737-8V3/W | 29667/3151 | ex N1786B | 491 | |
| ☐ HP-1711CMP | Boeing 737-8V3/W | 40663/3265 | | 492 | |
| ☐ HP-1712CMP | Boeing 737-8V3/W | 40664/3267 | ex N1796B | 493 | |
| ☐ HP-1713CMP | Boeing 737-8V3/W | 40890/3455 | | 494 | |
| ☐ HP-1714CMP | Boeing 737-8V3/W | 40891/3476 | | 495 | |
| ☐ HP-1715CMP | Boeing 737-8V3/W | 40361/3500 | | 496 | |
| ☐ HP-1716CMP | Boeing 737-8V3/W | 40666/3567 | | 497 | ♦ |
| ☐ HP-1717CMP | Boeing 737-8V3/W | 40665/3595 | | 498 | ♦ |
| ☐ HP-1718CMP | Boeing 737-8V3/W | 38139/3611 | | 499 | ♦ |
| ☐ HP-1719CMP | Boeing 737-8V3/W | 37957/3695 | | 550 | ♦ |
| ☐ HP-1720CMP | Boeing 737-8V3/W | 37958/3739 | | 551 | ♦ |
| ☐ HP-1721CMP | Boeing 737-8V3/W | 40362/3791 | | 552 | ♦ |
| ☐ HP-1722CMP | Boeing 737-8V3/W | 38100/3761 | | 533 | ♦ |
| ☐ HP-1723CMP | Boeing 737-8V3/W | 37959/3781 | | 554 | ♦ |
| ☐ HP-1724CMP | Boeing 737-8V3/W | 38140/3810 | | 555 | ♦ |
| ☐ HP-1725CMP | Boeing 737-8V3/W | 38102/3839 | ex N1787B | 556 | ♦ |
| ☐ HP-1726CMP | Boeing 737-86N/W | 38024/3919 | | | ♦ |
| ☐ HP-1727CMP | Boeing 737-8V3/W | 40778/3956 | | | ♦ |
| ☐ HP-1728CMP | Boeing 737-86N/W | 39396/3871 | | | ♦ |
| ☐ HP-1729CMP | Boeing 737-86N/W | 41088/3977 | | | ♦ |
| ☐ HP-1730CMP | Boeing 737-8V3/W | 38141/3988 | | | |
| ☐ HP-1821CMP | Boeing 737-8V3/W | 41089 | | | o/o♦ |
| ☐ HP-1822CMP | Boeing 737-8V3/W | 40779 | | | o/o♦ |
| ☐ HP-1823CMP | Boeing 737-86N/W | 39398 | | | o/o♦ |
| ☐ HP-1824CMP | Boeing 737-86N/W | 39399 | | | o/o♦ |
| | | | | | |
| ☐ HP-1540CMP | Embraer ERJ-190AR | 19000012 | ex PT-STL | | |
| ☐ HP-1556CMP | Embraer ERJ-190AR | 19000016 | ex PT-STQ | | |
| ☐ HP-1557CMP | Embraer ERJ-190AR | 19000034 | ex PT-SGI | | |
| ☐ HP-1558CMP | Embraer ERJ-190AR | 19000038 | ex PT-SGN | | |
| ☐ HP-1559CMP | Embraer ERJ-190AR | 19000053 | ex PT-SIC | | |
| ☐ HP-1560CMP | Embraer ERJ-190AR | 19000056 | ex PT-SIF | | |
| ☐ HP-1561CMP | Embraer ERJ-190AR | 19000089 | ex PT-SNI | | |
| ☐ HP-1562CMP | Embraer ERJ-190AR | 19000095 | ex PT-SNP | | >RPB |
| ☐ HP-1563CMP | Embraer ERJ-190AR | 19000098 | ex PT-SNS | | >RPB |
| ☐ HP-1564CMP | Embraer ERJ-190AR | 19000100 | ex PT-SNU | | |
| ☐ HP-1565CMP | Embraer ERJ-190AR | 19000126 | ex PT-SQV | | >RPB |
| ☐ HP-1566CMP | Embraer ERJ-190AR | 19000165 | ex PT-SAX | | |
| ☐ HP-1567CMP | Embraer ERJ-190AR | 19000174 | ex PT-SDJ | | |
| ☐ HP-1568CMP | Embraer ERJ-190AR | 19000212 | ex PT-SGV | | |
| ☐ HP-1569CMP | Embraer ERJ-190AR | 19000222 | ex PT-SHG | | |

| **DHL AERO EXPRESSO** | | **Yellow (D5/DAE)** | | **Panama City-Tocumen Intl (PTY)** |
|---|---|---|---|---|
| ☐ HP-1610DAE | Boeing 727-264F (FedEx 3) | 20780/986 | ex N625DH | |
| ☐ HP-1810DAE | Boeing 757-27APCF | 29611/910 | ex N646AL | |
| ☐ HP-1910DAE | Boeing 757-27APCF | 29607/832 | ex N644AL | |
| ☐ HP-2010DAE | Boeing 757-27APCF | 29610/904 | ex N645AL | |

| **PANAIR CARGO** | | | | **Panama City-Tocumen Intl (PTY)** |
|---|---|---|---|---|
| ☐ HP-1653CTW | Boeing 727-277F (FedEx 3) | 21695/1481 | ex N982JM | |

## HR-    HONDURAS (Republic of Honduras)

| **AEROLINEAS SOSA** | | **Sosa (P4/VSO)** | | **La Ceiba (LCE)** |
|---|---|---|---|---|
| ☐ HR-AIH | Britten-Norman BN-2A-21 Islander | 513 | ex C-GVZY | |
| ☐ HR-ARE | LET L-410UVP | 841312 | ex S9-TBL | |
| ☐ HR-ARJ | Nord 262A-14 | 15 | ex N417SA | [LCE] |
| ☐ HR-ARP | Nord 262A-27 | 33 | ex N274A | wfs |
| ☐ HR-ARU | Nord 262A-21 | 21 | ex TG-ANP | [LCE] |
| ☐ HR-ASI | LET L-410UVP-E3 | 871925 | ex N888LT | |

| | | | | |
|---|---|---|---|---|
| ☐ HR-ASR | Fairchild F-27F | 84 | ex 3C-QQA | |
| ☐ HR-ASZ | LET L-410UVP | 851530 | ex HR-AQO | |
| ☐ HR-ATA | British Aerospace Jetstream 31 | 725 | ex N833JS | |
| ☐ HR-ATB | British Aerospace Jetstream 31 | 726 | ex N834JS | |
| ☐ HR-ATE | British Aerospace Jetstream 31 | 757 | ex N843JS | |
| ☐ HR-AUE | LET L-410UVP-E3 | 882029 | ex TG-TAY | |
| ☐ HR-AWW | Canadair CRJ-100ER | 7037 | ex N931CA | ♦ |
| ☐ HR-AXJ | British Aerospace Jetstream 32 | 896 | ex C-GQJV | ♦ |
| ☐ N366PX | SAAB SF.340B | 340B-267 | | ♦ |

### ATLANTIC AIRLINES — Atlantic Honduras (ZF/HHA) — La Ceiba (LCE)

| | | | | |
|---|---|---|---|---|
| ☐ HR-ASD | LET L-410UVP-E3 | 882034 | ex YS-15C | |
| ☐ HR-ASH | LET L-410UVP-E | 861716 | ex YS-13C? | |
| ☐ HR-ASJ | LET L-410UVP-E | 861724 | ex YS-12C | |
| ☐ HR-ASM | LET L-410UVP-E | 861711 | ex YS-05C | |
| ☐ HR-ASN | LET L-410UVP-E | 861701 | ex YS-06C | |
| ☐ HR-ASW | LET L-410UVP-E3 | 871910 | ex CU-T1193 | |
| ☐ HR-ASX | LET L-410UVP-E3 | 871915 | ex CU-T1194 | |
| ☐ HR-AWA | LET L-410UVP-E3 | 882025 | ex HI-681CT | ♦ |
| | | | | |
| ☐ HR-ATC | Hawker Siddeley HS.748 Srs 2B/424 | 1801 | ex C-GBCS | |
| ☐ HR-ATI | Fairchild F-27F | 95 | ex N19FF | |
| ☐ HR-ATL | Fokker F.27 Friendship 500F | 10522 | ex N283EA | |
| Ceased ops Jan09 | | | | |

### CM AIRLINES

| | | | | |
|---|---|---|---|---|
| ☐ HR-AXC | LET L-410UVP-20 | | | ♦ |

### ISLENA AIRLINES — (WC/ISV) — La Ceiba (LCE)

| | | | | |
|---|---|---|---|---|
| ☐ HR-ARY | ATR 42-300 | 0030 | ex N423MQ | ♦ |
| ☐ HR-AUX | ATR 42-320 (QC) | 0394 | ex 9A-CTU | |
| ☐ HR-AVA | ATR 42-320 | 0388 | ex F-WQNC | |
| ☐ HR-AXA | ATR 42-320 | 0337 | ex D-BZZV | ♦ |
| ☐ HR-AXH | ATR 42-320 | 0291 | ex D-BZZS | ♦ |
| ☐ HR- | ATR 42-320 | 0378 | ex N378NA | ♦ |
| | | | | |
| ☐ HR-IAP | Short SD.3-60 | SH3616 | ex N345MV | |
| ☐ HR-IAW | Short SD.3-60 | SH3669 | ex N361PA | |
| ☐ HR-IBD | Cessna 208B Caravan I | 208B.... | | ♦ |
| ☐ HR-IBE | de Havilland DHC-6 Twin Otter | | | ♦ |
| ☐ HR-IBH | Cessna 208B Caravan I | | | |

### LANHSA — La Ceiba (LCE)

| | | | | |
|---|---|---|---|---|
| ☐ HR-AWS | Cessna 402C | 402C0069 | ex N390TM | ♦ |
| ☐ HR-AXG | British Aerospace Jetstream 3112 | 791 | ex C-GNRG | ♦ |

### ROLLINS AIR — La Ceiba (LCE)

| | | | | |
|---|---|---|---|---|
| ☐ HR-ASC | Yakovlev Yak-40 | 9332029 | ex`RA-87321 | |
| ☐ HR-AVR | Boeing 737-232 | 23104/1062 | ex N332DL | |
| ☐ HR-AVU | Cessna U206G | U20605128 | ex N206CF | ♦ |
| ☐ HR-AWG | British Aerospace Jetstream 31 | 764 | ex C-FSEW | |
| ☐ HR-AWH | British Aerospace Jetstream 31 | 766 | ex C-GPDC | |
| ☐ HR-AWM | Lockheed L1011-500 Tristar | 193C-1229 | ex N163AT | [AQJ] |
| ☐ HR- | GAF N.22 Nomad | | | |

### SETCO — Tegucigalpa (TGU)

| | | | | |
|---|---|---|---|---|
| ☐ HR-AFB | Rockwell 500S Shrike Commander | 3268 | ex HR-315 | [TGU] |
| ☐ HR-AFC | Rockwell 500S Shrike Commander | 3271 | ex HR-317 | [TGU] |
| ☐ HR-AJY | Douglas DC-3 | 6068 | ex HP-685 | [TGU] |
| ☐ HR-AKM | Rockwell 500S Shrike Commander | 3098 | ex HR-CNA | |
| ☐ HR-ALU | Douglas DC-3 | | | [TGU] |
| ☐ HR-ATH | Douglas DC-3 | 6102 | ex HR-SAH no titles | |

## HS-    THAILAND (Kingdom of Thailand)

### BANGKOK AIRWAYS — Bangkok Air (PG/BKP) — Bangkok-Suvarnabhumi (BKK)

| | | | | |
|---|---|---|---|---|
| ☐ HS-PGN | Airbus A319-132 | 3759 | ex D-AVXD | Luang Prabang |
| ☐ HS-PGT | Airbus A319-132 | 3421 | ex D-AVYM | Sukhothai |
| ☐ HS-PGX | Airbus A319-132 | 3424 | ex D-AVYO | Hirsoshima |
| ☐ HS-PGY | Airbus A319-132 | 3454 | ex D-AVWH | Angkor Wat |
| ☐ HS-PGZ | Airbus A319-132 | 3694 | ex D-AVWH | Phnom Penh |

| | | | | | |
|---|---|---|---|---|---|
| ☐ HS-PPA | Airbus A319-132 | 3911 | ex D-AVYN | Si Satchanali | |
| ☐ HS-PPB | Airbus A319-132 | 2648 | ex N648BV | Bangkok | ♦ |
| ☐ HS-PPC | Airbus A319-132 | 2660 | ex N660BV | Chiang Mai | ♦ |
| | | | | | |
| ☐ HS-PGA | ATR 72-212A | 0710 | ex F-WWEJ | Kut | wfs |
| ☐ HS-PGB | ATR 72-212A | 0708 | ex F-WWEH | Phuket | |
| ☐ HS-PGC | ATR 72-212A | 0715 | ex F-WWEO | Nangyuan | |
| ☐ HS-PGD | ATR 72-212A | 0833 | ex F-WWEZ | | |
| ☐ HS-PGF | ATR 72-212A | 0700 | ex F-WWEW | Hua Hin | |
| ☐ HS-PGG | ATR 72-212A | 0692 | ex F-WWEO | Chang | |
| ☐ HS-PGK | ATR 72-212A | 0680 | ex F-WWEV | Apsara | |
| ☐ HS-PGM | ATR 72-212A | 0704 | ex F-WWEC | Tao | |
| ☐ HS- | ATR 72-600 | | ex | | o/o |
| ☐ HS- | ATR 72-600 | | ex | | o/o |
| | | | | | |
| ☐ HS-PGU | Airbus A320-232 | 2254 | ex F-WWDC | Guilin | |
| ☐ HS-PGV | Airbus A320-232 | 2310 | ex F-WWDS | Krabi | |
| ☐ HS-PGW | Airbus A320-232 | 2509 | ex F-WWIQ | Samui | |

## BUSINESS AIR (BCC) Bangkok-Suvarnabhumi (BKK)

| | | | | | |
|---|---|---|---|---|---|
| ☐ HS-BIB | Boeing 767-341ER | 24753/291 | ex N753SJ | | |
| ☐ HS-BIC | Boeing 767-341ER | 24752/289 | ex N752SJ | Tevee 2 | |
| ☐ HS-BID | Boeing 767-383ER | 24848/325 | ex PH-AHY | | ♦ |
| ☐ HS-BIE | Boeing 767-383ER | 25088/359 | ex 5R-MFG | | ♦ |

## DESTINATION AIR Phuket (HKT)

| | | | | | |
|---|---|---|---|---|---|
| ☐ HS-DAB | Cessna 206H Stationair 6 | 20608046 | ex N2312V | | FP |

## HAPPY AIR (HPY) Phuket (HKT)

| | | | | |
|---|---|---|---|---|
| ☐ HS-HPA | SAAB SF.340B | 340A-255 | ex N255AJ | |

## JET ASIA AIRWAYS

| | | | | | |
|---|---|---|---|---|---|
| ☐ HS-JAB | Boeing 767-222ER | 21868/10 | ex HS-BIA | | ♦ |
| ☐ HS-JAC | Boeing 767-222EM | 21871/15 | ex HS-SSA | | [SEL]♦ |
| ☐ HS-JAD | Boeing 767-246 | 23214/122 | ex N738DA | | [RKT]♦ |
| ☐ HS-JAG | Boeing 767-222em | 21872/20 | ex HS-SSB | | [SEL]♦ |

## K-MILE AIR (8K/KMI) Bangkok-Suvarnabhumi (BKK)

| | | | | | |
|---|---|---|---|---|---|
| ☐ HS-SCH | Boeing 727-247F (FedEx 3) | 21700/1489 | ex 9M-TGJ | | <TSE |
| ☐ HS-SCJ | Boeing 727-247F (FedEx 3) | 21392/1305 | ex 9M-TGK | | <TSE |
| ☐ HS-SCK | Boeing 727-2J4F (FedEx 3) | 22080/1598 | ex VH-DHE | | ♦ |

## NOK AIR Nok Air (DD/NOK) Bangkok Don Muang (BMK)

| | | | | | |
|---|---|---|---|---|---|
| ☐ HS-DDL | Boeing 737-4Y0 | 24917/2071 | ex TC-JDF | | |
| ☐ HS-DDM | Boeing 737-4Y0 | 26065/2284 | ex TC-JDY | | |
| ☐ HS-DDO | Boeing 737-4Y0 | 26081/2442 | ex UR-GAR | | |
| ☐ HS-DDP | Boeing 737-406 | 25355/2132 | ex PH-BDZ | | |
| ☐ HS-DDQ | Boeing 737-4M0 | 29204/3051 | ex PK-GZI | | |
| ☐ HS-TDA | Boeing 737-4D7 | 24830/1899 | | Songkhla | |
| ☐ HS-TDB | Boeing 737-4D7 | 24831/1922 | | Phuket | |
| ☐ HS-TDE | Boeing 737-4D7 | 26612/2330 | | Surin | |
| ☐ HS-TDF | Boeing 737-4D7 | 26613/2338 | | | ♦ |
| | | | | | |
| ☐ HS-DBA | Boeing 737-8AS | 33813/1617 | ex N840AC | Nok Yim Wan | ♦ |
| ☐ HS-DBB | Boeing 737-8AS | 33814/1618 | ex N845AC | Nok Rak Yim | ♦ |
| ☐ HS-DBC | Boeing 737-85P | 28386/426 | ex EC-HGQ | Nok Om Yim | ♦ |
| ☐ HS-TRA | ATR72-201 | 0164 | | | ♦ |
| ☐ HS-TRB | ATR72-201 | 0167 | | | ♦ |

## NOK MINI

| | | | | | |
|---|---|---|---|---|---|
| ☐ HS-GBC | SAAB SF340B | 340B-422 | ex N422XJ | | ♦ |
| ☐ HS-GBD | SAAB SF340B | 340B-423 | ex N423XJ | | ♦ |
| ☐ HS-GBE | SAAB SF.340B | 340B-426 | ex N426XJ | | ♦ |
| ☐ HS- | SAAB SF.340B | 340B-435 | ex N435XJ | | o/o♦ |
| ☐ HS- | SAAB SF.340B | 340B-449 | ex N449XJ | | o/o♦ |

## KAN AIR

| | | | | | |
|---|---|---|---|---|---|
| ☐ HS-KAB | Cessna 208B Caravan I | 208B2222 | ex N6034P | | ♦ |

## ORIENT THAI AIRLINES — Orient Express (OX/OEA) — Bangkok-Suvarnabhumi (BKK)

| | | | | |
|---|---|---|---|---|
| ☐ HS-MDI | McDonnell-Douglas MD-81 | 53298/2045 | ex N822TH | ♦ |
| ☐ HS-MDJ | McDonnell-Douglas MD-81 | 53297/2040 | ex N821TH | ♦ |
| ☐ HS-MDK | McDonnell-Douglas MD-82 | 49113/1069 | ex 9A-CDD | ♦ |
| ☐ HS-MDL | McDonnell-Douglas MD-82 | 49853/1981 | ex N853JF | ♦ |
| ☐ HS-OMD | McDonnell-Douglas MD-82 | 49485/1316 | ex N72825 | [DMK]♦ |
| ☐ HS-OME | McDonnell-Douglas MD-82 | 49182/1128 | ex N911TW | |
| ☐ HS-OMI | McDonnell-Douglas MD-87 | 49464/1476 | ex JA8278 | [DMK]♦ |
| ☐ HS-OMJ | McDonnell-Douglas MD-87 | 49465/1604 | ex JA8279 | [DMK]♦ |
| ☐ HS- | McDonnell-Douglas MD-82 | 49112/1068 | ex 9A-CDC | [TNN]♦ |
| | | | | |
| ☐ HS-BKA | Boeing 767-3W0ER | 28148/620 | ex B-2568 | ♦ |
| ☐ HS-BKB | Boeing 767-346 | 23961/192 | ex JA8265 | ♦ |
| ☐ HS-BRA | Boeing 737-324/W | 23374/1204 | ex N10323 | ♦ |
| ☐ HS-BRB | Boeing 737-3T0/W | 23375/1207 | ex N14324 | ♦ |
| ☐ HS-BRC | Boeing 737-3T0/W | 23371/1191 | ex N14320 | ♦ |
| ☐ HS-STA | Boeing 747-422 | 26876/939 | ex N187UA | >SVA♦ |
| ☐ HS-STC | Boeing 747-412 | 26548/923 | ex N584MD | |
| ☐ HS-UTN | Boeing 747-346 | 23149/599 | ex JA8136 | ♦ |
| ☐ HS-UTV | Boeing 747-346 | 23151/607 | ex JA8166 | |
| ☐ HS-UTW | Boeing 747-346 | 23067/588 | ex JA812J | |

## PC AIR

| | | | | | |
|---|---|---|---|---|---|
| ☐ HS-PCC | Airbus A310-222 | 419 | ex XY-AGD | Klamkomol | ♦ |

## PHUKET AIRLINES — (9R/VAP) — Phuket (HKT)

| | | | | |
|---|---|---|---|---|
| ☐ HS-AVA | Boeing 747-446 | 25212/871 | ex N151AS | wfs♦ |
| ☐ HS-VAC | Boeing 747-306 | 23056/587 | ex (HS-TSA) | [CAI] |
| ☐ HS-VAN | Boeing 747-312 | 23245/626 | ex (HS-TSB) | wfs |
| ☐ HS-VAO | Boeing 747-2U3 | 22246/452 | ex PK-GSA | [JKT]♦ |

## SGA AIRLINES (SIAM GENERAL AVIATION) — (5E) — Bangkok-Suvarnabhumi (BKK)

| | | | |
|---|---|---|---|
| ☐ HS-SKR | Cessna 208B Caravan I | 208B1241 | ex N208AE |

## SOLAR AVIATION — (SRB)

| | | | | |
|---|---|---|---|---|
| ☐ HS-SAA | Dornier 228-200 | 8019 | ex RP-C2814 | ♦ |
| ☐ HS-SAB | Dornier 228-200 | 8007 | ex D-ISIS | ♦ |
| ☐ HS-SAC | SAAB SF.340A | 340A-115 | ex HS-HPY | ♦ |

## SUNNY AIRWAYS — (SUW)

| | | | | | |
|---|---|---|---|---|---|
| ☐ HS-KOA | Boeing 767-269ER | 23280/131 | ex N251MY | Suriya | ♦ |

## THAI AIRASIA — (FD/AIQ) — Bangkok-Suvarnabhumi (BKK)

| | | | | |
|---|---|---|---|---|
| ☐ HS-ABA | Airbus A320-216 | 3277 | ex F-WWDH | |
| ☐ HS-ABB | Airbus A320-216 | 3299 | ex F-WWDZ | |
| ☐ HS-ABC | Airbus A320-216 | 3338 | ex F-WWBM | |
| ☐ HS-ABD | Airbus A320-216 | 3394 | ex F-WWBQ | |
| ☐ HS-ABE | Airbus A320-216 | 3489 | ex F-WWIR | |
| ☐ HS-ABF | Airbus A320-216 | 3505 | ex F-WWBS | |
| ☐ HS-ABG | Airbus A320-216 | 3576 | ex F-WWBN | |
| ☐ HS-ABH | Airbus A320-216 | 3679 | ex F-WWBD | |
| ☐ HS-ABI | Airbus A320-216 | 3729 | ex F-WWDK | |
| ☐ HS-ABJ | Airbus A320-216 | 4019 | ex F-WWDF | |
| ☐ HS-ABK | Airbus A320-216 | 4088 | ex F-WWBV | |
| ☐ HS-ABL | Airbus A320-216 | 4126 | ex F-WWIO | |
| ☐ HS-ABM | Airbus A320-216 | 4278 | ex F-WWID | |
| ☐ HS-ABN | Airbus A320-216 | 4302 | ex F-WWDM | |
| ☐ HS-ABO | Airbus A320-216 | 4333 | ex F-WWIM | |
| ☐ HS-ABP | Airbus A320-216 | 4367 | ex F-WWDR | |
| ☐ HS-ABQ | Airbus A320-216 | 4386 | ex F-WWDE | |
| ☐ HS-ABR | Airbus A320-216 | 4390 | ex F-WWDK | |
| ☐ HS-ABS | Airbus A320-216 | 4426 | ex F-WWBP | |
| ☐ HS-ABT | Airbus A320-216 | 4557 | ex F-WWDT | |
| ☐ HS-ABU | Airbus A320-216 | 4807 | ex F-WWBM | |
| ☐ HS-ABV | Airbus A320-216 | 4979 | ex D-AVVM | ♦ |
| ☐ HS-ABW | Airbus A320-216 | 4980 | ex F-WWIZ | ♦ |
| ☐ HS-ABX | Airbus A320-216 | 4917 | ex 9M-AQJ | ♦ |
| ☐ HS-ABY | Airbus A320-214 | 4964 | ex 9M-AQK | ♦ |

## THAI AIRWAYS INTERNATIONAL     Thai (TG/THA)     Bangkok-Suvarnabhumi (BKK)

Member of Star Alliance

| | | | | | | |
|---|---|---|---|---|---|---|
| ☐ HS-TAK | Airbus A300B4-622R | 566 | ex F-WWAB | Phaya Thai | | |
| ☐ HS-TAL | Airbus A300B4-622R | 569 | ex F-WWAD | Sri Trang | | |
| ☐ HS-TAM | Airbus A300B4-622R | 577 | ex F-WWAG | Chiang Mai | | |
| ☐ HS-TAN | Airbus A300B4-622R | 628 | ex F-WWAE | Chiang Rai | | |
| ☐ HS-TAO | Airbus A300B4-622R | 629 | ex F-WWAF | Chanthaburi | Star Alliance c/s | |
| ☐ HS-TAP | Airbus A300B4-622R | 635 | ex F-WWAP | Pathum Thani | | |
| ☐ HS-TAR | Airbus A300B4-622R | 681 | ex F-WWAB | Yasothon | | |
| ☐ HS-TAS | Airbus A300B4-622R | 705 | ex F-WWAT | Yala | | |
| ☐ HS-TAT | Airbus A300B4-622R | 782 | ex F-WWAY | Srimuang | | |
| ☐ HS-TAW | Airbus A300B4-622R | 784 | ex F-WWAL | Suranaree | | |
| ☐ HS-TAX | Airbus A300B4-622R | 785 | ex F-WWAO | Thepsatri | | |
| ☐ HS-TAY | Airbus A300B4-622R | 786 | ex F-WWAQ | Srisoonthorn | | |
| ☐ HS-TAZ | Airbus A300B4-622R | 787 | ex F-WWAB | Srisubhan | | |
| | | | | | | |
| ☐ HS-TBA | Airbus A330-343E | 1263 | ex F-WWYC | | | ♦ |
| ☐ HS-TBB | Airbus A330-343E | 1269 | ex F-WWKV | | | ♦ |
| ☐ HS-TBC | Airbus A330-343E | 1289 | ex F-WW | Kanchanaburi | | ♦ |
| ☐ HS-TEA | Airbus A330-321 | 050 | ex F-WWKI | Manorom | | |
| ☐ HS-TEB | Airbus A330-321 | 060 | ex F-WWKQ | Sri Sakhon | | |
| ☐ HS-TEC | Airbus A330-321 | 062 | ex F-WWKR | Bang Rachan | | |
| ☐ HS-TED | Airbus A330-321 | 064 | ex F-WWKS | Donchedi | | |
| ☐ HS-TEE | Airbus A330-321 | 065 | ex F-WWKT | Kusuman | | |
| ☐ HS-TEF | Airbus A330-321 | 066 | ex F-WWKJ | Song Dao | | |
| ☐ HS-TEG | Airbus A330-321 | 112 | ex F-WWKM | Lam Plai Mat | | |
| ☐ HS-TEH | Airbus A330-321 | 122 | ex F-WWKG | Sai Buri | | |
| ☐ HS-TEJ | Airbus A330-322 | 209 | ex F-WWKN | Sudawadi | | |
| ☐ HS-TEK | Airbus A330-322 | 224 | ex F-WWKD | Srichulalak | Royal Barge c/s | |
| ☐ HS-TEL | Airbus A330-322 | 231 | ex F-WWKU | Thepamart | Star Alliance c/s | |
| ☐ HS-TEM | Airbus A330-323X | 346 | ex F-WWYE | Jiraprabha | | |
| ☐ HS-TEN | Airbus A330-343E | 990 | ex F-WWKK | Suchada | | |
| ☐ HS-TEO | Airbus A330-343E | 1003 | ex F-WWKR | Chutamas | | |
| ☐ HS-TEP | Airbus A330-343E | 1035 | ex F-WWKS | Srianocha | | |
| ☐ HS-TEQ | Airbus A330-343E | 1037 | ex F-WWYA | Si Ayutthaya | [BOD] | |
| ☐ HS-TER | Airbus A330-343E | 1060 | ex F-WWYQ | U Thong | | |
| ☐ HS-TES | Airbus A330-343E | 1074 | ex F-WWKJ | | | |
| ☐ HS-TET | Airbus A330-343E | 1086 | ex F-WWYV | | | |
| ☐ HS-TEU | Airbus A330-343E | 1090 | ex F-WWYB | | | |
| | | | | | | |
| ☐ HS-TLA | Airbus A340-541 | 624 | ex F-WWTN | Chiang Kham | | |
| ☐ HS-TLB | Airbus A340-541 | 628 | ex F-WWTO | Uttaradit | | |
| ☐ HS-TLC | Airbus A340-541 | 698 | ex F-WWTR | Phitsanulok | | |
| ☐ HS-TLD | Airbus A340-541HGW | 775 | ex F-WWTX | | | |
| ☐ HS-TNA | Airbus A340-642 | 677 | ex F-WWCJ | Watthana Nakhon | | |
| ☐ HS-TNB | Airbus A340-642 | 681 | ex F-WWCK | Saraburi | | |
| ☐ HS-TNC | Airbus A340-642 | 689 | ex F-WWCN | Chon Buri | | |
| ☐ HS-TND | Airbus A340-642 | 710 | ex F-WWCX | Phetchaburi | | |
| ☐ HS-TNE | Airbus A340-642 | 719 | ex F-WWCH | | | |
| ☐ HS-TNF | Airbus A340-642 | 953 | ex F-WWCM | Mae Hong Son | | |
| | | | | | | |
| ☐ HS-TDD | Boeing 737-4D7 | 26611/2318 | | | | |
| ☐ HS-TDG | Boeing 737-4D7 | 26614/2481 | | Kalasin | | |
| ☐ HS-TDH | Boeing 737-4D7 | 28703/2962 | | Lopburi | | |
| ☐ HS-TDJ | Boeing 737-4D7 | 28704/2968 | | Nakhon Chaisi | | |
| ☐ HS-TDK | Boeing 737-4D7 | 28701/2977 | | Sri Surat | | |
| ☐ HS-TGA | Boeing 747-4D7 | 32369/1273 | | Srisuriyothai | | |
| ☐ HS-TGB | Boeing 747-4D7 | 32370/1278 | | Si Satchanalai | | |
| ☐ HS-TGF | Boeing 747-4D7 | 33770/1335 | | Sri Ubon | | |
| ☐ HS-TGG | Boeing 747-4D7 | 33771/1337 | | Pathoomawadi | | |
| ☐ HS-TGH | Boeing 747-4D7 | 24458/769 | | Chaiprakarn | | |
| ☐ HS-TGJ | Boeing 747-4D7BCF | 24459/777 | | Hariphunchai | | ♦ |
| ☐ HS-TGK | Boeing 747-4D7 | 24993/833 | | Alongkorn | | |
| ☐ HS-TGL | Boeing 747-4D7 | 25366/890 | | Theparat | | |
| ☐ HS-TGM | Boeing 747-4D7 | 27093/945 | | Chao Phraya | | |
| ☐ HS-TGN | Boeing 747-4D7 | 26615/950 | | Simongkhon | | |
| ☐ HS-TGO | Boeing 747-4D7 | 26609/1001 | | Bowonrangsi | | |
| ☐ HS-TGP | Boeing 747-4D7 | 26610/1047 | | Thepprasit | | |
| ☐ HS-TGR | Boeing 747-4D7 | 27723/1071 | | Siriwatthna | | |
| ☐ HS-TGT | Boeing 747-4D7 | 26616/1097 | | Watthanothai | | |
| ☐ HS-TGW | Boeing 747-4D7 | 27724/1111 | | Visuthakasatriya | | |
| ☐ HS-TGX | Boeing 747-4D7 | 27725/1134 | | Sirisobhakya | | |
| ☐ HS-TGY | Boeing 747-4D7 | 28705/1164 | ex N60697 | Dararasmi | | |
| ☐ HS-TGZ | Boeing 747-4D7 | 28706/1214 | | Phimara | | |
| | | | | | | |
| ☐ HS-TJA | Boeing 777-2D7 | 27726/25 | | Lamphun | | |
| ☐ HS-TJB | Boeing 777-2D7 | 27727/32 | | U Thaithani | | |
| ☐ HS-TJC | Boeing 777-2D7 | 27728/44 | | Nakhon Nayok | | |

| | | | | | | |
|---|---|---|---|---|---|---|
| ☐ HS-TJD | Boeing 777-2D7 | 27729/51 | | | Mukdahan | |
| ☐ HS-TJE | Boeing 777-2D7 | 27730/89 | | | Chaiyaphum | |
| ☐ HS-TJF | Boeing 777-2D7 | 27731/95 | | | Phanom Sarakham | |
| ☐ HS-TJG | Boeing 777-2D7 | 27732/100 | | | Pattani | |
| ☐ HS-TJH | Boeing 777-2D7 | 27733/113 | | | Suphan Buri | |
| ☐ HS-TJR | Boeing 777-2D7ER | 34586/588 | | | Nakhon Sawan | |
| ☐ HS-TJS | Boeing 777-2D7ER | 34587/595 | | | Phra Nakhon | |
| ☐ HS-TJT | Boeing 777-2D7ER | 34588/596 | | | Pathum Wan | |
| ☐ HS-TJU | Boeing 777-2D7ER | 34589/599 | | | Phichit | |
| ☐ HS-TJV | Boeing 777-2D7ER | 34590/665 | | | Nakhon Pathom | |
| ☐ HS-TJW | Boeing 777-2D7ER | 34591/672 | | | Phetchabun | |
| | | | | | | |
| ☐ HS-TKA | Boeing 777-3D7 | 29150/156 | ex N5028Y | | Sriwanna | |
| ☐ HS-TKB | Boeing 777-3D7 | 29151/170 | | | Chainarai | |
| ☐ HS-TKC | Boeing 777-3D7 | 29211/250 | | | Kwanmuang | |
| ☐ HS-TKD | Boeing 777-3D7 | 29212/260 | | | Thepalai | |
| ☐ HS-TKE | Boeing 777-3D7 | 29213/304 | | | Sukhirin | |
| ☐ HS-TKF | Boeing 777-3D7 | 29214/310 | | | Chutamai | |
| ☐ HS-TKG | Boeing 777-35RER | 35157/627 | ex VT-JEA | | | ♦ |
| ☐ HS-TKH | Boeing 777-35RER | 35158/637 | ex VT-JEB | | | ♦ |
| ☐ HS-TKJ | Boeing 777-35RER | 35161/693 | ex VT-JEJ | | | ♦ |
| ☐ HS-TKK | Boeing 777-3ALER | 41520 | | | | o/o♦ |
| ☐ HS-TKL | Boeing 777-3ALER | 41521 | | | | o/o♦ |
| ☐ HS-TKS | Boeing 777-35RER | 35160/653 | ex TC-JAA | | | <JAI♦ |
| ☐ HS-TKT | Boeing 777-35RER | 35159/650 | ex TC-JJD | | Sri Vibha | ♦ |
| | | | | | | |
| ☐ HS-TUA | Airbus A380-841 | 087 | ex F-WWAO | | | o/o♦ |
| ☐ HS-TUB | Airbus A380-841 | 093 | ex F-WWAN | | | o/o♦ |
| ☐ N774SA | Boeing 777-FZB | 37986/844 | ex N5023Q | | | Op by SOO |
| ☐ N775SA | Boeing 777-FZB | 37987/852 | | | | Op by SOO |

| THAI AVIATION SERVICES | | | | | Songkhla (SGZ) |
|---|---|---|---|---|---|

| | | | | | |
|---|---|---|---|---|---|
| ☐ HS-HTE | Sikorsky S-76A++ | 760706 | ex N2584R | | <CHC Helicopters |
| ☐ HS-HTJ | Sikorsky S-76A++ | 760720 | ex N720G | | <CHC Helicopters |
| ☐ HS-HTN | Sikorsky S-76C++ | 760731 | ex C-FZSZ | | ♦ |
| ☐ HS-HTP | Sikorsky S-76A++ | 760697 | ex N25811 | | <CHC Helicopters |
| ☐ HS-HTT | Sikorsly S-76C++ | 760691 | ex C-FRSA | | ♦ |
| ☐ HS-HTU | Sikorsky S-76A++ | 760010 | ex VH-HUB | | <CHC Helicopters |
| ☐ HS-HTW | Sikorsky S-76C++ | 760724 | ex C-FUWP | | <CHC Helicopters |
| ☐ HS-HTY | Sikorsky S-76A | 760011 | ex C-GIHY | | <CHC Helicopters |
| ☐ HS-HTZ | Sikorsky S-76C+ | 760561 | ex C-GHRZ | | <CHC Helicopters |

| THAI FLYING SERVICE | | Thai Flying (TFT) | | Bangkok-Don Muang (DMK) |
|---|---|---|---|---|

| | | | | |
|---|---|---|---|---|
| ☐ HS-ITD | Beech 300 Super King Air | FL-151 | ex N10817 | |

## HZ- SAUDI ARABIA (Kingdom of Saudi Arabia)

### AL KHAYALA

Wholly owned by National Air Services and ops business class services between Jeddah and Riyadh

| ALWAFEER AIR | | (AW/WFR) | | Jeddah (JED) |
|---|---|---|---|---|

| | | | | |
|---|---|---|---|---|
| ☐ HZ-AWA3 | Boeing 747-4H6 | 25701/997 | ex 9M-MPD | |

| NAS AIR | | (2N/KNE) | | Jeddah (JED) |
|---|---|---|---|---|

| | | | | |
|---|---|---|---|---|
| ☐ VP-CXR | Airbus A320-214 | 3894 | ex F-WWDF | |
| ☐ VP-CXS | Airbus A320-214 | 3787 | ex F-WWBB | |
| ☐ VP-CXT | Airbus A320-214 | 3817 | ex F-WWIN | |
| ☐ VP-CXU | Airbus A320-214 | 2123 | ex SU-KBC | |
| ☐ VP-CXW | Airbus A320-214 | 3475 | ex F-WWDF | ♦ |
| ☐ VP-CXX | Airbus A320-214 | 3425 | ex F-WWIZ | |
| ☐ VP-CXY | Airbus A320-214 | 3396 | ex F-WWBR | |
| ☐ VP-CXZ | Airbus A320-214 | 3361 | ex F-WWIK | |
| | | | | |
| ☐ VP-CQT | Embraer ERJ-190LR | 19000403 | ex PT- | ♦ |
| ☐ VP-CQV | Embraer ERJ-190LR | 19000367 | ex PT-XNF | |
| ☐ VP-CQW | Embraer ERJ-190LR | 19000232 | ex PT-SID | |
| ☐ VP-CQX | Embraer ERJ-190LR | 19000233 | ex PT-SIE | |
| ☐ VP-CQY | Embraer ERJ-190LR | 19000227 | ex PT-SHQ | |
| ☐ VP-CQZ | Embraer ERJ-190LR | 19000217 | ex PT-SHA | |
| ☐ | Embraer ERJ-190LR | | ex PT- | o/o |
| ☐ | Embraer ERJ-190LR | | ex PT- | o/o |
| ☐ | Embraer ERJ-190LR | | ex PT- | o/o |
| ☐ | Embraer ERJ-190LR | | ex PT- | o/o |
| ☐ | Embraer ERJ-190LR | | ex PT- | o/o |
| ☐ | Embraer ERJ-190LR | | ex PT- | o/o |

| | | | | |
|---|---|---|---|---|
| ☐ | Embraer ERJ-190LR | | ex PT- | o/o |
| ☐ VP-CAN | Airbus A319-112 | 1886 | ex C-GKOC | |

## SAUDI ARABIAN AIRLINES — Saudia (SV/SVA) — Jeddah (JED)

| | | | | |
|---|---|---|---|---|
| ☐ HZ-ASA | Airbus A320-214 | 4081 | ex F-WWBR | |
| ☐ HZ-ASB | Airbus A320-214 | 4090 | ex F-WWBZ | |
| ☐ HZ-ASC | Airbus A320-214 | 4337 | ex F-WWIV | |
| ☐ HZ-ASD | Airbus A320-214 | 4364 | ex F-WWDI | |
| ☐ HZ-ASE | Airbus A320-214 | 4408 | ex F-WWIE | |
| ☐ HZ-ASF | Airbus A320-214 | 4955 | ex D-AXAW | ♦ |
| ☐ HZ-AS11 | Airbus A320-214 | 4015 | ex F-WWBS | |
| ☐ HZ-AS12 | Airbus A320-214 | 4057 | ex F-WWBC | |
| ☐ HZ-AS13 | Airbus A320-214 | 4104 | ex F-WWDQ | |
| ☐ HZ-AS14 | Airbus A320-214 | 4115 | ex F-WWDX | |
| ☐ HZ-AS15 | Airbus A320-214 | 4122 | ex F-WWIF | |
| ☐ HZ-AS16 | Airbus A320-214 | 4135 | ex F-WWIU | |
| ☐ HZ-AS17 | Airbus A320-214 | 4349 | ex F-WWBV | |
| ☐ HZ-AS18 | Airbus A320-214 | 4357 | ex F-WWDH | |
| ☐ HZ-AS19 | Airbus A320-214 | 4376 | ex F-WWIN | |
| ☐ HZ-AS20 | Airbus A320-214 | 4392 | ex F-WWDO | |
| ☐ HZ-AS21 | Airbus A320-214 | 4414 | ex D-AVVI | |
| ☐ HZ-AS22 | Airbus A320-214 | 4484 | ex F-WWDN | |
| ☐ HZ-AS23 | Airbus A320-214 | 4519 | ex F-WWDE | |
| ☐ HZ-AS31 | Airbus A320-214 | 4092 | ex F-WWDE | |
| ☐ HZ-AS32 | Airbus A320-214 | 4273 | ex F-WWBY | |
| ☐ HZ-AS33 | Airbus A320-214 | 4314 | ex F-WWBP | |
| ☐ HZ-AS34 | Airbus A320-214 | 4397 | ex F-WWIL | |
| ☐ HZ-AS35 | Airbus A320-214 | 4391 | ex D-AVVG | |
| ☐ HZ-AS36 | Airbus A320-214 | 4393 | ex D-AVVJ | |
| ☐ HZ-AS37 | Airbus A320-214 | 4394 | ex F-WWDX | |
| ☐ HZ-AS38 | Airbus A320-214 | 4432 | ex D-AVVP | |
| ☐ HZ-AS39 | Airbus A320-214 | 4442 | ex F-WWIA | |
| ☐ HZ-AS40 | Airbus A320-214 | 4419 | ex F-WWDU | |
| ☐ HZ-AS41 | Airbus A320-214 | 4454 | ex F-WWBE | |
| ☐ HZ-AS42 | Airbus A320-214 | 4501 | ex F-WWIM | |
| ☐ HZ-AS43 | Airbus A320-214 | 4517 | ex F-WWBO | |
| ☐ HZ-AS44 | Airbus A320-214 | 4564 | ex F-WWBD | |
| ☐ HZ-AS45 | Airbus A320-214 | 4823 | ex F-WWII | ♦ |
| ☐ HZ- | Airbus A320-214 | | ex | o/o |
| ☐ HZ- | Airbus A320-214 | | ex | o/o |
| ☐ HZ- | Airbus A320-214 | | ex | o/o |
| ☐ HZ- | Airbus A320-214 | | ex | o/o |
| ☐ HZ- | Airbus A320-214 | | ex | o/o |
| ☐ HZ-ASH | Airbus A321-211 | 4467 | ex D-AVZD | |
| ☐ HZ-ASI | Airbus A321-211 | 4542 | ex D-AVZR | |
| ☐ HZ-ASJ | Airbus A321-211 | 4577 | ex D-AZAG | |
| ☐ HZ-ASK | Airbus A321-211 | 4590 | ex D-AZAJ | |
| ☐ HZ-ASL | Airbus A321-211 | 4838 | ex D-AVZY | ♦ |
| ☐ HZ-ASM | Airbus A321-211 | 4811 | ex D-AVZP | ♦ |
| ☐ HZ-ASN | Airbus A321-211 | 4925 | ex D-AVZJ | ♦ |
| ☐ HZ-ASO | Airbus A321-211 | 4962 | ex D-AZAG | ♦ |
| ☐ HZ-ASP | Airbus A321-211 | 5009 | ex D-AZAK | ♦ |
| ☐ HZ-ASQ | Airbus A321-211 | 5065 | ex D-AVZM | ♦ |
| ☐ HZ-AQA | Airbus A330-343X | 1108 | ex F-WWKZ | |
| ☐ HZ-AQB | Airbus A330-343X | 1127 | ex F-WWYP | |
| ☐ HZ-AQC | Airbus A330-343X | 1137 | ex F-WWKM | |
| ☐ HZ-AQD | Airbus A330-343X | 1141 | ex F-WWKL | |
| ☐ HZ-AQE | Airbus A330-343X | 1147 | ex F-WWYB | |
| ☐ HZ-AQF | Airbus A330-343X | 1153 | ex F-WWYT | |
| ☐ HZ-AQG | Airbus A330-343X | 1192 | ex F-WWKO | |
| ☐ HZ-AQH | Airbus A330-343X | 1189 | ex F-WWKA | |
| ☐ TC-OCC | Airbus A330-322 | 143 | ex 9M-MKS | <OHY |
| ☐ EK-74799 | Boeing 747-281BF | 24399/750 | ex N281RF | <VPB♦ |
| ☐ HZ-AIB | Boeing 747-168B | 22499/517 | | [JED] |
| ☐ HZ-AIC | Boeing 747-168B | 22500/522 | | [JED] |
| ☐ HZ-AID | Boeing 747-168B | 22501/525 | | [JED] |
| ☐ HZ-AIE | Boeing 747-168B | 22502/530 | ex N8284V | [JED] |
| ☐ HZ-AIF | Boeing 747SP-68 | 22503/529 | | ♦ |
| ☐ HZ-AII | Boeing 747-168B | 22749/557 | | [JED] |
| ☐ HZ-AIK | Boeing 747-368 | 23262/616 | ex N6005C | |
| ☐ HZ-AIL | Boeing 747-368 | 23263/619 | ex N6009F | [JED] |
| ☐ HZ-AIM | Boeing 747-368 | 23264/620 | ex N6046P | [JED] |
| ☐ HZ-AIN | Boeing 747-368 | 23265/622 | ex N6046P | |
| ☐ HZ-AIP | Boeing 747-368 | 23267/630 | ex N6055X | |
| ☐ HZ-AIQ | Boeing 747-368 | 23268/631 | ex N6005C | [JED] |
| ☐ HZ-AIR | Boeing 747-368 | 23269/643 | ex N6038E | |
| ☐ HZ-AIT | Boeing 747-368 | 23271/652 | ex N6038N | |

| | | | | |
|---|---|---|---|---|
| ☐ HZ-AIU | Boeing 747-268F | 24359/724 | ex N6018N | [JED] |
| ☐ N783SA | Boeing 747-281F | 23919/689 | ex JA8188 | <SOO♦ |
| | | | | |
| ☐ HS-STA | Boeing 747-422 | 26876/939 | ex N187UA | <OEA♦ |
| ☐ HZ-AIV | Boeing 747-468 | 28339/1122 | ex N6005C | |
| ☐ HZ-AIW | Boeing 747-468 | 28340/1138 | | |
| ☐ HZ-AIX | Boeing 747-468 | 28341/1182 | | |
| ☐ HZ-AIY | Boeing 747-468 | 28342/1216 | ex N6009F | |
| ☐ N491EV | Boeing 747-412F | 26561/1042 | ex 9V-SFB | <EIA♦ |
| ☐ TF-AMI | Boeing 747-412 (SF) | 27066/940 | ex N706RB | <ABD |
| ☐ TF-AMS | Boeing 747-481 | 24920/832 | ex JA8096 | <ABD |
| ☐ TF-AMT | Boeing 747-481 | 25135/863 | ex JA8097 | <ABD |
| ☐ TF-AMU | Boeing 747-48EF | 27603/1210 | ex HL7426 | <ABD |
| ☐ TF-AMV | Boeing 747-412 | 28022/1082 | ex 9V-SPI | <ABD |
| ☐ TF-AMX | Boeing 747-441 | 24957/971 | ex ZS-SUI | <ABD♦ |
| | | | | |
| ☐ HZ-AKA | Boeing 777-268ER | 28344/98 | ex N50217 | |
| ☐ HZ-AKB | Boeing 777-268ER | 28345/99 | ex N5023Q | |
| ☐ HZ-AKC | Boeing 777-268ER | 28346/101 | | |
| ☐ HZ-AKD | Boeing 777-268ER | 28347/103 | | |
| ☐ HZ-AKE | Boeing 777-268ER | 28348/109 | | |
| ☐ HZ-AKF | Boeing 777-268ER | 28349/114 | | |
| ☐ HZ-AKG | Boeing 777-268ER | 28350/119 | | |
| ☐ HZ-AKH | Boeing 777-268ER | 28351/124 | | |
| ☐ HZ-AKI | Boeing 777-268ER | 28352/143 | | |
| ☐ HZ-AKJ | Boeing 777-268ER | 28353/147 | | |
| ☐ HZ-AKK | Boeing 777-268ER | 28354/154 | | |
| ☐ HZ-AKL | Boeing 777-268ER | 28355/166 | | |
| ☐ HZ-AKM | Boeing 777-268ER | 28356/175 | | |
| ☐ HZ-AKN | Boeing 777-268ER | 28357/181 | | |
| ☐ HZ-AKO | Boeing 777-268ER | 28358/186 | | |
| ☐ HZ-AKP | Boeing 777-268ER | 28359/194 | | |
| ☐ HZ-AKQ | Boeing 777-268ER | 28360/219 | ex N5016R | |
| ☐ HZ-AKR | Boeing 777-268ER | 28361/230 | ex N5017V | |
| ☐ HZ-AKS | Boeing 777-268ER | 28362/255 | | |
| ☐ HZ-AKT | Boeing 777-268ER | 28363/298 | | |
| ☐ HZ-AKU | Boeing 777-268ER | 28364/306 | | |
| ☐ HZ-AKV | Boeing 777-268ER | 28365/323 | | |
| ☐ HZ-AKW | Boeing 777-268ER | 28366/351 | | |
| | | | | |
| ☐ HZ-AK11 | Boeing 777-368ER | 41048/982 | | ♦ |
| ☐ HZ-AK12 | Boeing 777-368ER | 41050/986 | | ♦ |
| ☐ HZ-AK13 | Boeing 777-368ER | 41049/992 | | ♦ |
| ☐ HZ-AK14 | Boeing 777-368ER | 41051/999 | | ♦ |
| ☐ HZ-AK15 | Boeing 777-368ER | 41052 | | o/o♦ |
| ☐ HZ-AK16 | Boeing 777-368ER | 41053 | | o/o♦ |
| | | | | |
| ☐ HZ-AEA | Embraer ERJ-170LR | 17000108 | ex PT-SAQ | |
| ☐ HZ-AEB | Embraer ERJ-170LR | 17000114 | ex PT-SAZ | |
| ☐ HZ-AEC | Embraer ERJ-170LR | 17000118 | ex PT-SDF | |
| ☐ HZ-AED | Embraer ERJ-170LR | 17000119 | ex PT-SDG | |
| ☐ HZ-AEE | Embraer ERJ-170LR | 17000121 | ex PT-SDJ | |
| ☐ HZ-AEF | Embraer ERJ-170LR | 17000123 | ex PT-SDM | |
| ☐ HZ-AEG | Embraer ERJ-170LR | 17000124 | ex PT-SDN | |
| ☐ HZ-AEH | Embraer ERJ-170LR | 17000135 | ex PT-SDY | |
| ☐ HZ-AEI | Embraer ERJ-170LR | 17000142 | ex PT-SEG | |
| ☐ HZ-AEJ | Embraer ERJ-170LR | 17000145 | ex PT-SEJ | |
| ☐ HZ-AEK | Embraer ERJ-170LR | 17000149 | ex PT-SEN | |
| ☐ HZ-AEL | Embraer ERJ-170LR | 17000152 | ex PT-SEQ | |
| ☐ HZ-AEM | Embraer ERJ-170LR | 17000155 | ex PT-SES | |
| ☐ HZ-AEN | Embraer ERJ-170LR | 17000158 | ex PT-SEW | |
| ☐ HZ-AEO | Embraer ERJ-170LR | 17000161 | ex PT-SMB | |
| | | | | |
| ☐ HZ-APA | McDonnell-Douglas MD-90-30 | 53491/2191 | | [JED] |
| ☐ HZ-APB | McDonnell-Douglas MD-90-30 | 53492/2205 | ex N9012S | [JED] |
| ☐ HZ-APC | McDonnell-Douglas MD-90-30 | 53493/2209 | ex N9014S | |
| ☐ HZ-APD | McDonnell-Douglas MD-90-30 | 53494/2213 | ex N9010L | |
| ☐ HZ-APE | McDonnell-Douglas MD-90-30 | 53495/2215 | ex N6203D | [JED] |
| ☐ HZ-APF | McDonnell-Douglas MD-90-30 | 53496/2216 | ex N9012S | |
| ☐ HZ-APG | McDonnell-Douglas MD-90-30 | 53497/2219 | | [JED] |
| ☐ HZ-APH | McDonnell-Douglas MD-90-30 | 53498/2221 | ex N6202D | |
| ☐ HZ-API | McDonnell-Douglas MD-90-30 | 53499/2223 | | [JED] |
| ☐ HZ-APJ | McDonnell-Douglas MD-90-30 | 53500/2225 | | |
| ☐ HZ-APK | McDonnell-Douglas MD-90-30 | 53501/2226 | | |
| ☐ HZ-APL | McDonnell-Douglas MD-90-30 | 53502/2227 | | |
| ☐ HZ-APM | McDonnell-Douglas MD-90-30 | 53503/2229 | | [JED] |
| ☐ HZ-APN | McDonnell-Douglas MD-90-30 | 53504/2230 | | |
| ☐ HZ-APO | McDonnell-Douglas MD-90-30 | 53505/2231 | ex N9012S | |
| ☐ HZ-APQ | McDonnell-Douglas MD-90-30 | 53507/2235 | | [JED] |
| ☐ HZ-APR | McDonnell-Douglas MD-90-30 | 53508/2237 | | |
| ☐ HZ-APS | McDonnell-Douglas MD-90-30 | 53509/2250 | ex N6203D | [JED] |
| ☐ HZ-APT | McDonnell-Douglas MD-90-30 | 53510/2251 | ex N6203U | [JED] |

| | | | | |
|---|---|---|---|---|
| ☐ HZ-APU | McDonnell-Douglas MD-90-30 | 53511/2255 | | [JED] |
| ☐ HZ-APV | McDonnell-Douglas MD-90-30 | 53512/2256 | | [JED] |
| ☐ HZ-APW | McDonnell-Douglas MD-90-30 | 53513/2257 | ex N9010L | [RUH] |
| ☐ HZ-APX | McDonnell-Douglas MD-90-30 | 53514/2260 | ex N6200N | |
| ☐ HZ-APY | McDonnell-Douglas MD-90-30 | 53515/2262 | ex N9014S | [JED] |
| ☐ HZ-APZ | McDonnell-Douglas MD-90-30 | 53516/2263 | ex N9075H | |
| ☐ HZ-AP3 | McDonnell-Douglas MD-90-30 | 53518/2289 | ex N6203D | [RUH] |
| ☐ HZ-AP4 | McDonnell-Douglas MD-90-30 | 53519/2290 | ex N9075H | [RUH] |
| ☐ HZ-AP7 | McDonnell-Douglas MD-90-30 | 53517/2288 | ex HZ-AP2 | [RUH] |
| | | | | |
| ☐ HZ-ANA | McDonnell-Douglas MD-11F | 48773/609 | ex N90187 | |
| ☐ HZ-ANB | McDonnell-Douglas MD-11F | 48775/616 | ex N91566 | |
| ☐ HZ-ANC | McDonnell-Douglas MD-11F | 48776/617 | ex N91078 | |
| ☐ HZ-AND | McDonnell-Douglas MD-11F | 48777/618 | ex N9166N | |
| ☐ TC-OGT | Boeing 757-256 | 29308/935 | ex EC-HIR | <KKK |

## SNAS AVIATION — Red Sea (RSE) — Riyadh/Bahrain (RUH/BAH)

| | | | | |
|---|---|---|---|---|
| ☐ HZ-SNA | Boeing 727-264F (FedEx 3) | 20896/1051 | ex EC-HLP | all-white |
| ☐ HZ-SNB | Boeing 727-223F (FedEx 3) | 21084/1199 | ex EC-HAH | all-white |
| ☐ HZ-SNC | Boeing 727-230F (FedEx 3) | 20905/1091 | ex EC-IVF | <BCS |
| ☐ HZ-SND | Boeing 727-223F (FedEx 3) | 20994/1190 | ex EC-IVE | all-white  <BCS |
| ☐ HZ-SNF | Boeing 727-230F (FedEx 3) | 22643/1762 | ex ZS-DPE | |
| | | | | |
| ☐ A9C-DHC | Boeing 757-225 (PCF) | 22211/74 | ex N314ST | ♦ |
| ☐ A9C-DHD | Boeing 757-225 (PCF) | 22611/75 | ex (N243AL) | ♦ |

Ops in association with DHL Worldwide (Bahrain)

## H4- SOLOMON ISLANDS

## PACIFIC AIR EXPRESS — Solpac (PAQ) — Honiara / Brisbane, QLD (HIR/BNE)

Ops cargo flights using aircraft leased from HeavyLift Cargo as required

## SOLOMONS — Solomon (IE/SOL) — Honiara (HIR)

| | | | | |
|---|---|---|---|---|
| ☐ H4-AAI | Britten-Norman BN-2A-9 Islander | 355 | ex N355BN | |
| ☐ H4-BUS | Airbus A320-211 | 0302 | ex N957PG | ♦ |
| ☐ H4-NNP | de Havilland DHC-6 Twin Otter 300 | 491 | ex YJ-RV1 | |
| ☐ H4-SID | de Havilland DHC-6 Twin Otter 300 | 442 | ex VH-XFE | |
| ☐ P2-MCP | de Havilland DHC-8-102 | 033 | ex VH-TNX | <TOK♦ |

## I - ITALY (Italian Republic)

## AIR DOLOMITI — Dolomiti (EN/DLA) — Trieste (TRS)

| | | | | |
|---|---|---|---|---|
| ☐ I-ADCA | ATR 72-212A | 0658 | ex D-ANFG | |
| ☐ I-ADCB | ATR 72-212A | 0660 | ex D-ANFH | |
| ☐ I-ADCC | ATR 72-212A | 0662 | ex D-ANFI | |
| ☐ I-ADCD | ATR 72-212A | 0664 | ex D-ANFJ | |
| ☐ I-ADCE | ATR 72-212A | 0668 | ex D-ANFL | |
| ☐ I-ADLJ | ATR 72-212A | 0686 | ex F-WQMO | Il Trovatore di Giuseppe Verdi |
| ☐ I-ADLK | ATR 72-212A | 0706 | ex F-WWEF | Il Barbiere de Siviglia di Gioacchino Rossini |
| ☐ I-ADLO | ATR 72-212A | 0585 | ex F-WQJH | La Bohème di Giacomo Puccini |
| ☐ I-ADLS | ATR 72-212A | 0634 | ex F-WQMB | Ernani di Giuseppe Verdi |
| ☐ I-ADLT | ATR 72-212A | 0638 | ex F-WQME | Otello di Giuseppe Verdi |
| ☐ I-ADLW | ATR 72-212A | 0707 | ex F-WWEG | La Gazza Ladra di Gioacchino Rossini |
| | | | | |
| ☐ I-ADJK | Embraer ERJ-195LR | 19000245 | ex PT-SIQ | |
| ☐ I-ADJL | Embraer ERJ-195LR | 19000256 | ex PT-STE | |
| ☐ I-ADJM | Embraer ERJ-195LR | 19000258 | ex PT-STG | |
| ☐ I-ADJN | Embraer ERJ-195LR | 19000270 | ex PT-TLK | |
| ☐ I-ADJO | Embraer ERJ-195LR | 19000280 | ex PT-TLU | |
| | | | | |
| ☐ D-AEMG | Embraer ERJ-190LR | 19000404 | ex PT-TYX | <AUB♦ |

## AIR EUROPE ITALY — Air Europe (VA/VLE) — Milan-Malpensa (MXP)

Wholly owned subsidiary of Volare Group, parent of Volareweb

## AIR ITALY — Air Italy (I9/AEY) — Milan-Malpensa (MXP)

| | | | | |
|---|---|---|---|---|
| ☐ EI-IGP | Boeing 737-76N/W | 37233/2578 | ex I-AIGP | ♦ |
| ☐ EI-IGR | Boeing 737-36N/W | 28561/2896 | ex N561SM | |
| ☐ EI-IGS | Boeing 737-36N/W | 28562/2908 | ex N562SM | |
| ☐ EI-IGT | Boeing 737-73V | 32421/1357 | ex G-EZJZ | ♦ |
| ☐ EI-IGU | Boeing 737-73V | 32422/1363 | ex G-AZKA | ♦ |
| ☐ I-AIGG | Boeing 767-304ER | 28041/614 | ex G-OBYC | |

| | | | | |
|---|---|---|---|---|
| ☐ I-AIGH | Boeing 767-23BER | 23973/208 | ex N252MY | |
| ☐ I-AIGI | Boeing 767-23BER | 23974/214 | ex N253MY | |
| ☐ I-AIGJ | Boeing 767-304ER | 28039/610 | ex N769NA | |
| ☐ I-AIGM | Boeing 737-33A | 24299/1598 | ex SE-RCS | |
| ☐ I-AIMR | Boeing 737-430 | 27007/2367 | ex D-AGMR | ♦ |

## AIR VALLÉE — *Air Vallée (DO/RVL)* — Aosta (AOT)

| | | | | |
|---|---|---|---|---|
| ☐ I-AIRJ | Dornier 328-310 (328JET) | 3186 | | |
| ☐ I-AIRX | Dornier 328-300 (328JET) | 3142 | ex D-BDXS | Casino de la Vallée c/s |
| ☐ YR-HBE | McDonnell-Douglas MD-83 | 49396/1305 | ex EC-GNY | <MDB♦ |
| ☐ 9H-AEY | de Havilland DHC-8-315 | 508 | ex G-BRYX | <AMC♦ |
| Ceased ops 04Nov09, restarted 03Jly10 | | | | |

## ALIDAUNIA — *Lid (D4/LID)* — Foggia (FOG)

| | | | |
|---|---|---|---|
| ☐ I-AGSE | Agusta A.109A II | 7354 | |
| ☐ I-AGSH | Agusta A.109A II | 7384 | |
| ☐ I-LIDC | MBB BK-117C-1 | 7529 | ex D-HMB. |
| ☐ I-LIDD | Agusta A.109E Power | 11107 | |
| ☐ I-RMDV | Sikorsky S-76A | 760235 | ex (N721CD) |
| ☐ I- | Agusta AW139 | | o/o |
| ☐ I- | Agusta AW139 | | o/o |

## ALITALIA — *Alitalia (AZ/AZA)* — Rome-Fiumicino (FCO)

Member of Skyteam

| | | | | | |
|---|---|---|---|---|---|
| ☐ EI-IMB | Airbus A319-112 | 2033 | ex I-BIMB | Isola del Giglio | ♦ |
| ☐ EI-IMC | Airbus A319-112 | 2057 | ex I-BIMC | Isola di Lipari | |
| ☐ EI-EMD | Airbus A319-112 | 2074 | ex I-BIMD | Isola di Capri | ♦ |
| ☐ EI-IME | Airbus A319-112 | 1740 | ex I-BIME | Isola di Panarea | |
| ☐ EI-IMF | Airbus A319-112 | 2083 | ex I-BIMF | Isola Tremiti | |
| ☐ EI-IMG | Airbus A319-112 | 2086 | ex I-BIMG | Isola di Pantelleria | |
| ☐ EI-IMH | Airbus A319-112 | 2101 | ex I-BIMH | Isola di Ventotene | |
| ☐ EI-IMI | Airbus A319-112 | 1745 | ex I-BIMI | Isola di Ponza | |
| ☐ EI-IMJ | Airbus A319-112 | 1779 | ex I-BIMJ | Isola di Caprera | |
| ☐ EI-IML | Airbus A319-112 | 2127 | ex I-BIML | Isola La Maddalena | |
| ☐ EI-IMM | Airbus A319-112 | 4759 | ex D-AYVE | Vittorio Alfieri | ♦ |
| ☐ EI-IMN | Airbus A319-122 | 4764 | ex D-AVYG | | ♦ |
| ☐ EI-IMO | Airbus A319-112 | 1770 | ex I-BIMO | Isola d'Ischia | ♦ |
| ☐ EI-IMP | Airbus A319-112 | 4859 | ex D-AVWR | Italo Svevo | ♦ |
| ☐ EI-IMR | Airbus A319-112 | 4875 | ex D-AVYB | Italo Calvino | ♦ |
| ☐ EI-IMS | Airbus A319-112 | 4910 | ex D-AVYC | | |
| ☐ EI-IMT | Airbus A319-111 | 5018 | ex D-AVyi | | o/o♦ |
| ☐ EI-IMU | Airbus A319-111 | 5130 | ex | | o/o ♦ |
| ☐ I-BIMA | Airbus A319-112 | 1722 | ex D-AVWP | Isola d'Elba | |
| | | | | | |
| ☐ EI-IKB | Airbus A320-214 | 1226 | ex I-BIKB | Wolfgang Amadeus Mozart | |
| ☐ EI-IKF | Airbus A320-214 | 1473 | ex I-BIKF | Mole Antonelliana | |
| ☐ EI-IKG | Airbus A320-214 | 1480 | ex I-BIKG | Scirocco | |
| ☐ EI-IKL | Airbus A320-214 | 1489 | ex I-BIKL | Libeccio | |
| ☐ EI-IKU | Airbus A320-214 | 1217 | ex I-BIKU | Fryderyk Chopin | |
| ☐ I-BIKA | Airbus A320-214 | 0951 | ex F-WWBT | Johann Sebastian Bach | |
| ☐ I-BIKC | Airbus A320-214 | 1448 | ex F-WWBV | Torre di Pisa | |
| ☐ I-BIKD | Airbus A320-214 | 1457 | ex F-WWDE | Maschio Angioino Napoli | |
| ☐ I-BIKE | Airbus A320-214 | 0999 | ex F-WWBZ | Franz Liszt | |
| ☐ I-BIKI | Airbus A320-214 | 1138 | ex F-WWDJ | Girolamo Frescobaldi | |
| ☐ I-BIKO | Airbus A320-214 | 1168 | ex F-WWDL | George Bizet | |
| ☐ I-WEBA | Airbus A320-214 | 3138 | ex F-WWDI | | |
| ☐ I-WEBB | Airbus A320-214 | 3161 | ex F-WWIC | | |
| | | | | | |
| ☐ EI-DSA | Airbus A320-216 | 2869 | ex F-WWBE | | |
| ☐ EI-DSB | Airbus A320-216 | 2932 | ex F-WWBX | Tomasi di Lampedusa | |
| ☐ EI-DSC | Airbus A320-216 | 2995 | ex F-WWIY | Lorenzo de'Medici | |
| ☐ EI-DSD | Airbus A320-216 | 3076 | ex F-WWIP | Edmondo de Amicis | |
| ☐ EI-DSE | Airbus A320-216 | 3079 | ex F-WWIL | Antonio Fogazzaro | |
| ☐ EI-DSF | Airbus A320-216 | 3080 | ex F-WWIV | Emilio Salgari | |
| ☐ EI-DSG | Airbus A320-216 | 3115 | ex F-WWIZ | Elio Vittorini | |
| ☐ EI-DSH | Airbus A320-216 | 3178 | ex F-WWDS | | |
| ☐ EI-DSI | Airbus A320-216 | 3213 | ex F-WWIU | Carlo Emilio Gadda | |
| ☐ EI-DSJ | Airbus A320-216 | 3295 | ex F-WWDV | Ignazio Silone | |
| ☐ EI-DSK | Airbus A320-216 | 3328 | ex F-WWIX | | |
| ☐ EI-DSL | Airbus A320-216 | 3343 | ex F-WWBO | | |
| ☐ EI-DSM | Airbus A320-216 | 3362 | ex F-WWIR | | |
| ☐ EI-DSN | Airbus A320-216 | 3412 | ex F-WWIL | | |
| ☐ EI-DSO | Airbus A320-216 | 3464 | ex F-WWBM | Luigi Capuana | |
| ☐ EI-DSP | Airbus A320-216 | 3482 | ex F-WWDM | Ippolito Nievo | |
| ☐ EI-DSR | Airbus A320-216 | 3502 | ex F-WWBR | | |
| ☐ EI-DSS | Airbus A320-216 | 3515 | ex F-WWDP | | |
| ☐ EI-DST | Airbus A320-216 | 3532 | ex F-WWDY | | |

| | | | | | | |
|---|---|---|---|---|---|---|
| ☐ EI-DSU | Airbus A320-216 | 3563 | ex F-WWBI | Beppe Fenoglio | | |
| ☐ EI-DSV | Airbus A320-216 | 3598 | ex F-WWDJ | | | |
| ☐ EI-DSW | Airbus A320-216 | 3609 | ex F-WWIE | | | |
| ☐ EI-DSX | Airbus A320-216 | 3643 | ex F-WWBT | | | |
| ☐ EI-DSY | Airbus A320-216 | 3666 | ex F-WWDY | | | |
| ☐ EI-DSZ | Airbus A320-216 | 3695 | ex F-WWBI | | | |
| ☐ EI-DTA | Airbus A320-216 | 3732 | ex F-WWDM | Ada Negri | | |
| ☐ EI-DTB | Airbus A320-216 | 3815 | ex F-WWIF | Giacomo Leopardi | | |
| ☐ EI-DTC | Airbus A320-216 | 3831 | ex F-WWBD | | | |
| ☐ EI-DTD | Airbus A320-216 | 3846 | ex F-WWBY | | | |
| ☐ EI-DTE | Airbus A320-216 | 3885 | ex F-WWIY | Francesco Petrarca | | |
| ☐ EI-DTF | Airbus A320-216 | 3906 | ex F-WWIM | Giovanni Boccaccio | | |
| ☐ EI-DTG | Airbus A320-216 | 3921 | ex F-WWBK | Ludovico Ariosto | | |
| ☐ EI-DTH | Airbus A320-216 | 3956 | ex F-WWBZ | Torquato Tasso | | |
| ☐ EI-DTI | Airbus A320-216 | 3976 | ex F-WWIV | Niccolo Machiavelli | | |
| ☐ EI-DTJ | Airbus A320-216 | 3978 | ex F-WWIX | Giovanni Pascoli | | |
| ☐ EI-DTK | Airbus A320-216 | 4075 | ex F-WWBN | Giovanni Verga | | |
| ☐ EI-DTL | Airbus A320-216 | 4108 | ex F-WWDS | | | |
| ☐ EI-DTM | Airbus A320-216 | 4119 | ex F-WWIE | | | |
| ☐ EI-DTN | Airbus A320-216 | 4143 | ex F-WWBB | | | |
| ☐ EI-DTO | Airbus A320-216 | 4152 | ex F-WWBJ | | | |
| ☐ EI-EIA | Airbus A320-216 | 4195 | ex F-WWIL | Elsa Morante | | |
| ☐ EI-EIB | Airbus A320-216 | 4249 | ex F-WWDX | | | |
| ☐ EI-EIC | Airbus A320-216 | 4520 | ex D-AXAI | | | |
| ☐ EI-EID | Airbus A320-216 | 4523 | ex D-AUBU | Umberto Saba | | |
| ☐ EI-EIE | Airbus A320-216 | 4536 | ex D-AXAL | | | |
| ☐ EI- | Airbus A320-216 | 5130 | | | | o/o♦ |
| | | | | | | |
| ☐ EI-IXB | Airbus A321-112 | 0524 | ex I-BIXB | Piazza Castello-Torino | | ♦ |
| ☐ EI-IXC | Airbus A321-112 | 0526 | ex I-BIXC | Piazza del Campo Siena | | |
| ☐ EI-IXD | Airbus A321-112 | 0532 | ex I-BIXD | Piazza Pretoria-Palermo | | ♦ |
| ☐ EI-IXF | Airbus A321-112 | 0515 | ex I-BIXF | Piazza Maggiore-Bologna | | ♦ |
| ☐ EI-IXG | Airbus A321-112 | 0516 | ex I-BIXG | Piazza del Miracoli-Pisa | | |
| ☐ EI-IXH | Airbus A321-112 | 0940 | ex I-BIXH | Piazza della Signoria-Gubbio | | |
| ☐ EI-IXI | Airbus A321-112 | 0494 | ex I-BIXI | Piazza San Marco-Venezia | | |
| ☐ EI-IXJ | Airbus A321-112 | 0959 | ex I-BIXJ | Piazza del Municipio-Noto | | |
| ☐ EI-IXO | Airbus A321-112 | 0495 | ex I-BIXO | Piazza Plebiscito-Napoli | | ♦ |
| ☐ EI-IXU | Airbus A321-112 | 0434 | ex I-BIXU | Piazza della Signoria-Firenze | | ♦ |
| ☐ EI-IXV | Airbus A321-112 | 0819 | ex I-BIXV | Piazza del Rinascimento-Urbino | | |
| ☐ EI-IXZ | Airbus A321-112 | 0848 | ex I-BIXZ | Piazza del Duomo Orvieto | | |
| ☐ I-BIXA | Airbus A321-112 | 0477 | ex D-AVZE | Piazza del Duomo-Milano | | |
| ☐ I-BIXE | Airbus A321-112 | 0488 | ex D-AVZG | Piazza di Spagna-Roma | | |
| ☐ I-BIXK | Airbus A321-112 | 1220 | ex D-AVZC | Piazza Ducale Vigevano | | |
| ☐ I-BIXL | Airbus A321-112 | 0513 | ex D-AVZO | Piazza del Duomo-Lecce | | |
| ☐ I-BIXM | Airbus A321-112 | 0514 | ex D-AVZP | Piazza di San Francesco-Assisi | | |
| ☐ I-BIXN | Airbus A321-112 | 0576 | ex D-AVZR | Piazza del Duomo-Catania | | |
| ☐ I-BIXP | Airbus A321-112 | 0583 | ex D-AVZT | Carlo Morelli | | |
| ☐ I-BIXQ | Airbus A321-112 | 0586 | ex D-AVZU | Domenico Colapietro | | |
| ☐ I-BIXR | Airbus A321-112 | 0593 | ex D-AVZW | Piazza del Campidoglio-Roma | | |
| ☐ I-BIXS | Airbus A321-112 | 0599 | ex D-AVZZ | Piazza San Martino-Lucca | | |
| ☐ I-BIXT | Airbus A321-112 | 0765 | ex D-AVZW | Piazza del Signori-Vicenza | | |
| | | | | | | |
| ☐ EI-DIP | Airbus A330-202 | 339 | ex A6-EYW | Gian Lorenzo Bernini | | |
| ☐ EI-DIR | Airbus A330-202 | 272 | ex A6-EYV | | | |
| ☐ EI-EJG | Airbus A330-202 | 1123 | ex F-WWKY | Raffaello Sanzio | | |
| ☐ EI-EJH | Airbus A330-202 | 1135 | ex F-WWYU | Sandro Botticelli | | |
| ☐ EI-EJI | Airbus A330-202 | 1218 | ex F-WWYT | | | ♦ |
| ☐ EI-EJJ | Airbus A330-202 | 1225 | ex F-WWKV | | | ♦ |
| ☐ EI-EJK | Airbus A330-202 | 1252 | ex F-WWKP | | | ♦ |
| ☐ EI-EJL | Airbus A330-202 | 1283 | ex F-WWKA | Piero della Francesca | | ♦ |
| ☐ EI-EJM | Airbus A330-202 | 1308 | ex F-WWKH | Giovanni Battista Tiepolo | o/o♦ | |
| ☐ EI-EJN | Airbus A330-202 | 1313 | ex F-WWYM | Il Tintoretto | o/o♦ | |
| ☐ EI- | Airbus A330-202 | 1327 | ex F-WW | Tiziano | o/o♦ | |
| ☐ EI- | Airbus A330-202 | 1354 | ex F-WW | Michelangelo Buonarroti | o/o♦ | |
| | | | | | | |
| ☐ EI-DBK | Boeing 777-243ER | 32783/455 | | Ostuni | | |
| ☐ EI-DBL | Boeing 777-243ER | 32781/459 | | Sestriere | | |
| ☐ EI-DBM | Boeing 777-243ER | 32782/463 | | Argentario | | |
| ☐ EI-DDH | Boeing 777-243ER | 32784/477 | | Tropea | | |
| ☐ EI-ISB | Boeing 777-243ER | 32859/426 | ex I-DISB | Porto Rotondo | | ♦ |
| ☐ EI-ISD | Boeing 777-243ER | 32860/439 | ex I-DISD | Cortina d'Ampezzo | | ♦ |
| ☐ I-DISA | Boeing 777-243ER | 32855/413 | | Taormina | | |
| ☐ I-DISE | Boeing 777-243ER | 32856/421 | | Portofino | | |
| ☐ I-DISO | Boeing 777-243ER | 32857/424 | ex N5014K | Positano | | |
| ☐ I-DISU | Boeing 777-243ER | 32858/425 | | Madonna de Campiglio | | |
| | | | | | | |
| ☐ I-DACR | McDonnell-Douglas MD-82 | 49975/1775 | | Carrara | | |
| ☐ I-DACS | McDonnell-Douglas MD-82 | 53053/1806 | | Maratea | | |
| ☐ I-DACT | McDonnell-Douglas MD-82 | 53054/1856 | | Valtellina | wfs | |
| ☐ I-DACU | McDonnell-Douglas MD-82 | 53055/1857 | | Brindisi | wfs | |
| ☐ I-DACV | McDonnell-Douglas MD-82 | 53056/1880 | | Riccione | | |
| ☐ I-DACZ | McDonnell-Douglas MD-82 | 53058/1927 | | Castelfidardo | | |

| ☐ I-DAND | McDonnell-Douglas MD-82 | 53061/1957 | | Trani | |
|---|---|---|---|---|---|
| ☐ I-DANF | McDonnell-Douglas MD-82 | 53062/1960 | | Sassari | |
| ☐ I-DANG | McDonnell-Douglas MD-82 | 53176/1972 | | Benevento | |
| ☐ I-DANH | McDonnell-Douglas MD-82 | 53177/1973 | | Messina | |
| ☐ I-DANQ | McDonnell-Douglas MD-82 | 53181/2005 | | Lecce | |
| ☐ I-DANU | McDonnell-Douglas MD-82 | 53204/2009 | | Trapani | |
| ☐ I-DANW | McDonnell-Douglas MD-82 | 53206/2034 | | Siena | |
| ☐ I-DATC | McDonnell-Douglas MD-82 | 53222/2080 | | Foggia | |
| ☐ I-DATE | McDonnell-Douglas MD-82 | 53217/2053 | | Grosseto | |
| ☐ I-DATG | McDonnell-Douglas MD-82 | 53225/2086 | | Arezzo | |
| ☐ I-DATI | McDonnell-Douglas MD-82 | 53218/2060 | | Siracusa | |
| ☐ I-DATM | McDonnell-Douglas MD-82 | 53230/2106 | | Cividale del Friuli | |
| ☐ I-DAVT | McDonnell-Douglas MD-82 | 49552/1597 | | Como | |
| ☐ I-DAWB | McDonnell-Douglas MD-82 | 49197/1138 | | | [FCO]♦ |
| | | | | | |
| ☐ EI-CRF | Boeing 767-31BER | 25170/542 | ex B-2566 | | |
| ☐ EI-DBP | Boeing 767-35HER | 26389/459 | ex C-GGBJ | Duca degli Abruzzi | |
| ☐ EI-DDW | Boeing 767-3S1ER | 26608/559 | ex N979PG | Sebastiano Caboto | |
| ☐ I-DEIG | Boeing 767-33AER | 27918/603 | ex G-OITG | Francesco Agello | |

## ALITALIA CITYLINER      (CYL)

| ☐ EI-DOT | Canadair CRJ-900ER | 15066 | ex C- | | ♦ |
|---|---|---|---|---|---|
| ☐ EI-DOU | Canadair CRJ-900ER | 15068 | ex C- | | ♦ |
| ☐ EI-DRI | Canadair CRJ-900ER | 15076 | ex C- | | ♦ |
| ☐ EI-DRJ | Canadair CRJ-900ER | 15077 | ex C- | | ♦ |
| ☐ EI-DRK | Canadair CRJ-900ER | 15075 | ex C- | | ♦ |
| ☐ EI-DUK | Canadair CRJ-900ER | 15104 | ex C- | | ♦ |
| ☐ EI-DVP | Canadair CRJ-900ER | 15116 | ex C- | | ♦ |
| ☐ EI-DVR | Canadair CRJ-900ER | 15118 | ex C- | | ♦ |
| ☐ EI-DVS | Canadair CRJ-900ER | 15119 | ex C- | | ♦ |
| ☐ EI-DVT | Canadair CRJ-900ER | 15123 | ex C- | | ♦ |
| | | | | | |
| ☐ EI-RDA | Embraer ERJ-175LR | 17000330 | ex PT-TPD | Parco Nazionale del Gran Paradiso | ♦ |
| ☐ EI-RDB | Embraer ERJ-175LR | 17000331 | ex PT-TPR | | ♦ |
| ☐ EI-RDC | Embraer ERJ-175LR | 17000333 | ex PT-TSA | Parco Nazionale della Cinque Terre | ♦ |
| ☐ EI-RDD | Embraer ERJ-175LR | 17000334 | ex PT-TSP | | ♦ |
| ☐ EI-RDE | Embraer ERJ-175LR | 17000335 | ex PT-TUH | | o/o♦ |
| ☐ EI- | Embraer ERJ-175LR | 17000337 | ex PT-TUW | | o/o♦ |
| ☐ EI- | Embraer ERJ-175LR | 17000338 | ex PT-TVD | | o/o♦ |
| ☐ EI- | Embraer ERJ-175LR | 17000340 | | | o/o♦ |
| | | | | | |
| ☐ EI-RNA | Embraer ERJ-190LR | 19000470 | ex PT-TOQ | | ♦ |
| ☐ EI-RNB | Embraer ERJ-190LR | 19000479 | ex PT-TPC | Parco Nazionale del Pollino | ♦ |
| ☐ EI-RNC | Embraer ERJ-190LR | 19000503 | ex PT-TRL | Parco Nazionale Arcipelago Toscano | ♦ |
| ☐ EI-RND | Embraer ERJ-190LR | 19000512 | ex PT-TSQ | Parco Nazionale Dolomiti Bellunesi | ♦ |
| ☐ EI-RNE | Embraer ERJ-190LR | 19000520 | ex PT-TUI | | o/o♦ |

## ALITALIA EXPRESS    Ali Express (XM/SMX)      Rome-Fiumicino (FCO)

| ☐ EI-DFH | Embraer ERJ-170LR | 17000009 | ex PT-SKB | Via Aurélia | [EXT] |
|---|---|---|---|---|---|
| ☐ EI-DFJ | Embraer ERJ-170LR | 17000011 | ex PT-SKD | Via Flaminia | [EXT] |

## AQUA AIRLINES      Como

| ☐ I-SEAA | Cessna 208 Caravan I | 20800303 | exN904J | | FP♦ |
|---|---|---|---|---|---|

## BELLE AIR EUROPE    (L9/BAL)      Bergamo (AOI)

| ☐ EI-LIR | Airbus A319-132 | 2335 | ex EC-LIR | | ♦ |
|---|---|---|---|---|---|
| ☐ EI-LIS | Airbus A320-211 | 3492 | ex EK-32005 | | ♦ |
| ☐ I-LZAN | ATR 72-212A | 908 | ex F-ORAB | | |

## BLU EXPRESS.COM    (BV/BPA)      Rome-Fiumicino (FCO)

| ☐ EI-CUN | Boeing 737-4K5 | 27074/2281 | ex D-AHLS | | |
|---|---|---|---|---|---|
| ☐ EI-DXC | Boeing 737-4Q8 | 26300/2604 | ex TC-JKA | | |
| ☐ I-BPAG | Boeing 737-31S | 29059/2967 | ex EI-DVY | | ♦ |
| ☐ I-BPAI | Boeing 737-31S | 29060/2979 | ex EI-DXB | Citta di Roma | ♦ |

## BLUE PANORAMA AIRLINES    Blue Panorama (BV/BPA)      Rome-Fiumicino (FCO)

| ☐ EI-CUA | Boeing 737-4K5 | 24901/1854 | ex D-AHLR | | |
|---|---|---|---|---|---|
| ☐ EI-CUD | Boeing 737-4Q8 | 26298/2564 | ex TC-JEI | | |
| ☐ EI-CXO | Boeing 767-3G5ER | 28111/612 | ex (I-BPAB) | | |
| ☐ EI-CZH | Boeing 767-3G5ER | 29435/720 | ex (I-BPAD) | | |
| ☐ EI-DJL | Boeing 767-330ER | 25137/377 | ex I-LLAG | | ♦ |
| ☐ EI-DKL | Boeing 757-231 | 28482/770 | ex N714P | | |
| ☐ EI-DNA | Boeing 757-231 | 28483/777 | ex N715TW | | |
| ☐ EI-EED | Boeing 767-31AER | 27619/595 | ex N281LF | | ♦ |

## CARGOITALIA — White Pelican (2G/CRG) — Milan-Malpensa (MXP)

| | | | | |
|---|---|---|---|---|
| ☐ EI-EMS | McDonnell-Douglas MD-11BCF | 48766/600 | ex OH-LGF | [VCV] |
| ☐ EI-UPE | McDonnell-Douglas MD-11C | 48427/471 | ex I-DUPE | wfs |
| ☐ EI-UPI | McDonnell-Douglas MD-11C | 48428/474 | ex I-DUPI | wfs |

Ops suspended 21Dec11

## CARGOLUX ITALIA — (C8 / ICV) — Milan-Malpensa (MXP)

| | | | |
|---|---|---|---|
| ☐ LX-KCV | Boeing 747-4R7F | 25868/1125 | Lombardia |

## CITYFLY — City Fly (CII) — Rome-Urbe (ROM)

| | | | |
|---|---|---|---|
| ☐ I-LACO | Britten-Norman BN-2A-6 Islander | 17 | ex G-AWBY |

## CORPO FORESTALE DELLO STATO — Rome-Ciampino (CIA)

| | | | | | |
|---|---|---|---|---|---|
| ☐ I-CFAA | Agusta-Bell 412SP | 25610 | | CFS-20 | |
| ☐ I-CFAB | Agusta-Bell 412SP | 25614 | | CFS-21 | |
| ☐ I-CFAC | Agusta-Bell 412SP | 25615 | | CFS-22 | |
| ☐ I-CFAD | Agusta-Bell 412SP | 25618 | | CFS-23 | |
| ☐ I-CFAE | Agusta-Bell 412EP | 25918 | | CFS-24 | |
| ☐ I-CFAF | Agusta-Bell 412EP | 25919 | | CFS-25 | |
| ☐ I-CFAK | Agusta-Bell 412EP | 25926 | | CFS-26 | |
| ☐ I-CFAL | Agusta-Bell 412EP | 25978 | | CFS-27 | |
| ☐ I-CFSJ | Agusta-Bell 412 | 25561 | | CFS-14 | |
| ☐ I-CFSO | Agusta-Bell 412 | 25562 | | CFS-15 | |
| ☐ I-CFSP | Agusta-Bell 412 | 25563 | | CFS-16 | |
| ☐ I-CFSW | Agusta-Bell 412 | 25564 | | CFS-18 | |
| ☐ I-CFSX | Agusta-Bell 412 | 25572 | | CFS-19 | |
| ☐ I-CFAG | Erickson/Sikorsky S-64E Skycrane | 64088 | ex N213AC | CFS-100 | Op by European Air-Crane |
| ☐ I-CFAH | Erickson/Sikorsky S-64E Skycrane | 64080 | ex N174AC | CFS-101 | Op by European Air-Crane |
| ☐ I-CFAI | Erickson/Sikorsky S-64E Skycrane | 64067 | ex N197AC | CFS-102 | Op by European Air-Crane |
| ☐ I-CFAJ | Erickson/Sikorsky S-64E Skycrane | 64078 | ex N227AC | CFS-103 | Op by European Air-Crane |

## EAGLE AIRLINES — E3/EGS — Venice (VCE)

Renamed Prima Aero Trasporti Italiani ; ops terminated late 2011

## ELBAFLY — Elba-Island de Campo (EBA)

| | | | | |
|---|---|---|---|---|
| ☐ EY-WDT | LET L-410UVP-E | 912615 | ex OK-WDT | ♦ |

## ELIDOLOMITI — Elidolomiti (EDO) — Belluno (BLX)

| | | | | |
|---|---|---|---|---|
| ☐ EC-JKP | Agusta A.109E Power | 11637 | | EMS <HSE |
| ☐ I-AGKL | Agusta A.109K2 | 10020 | | EMS |
| ☐ I-REMJ | Agusta A.109S Grand | 22041 | | EMS |
| ☐ I-REMV | Agusta A.109E Power | 11119 | | EMS |

## ELIFRIULA — Elifriula (EFG) — Trieste (TRS)

| | | | | |
|---|---|---|---|---|
| ☐ I-ASAP | Aérospatiale AS350B3 Ecureuil | 7110 | | ♦ |
| ☐ I-HBLU | Aérospatiale AS350B3 Ecureuil | 3940 | ex F-WWPE | |
| ☐ I-HOLD | Aérospatiale AS350B3 Ecureuil | 3566 | | |
| ☐ I-HORT | Aérospatiale AS350B Ecureuil | 3699 | | |
| ☐ I-HPLC | Aérospatiale AS350B Ecureuil | 3702 | | |
| ☐ I-HALP | Eurocopter EC135T2 | 0469 | ex D-HDOL | |
| ☐ I-HFVG | Eurocopter EC135T2 | 1025 | | ♦ |
| ☐ I-ORAO | Aérospatiale AS355N Ecureuil 2 | 5583 | | |

## ELILARIO ITALIA — Lario (ELH) — Colico/Bergamo-Orio al Serio(-/BGY)

| | | | | |
|---|---|---|---|---|
| ☐ I-AICO | MBB BK-117C-1 | 7542 | ex D-HZBV | |
| ☐ I-DENI | MBB BK-117C-1 | 7539 | | |
| ☐ I-EITF | MBB BK-117C-1 | 9082 | ex D-HMBI | |
| ☐ I-EITG | MBB BK-117C-1 | 9086 | ex D-HMBN | |
| ☐ I-EITH | MBB BK-117C-1 | 9093 | ex D-HMBB | EMS |
| ☐ I-MESO | MBB BK-117C-1 | 7532 | ex D-HMB. | |
| ☐ I-DAMS | Aérospatiale AS365N3 Dauphin 2 | 6700 | ex F-WWQX | |
| ☐ I-EITB | Agusta-Bell 412SP | 25972 | | |
| ☐ I-EITC | Agusta A.109S Grand | 22007 | | |
| ☐ I-EITD | Agusta AW139 | 31054 | | |
| ☐ I-LOBE | Aérospatiale AS365N3 Dauphin 2 | 6699 | ex F-WWQX | |
| ☐ I-NUBJ | Agusta-Bell 412EP | 25913 | | |
| ☐ I-RCPM | Agusta A.109E Power Elite | 11172 | | |
| ☐ I-RMTI | Agusta-Bell 412EP | 25923 | | |

| | | | | | |
|---|---|---|---|---|---|
| ☐ I-RNBR | Agusta-Bell 412EP | 25921 | | | |
| ☐ I-ROCS | Agusta AW139 | 31005 | | | EMS |

## ELILOMBARDA (EQA) Calcinate del Pesce

| | | | | | |
|---|---|---|---|---|---|
| ☐ I-CEPA | Agusta AW139 | 31050 | | | |
| ☐ I-CESR | Agusta A.109S Grand | 22033 | | | |
| ☐ I-HELO | Agusta A.109E Power | 11605 | | | |
| ☐ I-MALF | Agusta-Bell 412EP | 25975 | | | EMS |
| ☐ I-MECE | Agusta-Bell 412EP | 25976 | | | EMS |
| ☐ I- | Agusta A.109E Power | 11100 | ex OE-XSA | | ♦ |
| ☐ I- | Agusta A.109E Power | 11148 | ex OE-XSB | | ♦ |

## ELITALIANA

| | | | | | |
|---|---|---|---|---|---|
| ☐ I-PNTE | Agusta AW.109SP | 22173 | | | ♦ |

## EUROPEAN AIR CRANE Florence (FLR)

European Air Crane is a subsidiary of Erikson Air Crane and ops Erickson/Sikorsky S-64E Skycranes for Corpo Forestale (I-)

## HELI-ITALIA Helitalia (HIT) Florence (FLR)

| | | | | | |
|---|---|---|---|---|---|
| ☐ I-HBHA | Agusta A.109K2 | 10023 | ex I-ECAM | | EMS |
| ☐ I-HBMS | MBB BK-117C-1 | 7531 | ex D-HMBB | | EMS |
| ☐ I-HDBX | MBB BK-117C-1 | 7546 | ex D-HDBX | | EMS |
| ☐ I-HDBZ | MBB BK-117C-1 | 7547 | ex D-HDBZ | | EMS |
| ☐ I-HDPR | Agusta A.109E | 11625 | | | EMS |
| ☐ I-HKAV | MBB BK-117C-1 | 7540 | ex D-HKAV | | EMS |
| ☐ I-RRMM | Agusta A.109E Power | 11667 | | | EMS |

## ITALIATOUR (OI/IAZ)

| | | | | | |
|---|---|---|---|---|---|
| ☐ I-CLBA | Avro 146-RJ85 | E2300 | ex EI-CNJ | | [SEN] |

## LIVINGSTON (LM/LVG)

| | | | | | |
|---|---|---|---|---|---|
| ☐ EI-ERH | Airbus A320-232 | 2157 | ex G-TTOJ | | ♦ |

## MERIDIANA FLY Merair (IG/EEZ) Olbia (OLB)

| | | | | | |
|---|---|---|---|---|---|
| ☐ EI-EZN | Airbus A320-232 | 1715 | ex I-EEZN | | ♦ |
| ☐ EI-EZO | Airbus A320-232 | 1723 | ex I-EEZO | | |
| ☐ EI-EZR | Airbus A320-214 | 1198 | ex N267AV | | |
| ☐ EI-EZS | Airbus A320-232 | 1823 | ex D-ANNH | | |
| ☐ EI-EZT | Airbus A320-214 | 1896 | ex D-ANNJ | | ♦ |
| ☐ I-EEZE | Airbus A320-214 | 1937 | ex F-WWIO | | ♦ |
| ☐ I-EEZF | Airbus A320-214 | 1983 | ex F-WWDM | | |
| ☐ I-EEZG | Airbus A320-214 | 2001 | ex F-WWBB | Domina titles | |
| ☐ I-EEZH | Airbus A320-214 | 0737 | ex F-GRSG | | |
| ☐ I-EEZI | Airbus A320-214 | 0749 | ex F-GRSH | | |
| ☐ I-EEZK | Airbus A320-214 | 1125 | ex I-VLEA | | |
| ☐ I-EEZP | Airbus A320-233 | 2102 | ex N489TA | | |
| | | | | | |
| ☐ EI-CRE | McDonnell-Douglas MD-83 | 49854/1601 | ex D-ALLL | Tavolara-Punta Coda Cavallo | wfs |
| ☐ I-SMEB | McDonnell-Douglas MD-82 | 53064/1908 | ex B-28001 | Parco di Baia | wfs |
| ☐ I-SMEL | McDonnell-Douglas MD-82 | 49247/1151 | ex HB-IKK | Parco Gaiola | |
| ☐ I-SMEM | McDonnell-Douglas MD-82 | 49248/1152 | ex HB-IKL | Penisola del sinis | |
| ☐ I-SMEN | McDonnell-Douglas MD-83 | 53013/1738 | ex EI-CRJ | Isole Egadi | [OLB] |
| ☐ I-SMEP | McDonnell-Douglas MD-82 | 49740/1618 | | Punta Campanella | |
| ☐ I-SMER | McDonnell-Douglas MD-82 | 49901/1766 | ex N6202S | Cinque Terre | [OLB] |
| ☐ I-SMES | McDonnell-Douglas MD-82 | 49902/1948 | | Isole Pelagie | |
| ☐ I-SMET | McDonnell-Douglas MD-82 | 49531/1362 | | Miramere nel Golfo di Trieste | |
| ☐ I-SMEV | McDonnell-Douglas MD-82 | 49669/1493 | | Isole di Ventotene e Santo Stefano | [OLB] |
| ☐ I-SMEZ | McDonnell-Douglas MD-82 | 49903/1949 | ex PH-SEZ | Secche di Tor Patemo | wfs |
| | | | | | |
| ☐ EI-DEZ | Airbus A319-112 | 1283 | ex F-WQQE | Capo Gallo | |
| ☐ EI-DFA | Airbus A319-112 | 1305 | ex D-ANDI | Capo Carbonara | |
| ☐ EI-DFP | Airbus A319-112 | 1048 | ex F-OHJV | Capo Caccia | |
| ☐ I-EEZJ | Airbus A330-223 | 665 | ex F-WWKO | Campari titles | |
| ☐ EI-EZL | Airbus A330-223 | 802 | ex I-EEZL | | |
| ☐ I-EEZM | Airbus A330-223 | 822 | ex 4X-ABE | | |

## MINILINER Miniliner (MNL) Bergamo-Orio al Serio (BGY)

| | | | | | |
|---|---|---|---|---|---|
| ☐ I-MLGT | Fokker F.27 Friendship 500 | 10379 | ex F-BPUG | | |
| ☐ I-MLHT | Fokker F.27 Friendship 500 | 10382 | ex F-BPUH | | |
| ☐ I-MLRT | Fokker F.27 Friendship 500 | 10377 | ex F-BPUE | | |
| ☐ I-MLTT | Fokker F.27 Friendship 500 | 10378 | ex F-BPUF | | |
| ☐ I-MLUT | Fokker F.27 Friendship 500 | 10369 | ex F-BPUA | | |

| | | | | | | |
|---|---|---|---|---|---|---|
| ☐ I-MLVT | Fokker F.27 Friendship 500 | 10373 | ex F-BPUC | | | |
| ☐ I-MLXT | Fokker F.27 Friendship 500 | 10374 | ex F-BPUD | | | |
| ☐ I-MLCT | Fokker 50 | 20191 | ex PH-KVC | Frtr | | [BGY] |
| ☐ I-MLDT | Fokker 50 | 20197 | ex PH-KVD | Frtr | | [BGY] |
| ☐ PH-LMB | Fokker 50 | 20119 | ex (PH-LCD) | Frtr | | >APF |

### MISTRAL AIR — Airmerci (MSA) — Rome-Ciampino (CIA)

| | | | | | |
|---|---|---|---|---|---|
| ☐ EI-DMR | Boeing 737-436 | 25851/2387 | ex G-DOCR | | ♦ |
| ☐ EI-DUS | Boeing 737-3M8 (QC) | 24021/1630 | ex TF-ELM | Maestrale | |
| ☐ EI-DVA | Boeing 737-36E (QC) | 25159/2068 | ex F-GIXM | | |
| ☐ EI-DVC | Boeing 737-33A (QC) | 25426/2172 | ex SE-DPC | Libeccio | |
| ☐ EI-ELZ | Boeing 737-4Q8 | 26308/2665 | ex SX-BGV | | |
| ☐ EI-SLA | ATR 42-300F | 0149 | ex SE-LST | | <ABR |

### NEOS — Moonflower (NO/NOS) — Milan-Malpensa (MXP)

| | | | | |
|---|---|---|---|---|
| ☐ I-NEOS | Boeing 737-86N/W | 32733/1078 | | Citta di Milano |
| ☐ I-NEOT | Boeing 737-86N/W | 33004/1144 | | Citta di Torino |
| ☐ I-NEOU | Boeing 737-86N/W | 29887/1263 | | Citta di Verona |
| ☐ I-NEOW | Boeing 737-86N/W | 32685/2186 | ex G-XLAN | Lago Maggiore |
| ☐ I-NEOX | Boeing 737-86N/W | 33677/1486 | | Citta di Bologna |
| ☐ I-NEOZ | Boeing 737-86N/W | 34257/2024 | ex SU-BPH | |
| ☐ I-NDMJ | Boeing 767-306ER/W | 27958/589 | ex EI-DMJ | |
| ☐ I-NDOF | Boeing 767-306ER | 27610/605 | ex EI-DOF | |

### ROTKOPF AVIATION ITALY

| | | | | |
|---|---|---|---|---|
| ☐ I-KOPF | Cessna 208B Caravan I | 208B2219 | | ♦ |

### SKYBRIDGE AIROPS — Rome-Ciampano (CIA)

| | | | | |
|---|---|---|---|---|
| ☐ F-GLRG | Embraer EMB.120ER Brasilia | 120149 | ex PH-MGX | ♦ |
| ☐ I-SKYB | Embraer EMB.120RT Brasilia | 120087 | ex F-GTSG | |

### SOREM / PROTEZIONE CIVILE — Rome-Ciampano/Urbe (CIA/ROM)

| | | | | |
|---|---|---|---|---|
| ☐ I-DPCC | Canadair CL415 | 2066 | ex C-FNLH | 27 |
| ☐ I-DPCD | Canadair CL415 | 2003 | ex C-FTUA | 7 |
| ☐ I-DPCE | Canadair CL415 | 2004 | ex C-FTUS | 8 |
| ☐ I-DPCF | Canadair CL415 | 2059 | ex C-GIWU | 23 |
| ☐ I-DPCG | Canadair CL415 | 2060 | ex C-GJHU | 24 |
| ☐ I-DPCH | Canadair CL415 | 2062 | ex C-GJLB | 25 |
| ☐ I-DPCI | Canadair CL415 | 2058 | ex C-GISM | 26 |
| ☐ I-DPCN | Canadair CL415 | 2070 | ex C-FUEP | 28 |
| ☐ I-DPCO | Canadair CL415 | 2009 | ex C-FVRA | 10 |
| ☐ I-DPCP | Canadair CL415 | 2020 | ex C-FYCY | 11 |
| ☐ I-DPCQ | Canadair CL415 | 2021 | ex C-FYDA | 12 |
| ☐ I-DPCR | Canadair CL415 | 2074 | ex C-FZTY | |
| ☐ I-DPCS | Canadair CL415 | 2073 | ex C-FZEG | |
| ☐ I-DPCT | Canadair CL415 | 2029 | ex C-FZYS | 18 |
| ☐ I-DPCU | Canadair CL415 | 2030 | ex C-GALV | 14 |
| ☐ I-DPCV | Canadair CL415 | 2035 | ex C-GCXG | 15 |
| ☐ I-DPCW | Canadair CL415 | 2036 | ex C-GDHW | 6 |
| ☐ I-DPCY | Canadair CL415 | 2047 | ex C-GFUS | 20 |
| ☐ I-DPCZ | Canadair CL415 | 2048 | ex C-GGCW | 21 |
| ☐ I-SRMA | Canadair CL215 | 1004 | ex I-SMRA | A1 |

### WINDJET — Ghibli (IV/JET) — Catania (CTA)

| | | | | |
|---|---|---|---|---|
| ☐ EI-DVD | Airbus A319-113 | 0647 | ex F-GPMH | |
| ☐ EI-DVU | Airbus A319-113 | 0660 | ex F-GPMI | |
| ☐ EI-ECX | Airbus A319-132 | 2698 | ex N515NK | |
| ☐ EI-ECY | Airbus A319-132 | 2723 | ex N519NK | |
| ☐ EI-ESG | Airbus A319-132 | 2797 | ex N611LF | ♦ |
| ☐ EI-CUM | Airbus A320-232 | 0542 | ex N721LF | |
| ☐ EI-DFN | Airbus A320-211 | 204 | ex F-GJVC | ♦ |
| ☐ EI-DFO | Airbus A320-211 | 0371 | ex A6-ABX | |
| ☐ EI-DNP | Airbus A320-212 | 0421 | ex A4O-EF | |
| ☐ EI-DOE | Airbus A320-211 | 0215 | ex F-GJVE | |
| ☐ EI-DOP | Airbus A320-232 | 0816 | ex B-HSF | |
| ☐ EI-ELG | Airbus A320-232 | 0877 | ex B-HSH | |
| ☐ F-GJVC | Airbus A320-211 | 0204 | ex EI-DFN | |
| ☐ I-LINH | Airbus A320-231 | 0163 | ex G-RDVE | |

## JA    JAPAN

### AIR DOLPHIN
Okinawa-Naha (OKA)

| | | | |
|---|---|---|---|
| ☐ JA3428 | Cessna P206C Super Skylane | P206-0517 | ex N1610C |
| ☐ JA5320 | Britten-Norman BN-2B-20 Islander | 2269 | ex G-BUBM |

### AIR JAPAN
Air Japan (NQ/AJX)    Osaka-Itami/Kansi (ITM/KIX)

| | | | |
|---|---|---|---|
| ☐ JA55OZ | Cessna 208B Caravan I | 208B0530 | ex N164SA |

### AIR NIPPON
ANK Air (EL/ANK)    Tokyo-Haneda (HND)

Fleet included under ANA – All Nippon

### AMAKUSA AIRLINES
(AHX)    Kumamoto (KMJ)

| | | | |
|---|---|---|---|
| ☐ JA81AM | de Havilland DHC-8Q-103 | 537 | ex C-FCSG |

### ANA - ALL NIPPON AIRWAYS
All Nippon (NH/ANA)    Tokyo-Haneda (HND)

Member of Star Alliance

| | | | | |
|---|---|---|---|---|
| ☐ JA205A | Airbus A320-214 | 3099 | ex F-WWIE | |
| ☐ JA206A | Airbus A320-214 | 3147 | ex F-WWBQ | |
| ☐ JA207A | Airbus A320-214 | 3148 | ex F-WWBR | |
| ☐ JA208A | Airbus A320-214 | 3189 | ex F-WWDZ | |
| ☐ JA8300 | Airbus A320-211 | 0549 | ex F-WWIT | |
| ☐ JA8304 | Airbus A320-211 | 0531 | ex F-WWDY | |
| ☐ JA8313 | Airbus A320-211 | 0534 | ex F-WWBC | |
| ☐ JA8382 | Airbus A320-211 | 0139 | ex F-WWDF | |
| ☐ JA8384 | Airbus A320-211 | 0151 | ex F-WWDR | |
| ☐ JA8385 | Airbus A320-211 | 0167 | ex F-WWIE | [SDJ] |
| ☐ JA8386 | Airbus A320-211 | 0170 | ex F-WWII | |
| ☐ JA8388 | Airbus A320-211 | 0212 | ex F-WWIG | |
| ☐ JA8390 | Airbus A320-211 | 0245 | ex F-WWDE | |
| ☐ JA8391 | Airbus A320-211 | 0300 | ex F-WWDD | |
| ☐ JA8392 | Airbus A320-211 | 0328 | ex F-WWDR | |
| ☐ JA8393 | Airbus A320-211 | 0365 | ex F-WWBZ | |
| ☐ JA8394 | Airbus A320-211 | 0383 | ex F-WWBF | |
| ☐ JA8395 | Airbus A320-211 | 0413 | ex F-WWIM | |
| ☐ JA8396 | Airbus A320-211 | 0482 | ex F-WWIO | |
| ☐ JA8400 | Airbus A320-211 | 0554 | ex F-WWIG | |
| ☐ JA8609 | Airbus A320-211 | 0501 | ex F-WWIN | |
| ☐ JA8654 | Airbus A320-211 | 0507 | ex F-WWBT | |
| ☐ JA8946 | Airbus A320-211 | 0669 | ex F-WWBD | |
| ☐ JA8947 | Airbus A320-211 | 0685 | ex F-WWDR | |
| ☐ JA8997 | Airbus A320-211 | 0658 | ex F-WWIU | |
| | | | | |
| ☐ JA301K | Boeing 737-54K | 27435/2875 | | >ADO |
| ☐ JA303K | Boeing 737-54K | 28991/3017 | | |
| ☐ JA305K | Boeing 737-54K | 28993/3075 | ex N1781B | >ADO |
| ☐ JA352K | Boeing 737-5Y0 | 26097/2534 | ex N97NK | |
| ☐ JA8196 | Boeing 737-54K | 27966/2824 | | >ADO |
| ☐ JA8404 | Boeing 737-54K | 27381/2708 | ex N35108 | >ADO |
| ☐ JA8419 | Boeing 737-54K | 27430/2723 | | |
| | | | | |
| ☐ JA01AN | Boeing 737-781/W | 33916/1781 | ex N6066U | |
| ☐ JA02AN | Boeing 737-781/W | 33872/1850 | | |
| ☐ JA03AN | Boeing 737-781/W | 33873/1871 | ex N1787B | |
| ☐ JA04AN | Boeing 737-781/W | 33874/1890 | ex N1781B | |
| ☐ JA05AN | Boeing 737-781/W | 33875/1971 | | |
| ☐ JA06AN | Boeing 737-781/W | 33876/1992 | | |
| ☐ JA07AN | Boeing 737-781/W | 33900/2071 | | |
| ☐ JA08AN | Boeing 737-781/W | 33877/2086 | | |
| ☐ JA09AN | Boeing 737-781/W | 33878/2145 | | |
| ☐ JA10AN | Boeing 737-781ER/W | 33879/2157 | ex N716BA | |
| ☐ JA11AN | Boeing 737-781/W | 33882/2268 | | |
| ☐ JA12AN | Boeing 737-781/W | 33881/2301 | | |
| ☐ JA13AN | Boeing 737-781ER/W | 33880/2232 | ex N717BA | |
| ☐ JA14AN | Boeing 737-781/W | 33883/2370 | | |
| ☐ JA15AN | Boeing 737-781/W | 33888/2394 | | |
| ☐ JA16AN | Boeing 737-781/W | 33889/2488 | | |
| ☐ JA17AN | Boeing 737-781/W | 33884/2513 | | |
| ☐ JA18AN | Boeing 737-781/W | 33885/2582 | | |
| | | | | |
| ☐ JA51AN | Boeing 737-881/W | 33886/2607 | ex N1786B | |
| ☐ JA52AN | Boeing 737-8781/W | 33887/2643 | | |
| ☐ JA53AN | Boeing 737-881/W | 33891/2739 | | |
| ☐ JA54AN | Boeing 737-881/W | 33890/2833 | | |

| □ | JA55AN | Boeing 737-881/W | 33892/2889 | | |
|---|--------|------------------|-----------|---|---|
| □ | JA56AN | Boeing 737-881/W | 33893/2926 | | |
| □ | JA57AN | Boeing 737-881/W | 33894/2975 | ex N1787B | |
| □ | JA58AN | Boeing 737-881/W | 33895/3029 | ex N1796B | |
| □ | JA59AN | Boeing 737-881/W | 33886/3073 | | |
| □ | JA60AN | Boeing 737-881/W | 33897/3126 | | |
| □ | JA61AN | Boeing 737-881/W | 33898/3379 | | |
| □ | JA62AN | Boeing 737-881/W | 33899/3414 | | |
| □ | JA63AN | Boeing 737-881/W | 33901/3449 | ex N1787B | |
| □ | JA64AN | Boeing 737-881/W | 33902/3478 | ex N1787B | |
| □ | JA65AN | Boeing 737-881/W | 33903/3502 | ex N1786B | |
| □ | JA66AN | Boeing 737-881/W | 33909/3598 | | |
| □ | JA67AN | Boeing 737-881/W | 33911/3682 | | |
| | | | | | |
| □ | JA8099 | Boeing 747-481D | 25292/891 | | [HND] |
| □ | JA8956 | Boeing 747-481D | 25640/920 | Pocket Monsters 2004 c/s | |
| □ | JA8957 | Boeing 747-481D | 25642/927 | Pocket Monsters c/s | |
| □ | JA8959 | Boeing 747-481D | 25646/952 | | |
| □ | JA8960 | Boeing 747-481D | 25643/972 | | |
| □ | JA8961 | Boeing 747-481D | 25644/975 | | |
| □ | JA8965 | Boeing 747-481D | 27436/1060 | | |
| □ | JA8966 | Boeing 747-481D | 27442/1066 | | |
| | | | | | |
| □ | JA602A | Boeing 767-381 | 27944/684 | | |
| □ | JA602F | Boeing 767-381F | 33509/937 | | |
| □ | JA603A | Boeing 767-381ER | 32972/877 | ex N6046P | |
| □ | JA604A | Boeing 767-381ER | 32973/881 | | |
| □ | JA604F | Boeing 767-381F | 35709/947 | | |
| □ | JA605A | Boeing 767-381ER | 32974/882 | | |
| □ | JA606A | Boeing 767-381ER | 32975/883 | Fly Panda c/s | |
| □ | JA607A | Boeing 767-381ER | 32976/884 | | |
| □ | JA608A | Boeing 767-381ER | 32977/886 | | |
| □ | JA609A | Boeing 767-381ER | 32978/888 | | |
| □ | JA610A | Boeing 767-381ER | 32979/895 | | |
| □ | JA611A | Boeing 767-381ER | 32980/914 | Star Cluster c/s | |
| □ | JA612A | Boeing 767-381ER | 33506/920 | | |
| □ | JA613A | Boeing 767-381ER | 33507/924 | | |
| □ | JA614A | Boeing 767-381ER | 33508/931 | Star Alliance c/s | |
| □ | JA615A | Boeing 767-381ER | 35877/951 | | |
| □ | JA616A | Boeing 767-381ER | 35876/953 | | |
| □ | JA617A | Boeing 767-381ER | 37719/971 | | |
| □ | JA618A | Boeing 767-381ER | 37720/976 | | |
| □ | JA619A | Boeing 767-381ER/W | 40564/993 | | |
| □ | JA620A | Boeing 767-381ER/W | 40565/996 | | |
| □ | JA621A | Boeing 767-381ER/W | 40566/998 | | |
| □ | JA622A | Boeing 767-381ER/W | 40567/1000 | | ♦ |
| □ | JA623A | Boeing 767-381ER/W | 40894/1001 | | ♦ |
| □ | JA624A | Boeing 767-381ER/W | 40895/1010 | | ♦ |
| □ | JA625A | Boeing 767-381ER/W | 40896/1012 | | ♦ |
| □ | JA626A | Boeing 767-381ER/W | 40897/1018 | | ♦ |
| □ | JA627A | Boeing 767-381ER | 40898/1023 | | ♦ |
| □ | JA8256 | Boeing 767-381 | 23756/176 | ex N6005C | |
| □ | JA8257 | Boeing 767-381 | 23757/177 | ex N6038E | |
| □ | JA8258 | Boeing 767-381 | 23758/179 | ex N6055X | |
| □ | JA8259 | Boeing 767-381 | 23759/185 | ex N6038E | |
| □ | JA8271 | Boeing 767-381 | 24002/199 | ex N60668 | |
| □ | JA8272 | Boeing 767-381 | 24003/212 | ex N6038E | |
| □ | JA8273 | Boeing 767-381 | 24004/218 | ex N6055X | |
| □ | JA8274 | Boeing 767-381 | 24005/222 | ex N6046P | |
| □ | JA8275 | Boeing 767-381 | 24006/223 | ex N6018N | |
| □ | JA8285 | Boeing 767-381 | 24350/245 | ex N1789B | |
| □ | JA8286 | Boeing 767-381ERBCF | 24400/269 | | |
| □ | JA8287 | Boeing 767-381 | 24351/271 | | |
| □ | JA8288 | Boeing 767-381 | 24415/276 | | |
| □ | JA8289 | Boeing 767-381 | 24416/280 | | |
| □ | JA8290 | Boeing 767-381 | 24417/290 | | |
| □ | JA8291 | Boeing 767-381 | 24755/295 | | |
| □ | JA8322 | Boeing 767-381 | 25618/458 | | |
| □ | JA8323 | Boeing 767-381ERBCF | 25654/463 | | |
| □ | JA8324 | Boeing 767-381 | 25655/465 | | |
| □ | JA8342 | Boeing 767-381 | 27445/573 | | |
| □ | JA8356 | Boeing 767-381ERBCF | 25136/379 | | |
| □ | JA8357 | Boeing 767-381 | 25293/401 | | |
| □ | JA8358 | Boeing 767-381ERBCF | 25616/432 | | |
| □ | JA8359 | Boeing 767-381 | 25617/439 | | >ADO |
| □ | JA8360 | Boeing 767-381 | 25055/352 | | |
| □ | JA8362 | Boeing 767-381ERBCF | 24632/285 | | |
| □ | JA8363 | Boeing 767-381 | 24756/300 | | |
| □ | JA8368 | Boeing 767-381 | 24880/336 | | |
| □ | JA8567 | Boeing 767-381 | 25656/510 | | |
| □ | JA8568 | Boeing 767-381 | 25657/515 | | |
| □ | JA8569 | Boeing 767-381 | 27050/516 | | |

| | | | | | |
|---|---|---|---|---|---|
| ☐ JA8578 | Boeing 767-381 | 25658/519 | | | |
| ☐ JA8579 | Boeing 767-381 | 25659/520 | | | |
| ☐ JA8664 | Boeing 767-381ER | 27339/556 | | | |
| ☐ JA8669 | Boeing 767-381 | 27444/567 | | | |
| ☐ JA8670 | Boeing 767-381 | 25660/539 | | | |
| ☐ JA8674 | Boeing 767-381 | 25661/543 | | | |
| ☐ JA8677 | Boeing 767-381 | 25662/551 | | | |
| ☐ JA8970 | Boeing 767-381ER | 25619/645 | | | |
| ☐ JA8971 | Boeing 767-381ER | 27942/651 | | | |
| | | | | | |
| ☐ JA701A | Boeing 777-281 | 27938/77 | | | |
| ☐ JA702A | Boeing 777-281 | 27033/75 | | | |
| ☐ JA703A | Boeing 777-281 | 27034/81 | ex N50217 | | |
| ☐ JA704A | Boeing 777-281 | 27035/131 | | | |
| ☐ JA705A | Boeing 777-281 | 29029/137 | | | |
| ☐ JA706A | Boeing 777-281 | 27036/141 | | | |
| ☐ JA707A | Boeing 777-281ER | 27037/247 | | | |
| ☐ JA708A | Boeing 777-281ER | 28277/278 | | | |
| ☐ JA709A | Boeing 777-281ER | 28278/286 | | | |
| ☐ JA710A | Boeing 777-281ER | 28279/302 | | | |
| ☐ JA711A | Boeing 777-281 | 33406/482 | | Star Alliance c/s | |
| ☐ JA712A | Boeing 777-281 | 33407/495 | | Star Alliance c/s | |
| ☐ JA713A | Boeing 777-281 | 32647/509 | | | |
| ☐ JA714A | Boeing 777-281 | 28276/523 | | | |
| ☐ JA715A | Boeing 777-281ER | 32646/563 | | | |
| ☐ JA716A | Boeing 777-281ER | 33414/574 | | | |
| ☐ JA717A | Boeing 777-281ER | 33415/580 | | | |
| ☐ JA741A | Boeing 777-281ER | 40900 | | | o/o♦ |
| ☐ JA742A | Boeing 777-281ER | 40901 | | | o/o♦ |
| ☐ JA8197 | Boeing 777-281 | 27027/16 | ex N5016R | | |
| ☐ JA8198 | Boeing 777-281 | 27028/21 | | | |
| ☐ JA8199 | Boeing 777-281 | 27029/29 | | | |
| ☐ JA8967 | Boeing 777-281 | 27030/37 | | | |
| ☐ JA8968 | Boeing 777-281 | 27031/38 | | | |
| ☐ JA8969 | Boeing 777-281 | 27032/50 | | | |
| | | | | | |
| ☐ JA731A | Boeing 777-381ER | 28281/488 | ex N240BA | Star Alliance c/s | |
| ☐ JA732A | Boeing 777-381ER | 27038/511 | | | |
| ☐ JA733A | Boeing 777-381ER | 32648/529 | ex N5014K | | |
| ☐ JA734A | Boeing 777-381ER | 32649/557 | | | |
| ☐ JA735A | Boeing 777-381ER | 34892/571 | | | |
| ☐ JA736A | Boeing 777-381ER | 34893/589 | | | |
| ☐ JA751A | Boeing 777-381 | 28272/142 | ex N5017Q | | |
| ☐ JA752A | Boeing 777-381 | 28274/160 | | | |
| ☐ JA753A | Boeing 777-381 | 28273/132 | | Sky Blue | |
| ☐ JA754A | Boeing 777-381 | 27939/172 | | Sky Lark | |
| ☐ JA755A | Boeing 777-381 | 28275/104 | ex N5017Q | | |
| ☐ JA756A | Boeing 777-381 | 27039/440 | | | |
| ☐ JA757A | Boeing 777-381 | 27040/442 | | | |
| ☐ JA777A | Boeing 777-381ER | 32650/593 | | | |
| ☐ JA778A | Boeing 777-381ER | 32651/606 | | | |
| ☐ JA779A | Boeing 777-381ER | 34894/631 | | | |
| ☐ JA780A | Boeing 777-381ER | 34895/639 | | | |
| ☐ JA781A | Boeing 777-381ER | 27041/667 | | | |
| ☐ JA782A | Boeing 777-381ER | 33416/691 | | | |
| ☐ JA783A | Boeing 777-381ER | 27940/737 | | | |
| ☐ JA784A | Boeing 777-381ER | 37950/833 | | | |
| ☐ JA785A | Boeing 777-381ER | 37951/855 | | | |
| ☐ JA786A | Boeing 777-381ER | 37948/866 | | | |
| ☐ JA787A | Boeing 777-381ER | 37949/870 | | | |
| ☐ JA788A | Boeing 777-381ER | 40686/873 | | | |
| ☐ JA789A | Boeing 777-381ER | 40687/878 | | | |
| | | | | | |
| ☐ JA801A | Boeing 787-8 | 34488/8 | | | ♦ |
| ☐ JA802A | Boeing 787-8 | 34497/24 | ex N1006F | | ♦ |
| ☐ JA803A | Boeing 787-8 | 34485/7 | | | ♦ |
| ☐ JA804A | Boeing 787-8 | 34486/9 | ex N1006F | | ♦ |
| ☐ JA805A | Boeing 787-8 | 34514/31 | | | ♦ |
| ☐ JA806A | Boeing 787-8 | 34515/40 | | | ♦ |
| ☐ JA807A | Boeing 787-8 | 34508/41 | | | ♦ |
| ☐ JA808A | Boeing 787-8 | 34990/ | | | o/o♦ |
| ☐ JA809A | Boeing 787-8 | 34494/47 | | | o/o♦ |
| ☐ JA810A | Boeing 787-8 | 34506/48 | | | o/o♦ |
| ☐ JA811A | Boeing 787-8 | 34487/18 | | | o/o♦ |
| ☐ JA812A | Boeing 787-8 | 40748/ | | | o/o♦ |
| ☐ JA815A | Boeing 787-8 | 34499/ | | | o/o♦ |
| ☐ JA816A | Boeing 787-8 | 34500/ | | | o/o♦ |
| ☐ JA817A | Boeing 787-8 | 34501/ | | | o/o♦ |
| | | | | | |
| ☐ JA392K | Boeing 737-46M | 28550/2847 | ex N8550F | | >SNJ |

## ANA WINGS (EH/AKX)

| | | | | | |
|---|---|---|---|---|---|
| ☐ | JA802K | de Havilland DHC-8Q-314 | 577 | ex C-FDHD | ♦ |
| ☐ | JA803K | de Havilland DHC-8Q-314 | 583 | ex C-FDHW | ♦ |
| ☐ | JA804K | de Havilland DHC-8Q-314 | 591 | ex C-GFUM | ♦ |
| ☐ | JA841A | de Havilland DHC-8-402Q | 4080 | ex C-GDLK | ♦ |
| ☐ | JA842A | de Havilland DHC-8-402Q | 4082 | ex C-GFOD | ♦ |
| ☐ | JA843A | de Havilland DHC-8-402Q | 4084 | ex C-GFQL | ♦ |
| ☐ | JA844A | de Havilland DHC-8-402Q | 4091 | ex C-GHRI | ♦ |
| ☐ | JA845A | de Havilland DHC-8-402Q | 4096 | ex C-FAQB | ♦ |
| ☐ | JA846A | de Havilland DHC-8-402Q | 4097 | ex C-FAQD | ♦ |
| ☐ | JA847A | de Havilland DHC-8-402Q | 4099 | ex C-FAQK | ♦ |
| ☐ | JA848A | de Havilland DHC-8-402Q | 4102 | ex C-FCQA | ♦ |
| ☐ | JA850A | de Havilland DHC-8-402Q | 4108 | ex C-FCVJ | ♦ |
| ☐ | JA851A | de Havilland DHC-8-402Q | 4109 | ex C-FCVK | ♦ |
| ☐ | JA852A | de Havilland DHC-8-402Q | 4131 | ex C-FGKC | ♦ |
| ☐ | JA853A | de Havilland DHC-8-402Q | 4135 | ex C-FGKN | ♦ |
| ☐ | JA854A | de Havilland DHC-8-402Q | 4151 | ex C-FJLH | ♦ |
| ☐ | JA855A | de Havilland DHC-8-402Q | 4292 | ex C-GAUB | ♦ |
| ☐ | JA856A | de Havilland DHC-8-402Q | 4335 | ex C-GGHS | ♦ |
| ☐ | JA857A | de Havilland DHC-8-402Q | 4362 | ex C-GISU | ♦ |
| ☐ | JA858A | de Havilland DHC-8-402Q | 4385 | ex C-GKVD | ♦ |
| ☐ | JA859A | de Havilland DHC-8-402Q | 4401 | ex C-GLKE | ♦ |
| ☐ | JA302K | Boeing 737-54K | 28990/3002 | ex N1787B | ♦ |
| ☐ | JA304K | Boeing 737-54K | 28992/3030 | | ♦ |
| ☐ | JA306K | Boeing 737-54K | 29794/3109 | ex N1786B | ♦ |
| ☐ | JA307K | Boeing 737-54K | 29795/3116 | ex N60436 | ♦ |
| ☐ | JA353K | Boeing 737-5Y0 | 26104/2552 | ex N104NK | ♦ |
| ☐ | JA354K | Boeing 737-5Y0 | 26105/2553 | ex N105NK | ♦ |
| ☐ | JA356K | Boeing 737-5L9 | 28083/2784 | ex N8083N | ♦ |
| ☐ | JA357K | Boeing 737-5L9 | 28131/2828 | ex N88131 | ♦ |
| ☐ | JA358K | Boeing 737-5L9 | 28130/2825 | ex N8130J | ♦ |
| ☐ | JA359K | Boeing 737-5L9 | 28128/2817 | ex N8128R | ♦ |
| ☐ | JA8195 | Boeing 737-54K | 27433/2815 | | ♦ |
| ☐ | JA8500 | Boeing 737-54K | 27431/2751 | | ♦ |

## FUJI DREAM AIRLINES (JH / FDA)

| | | | | | |
|---|---|---|---|---|---|
| ☐ | JA01FJ | Embraer ERJ-170STD | 17000271 | ex PT-SNB | |
| ☐ | JA02FJ | Embraer ERJ-170STD | 17000289 | ex PT-TQP | |
| ☐ | JA03FJ | Embraer ERJ-175STD | 17000304 | ex PT-XQD | |
| ☐ | JA04FJ | Embraer ERJ-170SU | 17000129 | ex N866RW | |
| ☐ | JA05FJ | Embraer ERJ-175STD | 17000317 | ex PT-XUL | |
| ☐ | JA06FJ | Embraer ERJ-175STD | 17000332 | ex PT-TPV | ♦ |

## HANKYU AIRLINES

| | | | | | |
|---|---|---|---|---|---|
| ☐ | JA8229 | Cessna 208 Caravan I | 20800137 | ex N1570C | ♦ |
| ☐ | JA8890 | Cessna 208 Caravan I | 20800195 | ex N9776F | ♦ |

## HOKKAIDO AIR SYSTEM — North Air (NTH) — Sapporo-Chitose (CTS)

| | | | | | |
|---|---|---|---|---|---|
| ☐ | JA01HC | SAAB SF.340B | 340B-432 | ex SE-B32 | |
| ☐ | JA02HC | SAAB SF.340B | 340B-440 | ex SE-B40 | |
| ☐ | JA03HC | SAAB SF.340B | 340B-458 | ex SE-B58 | |

## HOKKAIDO INTERNATIONAL AIRLINES (HD/ADO)

| | | | | | |
|---|---|---|---|---|---|
| ☐ | JA300K | Boeing 737-54K | 27434/2872 | | ♦ |
| ☐ | JA301K | Boeing 737-54K | 27435/2875 | | <ANA♦ |
| ☐ | JA305K | Boeing 737-54K | 28993/3075 | ex N1781B | <ANA♦ |
| ☐ | JA8196 | Boeing 737-54K | 27966/2824 | | <ANA♦ |
| ☐ | JA8404 | Boeing 737-54K | 27381/2708 | ex N35108 | <ANA♦ |
| ☐ | JA8504 | Boeing 737-54K | 27434/2783 | | ♦ |
| ☐ | JA8595 | Boeing 737-54K | 28461/2850 | | ♦ |
| ☐ | JA601A | Boeing 767-381 | 27943/669 | | ♦ |

## IBEX AIRLINES — Fair (FW/IBX) — Sendai (SDJ)

| | | | | | |
|---|---|---|---|---|---|
| ☐ | JA01RJ | Canadair CRJ-100ER | 7052 | ex OE-LRD | |
| ☐ | JA02RJ | Canadair CRJ-100ER | 7033 | ex OE-LRB | |
| ☐ | JA03RJ | Canadair CRJ-200ER | 7624 | ex C-GJZF | |
| ☐ | JA04RJ | Canadair CRJ-200ER | 7798 | ex C-FMLF | |
| ☐ | JA05RJ | Canadair CRJ-702NG | 10279 | ex C-FYDI | |
| ☐ | JA06RJ | Canadair CRJ-702NG | 10303 | ex C-GFFK | |
| ☐ | JA07RJ | Canadair CRJ-702NG | 10327 | ex C-GIBG | |

## J-AIR                                    (JLJLG)                    Nagoya-Komaki (NKM)

| | | | | |
|---|---|---|---|---|
| ☐ JA201J | Canadair CRJ-200ER | 7452 | ex C-FMND | |
| ☐ JA202J | Canadair CRJ-200ER | 7484 | ex C-FMLU | |
| ☐ JA203J | Canadair CRJ-200ER | 7626 | ex C-FMNW | |
| ☐ JA204J | Canadair CRJ-200ER | 7643 | ex C-FMNB | |
| ☐ JA205J | Canadair CRJ-200ER | 7767 | ex C-FMLB | |
| ☐ JA206J | Canadair CRJ-200ER | 7834 | ex C-FMMT | |
| ☐ JA207J | Canadair CRJ-200ER | 8050 | ex C-FFVJ | |
| ☐ JA208J | Canadair CRJ-200ER | 8059 | ex C-FMOW | |
| ☐ JA209J | Canadair CRJ-200ER | 8062 | ex C-FMNQ | |
| | | | | |
| ☐ JA211J | Embraer ERJ-170STD | 17000251 | ex PT-SJC | |
| ☐ JA212J | Embraer ERJ-170STD | 17000268 | ex PT-SJW | |
| ☐ JA213J | Embraer ERJ-170STD | 17000285 | ex PT-TQL | |
| ☐ JA214J | Embraer ERJ-170STD | 17000295 | ex PT-TQV | |
| ☐ JA215J | Embraer ERJ-170STD | 17000297 | ex PT-TQX | |
| ☐ JA216J | Embraer ERJ-170STD | 17000299 | ex PT-TQY | |
| ☐ JA217J | Embraer ERJ-170STD | 17000308 | ex PT-XQW | |
| ☐ JA218J | Embraer ERJ-170STD | 17000314 | ex PT-XUI | |
| ☐ JA219J | Embraer ERJ-170STD | 17000315 | ex PT-XUJ | |
| ☐ JA220J | Embraer ERJ-170STD | 17000322 | ex PT- | ◆ |

## JAL EXPRESS                              Janex (JC/JEX)            Osaka-Kansai (KIX)

| | | | | |
|---|---|---|---|---|
| ☐ JA8991 | Boeing 737-446 | 27916/2718 | | |
| ☐ JA8992 | Boeing 737-446 | 27917/2729 | ex N1792B | |
| ☐ JA8993 | Boeing 737-446 | 28087/2812 | | |
| ☐ JA8994 | Boeing 737-446 | 28097/2907 | ex N1786B | |
| ☐ JA8995 | Boeing 737-446 | 28831/2911 | | |
| ☐ JA8996 | Boeing 737-446 | 28832/2953 | ex N1786B | |
| | | | | |
| ☐ JA307J | Boeing 737-846/W | 35336/2450 | | |
| ☐ JA308J | Boeing 737-846/W | 35337/2479 | ex N1786B | <JAL |
| ☐ JA309J | Boeing 737-846/W | 35338/2522 | | <JAL |
| ☐ JA311J | Boeing 737-846/W | 35340/2571 | | <JAL |
| ☐ JA313J | Boeing 737-846/W | 35342/2633 | | |
| ☐ JA314J | Boeing 737-846/W | 35343/2701 | | |
| ☐ JA316J | Boeing 737-846/W | 35345/2762 | | <JAL |
| ☐ JA319J | Boeing 737-846/W | 35348/2867 | ex N1795B | |
| ☐ JA322J | Boeing 737-846/W | 35351/3002 | | |
| ☐ JA323J | Boeing 737-846/W | 35352/3057 | ex N1787B | <JAL |
| ☐ JA324J | Boeing 737-846/W | 35353/3105 | ex N1786B | <JAL |
| ☐ JA325J | Boeing 737-846/W | 35354/3117 | ex N1787B | <JAL |
| ☐ JA326J | Boeing 737-846/W | 35355/3159 | ex N1787B | |
| ☐ JA327J | Boeing 737-846/W | 35356/3201 | ex N1796B | |
| ☐ JA328J | Boeing 737-846/W | 35357/3279 | ex N1786B | |
| ☐ JA329J | Boeing 737-846/W | 35358/3315 | ex N1796B | |
| ☐ JA330J | Boeing 737-846/W | 35359/3341 | | |
| ☐ JA331J | Boeing 737-846/W | 40346/3366 | ex N1795B | |
| ☐ JA332J | Boeing 737-846/W | 40347/3385 | | |
| ☐ JA333J | Boeing 737-846/W | 40348/3465 | ex N1799B | |
| ☐ JA334J | Boeing 737-846/W | 40349/3489 | ex N1786B | |
| ☐ JA335J | Boeing 737-846/W | 40350/3525 | | ◆ |
| ☐ JA336J | Boeing 737-846/W | 40351/3543 | | ◆ |
| ☐ JA337J | Boeing 737-846/W | 40352/3604 | | ◆ |
| ☐ JA338J | Boeing 737-846/W | 40355/3609 | | ◆ |

## JAL WAYS                                 Jalways (JO/JAZ)          Tokyo-Narita (NRT)

Wholly owned by Japan Airlines and leases aircraft from the parent as required.

## JAPAN AIR COMMUTER                        Commuter (3X/JAC)         Amami (ASJ)

| | | | |
|---|---|---|---|
| ☐ JA841C | de Havilland DHC-8-402Q | 4072 | ex C-GEWI |
| ☐ JA842C | de Havilland DHC-8-402Q | 4073 | ex C-GFCA |
| ☐ JA843C | de Havilland DHC-8-402Q | 4076 | ex C-FDHZ |
| ☐ JA844C | de Havilland DHC-8-402Q | 4092 | ex C-GFEN |
| ☐ JA845C | de Havilland DHC-8-402Q | 4101 | ex C-FCPZ |
| ☐ JA846C | de Havilland DHC-8-402Q | 4107 | ex C-FCVI |
| ☐ JA847C | de Havilland DHC-8-402Q | 4111 | ex C-FCVS |
| ☐ JA848C | de Havilland DHC-8-402Q | 4121 | ex C-FFCO |
| ☐ JA849C | de Havilland DHC-8-402Q | 4133 | ex C-FGKJ |
| ☐ JA850C | de Havilland DHC-8-402Q | 4158 | ex C-FLKW |
| ☐ JA851C | de Havilland DHC-8-402Q | 4177 | ex C-FMTK |
| | | | |
| ☐ JA001C | SAAB SF.340B | 340B-419 | ex SE-B19 |
| ☐ JA002C | SAAB SF.340B | 340B-459 | ex SE-B59 |
| ☐ JA8594 | SAAB SF.340B | 340B-399 | ex SE-C99 |
| ☐ JA8642 | SAAB SF.340B | 340B-365 | ex SE-C65 |
| ☐ JA8649 | SAAB SF.340B | 340B-368 | ex SE-C68 |

| | | | | |
|---|---|---|---|---|
| ☐ JA8703 | SAAB SF.340B | 340B-355 | ex SE-C55 | |
| ☐ JA8704 | SAAB SF.340B | 340B-361 | ex SE-C61 | |
| ☐ JA8886 | SAAB SF.340B | 340B-281 | ex SE-G81 | |
| ☐ JA8887 | SAAB SF.340B | 340B-308 | ex SE-C08 | |
| ☐ JA8888 | SAAB SF.340B | 340B-331 | ex SE-C31 | |
| ☐ JA8900 | SAAB SF.340B | 340B-378 | ex SE-C78 | |

## JAPAN AIRLINES INTERNATIONAL          *Japanair (JL/JAL)*          *Tokyo-Haneda (HND)*

Member of Oneworld

| | | | | |
|---|---|---|---|---|
| ☐ JA301J | Boeing 737-846/W | 35330/2095 | | |
| ☐ JA302J | Boeing 737-846/W | 35331/2162 | | |
| ☐ JA303J | Boeing 737-846/W | 35332/2225 | ex N6066U | |
| ☐ JA304J | Boeing 737-846/W | 35333/2253 | | |
| ☐ JA305J | Boeing 737-846/W | 35334/2289 | | |
| ☐ JA306J | Boeing 737-846/W | 35335/2395 | ex N6065Y | |
| ☐ JA308J | Boeing 737-846/W | 35337/2479 | ex N1786B | >JEX |
| ☐ JA309J | Boeing 737-846/W | 35338/2522 | | >JEX |
| ☐ JA310J | Boeing 737-846/W | 35339/2510 | | |
| ☐ JA311J | Boeing 737-846/W | 35340/2571 | | >JEX |
| ☐ JA312J | Boeing 737-846/W | 35341/2584 | ex N1786B | |
| ☐ JA315J | Boeing 737-846/W | 35344/2731 | | |
| ☐ JA316J | Boeing 737-846/W | 35345/2762 | | >JEX |
| ☐ JA317J | Boeing 737-846/W | 35346/2824 | | |
| ☐ JA318J | Boeing 737-846/W | 35347/2830 | ex N1784B | >JEX |
| ☐ JA320J | Boeing 737-846/W | 35349/2953 | ex N1786B | |
| ☐ JA321J | Boeing 737-846/W | 35350/2977 | | |
| ☐ JA323J | Boeing 737-846/W | 35352/3057 | ex N1787B | >JEX |
| ☐ JA324J | Boeing 737-846/W | 35353/3105 | ex N1786B | >JEX |
| ☐ JA325J | Boeing 737-846/W | 35354/3117 | ex N1787B | >JEX |
| ☐ JA339J | Boeing 737-846/W | 40354/3687 | | ♦ |
| ☐ JA340J | Boeing 737-846/W | 39190/3882 | | ♦ |
| ☐ JA341J | Boeing 737-846/W | 40356/3906 | | ♦ |
| ☐ JA342J | Boeing 737-846/W | 39191 | | o/o♦ |
| ☐ JA343J | Boeing 737-846/W | 39192 | | o/o♦ |
| ☐ JA344J | Boeing 737-846/W | 39193 | | o/o♦ |
| ☐ JA345J | Boeing 737-846/W | 40947 | | o/o♦ |
| ☐ JA346J | Boeing 737-846/W | 40948 | | o/o♦ |
| ☐ JA349J | Boeing 737-846/W | 40950 | | o/o♦ |
| ☐ JA601J | Boeing 767-346ER | 32886/875 | ex N60697 | |
| ☐ JA602J | Boeing 767-346ER | 32887/879 | | |
| ☐ JA603J | Boeing 767-346ER | 32888/880 | ex N1794B | |
| ☐ JA604J | Boeing 767-346ER | 33493/905 | | |
| ☐ JA605J | Boeing 767-346ER | 33494/911 | | |
| ☐ JA606J | Boeing 767-346ER | 33495/915 | | |
| ☐ JA607J | Boeing 767-346ER | 33496/917 | | |
| ☐ JA608J | Boeing 767-346ER | 33497/919 | | |
| ☐ JA609J | Boeing 767-346ER | 33845/921 | | |
| ☐ JA610J | Boeing 767-346ER | 33846/925 | | |
| ☐ JA611J | Boeing 767-346ER | 33847/927 | | |
| ☐ JA612J | Boeing 767-346ER | 33848/929 | | |
| ☐ JA613J | Boeing 767-346ER | 33849/935 | | |
| ☐ JA614J | Boeing 767-346ER | 33851/938 | | |
| ☐ JA615J | Boeing 767-346ER | 33850/942 | ex N50217 | |
| ☐ JA616J | Boeing 767-346ER | 35813/954 | | |
| ☐ JA617J | Boeing 767-346ER | 35814/957 | ex N5023Q | |
| ☐ JA618J | Boeing 767-346ER | 35815/964 | | |
| ☐ JA619J | Boeing 767-346ER | 37550/969 | | |
| ☐ JA620J | Boeing 767-346ER | 37547/974 | | |
| ☐ JA621J | Boeing 767-346ER | 37548/975 | | |
| ☐ JA622J | Boeing 767-346ER | 37549/977 | | |
| ☐ JA623J | Boeing 767-346ER | 36131/978 | ex N1794B | |
| ☐ JA651J | Boeing 767-346ER | 40363/994 | | |
| ☐ JA652J | Boeing 767-346ER | 40364/995 | | |
| ☐ JA653J | Boeing 767-346ER | 40365/997 | | |
| ☐ JA654J | Boeing 767-346ER | 40366/999 | | |
| ☐ JA655J | Boeing 767-346ER | 40367/1007 | | ♦ |
| ☐ JA656J | Boeing 767-346ER | 40368/1009 | | ♦ |
| ☐ JA657J | Boeing 767-346ER | 40369/1013 | | ♦ |
| ☐ JA658J | Boeing 767-346ER | 40370/1015 | | ♦ |
| ☐ JA659J | Boeing 767-346ER | 40371/1017 | | ♦ |
| ☐ JA8264 | Boeing 767-346 | 23965/186 | ex N6018N | |
| ☐ JA8266 | Boeing 767-346 | 23966/191 | ex N6018N | |
| ☐ JA8267 | Boeing 767-346 | 23962/193 | ex N6038E | |
| ☐ JA8268 | Boeing 767-346 | 23963/224 | ex N6055X | |
| ☐ JA8269 | Boeing 767-346 | 23964/225 | ex N6046P | |
| ☐ JA8299 | Boeing 767-346 | 24498/277 | ex N6055X | |
| ☐ JA8364 | Boeing 767-346 | 24782/327 | | |
| ☐ JA8365 | Boeing 767-346 | 24783/329 | | |
| ☐ JA8397 | Boeing 767-346 | 27311/547 | | |

| | | | | | |
|---|---|---|---|---|---|
| ☐ | JA8398 | Boeing 767-346 | 27312/548 | | |
| ☐ | JA8399 | Boeing 767-346 | 27313/554 | | |
| ☐ | JA8975 | Boeing 767-346 | 27658/581 | | |
| ☐ | JA8976 | Boeing 767-346 | 27659/667 | | |
| ☐ | JA8980 | Boeing 767-346 | 28837/673 | | |
| ☐ | JA8986 | Boeing 767-346 | 28838/680 | | |
| ☐ | JA8987 | Boeing 767-346 | 28553/688 | | |
| ☐ | JA8988 | Boeing 767-346 | 29863/772 | | |
| | | | | | |
| ☐ | JA007D | Boeing 777-289 | 27639/134 | | |
| ☐ | JA008D | Boeing 777-289 | 27640/146 | | |
| ☐ | JA009D | Boeing 777-289 | 27641/159 | ex N5017V | |
| ☐ | JA010D | Boeing 777-289 | 27642/213 | | |
| ☐ | JA701J | Boeing 777-246ER | 32889/410 | ex (JA8989) | [HND] |
| ☐ | JA702J | Boeing 777-246ER | 32890/417 | ex (JA8990) | |
| ☐ | JA703J | Boeing 777-246ER | 32891/427 | ex N5023Q | |
| ☐ | JA704J | Boeing 777-246ER | 32892/435 | ex N50281 | Oneworld c/s |
| ☐ | JA705J | Boeing 777-246ER | 32893/446 | | |
| ☐ | JA706J | Boeing 777-246ER | 33394/464 | | |
| ☐ | JA707J | Boeing 777-246ER | 32894/475 | | |
| ☐ | JA708J | Boeing 777-246ER | 32895/483 | | |
| ☐ | JA709J | Boeing 777-246ER | 32896/489 | | |
| ☐ | JA710J | Boeing 777-246ER | 33395/525 | | |
| ☐ | JA711J | Boeing 777-246ER | 33396/533 | | |
| ☐ | JA712J | Boeing 777-246ER | 37879 | | o/o |
| ☐ | JA713J | Boeing 777-246ER | 37880 | | o/o |
| ☐ | JA714J | Boeing 777-246ER | 37881 | | o/o |
| ☐ | JA715J | Boeing 777-246ER | 37882 | | o/o |
| ☐ | JA716J | Boeing 777-246ER | 37883 | | o/o |
| ☐ | JA771J | Boeing 777-246 | 27656/437 | ex (JA711J) | |
| ☐ | JA772J | Boeing 777-246 | 27657/507 | | |
| ☐ | JA773J | Boeing 777-246 | 27653/635 | | |
| ☐ | JA8977 | Boeing 777-289 | 27636/45 | | |
| ☐ | JA8978 | Boeing 777-289 | 27637/79 | | |
| ☐ | JA8979 | Boeing 777-289 | 27638/107 | | |
| ☐ | JA8981 | Boeing 777-246 | 27364/23 | ex (JA8195) | |
| ☐ | JA8982 | Boeing 777-246 | 27365/26 | ex (JA8196) | |
| ☐ | JA8983 | Boeing 777-246 | 27366/39 | | |
| ☐ | JA8984 | Boeing 777-246 | 27651/68 | | |
| ☐ | JA8985 | Boeing 777-246 | 27652/72 | | |
| | | | | | |
| ☐ | JA731J | Boeing 777-346ER | 32431/429 | ex N5016R | |
| ☐ | JA732J | Boeing 777-346ER | 32430/423 | ex N5017V | |
| ☐ | JA733J | Boeing 777-346ER | 32432/521 | | |
| ☐ | JA734J | Boeing 777-346ER | 32433/527 | | |
| ☐ | JA735J | Boeing 777-346ER | 32434/577 | | |
| ☐ | JA736J | Boeing 777-346ER | 32435/583 | | |
| ☐ | JA737J | Boeing 777-346ER | 36126/668 | | |
| ☐ | JA738J | Boeing 777-346ER | 32436/724 | | |
| ☐ | JA739J | Boeing 777-346ER | 32437/736 | | |
| ☐ | JA740J | Boeing 777-346ER | 36127/744 | | |
| ☐ | JA741J | Boeing 777-346ER | 36128/812 | ex N50281 | |
| ☐ | JA742J | Boeing 777-346ER | 36129/816 | ex N1788B | |
| ☐ | JA743J | Boeing 777-346ER | 36130/821 | ex N6009F | |
| ☐ | JA751J | Boeing 777-346 | 27654/458 | | |
| ☐ | JA752J | Boeing 777-346 | 27655/460 | | |
| ☐ | JA8941 | Boeing 777-346 | 28393/152 | | |
| ☐ | JA8942 | Boeing 777-346 | 28394/158 | ex N50284 | |
| ☐ | JA8943 | Boeing 777-346 | 28395/196 | | |
| ☐ | JA8944 | Boeing 777-346 | 28396/212 | | |
| ☐ | JA8945 | Boeing 777-346 | 28397/238 | | |
| | | | | | |
| ☐ | JA821A | Boeing 787-8 | 34831/ | | o/o |
| ☐ | JA822A | Boeing 787-8 | 34832/23 | ex N1003W | ♦ |
| ☐ | JA823A | Boeing 787-8 | 34833/ | | o/o♦ |
| ☐ | JA824A | Boeing 787-8 | 34834/ | | o/o♦ |
| ☐ | JA825A | Boeing 787-8 | 34835/33 | ex N1006F | ♦ |
| ☐ | JA826A | Boeing 787-8 | 34836/ | | o/o♦ |
| ☐ | JA827A | Boeing 787-8 | 34827/ | | o/o♦ |
| ☐ | JA | Boeing 787-8 | | | o/o |
| | | | | | |
| ☐ | JA002D | McDonnell-Douglas MD-90-30 | 53556/2210 | | [HND] |
| ☐ | JA003D | McDonnell-Douglas MD-90-30 | 53557/2211 | | |
| ☐ | JA004D | McDonnell-Douglas MD-90-30 | 53558/2212 | | |
| ☐ | JA005D | McDonnell-Douglas MD-90-30 | 53559/2236 | | |
| ☐ | JA006D | McDonnell-Douglas MD-90-30 | 53560/2245 | | |
| ☐ | JA8004 | McDonnell-Douglas MD-90-30 | 53359/2164 | | |
| ☐ | JA8020 | McDonnell-Douglas MD-90-30 | 53360/2190 | | |
| ☐ | JA8029 | McDonnell-Douglas MD-90-30 | 53361/2202 | | |
| ☐ | JA8064 | McDonnell-Douglas MD-90-30 | 53354/2125 | | |
| ☐ | JA8065 | McDonnell-Douglas MD-90-30 | 53355/2131 | | |
| ☐ | JA8066 | McDonnell-Douglas MD-90-30 | 53356/2157 | | |

| | | | | | |
|---|---|---|---|---|---|
| ☐ | JA8069 | McDonnell-Douglas MD-90-30 | 53357/2164 | | |
| ☐ | JA8070 | McDonnell-Douglas MD-90-30 | 53358/2179 | | |
| | | | | | |
| ☐ | JA8998 | Boeing 737-446 | 28994/3044 | | >JEX |
| ☐ | JA8999 | Boeing 737-446 | 29864/3111 | ex N1786B | >JEX |

## JAPAN TRANSOCEAN AIR — JAI Ocean (NU/JTA) — Okinawa-Naha (OKA)

| | | | | | |
|---|---|---|---|---|---|
| ☐ | JA8523 | Boeing 737-4Q3 | 26603/2618 | | |
| ☐ | JA8524 | Boeing 737-4Q3 | 26604/2684 | | |
| ☐ | JA8525 | Boeing 737-4Q3 | 26605/2752 | | |
| ☐ | JA8526 | Boeing 737-4Q3 | 26606/2898 | | |
| ☐ | JA8597 | Boeing 737-4Q3 | 27660/3043 | | |
| ☐ | JA8931 | Boeing 737-429 | 25247/2106 | ex N931NU | [OKA] |
| ☐ | JA8932 | Boeing 737-429 | 25248/2120 | ex N932NU | [OKA] |
| ☐ | JA8938 | Boeing 737-4Q3 | 29485/3085 | | |
| ☐ | JA8939 | Boeing 737-4Q3 | 29486/3088 | ex N1800B | |
| ☐ | JA8940 | Boeing 737-4Q3 | 29487/3122 | | |

## JETSTAR JAPAN

| | | | | | |
|---|---|---|---|---|---|
| ☐ | JA01JJ | Airbus A320-232 | 5093 | ex F-WWIN | o/o♦ |

## NEW CENTRAL AVIATION / SHIN CHUO KOKU — Tokyo-Chofu

| | | | | | |
|---|---|---|---|---|---|
| ☐ | JA31CA | Dornier 228-212 | 8242 | ex D-CBDO | |
| ☐ | JA32CA | Dornier 228-212 | 8243 | ex D-CBDP | |
| ☐ | JA33CA | Dornier 228-212 | 8244 | ex D-CDRS | ♦ |
| ☐ | JA34CA | Dornier 228-212NG | 8300 | ex D-CRAQ | |
| ☐ | JA3453 | Cessna TU206C Super Skywagon | U206-1218 | ex N1775C | |
| ☐ | JA3669 | Cessna TU206F Turbo Stationair | U20601964 | ex N1704C | |
| ☐ | JA5305 | Britten-Norman BN-2B-20 Islander | 2239 | ex G-BSPS | |
| ☐ | JA5319 | Britten-Norman BN-2B-20 Islander | 2268 | ex G-BUBK | |

## NIPPON CARGO AIRLINES — Nippon Cargo (KZ/NCA) — Tokyo-Narita (NRT)

| | | | | | |
|---|---|---|---|---|---|
| ☐ | JA01KZ | Boeing 747-481F | 34016/1360 | NCA Pleiades | |
| ☐ | JA02KZ | Boeing 747-481F | 34017/1363 | NCA Progress | |
| ☐ | JA03KZ | Boeing 747-4KZF | 34018/1378 | NCA Phoenix | |
| ☐ | JA04KZ | Boeing 747-4KZF | 34283/1384 | NCA Pegasus | |
| ☐ | JA05KZ | Boeing 747-4KZF | 36132/1394 | NCA Apollo | |
| ☐ | JA06KZ | Boeing 747-4KZF | 36133/1397 | NCA Antares | |
| ☐ | JA07KZ | Boeing 747-4KZF | 36134/1405 | NCA Andromeda | |
| ☐ | JA08KZ | Boeing 747-4KZF | 36135/1408 | NCA Aries | |
| ☐ | JA11KZ | Boeing 747-8KZF | 36136/1421 | | o/o |
| ☐ | JA12KZ | Boeing 747-8KZF | 36137/1422 | | o/o |
| ☐ | JA13KZ | Boeing 747-8KZF | 36138/1431 | | o/o |

## ORIENTAL AIR BRIDGE — Oriental Bridge (NGK) — Nagasaki (NGS)

| | | | | | |
|---|---|---|---|---|---|
| ☐ | JA801B | de Havilland DHC-8Q-201 | 566 | ex C-GDNG | |
| ☐ | JA802B | de Havilland DHC-8Q-201 | 579 | ex C-FDHO | |

## PEACH

| | | | | | |
|---|---|---|---|---|---|
| ☐ | JA801P | Airbus A320-214 | 4887 | ex F-WWIQ | Peach Dream | ♦ |
| ☐ | JA802P | Airbus A320-214 | 4936 | ex F-WWBU | ♦ |
| ☐ | JA803P | Airbus A320-214 | 5015 | ex F-WWIG | ♦ |

## RYUKYU AIR COMMUTER — (RAC) — Okinawa-Naha (OKA)

| | | | | | |
|---|---|---|---|---|---|
| ☐ | JA8935 | de Havilland DHC-8Q-103B | 593 | ex C-GSAH | |
| ☐ | JA8936 | de Havilland DHC-8Q-314 | 635 | ex C-FIOX | |
| ☐ | JA8972 | de Havilland DHC-8Q-103 | 472 | ex C-GDKL | |
| ☐ | JA8973 | de Havilland DHC-8Q-103 | 501 | ex C-GDLD | |
| ☐ | JA8974 | de Havilland DHC-8Q-103B | 540 | ex C-FDHP | |
| | | | | | |
| ☐ | JA5324 | Britten-Norman BN-2B-20 Islander | 2297 | ex G-BWNG | |
| ☐ | JA5325 | Britten-Norman BN-2B-20 Islander | 2298 | ex G-BWYX | |

## SKYMARK AIRLINES — Skymark (BC/SKY) — Osaka-Itami (ITM)

| | | | | | |
|---|---|---|---|---|---|
| ☐ | JA73NA | Boeing 737-8HX/W | 36849/3372 | | |
| ☐ | JA73NB | Boeing 737-8HX/W | 36848/3394 | | |
| ☐ | JA73NC | Boeing 737-8FZ/W | 31743/3450 | ex N1787B | |
| ☐ | JA73ND | Boeing 737-8FZ/W | 33440/3474 | | |
| ☐ | JA73NE | Boeing 737-82Y/W | 40713/3501 | ex N1787B | |
| ☐ | JA73NF | Boeing 737-86N/W | 38019/3642 | | ♦ |
| ☐ | JA73NG | Boeing 737-86N/W | 36821/3738 | ex N1786B | ♦ |
| ☐ | JA73NH | Boeing 737-8HX/W | 38101/3803 | | ♦ |

| | | | | |
|---|---|---|---|---|
| ☐ JA73NJ | Boeing 737-86N/W | 39405/3845 | | ♦ |
| ☐ JA73NK | Boeing 737-86N/W | 38023/3883 | | ♦ |
| ☐ JA73NL | Boeing 737-8HX/W | 38104/3933 | | ♦ |
| ☐ JA73NM | Boeing 737-81D/W | 39421/3940 | | ♦ |
| ☐ JA73NN | Boeing 737-81D/W | 39422/3975 | | ♦ |
| ☐ JA73NP | Boeing 737-8HX/W | 38109 | | o/o♦ |
| ☐ JA737H | Boeing 737-86N | 34247/1830 | ex N1787B | |
| ☐ JA737K | Boeing 737-86N | 34249/1857 | ex N1786B | |
| ☐ JA737L | Boeing 737-86N | 32694/1960 | | |
| ☐ JA737M | Boeing 737-86N | 32683/2136 | | |
| ☐ JA737N | Boeing 737-8HX | 36845/2339 | | |
| ☐ JA737P | Boeing 737-8HX | 29681/2493 | ex N1795B | |
| ☐ JA737Q | Boeing 737-86N/W | 35228/2630 | | |
| ☐ JA737R | Boeing 737-86N/W | 35630/2666 | | |
| ☐ JA737T | Boeing 737-8Q8/W | 35290/2818 | | |
| ☐ JA737U | Boeing 737-8FZ/W | 29680/2888 | | |
| ☐ JA737X | Boeing 737-8AL/W | 36692/3088 | ex N1786B | |
| ☐ JA737Y | Boeing 737-8FZ/W | 29663/3113 | ex N1786B | |
| ☐ JA737Z | Boeing 737-82Y/W | 40712/3308 | ex N1786B | |

## SOLASEED AIR — Newsky (6J/SNJ) — Miyazaki (KMI)

| | | | | |
|---|---|---|---|---|
| ☐ JA392K | Boeing 737-46M | 28550/2847 | ex N8550F | <ANA♦ |
| ☐ JA737A | Boeing 737-46Q | 29000/3033 | ex N56CD | Miyazaki Intl c/s |
| ☐ JA737B | Boeing 737-46Q | 29001/3040 | ex N89CD | |
| ☐ JA737E | Boeing 737-4Y0 | 26069/2352 | ex N869DC | |
| ☐ JA737F | Boeing 737-43Q | 28492/2837 | ex N284CH | |
| ☐ JA737G | Boeing 737-43Q | 28491/2832 | ex N491MT | |
| ☐ JA737V | Boeing 737-4M0 | 29201/3018 | ex N391LS | |
| ☐ JA734H | Boeing 737-4M0 | 29203/3049 | ex N490MS | |
| ☐ JA801X | Boeing 737-81D/W | 39415/3666 | | ♦ |
| ☐ JA802X | Boeing 737-81D/W | 39418/3816 | | ♦ |
| ☐ JA803X | Boeing 737-86N/X | 39395/3915 | | ♦ |
| ☐ JA804X | Boeing 737-86N/W | 38026 | | o/o♦ |

## STAR FLYER — Starflyer (7G/SFJ) — Kitakyushu (KKJ)

| | | | | |
|---|---|---|---|---|
| ☐ JA01MC | Airbus A320-214 | 2620 | ex F-WWDM | |
| ☐ JA02MC | Airbus A320-214 | 2658 | ex F-WWIP | |
| ☐ JA03MC | Airbus A320-214 | 2695 | ex F-WWII | |
| ☐ JA04MC | Airbus A320-214 | 3025 | ex F-WWBI | |
| ☐ JA05MC | Airbus A320-214 | 4555 | ex F-WWDG | |
| ☐ JA06MC | Airbus A320-214 | 4720 | ex F-WWDF | ♦ |
| ☐ JA07MC | Airbus A320-214 | 5012 | ex F-WWIS | o/o♦ |

## JU - MONGOLIA (State of Mongolia)

## AERO MONGOLIA — Aero Mongolia (MNG) — Ulan Bator (ULN)

| | | | | |
|---|---|---|---|---|
| ☐ JU-8251 | Fokker 50 | 20251 | ex PH-WXH | |
| ☐ JU-8257 | Fokker 50 | 20257 | ex OY-PCI | |
| ☐ JU-8258 | Fokker 50 | 20258 | ex PH-KXU | |

## BLUE SKY AVIATION — Ulan Bator (ULN)

| | | | | |
|---|---|---|---|---|
| ☐ JU-2114 | Cessna 208B Caravan I | 208B0782 | ex N208BS | ♦ |

## CENTRAL MONGOLIAN AIRWAYS — Central Mongolia (CEM) — Ulan Bator (ULN)

| | | | | |
|---|---|---|---|---|
| ☐ JU-5444 | Mil Mi-8T | 20409 | ex JU-1024 | |
| ☐ JU-5445 | Mil Mi-8T | 98103227 | ex JU-1025 | |
| ☐ JU-5446 | Mil Mi-8T | 20411 | ex JU-1026 | |

## EZNIS AIRWAYS — (O7/EZA) — Ulan Bator (ULN)

| | | | | |
|---|---|---|---|---|
| ☐ JU-9901 | SAAB SF.340B | 340B-259 | ex N259AE | |
| ☐ JU-9903 | SAAB SF.340B | 340B-297 | ex N297AE | |
| ☐ JU-9905 | SAAB SF.340B | 340B-359 | ex LY-ESK | |
| ☐ JU-9907 | SAAB SF.340B | 340B-425 | ex N425XJ | |
| ☐ JU-9909 | Avro 146-RJ85 | E2257 | ex G-CGTP | ♦ |
| ☐ JU-9915 | Avro 146-RJ85 | E2261 | ex G-CGWJ | ♦ |

## MIAT MONGOLIAN AIRLINES — Mongol Air (OM/MGL) — Ulan Bator (ULN)

| | | | | |
|---|---|---|---|---|
| ☐ EI-CSG | Boeing 737-8AS/W | 29922/571 | | Ogedei Khaan |
| ☐ EI-CXV | Boeing 737-8CX/W | 32364/1166 | | Khubelai Khaan |
| ☐ JU-1006 | Antonov An-24RV | 47309807 | ex MT-1006 | [ULN] |

| | | | | | |
|---|---|---|---|---|---|
| ☐ JU-1009 | Antonov An-24RV | 57310104 | ex MT-1009 | | [ULN] |
| ☐ JU-1010 | Airbus A310-304 | 526 | ex F-OHPT | Chinggis Khan | |
| ☐ JU-1011 | Boeing 767-3W0ER | 28149/627 | ex B-2569 | | ♦ |
| ☐ JU-1012 | Boeing 767-3W0ER | 28264/644 | ex B-5001 | | ♦ |

## MONGOLIAN AIRLINES

| | | | | | |
|---|---|---|---|---|---|
| ☐ JU-8881 | Fokker 50 | 20183 | ex LN-RNF | Hunnu | ♦ |
| ☐ JU-8882 | Fokker 50 | 20184 | ex LN-RNG | Kidan | ♦ |
| ☐ JU-8888 | Airbus A319-112 | 1706 | ex N706MX | | ♦ |
| ☐ JU-8889 | Airbus A319-112 | 1750 | ex N750MX | | ♦ |

## SKY HORSE AVIATION / TENGERIN ELCH    Sky Horse (TNL)    Ulan Bator (ULN)

| | | | | |
|---|---|---|---|---|
| ☐ JU-2030 | LET L-410UVP-E1 | 861801 | ex OK-RDE | |
| ☐ JU-2032 | LET L-410UVP-E1 | 810602 | ex UR-67001 | |

## THOMAS AIR    Ulan Bator (ULN)

| | | | | |
|---|---|---|---|---|
| ☐ JU-1911 | Pilatus PC-6/B2-B4 Porter | 972 | ex HB-FNR | ♦ |

## JY-    JORDAN (Hashemite Kingdom of Jordan)

### BARQ AVIATION    Amman (AMM)

| | | | | |
|---|---|---|---|---|
| ☐ N162AT | Lockheed L-1011-500 Tristar | 193B-1220 | ex JY-AGC | |
| ☐ N164AT | Lockheed L-1011-500 Tristar | 193B-1238 | ex JY-AGE | |
| ☐ N194AT | Lockheed L-1011-100 Tristar | 193B-1230 | ex N8034T | |

### JORDAN AVIATION    Jordan Aviation (R5/JAV)    Amman-Marka (ADJ)

| | | | | | |
|---|---|---|---|---|---|
| ☐ JY-JAB | Boeing 737-33A | 23630/1312 | ex N169AW | Noor | |
| ☐ JY-JAD | Boeing 737-322 | 24662/1862 | ex N387UA | | |
| ☐ JY-JAN | Boeing 737-322 | 23956/1564 | ex N324UA | Amman | |
| ☐ JY-JAO | Boeing 737-322 | 24672/1915 | ex N672RY | | |
| ☐ JY-JAX | Boeing 737-322 | 23955/1550 | ex N323UA | | |
| ☐ JY-JAY | Boeing 737-3S3 | 29244/3059 | ex N244SJ | | |
| ☐ JY-JAC | Airbus A320-211 | 0029 | ex N290SE | | |
| ☐ JY-JAE | Boeing 727-2N4 | 21846/1549 | ex 7O-ACX | hanaviation.jo titles | |
| ☐ JY-JAG | Boeing 767-204ER | 24757/299 | ex G-SLVR | | |
| ☐ JY-JAH | Airbus A310-304 | 481 | ex VT-EVH | | |
| ☐ JY-JAI | Boeing 767-204ER | 24736/296 | ex G-SILC | | |
| ☐ JY-JAJ | Airbus A330-223 | 255 | ex VN-A369 | | ♦ |
| ☐ JY-JAL | Boeing 767-204ER | 24239/243 | ex G-BOPB | | |
| ☐ JY-JAP | Boeing 737-46B | 24124/1679 | ex SX-BGX | | |
| ☐ JY-JAQ | Boeing 737-46J | 27826/2694 | ex D-ABRE | | |
| ☐ JY-JAV | Airbus A310-222 | 357 | ex 3B-STK | Zuhair | op for UN |

### JORDAN INTERNATIONAL AIR CARGO    (J4/JCI)    Amman-Marka (ADJ)

| | | | | |
|---|---|---|---|---|
| ☐ JY-JIA | Ilyushin Il-76TD | 0023437093 | ex EX-86911 | |
| ☐ JY-JIC | Ilyushin Il-76MF | 1063421724 | | ♦ |

### MEELAD AIR    (MLW)

| | | | | |
|---|---|---|---|---|
| ☐ SX-BLL | McDonnell-Douglas MD-83 | 49933/1773 | ex JY-JRC | [ARN]♦ |

### PETRA AIRLINES    (9P/PTR)    Amman-Marka (ADJ)

| | | | | |
|---|---|---|---|---|
| ☐ JY-PTA | Airbus A320-212 | 0459 | ex A9C-EI | |
| ☐ JY-PTB | Airbus A320-212 | 0537 | ex A9C-EC | ♦ |

### ROYAL FALCON    (RL/RFJ)    Amman-Marka (ADJ)

| | | | | |
|---|---|---|---|---|
| ☐ JY-JRA | Boeing 737-201 (Nordam 3) | 22354/736 | ex J2-SHB | >6N♦ |
| ☐ JY-JRD | Boeing 767-3P6ER | 26237/544 | ex N90GZ | |
| ☐ JY-JRG | Airbus A320-212 | 814 | ex EI-DJH | ♦ |
| ☐ JY-RFF | Boeing 737-4K5 | 27831/2677 | ex OO-TUB | |

### ROYAL JORDANIAN    Jordanian (RJ/RJA)    Amman (AMM)

Member of Oneworld

| | | | | | |
|---|---|---|---|---|---|
| ☐ F-OHGV | Airbus A320-232 | 2649 | ex F-WWIL | Irbid | |
| ☐ F-OHGX | Airbus A320-231 | 2953 | ex F-WWIX | Madaba | |
| ☐ JY-AYQ | Airbus A320-232 | 4670 | ex F-WWBK | | ♦ |
| ☐ JY-AYR | Airbus A320-232 | 4817 | ex F-WWIA | | ♦ |
| ☐ JY-AYS | Airbus A320-232 | 4853 | ex F-WWBE | | ♦ |
| ☐ | Airbus A320-232 | 5128 | ex | | o/o♦ |

| | | | | | |
|---|---|---|---|---|---|
| ☐ JY-AYG | Airbus A321-231 | 2730 | ex D-AVZB | As-Salt | |
| ☐ JY-AYH | Airbus A321-231 | 2793 | ex D-AVZN | Karak | |
| ☐ JY-AYJ | Airbus A321-231 | 3458 | ex D-AVZM | Ramtha | |
| ☐ JY-AYK | Airbus A321-231 | 3522 | ex D-AVZW | Tafila | |
| ☐ JY-AYT | Airbus A321-231 | 5099 | ex D-AZAV | Karak | o/o♦ |
| | | | | | |
| ☐ JY-EMA | Embraer ERJ-195LR | 19000107 | ex PT-SQB | | |
| ☐ JY-EMB | Embraer ERJ-195LR | 19000131 | ex PT-SYJ | | |
| ☐ JY-EME | Embraer ERJ-195LR | 19000050 | ex PT-SGZ | Jerash | |
| ☐ JY-EMF | Embraer ERJ-195LR | 19000067 | ex PT-SJG | Petra | |
| ☐ JY-EMG | Embraer ERJ-195LR | 19000088 | ex PT-SNG | | |
| | | | | | |
| ☐ JY-AGM | Airbus A310-304 | 491 | ex F-ODVH | Prince Hamzeh | |
| ☐ JY-AGN | Airbus A310-304 | 531 | ex F-ODVI | Princess Haya | |
| ☐ JY-AGQ | Airbus A310-304F | 445 | ex F-ODVF | Princess Raiyah | |
| ☐ JY-AGR | Airbus A310-304F | 490 | ex F-ODVG | Prince Faisal | |
| ☐ JY-AIA | Airbus A340-212 | 038 | ex F-GLZE | Prince Hussein bin Abdullah | |
| ☐ JY-AIB | Airbus A340-212 | 043 | ex F-GLZF | Princess Iman Bint Abdullah | |
| ☐ JY-AIC | Airbus A340-212 | 014 | ex F-OHLP | Princess Salma Bint Abdullah | |
| ☐ JY-AID | Airbus A340-212 | 022 | ex F-OHLQ | Queen Rania Alabdulah | |
| ☐ JY-AIE | Airbus A330-223 | 970 | ex EI-EJY | Jordan River | |
| ☐ JY-AIF | Airbus A330-223 | 979 | ex EI-EJZ | Prince Ali Ibn Al Hussain | |
| ☐ JY-AIG | Airbus A330-223 | 1002 | ex EI-ESA | Prince Feisal Ibn Al-Hussein | ♦ |
| ☐ JY-AYL | Airbus A319-132 | 3428 | ex D-AVYQ | Mafraq | |
| ☐ JY-AYM | Airbus A319-132 | 3685 | ex D-AVWC | Ma'an | |
| ☐ JY-AYN | Airbus A319-132 | 3803 | ex D-AVYB | Shobak | |
| ☐ JY-AYP | Airbus A319-132 | 3832 | ex D-AVYL | Ajloun | |
| ☐ JY-EMC | Embraer ERJ-175LR | 17000223 | ex PT-SCZ | Zay | ♦ |
| ☐ JY-EMD | Embraer ERJ-175LR | 17000232 | ex PT-SFI | Dana | ♦ |
| ☐ JY-EMH | Embraer ERJ-175LR | 17000316 | ex PT-XUK | | ♦ |

## ROYAL JORDANIAN XPRESS                                                        *Amman (AMM)*

Wholly owned subsidiary of Royal Jordanian; leases aircraft from the parent as required.

## ROYAL WINGS AIRLINES          *Royal Wings (RY/RYW)*              *Amman (AMM)*

| | | | | |
|---|---|---|---|---|
| ☐ JY-AYI | Airbus A320-212 | 0569 | ex F-OGYC | |

# J2-     DJIBOUTI (Republic of Djibouti)

## DAALLO AIRLINES          *Dalo Airlines (D3/DAO)*          *Djibouti/Dubai (JIB/DAB)*

| | | | | |
|---|---|---|---|---|
| ☐ EY-47693 | Antonov An-24RV | 27307510 | | <TJK♦ |
| ☐ (J2-KCV) | Boeing 747-212B | 21938/436 | ex N938GA | [OPF], for IRA? |
| ☐ UP-I1802 | Ilyushin Il-18E | 185008603 | ex UN-75002 | <MGK |
| ☐ ZS-PUZ | British Aerospace 146 Srs.200 | E2074 | ex EI-CSL | JNB♦ |

## DJIBOUTI AIR          *(DZ)*

| | | | | |
|---|---|---|---|---|
| ☐ UP-B3701 | Boeing 737-230 (Nordam 3) | 22123/726 | ex 4L-VML | ♦ |

## DJIBOUTI AIRLINES          *Djibouti Air (D8/DJB)*          *Djibouti (JIB)*

Leases aircraft from other operators as required

## SILVER AIR          *(SVJ)*          *Djibouti / Dubai (JIB/DAB)*

Ceased ops 02Aug09

## TEEBAH AIRLINES          *Teebah (TBN)*          *Amman (AMM)*

| | | | | |
|---|---|---|---|---|
| ☐ YI-APW | Boeing 737-2B7 | 22885/966 | ex 9L-LEG | >IAW♦ |

# J8-     ST. VINCENT & GRENADINES (State of St. Vincent & Grenadines)

## MUSTIQUE AIRWAYS          *Mustique (MAW)*          *Mustique (MQS)*

| | | | | |
|---|---|---|---|---|
| ☐ J8-CIW | Britten-Norman BN-2B-26 Islander | 2018 | ex J8-VAH | |
| ☐ J8-KIM | Rockwell 500S Shrike Commander | 3253 | ex J8-VBE | |
| ☐ J8-MQS | Aero Commander 500B | 1400-144 | ex J8-SJK | |
| ☐ J8-PUG | Aero Commander 500U | 1670-18 | ex J8-VBD | |
| ☐ J6-SLU | Aero Commander 500B | 1146-80 | ex N6275X | |
| ☐ J8-UVF | Britten-Norman BN-2B-26 Islander | 2165 | ex J8-VAM | |

## SVG AIR / GRENADINE AIRWAYS          *Grenadines (SVD)*          *Kingston, St Vincent (SVD)*

| | | | | |
|---|---|---|---|---|
| ☐ J8-GAL | de Havilland DHC-6 Twin Otter 300 | 510 | ex V2-LFL | ♦ |
| ☐ J8-SUN | de Havilland DHC-6 Twin Otter 300 | 477 | ex 8P-MLK | all-white |

| | | | |
|---|---|---|---|
| ☐ J8-VAQ | Cessna 402B II STOL | 402B1038 | ex N400XY |
| ☐ J8-VBI | Britten-Norman BN-2B-26 Islander | 2025 | ex J3-GAF |
| ☐ J8-VBJ | Britten-Norman BN-2A Islander | 163 | ex J3-GAG |
| ☐ J8-VBK | Britten-Norman BN-2A-26 Islander | 570 | ex J3-GAH |
| ☐ J8-VBL | Cessna 402C II | 402C0640 | ex N404MN |
| ☐ J8-VBQ | de Havilland DHC-6 Twin Otter 300 | 604 | ex 8P-BGC   all-white |
| ☐ J8-VBS | de Havilland DHC-6 Twin Otter 300 | 249 | ex V2-LFG   Trans Island 2000 colours |

## LN-   NORWAY (Kingdom of Norway)

### AIRWING                                                                 Oslo-Gardermoen (OSL)

| | | | |
|---|---|---|---|
| ☐ LN-AWA | Beech A100 King Air | B-213 | ex SE-LDL |
| ☐ LN-AWD | Beech 350 Super King Air | FL-256 | ex D-CSKF |
| ☐ LN-FIX | Beech B200 Super King Air | BB-1898 | ex N199GA |

### BENAIR                          Scoop (HAX)                            Oslo-Gardermoen (OSL)

Fleet merged back into Benair Air Services (OY-)

### BERGEN AIR TRANSPORT        Bergen Air (BGT)                              Bergen (BGO)

| | | | |
|---|---|---|---|
| ☐ LN-BAA | Beech B200 Super King Air | BB-1327 | ex N67SD |
| ☐ LN-BAB | Beech 350 Super King Air | FL-590 | ex N590EU |
| ☐ LN-TWL | Beech B200 Super King Air | BB-1144 | ex N120AJ |

### BRISTOW NORWAY                 Norske (NOR)                            Stavanger (SVG)

| | | | | |
|---|---|---|---|---|
| ☐ LN-ONA | Sikorsky S-92A | 920144 | ex N1016R | ♦ |
| ☐ LN-ONB | Sikorsky S-92A | 920145 | ex N145MH | ♦ |
| ☐ LN-ONC | Sikorsky S-92A | 920148 | ex N148FF | ♦ |
| ☐ LN-ONN | Sikorsky S-92 | 920011 | ex N7107S   Mona Lisa | |
| ☐ LN-ONO | Sikorsky S-92 | 920012 | ex N7108Z   Madonna | |
| ☐ LN-ONP | Sikorsky S-92A | 920025 | ex N8011N | |
| ☐ LN-ONQ | Sikorsky S-92A | 920032 | ex N8036Q | |
| ☐ LN-ONR | Sikorsky S-92A | 920033 | ex N8021R | |
| ☐ LN-ONS | Sikorsky S-92A | 920043 | ex N8061E | |
| ☐ LN-ONU | Sikorsky S-92A | 920091 | ex N2000Q | |
| ☐ LN-ONV | Sikorsky S-92A | 920092 | ex N2010H | |
| ☐ LN-ONW | Sikorsky S-92A | 920090 | ex N921AL | |
| ☐ LN-ONX | Sikorsky S-92A | 920137 | ex N1133W | |
| ☐ LN-OMI | Aérospatiale AS.332L | 2123 | ex G-BLZJ | |
| ☐ LN-ONF | Eurocopter EC225LP 2 | 2750 | | |
| ☐ LN-ONG | Eurocopter EC225LP 2 | 2755 | | |

### CHC HELIKOPTER SERVICE       Helibus (L5/HKS)             Stavanger/Bergen (SVG/BGO)

| | | | | |
|---|---|---|---|---|
| ☐ LN-OAW | Aérospatiale AS.332L | 2053 | ex VH-LHD | |
| ☐ LN-OHA | Aérospatiale AS.332L | 2396 | ex F-WYMS | |
| ☐ LN-OHE | Aérospatiale AS.332L2 2 | 2474 | | |
| ☐ LN-OHG | Aérospatiale AS.332L2 2 | 2493 | | |
| ☐ LN-OHJ | Aérospatiale AS.332L2 2 | 2594 | | |
| ☐ LN-OHK | Aérospatiale AS.332L2 2 | 2613 | | |
| ☐ LN-OHW | Eurocopter EC225LP 2 | 2715 | ex F-WJXV | |
| ☐ LN-OJA | Eurocopter EC225LP 2 | 2692 | | |
| ☐ LN-OJB | Eurocopter EC225LP 2 | 2725 | | |
| ☐ LN-OJC | Eurocopter EC225LP 2 | 2739 | | |
| ☐ LN-OJD | Eurocopter EC225LP 2 | 2744 | ex F-WWOY | |
| ☐ LN-OJE | Eurocopter EC225LP 2 | 2716 | | |
| ☐ LN-OJF | Eurocopter EC225LP 2 | 2721 | ex F-WJXT | |
| ☐ LN-OJG | Eurocopter EC225LP 2 | 2747 | | |
| ☐ LN-OLB | Aérospatiale AS.332L | 2082 | ex OY-HMJ | |
| ☐ LN-OLD | Aérospatiale AS.332L | 2103 | ex OY-HMI | |
| ☐ LN-OME | Aérospatiale AS.332L | 2139 | ex C-GQCH | |
| ☐ LN-OMF | Aérospatiale AS.332L | 2067 | ex G-PUMK | |
| ☐ LN-OMH | Aérospatiale AS.332L | 2113 | ex HZ-RH4 | |
| ☐ LN-OPH | Aérospatiale AS.332L1 | 2347 | | |
| ☐ LN-OPX | Aérospatiale AS.332L1 | 9009 | | |
| ☐ LN-OXX | Aérospatiale AS.332L | 2015 | ex PR-CHZ | ♦ |
| ☐ LN-OQA | Sikorsky S-92A | 920013 | ex (LN-ONO) | |
| ☐ LN-OQB | Sikorsky S-92A | 920014 | ex (LN-OQA) | |
| ☐ LN-OQC | Sikorsky S-92A | 920018 | ex N7118N | |
| ☐ LN-OQD | Sikorsky S-92A | 920022 | ex N8016T | |
| ☐ LN-OQE | Sikorsky S-92A | 920047 | ex N80071 | |
| ☐ LN-OQF | Sikorsky S-92A | 920056 | ex N4502R | |
| ☐ LN-OQG | Sikorsky S-92A | 920095 | ex N20168 | |
| ☐ LN-OQH | Sikorsky S-92A | 920097 | ex N2021Y | |
| ☐ LN-OQI | Sikorsky S-92A | 920098 | ex N2055A | |

| | | | | |
|---|---|---|---|---|
| ☐ LN-OQJ | Sikorsky S-92A | 920110 | ex N2126Z | |
| ☐ LN-OQK | Sikorsky S-92A | 920117 | ex N21285 | |
| ☐ LN-OQL | Sikorsky S-92A | 920132 | ex N132GN | |
| ☐ LN-OQN | Sikorsky S-92A | 920057 | ex VH-LYJ | ◆ |

## CYBRAIR — Nesøya

| | | | | |
|---|---|---|---|---|
| ☐ LN-NCC | de Havilland DHC-2 Beaver I | 1167 | ex N5CC | FP◆ |

## FONNAFLY — Fonna (NOF)

**Rosendal / Bergen / Oslo-Gardermoen / Voss (-/BGN/OSL/-)**

| | | | | | |
|---|---|---|---|---|---|
| ☐ LN-FFF | Cessna U206G Stationair 6 II | U20604497 | ex SE-GXB | Fonna 19 | FP |
| ☐ LN-HAI | Cessna U206F Stationair 6 II | U20603058 | | | FP |
| ☐ LN-HOO | Cessna TU206F Turbo Stationair 6 II | U20605490 | | Fonna 10 | FP |
| ☐ LN-IKA | Cessna TU206F Turbo Stationair 6 II | U20606251 | ex N6356Z | Fonna 11 | FP |

## HELITRANS — Scanbird (HTA) — Trondheim (TRD)

| | | | | | |
|---|---|---|---|---|---|
| ☐ LN-OAK | Aérospatiale AS350B3 Ecureuil | 3212 | | | |
| ☐ LN-OEB | Aérospatiale AS350B3 Ecureuil | 3312 | | | |
| ☐ LN-OFB | Aérospatiale AS350B3 Ecureuil | 4691 | | | |
| ☐ LN-OGL | Aérospatiale AS350B3 Ecureuil | 3792 | ex F-WQDD | | |
| ☐ LN-OGN | Aérospatiale AS350B3 Ecureuil | 3570 | | | |
| ☐ LN-OGO | Aérospatiale AS350B3+ Ecureuil | 7145 | | | ◆ |
| ☐ LN-OTR | Aérospatiale AS350B3 Ecureuil | 4751 | | | ◆ |
| ☐ LN-OMD | Aérospatiale AS350B3 Ecureuil | 3303 | ex HB-ZCL | | |
| ☐ LN-OMY | Aérospatiale AS350BA Ecureuil | 1017 | ex SE-HIA | | |
| ☐ LN-OPA | Aérospatiale AS350B3 Ecureuil | 3589 | | | |
| | | | | | |
| ☐ LN-ABO | Cessna 185A Skywagon | 185-0439 | ex SE-EEM | | |
| ☐ LN-FAN | British Aerospace Jetstream 32 | 864 | ex SE-LHK | | >BCI |
| ☐ LN-FAQ | British Aerospace Jetstream 32EP | 953 | ex UR-CET | | |
| ☐ LN-HTB | British Aerospace Jetstream 32EP | 795 | ex G-OAKJ | | |
| ☐ LN-HTI | Swearingen SA.226T Merlin III | T-294 | ex PH-DYB | | Op for Baltic Air Svs |
| ☐ LN-OPO | Bell 214B | 28053 | ex N18091 | | |
| ☐ LN-ORM | Bell 214B-1 | 28054 | ex SE-HLE | | |

## KATO AIRLINE

| | | | | |
|---|---|---|---|---|
| ☐ LN-KAT | Cessna 208B Caravan I | 208B0970 | ex N12295 | ◆ |
| ☐ LN-KJK | Cessna 208B Caravan I | 208B0554 | ex N1267A | ◆ |

## LUFTTRANSPORT — Luft Transport (L5/LTR) — Bardufoss (BDU)

| | | | | |
|---|---|---|---|---|
| ☐ LN-OLF | Agusta AW139 | 31148 | | |
| ☐ LN-OLO | Agusta AW139 | 31139 | | |
| ☐ LN-OLS | Agusta AW139 | 31136 | | |
| ☐ LN-OLU | Agusta AW139 | 31135 | | |
| ☐ LN-OLV | Agusta AW139 | 31023 | ex I-RAIB | Vaeroy |
| | | | | |
| ☐ LN-LTA | Beech B200 Super King Air | BB-1868 | ex N954RM | |
| ☐ LN-LTB | Beech B200 Super King Air | BB-2001 | ex N3501D | |
| ☐ LN-LTC | Beech B200 Super King Air | BB-2002 | ex N60102 | |
| ☐ LN-LTD | Beech B200 Super King Air | BB-2006 | ex N61806 | |
| ☐ LN-LTE | Beech B200 Super King Air | BB-2007 | ex N63007 | |
| ☐ LN-LTG | Beech B200 Super King Air | BB-2009 | | |
| ☐ LN-LTI | Beech B200 Super King Air | BB-2010 | | |
| ☐ LN-LTJ | Beech B200 Super King Air | BB-2011 | | |
| ☐ LN-LTK | Beech B200 Super King Air | BB-2004 | | |
| ☐ LN-LTL | Beech B200 Super King Air | BB-2005 | | |
| | | | | |
| ☐ LN-LTS | Dornier 228-212NG | 8301 | ex D-CNEW | |
| ☐ LN-LYR | Dornier 228-202K | 8166 | ex D-CICA | Kings Bay |
| ☐ LN-OLA | Agusta A.109E Power | 11117 | | |
| ☐ LN-OLE | Aérospatiale SA365N2 Dauphin 2 | 6405 | ex VT-CKR | |
| ☐ LN-OLI | Agusta A.109E Power | 11204 | | |
| ☐ LN-OLM | Aérospatiale AS365N3 Dauphin 2 | 6725 | ex F-WWOT | |
| ☐ LN-OLN | Aérospatiale AS365N3 Dauphin 2 | 6721 | ex F-WWOF | |

## NORSK LUFTAMBULANCE — Helidoc (DOC) — Oslo/Dröbak (OSL/-)

| | | | | |
|---|---|---|---|---|
| ☐ LN-OOC | Eurocopter EC135P2+ | 0350 | ex D-HECH | EMS |
| ☐ LN-OOD | Eurocopter EC135P2+ | 0356 | ex D-HECL | EMS |
| ☐ LN-OOE | Eurocopter EC135P2+ | 0357 | ex D-HECA | EMS |
| ☐ LN-OOF | Eurocopter EC135P2+ | 0390 | ex D-HECH | EMS |
| ☐ LN-OOG | Eurocopter EC135P2+ | 0393 | ex D-HECM | EMS |
| ☐ LN-OOH | Eurocopter EC135P2+ | 0399 | ex D-HECG | EMS |
| ☐ LN-OOI | Eurocopter EC135P2+ | 0580 | | EMS |
| ☐ LN-OOJ | Eurocopter EC135P2+ | 0588 | | EMS |

| □ LN-OOM | MBB BK-117C-2 | 9074 | ex D-HMBB | |
|---|---|---|---|---|

| **NORWEGIAN** | | **Nor Shuttle (DY/NAX)** | | **Oslo-Gardermoen (OSL)** | |
|---|---|---|---|---|---|
| □ LN-KHA | Boeing 737-31S/W | 29100/2984 | ex SX-BGY | | |
| □ LN-KHB | Boeing 737-31S/W | 29264/3070 | ex SX-BGW | | |
| □ LN-KHC | Boeing 737-31S/W | 29265/3073 | ex SX-BGX | | |
| □ LN-KKB | Boeing 737-33A | 27457/2756 | ex N457AN | | |
| □ LN-KKD | Boeing 737-33V | 29339/3119 | ex 5N-VNB | | |
| □ LN-KKI | Boeing 737-3K2 | 24329/1858 | ex PH-HVV | Helge Ingstad | |
| □ LN-KKJ | Boeing 737-36N | 28564/2936 | ex N564SR | Sonja Henie | |
| □ LN-KKL | Boeing 737-36N | 28671/2955 | ex N671SR | Roald Amundsen | |
| □ LN-KKM | Boeing 737-3Y0 | 24676/1829 | ex HA-LES | Thor Heyerdahl | |
| □ LN-KKN | Boeing 737-3Y0 | 24910/2030 | ex HA-LET | Sigrid Undset | |
| □ LN-KKO | Boeing 737-3Y0 | 24909/2021 | ex HA-LED | Henrik Ibsen | |
| □ LN-KKR | Boeing 737-3Y0 | 24256/1629 | ex OM-AAA | | |
| □ LN-KKS | Boeing 737-33A | 24094/1729 | ex ZK-PLU | | |
| □ LN-KKW | Boeing 737-3K9 | 24213/1794 | ex CS-TLL | | |
| □ LN-KKX | Boeing 737-33S/W | 29072/3012 | ex ZK-NGN | | |
| | | | | | |
| □ LN-DYA | Boeing 737-8JP/W | 39162/2994 | ex N1786B | | |
| □ LN-DYB | Boeing 737-8JP/W | 39163/3054 | | | |
| □ LN-DYC | Boeing 737-8JP/W | 39164/3196 | ex N1787B | | |
| □ LN-DYD | Boeing 737-8JP/W | 39002/3231 | ex N1787B | | |
| □ LN-DYE | Boeing 737-8JP/W | 39003/3401 | ex N1787B | Arne Jacbobsen | |
| □ LN-DYF | Boeing 737-8JP/W | 39004/3482 | ex N1787B | | |
| □ LN-DYG | Boeing 737-8JP/W | 39165/3507 | ex N1786B | | |
| □ LN-DYH | Boeing 737-8JP/W | 40865/3410 | | Soren Kierkegaard | |
| □ LN-DYI | Boeing 737-8JP/W | 40866/3432 | ex N1787B | Aasmund Olavson Vinje | |
| □ LN-DYJ | Boeing 737-8JP/W | 39045/3530 | | | |
| □ LN-DYK | Boeing 737-8JP/W | 39046/3557 | | | ♦ |
| □ LN-DYL | Boeing 737-8JP/W | 40867/3565 | | | ♦ |
| □ LN-DYM | Boeing 737-8JP/W | 39005/3572 | | | ♦ |
| □ LN-DYN | Boeing 737-8JP/W | 39006/3583 | | | ♦ |
| □ LN-DYO | Boeing 737-8JP/W | 40868/3591 | | | ♦ |
| □ LN-DYP | Boeing 737-8JP/W | 39047/3630 | | | ♦ |
| □ LN-DYQ | Boeing 737-8JP/W | 40869/3651 | | | ♦ |
| □ LN-DYR | Boeing 737-8JP/W | 40869/3651 | | | ♦ |
| □ LN-DYS | Boeing 737-8JP/W | 390073665 | | | ♦ |
| □ LN-DYT | Boeing 737-8JP/W | 39048/3686 | | | ♦ |
| □ LN-DYU | Boeing 737-8JP/W | 39008/3725 | | | ♦ |
| □ LN-DYV | Boeing 737-8JP/W | 39009/3790 | | | ♦ |
| □ LN-DYW | Boeing 737-8JP/W | 39010/3871 | | | ♦ |
| □ LN-DYX | Boeing 737-8JP/W | 39011/3946 | | | ♦ |
| □ LN-DYY | Boeing 737-8JP/W | 39012/3982 | | Vilhelm Bjørknes | ♦ |
| □ LN-DYZ | Boeing 737-8JP/W | 39013/ | | | o/o♦ |
| □ LN-NGA | Boeing 737-8JP/W | 39014/ | | | o/o♦ |
| □ LN-NGB | Boeing 737-8JP/W | 39015/ | | | o/o♦ |
| □ LN-NGC | Boeing 737-8JP/W | 39016/ | | | o/o♦ |
| □ LN-NGD | Boeing 737-8JP/W | 39049/ | | | o/o♦ |
| □ LN-NGE | Boeing 737-8JP/W | 39050/ | | | o/o♦ |
| □ LN-NGF | Boeing 737-8JP/W | 39017/ | | | o/o♦ |
| □ LN-NGG | Boeing 737-8JP/W | 39018/ | | | o/o♦ |
| □ LN-NIA | Boeing 737-8JP/W | 39444/3965 | | Johan Ludvig Runeberg | ♦ |
| □ LN-NIB | Boeing 737-86J/W | 36879/3805 | ex D-ABMA | | ♦ |
| □ LN-NOB | Boeing 737-8FZ/W | 34954/2483 | ex N1786B | Edvard Grieg | |
| □ LN-NOC | Boeing 737-81Q/W | 30785/1007 | ex EC-ICD | | |
| □ LN-NOD | Boeing 737-8Q8/W | 35280/2629 | | Sonja Henie | |
| □ LN-NOE | Boeing 737-8Q8/W | 35283/2742 | ex N1787B | | |
| □ LN-NOF | Boeing 737-86N/W | 36809/2647 | | | |
| □ LN-NOG | Boeing 737-86N/W | 35647/2927 | ex N1786B | | |
| □ LN-NOH | Boeing 737-86N/W | 36814/3015 | ex N1779B | | |
| □ LN-NOI | Boeing 737-86N/W | 36820/3131 | | | |
| □ LN-NOJ | Boeing 737-86N/W | 37884/3223 | ex N1796B | | |
| □ LN-NOL | Boeing 737-8Q8/W | 37159/2868 | | | |
| □ LN-NOM | Boeing 737-86N/W | 28642/813 | ex SE-RHA | | |
| □ LN-NON | Boeing 737-86N/W | 28620/542 | ex SE-RHB | | |
| □ LN-NOO | Boeing 737-86Q/W | 30289/1399 | ex N289CG | | |
| □ LN-NOP | Boeing 737-86N/W | 32655/1662 | ex EI-ECL | | |
| □ LN-NOQ | Boeing 737-86N/W | 32658/1695 | ex EI-ECM | | |
| □ LN-NOR | Boeing 737-881D/W | 39412/3553 | | | ♦ |
| □ LN-NOT | Boeing 737-8JP/W | 37816/3194 | ex N1796B | | |
| □ LN-NOU | Boeing 737-8FZ/W | 29674/3140 | ex N1787B | | |
| □ LN-NOV | Boeing 737-8FZ/W | 31713/3215 | | | |
| □ LN-NOW | Boeing 737-8FZ/W | 37817/3364 | ex N1796B | Oda Krohg | |
| □ LN-NOX | Boeing 737-8JP/W | 37818/3384 | | | ♦ |
| □ LN-NOY | Boeing 737-8JP/W | 39419/3878 | | Knud Rasmussen | ♦ |
| □ LN-NOZ | Boeing 737-8JP/W | 39420/3891 | | Gidsken Jakobsen | ♦ |

## SCANDINAVIAN AIRLINE SYSTEM    Scandinavian (SK/SAS)     Copenhagen-Kastrup (CPH)

For details see under Sweden (SE-)

## WIDERØE'S FLYVESELSKAP     Widerøe (WF/WIF)       Bodo (BOO)

| | | | | | |
|---|---|---|---|---|---|
| ☐ | LN-ILS | de Havilland DHC-8-103 | 396 | ex C-GHRI | |
| ☐ | LN-WIA | de Havilland DHC-8-103B | 359 | ex C-GHRI | Nordland |
| ☐ | LN-WIB | de Havilland DHC-8-103B | 360 | ex C-GFBW | Finnmark |
| ☐ | LN-WIC | de Havilland DHC-8-103B | 367 | ex C-GDNG | Sogn og Fjordane |
| ☐ | LN-WID | de Havilland DHC-8-103B | 369 | ex C-FDHD | More og Romsdal |
| ☐ | LN-WIE | de Havilland DHC-8-103B | 371 | ex C-GFYI | Hordaland |
| ☐ | LN-WIF | de Havilland DHC-8-103B | 372 | ex C-GFOD | Nord-Tröndelag |
| ☐ | LN-WIG | de Havilland DHC-8-103B | 382 | ex C-GLOT | Troms |
| ☐ | LN-WIH | de Havilland DHC-8-103B | 383 | ex C-GFYI | Oslo |
| ☐ | LN-WII | de Havilland DHC-8-103B | 384 | ex C-GFOD | Nordkapp |
| ☐ | LN-WIJ | de Havilland DHC-8-103B | 386 | ex C-GFQL | Hammerfest |
| ☐ | LN-WIL | de Havilland DHC-8-103B | 398 | ex C-GFCF | Narvik |
| ☐ | LN-WIM | de Havilland DHC-8-103B | 403 | ex C-GDIU | Vesterälen |
| ☐ | LN-WIN | de Havilland DHC-8-103B | 409 | ex C-GDNG | Alstadhaug/Lofoten |
| ☐ | LN-WIO | de Havilland DHC-8-103B | 417 | ex C-GFQL | Rost/Akershus |
| ☐ | LN-WIP | de Havilland DHC-8-103A | 239 | ex C-FXNE | Alstahaug |
| ☐ | LN-WIR | de Havilland DHC-8-103A | 273 | ex C-FZNU | Nordkyn |
| ☐ | LN-WIT | de Havilland DHC-8-103 | 310 | ex D-BIER | |
| ☐ | LN-WIU | de Havilland DHC-8-103 | 378 | ex C-FZKQ | |
| ☐ | LN-WIV | de Havilland DHC-8-103 | 343 | ex C-GJMQ | ♦ |
| | | | | | |
| ☐ | LN-WFC | de Havilland DHC-8-311A | 236 | ex D-BEYT | ♦ |
| ☐ | LN-WFD | de Havilland DHC-8-311 | 407 | ex C-FSIJ | ♦ |
| ☐ | LN-WFH | de Havilland DHC-8-311A | 238 | ex C-FZOH | all-white ♦ |
| ☐ | LN-WFO | de Havilland DHC-8Q-311 | 493 | ex C-GERC | |
| ☐ | LN-WFP | de Havilland DHC-8Q-311 | 495 | ex C-GFUM | |
| ☐ | LN-WFS | de Havilland DHC-8Q-311 | 535 | ex C-GEWI | |
| ☐ | LN-WFT | de Havilland DHC-8Q-311 | 532 | ex C-FATN | |
| | | | | | |
| ☐ | LN-WDE | de Havilland DHC-8-402Q | 4183 | ex C-FNEC | |
| ☐ | LN-WDF | de Havilland DHC-8-402Q | 4244 | ex C-FUTZ | |
| ☐ | LN-WDG | de Havilland DHC-8-402Q | 4266 | ex C-FXJF | |
| ☐ | LN-WDH | de Havilland DHC-8-402Q | 4273 | ex C-FYGI | |
| ☐ | LN-WDI | de Havilland DHC-8-402Q | 4286 | ex C-FZFX | |
| ☐ | LN-WDJ | de Havilland DHC-8-402Q | 4290 | ex C-GARX | |
| ☐ | LN-WDK | de Havilland DHC-8-402Q | 4337 | ex C-GGIR | |
| ☐ | LN-WDL | de Havilland DHC-8-402Q | 4392 | ex C-GLKA | ♦ |
| | | | | | |
| ☐ | LN-WSB | de Havilland DHC-8-202 | 440 | ex C-GLUF | o/o♦ |
| ☐ | LN-WSC | de Havilland DHC-8-202 | 441 | ex C-GLUG | o/o♦ |

## ARGENTINA (Republic of Argentina)

## AEROLINEAS ARGENTINAS     Argentina (AR/ARG)     Buenos Aires-Ezeiza (EZE)

| | | | | | |
|---|---|---|---|---|---|
| ☐ | LV-BIT | Airbus A340-313 | 093 | ex 9Y-TJN | |
| ☐ | LV-BMT | Airbus A340-312 | 048 | ex C-FDRO | |
| ☐ | LV-CEK | Airbus A340-313 | 094 | ex EI-EHZ | |
| ☐ | LV-CSD | Airbus A340-313X | 123 | ex B-HXM | ♦ |
| ☐ | LV-CSE | Airbus A340-313X | 126 | ex B-HXN | ♦ |
| ☐ | LV-CSF | Airbus A340-313X | 128 | ex B-HXO | ♦ |
| ☐ | LV-CSX | Airbus A340-313X | 373 | ex F-GNIH | ♦ |
| | | | | | |
| ☐ | LV-AYE | Boeing 737-5H6 | 26456/2527 | ex F-GJNY | |
| ☐ | LV-AYI | Boeing 737-528 | 25234/2411 | ex F-GJNI | |
| ☐ | LV-AZU | Boeing 737-528 | 25235/2428 | ex F-GJNJ | |
| ☐ | LV-BAT | Boeing 737-5H6 | 27356/2654 | ex F-GJNP | |
| ☐ | LV-BAX | Boeing 737-5H6 | 26448/2484 | ex F-GJNL | |
| ☐ | LV-BBN | Boeing 737-5H6 | 26454/2511 | ex F-GJNX | |
| ☐ | LV-BDD | Boeing 737-5Y0 | 24899/2093 | ex B-2544 | |
| ☐ | LV-BIH | Boeing 737-53A | 24786/1898 | ex N786AW | |
| ☐ | LV-BIM | Boeing 737-53A | 25425/2177 | ex N425AN | |
| ☐ | LV-BIX | Boeing 737-53A | 24788/1921 | ex N233BC | |
| ☐ | LV-BNM | Boeing 737-5K5 | 24926/1966 | ex D-AHLD | |
| ☐ | LV-BNS | Boeing 737-5K5 | 24776/1848 | ex D-AHLG | |
| | | | | | |
| ☐ | LV-BYY | Boeing 737-7BD | 33938/2863 | ex N357AT | |
| ☐ | LV-BZA | Boeing 737-76N/W | 32674/1952 | ex OK-GCA | |
| ☐ | LV-BZO | Boeing 737-76N/W | 32676/1974 | ex OK-GCB | |
| ☐ | LV-CAD | Boeing 737-76N/W | 32680/2089 | ex OK-GCC | |
| ☐ | LV-CAM | Boeing 737-73V/W | 30243/919 | ex N243CL | |
| ☐ | LV-CAP | Boeing 737-76N/W | 32695/1919 | ex OK-GCD | |
| ☐ | LV-CBF | Boeing 737-76N/W | 32696/1922 | ex OK-GCE | |
| ☐ | LV-CBG | Boeing 737-73V/W | 30235/672 | ex N384DF | |

| | | | | | |
|---|---|---|---|---|---|
| ☐ LV-CBS | Boeing 737-73V/W | 30236/715 | ex N385DF | | |
| ☐ LV-CBT | Boeing 737-76N/W | 34756/2208 | ex OK-GCF | | |
| ☐ LV-CCR | Boeing 737-73V/W | 30237/730 | ex N386DF | | |
| ☐ LV-CMK | Boeing 737-7Q8/W | 28240/832 | ex N721LF | | ♦ |
| ☐ LV-CPH | Boeing 737-7Q8/W | 28238/817 | ex N711LF | | ♦ |
| ☐ LV-CSC | Boeing 737-7Q8/W | 30630/1032 | ex N351LF | | ♦ |
| ☐ LV-CSI | Boeing 737-7Q8/W | 30707975 | ex N331LF | | ♦ |
| ☐ LV-CVX | Boeing 737-7Q8/W | 30641/1080 | ex N151LF | | ♦ |
| ☐ LV-GOO | Boeing 737-7BD | 35962/2932 | ex N358AT | | |
| ☐ LV-ALJ | Boeing 747-475 | 25422/912 | ex N971PG | | [EZE] |
| ☐ LV-AXF | Boeing 747-475 | 24895/837 | ex N895NC | | |
| ☐ LV-BBU | Boeing 747-475 | 24883/823 | ex N987PG | | [EZE] |
| ☐ LV-CTB | Boeing 737-85F | 30478/997 | ex D-ABBZ | | |
| ☐ LV-CTC | Boeing 737-86J/W | 30570/879 | ex N570MQ | | ♦ |
| ☐ LV-VAG | McDonnell-Douglas MD-83 | 53117/1951 | ex N6202D | | ♦ |
| ☐ LV-VBX | McDonnell-Douglas MD-88 | 53047/2016 | | Parque Nacional Lanin | |
| ☐ LV-VBZ | McDonnell-Douglas MD-88 | 53049/2031 | | Parque Baritu | |
| ☐ LV-ZPJ | Airbus A340-211 | 074 | ex F-OHPG | | |
| ☐ LV-ZPO | Airbus A340-211 | 063 | ex F-OHPF | | |
| ☐ LV-ZPX | Airbus A340-211 | 080 | ex F-OHPH | | |
| ☐ LV-ZRA | Airbus A340-211 | 085 | ex F-OHPI | | |

## AERO VIP (AOG) Buenos Aires-Aeroparque (AEP)

| | | | | |
|---|---|---|---|---|
| ☐ LV-BYW | Canadair CRJ-900 | 15209 | ex CX-CRG | |

## AIR TANGO Buenos Aires-Aeroparque (AEP)

| | | | | |
|---|---|---|---|---|
| ☐ LV-WEO | Swearingen SA.226TC Metro II | TC-346 | ex N52EA | |

## AMERICAN JET Buenos Aires-Aeroparque (AEP)

| | | | | |
|---|---|---|---|---|
| ☐ LV-BYJ | Swearingen SA.227DC Metro 23 | DC-889B | ex N889AJ | |
| ☐ LV-BYM | Swearingen SA.227DC Metro 23 | DC-856B | ex N3027B | |
| ☐ LV-BYN | Swearingen SA.227DC Metro 23 | DC-888B | ex N332AJ | |
| ☐ LV-WTD | Dornier 228-202 | 8094 | ex D-CBDR | |
| ☐ LV-WTV | Dornier 228-201 | 8093 | ex N228AM | |
| ☐ LV-ZXA | Swearingen SA.227DC Metro 23 | DC-901B | ex LV-PIR | no titles |

## ANDES LINEAS AEREAS Aeroandes (ANS) Salta International (SLA)

| | | | | |
|---|---|---|---|---|
| ☐ LV-ARF | McDonnell-Douglas MD-83 | 49252/1169 | ex LV-PJH | ♦ |
| ☐ LV-BAY | McDonnell-Douglas MD-83 | 49284/1209 | ex LV-PJJ | ♦ |
| ☐ LV-BTH | McDonnell-Douglas MD-83 | 49952/1934 | ex N995AC | |
| ☐ LV-BZR | McDonnell-Douglas MD-87 | 49706/1614 | ex XA-TWT | |
| ☐ LV-CCJ | McDonnell-Douglas MD-83 | 49621/1495 | ex EC-479 | ♦ |
| ☐ LV-CDD | McDonnell-Douglas MD-83 | 49579/1465 | ex EC-GOM | wfs |
| ☐ LV-CFJ | McDonnell-Douglas MD-87 | 49389/1333 | ex XA-TXC | wfs♦ |
| ☐ EC-LLJ | Airbus A320-216 | 4661 | ex F-WWII | <VLG♦ |

## AUSTRAL LINEAS AEREAS Austral (AU/AUT) Buenos Aires-Aeroparque (AEP)

| | | | | |
|---|---|---|---|---|
| ☐ LV-CDY | Embraer ERJ-190AR | 19000365 | ex PT- | ♦ |
| ☐ LV-CDZ | Embraer ERJ-190AR | 19000377 | ex PT- | ♦ |
| ☐ LV-CET | Embraer ERJ-190AR | 19000383 | ex PT-XNR | |
| ☐ LV-CEU | Embraer ERJ-190AR | 19000389 | ex PT-XNW | |
| ☐ LV-CEV | Embraer ERJ-190AR | 19000390 | ex PT-XNX | |
| ☐ LV-CHO | Embraer ERJ-190AR | 19000395 | ex PT-XUB | |
| ☐ LV-CHQ | Embraer ERJ-190AR | 19000397 | ex PT-XUC | |
| ☐ LV-CHR | Embraer ERJ-190AR | 19000400 | ex PT-TYF | |
| ☐ LV-CHS | Embraer ERJ-190AR | 19000402 | ex PT-TYV | |
| ☐ LV-CID | Embraer ERJ-190AR | 19000409 | ex PT-TBH | |
| ☐ LV-CIE | Embraer ERJ-190AR | 19000414 | ex PT-TBL | |
| ☐ LV-CIF | Embraer ERJ-190AR | 19000421 | ex PT- | ♦ |
| ☐ LV-CIG | Embraer ERJ-190AR | 19000427 | ex PT- | ♦ |
| ☐ LV-CIH | Embraer ERJ-190AR | 19000428 | ex PT- | ♦ |
| ☐ LV-CKZ | Embraer ERJ-190AR | 19000439 | ex PT- | ♦ |
| ☐ LV-CMA | Embraer ERJ-190AR | 19000445 | ex PT- | ♦ |
| ☐ LV-CMB | Embraer ERJ-190AR | 19000448 | ex PT- | ♦ |
| ☐ LV-CPI | Embraer ERJ-190AR | 19000457 | ex PT-TNY | ♦ |
| ☐ LV-CPJ | Embraer ERJ-190AR | 19000463 | ex PT-TOG | ♦ |
| ☐ LV-CPK | Embraer ERJ-190AR | 19000474 | ex PT- | ♦ |
| ☐ LV-AYD | McDonnell-Douglas MD-83 | 53015/1818 | ex N824NK | |
| ☐ LV-BEG | McDonnell-Douglas MD-83 | 49630/1591 | ex N320FV | [AEP] |
| ☐ LV-BGV | McDonnell-Douglas MD-83 | 49904/1680 | ex N960PG | |
| ☐ LV-BHH | McDonnell-Douglas MD-83 | 49741/1630 | ex N959PG | |
| ☐ LV-WGM | McDonnell-Douglas MD-83 | 49784/1627 | ex N509MD | |
| ☐ LV-WGN | McDonnell-Douglas MD-83 | 49934/1764 | ex N907MD | wfs |

| | | | | |
|---|---|---|---|---|
| ☐ LV-BGZ | McDonnell-Douglas MD-82 | 49906/1786 | ex EC-JZA | [AEP] |
| ☐ LV-BGC | McDonnell Douglas MD-88 | 53447/2064 | | |
| ☐ LV-BOA | McDonnell-Douglas MD-88 | 53174/1854 | ex N168PL | |
| ☐ LV-BOH | McDonnell-Douglas MD-88 | 53175/1868 | ex N169PL | |

### BAIRES FLY                                        Buenos Aires-Aeroparque (AEP)

| | | | | |
|---|---|---|---|---|
| ☐ LV-VDJ | Swearingen SA.227AC Metro III | AC-729 | ex N27823 | |
| ☐ LV-WJT | Swearingen SA.227AC Metro III | AC-776B | ex N776NE | |
| ☐ LV-WRA | Swearingen SA.227AC Metro III | AC-429 | ex C-FJLF | ♦ |
| ☐ LV-WTE | Swearingen SA.227AC Metro III | AC-584 | ex LV-PMF | |
| ☐ LV-ZMG | Swearingen SA.227AC Metro III | AC-425 | ex N721MA | |
| ☐ LV-WHG | Swearingen SA.226TC Metro II | TC-344 | ex N44CS | |

### FLYING AMERICA                                    Buenos Aires-Aeroparque (AEP)

| | | | | |
|---|---|---|---|---|
| ☐ LV-BGH | Swearingen SA.227AC Metro III | AC-467 | ex TF-JMK | |
| ☐ LV-YIC | Swearingen SA.227AC Metro III | AC-448 | ex LV-PNF | |

### HANGAR UNO                                        Buenos Aires-Don Torcuato

| | | | | |
|---|---|---|---|---|
| ☐ LV-WFR | Britten-Norman BN-2B-26 Islander | 2263 | ex G-BUBF | Puerto Carmelo titles |

### HAWK AIR                          Air Hawk (HKR)   Buenos Aires-Aeroparque (AEP)

| | | | | |
|---|---|---|---|---|
| ☐ LV-WHX | Piper PA-31 Turbo Navajo | 31-353 | ex N716DR | |
| ☐ LV-WIR | Swearingen SA.226T Merlin III | T-232 | ex N56TA | Frtr |
| ☐ LV-WNC | Swearingen SA.226AT Merlin IVA | AT-036 | ex N642TS | Frtr |
| ☐ LV-WXW | Swearingen SA.226TC Metro II | TC-419 | ex N7205L | Frtr |

### LADE - LINEAS AEREAS DEL ESTADO     Lade (5U/LDE)   Comodoro Rivadavia (CRD)

| | | | | |
|---|---|---|---|---|
| ☐ T-81 | de Havilland DHC-6 Twin Otter 200 | 165 | | |
| ☐ T-82 | de Havilland DHC-6 Twin Otter 200 | 167 | | |
| ☐ T-85 | de Havilland DHC-6 Twin Otter 200 | 173 | | |
| ☐ T-86 | de Havilland DHC-6 Twin Otter 200 | 225 | | Antarctic red c/s |
| ☐ T-87 | de Havilland DHC-6 Twin Otter 200 | 158 | ex LV-JMP | |
| ☐ T-89 | de Havilland DHC-6 Twin Otter 200 | 185 | ex LV-JPX | |
| ☐ T-90 | de Havilland DHC-6 Twin Otter 200 | 178 | ex LV-JMR | |
| ☐ T-44 | Fokker F.27 Friendship 600 | 10454 | ex PH-EXB | wfs |
| ☐ TC-71 | Fokker F.27 Friendship 400M | 10403 | ex PH-FOB | |
| ☐ TC-74 | Fokker F.27 Friendship 400M | 10408 | ex PH-FOG | |
| ☐ TC-75 | Fokker F.27 Friendship 500 | 10621 | ex PH-EXM | |
| ☐ TC-79 | Fokker F.27 Friendship 400M | 10575 | ex PH-EXG | |
| ☐ T-31 | SAAB SF.340B | 340B-270 | ex N284DC | |
| ☐ T-32 | SAAB SF.340B | 340B-226 | ex N285DC | |
| ☐ T-33 | SAAB SF.340B | 340B-288 | ex N288JJ | |
| ☐ T-34 | SAAB SF.340B | 340B-217 | ex N217JJ | |
| ☐ TC-52 | Fokker F.28 Fellowship 1000C | 11074 | ex LV-RCS | [COR] |
| ☐ TC-53 | Fokker F.28 Fellowship 1000C | 11020 | ex PH-EXX | wfs |
| ☐ TC-55 | Fokker F.28 Fellowship 1000C | 11024 | ex PH-EXZ | |
| ☐ TC-91 | Boeing 707-387B | 21070/897 | ex T-91 | wfs |

### LAN ARGENTINA                      LAN Ar (4M/DSM)   Buenos Aires-Aeroparque (AEP)

| | | | | |
|---|---|---|---|---|
| ☐ LV-BET | Airbus A320-233 | 1854 | ex CC-COO | |
| ☐ LV-BFO | Airbus A320-233 | 1877 | ex CC-COQ | |
| ☐ LV-BFY | Airbus A320-233 | 1858 | ex CC-COP | |
| ☐ LV-BGI | Airbus A320-233 | 1903 | ex CC-COT | |
| ☐ LV-BHU | Airbus A320-233 | 1512 | ex CC-COH | |
| ☐ LV-BOI | Airbus A320-233 | 1491 | ex CC-COG | |
| ☐ LV-BRA | Airbus A320-233 | 1304 | ex CC-COC | |
| ☐ LV-BRY | Airbus A320-233 | 1351 | ex CC-COE | |
| ☐ LV-BSJ | Airbus A320-233 | 1332 | ex CC-COD | |
| ☐ LV-BTM | Airbus A320-233 | 1548 | ex CC-COK | |
| ☐ LV-CKV | Airbus A320-233 | 1568 | ex CC-COL | ♦ |
| ☐ LV-CQS | Airbus A320-233 | 1526 | ex CC-COI | ♦ |
| ☐ LV-CDQ | Boeing 767-316ER/W | 35229/949 | ex CC-CWN | |
| ☐ LV-CKU | Boeing 767-316ER/W | 34628/945 | ex CC-CWH | ♦ |

### LINEAS AEREAS DE ARGENTINA

| | | | | |
|---|---|---|---|---|
| ☐ LV-BSC | McDonnell-Douglas MD-87 | 49727/1621 | ex N755RA | ♦ |
| ☐ LV-CIT | McDonnell-Douglas MD-83 | 49568/1380 | ex N963PG | ♦ |
| ☐ LV-CSW | McDonnell-Douglas MD-83 | 49845/1573 | ex N989PG | ♦ |

| | | | | |
|---|---|---|---|---|
| ☐ LV-ZPZ | British Aerospace Jetstream 32EP | 931 | ex N931AE | ♦ |

## MACAIR JET                                                                    Buenos Aires-Aeroparque (AEP)

| | | | |
|---|---|---|---|
| ☐ LV-ZOW | British Aerospace Jetstream 32EP | 869 | ex N869AE |
| ☐ LV-ZPW | British Aerospace Jetstream 32EP | 861 | ex N861AE |
| ☐ LV-ZRL | British Aerospace Jetstream 32EP | 928 | ex N928AE |
| ☐ LV-ZSB | British Aerospace Jetstream 32EP | 942 | ex N942AE |
| ☐ LV-ZST | British Aerospace Jetstream 32EP | 941 | ex N941AE |

## SERVICIOS AEREOS PATAGONICOS

| | | | | |
|---|---|---|---|---|
| ☐ LV-RPB | Swearingen SA.227AC Metro III | AC-415 | ex N173MA | ♦ |
| ☐ LV-RBR | Swearingen SA.227AC Metro III | AC-416 | ex N177MA | ♦ |

## SOL LINEAS AEREAS                      Flight Sol (8R/OLS)                      Rosario-Fisherton (ROS)

| | | | | |
|---|---|---|---|---|
| ☐ LV-BEW | SAAB SF.340A | 340A-150 | ex N150CN | |
| ☐ LV-BEX | SAAB SF.340A | 340A-014 | ex N14XS | |
| ☐ LV-BMD | SAAB SF.340A | 340A-123 | ex N123XS | |
| ☐ LV-BTP | SAAB SF.340A | 340A-131 | ex VH-KDI | |
| ☐ LV-CEI | SAAB SF.340A | 340A-012 | ex N108PX | ♦ |
| ☐ LV-CSK | SAAB SF.340B | 340B-168 | ex SE-LJR | ♦ |

## SUR LINEAS AEREAS

| | | | |
|---|---|---|---|
| ☐ LV-ZXC | Boeing 737-236 | 23160/1053 | ex N950PG |

## TAPSA AVIACION                           Tapsa (TPS)                         Buenos Aires-Aeroparque (AEP)

| | | | |
|---|---|---|---|
| ☐ LV-LSI | de Havilland DHC-6 Twin Otter 300 | 456 | ex LV-PTW |

## TRANSPORTES BRAGADO                                                           Buenos Aires-Aeroparque (AEP)

| | | | |
|---|---|---|---|
| ☐ LV-MGD | Piper PA-31T Cheyenne | 31T-7720059 | ex LV-PXD |
| ☐ LV-ZNU | Cessna 208B Caravan I | 208B0718 | ex LV-POC |

## UNION AIR

| | | | | |
|---|---|---|---|---|
| ☐ LV-BGR | Swearingen SA.227AC Metro III | AC-461B | ex EC-HXY | ♦ |

# LX-    LUXEMBOURG (Grand Duchy of Luxembourg)

## CARGOLUX INTERNATIONAL AIRLINES    Cargolux (CV/CLX)                             Luxembourg (LUX)

| | | | | | |
|---|---|---|---|---|---|
| ☐ LX-ACV | Boeing 747-4B5F | 24200/748 | ex D-ALLA | | |
| ☐ LX-DCV | Boeing 747-4B5BCF | 24619/793 | ex HL7480 | | ♦ |
| ☐ LX-OCV | Boeing 747-4R7F | 29731/1222 | | Differdange | |
| ☐ LX-PCV | Boeing 747-4R7F | 29732/1231 | | Diekirch | |
| ☐ LX-RCV | Boeing 747-4R7F | 30400/1235 | | Schengen | |
| ☐ LX-SCV | Boeing 747-4R7F | 29733/1281 | | Niederanven | |
| ☐ LX-TCV | Boeing 747-4R7F | 30401/1311 | ex N6046P | Sandweiler | |
| ☐ LX-UCV | Boeing 747-4R7F | 33827/1345 | | Bertrange | |
| ☐ LX-VCV | Boeing 747-4R7F | 34235/1366 | | Walferdange | |
| ☐ LX-WCV | Boeing 747-4R7F | 35804/1390 | ex N5022E | Pétange | |
| ☐ LX-YCV | Boeing 747-4R7F | 35805/1407 | | City of Contern | |
| ☐ LX-ZCV | Boeing 747-481BDSF | 24801/805 | ex F-GISF | | |
| | | | | | |
| ☐ LX-VCB | Boeing 747-8R7F | 35806/1423 | ex N5014K | City of Esch-sur-Aizette | ♦ |
| ☐ LX-VCC | Boeing 747-8R7F | 35807/1424 | ex N5573S | | ♦ |
| ☐ LX-VCD | Boeing 747-8R7F | 35809/1436 | | City of Luxembourg | ♦ |
| ☐ LX-VCE | Boeing 747-8R7F | 35810/ | | | o/o♦ |
| ☐ LX-VCF | Boeing 747-8R7F | 35811/ | | | o/o♦ |
| ☐ LX-VCG | Boeing 747-8R7F | 35812/ | | | o/o♦ |

## LUXAIR                                     Luxair (LG/LGL)                         Luxembourg (LUX)

| | | | | |
|---|---|---|---|---|
| ☐ LX-LGA | de Havilland DHC-8-402Q | 4159 | ex C-FLKX | |
| ☐ LX-LGC | de Havilland DHC-8-402Q | 4162 | ex C-FLTY | |
| ☐ LX-LGD | de Havilland DHC-8-402Q | 4171 | ex C-FMJC | |
| ☐ LX-LGE | de Havilland DHC-8-402Q | 4284 | ex C-FXYV | |
| ☐ LX-LGF | de Havilland DHC-8-402Q | 4349 | ex C- | ♦ |
| | | | | |
| ☐ LX-LGI | Embraer ERJ-145LU | 145369 | ex PT-SOU | |
| ☐ LX-LGJ | Embraer ERJ-145LU | 145395 | ex PT-SQS | |
| ☐ LX-LGW | Embraer ERJ-145LU | 145135 | ex PT-SDM | |
| ☐ LX-LGX | Embraer ERJ-145LU | 145147 | ex PT-SDX | |
| ☐ LX-LGY | Embraer ERJ-145LU | 145242 | ex PT-SIH | |
| ☐ LX-LGZ | Embraer ERJ-145LU | 145258 | ex PT-SIR | |

| | | | | |
|---|---|---|---|---|
| ☐ D-ABBI | Boeing 737-86J/W | 32920/1293 | | <GXL♦ |
| ☐ LX-LGK | Embraer ERJ-135LR | 14500886 | ex PT-SXY | ♦ |
| ☐ LX-LGL | Embraer ERJ-135LR | 14500893 | ex PT-SYF | 900th titles ♦ |
| ☐ LX-LGQ | Boeing 737-7C9/W | 33802/1442 | | Chateau de Berg |
| ☐ LX-LGR | Boeing 737-7C9/W | 33803/1468 | | Chateau de Fischbach |
| ☐ LX-LGS | Boeing 737-7C9/W | 33956/1634 | | Chateau de Senningen |
| ☐ LX-LGT | Boeing 737-8K5/W | 28228/484 | ex D-AHFN | |
| ☐ LX-LGU | Boeing 737-8C9/W | 41047 | | o/o♦ |

## STRATEGIC AIRLINES LUXEMBOURG        (STU)                        Luxembourg (LUX)

| | | | | |
|---|---|---|---|---|
| ☐ LX-STA | Airbus A320-212 | 0446 | ex YL-LCF | ♦ |
| ☐ LX-STB | Airbus A320-212 | 0436 | ex F-GSTR | ♦ |
| ☐ LX-STC | Airbus A320-212 | 0420 | ex F-GSTS | ♦ |

## WEST AIR LUXEMBOURG            West Lux (WLX)                    Luxembourg (LUX)

| | | | | |
|---|---|---|---|---|
| ☐ LX-WAD | British Aerospace ATP (LFD) | 2038 | ex SE-MAJ | ♦ |
| ☐ LX-WAE | British Aerospace ATP (LFD) | 2037 | ex SE-MAP | ♦ |
| ☐ LX-WAF | British Aerospace ATP (LFD) | 2056 | ex SE-KXP | ♦ |
| ☐ LX-WAK | British Aerospace ATP | 2061 | ex SE-LNX | ♦ |
| ☐ LX-WAL | British Aerospace ATPF | 2059 | ex SE-LHZ | ♦ |
| ☐ LX-WAN | British Aerospace ATPF | 2020 | ex SE-LHX | |
| ☐ LX-WAO | British Aerospace ATP (LFD) | 2043 | ex SE-LPS | |
| ☐ LX-WAP | British Aerospace ATPF | 2057 | ex SE-LPR | |
| ☐ LX-WAS | British Aerospace ATP | 2058 | ex SE-LPT | |
| ☐ LX-WAT | British Aerospace ATP (LFD) | 2011 | ex SE-MAO | |
| ☐ LX-WAV | British Aerospace ATP (LFD) | 2041 | ex SE-LPV | |
| ☐ LX-WAW | British Aerospace ATP (LFD) | 2021 | ex SE-LGZ | |
| ☐ LX-WAX | British Aerospace ATP | 2063 | ex SE-LPX | ♦ |
| | | | | |
| ☐ LX-WAB | ATR 72-201F | 0227 | ex OY-RUC | |

# LY-    LITHUANIA (Republic of Lithuania)

## APATAS / AP AIRLINES                Apatas (LYT)              Kaunus-Karmelava (KUN)

| | | | | |
|---|---|---|---|---|
| ☐ LY-AVA | LET L-410UVP-E3 | 882036 | ex Soviet AF 2036 | |
| ☐ LY-AVT | LET L-410UVP-E3 | 882033 | ex Soviet AF 2033 | |
| ☐ LY-AVZ | LET L-410UVP-E | 892336 | ex CCCP-67610 | ♦ |

## AURELA                            Aurela (LSK)                        Vilnius (VNO)

| | | | | |
|---|---|---|---|---|
| ☐ LY-SKA | Boeing 737-35B | 23972/1537 | ex N223DZ | |
| ☐ LY-SKW | Boeing 737-382 | 25162/2241 | ex N161LF | |

## AVIAVILSA                        Aviavilsa (LVR)                      Vilnius (VNO)

| | | | | |
|---|---|---|---|---|
| ☐ LY-APK | Antonov An-26B | 27312201 | ex RA-26114 | |
| ☐ LY-APN | Antonov An-26B | 27312010 | ex UR-BXF | |
| ☐ LY-ETM | ATR 42-300F | 0067 | ex (SE-MAS) | <DNU |

## AVION EXPRESS                        (N9/NVD)

| | | | | |
|---|---|---|---|---|
| ☐ LY-COS | Airbus A320-231 | 0415 | ex EI-ETM | o/o♦ |
| ☐ LY-NSA | SAAB SF-340A | 340A-055 | ex SE-KPE | ♦ |
| ☐ LY-NSB | SAAB SF.340A | 340A-045 | ex SE-ISV | ♦ |
| ☐ LY-NSC | SAAF SF-340A | 340A-037 | ex SE-KPD | ♦ |
| ☐ LY-VEX | Airbus A320-212 | 0375 | ex M-GAPA | ♦ |
| ☐ LY-VEY | Airbus A320-212 | 0419 | ex N419AG | ♦ |
| ☐ LY-VEZ | Airbus A320-212 | 0299 | ex PH-AAZ | >CUB♦ |

## DANU ORO TRANSPORTAS            Danu (R6/DNU)                     Vilnius (VNO)

| | | | | |
|---|---|---|---|---|
| ☐ F-HAEK | ATR 42-300 | 0148 | ex LY-LWH | |
| ☐ LY-ARI | ATR 42-300 | 012A | ex F-WQBT | |
| ☐ LY-DAT | ATR 42-500 | 0445 | ex F-WKVF | |
| ☐ LY-ETM | ATR 42-300F | 0067 | ex (SE-MAS) | >LVR♦ |
| ☐ LY-OOV | ATR 42-300F | 0005 | ex EI-SLD | |
| ☐ LY-RUM | ATR 42-300F | 0010 | ex OY-RUM | |
| | | | | |
| ☐ LY-MCA | ATR 72-212A | 0212 | ex SE-MCA | >ABV |
| ☐ LY-RUN | SAAB SF.340A | 340A-086 | ex G-RUNG | <DTR |
| ☐ LY-RUS | SAAB SF.340A | 340A-074 | ex SE-LTO | |

| SMALL PLANET AIRLINES | | (LLC) | | Vilnius (VNO) |
|---|---|---|---|---|
| ☐ LY-AQX | Boeing 737-322 | 24664/1877 | ex SP-HAA | ♦ |
| ☐ LY-AWH | Boeing 737-3Y0 | 23924/1542 | ex N924RM | |
| ☐ LY-FLB | Boeing 737-322/W | 24667/1893 | ex ES-LBA | ♦ |
| ☐ LY-FLC | Boeing 737-31S | 29055/2923 | ex EI-DNX | |
| ☐ LY-FLE | Boeing 737-3L9 | 27061/2347 | ex PK-AWG | |
| ☐ LY-FLH | Boeing 737-382 | 25161/2226 | ex N161AN | |
| ☐ LY-FLJ | Boeing 737-3K2 | 24327/1712 | ex LN-KKG | ♦ |
| ☐ LY-AWD | Boeing 737-522 | 26739/2494 | ex C-FDCU | |
| ☐ LY-AWE | Boeing 737-522 | 26684/2388 | ex C-FCFR | |
| ☐ LY-AWF | Boeing 737-522 | 26707/2512 | ex C-FDCZ | ♦ |
| ☐ LY-AWG | Boeing 737-522 | 26700/2490 | ex C-FDCH | |
| ☐ LY-FLG | Boeing 757-204 | 27237/602 | ex G-BYAR | |

| STAR1 AIRLINES | (HCW) | Vilnius (VNO) |
|---|---|---|

Began bankruptcy proceedings 01Oct10

## LZ-    BULGARIA (Republic of Bulgaria)

| AIR BRIGHT | | | | |
|---|---|---|---|---|
| ☐ YL-RAC | Antonov An-26 | 9903 | | <MTL♦ |

| AIR MAX | | Aeromax (RMX) | | Plovdiv (PDV) |
|---|---|---|---|---|
| ☐ LZ-MAN | LET L-410UVP | | | ♦ |
| ☐ LZ-RMC | LET L-410UVP-E12 | 882207 | | [SOF]♦ |
| ☐ LZ-RMK | LET L-410UVP | 851406 | ex UR-67502 | |
| ☐ LZ-RMV | LET L-410UVP-E | 892215 | ex HA-LAV | |
| ☐ LZ-RMW | LET L-410UVP-E | 902517 | ex HA-LAE | |

| AIR SCORPIO | | Scorpio Univers (SCU) | | Sofia (SOF) |
|---|---|---|---|---|
| ☐ LZ-BIA | Piper PA-34-220T | 24-49198 | ex N4185D | ♦ |
| ☐ LZ-CCB | Cessna 402B | 402B0581 | ex EC-HDF | ♦ |
| ☐ LZ-MNG | LET L-410UVP | 841326 | ex HA-LAY | ♦ |
| ☐ LZ-SAB | SAAB SF.340AF | 340A-020 | ex S5-BAM | ♦ |
| ☐ LZ-SAC | SAAB SF.340AF | 340A-011 | ex S5-BAO | ♦ |

| BH AIR | | Balkan Holidays (BGH) | | Sofia (SOF) |
|---|---|---|---|---|
| ☐ LZ-BHB | Airbus A320-212 | 0294 | ex OY-CNP | |
| ☐ LZ-BHC | Airbus A320-212 | 0349 | ex OY-CNR | |
| ☐ LZ-BHD | Airbus A320-212 | 0221 | ex CS-TQE | |
| ☐ LZ-BHE | Airbus A320-211 | 0305 | ex EI-DNK | |
| ☐ LZ-BHF | Airbus A320-214 | 1087 | ex EC-HDN | >ERT♦ |
| ☐ LZ-AOA | Airbus A319-112 | 3139 | ex D-ABGE | ♦ |

| BULGARIA AIR | | Flying Bulgaria (FB/LZB) | | Sofia (SOF) |
|---|---|---|---|---|
| ☐ LZ-BOW | Boeing 737-330 | 23834/1454 | ex N242DL | |
| ☐ LZ-FBA | Airbus A319-112 | 3564 | ex D-AVWS | ♦ |
| ☐ LZ-FBB | Airbus A319-112 | 3309 | ex EI-DZW | ♦ |
| ☐ LZ-FBC | Airbus A320-214 | 2540 | ex EC-JMB | ♦ |
| ☐ LZ-FBD | Airbus A320-214 | 2596 | ex EC-JNA | ♦ |
| ☐ LZ-FBE | Airbus A320-214 | 3780 | ex D-AVVI | |
| ☐ LZ-FBF | Airbus A319-111 | 3028 | ex N950FR | |
| ☐ LZ-SOF | Embraer ERJ-190ER | 19000492 | ex PT-TPQ | ♦ |
| ☐ LZ- | Embraer ERJ-190ER | 19000496 | ex PT-TPT | ♦ |

| BULGARIAN AIR CHARTER | | Bulgarian Charter (1T/BUC) | | Sofia (SOF) |
|---|---|---|---|---|
| ☐ LZ-LDC | McDonnell-Douglas MD-82 | 49217/1268 | ex I-DAVC | |
| ☐ LZ-LDF | McDonnell-Douglas MD-82 | 49219/1310 | ex I-DAVF | |
| ☐ LZ-LDK | McDonnell-Douglas MD-82 | 49432/1378 | ex I-DAVK | |
| ☐ LZ-LDN | McDonnell-Douglas MD-82 | 53216/2048 | ex I-DATA | [SOF]♦ |
| ☐ LZ-LDO | McDonnell-Douglas MD-82 | 53223/2081 | ex I-DATD | [SOF]♦ |
| ☐ LZ-LDP | McDonnell-Douglas MD-82 | 49973/1762 | ex I-DACP | |
| ☐ LZ-LDW | McDonnell-Douglas MD-82 | 49795/1639 | ex I-DAVV | |
| ☐ LZ-LDY | McDonnell-Douglas MD-82 | 49213/1243 | ex I-DAWY | |

| **CARGO AIR** | | *(CGF)* | | *Sofia (SOF)* |
|---|---|---|---|---|
| ☐ LZ-CGO | Boeing 737-301F | 23237/1222 | ex N503UW | |
| ☐ LZ-CGP | Boeing 737-35BF | 23970/1467 | ex N221DL | |
| ☐ LZ-CGQ | Boeing 737-3Y5F | 25614/2467 | ex N413BC | ♦ |

| **HELI AIR SERVICES** | | *Heli Bulgaria (HLR)* | | *Sofia (SOF)* |
|---|---|---|---|---|
| ☐ LZ-CCJ | LET L-410UVP-E9 | 022634 | ex OK-SLD | ♦ |
| ☐ LZ-CCP | LET L-410UVP-E8C | 912540 | ex 3D-BAF | |
| ☐ LZ-CCQ | LET L-410UVP-E20 | 072621 | ex OK-KIM | ♦ |
| ☐ LZ-CCR | LET L-410UVP-E10 | 892301 | ex SP-FTX | |
| ☐ LZ-CCS | LET L-410UVP-E | 902425 | ex 3D-EER | op for UN |
| ☐ LZ-CCT | LET L-410UVP-E10 | 912528 | ex ST-DND | op for UN |
| ☐ LZ-CCQ | LET L-410UVP-E20 | 072621 | ex OK-KIM | ♦ |
| ☐ LZ-CCQ | LET L-410UVP-E20 | 072621 | ex OK-KIM | ♦ |
| ☐ LZ-CCQ | LET L-410UVP-E20 | 072621 | ex OK-KIM | ♦ |
| ☐ LZ-CCV | LET L-410UVP-E20 | 2720 | ex OK-SLT | ♦ |
| ☐ LZ-CCW | LET L-410UVP-E | 912609 | ex ES-LLC | ♦ |
| ☐ LZ-LSB | LET L-410UVP-E2 | 861802 | no titles | op for UN |
| | | | | |
| ☐ LZ-CBG | Antonov An-12A | 2340804 | ex RA-11370 | [SOF] |

| **HEMUS AIR** | | *Hemus Air (DU/HMS)* | | *Sofia (SOF)* |
|---|---|---|---|---|
| ☐ LZ-HBA | British Aerospace 146 Srs.200 | E2072 | ex VH-NJQ | |
| ☐ LZ-HBB | British Aerospace 146 Srs.200 | E2073 | ex VH-NJU | |
| ☐ LZ-HBC | British Aerospace 146 Srs.200 | E2093 | ex VH-JJS | |
| ☐ LZ-HBD | British Aerospace 146 Srs.300 | E3141 | ex N615AW | |
| ☐ LZ-HBE | British Aerospace 146 Srs.300 | E3131 | ex EI-CLG | |
| ☐ LZ-HBF | British Aerospace 146 Srs.300 | E3159 | ex EI-CLI | |
| ☐ LZ-HBG | British Aerospace 146 Srs.300 | E3146 | ex EI-CLH | |
| ☐ LZ-HBZ | British Aerospace 146 Srs.200 | E2103 | ex G-JEAK | |
| | | | | |
| ☐ LZ-ATS | ATR 42-300 | 0130 | ex F-WQNO | |
| ☐ LZ-TIM | Avro 146-RJ70 | E1258 | ex EI-CPJ | op for Bulgarian Govt |

| **VIA - AIR VIA** | | *(VL/VIM)* | | *Varna (VAR)* |
|---|---|---|---|---|
| ☐ LZ-MDA | Airbus A320-232 | 2732 | ex F-WWBE | |
| ☐ LZ-MDB | Airbus A320-232 | 3125 | ex F-WWBF | |
| ☐ LZ-MDC | Airbus A320-232 | 4270 | ex F-WWBS | |
| ☐ LZ-MDD | Airbus A320-232 | 4305 | ex F-WWDZ | |
| ☐ LZ-MDM | Airbus A320-232 | 2804 | ex F-WWIM | |
| ☐ LZ- | Airbus A320-232 | | ex | o/o |
| ☐ LZ- | Airbus A320-232 | | ex | o/o |

| **N** | **UNITED STATES OF AMERICA** |
|---|---|

| **ABX AIR** | | *Abex (GB/ABX)* | | *Wilmington-Airborne Airpark, OH (ILN)* |
|---|---|---|---|---|
| ☐ N315AA | Boeing 767-223 (SF) | 22317/109 | | |
| ☐ N739AX | Boeing 767-232 (SCD) | 22216/26 | ex N104DA | |
| ☐ N740AX | Boeing 767-232 (SCD) | 22213/6 | ex N101DA | |
| ☐ N742AX | Boeing 767-232 (SCD) | 22217/27 | ex N105DA | |
| ☐ N744AX | Boeing 767-232 (SCD) | 22221/53 | ex N109DL | |
| ☐ N745AX | Boeing 767-232 (SCD) | 22222/56 | ex N110DL | |
| ☐ N747AX | Boeing 767-232 (SCD) | 22224/76 | ex N112DL | |
| ☐ N749AX | Boeing 767-232 (SCD) | 22226/78 | ex N114DL | |
| ☐ N750AX | Boeing 767-232 (SCD) | 22227/83 | ex N115DA | |
| ☐ N752AX | Boeing 767-281F | 23434/171 | ex JA8255 | |
| ☐ N767AX | Boeing 767-281F | 22785/51 | ex JA8479 | |
| ☐ N768AX | Boeing 767-281F | 22786/54 | ex JA8480 | |
| ☐ N769AX | Boeing 767-281F | 22787/58 | ex JA8481 | |
| ☐ N773AX | Boeing 767-281F | 22788/61 | ex JA8482 | |
| ☐ N774AX | Boeing 767-281F | 22789/67 | ex JA8483 | |
| ☐ N775AX | Boeing 767-281F | 22790/69 | ex JA8484 | |
| ☐ N783AX | Boeing 767-281F | 23016/80 | ex JA8485 | |
| ☐ N784AX | Boeing 767-281F | 23017/82 | ex JA8486 | |
| ☐ N785AX | Boeing 767-281F | 23018/84 | ex JA8487 | |
| ☐ N786AX | Boeing 767-281F | 23019/85 | ex JA8488 | |
| ☐ N787AX | Boeing 767-281F | 23020/96 | ex JA8489 | |
| ☐ N788AX | Boeing 767-281F | 23021/103 | ex JA8490 | |
| ☐ N790AX | Boeing 767-281F | 23140/106 | ex JA8238 | |
| ☐ N792AX | Boeing 767-281 (SCD) | 23142/110 | ex JA8240 | |
| ☐ N793AX | Boeing 767-281F | 23143/114 | ex JA8241 | |
| ☐ N794AX | Boeing 767-281F | 23144/115 | ex JA8242 | |
| ☐ N795AX | Boeing 767-281F | 23145/116 | ex JA8243 | |
| ☐ N797AX | Boeing 767-281F | 23147/123 | ex JA8245 | |

| | | | | |
|---|---|---|---|---|
| ☐ N798AX | Boeing 767-281 (SCD) | 23431/143 | ex JA8251 | DHL c/s |
| ☐ N219CY | Boeing 767-383F | 24358/263 | ex D-VKNY | ♦ |
| ☐ N317CM | Boeing 767-338ERF | 24317/246 | ex VH-OGC | ♦ |

## AERO FLITE — Kingman, AZ (IGM)

| | | | | | |
|---|---|---|---|---|---|
| ☐ N262NR | Canadair CL215 | 1081 | ex C-GDRS | 262 | op for Minnesota DNR |
| ☐ N263NR | Canadair CL215 | 1082 | ex C-GENU | 263 | Lsd fr/op for Minnesota DNR |
| ☐ N264V | Canadair CL215 | 1090 | ex C-GOFM | 264 | |
| ☐ N266NR | Canadair CL215 | 1102 | ex C-GOFO | 266 | Lsd fr/op for Minnesota DNR |
| ☐ N267V | Canadair CL215 | 1103 | ex C-GOFP | 267 | |

## AERO UNION — Chico-Municipal, CA (CIC)

| | | | | | |
|---|---|---|---|---|---|
| ☐ N900AU | Lockheed P-3A Orion | 185-5104 | ex N406TP | 00 | Tanker |
| ☐ N920AU | Lockheed P-3A Orion | 185-5039 | ex Spain P.3-6 | 20 | Tanker |
| ☐ N921AU | Lockheed P-3A Orion | 185-5098 | ex Bu151385 | 21 | Tanker |
| ☐ N922AU | Lockheed P-3A Orion | 185-5100 | ex N181AU | 22 | Tanker |
| ☐ N923AU | Lockheed P-3A Orion | 185-5085 | ex N185AU | 23 | Tanker |
| ☐ N925AU | Lockheed P-3A Orion | 185-5074 | ex N183AU | 25 | Tanker |
| ☐ N927AU | Lockheed P-3A Orion | 185-5082 | ex N182AU | 27 | Tanker |

## AEX AIR — Desert (DST)   Phoenix-Sky Harbor, AZ/La Verne, CA (PHX/POC)

| | | | |
|---|---|---|---|
| ☐ N49SA | Piper PA-34-200 Seneca | 34-7350057 | ex C-FDRW |
| ☐ N86PP | Piper PA-34-200 Seneca | 34-7250358 | ex N15054 |
| ☐ N1080U | Piper PA-34-200 Seneca | 34-7250083 | |
| ☐ N1656H | Piper PA-34-200T Seneca II | 34-7770131 | |
| ☐ N2817T | Piper PA-34-200 Seneca | 34-7250170 | |
| ☐ N4581T | Piper PA-34-200 Seneca | 34-7250139 | |
| ☐ N41298 | Piper PA-34-200 Seneca | 34-7450106 | |
| ☐ N55549 | Piper PA-34-200 Seneca | 34-7350228 | |
| ☐ N56795 | Piper PA-34-200 Seneca | 34-7450032 | |
| ☐ N56974 | Piper PA-34-200 Seneca | 34-7450044 | |
| ☐ N57368 | Piper PA-34-200 Seneca | 34-7450054 | |
| ☐ N75053 | Piper PA-34-200T Seneca II | 34-7670233 | |
| ☐ N14FB | Piper PA-31 Turbo Navajo | 31-351 | ex N93H |
| ☐ N57AS | Piper PA-31 Turbo Navajo | 31-113 | ex N585HW |
| ☐ N300WA | Piper PA-31 Turbo Navajo | 31-294 | ex N9227Y |

## AIR AMERICA — San Juan-Luis Munoz Marin Intl, PR (SJU)

| | | | | |
|---|---|---|---|---|
| ☐ N21WW | Piper PA-23-250 Aztec E | 27-7554066 | ex N54754 | |
| ☐ N30PT | Cessna 421C Golden Eagle | 421C0157 | ex N5284J | |
| ☐ N707TL | Beech 65-E90 King Air | LW-173 | | ♦ |
| ☐ N2395Z | Piper PA-23-250 Aztec F | 27-7954107 | ex (AN-LAS) | |
| ☐ N7049T | Britten-Norman BN-2A-21 Islander | 643 | ex C-GPAB | |
| ☐ N62749 | Piper PA-23-250 Aztec F | 27-7654198 | | |

## AIR ARCTIC — Fairbanks-Intl, AK (FAI)

| | | | | |
|---|---|---|---|---|
| ☐ N42WP | Piper PA-31-350 Chieftain | 31-8252038 | ex N41063 | ♦ |
| ☐ N234CE | Piper PA-31-350 Chieftain | 31-8052203 | | <Northern Alaska |
| ☐ N820FS | Piper PA-31-350 Chieftain | 31-7952185 | ex TF-VLA | |
| ☐ N4434D | Piper PA-31-350 Chieftain | 31-755-2020 | ex PH-ASC | ♦ |
| ☐ N7164D | Piper PA-31-350 Chieftain | 31-8052013 | ex C-GBGI | |
| ☐ N3582P | Piper PA-31-350 Chieftain | 31-8052103 | | ♦ |
| ☐ N3589B | Piper PA-31-350 Chieftain | 31-8052134 | | ♦ |
| ☐ N27758 | Piper PA-31-350 Chieftain | 31-7852148 | | ♦ |
| ☐ N59826 | Piper PA-31-350 Navajo Chieftain | 31-7652077 | | |

## AIR CARGO CARRIERS — Night Cargo (2Q/SNC)   Milwaukee-General Mitchell Intl, WI (MKE)

| | | | | |
|---|---|---|---|---|
| ☐ N58DD | Short SD.3-30 | SH3008 | ex TG-TJA | |
| ☐ N167RC | Short SD.3-30 | SH3038 | ex N690RA | |
| ☐ N334AC | Short SD.3-30 | SH3029 | ex VH-LSI | |
| ☐ N336MV | Short SD.3-30 | SH3018 | ex PJ-DDB | |
| ☐ N390GA | Short SD.3-30 | SH3077 | ex 4X-CSP | |
| ☐ N936MA | Short SD.3-30 | SH3036 | ex G-BGNI | |
| ☐ N2629P | Short SD.3-30 | SH3079 | ex G-BJLL | |
| ☐ N124CA | Short SD.3-60 | SH3652 | ex G-BLJS | |
| ☐ N136LR | Short SD.3-60 | SH3752 | ex VH-SUL | all-white |
| ☐ N151CA | Short SD.3-60 | SH3653 | ex G-BLJT | |
| ☐ N360AB | Short SD.3-60 | SH3756 | ex G-BPKZ | |
| ☐ N360RW | Short SD.3-60 | SH3613 | ex C-FCRB | |
| ☐ N360SA | Short SD.3-60 | SH3601 | ex G-WIDE | |
| ☐ N367AC | Short SD.3-60 | SH3626 | ex VH-MVW | |
| ☐ N368AC | Short SD.3-60 | SH3651 | ex VH-BWO | |

| | | | | |
|---|---|---|---|---|
| ☐ N376AC | Short SD.3-60 | SH3736 | ex G-VBAC | |
| ☐ N601CA | Short SD.3-60 | SH3623 | ex G-BKWM | |
| ☐ N617FB | Short SD.3-60 | SH3617 | ex G-BKUF | |
| ☐ N618AN | Short SD.3-60 | SH3691 | ex N881BC | ♦ |
| ☐ N642AN | Short SD.3-60 | SH3661 | ex C-GPCE | ♦ |
| ☐ N688AN | Short SD.3-60 | SH3633 | ex C-GPCJ | |
| ☐ N701A | Short SD.3-60 | SH3627 | ex G-BKZP | |
| ☐ N733CH | Short SD.3-60 | SH3733 | ex N569FU | [MKE]♦ |
| ☐ N742CC | Short SD.3-60 | SH3742 | ex D-CFXH | |
| ☐ N764JR | Short SD.3-60 | SH3764 | ex VH-SUF | |
| ☐ N972AA | Short SD.3-60 | SH3754 | ex N263GA | |
| ☐ N973AA | Short SD.3-60 | SH3749 | ex N749JT | |
| ☐ N3732X | Short SD.3-60 | SH3732 | ex PK-DSN | |
| ☐ N4498Y | Short SD.3-60 | SH3625 | ex G-BKZN | |
| | | | | |
| ☐ N960AA | AMD Falcon 20C | 144 | ex N385AC | |
| ☐ N961AA | AMD Falcon 20D | 205 | ex N585AC | |

## AIR DIRECT                                        Rhinelander-Oneida County, WI (RHI)

| | | | | |
|---|---|---|---|---|
| ☐ N223CA | Beech C99 | U-200 | ex SE-IZX | ♦ |
| ☐ N800L | Piper PA-31 Turbo Navajo | 31-426 | ex C-GSGA | |
| ☐ N6645K | Beech C99 | U-209 | | ♦ |
| ☐ N87395 | Cessna 310R | 310R0543 | | |

## AIR FLAMENCO                              San Juan-Fernando Luis Ribas Dominici, PR (SIG)

| | | | | |
|---|---|---|---|---|
| ☐ N821RR | Britten-Norman BN-2A-9 Islander | 338 | ex N146A | |
| ☐ N901GD | Britten-Norman BN-2A-26 Islander | 855 | ex XA-JEK | The Spirit of Culebra |
| ☐ N904GD | Britten-Norman BN-2B-26 Islander | 2128 | ex N902VL | |
| ☐ N905GD | Britten-Norman BN-2A-9 Islander | 339 | ex C-FTAM | |
| ☐ N906GD | Britten-Norman BN-2A-9 Islander | 3008 | ex VP-AAB | |
| ☐ N907GD | Britten-Norman BN-2A-9 Islander | 340 | ex N161A | |
| ☐ N908GD | Britten-Norman BN-2A-26 Islander | 2040 | ex C6-BUS | |
| ☐ N909GD | Britten-Norman BN-2A-6 Islander | 239 | ex N143BW | |
| ☐ N910GD | Britten-Norman BN-2A-9 Islander | 341 | | |
| ☐ N913GD | Britten-Norman BN-2A-6 Islander | 198 | | ♦ |

## AIR GRAND CANYON                               Grand Canyon-National Park, AZ (GCN)

| | | | | |
|---|---|---|---|---|
| ☐ N803AN | Cessna T207A Stationair 7 | 20700570 | ex N73204 | |
| ☐ N6308H | Cessna T207A Stationair 7 | 20700476 | | |
| ☐ N6491H | Cessna T207A Stationair 7 | 20700543 | | |
| ☐ N7311U | Cessna T207A Stationair 7 | 20700395 | | |
| ☐ N7351U | Cessna T207A Stationair 7 | 20700415 | | |

## AIR SUNSHINE                Air Sunshine (YI/RSI)        Fort Lauderdale-Hollywood Intl, FL (FLL)

| | | | | |
|---|---|---|---|---|
| ☐ N220RS | Cessna 402C | 402C0220 | ex N2716L | |
| ☐ N347AB | Cessna 402C | 402C0347 | ex N26548 | |
| ☐ N351AB | Cessna 402C | 402C0351 | ex N26629 | |
| ☐ N402RS | Cessna 402C | 402C0402 | ex N2663N | |
| ☐ N603AB | Cessna 402C | 402C0603 | ex N84PB | |
| | | | | |
| ☐ N123HY | Embraer EMB.110P1 Bandeirante | 110321 | ex N619KC | |
| ☐ N744BA | SAAB SF.340A | 340A-105 | ex SE-F05 | |

## AIR TAHOMA                      Tahoma (5C/HMA)        Columbus-Rickenbacker, OH (LCK)

Ceased ops

## AIR WISCONSIN                 Air Wisconsin (ZW/AWI)      Appleton-Outagamie Co, WI (ATW)

Ops Canadair CRJ-200LRs for US Airways Express; for details see that listing

## AIRBORNE SUPPORT                                    Houma-Terrebonne, LA (HUM)

| | | | | |
|---|---|---|---|---|
| ☐ N38WA | Rockwell 690A Turbo Commander | 11169 | ex XB-FLF | |
| ☐ N3969A | Bell 407 | 53787 | | ♦ |
| ☐ N4669P | Piper PA-23 Aztec 250 | 27-193 | | ♦ |
| ☐ N14183 | Piper PA-23 Aztec 250 | 27-4747 | | ♦ |
| ☐ N64766 | Douglas DC-3 | 27218 | ex CAF12910 | Sprayer |
| ☐ N64767 | Douglas DC-3 | 10199 | ex CAF12941 | Sprayer |
| ☐ N67024 | Douglas DC-4 | 10550 | ex Bu50871 | Sprayer |

## AIRNET SYSTEMS                         Star Check (USC)
### Columbus-Port Columbus Intl, OH / Dallas-Love Field, TX (CMH/DAL)

| | | | | |
|---|---|---|---|---|
| ☐ N21ES | Beech 58 Baron | TH-1123 | ex N6744V | |
| ☐ N26CC | Beech 58 Baron | TH-136 | | |

| | | | | |
|---|---|---|---|---|
| ☐ N27MT | Beech 58 Baron | TH-1120 | ex F-GDJY | |
| ☐ N33DK | Beech 58 Baron | TH-372 | ex N2CF | |
| ☐ N33WC | Beech 58 Baron | TH-170 | | |
| ☐ N58WA | Beech 58 Baron | TH-201 | ex N58TC | |
| ☐ N65FS | Beech 58 Baron | TH-1084 | ex N6681Y | |
| ☐ N78DM | Beech 58 Baron | TH-281 | ex N78MM | |
| ☐ N95BB | Beech 58 Baron | TH-333 | ex N95BD | |
| ☐ N140S | Beech 58 Baron | TH-1155 | ex N3677N | |
| ☐ N297AT | Beech 58 Baron | TH-1349 | ex F-GOGA | |
| ☐ N400RP | Beech 58 Baron | TH-319 | ex N1036W | |
| ☐ N456WW | Beech 58 Baron | TH-444 | ex N444TE | |
| ☐ N696BD | Beech 58 Baron | TH-352 | ex N43HK | |
| ☐ N858LG | Beech 58 Baron | TH-518 | ex N555GP | |
| ☐ N882MT | Beech 58 Baron | TH-1343 | ex F-WQFG | |
| ☐ N1653W | Beech 58 Baron | TH-252 | | |
| ☐ N1814W | Beech 58 Baron | TH-287 | | |
| ☐ N1847F | Beech 58 Baron | TH-1291 | | |
| ☐ N1859K | Beech 58 Baron | TH-1299 | | |
| ☐ N2027V | Beech 58 Baron | TH-965 | | |
| ☐ N2064V | Beech 58 Baron | TH-1004 | | |
| ☐ N3695V | Beech 58 Baron | TH-1183 | | |
| ☐ N3703Q | Beech 58 Baron | TH-1189 | | |
| ☐ N6573K | Beech 58 Baron | TH-1369 | | |
| ☐ N6650D | Beech 58 Baron | TH-1375 | | |
| ☐ N6758C | Beech 58 Baron | TH-1080 | | |
| ☐ N7383R | Beech 58 Baron | TH-502 | | |
| ☐ N9044V | Beech 58 Baron | TH-216 | | |
| ☐ N9189Q | Beech 58 Baron | TH-148 | | |
| ☐ N17708 | Beech 58 Baron | TH-813 | | |
| ☐ N36673 | Beech 58 Baron | TH-1143 | | |
| ☐ N36901 | Beech 58 Baron | TH-1173 | | |
| | | | | |
| ☐ N3RY | Cessna 208B Caravan I | 208B0436 | ex C-GSKR | |
| ☐ N102AN | Cessna 208B Caravan I | 208B0906 | ex N51666 | |
| ☐ N103AN | Cessna 208B Caravan I | 208B0928 | | |
| ☐ N105AN | Cessna 208B Caravan I | 208B0956 | | |
| ☐ N106AN | Cessna 208B Caravan I | 208B0917 | ex N5207V | |
| ☐ N107AN | Cessna 208B Caravan I | 208B0993 | | |
| ☐ N1026V | Cessna 208B Caravan I | 208B0319 | | |
| ☐ N9514F | Cessna 208 Caravan I | 20800079 | | |
| ☐ N9539F | Cessna 208 Caravan I | 20800092 | | |
| ☐ N9642F | Cessna 208 Caravan I | 20800110 | | |
| | | | | |
| ☐ N15WH | Learjet 35A | 35A-085 | | |
| ☐ N27BL | Learjet 35A | 35A-163 | ex YV-173CP | |
| ☐ N31WR | Learjet 35A | 35A-313 | ex TR-LZI | |
| ☐ N56EM | Learjet 35A | 35A-144 | ex N56HF | |
| ☐ N64CP | Learjet 35A | 35A-264 | ex VR-CDI | |
| ☐ N81FR | Learjet 35A | 35A-081 | ex N118DA | |
| ☐ N88BG | Learjet 35A | 35A-090 | ex I-FIMI | |
| ☐ N122JW | Learjet 35A | 35A-217 | ex N111RF | |
| ☐ N400JE | Learjet 35A | 35A-120 | | |
| ☐ N474AN | Learjet 35A | 35A-295 | ex N94AA | ♦ |
| ☐ N813AS | Learjet 35A | 35A-167 | ex N725P | |
| ☐ N900JC | Learjet 35 | 35-178 | ex N35GG | |
| ☐ N959SA | Learjet 35A | 35A-076 | | |
| ☐ N1140A | Learjet 35 | 35-045 | ex N304AT | |
| | | | | |
| ☐ N4UE | Piper PA-31-350 Chieftain | 31-8152061 | ex N4U | |
| ☐ N42HD | Piper PA-31-350 Chieftain | 31-8152031 | ex N42ND | |
| ☐ N106TG | Piper PA-31-350 Chieftain | 31-8052002 | ex N106FC | |
| ☐ N525AA | Piper PA-31-350 Chieftain | 31-8052111 | ex N3583U | |
| ☐ N711LH | Piper PA-31-350 Chieftain | 31-8152174 | ex N711BH | |
| ☐ N3547C | Piper PA-31-350 Chieftain | 31-8052018 | | |
| ☐ N3587P | Piper PA-31-350 Chieftain | 31-8052120 | | |
| ☐ N3590D | Piper PA-31-350 Chieftain | 31-8052144 | | |
| ☐ N4079Y | Piper PA-31-350 Chieftain | 31-8152079 | ex (N479MG) | |
| ☐ N22427 | Piper PA-31-350 Chieftain | 31-8152065 | ex (N4078S) | |
| ☐ N35584 | Piper PA-31-350 Chieftain | 31-8052076 | | |
| ☐ N35871 | Piper PA-31-350 Chieftain | 31-8052123 | ex (N191VF) | |
| ☐ N40919 | Piper PA-31-350 Chieftain | 31-8152162 | | |
| | | | | |
| ☐ N6892R | Piper PA-60 | 60-0887-8161251 | | |
| ☐ N7512 | Piper PA-60 | 60-0144-064 | | ♦ |

All are freighters

| **AIRNOW (BUSINESS AIR)** | *Sky Courier (RLR)* | | *Burlington-Intl, VT (BTV)* |
|---|---|---|---|
| ☐ N29AN | Cessna 208B Caravan I | 208B0753 | | ♦ |
| ☐ N415TT | Cessna 208B Caravan I | 208B0365 | ex N208TA | ♦ |
| ☐ N803TH | Cessna 208B Caravan I | 208B0321 | ex N1027G | ♦ |
| ☐ N804TH | Cessna 208B Caravan I | 208B0421 | ex N9551F | |

| | | | | |
|---|---|---|---|---|
| ☐ N805TH | Cessna 208B Caravan I | 208B0609 | ex N9551F | |
| ☐ N929TG | Cessna 208B Caravan I | 208B0371 | ex N207TA | |
| ☐ N9339B | Cessna 208B Caravan I | 208B0057 | | |
| ☐ N9612B | Cessna 208B Caravan I | 208B0136 | | |
| | | | | |
| ☐ N24AN | Embraer EMB.110P1 Bandeirante | 110318 | ex F-GBRM | |
| ☐ N31AN | Embraer EMB.110P1 Bandeirante | 110372 | ex C-FSXR | |
| ☐ N42AN | Embraer EMB.110P1 Bandeirante | 110456 | ex C-GHCA | |
| ☐ N51BA | Embraer EMB.110P1 Bandeirante | 110404 | ex N903FB | |
| ☐ N83BA | Embraer EMB.110P1 Bandeirante | 110351 | ex N405AS | |
| ☐ N97BA | Embraer EMB.110P1 Bandeirante | 110322 | ex N403AS | |
| ☐ N621KC | Embraer EMB.110P1 Bandeirante | 110335 | ex PT-SDL | |
| ☐ N710NH | Embraer EMB.110P1 Bandeirante | 110250 | ex PT-SAQ | |
| ☐ N830AC | Embraer EMB.110P1 Bandeirante | 110205 | ex N524MW | |

## AIRPAC AIRLINES — Airpac (APC) — Seattle-Boeing Field, WA (BFI)

| | | | | |
|---|---|---|---|---|
| ☐ N36PB | Piper PA-31-350 Navajo Chieftain | 31-7405128 | | |
| ☐ N627HA | Piper PA-31-350 Chieftain | 31-7952241 | | |
| ☐ N777KT | Piper PA-31-350 Navajo Chieftain | 31-7552053 | ex N1TW | |
| ☐ N3582X | Piper PA-31-350 Chieftain | 31-8052105 | | |
| ☐ N27594 | Piper PA-31-350 Chieftain | 31-7852070 | | |
| | | | | |
| ☐ N2117V | Piper PA-34-200T Seneca II | 34-7970160 | | |
| ☐ N4490F | Piper PA-34-200T Seneca II | 34-7670339 | | |
| ☐ N8107D | Piper PA-34-200T Seneca II | 34-8070010 | | |
| ☐ N36319 | Piper PA-34-200T Seneca II | 34-7870318 | | |

## AIRSERV INTERNATIONAL — Warrenton, VA

| | | | | |
|---|---|---|---|---|
| ☐ N8HZ | Cessna 208B Caravan I | 208B0980 | | |
| ☐ N899AS | de Havilland DHC-6 Twin Otter 300 | 347 | ex LN-FKB | Op for UN |

## AIRTRAN AIRWAYS — Citrus (FL/TRS) — Orlando-Intl, FL/Atlanta-Hartsfield Intl, GA (MCO/ATL)

| | | | | |
|---|---|---|---|---|
| ☐ N603AT | Boeing 717-22A | 55127/5074 | ex N482HA | 771 |
| ☐ N607AT | Boeing 717-231 | 55074/5030 | ex N599BC | 776 |
| ☐ N608AT | Boeing 717-231 | 55081/5045 | ex N766BC | 777 |
| ☐ N717JL | Boeing 717-2BD | 55042/5115 | ex N983AT | 740 |
| ☐ N891AT | Boeing 717-2BD | 55043/5131 | ex (N984AT) | 741 |
| ☐ N892AT | Boeing 717-2BD | 55044/5134 | ex N7071U | 742 |
| ☐ N893AT | Boeing 717-2BD | 55045/5136 | | 743 |
| ☐ N894AT | Boeing 717-2BD | 55046/5137 | | 744 |
| ☐ N895AT | Boeing 717-2BD | 55047/5139 | | 745 |
| ☐ N896AT | Boeing 717-2BD | 55048/5141 | | 746 |
| ☐ N899AT | Boeing 717-2BD | 55049/5143 | | 747 |
| ☐ N906AT | Boeing 717-231 | 55087/5060 | ex N420TW | 795 |
| ☐ N910AT | Boeing 717-231 | 55086/5056 | ex N2419C | 794 |
| ☐ N915AT | Boeing 717-231 | 55085/5055 | ex N418TW | 793 |
| ☐ N919AT | Boeing 717-231 | 55084/5052 | ex N2417F | 792 |
| ☐ N920AT | Boeing 717-231 | 55083/5049 | ex N416TW | 791 |
| ☐ N921AT | Boeing 717-231 | 55082/5046 | ex N415TW | 790 |
| ☐ N922AT | Boeing 717-2BD | 55050/5144 | | 748 |
| ☐ N923AT | Boeing 717-2BD | 55051/5148 | | 749 |
| ☐ N924AT | Boeing 717-231 | 55080/5043 | ex N413TW | 789 |
| ☐ N925AT | Boeing 717-231 | 55079/5042 | ex N412TW | 788 |
| ☐ N926AT | Boeing 717-231 | 55078/5039 | ex N411TW | 787 |
| ☐ N927AT | Boeing 717-231 | 55077/5038 | ex N2410W | 786 |
| ☐ N928AT | Boeing 717-231 | 55076/5035 | ex N409TW | 785 |
| ☐ N929AT | Boeing 717-231 | 55075/5032 | ex N408TW | 784 |
| ☐ N930AT | Boeing 717-231 | 55072/5025 | ex N405TW | 782 |
| ☐ N932AT | Boeing 717-231 | 55073/5028 | ex N406TW | 783 |
| ☐ N933AT | Boeing 717-231 | 55071/5024 | ex N2404A | 781 |
| ☐ N934AT | Boeing 717-231 | 55070/5022 | ex N403TW | 780 |
| ☐ N935AT | Boeing 717-231 | 55069/5019 | ex N402TW | 779 |
| ☐ N936AT | Boeing 717-231 | 55058/5017 | ex N401TW | 778 |
| ☐ N937AT | Boeing 717-231 | 55091/5075 | ex N424TW | 799 |
| ☐ N938AT | Boeing 717-2BD | 55098/5155 | | 751 |
| ☐ N939AT | Boeing 717-2BD | 55099/5156 | | 752 |
| ☐ N940AT | Boeing 717-2BD | 55004/5005 | ex N717XE | 702 |
| ☐ N942AT | Boeing 717-2BD | 55005/5006 | | 703 |
| ☐ N943AT | Boeing 717-2BD | 55006/5007 | | 704 |
| ☐ N944AT | Boeing 717-2BD | 55007/5008 | | 705 |
| ☐ N945AT | Boeing 717-2BD | 55008/5009 | | 706 |
| ☐ N946AT | Boeing 717-2BD | 55009/5010 | | 707 |
| ☐ N947AT | Boeing 717-2BD | 55010/5011 | | 708 |
| ☐ N948AT | Boeing 717-2BD | 55011/5012 | | 709 |
| ☐ N949AT | Boeing 717-2BD | 55003/5004 | ex N717XD | 701 |
| ☐ N950AT | Boeing 717-2BD | 55012/5018 | | 710 |

| | | | | |
|---|---|---|---|---|
| ☐ | N951AT | Boeing 717-2BD | 55013/5021 | 711 |
| ☐ | N952AT | Boeing 717-2BD | 55014/5027 | 712 |
| ☐ | N953AT | Boeing 717-2BD | 55015/5033 | 713 |
| ☐ | N954AT | Boeing 717-2BD | 55016/5036 | 714 |
| ☐ | N955AT | Boeing 717-2BD | 55017/5040 | 715 |
| ☐ | N956AT | Boeing 717-2BD | 55018/5044 | 716 |
| ☐ | N957AT | Boeing 717-2BD | 55019/5047 | 717 |
| ☐ | N958AT | Boeing 717-2BD | 55020/5051 | 718 |
| ☐ | N959AT | Boeing 717-2BD | 55021/5057 | 719 |
| ☐ | N960AT | Boeing 717-2BD | 55022/5058 | 720 |
| ☐ | N961AT | Boeing 717-2BD | 55023/5062 | 721 |
| ☐ | N963AT | Boeing 717-2BD | 55024/5066 | 722 |
| ☐ | N964AT | Boeing 717-2BD | 55025/5071 | 723 |
| ☐ | N965AT | Boeing 717-2BD | 55026/5076 | 724 |
| ☐ | N966AT | Boeing 717-2BD | 55027/5081 | 725 |
| ☐ | N967AT | Boeing 717-2BD | 55028/5082 | 726 |
| ☐ | N968AT | Boeing 717-2BD | 55029/5091 | 727 |
| ☐ | N969AT | Boeing 717-2BD | 55030/5094 | 728 |
| ☐ | N970AT | Boeing 717-2BD | 55031/5096 | 729 |
| ☐ | N971AT | Boeing 717-2BD | 55032/5097 | 730 |
| ☐ | N972AT | Boeing 717-2BD | 55033/5099 | 731 |
| ☐ | N974AT | Boeing 717-2BD | 55034/5101 | 732 |
| ☐ | N975AT | Boeing 717-2BD | 55035/5102 | 733 |
| ☐ | N977AT | Boeing 717-2BD | 55036/5106 | 734 |
| ☐ | N978AT | Boeing 717-2BD | 55037/5108 | 735 |
| ☐ | N979AT | Boeing 717-2BD | 55038/5109 | 736 |
| ☐ | N980AT | Boeing 717-2BD | 55039/5111 | 737 |
| ☐ | N981AT | Boeing 717-2BD | 55040/5113 | 738 |
| ☐ | N982AT | Boeing 717-2BD | 55041/5114 | 739 |
| ☐ | N983AT | Boeing 717-2BD | 55052/5150 | 750 |
| ☐ | N985AT | Boeing 717-231 | 55090/5068 | ex N423TW | 798 |
| ☐ | N986AT | Boeing 717-231 | 55089/5067 | ex N422TW | 797 |
| ☐ | N987AT | Boeing 717-231 | 55088/5063 | ex N2421A | 796 |
| ☐ | N988AT | Boeing 717-23S | 55068/5065 | ex (EI-CWJ) | 760 |
| ☐ | N989AT | Boeing 717-23S | 55152/5085 | ex (EI-CWK) | 761 |
| ☐ | N990AT | Boeing 717-23S | 55134/5088 | ex (EI-CWM) | 762 |
| ☐ | N991AT | Boeing 717-23S | 55135/5090 | ex N6202S | 763 |
| ☐ | N992AT | Boeing 717-2BD | 55136/5100 | ex N6202D | 764 |
| ☐ | N993AT | Boeing 717-2BD | 55137/5103 | 765 |
| ☐ | N994AT | Boeing 717-2BD | 55138/5104 | ex N6206F | 766 |
| ☐ | N995AT | Boeing 717-2BD | 55139/5105 | 767 |
| ☐ | N996AT | Boeing 717-2BD | 55140/5107 | 768 |
| ☐ | N997AT | Boeing 717-2BD | 55141/5110 | 769 |
| ☐ | N998AT | Boeing 717-2BD | 55142/5112 | 770 |
| | | | | | |
| ☐ | N149AT | Boeing 737-76N/W | 32681/1526 | | 301 |
| ☐ | N168AT | Boeing 737-76N/W | 32653/1566 | | 303 |
| ☐ | N169AT | Boeing 737-76N/W | 32744/1584 | | 305 |
| ☐ | N173AT | Boeing 737-76N/W | 32661/1593 | | 306 |
| ☐ | N174AT | Boeing 737-76N/W | 32667/1623 | ex N1787B | 307 |
| ☐ | N175AT | Boeing 737-76N/W | 32652/1627 | | 308 |
| ☐ | N176AT | Boeing 737-76N/W | 32654/1641 | | 309 |
| ☐ | N184AT | Boeing 737-76N/W | 32656/1671 | | 310 |
| ☐ | N240AT | Boeing 737-76N/W | 32657/1687 | | 311 |
| ☐ | N261AT | Boeing 737-76N/W | 32660/1710 | | 312 |
| ☐ | N267AT | Boeing 737-7BD/W | 33919/1730 | | 313 |
| ☐ | N272AT | Boeing 737-7BD/W | 33921/1778 | ex N1784B | 315 |
| ☐ | N273AT | Boeing 737-76N/W | 32662/1788 | | 316 |
| ☐ | N276AT | Boeing 737-76N/W | 32664/1804 | | 317 |
| ☐ | N278AT | Boeing 737-76N/W | 32665/1827 | | 318 |
| ☐ | N279AT | Boeing 737-76N/W | 32666/1833 | | 319 |
| ☐ | N281AT | Boeing 737-7BD/W | 33922/1845 | | 320 |
| ☐ | N283AT | Boeing 737-7BD/W | 34479/1874 | | 321 |
| ☐ | N284AT | Boeing 737-76N/W | 32668/1876 | | 322 |
| ☐ | N285AT | Boeing 737-76N/W | 32670/1898 | ex N5573L | 323 |
| ☐ | N287AT | Boeing 737-76N/W | 32671/1925 | | 325 |
| ☐ | N289AT | Boeing 737-76N/W | 32673/1943 | ex N1787B | 327 |
| ☐ | N290AT | Boeing 737-7BD/W | 33925/1967 | | 328 |
| ☐ | N291AT | Boeing 737-76N/W | 32675/1970 | | 329 |
| ☐ | N295AT | Boeing 737-76N/W | 32677/2002 | | 331 |
| ☐ | N299AT | Boeing 737-76N/W | 32678/2055 | | 333 |
| ☐ | N300AT | Boeing 737-7BD/W | 33923/2083 | | 334 |
| ☐ | N307AT | Boeing 737-7BD/W | 34862/2094 | | 335 |
| ☐ | N308AT | Boeing 737-7BD/W | 35109/2126 | ex N1787B | 336 |
| ☐ | N309AT | Boeing 737-7BD/W | 33929/2129 | | 337 |
| ☐ | N311AT | Boeing 737-7BD/W | 33930/2143 | | 338 |
| ☐ | N312AT | Boeing 737-7BD/W | 35110/2147 | | 339 |
| ☐ | N313AT | Boeing 737-7BD/W | 33927/2169 | | 340 |
| ☐ | N315AT | Boeing 737-7BD/W | 35788/2178 | | 341 |
| ☐ | N316AT | Boeing 737-7BD/W | 33928/2190 | | 342 |
| ☐ | N318AT | Boeing 737-7BD/W | 33931/2214 | | 344 |
| ☐ | N326AT | Boeing 737-7BD/W | 33933/2278 | ex N1786B | 345 |

| | | | | | |
|---|---|---|---|---|---|
| ☐ | N328AT | Boeing 737-7BD/W | 33934/2296 | | 346 |
| ☐ | N329AT | Boeing 737-7BD/W | 36091/2304 | | 347 |
| ☐ | N330AT | Boeing 737-7BD/W | 36399/2312 | | 348 |
| ☐ | N336AT | Boeing 737-7BD/W | 36716/2505 | ex N1787B | 350 |
| ☐ | N337AT | Boeing 737-7BD/W | 36717/2526 | ex N1786B | 351 |
| ☐ | N338AT | Boeing 737-7BD/W | 33943/2552 | | 352 |
| ☐ | N344AT | Boeing 737-7BD/W | 36718/2568 | ex N1786B | 353 |
| ☐ | N353AT | Boeing 737-7BD/W | 36724/2813 | ex N1787B | 356 |
| ☐ | N354AT | Boeing 737-7BD/W | 36725/2815 | ex N1787B | 357 |
| ☐ | N7702A | Boeing 737-7BD/W | 33917/1550 | ex N166AT | 302 |
| ☐ | N7704B | Boeing 737-7BD/W | 33918/1572 | ex N167AT | 304 |
| ☐ | N7714B | Boeing 737-76N/W | 32679/1514 | ex N126AT | 300 |
| ☐ | N7726A | Boeing 737-7BD/W | 33924/1940 | ex N288AT | 326 |
| ☐ | N7730A | Boeing 737-7BD/W | 33926/1997 | ex N292AT | 330 |
| ☐ | N7732A | Boeing 737-7BD/W | 34861/2041 | ex N296AT | 332 |

Acquired by Southwest Airlines; continues separate ops

## ALASKA AIRLINES — Alaska (AS/ASA) — Seattle-Tacoma Intl, WA (SEA)

| | | | | | |
|---|---|---|---|---|---|
| ☐ | N703AS | Boeing 737-490 | 28893/3039 | ex (N747AS) | |
| ☐ | N705AS | Boeing 737-490 | 29318/3042 | ex (N748AS) | |
| ☐ | N706AS | Boeing 737-490 | 28894/3050 | ex (N749AS) | Disneyworld titles |
| ☐ | N708AS | Boeing 737-490 | 28895/3098 | | |
| ☐ | N709AS | Boeing 737-490 (SF) | 28896/3099 | ex N1787B | |
| ☐ | N713AS | Boeing 737-490 | 30161/3110 | ex N1787B | |
| ☐ | N754AS | Boeing 737-4Q8 | 25095/2265 | | Spirit of Alaska |
| ☐ | N755AS | Boeing 737-4Q8 | 25096/2278 | | |
| ☐ | N756AS | Boeing 737-4Q8 | 25097/2299 | | |
| ☐ | N760AS | Boeing 737-4Q8 | 25098/2320 | | |
| ☐ | N762AS | Boeing 737-4Q8F | 25099/2334 | | |
| ☐ | N763AS | Boeing 737-4Q8F | 25100/2346 | | |
| ☐ | N764AS | Boeing 737-4Q8F | 25101/2348 | | |
| ☐ | N765AS | Boeing 737-4Q8F | 25102/2350 | | |
| ☐ | N767AS | Boeing 737-490 | 27081/2354 | | |
| ☐ | N768AS | Boeing 737-490F | 27082/2356 | | |
| ☐ | N769AS | Boeing 737-4Q8 | 25103/2452 | | |
| ☐ | N771AS | Boeing 737-4Q8 | 25104/2476 | | |
| ☐ | N778AS | Boeing 737-4Q8 | 25110/2586 | | |
| ☐ | N779AS | Boeing 737-4Q8 | 25111/2605 | | |
| ☐ | N786AS | Boeing 737-4S3 | 24795/1870 | ex TF-FIE | |
| ☐ | N788AS | Boeing 737-490 | 28885/2891 | | |
| ☐ | N791AS | Boeing 737-490 | 28886/2902 | | |
| ☐ | N792AS | Boeing 737-490 | 28887/2903 | | Salmon Thirty Seven |
| ☐ | N793AS | Boeing 737-490 | 28888/2990 | | |
| ☐ | N794AS | Boeing 737-490 | 28889/3000 | | |
| ☐ | N795AS | Boeing 737-490 | 28890/3006 | | |
| ☐ | N796AS | Boeing 737-490 | 28891/3027 | | |
| ☐ | N797AS | Boeing 737-490 | 28892/3036 | | |
| ☐ | N799AS | Boeing 737-490 | 29270/3038 | | |
| ☐ | N607AS | Boeing 737-790/W | 29751/313 | | |
| ☐ | N609AS | Boeing 737-790/W | 29752/350 | | |
| ☐ | N611AS | Boeing 737-790/W | 29753/385 | | |
| ☐ | N612AS | Boeing 737-790/W | 30162/406 | ex N1787B | |
| ☐ | N613AS | Boeing 737-790/W | 30163/430 | | |
| ☐ | N614AS | Boeing 737-790/W | 30343/439 | | |
| ☐ | N615AS | Boeing 737-790/W | 30344/472 | ex N1787B | |
| ☐ | N617AS | Boeing 737-790/W | 30542/532 | | |
| ☐ | N618AS | Boeing 737-790/W | 30543/536 | ex N1787B | |
| ☐ | N619AS | Boeing 737-790/W | 30164/597 | | |
| ☐ | N622AS | Boeing 737-790/W | 30165/661 | | |
| ☐ | N623AS | Boeing 737-790/W | 30166/700 | | |
| ☐ | N624AS | Boeing 737-790/W | 30778/724 | | |
| ☐ | N625AS | Boeing 737-790/W | 30792/754 | ex N1795B | |
| ☐ | N626AS | Boeing 737-790/W | 30793/763 | | |
| ☐ | N627AS | Boeing 737-790/W | 30794/796 | ex N1787B | |
| ☐ | N644AS | Boeing 737-790/W | 30795/1277 | | |
| ☐ | N506AS | Boeing 737-890/W | 35690/2627 | | |
| ☐ | N508AS | Boeing 737-890/W | 35691/2662 | ex N1786B | |
| ☐ | N512AS | Boeing 737-890/W | 39043/2711 | | |
| ☐ | N513AS | Boeing 737-890/W | 35192/2721 | ex N1786B | |
| ☐ | N514AS | Boeing 737-890/W | 35193/2727 | ex N1786B | |
| ☐ | N516AS | Boeing 737-890/W | 39044/2751 | | |
| ☐ | N517AS | Boeing 737-890/W | 35197/2770 | | |
| ☐ | N518AS | Boeing 737-890/W | 35693/2785 | | |
| ☐ | N519AS | Boeing 737-890/W | 36482/2800 | ex N1795B | |
| ☐ | N520AS | Boeing 737-890/W | 36481/2812 | ex N1786B | |
| ☐ | N523AS | Boeing 737-890/W | 35194/2816 | | |
| ☐ | N524AS | Boeing 737-890/W | 35195/2850 | ex N1796B | |
| ☐ | N525AS | Boeing 737-890/W | 35692/2859 | ex N1786B | |
| ☐ | N526AS | Boeing 737-890/W | 35196/2862 | ex N1796B | |

| | | | | |
|---|---|---|---|---|
| ☐ N527AS | Boeing 737-890/W | 35694/2913 | ex N1796B | |
| ☐ N528AS | Boeing 737-890/W | 35695/2930 | | |
| ☐ N529AS | Boeing 737-890/W | 35198/3229 | ex N1796B | |
| ☐ N530AS | Boeing 737-890/W | 36578/3257 | ex N1786B | |
| ☐ N531AS | Boeing 737-890/W | 35199/3287 | ex N1787B | |
| ☐ N532AS | Boeing 737-890/W | 36346/3317 | | |
| ☐ N533AS | Boeing 737-890/W | 35201/3511 | ex N1786B | |
| ☐ N534AS | Boeing 737-890/W | 35202/3523 | | |
| ☐ N535AS | Boeing 737-890/W | 35200/3558 | | ♦ |
| ☐ N536AS | Boeing 737-890/W | 35203/3893 | | ♦ |
| ☐ N537AS | Boeing 737-890/W | 35204/3913 | | ♦ |
| ☐ N538AS | Boeing 737-890/W | 41188/ | | o/o♦ |
| ☐ N546AS | Boeing 737-890/W | 30022/1640 | | |
| ☐ N548AS | Boeing 737-890/W | 30020/1738 | | |
| ☐ N549AS | Boeing 737-8FH/W | 30824/1664 | | |
| ☐ N551AS | Boeing 737-890/W | 34593/1860 | | |
| ☐ N552AS | Boeing 737-890/W | 34595/1882 | ex N1795B | |
| ☐ N553AS | Boeing 737-890/W | 34594/1906 | | |
| ☐ N556AS | Boeing 737-890/W | 35175/1980 | | |
| ☐ N557AS | Boeing 737-890/W | 35176/2010 | | |
| ☐ N558AS | Boeing 737-890/W | 35177/2031 | | |
| ☐ N559AS | Boeing 737-890/W | 35178/2026 | ex N6067E | ETOPS test aircraft |
| ☐ N560AS | Boeing 737-890/W | 35179/2072 | | |
| ☐ N562AS | Boeing 737-890/W | 35091/2084 | | |
| ☐ N563AS | Boeing 737-890/W | 35180/2090 | | |
| ☐ N564AS | Boeing 737-890/W | 35103/2099 | | |
| ☐ N565AS | Boeing 737-890/W | 35181/2134 | | |
| ☐ N566AS | Boeing 737-890/W | 35182/2164 | | |
| ☐ N568AS | Boeing 737-890/W | 35183/2166 | | |
| ☐ N569AS | Boeing 737-890/W | 35184/2192 | | 75th anniversary c/s |
| ☐ N570AS | Boeing 737-890/W | 35185/2212 | | |
| ☐ N577AS | Boeing 737-890/W | 35186/2221 | ex N1787B | |
| ☐ N579AS | Boeing 737-890/W | 35187/2226 | | |
| ☐ N581AS | Boeing 737-890/W | 35188/2259 | | |
| ☐ N583AS | Boeing 737-890/W | 35681/2333 | | |
| ☐ N584AS | Boeing 737-890/W | 35682/2365 | | |
| ☐ N585AS | Boeing 737-890/W | 35683/2385 | | |
| ☐ N586AS | Boeing 737-890/W | 35189/2393 | | |
| ☐ N587AS | Boeing 737-890/W | 35684/2422 | ex N1786B | |
| ☐ N588AS | Boeing 737-890/W | 35685/2454 | ex N1786B | |
| ☐ N589AS | Boeing 737-890/W | 35686/2458 | ex N1786B | |
| ☐ N590AS | Boeing 737-890/W | 35687/2478 | | |
| ☐ N592AS | Boeing 737-890/W | 35190/2511 | ex N1786B | |
| ☐ N593AS | Boeing 737-890/W | 35107/2545 | ex N1786B | |
| ☐ N594AS | Boeing 737-890/W | 35191/2560 | ex N1786B | |
| ☐ N596AS | Boeing 737-890/W | 35688/2587 | | |
| ☐ N597AS | Boeing 737-890/W | 35689/2601 | | |
| | | | | |
| ☐ N302AS | Boeing 737-990 | 30017/596 | ex N737X | |
| ☐ N303AS | Boeing 737-990 | 30016/683 | ex N672AS | |
| ☐ N305AS | Boeing 737-990 | 30013/774 | ex (N673AS) | |
| ☐ N306AS | Boeing 737-990/W | 30014/802 | ex (N674AS) | |
| ☐ N307AS | Boeing 737-990/W | 30015/838 | ex N1786B | |
| ☐ N309AS | Boeing 737-990/W | 30857/902 | ex N1786B | |
| ☐ N315AS | Boeing 737-990/W | 30019/1218 | | |
| ☐ N317AS | Boeing 737-990/W | 30856/1296 | ex N1786B | |
| ☐ N318AS | Boeing 737-990/W | 30018/1326 | | |
| ☐ N319AS | Boeing 737-990/W | 33679/1344 | | |
| ☐ N320AS | Boeing 737-990/W | 33680/1380 | | |
| ☐ N323AS | Boeing 737-990/W | 30021/1454 | | |

## ALASKA CENTRAL EXPRESS — Ace Air (KO/AER) — Anchorage-Intl, AK (ANC)

| | | | | |
|---|---|---|---|---|
| ☐ N111AX | Beech 1900C-1 | UC-81 | ex N5632C | |
| ☐ N113AX | Beech 1900C-1 | UC-41 | ex N41UE | |
| ☐ N114AX | Beech 1900C-1 | UC-36 | ex N1566C | |
| ☐ N115AX | Beech 1900C-1 | UC-2 | ex N19NG | |
| ☐ N116AX | Beech 1900C-1 | UC-17 | ex N116AX | |
| ☐ N119AX | Beech 1900C-1 | UC-43 | ex YV149T | ♦ |
| | | | | |
| ☐ N219VP | Beech 1900 | UB-14 | ex N188GA | ♦ |
| ☐ N9874M | Cessna 207A Stationair 8 II | 20700745 | | |
| ☐ N9957M | Cessna 207A Stationair 8 II | 20700764 | | |

## ALASKA SEAPLANE SERVICE — (J5) — Juneau-Int'l, AK (JNU)

| | | | | |
|---|---|---|---|---|
| ☐ N777DH | de Havilland DHC-2 Beaver | 47 | ex CF-FHN | FP |
| ☐ N4794C | de Havilland DHC-2 Beaver | 342 | ex 51-16545 | FP |
| ☐ N7687K | Cessna 180 Skywagon | 18052703 | | FP♦ |
| ☐ N60077 | de Havilland DHC-2 Beaver | 1419 | ex LV-GLJ | FP |

## ALASKA WEST AIR · Kenai Island Lake, AK (ENA)

| | | | | | |
|---|---|---|---|---|---|
| ☐ N49AW | de Havilland DHC-3 Otter | 310 | ex N21PG | | FP |
| ☐ N87AW | de Havilland DHC-3 Turbo Otter | 52 | ex C-FMPO | | FP |
| ☐ N222RL | de Havilland DHC-2 Turbo Beaver | 1570/TB5 | ex C-FOEB | | FP |
| ☐ N1432Z | de Havilland DHC-2 Beaver | 797 | ex 54-1668 | | FP |

## ALLEGIANT AIR · Allegiant (G4/AAY) · Las Vegas-McCarran Int'l, NV (LAS)

| | | | | |
|---|---|---|---|---|
| ☐ N425NV | McDonnell-Douglas MD-82 | 49438/1353 | ex SE-DFY | ♦ |
| ☐ N428NV | McDonnell-Douglas MD-82 | 49420/1254 | ex OY-KGY | |
| ☐ N886GA | McDonnell-Douglas MD-82 | 49931/1754 | ex N829NK | [IGM] |
| ☐ N887GA | McDonnell-Douglas MD-82 | 49932/1756 | ex N830NK | |
| ☐ N894GA | McDonnell-Douglas MD-82 | 49660/1445 | ex EI-BTX | |
| ☐ N895GA | McDonnell-Douglas MD-82 | 49667/1466 | ex EI-BTY | ♦ |
| ☐ N405NV | McDonnell-Douglas MD-83 | 49623/1499 | ex SE-RFA | |
| ☐ N406NV | McDonnell-Douglas MD-83 | 49900/1765 | ex SE-RFC | |
| ☐ N407NV | McDonnell-Douglas MD-83 | 53244/1901 | ex SE-RFD | |
| ☐ N408NV | McDonnell-Douglas MD-83 | 53246/1918 | ex SE-RFB | |
| ☐ N409NV | McDonnell-Douglas MD-83 | 49574/1413 | ex SE-RDV | |
| ☐ N410NV | McDonnell-Douglas MD-83 | 49965/2044 | ex SE-DLV | |
| ☐ N411NV | McDonnell-Douglas MD-83 | 53245/1978 | ex HK-4413 | |
| ☐ N415NV | McDonnell-Douglas MD-83 | 49909/1625 | ex SE-DII | |
| ☐ N416NV | McDonnell-Douglas MD-83 | 49555/1402 | ex SE-DIO | |
| ☐ N417NV | McDonnell-Douglas MD-83 | 53347/1979 | ex SE-DMD | ♦ |
| ☐ N418NV | McDonnell-Douglas MD-83 | 49615/1543 | ex SE-DID | |
| ☐ N419NV | McDonnell-Douglas MD-83 | 53366/1999 | ex SE-DME | |
| ☐ N420NV | McDonnell-Douglas MD-83 | 49424/1284 | ex SE-DFX | ♦ |
| ☐ N421NV | McDonnell-Douglas MD-83 | 53275/1896 | ex OY-KHR | |
| ☐ N422NV | McDonnell-Douglas MD-83 | 49381/1231 | ex OY-KGZ | |
| ☐ N423NV | McDonnell-Douglas MD-83 | 53008/1895 | ex SE-DIY | [IGM] |
| ☐ N424NV | McDonnell-Douglas MD-83 | 49421/1263 | ex LN-ROS | ♦ |
| ☐ N426NV | McDonnell-Douglas MD-83 | 49437/1345 | ex SE-DMI | [IGM]♦ |
| ☐ N427NV | McDonnell-Douglas MD-83 | 49436/1303 | ex OY-KHC | ♦ |
| ☐ N429NV | McDonnell-Douglas MD-83 | 49385/1244 | ex SE-DFT | |
| ☐ N860GA | McDonnell-Douglas MD-83 | 49786/1631 | ex 9Y-THW | |
| ☐ N861GA | McDonnell-Douglas MD-83 | 49557/1436 | ex SE-DPI | |
| ☐ N862GA | McDonnell-Douglas MD-83 | 49556/1415 | ex LN-RMF | |
| ☐ N863GA | McDonnell-Douglas MD-83 | 49911/1653 | ex OY-KHL | |
| ☐ N864GA | McDonnell-Douglas MD-83 | 49912/1659 | ex LN-RMJ | |
| ☐ N865GA | McDonnell-Douglas MD-83 | 49998/1800 | ex SE-DIX | |
| ☐ N866GA | McDonnell-Douglas MD-83 | 49910/1638 | ex OY-KHK | |
| ☐ N868GA | McDonnell-Douglas MD-83 | 49554/1379 | ex LN-RMA | |
| ☐ N869GA | McDonnell-Douglas MD-83 | 53294/1917 | ex SE-DIZ | |
| ☐ N871GA | McDonnell-Douglas MD-83 | 53296/1937 | ex OY-KHT | |
| ☐ N872GA | McDonnell-Douglas MD-83 | 53295/1922 | ex LN-RMN | |
| ☐ N873GA | McDonnell-Douglas MD-83 | 49658/1461 | ex N946AS | |
| ☐ N874GA | McDonnell-Douglas MD-83 | 49643/1423 | ex N945AS | |
| ☐ N875GA | McDonnell-Douglas MD-83 | 53468/2130 | ex C-GKLN | |
| ☐ N876GA | McDonnell-Douglas MD-83 | 53469/2116 | ex C-GKLR | |
| ☐ N877GA | McDonnell-Douglas MD-83 | 53467/2102 | ex C-GKLJ | |
| ☐ N878GA | McDonnell-Douglas MD-83 | 53487/2132 | ex C-GKLQ | |
| ☐ N879GA | McDonnell-Douglas MD-83 | 53486/2130 | ex C-GKLN | |
| ☐ N880GA | McDonnell-Douglas MD-83 | 49625/1503 | ex OH-LMG | |
| ☐ N881GA | McDonnell-Douglas MD-83 | 49708/1561 | ex SE-RGO | |
| ☐ N883GA | McDonnell-Douglas MD-83 | 49710/1547 | ex SE-RGP | |
| ☐ N884GA | McDonnell-Douglas MD-83 | 49401/1357 | ex SE-RDS | |
| ☐ N891GA | McDonnell-Douglas MD-83 | 49423/1283 | ex LN-RLG | |
| ☐ N892GA | McDonnell-Douglas MD-83 | 49826/1578 | ex N861LF | |
| ☐ N893GA | McDonnell-Douglas MD-83 | 53051/1718 | ex N881LF | |
| ☐ N532PT | McDonnell-Douglas MD-87 | 49611/1522 | ex EC-KHA | [IGM]♦ |
| ☐ N533PT | McDonnell-Douglas MD-87 | 49609/1517 | ex EC-KCZ | [IGM]♦ |
| ☐ N534PT | McDonnell-Douglas MD-87 | 53340/1967 | ex SE-DMC | [IGM]♦ |
| ☐ N945MA | McDonnell-Douglas MD-87 | 49725/1552 | ex VP-BOP | |
| ☐ N948MA | McDonnell-Douglas MD-87 | 49778/1646 | ex VP-BOO | |
| ☐ N949MA | McDonnell-Douglas MD-87 | 49779/1670 | ex N751RA | [IGM] |
| ☐ N952MA | McDonnell-Douglas MD-87 | 49673/1508 | ex N673HC | [IGM] |
| ☐ N401NV | McDonnell-Douglas MD-88 | 49761/1623 | ex N158PL | |
| ☐ N402NV | McDonnell-Douglas MD-88 | 49763/1626 | ex N160PL | |
| ☐ N403NV | McDonnell-Douglas MD-88 | 49764/1632 | ex N161PL | |
| ☐ N404NV | McDonnell-Douglas MD-88 | 49765/1645 | ex N162PL | |
| ☐ N412NV | McDonnell-Douglas MD-88 | 49759/1606 | ex N822ME | |
| ☐ N414NV | McDonnell-Douglas MD-88 | 49766/1657 | ex N823ME | |
| ☐ N901NV | Boeing 757-204 | 26963/450 | ex OH-AFL | [JAX]♦ |
| ☐ N902NV | Boeing 757-204 | 26964/452 | ex N964BV | |
| ☐ N905NV | Boeing 757-204 | 27235/598 | ex G-BYAO | [JAX]♦ |
| ☐ N906NV | Boeing 757-204 | 27236/600 | ex G-BYAP | [JAX]♦ |

## ALLWEST FREIGHT — Kenai-Municipal, AK (ENA)

| | | | | |
|---|---|---|---|---|
| ☐ N114LH | Short SC.7 Skyvan | SH1926 | | Frtr♦ |
| ☐ N549WB | Short SC.7 Skyvan | SH1911 | ex XA-SRD | Frtr |

## ALOHA AIR CARGO — Aloha (AQ/AAH) — Honolulu-Intl, HI (HNL)

| | | | | |
|---|---|---|---|---|
| ☐ N826AL | Boeing 737-282C | 23051/1002 | ex CS-TEQ | |
| ☐ N840AL | Boeing 737-2X6C | 23124/1046 | ex N747AS | |
| ☐ N841AL | Boeing 737-2X6C | 23123/1042 | ex N746AS | |
| ☐ N842AL | Boeing 737-290QC | 23136/1032 | ex N742AS | |
| ☐ N843KH | SAAB SF.340AF | 340A-046 | ex XA-STX | |
| ☐ N844KH | SAAB SF.340AF | 340A-108 | ex OK-CCE | ♦ |

## ALPINE AIR EXPRESS — Alpine Air (5A/AIP) — Provo-Municipal, UT (PVU)

| | | | | |
|---|---|---|---|---|
| ☐ N14MV | Beech 99 | U-59 | ex C-FGJT | |
| ☐ N24BH | Beech 99 | U-67 | ex C-GVNQ | |
| ☐ N95WA | Beech 99 | U-6 | ex N19RA | |
| ☐ N99CA | Beech 99A | U-127 | ex N22AT | |
| ☐ N99GH | Beech 99A | U-112 | ex N86569 | |
| ☐ N216CS | Beech C99 | U-216 | ex C-GGPP | based HNL |
| ☐ N236AL | Beech C99 | U-236 | ex RP-C2317 | based HNL |
| ☐ N237SL | Beech C99 | U-237 | ex RP-C2370 | based HNL |
| ☐ N238AL | Beech C99 | U-238 | ex RP-C2380 | based HNL |
| ☐ N239AL | Beech C99 | U-239 | ex RP-C2390 | based HNL |
| ☐ N326CA | Beech B99 | U-135 | ex N10RA | |
| ☐ N950AA | Beech B99 | U-159 | ex C-FCBU | |
| ☐ N4381Y | Beech 99 | U-71 | ex N216BH | |
| | | | | |
| ☐ N125BA | Beech 1900C | UB-6 | ex N125GP | |
| ☐ N127BA | Beech 1900C | UB-7 | ex N126GP | |
| ☐ N153GA | Beech 1900C | UB-34 | ex N734GL | based HNL |
| ☐ N172GA | Beech 1900C | UB-11 | ex N11ZR | |
| ☐ N190GA | Beech 1900C | UB-1 | ex N1YW | |
| ☐ N192GA | Beech 1900C | UB-17 | ex N17ZR | based HNL |
| ☐ N194GA | Beech 1900C | UB-8 | ex CC-CAF | |
| ☐ N197GA | Beech 1900C | UB-16 | ex N16ZR | |
| ☐ N198GA | Beech 1900C | UB-5 | ex CC-CAS | |
| | | | | |
| ☐ N60MJ | Beech 1900D | UE-60 | ex N85445 | ♦ |
| ☐ N139ZV | Beech 1900D | UE-139 | | ♦ |
| ☐ N155CJ | Beech 1900D | UE-55 | ex N85230 | |

## AMERICAN AIRLINES — American (AA/AAL) — Dallas-Fort Worth, TX (DFW)

Member of Oneworld

| | | | | |
|---|---|---|---|---|
| ☐ N800NN | Boeing 737-823/W | 29564/2964 | | 3DY |
| ☐ N801NN | Boeing 737-823/W | 29565/2972 | | 3EA |
| ☐ N802NN | Boeing 737-823/W | 31073/2982 | | 3EB |
| ☐ N803NN | Boeing 737-823/W | 29566/2995 | | 3EC |
| ☐ N804NN | Boeing 737-823/W | 29567/3004 | | 3ED |
| ☐ N805NN | Boeing 737-823/W | 31075/3013 | | 3EE |
| ☐ N806NN | Boeing 737-823/W | 29561/3028 | | 3EF |
| ☐ N807NN | Boeing 737-823/W | 31077/3035 | | 3EF |
| ☐ N808NN | Boeing 737-823/W | 33206/3042 | | 3EH |
| ☐ N809NN | Boeing 737-823/W | 33519/3050 | | 3EJ |
| ☐ N810NN | Boeing 737-823/W | 33207/3056 | | 3EK |
| ☐ N811NN | Boeing 737-823/W | 31079/3063 | | 3EL |
| ☐ N812NN | Boeing 737-823/W | 33520/3070 | | 3EM |
| ☐ N813NN | Boeing 737-823/W | 30918/3077 | | 3EN |
| ☐ N814NN | Boeing 737-823/W | 29562/3085 | | 3EP |
| ☐ N815NN | Boeing 737-823/W | 33208/3094 | | 3ER |
| ☐ N816NN | Boeing 737-823/W | 31081/3102 | | 3ES |
| ☐ N817NN | Boeing 737-823/W | 29558/3107 | | 3ET |
| ☐ N818NN | Boeing 737-823/W | 30910/3112 | | 3EU |
| ☐ N819NN | Boeing 737-823/W | 31083/3118 | | 3EV |
| ☐ N820NN | Boeing 737-823/W | 29559/3125 | | 3EW |
| ☐ N821NN | Boeing 737-823/W | 30912/3137 | | 3EX |
| ☐ N822NN | Boeing 737-823/W | 31085/3149 | | 3EY |
| ☐ N823NN | Boeing 737-823/W | 29560/3156 | | 3FA |
| ☐ N824NN | Boeing 737-823/W | 30916/3170 | | 3FB |
| ☐ N825NN | Boeing 737-823/W | 31087/3178 | | 3FC |
| ☐ N826NN | Boeing 737-823/W | 31089/3185 | | 3FD |
| ☐ N827NN | Boeing 737-823/W | 33209/3193 | ex N1786B | 3FE |
| ☐ N829NN | Boeing 737-823/W | 33210/3200 | ex N1787B | 3FF |
| ☐ N830NN | Boeing 737-823/W | 31091/3209 | ex N1786B | 3FG |
| ☐ N831NN | Boeing 737-823/W | 33211/3217 | ex N1796B | 3FH |
| ☐ N832NN | Boeing 737-823/W | 33521/3228 | ex N1786B | 3FJ |

| | Registration | Type | MSN/Line | ex | Code | |
|---|---|---|---|---|---|---|
| ☐ | N833NN | Boeing 737-823/W | 31093/3236 | ex N1786B | 3FK | |
| ☐ | N834NN | Boeing 737-823/W | 29576/3244 | ex N1787B | 3FL | |
| ☐ | N835NN | Boeing 737-823/W | 29577/3252 | ex N1796B | 3FM | |
| ☐ | N836NN | Boeing 737-823/W | 31095/3260 | ex N1786B | 3FN | |
| ☐ | N837NN | Boeing 737-823/W | 30908/3268 | ex N1786B | 3FP | |
| ☐ | N838NN | Boeing 737-823/W | 31097/3276 | | 3FR | |
| ☐ | N839NN | Boeing 737-823/W | 29557/3282 | ex N1786B | 3FS | |
| ☐ | N840NN | Boeing 737-823/W | 33518/3291 | ex N1786B | 3FT | |
| ☐ | N841NN | Boeing 737-823/W | 30914/3298 | | 3FU | |
| ☐ | N842NN | Boeing 737-823/W | 31099/3307 | ex N1786B | 3FV | |
| ☐ | N843NN | Boeing 737-823/W | 30906/3328 | ex N1787B | 3FW | |
| ☐ | N844NN | Boeing 737-823/W | 33212/3334 | | 3FX | |
| ☐ | N845NN | Boeing 737-823/W | 40579/3340 | ex N1786B | 3FY | |
| ☐ | N846NN | Boeing 737-823/W | 31101/3347 | | 3GA | |
| ☐ | N847NN | Boeing 737-823/W | 29575/3361 | | 3GB | |
| ☐ | N848NN | Boeing 737-823/W | 31103/3367 | | 3GC | |
| ☐ | N849NN | Boeing 737-823/W | 33213/3373 | | 3GD | |
| ☐ | N850NN | Boeing 737-823/W | 40580/3380 | | 3GE | |
| ☐ | N851NN | Boeing 737-823/W | 29556/3390 | | 3GF | |
| ☐ | N852NN | Boeing 737-823/W | 40581/3396 | | 3GG | |
| ☐ | N853NN | Boeing 737-823/W | 31105/3404 | | 3GH | |
| ☐ | N854NN | Boeing 737-823/W | 33214/3412 | | 3GJ | |
| ☐ | N855NN | Boeing 737-823/W | 40852/3422 | | 3GK | |
| ☐ | N856NN | Boeing 737-823/W | 31107/3427 | | 3GL | |
| ☐ | N857NN | Boeing 737-823/W | 30907/3434 | | 3GM | |
| ☐ | N858NN | Boeing 737-823/W | 30904/3440 | | 3GN | |
| ☐ | N859NN | Boeing 737-823/W | 29555/3456 | | 3GP | |
| ☐ | N860NN | Boeing 737-823/W | 40583/3462 | | 3GR | |
| ☐ | N861NN | Boeing 737-823/W | 31109/3468 | | 3GS | |
| ☐ | N862NN | Boeing 737-823/W | 30905/3475 | | 3GT | |
| ☐ | N863NN | Boeing 737-823/W | 30903/3481 | | 3GU | |
| ☐ | N864NN | Boeing 737-823/W | 31111/3487 | | 3GV | |
| ☐ | N865NN | Boeing 737-823/W | 29554/3493 | ex N1787B | 3GW | |
| ☐ | N866NN | Boeing 737-823/W | 40584/3499 | | 3GX | |
| ☐ | N867NN | Boeing 737-823/W | 40762/3634 | | 3GY | ♦ |
| ☐ | N868NN | Boeing 737-823/W | 40763/3668 | | 3HA | ♦ |
| ☐ | N869NN | Boeing 737-823/W | 40764/3689 | | 3HB | ♦ |
| ☐ | N870NN | Boeing 737-823/W | 40765/3748 | | 3HE | ♦ |
| ☐ | N871NN | Boeing 737-823/W | 31127/3731 | | 3HC | ♦ |
| ☐ | N872NN | Boeing 737-823/W | 33219/3740 | | 3HD | ♦ |
| ☐ | N873NN | Boeing 737-823/W | 40766/3775 | | 3HG | ♦ |
| ☐ | N874NN | Boeing 737-823/W | 31129/3764 | | 3HF | ♦ |
| ☐ | N875NN | Boeing 737-823/W | 33220/3782 | | 3HH | ♦ |
| ☐ | N876NN | Boeing 737-823/W | 40767/3793 | | 3HJ | ♦ |
| ☐ | N877NN | Boeing 737-823/W | 31127/3764 | | 3HF | ♦ |
| ☐ | N878NN | Boeing 737-823/W | 40768/3820 | | 3HL | ♦ |
| ☐ | N879NN | Boeing 737-823/W | 31133/3833 | | 3HM | ♦ |
| ☐ | N880NN | Boeing 737-823/W | 40769/3854 | | 3HN | ♦ |
| ☐ | M881NN | Boeing 737-823/W | 31135/3862 | | 3HP | ♦ |
| ☐ | N882NN | Boeing 737-823/W | 33221/3880 | | 3HR | ♦ |
| ☐ | N883NN | Boeing 737-823/W | 31137/3892 | | | ♦ |
| ☐ | N884NN | Boeing 737-823/W | 33222/3914 | | | ♦ |
| ☐ | N885NN | Boeing 737-823/W | 31139/3935 | | | ♦ |
| ☐ | N886NN | Boeing 737-823/W | 33223/3950 | | | ♦ |
| ☐ | N887NN | Boeing 737-823/W | 31141/3964 | | | ♦ |
| ☐ | N889NN | Boeing 737-823/W | 33314/3981 | | | ♦ |
| ☐ | N890NN | Boeing 737-823/W | 31143/3999 | | | ♦ |
| ☐ | N891NN | Boeing 737-823/W | 33315 | | | o/o♦ |
| ☐ | N892NN | Boeing 737-823/W | 31145 | | | o/o♦ |
| ☐ | N893NN | Boeing 737-823/W | 33316 | | | o/o♦ |
| ☐ | N894NN | Boeing 737-823/W | 31147 | | | o/o♦ |
| ☐ | N895NN | Boeing 737-823/W | 31149 | | | o/o♦ |
| ☐ | N896NN | Boeing 737-823/W | 33224 | | | o/o♦ |
| ☐ | N897NN | Boeing 737-823/W | 33318 | | | o/o♦ |
| ☐ | N898NN | Boeing 737-823/W | 33225 | | | o/o♦ |
| ☐ | N899NN | Boeing 737-823/W | 31151 | | | o/o♦ |
| ☐ | N901AN | Boeing 737-823/W | 29503/184 | | 3AA | |
| ☐ | N901NN | Boeing 737-823/W | 33226 | | | o/o♦ |
| ☐ | N902AN | Boeing 737-823/W | 29504/190 | | 3AB | |
| ☐ | N902NN | Boeing 737-323/W | 31154 | | | o/o♦ |
| ☐ | N903AN | Boeing 737-823/W | 29505/196 | | 3AC | |
| ☐ | N903NN | Boeing 737-823/W | 31153 | | | o/o♦ |
| ☐ | N904AN | Boeing 737-823/W | 29506/207 | | 3AD | |
| ☐ | N904NN | Boeing 737-823/W | 33317 | | | o/o♦ |
| ☐ | N905AN | Boeing 737-823/W | 29507/231 | | 3AE | |
| ☐ | N905NN | Boeing 737-323/W | 31156 | | | o/o♦ |
| ☐ | N906AN | Boeing 737-823/W | 29508/240 | | 3AF | |
| ☐ | N906NN | Boeing 737-823/W | 31153 | | | o/o♦ |
| ☐ | N907AN | Boeing 737-823/W | 29509/254 | | 3AG | |
| ☐ | N907NN | Boeing 737-823/W | 31158 | | | o/o♦ |
| ☐ | N908AN | Boeing 737-823/W | 29510/263 | | 3AH | |
| ☐ | N908NN | Boeing 737-823/W | 31157 | | | o/o♦ |

| | | | | | | |
|---|---|---|---|---|---|---|
| ☐ | N909AN | Boeing 737-823/W | 29511/267 | ex (N909AM) | 3AJ | |
| ☐ | N90NN | Boeing 737-823/W | 31159 | | | o/o♦ |
| ☐ | N910AN | Boeing 737-823/W | 29512/271 | | 3AK | |
| ☐ | N910NN | Boeing 737-823/W | 31160 | | | o/o♦ |
| ☐ | N912AN | Boeing 737-823/W | 29513/289 | | 3AL | |
| ☐ | N912NN | Boeing 737-823/W | 33319 | | | o/o♦ |
| ☐ | N913AN | Boeing 737-823/W | 29514/293 | | 3AM | |
| ☐ | N914AN | Boeing 737-823/W | 29515/316 | | 3AN | |
| ☐ | N915AN | Boeing 737-823/W | 29516/322 | | 3AP | |
| ☐ | N916AN | Boeing 737-823/W | 29517/332 | | 3AR | |
| ☐ | N917AN | Boeing 737-823/W | 29518/344 | | 3AS | |
| ☐ | N918AN | Boeing 737-823/W | 29519/353 | | 3AT | |
| ☐ | N919AN | Boeing 737-823/W | 29520/363 | | 3AU | |
| ☐ | N920AN | Boeing 737-823/W | 29521/378 | | 3AV | |
| ☐ | N921AN | Boeing 737-823/W | 29522/383 | | 3AW | |
| ☐ | N922AN | Boeing 737-823/W | 29523/398 | | 3AX | |
| ☐ | N923AN | Boeing 737-823/W | 29524/405 | | 3AY | |
| ☐ | N924AN | Boeing 737-823/W | 29525/434 | | 3BA | |
| ☐ | N925AN | Boeing 737-823/W | 29526/440 | | 3BB | |
| ☐ | N926AN | Boeing 737-823/W | 29527/453 | | 3BC | |
| ☐ | N927AN | Boeing 737-823/W | 30077/462 | | 3BD | |
| ☐ | N928AN | Boeing 737-823/W | 29528/473 | | 3BE | |
| ☐ | N929AN | Boeing 737-823/W | 30078/488 | | 3BF | |
| ☐ | N930AN | Boeing 737-823/W | 29529/503 | | 3BG | |
| ☐ | N931AN | Boeing 737-823/W | 30079/509 | | 3BH | |
| ☐ | N932AN | Boeing 737-823/W | 29530/527 | | 3BJ | |
| ☐ | N933AN | Boeing 737-823/W | 30080/531 | | 3BK | |
| ☐ | N934AN | Boeing 737-823/W | 29531/553 | | 3BL | |
| ☐ | N935AN | Boeing 737-823/W | 30081/559 | | 3BM | |
| ☐ | N936AN | Boeing 737-823/W | 29532/575 | | 3BN | |
| ☐ | N937AN | Boeing 737-823/W | 30082/579 | | 3BP | |
| ☐ | N938AN | Boeing 737-823/W | 29533/608 | | 3BR | |
| ☐ | N939AN | Boeing 737-823/W | 30083/612 | | 3BS | |
| ☐ | N940AN | Boeing 737-823/W | 30598/616 | | 3BT | |
| ☐ | N941AN | Boeing 737-823/W | 29534/624 | | 3BU | |
| ☐ | N942AN | Boeing 737-823/W | 30084/629 | | 3BV | |
| ☐ | N943AN | Boeing 737-823/W | 30599/635 | | 3BW | |
| ☐ | N944AN | Boeing 737-823/W | 29535/645 | | 3BX | |
| ☐ | N945AN | Boeing 737-823/W | 30085/649 | | 3BY | |
| ☐ | N946AN | Boeing 737-823/W | 30600/655 | | 3CA | |
| ☐ | N947AN | Boeing 737-823/W | 29536/671 | ex (N2292Z) | 3CB | |
| ☐ | N948AN | Boeing 737-823/W | 30086/679 | ex (N2294B) | 3CC | |
| ☐ | N949AN | Boeing 737-823/W | 29537/699 | | 3CD | |
| ☐ | N950AN | Boeing 737-823/W | 30087/704 | | 3CE | |
| ☐ | N951AA | Boeing 737-823/W | 29538/720 | | 3CF | Astrojet c/s |
| ☐ | N952AA | Boeing 737-823/W | 30088/726 | | 3CG | |
| ☐ | N953AN | Boeing 737-823/W | 29539/741 | | 3CH | |
| ☐ | N954AN | Boeing 737-823/W | 30089/745 | | 3CJ | |
| ☐ | N955AN | Boeing 737-823/W | 29540/762 | | 3CK | |
| ☐ | N956AN | Boeing 737-823/W | 30090/764 | | 3CL | |
| ☐ | N957AN | Boeing 737-823/W | 29541/788 | | 3CM | |
| ☐ | N958AN | Boeing 737-823/W | 30091/797 | | 3CN | |
| ☐ | N959AN | Boeing 737-823/W | 30828/801 | | 3CP | |
| ☐ | N960AN | Boeing 737-823/W | 29542/818 | | 3CR | |
| ☐ | N961AN | Boeing 737-823/W | 30092/822 | | 3CS | |
| ☐ | N962AN | Boeing 737-823/W | 30858/825 | | 3CT | |
| ☐ | N963AN | Boeing 737-823/W | 29543/834 | | 3CU | |
| ☐ | N964AN | Boeing 737-823/W | 30093/837 | | 3CV | |
| ☐ | N965AN | Boeing 737-823/W | 29544/860 | | 3CW | |
| ☐ | N966AN | Boeing 737-823/W | 30094/863 | | 3CX | |
| ☐ | N967AN | Boeing 737-823/W | 29545/883 | | 3CY | |
| ☐ | N968AN | Boeing 737-823/W | 30095/886 | | 3DA | |
| ☐ | N969AN | Boeing 737-823/W | 29546/910 | | 3DB | |
| ☐ | N970AN | Boeing 737-823/W | 30096/915 | | 3DC | |
| ☐ | N971AN | Boeing 737-823/W | 29547/937 | | 3DD | |
| ☐ | N972AN | Boeing 737-823/W | 30097/941 | | 3DE | |
| ☐ | N973AN | Boeing 737-823/W | 29548/971 | | 3DF | |
| ☐ | N974AN | Boeing 737-823/W | 30098/977 | | 3DG | |
| ☐ | N975AN | Boeing 737-823/W | 29549/992 | | 3DH | |
| ☐ | N976AN | Boeing 737-823/W | 30099/1001 | | 3DJ | |
| ☐ | N978AN | Boeing 737-823/W | 30100/1022 | | 3DL | |
| ☐ | N979AN | Boeing 737-823/W | 29568/2838 | | 3DM | |
| ☐ | N980AN | Boeing 737-823/W | 33203/2846 | | 3DN | |
| ☐ | N981AN | Boeing 737-823/W | 29569/2870 | | 3DP | |
| ☐ | N982AN | Boeing 737-823/W | 31067/2876 | | 3DR | |
| ☐ | N983AN | Boeing 737-823/W | 29570/2899 | | 3DS | |
| ☐ | N987AN | Boeing 737-823/W | 31069/2907 | | 3DT | |
| ☐ | N989AN | Boeing 737-823/W | 33205/2915 | | 3DU | |
| ☐ | N990AN | Boeing 737-823/W | 29563/2935 | | 3DV | |
| ☐ | N991AN | Boeing 737-823/W | 30920/2945 | | 3DW | |
| ☐ | N992AN | Boeing 737-823/W | 31071/2954 | | 3DX | |

| | | | | |
|---|---|---|---|---|
| ☐ N172AJ | Boeing 757-223/W | 32400/1012 | | 5FT |
| ☐ N173AN | Boeing 757-223/W | 32399/1005 | | 5FS |
| ☐ N174AA | Boeing 757-223/W | 31308/998 | | 5FR |
| ☐ N175AN | Boeing 757-223/W | 32394/992 | | 5FK |
| ☐ N176AA | Boeing 757-223/W | 32395/994 | | 5FL |
| ☐ N177AN | Boeing 757-223/W | 32396/996 | | 5FM |
| ☐ N178AA | Boeing 757-223/W | 32398/1002 | ex (N20171) | 5FN |
| ☐ N179AA | Boeing 757-223/W | 32397/1000 | ex (N20140) | 5FP |
| ☐ N181AN | Boeing 757-223/W | 29591/852 | ex N5573L | 5EN |
| ☐ N182AN | Boeing 757-223/W | 29592/853 | | 5EP |
| ☐ N183AN | Boeing 757-223ER/W | 29593/862 | | 5ER |
| ☐ N184AN | Boeing 757-223ER/W | 29594/866 | ex N1787B | 5ES |
| ☐ N185AN | Boeing 757-223/W | 32379/962 | | 5ET |
| ☐ N186AN | Boeing 757-223/W | 32380/964 | | 5EU |
| ☐ N187AN | Boeing 757-223/W | 32381/965 | | 5EV |
| ☐ N188AN | Boeing 757-223/W | 32382/969 | | 5EW |
| ☐ N189AN | Boeing 757-223/W | 32383/970 | | 5EX |
| ☐ N190AA | Boeing 757-223/W | 32384/973 | | 5EY |
| ☐ N191AN | Boeing 757-223/W | 32385/977 | | 5FA |
| ☐ N192AN | Boeing 757-223/W | 32386/979 | | 5FB |
| ☐ N193AN | Boeing 757-223/W | 32387/981 | | 5FC |
| ☐ N194AA | Boeing 757-223/W | 32388/983 | | 5FD |
| ☐ N195AN | Boeing 757-223/W | 32389/984 | | 5FE |
| ☐ N196AA | Boeing 757-223/W | 32390/986 | | 5FF |
| ☐ N197AN | Boeing 757-223/W | 32391/988 | | 5FG |
| ☐ N198AA | Boeing 757-223/W | 32392/989 | | 5FH |
| ☐ N199AN | Boeing 757-223/W | 32393/991 | | 5FJ |
| ☐ N601AN | Boeing 757-223/W | 27052/661 | | 5DU |
| ☐ N602AN | Boeing 757-223/W | 27053/664 | | 5DV |
| ☐ N603AA | Boeing 757-223/W | 27054/670 | | 5DW |
| ☐ N604AA | Boeing 757-223/W | 27055/677 | | 5DX |
| ☐ N605AA | Boeing 757-223/W | 27056/680 | | 5DY |
| ☐ N606AA | Boeing 757-223/W | 27057/707 | | 5EA |
| ☐ N607AM | Boeing 757-223/W | 27058/712 | | 5EB |
| ☐ N608AA | Boeing 757-223ER/W | 27446/720 | | 5EC |
| ☐ N609AA | Boeing 757-223ER/W | 27447/722 | | 5ED |
| ☐ N610AA | Boeing 757-223//W | 24486/234 | | 610 |
| ☐ N611AM | Boeing 757-223/W | 24487/236 | | 611 |
| ☐ N612AA | Boeing 757-223/W | 24488/240 | | 612 |
| ☐ N613AA | Boeing 757-223/W | 24489/242 | | 613 |
| ☐ N614AA | Boeing 757-223/W | 24490/243 | | 614 |
| ☐ N615AM | Boeing 757-223/W | 24491/245 | | 615 |
| ☐ N616AA | Boeing 757-223/W | 24524/248 | | 616 |
| ☐ N617AM | Boeing 757-223/W | 24525/253 | | 617 |
| ☐ N618AA | Boeing 757-223/W | 24526/260 | | 618 |
| ☐ N619AA | Boeing 757-223/W | 24577/269 | | 619 |
| ☐ N620AA | Boeing 757-223/W | 24578/276 | | 620 |
| ☐ N621AM | Boeing 757-223/W | 24579/283 | | 621 |
| ☐ N622AA | Boeing 757-223/W | 24580/289 | | 622 |
| ☐ N623AA | Boeing 757-223/W | 24581/296 | | 623 |
| ☐ N624AA | Boeing 757-223/W | 24582/297 | | 624 |
| ☐ N625AA | Boeing 757-223/W | 24583/303 | | 625 |
| ☐ N626AA | Boeing 757-223/W | 24584/304 | | 626 | [ROW] |
| ☐ N627AA | Boeing 757-223/W | 24585/308 | | 627 | [ROW] |
| ☐ N628AA | Boeing 757-223/W | 24586/309 | | 628 |
| ☐ N629AA | Boeing 757-223/W | 24587/315 | | 629 |
| ☐ N630AA | Boeing 757-223/W | 24588/316 | | 630 |
| ☐ N631AA | Boeing 757-223/W | 24589/317 | | 631 |
| ☐ N632AA | Boeing 757-223/W | 24590/321 | | 632 | [ROW] |
| ☐ N633AA | Boeing 757-223/W | 24591/324 | | 633 |
| ☐ N634AA | Boeing 757-223/W | 24592/327 | | 634 |
| ☐ N635AA | Boeing 757-223/W | 24593/328 | | 635 |
| ☐ N636AM | Boeing 757-223/W | 24594/336 | | 636 |
| ☐ N637AM | Boeing 757-223/W | 24595/337 | | 637 |
| ☐ N638AA | Boeing 757-223/W | 24596/344 | | 638 |
| ☐ N639AA | Boeing 757-223/W | 24597/345 | | 639 |
| ☐ N640A | Boeing 757-223/W | 24598/350 | | 640 |
| ☐ N641AA | Boeing 757-223/W | 24599/351 | | 641 |
| ☐ N642AA | Boeing 757-223/W | 24600/357 | | 642 |
| ☐ N643AA | Boeing 757-223/W | 24601/360 | | 643 |
| ☐ N645AA | Boeing 757-223/W | 24603/370 | | 5BR |
| ☐ N646AA | Boeing 757-223/W | 24604/375 | | 5BS |
| ☐ N647AM | Boeing 757-223/W | 24605/378 | | 5BT |
| ☐ N648AA | Boeing 757-223/W | 24606/379 | | 5BU | [ROW] |
| ☐ N649AA | Boeing 757-223/W | 24607/383 | | 5BV |
| ☐ N650AA | Boeing 757-223/W | 24608/384 | | 5BW |
| ☐ N652AA | Boeing 757-223/W | 24610/391 | | 5BY |
| ☐ N653A | Boeing 757-223/W | 24611/397 | | 5CA |
| ☐ N654A | Boeing 757-223/W | 24612/398 | | 5CB |
| ☐ N655AA | Boeing 757-223/W | 24613/402 | | 5CC |
| ☐ N656AA | Boeing 757-223/W | 24614/404 | | 5CD |
| ☐ N657AM | Boeing 757-223/W | 24615/409 | | 5CE |

| | Registration | Type | Serial | Notes | Fleet | |
|---|---|---|---|---|---|---|
| ☐ | N658AA | Boeing 757-223/W | 24616/410 | | 5CF | |
| ☐ | N659AA | Boeing 757-223/W | 24617/417 | | 5CG Pride of American | |
| ☐ | N660AM | Boeing 757-223/W | 25294/418 | | 5CH | |
| ☐ | N662AA | Boeing 757-223/W | 25296/425 | | 5CK | |
| ☐ | N663AM | Boeing 757-223/W | 25297/432 | | 5CL | |
| ☐ | N664AA | Boeing 757-223/W | 25298/433 | | 5CM | [ROW] |
| ☐ | N665AA | Boeing 757-223/W | 25299/436 | | 5CN | |
| ☐ | N666A | Boeing 757-223/W | 25300/451 | | 5CP | |
| ☐ | N668AA | Boeing 757-223/W | 25333/460 | | 5CS | |
| ☐ | N669AA | Boeing 757-223/W | 25334/463 | | 5CT | |
| ☐ | N670AA | Boeing 757-223/W | 25335/468 | | 5CU | |
| ☐ | N671AA | Boeing 757-223/W | 25336/473 | | 5CV | |
| ☐ | N672AA | Boeing 757-223/W | 25337/474 | | 5CW | |
| ☐ | N673AN | Boeing 757-223/W | 29423/812 | | 5EE | |
| ☐ | N674AN | Boeing 757-223/W | 29424/816 | | 5EF | |
| ☐ | N675AN | Boeing 757-223/W | 29425/817 | | 5EG | |
| ☐ | N676AN | Boeing 757-223/W | 29426/827 | ex N1798B | 5EH | |
| ☐ | N677AN | Boeing 757-223/W | 29427/828 | | 5EJ | |
| ☐ | N678AN | Boeing 757-223/W | 29428/837 | ex N1787B | 5EK | |
| ☐ | N679AN | Boeing 757-223/W | 29589/842 | ex N1800B | 5EL Astrojet c/s | |
| ☐ | N680AN | Boeing 757-223/W | 29590/847 | | 5EM | |
| ☐ | N681AA | Boeing 757-223/W | 25338/483 | | 5CX | |
| ☐ | N682AA | Boeing 757-223/W | 25339/484 | | 5CY | |
| ☐ | N683A | Boeing 757-223/W | 25340/491 | | 5DA | |
| ☐ | N684AA | Boeing 757-223/W | 25341/504 | | 5DB | |
| ☐ | N685AA | Boeing 757-223/W | 25342/507 | | 5DC | |
| ☐ | N686AA | Boeing 757-223/W | 25343/509 | | 5DD | |
| ☐ | N687AA | Boeing 757-223ER/W | 25695/536 | | 5DE | |
| ☐ | N688AA | Boeing 757-223ER/W | 25730/548 | | 5DF | |
| ☐ | N689AA | Boeing 757-223ER/W | 25731/562 | | 5DG | |
| ☐ | N690AA | Boeing 757-223ER/W | 25696/566 | | 5DH | |
| ☐ | N691AA | Boeing 757-223ER/W | 25697/568 | | 5DJ | |
| ☐ | N692AA | Boeing 757-223/W | 26972/578 | | 5DK | |
| ☐ | N693AA | Boeing 757-223/W | 26973/580 | | 5DL | |
| ☐ | N694AN | Boeing 757-223/W | 26974/582 | | 5DM | |
| ☐ | N695AN | Boeing 757-223/W | 26975/621 | | 5DN | |
| ☐ | N696AN | Boeing 757-223/W | 26976/627 | | 5DP | |
| ☐ | N697AN | Boeing 757-223/W | 26977/633 | | 5DR | |
| ☐ | N698AN | Boeing 757-223/W | 26980/635 | | 5DS | |
| ☐ | N699AN | Boeing 757-223/W | 27051/660 | | 5DT | |
| ☐ | N7667A | Boeing 757-223/W | 25301/459 | | 5CR | |
| | | | | | | |
| ☐ | N319AA | Boeing 767-223ER | 22320/128 | | 319 | |
| ☐ | N320AA | Boeing 767-223ER | 22321/130 | | 320 | |
| ☐ | N321AA | Boeing 767-223ER | 22322/139 | | 321 | |
| ☐ | N322AA | Boeing 767-223ER | 22323/140 | | 322 | |
| ☐ | N323AA | Boeing 767-223ER | 22324/146 | | 323 | |
| ☐ | N324AA | Boeing 767-223ER | 22325/147 | | 324 | |
| ☐ | N325AA | Boeing 767-223ER | 22326/157 | | 325 | |
| ☐ | N327AA | Boeing 767-223ER | 22327/159 | | 327 | |
| ☐ | N328AA | Boeing 767-223ER | 22328/160 | | 328 | |
| ☐ | N329AA | Boeing 767-223ER | 22329/164 | | 329 | |
| ☐ | N332AA | Boeing 767-223ER | 22331/168 | | 332 | |
| ☐ | N335AA | Boeing 767-223ER | 22333/194 | | 335 | |
| ☐ | N336AA | Boeing 767-223ER | 22334/195 | | 336 | |
| ☐ | N338AA | Boeing 767-223ER | 22335/196 | | 338 | |
| ☐ | N339AA | Boeing 767-223ER | 22336/198 | | 339 | |
| ☐ | N342AN | Boeing 767-323ER | 33081/896 | | 342 | |
| ☐ | N343AN | Boeing 767-323ER | 33082/899 | | 343 | |
| ☐ | N344AN | Boeing 767-323ER | 33083/900 | | 344 | |
| ☐ | N345AN | Boeing 767-323ER/W | 33084/906 | | 345 | |
| ☐ | N346AN | Boeing 767-323ER | 33085/907 | | 346 | |
| ☐ | N347AN | Boeing 767-323ER | 33086/908 | | 347 | |
| ☐ | N348AN | Boeing 767-323ER | 33087/910 | | 348 | |
| ☐ | N349AN | Boeing 767-323ER | 33088/913 | | 349 | |
| ☐ | N350AN | Boeing 767-323ER | 33089/916 | | 350 | |
| ☐ | N351AA | Boeing 767-323ER | 24032/202 | | 351 | |
| ☐ | N352AA | Boeing 767-323ER | 24033/205 | | 352 | |
| ☐ | N353AA | Boeing 767-323ER/W | 24034/206 | | 353 | |
| ☐ | N354AA | Boeing 767-323ER/W | 24035/211 | | 354 | |
| ☐ | N355AA | Boeing 767-323ER | 24036/221 | | 355 | |
| ☐ | N357AA | Boeing 767-323ER | 24038/227 | | 357 | |
| ☐ | N358AA | Boeing 767-323ER | 24039/228 | | 358 | |
| ☐ | N359AA | Boeing 767-323ER/W | 24040/230 | | 359 | |
| ☐ | N360AA | Boeing 767-323ER/W | 24041/232 | | 360 | |
| ☐ | N361AA | Boeing 767-323ER/W | 24042/235 | | 361 | |
| ☐ | N362AA | Boeing 767-323ER/W | 24043/237 | | 362 | |
| ☐ | N363AA | Boeing 767-323ER/W | 24044/238 | | 363 | |
| ☐ | N366AA | Boeing 767-323ER | 25193/388 | | 366 | |
| ☐ | N368AA | Boeing 767-323ER | 25195/404 | | 368 | |
| ☐ | N369AA | Boeing 767-323ER | 25196/422 | | 369 | |
| ☐ | N370AA | Boeing 767-323ER/W | 25197/425 | | 370 | |

| | | | | | |
|---|---|---|---|---|---|
| ☐ | N371AA | Boeing 767-323ER | 25198/431 | | 371 |
| ☐ | N372AA | Boeing 767-323ER | 25199/433 | | 372 |
| ☐ | N373AA | Boeing 767-323ER/W | 25200/435 | | 373 |
| ☐ | N374AA | Boeing 767-323ER | 25201/437 | | 374 |
| ☐ | N376AN | Boeing 767-323ER | 25445/447 | | 376 |
| ☐ | N377AN | Boeing 767-323ER/W | 25446/453 | | 377 |
| ☐ | N378AN | Boeing 767-323ER | 25447/469 | | 378 |
| ☐ | N379AA | Boeing 767-323ER | 25448/481 | | 379 |
| ☐ | N380AN | Boeing 767-323ER/W | 25449/489 | | 380 |
| ☐ | N381AN | Boeing 767-323ER/W | 25450/495 | | 381 |
| ☐ | N382AN | Boeing 767-323ER/W | 25451/498 | | 382 |
| ☐ | N383AN | Boeing 767-323ER/W | 26995/500 | | 383 |
| ☐ | N384AA | Boeing 767-323ER | 26996/512 | | 384 |
| ☐ | N385AM | Boeing 767-323ER/W | 27059/536 | | 385 |
| ☐ | N386AA | Boeing 767-323ER | 27060/540 | | 386 |
| ☐ | N387AM | Boeing 767-323ER/W | 27184/541 | | 387 |
| ☐ | N388AA | Boeing 767-323ER | 27448/563 | | 388 |
| ☐ | N389AA | Boeing 767-323ER/W | 27449/564 | | 389 |
| ☐ | N390AA | Boeing 767-323ER | 27450/565 | | 390 |
| ☐ | N391AA | Boeing 767-323ER | 27451/566 | | 391 |
| ☐ | N392AN | Boeing 767-323ER | 29429/700 | | 392 |
| ☐ | N393AN | Boeing 767-323ER | 29430/701 | | 393 |
| ☐ | N394AN | Boeing 767-323ER | 29431/703 | | 394 |
| ☐ | N395AN | Boeing 767-323ER | 29432/709 | | 395 |
| ☐ | N396AN | Boeing 767-323ER | 29603/739 | | 396 |
| ☐ | N397AN | Boeing 767-323ER | 29604/744 | | 397 |
| ☐ | N398AN | Boeing 767-323ER | 29605/748 | | 398 |
| ☐ | N399AN | Boeing 767-323ER/W | 29606/752 | | 399 |
| ☐ | N7375A | Boeing 767-323ER | 25202/441 | | 375 |
| ☐ | N39356 | Boeing 767-323ER/W | 24037/226 | | 356 |
| ☐ | N39364 | Boeing 767-323ER/W | 24045/240 | | 364 |
| ☐ | N39365 | Boeing 767-323ER/W | 24046/241 | | 365 |
| ☐ | N39367 | Boeing 767-323ER | 25194/394 | | 367 |
| | | | | | |
| ☐ | N750AN | Boeing 777-223ER | 30259/332 | ex (N798AN) | 7BJ |
| ☐ | N751AN | Boeing 777-223ER | 30798/333 | | 7BK |
| ☐ | N752AN | Boeing 777-223ER | 30260/339 | ex (N799AN) | 7BL |
| ☐ | N753AN | Boeing 777-223ER | 30261/341 | ex (N750AN) | 7BM |
| ☐ | N754AN | Boeing 777-223ER | 30262/345 | | 7BN |
| ☐ | N755AN | Boeing 777-223ER | 30263/354 | | 7BP |
| ☐ | N756AM | Boeing 777-223ER | 30264/358 | | 7BR |
| ☐ | N757AN | Boeing 777-223ER | 32636/363 | | 7BS |
| ☐ | N758AN | Boeing 777-223ER | 32637/371 | | 7BT |
| ☐ | N759AN | Boeing 777-223ER | 32638/376 | | 7BU Pink Ribbon c/s |
| ☐ | N760AN | Boeing 777-223ER | 31477/379 | | 7BV |
| ☐ | N761AJ | Boeing 777-223ER | 31478/393 | | 7BW |
| ☐ | N762AN | Boeing 777-223ER | 31479/399 | | 7BX |
| ☐ | N763AN | Boeing 777-223ER | 31477/379 | | 7BV |
| ☐ | N764AN | Boeing 777-223ER | 32439 | | ♦ o/o♦ |
| ☐ | N765AN | Boeing 777-223ER | 32879/433 | | 7BY |
| ☐ | N766AN | Boeing 777-223ER | 32880/445 | | 7CA |
| ☐ | N767AJ | Boeing 777-223ER | 33539/555 | | 7CB |
| ☐ | N768AA | Boeing 777-223ER | 33540/566 | | 7CC |
| ☐ | N770AN | Boeing 777-223ER | 29578/185 | | 7AA |
| ☐ | N771AN | Boeing 777-223ER | 29579/190 | | 7AB |
| ☐ | N772AN | Boeing 777-223ER | 29580/198 | | 7AC |
| ☐ | N773AN | Boeing 777-223ER | 29583/199 | | 7AD |
| ☐ | N774AN | Boeing 777-223ER | 29581/208 | | 7AE |
| ☐ | N775AN | Boeing 777-223ER | 29584/209 | | 7AF |
| ☐ | N776AN | Boeing 777-223ER | 29582/215 | | 7AG |
| ☐ | N777AN | Boeing 777-223ER | 29585/218 | | 7AH |
| ☐ | N778AN | Boeing 777-223ER | 29587/223 | | 7AJ |
| ☐ | N779AN | Boeing 777-223ER | 29955/225 | | 7AK |
| ☐ | N780AN | Boeing 777-223ER | 29956/241 | ex N6055X | 7AL |
| ☐ | N781AN | Boeing 777-223ER | 29586/266 | | 7AM |
| ☐ | N782AN | Boeing 777-223ER | 30003/270 | | 7AN |
| ☐ | N783AN | Boeing 777-223ER | 30004/271 | | 7AP |
| ☐ | N784AN | Boeing 777-223ER | 29588/272 | | 7AR |
| ☐ | N785AN | Boeing 777-223ER | 30005/274 | | 7AS |
| ☐ | N786AN | Boeing 777-223ER | 30250/276 | | 7AT |
| ☐ | N787AL | Boeing 777-223ER | 30010/277 | | 7AU |
| ☐ | N788AN | Boeing 777-223ER | 30011/283 | | 7AV |
| ☐ | N789AN | Boeing 777-223ER | 30252/285 | | 7AW |
| ☐ | N790AN | Boeing 777-223ER | 30251/287 | | 7AX |
| ☐ | N791AN | Boeing 777-223ER | 30254/289 | | 7AY |
| ☐ | N792AN | Boeing 777-223ER | 30253/292 | | 7BA |
| ☐ | N793AN | Boeing 777-223ER | 30255/299 | | 7BB |
| ☐ | N794AN | Boeing 777-223ER | 30256/313 | | 7BC |
| ☐ | N795AN | Boeing 777-223ER | 30257/315 | | 7BD |
| ☐ | N796AN | Boeing 777-223ER | 30796/316 | | 7BE |
| ☐ | N797AN | Boeing 777-223ER | 30012/321 | ex (N796AN) | 7BF American Spirit |
| ☐ | N798AN | Boeing 777-223ER | 30797/324 | | 7BG |

| | | | | |
|---|---|---|---|---|
| ☐ N799AN | Boeing 777-223ER | 30258/328 | ex (N797AN) 7BH | |
| ☐ N208AA | McDonnell-Douglas MD-82 | 49159/1107 | 208 | [ROW] |
| ☐ N214AA | McDonnell-Douglas MD-82 | 49162/1110 | 214 | [ROW] |
| ☐ N223AA | McDonnell-Douglas MD-82 | 49173/1114 | 223 | [ROW] |
| ☐ N233AA | McDonnell-Douglas MD-82 | 49180/1124 | 233 | [ROW] |
| ☐ N249AA | McDonnell-Douglas MD-82 | 49269/1164 | 249 | [ROW] |
| ☐ N251AA | McDonnell-Douglas MD-82 | 49270/1165 | 251 | [ROW] |
| ☐ N258AA | McDonnell-Douglas MD-82 | 49288/1187 | 258 | [ROW] |
| ☐ N262AA | McDonnell-Douglas MD-82 | 49290/1195 | 262 | |
| ☐ N266AA | McDonnell-Douglas MD-82 | 49291/1210 | 266 | [ROW] |
| ☐ N271AA | McDonnell-Douglas MD-82 | 49293/1212 | 271 | [ROW] |
| ☐ N274AA | McDonnell-Douglas MD-82 | 49271/1166 | 274 | [ROW] |
| ☐ N278AA | McDonnell-Douglas MD-82 | 49294/1213 | 278 | |
| ☐ N279AA | McDonnell-Douglas MD-82 | 49295/1214 | 279 | [ROW] |
| ☐ N283AA | McDonnell-Douglas MD-82 | 49296/1215 | 283 | [ROW] |
| ☐ N287AA | McDonnell-Douglas MD-82 | 49299/1218 | 287 | [ROW] |
| ☐ N291AA | McDonnell-Douglas MD-82 | 49303/1222 | 291 | [ROW] |
| ☐ N293AA | McDonnell-Douglas MD-82 | 49305/1226 | 293 | [ROW] |
| ☐ N298AA | McDonnell-Douglas MD-82 | 49310/1247 | 298 | [ROW] |
| ☐ N403A | McDonnell-Douglas MD-82 | 49314/1256 | 403 | |
| ☐ N408AA | McDonnell-Douglas MD-82 | 49319/1266 | 408 | [ROW] |
| ☐ N410AA | McDonnell-Douglas MD-82 | 49321/1273 | 410 | [ROW] |
| ☐ N411AA | McDonnell-Douglas MD-82 | 49322/1280 | 411 | [ROW] |
| ☐ N413AA | McDonnell-Douglas MD-82 | 49324/1289 | 413 | [ROW] |
| ☐ N415AA | McDonnell-Douglas MD-82 | 49326/1295 | 415 | [ROW] |
| ☐ N417AA | McDonnell-Douglas MD-82 | 49328/1301 | 417 | [ROW] |
| ☐ N418AA | McDonnell-Douglas MD-82 | 49329/1302 | 418 | [ROW] |
| ☐ N419AA | McDonnell-Douglas MD-82 | 49331/1306 | 419 | [ROW] |
| ☐ N423AA | McDonnell-Douglas MD-82 | 49335/1320 | 423 | [ROW] |
| ☐ N424AA | McDonnell-Douglas MD-82 | 49336/1321 | 424 | |
| ☐ N426AA | McDonnell-Douglas MD-82 | 49338/1327 | 426 | |
| ☐ N427AA | McDonnell-Douglas MD-82 | 49339/1328 | 427 | [ROW] |
| ☐ N429AA | McDonnell-Douglas MD-82 | 49341/1336 | 429 | [ROW] |
| ☐ N431AA | McDonnell-Douglas MD-82 | 49343/1339 | 431 | [ROW] |
| ☐ N432AA | McDonnell-Douglas MD-82 | 49350/1376 | 432 | [ROW] |
| ☐ N452AA | McDonnell-Douglas MD-82 | 49553/1450 | 452 | [ROW] |
| ☐ N453AA | McDonnell-Douglas MD-82 | 49558/1451 | 453 | [ROW] |
| ☐ N454AA | McDonnell-Douglas MD-82 | 49559/1460 | 454 | |
| ☐ N455AA | McDonnell-Douglas MD-82 | 49560/1462 | 455 | |
| ☐ N456AA | McDonnell-Douglas MD-82 | 49561/1474 | 456 | |
| ☐ N457AA | McDonnell-Douglas MD-82 | 49562/1475 | 457 | [ROW] |
| ☐ N458AA | McDonnell-Douglas MD-82 | 49563/1485 | 458 | [ROW] |
| ☐ N459AA | McDonnell-Douglas MD-82 | 49564/1486 | 459 | [ROW] |
| ☐ N460AA | McDonnell-Douglas MD-82 | 49565/1496 | 460 | [ROW] |
| ☐ N461AA | McDonnell-Douglas MD-82 | 49566/1497 | 461 | [ROW] |
| ☐ N462AA | McDonnell-Douglas MD-82 | 49592/1505 | 462 | [ROW] |
| ☐ N463AA | McDonnell-Douglas MD-82 | 49593/1506 | 463 | [ROW] |
| ☐ N464AA | McDonnell-Douglas MD-82 | 49594/1507 | 464 | [ROW] |
| ☐ N466AA | McDonnell-Douglas MD-82 | 49596/1510 | 466 | |
| ☐ N467AA | McDonnell-Douglas MD-82 | 49597/1511 | 467 | |
| ☐ N468AA | McDonnell-Douglas MD-82 | 49598/1513 | 468 | |
| ☐ N469AA | McDonnell-Douglas MD-82 | 49599/1515 | 469 | |
| ☐ N470AA | McDonnell-Douglas MD-82 | 49600/1516 | 470 | |
| ☐ N471AA | McDonnell-Douglas MD-82 | 49601/1518 | 471 | |
| ☐ N472AA | McDonnell-Douglas MD-82 | 49647/1520 | 472 | |
| ☐ N473AA | McDonnell-Douglas MD-82 | 49648/1521 | 473 | |
| ☐ N474 | McDonnell-Douglas MD-82 | 49649/1526 | 474 | |
| ☐ N475AA | McDonnell-Douglas MD-82 | 49650/1527 | 475 | |
| ☐ N476AA | McDonnell-Douglas MD-82 | 49651/1528 | 476 | |
| ☐ N477AA | McDonnell-Douglas MD-82 | 49652/1529 | 477 | |
| ☐ N478AA | McDonnell-Douglas MD-82 | 49653/1534 | 478 | |
| ☐ N479AA | McDonnell-Douglas MD-82 | 49654/1535 | 479 | |
| ☐ N480AA | McDonnell-Douglas MD-82 | 49655/1536 | 480 | |
| ☐ N481AA | McDonnell-Douglas MD-82 | 49656/1545 | 481 | |
| ☐ N482AA | McDonnell-Douglas MD-82 | 49675/1546 | 482 | |
| ☐ N483A | McDonnell-Douglas MD-82 | 49676/1550 | 483 | |
| ☐ N484AA | McDonnell-Douglas MD-82 | 49677/1551 | 484 | |
| ☐ N485AA | McDonnell-Douglas MD-82 | 49678/1555 | 485 | |
| ☐ N486AA | McDonnell-Douglas MD-82 | 49679/1557 | 486 | |
| ☐ N487AA | McDonnell-Douglas MD-82 | 49680/1558 | 487 | |
| ☐ N488AA | McDonnell-Douglas MD-82 | 49681/1560 | 488 | |
| ☐ N489AA | McDonnell-Douglas MD-82 | 49682/1562 | 489 | |
| ☐ N490AA | McDonnell-Douglas MD-82 | 49683/1563 | 490 | |
| ☐ N491AA | McDonnell-Douglas MD-82 | 49684/1564 | 491 | |
| ☐ N492AA | McDonnell-Douglas MD-82 | 49730/1565 | 492 | |
| ☐ N493AA | McDonnell-Douglas MD-82 | 49731/1566 | 493 | |
| ☐ N494AA | McDonnell-Douglas MD-82 | 49732/1567 | 494 | |
| ☐ N495AA | McDonnell-Douglas MD-82 | 49733/1607 | 495 | |
| ☐ N496AA | McDonnell-Douglas MD-82 | 49734/1619 | 496 | |
| ☐ N497AA | McDonnell-Douglas MD-82 | 49735/1635 | 497 | |
| ☐ N498AA | McDonnell-Douglas MD-82 | 49736/1640 | 498 | |

| | Registration | Type | c/n | ex | Fleet | |
|---|---|---|---|---|---|---|
| ☐ | N499AA | McDonnell-Douglas MD-82 | 49737/1641 | | 499 | |
| ☐ | N501AA | McDonnell-Douglas MD-82 | 49738/1648 | | 501 | |
| ☐ | N505AA | McDonnell-Douglas MD-82 | 49799/1652 | | 505 | |
| ☐ | N510AM | McDonnell-Douglas MD-82 | 49804/1669 | | 510 | |
| ☐ | N513AA | McDonnell-Douglas MD-82 | 49890/1686 | | 513 | |
| ☐ | N516AM | McDonnell-Douglas MD-82 | 49893/1696 | | 516 | |
| ☐ | N552AA | McDonnell-Douglas MD-82 | 53034/1826 | | 552 | |
| ☐ | N553AA | McDonnell-Douglas MD-82 | 53083/1828 | | 553 | |
| ☐ | N554AA | McDonnell-Douglas MD-82 | 53084/1830 | | 554 | |
| ☐ | N555AN | McDonnell-Douglas MD-82 | 53085/1839 | | 555 | |
| ☐ | N556AA | McDonnell-Douglas MD-82 | 53086/1840 | | 556 | |
| ☐ | N557AN | McDonnell-Douglas MD-82 | 53087/1841 | | 557 | |
| ☐ | N558AA | McDonnell-Douglas MD-82 | 53088/1852 | | 558 | |
| ☐ | N559AA | McDonnell-Douglas MD-82 | 53089/1853 | | 559 | |
| ☐ | N560AA | McDonnell-Douglas MD-82 | 53090/1858 | | 560 | |
| ☐ | N561AA | McDonnell-Douglas MD-82 | 53091/1863 | | 561 | |
| ☐ | N573AA | McDonnell-Douglas MD-82 | 53092/1864 | | 573 | |
| ☐ | N574AA | McDonnell-Douglas MD-82 | 53151/1866 | | 574 | |
| ☐ | N575AM | McDonnell-Douglas MD-82 | 53152/1875 | | 575 | |
| ☐ | N576AA | McDonnell-Douglas MD-82 | 53153/1876 | | 576 | |
| ☐ | N577AA | McDonnell-Douglas MD-82 | 53154/1878 | | 577 | |
| ☐ | N578AA | McDonnell-Douglas MD-82 | 53155/1883 | | 578 | |
| ☐ | N579AA | McDonnell-Douglas MD-82 | 53156/1884 | | 579 | |
| ☐ | N580AA | McDonnell-Douglas MD-82 | 53157/1885 | | 580 | |
| ☐ | N581AA | McDonnell-Douglas MD-82 | 53158/1891 | | 581 | |
| ☐ | N582AA | McDonnell-Douglas MD-82 | 53159/1892 | | 582 | |
| ☐ | N583AA | McDonnell-Douglas MD-82 | 53160/1893 | | 583 | |
| ☐ | N584AA | McDonnell-Douglas MD-82 | 53247/1902 | | 584 | |
| ☐ | N585AA | McDonnell-Douglas MD-82 | 53248/1903 | | 585 | |
| ☐ | N586AA | McDonnell-Douglas MD-82 | 53249/1904 | | 586 | |
| ☐ | N587AA | McDonnell-Douglas MD-82 | 53250/1907 | | 587 | |
| ☐ | N931TW | McDonnell-Douglas MD-82 | 49527/1382 | | 4WA | |
| ☐ | N953U | McDonnell-Douglas MD-82 | 49267/1239 | | 4UA | [ROW] |
| ☐ | N954U | McDonnell-Douglas MD-82 | 49426/1399 | ex N786JA | 4UB | |
| ☐ | N955U | McDonnell-Douglas MD-82 | 49427/1401 | ex N787JA | 4UC | |
| ☐ | N3507A | McDonnell-Douglas MD-82 | 49801/1661 | | 507 | |
| ☐ | N3515 | McDonnell-Douglas MD-82 | 49892/1695 | | 515 | |
| ☐ | N7506 | McDonnell-Douglas MD-82 | 49800/1660 | | 506 | |
| ☐ | N7508 | McDonnell-Douglas MD-82 | 49802/1662 | | 508 | |
| ☐ | N7509 | McDonnell-Douglas MD-82 | 49803/1663 | | 509 | |
| ☐ | N7512A | McDonnell-Douglas MD-82 | 49806/1673 | | 512 | |
| ☐ | N7514A | McDonnell-Douglas MD-82 | 49891/1694 | | 514 | |
| ☐ | N7517A | McDonnell-Douglas MD-82 | 49894/1697 | | 517 | |
| ☐ | N7518A | McDonnell-Douglas MD-82 | 49895/1698 | | 518 | |
| ☐ | N7519A | McDonnell-Douglas MD-82 | 49896/1707 | | 519 | |
| ☐ | N7520A | McDonnell-Douglas MD-82 | 49897/1708 | | 520 | |
| ☐ | N7521A | McDonnell-Douglas MD-82 | 49898/1709 | | 521 | |
| ☐ | N7522A | McDonnell-Douglas MD-82 | 49899/1722 | | 522 | |
| ☐ | N7525A | McDonnell-Douglas MD-82 | 49917/1735 | | 525 | |
| ☐ | N7526A | McDonnell-Douglas MD-82 | 49918/1743 | | 526 | |
| ☐ | N7527A | McDonnell-Douglas MD-82 | 49919/1744 | | 527 | |
| ☐ | N7528A | McDonnell-Douglas MD-82 | 49920/1750 | | 528 | |
| ☐ | N7530 | McDonnell-Douglas MD-82 | 49922/1753 | | 530 | |
| ☐ | N7531A | McDonnell-Douglas MD-82 | 49923/1758 | | 531 | |
| ☐ | N7532A | McDonnell-Douglas MD-82 | 49924/1759 | | 532 | |
| ☐ | N7535A | McDonnell-Douglas MD-82 | 49989/1769 | | 535 | |
| ☐ | N7536A | McDonnell-Douglas MD-82 | 49990/1770 | | 536 | |
| ☐ | N7537A | McDonnell-Douglas MD-82 | 49991/1780 | | 537 | |
| ☐ | N7538A | McDonnell-Douglas MD-82 | 49992/1781 | | 538 | |
| ☐ | N7539A | McDonnell-Douglas MD-82 | 49993/1782 | | 539 | |
| ☐ | N7540A | McDonnell-Douglas MD-82 | 49994/1790 | | 540 | |
| ☐ | N7541A | McDonnell-Douglas MD-82 | 49995/1791 | | 541 | |
| ☐ | N7542A | McDonnell-Douglas MD-82 | 49996/1792 | | 542 | |
| ☐ | N7543A | McDonnell-Douglas MD-82 | 53025/1802 | | 543 | |
| ☐ | N7544A | McDonnell-Douglas MD-82 | 53026/1804 | | 544 | |
| ☐ | N7546A | McDonnell-Douglas MD-82 | 53028/1813 | | 546 | |
| ☐ | N7547A | McDonnell-Douglas MD-82 | 53029/1814 | | 547 | |
| ☐ | N7548A | McDonnell-Douglas MD-82 | 53030/1816 | | 548 | |
| ☐ | N7549A | McDonnell-Douglas MD-82 | 53031/1819 | | 549 | |
| ☐ | N7550 | McDonnell-Douglas MD-82 | 53032/1820 | | 550 | |
| ☐ | N14551 | McDonnell-Douglas MD-82 | 53033/1822 | | 551 | |
| ☐ | N16545 | McDonnell-Douglas MD-82 | 53027/1805 | | 545 | |
| ☐ | N33502 | McDonnell-Douglas MD-82 | 49739/1649 | | 502 | |
| ☐ | N44503 | McDonnell-Douglas MD-82 | 49797/1650 | | 503 | |
| ☐ | N59523 | McDonnell-Douglas MD-82 | 49915/1723 | | 523 | [ROW] |
| ☐ | N70401 | McDonnell-Douglas MD-82 | 49312/1249 | | 401 | |
| ☐ | N70425 | McDonnell-Douglas MD-82 | 49337/1325 | | 425 | |
| ☐ | N70504 | McDonnell-Douglas MD-82 | 49798/1651 | | 504 | |
| ☐ | N70524 | McDonnell-Douglas MD-82 | 49916/1729 | | 524 | |
| ☐ | N70529 | McDonnell-Douglas MD-82 | 49921/1752 | | 529 | |
| ☐ | N90511 | McDonnell-Douglas MD-82 | 49805/1672 | | 511 | |

| | | | | | |
|---|---|---|---|---|---|
| ☐ N110HM | McDonnell-Douglas MD-83 | 49787/1636 | ex HL7274 | 4WU | |
| ☐ N433AA | McDonnell-Douglas MD-83 | 49451/1388 | | 433 | |
| ☐ N434AA | McDonnell-Douglas MD-83 | 49452/1389 | | 434 | |
| ☐ N435AA | McDonnell-Douglas MD-83 | 49453/1390 | | 435 | |
| ☐ N436AA | McDonnell-Douglas MD-83 | 49454/1391 | | 436 | |
| ☐ N437AA | McDonnell-Douglas MD-83 | 49455/1392 | | 437 | |
| ☐ N438AA | McDonnell-Douglas MD-83 | 49456/1393 | | 438 | |
| ☐ N439AA | McDonnell-Douglas MD-83 | 49457/1398 | | 439 | |
| ☐ N564AA | McDonnell-Douglas MD-83 | 49346/1372 | | 564 | |
| ☐ N565AA | McDonnell-Douglas MD-83 | 49347/1373 | | 565 | |
| ☐ N566AA | McDonnell-Douglas MD-83 | 49348/1374 | | 566 | |
| ☐ N567AM | McDonnell-Douglas MD-83 | 53293/2021 | | 567 | |
| ☐ N568AA | McDonnell-Douglas MD-83 | 49349/1375 | | 568 | |
| ☐ N569AA | McDonnell-Douglas MD-83 | 49351/1385 | | 569 | [TUL] |
| ☐ N570AA | McDonnell-Douglas MD-83 | 49352/1386 | | 570 | |
| ☐ N571AA | McDonnell-Douglas MD-83 | 49353/1387 | | 571 | [TUL] |
| ☐ N588AA | McDonnell-Douglas MD-83 | 53251/1909 | | 588 | |
| ☐ N589AA | McDonnell-Douglas MD-83 | 53252/1910 | | 589 | [ROW] |
| ☐ N590AA | McDonnell-Douglas MD-83 | 53253/1919 | | 590 | [ROW] |
| ☐ N591AA | McDonnell-Douglas MD-83 | 53254/1920 | | 591 | [ROW] |
| ☐ N592AA | McDonnell-Douglas MD-83 | 53255/1932 | | 592 | |
| ☐ N593AA | McDonnell-Douglas MD-83 | 53256/1933 | | 593 | |
| ☐ N594AA | McDonnell-Douglas MD-83 | 53284/1966 | | 594 | |
| ☐ N595AA | McDonnell-Douglas MD-83 | 53285/1989 | | 595 | |
| ☐ N596AA | McDonnell-Douglas MD-83 | 53286/2000 | | 596 | |
| ☐ N597AA | McDonnell-Douglas MD-83 | 53287/2006 | | 597 | |
| ☐ N598AA | McDonnell-Douglas MD-83 | 53288/2011 | | 598 | |
| ☐ N599AA | McDonnell-Douglas MD-83 | 53289/2012 | | 599 | |
| ☐ N941AS | McDonnell-Douglas MD-83 | 49925/1616 | | 4UK | [ROW] |
| ☐ N948TW | McDonnell-Douglas MD-83 | 49575/1414 | ex EI-BWD | 4WS | Wings of Pride |
| ☐ N951TW | McDonnell-Douglas MD-83 | 53470/2135 | ex N978AS | 4XA | |
| ☐ N961TW | McDonnell-Douglas MD-83 | 53611/2264 | | 4XT | |
| ☐ N962TW | McDonnell-Douglas MD-83 | 53612/2265 | | 4XU | |
| ☐ N963TW | McDonnell-Douglas MD-83 | 53613/2266 | | 4XV | |
| ☐ N964TW | McDonnell-Douglas MD-83 | 53614/2267 | | 4XW | |
| ☐ N965TW | McDonnell-Douglas MD-83 | 53615/2268 | | 4XX | |
| ☐ N966TW | McDonnell-Douglas MD-83 | 53616/2269 | | 4XY | |
| ☐ N967TW | McDonnell-Douglas MD-83 | 53617/2270 | | 4YA | |
| ☐ N968TW | McDonnell-Douglas MD-83 | 53618/2271 | | 4YB | |
| ☐ N969TW | McDonnell-Douglas MD-83 | 53619/2272 | | 4YC | |
| ☐ N970TW | McDonnell-Douglas MD-83 | 53620/2273 | | 4YD | [TUL] |
| ☐ N971TW | McDonnell-Douglas MD-83 | 53621/2274 | | 4YE | [TUL] |
| ☐ N972TW | McDonnell-Douglas MD-83 | 53622/2275 | | 4YF | |
| ☐ N973TW | McDonnell-Douglas MD-83 | 53623/2276 | | 4YG | |
| ☐ N974TW | McDonnell-Douglas MD-83 | 53624/2277 | | 4YH | |
| ☐ N975TW | McDonnell-Douglas MD-83 | 53625/2278 | | 4YJ | |
| ☐ N976TW | McDonnell-Douglas MD-83 | 53626/2279 | | 4YK | |
| ☐ N978TW | McDonnell-Douglas MD-83 | 53628/2281 | | 4YM | |
| ☐ N979TW | McDonnell-Douglas MD-83 | 53629/2282 | | 4YN | |
| ☐ N980TW | McDonnell-Douglas MD-83 | 53630/2283 | | 4YP | |
| ☐ N982TW | McDonnell-Douglas MD-83 | 53632/2285 | | 4YR | |
| ☐ N983TW | McDonnell-Douglas MD-83 | 53633/2286 | | 4YS | |
| ☐ N984TW | McDonnell-Douglas MD-83 | 53634/2287 | | 4YT | Spirit of Long Beach |
| ☐ N9302B | McDonnell-Douglas MD-83 | 49528/1383 | | 4WB | |
| ☐ N9304C | McDonnell-Douglas MD-83 | 49530/1397 | | 4WD | |
| ☐ N9401W | McDonnell-Douglas MD-83 | 53137/1872 | ex N9001L | 4WJ | |
| ☐ N9402W | McDonnell-Douglas MD-83 | 53138/1886 | ex N9001D | 4WK | |
| ☐ N9403W | McDonnell-Douglas MD-83 | 53139/1899 | ex N9035C | 4WL | |
| ☐ N9404V | McDonnell-Douglas MD-83 | 53140/1923 | ex N9075H | 4WM | |
| ☐ N9405T | McDonnell-Douglas MD-83 | 53141/1935 | | 4WN | |
| ☐ N9406W | McDonnell-Douglas MD-83 | 53126/2026 | ex N6203U | 4WP | |
| ☐ N9407R | McDonnell-Douglas MD-83 | 49400/1356 | ex EI-CKB | 4WR | |
| ☐ N9409F | McDonnell-Douglas MD-83 | 53121/1971 | ex N532MD | 4WT | |
| ☐ N9412W | McDonnell-Douglas MD-83 | 53187/2118 | | 4WV | |
| ☐ N9413T | McDonnell-Douglas MD-83 | 53188/2119 | | 4WW | |
| ☐ N9414W | McDonnell-Douglas MD-83 | 53189/2121 | | 4WX | [ROW] |
| ☐ N9420D | McDonnell-Douglas MD-83 | 49824/1554 | ex 9Y-THU | 4WY | |
| ☐ N9615W | McDonnell-Douglas MD-83 | 53562/2192 | | 4XB | |
| ☐ N9616G | McDonnell-Douglas MD-83 | 53563/2196 | | 4XC | |
| ☐ N9617R | McDonnell-Douglas MD-83 | 53564/2199 | | 4XD | |
| ☐ N9618A | McDonnell-Douglas MD-83 | 53565/2201 | | 4XE | |
| ☐ N9619V | McDonnell-Douglas MD-83 | 53566/2206 | | 4XF | |
| ☐ N9620D | McDonnell-Douglas MD-83 | 53591/2208 | | 4XG | |
| ☐ N9621A | McDonnell-Douglas MD-83 | 53592/2234 | | 4XH | |
| ☐ N9622A | McDonnell-Douglas MD-83 | 53593/2239 | | 4XJ | |
| ☐ N9624T | McDonnell-Douglas MD-83 | 53594/2241 | | 4XK | |
| ☐ N9625W | McDonnell-Douglas MD-83 | 53595/2244 | | 4XL | |
| ☐ N9626F | McDonnell-Douglas MD-83 | 53596/2247 | | 4XM | |
| ☐ N9627R | McDonnell-Douglas MD-83 | 53597/2249 | | 4XN | |
| ☐ N9628W | McDonnell-Douglas MD-83 | 53598/2252 | | 4XP | |
| ☐ N9629H | McDonnell-Douglas MD-83 | 53599/2254 | | 4XR | |
| ☐ N9630A | McDonnell-Douglas MD-83 | 53561/2174 | ex N90126 | 4XS | |

| | | | | |
|---|---|---|---|---|
| ☐ N9677W | McDonnell-Douglas MD-83 | 53627/2280 | | 4YL |
| ☐ N9681B | McDonnell-Douglas MD-83 | 53631/2284 | ex (N981TW) | 4XT |
| ☐ N76200 | McDonnell-Douglas MD-83 | 53290/2013 | | 200 |
| ☐ N76201 | McDonnell-Douglas MD-83 | 53291/2019 | | 201 |
| ☐ N76202 | McDonnell-Douglas MD-83 | 53292/2020 | | 202 |
| | | | | |
| ☐ N717AN | Boeing 777-323ER | 31543/ | | o/o♦ |
| ☐ N718AN | Boeing 777-323ER | 41665/ | | o/o♦ |

## AMERICAN CONNECTION — Waterski (AX/LOF)
### Indianapolis, IN/St Louis-Lambert Intl, MO (IND/STL)

| | | | | |
|---|---|---|---|---|
| ☐ N295SK | Embraer ERJ-140LR | 145513 | ex PT-SYF | Chautauqua |
| ☐ N297SK | Embraer ERJ-140LR | 145522 | ex PT-SYN | Chautauqua |
| ☐ N299SK | Embraer ERJ-140LR | 145532 | ex PT-STW | Chautauqua |
| ☐ N371SK | Embraer ERJ-140LR | 145535 | ex PT-STZ | Chautauqua |
| ☐ N372SK | Embraer ERJ-140LR | 145538 | ex PT-SZC | Chautauqua |
| ☐ N373SK | Embraer ERJ-140LR | 145543 | ex PT-SZG | Chautauqua |
| ☐ N374SK | Embraer ERJ-140LR | 145544 | ex PT-SZH | Chautauqua |
| ☐ N375SK | Embraer ERJ-140LR | 145569 | ex PT-SBF | Chautauqua |
| ☐ N376SK | Embraer ERJ-140LR | 145578 | ex PT-SBO | Chautauqua |
| ☐ N377SK | Embraer ERJ-140LR | 145579 | ex PT-SBP | Chautauqua |
| ☐ N378SK | Embraer ERJ-140LR | 145593 | ex PT-SCC | Chautauqua |
| ☐ N379SK | Embraer ERJ-140LR | 145606 | ex PT-SCP | Chautauqua |
| ☐ N380SK | Embraer ERJ-140LR | 145613 | ex PT-SCX | Chautauqua |
| ☐ N381SK | Embraer ERJ-140LR | 145619 | ex PT-SDH | Chautauqua |
| ☐ N382SK | Embraer ERJ-140LR | 145624 | ex PT-SDM | Chautauqua |

## AMERICAN EAGLE — Eagle Flight (MQ/EGF)
### Dallas-Fort Worth, TX (DFW)

| | | | |
|---|---|---|---|
| ☐ N288AM | ATR 72-212 | 0288 | ex F-WWLP |
| ☐ N322AC | ATR 72-212 | 0320 | ex N320AT |
| ☐ N342AT | ATR 72-212 | 0345 | ex N345AT |
| ☐ N348AE | ATR 72-212 | 0349 | ex N349AT |
| ☐ N355AT | ATR 72-212 | 0355 | ex F-WWEQ |
| ☐ N407AT | ATR 72-212 | 0407 | ex F-WWEL |
| ☐ N408AT | ATR 72-212 | 0408 | ex F-WWEM |
| ☐ N410AT | ATR 72-212 | 0410 | ex F-WWLS |
| ☐ N414WF | ATR 72-212 | 0414 | ex F-WWLD |
| ☐ N417AT | ATR 72-212 | 0417 | ex F-WWIT |
| ☐ N420AT | ATR 72-212 | 0420 | ex F-WWLY |
| ☐ N425MJ | ATR 72-212 | 0425 | ex F-WWEC |
| ☐ N426AT | ATR 72-212 | 0426 | ex F-WWED |
| ☐ N429AT | ATR 72-212 | 0429 | ex F-WWEH |
| ☐ N431AT | ATR 72-212 | 0431 | ex F-WWEI |
| ☐ N447AM | ATR 72-212 | 0447 | ex F-WWEC |
| ☐ N448AM | ATR 72-212 | 0448 | ex F-WWED |
| ☐ N451AT | ATR 72-212 | 0451 | ex F-WWES |
| | | | |
| ☐ N500AE | Canadair CRJ-701ER | 10025 | ex C-GJEX |
| ☐ N501BG | Canadair CRJ-701ER | 10017 | ex C-GIAH |
| ☐ N502AE | Canadair CRJ-701ER | 10018 | ex C-GJUI |
| ☐ N503AE | Canadair CRJ-701ER | 10021 | ex C-GIAP |
| ☐ N504AE | Canadair CRJ-701ER | 10044 | ex C-GHZZ |
| ☐ N505AE | Canadair CRJ-701ER | 10053 | ex C-GIAU |
| ☐ N506AE | Canadair CRJ-701ER | 10056 | ex C-GIAX |
| ☐ N507AE | Canadair CRJ-701ER | 10059 | ex C-GIBH |
| ☐ N508AE | Canadair CRJ-701ER | 10072 | ex C-GHZV |
| ☐ N509AE | Canadair CRJ-701ER | 10078 | ex C-GZUC |
| ☐ N510AE | Canadair CRJ-701ER | 10105 | |
| ☐ N511AE | Canadair CRJ-701ER | 10107 | |
| ☐ N512AE | Canadair CRJ-701ER | 10110 | |
| ☐ N513AE | Canadair CRJ-701ER | 10114 | |
| ☐ N514AE | Canadair CRJ-701ER | 10119 | |
| ☐ N515AE | Canadair CRJ-701ER | 10121 | |
| ☐ N516AE | Canadair CRJ-701ER | 10123 | |
| ☐ N517AE | Canadair CRJ-701ER | 10124 | |
| ☐ N518AE | Canadair CRJ-701ER | 10126 | |
| ☐ N519AE | Canadair CRJ-701ER | 10131 | |
| ☐ N520DC | Canadair CRJ-701ER | 10140 | |
| ☐ N521AE | Canadair CRJ-701ER | 10142 | |
| ☐ N522AE | Canadair CRJ-701ER | 10147 | |
| ☐ N523AE | Canadair CRJ-701ER | 10152 | |
| ☐ N524AE | Canadair CRJ-701ER | 10154 | |
| ☐ N525AE | Canadair CRJ-702ER | 10302 | ex C-GIAX |
| ☐ N526EA | Canadair CRJ-702ER | 10304 | ex C-GICL |
| ☐ N527EA | Canadair CRJ-702ER | 10305 | ex C-GIAP |
| ☐ N528EG | Canadair CRJ-702ER | 10306 | |
| ☐ N529EA | Canadair CRJ-702ER | 10307 | |
| ☐ N530EA | Canadair CRJ-702ER | 10308 | |
| ☐ N531EG | Canadair CRJ-702ER | 10309 | ex C-GIAO |

| | | | | | |
|---|---|---|---|---|---|
| ☐ | N532EA | Canadair CRJ-702ER | 10310 | ex C-GIBJ | |
| ☐ | N533AE | Canadair CRJ-702ER | 10311 | ex C-GIBR | |
| ☐ | N534AE | Canadair CRJ-702ER | 10312 | ex C-GZQA | |
| ☐ | N535EA | Canadair CRJ-702ER | 10313 | ex C-GZQX | |
| ☐ | N536EA | Canadair CRJ-702ER | 10315 | ex C-GIAH | |
| ☐ | N537EA | Canadair CRJ-702ER | 10316 | ex C-GIAP | |
| ☐ | N538EG | Canadair CRJ-702ER | 10317 | | |
| ☐ | N539EA | Canadair CRJ-702ER | 10318 | | |
| ☐ | N540EG | Canadair CRJ-702ER | 10319 | ex CGIAV- | |
| ☐ | N541EA | Canadair CRJ-702ER | 10320 | ex C-GZQF | ◆ |
| ☐ | N542EA | Canadair CRJ-702ER | 10321 | ex C-GZQI | ◆ |
| ☐ | N543EA | Canadair CRJ-702ER | 10323 | ex C-GZQV | ◆ |
| ☐ | N544EA | Canadair CRJ-702ER | 10324 | ex C-GICL | ◆ |
| ☐ | N545PB | Canadair CRJ-702ER | 10325 | ex C-GZQO | ◆ |
| ☐ | N546FF | Canadair CRJ-702ER | 10326 | ex C-GZQP | ◆ |
| | | | | | |
| ☐ | N700LE | Embraer ERJ-135LR | 145156 | ex PT-SFC | [IGM] |
| ☐ | N701MH | Embraer ERJ-135LR | 145162 | ex PT-SFD | [IGM] |
| ☐ | N702AE | Embraer ERJ-135LR | 145164 | ex PT-SFE | [IGM] |
| ☐ | N703MR | Embraer ERJ-135LR | 145173 | ex PT-SFG | [IGM] |
| ☐ | N704PG | Embraer ERJ-135LR | 145174 | ex PT-SFH | [IGM] |
| ☐ | N705AE | Embraer ERJ-135LR | 145184 | ex PT-SFJ | [IGM] |
| ☐ | N706RG | Embraer ERJ-135LR | 145194 | ex PT-SFO | [IGM] |
| ☐ | N707EB | Embraer ERJ-135LR | 145195 | ex PT-SFP | [IGM] |
| ☐ | N708AE | Embraer ERJ-135LR | 145205 | ex PT-SFR | [IGM] |
| ☐ | N709GB | Embraer ERJ-135LR | 145211 | ex PT-SFV | [IGM] |
| ☐ | N710TB | Embraer ERJ-135LR | 145224 | ex PT-SFZ | [IGM] |
| ☐ | N711PH | Embraer ERJ-135LR | 145235 | ex PT-SJC | |
| ☐ | N712AE | Embraer ERJ-135LR | 145247 | ex PT-SJG | |
| ☐ | N713AE | Embraer ERJ-135LR | 145249 | ex PT-SJH | |
| ☐ | N715AE | Embraer ERJ-135LR | 145262 | ex PT-SIV | [IGM] |
| ☐ | N716AE | Embraer ERJ-135LR | 145264 | ex PT-SIW | |
| ☐ | N717AE | Embraer ERJ-135LR | 145272 | ex PT-SJO | |
| ☐ | N718AE | Embraer ERJ-135LR | 145275 | ex PT-SJR | [IGM] |
| ☐ | N719AE | Embraer ERJ-135LR | 145276 | ex PT-SJS | |
| ☐ | N720AE | Embraer ERJ-135LR | 145279 | ex PT-SJV | |
| ☐ | N721HS | Embraer ERJ-135LR | 145283 | ex PT-S JZ | |
| ☐ | N722AE | Embraer ERJ-135LR | 145287 | ex PT-SKE | |
| ☐ | N723AE | Embraer ERJ-135LR | 145288 | ex PT-SKF | |
| ☐ | N724AE | Embraer ERJ-135LR | 145301 | ex PT-SKS | |
| ☐ | N725AE | Embraer ERJ-135LR | 145312 | ex PT-SMD | |
| ☐ | N726AE | Embraer ERJ-135LR | 145314 | ex PT-SMF | [IGM] |
| ☐ | N727AE | Embraer ERJ-135LR | 145326 | ex PT-SMS | [IGM] |
| ☐ | N728AE | Embraer ERJ-135LR | 145328 | ex PT-SMU | |
| ☐ | N729AE | Embraer ERJ-135LR | 145343 | ex PT-SNJ | [IGM] |
| ☐ | N730KW | Embraer ERJ-135LR | 145346 | ex PT-SNM | |
| ☐ | N731BE | Embraer ERJ-135LR | 145356 | ex PT-SNV | [IGM] |
| ☐ | N732DH | Embraer ERJ-135LR | 145358 | ex PT-SNX | [IGM] |
| ☐ | N733KR | Embraer ERJ-135LR | 145368 | ex PT-SOT | |
| ☐ | N734EK | Embraer ERJ-135LR | 145371 | ex PT-SOW | |
| ☐ | N735TS | Embraer ERJ-135LR | 145386 | ex PT-SQK | |
| ☐ | N736DT | Embraer ERJ-135LR | 145388 | ex PT-SQM | |
| ☐ | N737MW | Embraer ERJ-135LR | 145396 | ex PT-SQT | |
| ☐ | N738NR | Embraer ERJ-135LR | 145401 | ex PT-SQY | |
| ☐ | N739AE | Embraer ERJ-135LR | 145402 | ex PT-SQZ | |
| | | | | | |
| ☐ | N800AE | Embraer ERJ-140LR | 145425 | ex PT-XGF | |
| ☐ | N801AE | Embraer ERJ-140LR | 145469 | ex PT-SVO | |
| ☐ | N802AE | Embraer ERJ-140LR | 145471 | ex PT-SVQ | |
| ☐ | N803AE | Embraer ERJ-140LR | 145483 | ex PT-SXC | 100th RJ  Spirit of Eagle titles |
| ☐ | N804AE | Embraer ERJ-140LR | 145487 | ex PT-SXG | |
| ☐ | N805AE | Embraer ERJ-140LR | 145489 | ex PT-SXI | |
| ☐ | N806AE | Embraer ERJ-140LR | 145503 | ex PT-SXW | |
| ☐ | N807AE | Embraer ERJ-140LR | 145506 | ex PT-SXZ | Make A Wish c/s |
| ☐ | N808AE | Embraer ERJ-140LR | 145519 | ex PT-SYK | |
| ☐ | N809AE | Embraer ERJ-140LR | 145521 | ex PT-SYM | |
| ☐ | N810AE | Embraer ERJ-140LR | 145525 | ex PT-SYQ | |
| ☐ | N811AE | Embraer ERJ-140LR | 145529 | ex PT-STT | |
| ☐ | N812AE | Embraer ERJ-140LR | 145531 | ex PT-STV | |
| ☐ | N813AE | Embraer ERJ-140LR | 145539 | ex PT-SZD | |
| ☐ | N814AE | Embraer ERJ-140LR | 145541 | ex PT-SZF | |
| ☐ | N815AE | Embraer ERJ-140LR | 145545 | ex PT-SZI | |
| ☐ | N816AE | Embraer ERJ-140LR | 145552 | ex PT-SZO | |
| ☐ | N817AE | Embraer ERJ-140LR | 145554 | ex PT-SZQ | |
| ☐ | N818AE | Embraer ERJ-140LR | 145561 | ex PT-SZW | |
| ☐ | N819AE | Embraer ERJ-140LR | 145566 | ex PT-SBC | |
| ☐ | N820AE | Embraer ERJ-140LR | 145576 | ex PT-SBM | |
| ☐ | N821AE | Embraer ERJ-140LR | 145577 | ex PT-SBN | |
| ☐ | N822AE | Embraer ERJ-140LR | 145581 | ex PT-SBS | |
| ☐ | N823AE | Embraer ERJ-140LR | 145582 | ex PT-SBT | |
| ☐ | N824AE | Embraer ERJ-140LR | 145584 | ex PT-SBV | |
| ☐ | N825AE | Embraer ERJ-140LR | 145589 | ex PT-SBZ | |

| | | | |
|---|---|---|---|
| ☐ N826AE | Embraer ERJ-140LR | 145592 | ex PT-SCA |
| ☐ N827AE | Embraer ERJ-140LR | 145602 | ex PT-SCL |
| ☐ N828AE | Embraer ERJ-140LR | 145604 | ex PT-SCN |
| ☐ N829AE | Embraer ERJ-140LR | 145609 | ex PT-SCS |
| ☐ N830AE | Embraer ERJ-140LR | 145615 | ex PT-SDD |
| ☐ N831AE | Embraer ERJ-140LR | 145616 | ex PT-SDE |
| ☐ N832AE | Embraer ERJ-140LR | 145627 | ex PT-SDP |
| ☐ N833AE | Embraer ERJ-140LR | 145629 | ex PT-SDR |
| ☐ N834AE | Embraer ERJ-140LR | 145631 | ex PT-SDT |
| ☐ N835AE | Embraer ERJ-140LR | 145634 | ex PT-SDW |
| ☐ N836AE | Embraer ERJ-140LR | 145635 | ex PT-SDX |
| ☐ N837AE | Embraer ERJ-140LR | 145647 | ex PT-SEH |
| ☐ N838AE | Embraer ERJ-140LR | 145651 | ex PT-SEL |
| ☐ N839AE | Embraer ERJ-140LR | 145653 | ex PT-SEN |
| ☐ N840AE | Embraer ERJ-140LR | 145656 | ex PT-SEQ |
| ☐ N841AE | Embraer ERJ-140LR | 145667 | ex PT-SFB |
| ☐ N842AE | Embraer ERJ-140LR | 145673 | ex PT-SFG |
| ☐ N843AE | Embraer ERJ-140LR | 145680 | ex PT-SFM |
| ☐ N844AE | Embraer ERJ-140LR | 145682 | ex PT-SFO |
| ☐ N845AE | Embraer ERJ-140LR | 145685 | ex PT-SFR |
| ☐ N846AE | Embraer ERJ-140LR | 145692 | ex PT-SFY |
| ☐ N847AE | Embraer ERJ-140LR | 145707 | ex PT-SGK |
| ☐ N848AE | Embraer ERJ-140LR | 145710 | ex PT-SGO |
| ☐ N849AE | Embraer ERJ-140LR | 145716 | ex PT-SGT |
| ☐ N850AE | Embraer ERJ-140LR | 145722 | ex PT-SGY |
| ☐ N851AE | Embraer ERJ-140LR | 145734 | ex PT-SHK |
| ☐ N852AE | Embraer ERJ-140LR | 145736 | ex PT-SHM |
| ☐ N853AE | Embraer ERJ-140LR | 145742 | ex PT-SJB |
| ☐ N854AE | Embraer ERJ-140LR | 145743 | ex PT-SJC |
| ☐ N855AE | Embraer ERJ-140LR | 145747 | ex PT-SJG |
| ☐ N856AE | Embraer ERJ-140LR | 145748 | ex PT-SJH |
| ☐ N857AE | Embraer ERJ-140LR | 145752 | ex PT-SJL |
| ☐ N858AE | Embraer ERJ-140LR | 145754 | ex PT-SJN |
| | | | |
| ☐ N600BP | Embraer ERJ-145LR | 145044 | ex N813HK |
| ☐ N601DW | Embraer ERJ-145LR | 145046 | ex N814HK |
| ☐ N602AE | Embraer ERJ-145LR | 145048 | ex N815HK |
| ☐ N603KC | Embraer ERJ-145LR | 145055 | ex N816HK |
| ☐ N604AE | Embraer ERJ-145LR | 145058 | ex N604DG |
| ☐ N605KS | Embraer ERJ-145LR | 145059 | ex N818HK |
| ☐ N606AE | Embraer ERJ-145LR | 145062 | ex N819HK |
| ☐ N607AE | Embraer ERJ-145LR | 145064 | ex N820HK |
| ☐ N608LM | Embraer ERJ-145LR | 145068 | ex N821HK |
| ☐ N609DP | Embraer ERJ-145LR | 145069 | ex N822HK |
| ☐ N610AE | Embraer ERJ-145LR | 145073 | ex PT-SAR |
| ☐ N611AE | Embraer ERJ-145LR | 145074 | ex PT-SAS |
| ☐ N612AE | Embraer ERJ-145LR | 145079 | ex PT-SAX |
| ☐ N613AE | Embraer ERJ-145LR | 145081 | ex (N826HK) |
| ☐ N614AE | Embraer ERJ-145LR | 145086 | |
| ☐ N615AE | Embraer ERJ-145LR | 145087 | |
| ☐ N616AE | Embraer ERJ-145LR | 145092 | |
| ☐ N617AE | Embraer ERJ-145LR | 145093 | ex PT-SBP |
| ☐ N618AE | Embraer ERJ-145LR | 145097 | ex PT-SBT |
| ☐ N619AE | Embraer ERJ-145LR | 145101 | |
| ☐ N620AE | Embraer ERJ-145LR | 145102 | |
| ☐ N621AE | Embraer ERJ-145LR | 145105 | |
| ☐ N622AE | Embraer ERJ-145LR | 145108 | |
| ☐ N623AE | Embraer ERJ-145LR | 145109 | |
| ☐ N624AE | Embraer ERJ-145LR | 145111 | |
| ☐ N625AE | Embraer ERJ-145LR | 145115 | ex PT-SCR |
| ☐ N626AE | Embraer ERJ-145LR | 145117 | ex PT-SCT |
| ☐ N627AE | Embraer ERJ-145LR | 145121 | ex PT-SCX |
| ☐ N628AE | Embraer ERJ-145LR | 145124 | ex PT-SDA |
| ☐ N629AE | Embraer ERJ-145LR | 145130 | ex PT-SDH |
| ☐ N630AE | Embraer ERJ-145LR | 145132 | ex PT-SDJ |
| ☐ N631AE | Embraer ERJ-145LR | 145139 | ex PT-SDQ |
| ☐ N632AE | Embraer ERJ-145LR | 145143 | ex PT-SDT |
| ☐ N633AE | Embraer ERJ-145LR | 145148 | ex PT-SDY |
| ☐ N634AE | Embraer ERJ-145LR | 145150 | ex PT-SEB |
| ☐ N635AE | Embraer ERJ-145LR | 145158 | |
| ☐ N636AE | Embraer ERJ-145LR | 145160 | |
| ☐ N637AE | Embraer ERJ-145LR | 145170 | |
| ☐ N638AE | Embraer ERJ-145LR | 145172 | |
| ☐ N639AE | Embraer ERJ-145LR | 145182 | ex PT-SGE |
| ☐ N640AE | Embraer ERJ-145LR | 145183 | ex PT-SGF |
| ☐ N641AE | Embraer ERJ-145LR | 145191 | ex PT-SGJ |
| ☐ N642AE | Embraer ERJ-145LR | 145193 | ex PT-SGK |
| ☐ N643AE | Embraer ERJ-145LR | 145200 | 200th titles |
| ☐ N644AE | Embraer ERJ-145LR | 145204 | ex PT-SGW |
| ☐ N645AE | Embraer ERJ-145LR | 145212 | ex PT-SGZ |
| ☐ N646AE | Embraer ERJ-145LR | 145213 | ex PT-SHA |
| ☐ N647AE | Embraer ERJ-145LR | 145222 | ex PT-SHH |

| ☐ N648AE | Embraer ERJ-145LR | 145225 | ex PT-SHJ |
|---|---|---|---|
| ☐ N649PP | Embraer ERJ-145LR | 145234 | ex PT-SIB |
| ☐ N650AE | Embraer ERJ-145LR | 145417 | ex PT-STO |
| ☐ N651AE | Embraer ERJ-145LR | 145422 | ex PT-STT |
| ☐ N652RS | Embraer ERJ-145LR | 145432 | ex PT-SUD |
| ☐ N653AE | Embraer ERJ-145LR | 145433 | ex PT-SUE |
| ☐ N654AE | Embraer ERJ-145LR | 145437 | ex PT-SUI |
| ☐ N655AE | Embraer ERJ-145LR | 145452 | ex PT-SUX |
| ☐ N656AE | Embraer ERJ-145LR | 145740 | ex PT-SHV |
| ☐ N657AE | Embraer ERJ-145LR | 145744 | ex PT-SJD |
| ☐ N658AE | Embraer ERJ-145LR | 145760 | ex PT-SJO |
| ☐ N659AE | Embraer ERJ-145LR | 145762 | ex PT-SJT |
| ☐ N660CL | Embraer ERJ-145LR | 145764 | ex PT-SJV |
| ☐ N661JA | Embraer ERJ-145LR | 145766 | ex PT-SJX |
| ☐ N662EH | Embraer ERJ-145LR | 145777 | ex PT-SMG |
| ☐ N663AR | Embraer ERJ-145LR | 145778 | ex PT-SMH |
| ☐ N664MS | Embraer ERJ-145LR | 145779 | ex PT-SMI |
| ☐ N665BC | Embraer ERJ-145LR | 145783 | ex PT-SMK |
| ☐ N667GB | Embraer ERJ-145LR | 145784 | ex PT-SML |
| ☐ N668HH | Embraer ERJ-145LR | 145785 | ex PT-SMM |
| ☐ N669MB | Embraer ERJ-145LR | 145788 | ex PT-SMQ |
| ☐ N670AE | Embraer ERJ-145LR | 145790 | ex PT-SMR |
| ☐ N671AE | Embraer ERJ-145LR | 145793 | ex PT-SMU |
| ☐ N672AE | Embraer ERJ-145LR | 145794 | ex PT-SMV |
| ☐ N673AE | Embraer ERJ-145LR | 145797 | ex PT-SMX |
| ☐ N674RJ | Embraer ERJ-145LR | 14500801 | ex PT-SNF |
| ☐ N675AE | Embraer ERJ-145LR | 14500806 | ex PT-SNI |
| ☐ N676AE | Embraer ERJ-145LR | 14500807 | ex PT-SNJ |
| ☐ N677AE | Embraer ERJ-145LR | 14500810 | ex PT-SNL |
| ☐ N678AE | Embraer ERJ-145LR | 14500813 | ex PT-SNP |
| ☐ N679AE | Embraer ERJ-145LR | 14500814 | ex PT-SNQ |
| ☐ N680AE | Embraer ERJ-145LR | 14500820 | ex PT-SNU |
| ☐ N681AE | Embraer ERJ-145LR | 14500824 | ex PT-SNX |
| ☐ N682AE | Embraer ERJ-145LR | 14500826 | ex PT-SNY |
| ☐ N683AE | Embraer ERJ-145LR | 14500833 | ex PT-SQF |
| ☐ N684JW | Embraer ERJ-145LR | 14500835 | ex PT-SQH |
| ☐ N685AE | Embraer ERJ-145LR | 14500836 | ex PT-SQI |
| ☐ N686AE | Embraer ERJ-145LR | 14500843 | ex PT-SQN |
| ☐ N687JS | Embraer ERJ-145LR | 14500846 | ex PT-SQQ |
| ☐ N688AE | Embraer ERJ-145LR | 14500849 | ex PT-SQS |
| ☐ N689EC | Embraer ERJ-145LR | 14500853 | ex PT-SQV |
| ☐ N690AE | Embraer ERJ-145LR | 14500858 | ex PT-SXM |
| ☐ N691AE | Embraer ERJ-145LR | 14500860 | ex PT-SXA |
| ☐ N692AE | Embraer ERJ-145LR | 14500866 | ex PT-SXF |
| ☐ N693AE | Embraer ERJ-145LR | 14500868 | ex PT-SXG |
| ☐ N694AE | Embraer ERJ-145LR | 14500869 | ex PT-SXN |
| ☐ N695AE | Embraer ERJ-145LR | 14500870 | ex PT-SXH |
| ☐ N696AE | Embraer ERJ-145LR | 14500874 | ex PT-SXO |
| ☐ N697AB | Embraer ERJ-145LR | 14500875 | ex PT-SXQ |
| ☐ N698CB | Embraer ERJ-145LR | 14500877 | ex PT-SXS |
| ☐ N699AE | Embraer ERJ-145LR | 14500883 | ex PT-SXW |
| ☐ N900AE | Embraer ERJ-145LR | 14500885 | ex PT-SXX |
| ☐ N902BC | Embraer ERJ-145LR | 14500887 | ex PT-SXZ |
| ☐ N905JH | Embraer ERJ-145LR | 14500892 | ex PT-SYE |
| ☐ N906AE | Embraer ERJ-145LR | 14500894 | ex PT-SYG |
| ☐ N907AE | Embraer ERJ-145LR | 14500895 | ex PT-SYH |
| ☐ N908AE | Embraer ERJ-145LR | 14500897 | ex PT-SYJ |
| ☐ N909AE | Embraer ERJ-145LR | 14500899 | ex PT-SYK |
| ☐ N918AE | Embraer ERJ-145LR | 14500902 | ex PT-SYM |
| ☐ N922AE | Embraer ERJ-145LR | 14500906 | ex PT-SYO |
| ☐ N923AE | Embraer ERJ-145LR | 14500907 | ex PT-SYQ |
| ☐ N925AE | Embraer ERJ-145LR | 14500908 | ex PT-SYR |
| ☐ N928AE | Embraer ERJ-145LR | 14500911 | ex PT-SYT |
| ☐ N931AE | Embraer ERJ-145LR | 14500912 | ex PT-SYU |
| ☐ N932AE | Embraer ERJ-145LR | 14500915 | ex PT-SYW |
| ☐ N933JN | Embraer ERJ-145LR | 14500918 | ex PT-SYY |
| ☐ N935AE | Embraer ERJ-145LR | 14500920 | ex PT-SYZ |
| ☐ N939AE | Embraer ERJ-145LR | 14500923 | ex PT-SOU |
| ☐ N941LT | Embraer ERJ-145LR | 14500926 | ex PT-SOW |
| ☐ N942LL | Embraer ERJ-145LR | 14500930 | ex PT-SOZ |

## AMERIFLIGHT                    Ameriflight (AMF)        Burbank Glendale-Pasadena, CA (BUR)

| ☐ N20FW | Beech 99A | U-111 | |
|---|---|---|---|
| ☐ N21FW | Beech 99A | U-117 | |
| ☐ N34AK | Beech 99A | U-105 | ex N4099A |
| ☐ N51RP | Beech C99 | U-212 | |
| ☐ N52RP | Beech C99 | U-210 | ex N66305 |
| ☐ N53RP | Beech C99 | U-195 | ex N64997 |
| ☐ N55RP | Beech C99 | U-198 | ex N64002 |
| ☐ N68TA | Beech C99 | U-177 | ex N177EE |
| ☐ N96AV | Beech C99 | U-201 | |

| | | | | |
|---|---|---|---|---|
| ☐ | N102GP | Beech C99 | U-208 | ex(N114GE) |
| ☐ | N104BE | Beech C99 | U-221 | ex N7203L |
| ☐ | N106SX | Beech C99 | U-166 | |
| ☐ | N107SX | Beech C99 | U-176 | |
| ☐ | N108SX | Beech C99 | U-184 | ex N6787P |
| ☐ | N130GP | Beech C99 | U-222 | ex N818FL |
| ☐ | N131GP | Beech C99 | U-225 | ex J6-AAF |
| ☐ | N134PM | Beech B99 | U-34 | ex N852SA |
| ☐ | N164HA | Beech B99 | U-60 | ex N72TC |
| ☐ | N174AV | Beech C99 | U-174 | ex N99CJ |
| ☐ | N191AV | Beech C99 | U-191 | ex VR-CIB |
| ☐ | N193SU | Beech C99 | U-193 | ex C-GFAT |
| ☐ | N199AF | Beech B99 | U-161 | ex N12AK |
| ☐ | N204AF | Beech C99 | U-204 | ex N575W |
| ☐ | N213AV | Beech C99 | U-213 | ex N6656N |
| ☐ | N221BH | Beech C99 | U-168 | ex N18AK |
| ☐ | N223BH | Beech C99 | U-173 | ex N6460D |
| ☐ | N225BH | Beech C99 | U-181 | ex N62936 |
| ☐ | N226BH | Beech C99 | U-182 | ex N6263D |
| ☐ | N228BH | Beech C99 | U-229 | ex N3067L |
| ☐ | N227AV | Beech C99 | U-227 | ex N2225H |
| ☐ | N230BH | Beech C99 | U-233 | ex N72355 |
| ☐ | N234AV | Beech C99 | U-234 | ex N234BH |
| ☐ | N230BH | Beech C99 | U-233 | ex N72355 |
| ☐ | N235AV | Beech C99 | U-235 | ex N235BH |
| ☐ | N261SW | Beech C99 | U-202 | |
| ☐ | N330AV | Beech C99 | U-230 | ex N3063W |
| ☐ | N388AV | Beech C99 | U-188 | ex N799GL |
| ☐ | N802BA | Beech 99 | U-29 | ex N800BE |
| ☐ | N805BA | Beech 99A | U-147 | ex N803BE |
| ☐ | N949K | Beech 99A | U-36 | |
| ☐ | N990AF | Beech C99 | U-211 | ex N113GP |
| ☐ | N991AF | Beech C99 | U-214 | ex N112GP |
| ☐ | N992AF | Beech C99 | U-203 | ex N541JC |
| ☐ | N997SB | Beech C99 | U-192 | ex N6534A |
| ☐ | N1924T | Beech 99A | U-115 | ex N24AT |
| ☐ | N4199C | Beech C99 | U-50 | ex N7940 |
| ☐ | N4299A | Beech B99 | U-146 | |
| ☐ | N6199D | Beech C99 | U-169 | |
| ☐ | N6724D | Beech C99 | U-215 | |
| ☐ | N7200Z | Beech C99 | U-219 | |
| ☐ | N7209W | Beech C99 | U-224 | |
| ☐ | N7862R | Beech 99A | U-85 | |
| ☐ | N8226Z | Beech C99 | U-190 | ex 6Y-JVB |
| ☐ | N8227P | Beech C99 | U-194 | ex 6Y-JVA |
| ☐ | N62989 | Beech C99 | U-183 | |
| ☐ | N63978 | Beech C99 | U-171 | |
| ☐ | N81820 | Beech C99 | U-232 | exJ60AAG |
| | | | | |
| ☐ | N19RZ | Beech 1900C-1 | UC-75 | ex JA190C |
| ☐ | N21RZ | Beech 1900C-1 | UC-106 | ex JA190B |
| ☐ | N26RZ | Beech 1900C-1 | UC-134 | ex JA190D |
| ☐ | N34RZ | Beech 1900C-1 | UC-151 | ex JA190A |
| ☐ | N49UC | Beech 1900C-1 | UC-49 | ex C-GCMJ |
| ☐ | N111YV | Beech 1900C-1 | UC-111 | ex F-GPYX |
| ☐ | N112YV | Beech 1900C-1 | UC-112 | ex VH-AFR |
| ☐ | N330AF | Beech 1900C | UB-38 | ex N805BE |
| ☐ | N331AF | Beech 1900C | UB-44 | ex N807BE |
| ☐ | N575G | Beech 1900C-1 | UC-155 | ex N155YV |
| ☐ | N718AF | Beech 1900C-1 | UC-162 | ex N575Y |
| ☐ | N1568G | Beech 1900C-1 | UC-58 | ex F-GNAD |
| ☐ | N2049K | Beech 1900C-1 | UC-164 | ex J6-AAJ |
| ☐ | N3052K | Beech 1900C | UB-70 | |
| ☐ | N3071A | Beech 1900C | UB-46 | ex N10RA |
| ☐ | N3229A | Beech 1900C | UB-51 | |
| ☐ | N7203C | Beech 1900C | UB-28 | |
| ☐ | N31701 | Beech 1900C | UB-2 | ex N121CZ |
| ☐ | N31702 | Beech 1900C | UB-3 | ex N122CZ |
| ☐ | N31703 | Beech 1900C | UB-10 | ex N123CZ |
| ☐ | N31704 | Beech 1900C | UB-12 | ex N124CZ |
| ☐ | N31705 | Beech 1900C | UB-60 | |
| | | | | |
| ☐ | N179CA | Embraer EMB.120ER Brasilia | 120179 | ex PT-SQR |
| ☐ | N189CA | Embraer EMB.120ER Brasilia | 120189 | ex PT-SRC |
| ☐ | N201YW | Embraer EMB.120RT Brasilia | 120201 | ex N142EB |
| ☐ | N246AS | Embraer EMB.120ER Brasilia | 120100 | ex PP-SMS |
| ☐ | N247CA | Embraer EMB.120ER Brasilia | 120225 | ex PT-SSU |
| ☐ | N257AS | Embraer EMB.120ER Brasilia | 120126 | ex PT-SNS |
| ☐ | N258AS | Embraer EMB.120ER Brasilia | 120131 | ex PT-SNX |
| ☐ | N266AS | Embraer EMB.120ER Brasilia | 120188 | [SGF]♦ |
| | | | | |
| ☐ | N94AF | Learjet 35A | 35A-094 | ex (N35PF) |

| | | | |
|---|---|---|---|
| ☐ N128CA | Learjet 35A | 35A-248 | ex C-GBFA |
| ☐ N237AF | Learjet 35A | 35A-262 | ex N237GA |
| ☐ N535AF | Learjet 35A | 35A-191 | ex N35SE |
| ☐ N754WS | Learjet 35A | 35A-197 | ex N754GL |
| | | | |
| ☐ N199DS | Piper PA-31 Turbo Navajo B | 31-7400980 | ex N7588L |
| ☐ N500CF | Piper PA-31 Turbo Navajo | 31-425 | ex N6467L |
| ☐ N6480L | Piper PA-31 Turbo Navajo | 31-443 | |
| ☐ N6733L | Piper PA-31 Turbo Navajo | 31-636 | |
| ☐ N6759L | Piper PA-31 Turbo Navajo | 31-661 | ex N479SJ |
| ☐ N7434L | Piper PA-31 Turbo Navajo B | 31-822 | |
| ☐ N7441L | Piper PA-31 Turbo Navajo B | 31-844 | |
| ☐ N9132Y | Piper PA-31 Turbo Navajo | 31-178 | |
| ☐ N27275 | Piper PA-31 Navajo C | 31-7712066 | |
| | | | |
| ☐ N3BT | Piper PA-31-350 Navajo Chieftain | 31-7752172 | ex N27422 |
| ☐ N555RG | Piper PA-31-350 Navajo Chieftain | 31-7305103 | ex N555RC |
| ☐ N600TS | Piper PA-31-350 Navajo Chieftain | 31-7305047 | ex N537N |
| ☐ N777MP | Piper PA-31-350 Navajo Chieftain | 31-7552072 | ex N59983 |
| ☐ N961CA | Piper PA-31-350 Navajo Chieftain | 31-7652014 | ex N961PS |
| ☐ N3527D | Piper PA-31-350 Chieftain | 31-7952137 | |
| ☐ N3540N | Piper PA-31-350 Chieftain | 31-7952214 | |
| ☐ N3548B | Piper PA-31-350 Chieftain | 31-8052025 | |
| ☐ N3553F | Piper PA-31-350 Chieftain | 31-8052044 | |
| ☐ N4044P | Piper PA-31-350 Chieftain | 31-8152004 | |
| ☐ N4078B | Piper PA-31-350 Chieftain | 31-8152055 | |
| ☐ N4087J | Piper PA-31-350 Chieftain | 31-8152128 | |
| ☐ N4098A | Piper PA-31-350 Chieftain | 31-8152200 | |
| ☐ N4502Y | Piper PA-31-350 Chieftain | 31-8052189 | |
| ☐ N27426 | Piper PA-31-350 Navajo Chieftain | 31-7752175 | |
| ☐ N27677 | Piper PA-31-350 Chieftain | 31-7852101 | |
| ☐ N35336 | Piper PA-31-350 Chieftain | 31-7952189 | |
| ☐ N42076 | Piper PA-31-350 Navajo Chieftain | 31-7405209 | ex G-OSPT |
| ☐ N42079 | Piper PA-31-350 Navajo Chieftain | 31-7405488 | ex G-BCOD |
| ☐ N45004 | Piper PA-31-350 Chieftain | 31-8052163 | |
| ☐ N45014 | Piper PA-31-350 Chieftain | 31-8052171 | |
| ☐ N59820 | Piper PA-31-350 Navajo Chieftain | 31-7652073 | |
| ☐ N59973 | Piper PA-31-350 Navajo Chieftain | 31-7552079 | |
| ☐ N62858 | Piper PA-31-350 Navajo Chieftain | 31-7652115 | |
| ☐ N62959 | Piper PA-31-350 Navajo Chieftain | 31-7752008 | |
| ☐ N66859 | Piper PA-31-350 Navajo Chieftain | 31-7405168 | |
| | | | |
| ☐ N152AF | Swearingen SA.227AC Metro III | AC-520 | ex TG-49346 |
| ☐ N155AF | Swearingen SA.227AC Metro III | AC-455 | ex N356AE |
| ☐ N191AF | Swearingen SA.227AC Metro III | AC-491 | ex N209CA |
| ☐ N360AE | Swearingen SA.227AC Metro III | AC-675 | |
| ☐ N362AE | Swearingen SA.227AC Metro III | AC-677B | |
| ☐ N377PH | Swearingen SA.227AC Metro III | AC-574 | ex (D-CABG) |
| ☐ N421MA | Swearingen SA.227AC Metro III | AC-634 | ex N3119Q |
| ☐ N422MA | Swearingen SA.227AC Metro III | AC-635 | ex N3119T |
| ☐ N423MA | Swearingen SA.227AC Metro III | AC-636 | ex N26823 |
| ☐ N424MA | Swearingen SA.227AC Metro III | AC-639 | |
| ☐ N426MA | Swearingen SA.227AC Metro III | AC-645 | |
| ☐ N428MA | Swearingen SA.227AC Metro III | AC-646 | |
| ☐ N443AF | Swearingen SA.227AC Metro III | AC-443 | ex N443NE |
| ☐ N473AF | Swearingen SA.227AC Metro III | AC-473 | ex N473NE |
| ☐ N475AF | Swearingen SA.227AC Metro III | AC-475 | ex N475NE |
| ☐ N476AF | Swearingen SA.227AC Metro III | AC-476 | ex N476NE |
| ☐ N488AF | Swearingen SA.227AC Metro III | AC-488 | ex N488NE |
| ☐ N529AF | Swearingen SA.227AC Metro III | AC-752 | ex XA-TML |
| ☐ N578AF | Swearingen SA.227AC Metro III | AC-578 | ex C-FJLE |
| ☐ N671AV | Swearingen SA.227AC Metro III | AC-671 | |
| ☐ N672AV | Swearingen SA.227AC Metro III | AC-672 | |
| ☐ N673AV | Swearingen SA.227AC Metro III | AC-673 | |
| ☐ N698AF | Swearingen SA.227AC Metro III | AC-698 | ex N698FA |
| ☐ N801AF | Swearingen SA.227AC Metro III | AC-701 | ex C-GWXZ |
| ☐ N838AF | Swearingen SA.227AC Metro III | AC-738 | ex C-GWXX |
| | | | |
| ☐ N240DH | Swearingen SA.227AT Expediter | AT-602B | ex N3117P |
| ☐ N241DH | Swearingen SA.227AT Expediter | AT-607B | ex N3118A |
| ☐ N242DH | Swearingen SA.227AT Expediter | AT-608B | ex N3118G |
| ☐ N243DH | Swearingen SA.227AT Expediter | AT-609B | ex N3118H |
| ☐ N244DH | Swearingen SA.227AT Expediter | AT-618B | |
| ☐ N245DH | Swearingen SA.227AT Expediter | AT-624B | |
| ☐ N246DH | Swearingen SA.227AT Expediter | AT-625B | |
| ☐ N247DH | Swearingen SA.227AT Expediter | AT-626B | |
| ☐ N248DH | Swearingen SA.227AT Expediter | AT-630B | |
| ☐ N249DH | Swearingen SA.227AT Expediter | AT-631B | |
| ☐ N544UP | Swearingen SA.227AT Expediter | AT-544 | ex N68TA |
| ☐ N548UP | Swearingen SA.227AT Expediter | AT-548 | ex N548SA |
| ☐ N556UP | Swearingen SA.227AT Expediter | AT-556 | ex N3113B |
| ☐ N560UP | Swearingen SA.227AT Expediter | AT-560 | ex N3113A |

| | | | | | |
|---|---|---|---|---|---|
| ☐ N561UP | Swearingen SA.227AT Expediter | AT-561 | ex N3113F | | |
| ☐ N566UP | Swearingen SA.227AT Expediter | AT-566 | ex N3113N | | |
| ☐ N569UP | Swearingen SA.227AT Expediter | AT-569 | ex N31134 | | |
| ☐ N573G | Swearingen SA.227AT Merlin IVC | AT-446B | ex N3008L | | |
| ☐ N200AF | Beech 200 Super King Air | BB-102 | ex N997MA | | |
| ☐ N807M | Swearingen SA.227AT Merlin IVC | AT-454B | ex N3013T | | |

## AMERIJET INTERNATIONAL — Amerijet (M6/AJT) — Fort Lauderdale-Hollywood Intl, FL (FLL)

| | | | | | |
|---|---|---|---|---|---|
| ☐ N395AJ | Boeing 727-233F/W (Duganair 3) | 21100/1148 | ex N727SN | | |
| ☐ N495AJ | Boeing 727-233F/W (Duganair 3) | 20937/1103 | ex C-GAAD | | |
| ☐ N598AJ | Boeing 727-212F/W (Duganair 3) | 21947/1506 | ex N86430 | | [OPF] |
| ☐ N794AJ | Boeing 727-227F/W (Duganair 3) | 21243/1197 | ex N567PE | Nogravity.com 'G-Force-One' | |
| ☐ N994AJ | Boeing 727-233F/W (Duganair 3) | 20942/1130 | ex N727JH | | wfs |
| ☐ N741AX | Boeing 767-232 (SF) | 22215/17 | ex N103DA | | ♦ |
| ☐ N743AX | Boeing 767-232 (SF) | 22218/31 | ex N106DA | | ♦ |

## AMERISTAR JET CHARTER — Ameristar (AJI) — Dallas-Addison, TX (ADS)

| | | | | | |
|---|---|---|---|---|---|
| ☐ N148TW | AMD Falcon 20C | 148 | ex N148WC | | |
| ☐ N158TW | AMD Falcon 20C | 158 | ex N450MA | | |
| ☐ N204TW | AMD Falcon 20DC | 204 | ex EC-EGM | | |
| ☐ N221TW | AMD Falcon 20DC | 221 | ex EC-EIV | | |
| ☐ N223TW | AMD Falcon 20C | 123 | ex N45MR | | |
| ☐ N232TW | AMD Falcon 20C | 32 | ex F-GIVT | | |
| ☐ N236TW | AMD Falcon 20D | 236 | ex N936NW | | |
| ☐ N240TW | AMD Falcon 20C | 40 | ex C-GSKQ | | |
| ☐ N285TW | AMD Falcon 20EC | 285 | ex N285AP | | |
| ☐ N295TW | AMD Falcon 20C | 5 | ex F-GJPR | | |
| ☐ N314TW | AMD Falcon 20E | 314 | ex F-GDLU | | [ADS] |
| ☐ N699TW | AMD Falcon 20DC | 50 | ex EC-EDO | | |
| ☐ N977TW | AMD Falcon 20C | 13 | ex F-BTCY | | [ADS] |
| ☐ N147TW | Learjet 25 | 25-023 | ex N767SC | | |
| ☐ N157TW | Learjet 24 | 24-157 | ex N659AT | | |
| ☐ N222TW | Learjet 24 | 24-161 | ex N24KF | | [ADS |
| ☐ N233TW | Learjet 24B | 24B-221 | ex N59JG | | |
| ☐ N237TW | Learjet 24D | 24D-237 | ex N825DM | | |
| ☐ N265TW | Learjet 25D | 25D-265 | ex N69GF | | |
| ☐ N266TW | Learjet 24D | 24D-266 | ex N266BS | | [ADS] |
| ☐ N277TW | Learjet 24D | 24D-277 | ex N57BC | | |
| ☐ N299TW | Learjet 24D | 24D-299 | ex XB-GJS | | |
| ☐ N324TW | Learjet 24D | 24D-324 | ex XA-SCY | | |
| ☐ N330TW | Learjet 24E | 24E-330 | ex N511AT | | |
| ☐ N333TW | Learjet 24 | 24-168 | ex N155BT | | [ADS] |
| ☐ N525TW | Learjet 25 | 25-011 | ex N108GA | | |
| ☐ N888TW | Learjet 24D | 24D-292 | ex N800PC | | [ADS] |
| ☐ N176TW | Beech 65-E90 King Air | LW-76 | ex ZS-LJF | | |
| ☐ N733TW | Boeing 737-2H4 (AvAero 3) | 22732/877 | ex N83SW | | |
| ☐ N783TW | Douglas DC-9-15F (ABS 3) | 47010/97 | ex N916R | | |
| ☐ N784TW | Douglas DC-9-15F (ABS 3) | 47014/141 | ex N923R | | |
| ☐ N785TW | Douglas DC-9-15F (ABS 3) | 47015/156 | ex N5373G | | |
| ☐ N786TW | McDonnell-Douglas MD-83 | 53123/1987 | ex HK-4589 | | |
| ☐ N787TW | McDonnell-Douglas MD-83 | 49945/1889 | ex HK-4588X | | |

## ANDREW AIRWAYS — Kodiak-Municipal, AK (KDK)

| | | | | | |
|---|---|---|---|---|---|
| ☐ N1544 | de Havilland DHC-2 Beaver | 1230 | ex N67686 | | FP/WS |
| ☐ N1545 | de Havilland DHC-2 Beaver | 1493 | ex N123UA | | FP/WS |
| ☐ N5303X | Cessna U206G Stationair 6 II | U20605622 | | | FP/WS |

## ARCTIC CIRCLE AIR SERVICE — Air Arctic (5F/CIR)
### Aniak/Bethel/Dillingham-Municipal/Fairbanks-Intl, AK (ANI/BET/DLG/FAI)

| | | | | | |
|---|---|---|---|---|---|
| ☐ N168LM | Short SD.3-30 | SH3104 | ex N174Z | | Frtr |
| ☐ N261AG | Short SD.3-30 | SH3117 | ex 84-0470 | | Frtr |
| ☐ N675AC | Britten-Norman BN-2T Islander | 2183 | ex G-LEAP | | ♦ |

## ASIA PACIFIC AIRLINES — Magellan (MGE) — Guam (GUM)

| | | | | | |
|---|---|---|---|---|---|
| ☐ N319NE | Boeing 727-212F/W (Duganair 3) | 21349/1289 | ex N591DB | | |
| ☐ N705AA | Boeing 727-223F/W (Super 27) | 22462/1751 | | | |
| ☐ N86425 | Boeing 727-212F/W (Duganair 3) | 21459/1329 | ex N296AS | | |

## ASPEN HELICOPTERS — Aspen (AHF) — Oxnard, CA (OXR)

| | | | | | |
|---|---|---|---|---|---|
| ☐ N212AH | Bell 212 | 30959 | ex C-FYMJ | | |

| | | | | |
|---|---|---|---|---|
| ☐ N383SH | Bell 206L-3 LongRanger III | 51073 | ex N333SH | |
| ☐ N1085T | Bell 206L-1 LongRanger III | 45376 | | |
| ☐ N5012F | Bell 206B JetRanger III | 2559 | | |
| ☐ N8131 | Piper PA-31-350 Chieftain | 31-8152032 | ex LN-REM | |
| ☐ N39049 | Bell 206B JetRanger III | 3101 | | |

## ASTAR AIR CARGO — DHL (ER/DHL) — Cincinnati-Northern Kentucky Intl, OH (CVG)

| | | | | |
|---|---|---|---|---|
| ☐ N801DH | Douglas DC-8-73AF | 46033/431 | ex C-FTIK | |
| ☐ N802DH | Douglas DC-8-73AF | 46076/451 | ex C-FTIO | [IGM] |
| ☐ N803DH | Douglas DC-8-73F | 46123/508 | ex C-FTIQ | ♦ |
| ☐ N804DH | Douglas DC-8-73AF | 46124/511 | ex C-FTIR | |
| ☐ N805DH | Douglas DC-8-73AF | 46125/515 | ex C-FTIS | |
| ☐ N806DH | Douglas DC-8-73CF | 46002/394 | ex N815UP | |
| ☐ N807DH | Douglas DC-8-73CF | 45990/375 | ex N816UP | |
| ☐ N873SJ | Douglas DC-8-73F | 46091/519 | ex F-GESM | Billy J Benson |

## ATI - AIR TRANSPORT INTERNATIONAL — Air Transport (8C/ATN) — Little Rock-Adams Field, AR (LIT)

| | | | | |
|---|---|---|---|---|
| ☐ N312AA | Boeing 767-223 (SF) | 22315/94 | | ♦ |
| ☐ N316CM | Boeing 767-338ER (SF) | 24146/231 | ex VH-OGA | ♦ |
| ☐ N319CM | Boeing 767-338ER (SF) | 24407/247 | ex VH-OGD | ♦ |
| ☐ N712AX | Boeing 767-2J6ER | 23307/126 | ex B-2551 | ♦ |
| ☐ N761CX | Boeing 767-223 (SCD) | 22318/111 | ex N316AA | |
| ☐ N762CX | Boeing 767-232 (SCD) | 22225/77 | ex N748AX | |
| ☐ N763CX | Boeing 767-232 (SCD) | 22223/74 | ex N746AX | |
| | | | | |
| ☐ N602AL | Douglas DC-8-73F | 45991/380 | ex D-ADUI | |
| ☐ N603AL | Douglas DC-8-73F | 46003/401 | ex D-ADUA | [MHV] |
| ☐ N604BX | Douglas DC-8-73CF | 46046/444 | ex N792FT | |
| ☐ N605AL | Douglas DC-8-73F | 46106/490 | ex D-ADUC | |
| ☐ N606AL | Douglas DC-8-73F | 46044/432 | ex D-ADUE | |
| ☐ N721CX | Douglas DC-8-72CF | 46013/427 | ex 46013 | |
| ☐ N820BX | Douglas DC-8-71F | 46065/460 | ex N8098U | Larry LJ Johnston' |
| ☐ N821BX | Douglas DC-8-71F | 45811/262 | ex N8071U | |
| ☐ N822BX | Douglas DC-8-71F | 45813/284 | ex N8073U | |
| ☐ N823BX | Douglas DC-8-71F | 46064/459 | ex N8097U | [MHV] |
| ☐ N825BX | Douglas DC-8-71F | 45978/381 | ex N8088U | [MHV] |
| ☐ N828BX | Douglas DC-8-71F | 45993/392 | ex N8089U | [MHV] |
| ☐ N830BX | Douglas DC-8-71F | 45973/358 | ex N783UP | wfs |
| | | | | |
| ☐ N41CX | Douglas DC-8-62CF (BAC 3) | 46129/523 | ex N798AL | wfs |
| ☐ N71CX | Douglas DC-8-62F (BAC 3) | 45961/361 | ex N818CK | |
| ☐ N799AL | Douglas DC-8-62F (BAC 3) | 45922/335 | ex RTAF 60112 | |

## ATLANTIC AIR CARGO — Miami-Intl, FL (MIA)

| | | | | |
|---|---|---|---|---|
| ☐ N437GB | Douglas DC-3 | 19999 | ex HR-LAD | Frtr |
| ☐ N705GB | Douglas DC-3 | 13854 | ex TG-SAA | Frtr |

## ATLANTIC SOUTHEAST AIRLINES — Candler (EV/CAA) — Atlanta-Hartsfield Intl, GA/Orlando-Intl, FL (ATL/MCO)

Wholly owned subsidiary of SkyWest Airlines, merged with ExpressJet and ExpressJet Airlines and ops as Delta Connection; to be renamed Surejet

## ATLAS AIR — Giant (5Y/GTI) — New York-JFK Intl, NY (JFK)

| | | | | | |
|---|---|---|---|---|---|
| ☐ N517MC | Boeing 747-243B (SF) | 23300/613 | ex I-DEMT | | |
| ☐ N523MC | Boeing 747-2D7B (SF) | 21782/402 | ex N323MC | | |
| ☐ N524MC | Boeing 747-2D7B (SF) | 21784/424 | ex HS-TGC | | |
| ☐ N526MC | Boeing 747-2D7B (SF) | 22337/479 | ex HS-TGF | all-white | [ROW] |
| ☐ N528MC | Boeing 747-2D7B (SF) | 22472/597 | ex HS-TGS | | [ROW] |
| ☐ N537MC | Boeing 747-271C | 22403/524 | ex LX-BCV | all-white | [ROW] |
| | | | | | |
| ☐ N249BA | Boeing 747-409LCF | 24309/766 | ex B-18271 | | op for Boeing♦ |
| ☐ N263SG | Boeing 747-481 | 29263/1204 | ex B-LFC | | <SOR♦ |
| ☐ N322SG | Boeing 747-481 | 30322/1250 | ex B-LFD | | <SOR♦ |
| ☐ N408MC | Boeing 747-47UF | 29261/1192 | ex (N495MC) | | >UAE |
| ☐ N409MC | Boeing 747-47UF | 30558/1242 | | | |
| ☐ N412MC | Boeing 747-47UF | 30559/1244 | | | |
| ☐ N415MC | Boeing 747-47UF | 32837/1304 | | | >UAE |
| ☐ N416MC | Boeing 747-47UF | 32838/1307 | | | >PAC |
| ☐ N418MC | Boeing 747-47UF | 32840/1319 | | | |
| ☐ N419MC | Boeing 747-48EF | 28367/1096 | ex TF-AMO | | |
| ☐ N429MC | Boeing 747-481BCF | 24833/812 | ex JA8095 | | |
| ☐ N458MC | Boeing 747-446BCF | 26356/1026 | ex N356NA | | ♦ |
| ☐ N459MC | Boeing 747-446BCF | 26344/929 | ex N344NA | | ♦ |
| ☐ N464MC | Boeing 747-446 | 26341/902 | ex N349AS | | ♦ |

| | | | | |
|---|---|---|---|---|
| ☐ N465MC | Boeing 747-446 | 24784/798 | ex N287AS | ♦ |
| ☐ N475MC | Boeing 747-47UF | 29252/1165 | ex G-GSSB | ♦ |
| ☐ N476MC | Boeing 747-47UF | 29256/1213 | ex G-GSSA | ♦ |
| ☐ N477MC | Boeing 747-47UF | 29255/1184 | ex G-GSSC | ♦ |
| ☐ N492MC | Boeing 747-47UF | 29253/1169 | | |
| ☐ N493MC | Boeing 747-47UF | 29254/1179 | | |
| ☐ N496MC | Boeing 747-47UF | 29257/1217 | | |
| ☐ N497MC | Boeing 747-47UF | 29258/1220 | | >UAE |
| ☐ N498MC | Boeing 747-47UF | 29259/1227 | | >PAC |
| ☐ N499MC | Boeing 747-47UF | 29260/1240 | | |
| ☐ N718BA | Boeing 747-4H6LCF | 27042/932 | ex 9M-MPA | op for Boeing♦ |
| ☐ N747BC | Boeing 747-4J6LCF | 25879/904 | ex B-2464 | op for Boeing♦ |
| ☐ N780BA | Boeing 747-409LCF | 24310/778 | ex B-18272 | op for Boeing♦ |
| | | | | |
| ☐ G-GSSD | Boeing 747-87UF | 37561/1442 | | >GSS♦ |
| ☐ G-GSSE | Boeing 747-87UF | 37568/1444 | ex (N851GT) | >GSS♦ |
| ☐ G-GSSF | Boeing 747-87UF | 37569/1445 | ex (N852GT) | >GSS♦ |
| ☐ N851GT | Boeing 747-87UF | 37565 | | o/o♦ |
| ☐ N852GT | Boeing 747-87UF | 37471 | | o/o♦ |
| | | | | |
| ☐ N640GT | Boeing 767-3S1ER | 25221/384 | ex N585MS | ♦ |
| ☐ N641GT | Boeing 767-38EER | 25132/417 | ex PR-VAF | ♦ |
| ☐ N642GT | Boeing 767-3Y0ER | 26207/503 | ex C-GHPH | [ATL]♦ |
| ☐ N650GT | Boeing 767-231BDSD | 22566/29 | ex N703AX | |
| ☐ N652GT | Boeing 767-231PC | 22571/64 | ex N708AX | o/o♦ |
| | | | | |
| ☐ N355MC | Boeing 747-341 (SF) | 23395/629 | ex PP-VNI | [MHV]♦ |

## BAKER AVIATION — Baker Aviation (8Q/BAJ) — Kotzebue-Wien Memorial, AK (OTZ)

| | | | | |
|---|---|---|---|---|
| ☐ N6908M | Cessna 207A Stationair 8 | 20700672 | | |
| ☐ N7396U | Cessna 207A Stationair 8 | 20700438 | | |
| ☐ N9641M | Cessna 207A Stationair 8 | 20700774 | | ♦ |
| ☐ N9874M | Cessna 207A Stationair 8 | 20700745 | | ♦ |
| ☐ N9933M | Cessna 207A Stationair 8 | 20700750 | | ♦ |
| ☐ N9941M | Cessna 207A Stationair 8 | 20700748 | | ♦ |
| ☐ N9942M | Cessna 207A Stationair 8 | 20700756 | | ♦ |
| ☐ N9946M | Cessna 207A Stationair 8 | 20700588 | | ♦ |
| ☐ N9952M | Cessna 207A Stationair 8 | 20700345 | | ♦ |
| ☐ N9953M | Cessna 207A Stationair 8 | 20700656 | | ♦ |
| | | | | |
| ☐ N93943 | Cessna A185F Skywagon | 18503267 | | ♦ |

## BALTIA AIRLINES — (BTL)

| | | | | |
|---|---|---|---|---|
| ☐ N705BL | Boeing 747-282B | 21035/256 | ex N559EV | [KUL] |
| ☐ N706BL | Boeing 747-251B | 21705/374 | ex N623US | wfs |

## BANKAIR — Bankair (B4/BKA) — Columbia-Owens Field, SC (CUB)

| | | | | |
|---|---|---|---|---|
| ☐ N33PT | Learjet 25D | 25D-240 | ex N83EA | |
| ☐ N58EM | Learjet 35 | 35-046 | ex VH-LJL | |
| ☐ N58HC | Learjet 25D | 25D-341 | ex XA-SAE | |
| ☐ N67PA | Learjet 35A | 35A-208 | ex (N39DJ) | |
| ☐ N90WR | Learjet 35 | 35-022 | ex OY-BLG | |
| ☐ N135AG | Learjet 35A | 35A-132 | ex N37TJ | |
| ☐ N155AM | Learjet 35A | 35A-131 | ex N26GD | |
| ☐ N326DD | Learjet 35A | 35A-173 | ex YU-BPY | |
| ☐ N399BA | Learjet 35A | 35A-371 | ex LV-ALF | |
| ☐ N465NW | Learjet 35A | 35A-465 | | |
| ☐ N500ED | Learjet 35A | 35A-241 | ex N500EX | |
| ☐ N900BJ | Learjet 35A | 35A-123 | ex N900JE | |
| | | | | |
| ☐ N21CJ | Mitsubishi MU-2L | 789SA | ex N278MA | |
| ☐ N21JA | Mitsubishi MU-2J | 614 | ex N998CA | |
| ☐ N44KU | Mitsubishi MU-2J | 647 | ex N44KS | |
| ☐ N174MA | Mitsubishi MU-2B | 753SA | ex N100BY | |
| ☐ N334EB | Mitsubishi MU-2J | 568 | ex N99SL | |
| ☐ N535WM | Mitsubishi MU-2J | 655 | ex N535MA | |
| ☐ N610CA | Mitsubishi MU-2B | 788SA | ex N277MA | |
| ☐ N637WG | Mitsubishi MU-2J | 637 | ex N951MS | |
| ☐ N942ST | Mitsubishi MU-2B | 745SA | ex N942MA | |

## BARON AVIATION SERVICES — Show-Me (BVN) — Rolla-Vichy-National, MO (VIH)

Ops Cessna 208/208B Caravans on behalf of Federal Express

## BASLER AIRLINES — Basler (BFC) — Oshkosh-Wittman Regional, WI (OSH)

| | | | | |
|---|---|---|---|---|
| ☐ N300BF | Basler BT-67 | 15299/26744 | ex N300TX | Turbo-Express |
| ☐ N400BF | Basler BT-67 | 9415 | | ♦ |

## BEMIDJI AIRLINES — Bemidji (CH/BMJ) — Bemidji, MN (BJI)

| | Reg | Type | c/n | ex | Notes |
|---|---|---|---|---|---|
| ☐ | N55SA | Beech 65-A80 Queen Air | LD-243 | ex N794A | Queenaire 8800 conversion |
| ☐ | N80RR | Beech 65-B80 Queen Air | LD-296 | | Queenaire 8800 conversion |
| ☐ | N95LL | Beech 65-A80 Queen Air | LD-235 | ex N33TX | Queenaire 8800 conversion |
| ☐ | N103BA | Beech 65-B80 Queen Air | LD-435 | ex N103EE | Queenaire 8800 conversion |
| ☐ | N104BA | Beech 65-B80 Queen Air | LD-411 | ex N4258S | |
| ☐ | N106BA | Beech 65-B80 Queen Air | LD-409 | ex N1338T | Queenaire 8800 conversion |
| ☐ | N107BA | Beech 65-B80 Queen Air | LD-358 | ex N7838L | Queenaire 8800 conversion |
| ☐ | N110BA | Beech 65-B80 Queen Air | LD-279 | ex N102KK | Queenaire 8800 conversion |
| ☐ | N111AR | Beech 65-80 Queen Air | LF-68 | ex 62-3780 | |
| ☐ | N131BA | Beech 65-B80 Queen Air | LD-297 | ex N1555M | Queenaire 8800 conversion |
| ☐ | N132BA | Beech 65-B80 Queen Air | LD-331 | ex C-GRID | Queenaire 8800 conversion |
| ☐ | N134BA | Beech 65-A80 Queen Air | LD-202 | ex N848S | Queenaire 8800 conversion |
| ☐ | N135BA | Beech 65-80 Queen Air | LD-68 | ex N29RG | Queenaire 8800 conversion |
| ☐ | N138BA | Beech 65-80 Queen Air | LD-361 | ex N3344Z | |
| ☐ | N306D | Beech 65-80 Queen Air | LD-439 | ex N4258S | |
| ☐ | N441MC | Beech 65-80 Queen Air | LF-45 | | ♦ |
| ☐ | N5078E | Beech 65-80 Queen Air | LF-76 | ex 63-13637 | |
| ☐ | N5078G | Beech 65-80 Queen Air | LF-8 | | ♦ |
| ☐ | N5078N | Beech 65-80 Queen Air | LF-16 | ex 60-3467 | |
| ☐ | N5078U | Beech 65-80 Queen Air | LF-32 | ex 62-3834 | |
| ☐ | N5079E | Beech 65-80 Queen Air | LF-52 | ex 62-3854 | |
| ☐ | N5080L | Beech 65-80 Queen Air | LF-59 | ex 62-3861 | |
| ☐ | N5080H | Beech 65-80 Queen Air | LF-27 | | |
| ☐ | N70NP | Beech 99 | U-14 | ex N914Y | |
| ☐ | N108BA | Beech 99 | U-40 | ex C-GQFD | |
| ☐ | N125DP | Beech 99 | U-12 | ex C-GPCE | |
| ☐ | N130BA | Beech 99A | U-80 | ex N51PA | Frtr |
| ☐ | N137BA | Beech 99A | U-137 | ex C-GAWW | |
| ☐ | N175EE | Beech C99 | U-175 | ex N994SB | |
| ☐ | N7207E | Beech C99 | U-223 | | |
| ☐ | N7212P | Beech C99 | U-220 | | |
| ☐ | N60BA | Beech 65-E90 King Air | LW-79 | ex N12AK | |
| ☐ | N227LC | Swearingen SA.227AC Metro III | AC-707B | ex N84GM | ♦ |
| ☐ | N611BA | Swearingen SA.227AC Metro III | AC-611B | ex VH-EEX | ♦ |
| ☐ | N619BA | Swearingen SA.227AC Metro III | AC-619B | ex VH-EEU | ♦ |
| ☐ | N4016A | Beech 58 Baron | TH-9 | | |
| ☐ | N6513Y | Piper PA-23 Aztec 250 | 27-3804 | | ♦ |

## BERING AIR — Bering Air (8E/BRG) — Nome, AK (OME)

| | Reg | Type | c/n | ex | Notes |
|---|---|---|---|---|---|
| ☐ | N204B | Cessna 208B Caravan I | 208B0752 | | ♦ |
| ☐ | N205BA | Cessna 208B Caravan I | 208B0890 | | |
| ☐ | N806BA | Cessna 208B Caravan I | 208B0943 | | |
| ☐ | N1128L | Cessna 208B Caravan I | 208B0536 | | |
| ☐ | N1123R | Cessna 208B Caravan I | 208B1022 | | ♦ |
| ☐ | N988BA | Cessna 208B Caravan I | 208B2089 | | ♦ |
| ☐ | N141ME | Piper PA-31-350 Chieftain | 31-8152117 | ex N4086L | |
| ☐ | N4112D | Piper PA-31-350 T-1020 | 31-8353004 | | |
| ☐ | N4112E | Piper PA-31-350 T-1020 | 31-8353005 | | |
| ☐ | N4118G | Piper PA-31-350 T-1020 | 31-8453001 | | |
| ☐ | N41189 | Piper PA-31-350 T-1020 | 31-8553002 | | |
| ☐ | N45052 | Piper PA-31-350 Chieftain | 31-8152063 | | |
| ☐ | N15GA | Beech 1900D | UE-37 | ex F-HCHA | |
| ☐ | N79CF | Beech 200 Super King Air | BB-441 | | CatPass 250 conversion |
| ☐ | N148SK | Beech 1900D | UE-148 | | |
| ☐ | N326KW | Beech 200 Super King Air | BB-1360 | ex HK-3703X | CatPass 250 conversion |
| ☐ | N349TA | CASA 212-200 | CC60-9-349 | ex N316CA | Frtr dam 18Sep09 |
| ☐ | N9964M | Cessna 207A Stationair 8 | 20700766 | | |
| ☐ | N9988M | Cessna 207A Stationair 8 | 20700776 | | |

## BERRY AVIATION — Berry (BYA) — San Marcos-Municipal, TX (HYI)

| | Reg | Type | c/n | ex | Notes |
|---|---|---|---|---|---|
| ☐ | N227LJ | Swearingen SA.226AC Metro III | AC-522 | ex N3109B | ♦ |
| ☐ | N373PH | Swearingen SA.227AC Metro III | AC-538 | ex N732C | |
| ☐ | N589BA | Swearingen SA.227AC Metro III | AC-589 | ex XA-TSF | [HYI] |
| ☐ | N590BA | Swearingen SA.227AC Metro III | AC-590 | ex XA-TSG | [HYI] |
| ☐ | N680AX | Swearingen SA.227AC Metro III | AC-680 | ex N365AE | |
| ☐ | N691AX | Swearingen SA.227AC Metro III | AC-691 | ex N367AE | |
| ☐ | N697AX | Swearingen SA.227AC Metro III | AC-697 | ex N730C | |
| ☐ | N729C | Swearingen SA.227AC Metro III | AC-571 | ex N374PH | |
| ☐ | N789C | Swearingen SA.227AC Metro III | AC-540 | ex N389PH | |
| ☐ | N27442 | Swearingen SA.227AC Metro III | AC-750B | | |
| ☐ | N54EA | Swearngin SA.226TC Metro II | TC-398 | ex N601AS | ♦ |
| ☐ | N165BA | Swearingen SA.226TC Metro II | TC-215 | ex N911HF | |

| | | | | | |
|---|---|---|---|---|---|
| ☐ N226BA | Swearingen SA.226TC Metro II | TC-321 | ex N105UR | | |
| ☐ N323BA | Swearingen SA.226TC Metro II | TC-280 | ex N303TL | | Frtr |
| ☐ N335PH | Dornier 328-110 | 3013 | ex D-CALT | | |
| ☐ N338PH | Dornier 328-120 | 3029 | ex D-CDHO | | ♦ |
| ☐ N339PH | Dornier 328-110 | 3015 | ex D-CARR | | |
| ☐ N437YV | de Havilland DHC-8-202B | 437 | | | ♦ |
| ☐ N449YV | de Havilland DHC-8-202Q | 449 | | | ♦ |
| ☐ N473PS | Dornier 328-110 | 3010 | ex N332PH | | |
| ☐ N541AV | de Havilland DHC-8-201Q | 541 | ex C-FSQT | | ♦ |

## BIG ISLAND AIR                          Big Isle (BIG)          Kailua-Keahole Kona Intl, HI (KOA)

| | | | | |
|---|---|---|---|---|
| ☐ N281A | Cessna 208 Caravan I | 20800271 | ex LV-WYX | |

## BIGHORN AIRWAYS                          Bighorn Air (BHR)
## Sheridan-County, WY/Casper-Natrona Co, WY (SHR/CPR)

| | | | | |
|---|---|---|---|---|
| ☐ N107BH | CASA C.212-200 | CC20-4-165 | ex N212TH | |
| ☐ N109BH | CASA C.212-200 | CC35-1-192 | ex N192PL | |
| ☐ N110BH | Cessna 402A | 402A-1135 | | ♦ |
| ☐ N112BH | CASA C.212-200 | CC50-11-292 | ex N311ST | ♦ |
| ☐ N113BH | Cessna 180 | 18051844 | | |
| ☐ N114BH | Cessna 340A | 340A1230 | ex N6228X | ♦ |
| ☐ N115BH | Cessna 340A | 340A1531 | ex N2688Q | |
| ☐ N117BH | CASA C.212-200 | CC23-1-171 | ex N349CA | |
| ☐ N118BH | Cessna 340A | 340A0003 | ex N5168J | |
| ☐ N257MC | Dornier 228-202 | 8102 | ex YV-648C | |
| ☐ N263MC | Dornier 228-202 | 8141 | ex N116DN | |
| ☐ N266MC | Dornier 228-202 | 8150 | ex D-CBDL | |
| ☐ N543CC | Bell 206B JetRanger III | 3593 | ex N2295W | |
| ☐ N700WJ | Cessna 425 Conquest I | 425-0036 | ex F-GCQN | |
| ☐ N6266C | Cessna T210N Turbo Centurion II | 21063849 | | |

## BIMINI ISLAND AIR                          (BMY)          Fort Lauderdale-Executive, FL (FXE)

AOC revoked 27Jun11

## BRAVO AIRLINES                          Miami-Opa Locka, FL (OPF)

| | | | | | |
|---|---|---|---|---|---|
| ☐ N701AU | Lockheed P2V-7 Neptune Firestar | 726-7190 | ex N920AU | 01 | Tanker |
| ☐ N716AU | Lockheed P2V-7 Neptune Firestar | 726-7065 | ex N90YY | 16 | Tanker |
| ☐ N718AU | Lockheed P2V-7 Neptune Firestar | 726-7214 | ex N964L | 18 | Tanker |

## BRISTOW US                          Airlog (ALG)          New Iberia-Air Logistics Heliport, LA (-)

| | | | | |
|---|---|---|---|---|
| ☐ N133AL | Bell 206L-3 LongRanger III | 51133 | | based Alaska |
| ☐ N182AL | Bell 206L-3 LongRanger III | 52057 | ex D-HSDA | |
| ☐ N330P | Bell 206L-3 LongRanger III | 51295 | | |
| ☐ N346AL | Bell 206L-3 LongRanger III | 51378 | | based Alaska |
| ☐ N358AL | Bell 206L-3 LongRanger III | 51460 | | based Alaska |
| ☐ N360AL | Bell 206L-3 LongRanger III | 51462 | | based Alaska |
| ☐ N363AL | Bell 206L-3 LongRanger III | 51472 | ex C-GLZE | based Alaska |
| ☐ N69AL | Bell 206L-4 LongRanger IV | 52139 | ex PT-YBH | |
| ☐ N76AL | Bell 206L-4 LongRanger IV | 52165 | ex N15EW | |
| ☐ N176AL | Bell 206L-4 LongRanger IV | 52146 | ex C-FOFE | |
| ☐ N177AL | Bell 206L-4 LongRanger IV | 52157 | ex C-GLZU | |
| ☐ N188AL | Bell 206L-4 LongRanger IV | 52082 | ex N84TV | |
| ☐ N189AL | Bell 206L-4 LongRanger IV | 52340 | | |
| ☐ N192AL | Bell 206L-4 LongRanger IV | 52342 | | |
| ☐ N193AL | Bell 206L-4 LongRanger IV | 52344 | | |
| ☐ N196AL | Bell 206L-4 LongRanger IV | 52380 | ex N218K | |
| ☐ N206DB | Bell 206L-4 LongRanger IV | 52127 | | |
| ☐ N265AL | Bell 206L-4 LongRanger IV | 52280 | ex C-GFNY | |
| ☐ N266AL | Bell 206L-4 LongRanger IV | 52281 | | |
| ☐ N267AL | Bell 206L-4 LongRanger IV | 52282 | ex C-GAXE | |
| ☐ N268AL | Bell 206L-4 LongRanger IV | 52283 | | |
| ☐ N269AL | Bell 206L-4 LongRanger IV | 52284 | | |
| ☐ N271AL | Bell 206L-4 LongRanger IV | 52287 | | |
| ☐ N272AL | Bell 206L-4 LongRanger IV | 52288 | | |
| ☐ N275AL | Bell 206L-4 LongRanger IV | 52285 | | |
| ☐ N276AL | Bell 206L-4 LongRanger IV | 52312 | | |
| ☐ N278AL | Bell 206L-4 LongRanger IV | 52313 | | |
| ☐ N279AL | Bell 206L-4 LongRanger IV | 52314 | ex C-GAEP | |
| ☐ N280AL | Bell 206L-4 LongRanger IV | 52315 | | |
| ☐ N281AL | Bell 206L-4 LongRanger IV | 52319 | | |
| ☐ N403AL | Bell 407 | 53478 | ex N4041F | |
| ☐ N404AL | Bell 407 | 53479 | ex N40410 | |
| ☐ N405AL | Bell 407 | 53480 | ex N40414 | |

| | | | | |
|---|---|---|---|---|
| ☐ N406AL | Bell 407 | 53481 | ex N6146J | |
| ☐ N407AL | Bell 407 | 53044 | | |
| ☐ N407TZ | Bell 407 | 53204 | ex N487AL | |
| ☐ N408AL | Bell 407 | 53491 | ex N6148U | |
| ☐ N409AL | Bell 407 | 53494 | ex N9182V | |
| ☐ N410AL | Bell 407 | 53482 | ex N388RT | |
| ☐ N415AL | Bell 407 | 53182 | ex N415AG | |
| ☐ N431AL | Bell 407 | 53923 | ex C-FYPN | |
| ☐ N436AL | Bell 407 | 53069 | ex N58236 | |
| ☐ N447AL | Bell 407 | 53126 | ex PT-YNM | |
| ☐ N477AL | Bell 407 | 53203 | | |
| ☐ N497AL | Bell 407 | 53172 | | |
| ☐ N527AL | Bell 407 | 53211 | | |
| ☐ N557AL | Bell 407 | 53243 | | |
| ☐ N577AL | Bell 407 | 53247 | | |
| ☐ N587AL | Bell 407 | 53248 | | |
| ☐ N597AL | Bell 407 | 53091 | ex N427AL | |
| ☐ N607AL | Bell 407 | 53264 | | |
| ☐ N617AL | Bell 407 | 53265 | | |
| ☐ N627AL | Bell 407 | 53284 | | |
| ☐ N637AL | Bell 407 | 53293 | ex PT-YUW | based Alaska |
| ☐ N647AL | Bell 407 | 53357 | ex N60321 | |
| ☐ N657AL | Bell 407 | 53413 | ex N155ZS | |
| ☐ N667AL | Bell 407 | 53624 | ex XA-SKY | |
| ☐ N687AL | Bell 407 | 53366 | ex N6302B | |
| ☐ N697AL | Bell 407 | 53374 | ex N6112Q | |
| ☐ N727AL | Bell 407 | 53227 | ex N298RS | |
| ☐ N796RV | Bell 407 | 53037 | ex RP-C2468 | |
| ☐ N847AL | Bell 407 | 53150 | ex N407XS | |
| ☐ N937AL | Bell 407 | 53383 | ex N63894 | |
| | | | | |
| ☐ N519AL | Sikorsky S-76A | 760058 | ex G-EWEL | |
| ☐ N522AL | Sikorsky S-76A | 760236 | ex N202SR | |
| ☐ N707AL | Sikorsky S-76A | 760189 | ex N989QS | |
| ☐ N709AL | Sikorsky S-76A | 760278 | | |
| ☐ N860AL | Sikorsky S-76C+ | 760527 | ex N9024W | |
| ☐ N861AL | Sikorsky S-76C+ | 760529 | ex N2032W | |
| ☐ N862AL | Sikorsky S-76C+ | 760531 | ex N2021W | |
| ☐ N863AL | Sikorsky S-76C+ | 760536 | ex N5009K | |
| ☐ N864AL | Sikorsky S-76C+ | 760557 | ex N50093 | |
| ☐ N865AL | Sikorsky S-76C | 760564 | ex N70089 | |
| ☐ N866AL | Sikorsky S-76C | 760562 | ex N50085 | |
| ☐ N867AL | Sikorsky S-76C | 760579 | ex N7104Q | |
| ☐ N868AL | Sikorsky S-76C+ | 760580 | ex N7102S | |
| ☐ N871AL | Sikorsky S-76C+ | 760627 | ex N80907 | |
| ☐ N881AL | Sikorsky S-76C+ | 760673 | ex N4512G | |
| ☐ N883AL | Sikorsky S-76C | 760677 | ex N4514G | |
| ☐ N884AL | Sikorsky S-76C | 760721 | | |
| ☐ N31211 | Sikorsky S-76A | 760225 | | |
| | | | | |
| ☐ N1016R | Sikorsky S-92A | 920144 | | ♦ |
| ☐ N149FF | Sikorsky S-92A | 920148 | | ♦ |
| ☐ N157Q | Sikorsky S-92A | 920157 | | ♦ |
| ☐ N158G | Sikorsky S-92A | 920158 | | ♦ |
| ☐ N159Y | Sikorsky S-92A | 920159 | | ♦ |
| ☐ N932BG | Sikorsky S-92A | 920021 | ex N92UT | ♦ |
| ☐ N933BG | Sikorsky S-92A | 920155 | ex N155N | ♦ |
| | | | | |
| ☐ N206XS | Bell 206B JetRanger III | 3040 | | op by Bristow Academy |
| ☐ N239BG | Agusta AW139 | 41221 | | |
| ☐ N335BG | Eurocopter EC135P2+ | 0793 | | |
| ☐ N339BG | Agusta AW139 | 41234 | ex N208YS | |
| ☐ N397AL | Bell 412 | 36012 | ex XA-TLO | |
| ☐ N412BG | Bell 412SP | 33210 | ex XA-TYQ | |
| ☐ N460WB | Bell 412EP | 36588 | | ♦ |
| ☐ N494HL | MBB Bo.105CBS-4 | S-813 | ex N494HL | |
| ☐ N5008N | Bell 206B JetRanger III | 2518 | | op by Bristow Academy |
| ☐ N535AL | Eurocopter EC135P2+ | 0716 | | |
| ☐ N635AL | Eurocopter EC135P2+ | 0758 | | |
| ☐ N935AL | Eurocopter EC135P2+ | 0817 | | |

## BROOKS AVIATION                                Douglas-Municipal, GA (DQH)

| | | | | |
|---|---|---|---|---|
| ☐ N99FS | Douglas DC-3 | 12425 | ex (N89BF) | |

## BROOKS FUEL                                      Fairbanks-Intl, AK (FAI)

| | | | | |
|---|---|---|---|---|
| ☐ N708Z | Douglas C-54G | 36067 | ex USCG 5614 | |
| ☐ N3054V | Douglas DC-4 | 10547 | ex N76AU      162 | Tanker |
| ☐ N51802 | Douglas C-54G | 35930 | ex 45-0477 | [FAI] |
| ☐ N96358 | Douglas C-54E | 27284 | ex Bu90398 | |

## BUSINESS AVIATION COURIER — Dakota (DKT) — Sioux Falls-Joe Foss Field, SD (FSD)

| Reg | Type | Serial | ex | Notes |
|---|---|---|---|---|
| ☐ N314U | Cessna 310R II | 310R1852 | | ♦ |
| ☐ N500FS | Cessna 310R II | 310R0630 | | |
| ☐ N1203W | Cessna 310R II | 310R2106 | | ♦ |
| ☐ N1533T | Cessna 310R II | 310R0111 | | |
| ☐ N3286M | Cessna 310R II | 310R1894 | | ♦ |
| ☐ N3482G | Cessna 310R II | 310R0850 | | |
| ☐ N3597G | Cessna 310R II | 310R0875 | | ♦ |
| ☐ N3845G | Cessna 310R II | 310R0929 | | ♦ |
| ☐ N6122C | Cessna 310R II | 310R1290 | | ♦ |
| ☐ N8251G | Cessna 310R II | 310R0931 | | ♦ |
| ☐ N87239 | Cessna 310R II | 310R0314 | | ♦ |
| ☐ N98904 | Cessna 310R II | 310R1240 | | ♦ |
| ☐ N76MD | Cessna 402B II | 402B1055 | ex N987PF | |
| ☐ N402BP | Cessna 402B | 402B0353 | ex N5419M | |
| ☐ N402SS | Cessna 402B | 402B0562 | ex N402CC | |
| ☐ N624CA | Cessna 402B | 402B0876 | ex D-IJOS | |
| ☐ N780MB | Cessna 402B | 402B0249 | ex N402RT | |
| ☐ N1048 | Cessna 402B | 402B0628 | ex N104WM | |
| ☐ N3729C | Cessna 402B | 402B0589 | ex XB-EAC | |
| ☐ N3796C | Cessna 402B | 402B0803 | | |
| ☐ N3813 | Cessna 402B | 402B0807 | ex PK-VCE | |
| ☐ N366AE | Swearingen SA.227AC Metro III | AC-681B | | |
| ☐ N387PH | Swearingen SA.227AC Metro III | AC-531 | ex N31094 | |
| ☐ N685BA | Swearingen SA.227AC Metro III | AC-685 | ex N685AV | |
| ☐ N3108B | Swearingen SA.227AC Metro III | AC-509 | ex XA-TAK | |
| ☐ N3116N | Swearingen SA.227AC Metro III | AC-596 | | |
| ☐ N80BS | Cessna 404 Titan II | 404-0048 | ex G-ZAPB | |
| ☐ N126BP | Cessna 414A Chancellor | 414A-0214 | | ♦ |
| ☐ N401VA | Piper PA-31-350 Chieftain | 31-8275001 | | ♦ |
| ☐ N797CF | Beech 65-C90 King Air | LJ-797 | | ♦ |
| ☐ N7914Q | Cessna 414A Chancellor | 414A-0305 | | ♦ |

## BUTLER AIRCRAFT — Redmond, OR (RDM)

| Reg | Type | Serial | ex | | Notes |
|---|---|---|---|---|---|
| ☐ N401US | Douglas DC-7 | 45145/767 | ex N6331C | 62 | Tanker |
| ☐ N756Z | Douglas DC-7 | 45400 | | | ♦ |
| ☐ N838D | Douglas DC-7 | 45347/936 | | 60 | Tanker |
| ☐ N6353C | Douglas DC-7 | 45486/964 | | 66 | Tanker |
| ☐ N60018 | Cessna TU206F Stationair | U20602002 | | | |

## CAMACHO EXPRESS — Miami, FL (MIA)

| Reg | Type | Serial | ex | Notes |
|---|---|---|---|---|
| ☐ N578DD | Cessna 208B Caravan I | 208B00249 | ex 5N-CES | ♦ |
| ☐ N696RA | Beech 65-F90 King Air | LA-87 | | ♦ |
| ☐ N29884 | Britten-Norman BN-2A-26 Islander | 847 | ex G-HMCG | ♦ |

## C&M AIRWAYS — Red Wing (RWG) — El Paso-Intl, TX (ELP)

| Reg | Type | Serial | ex |
|---|---|---|---|
| ☐ N563PC | Douglas DC-9-15RC (ABS 3) | 47055/194 | ex N1305T |
| ☐ N640CM | Convair 640F | 104 | ex C-GCWY |

## CAPE AIR (HYANNIS AIR SERVICE) — Cair (9K/KAP)
### Hyannis-Barnstable Municipal, MA/Naples-Municipal, FL (HYA/APF)

| Reg | Type | Serial | ex | Notes |
|---|---|---|---|---|
| ☐ N69SC | Cessna 402C II | 402C0041 | ex N5778C | |
| ☐ N83PB | Cessna 402C II | 402C0350 | ex N26627 | |
| ☐ N106CA | Cessna 402C III | 402C1020 | ex TJ-AHQ | |
| ☐ N120PC | Cessna 402C II | 402C0079 | ex N2612L | |
| ☐ N121PB | Cessna 402C II | 402C0507 | ex N6874X | |
| ☐ N160PB | Cessna 402C II | 402C0493 | ex N6841M | ♦ |
| ☐ N161TA | Cessna 402C II | 402C0070 | ex N2611A | |
| ☐ N223PB | Cessna 402C II | 402C0105 | ex N261PB | |
| ☐ N247GS | Cessna 402C II | 402C0637 | ex N404BK | |
| ☐ N290CA | Cessna 402C II | 402C0297 | ex N401BK | |
| ☐ N300SN | Cessna 402C II | 402C0060 | | ♦ |
| ☐ N401TJ | Cessna 402C II | 402C0109 | ex TJ-AFV | ♦ |
| ☐ N402NS | Cessna 402C II | 402C0277 | | ♦ |
| ☐ N402VN | Cessna 402C II | 402C0488 | ex (N6840D) | |
| ☐ N406GA | Cessna 402C II | 402C0329 | ex N2642D | |
| ☐ N494BC | Cessna 402C II | 402C0308 | ex N67PB | |
| ☐ N499CA | Cessna 402C II | 402C1006 | ex N410BK | ♦ |
| ☐ N514NC | Cessna 402C II | 402C0514 | ex N125PB | |
| ☐ N524CA | Cessna 402C II | 402C0522 | ex C-GSKG | |
| ☐ N525RH | Cessna 402C II | 402C0525 | ex N68761 | |
| ☐ N548GA | Cessna 402C II | 402C0653 | ex N6773T | |

| | | | | |
|---|---|---|---|---|
| ☐ N618CA | Cessna 402C II | 402C0620 | ex VH-RGK | |
| ☐ N660CA | Cessna 402C II | 402C0406 | ex C-GHMI | |
| ☐ N678JG | Cessna 402C II | 402C0266 | | ♦ |
| ☐ N747WS | Cessna 402C II | 402C0080 | ex C-GHYZ | |
| ☐ N751CA | Cessna 402C II | 402C0217 | ex N402AT | ♦ |
| ☐ N762EA | Cessna 402C II | 402C0061 | ex N5872C | |
| ☐ N763EA | Cessna 402C II | 402C0497 | ex N763AN | |
| ☐ N764EA | Cessna 402C II | 402C0237 | ex N2719T | |
| ☐ N769EA | Cessna 402C II | 402C0303 | ex N3283M | |
| ☐ N770CA | Cessna 402C II | 402C0432 | | ♦ |
| ☐ N771EA | Cessna 402C II | 402C0046 | ex N5809C | |
| ☐ N781EA | Cessna 402C II | 402C0310 | ex N822AN | |
| ☐ N810BW | Cessna 402C II | 402C0279 | | ♦ |
| ☐ N812AN | Cessna 402C II | 402C0229 | ex N2718P | |
| ☐ N818AN | Cessna 402C II | 402C0501 | ex N6842Q | |
| ☐ N1055 | Cessna 402C II | 402C0249 | | ♦ |
| ☐ N1361G | Cessna 402C II | 402C0270 | | |
| ☐ N1376G | Cessna 402C II | 402C0271 | ex N156PB | special landscape c/s |
| ☐ N2611X | Cessna 402C II | 402C0072 | | |
| ☐ N2612C | Cessna 402C II | 402C0077 | | ♦ |
| ☐ N2615G | Cessna 402C II | 402C0101 | ex C-GHGM | |
| ☐ N2649Z | Cessna 402C II | 402C0333 | | |
| ☐ N2714B | Cessna 402C II | 402C0210 | | |
| ☐ N2714M | Cessna 402C II | 402C0211 | | |
| ☐ N3249M | Cessna 402C II | 402C0296 | | ♦ |
| ☐ N3292M | Cessna 402C II | 402C0304 | | |
| ☐ N4630N | Cessna 402C II | 402C0001 | | ♦ |
| ☐ N4652N | Cessna 402C II | 402C0011 | | ♦ |
| ☐ N6765T | Cessna 402C II | 402C0629 | | ♦ |
| ☐ N6813J | Cessna 402C II | 402C0641 | | |
| ☐ N6875D | Cessna 402C II | 402C0511 | | special Flagship Whalers c/s |
| ☐ N6879R | Cessna 402C II | 402C0611 | ex C-GJVC | |
| ☐ N7037E | Cessna 402C II | 402C0471 | ex C-GGXH | |
| ☐ N26150 | Cessna 402C II | 402C0111 | | ♦ |
| ☐ N26156 | Cessna 402C II | 402C0112 | | |
| ☐ N26514 | Cessna 402C II | 402C0344 | | |
| ☐ N26151 | Cessna 402C II | 402C0842 | | ♦ |
| ☐ N26632 | Cessna 402C II | 402C0404 | | |
| ☐ N36911 | Cessna 402C II | 402C0314 | | |
| ☐ N67786 | Cessna 402C II | 402C0631 | | special Key West Express c/s |
| ☐ N67886 | Cessna 402C II | 402C0435 | | |
| ☐ N68391 | Cessna 402C II | 402C0483 | | |
| ☐ N68752 | Cessna 402C II | 402C0518 | | |
| ☐ N88833 | Cessna 402C II | 402C0265 | | special flowers c/s |
| | | | | |
| ☐ N14834 | ATR 42-320 | 0193 | ex F-WWEG | |
| ☐ N42836 | ATR 42-320 | 0200 | ex F-WWEN | 836 |

## CAPITAL CARGO INTERNATIONAL AIRLINES  Cappy (PT/CCI)                    Orlando-Intl, FL (MCO)

| | | | | | |
|---|---|---|---|---|---|
| ☐ N286SC | Boeing 727-2A1F (FedEx 3) | 21601/1694 | ex N328AS | Beth | |
| ☐ N287SC | Boeing 727-2A1F (FedEx 3) | 21345/1673 | ex N327AS | Florence | |
| ☐ N308AS | Boeing 727-227F (FedEx 3) | 22002/1627 | ex N479BN | Eloise | |
| ☐ N357KP | Boeing 727-230F (FedEx 3) | 20675/924 | ex G-BPNY | Princess Kendall | |
| ☐ N708AA | Boeing 727-223F (FedEx 3) | 22465/1761 | | | |
| ☐ N713AA | Boeing 727-223F (FedEx 3) | 22469/1769 | | Jessica | |
| ☐ N715AA | Boeing 727-223F (FedEx 3) | 22470/1771 | | | |
| ☐ N755DH | Boeing 727-225F (FedEx 3) | 21857/1539 | ex N887MA | | |
| ☐ N801EA | Boeing 727-225F (FedEx 3) | 22432/1658 | | Miss Ashley | |
| ☐ N815EA | Boeing 727-225F (FedEx 3) | 22552/1773 | | Gudrund | |
| ☐ N899AA | Boeing 727-223F (FedEx 3) | 22015/1666 | | Angie | |
| | | | | | |
| ☐ N531UA | Boeing 757-222F | 25042/361 | | | [JAX]♦ |
| ☐ N605DL | Boeing 757-232F | 22812/46 | | | |
| ☐ N620DL | Boeing 757-232F | 22910/111 | | | |

## CARIBE RICO

| | | | |
|---|---|---|---|
| ☐ N274FS | Swearingen SA.226TC Metro II | TC-274 | ex C-FTJC |

## CARSON HELICOPTERS                         Perkasie-Heliport, PA/Jackonsville Heliport, OR

| | | | | |
|---|---|---|---|---|
| ☐ N61NH | Sikorsky S-61N | 61474 | | ♦ |
| ☐ N103WF | Sikorsky S-61N | 61766 | ex 9M-AVO | |
| ☐ N116AZ | Sikorsky S-61N | 61242 | ex VH-BHO | |
| ☐ N261F | Sikorsky S-61N | 61771 | | ♦ |
| ☐ N302Y | Sikorsky S-61N | 61472 | ex YV-323C | |
| ☐ N349FC | Sikorsky S-61 (UH-3H) | 61239 | | |
| ☐ N349RH | Sikorsky S-61 (UH-3H) | 61117 | ex Bu149702 | |
| ☐ N350DA | Sikorsky S-61 (SH-3H) | 61187 | | |
| ☐ N352DH | Sikorsky S-61 (SH-3H) | 61161 | ex N1048Y | |

| ☐ | Reg | Type | Serial | Ex | Notes |
|---|-----|------|--------|-----|-------|
| ☐ | N364FH | Sikorsky S-61N II | 61718 | ex G-BBVA | |
| ☐ | N364HH | Sikorsky S-61N II | 61712 | ex G-BBHL | |
| ☐ | N408FS | Sikorsky S-61N | 61361 | | |
| ☐ | N408HH | Sikorsky S-61N II | 61716 | | ♦ |
| ☐ | N408WC | Sikorsky S-61N II | 61764 | | ♦ |
| ☐ | N410GH | Sikorsky S-61N | 61749 | ex V8-BSP | |
| ☐ | N439LS | Sikorsky S-61N | 61704 | ex C-FDOH | |
| ☐ | N445HD | Sikorsky S-61N | 61489 | | ♦ |
| ☐ | N448JS | Sikorsky S-61N | 61428 | ex C-GJDR | ♦ |
| ☐ | N454PG | Sikorsky S-61D | | ex Bu151545 | ♦ |
| ☐ | B454US | Sikorsky S-61D | | ex Bu151553 | ♦ |
| ☐ | N454VA | Sikorsky S-61A | | ex Bu149682 | ♦ |
| ☐ | N454WG | Sikorsky S-61A | | ex Bu148996 | ♦ |
| ☐ | N454XS | Sikorsky S-61D | | ex Bu151555 | ♦ |
| ☐ | N454YS | Sikorsky S-61A | | ex Bu149922 | ♦ |
| ☐ | N454ZG | Sikorsky S-61D | | ex Bu151536 | ♦ |
| ☐ | N463ZC | Sikorsky S-61N II | 61721 | | ♦ |
| ☐ | N564EH | Sikorsky S-61N | 61365 | | ♦ |
| ☐ | N612AZ | Sikorsky S-61N | 61297 | | |
| ☐ | N612RM | Sikorsky S-61N | 61744 | ex C-FSYH | |
| ☐ | N617HM | Sikorsky S-61N | 61754 | ex C-GSBL | |
| ☐ | N618PA | Sikorsky S-61L | 61426 | | |
| ☐ | N725JH | Sikorsky S-61N | 61775 | ex V8-SAV | |
| ☐ | N905AL | Sikorsky S-61N | 61717 | ex V8-UDZ | |
| ☐ | N4263A | Sikorsky S-61R | 61551 | ex 65-5700 | |
| ☐ | N4263F | Sikorsky S-61R | 61533 | ex 64-14230 | |
| ☐ | N5102Z | Sikorsky S-61N | 61518 | | ♦ |
| ☐ | N6981R | Sikorsky S-61N | 61453 | | |
| ☐ | N8167B | Sikorsky S-61A | 61137 | ex Bu149720 | |
| ☐ | N8170V | Sikorsky S-61A | 61232 | | |
| ☐ | N8174J | Sikorsky S-61R | 61584 | ex 66-13286 | wfs |
| ☐ | N9260A | Sikorsky S-61D | 61442 | ex Bu156496 | |
| ☐ | N9271A | Sikorsky S-61D | 61449 | ex Bu156486 | |
| ☐ | N13491 | Sikorsky S-61A | 61129 | | |
| ☐ | N15456 | Sikorsky S-61N | 61826 | | ♦ |
| ☐ | N31733 | Sikorsky S-61A | 61236 | | ♦ |
| ☐ | N42626 | Sikorsky S-61R | 61522 | ex 63-9690 | |
| ☐ | N81664 | Sikorsky S-61A | 61063 | ex Bu148989 | |
| ☐ | N81692 | Sikorsky S-61A | 61074 | ex Bu149000 | |
| ☐ | N81701 | Sikorsky S-61R | 61529 | ex 64-14226 | wfs |
| ☐ | N81702 | Sikorsky S-61R | 61608 | ex 64-14706 | wfs |
| ☐ | N81725 | Sikorsky S-61A | | ex Bu148050 | ♦ |
| ☐ | N81743 | Sikorsky S-61R | 61575 | ex 65-12800 | wfs |
| ☐ | N82702 | Sikorsky S-61D | 61432 | ex N92592 | |
| ☐ | N87580 | Sikorsky S-61N | 61465 | | ♦ |
| ☐ | N92590 | Sikorsky S-61D | 61351 | ex Bu152691 | |
| | | | | | |
| ☐ | N239Z | de Havilland DHC-6 Twin Otter 300 | 239 | ex N15239 | based Argentina |
| ☐ | N920R | de Havilland DHC-6 Twin Otter 100 | 045 | ex HC-BYK | based Argentina |

## CASCADE AIR — Ephrata-Municipal, WA (EPH)

| ☐ | Reg | Type | Serial | Ex | Notes |
|---|-----|------|--------|-----|-------|
| ☐ | N30422 | Cessna A185F Skywagon | 18503129 | | ♦ |
| ☐ | N91314 | Douglas DC-3 | 4538 | ex NC17884 | |

## CASTLE AVIATION — Castle (CSJ) — Akron-Canton Regional, OH (CAK)

| ☐ | Reg | Type | Serial | Ex | Notes |
|---|-----|------|--------|-----|-------|
| ☐ | N24MG | Cessna 208B Caravan I | 208B0850 | ex N5261R | Frtr |
| ☐ | N27MG | Cessna 208B Caravan I | 208B0650 | ex N5262Z | Frtr |
| ☐ | N29MG | Cessna 208B Caravan I | 208B0812 | ex N52229 | Frtr |
| ☐ | N31MG | Cessna 208B Caravan I | 208B1065 | | Frtr |
| ☐ | N1029Y | Cessna 208B Caravan I | 208B0325 | | Frtr |
| | | | | | |
| ☐ | N49MG | Piper PA-60 Aerostar 600 | 60-0634-7961201 | ex N8232J | |
| ☐ | N52MG | Ted Smith Aerostar 600A | 60-0530-172 | ex N8047J | |

## CATALINA FLYING BOATS — Catalina Air (CBT) — Long Beach-Daugherty Field, CA (LGB)

| ☐ | Reg | Type | Serial | Ex | Notes |
|---|-----|------|--------|-----|-------|
| ☐ | N18R | Beech E-18S | BA-312 | | >PPG |
| ☐ | N103AF | Beech G-18S | BA-526 | ex N277S | >PPG |
| ☐ | N166H | Beech E-18S | BA-253 | | |
| ☐ | N403JB | Douglas DC-3 | 16943/34202 | ex N17778 | |
| ☐ | N2298C | Douglas DC-3 | 16453/33201 | ex (N352SA) | |
| ☐ | N9680B | Cessna 208B Caravan I | 208B0150 | | |

## CDF AVIATION — Sacramento-Mather, CA (MHR)

| ☐ | Reg | Type | Serial | Ex | | Notes |
|---|-----|------|--------|-----|---|-------|
| ☐ | N481DF | Bell UH-1H | 13318 | ex 72-21019 | 104 | |
| ☐ | N489DF | Bell UH-1H | 12224 | ex 69-15936 | 901 | standby |
| ☐ | N490DF | Bell UH-1H | 12375 | ex 70-15765 | 205 | |
| ☐ | N491DF | Bell UH-1H | 12146 | ex 69-15858 | 301 | |

| | | | | | | |
|---|---|---|---|---|---|---|
| ☐ N492DF | Bell UH-1H | 11433 | ex 69-15145 | | | standby |
| ☐ N493DF | Bell UH-1H | 12001 | ex 69-15713 | | | standby |
| ☐ N494DF | Bell UH-1H | 11303 | ex 69-15015 | 404 | | |
| ☐ N495DF | Bell UH-1H | 12218 | ex 69-15930 | 106 | | |
| ☐ N496DF | Bell UH-1H | 11964 | ex 69-15676 | 102 | | |
| ☐ N497DF | Bell UH-1H | 11553 | ex 69-15265 | 202 | | |
| ☐ N498DF | Bell UH-1H | 12153 | ex 69-15865 | 406 | | |
| ☐ N499DF | Bell UH-1H | 12846 | ex 71-20022 | 101 | | |
| | | | | | | |
| ☐ N422DF | Marsh S-2T Turbo Tracker | 286C | ex N518DF | 82 | | |
| ☐ N424DF | Marsh S-2T Turbo Tracker | 289C | ex N519DF | 83 | | |
| ☐ N425DF | Marsh S-2T Turbo Tracker | 294C | ex N522DF | 89 | | |
| ☐ N426DF | Marsh S-2T Turbo Tracker | 293C | ex N520DF | 88 | | |
| ☐ N427DF | Marsh S-2T Turbo Tracker | 326C | ex N524DF | 70 | | |
| ☐ N428DF | Marsh S-2T Turbo Tracker | 137C | ex N511DF | 91 | | |
| ☐ N431DF | Marsh S-2T Turbo Tracker | 109C | ex N504DF | 78 | | |
| ☐ N432DF | Marsh S-2T Turbo Tracker | 112C | ex N505DF | 71 | | |
| ☐ N433DF | Marsh S-2T Turbo Tracker | 130C | ex N510DF | 86 | | |
| ☐ N434DF | Marsh S-2T Turbo Tracker | 335C | ex N527DF | 90 | | |
| ☐ N435DF | Marsh S-2T Turbo Tracker | 329C | ex N526DF | 76 | | |
| ☐ N437DF | Marsh S-2T Turbo Tracker | 123C | ex N507DF | 73 | | |
| ☐ N438DF | Marsh S-2T Turbo Tracker | 173C | ex N513DF | 85 | | |
| ☐ N439DF | Marsh S-2T Turbo Tracker | 129C | ex N509DF | 74 | | |
| ☐ N440DF | Marsh S-2T Turbo Tracker | 148C | ex N512DF | 96 | | |
| ☐ N441DF | Marsh S-2T Turbo Tracker | 277C | ex N517DF | 100 | | |
| ☐ N442DF | Marsh S-2T Turbo Tracker | 295C | ex Bu152826 | 94 | | |
| ☐ N444DF | Marsh S-2T Turbo Tracker | 187C | ex N515DF | 75 | | |
| ☐ N445DF | Marsh S-2T Turbo Tracker | 232C | ex N516DF | 80 | | |
| ☐ N448DF | Marsh S-2T Turbo Tracker | | ex Bu152347 | | | ♦ |
| ☐ N449DF | Marsh S-2T Turbo Tracker | 307C | ex N523DF | 81 | | |
| ☐ N450DF | Marsh S-2T Turbo Tracker | 228C | ex Bu152341 | | | |
| | | | | | | |
| ☐ N400DF | Rockwell OV-10A Bronco | 305-122M-65 | ex Bu155454 | 440 | | |
| ☐ N401DF | Rockwell OV-10A Bronco | 305-128M-68 | ex Bu155457 | 310 | | standby |
| ☐ N402DF | Rockwell OV-10A Bronco | 305-132M-70 | ex Bu155459 | 210 | | |
| ☐ N403DF | Rockwell OV-10A Bronco | 305-148M-78 | ex Bu155467 | 240 | | standby |
| ☐ N407DF | Rockwell OV-10A Bronco | 305-164M-86 | ex Bu155475 | 430 | | |
| ☐ N408DF | Rockwell OV-10A Bronco | 305-178M-90 | ex Bu155480 | 230 | | |
| ☐ N409DF | Rockwell OV-10A Bronco | 305-18M-12 | ex Bu155401 | 330 | | |
| ☐ N410DF | Rockwell OV-10A Bronco | 305-158M-82 | ex Bu155471 | 110 | | |
| ☐ N413DF | Rockwell OV-10A Bronco | 305-20M-13 | ex Bu155402 | 120 | | |
| ☐ N414DF | Rockwell OV-10A Bronco | 305-26M-16 | ex Bu155415 | 140 | | |
| ☐ N415DF | Rockwell OV-10A Bronco | 305-68M-38 | ex Bu155427 | 460 | | |
| ☐ N418DF | Rockwell OV-10A Bronco | 305-70M-39 | ex Bu155428 | 340 | | |
| ☐ N419DF | Rockwell OV-10A Bronco | 305-104M-56 | | | | ♦ |
| ☐ N421DF | Rockwell OV-10A Bronco | 305-206M-107 | ex Bu155496 | 240 | | |
| ☐ N429DF | Rockwell OV-10A Bronco | 305A-17M-11 | ex Bu155400 | 310 | | |
| ☐ N430DF | Rockwell OV-10A Bronco | 305-127A-60 | | | | ♦ |
| | | | | | | |
| ☐ N443DF | Grumman S-2A Tracker | 195 | ex Bu133224 | 72 | | |

## CENTURION CARGO — Challenge Cargo (WE/CWC) — Miami-Intl, FL (MIA)

| | | | | | |
|---|---|---|---|---|---|
| ☐ N612GC | Douglas DC-10-30F | 47840/337 | ex G-BHDJ | | [SFB] |
| ☐ N984AR | McDonnell-Douglas MD-11BCF | 48429/500 | ex N429AN | | |
| ☐ N985AR | McDonnell-Douglas MD-11F | 48430/508 | ex EI-UPU | | ♦ |
| ☐ N986AR | McDonnell-Douglas MD-11F | 48426/468 | ex EI-UPA | | ♦ |
| ☐ N988AR | McDonnell-Douglas MD-11F | 48434/476 | ex N701GC | | |

## CHAMPION AIR

| | | | | | |
|---|---|---|---|---|---|
| ☐ N183DE | Embraer ERJ-145LR | 145129 | ex LX-LGV | | ♦ |
| ☐ N500DE | Embraer ERJ-145EP | 145084 | ex LX-LGU | | ♦ |

## CHAMPLAIN AIR — Plattsburg-Clinton County, NY (PLB)

| | | | | | |
|---|---|---|---|---|---|
| ☐ N59NA | Douglas DC-3 | 9043 | ex G-AKNB | | |
| ☐ N700CA | Douglas DC-3 | 12438 | ex N107AD | Mary Ann | |

## CHANNEL ISLANDS AVIATION — Channel (CHN) — Camarillo, CA (CMA)

| | | | | | |
|---|---|---|---|---|---|
| ☐ N848MA | Britten-Norman BN-2B-20 Islander | 2210 | ex 8P-TAJ | | ♦ |

## CHARTER AIR TRANSPORT

| | | | | | |
|---|---|---|---|---|---|
| ☐ N650CT | Embraer EMB.120RT Brasilia | 120198 | ex N267AS | | ♦ |
| ☐ N651CT | Embraer EMB.120RT Brasilia | 120197 | ex N58733 | | ♦ |
| ☐ N654CT | Embraer EMB.120ER Brasilia | 120251 | ex N251YV | | ♦ |
| ☐ N658CT | Embraer EMB.120ER Brasilia | 120328 | ex N298SW | | ♦ |

## CHAUTAUQUA AIRLINES — Chautauqua (RP/CHQ) — Indianapolis-Intl, IN (IND)

Ops as US Airways Express from Boston, ME, Indianapolis, IN, Pittsburgh, PA and New York-La Guardia, NY. Also ops as American Connection from St Louis, MO, as Delta Connection from Orlando, FL and as United Express from Chicago, IL and Washington, DC. Wholly owned subsidiary of Republic Airways Holdings.

## CHERRY-AIR — Cherry (CCY) — Dallas-Addison, TX (ADS)

| | | | | |
|---|---|---|---|---|
| ☐ N209CA | AMD Falcon 20C | 71 | ex N195AS | |
| ☐ N216CA | AMD Falcon 20C | 11 | ex N983AJ | |
| ☐ N217CA | AMD Falcon 20C | 75 | ex UR-EFB | |
| ☐ N218CA | AMD Falcon 20D | 218 | ex EC-EEU | CADS |
| ☐ N219CA | AMD Falcon 20D | 193 | ex XA- | |
| ☐ N234CA | AMD Falcon 20C | 17 | ex N55TH | CADS♦ |
| ☐ N235CA | AMD Falcon 20C | 139 | ex N900WB | |
| | | | | |
| ☐ N151WW | Learjet 24 | 24-170 | ex N200DH | |
| ☐ N238CA | Learjet 25 | 25-040 | ex N23FN | CADS |

Ceased ops 10Jan09 but resumed later

## CIMARRON AIRE — Cimmaron Aire (CMN) — McAlester-Regional, OK (MLC)

| | | | | |
|---|---|---|---|---|
| ☐ N737SW | Beech E-18S | BA-402 | ex N388W | Frtr |

## COASTAL AIR TRANSPORT — Coastal (DQ/CXT) — St Croix-Alexander Hamilton, VI (STX)

| | | | | |
|---|---|---|---|---|
| ☐ N676MF | Cessna 402B | 402B0106 | ex N7856Q | Cruzan Queen |
| ☐ N677MF | Cessna 404 Titan | 404-0421 | ex N96889 | |

## COLGAN AIR — Colgan (9L/CJC) — Manassas-Regional, VA (MNZ)

| | | | | |
|---|---|---|---|---|
| ☐ N202SR | SAAB SF.340B | 340B-202 | ex N305CE | |
| ☐ N210CJ | SAAB SF.340B | 340B-210 | ex N308CE | |
| ☐ N251CJ | SAAB SF.340B | 340B-251 | ex XA-TQO | |

## COLUMBIA HELICOPTERS — Columbia Heli (WCO) — Aurora-State, OR/Lake Charles-Regional, LA (UAO/LCH)

| | | | | |
|---|---|---|---|---|
| ☐ C-GHFF | Boeing Vertol 107 II | 406 | ex N195CH | >Helifor |
| ☐ C-GHFY | Boeing Vertol 107 II | 2002 | ex N190CH | >Helifor |
| ☐ N184CH | Kawasaki KV107-II | 4001 | ex Thai 4001 | |
| ☐ N185CH | Kawasaki KV107-II | 4003 | ex Thai 4003 | |
| ☐ N186CH | Kawasaki KV107-II | 4005 | ex P2-CHA | |
| ☐ N187CH | Kawasaki KV107-II | 4012 | ex HC-BZP | |
| ☐ N188CH | Boeing Vertol 107 II | 107 | ex C-FHFW | |
| ☐ N190CH | Boeing Vertol 107 II | 2002 | ex C-GHFY | |
| ☐ N191CH | Boeing Vertol 107 II | 2003 | ex P2-CHD | |
| ☐ N192CH | Kawasaki KV107-II | 4011 | ex JA9505 | ♦ |
| ☐ N196CH | Boeing Vertol 107 II | 407 | | ♦ |
| ☐ N6672D | Boeing Vertol 107 II | 2 | | |
| ☐ N6674D | Boeing Vertol 107 II | 4 | ex C-FHFV | |
| ☐ N6675D | Boeing Vertol 107 II | 5 | | ♦ |
| ☐ N6676D | Boeing Vertol 107 II | 6 | | |
| ☐ N6682D | Boeing Vertol 107 II | 101 | | ♦ |
| | | | | |
| ☐ C-FHFB | Boeing Vertol 234UT Chinook | MJ-005 | ex N238CH | >Helifor |
| ☐ N235CH | Boeing Vertol 234UT Chinook | MJ-002 | ex G-BISO | |
| ☐ N241CH | Boeing Vertol 234UT Chinook | MJ-016 | ex HC-CEN | |
| ☐ N242CH | Boeing Vertol 234UT Chinook | MJ-023 | ex HC-BYF | |
| ☐ N246CH | Boeing Vertol 234UT Chinook | MJ-017 | ex LN-OMK | |
| ☐ P2-CHI | Boeing Vertol 234UT Chinook | MJ-003 | ex N237CH | >TOK |
| | | | | |
| ☐ N111NS | Beech 200C Super King Air | BL-36 | | |
| ☐ N3697F | Beech 200C Super King Air | BL-14 | | |

## COMAIR — Comair (OH/COM) — Cincinnati-Northern Kentucky Intl, OH (CVG)

Wholly owned subsidiary of Delta Air Lines, ops as Delta Connection in full colours and using DL flight numbers from Cincinnati, OH and Orlando, FL.

## COMMUTAIR — Commutair (C5/UCA) — Plattsburgh-Clinton County, NY (PLB)

Ops as United Express in full colours and using UA flight numbers. Commutair is a trading name of Champlain Enterprises. Leases 16 de Havilland DHC-8Q-200s from Horizon Airlines for service from Cleveland.

## COMPASS AIRLINES — (CP/CPZ) — Washington-Dulles-Intl, DC (IAD)

Ops as Delta Connection

| CORPJET / MIDLINE AIR FREIGHT | | Beewee (CPJ) | | Baltimore-Martin State, MD (MTN) |
|---|---|---|---|---|
| ☐ N801TH | Cessna 208 Caravan I | 20800123 | ex N9680F | |
| ☐ N5YV | Beech 1900D | UE-5 | | |

| CORPORATE AIR | | Air Spur (CPT) | | Billings-Logan Intl, MT (BIL) |
|---|---|---|---|---|
| ☐ N101UE | Beech 1900C | UC-101 | ex N919GL | ♦ |
| ☐ N122GL | Beech 1900C | UC-122 | ex N195GL | ♦ |
| ☐ N172EE | Beech C99 | U-172 | ex N993SB | ♦ |
| ☐ N205CA | Beech 1900C-1 | UC-103 | ex C-GZTU | ♦ |
| ☐ N319BH | Beech 1900C | UB-36 | ex N19RA | Frtr |
| ☐ N330SB | Short SD.3-30 | SH3013 | ex N241CA | Frtr |
| ☐ N331SB | Short SD.3-30 | SH3015 | ex N331CA | Frtr; [HNL] |

| CORPORATE FLIGHT MANAGEMENT | | Volunteer (VTE) | | Smyrna, TN (MQY) |
|---|---|---|---|---|
| ☐ N569ST | British Aerospace Jetstream 32EP | 952 | | ♦ |
| ☐ N643JX | British Aerospace Jetstream 31 | 643 | ex N421MX | [MQY] |
| ☐ N657BA | British Aerospace Jetstream 31 | 657 | ex N412MX | |
| ☐ N858CY | British Aerospace Jetstream 3201 | 858 | ex N423AM | wfs♦ |
| ☐ N874CP | British Aerospace Jetstream 32 | 874 | ex N426AM | ♦ |
| ☐ N913AE | British Aerospace Jetstream 32 | 913 | | ♦ |
| ☐ N936AE | British Aerospace Jetstream 32EP | 936 | | ♦ |
| ☐ N325UE | British Aerospace Jetstream 4101 | 41063 | | {MQY}♦ |
| ☐ N564HK | British Aerospace Jetstream 4101 | 41081 | | ♦ |

| CSA AIR | Iron Air (IRO) | Iron Mountain--Ford, MI (IMT) |
|---|---|---|

Ops Cessna Caravans leased from and on behalf of Federal Express

| DELTA AIR LINES | Delta (DL/DAL) | Atlanta-Hartsfield Intl, GA (ATL) |
|---|---|---|

Member of Skyteam

| ☐ N301NB | Airbus A319-114 | 1058 | ex D-AVYP | 3101 City of Duluth |
|---|---|---|---|---|
| ☐ N302NB | Airbus A319-114 | 1062 | ex D-AVWA | 3102 |
| ☐ N314NB | Airbus A319-114 | 1191 | ex D-AVWO | 3114 |
| ☐ N315NB | Airbus A319-114 | 1230 | ex D-AVYM | 3115 |
| ☐ N316NB | Airbus A319-114 | 1249 | ex D-AVYW | 3116 |
| ☐ N317NB | Airbus A319-114 | 1324 | ex D-AVWT | 3117 |
| ☐ N318NB | Airbus A319-114 | 1325 | ex D-AVYF | 3118 |
| ☐ N319NB | Airbus A319-114 | 1346 | ex D-AVYR | 3119 |
| ☐ N320NB | Airbus A319-114 | 1392 | ex D-AVYT | 3120 |
| ☐ N321NB | Airbus A319-114 | 1414 | ex D-AVYL | 3121 |
| ☐ N322NB | Airbus A319-114 | 1434 | ex D-AVYO | 3122 |
| ☐ N323NB | Airbus A319-114 | 1453 | ex D-AVWE | 3123 |
| ☐ N324NB | Airbus A319-114 | 1456 | ex D-AVWF | 3124 |
| ☐ N325NB | Airbus A319-114 | 1483 | ex D-AVYU | 3125 |
| ☐ N326NB | Airbus A319-114 | 1498 | ex D-AVYC | 3126 |
| ☐ N327NB | Airbus A319-114 | 1501 | ex D-AVYD | 3127 |
| ☐ N328NB | Airbus A319-114 | 1520 | ex D-AVYN | 3128 |
| ☐ N329NB | Airbus A319-114 | 1543 | ex D-AVWJ | 3129 |
| ☐ N330NB | Airbus A319-114 | 1549 | ex D-AVWM | 3130 |
| ☐ N331NB | Airbus A319-114 | 1567 | ex D-AVYU | 3131 |
| ☐ N332NB | Airbus A319-114 | 1570 | ex D-AVWD | 3132 |
| ☐ N333NB | Airbus A319-114 | 1582 | ex D-AVYA | 3133 |
| ☐ N334NB | Airbus A319-114 | 1659 | ex D-AVYU | 3134 |
| ☐ N335NB | Airbus A319-114 | 1662 | ex D-AVYW | 3135 |
| ☐ N336NB | Airbus A319-114 | 1683 | ex D-AVWJ | 3136 |
| ☐ N337NB | Airbus A319-114 | 1685 | ex D-AVWL | 3137 |
| ☐ N338NB | Airbus A319-114 | 1693 | ex D-AVYD | 3138 |
| ☐ N339NB | Airbus A319-114 | 1709 | ex D-AVWG | 3139 |
| ☐ N340NB | Airbus A319-114 | 1714 | ex D-AVWN | 3140 |
| ☐ N341NB | Airbus A319-114 | 1738 | ex D-AVWV | 3141 |
| ☐ N342NB | Airbus A319-114 | 1746 | ex D-AVYA | 3142 |
| ☐ N343NB | Airbus A319-114 | 1752 | ex D-AVYH | 3143 |
| ☐ N344NB | Airbus A319-114 | 1766 | ex D-AVYU | 3144 |
| ☐ N345NB | Airbus A319-114 | 1774 | ex D-AVYD | 3145 |
| ☐ N346NB | Airbus A319-114 | 1796 | ex D-AVYX | 3146 |
| ☐ N347NB | Airbus A319-114 | 1800 | ex D-AVYZ | 3147 |
| ☐ N348NB | Airbus A319-114 | 1810 | ex D-AVWH | 3148 |
| ☐ N349NB | Airbus A319-114 | 1815 | ex D-AVWI | 3149 |
| ☐ N351NB | Airbus A319-114 | 1820 | ex D-AVWL | 3151 |
| ☐ N352NB | Airbus A319-114 | 1824 | ex D-AVWM | 3152 |
| ☐ N353NB | Airbus A319-114 | 1828 | ex D-AVWO | 3153 |
| ☐ N354NB | Airbus A319-114 | 1833 | ex D-AVWS | 3154 |
| ☐ N355NB | Airbus A319-114 | 1839 | ex D-AVWA | 3155 |
| ☐ N357NB | Airbus A319-114 | 1875 | ex D-AVYH | 3157 |

| | | | | |
|---|---|---|---|---|
| ☐ N358NB | Airbus A319-114 | 1897 | ex D-AVYK | 3158 |
| ☐ N359NB | Airbus A319-114 | 1923 | ex D-AVWC | 3159 |
| ☐ N360NB | Airbus A319-114 | 1959 | ex D-AVWL | 3160 |
| ☐ N361NB | Airbus A319-114 | 1976 | ex D-AVYB | 3161 |
| ☐ N362NB | Airbus A319-114 | 1982 | ex D-AVYF | 3162 |
| ☐ N363NB | Airbus A319-114 | 1990 | ex D-AVYL | 3163 |
| ☐ N364NB | Airbus A319-114 | 2002 | ex D-AVWA | 3164 |
| ☐ N365NB | Airbus A319-114 | 2013 | ex D-AVWS | 3165 |
| ☐ N366NB | Airbus A319-114 | 2026 | ex D-AVWX | 3166 |
| ☐ N368NB | Airbus A319-114 | 2039 | ex D-AVYT | 3168 |
| ☐ N369NB | Airbus A319-114 | 2047 | ex D-AVWC | 3169 |
| ☐ N370NB | Airbus A319-114 | 2087 | ex D-AVWI | 3170 |
| ☐ N371NB | Airbus A319-114 | 2095 | ex D-AVYI | 3171 |
| | | | | |
| ☐ N309US | Airbus A320-211 | 0118 | ex F-WWIM | 3209 |
| ☐ N310NW | Airbus A320-211 | 0121 | ex F-WWIO | 3210 |
| ☐ N311US | Airbus A320-211 | 0125 | ex F-WWIT | 3211 |
| ☐ N312US | Airbus A320-211 | 0152 | ex F-WWDT | 3212 |
| ☐ N313US | Airbus A320-211 | 0153 | ex F-WWDX | 3213 |
| ☐ N314US | Airbus A320-211 | 0160 | ex F-WWDZ | 3214 |
| ☐ N315US | Airbus A320-211 | 0171 | ex F-WWIJ | 3215 |
| ☐ N316US | Airbus A320-211 | 0192 | ex F-WWIY | 3216 |
| ☐ N317US | Airbus A320-211 | 0197 | ex F-WWDF | 3217 |
| ☐ N318US | Airbus A320-211 | 0206 | ex F-WWDK | 3218 |
| ☐ N319US | Airbus A320-211 | 0208 | ex F-WWDT | 3219 |
| ☐ N320US | Airbus A320-211 | 0213 | ex F-WWIB | 3220 |
| ☐ N321US | Airbus A320-211 | 0262 | ex F-WWDI | 3221 |
| ☐ N322US | Airbus A320-211 | 0263 | ex F-WWDQ | 3222 |
| ☐ N323US | Airbus A320-211 | 0272 | ex F-WWBP | 3223 |
| ☐ N324US | Airbus A320-211 | 0273 | ex F-WWDS | 3224 |
| ☐ N325US | Airbus A320-211 | 0281 | ex F-WWBS | 3225 |
| ☐ N326US | Airbus A320-211 | 0282 | ex F-WWIA | 3226 |
| ☐ N327NW | Airbus A320-211 | 0297 | ex F-WWIO | 3227 |
| ☐ N328NW | Airbus A320-211 | 0298 | ex F-WWIP | 3228 |
| ☐ N329NW | Airbus A320-211 | 0306 | ex F-WWDG | 3229 |
| ☐ N330NW | Airbus A320-211 | 0307 | ex F-WWDJ | 3230 |
| ☐ N331NW | Airbus A320-211 | 0318 | ex F-WWBF | 3231 |
| ☐ N332NW | Airbus A320-211 | 0319 | ex F-WWBG | 3232 |
| ☐ N333NW | Airbus A320-211 | 0329 | ex F-WWDY | 3233 |
| ☐ N334NW | Airbus A320-212 | 0339 | ex F-WWBP | 3234 |
| ☐ N335NW | Airbus A320-212 | 0340 | ex F-WWBQ | 3235 |
| ☐ N336NW | Airbus A320-212 | 0355 | ex F-WWIE | 3236 |
| ☐ N337NW | Airbus A320-212 | 0358 | ex F-WWIO | 3237 |
| ☐ N338NW | Airbus A320-212 | 0360 | ex F-WWBY | 3238 |
| ☐ N339NW | Airbus A320-212 | 0367 | ex F-WWDG | 3239 |
| ☐ N340NW | Airbus A320-212 | 0372 | ex F-WWIX | 3240 |
| ☐ N341NW | Airbus A320-212 | 0380 | ex F-WWIS | 3241 |
| ☐ N342NW | Airbus A320-212 | 0381 | ex F-WWIJ | 3242 |
| ☐ N343NW | Airbus A320-212 | 0387 | ex F-WWBV | 3243 |
| ☐ N344NW | Airbus A320-212 | 0388 | ex F-WWDC | 3244 |
| ☐ N345NW | Airbus A320-212 | 0399 | ex F-WWIG | 3245 |
| ☐ N347NW | Airbus A320-212 | 0408 | ex F-WWDN | 3247 |
| ☐ N348NW | Airbus A320-212 | 0410 | ex F-WWDV | 3248 |
| ☐ N349NW | Airbus A320-212 | 0417 | ex F-WWBR | 3249 |
| ☐ N350NA | Airbus A320-212 | 0418 | ex F-WWDG | 3250 |
| ☐ N351NW | Airbus A320-212 | 0766 | ex F-WWDG | 3251 |
| ☐ N352NW | Airbus A320-212 | 0778 | ex F-WWDO | 3252 |
| ☐ N353NW | Airbus A320-212 | 0786 | ex F-WWDP | 3253 |
| ☐ N354NW | Airbus A320-212 | 0801 | ex F-WWDY | 3254 |
| ☐ N355NW | Airbus A320-212 | 0807 | ex F-WWIC | 3255 |
| ☐ N356NW | Airbus A320-212 | 0818 | ex F-WWBD | 3256 |
| ☐ N357NW | Airbus A320-212 | 0830 | ex F-WWIN | 3257 |
| ☐ N358NW | Airbus A320-212 | 0832 | ex F-WWIO | 3258 |
| ☐ N359NW | Airbus A320-212 | 0846 | ex F-WWBH | 3259 |
| ☐ N360NW | Airbus A320-212 | 0903 | ex F-WWDO | 3260 |
| ☐ N361NW | Airbus A320-212 | 0907 | ex F-WWDQ | 3261 |
| ☐ N362NW | Airbus A320-212 | 0911 | ex F-WWDT | 3262 |
| ☐ N363NW | Airbus A320-212 | 0923 | ex F-WWDZ | 3263 |
| ☐ N364NW | Airbus A320-212 | 0962 | ex F-WWBF | 3264 |
| ☐ N365NW | Airbus A320-212 | 0964 | ex F-WWBJ | 3265 |
| ☐ N366NW | Airbus A320-212 | 0981 | ex F-WWDE | 3266 |
| ☐ N367NW | Airbus A320-212 | 0988 | ex F-WWIH | 3267 |
| ☐ N368NW | Airbus A320-212 | 0996 | ex F-WWBV | 3268 |
| ☐ N369NW | Airbus A320-212 | 1011 | ex F-WWDO | 3269 |
| ☐ N370NW | Airbus A320-212 | 1037 | ex F-WWDY | 3270 |
| ☐ N371NW | Airbus A320-212 | 1535 | ex F-WWIS | 3271 |
| ☐ N372NW | Airbus A320-212 | 1633 | ex F-WWDO | 3272 |
| ☐ N373NW | Airbus A320-212 | 1641 | ex F-WWIR | 3273 |
| ☐ N374NW | Airbus A320-212 | 1646 | ex F-WWDS | 3274 |
| ☐ N375NC | Airbus A320-212 | 1789 | ex F-WWDU | 3275 |
| ☐ N376NW | Airbus A320-212 | 1812 | ex F-WWBB | 3276 |
| ☐ N377NW | Airbus A320-212 | 2082 | ex F-WWIU | 3277 |

| | | | | | | |
|---|---|---|---|---|---|---|
| ☐ | N378NW | Airbus A320-212 | . | 2092 | ex F-WWBP | 3278 |
| ☐ | N851NW | Airbus A330-223 | | 609 | ex F-WWYZ | 3351 |
| ☐ | N852NW | Airbus A330-223 | | 614 | ex F-WWKU | 3352 |
| ☐ | N853NW | Airbus A330-223 | | 618 | ex F-WWKN | 3353 |
| ☐ | N854NW | Airbus A330-223 | | 620 | ex F-WWYA | 3354 |
| ☐ | N855NW | Airbus A330-223 | | 621 | ex F-WWYB | 3355 |
| ☐ | N856NW | Airbus A330-223 | | 631 | ex F-WWYG | 3356 |
| ☐ | N857NW | Airbus A330-223 | | 633 | ex F-WWYI | 3357 |
| ☐ | N858NW | Airbus A330-223 | | 718 | ex F-WWYY | 3358 |
| ☐ | N859NW | Airbus A330-223 | | 722 | ex F-WWKM | 3359 |
| ☐ | N860NW | Airbus A330-223 | | 778 | ex F-WWKL | 3360 |
| ☐ | N861NW | Airbus A330-223 | | 796 | ex F-WWKT | 3361 |
| ☐ | N801NW | Airbus A330-323E | | 524 | ex F-WWYZ | 3301 |
| ☐ | N802NW | Airbus A330-323E | | 533 | ex F-WWYD | 3302 |
| ☐ | N803NW | Airbus A330-323E | | 542 | ex F-WWYH | 3303 |
| ☐ | N804NW | Airbus A330-323E | | 549 | ex F-WWYJ | 3304 |
| ☐ | N805NW | Airbus A330-323E | | 552 | ex F-WWKQ | 3305 |
| ☐ | N806NW | Airbus A330-323E | | 578 | ex F-WWKD | 3306 |
| ☐ | N807NW | Airbus A330-323E | | 588 | ex F-WWKM | 3307 |
| ☐ | N808NW | Airbus A330-323E | | 591 | ex F-WWKO | 3308 |
| ☐ | N809NW | Airbus A330-323E | | 663 | ex F-WWKM | 3309 |
| ☐ | N810NW | Airbus A330-323E | | 674 | ex F-WWKT | 3310 |
| ☐ | N811NW | Airbus A330-323E | | 690 | ex F-WWKV | 3311 |
| ☐ | N812NW | Airbus A330-323E | | 784 | ex F-WWYX | 3312 |
| ☐ | N813NW | Airbus A330-323E | | 799 | ex F-WWKV | 3313 |
| ☐ | N814NW | Airbus A330-323E | | 806 | ex F-WWYN | 3314 |
| ☐ | N815NW | Airbus A330-323E | | 817 | ex F-WWYP | 3315 |
| ☐ | N816NW | Airbus A330-323E | | 827 | ex F-WWKG | 3316 |
| ☐ | N817NW | Airbus A330-323E | | 843 | ex F-WWYX | 3317 |
| ☐ | N818NW | Airbus A330-323E | | 857 | ex F-WWYD | 3318 |
| ☐ | N819NW | Airbus A330-323E | | 858 | ex F-WWYE | 3319 |
| ☐ | N820NW | Airbus A330-323E | | 859 | ex F-WWYF | 3320 |
| ☐ | N821NW | Airbus A330-323E | | 865 | ex F-WWYJ | 3321 |
| ☐ | N301DQ | Boeing 737-732/W | | 29687/2667 | ex N1795B | 3601 |
| ☐ | N302DQ | Boeing 737-732/W | | 29648/2683 | | 3602 |
| ☐ | N303DQ | Boeing 737-732/W | | 29688/2720 | ex N1786B | 3603 |
| ☐ | N304DQ | Boeing 737-732/W | | 29683/2724 | ex N1787B | 3604 |
| ☐ | N305DQ | Boeing 737-732/W | | 29645/2743 | | 3605 |
| ☐ | N306DQ | Boeing 737-732/W | | 29633/2758 | | 3606 |
| ☐ | N307DQ | Boeing 737-732/W | | 29679/2767 | | 3607 |
| ☐ | N308DE | Boeing 737-732/W | | 29656/3022 | ex N1786B | 3608 |
| ☐ | N309DE | Boeing 737-732/W | | 29634/3031 | ex N1796B | 3609 |
| ☐ | N310DE | Boeing 737-732/W | | 29665/3058 | ex N1786B | 3610 |
| ☐ | N371DA | Boeing 737-832/W | | 29619/115 | ex N1787B | 3701 |
| ☐ | N372DA | Boeing 737-832/W | | 29620/118 | ex N1782B | 3702 |
| ☐ | N373DA | Boeing 737-832/W | | 29621/123 | ex N1800B | 3703 |
| ☐ | N374DA | Boeing 737-832/W | | 29622/128 | ex N1787B | 3704 |
| ☐ | N375DA | Boeing 737-832/W | | 29623/145 | | 3705 |
| ☐ | N376DA | Boeing 737-832/W | | 29624/176 | | 3706 |
| ☐ | N377DA | Boeing 737-832/W | | 29625/264 | | 3707 |
| ☐ | N378DA | Boeing 737-832/W | | 30265/340 | | 3708 |
| ☐ | N379DA | Boeing 737-832/W | | 30349/351 | | 3709 |
| ☐ | N380DA | Boeing 737-832/W | | 30266/361 | | 3710 |
| ☐ | N381DN | Boeing 737-832/W | | 30350/365 | ex (N381DA) | 3711 |
| ☐ | N382DA | Boeing 737-832/W | | 30345/389 | | 3712 |
| ☐ | N383DN | Boeing 737-832/W | | 30346/393 | ex (N383DA) | 3713 |
| ☐ | N384DA | Boeing 737-832/W | | 30347/412 | | 3714 |
| ☐ | N385DN | Boeing 737-832/W | | 30348/418 | | 3715 |
| ☐ | N386DA | Boeing 737-832/W | | 30373/446 | ex N1780B | 3716 |
| ☐ | N387DA | Boeing 737-832/W | | 30374/457 | ex N1795B | 3717 |
| ☐ | N388DA | Boeing 737-832/W | | 30375/469 | | 3718 |
| ☐ | N389DA | Boeing 737-832/W | | 30376/513 | ex N1787B | 3719 |
| ☐ | N390DA | Boeing 737-832/W | | 30536/518 | ex N6063S | 3720 |
| ☐ | N391DA | Boeing 737-832/W | | 30560/535 | ex N1787B | 3721 |
| ☐ | N392DA | Boeing 737-832/W | | 30561/564 | | 3722 |
| ☐ | N393DA | Boeing 737-832/W | | 30377/584 | ex N1782B | 3723 |
| ☐ | N394DA | Boeing 737-832/W | | 30562/589 | | 3724 |
| ☐ | N395DN | Boeing 737-832/W | | 30773/604 | | 3725 |
| ☐ | N396DA | Boeing 737-832/W | | 30378/632 | ex N1795B | 3726 | Delta Shuttle |
| ☐ | N397DA | Boeing 737-832/W | | 30537/638 | | 3727 | Delta Shuttle |
| ☐ | N398DA | Boeing 737-832/W | | 30774/641 | | 3728 | Delta Shuttle |
| ☐ | N399DA | Boeing 737-832/W | | 30379/657 | | 3729 | Delta Shuttle |
| ☐ | N3730B | Boeing 737-832/W | | 30538/662 | | 3730 | Delta Shuttle |
| ☐ | N3731T | Boeing 737-832/W | | 30775/665 | | 3731 | Delta Shuttle |
| ☐ | N3732J | Boeing 737-832/W | | 30380/674 | | 3732 | Delta Shuttle |
| ☐ | N3733Z | Boeing 737-832/W | | 30539/685 | | 3733 | Delta Shuttle |
| ☐ | N3734B | Boeing 737-832/W | | 30776/689 | | 3734 | Delta Shuttle |
| ☐ | N3735D | Boeing 737-832/W | | 30381/694 | ex (N3735J) | 3735 | Delta Shuttle |

| | Registration | Type | Serial/Line | ex | Fleet No | Name | |
|---|---|---|---|---|---|---|---|
| ☐ | N3736C | Boeing 737-832/W | 30540/709 | | 3736 | | Delta Shuttle |
| ☐ | N3737C | Boeing 737-832/W | 30799/712 | | 3737 | | |
| ☐ | N3738B | Boeing 737-832/W | 30382/723 | | 3738 | | |
| ☐ | N3739P | Boeing 737-832/W | 30541/729 | | 3739 | | |
| ☐ | N3740C | Boeing 737-832/W | 30800/732 | | 3740 | | |
| ☐ | N3741S | Boeing 737-832/W | 30487/750 | | 3741 | | |
| ☐ | N3742C | Boeing 737-832/W | 30835/755 | ex N1781B | 3742 | | |
| ☐ | N3743H | Boeing 737-832/W | 30836/770 | ex N1795B | 3743 | | |
| ☐ | N3744F | Boeing 737-832/W | 30837/805 | | 3744 | | |
| ☐ | N3745B | Boeing 737-832/W | 32373/831 | | 3745 | | |
| ☐ | N3746H | Boeing 737-832/W | 30488/842 | | 3746 | | |
| ☐ | N3747D | Boeing 737-832/W | 32374/846 | ex N1787B | 3747 | | |
| ☐ | N3748Y | Boeing 737-832/W | 30489/865 | | 3748 | | |
| ☐ | N3749D | Boeing 737-832/W | 30490/867 | | 3749 | | |
| ☐ | N3750D | Boeing 737-832/W | 32375/870 | ex N1787B | 3750 | | |
| ☐ | N3751B | Boeing 737-832/W | 30491/892 | | 3751 | | |
| ☐ | N3752 | Boeing 737-832/W | 30492/894 | | 3752 | | |
| ☐ | N3753 | Boeing 737-832/W | 32626/899 | | 3753 | | |
| ☐ | N3754A | Boeing 737-832/W | 29626/907 | | 3754 | | |
| ☐ | N3755D | Boeing 737-832/W | 29627/914 | | 3755 | | |
| ☐ | N3756 | Boeing 737-832/W | 30493/917 | ex N1799B | 3756 | | |
| ☐ | N3757D | Boeing 737-832/W | 30813/921 | | 3757 | | |
| ☐ | N3758Y | Boeing 737-832/W | 30814/923 | | 3758 | | |
| ☐ | N3759 | Boeing 737-832/W | 30815/949 | | 3759 | | |
| ☐ | N3760C | Boeing 737-832/W | 30816/952 | ex N1787B | 3760 | | |
| ☐ | N3761R | Boeing 737-832/W | 29628/964 | ex N1784B | 3761 | | |
| ☐ | N3762Y | Boeing 737-832/W | 30817/968 | | 3762 | | |
| ☐ | N3763D | Boeing 737-832/W | 29629/1003 | ex N1787B | 3763 | | |
| ☐ | N3764D | Boeing 737-832/W | 30818/1006 | | 3764 | | |
| ☐ | N3765 | Boeing 737-832/W | 30819/1008 | ex N1795B | 3765 | | |
| ☐ | N3766 | Boeing 737-832/W | 30820/1029 | | 3766 | | |
| ☐ | N3767 | Boeing 737-832/W | 30821/1031 | | 3767 | | |
| ☐ | N3768 | Boeing 737-832/W | 29630/1053 | | 3768 | | |
| ☐ | N3769L | Boeing 737-832/W | 30822/1057 | | 3769 | | |
| ☐ | N3771K | Boeing 737-832/W | 29632/1103 | | 3771 | | |
| ☐ | N3772H | Boeing 737-832/W | 30823/3274 | | 3772 | | |
| ☐ | N3773D | Boeing 737-832/W | 30825/3338 | ex N1796B | 3773 | | |
| ☐ | N37700 | Boeing 737-832/W | 29631/1074 | | 3770 | | |
| | | | | | | | |
| ☐ | N661US | Boeing 747-451 | 23719/696 | ex N401PW | 6301 | | |
| ☐ | N662US | Boeing 747-451 | 23720/708 | ex (N302US) | 6302 | | |
| ☐ | N663US | Boeing 747-451 | 23818/715 | ex (N303US) | 6303 | | |
| ☐ | N664US | Boeing 747-451 | 23819/721 | ex (N304US) | 6304 | | |
| ☐ | N665US | Boeing 747-451 | 23820/726 | ex (N305US) | 6305 | | |
| ☐ | N666US | Boeing 747-451 | 23821/742 | ex (N306US) | 6306 | | |
| ☐ | N667US | Boeing 747-451 | 24222/799 | ex (N307US) | 6307 | | |
| ☐ | N668US | Boeing 747-451 | 24223/800 | ex (N308US) | 6308 | | |
| ☐ | N669US | Boeing 747-451 | 24224/803 | ex (N309US) | 6309 | | |
| ☐ | N670US | Boeing 747-451 | 24225/804 | ex (N311US) | 6310 | | |
| ☐ | N671US | Boeing 747-451 | 26477/1206 | | 6311 | | |
| ☐ | N672US | Boeing 747-451 | 30267/1223 | | 6312 | | |
| ☐ | N673US | Boeing 747-451 | 30268/1226 | | 6313 | | |
| ☐ | N674US | Boeing 747-451 | 30269/1232 | | 6314 | | |
| ☐ | N675NW | Boeing 747-451 | 33001/1297 | | 6315 | | |
| ☐ | N676NW | Boeing 747-451 | 33002/1303 | | 6316 | | |
| | | | | | | | |
| ☐ | N501US | Boeing 757-251 | 23190/53 | | 5501 | St Paul | |
| ☐ | N502US | Boeing 757-251 | 23191/55 | | 5502 | Minneapolis | |
| ☐ | N503US | Boeing 757-251 | 23192/59 | | 5503 | Detroit | |
| ☐ | N507US | Boeing 757-251 | 23196/68 | | 5507 | Seattle | |
| ☐ | N516US | Boeing 757-251 | 23204/104 | | 5516 | San Diego | [MZJ] |
| ☐ | N517US | Boeing 757-251 | 23205/105 | | 5517 | Portland | [MZJ] |
| ☐ | N518US | Boeing 757-251 | 23206/107 | | 5518 | Milwaukee | [MZJ] |
| ☐ | N519US | Boeing 757-251 | 23207/108 | | 5519 | Cleveland | |
| ☐ | N520US | Boeing 757-251 | 23208/109 | | 5520 | Philadelphia | [MZJ] |
| ☐ | N521US | Boeing 757-251 | 23209/110 | | 5521 | Denver | |
| ☐ | N522US | Boeing 757-251 | 23616/119 | | 5522 | | |
| ☐ | N523US | Boeing 757-251 | 23617/121 | | 5523 | Dallas | |
| ☐ | N525US | Boeing 757-251 | 23619/124 | | 5525 | Miami | |
| ☐ | N526US | Boeing 757-251 | 23620/131 | | 5526 | Memphis | [MZJ] |
| ☐ | N527US | Boeing 757-251 | 23842/136 | | 5527 | | [MZJ]♦ |
| ☐ | N528US | Boeing 757-251 | 23843/137 | | 5528 | | [MZJ] |
| ☐ | N529US | Boeing 757-251 | 23844/140 | | 5529 | New Orleans | |
| ☐ | N530US | Boeing 757-251 | 23845/188 | | 5530 | Omaha | |
| ☐ | N531US | Boeing 757-251 | 23846/190 | | 5531 | Newark | |
| ☐ | N532US | Boeing 757-251 | 24263/192 | | 5532 | Fort Myers | |
| ☐ | N533US | Boeing 757-251 | 24264/194 | | 5533 | Orange County | |
| ☐ | N534US | Boeing 757-251 | 24265/196 | | 5534 | Winnipeg | |
| ☐ | N535US | Boeing 757-251/W | 26482/693 | | 5635 | | |
| ☐ | N536US | Boeing 757-251/W | 26483/695 | | 5636 | | |
| ☐ | N537US | Boeing 757-251/W | 26484/697 | | 5637 | | |
| ☐ | N538US | Boeing 757-251/W | 26485/699 | | 5638 | | |

| | | | | |
|---|---|---|---|---|
| ☐ N539US | Boeing 757-251/W | 26486/700 | 5639 Delta c/s | |
| ☐ N540US | Boeing 757-251/W | 26487/701 | 5640 | |
| ☐ N541US | Boeing 757-251 | 26488/703 | 5641 | |
| ☐ N542US | Boeing 757-251 | 26489/705 | 5642 | |
| ☐ N543US | Boeing 757-251 | 26490/709 | 5643 | |
| ☐ N544US | Boeing 757-251/W | 26491/710 | 5644 | |
| ☐ N545US | Boeing 757-251/W | 26492/711 | 5645 | |
| ☐ N546US | Boeing 757-251/W | 26493/713 | 5646 | |
| ☐ N547US | Boeing 757-251/W | 26494/714 | 5647 | |
| ☐ N548US | Boeing 757-251/W | 26495/715 | 5648 | |
| ☐ N549US | Boeing 757-251/W | 26496/716 | 5649 | |
| ☐ N550NW | Boeing 757-251 | 26497/968 | 5550 | |
| ☐ N551NW | Boeing 757-251 | 26498/971 | 5551 | |
| ☐ N552NW | Boeing 757-251/W | 26499/975 | 5552 | |
| ☐ N553NW | Boeing 757-251/W | 26500/982 | 5553 | |
| ☐ N554NW | Boeing 757-251/W | 26501/987 | 5554 | |
| ☐ N555NW | Boeing 757-251/W | 33391/1011 | 5555 | |
| ☐ N556NW | Boeing 757-251/W | 33392/1013 | 5556 | |
| ☐ N557NW | Boeing 757-251/W | 33393/1016 | 5557 | |

Names prefixed 'City of'

| | | | | |
|---|---|---|---|---|
| ☐ N602DL | Boeing 757-232 | 22809/39 | 602 | |
| ☐ N603DL | Boeing 757-232 | 22810/41 | 603 | |
| ☐ N604DL | Boeing 757-232 | 22811/43 | 604 | |
| ☐ N608DA | Boeing 757-232 | 22815/64 | 608 | |
| ☐ N609DL | Boeing 757-232/W | 22816/65 | 609 | |
| ☐ N610DL | Boeing 757-232 | 22817/66 | 610 pink c/s | |
| ☐ N612DL | Boeing 757-232 | 22819/73 | 612 | |
| ☐ N613DL | Boeing 757-232 | 22820/84 | 613 | |
| ☐ N614DL | Boeing 757-232 | 22821/85 | 614 | |
| ☐ N615DL | Boeing 757-232 | 22822/87 | 615 | |
| ☐ N616DL | Boeing 757-232 | 22823/91 | 616 | |
| ☐ N617DL | Boeing 757-232 | 22907/92 | 617 | |
| ☐ N618DL | Boeing 757-232 | 22908/95 | 618 | |
| ☐ N623DL | Boeing 757-232 | 22913/118 | 623 | |
| ☐ N624AG | Boeing 757-2Q8/W | 25624/541 | ex F-GTIP | [ATL]♦ |
| ☐ N624DL | Boeing 757-232/W | 22914/120 | 624 | [MZJ] |
| ☐ N625DL | Boeing 757-232 | 22915/126 | 625 | [MZJ] |
| ☐ N626DL | Boeing 757-232 | 22916/128 | 626 | [MZJ] |
| ☐ N627DL | Boeing 757-232 | 22917/129 | 627 | [MZJ] |
| ☐ N628DL | Boeing 757-232 | 22918/133 | 628 | |
| ☐ N629DL | Boeing 757-232 | 22919/134 | 629 | |
| ☐ N630DL | Boeing 757-232 | 22920/135 | 630 | |
| ☐ N631DL | Boeing 757-232 | 23612/138 | 631 | [MZJ] |
| ☐ N632DL | Boeing 757-232 | 23613/154 | 632 | |
| ☐ N633DL | Boeing 757-232 | 23614/157 | 633 | |
| ☐ N634DL | Boeing 757-232 | 23615/158 | 634 | |
| ☐ N635DL | Boeing 757-232 | 23762/159 | ex 'N635DA' 635 | |
| ☐ N636DL | Boeing 757-232 | 23763/164 | 636 | |
| ☐ N637DL | Boeing 757-232 | 23760/171 | 637 | |
| ☐ N638DL | Boeing 757-232/W | 23761/177 | 638 | |
| ☐ N639DL | Boeing 757-232 | 23993/198 | 639 | |
| ☐ N640DL | Boeing 757-232/W | 23994/201 | 640 | |
| ☐ N641DL | Boeing 757-232/W | 23995/202 | 641 | |
| ☐ N642DL | Boeing 757-232 | 23996/205 | 642 | |
| ☐ N643DL | Boeing 757-232 | 23997/206 | 643 | |
| ☐ N644DL | Boeing 757-232 | 23998/207 | 644 | |
| ☐ N645DL | Boeing 757-232 | 24216/216 | 645 | |
| ☐ N646DL | Boeing 757-232 | 24217/217 | 646 | [VCV] |
| ☐ N647DL | Boeing 757-232 | 24218/222 | 647 | |
| ☐ N648DL | Boeing 757-232/W | 24372/223 | 648 | |
| ☐ N649DL | Boeing 757-232/W | 24389/229 | 649 | |
| ☐ N650DL | Boeing 757-232/W | 24390/230 | 650 | |
| ☐ N651DL | Boeing 757-232 | 24391/238 | 651 | |
| ☐ N652DL | Boeing 757-232 | 24392/239 | 652 | |
| ☐ N653DL | Boeing 757-232 | 24393/261 | 653 | [MZJ] |
| ☐ N654DL | Boeing 757-232 | 24394/264 | 654 | |
| ☐ N655DL | Boeing 757-232 | 24395/265 | 655 | [MZJ] |
| ☐ N656DL | Boeing 757-232 | 24396/266 | 656 | |
| ☐ N657DL | Boeing 757-232 | 24419/286 | 657 | [MZJ] |
| ☐ N658DL | Boeing 757-232/W | 24420/287 | 658 | |
| ☐ N659DL | Boeing 757-232/W | 24421/293 | 659 | |
| ☐ N660DL | Boeing 757-232/W | 24422/294 | 660 | |
| ☐ N661DN | Boeing 757-232/W | 24972/335 | 661 | |
| ☐ N662DN | Boeing 757-232/W | 24991/342 | 662 | |
| ☐ N663DN | Boeing 757-232/W | 24992/343 | 663 | |
| ☐ N664DN | Boeing 757-232/W | 25012/347 | 664 | |
| ☐ N665DN | Boeing 757-232/W | 25013/349 | 665 | |
| ☐ N666DN | Boeing 757-232/W | 25034/354 | 666 | |
| ☐ N667DN | Boeing 757-232/W | 25035/355 | 667 | |
| ☐ N668DN | Boeing 757-232 | 25141/376 | 668 | |
| ☐ N669DN | Boeing 757-232 | 25142/377 | 669 | |

| | Registration | Type | c/n–l/n | ex | Fleet | Notes |
|---|---|---|---|---|---|---|
| ☐ | N670DN | Boeing 757-232 | 25331/415 | | 670 | |
| ☐ | N671DN | Boeing 757-232 | 25332/416 | | 671 | |
| ☐ | N672DL | Boeing 757-232 | 25977/429 | | 672 | [GSO] |
| ☐ | N673DL | Boeing 757-232 | 25978/430 | | 673 | |
| ☐ | N674DL | Boeing 757-232 | 25979/439 | | 674 | [MZJ] |
| ☐ | N675DL | Boeing 757-232 | 25980/448 | | 675 | |
| ☐ | N676DL | Boeing 757-232 | 25981/455 | | 676 | |
| ☐ | N677DL | Boeing 757-232 | 25982/456 | | 677 | [MZJ] |
| ☐ | N678DL | Boeing 757-232 | 25983/465 | | 678 | |
| ☐ | N679DA | Boeing 757-232 | 26955/500 | | 679 | |
| ☐ | N680DA | Boeing 757-232 | 26956/502 | | 680 | |
| ☐ | N681DA | Boeing 757-232 | 26957/516 | | 681 | |
| ☐ | N682DA | Boeing 757-232 | 26958/518 | | 682 | |
| ☐ | N683DA | Boeing 757-232 | 27103/533 | | 683 | |
| ☐ | N684DA | Boeing 757-232 | 27104/535 | | 684 | |
| ☐ | N685DA | Boeing 757-232 | 27588/667 | | 685 | |
| ☐ | N686DA | Boeing 757-232 | 27589/689 | | 686 | |
| ☐ | N687DL | Boeing 757-232/W | 27586/800 | | 687 | |
| ☐ | N688DL | Boeing 757-232/W | 27587/803 | | 688 | |
| ☐ | N689DL | Boeing 757-232/W | 27172/807 | | 689 | |
| ☐ | N690DL | Boeing 757-232/W | 27585/808 | | 690 | |
| ☐ | N692DL | Boeing 757-232/W | 29724/820 | ex N1799B | 692 | |
| ☐ | N693DL | Boeing 757-232 | 29725/826 | ex N1799B | 693 | |
| ☐ | N694DL | Boeing 757-232 | 29726/831 | | 694 | |
| ☐ | N695DL | Boeing 757-232/W | 29727/838 | ex N1795B | 695 | |
| ☐ | N696DL | Boeing 757-232 | 29728/845 | ex N1795B | 696 | |
| ☐ | N697DL | Boeing 757-232 | 30318/880 | ex N1795B | 697 | |
| ☐ | N698DL | Boeing 757-232 | 29911/885 | | 698 | |
| ☐ | N699DL | Boeing 757-232 | 29970/887 | ex N1795B | 699 | |
| ☐ | N702TW | Boeing 757-2Q8/W | 28162/732 | | 6801 | |
| ☐ | N703TW | Boeing 757-2Q8ER/W | 27620/736 | | 6802 | |
| ☐ | N704X | Boeing 757-2Q8/W | 28163/741 | | 6803 | |
| ☐ | N705TW | Boeing 757-231/W | 28479/742 | | 6811 | |
| ☐ | N706TW | Boeing 757-2Q8/W | 28165/743 | | 6804 | |
| ☐ | N707TW | Boeing 757-2Q8ER/W | 27625/744 | | 6805 | |
| ☐ | N709TW | Boeing 757-2Q8/W | 28168/754 | | 6806 | |
| ☐ | N710TW | Boeing 757-2Q8/W | 28169/757 | | 6807 | |
| ☐ | N711ZX | Boeing 757-231/W | 28481/758 | | 6814 | |
| ☐ | N712TW | Boeing 757-2Q8ER/W | 27624/760 | | 6808 | |
| ☐ | N713TW | Boeing 757-2Q8/W | 28173/764 | | 6809 | |
| ☐ | N717TW | Boeing 757-231/W | 28485/854 | | 6812 | |
| ☐ | N718TW | Boeing 757-231/W | 28486/869 | | 6815 | |
| ☐ | N721TW | Boeing 757-231/W | 29954/874 | | 6810 | |
| ☐ | N722TW | Boeing 757-231/W | 29385/893 | ex N1795B | 6816 | |
| ☐ | N723TW | Boeing 757-231/W | 29378/907 | | 6817 | |
| ☐ | N727TW | Boeing 757-231/W | 30340/901 | | 6813 | |
| ☐ | N750AT | Boeing 757-212ER | 23126/45 | ex 9V-SGL | 6902 | |
| ☐ | N751AT | Boeing 757-212ER | 23125/44 | ex 9V-SGK | 6901 | |
| ☐ | N752AT | Boeing 757-212ER | 23128/48 | ex 9V-SGN | 6904 | |
| ☐ | N757AT | Boeing 757-212ER | 23127/47 | ex 9V-SGM | 6903 | |
| ☐ | N900PC | Boeing 757-26D/W | 28446/740 | | 691 | |
| ☐ | N6700 | Boeing 757-232 | 30337/890 | | 6700 | |
| ☐ | N6701 | Boeing 757-232 | 30187/892 | | 6701 | |
| ☐ | N6702 | Boeing 757-232 | 30188/898 | | 6702 | |
| ☐ | N6703D | Boeing 757-232 | 30234/908 | ex N1795B | 6703 | |
| ☐ | N6704Z | Boeing 757-232 | 30396/914 | ex N1795B | 6704 | |
| ☐ | N6705Y | Boeing 757-232 | 30397/917 | | 6705 | |
| ☐ | N6706Q | Boeing 757-232 | 30422/921 | | 6706 | |
| ☐ | N6707A | Boeing 757-232 | 30395/927 | | 6707 | |
| ☐ | N6708D | Boeing 757-232 | 30480/934 | | 6708 | |
| ☐ | N6709 | Boeing 757-232 | 30481/937 | | 6709 | |
| ☐ | N6710E | Boeing 757-232 | 30482/939 | | 6710 | |
| ☐ | N6711M | Boeing 757-232 | 30483/941 | | 6711 | |
| ☐ | N6712B | Boeing 757-232 | 30484/942 | | 6712 | |
| ☐ | N6713Y | Boeing 757-232 | 30777/944 | | 6713 | |
| ☐ | N6714Q | Boeing 757-232 | 30485/949 | | 6714 | |
| ☐ | N6715C | Boeing 757-232 | 30486/953 | | 6715 | |
| ☐ | N6716C | Boeing 757-232 | 30838/955 | | 6716 | |
| ☐ | N67171 | Boeing 757-232 | 30839/959 | | 6717 | |
| ☐ | N581NW | Boeing 757-351 | 32982/1001 | ex N753JM | 5801 | |
| ☐ | N582NW | Boeing 757-351 | 32981/1014 | | 5802 | The Bernie Epple |
| ☐ | N583NW | Boeing 757-351 | 32983/1019 | | 5803 | |
| ☐ | N584NW | Boeing 757-351 | 32984/1020 | | 5804 | |
| ☐ | N585NW | Boeing 757-351 | 32985/1021 | | 5805 | |
| ☐ | N586NW | Boeing 757-351 | 32987/1022 | | 5806 | |
| ☐ | N587NW | Boeing 757-351 | 32986/1023 | | 5807 | |
| ☐ | N588NW | Boeing 757-351 | 32988/1024 | | 5808 | |
| ☐ | N589NW | Boeing 757-351 | 32989/1025 | | 5809 | |
| ☐ | N590NW | Boeing 757-351 | 32990/1027 | ex N1795B | 5810 | |
| ☐ | N591NW | Boeing 757-351 | 32991/1030 | | 5811 | |
| ☐ | N592NW | Boeing 757-351 | 32992/1033 | | 5812 | |

| | | | | | |
|---|---|---|---|---|---|
| ☐ N593NW | Boeing 757-351 | 32993/1034 | ex N1795B | 5813 | |
| ☐ N594NW | Boeing 757-351 | 32994/1035 | | 5814 | |
| ☐ N595NW | Boeing 757-351 | 32995/1036 | ex N1795B | 5815 | |
| ☐ N596NW | Boeing 757-351 | 32996/1037 | | 5816 | |
| | | | | | |
| ☐ N121DE | Boeing 767-332 | 23435/162 | | 121 | |
| ☐ N124DE | Boeing 767-332 | 23438/189 | | 124 | |
| ☐ N125DL | Boeing 767-332 | 24075/200 | | 125 | |
| ☐ N126DL | Boeing 767-332 | 24076/201 | | 126 | |
| ☐ N127DL | Boeing 767-332 | 24077/203 | | 127 | |
| ☐ N128DL | Boeing 767-332 | 24078/207 | | 128 | |
| ☐ N129DL | Boeing 767-332 | 24079/209 | | 129 | |
| ☐ N130DL | Boeing 767-332 | 24080/216 | | 130 | |
| ☐ N131DN | Boeing 767-332 | 24852/320 | | 131 | [MZJ] |
| ☐ N132DN | Boeing 767-332 | 24981/345 | | 132 | [VCV] |
| ☐ N133DN | Boeing 767-332 | 24982/348 | | 133 | [VCV] |
| ☐ N134DL | Boeing 767-332 | 25123/353 | | 134 | [VCV] |
| ☐ N135DL | Boeing 767-332 | 25145/356 | | 135 | [MZJ] |
| ☐ N136DL | Boeing 767-332 | 25146/374 | | 136 | |
| ☐ N137DL | Boeing 767-332 | 25306/392 | | 137 | |
| ☐ N138DL | Boeing 767-332 | 25409/410 | | 138 | |
| ☐ N139DL | Boeing 767-332 | 25984/427 | | 139 | |
| ☐ N140LL | Boeing 767-332 | 25988/499 | | 1401 | |
| ☐ N143DA | Boeing 767-332 | 25991/721 | | 1403 | |
| ☐ N144DA | Boeing 767-332 | 27584/751 | | 1404 | |
| ☐ N152DL | Boeing 767-3P6ER | 24984/339 | ex A4O-GM | 1502 | |
| ☐ N153DL | Boeing 767-3P6ER | 24985/340 | ex A4O-GN | 1503 | |
| ☐ N154DL | Boeing 767-3P6ER | 25241/389 | ex A4O-GO | 1504 | |
| ☐ N155DL | Boeing 767-3P6ER | 25269/390 | ex A4O-GP | 1505 | |
| ☐ N156DL | Boeing 767-3P6ER | 25354/406 | ex A4O-GR | 1506 | |
| ☐ N169DZ | Boeing 767-332ER/W | 29689/706 | | 1601 | |
| ☐ N171DN | Boeing 767-332ER | 24759/304 | | 171 | |
| ☐ N171DZ | Boeing 767-332ER/W | 29690/717 | | 1701 Habitat for Humanity c/s | |
| ☐ N172DN | Boeing 767-332ER/W | 24775/312 | | 172 | |
| ☐ N172DZ | Boeing 767-332ER/w | 29691/719 | | 1702 | |
| ☐ N173DN | Boeing 767-332ER | 24800/313 | | 173 | [VCV] |
| ☐ N173DZ | Boeing 767-332ER/W | 29692/723 | | 1703 | |
| ☐ N174DN | Boeing 767-332ER/W | 24802/317 | | 174 | |
| ☐ N174DZ | Boeing 767-332ER | 29693/725 | | 1704 | |
| ☐ N175DN | Boeing 767-332ER/W | 24803/318 | | 175 | |
| ☐ N175DZ | Boeing 767-332ER/W | 29696/740 | | 1705 | |
| ☐ N176DN | Boeing 767-332ER/W | 25061/341 | | 176 | |
| ☐ N176DZ | Boeing 767-332ER | 29697/745 | | 1706 | |
| ☐ N177DN | Boeing 767-332ER | 25122/346 | | 177 | |
| ☐ N177DZ | Boeing 767-332ER | 29698/750 | | 1707 | |
| ☐ N178DN | Boeing 767-332ER/W | 25143/349 | | 178 | |
| ☐ N178DZ | Boeing 767-332ER | 30596/795 | | 1708 | |
| ☐ N179DN | Boeing 767-332ER/W | 25144/350 | | 179 | |
| ☐ N180DN | Boeing 767-332ER | 25985/428 | | 180 | |
| ☐ N181DN | Boeing 767-332ER | 25986/446 | | 181 | |
| ☐ N182DN | Boeing 767-332ER | 25987/461 | | 182 | |
| ☐ N183DN | Boeing 767-332ER | 27110/492 | | 183 | |
| ☐ N184DN | Boeing 767-332ER | 27111/496 | | 184 | |
| ☐ N185DN | Boeing 767-332ER/W | 27961/576 | | 185 | |
| ☐ N186DN | Boeing 767-332ER/W | 27962/585 | | 186 | |
| ☐ N187DN | Boeing 767-332ER/W | 27582/617 | | 187 | |
| ☐ N188DN | Boeing 767-332ER | 27583/631 | | 188 | |
| ☐ N189DN | Boeing 767-332ER | 25990/646 | | 189 | |
| ☐ N190DN | Boeing 767-332ER | 28447/653 | | 190 | |
| ☐ N191DN | Boeing 767-332ER/W | 28448/654 | | 191 | |
| ☐ N192DN | Boeing 767-332ER/W | 28449/664 | | 192 | |
| ☐ N193DN | Boeing 767-332ER/W | 28450/671 | | 193 | |
| ☐ N194DN | Boeing 767-332ER/W | 28451/675 | | 194 | |
| ☐ N195DN | Boeing 767-332ER/W | 28452/676 | | 195 | |
| ☐ N196DN | Boeing 767-332ER/W | 28453/679 | | 196 | |
| ☐ N197DN | Boeing 767-332ER/W | 28454/683 | | 197 | |
| ☐ N198DN | Boeing 767-332ER/W | 28455/685 | | 198 | |
| ☐ N199DN | Boeing 767-332ER/W | 28456/690 | | 199 | |
| ☐ N394DL | Boeing 767-324ER | 27394/572 | ex HL7505 | 1521 | |
| ☐ N1200K | Boeing 767-332ER/W | 28457/696 | | 1200 | |
| ☐ N1201P | Boeing 767-332ER/W | 28458/697 | | 1201 | |
| ☐ N1402A | Boeing 767-332 | 25989/506 | | 1402 | |
| ☐ N1501P | Boeing 767-3P6ER | 24983/334 | ex A4O-GL | 1501 | |
| ☐ N1602 | Boeing 767-332ER | 29694/735 | | 1602 | |
| ☐ N1603 | Boeing 767-332ER | 29695/736 | | 1603 | |
| ☐ N1604R | Boeing 767-332ER | 30180/749 | | 1604 | |
| ☐ N1605 | Boeing 767-332ER | 30198/753 | | 1605 | |
| ☐ N1607B | Boeing 767-332ER/W | 30388/787 | | 1607 | |
| ☐ N1608 | Boeing 767-332ER/W | 30573/788 | | 1608 | |
| ☐ N1609 | Boeing 767-332ER/W | 30574/789 | | 1609 | |
| ☐ N1610D | Boeing 767-332ER/W | 30594/790 | | 1610 | |
| ☐ N1611B | Boeing 767-332ER/W | 30595/794 | | 1611 | |

| | | | | | |
|---|---|---|---|---|---|
| ☐ | N1612T | Boeing 767-332ER/W | 30575/838 | | 1612 |
| ☐ | N1613B | Boeing 767-332ER/W | 32776/847 | | 1613 |
| ☐ | N16065 | Boeing 767-332ER | 30199/755 | | 1606 |
| | | | | | |
| ☐ | N825MH | Boeing 767-432ER | 29703/758 | ex N6067U | 1801 |
| ☐ | N826MH | Boeing 767-432ER | 29713/769 | | 1802 |
| ☐ | N827MH | Boeing 767-432ER | 29705/773 | ex N76400 | 1803 |
| ☐ | N828MH | Boeing 767-432ER | 29699/791 | | 1804 |
| ☐ | N829MH | Boeing 767-432ER | 29700/801 | | 1805 |
| ☐ | N830MH | Boeing 767-432ER | 29701/803 | | 1806 |
| ☐ | N831MH | Boeing 767-432ER | 29702/804 | | 1807 |
| ☐ | N832MH | Boeing 767-432ER | 29704/807 | | 1808 |
| ☐ | N833MH | Boeing 767-432ER | 29706/810 | | 1809 |
| ☐ | N834MH | Boeing 767-432ER | 29707/813 | | 1810 |
| ☐ | N835MH | Boeing 767-432ER | 29708/814 | | 1811 |
| ☐ | N836MH | Boeing 767-432ER | 29709/818 | | 1812 |
| ☐ | N837MH | Boeing 767-432ER | 29710/820 | | 1813 |
| ☐ | N838MH | Boeing 767-432ER | 29711/821 | | 1814 |
| ☐ | N839MH | Boeing 767-432ER | 29712/824 | | 1815 |
| ☐ | N840MH | Boeing 767-432ER | 29718/830 | | 1816 |
| ☐ | N841MH | Boeing 767-432ER | 29714/855 | | 1817 |
| ☐ | N842MH | Boeing 767-432ER | 29715/856 | | 1818 |
| ☐ | N843MH | Boeing 767-432ER | 29716/865 | | 1819 |
| ☐ | N844MH | Boeing 767-432ER | 29717/871 | | 1820 |
| ☐ | N845MH | Boeing 767-432ER | 29719/874 | | 1821 |
| | | | | | |
| ☐ | N701DN | Boeing 777-232LR | 29740/697 | ex N5016R | 7101 |
| ☐ | N702DN | Boeing 777-232LR | 29741/704 | | 7102 |
| ☐ | N703DN | Boeing 777-232LR | 32222/767 | | 7103 |
| ☐ | N704DK | Boeing 777-232LR | 29739/772 | ex N5016R | 7104 |
| ☐ | N705DN | Boeing 777-232LR | 29742/773 | | 7105 |
| ☐ | N706DN | Boeing 777-232LR | 30440/776 | ex N5023Q | 7106 |
| ☐ | N707DN | Boeing 777-232LR | 39091/781 | | 7107 |
| ☐ | N708DN | Boeing 777-232LR | 39254/789 | | 7108 |
| ☐ | N709DN | Boeing 777-232LR | 40559/854 | | 7109 |
| ☐ | N710DN | Boeing 777-232LR | 40560/857 | | 7110 |
| ☐ | N860DA | Boeing 777-232ER | 29951/202 | | 7001 |
| ☐ | N861DA | Boeing 777-232ER | 29952/207 | | 7002 |
| ☐ | N862DA | Boeing 777-232ER | 29734/235 | ex N5022E | 7003 |
| ☐ | N863DA | Boeing 777-232ER | 29735/245 | ex N5014K | 7004 |
| ☐ | N864DA | Boeing 777-232ER | 29736/249 | ex N50217 | 7005 |
| ☐ | N865DA | Boeing 777-232ER | 29737/257 | | 7006 |
| ☐ | N866DA | Boeing 777-232ER | 29738/261 | | 7007 |
| ☐ | N867DA | Boeing 777-232ER | 29743/387 | | 7008 |
| | | | | | |
| ☐ | N90S | Douglas DC-9-31 | 47244/498 | | 9931 | [MZJ] |
| ☐ | N914RW | Douglas DC-9-31 | 47362/492 | ex N907H | 9962 | [MZJ] |
| ☐ | N915RW | Douglas DC-9-31 | 47139/169 | ex N8930E | 9957 | [MZJ] |
| ☐ | N923RW | Douglas DC-9-31 | 47183/272 | ex N8947E | 9956 | [MZJ] |
| ☐ | N964N | Douglas DC-9-31 | 47416/512 | | 9914 | [MZJ] |
| ☐ | N965N | Douglas DC-9-31 | 47417/518 | | 9915 | [MZJ] |
| ☐ | N1309T | Douglas DC-9-31 | 47316/439 | | 9944 | [MZJ] |
| ☐ | N1334U | Douglas DC-9-31 | 47280/597 | | 9933 | [MZJ] |
| ☐ | N8920E | Douglas DC-9-31 | 45835/95 | | 9927 | [MZJ] |
| ☐ | N8921E | Douglas DC-9-31 | 45836/96 | | 9928 | [MZJ] |
| ☐ | N8929E | Douglas DC-9-31 | 45866/138 | | 9948 | [MZJ] |
| ☐ | N8932E | Douglas DC-9-31 | 47141/227 | | 9996 | [MZJ] |
| ☐ | N8938E | Douglas DC-9-31 | 47161/249 | ex 5N-GIN | 9947 | [MZJ] |
| ☐ | N8944E | Douglas DC-9-31 | 47167/266 | | 9988 | [MZJ] |
| ☐ | N8960E | Douglas DC-9-31 | 45869/331 | | 9992 | [MZJ] |
| ☐ | N8986E | Douglas DC-9-31 | 47402/482 | ex 5N-INZ | 9993 | [MZJ] |
| ☐ | N9332 | Douglas DC-9-31 | 47264/329 | ex (N9107) | 9968 | [MZJ] |
| ☐ | N9341 | Douglas DC-9-31 | 47390/490 | | 9977 | [MZJ] |
| ☐ | N9342 | Douglas DC-9-31 | 47391/491 | | 9978 | [MZJ] |
| ☐ | N9343 | Douglas DC-9-31 | 47439/501 | | 9979 | [MZJ] |
| ☐ | N9344 | Douglas DC-9-31 | 47440/502 | | 9980 | [MZJ] |
| | | | | | |
| ☐ | N623NW | Douglas DC-9-32 | 47591/706 | ex I-RIFT | 9623 | [MZJ] |
| ☐ | N940N | Douglas DC-9-32 | 47572/708 | | 9918 | [MZJ] |
| ☐ | N943N | Douglas DC-9-32 | 47647/773 | | 9921 | [MZJ] |
| ☐ | N984US | Douglas DC-9-32 | 47383/538 | ex HB-IFV | 9984 | [MZJ] |
| ☐ | N987US | Douglas DC-9-32 | 47458/646 | ex OE-LDF | 9987 | [MZJ] |
| ☐ | N994Z | Douglas DC-9-32 | 47097/193 | ex N979NE | 9981 | [MZJ] |
| ☐ | N3324L | Douglas DC-9-32 | 47103/205 | ex YV-70C | 9941 | [MZJ] |
| ☐ | N9346 | Douglas DC-9-32 | 47376/517 | ex N394PA | 9950 | [MZJ] |
| ☐ | N9347 | Douglas DC-9-32 | 45827/135 | ex HL7201 | 9951 | [MZJ] |
| | | | | | |
| ☐ | N750NW | Douglas DC-9-41 | 47114/218 | ex SE-DBX | 9750 | [MZJ] |
| ☐ | N753NW | Douglas DC-9-41 | 47117/319 | ex SE-DBW | 9753 | [MZJ] |
| ☐ | N754NW | Douglas DC-9-41 | 47178/323 | ex OY-KGB | 9754 | [MZJ] |
| ☐ | N756NW | Douglas DC-9-41 | 47180/354 | ex SE-DBU | 9756 | [MZJ] |
| ☐ | N758NW | Douglas DC-9-41 | 47286/359 | ex OY-KGC | 9758 | [MZJ] |

| | Reg | Type | msn/ln | ex | fleet | notes |
|---|---|---|---|---|---|---|
| ☐ | N401EA | Douglas DC-9-51 | 47682/788 | ex N920VJ | 9885 | |
| ☐ | N600TR | Douglas DC-9-51 | 47783/899 | ex YV-40C | 9886 | |
| ☐ | N670MC | Douglas DC-9-51 | 47659/807 | ex HB-ISP | 9882 | [MZJ] |
| ☐ | N671MC | Douglas DC-9-51 | 47660/810 | ex HB-ISR | 9883 | |
| ☐ | N675MC | Douglas DC-9-51 | 47651/780 | ex OE-LDK | 9880 | [MZJ] |
| ☐ | N676MC | Douglas DC-9-51 | 47652/798 | ex OE-LDL | 9881 | |
| ☐ | N677MC | Douglas DC-9-51 | 47756/873 | ex OE-LDO | 9884 | |
| ☐ | N760NC | Douglas DC-9-51 | 47708/813 | | 9851 | [MZJ] |
| ☐ | N761NC | Douglas DC-9-51 | 47709/814 | | 9852 | [MZJ] |
| ☐ | N762NC | Douglas DC-9-51 | 47710/818 | | 9853 | |
| ☐ | N764NC | Douglas DC-9-51 | 47717/833 | | 9855 | |
| ☐ | N765NC | Douglas DC-9-51 | 47718/834 | | 9856 | [MSP] |
| ☐ | N766NC | Douglas DC-9-51 | 47739/852 | | 9857 | |
| ☐ | N767NC | Douglas DC-9-51 | 47724/853 | | 9858 | |
| ☐ | N768NC | Douglas DC-9-51 | 47729/854 | | 9859 | [MZJ] |
| ☐ | N769NC | Douglas DC-9-51 | 47757/877 | | 9860 | [MZJ] |
| ☐ | N770NC | Douglas DC-9-51 | 47758/880 | | 9861 | |
| ☐ | N771NC | Douglas DC-9-51 | 47769/881 | | 9862 | [MZJ] |
| ☐ | N772NC | Douglas DC-9-51 | 47774/884 | | 9863 | [MZJ] |
| ☐ | N773NC | Douglas DC-9-51 | 47775/888 | | 9864 | |
| ☐ | N774NC | Douglas DC-9-51 | 47776/889 | | 9865 | |
| ☐ | N775NC | Douglas DC-9-51 | 47785/904 | | 9866 | |
| ☐ | N776NC | Douglas DC-9-51 | 47786/905 | | 9867 | [MZJ] |
| ☐ | N777NC | Douglas DC-9-51 | 47787/912 | | 9868 | |
| ☐ | N778NC | Douglas DC-9-51 | 48100/927 | | 9869 | [MZJ] |
| ☐ | N779NC | Douglas DC-9-51 | 48101/931 | | 9870 | |
| ☐ | N780NC | Douglas DC-9-51 | 48102/932 | | 9871 | |
| ☐ | N781NC | Douglas DC-9-51 | 48121/935 | | 9872 | [MZJ] |
| ☐ | N782NC | Douglas DC-9-51 | 48107/936 | | 9873 | |
| ☐ | N783NC | Douglas DC-9-51 | 48108/937 | | 9874 | wfs |
| ☐ | N784NC | Douglas DC-9-51 | 48109/939 | | 9875 | |
| ☐ | N785NC | Douglas DC-9-51 | 48110/945 | | 9876 | [MZJ] |
| ☐ | N786NC | Douglas DC-9-51 | 48148/984 | | 9877 | |
| ☐ | N787NC | Douglas DC-9-51 | 48149/990 | | 9878 | |
| ☐ | N900DE | McDonnell-Douglas MD-88 | 53372/1970 | | 9000 | |
| ☐ | N901DE | McDonnell-Douglas MD-88 | 53378/1980 | | 9001 | |
| ☐ | N902DE | McDonnell-Douglas MD-88 | 53379/1983 | | 9002 | |
| ☐ | N903DE | McDonnell-Douglas MD-88 | 53380/1986 | | 9003 | |
| ☐ | N904DE | McDonnell-Douglas MD-88 | 53409/1990 | | 9004 | |
| ☐ | N904DL | McDonnell-Douglas MD-88 | 49535/1347 | | 904 | |
| ☐ | N905DE | McDonnell-Douglas MD-88 | 53410/1992 | | 9005 | |
| ☐ | N905DL | McDonnell-Douglas MD-88 | 49536/1348 | | 905 | |
| ☐ | N906DE | McDonnell-Douglas MD-88 | 53415/2027 | | 9006 | |
| ☐ | N906DL | McDonnell-Douglas MD-88 | 49537/1355 | | 906 | |
| ☐ | N907DE | McDonnell-Douglas MD-88 | 53416/2029 | | 9007 | |
| ☐ | N907DL | McDonnell-Douglas MD-88 | 49538/1365 | | 907 | |
| ☐ | N908DE | McDonnell-Douglas MD-88 | 53417/2032 | | 9008 | |
| ☐ | N908DL | McDonnell-Douglas MD-88 | 49539/1366 | | 908 | |
| ☐ | N909DE | McDonnell-Douglas MD-88 | 53418/2033 | | 9009 | |
| ☐ | N909DL | McDonnell-Douglas MD-88 | 49540/1395 | | 909 | |
| ☐ | N910DE | McDonnell-Douglas MD-88 | 53419/2036 | | 9010 | |
| ☐ | N910DL | McDonnell-Douglas MD-88 | 49541/1416 | | 910 | |
| ☐ | N911DE | McDonnell-Douglas MD-88 | 49967/2037 | | 9011 | |
| ☐ | N911DL | McDonnell-Douglas MD-88 | 49542/1433 | | 911 | |
| ☐ | N912DE | McDonnell-Douglas MD-88 | 49997/2038 | | 9012 | |
| ☐ | N912DL | McDonnell-Douglas MD-88 | 49543/1434 | | 912 | |
| ☐ | N913DE | McDonnell-Douglas MD-88 | 49956/2039 | | 9013 | |
| ☐ | N913DL | McDonnell-Douglas MD-88 | 49544/1443 | | 913 | |
| ☐ | N914DE | McDonnell-Douglas MD-88 | 49957/2049 | | 9014 | |
| ☐ | N914DL | McDonnell-Douglas MD-88 | 49545/1444 | | 914 | |
| ☐ | N915DE | McDonnell-Douglas MD-88 | 53420/2050 | | 9015 | |
| ☐ | N915DL | McDonnell-Douglas MD-88 | 49546/1447 | | 915 | |
| ☐ | N916DE | McDonnell-Douglas MD-88 | 53421/2051 | | 9016 | |
| ☐ | N916DL | McDonnell-Douglas MD-88 | 49591/1448 | | 916 | |
| ☐ | N917DE | McDonnell-Douglas MD-88 | 49958/2054 | | 9017 | |
| ☐ | N917DL | McDonnell-Douglas MD-88 | 49573/1469 | | 917 | |
| ☐ | N918DE | McDonnell-Douglas MD-88 | 49959/2055 | | 9018 | |
| ☐ | N918DL | McDonnell-Douglas MD-88 | 49583/1470 | | 918 | [VCV] |
| ☐ | N919DE | McDonnell-Douglas MD-88 | 53422/2058 | | 9019 | |
| ☐ | N919DL | McDonnell-Douglas MD-88 | 49584/1471 | | 919 | |
| ☐ | N920DE | McDonnell-Douglas MD-88 | 53423/2059 | | 9020 | |
| ☐ | N920DL | McDonnell-Douglas MD-88 | 49644/1473 | | 920 | |
| ☐ | N921DL | McDonnell-Douglas MD-88 | 49645/1480 | | 921 | |
| ☐ | N922DL | McDonnell-Douglas MD-88 | 49646/1481 | | 922 | |
| ☐ | N923DL | McDonnell-Douglas MD-88 | 49705/1491 | | 923 | |
| ☐ | N924DL | McDonnell-Douglas MD-88 | 49711/1492 | | 924 | [VCV] |
| ☐ | N925DL | McDonnell-Douglas MD-88 | 49712/1500 | | 925 | |
| ☐ | N926DL | McDonnell-Douglas MD-88 | 49713/1523 | | 926 | |
| ☐ | N927DA | McDonnell-Douglas MD-88 | 49714/1524 | | 927 | |
| ☐ | N928DL | McDonnell-Douglas MD-88 | 49715/1530 | | 928 | |

| | | | | |
|---|---|---|---|---|
| ☐ N929DL | McDonnell-Douglas MD-88 | 49716/1531 | | 929 |
| ☐ N930DL | McDonnell-Douglas MD-88 | 49717/1532 | | 930 |
| ☐ N931DL | McDonnell-Douglas MD-88 | 49718/1533 | | 931 |
| ☐ N932DL | McDonnell-Douglas MD-88 | 49719/1570 | | 932 |
| ☐ N933DL | McDonnell-Douglas MD-88 | 49720/1571 | | 933 |
| ☐ N934DL | McDonnell-Douglas MD-88 | 49721/1574 | | 934 |
| ☐ N935DL | McDonnell-Douglas MD-88 | 49722/1575 | | 935 |
| ☐ N936DL | McDonnell-Douglas MD-88 | 49723/1576 | | 936 |
| ☐ N937DL | McDonnell-Douglas MD-88 | 49810/1588 | | 937 |
| ☐ N938DL | McDonnell-Douglas MD-88 | 49811/1590 | | 938 |
| ☐ N939DL | McDonnell-Douglas MD-88 | 49812/1593 | | 939 |
| ☐ N940DL | McDonnell-Douglas MD-88 | 49813/1599 | | 940 |
| ☐ N941DL | McDonnell-Douglas MD-88 | 49814/1602 | | 941 |
| ☐ N942DL | McDonnell-Douglas MD-88 | 49815/1605 | | 942 |
| ☐ N943DL | McDonnell-Douglas MD-88 | 49816/1608 | | 943 |
| ☐ N944DL | McDonnell-Douglas MD-88 | 49817/1612 | | 944 |
| ☐ N945DL | McDonnell-Douglas MD-88 | 49818/1613 | | 945 |
| ☐ N946DL | McDonnell-Douglas MD-88 | 49819/1629 | | 946 |
| ☐ N947DL | McDonnell-Douglas MD-88 | 49878/1664 | | 947 |
| ☐ N948DL | McDonnell-Douglas MD-88 | 49879/1666 | | 948 |
| ☐ N949DL | McDonnell-Douglas MD-88 | 49880/1676 | | 949 |
| ☐ N950DL | McDonnell-Douglas MD-88 | 49881/1677 | | 950 |
| ☐ N951DL | McDonnell-Douglas MD-88 | 49882/1679 | | 951 |
| ☐ N952DL | McDonnell-Douglas MD-88 | 49883/1683 | | 952 |
| ☐ N953DL | McDonnell-Douglas MD-88 | 49884/1685 | | 953 |
| ☐ N954DL | McDonnell-Douglas MD-88 | 49885/1689 | | 954 |
| ☐ N955DL | McDonnell-Douglas MD-88 | 49886/1691 | | 955 |
| ☐ N956DL | McDonnell-Douglas MD-88 | 49887/1699 | | 956 |
| ☐ N957DL | McDonnell-Douglas MD-88 | 49976/1700 | | 957 |
| ☐ N958DL | McDonnell-Douglas MD-88 | 49977/1701 | | 958 |
| ☐ N959DL | McDonnell-Douglas MD-88 | 49978/1710 | | 959 |
| ☐ N960DL | McDonnell-Douglas MD-88 | 49979/1711 | | 960 |
| ☐ N961DL | McDonnell-Douglas MD-88 | 49980/1712 | | 961 |
| ☐ N962DL | McDonnell-Douglas MD-88 | 49981/1725 | | 962 |
| ☐ N963DL | McDonnell-Douglas MD-88 | 49982/1726 | | 963 |
| ☐ N964DL | McDonnell-Douglas MD-88 | 49983/1747 | | 964 |
| ☐ N965DL | McDonnell-Douglas MD-88 | 49984/1748 | | 965 |
| ☐ N966DL | McDonnell-Douglas MD-88 | 53115/1795 | | 966 |
| ☐ N967DL | McDonnell-Douglas MD-88 | 53116/1796 | | 967 |
| ☐ N968DL | McDonnell-Douglas MD-88 | 53161/1808 | | 968 |
| ☐ N969DL | McDonnell-Douglas MD-88 | 53172/1810 | | 969 |
| ☐ N970DL | McDonnell-Douglas MD-88 | 53173/1811 | | 970 |
| ☐ N971DL | McDonnell-Douglas MD-88 | 53214/1823 | | 971 |
| ☐ N972DL | McDonnell-Douglas MD-88 | 53215/1824 | | 972 |
| ☐ N973DL | McDonnell-Douglas MD-88 | 53241/1832 | | 973 |
| ☐ N974DL | McDonnell-Douglas MD-88 | 53242/1833 | | 974 |
| ☐ N975DL | McDonnell-Douglas MD-88 | 53243/1834 | | 975 |
| ☐ N976DL | McDonnell-Douglas MD-88 | 53257/1845 | | 976 |
| ☐ N977DL | McDonnell-Douglas MD-88 | 53258/1848 | | 977 |
| ☐ N978DL | McDonnell-Douglas MD-88 | 53259/1849 | | 978 |
| ☐ N979DL | McDonnell-Douglas MD-88 | 53266/1859 | | 979 |
| ☐ N980DL | McDonnell-Douglas MD-88 | 53267/1860 | | 980 |
| ☐ N981DL | McDonnell-Douglas MD-88 | 53268/1861 | | 981 |
| ☐ N982DL | McDonnell-Douglas MD-88 | 53273/1870 | | 982 |
| ☐ N983DL | McDonnell-Douglas MD-88 | 53274/1873 | | 983 |
| ☐ N984DL | McDonnell-Douglas MD-88 | 53311/1912 | | 984 |
| ☐ N985DL | McDonnell-Douglas MD-88 | 53312/1914 | | 985 |
| ☐ N986DL | McDonnell-Douglas MD-88 | 53313/1924 | | 986 |
| ☐ N987DL | McDonnell-Douglas MD-88 | 53338/1926 | | 987 |
| ☐ N988DL | McDonnell-Douglas MD-88 | 53339/1928 | | 988 |
| ☐ N989DL | McDonnell-Douglas MD-88 | 53341/1936 | | 989 |
| ☐ N990DL | McDonnell-Douglas MD-88 | 53342/1939 | | 990 |
| ☐ N991DL | McDonnell-Douglas MD-88 | 53343/1941 | | 991 |
| ☐ N992DL | McDonnell-Douglas MD-88 | 53344/1943 | | 992 |
| ☐ N993DL | McDonnell-Douglas MD-88 | 53345/1950 | | 993 |
| ☐ N994DL | McDonnell-Douglas MD-88 | 53346/1952 | | 994 |
| ☐ N995DL | McDonnell-Douglas MD-88 | 53362/1955 | | 995 |
| ☐ N996DL | McDonnell-Douglas MD-88 | 53363/1958 | | 996 |
| ☐ N997DL | McDonnell-Douglas MD-88 | 53364/1961 | | 997 |
| ☐ N998DL | McDonnell-Douglas MD-88 | 53370/1963 | | 998 |
| ☐ N999DN | McDonnell-Douglas MD-88 | 53371/1965 | | 999 |
| | | | | |
| ☐ N901DA | McDonnell-Douglas MD-90-30 | 53381/2100 | ex N902DC | 9201 |
| ☐ N902DA | McDonnell-Douglas MD-90-30 | 53382/2094 | | 9202 |
| ☐ N903DA | McDonnell-Douglas MD-90-30 | 53383/2095 | | 9203 |
| ☐ N904DA | McDonnell-Douglas MD-90-30 | 53384/2096 | | 9204 |
| ☐ N905DA | McDonnell-Douglas MD-90-30 | 53385/2097 | | 9205 |
| ☐ N906DA | McDonnell-Douglas MD-90-30 | 53386/2099 | | 9206 |
| ☐ N907DA | McDonnell-Douglas MD-90-30 | 53387/2115 | | 9207 |
| ☐ N908DA | McDonnell-Douglas MD-90-30 | 53388/2117 | | 9208 |
| ☐ N909DA | McDonnell-Douglas MD-90-30 | 53389/2122 | | 9209 |
| ☐ N910DN | McDonnell-Douglas MD-90-30 | 53390/2123 | | 9210 |

| | | | | | | |
|---|---|---|---|---|---|---|
| ☐ N911DA | McDonnell-Douglas MD-90-30 | 53391/2126 | | 9211 | | |
| ☐ N912DN | McDonnell-Douglas MD-90-30 | 53392/2136 | | 9212 | | |
| ☐ N913DN | McDonnell-Douglas MD-90-30 | 53393/2154 | | 9213 | | |
| ☐ N914DN | McDonnell-Douglas MD-90-30 | 53394/2156 | | 9214 | | |
| ☐ N915DN | McDonnell-Douglas MD-90-30 | 53395/2159 | | 9215 | | |
| ☐ N916DN | McDonnell-Douglas MD-90-30 | 53396/2161 | | 9216 | | |
| ☐ N917DN | McDonnell-Douglas MD-90-30 | 53552/2163 | ex N593BC | 9217 | | |
| ☐ N918DH | McDonnell-Douglas MD-90-30 | 53553/2165 | ex N648NW | 9218 | | |
| ☐ N919DN | McDonnell-Douglas MD-90-30ER | 53576/2195 | ex N647NW | 9219 | | |
| ☐ N920DN | McDonnell-Douglas MD-90-30 | 53582/2198 | ex B-2256 | 9220 | | |
| ☐ N921DN | McDonnell-Douglas MD-90-30 | 53583/2200 | ex B-2257 | 9221 | | |
| ☐ N922DX | McDonnell-Douglas MD-90-30 | 53584/2203 | ex B-2258 | 9222 | | |
| ☐ N923DN | McDonnell-Douglas MD-90-30 | 53585/2224 | ex B-2262 | 9223 | | |
| ☐ N924DN | McDonnell-Douglas MD-90-30 | 53586/2233 | ex B-2263 | 9224 | | |
| ☐ N925DN | McDonnell-Douglas MD-90-30 | 53587/2240 | ex B-2265 | 9225 | | |
| ☐ N926DH | McDonnell-Douglas MD-90-30 | 53588/2248 | ex B-2268 | 9226 | | |
| ☐ N927DN | McDonnell-Douglas MD-90-30 | 53589/2259 | ex B-2269 | 9227 | | |
| ☐ N928DN | McDonnell-Douglas MD-90-30 | 53590/2261 | ex B-2270 | 9228 | | |
| ☐ N929DN | McDonnell-Douglas MD-90-30 | 53459/2141 | ex OH-BLC | 9229 | | |
| ☐ N930DN | McDonnell-Douglas MD-90-30 | 53458/2140 | ex OH-BLU | 9230 | | [ATL] |
| ☐ N931DN | McDonnell-Douglas MD-90-30 | 53544/2197 | ex OH-BLD | 9231 | | ♦ |
| ☐ N932DN | McDonnell-Douglas MD-90-30 | 53457/2138 | ex OH-BLE | 9232 | | ♦ |
| ☐ N933DN | McDonnell-Douglas MD-90-30 | 53543/2194 | ex OH-BLF | 9233 | | [MZJ]♦ |
| ☐ N934DN | McDonnell-Douglas MD-90-30 | 53462/2149 | ex HB-JIF | 9234 | | [MIA]♦ |
| ☐ N935DN | McDonnell-Douglas MD-90-30 | 53460/2142 | ex HB-JID | 9235 | | ♦ |
| ☐ N936DN | McDonnell-Douglas MD-90-30 | 53461/2147 | ex HB-JIE | 9236 | | [MZJ]♦ |
| ☐ N937DN | McDonnell-Douglas MD-90-30 | 53352/2098 | ex JA8062 | | | [MZJ]♦ |
| ☐ N938DN | McDonnell-Douglas MD-90-30 | 53353/2120 | ex JA8063 | | | [MZJ]♦ |
| ☐ N941DN | McDonnell-Douglas MD-90-30 | 53555/2207 | ex JA001D | | | [MZJ]♦ |
| ☐ N953DN | McDonnell-Douglas MD-90-30 | 53523/2143 | ex B-2250 | 9253[MZJ] | | |
| ☐ N954DN | McDonnell-Douglas MD-90-30 | 53524/2146 | ex B-2251 | 9254 | | [MZJ]♦ |
| ☐ N955DN | McDonnell-Douglas MD-90-30 | 53525/2150 | ex B-2252 | 9255 | | [MIA]♦ |
| ☐ N956DN | McDonnell-Douglas MD-90-30 | 53526/2170 | ex B-2253 | 9256 | | [MZJ] |
| ☐ N957DN | McDonnell-Douglas MD-90-30 | 53527/2175 | ex B-2254 | 9257 | | [MZJ♦ |
| ☐ N958DN | McDonnell-Douglas MD-90-30 | 53528/2177 | ex B-2255 | 9258 | | [ATL]♦ |
| ☐ N959DN | McDonnell-Douglas MD-90-30 | 53529/2220 | ex B-2259 | 9259 | | ♦ |
| ☐ N960DN | McDonnell-Douglas MD-90-30 | 53530/2222 | ex B-2260 | 9260 | | [MZJ]♦ |
| ☐ N961DN | McDonnell-Douglas MD-90-30 | 53531/2228 | ex B-2261 | 9261 | | [ATL]♦ |
| ☐ N962DN | McDonnell-Douglas MD-90-30 | 53532/2253 | ex B-2266 | 9262 | | ♦ |
| ☐ N963DN | McDonnell-Douglas MD-90-30 | 53533/2258 | ex B-2267 | 9263 | | [MZJ]♦ |
| ☐ N964DN | McDonnell-Douglas MD-90-30 | 60001/4001 | ex B-2100 | 9264 AVIC II assembled | | [MZJ]♦ |
| ☐ N965DN | McDonnell-Douglas MD-90-30 | 60002/4002 | ex B-2103 | 9265 AVIC II assembled | | [MZJ]♦ |

## DELTA CONNECTION (DL/DAL)
### Cincinnati-Northern Kentucky Intl, OH/Atlanta-Hartsfield Intl, GA/Orlando-Intl, FL (CVG/ATL/MCO)

| | | | | | |
|---|---|---|---|---|---|
| ☐ N587SW | Canadair CRJ-100ER | 7062 | ex N943CA | 7062 | Comair |
| ☐ N588SW | Canadair CRJ-100ER | 7069 | ex N945CA | 7069 | Comair |
| ☐ N594SW | Canadair CRJ-100ER | 7285 | ex N767CA | 7285 | Comair [IGM] |
| ☐ N595SW | Canadair CRJ-100ER | 7292 | ex N769CA | 7292 | Comair [IGM] |
| ☐ N597SW | Canadair CRJ-100ER | 7293 | ex N776CA | 7293 | Comair [IGM] |
| ☐ N710CA | Canadair CRJ-100ER | 7241 | ex C-FVAZ | 7241 | Comair [IGM] |
| ☐ N712CA | Canadair CRJ-100ER | 7244 | ex C-FMLU | 7244 | Comair [IGM] |
| ☐ N713CA | Canadair CRJ-100ER | 7245 | ex C-FMOI | 7245 | Comair |
| ☐ N716CA | Canadair CRJ-100ER | 7250 | ex C-FMMW | 7250 | Comair |
| ☐ N721CA | Canadair CRJ-100ER | 7259 | ex C-FMLI | 7259 | Comair [IGM] |
| ☐ N739CA | Canadair CRJ-100ER | 7273 | ex C-FMNQ | 7273 | Comair |
| ☐ N784CA | Canadair CRJ-100ER | 7319 | ex C-FMLI | 7319 | Comair |
| ☐ N785CA | Canadair CRJ-100ER | 7326 | ex C-FMNW | 7326 | Comair [IGM] |
| ☐ N786CA | Canadair CRJ-100ER | 7333 | ex C-FMNQ | 7333 | Comair |
| ☐ N797CA | Canadair CRJ-100ER | 7344 | ex C-FMKV | 7344 | Comair |
| ☐ N868CA | Canadair CRJ-100LR | 7427 | ex C-FMML | 7427 | Comair |
| ☐ N936CA | Canadair CRJ-100ER | 7043 | ex C-FMLF | 7043 | Comair |
| ☐ N937CA | Canadair CRJ-100ER | 7044 | ex C-FMLI | 7044 | Comair |
| ☐ N938CA | Canadair CRJ-100ER | 7046 | ex C-FMLS | 7046 | Comair [IGM] |
| ☐ N940CA | Canadair CRJ-100ER | 7048 | ex C-FMLU | 7048 | Comair [IGM] |
| ☐ N941CA | Canadair CRJ-100ER | 7050 | ex C-FMMB | 7050 | Comair |
| ☐ N954CA | Canadair CRJ-100ER | 7100 | ex C-FXFB | 7100 | Comair [IGM] |
| ☐ N956CA | Canadair CRJ-100ER | 7105 | ex C-FMNH | 7105 | Comair [IGM] |
| ☐ N957CA | Canadair CRJ-100ER | 7109 | ex C-FMLV | 7109 | Comair |
| ☐ N958CA | Canadair CRJ-100ER | 7111 | ex C-FMML | 7111 | Comair |
| ☐ N959CA | Canadair CRJ-100ER | 7116 | ex C-FMMX | 7116 | Comair |
| ☐ N960CA | Canadair CRJ-100ER | 7117 | ex C-FMMY | 7117 | Comair |
| ☐ N962CA | Canadair CRJ-100ER | 7123 | ex C-FMLU | 7123 | Comair |
| ☐ N963CA | Canadair CRJ-100ER | 7127 | ex C-FMMN | 7127 | Comair |
| ☐ N964CA | Canadair CRJ-100ER | 7129 | ex C-FMMT | 7129 | Comair |
| ☐ N965CA | Canadair CRJ-100ER | 7131 | ex C-FMMX | 7131 | Comair |
| ☐ N966CA | Canadair CRJ-100ER | 7132 | ex C-FMMY | 7132 | Comair |
| ☐ N967CA | Canadair CRJ-100ER | 7134 | ex C-FMND | 7134 | Comair |
| ☐ N969CA | Canadair CRJ-100ER | 7141 | ex C-FMML | 7141 | Comair |
| ☐ N971CA | Canadair CRJ-100ER | 7145 | ex C-FMMW | 7145 | Comair |

| | N973CA | Canadair CRJ-100ER | 7146 | ex C-FMMX | 7146 | Comair |
|---|---|---|---|---|---|---|
| ☐ | N989CA | Canadair CRJ-100ER | 7215 | ex C-FMOI | 7215 | Comair [IGM] |
| | | | | | | |
| ☐ | N492SW | Canadair CRJ-100ER | 7168 | ex N982CA | 7168 | SkyWest |
| ☐ | N589SW | Canadair CRJ-100ER | 7072 | ex N946CA | 7072 | Skywest [IGM] |
| ☐ | N591SW | Canadair CRJ-100ER | 7079 | ex N948CA | 7079 | SkyWest [IGM] |
| ☐ | N779CA | Canadair CRJ-100ER | 7306 | ex C-FMMB | 7306 | Skywest |
| ☐ | N781CA | Canadair CRJ-100ER | 7312 | ex C-FMMY | 7312 | Skywest |
| ☐ | N783CA | Canadair CRJ-100ER | 7315 | ex C-FMKW | 7315 | Skywest <COM |
| ☐ | N809CA | Canadair CRJ-100ER | 7366 | ex C-FMMB | 7366 | Skywest <COM |
| | | | | | | |
| ☐ | N408CA | Canadair CRJ-200ER | 7440 | ex C-FMLQ | 7440 | Comair |
| ☐ | N409CA | Canadair CRJ-200ER | 7441 | ex C-FMLS | 7441 | Comair |
| ☐ | N420CA | Canadair CRJ-200ER | 7451 | ex C-FVAZ | 7451 | Comair |
| ☐ | N427CA | Canadair CRJ-200ER | 7460 | ex N897AS | 7460 | Comair [YYZ] |
| ☐ | N430CA | Canadair CRJ-200ER | 7461 | ex N898AS | 7461 | Comair [YYZ] |
| ☐ | N720SW | Canadair CRJ-200ER | 7297 | ex N778CA | 7297 | Comair [IGM] |
| ☐ | N810CA | Canadair CRJ-200ER | 7370 | ex C-FMMW | 7370 | Comair |
| ☐ | N811CA | Canadair CRJ-200ER | 7380 | ex C-FMLQ | 7380 | Comair |
| ☐ | N812CA | Canadair CRJ-200ER | 7381 | ex C-FMLS | 7381 | Comair |
| ☐ | N814CA | Canadair CRJ-200ER | 7387 | ex C-GFVM | 7387 | Comair |
| ☐ | N815CA | Canadair CRJ-200ER | 7397 | ex C-FMML | 7397 | Comair |
| ☐ | N818CA | Canadair CRJ-200ER | 7408 | ex C-FMLF | 7408 | Comair |
| ☐ | N819CA | Canadair CRJ-200ER | 7415 | ex C-FMNH | 7415 | Comair |
| | | | | | | |
| ☐ | N447CA | Canadair CRJ-200ER | 7552 | ex C-GJLL | 7552 | ExpressJet |
| ☐ | N451CA | Canadair CRJ-200ER | 7562 | ex C-GJVH | 7562 | ExpressJet |
| ☐ | N528CA | Canadair CRJ-200ER | 7841 | ex C-FVAZ | 7841 | ExpressJet |
| ☐ | N680BR | Canadair CRJ-200ER | 7679 | ex C-FMLI | | ExpressJet |
| ☐ | N681BR | Canadair CRJ-200ER | 7680 | ex C-FMLQ | | ExpressJet |
| ☐ | N682BR | Canadair CRJ-200ER | 7691 | ex C-FVAZ | | ExpressJet |
| ☐ | N683BR | Canadair CRJ-200ER | 7692 | ex C-FMND | | ExpressJet |
| ☐ | N684BR | Canadair CRJ-200ER | 7708 | ex C-FMLF | | ExpressJet |
| ☐ | N686BR | Canadair CRJ-200ER | 7715 | ex C-FMNH | | ExpressJet |
| ☐ | N820AS | Canadair CRJ-200ER | 7188 | ex C-FMMQ | 820 | ExpressJet |
| ☐ | N821AS | Canadair CRJ-200ER | 7194 | ex C-FMKV | 821 | ExpressJet |
| ☐ | N823AS | Canadair CRJ-200ER | 7196 | ex C-FMKZ | 823 | ExpressJet |
| ☐ | N824AS | Canadair CRJ-200ER | 7203 | ex C-FMLB | 824 | ExpressJet |
| ☐ | N825AS | Canadair CRJ-200ER | 7207 | ex C-FMNX | 825 | ExpressJet |
| ☐ | N826AS | Canadair CRJ-200ER | 7210 | ex C-FMOW | 826 | ExpressJet |
| ☐ | N827AS | Canadair CRJ-200ER | 7212 | ex C-FMND | 827 | ExpressJet |
| ☐ | N828AS | Canadair CRJ-200ER | 7213 | ex C-FMNQ | 828 | ExpressJet |
| ☐ | N829AS | Canadair CRJ-200ER | 7232 | ex C-FMLT | 829 | ExpressJet |
| ☐ | N833AS | Canadair CRJ-200ER | 7246 | ex C-FMMB | 833 | ExpressJet |
| ☐ | N835AS | Canadair CRJ-200ER | 7258 | ex C-FMLF | 835 | ExpressJet |
| ☐ | N837AS | Canadair CRJ-200ER | 7271 | ex C-FVAZ | 837 | ExpressJet |
| ☐ | N838AS | Canadair CRJ-200ER | 7276 | ex C-FMMB | 838 | ExpressJet |
| ☐ | N839AS | Canadair CRJ-200ER | 7284 | ex C-FMKV | 839 | ExpressJet |
| ☐ | N840AS | Canadair CRJ-200ER | 7290 | ex C-FMLQ | 840 | ExpressJet |
| ☐ | N841AS | Canadair CRJ-200ER | 7300 | ex C-FMOW | 841 | ExpressJet |
| ☐ | N842AS | Canadair CRJ-200ER | 7304 | ex C-FMLU | 842 | ExpressJet |
| ☐ | N843AS | Canadair CRJ-200ER | 7310 | ex C-FMMW | 843 | ExpressJet |
| ☐ | N844AS | Canadair CRJ-200ER | 7317 | ex C-FMLB | 844 | ExpressJet |
| ☐ | N845AS | Canadair CRJ-200ER | 7324 | ex C-FMMT | 845 | ExpressJet |
| ☐ | N846AS | Canadair CRJ-200ER | 7328 | ex C-FMNY | 846 | ExpressJet |
| ☐ | N847AS | Canadair CRJ-200ER | 7335 | ex C-FMOI | 847 | ExpressJet |
| ☐ | N848AS | Canadair CRJ-200ER | 7339 | ex C-FMMQ | 848 | ExpressJet |
| ☐ | N849AS | Canadair CRJ-200ER | 7347 | ex C-FMLB | 849 | ExpressJet |
| ☐ | N850AS | Canadair CRJ-200ER | 7355 | ex C-FMNH | 850 | ExpressJet |
| ☐ | N851AS | Canadair CRJ-200ER | 7360 | ex C-FMOW | 851 | ExpressJet |
| ☐ | N852AS | Canadair CRJ-200ER | 7369 | ex C-FMMQ | 852 | ExpressJet |
| ☐ | N853AS | Canadair CRJ-200ER | 7374 | ex C-FMKV | 853 | ExpressJet |
| ☐ | N854AS | Canadair CRJ-200ER | 7382 | ex C-FMLT | 854 | ExpressJet |
| ☐ | N855AS | Canadair CRJ-200ER | 7395 | ex C-GGKY | 855 | ExpressJet |
| ☐ | N856AS | Canadair CRJ-200ER | 7404 | ex C-FMKV | 856 | ExpressJet |
| ☐ | N857AS | Canadair CRJ-200ER | 7411 | ex C-FMLS | 857 | ExpressJet |
| ☐ | N858AS | Canadair CRJ-200ER | 7417 | ex C-FMNX | 858 | ExpressJet |
| ☐ | N859AS | Canadair CRJ-200ER | 7421 | ex C-FVAZ | 859 | ExpressJet |
| ☐ | N860AS | Canadair CRJ-200ER | 7433 | ex C-FMNB | 860 | ExpressJet |
| ☐ | N861AS | Canadair CRJ-200ER | 7445 | ex C-FMNH | 861 | ExpressJet |
| ☐ | N862AS | Canadair CRJ-200ER | 7476 | ex C-FMNW | 7476 | ExpressJet |
| ☐ | N863AS | Canadair CRJ-200ER | 7487 | ex C-FMML | 7487 | ExpressJet |
| ☐ | N864AS | Canadair CRJ-200ER | 7502 | ex C-FMLT | 864 | ExpressJet |
| ☐ | N865AS | Canadair CRJ-200ER | 7507 | ex C-FMNX | 865 | ExpressJet |
| ☐ | N866AS | Canadair CRJ-200ER | 7517 | ex C-FMML | 7517 | ExpressJet |
| ☐ | N867AS | Canadair CRJ-200ER | 7463 | ex C-FMNB | 867 | ExpressJet |
| ☐ | N868AS | Canadair CRJ-200ER | 7474 | ex C-FMMT | 868 | ExpressJet |
| ☐ | N869AS | Canadair CRJ-200ER | 7479 | ex C-FMOS | 869 | ExpressJet |
| ☐ | N870AS | Canadair CRJ-200ER | 7530 | ex C-FMLQ | 870 | ExpressJet |
| ☐ | N871AS | Canadair CRJ-200ER | 7537 | ex C-FMNX | 871 | ExpressJet |
| ☐ | N872AS | Canadair CRJ-200ER | 7542 | ex C-FMND | 872 | ExpressJet |
| ☐ | N873AS | Canadair CRJ-200ER | 7549 | ex C-GJLI | 873 | ExpressJet |

| | | | | | |
|---|---|---|---|---|---|
| ☐ N874AS | Canadair CRJ-200ER | 7551 | ex C-GJLK | 874 | ExpressJet>SKW |
| ☐ N875AS | Canadair CRJ-200ER | 7559 | ex C-GJLQ | 875 | ExpressJet |
| ☐ N876AS | Canadair CRJ-200ER | 7576 | ex C-FMMB | 876 | ExpressJet |
| ☐ N877AS | Canadair CRJ-200ER | 7579 | ex C-FMMQ | 877 | ExpressJet |
| ☐ N878AS | Canadair CRJ-200ER | 7590 | ex C-FMLQ | 878 | ExpressJet |
| ☐ N879AS | Canadair CRJ-200ER | 7600 | ex C-FMOW | 879 | ExpressJet |
| ☐ N880AS | Canadair CRJ-200ER | 7606 | ex C-FMMB | 880 | ExpressJet |
| ☐ N881AS | Canadair CRJ-200ER | 7496 | ex C-GIXF | 881 | ExpressJet |
| ☐ N882AS | Canadair CRJ-200ER | 7503 | ex C-GJAO | 882 | ExpressJet |
| ☐ N883AS | Canadair CRJ-200ER | 7504 | ex C-GIZD | 883 | ExpressJet |
| ☐ N884AS | Canadair CRJ-200ER | 7513 | ex C-GIZF | 884 | ExpressJet |
| ☐ N885AS | Canadair CRJ-200ER | 7521 | ex C-GJDX | 885 | ExpressJet>SKW |
| ☐ N886AS | Canadair CRJ-200ER | 7531 | ex C-GJJC | 886 | ExpressJet>SKW |
| ☐ N889AS | Canadair CRJ-200ER | 7538 | ex C-GJJG | 889 | ExpressJet |
| ☐ N900EV | Canadair CRJ-200ER | 7608 | ex C-FMMN | 900 | ExpressJet |
| ☐ N901EV | Canadair CRJ-200ER | 7616 | ex C-FMKZ | 901 | ExpressJet |
| ☐ N902EV | Canadair CRJ-200ER | 7620 | ex C-FMLQ | 902 | ExpressJet |
| ☐ N903EV | Canadair CRJ-200ER | 7621 | ex C-FMLS | 903 | ExpressJet |
| ☐ N904EV | Canadair CRJ-200ER | 7628 | ex C-FMNY | 904 | ExpressJet |
| ☐ N905EV | Canadair CRJ-200ER | 7632 | ex C-FMND | 905 | ExpressJet |
| ☐ N906EV | Canadair CRJ-200ER | 7642 | ex C-FMMY | 906 | ExpressJet |
| ☐ N907EV | Canadair CRJ-200ER | 7648 | ex C-FMLF | 907 | ExpressJet |
| ☐ N908EV | Canadair CRJ-200ER | 7654 | ex C-FMMT | 908 | ExpressJet |
| ☐ N909EV | Canadair CRJ-200ER | 7658 | ex C-FMNY | 909 | ExpressJet |
| ☐ N910EV | Canadair CRJ-200ER | 7727 | ex C-FMML | 7727 | ExpressJet |
| ☐ N913EV | Canadair CRJ-200ER | 7731 | ex C-FMMX | 7731 | ExpressJet |
| ☐ N914EV | Canadair CRJ-200ER | 7752 | ex C-FMND | 914 | ExpressJet |
| ☐ N915EV | Canadair CRJ-200ER | 7754 | ex C-FMLU | 7754 | ExpressJet>SKW |
| ☐ N916EV | Canadair CRJ-200ER | 7757 | ex C-FMML | 916 | ExpressJet |
| ☐ N917EV | Canadair CRJ-200ER | 7769 | ex C-FMLI | 917 | ExpressJet |
| ☐ N919EV | Canadair CRJ-200ER | 7780 | ex C-FMOW | 919 | ExpressJet |
| ☐ N920EV | Canadair CRJ-200ER | 7810 | ex C-FMOW | 920 | ExpressJet |
| ☐ N921EV | Canadair CRJ-200ER | 7819 | ex C-FMMQ | 921 | ExpressJet |
| ☐ N922EV | Canadair CRJ-200ER | 7822 | ex C-FMMY | 922 | ExpressJet |
| ☐ N923EV | Canadair CRJ-200ER | 7826 | ex C-FMKZ | 923 | ExpressJet |
| ☐ N924EV | Canadair CRJ-200ER | 7830 | ex C-FMLQ | 924 | ExpressJet |
| ☐ N925EV | Canadair CRJ-200ER | 7831 | ex C-FMLS | 925 | ExpressJet |
| ☐ N926EV | Canadair CRJ-200ER | 7843 | ex C-FMNQ | 926 | ExpressJet |
| ☐ N927EV | Canadair CRJ-200ER | 7844 | ex C-FMLU | 927 | ExpressJet |
| ☐ N928EV | Canadair CRJ-200ER | 8006 | ex C-FMMB | 928 | ExpressJet |
| ☐ N929EV | Canadair CRJ-200ER | 8007 | ex C-FMMN | 929 | ExpressJet |
| ☐ N930EV | Canadair CRJ-200ER | 8014 | ex C-FMKW | 930 | ExpressJet |
| ☐ N931EV | Canadair CRJ-200ER | 8015 | ex C-FMKZ | 931 | ExpressJet |
| ☐ N932EV | Canadair CRJ-200ER | 8016 | ex C-FMLB | 932 | ExpressJet |
| ☐ N933EV | Canadair CRJ-200ER | 8022 | ex C-FEHV | 933 | ExpressJet |
| ☐ N934EV | Canadair CRJ-200ER | 8028 | ex C-FMOS | 934 | ExpressJet |
| ☐ N935EV | Canadair CRJ-200ER | 8037 | ex C-FMMN | 935 | ExpressJet |
| ☐ N936EV | Canadair CRJ-200ER | 8038 | ex C-FEZT | 936 | ExpressJet |
| ☐ N937EV | Canadair CRJ-200ER | 8042 | ex C-FFAB | 937 | ExpressJet |
| ☐ N970EV | Canadair CRJ-200ER | 7527 | ex N663BR | 970 | ExpressJet |
| ☐ N971EV | Canadair CRJ-200ER | 7528 | ex N664BR | 971 | ExpressJet |
| ☐ N972EV | Canadair CRJ-200ER | 7534 | ex N665BR | 972 | ExpressJet |
| ☐ N973EV | Canadair CRJ-200ER | 7575 | ex N708BR | 973 | ExpressJet |
| ☐ N974EV | Canadair CRJ-200ER | 7594 | ex N672BR | 974 | ExpressJet |
| ☐ N975EV | Canadair CRJ-200ER | 7599 | ex N673BR | 975 | ExpressJet |
| ☐ N976EV | Canadair CRJ-200ER | 7601 | ex N674BR | 976 | ExpressJet |
| ☐ N977EV | Canadair CRJ-200ER | 7720 | ex N687BR | 977 | ExpressJet |
| ☐ N978EV | Canadair CRJ-200ER | 7723 | ex N688BR | 978 | ExpressJet |
| ☐ N979EV | Canadair CRJ-200ER | 7737 | ex N689BR | 979 | ExpressJet |
| ☐ N980EV | Canadair CRJ-200ER | 7759 | ex N692BR | 980 | ExpressJet |
| ☐ N981EV | Canadair CRJ-200ER | 7768 | ex N694BR | 981 | ExpressJet |
| ☐ N825AY | Canadair CRJ-200LR | 8025 | ex C-FMNW | 8025 | Mesaba |
| ☐ N601XJ | Canadair CRJ-200LR | 8044 | ex C-FFHW | | Pinnacle |
| ☐ N602XJ | Canadair CRJ-200LR | 8045 | ex C-FMKZ | | Pinnacle |
| ☐ N805AY | Canadair CRJ-200LR | 8005 | ex C-FDQP | 8005 | Pinnacle |
| ☐ N812AY | Canadair CRJ-200LR | 8012 | ex C- | 8012 | Pinnacle |
| ☐ N813AY | Canadair CRJ-200LR | 8013 | ex C- | 8013 | Pinnacle |
| ☐ N831AY | Canadair CRJ-200LR | 8031 | ex C-FETZ | 8031 | Pinnacle |
| ☐ N832AY | Canadair CRJ-200LR | 8032 | ex C-FMNQ | 8032 | Pinnacle |
| ☐ N833AY | Canadair CRJ-200LR | 8033 | ex C-FMLU | 8033 | Pinnacle |
| ☐ N834AY | Canadair CRJ-200LR | 8034 | ex C-FEXV | 8034 | Pinnacle |
| ☐ N835AY | Canadair CRJ-200LR | 8035 | ex C-FMMB | 8035 | Pinnacle |
| ☐ N836AY | Canadair CRJ-200LR | 8036 | ex C-FMML | 8036 | Pinnacle |
| ☐ N840AY | Canadair CRJ-200LR | 8040 | ex C-FEZX | 8040 | Pinnacle |
| ☐ N819AY | Canadair CRJ-200LR | 8019 | ex C-FMLQ | 8019 | Pinnacle |
| ☐ N820AY | Canadair CRJ-200LR | 8020 | ex C-FMLS | 8020 | Pinnacle |
| ☐ N821AY | Canadair CRJ-200LR | 8021 | ex C-FMLT | 8021 | Pinnacle |
| ☐ N823AY | Canadair CRJ-200LR | 8023 | ex C-FMMT | 8023 | Pinnacle |
| ☐ N824AY | Canadair CRJ-200LR | 8024 | ex C-FMNH | 8024 | Pinnacle |
| ☐ N826AY | Canadair CRJ-200LR | 8026 | ex C-FMNX | 8026 | Pinnacle |

| | | | | | | | | |
|---|---|---|---|---|---|---|---|---|
| ☐ | N827AY | Canadair CRJ-200LR | 8027 | ex C-FMNY | 8027 | | | Pinnacle |
| ☐ | N829AY | Canadair CRJ-200LR | 8029 | ex C-FMOW | 8029 | | | Pinnacle |
| ☐ | N8390A | Canadair CRJ-200LR | 7390 | ex C-FMOW | 8390 | Spirit of Memphis Belle | | Pinnacle |
| ☐ | N8409N | Canadair CRJ-200LR | 7409 | ex C-FMLI | 8409 | | | Pinnacle |
| ☐ | N8412F | Canadair CRJ-200LR | 7412 | ex C-FMLT | 8412 | | | Pinnacle |
| ☐ | N8416B | Canadair CRJ-200LR | 7416 | ex C-FMNW | 8416 | | | Pinnacle |
| ☐ | N8423C | Canadair CRJ-200LR | 7423 | ex C-FMNQ | 8423 | | | Pinnacle |
| ☐ | N8432A | Canadair CRJ-200LR | 7432 | ex C-GHRR | 8432 | | | Pinnacle |
| ☐ | N8444F | Canadair CRJ-200LR | 7444 | ex C-FMMT | 8444 | | | Pinnacle |
| ☐ | N8458A | Canadair CRJ-200LR | 7458 | ex C-FMMN | 8458 | | | Pinnacle |
| ☐ | N8475B | Canadair CRJ-200LR | 7475 | ex C-FMNH | 8475 | | | Pinnacle |
| ☐ | N8477R | Canadair CRJ-200LR | 7477 | ex C-FMNX | 8477 | | | Pinnacle |
| ☐ | N8488D | Canadair CRJ-200LR | 7488 | ex C-FMMN | 8488 | | | Pinnacle |
| ☐ | N8492C | Canadair CRJ-200LR | 7492 | ex C-FMMY | 8492 | | | Pinnacle |
| ☐ | N8495B | Canadair CRJ-200LR | 7495 | ex C-FMKW | 8495 | | | Pinnacle |
| ☐ | N8501F | Canadair CRJ-200LR | 7501 | ex C-FMLS | 8501 | | | Pinnacle |
| ☐ | N8505Q | Canadair CRJ-200LR | 7505 | ex C-FMNH | 8505 | | | Pinnacle |
| ☐ | N8506C | Canadair CRJ-200LR | 7506 | ex C-FMNW | 8506 | | | Pinnacle |
| ☐ | N8515F | Canadair CRJ-200LR | 7515 | ex C-FMOI | 8515 | | | Pinnacle |
| ☐ | N8516C | Canadair CRJ-200LR | 7516 | ex C-FMMB | 8516 | | | Pinnacle |
| ☐ | N8524A | Canadair CRJ-200LR | 7524 | ex C-FMKV | 8524 | | | Pinnacle |
| ☐ | N8525B | Canadair CRJ-200LR | 7525 | ex C-FMKW | 8525 | | | Pinnacle |
| ☐ | N8532G | Canadair CRJ-200LR | 7532 | ex C-FMLT | 8532 | | | Pinnacle |
| ☐ | N8533D | Canadair CRJ-200LR | 7533 | ex C-FMLV | 8533 | | | Pinnacle |
| ☐ | N8541D | Canadair CRJ-200LR | 7541 | ex C-FVAZ | 8541 | | | Pinnacle |
| ☐ | N8543F | Canadair CRJ-200LR | 7543 | ex C-FMNQ | 8543 | | | Pinnacle |
| ☐ | N8554A | Canadair CRJ-200LR | 7554 | ex C-FMKV | 8554 | | | Pinnacle |
| ☐ | N8560F | Canadair CRJ-200LR | 7560 | ex C-FMLQ | 8560 | | | Pinnacle |
| ☐ | N8577D | Canadair CRJ-200LR | 7577 | ex C-FMML | 8577 | | | Pinnacle |
| ☐ | N8580A | Canadair CRJ-200LR | 7580 | ex C-FMMW | 8580 | | | Pinnacle |
| ☐ | N8587E | Canadair CRJ-200LR | 7587 | ex C-FMLB | 8587 | | | Pinnacle |
| ☐ | N8665A | Canadair CRJ-200LR | 7665 | ex C-FMOI | 8665 | | | Pinnacle |
| ☐ | N8673D | Canadair CRJ-200LR | 7673 | ex C-FMNB | 8673 | | | Pinnacle |
| ☐ | N8674A | Canadair CRJ-200LR | 7674 | ex C-FMKV | 8674 | | | Pinnacle |
| ☐ | N8894A | Canadair CRJ-200LR | 7894 | ex C-FMMT | 8894 | | | Pinnacle |
| ☐ | N8896A | Canadair CRJ-200LR | 7896 | ex C-FMNW | 8896 | | | Pinnacle |
| ☐ | N8903A | Canadair CRJ-200LR | 7903 | ex C-FMNQ | 8903 | | | Pinnacle |
| ☐ | N8907A | Canadair CRJ-200LR | 7907 | ex C-FMML | 8907 | | | Pinnacle |
| ☐ | N8908D | Canadair CRJ-200LR | 7908 | ex C-FMMN | 8908 | | | Pinnacle |
| ☐ | N8914A | Canadair CRJ-200LR | 7914 | ex C-FMKV | 8914 | | | Pinnacle |
| ☐ | N8918B | Canadair CRJ-200LR | 7918 | ex C-FMLF | 8918 | | | Pinnacle |
| ☐ | N8936A | Canadair CRJ-200LR | 7936 | ex C-FMMB | 8936 | | | Pinnacle |
| ☐ | N8943A | Canadair CRJ-200LR | 7943 | ex C-FMNB | 8943 | | | Pinnacle |
| ☐ | N8944B | Canadair CRJ-200LR | 7944 | ex C-FMKV | 8944 | Spirit of Beale St | | Pinnacle |
| ☐ | N8946A | Canadair CRJ-200LR | 7946 | ex C-FMKZ | 8946 | | | Pinnacle |
| ☐ | N8948B | Canadair CRJ-200LR | 7948 | ex C-FMLF | 8948 | | | Pinnacle |
| ☐ | N8965E | Canadair CRJ-200LR | 7965 | ex C-FMOI | 8965 | | | Pinnacle |
| ☐ | N8970D | Canadair CRJ-200LR | 7970 | ex C-FMMW | 8970 | | | Pinnacle |
| ☐ | N8971A | Canadair CRJ-200LR | 7971 | ex C-FMMX | 8971 | | | Pinnacle |
| ☐ | N8974C | Canadair CRJ-200LR | 7974 | ex C-FMKV | 8974 | | | Pinnacle |
| ☐ | N8976E | Canadair CRJ-200LR | 7976 | ex C-FMKZ | 8976 | | | Pinnacle |
| | | | | | | | | |
| ☐ | N405SW | Canadair CRJ-200ER | 7029 | ex C-FMND | 7029 | | | SkyWest |
| ☐ | N406SW | Canadair CRJ-200ER | 7030 | ex C-FMNH | 7030 | | | SkyWest |
| ☐ | N408SW | Canadair CRJ-200ER | 7055 | ex C-FMMW | 7055 | | | SkyWest |
| ☐ | N409SW | Canadair CRJ-200ER | 7056 | ex C-FMMX | 7056 | | | SkyWest |
| ☐ | N410SW | Canadair CRJ-200ER | 7066 | ex C-FMOL | 7066 | | | SkyWest |
| ☐ | N411SW | Canadair CRJ-200ER | 7067 | ex C-FMOS | 7067 | | | SkyWest |
| ☐ | N412SW | Canadair CRJ-200ER | 7101 | ex C-FMMX | 7101 | | | SkyWest |
| | | | | | | SkyWest 30th anniversary c/s | | |
| ☐ | N416SW | Canadair CRJ-200ER | 7089 | ex N60SR | 7089 | | | SkyWest |
| ☐ | N417SW | Canadair CRJ-200ER | 7400 | ex C-FMMW | 7400 | | | SkyWest |
| ☐ | N418SW | Canadair CRJ-200ER | 7446 | ex C-FMNW | 7446 | | | SkyWest |
| ☐ | N423SW | Canadair CRJ-200ER | 7456 | ex C-FMMB | 7456 | | | SkyWest |
| ☐ | N426SW | Canadair CRJ-200ER | 7468 | ex C-FMLF | 7468 | | | SkyWest |
| ☐ | N427SW | Canadair CRJ-200ER | 7497 | ex C-FMLB | 7497 | | | SkyWest |
| ☐ | N429SW | Canadair CRJ-200ER | 7518 | ex C-FMMN | 7518 | | | SkyWest |
| ☐ | N430SW | Canadair CRJ-200ER | 7523 | ex C-FMNB | 7523 | | | SkyWest |
| ☐ | N431SW | Canadair CRJ-200ER | 7536 | ex C-FMNW | 7536 | | | SkyWest |
| ☐ | N432SW | Canadair CRJ-200ER | 7548 | ex C-GJFG | 7548 | | | SkyWest |
| ☐ | N433SW | Canadair CRJ-200ER | 7550 | ex C-GJFH | 7550 | | | SkyWest |
| ☐ | N435SW | Canadair CRJ-200ER | 7555 | ex C-GJHK | 7555 | | | SkyWest |
| ☐ | N437SW | Canadair CRJ-200ER | 7564 | ex C-GJIA | 7564 | | | SkyWest |
| ☐ | N438SW | Canadair CRJ-200ER | 7574 | ex C-FMLU | 7574 | | | SkyWest |
| ☐ | N439SW | Canadair CRJ-200ER | 7578 | ex C-FMMN | 7578 | | | SkyWest |
| ☐ | N440SW | Canadair CRJ-200ER | 7589 | ex C-FMLI | 7589 | | | SkyWest |
| ☐ | N441SW | Canadair CRJ-200ER | 7602 | ex C-FMND | 7602 | | | SkyWest |
| ☐ | N442SW | Canadair CRJ-200ER | 7609 | ex C-FMMQ | 7609 | | | SkyWest |
| ☐ | N443SW | Canadair CRJ-200ER | 7638 | ex C-FMMN | 7638 | | | SkyWest |
| ☐ | N445SW | Canadair CRJ-200ER | 7651 | ex C-FMLS | 7651 | | | SkyWest |
| ☐ | N446SW | Canadair CRJ-200ER | 7666 | ex C-FMMB | 7666 | | | SkyWest |
| ☐ | N447SW | Canadair CRJ-200ER | 7677 | ex C-FMLB | 7677 | | | SkyWest |

| | | | | | | | |
|---|---|---|---|---|---|---|---|
| ☐ | N448SW | Canadair CRJ-200ER | 7678 | ex C-FMLF | 7678 | | SkyWest |
| ☐ | N449SW | Canadair CRJ-200ER | 7699 | ex C-FMMQ | 7699 | | SkyWest |
| ☐ | N452SW | Canadair CRJ-200ER | 7716 | ex C-FMNW | 7716 | | SkyWest |
| ☐ | N453SW | Canadair CRJ-200ER | 7743 | ex C-FMLV | 7743 | | SkyWest |
| ☐ | N454SW | Canadair CRJ-200ER | 7749 | ex C-FMOS | 7749 | | SkyWest |
| ☐ | N455CA | Canadair CRJ-200ER | 7592 | ex C-FMLT | 7592 | | SkyWest |
| ☐ | N455SW | Canadair CRJ-200ER | 7760 | ex C-FMMW | 7760 | | SkyWest |
| ☐ | N457SW | Canadair CRJ-200ER | 7773 | ex C-FMLV | 7773 | | SkyWest |
| ☐ | N459SW | Canadair CRJ-200ER | 7782 | ex C-FMND | 7782 | | SkyWest |
| ☐ | N460SW | Canadair CRJ-200ER | 7803 | ex C-FMLV | 7803 | | SkyWest |
| ☐ | N461SW | Canadair CRJ-200ER | 7811 | ex C-FVAZ | 7811 | | SkyWest |
| ☐ | N463SW | Canadair CRJ-200ER | 7820 | ex C-FMMW | 7820 | | SkyWest |
| ☐ | N464SW | Canadair CRJ-200ER | 7827 | ex C-FMLB | 7827 | | SkyWest |
| ☐ | N465SW | Canadair CRJ-200ER | 7845 | ex C-FMOI | 7845 | | SkyWest |
| ☐ | N466SW | Canadair CRJ-200ER | 7856 | ex C-FMKZ | 7856 | | SkyWest |
| ☐ | N477CA | Canadair CRJ-200ER | 7670 | ex C-FMMW | 7670 | | SkyWest |
| ☐ | N487CA | Canadair CRJ-200ER | 7729 | ex C-FMMQ | 7729 | | SkyWest |
| ☐ | N629BR | Canadair CRJ-200ER | 7251 | ex (N533CA) | 7251 | | SkyWest |
| ☐ | N659BR | Canadair CRJ-200ER | 7509 | ex C-FMOS | 7509 | | SkyWest |
| ☐ | N675BR | Canadair CRJ-200ER | 7635 | ex (N536CA) | 7635 | | SkyWest |
| ☐ | N685BR | Canadair CRJ-200ER | 7712 | ex (N532CA) | 7712 | | SkyWest |
| ☐ | N912EV | Canadair CRJ-200ER | 7728 | ex C-FMMN | 7728 | | SkyWest |
| ☐ | N915EV | Canadair CRJ-200ER | 7754 | ex C-FMLU | 7754 | | SkyWest <ExpressJet |
| | | | | | | | |
| ☐ | N800AY | Canadair CRJ-440LR | 8000 | ex C-FMMW | 8000 | | Pinnacle |
| ☐ | N801AY | Canadair CRJ-440LR | 8001 | ex C-FMMX | 8001 | | Pinnacle |
| ☐ | N830AY | Canadair CRJ-440LR | 8030 | ex C-FVAZ | 8030 | | Pinnacle |
| ☐ | N839AY | Canadair CRJ-440LR | 8039 | ex C-FMMW | 8039 | | Pinnacle |
| ☐ | N841AY | Canadair CRJ-440LR | 8041 | ex C-FMMY | 8041 | | Pinnacle |
| ☐ | N8588D | Canadair CRJ-440LR | 7588 | ex C-GJSZ | 8588 | | Pinnacle |
| ☐ | N8598B | Canadair CRJ-440LR | 7598 | ex C-FMNY | 8598 | | Pinnacle |
| ☐ | N8604C | Canadair CRJ-440LR | 7604 | ex C-FMLU | 8604 | | Pinnacle |
| ☐ | N8611A | Canadair CRJ-440LR | 7611 | ex C-FMMX | 8611 | | Pinnacle |
| ☐ | N8623A | Canadair CRJ-440LR | 7623 | ex C-FMLV | 8623 | | Pinnacle |
| ☐ | N8631E | Canadair CRJ-440LR | 7631 | ex C-FVAZ | 8631 | | Pinnacle |
| ☐ | N8646A | Canadair CRJ-440LR | 7646 | ex C-FMKZ | 8646 | | Pinnacle |
| ☐ | N8659B | Canadair CRJ-440LR | 7659 | ex C-FMOS | 8659 | | Pinnacle |
| ☐ | N8672A | Canadair CRJ-440LR | 7672 | ex C-FMMY | 8672 | | Pinnacle |
| ☐ | N8683B | Canadair CRJ-440LR | 7683 | ex C-FMLV | 8683 | | Pinnacle |
| ☐ | N8688C | Canadair CRJ-440LR | 7688 | ex C-FMNY | 6888 | | Pinnacle |
| ☐ | N8694A | Canadair CRJ-440LR | 7694 | ex C-FMLU | 8694 | | Pinnacle |
| ☐ | N8696C | Canadair CRJ-440LR | 7696 | ex C-FMMB | 8696 | | Pinnacle |
| ☐ | N8698A | Canadair CRJ-440LR | 7698 | ex C-FMMN | 8698 | | Pinnacle |
| ☐ | N8709A | Canadair CRJ-440LR | 7709 | ex C-FMLI | 8709 | | Pinnacle |
| ☐ | N8710A | Canadair CRJ-440LR | 7710 | ex C-FMLQ | 8710 | | Pinnacle |
| ☐ | N8718E | Canadair CRJ-440LR | 7718 | ex C-FMNY | 8718 | | Pinnacle |
| ☐ | N8721B | Canadair CRJ-440LR | 7721 | ex C-FVAZ | 8721 | | Pinnacle |
| ☐ | N8733G | Canadair CRJ-440LR | 7733 | ex C-FMNB | 8733 | | Pinnacle |
| ☐ | N8736A | Canadair CRJ-440LR | 7736 | ex C-FMKZ | 8736 | | Pinnacle |
| ☐ | N8745B | Canadair CRJ-440LR | 7745 | ex C-FMNH | 8745 | | Pinnacle |
| ☐ | N8747B | Canadair CRJ-440LR | 7747 | ex C-FMNX | 8747 | | Pinnacle |
| ☐ | N8751D | Canadair CRJ-440LR | 7751 | ex C-FVAZ | 8751 | | Pinnacle |
| ☐ | N8758D | Canadair CRJ-440LR | 7758 | ex C-FMMN | 8758 | | Pinnacle |
| ☐ | N8771A | Canadair CRJ-440LR | 7771 | ex C-FMLS | 8771 | | Pinnacle |
| ☐ | N8775A | Canadair CRJ-440LR | 7775 | ex C-FMNH | 8775 | | Pinnacle |
| ☐ | N8783E | Canadair CRJ-440LR | 7783 | ex C-FMNQ | 8783 | | Pinnacle |
| ☐ | N8790A | Canadair CRJ-440LR | 7790 | ex C-FMMW | 8790 | | Pinnacle |
| ☐ | N8794B | Canadair CRJ-440LR | 7794 | ex C-FMKV | 8794 | | Pinnacle |
| ☐ | N8797A | Canadair CRJ-440LR | 7797 | ex C-FMLB | 8797 | | Pinnacle |
| ☐ | N8800G | Canadair CRJ-440LR | 7800 | ex C-FMLQ | 8800 | | Pinnacle |
| ☐ | N8808H | Canadair CRJ-440LR | 7808 | ex C-FMNY | 8808 | | Pinnacle |
| ☐ | N8828D | Canadair CRJ-440LR | 7828 | ex C-FMLF | 8828 | | Pinnacle |
| ☐ | N8836A | Canadair CRJ-440LR | 7836 | ex C-FMNW | 8836 | | Pinnacle |
| ☐ | N8837B | Canadair CRJ-440LR | 7837 | ex C-FMNX | 8837 | | Pinnacle |
| ☐ | N8839E | Canadair CRJ-440LR | 7839 | ex C-FMOS | 8839 | | Pinnacle |
| ☐ | N8847A | Canadair CRJ-440LR | 7847 | ex C-FMML | 8847 | | Pinnacle |
| ☐ | N8855A | Canadair CRJ-440LR | 7855 | ex C-FMKW | 8855 | | Pinnacle |
| ☐ | N8869B | Canadair CRJ-440LR | 7869 | ex C-FMOS | 8869 | | Pinnacle |
| ☐ | N8877A | Canadair CRJ-440LR | 7877 | ex C-FMML | 8877 | | Pinnacle |
| ☐ | N8883E | Canadair CRJ-440LR | 7883 | ex C-FMNB | 8883 | | Pinnacle |
| ☐ | N8884E | Canadair CRJ-440LR | 7884 | ex C-FMKV | 8884 | | Pinnacle |
| ☐ | N8886A | Canadair CRJ-440LR | 7886 | ex C-FMKZ | 8886 | | Pinnacle |
| ☐ | N8888D | Canadair CRJ-440LR | 7888 | ex C-FMLF | 8888 | | Pinnacle |
| ☐ | N8891A | Canadair CRJ-440LR | 7891 | ex C-FMLS | 8891 | | Pinnacle |
| ☐ | N8913A | Canadair CRJ-440LR | 7913 | ex C-FMNB | 8913 | | Pinnacle |
| ☐ | N8921B | Canadair CRJ-440LR | 7921 | ex C-FMLS | 8921 | | Pinnacle |
| ☐ | N8923A | Canadair CRJ-440LR | 7923 | ex C-FMLV | 8923 | | Pinnacle |
| ☐ | N8924B | Canadair CRJ-440LR | 7924 | ex C-FMMT | 8924 | | Pinnacle |
| ☐ | N8928A | Canadair CRJ-440LR | 7928 | ex C-FMNY | 8928 | | Pinnacle |
| ☐ | N8930E | Canadair CRJ-440LR | 7930 | ex C-FMOW | 8930 | | Pinnacle |
| ☐ | N8932C | Canadair CRJ-440LR | 7932 | ex C-FMND | 8932 | | Pinnacle |
| ☐ | N8933B | Canadair CRJ-440LR | 7933 | ex C-FMNQ | 8933 | | Pinnacle |

| | | | | | | |
|---|---|---|---|---|---|---|
| ☐ | N8938A | Canadair CRJ-440LR | 7938 | ex C-FMMN | 8938 | Pinnacle |
| ☐ | N8940E | Canadair CRJ-440LR | 7940 | ex C-FMMW | 8940 | Pinnacle |
| ☐ | N8942A | Canadair CRJ-440LR | 7942 | ex C-FMMY | 8942 | Pinnacle |
| ☐ | N8960A | Canadair CRJ-440LR | 7960 | ex C-FMOW | 8960 | Pinnacle |
| ☐ | N8964E | Canadair CRJ-440LR | 7964 | ex C-FMLU | 8964 | Pinnacle |
| ☐ | N8968E | Canadair CRJ-440LR | 7968 | ex C-FMMN | 8968 | Pinnacle |
| ☐ | N8969A | Canadair CRJ-440LR | 7969 | ex C-FMMQ | 8969 | Pinnacle |
| ☐ | N8972E | Canadair CRJ-440LR | 7972 | ex C-FMMY | 8972 | Pinnacle |
| ☐ | N8977A | Canadair CRJ-440LR | 7977 | ex C-FMLB | 8977 | Pinnacle |
| ☐ | N8980A | Canadair CRJ-440LR | 7980 | ex C-FMLQ | 8980 | Pinnacle |
| ☐ | N8982A | Canadair CRJ-440LR | 7982 | ex C-FMLT | 8982 | Pinnacle |
| ☐ | N8986B | Canadair CRJ-440LR | 7986 | ex C-FMNW | 8986 | Pinnacle |
| | | | | | | |
| ☐ | N369CA | Canadair CRJ-701ER | 10079 | ex C-GZUD | 10079 | Comair |
| ☐ | N371CA | Canadair CRJ-701ER | 10082 | ex C-GIAR | 10082 | Comair |
| ☐ | N374CA | Canadair CRJ-701ER | 10090 | ex C- | 10090 | Comair |
| ☐ | N378CA | Canadair CRJ-701ER | 10097 | ex C-GIAJ | 10097 | Comair |
| ☐ | N391CA | Canadair CRJ-701ER | 10108 | ex C- | 10108 | Comair |
| ☐ | N398CA | Canadair CRJ-701ER | 10112 | ex C- | 10112 | Comair |
| ☐ | N625CA | Canadair CRJ-701ER | 10113 | ex C- | 10113 | Comair |
| ☐ | N641CA | Canadair CRJ-701ER | 10122 | ex C- | 10122 | Comair |
| ☐ | N642CA | Canadair CRJ-701ER | 10125 | ex C- | 10125 | Comair |
| ☐ | N653CA | Canadair CRJ-701ER | 10129 | ex C-GZUC | 10129 | Comair |
| ☐ | N655CA | Canadair CRJ-701ER | 10134 | ex C- | 10134 | Comair |
| ☐ | N656CA | Canadair CRJ-701ER | 10143 | ex C-GIAU | 10143 | Comair |
| ☐ | N658CA | Canadair CRJ-701ER | 10148 | ex C-GIAU | 10148 | Comair |
| ☐ | N669CA | Canadair CRJ-701ER | 10176 | ex C- | 10176 | Comair |
| ☐ | N690CA | Canadair CRJ-701ER | 10182 | ex C- | 10182 | Comair |
| | | | | | | |
| ☐ | N317CA | Canadair CRJ-701ER | 10055 | ex C-GZXI | 10055 | ExpressJet |
| ☐ | N355CA | Canadair CRJ-701ER | 10067 | ex C-GIBT | 10067 | ExpressJet |
| ☐ | N376CA | Canadair CRJ-701ER | 10092 | ex C- | 10092 | ExpressJet |
| ☐ | N390CA | Canadair CRJ-701ER | 10106 | ex C- | 10106 | ExpressJet |
| ☐ | N609SK | Canadair CRJ-701ER | 10020 | ex N701EV | 10020 | ExpressJet>SKW |
| ☐ | N611SK | Canadair CRJ-701ER | 10035 | ex N702EV | 10035 | ExpressJet>SKW |
| ☐ | N613SK | Canadair CRJ-701ER | 10038 | ex N703EV | 10038 | ExpressJet>SKW |
| ☐ | N614SK | Canadair CRJ-701ER | 10051 | ex N705EV | 10051 | ExpressJet>SKW |
| ☐ | N750EV | Canadair CRJ-701ER | 10161 | ex C- | | ExpressJet |
| ☐ | N707EV | Canadair CRJ-701ER | 10057 | ex C-GIAZ | | ExpressJet |
| ☐ | N708EV | Canadair CRJ-701ER | 10060 | ex C-GIBI | | ExpressJet |
| ☐ | N709EV | Canadair CRJ-701ER | 10068 | ex C-GICB | | ExpressJet |
| ☐ | N710EV | Canadair CRJ-701ER | 10071 | ex C-GICP | | ExpressJet |
| ☐ | N712EV | Canadair CRJ-701ER | 10074 | ex C-GHZZ | | ExpressJet |
| ☐ | N713EV | Canadair CRJ-701ER | 10081 | ex C-GIAP | | ExpressJet |
| ☐ | N716EV | Canadair CRJ-701ER | 10084 | ex C-GIAV | | ExpressJet |
| ☐ | N717EV | Canadair CRJ-701ER | 10088 | ex C-GIBH | | ExpressJet |
| ☐ | N718EV | Canadair CRJ-701ER | 10095 | ex C- | | ExpressJet |
| ☐ | N719EV | Canadair CRJ-701ER | 10099 | ex C-GICL | | ExpressJet |
| ☐ | N720EV | Canadair CRJ-701ER | 10115 | ex C-GIAW | | ExpressJet |
| ☐ | N722EV | Canadair CRJ-701ER | 10127 | ex C- | | ExpressJet |
| ☐ | N723EV | Canadair CRJ-701ER | 10132 | ex C- | | ExpressJet |
| ☐ | N724EV | Canadair CRJ-701ER | 10138 | ex C-GIBT | | ExpressJet |
| ☐ | N730EV | Canadair CRJ-701ER | 10141 | ex C-GIAP | | ExpressJet |
| ☐ | N738EV | Canadair CRJ-701ER | 10146 | ex C- | | ExpressJet |
| ☐ | N740EV | Canadair CRJ-701ER | 10151 | ex C- | | ExpressJet |
| ☐ | N744EV | Canadair CRJ-701ER | 10157 | ex C- | | ExpressJet |
| ☐ | N748EV | Canadair CRJ-701ER | 10158 | ex C- | | ExpressJet |
| ☐ | N751EV | Canadair CRJ-701ER | 10163 | ex C- | | ExpressJet |
| ☐ | N752EV | Canadair CRJ-701ER | 10166 | ex C- | | ExpressJet |
| ☐ | N753EV | Canadair CRJ-701ER | 10169 | ex C- | | ExpressJet |
| ☐ | N754EV | Canadair CRJ-701ER | 10173 | ex C-FCRJ | | ExpressJet |
| ☐ | N755EV | Canadair CRJ-701ER | 10185 | ex C- | | ExpressJet |
| ☐ | N758EV | Canadair CRJ-701ER | 10210 | ex C- | | ExpressJet |
| ☐ | N759EV | Canadair CRJ-701ER | 10211 | ex C- | | ExpressJet |
| ☐ | N760EV | Canadair CRJ-701ER | 10212 | ex C- | | ExpressJet |
| ☐ | N761ND | Canadair CRJ-701ER | 10213 | ex C- | | ExpressJet |
| | | | | | | |
| ☐ | N668CA | Canadair CRJ-701ER | 10162 | ex C- | | GoJet♦ |
| ☐ | N741EV | Canadair CRJ-701ER | 10155 | ex C-FBQS | | GoJet♦ |
| | | | | | | |
| ☐ | N215AG | Canadair CRJ-701ER | 10009 | ex N601QX | | SkyWest |
| ☐ | N216AG | Canadair CRJ-701ER | 10023 | ex N606QX | | SkyWest |
| ☐ | N331CA | Canadair CRJ-701ER | 10061 | ex C-GIBJ | 10061 | SkyWest |
| ☐ | N340CA | Canadair CRJ-701ER | 10062 | ex C-GIBL | 10062 | SkyWest |
| ☐ | N368CA | Canadair CRJ-701ER | 10075 | ex C-GIAD | 10075 | SkyWest |
| ☐ | N603SK | Canadair CRJ-702ER | 10248 | ex C-FHUC | 10248 | SkyWest |
| ☐ | N603QX | Canadair CRJ-701ER | 10011 | ex C-GHCZ | | SkyWest<QXE |
| ☐ | N604SK | Canadair CRJ-702ER | 10249 | ex C- | 10239 | SkyWest |
| ☐ | N606SK | Canadair CRJ-702ER | 10250 | ex C- | 10250 | SkyWest |
| ☐ | N607SK | Canadair CRJ-702ER | 10251 | ex C-FIBQ | 10251 | SkyWest |
| ☐ | N608SK | Canadair CRJ-702ER | 10252 | ex C- | 10252 | SkyWest |
| ☐ | N609SK | Canadair CRJ-701ER | 10020 | ex N701EV | 10020 | SkyWest<BTA♦ |

| | | | | | | |
|---|---|---|---|---|---|---|
| ☐ N611SK | Canadair CRJ-701ER | 10035 | ex N702EV | 10035 | | SkyWest<BTA♦ |
| ☐ N613SK | Canadair CRJ-701ER | 10038 | ex N703EV | 10038 | | SkyWest<BTA♦ |
| ☐ N614SK | Canadair CRJ-701ER | 10051 | ex N705EV | 10051 | | SkyWest<BTA♦ |
| ☐ N630SK | Canadair CRJ-701ER | 10328 | ex C-GIBQ | | | SkyWest |
| ☐ N632SK | Canadair CRJ-702ER | 10330 | ex C-G | | | SkyWest |
| ☐ N633SK | Canadair CRJ-702ER | 10331 | ex C- | | | SkyWest |
| | | | | | | |
| ☐ N538CA | Canadair CRJ-900ER | 15157 | ex C- | | | Comair |
| ☐ N548CA | Canadair CRJ-900ER | 15159 | ex C- | | | Comair |
| ☐ N549CA | Canadair CRJ-900ER | 15164 | ex C- | | | Comair |
| ☐ N554CA | Canadair CRJ-900ER | 15168 | ex C- | | | Comair |
| ☐ N582CA | Canadair CRJ-900ER | 15171 | ex C- | | | Comair |
| ☐ N676CA | Canadair CRJ-900ER | 15127 | ex C- | | | Comair |
| ☐ N678CA | Canadair CRJ-900ER | 15125 | ex C- | | | Comair |
| ☐ N679CA | Canadair CRJ-900ER | 15132 | ex C- | | | Comair |
| ☐ N689CA | Canadair CRJ-900ER | 15133 | ex C- | | | Comair |
| ☐ N691CA | Canadair CRJ-900ER | 15136 | ex C- | | | Comair |
| ☐ N692CA | Canadair CRJ-900ER | 15092 | ex C- | | | Comair |
| ☐ N693CA | Canadair CRJ-900ER | 15096 | ex C- | | | Comair |
| ☐ N695CA | Canadair CRJ-900ER | 15097 | ex C- | | 30th Anniversary c/s | Comair |
| | | | | | | |
| ☐ N131EV | Canadair CRJ-900ER | 15217 | ex C- | | | ExpressJet |
| ☐ N132EV | Canadair CRJ-900ER | 15219 | ex C- | | | ExpressJet |
| ☐ N133EV | Canadair CRJ-900ER | 15222 | ex C- | | | ExpressJet |
| ☐ N134EV | Canadair CRJ-900ER | 15223 | ex C- | | | ExpressJet |
| ☐ N135EV | Canadair CRJ-900ER | 15225 | ex C-GIBI | | | ExpressJet |
| ☐ N136EV | Canadair CRJ-900ER | 15226 | ex C- | | | ExpressJet |
| ☐ N137EV | Canadair CRJ-900ER | 15227 | ex C- | | | ExpressJet |
| ☐ N138EV | Canadair CRJ-900ER | 15235 | ex C-GZQW | | | ExpressJet |
| ☐ N606LR | Canadair CRJ-900ER | 15173 | ex C- | | | ExpressJet |
| ☐ N607LR | Canadair CRJ-900ER | 15178 | ex C- | | | ExpressJet |
| | | | | | | |
| ☐ N901XJ | Canadair CRJ-900 | 15130 | ex C- | | | Mesaba |
| ☐ N902XJ | Canadair CRJ-900 | 15131 | ex C-FNWB | | | Mesaba |
| ☐ N903XJ | Canadair CRJ-900 | 15134 | ex C-FOFO | | | Mesaba |
| ☐ N904XJ | Canadair CRJ-900 | 15135 | ex C- | | | Mesaba |
| ☐ N905XJ | Canadair CRJ-900 | 15137 | ex C- | | | Mesaba |
| ☐ N906XJ | Canadair CRJ-900 | 15138 | ex C- | | | Mesaba |
| ☐ N907XJ | Canadair CRJ-900 | 15139 | ex C-FOVM | | | Mesaba |
| ☐ N908XJ | Canadair CRJ-900 | 15140 | ex C-FOWF | | | Mesaba |
| ☐ N909XJ | Canadair CRJ-900 | 15141 | ex C- | | | Mesaba |
| ☐ N910XJ | Canadair CRJ-900 | 15143 | ex C- | | | Mesaba |
| ☐ N912XJ | Canadair CRJ-900 | 15144 | ex C- | | | Mesaba |
| ☐ N913XJ | Canadair CRJ-900 | 15148 | ex C-FQYX | | | Mesaba |
| ☐ N914XJ | Canadair CRJ-900 | 15149 | ex C- | | | Mesaba |
| ☐ N915XJ | Canadair CRJ-900 | 15150 | ex C- | | | Mesaba |
| ☐ N916XJ | Canadair CRJ-900 | 15154 | ex C- | | | Mesaba |
| ☐ N917XJ | Canadair CRJ-900 | 15155 | ex C- | | | Mesaba |
| ☐ N918XJ | Canadair CRJ-900 | 15156 | ex C- | | | Mesaba |
| ☐ N919XJ | Canadair CRJ-900 | 15163 | ex C- | | | Mesaba |
| ☐ N920XJ | Canadair CRJ-900 | 15167 | ex C- | | | Mesaba |
| ☐ N921XJ | Canadair CRJ-900 | 15172 | ex C- | | | Mesaba |
| ☐ N922XJ | Canadair CRJ-900 | 15174 | ex C-FTTY | | | Mesaba |
| ☐ N923XJ | Canadair CRJ-900 | 15177 | ex C- | | | Mesaba |
| ☐ N924XJ | Canadair CRJ-900 | 15179 | ex C- | | | Mesaba |
| ☐ N925XJ | Canadair CRJ-900 | 15183 | ex C- | | | Mesaba |
| ☐ N926XJ | Canadair CRJ-900 | 15184 | ex C- | | | Mesaba |
| ☐ N927XJ | Canadair CRJ-900 | 15188 | ex C- | | | Mesaba |
| ☐ N928XJ | Canadair CRJ-900 | 15190 | ex C- | | | Mesaba |
| ☐ N929XJ | Canadair CRJ-900 | 15191 | ex C- | | | Mesaba |
| ☐ N930XJ | Canadair CRJ-900 | 15192 | ex C- | | | Mesaba |
| ☐ N931XJ | Canadair CRJ-900 | 15193 | ex C- | | | Mesaba |
| ☐ N932XJ | Canadair CRJ-900 | 15194 | ex C- | | | Mesaba |
| ☐ N933XJ | Canadair CRJ-900 | 15196 | ex C- | | | Mesaba |
| ☐ N934XJ | Canadair CRJ-900 | 15198 | ex C- | | | Mesaba |
| ☐ N935XJ | Canadair CRJ-900 | 15199 | ex C- | | | Mesaba |
| ☐ N936XJ | Canadair CRJ-900 | 15201 | ex C- | | | Mesaba |
| ☐ N937XJ | Canadair CRJ-900 | 15210 | ex C- | | | Mesaba |
| | | | | | | |
| ☐ N146PQ | Canadair CRJ-900ER | 15146 | ex C- | | | Pinnacle |
| ☐ N147PQ | Canadair CRJ-900ER | 15147 | ex C- | | | Pinnacle |
| ☐ N153PQ | Canadair CRJ-900ER | 15153 | ex C- | | | Pinnacle |
| ☐ N161PQ | Canadair CRJ-900ER | 15161 | ex C- | | | Pinnacle |
| ☐ N162PQ | Canadair CRJ-900ER | 15162 | ex C- | | | Pinnacle |
| ☐ N166PQ | Canadair CRJ-900ER | 15166 | ex C- | | | Pinnacle |
| ☐ N170PQ | Canadair CRJ-900ER | 15170 | ex C- | | | Pinnacle |
| ☐ N176PQ | Canadair CRJ-900ER | 15176 | ex C- | | | Pinnacle |
| ☐ N181PQ | Canadair CRJ-900ER | 15181 | ex C- | | | Pinnacle |
| ☐ N186PQ | Canadair CRJ-900ER | 15186 | ex C- | | | Pinnacle |
| ☐ N187PQ | Canadair CRJ-900ER | 15187 | ex C- | | | Pinnacle |
| ☐ N195PQ | Canadair CRJ-900ER | 15195 | ex C-FVWD | | | Pinnacle |
| ☐ N197PQ | Canadair CRJ-900ER | 15197 | ex C-GZQV | | | Pinnacle |

| | | | | | | |
|---|---|---|---|---|---|---|
| ☐ | N200PQ | Canadair CRJ-900ER | 15200 | ex C-GWVU | | Pinnacle |
| ☐ | N228PQ | Canadair CRJ-900ER | 15228 | ex C- | | Pinnacle |
| ☐ | N232PQ | Canadair CRJ-900ER | 15232 | ex C-GZQR | | Pinnacle |
| ☐ | N600LR | Canadair CRJ-900ER | 15142 | ex C- | | Pinnacle |
| ☐ | N601LR | Canadair CRJ-900ER | 15145 | ex C- | | Pinnacle |
| ☐ | N602LR | Canadair CRJ-900ER | 15151 | ex C- | | Pinnacle |
| ☐ | N604LR | Canadair CRJ-900ER | 15152 | ex C- | | Pinnacle |
| ☐ | N605LR | Canadair CRJ-900ER | 15160 | ex C- | | Pinnacle |
| | | | | | | |
| ☐ | N800SK | Canadair CRJ-900ER | 15060 | ex C- | | SkyWest |
| ☐ | N802SK | Canadair CRJ-900ER | 15061 | ex C- | | SkyWest |
| ☐ | N803SK | Canadair CRJ-900ER | 15062 | ex C-FJTQ | | SkyWest |
| ☐ | N804SK | Canadair CRJ-900ER | 15067 | ex C- | | SkyWest |
| ☐ | N805SK | Canadair CRJ-900ER | 15069 | ex C-GZQT | | SkyWest |
| ☐ | N806SK | Canadair CRJ-900ER | 15070 | ex C-GZQV | | SkyWest |
| ☐ | N807SK | Canadair CRJ-900ER | 15082 | ex C- | | SkyWest |
| ☐ | N809SK | Canadair CRJ-900ER | 15086 | ex C-FLCX | | SkyWest |
| ☐ | N810SK | Canadair CRJ-900ER | 15093 | ex C- | | SkyWest |
| ☐ | N812SK | Canadair CRJ-900ER | 15098 | ex C- | | SkyWest |
| ☐ | N813SK | Canadair CRJ-900ER | 15099 | ex C- | | SkyWest |
| ☐ | N814SK | Canadair CRJ-900ER | 15100 | ex C- | | SkyWest |
| ☐ | N815SK | Canadair CRJ-900ER | 15101 | ex C- | | SkyWest |
| ☐ | N816SK | Canadair CRJ-900ER | 15105 | ex C- | | SkyWest |
| ☐ | N817SK | Canadair CRJ-900ER | 15107 | ex C- | | SkyWest |
| ☐ | N820SK | Canadair CRJ-900ER | 15108 | ex C- | | SkyWest |
| ☐ | N821SK | Canadair CRJ-900ER | 15109 | ex C- | 35th anniversary c/s | SkyWest |
| ☐ | N822SK | Canadair CRJ-900ER | 15203 | ex C- | | SkyWest |
| ☐ | N823SK | Canadair CRJ-900ER | 15205 | ex C- | | SkyWest |
| ☐ | N824SK | Canadair CRJ-900ER | 15208 | ex C- | | SkyWest |
| ☐ | N825SK | Canadair CRJ-900ER | 15212 | ex C- | | SkyWest |
| | | | | | | |
| ☐ | N272SK | Embraer ERJ-145LR | 145306 | ex PT-SKX | 8272 | Chautauqua |
| ☐ | N273SK | Embraer ERJ-145LR | 145331 | ex PT-SMX | 8273 | Chautauqua |
| ☐ | N274SK | Embraer ERJ-145LR | 145344 | ex PT-SNK | 8274 | Chautauqua |
| ☐ | N561RP | Embraer ERJ-145LR | 145447 | ex PT-SUS | 8561 | Chautauqua |
| ☐ | N562RP | Embraer ERJ-145LR | 145451 | ex PT-SUW | 8562 | Chautauqua |
| ☐ | N563RP | Embraer ERJ-145LR | 145509 | ex PT-SYB | 8563 | Chautauqua |
| ☐ | N564RP | Embraer ERJ-145LR | 145524 | ex PT-SYP | 8564 | Chautauqua |
| ☐ | N565RP | Embraer ERJ-145LR | 145679 | ex PT-SFL | 8565 | Chautauqua |
| ☐ | N566RP | Embraer ERJ-145LR | 145691 | ex PT-SFX | 8566 | Chautauqua |
| ☐ | N567RP | Embraer ERJ-145LR | 145698 | ex PT-SGD | 8567 | Chautauqua |
| ☐ | N568RP | Embraer ERJ-145LR | 145800 | ex PT-SNE | 8568 | Chautauqua |
| ☐ | N569RP | Embraer ERJ-145LR | 14500816 | ex PT-SNR | 8569 | Chautauqua |
| ☐ | N570RP | Embraer ERJ-145LR | 14500821 | ex PT-SNV | 8570 | Chautauqua |
| ☐ | N571RP | Embraer ERJ-145LR | 14500827 | ex PT-SNZ | 8571 | Chautauqua |
| ☐ | N572RP | Embraer ERJ-145LR | 14500828 | ex PT-SQB | 8572 | Chautauqua |
| ☐ | N573RP | Embraer ERJ-145LR | 14500837 | ex PT-SQJ | 8573 | Chautauqua |
| ☐ | N574RP | Embraer ERJ-145LR | 14500845 | ex PT-SQP | 8574 | Chautauqua |
| ☐ | N575RP | Embraer ERJ-145LR | 14500847 | ex PT-SQR | 8575 | Chautauqua |
| ☐ | N576RP | Embraer ERJ-145LR | 14500856 | ex PT-SQX | 8576 | Chautauqua |
| ☐ | N577RP | Embraer ERJ-145LR | 14500862 | ex PT-SXC | 8577 | Chautauqua |
| ☐ | N578RP | Embraer ERJ-145LR | 14500865 | ex PT-SXE | 8578 | Chautauqua |
| ☐ | N579RP | Embraer ERJ-145LR | 14500871 | ex PT-SXI | 8579 | Chautauqua |
| | | | | | | |
| ☐ | N10575 | Embraer ERJ-145LR | 145640 | ex PT-SEC | | ExpressJet |
| ☐ | N11137 | Embraer ERJ-145XR | 145721 | ex PT-SGX | | ExpressJet |
| ☐ | N11544 | Embraer ERJ-145LR | 145557 | ex PT-SZS | | ExpressJet |
| ☐ | N11551 | Embraer ERJ-145LR | 145411 | ex PT-STI | | ExpressJet |
| ☐ | N11193 | Embraer ERJ-145XR | 14500938 | ex PT-SCJ | | ExpressJet |
| ☐ | N11165 | Embraer ERJ-145XR | 14500819 | ex PT-SNT | | ExpressJet |
| ☐ | N11176 | Embraer ERJ-145XR | 14500881 | ex PT-SXV | | ExpressJet |
| ☐ | N11181 | Embraer ERJ-145XR | 14500904 | ex PT-SYN | | ExpressJet |
| ☐ | N11184 | Embraer ERJ-145XR | 14500917 | ex PT-SVX | | ExpressJet |
| ☐ | N11189 | Embraer ERJ-145XR | 14500931 | ex PT-SCA | | ExpressJet |
| ☐ | N11192 | Embraer ERJ-145XR | 14500936 | ex PT-SCI | | ExpressJet |
| ☐ | N11199 | Embraer ERJ-145XR | 14500953 | ex PT-SFA | | ExpressJet |
| ☐ | N12163 | Embraer ERJ-145XR | 14500811 | ex PT-SNN | | ExpressJet |
| ☐ | N12167 | Embraer ERJ-145XR | 14500834 | ex PT-SQG | | ExpressJet |
| ☐ | N12175 | Embraer ERJ-145XR | 14500878 | ex PT-SXT | | ExpressJet |
| ☐ | N12201 | Embraer ERJ-145XR | 14500959 | ex PT-SFG | | ExpressJet |
| ☐ | N12569 | Embraer ERJ-145LR | 145630 | ex PT-SDS | | ExpressJet |
| ☐ | N14162 | Embraer ERJ-145XR | 14500808 | ex PT-SNK | | ExpressJet |
| ☐ | N14168 | Embraer ERJ-145XR | 14500840 | ex PT-SQL | | ExpressJet |
| ☐ | N14171 | Embraer ERJ-145XR | 14500859 | ex PT-SQZ | | ExpressJet |
| ☐ | N14173 | Embraer ERJ-145XR | 14500872 | ex PT-SXK | | ExpressJet |
| ☐ | N14174 | Embraer ERJ-145XR | 14500876 | ex PT-SXR | | ExpressJet |
| ☐ | N14179 | Embraer ERJ-145XR | 14500896 | ex PT-SYI | | ExpressJet |
| ☐ | N14188 | Embraer ERJ-145XR | 14500929 | ex PT-SOY | | ExpressJet |
| ☐ | N14198 | Embraer ERJ-145XR | 14500951 | ex PT-SCZ | | ExpressJet |
| ☐ | N14570 | Embraer ERJ-145LR | 145632 | ex PT-SDU | | ExpressJet |
| ☐ | N14907 | Embraer ERJ-145LR | 145468 | ex PT-SVN | | ExpressJet |
| ☐ | N16170 | Embraer ERJ-145XR | 14500850 | ex PT-SQT | | ExpressJet |

| | Registration | Type | MSN | Ex | | Operator |
|---|---|---|---|---|---|---|
| ☐ | N16178 | Embraer ERJ-145XR | 14500889 | ex PT-SYC | | ExpressJet |
| ☐ | N16183 | Embraer ERJ-145XR | 14500914 | ex PT-SYV | | ExpressJet |
| ☐ | N18557 | Embraer ERJ-145LR | 145596 | ex PT-SCF | | ExpressJet |
| ☐ | N19554 | Embraer ERJ-145LR | 145587 | ex PT-SBX | | ExpressJet |
| ☐ | N22909 | Embraer ERJ-145LR | 145459 | ex PT-SVE | | ExpressJet |
| ☐ | N33182 | Embraer ERJ-145XR | 14500909 | ex PT-SYS | | ExpressJet |
| | | | | | | |
| ☐ | N826MJ | Embraer ERJ-145LR | 145214 | ex PT-SHB | | Freedom |
| ☐ | N829MJ | Embraer ERJ-145LR | 145228 | ex PT-SHQ | | Freedom |
| ☐ | N830MJ | Embraer ERJ-145LR | 145259 | ex PT-SIS | | Freedom |
| ☐ | N832MJ | Embraer ERJ-145LR | 145310 | ex PT-SMB | | Freedom |
| ☐ | N836MJ | Embraer ERJ-145LR | 145359 | ex PT-SNY | | Freedom |
| ☐ | N837MJ | Embraer ERJ-145LR | 145367 | ex PT-SOR | | Freedom |
| ☐ | N838MJ | Embraer ERJ-145LR | 145384 | ex PT-SQI | | Freedom |
| ☐ | N842MJ | Embraer ERJ-145LR | 145457 | ex PT-SVC | | Freedom |
| ☐ | N845MJ | Embraer ERJ-145LR | 145502 | ex PT-SXV | | Freedom |
| ☐ | N851MJ | Embraer ERJ-145LR | 145572 | ex PT-SBI | | Freedom |
| ☐ | N853MJ | Embraer ERJ-145LR | 145464 | ex PT-SVJ | | Freedom |
| ☐ | N856MJ | Embraer ERJ-145LR | 145626 | ex PT-SDO | | Freedom |
| | | | | | | |
| ☐ | N825MJ | Embraer ERJ-145LR | 145179 | ex PT-SGB | | Mesa |
| ☐ | N827MJ | Embraer ERJ-145LR | 145217 | ex PT-SHD | | Mesa |
| ☐ | N828MJ | Embraer ERJ-145LR | 145218 | ex PT-SHE | | Mesa |
| ☐ | N831MJ | Embraer ERJ-145LR | 145273 | ex PT-SJP | | Mesa |
| ☐ | N833MJ | Embraer ERJ-145LR | 145327 | ex PT-SMT | | Mesa |
| ☐ | N841MJ | Embraer ERJ-145LR | 145448 | ex PT-SUT | | Mesa |
| ☐ | N843MJ | Embraer ERJ-145LR | 145478 | ex PT-SVX | YRT | Mesa wfs |
| ☐ | N844MJ | Embraer ERJ-145LR | 145481 | ex PT-SXA | | Mesa |
| ☐ | N846MJ | Embraer ERJ-145LR | 145507 | ex PT-SXZ | YRW | Mesa wfs |
| ☐ | N847MJ | Embraer ERJ-145LR | 145517 | ex PT-SYI | | Mesa |
| ☐ | N848MJ | Embraer ERJ-145LR | 145530 | ex PT-STU | | Mesa |
| ☐ | N849MJ | Embraer ERJ-145LR | 145534 | ex PT-STY | | Mesa |
| ☐ | N850MJ | Embraer ERJ-145LR | 145568 | ex PT-SBE | | Mesa |
| ☐ | N852MJ | Embraer ERJ-145LR | 145567 | ex PT-SBD | | Mesa |
| ☐ | N854MJ | Embraer ERJ-145LR | 145490 | ex PT-SXJ | | Mesa |
| ☐ | N855MJ | Embraer ERJ-145LR | 145614 | ex PT-SCZ | | Mesa |
| ☐ | N857MJ | Embraer ERJ-145LR | 145765 | ex PT-SJW | | Mesa |
| ☐ | N860MJ | Embraer ERJ-145LR | 145773 | ex PT-SMD | | Mesa |
| | | | | | | |
| ☐ | N746CZ | Embraer ERJ-170LR | 17000180 | ex VH-ZHA | | Compass |
| ☐ | N747CZ | Embraer ERJ-170LR | 17000187 | ex VH-ZHB | | Compass |
| ☐ | N748CZ | Embraer ERJ-170LR | 17000191 | ex VH-ZHC | | Compass |
| ☐ | N749CZ | Embraer ERJ-170LR | 17000227 | ex VH-ZHD | | Compass |
| ☐ | N751CZ | Embraer ERJ-170LR | 17000247 | ex VH-ZHE | | Compass |
| ☐ | N752CZ | Embraer ERJ-170LR | 17000255 | ex VH-ZHF | | Compass [BNA] |
| | | | | | | |
| ☐ | N868RW | Embraer ERJ-170SU | 17000131 | ex PT-SDU | | Republic |
| ☐ | N870RW | Embraer ERJ-170SE | 17000138 | ex PT-SEC | | Republic |
| | | | | | | |
| ☐ | N823MD | Embraer ERJ-170SU | 17000044 | ex PT-SUO | | Shuttle America |
| ☐ | N824MD | Embraer ERJ-170SU | 17000045 | ex PT-SUO | | Shuttle America |
| ☐ | N855RW | Embraer ERJ-170SE | 17000077 | ex PT-SZC | | Shuttle America |
| ☐ | N859RW | Embraer ERJ-170SE | 17000082 | ex PT-SZH | | Shuttle America |
| ☐ | N860RW | Embraer ERJ-170SE | 17000084 | ex PT-SZJ | | Shuttle America |
| ☐ | N862RW | Embraer ERJ-170SE | 17000098 | ex PT-SZY | | Shuttle America |
| ☐ | N867RW | Embraer ERJ-170SU | 17000130 | ex PT-SDT | | Shuttle America |
| ☐ | N869RW | Embraer ERJ-170SE | 17000133 | ex PT-SDW | | Shuttle America |
| | | | | | | |
| ☐ | N602CZ | Embraer ERJ-175LR | 17000171 | ex PT-SMN | | Compass |
| ☐ | N603CZ | Embraer ERJ-175LR | 17000176 | ex PT-SMT | | Compass |
| ☐ | N604CZ | Embraer ERJ-175LR | 17000181 | ex PT-SMY | | Compass |
| ☐ | N605CZ | Embraer ERJ-175LR | 17000186 | ex PT-SUD | | Compass |
| ☐ | N606CZ | Embraer ERJ-175LR | 17000188 | ex PT-SUH | | Compass |
| ☐ | N607CZ | Embraer ERJ-175LR | 17000192 | ex PT-SUT | | Compass |
| ☐ | N608CZ | Embraer ERJ-175LR | 17000195 | ex PT-SXA | | Compass |
| ☐ | N609CZ | Embraer ERJ-175LR | 17000197 | ex PT-SXJ | | Compass |
| ☐ | N610CZ | Embraer ERJ-175LR | 17000198 | ex PT-SXK | | Compass |
| ☐ | N612CZ | Embraer ERJ-175LR | 17000201 | ex PT-SXQ | | Compass |
| ☐ | N613CZ | Embraer ERJ-175AR | 17000203 | ex PT-SXS | | Compass |
| ☐ | N614CZ | Embraer ERJ-175AR | 17000205 | ex PT-SCA | | Compass |
| ☐ | N615CZ | Embraer ERJ-175LR | 17000207 | ex PT-SCC | | Compass |
| ☐ | N616CZ | Embraer ERJ-175LR | 17000209 | ex PT-SCG | | Compass |
| ☐ | N617CZ | Embraer ERJ-175LR | 17000210 | ex PT-SCH | | Compass |
| ☐ | N619CZ | Embraer ERJ-175LR | 17000213 | ex PT-SCK | | Compass |
| ☐ | N620CZ | Embraer ERJ-175LR | 17000214 | ex PT-SCL | | Compass |
| ☐ | N621CZ | Embraer ERJ-175LR | 17000218 | ex PT-SCP | | Compass |
| ☐ | N622CZ | Embraer ERJ-175LR | 17000219 | ex PT-SCQ | | Compass |
| ☐ | N623CZ | Embraer ERJ-175LR | 17000221 | ex PT-SCT | | Compass |
| ☐ | N624CZ | Embraer ERJ-175LR | 17000222 | ex PT-SCX | | Compass |
| ☐ | N625CZ | Embraer ERJ-175AR | 17000225 | ex PT-SFB | | Compass |
| ☐ | N626CZ | Embraer ERJ-175AR | 17000226 | ex PT-SFC | | Compass |
| ☐ | N627CZ | Embraer ERJ-175AR | 17000229 | ex PT-SFF | | Compass |

| ☐ N628CZ | Embraer ERJ-175AR | 17000233 | ex PT-SFJ | | Compass |
| ☐ N629CZ | Embraer ERJ-175AR | 17000236 | ex PT-SFM | | Compass |
| ☐ N630CZ | Embraer ERJ-175AR | 17000238 | ex PT-SFO | | Compass |
| ☐ N631CZ | Embraer ERJ-175AR | 17000239 | ex PT-SFP | | Compass |
| ☐ N632CZ | Embraer ERJ-175AR | 17000244 | ex PT-SFV | | Compass |
| ☐ N633CZ | Embraer ERJ-175AR | 17000245 | ex PT-SFW | | Compass |
| ☐ N634CZ | Embraer ERJ-175AR | 17000246 | ex PT-SFX | | Compass |
| ☐ N635CZ | Embraer ERJ-175AR | 17000252 | ex PT-SJD | | Compass |
| ☐ N636CZ | Embraer ERJ-175AR | 17000253 | ex PT-SJE | | Compass |
| ☐ N637CZ | Embraer ERJ-175AR | 17000256 | ex PT-SJI | | Compass |
| ☐ N638CZ | Embraer ERJ-175AR | 17000259 | ex PT-SJL | | Compass |
| ☐ N639CZ | Embraer ERJ-175AR | 17000262 | ex PT-SJP | | Compass |
| | | | | | |
| ☐ N201JQ | Embraer ERJ-175LR | 17000235 | ex PT-SFL | | Shuttle America |
| ☐ N202JQ | Embraer ERJ-175LR | 17000240 | ex PT-SFQ | | Shuttle America |
| ☐ N203JQ | Embraer ERJ-175LR | 17000242 | ex PT-SFT | | Shuttle America |
| ☐ N204JQ | Embraer ERJ-175LR | 17000243 | ex PT-SFU | | Shuttle America |
| ☐ N206JQ | Embraer ERJ-175LR | 17000249 | ex PT-SJA | | Shuttle America |
| ☐ N207JQ | Embraer ERJ-175LR | 17000254 | ex PT-SJG | | Shuttle America |
| ☐ N208JQ | Embraer ERJ-175LR | 17000257 | ex PT-SJJ | | Shuttle America |
| ☐ N209JQ | Embraer ERJ-175LR | 17000258 | ex PT-SJK | | Shuttle America |
| ☐ N210JQ | Embraer ERJ-175LR | 17000260 | ex PT-SJN | | Shuttle America |
| ☐ N211JQ | Embraer ERJ-175LR | 17000261 | ex PT-SJO | | Shuttle America |
| ☐ N212JQ | Embraer ERJ-175LR | 17000264 | ex PT-SJS | | Shuttle America |
| ☐ N213JQ | Embraer ERJ-175LR | 17000265 | ex PT-SJT | | Shuttle America |
| ☐ N214JQ | Embraer ERJ-175LR | 17000267 | ex PT-SJV | | Shuttle America |
| ☐ N215JQ | Embraer ERJ-175LR | 17000270 | ex PT-SNA | | Shuttle America |
| ☐ N216JQ | Embraer ERJ-175LR | 17000273 | ex PT-SNH | | Shuttle America |
| ☐ N958WH | Embraer ERJ-175LR | 17000248 | ex PT-SFZ | 8205 | Shuttle America |
| | | | | | |
| ☐ N412XJ | SAAB SF.340B | 340B-412 | ex SE-B12 | | Mesaba |
| ☐ N413XJ | SAAB SF.340B | 340B-413 | ex SE-B13 | | Mesaba |
| ☐ N416XJ | SAAB SF.340B | 340B-416 | ex SE-B16 | | Mesaba |
| ☐ N418XJ | SAAB SF.340B | 340B-418 | ex SE-B18 | | Mesaba |
| ☐ N449XJ | SAAB SF.340B | 340B-449 | ex SE-B49 | | Mesaba |
| ☐ N451XJ | SAAB SF.340B | 340B-451 | ex SE-B51 | | Mesaba |
| ☐ N453XJ | SAAB SF.340B | 340B-453 | ex SE-B53 | | Mesaba |
| ☐ N454XJ | SAAB SF.340B | 340B-454 | ex SE-B54 | | Mesaba |
| ☐ N456XJ | SAAB SF.340B | 340B-456 | ex SE-B56 | | Mesaba |
| ☐ N457XJ | SAAB SF.340B | 340B-457 | ex SE-B57 | | Mesaba |

## DESERT AIR    Anchorage, AK (ANC)

| ☐ N105CA | Douglas DC-3 | 14275/25720 | ex N85FA | [CLK] |
| ☐ N153PA | Convair 240-27 | 304 | ex 51-7892 | |
| ☐ N272R | Douglas DC-3 | 13678 | ex NC88824 | ♦ |
| ☐ N315JT | Piper PA-34-200 Seneca | 34-7870045 | | ♦ |
| ☐ N19906 | Douglas DC-3 | 4747 | ex 41-38644 | [ANC] |
| ☐ N44587 | Douglas DC-3 | 12857 | ex N353SA | [ANC] |

## DODITA AIR CARGO    San Juan-Munoz Marin Intl, PR (SJU)

| ☐ N912AL | Convair 440-78 | 353 | ex PZ-TGA | [SJU] |
| ☐ N31325 | Convair 240-52 | 52-8 | ex 52-1183 | [SJU] |

## DOLPHIN AIRLINES

| ☐ N271SA | de Havilland DHC-6 Twin Otter 300 | 524 | | ♦ |
| ☐ N288SA | de Havilland DHC-6 Twin Otter 300 | 389 | ex VQ-LEY | ♦ |

## DYNAMIC AVIATION

| ☐ N1000 | de Havilland DHC-8-102 | 024 | ex C-FZCC | ♦ |
| ☐ N8200L | de Havilland DHC-8-202Q | 455 | ex N455YV | |
| ☐ N8300F | de Havilland DHC-8-314 | 338 | ex ZS-NLW | [SHD]♦ |
| ☐ N8300G | de Havilland DHC-8-315 | 348 | ex ZS-NLX | [SHD]♦ |
| ☐ N8300L | de Havilland DHC-8-314 | 352 | ex ZS-NLY | [SHD]♦ |
| ☐ N8300T | de Havilland DHC-8-314 | 358 | ex ZS-NMA | [INT]♦ |
| | | | | |
| ☐ N767DA | Boeing 767-246 | 23213/118 | ex JA8232 | ♦ |
| ☐ N769DA | Boeing 767-246 | 23212/117 | ex JA8231 | [SHD]♦ |
| ☐ N880DA | McDonnell-Douglas MD-88 | 49760/1620 | ex N701ME | [GSO] |
| ☐ N884DA | McDonnell-Douglas MD-88 | 49762/1624 | ex N601ME | [GSO]♦ |
| ☐ N897JM | Douglas DC-9-32 | 47592/712 | ex C-FTMY | [MHV]♦ |
| ☐ N909AX | Douglas DC-9-32CF | 47148/246 | ex N934F | [ROW]♦ |

## EAGLE AIR TRANSPORT

| ☐ N40EA | Cessna 208A Caravan I | 208A00065 | ex N799FE | ♦ |
| ☐ N200EA | Cessna 208B Caravan I | 208B0151 | ex N9697B | ♦ |

## EG & G

| | | | |
|---|---|---|---|
| ☐ N273RH | Boeing 737-66N | 29890/1276 | ex N824SR |
| ☐ N288DP | Boeing 737-66N | 29892/1305 | ex N892SR |
| ☐ N319BD | Boeing 737-66N | 28649/887 | ex N649MT |
| ☐ N365SR | Boeing 737-66N | 29891/1294 | ex N891RD |
| ☐ N859WP | Boeing 737-66N | 28652/938 | ex N645DM |
| ☐ N869HH | Boeing 737-66N | 28650/932 | ex N628SR |
| | | | |
| ☐ N20RA | Beech 1900C | UB-42 | |
| ☐ N623RA | Beech 1900C-1 | UC-163 | ex N3043L |

## EMERALD COAST AIR

| | | | | |
|---|---|---|---|---|
| ☐ N71EC | de Havilland DHC-6 Twin Otter 100 | 037 | ex C-FTDJ | ♦ |

## EMPIRE AIRLINES   Empire Air  (EM/CFS)   Coeur d'Alene, ID/Spokane-Intl, WA (COE/GEG)

Ops Cessna 208 Caravans and ATR 42/72s plus Fokker F.27 Friendship 500s leased from, and operated on behalf of, FedEx

## EPPS AVIATION CHARTER   Epps Air (EPS)   Atlanta-De Kalb-Peachtree, GA (PDK)

| | | | |
|---|---|---|---|
| ☐ N10HT | Mitsubishi MU-2B-60 | 778SA | ex N264MA |
| ☐ N46AK | Mitsubishi MU-2B-60 | 754SA | ex N942ST |
| ☐ N888RH | Mitsubishi MU-2B-60 | 737SA | ex N315MA |
| ☐ N888SE | Mitsubishi MU-2B-60 | 1549SA | ex N475MA |
| ☐ N941MA | Mitsubishi MU-2B-60 | 744SA | |
| ☐ N1164F | Mitsubishi MU-2B-60 | 1562SA | ex D-ICDG |
| ☐ N8083A | Mitsubishi MU-2B-60 | 739SA | ex N707EZ |
| | | | |
| ☐ N23WJ | Beech 200 Super King Air | BB-1297 | ex N21VF |
| ☐ N57GA | Beech 200 Super King Air | BB-477 | ex F-GILB |
| ☐ N795CA | Beech 200 Super King Air | BB-559 | ex N559BM |

## ERA AVIATION   Erah (7H/ERR)   Anchorage-Intl South, AK (ANC)

| | | | | |
|---|---|---|---|---|
| ☐ N881EA | de Havilland DHC-8-106 | 233 | ex C-GFOD | |
| ☐ N882EA | de Havilland DHC-8-103 | 098 | ex D-BERT | |
| ☐ N883EA | de Havilland DHC-8-106 | 260 | ex C-GGEW | |
| ☐ N884EA | de Havilland DHC-8-106 | 387 | ex N824EX | ♦ |
| ☐ N889EA | de Havilland DHC-8-106 | 322 | ex N803LR | ♦ |

## ERA HELICOPTERS   Anchorage-Intl South, AK/Lake Charles-Regional, LA (ANC/LCH)

| | | | | |
|---|---|---|---|---|
| ☐ N108TA | Aérospatiale AS350BA AStar | 3080 | | |
| ☐ N109TA | Aérospatiale AS350B2 AStar | 3103 | | |
| ☐ N118TA | Aérospatiale AS350B2 AStar | 3110 | | |
| ☐ N159JK | Aérospatiale AS350B2 AStar | 3253 | | |
| ☐ N161EH | Aérospatiale AS350B2 AStar | 2144 | | |
| ☐ N162EH | Aérospatiale AS350B2 AStar | 2147 | | |
| ☐ N165EH | Aérospatiale AS350B1 AStar | 2185 | | |
| ☐ N166EH | Aérospatiale AS350B2 AStar | 2194 | | |
| ☐ N178EH | Aérospatiale AS350B2 AStar | 2264 | | |
| ☐ N181EH | Aérospatiale AS350B2 AStar | 2680 | | |
| ☐ N182EH | Aérospatiale AS350B2 AStar | 2681 | | |
| ☐ N183EH | Aérospatiale AS350B2 AStar | 2752 | | |
| ☐ N185EH | Aérospatiale AS350B2 AStar | 2823 | | |
| ☐ N186EH | Aérospatiale AS350B2 AStar | 2844 | | |
| ☐ N187EH | Aérospatiale AS350B2 AStar | 2839 | | |
| ☐ N188EH | Aérospatiale AS350B2 AStar | 2954 | | |
| ☐ N190EH | Aérospatiale AS350B2 AStar | 2974 | | |
| ☐ N191EH | Aérospatiale AS350B2 AStar | 2505 | | |
| ☐ N192EH | Aérospatiale AS350B2 AStar | 2582 | | |
| ☐ N193EH | Aérospatiale AS350B2 AStar | 2599 | | |
| ☐ N194EH | Aérospatiale AS350B2 AStar | 2608 | | |
| ☐ N195EH | Aérospatiale AS350B2 AStar | 2615 | | |
| ☐ N196EH | Aérospatiale AS350B2 AStar | 2976 | | |
| ☐ N212EH | Aérospatiale AS350B2 AStar | 3151 | | |
| ☐ N213EH | Aérospatiale AS350B2 AStar | 3158 | | ♦ |
| ☐ N214EH | Aérospatiale AS350B2 AStar | 3163 | | |
| ☐ N215EH | Aérospatiale AS350B2 AStar | 3172 | | |
| ☐ N216EH | Aérospatiale AS350B2 AStar | 3184 | | |
| ☐ N217EH | Aérospatiale AS350B2 AStar | 3197 | | |
| ☐ N217FD | Aérospatiale AS350B2 AStar | 4221 | ex N646PT | |
| ☐ N328BF | Aérospatiale AS350B2 AStar | 4284 | | |
| ☐ N420JA | Aérospatiale AS350B2 AStar | 4212 | | |
| ☐ N603WB | Aérospatiale AS350B2 AStar | 4225 | | |
| ☐ N747WB | Aérospatiale AS350B2 AStar | 2768 | | |
| ☐ N4061G | Aérospatiale AS350BA AStar | 3051 | ex F-OHVB | |
| ☐ N40584 | Aérospatiale AS350B2 AStar | 2924 | ex F-OHNT | |

| | | | |
|---|---|---|---|
| ☐ N18EA | Agusta A.109E Power | 11210 | ex N261CF |
| ☐ N334JT | Agusta A.109E Power | 11738 | |
| ☐ N512LD | Agusta A.109E Power | 11683 | |
| ☐ N530KS | Agusta A.109E Power | 11694 | |
| ☐ N820FT | Agusta A.109E Power | 11701 | |
| ☐ N903RW | Agusta A.109E Power | 11601 | ex N3ZJ |
| ☐ N910LB | Agusta A.109E Power | 11682 | |
| | | | |
| ☐ N108AG | Agusta A.119 Koala | 14053 | ex N911AM |
| ☐ N126RD | Agusta A.119 Koala | 14504 | ex N6QY |
| ☐ N149JM | Agusta A.119 Koala | 14533 | |
| ☐ N203JP | Agusta A.119 Koala | 14535 | |
| ☐ N330JN | Agusta A.119 Koala | 14510 | |
| ☐ N514RE | Agusta A.119 Koala II | 14701 | |
| ☐ N602FB | Agusta A.119 Koala | 14528 | |
| ☐ N628RL | Agusta A.119 Koala II | 14713 | |
| ☐ N709CG | Agusta A.119 Koala | 14052 | ex N18YC |
| ☐ N715RT | Agusta A.119 Koala | 14516 | |
| ☐ N802SM | Agusta A.119 Koala II | 14711 | |
| ☐ N803EB | Agusta A.119 Koala | 14033 | ex N7KN |
| ☐ N822MM | Agusta A.119 Koala | 14055 | ex N6QX |
| ☐ N907AG | Agusta A.119 Koala | 14045 | ex N119MW |
| ☐ N915BE | Agusta A.119 Koala | 14519 | |
| ☐ N920JD | Agusta A.119 Koala II | 14754 | |
| ☐ N927JK | Agusta A.119 Koala | 14517 | |
| | | | |
| ☐ N109DR | Agusta AW139 | 31311 | |
| ☐ N149DH | Agusta AW139 | 41004 | |
| ☐ N355RH | Agusta AW139 | 41013 | |
| ☐ N403CB | Agusta AW139 | 41206 | |
| ☐ N415JH | Agusta AW139 | 41224 | |
| ☐ N482LA | Agusta AW139 | 41272 | |
| ☐ N561RV | Agusta AW139 | 41263 | |
| ☐ N609PW | Agusta AW139 | 31309 | |
| ☐ N804CB | Agusta AW139 | 41277 | |
| ☐ N811TA | Agusta AW139 | 41269 | |
| ☐ N813DG | Agusta AW139 | 31032 | |
| ☐ N829SN | Agusta AW139 | 41244 | |
| | | | |
| ☐ N357EH | Bell 212 | 31209 | |
| ☐ N358EH | Bell 212 | 31211 | |
| ☐ N359EH | Bell 212 | 31212 | ex C-GRVN |
| ☐ N361EH | Bell 212 | 30554 | ex XA-TRY |
| ☐ N362EH | Bell 212 | 30853 | ex XA-TRX |
| ☐ N370EH | Bell 212 | 30624 | |
| ☐ N399EH | Bell 212 | 30810 | ex XA-AAM |
| ☐ N500EH | Bell 212 | 30945 | |
| ☐ N508EH | Bell 212 | 30908 | |
| ☐ N509EH | Bell 212 | 30925 | |
| ☐ N510EH | Bell 212 | 31113 | ex C-GNCH |
| ☐ N523EH | Bell 212 | 31214 | ex C-GRWX |
| | | | |
| ☐ N167EH | Bell 412 | 33089 | ex VH-NSO |
| ☐ N168EH | Bell 412 | 33058 | ex VH-NSI |
| ☐ N169EH | Bell 412 | 33064 | ex XA-BDD |
| ☐ N417EH | Bell 412 | 33031 | ex N3911E |
| ☐ N421EH | Bell 412 | 33067 | ex N57413 |
| | | | |
| ☐ N89EM | Eurocopter EC135P1 | 0049 | ex N94387 |
| ☐ N156MC | Eurocopter EC135P2 | 0613 | |
| ☐ N320TV | Eurocopter EC135P2 | 0467 | |
| ☐ N357TC | Eurocopter EC135P2+ | 0626 | |
| ☐ N430TM | Eurocopter EC135P2 | 0457 | |
| ☐ N551BA | Eurocopter EC135P2 | 0188 | |
| ☐ N605SS | Eurocopter EC135P2 | 0461 | |
| ☐ N611LS | Eurocopter EC135P2 | 0472 | |
| ☐ N812LV | Eurocopter EC135P2+ | 0614 | |
| | | | |
| ☐ N124EH | MBB Bo.105CBS | S-559 | ex 9Y-TJE |
| ☐ N125EH | MBB Bo.105CBS | S-562 | ex N9376Y |
| ☐ N130EH | MBB Bo.105CBS | S-588 | ex N2910H |
| ☐ N135EH | MBB Bo.105CBS | S-675 | ex N4573D |
| ☐ N149EH | MBB Bo.105CBS | S-705 | ex N968MB |
| ☐ N152EH | MBB Bo.105CBS | S-701 | ex N954MB |
| ☐ N290EH | MBB Bo.105CBS-4 | S-850 | ex N6554Y |
| ☐ N291EH | MBB Bo.105CBS-4 | S-842 | ex N65962 |
| ☐ N294EH | MBB Bo.105CBS-4 | S-846 | ex N6559A |
| ☐ N296EH | MBB Bo.105CBS-4 | S-849 | ex N65385 |
| ☐ N298EH | MBB Bo.105CBS-4 | S-845 | ex N4186F |
| ☐ N423EH | MBB Bo.105CBS | S-543 | ex N42018 |
| ☐ N424EH | MBB Bo.105CBS | S-548 | ex N42001 |

| | | | | |
|---|---|---|---|---|
| ☐ N427EH | MBB Bo.105CBS | S-554 | ex N93205 | |
| | | | | |
| ☐ N531BH | Sikorsky S-76C++ | 760725 | | ♦ |
| ☐ N547WM | Sikorsky S-76C++ | 760722 | ex N2579P | |
| ☐ N573EH | Sikorsky S-76A++ | 760373 | ex B- | |
| ☐ N574EH | Sikorsky S-76A++ | 760369 | ex N369AG | |
| ☐ N575EH | Sikorsky S-76A++ | 760366 | ex N621LH | |
| ☐ N577EH | Sikorsky S-76A++ | 760222 | ex N15459 | |
| ☐ N578EH | Sikorsky S-76A++ | 760099 | ex N223BF | |
| ☐ N761EH | Sikorsky S-76C++ | 760736 | ex N20302 | |
| ☐ N886AH | Sikorsky S-76A++ | 760153 | | ♦ |
| ☐ N905RD | Sikorsky S-76C+ | 760610 | ex N8109K | |
| ☐ N911LV | Sikorsky S-76A++ | 760281 | | ♦ |
| ☐ N928DZ | Sikorsky S-76C | 760609 | | ♦ |
| | | | | |
| ☐ N109RR | Eurocopter EC225LP | 2777 | | |

## ERICKSON AIR CRANE                  Central Point, OR

| | | | | | |
|---|---|---|---|---|---|
| ☐ N154AC | Erickson/Sikorsky S-64E Skycrane | 64037 | ex 68-18435 | 733 Georgia Peach | |
| ☐ N159AC | Erickson/Sikorsky S-64F Skycrane | 64084 | ex 68-18476 | 741 | |
| ☐ N163AC | Erickson/Sikorsky S-64F Skycrane | 64093 | ex 70-18485 | 738 Hurricane Bubba | |
| ☐ N164AC | Erickson/Sikorsky S-64E Skycrane | 64034 | ex C-FCRN | 730 The Incredible Hulk | |
| ☐ N171AC | Erickson/Sikorsky S-64F Skycrane | 64090 | ex 69-18482 | | [Central Point] |
| ☐ N172AC | Erickson/Sikorsky S-64F Skycrane | 64061 | ex C-FCRN | | ♦ |
| ☐ N173AC | Erickson/Sikorsky S-64E Skycrane | 64015 | ex 68-18413 | 736 Christina | |
| ☐ N176AC | Erickson/Sikorsky S-64E Skycrane | 64003 | | | ♦ |
| ☐ N178AC | Erickson/Sikorsky S-64F Skycrane | 64097 | ex 70-18489 | 748 Isabelle | |
| ☐ N179AC | Erickson/Sikorsky S-64E Skycrane | 64091 | ex C-GFAH | 733 Elvis | |
| ☐ N194AC | Erickson/Sikorsky S-64E Skycrane | 64017 | ex C-GFLH | 746 | |
| ☐ N217AC | Erickson/Sikorsky S-64E Skycrane | 64064 | ex N542SB | 732 Malcolm | |
| ☐ N218AC | Erickson/Sikorsky S-64E Skycrane | 64033 | ex N545SB | 749 Elsie | |
| ☐ N229AC | Erickson/Sikorsky S-64E Skycrane | 64018 | | | ♦ |
| ☐ N236AC | Erickson/Sikorsky S-64E Skycrane | 64089 | | | |
| ☐ N238AC | Erickson/Sikorsky S-64F Skycrane | 64016 | ex N543CH | | [Central Point]♦ |
| ☐ N243AC | Erickson/Sikorsky S-64E Skycrane | 64022 | ex N544CH | | [Central Point] |
| ☐ N247AC | Erickson/Sikorsky S-64E Skycrane | 64052 | ex C-GJRY | | ♦ |
| ☐ N957AC | Erickson/Sikorsky S-64E Skycrane | 64065 | ex C-GESG | 745 | |
| ☐ N4099M | Erickson/Sikorsky S-64F Skycrane | 64028 | ex 67-18426 | | [Central Point] |
| ☐ N6962R | Erickson/Sikorsky S-64E Skycrane | 64058 | ex HC-CAT | 741 Olga | [Central Point] |
| ☐ N7073C | Erickson/Sikorsky S-64E Skycrane | 64042 | ex N7073C | | [Central Point] |

## EVERGREEN HELICOPTERS       (7E)
### McMinnville, OR/Anchorage-Merrill, AK/ Galveston, TX (RNC/MRI/GLS)

| | | | | |
|---|---|---|---|---|
| ☐ N350EV | Aérospatiale AS350B AStar | 2961 | | ♦ |
| ☐ N351EV | Aérospatiale AS350B2 AStar | 2930 | ex SE-JCX | <GC Air |
| ☐ N352EV | Aérospatiale AS350B2 AStar | 2555 | ex JA6112 | |
| ☐ N353EV | Aérospatiale AS350B2 AStar | 2444 | ex C-GJVG | |
| ☐ N354EV | Aérospatiale AS350B3 AStar | 3664 | ex SE-JHG | |
| ☐ N356EV | Aérospatiale AS350B3 AStar | 3649 | ex SE-JHF | |
| ☐ N359EV | Aérospatiale AS350B3 AStar | 3797 | ex I-BALO | |
| ☐ N917JT | Aérospatiale AS350B2 AStar | 2759 | ex N6096P | |
| | | | | |
| ☐ N300EV | Aérospatiale SA.330J Puma | 1301 | ex F-GSYF | |
| ☐ N330J | Aérospatiale SA.330J Puma | 1647 | ex XA-SKT | |
| ☐ N330JF | Aérospatiale SA.330J Puma | 1514 | ex 9M-SSD | |
| ☐ N337EV | Aérospatiale SA.330J Puma | 1549 | ex D-HAXQ | ♦ |
| ☐ N338EV | Aérospatiale SA.330J Puma | 1573 | ex D-HAXS | ♦ |
| ☐ N366EV | Aérospatiale SA.330J Puma | 1201 | ex D-HAXA | |
| ☐ N367EV | Aérospatiale SA.330J Puma | 1332 | ex D-HAXG | |
| ☐ N405R | Aérospatiale SA.330J Puma | 1475 | ex PP-MGB | |
| | | | | |
| ☐ N104EV | Beech 1900D | UE-166 | ex N166YV | ♦ |
| ☐ N105EV | Beech 1900D | UE-064 | ex N1900R | |
| ☐ N171CJ | Beech 1900D | UE-71 | ex N95704 | ♦ |
| ☐ N172MJ | Beech 1900D | UE-72 | ex N85804 | ♦ |
| ☐ N191EV | Beech 1900D | UE-114 | ex N114YV | |
| | | | | |
| ☐ N212EV | Bell 212 | 30881 | ex HK-4064X | |
| ☐ N398EH | Bell 212 | 30766 | ex HK-4059X | |
| ☐ N420EP | Bell 212EP | 36552 | | ♦ |
| ☐ N827MS | Bell 212 | 31205 | | ♦ |
| ☐ N5410N | Bell 212 | 31206 | ex VH-CUZ | |
| ☐ N16973 | Bell 212 | 30882 | ex VH-CRO | |
| ☐ N16974 | Bell 212 | 30882 | ex N31BR | ♦ |
| ☐ N59633 | Bell 212 | 30676 | | |
| | | | | |
| ☐ N3CA | CASA C.212-200 | CC20-7-175 | | ♦ |
| ☐ N346CA | CASA C.212-200 | 172 | | ♦ |
| ☐ N348CA | CASA C.212-200 | CC20-7-175 | | |

| | | | | | |
|---|---|---|---|---|---|
| ☐ N392CA | CASA C.212-300 | DF72-1-398 | ex TN-AFD | | ♦ |
| ☐ N422CA | CASA C.212-200 | CC40-5-238 | | | |
| ☐ N423CA | CASA C.212-200 | CC40-6-240 | | >US Air Force | |
| ☐ N437CA | CASA C.212-200 | CC29-1-180 | ex ZS-PRL | | ♦ |
| ☐ N502FS | CASA C.212-200 | CD58-1-294 | ex N31BR | | ♦ |
| | | | | | |
| ☐ N22MS | Learjet 35A | 35A-209 | ex N711DS | | |
| ☐ N33AZ | Bell 206L-3 LongRanger III | 51110 | | | |
| ☐ N60EV | Sikorsky S-61 (H-3E) | 61643 | ex 69-5799 | | |
| ☐ N61EV | Sikorsky S-61 (H-3E) | 61566 | ex 65-12791 | | |
| ☐ N62EV | Sikorsky S-61 (HH-3F) | 61670 | ex USCG 1493 | | |
| ☐ N63EV | Sikorsky S-61 (HH-3F) | 61674 | ex USCG 1497 | | |
| ☐ N70DB | Bell 206B JetRanger | 1730 | | | |
| ☐ N105EV | Beech 1900D | UE-64 | ex N1900R | | ♦ |
| ☐ N134WJ | Beech B200C Super King Air | BL-134 | ex SE-LMP | | |
| ☐ N139EV | Agusta AW139 | 31006 | ex UAE 4003 | | |
| ☐ N140EV | Agusta AW139 | 31025 | ex UAE 4004 | | |
| ☐ N202EV | Lockheed P2V-5 Neptune | 726-5387 | ex Bu131502 141 | | Tanker |
| ☐ N204BB | MBB B0.105C | S-57 | ex D-HDBH | | |
| ☐ N368EV | Aérospatiale AS.332L | 2179 | | | ♦ |
| ☐ N405PC | Learjet 35A | 35A-651 | ex HB-VJK | | |
| ☐ N419EV | Bell 412EP | 36464 | ex C-FSOD | | |
| ☐ N500KM | MBB Bo.105C | S-76 | ex N500KV | | |
| ☐ N3195S | Bell 206L-3 LongRanger III | 51136 | | | |
| ☐ N5007F | Bell 206L-1 LongRanger III | 45186 | | | |
| ☐ N6979R | Sikorsky S-64E | 64079 | | | |
| ☐ N9688G | Cessna U206F Stationair | U20601888 | | | |
| ☐ N10729 | Bell 206B JetRanger III | 2876 | | | |

## EVERGREEN INTERNATIONAL AIRLINES  Evergreen (EZ/EIA)
### McMinnville, OR/Marana-Pinal Airpark, AZ (RNC/MZJ)

| | | | | | |
|---|---|---|---|---|---|
| ☐ N470EV | Boeing 747-273C | 20653/237 | ex N749WA | 947 Super Tanker | |
| ☐ N471EV | Boeing 747-273C | 20651/209 | ex N747WR | | |
| ☐ N478EV | Boeing 747SR-46 (SCD) | 21033/254 | ex PT-TDE | | [MZJ] |
| ☐ N479EV | Boeing 747-132 (SCD) | 19898/94 | ex N725PA | 979 Water Bomber | [MZJ] |
| ☐ N482EV | Boeing 747-212B (SCD) | 20713/219 | ex N729PA | | |
| ☐ N485EV | Boeing 747-212B (SCD) | 20712/218 | ex N728PA | | |
| ☐ N486EV | Boeing 747-212B (SCD) | 20888/240 | ex N745SJ | | |
| ☐ N487EV | Boeing 747-230B (SCD) | 23286/614 | ex TF-AMF | | |
| ☐ N488EV | Boeing 747-230B (SCD) | 23287/617 | ex D-ABZA | | |
| ☐ N489EV | Boeing 747-230B (SF) | 23393/633 | ex TF-AMH | | |
| ☐ N490EV | Boeing 747-230F | 24138/706 | ex TF-ARV | | |
| | | | | | |
| ☐ N491EV | Boeing 747-412F | 26561/1042 | ex 9V-SFB | | >SVA |
| ☐ N492EV | Boeing 747-446 | 25308/885 | ex N238AS | | for frt [TLV]♦ |

## EVERTS AIR ALASKA  Everts (3Z/VTS)  Fairbanks-Intl, AK (FAI)

| | | | | | |
|---|---|---|---|---|---|
| ☐ N108NS | Piper PA-32R-300 Lance | 32R-7680288 | | | |
| ☐ N148RF | Piper PA-32R-300 Lance | 32R-7680076 | | | |
| ☐ N462CA | Embraer EMB.120QC Brasilia | 120264 | | | ♦ |
| ☐ N463CA | Embraer EMB.120RT Brasilia | 120267 | | | ♦ |
| ☐ N575JD | Cessna 208B Caravan I | 208B0595 | ex N5268V | | |
| ☐ N1063H | Piper PA-32R-300 Lance | 32R-7780129 | | | |
| ☐ N5180 | Cessna 180 Skywagon | 18051077 | | | ♦ |
| ☐ N6969J | Piper PA-32R-300 Lance | 32R-7680398 | | | |

## EVERTS AIR CARGO  Everts (3K/VTS)  Fairbanks-Intl, AK (FAI)

| | | | | | |
|---|---|---|---|---|---|
| ☐ N151 | Douglas DC-6B | 45496/992 | ex C-GICD | | |
| ☐ N251CE | Douglas C-118A | 44612/532 | ex Bu153693 | | |
| ☐ N351CE | Douglas C-118A | 44599/505 | ex 53-3228 | | |
| ☐ N400UA | Douglas DC-6A | 44258/467 | ex YV-296C | | |
| ☐ N555SQ | Douglas DC-6B | 45137/830 | ex N37585 | | |
| ☐ N1036F | Douglas C-118A | 43581/295 | ex 51-3834 | | [FAI] |
| ☐ N1377K | Douglas C-118A | 44596/499 | ex 53-3225 | | [FAI] |
| ☐ N6174C | Douglas DC-6A | 44075/451 | ex C-GBYN | | |
| ☐ N6586C | Douglas DC-6BF | 45222/849 | | | |
| ☐ N9056R | Douglas DC-6A/B | 45498/1005 | ex C-FCZZ | | |
| | | | | | |
| ☐ N904AX | Douglas DC-9-32CF | 47040/172 | ex N931F | | [FAI]♦ |
| ☐ N930CE | Douglas DC-9-33F | 47363/445 | ex N930AX | | [FAI]♦ |
| ☐ N932CE | Douglas DC-9-33CF (ABS 3) | 47465/584 | ex N932AX | | ♦ |
| ☐ N935AX | Douglas DC-9-33RC (ABS 3) | 47413/521 | ex N935X | | [PAE]♦ |
| ☐ N952AX | Douglas DC-9-41F (ABS 3) | 47615/751 | ex JA8432 | | [FAI]♦ |
| | | | | | |
| ☐ N1105G | Embraer EMB.120FC Brasilia | 120105 | ex PT-SMX | | |
| ☐ N1110J | Embraer EMB.120FC Brasilia | 120110 | ex PT-SNC | | |
| ☐ N7848B | Curtiss C-46R Commando | 273 | ex HP-238 | Dumbo | |

| ☐ N54514 | Curtiss C-46D Commando | 33285 | ex 51-1122 | Maid in Japan |

Tatonduk Outfitters is an associated partner

## EVERTS AIR FUEL · Fairbanks-Intl, AK (FAI)

| ☐ N100CE | Douglas C-118A | 44662/629 | ex N51599 | |
| ☐ N444CE | Douglas DC-6B | 45478/962 | ex C-GHLZ | Spirit of America |
| ☐ N451CE | Douglas C-118B | 43712/358 | ex N840CS | |
| ☐ N747CE | Douglas C-118A | 44661/628 | ex N233HP | |
| ☐ N1822M | Curtiss C-46F Commando | 22521 | ex 44-18698 | Salmon Ella |
| ☐ N1837M | Curtiss C-46F Commando | 22388 | ex CF-FNC | Hot Stuff |
| ☐ N171CJ | Beech 1900D | UE-71 | ex N95704 | ♦ |
| ☐ N172MJ | Beech 1900D | UE-72 | ex N85804 | ♦ |
| ☐ N191EV | Beech 1900D | UE-114 | ex N114YV | ♦ |
| ☐ N6586C | Douglas DC-6B | 45222 | | ♦ |
| ☐ N7780B | Douglas DC-6A | 45372/875 | | |

## EXECUTIVE AIRLINES · Executive Eagle (OW/EXK)
### San Juan-Luis Munoz Marin Intl, PR/Miami Intl, FL (SJU/MIA)

A wholly owned subsidiary of American Eagle Airlines and ops as American Eagle

## EXPRESSJET AIRLINES · Jet Link (CO/BTA)
### Cleveland, OH/Houston-Intercontinental, TX/Newark, NJ (CLE/IAH/EWR)

Merged with Atlantic Southeast Airlines and ops as Surejet

## FALCON AIR EXPRESS · (6F)

| ☐ N120MN | McDonnell-Douglas MD-83 | 53120/1964 | ex EI-CFZ | ♦ |
| ☐ N125MN | McDonnell-Douglas MD-83 | 53125/1993 | ex EI-CER | ♦ |
| ☐ N305FA | McDonnell-Douglas MD-83 | 49398/1332 | ex N566MS | ♦ |

## FALCON AIR SERVICE

| ☐ N128ST | Cessna 208B Caravan I | 208B1133 | | ♦ |
| ☐ N213LA | Cessna 208B Caravan I | 208B1096 | ex N777VW | ♦ |
| ☐ N688FA | Cessna 208B Caravan I | 208B1103 | ex N688RP | ♦ |
| ☐ N891DF | Cessna 208B Caravan I | 208B1148 | | ♦ |

## FEDEX EXPRESS · FedEx (FX/FDX) · Memphis-Intl, TN (MEM)

| ☐ N650FE | Airbus A300F4-605R | 726 | ex F-WWAP | Molly Mickler |
| ☐ N651FE | Airbus A300F4-605R | 728 | ex F-WWAJ | Diane Kathleen |
| ☐ N652FE | Airbus A300F4-605R | 735 | ex F-WWAN | Rachel Patricia |
| ☐ N653FE | Airbus A300F4-605R | 736 | ex F-WWAD | Samantha Massey |
| ☐ N654FE | Airbus A300F4-605R | 738 | ex F-WWAX | Richard |
| ☐ N655FE | Airbus A300F4-605R | 742 | ex F-WWAJ | Dion |
| ☐ N656FE | Airbus A300F4-605R | 745 | ex F-WWAP | Devin |
| ☐ N657FE | Airbus A300F4-605R | 748 | ex F-WWAM | Lizzie |
| ☐ N658FE | Airbus A300F4-605R | 752 | ex F-WWAE | Tristian |
| ☐ N659FE | Airbus A300F4-605R | 757 | ex F-WWAF | Calvin |
| ☐ N660FE | Airbus A300F4-605R | 759 | ex F-WWAG | Zack |
| ☐ N661FE | Airbus A300F4-605R | 760 | ex F-WWAL | Whitney |
| ☐ N662FE | Airbus A300F4-605R | 761 | ex F-WWAK | Tessa |
| ☐ N663FE | Airbus A300F4-605R | 766 | ex F-WWAO | Domenick |
| ☐ N664FE | Airbus A300F4-605R | 768 | ex F-WWAA | Amanda |
| ☐ N665FE | Airbus A300F4-605R | 769 | ex F-WWAM | Ethan |
| ☐ N667FE | Airbus A300F4-605R | 771 | ex F-WWAF | Sean |
| ☐ N668FE | Airbus A300F4-605R | 772 | ex F-WWAP | Tianna |
| ☐ N669FE | Airbus A300F4-605R | 774 | ex F-WWAE | Kaitlyn |
| ☐ N670FE | Airbus A300F4-605R | 777 | ex F-WWAQ | Amrit |
| ☐ N671FE | Airbus A300F4-605R | 778 | ex F-WWAV | Drew |
| ☐ N672FE | Airbus A300F4-605R | 779 | ex F-WWAZ | Young Joe |
| ☐ N673FE | Airbus A300F4-605R | 780 | ex F-WWAU | Mark |
| ☐ N674FE | Airbus A300F4-605R | 781 | ex F-WWAN | Thea |
| ☐ N675FE | Airbus A300F4-605R | 789 | ex F-WWAZ | Byron |
| ☐ N676FE | Airbus A300F4-605R | 790 | ex F-WWAV | Jade |
| ☐ N677FE | Airbus A300F4-605R | 791 | ex F-WWAD | Clifford |
| ☐ N678FE | Airbus A300F4-605R | 792 | ex F-WWAF | Allison |
| ☐ N679FE | Airbus A300F4-605R | 793 | ex F-WWAG | Ty |
| ☐ N680FE | Airbus A300F4-605R | 794 | ex F-WWAH | Tierney |
| ☐ N681FE | Airbus A300F4-605R | 799 | ex F-WWAJ | Kaci |
| ☐ N682FE | Airbus A300F4-605R | 800 | ex F-WWAK | Gabrial |
| ☐ N683FE | Airbus A300F4-605R | 801 | ex F-WWAL | Xenophon |
| ☐ N684FE | Airbus A300F4-605R | 802 | ex F-WWAM | Daniel |
| ☐ N685FE | Airbus A300F4-605R | 803 | ex F-WWAB | Landon Ostlie |
| ☐ N686FE | Airbus A300F4-605R | 804 | ex F-WWAO | Alex |
| ☐ N687FE | Airbus A300F4-605R | 873 | ex F-WWAO | |
| ☐ N688FE | Airbus A300F4-605R | 874 | ex F-WWAP | |

| | | | | | | |
|---|---|---|---|---|---|---|
| ☐ | N689FE | Airbus A300F4-605R | 875 | ex F-WWAQ | | |
| ☐ | N690FE | Airbus A300F4-605R | 876 | ex F-WWAR | | |
| ☐ | N691FE | Airbus A300F4-605R | 877 | ex F-WWAS | | |
| ☐ | N692FE | Airbus A300F4-605R | 878 | ex F-WWAT | Gabriel | |
| ☐ | N716FD | Airbus A300B4-622F | 358 | ex HL7287 | Halle | |
| ☐ | N717FD | Airbus A300B4-622F | 361 | ex HL7280 | Roben | |
| ☐ | N718FD | Airbus A300B4-622F | 365 | ex HL7281 | Anna | |
| ☐ | N719FD | Airbus A300B4-622F | 388 | ex HL7290 | Cale | |
| ☐ | N720FD | Airbus A300B4-622F | 417 | ex HL7291 | Kristin Marie | |
| ☐ | N721FD | Airbus A300B4-622RF | 477 | ex D-ASAE | Kathryn | |
| ☐ | N722FD | Airbus A300B4-622RF | 479 | ex HL7535 | Terry | |
| ☐ | N723FD | Airbus A300B4-622RF | 543 | ex HL7536 | Cody | |
| ☐ | N724FD | Airbus A300B4-622RF | 530 | ex F-OIHA | Anacarina | |
| ☐ | N725FD | Airbus A300B4-622RF | 572 | ex SU-GAT | Zebradedra | |
| ☐ | N726FD | Airbus A300B4-622RF | 575 | ex SU-GAU | | |
| ☐ | N727FD | Airbus A300B4-622RF | 579 | ex SU-GAV | Mira | |
| ☐ | N728FD | Airbus A300B4-622RF | 581 | ex SU-GAW | Cassie | |
| ☐ | N729FD | Airbus A300B4-622RF | 657 | ex TF-ELU | Kaylee | |
| ☐ | N730FD | Airbus A300B4-622RF | 659 | ex TF-ELB | Kailey | |
| ☐ | N731FD | Airbus A300B4-605RF | 709 | ex B-2320 | | |
| ☐ | N732FD | Airbus A300B4-605RF | 713 | ex B-2321 | | |
| ☐ | N733FD | Airbus A300B4-605RF | 715 | ex B-2322 | | |
| ☐ | N740FD | Airbus A300B4-622RF | 559 | ex F-WQTD | | |
| ☐ | N741FD | Airbus A300B4-622RF | 611 | ex A7-AFC | | |
| ☐ | N742FD | Airbus A300B4-622RF | 613 | ex A7-AFD | Britton | |
| ☐ | N743FD | Airbus A300B4-622RF | 630 | ex A7-AFA | | |
| ☐ | N744FD | Airbus A300B4-622RF | 664 | ex A7-ABN | Grace | |
| ☐ | N745FD | Airbus A300B4-622RF | 668 | ex A7-ABO | Vale | |
| ☐ | N746FD | Airbus A300B4-622RF | 688 | ex A7-ABW | | |
| ☐ | N748FD | Airbus A300B4-622RF | 633 | ex N633AN | | |
| ☐ | N749FD | Airbus A300B4-622RF | 536 | ex TF-ELD | | |
| ☐ | N750FD | Airbus A300B4-622RF | 555 | ex F-HEEE | | |
| ☐ | N751FD | Airbus A300B4-622RF | 625 | ex F-HDDD | Tey | |
| | | | | | | |
| ☐ | N401FE | Airbus A310-203F | 191 | ex D-AICA | David | [VCV] |
| ☐ | N402FE | Airbus A310-203F | 201 | ex D-AICB | Carlye | |
| ☐ | N403FE | Airbus A310-203F | 230 | ex D-AICC | Maddison | |
| ☐ | N404FE | Airbus A310-203F | 233 | ex D-AICD | Collin | |
| ☐ | N405FE | Airbus A310-203F | 237 | ex D-AICF | Mariah | |
| ☐ | N407FE | Airbus A310-203F | 254 | ex D-AICH | Stacey Denise | [VCV] |
| ☐ | N408FE | Airbus A310-203F | 257 | ex D-AICK | Kealoha | [VCV] |
| ☐ | N409FE | Airbus A310-203F | 273 | ex D-AICL | Jake | [VCV] |
| ☐ | N410FE | Airbus A310-203F | 356 | ex D-AICM | Carolyn | |
| ☐ | N411FE | Airbus A310-203F | 359 | ex D-AICN | Barbra | |
| ☐ | N412FE | Airbus A310-203F | 360 | ex D-AICP | Corina | [VCV] |
| ☐ | N414FE | Airbus A310-203F | 400 | ex D-AICS | Tanner | [VCV] |
| ☐ | N416FE | Airbus A310-222F | 288 | ex F-WGYR | Patrick | |
| ☐ | N417FE | Airbus A310-222F | 333 | ex N802PA | Kyle | |
| ☐ | N418FE | Airbus A310-222F | 343 | ex N803PA | Rachel | |
| ☐ | N419FE | Airbus A310-222F | 345 | ex N804PA | Krystle | |
| ☐ | N421FE | Airbus A310-222F | 342 | ex N806PA | Caitlin | |
| ☐ | N423FE | Airbus A310-203F | 281 | ex PH-MCA | Trey | |
| ☐ | N425FE | Airbus A310-203F | 264 | ex PH-AGD | Jerome | |
| ☐ | N426FE | Airbus A310-203F | 245 | ex PH-AGB | Shana | |
| ☐ | N427FE | Airbus A310-203F | 362 | ex PH-AGH | Zackary | |
| ☐ | N428FE | Airbus A310-203F | 248 | ex PH-AGC | Kristina | |
| ☐ | N429FE | Airbus A310-203F | 364 | ex PH-AGI | Conner | |
| ☐ | N430FE | Airbus A310-203F | 394 | ex PH-AGK | Kelleen | |
| ☐ | N431FE | Airbus A310-203F | 316 | ex F-WWAD | Asumi | |
| ☐ | N435FE | Airbus A310-203F | 369 | ex F-GEME | Ceara | |
| ☐ | N436FE | Airbus A310-203F | 454 | ex F-GEMG | Gillian | |
| ☐ | N443FE | Airbus A310-203F | 283 | ex PH-AGE | Katelin | |
| ☐ | N445FE | Airbus A310-203F | 297 | ex PH-AGF | Nicholas | |
| ☐ | N446FE | Airbus A310-222F | 224 | ex HB-IPA | Makenna | [VCV] |
| ☐ | N447FE | Airbus A310-222F | 251 | ex HB-IPB | Shaunna | |
| ☐ | N448FE | Airbus A310-222F | 260 | ex HB-IPD | Augustine | [VCV] |
| ☐ | N450FE | Airbus A310-222F | 162 | ex F-GPDJ | Selna | |
| ☐ | N451FE | Airbus A310-222F | 303 | ex OO-SCA | Reis | [VCV] |
| ☐ | N453FE | Airbus A310-222F | 267 | ex D-ASAL | Rush | |
| ☐ | N454FE | Airbus A310-222F | 278 | ex D-ASAK | Marissa | |
| ☐ | N455FE | Airbus A310-222F | 331 | ex F-WWAH | Sara | |
| ☐ | N456FE | Airbus A310-222F | 318 | ex F-OHPQ | Simon | |
| ☐ | N801FD | Airbus A310-324F | 539 | ex D-ASAD | Amos | |
| ☐ | N802FD | Airbus A310-324F | 542 | ex D-ASAD | Saeed | |
| ☐ | N803FD | Airbus A310-324F | 378 | ex N853CH | Rylan | |
| ☐ | N804FD | Airbus A310-324F | 549 | ex N101MP | Paige | |
| ☐ | N805FD | Airbus A310-324F | 456 | ex F-OGYR | Fernando | |
| ☐ | N806FD | Airbus A310-324F | 458 | ex F-OGYN | Addisyn | |
| ☐ | N807FD | Airbus A310-324F | 492 | ex F-WQTA | Joshua | |
| ☐ | N808FD | Airbus A310-324F | 439 | ex F-OHPU | Berkeley | |
| ☐ | N809FD | Airbus A310-324F | 449 | ex F-OHPV | Gavin | |
| ☐ | N810FD | Airbus A310-324F | 452 | ex F-OHPY | Sebastian | |

| | | | | | |
|---|---|---|---|---|---|
| ☐ N811FD | Airbus A310-324F | 457 | ex F-OGYM | | |
| ☐ N812FD | Airbus A310-324F | 467 | ex F-OGYS | Agyei | |
| ☐ N813FD | Airbus A310-324F | 500 | ex N501RR | | |
| ☐ N814FD | Airbus A310-324F | 534 | ex N534RR | | [VCV] |
| ☐ N815FD | Airbus A310-324F | 638 | ex F-OJAF | Tommy | |
| ☐ N816FD | Airbus A310-304F | 593 | ex F-OGQR | | |
| ☐ N817FD | Airbus A310-304F | 552 | ex TF-ELS | | |
| | | | | | |
| ☐ N900FX | ATR 42-320F | 0170 | ex N14825 | | op by CFS |
| ☐ N901FX | ATR 42-320F | 0172 | ex N26826 | | op by CFS |
| ☐ N903FX | ATR 42-320F | 0179 | ex N14828 | | op by CFS |
| ☐ N906FX | ATR 42-320F | 0280 | ex N97841 | | op by MTN |
| ☐ N907FX | ATR 42-320F | 0286 | ex N86842 | | op by MTN |
| ☐ N908FX | ATR 42-300F | 0023 | ex N972NA | | op by CFS |
| ☐ N909FX | ATR 42-300F | 0275 | ex N275BC | | op by MTN |
| ☐ N910FX | ATR 42-300F | 0277 | ex N277AT | | op by MTN |
| ☐ N911FX | ATR 42-300F | 0045 | ex N424MQ | | op by CFS |
| ☐ N912FX | ATR 42-300F | 0047 | ex N47AE | | op by CFS |
| ☐ N913FX | ATR 42-320F | 0250 | ex N251AE | | op by CFS |
| ☐ N914FX | ATR 42-300F | 0293 | ex N293AT | | op by MTN |
| ☐ N915FX | ATR 42-320F | 0269 | ex N269AT | | op by CFS |
| ☐ N916FX | ATR 42-300F | 0314 | ex N314AM | | op by MTN |
| ☐ N917FX | ATR 42-320F | 0354 | ex N351AT | | op by CFS |
| ☐ N918FX | ATR 42-320F | 0262 | ex N262AT | | op by MTN |
| ☐ N919FX | ATR 42-320F | 0266 | ex N265AE | | op by CFS |
| ☐ N920FX | ATR 42-320F | 0325 | ex N325AT | | op by MTN |
| ☐ N921FX | ATR 42-300F | 0319 | ex N319AM | | op by CFS |
| | | | | | |
| ☐ EI-FXK | ATR 72-202F | 0256 | ex N817FX | | >ABR |
| ☐ N800FX | ATR 72-212 | 0336 | ex N630AS | | [ISO] |
| ☐ N801FX | ATR 72-212 | 0338 | ex N632AS | | op by CFS |
| ☐ N802FX | ATR 72-212 | 0344 | ex N633AS | | op by MTN |
| ☐ N803FX | ATR 72-212 | 0362 | ex N631AS | | op by CFS |
| ☐ N804FX | ATR 72-212 | 0370 | ex N634AS | | [ISO] |
| ☐ N805FX | ATR 72-212F | 0372 | ex N635AS | | op by CFS |
| ☐ N806FX | ATR 72-212 | 0375 | ex N636AS | | op by MTN |
| ☐ N807FX | ATR 72-212 | 0383 | ex N637AS | | op by CFS |
| ☐ N809FX | ATR 72-202F | 0217 | ex N721TE | | op by MTN |
| ☐ N810FX | ATR 72-202F | 0220 | ex N722TE | | op by MTN |
| ☐ N811FX | ATR 72-202F | 0283 | ex N723TE | | op by MTN |
| ☐ N812FX | ATR 72-212F | 0404 | ex D-AEWI | | op by MTN |
| ☐ N816FX | ATR 72-212F | 0347 | ex D-AEWG | | op by CFS |
| ☐ N819FX | ATR 72-212F | 0359 | ex D-AEWH | | op by CFS |
| ☐ N820FX | ATR 72-212F | 0248 | ex N248AT | | op by MTN |
| ☐ N821FX | ATR 72-212F | 0253 | ex N252AM | | op by CFS |
| | | | | | |
| ☐ N203FE | Boeing 727-2S2F (FedEx 3) | 22925/1819 | | Jonathan | |
| ☐ N204FE | Boeing 727-2S2F (FedEx 3) | 22926/1820 | | Rebecca | |
| ☐ N207FE | Boeing 727-2S2F (Super 27) | 22929/1823 | | Vivian | |
| ☐ N211FE | Boeing 727-2S2F (FedEx 3) | 22933/1827 | | Bobby | |
| ☐ N213FE | Boeing 727-2S2F (FedEx 3) | 22935/1829 | | Cagen | |
| ☐ N217FE | Boeing 727-2S2F (Super 27) | 22938/1832 | | Sonja | |
| ☐ N218FE | Boeing 727-233F (FedEx 3) | 21101/1150 | ex C-GAAM | Christin | [VCV] |
| ☐ N220FE | Boeing 727-233F (FedEx 3) | 20934/1074 | ex C-GAAC | Emily | [VCV] |
| ☐ N221FE | Boeing 727-233F (FedEx 3) | 20932/1069 | ex C-GAAA | Megan Nicole | |
| ☐ N222FE | Boeing 727-233F (FedEx 3) | 20933/1071 | ex C-GAAB | Michael | [VCV] |
| ☐ N223FE | Boeing 727-233F (FedEx 3) | 20935/1076 | ex C-GAAD | Dustin | |
| ☐ N233FE | Boeing 727-247F (FedEx 3) | 21327/1249 | ex C-FMEI | | |
| ☐ N234FE | Boeing 727-247F (FedEx 3) | 21328/1251 | ex C-FMEY | | ♦ |
| ☐ N235FE | Boeing 727-247F (FedEx 3) | 21329/1254 | ex C-FMEA | Stephanie | |
| ☐ N236FE | Boeing 727-247F (FedEx 3) | 21330/1260 | ex C-FMEE | | |
| ☐ N237FE | Boeing 727-247F (FedEx 3) | 21331/1266 | ex N2826W | Tristan | [VCV] |
| ☐ N240FE | Boeing 727-277F (FedEx 3) | 20978/1083 | ex VH-RMY | Baron | [VCV] |
| ☐ N241FE | Boeing 727-277F (FedEx 3) | 20979/1098 | ex VH-RMZ | Jill | |
| ☐ N243FE | Boeing 727-277F (FedEx 3) | 21480/1352 | ex VH-RML | Braden | [VCV] |
| ☐ N244FE | Boeing 727-277F (FedEx 3) | 21647/1436 | ex VH-RMM | Crystal | |
| ☐ N245FE | Boeing 727-277F (FedEx 3) | 22016/1566 | ex VH-RMO | Kelsey | [VCV] |
| ☐ N254FE | Boeing 727-233F (FedEx 3) | 20936/1078 | ex C-GAAE | Courtney | [VCV] |
| ☐ N257FE | Boeing 727-233F (FedEx 3) | 20939/1112 | ex C-GAAH | Felicia | |
| ☐ N262FE | Boeing 727-233F (FedEx 3) | 21624/1468 | ex C-GAAO | Betsy | |
| ☐ N263FE | Boeing 727-233F (FedEx 3) | 21625/1470 | ex C-GAAP | Marc | |
| ☐ N264FE | Boeing 727-233F (FedEx 3) | 21626/1472 | ex C-GAAQ | Brennan | |
| ☐ N265FE | Boeing 727-233F (FedEx 3) | 21671/1523 | ex C-GBZB | Paul | |
| ☐ N266FE | Boeing 727-233F (FedEx 3) | 21672/1538 | ex C-GAAS | Steven | |
| ☐ N267FE | Boeing 727-233F (FedEx 3) | 21673/1541 | ex C-GMSX | Jolene | |
| ☐ N268FE | Boeing 727-233F (FedEx 3) | 21674/1543 | ex C-GAAU | Ginger | |
| ☐ N269FE | Boeing 727-233F (FedEx 3) | 21675/1555 | ex C-GAAV | Alexander | |
| ☐ N271FE | Boeing 727-233F (FedEx 3) | 22036/1596 | ex C-GAAX | Andrew | [VCV] |
| ☐ N273FE | Boeing 727-233F (FedEx 3) | 22038/1612 | ex C-GAAZ | Samantha | |
| ☐ N274FE | Boeing 727-233F (FedEx 3) | 22039/1614 | ex C-GYNA | Jessica | [VCV] |
| ☐ N276FE | Boeing 727-233F (FedEx 3) | 22041/1628 | ex C-GYNC | Devan | |
| ☐ N278FE | Boeing 727-233F (FedEx 3) | 22345/1699 | ex C-GYNE | Jeffrey | [VCV] |

| | | | | | | |
|---|---|---|---|---|---|---|
| ☐ | N280FE | Boeing 727-223F (FedEx 3) | 22347/1708 | ex C-GYNG | Chad | [VCV] |
| ☐ | N283FE | Boeing 727-233F (FedEx 3) | 22350/1745 | ex C-GYNJ | Randall | [VCV] |
| ☐ | N284FE | Boeing 727-233F (FedEx 3) | 22621/1791 | ex C-GYNK | Victoria | |
| ☐ | N285FE | Boeing 727-233F (FedEx 3) | 22622/1792 | ex C-GYNL | Jordann | |
| ☐ | N286FE | Boeing 727-233F (FedEx 3) | 22623/1803 | ex C-GYNM | Charlsi | |
| ☐ | N287FE | Boeing 727-2D4F (FedEx 3) | 21849/1527 | ex N361PA | Alexa | |
| ☐ | N288FE | Boeing 727-2D4F (FedEx 3) | 21850/1536 | ex N362PA | Michelle | |
| ☐ | N461FE | Boeing 727-225F (FedEx 3) | 22548/1734 | ex C-FMES | | |
| ☐ | N462FE | Boeing 727-225F (FedEx 3) | 22550/1739 | ex N813EA | Daven | ♦ |
| ☐ | N463FE | Boeing 727-225F (FedEx 3) | 22551/1744 | ex N814EA | Tonga | |
| ☐ | N464FE | Boeing 727-225F (FedEx 3) | 21288/1234 | ex N8870Z | Blake | |
| ☐ | N466FE | Boeing 727-225F (FedEx 3) | 21292/1240 | ex N8874Z | Gideon | |
| ☐ | N467FE | Boeing 727-225F (FedEx 3) | 21449/1306 | ex N8876Z | Joy | |
| ☐ | N468FE | Boeing 727-225F (FedEx 3) | 21452/1312 | ex N8879Z | Chad | |
| ☐ | N469FE | Boeing 727-225F (FedEx 3) | 21581/1437 | ex N8884Z | Ray | |
| ☐ | N479FE | Boeing 727-227F (FedEx 3) | 21461/1337 | ex N455BN | Norah | |
| ☐ | N480FE | Boeing 727-227F (FedEx 3) | 21462/1342 | ex N456BN | Warren | [VCV] |
| ☐ | N481FE | Boeing 727-227F (FedEx 3) | 21463/1353 | ex N457BN | Tiffany | |
| ☐ | N482FE | Boeing 727-227F (FedEx 3) | 21464/1355 | ex N458BN | Natalie | |
| ☐ | N483FE | Boeing 727-227F (FedEx 3) | 21465/1363 | ex N459BN | David | |
| ☐ | N484FE | Boeing 727-227F (FedEx 3) | 21466/1372 | ex N460BN | Hallie | [VCV] |
| ☐ | N485FE | Boeing 727-227F (FedEx 3) | 21488/1388 | ex N461BN | Kristen | |
| ☐ | N486FE | Boeing 727-227F (FedEx 3) | 21489/1390 | ex N462BN | Hunter | |
| ☐ | N487FE | Boeing 727-227F (FedEx 3) | 21490/1396 | ex N463BN | Britney | |
| ☐ | N488FE | Boeing 727-227F (FedEx 3) | 21491/1402 | ex N464BN | Olivia | |
| ☐ | N489FE | Boeing 727-227F (FedEx 3) | 21492/1440 | ex N465BN | Timothy | |
| ☐ | N490FE | Boeing 727-227F (FedEx 3) | 21493/1442 | ex N466BN | Chase | |
| ☐ | N491FE | Boeing 727-227F (FedEx 3) | 21529/1444 | ex N467BN | Noel | |
| ☐ | N492FE | Boeing 727-227F (FedEx 3) | 21530/1446 | ex N468BN | Two Bears | |
| ☐ | N493FE | Boeing 727-227F (FedEx 3) | 21531/1450 | ex N469BN | Maxx | |
| ☐ | N494FE | Boeing 727-227F (FedEx 3) | 21532/1453 | ex N470BN | Ebony | |
| ☐ | N495FE | Boeing 727-227F (FedEx 3) | 21669/1484 | ex N471BN | Leslie | |
| ☐ | N499FE | Boeing 727-232F (FedEx 3) | 21018/1095 | ex CS-TCJ | Sierra | [VCV] |
| ☐ | N901FD | Boeing 757-2B7F | 27122/525 | ex N610AU | | |
| ☐ | N902FD | Boeing 757-2B7SF | 27123/534 | ex N927UW | | |
| ☐ | N903FD | Boeing 757-2B7SF | 27124/540 | ex N928UW | | >MAL |
| ☐ | N905FD | Boeing 757-2B7SF | 27145/546 | ex N930UW | | |
| ☐ | N906FD | Boeing 757-2B7SF | 27148/564 | ex N931UW | | |
| ☐ | N909FD | Boeing 757-2B7SF | 27200/589 | ex N934UW | | >MAL |
| ☐ | N910FD | Boeing 757-236SF | 25054/362 | ex G-OOOK | | |
| ☐ | N912FD | Boeing 757-28ASF | 24260/204 | ex N517NA | | |
| ☐ | N913FD | Boeing 757-28ASF | 24017/162 | ex C-FTDV | | |
| ☐ | N914FD | Boeing 757-28A | 24367/208 | ex C-FCLG | | |
| ☐ | N915FD | Boeing 757-236SF | 24120/174 | ex 4X-EBO | | |
| ☐ | N916FD | Boeing 757-27BSF | 24137/178 | ex 4X-EBY | | |
| ☐ | N917FD | Boeing 757-23AF | 24291/215 | ex CX-PUD | | |
| ☐ | N918FD | Boeing 757-23AERF | 24290/212 | ex N290AN | Dexter | |
| ☐ | N919FD | Boeing 757-23ASF | 24636/259 | ex G-FJEA | Evan | |
| ☐ | N920FD | Boeing 757-23AERF | 24289/209 | ex G-OAVB | | |
| ☐ | N921FD | Boeing 757-23ASF | 24924/333 | ex N924AW | | |
| ☐ | N922FD | Boeing 757-23ASF | 24293/220 | ex N293AW | | |
| ☐ | N923FD | Boeing 757-228ASF | 26266/514 | ex G-BYAF | | |
| ☐ | N924FD | Boeing 757-28ASF | 26267/538 | ex G-BYAK | | |
| ☐ | N925FD | Boeing 757-204SF | 27238/604 | ex G-BYAS | | |
| ☐ | N926FD | Boeing 757-2S7 | 23323/80 | ex N903AW | | [VCV]♦ |
| ☐ | N928FD | Boeing 757-28ASF | 24369/226 | ex G-JMCF | | |
| ☐ | N930FD | Boeing 757-2Y0SF | 25240/388 | ex N240MQ | | ♦ |
| ☐ | N933FD | Boeing 757-21BSF | 24330/200 | ex B-2804 | | |
| ☐ | N934FD | Boeing 757-21BSF | 24331/203 | ex B-2805 | | |
| ☐ | N935FD | Boeing 757-2T7ERSF | 22780/15 | ex G-MONB | Desirée | |
| ☐ | N936FD | Boeing 757-2T7ERSF | 23293/56 | ex G-MONE | | |
| ☐ | N937FD | Boeing 757-2T7SF | 23895/132 | ex N513NA | | |
| ☐ | N938FD | Boeing 757-23AER | 24292/219 | ex G-OJIB | | [VCV]♦ |
| ☐ | N939FD | Boeing 757-23A | 24528/250 | ex N549AX | | [SIN] |
| ☐ | N940FD | Boeing 757-236SF | 24772/271 | ex N247SS | | ♦ |
| ☐ | N941FD | Boeing 757-225 | 22691/155 | ex TF-LLY | | [MOB] |
| ☐ | N942FD | Boeing 757-225 | 22612/114 | ex N226LC | | [VCV]♦ |
| ☐ | N943FD | Boeing 757-2G5SF | 23929/153 | ex N929RD | | ♦ |
| ☐ | N944FD | Boeing 757-2G5SF | 24497/228 | ex N497EA | | ♦ |
| ☐ | N946FD | Boeing 757-236SF | 24398/224 | ex G-CPEL | | |
| ☐ | N947FD | Boeing 757-236SF | 24882/323 | ex G-BPEC | | |
| ☐ | N948FD | Boeing 757-236SF | 25059/363 | ex G-BPED | | |
| ☐ | N949FD | Boeing 757-236SF | 25060/364 | ex G-BPEE | | |
| ☐ | N950FD | Boeing 757-236SF | 25806/601 | ex G-BPEI | | |
| ☐ | N951FD | Boeing 757-236SF | 28665/747 | ex G-CPEM | | ♦ |
| ☐ | N952FD | Boeing 757-236 | 28666/751 | ex G-CPEN | | [SIN]♦ |
| ☐ | N953FD | Boeing 757-236 | 28667/762 | ex G-CPEO | | [SIN]♦ |
| ☐ | N954FD | Boeing 757-236 | 29113/784 | ex G-CPER | | [VCV] |
| ☐ | N955FD | Boeing 757-236 | 29114/793 | ex G-CPES | | [VCV] |
| ☐ | N956FD | Boeing 757-236 | 29115 | ex G-CPET | | [VCV]♦ |
| ☐ | N957FD | Boeing 757-21BSF | 24774/288 | ex N802PG | | [SIN] |

| | | | | | | |
|---|---|---|---|---|---|---|
| ☐ | N958FD | Boeing 757-236 | 24371//225 | ex N579SH | | [VCV]♦ |
| ☐ | N958SH | Boeing 757-236 | 24371/225 | ex OM-ASB | | [VCV]♦ |
| ☐ | N959FD | Boeing 757-236 | 25133/374 | ex N522NA | | [SIN]♦ |
| ☐ | N960FD | Boeing 757-236 | 25593/466 | ex G-OOOZ | | [VCV] |
| ☐ | N961FD | Boeing 757-2Y0 | 25268/400 | ex G-CPEP | | [VCV]♦ |
| ☐ | N962FD | Boeing 757-2G5 | 24176/173 | ex CS-TLX | | [VCV]♦ |
| ☐ | N964FD | Boeing 757-258ER | 24884/325 | ex 4X-EBS | | [VCV]♦ |
| ☐ | N965FD | Boeing 757-258 | 27622/745 | ex G-STRZ | | [VCV]♦ |
| ☐ | N973FD | Boeing 757-2Y0 | 26151/472 | ex TF-FIK | | wfs♦ |
| ☐ | N989FD | Boeing 757-231 | 28480/750 | ex N529SH | | [VCV]♦ |
| ☐ | N990FD | Boeing 757-232SF | 22909/101 | ex N619DL | | ♦ |
| ☐ | N991FD | Boeing 757-232SF | 22911/112 | ex N621DL | | ♦ |
| ☐ | N992FD | Boeing 757-232 | 22912/113 | ex N622DL | | [SAT]♦ |
| ☐ | N993FD | Boeing 757-2Q8SF | 24965/438 | ex SU-BPY | | ♦ |
| ☐ | N994FD | Boeing 757-23ASF | 25490/510 | ex N490AN | | ♦ |
| ☐ | N995FD | Boeing 757-2Q8SF | 25131/458 | ex N594BC | | ♦ |
| ☐ | N996FD | Boeing 757-2Q8SF | 26270/558 | ex N595BC | | ♦ |
| ☐ | N997FD | Boeing 757-230SF | 24738/274 | ex N473AC | | ♦ |
| ☐ | N998FD | Boeing 757-230 | 24747/275 | ex EI-IGC | | wfs♦ |
| ☐ | N999FD | Boeing 757-230SF | 24748/285 | ex N493AC | | ♦ |
| | | | | | | |
| ☐ | N850FD | Boeing 777-FS2 | 37721/813 | | Saad | |
| ☐ | N851FD | Boeing 777-FS2 | 37722/834 | | | |
| ☐ | N852FD | Boeing 777-FS2 | 37723/848 | | | |
| ☐ | N853FD | Boeing 777-FS2 | 37724/829 | | Talon | |
| ☐ | N854FD | Boeing 777-FS2 | 37725/890 | | Faith | |
| ☐ | N855FD | Boeing 777-FS2 | 37726/892 | | | |
| ☐ | N856FD | Boeing 777-FS2 | 37727/884 | | Shae | |
| ☐ | N857FD | Boeing 777-FS2 | 37728/886 | | Braydon | |
| ☐ | N858FD | Boeing 777-FS2 | 37729/936 | | | ♦ |
| ☐ | N859FD | Boeing 777-FS2 | 37730/ | | | o/o♦ |
| ☐ | N860FD | Boeing 777-FS2 | 37731/ | | | o/o♦ |
| ☐ | N861FD | Boeing 777-FS2 | 37732/973 | | | ♦ |
| ☐ | N862FD | Boeing 777-FS2 | 37733/975 | | | ♦ |
| ☐ | N863FD | Boeing 777-F28 | 37734/998 | | | ♦ |
| ☐ | N864FD | Boeing 777-F28 | 37735/ | | | o/o♦ |
| ☐ | N880FD | Boeing 777-F28 | 32967/718 | ex F-GUOA | | |
| ☐ | N882FD | Boeing 777-F28 | 32969/827 | ex N449BA | LeeAnna | |
| ☐ | N883FD | Boeing 777-FHT | 39285/897 | ex N5022E | Abbi | |
| ☐ | N884FD | Boeing 777-FS2 | 37137/917 | | | ♦ |
| ☐ | N885FD | Boeing 777-FS2 | 41064/967 | | | ♦ |
| ☐ | N886FD | Boeing 777-FS2 | 41065/ | | | o/o♦ |
| ☐ | N887FD | Boeing 777-FS2 | 41066/ | | | o/o♦ |
| ☐ | N890FD | Boeing 777-FS2 | 41439/ | | | o/o♦ |
| ☐ | N892FD | Boeing 777-FS2 | 38707/960 | | | ♦ |
| | | | | | | |
| ☐ | C-FEXB | Cessna 208B Caravan I | 208B0539 | ex N758FX | | >MAL |
| ☐ | C-FEXF | Cessna 208B Caravan I | 208B0508 | ex N749FX | | >MAL |
| ☐ | C-FEXV | Cessna 208B Caravan I | 208B0482 | ex N738FX | | >MAL |
| ☐ | C-FEXY | Cessna 208B Caravan I | 208B0226 | ex N896FE | | >MAL |
| ☐ | N700FX | Cessna 208B Caravan I | 208B0419 | | | op by CFS |
| ☐ | N701FX | Cessna 208B Caravan I | 208B0420 | | | op by WIG |
| ☐ | N702FX | Cessna 208B Caravan I | 208B0422 | | | op by BVN |
| ☐ | N703FX | Cessna 208B Caravan I | 208B0423 | | | op by IRO |
| ☐ | N705FX | Cessna 208B Caravan I | 208B0425 | | | op by CFS |
| ☐ | N706FX | Cessna 208B Caravan I | 208B0426 | | | op by IRO |
| ☐ | N707FX | Cessna 208B Caravan I | 208B0427 | | | op by PCM |
| ☐ | N709FX | Cessna 208B Caravan I | 208B0430 | | | op by CFS |
| ☐ | N710FX | Cessna 208B Caravan I | 208B0431 | | | op by CPT |
| ☐ | N711FX | Cessna 208B Caravan I | 208B0433 | | | op by CFS |
| ☐ | N712FX | Cessna 208B Caravan I | 208B0435 | | | op by IRO |
| ☐ | N713FX | Cessna 208B Caravan I | 208B0438 | | | op by PCM |
| ☐ | N715FX | Cessna 208B Caravan I | 208B0440 | | | op by MTN |
| ☐ | N716FX | Cessna 208B Caravan I | 208B0442 | | | op by CPT |
| ☐ | N717FX | Cessna 208B Caravan I | 208B0445 | | | op by IRO |
| ☐ | N718FX | Cessna 208B Caravan I | 208B0448 | | | op by BVN |
| ☐ | N719FX | Cessna 208B Caravan I | 208B0450 | | | op by BVN |
| ☐ | N720FX | Cessna 208B Caravan I | 208B0452 | ex N5132T | | op by CFS |
| ☐ | N721FX | Cessna 208B Caravan I | 208B0453 | ex N5133E | | op by MTN |
| ☐ | N722FX | Cessna 208B Caravan I | 208B0454 | ex N5135A | | op by PCM |
| ☐ | N723FX | Cessna 208B Caravan I | 208B0456 | | | op by BVN |
| ☐ | N724FX | Cessna 208B Caravan I | 208B0458 | | | op by CPT |
| ☐ | N725FX | Cessna 208B Caravan I | 208B0460 | | | op by WIG |
| ☐ | N726FX | Cessna 208B Caravan I | 208B0465 | | | op by PCM |
| ☐ | N727FX | Cessna 208B Caravan I | 208B0468 | | | op by IRO |
| ☐ | N728FX | Cessna 208B Caravan I | 208B0471 | ex N5061W | | op by CFS |
| ☐ | N729FX | Cessna 208B Caravan I | 208B0474 | ex N2617Z | | op by MTN |
| ☐ | N730FX | Cessna 208B Caravan I | 208B0477 | ex N5066U | | op by CPT |
| ☐ | N731FX | Cessna 208B Caravan I | 208B0480 | | | op by WIG |
| ☐ | N740FX | Cessna 208B Caravan I | 208B0484 | | | op by MTN |
| ☐ | N741FX | Cessna 208B Caravan I | 208B0486 | ex N5145P | | op by BVN |
| ☐ | N742FX | Cessna 208B Caravan I | 208B0489 | | | op by MTN |

| | | | | |
|---|---|---|---|---|
| ☐ N744FX | Cessna 208B Caravan I | 208B0492 | ex N5148B | op by PCM |
| ☐ N745FX | Cessna 208B Caravan I | 208B0495 | ex N5162W | op by BVN |
| ☐ N746FX | Cessna 208B Caravan I | 208B0498 | ex N51743 | op by CFS |
| ☐ N747FE | Cessna 208B Caravan I | 208B0238 | | op by MTN |
| ☐ N747FX | Cessna 208B Caravan I | 208B0501 | ex N51017 | op by MTN |
| ☐ N748FE | Cessna 208B Caravan I | 208B0241 | | op by WIG |
| ☐ N748FX | Cessna 208B Caravan I | 208B0503 | ex N52609 | op by PCM |
| ☐ N749FE | Cessna 208B Caravan I | 208B0242 | | op by BVN |
| ☐ N750FX | Cessna 208B Caravan I | 208B0511 | ex N5211Q | op by PCM |
| ☐ N751FE | Cessna 208B Caravan I | 208B0245 | | op by CPT |
| ☐ N751FX | Cessna 208B Caravan I | 208B0514 | ex N5262W | op by BVN |
| ☐ N752FE | Cessna 208B Caravan I | 208B0247 | | op by IRO |
| ☐ N752FX | Cessna 208B Caravan I | 208B0517 | ex N5214J | op by CFS |
| ☐ N753FX | Cessna 208B Caravan I | 208B0520 | ex N51942 | op by BVN |
| ☐ N754FX | Cessna 208B Caravan I | 208B0526 | ex N5201M | op by PCM |
| ☐ N755FE | Cessna 208B Caravan I | 208B0250 | | op by MTN |
| ☐ N755FX | Cessna 208B Caravan I | 208B0529 | ex N5264E | op by WIG |
| ☐ N756FE | Cessna 208B Caravan I | 208B0251 | | op by BVN |
| ☐ N756FX | Cessna 208B Caravan I | 208B0532 | | op by CFS |
| ☐ N760FE | Cessna 208B Caravan I | 208B0252 | | op by CPT |
| ☐ N761FE | Cessna 208B Caravan I | 208B0254 | | op by IRO |
| ☐ N762FE | Cessna 208B Caravan I | 208B0255 | | op by PCM |
| ☐ N763FE | Cessna 208B Caravan I | 208B0256 | | op by PCM |
| ☐ N764FE | Cessna 208B Caravan I | 208B0258 | | op by MTN |
| ☐ N765FE | Cessna 208B Caravan I | 208B0259 | | op by BVN |
| ☐ N766FE | Cessna 208B Caravan I | 208B0260 | | op by CPT |
| ☐ N767FE | Cessna 208B Caravan I | 208B0262 | | op by IRO |
| ☐ N768FE | Cessna 208B Caravan I | 208B0263 | | op by PCM |
| ☐ N769FE | Cessna 208B Caravan I | 208B0264 | | op by MTN |
| ☐ N770FE | Cessna 208B Caravan I | 208B0265 | | op by BVN |
| ☐ N771FE | Cessna 208B Caravan I | 208B0267 | | op by PCM |
| ☐ N772FE | Cessna 208B Caravan I | 208B0268 | | op by PCM |
| ☐ N773FE | Cessna 208B Caravan I | 208B0269 | | op by BVN |
| ☐ N774FE | Cessna 208B Caravan I | 208B0271 | | op by BVN |
| ☐ N775FE | Cessna 208B Caravan I | 208B0272 | | op by CFS |
| ☐ N776FE | Cessna 208B Caravan I | 208B0273 | | op by MTN |
| ☐ N778FE | Cessna 208B Caravan I | 208B0275 | | op by CFS |
| ☐ N779FE | Cessna 208B Caravan I | 208B0276 | | op by CFS |
| ☐ N780FE | Cessna 208B Caravan I | 208B0277 | | op by WIG |
| ☐ N781FE | Cessna 208B Caravan I | 208B0278 | | op by PCM |
| ☐ N782FE | Cessna 208B Caravan I | 208B0280 | | op by PCM |
| ☐ N783FE | Cessna 208B Caravan I | 208B0281 | | op by WIG |
| ☐ N784FE | Cessna 208B Caravan I | 208B0282 | | op by IRO |
| ☐ N785FE | Cessna 208B Caravan I | 208B0283 | | op by PCM |
| ☐ N786FE | Cessna 208B Caravan I | 208B0284 | | op by BVN |
| ☐ N787FE | Cessna 208B Caravan I | 208B0285 | | op by MTN |
| ☐ N788FE | Cessna 208B Caravan I | 208B0286 | | op by CFS |
| ☐ N789FE | Cessna 208B Caravan I | 208B0287 | | op by WIG |
| ☐ N790FE | Cessna 208B Caravan I | 208B0288 | | op by PCM |
| ☐ N792FE | Cessna 208B Caravan I | 208B0290 | | op by MTN |
| ☐ N793FE | Cessna 208B Caravan I | 208B0291 | | op by BVN |
| ☐ N794FE | Cessna 208B Caravan I | 208B0292 | | op by CPT |
| ☐ N795FE | Cessna 208B Caravan I | 208B0293 | | op by IRO |
| ☐ N796FE | Cessna 208B Caravan I | 208B0212 | ex C-FEXY | op by CPT |
| ☐ N797FE | Cessna 208B Caravan I | 208B0042 | ex C-FEXH | op by CPT |
| ☐ N798FE | Cessna 208B Caravan I | 208B0174 | ex C-FEDY | op by CPT |
| ☐ N804FE | Cessna 208B Caravan I | 208B0039 | ex F-GETN | op by WIG |
| ☐ N807FE | Cessna 208B Caravan I | 208B0041 | ex F-GETO | op by WIG |
| ☐ N820FE | Cessna 208B Caravan I | 208B0111 | ex F-GHHC | op by MTN |
| ☐ N828FE | Cessna 208B Caravan I | 208B0122 | ex F-GHHD | op by IRO |
| ☐ N831FE | Cessna 208B Caravan I | 208B0225 | ex F-GHHE | op by MTN |
| ☐ N841FE | Cessna 208B Caravan I | 208B0144 | | op by BVN |
| ☐ N842FE | Cessna 208B Caravan I | 208B0146 | | op by MTN |
| ☐ N843FE | Cessna 208B Caravan I | 208B0147 | | op by IRO |
| ☐ N844FE | Cessna 208B Caravan I | 208B0149 | | op by PCM |
| ☐ N845FE | Cessna 208B Caravan I | 208B0152 | | op by BVN |
| ☐ N846FE | Cessna 208B Caravan I | 208B0154 | | op by CPT |
| ☐ N847FE | Cessna 208B Caravan I | 208B0156 | | op by MTN |
| ☐ N848FE | Cessna 208B Caravan I | 208B0158 | | op by MTN |
| ☐ N849FE | Cessna 208B Caravan I | 208B0162 | | op by MTN |
| ☐ N850FE | Cessna 208B Caravan I | 208B0164 | | op by CFS |
| ☐ N851FE | Cessna 208B Caravan I | 208B0166 | | op by CPT |
| ☐ N852FE | Cessna 208B Caravan I | 208B0168 | | op by MTN |
| ☐ N853FE | Cessna 208B Caravan I | 208B0170 | | op by MTN |
| ☐ N855FE | Cessna 208B Caravan I | 208B0203 | | op by MTN |
| ☐ N856FE | Cessna 208B Caravan I | 208B0176 | | op by CFS |
| ☐ N857FE | Cessna 208B Caravan I | 208B0177 | | op by PCM |
| ☐ N858FE | Cessna 208B Caravan I | 208B0178 | | op by IRO |
| ☐ N859FE | Cessna 208B Caravan I | 208B0181 | | op by CFS |
| ☐ N860FE | Cessna 208B Caravan I | 208B0182 | | op by CPT |
| ☐ N861FE | Cessna 208B Caravan I | 208B0183 | | op by BVN |
| ☐ N862FE | Cessna 208B Caravan I | 208B0184 | | op by MTN |

| | | | | |
|---|---|---|---|---|
| ☐ | N863FE | Cessna 208B Caravan I | 208B0186 | | op by CPT |
| ☐ | N864FE | Cessna 208B Caravan I | 208B0187 | | op by CPT |
| ☐ | N865FE | Cessna 208B Caravan I | 208B0188 | | op by WIG |
| ☐ | N866FE | Cessna 208B Caravan I | 208B0189 | ex HK-3924X | op by BVN |
| ☐ | N867FE | Cessna 208B Caravan I | 208B0191 | | op by CPT |
| ☐ | N869FE | Cessna 208B Caravan I | 208B0195 | | op by MTN |
| ☐ | N870FE | Cessna 208B Caravan I | 208B0196 | | op by WIG |
| ☐ | N871FE | Cessna 208B Caravan I | 208B0198 | | op by IRO |
| ☐ | N872FE | Cessna 208B Caravan I | 208B0200 | | op by PCM |
| ☐ | N873FE | Cessna 208B Caravan I | 208B0202 | | op by CFS |
| ☐ | N874FE | Cessna 208B Caravan I | 208B0205 | | op by MTN |
| ☐ | N875FE | Cessna 208B Caravan I | 208B0206 | | op by CFS |
| ☐ | N876FE | Cessna 208B Caravan I | 208B0207 | | op by CFS |
| ☐ | N877FE | Cessna 208B Caravan I | 208B0232 | | op by CPT |
| ☐ | N878FE | Cessna 208B Caravan I | 208B0211 | | op by MTN |
| ☐ | N879FE | Cessna 208B Caravan I | 208B0213 | | op by PCM |
| ☐ | N880FE | Cessna 208B Caravan I | 208B0215 | | op by CFS |
| ☐ | N881FE | Cessna 208B Caravan I | 208B0204 | | op by MTN |
| ☐ | N882FE | Cessna 208B Caravan I | 208B0208 | | op by CFS |
| ☐ | N884FE | Cessna 208B Caravan I | 208B0233 | | op by IRO |
| ☐ | N885FE | Cessna 208B Caravan I | 208B0185 | | op by CPT |
| ☐ | N886FE | Cessna 208B Caravan I | 208B0190 | | op by PCM |
| ☐ | N887FE | Cessna 208B Caravan I | 208B0216 | | op by MTN |
| ☐ | N888FE | Cessna 208B Caravan I | 208B0217 | | op by WIG |
| ☐ | N889FE | Cessna 208B Caravan I | 208B0218 | | op by BVN |
| ☐ | N890FE | Cessna 208B Caravan I | 208B0219 | | op by CPT |
| ☐ | N891FE | Cessna 208B Caravan I | 208B0221 | | op by PCM |
| ☐ | N894FE | Cessna 208B Caravan I | 208B0224 | | op by BVN |
| ☐ | N895FE | Cessna 208B Caravan I | 208B0015 | ex C-FEXG | op by CFS |
| ☐ | N897FE | Cessna 208B Caravan I | 208B0227 | | op by CFS |
| ☐ | N898FE | Cessna 208B Caravan I | 208B0228 | | op by WIG |
| ☐ | N899FE | Cessna 208B Caravan I | 208B0235 | | op by CFS |
| ☐ | N900FE | Cessna 208B Caravan I | 208B0054 | ex (F-GJHL) | op by BVN |
| ☐ | N901FE | Cessna 208B Caravan I | 208B0001 | ex N9767F | op by WIG |
| ☐ | N902FE | Cessna 208B Caravan I | 208B0002 | | op by BVN |
| ☐ | N903FE | Cessna 208B Caravan I | 208B0003 | | op by CPT |
| ☐ | N904FE | Cessna 208B Caravan I | 208B0004 | | op by CPT |
| ☐ | N905FE | Cessna 208B Caravan I | 208B0005 | | op by MTN |
| ☐ | N906FE | Cessna 208B Caravan I | 208B0006 | | op by IRO |
| ☐ | N907FE | Cessna 208B Caravan I | 208B0007 | | op by IRO |
| ☐ | N908FE | Cessna 208B Caravan I | 208B0008 | | op by PCM |
| ☐ | N909FE | Cessna 208B Caravan I | 208B0009 | | op by WIG |
| ☐ | N910FE | Cessna 208B Caravan I | 208B0010 | | op by CPT |
| ☐ | N911FE | Cessna 208B Caravan I | 208B0011 | | op by WIG |
| ☐ | N912FE | Cessna 208B Caravan I | 208B0012 | | op by BVN |
| ☐ | N914FE | Cessna 208B Caravan I | 208B0014 | | op by IRO |
| ☐ | N916FE | Cessna 208B Caravan I | 208B0016 | | op by CPT |
| ☐ | N917FE | Cessna 208B Caravan I | 208B0017 | | op by MTN |
| ☐ | N918FE | Cessna 208B Caravan I | 208B0018 | | op by CFS |
| ☐ | N919FE | Cessna 208B Caravan I | 208B0019 | | op by WIG |
| ☐ | N920FE | Cessna 208B Caravan I | 208B0020 | | op by PCM |
| ☐ | N921FE | Cessna 208B Caravan I | 208B0021 | | op by MTN |
| ☐ | N922FE | Cessna 208B Caravan I | 208B0022 | | op by BVN |
| ☐ | N923FE | Cessna 208B Caravan I | 208B0023 | | op by IRO |
| ☐ | N924FE | Cessna 208B Caravan I | 208B0024 | | op by CPT |
| ☐ | N925FE | Cessna 208B Caravan I | 208B0025 | | op by IRO |
| ☐ | N926FE | Cessna 208B Caravan I | 208B0026 | | op by CPT |
| ☐ | N927FE | Cessna 208B Caravan I | 208B0027 | | op by IRO |
| ☐ | N928FE | Cessna 208B Caravan I | 208B0028 | | op by BVN |
| ☐ | N929FE | Cessna 208B Caravan I | 208B0029 | | op by BVN |
| ☐ | N930FE | Cessna 208B Caravan I | 208B0030 | | op by PCM |
| ☐ | N931FE | Cessna 208B Caravan I | 208B0031 | | op by WIG |
| ☐ | N933FE | Cessna 208B Caravan I | 208B0033 | | op by CPT |
| ☐ | N934FE | Cessna 208B Caravan I | 208B0034 | | op by BVN |
| ☐ | N935FE | Cessna 208B Caravan I | 208B0035 | | op by WIG |
| ☐ | N936FE | Cessna 208B Caravan I | 208B0036 | | op by CPT |
| ☐ | N937FE | Cessna 208B Caravan I | 208B0037 | | op by WIG |
| ☐ | N938FE | Cessna 208B Caravan I | 208B0038 | | op by MTN |
| ☐ | N939FE | Cessna 208B Caravan I | 208B0180 | | op by BVN |
| ☐ | N940FE | Cessna 208B Caravan I | 208B0040 | | op by CFS |
| ☐ | N943FE | Cessna 208B Caravan I | 208B0043 | | op by MTN |
| ☐ | N946FE | Cessna 208B Caravan I | 208B0048 | ex (N948FE) | op by IRO |
| ☐ | N947FE | Cessna 208B Caravan I | 208B0050 | ex (N950FE) | op by WIG |
| ☐ | N950FE | Cessna 208B Caravan I | 208B0056 | ex (N956FE) | op by BVN |
| ☐ | N952FE | Cessna 208B Caravan I | 208B0060 | ex (N960FE) | op by CPT |
| ☐ | N953FE | Cessna 208B Caravan I | 208B0062 | ex (N962FE) | op by CFS |
| ☐ | N954FE | Cessna 208B Caravan I | 208B0064 | ex (N964FE) | op by IRO |
| ☐ | N955FE | Cessna 208B Caravan I | 208B0066 | ex (N966FE) | op by MTN |
| ☐ | N956FE | Cessna 208B Caravan I | 208B0068 | ex (N968FE) | op by CFS |
| ☐ | N957FE | Cessna 208B Caravan I | 208B0070 | ex (N970FE) | op by BVN |
| ☐ | N958FE | Cessna 208B Caravan I | 208B0071 | | op by WIG |
| ☐ | N959FE | Cessna 208B Caravan I | 208B0073 | | op by WIG |

| | | | | | |
|---|---|---|---|---|---|
| ☐ | N960FE | Cessna 208B Caravan I | 208B0075 | | op by CFS |
| ☐ | N961FE | Cessna 208B Caravan I | 208B0077 | | op by BVN |
| ☐ | N962FE | Cessna 208B Caravan I | 208B0078 | | op by MTN |
| ☐ | N963FE | Cessna 208B Caravan I | 208B0080 | | op by WIG |
| ☐ | N964FE | Cessna 208B Caravan I | 208B0083 | | op by CPT |
| ☐ | N965FE | Cessna 208B Caravan I | 208B0084 | | op by CFS |
| ☐ | N966FE | Cessna 208B Caravan I | 208B0086 | | op by WIG |
| ☐ | N967FE | Cessna 208B Caravan I | 208B0088 | | op by MTN |
| ☐ | N968FE | Cessna 208B Caravan I | 208B0090 | | op by PCM |
| ☐ | N969FE | Cessna 208B Caravan I | 208B0092 | | op by PCM |
| ☐ | N970FE | Cessna 208B Caravan I | 208B0093 | | op by BVN |
| ☐ | N971FE | Cessna 208B Caravan I | 208B0094 | | op by CPT |
| ☐ | N972FE | Cessna 208B Caravan I | 208B0096 | | op by CPT |
| ☐ | N973FE | Cessna 208B Caravan I | 208B0098 | | op by MTN |
| ☐ | N975FE | Cessna 208B Caravan I | 208B0101 | | op by MTN |
| ☐ | N976FE | Cessna 208B Caravan I | 208B0103 | | op by CFS |
| ☐ | N977FE | Cessna 208B Caravan I | 208B0104 | | op by CPT |
| ☐ | N979FE | Cessna 208B Caravan I | 208B0106 | | op by MTN |
| ☐ | N980FE | Cessna 208B Caravan I | 208B0108 | | op by CPT |
| ☐ | N981FE | Cessna 208B Caravan I | 208B0110 | | op by WIG |
| ☐ | N983FE | Cessna 208B Caravan I | 208B0113 | | op by CFS |
| ☐ | N984FE | Cessna 208B Caravan I | 208B0115 | | op by PCM |
| ☐ | N985FE | Cessna 208B Caravan I | 208B0117 | | op by PCM |
| ☐ | N986FE | Cessna 208B Caravan I | 208B0194 | | op by IRO |
| ☐ | N987FE | Cessna 208B Caravan I | 208B0201 | | op by PCM |
| ☐ | N989FE | Cessna 208B Caravan I | 208B0124 | | op by WIG |
| ☐ | N990FE | Cessna 208B Caravan I | 208B0125 | | op by CPT |
| ☐ | N990FX | Cessna 208B Caravan I | 208B2276 | | ♦ |
| ☐ | N991FE | Cessna 208B Caravan I | 208B0127 | | op by CPT |
| ☐ | N991FX | Cessna 208B Caravan I | 208B2279 | | ♦ |
| ☐ | N992FE | Cessna 208B Caravan I | 208B0128 | | op by CFS |
| ☐ | N992FX | Cessna 208B Caravan I | 208B2288 | | ♦ |
| ☐ | N993FE | Cessna 208B Caravan I | 208B0130 | | op by IRO |
| ☐ | N993FX | Cessna 208B Caravan i | 208B2289 | | ♦ |
| ☐ | N994FE | Cessna 208B Caravan I | 208B0132 | | op by BVN |
| ☐ | N994FX | Cessna 208B Caravan I | 208B2315 | | ♦ |
| ☐ | N995FE | Cessna 208B Caravan I | 208B0133 | | op by PCM |
| ☐ | N996FE | Cessna 208B Caravan I | 208B0135 | | op by WIG |
| ☐ | N997FE | Cessna 208B Caravan I | 208B0197 | | op by CPT |
| ☐ | N998FE | Cessna 208B Caravan I | 208B0139 | | op by WIG |
| ☐ | N999FE | Cessna 208B Caravan I | 208B0231 | | op by MTN |
| | | | | | |
| ☐ | N302FE | McDonnell-Douglas MD-10-30CF | 46801/103 | ex N102TV | Cori |
| ☐ | N303FE | McDonnell-Douglas MD-10-30CF | 46802/110 | ex N103TV | Amanda |
| ☐ | N304FE | McDonnell-Douglas MD-10-30CF | 46992/257 | ex EC-DSF | Claire |
| ☐ | N306FE | McDonnell-Douglas MD-10-30F | 48287/409 | | John |
| ☐ | N307FE | McDonnell-Douglas MD-10-30F | 48291/412 | | Erin Lee |
| ☐ | N308FE | McDonnell-Douglas MD-10-30F | 48297/416 | | Ann |
| ☐ | N311FE | McDonnell-Douglas MD-10-30CF | 46871/219 | ex LN-RKB | Abraham |
| ☐ | N312FE | McDonnell-Douglas MD-10-30CF | 48300/433 | | Angela |
| ☐ | N313FE | McDonnell-Douglas MD-10-30F | 48311/440 | | Ameyali |
| ☐ | N314FE | McDonnell-Douglas MD-10-30F | 48312/442 | | Caitlan |
| ☐ | N315FE | McDonnell-Douglas MD-10-30F | 48313/443 | | Kevin |
| ☐ | N316FE | McDonnell-Douglas MD-10-30F | 48314/444 | | Brandon |
| ☐ | N317FE | McDonnell-Douglas MD-10-30CF | 46835/277 | ex N106WA | Madison |
| ☐ | N318FE | McDonnell-Douglas MD-10-30CF | 46837/282 | ex N108WA | Mason |
| ☐ | N319FE | McDonnell-Douglas MD-10-30CF | 47820/317 | ex N112WA | Sheridan |
| ☐ | N320FE | McDonnell-Douglas MD-10-30F | 47835/326 | ex OO-SLD | Maura |
| ☐ | N321FE | McDonnell-Douglas MD-10-30F | 47836/330 | ex OO-SLE | Athena |
| ☐ | N357FE | McDonnell-Douglas MD-10-10F | 46939/203 | ex N1849U | Channelle |
| ☐ | N358FE | McDonnell-Douglas MD-10-10F | 46633/297 | ex N1839U | Kurt |
| ☐ | N359FE | McDonnell-Douglas MD-10-10F | 46635/307 | ex N1842U | Michaela |
| ☐ | N360FE | McDonnell-Douglas MD-10-10F | 46636/309 | ex N1843U | Phillip |
| ☐ | N361FE | McDonnell-Douglas MD-10-10F | 48260/344 | ex N1844U | Lucas |
| ☐ | N362FE | McDonnell-Douglas MD-10-10F | 48261/347 | ex N1845U | Cole |
| ☐ | N363FE | McDonnell-Douglas MD-10-10F | 48263/353 | ex N1847U | Carter |
| ☐ | N365FE | McDonnell-Douglas MD-10-10F | 46601/6 | ex N1802U | Joey |
| ☐ | N366FE | McDonnell-Douglas MD-10-10F | 46602/8 | ex N1803U | Gretchen |
| ☐ | N367FE | McDonnell-Douglas MD-10-10F | 46605/15 | ex N1806U | Lathan |
| ☐ | N368FE | McDonnell-Douglas MD-10-10F | 46606/17 | ex N1807U | Cindy |
| ☐ | N369FE | McDonnell-Douglas MD-10-10F | 46607/25 | ex N1808U | Jessie | [VCV] |
| ☐ | N370FE | McDonnell-Douglas MD-10-10F | 46608/26 | ex N1809U | Jay |
| ☐ | N371FE | McDonnell-Douglas MD-10-10F | 46609/27 | ex N1810U | Vincent |
| ☐ | N372FE | McDonnell-Douglas MD-10-10F | 46610/32 | ex N1811U | Gus |
| ☐ | N373FE | McDonnell-Douglas MD-10-10F | 46611/35 | ex N1812U | |
| ☐ | N374FE | McDonnell-Douglas MD-10-10F | 46612/39 | ex N1813U | Brittnie | [VCV] |
| ☐ | N375FE | McDonnell-Douglas MD-10-10F | 46613/42 | ex N1814U | |
| ☐ | N377FE | McDonnell-Douglas MD-10-10F | 47965/59 | ex N1833U | Shelby |
| ☐ | N381FE | McDonnell-Douglas MD-10-10F | 46615/76 | ex N1816U | Duval |
| ☐ | N383FE | McDonnell-Douglas MD-10-10F | 46616/86 | ex N1817U | Cody |
| ☐ | N384FE | McDonnell-Douglas MD-10-10F | 46617/89 | ex N1818U | Kelly |
| ☐ | N385FE | McDonnell-Douglas MD-10-10F | 46619/119 | ex N1820U | Lindsay |

| | Registration | Type | c/n | ex | Name | Notes |
|---|---|---|---|---|---|---|
| ☐ | N386FE | McDonnell-Douglas MD-10-10F | 46620/138 | ex N1821U | TJ | first MD-10 conversion |
| ☐ | N387FE | McDonnell-Douglas MD-10-10F | 46621/140 | ex N1822U | Joel | |
| ☐ | N388FE | McDonnell-Douglas MD-10-10F | 46622/144 | ex N1823U | Izzul | |
| ☐ | N389FE | McDonnell-Douglas MD-10-10F | 46623/154 | ex N1824U | Kayla | |
| ☐ | N390FE | McDonnell-Douglas MD-10-10F | 46624/155 | ex N1825U | Rasik | |
| ☐ | N392FE | McDonnell-Douglas MD-10-10F | 46626/198 | ex N1827U | Axton | |
| ☐ | N394FE | McDonnell-Douglas MD-10-10F | 46628/207 | ex N1829U | Parker | |
| ☐ | N395FE | McDonnell-Douglas MD-10-10F | 46629/208 | ex N1830U | Audreon | |
| ☐ | N396FE | McDonnell-Douglas MD-10-10F | 46630/209 | ex N1831U | Adrienne | |
| ☐ | N397FE | McDonnell-Douglas MD-10-10F | 46631/210 | ex N1832U | Stefani | |
| ☐ | N398FE | McDonnell-Douglas MD-10-10F | 46634/298 | ex N1841U | Kacie | |
| ☐ | N399FE | McDonnell-Douglas MD-10-10F | 48262/351 | ex N1846U | Tariq | |
| ☐ | N550FE | McDonnell-Douglas MD-10-10F | 46521/55 | ex N121AA | Adam | |
| ☐ | N554FE | McDonnell-Douglas MD-10-10F | 46708/62 | ex N153AA | | |
| ☐ | N556FE | McDonnell-Douglas MD-10-10F | 46710/70 | ex N160AA | Kirsten | |
| ☐ | N559FE | McDonnell-Douglas MD-10-10F | 46930/112 | ex N167AA | Francesca | |
| ☐ | N560FE | McDonnell-Douglas MD-10-10F | 46938/153 | ex N168AA | Deonna | |
| ☐ | N562FE | McDonnell-Douglas MD-10-10F | 46947/247 | ex N126AA | Janai | |
| ☐ | N563FE | McDonnell-Douglas MD-10-10F | 46948/249 | ex N127AA | Kristine | |
| ☐ | N564FE | McDonnell-Douglas MD-10-10F | 46984/250 | ex N128AA | Ava | |
| ☐ | N566FE | McDonnell-Douglas MD-10-10F | 46989/271 | ex N130AA | Ben | |
| ☐ | N567FE | McDonnell-Douglas MD-10-10F | 46994/273 | ex N131AA | | |
| ☐ | N569FE | McDonnell-Douglas MD-10-10F | 47828/319 | ex N133AA | Stas | |
| ☐ | N570FE | McDonnell-Douglas MD-10-10F | 47829/321 | ex N134AA | Joelle | |
| ☐ | N571FE | McDonnell-Douglas MD-10-10F | 47830/323 | ex N135AA | Ella | |
| ☐ | N10060 | McDonnell-Douglas MD-10-10F | 46970/269 | ex N581LF | Haylee | |
| ☐ | N40061 | McDonnell-Douglas MD-10-10F | 46973/272 | ex N591LF | Garrett | |
| ☐ | N68049 | McDonnell-Douglas MD-10-10CF | 47803/139 | | Dusty | |
| ☐ | N68050 | McDonnell-Douglas MD-10-10CF | 47804/142 | | Merideth Allison | |
| ☐ | N68051 | McDonnell-Douglas MD-10-10CF | 47805/145 | | Todd | |
| ☐ | N68052 | McDonnell-Douglas MD-10-10CF | 47806/148 | | Brock | |
| ☐ | N68053 | McDonnell-Douglas MD-10-10CF | 47807/173 | | Chayne | |
| ☐ | N68054 | McDonnell-Douglas MD-10-10CF | 47808/177 | | Eren | |
| ☐ | N68057 | McDonnell-Douglas MD-10-10CF | 48264/379 | ex N1848U | Nelson | |
| ☐ | N68058 | McDonnell-Douglas MD-10-10F | 46705/33 | ex TC-JAU | Lauren | [VCV] |
| ☐ | N68059 | McDonnell-Douglas MD-10-10F | 46907/78 | ex TC-JAY | Mary Rea | |
| | | | | | | |
| ☐ | N521FE | McDonnell-Douglas MD-11F | 48478/514 | ex N807DE | | |
| ☐ | N522FE | McDonnell-Douglas MD-11F | 48476/510 | ex N805DE | | |
| ☐ | N523FE | McDonnell-Douglas MD-11F | 48479/536 | ex N808DE | | |
| ☐ | N524FE | McDonnell-Douglas MD-11F | 48480/538 | ex N809DE | | |
| ☐ | N525FE | McDonnell-Douglas MD-11F | 48565/542 | ex N810DE | | |
| ☐ | N527FE | McDonnell-Douglas MD-11F | 48601/562 | ex N812DE | | |
| ☐ | N528FE | McDonnell-Douglas MD-11F | 48623/605 | ex N814DE | | |
| ☐ | N529FE | McDonnell-Douglas MD-11F | 48624/622 | ex N815DE | | |
| ☐ | N572FE | McDonnell-Douglas MD-11ER | 48755/613 | ex N730BC | | |
| ☐ | N573FE | McDonnell-Douglas MD-11BCF | 48769/603 | ex N746BC | | |
| ☐ | N574FE | McDonnell-Douglas MD-11F | 48499/486 | ex N499HE | | |
| ☐ | N575FE | McDonnell-Douglas MD-11F | 48500/493 | ex N485LS | Sonni | |
| ☐ | N576FE | McDonnell-Douglas MD-11F | 48501/513 | ex N501FR | Keeley | |
| ☐ | N577FE | McDonnell-Douglas MD-11F | 48469/519 | ex B-18172 | Tobias | |
| ☐ | N578FE | McDonnell-Douglas MD-11F | 48458/449 | ex N489GX | Stephen | |
| ☐ | N579FE | McDonnell-Douglas MD-11F | 48470/546 | ex B-18151 | Nash | |
| ☐ | N580FE | McDonnell-Douglas MD-11F | 48471/558 | ex B-18152 | Ashton | |
| ☐ | N582FE | McDonnell-Douglas MD-11F | 48420/451 | ex N1751A | Jamie | |
| ☐ | N583FE | McDonnell-Douglas MD-11F | 48421/452 | ex N1752K | Nnacy | |
| ☐ | N584FE | McDonnell-Douglas MD-11F | 48436/483 | ex N1768D | Jeffrey Wellington | |
| ☐ | N585FE | McDonnell-Douglas MD-11F | 48481/482 | ex N1759 | Katherine | |
| ☐ | N586FE | McDonnell-Douglas MD-11F | 48487/469 | ex N1753 | Dylan | |
| ☐ | N587FE | McDonnell-Douglas MD-11F | 48489/492 | ex N1754 | Jeanno | |
| ☐ | N588FE | McDonnell-Douglas MD-11F | 48490/499 | ex N1755 | Kendra | |
| ☐ | N589FE | McDonnell-Douglas MD-11F | 48491/503 | ex N1756 | Shaun | |
| ☐ | N590FE | McDonnell-Douglas MD-11F | 48505/462 | ex N1757A | Stan | |
| ☐ | N591FE | McDonnell-Douglas MD-11F | 48527/504 | ex N1758B | Giovanni | |
| ☐ | N592FE | McDonnell-Douglas MD-11F | 48550/526 | ex N1760A | Joshua | |
| ☐ | N593FE | McDonnell-Douglas MD-11F | 48551/527 | ex N1761R | Harrison | |
| ☐ | N594FE | McDonnell-Douglas MD-11F | 48552/530 | ex N1762B | Derek | |
| ☐ | N595FE | McDonnell-Douglas MD-11F | 48553/531 | ex N1763 | Avery | |
| ☐ | N596FE | McDonnell-Douglas MD-11F | 48554/535 | ex N1764B | Peyton | |
| ☐ | N597FE | McDonnell-Douglas MD-11F | 48596/537 | ex N1765B | Corbin | |
| ☐ | N598FE | McDonnell-Douglas MD-11F | 48597/540 | ex N1766A | Kate | |
| ☐ | N599FE | McDonnell-Douglas MD-11F | 48598/550 | ex N1767A | Mariana | |
| ☐ | N601FE | McDonnell-Douglas MD-11F | 48401/447 | ex N111MD | Jim Riedmeyer | |
| ☐ | N602FE | McDonnell-Douglas MD-11F | 48402/448 | ex N211MD | Malcolm Baldrige 1990 | |
| ☐ | N603FE | McDonnell-Douglas MD-11F | 48459/470 | | Elizabeth | |
| ☐ | N604FE | McDonnell-Douglas MD-11F | 48460/497 | | Hollis | |
| ☐ | N605FE | McDonnell-Douglas MD-11F | 48514/515 | | April Star | |
| ☐ | N606FE | McDonnell-Douglas MD-11F | 48602/549 | | Charles & Teresa | |
| ☐ | N607FE | McDonnell-Douglas MD-11F | 48547/517 | | Christina | |
| ☐ | N608FE | McDonnell-Douglas MD-11F | 48548/521 | | Colton | |
| ☐ | N609FE | McDonnell-Douglas MD-11F | 48549/545 | | Scott | |
| ☐ | N610FE | McDonnell-Douglas MD-11F | 48603/551 | | Marisa | |

| | | | | | |
|---|---|---|---|---|---|
| ☐ N612FE | McDonnell-Douglas MD-11F | 48605/555 | | Alyssa | |
| ☐ N613FE | McDonnell-Douglas MD-11F | 48749/598 | | Krista | |
| ☐ N614FE | McDonnell-Douglas MD-11F | 48528/507 | | Cristy | |
| ☐ N615FE | McDonnell-Douglas MD-11F | 48767/602 | | Max | |
| ☐ N616FE | McDonnell-Douglas MD-11F | 48747/594 | | Shanita | |
| ☐ N617FE | McDonnell-Douglas MD-11F | 48748/595 | | Travis | |
| ☐ N618FE | McDonnell-Douglas MD-11F | 48754/604 | | Justin | |
| ☐ N619FE | McDonnell-Douglas MD-11F | 48770/607 | | Lyndon | |
| ☐ N620FE | McDonnell-Douglas MD-11F | 48791/635 | | Grady | |
| ☐ N621FE | McDonnell-Douglas MD-11F | 48792/636 | | Connor | |
| ☐ N623FE | McDonnell-Douglas MD-11F | 48794/638 | | Meghan | |
| ☐ N624FE | McDonnell-Douglas MD-11F | 48443/458 | ex HB-IWA | Corinne | |
| ☐ N625FE | McDonnell-Douglas MD-11BCF | 48753/608 | ex N785BC | | |
| ☐ N628FE | McDonnell-Douglas MD-11F | 48447/464 | ex HB-IWE | Noah | |
| ☐ N631FE | McDonnell-Douglas MD-11F | 48454/477 | ex HB-IWI | | |
| ☐ N642FE | McDonnell-Douglas MD-11F | 48485/502 | ex 9M-TGR | | |
| ☐ N643FE | McDonnell-Douglas MD-11F | 48486/509 | ex 9M-TGS | | ♦ |
| ☐ N644FE | McDonnell-Douglas MD-11F | 48444/459 | ex 9M-TGP | | ♦ |
| ☐ N645FE | McDonnell-Douglas MD-11F | 48446/463 | ex 9M-TGQ | | ♦ |

## FLIGHT ALASKA     Tundra (4Y/UYA)     Dillingham-Memorial, AK (DLG)

| | | | |
|---|---|---|---|
| ☐ N755AB | Cessna 207A Stationair 8 II | 20700622 | ex HP-916 |
| ☐ N1704U | Cessna 207 Skywagon | 20700304 | |
| ☐ N6470H | Cessna 207A Stationair 7 II | 20700534 | |
| ☐ N7336U | Cessna 207A Skywagon | 20700405 | |

## FLIGHT INTERNATIONAL AVIATION     Flight International (FNT)

### Newport News-Williamsburg Intl, VA (PHF)

| | | | |
|---|---|---|---|
| ☐ N10FN | Learjet 36 | 36-015 | ex N14CF |
| ☐ N12FN | Learjet 36 | 36-016 | ex N616DJ |
| ☐ N16FN | Learjet 36A | 36A-027 | ex N27MJ |
| ☐ N26FN | Learjet 36 | 36-011 | ex N26MJ |
| ☐ N39FN | Learjet 35 | 35-006 | ex N39DM |
| ☐ N50FN | Learjet 35A | 35A-070 | ex N543PA |
| ☐ N51FN | Learjet 35A | 35A-069 | ex N48GP |
| ☐ N52FN | Learjet 35A | 35A-424 | ex N508GP |
| ☐ N54FN | Learjet 25C | 25C-083 | ex N200MH |
| ☐ N55FN | Learjet 35A | 35A-202 | ex D-CGPD |
| ☐ N83FN | Learjet 36 | 36-007 | ex N83DM |
| ☐ N84FN | Learjet 36 | 36-002 | ex N84DM |
| ☐ N96FN | Learjet 35A | 35A-186 | ex (N317JD) |
| ☐ N118FN | Learjet 35A | 35A-118 | ex N88JA |
| ☐ N710GS | Learjet 35 | 35-032 | ex N711MA |
| | | | |
| ☐ N175SW | Swearingen SA.227AC Metro III | AC-621 | |
| ☐ N782C | Swearingen SA.227AC Metro III | AC-525 | ex N31078 |
| ☐ N26974 | Swearingen SA.227AC Metro III | AC-664 | |
| | | | |
| ☐ N707ML | Piper PA-31T Cheyenne | 31T-7520017 | ex N502RH |

## FLORIDA AIR CARGO     Miami-Opa Locka, FL (OPF)

| | | | | |
|---|---|---|---|---|
| ☐ N15MA | Douglas DC-3 | 19286 | ex F-WSGV | no titles |

## FLORIDA AIR TRANSPORT     Fort Lauderdale-Executive, FL (FXE)

| | | | | |
|---|---|---|---|---|
| ☐ N70BF | Douglas C-118B | 43720/373 | ex XA-SCZ | dam Jun07 |
| ☐ N381AA | Douglas DC-7BF | 44921/666 | ex N101LM | jt ops with Turks Air [OPF] |
| ☐ N9015Q | Douglas C-54D | 22178 | | ♦ |

## FLORIDA COASTAL AIRLINES     Florida Coastal (PA/FCL)     Fort Pierce-St Lucie, FL (FPR)

| | | | |
|---|---|---|---|
| ☐ N77FC | Cessna 402C II | 402C0044 | ex N440RC |
| ☐ N78FC | Cessna 402C II | 402C0496 | ex C-FFCH |
| ☐ N567JS | Cessna 402B II | 402B1090 | ex N87216 |
| ☐ N856D | Cessna 402B II | 402B1339 | ex N40EM |

## FLORIDA GULF AIRLINES

| | | | |
|---|---|---|---|
| ☐ N144ZV | Beech 1900D | UE-144 | ops for US Airways Express♦ |

## FLORIDA WEST INTERNATIONAL AIRLINES     Flo West (RF/FWL)     Miami-Intl, FL (MIA)

| | | | | |
|---|---|---|---|---|
| ☐ N316LA | Boeing 767-316F/W | 30842/860 | | <LCO |
| ☐ N422LA | Boeing 767-346F/W | 35818/960 | ex JA633J | |

## FOCUS AIR     Focus (F2/FKS)     Fort Lauderdale-Hollywood Intl, FL (FLL)

Focus Air is a subsidiary of Omega Air Holdings

### 40 MILE AIR — Mile-Air (Q5/MLA) — Tok-Junction, AK (TKJ)

| | Reg | Type | Serial | ex | Notes |
|---|---|---|---|---|---|
| ☐ | N87TS | Piper PA-31 Turbo Navajo B | 31-7300969 | ex N4426Y | |
| ☐ | N207DG | Cessna T207 Turbo Skywagon | 20700070 | ex N91902 | |
| ☐ | N734GW | Cessna U206G Stationair 6 | U20604832 | | |
| ☐ | N1541F | Cessna 185D Skywagon | 185-0896 | | |
| ☐ | N3125N | de Havilland DHC-3 Turbo Otter | 394 | | ♦ |
| ☐ | N4978C | Cessna U206G Stationair | U20603870 | | ♦ |

### FOUR STAR AIR CARGO — Four Star (HK/FSC) — St Thomas-Cyril E King, VI (STT)

| | Reg | Type | Serial | ex | Notes |
|---|---|---|---|---|---|
| ☐ | N131FS | Douglas DC-3 | 16172/32920 | ex N67PA | Frtr |
| ☐ | N132FS | Douglas DC-3 | 14333/25778 | ex N333EF | Frtr |
| ☐ | N133FS | Douglas DC-3 | 15757/27202 | ex N53NA | Frtr |
| ☐ | N135FS | Douglas DC-3 | 20063 | ex NC63107 | Frtr |
| ☐ | N138FS | Douglas DC-3 | 9967 | ex N303SF | Frtr |

### FREEDOM AIR — Freedom (FP/FRE) — Guam, GU (GUM)

| | Reg | Type | Serial | ex | Notes |
|---|---|---|---|---|---|
| ☐ | N4060R | Piper PA-32-300 Cherokee Six C | 32-40366 | | ♦ |
| ☐ | N4168R | Piper PA-32-300 Cherokee Six C | 32-40484 | | |
| ☐ | N4171R | Piper PA-32-300 Cherokee Six C | 32-40504 | | |
| ☐ | N8628N | Piper PA-32-300 Cherokee Six | 32-7140021 | | |
| ☐ | N8938N | Piper PA-32-300 Cherokee Six C | 32-40736 | | |
| ☐ | N8969N | Piper PA-32-300 Cherokee Six | 32-40769 | | |
| ☐ | N44FA | Cessna 207A Stationair 8 | 20700659 | ex N75975 | |
| ☐ | N72FA | Piper PA-31 Navajo C | 31-7812023 | ex JA5278 | |
| ☐ | N74NF | Short SD.3-60 | SH3721 | ex N121PC | |
| ☐ | N131FA | Piper PA-23-250 Aztec D | 27-4097 | ex N234SP | |
| ☐ | N330FA | Short SD.3-30 | SH3112 | ex N188LM | |
| ☐ | N2843F | Short SD.3-60 | SH3739 | ex SX-BFW | |
| ☐ | N7576C | Cessna U206G Stationair | U20606375 | | ♦ |

### FREEDOM AIRLINES — (FRL) — New York-JFK, NY/Orlando, FL (JFK/MCO)

A division of Mesa Airlines; provides Delta Connection services from Orlando-MCO, FL and New York, NY

### FREIGHT RUNNERS EXPRESS — Freight Runners (FRG) — Milwaukee-General Mitchell Intl, WI (MKE)

| | Reg | Type | Serial | ex | Notes |
|---|---|---|---|---|---|
| ☐ | N109CZ | Beech 99 | U-109 | ex N2880A | Frtr♦ |
| ☐ | N199CZ | Beech 99 | U-30 | ex N3RP | Frtr |
| ☐ | N299CZ | Beech 99 | U-74 | ex C-FCVJ | Frtr |
| ☐ | N399CZ | Beech 99 | U-91 | ex N195WA | Frtr |
| ☐ | N499CZ | Beech 99A | U-81 | ex N36AK | Frtr |
| ☐ | N599CZ | Beech 99A | U-89 | ex 5Y-BJW | Frtr |
| ☐ | N699CZ | Beech 99 | U-10 | ex N99NN | Frtr♦ |
| ☐ | N799CZ | Beech 99 | U-68 | ex N196WA | Frtr |
| ☐ | N899CZ | Beech 99A | U-96 | ex N199CA | Frtr |
| ☐ | N999CZ | Beech 99A | U-116 | ex C-GZAM | |
| ☐ | N75GB | Cessna 402B | 402B0912 | | |
| ☐ | N191CZ | Beech 1900C | UB-59 | ex D-CARA | |
| ☐ | N192CZ | Beech 1900C-1 | UC-118 | ex N439QA | ♦ |
| ☐ | N402CZ | Cessna 402B | 402B0213 | | ♦ |
| ☐ | N727CA | Cessna 402A | 402A0102 | ex N7802Q | Frtr |
| ☐ | N7886Q | Cessna 402B | 402B0214 | | ♦ |
| ☐ | N1517U | Cessna 207 Skywagon | 20700117 | | Frtr |
| ☐ | N1518U | Cessna 207 Skywagon | 20700118 | | Frtr |
| ☐ | N4504B | Cessna 402B | 402B1370 | ex C-GSMN | |

### FRONTIER AIRLINES — Frontier Flight (F9/FFT) — Denver-International, CO (DEN)

| | Reg | Type | Serial | ex | Name |
|---|---|---|---|---|---|
| ☐ | N902FR | Airbus A319-111 | 1515 | ex D-AVYM | |
| ☐ | N904FR | Airbus A319-111 | 1579 | ex D-AVWS | Trumpeter Swan |
| ☐ | N905FR | Airbus A319-111 | 1583 | ex D-AVYC | Seal |
| ☐ | N906FR | Airbus A319-111 | 1684 | ex D-AVWK | Pronghorn Antelope |
| ☐ | N908FR | Airbus A319-111 | 1759 | ex D-AVYL | Blue Heron |
| ☐ | N910FR | Airbus A319-112 | 1781 | ex D-AVYK | Cougar |
| ☐ | N912FR | Airbus A319-111 | 1803 | ex D-AVWE | Red Fox Pup |
| ☐ | N914FR | Airbus A319-111 | 1841 | ex D-AVWT | Great Egret |
| ☐ | N918FR | Airbus A319-111 | 1943 | ex D-AVWH | Whitetail Deer |
| ☐ | N919FR | Airbus A319-111 | 1980 | ex D-AVYD | Ocelot |
| ☐ | N920FR | Airbus A319-111 | 1997 | ex D-AVYO | Coyote |
| ☐ | N921FR | Airbus A319-111 | 2010 | ex D-AVWO | Mountain Goat |
| ☐ | N922FR | Airbus A319-111 | 2012 | ex D-AVWR | Red Fox |
| ☐ | N923FR | Airbus A319-111 | 2019 | ex D-AVWV | Racoon |
| ☐ | N924FR | Airbus A319-111 | 2030 | ex D-AVYG | Polar Bear Cubs |
| ☐ | N925FR | Airbus A319-111 | 2103 | ex D-AVWH | Dall's Sheep |

| | | | | | |
|---|---|---|---|---|---|
| ☐ N926FR | Airbus A319-111 | 2198 | ex D-AVYD | Black-tailed Deer Fawn | |
| ☐ N927FR | Airbus A319-111 | 2209 | ex D-AVYL | Bottle-nosed Dolphin | |
| ☐ N928FR | Airbus A319-111 | 2236 | ex D-AVWK | Bobcat | |
| ☐ N929FR | Airbus A319-111 | 2240 | ex D-AVWP | Lynx | |
| ☐ N930FR | Airbus A319-111 | 2241 | ex D-AVWU | Cougar & cub | |
| ☐ N931FR | Airbus A319-111 | 2253 | ex D-AVYR | Bear cub | |
| ☐ N932FR | Airbus A319-111 | 2258 | ex D-AVYK | Bald Eagle | |
| ☐ N933FR | Airbus A319-111 | 2260 | ex D-AVYX | Hawk | |
| ☐ N934FR | Airbus A319-111 | 2287 | ex D-AVYU | Lynx pup | |
| ☐ N935FR | Airbus A319-111 | 2318 | ex D-AVYJ | Sea Otter | |
| ☐ N936FR | Airbus A319-111 | 2392 | ex D-AVYK | Walrus | |
| ☐ N937FR | Airbus A319-111 | 2400 | ex D-AVYU | Blue crowned conure | |
| ☐ N938FR | Airbus A319-111 | 2406 | ex D-AVWA | Arctic Fox | |
| ☐ N939FR | Airbus A319-111 | 2448 | ex D-AVWL | Emperor Penguins | |
| ☐ N940FR | Airbus A319-111 | 2465 | ex D-AVWW | Snow Hare | |
| ☐ N941FR | Airbus A319-112 | 2483 | ex D-AVYY | Gray Wolf | |
| ☐ N942FR | Airbus A319-111 | 2497 | ex D-AVYT | Bighorn | |
| ☐ N943FR | Airbus A319-112 | 2518 | ex D-AVWT | Fawn | |
| ☐ N945FR | Airbus A319-112 | 2751 | ex D-AVWD | Bull Moose | |
| ☐ N947FR | Airbus A319-111 | 2806 | ex D-AVYK | Leopard | |
| ☐ N948FR | Airbus A319-112 | 2836 | ex D-AVXR | Pelican | |
| ☐ N949FR | Airbus A319-112 | 2857 | ex D-AVYL | White Ermine | |
| ☐ N951FR | Airbus A319-112 | 4127 | ex N412MX | | |
| ☐ N952FR | Airbus A319-112 | 4204 | ex N204MX | | |
| ☐ N953FR | Airbus A319-112 | 4254 | ex N254MX | | |
| | | | | | |
| ☐ N201FR | Airbus A320-214 | 3389 | ex F-WWDQ | Elk | |
| ☐ N202FR | Airbus A320-214 | 3431 | ex F-WWDT | Named 'Colorado' | |
| ☐ N203FR | Airbus A320-214 | 1806 | ex D-ALTI | | |
| ☐ N204FR | Airbus A320-214 | 2325 | ex N270AV | | |
| ☐ N205FR | Airbus A320-214 | 4253 | ex D-AXAB | Killer Whale | |
| ☐ N206FR | Airbus A320-214 | 4272 | ex F-WWBX | Polar Bear | |
| ☐ N207FR | Airbus A320-214 | 4307 | ex D-AXAK | | |
| ☐ N208FR | Airbus A320-214 | 4562 | ex D-AUBX | | |
| ☐ N209FR | Airbus A320-214 | 4641 | ex D-AVVO | | |
| ☐ N210FR | Airbus A320-214 | 4668 | ex F-WWBJ | | ♦ |
| ☐ N211FR | Airbus A320-214 | 4688 | ex F-WWIU | | ♦ |
| ☐ N213FR | Airbus A320-214 | 4704 | ex F-WWDQ | | ♦ |
| ☐ N214FR | Airbus A320-214 | 4727 | ex F-WWDZ | | ♦ |
| ☐ N216FR | Airbus A320-214 | 4745 | ex F-WWIS | | ♦ |
| ☐ N218FR | Airbus A320-214 | 1615 | ex N261AV | | ♦ |
| ☐ | Airbus A320-214 | | ex | | o/o |
| ☐ | Airbus A320-214 | | ex | | o/o |
| | | | | | |
| ☐ N510LX | de Havilland DHC-8-402Q | 4186 | ex C-FNER | Bobcat | |
| ☐ N801FR | Airbus A318-111 | 1939 | ex D-AUAA | Grizzly Bear | |
| ☐ N802FR | Airbus A318-111 | 1991 | ex D-AUAB | Elk | |
| ☐ N803FR | Airbus A318-111 | 2017 | ex D-AUAC | Hare 'Bugs' | |
| ☐ N805FR | Airbus A318-111 | 1660 | ex D-AUAA | Great Grey Owl | |

### FRONTIER ALASKA | (2F/FTA) | Fairbanks, AK (FAI)

| | | | | | |
|---|---|---|---|---|---|
| ☐ N404GV | Beech 1900C-1 | UC-154 | ex N154YV | | ♦ |
| ☐ N121WV | Beech 1900C-1 | UC-078 | ex N503RH | | ♦ |
| ☐ N575A | Beech 1900C-1 | UC-083 | ex N80334 | | |
| ☐ N575Q | Beech 1900C-1 | UC-160 | ex N160AM | | |
| ☐ N575U | Beech 1900C-1 | UC-093 | ex NN93YV | | ♦ |
| ☐ N575X | Beech 1900C-1 | UC-149 | ex N149YV | | |
| ☐ N575Z | Beech 1900C-1 | UC-136 | ex N21483 | | |
| ☐ N15503 | Beech 1900C-1 | UC-072 | | | |
| | | | | | |
| ☐ N17GN | Cessna 207A Stationair 8 II | 20700693 | ex C-GDFK | | |
| ☐ N104K | Cessna 207 Skywagon | 20700122 | ex C-GUHZ | | |
| ☐ N327CT | Cessna 207A Stationair 7 II | 20700535 | ex N6475H | | |
| ☐ N747SQ | Cessna 207A Skywagon | 20700387 | ex N1787U | | |
| ☐ N1668U | Cessna 207 Skywagon | 20700268 | | | |
| ☐ N5277J | Cessna 207A Stationair 8 II | 20700772 | ex N9975M | | |
| ☐ N6207H | Cessna 207A Stationair 7 II | 20700551 | ex C-FSEE | | |
| ☐ N6314H | Cessna 207A Stationair 7 II | 20700478 | | | |
| ☐ N7320U | Cessna 207A Skywagon | 20700397 | | | |
| ☐ N7384U | Cessna 207A Stationair 7 II | 20700431 | | | |
| ☐ N7389U | Cessna 207A Stationair 7 II | 20700432 | | | |
| ☐ N9399M | Cessna 207A Stationair 8 II | 20700652 | ex VH-UAA | | |
| ☐ N9400M | Cessna 207A Stationair 8 II | 20700687 | | | |
| ☐ N9869M | Cessna 207A Stationair 8 II | 20700744 | | | |
| ☐ N9996M | Cessna 207A Stationair 8 II | 20700779 | | | |
| ☐ N73067 | Cessna 207A Stationair 7 II | 20700558 | | | |
| | | | | | |
| ☐ N28AN | Cessna 208B Caravan I | 208B0751 | | | ♦ |
| ☐ N126AR | Cessna 208B Caravan I | 208B1004 | ex N5163K | | |
| ☐ N169LJ | Cessna 208B Caravan I | 208B0599 | ex N169BJ | | |
| ☐ N208RL | Cessna 208B Caravan I | 208B0865 | ex N5206T | | ♦ |

| | | | |
|---|---|---|---|
| ☐ N208SD | Cessna 208B Caravan I | 208B0491 | ex (N610DK) | |
| ☐ N215MC | Cessna 208B Caravan I | 208B0730 | ex N12328 | |
| ☐ N303GV | Cessna 208B Caravan I | 208B0581 | | |
| ☐ N405GV | Cessna 208B Caravan I | 208B0892 | ex C-GWCA | ♦ |
| ☐ N407GV | Cessna 208B Caravan I | 208B0616 | ex N5262X | |
| ☐ N409GV | Cessna 208B Caravan i | 208B1110 | ex N208BR | ♦ |
| ☐ N410GV | Cessna 208B Caravan I | 208B0632 | ex N5264U | |
| ☐ N411GV | Cessna 208B Caravan I | 208B0672 | | |
| ☐ N715HE | Cessna 208B Caravan I | 208B0603 | ex N715HL | |
| ☐ N717PA | Cessna 208B Caravan I | 208B0804 | ex N12890 | |
| ☐ N883GV | Cessna 208B Caravan I | 208B0838 | ex N833FB | ♦ |
| ☐ N1232Y | Cessna 208B Caravan I | 208B0566 | ex N5246Z | |
| ☐ N1242Y | Cessna 208B Caravan I | 208B0939 | ex N124LA | ♦ |
| ☐ N1275N | Cessna 208B Caravan I | 208B0756 | | |
| ☐ N12373 | Cessna 208B Caravan I | 208B0697 | ex N5268Z | |
| | | | | |
| ☐ N44AC | Piper PA-31-350 Chieftain | 31-8052147 | ex N3590M | |
| ☐ N137CS | Piper PA-31-350 Chieftain | 31-8152137 | ex C-GVPP | |
| ☐ N200AK | Piper PA-31-350 Chieftain | 31-8052180 | ex N8529T | |
| ☐ N3516A | Piper PA-31-350 Chieftain | 31-7952106 | | |
| ☐ N3535F | Piper PA-31-350 Chieftain | 31-7952200 | | |
| ☐ N3536B | Piper PA-31-350 Chieftain | 31-7952205 | | |
| ☐ N4112K | Piper PA-31-350 T-1020 | 31-8353006 | | |
| ☐ N4301C | Piper PA-31-350 T-1020 | 31-8353001 | ex C-FKGX | |
| ☐ N4501B | Piper PA-31-350 Chieftain | 31-8052168 | | |
| ☐ N4585U | Piper PA-31-350 Chieftain | 31-8052198 | ex C-GPIJ | |
| | | | | |
| ☐ N190WA | Beech C99 | U-207 | ex N207CS | |
| ☐ N196WA | Beech C99 | U-179 | ex N995SB | |
| ☐ N406GV | Reims Cessna F406 Caravan II | F406-0049 | ex 9M-PMS | |
| ☐ N6590Y | Reims Cessna F406 Caravan II | F406-0052 | | |
| ☐ N6591R | Reims Cessna F406 Caravan II | F406-0054 | | |
| ☐ N9620M | Cessna 207A Stationair 8 | 20700711 | | |
| ☐ N73100 | Cessna 207A Stationair 7 | 20700559 | | |
| ☐ N91361 | Cessna 180H Skywagon | 18052045 | | |

Also trades as Hageland Aviation Services

## GALLUP FLYING SERVICE　　　　　　　　　　　　　　Gallup-Municipal, NM (GUP)

| | | | |
|---|---|---|---|
| ☐ N425RM | Cessna 425 | 425-0180 | | ♦ |
| ☐ N986GM | Cessna 414A Chancellor | 414A0089 | ex N612CB | |
| ☐ N6640C | Cessna 414A Chancellor | 414A0044 | | |
| ☐ N7909Q | Cessna T310Q | 310Q0620 | | |
| ☐ N8840K | Cessna 414A Chancellor | 414A0236 | | |
| ☐ N29359 | Cessna 210L Centurion II | 21059858 | | |
| ☐ N68149 | Cessna 414A Chancellor | 414A0642 | | |

## GB AIRLINK　　　　　　　　Island Tiger (GBX)　　Fort Lauderdale-Hollywood Intl, FL (FLL)

| | | | | |
|---|---|---|---|---|
| ☐ N30GB | Beech H-18 | BA-688 | | Frtr♦ |
| ☐ N80GB | Short SC.7 Skyvan 3 | SH1888 | ex LX-ABC | Frtr |
| ☐ N431DK | Beech C-45H | AF-458 | | Frtr♦ |
| ☐ N911E | Beech E-18S | BA-10 | ex N501J | Frtr |

## GO!　　　　　　　　　　　　　　(YV)　　　　　　　Honolulu-Intl, HI (HNL)

| | | | | |
|---|---|---|---|---|
| ☐ N27318 | Canadair CRJ-440LR | 7318 | ex C-FMLF | [PHX] |
| ☐ N77302 | Canadair CRJ-440LR | 7302 | ex C-FMND | |

## GO! EXPRESS　　　　　　　　　　　　　　　　　　Honolulu-Intl, HI (HNL)

Op by Mokulele Airlines

## GOJET AIRLINES　　　　　　Gateway (G7/GJS)　　　St Louis-Lambert Intl, MO (STL)

GoJet Airlines is a wholly owned subsidiary of Trans State Airlines and ops feeder services for United Express.

## GRAND CANYON AIRLINES　　　　　Canyon View (CVU)
### Grand Canyon-National Park, AZ/Valle-J Robidoux, AZ (GCN/VLE)

| | | | | |
|---|---|---|---|---|
| ☐ N72GC | de Havilland DHC-6 Twin Otter 300 | 264 | ex N264Z | |
| ☐ N74GC | de Havilland DHC-6 Twin Otter 300 | 559 | ex J6-AAK | |
| ☐ N171GC | de Havilland DHC-6 Twin Otter 300 | 406 | ex J8-VBR | |
| ☐ N173GC | de Havilland DHC-6 Twin Otter 300 | 295 | ex C-GLAZ | |
| ☐ N177GC | de Havilland DHC-6 Twin Otter 300 | 263 | ex N102AC | |
| ☐ N178GC | de Havilland DHC-6 Twin Otter 300 | 697 | ex TI-AZD | |
| ☐ N190GC | de Havilland DHC-6 Twin Otter 300 | 285 | ex TI-BDM | |
| ☐ N227SA | de Havilland DHC-6 Twin Otter300 | 517 | | ♦ |
| ☐ N241SA | de Havilland DHC-6 Twin Otter 300 | 556 | | ♦ |

## GRANT AVIATION

**(GV/GUN)** — *Emmonak, AK (EMK)*

| | | | | | |
|---|---|---|---|---|---|
| ☐ N8NZ | Cessna 207A Stationair 7 II | 20700421 | ex VH-XXL | | |
| ☐ N48CF | Cessna T207A Turbo Skywagon | 20700366 | | | |
| ☐ N207DF | Cessna 207A Stationair 8 II | 20700728 | ex ZK-EAL | | |
| ☐ N207EX | Cessna 207 Stationair | 20700100 | | | ◆ |
| ☐ N562CT | Cessna 207A Stationair 7 II | 20700487 | ex HI-562CT | | |
| ☐ N2162C | Cessna 207A Stationair 8 II | 20700575 | ex HI-346 | | |
| ☐ N9651M | Cessna 207A Stationair 8 II | 20700715 | | | |
| ☐ N9728M | Cessna 207A Stationair 8 II | 20700721 | | | |
| ☐ N9973M | Cessna 207A Stationair 8 II | 20700771 | | | |
| | | | | | |
| ☐ N28KE | Piper PA-31-350 Chieftain | 31-8152049 | ex C-GVSX | | ◆ |
| ☐ N77HV | Piper PA-31-350 Chieftain | 31-8152193 | ex C-GLCN | | |
| ☐ N78GA | Piper PA-31-350 Chieftain | 31-8352030 | ex XA-DAM | | |
| ☐ N417PM | Piper PA-31-350 Chieftain | 31-8052051 | ex N357CT | | |
| ☐ N4105D | Piper PA-31-350 Chieftain | 31-8252027 | | | |
| ☐ N27739 | Piper PA-31-350 Chieftain | 31-7852135 | ex SE-KKS | | |
| | | | | | |
| ☐ N25JA | Cessna 208B Caravan I | 208B1212 | | | ◆ |
| ☐ N90PB | Beech 200 Super King Air | BB-125 | ex TG-UGA | | |
| ☐ N162GA | Cessna 208B Caravan I | 208B0667 | ex C-FPNG | | |

## GREAT LAKES AIRLINES

*Lakes Air (ZK/GLA)* — *Cheyenne, WY (CYS)*

| | | | | | |
|---|---|---|---|---|---|
| ☐ N100UX | Beech 1900D | UE-100 | | Fly Telluride | |
| ☐ N122UX | Beech 1900D | UE-122 | ex N122YV | | |
| ☐ N153GL | Beech 1900D | UE-153 | ex N153ZV | | |
| ☐ N154GL | Beech 1900D | UE-154 | ex N154ZV | Sierra Vista | |
| ☐ N165YV | Beech 1900D | UE-165 | | | ◆ |
| ☐ N169GL | Beech 1900D | UE-169 | | | |
| ☐ N170GL | Beech 1900D | UE-170 | ex N170YV | Garden City, NE | |
| ☐ N178YV | Beech 1900D | UE-178 | | | ◆ |
| ☐ N182YV | Beech 1900D | UE-182 | | | |
| ☐ N184UX | Beech 1900D | UE-184 | ex N184YV | | |
| ☐ N192GL | Beech 1900D | UE-192 | ex N192YV | Telluride, CO | |
| ☐ N195GL | Beech 1900D | UE-195 | ex N195YV | Miles City, MT | |
| ☐ N201GL | Beech 1900D | UE-201 | ex N201YQ | Ponca City, OK | |
| ☐ N202UX | Beech 1900D | UE-202 | ex N202ZK | | |
| ☐ N208GL | Beech 1900D | UE-208 | ex N208YV | Fly Telluride | |
| ☐ N210GL | Beech 1900D | UE-210 | ex N210UX | | |
| ☐ N211GL | Beech 1900D | UE-211 | ex N211UX | Laramie, WY | |
| ☐ N219GL | Beech 1900D | UE-219 | ex N219YV | | |
| ☐ N220GL | Beech 1900D | UE-220 | ex N220UX | Hays, KS | |
| ☐ N231YV | Beech 1900D | UE-231 | | | |
| ☐ N240GL | Beech 1900D | UE-240 | ex N240YV | Devil's Tower, WY | |
| ☐ N245GL | Beech 1900D | UE-245 | ex N245YV | | |
| ☐ N247GL | Beech 1900D | UE-247 | ex N247YV | | |
| ☐ N251GL | Beech 1900D | UE-251 | ex N251ZV | Grand Tetons | |
| ☐ N253GL | Beech 1900D | UE-253 | ex N253YV | | |
| ☐ N254GL | Beech 1900D | UE-254 | ex N10840 | Grand Island, NE | |
| ☐ N255GL | Beech 1900D | UE-255 | ex N10860 | | |
| ☐ N257GL | Beech 1900D | UE-257 | ex N257YV | | |
| ☐ N261GL | Beech 1900D | UE-261 | ex N261YV | Scotts Bluff, NE | |
| | | | | | |
| ☐ N71GL | Embraer EMB.120ER Brasilia | 120071 | ex N267UE | | |
| ☐ N96ZK | Embraer EMB.120ER Brasilia | 120096 | ex N452UE | | |
| ☐ N108UX | Embraer EMB.120ER Brasilia | 120108 | ex N451UE | | |
| ☐ N293UX | Embraer EMB.120ER Brasilia | 120293 | ex PT-SVN | | |
| ☐ N297UX | Embraer EMB.120ER Brasilia | 120297 | ex PT-SVQ | | |
| ☐ N299UX | Embraer EMB.120ER Brasilia | 120299 | ex PT-SVT | | |

## GRIFFING FLYING SERVICE

*Sandusky-Griffing, OH (SKY)*

| | | | | |
|---|---|---|---|---|
| ☐ N426S | Piper PA-31-350 Chieftain | 31-8152190 | ex N426SC | |
| ☐ N428S | Piper PA-32-301 Saratoga | 32-8106021 | | |
| ☐ N442S | Britten-Norman BN-2A-20 Islander | 770 | ex N6863G | |

## GUAM MARIANAS AIR

| | | | | |
|---|---|---|---|---|
| ☐ N5022 | CASA C.212-200 | 64N/CC4-16-224 | ex PK-XDM | ♦ |
| ☐ N5040 | CASA C.212-200 | 73N/CC4-25-253 | ex PK-XCV | |

## GUARDIAN AIR

*Flagstaff, AZ / Bullhead City, AZ (FLG/IFP)*

| | | | | | | |
|---|---|---|---|---|---|---|
| ☐ N92DV | Beech 65-E90 King Air | LW-292 | ex N7MA | EMSAir 4 | Lsd to/op by Air Methods |
| ☐ N407AM | Bell 407 | 53309 | | EMS | Lsd to/op by Air Methods |
| ☐ N407VV | Bell 407 | 53476 | | EMS | Lsd to/op by Air Methods |
| ☐ N987GM | Beech 65-E90 King Air | LW-65 | ex N3065W | EMSAir 2 | Lsd to/op by Air Methods |

## GULF AND CARIBBEAN AIR — Trans Auto (TSU) — Fort Lauderdale-Hollywood Intl, FL (FLL)

| | | | | | |
|---|---|---|---|---|---|
| ☐ N471FL | AMD Falcon 20 | 163 | ex N258PE | | |
| ☐ N481FL | AMD Falcon 20C-5 | 27 | ex N326VW | | |
| ☐ N511FL | AMD Falcon 20C-5 | 122 | ex N302TT | | |
| ☐ N521FL | AMD Falcon 20C-5 | 68 | ex N458SW | | |
| ☐ N531FL | AMD Falcon 20 | 113 | ex N22WJ | | |
| ☐ N541FL | AMD Falcon 20 | 48 | ex N23ND | | |
| ☐ N131FL | Convair 580 | 155 | ex N5804 | 13 | Frtr |
| ☐ N141FL | Convair 580F | 111 | ex N302K | 14 | Frtr |
| ☐ N151FL | Convair 580 | 51 | ex N5810 | 15 | Frtr |
| ☐ N171FL | Convair 580F | 318 | ex N300K | 17 | Frtr |
| ☐ N181FL | Convair 580 | 387 | ex N301K | 18 | Frtr |
| ☐ N191FL | Convair 580 | 326 | ex N923DR | 19 | Frtr |
| ☐ N361FL | Convair 5800 | 343 | ex C-FKFS | | |
| ☐ N371FL | Convair 5800 | 309 | ex C-FMKF | | Frtr |
| ☐ N381FL | Convair 5800 | 276 | ex C-FKFS | | Frtr |
| ☐ N391FL | Convair 5800 | 278 | ex C-GKFD | | Frtr |
| ☐ N991FL | Convair 580 | 508 | ex C-GTTG | | Frtr |
| ☐ N51211 | Convair 580 | 489 | ex N5121 | | wfs |
| ☐ N51255 | Convair 580 | 383 | ex N45LC | | wfs |
| ☐ N215WE | Boeing 727-2S2F | 22936/1830 | ex N215FE | | ♦ |
| ☐ N216WE | Boeing 727-2S2F | 22937/1831 | ex N216FE | | ♦ |
| ☐ N251FL | Boeing 727-277F/W (Duganair 3) | 20551/1054 | ex C-GYKF | 717 | |
| ☐ N281FL | Boeing 727-225F/W (Duganair 3) | 20153/779 | ex C-GKFH | 711 | |
| ☐ N7813B | Convair 340-70 | 265 | ex 53-7813 | | wfs |

## GULF ATLANTIC AIRWAYS

| | | | | | |
|---|---|---|---|---|---|
| ☐ N208LS | Cessna 208B Caravan I | 208B2256 | ex N52144 | | ♦ |
| ☐ N1243D | Cessna 208B Caravan I | 208B1003 | ex N5079V | | ♦ |

## HAGELAND AVIATION SERVICES — Hageland (H6/HAG) — St Mary's, Bethel, AK (KSM)

Trades as Frontier Alaska

## HAWAIIAN AIRLINES — Hawaiian (HA/HAL) — Honolulu-Intl, HI (HNL)

| | | | | | |
|---|---|---|---|---|---|
| ☐ N380HA | Airbus A330-243 | 1104 | ex F-WWYZ | | |
| ☐ N381HA | Airbus A330-243 | 1114 | ex F-WWYN | | |
| ☐ N382HA | Airbus A330-243 | 1171 | ex F-WWYA | Iwakeli'i | |
| ☐ N383HA | Airbus A330-243 | 1217 | ex F-WWJR | | |
| ☐ N384HA | Airbus A330-243 | 1259 | ex F-WWYV | Hokupa'a | ♦ |
| ☐ N385HA | Airbus A330-243 | 1295 | ex F-WWYD | Manalakalani | ♦ |
| ☐ N386HA | Airbus A330-243 | 1310 | ex F-WWKN | | o/o♦ |
| ☐ N389HA | Airbus A330-243 | 1317 | ex F-WWKR | | o/o♦ |
| ☐ N | Airbus A330-243 | 1302 | ex F-WWYO | | o/o♦ |
| ☐ N475HA | Boeing 717-22A | 55121/5050 | | I'Iwi | |
| ☐ N476HA | Boeing 717-22A | 55118/5053 | | Elepaio | |
| ☐ N477HA | Boeing 717-22A | 55122/5061 | | Apapane | |
| ☐ N478HA | Boeing 717-22A | 55123/5064 | | Amakihi | |
| ☐ N479HA | Boeing 717-22A | 55124/5069 | | Akepa | |
| ☐ N480HA | Boeing 717-22A | 55125/5070 | | Pueo | |
| ☐ N481HA | Boeing 717-22A | 55126/5073 | | Alauahio | |
| ☐ N483HA | Boeing 717-22A | 55128/5079 | ex N604AT | | |
| ☐ N484HA | Boeing 717-22A | 55129/5080 | | Oma'o | |
| ☐ N485HA | Boeing 717-22A | 55130/5089 | | Palila | |
| ☐ N486HA | Boeing 717-22A | 55131/5092 | | Akiki | |
| ☐ N487HA | Boeing 717-22A | 55132/5098 | | Lo | |
| ☐ N488HA | Boeing 717-23S | 55001/5002 | ex VH-NXF | | |
| ☐ N489HA | Boeing 717-23S | 55002/5003 | ex VH-NXB | | |
| ☐ N490HA | Boeing 717-23S | 55151/5041 | ex VH-NXC | | |
| ☐ N491HA | Boeing 717-2BL | 55175/5125 | ex N912ME | | [HNL]♦ |
| ☐ N492HA | Boeing 717-2BL | 55181/5135 | ex N919ME | | ♦ |
| ☐ N493HA | Boeing 717-2BL | 55184/5142 | ex N922ME | | ♦ |
| ☐ N580HA | Boeing 767-33AER/W | 28140/850 | | Kolea | |
| ☐ N581HA | Boeing 767-33AER/W | 28141/853 | | Manu o Ku | |
| ☐ N582HA | Boeing 767-33AER/W | 28139/857 | | Ake Ake | |
| ☐ N583HA | Boeing 767-33AER | 25531/423 | ex D-AMUP | A | |
| ☐ N584HA | Boeing 767-3G5ER | 24258/255 | ex D-AMUS | Kioea | |
| ☐ N585HA | Boeing 767-3G5ER | 24257/251 | ex D-AMUR | Noio | |
| ☐ N586HA | Boeing 767-3G5ER | 24259/268 | ex D-AMUN | Ou | |
| ☐ N587HA | Boeing 767-33AER/W | 33421/887 | | Pakalakala | |
| ☐ N588HA | Boeing 767-3CBER/W | 33466/890 | | Iwa | |
| ☐ N589HA | Boeing 767-33AER/W | 33422/892 | | Moli | |
| ☐ N590HA | Boeing 767-3CBER/W | 33467/894 | | Koa'e Ula | |

| ☐ N592HA | Boeing 767-3CBER/W | 33468/898 | | Hunakai |
| ☐ N594HA | Boeing 767-332 | 23275/136 | ex N116DL | |
| ☐ N596HA | Boeing 767-332 | 23276/151 | ex N117DL | |
| ☐ N597HA | Boeing 767-332 | 23277/152 | ex N118DL | |
| ☐ N598HA | Boeing 767-332 | 23278/153 | ex N119DL | |

## HOMER AIR
Homer, AK (HOM)

| ☐ N206DC | Cessna U206F Stationair II | U20603198 | ex N8337Q |
| ☐ N522HA | Cessna U206B Super Skywagon | U206-0755 | ex N3455L |
| ☐ N7138Q | Cessna U206F Stationair II | U20603074 | |
| ☐ N9815M | Cessna U206G Stationair 6 II | U20604572 | |

## HORIZON AIR
Horizon Air (QX/QXE) Seattle-Tacoma Intl, WA (SEA)

| ☐ N600QX | Canadair CRJ-701 | 10005 | ex C-GCRA | 600 | | >ASE |
| ☐ N601QX | Canadair CRJ-701 | 10009 | ex C-GHCS | 601 | | >SKW |
| ☐ N603QX | Canadair CRJ-701 | 10011 | ex C-GHCZ | 603 | | >SKW |
| ☐ N604QX | Canadair CRJ-701 | 10019 | ex C-GIAJ | 604 | | >ASE |
| ☐ N605QX | Canadair CRJ-701 | 10022 | ex C-GIAR | 605 | | >ASE |
| ☐ N606QX | Canadair CRJ-701 | 10023 | ex C-GISU | 606 | | >SKW |
| ☐ N608QX | Canadair CRJ-701 | 10026 | ex C-GIAX | 608 | | >ASE |
| ☐ N609QX | Canadair CRJ-701 | 10031 | ex C-GIBJ | 609 | | >SKW |
| ☐ N611QX | Canadair CRJ-701 | 10041 | ex C-GICP | 611 | | >ASE |
| ☐ N612QX | Canadair CRJ-701 | 10042 | ex C-GHZV | 612 | | >ASE |
| ☐ N613QX | Canadair CRJ-701 | 10045 | ex C-GIAD | 613 | | >ASE |
| ☐ N614QX | Canadair CRJ-701 | 10049 | ex C-GIAJ | 614 | | >ASE |
| ☐ N615QX | Canadair CRJ-701 | 10065 | ex C-GIBQ | 615 | | >ASE |
| ☐ N616QX | Canadair CRJ-701 | 10128 | ex C- | 616 | WSU Cougars c/s | >SKW |
| ☐ N617QX | Canadair CRJ-701 | 10130 | ex C- | 617 | | >SKW |
| ☐ N618QX | Canadair CRJ-701 | 10205 | ex C- | 618 | | >SKW |
| ☐ N619QX | Canadair CRJ-701 | 10246 | ex C- | 619 | | >SKW |
| | | | | | | |
| ☐ N358PH | de Havilland DHC-8Q-202 | 506 | ex C-FWBB | | | >UCA |
| ☐ N359PH | de Havilland DHC-8Q-202 | 514 | ex C-GEOA | City of Kelowna | | >UCA |
| ☐ N360PH | de Havilland DHC-8Q-202 | 515 | ex C-GEWI | City of Medford | | >UCA |
| ☐ N361PH | de Havilland DHC-8Q-202 | 516 | ex C-GFOD | City of Sun Valley | | >UCA |
| ☐ N362PH | de Havilland DHC-8Q-202 | 518 | ex C-FDHI | | | >UCA |
| ☐ N363PH | de Havilland DHC-8Q-202 | 520 | ex C-FDHP | City of Boise | | >UCA |
| ☐ N364PH | de Havilland DHC-8Q-202 | 524 | ex C-FDHX | Cities of Seattle/Tacoma | | >UCA |
| ☐ N365PH | de Havilland DHC-8Q-202 | 526 | ex C-FDHZ | City of Pocatello | | >UCA |
| ☐ N366PH | de Havilland DHC-8Q-202 | 510 | ex C-GELN | City of Redding | | >UCA |
| ☐ N367PH | de Havilland DHC-8Q-202 | 511 | ex C-GDLD | | | >UCA |
| ☐ N368PH | de Havilland DHC-8Q-202 | 512 | ex C-GDFT | City of Idaho Falls | | >UCA |
| ☐ N369PH | de Havilland DHC-8Q-202 | 513 | ex C-FWBB | | | >UCA |
| ☐ N374PH | de Havilland DHC-8Q-202 | 528 | ex C-GDIU | | | >UCA |
| ☐ N375PH | de Havilland DHC-8Q-202 | 529 | ex C-GDKL | | | >UCA |
| ☐ N379PH | de Havilland DHC-8Q-202 | 530 | ex C-GDLK | | | >UCA |
| | | | | | | |
| ☐ N400QX | de Havilland DHC-8-402Q | 4030 | ex C-GFCF | | |
| ☐ N401QX | de Havilland DHC-8-402Q | 4031 | ex C-GFCW | | |
| ☐ N402QX | de Havilland DHC-8-402Q | 4032 | ex C-GFOD | | |
| ☐ N403QX | de Havilland DHC-8-402Q | 4037 | ex C-FDHP | | |
| ☐ N404QX | de Havilland DHC-8-402Q | 4046 | ex C-GDKL | | |
| ☐ N405QX | de Havilland DHC-8-402Q | 4047 | ex C-GDLD | | |
| ☐ N406QX | de Havilland DHC-8-402Q | 4048 | ex C-GDLK | | |
| ☐ N407QX | de Havilland DHC-8-402Q | 4049 | ex C-GDNK | | |
| ☐ N408QX | de Havilland DHC-8-402Q | 4050 | ex C-GFCA | | |
| ☐ N409QX | de Havilland DHC-8-402Q | 4051 | ex C-GFCW | | |
| ☐ N410QX | de Havilland DHC-8-402Q | 4053 | ex C-GFQL | | |
| ☐ N411QX | de Havilland DHC-8-402Q | 4055 | ex C-GFUM | | |
| ☐ N412QX | de Havilland DHC-8-402Q | 4059 | ex C-FGNP | | |
| ☐ N413QX | de Havilland DHC-8-402Q | 4060 | ex C-FNGB | | |
| ☐ N414QX | de Havilland DHC-8-402Q | 4061 | ex C-GDFT | | |
| ☐ N415QX | de Havilland DHC-8-402Q | 4081 | ex C-GELN | | |
| ☐ N416QX | de Havilland DHC-8-402Q | 4083 | ex C-GDNK | | |
| ☐ N417QX | de Havilland DHC-8-402Q | 4086 | ex C-FCSG | | |
| ☐ N418QX | de Havilland DHC-8-402Q | 4143 | ex C-FHQX | | |
| ☐ N419QX | de Havilland DHC-8-402Q | 4145 | ex C-FHRD | | |
| ☐ N420QX | de Havilland DHC-8-402Q | 4147 | ex C-FJLA | | |
| ☐ N421QX | de Havilland DHC-8-402Q | 4149 | ex C-FJLF | | |
| ☐ N422QX | de Havilland DHC-8-402Q | 4150 | ex C-FJLG | | |
| ☐ N423QX | de Havilland DHC-8-402Q | 4153 | ex C-FJLO | | |
| ☐ N424QX | de Havilland DHC-8-402Q | 4006 | ex B-3568 | | |
| ☐ N425QX | de Havilland DHC-8-402Q | 4039 | ex B-3569 | 25 Years Jubilee c/s | |
| ☐ N426QX | de Havilland DHC-8-402Q | 4154 | ex C-FJLX | | |
| ☐ N427QX | de Havilland DHC-8-402Q | 4156 | ex C-FLKU | | |
| ☐ N428QX | de Havilland DHC-8-402Q | 4160 | ex C-FLTL | | |
| ☐ N429QX | de Havilland DHC-8-402Q | 4161 | ex C-FLTT | | |
| ☐ N430QX | de Havilland DHC-8-402Q | 4163 | ex C-FMES | | |
| ☐ N431QX | de Havilland DHC-8-402Q | 4164 | ex C-FMEU | | |

| | | | | | |
|---|---|---|---|---|---|
| ☐ N432QX | de Havilland DHC-8-402Q | 4166 | ex C-FMFH | | |
| ☐ N433QX | de Havilland DHC-8-402Q | 4210 | ex C-FPQB | | |
| ☐ N434MK | de Havilland DHC-8-402Q | 4227 | ex C-FTUQ | Milton G Koult II | |
| ☐ N435QX | de Havilland DHC-8-402Q | 4232 | ex C-FUCO | | |
| ☐ N436QX | de Havilland DHC-8-402Q | 4236 | ex C-FUOF | | |
| ☐ N437QX | de Havilland DHC-8-402Q | 4240 | ex C-FUSM | | |
| ☐ N438QX | de Havilland DHC-8-402Q | 4243 | ex C-FUTP | | |
| ☐ N439QX | de Havilland DHC-8-402Q | 4246 | ex C-FVGY | | |
| ☐ N440QX | de Havilland DHC-8-402Q | 4347 | ex C- | | ◆ |
| ☐ N441QX | de Havilland DHC-8-402Q | 4348 | ex C- | | ◆ |
| ☐ N442QX | de Havilland DHC-8-402Q | 4352 | ex C- | | ◆ |
| ☐ N443QX | de Havilland DHC-8-402Q | 4353 | ex C- | | ◆ |
| ☐ N444QX | de Havilland DHC-8-402Q | 4355 | ex C- | | ◆ |
| ☐ N445QX | de Havilland DHC-8-402Q | 4358 | ex C- | | ◆ |
| ☐ N446QX | de Havilland DHC-8-402Q | 4363 | ex C-GISZ | | ◆ |
| ☐ N447QX | de Havilland DHC-8-402Q | 4364 | ex C-GITK | | ◆ |

## IBC AIRWAYS — Chasqui (II/CSQ) — Miami-Intl, FL (MIA)

| | | | | | |
|---|---|---|---|---|---|
| ☐ N367PX | SAAB SF.340B | 340B-271 | | | ◆ |
| ☐ N431BC | SAAB SF.340B | 340B-260 | ex N363PX | | |
| ☐ N481BC | SAAB SF.340B | 340B-274 | ex N368PX | | |
| ☐ N541BC | SAAB SF.340A | 340A-029 | ex N184K | | |
| ☐ N611BC | SAAB SF.340A | 340A-060 | ex N403BH | | Frtr |
| ☐ N631BC | SAAB SF.340A | 340A-061 | ex N404BH | | Frtr |
| ☐ N641BC | SAAB SF.340A | 340A-069 | ex N340SL | | Frtr |
| ☐ N651BC | SAAB SF.340A | 340A-076 | ex N76XJ | | Frtr |
| ☐ N661BC | SAAB SF.340A | 340A-125 | ex N125CH | | Frtr |
| ☐ N671BC | SAAB SF.340A | 340A-084 | ex N163PW | | Frtr |
| ☐ N691BC | SAAB SF.340A | 340A-041 | ex XA-BML | | Frtr |
| ☐ N901BC | SAAB SF.340A | 340A-088 | ex XA-MDG | | Frtr◆ |
| | | | | | |
| ☐ N831BC | Swearingen SA.227AC Metro III | AC-654B | ex N26906 | | |
| ☐ N841BC | Swearingen SA.227TC Metro II | TC-282 | ex N248AM | | |
| ☐ N851BC | Swearingen SA.227AT Merlin IVC | AT-495B | ex N9UA | | |
| ☐ N861BC | Swearingen SA.227AC Metro III | AC-487B | ex N550TD | | |
| ☐ N871BC | Swearingen SA.227AC Metro III | AC-659B | ex N2693C | | |
| ☐ N891BC | Swearingen SA.227AC Metro III | AC-709B | ex N2708D | | |

## ILIAMNA AIR TAXI — Iliamna Air (V8/IAR) — Iliamna, AK (ILI)

| | | | | | |
|---|---|---|---|---|---|
| ☐ N715HL | Pilatus PC-12/45 | 292 | ex N292PB | | |
| ☐ N715TL | Pilatus PC-12/45 | 548 | ex HB-FST | | |
| ☐ N3682Z | Beech 58 Baron | TH-1159 | | | |
| ☐ N1748U | Cessna 207 Skywagon | 20700348 | | | |
| ☐ N7379U | Cessna 207A Stationair 7 II | 20700427 | | | |
| ☐ N9720M | Cessna 207A Stationair 8 II | 20700720 | | | |
| ☐ N62230 | de Havilland DHC-2 Beaver | 707 | ex 53-7899 | | FP |
| ☐ N68088 | de Havilland DHC-2 Beaver | 1197 | ex 56-4447 | | FP |

## INLAND AVIATION SERVICES — (7N) — Aniak, AK (ANI)

| | | | |
|---|---|---|---|
| ☐ N1673U | Cessna 207 Skywagon | 20700273 | |
| ☐ N1701U | Cessna 207 Skywagon | 20700301 | |
| ☐ N1754U | Cessna T207 Turbo Skywagon | 20700354 | |
| ☐ N91002 | Cessna 207 Skywagon | 20700003 | |
| ☐ N91099 | Cessna 207 Skywagon | 20700073 | |

## INTER-ARCHIPELAGO AIRWAYS

| | | | | |
|---|---|---|---|---|
| ☐ N77X | Cessna 208B Caravan I | 208B0904 | | ◆ |

## INTER COASTAL AIR — Bayamon, PR

| | | | | |
|---|---|---|---|---|
| ☐ N402AJ | Cessna 402B | 402B0884 | ex N884RC | ◆ |

## INTER ISLAND AIRWAYS — Pago Pago International (PPG)

| | | | | | |
|---|---|---|---|---|---|
| ☐ N27BN | Britten-Norman BN-2B-26 Islander | 2220 | ex ZK-JOC | | |
| ☐ N228ST | Dornier 228-212 | 8240 | ex D-CBDJ | Islands of Manu'a | |
| ☐ N229ST | Dornier 228-212 | 8199 | ex F-OHAF | | ◆ |
| ☐ N328ST | Dornier 328-120 | 3086 | ex N502CG | | ◆ |

## INTERNATIONAL AIR RESPONSE — Coolidge-Municipal, AZ(CHD)

| | | | | | |
|---|---|---|---|---|---|
| ☐ N117TG | Lockheed C-130A-1A Hercules | 3018 | ex 54-1631 | 31 Iron Butterfly | |
| ☐ N118TG | Lockheed C-130A-1A Hercules | 3219 | ex 57-0512 | 32 | |
| ☐ N119TG | Lockheed C-130A Hercules | 3227 | ex N138FF | 88 | [CHD] |
| ☐ N121TG | Lockheed C-130A Hercules | 3119 | ex N132FF | 83 | |
| ☐ N125TG | Lockheed C-130A Hercules | 3138 | ex N131FF | 81 | [CHD] |

| | N126TG | Lockheed C-130A-1A Hercules | 3142 | ex N131HP | 131 | [CHD] |
|---|---|---|---|---|---|---|
| ☐ | N133HP | Lockheed C-130A-1A Hercules | 3189 | ex N8026J | | |
| | | | | | | |
| ☐ | N4887C | Douglas DC-7B | 45351/903 | | 33 | |

## ISLAND AIR — Moku (WP/MKU) — Honolulu-Intl, HI (HNL)

| | | | | | |
|---|---|---|---|---|---|
| ☐ | N805WP | de Havilland DHC-8-103 | 353 | ex N853MA | |
| ☐ | N806WP | de Havilland DHC-8-103 | 357 | ex N854MA | |
| ☐ | N808WP | de Havilland DHC-8-103 | 026 | ex N812PH | [HNL] |
| ☐ | N809WP | de Havilland DHC-8-103 | 032 | ex N813SN | |
| ☐ | N829EX | de Havilland DHC-8-103 | 146 | ex N805AW | |

## ISLAND AIR CHARTERS — Barracuda (ILF) — Fort Lauderdale-Hollywood Intl, FL (FLL)

| | | | | | |
|---|---|---|---|---|---|
| ☐ | N138LW | Britten-Norman BN-2A-27 Islander | 138 | ex YR-BNF | |
| ☐ | N779KS | Britten-Norman BN-2A-27 Islander | 779 | ex YR-BNE | |
| ☐ | N5775C | Cessna 402C | 402C0040 | | ♦ |

## ISLAND AIR SERVICE — (2O) — Kodiak-Municipal, AK (ADQ)

| | | | | | |
|---|---|---|---|---|---|
| ☐ | N27MR | Britten-Norman BN-2A-26 Islander | 884 | ex XC-DUN | |
| ☐ | N1162W | Beech B80 Queen Air | LD-350 | | |
| ☐ | N5891V | Britten-Norman BN-2A-26 Islander | 3011 | ex J8-VAN | |

## ISLAND AIRLINES — Island (IS/ISA) — Nantucket-Memorial, MA (ACK)

| | | | | | |
|---|---|---|---|---|---|
| ☐ | N402BK | Cessna 402C II | 402C689 | ex N550CQ | |
| ☐ | N402NS | Cessna 402C II | 402C02777 | | ♦ |
| ☐ | N404NS | Cessna 402C II | 402C0421 | | ♦ |
| ☐ | N406BK | Cessna 402C III | 402C0807 | ex N1235A | |
| ☐ | N407BK | Cessna 402C II | 402C0238 | ex N279CB | |
| ☐ | N409BK | Cessna 402C II | 402C0651 | ex N67220 | |
| ☐ | N810BW | Cessna 402C II | 402C0279 | | |
| ☐ | N26150 | Cessna 402C II | 402C0111 | | ♦ |

## ISLAND AIRWAYS — Charlevoix-Municipal, MI (CVX)

| | | | | | |
|---|---|---|---|---|---|
| ☐ | N19WA | Britten-Norman BN-2A-8 Islander | 524 | ex N307SK | |
| ☐ | N80KM | Britten-Norman BN-2A Islander | 80 | ex G-BNXA | |
| ☐ | N95BN | Britten-Norman BN-2A-8 Islander | 95 | ex G-AXKB | |
| ☐ | N137MW | Britten-Norman BN-2A Islander | 137 | ex G-AXWH | |
| ☐ | N866JA | Britten-Norman BN-2A-6 islander | 185 | ex G-31-185 | |
| ☐ | N63750 | Piper PA-23-250 Aztec | 27-7754117 | | ♦ |

## ISLAND SEAPLANE SERVICE — Honolulu-Keehi Lagoon SPB, HI

| | | | | | | |
|---|---|---|---|---|---|---|
| ☐ | N110AW | de Havilland DHC-2 Beaver | 690 | ex N11015 | Fantasy Islands c/s | FP |

## ISLAND WINGS AIR SERVICE — Ketchikan-Waterfront SPB, AK (WFB)

| | | | | | |
|---|---|---|---|---|---|
| ☐ | N1117F | de Havilland DHC-2 Beaver | 1369 | ex N6783L | FP |

## JETBLUE AIRWAYS — JetBlue (B6/JBU) — New York-JFK Intl, NY (JFK)

| | | | | | | |
|---|---|---|---|---|---|---|
| ☐ | N503JB | Airbus A320-232 | 1123 | ex F-WWBR | Blue Bird | |
| ☐ | N504JB | Airbus A320-232 | 1156 | ex F-WWBV | Shades Of Blue | |
| ☐ | N505JB | Airbus A320-232 | 1173 | ex F-WWDN | Blue Skies | |
| ☐ | N506JB | Airbus A320-232 | 1235 | ex F-WWIN | Wild Blue Yonder | |
| ☐ | N507JT | Airbus A320-232 | 1240 | ex D-ANNB | Blue Crew | ♦ |
| ☐ | N508JL | Airbus A320-232 | 1257 | ex D-ANNC | May the Force be with Blue | ♦ |
| ☐ | N509JB | Airbus A320-232 | 1270 | ex F-WWDF | True Blue | |
| ☐ | N510JB | Airbus A320-232 | 1280 | ex F-WWBA | Out Of The Blue | |
| ☐ | N516JB | Airbus A320-232 | 1302 | ex F-WWBQ | Royal Blue | |
| ☐ | N517JB | Airbus A320-232 | 1327 | ex F-WWDU | Blue Moon | |
| ☐ | N519JB | Airbus A320-232 | 1398 | ex F-WWIY | It Had To Be Blue | |
| ☐ | N520JB | Airbus A320-232 | 1446 | ex F-WWBT | Blue Velvet | |
| ☐ | N521JB | Airbus A320-232 | 1452 | ex F-WWBY | Baby Blue | |
| ☐ | N523JB | Airbus A320-232 | 1506 | ex F-WWII | Born To Be Blue | |
| ☐ | N524JB | Airbus A320-232 | 1528 | ex F-WWIN | Blue Belle | |
| ☐ | N526JL | Airbus A320-232 | 1546 | ex D-ANND | Blues Just Want To Have Fun | ♦ |
| ☐ | N527JL | Airbus A320-232 | 1557 | ex D-ANNE | Blue Bayou | |
| ☐ | N529JB | Airbus A320-232 | 1610 | ex F-WWDE | Ole Blue Eyes | |
| ☐ | N531JL | Airbus A320-232 | 1650 | ex D-ANNF | All Blue Can Jet | ♦ |
| ☐ | N534JB | Airbus A320-232 | 1705 | ex F-WWIU | Bada Bing, Bada Blue | |
| ☐ | N535JB | Airbus A320-232 | 1739 | ex F-WWBQ | Estrella Azul | |
| ☐ | N536JB | Airbus A320-232 | 1784 | ex F-WWDS | Canyon Blue | |
| ☐ | N537JT | Airbus A320-232 | 1785 | ex D-ANNI | Red White and Blue | |
| ☐ | N547JB | Airbus A320-232 | 1849 | ex F-WWDF | Forever Blue | |
| ☐ | N552JB | Airbus A320-232 | 1861 | ex F-WWDM | Blue Jay | |

| | | | | | |
|---|---|---|---|---|---|
| ☐ N554JB | Airbus A320-232 | 1898 | ex F-WWBK | Sacre' Bleu! |
| ☐ N556JB | Airbus A320-232 | 1904 | ex F-WWDD | Betty Blue |
| ☐ N558JB | Airbus A320-232 | 1915 | ex F-WWIF | Song Sung Blue |
| ☐ N559JB | Airbus A320-232 | 1917 | ex F-WWIR | Here's Looking At Blue, Kid |
| ☐ N561JB | Airbus A320-232 | 1927 | ex F-WWIC | La Vie En Blue |
| ☐ N562JB | Airbus A320-232 | 1948 | ex F-WWDF | The Name Is Blue, jetBlue |
| ☐ N563JB | Airbus A320-232 | 2006 | ex F-WWBY | Blue Chip |
| ☐ N564JB | Airbus A320-232 | 2020 | ex F-WWBZ | Absolute Blue |
| ☐ N565JB | Airbus A320-232 | 2031 | ex F-WWDT | Bippity Boppity Blue |
| ☐ N566JB | Airbus A320-232 | 2042 | ex F-WWDU | Blue Suede Shoes |
| ☐ N568JB | Airbus A320-232 | 2063 | ex F-WWDE | Blue Sapphire |
| ☐ N569JB | Airbus A320-232 | 2075 | ex F-WWDF | Blues Brothers |
| ☐ N570JB | Airbus A320-232 | 2099 | ex F-WWBD | Devil With A Blue Dress On |
| ☐ N571JB | Airbus A320-232 | 2125 | ex F-WWIX | Blue Monday |
| ☐ N579JB | Airbus A320-232 | 2132 | ex F-WWDB | Can't Stop Lovin' Blue |
| ☐ N580JB | Airbus A320-232 | 2136 | ex F-WWBB | Mo Better Blue |
| ☐ N583JB | Airbus A320-232 | 2150 | ex F-WWII | Bluesville |
| ☐ N584JB | Airbus A320-232 | 2149 | ex F-WWID | Blue Fox |
| ☐ N585JB | Airbus A320-232 | 2159 | ex F-WWIC | I Got Blue Babe |
| ☐ N586JB | Airbus A320-232 | 2160 | ex F-WWIN | Blue Flight Special |
| ☐ N587JB | Airbus A320-232 | 2177 | ex F-WWIL | Blue Kid In Town |
| ☐ N588JB | Airbus A320-232 | 2201 | ex F-WWBJ | Hopelessly Devoted To Blue |
| ☐ N589JB | Airbus A320-232 | 2215 | ex F-WWIH | Blue Skies Ahead |
| ☐ N590JB | Airbus A320-232 | 2231 | ex F-WWIH | Liberty Blue |
| ☐ N591JB | Airbus A320-232 | 2246 | ex F-WWIS | Tale Of Blue Cities |
| ☐ N592JB | Airbus A320-232 | 2259 | ex F-WWBI | American Blue |
| ☐ N593JB | Airbus A320-232 | 2280 | ex F-WWDT | I Only Have Eyes For Blue |
| ☐ N594JB | Airbus A320-232 | 2284 | ex F-WWBQ | Whole Lotta Blue |
| ☐ N595JB | Airbus A320-232 | 2286 | ex F-WWBR | Rhythm & Blues |
| ☐ N597JB | Airbus A320-232 | 2307 | ex F-WWIC | For The Love Of Blue |
| ☐ N598JB | Airbus A320-232 | 2314 | ex F-WWDK | Me & You & A Plane Named Blue |
| ☐ N599JB | Airbus A320-232 | 2336 | ex F-WWIN | If The Blue Fits |
| ☐ N603JB | Airbus A320-232 | 2352 | ex F-WWIL | Viva La Blue |
| ☐ N605JB | Airbus A320-232 | 2368 | ex F-WWDO | Blue Yorker |
| ☐ N606JB | Airbus A320-232 | 2384 | ex F-WWIE | Idlewild Blue |
| ☐ N607JB | Airbus A320-232 | 2386 | ex F-WWIG | Beantown Blue |
| ☐ N608JB | Airbus A320-232 | 2415 | ex F-WWDP | ..And Along Came Blue |
| ☐ N612JB | Airbus A320-232 | 2447 | ex F-WWBU | Blue Look Maaahvelous |
| ☐ N613JB | Airbus A320-232 | 2449 | ex F-WWBX | Bahama Blue |
| ☐ N615JB | Airbus A320-232 | 2461 | ex F-WWDR | I Love Blue |
| ☐ N618JB | Airbus A320-232 | 2489 | ex F-WWDX | Can't Get Enough Of Blue |
| ☐ N621JB | Airbus A320-232 | 2491 | ex F-WWDY | Do-be-do-be Blue |
| ☐ N623JB | Airbus A320-232 | 2504 | ex F-WWBM | All We Need Is Blue |
| ☐ N624JB | Airbus A320-232 | 2520 | ex F-WWBN | Blue-T-Ful |
| ☐ N625JB | Airbus A320-232 | 2535 | ex F-WWII | CompanyBlue |
| ☐ N627JB | Airbus A320-232 | 2577 | ex F-WWDB | A Friend Like Blue |
| ☐ N629JB | Airbus A320-232 | 2580 | ex F-WWBH | Bright Lights, Blue City |
| ☐ N630JB | Airbus A320-232 | 2640 | ex F-WWBY | Honk If You love Blue |
| ☐ N632JB | Airbus A320-232 | 2647 | ex F-WWIF | Clear Blue Sky |
| ☐ N633JB | Airbus A320-232 | 2671 | ex F-WWDF | Major Blue |
| ☐ N634JB | Airbus A320-232 | 2710 | ex F-WWIZ | |
| ☐ N635JB | Airbus A320-232 | 2725 | ex F-WWDQ | All Because of Blue |
| ☐ N636JB | Airbus A320-232 | 2755 | ex F-WWDL | All Wrapped Up In Blue |
| ☐ N637JB | Airbus A320-232 | 2781 | ex F-WWDY | Big Blue Bus |
| ☐ N638JB | Airbus A320-232 | 2802 | ex F-WWIL | Blue begins with you |
| ☐ N639JB | Airbus A320-232 | 2814 | ex F-WWIV | A Little Blue Will Do |
| ☐ N640JB | Airbus A320-232 | 2832 | ex F-WWBD | Blue Better Believe It |
| ☐ N641JB | Airbus A320-232 | 2848 | ex F-WWIK | Blue Come Back Now Ya Hear |
| ☐ N643JB | Airbus A320-232 | 2871 | ex F-WWBF | Blue Jersey |
| ☐ N644JB | Airbus A320-232 | 2880 | ex F-WWBO | Blue Loves Ya, Baby |
| ☐ N645JB | Airbus A320-232 | 2900 | ex F-WWDE | Blues Have More Fun |
| ☐ N646JB | Airbus A320-232 | 2945 | ex F-WWIP | Bravo Lima Uniform Echo |
| ☐ N648JB | Airbus A320-232 | 2970 | ex F-WWDI | That's What I Like About Blue |
| ☐ N649JB | Airbus A320-232 | 2977 | ex F-WWBD | Fancy Meeting Blue Here |
| ☐ N651JB | Airbus A320-232 | 2992 | ex F-WWIS | I'm Having a Blue Moment |
| ☐ N652JB | Airbus A320-232 | 3029 | ex F-WWBT | Out With The Old, In With The Blue |
| ☐ N653JB | Airbus A320-232 | 3039 | ex F-WWDH | Breath of Fresh Blue |
| ☐ N655JB | Airbus A320-232 | 3072 | ex F-WWIN | special colours, Blue 100 |
| ☐ N656JB | Airbus A320-232 | 3091 | ex F-WWIQ | California Blue |
| ☐ N657JB | Airbus A320-232 | 3119 | ex F-WWBC | Denim Blue |
| ☐ N658JB | Airbus A320-232 | 3150 | ex F-WWBT | Woo-Hoo JetBlue |
| ☐ N659JB | Airbus A320-232 | 3190 | ex F-WWIQ | Simply Blue |
| ☐ N661JB | Airbus A320-232 | 3228 | ex F-WWBD | Let the Blue Times Roll |
| ☐ N662JB | Airbus A320-232 | 3263 | ex F-WWDO | Glad to be Blue |
| ☐ N663JB | Airbus A320-232 | 3287 | ex F-WWDG | Paint the town blue |
| ☐ N665JB | Airbus A320-232 | 3348 | ex F-WWBV | Something about blue |
| ☐ N703JB | Airbus A320-232 | 3381 | ex F-WWDM | It's up to blue, New York, New York |
| ☐ N705JB | Airbus A320-232 | 3416 | ex F-WWIN | Big Blue People Seater |
| ☐ N706JB | Airbus A320-232 | 3451 | ex F-WWBE | As blue as it gets |
| ☐ N708JB | Airbus A320-232 | 3479 | ex F-WWDJ | All that and a bag of blue chips |
| ☐ N709JB | Airbus A320-232 | 3488 | ex F-WWIK | Brand Spanking Blue |
| ☐ N712JB | Airbus A320-232 | 3517 | ex F-WWDQ | Enough about me..Let's talk about Blue |

| | Reg | Type | C/N | ex | Name | |
|---|---|---|---|---|---|---|
| ☐ | N715JB | Airbus A320-232 | 3554 | ex F-WWBB | How's My Flying? Call 1-800-JetBlue | |
| ☐ | N729JB | Airbus A320-232 | 3572 | ex F-WWBJ | If You Can Read This, Your Blue Close | |
| ☐ | N746JB | Airbus A320-232 | 3622 | ex F-WWIL | Some Like It Blue | |
| ☐ | N760JB | Airbus A320-232 | 3659 | ex F-WWDU | The Blues Were Made For Flying | |
| ☐ | N763JB | Airbus A320-232 | 3707 | ex F-WWIQ | Unforgetably blue | |
| ☐ | N766JB | Airbus A320-232 | 3724 | ex F-WWDG | Etjay Luebay | |
| ☐ | N768JB | Airbus A320-232 | 3760 | ex F-WWDC | Blue Crew | |
| ☐ | N775JB | Airbus A320-232 | 3800 | ex F-WWBT | Canard Bleu | |
| ☐ | N779JB | Airbus A320-232 | 3811 | ex F-WWID | Real Blue | |
| ☐ | N784JB | Airbus A320-232 | 4578 | ex F-WWDZ | Blue Infinity and Beyond | ♦ |
| ☐ | N789JB | Airbus A320-232 | 4612 | ex F-WWDC | What's Blue and White and Flies All Over | ♦ |
| ☐ | N793JB | Airbus A320-232 | 4647 | ex F-WWDN | | ♦ |
| ☐ | N794JB | Airbus A320-232 | 4904 | ex F-WWBX | Pretty Fly for a Blue Guy | ♦ |
| ☐ | N796JB | Airbus A320-232 | 5060 | ex F-WWBQ | | ♦ |
| ☐ | N805JB | Airbus A320-232 | 5148 | ex | | o/o♦ |
| ☐ | N | Airbus A320-232 | 5142 | ex | | o/o♦ |
| | | | | | | |
| ☐ | N178JB | Embraer ERJ-190AR | 19000004 | ex PT-STD | It's A Blue Thing | |
| ☐ | N179JB | Embraer ERJ-190AR | 19000006 | ex PT-STF | Come Fly With Blue | |
| ☐ | N183JB | Embraer ERJ-190AR | 19000007 | ex PT-STG | Azul Brasileiro | |
| ☐ | N184JB | Embraer ERJ-190AR | 19000008 | ex PT-STH | Outta the Blue | |
| ☐ | N187JB | Embraer ERJ-190AR | 19000009 | ex PT-STI | Dream Come Blue | |
| ☐ | N190JB | Embraer ERJ-190AR | 19000011 | ex PT-STK | Luiz F Kahl | |
| ☐ | N192JB | Embraer ERJ-190AR | 19000014 | ex PT-STO | Yes, I'm A Natural Blue | |
| ☐ | N193JB | Embraer ERJ-190AR | 19000017 | ex PT-STR | Peek-a-Blue | |
| ☐ | N197JB | Embraer ERJ-190AR | 19000020 | ex PT-STU | Color Me Blue | |
| ☐ | N198JB | Embraer ERJ-190AR | 19000021 | ex PT-STV | Big Apple Blue | |
| ☐ | N203JB | Embraer ERJ-190AR | 19000023 | ex PT-STX | Look at Blue now | |
| ☐ | N206JB | Embraer ERJ-190AR | 19000025 | ex PT-STZ | Blue-It's the New Black | |
| ☐ | N216JB | Embraer ERJ-190AR | 19000026 | ex PT-SGA | Blue Getaway | |
| ☐ | N228JB | Embraer ERJ-190AR | 19000030 | ex PT-SGE | Blue 4 You | |
| ☐ | N229JB | Embraer ERJ-190AR | 19000032 | ex PT-SGG | Blue Amigo | |
| ☐ | N231JB | Embraer ERJ-190AR | 19000033 | ex PT-SGH | Blue Bonnet | |
| ☐ | N236JB | Embraer ERJ-190AR | 19000035 | ex PT-SGJ | Blue by Design | |
| ☐ | N238JB | Embraer ERJ-190AR | 19000039 | ex PT-SGO | Blue Clipper | |
| ☐ | N239JB | Embraer ERJ-190AR | 19000040 | ex PT-SGP | Blissfully Blue | |
| ☐ | N247JB | Embraer ERJ-190AR | 19000042 | ex PT-SGR | Blue is so You | |
| ☐ | N249JB | Embraer ERJ-190AR | 19000045 | ex PT-SGU | Blueprint | |
| ☐ | N258JB | Embraer ERJ-190AR | 19000047 | ex PT-SGW | Blue Send Me | |
| ☐ | N265JB | Embraer ERJ-190AR | 19000049 | ex PT-SGY | Blue Streak | |
| ☐ | N266JB | Embraer ERJ-190AR | 19000054 | ex PT-SID | Blue Sweet Blue | |
| ☐ | N267JB | Embraer ERJ-190AR | 19000065 | ex PT-SJD | Bluesmobile | |
| ☐ | N273JB | Embraer ERJ-190AR | 19000073 | ex PT-SJM | Carribean Blue | |
| ☐ | N274JB | Embraer ERJ-190AR | 19000082 | ex PT-SJY | Good, Better, Blue | |
| ☐ | N279JB | Embraer ERJ-190AR | 19000090 | ex PT-SNJ | Indigo Blue | |
| ☐ | N281JB | Embraer ERJ-190AR | 19000103 | ex PT-SNX | Lady in Blue | |
| ☐ | N283JB | Embraer ERJ-190AR | 19000125 | ex PT-SQU | Pretty in Blue | |
| ☐ | N284JB | Embraer ERJ-190AR | 19000144 | ex PT-SVY | Sincerely Blue | |
| ☐ | N292JB | Embraer ERJ-190AR | 19000179 | ex PT-SDN | Parlez-Blue? | |
| ☐ | N294JB | Embraer ERJ-190AR | 19000185 | ex PT-SDT | Room with a blue | |
| ☐ | N296JB | Embraer ERJ-190AR | 19000219 | ex PT-SHC | Blue's your daddy | |
| ☐ | N298JB | Embraer ERJ-190AR | 19000249 | ex PT-SIT | Cool Blue | |
| ☐ | N304JB | Embraer ERJ-190AR | 19000257 | ex PT-STF | Midnight Blue | |
| ☐ | N306JB | Embraer ERJ-190AR | 19000272 | ex PT-TLM | Blue Orleans | |
| ☐ | N307JB | Embraer ERJ-190AR | 19000286 | ex PT-TZA | Mi Corazon Azul | |
| ☐ | N309JB | Embraer ERJ-190AR | 19000289 | ex PT-TZD | Rhapsody in Blue | |
| ☐ | N316JB | Embraer ERJ-190AR | 19000292 | ex PT-TZG | Usto Schulz | |
| ☐ | N317JB | Embraer ERJ-190AR | 19000363 | ex PT-XNC | Deja Blue | |
| ☐ | N318JB | Embraer ERJ-190AR | 19000364 | ex PT-XND | Blue Jean Baby | |
| ☐ | N323JB | Embraer ERJ-190AR | 19000384 | ex PT-XNS | Only Blue | |
| ☐ | N324JB | Embraer ERJ-190AR | 19000388 | ex PT-XNV | Blue Traveller | |
| ☐ | N328JB | Embraer ERJ-190AR | 19000422 | ex PT-TGY | Blue Warrior | |
| ☐ | N329JB | Embraer ERJ-190AR | 19000433 | ex PT-TCT | | ♦ |
| ☐ | N334JB | Embraer ERJ-190AR | 19000446 | ex PT-TJG | | ♦ |
| ☐ | N337JB | Embraer ERJ-190AR | 19000473 | ex PT-TOU | I'm with Blue | ♦ |
| ☐ | N339JB | Embraer ERJ-190AR | 19000490 | ex PT-TPP | BYO Blue | ♦ |
| ☐ | N346JB | Embraer ERJ-190AR | 19000504 | ex PT-TRO | | ♦ |
| ☐ | N348JB | Embraer ERJ-190AR | 19000511 | ex PT-TSH | Mystic Blue | ♦ |

## JIM HANKINS AIR SERVICE — Hankins (HKN) — Jackson-Hawkins Field, MS (JAN)

| | Reg | Type | C/N | ex | | |
|---|---|---|---|---|---|---|
| ☐ | N22BR | Beech H-18 | BA-729 | ex N402AP | | Frtr |
| ☐ | N81CK | Volpar Turboliner | BA-509 | ex F-ODHJ | | Frtr |
| ☐ | N231SK | Volpar Turboliner | AF-856 | ex N346V | | Frtr |
| ☐ | N368HC | Beech H-18 | BA-630 | | | Frtr♦ |
| ☐ | N4209V | Volpar Turboliner | AF-884 | ex HB-GFX | | Frtr |
| ☐ | N92756 | Beech H-18 | BA-728 | ex JA5133 | | Frtr |
| | | | | | | |
| ☐ | N3BA | Douglas DC-3 | 12172 | ex N94530 | | Frtr |
| ☐ | N40XL | Beech 58 Baron | TH-400 | ex N80LM | | |
| ☐ | N366MQ | Short SD.3-60 | SH3639 | ex G-BLEH | | |
| ☐ | N899DD | Beech 58 Baron | TH-899 | ex VH-BWJ | | |

| | | | | |
|---|---|---|---|---|
| ☐ N958JH | Beech 65-C90A King Air | LJ-1108 | ex N438SP | |
| ☐ N3106W | Beech 58 Baron | TH-408 | | |
| ☐ N6652A | Beech 58 Baron | TH-1045 | | |
| ☐ N8061A | Douglas DC-3 | 6085 | ex (N351SA) | Frtr |

## KALITTA AIR — Connie (K4/CKS) — Detroit-Willow Run, MI (YIP)

| | | | | |
|---|---|---|---|---|
| ☐ N110TR | Boeing 747-256B (SF) | 24071/699 | ex Z3-CAC | [OSC]♦ |
| ☐ N616US | Boeing 747-251F | 21120/258 | | [OSC] |
| ☐ N624US | Boeing 747-251B | 21706/377 | | [OSC]♦ |
| ☐ N629US | Boeing 747-251F | 22388/444 | | [OSC] |
| ☐ N630US | Boeing 747-2J9F | 21668/400 | ex N1288E | [OSC] |
| ☐ N700CK | Boeing 747-246B (SF) | 22990/579 | ex JA8161 | |
| ☐ N701CK | Boeing 747-259B (SCD) | 21730/372 | ex N924FT | |
| ☐ N703CK | Boeing 747-212B (SF) | 21939/449 | ex N319FV | |
| ☐ N704CK | Boeing 747-246F | 23391/654 | ex JA8171 | |
| ☐ N705CK | Boeing 747-246B (SCD) | 21034/243 | ex JA8123 | [OSC] |
| ☐ N706CK | Boeing 747-249F | 21827/406 | ex N806FT | [OSC] |
| ☐ N707CK | Boeing 747-246F | 21681/382 | ex JA8132 | [OSC] |
| ☐ N708CK | Boeing 747-212B (SF) | 21937/419 | ex N526UP | |
| ☐ N712CK | Boeing 747-122 (SCD) | 19754/60 | ex N854FT | [OSC] |
| ☐ N713CK | Boeing 747-2B4M | 21099/264 | ex OD-AGH | |
| ☐ N715CK | Boeing 747-209B (SF) | 22447/556 | ex B-18755 | |
| ☐ N716CK | Boeing 747-122 (SCD) | 19753/52 | ex N853FT | [OSC] |
| ☐ N717CK | Boeing 747-123 (SCD) | 20325/125 | ex N673UP | [OSC] |
| ☐ N719CK | Boeing 747-251F | 21321/308 | ex N619US | [OSC]♦ |
| ☐ N746CK | Boeing 747-246F | 22989/571 | ex JA811J | |
| ☐ N747CK | Boeing 747-221F | 21743/384 | ex JA8165 | |
| ☐ N748CK | Boeing 747-221F | 21744/392 | ex JA8160 | |
| ☐ N790CK | Boeing 747-251B (SF) | 23112/595 | ex N632NW | |
| ☐ N791CK | Boeing 747-251F | 23888/682 | ex N640US | |
| ☐ N792CK | Boeing 747-212B | 24177/710 | ex N644NW | |
| ☐ N793CK | Boeing 747-222B (SF) | 23736/673 | ex N645NW | [OSC] |
| ☐ N794CK | Boeing 747-222B (SF) | 23737/675 | exN646NW | ♦ |
| ☐ N795CK | Boeing 747-251B (SF) | 23111/594 | ex N631NW | [OSC]♦ |
| ☐ N923FT | Boeing 747-2U3B | 22769/562 | ex Z3-CAA | [OSC]♦ |
| | | | | |
| ☐ N740CK | Boeing 747-4H6FCF | 24405/745 | ex N73714 | |
| ☐ N741CK | Boeing 747-4H6FCF | 24315/738 | ex N73713 | |
| ☐ N742CK | Boeing 747-446BCF | 24424/760 | ex JA8072 | |
| ☐ N743CK | Boeing 747-446BCF | 26350/961 | ex JA8906 | |
| ☐ N744CK | Boeing 747-446BCF | 26353/980 | ex JA8909 | |
| ☐ N745CK | Boeing 747-446BCF | 26361/1188 | ex JA8915 | |
| | | | | |
| ☐ N782CK | Boeing 747-4HQERF | 37304/1419 | ex N798BA | ♦ |

## KALITTA CHARTERS — Kalitta (KFS) — Detroit-Willow Run, MI (YIP)

| | | | | |
|---|---|---|---|---|
| ☐ N720CK | Boeing 727-2B6F (Raisbeck 3) | 21298/1246 | ex N721SK | |
| ☐ N722CK | Boeing 727-2H3F (Raisbeck 3) | 20948/1084 | ex N722SK | |
| ☐ N723CK | Boeing 727-2H3F (Raisbeck 3) | 20545/877 | ex N723SK | |
| ☐ N724CK | Boeing 727-225F (Raisbeck 3) | 20383/831 | ex N8840E | |
| ☐ N725CK | Boeing 727-224F (Raisbeck 3) | 22252/1697 | ex N746DH | |
| ☐ N726CK | Boeing 727-2M7 (FedEx 3) | 21951/1680 | ex N750DH | |
| | | | | |
| ☐ N709CK | Boeing 747-132 (SCD) | 20247/159 | ex N625PL | [OSC]♦ |
| ☐ N915CK | Douglas DC-9-15RC | 47086/219 | ex N915R | |
| ☐ N933AX | Douglas DC-9-33RC | 47291/343 | ex N94454 | |

## KALITTA FLYING SERVICES — Kalitta (KFS) — Detroit-Willow Run, MI/Morristown, TN/El Paso, TX (YIP/MRX/ESP)

| | | | | |
|---|---|---|---|---|
| ☐ N70CK | AMD Falcon 20C | 128 | ex N228CK | |
| ☐ N108R | AMD Falcon 20DC | 108 | ex N101ZE | |
| ☐ N192CK | AMD Falcon 20C | 192 | ex N192R | |
| ☐ N212R | AMD Falcon 20DC | 212 | ex N31FE | |
| ☐ N226CK | AMD Falcon 20DC | 226 | ex N226R | |
| ☐ N227CK | AMD Falcon 20DC | 227 | ex N227R | |
| ☐ N229CK | AMD Falcon 20DC | 229 | ex N229R | |
| ☐ N230RA | AMD Falcon 20DC | 230 | ex N26EV | |
| ☐ N240CK | AMD Falcon 20C-5 | 24 | ex N240TJ | |
| ☐ N301R | AMD Falcon 20C | 3 | ex N92MH | |
| ☐ N810RA | AMD Falcon 20C | 81 | ex N93RS | |
| ☐ N995CK | AMD Falcon 20C | 95 | ex N950RA | |
| ☐ N998CK | AMD Falcon 20C | 98 | ex N980R | |
| | | | | |
| ☐ N11UF | Learjet 35A | 35A-237 | | ♦ |
| ☐ N39CK | Learjet 25 | 25-005 | ex XA-SDQ | |
| ☐ N50CK | Learjet 25B | 25B-157 | ex N57CK | |
| ☐ N71CK | Learjet 36A | 36A-035 | ex VH-BIB | |
| ☐ N72CK | Learjet 35A | 35A-165 | ex N16BJ | |

| | | | | | | |
|---|---|---|---|---|---|---|
| ☐ N73CK | Learjet 35A | 35A-092 | ex N39WA | | | |
| ☐ N75CK | Learjet 25D | 25D-256 | ex N6LL | | | |
| ☐ N76CK | Learjet 25 | 25-020 | ex N500JS | | | |
| ☐ N150CK | Learjet 25D | 25D-150 | ex N251JA | | | |
| ☐ N222B | Learjet 25 | 25-047 | | | | |
| ☐ N237CK | Learjet 35A | 35A-237 | ex N11UF | | | |
| ☐ N248CK | Learjet 25D | 25D-248 | ex (N248LJ) | | | ♦ |
| ☐ N298CK | Learjet 35A | 35A-298 | ex N298NW | | | |
| ☐ N818CK | Learjet 25B | 25B-118 | ex N118MB | | | ♦ |
| ☐ N905CK | Learjet 36 | 36-005 | ex N9108Z | | | |
| ☐ N913CK | Learjet 35 | 35-013 | ex N535TA | | | |

All freighters. A sister company of Kalitta Charters

## KAMAKA AIR
Honolulu-Intl, HI (HNL)

| | | | | | |
|---|---|---|---|---|---|
| ☐ N145KA | Cessna 208B Caravan I | 208B2019 | | | ♦ |
| ☐ N231H | Beech E-18S | BA-281 | ex N23Y | | |
| ☐ N933T | Beech Super H-18 | BA-665 | | | |
| ☐ N9796N | Douglas C-117D | 43375 | ex C-FLED | | |

## KATMAI AIR
King Salmon, AK/Anchorage-Lake Hood SPB, AK (AKN/LHD)

| | | | | | |
|---|---|---|---|---|---|
| ☐ N31TN | Beech B99 | U-49 | ex N98RZ | | |
| ☐ N45GB | de Havilland DHC-2 Turbo Beaver | 1623/TB14 | ex C-FNPW | | FP♦ |
| ☐ N491K | de Havilland DHC-3 Turbo Otter | 434 | ex N49KA | | FP |
| ☐ N492K | Piper PA-31-350 Chieftain | 31-8052176 | ex C-GAWL | | |
| ☐ N495K | Cessna U206F Stationair II | U20602549 | ex N1274V | | FP |
| ☐ N496K | Cessna U206G Stationair | U20603953 | ex N756BE | | FP |
| ☐ N498K | Cessna T207A Stationair 8 | 20700624 | ex N73762 | | FP |
| ☐ N499K | Cessna T207A Stationair 8 | 20700632 | ex N73835 | | FP |
| ☐ N9644G | Cessna U206F Stationair | U20601844 | | | FP |
| ☐ N17689 | de Havilland DHC-3 Turbo Otter | 431 | | | FP♦ |

## KENMORE AIR
Kenmore (M5/KEN)
Kenmore SPB, WA (KEH)

| | | | | | |
|---|---|---|---|---|---|
| ☐ N41F | de Havilland DHC-2 Beaver | 1352 | ex 58-2022 | | FP |
| ☐ N900KA | de Havilland DHC-2 Beaver | 1676 | ex LN-BFH | Maggie Evening Magazine | FP |
| ☐ N1018F | de Havilland DHC-2 Beaver | 710 | ex N62SJ | | FP |
| ☐ N1455T | de Havilland DHC-2 Turbo Beaver III | 1647/TB26 | ex C-FOEI | | FP |
| ☐ N6781L | de Havilland DHC-2 Beaver | 788 | ex N10LU | | FP |
| ☐ N9744T | de Havilland DHC-2 Turbo Beaver III | 1692/TB60 | ex N1944 | | FP |
| ☐ N9766Z | de Havilland DHC-2 Beaver | 504 | ex N13454 | | FP |
| ☐ N17598 | de Havilland DHC-2 Beaver | 1129 | ex VP-FAH | | FP |
| ☐ N57576 | de Havilland DHC-2 Beaver | 1168 | ex C-GNPQ | | FP |
| ☐ N72355 | de Havilland DHC-2 Beaver | 1164 | ex N62355 | | FP |
| ☐ N50KA | de Havilland DHC-3 Turbo Otter | 221 | ex C-GLMT | K5 Evening c/s | FP |
| ☐ N58JH | de Havilland DHC-3 Turbo Otter | 131 | ex N8510Q | | FP |
| ☐ N87KA | de Havilland DHC-3 Turbo Otter | 11 | ex N8262V | | FP |
| ☐ N606KA | de Havilland DHC-3 Turbo Otter | 37 | ex N8260L | | FP |
| ☐ N707KA | de Havilland DHC-3 Turbo Otter | 106 | ex N888KA | | FP |
| ☐ N3125S | de Havilland DHC-3 Turbo Otter | 407 | ex RCAF 9424 | Seattle Hospital c/s | FP |
| ☐ N90422 | de Havilland DHC-3 Turbo Otter | 152 | ex 55-3296 | Expedia.com titles | FP |
| ☐ N72KA | Cessna 208B Caravan I | 208B0326 | ex N1030N | | FP♦ |
| ☐ N426KM | Cessna 208 Caravan I | 20800306 | ex N12656 | | FP |
| ☐ N2803K | Cessna 180 Skywagon | 18053074 | | | FP♦ |
| ☐ N2849K | Cessna 180 Skywagon | 18053096 | | | FP♦ |

## KENAI RIVER XPRESS

| | | | | | |
|---|---|---|---|---|---|
| ☐ N150BA | de Havilland DHC-3 Turbo Otter | 15 | | | ♦ |

## KEY LIME AIR
Key Lime (LYM)
Denver-International, CO (DEN)

| | | | | | |
|---|---|---|---|---|---|
| ☐ N313RA | Piper PA-31-350 Chieftain | 31-8052069 | ex N333BM | | |
| ☐ N411BJ | Piper PA-31-350 Chieftain | 31-7952043 | ex C-GPQR | | |
| ☐ N3549X | Piper PA-31-350 Chieftain | 31-8052034 | ex C-FAWT | | |
| ☐ N9247L | Piper PA-31-350 Chieftain | 31-8152160 | ex G-BWAS | | |
| ☐ N27989 | Piper PA-31-350 Chieftain | 31-7952077 | | | |
| ☐ N62Z | Swearingen SA.226TC Metro II | TC-237 | ex N5437M | | |
| ☐ N276CA | Swearingen SA.226TC Metro II | TC-276 | ex N103GS | | ♦ |
| ☐ N326BA | Swearingen SA.226TC Metro II | TC-269 | ex C-GYXC | | |
| ☐ N509SS | Swearingen SA.226TC Metro II | TC-206 | ex N261S | | |
| ☐ N770S | Swearingen SA.226TC Metro II | TC-248 | | | |
| ☐ N81418 | Swearingen SA.226TC Metro II | TC-223 | ex EC-GNM | | |
| ☐ N184SW | Swearingen SA.227AC Metro III | AC-647 | ex CX-TAA | | |
| ☐ N508FA | Swearingen SA.227AC Metro III | AC-508 | ex ZK-NSW | | |
| ☐ N542FA | Swearingen SA.227AC Metro III | AC-542 | ex ZK-NSX | | |

| | | | | | |
|---|---|---|---|---|---|
| ☐ N640KL | Swearingen SA.227AC Metro III | AC-640 | ex N425MA | | ♦ |
| ☐ N655KL | Swearingen SA.227AC Metro III | AC-655B | ex N2691W | | ♦ |
| ☐ N731KY | Swearingen SA.227AC Metro III | AC-731 | ex N2728G | | ♦ |
| ☐ N765FA | Swearingen SA.227AC Metro III | AC-765 | ex ZK-NSI | | |
| ☐ N769KL | Swearingen SA.227AC Metro III | AC-769B | ex HZ-SN10 | | |
| ☐ N779BC | Swearingen SA.227AC Metro III | BC-779B | ex XA-RXW | | |
| ☐ N787C | Swearingen SA.227AC Metro III | AC-550 | ex N31110 | | ♦ |
| ☐ N787KL | Swearingen SA.227BC Metro III | BC-787B | ex XA-SAQ | | |
| ☐ N788KL | Swearingen SA.227AC Metro III | AC-788B | ex A9C-DHA | | |
| | | | | | |
| ☐ N366DC | Embraer EMB.120ER Brasilia | 120288 | ex N220SW | | ♦ |
| ☐ N394DC | Dornier 328-310 (328JET) | 3174 | ex N38VP | | ♦ |
| ☐ N395DC | Dornier 328-310 (328JET) | 3178 | ex N905HB | | ♦ |
| ☐ N404MG | Cessna 404 Titan | 404-0813 | ex 3X-GCF | | |
| ☐ N820DC | Swearingen SA.227DC Metro 23 | DC-820B | ex XA-SHD | | |
| ☐ N882DC | Swearingen SA.227DC Metro 23 | DC-882B | ex C-GAFQ | | |
| ☐ N37127 | Cessna 404 Titan | 404-0114 | | | |

## KING AIRELINES — Las Vegas-Henderson Executive, NV (HSH)

| | | | | |
|---|---|---|---|---|
| ☐ N57SA | Cessna 402A | 402A0101 | ex N7801Q | |
| ☐ N69PB | Cessna 402B II | 402B1248 | | |
| ☐ N82TA | Cessna 402 | 402-0156 | ex N402DK | |
| ☐ N402SW | Cessna 402 | 402-0036 | ex N8236Q | |
| ☐ N2966Q | Cessna 402B | 402B0321 | ex RP-C1998 | |
| ☐ N5098G | Cessna 402A | 402A0056 | ex C-FPDH | |
| ☐ N9901F | Cessna 402B | 402B0402 | ex C-GXHC | |

## KOLOB CANYON AIR SERVICE — Cedar City, UT (CDC)

| | | | | |
|---|---|---|---|---|
| ☐ N2BZ | Aero Commander 500S Shrike | 3227 | ex N57150 | |
| ☐ N57RS | Rockwell 690A Turbo Commander | 11149 | ex N5KW | |
| ☐ N66GW | Rockwell 690A Turbo Commander | 11174 | ex N6B | |
| ☐ N90AT | Rockwell 690A Turbo Commander | 11272 | ex N888PB | |
| ☐ N98PJ | Rockwell 690A Turbo Commander | 11320 | ex N220HC | |
| ☐ N900DT | Aero Commander 500S Shrike | 3056 | ex N9008N | |
| | | | | |
| ☐ N649KA | Swearingen SA.227AC Metro III | AC-649 | ex C6-REX | ♦ |
| ☐ N652KA | Swearingen SA.227AC Metro III | AC-652B | | ♦ |
| ☐ N690TR | Rockwell 690A Turbo Commander | 11034 | | ♦ |
| ☐ N746KA | Swearingen SA.227AC Metro III | AC-746B | ex C6-SDA | ♦ |
| ☐ N773DL | Learjet 35A | 35A-174 | | ♦ |
| ☐ N6851J | Piper PA-32R-300 Lance | 32R-7680870 | | ♦ |
| ☐ N75195 | Piper PA-32R-300 Lance | 32R-7680277 | | ♦ |

## LAB FLYING SERVICE — LAB (JF/LAB) — Juneau-Intl, AK/Haines-Municipal, AK (JNU/HNS)

| | | | | |
|---|---|---|---|---|
| ☐ N54KA | Piper PA-32-300 Cherokee Six | 32-7840197 | | |
| ☐ N666EB | Piper PA-32-300 Six | 32-7940115 | ex N2116G | |
| ☐ N2181Z | Piper PA-32-300 Six | 32-7940104 | | |
| ☐ N2897X | Piper PA-32-300 Six | 32-7940187 | | |
| ☐ N2930Q | Piper PA-32R-300 Lance | 32R-7780269 | | |
| ☐ N4485X | Piper PA-32-300 Cherokee Six | 32-7640026 | | |
| ☐ N5686V | Piper PA-32R-300 Lance | 32R-7780361 | | |
| ☐ N6117J | Piper PA-32-300 Cherokee Six | 32-7640095 | | |
| ☐ N6968J | Piper PA-32R-300 Lance | 32R-7680397 | | |
| ☐ N7718C | Piper PA-32-300 Cherokee Six | 32-7640049 | | |
| ☐ N8127Q | Piper PA-32-300 Six | 32-7940269 | | |
| ☐ N8493C | Piper PA-32R-300 Lance | 32R-7680118 | | |
| ☐ N9795C | Piper PA-32-300 Cherokee Six | 32-7840118 | | |
| ☐ N39636 | Piper PA-32-300 Cherokee Six | 32-7840172 | | |
| | | | | |
| ☐ N3523Y | Piper PA-31-350 Chieftain | 31-7952115 | | |
| ☐ N6314V | Helio H-295 Courier II | 2534 | | |
| ☐ N7333L | Piper PA-34-200T Seneca II | 34-7670099 | | |
| ☐ N27513 | Piper PA-31-350 Chieftain | 31-7852033 | | |
| ☐ N54732 | Piper PA-31-350 Navajo Chieftain | 31-7405254 | | |
| ☐ N55951 | Piper PA-34-200 Seneca | 34-7350264 | | ♦ |

## LAKE & PENINSULA AIRLINES — Port Alsworth, AK (PTA)

| | | | | |
|---|---|---|---|---|
| ☐ N454SF | Cessna 208B Caravan I | 208B0797 | ex N5180C | ♦ |
| ☐ N756BW | Cessna U206G Stationair | U20603969 | | FP/WS |
| ☐ N9530F | Cessna 208 Caravan I | 20800088 | | |
| ☐ N9602F | Cessna 208 Caravan I | 20800103 | | |

## LAKE CLARK AIR — Port Alsworth, AK (PTA)

| | | | | |
|---|---|---|---|---|
| ☐ N76RA | Piper PA-31-350 Navajo Chieftain | 31-7752089 | ex N27212 | |
| ☐ N991AK | Beech 99 | U-28 | ex N33TN | |

| | | | | |
|---|---|---|---|---|
| ☐ N993AK | PA-31-350 Navajo Chieftain | 31-7305015 | ex N7146T | |
| ☐ N996AK | Cessna U206E Stationair | U20601519 | | ◆ |
| ☐ N8300Q | Cessna U206F Stationair II | U20603161 | | FP |
| ☐ N27231 | Piper PA-31-350 Navajo Chieftain | 31-7752106 | | |
| ☐ N70076 | Cessna 207A Stationair 7 II | 20700547 | | |
| ☐ N91028 | Cessna 207 Skywagon | 20700019 | | |

## LOGISTIC AIR — Reno, NV (RNO)

| | | | | |
|---|---|---|---|---|
| ☐ N617US | Boeing 747-251F | 21121/261 | | [MZJ]◆ |
| ☐ N618US | Boeing 747-251F | 21122/269 | | [MZJ]◆ |
| ☐ S2-AFA | Boeing 747-121F | 19650/24 | ex N617FF | [JHB]◆ |
| ☐ 5U-ACF | Boeing 747-146B | 23150/601 | ex (CP-2480) | wfs |
| ☐ 5U-ACG | Boeing 747-146B | 22067/427 | ex N553SW | wfs |
| ☐ N722LA | Boeing 727-2F2F | 22992/1804 | ex TC-JCA | wfs◆ |
| ☐ N908AX | Douglas DC-9-31 | 47008/98 | ex VH-TJK | [MZJ]◆ |
| ☐ N941AX | Douglas DC-9-31 | 47419/602 | ex VH-TJQ | [MZJ]◆ |
| ☐ N982AX | Douglas DC-9-32 | 47317/385 | ex N1261L | [MZJ]◆ |

## LYNDEN AIR CARGO — Lynden (L2/LYC) — Anchorage-Intl, AK (ANC)

| | | | | |
|---|---|---|---|---|
| ☐ N401LC | Lockheed L-382G-31C Hercules | 4606 | ex ZS-RSJ | |
| ☐ N402LC | Lockheed L-382G-35C Hercules | 4698 | ex ZS-JJA | |
| ☐ N403LC | Lockheed L-382G-31C Hercules | 4590 | ex N903SJ | |
| ☐ N404LC | Lockheed L-382G-38C Hercules | 4763 | ex N909SJ | |
| ☐ N405LC | Lockheed L-382G-69C Hercules | 5025 | ex ZS-OLG | |
| ☐ N407LC | Lockheed L-382G Hercules | 5225 | ex N425GF | ◆ |

## LYNX AIR INTERNATIONAL — Lynx Flight (LXF) — Fort Lauderdale-Executive, FL (FXE)

| | | | |
|---|---|---|---|
| ☐ N61NE | Swearingen SA.227AC Metro III | AC-761B | |

## LYNX AVIATION — (SHA) — Denver, CO (DEN)

Ops de Havilland DHC-8-402Qs on behalf of Frontier Airlines, of which it is a wholly owned subsidiary.

## M & N AVIATION — (W4) — San Juan-Munoz Marin Intl, PR (SJU)

| | | | | |
|---|---|---|---|---|
| ☐ N409MN | Cessna 208B Caravan I | 208B0846 | ex N51666 | |
| ☐ N410MN | Beech 1900C | UC-167 | ex N167GL | |
| ☐ N787RA | Cessna 208B Caravan I | 208B1019 | ex N52144 | |
| ☐ N1131G | Cessna 208B Caravan I | 208B0661 | | |
| ☐ N1241X | Cessna 208B Caravan I | 208B0657 | ex N52601 | |

## MAJESTIC AIR CARGO

| | | | |
|---|---|---|---|
| ☐ N851SA | Beech 99A | U-25 | ◆ |

## MARTINAIRE — Martex (MRA) — Dallas-Addison, TX (ADS)

| | | | | |
|---|---|---|---|---|
| ☐ N78SA | Cessna 208B Caravan I | 208B0467 | ex N5058J | |
| ☐ N162SA | Cessna 208B Caravan I | 208B0548 | ex N1219N | |
| ☐ N1031P | Cessna 208B Caravan I | 208B0404 | | |
| ☐ N1037N | Cessna 208B Caravan I | 208B0334 | ex (C-GWFN) | |
| ☐ N1115M | Cessna 208B Caravan I | 208B0356 | | ◆ |
| ☐ N1116W | Cessna 208B Caravan I | 208B0411 | | |
| ☐ N1119V | Cessna 208B Caravan I | 208B0383 | | |
| ☐ N1120N | Cessna 208B Caravan I | 208B0386 | | |
| ☐ N1120W | Cessna 208B Caravan I | 208B0388 | | |
| ☐ N1324G | Cessna 208B Caravan I | 208B0777 | ex N5262Z | |
| ☐ N4591B | Cessna 208B Caravan I | 208B0137 | ex (N997FE) | |
| ☐ N4602B | Cessna 208B Caravan I | 208B0140 | ex (N999FE) | |
| ☐ N4625B | Cessna 208B Caravan I | 208B0159 | | |
| ☐ N4655B | Cessna 208B Caravan I | 208B0160 | | |
| ☐ N4662B | Cessna 208B Caravan I | 208B0161 | | |
| ☐ N4674B | Cessna 208B Caravan I | 208B0165 | | |
| ☐ N4687B | Cessna 208B Caravan I | 208B0167 | | ◆ |
| ☐ N4698B | Cessna 208B Caravan I | 208B0175 | | |
| ☐ N9331B | Cessna 208B Caravan I | 208B0055 | ex (N995FE) | |
| ☐ N9469B | Cessna 208B Caravan I | 208B0079 | | ◆ |
| ☐ N9471B | Cessna 208B Caravan I | 208B0081 | | |
| ☐ N9505B | Cessna 208B Caravan I | 208B0085 | | |
| ☐ N9525B | Cessna 208B Caravan I | 208B0087 | | |
| ☐ N9529G | Cessna 208B Caravan I | 208B0091 | ex (N9546B) | ◆ |
| ☐ N9546B | Cessna 208B Caravan I | 208B0126 | | |
| ☐ N9623B | Cessna 208B Caravan I | 208B0138 | | |
| ☐ N9714B | Cessna 208B Caravan I | 208B0153 | | |
| ☐ N9738B | Cessna 208B Caravan I | 208B0097 | | |
| ☐ N9760B | Cessna 208B Caravan I | 208B0102 | | |

| | | | | |
|---|---|---|---|---|
| ☐ N9761B | Cessna 208B Caravan I | 208B0107 | | |
| ☐ N9762B | Cessna 208B Caravan I | 208B0109 | | |
| ☐ N9766B | Cessna 208B Caravan I | 208B0112 | | |
| ☐ N9956B | Cessna 208B Caravan I | 208B0119 | | |
| ☐ N12155 | Cessna 208B Caravan I | 208B0562 | ex (C-FKAX) | ♦ |
| | | | | |
| ☐ N354AE | Swearingen SA.227AC Metro III | AC-633 | ex N3113C | |
| ☐ N370AE | Swearingen SA.227AC Metro III | AC-506 | ex N87FM | |
| ☐ N575F | Beech 1900C-1 | UC-99 | ex N80598 | ♦ |
| ☐ N575P | Beech 1900C-1 | UC-95 | ex N80532 | ♦ |
| ☐ N592BA | Swearingen SA.227AC Metro III | AC-592 | ex N384PH | |
| ☐ N821SF | Beech 1900C-1 | UC-121 | ex ZS-PKX | ♦ |
| ☐ N26932 | Swearingen SA.227AC Metro III | AC-660 | ex (N660AV) | |

## MAVERICK HELICOPTERS     Las Vegas-McCarran Intl/Grand Canyon-National Park (LAS/GCN)

| | | | |
|---|---|---|---|
| ☐ N805MH | Eurocopter EC130B4 | 3799 | |
| ☐ N806MH | Eurocopter EC130B4 | 3833 | |
| ☐ N807MH | Eurocopter EC130B4 | 3912 | |
| ☐ N808MH | Eurocopter EC130B4 | 3914 | |
| ☐ N809MH | Eurocopter EC130B4 | 3927 | |
| ☐ N810MH | Eurocopter EC130B4 | 3949 | |
| ☐ N812MH | Eurocopter EC130B4 | 3956 | |
| ☐ N813MH | Eurocopter EC130B4 | 3967 | |
| ☐ N814MH | Eurocopter EC130B4 | 4020 | |
| ☐ N815MH | Eurocopter EC130B4 | 4022 | |
| ☐ N816MH | Eurocopter EC130B4 | 4038 | |
| ☐ N817MH | Eurocopter EC130B4 | 4125 | |
| ☐ N818MH | Eurocopter EC130B4 | 4131 | |
| ☐ N821MH | Eurocopter EC130B4 | 4134 | |
| ☐ N822MH | Eurocopter EC130B4 | 4142 | |
| ☐ N823MH | Eurocopter EC130B4 | 4158 | |
| ☐ N824MH | Eurocopter EC130B4 | 4173 | |
| ☐ N846MH | Eurocopter EC130B4 | 4248 | |
| ☐ N847MH | Eurocopter EC130B4 | 4266 | |
| ☐ N848MH | Eurocopter EC130B4 | 4290 | |
| ☐ N849MH | Eurocopter EC130B4 | 4313 | |
| ☐ N850MH | Eurocopter EC130B4 | 4327 | |
| ☐ N851MH | Eurocopter EC130B4 | 4340 | |
| ☐ N852MH | Eurocopter EC130B4 | 4356 | |
| ☐ N853MH | Eurocopter EC130B4 | 4417 | |
| ☐ N854MH | Eurocopter EC130B4 | 4433 | |
| ☐ N856MH | Eurocopter EC130B4 | 4437 | |
| ☐ N857MH | Eurocopter EC130B4 | 4457 | |
| ☐ N858MH | Eurocopter EC130B4 | 4503 | |
| ☐ N862MH | Eurocopter EC130B4 | 4545 | |
| ☐ N863MH | Eurocopter EC130B4 | 4570 | |
| ☐ N864MH | Eurocopter EC130B4 | 4616 | ♦ |
| ☐ N867MH | Eurocopter EC130B4 | 4770 | ♦ |
| ☐ N868MH | Eurocopter EC130B4 | 4797 | ♦ |

## MAXFLY AVIATION

| | | | | |
|---|---|---|---|---|
| ☐ N208JH | Cessna 208B Caravan I | 208B1144 | ex N1273E | ♦ |

## MCNEELY CHARTER SERVICE     Mid-South (MDS)
West Memphis-Municipal, AR/Malden, MO (AWM/MAW)

| | | | |
|---|---|---|---|
| ☐ N106GA | Beech Baron 58 | TH-437 | ex N4379W |
| ☐ N120SC | Swearingen SA.226TC Merlin IVA | AT-067 | ex C-FJTL |
| ☐ N212SA | Cessna 208B Caravan I | 208B0466 | ex N5000R |
| ☐ N262AG | Short SD.3-30 | SH3120 | ex 84-0473 |
| ☐ N866D | Mitsubishi MU-2B-36 (MU-2L) | 656 | ex N666D |
| ☐ N2699Y | Swearingen SA.227AC Metro III | AC-666 | |

## MERLIN AIRWAYS

| | | | | |
|---|---|---|---|---|
| ☐ N708EG | Swearingen SA.227AC Metro III | AC-708B | ex N27188 | ♦ |

## MESA AIRLINES     Air Shuttle (YV/ASH)     Phoenix-Sky Harbor Intl, AZ/Albuquerque-Intl, NM (PHX/ABQ)

Ops for US Airways Express with de Havilland DHC-8s

## MESABA AIRLINES     Mesaba (XJ/MES)     Minneapolis-St Paul Intl, MN (MSP)

Ops services as part of the Delta Connection network, using flight numbers in the range 3000-3439.

## MIAMI AIR INTERNATIONAL     Biscayne (LL/BSK)     Miami-Intl, FL (MIA)

| | | | |
|---|---|---|---|
| ☐ N732MA | Boeing 737-81Q/W | 30618/830 | ex D-AXLI |
| ☐ N733MA | Boeing 737-81Q/W | 30619/856 | ex D-AXLJ |

| | N734MA | Boeing 737-8Q8/W | 30039/701 | ex 5W-SAM | Billie | |
|---|---|---|---|---|---|---|
| | N738MA | Boeing 737-8Q8/W | 32799/1467 | | Diane | |
| | N739MA | Boeing 737-8Q8/W | 30670/1481 | | Ely | |
| | N740EH | Boeing 737-8DC/W | 34596/1875 | | | |
| | N742MA | Boeing 737-83N/W | 30675/898 | ex N304TZ | | |
| | N752MA | Boeing 737-48E | 28198/2806 | ex HL7509 | | |
| | N753MA | Boeing 737-48E | 28053/2954 | ex HL7518 | Miami Heat c/s | |

## MIAMI AIR LEASE — Miami-Opa Locka, FL (OPF)

| | N41527 | Convair 440-72 | 346 | ex C-FPUM | |

## MID-ATLANTIC FREIGHT / ATLANTIC AERO — (MDC) — Greensboro-Piedmont Triad Intl, NC (GSO)

| | N1041L | Cessna 208B Caravan I | 208B0337 | | |
| | N1058N | Cessna 208B Caravan I | 208B0347 | | ♦ |
| | N4698B | Cessna 208B Caravan I | 208B0175 | | |
| | N9820F | Cessna 208B Caravan I | 208B0410 | | ♦ |

## MIDWEST CONNECT — Skyway-Ex (AL/SYX) — Milwaukee-General Mitchell Intl, WI (MKE)

| | N403SW | Canadair CRJ-200ER | 7028 | ex C-FMNB | SkyWest |
|---|---|---|---|---|---|
| | N407SW | Canadair CRJ-200ER | 7034 | ex C-FMNY | Mesa |
| | N471CA | Canadair CRJ-200ER | 7655 | ex C-FMNH | SkyWest |
| | N472CA | Canadair CRJ-200ER | 7667 | ex C-FMML | SkyWest |
| | N479CA | Canadair CRJ-200ER | 7675 | ex C-FMKW | SkyWest |
| | N494CA | Canadair CRJ-200ER | 7765 | ex C-FMKW | SkyWest |
| | N495CA | Canadair CRJ-200ER | 7774 | ex C-FMMT | SkyWest |
| | N498CA | Canadair CRJ-200ER | 7792 | ex C-FMMY | SkyWest |
| | N507CA | Canadair CRJ-200ER | 7796 | ex C-GZFC | SkyWest |
| | N699BR | Canadair CRJ-200ER | 7801 | ex C-FMLS | SkyWest |
| | N709BR | Canadair CRJ-200ER | 7850 | ex C-FMMW | SkyWest |
| | N983CA | Canadair CRJ-100ER | 7169 | ex C-FMNX | SkyWest |
| | N984CA | Canadair CRJ-100ER | 7171 | ex C-FMML | SkyWest |
| | N986CA | Canadair CRJ-100ER | 7174 | ex C-FMNX | SkyWest |
| | N988CA | Canadair CRJ-100ER | 7204 | ex C-FMMT | SkyWest |
| | N836RP | Embraer ERJ-135LR | 145713 | ex PT-SGQ | Chautauqua |

## MINDEN AIR — Minden, NV (MEV)

| | N446MA | British Aerospace 146 Srs.200 | E2111 | ex C-FBAO | | Tanker |
|---|---|---|---|---|---|---|
| | N556MA | British Aerospace 146 Srs.200 | E2106 | ex C-GRNZ | | Tanker |
| | N355MA | Lockheed P2V-7 Neptune (P-2H) | 726-7229 | ex 148344 | 55 red c/s | Tanker |
| | N1427M | Cessna 337E Super Skymaster | 33701247 | | | ♦ |
| | N4692A | Lockheed P2V-7 Neptune (P-2H) | 726-7247 | ex 148357 | 48 yellow c/s | Tanker |

## MOKULELE AIRLINES — Kailua/Kona-Keahole-Kona Intl, HI (KOA)

| | N861MA | Cessna 208B Caravan I | 208B0825 | ex N98RR |
| | N862MA | Cessna 208B Caravan I | 208B1138 | ex N115KW |
| | N863MA | Cessna 208B Caravan I | 208B1049 | ex N208LR |
| | N864MA | Cessna 208B Caravan I | 208B1275 | ex N4115J |

## MOUNTAIN AIR CARGO — Mountain (MTN) — Kinston-Regional Jetport, NC (ISO)

| | N2679U | Short SD.3-30 | SH3071 | ex (N330AE) |
| | N26288 | Short SD.3-30 | SH3074 | ex G-BIYF |

## NATIONAL AIRLINES — (N8/NLE) — Detroit-Willow Run, MI (YIP)

| | N151GX | Boeing 757-2G5 | 24451/227 | ex OB-1788P | [DHN]♦ |
|---|---|---|---|---|---|
| | N168CA | Boeing 757-2Z0 | 27259/609 | ex B-2837 | ♦ |
| | N169CA | Boeing 757-236 | 25592/453 | ex HC-CHC | ♦ |
| | N259CA | Boeing 757-2Y0ER | 26152/478 | ex EI-CEY | |
| | N763CA | Boeing 757-2Y0ERCF | 26154/486 | ex EI-CEZ | |
| | N155CA | Douglas DC-8-73CF | 46073/485 | ex N803UP | |
| | N865F | Douglas DC-8-63F (BAC 3) | 46088/464 | ex TF-FLC | |
| | N872CA | Douglas DC-8-71F | 46040/449 | ex N872SJ | |
| | N919CA | Boeing 747-428BCF | 25302/884 | ex F-GISB | |
| | N949CA | Boeing 747-428BCF | 25630 | ex TF-NAD | ♦ |
| | N952CA | Boeing 747-428MBCF | 25238/872 | exTF-NAC | ♦ |

## NATIVE AMERICAN AIR SERVICE — Phoenix-Williams Gateway, AZ (CHD)

| | N317NA | Pilatus PC-12/45 | 223 | ex N223PD | Air Ambulance |
| | N562NA | Pilatus PC-12/45 | 174 | ex N174PC | Air Ambulance |
| | N613NA | Pilatus PC-12/45 | 197 | ex N197PC | Air Ambulance |

| | | | | |
|---|---|---|---|---|
| ☐ N617LH | Aérospatiale AS350B2 AStar | 2140 | | EMS |
| ☐ N827NA | Aérospatiale AS350B3 AStar | 3144 | | EMS |
| ☐ N970NA | Pilatus PC-12/45 | 226 | ex N308NA | Air Ambulance |
| ☐ N41299 | Aérospatiale AS350B3 AStar | 3806 | | EMS |

## NAVAIR
Minneapolis-Flying Cloud, MN (FCM)

| | | | | |
|---|---|---|---|---|
| ☐ N16U | Beech E-18S | BA-394 | ex N5660D | Frtr |

## NEPTUNE AVIATION SERVICES
Missoula-Intl, MT (MSO)

| | | | | |
|---|---|---|---|---|
| ☐ N122HP | Lockheed P2V-7 Neptune | 726-7226 | ex Bu148341 | |
| ☐ N128HP | Lockheed P2V-7 Neptune | 726-7074 | ex Bu140972 | |
| ☐ N203EV | Lockheed P2V-7 Neptune | | ex Bu128382 | ♦ |
| ☐ N410NA | Lockheed P2V-5F Neptune | | ex Bu131482 | ♦ |
| ☐ N443NA | Lockheed P2V-7 Neptune | 726-7168 | ex N139HP | |
| ☐ N445NA | Lockheed P2V-7 Neptune | 726-7102 | ex N140HP | |
| ☐ N807NA | Lockheed P2V-5 Neptune | 426-5305 | ex N1386K | 07 |
| ☐ N1386C | Lockheed P2V-5 Neptune | 426-5268 | ex Bu128422 | 44 |
| ☐ N4235N | Lockheed SP-2H Neptune | 726-7158 | ex Bu144681 | 10 |
| ☐ N2216S | Lockheed P2V-7 Neptune | 726-7231 | ex Bu148346 | |
| ☐ N2218E | Lockheed P2V-7 Neptune | 726-7246 | ex Bu148356 | |
| ☐ N2218Q | Lockheed P2V-7 Neptune | 726-7255 | ex Bu148359 | |
| ☐ N9855F | Lockheed P2V-5 Neptune | 426-5326 | ex Bu131445 | 06 |
| ☐ N13859 | Lockheed P2V-5 Neptune | | ex Bu131463 | ♦ |
| ☐ N14447 | Lockheed P2V-7 Neptune | 826-8010 | ex RCAF 24110 | 11 |
| ☐ N96264 | Lockheed P2V-5 Neptune | 426-5192 | ex Bu128346 | 12 |
| ☐ N96278 | Lockheed P2V-5 Neptune | 426-5340 | ex Bu131459 | 05 |

## NEW ENGLAND AIRLINES
New England (EJ/NEA)                    Westerly-State, RI (WST)

| | | | | |
|---|---|---|---|---|
| ☐ N403WB | Britten-Norman BN-2A-26 Islander | 46 | ex N123NE | |
| ☐ N404WB | Britten-Norman BN-2A-26 Islander | 564 | ex N304SK | |
| ☐ N406WB | Piper PA-32-300 Cherokee Six | 32-7640058 | ex N8303C | |
| ☐ N408WB | Piper PA-32-300 Cherokee Six | 32-7240092 | ex N4885T | |
| ☐ N598JA | Britten-Norman BN-2A Islander | 66 | | |

## NEW MEXICO AIRLINES

| | | | | |
|---|---|---|---|---|
| ☐ N306PW | Cessna 208B Caravan I | 208B1240 | ex N208TD | |
| ☐ N307PW | Cessna 208B Caravan I | 208B1254 | ex N12959 | ♦ |
| ☐ N308PW | Cessna 208B Caravan I | 208B1273 | ex N5166T | ♦ |

## NORD AVIATION
Santa Teresa-Dona Ana County, NM (EPZ)

| | | | | |
|---|---|---|---|---|
| ☐ N321L | Douglas C-117D | 43345 | ex N307SF | Frtr |
| ☐ N620NA | Douglas DC-6A | 44677/527 | ex N32RU | Frtr |
| ☐ N738WB | Beech D50C Twin Bonanza | DH-286 | | Frtr |
| ☐ N9375Y | Beech H18 | BA-564 | | ♦ |
| ☐ N57626 | Douglas DC-3 | 4564 | ex NC57626 | Frtr |

## NORTH AMERICAN AIRLINES
North American (NA/NAO)                    New York-JFK Intl, NY (JFK)

| | | | | | |
|---|---|---|---|---|---|
| ☐ N760NA | Boeing 767-39HER | 26257/488 | ex N164LF | Tom Cygan | |
| ☐ N762NA | Boeing 767-319ER | 24876/413 | ex SP-LPF | | ♦ |
| ☐ N764NA | Boeing 767-328ER | 27135/493 | ex N135EL | | |
| ☐ N767NA | Boeing 767-324ER | 27569/601 | ex N569NB | Janice M | |
| ☐ N768NA | Boeing 767-36NER | 29898/754 | ex N898GE | Lisa Caroline | |
| ☐ N750NA | Boeing 757-28A | 26277/658 | | Deidre Stiehm | [GYE] |
| ☐ N752NA | Boeing 757-28A | 28174/865 | ex N1795B | Alisa Ferrara | |
| ☐ N754NA | Boeing 757-28A | 29381/958 | | | |
| ☐ N755NA | Boeing 757-28A | 30043/925 | ex N523NA | John Plueger | |

## NORTH STAR AIR CARGO
Sky Box (SBX)    Milwaukee-General Mitchell Intl, WI (MKE)

| | | | | |
|---|---|---|---|---|
| ☐ N50DA | Short SC.7 Skyvan | SH1852 | | Frtr♦ |
| ☐ N50NS | Short SC.7 Skyvan | SH1856 | ex N50GA | Frtr |
| ☐ N51NS | Short SC.7 Skyvan | SH1843 | ex N20DA | Frtr |
| ☐ N114LH | Short SC.7 Skyvan | SH1926 | | Frtr♦ |
| ☐ N731E | Short SC.7 Skyvan | SH1853 | ex N80JJ | Frtr |
| ☐ N754BD | Short SC.7 Skyvan | SH1907 | | Frtr♦ |
| ☐ N549WB | Short SC.7 Skyvan | SH1911 | | Frtr♦ |

## NORTHERN AIR CARGO
Yukon (NC/NAC)                    Anchorage-Intl, AK (ANC)

Ceased ops

## NORTHWEST SEAPLANES — Mariner (2G/MRR) — Seattle-Lake Union, WA/Seattle-Renton (LKS/RNT)

| | | | | |
|---|---|---|---|---|
| ☐ N90YC | de Havilland DHC-2 Beaver | 1338 | ex N127WA | FP |
| ☐ N67681 | de Havilland DHC-2 Beaver | 1158 | ex N215LU | FP |
| ☐ N67684 | de Havilland DHC-2 Beaver | 1208 | ex N67894 | FP |
| ☐ N67685 | de Havilland DHC-2 Beaver | 1250 | ex N128WA | FP |
| ☐ N67689 | de Havilland DHC-2 Beaver | 1242 | ex N67675 | FP |

## OMNI AIR INTERNATIONAL — Omni (OY/OAE) — Tulsa-Intl, OK (TUL)

| | | | | |
|---|---|---|---|---|
| ☐ N225AX | Boeing 767-224ER | 30434/825 | ex N68155 | ♦ |
| ☐ N234AX | Boeing 767-224ER | 30436/833 | ex N67157 | ♦ |
| ☐ N342AX | Boeing 767-328ER | 27136/497 | ex N225LF | |
| ☐ N351AX | Boeing 767-33AER | 27908/578 | ex I-DEIF | |
| ☐ N378AX | Boeing 767-33AER | 28147/622 | ex I-DEIL | |
| ☐ N387AX | Boeing 767-319ER | 24875/371 | ex N875AW | ♦ |
| ☐ N396AX | Boeing 767-319ER | 26264/555 | ex N411LF | |
| ☐ N522AX | Douglas DC-10-30ER | 48315/436 | ex N243NW | [GYE] |
| ☐ N531AX | Douglas DC-10-30ERF | 48316/437 | ex N244NW | |
| ☐ N540AX | Douglas DC-10-30 | 46595/299 | ex D-ADPO | [VCV] |
| ☐ N603AX | Douglas DC-10-30 | 48267/434 | ex N238NW | [PHX] |
| ☐ N612AX | Douglas DC-10-30ER | 48290/435 | ex N239NW | [GYE] |
| ☐ N621AX | Douglas DC-10-30ER | 48319/438 | ex N240NW | [GYE] |
| ☐ N630AX | Douglas DC-10-30 | 46596/301 | ex D-ADQO | [VCV] |
| ☐ N639AX | Boeing 757-28A | 24368/213 | ex N368CG | |
| ☐ N918AX | Boeing 777-222ER | 26935/88 | ex N789UA | |
| ☐ N927AX | Boeing 777-222ER | 26943/92 | ex N790UA | ♦ |

## OMNIFLIGHT HELICOPTERS — Dallas-Addison, TX (ADS)

| | | | | |
|---|---|---|---|---|
| ☐ N93CH | Bell 206L-3 LongRanger III | 51314 | | |
| ☐ N94CH | Bell 206L-4 LongRanger IV | 52070 | | |
| ☐ N95CH | Bell 206L-4 LongRanger IV | 52195 | | |
| ☐ N206AZ | Bell 206L-3 LongRanger III | 51007 | ex N725RE | |
| ☐ N314LS | Bell 206L-3 LongRanger III | 51006 | ex N2210H | EMS |
| ☐ N112LL | MBB BK-117A-3 | 7038 | ex N4493X | |
| ☐ N117M | MBB BK-117A-3 | 7023 | ex N39251 | EMS |
| ☐ N117MK | MBB BK-117B-2 | 7196 | ex N117BK | EMS |
| ☐ N117NG | MBB BK-117A-4 | 7083 | ex N312LF | EMS |
| ☐ N117VU | MBB BK-117B-1 | 7211 | ex N8194S | |
| ☐ N118LL | MBB BK-117A-3 | 7097 | ex N117SJ | |
| ☐ N170MC | MBB BK-117B-1 | 7217 | ex N7161S | |
| ☐ N171MU | MBB BK-117A-4 | 7138 | ex N313LF | |
| ☐ N195LL | MBB BK-117C-1 | 7505 | exN317MC | EMS op for Mayo Foundation |
| ☐ N217MC | MBB BK-117B-1 | 7195 | ex N54113 | EMS op for Mayo Foundation |
| ☐ N250KF | MBB BK-117B-1 | 7206 | ex N117VU | EMS |
| ☐ N504LH | MBB BK-117A-3 | 7061 | ex N312LS | |
| ☐ N527MB | MBB BK-117A-3 | 7103 | ex D-HBPX | |
| ☐ N711FC | MBB BK-117A-4 | 7070 | ex N311LF | EMS |
| ☐ N909LC | MBB BK-117B-1 | 7013 | ex N113LL | |
| ☐ N911MZ | MBB BK-117A-3 | 7098 | ex N117UC | |
| ☐ N1140H | MBB BK-117A-3 | 7078 | ex N212AE | |
| ☐ N75LV | Beech B200 Super King Air | BB-1075 | ex C-GTDY | EMS |
| ☐ N350AZ | Aérospatiale AS350B2 AStar | 3127 | ex N4073A | |
| ☐ N350GR | Aérospatiale AS350B AStar | 3140 | ex N911GF | EMS |
| ☐ N195LL | MBB BK-117C-1 | 7505 | exN317MC | EMS op for Mayo Foundation |
| ☐ N5230J | Aérospatiale AS350B2 Astar | 3256 | | ♦ |
| ☐ N40751 | Aérospatiale AS350B2 AStar | 3154 | | |

## PACE AIRLINES — Pace (Y5/PCE) — Winston-Salem/Smith Reynolds, NC (INT)

Ops suspended 11Sep09

## PACIFIC AIR EXPRESS

| | | | | |
|---|---|---|---|---|
| ☐ N865MA | Cessna 208B Caravan I | 208B0996 | ex N747CG | ♦ |
| ☐ N866MA | Cessna 208B Caravan i | 208B0934 | ex N108JA | ♦ |
| ☐ N867MA | Cessna 208B Caravan I | 208B1002 | ex N501LA | ♦ |

## PACIFIC AIRWAYS — (3F) — Ketchikan-Harbor SPB, AK (WFB)

| | | | | |
|---|---|---|---|---|
| ☐ N12UA | de Havilland DHC-2 Beaver | 700 | ex C-GSIN | FP |
| ☐ N96DG | de Havilland DHC-2 Beaver | 702 | ex N99132 | FP |
| ☐ N264P | de Havilland DHC-2 Beaver | 464 | ex N23RF | FP |
| ☐ N5595M | de Havilland DHC-2 Beaver | 1571 | ex 105 | FP |
| ☐ N9294Z | de Havilland DHC-2 Beaver | 1379 | ex 58-2047 | FP |

328

## PACIFIC WINGS — Tsunami (LW/NMI) — Kahului-Intl, HI (OGG)

| Reg | Type | Serial | Notes |
|---|---|---|---|
| ☐ N301PW | Cessna 208B Caravan I | 208B0983 | |
| ☐ N302PW | Cessna 208B Caravan I | 208B0984 | |
| ☐ N303PW | Cessna 208B Caravan I | 208B0985 | |
| ☐ N304PW | Cessna 208B Caravan I | 208B0833 | ex N699BA |
| ☐ N305PW | Cessna 208B Caravan I | 208B0828 | ex N297DF |

## PAN AM CLIPPER CONNECTION

| Reg | Type | Serial | Notes | |
|---|---|---|---|---|
| ☐ N529PA | British Aerospace Jetstream 31 | 771 | ex N846JS | ♦ |
| ☐ N539PA | British Aerospace Jetstream 31 | 741 | ex N838JS | wfs♦ |

## PAPILLON GRAND CANYON AIRWAYS — (HI) — Grand Canyon-National Park, AZ, (GCN)

| Reg | Type | Serial | Notes | # |
|---|---|---|---|---|
| ☐ N178PA | Bell 206L-1 LongRanger III | 45319 | ex F-ODUB | 8 |
| ☐ N333ER | Bell 206L-1 LongRanger III | 45203 | | 12 |
| ☐ N2072M | Bell 206L-1 LongRanger II | 45720 | | 2 |
| ☐ N3893U | Bell 206L-3 LongRanger III | 51020 | | 9 |
| ☐ N3895D | Bell 206L-1 LongRanger II | 45590 | | 1 |
| ☐ N4227E | Bell 206L-1 LongRanger III | 45702 | ex N725RE | 18 |
| ☐ N5743C | Bell 206L-1 LongRanger II | 45474 | | 23 |
| ☐ N5745Y | Bell 206L-1 LongRanger II | 45531 | | 11 |
| ☐ N20316 | Bell 206L-1 LongRanger II | 45687 | | 21 |
| ☐ N22425 | Bell 206L-1 LongRanger II | 45743 | | 29 |
| ☐ N27694 | Bell 206L-1 LongRanger II | 45282 | | 4 |
| ☐ N38885 | Bell 206L-1 LongRanger II | 45726 | | 20 |
| ☐ N50046 | Bell 206L-1 LongRanger II | 45173 | | 28 |
| ☐ N57491 | Bell 206L-1 LongRanger II | 45505 | | 15 |
| ☐ N130GC | Eurocopter EC130B4 | 3562 | | 41 |
| ☐ N130PH | Eurocopter EC130B4 | 3670 | | 38 |
| ☐ N132GC | Eurocopter EC130B4 | 3756 | | 43 |
| ☐ N133GC | Eurocopter EC130B4 | 3883 | | 48 |
| ☐ N133PH | Eurocopter EC130B4 | 3939 | | 49 |
| ☐ N135PH | Eurocopter EC130B4 | 3695 | | 39 |
| ☐ N136PH | Eurocopter EC130B4 | 3896 | | 46 |
| ☐ N137PH | Eurocopter EC130B4 | 3775 | | 40 |
| ☐ N138PH | Eurocopter EC130B4 | 3790 | | 44 |
| ☐ N151GC | Eurocopter EC130B4 | 4402 | | 51 |
| ☐ N152GC | Eurocopter EC130B4 | 4448 | | 52 |
| ☐ N175PA | Bell 407 | 53154 | | |
| ☐ N197AE | Aérospatiale AS350B2 AStar | 3909 | | 36 |
| ☐ N368PA | MD Helicopters MD900 Explorer | 900-00012 | ex N901CF | |
| ☐ N407PA | Bell 407 | 53567 | ex N16FR | |
| ☐ N425EH | Aérospatiale AS350B2 AStar | 4197 | | 35 |
| ☐ N616AC | Bell 407 | 53354 | ex N407BR | |
| ☐ N195LL | MBB BK-117C-1 | 7505 | exN317MC | EMS op for Mayo Foundation |
| ☐ N617AC | Bell 407 | 53570 | | ♦ |
| ☐ N890PA | Aérospatiale AS350B2 AStar | 4554 | | 37 |
| ☐ N891PA | Aérospatiale AS350B2 AStar | 4557 | | 33 |

## PARAGON AIR EXPRESS — Paragon Express (PGX) — Nashville-Intl, TN (BNA)

| Reg | Type | Serial | Notes | |
|---|---|---|---|---|
| ☐ N703PA | Cessna 208B Caravan I | 208B0776 | ex N5262B | Frtr |
| ☐ N9612B | Cessna 208B Caravan I | 208B0138 | | ♦ |

## PARAMOUNT JET — Little Rock-Adams Field, AR (LIT)

| Reg | Type | Serial | Notes | |
|---|---|---|---|---|
| ☐ N406BN | Boeing 727-291F (Raisbeck 3) | 19991/521 | ex HI-630CA  no titles | [SAT] |

## PENAIR / PENINSULAR AIRWAYS — Peninsula (KS/PEN) — Anchorage-Intl, AK (ANC)

| Reg | Type | Serial | Notes | |
|---|---|---|---|---|
| ☐ N4327P | Piper PA-32-301 Saratoga | 32-8406002 | | |
| ☐ N8212H | Piper PA-32-301 Saratoga | 32-8006046 | | |
| ☐ N8305H | Piper PA-32-301 Saratoga | 32-8106017 | | |
| ☐ N8402S | Piper PA-32-301 Saratoga | 32-8106075 | | |
| ☐ N8470Y | Piper PA-32-301 Saratoga | 32-8206012 | | |
| ☐ N81052 | Piper PA-32-301 Saratoga | 32-8206023 | | |
| ☐ N81844 | Piper PA-32-301 Saratoga | 32-8006012 | | |
| ☐ N82455 | Piper PA-32-301 Saratoga | 32-8006079 | | |
| ☐ N340AQ | SAAB SF.340AF | 340A-019 | ex C-GYQM | <ÇJT♦ |
| ☐ N364PX | SAAB SF.340B | 340B-262 | | ♦ |
| ☐ N365PX | SAAB SF.340B | 340B-265 | ex SE-G65 | ♦ |
| ☐ N403XJ | SAAB SF.340B | 340B-403 | | ♦ |
| ☐ N404XJ | SAAB SF.340B | 340B-404 | | ♦ |
| ☐ N662PA | SAAB SF.340A | 340A-109 | ex N109XJ | |
| ☐ N665PA | SAAB SF.340B | 340B-181 | ex N590MA | |

| | | | | |
|---|---|---|---|---|
| ☐ N675PA | SAAB SF.340B | 340B-206 | ex N593MA | Spirit of Bristol Bay |
| ☐ N677PA | SAAB SF.340B | 340B-328 | ex VH-XDZ | |
| ☐ N679PA | SAAB SF.340B | 340B-345 | ex N345CV | |
| ☐ N685PA | SAAB SF.340B | 340B-212 | ex N594MA | Spirit of the Aleutians |
| | | | | |
| ☐ N750PA | Cessna 208B Caravan I | 208B0628 | | |
| ☐ N195LL | MBB BK-117C-1 | 7505 | exN317MC | EMS op for Mayo Foundation |
| ☐ N985R | Grumman G-21A Goose | B-86 | | ◆ |
| ☐ N7811 | Grumman G-21A Goose | B-122 | | |
| ☐ N9304F | Cessna 208 Caravan I | 20800008 | | |
| ☐ N9481F | Cessna 208 Caravan I | 20800070 | | |
| ☐ N22932 | Grumman G-21A Goose | B-139 | ex CF-WCP | |

## PHI - PETROLEUM HELICOPTERS — Petroleum (PHM) — Lafayette-Regional, LA (LFT)

| | | | | |
|---|---|---|---|---|
| ☐ N151AE | Aérospatiale AS350B3 AStar | 3814 | | |
| ☐ N153AE | Aérospatiale AS350B3 AStar | 3829 | | |
| ☐ N350LG | Aérospatiale AS350B3 AStar | 3690 | ex N499AE | |
| ☐ N351LG | Aérospatiale AS350B3 AStar | 3722 | ex N580AE | |
| ☐ N352LG | Aérospatiale AS350B3 AStar | 3777 | ex N142AE | |
| ☐ N353P | Aérospatiale AS350B2 AStar | 3885 | ex N194AE | |
| ☐ N354P | Aérospatiale AS350B2 AStar | 3886 | ex N196AE | |
| ☐ N498AE | Aérospatiale AS350B3 AStar | 3687 | | |
| ☐ N585AE | Aérospatiale AS350B3 AStar | 3736 | | |
| ☐ N587AE | Aérospatiale AS350B3 AStar | 3730 | | |
| ☐ N590AE | Aérospatiale AS350B3 AStar | 3733 | | |
| ☐ N946AE | Aérospatiale AS350B2 AStar | 3351 | ex N855PH | EMS |
| ☐ N945AE | Aérospatiale AS350B2 AStar | 3004 | ex N40466 | EMS |
| ☐ N954AE | Aérospatiale AS350B2 AStar | 3248 | ex N854PH | EMS |
| ☐ N956AE | Aérospatiale AS350B2 AStar | 3352 | ex N856PH | |
| ☐ N970AE | Aérospatiale AS350B2 AStar | 3235 | | ◆ |
| ☐ N972AE | Aérospatiale AS350B3 AStar | 3234 | | EMS |
| ☐ N973AE | Aérospatiale AS350B3 AStar | 3229 | ex C-GFIH | EMS |
| ☐ N975AE | Aérospatiale AS350B2 AStar | 2777 | ex N6095S | |
| ☐ N4031L | Aérospatiale AS350B2 AStar | 2907 | | based Antarctica |
| ☐ N4036H | Aérospatiale AS350B2 AStar | 2919 | | based Antarctica |
| | | | | |
| ☐ N139PH | Agusta AW139 | 41253 | | |
| ☐ N140PH | Agusta AW139 | 41254 | ex N380SH | |
| ☐ N141PH | Agusta AW139 | 41266 | | |
| ☐ N145PH | Agusta AW139 | 41271 | | |
| ☐ N146PH | Agusta AW139 | 41280 | | ◆ |
| ☐ N998AA | Agusta AW139 | 31142 | ex N140PH | ◆ |
| | | | | |
| ☐ N49EA | Bell 206L-3 LongRanger III | 51507 | ex D-HHSG | |
| ☐ N92MT | Bell 206L-3 LongRanger III | 51175 | ex CC-ETG | |
| ☐ N202PH | Bell 206L-3 LongRanger III | 51076 | ex N31821 | |
| ☐ N203PH | Bell 206L-3 LongRanger III | 51520 | ex N31077 | |
| ☐ N204PH | Bell 206L-3 LongRanger III | 51465 | ex N41791 | |
| ☐ N205FC | Bell 206L-3 LongRanger III | 51130 | | |
| ☐ N207PH | Bell 206L-3 LongRanger III | 51495 | ex N8591X | |
| ☐ N209PH | Bell 206L-3 LongRanger III | 51531 | ex N8594X | |
| ☐ N214PH | Bell 206L-3 LongRanger III | 51131 | ex N4835 | |
| ☐ N215PH | Bell 206L-3 LongRanger III | 51575 | ex N53119 | |
| ☐ N219PH | Bell 206L-3 LongRanger III | 51509 | ex N8593X | |
| ☐ N221PH | Bell 206L-3 LongRanger III | 51494 | ex N8590X | |
| ☐ N225PH | Bell 206L-3 LongRanger III | 51556 | ex N6251Y | |
| ☐ N228PH | Bell 206L-4 LongRanger IV | 52033 | ex N7074W | |
| ☐ N229PH | Bell 206L-3 LongRanger III | 51184 | ex N54641 | |
| ☐ N230PH | Bell 206L-3 LongRanger III | 51506 | ex N206FS | |
| ☐ N266P | Bell 206L-4 LongRanger IV | 52271 | ex N3020J | |
| ☐ N306PH | Bell 206L-1 LongRanger II | 45411 | ex N11027 | |
| ☐ N363BH | Bell 206L-3 LongRanger III | 51345 | ex N997PT | |
| ☐ N436PH | Bell 206L-3 LongRanger III | 51436 | ex EI-CIO | |
| ☐ N668PH | Bell 206L-3 LongRanger III | 51487 | ex N8589X | |
| ☐ N979BH | Bell 206L-3 LongRanger III | 51403 | ex N998PT | |
| ☐ N3107N | Bell 206L-3 LongRanger III | 51512 | | |
| ☐ N3108E | Bell 206L-3 LongRanger III | 51498 | | |
| ☐ N3116L | Bell 206L-3 LongRanger III | 51529 | | |
| ☐ N3207Q | Bell 206L-3 LongRanger III | 51540 | ex C-FLYD | |
| ☐ N4180F | Bell 206L-3 LongRanger III | 51469 | | |
| ☐ N4282Z | Bell 206L-3 LongRanger III | 51499 | | |
| ☐ N5014V | Bell 206L-1 LongRanger II | 45217 | | |
| ☐ N6160Z | Bell 206L-3 LongRanger III | 51610 | | |
| ☐ N6603X | Bell 206L-3 LongRanger III | 51412 | | |
| ☐ N6610C | Bell 206L-3 LongRanger III | 51425 | | |
| ☐ N6748D | Bell 206L-3 LongRanger III | 51106 | ex HC-BVB | |
| ☐ N7077F | Bell 206L-4 LongRanger IV | 52038 | | |
| ☐ N8587X | Bell 206L-3 LongRanger III | 51464 | | |
| ☐ N8588X | Bell 206L-3 LongRanger III | 51486 | | |
| ☐ N21497 | Bell 206L-3 LongRanger III | 51518 | | |
| ☐ N32041 | Bell 206L-3 LongRanger III | 51539 | ex C-FLXL | |

| | | | | | |
|---|---|---|---|---|---|
| ☐ N62127 | Bell 206L-4 LongRanger IV | 52023 | | | |
| | | | | | |
| ☐ N401PH | Bell 407 | 53615 | ex N407MD | | |
| ☐ N402PH | Bell 407 | 53159 | | | |
| ☐ N403PH | Bell 407 | 53267 | ex N8595X | | |
| ☐ N404PH | Bell 407 | 53188 | | | |
| ☐ N406PH | Bell 407 | 53198 | | | |
| ☐ N407H | Bell 407 | 53464 | ex N407XM | | |
| ☐ N407PH | Bell 407 | 53003 | ex C-FWRD | | |
| ☐ N408PH | Bell 407 | 53228 | | | |
| ☐ N409PH | Bell 407 | 53626 | ex N45655 | | |
| ☐ N410PH | Bell 407 | 53636 | ex C-FDXK | | |
| ☐ N411PH | Bell 407 | 53637 | | | |
| ☐ N415PH | Bell 407 | 53390 | ex N492PH | | |
| ☐ N417PH | Bell 407 | 53038 | | | |
| ☐ N418PH | Bell 407 | 53640 | ex N418PH | | |
| ☐ N420PH | Bell 407 | 53747 | ex C-FLZR | | |
| ☐ N421PH | Bell 407 | 53749 | ex C-FLZP | | |
| ☐ N422PH | Bell 407 | 53675 | | | |
| ☐ N424PH | Bell 407 | 53682 | | | |
| ☐ N424QA | Bell 412 | 53999 | | | ♦ |
| ☐ N426PH | Bell 407 | 53751 | | | |
| ☐ N428PH | Bell 407 | 53754 | | | |
| ☐ N429PH | Bell 407 | 53772 | | | |
| ☐ N432PH | Bell 407 | 53681 | ex N431P | | |
| ☐ N433PH | Bell 407 | 53679 | ex N433P | | |
| ☐ N434PH | Bell 407 | 53773 | | | |
| ☐ N438PH | Bell 407 | 53994 | ex N424JA | | ♦ |
| ☐ N439PH | Bell 407 | 53999 | ex N424QA | | ♦ |
| ☐ N440PH | Bell 407 | 53327 | ex N724PH | | |
| ☐ N447PH | Bell 407 | 53114 | | | |
| ☐ N467PH | Bell 407 | 53142 | | | |
| ☐ N490PH | Bell 407 | 53378 | ex N6387C | | |
| ☐ N491PH | Bell 407 | 53386 | ex N6390Y | | |
| ☐ N493PH | Bell 407 | 53393 | | | |
| ☐ N494PH | Bell 407 | 53396 | | | |
| ☐ N495PH | Bell 407 | 53397 | | | |
| ☐ N496PH | Bell 407 | 53398 | | | |
| ☐ N498PH | Bell 407 | 53399 | | | |
| ☐ N501PH | Bell 407 | 53401 | | | |
| ☐ N510PH | Bell 407 | 53209 | | | |
| ☐ N612PH | Bell 407 | 53199 | | | |
| ☐ N719PH | Bell 407 | 53266 | | | |
| ☐ N720PH | Bell 407 | 53277 | | | |
| ☐ N721PH | Bell 407 | 53278 | | | |
| ☐ N722PH | Bell 407 | 53288 | | | |
| ☐ N723PH | Bell 407 | 53283 | | | |
| ☐ N740PH | Bell 407 | 53435 | ex N6077V | | |
| ☐ N741PH | Bell 407 | 53457 | | | |
| ☐ N742PH | Bell 407 | 53461 | | | |
| ☐ N4999 | Bell 407 | 53323 | | | |
| | | | | | |
| ☐ N412SM | Bell 412EP | 36213 | ex N426DR | EMS | |
| ☐ N412UM | Bell 412SP | 33023 | ex N3911L | | |
| ☐ N2014K | Bell 412 | 33020 | ex YV-922C | | |
| ☐ N22347 | Bell 412SP | 36005 | ex XA-RSL | | |
| ☐ 4X-BDT | Bell 412SP | 33150 | ex N142PH | | ♦ |
| | | | | | |
| ☐ N301PH | Eurocopter EC135P2 | 0355 | | | |
| ☐ N302PH | Eurocopter EC135P2 | 0364 | | EMS | |
| ☐ N303PH | Eurocopter EC135P2 | 0372 | | | |
| ☐ N304PH | Eurocopter EC135P2 | 0386 | | | |
| ☐ N305PH | Eurocopter EC135P2 | 0395 | | | |
| ☐ N307PH | Eurocopter EC135P2 | 0398 | | | |
| ☐ N308PH | Eurocopter EC135P2 | 0401 | | | |
| ☐ N309PH | Eurocopter EC135P2 | 0403 | | | |
| ☐ N311PH | Eurocopter EC135P2 | 0413 | | | |
| ☐ N312PH | Eurocopter EC135P2 | 0404 | | PHi Air Medical | |
| ☐ N314PH | Eurocopter EC135P2 | 0409 | | | |
| ☐ N317PH | Eurocopter EC135P2 | 0423 | | | |
| ☐ N320PH | Eurocopter EC135P2 | 0430 | | | |
| ☐ N323PH | Eurocopter EC135P2 | 0434 | | | |
| ☐ N324PH | Eurocopter EC135P2 | 0571 | | | |
| ☐ N325PH | Eurocopter EC135P2 | 0576 | | | ♦ |
| ☐ N326PH | Eurocopter EC135P2 | 0435 | | | ♦ |
| ☐ N327PH | Eurocopter EC135P2 | 0445 | ex D-HECB | | |
| ☐ N328PH | Eurocopter EC135P2 | 0450 | ex D-HECG | | |
| ☐ N329PH | Eurocopter EC135P2 | 0489 | | | ♦ |
| ☐ N330PH | Eurocopter EC135P2 | 0514 | | | |
| ☐ N332PH | Eurocopter EC135P2 | 0519 | | | |
| ☐ N343PH | Eurocopter EC135P2 | 0456 | | | |
| ☐ N344PH | Eurocopter EC135P2 | 0459 | | | |

| | Reg | Type | Serial | Notes | | |
|---|---|---|---|---|---|---|
| ☐ | N370PH | Eurocopter EC135P2 | 0464 | | | ◆ |
| ☐ | N376PH | Eurocopter EC135P2 | 0523 | | | |
| ☐ | N380PH | Eurocopter EC135P2 | 0593 | | | |
| ☐ | N381PH | Eurocopter EC135P2 | 0611 | | | |
| ☐ | N382PH | Eurocopter EC135P2 | 0618 | | | |
| ☐ | N383PH | Eurocopter EC135P2 | 0622 | | | |
| ☐ | N384PH | Eurocopter EC135P2 | 0653 | | | |
| ☐ | N385PH | Eurocopter EC135P2 | 0670 | | | ◆ |
| ☐ | N388PH | Eurocopter EC135P2 | 0701 | | | ◆ |
| ☐ | N389PH | Eurocopter EC135P2 | 0710 | | | ◆ |
| ☐ | N390PH | Eurocopter EC135P2 | 0733 | | | ◆ |
| ☐ | N391PH | Eurocopter EC135P2 | 0748 | | | ◆ |
| | | | | | | |
| ☐ | N709P | Sikorsky S-76C-2 | 760716 | | | |
| ☐ | N714P | Sikorsky S-76C+ | 760719 | | | |
| ☐ | N718P | Sikorsky S-76C-2 | 760686 | | | ◆ |
| ☐ | N725P | Sikorsky S-76C-2 | 760688 | | | |
| ☐ | N734P | Sikorsky S-76C | 760600 | ex N70936 | | |
| ☐ | N738P | Sikorsky S-76C-2 | 760668 | | | |
| ☐ | N745P | Sikorsky S-76C | 760619 | | | |
| ☐ | N746P | Sikorsky S-76C | 760623 | | | |
| ☐ | N753P | Sikorsky S-76C+ | 760726 | | | |
| ☐ | N759P | Sikorsky S-76C-2 | 760690 | | | ◆ |
| ☐ | N760PH | Sikorsky S-76A | 760078 | ex VH-BJR | | |
| ☐ | N761PH | Sikorsky S-76A | 760224 | ex VH-BJS | | |
| ☐ | N762P | Sikorsky S-76A | 760060 | ex N76NY | | |
| ☐ | N763P | Sikorsky S-76A | 760166 | ex C-GHJT | | |
| ☐ | N764P | Sikorsky S-76A | 760276 | ex N913UK | | |
| ☐ | N766P | Sikorsky S-76C | 760594 | | | |
| ☐ | N769P | Sikorsky S-76C | 760671 | | | |
| ☐ | N776P | Sikorsky S-76A | 760275 | ex N911UK | | |
| ☐ | N778P | Sikorsky S-76A | 760035 | ex N4253S | | |
| ☐ | N779P | Sikorsky S-76C+ | 760655 | ex N4501G | | |
| ☐ | N781P | Sikorsky S-76C+ | 760630 | | | |
| ☐ | N784P | Sikorsky S-76C | 760634 | | | |
| ☐ | N785P | Sikorsky S-76C | 760635 | | | |
| ☐ | N786P | Sikorsky S-76C | 760643 | | | |
| ☐ | N787P | Sikorsky S-76C-2 | 760692 | | | |
| ☐ | N790P | Sikorsky S-76C | 760675 | ex N45138 | | |
| ☐ | N792P | Sikorsky S-76A | 760193 | ex N792CH | | |
| ☐ | N796P | Sikorsky S-76C-2 | 760681 | | | |
| ☐ | N797P | Sikorsky S-76C+ | 760742 | | | ◆ |
| ☐ | N798P | Sikorsky S-76C-2 | 760685 | | | |
| ☐ | N911MJ | Sikorsky S-76A | 760231 | ex N3122D | | |
| ☐ | N932FF | Sikorsky S-76C | 761505 | | | ◆ |
| ☐ | N1545K | Sikorsky S-76A | 760047 | | | |
| ☐ | N1545X | Sikorsky S-76A | 760050 | | | |
| ☐ | N1546G | Sikorsky S-76A | 760076 | | | |
| ☐ | N1546K | Sikorsky S-76A | 760082 | | | |
| ☐ | N5435V | Sikorsky S-76A | 760158 | | | |
| ☐ | PP-MCS | Sikorsky S-76A | 760077 | ex N1547D | | |
| ☐ | PR-CHG | Sikorsky S-76C+ | 760658 | ex N658A | based Brazil | |
| ☐ | PR-CHI | Sikorsky S-76C+ | 760670 | ex N4514K | based Brazil | |
| | | | | | | |
| ☐ | N149LY | Sikorsky S-92 | 920149 | | | ◆ |
| ☐ | N192PH | Sikorsky S-92 | 920006 | | | |
| ☐ | N292PH | Sikorsky S-92 | 920008 | | | |
| ☐ | N392PH | Sikorsky S-92 | 920015 | | | |
| ☐ | N492PH | Sikorsky S-92 | 920016 | ex N592PH | | |
| ☐ | N592PH | Sikorsky S-92A | 920027 | | | |
| ☐ | N692PH | Sikorsky S-92A | 920028 | | | |
| ☐ | N921PH | Sikorsky S-92A | 920073 | | | |
| ☐ | N925PH | Sikorsky S-92A | 920118 | | | ◆ |
| ☐ | N923PH | Sikorsky S-92A | 920104 | | | ◆ |
| ☐ | N926PH | Sikorsky S-92A | 920121 | | | ◆ |
| ☐ | N2199M | Sikorsky S-92A | 920151 | | | ◆ |
| | | | | | | |
| ☐ | N217AE | MBB BK-117B-2 | 7152 | ex N217UC | | |
| ☐ | N217PH | MBB BK-117A-4 | 7092 | ex N911RZ | | |
| ☐ | N226PH | Bell 212 | 31106 | ex N27805 | | |
| ☐ | N227PH | Bell 212 | 30953 | ex N3131S | | |
| ☐ | N230H | Bell 230 | 23004 | ex N500HG | | |
| ☐ | N232PH | Cessna U206G Stationair | U20606068 | | | |
| ☐ | N241PH | Beech B200 Super King Air | BB-1182 | ex N416CS | | ◆ |
| ☐ | N246PH | Beech B200 Super King Air | BB-1373 | | | ◆ |
| ☐ | N248PH | Beech B200 Super King Air | BB-1618 | ex N827HT | | ◆ |
| ☐ | N380SH | Agusta AW139 | 41254 | | | |
| ☐ | N393AA | Bell 230 | 23028 | ex N14UH | | |
| ☐ | N851PH | MBB Bo.105CBS-4 | S-851 | ex N137AE | | |
| ☐ | N911CM | Beech B200 Super King Air | BB-1551 | ex N247PH | | ◆ |
| ☐ | N911TL | MBB BK-117B-1 | 7198 | ex N911AF | | |
| ☐ | N998AA | Agusta AW139 | 31142 | ex N140PH | | ◆ |

| | | | | |
|---|---|---|---|---|
| ☐ N2753F | Bell 206B JetRanger III | 2729 | | |
| ☐ N3208H | Bell 212 | 31304 | | |
| ☐ N5736J | Bell 212 | 31140 | | |
| ☐ N6607K | MBB Bo.105CBS-4 | S-841 | | |
| ☐ N6992 | Bell 222U | 47521 | ex N911WY | |
| ☐ N8765J | MBB BK-117A-3 | 7054 | ex ZS-HRP | |

## PHILLIPS AIR CHARTER — Beachball (BCH) — Del Rio Intl, TX (DRT)

| | | | | |
|---|---|---|---|---|
| ☐ N666AK | Beech E-18S | BA-18 | ex N3602B | Frtr |

## PHOENIX AIR — Gray Bird (PHA) — Cartersville, GA (VPC)

| | | | | |
|---|---|---|---|---|
| ☐ N164PA | Grumman G-159 Gulfstream I | 54 | ex N26AJ | |
| ☐ N167PA | Grumman G-159 Gulfstream I | 199 | ex N183PA | |
| ☐ N171PA | Grumman G-159 Gulfstream I | 192 | ex YV-76CP | |
| ☐ N185PA | Grumman G-159 Gulfstream I | 26 | ex YV-82CP | |
| ☐ N190PA | Grumman G-159 Gulfstream I (LFD) | 195 | ex N1900W | Frtr |
| ☐ N192PA | Grumman G-159 Gulfstream I | 149 | ex N684FM | [VPC] |
| ☐ N193PA | Grumman G-159 Gulfstream I (LFD) | 125 | ex N5NA | Frtr |
| ☐ N195PA | Grumman G-159C Gulfstream I | 88 | ex C-GPTN | |
| ☐ N196PA | Grumman G-159C Gulfstream I | 139 | ex C-FRTU | |
| ☐ N198PA | Grumman G-159C Gulfstream I | 27 | ex N415CA | |
| | | | | |
| ☐ N32PA | Learjet 36A | 36A-025 | ex N800BL | |
| ☐ N56PA | Learjet 36A | 36A-023 | ex N6YY | |
| ☐ N62PG | Learjet 36A | 36A-031 | ex N20UG | |
| ☐ N71PG | Learjet 36 | 36-013 | ex D-CBRD | |
| ☐ N80PG | Learjet 35 | 35-063 | ex N663CA | |
| ☐ N524PA | Learjet 35 | 35-033 | ex N31FN | |
| ☐ N527PA | Learjet 36A | 36A-019 | ex N540PA | |
| ☐ N541PA | Learjet 35 | 35-053 | ex N53FN | |
| ☐ N542PA | Learjet 35 | 35-030 | ex C-GKPE | |
| ☐ N544PA | Learjet 35A | 35A-247 | ex N523PA | coded NY |
| ☐ N545PA | Learjet 36A | 36A-028 | ex N75TD | coded HI |
| ☐ N547PA | Learjet 36 | 36-012 | ex N712JE | coded AK |
| ☐ N549PA | Learjet 35A | 35A-119 | ex (N64DH) | coded GA |
| ☐ N568PA | Learjet 35A | 35A-205 | ex N59FN | |
| | | | | |
| ☐ N163PA | Gulfstream G-1159A Gulfstream III-SMA | 249 | ex F-249 | |
| ☐ N173PA | Gulfstream G-1159A Gulfstream III-SMA | 313 | ex F-313 | |

## PHOENIX AIRTRANSPORT — Papago (PPG) — Phoenix-Sky Harbor Intl, AZ (PHX)

| | | | | |
|---|---|---|---|---|
| ☐ N18R | Beech E-18S | BA-312 | | <CBT |
| ☐ N103AF | Beech G-18S | BA-526 | ex N277S | <CBT |

## PIEDMONT AIRLINES — Piedmont (US/PDT) — Salisbury-Wicomico Regional, MD (SBY)

A wholly owned subsidiary of US Airways and uses US Airways Express flight numbers in the range US3000-3399.

## PINNACLE AIRLINES — Flagship (9E/FLG) — Memphis-Intl, TN/Minneapolis-St Paul Intl, MN (MEM/MSP)

Ops for Delta Connection; Colgan Air is a wholly owned subsidiary.

## PLANEMASTERS — Planemaster (PMS) — Chicago-Du Page, IL (DPA)

| | | | | |
|---|---|---|---|---|
| ☐ N274PM | Cessna 208B Caravan I | 208B0705 | ex N9183L | Frtr |
| ☐ N279PM | Cessna 208B Caravan I | 208B0623 | ex N104VE | Frtr |
| ☐ N281PM | Cessna 208B Caravan I | 208B0902 | | Frtr |
| ☐ N282PM | Cessna 208B Caravan I | 208B0981 | | Frtr |
| ☐ N286PM | Cessna 208B Caravan I | 208B0631 | | Frtr |
| ☐ N1114A | Cessna 208B Caravan I | 208B0309 | (N279PM res) | Frtr |
| ☐ N1256P | Cessna 208B Caravan I | 208B0564 | ex N5162W | Frtr |

## PLAYERS AIR — Players Air (PYZ) — Atlanta-de Kalb Peachtree, GA (PDK)

| | | | | |
|---|---|---|---|---|
| ☐ N653CT | Embraer EMB.120ER | 120243 | ex N204SW | |

## POLAR AIR CARGO — Polar (PO/PAC) — New York-JFK Intl, NY (JFK)

| | | | | |
|---|---|---|---|---|
| ☐ N416MC | Boeing 747-47UF | 32838/1307 | | <GTI |
| ☐ N450PA | Boeing 747-46NF | 30808/1257 | The Spirit of Long Beach | |
| ☐ N451PA | Boeing 747-46NF | 30809/1259 | Wings of Change | |
| ☐ N452PA | Boeing 747-46NF | 30810/1260 | Polar Spirit | |
| ☐ N453PA | Boeing 747-46NF | 30811/1283 | | |
| ☐ N454PA | Boeing 747-46NF | 30812/1310 | | |
| ☐ N498MC | Boeing 747-47UF | 29259/1227 | | <GTI♦ |

## PRESIDENTIAL AIRWAYS / EP AVIATION — Melbourne-Intl, FL (MLB)

| | Reg | Type | c/n | ex | Notes |
|---|---|---|---|---|---|
| ☐ | N604AR | CASA C.212-200 | CC50-10-289 | ex N966BW | |
| ☐ | N961BW | CASA C.212-200 | CC40-8-248 | ex N202FN | |
| ☐ | N962BW | CASA C.212-200 | CC44-1-290 | ex N439CA | |
| ☐ | N963BW | CASA C.212-200 | CC60-3-320 | ex N204FN | |
| ☐ | N967BW | CASA C.212-200 | CD51-2-304 | ex N203PA | |
| ☐ | N969BW | CASA C.212-200 | CC50-1-262 | ex N262MA | Frtr |
| ☐ | N2357G | CASA C.212-200 | CD51-4-309 | ex N968BW | |
| ☐ | N4399T | CASA C.212-300 | DF-1-393 | ex N965BW | |
| ☐ | N6369C | CASA C.212-200 | MS03-08-379 | ex M964BW | |
| ☐ | N511AV | de Havilland DHC-8-103 | 051 | ex C-GAAN | |
| ☐ | N635AR | de Havilland DHC-8-103 | 047 | ex N801LR | ♦ |
| ☐ | N636AR | de Havilland DHC-8-103 | 086 | ex N150RN | ♦ |
| ☐ | N810LR | de Havilland DHC-8-103 | 003 | ex C-GGOM | ♦ |
| ☐ | N979HA | de Havilland DHC-8-103 | 373 | ex C-GFQL | ♦ |
| ☐ | N990AV | de Havilland DHC-8-102 | 099 | ex C-GZTC | ♦ |
| ☐ | N955BW | Swearingen SA.227DC Metro 23 | DC-821B | ex N821JB | |
| ☐ | N956BW | Swearingen SA.227DC Metro 23 | DC-864B | ex C-GKAF | |
| ☐ | N982BW | CASA CN-235-10 | 010 | ex ZS-OGE | [JNB] as ZS-OGE |

## PRIORITY AIR — New Orleans-Lakefront, LA (NEW)

| | Reg | Type | c/n | ex | Notes |
|---|---|---|---|---|---|
| ☐ | N46SA | Swearingen SA.226T Merlin III | T-231 | ex N20QN | EMS |

## PRIORITY AIR CHARTER — Priority Air (PRY) — Kidron-Stolzfus Airfield, OH

| | Reg | Type | c/n | ex | Notes |
|---|---|---|---|---|---|
| ☐ | N179SA | Cessna 208B Caravan Ii | 208B0594 | ex N5268M | ♦ |
| ☐ | N208TF | Cessna 208B Caravan I | 208B0592 | ex N208CR | |
| ☐ | N228PA | Cessna 208B Caravan I | 208B0930 | ex N2418W | |
| ☐ | N467KS | Douglas DC-3 | 20175 | ex N145RD | ♦ |
| ☐ | N716BT | Cessna 208B Caravan I | 208B0843 | ex N5260Y | ♦ |
| ☐ | N814PA | Pilatus PC-12 | 110 | ex N108U | ♦ |
| ☐ | N820B | Cessna 340A II | 340A0328 | ex YV-1268P | |

## PROMECH AIR — (Z3) — Ketchikan-Harbor SPB, AK (WFB)

| | Reg | Type | c/n | ex | Notes |
|---|---|---|---|---|---|
| ☐ | N1108Q | de Havilland DHC-2 Beaver | 416 | ex 51-16851 | FP |
| ☐ | N4787C | de Havilland DHC-2 Beaver | 1330 | ex C-FGMK | FP |
| ☐ | N64393 | de Havilland DHC-2 Beaver | 845 | ex 54-1701 | FP |
| ☐ | N64397 | de Havilland DHC-2 Beaver | 760 | ex 53-7943 | FP |
| ☐ | N270PA | de Havilland DHC-3 Turbo Otter | 270 | ex N51KA | FP |
| ☐ | N409PA | de Havilland DHC-3 Turbo Otter | 409 | ex C-FLDD | FP |
| ☐ | N435B | de Havilland DHC-3 Turbo Otter | 183 | ex C-GIGZ | FP |
| ☐ | N959PA | de Havilland DHC-3 Turbo Otter | 159 | ex N67KA | FP |
| ☐ | N3952B | de Havilland DHC-3 Turbo Otter | 225 | ex C-GGON | FP |

## PSA AIRLINES — Blue Streak (JIA) — Dayton-Cox Intl, OH (DAY)

A wholly owned subsidiary of US Airways, ops services as a US Airways Express commuter using US flight numbers in the range 4000-4299. All aircraft officially leased to US Airways from AFS Investments and sub-leased to PSA Airlines.

## RAM AIR SERVICES

| | Reg | Type | c/n | ex |
|---|---|---|---|---|
| ☐ | N702RS | SAAB SF.340B | 340B-233 | ex N233CJ |
| ☐ | N703RS | SAAB SF.340B | 340B-252 | ex N252CJ |

## REDDING AERO ENTERPRISES — Boxer (BXR) — Redding-Municipal, CA (RDD)

| | Reg | Type | c/n | ex | Notes |
|---|---|---|---|---|---|
| ☐ | N681RC | Cessna 402C II | 402C0002 | | ♦ |
| ☐ | N2610G | Cessna 402C II | 402C0064 | | |
| ☐ | N2613B | Cessna 402C II | 402C0083 | | |
| ☐ | N2712F | Cessna 402C II | 402C0121 | | |
| ☐ | N5849C | Cessna 402C II | 402C0052 | | |
| ☐ | N36908 | Cessna 402C II | 402C0313 | | |
| ☐ | N48SA | Cessna 404A Titan II | 404-0417 | ex C-GSPG | |
| ☐ | N121HA | Cessna 208B Caravan I | 208B0068 | ex N6540Q | |
| ☐ | N932C | Cessna 208B Caravan I | 208B0032 | ex N932FE | ♦ |
| ☐ | N6072V | Piper Aerostar 601P | 61P-0696-7963332 | | |

## RED LINE AIR

| | Reg | Type | c/n | ex | Notes |
|---|---|---|---|---|---|
| ☐ | N196NW | Beech 1900D | UE-362 | ex N23627 | ♦ |
| ☐ | N603WM | Beech 300 Super King Air | FA-198 | | ♦ |

| | | | | |
|---|---|---|---|---|
| **REEVE AIR ALASKA** | | | | **Anchorage, AK (ANC)** |
| ☐ N16PC | Piper PA-31 Navajo | 31-639 | | ◆ |

| | | | | |
|---|---|---|---|---|
| **REPUBLIC AIRWAYS** | | **Brickyard (RW/RPA)** | | |
| | | **Chicago-O'Hare, IL/Washington-Dulles, DC (ORD/DUL)** | | |
| ☐ N810MD | Embraer ERJ-170SU | 17000026 | ex PT-SKT | |
| ☐ N813MA | Embraer ERJ-170SU | 17000031 | ex PT-SKZ | |
| ☐ N815MD | Embraer ERJ-170SU | 17000034 | ex PT-SUD | |
| ☐ N818MD | Embraer ERJ-170SU | 17000039 | ex PT-SUI | |
| ☐ N821MD | Embraer ERJ-170SU | 17000042 | ex PT-SUL | |
| ☐ N826MD | Embraer ERJ-170SU | 17000046 | ex PT-SUP | |
| ☐ N871RW | Embraer ERJ-170SU | 17000140 | ex PT-SEE | |
| ☐ N872RW | Embraer ERJ-170SU | 17000143 | ex PT-SEH | |
| ☐ N873RW | Embraer ERJ-170SU | 17000144 | ex PT-SEI | |
| ☐ N874RW | Embraer ERJ-170SU | 17000148 | ex PT-SEM | |
| ☐ N161HL | Embraer ERJ-190AR | 19000154 | ex N161HQ | Frontier |
| ☐ N162HL | Embraer ERJ-190AR | 19000231 | ex N162HQ | Frontier |
| ☐ N163HQ | Embraer ERJ-190AR | 19000255 | ex PT-STD | Frontier |
| ☐ N164HQ | Embraer ERJ-190AR | 19000275 | ex PT-TLP | Frontier |
| ☐ N165HQ | Embraer ERJ-190AR | 19000291 | ex PT-TZF | Frontier |
| ☐ N166HQ | Embraer ERJ-190AR | 19000166 | ex N959UW | Frontier |
| ☐ N167HQ | Embraer ERJ-190AR | 19000173 | ex N960UW | Frontier |
| ☐ N168HQ | Embraer ERJ-190AR | 19000183 | ex N961UW | Frontier |
| ☐ N169HQ | Embraer ERJ-190AR | 19000188 | ex N962UW | Frontier |
| ☐ N170HQ | Embraer ERJ-190AR | 19000191 | ex N963UW | Frontier |
| ☐ N171HQ | Embraer ERJ-190AR | 19000197 | ex N964UW | Frontier |
| ☐ N172HQ | Embraer ERJ-190AR | 19000198 | ex N965UW | Frontier |
| ☐ N173HQ | Embraer ERJ-190AR | 19000206 | ex N966UW | Frontier |
| ☐ N174HQ | Embraer ERJ-190AR | 19000211 | ex N967UW | Frontier |
| ☐ N175HQ | Embraer ERJ-190AR | 19000216 | ex N968UW | Frontier |
| ☐ N176HQ | Embraer ERJ-190AR | 19000461 | ex PT-TOC | Frontier◆ |
| ☐ N177HQ | Embraer ERJ-190AR | 19000481 | ex PT-TPG | Frontier◆ |
| ☐ N178HQ | Embraer ERJ-190AR | 19000485 | ex PT-TPJ | o/o◆ |
| ☐ N | Embraer ERJ-190AR | | | o/o |
| ☐ N | Embraer ERJ-190AR | | | o/o |
| ☐ N | Embraer ERJ-190AR | | | o/o |
| ☐ N502LX | de Havilland DHC-8-402Q | 4168 | ex C-FMIU | Frontier |
| ☐ N507LX | de Havilland DHC-8-402Q | 4181 | | Frontier |
| ☐ N508LX | de Havilland DHC-8-402Q | 4182 | | Frontier |
| ☐ N510LX | de Havilland DHC-8-402Q | 4186 | | Frontier |

| | | | | |
|---|---|---|---|---|
| **RHOADES INTERNATIONAL** | | **Rhoades Express (RDS)** | | **Columbus-Municipal, IN (CLU)** |
| ☐ N132JR | Cessna 402B | 402B1363 | ex (N4606N) | |
| ☐ N134JR | Cessna 310R | 310R2117 | ex N6831X | Frtr |
| ☐ N376AS | AMI Turbo DC-3-65TP | 15602/27047 | ex ZS-OBU | Frtr |

| | | | | |
|---|---|---|---|---|
| **ROBLEX AVIATION** | | **Roblex (ROX)** | | **Isla Grande, PR ( SIG)** |
| ☐ N165DD | Short SD.3-60 | SH3740 | ex D-CFXF | [SJU] |
| ☐ N377AR | Short SD.3-60 | SH3755 | ex SE-LHY | |
| ☐ N411ER | Short SD.3-60 | SH3726 | ex G-BNMW | [SJU] |
| ☐ N875RR | Short SD.3-60 | SH3741 | ex G-ZAPD | |
| ☐ N948RR | Short SD.3-60 | SH3751 | ex G-BVMX | |
| ☐ N821RR | Britten-Norman BN-2A-9 Islander | 338 | ex N146A | El Beb |

| | | | | |
|---|---|---|---|---|
| **ROSS AVIATION** | | **Energy (NRG)** | | **Albuquerque-Kirkland AFB, NM** |
| ☐ N7232R | Beech B200C Super King Air | BL-69 | ex N2811B | |

| | | | | |
|---|---|---|---|---|
| **ROYAL AIR FREIGHT** | | **Air Royal (RAX)** | | **Pontiac-Oakland, MI (PTK)** |
| ☐ N120RA | AMD Falcon 20DC | 211 | ex N764LA | |
| ☐ N123RA | AMD Falcon 20C | 30 | ex N514SA | |
| ☐ N220WE | Dassault Falcon 20C | 349 | | ◆ |
| ☐ N277RA | AMD Falcon 20C | 8 | ex N612GA | |
| ☐ N724JC | Dassault Falcon 20 | 310 | | ◆ |
| ☐ N900RA | AMD Falcon 20C | 59 | ex N159MV | |
| ☐ N22DM | Cessna 310R | 310R0069 | ex N7593Q | |
| ☐ N22LE | Cessna 310R | 310R0033 | ex N1398G | |
| ☐ N728FR | Cessna 310R | 310R1248 | | ◆ |
| ☐ N1591T | Cessna 310R | 310R0112 | | |
| ☐ N1768E | Cessna 310R | 310R1566 | | ◆ |
| ☐ N2643D | Cessna 310R | 310R1686 | | |
| ☐ N87309 | Cessna 310R | 310R0510 | | |

| | | | | | |
|---|---|---|---|---|---|
| ☐ N87341 | Cessna 310R | 310R0520 | | | |
| | | | | | |
| ☐ N34A | Embraer EMB.110P1 Bandeirante | 110350 | ex N4361Q | | |
| ☐ N49RA | Embraer EMB.110P1 Bandeirante | 110424 | ex C-GPRV | | |
| ☐ N64DA | Embraer EMB.110P1 Bandeirante | 110385 | ex PT-SFC | | |
| ☐ N72RA | Embraer EMB.110P1 Bandeirante | 110377 | ex C-GHOV | [PTK] | |
| ☐ N73RA | Embraer EMB.110P1 Bandeirante | 110413 | ex C-GPNW | | |
| | | | | | |
| ☐ N9RA | Learjet 25D | 25D-277 | ex N81MW | | |
| ☐ N16KK | Learjet 25B | 25B-174 | ex N412SP | | |
| ☐ N25FM | Learjet 25 | 25-063 | ex N24LT | | |
| ☐ N25MD | Learjet 25 | 25-054 | ex N509G | | |
| ☐ N48L | Learjet 24A | 24A-107 | | | |
| ☐ N62RA | Learjet 35A | 35A-312 | ex N369BA | ♦ | |
| ☐ N110RA | Learjet 25 | 25-025 | ex (N111LM) | | |
| ☐ N235EA | Learjet 35A | 35A-061 | | ♦ | |
| ☐ N688GS | Learjet 25B | 25B-123 | ex N906SU | | |
| ☐ N710TV | Learjet 24 | 24-159 | ex N66MR | | |
| ☐ N876MC | Learjet 24B | 24B-217 | ex C-FZHT | | |
| ☐ N945W | Learjet 35A | 35A-301 | | ♦ | |
| ☐ N2094L | Learjet 25B | 25B-095 | ex C-GRCO | | |
| | | | | | |
| ☐ N74LA | Beech H18 | BA-603 | | ♦ | |
| ☐ N160PB | Cessna 402C | 402C0493 | ex N6841M | | |
| ☐ N200AJ | Beech A100 King Air | B-146 | ex N410SB | | |
| ☐ N5279J | Cessna 402B | 402B1202 | ex N6841M | | |
| ☐ N5373J | Cessna 402B | 402B0367 | ex C-GCXI | | |

## RUST'S FLYING SERVICE — Anchorage-Lake Hood SPB, AK (LHD)

| | | | | |
|---|---|---|---|---|
| ☐ N121KT | de Havilland DHC-2 Beaver | 1407 | ex N692F | FP/WS♦ |
| ☐ N323KT | de Havilland DHC-2 Beaver | 1022 | ex N10RM | FP/WS♦ |
| ☐ N2740X | de Havilland DHC-2 Beaver | 579 | ex C-GIJO | FP/WS |
| ☐ N4444Z | de Havilland DHC-2 Beaver | 1307 | ex N123PG | FP/WS |
| ☐ N68083 | de Havilland DHC-2 Beaver | 1254 | ex 57-2580 | FP/WS |
| | | | | |
| ☐ N122KT | Piper PA-32-300 Cherokee Six | 32-7940190 | ex N2898W | ♦ |
| ☐ N125KT | Cessna A185F Skywagon II | 18503494 | ex N1855Q | ♦ |
| ☐ N424KT | de Havilland DHC-3 Turbo Otter | 338 | | FP/WS♦ |
| ☐ N675HP | Cessna 208 Caravan I | 20800289 | | |
| ☐ N626KT | Cessna U206G Stationair 6 II | U20604426 | ex N756WY | FP |
| ☐ N727KT | de Havilland DHC-3 Turbo Otter | 419 | ex N427PM | FP/WS♦ |
| ☐ N828KT | Piper PA-32-350 Chieftain | 31-8052098 | ex SE-KDB | ♦ |
| ☐ N929KT | de Havilland DHC-3 Turbo Otter | 461 | ex N271PA | FP/WS♦ |
| ☐ N1292F | Cessna A185F Skywagon | 18502668 | ex N3263C | FP/WS♦ |
| ☐ N2899J | de Havilland DHC-3 Turbo Otter | 425 | ex C-GLCR | FP/WS |
| ☐ N4596U | Cessna U206G Stationair 6 II | U20604990 | | FP |
| ☐ N4661Z | Cessna U206G Stationair 6 II | U20605998 | | FP |
| ☐ N4891Z | Cessna U206G Stationair 6 II | U20606044 | | FP |

## RYAN AIR

| | | | | |
|---|---|---|---|---|
| ☐ N352CA | CASA C.212-200 | CC40-1-190 | | ♦ |
| ☐ N439RA | CASA C.212-200 | CC50-9-287 | ex N287MA | ♦ |

## RYAN AIR / ARCTIC TRANSPORTATION SERVICES
### Arctic Transport (7S/RCT) — Unalakleet-Municipal, AK (UNK)

| | | | | |
|---|---|---|---|---|
| ☐ N26TA | Cessna 207A Stationair 8 | 20700725 | ex N9759M | |
| ☐ N624DR | Cessna 207A Stationair 7 II | 20700517 | ex N917AC | |
| ☐ N624ER | Cessna 207A Stationair 8 II | 20700752 | ex N9936M | |
| ☐ N7305U | Cessna 207A Skywagon | 20700392 | | |
| ☐ N7605U | Cessna 207A Stationair 7 | 20700443 | | |
| ☐ N9475M | Cessna 207A Stationair 8 | 20700695 | | |
| ☐ N9736M | Cessna 207A Stationair 8 | 20700722 | | |
| ☐ N9829M | Cessna 207A Stationair 8 | 20700741 | | |
| ☐ N9956M | Cessna 207A Stationair 8 | 20700763 | | |
| ☐ N73217 | Cessna 207A Stationair 8 | 20700572 | | |
| ☐ N73467 | Cessna 207A Stationair 8 II | 20700594 | | |
| ☐ N73503 | Cessna 207A Stationair 8 | 20700599 | | |
| ☐ N73789 | Cessna 207A Stationair 8 | 20700629 | | |
| | | | | |
| ☐ N424CA | CASA 212-200 | CC40-7-242 | | |
| ☐ N1906 | Short SC.7 Skyvan 3A | SH1906 | ex HS-DCC | Frtr |
| ☐ N2719A | Cessna 402C | 402C0233 | | |

## RYAN INTERNATIONAL AIRLINES — Ryan International (RD/RYN) — Wichita-Mid Continent, KS (ICT)

| | | | | |
|---|---|---|---|---|
| ☐ N120DL | Boeing 767-332 | 23279/154 | | [ATL] |
| ☐ N123DN | Boeing 767-332 | 23437/188 | | |

| | | | | |
|---|---|---|---|---|
| ☐ N125RD | Boeing 767-383ER | 24849/330 | ex XA-MIR | |
| ☐ N637TW | Boeing 767-33AER | 25403/409 | ex PR-BRW | |
| ☐ N763BK | Boeing 767-3Z9ER | 23765/165 | ex G-VKNG | |
| ☐ N764RD | Boeing 767-3Y0ER | 26204/464 | ex PR-VAD | [MZJ] |
| | | | | |
| ☐ N593AN | McDonnell-Douglas MD-83 | 53093/2066 | ex S5-ACE | ◆ |
| ☐ N932RD | McDonnell-Douglas MD-83 | 49233/1203 | ex N932AS | |
| ☐ N950NS | McDonnell-Douglas MD-83 | 53023/1821 | ex N950AS | ◆ |
| ☐ N964AS | McDonnell-Douglas MD-83 | 53078/1996 | | |
| ☐ N965AS | McDonnell-Douglas MD-83 | 53079/2004 | | ◆ |
| ☐ N969NS | McDonnell-Douglas MD-83 | 53063/1851 | ex N969AS | |
| ☐ N974AS | McDonnell-Douglas MD-83 | 53450/2078 | | ◆ |
| ☐ N976AS | McDonnell-Douglas MD-83 | 53452/2109 | | |
| ☐ N979NS | McDonnell-Douglas MD-83 | 53471/2139 | ex N979AS | ◆ |
| | | | | |
| ☐ N526NA | Boeing 757-236 | 24794/278 | ex EC-HDG | wfs |
| ☐ N771RD | Airbus A330-343E | 1231 | ex G-VINE | <VIR◆ |

## SALMON AIR — Mountain Bird (S6/MBI) — Salmon-Lemhi County, ID (SMN)

| | | | | |
|---|---|---|---|---|
| ☐ N80GV | Piper PA-31-350 Navajo Chieftain | 31-7552003 | ex N61487 | |
| ☐ N376ME | Cessna T206H Turbo Stationair | T20608225 | | ◆ |
| ☐ N3528Y | Piper PA-31-350 Chieftain | 31-7952149 | | |
| ☐ N4237D | Piper PA-31-350 Navajo Chieftain | 31-7305055 | ex N800MW | |
| ☐ N6561B | Britten-Norman BN-2A-20 Islander | 520 | ex YV-0-GSF-6 | dam 15Jly07 |
| ☐ N7067Z | Cessna T210M Turbo Centurion II | 21062572 | ex C-GPTX | |
| ☐ N7261 | Cessna U206G Stationair | U20603591 | | ◆ |
| ☐ N8514C | Piper PA-34-200T Seneca II | 34-7670147 | | |
| ☐ N31932 | Piper PA-31-350 Navajo Chieftain | 31-7405144 | ex N888TV | |

## SANDBAR AIR

| | | | | |
|---|---|---|---|---|
| ☐ N524DB | Cessna 208 Caravan I | 20800389 | ex N5244W | ◆ |

## SCENIC AIRLINES — Scenic (YR/SCE) — Las Vegas-North, NV/Page, AZ (VGT/PGA)

| | | | | |
|---|---|---|---|---|
| ☐ N97AR | de Havilland DHC-6 Twin Otter 300 | 365 | ex PJ-TSE | ◆ |
| ☐ N142SA | de Havilland DHC-6 Twin Otter 300 | 241 | ex N385EX | |
| ☐ N146SA | de Havilland DHC-6 Twin Otter 300 | 514 | ex N27RA | |
| ☐ N148SA | de Havilland DHC-6 Twin Otter 300 | 409 | ex N548N | |
| ☐ N226SA | de Havilland DHC-6 Twin Otter 300 | 585 | ex Chile 934 | |
| ☐ N228SA | de Havilland DHC-6 Twin Otter 300 | 253 | ex N103AC | |
| ☐ N297SA | de Havilland DHC-6 Twin Otter 300 | 297 | ex N852TB | |
| ☐ N359AR | de Havilland DHC-6 Twin Otter 300 | 359 | ex N148SA | |
| ☐ N692AR | de Havilland DHC-6 Twin Otter 300 | 692 | ex N230SA | |
| | | | | |
| ☐ N255GL | Beech 1900D | UE-255 | | <GLA |

## SEABORNE VIRGIN ISLANDS — Seaborne (BB) — St Thomas-SPB, VI (SPB)

| | | | | |
|---|---|---|---|---|
| ☐ N288SA | de Havilland DHC-6 Twin Otter 300 | 389 | ex V2-LEY | VistaLiner |
| ☐ N562CP | de Havilland DHC-6 Twin Otter 300 | 562 | ex TI-BAL | |
| ☐ N888PV | de Havilland DHC-6 Twin Otter 300 | 620 | ex CF-TWW | |

## SEAPORT AIRLINES — Portland, OR

| | | | | |
|---|---|---|---|---|
| ☐ N321PL | Pilatus PC-12 | 321 | | ◆ |
| ☐ N950PA | Cessna 208B Caravan I | 208B1063 | ex N208ED | ◆ |

## SHUTTLE AMERICA — Shuttlecraft (S5/TCF)
### Wilmington-Newcastle, DE/Windsor Locks-Bradley Intl, CT (ILG/BDL)

Ops aircraft for Delta Connection and United Express in full colours. Wholly owned by Republic Airlines.

## SIERRA PACIFIC AIRLINES — Sierra Pacific (SI/SPA) — Tucson-Intl, AZ (TUS)

| | | | | |
|---|---|---|---|---|
| ☐ N703S | Boeing 737-2T4 (AvAero 3) | 22529/750 | ex N703ML | |
| ☐ N712S | Boeing 737-2Y5 (AvAero 3) | 23038/949 | ex ZK-NAF | |

## SIERRA WEST AIRLINES — Platinum West (PKW) — Oakdale, CA (SCK)

| | | | | |
|---|---|---|---|---|
| ☐ N563TR | Swearingen SA.227AT Expediter | AT-563 | ex VH-EER | Frtr◆ |
| ☐ N564TR | Swearingen SA.227AC Expediter | AT-564 | ex VH-EEO | Frtr◆ |
| ☐ N567TR | Swearingen SA.227AC Expediter | AT-567 | ex VH-EEP | Frtr◆ |
| ☐ N632TR | Swearingen SA.277AC Metro III | AC-632 | ex VH-RRT | |
| ☐ N681TR | Swearingen SA.227AC Metro III | AC-682 | ex N921BC | Frtr |
| | | | | |
| ☐ N63NE | Swearingen SA.227AC Metro III | AC-763B | | Frtr |
| | | | | |
| ☐ N221TR | Learjet 35A | 35A-221 | ex VH-FSY | Frtr |

| | | | | |
|---|---|---|---|---|
| ☐ N242DR | Learjet 35A | 35A-242 | ex VH-FSZ | Frtr |
| ☐ N283SA | AMD Falcon 20 | 83 | ex (N82SR) | Frtr |
| ☐ N8897Y | Swearingen SA.226AT Merlin IVC | AT-492 | ex C-FJTA | Frtr |

## SILVER AIRWAYS      (3M/GFT)      Fort Lauderdale-Hollwood, FL (FLL)

| | | | | | |
|---|---|---|---|---|---|
| ☐ N45AR | Beech 1900D | UE-12 | ex N138MA | | >CSC♦ |
| ☐ N46AR | Beech 1900D | UE-27 | | | >CSC♦ |
| ☐ N327AG | SAAB SF.340B | 340B-427 | ex N427XJ | | [FLL]♦ |
| ☐ N341AG | SAAB SF.340B | 340B-437 | ex N437XJ | | [FLL]♦ |
| ☐ N344AG | SAAB SF.340B | 340B-444 | ex N444XJ | Ellie's Dream | [FLL]♦ |
| ☐ N614HR | Piper PA-31-350 Navajo Chieftain | 31-7305121 | ex N74HP | | >Gulfstream Air Charter♦ |
| ☐ N27319 | Piper PA-31-350 Chieftain | 31-7852137 | | | >Gulfstream Air Charter♦ |

## SKAGWAY AIR SERVICE      Skagway Air (N5/SGY)      Skagway, AK (SGY)

| | | |
|---|---|---|
| ☐ N1132Q | Piper PA-32-300 Cherokee Six | 32-7740046 |
| ☐ N2884M | Piper PA-32-300 Cherokee Six | 32-7840058 |
| ☐ N8127K | Piper PA-32-300 Cherokee Six | 32-7940268 |
| ☐ N31589 | Piper PA-32-300 Cherokee Six | 32-7840135 |
| ☐ N40698 | Piper PA-32-300 Cherokee Six | 32-7440056 |
| | | |
| ☐ N8216T | Piper PA-32-301 Saratoga | 32-8206037 |
| ☐ N9540K | Piper PA-34-200T Seneca II | 34-7670208 |

## SKY CASTLE AVIATION      New Castle-Henry County, IN (MIE)

| | | | | |
|---|---|---|---|---|
| ☐ N686FR | Beech 58 Baron | TH-1015 | | ♦ |
| ☐ N4231V | Piper PA-31-350 Navajo Chieftain | 31-7652162 | ex C-GBHM | |

## SKY KING      Songbird (F3/SGB)      Sacramento-Metropolitan, CA (SMF)

| | | | | | |
|---|---|---|---|---|---|
| ☐ N147AW | Boeing 737-297 (Nordam 3) | 22630/860 | ex N729AL | no titles | |
| ☐ N249TR | Boeing 737-2K5 (Nordam 3) | 22598/792 | ex F-GFLX | | |
| ☐ N251TR | Boeing 737-228 (Nordam 3) | 23792/1397 | ex F-GBYP | | |
| ☐ N252TR | Boeing 737-228 (Nordam 3) | 23001/936 | ex F-GBYB | Boni Belle | |
| ☐ N465AT | Boeing 737-2L9 (AvAero 3) | 21528/517 | ex N359AS | no titles | |
| | | | | | |
| ☐ N238AG | Boeing 737-4Y0 | 23866/1589 | ex SX-BGH | | ♦ |
| ☐ N720VX | Boeing 737-4K5 | 24129/1783 | ex JA8953 | | ♦ |
| ☐ N741AS | Boeing 737-484 | 25417/2160 | ex SX-BKE | | ♦ |
| ☐ N773AS | Boeing 737-4Q8 | 25106/2518 | | | ♦ |
| ☐ N870AG | Boeing 737-4Y0 | 23870/1647 | ex ZS-SPA | | ♦ |
| ☐ N916SK | Boeing 737-4Q8 | 24706/1996 | ex SP-LLI | | ♦ |
| | | | | | |
| ☐ N307WA | Boeing 737-347 | 23440/1218 | | | ♦ |
| ☐ N308WA | Boeing 737-347 | 23441/1220 | | | ♦ |

## SKY LEASE CARGO      Greensboro-Piedmont Triad Intl, NC (GSO)

| | | | | | |
|---|---|---|---|---|---|
| ☐ N950AR | McDonnell-Douglas MD-11F | 48461/475 | ex B-2170 | | ♦ |
| ☐ N951AR | McDonnell-Douglas MD-11F | 48495/461 | ex B-2171 | | ♦ |
| ☐ N952AR | McDonnell-Douglas MD-11F | 48497/512 | ex B-2173 | | ♦ |
| ☐ N953AR | McDonnell-Douglas MD-11F | 48520/541 | ex B-2175 | | ♦ |
| ☐ N954AR | McDonnell-Douglas MD-11F | 48498/522 | ex B-2174 | | ♦ |
| | | | | | |
| ☐ N501TR | Airbus A300B4-203F | 053 | ex N6254X | | [LIM] |
| ☐ N504TA | Airbus A300B4-203F | 216 | ex N861PA | | wfs |
| ☐ N510TA | Airbus A300B4-203F | 100 | ex C-GICD | | wfs♦ |
| ☐ N821SC | Airbus A300B4-203F | 211 | ex N829SC | | ♦ |

## SKYWAY ENTERPRISES      Skyway Inc (SKZ)
### Orlando-Kissimmee, FL/Detroit-Willow Run, IL (ISM/YIP)

| | | | |
|---|---|---|---|
| ☐ N367MQ | Short SD.3-60 | SH3640 | ex G-BLGA |
| ☐ N377MQ | Short SD.3-60 | SH3699 | ex G-BMUY |
| ☐ N378MQ | Short SD.3-60 | SH3700 | ex G-BMXP |
| ☐ N380MQ | Short SD.3-60 | SH3702 | ex (G-BMXS) |
| ☐ N381MQ | Short SD.3-60 | SH3703 | ex G-14-3703 |
| ☐ N383MQ | Short SD.3-60 | SH3706 | ex (G-BNBB) |
| ☐ N385MQ | Short SD.3-60 | SH3707 | ex G-BNBC |
| | | | |
| ☐ N112PS | Douglas DC-9-15F (ABS 3) | 47013/129 | ex N557AS |
| ☐ N118SW | Short SD.3-30 | SH3100 | ex 83-0512 |

## SKYWEST AIRLINES      SkyWest (OO/SKW)
### Salt Lake City-Intl, UT/Los Angeles-Intl, CA (SLC/LAX)

| | | | |
|---|---|---|---|
| ☐ N216SW | Embraer EMB.120ER Brasilia | 120285 | ex PT-SVF |
| ☐ N217SW | Embraer EMB.120ER Brasilia | 120286 | ex PT-SVG |

| | | | | | |
|---|---|---|---|---|---|
| ☐ N224SW | Embraer EMB.120ER Brasilia | 120294 | ex PT-SVO | | |
| ☐ N271YV | Embraer EMB.120ER Brasilia | 120271 | ex PT-SUS | | |
| ☐ N296SW | Embraer EMB.120ER Brasilia | 120325 | ex PT-SXR | | |
| ☐ N299SW | Embraer EMB.120ER Brasilia | 120329 | ex PT-SXV | | |
| ☐ N301YV | Embraer EMB.120ER Brasilia | 120301 | ex PT-SVV | | |
| ☐ N576SW | Embraer EMB.120ER Brasilia | 120345 | ex PT-SBZ | | |
| ☐ N947SW | Canadair CRJ-200ER | 7786 | ex C-FMMB | 7786 | |

A US Airways Express carrier

## SMOKEY BAY AIR (2E) Homer, AK (HOM)

| | | | | |
|---|---|---|---|---|
| ☐ N36GB | Cessna U206F Stationair | U20601854 | | FP♦ |
| ☐ N282AL | Cessna U206G Stationair | U20603612 | | FP♦ |
| ☐ N734JM | Cessna U206G Stationair | U20604839 | | FP♦ |
| ☐ N756ZV | Cessna U206G Stationair | U20604495 | | FP♦ |
| ☐ N9049G | Cessna U206G Stationair | U206G03795 | | FP♦ |

## SOUTH AERO Albuquerque-Intl, NM (ABQ)

| | | | | |
|---|---|---|---|---|
| ☐ N42MG | Cessna 402C II | 402C0320 | ex N36992 | |
| ☐ N57PB | Cessna 402C II | 402C0300 | ex N3628M | |
| ☐ N305AT | Cessna 402C II | 402C0030 | ex C-GZVM | |
| ☐ N402MQ | Cessna 402C II | 402C0095 | ex N81PB | |
| ☐ N2711X | Cessna 402C II | 402C0116 | | |
| ☐ N2713X | Cessna 402C II | 402C0207 | | |
| ☐ N4643N | Cessna 402C II | 402C0006 | ex C-GIKA | |
| ☐ N5820C | Cessna 402C II | 402C0047 | | |
| ☐ N6880A | Cessna 402C II | 402C0616 | | |
| ☐ N54ZP | Cessna 404 Titan II | 404-0694 | ex N6764X | |
| ☐ N165SA | Cessna 404 Titan II | 404-0622 | | |
| ☐ N404EN | Cessna 404 Titan | 404-0234 | | ♦ |
| ☐ N809RQ | Cessna 404 Titan II | 404-0809 | | ♦ |
| ☐ N5388J | Cessna 404 Titan II | 404-0666 | | |
| ☐ N29AN | Cessna 208B Caravan I | 208B0753 | | ♦ |
| ☐ N108AS | Cessna 208B Caravan I | 208B0975 | | ♦ |
| ☐ N6479N | Cessna T210N Turbo Centurion II | 21063053 | | |
| ☐ N7213N | Cessna T210N Turbo Centurion II | 21063207 | | |

## SOUTH PACIFIC EXPRESS Pago Pago International (PPG)

| | | | | |
|---|---|---|---|---|
| ☐ N711MP | Short SD.3-60 | SH3698 | ex G-BMUX | |

## SOUTHERN AIR Southern Air (9S/SOO) Columbus-Rickenbacker, OH (LCK)

| | | | | | |
|---|---|---|---|---|---|
| ☐ N704SA | Boeing 747-2B5F | 24195/718 | ex N298JD | | |
| ☐ N708SA | Boeing 747-2B5F | 24196/720 | ex N299JD | | |
| ☐ N740SA | Boeing 747-230B (SF) | 21380/320 | ex N507MC | | [MHV] |
| ☐ N748SA | Boeing 747-206M (EUD/(SF)) | 21110/271 | ex PH-BUH | | [MHV] |
| ☐ N749SA | Boeing 747-3B5F | 24194/713 | ex N301JD | | [MHV] |
| ☐ N751SA | Boeing 747-228F | 22678/535 | ex F-GCBE | | [CGK] |
| ☐ N752SA | Boeing 747-228F | 21255/295 | ex F-BPVR | William Neff | [CGK] |
| ☐ N753SA | Boeing 747-228F | 21787/398 | ex F-BPVZ | Southern Dreams | |
| ☐ N754SA | Boeing 747-228F | 21576/334 | ex N536MC | | [MHV] |
| ☐ N758SA | Boeing 747-281F | 23138/604 | ex JA8167 | | |
| ☐ N760SA | Boeing 747-230M | 21221/299 | ex N509MC | | |
| ☐ N761SA | Boeing 747-2F6SF | 21832/421 | ex N534MC | | |
| ☐ N765SA | Boeing 747-2F6B (SCD) | 21833/423 | ex N535FC | | |
| ☐ N783SA | Boeing 747-281F | 23919/689 | ex JA8188 | | >SVA |
| ☐ N815SA | Boeing 747-2L5B(SF) | 22107/469 | ex B-HMF | | |
| ☐ N820SA | Boeing 747-243M | 23476/647 | ex TF-AMD | | [MHV]♦ |
| ☐ N400SA | Boeing 747-412F | 270681000 | ex N417AC | | ♦ |
| ☐ N401SA | Boeing 747-4H6SF | 27044/1041 | ex N420AC | | o/o♦ |
| ☐ N409SA | Boeing 747-4F6SF | 27602/1161 | ex N469AC | | ♦ |
| ☐ N410SA | Boeing 747-419F | 29375/1228 | ex ZK-NBW | | o/o♦ |
| ☐ N714SA | Boeing 777-FZB | 37988/1002 | | | ♦ |
| ☐ N774SA | Boeing 777-FZB | 37986/844 | ex N5023Q | | |
| ☐ N775SA | Boeing 777-FZB | 37987/852 | | | |
| ☐ N777SA | Boeing 777-FZB | 37989 | | | o/o♦ |

## SOUTHERN SEAPLANE Southern Skies (SSC) Belle Chase-Southern Seaplane SPB, LA (BCS)

| | | | | |
|---|---|---|---|---|
| ☐ N206WW | Cessna U206G Stationair | U20604525 | | ♦ |
| ☐ N522SS | Cessna A185P Skywagon | 18504388 | | FP♦ |
| ☐ N732EJ | Cessna 210L Centurion | 21061454 | | FP♦ |
| ☐ N945RW | Cessna 210L Centurion | 21061258 | | FP♦ |

| | | | | |
|---|---|---|---|---|
| ☐ N2272X | Cessna U206E Skywagon | U20601556 | | FP |
| ☐ N21058 | de Havilland DHC-2 Beaver | 630 | ex CF-HOE | FP |
| ☐ N61301 | Cessna A185F Skywagon | 18504144 | | FP |
| ☐ N70822 | Cessna U206F Stationair | U20602099 | | FP |

## SOUTHWEST AIRLINES — Southwest (WN/SWA) — Dallas-Love Field, TX (DAL)

| | | | | |
|---|---|---|---|---|
| ☐ N302SW | Boeing 737-3H4 | 22942/1052 | | The Spirit of Kitty Hawk |
| ☐ N303SW | Boeing 737-3H4 | 22943/1101 | | |
| ☐ N308SA | Boeing 737-3Y0 | 23498/1233 | ex G-EZYA | |
| ☐ N310SW | Boeing 737-3H4 | 22949/1161 | | |
| ☐ N311SW | Boeing 737-3H4 | 23333/1183 | | |
| ☐ N314SW | Boeing 737-3H4 | 23336/1229 | | |
| ☐ N315SW | Boeing 737-3H4 | 23337/1231 | | |
| ☐ N316SW | Boeing 737-3H4 | 23338/1232 | | |
| ☐ N317WN | Boeing 737-3Q8 | 24068/1506 | ex G-EZYE | |
| ☐ N318SW | Boeing 737-3H4 | 23339/1255 | | |
| ☐ N323SW | Boeing 737-3H4 | 23344/1378 | | |
| ☐ N326SW | Boeing 737-3H4 | 23690/1400 | | |
| ☐ N327SW | Boeing 737-3H4 | 23691/1407 | | |
| ☐ N328SW | Boeing 737-3H4 | 23692/1521 | | |
| ☐ N329SW | Boeing 737-3H4 | 23693/1525 | | |
| ☐ N330SW | Boeing 737-3H4 | 23694/1529 | | |
| ☐ N331SW | Boeing 737-3H4 | 23695/1536 | | |
| ☐ N333SW | Boeing 737-3H4 | 23697/1547 | | |
| ☐ N334SW | Boeing 737-3H4 | 23938/1549 | | |
| ☐ N335SW | Boeing 737-3H4 | 23939/1553 | | Shamu |
| ☐ N336SW | Boeing 737-3H4 | 23940/1557 | | |
| ☐ N337SW | Boeing 737-3H4 | 23959/1567 | | |
| ☐ N338SW | Boeing 737-3H4 | 23960/1571 | | |
| ☐ N339SW | Boeing 737-3H4 | 24090/1591 | | |
| ☐ N340LV | Boeing 737-3K2 | 23738/1360 | ex PH-HVJ | |
| ☐ N341SW | Boeing 737-3H4 | 24091/1593 | | |
| ☐ N342SW | Boeing 737-3H4 | 24133/1682 | | |
| ☐ N343SW | Boeing 737-3H4 | 24151/1686 | | |
| ☐ N344SW | Boeing 737-3H4 | 24152/1688 | | |
| ☐ N345SA | Boeing 737-3K2 | 23786/1386 | ex PH-HVK | |
| ☐ N346SW | Boeing 737-3H4 | 24153/1690 | | |
| ☐ N347SW | Boeing 737-3H4 | 24374/1708 | | |
| ☐ N348SW | Boeing 737-3H4 | 24375/1710 | | |
| ☐ N349SW | Boeing 737-3H4 | 24408/1734 | | |
| ☐ N350SW | Boeing 737-3H4 | 24409/1748 | | |
| ☐ N351SW | Boeing 737-3H4 | 24572/1790 | | |
| ☐ N352SW | Boeing 737-3H4 | 24888/1942 | | |
| ☐ N353SW | Boeing 737-3H4/W | 24889/1947 | | Lone Star One |
| ☐ N354SW | Boeing 737-3H4/W | 25219/2092 | | |
| ☐ N355SW | Boeing 737-3H4/W | 25250/2103 | | |
| ☐ N356SW | Boeing 737-3H4/W | 25251/2105 | | |
| ☐ N357SW | Boeing 737-3H4/W | 26594/2294 | | |
| ☐ N358SW | Boeing 737-3H4/W | 26595/2295 | | |
| ☐ N359SW | Boeing 737-3H4/W | 26596/2297 | | |
| ☐ N360SW | Boeing 737-3H4/W | 26571/2307 | | |
| ☐ N361SW | Boeing 737-3H4/W | 26572/2309 | | |
| ☐ N362SW | Boeing 737-3H4/W | 26573/2322 | | |
| ☐ N363SW | Boeing 737-3H4/W | 26574/2429 | | |
| ☐ N364SW | Boeing 737-3H4/W | 26575/2430 | | Heroes of the Heart |
| ☐ N365SW | Boeing 737-3H4/W | 26576/2433 | | |
| ☐ N366SW | Boeing 737-3H4/W | 26577/2469 | | |
| ☐ N367SW | Boeing 737-3H4/W | 26578/2470 | | |
| ☐ N368SW | Boeing 737-3H4/W | 26579/2473 | | |
| ☐ N369SW | Boeing 737-3H4/W | 26580/2477 | | |
| ☐ N370SW | Boeing 737-3H4/W | 26597/2497 | | |
| ☐ N371SW | Boeing 737-3H4/W | 26598/2500 | | |
| ☐ N372SW | Boeing 737-3H4/W | 26599/2504 | | |
| ☐ N373SW | Boeing 737-3H4/W | 26581/2509 | | |
| ☐ N374SW | Boeing 737-3H4/W | 26582/2515 | | |
| ☐ N375SW | Boeing 737-3H4/W | 26583/2520 | | |
| ☐ N376SW | Boeing 737-3H4/W | 26584/2570 | | |
| ☐ N378SW | Boeing 737-3H4/W | 26585/2579 | | |
| ☐ N379SW | Boeing 737-3H4/W | 26586/2580 | | |
| ☐ N380SW | Boeing 737-3H4/W | 26587/2610 | | |
| ☐ N382SW | Boeing 737-3H4/W | 26588/2611 | | |
| ☐ N383SW | Boeing 737-3H4/W | 26589/2612 | | Arizona One |
| ☐ N384SW | Boeing 737-3H4/W | 26590/2613 | | |
| ☐ N385SW | Boeing 737-3H4/W | 26600/2617 | | |
| ☐ N386SW | Boeing 737-3H4/W | 26601/2626 | | |
| ☐ N387SW | Boeing 737-3H4/W | 26602/2627 | | |
| ☐ N388SW | Boeing 737-3H4/W | 26591/2628 | | |
| ☐ N389SW | Boeing 737-3H4/W | 26592/2629 | | |
| ☐ N390SW | Boeing 737-3H4/W | 26593/2642 | | |
| ☐ N391SW | Boeing 737-3H4/W | 27378/2643 | | |
| ☐ N392SW | Boeing 737-3H4/W | 27379/2644 | | |

| ☐ N394SW | Boeing 737-3H4/W | 27380/2645 | |
| ☐ N395SW | Boeing 737-3H4/W | 27689/2667 | |
| ☐ N396SW | Boeing 737-3H4/W | 27690/2668 | |
| ☐ N397SW | Boeing 737-3H4/W | 27691/2695 | |
| ☐ N398SW | Boeing 737-3H4/W | 27692/2696 | |
| ☐ N399WN | Boeing 737-3H4/W | 27693/2697 | |
| ☐ N600WN | Boeing 737-3H4/W | 27694/2699 | |
| ☐ N601WN | Boeing 737-3H4/W | 27695/2702 | Jack Vidal |
| ☐ N602SW | Boeing 737-3H4/W | 27953/2713 | |
| ☐ N603SW | Boeing 737-3H4/W | 27954/2714 | |
| ☐ N604SW | Boeing 737-3H4/W | 27955/2715 | |
| ☐ N605SW | Boeing 737-3H4/W | 27956/2716 | |
| ☐ N606SW | Boeing 737-3H4/W | 27926/2740 | |
| ☐ N607SW | Boeing 737-3H4/W | 27927/2741 | June M Morris |
| ☐ N608SW | Boeing 737-3H4/W | 27928/2742 | |
| ☐ N609SW | Boeing 737-3H4/W | 27929/2744 | California One |
| ☐ N610WN | Boeing 737-3H4/W | 27696/2745 | |
| ☐ N611SW | Boeing 737-3H4/W | 27697/2750 | |
| ☐ N612SW | Boeing 737-3H4/W | 27930/2753 | |
| ☐ N613SW | Boeing 737-3H4/W | 27931/2754 | |
| ☐ N614SW | Boeing 737-3H4/W | 28033/2755 | |
| ☐ N615SW | Boeing 737-3H4/W | 27698/2757 | |
| ☐ N616SW | Boeing 737-3H4/W | 27699/2758 | |
| ☐ N617SW | Boeing 737-3H4/W | 27700/2759 | ex N1786B |
| ☐ N618WN | Boeing 737-3H4/W | 28034/2761 | |
| ☐ N619SW | Boeing 737-3H4/W | 28035/2762 | |
| ☐ N620SW | Boeing 737-3H4/W | 28036/2766 | |
| ☐ N621SW | Boeing 737-3H4/W | 28037/2767 | |
| ☐ N622SW | Boeing 737-3H4/W | 27932/2779 | |
| ☐ N623SW | Boeing 737-3H4/W | 27933/2780 | |
| ☐ N624SW | Boeing 737-3H4/W | 27934/2781 | |
| ☐ N625SW | Boeing 737-3H4/W | 27701/2787 | |
| ☐ N626SW | Boeing 737-3H4/W | 27702/2789 | |
| ☐ N627SW | Boeing 737-3H4/W | 27935/2790 | |
| ☐ N628SW | Boeing 737-3H4/W | 27703/2795 | |
| ☐ N629SW | Boeing 737-3H4/W | 27704/2796 | 25 Silver One |
| ☐ N630WN | Boeing 737-3H4/W | 27705/2797 | |
| ☐ N631SW | Boeing 737-3H4/W | 27706/2798 | |
| ☐ N632SW | Boeing 737-3H4/W | 27707/2799 | |
| ☐ N633SW | Boeing 737-3H4/W | 27936/2807 | |
| ☐ N634SW | Boeing 737-3H4/W | 27937/2808 | |
| ☐ N635SW | Boeing 737-3H4/W | 27708/2813 | |
| ☐ N636WN | Boeing 737-3H4/W | 27709/2814 | |
| ☐ N637SW | Boeing 737-3H4/W | 27710/2819 | |
| ☐ N638SW | Boeing 737-3H4/W | 27711/2820 | |
| ☐ N639SW | Boeing 737-3H4/W | 27712/2821 | |
| ☐ N640SW | Boeing 737-3H4/W | 27713/2840 | |
| ☐ N641SW | Boeing 737-3H4/W | 27714/2841 | |
| ☐ N642WN | Boeing 737-3H4/W | 27715/2842 | |
| ☐ N643SW | Boeing 737-3H4/W | 27716/2843 | |
| ☐ N644SW | Boeing 737-3H4/W | 28329/2869 | |
| ☐ N645SW | Boeing 737-3H4/W | 28330/2870 | |
| ☐ N646SW | Boeing 737-3H4/W | 28331/2871 | |
| ☐ N647SW | Boeing 737-3H4/W | 27717/2892 | Triple Crown c/s |
| ☐ N648SW | Boeing 737-3H4/W | 27718/2893 | |
| ☐ N649SW | Boeing 737-3H4/W | 27719/2894 | |
| ☐ N650SW | Boeing 737-3H4/W | 27720/2901 | |
| ☐ N651SW | Boeing 737-3H4/W | 27721/2915 | |
| ☐ N652SW | Boeing 737-3H4/W | 27722/2916 | |
| ☐ N653SW | Boeing 737-3H4/W | 28398/2917 | |
| ☐ N654SW | Boeing 737-3H4/W | 28399/2918 | |
| ☐ N655WN | Boeing 737-3H4/W | 28400/2931 | |
| ☐ N656SW | Boeing 737-3H4/W | 28401/2932 | |
| ☐ N657SW | Boeing 737-3L9 | 23331/1111 | ex N960WP |
| ☐ N658SW | Boeing 737-3L9 | 23332/1118 | ex N961WP |
| ☐ N659SW | Boeing 737-301 | 23229/1112 | ex N950WP |
| ☐ N660SW | Boeing 737-301 | 23230/1115 | ex N949WP |
| ☐ N661SW | Boeing 737-317 | 23173/1098 | ex N946WP |
| ☐ N662SW | Boeing 737-3Q8 | 23255/1125 | ex N327US |
| ☐ N663SW | Boeing 737-3Q8 | 23256/1128 | ex N329US |
| ☐ N664WN | Boeing 737-3Y0 | 23495/1206 | ex EC-FVT |
| ☐ N665WN | Boeing 737-3Y0 | 23497/1227 | ex G-MONF |
| ☐ N669SW | Boeing 737-3A4 | 23752/1484 | ex N758MA |
| ☐ N670SW | Boeing 737-3G7 | 23784/1533 | ex N779MA |
| ☐ N671SW | Boeing 737-3G7 | 23785/1535 | ex N778MA |
| ☐ N676SW | Boeing 737-3A4 | 23288/1100 | ex N742MA |
| ☐ N679AA | Boeing 737-3A4 | 23291/1211 | ex N306AC |
| ☐ N682SW | Boeing 737-3Y0 | 23496/1217 | ex N67AB |
| ☐ N683SW | Boeing 737-3G7 | 24008/1576 | ex N301AW |
| ☐ N684WN | Boeing 737-3T0 | 23941/1520 | ex EC-EID |
| ☐ N685SW | Boeing 737-3Q8 | 23401/1209 | ex G-BOWR |
| ☐ N686SW | Boeing 737-317 | 23175/1110 | ex EI-CHU |

| | | | | |
|---|---|---|---|---|
| ☐ N687SW | Boeing 737-3Q8 | 23388/1187 | ex N103GU | |
| ☐ N688SW | Boeing 737-3Q8 | 23254/1107 | ex N780MA | |
| ☐ N689SW | Boeing 737-3Q8 | 23387/1163 | ex N734MA | |
| ☐ N691WN | Boeing 737-3G7 | 23781/1494 | ex N784MA | |
| ☐ N692SW | Boeing 737-3T5 | 23062/1083 | ex N733MA | |
| ☐ N693SW | Boeing 737-317 | 23174/1104 | ex N775MA | |
| ☐ N694SW | Boeing 737-3T5 | 23061/1080 | ex N744MA | |
| ☐ N697SW | Boeing 737-3T0 | 23838/1505 | ex N764MA | |
| ☐ N698SW | Boeing 737-317 | 23176/1213 | ex EI-CHD | |
| ☐ N699SW | Boeing 737-3Y0 | 23826/1372 | ex EI-CHE | |
| | | | | |
| ☐ N501SW | Boeing 737-5H4 | 24178/1718 | ex N73700 | |
| ☐ N502SW | Boeing 737-5H4 | 24179/1744 | | |
| ☐ N503SW | Boeing 737-5H4 | 24180/1766 | | |
| ☐ N504SW | Boeing 737-5H4 | 24181/1804 | | |
| ☐ N505SW | Boeing 737-5H4 | 24182/1826 | | |
| ☐ N506SW | Boeing 737-5H4 | 24183/1852 | | |
| ☐ N507SW | Boeing 737-5H4 | 24184/1864 | | |
| ☐ N508SW | Boeing 737-5H4 | 24185/1932 | | |
| ☐ N509SW | Boeing 737-5H4 | 24186/1934 | | |
| ☐ N510SW | Boeing 737-5H4 | 24187/1940 | | |
| ☐ N511SW | Boeing 737-5H4 | 24188/2029 | | |
| ☐ N512SW | Boeing 737-5H4 | 24189/2056 | | |
| ☐ N513SW | Boeing 737-5H4 | 24190/2058 | | |
| ☐ N514SW | Boeing 737-5H4 | 25153/2078 | | |
| ☐ N515SW | Boeing 737-5H4 | 25154/2080 | | |
| ☐ N519SW | Boeing 737-5H4 | 25318/2121 | | |
| ☐ N520SW | Boeing 737-5H4 | 25319/2134 | | |
| ☐ N521SW | Boeing 737-5H4 | 25320/2136 | | |
| ☐ N522SW | Boeing 737-5H4 | 26564/2202 | | |
| ☐ N523SW | Boeing 737-5H4 | 26565/2204 | | |
| ☐ N524SW | Boeing 737-5H4 | 26566/2224 | | |
| ☐ N525SW | Boeing 737-5H4 | 26567/2283 | | |
| ☐ N526SW | Boeing 737-5H4 | 26568/2285 | | |
| ☐ N527SW | Boeing 737-5H4 | 26569/2287 | | |
| ☐ N528SW | Boeing 737-5H4 | 26570/2292 | | |
| | | | | |
| ☐ N200WN | Boeing 737-7H4/W | 32482/1638 | ex N1795B | |
| ☐ N201LV | Boeing 737-7H4/W | 29854/1650 | | Fred J Jones |
| ☐ N202WN | Boeing 737-7H4/W | 33999/1653 | | |
| ☐ N203WN | Boeing 737-7H4/W | 32483/1656 | | |
| ☐ N204WN | Boeing 737-7H4/W | 29855/1663 | | |
| ☐ N205WN | Boeing 737-7H4/W | 34010/1668 | ex N1784B | |
| ☐ N206WN | Boeing 737-7H4/W | 34011/1675 | | |
| ☐ N207WN | Boeing 737-7H4/W | 34012/1678 | | |
| ☐ N208WN | Boeing 737-7H4/W | 29856/1679 | | |
| ☐ N209WN | Boeing 737-7H4/W | 32484/1683 | ex N1787B | |
| ☐ N210WN | Boeing 737-7H4/W | 34162/1690 | | |
| ☐ N211WN | Boeing 737-7H4/W | 34163/1699 | | |
| ☐ N212WN | Boeing 737-7H4/W | 32485/1708 | | |
| ☐ N213WN | Boeing 737-7H4/W | 34217/1717 | | |
| ☐ N214WN | Boeing 737-7H4/W | 32486/1721 | | Maryland One |
| ☐ N215WN | Boeing 737-7H4/W | 32487/1723 | | Ron Chapman |
| ☐ N216WR | Boeing 737-7H4/W | 32488/1735 | ex N1784B | |
| ☐ N217JC | Boeing 737-7H4/W | 34232/1737 | ex (N217WN) | |
| ☐ N218WN | Boeing 737-7H4/W | 32489/1741 | | |
| ☐ N219WN | Boeing 737-7H4/W | 32490/1744 | ex N1786B | |
| ☐ N220WN | Boeing 737-7H4/W | 32491/1756 | | |
| ☐ N221WN | Boeing 737-7H4/W | 34259/1776 | ex N1786B | |
| ☐ N222WN | Boeing 737-7H4/W | 34290/1780 | | |
| ☐ N223WN | Boeing 737-7H4/W | 32492/1799 | ex N1795B | |
| ☐ N224WN | Boeing 737-7H4/W | 32493/1801 | ex N1786B | Slam Dunk One |
| ☐ N225WN | Boeing 737-7H4/W | 34333/1820 | | |
| ☐ N226WN | Boeing 737-7H4/W | 32494/1822 | ex N1786B | |
| ☐ N227WN | Boeing 737-7H4/W | 34450/1831 | ex N1786B | |
| ☐ N228WN | Boeing 737-7H4/W | 32496/1835 | ex N1780B | |
| ☐ N229WN | Boeing 737-7H4/W | 32498/1858 | | |
| ☐ N230WN | Boeing 737-7H4/W | 34592/1868 | | 5000th 737 built |
| ☐ N231WN | Boeing 737-7H4/W | 32499/1881 | ex N1787B | |
| ☐ N232WN | Boeing 737-7H4/W | 32500/1888 | | |
| ☐ N233LV | Boeing 737-7H4/W | 32501/1893 | | |
| ☐ N234WN | Boeing 737-7H4/W | 32502/1905 | | |
| ☐ N235WN | Boeing 737-7H4/W | 34630/1916 | ex N1787B | |
| ☐ N236WN | Boeing 737-7H4/W | 34631/1928 | ex N1786B | |
| ☐ N237WN | Boeing 737-7H4/W | 34632/1930 | | |
| ☐ N238WN | Boeing 737-7H4/W | 34713/1950 | | Spreading the LUV |
| ☐ N239WN | Boeing 737-7H4/W | 34714/1954 | ex N1786B | |
| ☐ N240WN | Boeing 737-7H4/W | 32503/1959 | ex N1786B | |
| ☐ N241WN | Boeing 737-7H4/W | 32504/1965 | | |
| ☐ N242WN | Boeing 737-7H4/W | 32505/1969 | | |
| ☐ N243WN | Boeing 737-7H4/W | 34863/1973 | | |
| ☐ N244WN | Boeing 737-7H4/W | 34864/1977 | | |

| | | | | |
|---|---|---|---|---|
| ☐ N245WN | Boeing 737-7H4/W | 32506/1982 | | |
| ☐ N246LV | Boeing 737-7H4/W | 32507/1984 | ex N1786B | |
| ☐ N247WN | Boeing 737-7H4/W | 32508/1989 | | |
| ☐ N248WN | Boeing 737-7H4/W | 32509/2000 | | |
| ☐ N249WN | Boeing 737-7H4/W | 34951/2005 | | |
| ☐ N250WN | Boeing 737-7H4/W | 34972/2019 | | |
| ☐ N251WN | Boeing 737-7H4/W | 32510/2025 | | |
| ☐ N252WN | Boeing 737-7H4/W | 34973/2027 | | |
| ☐ N253WN | Boeing 737-7H4/W | 32511/2038 | | |
| ☐ N254WN | Boeing 737-7H4/W | 32512/2040 | | |
| ☐ N255WN | Boeing 737-7H4/W | 32513/2049 | | |
| ☐ N256WN | Boeing 737-7H4/W | 32514/2059 | | |
| ☐ N257WN | Boeing 737-7H4/W | 32515/2062 | | |
| ☐ N258WN | Boeing 737-7H4/W | 32516/2076 | | |
| ☐ N259WN | Boeing 737-7H4/W | 35554/2092 | | |
| ☐ N260WN | Boeing 737-7H4/W | 32518/2114 | ex N1786B | |
| ☐ N261WN | Boeing 737-7H4/W | 32517/2133 | ex N1787B | |
| ☐ N262WN | Boeing 737-7H4/W | 32519/2139 | ex N1786B | |
| ☐ N263WN | Boeing 737-7H4/W | 32520/2153 | | |
| ☐ N264LV | Boeing 737-7H4/W | 32521/2161 | | |
| ☐ N265WN | Boeing 737-7H4/W | 32522/2174 | | |
| ☐ N266WN | Boeing 737-7H4/W | 32523/2182 | ex N1787B | Colleen Barrett |
| ☐ N267WN | Boeing 737-7H4/W | 32525/2193 | | |
| ☐ N268WN | Boeing 737-7H4/W | 32524/2199 | | |
| ☐ N269WN | Boeing 737-7H4/W | 32526/2204 | | |
| ☐ N270WN | Boeing 737-705/W | 29089/83 | ex VP-BBT | |
| ☐ N271LV | Boeing 737-705/W | 29090/109 | ex VP-BBU | |
| ☐ N272WN | Boeing 737-7H4/W | 32527/2224 | ex N1786B | |
| ☐ N273WN | Boeing 737-7H4/W | 32528/2238 | | |
| ☐ N274WN | Boeing 737-7H4/W | 32529/2244 | | |
| ☐ N275WN | Boeing 737-7H4/W | 36153/2256 | | |
| ☐ N276WN | Boeing 737-7H4/W | 32530/2262 | | |
| ☐ N277WN | Boeing 737-7H4/W | 32531/2274 | | |
| ☐ N278WN | Boeing 737-7H4/W | 36441/2281 | ex N1787B | |
| ☐ N279WN | Boeing 737-7H4/W | 32532/2284 | ex N1786B | |
| ☐ N280WN | Boeing 737-7H4/W | 32533/2294 | | |
| ☐ N281WN | Boeing 737-7H4/W | 36528/2307 | | Southwest's 500th Boeing 737 |
| ☐ N282WN | Boeing 737-7H4/W | 32534/2318 | | |
| ☐ N283WN | Boeing 737-7H4/W | 36610/2322 | | |
| ☐ N284WN | Boeing 737-7H4/W | 32535/2328 | ex N1786B | |
| ☐ N285WN | Boeing 737-7H4/W | 32536/2337 | | |
| ☐ N286WN | Boeing 737-7H4/W | 32471/1535 | ex N471WN | |
| ☐ N287WN | Boeing 737-7H4/W | 32537/2344 | ex N1786B | |
| ☐ N288WN | Boeing 737-7H4/W | 36611/2350 | ex N1786B | |
| ☐ N289CT | Boeing 737-7H4/W | 36633/2354 | ex N1786B | |
| ☐ N290WN | Boeing 737-7H4/W | 36632/2363 | | |
| ☐ N291WN | Boeing 737-7H4/W | 32539/2378 | | |
| ☐ N292WN | Boeing 737-7H4/W | 32538/2383 | | |
| ☐ N293WN | Boeing 737-7H4/W | 36612/2387 | | |
| ☐ N294WN | Boeing 737-7H4/W | 32540/2390 | ex N1786B | |
| ☐ N295WN | Boeing 737-7H4/W | 32541/2409 | | |
| ☐ N296WN | Boeing 737-7H4/W | 36613/2413 | | |
| ☐ N297WN | Boeing 737-7H4/W | 32542/2417 | | |
| ☐ N298WN | Boeing 737-7H4/W | 32543/2438 | | |
| ☐ N299WN | Boeing 737-7H4/W | 36614/2442 | | |
| ☐ N400WN | Boeing 737-7H4/W | 27891/806 | | |
| ☐ N401WN | Boeing 737-7H4/W | 29813/810 | | |
| ☐ N402WN | Boeing 737-7H4/W | 29814/811 | ex N1786B | |
| ☐ N403WN | Boeing 737-7H4/W | 29815/821 | ex N1786B | |
| ☐ N404WN | Boeing 737-7H4/W | 27892/880 | ex N1787B | |
| ☐ N405WN | Boeing 737-7H4/W | 27893/881 | ex N1786B | |
| ☐ N406WN | Boeing 737-7H4/W | 27894/885 | ex N1786B | |
| ☐ N407WN | Boeing 737-7H4/W | 29817/903 | ex N1786B | |
| ☐ N408WN | Boeing 737-7H4/W | 27895/934 | ex N1786B | |
| ☐ N409WN | Boeing 737-7H4/W | 27896/945 | ex N1787B | |
| ☐ N410WN | Boeing 737-7H4/W | 27897/946 | ex N1786B | |
| ☐ N411WN | Boeing 737-7H4/W | 29821/950 | ex N1786B | |
| ☐ N412WN | Boeing 737-7H4/W | 29818/956 | ex N1795B | |
| ☐ N413WN | Boeing 737-7H4/W | 29819/960 | | |
| ☐ N414WN | Boeing 737-7H4/W | 29820/967 | ex N1795B | |
| ☐ N415WN | Boeing 737-7H4/W | 29836/980 | ex N1787B | |
| ☐ N416WN | Boeing 737-7H4/W | 32453/990 | ex N1786B | |
| ☐ N417WN | Boeing 737-7H4/W | 29822/993 | ex N1786B | The Rollin W King |
| ☐ N418WN | Boeing 737-7H4/W | 29823/1000 | | The Winning Spirit |
| ☐ N419WN | Boeing 737-7H4/W | 29824/1017 | ex N1786B | |
| ☐ N420WN | Boeing 737-7H4/W | 29825/1039 | | |
| ☐ N421LV | Boeing 737-7H4/W | 32452/1040 | | |
| ☐ N422WN | Boeing 737-7H4/W | 29826/1093 | | |
| ☐ N423WN | Boeing 737-7H4/W | 29827/1101 | | |
| ☐ N424WN | Boeing 737-7H4/W | 29828/1105 | | |
| ☐ N425LV | Boeing 737-7H4/W | 29829/1109 | | |
| ☐ N426WN | Boeing 737-7H4/W | 29830/1114 | | |

| | | | | |
|---|---|---|---|---|
| ☐ N427WN | Boeing 737-7H4/W | 29831/1119 | | |
| ☐ N428WN | Boeing 737-7H4/W | 29844/1243 | | |
| ☐ N429WN | Boeing 737-7H4/W | 33658/1256 | | |
| ☐ N430WN | Boeing 737-7H4/W | 33659/1257 | | |
| ☐ N431WN | Boeing 737-7H4/W | 29845/1259 | | |
| ☐ N432WN | Boeing 737-7H4/W | 33715/1297 | ex N1786B | |
| ☐ N433LV | Boeing 737-7H4/W | 33716/1301 | | |
| ☐ N434WN | Boeing 737-7H4/W | 32454/1313 | | |
| ☐ N435WN | Boeing 737-7H4/W | 32455/1328 | | |
| ☐ N436WN | Boeing 737-7H4/W | 32456/1342 | | |
| ☐ N437WN | Boeing 737-7H4/W | 29832/1349 | | |
| ☐ N438WN | Boeing 737-7H4/W | 29833/1353 | | |
| ☐ N439WN | Boeing 737-7H4/W | 29834/1356 | | The Donald G Ogden |
| ☐ N440LV | Boeing 737-7H4/W | 29835/1358 | | |
| ☐ N441WN | Boeing 737-7H4/W | 29837/1360 | | |
| ☐ N442WN | Boeing 737-7H4/W | 32459/1365 | ex (N442LV) | |
| ☐ N443WN | Boeing 737-7H4/W | 29838/1369 | | The Spirit of Hope |
| ☐ N444WN | Boeing 737-7H4/W | 29839/1374 | ex N1786B | |
| ☐ N445WN | Boeing 737-7H4/W | 29841/1388 | | |
| ☐ N446WN | Boeing 737-7H4/W | 29842/1401 | ex N1787B | |
| ☐ N447WN | Boeing 737-7H4/W | 33720/1405 | | |
| ☐ N448WN | Boeing 737-7H4/W | 33721/1409 | | The Spirit of Kitty Hawk |
| ☐ N449WN | Boeing 737-7H4/W | 32469/1427 | | |
| ☐ N450WN | Boeing 737-7H4/W | 32470/1429 | ex N60668 | |
| ☐ N451WN | Boeing 737-7H4/W | 32495/1458 | | |
| ☐ N452WN | Boeing 737-7H4/W | 29846/1461 | | |
| ☐ N453WN | Boeing 737-7H4/W | 29847/1476 | | |
| ☐ N454WN | Boeing 737-7H4/W | 29851/1477 | | |
| ☐ N455WN | Boeing 737-7H4/W | 32462/1480 | | |
| ☐ N456WN | Boeing 737-7H4/W | 32463/1484 | | |
| ☐ N457WN | Boeing 737-7H4/W | 33856/1485 | | |
| ☐ N458WN | Boeing 737-7H4/W | 33857/1490 | | |
| ☐ N459WN | Boeing 737-7H4/W | 32497/1492 | | |
| ☐ N460WN | Boeing 737-7H4/W | 32464/1499 | | |
| ☐ N461WN | Boeing 737-7H4/W | 32465/1510 | | |
| ☐ N462WN | Boeing 737-7H4/W | 32466/1513 | | |
| ☐ N463WN | Boeing 737-7H4/W | 32467/1515 | | |
| ☐ N464WN | Boeing 737-7H4/W | 32468/1517 | | |
| ☐ N465WN | Boeing 737-7H4/W | 33829/1519 | | |
| ☐ N466WN | Boeing 737-7H4/W | 30677/1520 | | |
| ☐ N467WN | Boeing 737-7H4/W | 33830/1521 | | |
| ☐ N468WN | Boeing 737-7H4/W | 33858/1523 | | |
| ☐ N469WN | Boeing 737-7H4/W | 33859/1525 | | |
| ☐ N470WN | Boeing 737-7H4/W | 33860/1528 | | |
| ☐ N472WN | Boeing 737-7H4/W | 33831/1537 | | |
| ☐ N473WN | Boeing 737-7H4/W | 33832/1541 | | |
| ☐ N474WN | Boeing 737-7H4/W | 33861/1543 | ex N1786B | |
| ☐ N475WN | Boeing 737-7H4/W | 32474/1545 | | |
| ☐ N476WN | Boeing 737-7H4/W | 32475/1549 | | |
| ☐ N477WN | Boeing 737-7H4/W | 33988/1552 | | |
| ☐ N478WN | Boeing 737-7H4/W | 33989/1555 | | |
| ☐ N479WN | Boeing 737-7H4/W | 33990/1558 | | |
| ☐ N480WN | Boeing 737-7H4/W | 33998/1561 | | |
| ☐ N481WN | Boeing 737-7H4/W | 29853/1564 | | |
| ☐ N482WN | Boeing 737-7H4/W | 29852/1568 | | |
| ☐ N483WN | Boeing 737-7H4/W | 32472/1570 | | |
| ☐ N484WN | Boeing 737-7H4/W | 33841/1575 | ex N1786B | |
| ☐ N485WN | Boeing 737-7H4/W | 32473/1577 | ex N1786B | |
| ☐ N486WN | Boeing 737-7H4/W | 33852/1579 | | |
| ☐ N487WN | Boeing 737-7H4/W | 33854/1583 | | |
| ☐ N488WN | Boeing 737-7H4/W | 33853/1587 | | |
| ☐ N489WN | Boeing 737-7H4/W | 33855/1589 | ex N1780B | |
| ☐ N490WN | Boeing 737-7H4/W | 32476/1591 | | 100 H-E-B titles |
| ☐ N491WN | Boeing 737-7H4/W | 33867/1598 | | |
| ☐ N492WN | Boeing 737-7H4/W | 33866/1605 | | |
| ☐ N493WN | Boeing 737-7H4/W | 32477/1616 | | |
| ☐ N494WN | Boeing 737-7H4/W | 33868/1621 | | |
| ☐ N495WN | Boeing 737-7H4/W | 33869/1625 | | |
| ☐ N496WN | Boeing 737-7H4/W | 32478/1626 | | |
| ☐ N497WN | Boeing 737-7H4/W | 32479/1628 | | |
| ☐ N498WN | Boeing 737-7H4/W | 32480/1633 | | |
| ☐ N499WN | Boeing 737-7H4/W | 32481/1636 | | |
| ☐ N550WN | Boeing 737-76Q/W | 30279/1010 | ex VT-SIR | |
| ☐ N551WN | Boeing 737-76Q/W | 30280/1025 | ex VT-SIS | |
| ☐ N552WN | Boeing 737-7BX/W | 30744/989 | ex VH-VBQ | |
| ☐ N553WN | Boeing 737-7BX/W | 30745/1027 | ex VH-VBR | |
| ☐ N554WN | Boeing 737-7BX/W | 30746/1085 | ex VH-VBS | |
| ☐ N555LV | Boeing 737-7BD/W | 36726/3585 | | |
| ☐ N556WN | Boeing 737-7BD/W | 33936/3613 | | |
| ☐ N700GS | Boeing 737-7H4/W | 27835/4 | | |
| ☐ N701GS | Boeing 737-7H4/W | 27836/6 | ex N35108 | |
| ☐ N703SW | Boeing 737-7H4/W | 27837/12 | ex N1792B | |

| | Reg | Type | c/n | ex | Notes |
|---|---|---|---|---|---|
| ☐ | N704SW | Boeing 737-7H4/W | 27838/15 | | |
| ☐ | N705SW | Boeing 737-7H4/W | 27839/20 | | |
| ☐ | N706SW | Boeing 737-7H4/W | 27840/24 | | |
| ☐ | N707SA | Boeing 737-7H4/W | 27841/1 | ex N737X | |
| ☐ | N708SW | Boeing 737-7H4/W | 27842/2 | | |
| ☐ | N709SW | Boeing 737-7H4/W | 27843/3 | | |
| ☐ | N710SW | Boeing 737-7H4/W | 27844/34 | ex N1787B | |
| ☐ | N711HK | Boeing 737-7H4/W | 27845/38 | | The Herbert D Kelleher |
| ☐ | N712SW | Boeing 737-7H4/W | 27846/53 | | |
| ☐ | N713SW | Boeing 737-7H4/W | 27847/54 | | Shamu c/s |
| ☐ | N714CB | Boeing 737-7H4/W | 27848/61 | | Southwest Classic colours |
| ☐ | N715SW | Boeing 737-7H4/W | 27849/62 | | Shamu c/s |
| ☐ | N716SW | Boeing 737-7H4/W | 27850/64 | | |
| ☐ | N717SA | Boeing 737-7H4/W | 27851/70 | ex N1799B | |
| ☐ | N718SW | Boeing 737-7H4/W | 27852/71 | ex N3134C | |
| ☐ | N719SW | Boeing 737-7H4/W | 27853/82 | | |
| ☐ | N720WN | Boeing 737-7H4/W | 27854/121 | ex N1787B | |
| ☐ | N723SW | Boeing 737-7H4/W | 27855/199 | ex N1787B | |
| ☐ | N724SW | Boeing 737-7H4/W | 27856/201 | ex N1787B | |
| ☐ | N725SW | Boeing 737-7H4/W | 27857/208 | ex N1786B | |
| ☐ | N726SW | Boeing 737-7H4/W | 27858/213 | | |
| ☐ | N727SW | Boeing 737-7H4/W | 27859/274 | ex N1786B | Nevada One c/s |
| ☐ | N728SW | Boeing 737-7H4/W | 27860/276 | ex N1787B | |
| ☐ | N729SW | Boeing 737-7H4/W | 27861/278 | ex N1786B | |
| ☐ | N730SW | Boeing 737-7H4/W | 27862/284 | ex N1795B | |
| ☐ | N731SA | Boeing 737-7H4/W | 27863/318 | ex N1786B | |
| ☐ | N732SW | Boeing 737-7H4/W | 27864/319 | ex N1787B | |
| ☐ | N733SA | Boeing 737-7H4/W | 27865/320 | ex N1787B | |
| ☐ | N734SA | Boeing 737-7H4/W | 27866/324 | ex N1795B | |
| ☐ | N735SA | Boeing 737-7H4/W | 27867/354 | ex N1786B | |
| ☐ | N736SA | Boeing 737-7H4/W | 27868/357 | ex N1786B | |
| ☐ | N737JW | Boeing 737-7H4/W | 27869/358 | | |
| ☐ | N738CB | Boeing 737-7H4/W | 27870/360 | ex N1786B | |
| ☐ | N739GB | Boeing 737-7H4/W | 29275/144 | ex N1786B | |
| ☐ | N740SW | Boeing 737-7H4/W | 29276/155 | | |
| ☐ | N741SA | Boeing 737-7H4/W | 29277/157 | | |
| ☐ | N742SW | Boeing 737-7H4/W | 29278/172 | | Nolan Ryan Express |
| ☐ | N743SW | Boeing 737-7H4/W | 29279/175 | ex N60436 | |
| ☐ | N744SW | Boeing 737-7H4/W | 29490/232 | ex N1781B | |
| ☐ | N745SW | Boeing 737-7H4/W | 29491/237 | ex "N728SW" | |
| ☐ | N746SW | Boeing 737-7H4/W | 29798/299 | ex N1786B | |
| ☐ | N747SA | Boeing 737-7H4/W | 29799/306 | | |
| ☐ | N748SW | Boeing 737-7H4/W | 29800/331 | ex N1786B | |
| ☐ | N749SW | Boeing 737-7H4/W | 29801/343 | ex N1786B | |
| ☐ | N750SA | Boeing 737-7H4/W | 29802/366 | | |
| ☐ | N751SW | Boeing 737-7H4/W | 29803/373 | ex N1786B | |
| ☐ | N752SW | Boeing 737-7H4/W | 29804/387 | | |
| ☐ | N753SW | Boeing 737-7H4/W | 29848/400 | ex N1787B | |
| ☐ | N754SW | Boeing 737-7H4/W | 29849/416 | ex N1787B | |
| ☐ | N755SA | Boeing 737-7H4/W | 27871/419 | ex N1787B | |
| ☐ | N756SA | Boeing 737-7H4/W | 27872/422 | ex N1786B | |
| ☐ | N757LV | Boeing 737-7H4/W | 29850/425 | ex N1786B | |
| ☐ | N758SW | Boeing 737-7H4/W | 27873/437 | ex N1786B | |
| ☐ | N759GS | Boeing 737-7H4/W | 30544/448 | ex N1786B | |
| ☐ | N760SW | Boeing 737-7H4/W | 27874/468 | ex N1786B | |
| ☐ | N761RR | Boeing 737-7H4/W | 27875/495 | | |
| ☐ | N762SW | Boeing 737-7H4/W | 27876/512 | ex N1786B | |
| ☐ | N763SW | Boeing 737-7H4/W | 27877/520 | ex N1786B | |
| ☐ | N764SW | Boeing 737-7H4/W | 27878/521 | ex N1787B | |
| ☐ | N765SW | Boeing 737-7H4/W | 29805/525 | ex N1786B | |
| ☐ | N766SW | Boeing 737-7H4/W | 29806/537 | ex N1786B | |
| ☐ | N767SW | Boeing 737-7H4/W | 29807/541 | ex N1787B | |
| ☐ | N768SW | Boeing 737-7H4/W | 30587/580 | ex N1002R | |
| ☐ | N769SW | Boeing 737-7H4/W | 30588/592 | | |
| ☐ | N770SA | Boeing 737-7H4/W | 30589/595 | | |
| ☐ | N771SA | Boeing 737-7H4/W | 27879/599 | | |
| ☐ | N772SW | Boeing 737-7H4/W | 27880/601 | | |
| ☐ | N773SA | Boeing 737-7H4/W | 27881/603 | ex N1786B | |
| ☐ | N774SW | Boeing 737-7H4/W | 27882/609 | ex N1786B | |
| ☐ | N775SW | Boeing 737-7H4/W | 30590/617 | ex N1786B | |
| ☐ | N776WN | Boeing 737-7H4/W | 30591/620 | ex N1786B | |
| ☐ | N777QC | Boeing 737-7H4/W | 30592/621 | ex N1786B | |
| ☐ | N778SW | Boeing 737-7H4/W | 27883/626 | ex N1786B | |
| ☐ | N779SW | Boeing 737-7H4/W | 27884/628 | ex N1786B | |
| ☐ | N780SW | Boeing 737-7H4/W | 27885/643 | ex N1786B | |
| ☐ | N781WN | Boeing 737-7H4/W | 30601/646 | | New Mexico One |
| ☐ | N782SA | Boeing 737-7H4/W | 29808/670 | ex N1787B | |
| ☐ | N783SW | Boeing 737-7H4/W | 29809/675 | ex N1785B | |
| ☐ | N784SW | Boeing 737-7H4/W | 29810/677 | ex N1786B | |
| ☐ | N785SW | Boeing 737-7H4/W | 30602/693 | ex N1786B | |
| ☐ | N786SW | Boeing 737-7H4/W | 29811/698 | ex N1787B | |
| ☐ | N787SA | Boeing 737-7H4/W | 29812/705 | ex N1786B | |

| | | | | |
|---|---|---|---|---|
| ☐ N788SA | Boeing 737-7H4/W | 30603/707 | ex N1786B | |
| ☐ N789SW | Boeing 737-7H4/W | 29816/718 | ex N1786B | |
| ☐ N790SW | Boeing 737-7H4/W | 30604/721 | ex N1786B | |
| ☐ N791SW | Boeing 737-7H4/W | 27886/736 | ex N1786B | |
| ☐ N792SW | Boeing 737-7H4/W | 27887/737 | | |
| ☐ N793SA | Boeing 737-7H4/W | 27888/744 | ex N1786B | Spirit One |
| ☐ N794SW | Boeing 737-7H4/W | 30605/748 | ex N1781B | |
| ☐ N795SW | Boeing 737-7H4/W | 30606/780 | ex N1786B | |
| ☐ N796SW | Boeing 737-7H4/W | 27889/784 | ex N1786B | |
| ☐ N797MX | Boeing 737-7H4/W | 27890/803 | | |
| ☐ N798SW | Boeing 737-7AD/W | 28436/41 | ex N700EW | |
| ☐ N799SW | Boeing 737-7Q8/W | 28209/14 | ex 9Y-TJI | |
| ☐ N900WN | Boeing 737-7H4/W | 32544/2460 | | |
| ☐ N901WN | Boeing 737-7H4/W | 32545/2462 | | |
| ☐ N902WN | Boeing 737-7H4/W | 36615/2469 | | |
| ☐ N903WN | Boeing 737-7H4/W | 32457/2473 | | |
| ☐ N904WN | Boeing 737-7H4/W | 36616/2480 | ex N1780B | |
| ☐ N905WN | Boeing 737-7H4/W | 36617/2491 | ex N1786B | |
| ☐ N906WN | Boeing 737-7H4/W | 36887/2494 | | |
| ☐ N907WN | Boeing 737-7H4/W | 36619/2500 | | |
| ☐ N908WN | Boeing 737-7H4/W | 36620/2509 | ex N1786B | |
| ☐ N909WN | Boeing 737-7H4/W | 32458/2517 | | |
| ☐ N910WN | Boeing 737-7H4/W | 36618/2521 | ex N1786B | |
| ☐ N912WN | Boeing 737-7H4/W | 36621/2532 | ex N1786B | |
| ☐ N913WN | Boeing 737-7H4/W | 29840/2536 | ex N1787B | |
| ☐ N914WN | Boeing 737-7H4/W | 36622/2540 | ex N1787B | |
| ☐ N915WN | Boeing 737-7H4/W | 36888/2546 | | |
| ☐ N916WN | Boeing 737-7H4/W | 36623/2558 | | |
| ☐ N917WN | Boeing 737-7H4/W | 36624/2562 | ex N1787B | |
| ☐ N918WN | Boeing 737-7H4/W | 29843/2572 | | |
| ☐ N919WN | Boeing 737-7H4/W | 36625/2591 | | |
| ☐ N920WN | Boeing 737-7H4/W | 32460/2597 | ex N1796B | |
| ☐ N921WN | Boeing 737-7H4/W | 36626/2600 | | |
| ☐ N922WN | Boeing 737-7H4/W | 32461/2620 | | |
| ☐ N923WN | Boeing 737-7H4/W | 36627/2634 | | |
| ☐ N924WN | Boeing 737-7H4/W | 36628/2640 | | |
| ☐ N925WN | Boeing 737-7H4/W | 36630/2656 | ex N1786B | |
| ☐ N926WN | Boeing 737-7H4/W | 36629/2663 | ex N1786B | |
| ☐ N927WN | Boeing 737-7H4/W | 36889/2679 | | |
| ☐ N928WN | Boeing 737-7H4/W | 36890/2687 | | |
| ☐ N929WN | Boeing 737-7H4/W | 36631/2689 | | |
| ☐ N930WN | Boeing 737-7H4/W | 36636/2784 | ex N1786B | |
| ☐ N931WN | Boeing 737-7H4/W | 36637/2799 | ex N1799B | |
| ☐ N932WN | Boeing 737-7H4/W | 36639/2837 | ex N1786B | |
| ☐ N933WN | Boeing 737-7H4/W | 36640/2847 | | |
| ☐ N934WN | Boeing 737-7H4/W | 36642/2878 | | |
| ☐ N935WN | Boeing 737-7H4/W | 36641/2894 | | |
| ☐ N936WN | Boeing 737-7H4/W | 36643/2909 | ex N1787B | |
| ☐ N937WN | Boeing 737-7H4/W | 36644/2925 | ex N1787B | |
| ☐ N938WN | Boeing 737-7H4/W | 36645/2929 | ex N1786B | |
| ☐ N939WN | Boeing 737-7H4/W | 36646/2933 | ex N1787B | |
| ☐ N940WN | Boeing 737-7H4/W | 36900/2943 | ex N1786B | |
| ☐ N941WN | Boeing 737-7H4/W | 36647/2961 | ex N1796B | |
| ☐ N942WN | Boeing 737-7H4/W | 36648/2985 | ex N1787B | |
| ☐ N943WN | Boeing 737-7H4/W | 36913/3195 | ex N1786B | |
| ☐ N944WN | Boeing 737-7H4/W | 36659/3220 | | |
| ☐ N945WN | Boeing 737-7H4/W | 36660/3226 | ex N1787B | |
| ☐ N946WN | Boeing 737-7H4/W | 36918/3251 | ex N1786B | |
| ☐ N947WN | Boeing 737-7H4/W | 36924/3290 | ex N1787B | |
| ☐ N948WN | Boeing 737-7H4/W | 36662/3296 | | |
| ☐ N949WN | Boeing 737-7H4/W | 36663/3358 | ex N1786B | |
| ☐ N950WN | Boeing 737-7H4/W | 36664/3365 | ex N1799B | |
| ☐ N951WN | Boeing 737-7H4/W | 36665/3388 | | |
| ☐ N952WN | Boeing 737-7H4/W | 36667/3477 | | |
| ☐ N953WN | Boeing 737-7H4/W | 36668/3510 | ex N1786B | |
| ☐ N954WN | Boeing 737-7H4/W | 36669/2547 | | |
| ☐ N955WN | Boeing 737-7H4/W | 36671/3603 | | |
| ☐ N956WN | Boeing 737-7H4/W | 36672/3629 | | |
| ☐ N957WN | Boeing 737-7H4/W | 41528/3657 | | |
| ☐ N958WN | Boeing 737-7H4/W | 36673/3661 | | |
| ☐ N959WN | Boeing 737-7H4/W | 36674/3696 | | |
| ☐ N960WN | Boeing 737-7H4/W | 36675/3715 | | |
| ☐ N961WN | Boeing 737-7H4/W | 36962/3719 | | |
| ☐ N962WN | Boeing 737-7H4/W | 36963/3724 | | |
| ☐ N963WN | Boeing 737-7H4/W | 36676/3726 | | |
| ☐ N964WN | Boeing 737-7H4/W | 36965/3759 | | |
| ☐ N965WN | Boeing 737-7H4/W | 36677/3774 | | |
| ☐ N966WN | Boeing 737-7H4/W | 36966/3788 | | |
| ☐ N967WN | Boeing 737-7H4/W | 36967/3791 | | |
| ☐ N968WN | Boeing 737-7H4/W | 36679/3872 | | ♦ |
| ☐ N969WN | Boeing 737-7H4/W | 41777/3874 | | ♦ |

| | | | | | |
|---|---|---|---|---|---|
| ☐ N8301J | Boeing 737-8H4/W | 36980/3952 | | | ♦ |
| ☐ N8302F | Boeing 737-8H4/W | 36680/3979 | | | ♦ |
| ☐ N8303R | Boeing 737-8H4/W | 36681/3993 | | | ♦ |
| ☐ N8305E | Boeing 737-8H4/W | 36683/ | | | o/o♦ |
| ☐ N8306H | Boeing 737-8H4/W | 36983/ | | | o/o♦ |
| ☐ N8307K | Boeing 737-8H4/W | 36987/ | | | o/o♦ |
| ☐ N8308K | Boeing 737-8H4/W | 36682/ | | | o/o♦ |
| ☐ N8309C | Boeing 737-8H4/W | 36985/ | | | o/o♦ |
| ☐ N8310C | Boeing 737-8H4/W | 38807/ | | | o/o♦ |
| ☐ N8311Q | Boeing 737-8H4/W | 38808/ | | | o/o♦ |
| ☐ N8312C | Boeing 737-8H4/W | 38809/ | | | o/o♦ |
| ☐ N8313F | Boeing 737-8H4/W | 38810/ | | | o/o♦ |
| ☐ N8314L | Boeing 737-8H4/W | 36990/ | | | o/o♦ |
| ☐ N8315C | Boeing 737-8H4/W | 38811/ | | | o/o♦ |
| ☐ N8316H | Boeing 737-8H4/W | 36684/ | | | o/o♦ |
| ☐ N8317M | Boeing 737-8H4/W | 36992/ | | | o/o♦ |
| ☐ N8318F | Boeing 737-8H4/W | 36685/ | | | o/o♦ |
| ☐ N8319F | Boeing 737-8H4/W | 36994/ | | | o/o♦ |
| ☐ N8320J | Boeing 737-8H4/W | 36686/ | | | o/o♦ |
| ☐ N8600F | Boeing 737-8H4/W | 39882/ | | | o/o♦ |
| ☐ N8601C | Boeing 737-8H4/W | 38874/ | | | o/o♦ |
| ☐ N8602F | Boeing 737-8H4/W | 38110/ | | | o/o♦ |
| ☐ N8603F | Boeing 737-8H4/W | 38875/ | | | o/o♦ |
| ☐ N8604K | Boeing 737-8H4/W | 39883/ | | | o/o♦ |

## SPECTRUM AIR SERVICE

| | | | | |
|---|---|---|---|---|
| ☐ N675MS | Cessna 208 Caravan I | 20800370 | | ♦ |

## SPEEDSTAR EXPRESS

| | | | | |
|---|---|---|---|---|
| ☐ N923MA | de Havilland DHC-6 Twin Otter 200 | 168 | ex N923HM | ♦ |
| ☐ N926MA | de Havilland DHC-6 Twin Otter 200 | 133 | ex N953SM | ♦ |

## SPERNAK AIRWAYS　　　　　　　　　　　　　　　　　　Anchorage-Merrill, AK (MRI)

| | | | | |
|---|---|---|---|---|
| ☐ N29CF | Cessna 207 Skywagon | 20700353 | | FP |
| ☐ N6492H | Cessna 207A Stationair 7 II | 20700544 | | FP |
| ☐ N7392U | Cessna 207A Stationair 7 II | 20700435 | | FP |
| ☐ N73047 | Cessna 207A Stationair 7 II | 20700556 | ex XB-EXR | FP |
| ☐ N91038 | Cessna 207 Skywagon | 20700027 | | FP♦ |

## SPIRIT AIRLINES　　　　　　　Spirit Wings (NK/NKS)　　　　Fort Lauderdale-Hollywood Intl, FL (FLL)

| | | | | | |
|---|---|---|---|---|---|
| ☐ N502NK | Airbus A319-132 | 2433 | ex D-AVWX | St Maarten/St Martin | |
| ☐ N503NK | Airbus A319-132 | 2470 | ex D-AVYJ | The Caribbean | |
| ☐ N504NK | Airbus A319-132 | 2473 | ex D-AVYP | The Bahamas | |
| ☐ N505NK | Airbus A319-132 | 2485 | ex D-AVYI | | |
| ☐ N506NK | Airbus A319-132 | 2490 | ex D-AVWH | | |
| ☐ N507NK | Airbus A319-132 | 2560 | ex D-AVYV | | |
| ☐ N508NK | Airbus A319-132 | 2567 | ex D-AVWM | | |
| ☐ N509NK | Airbus A319-132 | 2603 | ex D-AVXO | | |
| ☐ N510NK | Airbus A319-132 | 2622 | ex D-AVYT | Fort Lauderdale | |
| ☐ N512NK | Airbus A319-132 | 2673 | ex D-AVYO | Turks & Caicos Islands | |
| ☐ N514NK | Airbus A319-132 | 2679 | ex D-AVYV | Cayman Islands | |
| ☐ N516NK | Airbus A319-132 | 2704 | ex D-AVXJ | Cancun | |
| ☐ N517NK | Airbus A319-132 | 2711 | ex D-AVYM | Orlando | |
| ☐ N522NK | Airbus A319-132 | 2893 | ex D-AVYY | Las Vegas | |
| ☐ N523NK | Airbus A319-132 | 2898 | ex D-AVWN | Tampa | |
| ☐ N524NK | Airbus A319-132 | 2929 | ex D-AVYU | Suncatcher | |
| ☐ N525NK | Airbus A319-132 | 2942 | ex D-AVWX | The Americas | |
| ☐ N526NK | Airbus A319-132 | 2963 | ex D-AVYM | | |
| ☐ N527NK | Airbus A319-132 | 2978 | ex D-AVXD | | |
| ☐ N528NK | Airbus A319-132 | 2983 | ex D-AVXI | | |
| ☐ N529NK | Airbus A319-132 | 3007 | ex D-AVYL | | |
| ☐ N530NK | Airbus A319-132 | 3017 | ex D-AVXL | | |
| ☐ N531NK | Airbus A319-132 | 3026 | ex D-AVWC | | |
| ☐ N532NK | Airbus A319-132 | 3165 | ex D-AVYX | | |
| ☐ N533NK | Airbus A319-132 | 3393 | ex D-AVWJ | | |
| ☐ N534NK | Airbus A319-132 | 3395 | ex D-AVWK | | |

All names prefixed 'Spirit of'

| | | | | | |
|---|---|---|---|---|---|
| ☐ N601NK | Airbus A320-232 | 4206 | ex D-AVVI | | |
| ☐ N602NK | Airbus A320-232 | 4264 | ex D-AXAD | | |
| ☐ N603NK | Airbus A320-232 | 4321 | ex D-AXAM | | |
| ☐ N604NK | Airbus A320-232 | 4431 | ex D-AVVO | | |
| ☐ N605NK | Airbus A320-232 | 4548 | ex F-WWIV | | |
| ☐ N606NK | Airbus A320-232 | 4592 | ex F-WWIR | | |
| ☐ N607NK | Airbus A320-232 | 4595 | ex F-WWIZ | | |
| ☐ N608NK | Airbus A320-232 | 4902 | ex F-WWBT | | ♦ |
| ☐ N609NK | Airbus A320-232 | 4951 | ex F-WWDI | | ♦ |

| ☐ N611NK | Airbus A320-232 | 4996 | ex F-WWBJ | | ◆ |
| ☐ N612NK | Airbus A320-232 | 5029 | ex F-WWBN | | ◆ |
| ☐ N613NK | Airbus A320-232 | 5042 | ex F-WWDO | | ◆ |
| ☐ N614NK | Airbus A320-232 | 5132 | ex | | o/o◆ |
| | | | | | |
| ☐ N587NK | Airbus A321-231 | 2476 | ex D-AVXB | Jamaica | |
| ☐ N588NK | Airbus A321-231 | 2590 | ex D-AVZK | | |

## STARS AND STRIPES AIR TOURS — Boulder City, AZ

Helicopter flights op by Las Vegas Helicopters

## SRX TRANSCONTINENTAL

| ☐ N199AJ | Boeing 727-2F9F/W (Duganair 3) | 21426/1285 | ex N83428 | ◆ |

## SUBURBAN AIR FREIGHT — Sub Air (SUB) — Omaha-Eppley Airfield, NE (OMA)

| ☐ N114MN | Aero Commander 680FL | 1553-107 | ex (N2611L) | |
| ☐ N290MP | Aero Commander 680FL | 1535-104 | | |
| ☐ N309VS | Aero Commander 680FL | 1659-128 | ex N6626V | |
| ☐ N2828S | Aero Commander 680FL | 1329-14 | | |
| ☐ N4983S | Aero Commander 680FL | 1427-70 | ex CF-LAC | |
| ☐ N5035E | Aero Commander 680FL | 1764-147 | | |
| ☐ N9011N | Aero Commander 680FL | 1836-153 | | |
| | | | | |
| ☐ N118SF | Beech 99 | U-32 | ex C-FESU | |
| ☐ N124GP | Beech 1900C | UB-23 | ex N23VK | |
| ☐ N128SF | Beech 99A | U-87 | ex N59CA | |
| ☐ N147SF | Beech 99 | U-47 | ex N204BH | |
| ☐ N208QC | Cessna 208B Caravan I | 208B0774 | ex N5261R | |
| ☐ N253SF | Beech 1900C-1 | UC-53 | ex N31764 | |
| ☐ N719GL | Beech 1900C | UB-19 | ex N314BH | |
| ☐ N821SF | Beech 1900C-1 | UC-121 | ex ZS-PKX | ◆ |
| ☐ N864SF | Cessna 208B Caravan I | 208B0864 | | |
| ☐ N895SF | Cessna 208B Caravan I | 208B0095 | ex N9662B | |
| ☐ N7994R | Beech 99 | U-103 | | |

## SUN COUNTRY AIRLINES — Sun Country (SY/SCX) — Minneapolis/St Paul Intl, MN (MSP)

| ☐ N801SY | Boeing 737-8Q8/W | 30332/777 | ex N1787B | The Phoenix | |
| ☐ N804SY | Boeing 737-8Q8/W | 30689/908 | | Laughlin Luck | |
| ☐ N805SY | Boeing 737-8Q8/W | 30032/985 | ex N1781B | The Spirit of Minnesota | |
| ☐ N806SY | Boeing 737-8Q8/W | 28215/75 | ex N800NA | | |
| ☐ N809SY | Boeing 737-8Q8/W | 30683/1669 | | | |
| ☐ N813SY | Boeing 737-8Q8 | 28237/769 | ex OY-SED | | |
| ☐ N814SY | Boeing 737-8BK/W | 30620/991 | ex VH-VOA | | ◆ |
| ☐ N815SY | Boeing 737-8BK/W | 30623/1136 | ex VH-VOC | | ◆ |
| ☐ N816SY | Boeing 737-8Q8/W | 30637/800 | ex N281LF | | ◆ |
| ☐ N817SY | Boeing 737-8K2/W | 30392/833 | ex PH-HZM | | ◆ |
| ☐ PH-HZI | Boeing 737-8K2/W | 28380/524 | | <TRA◆ | |
| ☐ N710SY | Boeing 737-73V | 30241/1034 | ex N241CL | | |
| ☐ N711SY | Boeing 737-73V | 30245/1058 | ex G-EZJJ | | |
| ☐ N712SY | Boeing 737-7Q8 | 28219/183 | ex PR-GOU | | |
| ☐ N713SY | Boeing 737-7Q8 | 30635/713 | ex PR-GIL | | ◆ |

## SUNSHINE HELICOPTERS — Kahului, HI)

| ☐ N801MH | Eurocopter EC130B4 | 3654 | ◆ |
| ☐ N802MH | Eurocopter EC130B4 | 3707 | ◆ |
| ☐ N803MH | Eurocopter EC130B4 | 3735 | ◆ |
| ☐ N804MH | Eurocopter EC130B4 | 3750 | ◆ |

## SUPERIOR AVIATION — Spend Air (SO/HKA) — Iron Mountain-Kingsford, MI (IMT)

| ☐ N329SA | Swearingen SA.226TC Metro II | TC-238 | ex N5436M | ◆ |
| ☐ N6851X | Cessna 441 Conquest II | 441-0212 | | |
| ☐ N31171 | Swearingen SA.227AC Metro III | AC-605 | | ◆ |

## SWIFT AIR — (Q7/SWQ)

| ☐ N250MY | Boeing 767-238ER | 23306/125 | ex N770WD | ◆ |
| ☐ N737DX | Boeing 737-408 | 24804/1851 | ex TF-FIC | ◆ |
| ☐ N767MW | Boeing 767-277 | 22694/32 | ex N767AT | ◆ |
| ☐ N801TJ | Boeing 737-4B7 | 24892/1944 | ex N448US | ◆ |
| ☐ N802TJ | Boeing 737-4B7 | 24874/1936 | ex N447US | ◆ |

## TALKEETNA AIR TAXI — Talkeetna, AK (TKA)

| ☐ N144Q | de Havilland DHC-2 Beaver | 1465 | | FP/WS |
| ☐ N185FK | Cessna A185F Skywagon | 18502513 | ex N1796R | FP/WS |

| | | | | | |
|---|---|---|---|---|---|
| ☐ N510PR | de Havilland DHC-3 Turbo Otter | 250 | ex VH-OTV | | FP/WS♦ |
| ☐ N561TA | de Havilland DHC-2 Beaver | 581 | ex CF-HGV | | FP/WS |
| ☐ N565TA | de Havilland DHC-3 Turbo Otter | 46 | ex C-FQOQ | | FP/WS |
| ☐ N1694M | Cessna A185F Skywagon | 18501879 | | | FP/WS |
| ☐ N8190Y | de Havilland DHC-2 Beaver | 824 | ex C-GPUP | | FP/WS |
| ☐ N70018 | Cessna A185E Skywagon | 18501893 | | | FP/WS♦ |

## TANANA AIR SERVICE — Tan Air (4E/TNR) — Ruby, AK (RBY)

| | | | | | |
|---|---|---|---|---|---|
| ☐ N97CR | Piper PA-32R-300 Lance | 32R-7780078 | ex JA3776 | | |
| ☐ N4352F | Piper PA-32R-300 Lance | 32R-7680441 | | | |
| ☐ N4803S | Piper PA-32-260 Cherokee Six B | 32-1188 | | | |
| ☐ N31606 | Piper PA-32-260 Cherokee Six E | 32-7840137 | | | |
| ☐ N75387 | Piper PA-32R-300 Lance | 32R-7680298 | | | |
| | | | | | |
| ☐ N866CS | Cessna A185F Skywagon | 18502866 | | | ♦ |
| ☐ N1587U | Cessna 207 Stationair | 20700187 | | | ♦ |

## TAQUAN AIR SERVICE — Taquan (K3)
### Metlakatla/Ketchikan-Waterfront SPB, AK (MTM/WFB)

| | | | | | |
|---|---|---|---|---|---|
| ☐ N1018A | de Havilland DHC-2 Beaver | 178 | ex N52409 | | FP |
| ☐ N5160G | de Havilland DHC-2 Beaver | 236 | ex 51-16483 | | FP |
| ☐ N37756 | de Havilland DHC-2 Beaver | 1456 | ex G-203 | | FP |
| ☐ N67673 | de Havilland DHC-2 Beaver | 1284 | ex 57-2586 | | FP |
| ☐ N67676 | de Havilland DHC-2 Beaver | 809 | ex N93AK | | FP |
| ☐ N68010 | de Havilland DHC-2 Beaver | 1243 | ex 57-6150 | | FP |

## TBM — Tulare-Mefford Field, CA/Visalia-Municipal, CA (TLR/VIS)

| | | | | | |
|---|---|---|---|---|---|
| ☐ N466TM | Lockheed C-130A-1A Hercules | 3173 | ex 57-0466 | 64 | Tanker |
| ☐ N473TM | Lockheed C-130A-1A Hercules | 3081 | ex 56-0473 | 63 | Tanker |
| ☐ N531BA | Lockheed C-130A-1A Hercules | 3139 | ex 56-0531 | 67 | [VIS]♦ |

## TEMSCO HELICOPTERS — Temsco (TMS) — Ketchikan-Temsco Heliport, AK

| | | | | | |
|---|---|---|---|---|---|
| ☐ N94TH | Aérospatiale AS350B AStar | 2548 | | | |
| ☐ N141TH | Aérospatiale AS350B2 AStar | 1167 | ex N98MB | | |
| ☐ N142AE | Aérospatiale AS350B3 AStar | 7035 | | | ♦ |
| ☐ N143TH | Aérospatiale AS350B2 AStar | 9043 | | | |
| ☐ N145TH | Aérospatiale AS350B2 AStar | 9060 | | | |
| ☐ N146TH | Aérospatiale AS350B2 AStar | 9065 | | | ♦ |
| ☐ N147TH | Aérospatiale AS350B2 AStar | 9070 | | | |
| ☐ N149TH | Aérospatiale AS350B2 AStar | 9071 | | | |
| ☐ N403AE | Aérospatiale AS350B3 AStar | 3281 | | | |
| ☐ N405AE | Aérospatiale AS350B3 AStar | 3286 | | | |
| ☐ N802TH | Aérospatiale AS350B3 AStar | 9023 | | | |
| ☐ N911CV | Aérospatiale AS350B3 AStar | 3142 | ex N40729 | | |
| ☐ N913LP | Aérospatiale AS350B2 AStar | 2383 | | | |
| ☐ N970TH | Aérospatiale AS350BA AStar | 9011 | | | |
| ☐ N4022D | Aérospatiale AS350B2 AStar | 2891 | | | |
| ☐ N6015S | Aérospatiale AS350BA AStar | 1884 | | | |
| ☐ N6080R | Aérospatiale AS350BA AStar | 2685 | | | |
| ☐ N6094E | Aérospatiale AS350BA AStar | 2750 | | | |
| ☐ N6094U | Aérospatiale AS350BA AStar | 2751 | | | |
| ☐ N6302Y | Aérospatiale AS350B2 AStar | 9007 | | | |
| ☐ N57954 | Aérospatiale AS350B AStar | 1127 | ex N35977 | | |
| ☐ N57958 | Aérospatiale AS350B AStar | 1512 | | | |
| | | | | | |
| ☐ N214TH | Bell 214B-1 | 28031 | ex N4374D | | |
| ☐ N502TH | Bell 205A-1 | 30030 | ex C-FKHQ | | |
| ☐ N16920 | Bell 212 | 30865 | | | |
| ☐ N83230 | Bell 212 | 30560 | | | |

## TEPPER AVIATION — Crestview-Bob Sikes, FL (CEW)

| | | | | | |
|---|---|---|---|---|---|
| ☐ N2679C | Lockheed L-382G-69C Hercules | 4796 | ex N8183J | | |
| ☐ N2731G | Lockheed L-382G-30C Hercules | 4582 | ex N2189M | | |
| ☐ N3796B | Lockheed L-382G-39C Hercules | 5027 | ex N4557C | | |
| Operates for various US Government agencies | | | | | |

## TOLAIR SERVICES — Tol Air (TI/TOL) — San Juan-Munoz Marin Intl, PR (SJU)

| | | | | | |
|---|---|---|---|---|---|
| ☐ N728T | Beech E-18S | BA-130 | ex N28V | | Frtr |
| ☐ N732T | Beech E-18S | BA-114 | ex N52A | | Frtr |
| ☐ N748T | Beech E-18S | BA-329 | ex N398B | | Frtr |
| ☐ N749T | Beech E-18S | BA-55 | ex N4641A | | Frtr |
| ☐ N779T | Beech H-18 | BA-618 | ex N220WH | | Frtr |

| | | | | |
|---|---|---|---|---|
| ☐ N87T | Douglas DC-3 | 6148 | ex N31MC | Frtr |
| ☐ N783T | Douglas DC-3 | 4219 | ex N783V | Frtr |
| ☐ N840T | Cessna 402B | 402B1099 | ex N87280 | |

## TRANS AIR

| | | | | |
|---|---|---|---|---|
| ☐ N306AL | Boeing 737-2T4 | 23066/992 | ex XA-RCB | [MCE]♦ |
| ☐ N587CA | Convair 640 | 463 | ex C-FPWO | ♦ |

## TRANS STATES AIRLINES · Waterski (AX/LOF) · St Louis-Lambert Intl, MO (STL)

Ops commuter services for American Airlines as American Connection, US Airways as US Airways Express and United Air Lines as United Express from St Louis, MO, Baltimore-Washington, MD, Newark, NJ, Chicago, IL and Pittsburgh, PA. Go Jet Airlines is a wholly owned subsidiary based in St Louis, MO operating CRJ-700s for United Express.

## TRANSAIR · Maui (P6/MUI) · Honolulu-Intl, HI (HNL)

| | | | | |
|---|---|---|---|---|
| ☐ N221LM | Short SD.3-60 | SH3722 | ex N722PC | |
| ☐ N351TA | Short SD.3-60 | SH3759 | ex N159CC | |
| ☐ N729PC | Short SD.3-60 | SH3729 | ex 6Y-JMY | |
| ☐ N808KR | Short SD.3-60 | SH3734 | ex D-CFAO | Frtr |
| ☐ N808TR | Short SD.3-60 | SH3718 | ex VQ-TSK | Frtr |
| ☐ N827BE | Short SD.3-60 | SH3746 | ex N746SA | Frtr |
| ☐ N4476F | Short SD.3-60 | SH3731 | ex 5N-BFT | |
| ☐ N808TA | Boeing 737-2B1C | 20536/289 | ex RP-C8015 | ♦ |

## TRANSNORTHERN AVIATION · Transnorthern (TNV) · Talkeetna/Fairbanks, AK (TKA/FAI)

| | | | | |
|---|---|---|---|---|
| ☐ N27TN | Douglas C-117D | 43332 | ex N99857 | |
| ☐ N30TN | Douglas C-117D | 43159 | ex N53315 | |
| ☐ N39TN | Beech 99 | U-2 | ex TI-AYM | Passenger |
| ☐ N3114G | Swearingen SA.227AC Metro III | AC-583 | | |

## TROPIC AIR CHARTERS · Fort Lauderdale Executive, FL (FXE)

| | | | | |
|---|---|---|---|---|
| ☐ N131JL | Britten-Norman BN-2A-6 Islander | 225 | ex G-51-225 | |
| ☐ N200MU | Britten-Norman BN-2A-27 Islander | 78 | ex 6Y-JSX | |
| ☐ N296TA | Britten-Norman BN-2A-26 Islander | 384 | ex J8-VBN | |
| ☐ N297TA | Britten-Norman BN-2A-26 Islander | 741 | ex N196TA | |

## TWIN CITIES AIR SERVICE · Twin City (TCY) · Auburn-Lewiston Municipal, ME (LEW)

| | | | | |
|---|---|---|---|---|
| ☐ N18VV | Cessna 402C | 402C0619 | ex N180PB | |
| ☐ N196TC | Cessna 310R | 310R1801 | | |
| ☐ N401SX | Cessna 402C | 402C0447 | ex 9A-BPV | |
| ☐ N402SX | Cessna 402C | 402C0606 | ex 9A-BPX | |
| ☐ N404SX | Cessna 402C | 402C0280 | | ♦ |

## UFLY AIRWAYS · (6F/FAO) · Miami, FL (MIA)

| | | | | |
|---|---|---|---|---|
| ☐ N836NK | McDonnell-Douglas MD-83 | 53045/1777 | ex N833RA | |
| ☐ N836RA | McDonnell-Douglas MD-83 | 53046/1794 | ex YV-44C | |

## UNION FLIGHTS · Union Flights (UNF) · Dayton-Carson City, NV (CSN)

| | | | | |
|---|---|---|---|---|
| ☐ N208N | Cessna 208B Caravan I | 208B0279 | ex F-OGRU | |
| ☐ N1116N | Cessna 208B Caravan I | 208B0417 | | |
| ☐ N9655B | Cessna 208B Caravan I | 208B0145 | | |
| ☐ N9334B | Cessna 208B Caravan I | 208B0141 | | ♦ |

## UNITED AIR LINES · United (UA/UAL) · Chicago-O'Hare Intl, IL/San Francisco-Intl, CA (ORD/SFO)

Member of Star Alliance. Ex Continental aircraft are listed by last 3 digits within types.

| | | | | |
|---|---|---|---|---|
| ☐ N801UA | Airbus A319-131 | 0686 | ex D-AVYI | 4001 |
| ☐ N802UA | Airbus A319-131 | 0690 | ex D-AVYO | 4002 |
| ☐ N803UA | Airbus A319-131 | 0748 | ex D-AVYL | 4003 |
| ☐ N804UA | Airbus A319-131 | 0759 | ex D-AVYR | 4004 |
| ☐ N805UA | Airbus A319-131 | 0783 | ex D-AVYY | 4005 |
| ☐ N806UA | Airbus A319-131 | 0788 | ex D-AVYW | 4006 |
| ☐ N807UA | Airbus A319-131 | 0798 | ex D-AVYX | 4007 |
| ☐ N808UA | Airbus A319-131 | 0804 | ex D-AVYF | 4008 |
| ☐ N809UA | Airbus A319-131 | 0825 | ex D-AVYZ | 4009 |
| ☐ N810UA | Airbus A319-131 | 0843 | ex D-AVYR | 4010 |
| ☐ N811UA | Airbus A319-131 | 0847 | ex D-AVYB | 4011 |
| ☐ N812UA | Airbus A319-131 | 0850 | ex D-AVYK | 4012 |
| ☐ N813UA | Airbus A319-131 | 0858 | ex D-AVYP | 4013 |

| | | | | |
|---|---|---|---|---|
| ☐ N814UA | Airbus A319-131 | 0862 | ex D-AVYT | 4014 |
| ☐ N815UA | Airbus A319-131 | 0867 | ex D-AVYU | 4015 |
| ☐ N816UA | Airbus A319-131 | 0871 | ex D-AVYY | 4016 |
| ☐ N817UA | Airbus A319-131 | 0873 | ex D-AVYX | 4017 |
| ☐ N818UA | Airbus A319-131 | 0882 | ex D-AVYE | 4018 |
| ☐ N819UA | Airbus A319-131 | 0893 | ex D-AVYV | 4019 |
| ☐ N820UA | Airbus A319-131 | 0898 | ex D-AVYZ | 4020 |
| ☐ N821UA | Airbus A319-131 | 0944 | ex D-AVYC | 4021 |
| ☐ N822UA | Airbus A319-131 | 0948 | ex D-AVYE | 4022 |
| ☐ N823UA | Airbus A319-131 | 0952 | ex D-AVYF | 4023 |
| ☐ N824UA | Airbus A319-131 | 0965 | ex D-AVYH | 4024 |
| ☐ N825UA | Airbus A319-131 | 0980 | ex D-AVYN | 4025 |
| ☐ N826UA | Airbus A319-131 | 0989 | ex D-AVYU | 4026 |
| ☐ N827UA | Airbus A319-131 | 1022 | ex D-AVYD | 4027 |
| ☐ N828UA | Airbus A319-131 | 1031 | ex D-AVYF | 4028 |
| ☐ N829UA | Airbus A319-131 | 1211 | ex D-AVYC | 4029 |
| ☐ N830UA | Airbus A319-131 | 1243 | ex D-AVWI | 4030 |
| ☐ N831UA | Airbus A319-131 | 1291 | ex D-AVWF | 4031 |
| ☐ N832UA | Airbus A319-131 | 1321 | ex D-AVWQ | 4032 |
| ☐ N833UA | Airbus A319-131 | 1401 | ex D-AVYA | 4033 |
| ☐ N834UA | Airbus A319-131 | 1420 | ex D-AVYM | 4034 |
| ☐ N835UA | Airbus A319-131 | 1426 | ex D-AVYN | 4035 |
| ☐ N836UA | Airbus A319-131 | 1460 | ex D-AVYI | 4036 |
| ☐ N837UA | Airbus A319-131 | 1474 | ex D-AVYS | 4037 |
| ☐ N838UA | Airbus A319-131 | 1477 | ex D-AVYG | 4038 |
| ☐ N839UA | Airbus A319-131 | 1507 | ex D-AVYX | 4039 |
| ☐ N840UA | Airbus A319-131 | 1522 | ex D-AVYZ | 4040 |
| ☐ N841UA | Airbus A319-131 | 1545 | ex D-AVWK | 4041 |
| ☐ N842UA | Airbus A319-131 | 1569 | ex D-AVWA | 4042 |
| ☐ N843UA | Airbus A319-131 | 1573 | ex D-AVWE | 4043 |
| ☐ N844UA | Airbus A319-131 | 1581 | ex D-AVWT | 4044 |
| ☐ N845UA | Airbus A319-131 | 1585 | ex D-AVYD | 4045 |
| ☐ N846UA | Airbus A319-131 | 1600 | ex D-AVWW | 4046 |
| ☐ N847UA | Airbus A319-131 | 1627 | ex D-AVYB | 4047 |
| ☐ N848UA | Airbus A319-131 | 1647 | ex D-AVYK | 4048 |
| ☐ N849UA | Airbus A319-131 | 1649 | ex D-AVYP | 4049 |
| ☐ N850UA | Airbus A319-131 | 1653 | ex D-AVYR | 4050 |
| ☐ N851UA | Airbus A319-131 | 1664 | ex D-AVYX | 4051 |
| ☐ N852UA | Airbus A319-131 | 1671 | ex D-AVWD | 4052 |
| ☐ N853UA | Airbus A319-131 | 1688 | ex D-AVWM | 4053 |
| ☐ N854UA | Airbus A319-131 | 1731 | ex D-AVWS | 4054 |
| ☐ N855UA | Airbus A319-131 | 1737 | ex D-AVWU | 4055 |
| | | | | |
| ☐ N401UA | Airbus A320-232 | 0435 | ex F-WWDD | 4501 |
| ☐ N402UA | Airbus A320-232 | 0439 | ex F-WWIJ | 4502 |
| ☐ N403UA | Airbus A320-232 | 0442 | ex F-WWIY | 4703 |
| ☐ N404UA | Airbus A320-232 | 0450 | ex F-WWII | 4704 |
| ☐ N405UA | Airbus A320-232 | 0452 | ex F-WWBF | 4705 |
| ☐ N406UA | Airbus A320-232 | 0454 | ex F-WWBJ | 4506 |
| ☐ N407UA | Airbus A320-232 | 0456 | ex F-WWDB | 4507 |
| ☐ N408UA | Airbus A320-232 | 0457 | ex F-WWDG | 4508 |
| ☐ N409UA | Airbus A320-232 | 0462 | ex F-WWDQ | 4709 |
| ☐ N410UA | Airbus A320-232 | 0463 | ex F-WWDV | 4910 |
| ☐ N411UA | Airbus A320-232 | 0464 | ex F-WWDX | 4711 |
| ☐ N412UA | Airbus A320-232 | 0465 | ex F-WWIM | 4712 |
| ☐ N413UA | Airbus A320-232 | 0470 | ex F-WWBM | 4713 |
| ☐ N414UA | Airbus A320-232 | 0472 | ex F-WWIU | 4814 |
| ☐ N415UA | Airbus A320-232 | 0475 | ex F-WWBP | 4615 |
| ☐ N416UA | Airbus A320-232 | 0479 | ex F-WWDH | 4616 |
| ☐ N417UA | Airbus A320-232 | 0483 | ex F-WWIT | 4617 |
| ☐ N418UA | Airbus A320-232 | 0485 | ex F-WWIZ | 4618 |
| ☐ N419UA | Airbus A320-232 | 0487 | ex F-WWDJ | 4619 |
| ☐ N420UA | Airbus A320-232 | 0489 | ex F-WWDM | 4620 |
| ☐ N421UA | Airbus A320-232 | 0500 | ex F-WWDZ | 4621 |
| ☐ N422UA | Airbus A320-232 | 0503 | ex F-WWIV | 4622 |
| ☐ N423UA | Airbus A320-232 | 0504 | ex F-WWBO | 4623 |
| ☐ N424UA | Airbus A320-232 | 0506 | ex F-WWBQ | 4624 |
| ☐ N425UA | Airbus A320-232 | 0508 | ex F-WWBY | 4625 |
| ☐ N426UA | Airbus A320-232 | 0510 | ex F-WWBZ | 4626 |
| ☐ N427UA | Airbus A320-232 | 0512 | ex F-WWDD | 4627 |
| ☐ N428UA | Airbus A320-232 | 0523 | ex F-WWDE | 4628 |
| ☐ N429UA | Airbus A320-232 | 0539 | ex F-WWIX | 4629 |
| ☐ N430UA | Airbus A320-232 | 0568 | ex F-WWDC | 4630 |
| ☐ N431UA | Airbus A320-232 | 0571 | ex F-WWDH | 4631 |
| ☐ N432UA | Airbus A320-232 | 0587 | ex F-WWBB | 4632 |
| ☐ N433UA | Airbus A320-232 | 0589 | ex F-WWBD | 4633 |
| ☐ N434UA | Airbus A320-232 | 0592 | ex F-WWBF | 4634 |
| ☐ N435UA | Airbus A320-232 | 0613 | ex F-WWBQ | 4635 |
| ☐ N436UA | Airbus A320-232 | 0638 | ex F-WWDE | 4636 |
| ☐ N437UA | Airbus A320-232 | 0655 | ex F-WWIK | 4637 |
| ☐ N438UA | Airbus A320-232 | 0678 | ex F-WWBJ | 4838 |
| ☐ N439UA | Airbus A320-232 | 0683 | ex F-WWDQ | 4839 |

| | | | | | |
|---|---|---|---|---|---|
| ☐ | N440UA | Airbus A320-232 | 0702 | ex F-WWDP | 4840 |
| ☐ | N441UA | Airbus A320-232 | 0751 | ex F-WWIU | 4841 |
| ☐ | N442UA | Airbus A320-232 | 0780 | ex F-WWDQ | 4842 |
| ☐ | N443UA | Airbus A320-232 | 0820 | ex F-WWBT | 4643 |
| ☐ | N444UA | Airbus A320-232 | 0824 | ex F-WWBZ | 4844 |
| ☐ | N445UA | Airbus A320-232 | 0826 | ex F-WWIL | 4845 |
| ☐ | N446UA | Airbus A320-232 | 0834 | ex F-WWIP | 4846 |
| ☐ | N447UA | Airbus A320-232 | 0836 | ex F-WWIR | 4847 |
| ☐ | N448UA | Airbus A320-232 | 0842 | ex F-WWBF | 4848 |
| ☐ | N449UA | Airbus A320-232 | 0851 | ex F-WWBJ | 4849 |
| ☐ | N451UA | Airbus A320-232 | 0865 | ex F-WWBR | 4851 |
| ☐ | N452UA | Airbus A320-232 | 0955 | ex F-WWBD | 4852 |
| ☐ | N453UA | Airbus A320-232 | 1001 | ex F-WWBH | 4853 |
| ☐ | N454UA | Airbus A320-232 | 1104 | ex F-WWDC | 4654 |
| ☐ | N455UA | Airbus A320-232 | 1105 | ex F-WWDE | 4655 |
| ☐ | N456UA | Airbus A320-232 | 1128 | ex F-WWIJ | 4656 |
| ☐ | N457UA | Airbus A320-232 | 1146 | ex F-WWBM | 4857 |
| ☐ | N458UA | Airbus A320-232 | 1163 | ex F-WWDK | 4858 |
| ☐ | N459UA | Airbus A320-232 | 1192 | ex F-WWDX | 4859 |
| ☐ | N460UA | Airbus A320-232 | 1248 | ex F-WWIS | 4860 |
| ☐ | N461UA | Airbus A320-232 | 1266 | ex F-WWDC | 4661 |
| ☐ | N462UA | Airbus A320-232 | 1272 | ex F-WWDI | 4962 |
| ☐ | N463UA | Airbus A320-232 | 1282 | ex F-WWBJ | 4663 Jim Briggs |
| ☐ | N464UA | Airbus A320-232 | 1290 | ex F-WWBR | 4664 |
| ☐ | N465UA | Airbus A320-232 | 1341 | ex F-WWDP | 4865 |
| ☐ | N466UA | Airbus A320-232 | 1343 | ex F-WWDQ | 4666 |
| ☐ | N467UA | Airbus A320-232 | 1359 | ex F-WWBH | 4867 |
| ☐ | N468UA | Airbus A320-232 | 1363 | ex F-WWIE | 4668 |
| ☐ | N469UA | Airbus A320-232 | 1409 | ex F-WWDF | 4869 |
| ☐ | N470UA | Airbus A320-232 | 1427 | ex F-WWBN | 4870 |
| ☐ | N471UA | Airbus A320-232 | 1432 | ex F-WWBA | 4871 |
| ☐ | N472UA | Airbus A320-232 | 1435 | ex F-WWBC | 4872 |
| ☐ | N473UA | Airbus A320-232 | 1469 | ex F-WWDL | 4873 |
| ☐ | N474UA | Airbus A320-232 | 1475 | ex F-WWDQ | 4874 |
| ☐ | N475UA | Airbus A320-232 | 1495 | ex F-WWIC | 4875 |
| ☐ | N476UA | Airbus A320-232 | 1508 | ex F-WWBB | 4876 |
| ☐ | N477UA | Airbus A320-232 | 1514 | ex F-WWBF | 4877 |
| ☐ | N478UA | Airbus A320-232 | 1533 | ex F-WWIQ | 4878 |
| ☐ | N479UA | Airbus A320-232 | 1538 | ex F-WWIT | 4879 |
| ☐ | N480UA | Airbus A320-232 | 1555 | ex F-WWBP | 4880 |
| ☐ | N481UA | Airbus A320-232 | 1559 | ex F-WWDH | 4881 |
| ☐ | N482UA | Airbus A320-232 | 1584 | ex F-WWBN | 4882 |
| ☐ | N483UA | Airbus A320-232 | 1586 | ex F-WWBR | 4883 |
| ☐ | N484UA | Airbus A320-232 | 1609 | ex F-WWBZ | 4884 |
| ☐ | N485UA | Airbus A320-232 | 1617 | ex F-WWDD | 4885 |
| ☐ | N486UA | Airbus A320-232 | 1620 | ex F-WWDG | 4886 |
| ☐ | N487UA | Airbus A320-232 | 1669 | ex F-WWIJ | 4887 |
| ☐ | N488UA | Airbus A320-232 | 1680 | ex F-WWBF | 4888 |
| ☐ | N489UA | Airbus A320-232 | 1702 | ex F-WWIT | 4889 |
| ☐ | N490UA | Airbus A320-232 | 1728 | ex F-WWBI | 4890 |
| ☐ | N491UA | Airbus A320-232 | 1741 | ex F-WWBU | 4891 |
| ☐ | N492UA | Airbus A320-232 | 1755 | ex F-WWDZ | 4892 |
| ☐ | N493UA | Airbus A320-232 | 1821 | ex F-WWIO | 4893 |
| ☐ | N494UA | Airbus A320-232 | 1840 | ex F-WWDC | 4894 |
| ☐ | N495UA | Airbus A320-232 | 1842 | ex F-WWBP | 4895 |
| ☐ | N496UA | Airbus A320-232 | 1845 | ex F-WWDR | 4896 |
| ☐ | N497UA | Airbus A320-232 | 1847 | ex F-WWDE | 4897 |
| ☐ | N498UA | Airbus A320-232 | 1865 | ex F-WWIK | 4898 |
| | | | | | |
| ☐ | N14604 | Boeing 737-524/W | 27317/2576 | | 0604 |
| ☐ | N58606 | Boeing 737-524/W | 27319/2590 | | 0606 |
| ☐ | N27610 | Boeing 737-524/W | 27323/2616 | | 0610 |
| ☐ | N11612 | Boeing 737-524/W | 27325/2630 | | 0612 |
| ☐ | N14613 | Boeing 737-524/W | 27326/2633 | | 0613 |
| ☐ | N17614 | Boeing 737-524/W | 27327/2634 | | 0614 |
| ☐ | N16617 | Boeing 737-524/W | 27330/2648 | | 0617 |
| ☐ | N17619 | Boeing 737-524/W | 27332/2659 | | 0619 |
| ☐ | N17620 | Boeing 737-524/W | 27333/2660 | ex N1790B | 0620 |
| ☐ | N19621 | Boeing 737-524/W | 27334/2661 | | 0621 |
| ☐ | N18622 | Boeing 737-524/W | 27526/2669 | | 0622 |
| ☐ | N19623 | Boeing 737-524/W | 27527/2672 | | 0623 |
| ☐ | N13624 | Boeing 737-524/W | 27528/2675 | | 0624 |
| ☐ | N46625 | Boeing 737-524/W | 27529/2683 | | 0625 |
| ☐ | N32626 | Boeing 737-524/W | 27530/2686 | | 0626 |
| ☐ | N17627 | Boeing 737-524/W | 27531/2700 | | 0627 |
| ☐ | N14628 | Boeing 737-524/W | 27532/2712 | | 0628 |
| ☐ | N14629 | Boeing 737-524/W | 27533/2725 | | 0629 |
| ☐ | N59630 | Boeing 737-524/W | 27534/2726 | | 0630 |
| ☐ | N62631 | Boeing 737-524/W | 27535/2728 | | 0631 |
| ☐ | N16632 | Boeing 737-524/W | 27900/2736 | | 0632 |
| ☐ | N24633 | Boeing 737-524/W | 27901/2743 | | 0633 |
| ☐ | N16647 | Boeing 737-524/W | 28908/2958 | | 0647 |

| | Reg | Type | c/n | ex | Fleet | Name |
|---|---|---|---|---|---|---|
| ☐ | N16701 | Boeing 737-724/W | 28762/29 | ex N1786B | 0701 | |
| ☐ | N24702 | Boeing 737-724/W | 28763/32 | | 0702 | |
| ☐ | N16703 | Boeing 737-724/W | 28764/37 | | 0703 | |
| ☐ | N14704 | Boeing 737-724/W | 28765/43 | | 0704 | |
| ☐ | N25705 | Boeing 737-724/W | 28766/46 | | 0705 | |
| ☐ | N24706 | Boeing 737-724/W | 28767/47 | | 0706 | |
| ☐ | N23707 | Boeing 737-724/W | 28768/48 | ex N1787B | 0707 | |
| ☐ | N23708 | Boeing 737-724/W | 28769/52 | | 0708 | |
| ☐ | N16709 | Boeing 737-724/W | 28779/93 | | 0709 | |
| ☐ | N15710 | Boeing 737-724/W | 28780/94 | | 0710 | |
| ☐ | N54711 | Boeing 737-724/W | 28782/97 | ex N1786B | 0711 | |
| ☐ | N15712 | Boeing 737-724/W | 28783/105 | ex N1786B | 0712 | |
| ☐ | N16713 | Boeing 737-724/W | 28784/107 | ex N1786B | 0713 | |
| ☐ | N33714 | Boeing 737-724/W | 28785/119 | ex N1786B | 0714 | |
| ☐ | N24715 | Boeing 737-724/W | 28786/125 | ex N1795B | 0715 | |
| ☐ | N13716 | Boeing 737-724/W | 28787/156 | ex N1782B | 0716 | |
| ☐ | N29717 | Boeing 737-724/W | 28936/182 | ex N1786B | 0717 | |
| ☐ | N13718 | Boeing 737-724/W | 28937/185 | ex N1786B | 0718 | |
| ☐ | N17719 | Boeing 737-724/W | 28938/195 | ex N1786B | 0719 | |
| ☐ | N13720 | Boeing 737-724/W | 28939/214 | ex N1786B | 0720 | |
| ☐ | N23721 | Boeing 737-724/W | 28940/219 | | 0721 | |
| ☐ | N27722 | Boeing 737-724/W | 28789/247 | ex N1786B | 0722 | |
| ☐ | N21723 | Boeing 737-724/W | 28790/253 | ex N1787B | 0723 | |
| ☐ | N27724 | Boeing 737-724/W | 28791/283 | ex N1787B | 0724 | |
| ☐ | N39726 | Boeing 737-724/W | 28796/315 | ex N1787B | 0726 | |
| ☐ | N38727 | Boeing 737-724/W | 28797/317 | ex N1786B | 0727 | |
| ☐ | N39728 | Boeing 737-724/W | 28944/321 | ex N1786B | 0728 | |
| ☐ | N24729 | Boeing 737-724/W | 28945/325 | ex N1784B | 0729 | |
| ☐ | N17730 | Boeing 737-724/W | 28798/338 | ex N1786B | 0730 | |
| ☐ | N14731 | Boeing 737-724/W | 28799/346 | ex N1786B | 0731 | |
| ☐ | N16732 | Boeing 737-724/W | 28948/352 | ex N60436 | 0732 | |
| ☐ | N27733 | Boeing 737-724/W | 28800/364 | ex N1786B | 0733 | Sir Samuel J LeFrak |
| ☐ | N27734 | Boeing 737-724/W | 28949/371 | ex N1786B | 0734 | |
| ☐ | N14735 | Boeing 737-724/W | 28950/376 | ex N1786B | 0735 | |
| ☐ | N24736 | Boeing 737-724/W | 28803/380 | ex N1786B | 0736 | |
| ☐ | N13750 | Boeing 737-724/W | 28941/286 | | 0750 | |
| | | | | | | |
| ☐ | N25201 | Boeing 737-824/W | 28958/443 | ex N1786B | 0201 | |
| ☐ | N24202 | Boeing 737-824/W | 30429/581 | ex N1786B | 0202 | |
| ☐ | N33203 | Boeing 737-824/W | 30613/591 | ex N1786B | 0203 | |
| ☐ | N35204 | Boeing 737-824/W | 30576/606 | ex N1795B | 0204 | |
| ☐ | N27205 | Boeing 737-824/W | 30577/615 | ex N1786B | 0205 | |
| ☐ | N11206 | Boeing 737-824/W | 30578/618 | ex N1786B | 0206 | |
| ☐ | N36207 | Boeing 737-824/W | 30579/627 | ex N1786B | 0207 | |
| ☐ | N26208 | Boeing 737-824/W | 30580/644 | ex N1786B | 0208 | |
| ☐ | N33209 | Boeing 737-824/W | 30581/647 | ex N1786B | 0209 | |
| ☐ | N26210 | Boeing 737-824/W | 28770/56 | | 0210 | |
| ☐ | N24211 | Boeing 737-824/W | 28771/58 | | 0211 | |
| ☐ | N24212 | Boeing 737-824/W | 28772/63 | | 0212 | |
| ☐ | N27213 | Boeing 737-824/W | 28773/65 | | 0213 | |
| ☐ | N14214 | Boeing 737-824/W | 28774/74 | | 0214 | |
| ☐ | N26215 | Boeing 737-824/W | 28775/76 | | 0215 | |
| ☐ | N12216 | Boeing 737-824/W | 28776/79 | | 0216 | |
| ☐ | N16217 | Boeing 737-824/W | 28777/81 | | 0217 | |
| ☐ | N12218 | Boeing 737-824/W | 28778/84 | | 0218 | |
| ☐ | N14219 | Boeing 737-824/W | 28781/88 | | 0219 | |
| ☐ | N18220 | Boeing 737-824/W | 28929/134 | ex N60436 | 0220 | |
| ☐ | N12221 | Boeing 737-824/W | 28930/153 | ex N1796B | 0221 | |
| ☐ | N34222 | Boeing 737-824/W | 28931/159 | | 0222 | |
| ☐ | N18223 | Boeing 737-824/W | 28932/162 | ex N1786B | 0223 | |
| ☐ | N24224 | Boeing 737-824/W | 28933/165 | ex N1782B | 0224 | |
| ☐ | N12225 | Boeing 737-824/W | 28934/168 | ex N1782B | 0225 | |
| ☐ | N26226 | Boeing 737-824/W | 28935/171 | ex N1787B | 0226 | |
| ☐ | N13227 | Boeing 737-824/W | 28788/262 | ex N1787B | 0227 | |
| ☐ | N14228 | Boeing 737-824/W | 28792/281 | ex N1787B | 0228 | |
| ☐ | N17229 | Boeing 737-824/W | 28793/287 | ex N1786B | 0229 | |
| ☐ | N14230 | Boeing 737-824/W | 28794/296 | ex N1787B | 0230 | |
| ☐ | N14231 | Boeing 737-824/W | 28795/300 | ex N1787B | 0231 | |
| ☐ | N26232 | Boeing 737-824/W | 28942/304 | | 0232 | |
| ☐ | N17233 | Boeing 737-824/W | 28943/328 | ex N1787B | 0233 | |
| ☐ | N16234 | Boeing 737-824/W | 28946/334 | ex N1787B | 0234 | |
| ☐ | N14235 | Boeing 737-824/W | 28947/342 | | 0235 | |
| ☐ | N35236 | Boeing 737-824/W | 28801/367 | ex N1786B | 0236 | |
| ☐ | N14237 | Boeing 737-824/W | 28802/374 | | 0237 | |
| ☐ | N12238 | Boeing 737-824/W | 28804/386 | ex N1786B | 0238 | |
| ☐ | N27239 | Boeing 737-824/W | 28951/391 | ex N1787B | 0239 | |
| ☐ | N14240 | Boeing 737-824/W | 28952/394 | ex N1786B | 0240 | |
| ☐ | N54241 | Boeing 737-824/W | 28953/395 | ex N1787B | 0241 | |
| ☐ | N14242 | Boeing 737-824/W | 28805/402 | ex N1786B | 0242 | |
| ☐ | N18243 | Boeing 737-824/W | 28806/403 | ex N1786B | 0243 | |
| ☐ | N17244 | Boeing 737-824/W | 28954/409 | ex N1787B | 0244 | |

| Reg | Type | MSN/Line | ex | Fleet | Notes |
|---|---|---|---|---|---|
| ☐ N17245 | Boeing 737-824/W | 28955/411 | ex N1786B | 0245 | |
| ☐ N27246 | Boeing 737-824/W | 28956/413 | ex N1786B | 0246 | |
| ☐ N36247 | Boeing 737-824/W | 28807/431 | ex N1786B | 0247 | |
| ☐ N13248 | Boeing 737-824/W | 28808/435 | ex N1786B | 0248 | |
| ☐ N14249 | Boeing 737-824/W | 28809/438 | ex N1786B | 0249 | |
| ☐ N14250 | Boeing 737-824/W | 28957/441 | ex N1786B | 0250 | |
| ☐ N73251 | Boeing 737-824/W | 30582/650 | ex N1786B | 0251 | |
| ☐ N37252 | Boeing 737-824/W | 30583/656 | ex N1787B | 0252 | |
| ☐ N37253 | Boeing 737-824/W | 30584/660 | | 0253 | |
| ☐ N76254 | Boeing 737-824/W | 30779/667 | ex N1786B | 0254 | |
| ☐ N37255 | Boeing 737-824/W | 30610/686 | ex N1787B | 0255 | |
| ☐ N73256 | Boeing 737-824/W | 30611/692 | ex N1787B | 0256 | |
| ☐ N38257 | Boeing 737-824/W | 30612/706 | ex N1786B | 0257 | |
| ☐ N77258 | Boeing 737-824/W | 30802/708 | ex N1786B | 0258 | |
| ☐ N73259 | Boeing 737-824/W | 30803/854 | ex N1786B | 0259 | |
| ☐ N35260 | Boeing 737-824/W | 30855/862 | ex N1786B | 0260 | |
| ☐ N77261 | Boeing 737-824/W | 31582/897 | ex N1786B | 0261 | |
| ☐ N33262 | Boeing 737-824/W | 32402/901 | ex N1786B | 0262 | |
| ☐ N37263 | Boeing 737-824/W | 31583/906 | ex N1786B | 0263 | |
| ☐ N33264 | Boeing 737-824/W | 31584/916 | ex N1786B | 0264 | |
| ☐ N76265 | Boeing 737-824/W | 31585/928 | ex N1786B | 0265 | |
| ☐ N33266 | Boeing 737-824/W | 32403/930 | | 0266 | |
| ☐ N37267 | Boeing 737-824/W | 31586/939 | ex N1786B | 0267 | |
| ☐ N38268 | Boeing 737-824/W | 31587/957 | ex N1786B | 0268 | |
| ☐ N76269 | Boeing 737-824/W | 31588/966 | ex N1786B | 0269 | |
| ☐ N73270 | Boeing 737-824/W | 31632/970 | ex N1787B | 0270 | |
| ☐ N35271 | Boeing 737-824/W | 31589/982 | ex N1786B | 0271 | |
| ☐ N36272 | Boeing 737-824/W | 31590/987 | ex N1795B | 0272 | |
| ☐ N37273 | Boeing 737-824/W | 31591/1012 | ex N1787B | 0273 | |
| ☐ N37274 | Boeing 737-824/W | 31592/1062 | | 0274 | |
| ☐ N73275 | Boeing 737-824/W | 31593/1077 | | 0275 | |
| ☐ N73276 | Boeing 737-824/W | 31594/1079 | | 0276 | |
| ☐ N37277 | Boeing 737-824/W | 31595/1099 | | 0277 | |
| ☐ N73278 | Boeing 737-824/W | 31596/1390 | | 0278 | |
| ☐ N79279 | Boeing 737-824/W | 31597/1411 | ex N1787B | 0279 | |
| ☐ N36280 | Boeing 737-824/W | 31598/1423 | | 0280 | |
| ☐ N37281 | Boeing 737-824/W | 31599/1425 | | 0281 | |
| ☐ N34282 | Boeing 737-824/W | 31634/1440 | | 0282 | |
| ☐ N73283 | Boeing 737-824/W | 31606/1456 | | 0283 | |
| ☐ N33284 | Boeing 737-824/W | 31635/1475 | | 0284 | |
| ☐ N78285 | Boeing 737-824/W | 33452/1540 | | 0285 | |
| ☐ N33286 | Boeing 737-824/W | 31600/1506 | | 0286 | |
| ☐ N37287 | Boeing 737-824/W | 31636/1509 | | 0287 | |
| ☐ N76288 | Boeing 737-824/W | 33451/1516 | | 0288 | |
| ☐ N33289 | Boeing 737-824/W | 31607/1542 | ex N1786B | 0289 | |
| ☐ N37290 | Boeing 737-824/W | 31601/1567 | | 0290 | |
| ☐ N73291 | Boeing 737-824/W | 33454/1611 | | 0291 | |
| ☐ N33292 | Boeing 737-824/W | 33455/1622 | | 0292 | |
| ☐ N37293 | Boeing 737-824/W | 33453/1743 | | 0293 | |
| ☐ N33294 | Boeing 737-824/W | 34000/1762 | | 0294 | |
| ☐ N77295 | Boeing 737-824/W | 34001/1779 | | 0295 | |
| ☐ N77296 | Boeing 737-824/W | 34002/1787 | | 0296 | |
| ☐ N39297 | Boeing 737-824/W | 34003/1791 | | 0297 | |
| ☐ N37298 | Boeing 737-824/W | 34004/1813 | | 0298 | |
| ☐ N73299 | Boeing 737-824/W | 34005/1821 | ex N1786B | 0299 | |
| ☐ N78501 | Boeing 737-824/W | 31602/1994 | ex N1786B | 0501 | |
| ☐ N76502 | Boeing 737-824/W | 31603/2017 | | 0502 | |
| ☐ N76503 | Boeing 737-824/W | 33461/2023 | | 0503 | |
| ☐ N76504 | Boeing 737-824/W | 31604/2035 | | 0504 | |
| ☐ N76505 | Boeing 737-824/W | 32834/2048 | ex N1786B | 0505 | |
| ☐ N78506 | Boeing 737-824/W | 32832/2065 | | 0506 | |
| ☐ N87507 | Boeing 737-824/W | 31637/2487 | ex N1786B | 0507 | |
| ☐ N76508 | Boeing 737-824/W | 31639/2514 | | 0508 | |
| ☐ N78509 | Boeing 737-824/W | 31638/2523 | ex N1787B | 0509 | |
| ☐ N77510 | Boeing 737-824/W | 32828/2579 | | 0510 | |
| ☐ N78511 | Boeing 737-824/W | 33459/2598 | | 0511 | |
| ☐ N87512 | Boeing 737-824/W | 33458/2602 | | 0512 | |
| ☐ N87513 | Boeing 737-824/W | 31621/2655 | | 0513 | |
| ☐ N76514 | Boeing 737-824/W | 31626/2680 | | 0514 | |
| ☐ N76515 | Boeing 737-824/W | 31623/2713 | | 0515 | |
| ☐ N76516 | Boeing 737-824/W | 37096/2718 | | 0516 | |
| ☐ N76517 | Boeing 737-824/W | 31628/2723 | | 0517 | |
| ☐ N77518 | Boeing 737-824/W | 31605/2768 | | 0518 | Capt Marlon Green |
| ☐ N76519 | Boeing 737-824/W | 30132/3138 | ex N1796B | 0519 | |
| ☐ N77520 | Boeing 737-824/W | 31658/3158 | ex N1786B | 0520 | |
| ☐ N79521 | Boeing 737-824/W | 31662/3169 | ex N1786B | 0521 | |
| ☐ N76522 | Boeing 737-824/W | 31660/3175 | ex N1786B | 0522 | |
| ☐ N76523 | Boeing 737-824/W | 37101/3216 | ex N1786B | 0523 | |
| ☐ N78524 | Boeing 737-824/W | 31642/3224 | | 0524 | |
| ☐ N77525 | Boeing 737-824/W | 31659/3253 | ex N1787B | 0525 | |
| ☐ N76526 | Boeing 737-824/W | 38700/3289 | | 0526 | |
| ☐ N87527 | Boeing 737-824/W | 38701/3305 | | 0527 | |

| | | | | | |
|---|---|---|---|---|---|
| ☐ N76528 | Boeing 737-824/W | 31663/3464 | | 0528 | |
| ☐ N76529 | Boeing 737-824/W | 31652/3490 | | 0529 | |
| ☐ N77530 | Boeing 737-824/W | 39998/3521 | | 0530 | |
| ☐ N87531 | Boeing 737-824/W | 39999/3549 | | 0531 | ♦ |
| ☐ N | Boeing 737-824/W | | | | o/o |
| ☐ N | Boeing 737-824/W | | | | o/o |
| | | | | | |
| ☐ N30401 | Boeing 737-924/W | 30118/820 | | 0401 | |
| ☐ N79402 | Boeing 737-924/W | 30119/857 | | 0402 | |
| ☐ N38403 | Boeing 737-924/W | 30120/884 | ex N1786B | 0403 | |
| ☐ N32404 | Boeing 737-924/W | 30121/893 | ex N1787B | 0404 | |
| ☐ N72405 | Boeing 737-924/W | 30122/911 | ex N1786B | 0405 | |
| ☐ N73406 | Boeing 737-924/W | 30123/943 | ex N1786B | 0406 | |
| ☐ N35407 | Boeing 737-924/W | 30124/951 | ex N1786B | 0407 | |
| ☐ N37408 | Boeing 737-924/W | 30125/962 | ex N1787B | 0408 | |
| ☐ N37409 | Boeing 737-924/W | 30126/1004 | ex N1787B | 0409 | |
| ☐ N75410 | Boeing 737-924/W | 30127/1021 | ex N1786B | 0410 | |
| ☐ N71411 | Boeing 737-924/W | 30128/1052 | | 0411 | |
| ☐ N31412 | Boeing 737-924/W | 30129/1112 | | 0412 | |
| ☐ N37413 | Boeing 737-924ER/W | 31664/2474 | | 0413 | |
| ☐ N47414 | Boeing 737-924ER/W | 32827/2490 | ex N1787B | 0414 | |
| ☐ N39415 | Boeing 737-924ER/W | 32826/2516 | | 0415 | |
| ☐ N39416 | Boeing 737-924ER/W | 37093/2528 | | 0416 | |
| ☐ N38417 | Boeing 737-924ER/W | 31665/2541 | | 0417 | |
| ☐ N39418 | Boeing 737-924ER/W | 33456/2547 | | 0418 | |
| ☐ N37419 | Boeing 737-924ER/W | 31666/2553 | | 0419 | |
| ☐ N37420 | Boeing 737-924ER/W | 33457/2565 | | 0420 | |
| ☐ N27421 | Boeing 737-924ER/W | 37094/2577 | | 0421 | |
| ☐ N37422 | Boeing 737-924ER/W | 31620/2614 | | 0422 | |
| ☐ N39423 | Boeing 737-924ER/W | 32829/2645 | | 0423 | |
| ☐ N38424 | Boeing 737-924ER/W | 37095/2651 | | 0424 | |
| ☐ N75425 | Boeing 737-924ER/W | 33460/2657 | | 0425 | |
| ☐ N75426 | Boeing 737-924ER/W | 31622/2676 | | 0426 | |
| ☐ N37427 | Boeing 737-924ER/W | 37097/2707 | | 0427 | |
| ☐ N75428 | Boeing 737-924ER/W | 31633/2737 | | 0428 | |
| ☐ N75429 | Boeing 737-924ER/W | 30130/2750 | | 0429 | |
| ☐ N77430 | Boeing 737-924ER/W | 37098/2774 | ex N1786B | 0430 | |
| ☐ N77431 | Boeing 737-924ER/W | 32833/2787 | | 0431 | |
| ☐ N75432 | Boeing 737-924ER/W | 32835/2817 | | 0432 | |
| ☐ N75433 | Boeing 737-924ER/W | 33527/2842 | | 0433 | |
| ☐ N37434 | Boeing 737-924ER/W | 33528/2891 | | 0434 | |
| ☐ N75435 | Boeing 737-924ER/W | 33529/2916 | | 0435 | |
| ☐ N75436 | Boeing 737-924ER/W | 33531/2947 | | 0436 | |
| ☐ N37437 | Boeing 737-924ER/W | 33532/2959 | | 0437 | |
| ☐ N78438 | Boeing 737-924ER/W | 33533/2971 | | 0438 | |
| ☐ N57439 | Boeing 737-924ER/W | 33534/2990 | ex N1786B | 0439 | |
| ☐ N45440 | Boeing 737-924ER/W | 33535/2996 | | 0440 | |
| ☐ N53441 | Boeing 737-924ER/W | 30131/3014 | ex N1787B | 0441 | |
| ☐ N53442 | Boeing 737-924ER/W | 33536/3027 | | 0442 | |
| ☐ N38443 | Boeing 737-924ER/W | 31655/3393 | ex N1786B | 0443 | |
| ☐ N36444 | Boeing 737-924ER/W | 31643/3417 | ex N1786B | 0444 | |
| ☐ N73445 | Boeing 737-924ER/W | 40000/3615 | | 0445 | |
| ☐ N38446 | Boeing 737-924ER/W | 31661/3894 | | 0446 | |
| ☐ N36447 | Boeing 737-924ER/W | 31650/3924 | | 0447 | |
| ☐ N78448 | Boeing 737-924ER/W | 40003/3942 | | 0448 | |
| ☐ N81449 | Boeing 737-924ER/W | 31651/3978 | | | |
| ☐ N39450 | Boeing 737-924ER/W | 40004/3984 | | | |
| ☐ N38451 | Boeing 737-924ER/W | 31646/ | | | ♦ |
| ☐ N68452 | Boeing 737-924ER/W | 40005/ | | | o/o♦ |
| ☐ N68453 | Boeing 737-924ER/W | 41742/ | | | o/o♦ |
| ☐ N38454 | Boeing 737-924ER/W | 31640/ | | | o/o♦ |
| ☐ N34455 | Boeing 737-924ER/W | 41743/ | | | o/o♦ |
| | | | | | |
| ☐ N104UA | Boeing 747-422 | 26902/1141 | | 8104 | |
| ☐ N105UA | Boeing 747-451 | 26473/985 | ex N60659 | 8105 | |
| ☐ N107UA | Boeing 747-422 | 26900/1168 | | 8107 | |
| ☐ N116UA | Boeing 747-422 | 26908/1193 | | 8116 | |
| ☐ N117UA | Boeing 747-422 | 28810/1197 | | 8117 | |
| ☐ N118UA | Boeing 747-422 | 28811/1201 | | 8118 | |
| ☐ N119UA | Boeing 747-422 | 28812/1207 | | 8119 | |
| ☐ N120UA | Boeing 747-422 | 29166/1209 | | 8120 | |
| ☐ N121UA | Boeing 747-422 | 29167/1211 | | 8121 | |
| ☐ N122UA | Boeing 747-422 | 29168/1218 | | 8122 | |
| ☐ N127UA | Boeing 747-422 | 28813/1221 | | 8127 | |
| ☐ N128UA | Boeing 747-422 | 30023/1245 | | 8128 | |
| ☐ N171UA | Boeing 747-422 | 24322/733 | | 8171 | |
| ☐ N174UA | Boeing 747-422 | 24381/762 | | 8174 | |
| ☐ N175UA | Boeing 747-422 | 24382/806 | | 8175 | |
| ☐ N177UA | Boeing 747-422 | 24384/819 | | 8177 | |
| ☐ N178UA | Boeing 747-422 | 24385/820 | | 8178 | |
| ☐ N179UA | Boeing 747-422 | 25158/866 | | 8179 | |
| ☐ N180UA | Boeing 747-422 | 25224/867 | | 8180 | |

| | | | | |
|---|---|---|---|---|
| ☐ N181UA | Boeing 747-422 | 25278/881 | ex N6005C | 8181 |
| ☐ N182UA | Boeing 747-422 | 25279/882 | | 8182 |
| ☐ N193UA | Boeing 747-422 | 26890/1085 | | 8193 |
| ☐ N195UA | Boeing 747-422 | 26899/1113 | | 8195 |
| ☐ N197UA | Boeing 747-422 | 26901/1121 | | 8197 |
| ☐ N199UA | Boeing 747-422 | 28717/1126 | | 8199 |
| | | | | |
| ☐ N501UA | Boeing 757-222 | 24622/241 | | 5401 |
| ☐ N502UA | Boeing 757-222/W | 24623/246 | | 5702 |
| ☐ N503UA | Boeing 757-222 | 24624/247 | | 5403 |
| ☐ N504UA | Boeing 757-222 | 24625/251 | | 5404 |
| ☐ N505UA | Boeing 757-222/W | 24626/254 | | 5705 |
| ☐ N506UA | Boeing 757-222 | 24627/263 | | 5406 |
| ☐ N507UA | Boeing 757-222 | 24743/270 | | 5407 |
| ☐ N508UA | Boeing 757-222 | 24744/277 | | 5708 |
| ☐ N509UA | Boeing 757-222 | 24763/284 | | 5409 |
| ☐ N510UA | Boeing 757-222/W | 24780/290 | | 5710 |
| ☐ N511UA | Boeing 757-222 | 24799/291 | | 5411 |
| ☐ N512UA | Boeing 757-222/W | 24809/298 | | 5712 |
| ☐ N513UA | Boeing 757-222 | 24810/299 | | 5413 |
| ☐ N514UA | Boeing 757-222 | 24839/305 | | 5414 |
| ☐ N515UA | Boeing 757-222 | 24840/306 | | 5415 |
| ☐ N516UA | Boeing 757-222 | 24860/307 | | 5416 |
| ☐ N517UA | Boeing 757-222/W | 24861/310 | | 5717 |
| ☐ N518UA | Boeing 757-222/W | 24871/311 | | 5718 |
| ☐ N519UA | Boeing 757-222 | 24872/312 | | 5419 |
| ☐ N520UA | Boeing 757-222 | 24890/313 | | 5420 |
| ☐ N521UA | Boeing 757-222 | 24891/319 | | 5421 |
| ☐ N522UA | Boeing 757-222 | 24931/320 | | 5422 |
| ☐ N523UA | Boeing 757-222 | 24932/329 | | 5423 |
| ☐ N524UA | Boeing 757-222 | 24977/331 | | 5424 |
| ☐ N525UA | Boeing 757-222/W | 24978/338 | | 5725 |
| ☐ N526UA | Boeing 757-222 | 24994/339 | | 5426 |
| ☐ N527UA | Boeing 757-222 | 24995/341 | | 5427 |
| ☐ N528UA | Boeing 757-222 | 25018/346 | | 5428 |
| ☐ N529UA | Boeing 757-222 | 25019/352 | | 5429 |
| ☐ N530UA | Boeing 757-222 | 25043/353 | | 5430 |
| ☐ N532UA | Boeing 757-222/W | 25072/366 | | 5732 |
| ☐ N533UA | Boeing 757-222 | 25073/367 | | 5433 |
| ☐ N534UA | Boeing 757-222 | 25129/372 | | 5434 |
| ☐ N535UA | Boeing 757-222 | 25130/373 | | 5435 |
| ☐ N536UA | Boeing 757-222 | 25156/380 | | 5436 |
| ☐ N537UA | Boeing 757-222 | 25157/381 | | 5437 |
| ☐ N538UA | Boeing 757-222 | 25222/385 | | 5438 |
| ☐ N539UA | Boeing 757-222 | 25223/386 | | 5439 |
| ☐ N540UA | Boeing 757-222 | 25252/393 | | 5440 |
| ☐ N541UA | Boeing 757-222 | 25253/394 | | 5441 |
| ☐ N543UA | Boeing 757-222ER | 25698/401 | | 5543 |
| ☐ N544UA | Boeing 757-222ER/W | 25322/405 | | 5544 |
| ☐ N545UA | Boeing 757-222ER | 25323/406 | | 5545 |
| ☐ N546UA | Boeing 757-222ER/W | 25367/413 | | 5546 |
| ☐ N547UA | Boeing 757-222ER | 25368/414 | | 5547 |
| ☐ N548UA | Boeing 757-222ER | 25396/420 | | 5548 |
| ☐ N549UA | Boeing 757-222ER/W | 25397/421 | | 5549 |
| ☐ N550UA | Boeing 757-222ER | 25398/426 | | 5550 |
| ☐ N551UA | Boeing 757-222ER | 25399/427 | | 5551 |
| ☐ N552UA | Boeing 757-222ER | 26641/431 | | 5552 |
| ☐ N553UA | Boeing 757-222 | 25277/434 | | 5453 |
| ☐ N554UA | Boeing 757-222/W | 26644/435 | | 5754 |
| ☐ N555UA | Boeing 757-222/W | 26647/442 | | 5755 |
| ☐ N556UA | Boeing 757-222 | 26650/447 | | 5456 |
| ☐ N557UA | Boeing 757-222 | 26653/454 | | 5757 |
| ☐ N558UA | Boeing 757-222 | 26654/462 | | 5458 |
| ☐ N559UA | Boeing 757-222 | 26657/467 | | 5459 |
| ☐ N560UA | Boeing 757-222 | 26660/469 | | 5760 |
| ☐ N561UA | Boeing 757-222 | 26661/479 | | 5461 |
| ☐ N562UA | Boeing 757-222 | 26664/487 | | 5462 |
| ☐ N563UA | Boeing 757-222 | 26665/488 | | 5463 |
| ☐ N564UA | Boeing 757-222 | 26666/490 | | 5464 |
| ☐ N565UA | Boeing 757-222 | 26669/492 | | 5465 |
| ☐ N566UA | Boeing 757-222 | 26670/494 | | 5466 |
| ☐ N567UA | Boeing 757-222 | 26673/497 | | 5467 |
| ☐ N568UA | Boeing 757-222 | 26674/498 | | 5468 |
| ☐ N569UA | Boeing 757-222 | 26677/499 | | 5469 |
| ☐ N570UA | Boeing 757-222 | 26678/501 | | 5470 |
| ☐ N571UA | Boeing 757-222 | 26681/506 | | 5471 |
| ☐ N572UA | Boeing 757-222 | 26682/508 | | 5472 |
| ☐ N573UA | Boeing 757-222 | 26685/512 | | 5473 |
| ☐ N574UA | Boeing 757-222 | 26686/513 | | 5474 |
| ☐ N575UA | Boeing 757-222 | 26689/515 | | 5475 |
| ☐ N576UA | Boeing 757-222 | 26690/524 | | 5676 |
| ☐ N577UA | Boeing 757-222 | 26693/527 | | 5677 |

[VCV]
[VCV]

| | | | | | |
|---|---|---|---|---|---|
| ☐ | N578UA | Boeing 757-222 | 26694/531 | | 5678 |
| ☐ | N579UA | Boeing 757-222 | 26697/539 | | 5679 |
| ☐ | N580UA | Boeing 757-222 | 26698/542 | | 5680 |
| ☐ | N581UA | Boeing 757-222 | 26701/543 | | 5681 |
| ☐ | N583UA | Boeing 757-222 | 26705/556 | | 5683 | [VCV] |
| ☐ | N584UA | Boeing 757-222 | 26706/559 | | 5684 |
| ☐ | N585UA | Boeing 757-222 | 26709/563 | | 5685 |
| ☐ | N586UA | Boeing 757-222 | 26710/567 | | 5686 |
| ☐ | N587UA | Boeing 757-222 | 26713/570 | | 5687 |
| ☐ | N588UA | Boeing 757-222 | 26717/571 | | 5688 |
| ☐ | N589UA | Boeing 757-222ER/W | 28707/773 | ex N3509J | 5589 |
| ☐ | N590UA | Boeing 757-222ER/W | 28708/785 | | 5590 |
| ☐ | N592UA | Boeing 757-222 | 28143/719 | | 5492 Richard Damron, Captain |
| ☐ | N593UA | Boeing 757-222 | 28144/724 | | 5493 |
| ☐ | N594UA | Boeing 757-222 | 28145/727 | | 5494 |
| ☐ | N595UA | Boeing 757-222ER/W | 28748/789 | | 5595 |
| ☐ | N596UA | Boeing 757-222ER/W | 28749/794 | | 5596 |
| ☐ | N597UA | Boeing 757-222ER | 28750/841 | | 5597 |
| ☐ | N598UA | Boeing 757-222ER | 28751/844 | ex N1787B | 5598 |
| ☐ | N58101 | Boeing 757-224/W | 27291/614 | | 0101 |
| ☐ | N14102 | Boeing 757-224/W | 27292/619 | | 0102 |
| ☐ | N33103 | Boeing 757-224/W | 27293/623 | | 0103 |
| ☐ | N17104 | Boeing 757-224/W | 27294/629 | | 104 |
| ☐ | N17105 | Boeing 757-224/W | 27295/632 | | 0105 |
| ☐ | N14106 | Boeing 757-224/W | 27296/637 | | 0106 Sam E Ashmore |
| ☐ | N14107 | Boeing 757-224/W | 27297/641 | | 107 |
| ☐ | N21108 | Boeing 757-224/W | 27298/645 | | 0108 |
| ☐ | N12109 | Boeing 757-224/W | 27299/648 | | 0109 |
| ☐ | N13110 | Boeing 757-224/W | 27300/650 | | 110 |
| ☐ | N57111 | Boeing 757-224/W | 27301/652 | | 0111 |
| ☐ | N18112 | Boeing 757-224/W | 27302/653 | | 0112 |
| ☐ | N13113 | Boeing 757-224/W | 27555/668 | | 0113 |
| ☐ | N12114 | Boeing 757-224/W | 27556/682 | | 0114 |
| ☐ | N14115 | Boeing 757-224/W | 27557/686 | | 0115 |
| ☐ | N12116 | Boeing 757-224/W | 27558/702 | | 0116 |
| ☐ | N19117 | Boeing 757-224/W | 27559/706 | | 0117 |
| ☐ | N14118 | Boeing 757-224/W | 27560/748 | ex (N19118) | 0118 |
| ☐ | N18119 | Boeing 757-224/W | 27561/753 | | 0119 |
| ☐ | N14120 | Boeing 757-224/W | 27562/761 | | 0120 |
| ☐ | N14121 | Boeing 757-224/W | 27563/766 | | 121 |
| ☐ | N17122 | Boeing 757-224/W | 27564/768 | | 0122 |
| ☐ | N26123 | Boeing 757-224/W | 28966/781 | | 123 |
| ☐ | N29124 | Boeing 757-224/W | 27565/786 | | 0124 |
| ☐ | N12125 | Boeing 757-224/W | 28967/788 | ex N1787B | 0125 |
| ☐ | N17126 | Boeing 757-224/W | 27566/790 | | 126 |
| ☐ | N48127 | Boeing 757-224/W | 28968/791 | | 0127 |
| ☐ | N17128 | Boeing 757-224/W | 27567/795 | | 128 |
| ☐ | N29129 | Boeing 757-224/W | 28969/796 | | 129 |
| ☐ | N19130 | Boeing 757-224/W | 28970/799 | | 0130 |
| ☐ | N34131 | Boeing 757-224/W | 28971/806 | | 131 |
| ☐ | N33132 | Boeing 757-224/W | 29281/809 | | 132 |
| ☐ | N17133 | Boeing 757-224/W | 29282/840 | | 133 |
| ☐ | N67134 | Boeing 757-224/W | 29283/848 | ex N1800B | 134 |
| ☐ | N41135 | Boeing 757-224/W | 29284/851 | | 0135 |
| ☐ | N19136 | Boeing 757-224/W | 29285/856 | | 0136 |
| ☐ | N34137 | Boeing 757-224/W | 30229/899 | | 0137 |
| ☐ | N13138 | Boeing 757-224/W | 30351/903 | ex N1795B | 0138 |
| ☐ | N17139 | Boeing 757-224/W | 30352/911 | | 0139 |
| ☐ | N41140 | Boeing 757-224/W | 30353/913 | | 0140 |
| ☐ | N19141 | Boeing 757-224/W | 30354/933 | | 0141 |
| ☐ | N75851 | Boeing 757-324/W | 32810/990 | | 0851 |
| ☐ | N57852 | Boeing 757-324/W | 32811/995 | | 852 |
| ☐ | N75853 | Boeing 757-324/W | 32812/997 | | 853 |
| ☐ | N75854 | Boeing 757-324/W | 32813/999 | | 854 |
| ☐ | N57855 | Boeing 757-324/W | 32814/1038 | | 855 |
| ☐ | N74856 | Boeing 757-324/W | 32815/1039 | | 0856 |
| ☐ | N57857 | Boeing 757-324/W | 32816/1040 | | 0857 |
| ☐ | N75858 | Boeing 757-324/W | 32817/1042 | | 0858 |
| ☐ | N56859 | Boeing 757-324/W | 32818/1043 | | 859 last 757-300 built |
| ☐ | N73860 | Boeing 757-33N/W | 32584/972 | ex N550TZ | 860 |
| ☐ | N75861 | Boeing 757-33N/W | 32585/976 | ex N551TZ | 861 |
| ☐ | N57862 | Boeing 757-33N/W | 32586/978 | ex N552TZ | 863 |
| ☐ | N57863 | Boeing 757-33N/W | 32587/980 | ex N553TZ | 863 |
| ☐ | N57864 | Boeing 757-33N/W | 32588/985 | ex N554TZ | 864 |
| ☐ | N77865 | Boeing 757-33N/W | 32589/1003 | ex N555TZ | 865 |
| ☐ | N78866 | Boeing 757-33N/W | 32591/1007 | ex N557TZ | 866 |
| ☐ | N77867 | Boeing 757-33N/W | 32592/1008 | ex N558TZ | 867 |
| ☐ | N57868 | Boeing 757-33N/W | 32590/1017 | ex N556TZ | 868 |
| ☐ | N57869 | Boeing 757-33N/W | 32593/1018 | ex N559TZ | 869 |
| ☐ | N57870 | Boeing 757-33N/W | 33525/1031 | ex N560TZ | 0870 |
| ☐ | N77871 | Boeing 757-33N/W | 33526/1032 | ex N561TZ | 871 |

| | | | | |
|---|---|---|---|---|
| ☐ N76151 | Boeing 767-224ER | 30430/811 | ex (N37165) | 151 |
| ☐ N73152 | Boeing 767-224ER | 30431/815 | ex (N37166) | 152 |
| ☐ N76153 | Boeing 767-224ER | 30432/819 | ex (N37167) | 153 |
| ☐ N69154 | Boeing 767-224ER | 30433/823 | ex (N37168) | 154 |
| ☐ N76156 | Boeing 767-224ER | 30435/827 | ex (N37170) | 156 |
| ☐ N67158 | Boeing 767-224ER | 30437/839 | | 158 |
| ☐ N68159 | Boeing 767-224ER | 30438/845 | | 159 |
| ☐ N68160 | Boeing 767-224ER | 30439/851 | | 160 |
| | | | | |
| ☐ N641UA | Boeing 767-322ER | 25091/360 | | 6341 |
| ☐ N642UA | Boeing 767-322ER | 25092/367 | | 6342 |
| ☐ N643UA | Boeing 767-322ER | 25093/368 | | 6343 |
| ☐ N644UA | Boeing 767-322ER | 25094/369 | | 6344 |
| ☐ N646UA | Boeing 767-322ER | 25283/420 | | 6346 |
| ☐ N647UA | Boeing 767-322ER | 25284/424 | | 6347 |
| ☐ N648UA | Boeing 767-322ER | 25285/443 | | 6348 |
| ☐ N649UA | Boeing 767-322ER | 25286/444 | | 6349 |
| ☐ N651UA | Boeing 767-322ER | 25389/452 | | 6351 |
| ☐ N652UA | Boeing 767-322ER | 25390/457 | | 6352 |
| ☐ N653UA | Boeing 767-322ER | 25391/460 | | 6353 Star Alliance c/s |
| ☐ N654UA | Boeing 767-322ER | 25392/462 | | 6354 |
| ☐ N655UA | Boeing 767-322ER | 25393/468 | | 6355 |
| ☐ N656UA | Boeing 767-322ER | 25394/472 | | 6356 |
| ☐ N657UA | Boeing 767-322ER | 27112/479 | | 6357 |
| ☐ N658UA | Boeing 767-322ER | 27113/480 | | 6358 |
| ☐ N659UA | Boeing 767-322ER | 27114/485 | | 6359 |
| ☐ N660UA | Boeing 767-322ER | 27115/494 | | 6360 |
| ☐ N661UA | Boeing 767-322ER | 27158/507 | | 6361 |
| ☐ N662UA | Boeing 767-322ER | 27159/513 | | 6362 |
| ☐ N663UA | Boeing 767-322ER | 27160/514 | | 6363 |
| ☐ N664UA | Boeing 767-322ER | 29236/707 | | 6764 |
| ☐ N665UA | Boeing 767-322ER | 29237/711 | | 6765 |
| ☐ N666UA | Boeing 767-322ER | 29238/715 | | 6766 |
| ☐ N667UA | Boeing 767-322ER | 29239/716 | | 6767 |
| ☐ N668UA | Boeing 767-322ER | 30024/742 | | 6768 |
| ☐ N669UA | Boeing 767-322ER | 30025/757 | | 6769 |
| ☐ N670UA | Boeing 767-322ER | 29240/763 | | 6770 |
| ☐ N671UA | Boeing 767-322ER | 30026/766 | | 6771 |
| ☐ N672UA | Boeing 767-322ER | 30027/773 | | 6772 |
| ☐ N673UA | Boeing 767-322ER | 29241/779 | | 6773 |
| ☐ N674UA | Boeing 767-322ER | 29242/782 | | 6774 |
| ☐ N675UA | Boeing 767-322ER | 29243/800 | | 6775 |
| ☐ N676UA | Boeing 767-322ER | 30028/834 | | 6776 |
| ☐ N677UA | Boeing 767-322ER | 30029/852 | | 6777 |
| | | | | |
| ☐ N66051 | Boeing 767-424ER | 29446/799 | ex (N76401) | 051 |
| ☐ N67052 | Boeing 767-424ER | 29447/805 | ex (N87402) | 052 |
| ☐ N59053 | Boeing 767-424ER | 29448/809 | ex (N47403) | 053 |
| ☐ N76054 | Boeing 767-424ER | 29449/816 | ex (N87404) | 054 |
| ☐ N76055 | Boeing 767-424ER | 29450/826 | | 0055 |
| ☐ N66056 | Boeing 767-424ER | 29451/842 | | 056 |
| ☐ N66057 | Boeing 767-424ER | 29452/859 | | 057 |
| ☐ N67058 | Boeing 767-424ER | 29453/862 | | 058 |
| ☐ N69059 | Boeing 767-424ER | 29454/864 | | 0059 |
| ☐ N78060 | Boeing 767-424ER | 29455/866 | | 060 |
| ☐ N68061 | Boeing 767-424ER | 29456/868 | | 061 |
| ☐ N76062 | Boeing 767-424ER | 29457/869 | | 062 |
| ☐ N69063 | Boeing 767-424ER | 29458/872 | | 063 |
| ☐ N76064 | Boeing 767-424ER | 29459/873 | | 064 |
| ☐ N76065 | Boeing 767-424ER | 29460/876 | | 065 |
| ☐ N77066 | Boeing 767-424ER | 29461/878 | | 066 |
| | | | | |
| ☐ N204UA | Boeing 777-222ER | 28713/191 | | 2904 |
| ☐ N206UA | Boeing 777-222ER | 30212/216 | | 2906 |
| ☐ N209UA | Boeing 777-222ER | 30215/259 | | 2609 |
| ☐ N210UA | Boeing 777-222 | 30216/264 | | 2510 |
| ☐ N211UA | Boeing 777-222 | 30217/282 | | 2511 |
| ☐ N212UA | Boeing 777-222 | 30218/293 | | 2512 |
| ☐ N213UA | Boeing 777-222 | 30219/295 | | 2513 |
| ☐ N214UA | Boeing 777-222 | 30220/296 | | 2514 |
| ☐ N215UA | Boeing 777-222 | 30221/297 | | 2515 |
| ☐ N216UA | Boeing 777-222ER | 30549/291 | | 2616 |
| ☐ N217UA | Boeing 777-222ER | 30550/294 | | 2617 |
| ☐ N218UA | Boeing 777-222ER | 30222/317 | | 2618 10 Years Star Alliance c/s |
| ☐ N219UA | Boeing 777-222ER | 30551/318 | | 2619 |
| ☐ N220UA | Boeing 777-222ER | 30223/340 | | 2620 |
| ☐ N221UA | Boeing 777-222ER | 30552/347 | | 2621 |
| ☐ N222UA | Boeing 777-222ER | 30553/352 | | 2622 |
| ☐ N223UA | Boeing 777-222ER | 30224/357 | | 2623 |
| ☐ N224UA | Boeing 777-222ER | 30225/375 | | 2624 |
| ☐ N225UA | Boeing 777-222ER | 30554/377 | | 2625 Spirit of United |

| | | | | | |
|---|---|---|---|---|---|
| ☐ N226UA | Boeing 777-222ER | 30226/380 | | 2626 | |
| ☐ N227UA | Boeing 777-222ER | 30555/381 | | 2627 | |
| ☐ N228UA | Boeing 777-222ER | 30556/384 | | 2628 | |
| ☐ N229UA | Boeing 777-222ER | 30557/388 | | 2629 | |
| ☐ N768UA | Boeing 777-222 | 26919/11 | | 2368 | |
| ☐ N769UA | Boeing 777-222 | 26921/12 | | 2369 | |
| ☐ N771UA | Boeing 777-222 | 26932/3 | ex N7773 | 2371 | |
| ☐ N772UA | Boeing 777-222 | 26930/5 | ex (N77775) | 2372 | |
| ☐ N773UA | Boeing 777-222 | 26929/4 | ex N7774 | 2373 Richard H Leung, Customer | |
| ☐ N774UA | Boeing 777-222 | 26936/2 | ex N7772 | 2374 | |
| ☐ N775UA | Boeing 777-222 | 26947/22 | | 2375 | |
| ☐ N776UA | Boeing 777-222 | 26937/27 | | 2376 | |
| ☐ N777UA | Boeing 777-222 | 26916/7 | | 2377 | |
| ☐ N778UA | Boeing 777-222 | 26940/34 | | 2378 | |
| ☐ N779UA | Boeing 777-222 | 26941/35 | | 2379 | |
| ☐ N780UA | Boeing 777-222 | 26944/36 | | 2380 | |
| ☐ N781UA | Boeing 777-222 | 26945/40 | | 2381 | |
| ☐ N782UA | Boeing 777-222ER | 26948/57 | | 2982 | |
| ☐ N783UA | Boeing 777-222ER | 26950/60 | | 2983 | |
| ☐ N784UA | Boeing 777-222ER | 26951/69 | | 2984 | |
| ☐ N785UA | Boeing 777-222ER | 26954/73 | | 2985 | |
| ☐ N786UA | Boeing 777-222ER | 26938/52 | | 2986 | |
| ☐ N787UA | Boeing 777-222ER | 26939/43 | | 2987 | |
| ☐ N788UA | Boeing 777-222ER | 26942/82 | | 2988 | |
| ☐ N791UA | Boeing 777-222ER | 26933/93 | | 2991 | |
| ☐ N792UA | Boeing 777-222ER | 26934/96 | | 2992 | |
| ☐ N793UA | Boeing 777-222ER | 26946/97 | | 2993 | |
| ☐ N794UA | Boeing 777-222ER | 26953/105 | | 2994 | |
| ☐ N795UA | Boeing 777-222ER | 26927/108 | | 2995 | |
| ☐ N796UA | Boeing 777-222ER | 26931/112 | | 2996 | |
| ☐ N797UA | Boeing 777-222ER | 26924/116 | | 2997 | |
| ☐ N798UA | Boeing 777-222ER | 26928/123 | | 2998 | |
| ☐ N799UA | Boeing 777-222ER | 26926/139 | | 2999 | |
| | | | | | |
| ☐ N78001 | Boeing 777-224ER | 27577/161 | | 0001 Gordon M Bethune | |
| ☐ N78002 | Boeing 777-224ER | 27578/165 | | 002 | |
| ☐ N78003 | Boeing 777-224ER | 27579/167 | | 003 | |
| ☐ N78004 | Boeing 777-224ER | 27580/169 | | 004 | |
| ☐ N78005 | Boeing 777-224ER | 27581/177 | | 005 | |
| ☐ N77006 | Boeing 777-224ER | 29476/183 | | 006 Robert F Six | |
| ☐ N74007 | Boeing 777-224ER | 29477/197 | | 0007 | |
| ☐ N78008 | Boeing 777-224ER | 29478/200 | | 0008 | |
| ☐ N78009 | Boeing 777-224ER | 29479/211 | | 0009 | |
| ☐ N76010 | Boeing 777-224ER | 29480/220 | | 010 | |
| ☐ N79011 | Boeing 777-224ER | 29859/227 | | 0011 | |
| ☐ N77012 | Boeing 777-224ER | 29860/234 | | 0012 | |
| ☐ N78013 | Boeing 777-224ER | 29861/243 | | 013 | |
| ☐ N77014 | Boeing 777-224ER | 29862/253 | | 014 | |
| ☐ N27015 | Boeing 777-224ER | 28678/273 | | 015 | |
| ☐ N57016 | Boeing 777-224ER | 28679/279 | | 016 | |
| ☐ N78017 | Boeing 777-224ER | 31679/391 | | 017 | |
| ☐ N37018 | Boeing 777-224ER | 31680/397 | | 0018 | |
| ☐ N77019 | Boeing 777-224ER | 35547/617 | | 0019 | |
| ☐ N69020 | Boeing 777-224ER | 31687/625 | | 0020 | |
| ☐ N76021 | Boeing 777-224ER | 39776/858 | | 021 | |
| ☐ N77022 | Boeing 777-224ER | 39777/868 | | 022 | |
| | | | | | |
| ☐ N | Boeing 787-8 | | | | o/o |
| ☐ N | Boeing 787-8 | | | | o/o |
| ☐ N | Boeing 787-8 | | | | o/o |
| ☐ N | Boeing 787-8 | | | | o/o |
| ☐ N | Boeing 787-8 | | | | o/o |
| ☐ N | Boeing 787-8 | | | | o/o |

| UNITED EXPRESS | United (UA) |
|---|---|
| | Chicago-O'Hare Intl, IL/San Francisco-Intl, CA/Denver, CO (ORD/SFO/DEN) |

| | | | | |
|---|---|---|---|---|
| ☐ N81533 | Beech 1900D | UE-137 | ex N137ZV | Gulfstream Intl |
| ☐ N81535 | Beech 1900D | UE-147 | | Gulfstream Intl |
| ☐ N81536 | Beech 1900D | UE-152 | | Gulfstream Intl |
| ☐ N38537 | Beech 1900D | UE-158 | | Gulfstream Intl |
| ☐ N81538 | Beech 1900D | UE-199 | | Gulfstream Intl |
| ☐ N82539 | Beech 1900D | UE-168 | | Gulfstream Intl |
| ☐ N16540 | Beech 1900D | UE-172 | | Gulfstream Intl |
| ☐ N17541 | Beech 1900D | UE-203 | | Gulfstream Intl |
| ☐ N47542 | Beech 1900D | UE-198 | | Gulfstream Intl |
| ☐ N49543 | Beech 1900D | UE-181 | | Gulfstream Intl |
| ☐ N53545 | Beech 1900D | UE-185 | | Gulfstream Intl |
| ☐ N81546 | Beech 1900D | UE-187 | | Gulfstream Intl |
| ☐ N69547 | Beech 1900D | UE-189 | | Gulfstream Intl |
| ☐ N69549 | Beech 1900D | UE-194 | | Gulfstream Intl |

| | | | | | |
|---|---|---|---|---|---|
| ☐ N87550 | Beech 1900D | UE-205 | | | Gulfstream Intl |
| ☐ N87551 | Beech 1900D | UE-206 | | | Gulfstream Intl |
| ☐ N87552 | Beech 1900D | UE-216 | | | Gulfstream Intl |
| ☐ N87554 | Beech 1900D | UE-227 | | | Gulfstream Intl |
| ☐ N87555 | Beech 1900D | UE-234 | | | Gulfstream Intl |
| ☐ N81556 | Beech 1900D | UE-239 | | | Gulfstream Intl |
| ☐ N87557 | Beech 1900D | UE-246 | | | Gulfstream Intl |
| ☐ N715SF | Canadair CRJ-100LR | 7115 | ex LV-WPF | | GoJet |
| ☐ N830AS | Canadair CRJ-200ER | 7236 | ex C-FMNW | | ExpressJet |
| ☐ N832AS | Canadair CRJ-200ER | 7243 | ex C-FMNQ | | ExpressJet |
| ☐ N834AS | Canadair CRJ-200ER | 7254 | ex C-FMKV | | ExpressJet |
| ☐ N836AS | Canadair CRJ-200ER | 7263 | ex C-FMLU | | ExpressJet |
| ☐ N473CA | Canadair CRJ-200ER | 7668 | ex C-FMMN | 472 | Chautauqua |
| ☐ N652BR | Canadair CRJ-200ER | 7429 | ex C-FMMQ | 458 | Chautauqua |
| ☐ N653BR | Canadair CRJ-200ER | 7438 | ex C-FMLF | 460 | Chautauqua |
| ☐ N667BR | Canadair CRJ-200ER | 7535 | ex C-FMNH | 461 | Chautauqua |
| ☐ N702BR | Canadair CRJ-200ER | 7462 | ex N851FJ | 459 | Chautauqua |
| ☐ N75995 | Canadair CRJ-200ER | 7361 | ex C-FZTW | | GoJet♦ |
| ☐ N903SW | Canadair CRJ-200ER | 7425 | ex C-FMOI | 7425 | SkyWest |
| ☐ N905SW | Canadair CRJ-200ER | 7437 | ex C-FMLB | 7437 | SkyWest |
| ☐ N908SW | Canadair CRJ-200ER | 7540 | ex C-FMOW | 7540 | SkyWest |
| ☐ N909SW | Canadair CRJ-200ER | 7558 | ex C-GJHL | 7558 | SkyWest |
| ☐ N910SW | Canadair CRJ-200ER | 7566 | ex C-GJHY | 7566 | SkyWest |
| ☐ N912SW | Canadair CRJ-200ER | 7595 | ex C-FMNH | 7595 | SkyWest |
| ☐ N913SW | Canadair CRJ-200ER | 7597 | ex C-FMNX | 7597 | SkyWest |
| ☐ N915SW | Canadair CRJ-200ER | 7615 | ex C-GKJQ | 7615 | SkyWest |
| ☐ N916SW | Canadair CRJ-200ER | 7634 | ex C-FMLU | 7634 | SkyWest |
| ☐ N917SW | Canadair CRJ-200ER | 7641 | ex C-FMMX | 7641 | SkyWest |
| ☐ N918SW | Canadair CRJ-200ER | 7645 | ex C-FMKW | 7645 | SkyWest |
| ☐ N919SW | Canadair CRJ-200ER | 7657 | ex C-FMNX | 7657 | SkyWest |
| ☐ N920SW | Canadair CRJ-200ER | 7660 | ex C-FMOW | 7660 | SkyWest |
| ☐ N923SW | Canadair CRJ-200ER | 7664 | ex C-FMLU | 7664 | SkyWest |
| ☐ N924SW | Canadair CRJ-200ER | 7681 | ex C-FMLS | 7681 | SkyWest |
| ☐ N925SW | Canadair CRJ-200ER | 7682 | ex C-FMLT | 7682 | SkyWest |
| ☐ N926SW | Canadair CRJ-200ER | 7687 | ex C-FMNX | 7687 | SkyWest |
| ☐ N927SW | Canadair CRJ-200ER | 7693 | ex C-FMNQ | 7693 | SkyWest |
| ☐ N928SW | Canadair CRJ-200ER | 7701 | ex C-FMMX | 7701 | SkyWest |
| ☐ N929SW | Canadair CRJ-200ER | 7703 | ex C-FMNB | 7703 | SkyWest |
| ☐ N930SW | Canadair CRJ-200ER | 7713 | ex C-FMLV | 7713 | SkyWest |
| ☐ N932SW | Canadair CRJ-200ER | 7714 | ex C-FMMT | 7714 | SkyWest |
| ☐ N934SW | Canadair CRJ-200ER | 7722 | ex C-FMND | 7722 | SkyWest |
| ☐ N935SW | Canadair CRJ-200ER | 7725 | ex C-FMOI | 7725 | SkyWest |
| ☐ N936SW | Canadair CRJ-200ER | 7726 | ex C-FMMB | 7726 | SkyWest |
| ☐ N937SW | Canadair CRJ-200ER | 7735 | ex C-FMKW | 7735 | SkyWest |
| ☐ N938SW | Canadair CRJ-200ER | 7741 | ex C-FMLS | 7741 | SkyWest |
| ☐ N939SW | Canadair CRJ-200ER | 7742 | ex C-FMLT | 7742 | SkyWest |
| ☐ N941SW | Canadair CRJ-200ER | 7750 | ex C-FMOW | 7750 | SkyWest |
| ☐ N943SW | Canadair CRJ-200ER | 7762 | ex C-FMMY | 7762 | SkyWest |
| ☐ N945SW | Canadair CRJ-200ER | 7770 | ex C-FMLQ | 7770 | SkyWest |
| ☐ N946SW | Canadair CRJ-200ER | 7776 | ex C-FMNW | 7776 | SkyWest |
| ☐ N948SW | Canadair CRJ-200ER | 7789 | ex C-GXTU | 7789 | SkyWest |
| ☐ N951SW | Canadair CRJ-200ER | 7795 | ex C-FMKW | 7795 30th anniversary c/s | SkyWest |
| ☐ N952SW | Canadair CRJ-200ER | 7805 | ex C-FMNH | 7805 | SkyWest |
| ☐ N953SW | Canadair CRJ-200ER | 7813 | ex C-GZGP | 7813 | SkyWest |
| ☐ N954SW | Canadair CRJ-200ER | 7815 | ex C-FMOI | 7815 | SkyWest |
| ☐ N955SW | Canadair CRJ-200ER | 7817 | ex C-FMML | 7817 | SkyWest |
| ☐ N956SW | Canadair CRJ-200ER | 7825 | ex C-FMKW | 7825 | SkyWest |
| ☐ N957SW | Canadair CRJ-200ER | 7829 | ex C-FMLI | 7829 | SkyWest |
| ☐ N958SW | Canadair CRJ-200ER | 7833 | ex C-FMLV | 7833 | SkyWest |
| ☐ N959SW | Canadair CRJ-200ER | 7840 | ex C-FMOW | 7840 | SkyWest |
| ☐ N960SW | Canadair CRJ-200ER | 7853 | ex C-FMNB | 7853 | SkyWest |
| ☐ N961SW | Canadair CRJ-200ER | 7857 | ex C-FMLB | 7857 | SkyWest |
| ☐ N962SW | Canadair CRJ-200ER | 7859 | ex C-FMLI | 7859 | SkyWest |
| ☐ N963SW | Canadair CRJ-200ER | 7865 | ex C-FMNH | 7865 | SkyWest |
| ☐ N964SW | Canadair CRJ-200ER | 7868 | ex C-GZTD | 7867 | SkyWest |
| ☐ N965SW | Canadair CRJ-200ER | 7871 | ex C-FVAZ | 7871 | SkyWest |
| ☐ N967SW | Canadair CRJ-200ER | 7872 | ex C-FMND | 7872 | SkyWest |
| ☐ N969SW | Canadair CRJ-200ER | 7876 | ex C-FMMB | 7876 | SkyWest |
| ☐ N970SW | Canadair CRJ-200ER | 7881 | ex C-GZUJ | 7881 | SkyWest |
| ☐ N971SW | Canadair CRJ-200ER | 7947 | ex C-FMLB | 7947 | SkyWest |
| ☐ N973SW | Canadair CRJ-200ER | 7949 | ex C-FMLI | 7949 | SkyWest |
| ☐ N975SW | Canadair CRJ-200ER | 7951 | ex C-FMLS | 7951 | SkyWest |
| ☐ N976SW | Canadair CRJ-200ER | 7952 | ex C-FMLT | 7952 | SkyWest |
| ☐ N978SW | Canadair CRJ-200ER | 7953 | ex C-FMLV | 7953 | SkyWest |
| ☐ N979SW | Canadair CRJ-200ER | 7954 | ex C-FMMT | 7954 | SkyWest |
| ☐ N980SW | Canadair CRJ-200ER | 7955 | ex C-FMNH | 7955 | SkyWest |
| ☐ N982SW | Canadair CRJ-200ER | 7956 | ex C-FMNW | 7956 | SkyWest |

| | | | | | | |
|---|---|---|---|---|---|---|
| ☐ | N983SW | Canadair CRJ-200ER | 7961 | ex C-FVAZ | 7961 | SkyWest |
| ☐ | N986SW | Canadair CRJ-200ER | 7967 | ex C-FMML | 7967 | SkyWest |
| | | | | | | |
| ☐ | N154SF | Canadair CRJ-440LR | 7154 | ex LV-WSB | 154 | Mesa |
| ☐ | N592ML | Canadair CRJ-440LR | 7410 | ex C-FMLQ | | Mesa |
| ☐ | N650ML | Canadair CRJ-440LR | 7137 | ex N261BD | | Mesa |
| ☐ | N715SF | Canadair CRJ-440LR | 7115 | ex LV-WPF | | Mesa |
| ☐ | N17175 | Canadair CRJ-440LR | 7175 | ex LV-WXB | | Mesa [TUS] |
| ☐ | N37208 | Canadair CRJ-440LR | 7208 | ex C-FMNY | | Mesa |
| ☐ | N37228 | Canadair CRJ-440LR | 7228 | ex B-7692 | | Mesa [TUS] |
| ☐ | N47202 | Canadair CRJ-440LR | 7202 | ex C-FMLT | | Mesa [TUS] |
| ☐ | N75994 | Canadair CRJ-440LR | 7367 | ex C-FZTY | | Mesa |
| ☐ | N75995 | Canadair CRJ-440LR | 7361 | ex C-FZTW | | Mesa |
| ☐ | N77195 | Canadair CRJ-440LR | 7195 | ex C-FMKW | | Mesa [TUS] |
| | | | | | | |
| ☐ | N151GJ | Canadair CRJ-702ER | 10216 | ex C- | | GoJet |
| ☐ | N152GJ | Canadair CRJ-702ER | 10218 | ex C- | | GoJet |
| ☐ | N153GJ | Canadair CRJ-702ER | 10219 | ex C- | | GoJet |
| ☐ | N154GJ | Canadair CRJ-702ER | 10224 | ex C- | | GoJet |
| ☐ | N155GJ | Canadair CRJ-702ER | 10225 | ex C- | | GoJet |
| ☐ | N156GJ | Canadair CRJ-702ER | 10227 | ex C- | | GoJet |
| ☐ | N157GJ | Canadair CRJ-702ER | 10230 | ex C- | | GoJet |
| ☐ | N158GJ | Canadair CRJ-702ER | 10237 | ex C- | | GoJet |
| ☐ | N159GJ | Canadair CRJ-702ER | 10238 | ex C- | | GoJet |
| ☐ | N160GJ | Canadair CRJ-702ER | 10239 | ex C- | | GoJet |
| ☐ | N161GJ | Canadair CRJ-702ER | 10253 | ex C- | | GoJet |
| ☐ | N162GJ | Canadair CRJ-702ER | 10254 | ex C- | | GoJet |
| ☐ | N163GJ | Canadair CRJ-702ER | 10255 | ex C- | | GoJet |
| ☐ | N164GJ | Canadair CRJ-702ER | 10256 | ex C- | | GoJet |
| ☐ | N165GJ | Canadair CRJ-702ER | 10257 | ex C- | | GoJet |
| ☐ | N166GJ | Canadair CRJ-702ER | 10266 | ex C- | | GoJet |
| ☐ | N167GJ | Canadair CRJ-702ER | 10269 | ex C- | | GoJet |
| ☐ | N168GJ | Canadair CRJ-702ER | 10272 | ex C-GHZZ | | GoJet |
| ☐ | N169GJ | Canadair CRJ-702ER | 10273 | ex C- | | GoJet |
| ☐ | N170GJ | Canadair CRJ-702ER | 10280 | ex C-GICN | | GoJet |
| ☐ | N171GJ | Canadair CRJ-702ER | 10282 | ex C-GIAR | | GoJet |
| ☐ | N172GJ | Canadair CRJ-702ER | 10283 | ex C- | | GoJet |
| ☐ | N173GJ | Canadair CRJ-702ER | 10287 | ex C- | | GoJet |
| ☐ | N174GJ | Canadair CRJ-702ER | 10296 | ex C- | | GoJet |
| ☐ | N175GJ | Canadair CRJ-702ER | 10297 | ex C- | | GoJet |
| ☐ | N354CA | Canadair CRJ-701ER | 10064 | ex C-GIBO | | GoJet |
| ☐ | N367CA | Canadair CRJ-701ER | 10069 | ex C-GICL | 10069 | GoJet♦ |
| ☐ | N379CA | Canadair CRJ-701ER | 10102 | ex C- | 10102 | GoJet♦ |
| ☐ | N659CA | Canadair CRJ-701ER | 10153 | ex C- | 10153 | GoJet♦ |
| | | | | | | |
| ☐ | N501MJ | Canadair CRJ-701ER | 10047 | ex C-FZVM | | Mesa |
| ☐ | N502MJ | Canadair CRJ-701ER | 10050 | ex C-GIAI | | Mesa |
| ☐ | N503MJ | Canadair CRJ-701ER | 10058 | ex C-GIBG | | Mesa |
| ☐ | N504MJ | Canadair CRJ-701ER | 10066 | ex C-GIBR | | Mesa |
| ☐ | N505MJ | Canadair CRJ-701ER | 10070 | ex C-GICN | | Mesa |
| ☐ | N506MJ | Canadair CRJ-701ER | 10073 | ex C-GHZY | | Mesa |
| ☐ | N507MJ | Canadair CRJ-701ER | 10077 | ex C-GIAH | | Mesa |
| ☐ | N508MJ | Canadair CRJ-701ER | 10087 | ex C-FZZE | | Mesa |
| ☐ | N509MJ | Canadair CRJ-701ER | 10094 | ex C- | | Mesa |
| ☐ | N510MJ | Canadair CRJ-701ER | 10101 | ex C- | | Mesa |
| ☐ | N511MJ | Canadair CRJ-701ER | 10104 | ex C- | | Mesa |
| ☐ | N512MJ | Canadair CRJ-701ER | 10109 | ex C- | | Mesa |
| ☐ | N513MJ | Canadair CRJ-701ER | 10111 | ex C- | | Mesa |
| ☐ | N514MJ | Canadair CRJ-701ER | 10116 | ex C- | | Mesa |
| ☐ | N515MJ | Canadair CRJ-701ER | 10117 | ex C- | | Mesa |
| ☐ | N516LR | Canadair CRJ-701ER | 10258 | ex C- | | Mesa |
| ☐ | N518LR | Canadair CRJ-701ER | 10259 | ex C- | | Mesa |
| ☐ | N519LR | Canadair CRJ-701ER | 10260 | ex C-FLGD | | Mesa |
| ☐ | N521LR | Canadair CRJ-701ER | 10261 | ex C-FMHJ | | Mesa |
| ☐ | N522LR | Canadair CRJ-701ER | 10262 | ex C- | | Mesa |
| | | | | | | |
| ☐ | N217AG | Canadair CRJ-701ER | 10031 | ex N609QX | | Skywest<QXE |
| ☐ | N219AG | Canadair CRJ-701ER | 10246 | ex N619QX | | Skywest<QXE |
| ☐ | N631SK | Canadair CRJ-702ER | 10329 | ex C-GIBR | | SkyWest |
| ☐ | N701SK | Canadair CRJ-701ER | 10133 | ex C- | 10133 | SkyWest |
| ☐ | N702SK | Canadair CRJ-701ER | 10136 | ex C- | 10136 | SkyWest |
| ☐ | N703SK | Canadair CRJ-701ER | 10139 | ex C- | 10139 | SkyWest |
| ☐ | N705SK | Canadair CRJ-701ER | 10145 | ex C- | 10145 | SkyWest |
| ☐ | N706SK | Canadair CRJ-701ER | 10149 | ex C- | 10149 | SkyWest |
| ☐ | N707SK | Canadair CRJ-701ER | 10003 | ex C-FBKA | 10003 | SkyWest |
| ☐ | N708SK | Canadair CRJ-701ER | 10156 | ex C- | 10156 | SkyWest |
| ☐ | N709SK | Canadair CRJ-701ER | 10159 | ex C- | 10159 | SkyWest |
| ☐ | N710SK | Canadair CRJ-701ER | 10170 | ex C- | 10170 | SkyWest |
| ☐ | N712SK | Canadair CRJ-701ER | 10172 | ex C-GIAR | 10172 | SkyWest |
| ☐ | N713SK | Canadair CRJ-701ER | 10174 | ex C- | 10174 | SkyWest |
| ☐ | N715SK | Canadair CRJ-701ER | 10179 | ex C- | 10179 | SkyWest |
| ☐ | N716SK | Canadair CRJ-701ER | 10180 | ex C- | 10180 | SkyWest |

| | | | | | |
|---|---|---|---|---|---|
| ☐ N718SK | Canadair CRJ-701ER | 10184 | ex C- | 10184 | SkyWest |
| ☐ N719SK | Canadair CRJ-701ER | 10188 | ex C- | 10188 | SkyWest |
| ☐ N724SK | Canadair CRJ-701ER | 10189 | ex C- | 10189 | SkyWest |
| ☐ N726SK | Canadair CRJ-701ER | 10190 | ex C- | 10190 | SkyWest |
| ☐ N727SK | Canadair CRJ-701ER | 10191 | ex C- | 10191 | SkyWest |
| ☐ N728SK | Canadair CRJ-701ER | 10192 | ex C- | 10192 | SkyWest |
| ☐ N730SK | Canadair CRJ-701ER | 10193 | ex C- | 10193 | SkyWest |
| ☐ N732SK | Canadair CRJ-701ER | 10194 | ex C- | 10194 | SkyWest |
| ☐ N738SK | Canadair CHR-701ER | 10195 | ex C- | 10195 | SkyWest |
| ☐ N740SK | Canadair CRJ-701ER | 10196 | ex C- | 10196 | SkyWest |
| ☐ N742SK | Canadair CRJ-701ER | 10197 | ex C- | 10197 | SkyWest |
| ☐ N743SK | Canadair CRJ-701ER | 10199 | ex C- | 10199 | SkyWest |
| ☐ N744SK | Canadair CRJ-701ER | 10200 | ex C- | 10200 | SkyWest |
| ☐ N745SK | Canadair CRJ-701ER | 10201 | ex C- | 10201 | SkyWest |
| ☐ N746SK | Canadair CRJ-701ER | 10202 | ex C-FEUP | 10202 | SkyWest |
| ☐ N748SK | Canadair CRJ-701ER | 10203 | ex C- | 10203 | SkyWest |
| ☐ N750SK | Canadair CRJ-701ER | 10207 | ex C- | 10207 | SkyWest |
| ☐ N751SK | Canadair CRJ-701ER | 10208 | ex C- | 10208 | SkyWest |
| ☐ N752SK | Canadair CRJ-701ER | 10209 | ex C- | 10209 | SkyWest |
| ☐ N753SK | Canadair CRJ-701ER | 10214 | ex C-FEVZ | 10214 | SkyWest |
| ☐ N754SK | Canadair CRJ-701ER | 10215 | ex C- | 10215 | SkyWest |
| ☐ N755SK | Canadair CRJ-701ER | 10220 | ex C-FFVZ | 10220 | SkyWest |
| ☐ N756SK | Canadair CRJ-701ER | 10221 | ex C- | 10221 | SkyWest |
| ☐ N758SK | Canadair CRJ-701ER | 10222 | ex C- | 10222 | SkyWest |
| ☐ N760SK | Canadair CRJ-701ER | 10223 | ex C- | 10223 | SkyWest |
| ☐ N762SK | Canadair CRJ-702ER | 10226 | ex C- | 10226 | SkyWest |
| ☐ N763SK | Canadair CRJ-702ER | 10228 | ex C- | 10228 | SkyWest |
| ☐ N764SK | Canadair CRJ-702ER | 10229 | ex C-FGRE | 10229 | SkyWest |
| ☐ N765SK | Canadair CRJ-702ER | 10231 | ex C- | 10231 | SkyWest |
| ☐ N766SK | Canadair CRJ-702ER | 10232 | ex C- | 10232 | SkyWest |
| ☐ N767SK | Canadair CRJ-702ER | 10233 | ex C- | 10233 | SkyWest |
| ☐ N768SK | Canadair CRJ-702ER | 10234 | ex C- | 10234 | SkyWest |
| ☐ N770SK | Canadair CRJ-702ER | 10243 | ex C- | 10243 | SkyWest |
| ☐ N771SK | Canadair CRJ-702ER | 10244 | ex C- | 10244 | SkyWest |
| ☐ N772SK | Canadair CRJ-702ER | 10235 | ex C- | 10235 | SkyWest |
| ☐ N773SK | Canadair CRJ-702ER | 10236 | ex C- | 10236 | SkyWest |
| ☐ N774SK | Canadair CRJ-702ER | 10240 | ex C- | 10240 | SkyWest |
| ☐ N776SK | Canadair CRJ-702ER | 10241 | ex C- | 10241 | SkyWest |
| ☐ N778SK | Canadair CRJ-702ER | 10242 | ex C- | 10242 | SkyWest |
| ☐ N779SK | Canadair CRJ-702ER | 10276 | ex C- | 10276 | SkyWest |
| ☐ N780SK | Canadair CRJ-702ER | 10277 | ex C- | 10277 | SkyWest |
| ☐ N782SK | Canadair CRJ-702ER | 10278 | ex C- | 10278 | SkyWest |
| ☐ N783SK | Canadair CRJ-702ER | 10281 | ex C-GICP | 10281 | SkyWest |
| ☐ N784SK | Canadair CRJ-702ER | 10284 | ex C- | 10284 | SkyWest |
| ☐ N785SK | Canadair CRJ-702ER | 10285 | ex C- | 10285 | SkyWest |
| ☐ N786SK | Canadair CRJ-702ER | 10286 | ex C- | 10286 | SkyWest |
| ☐ N787SK | Canadair CRJ-702ER | 10288 | ex C- | 10288 | SkyWest |
| ☐ N788SK | Canadair CRJ-702ER | 10290 | ex C- | 10290 | SkyWest |
| ☐ N789SK | Canadair CRJ-702ER | 10291 | ex C- | 10291 | SkyWest |
| ☐ N790SK | Canadair CRJ-702ER | 10292 | ex C- | 10292 | SkyWest |
| ☐ N791SK | Canadair CRJ-702ER | 10293 | ex C- | 10293 | SkyWest |
| ☐ N792SK | Canadair CRJ-702ER | 10294 | ex C- | 10294 | SkyWest |
| ☐ N793SK | Canadair CRJ-702ER | 10295 | ex C- | 10295 | SkyWest |
| ☐ N794SK | Canadair CRJ-702ER | 10298 | ex C- | 10298 | SkyWest |
| ☐ N795SK | Canadair CRJ-702ER | 10299 | ex C- | 10299 | SkyWest |
| ☐ N796SK | Canadair CRJ-702ER | 10300 | ex C- | 10300 | SkyWest |
| ☐ N797SK | Canadair CRJ-702ER | 10310 | ex C- | 10301 | SkyWest |
| ☐ N | Canadair CRJ-702ER | | ex C- | | SkyWest |
| ☐ N | Canadair CRJ-702ER | | ex C- | | SkyWest |
| ☐ N | Canadair CRJ-702ER | | ex C- | | SkyWest |
| ☐ N | Canadair CRJ-702ER | | ex C- | | SkyWest |
| ☐ N | Canadair CRJ-702ER | | ex C- | | SkyWest |
| ☐ N | Canadair CRJ-702ER | | ex C- | | SkyWest |
| ☐ N | Canadair CRJ-702ER | | ex C- | | SkyWest |
| ☐ N | Canadair CRJ-702ER | | ex C- | | SkyWest |
| | | | | | |
| ☐ N351PH | de Havilland DHC-8Q-202 | 490 | ex C-GFUM | 763 | Commutair<QXE |
| ☐ N358PH | de Havilland DHC-8Q-202 | 506 | ex C-FWBB | 775 | Commutair<QXE |
| ☐ N359PH | de Havilland DHC-8Q-202 | 514 | ex C-GEOA | 764 | Commutair<QXE |
| ☐ N360PH | de Havilland DHC-8Q-202 | 515 | ex C-GEWI | 762 | Commutair<QXE |
| ☐ N361PH | de Havilland DHC-8Q-202 | 516 | ex C-GFOD | 767 | Commutair<QXE |
| ☐ N362PH | de Havilland DHC-8Q-202 | 518 | ex C-FDHI | 766 | Commutair<QXE |
| ☐ N363PH | de Havilland DHC-8Q-202 | 520 | ex C-FDHP | 760 | Commutair<QXE |
| ☐ N364PH | de Havilland DHC-8Q-202 | 524 | ex C-FDHX | 765 | Commutair<QXE |
| ☐ N365PH | de Havilland DHC-8Q-202 | 526 | | 773 | Commutair<QXE |
| ☐ N366PH | de Havilland DHC-8Q-202 | 510 | ex C-GELN | 769 | Commutair<QXE |
| ☐ N367PH | de Havilland DHC-8Q-202 | 511 | ex C-GDLD | 774 | Commutair<QXE |
| ☐ N368PH | de Havilland DHC-8Q-202 | 512 | ex C-GDFT | 768 | Commutair<QXE |
| ☐ N369PH | de Havilland DHC-8Q-202 | 513 | ex C-FWBB | 770 | Commutair<QXE |
| ☐ N374PH | de Havilland DHC-8Q-202 | 528 | ex C-GDIU | 771 | Commutair<QXE |
| ☐ N375PH | de Havilland DHC-8Q-202 | 529 | ex C-GDKL | 761 | Commutair<QXE |
| ☐ N379PH | de Havilland DHC-8Q-202 | 530 | ex C-GDLK | 772 | Commutair<QXE |

| | | | | | | |
|---|---|---|---|---|---|---|
| ☐ N837CA | de Havilland DHC-8Q-314 | 554 | ex OE-LTN | 355 | | Commutair |
| ☐ N838CA | de Havilland DHC-8Q-314 | 527 | ex OE-LTM | 356 | | Commutair |
| ☐ N839CA | de Havilland DHC-8Q-311 | 553 | ex OE-LTO | 357 | | Commutair |
| ☐ N857CA | de Havilland DHC-8Q-314 | 531 | ex OE-LTN | 359 | | Commutair |
| ☐ N876CA | de Havilland DHC-8Q-314 | 438 | ex OE-LTG | 358 | | Commutair |
| | | | | | | |
| ☐ N33WQ | de Havilland DHC-8-402Q | 4033 | ex C-GLPE | | | Colgan Air |
| ☐ N34NG | de Havilland DHC-8-402Q | 4340 | ex C-GGSI | | | Colgan Air |
| ☐ N187WQ | de Havilland DHC-8-402Q | 4187 | ex C-FNQG | 777 | | Colgan Air |
| ☐ N188WQ | de Havilland DHC-8-402Q | 4188 | ex C-FNQH | 778 | | Colgan Air |
| ☐ N190WQ | de Havilland DHC-8-402Q | 4190 | ex C-FNQN | 779 | | Colgan Air |
| ☐ N191WQ | de Havilland DHC-8-402Q | 4191 | ex C-FNQQ | 780 | | Colgan Air |
| ☐ N195WQ | de Havilland DHC-8-402Q | 4195 | ex C-FOJM | 781 | | Colgan Air |
| ☐ N196WQ | de Havilland DHC-8-402Q | 4196 | ex C-FOJT | 782 | | Colgan Air |
| ☐ N199WQ | de Havilland DHC-8-402Q | 4199 | ex C-FOUO | 783 | | Colgan Air |
| ☐ N202WQ | de Havilland DHC-8-402Q | 4202 | ex C-FOUY | 785 | | Colgan Air |
| ☐ N203WQ | de Havilland DHC-8-402Q | 4203 | ex C-FPDY | 786 | | Colgan Air |
| ☐ N204WQ | de Havilland DHC-8-402Q | 4204 | ex C-FPEF | 787 | | Colgan Air |
| ☐ N208WQ | de Havilland DHC-8-402Q | 4208 | ex C-FPPW | 788 | | Colgan Air |
| ☐ N209WQ | de Havilland DHC-8-402Q | 4209 | ex C-FPQA | 789 | | Colgan Air |
| ☐ N213WQ | de Havilland DHC-8-402Q | 4213 | ex C-FQXO | 790 | | Colgan Air [IAH] |
| ☐ N214WQ | de Havilland DHC-8-402Q | 4214 | ex C-FQXP | 791 | | Colgan Air |
| ☐ N323NG | de Havilland DHC-8-402Q | 4323 | ex C-GEVP | | | Colgan Air |
| ☐ N328NG | de Havilland DHC-8-402Q | 4328 | ex C-GPNN | | | Colgan Air |
| ☐ N332NG | de Havilland DHC-8-402Q | 4332 | ex C-GFKK | | | Colgan Air |
| ☐ N333NG | de Havilland DHC-8-402Q | 4333 | ex C-GGFI | | | Colgan Air |
| ☐ N336NG | de Havilland DHC-8-402Q | 4336 | ex C-GGIF | | | Colgan Air |
| ☐ N338NG | de Havilland DHC-8-402Q | 4338 | ex C-GGQY | | | Colgan Air |
| ☐ N339NG | de Havilland DHC-8-402Q | 4339 | ex C-GGRI | | | Colgan Air |
| ☐ N341NG | de Havilland DHC-8-402Q | 4341 | ex C-GGSV | | | Colgan Air |
| ☐ N342NG | de Havilland DHC-8-402Q | 4342 | ex C-GGUB | | | Colgan Air |
| ☐ N345NG | de Havilland DHC-8-402Q | 4345 | ex C- | | | Colgan Air |
| ☐ N346NG | de Havilland DHC-8-402Q | 4346 | ex C-GHCO | | | Colgan Air |
| ☐ N351NG | de Havilland DHC-8-402Q | 4351 | ex C-GHVS | | | Colgan Air |
| ☐ N354NG | de Havilland DHC-8-402Q | 4354 | ex | | | Colgan Air |
| ☐ N356NG | de Havilland DHC-8-402Q | 4356 | ex C-GILK | | | Colgan Air |
| ☐ N380NG | de Havilland DHC-8-402Q | 4380 | ex C-GKNB | | | Colgan Air |
| | | | | | | |
| ☐ N221SW | Embraer EMB.120ER Brasilia | 120290 | ex PT-SVK | | | SkyWest |
| ☐ N223SW | Embraer EMB.120ER Brasilia | 120291 | ex PT-SVL | | | SkyWest |
| ☐ N229SW | Embraer EMB.120ER Brasilia | 120305 | ex PT-SVX | | | SkyWest |
| ☐ N233SW | Embraer EMB.120ER Brasilia | 120307 | ex PT-SVZ | | | SkyWest |
| ☐ N234SW | Embraer EMB.120ER Brasilia | 120308 | ex PT-SXA | | | SkyWest |
| ☐ N235SW | Embraer EMB.120ER Brasilia | 120310 | ex PT-SXC | | | SkyWest |
| ☐ N236SW | Embraer EMB.120ER Brasilia | 120312 | ex PT-SXE | | | SkyWest |
| ☐ N237SW | Embraer EMB.120ER Brasilia | 120314 | ex PT-SXG | | | SkyWest |
| ☐ N270YV | Embraer EMB.120ER Brasilia | 120270 | ex PT-SUR | | | SkyWest |
| ☐ N284YV | Embraer EMB.120ER Brasilia | 120284 | ex PT-SVE | | | SkyWest |
| ☐ N290SW | Embraer EMB.120ER Brasilia | 120317 | ex PT-SXJ | | | SkyWest |
| ☐ N292SW | Embraer EMB.120ER Brasilia | 120319 | ex PT-SXL | | | SkyWest |
| ☐ N294SW | Embraer EMB.120ER Brasilia | 120321 | ex PT-SXN | | | SkyWest |
| ☐ N295SW | Embraer EMB.120ER Brasilia | 120322 | ex PT-SXO | | | SkyWest |
| ☐ N297SW | Embraer EMB.120ER Brasilia | 120327 | ex PT-SXT | | | SkyWest |
| ☐ N308SW | Embraer EMB.120ER Brasilia | 120326 | ex PT-SXS | | | SkyWest |
| ☐ N560SW | Embraer EMB.120ER Brasilia | 120334 | ex PT-SXX | | | SkyWest |
| ☐ N561SW | Embraer EMB.120ER Brasilia | 120335 | ex PT-SXY | | | SkyWest |
| ☐ N562SW | Embraer EMB.120ER Brasilia | 120336 | ex PT-SXZ | | | SkyWest |
| ☐ N563SW | Embraer EMB.120ER Brasilia | 120338 | | | | SkyWest♦ |
| ☐ N564SW | Embraer EMB.120ER Brasilia | 120339 | ex PT-SAC | | | SkyWest |
| ☐ N565SW | Embraer EMB.120ER Brasilia | 120340 | ex PT-SAI | | | SkyWest |
| ☐ N566SW | Embraer EMB.120ER Brasilia | 120341 | ex PT-SAF | | | SkyWest |
| ☐ N567SW | Embraer EMB.120ER Brasilia | 120342 | ex PT-SAL | | | SkyWest |
| ☐ N568SW | Embraer EMB.120ER Brasilia | 120343 | ex PT-SAZ | | | SkyWest |
| ☐ N569SW | Embraer EMB.120ER Brasilia | 120344 | ex PT-SBY | | | SkyWest |
| ☐ N578SW | Embraer EMB.120ER Brasilia | 120346 | ex PT-SCA | | | SkyWest |
| ☐ N579SW | Embraer EMB.120ER Brasilia | 120347 | ex PT-SCB | | | SkyWest |
| ☐ N580SW | Embraer EMB.120ER Brasilia | 120348 | ex PT-SCC | | | SkyWest |
| ☐ N581SW | Embraer EMB.120ER Brasilia | 120349 | ex PT-SCZ | | | SkyWest |
| ☐ N582SW | Embraer EMB.120ER Brasilia | 120350 | ex PT-SDC | | | SkyWest |
| ☐ N583SW | Embraer EMB.120ER Brasilia | 120351 | ex PT-SEF | | | SkyWest |
| ☐ N584SW | Embraer EMB.120ER Brasilia | 120352 | ex PT-SEG | | | SkyWest |
| ☐ N585SW | Embraer EMB.120ER Brasilia | 120353 | ex PT-SEH | | | SkyWest |
| ☐ N586SW | Embraer EMB.120ER Brasilia | 120354 | ex PT-SEJ | | | SkyWest |
| | | | | | | |
| ☐ N16501 | Embraer ERJ-135ER | 145145 | ex PT-SDV | 501 | | [IGM] |
| ☐ N16502 | Embraer ERJ-135ER | 145166 | ex PT-SFF | 502 | | [IGM] |
| ☐ N19503 | Embraer ERJ-135ER | 145176 | ex PT-SFI | 503 | | [IGM] |
| ☐ N25504 | Embraer ERJ-135ER | 145186 | ex PT-SFK | 504 | | [CLE] |
| ☐ N14505 | Embraer ERJ-135ER | 145192 | ex PT-SFN | 505 | | [IGM] |
| ☐ N27506 | Embraer ERJ-135ER | 145206 | ex PT-SFT | 506 | | [IGM] |
| ☐ N17507 | Embraer ERJ-135ER | 145215 | ex PT-SFW | 507 | | [IGM] |
| ☐ N14508 | Embraer ERJ-135ER | 145220 | ex PT-SFY | 508 | | [IGM] |

| | | | | | | |
|---|---|---|---|---|---|---|
| ☐ N15509 | Embraer ERJ-135ER | 145238 | ex PT-SID | 509 | | [IGM] |
| ☐ N16510 | Embraer ERJ-135ER | 145251 | ex PT-SJI | 510 | | [IGM] |
| ☐ N16511 | Embraer ERJ-135ER | 145267 | ex PT-SIZ | 511 | | [IGM] |
| ☐ N27512 | Embraer ERJ-135ER | 145274 | ex PT-SJQ | 512 | | [IGM] |
| ☐ N17513 | Embraer ERJ-135LR | 145292 | ex PT-SKJ | 513 | | [IGM] |
| ☐ N14514 | Embraer ERJ-135LR | 145303 | ex PT-SKU | 514 | | [IGM] |
| ☐ N29515 | Embraer ERJ-135LR | 145309 | ex PT-SMA | 515 | | [IGM] |
| ☐ N14516 | Embraer ERJ-135LR | 145323 | ex PT-SMP | 516 | | [IGM] |
| ☐ N24517 | Embraer ERJ-135LR | 145332 | ex PT-SMY | 517 | | [IGM] |
| ☐ N28518 | Embraer ERJ-135LR | 145334 | ex PT-SNA | 518 | | [IGM] |
| ☐ N12519 | Embraer ERJ-135LR | 145366 | ex PT-SOQ | 519 | | [IGM] |
| ☐ N16520 | Embraer ERJ-135LR | 145372 | ex PT-SOX | 520 | | [IGM] |
| ☐ N17521 | Embraer ERJ-135LR | 145378 | ex PT-SQC | 521 | | [IGM] |
| ☐ N14522 | Embraer ERJ-135LR | 145383 | ex PT-SQH | 522 | | [IGM] |
| ☐ N27523 | Embraer ERJ-135LR | 145389 | ex PT-SQN | 523 | | [IGM] |
| ☐ N17524 | Embraer ERJ-135LR | 145399 | ex PT-SQW | 524 | | [IGM] |
| ☐ N16525 | Embraer ERJ-135LR | 145403 | ex PT-STA | 525 | | [IGM] |
| | | | | | | |
| ☐ N11526 | Embraer ERJ-135LR | 145410 | ex PT-STH | 526 | | Chautauqua wfs |
| ☐ N28529 | Embraer ERJ-135LR | 145512 | ex PT-SYE | 529 | | Chautauqua |
| ☐ N12530 | Embraer ERJ-135LR | 145533 | ex PT-STX | 530 | | Chautauqua |
| | | | | | | |
| ☐ N15527 | Embraer ERJ-135LR | 145413 | ex PT-STJ | | | ExpressJet♦ |
| ☐ N12528 | Embraer ERJ-135LR | 145504 | ex PT-SXX | 528 | | ExpressJet♦ |
| | | | | | | |
| ☐ N265SK | Embraer ERJ-145LR | 145226 | ex PT-SHL | | | Chautauqua |
| ☐ N266SK | Embraer ERJ-145LR | 145241 | ex PT-SIG | 436 | | Chautauqua |
| ☐ N267SK | Embraer ERJ-145LR | 145268 | ex PT-SJK | 437 | | Chautauqua |
| ☐ N268SK | Embraer ERJ-145LR | 145270 | ex PT-SJM | | | Chautauqua |
| ☐ N269SK | Embraer ERJ-145LR | 145293 | ex PT-SYG | | | Chautauqua |
| ☐ N270SK | Embraer ERJ-145LR | 145304 | ex PT-SKV | | | Chautauqua |
| ☐ N271SK | Embraer ERJ-145LR | 145305 | ex PT-SKW | | | Chautauqua |
| ☐ N275SK | Embraer ERJ-145LR | 145345 | ex PT-SNL | 439 | | Chautauqua |
| ☐ N276SK | Embraer ERJ-145LR | 145348 | ex PT-SNO | | | Chautauqua |
| ☐ N277SK | Embraer ERJ-145LR | 145355 | ex PT-SNU | 440 | | Chautauqua |
| ☐ N278SK | Embraer ERJ-145LR | 145370 | ex PT- | | | Chautauqua |
| ☐ N279SK | Embraer ERJ-145LR | 145379 | ex PT-SQD | | | Chautauqua |
| ☐ N281SK | Embraer ERJ-145LR | 145391 | ex PT- | | | Chautauqua |
| ☐ N283SK | Embraer ERJ-145LR | 145424 | ex PT-STV | 442 | | Chautauqua |
| ☐ N284SK | Embraer ERJ-145LR | 145427 | ex PT-STY | | | Chautauqua |
| ☐ N285SK | Embraer ERJ-145LR | 145435 | ex PT-SUG | 444 | | Chautauqua |
| ☐ N286SK | Embraer ERJ-145LR | 145443 | ex PT-SUO | | | Chautauqua |
| ☐ N287SK | Embraer ERJ-145LR | 145460 | ex PT-SVF | | | Chautauqua |
| ☐ N288SK | Embraer ERJ-145LR | 145461 | ex PT-SVG | | | Chautauqua |
| ☐ N289SK | Embraer ERJ-145LR | 145463 | ex PT-SVI | | | Chautauqua |
| ☐ N290SK | Embraer ERJ-145LR | 145474 | ex PT-SVT | | | Chautauqua |
| ☐ N292SK | Embraer ERJ-145LR | 145488 | ex PT-SXH | | | Chautauqua |
| ☐ N294SK | Embraer ERJ-145LR | 145497 | ex PT-SXQ | | | Chautauqua |
| ☐ N296SK | Embraer ERJ-145LR | 145514 | ex PT-SYG | | | Chautauqua |
| | | | | | | |
| ☐ N11535 | Embraer ERJ-145LR | 145518 | ex PT-SYJ | 535 | | ExpressJet |
| ☐ N11536 | Embraer ERJ-145LR | 145520 | ex PT-SYL | 536 | | ExpressJet |
| ☐ N21537 | Embraer ERJ-145LR | 145523 | ex PT-SYO | 537 | | ExpressJet |
| ☐ N13538 | Embraer ERJ-145LR | 145527 | ex PT-STS | 538 | | ExpressJet |
| ☐ N11539 | Embraer ERJ-145LR | 145536 | ex PT-SZA | 539 | | ExpressJet |
| ☐ N12540 | Embraer ERJ-145LR | 145537 | ex PT-SZB | 540 | | ExpressJet |
| ☐ N16541 | Embraer ERJ-145LR | 145542 | ex PT-SZF | 541 | | ExpressJet |
| ☐ N14542 | Embraer ERJ-145LR | 145547 | ex PT-SZK | 542 | | ExpressJet |
| ☐ N14543 | Embraer ERJ-145LR | 145553 | ex PT-SZP | 543 | | ExpressJet |
| ☐ N26545 | Embraer ERJ-145LR | 145558 | ex PT-SZT | 545 | | ExpressJet |
| ☐ N16546 | Embraer ERJ-145LR | 145562 | ex PT-SZX | 546 | | ExpressJet |
| ☐ N11547 | Embraer ERJ-145LR | 145563 | ex PT-SZY | 547 | | ExpressJet |
| ☐ N11548 | Embraer ERJ-145LR | 145565 | ex PT-SBB | 548 | | ExpressJet |
| ☐ N26549 | Embraer ERJ-145LR | 145571 | ex PT-SBH | 549 | | ExpressJet |
| ☐ N13550 | Embraer ERJ-145LR | 145575 | ex PT-SBL | 550 | | ExpressJet |
| ☐ N12552 | Embraer ERJ-145LR | 145583 | ex PT-SBU | 552 | | ExpressJet |
| ☐ N13553 | Embraer ERJ-145LR | 145585 | ex PT-SBW | 553 | | ExpressJet |
| ☐ N15555 | Embraer ERJ-145LR | 145594 | ex PT- (SCD) | 555 | | ExpressJet |
| ☐ N18556 | Embraer ERJ-145LR | 145595 | ex PT-SCE | 556 | | ExpressJet |
| ☐ N14558 | Embraer ERJ-145LR | 145598 | ex PT-SCG | 558 | | ExpressJet |
| ☐ N16559 | Embraer ERJ-145LR | 145603 | ex PT-SCM | 559 | | ExpressJet |
| ☐ N17560 | Embraer ERJ-145LR | 145605 | ex PT-SCO | 560 | | ExpressJet |
| ☐ N16561 | Embraer ERJ-145LR | 145610 | ex PT-SCT | 561 | | ExpressJet |
| ☐ N14562 | Embraer ERJ-145LR | 145611 | ex PT-SCV | 562 | | ExpressJet |
| ☐ N12563 | Embraer ERJ-145LR | 145612 | ex PT-SCW | 563 | | ExpressJet |
| ☐ N12564 | Embraer ERJ-145LR | 145618 | ex PT-SDG | 564 | | ExpressJet |
| ☐ N11565 | Embraer ERJ-145LR | 145621 | ex PT-SDJ | 565 | | ExpressJet |
| ☐ N13566 | Embraer ERJ-145LR | 145622 | ex PT-SDK | 566 | | ExpressJet |
| ☐ N12567 | Embraer ERJ-145LR | 145623 | ex PT-SDL | 567 | | ExpressJet |
| ☐ N14568 | Embraer ERJ-145LR | 145628 | ex PT-SDQ | 568 | | ExpressJet |
| ☐ N16571 | Embraer ERJ-145LR | 145633 | ex PT-SDV | 571 | | ExpressJet |
| ☐ N15572 | Embraer ERJ-145LR | 145636 | ex PT-SDY | 572 | | ExpressJet |

| | | | | | |
|---|---|---|---|---|---|
| ☐ N14573 | Embraer ERJ-145LR | 145638 | ex PT-SDZ | 573 | ExpressJet |
| ☐ N15574 | Embraer ERJ-145LR | 145639 | ex PT-SEB | 574 | ExpressJet |
| ☐ N12900 | Embraer ERJ-145LR | 145511 | ex PT-SYD | 900 | ExpressJet |
| ☐ N48901 | Embraer ERJ-145LR | 145501 | ex PT-SXU | 901 | ExpressJet |
| ☐ N14902 | Embraer ERJ-145LR | 145496 | ex PT-SXO | 902 | ExpressJet |
| ☐ N13903 | Embraer ERJ-145LR | 145479 | ex PT-SVY | 903 | ExpressJet |
| ☐ N14904 | Embraer ERJ-145LR | 145477 | ex PT-SVW | 904 | ExpressJet |
| ☐ N14905 | Embraer ERJ-145LR | 145476 | ex PT-SVV | 905 | ExpressJet |
| ☐ N29906 | Embraer ERJ-145LR | 145472 | ex PT-SVR | 906 | ExpressJet |
| ☐ N13908 | Embraer ERJ-145LR | 145465 | ex PT-SVK | 908 | ExpressJet |
| ☐ N15910 | Embraer ERJ-145LR | 145455 | ex PT-SVA | 910 | ExpressJet |
| ☐ N16911 | Embraer ERJ-145LR | 145446 | ex PT-SUR | 911 | ExpressJet |
| ☐ N15912 | Embraer ERJ-145LR | 145439 | ex PT-SUK | 912 | ExpressJet |
| ☐ N13913 | Embraer ERJ-145LR | 145438 | ex PT-SUJ | 913 | ExpressJet |
| ☐ N13914 | Embraer ERJ-145LR | 145430 | ex PT-SUB | 914 | ExpressJet |
| ☐ N36915 | Embraer ERJ-145LR | 145421 | ex PT-STS | 915 | ExpressJet |
| ☐ N14916 | Embraer ERJ-145LR | 145415 | ex PT-STL | 916 | ExpressJet |
| ☐ N29917 | Embraer ERJ-145LR | 145414 | ex PT-STK | 917 | ExpressJet |
| ☐ N16918 | Embraer ERJ-145LR | 145397 | ex PT-SQU | 918 | ExpressJet |
| ☐ N16919 | Embraer ERJ-145LR | 145393 | ex PT-SQQ | 919 | ExpressJet |
| ☐ N14920 | Embraer ERJ-145LR | 145380 | ex PT-SQE | 920 | ExpressJet |
| ☐ N12921 | Embraer ERJ-145LR | 145354 | ex PT-SNT | 921 | ExpressJet |
| ☐ N12922 | Embraer ERJ-145LR | 145338 | ex PT-SNE | 922 | ExpressJet |
| ☐ N14923 | Embraer ERJ-145LR | 145318 | ex PT-SMJ | 923 | ExpressJet |
| ☐ N12924 | Embraer ERJ-145LR | 145311 | ex PT-SMC | 924 | ExpressJet |
| ☐ N14925 | Embraer ERJ-145EP | 145004 | ex PT-SYA | 925 | ExpressJet |
| ☐ N15926 | Embraer ERJ-145EP | 145005 | ex PT-SYB | 926 | ExpressJet |
| ☐ N16927 | Embraer ERJ-145EP | 145006 | ex PT-SYC | 927 | ExpressJet |
| ☐ N17928 | Embraer ERJ-145EP | 145007 | ex PT-SYD | 928 | ExpressJet |
| ☐ N13929 | Embraer ERJ-145EP | 145009 | ex PT-SYF | 929 | ExpressJet |
| ☐ N14930 | Embraer ERJ-145EP | 145011 | ex PT-SYH | 930 | ExpressJet |
| ☐ N15932 | Embraer ERJ-145EP | 145015 | ex PT-SYL | 932 | ExpressJet |
| ☐ N14933 | Embraer ERJ-145EP | 145018 | ex PT-SYO | 933 | ExpressJet |
| ☐ N12934 | Embraer ERJ-145EP | 145019 | ex PT-SYP | 934 | ExpressJet |
| ☐ N13935 | Embraer ERJ-145EP | 145022 | ex PT-SYS | 935 | ExpressJet |
| ☐ N13936 | Embraer ERJ-145EP | 145025 | ex PT-SYV | 936 | ExpressJet |
| ☐ N14937 | Embraer ERJ-145EP | 145026 | ex PT-SYW | 937 | ExpressJet |
| ☐ N14938 | Embraer ERJ-145EP | 145029 | ex PT-SYX | 938 | ExpressJet |
| ☐ N14939 | Embraer ERJ-145EP | 145030 | ex PT-SYY | 939 | ExpressJet |
| ☐ N14940 | Embraer ERJ-145EP | 145033 | ex PT-SZA | 940 | ExpressJet |
| ☐ N15941 | Embraer ERJ-145EP | 145035 | ex PT-SZB | 941 | ExpressJet |
| ☐ N14942 | Embraer ERJ-145EP | 145037 | ex PT-SZD | 942 | ExpressJet |
| ☐ N14943 | Embraer ERJ-145EP | 145040 | ex PT-SZF | 943 | ExpressJet |
| ☐ N16944 | Embraer ERJ-145EP | 145045 | ex PT-SZK | 944 | ExpressJet |
| ☐ N14945 | Embraer ERJ-145EP | 145049 | ex PT-SZO | 945 | ExpressJet |
| ☐ N12946 | Embraer ERJ-145EP | 145052 | ex PT-SZR | 946 | ExpressJet |
| ☐ N14947 | Embraer ERJ-145EP | 145054 | ex PT-SZT | 947 | ExpressJet |
| ☐ N15948 | Embraer ERJ-145EP | 145056 | ex PT-SZV | 948 | ExpressJet |
| ☐ N13949 | Embraer ERJ-145LR | 145057 | ex PT-SZW | 949 | ExpressJet |
| ☐ N14950 | Embraer ERJ-145LR | 145061 | ex PT-SAE | 950 | ExpressJet |
| ☐ N16951 | Embraer ERJ-145LR | 145063 | ex PT-SAG | 951 | ExpressJet |
| ☐ N14952 | Embraer ERJ-145LR | 145067 | ex PT-SAL | 952 | ExpressJet |
| ☐ N14953 | Embraer ERJ-145LR | 145071 | ex PT-SAP | 953 | ExpressJet |
| ☐ N16954 | Embraer ERJ-145LR | 145072 | ex PT-SAQ | 954 | ExpressJet |
| ☐ N13955 | Embraer ERJ-145LR | 145075 | ex PT-SAT | 955 | ExpressJet |
| ☐ N13956 | Embraer ERJ-145LR | 145078 | ex PT-S | 956 | ExpressJet |
| ☐ N12957 | Embraer ERJ-145LR | 145080 | ex PT-S | 957 | ExpressJet |
| ☐ N13958 | Embraer ERJ-145LR | 145085 | ex PT-S | 958 | ExpressJet |
| ☐ N14959 | Embraer ERJ-145LR | 145091 | ex PT-S | 959 | ExpressJet |
| ☐ N14960 | Embraer ERJ-145LR | 145100 | ex PT-SBW | 960 100th c/s | ExpressJet |
| ☐ N16961 | Embraer ERJ-145LR | 145103 | ex PT-S | 961 | ExpressJet |
| ☐ N27962 | Embraer ERJ-145LR | 145110 | ex PT-S | 962 | ExpressJet |
| ☐ N16963 | Embraer ERJ-145LR | 145116 | ex PT-SCS | 963 | ExpressJet |
| ☐ N13964 | Embraer ERJ-145LR | 145123 | ex PT-SCZ | 964 | ExpressJet |
| ☐ N13965 | Embraer ERJ-145LR | 145125 | ex PT-SDC | 965 | ExpressJet |
| ☐ N19966 | Embraer ERJ-145LR | 145131 | ex PT-SDI | 966 | ExpressJet |
| ☐ N12967 | Embraer ERJ-145LR | 145133 | ex PT-SDK | 967 | ExpressJet |
| ☐ N13968 | Embraer ERJ-145LR | 145138 | ex PT-SDP | 968 | ExpressJet |
| ☐ N13969 | Embraer ERJ-145LR | 145141 | ex PT-SDR | 969 | ExpressJet |
| ☐ N13970 | Embraer ERJ-145LR | 145146 | ex PT-SDW | 970 | ExpressJet |
| ☐ N22971 | Embraer ERJ-145LR | 145149 | ex PT-SDZ | 971 | ExpressJet |
| ☐ N14972 | Embraer ERJ-145LR | 145151 | ex PT-SEC | 972 | ExpressJet |
| ☐ N15973 | Embraer ERJ-145LR | 145159 | ex PT-S | 973 | ExpressJet |
| ☐ N14974 | Embraer ERJ-145LR | 145161 | ex PT-S | 974 | ExpressJet |
| ☐ N13975 | Embraer ERJ-145LR | 145163 | ex PT-S | 975 | ExpressJet |
| ☐ N16976 | Embraer ERJ-145LR | 145171 | ex PT-SEV | 976 | ExpressJet |
| ☐ N14977 | Embraer ERJ-145LR | 145175 | ex PT-SEX | 977 | ExpressJet |
| ☐ N13978 | Embraer ERJ-145LR | 145180 | ex PT-SGC | 978 | ExpressJet |
| ☐ N13979 | Embraer ERJ-145LR | 145181 | ex PT-SGD | 979 | ExpressJet |
| ☐ N15980 | Embraer ERJ-145LR | 145202 | ex PT-SGT | 980 | ExpressJet |
| ☐ N16981 | Embraer ERJ-145LR | 145208 | ex PT-SGY | 981 | ExpressJet |
| ☐ N15983 | Embraer ERJ-145LR | 145239 | ex PT-SIE | 983 | ExpressJet |

| | | | | | |
|---|---|---|---|---|---|
| ☐ N17984 | Embraer ERJ-145LR | 145246 | ex PT-SIK | 984 | ExpressJet |
| ☐ N15985 | Embraer ERJ-145LR | 145248 | ex PT-SIL | 985 | ExpressJet |
| ☐ N15986 | Embraer ERJ-145LR | 145254 | ex PT-SIO | 986 | ExpressJet |
| ☐ N16987 | Embraer ERJ-145LR | 145261 | ex PT-SIU | 987 | ExpressJet |
| ☐ N13988 | Embraer ERJ-145LR | 145265 | ex PT-SIX | 988 | ExpressJet |
| ☐ N13989 | Embraer ERJ-145LR | 145271 | ex PT-SJN | 989 | ExpressJet |
| ☐ N14991 | Embraer ERJ-145LR | 145278 | ex PT-SJU | 991 | ExpressJet |
| ☐ N13992 | Embraer ERJ-145LR | 145284 | ex PT-SKB | 992 | ExpressJet |
| ☐ N14993 | Embraer ERJ-145LR | 145289 | ex PT-SKG | 993 | ExpressJet |
| ☐ N13994 | Embraer ERJ-145LR | 145291 | ex PT-SKI | 994 | ExpressJet |
| ☐ N13995 | Embraer ERJ-145LR | 145295 | ex PT-SKM | 995 | ExpressJet |
| ☐ N12996 | Embraer ERJ-145LR | 145296 | ex PT-SKN | 996 | ExpressJet |
| ☐ N13997 | Embraer ERJ-145LR | 145298 | ex PT-SKP | 997 | ExpressJet |
| ☐ N14998 | Embraer ERJ-145LR | 145302 | ex PT-SKT | 998 | ExpressJet |
| ☐ N16999 | Embraer ERJ-145LR | 145307 | ex PT-SKY | 999 | ExpressJet |
| ☐ N18101 | Embraer ERJ-145XR | 145590 | ex PT-SDC | 101 | ExpressJet |
| ☐ N18102 | Embraer ERJ-145XR | 145643 | ex PT-SEE | 102 | ExpressJet |
| ☐ N24103 | Embraer ERJ-145XR | 145645 | ex PT-SEF | 103 | ExpressJet |
| ☐ N41104 | Embraer ERJ-145XR | 145646 | ex PT-SEG | 104 | ExpressJet |
| ☐ N14105 | Embraer ERJ-145XR | 145649 | ex PT-SEJ | 105 | ExpressJet |
| ☐ N11106 | Embraer ERJ-145XR | 145650 | ex PT-SEK | 106 | ExpressJet |
| ☐ N11107 | Embraer ERJ-145XR | 145654 | ex PT-SEO | 107 | ExpressJet |
| ☐ N17108 | Embraer ERJ-145XR | 145655 | ex PT-SEP | 108 | ExpressJet |
| ☐ N11109 | Embraer ERJ-145XR | 145657 | ex PT-SER | 109 | ExpressJet |
| ☐ N34110 | Embraer ERJ-145XR | 145658 | ex PT-SES | 110 | ExpressJet |
| ☐ N34111 | Embraer ERJ-145XR | 145659 | ex PT-SET | 111 | ExpressJet |
| ☐ N16112 | Embraer ERJ-145XR | 145660 | ex PT-SEU | 112 | ExpressJet |
| ☐ N11113 | Embraer ERJ-145XR | 145662 | ex PT-SEW | 113 | ExpressJet |
| ☐ N18114 | Embraer ERJ-145XR | 145664 | ex PT-SEY | 114 | ExpressJet |
| ☐ N17115 | Embraer ERJ-145XR | 145666 | ex PT-SFA | 115 | ExpressJet |
| ☐ N14116 | Embraer ERJ-145XR | 145672 | ex PT-SFF | 116 | ExpressJet |
| ☐ N14117 | Embraer ERJ-145XR | 145674 | ex PT-SFH | 117 | ExpressJet |
| ☐ N13118 | Embraer ERJ-145XR | 145675 | ex PT-SFI | 118 | ExpressJet |
| ☐ N11119 | Embraer ERJ-145XR | 145677 | ex PT-SFK | 119 | ExpressJet |
| ☐ N18120 | Embraer ERJ-145XR | 145681 | ex PT-SFN | 120 | ExpressJet |
| ☐ N11121 | Embraer ERJ-145XR | 145683 | ex PT-SFP | 121 | ExpressJet |
| ☐ N12122 | Embraer ERJ-145XR | 145684 | ex PT-SFQ | 122 | ExpressJet |
| ☐ N13123 | Embraer ERJ-145XR | 145688 | ex PT-SFU | 123 | ExpressJet |
| ☐ N13124 | Embraer ERJ-145XR | 145689 | ex PT-SFV | 124 | ExpressJet |
| ☐ N14125 | Embraer ERJ-145XR | 145690 | ex PT-SFW | 125 | ExpressJet |
| ☐ N12126 | Embraer ERJ-145XR | 145693 | ex PT-SFZ | 126 | ExpressJet |
| ☐ N11127 | Embraer ERJ-145XR | 145697 | ex PT-SGC | 127 | ExpressJet |
| ☐ N24128 | Embraer ERJ-145XR | 145700 | ex PT-SGE | 128 | ExpressJet |
| ☐ N21129 | Embraer ERJ-145XR | 145703 | ex PT-SGH | 129 | ExpressJet |
| ☐ N21130 | Embraer ERJ-145XR | 145704 | ex PT-SGI | 130 | ExpressJet |
| ☐ N31131 | Embraer ERJ-145XR | 145705 | ex PT-SGJ | 131 | ExpressJet |
| ☐ N13132 | Embraer ERJ-145XR | 145708 | ex PT-SGL | 132 | ExpressJet |
| ☐ N13133 | Embraer ERJ-145XR | 145712 | ex PT-SGP | 133 | ExpressJet |
| ☐ N25134 | Embraer ERJ-145XR | 145714 | ex PT-SGR | 134 | ExpressJet |
| ☐ N12135 | Embraer ERJ-145XR | 145718 | ex PT-SGU | 135 | ExpressJet |
| ☐ N12136 | Embraer ERJ-145XR | 145719 | ex PT-SGV | 136 | ExpressJet |
| ☐ N17138 | Embraer ERJ-145XR | 145727 | ex PT-SHD | 138 | ExpressJet |
| ☐ N23139 | Embraer ERJ-145XR | 145731 | ex PT-SHH | 139 | ExpressJet |
| ☐ N11140 | Embraer ERJ-145XR | 145732 | ex PT-SHI | 140 | ExpressJet |
| ☐ N26141 | Embraer ERJ-145XR | 145733 | ex PT-SHJ | 141 | ExpressJet |
| ☐ N12142 | Embraer ERJ-145XR | 145735 | ex PT-SHL | 142 | ExpressJet |
| ☐ N14143 | Embraer ERJ-145XR | 145739 | ex PT-SHT | 143 | ExpressJet |
| ☐ N21144 | Embraer ERJ-145XR | 145741 | ex PT-SJA | 144 | ExpressJet |
| ☐ N12145 | Embraer ERJ-145XR | 145745 | ex PT-SJE | 145 | ExpressJet |
| ☐ N17146 | Embraer ERJ-145XR | 145746 | ex PT-SJF | 146 | ExpressJet |
| ☐ N16147 | Embraer ERJ-145XR | 145749 | ex PT-SJI | 147 | ExpressJet |
| ☐ N14148 | Embraer ERJ-145XR | 145751 | ex PT-SJK | 148 | ExpressJet |
| ☐ N16149 | Embraer ERJ-145XR | 145753 | ex PT-SJM | 149 | ExpressJet |
| ☐ N11150 | Embraer ERJ-145XR | 145756 | ex PT-SJP | 150 | ExpressJet |
| ☐ N16151 | Embraer ERJ-145XR | 145758 | ex PT-SJQ | 151 | ExpressJet |
| ☐ N27152 | Embraer ERJ-145XR | 145759 | ex PT-SJR | 152 | ExpressJet |
| ☐ N14153 | Embraer ERJ-145XR | 145761 | ex PT-SJS | 153 | ExpressJet |
| ☐ N21154 | Embraer ERJ-145XR | 145772 | ex PT-SMC | 154 | ExpressJet |
| ☐ N11155 | Embraer ERJ-145XR | 145782 | ex PT-SMJ | 155 | ExpressJet |
| ☐ N10156 | Embraer ERJ-145XR | 145786 | ex PT-SMN | 156 | ExpressJet |
| ☐ N12157 | Embraer ERJ-145XR | 145787 | ex PT-SMP | 157 | ExpressJet |
| ☐ N14158 | Embraer ERJ-145XR | 145791 | ex PT-SMS | 158 | ExpressJet |
| ☐ N17159 | Embraer ERJ-145XR | 145792 | ex PT-SMT | 159 | ExpressJet |
| ☐ N12160 | Embraer ERJ-145XR | 145799 | ex PT-SMZ | 160 | ExpressJet |
| ☐ N13161 | Embraer ERJ-145XR | 14500805 | ex PT-SNH | 161 | ExpressJet |
| ☐ N11164 | Embraer ERJ-145XR | 14500817 | ex PT-SNS | 164 | ExpressJet |
| ☐ N12166 | Embraer ERJ-145XR | 14500831 | ex PT-SQE | 166 | ExpressJet |
| ☐ N17169 | Embraer ERJ-145XR | 14500844 | ex PT-SQO | 169 | ExpressJet |
| ☐ N12172 | Embraer ERJ-145XR | 14500864 | ex PT-SXD | 172 | ExpressJet |
| ☐ N14177 | Embraer ERJ-145XR | 14500888 | ex PT-SYA | 177 | ExpressJet |
| ☐ N14180 | Embraer ERJ-145XR | 14500900 | ex PT-SYL | 180 | ExpressJet |

| | | | | | |
|---|---|---|---|---|---|
| ☐ N17185 | Embraer ERJ-145XR | 14500922 | ex PT-SOT | 185 | ExpressJet |
| ☐ N14186 | Embraer ERJ-145XR | 14500924 | ex PT-SOV | 186 | ExpressJet |
| ☐ N11187 | Embraer ERJ-145XR | 14500927 | ex PT-SOX | 187 | ExpressJet |
| ☐ N27190 | Embraer ERJ-145XR | 14500934 | ex PT-SCC | 190 | ExpressJet |
| ☐ N11191 | Embraer ERJ-145XR | 14500935 | ex PT-SCH | 191 | ExpressJet |
| ☐ N11194 | Embraer ERJ-145XR | 14500940 | ex PT-SCL | | ExpressJet |
| ☐ N12195 | Embraer ERJ-145XR | 14500943 | ex PT-SCO | 195 | ExpressJet |
| ☐ N17196 | Embraer ERJ-145XR | 14500945 | ex PT-SCQ | 196 | ExpressJet |
| ☐ N21197 | Embraer ERJ-145XR | 14500947 | ex PT-SCS | 197 | ExpressJet |
| ☐ N27200 | Embraer ERJ-145XR | 14500956 | ex PT-SFE | 200 | ExpressJet |
| ☐ N13202 | Embraer ERJ-145XR | 14500962 | ex PT-SFJ | 202 | ExpressJet |
| ☐ N14203 | Embraer ERJ-145XR | 14500964 | ex PT-SFL | 203 | ExpressJet |
| ☐ N14204 | Embraer ERJ-145XR | 14500968 | ex PT- | 204 | ExpressJet |
| | | | | | |
| ☐ N858MJ | Embraer ERJ-145LR | 145767 | ex PT-SJY | | Mesa |
| ☐ N859MJ | Embraer ERJ-145LR | 145769 | ex PT-SMA | | Mesa |
| | | | | | |
| ☐ N806HK | Embraer ERJ-145ER | 145112 | ex PT-SCO | | Trans State |
| ☐ N807HK | Embraer ERJ-145ER | 145119 | ex PT-SCV | | Trans State |
| ☐ N810HK | Embraer ERJ-145ER | 145231 | ex PT-SHV | | Trans State |
| ☐ N811HK | Embraer ERJ-145ER | 145256 | ex PT-SIQ | | Trans State |
| ☐ N832HK | Embraer ERJ-145LR | 145771 | ex PT- | | Trans State |
| ☐ N833HK | Embraer ERJ-145LR | 145240 | ex HB-JAB | | Trans State |
| ☐ N835HK | Embraer ERJ-145LR | 145670 | ex PT-SFE | | Trans Stare |
| ☐ N836HK | Embraer ERJ-145LR | 145695 | ex PT-SGA | | Trans State |
| ☐ N838HK | Embraer ERJ-145LR | 145321 | ex HB-JAG | | Trans State |
| ☐ N839HK | Embraer ERJ-145LR | 14500829 | ex PT-SQC | | Trans State |
| ☐ N841HK | Embraer ERJ-145LR | 145382 | ex HB-JAJ | | Trans State |
| ☐ N842HK | Embraer ERJ-145LR | 14500830 | ex PT-SQD | | Trans State |
| ☐ N843HK | Embraer ERJ-145LR | 14500822 | ex PT-SNW | | Trans State |
| ☐ N844HK | Embraer ERJ-145LR | 14500838 | ex PT-SQK | | Trans State |
| ☐ N845HK | Embraer ERJ-145LR | 14500842 | ex PT-SQM | | Trans State |
| ☐ N846HK | Embraer ERJ-145LR | 14500855 | ex PT-SQW | | Trans State |
| ☐ N847HK | Embraer ERJ-145LR | 14500857 | ex PT-SQY | | Trans State |
| ☐ N851HK | Embraer ERJ-145LR | 145340 | ex N834MJ | | Trans State |
| ☐ N852HK | Embraer ERJ-145LR | 145353 | ex N835MJ | | Trans State |
| | | | | | |
| ☐ N631RW | Embraer ERJ-170SE | 17000007 | ex PT-SKX | | Shuttle America |
| ☐ N632RW | Embraer ERJ-170SE | 17000050 | ex PT-SUU | | Shuttle America |
| ☐ N633RW | Embraer ERJ-170SE | 17000054 | ex PT-SUZ | | Shuttle America |
| ☐ N634RW | Embraer ERJ-170SE | 17000055 | ex PT-SVE | | Shuttle America |
| ☐ N635RW | Embraer ERJ-170SE | 17000056 | ex PT-SVF | | Shuttle America |
| ☐ N636RW | Embraer ERJ-170SE | 17000052 | ex PT-SVK | | Shuttle America |
| ☐ N637RW | Embraer ERJ-170SE | 17000051 | ex PT-SUV | | Shuttle America |
| ☐ N638RW | Embraer ERJ-170SE | 17000053 | ex PT-SUY | | Shuttle America |
| ☐ N639RW | Embraer ERJ-170SE | 17000057 | ex PT-SVG | | Shuttle America |
| ☐ N640RW | Embraer ERJ-170SE | 17000058 | ex PT-SVH | | Shuttle America |
| ☐ N641RW | Embraer ERJ-170SE | 17000062 | ex PT-SVN | | Shuttle America |
| ☐ N642RW | Embraer ERJ-170SE | 17000063 | ex PT-SVO | | Shuttle America |
| ☐ N643RW | Embraer ERJ-170SE | 17000060 | ex PT-SVL | | Shuttle America |
| ☐ N644RW | Embraer ERJ-170SE | 17000061 | ex PT-SVM | | Shuttle America |
| ☐ N645RW | Embraer ERJ-170SE | 17000064 | ex PT-SVP | | Shuttle America |
| ☐ N646RW | Embraer ERJ-170SE | 17000066 | ex PT-SVR | | Shuttle America |
| ☐ N647RW | Embraer ERJ-170SE | 17000067 | ex PT-SVS | | Shuttle America |
| ☐ N648RW | Embraer ERJ-170SE | 17000068 | ex PT-SVT | | Shuttle America |
| ☐ N649RW | Embraer ERJ-170SE | 17000070 | ex PT-SVV | | Shuttle America |
| ☐ N650RW | Embraer ERJ-170SE | 17000071 | ex PT-SVW | | Shuttle America |
| ☐ N651RW | Embraer ERJ-170SE | 17000072 | ex PT-SVX | | Shuttle America |
| ☐ N652RW | Embraer ERJ-170SE | 17000075 | ex PT-SZA | | Shuttle America |
| ☐ N653RW | Embraer ERJ-170SE | 17000076 | ex PT-SZB | | Shuttle America |
| ☐ N654RW | Embraer ERJ-170SE | 17000104 | ex PT-SAK | | Shuttle America |
| ☐ N655RW | Embraer ERJ-170SE | 17000105 | ex PT-SAM | | Shuttle America |
| ☐ N656RW | Embraer ERJ-170SE | 17000113 | ex PT-SAY | | Shuttle America |
| ☐ N657RW | Embraer ERJ-170SE | 17000115 | ex PT-SDC | | Shuttle America |
| ☐ N856RW | Embraer ERJ-170SE | 17000078 | ex PT-SZD | | Shuttle America |
| ☐ N857RW | Embraer ERJ-170SE | 17000079 | ex PT-SZE | | Shuttle America |
| ☐ N858RW | Embraer ERJ-170SE | 17000080 | ex PT-SZF | | Shuttle America |
| ☐ N861RW | Embraer ERJ-170SE | 17000094 | ex PT-SZU | | Shuttle America |
| ☐ N863RW | Embraer ERJ-170SE | 17000100 | ex PT-SAB | | Shuttle America |
| ☐ N864RW | Embraer ERJ-170SE | 17000117 | ex PT-SDE | | Shuttle America |
| ☐ N865RW | Embraer ERJ-170SE | 17000122 | ex PT-SDK | | Shuttle America |
| | | | | | |
| ☐ N184CJ | SAAB SF.340B | 340B-184 | ex N300CE | | Colgan Air |
| ☐ N191MJ | SAAB SF.340B | 340B-191 | ex N301AE | | Colgan Air |
| ☐ N193CJ | SAAB SF.340B | 340B-193 | ex N302CE | | Colgan Air |
| ☐ N194CJ | SAAB SF.340B | 340B-194 | ex N303CE | | Colgan Air |
| ☐ N196CJ | SAAB SF.340B | 340B-196 | ex N196JW | | Colgan Air |
| ☐ N198CJ | SAAB SF.340B | 340B-198 | ex N304CE | | Colgan Air |
| ☐ N204CJ | SAAB SF.340B | 340B-204 | ex N307CE | | Colgan Air |
| ☐ N220MJ | SAAB SF.340B | 340B-220 | ex N360PX | | Colgan Air |
| ☐ N237MJ | SAAB SF.340B | 340B-237 | ex N351BE | | Colgan Air |
| ☐ N239CJ | SAAB SF.340B | 340B-239 | ex N352BE | | Colgan Air |

| | | | | |
|---|---|---|---|---|
| ☐ N242CJ | SAAB SF.340B | 340B-242 | ex N353BE | Colgan Air |
| ☐ N277MJ | SAAB SF.340B | 340B-277 | ex N357BE | Colgan Air |
| ☐ N309CE | SAAB SF.340B | 340B-201 | ex N201AE | Colgan Air |
| ☐ N311CE | SAAB SF.340B | 340B-214 | ex SE-G14 | Colgan Air |
| ☐ N314CE | SAAB SF.340B | 340B-335 | ex N335AE | Colgan Air |
| ☐ N334CJ | SAAB SF.340B | 340B-334 | ex N312CE | Colgan Air |
| ☐ N343CJ | SAAB SF.340B | 340B-343 | ex N315CE | Colgan Air |
| ☐ N352CJ | SAAB SF.340B | 340B-352 | ex N317CE | Colgan Air |
| ☐ N356CJ | SAAB SF.340B | 340B-356 | ex N356SB | Colgan Air |

## UNIVERSAL AIRLINES — Pacific Northern (PNA) — Victoria-Regional, TX (VCT)

| | | | |
|---|---|---|---|
| ☐ N170UA | Douglas DC-6A | 45518/998 | ex N870TA |
| ☐ N500UA | Douglas DC-6A | 44597/501 | ex N766WC |
| ☐ N600UA | Douglas DC-6BF | 44894/651 | ex N37570 |

## UPS AIRLINES — UPS (5X/UPS) — Louisville-Intl, KY (SDF)

| | | | |
|---|---|---|---|
| ☐ N120UP | Airbus A300F4-622R | 805 | ex F-WWAR |
| ☐ N121UP | Airbus A300F4-622R | 806 | ex F-WWAP |
| ☐ N122UP | Airbus A300F4-622R | 807 | ex F-WWAX |
| ☐ N124UP | Airbus A300F4-622R | 808 | ex F-WWAT |
| ☐ N125UP | Airbus A300F4-622R | 809 | ex F-WWAU |
| ☐ N126UP | Airbus A300F4-622R | 810 | ex F-WWAB |
| ☐ N127UP | Airbus A300F4-622R | 811 | ex F-WWAD |
| ☐ N128UP | Airbus A300F4-622R | 812 | ex F-WWAE |
| ☐ N129UP | Airbus A300F4-622R | 813 | ex F-WWAF |
| ☐ N130UP | Airbus A300F4-622R | 814 | ex F-WWAG |
| ☐ N131UP | Airbus A300F4-622R | 815 | ex F-WWAH |
| ☐ N133UP | Airbus A300F4-622R | 816 | ex F-WWAJ |
| ☐ N134UP | Airbus A300F4-622R | 817 | ex F-WWAL |
| ☐ N135UP | Airbus A300F4-622R | 818 | ex F-WWAM |
| ☐ N136UP | Airbus A300F4-622R | 819 | ex F-WWAN |
| ☐ N137UP | Airbus A300F4-622R | 820 | ex F-WWAO |
| ☐ N138UP | Airbus A300F4-622R | 821 | ex F-WWAQ |
| ☐ N139UP | Airbus A300F4-622R | 822 | ex F-WWAS |
| ☐ N140UP | Airbus A300F4-622R | 823 | ex F-WWAV |
| ☐ N141UP | Airbus A300F4-622R | 824 | ex F-WWAY |
| ☐ N142UP | Airbus A300F4-622R | 825 | ex F-WWAA |
| ☐ N143UP | Airbus A300F4-622R | 826 | ex F-WWAB |
| ☐ N144UP | Airbus A300F4-622R | 827 | ex F-WWAD |
| ☐ N145UP | Airbus A300F4-622R | 828 | ex F-WWAE |
| ☐ N146UP | Airbus A300F4-622R | 829 | ex F-WWAG |
| ☐ N147UP | Airbus A300F4-622R | 830 | ex F-WWAJ |
| ☐ N148UP | Airbus A300F4-622R | 831 | ex F-WWAM |
| ☐ N149UP | Airbus A300F4-622R | 832 | ex F-WWAN |
| ☐ N150UP | Airbus A300F4-622R | 833 | ex F-WWAO |
| ☐ N151UP | Airbus A300F4-622R | 834 | ex F-WWAP |
| ☐ N152UP | Airbus A300F4-622R | 835 | ex F-WWAQ |
| ☐ N153UP | Airbus A300F4-622R | 839 | ex F-WWAR |
| ☐ N154UP | Airbus A300F4-622R | 840 | ex F-WWAS |
| ☐ N155UP | Airbus A300F4-622R | 841 | ex F-WWAT |
| ☐ N156UP | Airbus A300F4-622R | 845 | ex F-WWAU |
| ☐ N157UP | Airbus A300F4-622R | 846 | ex F-WWAV |
| ☐ N158UP | Airbus A300F4-622R | 847 | ex F-WWAX |
| ☐ N159UP | Airbus A300F4-622R | 848 | ex F-WWAZ |
| ☐ N160UP | Airbus A300F4-622R | 849 | ex F-WWAF |
| ☐ N161UP | Airbus A300F4-622R | 850 | ex F-WWAG |
| ☐ N162UP | Airbus A300F4-622R | 851 | ex F-WWAJ |
| ☐ N163UP | Airbus A300F4-622R | 852 | ex F-WWAK |
| ☐ N164UP | Airbus A300F4-622R | 853 | ex F-WWAL |
| ☐ N165UP | Airbus A300F4-622R | 854 | ex F-WWAM |
| ☐ N166UP | Airbus A300F4-622R | 861 | ex F-WWAU |
| ☐ N167UP | Airbus A300F4-622R | 862 | ex F-WWAH |
| ☐ N168UP | Airbus A300F4-622R | 863 | ex F-WWAV |
| ☐ N169UP | Airbus A300F4-622R | 864 | ex F-WWAX |
| ☐ N170UP | Airbus A300F4-622R | 865 | ex F-WWAZ |
| ☐ N171UP | Airbus A300F4-622R | 866 | ex F-WWAE |
| ☐ N172UP | Airbus A300F4-622R | 867 | ex F-WWAF |
| ☐ N173UP | Airbus A300F4-622R | 868 | ex F-WWAG |
| ☐ N174UP | Airbus A300F4-622R | 869 | ex F-WWAN |
| ☐ N570UP | Boeing 747-44AF | 35667/1388 | |
| ☐ N572UP | Boeing 747-44AF | 35669/1396 | |
| ☐ N573UP | Boeing 747-44AF | 35662/1401 | |
| ☐ N574UP | Boeing 747-44AF | 35663/1403 | |
| ☐ N575UP | Boeing 747-44AF | 35664/1406 | |
| ☐ N576UP | Boeing 747-44AF | 35665/1410 | |
| ☐ N577UP | Boeing 747-44AF | 35666/1412 | |
| ☐ N578UP | Boeing 747-45EM | 27154/994 | ex B-16461 |
| ☐ N579UP | Boeing 747-45EM | 26062/1016 | ex B-16465 |

| | | | |
|---|---|---|---|
| ☐ N580UP | Boeing 747-428F | 25632/968 | ex LX-ICV |
| ☐ N581UP | Boeing 747-4R7F | 25866/1002 | ex LX-FCV |
| ☐ N582UP | Boeing 747-4R7F | 29053/1139 | ex LX-LCV |
| ☐ N583UP | Boeing 747-4R7F | 25867/1008 | ex LX-GCV |
| | | | |
| ☐ N401UP | Boeing 757-24APF | 23723/139 | |
| ☐ N402UP | Boeing 757-24APF | 23724/141 | |
| ☐ N403UP | Boeing 757-24APF | 23725/143 | |
| ☐ N404UP | Boeing 757-24APF | 23726/147 | |
| ☐ N405UP | Boeing 757-24APF | 23727/149 | |
| ☐ N406UP | Boeing 757-24APF | 23728/176 | |
| ☐ N407UP | Boeing 757-24APF | 23729/181 | |
| ☐ N408UP | Boeing 757-24APF | 23730/184 | |
| ☐ N409UP | Boeing 757-24APF | 23731/186 | |
| ☐ N410UP | Boeing 757-24APF | 23732/189 | |
| ☐ N411UP | Boeing 757-24APF | 23851/191 | |
| ☐ N412UP | Boeing 757-24APF | 23852/193 | |
| ☐ N413UP | Boeing 757-24APF | 23853/195 | |
| ☐ N414UP | Boeing 757-24APF | 23854/197 | |
| ☐ N415UP | Boeing 757-24APF | 23855/199 | |
| ☐ N416UP | Boeing 757-24APF | 23903/318 | |
| ☐ N417UP | Boeing 757-24APF | 23904/322 | |
| ☐ N418UP | Boeing 757-24APF | 23905/326 | |
| ☐ N419UP | Boeing 757-24APF | 23906/330 | |
| ☐ N420UP | Boeing 757-24APF | 23907/334 | |
| ☐ N421UP | Boeing 757-24APF | 25281/395 | |
| ☐ N422UP | Boeing 757-24APF | 25324/399 | |
| ☐ N423UP | Boeing 757-24APF | 25325/403 | |
| ☐ N424UP | Boeing 757-24APF | 25369/407 | |
| ☐ N425UP | Boeing 757-24APF | 25370/411 | |
| ☐ N426UP | Boeing 757-24APF | 25457/477 | |
| ☐ N427UP | Boeing 757-24APF | 25458/481 | |
| ☐ N428UP | Boeing 757-24APF | 25459/485 | |
| ☐ N429UP | Boeing 757-24APF | 25460/489 | |
| ☐ N430UP | Boeing 757-24APF | 25461/493 | |
| ☐ N431UP | Boeing 757-24APF | 25462/569 | ex OY-USA |
| ☐ N432UP | Boeing 757-24APF | 25463/573 | ex OY-USB |
| ☐ N433UP | Boeing 757-24APF | 25464/577 | ex OY-USC |
| ☐ N434UP | Boeing 757-24APF | 25465/579 | ex OY-USD |
| ☐ N435UP | Boeing 757-24APF | 25466/581 | |
| ☐ N436UP | Boeing 757-24APF | 25467/625 | |
| ☐ N437UP | Boeing 757-24APF | 25468/628 | |
| ☐ N438UP | Boeing 757-24APF | 25469/631 | |
| ☐ N439UP | Boeing 757-24APF | 25470/634 | |
| ☐ N440UP | Boeing 757-24APF | 25471/636 | |
| ☐ N441UP | Boeing 757-24APF | 27386/638 | |
| ☐ N442UP | Boeing 757-24APF | 27387/640 | |
| ☐ N443UP | Boeing 757-24APF | 27388/642 | |
| ☐ N444UP | Boeing 757-24APF | 27389/644 | |
| ☐ N445UP | Boeing 757-24APF | 27390/646 | |
| ☐ N446UP | Boeing 757-24APF | 27735/649 | |
| ☐ N447UP | Boeing 757-24APF | 27736/651 | |
| ☐ N448UP | Boeing 757-24APF | 27737/654 | |
| ☐ N449UP | Boeing 757-24APF | 27738/656 | |
| ☐ N450UP | Boeing 757-24APF | 25472/659 | |
| ☐ N451UP | Boeing 757-24APF | 27739/675 | |
| ☐ N452UP | Boeing 757-24APF | 25473/679 | |
| ☐ N453UP | Boeing 757-24APF | 25474/683 | |
| ☐ N454UP | Boeing 757-24APF | 25475/687 | |
| ☐ N455UP | Boeing 757-24APF | 25476/691 | |
| ☐ N456UP | Boeing 757-24APF | 25477/728 | |
| ☐ N457UP | Boeing 757-24APF | 25478/729 | |
| ☐ N458UP | Boeing 757-24APF | 25479/730 | |
| ☐ N459UP | Boeing 757-24APF | 25480/733 | |
| ☐ N460UP | Boeing 757-24APF | 25481/734 | |
| ☐ N461UP | Boeing 757-24APF | 28265/755 | |
| ☐ N462UP | Boeing 757-24APF | 28266/759 | |
| ☐ N463UP | Boeing 757-24APF | 28267/763 | |
| ☐ N464UP | Boeing 757-24APF | 28268/765 | |
| ☐ N465UP | Boeing 757-24APF | 28269/767 | |
| ☐ N466UP | Boeing 757-24APF | 25482/769 | |
| ☐ N467UP | Boeing 757-24APF | 25483/771 | |
| ☐ N468UP | Boeing 757-24APF | 25484/774 | |
| ☐ N469UP | Boeing 757-24APF | 25485/776 | |
| ☐ N470UP | Boeing 757-24APF | 25486/778 | |
| ☐ N471UP | Boeing 757-24APF | 28842/813 | |
| ☐ N472UP | Boeing 757-24APF | 28843/815 | |
| ☐ N473UP | Boeing 757-24APF | 28846/823 | ex N5573L |
| ☐ N474UP | Boeing 757-24APF | 28844/879 | |
| ☐ N475UP | Boeing 757-24APF | 28845/882 | |
| | | | |
| ☐ N301UP | Boeing 767-34AF | 27239/580 | |

| | | | | |
|---|---|---|---|---|
| ☐ N302UP | Boeing 767-34AF | 27240/590 | | |
| ☐ N303UP | Boeing 767-34AF | 27241/594 | | |
| ☐ N304UP | Boeing 767-34AF | 27242/598 | | |
| ☐ N305UP | Boeing 767-34AF | 27243/600 | | |
| ☐ N306UP | Boeing 767-34AF | 27759/622 | | |
| ☐ N307UP | Boeing 767-34AF | 27760/624 | | |
| ☐ N308UP | Boeing 767-34AF | 27761/626 | | |
| ☐ N309UP | Boeing 767-34AF | 27740/628 | | |
| ☐ N310UP | Boeing 767-34AF | 27762/630 | | |
| ☐ N311UP | Boeing 767-34AF | 27741/632 | | |
| ☐ N312UP | Boeing 767-34AF | 27763/634 | | |
| ☐ N313UP | Boeing 767-34AF | 27764/636 | | |
| ☐ N314UP | Boeing 767-34AF | 27742/638 | | |
| ☐ N315UP | Boeing 767-34AF | 27743/640 | | |
| ☐ N316UP | Boeing 767-34AF | 27744/660 | | |
| ☐ N317UP | Boeing 767-34AF | 27745/666 | | |
| ☐ N318UP | Boeing 767-34AF | 27746/670 | | |
| ☐ N319UP | Boeing 767-34AF | 27758/672 | | |
| ☐ N320UP | Boeing 767-34AF | 27747/674 | | |
| ☐ N322UP | Boeing 767-34AF | 27748/678 | | |
| ☐ N323UP | Boeing 767-34AF | 27749/682 | | |
| ☐ N324UP | Boeing 767-34AF | 27750/724 | | |
| ☐ N325UP | Boeing 767-34AF | 27751/726 | | |
| ☐ N326UP | Boeing 767-34AF | 27752/728 | | |
| ☐ N327UP | Boeing 767-34AF | 27753/730 | | |
| ☐ N328UP | Boeing 767-34AF | 27754/732 | | |
| ☐ N329UP | Boeing 767-34AF | 27755/756 | | |
| ☐ N330UP | Boeing 767-34AF | 27756/760 | | |
| ☐ N331UP | Boeing 767-34AF | 27757/764 | | |
| ☐ N332UP | Boeing 767-34AF | 32843/854 | | |
| ☐ N334UP | Boeing 767-34AF | 32844/858 | | |
| ☐ N335UP | Boeing 767-34AF | 37856/979 | ex N5023Q | |
| ☐ N336UP | Boeing 767-34AF | 37857/983 | | |
| ☐ N337UP | Boeing 767-34AF | 37858/986 | | |
| ☐ N338UP | Boeing 767-34AF | 37944/988 | | |
| ☐ N339UP | Boeing 767-34AF | 37859/989 | | |
| ☐ N340UP | Boeing 767-34AF | 37860/991 | | |
| ☐ N341UP | Boeing 767-34AF | 37861/992 | | |
| ☐ N342UP | Boeing 767-34AF | 37865/1002 | | |
| ☐ N343UP | Boeing 767-34AF | 37945/1003 | | ♦ |
| ☐ N344UP | Boeing 767-34AF | 37866/1005 | | ♦ |
| ☐ N345UP | Boeing 767-34AF | 37867/1006 | | ♦ |
| ☐ N346UP | Boeing 767-34AF | 37868/1008 | | ♦ |
| ☐ N347UP | Boeing 767-34AF | 37871/1020 | | ♦ |
| ☐ N348UP | Boeing 767-34AF | 37872/1022 | | ♦ |
| ☐ N349UP | Boeing 767-34AF | 37947/1024 | | ♦ |
| ☐ N350UP | Boeing 767-34AF | 37873/ | | o/o♦ |
| ☐ N351UP | Boeing 767-34AF | 37874/ | | o/o♦ |
| ☐ N352UP | Boeing 767-34AF | 37875/ | | o/o♦ |
| ☐ N353UP | Boeing 767-34AF | 37877/ | | o/o♦ |
| ☐ | Boeing 767-34AF | | | o/o |
| ☐ | Boeing 767-34AF | | | o/o |
| | | | | |
| ☐ N250UP | McDonnell-Douglas MD-11F | 48745/596 | ex N798BA | |
| ☐ N251UP | McDonnell-Douglas MD-11F | 48744/592 | ex N797BA | |
| ☐ N252UP | McDonnell-Douglas MD-11F | 48768/601 | ex PP-SFA | |
| ☐ N253UP | McDonnell-Douglas MD-11F | 48439/554 | ex PP-VPM | |
| ☐ N254UP | McDonnell-Douglas MD-11F | 48406/547 | ex PP-VPL | |
| ☐ N255UP | McDonnell-Douglas MD-11F | 48404/523 | ex PP-VPJ | |
| ☐ N256UP | McDonnell-Douglas MD-11F | 48405/524 | ex PP-VPK | |
| ☐ N257UP | McDonnell-Douglas MD-11F | 48451/505 | ex HS-TMG | |
| ☐ N258UP | McDonnell-Douglas MD-11F | 48416/466 | ex HS-TMD | |
| ☐ N259UP | McDonnell-Douglas MD-11F | 48417/467 | ex HS-TME | |
| ☐ N260UP | McDonnell-Douglas MD-11F | 48418/501 | ex HS-TMF | |
| ☐ N270UP | McDonnell-Douglas MD-11F | 48576/574 | ex JA8585 | |
| ☐ N271UP | McDonnell-Douglas MD-11F | 48572/556 | ex JA8581 | |
| ☐ N272UP | McDonnell-Douglas MD-11F | 48571/552 | ex JA8580 | |
| ☐ N273UP | McDonnell-Douglas MD-11F | 48574/566 | ex JA8583 | |
| ☐ N274UP | McDonnell-Douglas MD-11F | 48575/568 | ex JA8584 | |
| ☐ N275UP | McDonnell-Douglas MD-11F | 48774/610 | ex JA8589 | |
| ☐ N276UP | McDonnell-Douglas MD-11F | 48579/599 | ex JA8588 | |
| ☐ N277UP | McDonnell-Douglas MD-11F | 48578/588 | ex JA8587 | |
| ☐ N278UP | McDonnell-Douglas MD-11F | 48577/583 | ex JA8586 | |
| ☐ N279UP | McDonnell-Douglas MD-11F | 48573/559 | ex JA8582 | |
| ☐ N280UP | McDonnell-Douglas MD-11F | 48634/614 | ex N38WF | |
| ☐ N281UP | McDonnell-Douglas MD-11F | 48538/533 | ex N48WF | |
| ☐ N282UP | McDonnell-Douglas MD-11F | 48452/472 | ex N74WF | |
| ☐ N283UP | McDonnell-Douglas MD-11F | 48484/484 | ex V5-NMC | |
| ☐ N284UP | McDonnell-Douglas MD-11F | 48541/621 | ex PP-VTU | |
| ☐ N285UP | McDonnell-Douglas MD-11F | 48457/498 | ex PP-VTH | |
| ☐ N286UP | McDonnell-Douglas MD-11F | 48453/473 | ex V5-NMD | |
| ☐ N287UP | McDonnell-Douglas MD-11F | 48539/571 | ex PP-VTP | |

| | | | | |
|---|---|---|---|---|
| ☐ N288UP | McDonnell-Douglas MD-11F | 48540/611 | ex PP-VTK | |
| ☐ N289UP | McDonnell-Douglas MD-11F | 48455/487 | ex PP-VTJ | |
| ☐ N290UP | McDonnell-Douglas MD-11F | 48456/494 | ex PP-VTI | |
| ☐ N291UP | McDonnell-Douglas MD-11F | 48477/511 | ex N806DE | |
| ☐ N292UP | McDonnell-Douglas MD-11F | 48566/543 | ex N811DE | |
| ☐ N293UP | McDonnell-Douglas MD-11F | 48473/481 | ex N802DE | |
| ☐ N294UP | McDonnell-Douglas MD-11F | 48472/480 | ex N801DE | |
| ☐ N295UP | McDonnell-Douglas MD-11F | 48475/489 | ex N804DE | |
| ☐ N296UP | McDonnell-Douglas MD-11F | 48474/485 | ex N803DE | |

## US AIRWAYS — U S Air (US/USA)
### Pittsburgh-Greater Pittsburgh Intl, PA/Phoenix-Sky Harbor Intl, AZ (PIT/PHX)

Member of Star Alliance

| | | | | |
|---|---|---|---|---|
| ☐ N700UW | Airbus A319-112 | 0885 | ex D-AVYF | Star Alliance c/s |
| ☐ N701UW | Airbus A319-112 | 0890 | ex D-AVYG | Star Alliance c/s |
| ☐ N702UW | Airbus A319-112 | 0896 | ex D-AVYH | Star Alliance c/s |
| ☐ N703UW | Airbus A319-112 | 0904 | ex D-AVYI | Star Alliance c/s |
| ☐ N704US | Airbus A319-112 | 0922 | ex D-AVYQ | |
| ☐ N705UW | Airbus A319-112 | 0929 | ex D-AVYA | |
| ☐ N708UW | Airbus A319-112 | 0972 | ex D-AVYT | |
| ☐ N709UW | Airbus A319-112 | 0997 | ex D-AVYV | Philadelphia Eagles c/s |
| ☐ N710UW | Airbus A319-112 | 1019 | ex D-AVYR | |
| ☐ N711UW | Airbus A319-112 | 1033 | ex D-AVYG | |
| ☐ N712US | Airbus A319-112 | 1038 | ex D-AVYW | |
| ☐ N713UW | Airbus A319-112 | 1040 | ex D-AVYH | |
| ☐ N714US | Airbus A319-112 | 1046 | ex D-AVYZ | |
| ☐ N715UW | Airbus A319-112 | 1051 | ex D-AVYV | |
| ☐ N716UW | Airbus A319-112 | 1055 | ex D-AVYM | |
| ☐ N717UW | Airbus A319-112 | 1069 | ex D-AVWC | Carolina Panthers c/s |
| ☐ N721UW | Airbus A319-112 | 1095 | ex D-AVYQ | |
| ☐ N722US | Airbus A319-112 | 1097 | ex D-AVYS | |
| ☐ N723UW | Airbus A319-112 | 1109 | ex D-AVWP | |
| ☐ N724UW | Airbus A319-112 | 1122 | ex D-AVYA | |
| ☐ N725UW | Airbus A319-112 | 1135 | ex D-AVWC | |
| ☐ N730US | Airbus A319-112 | 1182 | ex D-AVYD | |
| ☐ N732US | Airbus A319-112 | 1203 | ex D-AVYA | |
| ☐ N733UW | Airbus A319-112 | 1205 | ex D-AVYB | Pittsburgh Steelers c/s |
| ☐ N737US | Airbus A319-112 | 1245 | ex D-AVYN | |
| ☐ N738US | Airbus A319-112 | 1254 | ex D-AVYQ | |
| ☐ N740UW | Airbus A319-112 | 1265 | ex D-AVWO | |
| ☐ N741UW | Airbus A319-112 | 1269 | ex D-AVWP | |
| ☐ N742PS | Airbus A319-112 | 1275 | ex N742US | PSA c/s |
| ☐ N744P | Airbus A319-112 | 1287 | ex N744US | Piedmont c/s |
| ☐ N745VJ | Airbus A319-112 | 1289 | ex N745UW | Allegheny c/s 'Vistajet' |
| ☐ N746UW | Airbus A319-112 | 1297 | ex D-AVWV | |
| ☐ N747UW | Airbus A319-112 | 1301 | ex D-AVWM | |
| ☐ N748UW | Airbus A319-112 | 1311 | ex D-AVYA | |
| ☐ N749US | Airbus A319-112 | 1313 | ex D-AVWG | |
| ☐ N750UW | Airbus A319-112 | 1315 | ex D-AVWH | |
| ☐ N751UW | Airbus A319-112 | 1317 | ex D-AVWK | |
| ☐ N752US | Airbus A319-112 | 1319 | ex D-AVWS | |
| ☐ N753US | Airbus A319-112 | 1326 | ex D-AVYG | |
| ☐ N754UW | Airbus A319-112 | 1328 | ex D-AVYJ | |
| ☐ N755US | Airbus A319-112 | 1331 | ex D-AVYN | |
| ☐ N756US | Airbus A319-112 | 1340 | ex D-AVYO | |
| ☐ N757UW | Airbus A319-112 | 1342 | ex D-AVYP | |
| ☐ N758US | Airbus A319-112 | 1348 | ex D-AVYS | |
| ☐ N760US | Airbus A319-112 | 1354 | ex D-AVWI | |
| ☐ N762US | Airbus A319-112 | 1358 | ex D-AVWD | |
| ☐ N763US | Airbus A319-112 | 1360 | ex D-AVWF | |
| ☐ N764US | Airbus A319-112 | 1369 | ex D-AVWM | |
| ☐ N765US | Airbus A319-112 | 1371 | ex D-AVWO | |
| ☐ N766US | Airbus A319-112 | 1378 | ex D-AVWG | |
| ☐ N767UW | Airbus A319-112 | 1382 | ex D-AVWN | |
| ☐ N768US | Airbus A319-112 | 1389 | ex D-AVYI | |
| ☐ N769US | Airbus A319-112 | 1391 | ex D-AVYJ | |
| ☐ N770UW | Airbus A319-112 | 1393 | ex D-AVYU | |
| | | | | |
| ☐ N801AW | Airbus A319-132 | 0889 | ex D-AVYM | |
| ☐ N802AW | Airbus A319-132 | 0924 | ex D-AVYR | |
| ☐ N803AW | Airbus A319-132 | 0931 | ex D-AVYK | |
| ☐ N804AW | Airbus A319-132 | 1043 | ex D-AVYY | |
| ☐ N805AW | Airbus A319-132 | 1049 | ex D-AVYU | |
| ☐ N806AW | Airbus A319-132 | 1056 | ex D-AVYO | |
| ☐ N807AW | Airbus A319-132 | 1064 | ex D-AVWB | |
| ☐ N808AW | Airbus A319-132 | 1088 | ex D-AVWM | |
| ☐ N809AW | Airbus A319-132 | 1111 | ex D-AVWT | |
| ☐ N810AW | Airbus A319-132 | 1116 | ex D-AVWV | |
| ☐ N812AW | Airbus A319-132 | 1178 | ex D-AVWP | |

| | | | | |
|---|---|---|---|---|
| ☐ N813AW | Airbus A319-132 | 1223 | ex D-AVYH | |
| ☐ N814AW | Airbus A319-132 | 1281 | ex D-AVYC | |
| ☐ N815AW | Airbus A319-132 | 1323 | ex D-AVWW | |
| ☐ N816AW | Airbus A319-132 | 1350 | ex D-AVYV | |
| ☐ N817AW | Airbus A319-132 | 1373 | ex D-AVWA | |
| ☐ N818AW | Airbus A319-132 | 1375 | ex D-AVWB | |
| ☐ N819AW | Airbus A319-132 | 1395 | ex D-AVYX | |
| ☐ N820AW | Airbus A319-132 | 1397 | ex D-AVWQ | |
| ☐ N821AW | Airbus A319-132 | 1406 | ex D-AVYC | |
| ☐ N822AW | Airbus A319-132 | 1410 | ex D-AVYD | Nevada flag c/s |
| ☐ N823AW | Airbus A319-132 | 1463 | ex D-AVYJ | |
| ☐ N824AW | Airbus A319-132 | 1490 | ex D-AVYA | |
| ☐ N825AW | Airbus A319-132 | 1527 | ex D-AVWG | |
| ☐ N826AW | Airbus A319-132 | 1534 | ex D-AVYO | Arizona flag c/s |
| ☐ N827AW | Airbus A319-132 | 1547 | ex D-AVWL | |
| ☐ N828AW | Airbus A319-132 | 1552 | ex D-AVWO | America West Heritage c/s |
| ☐ N829AW | Airbus A319-132 | 1563 | ex D-AVYS | |
| ☐ N830AW | Airbus A319-132 | 1565 | ex D-AVYT | |
| ☐ N831AW | Airbus A319-132 | 1576 | ex D-AVWQ | |
| ☐ N832AW | Airbus A319-132 | 1643 | ex D-AVYA | |
| ☐ N833AW | Airbus A319-132 | 1844 | ex D-AVWV | |
| ☐ N834AW | Airbus A319-132 | 2302 | ex D-AVWM | |
| ☐ N835AW | Airbus A319-132 | 2458 | ex D-AVYN | |
| ☐ N836AW | Airbus A319-132 | 2570 | ex D-AVXB | |
| ☐ N837AW | Airbus A319-132 | 2595 | ex D-AVXM | Arizona Cardinals c/s |
| ☐ N838AW | Airbus A319-132 | 2615 | ex D-AVXT | America West Heritage c/s |
| ☐ N839AW | Airbus A319-132 | 2669 | ex D-AVYH | dam |
| ☐ N840AW | Airbus A319-132 | 2690 | ex D-AVXA | |
| | | | | |
| ☐ N102UW | Airbus A320-214 | 0844 | ex F-WWBG | |
| ☐ N103US | Airbus A320-214 | 0861 | ex F-WWBP | |
| ☐ N104UW | Airbus A320-214 | 0863 | ex F-WWBQ | |
| ☐ N105UW | Airbus A320-214 | 0868 | ex F-WWBU | |
| ☐ N107US | Airbus A320-214 | 1052 | ex F-WWIM | |
| ☐ N108UW | Airbus A320-214 | 1061 | ex F-WWBB | |
| ☐ N109UW | Airbus A320-214 | 1065 | ex F-WWBD | |
| ☐ N110UW | Airbus A320-214 | 1112 | ex F-WWBJ | |
| ☐ N111US | Airbus A320-214 | 1114 | ex F-WWBK | |
| ☐ N112US | Airbus A320-214 | 1134 | ex F-WWIV | |
| ☐ N113UW | Airbus A320-214 | 1141 | ex F-WWBC | |
| ☐ N114UW | Airbus A320-214 | 1148 | ex F-WWBQ | |
| ☐ N117UW | Airbus A320-214 | 1224 | ex F-WWBH | |
| ☐ N118US | Airbus A320-214 | 1264 | ex F-WWDE | |
| ☐ N119US | Airbus A320-214 | 1268 | ex F-WWDH | |
| ☐ N121UW | Airbus A320-214 | 1294 | ex F-WWBC | |
| ☐ N122US | Airbus A320-214 | 1298 | ex F-WWBM | |
| ☐ N123UW | Airbus A320-214 | 1310 | ex F-WWBX | |
| ☐ N124US | Airbus A320-214 | 1314 | ex F-WWDJ | |
| ☐ N125UW | Airbus A320-214 | 4086 | ex F-WWBU | |
| ☐ N126UW | Airbus A320-214 | 4149 | ex D-AVVJ | |
| ☐ N127UW | Airbus A320-214 | 4202 | ex D-AVVH | |
| ☐ N128UW | Airbus A320-214 | 4242 | ex F-WWDL | |
| | | | | |
| ☐ N601AW | Airbus A320-232 | 1935 | ex D-ALAU | |
| ☐ N602AW | Airbus A320-232 | 0565 | ex D-ALAA | |
| ☐ N604AW | Airbus A320-232 | 1196 | ex F-WWDZ | |
| ☐ N620AW | Airbus A320-231 | 0052 | ex N901BN | |
| ☐ N621AW | Airbus A320-231 | 0053 | ex N902BN | |
| ☐ N622AW | Airbus A320-231 | 0054 | ex N903BN | |
| ☐ N624AW | Airbus A320-231 | 0055 | ex N904BN | |
| ☐ N625AW | Airbus A320-231 | 0064 | ex N905BN | |
| ☐ N626AW | Airbus A320-231 | 0065 | ex N906BN | |
| ☐ N627AW | Airbus A320-231 | 0066 | ex N907GP | |
| ☐ N628AW | Airbus A320-231 | 0067 | ex N908GP | |
| ☐ N629AW | Airbus A320-231 | 0076 | ex N910GP | |
| ☐ N631AW | Airbus A320-231 | 0077 | ex N911GP | |
| ☐ N632AW | Airbus A320-231 | 0081 | ex N912GP | |
| ☐ N633AW | Airbus A320-231 | 0082 | ex N913GP | |
| ☐ N637AW | Airbus A320-231 | 0099 | ex N917GP | Arizona Cardinals c/s |
| ☐ N640AW | Airbus A320-232 | 0448 | ex N931LF | |
| ☐ N642AW | Airbus A320-232 | 0584 | ex F-WWDZ | |
| ☐ N644AW | Airbus A320-231 | 0317 | ex N300ML | |
| ☐ N647AW | Airbus A320-232 | 0762 | ex F-WWDE | |
| ☐ N648AW | Airbus A320-232 | 0770 | ex F-WWDJ | |
| ☐ N649AW | Airbus A320-232 | 0803 | ex F-WWDZ | |
| ☐ N650AW | Airbus A320-232 | 0856 | ex F-WWBM | |
| ☐ N651AW | Airbus A320-232 | 0866 | ex F-WWBS | |
| ☐ N652AW | Airbus A320-232 | 0953 | ex F-WWDR | |
| ☐ N653AW | Airbus A320-232 | 1003 | ex F-WWDK | |
| ☐ N654AW | Airbus A320-232 | 1050 | ex F-WWIL | |
| ☐ N655AW | Airbus A320-232 | 1075 | ex F-WWIG | |
| ☐ N656AW | Airbus A320-232 | 1079 | ex F-WWIQ | |

| | | | | |
|---|---|---|---|---|
| ☐ N657AW | Airbus A320-232 | 1083 | ex F-WWIU | |
| ☐ N658AW | Airbus A320-232 | 1110 | ex F-WWDI | |
| ☐ N659AW | Airbus A320-232 | 1166 | ex F-WWDG | |
| ☐ N660AW | Airbus A320-232 | 1234 | ex F-WWIO | |
| ☐ N661AW | Airbus A320-232 | 1284 | ex F-WWBK | |
| ☐ N662AW | Airbus A320-232 | 1274 | ex F-WWDR | |
| ☐ N663AW | Airbus A320-232 | 1419 | ex F-WWBJ | |
| ☐ N664AW | Airbus A320-232 | 1621 | ex F-WWDK | |
| ☐ N665AW | Airbus A320-232 | 1644 | ex F-WWDN | |
| ☐ N667AW | Airbus A320-232 | 1710 | ex F-WWIX | |
| ☐ N668AW | Airbus A320-232 | 1764 | ex F-WWBZ | |
| ☐ N669AW | Airbus A320-232 | 1792 | ex F-WWDX | |
| ☐ N672AW | Airbus A320-232 | 2193 | ex F-WWDZ | |
| ☐ N673AW | Airbus A320-232 | 2312 | ex F-WWDJ | |
| ☐ N675AW | Airbus A320-232 | 2405 | ex F-WWDA | |
| ☐ N676AW | Airbus A320-232 | 2422 | ex F-WWBB | |
| ☐ N677AW | Airbus A320-232 | 2430 | ex F-WWBJ | |
| ☐ N678AW | Airbus A320-232 | 2482 | ex F-WWIN | |
| ☐ N679AW | Airbus A320-232 | 2613 | ex F-WWIX | |
| ☐ N680AW | Airbus A320-232 | 2630 | ex F-WWDX | |
| ☐ | Airbus A320-232 | | ex | o/o |
| ☐ | Airbus A320-232 | | ex | o/o |
| ☐ | Airbus A320-232 | | ex | o/o |
| ☐ | Airbus A320-232 | | ex | o/o |
| ☐ | Airbus A320-232 | | ex | o/o |
| ☐ | Airbus A320-232 | | ex | o/o |
| | | | | |
| ☐ N161UW | Airbus A321-211 | 1403 | ex D-AVZD | |
| ☐ N162UW | Airbus A321-211 | 1412 | ex D-AVZF | |
| ☐ N163US | Airbus A321-211 | 1417 | ex D-AVZG | |
| ☐ N165US | Airbus A321-211 | 1431 | ex D-AVZB | |
| ☐ N167US | Airbus A321-211 | 1442 | ex D-AVXA | |
| ☐ N169UW | Airbus A321-211 | 1455 | ex D-AVXD | |
| ☐ N170US | Airbus A321-211 | 1462 | ex D-AVZM | |
| ☐ N171US | Airbus A321-211 | 1465 | ex D-AVZN | |
| ☐ N172US | Airbus A321-211 | 1472 | ex D-AVZO | |
| ☐ N173US | Airbus A321-211 | 1481 | ex D-AVZI | |
| ☐ N174US | Airbus A321-211 | 1492 | ex D-AVZR | |
| ☐ N176UW | Airbus A321-211 | 1499 | ex D-AVZT | |
| ☐ N177US | Airbus A321-211 | 1517 | ex D-AVZF | |
| ☐ N178US | Airbus A321-211 | 1519 | ex D-AVZH | |
| ☐ N179UW | Airbus A321-211 | 1521 | ex D-AVZJ | |
| ☐ N180US | Airbus A321-211 | 1525 | ex D-AVZV | |
| ☐ N181UW | Airbus A321-211 | 1531 | ex D-AVZW | |
| ☐ N182UW | Airbus A321-211 | 1536 | ex D-AVZB | |
| ☐ N183UW | Airbus A321-211 | 1539 | ex D-AVZC | |
| ☐ N184US | Airbus A321-211 | 1651 | ex D-AVZQ | |
| ☐ N185UW | Airbus A321-211 | 1666 | ex D-AVZI | |
| ☐ N186US | Airbus A321-211 | 1701 | ex D-AVZD | |
| ☐ N187US | Airbus A321-211 | 1704 | ex D-AVZE | |
| ☐ N188US | Airbus A321-211 | 1724 | ex D-AVXB | |
| ☐ N189UW | Airbus A321-211 | 1425 | ex N164UW | |
| ☐ N190UW | Airbus A321-211 | 1436 | ex N166US | |
| ☐ N191UW | Airbus A321-211 | 1447 | ex N168US | |
| ☐ N192UW | Airbus A321-211 | 1496 | ex N175US | |
| ☐ N193UW | Airbus A321-211 | 3584 | ex D-AVZL | |
| ☐ N194UW | Airbus A321-211 | 3629 | ex D-AVZI | |
| ☐ N195UW | Airbus A321-211 | 3633 | ex D-AVZJ | |
| ☐ N196UW | Airbus A321-211 | 3879 | ex D-AVZR | |
| ☐ N197UW | Airbus A321-211 | 3928 | ex D-AZAC | |
| | | | | |
| ☐ N507AY | Airbus A321-231 | 3712 | ex D-AVZP | |
| ☐ N508AY | Airbus A321-231 | 3740 | ex D-AZAL | |
| ☐ N509AY | Airbus A321-231 | 3796 | ex D-AZAS | |
| ☐ N510UW | Airbus A321-231 | 3858 | ex D-AVZI | |
| ☐ N519UW | Airbus A321-231 | 3881 | ex D-AVZT | |
| ☐ N520UW | Airbus A321-231 | 3924 | ex D-AZAA | |
| ☐ N521UW | Airbus A321-231 | 3944 | ex D-AZAJ | |
| ☐ N523UW | Airbus A321-231 | 3960 | ex D-AZAV | |
| ☐ N524UW | Airbus A321-231 | 3977 | ex F-WWIX | |
| ☐ N534UW | Airbus A321-231 | 3989 | ex D-AZAO | |
| ☐ N535UW | Airbus A321-231 | 3993 | ex D-AZAP | |
| ☐ N536UW | Airbus A321-231 | 4025 | ex D-AVZH | |
| ☐ N537UW | Airbus A321-231 | 4041 | ex D-AVZJ | |
| ☐ N538UW | Airbus A321-231 | 4050 | ex D-AZAK | |
| ☐ N539UW | Airbus A321-231 | 4082 | ex D-AVZV | |
| ☐ N540UW | Airbus A321-231 | 4107 | ex D-AZAD | |
| ☐ N541UW | Airbus A321-231 | 4123 | ex D-AZAI | |
| ☐ N542UW | Airbus A321-231 | 4134 | ex D-AZAL | |
| ☐ N543UW | Airbus A321-231 | 4843 | ex D-AVZW | ♦ |
| ☐ N544UW | Airbus A321-231 | 4847 | ex D-AVZX | ♦ |
| ☐ N545UW | Airbus A321-231 | 4850 | ex D-AVZY | ♦ |

| | | | | |
|---|---|---|---|---|
| ☐ N546UW | Airbus A321-231 | 4885 | ex D-AVZD | ♦ |
| ☐ N547UW | Airbus A321-231 | 4893 | ex D-AVZE | ♦ |
| ☐ N548UW | Airbus A321-231 | 4898 | ex D-AVZF | ♦ |
| ☐ N549UW | Airbus A321-231 | 4932 | ex D-AVZK | ♦ |
| ☐ N550UW | Airbus A321-231 | 4935 | ex D-AVZL | ♦ |
| ☐ N551UW | Airbus A321-231 | 4940 | ex D-AZAB | ♦ |
| ☐ N552UW | Airbus A321-231 | 4957 | ex D-AZAE | ♦ |
| ☐ N553UW | Airbus A321-231 | 4960 | ex D-AZAF | ♦ |
| ☐ N554UW | Airbus A321-231 | 4966 | ex D-AVZB | ♦ |
| | | | | |
| ☐ N270AY | Airbus A330-323X | 315 | ex N670UW | |
| ☐ N271AY | Airbus A330-323X | 323 | ex N671UW | |
| ☐ N272AY | Airbus A330-323X | 333 | ex N672UW | |
| ☐ N273AY | Airbus A330-323X | 337 | ex N673UW | |
| ☐ N274AY | Airbus A330-323X | 342 | ex N674UW | |
| ☐ N275AY | Airbus A330-323X | 370 | ex N675US | |
| ☐ N276AY | Airbus A330-323X | 375 | ex N676UW | |
| ☐ N277AY | Airbus A330-323X | 380 | ex N677UW | |
| ☐ N278AY | Airbus A330-323X | 388 | ex N678US | |
| ☐ N279AY | Airbus A330-243 | 1011 | ex F-WWYG | |
| ☐ N280AY | Airbus A330-243 | 1022 | ex F-WWYP | |
| ☐ N281AY | Airbus A330-243 | 1041 | ex F-WWYT | |
| ☐ N282AY | Airbus A330-243 | 1069 | ex F-WWYG | |
| ☐ N283AY | Airbus A330-243 | 1076 | ex F-WWKP | |
| ☐ N284AY | Airbus A330-243 | 1095 | ex F-WWYS | |
| ☐ N285AY | Airbus A330-243 | 1100 | ex F-WWYF | |
| | | | | |
| ☐ N332AW | Boeing 737-3B7 | 23384/1427 | ex N953WP | [MZJ] |
| ☐ N516AU | Boeing 737-3B7 | 23702/1475 | ex N385AU | |
| ☐ N529AU | Boeing 737-3B7 | 24411/1713 | | |
| ☐ N530AU | Boeing 737-3B7 | 24412/1735 | | |
| ☐ N531AU | Boeing 737-3B7 | 24478/1743 | | |
| ☐ N532AU | Boeing 737-3B7 | 24479/1745 | | |
| ☐ N533AU | Boeing 737-3B7 | 24515/1767 | | |
| ☐ N574US | Boeing 737-301 | 23739/1469 | ex N358US | |
| | | | | |
| ☐ N404US | Boeing 737-401 | 23886/1487 | ex (N402P) | |
| ☐ N405US | Boeing 737-401 | 23885/1512 | ex (N403P) | |
| ☐ N406US | Boeing 737-401 | 23876/1528 | ex (N404P) | |
| ☐ N409US | Boeing 737-401 | 23879/1573 | ex (N407P) | |
| ☐ N417US | Boeing 737-401 | 23984/1674 | | |
| ☐ N418US | Boeing 737-401 | 23985/1676 | | |
| ☐ N419US | Boeing 737-401 | 23986/1684 | | |
| ☐ N420US | Boeing 737-401 | 23987/1698 | | |
| ☐ N421US | Boeing 737-401 | 23988/1714 | | |
| ☐ N422US | Boeing 737-401 | 23989/1716 | | |
| ☐ N423US | Boeing 737-401 | 23990/1732 | | |
| ☐ N424US | Boeing 737-401 | 23991/1746 | | |
| ☐ N425US | Boeing 737-401 | 23992/1764 | | |
| | | | | |
| ☐ N426US | Boeing 737-4B7 | 24548/1789 | | |
| ☐ N427US | Boeing 737-4B7 | 24549/1791 | | |
| ☐ N430US | Boeing 737-4B7 | 24552/1797 | | |
| ☐ N432US | Boeing 737-4B7 | 24554/1817 | | |
| ☐ N433US | Boeing 737-4B7 | 24555/1819 | | |
| ☐ N434US | Boeing 737-4B7 | 24556/1821 | | |
| ☐ N435US | Boeing 737-4B7 | 24557/1835 | | |
| ☐ N438US | Boeing 737-4B7 | 24560/1849 | | |
| ☐ N439US | Boeing 737-4B7 | 24781/1874 | | |
| ☐ N440US | Boeing 737-4B7 | 24811/1890 | | |
| ☐ N441US | Boeing 737-4B7 | 24812/1892 | | |
| ☐ N442US | Boeing 737-4B7 | 24841/1906 | | |
| ☐ N443US | Boeing 737-4B7 | 24842/1908 | | |
| ☐ N444US | Boeing 737-4B7 | 24862/1910 | | |
| ☐ N445US | Boeing 737-4B7 | 24863/1914 | | |
| ☐ N449US | Boeing 737-4B7 | 24893/1946 | | |
| ☐ N450UW | Boeing 737-4B7 | 24933/1954 | ex N775AU | |
| ☐ N451UW | Boeing 737-4B7 | 24934/1956 | ex N776AU | |
| ☐ N452UW | Boeing 737-4B7 | 24979/1980 | ex N777AU | |
| ☐ N453UW | Boeing 737-4B7 | 24980/1982 | ex N778AU | |
| ☐ N454UW | Boeing 737-4B7 | 24996/1986 | ex N779AU | |
| ☐ N455UW | Boeing 737-4B7 | 24997/1990 | ex N780AU | |
| ☐ N456UW | Boeing 737-4B7 | 25020/1992 | ex N781AU | |
| ☐ N457UW | Boeing 737-4B7 | 25021/1995 | ex N782AU | |
| ☐ N458UW | Boeing 737-4B7 | 25022/2010 | ex N783AU | |
| ☐ N459UW | Boeing 737-4B7 | 25023/2020 | ex N784AU | |
| ☐ N460UW | Boeing 737-4B7 | 25024/2026 | ex N785AU | |
| | | | | |
| ☐ N200UU | Boeing 757-2B7/W | 27809/673 | ex N631AU | |
| ☐ N201UU | Boeing 757-2B7/W | 27810/678 | ex N632AU | |
| ☐ N202UW | Boeing 757-2B7/W | 27811/681 | ex N633AU | |
| ☐ N203UW | Boeing 757-23N/W | 30548/930 | ex N642UW | |

| | | | | |
|---|---|---|---|---|
| ☐ N204UW | Boeing 757-23N/W | 30886/945 | ex N643UW | |
| ☐ N205UW | Boeing 757-23N/W | 30887/946 | ex N644UW | |
| ☐ N206UW | Boeing 757-2B7/W | 27808/666 | ex N630AU | |
| ☐ N207UW | Boeing 757-28A | 32448/967 | ex N756NA | |
| ☐ N901AW | Boeing 757-2S7 | 23321/76 | ex N601RC | |
| ☐ N902AW | Boeing 757-2S7 | 23322/79 | ex N602RC | |
| ☐ N903AW | Boeing 757-2S7 | 23323/80 | ex N603RC | |
| ☐ N904AW | Boeing 757-2S7 | 23566/96 | ex N604RC | |
| ☐ N905AW | Boeing 757-2S7 | 23567/97 | ex N605RC | |
| ☐ N906AW | Boeing 757-2S7 | 23568/99 | ex N606RC | |
| ☐ N908AW | Boeing 757-2G7/W | 24233/244 | | |
| ☐ N909AW | Boeing 757-2G7/W | 24522/252 | | |
| ☐ N910AW | Boeing 757-2G7/W | 24523/256 | | |
| ☐ N935UW | Boeing 757-2B7/W | 27201/605 | ex N622AU | Star Alliance c/s |
| ☐ N936UW | Boeing 757-2B7/W | 27244/607 | ex N623AU | |
| ☐ N937UW | Boeing 757-2B7/W | 27245/630 | ex N624AU | |
| ☐ N938UW | Boeing 757-2B7/W | 27246/643 | ex N625VJ | |
| ☐ N939UW | Boeing 757-2B7/W | 27303/647 | ex N626AU | |
| ☐ N940UW | Boeing 757-2B7/W | 27805/655 | ex N627AU | |
| ☐ N941UW | Boeing 757-2B7/W | 27806/657 | ex N628AU | |
| ☐ N942UW | Boeing 757-2B7/W | 27807/662 | ex N629AU | |
| ☐ N245AY | Boeing 767-201ER | 23897/173 | ex N645US | |
| ☐ N246AY | Boeing 767-201ER | 23898/175 | ex N646US | |
| ☐ N248AY | Boeing 767-201ER | 23900/190 | ex N648UA | |
| ☐ N249AU | Boeing 767-201ER | 23901/197 | ex N649US | |
| ☐ N250AY | Boeing 767-201ER | 23902/217 | ex N650US | |
| ☐ N251AY | Boeing 767-2B7ER | 24764/306 | ex N651US | |
| ☐ N252AU | Boeing 767-2B7ER | 24765/308 | ex N652US | |
| ☐ N253AY | Boeing 767-2B7ER | 24894/338 | ex N653US | |
| ☐ N255AY | Boeing 767-2B7ER | 25257/383 | ex N655US | |
| ☐ N256AY | Boeing 767-2B7ER | 26847/486 | ex N656US | |
| ☐ N944UW | Embraer ERJ-190AR | 19000058 | ex PT-SIL | Republic♦ |
| ☐ N945UW | Embraer ERJ-190AR | 19000062 | ex PT-SJA | Republic♦ |
| ☐ N946UW | Embraer ERJ-190AR | 19000072 | ex PT-SJL | Republic♦ |
| ☐ N947UW | Embraer ERJ-190AR | 19000078 | ex PT-SJU | Republic♦ |
| ☐ N948UW | Embraer ERJ-190AR | 19000081 | ex PT-SJX | Republic♦ |
| ☐ N949UW | Embraer ERJ-190AR | 19000102 | ex PT-SNW | Republic♦ |
| ☐ N950UW | Embraer ERJ-190AR | 19000106 | ex PT-SQA | Republic♦ |
| ☐ N951UW | Embraer ERJ-190AR | 19000112 | ex PT-SQG | Republic♦ |
| ☐ N952UW | Embraer ERJ-190AR | 19000119 | ex PT-SQN | Republic♦ |
| ☐ N953UW | Embraer ERJ-190AR | 19000133 | ex PT- | Republic♦ |
| ☐ N954UW | Embraer ERJ-190AR | 19000139 | ex PT-SYS | Republic♦ |
| ☐ N955UW | Embraer ERJ-190AR | 19000152 | ex PT-SAH | Republic♦ |
| ☐ N956UW | Embraer ERJ-190AR | 19000156 | ex PT-SAM | Republic♦ |
| ☐ N957UW | Embraer ERJ-190AR | 19000161 | ex PT-SAQ | Republic♦ |
| ☐ N958UW | Embraer ERJ-190AR | 19000164 | ex PT-SAT | Republic♦ |

## US AIRWAYS EXPRESS — Air Express (USX)
### Charlotte, NC,/Philadelphia. PA/Pittsburgh, PA (CLT/PHL/PIT)

| | | | | | |
|---|---|---|---|---|---|
| ☐ N401AW | Canadair CRJ-200LR | 7280 | ex C-FMLQ | 401 | Air Wisconsin |
| ☐ N403AW | Canadair CRJ-200LR | 7288 | ex C-FMLF | 403 | Air Wisconsin |
| ☐ N404AW | Canadair CRJ-200LR | 7294 | ex C-FMMT | 404 | Air Wisconsin |
| ☐ N405AW | Canadair CRJ-200LR | 7362 | ex C-FMND | 405 | Air Wisconsin |
| ☐ N406AW | Canadair CRJ-200LR | 7402 | ex C-FMMY | 406 | Air Wisconsin |
| ☐ N407AW | Canadair CRJ-200LR | 7424 | ex C-FMLU | 407 | Air Wisconsin |
| ☐ N408AW | Canadair CRJ-200LR | 7568 | ex C-FMNY | 408 | Air Wisconsin |
| ☐ N409AW | Canadair CRJ-200LR | 7447 | ex C-FMNX | 409 | Air Wisconsin |
| ☐ N410AW | Canadair CRJ-200LR | 7490 | ex C-FMMW | 410 | Air Wisconsin |
| ☐ N411ZW | Canadair CRJ-200LR | 7569 | ex C-FMNZ | 411 | Air Wisconsin |
| ☐ N412AW | Canadair CRJ-200LR | 7582 | ex C-FMMY | 412 | Air Wisconsin |
| ☐ N413AW | Canadair CRJ-200LR | 7585 | ex C-FMKW | 413 | Air Wisconsin |
| ☐ N414ZW | Canadair CRJ-200LR | 7586 | ex C-FMKZ | 414 | Air Wisconsin |
| ☐ N415AW | Canadair CRJ-200LR | 7593 | ex C-FMLV | 415 | Air Wisconsin |
| ☐ N416AW | Canadair CRJ-200LR | 7603 | ex C-FMNQ | 416 | Air Wisconsin |
| ☐ N417AW | Canadair CRJ-200LR | 7610 | ex C-FMMW | 417 | Air Wisconsin |
| ☐ N418AW | Canadair CRJ-200LR | 7618 | ex C-FMLF | 418 | Air Wisconsin |
| ☐ N419AW | Canadair CRJ-200LR | 7633 | ex C-FMNQ | 419 | Air Wisconsin |
| ☐ N420AW | Canadair CRJ-200LR | 7640 | ex C-FMMW | 420 | Air Wisconsin |
| ☐ N421ZW | Canadair CRJ-200LR | 7346 | ex N587ML | 421 | Air Wisconsin |
| ☐ N422AW | Canadair CRJ-200LR | 7341 | ex N586ML | 422 | Air Wisconsin |
| ☐ N423AW | Canadair CRJ-200LR | 7636 | ex C-FMMB | 423 | Air Wisconsin |
| ☐ N424AW | Canadair CRJ-200LR | 7656 | ex C-FMNW | 424 | Air Wisconsin |
| ☐ N425AW | Canadair CRJ-200LR | 7663 | ex C-FMNQ | 425 | Air Wisconsin |
| ☐ N426AW | Canadair CRJ-200LR | 7669 | ex C-FMMQ | 426 | Air Wisconsin |
| ☐ N427ZW | Canadair CRJ-200LR | 7685 | ex C-FMNH | 427 | Air Wisconsin |
| ☐ N428AW | Canadair CRJ-200LR | 7695 | ex C-FMOI | 428 | Air Wisconsin |
| ☐ N429AW | Canadair CRJ-200LR | 7711 | ex CFMLS | 429 | Air Wisconsin |
| ☐ N430AW | Canadair CRJ-200LR | 7719 | ex C-FMOS | 430 | Air Wisconsin |

| | | | | | | |
|---|---|---|---|---|---|---|
| ☐ | N431AW | Canadair CRJ-200LR | 7256 | ex N575ML | 431 | Air Wisconsin |
| ☐ | N432AW | Canadair CRJ-200LR | 7257 | ex N576ML | 432 | Air Wisconsin |
| ☐ | N433AW | Canadair CRJ-200LR | 7289 | ex N580ML | 433 | Air Wisconsin |
| ☐ | N434AW | Canadair CRJ-200LR | 7322 | ex N582ML | 434 | Air Wisconsin |
| ☐ | N435AW | Canadair CRJ-200LR | 7724 | ex C-FMLU | 435 | Air Wisconsin |
| ☐ | N436AW | Canadair CRJ-200LR | 7734 | ex C-FMKV | 436 | Air Wisconsin |
| ☐ | N437AW | Canadair CRJ-200LR | 7744 | ex C-FMMT | 437 | Air Wisconsin |
| ☐ | N438AW | Canadair CRJ-200LR | 7748 | ex C-GFAX | 438 | Air Wisconsin |
| ☐ | N439AW | Canadair CRJ-200LR | 7753 | ex C-FZZO | 439 | Air Wisconsin |
| ☐ | N440AW | Canadair CRJ-200LR | 7766 | ex C-FMKZ | 440 | Air Wisconsin |
| ☐ | N441ZW | Canadair CRJ-200LR | 7777 | ex C-FMNX | 441 | Air Wisconsin |
| ☐ | N442AW | Canadair CRJ-200LR | 7778 | ex C-FMNY | 442 | Air Wisconsin |
| ☐ | N443AW | Canadair CRJ-200LR | 7781 | ex C-FVAZ | 443 | Air Wisconsin |
| ☐ | N444ZW | Canadair CRJ-200LR | 7788 | ex C-FMMN | 444 | Air Wisconsin |
| ☐ | N445AW | Canadair CRJ-200LR | 7804 | ex C-FMMT | 445 | Air Wisconsin |
| ☐ | N446AW | Canadair CRJ-200LR | 7806 | ex C-FMNW | 446 | Air Wisconsin |
| ☐ | N447AW | Canadair CRJ-200LR | 7812 | ex C-FMND | 447 | Air Wisconsin |
| ☐ | N448AW | Canadair CRJ-200LR | 7814 | ex C-FMLU | 448 | Air Wisconsin |
| ☐ | N449AW | Canadair CRJ-200LR | 7818 | ex C-FMMN | 449 | Air Wisconsin |
| ☐ | N450AW | Canadair CRJ-200LR | 7823 | ex C-FMNB | 450 | Air Wisconsin |
| ☐ | N451AW | Canadair CRJ-200LR | 7832 | ex C-FMLT | 451 | Air Wisconsin |
| ☐ | N452AW | Canadair CRJ-200LR | 7835 | ex C-FMNH | 452 | Air Wisconsin |
| ☐ | N453AW | Canadair CRJ-200LR | 7838 | ex C-FMNY | 453 | Air Wisconsin |
| ☐ | N454AW | Canadair CRJ-200LR | 7842 | ex C-FMND | 454 | Air Wisconsin |
| ☐ | N455AW | Canadair CRJ-200LR | 7848 | ex C-FMMN | 455 | Air Wisconsin |
| ☐ | N456ZW | Canadair CRJ-200LR | 7849 | ex C-FMMQ | 456 | Air Wisconsin |
| ☐ | N457AW | Canadair CRJ-200LR | 7854 | ex C-FMKV | 457 | Air Wisconsin |
| ☐ | N458AW | Canadair CRJ-200LR | 7861 | ex C-FMLS | 458 | Air Wisconsin |
| ☐ | N459AW | Canadair CRJ-200LR | 7863 | ex C-FMLV | 459 | Air Wisconsin |
| ☐ | N460AW | Canadair CRJ-200LR | 7867 | ex C-GZTD | 460 | Air Wisconsin |
| ☐ | N461AW | Canadair CRJ-200LR | 7870 | ex C-FMOW | 461 | Air Wisconsin |
| ☐ | N462AW | Canadair CRJ-200LR | 7875 | ex C-FMOI | 462 | Air Wisconsin |
| ☐ | N463AW | Canadair CRJ-200LR | 7878 | ex C-FMMN | 463 | Air Wisconsin |
| ☐ | N464AW | Canadair CRJ-200LR | 7890 | ex C-FMLQ | 464 | Air Wisconsin |
| ☐ | N465AW | Canadair CRJ-200LR | 7893 | ex C-FMLV | 465 | Air Wisconsin |
| ☐ | N466AW | Canadair CRJ-200LR | 7899 | ex C-FMOS | 466 | Air Wisconsin |
| ☐ | N467AW | Canadair CRJ-200LR | 7900 | ex C-FMOW | 467 | Air Wisconsin |
| ☐ | N468AW | Canadair CRJ-200LR | 7916 | ex C-FMKZ | 468 | Air Wisconsin |
| ☐ | N469AW | Canadair CRJ-200LR | 7917 | ex C-FMLB | 469 | Air Wisconsin |
| ☐ | N470ZW | Canadair CRJ-200LR | 7927 | ex C-FMNX | 470 | Air Wisconsin |
| ☐ | N471ZW | Canadair CRJ-200ER | 7457 | ex N655BR | | Air Wisconsin |
| | | | | | | |
| ☐ | N570ML | Canadair CRJ-200ER | 7206 | ex C-GBNO | YJX | Mesa |
| ☐ | N651ML | Canadair CRJ-200ER | 7139 | ex N787BC | YCD | Mesa |
| ☐ | N7264V | Canadair CRJ-200ER | 7264 | ex C-FMMT | | Mesa [PHX] |
| ☐ | N7291Z | Canadair CRJ-200ER | 7291 | ex C-FMLS | | Mesa |
| ☐ | N7305V | Canadair CRJ-200ER | 7305 | ex C-F | | Mesa |
| ☐ | N17231 | Canadair CRJ-200ER | 7231 | ex C-FMLS | | Mesa |
| ☐ | N17275 | Canadair CRJ-200ER | 7275 | ex C-FMOI | | Mesa |
| ☐ | N17358 | Canadair CRJ-200ER | 7358 | ex C-FMNY | | Mesa |
| ☐ | N27314 | Canadair CRJ-200ER | 7314 | ex C-FMKV | | Mesa |
| ☐ | N37178 | Canadair CRJ-200ER | 7178 | ex C-GAVO | | Mesa |
| ☐ | N75984 | Canadair CRJ-200ER | 7489 | ex C-GZGX | YJW | Mesa |
| ☐ | N77260 | Canadair CRJ-200ER | 7260 | ex C-FMLQ | | Mesa |
| ☐ | N77286 | Canadair CRJ-200ER | 7286 | ex C-FMKZ | | Mesa [TUS] |
| ☐ | N97325 | Canadair CRJ-200ER | 7325 | ex C-FMNH | | Mesa |
| | | | | | | |
| ☐ | N202PS | Canadair CRJ-200ER | 7858 | ex C-FMLF | 202 | PSA Airlines |
| ☐ | N206PS | Canadair CRJ-200ER | 7860 | ex C-FMLQ | 206 | PSA Airlines |
| ☐ | N207PS | Canadair CRJ-200ER | 7873 | ex C-FMNQ | 207 | PSA Airlines |
| ☐ | N209PS | Canadair CRJ-200ER | 7874 | ex C-FMLU | 209 | PSA Airlines |
| ☐ | N213PS | Canadair CRJ-200ER | 7879 | ex C-FMMQ | 213 | PSA Airlines |
| ☐ | N215PS | Canadair CRJ-200ER | 7880 | ex C-FMMW | 215 | PSA Airlines |
| ☐ | N216PS | Canadair CRJ-200ER | 7882 | ex C-FMMY | 216 | PSA Airlines |
| ☐ | N218PS | Canadair CRJ-200ER | 7885 | ex C-FMKW | 218 | PSA Airlines |
| ☐ | N220PS | Canadair CRJ-200ER | 7887 | ex C-FMLB | 220 | PSA Airlines |
| ☐ | N221PS | Canadair CRJ-200ER | 7889 | ex C-FMLI | 221 | PSA Airlines |
| ☐ | N223JS | Canadair CRJ-200ER | 7892 | ex C-FMLT | 223 | PSA Airlines |
| ☐ | N226JS | Canadair CRJ-200ER | 7895 | ex C-FMNH | 226 | PSA Airlines |
| ☐ | N228PS | Canadair CRJ-200ER | 7897 | ex C-FMNX | 228 | PSA Airlines |
| ☐ | N229PS | Canadair CRJ-200ER | 7898 | ex C-FMNY | 229 | PSA Airlines |
| ☐ | N230PS | Canadair CRJ-200ER | 7904 | ex C-FMLU | 230 | PSA Airlines |
| ☐ | N237PS | Canadair CRJ-200ER | 7906 | ex C-FMMB | 237 | PSA Airlines |
| ☐ | N241PS | Canadair CRJ-200ER | 7909 | ex C-FMMQ | 241 | PSA Airlines |
| ☐ | N242JS | Canadair CRJ-200ER | 7911 | ex C-FMMX | 242 | PSA Airlines |
| ☐ | N244PS | Canadair CRJ-200ER | 7912 | ex C-FMMY | 244 | PSA Airlines |
| ☐ | N245PS | Canadair CRJ-200ER | 7919 | ex C-FMLI | 245 | PSA Airlines |
| ☐ | N246PS | Canadair CRJ-200ER | 7920 | ex C-FMLQ | 246 | PSA Airlines |
| ☐ | N247JS | Canadair CRJ-200ER | 7922 | ex C-FMLT | 247 | PSA Airlines |
| ☐ | N248PS | Canadair CRJ-200ER | 7925 | ex C-FMNH | 248 | PSA Airlines |
| ☐ | N249PS | Canadair CRJ-200ER | 7926 | ex C-FMNW | 249 | PSA Airlines |
| ☐ | N250PS | Canadair CRJ-200ER | 7929 | ex C-FMOS | 250 | PSA Airlines |

| | | | | | | |
|---|---|---|---|---|---|---|
| ☐ N251PS | Canadair CRJ-200ER | 7931 | ex C-FVAZ | 251 | | PSA Airlines |
| ☐ N253PS | Canadair CRJ-200ER | 7934 | ex C-FMLU | 253 | | PSA Airlines |
| ☐ N254PS | Canadair CRJ-200ER | 7935 | ex C-FMOI | 254 | | PSA Airlines |
| ☐ N256PS | Canadair CRJ-200ER | 7937 | ex C-FMML | 256 | | PSA Airlines |
| ☐ N257PS | Canadair CRJ-200ER | 7939 | ex C-FMMQ | 257 | | PSA Airlines |
| ☐ N258PS | Canadair CRJ-200ER | 7941 | ex C-FMMX | 258 | | PSA Airlines |
| ☐ N259PS | Canadair CRJ-200ER | 7945 | ex C-FMKW | 259 | | PSA Airlines |
| ☐ N260JS | Canadair CRJ-200ER | 7957 | ex C-FMNX | 260 | | PSA Airlines |
| ☐ N261PS | Canadair CRJ-200ER | 7959 | ex C-FMOS | 261 | | PSA Airlines |
| ☐ N262PS | Canadair CRJ-200ER | 7962 | ex C-FMND | 262 | | PSA Airlines |
| | | | | | | |
| ☐ N468CA | Canadair CRJ-200ER | 7649 | ex C-FMLI | 7649 | | SkyWest♦ |
| ☐ N496CA | Canadair CRJ-200ER | 7791 | ex C-FMMX | 791 | | SkyWest |
| ☐ N506CA | Canadair CRJ-200ER | 7793 | ex C-FMNB | 793 | | SkyWest |
| ☐ N874AS | Canadair CRJ-200ER | 7551 | ex C-GJLK | 874 | | SkyWest<BTA♦ |
| ☐ N885AS | Canadair CRJ-200ER | 7521 | ex C-GJDX | 885 | | SkyWest<BTA♦ |
| ☐ N886AS | Canadair CRJ-200ER | 7531 | ex C-GJJC | 886 | | SkyWest<BTA♦ |
| ☐ N906SW | Canadair CRJ-200ER | 7510 | ex C-FMOW | 7510 | | SkyWest |
| ☐ N907SW | Canadair CRJ-200ER | 7511 | ex C-FVAZ | 7511 | | SkyWest |
| ☐ N944SW | Canadair CRJ-200ER | 7764 | ex C-FMKV | 7764 | | SkyWest |
| | | | | | | |
| ☐ N702PS | Canadair CRJ-701ER | 10135 | ex C- | 702 | | PSA Airlines |
| ☐ N703PS | Canadair CRJ-701ER | 10137 | ex C- | 703 | | PSA Airlines |
| ☐ N705PS | Canadair CRJ-701ER | 10144 | ex C- | 705 | | PSA Airlines |
| ☐ N706PS | Canadair CRJ-701ER | 10150 | ex C-FBLQ | 706 | | PSA Airlines |
| ☐ N708PS | Canadair CRJ-701ER | 10160 | ex C- | 708 | Star Alliance c/s | PSA Airlines |
| ☐ N709PS | Canadair CRJ-701ER | 10165 | ex N165MD | 709 | | PSA Airlines |
| ☐ N710PS | Canadair CRJ-701ER | 10167 | ex N167MD | 710 | | PSA Airlines |
| ☐ N712PS | Canadair CRJ-701ER | 10168 | ex N168MD | 712 | | PSA Airlines |
| ☐ N716PS | Canadair CRJ-701ER | 10171 | ex N171MD | 716 | | PSA Airlines |
| ☐ N718PS | Canadair CRJ-701ER | 10175 | ex C-FCQX | 718 | | PSA Airlines |
| ☐ N719PS | Canadair CRJ-701ER | 10177 | ex N177MD | 719 | | PSA Airlines |
| ☐ N720PS | Canadair CRJ-701ER | 10178 | ex N175MD | 720 | | PSA Airlines |
| ☐ N723PS | Canadair CRJ-701ER | 10181 | ex C-FCRE | 723 | | PSA Airlines |
| ☐ N725PS | Canadair CRJ-701ER | 10186 | ex C- | 725 | | PSA Airlines |
| ☐ N726PS | Canadair CRJ-701ER | | ex C- | 726 | | o/o PSA Airlines |
| ☐ N728PS | Canadair CRJ-701ER | | ex C- | 728 | | o/o PSA Airlines |
| ☐ N729PS | Canadair CRJ-701ER | | ex C- | 729 | | o/o PSA Airlines |
| ☐ N730PS | Canadair CRJ-701ER | | ex C- | 730 | | o/o PSA Airlines |
| ☐ N736PS | Canadair CRJ-701ER | | ex C- | 736 | | o/o PSA Airlines |
| ☐ N740PS | Canadair CRJ-701ER | | ex C- | 740 | | o/o PSA Airlines |
| ☐ N741PS | Canadair CRJ-701ER | | ex C- | 741 | | o/o PSA Airlines |
| ☐ N743PS | Canadair CRJ-701ER | | ex C- | 743 | | o/o PSA Airlines |
| | | | | | | |
| ☐ N902FJ | Canadair CRJ-900ER | 15002 | ex C-GDNH | | | Mesa |
| ☐ N903FJ | Canadair CRJ-900ER | 15003 | ex C-GZQA | | | Mesa |
| ☐ N904FJ | Canadair CRJ-900ER | 15004 | ex C-GZQB | | | Mesa |
| ☐ N905J | Canadair CRJ-900ER | 15005 | ex C-GZQC | | | Mesa |
| ☐ N906FJ | Canadair CRJ-900ER | 15006 | ex C-GZQE | | | Mesa |
| ☐ N907FJ | Canadair CRJ-900ER | 15007 | ex C-GZQF | | | Mesa |
| ☐ N908FJ | Canadair CRJ-900ER | 15008 | ex C-GZQG | | | Mesa |
| ☐ N909FJ | Canadair CRJ-900ER | 15009 | ex C-GZQI | | | Mesa |
| ☐ N910FJ | Canadair CRJ-900ER | 15010 | ex C-GZQJ | | | Mesa |
| ☐ N911FJ | Canadair CRJ-900ER | 15011 | ex C-GZQK | | | Mesa |
| ☐ N912FJ | Canadair CRJ-900ER | 15012 | ex C-GZQL | | | Mesa |
| ☐ N913FJ | Canadair CRJ-900ER | 15013 | ex C-GZQM | | | Mesa |
| ☐ N914FJ | Canadair CRJ-900ER | 15014 | ex C-GZQO | | | Mesa |
| ☐ N915FJ | Canadair CRJ-900ER | 15015 | ex C-GZQP | | | Mesa |
| ☐ N916FJ | Canadair CRJ-900ER | 15016 | ex C-GZQQ | | | Mesa |
| ☐ N917FJ | Canadair CRJ-900ER | 15017 | ex C-GZQR | | | Mesa |
| ☐ N918FJ | Canadair CRJ-900ER | 15018 | ex C- | | | Mesa |
| ☐ N919FJ | Canadair CRJ-900ER | 15019 | ex C- | | | Mesa |
| ☐ N920FJ | Canadair CRJ-900ER | 15020 | ex C- | | | Mesa |
| ☐ N921FJ | Canadair CRJ-900ER | 15021 | ex C- | | | Mesa |
| ☐ N922FJ | Canadair CRJ-900ER | 15022 | ex C- | | | Mesa |
| ☐ N923FJ | Canadair CRJ-900ER | 15023 | ex C- | | | Mesa |
| ☐ N924FJ | Canadair CRJ-900ER | 15024 | ex C- | | | Mesa |
| ☐ N925FJ | Canadair CRJ-900ER | 15025 | ex C- | | | Mesa |
| ☐ N926LR | Canadair CRJ-900ER | 15026 | ex C- | | | Mesa |
| ☐ N927LR | Canadair CRJ-900ER | 15027 | ex C- | | | Mesa |
| ☐ N928LR | Canadair CRJ-900ER | 15028 | ex C- | | | Mesa |
| ☐ N929LR | Canadair CRJ-900ER | 15029 | ex C- | | | Mesa |
| ☐ N930LR | Canadair CRJ-900ER | 15030 | ex C- | | | Mesa |
| ☐ N931LR | Canadair CRJ-900ER | 15031 | ex C- | | | Mesa |
| ☐ N932LR | Canadair CRJ-900ER | 15032 | ex C- | | | Mesa |
| ☐ N933LR | Canadair CRJ-900ER | 15033 | ex C- | | | Mesa |
| ☐ N934FJ | Canadair CRJ-900ER | 15034 | ex C- | | | Mesa |
| ☐ N935LR | Canadair CRJ-900ER | 15035 | ex C- | | | Mesa |
| ☐ N938LR | Canadair CRJ-900ER | 15038 | ex C- | | | Mesa |
| ☐ N939LR | Canadair CRJ-900ER | 15039 | ex C- | | | Mesa |
| ☐ N942LR | Canadair CRJ-900ER | 15042 | ex C- | | | Mesa |
| ☐ N956LR | Canadair CRJ-900ER | 15056 | ex C- | | | Mesa |

| | | | | | | |
|---|---|---|---|---|---|---|
| ☐ | N804EX | de Havilland DHC-8-102A | 227 | ex C-GFYI | ESA | Piedmont |
| ☐ | N805EX | de Havilland DHC-8-102A | 228 | ex C-GLOT | ESB | Piedmont |
| ☐ | N806EX | de Havilland DHC-8-102A | 263 | ex C-GEVP | ESC | Piedmont |
| ☐ | N807EX | de Havilland DHC-8-102A | 292 | ex C-GFQL | ESD | Piedmont |
| ☐ | N808EX | de Havilland DHC-8-102A | 299 | ex C-GDKL | ESE | Piedmont |
| ☐ | N809EX | de Havilland DHC-8-102A | 302 | ex PT-MFI | ESF | Piedmont |
| ☐ | N810EX | de Havilland DHC-8-102A | 308 | ex C-GDKL | ESG | Piedmont |
| ☐ | N812EX | de Havilland DHC-8-102A | 312 | ex C-GDNG | ESH | Piedmont |
| ☐ | N814EX | de Havilland DHC-8-102A | 318 | ex C-GDNG | ESI | Piedmont |
| ☐ | N815EX | de Havilland DHC-8-102A | 321 | ex C-GDFT | ESJ | Piedmont |
| ☐ | N816EX | de Havilland DHC-8-102A | 329 | ex C-GEVP | ESK | Piedmont |
| ☐ | N837EX | de Havilland DHC-8-102A | 217 | ex N976HA | ERH | Piedmont |
| ☐ | N838EX | de Havilland DHC-8-102A | 220 | ex N977HA | ERK | Piedmont |
| ☐ | N839EX | de Havilland DHC-8-102 | 226 | ex N803EX | ERL | Piedmont |
| ☐ | N906HA | de Havilland DHC-8-102 | 009 | ex C-GHRI | HAS | Piedmont |
| ☐ | N907HA | de Havilland DHC-8-102 | 011 | ex C-GESR | HSB | Piedmont |
| ☐ | N908HA | de Havilland DHC-8-102 | 015 | ex C-GIBQ | HSC | Piedmont |
| ☐ | N911HA | de Havilland DHC-8-102 | 034 | ex C-GEOA | HSF | Piedmont |
| ☐ | N912HA | de Havilland DHC-8-102 | 040 | ex C-GEOA | HSG | Piedmont |
| ☐ | N914HA | de Havilland DHC-8-102 | 053 | ex C-GETI | HSH | Piedmont |
| ☐ | N930HA | de Havilland DHC-8-102 | 126 | ex C-GFQL | HSW | Piedmont |
| ☐ | N931HA | de Havilland DHC-8-102 | 132 | ex C-GFOD | HSZ | Piedmont |
| ☐ | N933HA | de Havilland DHC-8-102 | 134 | ex C-GFUM | HBA | Piedmont |
| ☐ | N934HA | de Havilland DHC-8-102 | 139 | ex C-GETI | HBB | Piedmont |
| ☐ | N935HA | de Havilland DHC-8-102 | 142 | ex C-GLOT | HBC | Piedmont |
| ☐ | N936HA | de Havilland DHC-8-102 | 145 | ex C-GFQL | HRA | Piedmont |
| ☐ | N937HA | de Havilland DHC-8-102 | 148 | ex C-GLOT | HRB | Piedmont |
| ☐ | N938HA | de Havilland DHC-8-102 | 152 | ex C-GFUM | HRC | Piedmont |
| ☐ | N940HA | de Havilland DHC-8-102 | 156 | ex C-GLOT | HRE | Piedmont |
| ☐ | N941HA | de Havilland DHC-8-102 | 161 | ex C-GETI | HRF | Piedmont |
| ☐ | N942HA | de Havilland DHC-8-102 | 163 | ex C-GFUM | HRG | Piedmont |
| ☐ | N943HA | de Havilland DHC-8-102 | 167 | ex C-GFOD | HRH | Piedmont |
| ☐ | N975HA | de Havilland DHC-8-102 | 176 | | HRI | Piedmont |
| ☐ | N434YV | de Havilland DHC-8-202B | 434 | ex C- | MDI | Mesa |
| ☐ | N436YV | de Havilland DHC-8-202B | 436 | ex C-GDNG | MDJ | Mesa wfs |
| ☐ | N987HA | de Havilland DHC-8-201 | 425 | ex C-GFHZ | | Mesa |
| ☐ | N988HA | de Havilland DHC-8-201 | 426 | ex C-FDHD | | Mesa |
| ☐ | N989HA | de Havilland DHC-8-201 | 427 | ex C-GFEN | | Mesa |
| ☐ | N991HA | de Havilland DHC-8-201 | 431 | ex C-GLOT | | Mesa |
| ☐ | N326EN | de Havilland DHC-8-311 | 234 | ex N386DC | HDF | Piedmont |
| ☐ | N327EN | de Havilland DHC-8-311A | 261 | ex N379DC | HDD | Piedmont |
| ☐ | N328EN | de Havilland DHC-8-311A | 281 | ex N380DC | HDC | Piedmont |
| ☐ | N329EN | de Havilland DHC-8-311 | 290 | ex SU-UAD | HDG | Piedmont |
| ☐ | N330EN | de Havilland DHC-8-311A | 274 | ex N805SA | HDI | Piedmont |
| ☐ | N331EN | de Havilland DHC-8-311A | 279 | ex N806SA | HDJ | Piedmont |
| ☐ | N333EN | de Havilland DHC-8-311 | 221 | ex N803SA | HDK | Piedmont |
| ☐ | N335EN | de Havilland DHC-8-311 | 375 | ex N804SA | HDN | Piedmont |
| ☐ | N336EN | de Havilland DHC-8-311A | 336 | ex N284BC | HAD | Piedmont |
| ☐ | N337EN | de Havilland DHC-8-311A | 284 | ex SU-UAE | HDH | Piedmont |
| ☐ | N343EN | de Havilland DHC-8-311A | 340 | ex OE-LLZ | HDE | Piedmont |
| ☐ | N257JQ | Embraer ERJ-145LR | 14500812 | ex PT-SNO | JBJ | Chautauqua |
| ☐ | N258JQ | Embraer ERJ-145LR | 145768 | ex PT-SJZ | JBI | Chautauqua |
| ☐ | N259JQ | Embraer ERJ-145LR | 145763 | ex PT-SJU | JBH | Chautauqua |
| ☐ | N280SK | Embraer ERJ-145LR | 145381 | ex PT-SQF | JRM | Chautauqua |
| ☐ | N291SK | Embraer ERJ-145LR | 145486 | ex PT-SXF | JRX | Chautauqua |
| ☐ | N293SK | Embraer ERJ-145LR | 145500 | ex PT-SXT | JRY | Chautauqua |
| ☐ | N298SK | Embraer ERJ-145LR | 145508 | ex PT-SYA | JRZ | Chautauqua |
| ☐ | N370SK | Embraer ERJ-145LR | 145515 | ex PT-SYH | JBA | Chautauqua |
| ☐ | N977RP | Embraer ERJ-145MP | 145185 | ex SE-DZD | JBH | Chautauqua<SKX |
| ☐ | N839MJ | Embraer ERJ-145LR | 145416 | ex PT-STM | YRO | Mesa |
| ☐ | N840MJ | Embraer ERJ-145LR | 145429 | ex PT-SUA | YRP | Mesa |
| ☐ | N841MJ | Embraer ERJ-145LR | 145448 | ex PT | | Mesa wfs |
| ☐ | N801HK | Embraer ERJ-145ER | 145053 | ex PT-SZS | TRK | Trans State |
| ☐ | N803HK | Embraer ERJ-145ER | 145077 | ex PT-S | TRM | Trans State |
| ☐ | N804HK | Embraer ERJ-145ER | 145082 | ex PT-S | TRA | Trans State |
| ☐ | N805HK | Embraer ERJ-145ER | 145096 | ex PT-SBS | TRB | Trans State |
| ☐ | N808HK | Embraer ERJ-145ER | 145157 | ex PT-SEK | TRD | Trans State |
| ☐ | N809HK | Embraer ERJ-145ER | 145187 | ex PT-SGH | TRE | Trans State |
| ☐ | N812HK | Embraer ERJ-145ER | 145373 | ex PT-SOY | TRG | Trans State |
| ☐ | N801MA | Embraer ERJ-170SU | 17000012 | ex PT-SKE | 801 | Republic |
| ☐ | N802MD | Embraer ERJ-170SU | 17000013 | ex PT-SKF | 802 | Republic |
| ☐ | N803MD | Embraer ERJ-170SU | 17000015 | ex PT-SKI | 803 | Republic |
| ☐ | N805MD | Embraer ERJ-170SU | 17000018 | ex PT-SKL | 805 | Republic |
| ☐ | N806MD | Embraer ERJ-170SU | 17000019 | ex PT-SKM | 806 | Republic |
| ☐ | N807MD | Embraer ERJ-170SU | 17000020 | ex PT-SKN | 807 | Republic |
| ☐ | N808MD | Embraer ERJ-170SU | 17000021 | ex PT-SKO | 808 | Republic |

| | | | | | | |
|---|---|---|---|---|---|---|
| ☐ N809MD | Embraer ERJ-170SU | 17000022 | ex PT-SKP | 809 | | Republic |
| ☐ N811MD | Embraer ERJ-170SU | 17000028 | ex PT-SKV | 811 | | Republic |
| ☐ N812MD | Embraer ERJ-170SU | 17000030 | ex PT-SKY | 812 | | Republic |
| ☐ N813MA | Embraer ERJ-170SU | 17000031 | ex PT- | 813 | | Republic |
| ☐ N814MD | Embraer ERJ-170SU | 17000033 | ex PT-SUB | 814 | | Republic |
| ☐ N816MA | Embraer ERJ-170SU | 17000037 | ex PT-SUG | 816 | | Republic |
| ☐ N817MD | Embraer ERJ-170SU | 17000038 | ex PT-SUH | 817 | | Republic |
| ☐ N818MD | Embraer ERJ-170SU | 17000039 | ex PT- | 818 | | Republic |
| ☐ N819MD | Embraer ERJ-170SU | 17000040 | ex PT-SUJ | 819 | | Republic |
| ☐ N820MD | Embraer ERJ-170SU | 17000041 | ex PT-SUK | 820 | | Republic |
| ☐ N821MD | Embraer ERJ-170SU | 17000042 | ex PT- | 821 | | Republic |
| ☐ N822MD | Embraer ERJ-170SU | 17000043 | ex PT-SUM | 822 | | Republic |
| ☐ N826MD | Embraer ERJ-170SU | 17000046 | ex PT- | 826 | | Republic |
| ☐ N827MD | Embraer ERJ-170SU | 17000047 | ex PT-SUQ | 827 | | Republic |
| ☐ N828MD | Embraer ERJ-170SU | 17000048 | ex PT-SUR | 828 | | Republic |
| ☐ N829MD | Embraer ERJ-170SU | 17000049 | ex PT-SUT | 829 | | Republic |
| ☐ N873RW | Embraer ERJ-170SU | 17000144 | ex PT- | 703 | | Republic |
| ☐ N874RW | Embraer ERJ-170SU | 17000148 | ex PT- | 704 | | Republic |
| | | | | | | |
| ☐ N101HQ | Embraer ERJ-175LR | 17000156 | ex PT-SEU | | | Republic |
| ☐ N102HQ | Embraer ERJ-175LR | 17000157 | ex PT-SEV | | | Republic |
| ☐ N103HQ | Embraer ERJ-175LR | 17000159 | ex PT-SEX | | | Republic |
| ☐ N104HQ | Embraer ERJ-175LR | 17000160 | ex PT-SMA | | | Republic |
| ☐ N105HQ | Embraer ERJ-175LR | 17000163 | ex PT-SMF | | | Republic |
| ☐ N106HQ | Embraer ERJ-175LR | 17000164 | ex PT-SMG | | | Republic |
| ☐ N107HQ | Embraer ERJ-175LR | 17000165 | ex PT-SMH | | | Republic |
| ☐ N108HQ | Embraer ERJ-175LR | 17000166 | ex PT-SMI | | | Republic |
| ☐ N109HQ | Embraer ERJ-175LR | 17000168 | ex PT-SMK | | | Republic |
| ☐ N110HQ | Embraer ERJ-175LR | 17000172 | ex PT-SMP | | | Republic |
| ☐ N111HQ | Embraer ERJ-175LR | 17000173 | ex PT-SMQ | | | Republic |
| ☐ N112HQ | Embraer ERJ-175LR | 17000174 | ex PT-SMR | | | Republic |
| ☐ N113HQ | Embraer ERJ-175LR | 17000177 | ex PT-SMU | | | Republic |
| ☐ N114HQ | Embraer ERJ-175LR | 17000179 | ex PT-SMW | | | Republic |
| ☐ N115HQ | Embraer ERJ-175LR | 17000182 | ex PT-SMZ | | | Republic |
| ☐ N116HQ | Embraer ERJ-175LR | 17000183 | ex PT-SUA | | | Republic |
| ☐ N117HQ | Embraer ERJ-175LR | 17000184 | ex PT-SUB | | | Republic |
| ☐ N118HQ | Embraer ERJ-175LR | 17000189 | ex PT-SUI | | | Republic |
| ☐ N119HQ | Embraer ERJ-175LR | 17000190 | ex PT-SUQ | | | Republic |
| ☐ N120HQ | Embraer ERJ-175LR | 17000193 | ex PT-SUV | | | Republic |
| ☐ N121HQ | Embraer ERJ-175LR | 17000194 | ex PT-SUY | | | Republic |
| ☐ N122HQ | Embraer ERJ-175LR | 17000196 | ex PT-SXF | | | Republic |
| ☐ N123HQ | Embraer ERJ-175LR | 17000199 | ex PT-SXM | | | Republic |
| ☐ N124HQ | Embraer ERJ-175LR | 17000200 | ex PT-SXO | | | Republic |
| ☐ N125HQ | Embraer ERJ-175LR | 17000202 | ex PT-SXR | | | Republic |
| ☐ N126HQ | Embraer ERJ-175LR | 17000204 | ex PT-SXU | | | Republic |
| ☐ N127HQ | Embraer ERJ-175LR | 17000206 | ex PT-SCB | | | Republic |
| ☐ N128HQ | Embraer ERJ-175LR | 17000208 | ex PT-SCF | | | Republic |
| ☐ N129HQ | Embraer ERJ-175LR | 17000211 | ex PT-SCI | | | Republic |
| ☐ N130HQ | Embraer ERJ-175LR | 17000212 | ex PT-SCJ | | | Republic |
| ☐ N131HQ | Embraer ERJ-175LR | 17000215 | ex PT-SCM | | | Republic |
| ☐ N132HQ | Embraer ERJ-175LR | 17000216 | ex PT-SCN | | | Republic |
| ☐ N133HQ | Embraer ERJ-175LR | 17000217 | ex PT-SCO | | | Republic |
| ☐ N134HQ | Embraer ERJ-175LR | 17000220 | ex PT-SCS | | | Republic |
| ☐ N135HQ | Embraer ERJ-175LR | 17000224 | ex PT-SFA | | | Republic |
| ☐ N136HQ | Embraer ERJ-170LR | 17000228 | ex PT-SFE | | | Republic |
| ☐ N137HQ | Embraer ERJ-170LR | 17000231 | ex PT-SFH | | | Republic |
| ☐ N138HQ | Embraer ERJ-170LR | 17000234 | ex PT-SFK | | | Republic |
| | | | | | | |
| ☐ N9CJ | SAAB SF.340B | 340B-224 | ex N224TH | LVE | | Colgan Air |
| ☐ N203CJ | SAAB SF.340B | 340B-203 | ex N306CE | LNI | | Colgan Air |
| ☐ N249CJ | SAAB SF.340B | 340B-249 | ex N361PX | | | Colgan Air |
| ☐ N321CJ | SAAB SF.340B | 340B-321 | ex XA-TQX | LVH | | Colgan Air |
| ☐ N338CJ | SAAB SF.340B | 340B-338 | ex N338SB | LNG | | Colgan Air |
| ☐ N339CJ | SAAB SF.340B | 340B-339 | ex N339SB | LNA | | Colgan Air |
| ☐ N341CJ | SAAB SF.340B | 340B-341 | ex N341SB | LND | | Colgan Air |
| ☐ N344CJ | SAAB SF.340B | 340B-344 | ex N344SB | LNF | | Colgan Air |
| ☐ N346CJ | SAAB SF.340B | 340B-346 | ex N346SB | LNB | | Colgan Air |
| ☐ N347CJ | SAAB SF.340B | 340B-347 | ex N347SB | LNH | | Colgan Air |
| ☐ N350CJ | SAAB SF.340B | 340B-350 | ex N350CF | LNE | | Colgan Air |
| ☐ N362PX | SAAB SF.340B | 340B-258 | ex SE-G58 | | | ColganAir |
| ☐ N420XJ | SAAB SF.340B | 340B-420 | ex SE-B20 | | | Colgan Air |
| | | | | | | |
| ☐ N402XJ | SAAB SF.340B | 340B-402 | | XJE | | Mesaba |
| ☐ N407XJ | SAAB SF.340B | 340B-407 | | XJC | | Mesaba |
| ☐ N412XJ | SAAB SF.340B | 340B-412 | | XJG | | Mesaga |
| ☐ N413XJ | SAAB SF.340B | 340B-413 | | XJD | | Mesaba |
| ☐ N414XJ | SAAB SF.340B | 340B-414 | | XJF | | Mesaba |
| ☐ N416XJ | SAAB SF.340B | 340B-416 | | XJB | | Mesaba |
| ☐ N418XJ | SAAB SF.340B | 340B-418 | | XJA | | Mesaba |
| | | | | | | |
| ☐ N144ZV | Beech 1900D | UE-144 | | | | Florida Gulf |
| ☐ N191CJ | Beech 1900D | UE-19 | ex N83005 | LVW | | Colgan Air |

## USDA FOREST SERVICE

Boise, ID (BOI)

| | | | | | | |
|---|---|---|---|---|---|---|
| ☐ | N109FC | Piper PA-31-350 Chieftain | 31-8012073 | | | |
| ☐ | N109Z | Bell UH-1 | 20854 | | | ◆ |
| ☐ | N344WN | Bell UH-1H | | ex 69-16422 | | |
| ☐ | N345WN | Bell UH-1H | | ex 71-20329 | | |
| ☐ | N346WN | Bell UH-1H | | ex 72-21629 | | ◆ |
| ☐ | N347WN | Bell UH-1H | | ex 70-15708 | | ◆ |
| ☐ | N431LH | Bell UH-1H | | ex 73-22066 | | ◆ |
| | | | | ex N1-20257 | | ◆ |
| | | | | | | |
| ☐ | N106Z | Bell 206B JetRanger | 508 | ex N950NS | | |
| ☐ | N111Z | Cessna TU206F Stationair | U20602919 | | | |
| ☐ | N115Z | Basler Turbo-67 (DC-3TP) | 16819/33567 | ex N146Z | | |
| ☐ | N126Z | Cessna TU206F Stationair | U20602367 | ex N2399U | | |
| ☐ | N127Z | Beech A100 King Air | B-179 | ex N20EG | | |
| ☐ | N136Z | Cessna TU206G Stationair 6 | U20606923 | ex N9659R | | |
| ☐ | N141Z | de Havilland DHC-6 Twin Otter 300 | 803 | ex C-GDNG | | |
| ☐ | N142Z | Basler Turbo-67 (DC-3TP) | 20494 | ex N100Z | | |
| ☐ | N143Z | de Havilland DHC-6 Twin Otter 300 | 437 | ex N300LJ | | |
| ☐ | N144Z | Cessna 550 Citation Bravo | 550-0926 | ex N100Z | | |
| ☐ | N147Z | Aero Commander 500B | 1432-152 | | | |
| ☐ | N148Y | Beech 65-B90 King Air | LJ-472 | ex N148Z | | |
| ☐ | N149Z | Beech B200C Super King Air | BL-124 | ex N107Z | | |
| ☐ | N173Z | Short SD.3-30 | SH3116 | ex 84-0469 | | |
| ☐ | N175Z | Short SD.3-30 | SH3115 | ex 84-0468 | | |
| ☐ | N178Z | Short SD.3-30 | SH3119 | ex 84-0472 | | |
| ☐ | N179Z | Short SD.3-30 | SH3109 | ex 84-0462 | | |
| ☐ | N181Z | Beech 65-E90 King Air | LW-52 | ex N74171 | | |
| ☐ | N182Z | Beech 200 Super King Air | BB-402 | ex N318W | | |
| ☐ | N191Z | de Havilland DHC-2 Beaver | 1006 | | | |
| ☐ | N192Z | de Havilland DHC-2 Beaver | 1347 | | | |
| ☐ | N193Z | de Havilland DHC-2 Beaver | 1162 | ex N197Z | | |

## US HELICOPTERS

Wingate-US Heliport, NC

| | | | | | |
|---|---|---|---|---|---|
| ☐ | N23ME | Aérospatiale AS350B2 AStar | 3430 | | ◆ |
| ☐ | N36TV | Aérospatiale AS350B AStar | 1858 | ex N69TL | |
| ☐ | N119TV | Aérospatiale AS350B AStar | 2122 | ex N477HD | |
| ☐ | N129TV | Aérospatiale AS350BA AStar | 2897 | | |
| ☐ | N215TV | Aérospatiale AS350B2 AStar | 3167 | | |
| ☐ | N355TV | Aérospatiale AS350B AStar | 2647 | ex TG-JBG | |
| ☐ | N357TV | Aérospatiale AS350B AStar | 2376 | ex N795WC | |
| ☐ | N915HD | Aérospatiale AS350B2 AStar | 3583 | ex N311SJ | |
| | | | | | |
| ☐ | N73DP | Bell 206B JetRanger II | 2513 | | |
| ☐ | N79TV | Bell 206L-1 LongRanger III | 45718 | ex N84PC | |
| ☐ | N212TV | Bell 206B JetRanger II | 2048 | ex N97CW | |
| ☐ | N316TV | Bell 206B JetRanger III | 2704 | ex N188TV | |

## USA 3000 AIRLINES

Getaway (U5/GWY)

Philadelphia-Intl, PA (PHL)

| | | | | | | |
|---|---|---|---|---|---|---|
| ☐ | N262AV | Airbus A320-214 | 1725 | ex F-WWBP | Miss Doreen | [RME] |
| ☐ | N263AV | Airbus A320-214 | 1860 | ex D-AXLB | Chicago | [RME] |
| ☐ | N264AV | Airbus A320-214 | 1867 | ex F-WWIL | Bermuda | [SJO] |

## USA JET AIRLINES

Jet USA (JUS)

Detroit-Willow Run, MI (YIP)

| | | | | | |
|---|---|---|---|---|---|
| ☐ | N191US | Douglas DC-9-15 | 45718/17 | ex N300ME | VIP |
| ☐ | N192US | Douglas DC-9-15RC | 47156/228 | ex N9357 | VIP |
| ☐ | N194US | Douglas DC-9-15RC (ABS 3) | 47016/173 | ex N9349 | [YIP] |
| ☐ | N195US | Douglas DC-9-15RC (ABS 3) | 47017/186 | ex N9352 | VIP |
| ☐ | N196US | Douglas DC-9-15RC | 47155/216 | ex N9355 | |
| | | | | | |
| ☐ | N205US | Douglas DC-9-32CF | 47690/843 | ex N724HB | |
| ☐ | N208US | Douglas DC-9-32F (ABS 3) | 47220/296 | ex N935F | |
| ☐ | N215US | Douglas DC-9-32 (ABS 3) | 47480/607 | ex N986US | |
| ☐ | N231US | Douglas DC-9-32 (ABS 3) | 48114/919 | ex XA-TXG | |
| ☐ | N327US | Douglas DC-9-33F (ABS 3) | 47414/536 | ex N940F | |
| ☐ | N934US | Douglas DC-9-34 | 48124/954 | ex N928L | |
| | | | | | |
| ☐ | N822AA | AMD Falcon 20D | 195 | ex N195MP | |
| ☐ | N826AA | AMD Falcon 20C | 67 | ex N821AA | |
| ☐ | N827AA | AMD Falcon 20E | 298 | ex OE-GNN | |
| ☐ | N829AA | LearJet 25B | 25B-100 | ex N25TK | |
| ☐ | N831US | McDonnell-Douglas MD-83 | 49791/1644 | ex N791MD | |
| ☐ | N948AS | McDonnell-Douglas MD-83 | 53021/1801 | | [VCV] |
| ☐ | N949NS | McDonnell-Douglas MD-83 | 53022/1809 | ex N949AS | |

## VEE NEAL AVIATION

| | | | | |
|---|---|---|---|---|
| ☐ N646VN | British Aerospace Jetstream 31 | 646 | ex N646SA | ♦ |
| ☐ N651VN | British Aerospace Jetstream 31 | 651 | ex ZK-JSX | ♦ |
| ☐ N752VN | British Aerospace Jetstream 31 | 752 | ex N120HR | ♦ |

## VENT AIRLINES

| | | | | |
|---|---|---|---|---|
| ☐ N575EG | Swearingen SA.227AC Metro III | AC-575 | ex N378PH | ♦ |

## VIEQUES AIR LINK     Vieques (V4/VES)     Vieques, PR (VQS)

| | | | | | |
|---|---|---|---|---|---|
| ☐ N663VL | Britten-Norman BN-2B-26 Islander | 2110 | ex N663J | | |
| ☐ N861VL | Britten-Norman BN-2B-26 Islander | 2155 | ex N861JA | | |
| ☐ N902VL | Britten-Norman BN-2A-20 Islander | 685 | ex N148ES | | |
| ☐ N903VL | Britten-Norman BN-2A-26 Islander | 2019 | ex N2159X | | |
| ☐ N904VL | Britten-Norman BN-2A-26 Islander | 3014 | ex HK-3813 | no titles | |
| ☐ N907VL | Britten-Norman BN-2A-9 Islander | 343 | ex N723JM | | |
| ☐ N908VL | Britten-Norman BN-2B-26 Islander | 2187 | ex N728JM | | ♦ |
| | | | | | |
| ☐ N335VL | Cessna 208B Caravan I | 208B0964 | ex N5260Y | | |
| ☐ N741VL | Cessna 208B Caravan I | 208B1091 | ex N1272N | | |
| ☐ N742VL | Cessna 208B Caravan I | 208B1100 | ex N12727 | | |
| ☐ N905VL | Britten-Norman BN-2A Mk.III-2 Trislander | 1048 | ex N905GD | | |
| ☐ N906VL | Britten-Norman BN-2A Mk.III-2 Trislander | 1060 | ex N906GD | | |

## VINTAGE PROPS AND JETS     (VQ)     New Smyrna Beach-Municipal, FL

| | | | | |
|---|---|---|---|---|
| ☐ N211VP | Beech 100 King Air | B-2 | ex N11JJ | |
| ☐ N431R | Beech 100 King Air | B-71 | ex N431CH | |
| ☐ N577D | Beech 100 King Air | B-22 | ex N577L | |
| ☐ N5727 | Beech 100 King Air | B-48 | ex N572 | |

## VIRGIN AMERICA     (VX/VRD)     San Francisco, CA (SFO)

| | | | | | |
|---|---|---|---|---|---|
| ☐ N521VA | Airbus A319-112 | 2773 | ex D-AVWZ | let there be flight | |
| ☐ N522VA | Airbus A319-112 | 2811 | ex D-AVYP | | |
| ☐ N523VA | Airbus A319-112 | 3181 | ex D-AVYB | | |
| ☐ N524VA | Airbus A319-112 | 3204 | ex D-AVWK | dark horse | |
| ☐ N525VA | Airbus A319-112 | 3324 | ex D-AVYG | | |
| ☐ N526VA | Airbus A319-112 | 3347 | ex D-AVYW | | |
| ☐ N527VA | Airbus A319-112 | 3417 | ex D-AVYK | tubular belle | |
| ☐ N528VA | Airbus A319-112 | 3445 | ex D-AVYR | fog cutter | |
| ☐ N529VA | Airbus A319-112 | 3684 | ex D-AVWB | moodlights, camera, action | |
| ☐ N530VA | Airbus A319-112 | 3686 | ex D-AVWD | gogo dancer | |
| | | | | | |
| ☐ N621VA | Airbus A320-214 | 2616 | ex F-WWDJ | air colbert | |
| ☐ N622VA | Airbus A320-214 | 2674 | ex F-WWID | California Dreaming | |
| ☐ N623VA | Airbus A320-214 | 2740 | ex PR-MHH | three if by air | |
| ☐ N624VA | Airbus A320-214 | 2778 | ex F-WWDX | red, white & blue | |
| ☐ N625VA | Airbus A320-214 | 2800 | ex F-WWIJ | Jefferson Airplane | |
| ☐ N626VA | Airbus A320-214 | 2830 | ex F-WWDO | unicorn chaser | |
| ☐ N627VA | Airbus A320-214 | 2851 | ex F-WWIQ | | |
| ☐ N628VA | Airbus A320-214 | 2993 | ex F-WWIT | | |
| ☐ N629VA | Airbus A320-214 | 3037 | ex PR-MHL | Midnight Ride | |
| ☐ N630VA | Airbus A320-214 | 3101 | ex F-WWIG | superfly | |
| ☐ N631VA | Airbus A320-214 | 3135 | ex F-WWDL | chic mobile | |
| ☐ N632VA | Airbus A320-214 | 3155 | ex F-WWDH | youtube air | |
| ☐ N633VA | Airbus A320-214 | 3230 | ex F-WWBE | the tim clark express | |
| ☐ N634VA | Airbus A320-214 | 3359 | ex F-WWII | mach daddy | |
| ☐ N635VA | Airbus A320-214 | 3398 | ex F-WWBS | my other ride's a spaceship | |
| ☐ N636VA | Airbus A320-214 | 3460 | ex F-WWBJ | | |
| ☐ N637VA | Airbus A320-214 | 3465 | ex F-WWBN | an airplane named desire | |
| ☐ N638VA | Airbus A320-214 | 3503 | ex D-AVVB | san francisco pride | |
| ☐ N639VA | Airbus A320-214 | 3016 | ex 9K-CAE | | |
| ☐ N640VA | Airbus A320-214 | 3349 | ex 9K-CAF | | |
| ☐ N641VA | Airbus A320-214 | 3656 | ex 9K-CAG | | |
| ☐ N642VA | Airbus A320-214 | 3670 | ex 9K-CAH | | |
| ☐ N835VA | Airbus A320-214 | 4448 | ex D-AVVZ | | |
| ☐ N836VA | Airbus A320-214 | 4480 | ex D-AUBD | | |
| ☐ N837VA | Airbus A320-214 | 4558 | ex D-AUBT | | |
| ☐ N838VA | Airbus A320-214 | 4559 | ex F-WWDY | | |
| ☐ N839VA | Airbus A320-214 | 4610 | ex F-WWIY | | |
| ☐ N840VA | Airbus A320-214 | 4616 | ex F-WWBI | bytheway | |
| ☐ N841VA | Airbus A320-214 | 4655 | ex F-WWDS | #nerdbird | ♦ |
| ☐ N842VA | Airbus A320-214 | 4805 | ex F-WWBK | Real Steel | ♦ |
| ☐ N843VA | Airbus A320-214 | 4814 | ex F-WWDR | VAmanos! | ♦ |
| ☐ N844VA | Airbus A320-214 | 4851 | ex F-WWBB | sol plane | ♦ |
| ☐ N845VA | Airbus A320-214 | 4867 | ex F-WWDM | stay hungry, stay foolish | ♦ |
| ☐ N846VA | Airbus A320-214 | 4894 | ex F-WWIU | glitter girl | ♦ |

| | | | | | |
|---|---|---|---|---|---|
| ☐ N847VA | Airbus A320-214 | 4948 | ex F-WWDH | Scarlett O'Air | ♦ |
| ☐ N848VA | Airbus A320-214 | 4959 | ex F-WWDJ | bellapierre | ♦ |
| ☐ N849VA | Airbus A320-214 | 4991 | ex F-WWBB | fly bye baby | ♦ |
| ☐ N851VA | Airbus A320-214 | 4999 | ex F-WWBR | | ♦ |
| ☐ N852VA | Airbus A320-214 | 5004 | ex F-WWDL | | ♦ |
| ☐ N853VA | Airbus A320-214 | 5034 | ex F-WWIP | | ♦ |
| ☐ N854VA | Airbus A320-214 | 5058 | ex F-WWBG | | ♦ |

## VISIONAIR  (V2/RBY)  Las Vegas North, NV (VGT)

| | | | | |
|---|---|---|---|---|
| ☐ N402VA | Dornier 228-202K | 8085 | ex G-BWEX | |
| ☐ N403VA | Dornier 228-202 | 8171 | ex 9M-BAS | |
| ☐ N404VA | Dornier 228-203F | 8120 | ex N279MC | |
| ☐ N405VA | Dornier 228-203F | 8144 | ex N264MC | |
| ☐ N409VA | Dornier 228-202 | 8097 | ex N228ME | |
| | | | | |
| ☐ N328MX | Dornier 328-120 | 3071 | ex D-CDXX | ♦ |
| ☐ N329MX | Dornier 328-100 | 3049 | ex D-CAOS | |
| ☐ N330MX | Dornier 328-120 | 3067 | ex D-CDXN | |
| ☐ N331MX | Dornier 328-110 | 3074 | ex D-CDXA | |
| ☐ N906HB | Dornier 328-310 (328JET) | 3179 | ex N421FJ | |
| | | | | |
| ☐ N732VA | Boeing 737-3T0 | 23366/1174 | ex N34315 | |
| ☐ N742VA | Boeing 737-448 | 24773/1850 | ex TC-MNH | |
| ☐ N743VA | Boeing 737-4B6 | 25262/2088 | ex N252MQ | |
| ☐ N745VA | Boeing 737-405 | 24271/1738 | ex N427BV | |
| ☐ N766VA | Boeing 767-2Q8ER | 24448/272 | ex EI-DMP | ♦ |
| ☐ N767VA | Boeing 767-222ER | 21870/13 | ex N609UA | ♦ |
| ☐ N768VA | Boeing 767-222ER | 21869/11 | ex N608UA | ♦ |
| ☐ N769VA | Boeing 767-222ER | 21866/7 | ex N605UA | ♦ |

## WARBELOW'S AIR  Ventaire (4W/WAV)  Fairbanks-Intl, AK (FAI)

| | | | |
|---|---|---|---|
| ☐ N300ED | Piper PA-31-350 Chieftain | 31-7852008 | ex N27457 |
| ☐ N3527U | Piper PA-31-350 Chieftain | 31-7952141 | |
| ☐ N4082T | Piper PA-31-350 Chieftain | 31-8152089 | |
| ☐ N59764 | Piper PA-31-350 Navajo Chieftain | 31-7652037 | |
| ☐ N59829 | Piper PA-31-350 Navajo Chieftain | 31-7652081 | |
| | | | |
| ☐ N121WV | Beech 1900C-1 | UC-78 | ex N503RH |
| ☐ N767DM | Piper PA-31-T2 Cheyenne II XL | 31T-8166042 | ex N500XL |
| ☐ N999WV | Cessna 208B Caravan I | 2082082 | |
| ☐ N5200X | Cessna U206G Stationair 6 II | U20605591 | ♦ |

## WARD AIR  Juneau-Intl, AK (JNU)

| | | | | |
|---|---|---|---|---|
| ☐ N767RR | Cessna 310Q | 310Q0455 | | |
| ☐ N8773Q | Cessna U206G Stationair II | U20603526 | | FP♦ |
| ☐ N62353 | de Havilland DHC-2 Beaver | 1363 | ex 58-2031 | FP |
| ☐ N62355 | de Havilland DHC-2 Beaver | 1045 | ex N67897 | FP |
| ☐ N62357 | de Havilland DHC-2 Beaver | 1145 | ex N64391 | FP |
| ☐ N62358 | de Havilland DHC-2 Beaver | 627 | | FP♦ |
| ☐ N63354 | de Havilland DHC-3 Turbo Otter | 30 | ex C-FWAF | FP |
| ☐ N93024 | Cessna U206G Stationair II | U20604392 | | FP♦ |
| ☐ N93025 | Cessna A185F Skywagon | 18503163 | | FP |
| ☐ N93356 | de Havilland DHC-3 Turbo Otter | 144 | ex N62KA | FP |

## WEST AIR  PAC Valley (PCM)
## Fresno-Air Terminal, CA / Chico-Municipal, CA (FAT/CIC)

Ops Cessna Caravans leased from, and operated on behalf of, FedEx

## WESTERN AIR EXPRESS  Western Express (WAE)  Boise, ID (BOI)

| | | | |
|---|---|---|---|
| ☐ N158WA | Swearingen SA.226TC Metro II | TC-411 | ex N5974V |
| ☐ N160WA | Swearingen SA.226TC Metro IIA | TC-399 | ex N56EA |
| ☐ N162WA | Swearingen SA.226TC Metro IIA | TC-418 | ex C-GRET |
| ☐ N167WA | Cessna 402B II | 402B1044 | ex N98680 |
| ☐ N7947Q | Cessna 402B | 402B0397 | |

## WESTERN AVIATORS  Westavia (WTV)  Grand Junction-Walker Field, CO (GJT)

| | | | | |
|---|---|---|---|---|
| ☐ N106RE | Piper PA-31-350 Navajo Chieftain | 31-7752056 | | |
| ☐ N159SW | Piper PA-31-350 Navajo Chieftain | 31-7405229 | ex N400AA | |
| ☐ N494SC | Piper PA-31-350 Navajo Chieftain | 31-7752099 | ex N27199 | |
| ☐ N495SC | Piper PA-31-350 Chieftain | 31-8052062 | ex N3555Y | |
| ☐ N59798 | Piper PA-31-350 Navajo Chieftain | 31-7652071 | | ♦ |

## WESTWIND AVIATION — Phoenix-Deer Valley, AZ (DVT)

| | | | | | |
|---|---|---|---|---|---|
| ☐ N2AV | Cessna 208 Caravan I | 20800057 | ex N208NN | | ♦ |
| ☐ N81U | Cessna 208B Caravan I | 208B0266 | ex LN-TWD | | ♦ |
| ☐ N122JB | Cessna 208B Caravan I | 208B1025 | ex N5090V | | |
| ☐ N208WW | Cessna 208B Caravan I | 208B0721 | | | |
| ☐ N785WW | Cessna 208B Caravan I | 208B0792 | ex N5267T | | |
| ☐ N786WW | Cessna 208B Caravan I | 208B1099 | ex N12744 | | |
| | | | | | |
| ☐ N9317M | Cessna T207A Stationair 8 II | 20700680 | | | |
| ☐ N9482M | Cessna T207A Stationair 8 II | 20700698 | | | |

## WIGGINS AIRWAYS (PIPER EAST) — Wiggins (WIG) — Norwood-Memorial, MA (OWD)

| | | | | |
|---|---|---|---|---|
| ☐ N189WA | Beech 99 | U-76 | ex N139BA | ♦ |
| ☐ N190WA | Beech C99 | U-207 | ex N207CS | |
| ☐ N191WA | Beech 99A | U-136 | ex C-GPCF | |
| ☐ N192WA | Beech B99 | U-152 | ex C-GEOI | |
| ☐ N193WA | Beech 99 | U-17 | ex N10MV | |
| ☐ N194WA | Beech 99 | U-64 | ex C-FAWX | |
| ☐ N195WA | Beech 99 | U-38 | ex N202BH | |
| ☐ N196WA | Beech C99 | U-179 | ex N995SB | |
| ☐ N197WA | Beech 99A | U-130 | ex C-FOZU | |
| ☐ N198WA | Beech 99A | U-142 | ex N133BA | |
| ☐ N199WA | Beech B99 | U-154 | ex N99CH | |
| | | | | |
| ☐ N91RK | Beech A100 King Air | B-226 | ex N9126S | |
| ☐ N115WA | Embraer EMB.110P1 Bandeirante | 110451 | ex N36AN | ♦ |
| ☐ N116WA | Embraer EMB.110P1 Bandeirante | 110399 | ex N64CZ | ♦ |
| ☐ N117WA | Embraer EMB.110P1 Bandeirante | 110388 | ex N62CZ | ♦ |

## WILLIAMS AIR SERVICE

| | | | | |
|---|---|---|---|---|
| ☐ N659WF | Beech 1900D | UE-290 | ex N18153 | ♦ |

## WINGS OF ALASKA — Wings Alaska (K5/WAK) — Juneau-Intl, AK (JNU)

| | | | | |
|---|---|---|---|---|
| ☐ N335AK | de Havilland DHC-3 Otter | 263 | ex C-FOMS | FP |
| ☐ N336AK | de Havilland DHC-3 Turbo Otter | 333 | ex N567KA | FP |
| ☐ N337AK | de Havilland DHC-3 Turbo Otter | 418 | ex N2783J | FP |
| ☐ N338AK | de Havilland DHC-3 Turbo Otter | 262 | ex N62355 | FP |
| ☐ N339AK | de Havilland DHC-3 Turbo Otter | 454 | ex N28TH | FP |
| ☐ N753AK | de Havilland DHC-3 Turbo Otter | 7 | ex N342AK | FP |
| | | | | |
| ☐ N39AK | Cessna 207A Stationair 8 II | 20700597 | ex N73482 | FP/WS |
| ☐ N62AK | Cessna 207A Stationair 8 II | 20700780 | ex N9997M | FP/WS |
| ☐ N91AK | de Havilland DHC-2 Beaver | 737 | | ♦ |
| ☐ N92AK | de Havilland DHC-2 Beaver | 1031 | ex C-GFNR | FP/WS |
| ☐ N96AK | Cessna 207A Stationair 8 II | 20700782 | ex N1347Q | FP/WS |
| ☐ N331AK | Cessna 208B Caravan I | 208B0739 | ex N5264S | |
| ☐ N332AK | Cessna 208B Caravan I | 208B0779 | ex N5264S | FP/WS |

## WORLD AIRWAYS — World (WO/WOA) — Charleston-Intl, SC (CHS)

| | | | | | |
|---|---|---|---|---|---|
| ☐ N269WA | McDonnell-Douglas MD-11 | 48450/479 | ex OH-LGB | | |
| ☐ N270WA | McDonnell-Douglas MD-11 | 48449/455 | ex OH-LGA | | |
| ☐ N271WA | McDonnell-Douglas MD-11 | 48518/525 | | 271 | |
| ☐ N272WA | McDonnell-Douglas MD-11 | 48437/506 | | 272 | |
| ☐ N273WA | McDonnell-Douglas MD-11 | 48519/539 | | 273 | |
| ☐ N274WA | McDonnell-Douglas MD-11F | 48633/563 | | 274 | [GYE] |
| ☐ N275WA | McDonnell-Douglas MD-11CF | 48631/579 | | 275 | [GYE] |
| ☐ N276WA | McDonnell-Douglas MD-11CF | 48632/582 | | 276 | |
| ☐ N277WA | McDonnell-Douglas MD-11ER | 48743/590 | ex N6203D | 277 | [MIA] |
| ☐ N278WA | McDonnell-Douglas MD-11ER | 48746/597 | ex N9020Q | 278 | |
| ☐ N279WA | McDonnell-Douglas MD-11F | 48756/623 | ex P4-TKA | 279 | [VCV] |
| ☐ N380WA | McDonnell-Douglas MD-11F | 48407/456 | ex HL7371 | 380 | |
| ☐ N381WA | McDonnell-Douglas MD-11F | 48523/516 | ex HL7375 | 381 | |
| ☐ N382WA | McDonnell-Douglas MD-11F | 48411/453 | ex N703GC | | |
| ☐ N383WA | McDonnell-Douglas MD-11F | 48412/454 | ex N705GC | | |
| | | | | | |
| ☐ N740WA | Boeing 747-4H6 (BDSF) | 25700/974 | ex 9V-SPS | | |
| ☐ N741WA | Boeing 747-4H6 (BDSF) | 25702/999 | ex 9V-SPR | | [MZJ] |
| ☐ N742WA | Boeing 747-412BCF | 27071/1072 | ex N270RP | | |
| ☐ N743WA | Boeing 747-412SF | 26562/1074 | ex N265MS | | |

## WORLD ATLANTIC AIRLINES — (WAL)

| | | | | |
|---|---|---|---|---|
| ☐ N563AA | McDonnell-Douglas MD-83 | 49345/1371 | | o/o♦ |
| ☐ N802WA | McDonnell-Douglas MD-83 | 53052/1731 | ex N751LF | ♦ |
| ☐ N803WA | McDonnell-Douglas MD-82 | 49507/1425 | ex N507MT | ♦ |

## WRIGHT AIR SERVICE — Wright Air (8V/WRT) — Fairbanks-Intl, AK (FAI)

| | | | | |
|---|---|---|---|---|
| ☐ N32WA | Cessna 208B Caravan I | 208B0234 | ex C-FKEL | |
| ☐ N540ME | Cessna 208B Caravan I | 208B0540 | ex N1329G | |
| ☐ N900WA | Cessna 208B Caravan I | 208B0659 | ex N52613 | |
| ☐ N976E | Cessna 208B Caravan I | 208B0976 | ex N5263D | |
| ☐ N1323R | Cessna 208B Caravan I | 208B0745 | | |
| ☐ N1323Y | Cessna 208 Caravan I | 20800352 | ex N52623 | |
| ☐ N4365U | Cessna 208B Caravan I | 208B0253 | ex N208CC | ♦ |
| ☐ N9FW | Piper PA-31-350 Navajo Chieftain | 31-7405468 | ex N61441 | |
| ☐ N54WA | Piper PA-31-350 Navajo Chieftain | 31-7652067 | ex N942LU | |
| ☐ N7426L | Piper PA-31 Turbo Navajo B | 31-812 | | |
| ☐ N8795Q | Cessna U206G Stationair | U20603547 | | ♦ |

## XTRA AIRWAYS — Casino Express (XP/CXP) — Elko-JC Harris Field, NV (EKO)

| | | | | |
|---|---|---|---|---|
| ☐ N42XA | Boeing 737-429 | 25729/2217 | ex TF-ELP | |
| ☐ N43XA | Boeing 737-4S3 | 24796/1887 | ex TF-ELV | |
| ☐ N279AD | Boeing 737-4Q8 | 26279/2221 | ex SX-BGS | |
| ☐ N416BC | Boeing 737-4Q8 | 25109/2561 | ex JY-SOA | |
| ☐ N772AS | Boeing 737-4Q8 | 25105/2505 | | ♦ |
| | | | | ♦ |

## YUKON AVIATION — Bethel, AK (BET)

| | | | | |
|---|---|---|---|---|
| ☐ N150HH | Bell 206B JetRanger III | 701 | | |
| ☐ N205WA | Bell UH-1H | 12261 | ex 69-16663 | |
| ☐ N1322F | Cessna A185F Skywagon | 18502825 | | |
| ☐ N1653U | Cessna 207 Super Skywagon | 20700253 | | |
| ☐ N4237V | Bell 204 (UH-1B) | 261 | ex 60-0315 | |
| ☐ N7378U | Cessna 207A Skywagon | 20700396 | | |
| ☐ N24165 | Beech 58TC Baron | TK-78 | | |
| ☐ N29970 | Cessna A185F Skywagon II | 18504292 | ex (C-GMTU) | |
| ☐ N91060 | Cessna T207 Turbo Skywagon | 20700047 | | |

## OB-    PERU (Republic of Peru)

### AEROANDINA

| | | | | |
|---|---|---|---|---|
| ☐ OB-1963-P | Cessna 208B Caravan I | 208B2252 | ex N5073F | ♦ |

### AEROMASTER DEL PERU

| | | | | |
|---|---|---|---|---|
| ☐ OB-1994-P | Sikorsky S-61N | 61719 | ex N61NW | ♦ |
| ☐ OB-1995-P | Bell 214ST | 28196 | ex N726HT | ♦ |

### AERO TRANSPORTE - ATSA — ATSA (AMP) — Lima-Jorge Chavez Intl (LIM)

| | | | | |
|---|---|---|---|---|
| ☐ OB-1629 | Piper PA-42 Cheyenne III | 42-8001067 | ex N183CC | |
| ☐ OB-1633-P | Piper PA-42 Cheyenne III | 42-7801003 | ex N134KM | |
| ☐ OB-1687-P | Piper PA-42 Cheyenne III | 42-8001016 | ex N69PC | |
| ☐ OB-1803-P | Piper PA-42 Cheyenne III | 42-7800002 | ex N911VJ | |
| ☐ OB-1667-P | Beech 1900C | UB-54 | ex OB-1667 | |
| ☐ OB-1770-P | Fokker 50 | 20280 | ex N209AC | |
| ☐ OB-1778-P | Antonov An-26B-100 | 14205 | ex OB-1777-T | ♦ |
| ☐ OB-1875 | Beech 1900D | UE-68 | ex N168AZ | |
| ☐ OB-1903-P | Cessna 208B Caravan I | 208B2057 | ex OB-1903-T | ♦ |
| ☐ OB-1962-T | Antonov An-32A | 2602 | | ♦ |
| ☐ OB-1985 | Beech 1900D | UE-138 | ex N239SC | ♦ |
| ☐ OB-1992-P | Beech B200 Super King Air | BB-1632 | ex N888FV | ♦ |

### AEROCONDOR — Condor (Q6/CDP) — Lima-Jorge Chavez Intl (LIM)

| | | | | |
|---|---|---|---|---|
| ☐ OB-1693-P | Fokker F.27 Friendship 200 | 10181 | ex N863MA | [LIM] |
| ☐ OB-1829-P | Fokker50 | 20260 | ex SE-LLN | wfs |

### AERODIANA

| | | | | |
|---|---|---|---|---|
| ☐ OB-1870-T | Cessna 208B Caravan I | 208B1278 | ex OB-1870-P | |
| ☐ OB-1882-P | Cessna 208B Caravan I | 208B1306 | | ♦ |

### AIR MAJORO — Lima-Jorge Chavez Intl (LIM)

| | | | | |
|---|---|---|---|---|
| ☐ OB-1920-P | Cessna 402C II | 402C0442 | ex N6790B | |
| ☐ OB-1921-P | Cessna 402C II | 402C0419 | ex N419RC | |

### AMAZON SKY — Lima-Jorge Chavez Intl (LIM)

| | | | | |
|---|---|---|---|---|
| ☐ OB-1859-P | Antonov An-26B-100 | 6209 | ex UR-VYV | |

## CIELOS AIRLINES     Cielos (A2/CIU)     Lima-Jorge Chavez Intl (LIM)

| | | | | | | |
|---|---|---|---|---|---|---|
| ☐ | N305FE | Douglas DC-10-30F | 47870/339 | | | ◆ |
| ☐ | N614GC | Douglas DC-10-30F | 46931/137 | ex N832LA | Petete V | |
| ☐ | N900AR | Douglas DC-10-30F | 47888/291 | ex N47888 | Petete XI | [SFB]◆ |

## COYOTAIR PERU

| | | | | | |
|---|---|---|---|---|---|
| ☐ | OB-1969-P | Aérospatiale AS350B3 Ecureuil | 3727 | ex OY-HIZ | ◆ |
| ☐ | OB-1970-P | Aérospatiale AS350B3 Ecureuil | 3612 | ex OY-HGW | ◆ |
| ☐ | OB-1972-P | Bell 212 | 30639 | ex EC-HFX | ◆ |
| ☐ | OB-1973-P | Bell 212 | 30757 | ex EC-GXG | ◆ |

## HELISUR / HELICOPTEROS DEL SUR     Iquitos (IQT)

| | | | | | |
|---|---|---|---|---|---|
| ☐ | OB-1584 | Mil Mi-17 (Mi-8MTV-1) | 95432 | ex CCCP-70879 | |
| ☐ | OB-1585 | Mil Mi-17 (Mi-8MTV-1) | 223M103 | ex RA-70951 | |
| ☐ | OB-1586 | Mil Mi-17 (Mi-8MTV-1) | 223M104 | | |
| ☐ | OB-1663 | Mil Mi-17 (Mi-8MTV-1) | 94704 | ex OB-1725 | |
| ☐ | OB-1691 | Mil Mi-17 (Mi-8MTV-1) | 96153 | ex RA-27193 | |
| ☐ | OB-1760 | Mil Mi-17 (Mi-8MTV-1) | 93823 | | ◆ |
| ☐ | OB-1761 | Mil Mi-17 (Mi-8MTV-1) | 93477 | | ◆ |
| ☐ | OB-1878-P | Mil Mi-171 | 59489614258 | ex HK-4312 | ◆ |
| ☐ | OB-1935-P | Mil Mi-171C | 171C00643083909U | | ◆ |
| | | | | ex RA-22471 | ◆ |
| ☐ | OB-1987P | Mil Mi-171C | 171C00643083806U | | ◆ |
| | | | | ex RA-22438 | ◆ |
| ☐ | OB-1988-P | Mil Mi-171C | 171C00643083807U | | ◆ |
| | | | | ex RA-22437 | ◆ |
| ☐ | OB-1989P | Mil Mi-171C | 171C00643083808U | | ◆ |
| | | | | ex RA-22435 | ◆ |
| ☐ | OB-1990-P | Mil Mi-171C | 171C00643083809U | | ◆ |
| | | | | ex RA-22433 | ◆ |
| ☐ | OB-1998-P | Mil Mi-171C | 171C00643083807U | | ◆ |
| | | | | ex RA-22437 | ◆ |
| ☐ | OB-1639-P | Mil Mi-8AMT | 59489607212 | ex OB-1639-T | ◆ |
| ☐ | OB-1663 | Mil Mi-8AMT | 94704 | ex RA-27126 | ◆ |
| ☐ | OB-1826 | Mil Mi-8MTV-1 | 93281 | | ◆ |
| ☐ | OB-1934-P | Mil Mi-8MTV-1 | 96264 | ex RA-25809 | ◆ |

## LAN PERU     Linea Peru (LP/LPE)     Lima-Jorge Chavez Intl (LIM)

| | | | | |
|---|---|---|---|---|
| ☐ | CC-COU | Airbus A319-132 | 2089 | ex D-AVWL |
| ☐ | CC-CPE | Airbus A319-132 | 2321 | ex D-AVYO |
| ☐ | CC-CPF | Airbus A319-132 | 2572 | ex D-AVXC |
| ☐ | CC-CPI | Airbus A319-132 | 2585 | ex D-AVXH |
| ☐ | CC-CPM | Airbus A319-132 | 2864 | ex D-AVWC |
| ☐ | CC-CPO | Airbus A319-132 | 2872 | ex D-AVWJ |
| ☐ | CC-CPQ | Airbus A319-132 | 2886 | ex D-AVXP |
| ☐ | CC-CPX | Airbus A319-132 | 2887 | ex D-AVYF |
| ☐ | CC-CQK | Airbus A319-132 | 2892 | ex D-AVYV |
| ☐ | CC-CQL | Airbus A319-132 | 2894 | ex D-AVWE |

## LC BUSRE     Busre (LCB)     Lima-Jorge Chavez Intl (LIM)

| | | | | | |
|---|---|---|---|---|---|
| ☐ | N139LC | Swearingen SA.227TC Metro III | AC-732 | ex XA-TKE | |
| ☐ | N239LC | Swearingen SA.227TC Metro III | AC-735 | ex N523WA | |
| ☐ | N386PH | Swearingen SA.227TC Metro III | AC-597 | ex N3116T | |
| ☐ | N444YV | de Havilland DHC-8Q-202 | 444 | | ◆ |
| ☐ | N447YV | de Havilland DHC-8Q-202 | 447 | | ◆ |
| ☐ | N448YV | de Havilland DHC-8Q-202 | 448 | | ◆ |
| ☐ | N454YV | de Havilland DHC-8Q-202 | 454 | | ◆ |
| ☐ | N26974 | Swearingen SA.227AC Metro III | AC-664 | | ◆ |

## PERUVIAN AIR LINES     (P9/PVN)     Lima-Jorge Chavez Intl (LIM)

| | | | | | |
|---|---|---|---|---|---|
| ☐ | OB-1823-P | Boeing 737-2T2 9Nordam 3) | 22793/892 | ex OB-1823 | ◆ |
| ☐ | OB-1839-P | Boeing 737-204 | 22640/867 | ex N640AD | ◆ |
| ☐ | OB-1841-P | Boeing 737-204 | 22058/629 | ex N58AD | ◆ |
| ☐ | OB-1851-P | Boeing 737-230 (Nordam 3) | 22133/772 | ex N133AD | ◆ |
| ☐ | OB-1954-P | Boeing 737-247 (Nordam 3) | 23188/1071 | ex HC-CGA | ◆ |
| ☐ | OB-1955 | Boeing 737-2T7 | 22761/850 | ex N763SH | |
| ☐ | OB-1956 | Boeing 737-2T7 | 22762/856 | ex N762SH | |
| ☐ | OB-1957-P | Boeing 737-236 | 21806/699 | ex LV-ZTT | [EZE]◆ |
| ☐ | OB- | Boeing 737-217 | 21716/560 | ex N716SH | [LIM] |
| ☐ | OB- | Boeing 737-217 | 22256/672 | ex N764SH | [LIM]◆ |

| | | | | | | |
|---|---|---|---|---|---|---|
| ☐ | OB-1876-P | Antonov An-26B-100 | 17311506 | ex OB-1876-T | | ◆ |
| ☐ | OB-1893-P | Antonov An-26-100 | 97308401 | ex OB-1893-T | | ◆ |
| ☐ | OB-1960-P | Boeing 737-33A | 23627/1302 | ex N166AW | | ◆ |
| ☐ | OB-1961-P | Boeing 737-33A | 23629/1311 | ex N168AW | | ◆ |

## SERVICIOS AEREOS DE LOS ANDES — *Miraflores, Lima*

| | | | | | | |
|---|---|---|---|---|---|---|
| ☐ | OB-1813-P | Bell 212 | 30811 | ex OB-1762-T | | ◆ |
| ☐ | OB-1845-P | Bell 212 | 30926 | ex C-FHVC | | ◆ |
| ☐ | OB-1906-P | Bell 212 | 30544 | ex C-FLBF | | ◆ |
| ☐ | OB-1910-P | Bell 212 | 30798 | ex C-GSLL | | |
| ☐ | OB-1912-P | Bell 212 | 30820 | ex C-GZMQ | | |
| ☐ | OB-1965-P | Bell 212 | 30615 | ex 9Y-TIF | | |
| | | | | | | |
| ☐ | OB-1835-P | Bell 204B | 2010 | ex C-GEAW | | |
| ☐ | OB-1846-P | Aérospatiale AS350B-3 Ecureuil | 3698 | ex I-EWAY | | ◆ |
| ☐ | OB-1854-P | Bell 407 | 53732 | ex C-FLER | | ◆ |
| ☐ | OB-1864-P | de Havilland DHC-6 Twin Otter 300 | 282 | ex CC-PCI | | |
| ☐ | OB-1897-P | de Havilland DHC-6 Twin Otter 300 | 521 | ex C-FSXF | | |
| ☐ | OB-1904-P | Aérospatiale AS350B-3 Ecureuil | 4572 | | | |
| ☐ | OB-1913-P | de Havilland DHC-6 Twin Otter 300 | 391 | ex C-GHVV | | ◆ |
| ☐ | OB-1937-P | Aérospatiale AS350B-3 Ecureuil | 4800 | | | |
| ☐ | OB-1939-P | Bell 205A-1 | 30136 | ex C-GCZG | | ◆ |
| ☐ | OB-1940-P | Bell 204B | 2044 | ex C-GAHN | | |
| ☐ | OB-1949-B | Aérospatiale AS350B-3 Ecureuil | 4946 | | | ◆ |
| ☐ | OB-1958-B | Bell 412HP | 36065 | ex C-FDDI | | ◆ |

## STAR PERU — *Star Up (2I/SRU)* — *Lima-Jorge Chavez Intl (LIM)*

| | | | | | | |
|---|---|---|---|---|---|---|
| ☐ | OB-1877-P | British Aerospace 146 Srs.100 | E1199 | ex A5-RGE | | |
| ☐ | OB-1879-P | British Aerospace 146 Srs.100 | E1095 | ex A5-RGD | | |
| ☐ | OB-1885-P | British Aerospace 146 Srs.200 | E2087 | ex N292UE | | |
| ☐ | OB-1914-P | British Aerospace 146 Srs.300 | E3181 | ex G-JEBE | | |
| ☐ | OB-1923-P | British Aerospace 146 Srs.300 | E3185 | ex G-JEBB | | |
| ☐ | OB-1930-P | British Aerospace 146 Srs.200 | E2201 | ex D-AJET | | |
| ☐ | OB-1943-P | British Aerospace 146 Srs.200 | E2133 | ex C-GRNV | | |
| ☐ | OB-1948-P | British Aerospace 146 Srs.200 | E2156 | ex N156TR | | |
| ☐ | OB-1964-P | British Aerospace 146 Srs.200 | E2184 | ex G-BTKC | | ◆ |
| ☐ | OB-1978-P | British Aerospace 146 Srs.200QT | E2114 | ex OB-1978-T | | [LIM]◆ |
| | | | | | | |
| ☐ | OB-1717 | Antonov An-24RV | 27308010 | ex ER-AFU | Anna | wfs |
| ☐ | OB-1734-P | Antonov An-24RV | 17307006 | ex ER-AFC | | wfs |
| ☐ | OB-1769 | Antonov An-24RV | 57310110 | ex ER-AWX | Leonid | wfs |
| ☐ | OB-1772 | Antonov An-26B-100 | 10704 | ex OB-1772-P | | wfs |
| ☐ | OB-1794-P | Boeing 737-2Y5 (Nordam 3) | 23039/954 | ex HR-ATM | Best of Peru c/s | |
| ☐ | OB-1800-P | Boeing 737-291 (Nordam 3) | 21641/537 | ex HR-ATR | Machu Picchu c/s | |
| ☐ | OB-1823-P | Boeing 737-2T2 (Nordam 3) | 22793/892 | ex LY-BSG | Lord of Sipan c/s | |

## TACA PERU — *Trans Peru (T0/TPU)* — *Lima-Jorge Chavez Intl (LIM)*

| | | | | | |
|---|---|---|---|---|---|
| ☐ | N471TA | Airbus A319-132 | 1066 | ex D-AVWE | <TAI |
| ☐ | N472TA | Airbus A319-132 | 1113 | ex D-AVWU | <TAI |
| ☐ | N491TA | Airbus A320-233 | 2301 | ex F-WWDF | ◆ |
| ☐ | N521TA | Airbus A319-132 | 3276 | ex D-AVYK | ◆ |
| ☐ | N988TA | Embraer ERJ-190LR | 19000399 | ex PT-XUE | |

## TRANSPORTES AEREOS CIELOS ANDINOS (NDN) — *Lima-Jorge Chavez Intl (LIM)*

| | | | | | |
|---|---|---|---|---|---|
| ☐ | OB-1650-P | Antonov An-24RV | 37308802 | ex OB-1650 | ◆ |
| ☐ | OB-1651 | Antonov An-24RV | 27308303 | | ◆ |
| ☐ | OB-1828 | Antonov An-26 | 87307409 | ex OB-1828-P | wfs |
| ☐ | OB-1859-P | Antonov An-26 | | | |
| ☐ | OB-1876-T | Antonov An-26B-100 | 17311506 | ex EX-063 | |
| ☐ | OB-1887-P | Antonov An-26-100 | 87306606 | ex UR-VIG | |
| ☐ | OB-1893-P | Antonov An-26-100 | 8401 | | |

## OD-   LEBANON (Republic of Lebanon)

## BERYTOS AIRWAYS — *(BYR)* — *Beirut (BEY)*

Ops charter flights with Airbus A320 and Douglas DC-9-51 aircraft wet leased from UM Air as required

## IMPERIAL JET — *(IMJ)* — *Beirut (BEY)*

| | | | | | |
|---|---|---|---|---|---|
| ☐ | OD-NOR | Boeing 737-247 (Nordam 3) | 22754/870 | ex N247US | ◆ |

| **MED AIRWAYS** | | **Flying Carpet (7Y/MED)** | | | **Beirut (BEY)** |
|---|---|---|---|---|---|
| ☐ | OD-AMB | Boeing 737-2H4 (AvAero 3) | 23109/1016 | ex N103SW | ◆ |
| ☐ | OD-MAB | Swearingen SA.227AC Metro III | AC-604 | ex C-FNAL | ◆ |

| **MIDDLE EAST AIRLINES** | | **Cedar Jet (ME/MEA)** | | | **Beirut (BEY)** |
|---|---|---|---|---|---|
| ☐ | F-OMRN | Airbus A320-232 | 4339 | ex D-AXAR | |
| ☐ | F-OMRO | Airbus A320-232 | 4296 | ex D-AXAI | |
| ☐ | OD-MRL | Airbus A320-232 | 5000 | ex D-AVVV | ◆ |
| ☐ | OD-MRM | Airbus A320-232 | 4632 | ex D-AXAY | ◆ |
| ☐ | OD-MRR | Airbus A320-232 | 3837 | ex F-WWBJ | |
| ☐ | OD-MRS | Airbus A320-232 | 3804 | ex F-WWDJ | |
| ☐ | OD-MRT | Airbus A320-232 | 3736 | ex F-ORMK | |
| ☐ | F-ORMA | Airbus A330-243 | 926 | ex F-WWKD | |
| ☐ | F-ORMG | Airbus A321-231 | 1956 | ex D-AVZE | |
| ☐ | OD-MEA | Airbus A330-243 | 984 | ex F-WWKE | |
| ☐ | OD-MEB | Airbus A330-243 | 998 | ex F-WWYT | |
| ☐ | OD-MEC | Airbus A330-243 | 995 | ex F-WWKQ | |
| ☐ | OD-RMH | Airbus A321-231 | 1967 | ex F-ORMH | |
| ☐ | OD-RMI | Airbus A321-231 | 1977 | ex F-ORMI | |
| ☐ | OD-RMJ | Airbus A321-231 | 2055 | ex F-ORMJ | |

| **TMA** | | **(TMA)** | | | **Beirut (BEY)** |
|---|---|---|---|---|---|
| ☐ | OD-TMA | Airbus A300F4-622RF | 872 | ex N140MN | |

| **WINGS OF LEBANON AVIATION** | | **Wings Lebanon (WLB)** | | | **Beirut (BEY)** |
|---|---|---|---|---|---|
| ☐ | OD-HAJ | Boeing 737-3Q8 | 26313/2704 | ex G-THOE | |

# OE-  AUSTRIA (Republic of Austria)

| **AIR ALPS AVIATION** | | **Alpav (A6/LPV)** | | | **Innsbruck (INN)** |
|---|---|---|---|---|---|
| ☐ | OE-LKA | Dornier 328-110 | 3110 | ex D-COXI | Igls-Innsbruck | |
| ☐ | OE-LKB | Dornier 328-110 | 3036 | ex HB-AEH | Sudtirol colours | |
| ☐ | OE-LKH | Dornier 328-110 | 3055 | ex OY-NCG | | ◆ |

Declared insolvent 13Jan12

| **AMERER AIR** | | **Amer Air (AMK)** | | **Linz (LNZ)** |
|---|---|---|---|---|

Aircraft sold Oct11

| **AUSTRIAN AIRLINES** | | **Austrian (OS/AUA)** | | | **Vienna-Schwechat (VIE)** |
|---|---|---|---|---|---|

Member of Star Alliance

| ☐ | OE-LDA | Airbus A319-112 | 2131 | ex D-AVWS | Sofia | |
| ☐ | OE-LDB | Airbus A319-112 | 2174 | ex D-AVYP | Bucharest | |
| ☐ | OE-LDC | Airbus A319-112 | 2262 | ex D-AVWE | Kiev | |
| ☐ | OE-LDD | Airbus A319-112 | 2416 | ex D-AVWN | Moscow | |
| ☐ | OE-LDE | Airbus A319-112 | 2494 | ex D-AVYL | Baku | |
| ☐ | OE-LDF | Airbus A319-112 | 2547 | ex D-AVYA | Sarajevo | |
| ☐ | OE-LDG | Airbus A319-112 | 2652 | ex D-AVYF | Tbilisi | |
| ☐ | OE-LBN | Airbus A320-214 | 0768 | ex F-WWDH | | |
| ☐ | OE-LBO | Airbus A320-214 | 0776 | ex F-WWDM | Pyhrn-Eisenwürzen | |
| ☐ | OE-LBP | Airbus A320-214 | 0797 | ex F-WWDV | Neusiedlersee | Retro c/s |
| ☐ | OE-LBQ | Airbus A320-214 | 1137 | ex F-WWDF | Ray Charles | |
| ☐ | OE-LBR | Airbus A320-214 | 1150 | ex F-WWBP | Frida Kahlo | |
| ☐ | OE-LBS | Airbus A320-214 | 1189 | ex F-WWDV | Waldviertel | |
| ☐ | OE-LBT | Airbus A320-214 | 1387 | ex F-WWIS | Wörthersee | |
| ☐ | OE-LBU | Airbus A320-214 | 1478 | ex F-WWDS | Mühlvierter | |
| ☐ | OE-LBV | Airbus A320-214 | 1385 | ex D-ALTB | | ◆ |
| ☐ | OE-LBA | Airbus A321-111 | 0552 | ex D-AVZH | Salzkammergut | |
| ☐ | OE-LBB | Airbus A321-111 | 0570 | ex D-AVZQ | Pinzgau | |
| ☐ | OE-LBC | Airbus A321-111 | 0581 | ex D-AVZS | Südtirol | |
| ☐ | OE-LBD | Airbus A321-211 | 0920 | ex D-AVZN | Steirisches Weinland | |
| ☐ | OE-LBE | Airbus A321-211 | 0935 | ex D-AVZR | Wachau | |
| ☐ | OE-LBF | Airbus A321-211 | 1458 | ex D-AVXE | Wien | |
| ☐ | OE-LNJ | Boeing 737-8Z9/W | 28177/69 | | Wildspitze | |
| ☐ | OE-LNK | Boeing 737-8Z9/W | 28178/222 | | Freddie Mercury | |
| ☐ | OE-LNP | Boeing 737-8Z9/W | 30420/1100 | | Grossglockner | |
| ☐ | OE-LNQ | Boeing 737-8Z9/W | 30421/1345 | | Grossvenediger | |

| | | | | | | |
|---|---|---|---|---|---|---|
| ☐ | OE-LNR | Boeing 737-8Z9/W | 33833/1680 | | Piz Buin | |
| ☐ | OE-LNS | Boeing 737-8Z9/W | 34262/1720 | | Geshriebenstein | |
| ☐ | OE-LNT | Boeing 737-8Z9/W | 33834/1938 | | Gerlitzen | |
| | | | | | | |
| ☐ | OE-LAE | Boeing 767-3Z9ER/W | 30383/812 | | Wiener Sangerknaben | |
| ☐ | OE-LAT | Boeing 767-31AER | 25273/393 | ex PH-MCK | Thailand | |
| ☐ | OE-LAW | Boeing 767-3Z9ER | 26417/448 | | China | |
| ☐ | OE-LAX | Boeing 767-3Z9ER/W | 27095/467 | | Salzburger Festspiele | |
| ☐ | OE-LAY | Boeing 767-3Z9ER/W | 29867/731 | ex D-ABUV | Japan | |
| ☐ | OE-LAZ | Boeing 767-3Z9ER/W | 30331/759 | ex D-ABUW | India | |
| | | | | | | |
| ☐ | OE-LNL | Boeing 737-6Z9 | 30137/526 | ex N743NV | Kahlenberg | |
| ☐ | OE-LNM | Boeing 737-6Z9 | 30138/546 | ex N1795B | Albert Einstein | wfs |
| ☐ | OE-LNN | Boeing 737-7Z9/W | 30418/815 | | Maria Callas | |
| ☐ | OE-LNO | Boeing 737-7Z9/W | 30419/874 | | Greta Garbo | |
| ☐ | OE-LPA | Boeing 777-2Z9ER | 28698/87 | ex N5022E | Melbourne | |
| ☐ | OE-LPB | Boeing 777-2Z9ER | 28699/163 | | Sydney | |
| ☐ | OE-LPC | Boeing 777-2Z9ER | 29313/386 | | Don Bradman | |
| ☐ | OE-LPD | Boeing 777-2Z9ER | 35960/607 | | America | |

## FLYING BULLS                                                               Salzburg (SZG)

| | | | | | | |
|---|---|---|---|---|---|---|
| ☐ | OE-EDM | Cessna 208 Caravan I | 20800257 | ex N666CS | Amphibian | |
| ☐ | N996DM | Douglas DC-6B | 45563/1034 | ex V5-NCF | Red Bull | |
| ☐ | N6123C | North American B-25J Mitchell | 108-47647 | ex 44-86893A | | |

Ops some pleasure flights as well as airshow appearances

## INTERSKY                    Intersky (3L/ISK)          Freidrichschafen-Lowental (FDH)

| | | | | | |
|---|---|---|---|---|---|
| ☐ | OE-LIA | de Havilland DHC-8Q-314 | 505 | ex D-BHAT | |
| ☐ | OE-LIC | de Havilland DHC-8Q-314 | 503 | ex D-BHAS | |
| ☐ | OE-LSB | de Havilland DHC-8Q-314 | 525 | ex C-FDHY | Espace Mittelland |

## LAUDA AIR                   Lauda Air (NG/LDA)              Vienna-Schwechat (VIE)

Ops leisure services for Austrian Airlines using OS/AUA designators as 'Lauda Air-the Austrian way to holidays'. Leases aircraft as required from Austrian. Member of Star Alliance.

## MAPJET                       MapJet (MPJ)                  Vienna-Schwechat (VIE)

Ceased ops

## NIKI                         FlyNiki (HG/NLY)              Vienna-Schwecat (VIE)

| | | | | | | |
|---|---|---|---|---|---|---|
| ☐ | OE-LEA | Airbus A320-214 | 2529 | ex F-WWID | Rock'n Roll | |
| ☐ | OE-LEB | Airbus A320-214 | 4231 | ex D-AXAA | Polka | |
| ☐ | OE-LEC | Airbus A320-214 | 4316 | ex D-AXAL | | |
| ☐ | OE-LEE | Airbus A320-214 | 2749 | ex F-WWDB | | |
| ☐ | OE-LEF | Airbus A320-214 | 4368 | ex D-AXAY | | |
| ☐ | OE-LEO | Airbus A320-214 | 2668 | ex F-WWBP | Soul | [VIE] |
| ☐ | OE-LEG | Airbus A320-214 | 4581 | ex D-AXAP | | ♦ |
| ☐ | OE-LEH | Airbus A320-214 | 4594 | ex D-AVVG | | ♦ |
| ☐ | OE-LEJ | Airbus A320-214 | 5115 | ex D-AUBX | | ♦ |
| ☐ | OE-LEU | Airbus A320-214 | 2902 | ex F-WWDH | | |
| ☐ | OE-LEX | Airbus A320-214 | 2867 | ex F-WWBC | Jazz | |
| ☐ | OE- | Airbus A320-214 | | ex | | o/o |
| | | | | | | |
| ☐ | OE-IHA | Embraer ERJ-190LR | 19000285 | ex PT-TLZ | | |
| ☐ | OE-IHB | Embraer ERJ-190LR | 19000294 | ex PT-TZI | | |
| ☐ | OE-IHC | Embraer ERJ-190LR | 19000349 | ex PT-XQP | | |
| ☐ | OE-IHD | Embraer ERJ-190LR | 19000354 | ex PT-XQT | | |
| ☐ | OE-IHE | Embraer ERJ-190LR | 19000387 | ex PT- | | ♦ |
| ☐ | OE-IHF | Embraer ERJ-190LR | 19000420 | ex PT- | | ♦ |
| ☐ | OE-IHG | Embraer ERJ-190LR | 19000435 | ex PT-TCU | | ♦ |
| | | | | | | |
| ☐ | OE-LES | Airbus A321-211 | 3504 | ex D-AVZI | Boogie Woogie | |
| ☐ | OE-LET | Airbus A321-211 | 3830 | ex D-AVZG | Heavy Metal | |
| ☐ | OE-LEW | Airbus A321-211 | 4611 | ex D-AZAL | Cancan | |
| ☐ | OE-LEZ | Airbus A321-211 | 4648 | ex D-AZAV | | ♦ |

## ROBIN HOOD AVIATION              (RH/RHA)                        Graz (GRZ)

| | | | | | | |
|---|---|---|---|---|---|---|
| ☐ | OE-GIR | SAAB SF.340A | 340A-134 | ex SE-F34 | Graz-Zurich titles | wfs |
| ☐ | OE-GOD | SAAB SF.340A | 340A-153 | ex ZK-NLO | {LNZ} | |

## TYROLEAN AIRWAYS              Tyrolean (VO/TYR)               Innsbruck (INN)

| | | | | | |
|---|---|---|---|---|---|
| ☐ | OE-LCI | Canadair CRJ-200LR | 7133 | | ♦ |
| ☐ | OE-LCK | Canadair CRJ-200LR | 7188 | | ♦ |

| | | | | | |
|---|---|---|---|---|---|
| ☐ | OE-LCN | Canadair CRJ-200LR | 7365 | ex C-FMOI | Stadt Bremen |
| ☐ | OE-LCO | Canadair CRJ-200LR | 7371 | | |
| ☐ | OE-LCR | Canadair CRJ-200LR | 7910 | ex C-FMMW | Stadt Baden ♦ |
| | | | | | |
| ☐ | OE-LGA | de Havilland DHC-8-402Q | 4014 | ex C-GDNG | Kärnten |
| ☐ | OE-LGB | de Havilland DHC-8-402Q | 4015 | ex C-GDOE | Tirol |
| ☐ | OE-LGC | de Havilland DHC-8-402Q | 4026 | ex C-GEVP | Salzburg |
| ☐ | OE-LGD | de Havilland DHC-8-402Q | 4027 | ex C-GEWI | Land Steiermark |
| ☐ | OE-LGE | de Havilland DHC-8-402Q | 4042 | ex C-FNGB | Land Oberössterreich |
| ☐ | OE-LGF | de Havilland DHC-8-402Q | 4068 | ex C-GERC | Land Niederösterreich |
| ☐ | OE-LGG | de Havilland DHC-8-402Q | 4074 | ex C-GFCF | Stadt Budapest |
| ☐ | OE-LGH | de Havilland DHC-8-402Q | 4075 | ex C-GFCW | Vorarlberg |
| ☐ | OE-LGI | de Havilland DHC-8-402Q | 4100 | ex C-FAQR | Eisenstadt |
| ☐ | OE-LGJ | de Havilland DHC-8-402Q | 4104 | ex C-FCQH | St Pölten |
| ☐ | OE-LGK | de Havilland DHC-8-402Q | 4280 | ex C-FYMK | Burgenland |
| ☐ | OE-LGL | de Havilland DHC-8-402Q | 4310 | ex C-GCQB | Altenrhein |
| ☐ | OE-LGM | de Havilland DHC-8-402Q | 4319 | ex C-GEII | Villach |
| ☐ | OE-LGN | de Havilland DHC-8-402Q | 4326 | ex C-GEZY | Gmunden |
| | | | | | |
| ☐ | OE-LFG | Fokker 70 | 11549 | ex PH-EZW | Innsbruck |
| ☐ | OE-LFH | Fokker 70 | 11554 | ex PH-EZN | Stadt Salzburg |
| ☐ | OE-LFI | Fokker 70 | 11529 | ex PH-WXF | Stadt Klagenfurt |
| ☐ | OE-LFJ | Fokker 70 | 11532 | ex PH-WXG | Stadt Graz |
| ☐ | OE-LFK | Fokker 70 | 11555 | ex PH-EZP | Krems |
| ☐ | OE-LFL | Fokker 70 | 11573 | ex PH-WXE | Stadt Linz |
| ☐ | OE-LFP | Fokker 70 | 11560 | ex PH-EZW | Wels |
| ☐ | OE-LFQ | Fokker 70 | 11568 | ex PH-EZC | Dornbirn |
| ☐ | OE-LFR | Fokker 70 | 11572 | ex PH-EZD | Steyr |
| | | | | | |
| ☐ | OE-LVA | Fokker 100 | 11490 | ex PH-ZFB | Riga |
| ☐ | OE-LVB | Fokker 100 | 11502 | ex PH-ZFE | Vilnius |
| ☐ | OE-LVC | Fokker 100 | 11446 | ex PH-ZFF | Tirana |
| ☐ | OE-LVD | Fokker 100 | 11515 | ex PH-ZFG | Skopje |
| ☐ | OE-LVE | Fokker 100 | 11499 | ex PH-ZFH | Zagreb |
| ☐ | OE-LVF | Fokker 100 | 11483 | ex PH-ZFI | Yerevan |
| ☐ | OE-LVG | Fokker 100 | 11520 | ex PH-ZFJ | Krakow Star Alliance c/s |
| ☐ | OE-LVH | Fokker 100 | 11456 | ex PH-ZFK | Minsk |
| ☐ | OE-LVI | Fokker 100 | 11468 | ex PH-ZFL | Prague |
| ☐ | OE-LVJ | Fokker 100 | 11359 | ex PH-ZFM | Bratislava |
| ☐ | OE-LVK | Fokker 100 | 11397 | ex PH-ZFQ | Burgenland |
| ☐ | OE-LVL | Fokker 100 | 11404 | ex PH-ZFR | Odessa |
| ☐ | OE-LVM | Fokker 100 | 11361 | ex PH-ZFN | Krasnodar |
| ☐ | OE-LVN | Fokker 100 | 11367 | ex PH-ZFO | Dniepropetrovsk |
| ☐ | OE-LVO | Fokker 100 | 11460 | ex PH-ZFS | Chisinau |

Ops scheduled services using OS/ AUA designators in 5000 range and in full Austrian colours.

## TYROLEAN JET SERVICE — Tyroljet (TJS) — Innsbruck (INN)

| | | | | | |
|---|---|---|---|---|---|
| ☐ | OE-HMS | Dornier 328-300 (328JET) | 3121 | ex D-BDXI | |
| ☐ | OE-HRJ | Dornier 328-210 (328JET) | 3206 | ex D-BHRJ | ♦ |
| ☐ | OE-HTJ | Dornier 328-300 (328JET) | 3114 | ex D-BDXA | |
| ☐ | OE-LUX | Airbus A318-112CJ | 4169 | ex 9H-AFT | VIP♦ |

## WELCOME AIR — Welcomeair (2W/WLC) — Innsbruck (INN)

| | | | | | |
|---|---|---|---|---|---|
| ☐ | OE-GBB | Dornier 328-110 | 3078 | ex D-CDXG | Rotterdam |
| ☐ | OE-LIR | Dornier 328-110 | 3115 | ex D-CDXG | Phönix |

## VISTA JET — (VJS)

| | | | | | | |
|---|---|---|---|---|---|---|
| ☐ | OE-LRW | McDonnell-Douglas MD-83 | 49629/1583 | ex EC-HBP | all-white | [ARN]♦ |

## OH- FINLAND (Republic of Finland)

### AIR ALAND — Mariehamn (MHQ)

| | | | | | |
|---|---|---|---|---|---|
| ☐ | SE-KXE | SAAB SF.340A | 340A-111 | ex LY-KXE | [ORB]♦ |
| ☐ | SE-LJM | SAAB SF.340A | 340A-112 | ex LY-RIK | |
| ☐ | 5Y-FLB | SAAB SF.340B | 340B-171 | ex OM-UGT | [OSR]♦ |

### AIR FINLAND — Air Finland (OF/FIF) — Helsinki-Vantaa (HEL)

| | | | | | |
|---|---|---|---|---|---|
| ☐ | OH-AFI | Boeing 757-2K2/W | 26330/717 | ex PH-TKD | |
| ☐ | OH-AFJ | Boeing 757-28A | 26269/612 | ex N321LF | |
| ☐ | OH-AFM | Boeing 757-204/W | 25623/528 | ex SE-RFO | ♦ |

389

## BLUE1 — Bluefin (KF/BLF) — Helsinki-Vantaa (HEL)

Member of Star Alliance

| | Reg | Type | c/n | ex | Name | notes |
|---|---|---|---|---|---|---|
| ☐ | OH-SAJ | Avro 146-RJ85 | E2388 | ex G-6-388 | Pyhaselka | wfs |
| ☐ | OH-SAK | Avro 146-RJ85 | E2389 | ex G-6-389 | Nasijarvi | wfs |
| ☐ | OH-SAL | Avro 146-RJ85 | E2392 | ex G-6-390 | Orivesi | wfs |
| ☐ | OH-SAO | Avro 146-RJ85 | E2393 | ex G-CBMG | Oulunjärvi | wfs |
| ☐ | OH-SAP | Avro 146-RJ85 | E2394 | ex G-CBMH | Pielinen | wfs |
| ☐ | OH-BLG | Boeing 717-23S | 55059/5023 | ex SE-REN | Blue Flow | |
| ☐ | OH-BLH | Boeing 717-23S | 55060/5026 | ex SE-REO | Summer Spring | |
| ☐ | OH-BLI | Boeing 717-23S | 55061/5029 | ex SE-REP | Sky Trickle | |
| ☐ | OH-BLJ | Boeing 717-23S | 55065/5048 | ex SE-REL | Pearl Mist | |
| ☐ | OH-BLM | Boeing 717-23S | 55065/5054 | ex SE-REM | Spring Rain | |
| ☐ | OH-BLN | Boeing 717-2K9 | 55053/5016 | ex EC-KHX | Star Alliance c/s | |
| ☐ | OH-BLO | Boeing 717-2K9 | 55056/5015 | ex EC-KFR | | |
| ☐ | OH-BLP | Boeing 717-23S | 55064/5037 | ex EC-KNE | Star Alliance c/s | |
| ☐ | OH-BLQ | Boeing 717-23S | 55067/5059 | ex EC-KRO | | |

## FINNAIR — Finnair (AY/FIN) — Helsinki-Vantaa (HEL)

Member of Oneworld

| | Reg | Type | c/n | ex | notes | |
|---|---|---|---|---|---|---|
| ☐ | OH-LVA | Airbus A319-112 | 1073 | ex F-WWID | | |
| ☐ | OH-LVB | Airbus A319-112 | 1107 | ex D-AVWS | | |
| ☐ | OH-LVC | Airbus A319-112 | 1309 | ex D-AVWY | | |
| ☐ | OH-LVD | Airbus A319-112 | 1352 | ex D-AVYW | | |
| ☐ | OH-LVE | Airbus A319-112 | 1791 | ex D-AVYS | Retro c/s | |
| ☐ | OH-LVF | Airbus A319-112 | 1808 | ex D-AVWG | | |
| ☐ | OH-LVG | Airbus A319-112 | 1916 | ex D-AVYG | | |
| ☐ | OH-LVH | Airbus A319-112 | 1184 | ex EI-CZE | | |
| ☐ | OH-LVI | Airbus A319-112 | 1364 | ex F-WQQZ | | |
| ☐ | OH-LVK | Airbus A319-112 | 2124 | ex D-AVWB | | |
| ☐ | OH-LVL | Airbus A319-112 | 2266 | ex D-AVWS | | |
| ☐ | OH-LXA | Airbus A320-214 | 1405 | ex F-WWDH | | |
| ☐ | OH-LXB | Airbus A320-214 | 1470 | ex F-WWDO | | |
| ☐ | OH-LXC | Airbus A320-214 | 1544 | ex F-WWIX | | |
| ☐ | OH-LXD | Airbus A320-214 | 1588 | ex F-WWBQ | | |
| ☐ | OH-LXE | Airbus A320-214 | 1678 | ex F-WWIF | | |
| ☐ | OH-LXF | Airbus A320-214 | 1712 | ex F-WWIY | | |
| ☐ | OH-LXG | Airbus A320-214 | 1735 | ex F-WWBM | | |
| ☐ | OH-LXH | Airbus A320-214 | 1913 | ex F-WWIZ | | |
| ☐ | OH-LXI | Airbus A320-214 | 1989 | ex F-WWDN | | |
| ☐ | OH-LXK | Airbus A320-214 | 2065 | ex F-WWIQ | | |
| ☐ | OH-LXL | Airbus A320-214 | 2146 | ex F-WWDN | | |
| ☐ | OH-LXM | Airbus A320-214 | 2154 | ex F-WWDP | | |
| ☐ | OH-LZA | Airbus A321-211 | 0941 | ex D-AVZT | | |
| ☐ | OH-LZB | Airbus A321-211 | 0961 | ex D-AVZU | | |
| ☐ | OH-LZC | Airbus A321-211 | 1185 | ex D-AVZI | | |
| ☐ | OH-LZD | Airbus A321-211 | 1241 | ex D-AVZG | | |
| ☐ | OH-LZE | Airbus A321-211 | 1978 | ex D-AVZV | | |
| ☐ | OH-LZF | Airbus A321-211 | 2208 | ex D-AVZI | | |
| ☐ | OH-LTM | Airbus A330-302E | 994 | ex F-WWKO | | |
| ☐ | OH-LTN | Airbus A330-302E | 1007 | ex F-WWYC | | |
| ☐ | OH-LTO | Airbus A330-302E | 1013 | ex F-WWKD | | |
| ☐ | OH-LTP | Airbus A330-302E | 1023 | ex F-WWYQ | | |
| ☐ | OH-LTR | Airbus A330-302E | 1067 | ex F-WWKY | | |
| ☐ | OH-LTS | Airbus A330-302E | 1078 | ex F-WWYU | | |
| ☐ | OH-LTT | Airbus A330-302E | 1088 | ex F-WWKH | | |
| ☐ | OH-LTU | Airbus A330-302E | 1173 | ex F-WWYN | | |
| ☐ | OH-LQA | Airbus A340-311 | 058 | ex G-VFLY | | |
| ☐ | OH-LQB | Airbus A340-313E | 835 | ex F-WWJG | | |
| ☐ | OH-LQC | Airbus A340-313E | 844 | ex F-WWJI | | |
| ☐ | OH-LQD | Airbus A340-313E | 921 | ex F-WWJK | | |
| ☐ | OH-LQE | Airbus A340-313E | 938 | ex F-WWJL | | |
| ☐ | OH-LQF | Airbus A340-313X | 168 | ex F-GNIF | <AFR | |
| ☐ | OH-LEE | Embraer ERJ-170STD | 17000093 | ex PT-SZT | >ELL | |
| ☐ | OH-LEF | Embraer ERJ-170STD | 17000106 | ex PT-SAO | >ELL | |
| ☐ | OH-LEG | Embraer ERJ-170STD | 17000107 | ex PT-SAP | >ELL | |
| ☐ | OH-LEH | Embraer ERJ-170STD | 17000112 | ex PT-SAX | >ELL | |
| ☐ | OH-LEL | Embraer ERJ-170STD | 17000139 | ex PT-SED | | |
| ☐ | OH-LEO | Embraer ERJ-170STD | 17000150 | ex PT-SEO | | |
| ☐ | OH-LKE | Embraer ERJ-190LR | 19000059 | ex PT-SEW | | |
| ☐ | OH-LKF | Embraer ERJ-190LR | 19000066 | ex PT-SJE | | |
| ☐ | OH-LKG | Embraer ERJ-190LR | 19000079 | ex PT-SJV | | |

| | | | | | | |
|---|---|---|---|---|---|---|
| ☐ | OH-LKH | Embraer ERJ-190LR | 19000086 | ex PT-SNE | | |
| ☐ | OH-LKI | Embraer ERJ-190LR | 19000117 | ex PT-SQL | | |
| ☐ | OH-LKK | Embraer ERJ-190LR | 19000127 | ex PT-SQW | | |
| ☐ | OH-LKL | Embraer ERJ-190LR | 19000153 | ex PT-SAI | | |
| ☐ | OH-LKM | Embraer ERJ-190LR | 19000160 | ex PT-SAP | | |
| ☐ | OH-LKN | Embraer ERJ-190LR | 19000252 | ex PT-SIX | | |
| ☐ | OH-LKO | Embraer ERJ-190LR | 19000267 | ex PT- | | |
| ☐ | OH-LKP | Embraer ERJ-190LR | 19000416 | ex PT- | | ♦ |
| ☐ | OH-LKQ | Embraer ERJ-190LR | 19000436 | ex PT- | | ♦ |
| | | | | | | |
| ☐ | OH-LBO | Boeing 757-2Q8/W | 28172/772 | ex N1789B | | |
| ☐ | OH-LBR | Boeing 757-2Q8/W | 28167/775 | | | |
| ☐ | OH-LBS | Boeing 757-2Q8/W | 27623/792 | ex N5573K | | |
| ☐ | OH-LBT | Boeing 757-2Q8/W | 28170/801 | | | |

## FLYBE NORDIC — Westbird (FC/WBA) — Helsinki-Vantaa (HEL)

| | | | | | | |
|---|---|---|---|---|---|---|
| ☐ | OH-ATE | ATR 72-212A | 0741 | ex F-WWEB | | |
| ☐ | OH-ATF | ATR 72-212A | 0744 | ex F-WWEE | | |
| ☐ | OH-ATG | ATR 72-212A | 0757 | ex F-WWER | | |
| ☐ | OH-ATH | ATR 72-212A | 0769 | ex F-WWEH | | |
| ☐ | OH-ATI | ATR 72-212A | 0783 | ex F-WWEB | | |
| ☐ | OH-ATJ | ATR 72-212A | 0792 | ex F-WWEM | | |
| ☐ | OH-ATK | ATR 72-212A | 0848 | ex F-WWEN | | |
| ☐ | OH-ATL | ATR 72-212A | 0851 | ex F-WWEU | | |
| ☐ | OH-ATM | ATR 72-212A | 0916 | ex F-WW | | ♦ |
| ☐ | OH-ATN | ATR 72-212A | 0959 | ex F-WW | | ♦ |
| ☐ | OH-ATO | ATR 72-212A | 0977 | ex F-WWEV | | ♦ |
| ☐ | OH- | ATR 72-212A | | ex | | o/o |
| | | | | | | |
| ☐ | OH-ATA | ATR 42-500 | 0641 | ex F-WWLV | | ♦ |
| ☐ | OH-ATB | ATR 42-500 | 0643 | ex F-WWLA | | ♦ |
| ☐ | OH-ATC | ATR 42-500 | 0651 | ex F-WWLI | | ♦ |
| ☐ | OH-ATD | ATR 42-500 | 0655 | ex F-WWLM | | ♦ |
| ☐ | OK-JFJ | ATR 42-500 | 0623 | ex F-WWLD | Namest nad Oslavou | <CSA♦ |
| | | | | | | |
| ☐ | OH-LEI | Embraer ERJ-170STD | 17000120 | ex PT-SDI | | |
| ☐ | OH-LEK | Embraer ERJ-170STD | 17000127 | ex PT-SDQ | | |

## NORDIC GLOBAL AIRLINES — (NJ/NGB)

| | | | | | | |
|---|---|---|---|---|---|---|
| ☐ | OH-LGC | McDonnell-Douglas MD-11F | 48512/529 | ex N512SU | | ♦ |
| ☐ | OH-LGD | McDonnell-Douglas MD-11BCF | 48513/564 | ex N518AY | | ♦ |

## SCANWINGS — Skywings (ABF) — Helsinki-Vantaa (HEL)

| | | | | | |
|---|---|---|---|---|---|
| ☐ | OH-BAX | Beech 65-C90 King Air | LJ-948 | ex N4495U | |
| ☐ | OH-BEX | Beech 65-C90 King Air | LJ-978 | ex N725KR | |

## UTIN LENTO

| | | | | | |
|---|---|---|---|---|---|
| ☐ | OH-SIS | Cessna 208 Caravan I | 20800105 | ex LN-PBD | |
| ☐ | OH-USI | Cessna 208 Caravan I | 20800275 | ex N52639 | |

## OK-   CZECH REPUBLIC

## CENTRAL CONNECT AIRLINES — (3B/CCG) — Ostrava (OSR)

| | | | | | |
|---|---|---|---|---|---|
| ☐ | OK-CCC | SAAB SF.340B | 340B-208 | ex YR-VGM | |
| ☐ | OK-CCD | SAAB SF.340B | 340A-161 | ex SE-KXH | |
| ☐ | OK-CCF | SAAB SF.340A | 340A-101 | ex N101CN | Frtr; Op for UPS |
| ☐ | OK-CCG | SAAB SF.340A | 340A-104 | ex N104CQ | Frtr; Op for UPS |
| ☐ | OK-CCL | SAAB SF.340A | 340A-159 | ex LY-NSD | Frtr |
| ☐ | OK-CCO | SAAB SF.340B | 340B-188 | ex XA-TJI | |

Ops suspended 24Jan12

## CSA CZECH AIRLINES — CSA Lines (OK/CSA) — Prague-Ruzyne (PRG)

Member of Skyteam

| | | | | | |
|---|---|---|---|---|---|
| ☐ | OK-MEK | Airbus A319-112 | 3043 | ex D-AVWL | |
| ☐ | OK-MEL | Airbus A319-112 | 3094 | ex D-AVWN | |
| ☐ | OK-NEM | Airbus A319-112 | 3406 | ex D-AVYB | |
| ☐ | OK-NEN | Airbus A319-112 | 3436 | ex D-AVYJ | |
| ☐ | OK-NEO | Airbus A319-112 | 3452 | ex D-AVYY | |
| ☐ | OK-NEP | Airbus A319-112 | 3660 | ex D-AVYT | |
| ☐ | OK-OER | Airbus A319-112 | 3892 | ex D-AVWK | |
| ☐ | OK-PET | Airbus A319-112 | 4258 | ex D-AVWM | |

| | | | | | | |
|---|---|---|---|---|---|---|
| ☐ | OK-REQ | Airbus A319-112 | 4713 | ex D-AVYS | | ♦ |
| ☐ | OK- | Airbus A319-112 | | ex | | o/o |
| ☐ | OK- | Airbus A319-112 | | ex | | o/o |
| ☐ | OK- | Airbus A319-112 | | ex | | o/o |
| ☐ | OK-GEA | Airbus A320-214 | 1439 | ex CS-TQA | Roznov pod Radhostem | |
| ☐ | OK-GEB | Airbus A320-214 | 1450 | ex CS-TQB | Strakonice | |
| ☐ | OK-LEE | Airbus A320-214 | 2719 | ex F-WWDC | | |
| ☐ | OK-LEF | Airbus A320-214 | 2758 | ex F-WWDP | | |
| ☐ | OK-LEG | Airbus A320-214 | 2789 | ex F-WWBX | | |
| ☐ | OK-MEH | Airbus A320-214 | 3031 | ex F-WWBU | | |
| ☐ | OK-MEI | Airbus A320-214 | 3060 | ex F-WWDY | | |
| ☐ | OK-MEJ | Airbus A320-214 | 3097 | ex F-WWID | | |
| ☐ | OK-JFJ | ATR 42-500 | 0623 | ex F-WWLD | Namest nad Oslavou | >FCM |
| ☐ | OK-JFK | ATR 42-500 | 0625 | ex F-WWLF | Slavkov u Brna | |
| ☐ | OK-JFL | ATR 42-500 | 0629 | ex F-WWLJ | Susice | |
| ☐ | OK-KFM | ATR 42-500 | 0635 | ex F-WWLP | Benesov | |
| ☐ | OK-KFN | ATR 42-500 | 0637 | ex F-WWLR | Prerov | |
| ☐ | OK-KFO | ATR 42-500 | 0633 | ex F-WWLN | Sokolov | |
| ☐ | OK-KFP | ATR 42-500 | 0639 | ex F-WWLT | Svitavy | |
| ☐ | OK-DGL | Boeing 737-55S | 28472/3004 | | Tabor | >RNV |
| ☐ | OK-XGA | Boeing 737-55S | 26539/2300 | ex (OO-SYL) | Plzen | |
| ☐ | OK-XGB | Boeing 737-55S | 26540/2317 | ex (OO-SYM) | Olomouc | |
| ☐ | OK-XGC | Boeing 737-55S | 26541/2319 | ex (OO-SYN) | Ceske Budejovice | |
| ☐ | OK-XGD | Boeing 737-55S | 26542/2337 | ex (OO-SYO) | Poprad | |
| ☐ | OK-XGE | Boeing 737-55S | 26543/2339 | ex (OO-SYP) | Kosice | |
| ☐ | OK-CEC | Airbus A321-211 | 0674 | ex C-GKOH | Nove mesto nad Metuji | |
| ☐ | OK-CED | Airbus A321-211 | 0684 | ex C-GKOJ | Havlickuv Brod | |

## CZECH CONNECT AIRLINES

| | | | | | | |
|---|---|---|---|---|---|---|
| ☐ | OK-CCA | Boeing 737-31S | 29058/2946 | ex G-THOH | | ♦ |

## HOLIDAYS CZECH AIRLINES  (HCC)

| | | | | | |
|---|---|---|---|---|---|
| ☐ | OK-HCA | Airbus A320-214 | 4699 | ex F-WWDO | >FHE♦ |
| ☐ | OK-HCB | Airbus A320-214 | 2180 | ex G-OOPX | >FHE♦ |
| ☐ | OK-WGX | Boeing 737-436 | 25349/2156 | ex G-DOCD | ♦ |

## LR AIRLINES  Lady Racine (LRB)  Ostrava (OSR)

| | | | | | |
|---|---|---|---|---|---|
| ☐ | OK-LRA | LET L-410UVP-E | 892216 | ex CCCP-67605 | Lady Racine |

## SILVER AIR  Solid (SLD)  Prague-Ruzyne (PRG)

| | | | | | |
|---|---|---|---|---|---|
| ☐ | OK-SLD | LET L-410UVP-E9 | 902503 | ex LZ-CCG | Ceska Posta titles |
| ☐ | OK-WDC | LET L-410UVP-E8D | 912531 | | |

## SMARTWINGS  Skytravel (QS/TVS)  Prague-Ruzyne (PRG)

| | | | | | |
|---|---|---|---|---|---|
| ☐ | OK-SWV | Boeing 737-522 | 26696/2440 | ex N951UA | wfs |
| ☐ | OK-SWX | Boeing 737-76N/W | 29885/1120 | ex G-STRF | ♦ |

## TRAVEL SERVICE AIRLINES  Skytravel (QS/TVS)  Prague-Ruzyne (PRG)

| | | | | | |
|---|---|---|---|---|---|
| ☐ | OK-TVB | Boeing 737-8CX/W | 32362/1125 | | |
| ☐ | OK-TVD | Boeing 737-86N | 28595/285 | ex CN-RNO | Prague Airport |
| ☐ | OK-TVF | Boeing 737-8FH/W | 29669/1692 | | >SWG |
| ☐ | OK-TVG | Boeing 737-8Q8/W | 30719/2257 | ex C-GTVG | >SWG |
| ☐ | OK-TVH | Boeing 737-8Q8/W | 35275/2604 | | >SWG |
| ☐ | OK-TVK | Boeing 737-86N/W | 32740/1444 | ex N977RY | >SWG |
| ☐ | OK-TVL | Boeing 737-8FN/W | 37076/3147 | | |
| ☐ | OK-TVM | Boeing 737-8FN/W | 37077/3163 | | |
| ☐ | OK-TVN | Boeing 737-8BK/W | 29643/2303 | ex G-CEJO | |
| ☐ | OK-TVO | Boeing 737-8CX/W | 32360/1084 | ex PR-GOK | |
| ☐ | OK-TVP | Boeing 737-8K5/W | 32907/1117 | ex D-AHLR | |
| ☐ | OK-TVS | Boeing 737-86N/W | 39404/3633 | | ♦ |
| ☐ | OK-TVT | Boeing 737-86N/W | 39394/3899 | | .>SWG♦ |
| ☐ | OK-TVU | Boeing 737-86N/W | 38025/3968 | | ♦ |
| ☐ | OK-TV | Boeing 737-86N/W | 38027 | | o/o |

## VAN AIR EUROPE  (6Z/VAA)  Brno-Turany

| | | | | | |
|---|---|---|---|---|---|
| ☐ | OK-ASA | LET L-410UVP-E | 902439 | ex SP-KPY | Op for Manx2♦ |
| ☐ | OK-TCA | LET L-410UVP-E | 902431 | ex SP-KPZ | Op for Manx2 |
| ☐ | OK-UBA | LET L-410UVP-E19 | 892319 | ex SP-TXA | Op for Manx2 |

## OM-    SLOVAKIA (Slovak Republic)

### AIREXPLORE                                    (ED/AXE)

| | | | | |
|---|---|---|---|---|
| ☐ | OM-AEX | Boeing 737-4Y0 | 25178/2199 | ex D-AEFL |
| ☐ | OM-BEX | Boeing 737-382 | 24365/1695 | ex Z3-AAN | >K9♦ |

### DANUBE WINGS                                 (V5/VPA)                          Bratislava-MR Stefanik (BTS)

| | | | | |
|---|---|---|---|---|
| ☐ | OM-VRA | ATR 72-201 | 0373 | ex F-WAGR |
| ☐ | OM-VRB | ATR 72-202 | 0367 | ex EI-REG |
| ☐ | OM-VRC | ATR 72-202 | 0307 | ex F-WKVB | >NTJ |
| ☐ | OM-VRD | ATR 42-300 (QC) | 0158 | ex D-BCRP | ♦ |

### DUBNICA AIR                                                                   Slavnica

| | | | | |
|---|---|---|---|---|
| ☐ | OM-ODQ | LET L-410UVP | 841320 | ex OK-ODQ |
| ☐ | OM-PGB | LET L-410UVP | 810712 |
| ☐ | OM-PGD | LET L-410M | 750403 | | ♦ |
| ☐ | OM-SAB | LET L-410MA | 750405 | ex 0405 Slovak AF | ♦ |

### SAMAIR

| | | | | |
|---|---|---|---|---|
| ☐ | OM-SAA | Boeing 737-476 | 24439/2265 | ex N249SY | ♦ |

### SLOVAK GOVERNMENT FLYING SERVICE      Slovak Government (SSG)    Bratislava-MR Stefanik (BTS)

| | | | | |
|---|---|---|---|---|
| ☐ | OM-BYE | Yakovlev Yak-40 | 9440338 | ex OK-BYE | VIP |
| ☐ | OM-BYL | Yakovlev Yak-40 | 9940560 | ex OK-BYL | VIP |
| ☐ | OM-BYO | Tupolev Tu-154M | 89A803 | ex OK-BYO |
| ☐ | OM-BYR | Tupolev Tu-154M | 98A1012 | | VIP |

### SLOVAKIAN AIRLINES

| | | | | |
|---|---|---|---|---|
| ☐ | OM-BTS | Boeing 737-55S | 28471/2885 | ex EK-73771 | <RNV♦ |

### TRAVEL SERVICE SLOVAKIA                   (TVQ)

| | | | | |
|---|---|---|---|---|
| ☐ | OM-TVA | Boeing 737-86N/W | 32243/869 | ex OK-TVA |
| ☐ | OM-TVR | Boeing 737-86N/W | 38018/3618 | ex (OM-TVR) | ♦ |

## OO-    BELGIUM (Kingdom of Belgium)

### AIR SERVICE LIEGE                                                             Liege (LGG)

| | | | | |
|---|---|---|---|---|
| ☐ | OO-AFM | Beech C90A King Air | LJ-1405 | ex N59MS | ♦ |
| ☐ | OO-ASL | Beech B200A Super King Air | BL-49 | ex OK-LFB |
| ☐ | OO-ELI | Dornier 328-110 | 3060 | ex PH-SOX | ♦ |
| ☐ | OO-GMJ | Beech B300 Super King Air | FL-460 | ex D-CGMJ |
| ☐ | OO-LET | Beech B200 Super King Air | BB-1473 | ex N8210X |
| ☐ | OO-PHB | Beech 1900D | UE-106 | ex N106UE | Mr Blue Sky |

### AIRVENTURE                                 Venture Liner (RVE)              Antwerp-Deurne (ANR)

| | | | | |
|---|---|---|---|---|
| ☐ | OO-SXC | Embraer EMB.121A Xingu | 121042 | ex PT-MBJ | EMS |

### BRUSSELS AIRLINES                         Estail (SN/BEL)                  Brussels-National (BRU)

Member of Star Alliance

| | | | | |
|---|---|---|---|---|
| ☐ | OO-SSC | Airbus A319-112 | 1086 | ex F-OHJX |
| ☐ | OO-SSD | Airbus A319-112 | 1102 | ex EI-DEY |
| ☐ | OO-SSG | Airbus A319-112 | 1160 | ex EI-CZF |
| ☐ | OO-SSK | Airbus A319-112 | 1336 | ex F-WQRU |
| ☐ | OO-SSM | Airbus A319-112 | 1388 | ex F-WQRV |
| ☐ | OO-SSP | Airbus A319-111 | 0644 | ex F-GPMG |
| ☐ | OO-SSQ | Airbus A319-112 | 4275 | ex N275MX |
| ☐ | OO-SSR | Airbus A319-112 | 4275 | ex N275MX | ♦ |
| ☐ | OO-SSU | Airbus A319-111 | 2230 | ex G-EZEM | ♦ |
| ☐ | OO-SSV | Airbus A319-111 | 2196 | ex G-EZEI | ♦ |
| ☐ | OO-SSW | Airbus A319-111 | 3255 | ex EI-ETG | ♦ |
| | | | | | |
| ☐ | OO-SFM | Airbus A330-301 | 030 | ex F-GMDA |
| ☐ | OO-SFN | Airbus A330-301 | 037 | ex F-GMDB |

| | | | | | |
|---|---|---|---|---|---|
| ☐ | OO-SFO | Airbus A330-301 | 045 | ex F-GMDC | |
| ☐ | OO-SFV | Airbus A330-322 | 095 | ex 9M-MKR | |
| ☐ | OO-SFW | Airbus A330-322 | 082 | ex EI-DVB | |
| ☐ | OO-SFY | Airbus A330-223 | 229 | ex HB-IQA | <SWR♦ |
| ☐ | OO-SFZ | Airbus A330-223 | 249 | ex HB-IQC | <SWR♦ |
| | | | | | |
| ☐ | OO-DJP | Avro 146-RJ85 | E2287 | ex G-6-287 | |
| ☐ | OO-DJR | Avro 146-RJ85 | E2290 | ex G-6-290 | [SEN] |
| ☐ | OO-DJS | Avro 146-RJ85 | E2292 | ex G-6-292 | [SEN] |
| ☐ | OO-DJT | Avro 146-RJ85 | E2294 | ex G-6-294 | wfs |
| ☐ | OO-DJV | Avro 146-RJ85 | E2295 | ex G-6-295 | |
| ☐ | OO-DJW | Avro 146-RJ85 | E2296 | ex G-6-296 | |
| ☐ | OO-DJX | Avro 146-RJ85 | E2297 | ex G-6-297 | |
| ☐ | OO-DJY | Avro 146-RJ85 | E2302 | ex G-6-302 | |
| ☐ | OO-DJZ | Avro 146-RJ85 | E2305 | ex G-6-305 | |
| ☐ | OO-DWA | Avro 146-RJ100 | E3308 | ex G-BXEU | |
| ☐ | OO-DWB | Avro 146-RJ100 | E3315 | ex G-6-315 | |
| ☐ | OO-DWC | Avro 146-RJ100 | E3322 | ex G-6-322 | |
| ☐ | OO-DWD | Avro 146-RJ100 | E3324 | ex G-6-324 | |
| ☐ | OO-DWE | Avro 146-RJ100 | E3327 | ex G-6-327 | |
| ☐ | OO-DWF | Avro 146-RJ100 | E3332 | ex G-6-332 | |
| ☐ | OO-DWG | Avro 146-RJ100 | E3336 | ex G-6-336 | |
| ☐ | OO-DWH | Avro 146-RJ100 | E3340 | ex G-6-340 | |
| ☐ | OO-DWI | Avro 146-RJ100 | E3342 | ex G-6-342 | |
| ☐ | OO-DWJ | Avro 146-RJ100 | E3355 | ex G-6-355 | |
| ☐ | OO-DWK | Avro 146-RJ100 | E3360 | ex G-6-360 | |
| ☐ | OO-DWL | Avro 146-RJ100 | E3361 | ex G-6-361 | |
| | | | | | |
| ☐ | OO-LTM | Boeing 737-3M8 | 25070/2037 | ex F-GMTM | >ZC |
| ☐ | OO-VEG | Boeing 737-36N/W | 28568/2987 | ex EI-TVQ | |
| ☐ | OO-VEH | Boeing 737-36N/W | 28571/3022 | ex EI-TVR | |
| ☐ | OO-VEK | Boeing 737-405 | 24270/1726 | ex LN-BRA | |
| ☐ | OO-VEN | Boeing 737-36N | 28586/3090 | ex EI-TVN | |
| ☐ | OO-VEP | Boeing 737-43Q | 28489/2827 | ex VH-VGA | |
| ☐ | OO-VES | Boeing 737-43Q | 28493/2838 | ex VH-VGE | |
| ☐ | OO-VET | Boeing 737-4Q8 | 28202/3009 | ex VT-SJB | |
| | | | | | |
| ☐ | D-ADHD | de Havilland DHC-8-402Q | 4056 | ex C-GFYI | <AUB♦ |
| ☐ | G-ECOH | de Havilland DHC-8-402Q | 4221 | ex C-FSRW | <BEE♦ |
| ☐ | G-ECOI | de Havilland DHC-8-402Q | 4224 | ex C-FTIE | <BEE♦ |
| ☐ | OO-DJJ | British Aerospace 146 Srs.200 | E2196 | ex SE-DRM | >ZC |
| ☐ | OO-MJE | British Aerospace 146 Srs.200 | E2192 | ex G-6-192 | >ZC |
| ☐ | OO-SNA | Airbus A320-214 | 1441 | ex D-ALTC | |
| ☐ | OO-SNB | Airbus A320-214 | 1493 | ex D-ALTD | ♦ |
| ☐ | OO-SNC | Airbus A320-214 | 1797 | ex D-ALTH | ♦ |
| ☐ | OO-SND | Airbus A320-214 | 1838 | ex D-ALTJ | ♦ |

## JETAIRFLY — Beauty (TB/JAF) — Brussels-National (BRU)

| | | | | | | |
|---|---|---|---|---|---|---|
| ☐ | OO-JAD | Boeing 737-8K5/W | 39093/3601 | | | ♦ |
| ☐ | OO-JAF | Boeing 737-8K5/W | 35133/2313 | ex N1780B | Smile | |
| ☐ | OO-JAH | Boeing 737-8K5/W | 37260/3688 | | Perspective | |
| ☐ | OO-JAQ | Boeing 737-8K5/W | 35148/2790 | ex N1786B | Vision | >CJA♦ |
| ☐ | OO-JAX | Boeing 737-8K5/W | 37238/3452 | ex N1787B | Brightness | |
| ☐ | OO-JBG | Boeing 737-8K5/W | 35142/2660 | | Gerard Brackx | |
| ☐ | OO-JLO | Boeing 737-8K5/W | 34692/2249 | ex CN-RPG | | ♦ |
| ☐ | OO-JPT | Boeing 737-8K5/W | 34691/2246 | ex CN-RPF | | ♦ |
| ☐ | OO-VAC | Boeing 737-8BK/W | 33014/1367 | ex N334CT | Rising Sun | |
| ☐ | PH-TFF | Boeing 737-86N/W | 35220/2406 | ex EI-EPO | | <TFL♦ |
| | | | | | | |
| ☐ | OO-JAM | Boeing 737-46J | 28867/2879 | ex CN-RPH | | ♦ |
| ☐ | OO-JAN | Boeing 737-76N/W | 28609/417 | ex VT-JNT | Revelation | |
| ☐ | OO-JAO | Boeing 737-7K5/W | 35141/2603 | ex D-AHXI | Playing to Win | |
| ☐ | OO-JAP | Boeing 767-38EER | 30840/829 | ex N308MT | Crystal | |
| ☐ | OO-JAR | Boeing 737-7K5/W | 35150/2825 | | Enjoy | |
| ☐ | OO-JAS | Boeing 737-7K5/W | 35144/2652 | ex D-AHXK | | |
| ☐ | OO-TUC | Boeing 767-341ER | 24844/324 | ex N484TC | Discover | |
| ☐ | OO-JAT | Boeing 737-5K5 | 24927/1968 | ex D-AHLF | | |

## NOORDZEE HELIKOPTERS VLAANDEREN — Ostend/Antwerp-Deurne/Kortrijk-Wevelgem (OST/ANR/KJK)

| | | | | | | |
|---|---|---|---|---|---|---|
| ☐ | CS-HHR | Aérospatiale AS365N3 Dauphin 2 | | | | <HPL♦ |
| ☐ | OO-NHE | Aérospatiale AS365N3 Dauphin 2 | 6843 | | | |
| ☐ | OO-NHG | Aérospatiale AS365N3 Dauphin 2 | 6881 | | | |
| ☐ | OO-NHH | Aérospatiale AS365N3 Dauphin 2 | 6891 | | | |
| ☐ | OO-NHK | Aérospatiale AS365N3 Dauphin 2 | 6876 | | | |
| ☐ | OO-NHM | Aérospatiale SA365N Dauphin 3 | 6740 | ex C-FYRC | | |
| ☐ | OO-NHN | Aérospatiale AS365N3 Dauphin 2 | 6783 | ex D2-EWF | | op Liberia♦ |
| ☐ | OO-NHO | Aérospatiale AS365N2 Dauphin | 6809 | ex D2-EWH | | op Liberia♦ |
| ☐ | OO-NHU | Aérospatiale AS365SR Dauphin | 6665 | ex F-WWOS | Flipper 2 | |
| ☐ | OO-NHV | Aérospatiale AS.365N2 Dauphin 2 | 6510 | ex F-WWQZ | Flipper 1 | ♦ |
| ☐ | OO-NHX | Aérospatiale AS365N3 Dauphin 2 | 6706 | ex OY-HMO | | |

| | | | | | | |
|---|---|---|---|---|---|---|
| ☐ | OO-NHY | Aérospatiale AS365N3 Dauphin 2 | 6754 | | | |
| ☐ | OO-NHZ | Aérospatiale AS365N2 Dauphin 2 | 6450 | ex N4H | Flipper 3 | EMS |
| | | | | | | |
| ☐ | OO-ECB | Eurocopter EC120B Colibri | 1096 | ex F-WQDK | | |
| ☐ | OO-EMS | MD Helicopters MD900 Explorer | 900-00020 | ex SE-JCG | | EMS |
| ☐ | OO-NHB | Eurocopter EC145B | 9083 | ex D-HMBG | | EMS |
| ☐ | OO-NHF | MD Helicopters MD900 Explorer | 900-00015 | ex N9015P | | EMS |

## THOMAS COOK AIRLINES BELGIUM  —  Thomas Cook (FQ/TCW)  —  Brussels-National (BRU)

| | | | | | | |
|---|---|---|---|---|---|---|
| ☐ | OO-TCH | Airbus A320-214 | 1929 | ex D-AICM | Experience | |
| ☐ | OO-TCI | Airbus A320-214 | 1975 | ex EI-DBD | Mega Mindy | |
| ☐ | OO-TCJ | Airbus A320-214 | 1787 | ex EI-DBC | inspire | |
| ☐ | OO-TCN | Airbus A320-232 | 0425 | ex SX-BVA | | |
| ☐ | OO-TCP | Airbus A320-214 | 0653 | ex F-GRSD | | |
| | | | | | | |
| ☐ | OO-TCS | Airbus A319-132 | 2362 | ex M-ABEL | | ♦ |

## TNT AIRWAYS  —  Quality (3V/TAY)  —  Liege (LGG)

| | | | | | | |
|---|---|---|---|---|---|---|
| ☐ | OO-TNA | Boeing 737-3T0 (SF) | 23569/1258 | ex N13331 | | |
| ☐ | OO-TNB | Boeing 737-3T0 (SF) | 23578/1358 | ex N39340 | | |
| ☐ | OO-TNC | Boeing 737-301 (SF) | 23513/1327 | ex N559AU | | |
| ☐ | OO-TNH | Boeing 737-301 (SF) | 23930/1539 | ex N585US | | |
| ☐ | OO-TNL | Boeing 737-34S (SF) | 29109/3001 | ex N132MN | | |
| | | | | | | |
| ☐ | OE-IAP | Boeing 737-4M0 (SF) | 29206/3058 | ex OO-TNR | | ♦ |
| ☐ | OE-IAQ | Boeing 737-4M0 (SF) | 29207/3078 | ex PK-GZL | | ♦ |
| ☐ | OE-IAR | Boeing 737-4M0 (SF) | 29208/3081 | ex PK-GZM | | ♦ |
| ☐ | OE-IAS | Boeing 737-4M0 (SF) | 29209/3087 | ex PK-GZN | | ♦ |
| ☐ | OO-TNN | Boeing 737-45DF | 27131/2458 | ex EI-EMW | | ♦ |
| ☐ | OO-TNO | Boeing 737-49R | 28881/2833 | ex EI-DOS | | ♦ |
| ☐ | OO-TNP | Boeing 737-45DF | 27256/2589 | ex EI-EOD | | ♦ |
| ☐ | OO-TNQ | Boeing 737-4M0 (SF) | 29205/3056 | ex OE-IAO | | ♦ |
| | | | | | | |
| ☐ | OO-TAD | British Aerospace 146 Srs.300QT | E3166 | ex G-TNTM | | |
| ☐ | OO-TAE | British Aerospace 146 Srs.300QT | E3182 | ex G-TNTG | | |
| ☐ | OO-TAF | British Aerospace 146 Srs.300QT | E3186 | ex G-TNTK | | |
| ☐ | OO-TAH | British Aerospace 146 Srs.300QT | E3168 | ex G-TNTL | | |
| ☐ | OO-TAJ | British Aerospace 146 Srs.300QT | E3153 | ex G-TNTE | | |
| ☐ | OO-TAQ | British Aerospace 146 Srs.200QT | E2078 | ex G-BNPJ | | |
| ☐ | OO-TAR | British Aerospace 146 Srs.200QT | E2067 | ex G-TNTB | | [LGG] |
| ☐ | OO-TAS | British Aerospace 146 Srs.300QT | E3154 | ex EC-FFY | | |
| ☐ | OO-TAU | British Aerospace 146 Srs.200QT | E2100 | ex EC-GQP | | |
| ☐ | OO-TAW | British Aerospace 146 Srs.200QT | E2089 | ex EC-EPA | | |
| ☐ | OO-TAZ | British Aerospace 146 Srs.200 (QC) | E2188 | ex F-GLNI | | [NWI] |
| | | | | | | |
| ☐ | OO-TFA | Boeing 757-28AF | 25622/530 | ex OH-AFK | | op for NATO♦ |
| ☐ | OO-THA | Boeing 747-4HAERF | 35232/1381 | | Peter Abeles 1924-1999 | |
| ☐ | OO-THB | Boeing 747-4HAERF | 35234/1386 | | Ken Thomas 1913-1997 | |
| ☐ | OO-THC | Boeing 747-4HAERF | 35235/1389 | ex N50217 | | op for UAE |
| ☐ | OO-THD | Boeing 747-4HAERF | 35236/1399 | | | op for UAE |
| ☐ | OO-TSA | Boeing 777-FHT | 38969/944 | | | |
| ☐ | OO-TSB | Boeing 777-FHT | 39286/963 | ex N778SA | | ♦ |
| ☐ | OO-TSC | Boeing 777-FHT | 37138/977 | | | ♦ |
| ☐ | TF-ELF | Airbus A300B4-622RF | 529 | ex EI-DJN | | <ABD♦ |

## VLM AIRLINES  —  Rubens (VG/VLM)  —  Antwerp-Deurne (ANR)

| | | | | | |
|---|---|---|---|---|---|
| ☐ | OO-VLF | Fokker 50 | 20208 | ex PH-DMT | Panamarenko |
| ☐ | OO-VLI | Fokker 50 | 20226 | ex PH-JXC | |
| ☐ | OO-VLJ | Fokker 50 | 20105 | ex PH-ARE | Isle of Man |
| ☐ | OO-VLL | Fokker 50 | 20144 | ex TF-JMG | City of Groningen |
| ☐ | OO-VLM | Fokker 50 | 20135 | ex PH-VLM | Ville de Nantes |
| ☐ | OO-VLN | Fokker 50 | 20145 | ex PH-VLN | City of Reenstar |
| ☐ | OO-VLO | Fokker 50 | 20127 | ex ES-AFL | Angela Dirkin |
| ☐ | OO-VLP | Fokker 50 | 20209 | ex PH-DMS | |
| ☐ | OO-VLQ | Fokker 50 | 20159 | ex EC-GBH | City of Manchester |
| ☐ | OO-VLR | Fokker 50 | 20121 | ex PH-ARF | City of Brussels |
| ☐ | OO-VLS | Fokker 50 | 20109 | ex EC-GBG | City of Hamburg |
| ☐ | OO-VLV | Fokker 50 | 20160 | ex EC-GDD | Island of Jersey |
| ☐ | OO-VLY | Fokker 50 | 20181 | ex PH-ZFC | City of Liverpool |
| ☐ | OO-VLZ | Fokker 50 | 20264 | ex TF-JMU | City of Rotterdam |

## OY-   DENMARK (Kingdom of Denmark)

## AIR ALPHA GREENLAND  —  Air Alpha (GD/AHA)  —  Nuuk Godthaab (GOH)

| | | | | | |
|---|---|---|---|---|---|
| ☐ | OY-HIC | Bell 222U | 47522 | ex PT-HXC | |

## AIR GREENLAND — Greenlandair (GL/GRL) — Nuuk Godthaab (GOH)

| | Reg | Type | c/n | Notes | | |
|---|---|---|---|---|---|---|
| ☐ | OY-HGA | Aérospatiale AS350B2 Ecureuil | 2600 | | | |
| ☐ | OY-HGK | Aérospatiale AS350B2 Ecureuil | 2570 | ex C-FNJW | | |
| ☐ | OY-HGO | Aérospatiale AS350B3 Ecureuil | 3919 | | | |
| ☐ | OY-HGP | Aérospatiale AS350B3 Ecureuil | 4062 | | | |
| ☐ | OY-HGS | Aérospatiale AS350B3 Ecureuil | 4226 | | | |
| ☐ | OY-HUD | Aérospatiale AS350B Ecureuil | 7152 | | | ♦ |
| ☐ | OY-HVE | Aérospatiale AS350B Ecureuil | 7172 | | | ♦ |
| ☐ | OY-HCY | Bell 212 | 31166 | | Piseeq 2 | |
| ☐ | OY-HDM | Bell 212 | 31142 | ex N57545 | | |
| ☐ | OY-HDN | Bell 212 | 31136 | ex N5752K | Miteq | |
| ☐ | OY-HMD | Bell 212 | 31125 | ex LN-ORI | | |
| ☐ | OY-HIA | Bell 222UT | 47529 | ex TC-HCS | | |
| ☐ | OY-HID | Bell 222U | 47548 | ex D-HCAN | | |
| ☐ | OY-HIE | Bell 222U | 47501 | ex D-HUKM | | |
| ☐ | OY-HIF | Bell 222UT | 47512 | ex N256SP | | |
| ☐ | OY-GRG | de Havilland DHC-8Q-202 | 504 | ex C-FXBO | | |
| ☐ | OY-GRH | de Havilland DHC-8Q-202 | 488 | ex C-GCTX | | |
| ☐ | OY-GRI | de Havilland DHC-8Q-202 | 477 | ex C-GJXW | | |
| ☐ | OY-GRJ | de Havilland DHC-8Q-202 | 496 | ex C-GLVB | | ♦ |
| ☐ | OY-GRK | de Havilland DHC-8Q-202 | 498 | ex C-GLUZ | | ♦ ♦ |
| ☐ | OY-CBT | de Havilland DHC-7-103 | 010 | ex C-GRQB-X | Papikkaaq | |
| ☐ | OY-CBU | de Havilland DHC-7-103 | 020 | | Nipiki | |
| ☐ | OY-GRE | de Havilland DHC-7-103 | 106 | ex N54026 | Taateraaq | |
| ☐ | OY-GRF | de Havilland DHC-7-102 | 113 | ex OE-LLU | Sululik | |
| ☐ | OY-GRN | Airbus A330-223 | 230 | ex F-WIHL | Norsaq | |
| ☐ | OY-HAF | Sikorsky S-61N | 61267 | ex N10045 | Nattoralik | |
| ☐ | OY-HAG | Sikorsky S-61N | 61268 | ex N10046 | Kussak | |
| ☐ | OY-PCL | Beech B200 Super King Air | BB-1675 | ex N2355Z | | |
| ☐ | OY-POF | de Havilland DHC-6 Twin Otter 300 | 235 | ex N6868 | | |

## ATLANTIC AIRWAYS — Faroeline (RC/FLI) — Vagar (FAE)

| | Reg | Type | c/n | Notes | |
|---|---|---|---|---|---|
| ☐ | OY-HMB | Bell 212 | 30686 | ex LN-OSR | |
| ☐ | OY-HSJ | Bell 412 | 36069 | ex N412SX | |
| ☐ | OY-HSR | Bell 412EP | 36133 | ex N62734 | |
| ☐ | OY-RCC | Avro 146-RJ100 | E3357 | ex HB-IYX | |
| ☐ | OY-RCD | Avro 146-RJ85 | B | ex HB-IXK | |
| ☐ | OY-RCE | Avro 146-RJ85 | E2233 | ex HB-IXH | |
| ☐ | OY-RCG | Airbus A319-115 | 5079 | ex D-AVYN | |
| ☐ | OY-RCW | British Aerospace 146 Srs.200 | E2115 | ex G-BRXT | ♦ ♦ |

## BENAIR AIR SERVICE — Birdie (BDI) — Stauning (STA)

| | Reg | Type | c/n | Notes | | |
|---|---|---|---|---|---|---|
| ☐ | OY-ARJ | Cessna 414 | 414-0614 | ex D-IAWM | | |
| ☐ | OY-BJP | Swearingen SA.227AC Metro III | AC-499 | ex F-GHVG | | |
| ☐ | OY-HDD | Bell 206B JetRanger III | 3649 | ex N130S | | |
| ☐ | OY-MUG | Short SD.3-60 | SH3716 | ex G-BNDM | all-white | |
| ☐ | OY-PBF | Cessna 208B Caravan I | 208B0584 | ex LN-PBF | | ♦ |
| ☐ | OY-PBH | LET L-410UVP-E20 | 972736 | ex OK-EDA | | |
| ☐ | OY-PBI | LET L-410UVP-E20 | 871936 | ex OK-SDM | | |
| ☐ | OY-PBK | Cessna 208B Caravan I | 208B0914 | ex LN-PBK | | ♦ |
| ☐ | OY-PBO | Cessna 208B Caravan I | 208B1128 | ex LN-PBO | | ♦ |
| ☐ | OY-PBV | Short SD.3-60 | SH3747 | ex G-GPBV | | |
| ☐ | OY-PBW | Short SD.3-60 | SH3760 | ex VH-SEG | | |

## CHC DENMARK — Helibird (HBI) — Esbjerg (EBJ)

| | Reg | Type | c/n | Notes | |
|---|---|---|---|---|---|
| ☐ | OY-HDT | Aérospatiale AS.332L | 2017 | ex G-BWHN | <CHC Helicopters Intl |
| ☐ | OY-HKA | Sikorsky S-92A | 920046 | ex N8052Z | |
| ☐ | OY-HKB | Sikorsky S-92A | 920058 | ex N4502X | |
| ☐ | OY-HKC | Sikorsky S-92A | 920060 | ex N4503U | |

## CIMBER AIR — Cimber (QI/CIM) — Sonderborg (SGD)

| | Reg | Type | c/n | Notes | |
|---|---|---|---|---|---|
| ☐ | OY-CIM | ATR 72-212A | 0468 | ex EC-JCR | |
| ☐ | OY-CIN | ATR 72-212A | 0568 | ex F-WWEH | |
| ☐ | OY-CIO | ATR 72-212A | 0595 | ex 3B-NBK | |
| ☐ | OY-RTC | ATR 72-202 | 0508 | ex F-WQNK | |
| ☐ | OY-RTD | ATR 72-211 | 0509 | ex F-OHFQ | |
| ☐ | OY-RTF | ATR 72-202 | 0496 | ex F-WQNL | >AEW |
| ☐ | OY-MBT | Canadair CRJ-200LR | 7617 | ex C-GKDI | |
| ☐ | OY-RJA | Canadair CRJ-200LR | 7413 | ex D-ACIM | |
| ☐ | OY-RJB | Canadair CRJ-200LR | 7419 | ex D-ACIN | |

| | | | | | |
|---|---|---|---|---|---|
| ☐ | OY-RJC | Canadair CRJ-200LR | 7015 | ex D-ACLF | |
| ☐ | OY-RJD | Canadair CRJ-200LR | 7007 | ex D-ACLH | |
| ☐ | OY-RJE | Canadair CRJ-200LR | 7009 | ex C-FMUQ | |
| ☐ | OY-RJF | Canadair CRJ-200LR | 7019 | ex C-FMUR | |
| ☐ | OY-RJG | Canadair CRJ-200LR | 7104 | ex D-ACLU | |
| ☐ | OY-RJH | Canadair CRJ-200LR | 7090 | ex D-ACLS | |
| ☐ | OY-RJI | Canadair CRJ-200LR | 7093 | ex D-ACLT | |
| ☐ | OY-RJJ | Canadair CRJ-200ER | 7784 | ex HA-LNC | |
| | | | | | |
| ☐ | OY-CIJ | ATR 42-500 | 0497 | ex A4O-AL | |
| ☐ | OY-CIK | ATR 42-500 | 0501 | ex A4O-AM | >OMA |
| ☐ | OY-CIL | ATR 42-500 | 0514 | ex F-WWLO | |

## CIMBER STERLING (QI/CIM)

| | | | | | |
|---|---|---|---|---|---|
| ☐ | OY-MRE | Boeing 737-7L9/W | 28008/203 | | |
| ☐ | OY-MRF | Boeing 737-7L9/W | 28009/221 | | |
| ☐ | OY-MRG | Boeing 737-7L9/W | 28010/396 | | |
| ☐ | OY-MRH | Boeing 737-7L9/W | 28013/682 | | |
| ☐ | OY-MRS | Boeing 737-76N/W | 32737/1130 | ex G-STRH | |
| ☐ | OY-MRU | Boeing 737-73S/W | 29079/194 | | |

## COPENHAGEN AIRTAXI — Aircat (CAT) — Copenhagen-Roskilde (RKE)

| | | | | | |
|---|---|---|---|---|---|
| ☐ | OY-CAC | Partenavia P.68B | 179 | | |
| ☐ | OY-CAT | Britten-Norman BN-2B-26 Islander | 2224 | ex EC-FFZ | |
| ☐ | OY-CDC | Partenavia P.68C | 211 | ex D-GEMD | |

## DANCOPTER — Holsted Heliport & Esbjerg (-/EBJ)

| | | | | | |
|---|---|---|---|---|---|
| ☐ | OY-HJA | Eurocopter EC155B1 | 6828 | | |
| ☐ | OY-HJP | Eurocopter EC155B1 | 6655 | ex F-WWOI | |
| ☐ | OY-HSK | Eurocopter EC155B1 | 6660 | ex N155EW | |
| ☐ | OY-HSL | Eurocopter EC155B1 | 6658 | | |

## DANISH AIR TRANSPORT — Danish (DX/DTR) — Kolding-Vamdrup

| | | | | | |
|---|---|---|---|---|---|
| ☐ | OY-CIR | ATR 42-310 | 0107 | ex F-GHPX | |
| ☐ | OY-CIU | ATR 42-310 | 0112 | ex C-FIQB | |
| ☐ | OY-JRJ | ATR 42-320 | 0036 | ex F-WQIS | based BSG |
| ☐ | OY-JRY | ATR 42-300 | 0063 | ex F-WQOC | |
| ☐ | OY-RUF | ATR 42-500 | 0515 | ex F-GVIJ | ♦ |
| | | | | | |
| ☐ | OY-JRU | McDonnell-Douglas MD-87 | 49403/1404 | ex SE-RBA | |
| ☐ | OY-RUB | ATR 72-202 | 0301 | ex F-WQNS | |
| ☐ | OY-RUD | ATR 72-201 | 0162 | ex LY-ATR | |
| ☐ | OY-RUE | McDonnell-Douglas MD-83 | 49936/1778 | ex YR-HBZ | |
| ☐ | OY-RUI | de Havilland DHC-8-106 | 335 | ex TF-JAM | ♦ |
| ☐ | OY-RUW | de Havilland DHC8-102 | 060 | ex ZK-VAC | ♦ |

## JETTIME — Jettime (JTG) — Copenhagen-Kastrup (CPH)

| | | | | | |
|---|---|---|---|---|---|
| ☐ | OY-JTA | Boeing 737-33A | 23631/1337 | ex N371FA | |
| ☐ | OY-JTB | Boeing 737-3Y0 | 24464/1753 | ex RP-C4010 | |
| ☐ | OY-JTC | Boeing 737-3L9/W | 23718/1402 | ex 9M-AAB | |
| ☐ | OY-JTD | Boeing 737-3Y0/W | 24678/1853 | ex 9M-AAY | |
| ☐ | OY-JTE | Boeing 737-3L9 | 27834/2692 | ex G-OGBE | |
| ☐ | OY-JTF | Boeing 737-382QC | 24364/1657 | ex OK-GCG | |
| ☐ | OY-JTH | Boeing 737-3Y0 (QC) | 24255/1625 | ex OO-TNG | ♦ |
| | | | | | |
| ☐ | OY-JTV | Boeing 737-7L9/W | 28015/785 | ex TS-IEB | ♦ |
| ☐ | OY-JTY | Boeing 737-7Q8/W | 30727/1005 | ex VT-SJE | ♦ |
| ☐ | OY-JTZ | Boeing 737-73S/W | 29083/392 | ex LY-STG | ♦ |

## NORTH FLYING — North Flying (M3/NFA) — Aalborg (AAL)

| | | | | | |
|---|---|---|---|---|---|
| ☐ | OY-DLY | Piper PA-31 Turbo Navajo | 31-229 | ex G-AWOW | |
| ☐ | OY-FRE | Piper PA-31 Turbo Navajo | 31-632 | ex G-AXYA | |
| ☐ | OY-NPD | Swearingen SA.227DC Metro 23 | DC-865B | ex 9M-BCH | |
| ☐ | OY-NPE | Swearingen SA.227DC Metro 23 | DC-867B | ex N23VJ | |
| ☐ | OY-NPF | Swearingen SA.227DC Metro 23 | DC-880B | ex TF-JME | |

## PRIMERA AIR SCANDINAVIA (PF/PRI)

| | | | | | |
|---|---|---|---|---|---|
| ☐ | OY-PSA | Boeing 737-8Q8/W | 30688/2280 | ex TF-JXD | |
| ☐ | OY-PSB | Boeing 737-8Q8/W | 30722/2261 | ex TF-JXE | |
| ☐ | OY-PSC | Boeing 737-86N/W | 33419/1251 | ex TF-JXF | |
| ☐ | OY-PSD | Boeing 737-86N/W | 28618/514 | ex TF-JXH | |
| ☐ | OY-PSE | Boeing 737-809/W | 30664/743 | ex TF-JXI | |
| ☐ | OY-PSF | Boeing 737-7Q8/W | 28210/22 | ex TF-JXG | |

| | | | | | |
|---|---|---|---|---|---|
| **SCANDINAVIAN AIRLINE SYSTEM** | | *Scandinavian (SK/SAS)* | | **Copenhagen-Kastrup (CPH)** | |

For details see under Sweden (SE-)

| | | | | | |
|---|---|---|---|---|---|
| **STAR AIR** | | *Whitestar (S6/SRR)* | | **Copenhagen-Kastrup (CPH)** | |
| ☐ OY-SRF | Boeing 767-219ER (SF) | 23327/134 | ex N327MR | | |
| ☐ OY-SRG | Boeing 767-219ER (SF) | 23328/149 | ex N328MT | | |
| ☐ OY-SRH | Boeing 767-204ER (SF) | 24457/256 | ex N457GE | | |
| ☐ OY-SRI | Boeing 767-25E (SF) | 27193/527 | ex N622EV | | |
| ☐ OY-SRJ | Boeing 767-25E (SF) | 27195/535 | ex N625EV | | |
| ☐ OY-SRK | Boeing 767-204ER (SF) | 23072/107 | ex N307MT | | |
| ☐ OY-SRL | Boeing 767-232 (SF) | 22219/37 | ex N107DL | | |
| ☐ OY-SRM | Boeing 767-25E (SF) | 27192/524 | ex N621EV | | |
| ☐ OY-SRN | Boeing 767-219ER (SF) | 23326/124 | ex N326MR | | |
| ☐ OY-SRO | Boeing 767-25E (SF) | 27194/532 | ex N623EV | | |
| ☐ OY-SRP | Boeing 767-232 (SF) | 22220/38 | ex N108DL | | |

| | | | | | |
|---|---|---|---|---|---|
| **STENBERG AVIATION** | | | | **Thisted (TED)** | |
| ☐ OY-BHT | Embraer EMB.110P2 Bandeirante | 110161 | ex N4942S | flying dk titles | op by Flyvsmart |

| | | | | | |
|---|---|---|---|---|---|
| **SUN-AIR OF SCANDINAVIA** | | *Sunscan (EZ/SUS)* | | **Billund (BLL)** | |
| ☐ OY-NCA | Dornier 328-110 | 3047 | ex N433JS | | |
| ☐ OY-NCL | Dornier 328-310 (328JET) | 3192 | ex N427FJ | | |
| ☐ OY-NCM | Dornier 328-310 (328JET) | 3190 | ex N426FJ | | |
| ☐ OY-NCN | Dornier 328-310 (328JET) | 3193 | ex N428FJ | | |
| ☐ OY-NCO | Dornier 328-310 (328JET) | 3210 | ex OE-HAB | | |
| ☐ OY-NCP | Dornier 328-300 (328JET) | 3132 | ex N328AC | | |
| ☐ OY-NCT | Dornier 328-310 (328JET) | 3213 | ex OE-LJR | | ♦ |
| ☐ OY- | Dornier 328-300 (328JET0 | 3122 | ex N353SK | | |
| ☐ OY-SVB | British Aerospace Jetstream 31 | 985 | ex JA8591 | | |
| ☐ OY-SVF | British Aerospace Jetstream 31 | 686 | ex G-BSFG | Skien | |

| | | | | | |
|---|---|---|---|---|---|
| **THOMAS COOK SCANDINAVIA** | | *(DK/VKG)* | | **Copenhagen-Kastrup (CPH)** | |
| ☐ OY-VKA | Airbus A321-211 | 1881 | ex D-AVZO | | |
| ☐ OY-VKB | Airbus A321-211 | 1921 | ex D-AVZQ | | |
| ☐ OY-VKC | Airbus A321-211 | 1932 | ex D-AVXB | | |
| ☐ OY-VKD | Airbus A321-211 | 1960 | ex G-EFPA | | |
| ☐ OY-VKE | Airbus A321-211 | 1887 | ex G-CTLA | | |
| ☐ OY-VKT | Airbus A321-211 | 1972 | ex G-SMTJ | | |
| ☐ OY-VKF | Airbus A330-243 | 309 | ex G-CSJS | | |
| ☐ OY-VKG | Airbus A330-343X | 349 | ex F-WWYG | | |
| ☐ OY-VKH | Airbus A330-343X | 356 | ex F-WWYJ | | |
| ☐ OY-VKI | Airbus A330-343X | 357 | ex C-GVKI | | |
| ☐ OY-VKM | Airbus A320-214 | 1889 | ex F-WWBV | | ♦ |
| ☐ OY-VKS | Airbus A320-214 | 1954 | ex G-YLBM | | ♦ |

## P- KOREA (Democratic People's Republic of Korea)

| | | | | | |
|---|---|---|---|---|---|
| **AIR KORYO** | | *Air Koryo (JS/KOR)* | | **Pyongyang (FNJ)** | |
| ☐ P-527 | Antonov An-24B | 67302207 | | | |
| ☐ P-532 | Antonov An-24RV | 47309707 | | | |
| ☐ P-533 | Antonov An-24RV | 47309708 | | | |
| ☐ P-534 | Antonov An-24RV | 47309802 | | | |
| ☐ P-537 | Antonov An-24B | 67302408 | | | |
| ☐ P-551 | Tupolev Tu-154B | 75A129 | ex 551 | | |
| ☐ P-552 | Tupolev Tu-154B | 76A143 | ex 552 | | |
| ☐ P-553 | Tupolev Tu-154B | 77A191 | ex 553 | | |
| ☐ P-561 | Tupolev Tu-154B-2 | 83A573 | | | |
| ☐ P-618 | Ilyushin Il-62M | 2546624 | | no titles | Op for Govt |
| ☐ P-632 | Tupolev Tu-204-300 | 1450742364012 | ex RA-64012 | | |
| ☐ P-633 | Tupolev Tu-204-100 | 1450741964048 | ex RA-64048 | | |
| ☐ P-813 | Tupolev Tu-134B-3 | 66215 | | | |
| ☐ P-814 | Tupolev Tu-134B-3 | 66368 | | | |
| ☐ P-835 | Ilyushin Il-18D | 188011205 | ex 835 | | |
| ☐ P-836 | Ilyushin Il-18V | 185008204 | ex 836 | | |
| ☐ P-881 | Ilyushin Il-62M | 3647853 | | | |
| ☐ P-882 | Ilyushin Il-62M | 2850236 | | no titles | Op for Govt |
| ☐ P-885 | Ilyushin Il-62M | 3933913 | ex 885 | | |
| ☐ P-912 | Ilyushin Il-76MD | 1003403104 | | | |
| ☐ P-913 | Ilyushin Il-76MD | 1003404126 | | | |

| | | | | |
|---|---|---|---|---|
| ☐ | P-914 | Ilyushin Il-76MD | 1003404146 | |
| ☐ | P- | Tupolev Tu-204-300 | | o/o |

## PH-  NETHERLANDS (Kingdom of the Netherlands)

| **AMSTERDAM AIRLINES** | **Amstel (WD/AAN)** | **Amsterdam-Schiphol (AMS)** |
|---|---|---|

Suspended ops 31Oct11

| **ARKEFLY / TUI NETHERLANDS** | **(OR/TFL)** | **Amsterdam-Schiphol (AMS)** |
|---|---|---|

| | | | | | |
|---|---|---|---|---|---|
| ☐ | PH-TFA | Boeing 737-8FH/W | 35100/2424 | ex N1786B | Ferdinand Fransen |
| ☐ | PH-TFB | Boeing 737-8K5/W | 35149/2820 | ex N1781B | |
| ☐ | PH-TFC | Boeing 737-8K5/W | 35146/2875 | ex N1787B | |
| ☐ | PH-TFD | Boeing 737-86N/W | 38014/3588 | | ♦ |
| ☐ | PH-TFF | Boeing 737-86N/W | 35220/2406 | ex EI-EPO | >JAF♦ |
| | | | | | |
| ☐ | PH-AHQ | Boeing 767-383ER | 24477/337 | ex OY-KDL | |
| ☐ | PH-AHX | Boeing 767-383ER | 24847/315 | ex LN-RCD | |
| ☐ | PH-OYE | Boeing 767-304ER/W | 28979/691 | ex G-OBYE | <TOM♦ |
| ☐ | PH-OYI | Boeing 767-304ER/W | 29138/783 | ex G-OBYI | |
| ☐ | PH-OYJ | Boeing 767-304ER/W | 29384/784 | ex G-OBYJ | ♦ |

| **CHC AIRWAYS** | **Schreiner (AW/SCH)** | **Rotterdam (RTM)** |
|---|---|---|

| | | | | | |
|---|---|---|---|---|---|
| ☐ | 5A-DLX | de Havilland DHC-8-311A | 254 | ex PH-SDK | [MST] |

| **CHC HELICOPTERS NETHERLANDS** | | **den Helder (DHR)** |
|---|---|---|

| | | | | | |
|---|---|---|---|---|---|
| ☐ | PH-EAA | Agusta AW139 | 31141 | | |
| ☐ | PH-EUC | Agusta AW139 | 41210 | ex N246SM | |
| ☐ | PH-EUE | Agusta AW139 | 31387 | | ♦ |
| ☐ | PH-SHK | Agusta AW139 | 31030 | ex I-RAIA | |
| ☐ | PH-SHL | Agusta AW139 | 31041 | | |
| ☐ | PH-SHP | Agusta AW139 | 31099 | | |
| | | | | | |
| ☐ | PH-NZS | Sikorsky S-76B | 760325 | ex G-UKLS | |
| ☐ | PH-NZT | Sikorsky S-76B | 760326 | ex G-UKLT | |
| ☐ | PH-NZU | Sikorsky S-76B | 760329 | ex G-UKLU | |
| ☐ | PH-NZV | Sikorsky S-76B | 760336 | ex G-UKLM | |
| ☐ | PH-NZW | Sikorsky S-76B | 760381 | ex G-OKLE | |
| ☐ | PH-NZZ | Sikorsky S-76B | 760316 | ex N373G | |
| | | | | | |
| ☐ | PH-SHN | Eurocopter EC155B1 | 6755 | ex F-WQVV | |
| ☐ | PH-SHO | Eurocopter EC155B1 | 6739 | ex F-WWOV | |

| **CORENDON DUTCH AIRLINES** | **(CND)** | **Amsterdam-Schiphol (AMS)** |
|---|---|---|

| | | | | | |
|---|---|---|---|---|---|
| ☐ | PH-CDE | Boeing 737-8KN/W | 35795/2829 | ex A6-FDB | ♦ |
| ☐ | PH-CDF | Boeing 737-804 | 28227/452 | ex G-CDZH | [o/o♦ |

| **DENIM AIR ACMI** | **(J7)** | **Amsterdam-Schiphol (AMS)** |
|---|---|---|

| | | | | | |
|---|---|---|---|---|---|
| ☐ | PH-JXJ | Fokker 50 | 20232 | ex PT-SLV | ♦ |
| ☐ | PH-JXK | Fokker 50 | 20233 | ex PT-SLK | ♦ |
| ☐ | PH-JXN | Fokker 50 | 20239 | ex EC-GFP | ♦ |
| ☐ | PH-KXX | Fokker 50 | 20262 | ex EC-GHC | ♦ |
| ☐ | PH-LNE | Fokker 100 | 11322 | ex EC-JDN | ♦ |

| **JETISFACTION** | | |
|---|---|---|

| | | | | | |
|---|---|---|---|---|---|
| ☐ | PH-RNI | Beech 1900D | UE-338 | ex PK-TVE | ♦ |

| **JET NETHERLANDS** | | |
|---|---|---|

| | | | | | |
|---|---|---|---|---|---|
| ☐ | PH-AAG | Canadair CRJ-200ER | 7763 | ex N492CA | ♦ |

| **KLM CITYHOPPER** | **City (WA/KLC)** | **Amsterdam-Schiphol (AMS)** |
|---|---|---|

| | | | | | |
|---|---|---|---|---|---|
| ☐ | PH-EZA | Embraer ERJ-190LR | 19000224 | ex PT-SHI | |
| ☐ | PH-EZB | Embraer ERJ-190LR | 19000235 | ex PT-SIG | |
| ☐ | PH-EZC | Embraer ERJ-190LR | 19000250 | ex PT-SIU | |
| ☐ | PH-EZD | Embraer ERJ-190LR | 19000279 | ex PT-TLT | |
| ☐ | PH-EZE | Embraer ERJ-190LR | 19000288 | ex PT-TZC | |
| ☐ | PH-EZF | Embraer ERJ-190LR | 19000304 | ex PT-TZS | |
| ☐ | PH-EZG | Embraer ERJ-190LR | 19000315 | ex PT-TXD | |
| ☐ | PH-EZH | Embraer ERJ-190LR | 19000319 | ex PT-TXH | |

| | | | | | |
|---|---|---|---|---|---|
| ☐ | PH-EZI | Embraer ERJ-190LR | 19000322 | ex PT-TXK | |
| ☐ | PH-EZK | Embraer ERJ-190LR | 19000326 | ex PT-TXO | |
| ☐ | PH-EZL | Embraer ERJ-190LR | 19000334 | ex PT-TXU | |
| ☐ | PH-EZM | Embraer ERJ-190LR | 19000338 | ex PT-TXX | |
| ☐ | PH-EZN | Embraer ERJ-190LR | 19000342 | ex PT-XQJ | |
| ☐ | PH-EZO | Embraer ERJ-190LR | 19000345 | ex PT-XQL | |
| ☐ | PH-EZP | Embraer ERJ-190LR | 19000347 | ex PT-XQN | |
| ☐ | PH-EZR | Embraer ERJ-190LR | 19000375 | ex PT-XNL | |
| ☐ | PH-EZS | Embraer ERJ-190LR | 19000380 | ex PT-XNP | |
| ☐ | PH-EZT | Embraer ERJ-190LR | 19000519 | ex PT-TUG | |
| ☐ | PH-EZU | Embraer ERJ-190LR | 19000522 | ex PT-TUJ | ♦ |
| ☐ | PH- | Embraer ERJ-190LR | 19000533 | ex PT-TUX | o/o♦ |
| ☐ | PH- | Embraer ERJ-190LR | 19000545 | ex PT- | o/o♦ |
| | | | | | |
| ☐ | PH-JCH | Fokker 70 | 11528 | ex OE-LFS | |
| ☐ | PH-JCT | Fokker 70 | 11537 | ex OE-LFT | |
| ☐ | PH-KBX | Fokker 70 | 11547 | | |
| ☐ | PH-KZA | Fokker 70 | 11567 | | |
| ☐ | PH-KZB | Fokker 70 | 11562 | | |
| ☐ | PH-KZC | Fokker 70 | 11566 | | |
| ☐ | PH-KZD | Fokker 70 | 11582 | | |
| ☐ | PH-KZE | Fokker 70 | 11576 | | |
| ☐ | PH-KZF | Fokker 70 | 11577 | ex (G-BVTH) | |
| ☐ | PH-KZG | Fokker 70 | 11578 | ex (G-BWTI) | |
| ☐ | PH-KZH | Fokker 70 | 11583 | | |
| ☐ | PH-KZI | Fokker 70 | 11579 | ex (I-REJC) | |
| ☐ | PH-KZK | Fokker 70 | 11581 | ex (I-REJD) | |
| ☐ | PH-KZL | Fokker 70 | 11536 | ex 9V-SLK | |
| ☐ | PH-KZM | Fokker 70 | 11561 | ex 9V-SLL | |
| ☐ | PH-KZN | Fokker 70 | 11553 | ex PK-PFE | |
| ☐ | PH-KZO | Fokker 70 | 11538 | ex G-BVTE | |
| ☐ | PH-KZP | Fokker 70 | 11539 | ex G-BVTF | |
| ☐ | PH-KZR | Fokker 70 | 11551 | ex G-BVTG | |
| ☐ | PH-KZS | Fokker 70 | 11540 | ex F-GLIS | |
| ☐ | PH-KZT | Fokker 70 | 11541 | ex F-GLIT | |
| ☐ | PH-KZU | Fokker 70 | 11543 | ex F-GLIU | |
| ☐ | PH-KZV | Fokker 70 | 11556 | ex F-GLIV | |
| ☐ | PH-KZW | Fokker 70 | 11558 | ex F-GLIX | |
| ☐ | PH-WXA | Fokker 70 | 11570 | ex I-REJO | |
| ☐ | PH-WXC | Fokker 70 | 11574 | ex I-REJI | |
| ☐ | PH-WXD | Fokker 70 | 11563 | ex HA-LMD | |
| | | | | | |
| ☐ | PH-OFL | Fokker 100 | 11444 | ex F-OORG | |
| ☐ | PH-OFM | Fokker 100 | 11475 | ex F-OFRG | |
| ☐ | PH-OFN | Fokker 100 | 11477 | ex F-OHXA | |
| ☐ | PH-OFO | Fokker 100 | 11462 | ex PT-MRS | |
| ☐ | PH-OFP | Fokker 100 | 11472 | ex PT-MRP | |

## KLM ROYAL DUTCH AIRLINES  — KLM (KL/KLM)  — Amsterdam-Schiphol (AMS)

Member of Skyteam

| | | | | | | |
|---|---|---|---|---|---|---|
| ☐ | PH-AOA | Airbus A330-203 | 682 | ex F-WWYE | dam-Amsterdam | |
| ☐ | PH-AOB | Airbus A330-203 | 686 | ex F-WWYH | Potsdamer Platz-Berlin | |
| ☐ | PH-AOC | Airbus A330-203 | 703 | ex F-WWKE | Place de la Concorde-Paris | |
| ☐ | PH-AOD | Airbus A330-203 | 738 | ex F-WWYC | Piazza del Duomo-Milano | |
| ☐ | PH-AOE | Airbus A330-203 | 770 | ex F-WWKD | Parliament Square-Edinburgh | |
| ☐ | PH-AOF | Airbus A330-203 | 801 | ex F-WWYC | Federation Square-Melbourne | |
| ☐ | PH-AOH | Airbus A330-203 | 811 | ex F-WWYH | Senaatintori/Senate Square-Helsinki | |
| ☐ | PH-AOI | Airbus A330-203 | 819 | ex F-WWYR | Plaza de la Independencia-Madrid | |
| ☐ | PH-AOK | Airbus A330-203 | 834 | ex F-WWKZ | Radhuspladsen-Kobenhavn | |
| ☐ | PH-AOL | Airbus A330-203 | 900 | ex F-WWKP | Piccadilly Circus-London | |
| ☐ | PH-AOM | Airbus A330-203 | 1161 | ex F-WWKP | Piazza San Marco-Venezia | |
| ☐ | PH- | Airbus A330-203 | 925 | ex F-WWKB | | ♦ |
| | | | | | | |
| ☐ | PH-BGD | Boeing 737-7K2/W | 30366/2675 | | Goldcrest/Goadhaantje | |
| ☐ | PH-BGE | Boeing 737-7K2/W | 30371/2705 | | Ortolan Bunting/Ortolaan | |
| ☐ | PH-BGF | Boeing 737-7K2/W | 30365/2714 | | Great White Heron/Grote Zilverreiger | |
| ☐ | PH-BGG | Boeing 737-7K2/W | 30367/2835 | | King Eider/Koeningseider | |
| ☐ | PH-BGH | Boeing 737-7K2/W | 38053/3119 | | Godwit/Grutto | |
| ☐ | PH-BGI | Boeing 737-7K2/W | 30364/3172 | ex N1786B | Finch/Vink | |
| ☐ | PH-BGK | Boeing 737-7K2/W | 38054/3292 | ex N1786B | Fulmar/Noordse Stormvogel | |
| ☐ | PH-BGL | Boeing 737-7K2/W | 30369/3407 | | Tjiftjaf/Warbler | |
| ☐ | PH-BGM | Boeing 737-7K2/W | 39255/3569 | | | |
| ☐ | PH-BGN | Boeing 737-7K2/W | 38125/3584 | | | ♦ |
| ☐ | PH-BGO | Boeing 737-7K2/W | 38126/3590 | | | ♦ |
| ☐ | PH-BGP | Boeing 737-7K2/W | 38127/3632 | | Pelikaan/Pelican | ♦ |
| ☐ | PH-BGQ | Boeing 737-7K2/W | 39256/3675 | ex N1796B | | ♦ |
| ☐ | PH-BGR | Boeing 737-7K2/W | 39446/3728 | | Zwarte Wouw/Black Kite | ♦ |
| ☐ | PH-BGT | Boeing 737-7K2/W | 38634/3762 | | Zanglijster/Song Thrush | ♦ |
| ☐ | PH-BGU | Boeing 737-7K2/W | 39257/3779 | | Koekoek/Cuckoo | ♦ |

| | | | | | |
|---|---|---|---|---|---|
| ☐ | PH-BGW | Boeing 737-7K2/W | 38128/3797 | | Zanglijster/Songthrush | ♦ |
| ☐ | PH-BGX | Boeing 737-7K2/W | 38635/3811 | | Scholekster/Oystercatcher | ♦ |
| | | | | | | |
| ☐ | PH-BCA | Boeing 737-8K2/W | 37820/3480 | | Flamingo | |
| ☐ | PH-BCB | Boeing 737-8K2/W | 39443/3648 | | | ♦ |
| ☐ | PH-BCC | Boeing 737-8K2/W | 42148 | | | o/o♦ |
| ☐ | PH-BCD | Boeing 737-8K2/W | 42149 | | | o/o♦ |
| ☐ | PH-BCE | Boeing 737-8K2/W | 42150 | | | o/o♦ |
| ☐ | PH-BCF | Boeing 737-8K2/W | 42151 | | | o/o♦ |
| ☐ | PH-BGA | Boeing 737-8K2/W | 37593/2569 | ex N1786B | | |
| ☐ | PH-BGB | Boeing 737-8K2/W | 37594/2594 | | Whimbiel/Regenwulp | |
| ☐ | PH-BGC | Boeing 737-8K2/W | 30361/2619 | | Pintail/Pijlstaart | |
| ☐ | PH-BXA | Boeing 737-8K2/W | 29131/198 | ex N1786B | Zwann/Swan | Retro c/s |
| ☐ | PH-BXB | Boeing 737-8K2/W | 29132/261 | ex N1786B | Valk/Falcon | |
| ☐ | PH-BXC | Boeing 737-8K2/W | 29133/305 | | Karhoen/Grouse | |
| ☐ | PH-BXD | Boeing 737-8K2/W | 29134/355 | ex N1784B | Arend/Eagle | |
| ☐ | PH-BXE | Boeing 737-8K2/W | 29595/552 | ex N1787B | Havik/Hawk | |
| ☐ | PH-BXF | Boeing 737-8K2/W | 29596/583 | ex N1787B | Zwalluw/Swallow | |
| ☐ | PH-BXG | Boeing 737-8K2/W | 30357/605 | ex N1787B | Kraanvogel/Crane | |
| ☐ | PH-BXH | Boeing 737-8K2/W | 29597/630 | ex N1786B | Gans/Goose | |
| ☐ | PH-BXI | Boeing 737-8K2/W | 30358/633 | ex N1787B | Zilvermeeuw/Herring Gull | |
| ☐ | PH-BXK | Boeing 737-8K2/W | 29598/639 | ex N1015G | Gierzwalluw/Swift | |
| ☐ | PH-BXL | Boeing 737-8K2/W | 30359/659 | | Sperwer/Sparrow Hawk | |
| ☐ | PH-BXM | Boeing 737-8K2/W | 30355/714 | ex N1786B | Kluut/Avocet | |
| ☐ | PH-BXN | Boeing 737-8K2/W | 30356/728 | ex N1787B | Merel/Blackbird | |
| ☐ | PH-BXU | Boeing 737-8BK/W | 33028/1936 | | Albatross | |
| ☐ | PH-BXV | Boeing 737-8K2/W | 30370/2205 | ex N1786B | Roodborstje/Robin | |
| ☐ | PH-BXW | Boeing 737-8K2/W | 30360/2467 | ex N1784B | Partridge | |
| ☐ | PH-BXY | Boeing 737-8K2/W | 30372/2503 | | Grebe/Fuut | |
| ☐ | PH-BXZ | Boeing 737-8K2/W | 30288/2533 | ex N1786B | | |
| | | | | | | |
| ☐ | PH-BXO | Boeing 737-9K2/W | 29599/866 | ex N1786B | Plevier/Plover | |
| ☐ | PH-BXP | Boeing 737-9K2/W | 29600/924 | ex N1786B | Merkroet/Crested Coot | |
| ☐ | PH-BXR | Boeing 737-9K2/W | 29601/959 | ex N1786B | Nachtegaal/Nightingale | |
| ☐ | PH-BXS | Boeing 737-9K2/W | 29602/981 | ex N1786B | Buizard/Buzzard | |
| ☐ | PH-BXT | Boeing 737-9K2/W | 32944/1498 | | Zeestern/Sea Tern | |
| | | | | | | |
| ☐ | PH-BFA | Boeing 747-406 | 23999/725 | ex N6018N | City of Atlanta | |
| ☐ | PH-BFB | Boeing 747-406 | 24000/732 | | City of Bangkok | |
| ☐ | PH-BFC | Boeing 747-406M | 23982/735 | ex N6038E | City of Calgary | |
| ☐ | PH-BFD | Boeing 747-406M | 24001/737 | | City of Dubai/Doebai | |
| ☐ | PH-BFE | Boeing 747-406M | 24201/763 | ex N6046P | City of Melbourne | |
| ☐ | PH-BFF | Boeing 747-406M | 24202/770 | ex N6046P | City of Freetown | |
| ☐ | PH-BFG | Boeing 747-406 | 24517/782 | | City of Guayaquil | |
| ☐ | PH-BFH | Boeing 747-406M | 24518/783 | ex N60668 | City of Hong Kong | |
| ☐ | PH-BFI | Boeing 747-406M | 25086/850 | | City of Jakarta | |
| ☐ | PH-BFK | Boeing 747-406 | 25087/854 | | City of Karachi | |
| ☐ | PH-BFL | Boeing 747-406 | 25356/888 | | City of Lima | |
| ☐ | PH-BFM | Boeing 747-406M | 26373/896 | | City of Mexico | |
| ☐ | PH-BFN | Boeing 747-406 | 26372/969 | | City of Nairobi | |
| ☐ | PH-BFO | Boeing 747-406M | 25413/938 | | City of Orlando | |
| ☐ | PH-BFP | Boeing 747-406M | 26374/992 | | City of Paramaribo | |
| ☐ | PH-BFR | Boeing 747-406M | 27202/1014 | | City of Rio de Janeiro | |
| ☐ | PH-BFS | Boeing 747-406 | 28195/1090 | | City of Seoul | |
| ☐ | PH-BFT | Boeing 747-406 | 28459/1112 | | City of Tokyo | |
| ☐ | PH-BFU | Boeing 747-406 | 28196/1127 | | City of Beijing | |
| ☐ | PH-BFV | Boeing 747-406 | 28460/1225 | | City of Vancouver | |
| ☐ | PH-BFW | Boeing 747-406 | 30454/1258 | | City of Shanghai | |
| ☐ | PH-BFY | Boeing 747-406 | 30455/1302 | | City of Johannesburg | |
| | | | | | | |
| ☐ | PH-BQA | Boeing 777-206ER | 33711/454 | ex N5014K | Albert Plesman | |
| ☐ | PH-BQB | Boeing 777-206ER | 33712/457 | | Borobudur | |
| ☐ | PH-BQC | Boeing 777-206ER | 29397/461 | | Chichen-Itza | |
| ☐ | PH-BQD | Boeing 777-206ER | 33713/465 | | Darjeeling Highway | |
| ☐ | PH-BQE | Boeing 777-206ER | 28691/468 | | Epidaurus | |
| ☐ | PH-BQF | Boeing 777-206ER | 29398/474 | | Ferrara City | |
| ☐ | PH-BQG | Boeing 777-206ER | 32704/476 | | Galapagos Islands | |
| ☐ | PH-BQH | Boeing 777-206ER | 32705/493 | ex N5016R | Hadrian's Wall | |
| ☐ | PH-BQI | Boeing 777-206ER | 33714/497 | | Iguazu Falls | |
| ☐ | PH-BQK | Boeing 777-206ER | 29399/499 | | Mount Kilimanjaro | |
| ☐ | PH-BQL | Boeing 777-206ER | 34711/552 | | Litomyšl Castle | |
| ☐ | PH-BQM | Boeing 777-206ER | 34712/559 | | Machu Picchu | |
| ☐ | PH-BQN | Boeing 777-206ER | 32720/561 | | Nahanni National Park | |
| ☐ | PH-BQO | Boeing 777-206ER | 35295/609 | | Old Rauma | |
| ☐ | PH-BQP | Boeing 777-206ER | 32721/630 | | Pont du Gard | |
| | | | | | | |
| ☐ | PH-BVA | Boeing 777-306ER | 35671/694 | (ex PH-BQR) | De Hoge Veluwe National Park | |
| ☐ | PH-BVB | Boeing 777-306ER | 36145/706 | | Fulufjallet National Park | |
| ☐ | PH-BVC | Boeing 777-306ER | 37582/787 | | Sian Ka'an National Park | |
| ☐ | PH-BVD | Boeing 777-306ER | 35979/807 | | National Park Amboseli | |
| ☐ | PH-BVF | Boeing 777-306ER | 39972/915 | | | ♦ |
| ☐ | PH-BVG | Boeing 777-306ER | 38867 | | | o/o♦ |
| ☐ | PH-BVI | Boeing 777-306ER | 35947 | | | o/o♦ |

| | | | | | | |
|---|---|---|---|---|---|---|
| ☐ | PH-KCA | McDonnell-Douglas MD-11 | 48555/557 | ex N6202D | Amy Johnson | |
| ☐ | PH-KCB | McDonnell-Douglas MD-11 | 48556/561 | | Maria Montessori | |
| ☐ | PH-KCC | McDonnell-Douglas MD-11 | 48557/569 | | Marie Curie | |
| ☐ | PH-KCD | McDonnell-Douglas MD-11 | 48558/573 | | Florence Nightingale | |
| ☐ | PH-KCE | McDonnell-Douglas MD-11 | 48559/575 | ex N91566 | Audrey Hepburn | |
| ☐ | PH-KCF | McDonnell-Douglas MD-11 | 48560/578 | | Annie Romein | |
| ☐ | PH-KCG | McDonnell-Douglas MD-11 | 48561/585 | | Maria Callas | |
| ☐ | PH-KCH | McDonnell-Douglas MD-11 | 48562/591 | | Anna Pavlova | |
| ☐ | PH-KCI | McDonnell-Douglas MD-11 | 48563/593 | ex PP-SPM | Mother Theresa | |
| ☐ | PH-KCK | McDonnell-Douglas MD-11 | 48564/612 | | Ingrid Bergman | |
| | | | | | | |
| ☐ | PH-AKA | Airbus A330-303 | 1267 | ex F-WWYP | Times Square-New York | ♦ |
| ☐ | PH-AKB | Airbus A330-303 | 1294 | ex F-WWKK | Piazza Navonna-Roma | ♦ |
| ☐ | PH-AKC | Airbus A330-303 | 1300 | ex F-WWYC | Plaza de la Catedral-La Habana | o/o♦ |
| ☐ | PH-BDO | Boeing 737-306 | 24262/1642 | | Jacob van Heemskerck | [NWI] |
| ☐ | PH-BTA | Boeing 737-406 | 25412/2161 | | Fernao de Magelhaes | [NWI] |
| ☐ | PH-BTB | Boeing 737-406 | 25423/2184 | | Henry Hudson | [NWI] |
| ☐ | PH-BTF | Boeing 737-406 | 27232/2591 | | Alexander von Humboldt | [NWI] |
| ☐ | PH-BTG | Boeing 737-406 | 27233/2601 | | Sir Henry Morton Stanley | [AMS] |

## MARTINAIR — Martinair (MP/MPH) — Amsterdam-Schiphol (AMS)

| | | | | | | |
|---|---|---|---|---|---|---|
| ☐ | PH-CKA | Boeing 747-406ERF | 33694/1326 | | | ♦ |
| ☐ | PH-CKB | Boeing 747-406ERF | 33695/1328 | | | ♦ |
| ☐ | PH-CKC | Boeing 747-406ERF | 33696/1341 | | | ♦ |
| ☐ | PH-CKD | Boeing 747-406ERF | 35233/1382 | | | ♦ |
| ☐ | PH-MPR | Boeing 747-412BCF | 24226/809 | ex N242BA | | |
| ☐ | PH-MPS | Boeing 747-412BCF | 24066/791 | ex N728BA | | [MZJ] |
| | | | | | | |
| ☐ | PH-MCP | McDonnell-Douglas MD-11CF | 48616/577 | ex N90187 | | |
| ☐ | PH-MCR | McDonnell-Douglas MD-11CF | 48617/581 | | Cargo | |
| ☐ | PH-MCS | McDonnell-Douglas MD-11CF | 48618/584 | | | |
| ☐ | PH-MCT | McDonnell-Douglas MD-11CF | 48629/486 | | | |
| ☐ | PH-MCU | McDonnell-Douglas MD-11F | 48757/606 | | Prinses Maxima | |
| ☐ | PH-MCW | McDonnell-Douglas MD-11F | 48788/632 | | | |
| ☐ | PH-MCY | McDonnell-Douglas MD-11F | 48445/460 | ex N626FE | | |
| | | | | | | |
| ☐ | PH-MCL | Boeing 767-31AER | 26469/415 | | Koningin Beatrix | Retro c/s |
| ☐ | PH-MCM | Boeing 767-31AER | 26470/416 | | Prins Floris | |

## SOLID AIR

| | | | | | | |
|---|---|---|---|---|---|---|
| ☐ | PH-EVY | Dornier 328-120 | 3095 | ex N328FA | | [EIN]♦ |
| | Ceased ops | | | | | |

## TESSEL AIR

| | | | | | | |
|---|---|---|---|---|---|---|
| ☐ | PH-LBR | Cessna 208 Caravan I | 20800101 | ex N99U | | FP♦ |

## TRANSAVIA AIRLINES — Transavia (HV/TRA) — Amsterdam-Schiphol (AMS)

| | | | | | | |
|---|---|---|---|---|---|---|
| ☐ | PH-XRA | Boeing 737-7K2/W | 30784/873 | ex N1786B | Leontien van Moorsel | |
| ☐ | PH-XRB | Boeing 737-7K2/W | 28256/1298 | | | |
| ☐ | PH-XRC | Boeing 737-7K2/W | 29347/1318 | ex OY-TDZ | | |
| ☐ | PH-XRD | Boeing 737-7K2/W | 30659/1329 | | | |
| ☐ | PH-XRE | Boeing 737-7K2/W | 30668/1482 | | | |
| ☐ | PH-XRV | Boeing 737-7K2/W | 34170/1701 | | Rotterdam The Hague Airport | |
| ☐ | PH-XRW | Boeing 737-7K2/W | 33465/1316 | | | |
| ☐ | PH-XRX | Boeing 737-7K2/W | 33464/1299 | | Stadprins Akkedeer | |
| ☐ | PH-XRY | Boeing 737-7K2/W | 33463/1292 | | | |
| ☐ | PH-XRZ | Boeing 737-7K2/W | 33462/1278 | | | |
| | | | | | | |
| ☐ | PH-HSA | Boeing 737-8K2/W | 34171/2950 | ex N1786B | | >BWA |
| ☐ | PH-HSB | Boeing 737-8K2/W | 34172/3242 | ex N1786B | | |
| ☐ | PH-HSC | Boeing 737-8K2/W | 34173/3266 | | | |
| ☐ | PH-HSD | Boeing 737-8K2/W | 39260/3581 | ex N1787B | | ♦ |
| ☐ | PH-HSE | Boeing 737-8K2/W | 39259/3635 | | | |
| ☐ | PH-HSF | Boeing 737-8K2/W | 39262 | | | o/o♦ |
| ☐ | PH-HSG | Boeing 737-8K2/W | 39261 | | | o/o♦ |
| ☐ | PH-HSW | Boeing 737-8K2/W | 37160/2880 | | | >BWA |
| ☐ | PH-HZD | Boeing 737-8K2/W | 28376/252 | ex N1786B | | |
| ☐ | PH-HZE | Boeing 737-8K2/W | 28377/277 | ex N1786B | City of Rhodos | >AMX |
| ☐ | PH-HZF | Boeing 737-8K2/W | 28378/291 | ex N1796B | | |
| ☐ | PH-HZG | Boeing 737-8K2/W | 28379/498 | ex N1786B | | |
| ☐ | PH-HZI | Boeing 737-8K2/W | 28380/524 | | | >SCX |
| ☐ | PH-HZJ | Boeing 737-8K2/W | 30389/549 | ex N1796B | | |
| ☐ | PH-HZK | Boeing 737-8K2/W | 30390/555 | ex N1786B | | |
| ☐ | PH-HZL | Boeing 737-8K2/W | 30391/814 | ex N1786B | | >GAI |
| ☐ | PH-HZN | Boeing 737-8K2/W | 32943/1478 | | | |
| ☐ | PH-HZO | Boeing 737-8K2/W | 34169/2243 | | | >AMX |
| ☐ | PH-HZV | Boeing 737-8K2/W | 30650/1158 | ex OY-TDB | | |

| | | | | | |
|---|---|---|---|---|---|
| ☐ | PH-HZW | Boeing 737-8K2/W | 29345/1132 | ex VT-SPZ | Jumbo Supermarket |
| ☐ | PH-HZX | Boeing 737-8K2/W | 28248/1126 | | ♦ |

## PJ-    NETHERLANDS ANTILLES

### DIVI DIVI AIR | Divi divi (DVR) | Curacao (CUR)

| | | | | | |
|---|---|---|---|---|---|
| ☐ | PJ-BMV | Cessna 402B | 402B0865 | ex C-GCKB | |
| ☐ | PJ-SEA | Britten-Norman BN-2A-26 Islander | 311 | ex C-FFXS | FlyDivi.com titles |
| ☐ | PJ-SKY | Britten-Norman BN-2A-26 Islander | 885 | ex C-FDYT | |

### DUTCH ANTILLES EXPRESS | BonExpress (9H/DNL) | Kralendijk (BON)

| | | | | | |
|---|---|---|---|---|---|
| ☐ | PJ-DAA | Fokker 100 | 11310 | ex D-AGPI | FlyDAE titles ♦ |
| ☐ | PJ-DAB | Fokker 100 | 11331 | ex D-AGPM | ♦ |
| ☐ | PJ-DAH | ATR 42-320 | 0090 | ex PJ-SLH | ♦ |

### INSEL AIR INTERNATIONAL | Inselair (7I/INC) | Curacao (CUR)

| | | | | | |
|---|---|---|---|---|---|
| ☐ | PJ-MDA | McDonnell-Douglas MD-83 | 49449/1354 | ex 9A-CBJ | |
| ☐ | PJ-MDB | McDonnell-Douglas MD-82 | 48021/1078 | ex N812NK | <SFR |
| ☐ | PJ-MDC | McDonnell-Douglas MD-82 | 49434/1446 | ex N434AG | |
| ☐ | PJ-MDE | McDonnell-Douglas MD-82 | 49971/1755 | ex N971AG | |
| ☐ | PJ-VIA | Embraer EMB.110P1 Bandeirante | 110387 | ex E5-TAI | |
| ☐ | PJ-VIC | Embraer EMB.110P1 Bandeirante | 110261 | ex VH-BWC | ♦ |
| ☐ | PJ-VIP | Embraer EMB.110P1 Bandeirante | 110382 | ex YV-249C | Curacao |

### WINAIR / WINDWARD ISLANDS AIRWAYS INTERNATIONAL | Windward (WM/WIA) | St. Maarten (SXM)

| | | | | | |
|---|---|---|---|---|---|
| ☐ | PJ-AIW | Britten-Norman BN-2A-26 Islander | 2038 | ex C-GZKG | |
| ☐ | PJ-CIW | Britten-Norman BN-2B-26 Islander | 876 | ex C-GZTP | |
| ☐ | PJ-WIL | de Havilland DHC-6 Twin Otter 300 | 358 | ex C-FCSY | |
| ☐ | PJ-WIN | de Havilland DHC-6 Twin Otter 300 | 518 | ex 5Y-SKA | |
| ☐ | PJ-WIS | de Havilland DHC-6 Twin Otter 300 | 447 | ex C-GPAO | ♦ |
| ☐ | PJ-WJR | de Havilland DHC-6 Twin Otter 300 | 476 | ex N476R | ♦ |

### WINDWARD EXPRESS AIRWAYS | St Maarten (SXM)

| | | | | | |
|---|---|---|---|---|---|
| ☐ | PJ-WEA | Britten-Norman BN-2A-27 Islander | 659 | ex N659CM | |
| ☐ | PJ-WEB | Britten-Norman BN-2A-26 Islander | 2208 | ex 8P-TAG | |

## PK-    INDONESIA (Republic of Indonesia)

### AIR MALEO

| | | | | | |
|---|---|---|---|---|---|
| ☐ | PK-ZMM | Fokker F.27 Friendship 600 | 10349 | ex N19QQ | ♦ |
| ☐ | PK-ZMV | Fokker F.27 Friendship 600 | 10385 | ex N19NN | ♦ |

### AIR MARK INDONESIA AVIATION | Jakarta-Halim (HLP)

| | | | | | |
|---|---|---|---|---|---|
| ☐ | EW-262TK | Antonov An-32A | 2103 | ex ER-AWY | |

### AIRFAST INDONESIA | Airfast (AFE) | Balikpapan/Jayapura (BPN/DJJ)

| | | | | | |
|---|---|---|---|---|---|
| ☐ | PK-OAT | Agusta-Bell 204B | 3169 | ex PK-LBC | |
| ☐ | PK-OAW | Beech 65-B80 Queen Air | LD-308 | ex PK-JBF | |
| ☐ | PK-OBA | Bell 204B | 2050 | ex VH-UTW | |
| ☐ | PK-OCA | IPTN Bell 412 | 34009/NB09 | ex PK-XFJ | |
| ☐ | PK-OCB | IPTN Bell 412 | 34007/NB07 | ex PK-XFH | |
| ☐ | PK-OCC | CASA-Nurtanio C.212-200 | 50N/CC4-2-210 | ex PK-NZJ | |
| ☐ | PK-OCE | Bell 212 | 30981 | ex PK-VBZ | |
| ☐ | PK-OCJ | de Havilland DHC-6 Twin Otter 300 | 522 | ex A6-MBM | |
| ☐ | PK-OCK | de Havilland DHC-6 Twin Otter 310 | 616 | ex 9Q-CLE | all-white |
| ☐ | PK-OCL | de Havilland DHC-6 Twin Otter 300 | 689 | ex N689WJ | Santigi |
| ☐ | PK-OCP | Boeing 737-27A | 23794/1424 | ex B-2625 | |
| ☐ | PK-OCS | McDonnell-Douglas MD-83 | 53124/1991 | ex N786BC | ♦ |
| ☐ | PK-OCT | McDonnell-Douglas MD-82 | 49889/1761 | ex N823RA | |
| ☐ | PK-OCU | McDonnell-Douglas MD-82 | 53017/1797 | ex N824RA | |
| ☐ | PK-OCV | IPTN Bell 412SP | 34019/NB19 | ex PK-HNI | ♦ |
| ☐ | PK-OCY | Beech 1900D | UE-393 | ex N830CA | |
| ☐ | PK-OSP | British Aerospace 146 Srs.100 | E1124 | ex G-CBXY | op for Metro TV/VIP |

## ASIALINK CARGO AIRLINES (KP/AKC)

| | | | | | | |
|---|---|---|---|---|---|---|
| ☐ | PK-KRJ | Fokker F.27 Friendship 500 | 10660 | ex TC-MBB | | ◆ |
| ☐ | PK-KRL | Fokker F.27 Friendship 500 | 10654 | ex TC-MBA | | ◆ |
| ☐ | PK | Fokker F.27 Friendship 500 | 10632 | ex N19XF | | ◆ |

## AVIASTAR MANDIRI (VIT) Banjarmasin (BDJ)

| | | | | | | |
|---|---|---|---|---|---|---|
| ☐ | PK-BRE | British Aerospace 146 Srs.200 | E2139 | ex C-GRNU | | |
| ☐ | PK-BRF | British Aerospace 146 Srs.200 | E2210 | ex PK-LNJ | | |
| ☐ | PK-BRI | British Aerospace 146 Srs.200 | E2227 | ex G-BVMS | | ◆ |
| ☐ | PK-BRM | CASA-Nurtanio C.212-300 | 91N/4-411 | ex PK-VSD | | |
| ☐ | PK-BRN | CASA-Nurtanio C.212-300 | 90N/4-410 | ex PK-VSC | | dam 11Jan07 |
| ☐ | PK-BRP | de Havilland DHC-6 Twin Otter 300 | 356 | ex N972SW | | |
| ☐ | PK-BRQ | de Havilland DHC-6 Twin Otter 300 | 702 | ex N702PV | | |
| ☐ | PK-BRS | de Havilland DHC-6 Twin Otter 300 | 756 | ex C-FPNZ | | |
| ☐ | PK-BRT | de Havilland DHC-6 Twin Otter 300 | 380 | ex (F-GUTR) | | |
| ☐ | PK-TNC | Fokker 50 | 20240 | ex D2-ESR | | |

## BATAVIA AIR Batavia (7P/BTV) Jakarta-Soekarno Hatta (CGK)

| | | | | | | |
|---|---|---|---|---|---|---|
| ☐ | PK-YUC | Airbus A320-233 | 0460 | ex N951LF | | |
| ☐ | PK-YUE | Airbus A320-233 | 0461 | ex N941LF | | |
| ☐ | PK-YVD | Airbus A320-231 | 0449 | ex G-JOEM | | |
| ☐ | PK-YVE | Airbus A320-231 | 0441 | ex B-22306 | | |
| ☐ | PK-YVF | Airbus A320-233 | 1676 | ex N206CT | | |
| ☐ | PK-YVG | Airbus A320-231 | 0168 | ex N168BN | | |
| ☐ | PK-YVH | Airbus A320-232 | 0710 | ex B-2401 | | |
| ☐ | PK-YTC | Boeing 737-2M8 | 22090/664 | ex N220LS | | [CGK]◆ |
| ☐ | PK-YTF | Boeing 737-2T5 | 22397/737 | ex N31AU | | [CGK] |
| ☐ | PK-YTG | Boeing 737-2Q8 | 22453/748 | ex N453LS | | [CGK] |
| ☐ | PK-YTJ | Boeing 737-204 | 21693/541 | ex N693YT | | [CGK] |
| ☐ | PK-YTN | Boeing 737-217 (AvAero 3) | 22659/874 | ex N986PG | | [CGK] |
| ☐ | PK-YTR | Boeing 737-281 (AvAero 3) | 21766/583 | ex N738AP | | [CGK] |
| ☐ | PK-YTS | Boeing 737-2T4 (AvAero 3) | 22055/633 | ex N739AA | | [CGK] |
| ☐ | PK-YTV | Boeing 737-2M8 (AvAero 3) | 21955/659 | ex N742AP | | [CGK] |
| ☐ | PK-YTM | Boeing 737-3B7 | 22957/1127 | ex N384US | | |
| ☐ | PK-YTU | Boeing 737-3Y9 | 25604/2405 | ex N999CZ | | |
| ☐ | PK-YTW | Boeing 737-3B7 | 23318/1234 | ex N396US | | |
| ☐ | PK-YTX | Boeing 737-3B7 | 22953/1022 | ex N374US | | |
| ☐ | PK-YTY | Boeing 737-3B7 | 22955/1043 | ex N376US | | |
| ☐ | PK-YUA | Boeing 737-3Y0 | 24914/2054 | ex PK-GHV | | |
| ☐ | PK-YVK | Boeing 737-301 | 23233/1200 | ex N232AP | | ◆ |
| ☐ | PK-YVL | Boeing 737-322 | 24638/1784 | ex N373UA | | |
| ☐ | PK-YVM | Boeing 737-322 | 24253/1650 | ex N349UA | | |
| ☐ | PK-YVU | Boeing 737-33A | 24097/1741 | ex N497AN | | |
| ☐ | PK-YVV | Boeing 737-3B7 | 23316/1212 | ex N394US | | |
| ☐ | PK-YVW | Boeing 737-3B7 | 23319/1250 | ex N397US | | |
| ☐ | PK-YVX | Boeing 737-33A | 24093/1727 | ex N493AN | | |
| ☐ | PK-YVY | Boeing 737-3B7 | 22952/1015 | ex N373US | | |
| ☐ | PK-YVZ | Boeing 737-3B7 | 23317/1221 | ex N395US | | |
| ☐ | PK-YTE | Boeing 737-405 | 25303/2137 | ex LN-BRP | | |
| ☐ | PK-YTK | Boeing 737-4Y0 | 24687/1865 | ex TC-APT | | |
| ☐ | PK-YTP | Boeing 737-4Y0 | 24345/1731 | ex TC-APC | | |
| ☐ | PK-YTZ | Boeing 737-4Y0 | 23869/1639 | ex N869AP | | |
| ☐ | PK-YVN | Boeing 737-48E | 25766/2543 | ex N766SJ | | |
| ☐ | PK-YVO | Boeing 737-4Y0 | 23868/1616 | ex PK-RIH | | |
| ☐ | PK-YVP | Boeing 737-4Y0 | 23979/1661 | ex PK-RIT | | |
| ☐ | PK-YVQ | Boeing 737-4S3 | 25594/2223 | ex N594AB | | |
| ☐ | PK-YVR | Boeing 737-4Y0 | 24494/1757 | ex N494AC | | |
| ☐ | PK-YVS | Boeing 737-4H6 | 27352/2624 | ex HS-DDJ | | |
| ☐ | PK-YVT | Boeing 737-4H6 | 27191/2676 | ex HS-DDH | | |
| ☐ | PK-YUY | Boeing 737-476 | 24441/2363 | ex ZK-JTP | | |
| ☐ | PK-YUF | Airbus A321-111 | 1017 | ex F-OIVU | | ◆ |
| ☐ | PK-YUZ | Boeing 737-5Y0 | 25192/2262 | ex OE-IAH | | ◆ |
| ☐ | PK-YVI | Airbus A330-202 | 330 | ex EI-EWR | | ◆ |
| ☐ | PK-YVJ | Airbus A330-202 | 205 | ex N271LF | | |

## CARDIG AIR (8F/CAD)

| | | | | | | |
|---|---|---|---|---|---|---|
| ☐ | PK-BBB | Boeing 737-347SF | 23598/1289 | ex N312WA | Creativity | |
| ☐ | PK-BBS | Boeing 737-301F | 23258/1126 | ex OE-IAU | | ◆ |

## CITILINK Jakarta-Halim (HLP)

| | | | | | | |
|---|---|---|---|---|---|---|
| ☐ | PK-GLA | Airbus A320-233 | 1635 | ex HA-LPB | | ◆ |
| ☐ | PK-GLD | Airbus A320-233 | 0839 | ex HA-LPA | | ◆ |

## DERAYA AIR TAXI — *Deraya (DRY)* — Jakarta-Halim (HLP)

| | | | | | |
|---|---|---|---|---|---|
| ☐ | PK-DCC | Cessna 402C II | 402C0250 | ex N444DS | |
| ☐ | PK-DCJ | Cessna 402B | 402B0615 | ex N3759C | |
| ☐ | PK-DCQ | CASA-Nurtanio C.212-A4 | 16N/A4-13-112 | ex PK-XCO | |
| ☐ | PK-DCZ | Cessna 402B | 402B0890 | ex N5203J | |
| ☐ | PK-DGA | British Aerospace ATP(F) | 2026 | ex G-JEMD | |
| ☐ | PK-DGI | British Aerospace ATP(F) | 2027 | ex G-JEME | |
| ☐ | PK-DSB | Short SD.3-30 | SH3056 | ex DQ-SUN | |
| ☐ | PK-DSF | Short SC.7 Skyvan 3 | SH1881 | ex AF-702 | |
| ☐ | PK-DSH | Short SD.3-60 | SH3757 | ex N350TA | |
| ☐ | PK-DSR | Short SD.3-30 | SH3060 | ex DQ-FIJ | |
| ☐ | PK-DSS | Short SD.3-60 | SH3743 | ex N743RW | |
| ☐ | PK-DYR | Piper PA-31T Cheyenne II | 31T-7820054 | ex VH-MWT | |
| ☐ | PK-LPN | Cessna U206F Stationair II | U20602789 | ex PK-UFO | |

## DIRGANTARA AIR SERVICE — *Dirgantara (AW/DIR)*
### Jakarta-Halim/Bandarmasin/Pontianak (HLP/BDJ/PNK)

| | | | | | |
|---|---|---|---|---|---|
| ☐ | PK-VIB | Britten-Norman BN-2A-21 Islander | 545 | ex PK-TRC | |
| ☐ | PK-VIM | Britten-Norman BN-2A-3 Islander | 634 | ex 9V-BEB | |
| ☐ | PK-VIN | Britten-Norman BN-2A-3 Islander | 351 | ex G-BBJA | |
| ☐ | PK-VIS | Britten-Norman BN-2A-21 Islander | 485 | ex G-BEGB | |
| ☐ | PK-VIU | Britten-Norman BN-2A-21 Islander | 781 | ex PK-KNH | |
| ☐ | PK-VIW | Britten-Norman BN-2A-21 Islander | 2026 | ex G-BIPD | |
| ☐ | PK-VIX | Britten-Norman BN-2A-21 Islander | 2027 | ex G-BIUF | |
| ☐ | PK-VIY | Britten-Norman BN-2A-21 Islander | 2133 | ex G-BJOR | |
| | | | | | |
| ☐ | PK-VMB | Gippsland GA-8 Airvan | GA8-03-031 | ex VH-BOI | |
| ☐ | PK-VMC | Gippsland GA-8 Airvan | GA8-03-033 | ex VH-BNL | |
| ☐ | PK-VMD | Gippsland GA-8 Airvan | GA8-03-041 | ex VH-FDR | |
| ☐ | PK-VME | Gippsland GA-8 Airvan | GA8-03-042 | ex VH-JYN | |
| ☐ | PK-VSA | CASA-Nurtanio C.212-200 | 87N/CC4-38-282 | ex PK-HJA | |
| ☐ | PK-VSF | CASA-Nurtanio C.212-200 | 93N/4-413 | ex PK-HJI | |
| ☐ | PK-VSN | CASA-Nurtanio C.212-100 | 22N/A4-19-136 | ex PK-XCU | |
| ☐ | PK-VSP | CASA-Nurtanio C.212-100 | 7N/174-4-78 | ex PK-NCE | ◆ |

## EASTINDO — Jakarta-Halim (HLP)

| | | | | | |
|---|---|---|---|---|---|
| ☐ | PK-RGA | Beech 1900D | UE-376 | ex N31425 | |
| ☐ | PK-RGE | Fokker 100 | 11445 | ex F-WQVP | |
| ☐ | PK-RGP | Britten-Norman BN-2B-20 Islander | 2249 | ex PK-HNG | |
| ☐ | PK- | Britten-Norman BN-2T Turbo Islander | 2303 | ex N2536Y | ◆ |

## EXPRESSAIR — *(XN/XAR)* — Ujung Pandang

| | | | | | |
|---|---|---|---|---|---|
| ☐ | PK-TXL | Dornier 328-110 | 3037 | ex N425JS | ◆ |
| ☐ | PK-TXM | Dornier 328-110 | 3032 | ex N423JS | |
| ☐ | PK-TXN | Dornier 328-110 | 3030 | ex N328CH | |
| ☐ | PK-TXO | Dornier 328-110 | 3045 | ex N432JS | ◆ |
| ☐ | PK-TXP | Dornier 328-110 | 3043 | ex N429JS | |
| ☐ | PK-TXQ | Dornier 328-110 | 3038 | ex N426JS | |
| ☐ | PK-TXR | Dornier 328-120 | 3008 | ex N472PS | ◆ |
| ☐ | PK-TXT | Dornier 328-310 (328JET) | 3165 | ex N365SK | |
| | | | | | |
| ☐ | PK-TXD | Boeing 737-284 | 22400/766 | ex SX-BCK | Grace |
| ☐ | PK-TXF | Boeing 737-284 | 21302/475 | ex SX-BCD | |
| ☐ | PK-TXG | Boeing 737-5L9 | 25066/2038 | ex OY-MAE | |
| ☐ | PK-TXH | Boeing 737-529 | 25218/2111 | ex N22YH | ◆ |
| ☐ | PK-TXI | Boeing 737-322 | 24671/1913 | ex N396UA | ◆ |
| ☐ | PK-TXJ | Boeing 737-3M8 | 24413/1884 | ex N16EA | ◆ |

## GADING SARI AVIATION SERVICES

Ceased ops

## GARUDA INDONESIA — *Indonesia (GA/GIA)* — Jakarta-Soekarno Hatta (CGK)

| | | | | | |
|---|---|---|---|---|---|
| ☐ | PK-GPH | Airbus A330-243 | 1020 | ex F-WWYL | |
| ☐ | PK-GPI | Airbus A330-243 | 1052 | ex F-WWKQ | |
| ☐ | PK-GPJ | Airbus A330-243 | 988 | ex F-WWKI | |
| ☐ | PK-GPK | Airbus A330-243 | 1028 | ex F-WWYZ | |
| ☐ | PK-GPL | Airbus A330-243 | 1184 | ex F-WWKT | |
| ☐ | PK-GPM | Airbus A330-243 | 1214 | ex F-WWKH | |
| ☐ | PK-GPN | Airbus A330-243 | 1261 | ex F-WWKF | ◆ |
| ☐ | PK-GPO | Airbus A330-243 | 1288 | ex F-WWKL | ◆ |
| | | | | | |
| ☐ | PK-GPA | Airbus A330-341 | 138 | ex F-WWKH | |
| ☐ | PK-GPC | Airbus A330-341 | 140 | ex F-WWKU | |

| | | | | | |
|---|---|---|---|---|---|
| ☐ | PK-GPD | Airbus A330-341 | 144 | ex F-WWKG | |
| ☐ | PK-GPE | Airbus A330-341 | 148 | ex F-WWKD | |
| ☐ | PK-GPF | Airbus A330-341 | 153 | ex F-WWKY | |
| ☐ | PK-GPG | Airbus A330-341 | 165 | ex F-WWKL | |
| | | | | | |
| ☐ | PK-GCA | Boeing 737-3L9 | 24569/1775 | ex N569AG | |
| ☐ | PK-GCC | Boeing 737-3Q8 | 28200/2854 | ex 9M-AAC | |
| ☐ | PK-GGG | Boeing 737-3U3 | 28731/2949 | | |
| ☐ | PK-GGN | Boeing 737-3U3 | 28735/3029 | ex N5573K | |
| ☐ | PK-GGO | Boeing 737-3U3 | 28736/3032 | ex N3134C | |
| ☐ | PK-GGP | Boeing 737-3U3 | 28737/3037 | ex N1020L | |
| ☐ | PK-GGQ | Boeing 737-3U3 | 28739/3064 | ex N1024A | |
| ☐ | PK-GGR | Boeing 737-3U3 | 28741/3079 | ex N1026G | |
| ☐ | PK-GHW | Boeing 737-3M8 | 25039/2007 | ex N303FL | |
| ☐ | PK-GHX | Boeing 737-3L9 | 26440/2234 | ex N310FL | |
| | | | | | |
| ☐ | PK-GGA | Boeing 737-5U3 | 28726/2920 | | |
| ☐ | PK-GGC | Boeing 737-5U3 | 28727/2937 | ex N1786B | |
| ☐ | PK-GGD | Boeing 737-5U3 | 28728/2938 | ex N1786B | |
| ☐ | PK-GGE | Boeing 737-5U3 | 28729/2950 | ex N60436 | |
| ☐ | PK-GGF | Boeing 737-5U3 | 28730/2952 | | |
| | | | | | |
| ☐ | PK-GEE | Boeing 737-8CX/W | 32361/1098 | ex TC-IEA | |
| ☐ | PK-GEF | Boeing 737-8CX/W | 32363/1139 | ex N236GX | |
| ☐ | PK-GEG | Boeing 737-83N/W | 30033/1149 | ex N323TZ | |
| ☐ | PK-GEH | Boeing 737-83N/W | 30643/1106 | ex N319TZ | |
| ☐ | PK-GEI | Boeing 737-86N/W | 29883/1083 | ex N29883 | |
| ☐ | PK-GEJ | Boeing 737-86N/W | 33003/1121 | ex G-XLAG | |
| ☐ | PK-GEK | Boeing 737-85F/W | 30568/793 | ex N568MQ | |
| ☐ | PK-GEL | Boeing 737-8AS/W | 29927/727 | ex EI-CSN | |
| ☐ | PK-GEM | Boeing 737-8AS/W | 29928/735 | ex EI-CSO | |
| ☐ | PK-GEN | Boeing 737-8AS/W | 29929/753 | ex EI-CSP | |
| ☐ | PK-GEO | Boeing 737-8AS/W | 29930/757 | ex EI-CSQ | |
| ☐ | PK-GEP | Boeing 737-8AS/W | 29931/1020 | ex EI-CSR | |
| ☐ | PK-GEQ | Boeing 737-86N/W | 32659/1709 | ex EC-JEX | |
| ☐ | PK-GER | Boeing 737-86J/W | 30876/759 | ex D-ABAD | |
| ☐ | PK-GFA | Boeing 737-86N/W | 36549/3331 | | |
| ☐ | PK-GFC | Boeing 737-86N/W | 39390/3348 | | |
| ☐ | PK-GFD | Boeing 737-8U3/W | 40807/3337 | | |
| ☐ | PK-GFE | Boeing 737-86N/W | 36804/3374 | | |
| ☐ | PK-GFF | Boeing 737-8U3/W | 36436/3370 | | |
| ☐ | PK-GFG | Boeing 737-8BK/W | 37819/3402 | ex N1786B | |
| ☐ | PK-GFH | Boeing 737-8U3/W | 36850/3389 | | |
| ☐ | PK-GFI | Boeing 737-86N/W | 36805/3438 | | |
| ☐ | PK-GFJ | Boeing 737-86N/W | 37885/3445 | ex N1796B | |
| ☐ | PK-GFK | Boeing 737-86N/W | 37887/3463 | | |
| ☐ | PK-GFL | Boeing 737-86N/W | 36808/3505 | ex N1786B | |
| ☐ | PK-GFM | Boeing 737-8U3/W | 39920/3518 | | |
| ☐ | PK-GFN | Boeing 737-86N/W | 38033/3607 | | |
| ☐ | PK-GFO | Boeing 737-86N/W | 39403/3674 | ex N1795B | ♦ |
| ☐ | PK-GFP | Boeing 737-8U3/W | 38821/3684 | | ♦ |
| ☐ | PK-GFQ | Boeing 737-81D/W | 39416/3766 | | ♦ |
| ☐ | PK-GFR | Boeing 737-81D/W | 39417/3802 | | ♦ |
| ☐ | PK-GFS | Boeing 737-86N/W | 36830/3860 | | ♦ |
| ☐ | PK-GFT | Boeing 737-86N/W | 38032/3869 | | ♦ |
| ☐ | PK-GMA | Boeing 737-8U3/W | 30151/2942 | ex N1784B | |
| ☐ | PK-GMC | Boeing 737-8U3/W | 30155/3081 | ex N1786B | |
| ☐ | PK-GMD | Boeing 737-8U3/W | 30156/3100 | | |
| ☐ | PK-GME | Boeing 737-8U3/W | 30157/3123 | | |
| ☐ | PK-GMF | Boeing 737-8U3/W | 30140/3129 | | |
| ☐ | PK-GMG | Boeing 737-8U3/W | 30141/3166 | ex N1796B | |
| ☐ | PK-GMH | Boeing 737-8U3/W | 30142/3213 | ex N1786B | |
| ☐ | PK-GMI | Boeing 737-8U3/W | 30143/3243 | ex N1786B | |
| ☐ | PK-GMJ | Boeing 737-8U3/W | 30144/3249 | ex N1787B | |
| ☐ | PK-GMK | Boeing 737-8U3/W | 29666/3171 | ex N1787B | |
| ☐ | PK-GML | Boeing 737-8U3/W | 30145/3177 | ex N1787B | |
| ☐ | PK-GMM | Boeing 737-8U3/W | 30147/3285 | | |
| ☐ | PK-GMN | Boeing 737-8U3/W | 30146/3303 | | |
| ☐ | PK-GMO | Boeing 737-8U3/W | 30147/3327 | ex N1786B | |
| ☐ | PK-GMP | Boeing 737-8U3/W | 30148/3353 | ex N1787B | |
| ☐ | PK-GMQ | Boeing 737-8U3/W | 30149/3405 | ex N1787B | |
| ☐ | PK-GMR | Boeing 737-8U3/W | 30150/3429 | | |
| ☐ | PK-GMS | Boeing 737-8U3/W | 38071/3855 | | |
| ☐ | PK-GMU | Boeing 737-8U3/W | 38073/3930 | | ♦ |
| ☐ | PK-GMV | Boeing 737-8U3/W | 38074/3960 | | ♦ |
| ☐ | PK-GMW | Boeing 737-8U3/W | 38089/ | | o/o♦ |
| ☐ | PK-GMX | Boeing 737-8U3/W | 38079 | | o/o♦ |
| | | | | | |
| ☐ | PK-GSG | Boeing 747-4U3 | 25704/1011 | | |
| ☐ | PK-GSH | Boeing 747-4U3 | 25705/1029 | ex N6038E | |
| ☐ | PK-GSI | Boeing 747-441 | 24956/917 | ex N791LF | |
| ☐ | PK-GWO | Boeing 737-4U3 | 25717/2546 | | |
| ☐ | PK-GZP | Boeing 737-46Q | 28661/2910 | ex EI-CXI | |

| | | | | |
|---|---|---|---|---|
| ☐ | PK-GZQ | Boeing 737-4S3 | 25134/2083 | ex N534AG |
| ☐ | PK- | Boeing 777-3U3ER | | o/o |
| ☐ | PK- | Boeing 777-3U3ER | | o/o |
| ☐ | PK- | Boeing 777-3U3ER | | o/o |
| ☐ | PK- | Boeing 777-3U3ER | | o/o |

## GATARI AIR SERVICE — Gatari (GHS) — Jakarta-Halim (HLP)

| | | | | | |
|---|---|---|---|---|---|
| ☐ | PK-HMB | Bell 212 | 30502 | ex PK-DBY | |
| ☐ | PK-HMM | Bell 212 | 30958 | ex PK-PGF | |
| ☐ | PK-HNH | Fokker F.28 Fellowship 4000 | 11218 | ex PK-GQB | [HLP] |
| ☐ | PK-HNJ | Fokker F.28 Fellowship 3000RC | 11134 | ex PK-GFW | [HLP] |
| ☐ | PK-HNK | Fokker F.28 Fellowship 4000 | 11129 | ex PK-GFT | [JKT]♦ |
| ☐ | PK-HNP | Fokker F.28 Fellowship 4000 | 11216 | ex PK-GKZ | [HLP] |
| ☐ | PK-HNS | ATR 42-500 | 0601 | ex PK-TSQ | |
| ☐ | PK-HNT | ATR 42-500 | 0614 | ex OY-EDE | |
| ☐ | PK-HNY | Kawasaki/MBB BK-117B-1 | 1052 | ex JA6614 | |

## GT AIR — Jakarta-Halim (HLP)

| | | | | |
|---|---|---|---|---|
| ☐ | PK-LTT | Dornier 28D-1 Skyservant | 4031 | ex PK-VRB |
| ☐ | PK-LTU | Dornier 28D-1 Skyservant | 4026 | ex PK-VRA |

## INDONESIA AIR TRANSPORT — Intra (IDA) — Jakarta-Halim (HLP)

| | | | | | |
|---|---|---|---|---|---|
| ☐ | PK-TRD | Aérospatiale SA365C Dauphin 2 | 5058 | ex N3606Q | |
| ☐ | PK-TRE | Aérospatiale SA365C Dauphin 2 | 5004 | ex N3604G | |
| ☐ | PK-TSH | Aérospatiale SA365N Dauphin 2 | 6008 | ex N801BA | |
| ☐ | PK-TSI | Aérospatiale SA365N Dauphin 2 | 6026 | ex N87SV | |
| ☐ | PK-TSW | Aérospatiale AS365N2 Dauphin 2 | 6470 | ex HL9204 | |
| ☐ | PK-TSX | Aérospatiale AS365N2 Dauphin 2 | 6472 | ex HL9206 | |
| ☐ | PK-THT | ATR 42-500 | 0611 | ex I-ADLZ | |
| ☐ | PK-TRW | Beech 1900D | UE-177 | ex N3237H | |
| ☐ | PK-TRX | Beech 1900D | UE-186 | ex N3233J | |
| ☐ | PK-TSF | Bell 212 | 30974 | ex N27664 | |
| ☐ | PK-TSG | Bell 212 | 30753 | ex N81FC | |
| ☐ | PK-TSJ | Fokker F.27 Friendship 500RFC | 10525 | ex N702A | |
| ☐ | PK-TSN | Fokker 50 | 20185 | ex PH-ZDA | ♦ |
| ☐ | PK-TSO | Fokker 50 | 20186 | ex PH-ZDB | |
| ☐ | PK-TSP | Fokker 50 | 20316 | ex PK-TWJ | |
| ☐ | PK-TSY | ATR 42-300 | 0118 | ex LY-ARY | |
| ☐ | PK-TSZ | ATR 42-300 | 0059 | ex LY-ARJ | |

## INDONESIA AIRASIA — Wagon Air (QZ/AWQ) — Jakarta-Soekarno Hatta (CGK)

| | | | | | |
|---|---|---|---|---|---|
| ☐ | PK-AXA | Airbus A320-216 | 3610 | ex F-WWIG | |
| ☐ | PK-AXC | Airbus A320-216 | 3648 | ex F-WWBZ | |
| ☐ | PK-AXD | Airbus A320-216 | 3182 | ex 9M-AFX | |
| ☐ | PK-AXE | Airbus A320-216 | 3715 | ex F-WWIZ | |
| ☐ | PK-AXF | Airbus A320-216 | 3765 | ex F-WWDO | |
| ☐ | PK-AXG | Airbus A320-216 | 3813 | ex F-WWIE | |
| ☐ | PK-AXH | Airbus A320-216 | 3875 | ex F-WWII | |
| ☐ | PK-AXI | Airbus A320-216 | 3963 | ex F-WWID | |
| ☐ | PK-AXJ | Airbus A320-216 | 4035 | ex F-WWIJ | |
| ☐ | PK-AXK | Airbus A320-216 | 4147 | ex F-WWBC | |
| ☐ | PK-AXL | Airbus A320-216 | 4346 | ex F-WWBT | |
| ☐ | PK-AXM | Airbus A320-216 | 4462 | ex F-WWBI | |
| ☐ | PK-AXR | Airbus A320-216 | 2881 | ex 9M-AFJ | ♦ |
| ☐ | PK-AXS | Airbus A320-216 | 2885 | ex 9M-AFK | ♦ |
| ☐ | PK-AXT | Airbus A320-216 | 3486 | ex 9M-AHK | ♦ |
| ☐ | PK-AXU | Airbus A320-216 | 3549 | ex 9M-AHN | ♦ |
| ☐ | PK-AXV | Airbus A320-216 | 4889 | ex RP-C8190 | ♦ |
| ☐ | PK-AWO | Boeing 737-322 | 24659/1836 | ex 9M-AEA | |
| ☐ | PK-AWT | Boeing 737-3B7 | 23345/1170 | ex N304WA | |
| ☐ | PK-AWX | Boeing 737-3Y0 | 24547/1813 | ex 9M-AEC | |

## JATAYU AIR — Jatayu (VJ/JTY) — Jakarta-Soekarno Hatta (CGK)

Ceased ops

## KALSTAR — (KD) — Serpong

| | | | | | |
|---|---|---|---|---|---|
| ☐ | PK-KSE | ATR 42-320 | 0415 | ex N415AN | |
| ☐ | PK-KSI | ATR 42-320 | 0348 | ex N38AN | |
| ☐ | PK-KSM | Boeing 737-529 | 26537/2265 | ex PK-RAW | ♦ |
| ☐ | PK-KSN | Boeing 737-3MB | 25040/2017 | ex N119GA | ♦ |
| ☐ | PK-KSO | ATR 42-320 | 0202 | ex N21837 | ♦ |

## KARTIKA AIRLINES — Kartika (3Y/KAE) — Jakarta-Soekarno Hatta (CGK)

Asian launch customer for Sukhoi Superjet 100

## LION AIRLINES — Lion Inter (JT/LNI) — Jakarta-Soekarno Hatta (CGK)

| | Reg | Type | MSN | Notes | |
|---|---|---|---|---|---|
| ☐ | PK-LIF | Boeing 737-4Y0 | 24467/1733 | ex PK-MBL | |
| ☐ | PK-LIG | Boeing 737-4Y0 | 24513/1779 | ex PK-MBM | |
| ☐ | PK-LIH | Boeing 737-4Y0 | 24520/1803 | ex HL7260 | [CGK] |
| ☐ | PK-LII | Boeing 737-46B | 24123/1663 | ex EC-GRX | |
| ☐ | PK-LIR | Boeing 737-4Y0 | 24692/1963 | ex EC-IRA | |
| ☐ | PK-LIS | Boeing 737-4Y0 | 24693/1972 | ex OK-WGG | |
| ☐ | PK-LIT | Boeing 737-4Y0 | 24512/1777 | ex PK-GWV | |
| ☐ | PK-LIU | Boeing 737-3G7 | 23218/1076 | ex N380WL | [CGK] |
| ☐ | PK-LIV | Boeing 737-3G7 | 23219/1090 | ex N390WL | |
| ☐ | PK-LIW | Boeing 737-4Y0 | 24684/1841 | ex EI-CVN | |
| | | | | | |
| ☐ | PK-LJW | Boeing 737-8GP/W | 37295 | | o/o♦ |
| ☐ | PK-LJY | Boeing 737-8GP/W | 38722 | | o/o♦ |
| ☐ | PK-LKG | Boeing 737-8GP/W | 38681 | | o/o♦ |
| ☐ | PK-LKH | Boeing 737-8GP/W | 37297 | | o/o♦ |
| ☐ | PK-LKI | Boeing 737-8GP/W | 38724 | | o/o♦ |
| ☐ | PK-LKJ | Boeing 737-85N/W | 38682 | | o/o♦ |
| | | | | | |
| ☐ | PK-LFF | Boeing 737-9GPER/W | 35679/2093 | ex N6055X | |
| ☐ | PK-LFG | Boeing 737-9GPER/W | 35680/1981 | ex N900ER | |
| ☐ | PK-LFH | Boeing 737-9GPER/W | 35710/2285 | ex N1786B | |
| ☐ | PK-LFI | Boeing 737-9GPER/W | 35711/2319 | ex N1780B | |
| ☐ | PK-LFJ | Boeing 737-9GPER/W | 35712/2349 | ex (PK-LAJ) | |
| ☐ | PK-LFK | Boeing 737-9GPER/W | 35713/2437 | ex N1781B | |
| ☐ | PK-LFL | Boeing 737-9GPER/W | 35714/2461 | ex (PK-LAL) | |
| ☐ | PK-LFM | Boeing 737-9GPER/W | 35715/2485 | ex N1786B | |
| ☐ | PK-LFO | Boeing 737-9GPER/W | 35716/2504 | ex N1786B | |
| ☐ | PK-LFP | Boeing 737-9GPER/W | 35717/2455 | | |
| ☐ | PK-LFQ | Boeing 737-9GPER/W | 35718/2670 | | |
| ☐ | PK-LFR | Boeing 737-9GPER/W | 35719/2694 | | |
| ☐ | PK-LFS | Boeing 737-9GPER/W | 35720/2756 | | |
| ☐ | PK-LFT | Boeing 737-9GPER/W | 35721/2793 | | |
| ☐ | PK-LFU | Boeing 737-9GPER/W | 35722/2836 | ex N1784B | |
| ☐ | PK-LFV | Boeing 737-9GPER/W | 35723/2848 | ex N1787B | |
| ☐ | PK-LFW | Boeing 737-9GPER/W | 35724/2879 | | |
| ☐ | PK-LFY | Boeing 737-9GPER/W | 35725/2897 | ex N1786B | |
| ☐ | PK-LFZ | Boeing 737-9GPER/W | 35726/2904 | | |
| ☐ | PK-LGJ | Boeing 737-9GPER/W | 35727/2934 | ex N1796B | |
| ☐ | PK-LGK | Boeing 737-9GPER/W | 35728/2984 | ex N1786B | |
| ☐ | PK-LGL | Boeing 737-9GPER/W | 35729/3008 | | |
| ☐ | PK-LGM | Boeing 737-9GPER/W | 35730/3075 | | |
| ☐ | PK-LGO | Boeing 737-9GPER/W | 35731/3093 | | |
| ☐ | PK-LGP | Boeing 737-9GPER/W | 35732/3111 | | |
| ☐ | PK-LGQ | Boeing 737-9GPER/W | 35733/3135 | | |
| ☐ | PK-LGR | Boeing 737-9GPER/W | 35734/3153 | | |
| ☐ | PK-LGS | Boeing 737-9GPER/W | 35735/3183 | | |
| ☐ | PK-LGT | Boeing 737-9GPER/W | 35736/3207 | ex N1787B | |
| ☐ | PK-LGU | Boeing 737-9GPER/W | 35737/3225 | ex N1787B | |
| ☐ | PK-LGV | Boeing 737-9GPER/W | 37268/3297 | | |
| ☐ | PK-LGW | Boeing 737-9GPER/W | 37269/3321 | | |
| ☐ | PK-LGY | Boeing 737-9GPER/W | 37270/3333 | | |
| ☐ | PK-LGZ | Boeing 737-9GPER/W | 37271/3345 | ex N1786B | |
| ☐ | PK-LHH | Boeing 737-9GPER/W | 37275/3375 | | |
| ☐ | PK-LHI | Boeing 737-9GPER/W | 37276/3381 | | |
| ☐ | PK-LHJ | Boeing 737-9GPER/W | 37272/3411 | | |
| ☐ | PK-LHK | Boeing 737-9GPER/W | 37273/3423 | ex N1787B | |
| ☐ | PK-LHL | Boeing 737-9GPER/W | 37274/3441 | | |
| ☐ | PK-LHM | Boeing 737-9GPER/W | 37277/3513 | | |
| ☐ | PK-LHO | Boeing 737-9GPER/W | 37278/3555 | | ♦ |
| ☐ | PK-LHP | Boeing 737-9GPER/W | 37279/3573 | | ♦ |
| ☐ | PK-LHQ | Boeing 737-9GPER/W | 37280/3537 | | ♦ |
| ☐ | PK-LHR | Boeing 737-9GPER/W | 37281/362 | | ♦ |
| ☐ | PK-LHS | Boeing 737-9GPER/W | 37282/3663 | | ♦ |
| ☐ | PK-LHT | Boeing 737-9GPER/W | 37283/3699 | | ♦ |
| ☐ | PK-LHU | Boeing 737-9GPER/W | 38300/3717 | | ♦ |
| ☐ | PK-LHV | Boeing 737-9GPER/W | 37284/3735 | | ♦ |
| ☐ | PK-LHW | Boeing 737-9GPER/W | 38302/3753 | | ♦ |
| ☐ | PK-LHY | Boeing 737-9GPER/W | 37285/3765 | | ♦ |
| ☐ | PK-LHZ | Boeing 737-9GPER/W | 38305/3807 | | ♦ |
| ☐ | PK-LJF | Boeing 737-9GPER/W | 37286/3813 | | ♦ |
| ☐ | PK-LJG | Boeing 737-9GPER/W | 37287/3831 | | ♦ |
| ☐ | PK-LJH | Boeing 737-9PGER/W | 37288/3849 | | ♦ |
| ☐ | PK-LJI | Boeing 737-9GPER/W | 38310/3867 | | ♦ |
| ☐ | PK-LJJ | Boeing 737-9GPER/W | 37289/3888 | | ♦ |
| ☐ | PK-LJK | Boeing 737-9GPER/W | 38311/3900 | | ♦ |
| ☐ | PK-LJL | Boeing 737-9GPER/W | 37290/3918 | | ♦ |

| | | | | | | |
|---|---|---|---|---|---|---|
| ☐ | PK-LJM | Boeing 737-9GPER/W | 38313/3936 | | | ♦ |
| ☐ | PK-LJO | Boeing 737-9GPER/W | 38315/3954 | | | ♦ |
| ☐ | PK-LJP | Boeing 737-9GPER/W | 37291/3966 | | | ♦ |
| ☐ | PK-LJQ | Boeing 737-9GPER/W | 38317/3985 | | | ♦ |
| ☐ | PK-LJR | Boeing 737-9GPER/W | 37292 | | | o/o♦ |
| ☐ | PK-LJS | Boeing 737-9GPER/W | 37293 | | | o/o♦ |
| ☐ | PK-LJT | Boeing 737-9GPER/W | 38720 | | | o/o♦ |
| ☐ | PK-LJU | Boeing 737-9GPER/W | 37294 | | | o/o♦ |
| ☐ | PK-LJV | Boeing 737-9GPER/W | 38721 | | | o/o♦ |
| ☐ | PK-LJW | Boeing 737-9GPER/W | 37295 | | | o/o♦ |
| ☐ | PK-LJZ | Boeing 737-9GPER/W | 37296 | | | o/o♦ |
| ☐ | PK-LKF | Boeing 737-9GPER/W | 38723 | | | o/o♦ |
| ☐ | PK-LKM | Boeing 737-9GPER/W | 38726 | | | o/o |
| ☐ | PK- | Boeing 737-9GPER/W | | | | o/o |
| ☐ | PK- | Boeing 737-9GPER/W | | | | o/o |
| | | | | | | |
| ☐ | PK-LHF | Boeing 747-412 | 24063/736 | ex N240BA | | |
| ☐ | PK-LHG | Boeing 747-412 | 24065/761 | ex N465BB | | |
| ☐ | PK-LIK | McDonnell-Douglas MD-90-30 | 53570/2181 | ex N904RA | | |
| ☐ | PK-LIO | McDonnell-Douglas MD-90-30 | 53490/2133 | ex N902RA | | [CGK] |
| ☐ | PK-LIP | McDonnell-Douglas MD-90-30 | 53551/2144 | ex N903RA | | |

## MANDALA AIRLINES      Mandala (RI/MDL)      Jakarta-Soekarno Hatta (CGK)

| | | | | | | |
|---|---|---|---|---|---|---|
| ☐ | PK-RMN | Airbus A320-232 | 4918 | ex 9V-TRC | | ♦ |
| ☐ | PK-RMO | Airbus A320-232 | 4973 | ex 9V-TRE | | <TGW♦ |
| ☐ | PK-RMP | Airbus A320-232 | 5073 | ex D-AUBH | | <TGW♦ |

## MANUNGGAL AIR SERVICE      Jakarta-Halim (HLP)

| | | | | | | |
|---|---|---|---|---|---|---|
| ☐ | PK-VTA | British Aerospace 146 Srs.100 | E1015 | ex N146AP | | |
| ☐ | PK-VTM | British Aerospace 146 Srs.100 | E1009 | ex RP-C2999 | | |
| ☐ | PK-VTP | Aérospatiale/MBB Transall C-160P | 234 | ex PK-PTP | | ♦ |
| ☐ | PK-VTR | Aérospatiale/MBB Transall C-160P | 233 | ex PK-PTO | | [HLP] |
| ☐ | PK-VTS | Aérospatiale/MBB Transall C-160P | 207 | ex PK-PTY | | [HLP] |
| ☐ | PK-VTZ | Aérospatiale/MBB Transall C-160P | 208 | ex PK-PTZ | | ♦ |

## MERPATI NUSANTARA AIRLINES      Merpati (MZ/MNA)
### Jakarta-Soekarno Hatta/Surabaya (CGK/SUB)

| | | | | | | |
|---|---|---|---|---|---|---|
| ☐ | PK-MZA | AVIC I Y7-MA-60 | 0405 | | | |
| ☐ | PK-MZC | AVIC I Y7-MA-60 | 0407 | ex B-779L | | |
| ☐ | PK-MZD | AVIC I Y7-MA-60 | 0410 | | | |
| ☐ | PK-MZE | AVIC I Y7-MA-60 | 0501 | | | |
| ☐ | PK-MZF | AVIC I Y7-MA-60 | 0502 | | | on order |
| ☐ | PK-MZG | AVIC I Y7-MA-60 | 0505 | | | ♦ |
| ☐ | PK-MZH | AVIC I Y7-MA-60 | 0506 | | | ♦ |
| ☐ | PK-MZI | AVIC I Y7-MA-60 | 0601 | | | |
| ☐ | PK-MZJ | AVIC I Y7-MA-60 | 0601 | | | on order |
| ☐ | PK-MZL | AVIC I Y7-MA-60 | 0604 | | | ♦ |
| ☐ | PK-MZM | AVIC I Y7-MA-60 | 0605 | | | ♦ |
| ☐ | PK-MZN | AVIC I Y7-MA-60 | 0606 | | | ♦ |
| ☐ | PK-MZO | AVIC I Y7-MA-60 | 0608 | | | ♦ |
| ☐ | PK-MZP | AVIC I Y7-MA-60 | 0609 | | | ♦ |
| | | | | | | |
| ☐ | PK-MBP | Boeing 737-33A | 23632/1344 | ex N173AW | | |
| ☐ | PK-MDF | Boeing 737-3S1 | 24856/1911 | ex PK-AWS | | |
| ☐ | PK-MDH | Boeing 737-301 | 23932/1554 | ex N587US | | wfs |
| ☐ | PK-MDJ | Boeing 737-301 | 23931/1552 | ex N586US | | wfs |
| ☐ | PK-MDK | Boeing 737-3B7 | 23858/1509 | ex N140CT | | |
| ☐ | PK-MDQ | Boeing 737-3Q8 | 24300/1666 | ex N243AD | | |
| | | | | | | |
| ☐ | PK-NCD | CASA-Nurtanio C.212-A4 | 5N/A4-2-63 | ex PK-XCB | | ♦ |
| ☐ | PK-NCH | CASA-Nurtanio C.212-AB4 | 30N/AB4-2-173 | ex PK-XAD | Weh | |
| ☐ | PK-NCM | CASA-Nurtanio C.212-200 | 35N/AB4-7-188 | ex PK-XAI | | ♦ |
| ☐ | PK-NCN | CASA-Nurtanio C.212-AB4 | 36N/AB4-8-191 | ex PK-XAJ | Seribu | |
| ☐ | PK-NCP | CASA-Nurtanio c.212-200 | 38N/AB4-10-197 | ex PK-XAL | | ♦ |
| ☐ | PK-NCV | CASA-Nurtanio C.212-C4 | 75N/CC4-26-255 | ex PK-XDX | Misool | |
| ☐ | PK-NCW | CASA-Nurtanio C.212-200 | 76N/CC4-27-256 | ex PK-XDY | | ♦ |
| ☐ | PK-NCX | CASA-Nurtanio C.212-C4 | 77N/CC4-28-257 | ex PK-XDZ | Batudata | |
| | | | | | | |
| ☐ | PK-MND | CASA-Nurtanio CN-235 | 7/N003 | ex PK-XNE | Sermata | [SUB] |
| ☐ | PK-MNE | CASA-Nurtanio CN-235 | 9/N004 | ex PK-XNF | Letiall-white | [MES] |
| ☐ | PK-MNF | CASA-Nurtanio CN-235-200 | 10/N005 | ex PK-XNG | Wowoni | [SUB] |
| ☐ | PK-MNG | CASA-Nurtanio CN-235 | 14/N006 | ex PK-XNH | Timorall-white | [SUB] |
| ☐ | PK-MNK | CASA-Nurtanio CN-235 | 20/N010 | ex PK-XNL | Kobroor | [SUB] |
| ☐ | PK-MNL | CASA-Nurtanio CN-235 | 24/N011 | ex PK-XNM | | ♦ |
| ☐ | PK-MNM | CASA-Nurtanio CN-235 | 26/N012 | ex PK-XNN | Moa | |
| | | | | | | |
| ☐ | PK-NUH | de Havilland DHC-6 Twin Otter 300 | 383 | | Natuna | |
| ☐ | PK-NUI | de Havilland DHC-6 Twin Otter 300 | 386 | | | ♦ |

| | Reg | Type | C/n | Ex | Name | Notes |
|---|---|---|---|---|---|---|
| ☐ | PK-NUO | de Havilland DHC-6 Twin Otter 300 | 487 | | Singkep | [BIK] |
| ☐ | PK-NUR | de Havilland DHC-6 Twin Otter 300 | 484 | | Muna | [BIK] |
| ☐ | PK-NUS | de Havilland DHC-6 Twin Otter 300 | 481 | | Peleng | |
| ☐ | PK-NUV | de Havilland DHC-6 Twin Otter 300 | 472 | | Tanimbar | |
| ☐ | PK-NUZ | de Havilland DHC-6 Twin Otter 300 | 443 | ex PK-NUM | Alor | |
| ☐ | PK-NVA | de Havilland DHC-6 Twin Otter 300 | 551 | ex VH-UQY | | |
| | | | | | | |
| ☐ | PK-MBC | Boeing 737-230 | 22129/754 | ex D-ABFY | | [SUB] |
| ☐ | PK-MBE | Boeing 737-230 | 22142/797 | ex D-ABHS | Batanta | |
| ☐ | PK-MBS | Boeing 737-217 (AvAero 3) | 22342/810 | ex N288TR | | [SUB] |
| ☐ | PK-MBU | Boeing 737-217 (AvAero 3) | 22259/771 | ex N284TR | | [SUB] |
| ☐ | PK-MDO | Boeing 737-4Q8 | 24069/1635 | ex N240AD | | |
| ☐ | PK-MDS | Boeing 737-4Q8 | 24708/2076 | ex PK-GWU | | ♦ |
| ☐ | PK-MDT | Boeing 737-522 | 26704/2508 | ex OM-CCB | | ♦ |
| ☐ | PK-MDY | Boeing 737-4K5 | 26316/2711 | ex PK-GWT | | ♦ |
| ☐ | PK-MFY | Fokker F.27 Friendship 500 | 10629 | ex PK-GRK | Halmahera | wfs |
| ☐ | PK-MJA | Fokker 100 | 11453 | ex PH-MXO | Bawal | [SUB] |
| ☐ | PK-MJC | Fokker 100 | 11463 | ex PH-EZV | Sabu | |
| ☐ | PK-MJD | Fokker 100 | 11474 | ex PH-EZW | Rupat | |

## NUSANTARA AIR CHARTER
*Jakarta-Halim (HLP)*

| | Reg | Type | C/n | Ex | Name | Notes |
|---|---|---|---|---|---|---|
| ☐ | PK-JKC | British Aerospace 146 Srs.200 | E2113 | ex SE-DRN | | |
| ☐ | PK-JKW | British Aerospace 146 Srs.200 | E2204 | ex PK-LNI | Athirah | |

## NUSANTARA BUANA AIR

| | Reg | Type | C/n | Ex | Name | Notes |
|---|---|---|---|---|---|---|
| ☐ | PK-DCP | CASA C.212-A4 | 14N/A4-11-101 | ex PK-XCM | | ♦ |

## PACIFIC ROYALE AIRWAYS

| | Reg | Type | C/n | Ex | Name | Notes |
|---|---|---|---|---|---|---|
| ☐ | PK-PRA | Fokker 50 | 20313 | ex ET-AKR | | [BDO]♦ |
| ☐ | PK-PRB | Fokker 50 | 20328 | ex ET-AKS | | [BDO]♦ |
| ☐ | PK- | Fokker 50 | 20331 | ex ET-AKT | | o/o♦ |
| ☐ | PK- | Fokker 50 | 20333 | ex ET-AKU | | o/o♦ |
| ☐ | PK- | Fokker 50 | 20335 | ex ET-AKV | | o/o♦ |

## PELITA AIR
*Pelita (6D/PAS)*    *Jakarta-Halim/Pondok Cabe (HLP/PCB)*

| | Reg | Type | C/n | Ex | Name | Notes |
|---|---|---|---|---|---|---|
| ☐ | PK-PDT | Aérospatiale SA.330G Puma | 1264 | ex F-WTNB | | |
| ☐ | PK-PDY | Aérospatiale SA.330G Puma | 1160 | | | |
| ☐ | PK-PEI | Aérospatiale SA.330J Puma | 1299 | | | |
| ☐ | PK-PEK | Aérospatiale SA.330G Puma | 1283 | | | |
| ☐ | PK-PEO | Aérospatiale SA.330J Puma | 1261 | | | |
| ☐ | PK-PHW | Aérospatiale SA.330G Puma | 1082 | ex F-OCRQ | | |
| ☐ | PK-PUG | IPTN/Aérospatiale NAS.332C | NSP2/2020 | ex PK-XSB | | |
| ☐ | PK-PUH | IPTN/Aérospatiale NAS.332C | NSP3/2021 | ex PK-XSC | | |
| | | | | | | |
| ☐ | PK-PCN | CASA-Nurtanio C.212-A4 | 56N/CC4-8-216 | ex PK-XDE | | [PCB] |
| ☐ | PK-PCO | CASA-Nurtanio C.212-A4 | 55N/CC4-7-215 | ex PK-XDD | | |
| ☐ | PK-PCP | CASA-Nurtanio C.212-A4 | 48N/AB4-20-208 | ex PK-XAV | | |
| ☐ | PK-PCQ | CASA-Nurtanio C.212-A4 | 47N/AB4-19-207 | ex PK-XAU | | [PCB] |
| ☐ | PK-PCR | CASA-Nurtanio C.212-A4 | 46N/AB4-18-206 | ex PK-XAT | | |
| ☐ | PK-PCS | CASA-Nurtanio C.212-A4 | 45N/AB4-17-205 | ex PK-XAS | | |
| ☐ | PK-PCT | CASA-Nurtanio C.212-A4 | 44N/AB4-16-204 | ex PK-XAR | | |
| ☐ | PK-PCU | CASA-Nurtanio C.212-A4 | 43N/AB4-15-203 | ex PK-XAQ | | |
| ☐ | PK-PCV | CASA C.212-100 | 21N/A4-18-132 | ex PK-XCT | | ♦ |
| ☐ | PK-PCY | CASA C.212-100 | 2N/C4-2-39 | ex PK-PCL | | ♦ |
| | | | | | | |
| ☐ | PK-PKT | de Havilland DHC-7-110 | 054 | ex C-FYXV | | |
| ☐ | PK-PSV | de Havilland DHC-7-103 | 105 | ex C-GFOD | | |
| ☐ | PK-PSW | de Havilland DHC-7-103 | 100 | ex C-GFCF | | |
| ☐ | PK-PSX | de Havilland DHC-7-103 | 094 | ex C-GFYI | | |
| ☐ | PK-PSY | de Havilland DHC-7-103 | 086 | ex C-GFUM | | |
| ☐ | PK-PSZ | de Havilland DHC-7-103 | 075 | ex C-GFCF | | [PCB] |
| | | | | | | |
| ☐ | PK-PGQ | Nurtanio/MBB Bo.105CB | N60/S-458 | | | |
| ☐ | PK-PGR | Nurtanio/MBB Bo.105CB | N62/S-460 | | | |
| ☐ | PK-PGU | Nurtanio/MBB Bo.105C | N12/S-218 | ex PK-XZJ | | |
| ☐ | PK-PGZ | Nurtanio/MBB Bo.105CB | N65/S-553 | | | |
| ☐ | PK-PIH | Nurtanio/MBB Bo.105CB | N68/S-556 | | | |
| ☐ | PK-PIJ | Nurtanio/MBB Bo.105CB | N70/S-558 | ex PK-XYN | | |
| ☐ | PK-PIM | Nurtanio/MBB Bo.105CB | N72/S-560 | ex PK-XYP | | |
| | | | | | | |
| ☐ | PK-PFZ | Fokker 100 | 11486 | ex PH-ZFA | | |
| ☐ | PK-PJJ | Avro 146-RJ85 | E2239 | ex G-6-239 | Wamena | VIP |
| ☐ | PK-PJK | Fokker F.28 Fellowship 4000 | 11192 | ex PH-EXW | Lengguru | [PCB] |
| ☐ | PK-PJL | Fokker F.28 Fellowship 4000 | 11111 | ex PH-EZA | Kurau | wfs |
| ☐ | PK-PJN | Fokker 100 | 11288 | ex PH-LMU | Minas | |
| ☐ | PK-PJY | Fokker F.28 Fellowship 4000 | 11146 | ex PH-EXN | Aceh | |
| ☐ | PK-PUA | Sikorsky S-76A | 76-0179 | ex N5446U | | >TVV |

| | | | | | | |
|---|---|---|---|---|---|---|
| ☐ | PK-PUD | Sikorsky S-76A | 76-0195 | ex N3121A | | >TVV |
| ☐ | PK-PUE | Sikorsky S-76A | 76-0200 | | | >TVV |
| ☐ | PK-PUJ | Bell 412EP | 36282 | ex N2012Y | | |
| ☐ | PK-PUK | Bell 412EP | 36288 | ex N2028L | | |
| ☐ | PK-PUL | Bell 430 | 49088 | ex N3005J | | |

## PREMIAIR · Jakarta-Halim (HLP)

| | | | | | | |
|---|---|---|---|---|---|---|
| ☐ | PK-RJC | Embraer EMB.120ER Brasilia | 120214 | ex VH-ANV | | |
| ☐ | PK-RJI | Fokker 100 | 11328 | ex G-BXWF | Imanuel | VIP |

## RIAU AIR · Riau (RIU) · Pekanbaru (PKU)

Ceased ops 06Apr11

## RPX AIRLINES · Public Express (RH/RPH) · Jakarta-Soekarno Hatta (CGK)

| | | | | | |
|---|---|---|---|---|---|
| ☐ | PK-RPH | Boeing 737-2K2C (AvAero 3) | 20943/405 | ex F-GGVP | |
| ☐ | PK-RPI | Boeing 737-2K2C (AvAero 3) | 20944/408 | ex F-GGVQ | |

## SABANG MERAUKE RAYA AIR CHARTER · Samer (SMC) · Medan (MES)

| | | | | | |
|---|---|---|---|---|---|
| ☐ | PK-ZAB | CAS-Nurtanio C.212-A4 | A4-20-140 | ex PK-XCV | ♦ |
| ☐ | PK-ZAE | Britten-Norman BN-2A-21 Islander | 565 | ex G-BEGH | [MES] |
| ☐ | PK-ZAK | Piper PA-31 Turbo Navajo | 31-407 | ex PK-FJA | |
| ☐ | PK-ZAN | CASA-Nurtanio C.212-A4 | 5N/A4-1-60 | ex A-2102 | |
| ☐ | PK-ZAO | CASA-Nurtanio C.212-A4 | 6N/A4-3-64 | ex A-2101 | |
| ☐ | PK-ZAQ | CASA-Nurtanio C.212-A4 | 82N/CC40330277 | ex PK-JSR | |
| ☐ | PK-ZAV | CASA-Nurtanio C.212-A4 | 81N/CC4-32-276 | ex PK-JSS | |

## SKY AVIATION

| | | | | | |
|---|---|---|---|---|---|
| ☐ | PK-ECD | Fokker 50 | 20271 | ex PH-LXK | ♦ |
| ☐ | PK-ECE | Fokker 50 | 20277 | ex PH-LXR | ♦ |
| ☐ | PK-ECF | Fokker 50 | 20279 | ex PH-LXT | ♦ |
| ☐ | PK-ECG | Fokker 50 | 20254 | ex PH-KXN | ♦ |
| ☐ | PK-ECH | Fokker 50 | 20255 | ex PH-KXS | ♦ |

## SRIWIJAYA AIR · Sriwijaya (SJ/SJY) · Jakarta-Soekarno Hatta (CGK)

| | | | | | | |
|---|---|---|---|---|---|---|
| ☐ | PK-CJA | Boeing 737-284 | 22301/683 | ex PK-IJS | Brenda | |
| ☐ | PK-CJD | Boeing 737-204 (Nordam 3) | 22057/621 | ex 9L-LFI | Emilio | |
| ☐ | PK-CJE | Boeing 737-2T4 | 23446/1165 | ex ET-ALE | Citra | |
| ☐ | PK-CJF | Boeing 737-284 | 22343/695 | ex SX-BCI | | |
| ☐ | PK-CJH | Boeing 737-2B7 (Nordam 3) | 22883/935 | ex N271AU | | |
| ☐ | PK-CJI | Boeing 737-2B7 (Nordam 3) | 23135/1054 | ex PK-ALV | Membalong | [CGK] |
| ☐ | PK-CJJ | Boeing 737-2B7 (Nordam 3) | 22880/927 | ex N268AU | | |
| ☐ | PK-CJK | Boeing 737-236 | 22032/742 | ex PK-ALK | | |
| ☐ | PK-CJL | Boeing 737-284 | 21301/474 | ex PK-TXE | | |
| ☐ | PK-CJM | Boeing 737-2B7 (Nordam 3) | 22884/956 | ex PK-TXC | | |
| ☐ | PK-CJN | Boeing 737-2B7 (Nordam 3) | 23134/1050 | ex PK-TXA | Sherly | |
| ☐ | PK-CJO | Boeing 737-284 | 22300/674 | ex PK-IJR | Lomasasta | |
| ☐ | PK-CJP | Boeing 737-2B7 (Nordam 3) | 23132/1044 | ex PK-ALN | Lenggang | |
| ☐ | PK-CJR | Boeing 737-284 | 21225/464 | ex SX-BCB | Perkasa | |
| ☐ | PK-CKP | Boeing 737-36N | 28559/2882 | ex B-2601 | | ♦ |
| ☐ | PK-CJC | Boeing 737-33A | 24025/1556 | ex SE-RCP | | ♦ |
| ☐ | PK-CJS | Boeing 737-3L9 | 27925/2763 | ex N104VR | | |
| ☐ | PK-CJT | Boeing 737-33A | 24791/1984 | ex N791AW | | |
| ☐ | PK-CJY | Boeing 737-3Q8 | 24698/1846 | ex PK-GHS | | ♦ |
| ☐ | PK-CKE | Boeing 737-3Q8 | 24987/2268 | ex N596BC | | ♦ |
| ☐ | PK-CKF | Boeing 737-3Y0 | 25179/2205 | ex N381DF | | ♦ |
| ☐ | PK-CKH | Boeing 737-3Y0 | 24907/2013 | ex N383DF | | ♦ |
| ☐ | PK-CKI | Boeing 737-3Y0 | 25187/2248 | ex N382DF | | ♦ |
| ☐ | PK-CKJ | Boeing 737-3L9 | 27337/2594 | ex N581MS | Kemurahan | ♦ |
| ☐ | PK-CKK | Boeing 737-3L9 | 27336/2587 | ex N308MS | Kejujura | ♦ |
| ☐ | PK-CKL | Boeing 737-3Q8 | 26293/2541 | ex PK-GGV | Keikhlasan | ♦ |
| ☐ | PK-CJU | Boeing 737-4Q8 | 24234/1627 | ex N234AN | | |
| ☐ | PK-CJV | Boeing 737-4Y0 | 24689/1883 | ex N689MD | | |
| ☐ | PK-CJW | Boeing 737-4Y0 | 24690/1885 | ex N690MD | | |
| ☐ | PK-CKA | Boeing 737-4Q8 | 25169/2237 | ex N483JC | | |
| ☐ | PK-CKC | Boeing 737-4Q8 | 26285/2416 | ex N587BC | | |
| ☐ | PK-CKD | Boeing 737-4Y0 | 25180/2201 | ex N251MD | | |
| ☐ | PK-CKN | Boeing 737-4Q8 | 26281/2380 | ex D-ABRF | | ♦ |

## SUSI AIR / ASI PUDJIASTUTI AVIATION · Medan (MES)

| | | | | | |
|---|---|---|---|---|---|
| ☐ | PK-BVA | Cessna 208B Caravan I | 208B2126 | ex N61905 | |
| ☐ | PK-BVD | Cessna 208B Caravan I | 208B2141 | ex N61932 | |

| | Reg | Type | c/n | ex | Notes |
|---|---|---|---|---|---|
| ☐ | PK-BVE | Cessna 208B Caravan I | 208B2142 | ex N6194X | |
| ☐ | PK-BVF | Cessna 208B Caravan I | 208B2143 | ex N61983 | |
| ☐ | PK-BVG | Cessna 208B Caravan I | 208B2146 | ex N6203C | |
| ☐ | PK-BVH | Cessna 208B Caravan I | 208B2151 | ex N6204C | |
| ☐ | PK-BVJ | Cessna 208B Caravan I | 208B2177 | ex N1015J | |
| ☐ | PK-BVK | Cessna 208B Caravan I | 208B2198 | ex N10200 | |
| ☐ | PK-BVL | Cessna 208B Caravan I | 208B2206 | ex N1021S | |
| ☐ | PK-BVN | Cessna 208B Caravan I | 208B2258 | ex N258CC | |
| ☐ | PK-BVO | Cessna 208B Caravan I | 208B2217 | ex N1022G | ♦ |
| ☐ | PK-BVQ | Cessna 208B Caravan I | 208B2225 | ex N10225 | ♦ |
| ☐ | PK-BV. | Cessna 208B Caravan I | 208B2194 | ex N1016M | ♦ |
| ☐ | PK-BV. | Cessna 208B Caravan I | 208B2163 | ex N208CC | ♦ |
| ☐ | PK-VVA | Cessna 208B Caravan I | 208B1066 | ex N12690 | |
| ☐ | PK-VVB | Cessna 208B Caravan I | 208B1285 | ex N4117B | |
| ☐ | PK-VVD | Cessna 208B Caravan I | 208B1303 | ex N20722 | |
| ☐ | PK-VVF | Cessna 208B Caravan I | 208B1177 | ex N1307K | |
| ☐ | PK-VVH | Cessna 208B Caravan I | 208B1078 | ex N278ST | |
| ☐ | PK-VVI | Cessna 208B Caravan I | 208B1205 | ex RP-C2929 | |
| ☐ | PK-VVJ | Cessna 208B Caravan I | 208B2086 | ex N2232Y | |
| ☐ | PK-VVM | Cessna 208B Caravan I | 208B2093 | ex N2154L | |
| ☐ | PK-VVO | Cessna 208B Caravan I | 208B2111 | ex N61611 | |
| ☐ | PK-VVR | Cessna 208B Caravan I | 208B1085 | ex N12722 | |
| ☐ | PK-VVS | Cessna 208B Caravan I | 208B1117 | ex N12775 | |
| ☐ | PK-VVT | Cessna 208B Caravan I | 208B2068 | ex N61413 | |
| ☐ | PK- | Cessna 208B Caravan I | 208B2218 | ex N1022Z | ♦ |
| ☐ | PK-BVM | Pilatus PC-6/B2-H4 Turbo Porter | 975 | ex HB-FNU | |
| ☐ | PK-BVT | Pilatus PC-6/B2-H4 Turbo Porter | 968 | | |
| ☐ | PK-BVY | Pilatus PC-6/B2-H4 Turbo Porter | 973 | ex HB-FNS | |
| ☐ | PK-VVK | Pilatus PC-6/B2-H4 Turbo Porter | 958 | | |
| ☐ | PK-VVP | Pilatus PC-6/B2-H4 Turbo Porter | 957 | | |
| ☐ | PK-VVQ | Pilatus PC-6/B2-H4 Turbo Porter | 965 | | |
| ☐ | PK-VVU | Pilatus PC-6/B2-H4 Turbo Porter | 967 | | |
| ☐ | PK-BVV | Piaggio F.180 Avanti | 1209 | ex N128PA | ♦ |
| ☐ | PK-BVX | Piaggio F.180 Avanti | 1204 | | ♦ |

## TRANSNUSA AIR SERVICES (TNU)

| | Reg | Type | c/n | ex | Notes |
|---|---|---|---|---|---|
| ☐ | PK-TNA | Fokker 50 | 20261 | ex PK-BRS | ♦ |
| ☐ | PK-TNB | Fokker 50 | 20282 | ex PK-BRY | ♦ |
| ☐ | PK-TNC | Fokker 50 | 20240 | ex D2-ESR | ♦ |
| ☐ | PK-TNS | Fokker 50 | 20307 | ex PK-BRW | ♦ |

## TRANSWISATA AIR (TWT) Jakarta-Halim (HLP)

| | Reg | Type | c/n | ex | Notes |
|---|---|---|---|---|---|
| ☐ | PK-TWA | Fokker F.28 Fellowship 4000 | 11234 | ex N484US | |
| ☐ | PK-TWM | Fokker F.28 Fellowship 4000 | 11183 | ex ZS-JAV | |
| ☐ | PK-TWN | Fokker 100 | 11335 | ex PH-SXI | |
| ☐ | PK-TWV | Bell 412 | 36153 | ex NL9251 | ♦ |

## TRAVIRA AIR (TR/TVV) Denpasar (DPS)

| | Reg | Type | c/n | ex | Notes |
|---|---|---|---|---|---|
| ☐ | PK-PUA | Sikorsky S-76A | 760179 | ex N5446U | <PAS |
| ☐ | PK-PUD | Sikorsky S-76A | 760195 | ex N3121A | <PAS |
| ☐ | PK-PUE | Sikorsky S-76A | 760200 | | <PAS |
| ☐ | PK-TVF | Sikorsky S-76A | 760154 | ex VH-CPH | |
| ☐ | PK-TVP | Sikorsky S-76C | 760421 | ex N899KK | |
| ☐ | PK-TVQ | Sikorsky S-76A | 760286 | ex N30DJ | |
| ☐ | PK-TVP | Sikorsky S-76C | 760436 | ex N476X | |
| ☐ | PK-TVU | Sikorsky S-76C | 760298 | ex N520AL | |
| ☐ | PK-NZU | IPTN/MBB Bo.105CB | N121/S-719 | ex PK-IWJ | |
| ☐ | PK-TUB | de Havilland DHC-8Q-315 | 590 | ex C-GJTR | |
| ☐ | PK-TVA | IPTN/MBB Bo.105CB | N1/S-124 | ex PK-PEE | |
| ☐ | PK-TVB | IPTN/MBB Bo.105CB | N6/S-177 | ex PK-PGV | |
| ☐ | PK-TVH | Beech 1900D | UE-364 | ex N30469 | |
| ☐ | PK-TVI | Cessna 208 Caravan I | 20800313 | ex C-FAMB | FP |
| ☐ | PK-TVJ | Beech 1900D | UE-352 | ex N352RA | |
| ☐ | PK-TVK | Beech 1900D | UE-375 | ex N31424 | Air Ambulance |
| ☐ | PK-TVN | Cessna 208 Caravan I | 20800358 | ex N1229N | FP |
| ☐ | PK-TVV | Beech 1900D | UE-308 | ex N803UE | ♦ |
| ☐ | PK-TVW | Cessna 208 Caravan I | 20800418 | ex N20869 | |
| ☐ | PK-TVX | Cessna 208 Caravan I | 20800421 | ex N2098U | |
| ☐ | PK-TVY | de Havilland DHC-8-315 | 549 | ex VH-AAY | |
| ☐ | PK-TVZ | Boeing 737-5L9 | 28996/2998 | ex N737RH | VIP |

## TRIGANA AIR SERVICE Trigana (TGN) Jakarta-Halim (HLP)

| | Reg | Type | c/n | ex | Notes |
|---|---|---|---|---|---|
| ☐ | PK-KSE | ATR 42-320 | 0415 | ex N415AN | ♦ |
| ☐ | PK-KSI | ATR 42-320 | 0348 | ex N38AN | ♦ |

| | | | | | | |
|---|---|---|---|---|---|---|
| ☐ | PK-KSO | ATR 42-320 | 0202 | ex N21837 | | ♦ |
| ☐ | PK-YRE | ATR 42-300 | 0027 | ex F-GPZB | <Martinique Aero Lease | |
| ☐ | PK-YRH | ATR 42-300 | 0097 | ex F-ODGN | | |
| ☐ | PK-YRK | ATR 42-300 | 0106 | ex N422TE | | |
| ☐ | PK-YRN | ATR 42-300 | 0102 | ex N421TE | | |
| ☐ | PK-YRR | ATR 42-310 | 0214 | ex F-GHPI | | |
| ☐ | PK-YRV | ATR 42-300 | 0190 | ex G-BYHA | | |
| | | | | | | |
| ☐ | PK-YRT | Boeing 737-2K5 | 22599/814 | ex PK-KJN | | |
| ☐ | PK-YSA | Boeing 737-228 (Nordam 3) | 23007/948 | ex PK-MBZ | | ♦ |
| ☐ | PK-YSB | Boeing 737-228 (Nordam 3) | 23005/943 | ex PK-MBX | | ♦ |
| ☐ | PK-YSC | Boeing 737-228 (Nordam 3) | 23004/941 | ex PK-MBY | | ♦ |
| ☐ | PK-YSD | Boeing 737-217 (AvAero 3) | 22260/784 | ex PK-MBQ | | ♦ |
| | | | | | | |
| ☐ | PK-YPA | Fokker F27 Friendship 200 | 10223 | ex PK-ZAY | | wfs♦ |
| ☐ | PK-YPX | de Havilland DHC-6 Twin Otter 300 | 684 | ex HB-LTF | | |
| ☐ | PK-YRC | Cessna TU206D Skywagon | U206-1269 | ex PK-MCA | | |
| ☐ | PK-YRF | de Havilland DHC-6 Twin Otter 300 | 462 | ex D-ISKY | | wfs |
| ☐ | PK-YRG | Fokker F.27 Friendship 500 | 10397 | ex PH-FNV | | wfs |
| ☐ | PK-YRI | ATR 72-202 | 0326 | ex F-WQUF | | |
| ☐ | PK-YRJ | de Havilland DHC-4A Caribou | 27 | ex N666NC | | |
| ☐ | PK-YRQ | Bell 206L-4 LongRanger IV | 52069 | ex F-GPGC | | |
| ☐ | PK-YRU | de Havilland DHC-6 Twin Otter 300 | 685 | ex VH-VHP | | |
| ☐ | PK-YRX | ATR 72-202 | 0342 | ex F-WQRY | | |
| ☐ | PK-YRY | ATR 72-202 | 0201 | ex F-WQAL | | |
| ☐ | PK-YRZ | Boeing 737-3Q8 (SF) | 24700/1924 | ex N470AG | | [WMX]♦ |
| ☐ | PK-YSY | Boeing 737-347SF | 23597/1287 | ex PK-BBA | | ♦ |
| ☐ | PK-YSZ | Boeing 737-3Z0F | 23451/1240 | ex N23451 | | ♦ |

### TRI-MG INTRA-ASIA AIRLINES — Trilines (GY/TMG) — Jakarta-Halim (HLP)

| | | | | | | |
|---|---|---|---|---|---|---|
| ☐ | PK-YGL | LET L-410UVP-E | 892342 | ex RP-C748 | | |
| ☐ | PK-YGN | LET L-410UVP-E | 902434 | ex RP-C728 | | ♦ |
| ☐ | PK-YGP | Boeing 737-210C (Nordam 3) | 21822/605 | ex 9M-NEA | Galactico | |
| ☐ | PK-YGR | Boeing 727-223F (FedEx 3) | 20993/1189 | ex N117JB | Zenith | |
| ☐ | PK-YGZ | Boeing 727-31F (FedEx 3) | 20112/700 | ex OO-DHO | Noble Witness | |

### WINGS ABADI AIR — Wings Abadi (IW/WON) — Jakarta-Soekarno Hatta (CGK)

| | | | | | | |
|---|---|---|---|---|---|---|
| ☐ | PK-WFF | ATR 72-212A | 0869 | ex F-WWET | | |
| ☐ | PK-WFG | ATR 72-212A | 0882 | ex F-WWEL | | |
| ☐ | PK-WFH | ATR 72-212A | 0883 | ex F-WWEM | | |
| ☐ | PK-WFI | ATR 72-212A | 0871 | ex F-WWEV | | |
| ☐ | PK-WFJ | ATR 72-212A | 0898 | ex F-WWEI | | |
| ☐ | PK-WFK | ATR 72-212A | 0905 | ex F-WWEV | | |
| ☐ | PK-WFL | ATR 72-212A | 0915 | ex F-WWEM | | |
| ☐ | PK-WFM | ATR 72-212A | 0922 | ex F-WWEV | | |
| ☐ | PK-WFO | ATR 72-212A | 0936 | ex F-WWEL | | |
| ☐ | PK-WFP | ATR 72-212A | 0937 | ex F-WWEM | | |
| ☐ | PK-WFQ | ATR 72-212A | 0943 | ex F-WW | | |
| ☐ | PK-WFR- | ATR 72-212A | 0946 | ex F-WWEW | | ♦ |
| ☐ | PK-WFS | ATR 72-212A | 0957 | ex F-WWEJ | | ♦ |
| ☐ | PK-WFT | ATR 72-212A | 0961 | ex F-WWEN | | ♦ |
| ☐ | PK-WFU | ATR 72-212A | 0964 | ex F-WWEQ | | ♦ |
| ☐ | PK-WFV | ATR 72-212A | 0985 | ex F-WWEF | | ♦ |
| ☐ | PK- | ATR 72-212A | 1024 | ex F-WWEK | | o/o♦ |
| | | | | | | |
| ☐ | PK-WIF | McDonnell-Douglas MD-82 | 49481/1308 | ex N72821 | | |
| ☐ | PK-WIH | McDonnell-Douglas MD-82 | 49582/1411 | ex N57837 | | |
| ☐ | PK-WII | McDonnell-Douglas MD-82 | 49263/1163 | ex PK-LMI | | ♦ |
| ☐ | PK-WIM | McDonnell-Douglas MD-82 | 49373/1201 | ex PK-LMO | | |
| ☐ | PK-WIO | McDonnell-Douglas MD-82 | 49102/1076 | ex PK-LMQ | | [CGK], |
| | | | | | | |
| ☐ | PK-WIA | de Havilland DHC-8-301 | 194 | ex N194TY | | {SUB} |
| ☐ | PK-WID | de Havilland DHC-8-301 | 116 | ex N116TY | | |
| ☐ | PK-WIE | de Havilland DHC-8-301 | 108 | ex N108TY | | |

## PP-, PR-, PT-   BRAZIL (Federative Republic of Brazil)

### ABAETE LINHAS AEREAS — (ABJ) — Salvador, BA (SSA)

| | | | | | |
|---|---|---|---|---|---|
| ☐ | PT-OGK | Cessna 208A Caravan I | 20800078 | ex PT-OZA | |
| ☐ | PT-OGP | Cessna 208A Caravan I | 20800050 | ex N817FE | |
| ☐ | PT-OGR | Cessna 208A Caravan I | 20800100 | ex N838FE | |
| ☐ | PT-OGS | Cessna 208A Caravan I | 20800034 | ex N811FE | |
| ☐ | PT-OGT | Cessna 208A Caravan I | 20800038 | ex N815FE | |
| ☐ | PT-OGU | Cessna 208A Caravan I | 20800066 | ex N826FE | |
| ☐ | PT-OZA | Cessna 208B Caravan I | 208B0157 | ex N4615B | |
| | | | | | |
| ☐ | PP-ATT | Cessna 402B | 402B0631 | ex N3786C | |

| | | | | | |
|---|---|---|---|---|---|
| ☐ | PT-JBD | Cessna 402B | 402B0404 | | |
| ☐ | PT-JRT | Cessna 402B | 402B0552 | ex N1634T | |
| ☐ | PT-JTZ | Cessna 402B | 402B0532 | | |
| ☐ | PT-LKZ | Cessna 402B | 402B1074 | ex N1554G | |
| | | | | | |
| ☐ | PT-GKO | Embraer EMB.110P Bandeirante | 110119 | | |
| ☐ | PT-MFN | Embraer EMB.110C Bandeirante | 110010 | ex FAB2148 | wfs♦ |
| ☐ | PT-MFO | Embraer EMB.110C Bandeirante | 110058 | ex FAB2158 | |
| ☐ | PT-MFP | Embraer EMB.110C Bandeirante | 110105 | ex FAB2181 | |
| ☐ | PT-MFQ | Embraer EMB.110C Bandeirante | 110121 | ex FAB2188 | |
| ☐ | PT-MFS | Embraer EMB.110C Bandeirante | 110054 | ex FAB2160 | |
| | | | | | |
| ☐ | PT-RGV | Embraer EMB.821 Caraja | 820136 | ex PT-ZNA | |
| ☐ | PT-VCH | Embraer EMB.821 Caraja | 821012 | | |
| ☐ | PT-VCI | Embraer EMB.821 Caraja | 820144 | | |
| ☐ | PT-VKD | Embraer EMB.821 Caraja | 820159 | | |
| ☐ | PT-WFL | Embraer EMB.821 Caraja | 820150 | | |
| | | | | | |
| ☐ | PT-ACM | Embraer EMB.121A Xingu | 121021 | ex PT-MAN | |
| ☐ | PT-MCA | Embraer EMB.121A1 Xingu | 121058 | | |

## ABSA CARGO  —  Absa Cargo (M3/TUS)  —  Sao Paulo-Viracopos, SP (VCP)

| | | | | | |
|---|---|---|---|---|---|
| ☐ | PR-ABB | Boeing 767-316F/W | 29881/778 | ex CC-CZX | <LAN |
| ☐ | PR-ABD | Boeing 767-316F/W | 34245/934 | | <LAN |
| ☐ | PR-ACG | Boeing 767-316F/W | 30780/806 | ex CC-CZY | <LAN |

## AERO RIO

| | | | | | |
|---|---|---|---|---|---|
| ☐ | PR-RJZ | Cessna 208B Caravan I | 208B2131 | ex (VH-NQB) | ♦ |

## AERO STAR TAXI AEREO  —  Salvador, BA (SSA)

| | | | | | |
|---|---|---|---|---|---|
| ☐ | PT-EDF | Embraer EMB-820C Navajo | 820014 | | |
| ☐ | PT-EZN | Embraer EMB-820C Navajo | 820106 | | |
| ☐ | PT-KTR | Britten-Norman BN-2A-27 Islander | 495 | ex G-BDNN | |

## AEROLEO TAXI AERO  —  Rio de Janeiro-Santos Dumont, RJ/Macae & Sao Tome, RJ (SDU/MEA)

| | | | | | |
|---|---|---|---|---|---|
| ☐ | PR-CHL | Sikorsky S-76A++ | 760160 | ex D2-EXF | |
| ☐ | PR-CHP | Sikorsky S-76C+ | 760743 | ex C-FYDD | |
| ☐ | PR-EDA | Sikorsky S-76A | 760279 | ex N710AL | <ALG |
| ☐ | PR-GPC | Sikorsky S-76A | 760266 | ex N703AL | <ALG |
| ☐ | PR-LBA | Sikorsky S-76C+ | 760705 | ex N2584Q | <ALG |
| ☐ | PR-LCT | Sikorsky S-76C+ | 760723 | ex N723Y | <ALG |
| ☐ | PR-LCL | Sikorsky S-76A | 760280 | ex N712AL | <ALG |
| ☐ | PR-LCV | Sikorsky S-76C+ | 760672 | ex N4508N | <ALG |
| ☐ | PR-LCX | Sikorsky S-76C+ | 760704 | ex N231Y | <ALG |
| ☐ | PR-LCZ | Sikorsky S-76C+ | 760707 | ex N415Y | <ALG |
| ☐ | PR-LDA | Sikorsky S-76C+ | 760756 | ex N756N | <ALG |
| ☐ | PR-LDB | Sikorsky S-76C+ | 760759 | ex N759L | <ALG |
| ☐ | PR-LDC | Sikorsky S-76C+ | 760783 | | |
| ☐ | PR-LDD | Sikorsky S-76C+ | 760679 | ex N882AL | <ALG |
| ☐ | PR-LDE | Sikorsky S-76C+ | 760784 | | |
| ☐ | PR-LDG | Sikorsky S-76C+ | 760785 | | |
| ☐ | PR-LDH | Sikorsky S-76C+ | 760777 | ex N777LQ | |
| ☐ | PR-LDK | Sikorsky S-76C | 760608 | ex N176PG | |
| ☐ | PR-LDJ | Sikorsky S-76C | 760530 | ex N22CP | ♦ |
| ☐ | PR-LDN | Sikorsky S-76C++ | 760654 | ex G-CEOR | ♦ |
| ☐ | PR-LDP | Sikorsky S-76C | 760534 | ex N115PD | ♦ |
| ☐ | PR-LDQ | Sikorsky S-76C++ | 760718 | ex VH-TZK | ♦ |
| ☐ | PR-LDT | Sikorsky S-76C+ | 760553 | ex N767LL | ♦ |
| ☐ | PR-LDU | Sikorsky S-76C++ | 760768 | ex G-CGRK | ♦ |
| ☐ | PR-LDV | Sikorsky s-76c++ | 760768 | ex (PR-LDU) | ♦ |
| ☐ | PR-NLF | Sikorsky S-76A | 760085 | ex N1547K | <ALG |
| ☐ | PT-HOR | Sikorsky S-76A | 760003 | ex N476AL | <ALG |
| ☐ | PT-YAY | Sikorsky S-76A | 760277 | ex N708AL | <ALG |
| | | | | | |
| ☐ | PR-JAA | Sikorsky S-92A | 920099 | ex N2059J | |
| ☐ | PR-JAE | Sikorsky S-92A | 920105 | ex N2082Q | |
| ☐ | PR-JAF | Sikorsky S-92A | 920093 | ex N922AL | |
| ☐ | PR-AEL | Sikorsky S-61N | 61808 | ex N563EH | |
| ☐ | PR-FNT | Aérospatiale AS.332L1 | 2468 | ex LN-OMT | |

## AIR AMAZONIA

| | | | | | |
|---|---|---|---|---|---|
| ☐ | PP-PSA | Embraer EMB.120ER Brasilia | 120302 | Tefé | ♦ |
| ☐ | PT-SLD | Embraer EMB.120ER Brasilia | 120147 | Juruá | ♦ |
| ☐ | PT-SLE | Embraer EMB.120ER Brasilia | 120161 | Solimões | ♦ |

414

## AIR BRASIL CARGO  (BSL)  Sao Paulo-Guarulhos, SP ( GRU)

| ☐ | PR-AIB | Boeing 727-227F (FedEx 3) | 21363/1258 | ex N79754 | |
| ☐ | PR-MTJ | Boeing 727-2M7F (FedEx 3) | 21952/1693 | ex N742RW | ♦ |

Ceased ops May10

## AMERICA DO SUL TAXI AEREO

| ☐ | PP-OSP | Cessna 208B Caravan i | 208B2236 | ex N5296X | ♦ |

## AMAZONAVES TAXI AEREO  Tefe/Manaus, AM (-/MAO)

| ☐ | PP-AMV | Cessna 208B Caravan I | 208B2179 | ex N5036Q | ♦ |
| ☐ | PP-AMX | Cessna 208B Caravan I | 208B2267 | ex N50549 | ♦ |
| ☐ | PP-AMZ | Cessna 208B Caravan I | 208B2073 | ex N2210K | ♦ |
| ☐ | PP-ITZ | Cessna 208B Caravan I | 208B0499 | ex N5188N | |
| ☐ | PT-MET | Cessna 208B Caravan I | 208B0509 | ex N5073G | |
| ☐ | PT-EUS | Embraer EMB.810C Seneca | 810230 | | |
| ☐ | PT-OLJ | Embraer EMB.810C Seneca | 810330 | | |
| ☐ | PT-WIG | Embraer EMB.810C Seneca | 810433 | | |

## APUI TAXI AEREO  Manaus-Ponta Pelada, AM (PLL)

| ☐ | PT-GKX | Embraer EMB.110P Bandeirante | 110129 | | |
| ☐ | PT-LRR | Embraer EMB.110P1 Bandeirante | 110315 | ex N695RA | |
| ☐ | PT-ODJ | Embraer EMB.110 Bandeirante | 110034 | ex FAB 2144 | |
| ☐ | PT-ODY | Embraer EMB.110 Bandeirante | 110039 | ex FAB 2147 | |
| ☐ | PT-RCV | Embraer EMB.810C Seneca | 810333 | | |

## ARIZONA TAXI AEREO

| ☐ | PR-ECC | Cessna 208B Caravan I | 208B2205 | | ♦ |

## ATA BRASIL  ATA Brasil (ABZ)  Fortaleza, CE (FOR)

Ceased ops

## ATLANTICO TRANSPORTE AEREO

| ☐ | PR-ATA | Cessna 208B Caravan I | 208B0880 | | ♦ |

## AVIANCA BRAZIL  (ONE)  Rio de Janeiro-Santos Dumont, RJ (SDU)

| ☐ | PR-AVH | Airbus A318-121 | 3001 | ex CC-CVA | | ♦ |
| ☐ | PR-AVJ | Airbus A318-121 | 3030 | ex CC-CVB | | ♦ |
| ☐ | PR-AVK | Airbus A318-121 | 3062 | ex CC-CVF | | ♦ |
| ☐ | PR-AVL | Airbus A318-121 | 3214 | ex CC-CVH | | ♦ |
| ☐ | PR-AVO | Airbus A318-121 | 3216 | ex CC-CVN | | ♦ |
| ☐ | PR-OAN | Embraer EMB.120RT Brasilia | 120051 | ex N237AS | | wfs |
| ☐ | PR-OAO | Embraer EMB.120RT Brasilia | 120057 | ex N239AS | Grey c/s | wfs |
| ☐ | PR-OAP | Embraer EMB.120RT Brasilia | 120060 | ex N240AS | Magenta c/s | [SOD] |
| ☐ | PT-SLC | Embraer EMB.120ER Brasilia | 120094 | ex PT-SML | Red c/s | [SOD] |
| ☐ | PT-SRF | Embraer EMB.120ER Brasilia | 120192 | | White c/s | [SOD] |
| ☐ | PR-OAD | Fokker 100 | 11370 | ex N1412A | | |
| ☐ | PR-OAE | Fokker 100 | 11426 | ex N1436A | | |
| ☐ | PR-OAF | Fokker 100 | 11415 | ex N1430D | | |
| ☐ | PR-OAG | Fokker 100 | 11412 | ex N1427A | | |
| ☐ | PR-OAI | Fokker 100 | 11417 | ex N1432A | | |
| ☐ | PR-OAJ | Fokker 100 | 11418 | ex N1433B | | |
| ☐ | PR-OAK | Fokker 100 | 11425 | ex N1435D | | |
| ☐ | PR-OAL | Fokker 100 | 11435 | ex N1440A | | |
| ☐ | PR-OAM | Fokker 100 | 11436 | ex N1441A | | |
| ☐ | PR-OAQ | Fokker 100 | 11467 | ex N1455K | | |
| ☐ | PR-OAR | Fokker 100 | 11481 | ex N1461C | | |
| ☐ | PR-OAS | Fokker 100 | 11405 | ex N1422J | | |
| ☐ | PR-OAT | Fokker 100 | 11411 | ex N1426A | | |
| ☐ | PR-OAU | Fokker 100 | 11427 | ex N1437B | | |
| ☐ | PR-AVB | Airbus A319-115 | 4222 | ex D-AVYJ | | |
| ☐ | PR-AVC | Airbus A319-115 | 4287 | ex D-AVWT | | |
| ☐ | PR-AVD | Airbus A319-115 | 4336 | ex D-AVXG | | |
| ☐ | PR-AVP | Airbus A320-214 | 4891 | ex F-WWIS | | ♦ |
| ☐ | PR-AVQ | Airbus A320-214 | 4913 | ex F-WWDA | | ♦ |
| ☐ | PR-AVR | Airbus A320-214 | 4941 | ex D-AXAP | | ♦ |
| ☐ | PR-AVU | Airbus A320-214 | 4942 | ex F-WWBV | | ♦ |

## AXE TAXI AEREO — Salvador, BA (SSA)

| | | | | | | |
|---|---|---|---|---|---|---|
| ☐ | PT-KRO | Britten-Norman BN-2A-21 Islander | 742 | ex G-BCVL | | ♦ |

## AZUL LINHAS AEREAS BRASILEIRAS — (AD / AZU) — Sao Paulo-Viracopos, SP (VCP)

| | | | | | | |
|---|---|---|---|---|---|---|
| ☐ | PR-ATR | ATR 72-202 | 0966 | ex F-WW | | ♦ |
| ☐ | PR-AZR | ATR 72-202 | 0519 | ex F-WKVB | | |
| ☐ | PR-AZS | ATR-72-202 | 0523 | ex F-WNUE | | ♦ |
| ☐ | PR-AZT | ATR-72-202 | 0450 | ex F-WKVE | | ♦ |
| ☐ | PR-AZV | ATR-72-202 | 0396 | ex F-WNUA | | ♦ |
| ☐ | PR-AZW | ATR-72-202 | 0316 | ex F-WKVF | | ♦ |
| ☐ | PR-AZX | ATR-72-202 | 0352 | ex F-WKVI | | ♦ |
| ☐ | PR-AZY | ATR-72-202 | 0365 | ex F-WKVB | | ♦ |
| ☐ | PR-AZZ | ATR 72-202 | 0192 | ex F-WKVC | Azulmania | ♦ |
| | | | | | | |
| ☐ | PR-ATB | ATR 72-600 | 0969 | ex F-WWLT | La Ville Rose | ♦ |
| ☐ | PR-ATE | ATR 72-600 | 0972 | ex F-WWLW | Azul Zulu Uniform Lima | ♦ |
| ☐ | PR-ATG | ATR 72-600 | 0988 | ex F-WWLO | Planeta Azul | ♦ |
| ☐ | PR-ATH | ATR 72-600 | 991 | ex F-WWLQ | Meu Coração é Azul | ♦ |
| ☐ | PR-ATJ | ATR 72-600 | 996 | ex F-WWLU | | ♦ |
| ☐ | PR-ATK | ATR 72-600 | 1020 | ex F-WWLN | Azul Viagens | ♦ |
| ☐ | PR-ATP | ATR 72-600 | 1026 | ex F-WWLS | | o/o♦ |
| ☐ | PR- | ATR 72-600 | 1027 | ex F-WW | | o/o♦ |
| | | | | | | |
| ☐ | PR-AZA | Embraer ERJ-190AR | 19000150 | ex N290JB | Azulville | |
| ☐ | PR-AZB | Embraer ERJ-190AR | 19000241 | ex N840JE | Azul Paulista | |
| ☐ | PR-AZC | Embraer ERJ-190AR | 19000242 | ex N841JS | Ceu Azul | |
| ☐ | PR-AZD | Embraer ERJ-190AR | 19000271 | ex PT-TLL | Passaro Azul | |
| ☐ | PR-AZE | Embraer ERJ-190AR | 19000282 | ex PT-TLW | Verda, Amarelo e Azul | |
| ☐ | PR-AZF | Embraer ERJ-190AR | 19000295 | | Voce que e Feito de Azul | |
| ☐ | PR-AZG | Embraer ERJ-190AR | 19000329 | | A Terra e Azul | |
| ☐ | PR-AZH | Embraer ERJ-190AR | 19000330 | | Azulcenter | |
| ☐ | PR-AZI | Embraer ERJ-190AR | 19000336 | | Adorinha Azul | |
| ☐ | PR-AZL | Embraer ERJ-190AR | 19000147 | ex N288JB | O Rio de Janeiro continua Azul | |
| | | | | | | |
| ☐ | PR-AXA | Embraer ERJ-195AR | 19000491 | | Azul Safira | ♦ |
| ☐ | PR-AXB | Embraer ERJ-195AR | 19000498 | | Céu Azul de Brasilia | ♦ |
| ☐ | PR-AXC | Embraer ERJ-195AR | 19000510 | | Azul Tropical | ♦ |
| ☐ | PR-AXD | Embraer ERJ-195AR | 19000514 | | Azulão | ♦ |
| ☐ | PR-AXE | Embraer ERJ-195AR | 19000521 | | Axé Azul | ♦ |
| ☐ | PR-AXF | Embraer ERJ-195AR | 19000530 | | | o/o♦ |
| ☐ | PR-AYA | Embraer ERJ-195AR | 19000237 | ex PT-SIK | Azul e Brasil | |
| ☐ | PR-AYB | Embraer ERJ-195AR | 19000239 | | Tudo Azul | |
| ☐ | PR-AYC | Embraer ERJ-195AR | 19000240 | | A Liberdade e Azul | |
| ☐ | PR-AYD | Embraer ERJ-195AR | 19000247 | | Azalou | |
| ☐ | PR-AYE | Embraer ERJ-195AR | 19000260 | ex PT-STI | Azul do Cor da Mar | |
| ☐ | PR-AYF | Embraer ERJ-195AR | 19000353 | | Tripulante Azul | |
| ☐ | PR-AYG | Embraer ERJ-195AR | 19000356 | | Tudo Novo, Tudo Azul | |
| ☐ | PR-AYH | Embraer ERJ-195AR | 19000361 | | Céu, Sol, Sul, Azul | |
| ☐ | PR-AYI | Embraer ERJ-195AR | 19000366 | | Azul Celeste | |
| ☐ | PR-AYJ | Embraer ERJ-195AR | 19000370 | | Azul Real | |
| ☐ | PR-AYK | Embraer ERJ-195AR | 19000374 | | Diamante Azul | |
| ☐ | PR-AYL | Embraer ERJ-195AR | 19000378 | | Amazonia Azul | |
| ☐ | PR-AYM | Embraer ERJ-195AR | 19000382 | | Cada Vez mais Azul | |
| ☐ | PR-AYN | Embraer ERJ-195AR | 19000386 | | Blue Angels | |
| ☐ | PR-AYO | Embraer ERJ-195AR | 19000391 | | Rosa e Azul | |
| ☐ | PR-AYP | Embraer ERJ-195AR | 19000396 | | Arara Azul | |
| ☐ | PR-AYQ | Embraer ERJ-195AR | 19000407 | | | |
| ☐ | PR-AYR | Embraer ERJ-195AR | 19000413 | | | |
| ☐ | PR-AYS | Embraer ERJ-195AR | 19000419 | | | ♦ |
| ☐ | PR-AYT | Embraer ERJ-195AR | 19000429 | | | ♦ |
| ☐ | PR-AYU | Embraer ERJ-195AR | 19000434 | | | ♦ |
| ☐ | PR-AYV | Embraer ERJ-195AR | 19000449 | | | ♦ |
| ☐ | PR-AYW | Embraer ERJ-195AR | 19000458 | | Vento Azul | ♦ |
| ☐ | PR-AYX | Embraer ERJ-195AR | 19000471 | | | ♦ |
| ☐ | PR-AYY | Embraer ERJ-195AR | 19000475 | | Sorriso Azul | ♦ |
| ☐ | PR-AYZ | Embraer ERJ-195AR | 19000484 | | Azul de A a Z | ♦ |

## BETA CARGO AIR — Beta Cargo (BET) — Sao Paulo-Guarulhos, SP (GRU)

| | | | | | |
|---|---|---|---|---|---|
| ☐ | PP-BEL | Douglas DC-8-73AF | 46047/447 | ex N809DH | wfs |

## BHS - BRAZILIAN HELICOPTER SERVICES
### Sao Paulo-Marte, SP, Farol de Sao Tome, SP, Macae & Sao Tome, RJ

| | | | | | |
|---|---|---|---|---|---|
| ☐ | PP-MEM | Sikorsky S-76A+ | 760092 | ex N176PA | |
| ☐ | PP-MET | Sikorsky S-76A | 760229 | ex N31217 | |
| ☐ | PP-MHM | Sikorsky S-76C | 760376 | ex N776AB | |
| ☐ | PP-MPM | Sikorsky S-76C | 760375 | ex N775AB | |

| | | | | | |
|---|---|---|---|---|---|
| ☐ | PR-BGC | Sikorsky S-76-2 | 760601 | ex C-GGIU | ◆ |
| ☐ | PR-BGD | Sikorsky S-76C+ | 760568 | ex C-GHRY | ◆ |
| ☐ | PR-BGE | Sikorsky S-76C+ | 760546 | ex C-FCHC | ◆ |
| ☐ | PR-BGG | Sikorsky S-76C+ | 760602 | ex C-FGDO | ◆ |
| ☐ | PR-BGI | Sikorsky S-76C+ | 760537 | ex C-GETL | ◆ |
| ☐ | PR-BGJ | Sikorsky S-76C+ | 760570 | ex C-GHRW | ◆ |
| ☐ | PR-CHA | Sikorsky S-76C+ | 760625 | ex C-GBQE | |
| ☐ | PR-CHB | Sikorsky S-76A++ | 760004 | ex C-GIME | |
| ☐ | PR-CHC | Sikorsky S-76C+ | 760632 | ex C-GBQF | |
| ☐ | PR-CHD | Sikorsky S-76C+ | 760636 | ex C-GBQG | |
| ☐ | PR-CHE | Sikorsky S-76C+ | 760642 | ex C-GBQH | |
| ☐ | PR-CHF | Sikorsky S-76C+ | 760657 | ex N4505G | |
| ☐ | PR-CHK | Sikorsky S-76C+ | 760687 | ex C-FRHF | <CHC Helicopters Intl |
| ☐ | PR-CJK | Sikorsky S-76C+ | 760674 | ex N4513G | <CHC Helicopters Intl |
| ☐ | PR-CHN | Sikorsky S-76A++ | 760187 | ex C-FIHD | |
| ☐ | PR-CHP | Sikorsky S-76C++ | 760743 | ex C-FYDD | |
| ☐ | PR-CHQ | Sikorsky S-76C++ | 760734 | ex C-FXFK | |
| ☐ | PT-YGM | Sikorsky S-76A | 760067 | ex ZS-RJK | <CHC Helicopters Africa |
| ☐ | PT-YIM | Sikorsky S-76A | 760144 | ex XA-SRS | |
| ☐ | PT-YQM | Sikorsky S-76A | 760051 | ex ZS-RGZ | <CHC Helicopters Africa |
| | | | | | |
| ☐ | PR-BGB | Sikorsky S-92A | 920141 | ex C-GJMY | ◆ |
| ☐ | PR-BGM | Sikorsky S-92A | 920153 | ex C-GNUA | ◆ |
| ☐ | PR-CHR | Sikorsky S-92A | 920112 | ex C-FRWL | |
| ☐ | PR-CHS | Sikorsky S-92A | 920113 | ex C-FPKW | |
| ☐ | PR-CHT | Sikorsky S-92A | 920119 | ex C-GDHU | |
| ☐ | PR-CHU | Sikorsky S-92A | 920127 | ex C-GFHO | |
| | | | | | |
| ☐ | PR-BGA | Eurocopter EC225LP | 2773 | ex G-LCAS | ◆ |
| ☐ | PR-BGH | Eurocopter EC225LP | 2798 | ex C-GLIS | ◆ |
| ☐ | PR-BGK | Eurocopter EC225LP | 2801 | ex C-GMJI | ◆ |
| ☐ | PR-BGL | Eurocopter EC225LP | 2822 | | ◆ |
| ☐ | PR-CHW | Eurocopter EC225LP | 2740 | ex G-DRIT | |
| ☐ | PR-CHX | Eurocopter EC225LP | 2729 | ex G-CLAR | |
| ☐ | PR-CHY | Eurocopter EC225LP | 2722 | ex G-LJAM | |
| ☐ | PR-PLL | Eurocopter EC225LP | 2680 | ex N225EH | |
| ☐ | PR-VLL | Eurocopter EC225LP | 2685 | ex N247CF | |
| ☐ | PR-YCL | Eurocopter EC225LP  2 | 2708 | ex LN-OHY | |
| | | | | | |
| ☐ | PP-MTM | Aérospatiale AS.332L2 | 2599 | | |
| ☐ | PP-MZM | Aérospatiale AS.332L2 | 2572 | ex F-WQDJ | |
| ☐ | PR-MEK | Aérospatiale SA365N Dauphin 2 | 6030 | ex PH-SSX | |
| ☐ | PT-HNZ | Helibras HS.350B Esquilo | B-1151-2486 | | |

## CRUISER TAXI AEREO BRASIL                    (J6)                    Curitiba, PR (CWB)

| | | | | | |
|---|---|---|---|---|---|
| ☐ | PT-WBR | Embraer EMB.110C Bandeirante | 110045 | ex FAB 2153 | |

## CTA – CLEITON TAXI AEREO

| | | | | | |
|---|---|---|---|---|---|
| ☐ | PT-PTA | Cessna 208B Caravan I | 208B0763 | ex N5165P | ◆ |
| ☐ | PT-PTB | Cessna 208B Caravan I | 208B0766 | ex N52086 | ◆ |

## FRETAX TAXI AEREO

| | | | | | |
|---|---|---|---|---|---|
| ☐ | PR-JOH | Cessna 208B Caravan I | 208B0323 | ex N465BA | |
| ☐ | PR-MSH | Cessna 208B Caravan I | 208B0700 | ex N700RH | dam 24Nov10 |
| ☐ | PR-SMG | Cessna 208B Caravan I | 208B2247 | ex PR-BAX | ◆ |
| ☐ | PR-SMM | Cessna 208B Caravan I | 208B1224 | | |
| ☐ | PT-OGQ | Cessna 208A Caravan | 208A00032 | ex N809FE | |

## GENSA                    Gensa Brasil (GEN)                    Campo Grande, MS (CGR)

| | | | | | |
|---|---|---|---|---|---|
| ☐ | PR-GSA | Embraer EMB.120ER Brasilia | 120119 | ex 5N-TCE | wfs |
| ☐ | PR-GSB | Embraer EMB.120ER Brasilia | 120127 | ex 5N-LCE | wfs |
| ☐ | PT-SHN | Embraer EMB.110P1A Bandeirante | 110460 | | |
| ☐ | PT-SOG | Embraer EMB.110P1 Bandeirante | 110490 | | |

## GOL TRANSPORTES AEREOS          Gol Transporte (G3/GLO)          Sao Paulo-Congonhas, SP (CGH)

| | | | | | |
|---|---|---|---|---|---|
| ☐ | PR-WJA | Boeing 737-322 | 24663/1875 | ex N401TZ | ◆ |
| ☐ | PR-WJB | Boeing 737-341 | 25050/2125 | ex PR-BRG | ◆ |
| ☐ | PR-WJC | Boeing 737-341 | 25051/2127 | ex PR-BRF | ◆ |
| ☐ | PR-WJD | Boeing 737-3Y0 | 23922/1538 | ex PT-SSK | ◆ |
| ☐ | PR-WJE | Boeing 737-33A | 25057/2046 | ex PT-MNJ | ◆ |
| ☐ | PR-WJF | Boeing 737-341 | 24936/1951 | ex PP-VOO | ◆ |
| ☐ | PR-WJG | Boeing 737-322 | 24452/1728 | ex N359UA | ◆ |
| ☐ | PR-WJH | Boeing 737-341 | 26856/2321 | ex PP-VPB | ◆ |
| ☐ | PR-WJI | Boeing 737-341 | 26857/2326 | ex PP-VPC | ◆ |
| ☐ | PR-WJJ | Boeing 737-341 | 24935/1935 | ex PP-VON | ◆ |

| | Registration | Type | c/n | ex | Notes | |
|---|---|---|---|---|---|---|
| ☐ | PR-WJK | Boeing 737-33A | 23830/1462 | ex N238MQ | | ♦ |
| ☐ | PR-WJL | Boeing 737-36N | 28590/3097 | ex SP-LME | | ♦ |
| ☐ | PR-WJM | Boeing 737-36Q | 28660/2883 | ex G-THOK | | ♦ |
| ☐ | PR-WJN | Boeing 737-36Q | 29327/3023 | ex G-THOI | | ♦ |
| ☐ | PR-WJO | Boeing 737-3Q8 | 26295/2557 | ex N295AN | | ♦ |
| ☐ | PR-WJP | Boeing 737-3Q8 | 26309/2674 | ex N309AN | | ♦ |
| ☐ | PR-WJQ | Boeing 737-3U3 | 28742/2992 | ex ZK-FRE | | ♦ |
| ☐ | PR-WJR | Boeing 737-36N | 28566/2964 | ex PK-GGT | | ♦ |
| ☐ | PR-WJS | Boeing 737-3Y0 | 24465/1755 | ex N465BV | | ♦ |
| ☐ | PR-WJT | Boeing 737-3Y0 | 24908/2015 | ex N908BV | | ♦ |
| ☐ | PR-WJU | Boeing 737-36N | 28560/2888 | ex SE-RHU | | ♦ |
| ☐ | PR-WJV | Boeing 737-36N | 28567/2971 | ex N558MS | | ♦ |
| ☐ | PR-WJW | Boeing 737-33A | 27267/2600 | ex N267AN | | ♦ |
| ☐ | PR-WJX | Boeing 737-33A | 25033/2025 | ex LN-KKA | | ♦ |
| | | | | | | |
| ☐ | PR-GEA | Boeing 737-7EH/W | 37595/3026 | | | ♦ |
| ☐ | PR-GEC | Boeing 737-7EH/W | 37608/3678 | | | ♦ |
| ☐ | PR-GED | Boeing 737-7EH/W | 37609/3799 | | | ♦ |
| ☐ | PR-GID | Boeing 737-76N/W | 29904/347 | ex N745AL | | |
| ☐ | PR-GIF | Boeing 737-73S | 29076/98 | ex OY-MLY | | |
| ☐ | PR-GIG | Boeing 737-73S | 29077/104 | ex OY-MLZ | | |
| ☐ | PR-GIH | Boeing 737-76N/W | 32743/1503 | ex N750AL | | |
| ☐ | PR-GII | Boeing 737-7L9 | 28011/1203 | ex OY-MRL | | |
| ☐ | PR-GIJ | Boeing 737-7L9 | 28012/1092 | ex OY-MRK | | |
| ☐ | PR-GIK | Boeing 737-7Q8 | 28224/369 | ex N161LF | | |
| ☐ | PR-GIM | Boeing 737-73V | 30238/913 | ex G-EZJE | | |
| ☐ | PR-GIN | Boeing 737-73V | 30242/690 | ex G-EZJD | | |
| ☐ | PR-GOA | Boeing 737-7L9 | 28005/11 | ex OY-MRB | special c/s | |
| ☐ | PR-GOB | Boeing 737-75B | 28099/13 | ex D-AGEM | | |
| ☐ | PR-GOC | Boeing 737-75B | 28101/17 | ex D-AGEO | | |
| ☐ | PR-GOD | Boeing 737-75B | 28105/66 | ex D-AGEV | | |
| ☐ | PR-GOE | Boeing 737-75B | 28106/68 | ex D-AGEW | | |
| ☐ | PR-GOF | Boeing 737-76Q | 30273/843 | ex N1786B | Aurea | |
| ☐ | PR-GOG | Boeing 737-76Q | 30275/900 | ex N795BA | | |
| ☐ | PR-GOH | Boeing 737-76N | 32440/954 | ex N1786B | | |
| ☐ | PR-GOI | Boeing 737-76N | 32574/983 | ex N1786B | | |
| ☐ | PR-GOL | Boeing 737-7L9 | 28004/10 | ex OY-MRA | | |
| ☐ | PR-GOM | Boeing 737-76N | 28613/463 | ex N312ML | | |
| ☐ | PR-GON | Boeing 737-76N | 30051/436 | ex N311ML | | |
| ☐ | PR-GOR | Boeing 737-76N | 33380/1231 | | | |
| ☐ | PR-GOV | Boeing 737-76N | 28580/135 | ex N580HE | | |
| ☐ | PR-GOW | Boeing 737-76N | 28584/170 | ex N584SR | | |
| ☐ | PR-GOX | Boeing 737-7K9 | 28088/19 | ex N100UN | | |
| ☐ | PR-GOY | Boeing 737-7K9 | 28089/25 | ex N101UN | | |
| ☐ | PR-VBH | Boeing 737-73V | 30239/944 | ex N239CG | | |
| ☐ | PR-VBI | Boeing 737-73V | 30246/1064 | ex N346CL | | |
| ☐ | PR-VBO | Boeing 737-73V | 30247/1066 | ex G-EZJL | | |
| ☐ | PR-VBW | Boeing 737-7BX | 30739/758 | ex 6V-AHO | | |
| ☐ | PR-VBX | Boeing 737-7BX/W | 30738/716 | ex 6V-AHN | | ♦ |
| | | | | | | |
| ☐ | PR-GGA | Boeing 737-8EH/W | 35063/2476 | ex N1787B | | |
| ☐ | PR-GGB | Boeing 737-8EH/W | 35064/2498 | | | |
| ☐ | PR-GGD | Boeing 737-8EH/W | 34275/2588 | | | |
| ☐ | PR-GGE | Boeing 737-8EH/W | 35824/2665 | ex N1786B | | |
| ☐ | PR-GGF | Boeing 737-8EH/W | 35826/2749 | | | |
| ☐ | PR-GGG | Boeing 737-8EH/W | 36566/2809 | | | |
| ☐ | PR-GGH | Boeing 737-8EH/W | 36147/2864 | ex N1787B | | |
| ☐ | PR-GGJ | Boeing 737-8EH/W | 35825/2786 | ex N1796B | | |
| ☐ | PR-GGK | Boeing 737-8EH/W | 35065/2561 | | | |
| ☐ | PR-GGL | Boeing 737-8EH/W | 36148/2890 | | | |
| ☐ | PR-GGM | Boeing 737-8EH/W | 36149/2920 | ex N1786B | | |
| ☐ | PR-GGN | Boeing 737-8EH/W | 35827/2991 | ex N1786B | | |
| ☐ | PR-GGO | Boeing 737-8EH/W | 35828/3025 | | | |
| ☐ | PR-GGP | Boeing 737-8EH/W | 35829/3076 | ex N1787B | | |
| ☐ | PR-GGQ | Boeing 737-8EH/W | 37596/3103 | ex N1786B | | |
| ☐ | PR-GGR | Boeing 737-8EH/W | 36150/3106 | ex N1787B | | |
| ☐ | PR-GGT | Boeing 737-8EH/W | 35830/3115 | | | |
| ☐ | PR-GGU | Boeing 737-8EH/W | 37597/3133 | | | |
| ☐ | PR-GGV | Boeing 737-8EH/W | 37598/3136 | | | |
| ☐ | PR-GGW | Boeing 737-8EH/W | 35831/3165 | ex PH-GGW | | |
| ☐ | PR-GGX | Boeing 737-8EH/W | 36596/3180 | ex N1787B | | |
| ☐ | PR-GGY | Boeing 737-8EH/W | 37599/3191 | | | |
| ☐ | PR-GGZ | Boeing 737-8EH/W | 37600/3205 | exPH-GGZ | | |
| ☐ | PR-GIE | Boeing 737-8BK/W | 33027/1918 | ex N1786B | | |
| ☐ | PR-GIO | Boeing 737-85F/W | 30477/976 | ex N477GX | | |
| ☐ | PR-GIP | Boeing 737-85F/W | 30571/936 | ex N571GX | | |
| ☐ | PR-GIQ | Boeing 737-86N/W | 28616/483 | ex TC-SUC | | |
| ☐ | PR-GIR | Boeing 737-8Q8 | 28213/50 | ex OY-SEA | | |
| ☐ | PR-GIU | Boeing 737-809 | 29103/129 | ex TC-APZ | | |
| ☐ | PR-GIV | Boeing 737-86N/W | 28578/89 | ex VT-JNA | | |
| ☐ | PR-GIW | Boeing 737-86N/W | 28575/91 | ex VT-JNB | | |
| ☐ | PR-GIX | Boeing 737-809 | 30636/768 | ex N330LF | | |
| ☐ | PR-GOP | Boeing 737-8BK | 30621/1194 | ex N461LF | Victoria | |

| | | | | |
|---|---|---|---|---|
| ☐ | PR-GOT | Boeing 737-8BK | 30625/1248 | |
| ☐ | PR-GTA | Boeing 737-8EH/W | 34474/1843 | ex N6067U |
| ☐ | PR-GTB | Boeing 737-8EH/W | 34475/2020 | |
| ☐ | PR-GTC | Boeing 737-8EH/W | 34277/2028 | ex N1786B |
| ☐ | PR-GTE | Boeing 737-8EH/W | 34278/2052 | |
| ☐ | PR-GTF | Boeing 737-8EH/W | 34279/2061 | |
| ☐ | PR-GTG | Boeing 737-8EH/W | 34654/2075 | |
| ☐ | PR-GTH | Boeing 737-8EH/W | 34655/2091 | |
| ☐ | PR-GTI | Boeing 737-8EH/W | 34280/2100 | |
| ☐ | PR-GTJ | Boeing 737-8EH/W | 34656/2110 | |
| ☐ | PR-GTK | Boeing 737-8EH/W | 34281/2116 | |
| ☐ | PR-GTL | Boeing 737-8EH/W | 34962/2215 | ex N1786B |
| ☐ | PR-GTM | Boeing 737-8EH/W | 34963/2240 | |
| ☐ | PR-GTN | Boeing 737-8EH/W | 34267/2311 | |
| ☐ | PR-GTO | Boeing 737-8EH/W | 34964/2332 | |
| ☐ | PR-GTP | Boeing 737-8EH/W | 34965/2341 | |
| ☐ | PR-GTQ | Boeing 737-8EH/W | 36146/2358 | |
| ☐ | PR-GTR | Boeing 737-8EH/W | 34966/2367 | |
| ☐ | PR-GTT | Boeing 737-8EH/W | 34268/2407 | |
| ☐ | PR-GTU | Boeing 737-8EH/W | 34269/2412 | ex N1786B |
| ☐ | PR-GTV | Boeing 737-8EH/W | 34270/2420 | |
| ☐ | PR-GTY | Boeing 737-8EH/W | 34273/2464 | |
| ☐ | PR-GTZ | Boeing 737-8EH/W | 34274/2468 | ex N1795B |
| ☐ | PR-GUA | Boeing 737-8EH/W | 37601/3301 | |
| ☐ | PR-GUB | Boeing 737-8EH/W | 35832/3309 | |
| ☐ | PR-GUC | Boeing 737-8EH/W | 35835/3430 | ex N1787B |
| ☐ | PR-GUD | Boeing 737-8EH/W | 35836/3466 | |
| ☐ | PR-GUE | Boeing 737-8EH/W | 35837/3473 | |
| ☐ | PR-GUF | Boeing 737-8EH/W | 35838/3508 | |
| ☐ | PR-GUG | Boeing 737-8EH/W | 35842/3639 | |
| ☐ | PR-GUH | Boeing 737-8EH/W | 35843/3667 | ex N17868 | ♦ |
| ☐ | PR-GUI | Boeing 737-8EH/W | 35844/3722 | | ♦ |
| ☐ | PR-GUJ | Boeing 737-8EH/W | 35845/3745 | | ♦ |
| ☐ | PR-GUK | Boeing 737-8EH/W | 35852/3760 | | ♦ |
| ☐ | PR-GUL | Boeing 737-8EH/W | 35845/3785 | | ♦ |
| ☐ | PR-GUM | Boeing 737-8EH/W | 35846//3823 | | ♦ |
| ☐ | PR-GUN | Boeing 737-8EH/W | 37610/3912 | | ♦ |

## HELISUL TAXI AEREO · Foz do Iguaçu, PR

| | | | | | |
|---|---|---|---|---|---|
| ☐ | PR-HTA | Helibras HS.350B2 Esquilo | AS3523 | | |
| ☐ | PR-KEB | Beech 200 Super King Air | BB-835 | ex N84PN | ♦ |
| ☐ | PT-HGB | Bell 206B JetRanger III | 4298 | ex C-FRIN | |
| ☐ | PT-HMI | Helibras HS.350B Esquilo | 1639/HB1046 | | |
| ☐ | PT-HML | Helibras HS.350B Esquilo | 1642/HB1049 | | |
| ☐ | PT-HOY | Bell 206B JetRanger III | 4171 | ex N4171J | |
| ☐ | PT-HTC | Bell 206B JetRanger III | 3449 | ex N2113Z | |
| ☐ | PT-YAP | Bell 206B JetRanger III | 3481 | ex N215RG | |
| ☐ | PT-YEL | Bell 206L-4 LongRanger IV | 52198 | ex N6593X | |

## INTERAVIA TAXI AEREO

| | | | | |
|---|---|---|---|---|
| ☐ | PR-JAT | Cessna 208B Caravan I | 208B1193 | ex N13189 |

## MAIS LINHAS AEREAS

| | | | | | |
|---|---|---|---|---|---|
| ☐ | PR-JFO | Fokker 100 | 11400 | ex XA-KXJ | wfs♦ |
| ☐ | PR-RMJ | Fokker 100 | 11390 | ex XA-JXW | wfs♦ |

## MAP LINHAS AEREAS · Manaus-Ponta Pelada, AM (PLL)

| | | | | | |
|---|---|---|---|---|---|
| ☐ | PR-MPE | Cessna 208 Caravan I | 20800510 | ex N6144K | FP |
| ☐ | PT-SOF | Embraer EMB.110P1A Bandeirante | 110486 | | ♦ |
| ☐ | PR-TTG | ATR 42-320 | 0020 | ex F-OHOT | ♦ |

## META - MESQUITA TRANSPORTES AEREO · Meta (MSQ) · Boa Vista, RR (BVB)

| | | | | |
|---|---|---|---|---|
| ☐ | PT-FLY | Embraer EMB.120ER Brasilia | 120044 | ex PT-SLI |
| ☐ | PT-LMZ | Cessna U206F Stationair | U20602184 | |
| ☐ | PT-LNW | Embraer EMB.110P1 Bandeirante | 110346 | ex N697RA |
| ☐ | PT-LXN | Embraer EMB.120ER Brasilia | 120052 | ex D-CEMG |
| ☐ | PT-OND | Cessna U206G Stationair 6 | U20606542 | ex N9529Z |

## MTA CARGO · Master (MST) · Sao Paulo-Viracopos, SP (VCP)

Ceased ops 2011

## NHR TAXI AEREO — Sorocaba, SP (SOD)

| | | | | | |
|---|---|---|---|---|---|
| ☐ | PR-KIN | Embraer EMB.110P1 Bandeirante | 110254 | ex P2-IAJ | wfs |
| ☐ | PR-NHR | Embraer EMB.110P1 Bandeirante | 110394 | ex P2-IAK | wfs |
| ☐ | PT-MAL | Embraer EMB.121A1 Xingu | 121019 | | |
| ☐ | PT-SHY | Embraer EMB.110P1 Bandeirante | 110470 | | |
| ☐ | PT-WAW | Embraer EMB.110 Bandeirante | 110122 | ex FAB 2189 | |

## NHT LINHAS AEREAS — (NHG) — Sorocaba, SP (SOD)

| | | | | | |
|---|---|---|---|---|---|
| ☐ | PR-CRX | LET L-410UVP-E20 | 912617 | ex OK-2617 | ♦ |
| ☐ | PR-NHA | LET L-410UVP-E20 | 062636 | | |
| ☐ | PR-NHB | LET L-410UVP-E20 | 062637 | | |
| ☐ | PR-NHC | LET L-410UVP-E20 | 072639 | | |
| ☐ | PR-NHD | LET L-410UVP-E20 | 072640 | | |
| ☐ | PR-NHE | LET L-410UVP-E20 | 082714 | ex OK-2714 | |

## NORDESTE LINHAS AEREAS REGIONAIS

| | | | | | |
|---|---|---|---|---|---|
| ☐ | PR-NOA | LET L-410UVP-E20 | 092719 | ex OK-SLP | ♦ |

## PANTANAL — Pantanal (GP/PTN) — Sao Paulo-Congonhas, SP (CGH)

| | | | | | |
|---|---|---|---|---|---|
| ☐ | PT-MFJ | ATR 42-320 | 0343 | ex F-WQHV | |
| ☐ | PT-MFM | ATR 42-300 | 0376 | ex F-GKNH | |
| ☐ | PT-MFT | ATR 42-320 | 0306 | ex G-BXEH | |
| ☐ | PT-MFU | ATR 42-310 | 0070 | ex F-GHJE | |
| ☐ | PT-MFV | ATR 42-300 | 0043 | ex F-GGLR | |
| ☐ | PT-MZD | Airbus A319-132 | 1096 | ex D-AVYR | <TAM♦ |
| ☐ | PT-MZE | Airbus A319-132 | 1103 | ex D-AVWD | <TAM♦ |

## PASSAREDO TRANSPORTES AEREOS — (PTB) — Ribeirao Preto, SP (RAO)

| | | | | | |
|---|---|---|---|---|---|
| ☐ | PR-PSF | Embraer ERJ-145EP | 145016 | ex N826HK | |
| ☐ | PR-PSG | Embraer ERJ-145EP | 145021 | ex N827HK | |
| ☐ | PR-PSH | Embraer ERJ-145LR | 145597 | ex N559MD | |
| ☐ | PR-PSI | Embraer ERJ-145LR | 145607 | ex N607MD | ♦ |
| ☐ | PR-PSK | Embraer ERJ-145LU | 145387 | ex OH-EBF | |
| ☐ | PR-PSL | Embraer ERJ-145LR | 145269 | ex N834HK | |
| ☐ | PR-PSM | Embraer ERJ-145LR | 145281 | ex N829HK | |
| ☐ | PR-PSN | Embraer ERJ-145MP | 145407 | ex F-GUJA | |
| ☐ | PR-PSO | Embraer ERJ-145MP | 145408 | ex OE-IAL | ♦ |
| ☐ | PR-PSP | Embraer ERJ-145MP | 145441 | ex OE-IAJ | ♦ |
| ☐ | PR-PSQ | Embraer ERJ-145MP | 145244 | ex G-CGJR | |
| ☐ | PR-PSR | Embraer ERJ-145MP | 145339 | ex G-RJXO | |
| ☐ | PR-PST | Embraer ERJ-145MP | 145385 | ex F-GVGS | ♦ |
| ☐ | PT-PSS | Embraer ERJ-145MP | 145336 | ex EI-EHW | ♦ |
| ☐ | PP-PSB | Embraer EMB.120ER Brasilia | 120303 | | |
| ☐ | PR-PSD | Embraer EMB.120ER Brasilia | 120118 | ex N507DM | |
| ☐ | P | ATR 72-600 | 1022 | ex F-WWLV | ♦ |

## PENTA - PENA TRANSPORTES AEREOS — Aero Pena (5P/PEP) — Santarem, PA (STM)

Ceased ops 2010

## PUMA AIR LINHAS AEREAS — Puma Brasil (PLY) — Belem, PA (BEL)

| | | | | | |
|---|---|---|---|---|---|
| ☐ | PP-PTB | Embraer EMB.120RT Brasilia | 120080 | ex F-GFEP | [ATM] |
| ☐ | PR-GLK | Boeing 737-322 | 24668/1905 | ex N393UA | |
| ☐ | PR-PMC | Cessna 208B Caravan I | 208B0909 | ex N12826 | |
| ☐ | PR-PUA | Boeing 737-322 | 24668/1905 | ex PR-GLK | ♦ |
| ☐ | PT-STN | Embraer EMB.120ER Brasilia | 120241 | | <TTL |

## RICO LINHAS AEREAS — Rico (C7/RLE) — Manaus-Eduardo Gomez, AM (MAO)

| | | | | | |
|---|---|---|---|---|---|
| ☐ | PP-VMM | Boeing 737-241 | 21008/402 | | [MAO] |
| ☐ | PR-RLA | Boeing 737-241 | 21009/417 | ex PP-VMN | [MAO] |
| ☐ | PT-WJA | Embraer EMB.110P1 Bandeirante | 110265 | ex PT-OHF | |
| ☐ | PT-WJG | Embraer EMB.120ER Brasilia | 120064 | ex PT-PCA | |
| ☐ | PT-WRU | Cessna 208 Caravan I | 20800284 | | FP |
| ☐ | PT-WZM | Embraer EMB.120ER Brasilia | 120041 | ex PP-IAD | wfs |

## RICO TAXI AEREO — Manaus-Eduardo Gomez, AM (MAO)

| | | | | | |
|---|---|---|---|---|---|
| ☐ | PT-GJC | Embraer EMB.110E Bandeirante | 110055 | | |
| ☐ | PT-MAA | Embraer EMB.121A Xingu II | 121001 | ex PT-ZCT | |

## RIO BRANCO TAXI AEREO

| | | | | | |
|---|---|---|---|---|---|
| ☐ | PT-OCW | Embraer EMB.110P1 Bandeirante | 110273 | ex N90PB | ♦ |
| ☐ | PT-WAP | Embraer EMB.110C Bandeirante | 110044 | ex Brazil 2152 | ♦ |
| ☐ | PR-SBR | Cessna 208B Caravan I | 208B2253 | ex N5163C | ♦ |

## RIO LINHAS AEREAS (R3/RIO)

| | | | | | |
|---|---|---|---|---|---|
| ☐ | PR-IOA | Boeing 727-214F | 21512/1343 | ex N750US | |
| ☐ | PR-IOB | Boeing 727-264F (FedEx 3) | 22983/1806 | ex N763AT | |
| ☐ | PR-IOC | Boeing 727-264F (FedEx 3) | 22984/1813 | ex N764AT | |
| ☐ | PR-IOD | Boeing 727-264F (FedEx 3) | 23014/1816 | ex N765AT | |
| ☐ | PR-IOF | Boeing 727-214F | 21692/1479 | ex N786AT | |
| ☐ | PR-IOG | Boeing 727-214F | 21691/1480 | ex N785AT | |
| ☐ | PR-RLJ | Boeing 727-214F | 21513/1365 | ex N751US | |
| | | | | | |
| ☐ | PR-IOE | Boeing 767-281BDSF | 23141/108 | ex N791AX | ♦ |
| ☐ | PR-IOH | Boeing 767-281BDSF | 23146/121 | ex N796AX | ♦ |

## SANTA BARBARA TAXI AEREO

| | | | | | |
|---|---|---|---|---|---|
| ☐ | PT-JES | Beech B200 Super King Air | BB-1937 | | ♦ |

## SETE TAXI AEREO — Sete — Goiania, GO (GYN)

| | | | | | |
|---|---|---|---|---|---|
| ☐ | PR-MEI | Cessna 208B Caravan I | 208B0358 | ex N1115P | |
| ☐ | PT-MEG | Cessna 208B Caravan I | 208B0352 | ex N1114N | |
| ☐ | PT-MEH | Cessna 208B Caravan I | 208B0354 | ex N1114W | |
| ☐ | PT-MEK | Cessna 208B Caravan I | 208B0360 | ex N1115W | |
| ☐ | PT-MEL | Cessna 208B Caravan I | 208B0361 | ex N1116G | |
| ☐ | PR-STE | Embraer EMB.120ER Brasilia | 120295 | ex N295UX | |
| ☐ | PR-TUH | Embraer EMB.120RT Brasilia | 120276 | ex N212SW | ♦ |
| ☐ | PT-EHE | Embraer EMB.820C Navajo | 820041 | | |
| ☐ | PT-LHH | Mitsubishi MU-2B-60 Marquise | 1508SA | ex N618RT | |
| ☐ | PT-WST | Mitsubishi MU-2B-36A | 711SA | ex N171CA | |
| ☐ | PT-WYT | Mitsubishi MU-2B-36A | 722SA | ex N722MU | |

## SIDERAL AIR CARGO

| | | | | | |
|---|---|---|---|---|---|
| ☐ | PR-SDL | Boeing 737-3S3F | 24060/1519 | ex N312AW | |

## SKYLIFT TAXI AEREO — Campinhas, SP (CPQ)

| | | | | | |
|---|---|---|---|---|---|
| ☐ | PT-PQD | Short SC.7 Skyvan 3 | SH1951 | ex C-FSDZ | |

## SOL LINHAS AEREAS

| | | | | | |
|---|---|---|---|---|---|
| ☐ | PR-VLA | LET L-410UVP-E3 | 882101 | ex OK-TDA | |

## TAF LINHAS AEREAS — Tafi (TSD) — Fortaleza, CE (FOR)

| | | | | | |
|---|---|---|---|---|---|
| ☐ | PR-MTD | Boeing 727-227F (Raisbeck 3) | 21248/1218 | ex N76752 | |
| ☐ | PR-MTG | Boeing 737-217 (AvAero 3) | 22255/666 | ex N5JY | Gracinha |
| ☐ | PR-MTH | Boeing 737-232 (Nordam 3) | 23102/1045 | ex N330DL | |
| ☐ | PR-MTL | Boeing 727-2J7F | 20879/1033 | ex N128NA | |
| ☐ | PT-GJD | Embraer EMB.110EJ Bandeirante | 110056 | | |
| ☐ | PT-MTC | Boeing 727-228F (FedEx 3) | 20409/845 | ex N726DH | Comte Dilsonr |
| ☐ | PT-MTF | Boeing 737-241 | 21007/400 | ex PP-VML | |
| ☐ | PT-OGG | Cessna 208A Caravan I | 208A00041 | ex N813FE | |
| ☐ | PT-OGL | Cessna 208A Caravan I | 20800102 | ex N839FE | |
| ☐ | PT-OGV | Cessna 208A Caravan I | 20800019 | ex N805FE | |
| ☐ | PT-OQT | Cessna 208B Grand Caravan | 208B0314 | ex N1018X | |
| ☐ | PT-YTF | Helibras AS350B2 Esquilo | AS.3149 | | |

## TAM LINHAS AEREAS — TAM (JJ/TAM) — Sao Paulo-Congonhas, SP (GGH)

| | | | | | |
|---|---|---|---|---|---|
| ☐ | PR-MAH | Airbus A319-132 | 1608 | ex D-AIJO | |
| ☐ | PR-MAI | Airbus A319-132 | 1703 | ex D-AIMM | |
| ☐ | PR-MAL | Airbus A319-132 | 1801 | ex D-AVWD | |
| ☐ | PR-MAM | Airbus A319-132 | 1826 | ex D-AVWN | |
| ☐ | PR-MAN | Airbus A319-132 | 1831 | ex D-AVWR | |
| ☐ | PR-MAO | Airbus A319-132 | 1837 | ex D-AVYQ | |
| ☐ | PR-MAQ | Airbus A319-132 | 1855 | ex D-AVYA | |
| ☐ | PR-MBI | Airbus A319-132 | 1575 | ex N475TA | |
| ☐ | PR-MBN | Airbus A319-132 | 3032 | ex D-AVWG | |
| ☐ | PR-MBU | Airbus A319-132 | 3588 | ex D-AVYG | |
| ☐ | PR-MBV | Airbus A319-132 | 3595 | ex D-AVYC | |
| ☐ | PR-MBW | Airbus A319-132 | 3710 | ex D-AVWQ | |

| | | | | | |
|---|---|---|---|---|---|
| ☐ | PR-MYB | Airbus A319-112 | 3727 | ex D-AVWT | |
| ☐ | PR-MYC | Airbus A319-112 | 3733 | ex D-AVWW | |
| ☐ | PR-MYL | Airbus A319-112 | 4734 | ex D-AVYA | |
| ☐ | PR-MYM | Airbus A319-112 | 4756 | ex D-AVYD | ◆ |
| ☐ | PT-MZA | Airbus A319-132 | 0976 | ex D-AVYI | ◆ |
| ☐ | PT-MZB | Airbus A319-132 | 1010 | ex D-AVYA | |
| ☐ | PT-MZC | Airbus A319-132 | 1092 | ex D-AVYD | |
| ☐ | PT-MZD | Airbus A319-132 | 1096 | ex D-AVYR | >PTN |
| ☐ | PT-MZE | Airbus A319-132 | 1103 | ex D-AVWD | >PTN |
| ☐ | PT-MZF | Airbus A319-132 | 1139 | ex D-AVYO | |
| ☐ | PT-TMA | Airbus A319-132 | 4000 | ex D-AVYA | |
| ☐ | PT-TMB | Airbus A319-132 | 4163 | ex D-AVYF | |
| ☐ | PT-TMC | Airbus A319-132 | 4171 | ex D-AVWJ | |
| ☐ | PT-TMD | Airbus A319-132 | 4192 | ex D-AVYA | |
| ☐ | PT-TME | Airbus A319-132 | 4389 | ex D-AVXH | |
| ☐ | PT-TMF | Airbus A319-132 | 2467 | ex D-ABGB | |
| ☐ | PT-TMG | Airbus A319-132 | 4773 | | |
| ☐ | PT-TMH | Airbus A319-132 | 2784 | ex N601LF | ◆ |
| | | | | | |
| ☐ | PR-MAA | Airbus A320-232 | 1595 | ex F-WWBU | |
| ☐ | PR-MAB | Airbus A320-232 | 1663 | ex F-WWIE | |
| ☐ | PR-MAC | Airbus A320-232 | 1672 | ex F-WWIK | 450 anos |
| ☐ | PR-MAD | Airbus A320-232 | 1771 | ex F-WWDD | |
| ☐ | PR-MAE | Airbus A320-232 | 1804 | ex F-WWII | |
| ☐ | PR-MAG | Airbus A320-232 | 1832 | ex F-WWBD | Sao Paulo 450 Anos |
| ☐ | PR-MAJ | Airbus A320-232 | 1818 | ex F-WWIN | |
| ☐ | PR-MAK | Airbus A320-232 | 1825 | ex F-WWIX | |
| ☐ | PR-MAP | Airbus A320-232 | 1857 | ex F-WWBZ | |
| ☐ | PR-MAR | Airbus A320-232 | 1888 | ex F-WWBS | |
| ☐ | PR-MAS | Airbus A320-232 | 2372 | ex F-WWDQ | |
| ☐ | PR-MAV | Airbus A320-232 | 2393 | ex F-WWIR | |
| ☐ | PR-MAW | Airbus A320-232 | 2417 | ex F-WWDT | |
| ☐ | PR-MAX | Airbus A320-232 | 2602 | ex F-WWBO | |
| ☐ | PR-MAY | Airbus A320-232 | 2661 | ex F-WWIV | |
| ☐ | PR-MAZ | Airbus A320-232 | 2513 | ex F-WWIY | |
| ☐ | PR-MBA | Airbus A320-232 | 2734 | ex F-WWBF | |
| ☐ | PR-MBB | Airbus A320-232 | 2737 | ex F-WWBH | |
| ☐ | PR-MBC | Airbus A320-232 | 2783 | ex F-WWDZ | |
| ☐ | PR-MBD | Airbus A320-232 | 2838 | ex F-WWID | |
| ☐ | PR-MBE | Airbus A320-232 | 2859 | ex F-WWIU | |
| ☐ | PR-MBF | Airbus A320-232 | 2896 | ex F-WWBZ | |
| ☐ | PR-MBG | Airbus A320-232 | 1459 | ex OE-LOR | |
| ☐ | PR-MBH | Airbus A320-232 | 2904 | ex F-WWDP | |
| ☐ | PR-MBL | Airbus A320-233 | 2044 | ex HC-CDZ | |
| ☐ | PR-MBM | Airbus A320-233 | 1339 | ex N463TA | |
| ☐ | PR-MBO | Airbus A320-232 | 3156 | ex F-WWDK | |
| ☐ | PR-MBP | Airbus A320-232 | 1215 | ex G-TTOA | |
| ☐ | PR-MBQ | Airbus A320-232 | 1652 | ex N533JB | |
| ☐ | PR-MBR | Airbus A320-232 | 1802 | ex N542JB | |
| ☐ | PR-MBS | Airbus A320-232 | 1835 | ex N544JB | |
| ☐ | PR-MBT | Airbus A320-233 | 2014 | ex HC-CDY | ◆ |
| ☐ | PR-MBX | Airbus A320-232 | 1591 | ex N528JB | |
| ☐ | PR-MBY | Airbus A320-232 | 1891 | ex N550JB | |
| ☐ | PR-MBZ | Airbus A320-232 | 1827 | ex N546JB | |
| ☐ | PR-MHA | Airbus A320-214 | 2924 | ex F-WWDV | |
| ☐ | PR-MHB | Airbus A320-214 | 1692 | ex F-GRSN | |
| ☐ | PR-MHC | Airbus A320-214 | 1717 | ex EC-ICN | |
| ☐ | PR-MHD | Airbus A320-214 | 1775 | ex EC-JHJ | |
| ☐ | PR-MHE | Airbus A320-214 | 3111 | ex F-WWIS | |
| ☐ | PR-MHF | Airbus A320-214 | 3180 | ex F-WWDT | |
| ☐ | PR-MHG | Airbus A320-214 | 3002 | ex F-WWBB | |
| ☐ | PR-MHI | Airbus A320-214 | 3035 | ex F-WWDE | |
| ☐ | PR-MHJ | Airbus A320-214 | 3047 | ex F-WWDQ | |
| ☐ | PR-MHK | Airbus A320-214 | 3058 | ex F-WWDX | |
| ☐ | PR-MHM | Airbus A320-214 | 3211 | ex F-WWIR | |
| ☐ | PR-MHN | Airbus A320-214 | 3240 | ex F-WWBM | |
| ☐ | PR-MHO | Airbus A320-214 | 3278 | ex F-WWDK | |
| ☐ | PR-MHP | Airbus A320-214 | 3266 | ex F-WWBS | |
| ☐ | PR-MHQ | Airbus A320-214 | 3284 | ex F-WWDQ | |
| ☐ | PR-MHR | Airbus A320-214 | 3313 | ex F-WWIQ | |
| ☐ | PR-MHS | Airbus A320-214 | 3325 | ex F-WWBF | |
| ☐ | PR-MHT | Airbus A320-214 | 1757 | ex EI-DJI | |
| ☐ | PR-MHU | Airbus A320-214 | 3391 | ex F-WWDR | |
| ☐ | PR-MHV | Airbus A320-214 | 3540 | ex F-WWIO | |
| ☐ | PR-MHW | Airbus A320-214 | 3630 | ex F-WWBQ | |
| ☐ | PR-MHX | Airbus A320-214 | 3565 | ex F-WWBM | |
| ☐ | PR-MHY | Airbus A320-214 | 3594 | ex F-WWDG | |
| ☐ | PR-MHZ | Airbus A320-214 | 3658 | ex F-WWDT | |
| ☐ | PR-MYA | Airbus A320-214 | 3662 | ex F-WWDV | |
| ☐ | PR-MYD | Airbus A320-214 | 3750 | ex F-WWBR | |
| ☐ | PR-MYE | Airbus A320-214 | 3908 | ex F-WWIR | |
| ☐ | PR-MYF | Airbus A320-214 | 3972 | ex F-WWIQ | |
| ☐ | PR-MYG | Airbus A320-214 | 4320 | ex F-WWDJ | |

| | | | | | |
|---|---|---|---|---|---|
| ☐ | PR-MYH | Airbus A320-214 | 4441 | ex F-WWDY | |
| ☐ | PR-MYI | Airbus A320-214 | 4446 | ex D-AVVY | |
| ☐ | PR-MYJ | Airbus A320-214 | 4465 | ex D-AVVL | |
| ☐ | PR-MYK | Airbus A320-214 | 4544 | ex D-AXAN | |
| ☐ | PR-MYN | Airbus A320-214 | 4953 | ex D-AXAU | ♦ |
| ☐ | PR-MYO | Airbus A320-214 | 4974 | ex D-AVVK | ♦ |
| ☐ | PR-MYP | Airbus A320-214 | 5066 | ex D-AUBE | o/o♦ |
| ☐ | PR-MYQ | Airbus A320-214 | 5101 | ex D-AUBQ | ♦ |
| ☐ | PR-MYR | Airbus A320-214 | 5107 | ex D-AUBT | ♦ |
| ☐ | PR-MYS | Airbus A320-214 | 5109 | ex D-AUBU | ♦ |
| ☐ | PT-MZG | Airbus A320-232 | 1143 | ex F-WWBG | |
| ☐ | PT-MZH | Airbus A320-232 | 1158 | ex F-WWBY | |
| ☐ | PT-MZI | Airbus A320-232 | 1246 | ex F-WWIR | |
| ☐ | PT-MZJ | Airbus A320-232 | 1251 | ex F-WWIV | |
| ☐ | PT-MZK | Airbus A320-232 | 1368 | ex F-WWIJ | |
| ☐ | PT-MZL | Airbus A320-232 | 1376 | ex F-WWIN | |
| ☐ | PT-MZN | Airbus A320-231 | 0440 | ex ZS-SHG | |
| ☐ | PT-MZO | Airbus A320-231 | 0250 | ex ZS-SHC | |
| ☐ | PT-MZQ | Airbus A320-231 | 0335 | ex ZS-SHF | |
| ☐ | PT-MZR | Airbus A320-231 | 0334 | ex ZS-SHE | |
| ☐ | PT-MZT | Airbus A320-232 | 1486 | ex F-WWDV | |
| ☐ | PT-MZU | Airbus A320-232 | 1518 | ex F-WWIJ | |
| ☐ | PT-MZV | Airbus A320-232 | 0758 | ex N758SL | |
| ☐ | PT-MZW | Airbus A320-232 | 1580 | ex F-WWBK | |
| ☐ | PT-MZX | Airbus A320-232 | 1613 | ex F-WWDI | |
| ☐ | PT-MZY | Airbus A320-232 | 1628 | ex F-WWDO | |
| ☐ | PT-MZZ | Airbus A320-232 | 1593 | ex F-WWBT | |
| | | | | | |
| ☐ | PT-MXA | Airbus A321-231 | 3222 | ex D-AVZF | |
| ☐ | PT-MXB | Airbus A321-231 | 3229 | ex D-AVZG | |
| ☐ | PT-MXC | Airbus A321-231 | 3294 | ex D-AVZE | |
| ☐ | PT-MXD | Airbus A321-231 | 3761 | ex D-AZAP | |
| ☐ | PT-MXE | Airbus A321-231 | 3816 | ex D-AVZB | |
| ☐ | PT-MXF | Airbus A321-231 | 4352 | ex D-AVZC | |
| ☐ | PT-MXG | Airbus A321-231 | 4358 | ex D-AVZK | |
| ☐ | PT-MXH | Airbus A321-231 | 4570 | ex D-AZAK | ♦ |
| ☐ | PT-MXI | Airbus A321-231 | 4662 | ex D-AZAD | ♦ |
| | | | | | |
| ☐ | PT-MVA | Airbus A330-223 | 232 | ex A6-EYX | |
| ☐ | PT-MVB | Airbus A330-223 | 238 | ex A6-EYY | |
| ☐ | PT-MVC | Airbus A330-223 | 247 | ex F-WWKH | |
| ☐ | PT-MVD | Airbus A330-223 | 259 | ex A6-EYB | |
| ☐ | PT-MVE | Airbus A330-223 | 361 | ex A6-EYA | |
| ☐ | PT-MVF | Airbus A330-203 | 466 | ex F-WWKP | |
| ☐ | PT-MVG | Airbus A330-203 | 472 | ex F-WWKQ | |
| ☐ | PT-MVH | Airbus A330-203 | 477 | ex F-WWKS | |
| ☐ | PT-MVK | Airbus A330-203 | 486 | ex F-WWYL | |
| ☐ | PT-MVL | Airbus A330-203 | 700 | ex F-WWKB | |
| ☐ | PT-MVM | Airbus A330-223 | 869 | ex F-WWYR | |
| ☐ | PT-MVN | Airbus A330-223 | 876 | ex F-WWKE | |
| ☐ | PT-MVO | Airbus A330-223 | 949 | ex F-WWKP | |
| ☐ | PT-MVP | Airbus A330-223 | 961 | ex F-WWYF | |
| ☐ | PT-MVQ | Airbus A330-223 | 968 | ex F-WWYN | |
| ☐ | PT-MVR | Airbus A330-223 | 977 | ex F-WWKV | |
| ☐ | PT-MVS | Airbus A330-223 | 1112 | ex F-WWYJ | |
| ☐ | PT-MVT | Airbus A330-223 | 1118 | ex F-WWKS | |
| ☐ | PT-MVU | Airbus A330-223 | 1213 | ex F-WWKF | ♦ |
| ☐ | PT-MVV | Airbus A330-223 | 1221 | ex F-WWKT | ♦ |
| ☐ | PT- | Airbus A330-233 | 1068 | | o/o♦ |
| | | | | | |
| ☐ | PT-MUA | Boeing 777-32WER | 37664/727 | ex N5573S | |
| ☐ | PT-MUB | Boeing 777-32WER | 37665/733 | ex N6009F | |
| ☐ | PT-MUC | Boeing 777-32WER | 37666/740 | | |
| ☐ | PT-MUD | Boeing 777-32WER | 37667/751 | | |
| ☐ | PT-MUE | Boeing 777-32WER | 38886/ | | o/o♦ |
| ☐ | PT-MUF | Boeing 777-32WER | 38887/ | | o/o♦ |
| ☐ | PT-MUG | Boeing 777-32WER | 38888/ | | o/o♦ |
| | | | | | |
| ☐ | PT-MSL | Airbus A340-541 | 464 | ex C-GKOM | |
| ☐ | PT-MSN | Airbus A340-541 | 445 | ex C-GKOL | <ACA [MLA] |
| ☐ | PT-MSQ | Boeing 767-33AER | 27468/584 | ex I-DEID | |
| ☐ | PT-MSR | Boeing 767-33AER | 27377/561 | ex I-DEIC | |
| ☐ | PT-MSU | Boeing 767-33AER | 27376/560 | ex PR-VAG | |

## TAM - TAXI AEREO MARILIA — Sao Paulo-Congonhas, SP (GGH)

| | | | | | |
|---|---|---|---|---|---|
| ☐ | PP-ITY | Cessna 208B Caravan I | 208B0560 | ex N1301B | |
| ☐ | PR-MAU | Cessna 208B Caravan I | 208B0621 | ex ZP-CAD | |
| ☐ | PT-MEA | Cessna 208B Caravan I | 208B0333 | ex N1037L | |
| ☐ | PT-MEB | Cessna 208B Caravan I | 208B0335 | ex N1038G | |
| ☐ | PT-MEC | Cessna 208B Caravan I | 208B0342 | ex N1045C | |
| ☐ | PT-MED | Cessna 208B Caravan I | 208B0343 | ex N1052C | |

| | | | | | |
|---|---|---|---|---|---|
| ☐ | PT-MEJ | Cessna 208B Caravan I | 208B0359 | ex N1115V | |
| ☐ | PT-MEM | Cessna 208B Caravan I | 208B0405 | | |
| ☐ | PT-MEN | Cessna 208B Caravan I | 208B0408 | | |
| ☐ | PT-MEO | Cessna 208B Caravan I | 208B0412 | | |
| ☐ | PT-MEP | Cessna 208B Caravan I | 208B0413 | | |
| ☐ | PT-MES | Cessna 208B Caravan I | 208B0507 | | ♦ |
| ☐ | PT-MEX | Cessna 208B Caravan I | 208B0515 | ex N50280 | |
| ☐ | PT-MEY | Cessna 208B Caravan I | 208B0518 | | ♦ |
| ☐ | PT-MHC | Cessna 208B Caravan I | 208B0543 | | |
| ☐ | PT-MLR | Cessna 208B Caravan i | 208B2119 | ex N61466 | ♦ |
| ☐ | PT-WIO | Cessna 208B Caravan I | 208B0521 | ex N5058J | ♦ |

## TAVAJ LINHAS AEREAS — Tavaj (4U/TVJ) — Rio Branco, AC (RBR)

Ceased ops

## TAXI AEREO ITAITUBA — Santarem, PA (STM)

| | | | | | |
|---|---|---|---|---|---|
| ☐ | PT-GJR | Embraer EMB.110EJ Bandeirante | 110070 | | |
| ☐ | PT-GKE | Embraer EMB.110B1 Bandeirante | 110096 | ex PP-ZKE | |
| ☐ | PT-WTL | Embraer EMB-110P1 Bandeirante | 110104 | ex Brazil 2180 | ♦ |

## TAXI AEREO WEISS — Curitiba, PR (CWB)

| | | | | | |
|---|---|---|---|---|---|
| ☐ | PR-ELT | Embraer EMB.110P1 Bandeirante | 110412 | ex P2-IAL | ♦ |
| ☐ | PT-EFU | Embraer EMB.820C Navajo | 820031 | | |
| ☐ | PT-ELY | Embraer EMB.820C Navajo | 820063 | | |
| ☐ | PT-SFS | Embraer EMB.110P1 Bandeirante | 110401 | | |
| ☐ | PT-TAW | Embraer EMB.110P1 Bandeirante | 110258 | ex CX-VIP | ♦ |

## TEAM AIRLINES – TEAM TRANSPORTES AEREOS
### Team Brasil (TIM) Rio de Janeiro-Santos Dumont, RJ (SDU)

| | | | | | |
|---|---|---|---|---|---|
| ☐ | PR-AIA | LET L-410UVP-E | 912611 | ex CCCP-67680 | |
| ☐ | PR-CRA | LET L-410UVP-E20 | 902514 | ex OK-VDP | |
| ☐ | PR-IMO | LET L-410UVP-E20 | 922701 | ex OK-XDJ | |

## TOTAL LINHAS AEREAS — (TTL)

| | | | | | |
|---|---|---|---|---|---|
| ☐ | PR-TTB | Boeing 727-223 (FedEx 3) | 22007/1643 | ex N891AA | |
| ☐ | PR-TTO | Boeing 727-2M7F (FedEx 3) | 21200/1206 | ex N721RW | |
| ☐ | PR-TTP | Boeing 727-2M7F (FedEx 3) | 1339/21502 | ex N998PG | |
| ☐ | PT-TTW | Boeing 727-225F | 22438/1685 | ex N743DH | |
| ☐ | PT-MTQ | Boeing 727-243F | 22053/1620 | ex N198PC | |
| ☐ | PT-MTT | Boeing 727-243F | 22167/1752 | ex N270PC | |
| ☐ | PT-STN | Embraer EMB.120ER Brasilia | 120241 | | >PLY♦ |
| ☐ | PR-TTH | ATR 42-500 | 0506 | ex F-WQNL | ♦ |
| ☐ | PR-TTK | ATR 42-500 | 0504 | ex F-WQNK | ♦ |
| ☐ | PR-TTM | ATR 42-500 | 0551 | ex D-BNNN | ♦ |

## TRIP LINHAS AEREAS — (T4/TIB) — Sao Paulo-Viracopos, SP (VCP)

| | | | | | |
|---|---|---|---|---|---|
| ☐ | PP-ATV | ATR 42-300 | 0298 | ex F-WQHA | |
| ☐ | PP-PTC | ATR 42-300 | 0035 | ex F-ODUD | |
| ☐ | PP-PTD | ATR 42-320 | 0091 | ex F-WQNS | |
| ☐ | PP-PTF | ATR 42-300 | 0072 | ex LV-ZNV | |
| ☐ | PP-PTG | ATR 42-320 | 0128 | ex F-WQNA | |
| ☐ | PP-PTI | ATR 42-320 | 0374 | ex F-WQNP | |
| ☐ | PP-PTJ | ATR 42-320 | 0284 | ex CX-PUC | |
| ☐ | PR-TTE | ATR 42-300 | 0400 | ex F-WQNG | |
| ☐ | PR-TTF | ATR 42-300 | 0021 | ex F-WQNS | |
| ☐ | PT-MFE | ATR 42-300 | 0295 | ex F-WWLU | |
| ☐ | PT-TTL | ATR 42-320 | 0380 | ex N988MA | |
| ☐ | PP-PTV | ATR 42-500 | 0503 | ex F-WNUA | |
| ☐ | PP-PTW | ATR 42-500 | 0510 | ex F-WNUB | |
| ☐ | PR-TKB | ATR 42-500 | 0610 | ex I-ADLV | |
| ☐ | PR-TKC | ATR 42-500 | 0609 | ex I-ADLU | |
| ☐ | PR-TKD | ATR 42-500 | 0604 | ex I-ADLP | |
| ☐ | PR-TKE | ATR 42-500 | 0556 | ex F-WKVC | |
| ☐ | PR-TKF | ATR 42-500 | 0579 | ex F-OIJB | ♦ |
| ☐ | PR-TKG | ATR 42-500 | 0581 | ex D-BPPP | ♦ |
| ☐ | PR-TKH | ATR 42-500 | 0584 | ex D-BQQQ | ♦ |
| ☐ | PP-PTL | ATR 72-212A | 0773 | ex F-WWEL | |
| ☐ | PP-PTM | ATR 72-212A | 0798 | ex F-WWEO | |
| ☐ | PP-PTN | ATR 72-212A | 0832 | ex F-WWEI | |
| ☐ | PP-PTO | ATR 72-212A | 0837 | ex F-WWEO | |

| | | | | | |
|---|---|---|---|---|---|
| ☐ | PP-PTP | ATR 72-212A | 0865 | ex F-WWEO | |
| ☐ | PP-PTQ | ATR 72-212A | 0874 | ex F-WWEZ | |
| ☐ | PP-PTR | ATR 72-212A | 0785 | ex F-WWED | |
| ☐ | PP-PTT | ATR 72-212A | 0846 | ex F-WWEL | |
| ☐ | PP-PTU | ATR 72-212A | 0891 | ex F-WWEW | |
| ☐ | PP-PTX | ATR 72-212A | 0666 | ex F-WKVE | |
| ☐ | PP-PTY | ATR 72-212A | 0911 | ex F-WWEE | |
| ☐ | PP-PTZ | ATR 72-212A | 0918 | ex F-WWEP | |
| ☐ | PR-TKA | ATR 72-212A | 0926 | ex F-WWEB | |
| ☐ | PR-TTJ | ATR 72-212 | 0463 | ex N534AS | |
| | | | | | |
| ☐ | PR-TKI | ATR 72-600 | 0967 | ex F-WWLR | ♦ |
| ☐ | PR-TKJ | ATR 72-600 | 0971 | ex F-WWLV | ♦ |
| ☐ | PR-TKK | ATR 72-600 | 987 | ex F-WWLN | ♦ |
| ☐ | PR-TKL | ATR 72-600 | 992 | ex F-WWLR | ♦ |
| ☐ | PR-TKM | ATR 72-600 | 998 | ex F-WWLW | ♦ |
| ☐ | PR- | ATR 72-600 | 1028 | ex F-WW | o/o♦ |
| | | | | | |
| ☐ | PP-PJA | Embraer ERJ-175LR | 17000272 | ex PT-SNF | |
| ☐ | PP-PJB | Embraer ERJ-175LR | 17000277 | ex PT-TQD | |
| ☐ | PP-PJC | Embraer ERJ-175LR | 17000287 | ex PT-TQN | |
| ☐ | PP-PJD | Embraer ERJ-175LR | 17000017 | ex D-ALIB | |
| ☐ | PP-PJE | Embraer ERJ-175LR | 17000291 | | |
| ☐ | PP-PJF | Embraer ERJ-175LR | 17000309 | | |
| ☐ | PP-PJG | Embraer ERJ-175LR | 17000137 | ex M-YRGM | |
| ☐ | PP-PJH | Embraer ERJ-175LR | 17000147 | ex M-YRGN | |
| ☐ | PP-PJI | Embraer ERJ-175LR | 17000126 | | ♦ |
| | | | | | |
| ☐ | PP-PJJ | Embraer ERJ-190LR | 19000163 | ex HB-JQE | |
| ☐ | PP-PJK | Embraer ERJ-190LR | 19000178 | ex HB-JQF | |
| ☐ | PP-PJL | Embraer ERJ-190LR | 19000189 | ex HB-JQG | |
| ☐ | PP-PJM | Embraer ERJ-190LR | 19000432 | | ♦ |
| ☐ | PP-PJN | Embraer ERJ-190LR | 19000441 | | ♦ |
| ☐ | PP-PJO | Embraer ERJ-190LR | 19000450 | | ♦ |
| ☐ | PP-PJP | Embraer ERJ-190LR | 19000460 | | ♦ |
| ☐ | PP-PJQ | Embraer ERJ-190LR | 19000493 | | ♦ |
| ☐ | PP-PJR | Embraer ERJ-190LR | 19000495 | | ♦ |
| ☐ | PP-PJT | Embraer ERJ-190LR | 19000506 | | ♦ |
| ☐ | PP- | Embraer ERJ-190LR | 19000541 | | o/o♦ |
| | | | | | |
| ☐ | PT-WJG | Embraer EMB.120ER Brasilia | 120061 | ex F-GFEN | wfs♦ |

## TWO TAXI AERO                                                                           Itapeva

| | | | | | |
|---|---|---|---|---|---|
| ☐ | PR-BAT | Cessna 208B Caravan I | 208B2169 | ex N5180K | ♦ |
| ☐ | PR-CRF | Cessna 208B Caravan I | 208B2227 | | ♦ |
| ☐ | PR-WOT | Cessna 208B Caravan I | 208B2240 | | ♦ |

## VARIG
### Varig (RG/VRN)
### Rio de Janeiro-Galeao, RJ/Porto Alegre-Canoas, RS (GIG/POA)

| | | | | | |
|---|---|---|---|---|---|
| ☐ | PR-GOQ | Boeing 737-76N | 33417/1215 | | ♦ |
| ☐ | PR-VBM | Boeing 737-7EA | 32406/859 | ex N815PG | |
| ☐ | PR-VBN | Boeing 737-76N | 28577/124 | ex N966PG | |
| ☐ | PR-VBP | Boeing 737-7EA | 32407/904 | ex N160CK | |
| ☐ | PR-VBQ | Boeing 737-76N | 30135/1068 | ex PR-GOO | ♦ |
| ☐ | PR-VBU | Boeing 737-76N/W | 29905/372 | ex N746AL | |
| ☐ | PR-VBV | Boeing 737-76N/W | 30050/429 | ex N748AL | |
| ☐ | PR-VBY | Boeing 737-73A/W | 28499/390 | ex N738AL | ♦ |
| ☐ | PR-VBZ | Boeing 737-73A/W | 28500/414 | ex N739AL | ♦ |
| | | | | | |
| ☐ | PR-GIT | Boeing 737-809 | 28403/117 | ex TC-APM | ♦ |
| ☐ | PR-VBA | Boeing 737-8AS/W | 29916/210 | ex EI-CSA | |
| ☐ | PR-VBB | Boeing 737-8AS/W | 29917/298 | ex EI-CSB | |
| ☐ | PR-VBC | Boeing 737-8AS/W | 29918/307 | ex EI-CSC | |
| ☐ | PR-VBD | Boeing 737-8AS/W | 29919/341 | ex EI-CSD | |
| ☐ | PR-VBE | Boeing 737-8AS/W | 29920/362 | ex EI-CSE | |
| ☐ | PR-VBF | Boeing 737-8EH/W | 34276/2716 | | |
| ☐ | PR-VBG | Boeing 737-8EH/W | 35066/2700 | | |
| ☐ | PR-VBJ | Boeing 737-86N/W | 36434/2706 | | |
| ☐ | PR-VBK | Boeing 737-8EH/W | 34271/2445 | ex PR-GTX | |
| ☐ | PR-VBL | Boeing 737-8EH/W | 34272/2449 | ex PR-GTW | |
| | | | | | |
| ☐ | PR-VAC | Boeing 767-27GER | 27048/475 | ex N48SN | [MIA] |
| ☐ | PR-VAO | Boeing 767-383ER | 24846/309 | ex TF-FIC | [GYE]♦ |

## VARIG LOG                            (LC/VLO)            Sao Paulo-Guarulhos, SP/ (GRU)

| | | | | | |
|---|---|---|---|---|---|
| ☐ | PP-VQU | Boeing 727-2J7F | 20880/1037 | ex N129NA | wfs♦ |
| ☐ | PP-VQV | Boeing 727-243F | 22166/1725 | ex PP-SFE | |
| ☐ | PR-LGN | Boeing 757-236 (PCF) | 25597/441 | ex N597AG | ♦ |

| | | | | | | |
|---|---|---|---|---|---|---|
| ☐ | PR-LGR | Boeing 737-408SF | 25063/2032 | ex N563AC | | [MIA]♦ |
| ☐ | PR-LGS | Boeing 737-4S3SF | 25595/2233 | ex N595AG | | [MIA]♦ |

## VERA CRUZ TAXI AEREO | Vera Cruz

| | | | | | |
|---|---|---|---|---|---|
| ☐ | PR-CFJ | Cessna 208B Caravan I | 208B1217 | ex N52136 | ♦ |
| ☐ | PR-SLD | Cessna 208B Caravan I | 208B1154 | | ♦ |
| ☐ | PR-VCB | Cessna 208B Caravan I | 208B1236 | ex N208GH | ♦ |
| ☐ | PR-VCE | Cessna 208B Caravan I | 208B1256 | ex N5147B | ♦ |
| ☐ | PR-VCI | Cessna 208B Caravan I | 208B2034 | | ♦ |
| ☐ | PT-MEV | Cessna 208B Caravan I | 208B0512 | ex N5076K | ♦ |
| ☐ | PT-OGE | Cessna 208 Caravan I | 20800184 | ex N9765F | ♦ |
| ☐ | PT-OGF | Cessna 208 Caravan I | 20800187 | ex N9768F | ♦ |
| ☐ | PT-OGY | Cessna 208A Caravan I | 208A00094 | ex N836FE | ♦ |
| ☐ | PT-OPA | Cessna 208 Caravan I | 20800214 | ex N9799F | ♦ |
| ☐ | PT-OTM | Cessna 208B Caravan I | 208B0318 | ex N1025Y | ♦ |
| ☐ | PT-WYP | Cessna 208B Caravan I | 208B0696 | | ♦ |
| ☐ | PT-WZN | Cessna 208B Caravan I | 208B0698 | | ♦ |

## WEBJET LINHAS AEREAS | (WEB) | | Curitiba (CWB)

Taken over by GOL Transportes Aereos Sep11

## WHITEJETS | (WTJ)

| | | | | | |
|---|---|---|---|---|---|
| ☐ | PR-WTB | Airbus A320-214 | 0548 | ex CS-TQO | ♦ |

## XP TAXI AEREO

| | | | | | |
|---|---|---|---|---|---|
| ☐ | PR-VXP | Cessna 208B Caravan I | 208B1281 | ex N5249W | ♦ |

# PZ- SURINAME (Republic of Suriname)

## BLUE WING AIRLINES | (BWI) | | Paramaribo-Zorg en Hoop (ORG)

| | | | | | |
|---|---|---|---|---|---|
| ☐ | PZ-TGQ | Cessna U206G Stationair 6 | U20605917 | ex PZ-TAO | |
| ☐ | PZ-TLV | Cessna U206G Stationair 6 | U20606951 | | |
| ☐ | PZ-TSA | WSK/PZL Antonov An-28 | 1AJ007-21 | ex PZ-TGW | |
| ☐ | PZ-TSB | Cessna 208 Caravan I | 20800098 | ex N207RM | |
| ☐ | PZ-TSD | de Havilland DHC-6 Twin Otter 200 | 117 | ex VH-JEA | |
| ☐ | PZ-TSH | de Havilland DHC-6 Twin Otter 200 | 145 | ex VH-TZR | |
| ☐ | PZ-TSN | WSK/PZL Antonov An-28 | 1AJ007-20 | ex YV-528C | |
| ☐ | PZ- | Reims Cessna F406 Caravan II | F406-0033 | ex VH-JVN | |
| ☐ | PZ- | Cessna 208B Caravan | 208B0488 | ex N1301K | ♦ |

## CARIBBEAN COMMUTER AIRLINES

| | | | | | |
|---|---|---|---|---|---|
| ☐ | PZ-TYD | Britten-Norman BN-2A Islander | 3009 | | ♦ |
| ☐ | PZ-TYL | Britten-Norman BN-2A Islander | 2211 | | ♦ |

## GUM AIR | (GUM) | | Paramaribo-Zorg en Hoop (ORG)

| | | | | | |
|---|---|---|---|---|---|
| ☐ | PZ-TBA | GAF Nomad N22B | N22B-66 | | ♦ |
| ☐ | PZ-TBD | Cessna U206G Stationair | U20603786 | ex N8286G | |
| ☐ | PZ-TBE | Cessna U206G Stationair 6 | U20606776 | ex N9959Z | |
| ☐ | PZ-TBG | Cessna U206B Super Skywagon | U206-0832 | ex N3832G | |
| ☐ | PZ-TBH | Cessna 208B Caravan I | 208B0923 | ex N1132W | Spirit of Pike |
| ☐ | PZ-TBL | Britten-Norman BN-2B-26 Islander | 2153 | ex N633BB | |
| ☐ | PZ-TBS | Cessna 208B Caravan I | 208B1284 | ex N4114A | ♦ |
| ☐ | PZ-TBW | de Havilland DHC-6 Twin Otter 300 | 601 | ex N28SP | |
| ☐ | PZ-TBY | de Havilland DHC-6 Twin Otter 300 | 646 | ex N7015A | |
| ☐ | PZ-TVC | Cessna 404 Titan | 404-0243 | ex YV-236CP | |
| ☐ | PZ-TVU | Cessna TU206G Stationair 6 | U20604783 | ex PZ-PVU | |

## SURINAM AIRWAYS | Surinam (PY/SLM)
## Paramaribo-Zanderij International/Zorg en Hoop (PBM/ORG)

| | | | | | | |
|---|---|---|---|---|---|---|
| ☐ | PZ-TCM | Boeing 747-306M | 23508/657 | ex PH-BUW | Ronald Elwin Kappel | [MZJ] |
| ☐ | PZ-TCN | Boeing 737-36N | 28668/2890 | ex N668AN | | |
| ☐ | PZ-TCO | Boeing 737-36N | 28669/2897 | ex N669AN | | |
| ☐ | PZ-TCP | Airbus A340-311 | 049 | ex F-GLZG | | |

## P2- PAPUA NEW GUINEA (Independent State of Papua New Guinea)

### AIR NIUGINI | Niugini (PX/ANG) | Port Moresby (POM)

| | | | | |
|---|---|---|---|---|
| ☐ | P2-ANK | de Havilland DHC-8Q-202 | 461 | ex C-GFBW |
| ☐ | P2-ANL | de Havilland DHC-8-102 | 153 | ex D-BOBO |
| ☐ | P2-ANM | de Havilland DHC-8Q-314 | 523 | ex D-BPAD |
| ☐ | P2-ANN | de Havilland DHC-8-315 | 401 | ex JY-RWB |
| ☐ | P2-ANO | de Havilland DHC-8-311A | 252 | ex D-BOBU |
| ☐ | P2-ANP | de Havilland DHC-8-102 | 177 | ex D-BOBY |
| ☐ | P2-ANX | de Havilland DHC-8Q-202 | 463 | ex D-BHAL |
| ☐ | P2-ANZ | de Havilland DHC-8Q-201 | 421 | ex N986HA |
| ☐ | P2-PXS | de Havilland DHC-8-402 | 4262 | ex C-FXAW | ♦ |
| ☐ | P2-PXT | de Havilland DHC-8-402Q | 4329 | ex C-GNIU |
| ☐ | P2-PXU | de Havilland DHC-8-402Q | 4316 | ex C-GEHE |
| ☐ | P2-ANC | Fokker 100 | 11471 | ex PH-MXW |
| ☐ | P2-AND | Fokker 100 | 11473 | ex PT-MRQ |
| ☐ | P2-ANE | Fokker 100 | 11264 | ex PH-THY |
| ☐ | P2-ANF | Fokker 100 | 11351 | ex PH-FDI |
| ☐ | P2-ANH | Fokker 100 | 11301 | ex C-GPNL |
| ☐ | P2-ANQ | Fokker 100 | 11451 | ex PH-ZDJ |
| ☐ | P2-ANA | Boeing 767-366ER | 24541/275 | ex TF-LLA | <ICE |
| ☐ | P2-PXV | Boeing 767-341ER | 30341/768 | ex A6-JBD | <ICE♦ |
| ☐ | P2-PXW | Boeing 767-383ER | 25365/395 | ex TF-FIB | <ICE♦ |
| ☐ | TF-FIC | Boeing 757-23N | 30735/931 | ex M-ABDG | .<ICE♦ |

### AIR SANGA | | Port Moresby (POM)

| | | | | | |
|---|---|---|---|---|---|
| ☐ | P2-ASZ | Pacific Aerospace 750XL | 179 | ex ZK-KBQ | ♦ |

### AIRLINES OF PAPUA NEW GUINEA | (CG/TOK) | Port Moresby (POM)

| | | | | | |
|---|---|---|---|---|---|
| ☐ | P2-EMO | de Havilland DHC-6 Twin Otter 300 | 726 | ex N726JM | ♦ |
| ☐ | P2-MCC | de Havilland DHC-6 Twin Otter 200 | 218 | ex VH-IPD |
| ☐ | P2-MCD | de Havilland DHC-6 Twin Otter 300 | 592 | ex C-GOVG |
| ☐ | P2-MCE | de Havilland DHC-6 Twin Otter 300 | 673 | ex C-GHRB |
| ☐ | P2-MCF | de Havilland DHC-6 Twin Otter 300 | 741 | ex C-GRBY |
| ☐ | P2-MCR | de Havilland DHC-6 Twin Otter 310 | 219 | ex P2-MFY |
| ☐ | P2-MCS | de Havilland DHC-6 Twin Otter 310 | 516 | ex 5W-PAH |
| ☐ | P2-MCV | de Havilland DHC-6 Twin Otter 300 | 280 | ex H4-FNT | ♦ |
| ☐ | P2-MCX | de Havilland DHC-6 Twin Otter 300 | 703 | ex YJ-RV8 | ♦ |
| ☐ | P2- | de Havilland DHC-6 Twin Otter 300 | 330 | ex N901WW | ♦ |
| ☐ | P2-MCG | de Havilland DHC-8-102 | 006 | ex C-GJCB |
| ☐ | P2-MCH | de Havilland DHC-8-102 | 012 | ex C-GPYD |
| ☐ | P2-MCI | de Havilland DHC-8-102 | 197 | ex ZK-NET |
| ☐ | P2-MCK | de Havilland DHC-8-102 | 041 | ex VH-QQD | ♦ |
| ☐ | P2-MCL | de Havilland DHC-8-102 | 027 | ex VH-WZJ |
| ☐ | P2-MCP | de Havilland DHC-8-102 | 033 | ex VH-TNX | >SOL |
| ☐ | P2-MCQ | de Havilland DHC-8-103A | 243 | ex VH-TNW |
| ☐ | P2-MCT | de Havilland DHC-8-102 | 135 | ex VH-QQH |
| ☐ | P2-MCU | de Havilland DHC-8-102 | 208 | ex VH-QQJ |
| ☐ | P2-MCW | de Havilland DHC-8-102 | 067 | ex VH-QQI | ♦ |
| ☐ | P2- | de Havilland DHC-8-102 | 211 | ex C-FNCG | ♦ |
| ☐ | P2-CHI | Boeing Vertol 234UT Chinook | MJ-003 | ex N237CH | <WCO |

### ASIA PACIFIC AIRLINES | | Tabubil (TBG)

| | | | | | | |
|---|---|---|---|---|---|---|
| ☐ | P2-NAX | de Havilland DHC-8-103 | 229 | ex VH-JSI | |
| ☐ | P2-NAZ | de Havilland DHC-8-102 | 316 | ex C-GFUM | Spirit of Tabubil | <NJS |

### CENTRAL AIR TRANSPORT | | Port Moresby (POM)

| | | | | | |
|---|---|---|---|---|---|
| ☐ | P2-ALM | Britten-Norman BN-2A-26 Islander | 124 | ex P2-NAA | |

### CENTRAL AVIATION SERVICES

| | | | | | |
|---|---|---|---|---|---|
| ☐ | P2-BWC | Pacific Aerospace 750XL | 136 | ex ZK-JQQ | ♦ |
| ☐ | P2-BWE | Pacific Aerospace 750XL | 161 | ex ZK-KAU | ♦ |
| ☐ | P2-BWF | Pacific Aerospace 750XL | 159 | ex ZK-KAX | ♦ |

### COLUMBIA HELICOPTERS

| | | | | | |
|---|---|---|---|---|---|
| ☐ | P2-CHJ | Boeing-Vertol BV-234UT | MJ-022 | | |
| ☐ | P2-CHK | Boeing-Vertol BV-234UT | MJ-006 | | ♦ |

## EMERALD AIR

| | | | | |
|---|---|---|---|---|
| ☐ | P2-EMO | de Havilland DHC-6 Twin Otter 300 | 726 | ex N726JM |

## HEVI-LIFT (IU) Mount Hagen/Cairns (HGU/CNS)

| | | | | | |
|---|---|---|---|---|---|
| ☐ | P2-HCA | Bell 206L-1 LongRanger II | 45337 | ex VH-BJX | |
| ☐ | P2-HCB | Bell 206L-1 LongRanger II | 45404 | ex VH-HHS | |
| ☐ | P2-HCC | Bell 206L-1 LongRanger III | 45427 | ex N5019T | |
| ☐ | P2-HCD | Bell 206L-1 LongRanger III | 45528 | ex C-GGHZ | |
| ☐ | P2-HCM | Bell 206L-1 LongRanger III | 45608 | ex P2-NHE | |
| ☐ | P2-HCO | Bell 206L-3 LongRanger III | 51178 | ex N3204K | |
| ☐ | P2-HCU | Bell 206L-3 LongRanger III | 51416 | ex N254EV | |
| ☐ | P2-HCY | Bell 206L-3 LongRanger III | 45333 | ex P2-IHA | |
| ☐ | P2-HLT | Bell 206L-3 LongRanger III | 51387 | ex VH-HQT | ♦ |
| ☐ | P2-HCJ | Bell 212 | 30799 | ex VH-EMJ | |
| ☐ | P2-HCK | Bell 212 | 30583 | ex N212SX | |
| ☐ | P2-HCQ | Bell 212 | 30860 | ex JA9528 | |
| ☐ | P2-HCW | Bell 212 | 30520 | ex PK-EBO | |
| ☐ | P2-HLV | Bell 212 | 30508 | ex VH-SYV | |
| ☐ | P2-KSB | de Havilland DHC-6 Twin Otter 300 | 485 | ex VH-RPU | ♦ |
| ☐ | P2-KSF | de Havilland DHC-6 Twin Otter 300 | 528 | ex PK-HCF | |
| ☐ | P2-KSG | de Havilland DHC-6 Twin Otter 300 | 509 | ex VH-WPT | ♦ |
| ☐ | P2-KSI | de Havilland DHC-6 Twin Otter 300 | 706 | ex VH-HPY | ♦ |
| ☐ | P2-KSS | de Havilland DHC-6 Twin Otter 300 | 634 | ex PK-LTV | ♦ |
| ☐ | P2-KST | de Havilland DHC-6 Twin Otter 300 | 520 | ex YJ-RVS | ♦ |
| ☐ | ER-MHL | Mil Mi-8MTV-1 | 95721 | ex RA-25105 | |
| ☐ | P2-HCA | Bell 407 | 53054 | ex N417AL | |
| ☐ | P2-HCB | Bell 407 | 53141 | ex N437AL | |
| ☐ | P2-HCL | Aérospatiale AS.350B2 Ecureuil | 3374 | ex SE-JFO | |
| ☐ | P2-HCS | Bell 412HP | 33160 | ex VH-HQQ | |
| ☐ | P2-HCV | Bell 412EP | 36424 | ex N416EV | |
| ☐ | P2-HCY | Aérospatiale AS.350B3 Ecureuil | 3242 | ex JA6292 | |
| ☐ | P2-HCZ | Bell 412HP | 36024 | ex VT-AZE | |
| ☐ | P2-KSJ | ATR42-320 | 0096 | ex (P2-HLB) | ♦ |
| ☐ | P2-MHM | Mil Mi-8MTV-1 | 95881 | ex ER-MHM | ♦ |
| ☐ | P2- | Bell 412EP | 30381 | ex N413EV | |

## LYNDEN AIR CARGO NIUGINI Lae (LAE)

| | | | | | |
|---|---|---|---|---|---|
| ☐ | P2-LAC | Lockheed L-382G Hercules | 4676 | ex N406LC | ♦ |

## NATIONAL AVIATION SERVICES

| | | | | | |
|---|---|---|---|---|---|
| ☐ | P2-MBH | Bell 214B-1 | 28063 | ex N214BH | ♦ |
| ☐ | P2-MLJ | Bell 214B-1 | 28066 | ex N214JL | ♦ |
| ☐ | P2-MSA | Bell 214B-1 | 28065 | ex N28065 | ♦ |
| ☐ | P2-NAV | Britten-Norman BN-2A-26 Islander | 81 | ex VH-CSU | ♦ |
| ☐ | P2-NCA | Pacific Aerospace 750XL | 134 | ex ZK-JQO | ♦ |

## NORTH COAST AVIATION (N9/AOH) Madang (MAG)

| | | | | | |
|---|---|---|---|---|---|
| ☐ | P2-DWA | Britten-Norman BN-2A-26 Islander | 113 | ex VH-EQE | |
| ☐ | P2-IAC | Britten-Norman BN-2A-21 Islander | 425 | ex P2-KAF | |
| ☐ | P2-ISA | Britten-Norman BN-2A-20 Islander | 758 | ex P2-SWB | |
| ☐ | P2-ISB | Britten-Norman BN-2A-20 Islander | 709 | ex P2-MKW | wfs |
| ☐ | P2-ISM | Britten-Norman BN-2A-20 Islander | 227 | ex VH-EDI | |
| ☐ | P2-NCE | Britten-Norman BN-2A-20 Islander | 768 | ex P2-IAD | |
| ☐ | P2-SAC | Britten-Norman BN-2A-20 Islander | 94 | ex P2-DNY | |
| ☐ | P2-DQU | Cessna U206B Super Skywagon | U206-0892 | ex VH-DQU | |
| ☐ | P2-GKB | Cessna 402 | 402-0141 | ex VH-GKB | |
| ☐ | P2-IDK | Cessna U206G Super Skywagon | U206-1418 | ex P2-TNK | |
| ☐ | P2-IDM | Cessna U206F Stationair | U20603126 | ex P2-SIA | |
| ☐ | P2-NCD | Cessna 402B | 402B1027 | ex VH-USV | |
| ☐ | P2-OHS | Cessna P206B Super Skylane | P206-0392 | ex P2-HCM | |

## REGIONAL AIR (QT) Madang (MAG)

| | | | | | |
|---|---|---|---|---|---|
| ☐ | P2-KSA | Beech 200 Super King Air | BB-1527 | ex N170W | |
| ☐ | P2-KST | de Havilland DHC-6 Twin Otter 300 | 520 | ex YJ-RV5 | |

## SIL AVIATION Aiyura (AYU)

| | | | | | |
|---|---|---|---|---|---|
| ☐ | P2-SIA | Beech B200C Super King Air | BL-39 | ex VH-FDR | |
| ☐ | P2-SIG | Cessna TU206G Stationair 6 | U20606029 | ex VH-XAA | Robertson STOL conversion |

| | | | | | |
|---|---|---|---|---|---|
| ☐ | P2-SIJ | Cessna TU206G Stationair 6 | U20605805 | ex N5491X | Robertson STOL conversion |
| ☐ | P2-SIT | Cessna TU206G Stationair 6 | U20606158 | ex N181PK | Robertson STOL conversion |

## SOUTHWEST AIR — Mendi (MDU)

| | | | | | |
|---|---|---|---|---|---|
| ☐ | P2-SHA | Bell 206L-3 LongRanger III | 51533 | ex VH-IRE | |
| ☐ | P2-SWE | de Havilland DHC-6 Twin Otter 300 | 480 | ex P2-RDL | |
| ☐ | P2-SWF | Embraer EMB.110P1 Bandeirante | 110237 | ex N691RA | [BNE] |

## SUNBIRD AVIATION — Port Moresby (POM)

| | | | | | |
|---|---|---|---|---|---|
| ☐ | P2-SBA | Britten-Norman BN-2T Islander | 2138 | ex P2-SIV | ♦ |
| ☐ | P2-SBB | Britten-Norman BN-2T Islander | 880 | ex N121MT | ♦ |

## TRANSNIUGINI AIRWAYS — Port Moresby (POM)

| | | | | | |
|---|---|---|---|---|---|
| ☐ | P2-TND | Britten-Norman BN-2A-21 Islander | 813 | ex P2-COD | |
| ☐ | P2-TNT | Pacific Aerospace 750XL | 143 | ex ZK-JNG | ♦ |

## TRAVEL AIR

| | | | | | |
|---|---|---|---|---|---|
| ☐ | P2-TAH | Fokker 50 | 20122 | ex PH-FZF | ♦ |
| ☐ | P2-TAG | Fokker 50 | 20177 | ex PH-TAG | ♦ |
| ☐ | P2-TAF | Fokker 50 | 20192 | ex PH-LMT | ♦ |
| ☐ | P2-TAE | Fokker 50 | 20202 | ex PH-FZG | ♦ |

## TROPICAIR — Port Moresby (POM)

| | | | | | |
|---|---|---|---|---|---|
| ☐ | P2-AMH | Cessna 208B Caravan I | 208B0785 | ex N785SC | |
| ☐ | P2-BEN | Cessna 208B Caravan I | 208B0424 | ex VH-LSA | |
| ☐ | P2-MAX | Beech B200 Super King Air | BB-1695 | | ♦ |
| ☐ | P2-SAH | Cessna 208B Caravan I | 208B1263 | ex N41149 | |
| ☐ | P2-SMA | Cessna U206G Stationair 6 | U20604227 | ex P2-AAC | |

## VAN AIR — Vanimo (VAI)

| | | | | | |
|---|---|---|---|---|---|
| ☐ | P2-VAB | Britten-Norman BN-2A-20 Islander | 759 | ex P2-MFZ | |

## P4- ARUBA

### FLY ARUBA

| | | | | | |
|---|---|---|---|---|---|
| ☐ | P4-FAA | Airbus A320-212 | 407 | ex N407BV | [AUA]♦ |

### INSEL AIR ARUBA — (NLU)

| | | | | | |
|---|---|---|---|---|---|
| ☐ | PJ-KVG | Fokker 50 | 20211 | ex PH-KVG | ♦ |
| ☐ | PJ-KVH | Fokker 50 | 20217 | ex PH-KVH | wfs♦ |
| ☐ | PJ-KVI | Fokker 50 | 20218 | ex PH-KVI | ♦ |
| ☐ | PJ-KVK | Fokker 50 | 20219 | ex PH-KVK | ♦ |
| ☐ | PJ-MDD | McDonnell-Douglas MD-82 | 49972/1757 | ex N972AG | |

### TIARA AIR — (3P/TNM) — Aruba (AUA)

| | | | | | |
|---|---|---|---|---|---|
| ☐ | P4-TIA | Short SD.3-60 | SH3619 | ex C-GPCG | |
| ☐ | P4-TIB | Short SD.3-60 | SH3621 | ex C-GPCN | |
| ☐ | P4-TIC | Short SD.3-60 | SH3614 | ex HP-1315APP | [AUA]♦ |
| ☐ | P4-TID | Learjet 35A | 35A-200 | ex N200LJ | ♦ |
| ☐ | P4-TIE | Boeing 737-322 | 24249/1638 | ex N189AQ | ♦ |

## RA- RUSSIA (Russian Federation)

### ABAKAN-AVIA — Abakan-Avia (ABG) — Abakan (ABA)

| | | | | | |
|---|---|---|---|---|---|
| ☐ | RA-76457 | Ilyushin Il-76T | 093421621 | ex CCCP-76457 | |
| ☐ | RA-76504 | Ilyushin Il-76T | 073411328 | | ♦ |
| ☐ | RA-76780 | Ilyushin Il-76T | 0013430901 | ex CCCP-76780 all-white | |
| ☐ | RA-76799 | Ilyushin Il-76TD | 1003403075 | | <ESL♦ |

### AERO RENT — Aeromaster (NRO) — Moscow-Vnukovo (VKO)

| | | | | | |
|---|---|---|---|---|---|
| ☐ | RA-21506 | Yakovlev Yak-40KD | 9840259 | ex CCCP-21506 | VIP |
| ☐ | RA-76484 | Ilyushin Il-76TD | 0063469081 | | ♦ |
| ☐ | RA-85551 | Tupolev Tu-154B-2 | 82A551 | | ♦ |
| ☐ | RA-85716 | Tupolev Tu-154M | 91A892 | | ♦ |

## AEROBRATSK — Aerobra (BRP) — Bratsk (BTK)

| | | | | |
|---|---|---|---|---|
| ☐ | RA-06114 | Mil Mi-8T | 7692 | | ◆ |
| ☐ | RA-22856 | Mil Mi-8T | 98415350 | ex CCCP-22856 |
| ☐ | RA-24261 | Mil Mi-8T | 98734147 | ex CCCP-24261 |
| ☐ | RA-87937 | Yakovlev Yak-40 | 9410933 |
| ☐ | RA-88205 | Yakovlev Yak-40 | 9630749 | ex CCCP-88205 |
| ☐ | RA-88215 | Yakovlev Yak-40K | 9630150 | ex CCCP-88215 |

## AEROFLOT PLUS — (PLS) — Moscow-Sheremetyevo (SVO)

| | | | | | |
|---|---|---|---|---|---|
| ☐ | RA-65559 | Tupolev Tu-134A | 7349909 | ex CCCP-65559 | VIP |
| ☐ | RA-65623 | Tupolev Tu-134AK | 7349985 | | ◆ |

## AEROFLOT RUSSIAN AIRLINES — Aeroflot (SU/AFL) — Moscow-Sheremetyevo (SVO)

Member of Skyteam

| | | | | | |
|---|---|---|---|---|---|
| ☐ | VP-BDM | Airbus A319-111 | 2069 | ex D-AVYJ | A Borodin |
| ☐ | VP-BDN | Airbus A319-111 | 2072 | ex D-AVYL | A Dargomyzhsky |
| ☐ | VP-BDO | Airbus A319-111 | 2091 | ex D-AVWU | I Stravinsky |
| ☐ | VP-BUK | Airbus A319-111 | 3281 | ex D-AVYP | YU Senkevich |
| ☐ | VP-BUN | Airbus A319-111 | 3298 | ex D-AVYI | |
| ☐ | VP-BUO | Airbus A319-111 | 3336 | ex D-AVYS | |
| ☐ | VP-BWA | Airbus A319-111 | 2052 | ex D-AVYA | S Prokofiev |
| ☐ | VP-BWG | Airbus A319-111 | 2093 | ex D-AVYE | A Aleksandrov |
| ☐ | VP-BWJ | Airbus A319-111 | 2179 | ex D-AVYU | A Shnitke |
| ☐ | VP-BWK | Airbus A319-111 | 2222 | ex D-AVYI | S Taneyev |
| ☐ | VP-BWL | Airbus A319-111 | 2243 | ex D-AVWV | A Grechaninov |
| ☐ | VQ-BBA | Airbus A319-111 | 3794 | ex D-AVXM | S Cheliuskin |
| ☐ | VQ-BBD | Airbus A319-111 | 3838 | ex D-AVYP | V Golovnin |
| ☐ | VQ-BCO | Airbus A319-111 | 3942 | ex D-AVWR | A Hachaturian |
| ☐ | VQ-BCP | Airbus A319-111 | 3998 | ex D-AVYZ | D Mendeleev |
| ☐ | VP-BDK | Airbus A320-214 | 2106 | ex F-WWDR | G Sviridov |
| ☐ | VP-BKC | Airbus A320-214 | 3545 | ex F-WWIT | I Kruzenshtern |
| ☐ | VP-BKX | Airbus A320-214 | 3410 | ex F-WWIJ | G Sedov |
| ☐ | VP-BKY | Airbus A320-214 | 3511 | ex F-WWBZ | M Rostropovich |
| ☐ | VP-BME | Airbus A320-214 | 3699 | ex F-WWBO | N Mikluho-Maklay |
| ☐ | VP-BMF | Airbus A320-214 | 3711 | ex F-WWIV | G Shelihov |
| ☐ | VP-BQP | Airbus A320-214 | 2875 | ex F-WWBJ | A Rublev |
| ☐ | VP-BQU | Airbus A320-214 | 3373 | ex F-WWDG | A Nikitin |
| ☐ | VP-BQV | Airbus A320-214 | 2920 | ex F-WWDY | V Vasnetsov |
| ☐ | VP-BQW | Airbus A320-214 | 2947 | ex F-WWBV | V Vereshchagin |
| ☐ | VP-BRX | Airbus A320-214 | 3063 | ex F-WWDZ | V Surikov |
| ☐ | VP-BRY | Airbus A320-214 | 3052 | ex F-WWDT | K Brulloff |
| ☐ | VP-BRZ | Airbus A320-214 | 3157 | ex F-WWDM | V Serov |
| ☐ | VP-BWD | Airbus A320-214 | 2116 | ex F-WWDY | A Aliabiev |
| ☐ | VP-BWE | Airbus A320-214 | 2133 | ex F-WWDX | N Rimsky-Korsakov |
| ☐ | VP-BWF | Airbus A320-214 | 2144 | ex F-WWBY | D Shostakovich |
| ☐ | VP-BWH | Airbus A320-214 | 2151 | ex F-WWIR | M Balakirev |
| ☐ | VP-BWI | Airbus A320-214 | 2163 | ex F-WWBD | A Glazunov |
| ☐ | VP-BWM | Airbus A320-214 | 2233 | ex F-WWII | S Rackhmaninov |
| ☐ | VP-BZO | Airbus A320-214 | 3574 | ex F-WWBK | V Bering |
| ☐ | VP-BZP | Airbus A320-214 | 3631 | ex D-AVYG | E Haborov |
| ☐ | VP-BZQ | Airbus A320-214 | 3627 | ex F-WWIS | Yu. Lisiansky |
| ☐ | VP-BZR | Airbus A320-214 | 3640 | ex F-WWBR | F Bellinghausen |
| ☐ | VP-BZS | Airbus A320-214 | 3644 | ex F-WWBU | M Lazarev |
| ☐ | VQ-BAX | Airbus A320-214 | 3778 | ex F-WWIM | G Nevelskoy |
| ☐ | VQ-BAY | Airbus A320-214 | 3786 | ex D-AVVL | S Krasheninnikov |
| ☐ | VQ-BAZ | Airbus A320-214 | 3789 | ex F-WWBC | V Obruchev |
| ☐ | VQ-BBB | Airbus A320-214 | 3823 | ex F-WWIT | Yu Gagarin |
| ☐ | VQ-BBC | Airbus A320-214 | 3835 | ex F-WWBI | N Przhevalsky |
| ☐ | VQ-BCM | Airbus A320-214 | 3923 | ex F-WWBN | G Titov |
| ☐ | VQ-BCN | Airbus A320-214 | 3954 | ex F-WWBV | V Chelomey |
| ☐ | VQ-BEH | Airbus A320-214 | 4133 | ex F-WWIS | I Pavlov |
| ☐ | VQ-BEJ | Airbus A320-214 | 4160 | ex D-AVVO | I Kurchatov |
| ☐ | VQ-BHL | Airbus A320-214 | 4453 | ex F-WWIX | S Vavilov |
| ☐ | VQ-BHN | Airbus A320-214 | 4498 | ex D-AUBL | N Lobachevsky |
| ☐ | VQ-BIR | Airbus A320-214 | 4625 | ex F-WWBZ | | ◆ |
| ☐ | VQ-BIT | Airbus A320-214 | 4656 | ex D-AXAB | | ◆ |
| ☐ | VQ-BIU | Airbus A320-214 | 4684 | ex D-AUBA | | ◆ |
| ☐ | VQ-BIV | Airbus A320-214 | 4649 | ex F-WWDP | A Kolmogorov | ◆ |
| ☐ | VQ-BIW | Airbus A320-214 | 4579 | ex D-AUBZ | V Glushko | ◆ |
| ☐ | VQ-BKS | Airbus A320-214 | 4692 | ex F-WWDI | | ◆ |
| ☐ | VQ-BKT | Airbus A320-214 | 4712 | ex F-WWBR | | ◆ |
| ☐ | VQ-BKU | Airbus A320-214 | 4835 | ex D-AXAN | | ◆ |
| ☐ | VP-BQR | Airbus A321-211 | 2903 | ex D-AVZD | I Repin |
| ☐ | VP-BQS | Airbus A321-211 | 2912 | ex D-AVZL | I Kramskoi |
| ☐ | VP-BQT | Airbus A321-211 | 2965 | ex D-AVZE | I Shishkin |

| | | | | | | |
|---|---|---|---|---|---|---|
| ☐ | VP-BQX | Airbus A321-211 | 2957 | ex D-AVZU | I Ayvazovsky | |
| ☐ | VP-BRW | Airbus A321-211 | 3191 | ex D-AVZW | N Rerih | |
| ☐ | VP-BUM | Airbus A321-211 | 3267 | ex D-AVZQ | A Deineka | |
| ☐ | VP-BUP | Airbus A321-211 | 3334 | ex D-AVZY | M Shagal | |
| ☐ | VP-BWN | Airbus A321-211 | 2330 | ex D-AVZR | A Skriabin | |
| ☐ | VP-BWO | Airbus A321-211 | 2337 | ex D-AVZS | P Chaikovsky | |
| ☐ | VP-BWP | Airbus A321-211 | 2342 | ex D-AVZT | M Musorgsky | |
| ☐ | VQ-BEA | Airbus A321-211 | 4058 | ex D-AZAS | I Michurin | |
| ☐ | VQ-BED | Airbus A321-211 | 4074 | ex D-AVZT | N Pirogov | |
| ☐ | VQ-BEE | Airbus A321-211 | 4099 | ex D-AZAA | I Sechenov | |
| ☐ | VQ-BEF | Airbus A321-211 | 4103 | ex D-AZAC | N Zhukovsky | |
| ☐ | VQ-BEG | Airbus A321-211 | 4116 | ex D-AZAF | K Tsiolkovsky | |
| ☐ | VQ-BEI | Airbus A321-211 | 4148 | ex D-AVZS | S Korelov | |
| ☐ | VQ-BHK | Airbus A321-211 | 4461 | ex D-AVZB | M Keldysh | |
| ☐ | VQ-BHM | Airbus A321-211 | 4500 | ex D-AVZG | N Vavilov | |
| ☐ | VQ-BOH | Airbus A321-211 | 5044 | ex D-AZAP | A Prokorov | ♦ |
| ☐ | VQ-BOI | Airbus A321-211 | 5059 | ex D-AZAS | N Semenov | ♦ |
| | | | | | | |
| ☐ | VP-BLX | Airbus A330-243 | 963 | ex F-WWYJ | E. Sveetlanov | |
| ☐ | VP-BLY | Airbus A330-243 | 973 | ex F-WWKA | V Vysctsky | |
| ☐ | VQ-BBE | Airbus A330-243 | 1014 | ex F-WWKU | I Brodsky | |
| ☐ | VQ-BBF | Airbus A330-243 | 1045 | ex F-WWYB | A Griboedov | |
| ☐ | VQ-BBG | Airbus A330-243 | 1047 | ex F-WWKD | N Gogol | |
| ☐ | VQ-BCQ | Airbus A330-343E | 1058 | ex F-WWYX | | |
| ☐ | VQ-BCU | Airbus A330-343E | 1065 | ex F-WWYJ | V Mayakovsky | |
| ☐ | VQ-BCV | Airbus A330-343E | 1072 | ex F-WWYK | B Pasternak | |
| ☐ | VQ-BEK | Airbus A330-343E | 1077 | ex F-WWKN | A Tvardovskiy | |
| ☐ | VQ-BEL | Airbus A330-343E | 1103 | ex F-WWYR | F Tyutchev | |
| ☐ | VQ-BMV | Airbus A330-343E | 1284 | ex F-WWYA | P Kapitsa | |
| ☐ | VQ-BMX | Airbus A330-343E | 1299 | ex F-WWKQ | A Sakharov | ♦ |
| ☐ | VQ-BMY | Airbus A330-343E | 1301 | ex F-WWYL | I Frank | o/o♦ |
| ☐ | VQ-BNS | Airbus A330-343E | 1264 | ex F-WWYT | A Bakulev | ♦ |
| ☐ | VQ-BQX | Airbus A330-343E | 1212 | ex F-WWYI | | ♦ |
| ☐ | VQ-BQY | Airbus A330-343E | 1247 | ex F-WWYQ | | ♦ |
| ☐ | VQ-BQZ | Airbus A330-343E | 1270 | ex F-WWYG | N Burdenko | ♦ |
| | | | | | | |
| ☐ | VP-BAV | Boeing 767-36NER | 30107/761 | | L Tolstoy | |
| ☐ | VP-BAX | Boeing 767-36NER | 30109/767 | | F Dostoevsky | |
| ☐ | VP-BAY | Boeing 767-36NER | 30110/775 | | I Turgenev | |
| ☐ | VP-BAZ | Boeing 767-36NER | 30111/776 | | N Nekrasov | |
| ☐ | VP-BDI | Boeing 767-38AER | 29618/792 | ex N618SH | A Pushkin | |
| ☐ | VP-BWU | Boeing 767-3T7ER | 25076/366 | ex N601EV | I Bunin | |
| ☐ | VP-BWV | Boeing 767-3T7ER | 25117/370 | ex N602EV | A Kuprin | |
| ☐ | VP-BWW | Boeing 767-306ER | 27959/609 | ex PH-BZF | | |
| ☐ | VP-BWX | Boeing 767-306ER | 27960/625 | ex PH-BZG | | |
| | | | | | | |
| ☐ | RA-96005 | Ilyushin Il-96-300 | 74393201002 | ex CCCP-96005 | V Chkalov | |
| ☐ | RA-96007 | Ilyushin Il-96-300 | 74393201004 | | A Mayorov | |
| ☐ | RA-96008 | Ilyushin Il-96-300 | 74393201005 | | IA Moiseyev | |
| ☐ | RA-96010 | Ilyushin Il-96-300 | 74393201007 | | Nikolaj Karpajev | |
| ☐ | RA-96011 | Ilyushin Il-96-300 | 74393201008 | | K Kokkinaki | |
| ☐ | RA-96015 | Ilyushin Il-96-300 | 74393201012 | | M Gromov | |
| ☐ | RA- | Ilyushin Il-96-300 | | | | o/o |
| ☐ | RA- | Ilyushin Il-96-300 | | | | o/o |
| ☐ | RA- | Ilyushin Il-96-300 | | | | o/o |
| ☐ | RA- | Ilyushin Il-96-300 | | | | o/o |
| ☐ | RA- | Ilyushin Il-96-300 | | | | o/o |
| ☐ | RA- | Ilyushin Il-96-300 | | | | o/o |
| | | | | | | |
| ☐ | RA-89001 | Sukhoi Superjet 100-95 | 95008 | | M Vodopyanov | |
| ☐ | RA-89002 | Sukhoi Superjet 100 | 95010 | | | |
| ☐ | RA-89003 | Sukhoi Superjet 100 | 95011 | | | |
| ☐ | RA-89004 | Sukhoi Superjet 100 | 95012 | | | |
| ☐ | RA-89005 | Sukhoi Superjet 100 | 95013 | | | ♦ |
| ☐ | RA-89006 | Sukhoi Superjet 100 | 95014 | | | o/o♦ |
| ☐ | RA-89007 | Sukhoi Superjet 100 | 95015 | | | o/o♦ |
| ☐ | RA- | Sukhoi Superjet 100 | | | | o/o |
| ☐ | RA- | Sukhoi Superjet 100 | | | | o/o |
| | | | | | | |
| ☐ | RA-85627 | Tupolev Tu-154M | 87A756 | ex CCCP-85627 | | |
| ☐ | RA-85735 | Tupolev Tu-154M | 92A917 | ex B-2627 | | |
| ☐ | RA-85760 | Tupolev Tu-154M | 92A942 | ex EW-85760 | | |
| ☐ | RA-85765 | Tupolev Tu-154M | 90A832 | ex LZ-HMN | | |
| ☐ | VP-BDP | McDonnell-Douglas MD-11F | 48502/520 | ex N774BC | | |
| ☐ | VP-BDQ | McDonnell-Douglas MD-11F | 48504/548 | ex N702BC | | |
| ☐ | VP-BDR | McDonnell-Douglas MD-11F | 48503/528 | ex N725BC | | |

## AEROKUZBASS  Novokuznetsk (NKZ)  Novokuznetsk (NOZ)

| | | | | | |
|---|---|---|---|---|---|
| ☐ | RA-85747 | Tupolev Tu-154M | 92A930 | ex EP-EAD | >IRB as EP-MBT |
| ☐ | RA-85749 | Tupolev Tu-154M | 92A931 | ex EP-MBM | >IRB as EP-MBQ |

| | | | | | |
|---|---|---|---|---|---|
| ☐ | RA-22725 | Mil Mi-8T | 98308700 | ex CCCP-22725 | |
| ☐ | RA-24140 | Mil Mi-8T | 98841391 | ex CCCP-24140 | |
| ☐ | RA-24430 | Mil Mi-8T | 98625661 | ex CCCP-24430 | |

## AEROMOSKOVIA

| | | | | | |
|---|---|---|---|---|---|
| ☐ | RA-65065 | Tupolev Tu-134AK-3 | 49890 | | ♦ |
| ☐ | RA-65096 | Tupolev Tu-134A-3 | 60257 | | ♦ |
| ☐ | RA-65102 | Tupolev Tu-134A-3 | 60267 | | ♦ |
| ☐ | RA-65108 | Tupolev Tu-134A-3 | 60332 | | ♦ |
| ☐ | RA-65721 | Tupolev Tu-134A-3M | 66130 | | ♦ |
| ☐ | RA-65784 | Tupolev Tu-134A-3 | 62715 | | ♦ |

## AIR BASHKORTOSTAN · (BBT) · Ufa (UFA)

| | | | | | |
|---|---|---|---|---|---|
| ☐ | RA-73011 | Boeing 757-230 | 25439/437 | ex D-ABNL | <MOV |
| ☐ | RA-73012 | Boeing 757-230 | 25440/443 | ex D-ABNM | <MOV |
| ☐ | RA-73015 | Boeing 757-230 | 25901/464 | ex D-ABNO | <MOV |

## AIRBRIDGE CARGO · Volga Dnepr (RU/ABW) · MoscowSheremetyevo(SVO)

| | | | | | |
|---|---|---|---|---|---|
| ☐ | VP-BIG | Boeing 747-46NERF | 35420/1395 | ex N5022E | |
| ☐ | VP-BIK | Boeing 747-46NERF | 35421/1400 | | |
| ☐ | VP-BIM | Boeing 747-4HAERF | 35237/1402 | | |
| ☐ | VQ-BFX | Boeing 747-428ERF | 33096/1317 | ex F-GIUB | |
| ☐ | VQ-BGY | Boeing 747-428ERF | 33097/1361 | ex F-GIUE | |
| ☐ | VQ-BHE | Boeing 747-4KZF | 36784/1411 | ex N384NC | |
| ☐ | VQ-BIA | Boeing 747-4KZF | 36785/1418 | ex N385NY | |
| ☐ | VQ-BJB | Boeing 747-446F | 33749/1352 | ex N402AL | ♦ |
| ☐ | VQ-BGZ | Boeing 747-8HVF | 37580/1430 | | o/o |
| ☐ | VP-BIC | Boeing 747-329 (SF) | 24837/810 | ex TF-ARY | |
| ☐ | VP-BII | Boeing 747-281F | 24576/818 | ex JA8191 | |
| ☐ | VP-BIJ | Boeing 747-281F | 25171/886 | ex JA8194 | |
| ☐ | VQ-BLQ | Boeing 747-8HVF | 37581/1448 | | ♦ |
| ☐ | VQ-BLR | Boeing 747-8HVF | 37668/1452 | ex N1788B | ♦ |
| ☐ | VQ-BRH | Boeing 747-8HVF | 37669/ | | o/o♦ |
| ☐ | RA-64051 | Tupolev Tu-204-120C | 64051 | | o/o |
| ☐ | RA-64052 | Tupolev Tu-204-120C | 64052 | | o/o |

## AIRSTARS AIRWAYS · Morozov (PL/ASE) · Moscow-Domodedovo (DME)

| | | | | | |
|---|---|---|---|---|---|
| ☐ | RA-76476 | Ilyushin Il-76TD | 0043451528 | ex CCCP-76476 | |
| ☐ | RA-76750 | Ilyushin Il-76TD | 0083485561 | ex CCCP-76750 | |
| ☐ | RA-76843 | Ilyushin Il-76TD | 1013408269 | | |
| ☐ | RA-96002 | Ilyushin Il-96-300 | 74393201001 | | ♦ |

## AIR TRANZIT

| | | | | | |
|---|---|---|---|---|---|
| ☐ | RA-67678 | LET L-410UVP-E3 | 871307 | ex RA-0144G | ♦ |
| ☐ | RA-67681 | LET L-410UVP-E3 | 871913 | ex RA-1106G | ♦ |

## AK BARS AERO · (2B/BGM) · Bugulma (UUA)

| | | | | | |
|---|---|---|---|---|---|
| ☐ | VQ-BHF | Canadair CRJ-200LR | 7802 | ex N510CA | |
| ☐ | VQ-BHG | Canadair CRJ-200LR | 7816 | ex N518CA | ♦ |
| ☐ | VQ-BHH | Canadair CRJ-200LR | 7824 | ex N526CA | |
| ☐ | VQ-BHI | Canadair CRJ-200LR | 7809 | ex N514CA | |
| ☐ | VQ-BHJ | Canadair CRJ-200LR | 7821 | ex N523CA | |
| ☐ | VQ-BJZ | Canadair CRJ-200ER | 7500 | ex N130MN | ♦ |
| ☐ | VQ-BLZ | Canadair CRJ-200LR | 7520 | ex N129MN | ♦ |
| ☐ | VQ-BOM | Canadair CRJ-200ER | 7707 | ex N486CA | ♦ |
| ☐ | VQ-BOP | Canadair CRJ-200ER | 7689 | ex N483CA | ♦ |
| ☐ | VQ- | Canadair CRJ-200ER | 7739 | ex N677SA | ♦ |
| ☐ | RA-87209 | Yakovlev Yak-40K | 9810657 | ex CCCP-87209 all-white | |
| ☐ | RA-87447 | Yakovlev Yak-40 | 9430436 | ex CCCP-87447 AK Bars Bank titles | VIP |
| ☐ | RA-87494 | Yakovlev Yak-40 | 9541745 | | ♦ |
| ☐ | RA-87517 | Yakovlev Yak-40 | 9521940 | ex CCCP-87517 | VIP |
| ☐ | RA-87849 | Yakovlev Yak-40 | 9331830 | ex CCCP-87849 | |
| ☐ | RA-88165 | Yakovlev Yak-40 | 9611946 | ex CCCP-88165 | |
| ☐ | RA-88231 | Yakovlev Yak-40 | 9642050 | | ♦ |

## ALANIA AIRLINE · Alania (2D/OST) · Vladikavkaz (OGZ)

| | | | | |
|---|---|---|---|---|
| ☐ | RA-42435 | Yakovlev Yak-42D | 4520424306017 | ex ER-YCA |

## ALROSA AVIA — Alrosa (LRO) — Moscow-Zhukovsky / Vnukovo

| | | | | | |
|---|---|---|---|---|---|
| ☐ | RA-65693 | Tupolev Tu-134B-3 | 63221 | ex YL-LBC | Executive |
| ☐ | RA-65907 | Tupolev Tu-134A | 63996 | ex CCCP-65907 | Executive |

## ALROSA AVIATION — Mirny (6R/DRU) — Mirny (MJZ)

| | | | | | |
|---|---|---|---|---|---|
| ☐ | RA-46358 | Antonov An-24B | 07305808 | | ♦ |
| ☐ | RA-46488 | Antonov An-24RV | 27308106 | ex CCCP-46488 | |
| ☐ | RA-46621 | Antonov An-24RV | 37308708 | ex CCCP-46621 | |
| ☐ | RA-47272 | Antonov An-24B | 07306402 | ex CCCP-47272 | |
| ☐ | RA-47694 | Antonov An-24B | 27307601 | ex CCCP-47694 | |
| | | | | | |
| ☐ | RA-22394 | Mil Mi-8T | 7296 | ex CCCP-22394 | |
| ☐ | RA-22570 | Mil Mi-8T | 7816 | ex CCCP-22570 | |
| ☐ | RA-22571 | Mil Mi-8T | 7817 | ex CCCP-22571 | |
| ☐ | RA-22731 | Mil Mi-8T | 98308847 | ex CCCP-22731 | |
| ☐ | RA-22744 | Mil Mi-8T | 98311127 | ex CCCP-22744 | |
| ☐ | RA-22879 | Mil Mi-8T | 98415832 | ex CCCP-22879 | |
| ☐ | RA-22899 | Mil Mi-8T | 98417179 | ex CCCP-22899 | |
| ☐ | RA-22902 | Mil Mi-8T | 98420099 | ex CCCP-22902 | |
| ☐ | RA-24256 | Mil Mi-8T | 98734114 | ex CCCP-24256 | |
| ☐ | RA-24257 | Mil Mi-8T | 98734121 | ex CCCP-24257 | |
| ☐ | RA-24435 | Mil Mi-8T | 98625845 | ex CCCP-24435 | |
| ☐ | RA-24451 | Mil Mi-8T | 98628263 | ex CCCP-24451 | |
| ☐ | RA-24506 | Mil Mi-8T | 98520843 | ex CCCP-24506 | |
| ☐ | RA-24536 | Mil Mi-8T | 98522588 | ex CCCP-24536 | |
| ☐ | RA-24741 | Mil Mi-8T | 98417837 | ex CCCP-24741 | |
| ☐ | RA-25228 | Mil Mi-8T | 7763 | ex CCCP-25228 | |
| ☐ | RA-25313 | Mil Mi-8T | 98203720 | ex CCCP-25313 | |
| ☐ | RA-25333 | Mil Mi-8T | 98206010 | ex CCCP-25333 | |
| ☐ | RA-25376 | Mil Mi-8T | 98209062 | ex CCCP-25376 | |
| ☐ | RA-25606 | Mil Mi-8T | 99150564 | ex CCCP-25606 | |
| | | | | | |
| ☐ | RA-85654 | Tupolev Tu-154M | 89A796 | ex CCCP-86654 | |
| ☐ | RA-85675 | Tupolev Tu-154M | 90A835 | ex CCCP-85675 | |
| ☐ | RA-85684 | Tupolev Tu-154M | 90A851 | ex CCCP-85684 | dam 07Sep2009 |
| ☐ | RA-85728 | Tupolev Tu-154M | 92A910 | ex CCCP-85728 | |
| ☐ | RA-85782 | Tupolev Tu-154M | 93A966 | ex UN-85782 | |
| | | | | | |
| ☐ | RA-06036 | Mil Mi-26 | 34001212426 | ex CCCP-06036 | |
| ☐ | RA-06081 | Mil Mi-26 | 34001212471 | ex CCCP-06081 | |
| ☐ | RA-26552 | Antonov An-26 | 3107 | ex CCCP-26552 | [YKS] |
| ☐ | RA-26606 | Antonov An-26 | 4704 | | ♦ |
| ☐ | RA-26628 | Antonov An-26 | 5309 | | ♦ |
| ☐ | RA-26668 | Antonov An-26B-100 | 8201 | ex CCCP-26668 | |
| ☐ | RA-65146 | Tupolev Tu-134B-3 | 61000 | ex YL-LBA | |
| ☐ | RA-65653 | Tupolev Tu-134A | 0351009 | | ♦ |
| ☐ | RA-65715 | Tupolev Tu-134B-3 | 63536 | ex 4L-AAC | |
| ☐ | RA-76357 | Ilyushin Il-76TD | 1023414467 | | |
| ☐ | RA-76360 | Ilyushin Il-76TD | 1033414492 | | |
| ☐ | RA-76373 | Ilyushin Il-76TD | 1033415507 | | |
| ☐ | RA-76420 | Ilyushin Il-76TD | 1023413446 | | Jt ops with TIS |

## AMUR ARTEL STARATELEI AVIAKOMPANIA — Khabarovsk-Novy (KHV)

| | | | | | |
|---|---|---|---|---|---|
| ☐ | RA-26001 | Antonov An-26 | 9705 | ex CCCP-26001 | |
| ☐ | RA-26048 | Antonov An-26B | 10901 | ex CCCP-26048 | |
| ☐ | RA-26082 | Antonov An-26B-100 | 11705 | | ♦ |
| ☐ | RA-87395 | Yakovlev Yak-40 | 9410733 | | ♦ |
| ☐ | RA-87938 | Yakovlev Yak-40K | 9710153 | ex CCCP-87936 | ♦ |
| ☐ | RA-88153 | Yakovlev Yak-40 | 9610746 | | ♦ |

## ANGARA AIRLINES — Sarma (AGU) — Irkutsk-One (IKT)

| | | | | | |
|---|---|---|---|---|---|
| ☐ | RA-46625 | Antonov An-24RV | 37308804 | ex CCCP-46625 | |
| ☐ | RA-46662 | Antonov An-24RV | 47309410 | ex CCCP-46662 | |
| ☐ | RA-46697 | Antonov An-24RV | 47309908 | ex CCCP-46697 | |
| ☐ | RA-46712 | Antonov An-24RV | 57310408 | ex EK-24408 | |
| ☐ | RA-47818 | Antonov An-24RV | 17307107 | ex CCCP-47818 | |
| ☐ | RA-47848 | Antonov An-24B | 17307410 | ex CCCP-47848 | |
| | | | | | |
| ☐ | RA-26040 | Antonov An-26B | 10703 | | ♦ |
| ☐ | RA-26511 | Antonov An-26-100 | 6808 | ex CCCP-26511 | |
| ☐ | RA-26543 | Antonov An-26 | 2709 | | ♦ |
| ☐ | RA-26655 | Antonov An-26-100 | 7802 | ex CCCP-26655 | |

## ARKHANGELSK 2ND AVIATION ENTERPRISE — Dvina (5N/OAO) — Arkhangelsk-Vaslearo

| | | | | | |
|---|---|---|---|---|---|
| ☐ | RA-67553 | LET L-410UVP-E | 851430 | ex CCCP-67553 | |
| ☐ | RA-67564 | LET L-410UVP-E | 851604 | ex CCCP-67564 | |

| | | | | |
|---|---|---|---|---|
| ☐ | RA-67567 | LET L-410UVP-E | 861607 | ex CCCP-67567 |
| ☐ | RA-67602 | LET L-410UVP-E | 892229 | ex CCCP-67602 |
| ☐ | RA-67603 | LET L-410UVP-E | 892214 | ex CCCP-67603 ♦ |
| ☐ | RA-67606 | LET L-410UVP-E | 892322 | ex CCCP-67606 ♦ |
| | | | | |
| ☐ | RA-22341 | Mil Mi-8T | 7166 | ex CCCP-22341 |
| ☐ | RA-22762 | Mil Mi-8T | 98311485 | ex CCCP-22762 |
| ☐ | RA-24012 | Mil Mi-8MTV-1 | 95713 | ex CCCP-24012 |
| ☐ | RA-24485 | Mil Mi-8T | 98628927 | ex CCCP-24485 |
| | | | | |
| ☐ | RA-06039 | Mil Mi-26T | 34001212429 | ex CCCP-06039 |
| ☐ | RA-06042 | Mil Mi-26T | 34001212432 | ex CCCP-06042 |
| ☐ | RA-06044 | Mil Mi-26T | 34001212434 | ex CCCP-06044 |
| ☐ | RA-21077 | Mil Mi-6T | 7065302B | ex CCCP-21077 |
| ☐ | RA-21161 | Mil Mi-6T | 0533 | ex CCCP-21161 |

## ARKHANGELSK AIRLINES                                                                 Arkhangelsk-Vaslearo

| | | | | |
|---|---|---|---|---|
| ☐ | RA-46667 | Antonov An-24RV | 47309508 | ex CCCP-46667 |

## ASTAIR

| | | | | |
|---|---|---|---|---|
| ☐ | RA-85031 | Tupolev Tu-154M | 87A751 | ex EX-087 |

## ATRAN - AVIATRANS CARGO AIRLINES        Atran (V8/VAS)   Moscow-Domodedovo / Myachkovo (DME/-)

| | | | | |
|---|---|---|---|---|
| ☐ | RA-11868 | Antonov An-12B | 9346310 | ex OB-1448 |
| ☐ | RA-12990 | Antonov An-12B | 00347304 | ex OB-1449 |
| ☐ | RA-93913 | Antonov An-12B | 4342609 | ex CCCP-93913 |

## AVIACON ZITOTRANS            Zitotrans (ZR/AZS)          Ekaterinburg-Koltsovo (SVX)

| | | | | |
|---|---|---|---|---|
| ☐ | EW-78843 | Ilyushin Il-76TD | 1003403082 | | <TXC♦ |
| ☐ | RA-76352 | Ilyushin Il-76TD | 1023411378 | ex EP-SFB | op for UN WFP |
| ☐ | RA-76386 | Ilyushin Il-76TD | 1033418600 | ex UK 76386 | |
| ☐ | RA-76445 | Ilyushin Il-76TD | 1023410330 | | |
| ☐ | RA-76483 | Ilyushin Il-76TD | 0063468042 | | ♦ |
| ☐ | RA-76502 | Ilyushin Il-76TD | 1003401004 | | ♦ |
| ☐ | RA-76807 | Ilyushin Il-76TD | 1013405176 | ex CCCP-76807 | op for UN WFP |
| ☐ | RA-76842 | Ilyushin Il-76TD | 1033418616 | | |
| ☐ | RA-76846 | Ilyushin Il-76TD | 0093497936 | | ♦ |

## AVIAENERGO                   Aviaenergo (7U/ERG)        Moscow-Sheremetyevo (SVO)

| | | | | |
|---|---|---|---|---|
| ☐ | RA-65962 | Tupolev Tu-134A-3 | 3351901 | ex CCCP-65962 | VIP |
| ☐ | RA-86583 | Ilyushin Il-62M | 1356851 | ex CCCP-86583 | VIP |

## AVIAL AVIATION CO            New Avial (NVI)            Moscow-Domodedovo (DME)

| | | | | |
|---|---|---|---|---|
| ☐ | RA-11115 | Antonov An-12BP | 01348003 | ex CCCP-11115 |
| ☐ | RA-11130 | Antonov An-12BP | 02348205 | |
| ☐ | RA-11372 | Antonov An-12BP | 401912 | ex EW-252TI ♦ |
| ☐ | RA-11906 | Antonov An-12BP | 2340802 | ex CCCP-11906 |

## AVIALESOOKHRANA VLADIMIR AIR ENTERPRISE       (FFA)                          Vladimir

| | | | | |
|---|---|---|---|---|
| ☐ | RA-26002 | Antonov An-26 | 07309706 | ex CCCP-26002 |
| ☐ | RA-26005 | Antonov An-26 | 9809 | ex CCCP-26005 |
| ☐ | RA-26532 | Antonov An-26 | 7410 | ex CCCP-26532 |

## AVIAPRAD

| | | | | |
|---|---|---|---|---|
| ☐ | RA-85795 | Tupolev Tu-154M | 06A979 | |

Ceased ops Feb08

## AVIAST AIR                    Ialsi (6I/VVA)             Moscow-Vnukovo (VKO)

| | | | | |
|---|---|---|---|---|
| ☐ | RA-11756 | Antonov An-12BP | 4342208 | ex CCCP-11756 | >SHU |
| ☐ | RA-11962 | Antonov An-12BP | 5343007 | ex CCCP-11962 | |
| ☐ | RA-76843 | Ilyushin Il-76TD | 1013408269 | | op for UN WFP |
| ☐ | RA-76849 | Ilyushin Il-76TD | 23440161 | | ♦ |

## AVIASTAR – TUPOLEV          Tupolev Air (4B/TUP)   Moscow-Zhukovsky/Domodedovo (-/DME)

| | | | | |
|---|---|---|---|---|
| ☐ | RA-64021 | Tupolev Tu-204-100C | 2964021 | |
| ☐ | RA-64024 | Tupolev Tu-204-100C | 1364024 | ex LY-AGT   DHL c/s |
| ☐ | RA-64032 | Tupolev Tu-204-100C | 2264032 | |

434

| | | | | | |
|---|---|---|---|---|---|
| ☐ | RA-64051 | Tupolev Tu-204-100c | 2964051 | | ♦ |
| ☐ | RA-64052 | Tupolev Tu-204-100C | 2964052 | | ♦ |
| | | | | | |
| ☐ | RA-26625 | Antonov An-26ALSK | 5203 | | ♦ |

## BARKOL AVIAKOMPANIA — Moscow-Byokovo/Volgograd-Gurmak (BKA/VOG)

| | | | | | |
|---|---|---|---|---|---|
| ☐ | RA-87280 | Yakovlev Yak-40 | 9322025 | ex CCCP-87280 | Executive |
| ☐ | RA-87353 | Yakovlev Yak-40 | 9330231 | | ♦ |
| ☐ | RA-87828 | Yakovlev Yak-40 | 9242024 | | |
| ☐ | RA-87957 | Yakovlev Yak-40K | 9821857 | ex CCCP-87957 | Executive |
| ☐ | RA-88228 | Yakovlev Yak-40 | 9641750 | | Executive |

## BURYAT AVIA — Bural (BUN) — Ulan Ude-Mukhino (UUD)

| | | | | | |
|---|---|---|---|---|---|
| ☐ | RA-46408 | Antonov An-24B | 77304003 | ex CCCP-46408 | |
| ☐ | RA-46506 | Antonov An-24RV | 37308402 | | ♦ |
| ☐ | RA-46614 | Antonov An-24RV | 37308701 | ex CCCP-46614 | |
| ☐ | RA-47361 | Antonov An-24RV | 67310705 | | ♦ |
| ☐ | RA-47799 | Antonov An-24RV | 17306808 | | ♦ |

## BYLINA — Bylina (BYL) — Moscow-Vnukovo (VKO)

| | | | | | |
|---|---|---|---|---|---|
| ☐ | RA-87334 | Yakovlev Yak-40 | 9510738 | | ♦ |
| ☐ | RA-88263 | Yakovlev Yak-40 | 9711852 | ex CCCP-88263 | VIP |
| ☐ | RA-88274 | Yakovlev Yak-40 | 9721253 | ex CCCP-88274 | VIP |

## CENTER-SOUTH AIRLINES — Center-South (CTS) — Belgorod (EGO)

| | | | | |
|---|---|---|---|---|
| ☐ | RA-87655 | Yakovlev Yak-40 | 9211820 | ex CCCP-87655 |
| ☐ | RA-87966 | Yakovlev Yak-40 | 9820958 | ex CCCP-87966 |
| ☐ | RA-88236 | Yakovlev Yak-40 | 9640551 | ex CCCP-88236 |

## CENTRE-AVIA AIRLINES — Aviacentre (J7/CVC) — Moscow-Bykovo (BKA)

| | | | | | |
|---|---|---|---|---|---|
| ☐ | RA-42325 | Yakovlev Yak-42D | 4520424402148 | ex CCCP-42325 | |
| ☐ | RA-42341 | Yakovlev Yak-42D | 4520421706292 | ex CCCP-42341 | |
| ☐ | RA-42353 | Yakovlev Yak-42D | 4520424711396 | ex LY-AAT | |
| ☐ | RA-42385 | Yakovlev Yak-42D | 4520423016309 | ex ER-YCC | |
| ☐ | RA-42423 | Yakovlev Yak-42 | 4520424216606 | ex CCCP-42423 | VIP |
| ☐ | RA-42542 | Yakovlev Yak-42D | 11140804 | ex CCCP-42542 | |
| ☐ | RA-87507 | Yakovlev Yak-40 | 9520940 | ex LY-AAB | |

## CHUKOTAVIA — Anadyr (DYR)

| | | | | |
|---|---|---|---|---|
| ☐ | RA-22728 | Mil Mi-8T | 98308799 | ex CCCP-22728 |
| ☐ | RA-24199 | Mil Mi-8T | 98943825 | ex CCCP-24199 |
| ☐ | RA-24422 | Mil Mi-8T | 98625391 | ex CCCP-24422 |
| ☐ | RA-24497 | Mil Mi-8T | 98734707 | ex CCCP-24497 |
| ☐ | RA-24498 | Mil Mi-8T | 98734729 | ex CCCP-24498 |
| ☐ | RA-24503 | Mil Mi-8T | 96520730 | ex CCCP-24503 |
| ☐ | RA-24531 | Mil Mi-8T | 98522401 | ex CCCP-24531 |
| ☐ | RA-24719 | Mil Mi-8T | 98417340 | ex CCCP-24719 |
| ☐ | RA-24738 | Mil Mi-8T | 98417759 | ex CCCP-24738 |
| ☐ | RA-25158 | Mil Mi-8T | 99047875 | ex CCCP-25158 |
| ☐ | RA-25189 | Mil Mi-8T | 98943829 | ex CCCP-25189 |
| ☐ | RA-25470 | Mil Mi-8MTV-1 | 95614 | ex CCCP-25470 |
| ☐ | RA-25988 | Mil Mi-8T | 7520 | ex CCCP-25988 |
| ☐ | RA-27014 | Mil Mi-8MTV-1 | 96352 | |
| ☐ | RA-27025 | Mil Mi-8PS | 8730 | |
| | | | | |
| ☐ | RA-26099 | Antonov An-26B-100 | 11905 | ex CCCP-26099 |
| ☐ | RA-26128 | Antonov An-26B | 12702 | ex CCCP-26128 |
| ☐ | RA-26590 | Antonov An-26B | 13910 | ex CCCP-26590 |
| ☐ | RA-46616 | Antonov An-24RV | 37308703 | ex CCCP-46616 |
| ☐ | RA-47159 | Antonov An-24B | 89901701 | ♦ |

## CONTINENTAL AIRWAYS — Contair (PC/PVV) — Moscow-Sheremetyevo (SVO)

Ceased ops 29Jly11

## DAGHESTAN AIRLINES — Dagal (N2/DAG) — Makhachkala (MCX)

AOC revoked 2011

## DALAVIA — Khabarovsk Air (H8/KHB) — Khabarovsk-Novy (KHV)

| | | | | | |
|---|---|---|---|---|---|
| ☐ | RA-86128 | Ilyushin Il-62M | 2255719 | | [KHV]♦ |
| ☐ | RA-86131 | Ilyushin Il-62M | 4255244 | ex CCCP-86131 | |

| | | | | | |
|---|---|---|---|---|---|
| ☐ | RA-86479 | Ilyushin Il-62M | 4728118 | | [KHV]♦ |
| ☐ | RA-86493 | Ilyushin Il-62M | 4140748 | ex CU-T1248 | |
| ☐ | RA-86525 | Ilyushin Il-62M | 4851612 | ex CCCP-86525 | |
| ☐ | RA-86560 | Ilyushin Il-62M | 2153347 | ex CCCP-86560 | |
| ☐ | RA-85114 | Tupolev Tu-154M | 89A814 | ex EP-EAC | [KHV] |
| ☐ | RA-85477 | Tupolev Tu-154B-2 | 81A477 | ex CCCP-85477 | [KHV] |
| ☐ | RA-85607 | Tupolev Tu-154M | 84A702 | | [KHV]♦ |
| ☐ | RA-85752 | Tupolev Tu-154M | 92A934 | ex EP-MAT | [[KHV] |
| ☐ | RA-85797 | Tupolev Tu-154M | 93A981 | | |
| ☐ | RA-85802 | Tupolev Tu-154M | 93A961 | ex EP-MAN | [KHV] |
| ☐ | RA-64502 | Tupolev Tu-214 | 42625002 | Yuri Vorob'yoy | |
| ☐ | RA-64503 | Tupolev Tu-214 | 43103003 | | |
| ☐ | RA-64507 | Tupolev Tu-214 | 42305007 | | |
| ☐ | RA-64510 | Tupolev Tu-214 | 42305010 | | |
| ☐ | RA-64512 | Tupolev Tu-214 | 42305012 | | |
| | | | | | |
| ☐ | RA-26000 | Antonov An-26 | 7309604 | ex CCCP-26000 | |
| ☐ | RA-26058 | Antonov An-26B | 11101 | ex CCCP-26058 | |
| ☐ | RA-46474 | Antonov An-24RV | 27308002 | ex CCCP-46474 | |
| ☐ | RA-46522 | Antonov An-24RV | 47310001 | ex CCCP-46522 | |
| ☐ | RA-47354 | Antonov An-24RV | 67310603 | ex CCCP-47354 | |

### DAURIA — Chita-Kadala (HTA)

| | | | | | |
|---|---|---|---|---|---|
| ☐ | RA-26543 | Antonov An-26 | 57302709 | ex CCCP-26543 | [IKT] |
| ☐ | RA-47268 | Antonov An-24B | 07306306 | ex CCCP-47268 | |
| ☐ | RA-47838 | Antonov An-24B | 17307310 | ex CCCP-47838 | Avialinii Zabaikalaya titles |

### DOMODEDOVO AIRLINES — Domodedovo (E3/DMO) — Moscow-Domodedovo (DME)

| | | | | | |
|---|---|---|---|---|---|
| ☐ | RA-86519 | Ilyushin Il-62M | 4140212 | ex CCCP-86519 | |
| ☐ | RA-76799 | Ilyushin Il-76TD | 1003403075 | ex CCCP-76799 | >ESL |
| ☐ | RA-96006 | Ilyushin Il-96-300 | 74393201003 | ex CCCP-96006 | |
| ☐ | RA-96009 | Ilyushin Il-96-300 | 74393201006 | | [DME] |
| ☐ | RA-96013 | Ilyushin Il-96-300 | 74393202013 | | [DME] |

### DONAVIA — Donavia (D9/DNV) — Rostov-on-Don (ROV)

| | | | | | |
|---|---|---|---|---|---|
| ☐ | VP-BVU | Boeing 737-5Q8 | 25166/2129 | ex G-BVZH | |
| ☐ | VP-BWY | Boeing 737-528 | 27305/2574 | ex F-GJNO | |
| ☐ | VP-BWZ | Boeing 737-528 | 27304/2572 | ex F-GJNN | |
| ☐ | VP-BYU | Boeing 737-5Q8 | 25167/2173 | ex G-BVZI | |
| ☐ | VP-BYV | Boeing 737-5Q8 | 25160/2114 | ex G-BVZG | |
| | | | | | |
| ☐ | VP-BBU | Airbus A319-112 | 1630 | ex C-FBLJ | o/o♦ |
| ☐ | VQ-BAN | Boeing 737-4Q8 | 25113/2656 | ex N782AS | |
| ☐ | VQ-BAO | Boeing 737-4Q8 | 25114/2666 | ex N783AS | |
| ☐ | VQ-BCS | Boeing 737-43Q | 28494/2839 | ex SX-BTN | |
| ☐ | RA-85626 | Tupolev Tu-154M | 87A753 | ex CCCP-85626 | |
| ☐ | RA-85630 | Tupolev Tu-154M | 87A759 | ex CCCP-85630 | |
| ☐ | RA-86141 | Ilyushin Il-86 | 51483211103 | | |

### EVENKIA AVIA — Tura

| | | | | | |
|---|---|---|---|---|---|
| ☐ | RA-26008 | Antonov An-26B-100 | 9902 | ex CCCP-26008 | |
| ☐ | RA-87900 | Yakovlev Yak-40K | 9720254 | ex CCCP-87900 | VIP |

### FLIGHT INSPECTIONS & SYSTEMS — Aviaspec (LTS) — Moscow-Bykovo/Khabarovsk-Novy (BKA/KHV)

| | | | | | |
|---|---|---|---|---|---|
| ☐ | RA-26571 | Antonov An-26 | 67303909 | ex CCCP-26571 | Calibrator/Flying laboratory |
| ☐ | RA-26631 | Antonov An-26ASLK | 77305503 | ex CCCP-26631 | Calibrator/Flying laboratory |
| ☐ | RA-26673 | Antonov An-26ASLK | 97308408 | ex CCCP-26673 | Calibrator/Flying laboratory |
| ☐ | RA-46395 | Antonov An-24ALK | 07306209 | ex CCCP-46395 | Calibrator/Flying laboratory |

### GAZPROMAVIA — Gazprom (4G/GZP) — Moscow-Ostafyevo/Moscow-Vnukovo (-/VKO)

| | | | | | |
|---|---|---|---|---|---|
| ☐ | RA-74005 | Antonov An-74TK-100C | 36547095892 | ex CCCP-74005 | EMS |
| ☐ | RA-74008 | Antonov An-74TK-100 | 36547095900 | ex UR-74008 | |
| ☐ | RA-74032 | Antonov An-74TK-100 | 36547098962 | ex UR-74032 | |
| ☐ | RA-74035 | Antonov An-74TK-100 | 36547098963 | | |
| ☐ | RA-74056 | Antonov An-74-200 | 36547098951 | | |
| | | | | | |
| ☐ | RA-04090 | Eurocopter EC135T2+ | 0899 | | ♦ |
| ☐ | RA-04091 | Eurocopter EC135T2+ | 0904 | | ♦ |
| ☐ | RA-04093 | Eurocopter EC135T2+ | 0906 | | ♦ |
| ☐ | RA-04086 | Eurocopter EC135T2+ | 0924 | | ♦ |
| ☐ | RA-04087 | Eurocopter EC135T2+ | 0927 | | ♦ |
| ☐ | RA-04088 | Eurocopter EC135T2+ | 0952 | | ♦ |
| ☐ | RA-04089 | Eurocopter EC135T2+ | 0955 | | ♦ |

| | | | | | |
|---|---|---|---|---|---|
| ☐ | RA-21505 | Yakovlev Yak-40K | 9830159 | ex CCCP-21505 | |
| ☐ | RA-87511 | Yakovlev Yak-40 | 9521340 | ex CCCP-87511 | |
| ☐ | RA-88186 | Yakovlev Yak-40K | 9620648 | ex CCCP-88186 | |
| ☐ | RA-88300 | Yakovlev Yak-40K | 9641451 | ex OK-GEO | |
| ☐ | RA-98109 | Yakovlev Yak-40 | 9740956 | | ♦ |
| ☐ | RA-98113 | Yakovlev Yak-40 | 9710253 | ex CCCP-98113 | VIP |
| | | | | | |
| ☐ | RA-42425 | Yakovlev Yak-42D | 4520423303016 | ex CU-T1243 | |
| ☐ | RA-42436 | Yakovlev Yak-42D | 4520421605018 | | |
| ☐ | RA-42437 | Yakovlev Yak-42D | 4520423606018 | | |
| ☐ | RA-42438 | Yakovlev Yak-42D | 4520423609018 | | VIP |
| ☐ | RA-42439 | Yakovlev Yak-42D | 4520423904019 | | |
| ☐ | RA-42442 | Yakovlev Yak-42D | 4520421402019 | | VIP |
| ☐ | RA-42451 | Yakovlev Yak-42D | 4520422708018 | | VIP |
| ☐ | RA-42452 | Yakovlev Yak-42D | 409016 | ex RA-42431 | |
| | | | | | |
| ☐ | RA-24143 | Mil Mi-8T | 98841441 | ex UN-24143 | ♦ |
| ☐ | RA-73000 | Boeing 737-76N | 28630/664 | ex VT-JNP | |
| ☐ | RA-73004 | Boeing 737-76N | 28635/734 | ex VT-JNQ | |

## GLOBUS (GH/GLP)

| | | | | | |
|---|---|---|---|---|---|
| ☐ | VP-BDF | Boeing 737-8Q8 | 30672/1497 | ex HA-LOM | ♦ |
| ☐ | VP-BDG | Boeing 737-8Q8 | 30669/1479 | ex HA-LOK | ♦ |
| ☐ | VP-BDH | Boeing 737-8Q8 | 30667/1448 | ex HA-LOH | ♦ |
| ☐ | VP-BND | Boeing 737-83N/W | 28245/1054 | ex N315TZ | ♦ |
| ☐ | VP-BNG | Boeing 737-83N/W | 30640/1035 | ex N314TZ | ♦ |
| ☐ | VP-BQD | Boeing 737-83N/W | 28239/847 | ex N301TZ | ♦ |
| ☐ | VP-BQF | Boeing 737-83N/W | 28243/984 | ex N310TZ | ♦ |
| ☐ | VQ-BKV | Boeing 737-8ZS/W | 37084/3605 | | ♦ |
| ☐ | VQ-BKW | Boeing 737-8ZS/W | 37085/3654 | | ♦ |
| | | | | | |
| ☐ | RA-85611 | Tupolev Tu-154M | 85A715 | ex CCCP-85611 | |
| ☐ | RA-85612 | Tupolev Tu-154M | 86A721 | ex CCCP-85612 | |
| ☐ | RA-85623 | Tupolev Tu-154M | 87A749 | ex CCCP-85623 | [DME] |
| ☐ | VP-BAN | Boeing 737-4Y0 | 26071/2361 | ex N314PW | ♦ |
| ☐ | VP-BQG | Boeing 737-46J | 27171/2465 | ex EI-DGL | ♦ |
| ☐ | VP-BTA | Boeing 737-4Q8 | 25168/2210 | ex TF-ELY | |
| ☐ | VP-BTH | Boeing 737-42C | 24231/1871 | ex N60669 | |

## GROZNYYAVIA      Grozny (GRV)

| | | | | | |
|---|---|---|---|---|---|
| ☐ | RA-42353 | Yakovlev Yak-42 | 4520424711396 | | ♦ |
| ☐ | RA-42379 | Yakovlev Yak-42D | 4520421014543 | ex EP-YAE | |
| ☐ | RA-42418 | Yakovlev Yak-42D | 4520423219118 | ex CCCP-42418 | |
| ☐ | RA-42542 | Yakovlev Yak-42D | 11140804 | | ♦ |

## IFLY (H5/RSY)

| | | | | | |
|---|---|---|---|---|---|
| ☐ | EI-DUA | Boeing 757-256 | 26247/860 | ex N241LF | |
| ☐ | EI-DUC | Boeing 757-256 | 26248/863 | ex N263LF | |
| ☐ | EI-DUD | Boeing 757-256 | 26249/881 | ex N271LF | |
| ☐ | EI-ERF | Boeing 757-256 | 26254/905 | ex TC-ETG | ♦ |

## IKAR      Magadan-Sokol (GDX)

| | | | | |
|---|---|---|---|---|
| ☐ | RA-28723 | WSK-PZL/Antonov An-28 | 1AJ007-08 | ex CCCP-26105 |
| ☐ | RA-26726 | WSK-PZL/Antonov An-28 | 1AJ007-11 | ex CCCP-26105 |

## ILIN AVIAKOMPANIA      Yakutsk-Magan

| | | | | |
|---|---|---|---|---|
| ☐ | RA-67664 | LET L-410UVP-E | 902526 | ex CCCP-67664 |

## INTERAVIA AIRLINES    Astair (8D/SUW)    Moscow-Domodedovo (DME)

| | | | | |
|---|---|---|---|---|
| ☐ | RA-86533 | Ilyushin Il-62M | 1343123 | ex CCCP-86533 Novowilov |
| ☐ | RA-86567 | Ilyushin Il-62M | 4256314 | |
| ☐ | RA-86575 | Ilyushin Il-62M | 1647928 | ex UK 86575 |
| ☐ | RA-86577 | Ilyushin Il-62M | 2748552 | ex UK 86577 |
| | | | | |
| ☐ | RA-42339 | Yakovlev Yak-42D | 4520424606267 | ex LY-AAO |
| ☐ | RA-42356 | Yakovlev Yak-42D | 4520422811400 | ex CCCP-42356 |
| ☐ | RA-42359 | Yakovlev Yak-42D | 4520424811417 | ex LY-AAW |

## IRAERO    (IO/IAE)    Irkutsk-One (IKT)

| | | | | | |
|---|---|---|---|---|---|
| ☐ | RA-46480 | Antonov An-24RV | 27308008 | | ♦ |
| ☐ | RA-46846 | Antonov An-24RV | 27307504 | ex ER-AWC | |

| | | | | | |
|---|---|---|---|---|---|
| ☐ | RA-47321 | Antonov An-24RV | 67310507 | | ♦ |
| ☐ | RA-47804 | Antonov An-24RV | 17306903 | ex CCCP-47804 | |
| ☐ | RA-47805 | Antonov An-24RV | 17306907 | ex ER-AWD | |
| ☐ | RA-48096 | Antonov An-24RV | 57310406 | | ♦ |
| ☐ | RA-93934 | Antonov An-24B | 099002310 | | ♦ |
| | | | | | |
| ☐ | RA-26051 | Antonov An-26B | 10906 | ex CCCP-26051 | |
| ☐ | RA-26105 | Antonov An-26B-100 | 12003 | | ♦ |
| ☐ | RA-26131 | Antonov An-26B | 12707 | ex CCCP-26131 | |
| ☐ | RA-26138 | Antonov An-26B | 37312810 | | ♦ |
| ☐ | RA-26515 | Antonov An-26 | 87306910 | | ♦ |
| ☐ | RA-26665 | Antonov An-26 | 97308108 | | ♦ |
| ☐ | RA-26692 | Antonov An-26B-100 | 9409 | ex CCCP-26692 | |
| | | | | | |
| ☐ | VQ-BIX | Canadair CRJ-200ER | 7546 | ex N446CA | <RLU♦ |
| ☐ | VQ-BIY | Canadair CRJ-200ER | 7539 | ex N443CA | ♦ |
| ☐ | VQ-BMK | Canadair CRJ-200ER | 7668 | ex N473CA | <RLU♦ |
| ☐ | VQ-BML | Canadair CRJ-200ER | 7650 | ex N469SM | |

## IZHAVIA — Izhavia (IZA) — Izhevsk (IJK)

| | | | | | |
|---|---|---|---|---|---|
| ☐ | RA-42385 | Yakovlev Yak-42D | 4520423016309 | | ♦ |
| ☐ | RA-42450 | Yakovlev Yak-42 | 4520424601019 | | ♦ |
| ☐ | RA-42455 | Yakovlev Yak-42D | 4520424404018 | | ♦ |
| ☐ | RA-42524 | Yakovlev Yak-42D | 11030603 | ex EP-TAK | ♦ |
| ☐ | RA-42549 | Yakovlev Yak-42 | 11040105 | | ♦ |
| | | | | | |
| ☐ | RA-26245 | Antonov An-26-100 | 6206 | | ♦ |
| ☐ | RA-26529 | Antonov An-26-100 | 7310 | | ♦ |
| ☐ | RA-26683 | Antonov An-26-100 | 8707 | | ♦ |
| ☐ | RA-46620 | Antonov An-24RV | 37308707 | ex CCCP-46620 | |
| ☐ | RA-46637 | Antonov An-24RV | 37308903 | ex CCCP-46637 | |
| ☐ | RA-47315 | Antonov An-24RV | 67310502 | ex CCCP-47315 | |
| ☐ | RA-65056 | Tupolev Tu-134A-3 | 49860 | ex CCCP-65056 | |
| ☐ | RA-65577 | Tupolev Tu-134A-3 | 60475 | | ♦ |

## JET 2000

| | | | | | |
|---|---|---|---|---|---|
| ☐ | RA-87216 | Yakovlev Yak-40 | 9510440 | ex CCCP-87216 | |

## JET AIR GROUP — Sistema (JSI) — Moscow-Sheremetyevo (SME)

| | | | | | |
|---|---|---|---|---|---|
| ☐ | RA-65723 | Tupolev Tu-134A-3M | 66440 | ex CCCP-65723 | Executive |
| ☐ | RA-65930 | Tupolev Tu-134A-3M | 66500 | ex CCCP-65930 | Executive |

## KAPO — Kazavia (KAO) — Kazan-Bonsoglebskow (KZN)

| | | | | | |
|---|---|---|---|---|---|
| ☐ | RA-86126 | Ilyushin Il-62MF | 4154535 | | |
| ☐ | RA-86576 | Ilyushin Il-62MF | 4546257 | ex UK 86576 | Frtr |
| ☐ | RA-86579 | Ilyushin Il-62MF | 2951636 | ex UK 86579 | Frtr Govt of Amur Region |
| ☐ | RA-86945 | Ilyushin Il-62M | 3850145 | ex OK-BYV | VIP Govt of Amur Region |

## KATEKAVIA — Katekavia (KTK) — Sharypovo/Krasnoyarsk-Yernelyanovo (-/KJA)

| | | | | | |
|---|---|---|---|---|---|
| ☐ | RA-46491 | Antonov An-24RV | 27308204 | ex 3X-GEB | |
| ☐ | RA-46493 | Antonov An-24RV | 27308206 | ex CCCP-46493 | |
| ☐ | RA-46497 | Antonov An-24RV | 27308210 | ex CCCP-46497 | |
| ☐ | RA-46520 | Antonov An-24RV | 37308506 | ex CCCP-46520 | no titles |
| ☐ | RA-46604 | Antonov An-24RV | 37308601 | ex CCCP-46604 | |
| ☐ | RA-46674 | Antonov An-24RV | 47309606 | | ♦ |
| ☐ | RA-46683 | Antonov An-24RV | 47309706 | | ♦ |
| ☐ | RA-46689 | Antonov An-24RV | 47309806 | ex CCCP-46689 | |
| ☐ | RA-46693 | Antonov An-24RV | 47309904 | ex CCCP-46693 | |
| ☐ | RA-47279 | Antonov An-24RV | 17306905 | | ♦ |
| ☐ | RA-47351 | Antonov An-24RV | 67310510 | ex YL-LCI | |
| ☐ | RA-47358 | Antonov An-24RV | 67310607 | ex CCCP-47358 | |
| ☐ | RA-48102 | Antonov An-24RT | 1911804 | ex CCCP-48102 | |
| | | | | | |
| ☐ | RA-65052 | Tupolev Tu-134A-3 | 49825 | ex CCCP-65052 | |
| ☐ | RA-65083 | Tupolev Tu-134A-3 | 60090 | | |

## KAZAN AIR ENTERPRISES — Kazan Osnovnoi/Khanty Mansisk (KZN/-)

| | | | | | |
|---|---|---|---|---|---|
| ☐ | RA-06171 | Mil Mi-8T | 98420128 | ex CCCP-06171 | |
| ☐ | RA-22674 | Mil Mi-8T | 8127 | ex CCCP-22674 | |
| ☐ | RA-22679 | Mil Mi-8T | 8133 | ex CCCP-22679 | |
| ☐ | RA-22734 | Mil Mi-8T | 98308901 | ex CCCP-22734 | |
| ☐ | RA-22873 | Mil Mi-8T | 98415711 | ex CCCP-22873 | |
| ☐ | RA-25408 | Mil Mi-8T | 98233135 | ex CCCP-25408 | |

438

| | | | | | |
|---|---|---|---|---|---|
| ☐ | RA-25519 | Mil Mi-8T | 9775214 | ex CCCP-25519 | |
| ☐ | RA-25599 | Mil Mi-8T | 99150362 | ex CCCP-25599 | |
| ☐ | RA-27023 | Mil Mi-8T | 9754622 | ex CCCP-27023 | |
| ☐ | RA-27176 | Mil Mi-8PS | 8710 | ex TC-HSA | |
| ☐ | RA-67667 | LET L-410UVP-E3 | 902408 | ex Soviet AF 2408 | ♦ |
| ☐ | RA-67672 | LET L-410UVP-E | 872013 | ex Soviet AF 2013 | no titles |
| ☐ | RA-67675 | LET L-410UVP-E | 882027 | ex Soviet AF 2027 | [Kazan] |
| ☐ | RA-67694 | LET L-410UVP-E | 952625 | ex OK-ADU | |

## KHABAROVSK AIRLINES — Nikolaevsk-na-Amure

| | | | | | |
|---|---|---|---|---|---|
| ☐ | RA-87303 | Yakovlev Yak-40 | 9321928 | | ♦ |
| ☐ | RA-87376 | Yakovlev Yak-40 | 9411032 | | ♦ |
| ☐ | RA-87400 | Yakovlev Yak-40 | 9421233 | | ♦ |
| ☐ | RA-87647 | Yakovlev Yak-40 | 9140820 | | ♦ |
| ☐ | RA-87651 | Yakovlev Yak-40 | 9141220 | ex CCCP-87651 Nikolaevsk titles | |
| ☐ | RA-88251 | Yakovlev Yak-40K | 9710552 | ex CCCP-88251 | |
| ☐ | RA-24532 | Mil Mi-8T | 98522422 | ex CCCP-24532 | |
| ☐ | RA-24722 | Mil Mi-8T | 98417398 | ex CCCP-24722 | |
| ☐ | RA-25196 | Mil Mi-8T | 99047381 | ex CCCP-25196 | |
| ☐ | RA-26174 | Antonov An-26B-100 | 97308304 | ex CCCP-26174 | |
| ☐ | RA-46367 | Antonov An-24RV | 77310806 | | ♦ |

## KIROV AVIA ENTERPRISE — Vyatka-Avia (KTA) — Kirov (KVX)

| | | | | | |
|---|---|---|---|---|---|
| ☐ | RA-46660 | Antonov An-24RV | 47309307 | ex CCCP-46660 | |
| ☐ | RA-47154 | Antonov An-24B | 89901606 | | [KVX]♦ |
| ☐ | RA-47264 | Antonov An-24RV | 27307806 | | >KMV♦ |
| ☐ | RA-47295 | Antonov An-24RV | 07306608 | ex CCCP-47295 | >KMV |
| ☐ | RA-26086 | Antonov An-26B | 12302 | ex CCCP-26086 | |
| ☐ | RA-26101 | Antonov An-26B | 11908 | | ♦ |
| ☐ | RA-26664 | Antonov An-26 | 97307905 | | ♦ |
| ☐ | RA-26677 | Antonov An-26B | 8603 | | ♦ |

## KMV MINERALNYE VODY AIRLINES — Air Minvody (KV/MVD) — Mineralnye Vody (MRV)

Ceased ops 28Sep11

## KNAAPO — Knaapo (KNM) — Komsomolsk na Amur (KXK)

| | | | | | |
|---|---|---|---|---|---|
| ☐ | RA-11230 | Antonov An-12BP | 5342708 | | ♦ |
| ☐ | RA-11371 | Antonov An-12BP | 00347406 | ex 22 red | |
| ☐ | RA-11789 | Antonov An-12BP | 6343905 | ex LZ-BFB | |

## KOLAVIA — Kogalym (7K/KGL) — Kogalym (KGP)

| | | | | | |
|---|---|---|---|---|---|
| ☐ | RA-22501 | Mil Mi-8T | 99357415 | | |
| ☐ | RA-26641 | Mil Mi-8T | 8026 | ex CCCP-22641 | |
| ☐ | RA-22980 | Mil Mi-8AMT | 59489607603 | ex RA-22509 | |
| ☐ | RA-24588 | Mil Mi-8T | 98839385 | ex CCCP-24588 | |
| ☐ | RA-25328 | Mil Mi-8T | 98203998 | ex CCCP-25328 | |
| ☐ | RA-25342 | Mil Mi-8T | 98206652 | ex CCCP-25342 | |
| ☐ | RA-25761 | Mil Mi-8MTV-1 | 96073 | | |
| ☐ | RA-27066 | Mil Mi-8MTV-1 | 95902 | ex CCCP-27066 | |
| ☐ | RA-85427 | Tupolev Tu-154b-2 | 80A427 | | ♦ |
| ☐ | RA-85522 | Tupolev Tu-154B-2 | 82A522 | ex CCCP-85522 | |
| ☐ | RA-85757 | Tupolev Tu-156M | 92A939 | | ♦ |
| ☐ | RA-85761 | Tupolev Tu-154M | 93A944 | | >TBM |
| ☐ | RA-85784 | Tupolev Tu-154M | 93A968 | | |
| ☐ | RA-85768 | Tupolev Tu-154M | 93A970 | | ♦ |
| ☐ | RA-85829 | Tupolev Tu-154M | 87A755 | ex SP-LCD | |
| ☐ | EI-ETH | Airbus A321-231 | 0668 | ex TC-OAF | ♦ |
| ☐ | EI-ETK | Airbus A321-231 | 0787 | ex TC-OAI | ♦ |
| ☐ | EI-ETJ | Airbus A321-231 | 0663 | ex TC-OAE | o/o♦ |
| ☐ | TC-KLA | Airbus A320-232 | 2029 | ex N615SA | |
| ☐ | TC-KLB | Airbus A320-232 | 2077 | ex N607SA | |

## KORYAKAVIA — Tilichiki

| | | | | | |
|---|---|---|---|---|---|
| ☐ | RA-28714 | WSK-PZL/Antonov An-28 | 1AJ006-24 | ex CCCP-28714 | |
| ☐ | RA-28715 | WSK-PZL/Antonov An-28 | 1AJ006-25 | ex CCCP-28715 | |
| ☐ | RA-28716 | WSK-PZL/Antonov An-28 | 1AJ007-01 | ex CCCP-28716 | |
| ☐ | RA-28722 | WSK-PLZ/Antonov An-28 | 1AJ007-07 | | |
| ☐ | RA-74039 | Antonov An-74 | 36547097931 | | ♦ |
| ☐ | RA-74050 | Antonov An-74 | 47181011 | | ♦ |

## KOSMOS AIRLINES · Kosmos (KSM) · Moscow-Vnukovo (VKO)

| | Reg | Type | c/n | Notes | |
|---|---|---|---|---|---|
| ☐ | RA-65010 | Tupolev Tu-134A | 46130 | ex CCCP-65010 | Yelena |
| ☐ | RA-65097 | Tupolev Tu-134AK | 60540 | ex CCCP-65097 | |
| ☐ | RA-65557 | Tupolev Tu-134AK-3 | 66380 | | ♦ |
| ☐ | RA-65566 | Tupolev Tu-134AK-1 | 63952 | | |
| ☐ | RA-65719 | Tupolev Tu-134AK | 63637 | ex CCCP-65719 | VIP |
| ☐ | RA-65726 | Tupolev Tu-134AK | 63720 | ex CCCP-65726 | VIP |
| ☐ | RA-65727 | Tupolev Tu-134B-3 | 03564820 | ex CCCP-65727 | VIP,Bank Moscovski Kapital |
| ☐ | RA-65771 | Tupolev Tu-134A-3 | 62445 | | ♦ |
| ☐ | RA-65919 | Tupolev Tu-134AK | 66168 | | |
| ☐ | RA-65935 | Tupolev Tu-134A-3 | 66180 | ex CCCP-65935 | VIP |
| ☐ | RA-65941 | Tupolev Tu-134A-3 | 60642 | | ♦ |
| ☐ | RA-65956 | Tupolev Tu-134AK | 2351709 | | ♦ |
| ☐ | RA-11025 | Antonov An-12TB | 6344103 | ex CCCP-11025 | |
| ☐ | RA-12988 | Antonov An-12TB | 00347206 | | |
| ☐ | RA-11363 | Antonov An-12BK | 00347505 | | ♦ |

## KOSTROMA AIR ENTERPRISE · Kostroma (KMW)

| | Reg | Type | c/n | Notes | |
|---|---|---|---|---|---|
| ☐ | RA-26081 | Antonov An-26B-100 | 11703 | | ♦ |
| ☐ | RA-26595 | Antonov An-26 | 47313401 | ex CCCP-26595 | |
| ☐ | RA-27210 | Antonov An-26-100 | 5410 | ex CCCP-27210 Marshal Novikov | |

## KUBAN AIRLINES · Air Kuban (GW/KIL) · Krasnodar-Pashkovskaya (KRR)

| | Reg | Type | c/n | Notes | |
|---|---|---|---|---|---|
| ☐ | VQ-BHB | Boeing 737-3Q8 | 26310/2680 | ex G-TOYA | |
| ☐ | VQ-BHC | Boeing 737-3Q8 | 26311/2681 | ex G-TOYB | |
| ☐ | VQ-BHD | Boeing 737-3Q8 | 26312/2693 | ex G-TOYC | |
| ☐ | VP-BOT | Boeing 737-341 | 25048/2085 | ex N728BC | |
| ☐ | VP-BOU | Boeing 737-341 | 25049/2091 | ex N729BC | ♦ |
| ☐ | RA-42331 | Yakovlev Yak-42 | 4520424505128 | ex CCCP-42331 | |
| ☐ | RA-42336 | Yakovlev Yak-42 | 4250422606220 | ex CCCP-42336 | |
| ☐ | RA-42342 | Yakovlev Yak-42 | 4520421706302 | ex EK-42342 | |
| ☐ | RA-42350 | Yakovlev Yak-42 | 4520424711372 | ex CCCP-42350 | |
| ☐ | RA-42363 | Yakovlev Yak-42D | 4520424811438 | ex CCCP-42363 | |
| ☐ | RA-42367 | Yakovlev Yak-42D | 4520421914133 | ex CCCP-42367 | |
| ☐ | RA-42375 | Yakovlev Yak-42D | 4520424914410 | ex CCCP-42375 | |
| ☐ | RA-42386 | Yakovlev Yak-42D | 4520424016310 | ex CCCP-42386 | |
| ☐ | RA-42406 | Yakovlev Yak-42D | 4520424116683 | | |
| ☐ | RA-42421 | Yakovlev Yak-42D | 4520422303017 | ex CCCP-42421 | ♦ |
| ☐ | RA-42526 | Yakovlev Yak-42 | 11040803 | | |
| ☐ | RA-42538 | Yakovlev Yak-42 | 11130404 | | ♦ |
| ☐ | RA-42541 | Yakovlev Yak-42 | 11140704 | ex CCCP-42541 | ♦ |
| ☐ | VP-BFJ | Boeing 737-53A | 24859/1919 | ex G-THOA | wfs♦ |
| ☐ | VP-BFK | Boeing 737-5L9 | 24928/1961 | ex G-THOB | ♦ |
| ☐ | VP-BHA | Boeing 737-529 | 26538/2298 | ex C-GAHB | ♦ |
| ☐ | VQ-BLY | Airbus A319-111 | 2224 | ex G-EZEK | ♦ |
| ☐ | VQ-BMN | Airbus A319-111 | 2249 | ex G-EZEO | ♦ |
| ☐ | VQ-BMO | Airbus A319-111 | 2214 | ex G-EZEJ | ♦ |

## LIPETSK AVIA

| | Reg | Type | c/n | Notes | |
|---|---|---|---|---|---|
| ☐ | RA-87281 | Yakovlev Yak-40 | 9311627 | | ♦ |
| ☐ | RA-87372 | Yakovlev Yak-40 | 9340332 | ex CCCP-87372 | |
| ☐ | RA-87406 | Yakovlev Yak-40 | 9421833 | | ♦ |

## LUKIAVIATRANS · Velikie Luki/Pskov-Kresty (VLU/PKV)

| | Reg | Type | c/n | Notes | |
|---|---|---|---|---|---|
| ☐ | RA-30007 | Antonov An-30D | 1408 | ex CCCP-30007 | |
| ☐ | RA-30039 | Antonov An-30 | 0710 | | ♦ |
| ☐ | RA-30042 | Antonov An-30 | 0901 | ex CCCP-30042 | no titles |
| ☐ | RA-30053 | Antonov An-30D | 1008 | ex CCCP-30053 | |
| ☐ | RA-46632 | Antonov An-30 | 0201 | ex CCCP-46632 | |

## MCHS ROSSII · Sumes (SUM) · Moscow-Zhukovsky

| | Reg | Type | c/n | Notes | |
|---|---|---|---|---|---|
| ☐ | RF-31120 | Beriev Be-200ES | 76820002501 | | ♦ |
| ☐ | RF-31121 | Beriev Be-200ES | 76820003001 | | ♦ |
| ☐ | RF-31361 | Beriev Be-200ES | 76820003102 | | ♦ |
| ☐ | RF-32765 | Beriev Be-200ES | 76820001301 | ex RA-21515 | |
| ☐ | RF-32766 | Beriev Be-200ES | 76820001402 | ex RA-21516 | |
| ☐ | RF-32767 | Beriev Be-200ES | 76820002501 | ex RA-21517 | |
| ☐ | RF-32768 | Beriev Be-200ES | 76820002602 | | |
| ☐ | RA-76362 | Ilyushin Il-76TD | 1033416533 | Anatoliy Lyapidevskiy | |
| ☐ | RA-76363 | Ilyushin Il-76TD | 1033417540 | Vasiliy Molokov | |

| | | | | | | |
|---|---|---|---|---|---|---|
| ☐ | RA-76429 | Ilyushin Il-76TD | 1043419639 | | | |
| ☐ | RA-76840 | Ilyushin Il-76TD | 1033417553 | | Nikolay Kamanin | |
| ☐ | RA-76841 | Ilyushin Il-76TD | 1033418601 | | Mavrikiy Slepnev | |
| ☐ | RA-76845 | Ilyushin Il-76TDP | 1043420696 | | Mikhail Vodop'yanov | |
| | | | | | | |
| ☐ | RA-06075 | Mil Mi-26T | 34001212465 | | | |
| ☐ | RA-06278 | Mil Mi-26T | 34001212522 | | | |
| ☐ | RA-06279 | Mil Mi-26T | 34001212603 | | | |

Above three now believed to be RF-31110, RF-31124 and RF-32821 but order unknown

| | | | | | | |
|---|---|---|---|---|---|---|
| ☐ | RA-42441 | Yakovlev Yak-42D | 4520421402018 | ex EP-LAN | Velerij Chkalov | VIP |
| ☐ | RA-42446 | Yakovlev Yak-42D | 4520423308017 | ex UN-42446 | Vladimir Kokkinaki | |
| ☐ | RA-86570 | Ilyushin Il-62M | 1356344 | | Mikhail Gromov | |

## MORDOVIA AIR — Saransk (SKX)

| | | | | | |
|---|---|---|---|---|---|
| ☐ | RA-08824 | Antonov An-24RV | 97310810V | | ♦ |
| ☐ | RA-26247 | Antonov An-26B-100 | 4103 | ex CCCP-26247 | |
| ☐ | RA-46505 | Antonov An-24RV | 37308309 | ex CCCP-46505 | |
| ☐ | RA-47834 | Antonov An-24B | 17307306 | | ♦ |

## MOSKOVIA — Gromov Airline (3R/GAI) — Moscow-Zhukovsky

| | | | | | |
|---|---|---|---|---|---|
| ☐ | RA-11309 | Antonov An-12BP | 00347510 | ex CCCP-11309 | op for Irkut |
| ☐ | RA-11310 | Antonov An-12BP | 4342601 | ex CCCP-11310 | op for Irkut |
| ☐ | RA-12162 | Antonov An-12BP | 3341509 | ex CCCP-12162 | op for Irkut |
| ☐ | RA-12193 | Antonov An-12BK | 9346805 | | ♦ |
| ☐ | RA-12194 | Antonov An-12BK | 00347203 | | ♦ |
| ☐ | RA-12195 | Antonov An-12BK | 00347410 | | ♦ |
| | | | | | |
| ☐ | RA-85615 | Tupolev Tu-154M | 86A731 | ex CCCP-85615 | |
| ☐ | RA-85699 | Tupolev Tu-154M | 91A874 | | ♦ |
| ☐ | RA-85736 | Tupolev Tu-154M | 92A918 | ex CCCP-85736 Yuri Morozov | |
| ☐ | RA-85743 | Tupolev Tu-154M | 92A926 | ex CCCP-85743 Yuri Sheffer | |
| ☐ | RA-85851 | Tupolev Tu-154M | 82A531 | | ♦ |
| | | | | | |
| ☐ | RA-30028 | Antonov An-30 | 0510 | ex CCCP-30028 | |
| ☐ | VQ-BDI | Boeing 737-73A | 28497/216 | ex N497TF | |
| ☐ | VQ-BER | Boeing 737-7L9/W | 28006/26 | ex N280AG | |
| ☐ | VQ-BPF | Boeing 737-8K2/W | 30391/814 | ex PH-HZL | <TRA♦ |

## MOSKVA AIR COMPANY — (3G/AYZ) — Moscow-Domodedovo (DME)

Ceased ops 27Jan11

## NAPO AVIATRANS — Novsib (NPO) — Novosibirsk-Yeltsovka

| | | | | | |
|---|---|---|---|---|---|
| ☐ | RA-12193 | Antonov An-12BK | 9346805 | ex CCCP-12193 | |
| ☐ | RA-12194 | Antonov An-12BK | 00347203 | ex CCCP-12194 | |
| ☐ | RA-12195 | Antonov An-12BK | 00347410 | ex CCCP-12195 | |
| ☐ | RA-41900 | Antonov An-38-120 | 4160381607003 | | >LAY |
| ☐ | RA-41902 | Antonov An-38-120 | 4163847010002 | | >VTK |

Status uncertain

## NORDAVIA REGIONAL AIRLINES — Dvina (5N/AUL) — Arkhangelsk-Talegi (ARH)

| | | | | | |
|---|---|---|---|---|---|
| ☐ | RA-46528 | Antonov An-24RV | 47310007 | ex CCCP-46528 | |
| ☐ | RA-46651 | Antonov An-24RV | 47309202 | ex CCCP-46651 | |
| ☐ | RA-46667 | Antonov An-24RV | 47309508 | | ♦ |
| ☐ | RA-47199 | Antonov An-24RV | 27307703 | | ♦ |
| ☐ | RA-47305 | Antonov An-24RV | 57310305 | | ♦ |
| | | | | | |
| ☐ | LY-AYU | Boeing 737-505 | 24646/2138 | ex ES-ABO | ♦ |
| ☐ | VP-BKP | Boeing 737-59D | 25065/2028 | ex OK-WGD | |
| ☐ | VP-BKT | Boeing 737-33R | 28871/2900 | ex PP-VPY | |
| ☐ | VP-BKU | Boeing 737-505 | 25789/2229 | ex G-GFFB | |
| ☐ | VP-BKV | Boeing 737-505 | 27155/2449 | ex N215BV | |
| ☐ | VP-BOH | Boeing 737-59D | 25038/1969 | ex G-GFFA | |
| ☐ | VP-BOI | Boeing 737-505 | 24650/1792 | ex G-GFFG | |
| ☐ | VP-BQI | Boeing 737-5Y0 | 25186/2236 | ex OM-SEA | |
| ☐ | VP-BQL | Boeing 737-5Y0 | 25185/2220 | ex OM-SEF | |
| ☐ | VP-BRE | Boeing 737-53C | 24827/2243 | ex OM-SEE | |
| ☐ | VP-BRG | Boeing 737-53C | 24826/2041 | ex OM-SED | |
| ☐ | VP-BRI | Boeing 737-5Y0 | 25289/2288 | ex OM-SEG | >AFL |
| ☐ | VP-BRK | Boeing 737-5Y0 | 25288/2286 | ex OM-SEC | |
| ☐ | VP-BRN | Boeing 737-5Y0 | 25191/2260 | ex OM-SEB | |
| ☐ | VP-BRP | Boeing 737-505 | 24651/1842 | ex LN-BRD | |
| ☐ | VP-BXN | Boeing 737-53A | 24754/1868 | ex G-GFFF | |
| | | | | | |
| ☐ | RA-26135 | Antonov An-26B | 12806 | | ♦ |

## NORDSTAR (Y7/TYA)

| | | | | | |
|---|---|---|---|---|---|
| ☐ | VQ-BKN | ATR 42-500 | 0823 | ex F-WWBL | ♦ |
| ☐ | VQ-BKO | ATR 42-500 | 0827 | ex F-WNUC | ♦ |
| ☐ | VQ-BKP | ATR 42-500 | 0835 | ex F-WW | ♦ |
| ☐ | VQ-BKQ | ATR 42-500 | 0839 | ex F-WW | ♦ |
| ☐ | VQ-BPE | ATR 42-500 | 0641 | ex OH-ATA | ♦ |
| ☐ | VQ-BDN | Boeing 737-8K5/W | 32905/1046 | ex D-AHLP | |
| ☐ | VQ-BDO | Boeing 737-8K5/W | 32906/1087 | ex D-AHLQ | |
| ☐ | VQ-BDP | Boeing 737-8Q8/W | 28221/226 | ex N282AG | |
| ☐ | VQ-BDW | Boeing 737-8K5/W | 27977/9 | ex D-AHFC | |
| ☐ | VQ-BDZ | Boeing 737-8K5/W | 27978/40 | ex D-AHFD | |
| ☐ | VQ-BKR | Boeing 737-8AS/W | 33559/1443 | ex N292MS | ♦ |
| ☐ | VQ-BNG | Boeing 737-86J/W | 37747/3120 | ex D-ABKH | ♦ |
| ☐ | VQ-BPM | Boeing 737-8AS/W | 33812/1615 | ex EI-DCS | ♦ |
| ☐ | VQ-BQT | Boeing 737-8AS/W | 33561/1463 | ex N591MS | ♦ |

## NORDWIND (N4/NWS) Moscow-Sheremetyevo (SVO)

| | | | | | |
|---|---|---|---|---|---|
| ☐ | VQ-BAK | Boeing 757-2Q8 | 26332/688 | ex N401JS | |
| ☐ | VQ-BAL | Boeing 757-2Q8 | 27351/639 | ex N403JS | |
| ☐ | VQ-BBT | Boeing 757-2Q8 | 29443/821 | ex N763MX | |
| ☐ | VQ-BBU | Boeing 757-2Q8 | 29442/819 | ex N762MX | |
| ☐ | VQ-BHR | Boeing 757-2Q8/W | 30046/1006 | ex OH-LBV | |
| ☐ | VQ-BJK | Boeing 757-2Q8 | 29380/836 | ex N380RM | |
| ☐ | VQ-BKE | Boeing 757-231/W | 28484/825 | ex N716TW | |
| ☐ | VQ-BKM | Boeing 757-29J/W | 27203/588 | ex LY-FLA | ♦ |
| ☐ | VQ-BMQ | Boeing 767-306ER | 28098/607 | ex N765NA | ♦ |
| ☐ | VQ-BMU | Boeing 767-328ER | 27427/579 | ex PR-VAN | ♦ |
| ☐ | VQ-BOG | Boeing 767-341ER | 30342/774 | ex VP-BWQ | |
| ☐ | VQ-BPT | Boeing 767-306ER | 27957/587 | ex N281LF | ♦ |
| ☐ | VQ-BRA | Boeing 767-33AER | 27310/545 | ex N310AN | |
| ☐ | VQ-BOD | Airbus A321-211 | 1233 | ex M-ABEE | |
| ☐ | VQ-BOE | Airbus A321-211 | 1219 | ex M-ABED | ♦ |

## NOVOSIBIRSK AIR ENTERPRISE Nakair (NBE) Novosibirsk-Severny

| | | | | | |
|---|---|---|---|---|---|
| ☐ | RA-46642 | Antonov An-24RV | 37308910 | ex CCCP-46642 | |
| ☐ | RA-46659 | Antonov An-24RV | 47309306 | ex CCCP-46659 | |
| ☐ | RA-46682 | Antonov An-24RV | 47309704 | ex CCCP-46682 | |

## ORENAIR Orenburg (R2/ORB) Orenburg-Tsentralny (REN)

| | | | | | | |
|---|---|---|---|---|---|---|
| ☐ | VP-BPG | Boeing 737-8AS/W | 29924/578 | ex EI-CSI | | |
| ☐ | VP-BPI | Boeing 737-83N/W | 28244/958 | ex N308TZ | | |
| ☐ | VP-BPY | Boeing 737-83N/W | 28247/1091 | ex N318TZ | | |
| ☐ | VQ-BCJ | Boeing 737-8AS/W | 29932/1030 | ex EI-CSS | | |
| ☐ | VQ-BEM | Boeing 737-85R/W | 29036/164 | ex N636AC | Michael | |
| ☐ | VQ-BEN | Boeing 737-85R/W | 29037/177 | ex N637AC | | |
| ☐ | VQ-BFY | Boeing 737-86N/W | 29884/1094 | ex N117MN | | |
| ☐ | VQ-BFZ | Boeing 737-86N/W | 28644/839 | ex N116MN | | |
| ☐ | VQ-BIZ | Boeing 737-86N/W | 28645/840 | ex N548MS | | ♦ |
| ☐ | VQ-BJC | Boeing 737-8K5/W | 27992/523 | ex D-AHFQ | | |
| ☐ | VQ-BJX | Boeing 737-86N/W | 32735/1104 | ex TC-APJ | | ♦ |
| ☐ | VQ-BLW | Boeing 737-85P/W | 28381/250 | ex EC-HBL | | ♦ |
| ☐ | VQ-BLX | Boeing 737-85P/W | 28384/420 | ex EC-HGO | | ♦ |
| ☐ | VQ-BNK | Boeing 737-8K5/W | 30414/703 | ex D-AHFU | | ♦ |
| ☐ | VQ- | Boeing 737-808 | 34969/2293 | ex D-ABBX | | o/o♦ |
| ☐ | VQ- | Boeing 737-808 | 34970/2379 | ex D-ABBY | | o/o♦ |
| ☐ | RA-65049 | Tupolev Tu-134A-3 | 49755 | ex EW-65049 | | |
| ☐ | RA-65054 | Tupolev Tu-134A | 49840 | ex CCCP-65054 | | |
| ☐ | RA-65090 | Tupolev Tu-134A | 60185 | ex CCCP-65090 | | |
| ☐ | RA-65101 | Tupolev Tu-134A-3 | 60260 | ex CCCP-65101 | | |
| ☐ | RA-65110 | Tupolev Tu-134A-3 | 60343 | ex (HA-LBT) | | |
| ☐ | RA-65117 | Tupolev Tu-134A-3 | 60450 | ex (HA-LBU) | | |
| ☐ | RA-65136 | Tupolev Tu-134A-3 | 60885 | ex CCCP-65136 | | |
| ☐ | RA-64016 | Tupolev Tu-204-100 | 1450742564017 | | | ♦ |
| ☐ | RA-85602 | Tupolev Tu-154B-2 | 84A602 | ex CCCP-85602 | | |
| ☐ | RA-85603 | Tupolev Tu-154B-2 | 84A603 | ex CCCP-85603 no titles | | |
| ☐ | RA-85604 | Tupolev Tu-154B-2 | 85A604 | ex CCCP-85604 | | |
| ☐ | RA-85768 | Tupolev Tu-154M | 94A949 | Konstantine Brexos | | |
| ☐ | VP-BEW | Boeing 737-505 | 26297/2578 | ex N371LF | | |
| ☐ | VP-BGP | Boeing 737-4Y0 | 24691/1904 | ex N691GE | | |
| ☐ | VP-BGQ | Boeing 737-4Y0 | 24683/1901 | ex N683GE | | |
| ☐ | VP-BPE | Boeing 737-5H6 | 26445/2327 | ex OK-XGV | Aleksandr Kukishev | |
| ☐ | VP-BPF | Boeing 737-5H6 | 26446/2358 | ex OK-XGW | | |

442

| | VQ-BNU | Boeing 777-2Q8ER | 29908/229 | ex F-OPAR | ◆ |

## PERM AIRLINES  Perm Air (P9/PGP)  Perm-Bolshoe Savina (PEE)

| | | | | |
|---|---|---|---|---|
| ☐ | RA-26520 | Antonov An-26-100 | 87307101 | ex CCCP-26520 |
| ☐ | RA-26636 | Antonov An-26-100 | 87306306 | ex EP-TQB |
| ☐ | RA-47756 | Antonov An-24B | 79901209 | ex CCCP-47756 |
| ☐ | RA-65064 | Tupolev Tu-134A-3 | 49886 | ex CCCP-65064 |
| ☐ | RA-65751 | Tupolev Tu-134A-3 | 61066 | ex CCCP-65751 Sverbank titles |
| ☐ | RA-65775 | Tupolev Tu-134A-3 | 62530 | ex CCCP-65775 |

## PETROPAVLOVSK-KAMCHATSKY AIR ENTERPRISE
## Petrokam (PTK) Petropavlovsk Kamchatsky-Yelixovo (PKC)

| | | | | | |
|---|---|---|---|---|---|
| ☐ | RA-67007 | LET L-410UVP-E20 | 2723 | ex OK-SLV | ◆ |
| ☐ | RA-67008 | LET L-410UVP-E20 | 2724 | ex OK-SDT | ◆ |
| ☐ | RA-67009 | LET L-410UVP-E20 | 2725 | ex OK-SDU | ◆ |
| ☐ | RA-67645 | LET L-410UVP-E | 902438 | ex CCCP-67645 | |
| ☐ | RA-67662 | LET L-410UVP-E | 902520 | ex CCCP-67662 | |
| | | | | | |
| ☐ | RA-26122 | Antonov An-26B | 12401 | ex CCCP-26122 | |
| ☐ | RA-26251 | Antonov An-26-100 | 9109 | | |
| ☐ | RA-87385 | Yakovlev Yak-40K | 9411632 | ex CCCP-87385 | |
| ☐ | RA-87947 | Yakovlev Yak-40K | 9621145 | ex CCCP-87947 | |
| ☐ | RA-87949 | Yakovlev Yak-40K | 9621345 | ex CCCP-87949 | |
| ☐ | RA-87988 | Yakovlev Yak-40 | 9541244 | ex CCCP-87988 | |

## POLAR AIRLINES  (RKA)  Batagai

| | | | | | |
|---|---|---|---|---|---|
| ☐ | RA-46333 | Antonov An-24B | 97305510 | ex CCCP-46333 | |
| ☐ | RA-46374 | Antonov An-24B | 07306005 | ex CCCP-46374 | |
| ☐ | RA-47161 | Antonov An-24B | 89901703 | ex CCCP-47161 | |
| ☐ | RA-47195 | Antonov An-24LRI | 07306202 | | |
| ☐ | RA-47260 | Antonov An-24B | 27307802 | ex CCCP-47260 | |
| ☐ | RA-47786 | Antonov An-24B | 89901601 | | ◆ |
| | | | | | |
| ☐ | RA-26030 | Antonov An-26B | 10501 | ex CCCP-26030 | |
| ☐ | RA-26061 | Antonov An-26B | 11108 | ex CCCP-26061 | |
| ☐ | RA-26538 | Antonov An-26-100 | 47302102 | ex CCCP-26538 | |
| ☐ | RA-26604 | Antonov An-26 | 4506 | | ◆ |
| ☐ | RA-67623 | LET L-410UVP-E | 902405 | | ◆ |
| ☐ | RA-67670 | LET L-410UVP-E3 | 902416 | | ◆ |
| ☐ | RA-67676 | LET L-410UVP-E | 872007 | | ◆ |
| ☐ | RA-67693 | LET L-410UVP-E | 952624 | | ◆ |

## POLET AVIAKOMPANIA  Polet (YQ/POT)  Voronezh (VOZ)

| | | | | | |
|---|---|---|---|---|---|
| ☐ | RA-82010 | Antonov An-124-100 Ruslan | 9773053616017 | ex CCCP-82010 | |
| ☐ | RA-82014 | Antonov An-124-100 Ruslan | 9773054732039 | ex CCCP-82014 | |
| ☐ | RA-82068 | Antonov An-124-100 Ruslan | 9773051359127 | ex RA-82070 | |
| ☐ | RA-82075 | Antonov An-124-100 Ruslan | 9773053459147 | Boris Naginski | |
| ☐ | RA-82077 | Antonov An-124-100 Ruslan | 9773054459151 | Fedor Muravchenko | |
| ☐ | RA-82080 | Antonov An-124-100 Ruslan | 9773051462161 | | |
| | | | | | |
| ☐ | RA-61709 | Antonov An-148 | 27015040009 | | |
| ☐ | RA-61710 | Antonov An-148 | 27015040010 | | |
| ☐ | RA-61711 | Antonov An-148 | 27015040011 | | ◆ |
| ☐ | RA-61713 | Antonov An-148 | | | ◆ |
| ☐ | RA- | Antonov An-148 | | | o/o |
| ☐ | RA- | Antonov An-148 | | | o/o |
| | | | | | |
| ☐ | RA-96101 | Ilyushin Il-96-400T | 74393201001 | | Frtr |
| ☐ | RA-96102 | Ilyushin Il-96-400T | 73439201002 | | Frtr |
| ☐ | RA-96103 | Ilyushin Il-96-400T | 97693201003 | | Frtr |
| ☐ | RA-96104 | Ilyushin Il-96-400T | | | o/o |
| ☐ | RA-96105 | Ilyushin Il-96-400T | | | o/o◆ |
| | | | | | |
| ☐ | VQ-BGB | SAAB SF.340B | 340B-211 | ex N211NE | ◆ |
| ☐ | VQ-BGC | SAAB SF.340B | 340B-232 | ex N232AE | |
| ☐ | VQ-BGD | SAAB SF.340B | 340B-250 | ex N250AE | |
| ☐ | VQ-BGE | SAAB SF.340B | 340B-273 | ex N273AE | |
| ☐ | VQ-BGF | SAAB SF.340B | 340B-218 | ex N218AE | |
| | | | | | |
| ☐ | VP-BPL | SAAB 2000 | 2000-029 | ex HB-IZO | |
| ☐ | VP-BPM | SAAB 2000 | 2000-057 | ex HB-IYB | |
| ☐ | VP-BPN | SAAB 2000 | 2000-058 | ex HB-IYC | |
| ☐ | VP-BPQ | SAAB 2000 | 2000-060 | ex HB-IYE | |
| ☐ | VP-BPR | SAAB 2000 | 2000-061 | ex HB-IYF | |
| | | | | | |
| ☐ | RA-30024 | Antonov An-30 | 0502 | ex CCCP-30024 | |
| ☐ | RA-30048 | Antonov An-30 | 0910 | ex CCCP-30048 | |

| | | | | | |
|---|---|---|---|---|---|
| ☐ | RA-46676 | Antonov An-24RV | 47309608 | ex CCCP-46676 | |
| ☐ | RA-46690 | Antonov An-24RV | 47309901 | ex CCCP-46690 Nikolai Pribilov | |
| ☐ | RA-87436 | Yakovlev Yak-40 | 9431235 | | |
| ☐ | RA-88304 | Yakovlev Yak-40S2 | 9510439 | ex ST-YAK | ♦ |

## POLYARNYA AVIA
*Yakutsk (YKS)*

| | | | | | |
|---|---|---|---|---|---|
| ☐ | RA-46834 | Antonov An-24RV | 17306801 | | |
| ☐ | RA-67623 | LET L-410UVP-E | 902405 | ex CCCP-67623 | ♦ |
| ☐ | RA-67670 | LET L-410UVP-E3 | 902416 | ex ES-LLA | ♦ |
| ☐ | RA-67676 | LET L-410UVP-E3 | 872007 | ex Soviet AF 2007 | ♦ |
| ☐ | RA-67693 | LET L-410UVP-E | 952624 | ex OK-ADT | ♦ |

## PROGRESS AVIAKOMPANIA
*Progress (PSS)*     *Samara-Bezymyanka (KUF)*

| | | | | | |
|---|---|---|---|---|---|
| ☐ | RA-26180 | Antonov An-26 | 9737810 | ex CCCP-26180 | |
| ☐ | RA-26192 | Antonov An-24RT | 1911805 | ex CCCP-26192 | |

## PSKOVAVIA
*Pskovavia (PSW)*     *Pskov-Kresty (PKV)*

| | | | | | |
|---|---|---|---|---|---|
| ☐ | RA-26041 | Antonov An-26B | 10707 | | ♦ |
| ☐ | RA-26086 | Antonov An-26B | 12302 | | ♦ |
| ☐ | RA-26134 | Antonov An-26B | 12805 | ex CCCP-26134 | |
| ☐ | RA-26142 | Antonov An-26B | 37312904 | ex CCCP-26142 | |
| ☐ | RA-26209 | Antonov An-26B | 14302 | | |

## RED WINGS
*Remont Air (WZ/RWZ)*     *Moscow-Vnukovo (VKO)*

| | | | | | |
|---|---|---|---|---|---|
| ☐ | RA-64018 | Tupolev Tu-204-100 | 1450741964018 | | |
| ☐ | RA-64019 | Tupolev Tu-204-100 | 1450741064019 | | |
| ☐ | RA-64020 | Tupolev Tu-204-100 | 1450743164020 | | |
| ☐ | RA-64043 | Tupolev Tu-204-100 | 64043 | | |
| ☐ | RA-64046 | Tupolev Tu-204-100 | 64046 | | o/o |
| ☐ | RA-64047 | Tupolev Tu-204-100 | 64047 | | |
| ☐ | RA-64049 | Tupolev Tu-204-100 | 64049 | | |
| ☐ | RA-64050 | Tupolev Tu-204-100 | 64050 | | |

## REGION-AVIA

| | | | | | |
|---|---|---|---|---|---|
| ☐ | VQ-BCL | Embraer EMB.120ER Brasilia | 120304 | ex N227SW | ♦ |

## ROSNEFT-BALTIKA
*Rosbalt (RNB)*     *St Petersburg-Pulkovo (LED)*

| | | | | | |
|---|---|---|---|---|---|
| ☐ | RA-21500 | Yakovlev Yak-40K | 9741356 | ex CCCP-21500 | |

## ROSSIYA RUSSIAN AIRLINES
*Russia (FV/SDM)*
*Moscow-Vnukovo/St Petersburg-Pulkovo (VKO/LED)*

| | | | | | |
|---|---|---|---|---|---|
| ☐ | VP-BIQ | Airbus A319-111 | 1890 | ex N917FR | |
| ☐ | VP-BIT | Airbus A319-112 | 1761 | ex N909FR | |
| ☐ | VP-BIU | Airbus A319-114 | 0649 | ex N574SX | |
| ☐ | VQ-BAQ | Airbus A319-111 | 1560 | ex N903FR | |
| ☐ | VQ-BAR | Airbus A319-111 | 1488 | ex N901FR | |
| ☐ | VQ-BAS | Airbus A319-111 | 1863 | ex N913FR | |
| ☐ | VQ-BAT | Airbus A319-112 | 1876 | ex N916FR | |
| ☐ | VQ-BAU | Airbus A319-112 | 1851 | ex N915FR | |
| ☐ | VQ-BAV | Airbus A319-111 | 1743 | ex N907FR | |
| | | | | | |
| ☐ | EI-DXY | Airbus A320-212 | 0525 | ex D-AKNX | |
| ☐ | EI-DZR | Airbus A320-212 | 0427 | ex N265AV | |
| ☐ | VQ-BBM | Airbus A320-214 | 1578 | ex EC-HZU | |
| ☐ | VQ-BDQ | Airbus A320-214 | 1767 | ex EC-KDD | |
| ☐ | VQ-BDR | Airbus A320-214 | 1130 | ex EC-IMU | |
| ☐ | VQ-BDY | Airbus A320-214 | 1657 | ex EC-KBQ | |
| | | | | | |
| ☐ | RA-61701 | Antonov An-148-100B | 2701504001 | | |
| ☐ | RA-61702 | Antonov An-148-100B | 2701504002 | | |
| ☐ | RA-61703 | Antonov An-148-100B | 2701504003 | | |
| ☐ | RA-61704 | Antonov An-148-100B | 2701504004 | | |
| ☐ | RA-61705 | Antonov An-148-100B | 2701504005 | | |
| ☐ | RA-61706 | Antonov An-148-100B | 2701504006 | | |
| | | | | | |
| ☐ | EI-CDD | Boeing 737-548 | 24989/1989 | ex EI-BXH | |
| ☐ | EI-CDE | Boeing 737-548 | 25115/2050 | ex PT-SLM | |
| ☐ | EI-CDF | Boeing 737-548 | 25737/2232 | | |
| ☐ | EI-CDG | Boeing 737-548 | 25738/2261 | | |
| ☐ | EI-CDH | Boeing 737-548 | 25739/2271 | | |
| | | | | | |
| ☐ | EC-HSV | Boeing 767-3Q8ER | 29387/840 | | <AEA♦ |

| | | | | | |
|---|---|---|---|---|---|
| ☐ | EI-DZH | Boeing 767-3Q8ER | 29390/870 | ex N101LF | |
| ☐ | EI-EAR | Boeing 767-3Q8ER | 27616/714 | ex N364LF | |
| ☐ | EI-ECB | Boeing 767-3Q8ER | 27617/722 | ex N151LF | |

## RUSAIR | CGI-Rusair (CGI) | Moscow-Sheremetyevo (SVO)

| | | | | | |
|---|---|---|---|---|---|
| ☐ | RA-42368 | Yakovlev Yak-42D | 4520422914166 | ex EP-LBT | |
| ☐ | RA-42387 | Yakovlev Yak-42 | 4520424016436 | | |
| ☐ | RA-42402 | Yakovlev Yak-42D | 4520422116583 | | ♦ |
| ☐ | RA-65087 | Tupolev Tu-134A-3 | 60155 | | wfs♦ |
| ☐ | RA-65124 | Tupolev Tu-134A | 60560 | ex ES-AAN | VIP |
| ☐ | RA-65576 | Tupolev Tu-134B-3 | 63285 | | ♦ |
| ☐ | RA-65790 | Tupolev Tu-134A-3 | 63100 | | ♦ |
| ☐ | RA-87502 | Yakovlev Yak-40 | 9510140 | ex CCCP-87502 | VIP |

## RUSJET | (RSJ) | Moscow-Vnukovo (VKO)

| | | | | | |
|---|---|---|---|---|---|
| ☐ | RA-42365 | Yakovlev Yak-42D | 4520424811447 | ex CCCP-42365 | |
| ☐ | RA-42411 | Yakovlev Yak-42D | 4520421219043 | ex CCCP-42411 | VIP |
| ☐ | RA-42415 | Yakovlev Yak-42D | 4520422219089 | | ♦ |
| ☐ | RA-42423 | Yakovlev Yak-42D | 4520424216606 | | ♦ |
| ☐ | RA-42468 | Yakovlev Yak-42D | 4520422914166 | | ♦ |
| ☐ | RA-65701 | Tupolev Tu-134B-3 | 63365 | | |
| ☐ | RA-65737 | Tupolev Tu-134B-3 | 64195 | ex CCCP-65737 | converted Tu-134UBL |
| ☐ | RA-65747 | Tupolev Tu-134B-3 | 03564715 | | ♦ |
| ☐ | RA-87418 | Yakovlev Yak-40 | 9421034 | ex CCCP-87418 | VIP [PEE] |
| ☐ | RA-88240 | Yakovlev Yak-40K | 9641151 | ex CCCP-88240 | Executive |

## RUSLINE AIR | Rusline Air (7R/RLU) | Moscow-Sheremetyevo (SVO)

| | | | | | |
|---|---|---|---|---|---|
| ☐ | VP-BAO | Canadair CRJ-100 | 7177 | ex F-GPTB | |
| ☐ | VQ-BNB | Canadair CRJ-100ER | 7364 | ex N807CA | |
| ☐ | VQ-BND | Canadair CRJ-100LR | 7483 | ex N442CA | ♦ |
| ☐ | VQ-BNE | Canadair CRJ-100ER | 7482 | ex N436CA | ♦ |
| ☐ | VQ-BNL | Canadair CRJ-100ER | 7106 | ex F-GRJE | ♦ |
| ☐ | VQ-BNY | Canadair CRJ-100ER | 7108 | ex F-GRJF | ♦ |
| ☐ | VP-BMN | Canadair CRJ-200 | 7179 | ex N620BR | ♦ |
| ☐ | VP-BMR | Canadair CRJ-200 | 7192 | ex N623BR | ♦ |
| ☐ | VQ-BBW | Canadair CRJ-200 | 7426 | ex N651BR | |
| ☐ | VQ-BEV | Canadair CRJ-200ER | 7467 | ex N703BR | ♦ |
| ☐ | VQ-BFA | Canadair CRJ-200ER | 7627 | ex N466CA | ♦ |
| ☐ | VQ-BFB | Canadair CRJ-200ER | 7637 | ex N467CA | ♦ |
| ☐ | VQ-BFF | Canadair CRJ-200LR | 7470 | ex N705BR | ♦ |
| ☐ | VQ-BFI | Canadair CRJ-200ER | 7671 | ex N478CA | ♦ |
| ☐ | VQ-BIX | Canadair CRJ-200ER | 7539 | ex N443CA | >IAE♦ |
| ☐ | VQ-BMK | Canadair CRJ-200ER | 7668 | ex N473CA | >IAE♦ |
| ☐ | VQ-BNA | Canadair CRJ-200ER | 7473 | ex N435CA | ♦ |
| ☐ | RA-65035 | Tupolev Tu-134A-3 | 48590 | | ♦ |
| ☐ | RA-65087 | Tupolev Tu-134A-3 | 60155 | ex CCCP-65087 | VIP |
| ☐ | RA-65756 | Tupolev Tu-134A | 62179 | ex CCCP-65756 | |
| ☐ | RA-65903 | Tupolev Tu-134A | 63750 | ex CCCP-65903 | |
| ☐ | RA-65934 | Tupolev Tu-134A | 66143 | ex CCCP-65934 | |
| ☐ | RA-87248 | Yakovlev Yak-40K | 9540144 | ex CCCP-87248 | |
| ☐ | RA-87380 | Yakovlev Yak-40 | 9421225 | ex 5N-MAR | |
| ☐ | RA-87429 | Yakovlev Yak-40 | 9420535 | | ♦ |
| ☐ | RA-88293 | Yakovlev Yak-40 | 9510138 | | ♦ |
| ☐ | VQ-BBX | Embraer EMB.120ER Brasilia | 120205 | ex N205CA | |
| ☐ | VQ-BCB | Embraer EMB.120ER Brasilia | 120231 | ex N280AS | |
| ☐ | VQ-BCL | Embraer EMB.120ER Brasilia | 120304 | ex N227SW | |

## RUSSIAN SKY AIRLINES | Ruduga (P7/ESL) | Moscow-Domodedovo (DME)

| | | | | | |
|---|---|---|---|---|---|
| ☐ | EW-78848 | Ilyushin Il-76TD | 1013405159 | | <TXC♦ |
| ☐ | RA-76799 | Ilyushin Il-76TD | 10034030375 | ex CCCP-76799 | >ABG |
| ☐ | RA-76817 | Ilyushin Il-76TD | 1023412387 | ex CCCP-76817 | |

## RUSSIAN STATE TRANSPORT

| | | | | | |
|---|---|---|---|---|---|
| ☐ | RA-86466 | Ilyushin Il-62M | 2749316 | ex CCCP-86466 | |
| ☐ | RA-86467 | Ilyushin Il-62M | 3749733 | ex CCCP-86467 | VIP |
| ☐ | RA-86468 | Ilyushin Il-62M | 4749857 | ex CCCP-86468 | VIP |
| ☐ | RA-86536 | Ilyushin Il-62M | 4445948 | ex CCCP-86536 | |
| ☐ | RA-86540 | Ilyushin Il-62M | 3546548 | ex CCCP-86540 | VIP |
| ☐ | RA-86559 | Ilyushin Il-62M | 2153258 | ex CCCP-86559 | VIP |
| ☐ | RA-86561 | Ilyushin Il-62M | 4154842 | ex CCCP-86561 | VIP |

| | | | | |
|---|---|---|---|---|
| ☐ | RA-86710 | Ilyushin Il-62M | 2647646 | ex CCCP-86710 | |
| ☐ | RA-86712 | Ilyushin Il-62M | 4648339 | ex CCCP-86712 | VIP |

| | | | | | |
|---|---|---|---|---|---|
| ☐ | RA-96012 | Ilyushin Il-96-300 | 74393201009 | | Presidential a/c |
| ☐ | RA-96014 | Ilyushin Il-96-300 | 74393202014 | | o/o♦ |
| ☐ | RA-96016 | Ilyushin Il-96-300PU | 74393202010 | ex (RA-96013) | Presidential a/c |
| ☐ | RA-96017 | Ilyushin Il-96-300S | 74393202011 | | ♦ |
| ☐ | RA-96018 | Ilyushin Il-96-300PU | 74393202018 | | VIP |
| ☐ | RA-96019 | Ilyushin Il-96-300 | 74393202019 | | ♦ |
| ☐ | RA-96020 | Ilyushin Il-96-300PU | 74393202020 | | o/o♦ |
| ☐ | RA-96021 | Ilyushin Il-96-300 | 73392302021 | | o/o♦ |

| | | | | | |
|---|---|---|---|---|---|
| ☐ | RA-65555 | Tupolev Tu-134A-3 | 66350 | ex CCCP-65555 | VIP |
| ☐ | RA-65904 | Tupolev Tu-134A-3 | 63953 | | ♦ |
| ☐ | RA-65905 | Tupolev Tu-134A-3 | 63965 | | ♦ |
| ☐ | RA-65911 | Tupolev Tu-134A-3 | 63972 | | ♦ |
| ☐ | RA-65921 | Tupolev Tu-134A-3 | 63997 | ex CCCP-65921 | |

| | | | | | |
|---|---|---|---|---|---|
| ☐ | RA-64504 | Tupolev Tu-214 | 41203004 | | |
| ☐ | RA-64505 | Tupolev Tu-214 | 42204005 | | |
| ☐ | RA-64506 | Tupolev Tu-214 | 44204006 | | |
| ☐ | RA-64515 | Tupolev Tu-214SR | 42305015 | | |
| ☐ | RA-64516 | Tupolev Tu-214SR | 42709016 | | |
| ☐ | RA-64517 | Tupolev Tu-214SR | 41709017 | | ♦ |
| ☐ | RA-64520 | Tupolev Tu-214PU | 020 | | ♦ |

| | | | | | |
|---|---|---|---|---|---|
| ☐ | RA-87203 | Yakovlev Yak-40 | 9741456 | ex CCCP-87203 | VIP |
| ☐ | RA-87968 | Yakovlev Yak-40 | 9841258 | | ♦ |
| ☐ | RA-87969 | Yakovlev Yak-40 | 9831358 | ex CCCP-87969 | VIP |
| ☐ | RA-87971 | Yakovlev Yak-40D | 9831558 | ex CCCP-87971 | VIP |
| ☐ | RA-87972 | Yakovlev Yak-40 | 9921658 | | ♦ |
| ☐ | RA-88200 | Yakovlev Yak-40 | 9630149 | ex CCCP-88200 | |

| | | | | | |
|---|---|---|---|---|---|
| ☐ | RA-64057 | Tupolev Tu-204-300A | 64057 | | ♦ |
| ☐ | RA-64058 | Tupolev Tu-204-300A | 64058 | | ♦ |
| ☐ | RA-75454 | Ilyushin Il-18D | 187010104 | | ♦ |
| ☐ | RA-75464 | Ilyushin Il-18D | 187010401 | | ♦ |
| ☐ | RA-85629 | Tupolev Tu-154M | 87A758 | ex CCCP-85629 | |
| ☐ | RA-85645 | Tupolev Tu-154M | 88A782 | ex CCCP-85645 | |
| ☐ | RA-85659 | Tupolev Tu-154M | 89A809 | ex CCCP-85659 | |
| ☐ | RA-85843 | Tupolev Tu-154M | 95A991 | ex RA-85811 | VIP |

## RYAZANAVIA TRANS      Ryazan Air (RYZ)     Ryazan (RZN)

| | | | | |
|---|---|---|---|---|
| ☐ | RA-47359 | Antonov An-24RV | 67310608 | ex UR-47359 |
| ☐ | RA-47362 | Antonov An-24RV | 67310706 | ex UR-47362 |

## S-AIR      S-Air (RLS)     Ermolino

| | | | | |
|---|---|---|---|---|
| ☐ | RA-65550 | Tupolev Tu-134A-3 | 66200 | ex CCCP-65550 |
| ☐ | RA-65692 | Tupolev Tu-134A-3 | 63215 | ex YL-LBB |
| ☐ | RA-65721 | Tupolev Tu-134A-3M | 66130 | ex CCCP-65721 |
| ☐ | RA-65926 | Tupolev Tu-134A-3 | 66101 | ex CCCP-65926 |
| ☐ | RA-65932 | Tupolev Tu-134A-3 | 66405 | ex 65932 |

| | | | | |
|---|---|---|---|---|
| ☐ | RA-42402 | Yakovlev Yak-42D | 4520422116583 | ex CCCP-42402 |
| ☐ | RA-42427 | Yakovlev Yak-42D | 4520422305016 | Marco Group |

## S7 AIRLINES      Siberia Airlines (S7/SBI)     Novosibirsk-Tolmachevo (OVB)

| | | | | | |
|---|---|---|---|---|---|
| ☐ | VP-BHF | Airbus A319-114 | 1819 | ex N350NB | |
| ☐ | VP-BHG | Airbus A319-114 | 1870 | ex N356NB | |
| ☐ | VP-BHI | Airbus A319-114 | 2028 | ex N367NB | |
| ☐ | VP-BHJ | Airbus A319-114 | 2369 | ex N372NB | |
| ☐ | VP-BHK | Airbus A319-114 | 2373 | ex N373NB | |
| ☐ | VP-BHL | Airbus A319-114 | 2464 | ex N374NB | |
| ☐ | VP-BHP | Airbus A319-114 | 2618 | ex N376NB | |
| ☐ | VP-BHQ | Airbus A319-114 | 2641 | ex N377NB | |
| ☐ | VP-BHV | Airbus A319-114 | 2474 | ex N375NB | |
| ☐ | VP-BTN | Airbus A319-114 | 1126 | ex N307NB | |
| ☐ | VP-BTO | Airbus A319-114 | 1129 | ex N308NB | |
| ☐ | VP-BTP | Airbus A319-114 | 1131 | ex N309NB | |
| ☐ | VP-BTQ | Airbus A319-114 | 1149 | ex N310NB | |
| ☐ | VP-BTS | Airbus A319-114 | 1164 | ex N311NB | |
| ☐ | VP-BTT | Airbus A319-114 | 1167 | ex N312NB | |
| ☐ | VP-BTU | Airbus A319-114 | 1071 | ex N303NB | |
| ☐ | VP-BTV | Airbus A319-114 | 1078 | ex N304NB | |
| ☐ | VP-BTW | Airbus A319-114 | 1090 | ex N305NB | |
| ☐ | VP-BTX | Airbus A319-114 | 1091 | ex N306NB | |
| ☐ | VQ-BQW | Airbus A319-115LR | 2279 | ex F-GRXI | ♦ |

| | | | | | |
|---|---|---|---|---|---|
| □ | VP-BCP | Airbus A320-214 | 3473 | ex F-WWBY | |
| □ | VP-BCS | Airbus A320-214 | 3490 | ex F-WWIS | |
| □ | VP-BCZ | Airbus A320-214 | 3446 | ex F-WWIT | |
| □ | VP-BDT | Airbus A320-214 | 3494 | ex F-WWIC | |
| □ | VQ-BCI | Airbus A320-214 | 2623 | ex EC-JNT | |
| □ | VQ-BDE | Airbus A320-214 | 3866 | ex F-WWDZ | |
| □ | VQ-BDF | Airbus A320-214 | 3880 | ex F-WWIL | |
| □ | VQ-BES | Airbus A320-214 | 4032 | ex F-WWIH | |
| □ | VQ-BET | Airbus A320-214 | 4150 | ex F-WWBG | |
| □ | VQ-BOA | Airbus A320-214 | 5001 | ex F-WWBM | ♦ |
| □ | VQ-BPL | Airbus A320-214 | 5026 | ex F-WWBK | ♦ |
| □ | VQ-BRC | Airbus A320-214 | 5106 | ex F-WWIU | o/o♦ |
| □ | VQ-BRD | Airbus A320-214 | 5031 | ex F-WWBE | ♦ |
| □ | VQ- | Airbus A320-214 | | ex | o/o |
| □ | VQ- | Airbus A320-214 | | ex | o/o |
| □ | VQ- | Airbus A320-214 | | ex | o/o |
| □ | VQ- | Airbus A320-214 | | ex | o/o |
| □ | VQ- | Boeing 737-800 | | ex | o/o |
| □ | VQ- | Boeing 737-800 | | ex | o/o |
| □ | VQ- | Boeing 737-800 | | ex | o/o |
| □ | VQ- | Boeing 737-800 | | ex | o/o |
| □ | VQ- | Boeing 737-800 | | ex | o/o |
| □ | RA-85613 | Tupolev Tu-154M | 86A722 | ex CCCP-85613 | [OVB] |
| □ | RA-85620 | Tupolev Tu-154M | 86A739 | ex TC-ACT | [OVB] |
| □ | RA-85622 | Tupolev Tu-154M | 87A746 | ex CCCP-85622 | |
| □ | RA-85628 | Tupolev Tu-154M | 87A757 | ex CCCP-85628 | [OVB] |
| □ | RA-85674 | Tupolev Tu-154M | 90A834 | ex TC-ACI | |
| □ | RA-85724 | Tupolev Tu-154M | 92A906 | ex EP-MHD | [OVB] |
| □ | RA-85827 | Tupolev Tu-154M | 87A745 | ex SP-LCC | [OVB] |
| □ | VP-BTJ | Airbus A310-304 | 520 | ex D-AHLA | |
| □ | VP-BVH | Boeing 767-33AER | 28495/643 | ex N495AN | |
| □ | VQ-BBI | Boeing 767-328ER | 27428/586 | ex EC-JJJ | |

## SAMARA AIRLINES — Beryoza (E5/BRZ) — Samara-Kurumotch (KUF)

| | | | | | |
|---|---|---|---|---|---|
| □ | RA-65105 | Tupolev Tu-134A | 60308 | ex LY-ABH | |
| □ | RA-65122 | Tupolev Tu-134A-3 | 60518 | ex CCCP-65122 | |
| □ | RA-65753 | Tupolev Tu-134A-3 | 61099 | ex CCCP-65753 | |
| □ | RA-65758 | Tupolev Tu-134A-3 | 62230 | ex CCCP-65758 | |
| □ | RA-65792 | Tupolev Tu-134A-3 | 63121 | ex CCCP-65792 | |
| □ | RA-65797 | Tupolev Tu-134A-3 | 63173 | ex CCCP-65797 | |
| □ | RA-85057 | Tupolev Tu-154M | 07A1001 | | > Avialinii Dagestana |
| □ | RA-85332 | Tupolev Tu-154B-2 | 79A332 | ex ER-85585 | |
| □ | RA-85585 | Tupolev Tu-154B-2 | 83A585 | ex CCCP-85585 | |
| □ | RA-85601 | Tupolev Tu-154B-2 | 84A601 | ex 85601 | op for Samara Oblast |
| □ | RA-85707 | Tupolev Tu-154M | 91A882 | ex UR-85707 | |
| □ | RA-85716 | Tupolev Tu-154M | 91A892 | ex EP-MCI | AiRUnion colours |
| □ | RA-85723 | Tupolev Tu-154M | 92A905 | ex HA-LGB | |
| □ | RA-85731 | Tupolev Tu-154M | 92A913 | ex EP-LBH | |
| □ | RA-85817 | Tupolev Tu-154M | 95A1007 | ex EP-LBM | >KJC |
| □ | RA-85818 | Tupolev Tu-154M | 85A719 | ex EP-MAJ   AiRUnion colours | |
| □ | RA-85821 | Tupolev Tu-154M | 89A805 | ex SP-LCI   AiRUnion colours | |
| □ | RA-85822 | Tupolev Tu-154M | 89A806 | ex HA-LGC | |
| □ | RA-85823 | Tupolev Tu-154M | 88A775 | ex HA-LGA | |
| □ | RA-76475 | Ilyushin Il-76TD | 0043451523 | ex EP-TPV | [KUF] as EP-TPV |
| □ | RA-76791 | Ilyushin Il-76TD | 0093497936 | ex EP-TPU | [KUF] as EP-TPU |

## SARAVIA — Saratov Air (6W/SOV) — Saratov-Tsentralny (RTW)

| | | | | | |
|---|---|---|---|---|---|
| □ | RA-42316 | Yakovlev Yak-42 | 4520422202030 | ex CCCP-42316 | [RTW] |
| □ | RA-42326 | Yakovlev Yak-42D | 4520424402154 | ex CCCP-42326 | |
| □ | RA-42328 | Yakovlev Yak-42 | 4520421505058 | ex CCCP-42328 | |
| □ | RA-42329 | Yakovlev Yak-42 | 4520422505093 | | ♦ |
| □ | RA-42343 | Yakovlev Yak-42 | 4520421708285 | | ♦ |
| □ | RA-42356 | Yakovlev Yak-42 | 4520422811400 | | ♦ |
| □ | RA-42361 | Yakovlev Yak-42 | 4520423811427 | | ♦ |
| □ | RA-42378 | Yakovlev Yak-42D | 4520421014494 | ex TC-FAR | |
| □ | RA-42389 | Yakovlev Yak-42D | 4520424016542 | ex CCCP-42389 | |
| □ | RA-42432 | Yakovlev Yak-42D | 4520424410016 | ex TC-ALY   no titles | |
| □ | RA-42550 | Yakovlev Yak-42D | 11140205 | ex CCCP-42550 | |

## SAT AIRLINES — Satair (HZ/SHU) — Yuzhno-Sakhalinsk Khomutovo (UUZ)

| | | | | | |
|---|---|---|---|---|---|
| □ | RA-46929 | Antonov An-24RV | 57310008 | | ♦ |
| □ | RA-46530 | Antonov An-24B | 57310009 | ex CCCP-46530 | |
| □ | RA-46618 | Antonov An-24RV | 37308705 | ex CCCP-46618 | |

| | | | | |
|---|---|---|---|---|
| ☐ | RA-46639 | Antonov An-24RV | 37308905 | ex CCCP-46639 |
| ☐ | RA-47198 | Antonov An-24RV | 27307702 | ex CCCP-47198 |
| ☐ | RA-47317 | Antonov An-24RV | 67310504 | ex CCCP-47317 |
| ☐ | RA-47366 | Antonov An-24RV | 77310804 | ex CCCP-47366 |
| | | | | |
| ☐ | RA-67251 | de Havilland DHC-8-311 | 533 | ex C-FWFH |
| ☐ | RA-67253 | de Havilland DHC-8-311 | 451 | ex C-GAPW |
| ☐ | RA-67255(2) | de Havilland DHC-8-315 | 581 | ex C-GLKW |
| ☐ | RA-67257 | de Havilland DHC-8-201 | 457 | ex C-FJFW |
| ☐ | RA-67259 | de Havilland DHC-8-201 | 459 | ex C-FNOP |

* (♦ beside RA-67255(2) row)
Op for Exxon Neftegas (RA-67257, RA-67259)

| | | | | |
|---|---|---|---|---|
| ☐ | RA-11364 | Antonov An-12V | 347601 | ex CCCP-11364 |
| ☐ | RA-26132 | Antonov An-26B | 37312708 | ex CCCP-26132 |
| ☐ | RA-48984 | Antonov An-12BP | 402913 | ex UR-48984 | [UUS] |
| ☐ | RA-73003 | Boeing 737-2J8 (Nordam 3) | 22859/890 | ex N235WA |
| ☐ | RA-73005 | Boeing 737-232 (Nordam 3) | 23100/1038 | ex N328DL |
| ☐ | RA-73013 | Boeing 737-5L9 | 28721/2856 | ex OY-APH |

## SATURN AVIAKOMPANIA — Rybmotors (RMO) — Rybinsk-Starosel'ye (RYB)

| | | | | |
|---|---|---|---|---|
| ☐ | RA-87225 | Yakovlev Yak-40K | 9841359 | ex CCCP-87225 |
| ☐ | RA-87936 | Yakovlev Yak-40K | 9740756 | ex CCCP-87936 |
| ☐ | RA-88289 | Antonov An-26B | 11804 | ex CCCP-88289 |

## SEVERSTAL AIRCOMPANY — Severstal (D2/SSF) — Cherepovets (CEE)

| | | | | | |
|---|---|---|---|---|---|
| ☐ | RA-87224 | Yakovlev Yak-40K | 9841259 | ex CCCP-87224 | VIP Op for Yava Group |
| ☐ | RA-87954 | Yakovlev Yak-40 | 9811357 | ex CCCP-87954 | |
| ☐ | RA-88180 | Yakovlev Yak-40 | 9622047 | ex CCCP-88180 | |
| ☐ | RA-88188 | Yakovlev Yak-40 | 9620848 | ex CCCP-88188 | |
| ☐ | RA-88296 | Yakovlev Yak-40 | 9421634 | ex VN-A445 | VIP |
| | | | | | |
| ☐ | RA-67229 | Canadair CRJ-200LR | 7403 | ex D-ACHD | ♦ |
| ☐ | RA-67230 | Canadair CRJ-200LR | 7407 | ex D-ACHE | ♦ |
| ☐ | RA-67231 | Canadair CRJ-200LR | 7464 | ex D-ACHI | ♦ |

## SHAR INK — Sharink (UGP) — Moscow-Ostafyevo

| | | | | | |
|---|---|---|---|---|---|
| ☐ | RA-74001 | Antonov An-74TK-100 | 36547070655 | ex CCCP-74001 | |
| ☐ | RA-74014 | Antonov An-74-200 | 36547098968 | ex ST-BDA | |
| ☐ | RA-74015 | Antonov An-74-200 | 36547098969 | | |
| ☐ | RA-74020 | Antonov An-74TK-100 | 36547195014 | | |
| ☐ | RA-74047 | Antonov An-74-200 | 36547097941 | | on rebuild |
| | | | | | |
| ☐ | RA-25770 | Mil Mi-8PS-11 | 8709 | ex CCCP-25770 | VIP |

## SIBAVIATRANS — Sibavia (5M/SIB) — Krasnoyarsk-Yemelyanovo (KJA)

| | | | | | |
|---|---|---|---|---|---|
| ☐ | RA-21503 | Yakovlev Yak-40K | 9820358 | ex CCCP-21503 | |
| ☐ | RA-46674 | Antonov An-24RV | 47309606 | ex CCCP-46674 | <OMS |
| ☐ | RA-48113 | Antonov An-32 | 1709 | ex CCCP-48113 | |
| ☐ | RA-49278 | Antonov An-24RV | 47309808 | ex YR-AMJ | |
| ☐ | RA-49279 | Antonov An-24RV | 17306905 | ex YR-AMB  AiRUnion colours | |
| ☐ | RA-49287 | Antonov An-24RV | 27307607 | ex YR-AME | |
| ☐ | RA-65571 | Tupolev Tu-134AK | 63955 | ex EW-63955 | |
| ☐ | RA-65605 | Tupolev Tu-134A | 09070 | ex EW-65605 | |
| ☐ | RA-65615 | Tupolev Tu-134A-3 | 4352205 | ex D-AOBE | |
| ☐ | RA-65881 | Tupolev Tu-134A-3 | 35220 | ex CCCP-65881 | |
| ☐ | RA-65694 | Tupolev Tu-134B-3 | 63235 | ex UN-65694  AiRUnion colours | |

## SIRIUS AERO — Sirius Aero (CIG) — Moscow-Vnukovo (VKO)

| | | | | | |
|---|---|---|---|---|---|
| ☐ | RA-65079 | Tupolev Tu-134A-3 | 60054 | ex LY-ASK | VIP |
| ☐ | RA-65099 | Tupolev Tu-134A-3 | 63700 | ex CCCP-65099 | VIP |
| ☐ | RA-65604 | Tupolev Tu-134AK | 62561 | ex CCCP-65604 | VIP |
| ☐ | RA-65722 | Tupolev Tu-134A-3M | 66420 | ex CCCP-65722 | VIP |
| ☐ | RA-65928 | Tupolev Tu-134A-3M | 66491 | ex CCCP-65928 | VIP |
| ☐ | RA-65978 | Tupolev Tu-134A-3 | 63357 | ex CCCP-65978  Svetlana | VIP |
| | | | | | |
| ☐ | RA-87669 | Yakovlev Yak-40 | 9021760 | | ♦ |

## SKOL AVIAKOMPANIA — (CDV) — Surgut (SGC)

| | | | | | |
|---|---|---|---|---|---|
| ☐ | RA-06033 | Mil Mi-26T | 34001212423 | ex CCCP-06033 | |
| ☐ | RA-06394 | Mil Mi-26T | 34001212123 | | |
| ☐ | RA-87940 | Yakovlev Yak-40 | 9540444 | ex CCCP-87940 | |
| ☐ | RA-88226 | Yakovlev Yak-40 | 9641350 | | ♦ |
| ☐ | RA-88306 | Yakovlev Yak-40 | 9640651 | | ♦ |

## SKYEXPRESS  (XW/SXR)  Moscow-Vnukovo (VNO)

Ceased ops 29Oct11, fleet merged into Kuban Airlines

## SOUTH EAST AIRLINES  (N2/DAG)

| | | | | |
|---|---|---|---|---|
| ☐ | RA-85332 | Tupolev Tu-154B-2 | 79A332 | ♦ |
| ☐ | RA-85495 | Tupolev Tu-154B-2 | 81A495 | ♦ |
| ☐ | RA-85725 | Tupolev Tu-154M | 92A725 | ♦ |
| ☐ | RA-85756 | Tupolev Tu-154M | 92A938 | ♦ |
| ☐ | RA-85828 | Tupolev Tu-154M | 97A1009 | ♦ |
| ☐ | RA-85840 | Tupolev Tu-154M | 98A1011 | ♦ |
| ☐ | RA-85849 | Tupolev Tu-154M | 89A815 | ♦ |
| ☐ | RA-46654 | Antonov An-24RV | 47309209 | ♦ |
| ☐ | RA-65569 | Tupolev Tu-134B-3 | 63340 | ♦ |
| ☐ | RA-65570 | Tupolev Tu-134A-3 | 66550 | ♦ |
| ☐ | RA-65579 | Tupolev Tu-134B-3 | 63295 | ♦ |
| ☐ | RA-65682 | Tupolev Tu-134AK | 62120 | ♦ |

## SVERDLOVSK 2ND AIR ENTERPRISE  Pyshma (UKU)  Yekaterinburg-Koltsovo (SVX)

| | | | | | |
|---|---|---|---|---|---|
| ☐ | RA-87253 | Yakovlev Yak-40 | 9321026 | ex CCCP-87253 | all-whiteVIP |
| ☐ | RA-87503 | Yakovlev Yak-40 | 9520240 | ex CCCP-87503 | VIP. op for Kolsto Ural |
| ☐ | RA-87524 | Yakovlev Yak-40 | 9520641 | ex CCCP-87524 | VIP |
| ☐ | RA-87974 | Yakovlev Yak-40K | 9621346 | ex CCCP-87974 | no titlesVIP |
| ☐ | RA-88159 | Yakovlev Yak-40 | 9611346 | ex CCCP-88159 | all-whiteVIP |
| ☐ | RA-88234 | Yakovlev Yak-40 | 9640351 | ex CCCP-82834 | all-whiteVIP |
| ☐ | RA-74004 | Antonov An-74 | 36547094890 | ex CCCP-74004 | VIP |
| ☐ | RA-74006 | Antonov An-74 | 36547095896 | ex CCCP-74006 | |
| ☐ | RA-74048 | Antonov An-74D | 36547098943 | all-white, no titles | VIP |

## TATARSTAN AIR  Air Tatarstan (U9/TAK)  Kazan-Osnovnoi (KZN)

| | | | | | |
|---|---|---|---|---|---|
| ☐ | VQ-BAP | Boeing 737-322 | 24665/1889 | ex LZ-BOT | |
| ☐ | VQ-BBN | Boeing 737-53A | 24785/1882 | ex LZ-BOY | |
| ☐ | VQ-BBO | Boeing 737-548 | 25165/2463 | ex LZ-BOR | |
| ☐ | VQ-BDB | Boeing 737-4D7 | 28702/2978 | ex HS-TDL | |
| ☐ | VQ-BDC | Boeing 737-341 | 26852/2273 | ex LZ-BOO | |
| ☐ | RA-85101 | Tupolev Tu-154M | 88A783 | ex B-608L | [KZN] |
| ☐ | RA-85109 | Tupolev Tu-154M | 88A790 | ex B-609L | [KZN] |
| ☐ | RA-85136 | Tupolev Tu-154M | 88A791 | ex B-607L | [KZN] |
| ☐ | RA-85798 | Tupolev Tu-154M | 93A982 | ex EP-MBO | |
| ☐ | RA-85799 | Tupolev Tu-154M | 94A983 | | |
| ☐ | RA-42332 | Yakovlev Yak-42 | 4520424505135 | | [KZN]♦ |
| ☐ | RA-42335 | Yakovlev Yak-42 | 4520422606204 | ex CU-T1274 | |
| ☐ | RA-42357 | Yakovlev Yak-42 | 4520422811408 | ex CCCP-42357 | [KZN] |
| ☐ | RA-42374 | Yakovlev Yak-42D | 4520423914340 | ex CU-T1273 | |
| ☐ | RA-42380 | Yakovlev Yak-42D | 4520422014549 | ex CU-T1242 | |
| ☐ | RA-42433 | Yakovlev Yak-42D | 4520421301017 | | |
| ☐ | RA-65970 | Tupolev Tu-134A | 3351910 | ex CCCP-65970 | |
| ☐ | RA-86142 | Ilyushin Il-86 | 51483210097 | ex B-2016 | [DME] |
| ☐ | RA-86143 | Ilyushin Il-86 | 51483210099 | ex B-2018 | |
| ☐ | RA-86926 | Ilyushin Il-86 | 51463210100 | ex B-2019 | |
| ☐ | VQ-BMM | Airbus A319-112 | 3171 | ex EI-EAF | ♦ |
| ☐ | VQ-BNF | Airbus A319-112 | 3331 | ex N331BV | ♦ |

## TOMSKAVIA  Tomsk Avia (TSK)  Tomsk (TOF)

| | | | | | |
|---|---|---|---|---|---|
| ☐ | RA-46627 | Antonov An-24RV | 37308806 | | ♦ |
| ☐ | RA-46650 | Antonov An-24RV | 47309201 | | ♦ |
| ☐ | RA-46679 | Antonov An-24RV | 47309701 | ex CCCP-46679 | |
| ☐ | RA-47254 | Antonov An-24RV | 27307706 | ex CCCP-47254 | |
| ☐ | RA-47255 | Antonov An-24RV | 27307707 | | ♦ |
| ☐ | RA-47355 | Antonov An-24RV | 67310604 | ex CCCP-47355 | |
| ☐ | RA-26039 | Antonov An-26B-100 | 10702 | ex CCCP-26039 | [TOF] |
| ☐ | RA-26518 | Antonov An-26-100 | 87307009 | | ♦ |
| ☐ | RA-26688 | Antonov An-26-100 | 97309004 | | ♦ |

## TRANSAERO AIRLINES  Transoviet (UN/TSO)  Moscow-Domodedovo (DME)

| | | | | | |
|---|---|---|---|---|---|
| ☐ | EI-CXK | Boeing 737-4S3 | 25596/2255 | ex G-OGBA | |
| ☐ | EI-CZK | Boeing 737-4Y0 | 24519/1781 | ex N519AP | |

| | | | | |
|---|---|---|---|---|
| ☐ | EI-DDK | Boeing 737-4S3 | 24165/1720 | ex N758BC | |
| ☐ | EI-DDY | Boeing 737-4Y0 | 24904/1988 | ex HA-LEV | |
| ☐ | EI-DNM | Boeing 737-4S3 | 24166/1722 | ex EC-JHX | |
| | | | | | |
| ☐ | EI-DTV | Boeing 737-5Y0 | 25183/2218 | ex B-2549 | |
| ☐ | EI-DTW | Boeing 737-5Y0 | 25188/2238 | ex B-2550 | |
| ☐ | EI-DTX | Boeing 737-5Q8 | 28052/2965 | ex LY-AZX | |
| ☐ | EI-UNG | Boeing 737-524 | 28915/2993 | ex N14654 | |
| ☐ | EI-UNH | Boeing 737-524 | 28916/2994 | ex N14655 | ♦ |
| ☐ | VP-BPA | Boeing 737-5K5 | 25037/2022 | ex D-AHLI | |
| ☐ | VP-BPD | Boeing 737-5K5 | 25062/2044 | ex D-AHLN | |
| ☐ | VP-BYI | Boeing 737-524 | 28921/3052 | ex N14660 | |
| ☐ | VP-BYJ | Boeing 737-524 | 28923/3060 | ex N14662 | |
| ☐ | VP-BYN | Boeing 737-524 | 28924/3063 | ex N17663 | |
| ☐ | VP-BYO | Boeing 737-524 | 28922/3055 | ex N23661 | |
| ☐ | VP-BYP | Boeing 737-524 | 28927/3074 | ex N14667 | |
| ☐ | VP-BYQ | Boeing 737-524 | 28919/3045 | ex N18658 | |
| ☐ | VP-BYT | Boeing 737-524 | 28928/3077 | ex N14668 | |
| | | | | | |
| ☐ | EI-EDZ | Boeing 737-8K5/W | 27980/45 | ex D-AHFF | |
| ☐ | EI-EEA | Boeing 737-8K5/W | 27989/59 | ex D-AHFG | |
| ☐ | EI-RUA | Boeing 737-86J/W | 30498/450 | ex D-ABAV | ♦ |
| ☐ | EI-RUB | Boeing 737-85P/W | 33982/2338 | ex EC-KEO | ♦ |
| ☐ | EI-RUE | Boeing 737-85P/W | 28388/533 | ex EC-HKQ | ♦ |
| ☐ | EI-UNJ | Boeing 737-86J/W | 36883/3709 | ex D-ABKV | o/o♦ |
| ☐ | EI-UNK | Boeing 737-86J/W | 36119/3750 | ex D-ABKX | ♦ |
| | | | | | |
| ☐ | EI-XLB | Boeing 747-446 | 26359/1153 | ex N913UN | |
| ☐ | EI-XLC | Boeing 747-446 | 27100/1236 | ex N919UN | |
| ☐ | EI-XLD | Boeing 747-446 | 26360/1166 | ex N914UN | ♦ |
| ☐ | EI-XLE | Boeing 747-446 | 26362/1202 | ex N916UN | o/o♦ |
| ☐ | EI-XLF | Boeing 747-446 | 27645/1282 | ex N921MM | ♦ |
| ☐ | EI-XLG | Boeing 747-446 | 29899/1208 | ex N917UN | ♦ |
| ☐ | EI-XLH | Boeing 747-446 | 27650/1234 | ex N918UN | ♦ |
| ☐ | EI-XLI | Boeing 747-446 | 27648/1253 | ex N920UN | ♦ |
| ☐ | EI-XLJ | Boeing 747-446 | 27646/1280 | ex N922UN | [ROM]♦ |
| ☐ | EI-XLK | Boeing 747-412 | 29950/1241 | ex N747NB | ♦ |
| ☐ | EI-XLL | Boeing 747-412 | 28031/1266 | ex N747NP | ♦ |
| ☐ | EI-XLM | Boeing 747-412 | 28028/1270 | ex N747WV | [ROM]♦ |
| ☐ | N747ZA | Boeing 747-444 | 29119/1187 | ex ZS-SAZ | ♦ |
| ☐ | VP-BKJ | Boeing 747-444 | 26638/995 | ex N7716Q | ♦ |
| ☐ | VP-BKL | Boeing 747-444 | 28468/1162 | ex N3508M | ♦ |
| ☐ | VP-BVR | Boeing 747-444 | 26637/943 | ex (VP-BKG) | ♦ |
| ☐ | VQ-BHW | Boeing 747-4F6 | 28959/1158 | ex ZS-SBK | |
| ☐ | VQ-BHX | Boeing 747-4F6 | 28960/1167 | ex ZS-SBS | |
| | | | | | |
| ☐ | EI-CXZ | Boeing 767-216ER | 24973/347 | ex N502GX | |
| ☐ | EI-CZD | Boeing 767-216ER | 23623/142 | ex N762TA | |
| ☐ | EI-DBF | Boeing 767-3Q8ER | 24745/355 | ex F-GHGF | |
| ☐ | EI-DBG | Boeing 767-3Q8ER | 24746/378 | ex F-GHGG | |
| ☐ | EI-DBU | Boeing 767-37EER | 25077/385 | ex F-GHGH | |
| ☐ | EI-DBW | Boeing 767-201ER | 23899/182 | ex N647US | |
| ☐ | EI-DFS | Boeing 767-33AER | 25346/403 | ex ET-AKW | |
| ☐ | EI-RUZ | Boeing 767-3Q8ER | 30048/828 | ex EC-HPU | ♦ |
| ☐ | EI-UNA | Boeing 767-3P6ER | 26233/501 | ex A4O-GU | |
| ☐ | EI-UNB | Boeing 767-3P6ER | 26234/538 | ex A4O-GY | |
| ☐ | EI-UNC | Boeing 767-319ER | 29388/785 | ex N381LF | |
| ☐ | EI-UND | Boeing 767-3P6ER | 26236/436 | ex A4O-GX | |
| ☐ | EI-UNE | Boeing 767-3Q8ER | 29383/747 | ex 5Y-KYY | ♦ |
| ☐ | EI-UNF | Boeing 767-3P6ER | 26238/440 | ex A4O-GT | |
| | | | | | |
| ☐ | EI-UNL | Boeing 777-312 | 28515/180 | ex 9V-SYA | ♦ |
| ☐ | EI-UNM | Boeing 777-312 | 28534/192 | ex 9V-SYD | ♦ |
| ☐ | EI-UNN | Boeing 777-312 | 28517/188 | ex 9V-SYC | ♦ |
| ☐ | EI-UNP | Boeing 777-312 | 28516/184 | ex 9V-SYB | ♦ |
| ☐ | EI-UNR | Boeing 777-212ER | 28523/239 | ex 9V-SRE | |
| ☐ | EI-UNS | Boeing 777-212ER | 28514/153 | ex 9V-SRD | ♦ |
| ☐ | EI-UNT | Boeing 777-212ER | 28999/150 | ex 9V-SRC | |
| ☐ | EI-UNU | Boeing 777-212ER | 28998/149 | ex 9V-SRB | |
| ☐ | EI-UNV | Boeing 777-222ER | 28714/205 | ex N205UA | |
| ☐ | EI-UNW | Boeing 777-222ER | 30214/254 | ex N208UA | |
| ☐ | EI-UNX | Boeing 777-222ER | 30213/232 | ex N207UA | |
| ☐ | EI-UNY | Boeing 777-222 | 26918/9 | ex N767UA | ♦ |
| ☐ | EI-UNZ | Boeing 777-222 | 26925/13 | ex N770UA | o/o |
| | | | | | |
| ☐ | EI-CXN | Boeing 737-329 | 23772/1432 | ex OO-SDW | |
| ☐ | EI-CXR | Boeing 737-329 | 24355/1709 | ex OO-SYA | |
| ☐ | EI-DOH | Boeing 737-31S | 29056/2928 | ex VT-SAX | ♦ |
| ☐ | EI-ERP | Boeing 737-3S3 | 29245/3061 | ex LN-KKY | ♦ |
| ☐ | EI-ETX | Boeing 737-7Q8 | 29359/1659 | ex HA-LOS | o/o♦ |
| ☐ | EI-EUW | Boeing 737-7Q8 | 29350/1452 | ex HA-LOI | o/o♦ |
| ☐ | EI-EUY | Boeing 737-7Q8 | 29354/1581 | ex HA-LOP | o/o♦ |
| ☐ | RA-64509 | Tupolev Tu-214 | 42305009 | | |

| | | | | | |
|---|---|---|---|---|---|
| ☐ | RA-64518 | Tupolev Tu-214 | 42305018 | | |
| ☐ | RA-64549 | Tupolev Tu-214 | 42305013 | ex RA-64513 | |
| ☐ | VP-BGU | Boeing 747-346 | 23482/640 | ex N740UN | |
| ☐ | VP-BGW | Boeing 747-346 | 24019/695 | ex N742UN | |
| ☐ | VP-BGX | Boeing 747-346 | 24156/716 | ex N741UN | |
| ☐ | VP-BGY | Boeing 747-346 | 23640/668 | ex N743UN | |
| ☐ | VP-BPX | Boeing 747-267B | 22872/566 | ex N747VC | wfs |
| ☐ | VP-BQC | Boeing 747-219B | 22725/563 | ex N705TA | [ROM] |
| ☐ | VP-BQE | Boeing 747-219B | 22722/523 | ex N702TA | [DME] |
| ☐ | VP-BQH | Boeing 747-219B | 22791/568 | ex N701TA | [ROM] |

## TRANSAVIA GARANTIA                              Arkhangelsk-Talagi (ARH)

| | | | | | |
|---|---|---|---|---|---|
| ☐ | RA-26024 | Antonov An-26B-100 | 10306 | ex CCCP-26024 | |
| ☐ | RA-26682 | Antonov An-26B-100 | 97308706 | ex CCCP-26682 | Frtr |
| ☐ | RA-26687 | Antonov An-26B-100 | 8902 | ex CCCP-26687 | |
| ☐ | RA-87336 | Yakovlev Yak-40 | 9610539 | ex CCCP-87336 | |

## TULPAR AIR              (TUL)    Kazan-Osnovnoi / Orenburg-Tsentralny (KZN/REN)

| | | | | | |
|---|---|---|---|---|---|
| ☐ | RA-21504 | Yakovlev Yak-40K | 9831758 | ex CCCP-21504 | Executive |
| ☐ | RA-87535 | Yakovlev Yak-40 | 9521941 | ex CCCP-87535 | Vasili Nesterov |
| ☐ | RA-87977 | Yakovlev Yak-40 | 9321128 | ex OK-BYH | |
| ☐ | RA-88269 | Yakovlev Yak-40 | 9720753 | ex LY-AAY | Kamaz titles |
| ☐ | RA-88287 | Yakovlev Yak-40K | 9940360 | | ♦ |
| ☐ | RA-42330 | Yakovlev Yak-42D | 4520422505122 | ex UR-42330 | |
| ☐ | RA-42333 | Yakovlev Yak-42 | 4520422606156 | ex CCCP-42333 | ♦ |
| ☐ | RA-42347 | Yakovlev Yak-42D | 4520423711322 | | ♦ |
| ☐ | RA-42408 | Yakovlev Yak-42D | 4520424116698 | | ♦ |
| ☐ | RA-42440 | Yakovlev Yak-42D | 4520424210018 | ex 9L-LDT    all-white | ♦ |
| ☐ | RA-42445 | Yakovlev Yak-42D | 4520424116669 | | ♦ |

## TUVA AIRLINES                                           Kyzyl (KYZ)

| | | | | | |
|---|---|---|---|---|---|
| ☐ | RA-87425 | Yakovlev Yak-40 | 9420135 | ex CCCP-87425 | |
| ☐ | RA-87443 | Yakovlev Yak-40 | 9432035 | | ♦ |
| ☐ | RA-87476 | Yakovlev Yak-40 | 9440438 | | ♦ |
| ☐ | RA-87495 | Yakovlev Yak-40 | 9541845 | | ♦ |
| ☐ | RA-87519 | Yakovlev Yak40 | 9520141 | | ♦ |
| ☐ | RA-87915 | Yakovlev Yak-40 | 9730455 | | ♦ |
| ☐ | RA-87925 | Yakovlev Yak-40 | 9731655 | ex CCCP-87925 | |
| ☐ | RA-88212 | Yakovlev Yak-40 | 9631849 | ex CCCP-88212 | |

## TYUMENSPECAVIA                  (TUM)              Tyumen-Roshchino (TJM)

| | | | | | |
|---|---|---|---|---|---|
| ☐ | RA-26088 | Antonov An-26 | 17311209 | ex CCCP-26088 | |
| ☐ | RA-26102 | Antonov An-26 | 17311909 | ex CCCP-26102 | |
| ☐ | RA-26662 | Antonov An-26 | 97308101 | | all-white |

## URAL AIRLINES            Sverdlovsk Air (U6/SVR)    Yekaterinburg-Koltsovo (SVX)

| | | | | | |
|---|---|---|---|---|---|
| ☐ | VP-BBQ | Airbus A320-214 | 2278 | ex A6-ABC | ♦ |
| ☐ | VP-BFZ | Airbus A320-214 | 0735 | ex G-BXKD | |
| ☐ | VP-BPU | Airbus A320-211 | 0220 | ex F-GLGH | |
| ☐ | VP-BPV | Airbus A320-211 | 0203 | ex F-GLGG | |
| ☐ | VP-BQY | Airbus A320-211 | 0140 | ex TS-ING | |
| ☐ | VP-BQZ | Airbus A320-211 | 0157 | ex TS-INH | |
| ☐ | VQ-BAG | Airbus A320-214 | 1063 | ex EC-KLU | |
| ☐ | VQ-BCY | Airbus A320-214 | 1484 | ex EC-HQM | |
| ☐ | VQ-BCZ | Airbus A320-214 | 1777 | ex G-OOPW | |
| ☐ | VQ-BDJ | Airbus A320-214 | 2175 | ex N268AV | |
| ☐ | VQ-BDM | Airbus A320-214 | 2187 | ex N269AV | |
| ☐ | VQ-BFV | Airbus A320-214 | 1152 | ex N266AV | |
| ☐ | VQ-BFW | Airbus A320-214 | 2327 | ex N271AV | |
| ☐ | VQ-BLO | Airbus A320-214 | 1751 | ex 6Y-JMJ | ♦ |
| ☐ | VQ-BRE | Airbus A320-214 | 2998 | ex JA204A | ♦ |
| ☐ | VQ-BCX | Airbus A321-211 | 1720 | ex G-OOAV | |
| ☐ | VQ-BDA | Airbus A321-211 | 1012 | ex TC-KTY | |
| ☐ | VQ-BKG | Airbus A321-211 | 0991 | ex EI-CPF | ♦ |
| ☐ | VQ-BKH | Airbus A321-211 | 0841 | ex EI-CPD | ♦ |
| ☐ | VQ-BKJ | Airbus A321-211 | 0815 | ex EI-CPC | ♦ |
| ☐ | VQ-BOB | Airbus A321-211 | 1905 | ex EI-ERT | ♦ |
| ☐ | VQ-BOC | Airbus A321-231 | 1199 | ex EI-ERS | ♦ |
| ☐ | VQ-BOF | Airbus A321-211 | 0775 | ex EI-EPM | ♦ |
| ☐ | VQ-BOZ | Airbus A321-211 | 2117 | ex EI-ERU | ♦ |
| ☐ | RA-85508 | Tupolev Tu-154B-2 | 81A508 | ex CCCP-85508 | |
| ☐ | RA-85807 | Tupolev Tu-154M | 94A988 | | |

| | | | | | |
|---|---|---|---|---|---|
| ☐ | RA-85814 | Tupolev Tu-154M | 95A994 | | |
| ☐ | RA-85833 | Tupolev Tu-154M | 01A1020 | | |
| ☐ | RA-85844 | Tupolev Tu-154M | 03A992 | | |
| | | | | | |
| ☐ | RA-47182 | Antonov An-24B | 99901907 | ex CCCP-47182 | |
| ☐ | RA-47187 | Antonov An-24B | 99902002 | ex CCCP-47187 | |

## UTAIR AIRLINES — UTair (UT/UTA) — Tyumen-Roshchino (TJM)

| | | | | | |
|---|---|---|---|---|---|
| ☐ | VP-BCA | ATR 42-300 | 0051 | ex I-NOWA | |
| ☐ | VP-BCB | ATR 42-300 | 0054 | ex I-NOWT | |
| ☐ | VP-BLI | ATR 42-300 | 0233 | ex D-BCRQ | |
| ☐ | VP-BLJ | ATR 42-300 | 0255 | ex D-BCRR | |
| ☐ | VP-BLN | ATR 42-300 | 0278 | ex D-BJJJ | |
| ☐ | VP-BLO | ATR 42-300 | 0289 | ex D-BCRT | |
| ☐ | VP-BLU | ATR 42-300 | 0287 | ex D-BCRS | |
| ☐ | VP-BPJ | ATR 42-300 | 0165 | ex N15823 | |
| ☐ | VP-BPK | ATR 42-300 | 0166 | ex N16824 | |
| | | | | | |
| ☐ | UR-UTH | ATR 72-212A | 994 | ex F-WWEI | o/o♦ |
| ☐ | UR-UTI | ATR 42-212A | 1000 | ex F-WWEJ | o/o♦ |
| ☐ | VP-BYW | ATR 72-201 | 0174 | ex ES-KRE | |
| ☐ | VP-BYX | ATR 72-201 | 0251 | ex ES-KRK | |
| ☐ | VQ-BLC | ATR 72-212A | 0942 | | ♦ |
| ☐ | VQ-BLD | ATR 72-212A | 0945 | | ♦ |
| ☐ | VQ-BLE | ATR 72-212A | 0950 | | ♦ |
| ☐ | VQ-BLF | ATR 72-212A | 0951 | | ♦ |
| ☐ | VQ-BLG | ATR 72-212A | 0952 | | ♦ |
| ☐ | VQ-BLH | ATR 72-212A | 0953 | | ♦ |
| ☐ | VQ-BLI | ATR 72-212A | 0963 | ex F-WWEP | ♦ |
| ☐ | VQ-BLJ | ATR 72-212A | 0965 | ex F-WWER | ♦ |
| ☐ | VQ-BLK | ATR 72-212A | 0975 | | ♦ |
| ☐ | VQ-BLL | ATR 72-212A | 0976 | ex F-WWEU | ♦ |
| ☐ | VQ-BLM | ATR 72-212A | 0980 | ex F-WWEZ | ♦ |
| ☐ | VQ-BLN | ATR 72-212A | 0981 | ex F-WWEB | ♦ |
| ☐ | VQ-BMA | ATR 72-212A | 0983 | ex F-WWED | ♦ |
| ☐ | VQ-BMB | ATR 72-212A | 0984 | ex F-WWEE | ♦ |
| ☐ | VQ-BMD | ATR 72-212A | 990 | ex F-WWEH | ♦ |
| ☐ | VQ- | ATR 72-212A | 1029 | ex F-WW | o/o♦ |
| | | | | | |
| ☐ | VQ-BHZ | Boeing 737-46M | 28549/2844 | ex OK-CGT | ♦ |
| ☐ | VQ-BIC | Boeing 737-45S | 28478/3132 | ex OK-FGS | |
| ☐ | VQ-BID | Boeing 737-45S | 28477/3131 | ex OK-FGR | |
| ☐ | VQ-BIE | Boeing 737-45S | 28476/3103 | ex OK-EGP | |
| ☐ | VQ-BIF | Boeing 737-45S | 28474/3028 | ex OK-DGN | op for UN |
| ☐ | VQ-BIG | Boeing 737-45S | 28473/3014 | ex OK-DGM | ♦ |
| | | | | | |
| ☐ | VP-BVL | Boeing 737-524 | 28926/3069 | ex N13665 | |
| ☐ | VP-BVN | Boeing 737-524 | 27540/2776 | ex N33637 | |
| ☐ | VP-BVZ | Boeing 737-524 | 28925/3066 | ex N14664 | |
| ☐ | VP-BXO | Boeing 737-524/W | 27314/2566 | ex N14601 | |
| ☐ | VP-BXQ | Boeing 737-524/W | 27315/2571 | ex N69602 | |
| ☐ | VP-BXR | Boeing 737-524/W | 27316/2573 | ex N69603 | |
| ☐ | VP-BXU | Boeing 737-524/W | 27318/2582 | ex N14605 | |
| ☐ | VP-BXV | Boeing 737-524/W | 27322/2607 | ex N14609 | |
| ☐ | VP-BXY | Boeing 737-524/W | 27328/2640 | ex N37615 | |
| ☐ | VP-BXZ | Boeing 737-524/W | 27329/2641 | exN52616 | |
| ☐ | VP-BYK | Boeing 737-524 | 28918/3026 | ex N23657 | |
| ☐ | VP-BYL | Boeing 737-524 | 28920/3048 | ex N15659 | |
| ☐ | VP-BYM | Boeing 737-524 | 28917/3019 | ex N11656 | |
| ☐ | VQ-BAC | Boeing 737-524/W | 27321/2597 | ex N33608 | |
| ☐ | VQ-BAD | Boeing 737-524/W | 27331/2652 | ex N16618 | |
| ☐ | VQ-BAE | Boeing 737-524/W | 27320/2596 | ex N16607 | |
| ☐ | VQ-BJL | Boeing 737-524/W | 28913/2985 | ex N14652 | ♦ |
| ☐ | VQ-BJM | Boeing 737-524/W | 28912/2980 | ex N11651 | ♦ |
| ☐ | VQ-BJN | Boeing 737-524/W | 28911/2973 | ex N16650 | ♦ |
| ☐ | VQ-BJO | Boeing 737-524/W | 28910/2972 | ex N16649 | ♦ |
| ☐ | VQ-BJP | Boeing 737-524/W | 28905/2934 | ex N17644 | ♦ |
| ☐ | VQ-BJQ | Boeing 737-524/W | 28902/2926 | ex N11641 | ♦ |
| ☐ | VQ-BJS | Boeing 737-524/W | 28901/2924 | ex N17640 | ♦ |
| ☐ | VQ-BJT | Boeing 737-524/W | 28900/2913 | ex N14693 | ♦ |
| ☐ | VQ-BJU | Boeing 737-524/W | 28899/2912 | ex N19638 | ♦ |
| ☐ | VQ-BJV | Boeing 737-524/W | 28914/2986 | ex N14653 | ♦ |
| ☐ | VQ-BPO | Boeing 737-524/W | 28903/2927 | ex N16642 | ♦ |
| ☐ | VQ-BPP | Boeing 737-524/W | 28906/2935 | ex N14654 | ♦ |
| ☐ | VQ- | Boeing 737-524/W | 28907/2956 | ex N16646 | wfs♦ |
| ☐ | VQ- | Boeing 737-524/W | 28909/2960 | ex N16648 | wfs♦ |
| | | | | | |
| ☐ | VQ-BJF | Boeing 737-8AS/W | 32778/1140 | ex VQ-BBR | ♦ |
| ☐ | VQ-BJG | Boeing 737-8AS/W | 32779/1167 | ex VQ-BBS | ♦ |
| ☐ | VQ-BJH | Boeing 737-8AS/W | 32780/1178 | ex VQ-BCH | ♦ |
| ☐ | VQ-BJI | Boeing 737-8AS/W | 29937/1238 | ex VQ-BDV | ♦ |

| | | | | | |
|---|---|---|---|---|---|
| ☐ | VQ-BJJ | Boeing 737-8AS/W | 29936/1236 | ex VQ-BDU | ♦ |
| ☐ | VQ-BQP | Boeing 737-8GU/W | 37553/3646 | | ♦ |
| ☐ | VQ-BQQ | Boeing 737-8GU/W | 37552/3620 | | ♦ |
| ☐ | VQ-BQR | Boeing 737-8GU/W | 36386/3710 | | ♦ |
| ☐ | VQ-BQS | Boeing 737-8GU/W | 36387/3729 | | ♦ |
| | | | | | |
| ☐ | VQ-BGH | Canadair CRJ-200LR | 7114 | ex C-GGDU | |
| ☐ | VQ-BGI | Canadair CRJ-200LR | 7119 | ex C-GGDW | |
| ☐ | VQ-BGJ | Canadair CRJ-200LR | 7121 | ex C-GFNF | |
| ☐ | VQ-BGK | Canadair CRJ-200LR | 7122 | ex C-GFNB | |
| ☐ | VQ-BGL | Canadair CRJ-200LR | 7128 | ex C-GFNJ | |
| ☐ | VQ-BGM | Canadair CRJ-200LR | 7130 | ex C-GGEV | |
| ☐ | VQ-BGO | Canadair CRJ-200LR | 7135 | ex D-ACJD | |
| ☐ | VQ-BGP | Canadair CRJ-200LR | 7165 | ex C-GGDO | |
| ☐ | VQ-BGQ | Canadair CRJ-200LR | 7200 | ex D-ACJF | |
| ☐ | VQ-BGR | Canadair CRJ-200LR | 7220 | ex D-ACJG | op for UN |
| ☐ | VQ-BGT | Canadair CRJ-200LR | 7266 | ex C-GGDQ | |
| ☐ | VQ-BGU | Canadair CRJ-200LR | 7298 | ex C-GEDO | |
| ☐ | VQ-BGV | Canadair CRJ-200LR | 7378 | ex C-GFMQ | |
| ☐ | VQ-BGW | Canadair CRJ-200LR | 7391 | ex C-GFLZ | |
| ☐ | VQ-BGX | Canadair CRJ-200LR | 7394 | ex C-GGDR | |
| | | | | | |
| ☐ | RA-65005 | Tupolev Tu-134A-3 | 44065 | ex CCCP-65005 | |
| ☐ | RA-65024 | Tupolev Tu-134A | 48420 | ex CCCP-65024 | |
| ☐ | RA-65033 | Tupolev Tu-134A-3 | 48540 | ex CCCP-65033 | |
| ☐ | RA-65055 | Tupolev Tu-134A | 49856 | ex CCCP-65055 | |
| ☐ | RA-65127 | Tupolev Tu-134A-3 | 60627 | ex EY-65127 | |
| ☐ | RA-65148 | Tupolev Tu-134A-3 | 61025 | ex CCCP-65148 | |
| ☐ | RA-65560 | Tupolev Tu-134A | 60321 | ex YU-AJW | |
| ☐ | RA-65565 | Tupolev Tu-134A-1 | 63998 | ex CCCP-65565 | |
| ☐ | RA-65572 | Tupolev Tu-134AK-3 | 63960 | ex UR-CCG | |
| ☐ | RA-65607 | Tupolev Tu-134A | 48560 | ex CCCP-65607 | VIP |
| ☐ | RA-65608 | Tupolev Tu-134A | 38040 | ex CCCP-65608 | VIP |
| ☐ | RA-65609 | Tupolev Tu-134A-3 | 46155 | ex CCCP-65609 | |
| ☐ | RA-65611 | Tupolev Tu-134A-3 | 3351903 | ex CCCP-65611 | |
| ☐ | RA-65614 | Tupolev Tu-134A | 4352207 | ex CCCP-65614 | |
| ☐ | RA-65620 | Tupolev Tu-134A-3 | 35180 | ex CCCP-65620 | |
| ☐ | RA-65621 | Tupolev Tu-134A-3 | 48320 | ex CCCP-65621 | |
| ☐ | RA-65716 | Tupolev Tu-134B-3 | 63595 | ex CCCP-65716 | |
| ☐ | RA-65728 | Tupolev Tu-134B-3 | 49858 | ex LZ-TUG | |
| ☐ | RA-65755 | Tupolev Tu-134A-3 | 62165 | ex CCCP-65755 | |
| ☐ | RA-65777 | Tupolev Tu-134A-3 | 62552 | ex CCCP-65777 | |
| ☐ | RA-65780 | Tupolev Tu-134A-3 | 62622 | ex CCCP-65780 | |
| ☐ | RA-65793 | Tupolev Tu-134A-3 | 63128 | ex CCCP-65793 | |
| ☐ | RA-65901 | Tupolev Tu-134A-3 | 63731 | ex CCCP-65901 | |
| ☐ | RA-65977 | Tupolev Tu-134A | 63245 | ex CCCP-65977 | |
| | | | | | |
| ☐ | RA-85013 | Tupolev Tu-154M | 90A840 | ex LZ-MIG | |
| ☐ | RA-85016 | Tupolev Tu-154M | 90A844 | ex LZ-MIH | |
| ☐ | RA-85018 | Tupolev Tu-154M | 90A852 | ex LZ-MIR | |
| ☐ | RA-85056 | Tupolev Tu-154M | 90A845 | ex LZ-MIL | Nikolai Baibakov |
| ☐ | RA-85069 | Tupolev Tu-154M | 90A863 | ex LZ-MIS | |
| ☐ | RA-85595 | Tupolev Tu-154B-2 | 84A595 | ex CCCP-85595 | |
| ☐ | RA-85681 | Tupolev Tu-154M | 90A848 | ex LZ-LTE | Abakan | wfs |
| ☐ | RA-85685 | Tupolev Tu-154M | 90A853 | | ♦ |
| ☐ | RA-85727 | Tupolev Tu-154M | 92A909 | ex ES-LTP | |
| ☐ | RA-85733 | Tupolev Tu-154M | 92A915 | ex EP-MAL | Antonina Grigoreva |
| ☐ | RA-85755 | Tupolev Tu-154M | 92A937 | | Vasilij Bachilov |
| ☐ | RA-85788 | Tupolev Tu-154M | 93A972 | ex EP-ITS | |
| ☐ | RA-85789 | Tupolev Tu-154M | 93A973 | | |
| ☐ | RA-85796 | Tupolev Tu-154M | 94A980 | | Victor Muravlenko |
| ☐ | RA-85805 | Tupolev Tu-154M | 94A986 | | Farman Salmanov |
| ☐ | RA-85806 | Tupolev Tu-154M | 94A987 | | [TJM] |
| ☐ | RA-85808 | Tupolev Tu-154M | 94A989 | | Shetr Panov |
| ☐ | RA-85813 | Tupolev Tu-154M | 95A990 | | |
| ☐ | RA-85820 | Tupolev Tu-154M | 98A995 | | Roman Marchenko | [TJM] |
| | | | | | |
| ☐ | EI-EUW | Boeing 737-7Q8 | 29350/1452 | ex HA-LOI | o/o♦ |
| ☐ | EI-EUX | Boeing 737-7Q8 | 29352/1491 | ex HA-LOL | o/o♦ |
| ☐ | EI-EUY | Boeing 737-7Q8 | 29354 | ex HA-LOP | o/o♦ |
| ☐ | EI-EUZ | Boeing 737-7Q8 | 29355/1609 | ex HA-LOR | o/o♦ |
| | | | | | |
| ☐ | RA-87907 | Yakovlev Yak-40 | 9731254 | ex CCCP-87907 | |
| ☐ | RA-87941 | Yakovlev Yak-40 | 9540545 | ex CCCP-87941 | |
| ☐ | RA-87997 | Yakovlev Yak-40 | 9540145 | ex CCCP-87997 | |
| ☐ | RA-88209 | Yakovlev Yak-40K | 9730353 | ex CCCP-88209 | |
| | | | | | |
| ☐ | VQ-BEY | Boeing 757-2Q8/W | 29382/1010 | ex OH-LBX | |
| ☐ | VQ-BEZ | Boeing 757-2Q8/W | 29377/857 | ex OH-LBU | |
| ☐ | VQ-BKB | Boeing 757-2Q8/W | 26271/592 | ex TC-SNB | ♦ |
| ☐ | VQ-BKF | Boeing 757-2Q8/W | 26268/590 | ex TC-SND | ♦ |

## UTAIR CARGO

**(TUM)**

| | | | | |
|---|---|---|---|---|
| ☐ | RA-26088 | Antonov An-26 | 17311209 | ♦ |
| ☐ | RA-26102 | Antonov An-26 | 11909 | ♦ |
| ☐ | RA-26636 | Antonov An-26-100 | 87306306 | ♦ |
| ☐ | RA-26520 | Antonov An-26-100 | 87307101 | ♦ |
| ☐ | RA-26662 | Antonov An-26 | 97308101 | ♦ |
| ☐ | RA-88289 | Antonov An-26B | 11804 | ♦ |

## UTAIR EXPRESS

**Komiinter (UR/KMV)** — **Syktyvkar (SCW)**

| | | | | | |
|---|---|---|---|---|---|
| ☐ | RA-13344 | Antonov An-24RV | 37308310 | ex CCCP-13344 | |
| ☐ | RA-46362 | Antonov An-24B | 07305903 | | |
| ☐ | RA-46388 | Antonov An-24B | 07306201 | | ♦ |
| ☐ | RA-46468 | Antonov An-24RV | 27307906 | ex CCCP-46468 | ♦ |
| ☐ | RA-46481 | Antonov An-24RV | 27308009 | | |
| ☐ | RA-46494 | Antonov An-24RV | 27308207 | ex CCCP-46494 | ♦ |
| ☐ | RA-46509 | Antonov An-24RV | 37308405 | | |
| ☐ | RA-46519 | Antonov An-24RV | 37308505 | | ♦ |
| ☐ | RA-46532 | Antonov An-24RV | 57310101 | | ♦ |
| ☐ | RA-46603 | Antonov An-24RV | 37308510 | ex CCCP-46603 | |
| ☐ | RA-46609 | Antonov An-24RV | 37308606 | ex CCCP-46609 | |
| ☐ | RA-46610 | Antonov An-24RV | 37308607 | ex CCCP-46610 | |
| ☐ | RA-46619 | Antonov An-24RV | 37308706 | ex CCCP-46619 | |
| ☐ | RA-46640 | Antonov An-24RV | 37308908 | ex CCCP-46640 | |
| ☐ | RA-46692 | Antonov An-24RV | 47309903 | ex CCCP-46692 | |
| ☐ | RA-46848 | Antonov An-24RV | 27307506 | | ♦ |
| ☐ | RA-47264 | Antonov An-24RV | 27307806 | | <KTA♦ |
| ☐ | RA-47271 | Antonov An-24RV | 07306401 | ex BNMAU-47271 | |
| ☐ | RA-47273 | Antonov An-24B | 07306403 | | ♦ |
| ☐ | RA-47289 | Antonov An-24B | 07306509 | | ♦ |
| ☐ | RA-47295 | Antonov An-24RV | 07306608 | | <KTA |
| ☐ | RA-47357 | Antonov An-24RV | 67310606 | ex CCCP-47357 | |
| ☐ | RA-47800 | Antonov An-24RV | 17306809 | | ♦ |
| ☐ | RA-47820 | Antonov An-24RV | 17307201 | ex CCCP-47820 | |
| ☐ | RA-47821 | Antonov An-24RV | 17307202 | | |
| ☐ | RA-47827 | Antonov An-24B | 17307208 | | ♦ |
| ☐ | RA-47829 | Antonov An-24B | 17307210 | | ♦ |
| ☐ | RA-47847 | Antonov An-24B | 17307409 | | ♦ |

## UVAUGA

**Pilot Air (UHS)** — **Ulyanovsk-Tsentralny (ULY)**

| | | | | | |
|---|---|---|---|---|---|
| ☐ | RA-26025 | Antonov An-26B | 10308 | ex CCCP-26025 | |
| ☐ | RA-26513 | Antonov An-26 | 6810 | ex CCCP-26513 | |
| ☐ | RA-26544 | Antonov An-26 | 2710 | ex CCCP-26544 | |
| ☐ | RA-42528 | Yakovlev Yak-42D | 11041003 | ex CCCP-42528 | [ULY] |
| ☐ | RA-85470 | Tupolev Tu-154B-2 | 81A470 | ex CCCP-85470 | |
| ☐ | RA-85609 | Tupolev Tu-154M | 84A704 | ex CCCP-85609 | no titles |
| ☐ | RA-87299 | Yakovlev Yak-40 | 9341528 | ex CCCP-87299 | |
| ☐ | RA-87315 | Yakovlev Yak-40 | 9331429 | ex CCCP-87315 | |
| ☐ | RA-87580 | Yakovlev Yak-40 | 9221222 | ex CCCP-87580 | |

## VIM AIRLINES

**MovAir (NN/MOV)** — **Moscow-Domodedovo (DME)**

| | | | | | |
|---|---|---|---|---|---|
| ☐ | RA-73007 | Boeing 757-230 | 24749/295 | ex D-ABNE | |
| ☐ | RA-73008 | Boeing 757-230 | 25436/419 | ex D-ABNH | |
| ☐ | RA-73009 | Boeing 757-230 | 25437/422 | ex D-ABNI | |
| ☐ | RA-73010 | Boeing 757-230 | 25438/428 | ex D-ABNK | |
| ☐ | RA-73011 | Boeing 757-230 | 25439/437 | ex D-ABNL | >BBT |
| ☐ | RA-73012 | Boeing 757-230 | 25440/443 | ex D-ABNM | >BBT |
| ☐ | RA-73014 | Boeing 757-230 | 25441/446 | ex D-ABNN | |
| ☐ | RA-73015 | Boeing 757-230 | 25901/464 | ex D-ABNO | >BBT |
| ☐ | RA-73016 | Boeing 757-230 | 26433/521 | ex D-ABNP | |
| ☐ | RA-73017 | Boeing 757-230 | 26434/532 | ex D-ABNR | |
| ☐ | RA-73018 | Boeing 757-230 | 26435/537 | ex D-ABNS | |

## VLADIVOSTOK AIR

**Vladair (XF/VLK)** — **Vladivostok-Knevichi (VVO)**

| | | | | | |
|---|---|---|---|---|---|
| ☐ | VP-BEQ | Airbus A320-212 | 0422 | ex 6Y-JMB | |
| ☐ | VP-BFX | Airbus A320-214 | 0714 | ex G-BXKA | |
| ☐ | VP-BFY | Airbus A320-214 | 0730 | ex G-BXKC | |
| ☐ | VP-BRB | Airbus A320-212 | 0528 | ex 6Y-JMA | |
| ☐ | VQ-BCG | Airbus A320-214 | 1200 | ex EC-HGY | |
| ☐ | VQ-BFM | Airbus A320-214 | 1379 | ex EC-HQG | ♦ |
| ☐ | VQ-BHS | Airbus A320-214 | 1213 | ex 6Y-JMF | ♦ |
| | | | | | |
| ☐ | RA-64026 | Tupolev Tu-204-300 | 1450743164026 | | |
| ☐ | RA-64038 | Tupolev Tu-204-300 | 1450744464038 | Sberbank Rossii titles | |
| ☐ | RA-64039 | Tupolev Tu-204-300 | 1450741564039 | Sberbank Rossii titles | |
| ☐ | RA-64040 | Tupolev Tu-204-300 | 1450744565040 | | |

| | | | | |
|---|---|---|---|---|
| ☐ | RA-64044 | Tupolev Tu-204-300 | 1450744564044 | |
| ☐ | RA-64045 | Tupolev Tu-204-300 | 1450744564045 | |
| | | | | |
| ☐ | RA-85676 | Tupolev Tu-154M | 90A836 | ex EP-MAM Sayanogorsk |
| ☐ | RA-85766 | Tupolev Tu-154M | 92A923 | ex EP-MAP |
| ☐ | RA-85803 | Tupolev Tu-154M | 89A822 | ex EK-85803 Spassk-Dalny |
| ☐ | RA-85837 | Tupolev Tu-154M | 91A876 | ex UR-85701 Khakasia |
| ☐ | RA-87958 | Yakovlev Yak-40K | 9821957 | ex CCCP-87958 |
| ☐ | RA-88216 | Yakovlev Yak-40 | 9630250 | ex CCCP-88216 |
| ☐ | VQ-BCW | Airbus A330-301 | 070 | ex EI-CRK |
| ☐ | VQ-BEQ | Airbus A330-301 | 086 | ex EI-JFK |
| ☐ | VQ-BEU | Airbus A330-301 | 055 | ex EI-DUB |

Dveuk (RA-88216), o/o (VQ-BEU)

## VOLGA AVIAEXPRESS — Goumrak (WLG) — Volgograd-Goomrak (VOG)

| | | | | |
|---|---|---|---|---|
| ☐ | RA-42384 | Yakovlev Yak-42D | 4520423016230 | ex CCCP-42384 |
| ☐ | RA-42406 | Yakovlev Yak-42D | 4520424116683 | ex CCCP-42406 |
| ☐ | RA-42549 | Yakovlev Yak-42D | 11040105 | ex ER-YCD Yevgeni Kucher |
| ☐ | RA-65019 | Tupolev Tu-134A | 48375 | ex CCCP-65019 |
| ☐ | RA-65086 | Tupolev Tu-134A-3 | 60130 | ex CCCP-65086 |
| ☐ | RA-76484 | Ilyushin Il-76TD | 0063469081 | ex CCCP-76484 |
| ☐ | RA-88171 | Yakovlev Yak-40 | 9620947 | ex EP-LBK |
| ☐ | RA-88228 | Yakovlev Yak-40 | 9641750 | ex CCCP-88228 |

wfs (RA-42406)

## VOLGA-DNEPR AIRLINES — Volga Dnepr (VI/VDA) — Ulyanovsk-Vostochniy East

| | | | | |
|---|---|---|---|---|
| ☐ | RA-82042 | Antonov An-124-100 | 9773054055093 | ex CCCP-82042 |
| ☐ | RA-82043 | Antonov An-124-100 | 9773054155101 | ex CCCP-82043 |
| ☐ | RA-82044 | Antonov An-124-100 | 9773054155109 | ex CCCP-82044 |
| ☐ | RA-82045 | Antonov An-124-100 | 9773052255113 | ex CCCP-82045 |
| ☐ | RA-82046 | Antonov An-124-100 | 9773052255117 | ex RA-82067 |
| ☐ | RA-82047 | Antonov An-124-100 | 9773053259121 | |
| ☐ | RA-82074 | Antonov An-124-100 | 9773051459142 | |
| ☐ | RA-82078 | Antonov An-124-100 | 9773054559153 | |
| ☐ | RA-82079 | Antonov An-124-100 | 9773052062157 | |
| ☐ | RA-82081 | Antonov An-124-100M | 9773051462165 | |
| | | | | |
| ☐ | EW-76734 | Ilyushin Il-76TD | 0073476312 | ex RA-76734 |
| ☐ | RA-76502 | Ilyushin Il-76-90VD | .0.3422748 | ◆ |
| ☐ | RA-76950 | Ilyushin Il-76-90VD | 2053420697 | Vladimir Kokkinaki |
| ☐ | RA-76951 | Ilyushin Il-76-90VD | 2073421704 | |
| ☐ | RA-76952 | Ilyushin Il-76-90VD | 2093422743 | ◆ |
| | | | | |
| ☐ | RA-88231 | Yakovlev Yak-40K | 9642050 | ex CCCP-88231 |

## VOLOGDA AIR ENTERPRISE — Vologda Air (VGV) — Vologda-Grishino (VGD)

| | | | | |
|---|---|---|---|---|
| ☐ | RA-87284 | Yakovlev Yak-40 | 9311927 | ex CCCP-87277 |
| ☐ | RA-87484 | Yakovlev Yak-40 | 9441238 | ex CCCP-87484 |
| ☐ | RA-87665 | Yakovlev Yak-40 | 9240925 | ex CCCP-87665 |
| ☐ | RA-87842 | Yakovlev Yak-40 | 9321030 | ex CCCP-87842 |
| ☐ | RA-87844 | Yakovlev Yak-40 | 9331330 | |
| ☐ | RA-88231 | Yakovlev Yak-40 | 9642050 | |
| ☐ | RA-88247 | Yakovlev Yak-40 | 9642051 | ex EP-LBJ |

no titles (RA-87665), ◆ (RA-87844, RA-88231)

## VOSTOK AIRLINES — Vostok (VTK) — Khabarovsk-Novy (KHV)

| | | | | |
|---|---|---|---|---|
| ☐ | RA-28920 | WSK/PZL Antonov An-28 | 1AJ008-06 | ex CCCP-28920 |
| ☐ | RA-28929 | WSK/PZL Antonov An-28 | 1AJ008-16 | ex CCCP-28929 |
| ☐ | RA-28931 | WSK/PZL Antonov An-28 | 1AJ008-18 | |
| ☐ | RA-28933 | WSK/PZL Antonov An-28 | 1AJ008-20 | ex CCCP-28933 |
| ☐ | RA-28941 | WSK/PZL Antonov An-28 | 1AJ009-07 | ex CCCP-28941 |
| ☐ | RA-28942 | WSK/PZL Antonov An-28 | 1AJ009-08 | ex CCCP-28942 |
| | | | | |
| ☐ | RA-41901 | Antonov An-38-100 | 4163847010001 | Vera |
| ☐ | RA-41902 | Antonov An-38-100 | 4163847010002 | |
| ☐ | RA-41903 | Antonov An-38-100 | 4163838010003 | Lyubov |
| ☐ | RA-67038 | LET L-410UVP | 820808 | ex CCCP-67038 |
| ☐ | RA-67636 | LET L-410UVP-E | 902429 | ex CCCP-67636 |

◆ (RA-28931, RA-41902, RA-67038)

## VYBORG AIRLINES — Vyborg Air (VBG) — St Petersburg-Pulkovo (LED)

| | | | | |
|---|---|---|---|---|
| ☐ | RA-91014 | Ilyushin Il-114 | 1023823024 | |
| ☐ | RA-91015 | Ilyushin Il-114 | 1033828025 | ex UK 91015 |

## YAK SERVICE — Yak-Service (AKY) — Moscow-Bykovo (BKA)

| | | | | |
|---|---|---|---|---|
| ☐ | RA-87648 | Yakovlev Yak-40 | 9140920 | ex CCCP-87648 | VIP |
| ☐ | RA-87659 | Yakovlev Yak-40 | 9240325 | ex CCCP-87659 | VIP |

| | | | | | |
|---|---|---|---|---|---|
| ☐ | RA-88294 | Yakovlev Yak-40 | 9331029 | ex UN-88294 | VIP |
| ☐ | RA-88295 | Yakovlev Yak-40 | 9331329 | ex 035 | VIP |
| ☐ | RA-88308 | Yakovlev Yak-40 | 9230224 | | ◆ |
| ☐ | RA-42412 | Yakovlev Yak-42D | 4520422219055 | ex EP-YAA | |

## YAKUTIA AIRLINES — Air Yakutia (K7/SYL) — Yakutsk (YKS)

| | | | | | |
|---|---|---|---|---|---|
| ☐ | RA-46496 | Antonov An-24RV | 27308209 | ex CCCP-47496 | |
| ☐ | RA-46510 | Antonov An-24RV | 37308406 | ex CCCP-46510 | |
| ☐ | RA-46665 | Antonov An-24RV | 47309506 | ex CCCP-46665 | |
| ☐ | RA-47352 | Antonov An-24RV | 67310601 | ex CCCP-47352 | |
| ☐ | RA-47353 | Antonov An-24RV | 67310602 | ex CCCP-47353 | |
| ☐ | RA-47360 | Antonov An-24RV | 67310704 | ex CCCP-47360 | |
| ☐ | RA-47819 | Antonov An-24RV | 17307108 | ex CCCP-47819 | |
| ☐ | VQ-BEO | Boeing 737-76Q/W | 30293/1496 | ex D-ABBN | |
| ☐ | VQ-BLS | Boeing 737-76Q | 30277/947 | ex D-ABAB | |
| ☐ | VQ-BLT | Boeing 737-76Q | 30271/740 | ex D-ABAA | ◆ |
| ☐ | VQ-BMP | Boeing 737-86N/W | 28617/504 | ex SE-RHS | ◆ |
| ☐ | VQ-BOY | Boeing 737-85F | 28825/188 | ex D-ABBR | |
| ☐ | VP-BFG | Boeing 757-256/W | 26244/616 | ex TF-FIT | |
| ☐ | VP-BFI | Boeing 757-27B | 24838/302 | ex TF-FIW | |
| ☐ | VQ-BCF | Boeing 757-23N/W | 27974/737 | ex N518AT | |
| ☐ | VQ-BCK | Boeing 757-256/W | 26245/617 | ex TF-FIS | |
| ☐ | VQ-BMW | Boeing 757-23N/W | 29330/843 | ex N522AT | |
| ☐ | VQ-BOX | Boeing 757-23APF | 24868/314 | ex N868AN | ◆ |
| ☐ | RA-85007 | Tupolev Tu-154M | 88A777 | ex LZ-HMF | |
| ☐ | RA-85700 | Tupolev Tu-154M | 91A875 | ex LZ-HMY | |
| ☐ | RA-857707 | Tupolev Tu-154M | 91A882 | | |
| ☐ | RA-85791 | Tupolev Tu-154M | 93A975 | ex EP-MBR | ◆ |
| ☐ | RA-85794 | Tupolev Tu-154M | 93A978 | | [YKS] |
| ☐ | RA-85812 | Tupolev Tu-154M | 94A1005 | AirUnion c/s | |
| ☐ | RA-26660 | Antonov An-26-100 | 97308008 | ex CCCP-26660 | |
| ☐ | RA-41250 | Antonov An-140-100 | 05A001 | | wfs |
| ☐ | RA-41251 | Antonov An-140-100 | 07A012 | | |
| ☐ | RA-41252 | Antonov An-140-100 | 09A014 | | |
| ☐ | RA-41253 | Antonov An-140-100 | 36525305032 | ex UR-14008 | |

## YAMAL AIRLINES — Yamal (YL/LLM) — Salekhard-Nepalkovo (SLY)

| | | | | | |
|---|---|---|---|---|---|
| ☐ | VP-BRQ | Boeing 737-528 | 25230/2191 | ex F-GJNE | |
| ☐ | VP-BRS | Boeing 737-528 | 25231/2208 | ex F-GJNF | |
| ☐ | VP-BRU | Boeing 737-528 | 25206/2099 | ex F-GJNA | |
| ☐ | VP-BRV | Boeing 737-528 | 25227/2108 | ex F-GJNB | |
| ☐ | VQ-BAB | Boeing 737-56N | 28565/2944 | ex N565LS | |
| ☐ | VQ-BNM | Boeing 737-5Q8 | 28201/2999 | ex N171LF | |
| ☐ | VQ- | Boeing 737-5Q8 | 28052/2965 | ex EI-DTX | ◆ |
| ☐ | VP-BBA | Canadair CRJ-200LR | 7607 | ex D-ACRE | ◆ |
| ☐ | VQ-BBC | Canadair CRJ-200LR | 7619 | ex D-ACRF | ◆ |
| ☐ | VQ-BBV | Canadair CRJ-200ER | 7454 | ex N654BR | ◆ |
| ☐ | VQ-BPA | Canadair CRJ-200LR | 7583 | ex D-ACRD | ◆ |
| ☐ | VQ-BPB | Canadair CRJ-200LR | 7573 | ex D-ACRC | ◆ |
| ☐ | VQ-BPC | Canadair CRJ-200LR | 7570 | ex D-ACRB | ◆ |
| ☐ | VQ-BPD | Canadair CRJ-200LR | 7567 | ex D-ACRA | ◆ |
| ☐ | VQ- | Canadair CRJ-200LR | 7630 | ex D-ACRG | o/o◆ |
| ☐ | RA-65132 | Tupolev Tu-134A-3 | 60639 | ex CCCP-65132 | |
| ☐ | RA-65143 | Tupolev Tu-134A | 60967 | ex CCCP-65143 | |
| ☐ | RA-65552 | Tupolev Tu-134A-3 | 66270 | ex CCCP-65552 | |
| ☐ | RA-65554 | Tupolev Tu-134A-3 | 66320 | ex CCCP-65554 | |
| ☐ | RA-65906 | Tupolev Tu-134A | 66175 | ex CCCP-65906 | Salekhard |
| ☐ | RA-65914 | Tupolev Tu-134A-3 | 66109 | ex CCCP-65914 | |
| ☐ | RA-65915 | Tupolev Tu-134A-3 | 66120 | ex TC-GRE | |
| ☐ | RA-65916 | Tupolev Tu-134A-3 | 66152 | | ◆ |
| ☐ | RA-65983 | Tupolev Tu-134A-3 | 63350 | ex CCCP-65983 | |
| ☐ | RA-87222 | Yakovlev Yak-40K | 9832058 | ex CCCP-87222 | |
| ☐ | RA-87340 | Yakovlev Yak-40 | 9510939 | ex YL-TRA | |
| ☐ | RA-87381 | Yakovlev Yak-40 | 9411232 | ex CCCP-87381 | |
| ☐ | RA-87416 | Yakovlev Yak-40 | 9420834 | ex CCCP-87416 | |
| ☐ | RA-88264 | Yakovlev Yak-40K | 9711952 | ex CCCP-88264 | |
| ☐ | EI-DTX | Boeing 737-5Q8 | 28052/2965 | ex LY-AZX | ◆ |
| ☐ | RA-26133 | Antonov An-26B | 37312709 | ex CCCP-26133 | |
| ☐ | RA-46694 | Antonov An-24RV | 47309905 | ex CCCP-46694 | |
| ☐ | RA-46695 | Antonov An-24RV | 47309906 | ex UN 46695 | |
| ☐ | VQ-BII | Boeing 737-48E | 25773/2905 | ex N773SJ | |

| | | | | | |
|---|---|---|---|---|---|
| ☐ | VQ-BIK | Boeing 737-48E | 25775/2925 | ex N775SJ | ♦ |
| ☐ | VQ-BNR | Airbus A320-214 | 1054 | ex N105SR | ♦ |
| ☐ | VQ- | Airbus A319-232 | 1918 | ex EI-ELD | o/o♦ |

## ZAPOLYARYE AVIAKOMPANIA
Norlisk-Alykel (NSK)

| | | | | | |
|---|---|---|---|---|---|
| ☐ | RA-85562 | Tupolev Tu-154B-2 | 82A562 | | ♦ |

## RDPL- LAOS (Lao People's Democratic Republic

### LAO AIRLINES
Lao (QV/LAO)                          Vientiane (VTE)

| | | | | | |
|---|---|---|---|---|---|
| ☐ | RDPL-34149 | Cessna 208B Caravan I | 208B1159 | ex N12879 | |
| ☐ | RDPL-34150 | Mil Mi-8T | | | ♦ |
| ☐ | RDPL-34173 | ATR 72-202 | 0870 | ex F-WNUD | |
| ☐ | RDPL-34174 | ATR 72-202 | 0878 | ex F-WNUF | |
| ☐ | RDPL-34175 | ATR 72-202 | 0929 | ex F-WKVF | |
| ☐ | RDPL-34176 | ATR 72-202 | 0938 | ex F-WKVJ | |
| ☐ | RDPL-34179 | de Havilland DHC-6 Twin Otter 300 | 593 | ex N169SG | ♦ |
| ☐ | RDPL-34182 | Aérospatiale AS350B2 Ecureuil | | | ♦ |
| ☐ | RDPL-34188 | Airbus A320-214 | 4596 | ex F-WWIX | ♦ |
| ☐ | RDPL-34199 | Airbus A320-214 | 4639 | ex F-WWBN | ♦ |

### LAO AVIATION
Lavie (LLL)                          Vientiane (VTE)

| | | | | | |
|---|---|---|---|---|---|
| ☐ | RDPL-34120 | Harbin Y7-100C | | | ♦ |
| ☐ | RDPL-34128 | Harbin Y7-100C | | | |
| ☐ | RDPL-34140 | Mil Mi-17 (Mi-8MTV-1) | 95984 | ex CCCP-27121 | |
| ☐ | RDPL-34145 | Aérospatiale AS350BA Ecureuil | 2532 | ex D-HLEA | |
| ☐ | RDPL-34156 | Antonov An-12BP | 402001 | ex LZ-VEF | |
| ☐ | RDPL-34168 | CAIC MA60 | 0402 | | ♦ |
| ☐ | RDPL-34169 | CAIC MA60 | 0403 | | ♦ |
| ☐ | RDPL-34171 | CAIC MA60 | 0507 | | ♦ |
| ☐ | RDPL-34172 | CAIC MA60 | 0508 | | ♦ |

### LAO CAPRICORN AIR
(LKA)

| | | | | | |
|---|---|---|---|---|---|
| ☐ | RDPL-34158 | LET L-410UVP-E | 902437 | ex ER-LID | ♦ |
| ☐ | RDPL-34163 | Ilyushin Il-76TD | 0053460832 | ex UP-I7610 | |

### LAO CENTRAL AIRLINES

| | | | | | |
|---|---|---|---|---|---|
| ☐ | RDPL-34183 | Boeing 737-4K5 | 24127/1707 | ex OO-TUA | ♦ |
| ☐ | RDPL-34189 | Boeing 737-4Y0 | 24314/1680 | ex YR-BAI | [VTE]♦ |

## RP- PHILIPPINES (Republic of the Philippines)

### AIRASIA PHILIPPINES
(PQ)

| | | | | | |
|---|---|---|---|---|---|
| ☐ | RP-C8189 | Airbus A320-216 | 4797 | ex F-WWIH | ♦ |
| ☐ | RP-C8191 | Airbus A320-216 | 4989 | ex F-WWDU | ♦ |

### AIR LINK INTERNATIONAL AIRWAYS
Manila-Sangley Point (SGL)

| | | | | | |
|---|---|---|---|---|---|
| ☐ | RP-C180 | Cessna 414 | 414-0402 | ex RP.180 | |
| ☐ | RP-C1102 | Beech 88 Queen Air | LP-44 | ex RP-94 | |
| ☐ | RP-C2252 | NAMC YS-11A-212 | 2079 | ex RP-C1931 | |

### AIRPHIL EXPRESS
Orient Pacific (2P/GAP)   Manila-Ninoy Aquino Intl (MNL)

| | | | | | |
|---|---|---|---|---|---|
| ☐ | RP-C3227 | Airbus A320-214 | 2183 | ex OY-VKP | |
| ☐ | RP-C3228 | Airbus A320-214 | 2162 | ex RP-C3226 | |
| ☐ | RP-C8388 | Airbus A320-214 | 4415 | ex F-WWIZ | |
| ☐ | RP-C8389 | Airbus A320-214 | 4475 | ex D-AUBA | |
| ☐ | RP-C8390 | Airbus A320-214 | 4504 | ex D-AUBM | |
| ☐ | RP-C8391 | Airbus A320-214 | 4512 | ex D-AXAE | |
| ☐ | RP-C8393 | Airbus A320-214 | 4777 | ex F-WWDN | ♦ |
| ☐ | RP-C8394 | Airbus A320-214 | 4907 | ex D-AVVL | ♦ |
| ☐ | RP-C8395 | Airbus A320-214 | 4984 | ex D-AVVR | ♦ |
| ☐ | RP-C8396 | Airbus A320-214 | 5007 | ex D-AVVY | ♦ |
| ☐ | RP-C8397 | Airbus A320-214 | 5012 | ex D-AVVZ | ♦ |
| ☐ | RP-C8398 | Airbus A320-214 | 5103 | ex D-AUBR | o/o♦ |
| ☐ | RP-C8616 | Airbus A320-214 | 5081 | ex D-AUBJ | ♦ |
| ☐ | RP-C | Airbus A320-214 | 5140 | ex | o/o♦ |
| ☐ | RP-C3016 | de Havilland DHC-8Q-314 | 653 | ex C-FNEA | |

| | | | | | |
|---|---|---|---|---|---|
| ☐ | RP-C3017 | de Havilland DHC-8Q-314 | 657 | ex C-FOUN | |
| ☐ | RP-C3018 | de Havilland DHC-8Q-314 | 658 | ex C-FPDR | |
| ☐ | RP-C3030 | de Havilland DHC-8-402Q | 4064 | ex LN-WDD | |
| ☐ | RP-C3031 | de Havilland DHC-8-402Q | 4069 | ex LN-WDA | |
| ☐ | RP-C3032 | de Havilland DHC-8-402Q | 4070 | ex LN-WDB | |
| ☐ | RP-C3033 | de Havilland DHC-8-402Q | 4071 | ex LN-WDC | |
| ☐ | RP-C3036 | de Havilland DHC-8-402Q | 4023 | ex LN-RDH | |
| | | | | | |
| ☐ | RP-C8007 | Boeing 737-2B7 (Nordam 3) | 22878/921 | ex N266AU | [MNL] |
| ☐ | RP-C8011 | Boeing 737-247 (Nordam 3) | 23606/1379 | ex N379DL | wfs |
| ☐ | RP-C8022 | Boeing 737-247 (Nordam 3) | 23607/1387 | ex N380DL | [MNL] |

## ASIAN SPIRIT

| | | | | | |
|---|---|---|---|---|---|
| ☐ | RP-C3588 | NAMC YS-11A-214 | 2168 | ex N12035 | ♦ |

## CARGOHOUSE

| | | | | | |
|---|---|---|---|---|---|
| ☐ | RP-C6021 | Cessna 208B Caravan I | 208B2263 | ex N3042E | ♦ |

## CEBU PACIFIC AIR
Cebu Air (5J/CEB)  Manila-Sangley Point (SGL)

| | | | | | |
|---|---|---|---|---|---|
| ☐ | RP-C3189 | Airbus A319-111 | 2556 | ex D-AVYG | |
| ☐ | RP-C3190 | Airbus A319-111 | 2586 | ex D-AVXI | |
| ☐ | RP-C3191 | Airbus A319-111 | 2625 | ex D-AVYZ | |
| ☐ | RP-C3192 | Airbus A319-111 | 2638 | ex D-AVWJ | |
| ☐ | RP-C3193 | Airbus A319-111 | 2786 | ex D-AVYV | |
| ☐ | RP-C3194 | Airbus A319-111 | 2790 | ex D-AVWN | |
| ☐ | RP-C3195 | Airbus A319-111 | 2831 | ex D-AVXH | |
| ☐ | RP-C3196 | Airbus A319-111 | 2821 | ex D-AVXC | |
| ☐ | RP-C3197 | Airbus A319-111 | 2852 | ex D-AVXL | |
| ☐ | RP-C3198 | Airbus A319-111 | 2876 | ex D-AVWL | |
| | | | | | |
| ☐ | RP-C3240 | Airbus A320-214 | 2419 | ex F-WWID | |
| ☐ | RP-C3241 | Airbus A320-214 | 2439 | ex F-WWBO | |
| ☐ | RP-C3242 | Airbus A320-214 | 2994 | ex F-WWIU | |
| ☐ | RP-C3243 | Airbus A320-214 | 3048 | ex F-WWDR | |
| ☐ | RP-C3244 | Airbus A320-214 | 3272 | ex F-WWBZ | |
| ☐ | RP-C3245 | Airbus A320-214 | 3433 | ex F-WWDU | |
| ☐ | RP-C3246 | Airbus A320-214 | 3472 | ex F-WWBV | |
| ☐ | RP-C3247 | Airbus A320-214 | 3487 | ex F-WWII | |
| ☐ | RP-C3248 | Airbus A320-214 | 3646 | ex F-WWBX | |
| ☐ | RP-C3249 | Airbus A320-214 | 3762 | ex F-WWDI | |
| ☐ | RP-C3250 | Airbus A320-214 | 3767 | ex F-WWDP | |
| ☐ | RP-C3260 | Airbus A320-214 | 4447 | ex F-WWII | |
| ☐ | RP-C3261 | Airbus A320-214 | 4508 | ex F-WWBJ | |
| ☐ | RP-C3262 | Airbus A320-214 | 4537 | ex F-WWIF | ♦ |
| ☐ | RP-C3263 | Airbus A320-214 | 4574 | ex D-AVVJ | ♦ |
| ☐ | RP-C3264 | Airbus A320-214 | 4852 | ex D-AUBM | ♦ |
| ☐ | RP-C3265 | Airbus A320-214 | 4861 | ex D-AUBO | ♦ |
| ☐ | RP-C3266 | Airbus A320-214 | 4870 | ex D-AUBR | ♦ |
| ☐ | RP-C3267 | Airbus A320-214 | 4927 | ex F-WWBH | ♦ |
| ☐ | RP-C3268 | Airbus A320-214 | 4993 | ex F-WWBF | ♦ |
| ☐ | RP-C3236 | Airbus A320-214 | 5067 | ex F-WWBX | ♦ |
| ☐ | RP-C3237 | Airbus A320-214 | 5045 | ex F-WWDZ | ♦ |
| ☐ | RP-C3238 | Airbus A320-214 | 5067 | ex F-WWBX | ♦ |
| | | | | | |
| ☐ | RP-C7250 | ATR 72-212A | 0779 | ex F-WWER | |
| ☐ | RP-C7251 | ATR 72-212A | 0784 | ex F-WWEC | |
| ☐ | RP-C7252 | ATR 72-212A | 0820 | ex F-WWEJ | |
| ☐ | RP-C7253 | ATR 72-212A | 0828 | ex F-WWEV | |
| ☐ | RP-C7255 | ATR 72-212A | 0842 | ex F-WWEH | |
| ☐ | RP-C7256 | ATR 72-212A | 0847 | ex F-WWEI | |
| ☐ | RP-C7257 | ATR 72-212A | 0857 | ex F-WWEB | |
| ☐ | RP-C7258 | ATR 72-212A | 0944 | ex | ♦ |

## CHEMTRAD AVIATION
Manila-Sangley Point (SGL)

| | | | | | |
|---|---|---|---|---|---|
| ☐ | RP-C28 | Britten-Norman BN-2A-21 Islander | 409 | ex G-BCLF | |
| ☐ | RP-C1262 | Britten-Norman BN-2A-21 Islander | 408 | ex G-BCLE | |
| ☐ | RP-C2207 | Britten-Norman BN-2A-26 Islander | 718 | ex G-BCAF | |

## INTERISLAND AIRLINES
(ISN)  Manila-Ninoy Aquino Intl (MNL)

| | | | | | |
|---|---|---|---|---|---|
| ☐ | RP-C2639 | Antonov An-26 | 77305509 | ex EK-26227 | |
| ☐ | RP-C2803 | Yakovlev Yak-40 | 9430537 | | ♦ |
| ☐ | RP-C2805 | Yakovlev Yak-40 | 9342031 | ex 4L-AVC | |
| ☐ | RP-C3338 | NAMC YS-11A-227 | 2142 | ex JA8766 | ♦ |

## ISLAND AVIATION — Soriano (SOY) — Manila-Sangley Point (SGL)

| | | | | |
|---|---|---|---|---|
| ☐ | RP-C2282 | Dornier 228-202K | 8173 | ex N23UA |
| ☐ | RP-C2283 | Dornier 228-202K | 8077 | ex F-ODZH |
| ☐ | RP-C2287 | Dornier 228-202K | 8174 | ex VH-YJD |

## ISLAND TRANSVOYAGER — Manila-Sangley Point (SGL)

| | | | | |
|---|---|---|---|---|
| ☐ | RP-C1008 | Dornier 228-212 | 8193 | ex D-CARD |
| ☐ | RP-C2289 | Dornier 228-212 | 8177 | ex B-11150 |

## JET EAGLE INTERNATIONAL

| | | | | | |
|---|---|---|---|---|---|
| ☐ | RP-C7573 | Cessna 208B Caravan I | 208B2266 | ex N30197 | ♦ |

## LIONAIR

| | | | | |
|---|---|---|---|---|
| ☐ | RP-C5525 | British Aerospace 146 Srs.200 | E2031 | ex N66LN |

## MID-SEA EXPRESS

| | | | | | |
|---|---|---|---|---|---|
| ☐ | RP-C863 | British Aerospace Jetstream 32 | 974 | ex VH-OTP | ♦ |
| ☐ | RP-C5700 | Beech B200 Super King Air | BB-1175 | ex N515CP | ♦ |

## NORTH SOUTH AIRLINES — Manila-Ninoy Aquino Intl (MNL)

| | | | | |
|---|---|---|---|---|
| ☐ | RP-C8258 | LET L-410UVP-E10 | 882038 | ex 3D-RTV |

## PACIFIC EAST ASIA CARGO AIRLINES — Pac-East Cargo (Q8/PEC) — Manila-Ninoy Aquino Intl (MNL)

| | | | | | |
|---|---|---|---|---|---|
| ☐ | RP-C5354 | Learjet 35A | 35A-185 | ex ZS-SES | |
| ☐ | RP-C5355 | Boeing 727-223F (FedEx 3) | 20185/710 | ex PK-YGT | wfs |

## PACIFICAIR — Pacific West (GX/PFR) — Manila-Sangley Point (SGL)

| | | | | |
|---|---|---|---|---|
| ☐ | RP-C1321 | Britten-Norman BN-2A-21 Islander | 547 | ex PAF-547 |
| ☐ | RP-C1801 | Britten-Norman BN-2A-21 Islander | 739 | ex G-BCNI |
| ☐ | RP-C2132 | Britten-Norman BN-2A-21 Islander | 422 | ex G-BCSG |
| ☐ | RP-C2137 | Britten-Norman BN-2A-21 Islander | 443 | ex G-BCZU |
| ☐ | RP-C1103 | Beech H-18 | BA-660 | ex N638CZ |
| ☐ | RP-C1358 | Beech H-18 Tri-Gear | BA-750 | ex RP-C1986 |
| ☐ | RP-C1611 | Cessna 421C Golden Eagle | 421C0155 | ex N5282J |

## PHILIPPINE AIRLINES — Philippine (PR/PAL) — Manila-Ninoy Aquino Intl (MNL)

| | | | | |
|---|---|---|---|---|
| ☐ | RP-C3221 | Airbus A320-214 | 0706 | ex F-WWIM |
| ☐ | RP-C3223 | Airbus A320-214 | 0745 | ex F-WWIR |
| ☐ | RP-C8604 | Airbus A320-214 | 3087 | ex F-WWBV |
| ☐ | RP-C8605 | Airbus A320-214 | 3107 | ex F-WWIK |
| ☐ | RP-C8606 | Airbus A320-214 | 3187 | ex F-WWDY |
| ☐ | RP-C8607 | Airbus A320-214 | 3205 | ex F-WWIH |
| ☐ | RP-C8609 | Airbus A320-214 | 3273 | ex F-WWIC |
| ☐ | RP-C8610 | Airbus A320-214 | 3310 | ex F-WWIO |
| ☐ | RP-C8611 | Airbus A320-214 | 3455 | ex F-WWBH |
| ☐ | RP-C8612 | Airbus A320-214 | 3553 | ex F-WWIZ |
| ☐ | RP-C8613 | Airbus A320-214 | 3579 | ex F-WWBY |
| ☐ | RP-C8614 | Airbus A320-214 | 3652 | ex F-WWDQ |
| ☐ | RP-C8615 | Airbus A320-214 | 3731 | ex F-WWDL |
| ☐ | RP-C3330 | Airbus A330-301 | 183 | ex F-OHZM |
| ☐ | RP-C3331 | Airbus A330-301 | 184 | ex F-OHZN |
| ☐ | RP-C3332 | Airbus A330-301 | 188 | ex F-OHZO |
| ☐ | RP-C3333 | Airbus A330-301 | 191 | ex F-OHZP |
| ☐ | RP-C3335 | Airbus A330-301 | 189 | ex F-OHZQ |
| ☐ | RP-C3336 | Airbus A330-301 | 198 | ex F-OHZR |
| ☐ | RP-C3337 | Airbus A330-301 | 200 | ex F-OHZS |
| ☐ | RP-C3340 | Airbus A330-301 | 203 | ex F-OHZT |
| ☐ | RP-C7471 | Boeing 747-4F6 | 27261/1005 | ex N751PR |
| ☐ | RP-C7472 | Boeing 747-4F6 | 27262/1012 | ex N752PR |
| ☐ | RP-C7473 | Boeing 747-4F6 | 27828/1039 | ex N753PR |
| ☐ | RP-C7475 | Boeing 747-469M | 27663/1068 | ex N754PR |
| ☐ | RP-C8168 | Boeing 747-4F6 | 27827/1038 | ex C-FGHZ |
| ☐ | RP-C3430 | Airbus A340-313X | 173 | ex F-OHPJ |
| ☐ | RP-C3431 | Airbus A340-313X | 176 | ex F-OHPK |
| ☐ | RP-C3432 | Airbus A340-313X | 187 | ex F-OHPL |

| | | | | | |
|---|---|---|---|---|---|
| ☐ | RP-C3434 | Airbus A340-313X | 196 | ex F-OHPM | |
| ☐ | RP-C7775 | Boeing 777-3F6ER | 35555 | | o/o♦ |
| ☐ | RP-C7776 | Boeing 777-36NER | 37712/841 | | |
| ☐ | RP-C7777 | Boeing 777-36NER | 37709/826 | | |
| ☐ | RP-C8600 | Airbus A319-112 | 2878 | ex D-AVWO | |
| ☐ | RP-C8601 | Airbus A319-112 | 2925 | ex D-AVYP | |
| ☐ | RP-C8602 | Airbus A319-112 | 2954 | ex D-AVXE | |
| ☐ | RP-C8603 | Airbus A319-112 | 3108 | ex D-AVYM | |

## ROYAL STAR AVIATION — Manila-Sangley Point (SGL)

| | | | | | |
|---|---|---|---|---|---|
| ☐ | RP-C1098 | Agusta A109E Power | 11041 | ex CS-HEM | ♦ |
| ☐ | RP-C2812 | British Aerospace Jetstream 3217 | 923 | ex N93BA | |
| ☐ | RP-C8298 | British Aerospace Jetstream 4101 | 41013 | ex N302UE | |
| ☐ | RP-C8299 | British Aerospace Jetstream 4101 | 41080 | ex N327UE | |
| ☐ | RP-C8328 | Dornier 328-300 (328JET) | 3136 | ex N360SK | |

## SEAIR — Seair (DG/SRQ)
### Manila- Ninoy Aquino Intl/Diosdado Macapagal Intl (MNL/CRK)

| | | | | | |
|---|---|---|---|---|---|
| ☐ | RP-C2128 | LET L-410UVP-E3 | 882102 | ex S9-BOX | |
| ☐ | RP-C2328 | LET L-410UVP-E3 | 872004 | ex S9-BOY | |
| ☐ | RP-C2428 | LET L-410UVP-E3 | 871909 | ex 3D-DAM | |
| ☐ | RP-C2628 | LET L-410UVP-E3 | 871931 | ex Russ AF 1931 | |
| ☐ | RP-C2728 | LET L-410UVP-E | 861708 | ex RA-67588  jungle c/s | |
| ☐ | RP-C2928 | LET L-410UVP-E | 871821 | ex Russ AF 1821 | |
| ☐ | RP-C3318 | LET L-410UVP-E3 | 871934 | ex 3C-QRH | |
| ☐ | RP-C3328 | LET L-410UVP-E3 | 872003 | ex RP-C528 | ♦ |
| | | | | | |
| ☐ | RP-C4328 | Dornier 328-120 | 3042 | ex D-CPRT | |
| ☐ | RP-C5328 | Dornier 328-110 | 3046 | ex D-CPRS | |
| ☐ | RP-C6328 | Dornier 328-110 | 3027 | ex N653JC | |
| ☐ | RP-C7328 | Dornier 328-110 | 3069 | ex G-BYML | |
| ☐ | RP-C9328 | Dornier 328-110 | 3003 | ex D-CDOL    all-white | |
| | | | | | |
| ☐ | RP-C1179 | Dornier 28D-2 Skyservant | 4127 | ex D-IDRH | ♦ |
| ☐ | RP-C4319 | Airbus A319-132 | 3757 | ex 9V-TRA | <TGW♦ |
| ☐ | RP-C4737 | Boeing 737-2T4C | 23065/989 | ex JY-TWC | ♦ |
| ☐ | RP-C5320 | Airbus A319-132 | 3801 | ex 9V-TRB | <TGW♦ |

## SPIRIT OF MANILA AIRLINES

Ceased ops

## TRANSGLOBAL AIRWAYS — Diosdado Macapagal IntL (CRK)

| | | | | | |
|---|---|---|---|---|---|
| ☐ | RP-C8017 | Boeing 727-51F | 19289/403 | ex 9L-LFJ | ♦ |

## VICTORIA AIR — Manila-Sangley Point (SGL)

| | | | | | |
|---|---|---|---|---|---|
| ☐ | RP-C535 | Douglas DC-3 | 15571/27016 | ex RP-C95 | |

## ZEST AIRWAYS — (Z2/EZD) — Manila-Sangley Point (SGL)

| | | | | | |
|---|---|---|---|---|---|
| ☐ | RP-C8897 | Airbus A320-232 | 2141 | ex N581JB | |
| ☐ | RP-C8988 | Airbus A320-232 | 2147 | ex RP-C8898 | |
| ☐ | RP-C8989 | Airbus A320-232 | 3621 | ex F-WWIK | |
| ☐ | RP-C8991 | Airbus A320-232 | 4533 | ex D-AXAK | |
| ☐ | RP-C8992 | Airbus A320-232 | 2137 | ex G-TTOI | |
| ☐ | RP-C8993 | Airbus A320-232 | 0667 | ex N403AC | ♦ |
| ☐ | RP-C8994 | Airbus A320-233 | 0743 | ex N416AC | ♦ |
| ☐ | RP-C | Airbus A320-232 | 0872 | ex N593SH | ♦ |
| | | | | | |
| ☐ | RP-C2918 | LET L-410UVP | 902510 | ex 9A-BNZ    Fleuris titles | |
| ☐ | RP-C2996 | British Aerospace 146-100 | E1005 | ex VH-NJY    Fleuris titles | ♦ |
| ☐ | RP-C3880 | LET L-410UVP-E | 892228 | ex RA-67601  Fleuris titles | |
| ☐ | RP-C3889 | LET L-410UVP-E | 851511 | ex RA-67544  Fleuris titles | |
| ☐ | RP-C5000 | ITPN CASA CN-235 | 2/N001 | ex PK-MNA | |
| ☐ | RP-C8892 | CAIC MA60 | 0703 | ex B-956L | |
| ☐ | RP-C8894 | CAIC MA60 | 0710 | ex B-956L | |
| ☐ | RP-C8895 | CAIC MA60 | 0711 | ex B-963L | |
| ☐ | RP-C8896 | CAIC MA60 | 0712 | ex B-964L | |
| ☐ | RP-C8990 | Airbus A319-132 | 1074 | ex SE-RIB | |

## SE-    SWEDEN (Kingdom of Sweden)

### AIR SWEDEN    (SXN)

| | | | | | |
|---|---|---|---|---|---|
| ☐ | SE-DMT | McDonnell-Douglas MD-81 | 48003/944 | ex N480LT | wfs |
| ☐ | SE-RJM | Airbus A320-212 | 0289 | ex F-WBGE | [SAW] |
| ☐ | SE-RJP | McDonnell-Douglas MD-82 | 49209/1191 | ex I-DAWS | [ARN] |

### AMAPOLA FLYG    Amapola (APF)    Stockholm-Arlanda (ARN)

| | | | | | |
|---|---|---|---|---|---|
| ☐ | PH-LMB | Fokker 50 | 20119 | ex OY-EBD | ♦ |
| ☐ | SE-KTC | Fokker 50 | 20124 | ex OY-MMG | |
| ☐ | SE-KTD | Fokker 50 | 20125 | ex OY-MMH | |
| ☐ | SE-LEU | Fokker 50 | 20115 | ex 9M-MGZ | ♦ |
| ☐ | SE-LIP | Fokker 50 | 20147 | ex PH-PRD | |
| ☐ | SE-LIS | Fokker 50 | 20152 | ex PH-PRF | ♦ |
| ☐ | SE-LJG | Fokker 50 | 20168 | ex LX-LGC | |
| ☐ | SE-LJH | Fokker 50 | 20171 | ex LX-LGD | |
| ☐ | SE-LJI | Fokker 50 | 20180 | ex LX-LGE | |
| ☐ | SE-LJV | Fokker 50 | 20103 | ex VT-CAA | |
| ☐ | SE-LJY | Fokker 50 | 20259 | ex OY-PAA | |
| ☐ | SE-MFA | Fokker 50 | 20118 | ex PH-LMA | ♦ |
| ☐ | SE-MFB | Fokker 50 | 20252 | ex PH-KXM | ♦ |

### AVIA EXPRESS SWEDEN    Sky Express (JZ/SKX)
#### Jönköping/Stockholm-Arlanda (JKG/ARN)

| | | | | | |
|---|---|---|---|---|---|
| ☐ | SE-DZB | Embraer ERJ-145EP | 145113 | ex PT-SCP | ♦ |
| ☐ | SE-RAC | Embraer ERJ-145LR | 145098 | ex N285CD | ♦ |
| ☐ | SE-RAD | Embraer ERJ-145EU | 145458 | ex G-EMBU | ♦ |
| ☐ | SE-RAE | Embraer ERJ-145EU | 145482 | ex G-EMBV | ♦ |
| ☐ | SE-RAF | Embraer ERJ-145LR | 145286 | ex UR-DNX | ♦ |
| ☐ | SE-RAG | Embraer ERJ-145LR | 145709 | ex UR-DNT | [CFE]♦ |
| ☐ | SE-RIA | Embraer ERJ-145MP | 145320 | ex PH-RXB | ♦ |
| ☐ | SE-LEA | Fokker 50 | 20116 | ex PH-GHK | ♦ |
| ☐ | SE-LEC | Fokker 50 | 20112 | ex VH-FNG | ♦ |
| ☐ | SE-LED | Fokker 50 | 20111 | ex VH-FNF | ♦ |
| ☐ | SE-LEH | Fokker 50 | 20108 | ex VH-FNC | ♦ |
| ☐ | SE-LEL | Fokker 50 | 20110 | ex VH-FNE | ♦ |
| ☐ | SE-LEU | Fokker 50 | 20115 | ex 9M-MGZ | ♦ |
| ☐ | SE-LEZ | Fokker 50 | 20128 | ex PH-PRA | ♦ |
| ☐ | SE-LIO | Fokker 50 | 20146 | ex PH-PRC | ♦ |
| ☐ | SE-LIR | Fokker 50 | 20151 | ex PH-PRE | ♦ |
| ☐ | SE-LIT | Fokker 50 | 20194 | ex PH-ZDF | ♦ |
| ☐ | SE-MEI | Fokker 50 | 20210 | ex PH-FZH | ♦ |
| ☐ | SE-RAA | Embraer ERJ-135ER | 145210 | ex PT-SFU | ♦ |
| ☐ | SE-RAB | Embraer ERJ-135LR | 145453 | ex PT-SUY | ♦ |

### AVITRANS NORDIC    Extrans (2Q/ETS)    Nyköping (NYO)

Ceased ops Aug10

### BARENTS AIRLINK    Nordflight (8N/NKF)    Lulea (LLA)

| | | | | | |
|---|---|---|---|---|---|
| ☐ | SE-IUX | Beech 200 Super King Air | BB-675 | ex N26SD | |
| ☐ | SE-LTL | Beech 200 Super King Air | BB-582 | ex LN-MOA | |

### CITY AIRLINE    Swedestar (CF/SDR)    Gothenburg-Landvetter (GOT)

Acquired by Skyways 29Apr11

### DIREKTFLYG    Skyreg (HS/HSV)    Borlänge (BLE)

| | | | | | |
|---|---|---|---|---|---|
| ☐ | SE-LHB | British Aerospace Jetstream 32EP | 844 | ex N844JX | |
| ☐ | SE-LHC | British Aerospace Jetstream 32EP | 846 | ex N846JX | |
| ☐ | SE-LHE | British Aerospace Jetstream 32EP | 854 | ex N854JX | |
| ☐ | SE-LHF | British Aerospace Jetstream 32EP | 855 | ex N855JX | |
| ☐ | SE-LHG | British Aerospace Jetstream 32EP | 857 | ex N857JX | |
| ☐ | SE-LHH | British Aerospace Jetstream 32EP | 848 | ex N848JX | |
| ☐ | SE-LHI | British Aerospace Jetstream 32EP | 841 | ex N841JX | |
| ☐ | SE-LNV | British Aerospace Jetstream 32EP | 951 | ex N566HK | wfs♦ |
| ☐ | SE-LXD | British Aerospace Jetstream 32 | 977 | ex G-BUVD | |
| ☐ | SE-LXE | British Aerospace Jetstream 32 | 970 | ex G-BUVC | |

## FLY LOGIC SWEDEN · Logic (LOD) · Malmö-Sturup (MMX)

| | | | | | |
|---|---|---|---|---|---|
| ☐ | SE-GIN | Piper PA-31 Navajo C | 31-7512039 | | |
| ☐ | SE-IDR | Piper PA-31 Navajo C | 31-7712085 | ex LN-DAB | |
| ☐ | SE-IKV | Piper PA-31-350 Navajo Chieftain | 31-7405148 | ex G-BDFN | |
| ☐ | SE-KCP | Swearingen SA.226TCMetro II | TC-330 | ex N7217N | |

## GOLDEN AIR · Golden (DC/GAO) · Trollhattan (THN)

| | | | | | |
|---|---|---|---|---|---|
| ☐ | SE-MDA | ATR 72-212A | 0778 | ex EI-REN | |
| ☐ | SE-MDB | ATR 72-212A | 0822 | ex EI-RER | |
| ☐ | SE-MDC | ATR 72-212A | 0894 | ex F-WWED | |
| ☐ | SE-MDH | ATR 72-212A | 0917 | ex F-WWEO | |
| ☐ | SE-MDI | ATR 72-212A | 0930 | ex F-WWEF | |
| ☐ | SE-KXK | SAAB 2000 | 2000-012 | ex F-GOZI | |
| ☐ | SE-LOM | SAAB 2000 | 2000-035 | ex LY-SBK | |
| ☐ | SE-LOT | SAAB 2000 | 2000-013 | ex YR-SBL | |
| ☐ | SE-LSB | SAAB 2000 | 2000-043 | ex OH-SAU | ♦ |
| ☐ | SE-LTU | SAAB 2000 | 2000-062 | ex HB-IYG | ♦ |
| ☐ | SE-LTV | SAAB 2000 | 2000-063 | ex HB-IYH | |
| ☐ | SE-LTX | SAAB 2000 | 2000-024 | ex HB-IZM | |
| ☐ | SE-LXH | SAAB 2000 | 2000-007 | ex LY-SBQ | |
| ☐ | SE-LXK | SAAB 2000 | 2000-056 | ex ER-SFA | ♦ |
| ☐ | SE-MFF | SAAB 2000 | 2000-038 | ex YR-SBA | ♦ |
| ☐ | SE-ISG | SAAB SF.340B | 340B-162 | ex SE-F62 | |
| ☐ | SE-KTE | SAAB SF.340B | 340B-230 | ex OK-CCN | |
| ☐ | SE-KXG | SAAB SF.340B | 340B-164 | ex XA-AAO | |

## MALMÖ AVIATION · Scanwing (TF/SCW) · Stockholm-Arlanda/Malmö-Sturup (ARN/MMX)

| | | | | | |
|---|---|---|---|---|---|
| ☐ | SE-DJN | Avro 146-RJ85 | E2231 | ex HB-IXG | |
| ☐ | SE-DJO | Avro 146-RJ85 | E2226 | ex HB-IXF | |
| ☐ | SE-DSO | Avro 146-RJ100 | E3221 | ex N504MM | |
| ☐ | SE-DSP | Avro 146-RJ100 | E3242 | ex N505MM | |
| ☐ | SE-DSR | Avro 146-RJ100 | E3244 | ex N506MM | Inga Omvägar |
| ☐ | SE-DSS | Avro 146-RJ100 | E3245 | ex N507MM | |
| ☐ | SE-DST | Avro 146-RJ100 | E3247 | ex N508MM | |
| ☐ | SE-DSU | Avro 146-RJ100 | E3248 | ex N509MM | |
| ☐ | SE-DSV | Avro 146-RJ100 | E3250 | ex N510MM | Stig Ombord |
| ☐ | SE-DSX | Avro 146-RJ100 | E3255 | ex N511MM | Bill Jet |
| ☐ | SE-DSY | Avro 146-RJ100 | E3263 | ex N512MM | |

## NEXTIME JET · Nextjet (2N/NTJ) · Stockholm-Bromma (BMA)

| | | | | | |
|---|---|---|---|---|---|
| ☐ | SE-ISE | SAAB SF.340A | 340A-156 | ex YL-BAP | ♦ |
| ☐ | SE-ISY | SAAB SF.340A | 340A-080 | ex SE-E80 | ♦ |
| ☐ | SE-KCS | SAAB SF.340A (QC) | 340A-066 | ex (SP-KPH) | ♦ |
| ☐ | SE-KXI | SAAB SF.340B | 340B-176 | ex XA-AFR | ♦ |
| ☐ | SE-KXJ | SAAF SF.340B | 340B-189 | ex XA-TKT | ♦ |
| ☐ | SE-LEP | SAAB SF.340A | 340A-127 | ex B-12200 | |
| ☐ | SE-LJN | SAAB SF.340A | 340A-114 | ex LY-DIG | |
| ☐ | SE-LJS | SAAB SF.340B | 340B-215 | ex D-CDEO | ♦ |
| ☐ | SE-LJT | SAAB SF.340B | 340B-221 | ex D-CASD | ♦ |
| ☐ | SE-LMR | SAAB SF.340A | 340A-141 | ex OK-UFO | |
| ☐ | OM-VRC | ATR 72-202 | 0307 | ex F-WKVB | <VPA |
| ☐ | SE-LLO | British Aerospace ATP | 2023 | ex G-MANP | |
| ☐ | SE-MAK | British Aerospace ATP | 2040 | ex G-MANF | |
| ☐ | SE-MAL | British Aerospace ATP | 2045 | ex G-MANE | |
| ☐ | SE-MEE | British Aerospace ATP | 2019 | ex CS-TGL | ♦ |

## NORRLANDSFLYG · Lifeguard Sweden (HMF) · Gallivare/Kiruna (GEV/KRN)

| | | | | | |
|---|---|---|---|---|---|
| ☐ | SE-HAJ | Sikorsky S-76C | 760510 | ex OH-HCJ | SAR |
| ☐ | SE-HAV | Sikorsky S-76C | 760377 | ex N50KH | SAR |
| ☐ | SE-HEJ | Sikorsky S-76C+ | 760604 | ex N71141 | SAR |
| ☐ | SE-HOJ | Sikorsky S-76C+ | 760605 | ex N8125H | SAR |
| ☐ | SE-JEZ | Sikorsky S-76A | 760215 | ex N72WW | EMS |
| ☐ | SE-JUC | Sikorsky S-76A | 760219 | ex N18KH | EMS |
| ☐ | SE-JUS | Sikorsky S-76A | 760172 | ex N876TC | EMS |
| ☐ | SE-JUX | Sikorsky S-76C | 760518 | ex N552J | SAR |
| ☐ | SE-JUY | Sikorsky S-76C | 760407 | ex N154AE | SAR |

## NOVAIR · Navigator (1I/NVR) · Stockholm-Arlanda (ARN)

| | | | | | |
|---|---|---|---|---|---|
| ☐ | SE-RDN | Airbus A321-231 | 2211 | ex D-AVZK | |
| ☐ | SE-RDO | Airbus A321-231 | 2216 | ex D-AVZN | |
| ☐ | SE-RDP | Airbus A321-231 | 2410 | ex D-AVZK | |

## SCANDINAVIAN AIRLINES SYSTEM — Scandinavian (SK/SAS)
### Copenhagen-Kastrup/Oslo-Gardermoen/Stockholm-Arlanda (CPH/OSL/ARN)

Member of Star Alliance

| | | | | | |
|---|---|---|---|---|---|
| ☐ | LN-RKI | Airbus A321-232 | 1817 | ex D-AVZK | Gunnhild Viking |
| ☐ | LN-RKK | Airbus A321-232 | 1848 | ex SE-REG | Svipdag Viking |
| ☐ | OY-KBB | Airbus A321-232 | 1642 | ex D-AVZN | Hjörulf Viking |
| ☐ | OY-KBE | Airbus A321-232 | 1798 | ex D-AVZG | Emma Viking |
| ☐ | OY-KBF | Airbus A321-232 | 1807 | ex D-AVZH | Skapti Viking |
| ☐ | OY-KBH | Airbus A321-232 | 1675 | ex D-AVZV | Sulke Viking |
| ☐ | OY-KBK | Airbus A321-232 | 1587 | ex D-AVZK | Arne Viking |
| ☐ | OY-KBL | Airbus A321-232 | 1619 | ex D-AVZB | Gunnbjörn Viking |
| ☐ | LN-RKF | Airbus A340-313X | 413 | ex SE-REA | Godfred Viking |
| ☐ | LN-RKG | Airbus A340-313X | 424 | ex SE-REB | Gudrod Viking |
| ☐ | OY-KBA | Airbus A340-313X | 435 | ex F-WWJU | Adalstein Viking |
| ☐ | OY-KBC | Airbus A340-313X | 467 | ex F-WWJE | Freydis Viking |
| ☐ | OY-KBD | Airbus A340-313X | 470 | ex F-WWJF | Toste Viking |
| ☐ | OY-KBI | Airbus A340-313X | 430 | ex F-WWJR | Rurik Viking |
| ☐ | OY-KBM | Airbus A340-313X | 450 | ex F-WWJD | Astrid Viking |
| ☐ | LN-BRH | Boeing 737-505 | 24828/1925 | ex D-ACBB | Haakon den Gode |
| ☐ | LN-BRV | Boeing 737-505 | 25791/2351 | | Hakon Sverresson |
| ☐ | LN-BRX | Boeing 737-505 | 25797/2434 | | Sigurd Munn |
| ☐ | LN-BUC | Boeing 737-505 | 26304/2649 | | Magnus Erlingsson |
| ☐ | LN-BUD | Boeing 737-505 | 25794/2803 | | Inge Krokrygg |
| ☐ | LN-BUE | Boeing 737-505 | 27627/2800 | | Erling Skjalgsson |
| ☐ | LN-BUG | Boeing 737-505 | 27631/2866 | | Øystein Haraldsson |
| ☐ | LN-RCT | Boeing 737-683 | 30189/303 | ex OY-KKF | Fridlev Viking |
| ☐ | LN-RCU | Boeing 737-683 | 30190/335 | ex SE-DNZ | Sigfrid Viking |
| ☐ | LN-RCW | Boeing 737-683 | 28308/333 | ex SE-DNY | Yngvar Viking |
| ☐ | LN-RPA | Boeing 737-683 | 28290/100 | ex N5002K | Amljot Viking |
| ☐ | LN-RPB | Boeing 737-683 | 28294/137 | ex N1787B | Bure Viking |
| ☐ | LN-RPE | Boeing 737-683 | 28306/329 | ex SE-DOT | Edla Viking |
| ☐ | LN-RPF | Boeing 737-683 | 28307/330 | ex N1784B | Frede Viking |
| ☐ | LN-RPG | Boeing 737-683 | 28310/255 | ex N1787B | Geirmund Viking |
| ☐ | LN-RPH | Boeing 737-683 | 28605/375 | | Hamder Viking |
| ☐ | LN-RPS | Boeing 737-683 | 28298/191 | ex OY-KKC | Gautrek Viking |
| ☐ | LN-RPT | Boeing 737-683 | 28299/193 | ex OY-KKD | Ellida Viking |
| ☐ | LN-RPU | Boeing 737-683 | 28312/407 | ex OY-KKP | Ragna Viking |
| ☐ | LN-RPW | Boeing 737-683 | 28289/92 | ex OY-KKA | Alvid Viking |
| ☐ | LN-RPX | Boeing 737-683 | 28291/112 | ex SE-DNN | Nanna Viking |
| ☐ | LN-RPY | Boeing 737-683 | 28292/116 | ex SE-DNO | Olof Viking |
| ☐ | LN-RPZ | Boeing 737-683 | 28293/120 | ex OY-KKB | Bera Viking |
| ☐ | LN-RRC | Boeing 737-683 | 28300/209 | ex OY-KKG | Sindre Viking |
| ☐ | LN-RRD | Boeing 737-683 | 28301/227 | ex OY-KKH | Embla Viking |
| ☐ | LN-RRO | Boeing 737-683 | 28288/49 | ex SE-DNM | Bernt Viking |
| ☐ | LN-RRP | Boeing 737-683 | 28311/382 | ex SE-DTU | Vilborg Viking |
| ☐ | LN-RRR | Boeing 737-683 | 28309/368 | ex SE-DTF | Torbjörn Viking |
| ☐ | LN-RRX | Boeing 737-683 | 28296/21 | ex SE-DNR | Ragnfast Viking |
| ☐ | LN-RRY | Boeing 737-683 | 28297/30 | ex SE-DNS | Signe Viking |
| ☐ | LN-RRZ | Boeing 737-683 | 28295/149 | ex SE-DNP | Gisla Viking |
| ☐ | OY-KKS | Boeing 737-683 | 28322/614 | ex LN-RPC | Ramveig Viking |
| ☐ | SE-DNX | Boeing 737-683 | 28304/270 | ex G-CDRA | Torvald Viking |
| ☐ | SE-DOR | Boeing 737-683 | 28305/290 | ex G-CDRB | Elisabeth Viking |
| ☐ | SE-DTH | Boeing 737-683 | 28313/447 | ex (OY-KKI) | Vile Viking |
| ☐ | LN-RNN | Boeing 737-783 | 28315/464 | ex OY-KKI | Borgny Viking |
| ☐ | LN-RNO | Boeing 737-783 | 28316/476 | ex OY-KKR | Gjuke Viking |
| ☐ | LN-RNU | Boeing 737-783/W | 34548/3116 | ex N1786B | Hans Viking |
| ☐ | LN-RNW | Boeing 737-783/W | 34549/3210 | | Granmar Viking |
| ☐ | LN-RPJ | Boeing 737-783 | 30192/486 | ex N1786B | Grimhild Viking |
| ☐ | LN-RPK | Boeing 737-783 | 28317/500 | ex N1786B | Heimer Viking |
| ☐ | LN-RRA | Boeing 737-783/W | 30471/2288 | ex (SE-DYD) | Steinar Viking |
| ☐ | LN-RRB | Boeing 737-783/W | 32276/2331 | | Dag Viking |
| ☐ | LN-RRM | Boeing 737-783 | 28314/458 | ex SE-DTI | Erland Viking |
| ☐ | LN-RRN | Boeing 737-783 | 30191/404 | ex SE-DTG | Solveig Viking |
| ☐ | LN-TUA | Boeing 737-705 | 28211/33 | | Ingeborg Eriksdatter |
| ☐ | LN-TUD | Boeing 737-705 | 28217/142 | | Magrete Skulesdatter |
| ☐ | LN-TUF | Boeing 737-705 | 28222/245 | | Tyra Haraldsdatter |
| ☐ | LN-TUH | Boeing 737-705 | 29093/471 | | Margrete Ingesdatter |
| ☐ | LN-TUI | Boeing 737-705 | 29094/507 | ex N1787B | Kristin Knudsdatter |
| ☐ | LN-TUJ | Boeing 737-705/W | 29095/773 | | Eirik Blodöks |
| ☐ | LN-TUK | Boeing 737-705/W | 29096/794 | | Inge Bärdsson |
| ☐ | LN-TUL | Boeing 737-705/W | 29097/1072 | ex N1786B | Hakon IV Hakonsson |
| ☐ | LN-TUM | Boeing 737-705/W | 29098/1116 | | Øystein Magnusson |
| ☐ | SE-RER | Boeing 737-7BX | 30736/658 | ex B-5064 | Svein Viking ♦ |
| ☐ | SE-RES | Boeing 737-7BX | 30737/687 | ex N343MS | Rut Viking ♦ |
| ☐ | SE-RET | Boeing 737-7BX | 32734/1090 | ex N588SC | o/o♦ |

| | | | | | | |
|---|---|---|---|---|---|---|
| ☐ | LN-RCN | Boeing 737-883 | 28318/529 | ex SE-DTK | Hedrun Viking | |
| ☐ | LN-RCX | Boeing 737-883 | 30196/733 | ex SE-DYH | Höttur Viking | |
| ☐ | LN-RCY | Boeing 737-883 | 28324/767 | ex SE-DTT | Eylime Viking | |
| ☐ | LN-RCZ | Boeing 737-883 | 30197/798 | ex SE-DTS | Glitne Viking | |
| ☐ | LN-RGA | Boeing 737-86N/W | 39397 | | | o/o♦ |
| ☐ | LN-RGB | Boeing 737-86N/W | 38034 | | | o/oä |
| ☐ | LN-RGC | Boeing 737-86N/W | 41257 | | | o/o♦ |
| ☐ | LN-RGD | Boeing 737-86N/W | 41258 | | | o/o♦ |
| ☐ | LN-RGE | Boeing 737-86N/W | 38037 | | | o/o♦ |
| ☐ | LN-RGF | Boeing 737-86N/W | 38038 | | | o/o♦ |
| ☐ | LN-RGG | Boeing 737-86N/W | 38039 | | | o/o♦ |
| ☐ | LN-RGH | Boeing 737-86N/W | 41266 | | | o/o♦ |
| ☐ | LN-RPL | Boeing 737-883 | 30469/673 | ex (SE-DYC) | Svanevit Viking | |
| ☐ | LN-RPM | Boeing 737-883 | 30195/696 | ex (SE-DYD) | Frigg Viking | |
| ☐ | LN-RPN | Boeing 737-883 | 30470/717 | ex (SE-DYG) | Bergfora Viking | |
| ☐ | LN-RPO | Boeing 737-883 | 30467/634 | ex VQ-BFU | | ♦ |
| ☐ | LN-RPR | Boeing 737-883 | 30468/668 | ex VQ-BFR | | ♦ |
| ☐ | LN-RRE | Boeing 737-85P/W | 35706/2586 | | Knut Viking | |
| ☐ | LN-RRF | Boeing 737-85P/W | 35707/2610 | | Froydis Viking | |
| ☐ | LN-RRG | Boeing 737-85P/W | 35708/2653 | | Einar Viking | |
| ☐ | LN-RRH | Boeing 737-883/W | 34546/2898 | ex N1786B | Freja Viking | |
| ☐ | LN-RRJ | Boeing 737-883/W | 34547/2956 | ex N5573L | Frida Viking | |
| ☐ | LN-RRK | Boeing 737-883 | 32278/1169 | ex SE-DYG | Gerud Viking | |
| ☐ | LN-RRL | Boeing 737-883/W | 28328/1424 | ex SE-DYT | Jarlabanke Viking | Star Alliance c/s |
| ☐ | LN-RRS | Boeing 737-883 | 28325/1014 | ex (SE-DYM) | Ymer Viking | |
| ☐ | LN-RRT | Boeing 737-883 | 28326/1036 | ex (SE-DYN) | Lodyn Viking | |
| ☐ | LN-RRU | Boeing 737-883 | 28327/1070 | ex (SE-DYP) | Vingolf Viking | |
| ☐ | LN-RRW | Boeing 737-883 | 32277/1554 | ex SE-DTR | Saga Viking | |
| ☐ | LN-RNL | Canadair CRJ-900 | 15250 | ex C- | Fafner Viking | |
| ☐ | OY-KFA | Canadair CRJ-900 | 15206 | ex C-GIAW | Johan Viking | |
| ☐ | OY-KFB | Canadair CRJ-900 | 15211 | ex C- | Alfhild Viking | |
| ☐ | OY-KFC | Canadair CRJ-900 | 15218 | ex C- | Bertil Viking | |
| ☐ | OY-KFD | Canadair CRJ-900 | 15221 | ex C- | Estrid Viking | |
| ☐ | OY-KFE | Canadair CRJ-900 | 15224 | ex C-GIBH | Ingemar Viking | |
| ☐ | OY-KFF | Canadair CRJ-900 | 15231 | ex C-GZQO | Karl Viking | |
| ☐ | OY-KFG | Canadair CRJ-900 | 15237 | ex C- | Maria Viking | |
| ☐ | OY-KFH | Canadair CRJ-900 | 15240 | ex C-GZQU | Ella Viking | |
| ☐ | OY-KFI | Canadair CRJ-900 | 15242 | ex C-GIAP | Rolf Viking | |
| ☐ | OY-KFK | Canadair CRJ-900 | 15244 | ex C-GBSZ | Hardenknud Viking | |
| ☐ | OY-KFL | Canadair CRJ-900 | 15246 | ex C- | Regin Viking | |
| ☐ | LN-RLE | McDonnell-Douglas MD-82 | 49382/1232 | | Kettil Viking | |
| ☐ | LN-RLF | McDonnell-Douglas MD-82 | 49383/1236 | ex VH-LNJ | Finn Viking | |
| ☐ | LN-RML | McDonnell-Douglas MD-82 | 53002/1835 | | Aud Viking | |
| ☐ | LN-RMM | McDonnell-Douglas MD-82 | 53005/1855 | | Blenda Viking | |
| ☐ | LN-RMO | McDonnell-Douglas MD-82 | 53315/1947 | | Bergljot Viking | |
| ☐ | LN-RMR | McDonnell-Douglas MD-82 | 53365/1998 | | Olav Viking | |
| ☐ | LN-RMS | McDonnell-Douglas MD-82 | 53368/2003 | | Nial Viking | |
| ☐ | LN-RMT | McDonnell-Douglas MD-82 | 53001/1815 | ex OY-KHS | Jarl Viking | |
| ☐ | LN-ROP | McDonnell-Douglas MD-82 | 49384/1237 | ex SE-DFS | Bjorn Viking | |
| ☐ | LN-ROT | McDonnell-Douglas MD-82 | 49422/1264 | ex SE-DFR | Ingjald Viking | |
| ☐ | LN-ROX | McDonnell-Douglas MD-82 | 49603/1442 | ex SE-DIA | Ulvrik Viking | |
| ☐ | OY-KGT | McDonnell-Douglas MD-82 | 49380/1225 | ex N845RA | Hake Viking | |
| ☐ | OY-KHE | McDonnell-Douglas MD-82 | 49604/1456 | ex N842RA | Saxo Viking | Star Alliance c/s |
| ☐ | OY-KHG | McDonnell-Douglas MD-82 | 49613/1519 | | Alle Viking | |
| ☐ | OY-KHM | McDonnell-Douglas MD-82 | 49914/1693 | | Mette Viking | |
| ☐ | OY-KHN | McDonnell-Douglas MD-82 | 53000/1812 | | Dan Viking | |
| ☐ | OY-KHP | McDonnell-Douglas MD-82 | 53007/1882 | | Arild Viking | Star Alliance c/s |
| ☐ | SE-DIK | McDonnell-Douglas MD-82 | 49728/1553 | ex (SE-DIE) | Stenkil Viking | |
| ☐ | SE-DIL | McDonnell-Douglas MD-82 | 49913/1665 | | Tord Viking | |
| ☐ | SE-DIN | McDonnell-Douglas MD-82 | 49999/1803 | | Eskil Viking | |
| ☐ | SE-DIR | McDonnell-Douglas MD-82 | 53004/1846 | | Nora Viking | |
| ☐ | SE-DIS | McDonnell-Douglas MD-82 | 53006/1869 | | Adis Viking | |
| ☐ | SE-DMB | McDonnell-Douglas MD-82 | 53314/1946 | | Bjarne Viking | |
| ☐ | OY-KHU | McDonnell-Douglas MD-87 | 53336/1953 | | Ravn Viking | |
| ☐ | SE-DIB | McDonnell-Douglas MD-87 | 49605/1501 | | Varin Viking | wfs♦ |
| ☐ | SE-DIC | McDonnell-Douglas MD-87 | 49607/1512 | | Grane Viking | [OSL] |
| ☐ | SE-DIF | McDonnell-Douglas MD-87 | 49606/1569 | ex EC-KJE | | [ARN]♦ |
| ☐ | SE-DIP | McDonnell-Douglas MD-87 | 53010/1921 | ex N6202D | | |
| ☐ | SE-DIU | McDonnell-Douglas MD-87 | 53011/1931 | | Margret Viking | [IGM] |
| ☐ | SE-DMK | McDonnell-Douglas MD-87 | 53337/1962 | ex LN-RMP | Torsten Viking | ♦ |
| ☐ | SE-DMM | McDonnell-Douglas MD-87 | 53208/1865 | ex EC-FEY | | [IGM]♦ |
| ☐ | SE-DMN | McDonnell-Douglas MD-87 | 53211/1874 | ex EC-FFH | | [MAD]♦ |
| ☐ | SE-DMP | McDonnell-Douglas MD-87 | 53210/1871 | ex EC-FFI | | [MAD]♦ |
| ☐ | SE-DMS | McDonnell-Douglas MD-87 | 53212/1877 | ex EC-FHD | | [MAD]♦ |
| ☐ | LN-BRE | Boeing 737-405 | 24643/1860 | | Hakon V Magnusson | |
| ☐ | LN-BRI | Boeing 737-405 | 24644/1938 | ex 9M-MLL | Harald Hårfagre | |
| ☐ | LN-BRQ | Boeing 737-405 | 25348/2148 | | Harald Gråfell | |
| ☐ | LN-RDA | de Havilland DHC-8-402Q | 4013 | ex C-GDFT | | [NYO] |
| ☐ | LN-RDP | de Havilland DHC-8-402Q | 4012 | ex OY-KCA | | [NYO] |

| | | | | | | |
|---|---|---|---|---|---|---|
| ☐ | LN-RKH | Airbus A330-343X | 497 | ex F-WWYP | Emund Viking | |
| ☐ | OY-KBN | Airbus A330-343X | 496 | ex F-WWKK | Eystein Viking | |
| ☐ | OY-KBO | Airbus A319-132 | 2850 | ex D-AVXK | Christian Valdemar Viking | retro c/s |
| ☐ | OY-KBP | Airbus A319-132 | 2888 | ex D-AVYG | Viger Viking | |
| ☐ | OY-KBR | Airbus A319-131 | 3231 | ex D-AVYV | Sten Viking | |
| ☐ | OY-KBT | Airbus A319-131 | 3292 | ex D-AVYC | Ragnvald Viking | |
| ☐ | SE-REE | Airbus A330-343X | 515 | ex F-WWYY | Sigrid Viking | |
| ☐ | SE-REF | Airbus A330-343X | 568 | ex F-WWYS | Erik Viking | Star Alliance c/s |
| ☐ | SE-RJE | Airbus A320-232 | 1183 | ex EC-KEC | | ♦ |
| ☐ | SE-RJF | Airbus A320-232 | 1383 | exEC-KOX | | ♦ |
| ☐ | SE- | Airbus A320-232 | 2883 | ex VT-INC | | o/o♦ |

## SKYWAYS EXPRESS — Sky Express (JZ/SKX)   Jönköping /Stockholm-Arlanda (JKG/ARN)

Acquired City Airlines 29Apr11; renamed Avia Express Sweden

## SWEDEN AIRWAYS — Nyköping (NYO)

| | | | | | |
|---|---|---|---|---|---|
| ☐ | SE-KCY | Piper PA-31-350 Navajo Chieftain | 31-7752061 | ex LY-AXC | ♦ |

## TOR AIR — (OD/OAI)

AOC suspended 19Dec11

## TUIFLY NORDIC — Bluescan (6B/BLX)   Stockholm-Arlanda (ARN)

| | | | | | |
|---|---|---|---|---|---|
| ☐ | SE-DZK | Boeing 737-804/W | 28231/538 | | |
| ☐ | SE-DZN | Boeing 737-804/W | 32903/1127 | ex PH-AAW | |
| ☐ | SE-DZV | Boeing 737-804/W | 32904/1302 | | |
| ☐ | SE-RFT | Boeing 737-8K5/W | 38097/3548 | | ♦ |
| ☐ | SE-RFU | Boeing 737-8K5/W | 37259/3673 | | ♦ |
| ☐ | SE-RFV | Boeing 737-86N/W | 32669/1895 | ex EI-EOX | ♦ |
| ☐ | SE-RFR | Boeing 767-38AER/W | 29617/741 | ex VP-BWT | ♦ |
| ☐ | SE-RFS | Boeing 767-304ER/W | 28040/613 | ex G-OBYB | |
| ☐ | SE-RFX | Boeing 737-8K5/W | 37246/ | | o/o♦ |

## WEST AIR SWEDEN — Air Sweden (PT/SWN)   Lidköping (LDK)

| | | | | | |
|---|---|---|---|---|---|
| ☐ | G-BTPL | British Aerospace ATP | 2042 | ex EC-HES | [CVT]♦ |
| ☐ | G-MANC | British Aerospace ATPF | 2054 | ex VT-FAA | [CVT]♦ |
| ☐ | SE-LGU | British Aerospace ATP | 2022 | ex N853AW | [MMX] |
| ☐ | SE-LGV | British Aerospace ATP | 2034 | ex N857AW | [IOM] |
| ☐ | SE-LGX | British Aerospace ATP | 2036 | ex N859AW | [MMX] |
| ☐ | SE-LGY | British Aerospace ATP | 2035 | ex N858AW | |
| ☐ | SE-LNY | British Aerospace ATP | 2062 | ex OY-SVT | op for Posten Norge |
| ☐ | SE-LPU | British Aerospace ATP | 2060 | ex LX-WAM | |
| ☐ | SE-MAF | British Aerospace ATP | 2002 | ex G-MAUD | |
| ☐ | SE-MAH | British Aerospace ATP | 2004 | ex G-MANJ | |
| ☐ | SE-MAR | British Aerospace ATP | 2053 | ex G-OBWR | |
| ☐ | SE-MAY | British Aerospace ATP | 2044 | ex G-BTPN | ♦ |
| ☐ | SE-MEG | British Aerospace ATP | 2031 | ex CS-TGN | [MMX] |
| ☐ | SE-DUX | Canadair CRJ-200F | 7010 | ex C-FJGI | |
| ☐ | SE-DUY | Canadair CRJ-200F | 7023 | ex C-FJGK | |
| ☐ | SE-RIF | Canadair CRJ-200F | 7142 | ex OE-LCJ | ♦ |

## SP- POLAND (Republic of Poland)

## AIR ITALY POLSKA — Polish Bird (4Q/AEI)   Warsaw-Okecie (WAW)

| | | | | | |
|---|---|---|---|---|---|
| ☐ | EI-EOJ | Boeing 737-8BK/W | 33022/1672 | ex LN-KHD | |
| ☐ | SP-IGN | Boeing 737-84P/W | 35074/2217 | ex I-AIGN | ♦ |

## ENTER AIR — (ENT)   Warsaw-Okecie (WAW)

| | | | | | |
|---|---|---|---|---|---|
| ☐ | SP-ENA | Boeing 737-4Q8 | 26320/2563 | ex HL7592 | |
| ☐ | SP-ENB | Boeing 737-4Q8 | 26299/2602 | ex HL7527 | |
| ☐ | SP-ENC | Boeing 737-4Q8 | 25376/2689 | ex EI-DXG | |
| ☐ | SP-ENE | Boeing 737-4Q8 | 25374/2562 | ex TC-TJC | |
| ☐ | SP-ENF | Boeing 737-4C9 | 25429/2215 | ex YR-BAD | ♦ |
| ☐ | SP-ENH | Boeing 737-405 | 25795/2867 | LN-BUF | ♦ |
| ☐ | SP-ENX | Boeing 737-8Q8 | 30627/752 | ex D-AABU | ♦ |
| ☐ | SP-ENY | Boeing 737-86N/W | 28592/258 | ex SE-RHX | ♦ |
| ☐ | SP-ENZ | Boeing 737-85F | 28823/174 | ex D-ABBM | |

## EUROLOT

**Eurolot (K2/ELO)** — **Warsaw-Okecie (WAW)**

| | Reg | Type | Serial | Ex | |
|---|---|---|---|---|---|
| ☐ | SP-EDE | ATR 42-500 | 0443 | ex F-WWEZ | |
| ☐ | SP-EDF | ATR 42-500 | 0559 | ex D-BOOO | |
| ☐ | SP-EDG | ATR 42-500 | 0603 | ex D-BTTT | |
| ☐ | SP-EDH | ATR 42-500 | 0602 | ex D-BSSS | ♦ |
| ☐ | SP-EFI | ATR 72-202 | 0297 | ex OK-XBF | ♦ |
| ☐ | SP-EFK | ATR 72-202 | 0299 | ex OK-XFC | ♦ |
| ☐ | SP-LFA | ATR 72-202 | 0246 | ex F-WWEM | ♦ |
| ☐ | SP-LFB | ATR 72-202 | 0265 | ex F-WWEJ | |
| ☐ | SP-LFC | ATR 72-202 | 0272 | ex F-WWEN | |
| ☐ | SP-LFD | ATR 72-202 | 0279 | ex F-WWLD | |
| ☐ | SP-LFE | ATR 72-202 | 0328 | ex F-WWLJ | |
| ☐ | SP-LFF | ATR 72-202 | 0402 | ex F-WWLM | |
| ☐ | SP-LFG | ATR 72-202 | 0411 | ex F-WWEO | |
| | | | | | |
| ☐ | SP-EQA | de Havilland DHC-8-402Q | 4406 | ex C-GMXB | o/o♦ |
| ☐ | SP-EQB | de Havilland DHC-8-402Q | 4407 | ex C-GMXR | o/o♦ |
| ☐ | SP-EQC | de Havilland DHC-8-402Q | 4409 | ex C-GMYD | o/o♦ |

## EXIN

**Exin (EXN)** — **Katowice-Muchoeiec (KTW)**

| | Reg | Type | Serial | Ex | |
|---|---|---|---|---|---|
| ☐ | SP-EKA | Antonov An-26B | 12008 | | ♦ |
| ☐ | SP-EKB | Antonov An-26 | 1310 | | ♦ |
| ☐ | SP-EKC | Antonov An-26 | 1407 | | ♦ |
| ☐ | SP-EKD | Antonov An-26 | 1402 | ex 1402 Polish AF | ♦ |
| ☐ | SP-EKE | Antonov An-26 | 1509 | ex 1509 Polish AF | ♦ |
| ☐ | SP-EKF | Antonov An-26 | 1604 | ex 1604 Polish AF | ♦ |
| ☐ | SP-FDR | Antonov An-26B | 11305 | ex RA-26067 | |
| ☐ | SP-FDS | Antonov An-26B | 12205 | ex RA-26116 | |
| ☐ | SP-FDT | Antonov An-26B | 12102 | ex RA-26110 | |

## LOT - POLISH AIRLINES

**LOT (LO/LOT)** — **Warsaw-Okecie (WAW)**

Member of Star Alliance

| | Reg | Type | Serial | Ex | Notes | |
|---|---|---|---|---|---|---|
| ☐ | SP-LPA | Boeing 767-35DER | 24865/322 | | Warszawa | |
| ☐ | SP-LPB | Boeing 767-35DER | 27902/577 | | Gdansk | |
| ☐ | SP-LPC | Boeing 767-35DER | 28656/659 | | Poznan | [WAW] |
| ☐ | SP-LPE | Boeing 767-341ER | 24843/314 | ex N483TC | Star Alliance c/s | |
| ☐ | SP-LPG | Boeing 767-306ER | 26263/592 | ex N261LF | | |
| ☐ | UR-AAJ | Boeing 767-33AER | 25533/454 | ex V8-RBJ | | <AEW♦ |
| | | | | | | |
| ☐ | SP-LDA | Embraer ERJ-170STD | 17000023 | ex PT-SKQ | | |
| ☐ | SP-LDB | Embraer ERJ-170STD | 17000024 | ex PT-SKR | | |
| ☐ | SP-LDC | Embraer ERJ-170STD | 17000025 | ex PT-SKS | Star Alliance c/s | |
| ☐ | SP-LDD | Embraer ERJ-170STD | 17000027 | ex PT-SKU | | |
| ☐ | SP-LDE | Embraer ERJ-170LR | 17000029 | ex PT-SKW | | |
| ☐ | SP-LDF | Embraer ERJ-170LR | 17000035 | ex PT-SUE | | |
| ☐ | SP-LDG | Embraer ERJ-170LR | 17000065 | ex PT-SVQ | | |
| ☐ | SP-LDH | Embraer ERJ-170LR | 17000069 | ex PT-SVU | | |
| ☐ | SP-LDI | Embraer ERJ-170LR | 17000073 | ex PT-SVY | | |
| ☐ | SP-LDK | Embraer ERJ-170LR | 17000074 | ex PT-SVZ | | |
| | | | | | | |
| ☐ | SP-LIA | Embraer ERJ-175LR | 17000125 | ex PT-SDO | | |
| ☐ | SP-LIB | Embraer ERJ-175LR | 17000132 | ex PT-SDV | | |
| ☐ | SP-LIC | Embraer ERJ-175LR | 17000134 | ex PT-SDX | | |
| ☐ | SP-LID | Embraer ERJ-175LR | 17000136 | ex PT-SDZ | | |
| ☐ | SP-LIE | Embraer ERJ-175LR | 17000153 | ex EI-DVW | | |
| ☐ | SP-LIF | Embraer ERJ-175LR | 17000154 | ex EI-DVV | | |
| ☐ | SP-LIG | Embraer ERJ-175LR | 17000283 | ex PT-TQJ | | |
| ☐ | SP-LIH | Embraer ERJ-175LR | 17000288 | ex PT-TQO | | |
| ☐ | SP-LII | Embraer ERJ-175LR | 17000290 | ex PT-TQQ | | |
| ☐ | SP-LIK | Embraer ERJ-175LR | 17000303 | ex PT-XQC | | |
| ☐ | SP-LIL | Embraer ERJ-175LR | 17000306 | ex PT-XQF | | |
| ☐ | SP-LIM | Embraer ERJ-175LR | 17000311 | ex PT-XQY | | |
| ☐ | SP-LIN | Embraer ERJ-175LR | 17000313 | ex PT-XUH | | |
| ☐ | SP-LIO | Embraer ERJ-175LR | 17000321 | ex PT-XUP | | |
| | | | | | | |
| ☐ | SP-LGG | Embraer ERJ-145MP | 145319 | ex PT-SMK | | |
| ☐ | SP-LGH | Embraer ERJ-145MP | 145329 | ex PT-SMV | | |
| ☐ | SP-LGO | Embraer ERJ-145MP | 145560 | ex PT-SZV | Pomocy logo | |
| ☐ | SP-LKE | Boeing 737-55D | 27130/2448 | | Star Alliance c/s | |
| ☐ | SP-LKF | Boeing 737-55D | 27368/2603 | | | |
| ☐ | SP-LLB | Boeing 737-45D | 27156/2492 | ex UR-VVH | | |
| ☐ | SP-LLC | Boeing 737-45D | 27157/2502 | | | |
| ☐ | SP-LNA | Embraer ERJ-195LR | 19000415 | ex PT-TBM | | |
| ☐ | SP-LNB | Embraer ERJ-195LR | 19000444 | ex PT-TJE | | |
| ☐ | SP-LNC | Embraer ERJ-195LR | 19000462 | ex PT-TOD | | |
| ☐ | SP-LND | Embraer ERJ-195LR | 19000516 | ex PT-TUD | | ♦ |
| ☐ | SP- | Boeing 787-8 | | | | o/o |

| | | | | | |
|---|---|---|---|---|---|
| ☐ | SP- | Boeing 787-8 | | | o/o |
| ☐ | SP- | Boeing 787-8 | | | o/o |

## LOT CHARTERS

| | | | | | |
|---|---|---|---|---|---|
| ☐ | SP-LLE | Boeing 737-45D | 27914/2804 | | ♦ |
| ☐ | SP-LLF | Boeing 737-45D | 28752/2874 | | ♦ |
| ☐ | SP-LLG | Boeing 737-45D | 28753/2895 | ex SX-BGN | ♦ |
| ☐ | SP-LLK | Boeing 737-4Q8 | 25740/2461 | ex EI-CZG | ♦ |
| ☐ | SP-LLL | Boeing 737-4Q8 | 25164/2447 | ex EI-CXJ | ♦ |

## OLT EXPRESS  (YAP)  Warsaw-Okecie (WAW)

| | | | | | |
|---|---|---|---|---|---|
| ☐ | SP-IAA | Airbus A320-214 | 0533 | ex EI-BDL | ♦ |
| ☐ | SP-IAB | Airbus A320-214 | 0566 | ex EI-ERV | ♦ |
| ☐ | SP-IAC | Airbus A320-214 | 0973 | ex F-GRSI | ♦ |
| ☐ | SP-IAD | Airbus A320-214 | 2142 | ex SP-IAD | <AMC♦ |
| ☐ | SP-IAE | Airbus A320-214 | 1454 | ex EI=EPX | ♦ |

Formerly Yes Airways

## OLT JETAIR  Jeta (O2/JEA)  Warsaw-Okecie (WAW)

| | | | | | |
|---|---|---|---|---|---|
| ☐ | SP-KTF | ATR 42-320 | 0257 | ex OY-PCE | ♦ |
| ☐ | SP-KTR | ATR 42-300 | 0092 | ex D-BAAA | ♦ |
| ☐ | SP-KWE | British Aerospace Jetstream 3201 | 842 | ex G-CBCS | op for LOT [BRE]♦ |
| ☐ | SP-KWF | British Aerospace Jetstream 3201 | 845 | ex G-BYRA | op for LOT♦ |
| ☐ | SP-KWN | British Aerospace Jetstream 3201 | 856 | ex LN-FAC | wfs♦ |

## SKY TAXI  Iguana (IGA)  Wroclaw (WRO)

| | | | | | | |
|---|---|---|---|---|---|---|
| ☐ | SP-MRB | SAAB SF.340A (QC) | 340A-100 | ex OE-GIF | all white | |
| ☐ | SP-MRC | SAAB SF.340A | 340A-143 | ex EC-IRR | | |
| ☐ | SP-MRD | SAAB SF.340A | 340A-111 | ex SE-KXE | | o/o♦ |

## SMALL PLANET AIRLINES POLAND  (LLP)

| | | | | | |
|---|---|---|---|---|---|
| ☐ | SP-HAB | Airbus A320-232 | 1411 | ex G-TCAC | ♦ |
| ☐ | SP-HAC | Airbus A320-233 | 0739 | ex N413AC | ♦ |
| ☐ | YL-LCE | Airbus A320-211 | 0311 | ex F-HDCE | <ART♦ |

## SPRINT AIR  (SRN)  Warsaw-Okecie (WAW)

| | | | | | |
|---|---|---|---|---|---|
| ☐ | SP-KPC | SAAB SF.340A | 340A-070 | ex SE-KCT | ♦ |
| ☐ | SP-KPE | SAAB SF.340A (QC) | 340A-130 | ex SE-ISL | |
| ☐ | SP-KPF | SAAB SF.340A (QC) | 340A-135 | ex SE-KCU | |
| ☐ | SP-KPG | SAAB SF.340A (QC) | 340A-065 | ex SE-KCR | |
| ☐ | SP-KPH | SAAB SF.340A (QC) | 340A-015 | ex SE-ISP | op for Farnair |
| ☐ | SP-KPK | SAAB SF.340AF | 340A-026 | ex VH-ZLY | |
| ☐ | SP-KPL | SAAB SF.340A | 340A-038 | ex VH-ZRX | |
| ☐ | SP-KPN | SAAB SF.340A | 340A-118 | ex SE-F18 | |
| ☐ | SP-KPO | SAAB SF.340A (QC) | 340A-010 | ex SE-LTI | |
| ☐ | SP-KPR | SAAB SF.340A (QC) | 340A-139 | ex OH-FAE | |
| ☐ | SP-KPU | SAAB SF.340AF | 340A-145 | ex SE-ISD | |
| ☐ | SP-KPV | SAAB SF.340A | 340A-071 | ex SE-LGS | |
| ☐ | SP-KPZ | SAAB SF.340AF | 340A-087 | ex SE-KUT | ♦ |
| ☐ | SP-KTL | LET L-410UVP-E16A | 902414 | ex SP-TXB | ♦ |

## ST-  SUDAN (Republic of the Sudan)

## ABABEEL AVIATION  Khartoum (KRT)

| | | | | | |
|---|---|---|---|---|---|
| ☐ | EX-036 | Ilyushin Il-76TD | 0093495863 | ex RA-76785 | wfs |

Ceased ops 2009

## AIR TAXI & CARGO  (WAM)  Khartoum (KRT)

| | | | | | | |
|---|---|---|---|---|---|---|
| ☐ | ST-TKO | Antonov An-32B | 3110 | ex ER-AWL | Deena | <PXA |

## AIR WEST CARGO  (AWZ)  Sharjah (SHJ)

| | | | | | |
|---|---|---|---|---|---|
| ☐ | ST-AWH | WSK-PZL/Antonov An-28 | 1AJ004-07 | ex ER-AJH | |
| ☐ | ST-AWN | WSK-PZL/Antonov An-28 | 1AJ004-06 | ex ER-AIP | |
| ☐ | ST-AWR | Ilyushin Il-76TD | 0033447365 | ex RDPL-11308 | [FJR] |
| ☐ | ST-EWC | Ilyushin Il-76TD | 0023438129 | ex EX-86919 | |
| ☐ | ST-EWX | Ilyushin Il-76TD | 1013409282 | ex UN-76810 | |

## ALFA AIRLINES

| | | | | | |
|---|---|---|---|---|---|
| ☐ | EK-74027 | Antonov An-74-200 | 36547096920 | | ◆ |
| ☐ | ST-ARL | Antonov An-26-100 | 2606 | | ◆ |
| ☐ | ST-ARP | Antonov An-24RV | 37308809 | | ◆ |
| ☐ | ST-AQR | Ilyushin Il-76TD | 0043453575 | | ◆ |
| ☐ | ST-AWR | Ilyushin Il-76TD | 0033447365 | | ◆ |
| ☐ | ST-AWT | Antonov An-26-100 | 3508 | | ◆ |
| ☐ | ST-EWD | Ilyushin Il-76TD | 0063466989 | ex UR-CAP | ◆ |
| ☐ | ST-EWX | Ilyushin Il-76TD | 1013409282 | | ◆ |

## ALMAJARA AVIATION — (MJA)

| | | | | |
|---|---|---|---|---|
| ☐ | ST-ATH | Ilyushin Il-76MD | 0063472158 | ex EK-76705 |

## ALOK AIR — (LOK)

| | | | | | |
|---|---|---|---|---|---|
| ☐ | ST-ATF | Antonov An-32B | 3205 | | ◆ |
| ☐ | ST-AWZ | Antonov An-24RV | 77310808 | | ◆ |
| ☐ | ST-SMS | Yakovlev Yak-40 | 9311526 | | ◆ |

## AYR AVIATION

| | | | | | |
|---|---|---|---|---|---|
| ☐ | ST-SMZ | Antonov An-32 | 3205 | ex ER-AFI | AMIS titles |

## AZZA AIR TRANSPORT — Azza Transport (AZZ) — Khartoum (KRT)

| | | | | | |
|---|---|---|---|---|---|
| ☐ | ST-APS | Ilyushin Il-76TD | 1023409316 | ex RA-76837 | |
| ☐ | ST-ARV | Antonov An-12BP | 8345310 | ex EK-11028 | |
| ☐ | ST-AZN | Antonov An-12 | 9346808 | ex UR-CFC | status? |
| ☐ | ST-AZZ | Ilyushin Il-76TD | 1023408265 | ex XT-FCB | op by Sudanese AF as 956 |
| ☐ | ST-JAC | Antonov An-26B-100 | 10203 | ex EX-003 | |
| ☐ | ST-JCC | Boeing 707-384C (Comtran 2) | 18948/495 | ex P4-JCC | [KRT] |

## BADR AIRLINES — Badr Air (J4/BDR) — Khartoum (KRT)

| | | | | | |
|---|---|---|---|---|---|
| ☐ | ST-BDA | Antonov An-74-200 | 3654709868 | | wfs?◆ |
| ☐ | ST-BDE | Ilyushin Il-76TD | 1013408252 | ex RA-76809 | |
| ☐ | ST-BDK | Antonov An-72-100 | 36572060642 | ex 4L-SAS | AMIS titles |
| ☐ | ST-BDN | Ilyushin Il-76TD | 1023413443 | ex UK 76448 | |
| ☐ | ST-BDS | Antonov An-74 | 36547070655 | ex RA-74001? | ◆ |
| ☐ | ST-SAL | Antonov An-26B | 17311907 | ex RA-26100 | |

## BENTIU AIR TRANSPORT — Bentiu Air (BNT) — Sharjah/Khartoum (SHJ/KRT)

| | | | | |
|---|---|---|---|---|
| ☐ | ST-NDC | Antonov An-26 | 17310908 | ex RA-26052 |
| ☐ | ST-SRA | Antonov An-26 | 17311807 | ex RA-08827 |

## BLUE BIRD AIRLINES — (BLB) — Khartoum (KRT)

| | | | | | |
|---|---|---|---|---|---|
| ☐ | ST-AFP | de Havilland DHC-6 Twin Otter 300 | 479 | ex C-GDVN-X | |
| ☐ | ZS-TIL | Beech 1900D | UE-21 | ex 5Y-RAE | op for Red Cross |

## DOVE AIR

| | | | | |
|---|---|---|---|---|
| ☐ | ST-HIS | Antonov An-26B-100 | 10310 | ◆ |
| ☐ | ST-MRS | Tupolev Tu-134B-3 | 63333 | ◆ |

## EL MAGAL AVIATION — El Magal (MGG) — Khartoum (KRT)

| | | | | | |
|---|---|---|---|---|---|
| ☐ | ST-APJ | Antonov An-12BP | 2400701 | ex RA-11308 | |
| ☐ | ST-AQQ | Antonov An-12B | 9346504 | | |
| ☐ | ST-BEN | Antonov An-26 | 6907 | | ◆ |
| ☐ | ST-EIB | Antonov An-32B | 2903 | ex D2-FAP | ◆ |
| ☐ | ST-ISG | WSK-PZL/Antonov An-28 | 1AJ005-01 | ex EK-28501 | |
| ☐ | S9-PSE | Antonov An-32 | 2803 | ex UR-48053 | <GLE |

## FEEDER AIRLINES — (FDD)

| | | | | | |
|---|---|---|---|---|---|
| ☐ | ST-DMS | LET L-410UVP-E | 902438 | ex 5A-DMS | ◆ |
| ☐ | ST-NEW | Fokker 50 | 20138 | ex PH-PRB | |

## GREEN FLAG AVIATION

| | | | | |
|---|---|---|---|---|
| ☐ | ST-BDT | Antonov An-74 | 36547097935 | ◆ |
| ☐ | ST-GFD | Antonov An-30A-100 | 0605 | ◆ |
| ☐ | ST-GFF | Antonov An-74 | 36547097932 | ◆ |

## KATA TRANSPORTATION COMPANY · *Khartoum (KRT)*

| | | | | |
|---|---|---|---|---|
| ☐ ST-AQD | Antonov An-26B | 11008 | | ♦ |
| ☐ ST-AZM | Antonov An-12BK | 00346907 | ex 05 red | |

## MARSLAND AVIATION · *Marslandair (M7/MSL)* · *Khartoum (KRT)*

| | | | |
|---|---|---|---|
| ☐ ST-ARJ | Antonov An-26 | 77305602 | ex ER-AZC |
| ☐ ST-ARP | Antonov An-24RV | 37308809 | ex EK-46630 |

## MID AIRLINES · *Nile (7Y/NYL)* · *Khartoum (KRT)*

| | | | | |
|---|---|---|---|---|
| ☐ ST-ARG | Fokker 50 | 20130 | ex LN-BBA | |
| ☐ ST-ARH | Fokker 50 | 20131 | ex LN-BBB | |
| ☐ ST-ARZ | Fokker 50 | 20134 | ex LN-BBC | [KRT] |

## NOVA AIRLINES · *(O9/NOV)* · *Khartoum (KRT)*

| | | | | |
|---|---|---|---|---|
| ☐ ST-NVB | Canadair CRJ-200ER | 7807 | ex HA-LND | |
| ☐ ST-NVC | Canadair CRJ-200ER | 7686 | ex HA-LNB | |
| ☐ ST-SDB | Boeing 737-2T4 | 23273/1097 | ex B-2507 | ♦ |

## SOUTHERN SUDAN AIRWAYS · *Juba*

| | | | | |
|---|---|---|---|---|
| ☐ S9-PAC | Boeing 727-44C (FedEx 3) | 20475/854 | ex C-GVFA | >TFK♦ |

## SUDAN AIRWAYS · *Sudanair (SD/SUD)* · *Khartoum (KRT)*

| | | | | | |
|---|---|---|---|---|---|
| ☐ ST-AFA | Boeing 707-3J8C | 20897/885 | | Blue Nile | |
| ☐ ST-ASF | Fokker 50 | 20155 | ex PH-PRG | | |
| ☐ ST-ASI | Fokker 50 | 20247 | ex G-UKTB | | |
| ☐ ST-ASO | Fokker 50 | 20256 | ex G-UKTD | | |
| ☐ ST-AST | Airbus A310-322 | 437 | ex SU-BOW | | |
| ☐ ST-ATA | Airbus A300B4-622R | 775 | ex TF-ELC | Alqaswa | <NAS |
| ☐ ST-ATB | Airbus A300B4-622R | 666 | ex TF-ELB | Elburag | |
| ☐ ST-MRL | Yakovlev Yak-42 | 4520424116690 | ex UN-42703 | | ♦ |

## SUDANESE STATES AVIATION · *Khartoum (KRT)*

| | | | | |
|---|---|---|---|---|
| ☐ ST-AQW | Boeing 707-336C | 20517/854 | ex 3D-GFG | [KRT] |

## SUN AIR · *(S6/SNR)* · *Khartoum (KRT)*

| | | | |
|---|---|---|---|
| ☐ ST-SDA | Boeing 737-2T4 | 23274/1099 | ex B-2508 |

## TARCO AIR

| | | | |
|---|---|---|---|
| ☐ ST-NSP | Antonov An-32B | 2109 | ♦ |
| ☐ ST-TAB | Yakovlev Yak-42D | 4520421401018 | ♦ |

## TRANS ATTICO · *Tranattico Sudan (ML/ETC)* · *Khartoum/Sharjah (KRT/SHJ)*

| | | | | |
|---|---|---|---|---|
| ☐ ST-AQU | Antonov An-32B | 2009 | ex RA-69344 | |
| ☐ ST-ASX | Ilyushin Il-76 | 0073479392 | ex 5A-DMQ | |
| ☐ ST-LRN | de Havilland DHC-6 Twin Otter 300 | 636 | ex HB-LRN | ♦ |

# SU- EGYPT (Arab Republic of Egypt)

## AIR ARABIA EGYPT · *(E5/RBG)* · *Alexandria (ALY)*

| | | | | |
|---|---|---|---|---|
| ☐ SU-AAA | Airbus A320-214 | 2764 | ex A6-ABF | |
| ☐ SU-AAB | Airbus A320-214 | 3152 | ex A6-ABN | |
| ☐ SU-AAC | Airbus A320-214 | 3246 | ex A6-ABM | <ABY |

## AIR CAIRO · *(MSC)* · *Cairo-Intl (CAI)*

| | | | |
|---|---|---|---|
| ☐ SU-BPU | Airbus A320-214 | 2937 | ex F-WWIJ |
| ☐ SU-BPV | Airbus A320-214 | 2966 | ex F-WWDC |
| ☐ SU-BPW | Airbus A320-214 | 3282 | ex F-WWDP |
| ☐ SU-BPX | Airbus A320-214 | 3323 | ex F-WWBE |

## AIR MEMPHIS · *Air Memphis (MHS)* · *Cairo-Intl (CAI)*

| | | | |
|---|---|---|---|
| ☐ SU-BME | McDonnell-Douglas MD-83 | 49628/1582 | ex F-GRML |

| | | | | | | |
|---|---|---|---|---|---|---|
| ☐ | SU-PBG | Airbus A320-233 | | 1353 | ex N464TA | |
| ☐ | SU-PBH | Airbus A320-233 | | 1300 | ex N461TA | |
| ☐ | SU-PBO | Douglas DC-9-31 (ABS 3) | | 48131/940 | ex N928VJ | |
| ☐ | SU-YAI | Fokker 50 | | 20143 | ex PH-FZI | |
| ☐ | TC-TJK | Boeing 737-8KN/W | | 35794/2794 | ex A6-FDA | <CAI♦ |

## AIR SINAI — Air Sinai (4D/ASD) — Cairo-Intl (CAI)

A wholly owned subsidiary of Egyptair; ops services with aircraft leased from the parent

## ALEXANDRIA AIRLINES — (ZR/KHH) — Alexandria (ALY)

| | | | | | | |
|---|---|---|---|---|---|---|
| ☐ | SU-KHM | Boeing 737-5C9 | | 26438/2413 | ex JY-JA1 | <JAV |

## ALMASRIA UNIVERSAL AIRLINES — AMC (UJ/LMU) — Cairo-Intl (CAI)

| | | | | | | |
|---|---|---|---|---|---|---|
| ☐ | SU-TCA | Airbus A320-232 | | 0932 | ex VT-ADX | |
| ☐ | SU-TCB | Airbus A320-232 | | 0943 | ex VT-ADY | |
| ☐ | SU-TCC | Airbus A321-211 | | 0666 | ex EI-ESI | ♦ |

## AMC AIRLINES — AMC (AMV) — Cairo-Intl (CAI)

| | | | | | | |
|---|---|---|---|---|---|---|
| ☐ | SU-BOZ | McDonnell-Douglas MD-83 | | 53192/2155 | ex N192AJ | |
| ☐ | SU-BPZ | Boeing 737-86N/W | | 35213/2300 | | >Sham Wings [KHI] |

## CAIRO AVIATION — Cairo Air (CCE) — Cairo-Intl (CAI)

| | | | | | | |
|---|---|---|---|---|---|---|
| ☐ | SU-EAF | Tupolev Tu-204-120 | | 1450742764027 | ex RA-64027 | |
| ☐ | SU-EAG | Tupolev Tu-204-120S | | 1450744764028 | ex RA-64028  TNT c/s | [CAI] |
| ☐ | SU-EAH | Tupolev Tu-204-120 | | 1450744864023 | | [CAI] |
| ☐ | SU-EAI | Tupolev Tu-204-120 | | 1450744964025 | | [CAI] |
| ☐ | SU-EAJ | Tupolev Tu-204-120S | | 1450742264029 | ex RA-64029  TNT c/s | [CAI} |

## EGYPTAIR — Egyptair (MS/MSR) — Cairo-Intl (CAI)

Member of Star Alliance

| | | | | | | |
|---|---|---|---|---|---|---|
| ☐ | SU-GBA | Airbus A320-231 | | 0165 | ex F-WWDV | Aswan |
| ☐ | SU-GBB | Airbus A320-231 | | 0166 | ex F-WWID | Luxor |
| ☐ | SU-GBC | Airbus A320-231 | | 0178 | ex F-WWIQ | Hurghada |
| ☐ | SU-GBD | Airbus A320-231 | | 0194 | ex F-WWIZ | Taba |
| ☐ | SU-GBE | Airbus A320-231 | | 0198 | ex F-WWDG | El Alamein |
| ☐ | SU-GBF | Airbus A320-231 | | 0351 | ex F-WWDM | Sharm El Sheikh |
| ☐ | SU-GBG | Airbus A320-231 | | 0366 | ex F-WWDD | Saint Catherine |
| ☐ | SU-GBZ | Airbus A320-232 | | 2070 | ex F-WWDJ | |
| ☐ | SU-GCA | Airbus A320-232 | | 2073 | ex F-WWIO | |
| ☐ | SU-GCB | Airbus A320-232 | | 2079 | ex F-WWDV | |
| ☐ | SU-GCC | Airbus A320-232 | | 2088 | ex F-WWBH | |
| ☐ | SU-GCD | Airbus A320-232 | | 2094 | ex F-WWBX | |
| ☐ | SU-GCL | Airbus A320-231 | | 0322 | ex SU-RAA | |
| ☐ | SU-GCE | Airbus A330-243 | | 600 | ex F-WWYK | |
| ☐ | SU-GCF | Airbus A330-243 | | 610 | ex F-WWKS | |
| ☐ | SU-GCG | Airbus A330-243 | | 666 | ex F-WWKQ | |
| ☐ | SU-GCH | Airbus A330-243 | | 683 | ex F-WWYF | |
| ☐ | SU-GCI | Airbus A330-243 | | 696 | ex F-WWYR | |
| ☐ | SU-GCJ | Airbus A330-243 | | 709 | ex F-WWKK | |
| ☐ | SU-GCK | Airbus A330-243 | | 726 | ex F-WWKP | |
| ☐ | SU-GDS | Airbus A330-343X | | 1143 | ex F-WWKQ | |
| ☐ | SU-GDT | Airbus A330-343X | | 1230 | ex F-WWYR | ♦ |
| ☐ | SU-GDU | Airbus A330-343X | | 1238 | ex F-WWKI | ♦ |
| ☐ | SU-GDV | Airbus A330-343X | | 1246 | ex F-WWKY | ♦ |
| ☐ | SU-GCM | Boeing 737-866/W | | 35558/2054 | | |
| ☐ | SU-GCN | Boeing 737-866/W | | 35559/2113 | ex N1795B | |
| ☐ | SU-GCO | Boeing 737-866/W | | 35561/2369 | ex N1795B | |
| ☐ | SU-GCP | Boeing 737-866/W | | 35560/2434 | ex N1786B | |
| ☐ | SU-GCR | Boeing 737-866/W | | 35562/2826 | ex N1786B | |
| ☐ | SU-GCS | Boeing 737-866/W | | 35563/2695 | | |
| ☐ | SU-GCZ | Boeing 737-866/W | | 35568/2795 | | |
| ☐ | SU-GDA | Boeing 737-866/W | | 35565/2999 | ex N1796B | |
| ☐ | SU-GDB | Boeing 737-866/W | | 35567/3017 | ex N1786B | |
| ☐ | SU-GDC | Boeing 737-866/W | | 35564/3040 | ex N1779B | |
| ☐ | SU-GDD | Boeing 737-866/W | | 35566/3061 | | |
| ☐ | SU-GDE | Boeing 737-866/W | | 35569/3043 | ex N1786B | |
| ☐ | SU-GDX | Boeing 737-866/W | | 40757/3409 | ex N1786B | |
| ☐ | SU-GDY | Boeing 737-866/W | | 40758/3442 | | |
| ☐ | SU-GDZ | Boeing 737-866/W | | 40759/3472 | | |
| ☐ | SU-GEA | Boeing 737-866/W | | 40760/3492 | ex N1786B | |

| | | | | | | |
|---|---|---|---|---|---|---|
| ☐ | SU-GEB | Boeing 737-866/W | 40800/3677 | ex N1786B | | ◆ |
| ☐ | SU-GEC | Boeing 737-866/W | 40801/3819 | | | ◆ |
| ☐ | SU-GED | Boeing 737-866/W | 40802/ | | | o/o◆ |
| | | | | | | |
| ☐ | SU-GBR | Boeing 777-266 | 28424/80 | | Nefertari | |
| ☐ | SU-GBS | Boeing 777-266 | 28425/85 | | Tiye | |
| ☐ | SU-GBX | Boeing 777-266ER | 32629/362 | | Neit | |
| ☐ | SU-GBY | Boeing 777-266ER | 32630/368 | | | |
| ☐ | SU-GDL | Boeing 777-36NER | 38284850 | | | |
| ☐ | SU-GDM | Boeing 777-36NER | 38285/862 | | | |
| ☐ | SU-GDN | Boeing 777-36NER | 38288/896 | | | |
| ☐ | SU-GDO | Boeing 777-36NER | 38289/907 | ex N5023Q | | |
| ☐ | SU-GDP | Boeing 777-36NER | 38290/918 | | | ◆ |
| ☐ | SU-GDR | Boeing 777-36NER | 38291/926 | | | ◆ |
| | | | | | | |
| ☐ | SU-BDG | Airbus A300B4-203F | 200 | ex F-WZMN | Toshki | [CAI] |
| ☐ | SU-GAC | Airbus A300B4-203F | 255 | ex F-WZMY | New Valley | |
| ☐ | SU-GAS | Airbus A300B4-622RF | 561 | ex F-WWAN | Cheops | |
| ☐ | SU-GAY | Airbus A300B4-622RF | 607 | ex F-WWAB | Seti 1 | |
| ☐ | SU-GBH | Boeing 737-566 | 25084/2019 | | Karnakno titles | |
| ☐ | SU-GBJ | Boeing 737-566 | 25352/2169 | | Philae | |
| ☐ | SU-GBK | Boeing 737-566 | 26052/2276 | | Kalabshano titles | |
| ☐ | SU-GBL | Boeing 737-566 | 26051/2282 | | Ramesseum | |
| ☐ | SU-GBM | Airbus A340-212 | 156 | ex F-WWJK | Osiris Express | |
| ☐ | SU-GBN | Airbus A340-212 | 159 | ex F-WWJV | Cleo Express | |
| ☐ | SU-GBO | Airbus A340-212 | 178 | ex F-WWJD | Hathor Express | |
| ☐ | SU-GBT | Airbus A321-231 | 0680 | ex D-AVZB | Red Sea | |
| ☐ | SU-GBU | Airbus A321-231 | 0687 | ex D-AVZR | Sinai | |
| ☐ | SU-GBV | Airbus A321-231 | 0715 | ex D-AVZX | Mediterranean | |
| ☐ | SU-GBW | Airbus A321-231 | 0725 | ex D-AVZA | The Nileno titles | |

### EGYPTAIR EXPRESS  (MSE)  Cairo-Intl (CAI)

| | | | | | |
|---|---|---|---|---|---|
| ☐ | SU-GCT | Embraer ERJ-170LR | 17000167 | ex PT-SMJ | |
| ☐ | SU-GCU | Embraer ERJ-170LR | 17000169 | ex PT-SML | |
| ☐ | SU-GCV | Embraer ERJ-170LR | 17000170 | ex PT-SMM | |
| ☐ | SU-GCW | Embraer ERJ-170LR | 17000175 | ex PT-SMR | |
| ☐ | SU-GCX | Embraer ERJ-170LR | 17000178 | ex PT-SMV | |
| ☐ | SU-GCY | Embraer ERJ-170LR | 17000185 | ex PT-SUC | |
| ☐ | SU-GDF | Embraer ERJ-170LR | 17000266 | ex PT-SJU | |
| ☐ | SU-GDG | Embraer ERJ-170LR | 17000269 | ex PT-SJZ | |
| ☐ | SU-GDH | Embraer ERJ-170LR | 17000274 | ex PT-TQA | |
| ☐ | SU-GDI | Embraer ERJ-170LR | 17000276 | ex PT-TQC | |
| ☐ | SU-GDJ | Embraer ERJ-170LR | 17000282 | ex PT-TQI | |
| ☐ | SU-GDK | Embraer ERJ-170LR | 17000284 | ex PT-TQK | |

### KORAL BLUE  (KBR)  Sharm el Sheikh (SSH)

Ceased ops 2011

### LOTUS AIR  Lotus Flower (TAS)  Cairo-Intl (CAI)

Ceased ops 2011

### MIDWEST AIRLINES EGYPT  (MY/MWA)  Cairo-Intl (CAI)

| | | | | | |
|---|---|---|---|---|---|
| ☐ | SU-MWD | Boeing 737-86N/W | 28591/233 | ex N112MN | |
| ☐ | SU-MWE | Boeing 737-8Q8/W | 30040/1693 | ex G-DLCH | |
| ☐ | SU-MWF | Boeing 737-8Q8/W | 32841/1705 | ex EI-EOP | |

### NESMA AIRLINES  (NE/NMA)

| | | | | | |
|---|---|---|---|---|---|
| ☐ | SU-NMA | Airbus A320-232 | 1697 | ex G-MIDR | |
| ☐ | SU-NMB | Airbus A320-232 | 1732 | ex G-MIDP | ◆ |

### NILE AIR  (NIA)

| | | | | |
|---|---|---|---|---|
| ☐ | SU-BQB | Airbus A320-232 | 3183 | ex N621SA |
| ☐ | SU-BQC | Airbus A320-232 | 3219 | ex N623SA |

### PETROLEUM AIR SERVICES  (VPS)  Al Arish/Hurghada (AAC/HRG)

| | | | |
|---|---|---|---|
| ☐ | SU-CAC | Bell 206L-3 LongRanger III | 51004 |
| ☐ | SU-CAE | Bell 206L-3 LongRanger III | 51030 |
| ☐ | SU-CAF | Bell 206L-3 LongRanger III | 51031 |
| ☐ | SU-CAG | Bell 206B JetRanger III | 3574 |
| ☐ | SU-CAH | Bell 206B JetRanger III | 3581 |
| ☐ | SU-CAI | Bell 206L-3 LongRanger III | 51018 |

| | | | | | | |
|---|---|---|---|---|---|---|
| ☐ | SU-CAB | Bell 212 | 31223 | | | |
| ☐ | SU-CAJ | Bell 212 | 31247 | | | |
| ☐ | SU-CAL | Bell 212 | 31215 | ex N3889A | | |
| ☐ | SU-CAM | Bell 212 | 31249 | | | |
| ☐ | SU-CAN | Bell 212 | 31250 | | | |
| ☐ | SU-CAO | Bell 212 | 31260 | | | |
| ☐ | SU-CAQ | Bell 212 | 31262 | | | |
| ☐ | SU-CAR | Bell 212 | 31263 | | | |
| ☐ | SU-CAS | Bell 212 | 31264 | | | |
| ☐ | SU-CAU | Bell 212 | 35036 | | | |
| ☐ | SU-CAV | Bell 412HP | 36037 | ex XA-TNO | | |
| ☐ | SU-CAX | Bell 412HP | 36081 | ex N2156S | | |
| ☐ | SU-CAY | Bell 412EP | 36158 | ex N6489P | | |
| ☐ | SU-CAZ | Bell 412EP | 36184 | ex N55248 | | |
| ☐ | SU-CBI | Bell 412EP | 36353 | ex C-FCSC | | |
| ☐ | SU-CBL | Bell 412EP | 36377 | ex C-FENJ | | |
| ☐ | SU-CBM | Bell 412EP | 36379 | ex C-FEON | | |
| ☐ | SU-CBO | Bell 412EP | 36410 | ex C-FIRW | | |
| ☐ | SU-CBR | Bell 412EP | 36432 | ex C-FMQV | | |
| ☐ | SU-CBS | Bell 412EP | 36468 | ex C-FTCJ | | |
| ☐ | SU-CBT | Bell 412EP | 36492 | ex C-FVDY | | |
| ☐ | SU-CBA | de Havilland DHC-7-102 | 093 | ex C-GFYI | | |
| ☐ | SU-CBB | de Havilland DHC-7-102 | 096 | ex C-GEWQ | | |
| ☐ | SU-CBC | de Havilland DHC-7-102 | 097 | ex C-GFQL | | |
| ☐ | SU-CBD | de Havilland DHC-7-102 | 098 | ex C-GEWQ | | |
| ☐ | SU-CBE | de Havilland DHC-7-102 | 099 | ex C-GFBW | | |
| ☐ | SU-CBF | de Havilland DHC-8Q-315 | 584 | ex C-FDHX | | |
| ☐ | SU-CBG | de Havilland DHC-8Q-315 | 585 | ex C-FDHY | | |
| ☐ | SU-CBH | de Havilland DHC-8Q-315 | 594 | ex C-FPJH | | |
| ☐ | SU-CBJ | de Havilland DHC-8Q-315 | 607 | ex C-FBNT | | |
| ☐ | SU-CBN | de Havilland DHC-8Q-315 | 632 | ex C-FIOY | | |
| ☐ | SU-CBP | Eurocopter EC135P2+ | 0604 | | | |
| ☐ | SU-CBQ | Eurocopter EC135P2+ | 0607 | | | |
| ☐ | SU-CBY | Canadair CRJ-900ER | 15278 | ex C-GIBL | | ♦ |

## SMART AVIATION  (M4/SME)

| | | | | | |
|---|---|---|---|---|---|
| ☐ | SU-SMG | Beech B300 Super King Air | FL-721 | ex N6021C | ♦ |
| ☐ | SU-SMH | de Havilland DHC-8Q-400 | 4367 | ex C-GJFG | ♦ |
| ☐ | SU-SMI | de Havilland DHC-8Q-400 | 4368 | ex C-GJFP | ♦ |

## TRISTAR AIR  Triple Star (TSY)  Cairo-Intl (CAI)

| | | | | | |
|---|---|---|---|---|---|
| ☐ | SU-BMZ | Airbus A300B4-203F | 129 | ex N825SC | |

## SU-Y  PALESTINE

## PALESTINIAN AIRLINES  (PF/PNW)

| | | | | | |
|---|---|---|---|---|---|
| ☐ | SU-YAH | Fokker 50 | 20123 | ex PH-FZJ | ♦ |

## SX-  GREECE (Hellenic Republic)

## AEGEAN AIRLINES  Aegean (A3/AEE)  Athens-Eleftherios Venizelos Intl (ATH)

| | | | | | | |
|---|---|---|---|---|---|---|
| ☐ | SX-DGB | Airbus A320-232 | 4165 | ex F-WWBX | | |
| ☐ | SX-DGC | Airbus A320-232 | 4094 | ex SX-OAS | | |
| ☐ | SX-DGD | Airbus A320-232 | 4065 | ex SX-OAP | | <OAL♦ |
| ☐ | SX-DGE | Airbus A320-232 | 3990 | ex SX-OAM | | <OAL♦ |
| ☐ | SX-DGI | Airbus A320-232 | 3162 | ex VT-DNY | | <OAL♦ |
| ☐ | SX-DVG | Airbus A320-232 | 3033 | ex F-WWBX | Ethos | <OAL♦ |
| ☐ | SX-DVH | Airbus A320-232 | 3066 | ex F-WWIF | Nostos | |
| ☐ | SX-DVI | Airbus A320-232 | 3074 | ex F-WWIO | Kinesis | |
| ☐ | SX-DVJ | Airbus A320-232 | 3365 | ex F-WWIS | Exelixis | |
| ☐ | SX-DVK | Airbus A320-232 | 3392 | ex F-WWDS | | |
| ☐ | SX-DVL | Airbus A320-232 | 3423 | ex F-WWIV | | |
| ☐ | SX-DVM | Airbus A320-232 | 3439 | ex F-WWDY | | |
| ☐ | SX-DVN | Airbus A320-232 | 3478 | ex F-WWDI | | |
| ☐ | SX-DVQ | Airbus A320-232 | 3526 | ex F-WWDU | | |
| ☐ | SX-DVR | Airbus A320-232 | 3714 | ex D-AVVB | | |
| ☐ | SX-DVS | Airbus A320-232 | 3709 | ex F-WWIT | | |
| ☐ | SX-DVT | Airbus A320-232 | 3745 | ex F-WWIJ | | |
| ☐ | SX-DVU | Airbus A320-232 | 3753 | ex F-WWBS | Pheidias | |
| ☐ | SX-DVV | Airbus A320-232 | 3773 | ex F-WWDT | Cleisthenes | |

| | | | | | |
|---|---|---|---|---|---|
| ☐ | SX-DVW | Airbus A320-232 | 3785 | ex F-WWIU | Nikos Kazantzakis |
| ☐ | SX-DVX | Airbus A320-232 | 3829 | ex F-WWIZ | |
| ☐ | SX-DVY | Airbus A320-232 | 3850 | ex F-WWDG | |
| | | | | | |
| ☐ | SX-DGA | Airbus A321-231 | 3878 | ex D-AVZP | |
| ☐ | SX-DGF | Airbus A319-132 | 2468 | ex D-ABGC | <BER♦ |
| ☐ | SX-DGG | Airbus A319-132LR | 1727 | ex SX-OAN | <OAL♦ |
| ☐ | SX-DGH | Airbus A319-133 | 1880 | ex SX-OAO | <OAL♦ |
| ☐ | SX-DVO | Airbus A321-231 | 3462 | ex D-AVZU | Philoxenia |
| ☐ | SX-DVP | Airbus A321-231 | 3527 | ex D-AVZZ | |
| ☐ | SX-DVZ | Airbus A321-231 | 3820 | ex D-AVZF | |

## AEOLIAN AIRLINES

| | | | | |
|---|---|---|---|---|
| SX-BTM | McDonnell-Douglas MD-83 | 49627/1580 | ex TF-JXC | o/o |

## AEROLAND AIRWAYS  (3S/AEN)  Athens-Eleftherios Venizelos Intl (ATH)

| | | | | | |
|---|---|---|---|---|---|
| ☐ | SX-ARW | Cessna 208B Caravan I | 208B1174 | ex N13080 | Isle of Chios |
| ☐ | SX-ARX | Cessna 208B Caravan I | 208B1182 | ex N1300G | Isle of Lesvos |
| ☐ | SX-ARY | Cessna 208B Caravan I | 208B1301 | ex N2028N | Isle of Paros |
| ☐ | SX-BVE | de Havilland DHC-8-106 | 351 | ex C-FRIY | Island of Mykonos |

## ASTRA AIRLINES  (A2/AZI)

| | | | | | |
|---|---|---|---|---|---|
| ☐ | SX-DIO | Airbus A320-232 | 0527 | ex PH-AAY | [DUB]♦ |
| ☐ | SX-DIX | British Aerospace 146 Srs.300 | E3193 | ex I-ADJF | |
| ☐ | SX-DIZ | British Aerospace 146 Srs.300 | E3206 | ex G-JEBE | |

## AVIATOR AIRWAYS  Aviator (AVW)  Athens-Eleftherios Venizelos Intl (ATH)

| | | | | |
|---|---|---|---|---|
| ☐ | SX-APJ | Beech 200 Super King Air | BB-401 | ex OY-JAO |

## BLUEBIRD AIRWAYS  (BZ/BBG)

| | | | | | |
|---|---|---|---|---|---|
| ☐ | SX-DAV | Boeing 737-4Q8 | 24704/1855 | ex N744VA | |
| ☐ | SX-TZE | Boeing 737-48E | 27632/2857 | ex EI-DOV | ♦ |

## EPSILON AVIATION

Became Ver-Avia, see below

## EUROAIR  Eurostar (6I/EUP)  Athens-Eleftherios Venizelos Intl (ATH)

| | | | | |
|---|---|---|---|---|
| ☐ | SX-APP | Piper PA-31-350 Chieftain | 31-8152171 | ex N4093G |
| ☐ | SX-BFL | Piper PA-31-350 Chieftain | 31-7952171 | ex N64TT |
| ☐ | SX-BMS | Piper PA-31-350 Navajo Chieftain | 31-7752122 | ex HP-1049PS |

## FLY HELLAS  (VQ/VKH)

| | | | | |
|---|---|---|---|---|
| ☐ | SX-SMS | McDonnell-Douglas MD-83 | 49631/1596 | ex SE-RDI | [IEV]♦ |

## GAINJET  (GNJ)  Athens-Eleftherios Venizelos Intl (ATH)

| | | | | | |
|---|---|---|---|---|---|
| ☐ | SX-RFA | Boeing 757-23N/W | 30232/888 | ex EI-LTO | |
| ☐ | SX-MTF | Boeing 737-329 | 23774/1443 | ex N473CT | ♦ |

## HELLENIC IMPERIAL AIRWAYS  (IMP)  Athens-Eleftherios Venizelos Intl (ATH)

| | | | | |
|---|---|---|---|---|
| ☐ | SX-TIB | Boeing 747-230B | 23622/665 | ex JY-AUB |
| ☐ | SX-TIC | Boeing 747-281B | 23501/648 | ex AP-BIC |
| ☐ | SX-TID | Boeing 747-281B | 23502/649 | ex (SX-DID) |
| ☐ | SX-TIE | Boeing 747-230M | 23509/663 | ex 5T-AUE |

## HERMES AIRLINES

| | | | | | |
|---|---|---|---|---|---|
| ☐ | SX-BHR | Boeing 737-5L9 | 29234/3068 | ex TC-AAG | <BIE♦ |
| ☐ | SX-BHS | Airbus A321-111 | 0642 | ex F-GYAO | <BIE♦ |
| ☐ | SX-BHV | Airbus A320-211 | 0293 | ex F-GYAI | <BIE♦ |

## KAPA AIR

| | | | | |
|---|---|---|---|---|
| ☐ | SX-BFM | PA-31-350 Chieftain | 31-8052024 | ♦ |

## OLYMPIC AIR | Olympic (OA/OAL) | Athens-Eleftherios Venizelos Intl (ATH)

| ☐ | SX-OAF | Airbus A319-111 | 3895 | ex D-AHIP | | |
| ☐ | SX-OAG | Airbus A319-112 | 3950 | ex D-AHIQ | | |
| ☐ | SX-OAJ | Airbus A319-112 | 3905 | ex D-AVWS | | |
| ☐ | SX-OAN | Airbus A319-133 | 1727 | ex D-APAC | | >AEE |
| ☐ | SX-OAO | Airbus A319-133 | 1880 | ex D-APAD | | >AEE |
| ☐ | SX-OAH | Airbus A320-232 | 3316 | ex VT-DNV | | |
| ☐ | SX-OAI | Airbus A320-232 | 3162 | ex VT-DNY | | >AEE |
| ☐ | SX-OAM | Airbus A320-232 | 3990 | ex F-WWBY | | >AEE |
| ☐ | SX-OAP | Airbus A320-232 | 4065 | ex D-AVVL | | >AEE |
| ☐ | SX-OAQ | Airbus A320-232 | 3748 | ex F-WWBQ | | |
| ☐ | SX-OAR | Airbus A320-232 | 3812 | ex D-AVVE | | |
| ☐ | SX-OAS | Airbus A320-232 | 4094 | ex D-AVVB | | >AEE |
| ☐ | SX-OAT | Airbus A320-232 | 4190 | ex F-WWII | | |
| ☐ | SX-OAU | Airbus A320-232 | 4193 | ex F-WWIJ | | |
| ☐ | SX-BIO | de Havilland DHC-8-102 | 330 | ex C-GZQZ | Katerina Thanou | |
| ☐ | SX-BIP | de Havilland DHC-8-102 | 347 | ex C-GZRA | Voula Patoulidou | |
| ☐ | SX-BIQ | de Havilland DHC-8-102 | 361 | ex C-GZRD | Kahi Kahiasvili | |
| ☐ | SX-BIR | de Havilland DHC-8-102 | 364 | ex C-GZRF | Kostas Kenteris | |
| ☐ | SX-BIW | de Havilland DHC-8-102 | 289 | ex OE-HWG | | |
| ☐ | SX-BIT | de Havilland DHC-8-402Q | 4148 | ex G-JECV | | |
| ☐ | SX-BIU | de Havilland DHC-8-402Q | 4152 | ex G-JECW | | |
| ☐ | SX-OBA | de Havilland DHC-8-402Q | 4267 | ex G-PTHA | | |
| ☐ | SX-OBB | de Havilland DHC-8-402Q | 4268 | ex G-PTHB | | |
| ☐ | SX-OBC | de Havilland DHC-8-402Q | 4276 | ex G-PTHC | | |
| ☐ | SX-OBD | de Havilland DHC-8-402Q | 4311 | ex G-PTHD | | |
| ☐ | SX-OBE | de Havilland DHC-8-402Q | 4314 | ex G-PTHE | | |
| ☐ | SX-OBF | de Havilland DHC-8-402Q | 4318 | ex G-PTHF | | |
| ☐ | SX-OBG | de Havilland DHC-8-402Q | 4321 | ex G-PTHG | | |
| ☐ | SX-OBH | de Havilland DHC-8-402Q | 4327 | ex G-PTHH | | |
| ☐ | SX-BPA | ATR 42-300 | 0033 | ex EI-CVS | | |

## SKY EXPRESS | Air Crete (G3/SEH) | Heraklion (HER)

| ☐ | SX-DIA | British Aerospace Jetstream 41 | 41075 | ex G-CEYV |
| ☐ | SX-IDI | British Aerospace Jetstream 32 | 947 | ex N149JH |
| ☐ | SX-ROD | British Aerospace Jetstream 41 | 41076 | ex G-CEYW |
| ☐ | SX-SEC | British Aerospace Jetstream 41 | 41040 | ex G-MAJT |
| ☐ | SX-SEH | British Aerospace Jetstream 41 | 41014 | ex G-ISAY |

## SKY WINGS AIRLINES | (GSW) | Heraklion (HER)

| ☐ | SX-BTG | McDonnell-Douglas MD-83 | 49856/1675 | ex SE-RDG | |
| ☐ | SX-BTL | McDonnell-Douglas MD-82 | 53232/2108 | ex N598BC | ♦ |
| ☐ | SX-BTM | McDonnell-Douglas MD-83 | 49627/1580 | ex TF-JXC | ♦ |
| ☐ | SX-BTP | Airbus A320-231 | 0376 | ex N376BV | [ATH]♦ |
| ☐ | SX-DMA | Avro 146-RJ100 | E3341 | ex SX-DVA | ♦ |
| ☐ | SX-DMB | Avro 146-RJ100 | E3343 | ex SX-DVB | ♦ |
| ☐ | SX-DMC | Avro 146-RJ100 | E3358 | ex SX-DVC | ♦ |
| ☐ | SX-DMD | Avro 146-RJ100 | E3362 | ex SX-DVD | ♦ |

## SWIFTAIR HELLAS | Med-Freight (MDF) | Athens-Eleftherios Venizelos Intl (ATH)

| ☐ | SX-BGU | Swearingen SA.227AC Metro III | AC-615B | ex EC-HJO |
| ☐ | SX-BKZ | Swearingen SA.227AC Metro III | AC-694B | ex SX-BKW |
| ☐ | SX-BMT | Swearingen SA.227AC Metro III | AC-699B | ex EC-GYB |

## VER-AVIA | Night Rider (GRV) | Athens-Eleftherios Venizelos Intl (ATH)

| ☐ | SX-BMM | Swearingen SA.227AC Metro III | BC-774B | ex N774MW | Mike | ♦ |
| ☐ | SX-BNN | Swearingen SA.227AC Metro III | BC-771B | ex N771MW | Nick | ♦ |

## S2- BANGLADESH (People's Republic of Bangladesh)

## BEST AIR | Best Air (5Q/BEA) | Dhaka (DAC)

Ceased ops Jan10

## BIMAN BANGLADESH AIRLINES | Bangladesh (BG/BBC) | Dhaka (DAC)

| ☐ | S2-ACO | Douglas DC-10-30 | 46993/263 | ex 9V-SDB | City of Hazrat Shah Makhdoom (RA) |
| ☐ | S2-ACR | Douglas DC-10-30 | 48317/445 | | The New Era |
| ☐ | S2-ACV | Fokker F.28 Fellowship 4000 | 11124 | ex PK-YPV | |

| | | | | | | |
|---|---|---|---|---|---|---|
| ☐ | S2-ACW | Fokker F.28 Fellowship 4000 | 11148 | ex PK-YPJ | | |
| ☐ | S2-ADF | Airbus A310-325 | 700 | ex F-WWCB | City of Chittagong | |
| ☐ | S2-ADK | Airbus A310-325 | 594 | ex N594RC | | |
| ☐ | S2-AFL | Boeing 737-83N/W | 28648/888 | ex PR-GOZ | | |
| ☐ | S2-AFM | Boeing 737-83N/W | 28653/948 | ex PR-GIA | | |
| ☐ | S2-AFO | Boeing 777-3E9ER | 40122/964 | | The Palki | |
| ☐ | S2-AFP | Boeing 777-3E9ER | 40123/971 | | Arun Alo | |
| ☐ | S2-AFT | Airbus A310-325ET | 642 | ex N301LF | | |
| ☐ | TF-AMY | Boeing 747-446 | 25260/876 | ex N269AS | | <ABD♦ |

## BISMILLAH AIRLINES — Bismillah (5Z/BML) — Dhaka/Sharjah (DAC/SHJ)

| | | | | | | |
|---|---|---|---|---|---|---|
| ☐ | S2-ADW | Hawker Siddeley HS.748 Srs 2A/347 | 1766 | ex G-BGMN | | Frtr |
| ☐ | S2-AEE | Hawker Siddeley HS.748 Srs 2A/242 | 1647 | ex G-ORCP | | Frtr♦ |

## EASY FLY EXPRESS — Dhaka (DAC)

| | | | | | |
|---|---|---|---|---|---|
| ☐ | S2-AAX | Hawker Siddeley HS.748 Srs.2A/242 | 1767 | ex G-BGMO | [DAC] |

## GMG AIRLINES — (Z5/GMG) — Dhaka (DAC)

| | | | | | | |
|---|---|---|---|---|---|---|
| ☐ | S2-AAA | de Havilland DHC-8-102 | 245 | ex N802MA | In memory of Bangabondu | [DAC] |
| ☐ | S2-ACT | de Havilland DHC-8-311 | 307 | ex OE-LRW | | [DAC] |
| ☐ | S2-ADM | McDonnell-Douglas MD-82 | 53147/2069 | ex PK-LMF | | [DAC] |
| ☐ | S2-ADO | McDonnell-Douglas MD-82 | 53481/2145 | ex S7-ASK | | |
| ☐ | S2-ADP | McDonnell-Douglas MD-83 | 53044/1776 | ex N835NK | | |
| ☐ | S2-ADX | de Havilland DHC-8Q-311A | 464 | ex G-BRYZ | In memory of HZT Saha Jalal | [DAC] |
| ☐ | S2-AFR | Boeing 767-3Y0ER | 24948/380 | ex N948AV | | [DAC]♦ |
| ☐ | S2-AFX | Boeing 767-33AER | 25535/491 | ex PH-MCJ | | [DAC]♦ |

## REGENT AIRWAYS — (RX)

| | | | | | |
|---|---|---|---|---|---|
| ☐ | S2-AHA | de Havilland DHC-8Q-314 | 521 | ex D-BLEJ | |
| ☐ | S2-AHB | de Havilland DHC-8Q-314 | 543 | ex D-BEBA | |

## ROYAL BENGAL AIRLINES — (4A)

Ceased ops

## UNITED AIRWAYS — United Bangladesh (4H/UBD)

| | | | | | | |
|---|---|---|---|---|---|---|
| ☐ | S2-AEH | McDonnell-Douglas MD-83 | 49937/1784 | ex YR-HBA | | |
| ☐ | S2-AER | de Havilland DHC-8-103 | 366 | ex N811WP | | |
| ☐ | S2-AES | de Havilland DHC-8-103 | 363 | ex N810WP | | wfs |
| ☐ | S2-AEU | McDonnell-Douglas MD-83 | 49790/1643 | ex G-FLTL | | |
| ☐ | S2-AFE | ATR 72-212 | 0385 | ex N385FA | | ♦ |
| ☐ | S2-AFF | Airbus A310-325 | 672 | ex M-ABCX | | |
| ☐ | S2-AFN | ATR 72-212 | 0379 | ex PK-MFA | | ♦ |
| ☐ | S2-AFV | McDonnell-Douglas MD-83 | 53377/2057 | ex SX-BPP | | ♦ |
| ☐ | S2-AFW | Airbus A310-325 | 674 | ex F-HBOS | | ♦ |

## VOYAGER AIRLINES — Voyager Air (V6/VOG) — Dhaka (DAC)

| | | | | | |
|---|---|---|---|---|---|
| ☐ | S2-AEM | Fokker F-27 Friendship 500RF | 10630 | ex 4R-EXG | [CGP]♦ |

## YOUNGONE

| | | | | | |
|---|---|---|---|---|---|
| ☐ | S2-ACU | Cessna 208B Caravan I | 208B0612 | ex N1215A | |
| ☐ | S2-AEK | Piaggio P.180 Avanti | 1212 | ex D-IMIA | ♦ |
| ☐ | S2-AEV | Piaggio P.180 Avanti | 1193 | | ♦ |

## ZOOM AIRWAYS — Zed Air (3Z/ZAW) — Dhaka (DAC)

| | | | | | |
|---|---|---|---|---|---|
| ☐ | S2-AET | Lockheed L-1011-1F Tristar | 193-1012 | ex HS-AXF | [DAC] |

# S5-  SLOVENIA (Republic of Slovenia)

## ADRIA AIRWAYS — Adria (JP/ADR) — Ljubljana (LJU)

Member of Star Alliance

| | | | | | | |
|---|---|---|---|---|---|---|
| ☐ | S5-AAD | Canadair CRJ-200LR | 7166 | ex C-FZWS | | |
| ☐ | S5-AAE | Canadair CRJ-200LR | 7170 | ex C-GAIK | | >RUS |
| ☐ | S5-AAF | Canadair CRJ-200LR | 7272 | ex C-FMND | | |
| ☐ | S5-AAG | Canadair CRJ-200LR | 7384 | ex C-FMMT | Star Alliance c/s | |
| ☐ | S5-AAI | Canadair CRJ-200LR | 7248 | ex G-DUOH | | |
| ☐ | S5-AAJ | Canadair CRJ-200LR | 8010 | ex C- | | |

| | | | | | | |
|---|---|---|---|---|---|---|
| ☐ | S5-AAA | Airbus A320-231 | 0043 | ex SX-BAS | | [LJU] |
| ☐ | S5-AAK | Canadair CRJ-900ER | 15128 | ex C- | | |
| ☐ | S5-AAL | Canadair CRJ-900ER | 15129 | ex C- | | |
| ☐ | S5-AAN | Canadair CRJ-900ER | 15207 | ex C- | | |
| ☐ | S5-AAO | Canadair CRJ-900ER | 15215 | ex C- | | |
| ☐ | S5-AAP | Airbus A319-132 | 4282 | ex D-AVWR | | |
| ☐ | S5-AAR | Airbus A319-132 | 4301 | ex D-AVXB | | |
| ☐ | S5-AAS | Airbus A320-231 | 0444 | ex EI-DOD | | ♦ |

## AURORA AIRLINES (URR) Ljubljana (LJU)

Ceased ops

## LINXAIR BUSINESS AIRLINES (LIX)

| | | | | | |
|---|---|---|---|---|---|
| ☐ | F-HAFS | Embraer ERJ-145EU | 145177 | ex F-WAFS | ♦ |
| ☐ | UP-EM003 | Embraer ERJ-145EU | 145167 | ex SX-CMB | ♦ |

## SOLINAIR Solinair (SOP) Portoroz (POW)

| | | | | | |
|---|---|---|---|---|---|
| ☐ | S5-ABS | Airbus A300B4-203F | 126 | ex TC-MNN | <MNB |
| ☐ | S5-ABV | Boeing 737-4K5SF | 24128/1715 | ex TC-MNG | <MNB♦ |
| ☐ | S5-BBS | SAAB SF.340A | 340A-064 | ex SE-E64 | ♦ |

# S7-    SEYCHELLES (Republic of Seychelles)

## AIR SEYCHELLES Seychelles (HM/SEY) Mahe (SEZ)

| | | | | | | |
|---|---|---|---|---|---|---|
| ☐ | S7-AAF | de Havilland DHC-6 Twin Otter 300 | 623 | ex S7-AAO | Isle of Praslin | |
| ☐ | S7-AAJ | de Havilland DHC-6 Twin Otter 310 | 499 | ex PH-STB | Isle of Desroches | |
| ☐ | S7-AAR | de Havilland DHC-6 Twin Otter 300 | 539 | ex PH-STF | Isle of Farquhar | |
| ☐ | S7-CUR | de Havilland DHC-6 Twin Otter 400 | 846 | ex C-GLVA | | |
| ☐ | S7- | de Havilland DHC-6 Twin Otter 400 | | ex | | o/o |
| ☐ | S7- | de Havilland DHC-6 Twin Otter 400 | | ex | | o/o |
| ☐ | S7-AAA | Britten-Norman BN-2A-27 Islander | 540 | ex G-BDZP | Isle of Remire | wfs |
| ☐ | S7-AHM | Boeing 767-37DER | 26328/637 | ex (S7-AAZ) | Vailee de Mai | [MIA] |
| ☐ | S7-ASY | Boeing 767-3Q8ER | 29386/831 | | Aldabra | [MIA] |
| ☐ | S7-FCS | Boeing 767-306ER | 28884/738 | ex HA-LHC | | |
| ☐ | S7-PAL | Short SD.3-60 | SH3758 | ex G-KBAC | Isle de Palme | |
| ☐ | S7-PRI | Short SD.3-60 | SH3724 | ex G-BNMU | Isle of La Digue | |

## HELICOPTER SEYCHELLES

| | | | | | |
|---|---|---|---|---|---|
| ☐ | S7-NEL | Agusta A.109C | 7630 | | ♦ |

## IDC AIRCRAFT Mahe (SEZ)

| | | | | | |
|---|---|---|---|---|---|
| ☐ | S7-AAI | Reims Cessna F406 Caravan II | F406-0051 | ex N7148P | |
| ☐ | S7-AAU | Britten-Norman BN-2A-21 Islander | 589 | ex A2-01M | op for Coast Guard |
| ☐ | S7-IDC | Beech 1900D | UE-212 | ex N3217U | op for Coast Guard |

# S9-    SAO TOME (Democratic Republic of São Tomé & Principe)

## AFRICA'S CONNECTION (AUN)

| | | | | | |
|---|---|---|---|---|---|
| ☐ | S9-AUN | Dornier 228-201 | 8076 | ex 5N-AUN | ♦ |
| ☐ | S9-LGM | Dornier 228-212 | 8155 | ex TR-LGM | wfs♦ |
| ☐ | S9-RAS | Dornier 228-201 | 8068 | ex TR-LHE | ♦ |

## GOLFO INTERNATIONAL São Tomé/Luanda (TMS/LAD)

Aircraft sold to Angola

## GOLIAF AIR Goliaf Air (GLE) São Tomé (TMS)

| | | | | | |
|---|---|---|---|---|---|
| ☐ | S9-BOH | Antonov An-32 | 2108 | ex T-256 | |
| ☐ | S9-BOZ | Antonov An-12A | 2340803 | ex RA-122375 | >Africa West |
| ☐ | S9-DAF | Antonov An-12A | 2340606 | ex RA-12971  Principe | |
| ☐ | S9-DBA | Antonov An-12AP | 2400802 | ex UR-11326 | |
| ☐ | S9-GAR | Lockheed L-1011-200 Tristar | 193U-1201 | ex EX-102 | [DAK] |
| ☐ | S9-PSE | Antonov An-32 | 2803 | ex UR-48053 | >MGG |
| ☐ | S9-PSO | Antonov An-12BP | 5343109 | ex EW-11365 | |

## TRANSAFRIK INTERNATIONAL                     (TFK)                    São Tomé/Luanda (TMS/LAD)

| | | | | | |
|---|---|---|---|---|---|
| ☐ | 5X-TUA | Lockheed L-382G-11C Hercules | 4301 | ex S9-CAV | |
| ☐ | 5X-TUB | Lockheed L-382G-13C Hercules | 4300 | ex S9-CAW | |
| ☐ | 5X-TUD | Lockheed L-382G Hercules | 4299 | ex S9-DBF | op for UN♦ |
| ☐ | 5X-TUE | Lockheed L-382E-25C Hercules | 4385 | ex S9-NAL | |
| ☐ | 5X-TUF | Lockheed L-328G Hercules | 4383 | ex N910SJ | ♦ |
| | | | | | |
| ☐ | S9-BAE | Boeing 727-31F | 18903/147 | ex N210NE | |
| ☐ | S9-PAC | Boeing 727-44C (FedEx 3) | 20475/854 | ex C-GVFA | >Southern Sudan |
| ☐ | 5X-PST | Boeing 727-171C | 19859/559 | ex S9-PST | wfs |

## TRANSLIZ AVIATION                                                      São Tomé (TMS)

| | | | | | |
|---|---|---|---|---|---|
| ☐ | S9-KHC | Antonov An-12B | 00347306 | ex ER-ACY | |
| ☐ | S9-KHD | Antonov An-12B | 01347908 | ex ER-ACQ | [KIN] |
| ☐ | S9-KHE | Antonov An-12BK | 9346302 | | ♦ |
| ☐ | S9-KHF | Antonov An-12V | 00347109 | ex ER-ADG | |
| ☐ | S9-KHL | Antonov An-12B | 00347401 | ex ER-ACS | |

## TC-   TURKEY (Republic of Turkey)

### AIRBERLIN TURKEY                          Izmir (4I/IZM)                        Izmir (ADB)

| | | | | | | |
|---|---|---|---|---|---|---|
| ☐ | TC-IZA | Airbus A320-233 | 2118 | ex N488TA | | [SEN]♦ |
| ☐ | TC-IZB | Boeing 737-86J/W | 37743/2834 | ex D-ABKE | | <BER♦ |
| ☐ | TC-IZC | Boeing 737-86J/W | 37745/3044 | ex D-ABKF | | <BER♦ |
| ☐ | TC-IZF | Boeing 737-86J/W | 30880/1043 | ex D-ABBD | | <BER♦ |
| ☐ | TC-IZH | Airbus A319-132 | 2452 | ex N812BR | Goztepe | |
| ☐ | TC-IZM | Airbus A319-132 | 2404 | ex N809BR | Alsancak | |
| ☐ | TC-IZR | Airbus A319-132 | 2414 | ex N810BR | Karsiyaka | |

### ANADOLU JET                              Ankara/Esenboga International (ESB)

| | | | | | | |
|---|---|---|---|---|---|---|
| ☐ | TC-JKH | Boeing 737-76N/W | 34757/2241 | ex OM-NGL | Ihlara | |
| ☐ | TC-JKI | Boeing 737-76N/W | 34758/2266 | ex EI-EDU | Abant | |
| ☐ | TC-JKL | Boeing 737-76N/W | 34753/2165 | ex OM-NGG | Anamur | |
| ☐ | TC-JKM | Boeing 737-76N/W | 34755/2187 | ex OM-NGJ | | |
| ☐ | TC-JKP | Boeing 737-7GL/W | 34759/2320 | ex G-CGFV | | ♦ |
| ☐ | TC-JKR | Boeing 737-7GL/W | 34760/2352 | ex G-CGFW | Gelibolu | ♦ |
| ☐ | TC-JKS | Boeing 737-73V | 32419/1321 | ex G-EZJX | | |
| ☐ | TC-JKT | Boeing 737-73V | 32420/1341 | ex G-EZJY | | |
| ☐ | TC-SAC | Boeing 737-76N/W | 32684/1889 | ex TC-JKF | | <SXS♦ |
| ☐ | TC-SAD | Boeing 737-76N/W | 34754/2172 | ex TC-JKG | Mugla | <SXS♦ |
| | | | | | | |
| ☐ | TC-JFK | Boeing 737-8F2/W | 29773/259 | ex N1786B | Zonguldak | ♦ |
| ☐ | TC-JGC | Boeing 737-8F2/W | 29787/771 | ex N1786B | Kocaeli | |
| ☐ | TC-JGF | Boeing 737-8F2/W | 29790/1088 | ex N1786B | Ardahan | |
| ☐ | TC-JGJ | Boeing 737-8F2/W | 34408/1880 | | Aydin | ♦ |
| ☐ | TC-JGK | Boeing 737-8F2/W | 34409/1924 | ex N1786B | Kirsehir | ♦ |
| ☐ | TC-JGL | Boeing 737-8F2/W | 34410/1927 | ex N1787B | Karaman | ♦ |
| ☐ | TC-JGM | Boeing 737-8F2/W | 34411/1944 | | Hakkari | ♦ |
| ☐ | TC-JGN | Boeing 737-8F2/W | 34412/1949 | | Bilecik | ♦ |
| ☐ | TC-JGO | Boeing 737-8F2/W | 34413/1972 | ex N1786B | Kilis | ♦ |
| ☐ | TC-JHG | Boeing 737-8GJ/W | 34958/2688 | ex VT-SGD | Pamukkale | |
| ☐ | TC-JHH | Boeing 737-8GJ/W | 34959/2719 | | Kemer | |
| ☐ | TC-JHI | Boeing 737-8FH/W | 35092/2160 | ex G-XLAK | Hendek | |
| ☐ | TC-JHJ | Boeing 737-86Q | 30296/1647 | ex VT-AXA | | |
| | | | | | | |
| ☐ | TC-JAI | Airbus A320-232 | 3259 | ex N569MS | | ♦ |
| ☐ | TC-JBI | Airbus A320-232 | 3308 | ex N568MS | | ♦ |

### ATLASJET INTERNATIONAL              Atlasjet (KK/KKK)                    Antalya (AYT)

| | | | | | |
|---|---|---|---|---|---|
| ☐ | TC-ATB | Airbus A321-211 | 1503 | ex 6Y-JMH | ♦ |
| ☐ | TC-ATE | Airbus A321-211 | 0675 | ex F-WTAX | ♦ |
| ☐ | TC-ATF | Airbus A321-211 | 0761 | ex F-WTAV | ♦ |
| ☐ | TC-ATG | Airbus A321-231 | 1878 | ex F-ORME | ♦ |
| ☐ | TC-ATH | Airbus A321-231 | 1953 | ex F-ORMF | ♦ |
| ☐ | TC-ETF | Airbus A321-231 | 1438 | ex N585NK | |
| ☐ | TC-ETH | Airbus A321-231 | 0968 | ex TC-IEF | |
| ☐ | TC-ETJ | Airbus A321-231 | 0974 | ex TC-IEG | |
| ☐ | TC-ETM | Airbus A321-131 | 0604 | ex TC-TUB | |
| ☐ | TC-ETN | Airbus A321-131 | 0614 | ex TC-TUC | |
| ☐ | TC-ETV | Airbus A321-221 | 1950 | ex EI-LVA | |
| | | | | | |
| ☐ | TC-ATD | Airbus A319-112 | 1124 | ex EI-ELO | ♦ |
| ☐ | TC-ATJ | Airbus A320-233 | 1730 | ex TC-IZL | o/o♦ |
| ☐ | TC-ETK | Airbus A330-223 | 358 | ex I-EEZA | |

| | | | | | | |
|---|---|---|---|---|---|---|
| ☐ | TC-ETE | Boeing 757-2Q8 | 30044/954 | ex TC-GLA | | |
| ☐ | TC-ETP | Airbus A330-223 | 343 | ex HB-IQO | | |
| ☐ | TC-OGS | Boeing 757-256 | 29307/924 | ex EC-HIQ | | |
| ☐ | TC-OGT | Boeing 757-256 | 29308/935 | ex EC-HIR | | >SVA |
| ☐ | TC- | Airbus A320-232 | 2747 | ex OE-IBD | | o/o♦ |
| ☐ | TC- | Airbus A320-232 | 2753 | ex OE-IBE | | o/o♦ |

### BEST AIR
**(5F/BST)** — *Istanbul-Ataturk (IST)*

Ceased ops Feb10

### BORAJET
**(BJ/BRJ)**

| | | | | | | |
|---|---|---|---|---|---|---|
| ☐ | TC-YAB | ATR 72-212A | 0588 | ex G-CGFT | | |
| ☐ | TC-YAC | ATR 72-212A | 0701 | ex OY-EDC | | |
| ☐ | TC-YAD | ATR 72-212A | 0702 | ex OY-EDD | | |
| ☐ | TC-YAE | ATR 72-212A | 0705 | ex G-CGFX | | ♦ |
| ☐ | TC-YAF | ATR 72-212A | 0982 | ex F-WWEC | | VIP♦ |

### CORENDON AIR
**Corendon (7H/CAI)** — *Istanbul-Sabiha Gokcen Int'l (SAW)*

| | | | | | | |
|---|---|---|---|---|---|---|
| ☐ | TC-TJG | Boeing 737-86J/W | 29120/202 | ex D-ABAT | | |
| ☐ | TC-TJH | Boeing 737-86J/W | 29121/239 | ex D-ABAU | | |
| ☐ | TC-TJI | Boeing 737-8S3/W | 29246/475 | ex TC-SGK | | |
| ☐ | TC-TJJ | Boeing 737-8S3/W | 29247/493 | ex TC-SGL | | ♦ |
| ☐ | TC-TJK | Boeing 737-8KN/W | 35794/2794 | ex A6-FDA | | >MHS♦ |
| | | | | | | |
| ☐ | TC-TJB | Boeing 737-3Q8 | 27633/2878 | ex N304FL | Ayhan Saracoglu | |
| ☐ | TC-TJE | Boeing 737-4Y0 | 26073/2375 | ex TC-JER | | |
| ☐ | TC-TJF | Boeing 737-4Y0 | 26078/2431 | ex TC-JEU | | |

### FREEBIRD AIRLINES
**Free Turk (FHY)** — *Istanbul-Ataturk (IST)*

| | | | | | |
|---|---|---|---|---|---|
| ☐ | TC-FBH | Airbus A320-214 | 4207 | ex F-WWBP | |
| ☐ | TC-FBJ | Airbus A320-232 | 0580 | ex N580CG | |
| ☐ | TC-FBO | Airbus A320-214 | 5096 | ex F-WWIO | |
| ☐ | TC-FBR | Airbus A320-232 | 2524 | ex VT-DKZ | o/o♦ |
| ☐ | TC-FBV | Airbus A320-214 | 4658 | ex F-WWIM | ♦ |
| | | | | | |
| ☐ | TC-FBG | Airbus A321-231 | 0771 | ex HL7588 | |
| ☐ | TC-FBT | Airbus A321-231 | 0855 | ex HL7589 | |

### MARIN AIR
*Antalya/Bodrum-Marina/Marmaris-Marina (AYT/-/-)*

| | | | | | |
|---|---|---|---|---|---|
| ☐ | TC-KEU | Cessna 208 Caravan I | 20800317 | ex N52234 | FP |

### MNG CARGO AIRLINES
**Black Sea (MB/MNB)** — *Istanbul-Ataturk (IST)*

| | | | | | |
|---|---|---|---|---|---|
| ☐ | TC-MCA | Airbus A300C4-605R | 755 | ex TF-ELW | |
| ☐ | TC-MCB | Airbus A300B4-203F | 304 | ex N308FV | |
| ☐ | TC-MNB | Airbus A300B4-203F | 292 | ex HL7279 | |
| ☐ | TC-MND | Airbus A300C4-203F | 212 | ex ZS-SDG | >Ceiba Cargo |
| ☐ | TC-MNJ | Airbus A300B4-203F | 123 | ex PH-JLH | |
| ☐ | TC-MNU | Airbus A300B4-203F | 047 | ex N740SC | |
| ☐ | TC-MNV | Airbus A300C4-605R | 758 | ex TF-ELG | |
| ☐ | TC- | Airbus A300B4-622R | 739 | ex N739AA | [IST]♦ |
| ☐ | TC- | Airbus A300B4-622R | 756 | ex N756ZG | [SHE]♦ |
| | | | | | |
| ☐ | TC-MCF | Boeing 737-4K5SF | 24126/1697 | ex N726CF | |
| ☐ | TC-MNG | Boeing 737-4K5SF | 24128/1715 | ex N728CF | >SOP |

### MYCARGO AIRLINES
**(9T/RUN)** — *Istanbul-Ataturk (IST)*

| | | | | | |
|---|---|---|---|---|---|
| ☐ | TC-ACD | Airbus A300B4-203F | 075 | ex N502TA | op for Empost |
| ☐ | TC-ACE | Airbus A300B4-203F | 154 | ex N320SC | |
| ☐ | TC-ACK | Airbus A300B4-622RF | 743 | ex B-MAS | ♦ |
| ☐ | TC-ACU | Airbus A300B4-203F | 183 | ex N512TA | |
| ☐ | TC-ACY | Airbus A300B4-203F | 107 | ex N59107 | [SAW] |
| ☐ | TC-ACZ | Airbus A300B4-203F | 105 | ex N317FV | |
| ☐ | TC-ACF | Boeing 747-400481SF | 25645/979 | ex N596MS | ♦ |
| ☐ | TC-ACM | Airbus A300B4-622RF | 677 | ex b-mbj | o/o♦ |

### ONUR AIR
**Onur Air (8Q/OHY)** — *Istanbul-Ataturk (IST)*

| | | | | | |
|---|---|---|---|---|---|
| ☐ | TC-OAA | Airbus A300B4-605R | 744 | ex F-WQRD | |
| ☐ | TC-OAB | Airbus A300B4-605R | 749 | ex F-WQRC | Safuan 1 |
| ☐ | TC-OAG | Airbus A300B4-605R | 747 | ex F-OHLN | |
| ☐ | TC-OAH | Airbus A300B4-605R | 584 | ex S7-RGO | |

| | | | | | | |
|---|---|---|---|---|---|---|
| ☐ | TC-OAO | Airbus A300B4-605R | 764 | ex D-AIAW | | |
| ☐ | TC-OAZ | Airbus A300B4-605R | 603 | ex SX-BEM | | |
| | | | | | | |
| ☐ | TC-OBD | Airbus A320-232 | 0455 | ex N11112 | Kaspersky | |
| ☐ | TC-OBE | Airbus A320-232 | 0471 | ex VT-WAB | | |
| ☐ | TC-OBG | Airbus A320-233 | 0916 | ex N590SH | | ♦ |
| ☐ | TC-OBH | Airbus A320-233 | 1482 | ex PK-RMJ | | ♦ |
| ☐ | TC-OBI | Airbus A320-233 | 1509 | ex N380DF | | ♦ |
| ☐ | TC-OBL | Airbus A320-232 | 0640 | ex TC-OGI | | ♦ |
| ☐ | TC-OBM | Airbus A320-232 | 0676 | ex TC-OGJ | | ♦ |
| ☐ | TC-OBN | Airbus A320-232 | 2571 | ex LZ-WZA | | ♦ |
| ☐ | TC-OBO | Airbus A320-232 | 2688 | ex HA-LPH | | ♦ |
| ☐ | TC-OBP | Airbus A320-231 | 0496 | ex N201LF | | ♦ |
| ☐ | TC- | Airbus A320-232 | 0543 | ex EI-EEL | | o/o♦ |
| | | | | | | |
| ☐ | TC-OAK | Airbus A321-231 | 0954 | ex D-ALAI | | |
| ☐ | TC-OAL | Airbus A321-231 | 1004 | ex D-ALAK | | |
| ☐ | TC-OAN | Airbus A321-231 | 1421 | ex D-ALAP | | >BGH |
| ☐ | TC-OBF | Airbus A321-231 | 0963 | ex OE-IAA | | |
| ☐ | TC-OBJ | Airbus A321-231 | 0835 | ex N835AG | | ♦ |
| ☐ | TC-OBK | Airbus A321-231 | 0792 | ex EI-LVD | | ♦ |
| ☐ | TC-OBR | Airbus A321-231 | 1008 | ex N108DE | | ♦ |
| ☐ | TC-ONJ | Airbus A321-131 | 0385 | ex D-AVZG | Kaptan Koray Sahin | |
| ☐ | TC-ONS | Airbus A321-131 | 0364 | ex D-AVZD | Funda | |
| | | | | | | |
| ☐ | TC-OCA | Airbus A330-322 | 072 | ex EC-IJH | | |
| ☐ | TC-OCB | Airbus A330-342 | 098 | ex B-HYA | | |
| ☐ | TC-OCC | Airbus A330-322 | 143 | ex 9M-MKS | | >SVA♦ |
| ☐ | TC-OCD | Airbus A330-322 | 087 | ex VN-A368 | | ♦ |

## PEGASUS AIRLINES — Sunturk (1I/PGT) — Istanbul-Ataturk (IST)

| | | | | | | |
|---|---|---|---|---|---|---|
| ☐ | TC-AAE | Boeing 737-82R/W | 35700/2435 | | Hayirli | |
| ☐ | TC-AAH | Boeing 737-82R/W | 35701/2496 | | Hanim | |
| ☐ | TC-AAI | Boeing 737-82R/W | 35699/2712 | | | |
| ☐ | TC-AAJ | Boeing 737-82R/W | 35702/2810 | ex N1787B | Ece | |
| ☐ | TC-AAK | Boeing 737-8FH/W | 35094/2195 | | | |
| ☐ | TC-AAL | Boeing 737-82R/W | 35984/2937 | ex N1786B | | |
| ☐ | TC-AAN | Boeing 737-82R/W | 38173/3011 | | | |
| ☐ | TC-AAO | Boeing 737-86N/W | 28619/534 | ex EI-DJU | | |
| ☐ | TC-AAR | Boeing 737-86N/W | 28624/585 | ex EI-DGZ | | |
| ☐ | TC-AAS | Boeing 737-82R/W | 40871/3212 | ex N1787B | | |
| ☐ | TC-AAT | Boeing 737-82R/W | 40872/3227 | ex N1786B | | |
| ☐ | TC-AAU | Boeing 737-882R/W | 40873/3238 | | | ♦ |
| ☐ | TC-AAV | Boeing 737-82R/W | 40696/3295 | ex N1787B | | |
| ☐ | TC-AAY | Boeing 737-82R/W | 40874/3316 | | | |
| ☐ | TC-AAZ | Boeing 737-82R/W | 40875/3325 | | | |
| ☐ | TC-ABP | Boeing 737-82R/W | 40876/3326 | ex N1786B | | |
| ☐ | TC-ACP | Boeing 737-82R/W | 40697/3354 | | | |
| ☐ | TC-ADP | Boeing 737-82R/W | 40720/3526 | | | ♦ |
| ☐ | TC-AEP | Boeing 737-82R/W | 40724/3563 | | | ♦ |
| ☐ | TC-AGP | Boeing 737-82R/W | 40728/3579 | | | ♦ |
| ☐ | TC-AHP | Boeing 737-82R/W | 40721/3600 | ex N1787B | Iram Naz | ♦ |
| ☐ | TC-AIP | Boeing 737-82R/W | 40877/3602 | ex N1787B | Hante | ♦ |
| ☐ | TC-AIS | Boeing 737-82R/W | 38174/3857 | | Sevde Nil D | ♦ |
| ☐ | TC-AJP | Boeing 737-82R/W | 35983/3617 | ex N1787B | Masal | ♦ |
| ☐ | TC-AMP | Boeing 737-82R/W | 40723/3622 | | Nil | ♦ |
| ☐ | TC-ANP | Boeing 737-82R/W | 40722/3637 | | Sena | ♦ |
| ☐ | TC-APH | Boeing 737-8S3/W | 29250/792 | ex N1787B | | |
| ☐ | TC-ARP | Boeing 737-82R/W | 40272/3652 | | Nehir | |
| ☐ | TC-ASP | Boeing 737-82R/W | 40011/3662 | | Ipek | ♦ |
| ☐ | TC-AVP | Boeing 737-82R/W | 38175/3877 | | Yagmur A | ♦ |
| ☐ | TC-AZP | Boeign 737-82R/W | 38176/3896 | | Maya | ♦ |
| ☐ | TC-CCP | Boeing 737-86J/W | 37746/3109 | ex D-ABKG | | ♦ |
| ☐ | TC-CPA | Boeing 737-82R/W | 40725/3909 | | Sena | ♦ |
| ☐ | TC-CPB | Boeing 737-82R/W | 38177/3947 | | Doğa | ♦ |
| ☐ | TC-CPC | Boeing 737-82R/W | 408783972 | | Öykü | ♦ |
| ☐ | TC-CPE | Boeing 737-82R/W | 38178/ | | | o/o♦ |
| | | | | | | |
| ☐ | TC-APD | Boeing 737-42R | 29107/2997 | | | |
| ☐ | TC-APR | Boeing 737-4Y0 | 24685/1859 | ex EC-GXR | | |

## REDSTAR AVIATION — Istanbul-Sabiha Gokcen (SAW)

| | | | | | |
|---|---|---|---|---|---|
| ☐ | TC-RSA | British Aerospace Jetstream 32EP | 986 | ex G-CBDA | |

## SAGA AIRLINES — (SGX) — Istanbul-Ataturk (IST)

| | | | | | | |
|---|---|---|---|---|---|---|
| ☐ | TC-SGB | Airbus A310-304 | 562 | ex N351LF | Akçaabat | >AFG |
| ☐ | TC-SGC | Airbus A310-304 | 519 | ex VT-EVI | Fethiya Kolot | |

## SEA BIRD AIRLINES

| | | | | | |
|---|---|---|---|---|---|
| ☐ | TC-SBA | de Havilland DHC-6 Twin Otter 300 | 382 | ex C-FUGT | FP♦ |

## SKY AIRLINES — Antalya Bird (SHY) — Antalya (AYT)

| | | | | | |
|---|---|---|---|---|---|
| ☐ | TC-SKD | Boeing 737-4Q8 | 25372/2280 | ex TC-JDI | Black Eagle |
| ☐ | TC-SKE | Boeing 737-4Q8 | 25163/2264 | ex VH-TJV | Milky Way |
| ☐ | TC-SKG | Boeing 737-4Q8 | 25371/2195 | ex SX-BKK | Gold |
| ☐ | TC-SKH | Boeing 737-8BK | 29644/2231 | ex N1786B | Rainbow |
| ☐ | TC-SKI | Airbus A321-231 | 0811 | ex D-ALAA | Antalya |
| ☐ | TC-SKJ | Airbus A320-211 | 0138 | ex N138LC | Jupiter |
| ☐ | TC-SKK | Airbus A320-211 | 0148 | ex N148LC | Side |
| ☐ | TC-SKM | Boeing 737-49R | 28882/2845 | ex OK-CGI | |
| ☐ | TC-SKN | Boeing 737-94XER/W | 36086/2910 | ex N1787B | Alanya Smile in the Sky |
| ☐ | TC-SKP | Boeing 737-94XER/W | 36087/2928 | ex N1786B | Kapadokya |
| ☐ | TC-SKR | Boeing 737-83N/W | 32576/875 | ex PR-GIC | |
| ☐ | TC-SKS | Boeing 737-83N/W | 32348/933 | ex PR-GIB | |
| ☐ | TC-SKT | Airbus A320-232 | 1194 | ex G-MEDE | |

## SUNEXPRESS — Sunexpress (XQ/SXS) — Antalya (AYT)

| | | | | | |
|---|---|---|---|---|---|
| ☐ | TC-SAD | Boeing 737-76N/W | 34754/2172 | ex TC-JKG | op for Anadolu<THY♦ |
| ☐ | TC-SNE | Boeing 737-8HX/W | 29684/2539 | ex N1786B | |
| ☐ | TC-SNF | Boeing 737-8HC/W | 36529/2566 | ex N1787B | |
| ☐ | TC-SNG | Boeing 737-8HC/W | 36530/2622 | ex N1786B | |
| ☐ | TC-SNH | Boeing 737-8FH/W | 30826/1732 | ex EI-ECD | |
| ☐ | TC-SNI | Boeing 737-8FH/W | 29671/1700 | ex EI-DMZ | |
| ☐ | TC-SNJ | Boeing 737-86J/W | 30827/1632 | ex D-ABBO | |
| ☐ | TC-SNL | Boeing 737-86N/W | 34251/1817 | ex EC-JKZ | |
| ☐ | TC-SNM | Boeing 737-8BK/W | 33023/1682 | ex VT-AXB | |
| ☐ | TC-SNN | Boeing 737-8HC/W | 40775/3250 | | |
| ☐ | TC-SNO | Boeing 737-8HC/W | 40776/3273 | ex N1795B | |
| ☐ | TC-SNP | Boeing 737-8HC/W | 40777/3320 | ex N1786B | |
| ☐ | TC-SNR | Boeing 737-8HC/W | 40754/3352 | ex N1795B | |
| ☐ | TC-SNT | Boeing 737-8HC/W | 40755/3400 | ex N1786B | |
| ☐ | TC-SNU | Boeing 737-8HC/W | 40756/3457 | ex N1796B | |
| ☐ | TC-SUG | Boeing 737-8CX/W | 32365/1209 | | >SXD |
| ☐ | TC-SUH | Boeing 737-8CX/W | 32366/1235 | | >SXD |
| ☐ | TC-SUI | Boeing 737-8CX/W | 32367/1253 | | |
| ☐ | TC-SUJ | Boeing 737-8CX/W | 32368/1289 | | >SXD |
| ☐ | TC-SUL | Boeing 737-85F/W | 28822/166 | ex SE-DVO | |
| ☐ | TC-SUM | Boeing 737-85F/W | 28826/238 | ex SE-DVR | |
| ☐ | TC-SUO | Boeing 737-86Q/W | 30272/824 | ex VH-VOE | |
| ☐ | TC-SUU | Boeing 737-86Q/W | 30274/845 | ex VH-VOF | |
| ☐ | TC-SUV | Boeing 737-86N/W | 30807/829 | ex N50089 | |
| ☐ | TC-SUY | Boeing 737-86N/W | 30806/790 | ex G-OXLB | |
| ☐ | TC-SUZ | Boeing 737-8HXS/W | 29649/2515 | ex N1786B | |
| ☐ | TC-SAC | Boeing 737-76N/W | 32684/1889 | ex TC-JKF | op for Anadolu<THY |

## TAILWIND AIRLINES — (TI/TWI)

| | | | | | |
|---|---|---|---|---|---|
| ☐ | TC-TLA | Boeing 737-4Q8 | 25107/2526 | ex N774AS | |
| ☐ | TC-TLB | Boeing 737-4Q8 | 25108/2551 | ex N775AS | |
| ☐ | TC-TLC | Boeing 737-4Q8 | 25112/2638 | ex N780AS | Capt Z Kllic |
| ☐ | TC-TLD | Boeing 737-4Q8 | 28199/2826 | ex N784AS | |
| ☐ | TC-TLE | Boeing 737-4Q8 | 27628/2858 | ex N785AS | |

## TARHAN AIR — (TTH) — Istanbul-Ataturk (IST)

AOC revoked Mar08

## THK - TURK HAVA KURUMU — Hur Kus (THK) — Ankara (ANK)

| | | | | | |
|---|---|---|---|---|---|
| ☐ | TC-TKH | Canadair CL215 | 1104 | ex C-GOFR | ♦ |
| ☐ | TC-TKK | Canadair CL215 | 1030 | ex C-FTUW | ♦ |
| ☐ | TC-TKL | Canadair CL215 | 1011 | ex C-FTUU | ♦ |
| ☐ | TC-TKM | Canadair CL215 | 1097 | ex I-SRMD | ♦ |
| ☐ | TC-TKV | Canadair CL215 | 1072 | ex I-CFST | ♦ |
| ☐ | TC-TKY | Canadair CL215 | 1108 | ex I-CFSZ | ♦ |
| ☐ | TC-TKZ | Canadair CL215 | 1076 | ex I-SRMC | ♦ |
| ☐ | TC-CAU | Cessna 208 Caravan I | 20800248 | ex N1123X | |
| ☐ | TC-CAV | Cessna 208 Caravan I | 20800256 | ex N1249T | |
| ☐ | TC-CAY | Cessna 402B | 402B1073 | ex 10007 | |
| ☐ | TC-CAZ | Cessna 421C Golden Eagle II | 421C0089 | ex 10006 | |
| ☐ | TC-FAH | Piper PA-42-720 Cheyenne IIIA | 42-5501033 | | |
| ☐ | TC-THK | Piper PA-42-720 Cheyenne IIIA | 42-5501031 | ex TC-FAG | |

| | | | | | |
|---|---|---|---|---|---|
| ☐ | TC-ZTP | Cessna 402B | 402B0412 | ex N69289 | |
| ☐ | TC-ZVJ | Cessna 402B | 402B1084 | ex N1906G | |

| | | |
|---|---|---|
| **TURKISH AIRLINES** | **Turkair (TK/THY)** | **Istanbul-Ataturk (IST)** |

Member of Star Alliance

| | | | | | | |
|---|---|---|---|---|---|---|
| ☐ | TC-JLM | Airbus A319-132 | 2738 | ex D-AVXN | Sinop | |
| ☐ | TC-JLN | Airbus A319-132 | 2739 | ex D-AVXO | Karabuk | |
| ☐ | TC-JLO | Airbus A319-132 | 2631 | ex TC-OGU | Ahlat | |
| ☐ | TC-JLP | Airbus A319-132 | 2655 | ex TC-OGV | Koycegiz | |
| ☐ | TC-JLR | Airbus A319-132 | 3142 | ex SX-OAV | | [IST] |
| ☐ | TC-JLS | Airbus A319-132 | 4629 | ex D-AVWM | Salihli | ♦ |
| ☐ | TC-JLT | Airbus A319-132 | 4665 | ex D-AVYLAdilcevaz | | ♦ |
| ☐ | TC-JLU | Airbus A319-132 | 4695 | ex D-AVYQ | | ♦ |
| ☐ | TC-JLV | Airbus A319-132 | 4755 | ex D-AVYC | | ♦ |
| ☐ | TC-JLY | Airbus A319-132 | 4774 | ex D-AVYK | | ♦ |
| ☐ | TC-JLZ | Airbus A319-132 | 4790 | ex D-AVYY | | ♦ |
| | | | | | | |
| ☐ | TC-JLJ | Airbus A320-232 | 1856 | ex EI-DIV | Sirnak | |
| ☐ | TC-JLK | Airbus A320-232 | 1909 | ex EI-DIW | Kirklareli | |
| ☐ | TC-JLL | Airbus A320-232 | 1956 | ex EI-DIX | Duzce | |
| ☐ | TC-JPA | Airbus A320-232 | 2609 | ex F-WWBU | Mus | |
| ☐ | TC-JPB | Airbus A320-232 | 2626 | ex F-WWDS | Rize | |
| ☐ | TC-JPC | Airbus A320-232 | 2928 | ex F-WWDZ | Hasankeyf | |
| ☐ | TC-JPD | Airbus A320-232 | 2934 | ex F-WWIC | Isparta | |
| ☐ | TC-JPE | Airbus A320-232 | 2941 | ex F-WWIF | Gumushane | |
| ☐ | TC-JPF | Airbus A320-232 | 2984 | ex F-WWIE | Yozgat | |
| ☐ | TC-JPG | Airbus A320-232 | 3010 | ex F-WWBJ | Osmaniye | |
| ☐ | TC-JPH | Airbus A320-232 | 3185 | ex F-WWDX | Kars | |
| ☐ | TC-JPI | Airbus A320-232 | 3208 | ex F-WWIS | Dogubevazit | |
| ☐ | TC-JPJ | Airbus A320-232 | 3239 | ex F-WWBK | Edremit | |
| ☐ | TC-JPK | Airbus A320-232 | 3257 | ex F-WWDI | Erdek | |
| ☐ | TC-JPL | Airbus A320-232 | 3303 | ex F-WWIJ | Göreme | |
| ☐ | TC-JPM | Airbus A320-232 | 3341 | ex F-WWBN | Harput | |
| ☐ | TC-JPN | Airbus A320-232 | 3558 | ex F-WWBE | Sarikamis | |
| ☐ | TC-JPO | Airbus A320-232 | 3567 | ex F-WWBP | Kemer | |
| ☐ | TC-JPP | Airbus A320-232 | 3603 | ex F-WWDL | Harran | |
| ☐ | TC-JPR | Airbus A320-232 | 3654 | ex F-WWDR | Kusadasi | |
| ☐ | TC-JPS | Airbus A320-232 | 3718 | ex F-WWBK | Adilcevaz | |
| ☐ | TC-JPT | Airbus A320-232 | 3719 | ex D-AVVC | Urgup | |
| ☐ | TC-JPU | Airbus A320-214 | 3896 | ex A9C-BAT | Salihli | |
| ☐ | TC-JPV | Airbus A320-214 | 3931 | ex A9C-BAS | Sisli | |
| ☐ | TC-JPY | Airbus A320-214 | 3949 | ex A9C-BAP | Beykoz | |
| | | | | | | |
| ☐ | TC-JMC | Airbus A321-231 | 0806 | ex G-MIDA | Aksaray | |
| ☐ | TC-JMD | Airbus A321-231 | 0810 | ex G-MIDF | Cankiri | |
| ☐ | TC-JMH | Airbus A321-231 | 3637 | ex D-AVZM | Didim | |
| ☐ | TC-JMI | Airbus A321-231 | 3673 | ex D-AVZZ | Milas | |
| ☐ | TC-JMJ | Airbus A321-231 | 3688 | ex D-AZAG | Tekirdag | |
| ☐ | TC-JMK | Airbus A321-231 | 3738 | ex D-AZAK | Uskudar | |
| ☐ | TC-JML | Airbus A321-231 | 3382 | ex G-TTIG | Eminonu | |
| ☐ | TC-JRA | Airbus A321-231 | 2823 | ex D-AVZE | Kutahya | |
| ☐ | TC-JRB | Airbus A321-231 | 2868 | ex D-AVZI | Sanliurfa | |
| ☐ | TC-JRC | Airbus A321-231 | 2999 | ex D-AVZV | Sakarya | |
| ☐ | TC-JRD | Airbus A321-231 | 3015 | ex D-AVZX | Balikesir | |
| ☐ | TC-JRE | Airbus A321-231 | 3126 | ex D-AVZS | Trabzon | |
| ☐ | TC-JRF | Airbus A321-231 | 3207 | ex D-AVZY | Fethiye | |
| ☐ | TC-JRG | Airbus A321-231 | 3283 | ex D-AVZZ | Finike | |
| ☐ | TC-JRH | Airbus A321-231 | 3350 | ex D-AVZI | Yalova | |
| ☐ | TC-JRI | Airbus A321-231 | 3405 | ex D-AVZS | Adiyaman | |
| ☐ | TC-JRJ | Airbus A321-231 | 3429 | ex D-AVZC | Corum | |
| ☐ | TC-JRK | Airbus A321-231 | 3525 | ex D-AVZY | Batman | |
| ☐ | TC-JRL | Airbus A321-231 | 3539 | ex D-AVZB | Tarsus | |
| ☐ | TC-JRM | Airbus A321-231 | 4643 | ex D-AZAU | Afyonkarahisar | ♦ |
| ☐ | TC-JRN | Airbus A321-231 | 4654 | ex D-AZAC | Sariyer | ♦ |
| ☐ | TC-JRO | Airbus A321-231 | 4682 | ex D-AZAI | | ♦ |
| ☐ | TC-JRP | Airbus A321-231 | 4698 | ex D-AZAP | | ♦ |
| ☐ | TC-JRR | Airbus A321-231 | 4706 | ex D-AZAR | | ♦ |
| ☐ | TC-JRS | Airbus A321-231 | 4761 | ex D-AVZJ | | ♦ |
| ☐ | TC-JRT | Airbus A321-231 | 4779 | ex D-AVZL | | ♦ |
| ☐ | TC-JRU | Airbus A321-231 | 4788 | ex D-AVZB | | ♦ |
| ☐ | TC-JRV | Airbus A321-231 | 5077 | ex D-AVZO | | ♦ |
| ☐ | TC-JRY | Airbus A321-231 | 5083 | ex D-AZAT | | ♦ |
| ☐ | TC-JRZ | Airbus A321-231 | 5118 | ex D-AZAW | | o/o♦ |
| ☐ | TC-JSA | Airbus A321-231 | 5154 | ex D-AVZE | | o/o♦ |
| ☐ | TC-JSC | Airbus A321-231 | 5254 | ex | | o/o♦ |
| | | | | | | |
| ☐ | TC-JDO | Airbus A330-223F | 1004 | ex F-WWYE | Meric | |
| ☐ | TC-JDP | Airbus A330-223F | 1092 | ex F-WWKS | Firat | ♦ |
| ☐ | TC-JDR | Airbus A330-243F | 1344 | ex F-WW | | o/o♦ |
| ☐ | TC-JNA | Airbus A330-203 | 697 | ex F-WWYS | Gaziantep | |

| | | | | | | |
|---|---|---|---|---|---|---|
| ☐ | TC-JNB | Airbus A330-203 | 704 | ex F-WWKF | Konya | |
| ☐ | TC-JNC | Airbus A330-203 | 742 | ex F-WWYF | Bursa | |
| ☐ | TC-JND | Airbus A330-203 | 754 | ex F-WWYL | Antalya | |
| ☐ | TC-JNE | Airbus A330-203 | 774 | ex F-WWKG | Kayseri | |
| ☐ | TC-JNF | Airbus A330-202 | 463 | ex A7-AFN | Canakkale | |
| ☐ | TC-JNG | Airbus A330-202 | 504 | ex A7-AFO | Esklsehir | |
| | | | | | | |
| ☐ | TC-JNH | Airbus A330-343E | 1150 | ex F-WWYM | Topkapi | |
| ☐ | TC-JNI | Airbus A330-343E | 1160 | ex F-WWKH | Konak | |
| ☐ | TC-JNJ | Airbus A330-343E | 1170 | ex F-WWKZ | Kapadokya | |
| ☐ | TC-JNK | Airbus A330-343E | 1172 | ex F-WWYK | Sanliurfa | |
| ☐ | TC-JNL | Airbus A330-343E | 1204 | ex F-WWYF | | |
| ☐ | TC-JNM | Airbus A330-343E | 1212 | ex F-WWYY | | ♦ |
| ☐ | TC-JNN | Airbus A330-343E | 1228 | ex F-WWKZ | | ♦ |
| ☐ | TC-JNO | Airbus A330-343E | 1298 | ex F-WWKG | Boğaziçi | ♦ |
| ☐ | TC-JNP | Airbus A330-343E | 1307 | ex F-WWYX | | o/o♦ |
| ☐ | TC-JNR | Airbus A330-343E | 1311 | ex F-WWKY | | o/o♦ |
| | | | | | | |
| ☐ | TC-JDJ | Airbus A340-311 | 023 | ex F-WWJN | Istanbul | |
| ☐ | TC-JDK | Airbus A340-311 | 025 | ex F-WWJP | Isparta | |
| ☐ | TC-JDL | Airbus A340-311 | 057 | ex F-WWJF | Ankara | |
| ☐ | TC-JDM | Airbus A340-311 | 115 | ex F-WWJN | Izmir | |
| ☐ | TC-JDN | Airbus A340-313X | 180 | ex F-WWJU | Adana | |
| ☐ | TC-JIH | Airbus A340-313X | 270 | ex F-WWJP | Kocaeli | |
| ☐ | TC-JII | Airbus A340-313X | 331 | ex F-WWJQ | Aydin | |
| ☐ | TC-JIJ | Airbus A340-313X | 216 | ex 6Y-JMM | Selcuk | |
| ☐ | TC-JIK | Airbus A340-313X | 257 | ex 6Y-JMP | Kas | wfs |
| | | | | | | |
| ☐ | TC-JFC | Boeing 737-8F2/W | 29765/80 | | Diyarbakir | |
| ☐ | TC-JFD | Boeing 737-8F2/W | 29766/87 | | Artvin | |
| ☐ | TC-JFE | Boeing 737-8F2/W | 29767/95 | ex N1786B | Hatay | |
| ☐ | TC-JFF | Boeing 737-8F2/W | 29768/99 | ex N1786B | Afyonkarahisar | |
| ☐ | TC-JFG | Boeing 737-8F2/W | 29769/102 | ex N1787B | Mardin | |
| ☐ | TC-JFH | Boeing 737-8F2/W | 29770/114 | ex N1787B | Igdir | |
| ☐ | TC-JFI | Boeing 737-8F2/W | 29771/228 | ex N1795B | Sivas | |
| ☐ | TC-JFJ | Boeing 737-8F2/W | 29772/242 | ex N1786B | Agri | |
| ☐ | TC-JFL | Boeing 737-8F2/W | 29774/269 | ex N1786B | Ordu | |
| ☐ | TC-JFM | Boeing 737-8F2/W | 29775/279 | ex N1786B | Nigde | |
| ☐ | TC-JFN | Boeing 737-8F2/W | 29776/308 | | Bitlis | |
| ☐ | TC-JFO | Boeing 737-8F2/W | 29777/309 | | Batman | |
| ☐ | TC-JFP | Boeing 737-8F2/W | 29778/349 | ex N1787B | Amasya | |
| ☐ | TC-JFR | Boeing 737-8F2/W | 29779/370 | ex N1786B | Giresun | |
| ☐ | TC-JFT | Boeing 737-8F2/W | 29780/454 | ex N1787B | Kastamonu | |
| ☐ | TC-JFU | Boeing 737-8F2/W | 29781/461 | ex N1795B | Elazig | |
| ☐ | TC-JFV | Boeing 737-8F2/W | 29782/490 | ex N1786B | Tuncell | |
| ☐ | TC-JFY | Boeing 737-8F2/W | 29783/497 | ex N1786B | Manisa | |
| ☐ | TC-JFZ | Boeing 737-8F2/W | 29784/539 | | Bolu | |
| ☐ | TC-JGA | Boeing 737-8F2/W | 29785/544 | ex N1786B | Malatya | |
| ☐ | TC-JGB | Boeing 737-8F2/W | 29786/566 | ex N1786B | Foca | |
| ☐ | TC-JGD | Boeing 737-8F2/W | 29788/791 | ex N1787B | Nevsehir | |
| ☐ | TC-JGG | Boeing 737-8F2/W | 34405/1828 | | Erzincan | |
| ☐ | TC-JGH | Boeing 737-8F2/W | 34406/1852 | | Tokat | |
| ☐ | TC-JGI | Boeing 737-8F2/W | 34407/1873 | | Siirt | |
| ☐ | TC-JGP | Boeing 737-8F2/W | 34414/1978 | ex N1786B | Bartin | |
| ☐ | TC-JGR | Boeing 737-8F2/W | 34415/1988 | ex N1786B | Usak | |
| ☐ | TC-JGS | Boeing 737-8F2/W | 34416/1996 | | Kahramanmaras | |
| ☐ | TC-JGT | Boeing 737-8F2/W | 34417/2009 | | Avanos | |
| ☐ | TC-JGU | Boeing 737-8F2/W | 34418/2012 | | Bodrum | |
| ☐ | TC-JGV | Boeing 737-8F2/W | 34419/2021 | ex N60668 | Cesme | |
| ☐ | TC-JGY | Boeing 737-8F2/W | 35738/2592 | | Manavgat | |
| ☐ | TC-JGZ | Boeing 737-8F2/W | 35739/2654 | | Midyat | |
| ☐ | TC-JHA | Boeing 737-8F2/W | 35740/2673 | | Mudanya | |
| ☐ | TC-JHB | Boeing 737-8F2/W | 35741/2685 | | Safranbolu | |
| ☐ | TC-JHC | Boeing 737-8F2/W | 35742/2708 | | Iskenderun | |
| ☐ | TC-JHD | Boeing 737-8F2/W | 35743/2717 | | Serik | |
| ☐ | TC-JHE | Boeing 737-8F2/W | 357442733 | ex N1786B | Burhanlye | |
| ☐ | TC-JHF | Boeing 737-8F2/W | 35745/2748 | | Ayvalik | |
| ☐ | TC-JHK | Boeing 737-8F2/W | 40975/3824 | | Yesilköy | ♦ |
| ☐ | TC-JHL | Boeing 737-8F2/W | 40976/3870 | | Unye | ♦ |
| ☐ | TC-JHM | Boeing 737-8F2/W | 40980 | | | o/o♦ |
| ☐ | TC-JKG | Boeing 737-76N/W | 34754/2172 | ex OM-NGH | | >SXS♦ |
| ☐ | TC- | Boeing 737-8F2/W | | | | o/o |
| ☐ | TC- | Boeing 737-8F2/W | | | | |
| | | | | | | |
| ☐ | TC-JYA | Boeing 737-9F2ER/W | 40973/3669 | ex N973TK | Amasya | ♦ |
| ☐ | TC-JYB | Boeing 737-9F2ER/W | 40974/3693 | ex N974TK | Denizii | ♦ |
| ☐ | TC-JYC | Boeing 737-9FRER/W | 40977 | ex N977TK | | o/o♦ |
| ☐ | TC-JYD | Boeing 737-9F2ER/W | 40978 | ex N978TK | | o/o♦ |
| ☐ | TC-JYE | Boeing 737-9F2ER/W | 40979 | ex N981TK | | o/o♦ |
| ☐ | TC- | Boeing 737-9F2ER/W | 40982 | ex N982TK | | o/o♦ |
| ☐ | TC- | Boeing 737-9F2ER/W | 40983 | ex N983TK | | o/o♦ |
| ☐ | TC- | Boeing 737-9F2ER/W | 40984 | ex N984TK | | o/o♦ |
| ☐ | TC- | Boeing 737-9F2ER/W | 40985 | ex N985TK | | o/o♦ |

482

| | | | | | | |
|---|---|---|---|---|---|---|
| ☐ | TC- | Boeing 737-9F2ER/W | 40986 | ex N986TK | | o/o♦ |
| ☐ | TC-JJE | Boeing 777-3F2ER | 40707/895 | ex N5020K | Dolmabahce | |
| ☐ | TC-JJF | Boeing 777-3F2ER | 40708/899 | ex N6009F | Beylerbeyi | |
| ☐ | TC-JJG | Boeing 777-3F2ER | 40791/903 | ex N50281 | Yildiz | |
| ☐ | TC-JJH | Boeing 777-3F2ER | 40792/906 | ex N5016R | Rumeli | |
| ☐ | TC-JJI | Boeing 777-3F2ER | 40709/909 | ex N5020K | Ege | |
| ☐ | TC-JJJ | Boeing 777-3F2ER | 40710/913 | | | ♦ |
| ☐ | TC-JJK | Boeing 777-3F2ER | 40711/916 | | | ♦ |
| ☐ | TC-JJL | Boeing 777-3F2ER | 40793/919 | | | ♦ |
| ☐ | TC-JJM | Boeing 777-3F2ER | 40794/923 | | | ♦ |
| ☐ | TC-JJN | Boeing 777-3F2ER | 40795/940 | | Anadolu | ♦ |
| ☐ | TC-JJO | Boeing 777-3F2ER | 40796/953 | | Istanbul | ♦ |
| ☐ | TC-JJP | Boeing 777-3F2ER | 40797/959 | | | ♦ |
| ☐ | TC-JCT | Airbus A310-304F | 502 | ex TF-ELE | Samsun | |
| ☐ | TC-JCV | Airbus A310-304F | 476 | ex F-WWCT | Aras | |
| ☐ | TC-JCY | Airbus A310-304F | 478 | ex F-WWCX | Coruh | |
| ☐ | TC-JCZ | Airbus A310-304F | 480 | ex F-WWCZ | Ergene | |
| ☐ | TC-JDG | Boeing 737-4Y0 | 25181/2203 | | Marmaris | |
| ☐ | TC-JDH | Boeing 737-4Y0 | 25184/2227 | | Amasra | |
| ☐ | TC-JDT | Boeing 737-4Y0 | 25261/2258 | ex N600SK | Alanya | ♦ |
| ☐ | TC-JKJ | Boeing 737-752/W | 34297/1808 | ex N297MD | | |
| ☐ | TC-JKK | Boeing 737-752/W | 34298/1812 | ex N298MD | | |
| ☐ | TC-JKN | Boeing 737-752/W | 34299/1829 | ex N342CT | | |
| ☐ | TC-JKO | Boeing 737-752/W | 34300/1848 | ex N343CT | | |

| TURKUAZ AIR | (TRK) | Istanbul-Ataturk (IST) |
|---|---|---|

Ceased ops 2011

| UNSPED PAKET SERVISI/ UPS | Unsped (UNS) | Istanbul-Ataturk (IST) |
|---|---|---|

| | | | | | | |
|---|---|---|---|---|---|---|
| ☐ | TC-APS | Cessna 340A | 340A0247 | ex N3964G | | |
| ☐ | TC-UPS | Swearingen SA.226TC Merlin IVA | AT-044 | ex TC-BPS | Beril | op for UPS |

| ULS CARGO | (GO/KZU) | Istanbul-Ataturk (IST) |
|---|---|---|

| | | | | | |
|---|---|---|---|---|---|
| ☐ | TC-ABK | Airbus A300B4-203 | 101 | ex N59101 | Adiyaman |
| ☐ | TC-AGK | Airbus A300B4-203F | 117 | ex G-CEXH | Siirt 5 |
| ☐ | TC-KZV | Airbus A300B4-103F | 041 | ex PH-EAN | Siirt 4 |
| ☐ | TC-LER | Airbus A310-304F | 646 | ex A6-EFA | |
| ☐ | TC-SGM | Airbus A310-304F | 592 | ex A6-EFB | |
| ☐ | TC-VEL | Airbus A310-304F | 622 | ex A6-EFC | |

## TF- ICELAND (Republic of Iceland)

| AIR ATLANTA | Atlanta (CC/ABD) | Keflavik (KEF) |
|---|---|---|

| | | | | | | |
|---|---|---|---|---|---|---|
| ☐ | TF-AAC | Boeing 747-481 | 29262/1199 | ex N262SG | | [KUL]♦ |
| ☐ | TF-AAD | Boeing 747-4H6 | 28426/1130 | ex HZ-AWA2 | | [KUL]♦ |
| ☐ | TF-AEE | Boeing 747-4H6 | 27672/1091 | ex 9M-MPI | | [KUL]♦ |
| ☐ | TF-AMI | Boeing 747-412 (SF) | 27066/940 | ex N706RB | | >SVA |
| ☐ | TF-AMS | Boeing 747-481 | 24920/832 | ex JA8096 | | >SVA |
| ☐ | TF-AMT | Boeing 747-481 | 25135/863 | ex JA8097 | | >SVA |
| ☐ | TF-AMU | Boeing 747-48EF | 27603/1210 | ex HL7426 | | >SVA |
| ☐ | TF-AMV | Boeing 747-412 | 28022/1082 | ex 9V-SPI | | >SVA |
| ☐ | TF-AMX | Boeing 747-441 | 24957/971 | ex ZK-SUI | | >SVA♦ |
| ☐ | TF-AMY | Boeing 747-446 | 25260/876 | ex N269AS | | >BBC♦ |
| ☐ | TF-AMZ | Boeing 747-446 | 24423/758 | ex N344AS | | ♦ |
| ☐ | TF-AAA | Boeing 747-236B (SCD) | 22442/526 | ex N361FC | | |
| ☐ | TF-AAB | Boeing 747-236M | 22304/502 | ex N362FM | | ♦ |
| ☐ | TF-AME | Boeing 747-312 | 23032/603 | ex F-GSEA | | |
| ☐ | TF-AMJ | Boeing 747-312 | 23030/593 | ex CP-2525 | | [ILM] |
| ☐ | TF-ARJ | Boeing 747-236M | 23735/674 | ex G-BDXN | | |
| ☐ | TF-ATX | Boeing 747-236B (SF) | 23711/672 | ex G-BDXM | | [KUL]♦ |
| ☐ | TF-ELF | Airbus A300B4-622RF | 529 | ex EI-DJN | | >TAY |
| ☐ | TF-ELK | Airbus A300B4-622RF | 557 | ex EI-DGU | | |

| AIR ICELAND | Iceland (NY/FXI) | Akureyri/Reykjavik (AEY/REK) |
|---|---|---|

| | | | | | |
|---|---|---|---|---|---|
| ☐ | TF-JMM | Fokker 50 | 20214 | ex D-AFKM | |
| ☐ | TF-JMN | Fokker 50 | 20223 | ex D-AFKN | |
| ☐ | TF-JMO | Fokker 50 | 20205 | ex D-AFKK | |
| ☐ | TF-JMR | Fokker 50 | 20243 | ex TF-FIR | Asdis |
| ☐ | TF-JMS | Fokker 50 | 20244 | ex TF-FIS | Sigdis |
| ☐ | TF-JMT | Fokker 50 | 20250 | ex TF-FIT | Freydis |

| | | | | | | |
|---|---|---|---|---|---|---|
| ☐ | TF-JMB | de Havilland DHC-8-106 | 337 | ex C-FHYQ | | |
| ☐ | TF-JMK | de Havilland DHC-8-202 | 446 | ex C-GLSG | | ♦ |

## BLUEBIRD CARGO | Blue Cargo (BF/BBD) | Keflavik (KEF)

| | | | | | |
|---|---|---|---|---|---|
| ☐ | TF-BBD | Boeing 737-3Y0 (SF) | 24463/1701 | ex OY-SEE | |
| ☐ | TF-BBE | Boeing 737-36E (SF) | 25256/2123 | ex N314FL | |
| ☐ | TF-BBF | Boeing 737-36E (SF) | 25264/2194 | ex N316FL | |
| ☐ | TF-BBG | Boeing 737-36E (SF) | 25263/2187 | ex N317FL | |
| ☐ | TF-BBI | Boeing 737-301 (SF) | 23260/1146 | ex OO-TNJ | |
| ☐ | TF-TNM | Boeing 737-34S | 29108/2983 | ex N491MS | ♦ |
| | | | | | ♦ |
| ☐ | TF-BBH | Boeing 737-4Y0F | 23865/1582 | ex N865FC | |

## ERNIR AIR | Artic Eagle (FEI) | Reykjavik (REK)

| | | | | | |
|---|---|---|---|---|---|
| ☐ | TF-ORA | British Aerospace Jetstream 32 | 925 | ex OY-SVR | |
| ☐ | TF-ORB | Cessna 207A Stationair 8 II | 20700781 | ex OY-SUC | |
| ☐ | TF-ORC | British Aerospace Jetstream 3212 | 981 | ex OY-SVY | |
| ☐ | TF-ORD | Reims Cessna F406 Caravan II | F406-0047 | ex D-IAAD | |
| ☐ | TF-ORF | Cessna 441 Conquest II | 441-0057 | ex N441AK | |

## ICEJET | Icejet (ICJ)

Ceased ops 2010

## ICELANDAIR | Iceair (FI/ICE) | Keflavik/Reykjavik (KEF/REK)

| | | | | | | |
|---|---|---|---|---|---|---|
| ☐ | TF-FIA | Boeing 757-256/W | 29310/938 | ex EC-HIT | Herdubreid | |
| ☐ | TF-FIC | Boeing 757-23N | 30735/931 | ex M-ABDG | | >ANG |
| ☐ | TF-FID | Boeing 757-23A (PCF) | 24567/257 | ex N757NA | | TNT c/s |
| ☐ | TF-FIE | Boeing 757-23A (PCF) | 24566/255 | ex N566AN | | |
| ☐ | TF-FIG | Boeing 757-23APF | 24456/237 | ex N571CA | | |
| ☐ | TF-FIH | Boeing 757-208 (PCF) | 24739/273 | | Hafdis | |
| ☐ | TF-FII | Boeing 757-208 | 24760/281 | | Fanndis | |
| ☐ | TF-FIJ | Boeing 757-208/W | 25085/368 | ex G-BTEJ | Surtsey | |
| ☐ | TF-FIN | Boeing 757-208/W | 28989/780 | ex N1790B | Eldborg | |
| ☐ | TF-FIO | Boeing 757-208/W | 29436/859 | | Krafla | |
| ☐ | TF-FIP | Boeing 757-208/W | 30423/916 | ex N1006K | Leifur Eriksson | |
| ☐ | TF-FIR | Boeing 757-256/W | 26242/593 | ex EC-FYJ | Askja | |
| ☐ | TF-FIU | Boeing 757-256/W | 26243/603 | ex PH-ITA | Hekla | |
| ☐ | TF-FIV | Boeing 757-208/W | 30424/956 | | Katla | |
| ☐ | TF-FIX | Boeing 757-308/W | 29434/1004 | ex N60659 | Hengill | |
| ☐ | TF-FIY | Boeing 757-256/W | 29312/943 | ex P2-ANB | | ♦ |
| ☐ | TF-FIZ | Boeing 757-256/W | 30052/948 | ex EC-HIX | Keilir | |
| ☐ | TF-ISL | Boeing 757-223/W | 25295/423 | ex N661AA | | ♦ |
| ☐ | TF-LLX | Boeing 757-256 | 29311/940 | ex A6-RKA | Skjaldbreidur | ♦ |
| | | | | | | |
| ☐ | TF-FIB | Boeing 767-383ER | 25365/395 | ex N365SR | | >ANG♦ |
| ☐ | P2-PXV | Boeing 767-341ER | 30341/768 | ex A6-JBD | | >ANG♦ |

## ICELAND EXPRESS | (HW/FHE) | Reykjavik (REK)

| | | | | | |
|---|---|---|---|---|---|
| ☐ | OK-HCA | Airbus A320-214 | 4699 | ex F-WWDO | <HCC♦ |
| ☐ | OK-HCB | Airbus A320-214 | 2180 | ex G-OOPX | <HCC♦ |

## LOFTLEIDIR ICELANDIC

Ops charter flights and ACMI leases using the AOC of its parent, Icelandair, from whom the aircraft are leased

## MYFLUG | Myflug (MYA) | Myvatn (MVA)

| | | | | | |
|---|---|---|---|---|---|
| ☐ | TF-MYF | Cessna U206G Stationair 6 II | U20606614 | ex TC-FAE | |
| ☐ | TF-MYX | Beech B200 Super King Air | BB-1136 | ex LN-VIZ | |
| ☐ | TF-MYY | Cessna U206F Stationair | U20602831 | ex N35960 | |

## NORLANDAIR | | Akureyri (AEY)

| | | | | | |
|---|---|---|---|---|---|
| ☐ | TF-LNB | Beech B200 Super King Air | BB-1689 | ex N225TL | ♦ |
| ☐ | TF-NLC | de Havilland DHC-6 Twin Otter 300 | 413 | ex TF-JMC | |
| ☐ | TF-NLD | de Havilland DHC-6 Twin Otter 300 | 475 | ex TF-JMD | |

## WESTMANN ISLANDS AIRLINES | | Reykjavik (REK)

| | | | | |
|---|---|---|---|---|
| ☐ | TF-VEV | Piper PA-31-350 Chieftain | 31-8152007 | ex N4051Q |
| ☐ | TF-VEY | Partenavia P.68B | 109 | ex G-JVMR |

## TG-    GUATEMALA (Republic of Guatemala)

### AEREO RUTA MAYA / JUNGLE FLYING          (MMG)                    Guatemala City-La Aurora (GUA)

| | | | | |
|---|---|---|---|---|
| ☐ | TG-AGV | LET L-410UVP | 790212 | | ♦ |
| ☐ | TG-AGW | LET L-410UVP | 831137 | | ♦ |
| ☐ | TG-AGY | LET L-410UVP | 851404 | ex HR-IBC | ♦ |
| ☐ | TG-TJD | LET L-410UVP | 851421 | ex CCCP-67517 | ♦ |
| ☐ | TG-TJG | LET L-410UVP-E | 902419 | ex CCCP-67626 | |
| ☐ | TG-TJH | LET L-410UVP-E | 902418 | ex CCCP-67625 | |
| | | | | | |
| ☐ | TG-ARM | Cessna 208B Caravan I | 208B0768 | ex N5152X | |
| ☐ | TG-JCA | de Havilland DHC-6 Twin Otter 300 | 647 | ex N300WH | |
| ☐ | TG-JCC | Embraer EMB.110P2 Bandeirante | 110348 | ex N57DA | |
| ☐ | TC-JCE | DHC-6 Twin Otter 300 | 420 | ex TI-AYQ | ♦ |
| ☐ | TG-JCO | Embraer EMB.110P2 Bandeirante | 110354 | ex N102EB | |
| ☐ | TG-JFT | Cessna 208B Caravan I | 208B0622 | ex N52601 | ♦ |

### AVIATECA                                    (GU/GUG)                     Guatemala City-La Aurora (GUA)

| | | | | | |
|---|---|---|---|---|---|
| ☐ | TG-MYH | ATR 42-300 | 0113 | ex G-ZAPJ | ♦ |
| ☐ | TG-RYM | ATR 42-300 | 0109 | ex G-BUPS | ♦ |
| ☐ | TG-TRA | ATR 42-300 (QC) | 0312 | ex 9A-CTS | |
| ☐ | TG-TRB | ATR 42-300 (QC) | 0317 | ex 9A-CTT | |

### AVCOM                                                                   Guatemala City-La Aurora (GUA)

| | | | | |
|---|---|---|---|---|
| ☐ | TG-JAB | Rockwell 500S Shrike Commander | 3303 | |
| ☐ | TG-JAD | Rockwell 500S Shrike Commander | 3123 | ex N500MT |
| ☐ | TG-JAM | Aero Commander 500B | 1594-205 | ex TG-HIA |
| ☐ | TG-JWC | Rockwell 500S Shrike Commander | 3209 | |

### DHL DE GUATEMELA                          (L3/JOS)                     Guatemala City-La Aurora (GUA)

| | | | | | |
|---|---|---|---|---|---|
| ☐ | TG-DHP | ATR 42-300 | 0052 | ex YV-876C | ops in DHL colours |

### INTER - TRANSPORTES AEREOS INTER     Transpo-Inter (9O/TSP)     Guatemala City-La Aurora (GUA)

| | | | | | |
|---|---|---|---|---|---|
| ☐ | TG-MYH | ATR 42-300 | 0113 | ex G-ZAPJ | >APP |

### MESOAMERICA AIR SERVICES

| | | | | | |
|---|---|---|---|---|---|
| ☐ | TG-JCB | Cessna 404 | 0235 | ex N88719 | ♦ |

### MILLENIUM AVIATION TRANSPORTES

| | | | | | |
|---|---|---|---|---|---|
| ☐ | TG-MMM | Cessna 208 Caravan I | 20800014 | ex YV-1122P | ♦ |

### RACSA (RUTAS AEREAS CENTRO AMERICANOS)          (R6)          Guatemala City-La Aurora (GUA)

| | | | | |
|---|---|---|---|---|
| ☐ | TG-JSG | Nord 262A-30 | 37 | ex HK-3878X |

### TRANSPORTES AEREOS GUATEMALTECOS     (GUM)                    Guatemala City-La Aurora (GUA)

| | | | | | |
|---|---|---|---|---|---|
| ☐ | TG-TAG | Embraer EMB.110P1 Bandeirante | 110441 | ex VH-LNB | |
| ☐ | TG-TAK | Embraer EMB.110P1 Bandeirante | 110405 | ex C-FPCO | |
| ☐ | TG-TAM | Embraer EMB.110P1 Bandeirante | 110220 | ex N101RA | |
| ☐ | TG-TAN | Embraer EMB.110P1 Bandeirante | 110342 | ex C-GPCQ | |
| ☐ | TG-TAY | Embraer EMB.110P1 Bandeirante | 110218 | ex TG-JCU | ♦ |
| | | | | | |
| ☐ | TG-BJO | SAAB SF.340A | 340A-142 | ex N142XJ | |
| ☐ | TC-CAO | British Aerospace Jetstream 31 | 722 | ex TG-TAN | ♦ |
| ☐ | TG-TAA | Piper PA-23-250 Aztec E | 27-7304965 | ex TG-PYM | |
| ☐ | TG-TAB | Bell 206L LongRanger I | 45315 | ex N2775G | |
| ☐ | TG-TAT | Piper PA-31 Turbo Najavo B | 31-826 | ex N7438L | |
| ☐ | TG-TAW | British Aerospace Jetstream 31 | 697 | ex YV216T | ♦ |

## TI-    COSTA RICA (Republic of Costa Rica)

### AEROBELL AIR CHARTER                                        San José-Tobias Bolanos (SYQ)

| | | | | |
|---|---|---|---|---|
| ☐ | TI-BAD | Bell 407 | 53403 | ex N501TH |
| ☐ | TI-BAJ | Cessna 208B Caravan I | 208B1180 | ex N5058J |
| ☐ | TI-BAY | Cessna 208B Caravan I | 208B1218 | |

## AVIONES TAXI AEREO — San José-Juan Santamaria (SJO)

| | | | | | |
|---|---|---|---|---|---|
| ☐ | TI-ABA | Piper PA-23-250 Aztec D | 27-4229 | ex TI-1089C | stored |
| ☐ | TI-ACA | Piper PA-23-250 Aztec C | 27-3515 | ex TI-1058C | |
| ☐ | TI-AST | Piper PA-23-250 Aztec E | 27-7554074 | ex N54763 | |
| ☐ | TI-ATZ | de Havilland DHC-6 Twin Otter 200 | 169 | ex N931MA | |

## NATUREAIR — (5C/NRR) — San José-Tobias Bolanos (SYQ)

| | | | | | |
|---|---|---|---|---|---|
| ☐ | TI-AZC | de Havilland DHC-6 Twin Otter 300 | 433 | ex N239SA | VistaLiner |
| ☐ | TI-BBC | Cessna 208B Caravan I | 208B1210 | ex N183GC | ♦ |
| ☐ | TI-BBQ | de Havilland DHC-6 Twin Otter 300 | 537 | ex N147SA | VistaLiner |
| ☐ | TI-BCS | Dornier 228-212 | 8236 | ex XA-AIR | ♦ |
| ☐ | TI-BDZ | de Havilland DHC-6 Twin Otter 300 | 267 | ex N140SA | ♦ |
| ☐ | TI-BEI | Cessna 208B Caravan I | 208b0900 | ex N181GC | ♦ |
| ☐ | TI-BBN | Beech 65-E90 King Air | LW-250 | ex N321DM | ♦ |

## PARADISE AIR — San José-Tobias Bolanos (SYQ)

| | | | | | |
|---|---|---|---|---|---|
| ☐ | N13AV | Gippsland GA-8 Airvan | GA8-03-028 | ex VH-ARW | |
| ☐ | TI-AZY | Gippsland GA-8 Airvan | GA8-02-021 | ex N530AV | |

## SANSA REGIONAL — Sansa (RZ/LRS) — San José-Juan Santamaria (SJO)

| | | | | | |
|---|---|---|---|---|---|
| ☐ | TI-BAK | Cessna 208B Caravan I | 208B0681 | ex HP-1355APP | |
| ☐ | TI-BAP | Cessna 208B Caravan I | 208B0789 | ex HP-1402APP | |
| ☐ | TI-BAQ | Cessna 208B Caravan I | 208B0790 | ex HP-1403APP | |
| ☐ | TI-BCU | Cessna 208B Caravan I | 208B2045 | ex N23045 | |
| ☐ | TI-BCV | Cessna 208B Caravan I | 208B2050 | ex N5148B | |
| ☐ | TI-BCX | Cessna 208B Caravan I | 208B2058 | ex N5040E | |
| ☐ | TI-BCY | Cessna 208B Caravan I | 208B2064 | ex N5214L | |
| ☐ | TI-BDL | Cessna 208B Caravan I | 208B2097 | ex N208LD | |
| ☐ | TI-BDW | Cessna 208B Caravan I | 208B2176 | ex N208LD | ♦ |
| ☐ | TI-BDX | Cessna 208B Caravan I | 208B2246 | ex N5091J | ♦ |
| ☐ | TI-BDY | Cessna 208B Caravan I | 208B2248 | | ♦ |

## TACA COSTA RICA — TACA CostaRica (TI/TAT) — San José-Juan Santamaria (SJO)

Ops aircraft of TACA International (YS-)

# TJ-    CAMEROON (Republic of Cameroon)

## AIR LEASING CAMEROON — Douala (DLA)

| | | | | | |
|---|---|---|---|---|---|
| ☐ | TJ-ALD | Fokker F.28 Fellowship 4000 | 11226 | ex N477AU | |
| ☐ | TJ-ALG | Fokker F.28 Fellowship 4000 | 11227 | ex N159AD | ♦ |

## CAMAIR — Douala (DLA)

| | | | | | |
|---|---|---|---|---|---|
| ☐ | TJ-CAC | Boeing 767-33AER | 28138/822 | | Le Dja | ♦ |
| ☐ | TJ-QCA | Boeing 737-7BD/W | 34480/1900 | ex N480AC | ♦ |
| ☐ | TJ-QCB | Boeing 737-7BD/W | 33920/1753 | ex N339AG | ♦ |

## CAMEROON AIRLINES — Cam-Air (UY/UYC) — Douala (DLA)

Ceased ops 2009

## CHC CAMEROON — Douala (DLA)

| | | | | | |
|---|---|---|---|---|---|
| ☐ | TJ-ALL | de Havilland DHC-6 Twin Otter 300 | 572 | ex (5B-CJN) | |
| ☐ | TJ-CQD | Aérospatiale SA365N Dauphin 2 | 6062 | ex 5N-ARM | |
| ☐ | TJ-CQE | de Havilland DHC-6 Twin Otter 300 | 662 | ex 5N-EVS | |
| ☐ | TJ-SAF | de Havilland DHC-6 Twin Otter 310 | 529 | ex 9M-MDZ | |
| ☐ | TJ-SAY | Aérospatiale AS365N3 Dauphin 2 | 6571 | ex PH-SLW | ♦ |

## JETFLY AVIATION

| | | | | | |
|---|---|---|---|---|---|
| ☐ | TJ-PHT | Dornier 228-202K | 8143 | ex F-OGOF | ♦ |

## NATIONAL AIRWAYS CAMEROON — (9O) — Yaounde (YAO)

| | | | | | |
|---|---|---|---|---|---|
| ☐ | ZS-NTT | Beech 200 Super King Air | BB-350 | ex N125MS | |

## TL-    CENTRAL AFRICAN REPUBLIC

### CENTRAFRIQUE AIR EXPRESS                      (6C/CAE)

| | | | | | |
|---|---|---|---|---|---|
| ☐ | TL-ADR | Boeing 737-268 | 21281/472 | ex HZ-AGL | wfs |
| ☐ | TL-ADY | Boeing 727-223 (Raisbeck 3) | 21385/1331 | ex YK-DGL | [CAI] |

### MINAIR                              Ormine (OMR)                              Bangui (BGF)

| | | | | | |
|---|---|---|---|---|---|
| ☐ | TL-AEE | LET L-410UVP | | | ♦ |
| ☐ | ZS-TAS | Cessna 208B Caravan I | 208B0378 | ex N208SA | |

## TN-    CONGO BRAZZAVILLE (People's Republic of Congo)

### AERO FRET BUSINESS                                Brazzaville/Pointe Noir (BZV/PNR)

| | | | | | |
|---|---|---|---|---|---|
| ☐ | EX-124 | Antonov An-12BK | 7345403 | ex TN-AGZ | |
| ☐ | TN-AHH | Antonov An-24RV | 47309705 | ex 9XR-DB | |
| ☐ | TN-AIW | Yakovlev Yak-40 | | | ♦ |

### AEROSERVICE                    Congoserv (BF/RSR)    Brazzaville/Pointe Noire (BZV/PNR)

| | | | | | |
|---|---|---|---|---|---|
| ☐ | TN-ACY | Cessna 402B | 402B0810 | ex TR-LTN | |
| ☐ | TN-ADN | Britten-Norman BN-2A-9 Islander | 647 | ex TL-AAQ | |
| ☐ | TN-ADY | Britten-Norman BN-2A-9 Islander | 764 | ex TR-LWL | |
| ☐ | TN-AEK | Cessna 404 Titan II | 404-0132 | ex TR-LXI | |
| ☐ | TN-AFC | CASA C.212-300 | DF72-1-397 | ex D4-CBA | ♦ |
| ☐ | TN-AFD | CASA C.212-300 | DF72-2-398 | ex D4-CBB | |

### AIR CONGO INTERNATIONAL                              Brazzaville (BZV)

| | | | | |
|---|---|---|---|---|
| ☐ | TN-AHL | AVIC 1 MA-60 | 0405 | ex B-762L |
| ☐ | TN-AHN | AVIC 1 MA-60 | 0406 | ex B-800L |
| ☐ | TN-AHO | AVIC 1 MA-60 | 0408 | ex B-800L |

### EQUAFLIGHT SERVICE                    (EKA)                    Brazzaville (BZV)

| | | | | | |
|---|---|---|---|---|---|
| ☐ | F-HEKF | ATR 42-300 | 0173 | ex F-WEKF | <Regourd♦ |
| ☐ | TN-AIJ | Embraer EMB.120ER Brasilia | 120209 | ex F-HBBB | ♦ |
| ☐ | 5Y-EKA | Dornier 228-201 | 8105 | ex LN-AAO | |

### TRANSAIR CONGO            Trans-Congo (Q8/TSG)    Brazzaville/Pointe Noire (BZV/PNR)

| | | | | | |
|---|---|---|---|---|---|
| ☐ | TN-AHI | Boeing 737-247 (Nordam 3) | 23609/1403 | ex N328DL | |
| ☐ | TN-AHK | Boeing 737-2Q8 | 21687/554 | ex EX-132 | |
| ☐ | TN-AHM | LET L-410UVP | 820830 | ex UR-MLD | ♦ |
| ☐ | TN-AIM | Boeing 737-232 (AvAero 3) | 23083/1008 | ex OD-WOL | ♦ |
| ☐ | TN-AIN | Boeing 737-236 | 23172/1091 | ex N843AL | ♦ |
| ☐ | TN-AIZ | Boeing 737-33A | 25138/2153 | ex N552MS | ♦ |

## TR-    GABON (Gabonese Republic)

### AFRIC AVIATION

| | | | | | |
|---|---|---|---|---|---|
| ☐ | TR-LIT | Embraer EMB.120ER Brasilia | 120213 | ex EC-LHY | ♦ |

### AIR SERVICE GABON                    (X7/AGB)                    Libreville (LBV)

Ceased ops Aug10

### AVIREX                    Avirex-Gabon (G2/AVX)                    Libreville (LBV)

| | | | | |
|---|---|---|---|---|
| ☐ | TR-LEB | Cessna 402B | 402B1078 | ex TN-AEZ |
| ☐ | TR-LEI | Piper PA-31 Turbo Navajo B | 31-7300904 | ex N4330B |
| ☐ | TR-LEQ | Reims Cessna F406 Caravan II | F406-0007 | ex LX-LMS |
| ☐ | TR-LFG | Cessna 404 Titan II | 404-0844 | ex TJ-AHY |
| ☐ | TR-LVR | Cessna 207 Skywagon | 20700310 | ex N1710U |

### GABON AIRLINES                    (GY/GBK)                    Libreville (LBV)

| | | | | | |
|---|---|---|---|---|---|
| ☐ | TR-LHP | Boeing 767-222 | 21877/46 | ex N617UA | [ADD] |
| ☐ | TR-LHQ | Boeing 767-222 | 21878/48 | ex N618UA | |
| ☐ | TR-LSU | Fokker -28 Fellowship 2000 | 11081 | | ♦ |

## JETEXPRESS (G2/VXG)

| | | | | |
|---|---|---|---|---|
| ☐ 5Y-TAZ | Douglas DC-9-32 | 47198/302 | ex TR-LHG | >PNF♦ |

## LA NATIONALE — Libreville (LBV)

| | | | | |
|---|---|---|---|---|
| ☐ ZS-DOC | Dornier 228-202 | 8104 | ex MAAW-R1 | |

## MESOAMERICA AIR SERVICE

| | | | | |
|---|---|---|---|---|
| ☐ TR-AGV | LET L-410UVP | 790212 | ex TR-AGZ | ♦ |

## NOUVELLES AIR AFFAIRES GABON — Nouvelle Affaires (NVS) — Libreville (LBV)

| | | | | |
|---|---|---|---|---|
| ☐ TR-CLB | de Havilland DHC-8Q-314 | 545 | ex D-BDTM | |
| ☐ TR-LBV | Beech 1900D | UE-321 | ex ZS-OCX | |
| ☐ TR-LFO | Beech 1900D | UE-313 | ex ZS-OCV | ♦ |
| ☐ TR-LFX | Cessna 208B Caravan I | 208B0796 | ex N99FX | |
| ☐ TR-LGQ | Fokker 100 | 11424 | ex F-GIOH | |

## SCD AVIATION / AFRICA CONNECTION

| | | | | |
|---|---|---|---|---|
| ☐ TR-LRS | Embraer EMB.120 Brasilia | 120239 | ex F-GTBG | wfs♦ |
| ☐ TR-NRT | Embraer EMB.120ER Brasilia | 120184 | ex SX-BHW | wfs |

## SKY GABON SA (GV)

| | | | | |
|---|---|---|---|---|
| ☐ C-FHNM | Convair 580F | 454 | ex N583P | <NRL |

## SOLENTA AVIATION GABON

| | | | | |
|---|---|---|---|---|
| ☐ TR-LID | Antonov An-26 | 47302203 | ex LZ-MNS | |
| ☐ TR-LIE | Antonov An-26 | 87307504 | ex LZ-MNR | |

## TS- TUNISIA

## KARTHAGO AIRLINES — Karthago (5R/KAJ) — Tunis-Carthage/Djerba-Zarzis (TUN/DJE)

Merged into Nouvelair by Jan11

## NOUVELAIR — Nouvelair (BJ/LBT) — Monastir (MIB)

| | | | | | |
|---|---|---|---|---|---|
| ☐ TS-INA | Airbus A320-214 | 1121 | ex F-WWBT | Dora | |
| ☐ TS-INB | Airbus A320-214 | 1175 | ex F-WWDO | | |
| ☐ TS-INC | Airbus A320-214 | 1744 | ex F-WWBS | Youssef | |
| ☐ TS-INF | Airbus A320-212 | 0937 | ex SU-KBA | | |
| ☐ TS-INH | Airbus A320-214 | 4623 | ex F-WWBY | | ♦ |
| ☐ TS-INI | Airbus A320-212 | 0301 | ex OY-CNM | | |
| ☐ TS-INL | Airbus A320-212 | 0400 | ex N346NW | | |
| ☐ TS-INN | Airbus A320-212 | 0793 | ex D-AICB | | |
| ☐ TS-INO | Airbus A320-214 | 3480 | ex F-WWDK | | |
| ☐ TS-INP | Airbus A320-214 | 1597 | ex SU-KBD | | ♦ |
| ☐ TS-IAX | Airbus A300B4-622R | 601 | ex 5A-DLY | | >LAA ♦ |
| ☐ TS-IQA | Airbus A321-211 | 0970 | ex OO-SUA | | |
| ☐ TS-IQB | Airbus A321-211 | 0995 | ex OO-SUB | | |

## SYPHAX AIRLINES

| | | | | |
|---|---|---|---|---|
| ☐ TS-IEF | Airbus A319-112 | 3853 | ex D-AHIN | ♦ |
| ☐ TS-IEG | Airbus A319-112 | 3872 | ex D-AHIO | ♦ |

## TUNISAIR — Tunair (TU/TAR) — Tunis-Carthage (TUN)

| | | | | | |
|---|---|---|---|---|---|
| ☐ TS-IMB | Airbus A320-211 | 0119 | ex F-WWIJ | Fahrat Hached | |
| ☐ TS-IMC | Airbus A320-211 | 0124 | ex F-WWIS | 7 Novembre | |
| ☐ TS-IMD | Airbus A320-211 | 0205 | ex F-WWDO | Khereddine | |
| ☐ TS-IME | Airbus A320-211 | 0123 | ex F-OGYC | Tabarka | |
| ☐ TS-IMF | Airbus A320-211 | 0370 | ex F-WWIP | Djerba | |
| ☐ TS-IMG | Airbus A320-211 | 0390 | ex F-WWDL | Abou el Kacem Chebbi | |
| ☐ TS-IMH | Airbus A320-211 | 0402 | ex F-WWBN | Ali Belhaouane | >MTW |
| ☐ TS-IMI | Airbus A320-211 | 0511 | ex F-WWDC | Jugurtha | |
| ☐ TS-IML | Airbus A320-211 | 0958 | ex F-WWBI | Gafsa El Ksar | |
| ☐ TS-IMM | Airbus A320-211 | 0975 | ex F-WWIR | Le Bardo | |
| ☐ TS-IMN | Airbus A320-211 | 1187 | ex F-WWDU | Ibn Khaldoun | |

| | | | | | | |
|---|---|---|---|---|---|---|
| ☐ | TS-IMP | Airbus A320-211 | 1700 | ex F-WWIS | La Galite | |
| ☐ | TS-IMR | Airbus A320-214 | 4344 | ex D-AXAS | Habib Bourguiba | |
| ☐ | TS-IMS | Airbus A320-214 | 4689 | ex D-AUBC | | ◆ |
| ☐ | TU-IMT | Airbus A320-214 | 5240 | | | o/o◆ |
| | | | | | | |
| ☐ | TS-IOK | Boeing 737-6H3 | 29496/268 | ex N1786B | Kairouan | |
| ☐ | TS-IOL | Boeing 737-6H3 | 29497/282 | ex N1786B | Tozeur Nefta | |
| ☐ | TS-IOM | Boeing 737-6H3 | 29498/310 | ex N1786B | Carthage | |
| ☐ | TS-ION | Boeing 737-6H3 | 29499/510 | ex N1786B | Utique | |
| ☐ | TS-IOP | Boeing 737-6H3 | 29500/543 | | El Jem | |
| ☐ | TS-IOQ | Boeing 737-6H3 | 29501/563 | ex N1787B | Bizerte | |
| ☐ | TS-IOR | Boeing 737-6H3 | 29502/816 | ex N1786B | Tahar Haddad | |
| | | | | | | |
| ☐ | TS-IMJ | Airbus A319-114 | 0869 | ex D-AVYW | El Kantaoui | |
| ☐ | TS-IMK | Airbus A319-114 | 0880 | ex D-AVYD | Kerkenah | |
| ☐ | TS-IMO | Airbus A319-114 | 1479 | ex D-AVYT | Hannibal | |
| ☐ | TS-IMQ | Airbus A319-112 | 3096 | ex D-AVWZ | Alyssa | |
| ☐ | TS-IOG | Boeing 737-5H3 | 26639/2253 | | Sfax | |
| ☐ | TS-IOH | Boeing 737-5H3 | 26640/2474 | | Hammamet | |
| ☐ | TS-IOI | Boeing 737-5H3 | 27257/2583 | | Mahdia | |
| ☐ | TS-IOJ | Boeing 737-5H3 | 27912/2701 | | Monastir | |
| ☐ | TS-IPA | Airbus A300B4-605R | 558 | ex A6-EKD | Sidi Bou Said | |
| ☐ | TS-IPB | Airbus A300B4-605R | 563 | ex A6-EKE | Tunis | |
| ☐ | TS-IPC | Airbus A300B4-605R | 505 | ex F-OIHB | Amilcar | |

## TUNISAIR EXPRESS — (UG/SEN) — Tunis-Carthage (TUN)

| | | | | | | |
|---|---|---|---|---|---|---|
| ☐ | TS-ISA | Canadair CRJ-900 | 15091 | ex C- | Didon | ◆ |
| ☐ | TS-LBA | ATR 42-300 | 0245 | ex G-BXBV | Alyssa | >MTW◆ |
| ☐ | TS-LBC | ATR 72-202 | 0281 | ex F-WWLK | Tahar Haddad | ◆ |
| ☐ | TS-LBD | ATR 72-202 | 0756 | ex F-WWEQ | Hasdrubal | ◆ |
| ☐ | TS-LBE | ATR 72-202 | 0794 | ex F-WWEU | | ◆ |
| ☐ | ZS-PYU | Beech 1900D | UE-107 | ex N107YV | | ◆ |

## TUNISAVIA — Tunisavia (TAJ) — Tunis-Carthage (TUN)

| | | | | | |
|---|---|---|---|---|---|
| ☐ | TS-HSD | Aérospatiale SA365N Dauphin 2 | 6117 | ex F-WXFC | |
| ☐ | TS-HSE | Aérospatiale SA365N Dauphin 2 | 6150 | ex F-WYMN | |
| ☐ | TS-LIB | de Havilland DHC-6 Twin Otter 300 | 716 | ex TS-DIB | |
| ☐ | TS-LSF | de Havilland DHC-6 Twin Otter 300 | 575 | ex TS-DSF | |

## TT-   TCHAD (Republic of Chad)

## AIR HORIZON AFRIQUE — Tchad-Horizon (TPK) — N'Djamena (NDJ)

Ops cargo flights with Antonov An-12 frtrs leased from other operators as required

## AMW TCHAD — (MCW) — N'Djamena (NDJ)

Aircraft retired

## MID EXPRESS TCHAD — N'Djamena (NDJ)

Aircraft retired

## TOUMAI AIR TCHAD — Toumai Air (9D/THE) — N'Djamena (NDJ)

| | | | | | |
|---|---|---|---|---|---|
| ☐ | TT-EAS | Fokker F.28 Fellowship 4000 | 11204 | ex TJ-ALC | |

## TU-   IVORY COAST (Republic of the Ivory Coast)

## AIR INTER IVOIRE — Inter Ivoire (NTV) — Abidjan (ABJ)

| | | | | | |
|---|---|---|---|---|---|
| ☐ | TU-TDM | Grumman G.159 Gulfstream I | 20 | ex TJ-WIN | [MAD] |
| ☐ | TU-TGF | Piper PA-31-350 Navajo Chieftain | 31-7305072 | ex N74930 | |
| ☐ | TU-TJF | Piper PA-23-250 Aztec F | 27-7654072 | ex N62594 | |
| ☐ | TU-TJN | Beech 58 Baron | TH-776 | ex HB-GGE | |

## AIR IVOIRE — Air Ivoire (VU/VUN) — Abidjan (ABJ)

| | | | | | |
|---|---|---|---|---|---|
| ☐ | TU-TIX | Fokker F.28 Fellowship 4000 | 11237 | ex N486US | [ABJ]Ceased ops Apr11 |

## IVOIRIENNE DE TRANSPORTS AERIENS

| | | | | | |
|---|---|---|---|---|---|
| ☐ | TU-PAD | Hawker Siddeley HS.748 Srs.2B/426 | 1799 | ex 4R-SER | Frtr◆ |

## SHUTTLE BIRD

| ☐ | TU-TCV | LET L-410UVP | 851507 | ex UR-SEV | ♦ |

## SOPHIA AIRLINES / COTAIR

| ☐ | TU-TBG | LET L-410UVP | 851423 | ex 3D-GAM | |
| ☐ | TU-TBS | LET L-410UVP | 810724 | ex 3D-BHK | |

## WESTAIR CARGO AIRLINES   (WSC)

| ☐ | 3D-RED | Boeing 737-268C | 20575/295 | ex HZ-AGB | ♦ |

## TY-   BENIN (Republic of Benin)

### AERO BENIN   AeroBen (EM/AEB)   Cotonou (COO)

Ops services with Boeing 727 and Boeing 737 aircraft leased from Interair or Aero Africa when required

### BENIN GOLF AIR   Benin Golf (A8/BGL)   Cotonou (COO)

Status uncertain

### ROYAL AIR

Aircraft retired

### TRANS AIR BENIN   Trans-Benin (N4/TNB)   Cotonou (COO)

Ops services with aircraft leased from Airquarius Aviation or TransAir Congo as required

## TZ-   MALI (Republic of Mali)

### ASKARI AVIATION

Status uncertain

### AIR MALI   (I5/MLI)   Bamako (BKO)

| ☐ | TZ-RCA | Canadair CRJ-200ER | 7392 | ex N646BR | |
| ☐ | TZ-RMA | McDonnell-Douglas MD-87 | 49832/1703 | ex I-AFRB | |
| ☐ | TZ-RMB | McDonnell-Douglas MD-87 | 49841/1751 | ex EC-EYZ | |
| ☐ | TZ-RMC | McDonnell-Douglas MD-87 | 49842/1763 | ex EC-EZA | ♦ |
| ☐ | TZ-RMK | McDonnell-Douglas MD-83 | 53463/2089 | ex N160BS | |

### MALI AIR EXPRESS   Avion Express (VXP)   Bamako (BKO)

| ☐ | 3X-GED | SAAB SF.340A | 340A-051 | ex ZS-PMN | [BKO] |
| ☐ | 3X-GEJ | SAAB SF.340A | 340A-136 | ex ZK-NLN | wfs |

### MALI AIR TRANSPORT   Bamako (BKO)

| ☐ | TZ-NBA | Boeing 727-2K5/W (Duganair 3) | 21853/1640 | ex P4-JLI | |

### SAM INTERCONTINENTAL

| ☐ | TZ-MHI | Lockheed L-1011-100 Tristar | 193B-1221 | ex EX-35000 | [NBO]♦ |
| ☐ | TZ-SPA | Lockheed L1011-250 Tristar | 193C-1237 | ex EX-056 | wfs♦ |

### SKY PEARL AVIATION

| ☐ | TZ-SGI | Lockheed L1011-250 Tristar | 193C-1245 | ex EX-044 | ♦ |

### STA MALI

| ☐ | 3D-KKT | LET L-410UVP | | | ♦ |
| ☐ | 9L-LCV | LET L-410UVP | | | ♦ |

### TOMBOUCTOU AVIATION

| ☐ | TZ-BSB | BAC One-Eleven 401AK | 086 | ex YR-CJL | ♦ |

## T3- KIRIBATI (Republic of Kiribati)

### AIR KIRIBATI (4A) Tarawa-Bonriki Intl (TRW)

| | | | | |
|---|---|---|---|---|
| ☐ | T3-ATC | CASA C.212-200 | CC30-1-236 | | ♦ |
| ☐ | T3-ATI | Harbin Y-12 II | 0077 | |
| ☐ | T3-ATJ | CASA C.212-200 | CD67-01-356 | ex N398FL |

### CORAL SUN AIRWAYS

| | | | | |
|---|---|---|---|---|
| ☐ | T3-VIN | Britten-Norman BN-2B-26 Islander | 2154 | ex VH-YIE |

## T8A- PALAU

### PACIFICFLYER (PI/PFL)

| | | | | |
|---|---|---|---|---|
| ☐ | CS-TEI | Airbus A310-304 | 495 | ex F-WWCO | <HFY |

## UK UZBEKISTAN (Republic of Uzbekistan)

### AVIALEASING Twinarrow (EC/TWN)
Tashkent-Vostochny/Miami-Opa Locka, FL (TAS/OPF)

| | | | | | |
|---|---|---|---|---|---|
| ☐ | N5057E | Antonov An-26 | 6101 | ex 57 red | based OPF |
| ☐ | UK 11418 | Antonov An-12B | 402504 | ex RA-11996 | based OPF |
| ☐ | UK 12002 | Antonov An-12B | 402002 | ex RA-11373 | |
| ☐ | UK 26001 | Antonov An-26B | 67314402 | ex UK 26213 | [OPF] |
| ☐ | UK 26003 | Antonov An-26 | 07310406 | ex S9-BOW The Sky's the Limit | [OPF] |

Those based at Opa Locka, FL op cargo flights for Bahamasair and DHL

### QANOT SHARQ Qanot Sharq (QNT) Tashkent-Vostochny (TAS)

| | | | | |
|---|---|---|---|---|
| ☐ | UK 76353 | Ilyushin Il-76TD | 102314454 | ex 76353 |

### SAMARKAND AIRWAYS Sogdiana (C7/UZS) Tashkent-Vostochny (TAS)

Ops services with Antonov An-12/26 and Ilyushin Il-76 aircraft leased from other operators as required

### SILK ROAD CARGO

| | | | | |
|---|---|---|---|---|
| ☐ | VQ-BNW | Airbus A300-622RF | 0733 | ex N733MY | ♦ |

### TAPO-AVIA Cortas (4C/CTP) Tashkent-Vostochny (TAS)

| | | | | |
|---|---|---|---|---|
| ☐ | UK 11807 | Antonov An-12BK | 00346910 | ex CCCP-11807 |
| ☐ | UK 58644 | Antonov An-12BP | 2340303 | ex CCCP-58644 |
| ☐ | UK 76375 | Ilyushin Il-76TD | 1033414496 | |
| ☐ | UK 76821 | Ilyushin Il-76TD | 0023441200 | ex 4K-AZ62 |

### UZBEKISTAN AIRWAYS Uzbek (HY/UZB) Tashkent-Vostochny/Samarkand (TAS/SKD)

| | | | | | |
|---|---|---|---|---|---|
| ☐ | UK 32000 | Airbus A320-214 | 4528 | ex D-AUBV | [SAT]♦ |
| ☐ | UK 32011 | Airbus A320-214 | 4371 | ex D-AVVA | |
| ☐ | UK 32012 | Airbus A320-214 | 4395 | ex D-AVVK | |
| ☐ | UK 32014 | Airbus A320-214 | 4417 | ex F-WWDM | |
| ☐ | UK 32015 | Airbus A320-214 | 4485 | ex D-AUBF | |
| ☐ | UK 32016 | Airbus A320-214 | 4492 | ex D-AUBJ | |
| ☐ | UK 32017 | Airbus A320-214 | 4651 | ex D-AXAA | ♦ |
| ☐ | UK 32018 | Airbus A320-214 | 4724 | ex D-AUBK | ♦ |
| ☐ | UK 32019 | Airbus A320-214 | 4770 | ex F-WWDC | ♦ |
| ☐ | UK 32020 | Airbus A320-214 | 4952 | ex D-AXAT | ♦ |
| | | | | | |
| ☐ | UK 46223 | Antonov An-24B | 77303102 | ex CCCP-46223 | |
| ☐ | UK 46360 | Antonov An-24B | 07305901 | ex RA-46360 | |
| ☐ | UK 46373 | Antonov An-24B | 07306004 | ex CCCP-46373 | |
| ☐ | UK 46387 | Antonov An-24B | 07306110 | ex 46387 | |
| ☐ | UK 46392 | Antonov An-24B | 07306205 | ex CCCP-46392 | |
| ☐ | UK 46573 | Antonov An-24B | 87304807 | ex CCCP-46573 | |
| ☐ | UK 46594 | Antonov An-24B | 97305104 | ex CCCP-46594 | wfs |
| ☐ | UK 46623 | Antonov An-24RV | 37308710 | ex CCCP-46623 | |
| ☐ | UK 47274 | Antonov An-24B | 07306404 | ex CCCP-47274 | |
| | | | | | |
| ☐ | UK 75700 | Boeing 757-23P | 28338/731 | | op for Govt |
| ☐ | UK 75701 | Boeing 757-23P | 30060/875 | ex VP-BUB Urgench | |

| | | | | | |
|---|---|---|---|---|---|
| ☐ | UK 75702 | Boeing 757-23P | 30061/886 | ex VP-BUD | Shahrisabz |
| ☐ | VP-BUH | Boeing 757-231 | 30339/896 | ex N726TW | |
| ☐ | VP-BUI | Boeing 757-231 | 28487/878 | ex N719TW | |
| ☐ | VP-BUJ | Boeing 757-231 | 28488/884 | ex N724TW | |
| | | | | | |
| ☐ | UK 67000 | Boeing 767-33PER | 35796/958 | ex N5014K | VIP a/c op for Govt |
| ☐ | UK 67001 | Boeing 767-33PER | 28370/635 | ex VP-BUA | Samarkand |
| ☐ | UK 67002 | Boeing 767-33PER | 28392/650 | ex VP-BUZ | Khiva |
| ☐ | UK 67003 | Boeing 767-33PER | 40534/1019 | | ♦ |
| ☐ | UK 67004 | Boeing 767-33PER | 40536/1021 | | ♦ |
| ☐ | VP-BUE | Boeing 767-3CBER | 33469/904 | ex N594HA | ♦ |
| ☐ | VP-BUF | Boeing 767-33PER | 33078/928 | | |
| | | | | | |
| ☐ | UK 76351 | Ilyushin Il-76TD | 1013408240 | ex RA-76351 | [TAS] |
| ☐ | UK 76353 | Ilyushin Il-76TD | 1023414454 | | ♦ |
| ☐ | UK 76358 | Ilyushin Il-76TD | 1023410339 | | |
| ☐ | UK 76359 | Ilyushin Il-76TD | 1033414483 | | |
| ☐ | UK 76426 | Ilyushin Il-76TD | 1043419644 | | |
| ☐ | UK 76428 | Ilyushin Il-76TD | 1043419648 | ex 76428 | |
| ☐ | UK 76449 | Ilyushin Il-76TD | 1023403058 | ex 76449 | |
| ☐ | UK 76782 | Ilyushin Il-76TD | 0093498971 | ex CCCP-76782 | |
| ☐ | UK 76793 | Ilyushin Il-76TD | 0093498951 | ex CCCP-76793 | |
| ☐ | UK 76794 | Ilyushin Il-76TD | 0093498954 | ex CCCP-76794 | [TAS] |
| ☐ | UK 76805 | Ilyushin Il-76TD | 1003403109 | ex CCCP-76805 | [TAS] |
| ☐ | UK 76824 | Ilyushin Il-76TD | 1023410327 | ex CCCP-76824 | [TAS] |
| | | | | | |
| ☐ | UK 91102 | Ilyushin Il-114-100 | 1063800202 | | ♦ |
| ☐ | UK 91104 | Ilyushin Il-114-100 | 2093800204 | | |
| ☐ | UK 91105 | Ilyushin Il-114-100 | 2063800205 | ex 91105 | |
| ☐ | UK 91106 | Ilyushin Il-114-100 | 2083800206 | ex 91106 | |
| ☐ | UK 91107 | Ilyushin Il-114-100 | 2103800207 | | ♦ |
| ☐ | UK 91108 | Ilyushin Il-114-100 | 10.3800206 | | ♦ |
| | | | | | |
| ☐ | UK 85575 | Tupolev Tu-154B-2 | 83A575 | ex 85575 | [TAS] |
| ☐ | UK 85578 | Tupolev Tu-154B-2 | 83A578 | ex 85578 | [TAS] |
| ☐ | UK 85600 | Tupolev Tu-154B-2 | 84A600 | ex 85600 | [TAS] |
| ☐ | UK 85711 | Tupolev Tu-154M | 91A887 | ex 85711 | [TAS] |
| ☐ | UK 85764 | Tupolev Tu-154M | 93A947 | ex RA-85764 | [TAS] |
| ☐ | UK 85776 | Tupolev Tu-154M | 93A958 | | [TAS] |
| | | | | | |
| ☐ | UK 31001 | Airbus A310-324 | 574 | ex F-OGQY | Tashkent |
| ☐ | UK 31002 | Airbus A310-324 | 576 | ex F-OGQZ | Fergana |
| ☐ | UK 31003 | Airbus A310-324 | 706 | ex F-WWCM | Bukhara |
| ☐ | UK 31004 | Airbus A300B4-622RF | 717 | ex HL7299 | |
| ☐ | UK 31005 | Airbus A300B4-622RF | 722 | ex HL7244 | |
| ☐ | UK 80001 | Avro 146-RJ85 | E2312 | ex G-6-312 | VIP op for Govt |
| ☐ | UK 80002 | Avro 146-RJ85 | E2309 | ex G-6-309 | |
| ☐ | UK 80003 | Avro 146-RJ85 | E2319 | ex G-6-319 | |
| ☐ | UK 86056 | Ilyushin Il-86 | 51483203023 | ex CCCP-86056 | [TAS] |
| ☐ | UK 86064 | Ilyushin Il-86 | 51483203031 | ex CCCP-86064 | [TAS] |
| ☐ | UK 86090 | Ilyushin Il-86 | 51483207061 | ex CCCP-86090 | [TAS] |
| ☐ | UK 87923 | Yakovlev Yak-40 | 9741455 | ex CCCP-87923 | VIP |
| ☐ | UK 88194 | Yakovlev Yak-40 | 9621448 | ex CCCP-88194 | VIP |
| ☐ | UK 88217 | Yakovlev Yak-40 | 9630350 | ex CCCP-88217 | VIP |

## UP-    KAZAKHSTAN (Republic of Kazakhstan)

### AEROTUR-KZ/SKYBUS      Diasa (RAN)      Astana (TSE)

| | | | | | |
|---|---|---|---|---|---|
| ☐ | UN-85521 | Tupolev Tu-154B-2 | 81A521 | | ♦ |
| ☐ | UP-T5407 | Tupolev Tu-154M | 87A754 | ex UN-85570 | |
| ☐ | UP-T5408 | Tupolev Tu-154B-2 | 82A569 | | ♦ |

### AIR ALMATY      Agleb (LMY)      Almaty (ALA)

| | | | | | |
|---|---|---|---|---|---|
| ☐ | UP-I7601 | Ilyushin Il-76TD | 1013409295 | ex YL-LAJ | |
| ☐ | UP-I7618 | Ilyushin Il-76TD | 0013428831 | | ♦ |

### AIR ASTANA      Astanaline (KC/KZR)      Astana/Almaty(TSE/ALA)

| | | | | |
|---|---|---|---|---|
| ☐ | P4-PAS | Airbus A320-232 | 2128 | ex D-ARFF |
| ☐ | P4-SAS | Airbus A320-232 | 2016 | ex SX-BVC |
| ☐ | P4-TAS | Airbus A320-232 | 2828 | ex F-WWDN |
| ☐ | P4-UAS | Airbus A320-232 | 2987 | ex F-WWIH |
| ☐ | P4-VAS | Airbus A320-232 | 3141 | ex F-WWDO |
| ☐ | P4-WAS | Airbus A320-232 | 3484 | ex F-WWIE |
| ☐ | P4-XAS | Airbus A320-232 | 3519 | ex F-WWDR |
| | | | | |
| ☐ | P4-EAS | Boeing 757-2G5/W | 29488/830 | ex D-AMUG |
| ☐ | P4-FAS | Boeing 757-2G5/W | 29489/834 | ex D-AMUH |

492

| | | | | | |
|---|---|---|---|---|---|
| ☐ | P4-GAS | Boeing 757-2G5/W | 28112/708 | ex D-AMUI | |
| ☐ | P4-KCU | Boeing 757-23N/W | 27971/690 | ex N558AX | ♦ |
| ☐ | P4-MAS | Boeing 757-28A/W | 28833/782 | ex B-2852 | |
| ☐ | P4-HAS | Fokker 50 | 20198 | ex PH-ZDH | |
| ☐ | P4-IAS | Fokker 50 | 20188 | ex PH-ZDD | |
| ☐ | P4-JAS | Fokker 50 | 20195 | ex PH-ZDG | |
| ☐ | P4-KAS | Fokker 50 | 20187 | ex PH-ZDC | |
| ☐ | P4-LAS | Fokker 50 | 20193 | ex PH-ZDE | |
| ☐ | P4-RAS | Fokker 50 | 20237 | ex OO-VLT | ♦ |
| ☐ | P4-KCA | Boeing 767-306ER | 27612/647 | ex PH-BZI | |
| ☐ | P4-KCB | Boeing 767-306ER | 27614/661 | ex PH-BZK | |
| ☐ | P4-KCC | Embraer ERJ-190LR | 19000418 | ex PT-TBP | ♦ |
| ☐ | P4-KCD | Embraer ERJ-190LR | 19000431 | ex PT-TCR | ♦ |
| ☐ | P4-KCE | Embraer ERJ-190LR | 19000487 | ex PT-TPL | ♦ |
| ☐ | P4-NAS | Airbus A321-231 | 1042 | ex N104AQ | |
| ☐ | P4-OAS | Airbus A321-231 | 1204 | ex N120ED | |
| ☐ | P4-YAS | Airbus A319-132 | 3614 | ex D-AVYL | |
| ☐ | P4- | Embraer ERJ-190LR | 19000543 | ex PT- | o/o♦ |

## AIR MARK

| | | | | | |
|---|---|---|---|---|---|
| ☐ | UP-AN215 | Antonov An-12BP | 6344305 | | ♦ |

## ARIA AIR    (SYM)

| | | | | | |
|---|---|---|---|---|---|
| ☐ | UP-I6204 | Ilyushin Il-62M | 4255152 | | [THR]♦ |
| ☐ | UP-I6205 | Ilyushin Il-62M | 3357947 | | [THR]♦ |

## ATMA    (AMA)

| | | | | | |
|---|---|---|---|---|---|
| ☐ | UP-AN211 | Antonov An-12B | 02348207 | ex UN-11017 | |
| ☐ | UP-AN212 | Antonov An-12TB | 01347701 | ex UN-11019 | |
| ☐ | UP-AN213 | Antonov An-12BP | 2340806 | ex UN-11015 | |
| ☐ | UP-AN217 | Antonov An-12B | 8345507 | ex TN-AHZ | ♦ |
| ☐ | UP-I7632 | Ilyushin Il-76TD | 0023441186 | ex UN-76499 | ♦ |

## ATYRAU AIRWAYS    Edil (IP/JOL)    Atyrau (GUW)

| | | | | | |
|---|---|---|---|---|---|
| ☐ | UP-T3407 | Tupolev Tu 134A-3 | 49912 | ex UN-65070 | ♦ |
| ☐ | UN-T3408 | Tupolev Tu 134A-3 | 49908 | ex UN-65069 | ♦ |

## AVIA-JAYNAR    Tobol (SAP)    Kostanay (KSN)

| | | | | | |
|---|---|---|---|---|---|
| ☐ | UP-AN401 | Antonov An-24B | 88901605 | ex UN-47153 | |
| ☐ | UP-AN402 | Antonov An-24RV | 37308608 | | ♦ |
| ☐ | UN-AN403 | Antonov An-24RV | 27308205 | | ♦ |

## BEIBARS

| | | | | | |
|---|---|---|---|---|---|
| ☐ | UP-I7625 | Ilyushin Il-76TD | 0033446350 | ex UN-76472 | |
| ☐ | UP-I7626 | Ilyushin Il-76M | 1013409303 | ex YU-AMJ | |

## BERKUT AIR    Berkut (BEK)    Almaty (ALA)

| | | | | | |
|---|---|---|---|---|---|
| ☐ | UP-Y4021 | Yakovlev Yak-40 | 9302229 | ex UN-87306 | wfs?♦ |
| ☐ | UP-Y4022 | Yakovlev Yak-40 | 9411533 | ex UP-Y4023(1) | ♦ |
| ☐ | UP-Y4023(2) | Yakovlev Yak-40 | 9621148 | ex UN-88191 | ♦ |
| ☐ | UP-Y4024 | Yakovlev Yak-40 | 9711552 | ex UN-88260 | ♦ |

## BERKUT STATE AIR COMPANY    (BEC)    Almaty (ALA)

| | | | | | |
|---|---|---|---|---|---|
| ☐ | UP-AN205 | Antonov An-12BP | 02348304 | ex UN-11373 | |
| ☐ | UP-B5701 | Boeing 757-2M6ER | 23454/102 | ex P4-NSN | VIP |
| ☐ | UP-I7605 | Ilyushin Il-76TD | 1033416520 | ex UN-76374 | |
| ☐ | UP-MI702 | Mil Mi-172 (Mi-8MTV-3) | 398C01 | ex UN-17201 | VIP |
| ☐ | UP-MI814 | Mil Mi-8MTV-1 | 96275 | ex UN-25401 | VIP |
| ☐ | UN-85464 | Tupolev Tu-154B-2 | 80A464 | ex 85464 | VIP |

## CASPIY    (TLG)

| | | | | | |
|---|---|---|---|---|---|
| ☐ | UP-F1001 | Fokker 100 | 11384 | ex N110MN | ♦ |
| ☐ | UP-F1002 | Fokker 100 | 11371 | ex N371MX | ♦ |
| ☐ | UP-F1003 | Fokker 100 | 11375 | ex N375MX | ♦ |

## DETA AIR  (DET)  Almaty (ALA)

| | | | | | |
|---|---|---|---|---|---|
| ☐ | UP-DC101 | Douglas DC-10-40F | 47823/306 | ex VP-BDE | |
| ☐ | UP-DC102 | Douglas DC-10-40F | 47855/349 | ex VP-BDF | |
| ☐ | UP-I6206 | Ilyushin Il-62M | 3242321 | ex UN-86524  Galina | |
| ☐ | UP-I6207 | Ilyushin Il-62M | 1545951 | ex UN-86935 | |
| ☐ | UP-I6209 | Ilyushin Il-62M | 3139956 | ex RA-86518 | |

## EAST KAZAKHSTAN AVIA

| | | | | | |
|---|---|---|---|---|---|
| ☐ | UP-Y4009 | Yakovlev Yak-40K | 9640252 | | ♦ |

## EAST WING  E Wing (EWZ)  Taraz / Fujairah, UAE (DMB/FJR)

| | | | | | |
|---|---|---|---|---|---|
| ☐ | UN-B1110 | BAC One-Eleven 401AK | 078 | ex UN-B1111 | East Wing titles |
| ☐ | UP-AN206 | Antonov An-12BP | 4341705 | ex -UN-11004(2) | ♦ |
| ☐ | UP-AN207 | Antonov An-12TB | 4342505 | ex UN-11006 | |
| ☐ | UP-AN209 | Antonov An-12B | 5343408 | ex -UN-11009 | |
| ☐ | UP-AN210 | Antonov An-12B | 6344104 | ex -UN-11016 | ♦ |
| ☐ | UP-AN604 | Antonov An-26B | 12601 | | ♦ |
| ☐ | UP-I7621 | Ilyushin Il-76TD | 0013434018 | ex UN-76008 | |
| ☐ | UP-I7623 | Ilyushin Il-76TD | 0033448404 | ex UN-76010 | |
| ☐ | UP-I7624 | Ilyushin Il-76TD | 0023442218 | ex UN-76033 | |

## EASTERN EXPRESS

| | | | | | |
|---|---|---|---|---|---|
| ☐ | UP-I7606 | Ilyushin Il-76T | 0033446325 | ex UN-76026 | |
| ☐ | UN-I7609 | Ilyushin Il-76TD | 1013406294 | | ♦ |
| ☐ | UP-I7612 | Ilyushin Il-76T | 0003425746 | ex UN-76032 | |
| ☐ | UP-I7628 | Ilyushin Il-76TD | 0053460790 | ex EW-264TH | |

## EURO-ASIA INTERNATIONAL  Eakaz (5B/EAK)  Almaty/Sharjah (ALA/SHJ)

| | | | | | |
|---|---|---|---|---|---|
| ☐ | UP-Y4026 | Yakovlev Yak-40 | 9510639 | ex UN-87337  Aibike titles | VIP |
| ☐ | UP-Y4027 | Yakovlev Yak-40K | 9741856 | ex UN-87935 | VIP |
| ☐ | UP-Y4028 | Yakovlev Yak-40K | 9710453 | ex UN-88266 | |
| ☐ | UP-Y4030 | Yakovlev Yak-40 | 9541444 | | ♦ |

## EXCELLENT GLIDE

| | | | | |
|---|---|---|---|---|
| ☐ | UP-Y4208 | Yakovlev Yak-42D | 4520423116650 | ex UN-42642 |

## GST AERO

| | | | | | |
|---|---|---|---|---|---|
| ☐ | UN-76497 | Ilyushin Il-76T | 0434023116650 | | ♦ |
| ☐ | UN85558 | Tupolev Tu-154B-2 | 82A558 | | ♦ |

## INVESTAVIA  (TLG)  Almaty (ALA)

| | | | | | |
|---|---|---|---|---|---|
| ☐ | UP-I6210 | Ilyushin Il-62M | 3255333 | ex UN-86130 | NRG titles |

## KAZAIR WEST  Kazwest (KAW)  Atyrau (GUW)

| | | | | | |
|---|---|---|---|---|---|
| ☐ | UP-L4104 | LET L-410UVP-E | 861606 | ex UN-67566 | |
| ☐ | UP-T3402 | Tupolev Tu-134B-3 | 63187 | ex UN-65799 | VIP |
| ☐ | UP-Y4015 | Yakovlev Yak-40K | 9831958 | ex UN-87221 | |
| ☐ | UN-25358 | Mil Mi-8T | 98206781 | ex CCCP-25358 | jt ops with JOL |
| ☐ | UN-25517 | Mil Mi-8PS-9 | 8687 | ex CCCP-25517 | |
| ☐ | UP-L4103 | LET L-410UVP-E | 892339 | ex UN-67611 | |

## KAZAKHMYS

| | | | | | |
|---|---|---|---|---|---|
| ☐ | UP-Y4014 | Yakovlev Yak-40K | 9732054 | ex UN-87912 | |

## KAZAVIASPAS

| | | | | | |
|---|---|---|---|---|---|
| ☐ | UP-AN205 | Antonov An-12BP | 02348304 | | ♦ |
| ☐ | UP-I7604 | Ilyushin Il-76TD | 1033414485 | ex UN-76371 | ♦ |
| ☐ | UP-I7605 | Ilyushin Il-76TD | 1033416520 | | ♦ |

## KOKSHETAU AIRLINES  Kokta (KRT)  Kokchetav (KOV)

| | | | | | |
|---|---|---|---|---|---|
| ☐ | UP-Y4001 | Yakovlev Yak-40 | 9721953 | ex UN-88277 | |
| ☐ | UP-Y4002 | Yakovlev Yak-40 | 9630750 | ex UN-88221 | |
| ☐ | UP-Y4003 | Yakovlev Yak-40 | 9632048 | | ♦ |

| | | | | | |
|---|---|---|---|---|---|
| ☐ | UN-Y4004 | Yakovlev Yak-40 | 9740356 | | ◆ |
| ☐ | UP-Y4005 | Yakovlev Yak-40 | 9730255 | ex UN-87913 | |
| | | | | | |
| ☐ | UP-I6201 | Ilyushin Il-62M | 1748445 | ex UN-86505  no titles | [ALA] |
| ☐ | UP-I6202 | Ilyushin Il-62M | 1138234 | exUN-86506 | [ALA] |

## MAKAIR  (AKM)  *Almaty (ALA)*

| | | | | | |
|---|---|---|---|---|---|
| ☐ | UP-T5405 | Tupolev Tu-154M | 89A823 | ex UN-85855 | |

## MEGA AIRCOMPANY  *Mega (MGK)*  *Almaty (ALA)*

| | | | | | |
|---|---|---|---|---|---|
| ☐ | UP-AN607 | Antonov An-26 | 7002 | ex UN-26517 | [ALA] |
| ☐ | UP-B2701 | Boeing 727-232 (FedEx 3) | 22045/1602 | ex UN-B2701 | [FJR] |
| ☐ | UP-B2702 | Boeing 727-232 (FedEx 3) | 21861/1554 | ex UN-B2702 | |
| ☐ | UP-B2703 | Boeing 727-232 (FedEx 3) | 21584/1478 | ex UN-B2703 | [FJR] |
| ☐ | UP-B2704 | Boeing 727-232 (FedEx 3) | 22046/1604 | ex A6-RSA | [FJR]◆ |
| ☐ | UP-I1801 | Ilyushin Il-18D | 187010204 | ex UN-75005 | |
| ☐ | UP-I1802 | Ilyushin Il-18E | 185008603 | ex UN-75002 | |
| ☐ | UP-I1803 | Ilyushin Il-18V | 184006903 | ex UN-75003 | |
| ☐ | UP-I1804 | Ilyushin Il-18GrM | 186009202 | ex UN-75004 | |

## MIRAS CARGO  *Miras (MIF)*  *Almaty (ALA)*

| | | | | | |
|---|---|---|---|---|---|
| ☐ | UP-AN201 | Antonov An-12BP | 01348007 | ex YU-AIA | |

## SAMAL AIR  (SAV)  *Almaty (ALA)*

| | | | | | |
|---|---|---|---|---|---|
| ☐ | UP-T3401 | Tupolev Tu-134AK-3 | 63684 | ex UN-65900 | [ALA] |

## SAT AIRLINES  *Satco (SOZ)*  *Almaty (ALA)*

| | | | | | |
|---|---|---|---|---|---|
| ☐ | UP-T3403 | Tupolev Tu-134A-3 | 62545 | ex UN-65776 | VIP |
| ☐ | UP-T3404 | Tupolev Tu-134A-3 | 66212 | ex UN-65551 | VIP |

## SAYAKHAT  *Sayakhat (W7/SAH)*  *Almaty (ALA)*

| | | | | | |
|---|---|---|---|---|---|
| ☐ | UP-I7615 | Ilyushin Il-76TD | 1003401015 | ex UN-76384 | |
| ☐ | UP-T5402 | Tupolev Tu-154M | 86A726 | ex UN-85852 | |
| ☐ | UP-T5403 | Tupolev Tu-154M | 86A728 | ex UN-85853 | |
| ☐ | UP-T5404 | Tupolev Tu-154M | 86A729 | ex UN-85854 | |

## SCAT AIRCOMPANY  *Vlasta (DV/VSV)*  *Shymkent*

| | | | | | |
|---|---|---|---|---|---|
| ☐ | UP-AN404 | Antonov An-24B | 17307303 | ex UN-26196 | |
| ☐ | UP-AN405 | Antonov An-24B | 77303508 | ex UN-46265 | |
| ☐ | UP-AN406 | Antonov An-24B | 77303604 | ex UN-46271 | |
| ☐ | UP-AN407 | Antonov An-24B | 87305305 | ex UN-46310 | |
| ☐ | UP-AN408 | Antonov An-24B | 97305608 | ex UN-46340 | |
| ☐ | UP-AN409 | Antonov An-24B | 07305909 | ex UN-46368 | |
| ☐ | UP-AN410 | Antonov An-24B | 07306104 | ex UN-46381 | |
| ☐ | UP-AN411 | Antonov An-24B | 87304106 | ex UN-46421 | |
| ☐ | UP-AN412 | Antonov An-24B | 87304309 | ex UN-46438 | |
| ☐ | UP-AN413 | Antonov An-24RV | 37309305 | ex UN-46500 | |
| ☐ | UP-AN414 | Antonov An-24RV | 37308305 | ex UN-46626 | |
| ☐ | UP-AN415 | Antonov An-24RV | 47309505 | ex UN-46664 | |
| ☐ | UP-AN416 | Antonov An-24RV | 47309604 | ex UN-46672 | |
| ☐ | UP-AN417 | Antonov An-24RV | 47309910 | ex UN-46699 | |
| ☐ | UP-AN418 | Antonov An-24B | 89901810 | ex UN-47176 | |
| ☐ | UP-AN419 | Antonov An-24RV | 27307609 | ex UN-47258 | |
| ☐ | UP-AN420 | Antonov An-24B | 07306308 | ex UN-47270 | |
| ☐ | UP-AN421 | Antonov An-24B | 07306407 | ex UN-47277 | |
| ☐ | UP-AN422 | Antonov An-24B | 07306504 | ex UN-47284 | |
| ☐ | UP-AN423 | Antonov An-24RV | 67310509 | ex UN-47350 | |
| ☐ | UP-AN424 | Antonov An-24RV | 27307509 | ex UN-47692 | |
| ☐ | UP-AN425 | Antonov An-24B | 79901307 | ex UN-47763 | |
| ☐ | UP-AN426 | Antonov An-24B | 17307406 | ex UN-47844 | |
| | | | | | |
| ☐ | UP-AN202 | Antonov An-12BP | 3341201 | ex UN-11367 | |
| ☐ | UP-AN601 | Antonov An-26 | 0503 | ex UN-26027 | |
| ☐ | UP-B3710 | Boeing 737-505 | 29116/3005 | ex 4L-TGF | >TGZ◆ |
| ☐ | UP-B5702 | Boeing 757-21B | 25083/359 | ex N508AG | ◆ |
| ☐ | UP-CJ004 | Canadair CRJ-200LR | 7901 | ex LY-AYJ | ◆ |
| ☐ | UP-CJ005 | Canadair CRJ-200LR | 7902 | ex LY-AYK | ◆ |
| ☐ | UP-Y4203 | Yakovlev Yak-42D | 4250421116567 | ex UN-42401 | |
| ☐ | UP-Y4205 | Yakovlev Yak-42D | 4520421219029 | ex UN-42410 | |
| ☐ | UP-Y4210 | Yakovlev Yak-42D | 4520422306016 | ex UN-42428 | <MSI |

## SEMEYAVIA  —  Ertis (SMK)  —  Semipalatinsk (PLX)

| | | | |
|---|---|---|---|
| ☐ UP-Y4016 | Yakovlev Yak-40K | 9810557 | ex UN-87208 |
| ☐ UP-Y4017 | Yakovlev Yak-40K | 9810157 | ex UN-87204 |

## TULPAR AIR SERVICE  —  Tulpa (2T/TUX)  —  Qaraghandy-Sary Arka (KGF)

| | | | |
|---|---|---|---|
| ☐ UN-46492 | Antonov An-24RV | 27305001 | ex CCCP-46492 |
| ☐ UN-46611 | Antonov An-24RV | 37308608 | ex CCCP-46611 |
| ☐ UP-AN427 | Antonov An-24B | 97305001 | ex UN -46582 |
| ☐ UP-AN428 | Antonov An-24B | 87304410 | ex UN-46448 |

## ZHETYSU AVIA  —  Zhetysu Avia (JTU)  —  Almaty (ALA)

| | | | |
|---|---|---|---|
| ☐ UP-Y4019 | Yakovlev Yak-40K | 9741855 | ex UN-87927 |
| ☐ UP-Y4020 | Yakovlev Yak-40 | 9740256 | ex UN-87931 |

## ZHEZKAZGAN AIR  —  (KZH)

| | | | | |
|---|---|---|---|---|
| ☐ UP-L4102 | LET L-410UVP-E | 902512 | ex UR-SVI | ♦ |
| ☐ UP-Y4012 | Yakovlev Yak-40K | 9741755 | | ♦ |
| ☐ UP-Y4014 | Yakovlev Yak-40K | 9732054 | | ♦ |

# UR-  UKRAINE

## AERO-CHARTER UKRAINE  —  Charter Ukraine (DW/UCR)  —  Kiev-Borispol (KBP)

| | | | | |
|---|---|---|---|---|
| ☐ UR-CDW | Yakovlev Yak-40 | 9610546 | ex UR-88151 | |
| ☐ UR-CJN | Antonov An-12B | 01348007 | | ♦ |
| ☐ UR-DWB | Antonov An-26B | 6207 | ex UR-BXB | |
| ☐ UR-DWC | Yakovlev Yak-40 | 9541144 | ex UR-87987 | |
| ☐ UR-DWD | Antonov An-26B | 10103 | ex ER-AFF | |
| ☐ UR-DWG | Antonov An-12BP | 8345710 | ex LZ-MNP | |
| ☐ UR-LRZ | Yakovlev Yak-40K | 9641851 | ex LY-ARZ | |
| ☐ UR-88290 | Yakovlev Yak-40K | 9840459 | ex CCCP-88290 | |

## AEROMOST KHARKOV  —  Aeromist (HT/AHW)  —  Kharkov-Osnova (HRK)

| | | |
|---|---|---|
| ☐ UR-14002 | Antonov An-140 | 36525302006 |

## AEROSTAR  —  Aerostar (UAR)  —  Kiev-Zhulyany/Kiev-Borispol (IEV/KBP)

| | | | | |
|---|---|---|---|---|
| ☐ UR-AER | Dornier 328-310 (328JET) | 3176 | ex N328DR | ♦ |
| ☐ UR-DAV | Dornier 328-310 (328JET) | 3169 | ex N328DP | ♦ |
| ☐ UR-WOG | Dornier 328-300QC | 3118 | ex 5A- | ♦ |

## AEROSVIT AIRLINES  —  Aerosvit (VV/AEW)  —  Kiev-Borispol (KBP)

| | | | | |
|---|---|---|---|---|
| ☐ UR-VVE | Boeing 737-448 | 24521/1788 | ex EI-BXB | |
| ☐ UR-VVL | Boeing 737-448 | 25052/2036 | ex EI-BXI | |
| ☐ UR-VVM | Boeing 737-448 | 25736/2269 | ex EI-BXK | |
| ☐ UR-VVN | Boeing 737-4Y0 | 24903/1978 | ex M-ABCO | |
| ☐ UR-VVP | Boeing 737-4Q8 | 26290/2482 | ex OK-YGA | |
| ☐ UR-AAK | Boeing 737-548/W | 24968/1975 | ex YL-BBH | |
| ☐ UR-AAL | Boeing 737-548/W | 24878/1939 | ex YL-BBF | |
| ☐ UR-AAM | Boeing 737-548/W | 24919/1970 | ex UP-B3708 | |
| ☐ UR-VVQ | Boeing 737-5L9 | 29235/3076 | ex OK-DGC | |
| ☐ UR-VVS | Boeing 737-5Q8 | 26324/2735 | ex ES-ABC | |
| ☐ UR-VVU | Boeing 737-5Q8 | 26323/2770 | ex ES-ABD | |
| | | | | |
| ☐ UR-AAG | Boeing 767-33AER | 25532/442 | ex V8-RBG | |
| ☐ UR-AAH | Boeing 767-33AER/W | 25534/477 | ex V8-RBH | |
| ☐ UR-AAI | Boeing 767-33AER/W | 25530/414 | ex V8-RBF | ♦ |
| ☐ UR-AAJ | Boeing 767-33AER | 25533/454 | ex V8-RBJ | >LOT |
| ☐ UR-DNM | Boeing 767-322ER/W | 25280/391 | ex N202AC | <UDN |
| ☐ UR-VVF | Boeing 767-383ER | 24476/274 | ex N4476F | |
| ☐ UR-VVV | Boeing 767-33AER/W | 25536/504 | ex V8-RBK | |
| ☐ UR-VVW | Boeing 767-33AER | 27189/521 | ex V8-RBL | |
| | | | | |
| ☐ UR-DSA | Embraer ERJ-190 | 19000494 | ex PT-TPS | o/o♦ |
| ☐ UR- | Embraer ERJ-190 | 19000501 | ex PT-TRI | o/o♦ |
| ☐ UR- | Embraer ERJ-190 | 19000505 | ex PT- | o/o♦ |
| ☐ UR- | Embraer ERJ-190 | 19000509 | ex PT-TQG | o/o♦ |
| ☐ UR- | Embraer ERJ-190 | 19000515 | ex PT- | o/o♦ |
| | | | | |
| ☐ OY-RTF | ATR 72-202 | 0496 | ex F-WQNL | <CIM♦ |
| ☐ UR-AAN | Boeing 737-84R/W | 38119/3962 | | ♦ |

| | | | | | |
|---|---|---|---|---|---|
| ☐ | UR-AAO | Boeing 737-84R/W | 38120/ | | o/o♦ |
| ☐ | UR-BVY | Boeing 737-2Q8 | 22760/852 | ex F-GEXJ | [KBP] |
| ☐ | UR-CGR | SAAB SF.340A | 340A-124 | ex N340JW | <MRW♦ |
| ☐ | UR-DAE | Airbus A320-212 | 0235 | ex F-GKXB | <UDC♦ |
| ☐ | UR-DAH | Airbus A320-212 | 0579 | ex A9C-BAY | ♦ |
| ☐ | UR-VVA | Boeing 737-3Q8 | 24492/1808 | ex N492GD | |
| ☐ | UR-VVR | Boeing 737-3Q8 | 24699/1886 | ex TC-TJA | |

## AEROVIS AIRLINES / AVFL LOGISTICS — Aeroviz (VIZ) — Rivnu (RWN)

| | | | | |
|---|---|---|---|---|
| ☐ | UR-CBF | Antonov An-12BP | 2340507 | ex LZ-SFW |
| ☐ | UR-CBG | Antonov An-12BP | 6343705 | ex UR-11302 |
| ☐ | UR-CCP | Antonov An-12AP | 2340505 | ex LZ-CBM |
| ☐ | UR-CEZ | Antonov An-12B | 6344304 | ex RA-98118 |
| ☐ | UR-CFB | Antonov An-12BP | 6343802 | ex 02 red |
| ☐ | UR-CGU | Antonov An-12BK | 7345203 | ex 09 red |

## AIR URGA — Urga (3N/URG) — Kirovograd-Khmelyovoye (KGO)

| | | | | | |
|---|---|---|---|---|---|
| ☐ | UR-ELC | Antonov An-24RV | 57310410 | ex UR-47313 | op for UN |
| ☐ | UR-ELK | Antonov An-24RV | 57310203 | ex UR-47300 all-white | |
| ☐ | UR-ELL | Antonov An-24RV | 67310503 | ex UR-47316 | |
| ☐ | UR-ELM | Antonov An-24RV | 67310506 | ex UR-47319 | |
| ☐ | UR-ELN | Antonov An-24B | 89901607 | ex UR-47155 | op for UN as UN-967 |
| ☐ | UR-ELO | Antonov An-24RV | 47309507 | ex UR-46666 | op for UN as UN-628 |
| ☐ | UR-ELT | Antonov An-24RV | 27307809 | ex XU-054 | op for UN |
| ☐ | UR-ELW | Antonov An-24RV | 57310109 | ex XU-375 | wfs |
| ☐ | UR-46311 | Antonov An-24B | 97305307 | ex LZ-MND | op for UN as UN-969 |
| ☐ | UR-46464 | Antonov An-24RV | 27307810 | ex ER-46464 | op for UN |
| ☐ | UR-ELB | Antonov An-26B | 14005 | ex UR-26201 | op for UN as UN-687 |
| ☐ | UR-ELD | Antonov An-26B | 14010 | ex UR-26203 | |
| ☐ | UR-ELE | Antonov An-26B | 12108 | ex UR-26111 | op for UN |
| ☐ | UR-ELF | Antonov An-26B | 12204 | ex UR-26115 | |
| ☐ | UR-ELG | Antonov An-26B | 12902 | ex UR-26140 | op for UN as UN-698 |
| ☐ | UR-ELH | Antonov An-26B | 12908 | ex UR-26143 | >/op for Air Boyoma |
| ☐ | UR-ELP | Antonov An-26B | 47313408 | ex UR-26580 | |
| ☐ | UR-ELR | Antonov An-26B | 9807 | ex UR-26004 | op for UN as UNO-967 |

## ANTONOV AIRLINES — Antonov Bureau (ADB) — Kiev-Gostomel

| | | | | | |
|---|---|---|---|---|---|
| ☐ | UR-82007 | Antonov An-124-100 | 19530501005 | ex CCCP-82007 | |
| ☐ | UR-82008 | Antonov An-124-100M-150 | 19530501006 | ex CCCP-82008 | |
| ☐ | UR-82009 | Antonov An-124-100 | 19530501007 | ex CCCP-82009 | |
| ☐ | UR-82027 | Antonov An-124-100 | 19530502288 | ex CCCP-82027 | |
| ☐ | UR-82029 | Antonov An-124-100 | 19530502630 | ex CCCP-82029 | |
| ☐ | UR-82072 | Antonov An-124-100 | 9773053359136 | ex RA-82072 | |
| ☐ | UR-82073 | Antonov An-124-100 | 9773054359139 | ex RA-82073 | |
| ☐ | UR-09307 | Antonov An-22A | 043481244 | ex CCCP-09307 | |
| ☐ | UR-74010 | Antonov An-74T | 36547030450 | ex CCCP-74010 | VIP |
| ☐ | UR-82060 | Antonov An-225 Mriya | 19530503763 | ex CCCP-82060 | |

## ARP 410 AIRLINES — Air-Arp (URP) — Kiev-Zhulyany (IEV)

| | | | | |
|---|---|---|---|---|
| ☐ | UR-BWZ | Antonov An-26B | 12208 | ex UR-26119 |
| ☐ | UR-CBJ | Antonov An-26B | 11401 | ex UR-26069 |
| ☐ | UR-CDY | Antonov An-24RV | 47309305 | ex ST-SHE |
| ☐ | UR-PWA | Antonov An-24RV | 67302608 | ex RA-46820 |
| ☐ | UR-26581 | Antonov An-26B | 57313503 | ex RA-26581 |
| ☐ | UR-47294 | Antonov An-24RV | 07306604 | ex RA-47294 |
| ☐ | UR-47297 | Antonov An-24RV | 07306610 | ex CCCP-47297 |

## ATA AIRLINES

| | | | | | |
|---|---|---|---|---|---|
| ☐ | UR-CDN | McDonnell-Douglas MD-83 | 53520/2137 | ex TC-OAV | <KHO♦ |
| ☐ | UR-CHP | McDonnell-Douglas MD-83 | 53466/2101 | ex TC-OAT | <KHO♦ |
| ☐ | UR-CHQ | McDonnell-Douglas MD-83 | 53488/2134 | ex TC-OAU | <KHO♦ |
| ☐ | UR-CJO | Airbus A320-231 | 0354 | ex N354BV | <KHO♦ |

## AVIANT — Aviation Plant (UAK) — Kiev-Gostomel

| | | | | | |
|---|---|---|---|---|---|
| ☐ | UR-ZYD | Antonov An-124-100 | 19530502843 | ex UR-CCX | >MXU |
| ☐ | UR-48086 | Antonov An-32P | 2901 | ex CCCP-48086 | |
| ☐ | UR-48087 | Antonov An-32B | 2904 | ex CCCP-48087 | |

## AVIATRANS

| | | | | | |
|---|---|---|---|---|---|
| ☐ | UR-CHL | McDonnell-Douglas MD-83 | 49395/1286 | ex XU-U4E | <KHO♦ |

## BUKOVYNA AIRLINES | Bukovyna (BQ/BKV) | Chernovtsy (CWC)

| | Reg | Type | c/n | Previous | Notes |
|---|---|---|---|---|---|
| ☐ | UR-BXI | McDonnell-Douglas MD-82 | 53170/2065 | ex G-CEPJ | ♦ |
| ☐ | UR-BXL | McDonnell-Douglas MD-82 | 49512/1548 | ex G-CEPG | >IRB♦ |
| ☐ | UR-BXM | McDonnell-Douglas MD-82 | 49505/1381 | ex G-CEPD | >IRB♦ |
| ☐ | UR-CGS | McDonnell-Doulgas MD-82 | 49425/1240 | ex G-CEPA | [THR]♦ |
| ☐ | UR-CGT | McDonnell-Douglas MD-82 | 49428/1241 | ex G-CEPB | [THR]♦ |
| ☐ | UR-CHW | McDonnell-Douglas MD-82 | 49510/1514 | ex S5-ACY | ♦ |
| ☐ | UR-CHX | McDonnell-Douglas MD-82 | 53162/2010 | ex G-CEPH | wfs♦ |
| ☐ | UR-CHZ | McDonnell-Douglas MD-82 | 53169/2063 | ex G-CEPI | ♦ |
| ☐ | UR-CIK | McDonnell-Douglas MD-82 | 49519/1658 | ex N915MD | [ARN]♦ |
| ☐ | UR-CJA | McDonnell-Douglas MD-82 | 49277/1181 | ex LZ-LDR | ♦ |
| ☐ | UR-CJQ | McDonnell-Douglas MD-82 | 49502/1300 | ex G-CEPC | >IRB♦ |
| ☐ | UR-BHJ | McDonnell-Douglas MD-83 | 53184/2088 | ex TC-AKL | >CPN♦ |
| ☐ | UR-BXN | McDonnell-Douglas MD-83 | 49569/1405 | ex LZ-LDV | ♦ |
| ☐ | UR-BXO | McDonnell-Douglas MD-83 | 53150/1831 | ex LZ-LDH | ♦ |
| ☐ | UR-CIX | McDonnell-Douglas MD-88 | 53546/2167 | ex TC-ONM | >TBM♦ |
| ☐ | UR-CIY | McDonnell-Douglas MD-88 | 53547/2176 | ex TC-ONN | >TBM♦ |
| ☐ | UR-CIZ | McDonnell-Douglas MD-88 | 53549/2185 | ex TC-ONP | >TBM♦ |

## BURYAT AVIA

| | Reg | Type | c/n | Previous | Notes |
|---|---|---|---|---|---|
| ☐ | UR-CDY | Antonov An-24RV | 47309305 | | ♦ |

## BUSINESS AVIATION CENTRE

| | Reg | Type | c/n | Previous | Notes |
|---|---|---|---|---|---|
| ☐ | UR-ARO | SAAB SF.340B | 340B-276 | ex SE-KTK | ♦ |

## CONSTANTA AIRLINES | Constanta (UZA) | Zaporozhye (OZH)

| | Reg | Type | c/n | Previous | Notes |
|---|---|---|---|---|---|
| ☐ | UR-ETG | Yakovlev Yak-40 | 9531143 | ex RA-87243 | VIP |
| ☐ | UR-FRU | Yakovlev Yak-40 | 9440737 | ex RA-87211 | VIP op for Sumy Frunze |

## DNEPR-AIR | Dniepro (Z6/UDN) | Dnepropetrovsk-Kodaki (DNK)

| | Reg | Type | c/n | Previous | Notes |
|---|---|---|---|---|---|
| ☐ | UR-DNA | Embraer ERJ-145EU | 145088 | ex G-EMBF | |
| ☐ | UR-DNB | Embraer ERJ-145EU | 145094 | ex G-EMBG | |
| ☐ | UR-DNE | Embraer ERJ-145EU | 145357 | ex G-EMBS | |
| ☐ | UR-DNF | Embraer ERJ-145EU | 145404 | ex G-EMBT | |
| ☐ | UR-DNG | Embraer ERJ-145EP | 145394 | ex G-ERJG | |
| ☐ | UR-DNI | Embraer ERJ-145EP | 145325 | ex G-ERJF | |
| ☐ | UR-DNL | Embraer ERJ-145EU | 145042 | ex G-EMBE | wfs |
| ☐ | UR-DNN | Embraer ERJ-145LR | 145665 | ex I-EXMH | ♦ |
| ☐ | UR-DNO | Embraer ERJ-145EP | 145237 | ex G-ERJB | |
| ☐ | UR-DNP | Embraer ERJ-145EP | 145290 | ex G-ERJD | |
| ☐ | UR-DNQ | Embraer ERJ-145EP | 145315 | ex G-ERJE | |
| ☐ | UR-DNR | Embraer ERJ-145LR | 145641 | ex F-WKXA | |
| ☐ | UR-DNS | Embraer ERJ-145LR | 145652 | ex I-EXMG | ♦ |
| ☐ | UR-DNU | Embraer ERJ-145LR | 145738 | ex F-WKXF | ♦ |
| ☐ | UR-DNV | Embraer ERJ-145LR | 145445 | ex I-EXM | ♦ |
| ☐ | UR-DNW | Embraer ERJ-145LR | 145316 | ex I-EXMU | ♦ |
| ☐ | UR-DNX | Embraer ERJ-145LR | 145436 | ex F-WKXL | ♦ |
| ☐ | UR-DNY | Embraer ERJ-145LR | 145282 | ex I-EXME | wfs♦ |
| ☐ | UR-DPA | Embraer ERJ-145LR | 145330 | ex I-EXMB | ♦ |
| ☐ | UR-DPB | Embraer ERJ-145LR | 145250 | ex F-WKXI | ♦ |
| ☐ | UR-DNC | Boeing 737-5L9 | 28995/2947 | ex OY-APK | |
| ☐ | UR-DND | Boeing 737-5L9 | 28722/2868 | ex OY-API | |
| ☐ | UR-DNH | Boeing 737-5Y0 | 24696/1960 | ex N246ST | |
| ☐ | UR-DNJ | Boeing 737-36Q | 28659/2680 | ex G-THOJ | |
| ☐ | UR-IVK | Boeing 737-3L9 | 24571/1815 | ex G-IGOT | ♦ |
| ☐ | UR-KIV | Boeing 737-4Y0 | 24686/1861 | ex F-GQQJ | ♦ |

## DONBASSAERO | Donbassaero (7D/UDC) | Donetsk (DOK)

| | Reg | Type | c/n | Previous | Notes |
|---|---|---|---|---|---|
| ☐ | UR-DAA | Airbus A320-211 | 0085 | ex EI-CTD | |
| ☐ | UR-DAB | Airbus A320-231 | 0230 | ex G-SSAS | |
| ☐ | UR-DAC | Airbus A320-233 | 0733 | ex N451TA | |
| ☐ | UR-DAD | Airbus A320-233 | 0747 | ex N453TA | |
| ☐ | UR-DAE | Airbus A320-212 | 0235 | ex F-GKXB | >AEW♦ |
| ☐ | UR-DAI | Airbus A320-212 | 0645 | ex N241LF | ♦ |
| ☐ | UR-DAJ | Airbus A320-232 | 0760 | ex N263LF | ♦ |
| ☐ | UR-DAK | Airbus A320-211 | 0662 | ex F-WTAU | ♦ |
| ☐ | UR-42327 | Yakovlev Yak-42 | 4520424402161 | ex T9-ABF | |
| ☐ | UR-42372 | Yakovlev Yak-42D | 4520423914266 | ex CCCP-42372 | no titles |
| ☐ | UR-42377 | Yakovlev Yak-42D | 4520421014479 | ex CCCP-42377 | |
| ☐ | UR-42381 | Yakovlev Yak-42D | 4520422014576 | ex CU-T1705 | |

| | | | | |
|---|---|---|---|---|
| ☐ | UR-42383 | Yakovlev Yak-42D | 4520422016201 | ex T9-ABD |
| ☐ | UR-DAF | Airbus A321-231 | 1869 | ex G-TTIC ♦ |

## ILYICH AVIA          Marlupol (MPW)

| | | | | | |
|---|---|---|---|---|---|
| ☐ | UR-MMK | Yakovlev Yak-40 | 9521540 | ex RA-87513 Ilyichevets 3 | VIP |

## ISD AVIA      Isdavia (ISD)      Donetsk (DOK)

| | | | | | |
|---|---|---|---|---|---|
| ☐ | UR-CAR | Yakovlev Yak-40K | 9741756 | ex RA-21501 | VIP |

## KHORS AIR      Aircompany Khors (X9/KHO)      Kiev-Borispol (KBP)

| | | | | | |
|---|---|---|---|---|---|
| ☐ | UR-CBN | McDonnell-Douglas MD-82 | 49490/1352 | ex N72830 | [IEV] |
| ☐ | UR-CBO | McDonnell-Douglas MD-82 | 49483/1314 | ex RP-C2986 | >CPN |
| ☐ | UR-CDA | McDonnell-Douglas MD-82 | 49278/1183 | ex SE-RDT | >WRC♦ |
| ☐ | UR-CDI | McDonnell-Douglas MD-82 | 49279/1230 | ex SX-BMP | ♦ |
| ☐ | UR-CDM | McDonnell-Douglas MD-82 | 53119/1956 | ex N481JC | ♦ |
| ☐ | UR-CDN | McDonnell-Douglas MD-83 | 53520/2137 | ex TC-OAV | >ATA Air |
| ☐ | UR-CDP | McDonnell-Douglas MD-83 | 49769/1559 | ex SE-RDF | |
| ☐ | UR-CDQ | McDonnell-Douglas MD-82 | 49372/1252 | ex SX-BSQ | >IZG♦ |
| ☐ | UR-CDR | McDonnell-Douglas MD-83 | 49949/1906 | ex SX-BSW | |
| ☐ | UR-CEL | McDonnell-Douglas MD-83 | 49390/1269 | ex XU-U4D | >SWM |
| ☐ | UR-CEW | McDonnell-Douglas MD-82 | 49634/1419 | ex N34838 | [THR]♦ |
| ☐ | UR-CHJ | McDonnell-Douglas MD-82 | 53066/1938 | ex N482JC | |
| ☐ | UR-CHK | McDonnell-Douglas MD-82 | 49188/1172 | ex N501AM | |
| ☐ | UR-CHL | McDonnell-Douglas MD-83 | 49395/1286 | ex XU-U4E | >Aviatrans♦ |
| ☐ | UR-CHM | McDonnell-Douglas MD-83 | 53465/2093 | ex TC-OAS | |
| ☐ | UR-CHO | McDonnell-Douglas MD-82 | 53231/2107 | ex N597BC | ♦ |
| ☐ | UR-CHP | McDonnell-Douglas MD-83 | 53466/2101 | ex TC-OAT | >ATA Air |
| ☐ | UR-CHQ | McDonnell-Douglas MD-83 | 53488/2134 | ex TC-OAU | >ATA Air |
| ☐ | UR-CIK | McDonnell-Douglas MD-83 | 53198/1847 | ex N198MD | [IEV]♦ |
| ☐ | UR-CJB | McDonnell-Douglas MD-83 | 49930/1720 | ex LZ-LDZ | >IZG♦ |
| ☐ | UR-CJC | McDonnell-Douglas MD-83 | 49986/1842 | ex 9A-CDB | |
| ☐ | UR-CJE | McDonnell-Douglas MD-83 | 49857/1687 | ex SX-BTF | ♦ |
| ☐ | UR-CFW | Airbus A320-231 | 0361 | ex N361DA | ♦ |
| ☐ | UR-CJD | Airbus A320-231 | 0362 | ex N362BV | ♦ |
| ☐ | UR-CJF | Airbus A320-231 | 0405 | ex N405MX | ♦ |
| ☐ | UR-CJO | Airbus A320-231 | 0354 | ex N354BV | >TBZ |

## KOSTROMA AIR

| | | | | | |
|---|---|---|---|---|---|
| ☐ | UR-BXU | Antonov An-26B-100 | 11703 | | ♦ |

## LUGANSK AVIATION ENTERPRISE      (LE/LHS)

| | | | | |
|---|---|---|---|---|
| ☐ | UR-46677 | Antonov An-24RV | 47309609 | ♦ |
| ☐ | UR-47312 | Antonov An-24RV | 57310403 | ♦ |

## LVIV AIRLINES      Ukraine West (5V/UKW)      Lviv-Snilow (LWO)

| | | | | | |
|---|---|---|---|---|---|
| ☐ | UR-42317 | Yakovlev Yak-42 | 4520422202039 | ex 42317 | [BKA] |
| ☐ | UR-42369 | Yakovlev Yak-42D | 4520422914190 | ex CCCP-42369 | all-white |
| ☐ | UR-42403 | Yakovlev Yak-42D | 4520422116588 | ex CCCP-42403 | no titles |

## MARS RK AIRLINES      (6V/MRW)      Kiev-Borispol (KBP)

| | | | | | |
|---|---|---|---|---|---|
| ☐ | UR-CGQ | SAAB SF.340A | 340A-097 | ex N771DF | |
| ☐ | UR-CGR | SAAB SF.340A | 340A-124 | ex N340JW | >AEW♦ |

## MERIDIEN / CARGO AIR CHARTERING      (MEM)      Poltava (PLV)

| | | | | | |
|---|---|---|---|---|---|
| ☐ | UR-CAG | Antonov An-12BK | 9346904 | ex ER-AXY | |
| ☐ | UR-CAH | Antonov An-12BK | 8345604 | ex ER-AXX | |
| ☐ | UR-CAJ | Antonov An-12BK | 8346106 | ex ER-AXZ | |
| ☐ | UR-CAK | Antonov An-12BP | 6343707 | ex ER-ACI | |
| ☐ | UR-CGV | Antonov An-12BP | 6344610 | ex EW-266TI | |
| ☐ | UR-CGW | Antonov An-12B | 402410 | ex EW-265TI | |
| ☐ | UR-DWF | Antonov An-12BK | 8345802 | ex LZ-MNK | ♦ |
| ☐ | UR-CHT | Antonov An-26B | 77305901 | ex UR-VIV | |
| ☐ | UR-MDA | Antonov An-26-100 | 87307108 | | |

## MOTOR SICH AIRLINES      Motor Sich (M9/MSI)      Zaporozhye (OZH)

| | | | | |
|---|---|---|---|---|
| ☐ | UR-BXC | Antonov An-24RV | 37308902 | ex UR-46636 |
| ☐ | UR-MSI | Antonov An-24RV | 27307608 | ex UR-47699 |

| | | | | | |
|---|---|---|---|---|---|
| ☐ | UR-06130 | Mil Mi-8T | 22686 | | |
| ☐ | UR-06131 | Mil-Mi-8T | 22688 | | |
| ☐ | UR-11316 | Antonov An-12BK | 9346810 | ex RA-11316 | |
| ☐ | UR-11819 | Antonov An-12B | 6344009 | ex CCCP-11819 | no titles |
| ☐ | UR-14005 | Antonov An-140 | 36525305021 | | |
| ☐ | UR-14006 | Antonov An-140K | 36525305025 | | |
| ☐ | UR-74026 | Antonov An-74TK-200 | 36547096919 | ex HK-3810X | op for UN |
| ☐ | UR-87215 | Yakovlev Yak-40 | 9510540 | ex OK-FEJ | |
| ☐ | UR-88310 | Yakovlev Yak-40 | 9940760 | ex 5R-MUB | ♦ |

## PODILLA AVIA — Podilia (PDA) — Khmelnitsky-Ruzuchaya (HMJ)

| | | | | | |
|---|---|---|---|---|---|
| ☐ | UR-46397 | Antonov An-24B | 07306301 | ex RA-46397 | [HMJ] |

## SHOVKOVY SKLYAH — Way Aero (S8/SWW) — Kiev-Zhulyany (IEV)

| | | | | |
|---|---|---|---|---|
| ☐ | UR-CAF | Antonov An-12BP | 3341209 | ex 4K-AZ56 |
| ☐ | UR-CGX | Antonov An-12BP | 5343510 | ex 4K-AZ60 |

## SOUTH AIRLINES — Southline (YG/OTL) — Odessa-Tsentralny (ODS)

| | | | | | |
|---|---|---|---|---|---|
| ☐ | UR-CER | Yakovlev Yak-42D | | | ♦ |
| ☐ | UR-EEE | Yakovlev Yak-40 | 9340632 | ex 5N-DAN | |
| ☐ | UR-IMF | SAAB SF.340B | 340B-163 | ex 4L-EUI | |
| ☐ | UR-IMS | SAAB SF.340B | 340B-228 | ex HB-AKO | ♦ |
| ☐ | UR-IMX | SAAB SF.340B | 340B-225 | ex YR-VGR | ♦ |
| ☐ | UR-30036 | Antonov An-30 | 0703 | | ♦ |
| ☐ | UR-47256 | Antonov An-24RV | 27307708 | | ♦ |

## UKRAINE AIR ALLIANCE — Ukraine Airalliance (UKL) — Kiev-Borispol (KBP)

| | | | | | |
|---|---|---|---|---|---|
| ☐ | UR-BXQ | Ilyushin Il-76TD | 1023410360 | ex EX-832 | >MXU |
| ☐ | UR-BXS | Ilyushin Il-76TD | 1023411368 | ex EX-436 | >MXU |
| ☐ | UR-CID | Ilyushin Il-76TD | 0063465956 | ex UP-I7640 | |

## UKRAINE INTERNATIONAL AIRLINES — Ukraine International (PS/AUI) — Kiev-Borispol (KBP)

| | | | | | |
|---|---|---|---|---|---|
| ☐ | UR-FAA | Boeing 737-3Y0 (SF) | 24462/1691 | ex N105KH | |
| ☐ | UR-GAH | Boeing 737-32Q/W | 29130/3105 | ex N1779B | Mayrni |
| ☐ | UR-GAN | Boeing 737-36N/W | 28569/2996 | ex F-GRFC | |
| ☐ | UR-GAQ | Boeing 737-33R/W | 28869/2887 | ex SX-BLA | |
| ☐ | UR-GBA | Boeing 737-36N/W | 28670/2948 | ex OO-VEX | ♦ |
| ☐ | UR-GAM | Boeing 737-4Y0 | 25190/2256 | ex HA-LEU | |
| ☐ | UR-GAO | Boeing 737-4Z9 | 25147/2043 | ex OE-LNH | |
| ☐ | UR-GAP | Boeing 737-4Z9 | 27094/2432 | ex OE-LNI | |
| ☐ | UR-GAV | Boeing 737-4C9 | 26437/2249 | ex EI-DGM | |
| ☐ | UR-GAX | Boeing 737-4Y0 | 26066/2301 | ex LZ-HVA | |
| ☐ | UR-GAK | Boeing 737-5Y0/W | 26075/2374 | ex PT-SLN | |
| ☐ | UR-GAS | Boeing 737-528/W | 25236/2443 | ex S5-AAM | |
| ☐ | UR-GAT | Boeing 737-528/W | 25237/2464 | ex F-GJNM | |
| ☐ | UR-GAU | Boeing 737-5Y0/W | 25182/2211 | ex N182GE | |
| ☐ | UR-GAW | Boeing 737-5Y0/W | 24898/2079 | ex N898ED | |
| ☐ | UR-GAZ | Boeing 737-55D | 27418/2397 | ex SP-LKC | ♦ |
| ☐ | UR-NTA | Antonov An-148-100 | 0101 | | ♦ |
| ☐ | UR-NTC | Antonov An-148-100 | 0109 | | ♦ |
| ☐ | UR-NTD | Antonov An-148-100 | 0110 | | ♦ |
| ☐ | UR-PSA | Boeing 737-8HX/W | 29658/2970 | ex N1787B | |
| ☐ | UR-PSB | Boeing 737-8HX/W | 29654/3018 | | |
| ☐ | UR-PSC | Boeing 737-8HX/W | 29662/3182 | ex N1787B | |
| ☐ | UR-PSD | Boeing 737-8HX/W | 29686/3259 | | |

## UKRAINIAN CARGO AIRWAYS — Cargotrans (6Z/UKS) — Zaporozhye (OZH)

| | | | | |
|---|---|---|---|---|
| ☐ | UR-UCN | Antonov An-12BK | 00347604 | ex UR-11303 |
| ☐ | UR-UCU | Ilyushin Il-76MD | 0073476275 | ex UR-76729 |
| ☐ | UR-UDM | Antonov An-26 | 0909 | ex UR-26241 |
| ☐ | UR-UWA | Mil Mi-8MTV-1 | 93151 | ex LZ-MOT |
| ☐ | UR-UWC | Mil Mi-8MTV-1 | 95236 | ex UR-MOR |
| ☐ | UR-UWD | Mil Mi-8MTV-1 | 95235 | ex UR-MOQ |

## UKRAINIAN PILOT SCHOOL — Pilot School (UPL) — Kiev-Chaika

| | | | | | |
|---|---|---|---|---|---|
| ☐ | UR-28721 | WSK/PZL Antonov An-28 | 1AJ007-06 | ex RA-28721 | |
| ☐ | UR-VTV | LET L-410UVP | 810705 | | ♦ |

### UM AIR — Mediterranee Ukraine (UF/UKM) — Kiev-Borispol (KBP)

| | | | | | |
|---|---|---|---|---|---|
| ☐ | UR-CCT | Douglas DC-9-51 (ABS 3) | 47696/808 | ex OH-LYP Diana | [KBP] |
| ☐ | UR-CHN | McDonnell-Douglas MD-83 | 49938/1785 | ex N938MD | >CPN |
| ☐ | UR-CHY | McDonnell-Douglas MD-82 | 53171/2067 | ex G-CEPK | |
| ☐ | UR-CJJ | British Aerospace 146 Srs.300 | E3165 | ex G-BSNR | >IRM♦ |
| ☐ | UR-CJK | McDonnell-Douglas MD-88 | 53548/2180 | ex TC-ONO | ♦ |
| ☐ | UR-CJL | McDonnell-Douglas MD-88 | 53550/2187 | ex TC-ONR | ♦ |
| ☐ | UR-CJM | British Aerospace 146 Srs.300 | E3129 | ex G-BTXN | >IRM♦ |

### UNIVERSAL AVIA — Rivne Universal (UNR) — Rivnu (RWN)

| | | | | | |
|---|---|---|---|---|---|
| ☐ | UR-67439 | LET L-410UVP | 841204 | ex YL-KAH | based UK♦ |

### UTAIR UKRAINE — (UTN)

| | | | | | |
|---|---|---|---|---|---|
| ☐ | UR-UTA | ATR 42-320 | 0382 | ex VP-BLP | |
| ☐ | UR-UTB | ATR 42-320 | 0386 | ex VP-BLQ | |
| ☐ | UR-UTD | ATR 42-300 | 0068 | ex VP-BCF | |
| ☐ | UR-UTE | ATR 42-300 | 0057 | ex VP-BCG | ♦ |
| ☐ | UR-UTF | ATR 42-300 | 0042 | ex VP-BDC | ♦ |
| ☐ | UR-UTG | Boeing 737-4Q8 | 25377/2717 | ex EI-ELP | |

### VETERAN AIRLINES — Veteran (VPB) — Simferopol-Zavodstoye (SIP)

| | | | | | |
|---|---|---|---|---|---|
| ☐ | UR-CBZ | Antonov An-12BP | 402707 | ex RA-11117 all-white | |
| ☐ | UR-CDB | Antonov An-12BP | 401605 | ex RA-11766 all-white | |
| ☐ | UR-CEM | Antonov An-12BP | 3340908 | ex RA-11813 | |
| ☐ | UR-PAS | Antonov An-12AP | 2401105 | all-white | |

### WIND ROSE — Wind Rose 7W/WRC — Kiev-Borispol (BPL)

| | | | | | |
|---|---|---|---|---|---|
| ☐ | UR-WRA | Antonov An-24RV | 37308709 | ex UR-VIK | |
| ☐ | UR-WRB | McDonnell-Douglas MD-82 | 49364/1276 | ex N937AS | |
| ☐ | UR-WRE | McDonnell-Douglas MD-82 | 49278/1183 | ex UR-CDA | <KHO |
| ☐ | UR-WRF | Embraer ERJ-195AR | 19000169 | ex HZ-NQB | |
| ☐ | UR-WRG | Embraer ERJ-195AR | 19000157 | ex HZ-NQA Sophia Kylvska Ukraine | |
| ☐ | UR-WRH | Airbus A321-231 | 2462 | ex G-TTID | |
| ☐ | UR-WRI | Airbus A321-231 | 2682 | ex G-TTIE | |

### WIZZ AIR UKRAINE — Wizzair Ukraine (WU/WAU) — Kiev-Borispol (BPL)

| | | | | | |
|---|---|---|---|---|---|
| ☐ | UR-WUA | Airbus A320-232 | 3531 | ex F-WWDX | |
| ☐ | UR-WUB | Airbus A319-132 | 3741 | ex F-WWIB | |

### YUZMASHAVIA — Yuzmash (2N/UMK) — Dnepropetrovsk-Kodaki (DNK)

| | | | | |
|---|---|---|---|---|
| ☐ | UR-78785 | Ilyushin Il-76MD | 0083489691 | ex RA-78785 |
| ☐ | UR-78786 | Ilyushin Il-76TD | 0083490693 | ex CCCP-78786 |
| ☐ | UR-87951 | Yakovlev Yak-40K | 9810957 | ex CCCP-87951 |

### ZETAVIA

| | | | | | |
|---|---|---|---|---|---|
| ☐ | UR-CID | Ilyushin Il-76TD | 0063465956 | | ♦ |

## VH- AUSTRALIA (Commonwealth of Australia)

### AD-ASTRAL AVIATION SERVICES — Perth International, WA (PER)

| | | | | | |
|---|---|---|---|---|---|
| ☐ | VH-FWA | Beech 1900C | UB-061 | ex N818BE | ♦ |
| ☐ | VH-KFN | Beech 1900C-1 | UC-173 | ex N412CM | ♦ |
| ☐ | VH-NOA | Beech 1900D | UE-094 | ex N94GL | ♦ |
| ☐ | VH-VOA | Beech 1900C | UB-62 | ex ZS-NAV | ♦ |

### ADAGOLD AVIATION — Brisbane (BNE)

| | | | | | |
|---|---|---|---|---|---|
| ☐ | CS-TQM | Airbus A340-313X | 117 | ex A6-EYC | ops Australian DF charters <HFY |

### ADVANCE AVIATION — Emerald, QLD (EMD)

| | | | | | |
|---|---|---|---|---|---|
| ☐ | VH-BCQ | Piper PA-31-350 Chieftain | 31-7952134 | ex N35265 | |
| ☐ | VH-FLZ | Beech Baron 58 | TH-274 | ex VH-OTP | ♦ |
| ☐ | VH-FWJ | Piper PA-31 Navajo C | 31-7712092 | ex ZK-PNX | |
| ☐ | VH-LEW | Beech Baron 58 | TH-749 | ex N1860L | ♦ |

| ☐ | VH-LWW | Piper PA-31 Navajo C | 31-8112034 | ex VH-NMT | | |
| ☐ | VH-NWN | Piper PA-31-350 Chieftain | 31-8152197 | ex VH-SAQ | | |
| ☐ | VH-TQC | Cessna 210N Centurion | 21063325 | ex N44ZP | | |
| ☐ | VH-VJE | Dornier 228-202 | 8041 | ex 5N-DOC | | |

## AEROLINK AIR SERVICES
**Sydney-Bankstown, NSA (BWU)**

| ☐ | VH-OZF | Embraer EMB.110P1 Bandeirante | 110201 | ex G-EIIO | |
| ☐ | VH-UQA | Embraer EMB.110P1 Bandeirante | 110245 | ex VH-XFL | |
| ☐ | VH-WBR | Embraer EMB.110P2 Bandeirante | 110292 | ex DQ-WBI | |
| ☐ | VH-XMA | Cessna 310R | 310R0628 | ex N31HS | ♦ |

## AEROPELICAN AIR SERVICES
**Aeropelican (OT/PEL)**  **Newcastle-Belmont, NSW (BEO)**

| ☐ | VH-OTD | British Aerospace Jetstream 3202 | 978 | ex G-BZYP | City of Newcastle |
| ☐ | VH-OTE | British Aerospace Jetstream 3202 | 980 | ex G-CBEP | City of Port Stephens |
| ☐ | VH-OTF | British Aerospace Jetstream 3202 | 982 | ex G-CBER | Narrabri Shire |
| ☐ | VH-OTH | British Aerospace Jetstream 32EP | 967 | ex ZK-ECN | |
| ☐ | VH-OTQ | British Aerospace Jetstream 3202 | 975 | ex G-BUTW | |
| ☐ | VH-OTR | British Aerospace Jetstream 3202 | 976 | ex G-BUUZ | |

## AIR AUSTRALIA
**(VC/AGC)**

| ☐ | VH-YQA | Airbus A320-212 | 0190 | ex F-OHFU | The Kimberley | [MPL] |

Ceased ops Mar12

## AIR LINK
**(ZL)**  **Dubbo, NSW (DBO)**

| ☐ | VH-BWQ | Cessna 310R | 310R1401 | ex N4915A | |
| ☐ | VH-DVR | Piper PA-31-350 Chieftain | 31-7952052 | ex N27936 | |
| ☐ | VH-DVW | Piper PA-31-350 Chieftain | 31-7952011 | ex VH-LHH | |
| ☐ | VH-HSL | Cessna 310R | 310R0946 | ex N8643G | |
| ☐ | VH-JMP | Cessna 310R | 310R1270 | ex N125SP | |
| ☐ | VH-MWP | Piper PA-31-350 Chieftain | 31-8352005 | ex N4109C | |
| ☐ | VH-MZF | Piper PA-31-350 Chieftain | 31-8252039 | ex N41064 | |
| ☐ | VH-RUE | Beech 1900D | UE-53 | ex ZK-JNG | |
| ☐ | VH-TDL | Piper PA-39 Twin Comanche C/R | 39-152 | ex VH-NHC | |

## AIR SOUTH REGIONAL
**Adelaide, SA (ADL)**

| ☐ | VH-EMP | Beech Baron 58 | TH-1491 | ex VH-FEK | |
| ☐ | VH-EQB | Embraer EMB.110P1 Bandeirante | 110214 | ex ZK-MAS | |
| ☐ | VH-YOA | Beech 1900D | UE-143 | ex ZS-SSX | |
| ☐ | VH-ZOA | Beech 1900D | UE-85 | ex VH-VNT | ♦ |

## AIR WHITSUNDAY SEAPLANES
**(RWS)**  **Whitsunday/Airlie Beach, QLD (WSY)**

| ☐ | VH-AQV | de Havilland DHC-2 Beaver | 1257 | ex N67685 | FP wfs |
| ☐ | VH-AWD | de Havilland DHC-2 Beaver | 1066 | ex VH-AYS | FP |
| ☐ | VH-AWI | de Havilland DHC-2 Beaver | 298 | ex VH-HQE | FP |
| ☐ | VH-AWY | de Havilland DHC-2 Beaver | 1444 | ex VH-SSG | FP |
| ☐ | VH-PGA | Cessna 208 Caravan I | 20800312 | ex N1127W | FP |
| ☐ | VH-PGB | Cessna 208 Caravan I | 20800346 | ex N209E | FP |
| ☐ | VH-PGT | Cessna 208 Caravan I | 20800345 | ex N208E | FP |
| ☐ | VH-WTY | Cessna 208 Caravan I | 20800522 | ex 1027V | FP♦ |

## AIRLINES OF TASMANIA
**Airtas (FO/ATM)**  **Hobart, TAS (HBA)**

| ☐ | VH-BTD | Piper PA-31 Navajo C | 31-7912041 | ex VH-ATG | |
| ☐ | VH-BTI | Piper PA-31 Navajo C | 31-8212003 | ex ZK-VNA | |
| ☐ | VH-BTN | Aero Commander 680FL | 1695-35 | ex D-IBME | |
| ☐ | VH-CCN | Cessna 404 Titan II | 404-0801 | ex VH-WZK | |
| ☐ | VH-LCD | Cessna U206G Stationair 6 | 20604523 | ex N673AA | |
| ☐ | VH-MYS | Cessna U206G Stationair 6 | 20605162 | ex N4921U | |
| ☐ | VH-OBL | Britten-Norman BN-2A-20 Islander | 2035 | ex ZK-OBL | |
| ☐ | VH-RTP | Britten-Norman BN-2A-6 Islander | 79 | ex G-AXIN | ♦ |
| ☐ | VH-TRC | Cessna 404 Titan II | 404-0129 | ex HL2013 | ♦ |
| ☐ | VH-WZM | Cessna 404 Titan II | 404-0837 | ex N68075 | |

## AIRNORTH REGIONAL
**Topend (TL/ANO)**  **Darwin, NT**

| ☐ | VH-ANA | Swearingen SA.227DC Metro 23 | DC-871B | ex VH-HCB | |
| ☐ | VH-ANK | Embraer EMB.120ER Brasilia | 120155 | ex VH-YDD | |
| ☐ | VH-ANN | Embraer EMB.120ER Brasilia | 120203 | ex VH-BRP | |
| ☐ | VH-ANO | Embraer ERJ-170LR | 17000099 | ex B-KXB | Savannah |
| ☐ | VH-ANV | Embraer ERJ-170LR | 17000280 | ex PT-TQG | |
| ☐ | VH-ANW | Swearingen SA.227DC Metro 23 | DC-873B | ex N3031Q | |
| ☐ | VH-ANY | Swearingen SA.227DC Metro 23 | DC-840B | ex N3022L | |

| | | | | | |
|---|---|---|---|---|---|
| ☐ | VH-ANZ | Embraer EMB.120RT Brasilia | 120135 | ex VH-XFR | |
| ☐ | VH-DIL | Embraer EMB.120ER Brasilia | 120153 | ex N285UE | |
| ☐ | VH-SWO | Embraer ERJ-170LR | 17000081 | ex B-KXA | |

## ALLIANCE AIRLINES      Alli (QQ/UTY)      Brisbane-International, QLD (BNE)

| | | | | | | |
|---|---|---|---|---|---|---|
| ☐ | VH-FKP | Fokker 50 | 20161 | ex VH-AHX | | [ADL] |
| ☐ | VH-FKV | Fokker 50 | 20303 | ex B-12273 | | |
| ☐ | VH-FKW | Fokker 50 | 20306 | ex B-12275 | | |
| ☐ | VH-FKX | Fokker 50 | 20312 | ex B-12276 | | |
| ☐ | VH-FKY | Fokker 50 | 20284 | ex B-12271 | | |
| ☐ | VH-FKZ | Fokker 50 | 20286 | ex B-12272 | | |
| ☐ | VH-FKA | Fokker 100 | 11345 | ex N885US | | |
| ☐ | VH-FKC | Fokker 100 | 11349 | ex P2-ANB | | |
| ☐ | VH-FKD | Fokker 100 | 11357 | ex N888AU | | |
| ☐ | VH-FKF | Fokker 100 | 11365 | ex N890US | | |
| ☐ | VH-FKG | Fokker 100 | 11366 | ex N891US | | |
| ☐ | VH-FKJ | Fokker 100 | 11372 | ex N892US | | |
| ☐ | VH-FKK | Fokker 100 | 11379 | ex N894US | | |
| ☐ | VH-FKL | Fokker 100 | 11380 | ex N895US | | |
| ☐ | VH-FWH | Fokker 100 | 11316 | ex G-BXNF | City of Townsville | based PER |
| ☐ | VH-FWI | Fokker 100 | 11318 | ex G-FIOR | City of Rockhampton | based PER |
| ☐ | VH-XWM | Fokker 100 | 11276 | ex D-AGPA | | |
| ☐ | VH-XWN | Fokker 100 | 11278 | ex D-AGPB | | |
| ☐ | VH-XWP | Fokker 100 | 11281 | ex D-AGPD | | ♦ |
| ☐ | VH-XWQ | Fokker 100 | 11300 | ex D-AGPE | | ♦ |
| ☐ | VH-XWR | Fokker 100 | 11306 | ex D-AGPG | | |
| ☐ | VH-XWS | Fokker 100 | 11314 | ex D-AGPL | | [BNE] |
| ☐ | VH-XWT | Fokker 100 | 11338 | ex D-AGPQ | | |
| ☐ | VH-QQX | Fokker 70 | 11571 | ex 9H-AFS | | ♦ |
| ☐ | VH-QQY | Fokker 70 | 11575 | ex 9H-AFZ | | ♦ |
| ☐ | ZK-JTQ | Boeing 737-476 | 24442/2371 | ex VH-JTQ | | .>AWK♦ |

## ALLIGATOR AIRWAYS      Kununurra, WA (KNX)

| | | | | | | |
|---|---|---|---|---|---|---|
| ☐ | VH-RAS | Cessna 207 Skywagon | 20700158 | ex N1558U | | |
| ☐ | VH-WOT | Cessna 207 Skywagon | 20700267 | ex ZK-DEW | | |
| ☐ | VH-WOU | Cessna 207 Skywagon | 20700099 | ex N91164 | | |
| ☐ | VH-WOX | Cessna 207Skywagon | 20700099 | ex ZK-DEW | | ♦ |
| ☐ | VH-WOY | Cessna 207A Stationair 8 | 20700707 | ex N9592M | | |
| ☐ | VH-BJN | Piper PA-23-250D Aztec | 27-4460 | ex F-OCFU | | |
| ☐ | VH-EDE | Cessna 210L Centurion II | 21060517 | ex (N94140) | | |
| ☐ | VH-IXE | Partenavia P.68B | 178 | | | |
| ☐ | VH-KWP | Piper PA-34-220T Seneca | 34-8133024 | ex ZS-KWN | | |
| ☐ | VH-NOQ | Gippsland GA-8 Airvan | GA8-00-127 | ex VH-WOQ | | |
| ☐ | VH-OBJ | Britten Norman BN-2A-21 Islander | 458 | ex ZK-JSB | | |
| ☐ | VH-RDA | Piper PA-31-350 Navajo Chieftain | 31-7305032 | ex N74903 | | |
| ☐ | VH-WNI | Cessna 210M Centurion II | 21062462 | ex N761RR | | |
| ☐ | VH-WOG | GippsAero GA-8-TC320 Airvan | GA8-TC320-10-154 | | | ♦ |
| ☐ | VH-WOP | GippsAero GA-8-TC320 Airvan | GA8-TC320-09-145 | | | ♦ |
| ☐ | VH-WOQ | GippsAero GA-8-TC320 Airvan | GA8-TC320-09-152 | | Miss Jane | ♦ |
| ☐ | VH-WOS | GippsAero GA-8-TC320 Airvan | GA8-TC320-09-151 | | | ♦ |

## AVTEX AVIATION      Sydney-Bankstown, NSW (BWU)

| | | | | | |
|---|---|---|---|---|---|
| ☐ | VH-MKK | Piper PA-31-350 Navajo Chieftain | 31-7652068 | | ♦ |

## BARRIER AVIATION      Cairns, QLD (CNS)

| | | | | | |
|---|---|---|---|---|---|
| ☐ | VH-BSO | Britten-Norman BN-2B-26 Islander | 2129 | ex JA5282 | |
| ☐ | VH-BWO | Britten-Norman BN-2A-26 Islander | 2042 | ex T8A-103 | |
| ☐ | VH-CIR | Cessna 310R | 310R1813 | ex G-BPYC | ♦ |
| ☐ | VH-HGO | Cessna 310R II | 21061159 | ex N2198S | |
| ☐ | VH-JOH | Cessna 402C | 4020486 | ex VH-JOC | |
| ☐ | VH-LFU | Cessna 207 Super Skywagon | 20700296 | ex ZK-DXT | ♦ |
| ☐ | VH-LKC | Cessna 402C | 4020625 | ex N6386X | |
| ☐ | VH-MDU | Cessna 210M Centurion | 21061634 | ex (N732NB) | |
| ☐ | VH-MHL | Cessna 207 Skywagon | 20700059 | ex N91076 | |
| ☐ | VH-SKG | Britten-Norman BN-2A-27 Islander | 609 | ex ZK-CRA | ♦ |
| ☐ | VH-SKU | Beech 200 Super King Air | BB-165 | ex VH-XRF | |
| ☐ | VH-THX | Cessna 402C | 4020250 | ex PK-DCC | |
| ☐ | VH-UBW | Cessna 207 Super Skywagon | 20700137 | ex N1537U | ♦ |
| ☐ | VH-URJ | Britten-Norman BN-2A-21 Islander | 402 | ex VH-OIA | |
| ☐ | VH-VDK | Cessna 402C | 4020801 | ex PK-DCY | ♦ |

## BRINDABELLA AIRLINES (FQ) Canberra, ACT (CBR)

| | | | | | | |
|---|---|---|---|---|---|---|
| ☐ | VH-OZV | Swearingen SA.227AC Metro III | AC-610B | ex VH-TGQ | | |
| ☐ | VH-SEF | Swearingen SA.227AC Metro III | AC-641 | ex ZK-SDA | | |
| ☐ | VH-TAG | Swearingen SA.227AC Metro III | AC-705 | ex ZK-NSU | | |
| ☐ | VH-TAM | Swearingen SA.227AC Metro III | AC-665 | ex VH-OZN | | |
| ☐ | VH-TAO | Swearingen SA.227AC Metro III | AC-513 | ex N513FA | | ♦ |
| | | | | | | |
| ☐ | VH-TAH | British Aerospace Jetstream 41 | 41084 | ex N566HK | | |
| ☐ | VH-TAI | British Aerospace Jetstream 41 | 41082 | ex N565HK | | |
| ☐ | VH-TAM | Swearingen SA.227AC Metro III | AC-665 | ex VH-OZN | | ♦ |

Ops services for Qantas

## BRISTOW HELICOPTERS (AUSTRALIA)
### Perth-Jandakot/Karratha/Barrow Island, WA/Darwin, NT (-/KTA/BWB/DRW)

| | | | | | | |
|---|---|---|---|---|---|---|
| ☐ | VH-BHH | Aérospatiale AS.332L | 2059 | ex G-TIGW | Nairn | |
| ☐ | VH-BHK | Aérospatiale AS.332L | 2096 | ex G-TIGU | | |
| ☐ | VH-BHX | Aérospatiale AS.332L | 2079 | ex G-BRWE | City of Albany | |
| ☐ | VH-BHY | Aérospatiale AS.332L | 2129 | ex B-HZY | | [KTA] |
| ☐ | VH-BWJ | Aérospatiale AS.332L | 2023 | ex G-TIGB | | wfs |
| ☐ | VH-BXZ | Aérospatiale AS.332L | 2078 | ex G-TIGT | | |
| ☐ | VH-BYT | Aérospatiale AS.332L | 2083 | ex G-CEYJ | | |
| ☐ | VH-BYV | Aérospatiale AS.332L | 2061 | ex G-TIGO | | |
| ☐ | VH-BZB | Aérospatiale AS.332L | 2157 | ex LN-OND | | |
| ☐ | VH-BZC | Aérospatiale AS.332L | 2036 | ex 9M-BEM | | |
| ☐ | VH-BZF | Aérospatiale AS.332L | 2064 | ex G-TIGP | | |
| ☐ | VH-BZU | Aérospatiale AS.332L | 2045 | ex G-TIGM | | |
| ☐ | VH-TZD | Aérospatiale AS.332L | 2122 | ex G-BLPM | | |
| ☐ | VH-ZFC | Eurocopter EC225LP | 2709 | ex G-ZZSP | | |
| ☐ | VH-ZFD | Eurocopter EC225LP | 2724 | ex G-CFZE | | |
| ☐ | VH-ZFE | Eurocopter EC225LP | 2726 | ex G-CFZY | | |
| ☐ | VH-ZFH | Eurocopter EC225LP | 2723 | ex G-ZZSH | | |
| | | | | | | |
| ☐ | VH-BHL | Sikorsky S-76A+ | 760046 | ex G-BHLY | | |
| ☐ | VH-BHM | Sikorsky S-76A+ | 760107 | ex G-BVKO | | |
| ☐ | VH-BZR | Sikorsky S-76A++ | 760132 | ex EZ-S704 | | |
| ☐ | VH-TZI | Sikorsky S-76C++ | 760774 | ex G-CGLS | | |
| ☐ | VH-TZL | Sikorsky S-76C+ | 760735 | ex G-CFPY | | |
| ☐ | VH-TZN | Sikorsky S-76A | 760115 | ex G-BVKR | | |
| ☐ | VH-TZR | Sikorsky S-76C+ | 760775 | ex G-CGLU | | |
| ☐ | VH-ZFJ | Sikorsky S-76C+ | 760733 | ex G-CFPV | | |
| | | | | | | |
| ☐ | VH-BHO | Bell 206L-3 LongRanger | 51354 | ex JA9893 | | |
| ☐ | VH-BKE | Kawasaki/MBB BK-117B-2 | 1042 | ex ZK-HLI | | |
| ☐ | VH-BKK | Kawasaki/MBB BK-117B-1 | 1044 | ex JA9993 | | ♦ |
| ☐ | VH-ZFM | Agusta AW139 | 41233 | ex N370SH | | |
| ☐ | VH-ZFN | Agusta AW139 | 41228 | ex N368SH | | |

## BROOME AVIATION Broome, WA (BME)

| | | | | | | |
|---|---|---|---|---|---|---|
| ☐ | VH-CRN | Cessna 208B Caravan I | 208B0428 | ex VH-URT | | ♦ |
| ☐ | VH-MOX | Cessna 208 Caravan I | 20800227 | ex VH-NGD | | |
| ☐ | VH-NCK | Cessna 208B Caravan I | 208B1129 | ex N229CF | | ♦ |
| ☐ | VH-NDC | Cessna 208B Caravan I | 208B2215 | ex N2056W | | |
| ☐ | VH-NGS | Cessna 208B Caravan I | 208B0416 | ex N1114W | | |
| ☐ | VH-NTC | Cessna 208B Caravan I | 208B0418 | ex VH-DEX | | |
| ☐ | VH-TLD | Cessna 208B Caravan I | 208B0339 | ex P2-TSJ | | |
| ☐ | VH-TWX | Cessna 208B Caravan I | 208B0648 | ex VH-UZF | | |
| | | | | | | |
| ☐ | VH-AOI | Cessna 210N Centurion II | 21064609 | ex N9821Y | | ♦ |
| ☐ | VH-AMG | Cessna 210N Centurion II | 21064075 | ex C-GTSW | | ♦ |
| ☐ | VH-DZH | Cessna 210L Centurion II | 21061247 | ex VH-SJQ | | |
| ☐ | VH-EGB | Cessna 210M Centurion II | 21062858 | ex N6969B | | ♦ |
| ☐ | VH-FOK | Cessna 210N Centurion II | 21063041 | ex N6559N | | ♦ |
| ☐ | VH-KDM | Cessna 210N Centurion II | 21063041 | ex N6467N | | |
| ☐ | VH-PBV | Cessna 210M Centurion II | 21062350 | ex N761LW | | ♦ |
| ☐ | VH-KJL | Cessna 210L Centurion II | 21060776 | ex N1765C | | |
| ☐ | VH-RLP | Cessna 210-5 (205) | 21050213 | ex (N8213Z) | | |
| ☐ | VH-SJG | Cessna 210L Centurion II | 21063529 | ex N6450A | | |
| ☐ | VH-SKQ | Cessna 210L Centurion II | 21061243 | ex N1629C | | |
| ☐ | VH-TCI | Cessna 210L Centurion II | 21060548 | ex N94225 | | |
| ☐ | VH-TWD | Cessna 210L Centurion II | 21064356 | ex N6372Y | | ♦ |
| ☐ | VH-WTX | Cessna 210L Centurion II | 21060222 | ex (N93025) | | |
| ☐ | VH-BBU | Cessna U206G Stationair | 20604109 | ex N756HS | | |
| ☐ | VH-DAW | Cessna 310R II | 310R0148 | ex N5028J | | |
| ☐ | VH-DLF | Cessna 404 | 404-0683 | ex N6763K | | |
| ☐ | VH-DMN | Beech Baron 58 | TH-1103 | ex VH-HUG | | ♦ |
| ☐ | VH-ENT | Cessna 404 Titan II | 404-0818 | ex ZK-ECP | | ♦ |
| ☐ | VH-JOR | Cessna 404 | 404-0642 | ex D-IEEE | | |
| ☐ | VH-JOV | Cessna 402C | 402C0087 | | | ♦ |

| | | | | | |
|---|---|---|---|---|---|
| ☐ | VH-KEZ | Cessna 402C | 402C0262 | | ◆ |
| ☐ | VH-LBB | Cessna 402C | 402C0283 | ex N470A | ◆ |
| ☐ | VH-SKC | Cessna 404 Titan II | 404-0404 | ex VH-TWZ | ◆ |
| ☐ | VH-SHZ | Cessna U206G Stationair | 20603726 | ex (N9909N) | ◆ |
| ☐ | VH-TDQ | Cessna U206F Stationair | 20602801 | | ◆ |
| ☐ | VH-WSF | Beech Baron 58 | TH-549 | ex VH-WZG | ◆ |
| ☐ | VH-ZOR | Beech 200 Super King Air | BB-762 | ex N762KA | ◆ |

### CAIRNS SEAPLANES

**Cairns, QLD (CNS)**

| | | | | | |
|---|---|---|---|---|---|
| ☐ | VH-CXS | de Havilland DHC-2 Beaver | 1360 | ex N211AW | FP |
| ☐ | VH-PCF | de Havilland DHC-2 Beaver | 1348 | ex VH-CZS | FP |

### CASAIR

**Perth-International, WA (PER)**

| | | | | |
|---|---|---|---|---|
| ☐ | VH-KGX | Swearingen SA.226TC Metro II | TC-326 | ex VH-UUK |
| ☐ | VH-NGX | Swearingen SA.226TC Metro II | TC-287 | ex VH-WGV |
| ☐ | VH-OGX | Swearingen SA.226TC Metro II | TC-395 | ex VH-TFQ |
| ☐ | VH-WGX | Swearingen SA.226TC Metro II | TC-312 | ex N1015B |

### CHARTAIR

**(TL)**     **Alice Springs, NT (ASP)**

| | | | | |
|---|---|---|---|---|
| ☐ | VH-BYK | Cessna 210L Centurion | 21060435 | ex N2691W |
| ☐ | VH-IDZ | Cessna 210M Centurion II | 21062530 | ex N761UN |
| ☐ | VH-JLC | Cessna 210N Centurion II | 21063490 | ex VH-OKH |
| ☐ | VH-KST | Cessna 210M Centurion II | 21062521 | ex ZK-KLG |
| ☐ | VH-LTB | Cessna 210N Centurion II | 21064679 | ex N670A |
| ☐ | VH-NQP | Cessna 210N Centurion II | 21064572 | ex N9678Y |
| ☐ | VH-OKJ | Cessna 210M Centurion II | 21061602 | ex VH-FZO |
| ☐ | VH-RDH | Cessna 210N Centurion II | 21065374 | ex N5427Y |
| ☐ | VH-TFF | Cessna 210N Centurion II | 21064277 | ex N6169Y |
| ☐ | VH-TFL | Cessna 210M Centurion II | 21063678 | ex N671AA |
| ☐ | VH-TFT | Cessna 210N Centurion II | 21063448 | |
| ☐ | VH-TWP | Cessna 210M Centurion II | 21061841 | ex N1636C |
| ☐ | VH-WMP | Cessna 210M Centurion II | 21062731 | ex N6278B |

| | | | | | |
|---|---|---|---|---|---|
| ☐ | VH-BUY | Cessna 404 Titan | 4040611 | ex N2684R | |
| ☐ | VH-CAJ | Cessna 402C II | 402C0026 | ex N5717C | |
| ☐ | VH-COQ | Cessna 310R | 310R1643 | ex N2635Y | |
| ☐ | VH-FTW | Beech 95-B55 Baron | TC-2123 | ex N24097 | |
| ☐ | VH-HOR | Cessna 402C | 402C0108 | ex P2-KSR | |
| ☐ | VH-JJN | Beech Baron 58 | TH-1276 | ex N3837M | |
| ☐ | VH-LGX | Piper PA-31-350 Chieftain | 31-8452001 | ex N41160 | |
| ☐ | VH-LWA | Cessna 208B Caravan I | 208B1173 | ex N208JJ | |
| ☐ | VH-NGC | Cessna 208B Caravan I | 208B0916 | ex VH-SMH | ◆ |
| ☐ | VH-NGK | Cessna 208B Caravan I | 208B1203 | ex HB-CZE | ◆ |
| ☐ | VH-PBI | Cessna 310R | 310R0831 | ex N3423G | |
| ☐ | VH-SKN | Cessna 310R | 310R1681 | ex ZK-ETM | |
| ☐ | VH-SMW | Beech Baron 58 | TH-694 | ex N6076S | |
| ☐ | VH-TFM | Cessna 402C II | 402C0067 | ex N2610Y | |
| ☐ | VH-TZH | Cessna 402C II | 402C0617 | ex N6880Y | |
| ☐ | VH-UCD | Cessna 402C II | 402C0049 | ex N5825C | |
| ☐ | VH-WZT | Beech Baron 58 | TH-542 | ex VH-TYR | |

### CHC HELICOPTERS (AUSTRALIA)

**Hems (HEM)**     **Adelaide-International, SA (ADL)**

| | | | | | |
|---|---|---|---|---|---|
| ☐ | VH-LAF | Aérospatiale SA.332L1 | 2319 | ex LN-OBT | <CHC Scotia |
| ☐ | VH-LAG | Aérospatiale SA.332L1 | 2352 | ex LN-OBU | <CHC Scotia |
| ☐ | VH-LHG | Aérospatiale SA.332L1 | 2317 | ex LN-OBR | |
| ☐ | VH-LHH | Aérospatiale AS.332L1 | 2407 | ex 9M-STU | <CHC Intl |
| ☐ | VH-LHJ | Aérospatiale AS.332L | 2063 | ex G-BSOI | |
| ☐ | VH-LOF | Aérospatiale AS.332L | 2058 | ex G-CDSV | <CHC Intl |
| ☐ | VH-LOJ | Aérospatiale AS.332L | 2312 | ex C-FWPE | <CHC Intl |
| ☐ | VH-LYH | Aérospatiale AS.332L | 2468 | ex C-GGKX | ◆ |
| ☐ | VH-LYI | Aérospatiale AS.332L | 2381 | ex C-GGKY | ◆ |
| ☐ | VH-LYP | Aérospatiale AS.332L | 9008 | ex C-GOSA | ◆ |
| ☐ | VH-WEQ | Eurocopter EC.225LP | 2688 | ex LN-OHU | ◆ |
| ☐ | VH-WEV | Eurocopter EC.225LP | 2768 | ex G-NNCY | ◆ |
| ☐ | VH-WEX | Eurocopter EC.225LP | 2775 | ex G-CMJK | ◆ |
| ☐ | VH-WGV | Eurocopter EC225LP | 2794 | | ◆ |
| ☐ | VH-WSO | Eurocopter EC225LP | 2779 | | ◆ |

| | | | | | |
|---|---|---|---|---|---|
| ☐ | VH-SYJ | Agusta AW139 | 31114 | | Op for NSW Air Ambulance |
| ☐ | VH-SYV | Agusta AW139 | 31126 | | Op for NSW Air Ambulance |
| ☐ | VH-SYZ | Agusta AW139 | 31155 | | Op for NSW Air Ambulance |
| ☐ | VH-WEJ | Agusta AW139 | 31319 | ex G-CGRG | ◆ |
| ☐ | VH-WEK | Agusta AW139 | 31320 | ex G-CGRH | ◆ |

| | | | | | |
|---|---|---|---|---|---|
| ☐ | VH-BZH | Bell 412 | 33044 | ex N18098 | |
| ☐ | VH-EPH | Bell 412EP | 36419 | ex N3070R | Op for NSW Air Ambulance |
| ☐ | VH-EPK | Bell 412EP | 36100 | ex N412HH | Op for NSW Air Ambulance |

| | | | | | |
|---|---|---|---|---|---|
| ☐ | VH-EWA | Bell 412EP | 36312 | ex C-GUOP | |
| ☐ | VH-NSC | Bell 412 | 33029 | ex VH-CRQ | EMS, based CBR |
| ☐ | VH-NSP | Bell 412 | 33091 | ex N22976 | EMS |
| ☐ | VH-NSV | Bell 412 | 33084 | ex VH-AHH | EMS, based MKY |
| ☐ | VH-VAA | Bell 412EP | 36274 | ex C-GLZM | Op for Metropolitan Ambulance Sve |
| ☐ | VH-VAB | Bell 412EP | 36275 | | Op for Metropolitan Ambulance Sve |
| | | | | | |
| ☐ | VH-HRP | Sikorsky S-76A+ | 760122 | ex N176CH | based East Sale op for RAAF |
| ☐ | VH-LAH | Sikorsky S-76A+ | 760089 | ex RJAF 725 | based NTL |
| ☐ | VH-LAI | Sikorsky S-76A+ | 760103 | ex RJAF 727 | |
| ☐ | VH-LHN | Sikorsky S-76A++ | 760300 | ex B-HZE | |
| ☐ | VH-LHY | Sikorsky S-76A+ | 760105 | ex RJAF 729 | based Pearce |
| ☐ | VH-LHZ | Sikorsky S-76A+ | 760113 | ex RJAF 732 | RAAF rescue |
| | | | | | |
| ☐ | VH-LOH | Sikorsky S-92D | 920036 | ex N8068D | |
| ☐ | VH-PVD | Aérosapatiale SA.365N3 Dauphin | 6846 | ex F-WWOK | based MEN ♦ |
| ☐ | VH-PVE | Eurocopter EC135T2 | 0834 | | based MEN |
| ☐ | VH-PVG | Aérospatiale SA.365N3 Dauphin 2 | 6539 | ex (HB-XQS) | based MEN♦ |
| ☐ | VH-PVH | Aérospatiale AS365N3 Dauphin 2 | 6604 | ex F-WQDC | based MEN |
| ☐ | VH-SYB | Eurocopter EC145+ | 9203 | ex D-HMBZ | ♦ |
| ☐ | VH-SYG | Eurocopter EC145+ | 9235 | ex D-HMBJ | ♦ |

## COBHAM AVIATION SERVICES AUSTRALIA    National Jet (NC/NJS)    Adelaide-International, SA (ADL)

| | | | | | |
|---|---|---|---|---|---|
| ☐ | VH-NBU | Avro 146-RJ100 | E3243 | ex PK-RAY | [ADL] |
| ☐ | VH-NJI | Avro 146-RJ100 | E3265 | ex VH-NBK | [ADL] |
| ☐ | VH-NJP | Avro 146-RJ100 | E3354 | ex G-BZAW | |
| ☐ | VH-NJQ | Avro 146-RJ100 | E3328 | ex G-BZAU | |
| ☐ | VH-NJT | Avro 146-RJ70A | E1228 | ex G-OLXX | |
| ☐ | VH-NJY | Avro 146-RJ100 | E3331 | ex G-BZAV | |
| | | | | | |
| ☐ | VH-NXD | Boeing 717-23S | 55062/5031 | ex VH-VQD | ♦ |
| ☐ | VH-NXE | Boeing 717-23S | 55063/5034 | ex VH-VQE | ♦ |
| ☐ | VH-NXG | Boeing 717-2K9 | 55057/5020 | ex VH-LAX | ♦ |
| ☐ | VH-NXH | Boeing 717-2K9 | 55055/5014 | ex VH-IMD | ♦ |
| ☐ | VH-NXI | Boeing 717-2K9 | 55054/5013 | ex VH-IMP | ♦ |
| ☐ | VH-NXJ | Boeing 717-2BL | 55168/5116 | ex N904ME | ♦ |
| ☐ | VH-NXK | Boeing 717-231 | 55092/5077 | ex VH-YQF | ♦ |
| ☐ | VH-NXL | Boeing 717-231 | 55093/5083 | ex VH-YQG | ♦ |
| ☐ | VH-NXM | Boeing 717-231 | 55094/5084 | ex VH-YQH | ♦ |
| ☐ | VH-NXN | Boeing 717-231 | 55095/5087 | ex VH-YQI | ♦ |
| ☐ | VH-NXO | Boeing 717-231 | 55096/5093 | ex VH-YQJ | ♦ |
| ☐ | VH-NXQ | Boeing 717-231 | 55097/5095 | ex VH-YQK | ♦ |
| | | | | | |
| ☐ | VH-NJC | British Aerospace 146 Srs.100 | E1013 | ex G-6-013 | |
| ☐ | VH-NJF | British Aerospace 146 Srs.300QT | E3198 | ex G-BTLD | |
| ☐ | VH-NJG | British Aerospace 146 Srs.200 | E2170 | ex G-BSOH | |
| ☐ | VH-NJL | British Aerospace 146 Srs.300 | E3213 | ex G-BVPE | |
| ☐ | VH-NJM | British Aerospace 146 Srs.300QT | E3194 | ex G-BTHT | |
| ☐ | VH-NJN | British Aerospace 146 Srs.300 | E3217 | ex G-BUHW | |
| ☐ | VH-NJR | British Aerospace 146 Srs.100 | E1152 | ex G-BRLN | |
| ☐ | VH-NJV | British Aerospace 146 Srs.100QT | E1002 | ex G-BSTA | |
| ☐ | VH-NJX | British Aerospace 146 Srs.100 | E1003 | ex EI-CPY | [ADL] |
| ☐ | VH-NJZ | British Aerospace 146 Srs.300QT | E3126 | ex G-BPNT | |
| ☐ | VH-YAD | British Aerospace 146 Srs.200 | E2097 | ex N293UE | [ADL] |
| ☐ | VH-YAE | British Aerospace 146 Srs.200 | E2107 | ex N294UE | |
| | | | | | |
| ☐ | VH-JSJ | de Havilland DHC-8-103 | 170 | ex VH-NJD | |
| ☐ | VH-LCL | de Havilland DHC-8Q-202 | 492 | ex C-GEOA | op for RAN |
| ☐ | VH-SBJ | de Havilland DHC-8Q-315 | 578 | ex C-FDHI | |
| ☐ | VH-ZZA | de Havilland DHC-8-202MPA | 419 | ex C-FWWU | op for Custom Coastwatch |
| ☐ | VH-ZZB | de Havilland DHC-8-202MPA | 424 | ex C-FXBC | op for Custom Coastwatch |
| ☐ | VH-ZZC | de Havilland DHC-8-202MPA | 433 | ex C-FXFK | op for Custom Coastwatch |
| ☐ | VH-ZZE | de Havilland DHC-8Q-315MPA | 640 | ex C-FHQG | op for Custom Coastwatch |
| ☐ | VH-ZZF | de Havilland DHC-8Q-315MPA | 643 | ex C-FJKS | op for Custom Coastwatch |
| ☐ | VH-ZZG | de Havilland DHC-8Q-315MPA | 644 | ex C-FJKU | op for Custom Coastwatch |
| ☐ | VH-ZZI | de Havilland DHC-8-202MPA | 550 | ex C-GDLD | op for Custom Coastwatch |
| ☐ | VH-ZZJ | de Havilland DHC-8-202MPA | 551 | ex C-FDHI | op for Custom Coastwatch |
| ☐ | VH-ZZN | de Havilland DHC-8-315 | 399 | ex VH-JSQ | op for Custom Coastwatch |
| ☐ | VH-ZZP | de Havilland DHC-8-202 | 411 | ex VH-JSH | op for Custom Coastwatch |
| | | | | | |
| ☐ | VH-YZE | Reims Cessna F406 Vigilant | F406-0076 | ex VH-ZZE | op for Custom Coastwatch |
| ☐ | VH-YZF | Reims Cessna F406 Vigilant | F406-0078 | ex VH-ZZF | op for Custom Coastwatch |
| ☐ | VH-YZG | Reims Cessna F406 Vigilant | F406-0079 | ex VH-ZZG | op for Custom Coastwatch |

## CORPORATE AIR    Canberra, ACT (CBR)

| | | | | | |
|---|---|---|---|---|---|
| ☐ | VH-VED | Cessna 441 Conquest II | 441-0272 | ex N394G | |
| ☐ | VH-VEH | Cessna 441 Conquest II | 441-0238 | ex N3NC | |
| ☐ | VH-VEJ | Cessna 441 Conquest II | 441-0249 | ex N911ER | |
| ☐ | VH-VEW | Cessna 441 Conquest II | 441-0264 | ex C-FWCP | |
| ☐ | VH-VEY | Cessna 441 Conquest II | 441-0295 | ex N181MD | |

| | VH-VEZ | Cessna 441 Conquest II | 441-0182 | ex VH-AZB |
|---|---|---|---|---|

| | VH-VEA | Cessna 404 Titan II | 404-0219 | ex VH-ARQ |
|---|---|---|---|---|
| | VH-VEB | Beech Baron 58 | TH-399 | ex VH-CYT |
| | VH-VEC | Cessna 404 Titan II | 404-0217 | ex VH-CSV |
| | VH-VEG | Beech Baron 58 | TH-822 | ex VH-WIM |
| | VH-VEK | Swearingen SA.227DC Metro 23 | DC-845B | ex VH-KED |
| | VH-VEU | Swearingen SA.227TC Metro 23 | DC-797B | ex VH-KDJ |

## DE BRUIN AIR — Mount Gambier, SA (MGB)

| | VH-OAA | Cessna 441 Conquest II | 441-0102 | ex N4246Z | ♦ |
|---|---|---|---|---|---|
| | VH-OAB | British Aerospace Jetstream 32EP | 853 | ex N853JX | |
| | VH-OAE | British Aerospace Jetstream 32EP | 851 | ex N851JX | |
| | VH-OAM | British Aerospace Jetstream 32EP | 859 | ex N859AE | |
| | VH-OAV | Vulcanair P.68C | 460/C | | ♦ |

## EASTERN AUSTRALIA AIRLINES — (EAQ) — Sydney-Kingsford Smith, NSW (SYD)

A wholly-owned subsidiary of Qantas and ops scheduled services in full colours as QantasLink

## EXPRESS FREIGHTERS AUSTRALIA — (EFA) — Sydney-Kingsford Smith, NSW (SYD)

| | VH-XMB | Boeing 737-376 (SF) | 23478/1251 | ex ZK-JNG | |
|---|---|---|---|---|---|
| | VH-XML | Boeing 737-376 (SF) | 23486/1286 | ex ZK-JNF | |
| | VH-XMO | Boeing 737-376 (SF) | 23488/1352 | ex ZK-JNH | |
| | VH-XMR | Boeing 737-376 (SF) | 23490/1390 | ex ZK-JNA | |
| | VH-EFR | Boeing 767-381F | 33510/939 | ex | op for QF Freight♦ |

## GAM AIR SERVICES — Melbourne-Essendon, VIC (MEB)

| | VH-DZC | Rockwell 500S Shrike Commander | 3226 | ex G-BDAL |
|---|---|---|---|---|
| | VH-KAK | Rockwell 500S Shrike Commander | 3269 | ex N57163 |
| | VH-LET | Rockwell 500S Shrike Commander | 3264 | ex N70343 |
| | VH-LTP | Rockwell 500S Shrike Commander | 3323 | ex N12RS |
| | VH-MDW | Rockwell 500S Shrike Commander | 3158 | ex N801AC |
| | VH-MEH | Rockwell 500S Shrike Commander | 3258 | ex N57213 |
| | VH-UJI | Rockwell 500S Shrike Commander | 3301 | ex VH-TWS |
| | VH-UJL | Rockwell 500S Shrike Commander | 3088 | ex N9120N |
| | VH-UJM | Rockwell 500S Shrike Commander | 3117 | ex N5007H |
| | VH-UJN | Rockwell 500S Shrike Commander | 3151 | ex ZS-NRO |
| | VH-UJR | Rockwell 500S Shrike Commander | 3311 | ex VH-PAR |
| | VH-UJS | Rockwell 500S Shrike Commander | 1797-12 | ex VH-EXF |
| | VH-UJU | Rockwell 500S Shrike Commander | 3055 | ex VH-PWO |
| | VH-UJV | Rockwell 500S Shrike Commander | 3161 | ex N712PC |
| | VH-UJX | Aero Commander 500S Shrike | 1839-31 | ex VH-EXI |
| | VH-YJC | Rockwell 500S Shrike Commander | 3176 | ex VH-ACZ |
| | VH-YJJ | Rockwell 500S Shrike Commander | 3178 | ex VH-ACJ |
| | VH-YJL | Aero Commander 500S Shrike | 1875-48 | ex VH-ACL |
| | VH-YJM | Rockwell 500S Shrike Commander | 3186 | ex RP-C1268 |
| | VH-YJO | Aero Commander 500B | 1506-180 | ex VH-WRU |
| | VH-YJR | Rockwell 500S Shrike Commander | 3231 | ex VH-PCO |
| | VH-YJS | Rockwell 500S Shrike Commander | 3315 | ex VH-FGS |
| | VH-YJU | Aero Commander 500U Shrike | 1765-49 | ex F-ODHD |

| | VH-NBT | Rockwell Commander 681B | 6047 | ex VH-NYE |
|---|---|---|---|---|
| | VH-PCV | Rockwell 690A Turbo Commander | 11283 | ex N57228 |
| | VH-UJA | Aero Commander 680FL | 1521-100 | ex PK-MAG |
| | VH-YJA | Aero Commander 680FL | 1734-140 | ex RP-C699 |
| | VH-YJF | Aero Commander 680FL | 1642-122 | ex N1414S |
| | VH-YJG | Rockwell 690A Turbo Commander | 11308 | ex N99WC |

| | VH-IHA | Piper PA-31 Turbo Navajo | 31-136 | ex N9099Y |
|---|---|---|---|---|
| | VH-VJD | Dornier 228-202K | 8157 | ex D2-EBT |
| | VH-VJE | Dornier 228-202 | 8041 | ex 5N-DOC |
| | VH-VJF | Dornier 228-202 | 8047 | ex 5N-ARF |
| | VH-VJJ | Dornier 228-202 | 8025 | ex 5N-DOA |

## GOLD COAST SEAPLANES — Coolangatta, QLD (OOL)

| | VH-IDO | de Havilland DHC-2 Beaver | 1545 | FP |
|---|---|---|---|---|

## GOLDEN EAGLE AIRLINES — Port Hedland, WA (PHE)

| | VH-AEC | Britten-Norman BN-2B-26 Islander | 2164 | ex G-BKJO |
|---|---|---|---|---|
| | VH-AEU | Britten-Norman BN-2B-26 Islander | 2130 | ex G-BJON |
| | VH-AEX | Cessna U206G Stationair 6 II | U20606587 | ex N9635Z |
| | VH-EGE | Britten-Norman BN-2A-26 Islander | 3015 | ex VH-WRM |
| | VH-FML | Piper PA-31 Navajo C | 31-8112015 | ex N40540 |

| | | | | | |
|---|---|---|---|---|---|
| ☐ | VH-KTS | Piper PA-31 Navajo C | 31-7912014 | ex N27833 | |
| ☐ | VH-LCK | Piper PA-34-200 Seneca | 34-7350236 | ex N55663 | |
| ☐ | VH-NMK | Piper PA-31-350 Chieftain | 31-8152163 | ex P2-RHA | |
| ☐ | VH-NPA | Piper PA-31-350 Chieftain | 31-8452016 | ex N41171 | |
| ☐ | VH-PJY | Cessna U206G Stationair 6 II | U20605120 | ex N4829U | |
| ☐ | VH-UPK | Cessna U206G Stationair 6 II | U20605477 | ex (N6399U) | |

## GOLDFIELDS AIR SERVICES (GOS) Kalgoorlie, WA (KGI)

| | | | | | |
|---|---|---|---|---|---|
| ☐ | VH-NTE | Beech 200 Super King Air | BB-529 | ex VH-SWP | ♦ |
| ☐ | VH-TFT | Cessna 210N Centurion | 21063448 | ex N5456A | ♦ |

## HARDY AVIATION Darwin, NT (DRW)

| | | | | | |
|---|---|---|---|---|---|
| ☐ | VH-ANM | Cessna 404 Titan II | 404-0010 | ex VH-BPM | |
| ☐ | VH-HAZ | Cessna 404 Titan II | 404-0046 | ex G-BYLR | |
| ☐ | VH-HMA | Cessna 404 Titan II | 404-0122 | ex N37158 | |
| ☐ | VH-HVR | Cessna 404 Titan II | 404-0673 | ex N404MT | |
| ☐ | VH-UOP | Cessna 404 Titan II | 404-0636 | ex N5280J | |
| | | | | | |
| ☐ | VH-AZW | Cessna 441 Conquest II | 441-0028 | ex VH-FWA | |
| ☐ | VH-JVB | Cessna 441 Conquest | 441-0231 | ex N441YA | |
| ☐ | VH-JVL | Cessna 441 Conquest | 441-0352 | ex AP-BCQ | ♦ |
| ☐ | VH-JVN | Cessna 441 Conquest | 441-0247 | ex N5HG | ♦ |
| ☐ | VH-JVY | Cessna 441 Conquest | 441-0074 | ex N441RK | ♦ |
| | | | | | |
| ☐ | VH-ANS | Cessna 210M Centurion II | 21062784 | ex N784ED | |
| ☐ | VH-ARJ | Cessna 402B | 402B0629 | ex N3784C | |
| ☐ | VH-ASN | Embraer EMB.120ER Brasilia | 120056 | ex N334JS | ♦ |
| ☐ | VH-BEM | Cessna 402B | 404B0590 | ex N402HA | |
| ☐ | VH-CNH | Swearingen SA.227DC Metro 23 | DC-899B | ex YV-256T | ♦ |
| ☐ | VH-HPA | Cessna U206G Stationair 6 | U20605002 | ex VH-WIW | |
| ☐ | VH-HVH | Swearingen SA.227DC Metro 23 | DC-886B | ex N3006M | ♦ |
| ☐ | VH-JZL | Cessna TU206G Stationair 6 | U20604721 | ex N732TS | |
| ☐ | VH-MJN | Cessna 210M Centurion | 21061888 | ex N732YU | ♦ |
| ☐ | VH-MKS | Swearingen SA.226TC Metro II | TC-262 | ex N49GW | |
| ☐ | VH-MNH | Beech Baron 58 | TH-1137 | ex N67249 | ♦ |
| ☐ | VH-NOK | Cessna 210M Centurion II | 21062063 | ex N9127M | |
| ☐ | VH-RAP | Cessna U206F Stationair | U20602989 | ex VH-DXU | |
| ☐ | VH-RUY | Cessna 402C | 402C0273 | ex N1774G | |
| ☐ | VH-SGO | Beech 58 Baron | TH-1185 | ex N3702D | |
| ☐ | VH-SQL | Cessna 402C II | 402C0326 | ex VH-OAS | |
| ☐ | VH-TFG | Swearingen SA.227AC Metro III | AC-504 | ex N31072 | |
| ☐ | VH-TGD | Swearingen SA.227AC Metro III | AC-667B | ex C-FAFS | |
| ☐ | VH-TWC | Swearingen SA.227DC Metro 23 | DC-896B | ex D-CSWF | |
| ☐ | VH-TWL | Swearingen SA.227DC Metro 23 | DC-896B | ex D-CSWF | ♦ |
| ☐ | VH-XSM | Beech E55 Baron | TE-804 | ex P2-COE | ♦ |

## HEAVYLIFT CARGO AIRLINES HeavyCargo (HN/HVY) Brisbane-International, QLD (BNE)

| | | | | | |
|---|---|---|---|---|---|
| ☐ | RP-C8020 | Short SC.5 Belfast | SH1819 | ex 9L-LDQ | |

## HELIWEST Perth, WA (PER)

| | | | | | |
|---|---|---|---|---|---|
| ☐ | VH-BII | Aérospatiale AS.350B2 | 2267 | ex N13HF | ♦ |
| ☐ | VH-DEA | Aérospatiale AS.350BA | 1447 | ex N121US | ♦ |
| ☐ | VH-DHQ | Aérospatiale AS350B2 | 9057 | ex I-MCDT | ♦ |
| ☐ | VH-JVC | Aérospatiale AS.350BA | 1516 | ex P2-PHB | ♦ |
| ☐ | VH-LRW | Aérospatiale AS.350B2 | 1819 | ex N78KR | ♦ |
| ☐ | VH-NRW | Aérospatiale AS.350B2 | 3232 | ex N350JG | ♦ |
| | | | | | |
| ☐ | VH-BHO | Bell 206L3 LongRanger | 51354 | ex JA9893 | ♦ |
| ☐ | VH-BHT | Bell 206L1 LongRanger | 45223 | ex N4643E | ♦ |
| ☐ | VH-CYJ | Bell 206L3 LongRanger | 51245 | ex JA9767 | ♦ |
| ☐ | VH-LHP | Bell 206L3 LongRanger | 51002 | ex G-CJCB | ♦ |
| ☐ | VH-ZHP | Bell 206L3 LongRanger | 45308 | ex N2774V | op for Queensland Police ♦ |
| ☐ | VH-ZWV | Bell 206L3 LongRanger | 51040 | ex N209RM | ♦ |
| | | | | | |
| ☐ | VH-XRA | MBB Bo.105LSA-3 | 2015 | ex N31RX | ♦ |
| ☐ | VH-XRF | MBB Bo.105LSA-3 | 2032 | ex N999SA | ♦ |
| ☐ | VH-XRG | MBB Bo.105LSA-3 | 2037 | ex C-FRIQ | ♦ |
| ☐ | VH-XRI | MBB Bo.105LSA-3 | 2041 | ex N404AB | ♦ |
| ☐ | VH-XRQ | MBB Bo.105LSA-3 | 2016 | ex TC-HCR | ♦ |
| ☐ | VH-XRX | MBB Bo.105LSA-3 | 2033 | ex N315LS | ♦ |
| | | | | | |
| ☐ | VH-BIN | Bell 206B JetRanger III | 2019 | ex VH-UEE | ♦ |
| ☐ | VH-CFE | Bell 412EP | 36204 | ex N30Y | ♦ |
| ☐ | VH-VJG | Bell 206B JetRanger III | 2169 | ex 9M-AVM | ♦ |
| ☐ | VH-VJH | Bell 206B JetRanger III | 1047 | ex 9M-AVL | ♦ |
| ☐ | VH-XFM | DHC-6 Twin Otter 200 | 164 | ex P2-MBU | op for Fortescue Metals ♦ |
| ☐ | VH-ZMN | Bell 206B JetRanger III | 3591 | ex VH-UPT | ♦ |

## HINTERLAND AVIATION                                                                 Cairns, QLD (CNS)

| | | | | | |
|---|---|---|---|---|---|
| ☐ | VH-CVN | Cessna 208B Caravan I | 208B0676 | ex N12372 | |
| ☐ | VH-ETF | Cessna 208B Caravan I | 208B1175 | ex G-GOTF | ◆ |
| ☐ | VH-HLL | Cessna 208B Caravan I | 208B0615 | ex VH-AGS | |
| ☐ | VH-MRZ | Cessna 208B Caravan I | 208B1048 | ex N1266V | |
| ☐ | VH-TFQ | Cessna 208B Caravan I | 208B1216 | ex N84BP | |
| ☐ | VH-TFS | Cessna 208B Caravan I | 208B1006 | ex N1247N | |
| | | | | | |
| ☐ | VH-HLJ | Beech B200 Super King Air | BB-945 | ex RP-C11577 | |
| ☐ | VH-JOB | Cessna 310R | 310R1236 | ex G-BOAT | |
| ☐ | VH-NTM | Cessna 310R | 310R1213 | ex N13659 | ◆ |
| ☐ | VH-SKH | Cessna 310R | 310R1221 | | |
| ☐ | VH-TFK | Cessna 402C III | 402C1011 | ex VH-PVU | |
| ☐ | VH-TFO | Cessna 404 Titan II | 404-0076 | ex N32L | |
| ☐ | VH-TFU | Cessna 404 Titan | 404-0834 | ex VH-SZO | |
| ☐ | VH-TFY | Rockwell 500S Shrike Commander | 3057 | ex VH-IBY | |
| ☐ | VH-TFZ | Cessna 402C II | 402C0408 | ex VH-RMI | |
| ☐ | VH-TSI | Cessna 402C | 402C0492 | ex N6841L | |

## JETGO AUSTRALIA

| | | | | | |
|---|---|---|---|---|---|
| ☐ | VH-JTG | Embraer ERJ-135LR | 145687 | ex XA-AMM | ◆ |

## JETSTAR AIRWAYS                          Jetstar (JQ/JST)          Melbourne-Tullamarine, VIC (MEL)

| | | | | | |
|---|---|---|---|---|---|
| ☐ | VH-JQG | Airbus A320-232 | 2169 | ex F-WWDQ | |
| ☐ | VH-JQL | Airbus A320-232 | 2185 | ex F-WWDB | |
| ☐ | VH-JQX | Airbus A320-232 | 2197 | ex F-WWDH | |
| ☐ | VH-VFF | Airbus A320-232 | 5039 | ex F-WWDG | ◆ |
| ☐ | VH-VGA | Airbus A320-232 | 4899 | ex F-WWES | ◆ |
| ☐ | VH-VGD | Airbus A320-232 | 4527 | ex D-AXAJ | |
| ☐ | VH-VGF | Airbus A320-232 | 4497 | ex F-WWIK | |
| ☐ | VH-VGH | Airbus A320-232 | 4495 | ex D-AUBK | |
| ☐ | VH-VGI | Airbus A320-232 | 4466 | ex F-WWBU | |
| ☐ | VH-VGJ | Airbus A320-232 | 4460 | ex F-WWBH | |
| ☐ | VH-VGN | Airbus A320-232 | 4434 | ex D-AVVT | |
| ☐ | VH-VGO | Airbus A320-232 | 4356 | ex D-AXAV | |
| ☐ | VH-VGP | Airbus A320-232 | 4343 | ex F-WWBH | Powderfinger c/s |
| ☐ | VH-VGQ | Airbus A320-232 | 4303 | ex F-WWDY | |
| ☐ | VH-VGR | Airbus A320-232 | 4257 | ex F-WWIQ | |
| ☐ | VH-VGT | Airbus A320-232 | 4178 | ex F-WWDZ | |
| ☐ | VH-VGU | Airbus A320-232 | 4245 | ex F-WWDQ | |
| ☐ | VH-VGV | Airbus A320-232 | 4229 | ex F-WWBU | |
| ☐ | VH-VGY | Airbus A320-232 | 4177 | ex D-AVVW | |
| ☐ | VH-VGZ | Airbus A320-232 | 3917 | ex F-WWBF | Quicksilver c/s |
| ☐ | VH-VQA | Airbus A320-232 | 3783 | ex F-WWIS | |
| ☐ | VH-VQB | Airbus A320-232 | 3743 | ex F-WWII | |
| ☐ | VH-VQC | Airbus A320-232 | 3668 | ex F-WWID | |
| ☐ | VH-VQD | Airbus A320-232 | 3547 | ex F-WWIV | |
| ☐ | VH-VQE | Airbus A320-232 | 3495 | ex F-WWIJ | |
| ☐ | VH-VQF | Airbus A320-232 | 3474 | ex F-WWDE | |
| ☐ | VH-VQG | Airbus A320-232 | 2787 | ex F-WWBV | |
| ☐ | VH-VQH | Airbus A320-232 | 2766 | ex F-WWDG | Go Roos c/s |
| ☐ | VH-VQI | Airbus A320-232 | 2717 | ex F-WWBG | |
| ☐ | VH-VQJ | Airbus A320-232 | 2703 | ex F-WWIS | |
| ☐ | VH-VQK | Airbus A320-232 | 2651 | ex F-WWIM | |
| ☐ | VH-VQL | Airbus A320-232 | 2642 | ex F-WWBZ | |
| ☐ | VH-VQM | Airbus A320-232 | 2608 | ex F-WWBS | |
| ☐ | VH-VQN | Airbus A320-232 | 2600 | ex F-WWBK | |
| ☐ | VH-VQO | Airbus A320-232 | 2587 | ex F-WWDL | |
| ☐ | VH-VQP | Airbus A320-232 | 2573 | ex F-WWBD | |
| ☐ | VH-VQQ | Airbus A320-232 | 2537 | ex F-WWIJ | Sea World c/s |
| ☐ | VH-VQR | Airbus A320-232 | 2526 | ex F-WWDQ | |
| ☐ | VH-VQS | Airbus A320-232 | 2515 | ex F-WWIE | |
| ☐ | VH-VQT | Airbus A320-232 | 2475 | ex F-WWDS | |
| ☐ | VH-VQU | Airbus A320-232 | 2455 | ex F-WWDJ | |
| ☐ | VH-VQV | Airbus A320-232 | 2338 | ex F-WWIO | |
| ☐ | VH-VQW | Airbus A320-232 | 2329 | ex F-WWDZ | |
| ☐ | VH-VQX | Airbus A320-232 | 2322 | ex 9V-VQX | |
| ☐ | VH-VQY | Airbus A320-232 | 2299 | ex F-WWBV | |
| ☐ | VH-VQZ | Airbus A320-232 | 2292 | ex 9V-VQZ | |
| | | | | | |
| ☐ | VH-VWT | Airbus A321-231 | 3717 | ex D-AVZQ | |
| ☐ | VH-VWU | Airbus A321-231 | 3948 | ex D-AZAL | |
| ☐ | VH-VWW | Airbus A321-231 | 3916 | ex D-AVZX | |
| ☐ | VH-VWX | Airbus A321-231 | 3899 | ex D-AVZW | |
| ☐ | VH-VWY | Airbus A321-231 | 1408 | ex N584NK | |
| ☐ | VH-VWZ | Airbus A321-231 | 1195 | ex N583NK | |
| | | | | | |
| ☐ | VH-EBA | Airbus A330-202 | 508 | ex F-WWKM | |

| | | | | | |
|---|---|---|---|---|---|
| ☐ | VH-EBB | Airbus A330-202 | 522 | ex F-WWYQ | |
| ☐ | VH-EBC | Airbus A330-202 | 506 | ex F-WWYU | |
| ☐ | VH-EBD | Airbus A330-202 | 513 | ex F-WWYV | |
| ☐ | VH-EBE | Airbus A330-202 | 842 | ex F-WWYV | |
| ☐ | VH-EBF | Airbus A330-202 | 853 | ex F-WWYU | |
| ☐ | VH-EBJ | Airbus A330-203 | 940 | ex F-WWKL | |
| ☐ | VH-EBK | Airbus A330-202 | 945 | ex F-WWYV | ♦ |
| ☐ | VH-EBQ | Airbus A330-203 | 1198 | ex F-WWYZ | ♦ |
| ☐ | VH-EBR | Airbus A330-203 | 1251 | ex F-WWXK | ♦ |
| ☐ | VH-EBS | Airbus A330-202 | 1258 | ex F-WWYS | ♦ |

## KAKADU AIR SERVICES
Jabiru, NT (JAB)

| | | | | | |
|---|---|---|---|---|---|
| ☐ | VH-KNQ | Cessna 208B Caravan I | 208B2193 | ex N2028N | ♦ |

## KARRATHA FLYING SERVICES
Karratha, WA (KTA)

| | | | | | |
|---|---|---|---|---|---|
| ☐ | VH-KFE | Beech B200 Super King Air | BB-1172 | ex VH-FDG | ♦ |
| ☐ | VH-KFF | Piper PA-31-350 Chieftain | 31-7952125 | ex VH-UOT | |
| ☐ | VH-KFG | Beech 65-C90 King Air | LJ-777 | ex N9AN | |
| ☐ | VH-KFH | Beech B200 Super King Air | BB-1641 | ex VH-HWO | ♦ |
| ☐ | VH-KFQ | Piper PA-31 Turbo Navajo B | 31-7401250 | ex VH-SRZ | |
| ☐ | VH-KFW | Piper PA-31 Turbo Navajo | 31-366 | ex VH-WGU | |
| ☐ | VH-KFX | Beech B200 Super King Air | BB-1862 | ex N225WC | |
| ☐ | VH-ZKF | de Havilland DHC-6 Twin Otter 100 | 43 | ex VH-TZL | |

## KING ISLAND AIRLINES
Melbourne-Moorabbin, VIC (MBW)

| | | | | | |
|---|---|---|---|---|---|
| ☐ | VH-KGQ | Embraer EMB.110P1 Bandeirante | 110221 | ex VH-XFD | |
| ☐ | VH-KIB | Piper PA-31-350 Navajo Chieftain | 31-7305035 | ex VH-TXD | |
| ☐ | VH-KIG | Piper PA-31-350 Chieftain | 31-7852146 | ex VH-HRL | |
| ☐ | VH-KIO | Piper PA-31-350 Navajo Chieftain | 31-7405487 | ex VH-DMV | |
| ☐ | VH-KIY | Piper PA-31-350 Chieftain | 31-7952061 | ex VH-KGN | |

## LLOYD HELICOPTERS

| | | | | | |
|---|---|---|---|---|---|
| ☐ | VH-WEV | Eurocopter EC225LP | 2768 | ex G-NNCY | ♦ |
| ☐ | VH-WEX | Eurocopter EC225LP | 2775 | ex G-CMJK | ♦ |
| ☐ | VH-WSO | Eurocopter EC225LP | 2779 | | ♦ |
| ☐ | VH-WGV | Eurocopter EC225LP | 2794 | | ♦ |

## MAROOMBA AIRLINES
(KN)                    Perth-International, WA (PER)

| | | | | | |
|---|---|---|---|---|---|
| ☐ | VH-ITA | Beech B200 Super King Air | BB-1244 | ex F-OINC | |
| ☐ | VH-LOA | Beech B200 Super King Air | BB-1463 | ex ZS-PLK | |
| ☐ | VH-MQZ | Beech B200 Super King Air | BB-1961 | ex N74061 | |
| ☐ | VH-QQB | de Havilland DHC-8-102 | 004 | ex VH-TQO | <SKP |

## MILITARY SUPPORT SERVICES
Brisbane (BNE)

| | | | | | |
|---|---|---|---|---|---|
| ☐ | VH-MQD | CASA C.212-200 | CC50-7-272 | ex N433CA | |
| ☐ | VH-MQE | CASA C.212-200 | CD51-6-318 | ex N7241E | |

## NETWORK AVIATION AUSTRALIA
Perth-International, WA (PER)

| | | | | | |
|---|---|---|---|---|---|
| ☐ | VH-NHA | Embraer EMB.120ER Brasilia | 120269 | ex N209SW | |
| ☐ | VH-NHC | Embraer EMB.120ER Brasilia | 120152 | ex VH-TLZ | |
| ☐ | VH-NHY | Embraer EMB.120ER Brasilia | 120054 | ex VH-NIF | |
| ☐ | VH-NHZ | Embraer EMB.120ER Brasilia | 120034 | ex N186SW | ♦ |
| ☐ | VH-TFX | Embraer EMB.120RT Brasilia | 120079 | ex VH-RPA | |
| ☐ | VH-TWF | Embraer EMB.120ER Brasilia | 120186 | ex N197SW | |
| ☐ | VH-TWZ | Embraer EMB.120ER Brasilia | 120266 | ex N207SW | |
| ☐ | VH-NHG | Fokker 100 | 11514 | ex PH-ZFU | |
| ☐ | VH-NHO | Fokker 100 | 11312 | ex D-AGPJ | |
| ☐ | VH-NHP | Fokker 100 | 11399 | ex D-AGPS | |
| ☐ | VH-NHQ | Fokker 100 | 11506 | ex PH-ZFV | |
| ☐ | VH-NHV | Fokker 100 | 11482 | ex PH-ZFW | ♦ |
| ☐ | VH- | Fokker 100 | 11449 | ex HK-4445 | o/o♦ |
| ☐ | VH- | Fokker 100 | 11464 | ex PH-ZFY | [WOE]♦ |
| ☐ | VH- | Fokker 100 | 11469 | ex PH-ZFX | [WOE]♦ |
| ☐ | VH- | Fokker 100 | 11479 | ex HK-4443 | o/o♦ |

## NORFOLK AIR
Norfolk Island, NSW(NLK)

Ceased ops 26Feb12

## PEARL AVIATION — Perth-International, WA (PER)

| | | | | | |
|---|---|---|---|---|---|
| ☐ | VH-FII | Beech 200 Super King Air | BB-653 | ex VH-MXK | op for Flight Inspection Alliance |
| ☐ | VH-FIX | Beech 350 Super King Air | FL-90 | ex D-CKRA | Calibrator |
| ☐ | VH-NTG | Beech 200C Super King Air | BL-9 | ex VH-KZL | [DRW] |
| ☐ | VH-NTH | Beech 200C Super King Air | BL-12 | ex VH-SWO | [DRW] |
| ☐ | VH-NTS | Beech 200C Super King Air | BL-30 | ex VH-TNQ | [DRW] |
| ☐ | VH-OYA | Beech 200 Super King Air | BB-365 | ex P2-SML | >RAAF |
| ☐ | VH-OYD | Beech B200 Super King Air | BB-1041 | ex N200BK | |
| ☐ | VH-OYE | Beech 200 Super King Air | BB-355 | ex VH-SMB | |
| ☐ | VH-OYH | Beech 200 Super King Air | BB-148 | ex VH-WNH | |
| ☐ | VH-OYT☐ | Beech 200T Super King Air | BT-6/BB-489 | ex VH-PPJ | [BNE] |
| ☐ | VH-TLX | Beech 200 Super King Air | BB-550 | ex P2-MBM | [DRW] |
| | | | | | |
| ☐ | VH-PPF | Dornier 328-110 | 3057 | ex N439JS | based PER |
| ☐ | VH-PPG | Dornier 328-110 | 3053 | ex D-CIAB | based DRW |
| ☐ | VH-PPJ | Dornier 328-110 | 3059 | ex D-CCAD | based CNS |
| ☐ | VH-PPQ | Dornier 328-110 | 3051 | ex D-CEAD | based MEB |
| ☐ | VH-PPV | Dornier 328-110 | 3052 | ex D-CDAD | based BNE |
| | | | | | |
| ☐ | VH-OYB | Swearingen SA.227DC Metro 23 | DC-848B | ex N452LA | |
| ☐ | VH-OYG | Swearingen SA.227DC Metro 23 | DC-875B | ex VH-SWM | |
| ☐ | VH-OYI | Swearingen SA.227DC Metro 23 | DC-839B | ex VH-DMI | |
| ☐ | VH-OYN | Swearingen SA.227DC Metro 23 | DC-870B | ex VH-DMO | |

## PEL-AIR — Questair (QWA) — Sydney Kingsford-Smith, NSW / Brisbane, QLD (SYD/BNE)

| | | | | | |
|---|---|---|---|---|---|
| ☐ | VH-AJG | IAI 1124 Westwind | 281 | ex N1124F | EMS/Frtr |
| ☐ | VH-AJJ | IAI 1124 Westwind | 248 | ex N25RE | EMS/Frtr |
| ☐ | VH-AJK | IAI 1124 Westwind | 256 | ex 4X-CNB | EMS/Frtr |
| ☐ | VH-AJP | IAI 1124 Westwind | 238 | ex 4X-CMJ | EMS/Frtr |
| ☐ | VH-AJV | IAI 1124 Westwind | 282 | ex N186G | EMS/Frtr |
| ☐ | VH-KNR | IAI 1124A Westwind II | 340 | ex N118MP | Frtr |
| ☐ | VH-KNS | IAI 1124 Westwind | 323 | ex N816H | Frtr |
| ☐ | VH-KNU | IAI 1124 Westwind | 317 | ex VH-UUZ | EMS/Frtr |
| | | | | | |
| ☐ | VH-EKD | SAAB SF.340AF | 340A-155 | ex SE-F55 | |
| ☐ | VH-EKT | SAAB SF.340AF | 340A-085 | ex F-GGBJ | |
| ☐ | VH-KDB | SAAB SF.340AF | 340A-008 | ex PH-KJK | |
| ☐ | VH-KDK | SAAB SF.340AF | 340A-016 | ex SE-E16 | |
| ☐ | VH-ZXS | SAAB SF.340B | 340B-179 | ex HS-HPE | ♦ |
| | | | | | |
| ☐ | VH-EEB | Embraer EMB.120FC Brasilia | 120117 | ex N1117H | [WGA] |
| ☐ | VH-EEN | Swearingen SA.227AT Expediter | AT-563 | ex N563UP | Frtr Jt ops with XME [ADL] |
| ☐ | VH-KAN | Swearingen SA.227DC Metro 23 | DC-838B | ex N3021U | [ADL] |
| ☐ | VH-KDO | Swearingen SA.227DC Metro 23 | DC-837B | ex N3021N | [ADL] |
| ☐ | VH-KEX | Swearingen SA.227DC Metro 23 | DC-872B | ex N3030X | [ADL] |
| ☐ | VH-SLD | Learjet 35A | 35A-145 | ex (N166AG) | |
| ☐ | VH-SLE | Learjet 35A | 35A-428 | ex N17LH | |
| ☐ | VH-SLF | Learjet 36A | 36A-049 | ex N136ST | |
| ☐ | VH-SLJ | Learjet 36 | 36-014 | ex N200Y | Frtr |
| ☐ | VH-VAD | Beech B200C Super King Air | BL-154 | ex VH-ZKA | Victorian Ambulance Service |
| ☐ | VH-VAE | Beech B200C Super King Air | BL-155 | ex VH-ZKB | Victorian Ambulance Service |
| ☐ | VH-VAH | Beech B200C Super King Air | BL-156 | ex N6388B | Victorian Ambulance Service |
| ☐ | VH-VAI | Beech B200C Super King Air | BL-157 | ex N6350V | Victorian Ambulance Service |

## POLAR AVIATION — Port Hedland, WA (PHE)

| | | | | | |
|---|---|---|---|---|---|
| ☐ | VH-BIV | Cessna 210N Centurion II | 21063398 | ex N5373A | |
| ☐ | VH-BLW | Beech Baron 58 | TH-490 | ex N1349K | |
| ☐ | VH-CFL | Cessna 208B Caravan I | 208B0434 | ex N1203D | ♦ |
| ☐ | VH-ILD | Beech 95-E55 Baron | TE-788 | ex N4055A | |
| ☐ | VH-NSM | Beech 58 Baron | TH-1798 | ex N1098C | |
| ☐ | VH-NWT | Cessna 208B Caravan I | 208B0733 | ex N1269N | |
| ☐ | VH-YOT | Cessna U206G Stationair | 20605045 | ex VH-TEO | |
| ☐ | VH-YSS | Beech 58 Baron | TH-1583 | ex N56569 | |

## QANTAS AIRWAYS — Qantas (QF/QFA) — Sydney-Kingsford Smith, NSW (SYD)

Member of Oneworld

| | | | | | |
|---|---|---|---|---|---|
| ☐ | VH-EBG | Airbus A330-203 | 887 | ex F-WWKD | Barossa Valley |
| ☐ | VH-EBH | Airbus A330-203 | 892 | ex F-WWYT | Hunter Valley |
| ☐ | VH-EBI | Airbus A330-203 | 898 | ex F-WWKM | Yarra Valley |
| ☐ | VH-EBL | Airbus A330-203 | 976 | ex F-WWKU | Whitsundays |
| ☐ | VH-EBM | Airbus A330-202 | 1061 | ex F-WWKU | Tamar Valley |
| ☐ | VH-EBN | Airbus A330-202 | 1094 | ex F-WWKM | Clare Valley |
| ☐ | VH-EBO | Airbus A330-202 | 1169 | ex F-WWKJ | Kimberley |
| ☐ | VH-EBP | Airbus A330-202 | 1174 | ex F-WWKS | Ningaloo Reef |
| ☐ | VH-QPA | Airbus A330-303 | 553 | ex F-WWKS | Kununurra |
| ☐ | VH-QPB | Airbus A330-303 | 558 | ex F-WWYO | Freycinet Peninsula |

| | Registration | Type | Serial | ex | Name | Notes |
|---|---|---|---|---|---|---|
| ☐ | VH-QPC | Airbus A330-303 | 564 | ex F-WWYQ | Broken Hill | |
| ☐ | VH-QPD | Airbus A330-303 | 574 | ex F-WWYU | Port Macquarie | |
| ☐ | VH-QPE | Airbus A330-303 | 593 | ex F-WWKP | Port Lincoln | |
| ☐ | VH-QPF | Airbus A330-303 | 595 | ex F-WWKR | Esperance | |
| ☐ | VH-QPG | Airbus A330-303 | 603 | ex F-WWYN | Mount Gambier | |
| ☐ | VH-QPH | Airbus A330-303 | 695 | ex F-WWYQ | Noosa | |
| ☐ | VH-QPI | Airbus A330-303 | 705 | ex F-WWKG | Cairns | |
| ☐ | VH-QPJ | Airbus A330-303 | 712 | ex F-WWYM | Port Stephens | |
| | | | | | | |
| ☐ | VH-OQA | Airbus A380-842 | 014 | ex F-WWSK | Nancy Bird Walton | |
| ☐ | VH-OQB | Airbus A380-842 | 015 | ex F-WWSL | Hudson Fysh | |
| ☐ | VH-OQC | Airbus A380-842 | 022 | ex F-WWSR | Paul McGinness | |
| ☐ | VH-OQD | Airbus A380-842 | 026 | ex F-WWSX | Fergus McMaster | |
| ☐ | VH-OQE | Airbus A380-842 | 027 | ex F-WWSY | Lawrence Hargrave | |
| ☐ | VH-OQF | Airbus A380-842 | 029 | ex F-WWSA | Charles Kingsford Smith | |
| ☐ | VH-OQG | Airbus A380-842 | 047 | ex F-WWAD | Charles Ulm | |
| ☐ | VH-OQH | Airbus A380-842 | 050 | ex F-WWAE | Reginald Ansett | |
| ☐ | VH-OQI | Airbus A380-842 | 055 | ex F-WWAP | David Warren | |
| ☐ | VH-OQJ | Airbus A380-842 | 062 | ex F-WWAQ | Bert Hinkler | |
| ☐ | VH-OQK | Airbus A380-842 | 063 | ex F-WWSK | John/Reginald Duigen | |
| ☐ | VH-OQL | Airbus A380-842 | 074 | ex F-WWSL | Phyllis Arnott | |
| ☐ | VH-OQM | Airbus A380-842 | 091 | ex | | o/o |
| | | | | | | |
| ☐ | VH-TJE | Boeing 737-476 | 24430/1820 | | Kookaburra | |
| ☐ | VH-TJF | Boeing 737-476 | 24431/1863 | | Brolga | [VCV] |
| ☐ | VH-TJG | Boeing 737-476 | 24432/1879 | ex 9M-MLE | Eagle | |
| ☐ | VH-TJH | Boeing 737-476 | 24433/1881 | | Falcon | |
| ☐ | VH-TJI | Boeing 737-476 | 24434/1912 | ex 9M-MLD | Cloncurry | |
| ☐ | VH-TJJ | Boeing 737-476 | 24435/1959 | | Heron | |
| ☐ | VH-TJK | Boeing 737-476 | 24436/1998 | | Ibis | |
| ☐ | VH-TJL | Boeing 737-476 | 24437/2162 | | Swift | |
| ☐ | VH-TJO | Boeing 737-476 | 24440/2324 | | Lorikeet | [VCV] |
| ☐ | VH-TJR | Boeing 737-476 | 24443/2398 | | Cockatiel | |
| ☐ | VH-TJS | Boeing 737-476 | 24444/2454 | | Jabiru | |
| ☐ | VH-TJU | Boeing 737-476 | 24446/2569 | | Currawong | |
| ☐ | VH-TJW | Boeing 737-4L7 | 26961/2517 | ex C2-RN11 | Strahan | [VCV] |
| ☐ | VH-TJX | Boeing 737-476 | 28150/2773 | | Stawell | |
| ☐ | VH-TJY | Boeing 737-476 | 28151/2785 | | Marlborough | |
| ☐ | VH-TJZ | Boeing 737-476 | 28152/2829 | ex ZK-JTS | Tenacity | |
| | | | | | | |
| ☐ | VH-VXA | Boeing 737-838/W | 29551/1042 | ex (N979AN) | Broome | |
| ☐ | VH-VXB | Boeing 737-838/W | 30101/1045 | ex (N980AN) | Yanani Dreaming | |
| ☐ | VH-VXC | Boeing 737-838/W | 30897/1049 | ex (N981AN) | Gippsland | |
| ☐ | VH-VXD | Boeing 737-838/W | 29552/1063 | ex (N982AN) | Tenterfield | |
| ☐ | VH-VXE | Boeing 737-838/W | 30899/1071 | ex (N983AN) | Coffs Harbour | |
| ☐ | VH-VXF | Boeing 737-838/W | 29553/1096 | ex (N984AN) | Sunshine Coast | |
| ☐ | VH-VXG | Boeing 737-838/W | 30901/1102 | ex (N985AM) | Port Douglas | |
| ☐ | VH-VXH | Boeing 737-838/W | 33478/1137 | ex (N986AM) | Warrnambool | |
| ☐ | VH-VXI | Boeing 737-838/W | 33479/1141 | ex (N987AM) | Oonadatta | |
| ☐ | VH-VXJ | Boeing 737-838/W | 33480/1157 | ex (N988AM) | Coober Pedy | |
| ☐ | VH-VXK | Boeing 737-838/W | 33481/1160 | ex (N989AM) | Katherine | |
| ☐ | VH-VXL | Boeing 737-838/W | 33482/1172 | | Charleville | |
| ☐ | VH-VXM | Boeing 737-838/W | 33483/1177 | ex N6055X | Mount Hotham | |
| ☐ | VH-VXN | Boeing 737-838/W | 33484/1180 | | Freemantle | |
| ☐ | VH-VXO | Boeing 737-838/W | 33485/1183 | | Kakadu | Prostate Cancer c/s |
| ☐ | VH-VXP | Boeing 737-838/W | 33722/1324 | | Logan | |
| ☐ | VH-VXQ | Boeing 737-838/W | 33723/1335 | | Redlands | |
| ☐ | VH-VXR | Boeing 737-838/W | 33724/1340 | | Shepparton | |
| ☐ | VH-VXS | Boeing 737-838/W | 33725/1352 | | St Helens | |
| ☐ | VH-VXT | Boeing 737-838/W | 33760/1412 | ex N1787B | Townsville | |
| ☐ | VH-VXU | Boeing 737-838/W | 33761/1420 | | Wollongong | |
| ☐ | VH-VYA | Boeing 737-838/W | 33762/1532 | | Narooma | |
| ☐ | VH-VYB | Boeing 737-838/W | 33763/1534 | | Cape Otway | |
| ☐ | VH-VYC | Boeing 737-838/W | 33991/1612 | | Arnhem Land | |
| ☐ | VH-VYD | Boeing 737-838/W | 33992/1706 | | Eudunda | |
| ☐ | VH-VYE | Boeing 737-838/W | 33993/1712 | | Alice Springs | |
| ☐ | VH-VYF | Boeing 737-838/W | 33994/1727 | ex N1784B | Evandale | |
| ☐ | VH-VYG | Boeing 737-838/W | 33995/1736 | | Australind | |
| ☐ | VH-VYH | Boeing 737-838/W | 34180/1815 | | Queanbeyan | |
| ☐ | VH-VYI | Boeing 737-838/W | 34181/1840 | | Bathurst Island | |
| ☐ | VH-VYJ | Boeing 737-838/W | 34182/1842 | ex N1782B | Cann River | |
| ☐ | VH-VYK | Boeing 737-838/W | 34183/1846 | ex N1784B | Moree | |
| ☐ | VH-VYL | Boeing 737-838/W | 34184/1854 | | Wangaratta | |
| ☐ | VH-VZA | Boeing 737-838/W | 34195/2502 | ex N1779B | Port Augusta | |
| ☐ | VH-VZB | Boeing 737-838/W | 34196/2623 | ex N1786B | Lake Macquarie | |
| ☐ | VH-VZC | Boeing 737-838/W | 34197/2649 | | Innisfail | |
| ☐ | VH-VZD | Boeing 737-838/W | 34198/2659 | | Geelong | Optus c/s |
| ☐ | VH-VZE | Boeing 737-838/W | 34199/2661 | ex N1786B | Bunbury | |
| ☐ | VH-VZL | Boeing 737-838/W | 34194/3621 | | | ♦ |
| ☐ | VH-VZM | Boeing 737-838/W | 34192/3644 | | | ♦ |
| ☐ | VH-VZO | Boeing 737-838/W | 34191/3692 | | | ♦ |
| ☐ | VH-VZP | Boeing 737-383/W | 39362/3714 | | | ♦ |
| ☐ | VH-VZR | Boeing 737-838/W | 34193/3754 | | Coral Bay | ♦ |

| | | | | | |
|---|---|---|---|---|---|
| ☐ | VH-VZS | Boeing 737-838/W | 39358/3769 | | Tamworth | ♦ |
| ☐ | VH-VZT | Boeing 737-838/W | 34186/3798 | | Kalgoorlie | ♦ |
| ☐ | VH-VZU | Boeing 737-838/w | 34187/3826 | | Lorne | ♦ |
| ☐ | VH-VZV | Boeing 737-838/W | 34189/3856 | | Palm Cove | ♦ |
| ☐ | VH-VZW | Boeing 737-838/W | 39359/3881 | | Beaconfield | ♦ |
| ☐ | VH-VZY | Boeing 737-838/W | 39363/3944 | | Temora | ♦ |
| ☐ | VH-VZX | Boeing 737-838/W | 34188/3910 | | Daylesford | ♦ |
| ☐ | VH-VZZ | Boeing 737-838/W | 39445 | | | o/o♦ |
| ☐ | VH-XZA | Boeing 737-838/W | 39367 | | | o/o♦ |
| ☐ | VH-XZB | Boeing 737-838/W | 39360 | | | o/o♦ |
| ☐ | VH-XZC | Boeing 737-838/W | 39361 | | | o/o♦ |
| | | | | | | |
| ☐ | VH-OEB | Boeing 747-48E | 25778/983 | ex HL7416 | Phillip Island | |
| ☐ | VH-OEE | Boeing 747-438ER | 32909/1308 | ex N747ER | Nullarbor | |
| ☐ | VH-OEF | Boeing 747-438ER | 32910/1313 | ex N60659 | City of Sydney | |
| ☐ | VH-OEG | Boeing 747-438ER | 32911/1320 | | Parkes | |
| ☐ | VH-OEH | Boeing 747-438ER | 32912/1321 | ex N5020K | Hervey Bay | |
| ☐ | VH-OEI | Boeing 747-438ER | 32913/1330 | | Ceduna | |
| ☐ | VH-OEJ | Boeing 747-438ER | 32914/1331 | ex N60668 | Wanula Dreaming | |
| ☐ | VH-OJA | Boeing 747-438 | 24354/731 | ex N6046P | City of Canberra | |
| ☐ | VH-OJB | Boeing 747-438 | 24373/746 | | Mount Isa | |
| ☐ | VH-OJC | Boeing 747-438 | 24406/751 | | City of Melbourne | |
| ☐ | VH-OJD | Boeing 747-438 | 24481/764 | | City of Brisbane | |
| ☐ | VH-OJE | Boeing 747-438 | 24482/765 | | City of Adelaide | |
| ☐ | VH-OJF | Boeing 747-438 | 24483/781 | | City of Perth | |
| ☐ | VH-OJG | Boeing 747-438 | 24779/801 | ex N6009F | City of Hobart | |
| ☐ | VH-OJH | Boeing 747-438 | 24806/807 | | City of Darwin | |
| ☐ | VH-OJI | Boeing 747-438 | 24887/826 | ex N6009F | Longreach | |
| ☐ | VH-OJJ | Boeing 747-438 | 24974/835 | | Winton | |
| ☐ | VH-OJL | Boeing 747-438 | 25151/865 | | City of Ballarat | |
| ☐ | VH-OJM | Boeing 747-438 | 25245/875 | | Gosford | |
| ☐ | VH-OJN | Boeing 747-438 | 25315/883 | ex N6009F | City of Dubbo | [VCV] |
| ☐ | VH-OJO | Boeing 747-438 | 25544/894 | ex N6005C | City of Toowoomba[SYD] | |
| ☐ | VH-OJP | Boeing 747-438 | 25545/916 | | City of Albury | |
| ☐ | VH-OJQ | Boeing 747-438 | 25546/924 | ex N6005C | Mandurah | |
| ☐ | VH-OJS | Boeing 747-438 | 25564/1230 | | Hamilton Island | |
| ☐ | VH-OJT | Boeing 747-438 | 25565/1233 | | | |
| ☐ | VH-OJU | Boeing 747-438 | 25566/1239 | | Lord Howe Island | |
| | | | | | | |
| ☐ | VH-OGG | Boeing 767-338ER | 24929/343 | | City of Rockhampton | |
| ☐ | VH-OGH | Boeing 767-338ER | 24930/344 | | City of Parramatta | |
| ☐ | VH-OGI | Boeing 767-338ER | 25246/387 | | City of Port Augusta | |
| ☐ | VH-OGJ | Boeing 767-338ER | 25274/396 | | | |
| ☐ | VH-OGK | Boeing 767-338ER | 25316/397 | ex N6018N | Mackay | |
| ☐ | VH-OGL | Boeing 767-338ER | 25363/402 | ex N6018N | Wallabies Rugby World Cup c/s | |
| ☐ | VH-OGM | Boeing 767-338ER | 25575/451 | | Bundaberg | |
| ☐ | VH-OGN | Boeing 767-338ER | 25576/549 | | Partnership | |
| ☐ | VH-OGO | Boeing 767-338ER | 25577/550 | | Unity | |
| ☐ | VH-OGP | Boeing 767-338ER | 28153/615 | | Forbes | |
| ☐ | VH-OGQ | Boeing 767-338ER | 28154/623 | | Birdsville | |
| ☐ | VH-OGR | Boeing 767-338ER | 28724/662 | | | |
| ☐ | VH-OGS | Boeing 767-338ER | 28725/665 | | Roma | |
| ☐ | VH-OGT | Boeing 767-338ER | 29117/710 | | Maroochydore | |
| ☐ | VH-OGU | Boeing 767-338ER | 29118/713 | | Byron Bay | |
| ☐ | VH-OGV | Boeing 767-338ER | 30186/796 | | | |
| ☐ | VH-ZXA | Boeing 767-336ER | 24337/288 | ex G-BNWE | | |
| ☐ | VH-ZXB | Boeing 767-336ER | 24338/293 | ex G-BNWF | | |
| ☐ | VH-ZXC | Boeing 767-336ER | 24339/298 | ex G-BNWG | | |
| ☐ | VH-ZXD | Boeing 767-336ER | 24342/363 | ex G-BNWJ | | |
| ☐ | VH-ZXE | Boeing 767-336ER | 24343/364 | ex G-BNWK | | |
| ☐ | VH-ZXF | Boeing 767-336ER | 25203/365 | ex G-BNWL | | |
| ☐ | VH-ZXG | Boeing 767-336ER | 25443/419 | ex G-BNWP | | |

## QANTASLINK                                    (QF/QFA)                                              *various*

| | | | | | | |
|---|---|---|---|---|---|---|
| ☐ | VH-SDA | de Havilland DHC-8Q-202 | 482 | ex C-GFQL | Torres Straot | Eastern Australia |
| ☐ | VH-SDE | de Havilland DHC-8Q-202 | 453 | ex N453DS | | Eastern Australia |
| ☐ | VH-TQG | de Havilland DHC-8-201 | 430 | ex C-GDNG | Pixie Rourke | Eastern Australia |
| ☐ | VH-TQS | de Havilland DHC-8-202 | 418 | ex 9M-EKB | | Eastern Australia |
| ☐ | VH-TQX | de Havilland DHC-8-202 | 439 | ex N439SD | | Eastern Australia |
| | | | | | | |
| ☐ | VH-SBB | de Havilland DHC-8Q-315 | 539 | ex C-FDHO | | Eastern Australia |
| ☐ | VH-SBG | de Havilland DHC-8Q-315 | 575 | ex C-GSAH | | Eastern Australia |
| ☐ | VH-SBI | de Havilland DHC-8Q-315 | 605 | ex C-FZKU | | Eastern Australia |
| ☐ | VH-SBT | de Havilland DHC-8Q-315 | 580 | ex C-FDHP | | Eastern Australia |
| ☐ | VH-SBV | de Havilland DHC-8Q-315 | 595 | ex C-GIHK | | Eastern Australia |
| ☐ | VH-SBW | de Havilland DHC-8Q-315 | 599 | ex C-GZPN | | Eastern Australia |
| ☐ | VH-SCE | de Havilland DHC-8Q-315 | 602 | ex C-GZPP | | Eastern Australia |
| ☐ | VH-TQD | de Havilland DHC-8Q-315 | 598 | ex C-GZDO | | Eastern Australia |
| ☐ | VH-TQE | de Havilland DHC-8Q-315 | 596 | ex C-GDOE | | Eastern Australia |
| ☐ | VH-TQH | de Havilland DHC-8Q-315 | 597 | ex C-GZDM | | Eastern Australia |
| ☐ | VH-TQK | de Havilland DHC-8Q-315 | 600 | ex C-GZPO | | Eastern Australia |

| | | | | | | |
|---|---|---|---|---|---|---|
| ☐ | VH-TQL | de Havilland DHC-8Q-315 | 603 | ex C-GZPQ | | Eastern Australia |
| ☐ | VH-TQM | de Havilland DHC-8Q-315 | 604 | ex C-FZHW | | Eastern Australia |
| ☐ | VH-TQY | de Havilland DHC-8Q-315 | 552 | ex C-FDHP | | Eastern Australia |
| ☐ | VH-TQZ | de Havilland DHC-8Q-315 | 555 | ex C-GDNK | | Eastern Australia |
| ☐ | VH-LQB | de havilland DHC-8-402Q | 4343 | | | Sunstate♦ |
| ☐ | VH-LQD | de Havilland DHC-8-402Q | 4371 | ex C-GJFZ | City of Greater Geraldton | Sunstate♦ |
| ☐ | VH-LQF | de Havilland DHC-8-402Q | 4375 | ex C-GJKV | | Sunstate♦ |
| ☐ | VH-LQG | de Havilland DHC-8-402Q | 4376 | ex C-GJLE | Town of Exmouth | Sunstate♦ |
| ☐ | VH-QOA | de Havilland DHC-8-402Q | 4112 | ex C-FDHG | Gladstone: | Sunstate |
| ☐ | VH-QOB | de Havilland DHC-8-402Q | 4116 | ex C-FERF | Yeppoon | Sunstate |
| ☐ | VH-QOC | de Havilland DHC-8-402Q | 4117 | ex C-FFCD | Mackay | Sunstate |
| ☐ | VH-QOD | de Havilland DHC-8-402Q | 4123 | ex C-FFQL | Emerald | Sunstate |
| ☐ | VH-QOE | de Havilland DHC-8-402Q | 4125 | ex C-FFQE | | Sunstate |
| ☐ | VH-QOF | de Havilland DHC-8-402Q | 4128 | ex C-FFQM | | Sunstate |
| ☐ | VH-QOH | de Havilland DHC-8-402Q | 4132 | ex C-FGKH | Breast Cancer c/s | Sunstate |
| ☐ | VH-QOI | de Havilland DHC-8-402Q | 4189 | ex C-FNQL | Tamworth | Sunstate |
| ☐ | VH-QOJ | de Havilland DHC-8-402Q | 4192 | ex C-FNZU | Riverina | Sunstate |
| ☐ | VH-QOK | de Havilland DHC-8-402Q | 4215 | ex C-FQXU | | Sunstate |
| ☐ | VH-QOM | de Havilland DHC-8-402Q | 4217 | ex C-FRLL | | Sunstate |
| ☐ | VH-QON | de Havilland DHC-8-402Q | 4218 | ex C-FRLP | | Sunstate |
| ☐ | VH-QOP | de Havilland DHC-8-402Q | 4238 | ex C-FUOI | Coffs Harbour | Sunstate |
| ☐ | VH-QOR | de Havilland DHC-8-402Q | 4241 | ex C-FUST | Eyre Peninsula | Sunstate |
| ☐ | VH-QOS | de Havilland DHC-8-402Q | 4263 | ex C-FXAZ | Mildura | Sunstate |
| ☐ | VH-QOT | de Havilland DHC-8-402Q | 4269 | ex C-FXYP | | Sunstate |
| ☐ | VH-QOU | de Havilland DHC-8-402Q | 4275 | ex C-FYGQ | | Sunstate |
| ☐ | VH-QOV | de Havilland DHC-8-402Q | 4277 | ex C-FYIC | | Sunstate |
| ☐ | VH-QOW | de Havilland DHC-8-402Q | 4285 | ex C-FZFT | Taronga Zoo c/s | Sunstate |
| ☐ | VH-QOX | de Havilland DHC-8-402Q | 4287 | ex C-FZGC | | Sunstate |
| ☐ | VH-QOY | de Havilland DHC-8-402Q | 4288 | ex C-FZGG | | Sunstate |

## REX – REGIONAL EXPRESS   (ZL/RXA)   Orange, NSW/Wagga Wagga, NSW (OAG/WGA)

| | | | | | | |
|---|---|---|---|---|---|---|
| ☐ | VH-EKH | SAAB SF.340B | 340B-369 | ex SE-C69 | | |
| ☐ | VH-EKX | SAAB SF.340B | 340B-257 | ex (F-GNVQ) | | |
| ☐ | VH-KDQ | SAAB SF.340B | 340B-325 | ex SE-KVO | | |
| ☐ | VH-KDV | SAAB SF.340B | 340B-322 | ex SE-KVN | | |
| ☐ | VH-KRX | SAAB SF.340B | 340B-290 | ex N361BE | | |
| ☐ | VH-NRX | SAAB SF.340B | 340B-291 | ex N362BE | | |
| ☐ | VH-OLL | SAAB SF.340B | 340B-175 | ex N143NC | | |
| ☐ | VH-OLM | SAAB SF.340B | 340B-205 | ex SE-G05 | | |
| ☐ | VH-ORX | SAAB SF.340B | 340B-293 | ex N363BE | | |
| ☐ | VH-PRX | SAAB SF.340B | 340B-303 | ex N366BE | | |
| ☐ | VH-REX | SAAF SF.340B | 340B-384 | ex N384AE | | ♦ |
| ☐ | VH-RXE | SAAB SF.340B | 340B-275 | ex N275CJ | | |
| ☐ | VH-RXN | SAAB SF.340B | 340B-279 | ex N358BE | | |
| ☐ | VH-RXQ | SAAB SF.340B | 340B-200 | ex YR-VGN | | |
| ☐ | VH-RXS | SAAB SF.340B | 340B-285 | ex N359BE | | |
| ☐ | VH-RXX | SAAB SF.340B | 340B-209 | ex N355BE | | |
| ☐ | VH-SBA | SAAB SF.340B | 340B-311 | ex SE-KXA | | |
| ☐ | VH-TRX | SAAB SF.340B | 340B-287 | ex N360BE | Kay Hull Plane | |
| ☐ | VH-YRX | SAAB SF.340B | 340B-178 | ex N178CT | | |
| ☐ | VH-ZJS | SAAB SF.340B | 340B-186 | ex HS-HPI | | ♦ |
| ☐ | VH-ZLA | SAAB SF.340B | 340B-371 | ex N371AE | | |
| ☐ | VH-ZLC | SAAB SF.340B | 340B-373 | ex N373AE | | |
| ☐ | VH-ZLF | SAAB SF.340B | 340B-374 | ex N374AE | | |
| ☐ | VH-ZLG | SAAB SF.340B | 340B-375 | ex N375AE | | |
| ☐ | VH-ZLH | SAAB SF.340B | 340B-376 | ex N376AE | | |
| ☐ | VH-ZLJ | SAAB SF.340B | 340B-380 | ex N380AE | | |
| ☐ | VH-ZLK | SAAB SF.340B | 340B-381 | ex N381AE | | |
| ☐ | VH-ZLO | SAAB SF.340B | 340B-382 | ex N382AE | | |
| ☐ | VH-ZLQ | SAAB SF.340B | 340B-370 | ex N370AM | | |
| ☐ | VH-ZLR | SAAB SF.340B | 340B-229 | ex SE-KSK | | |
| ☐ | VH-ZLS | SAAB SF.340B | 340B-383 | ex N383AE | | |
| ☐ | VH-ZLV | SAAB SF.340B | 340B-386 | ex N386AE | | |
| ☐ | VH-ZLW | SAAB SF.340B | 340B-387 | ex N387AE | | |
| ☐ | VH-ZLX | SAAB SF.340B | 340B-182 | ex ER-SGB | | |
| ☐ | VH-ZRB | SAAB SF.340B | 340B-389 | ex N389AE | | |
| ☐ | VH-ZRC | SAAB SF.340B | 340B-390 | ex N390AE | | |
| ☐ | VH-ZRE | SAAB SF.340B | 340B-391 | ex N391AE | | |
| ☐ | VH-ZRH | SAAB SF.340B | 340B-392 | ex N392AE | | |
| ☐ | VH-ZRI | SAAB SF.340B | 340B-394 | ex N394AE | | |
| ☐ | VH-ZRJ | SAAB SF.340B | 340B-396 | ex N396AE | | |
| ☐ | VH-ZRK | SAAB SF.340B | 340B-397 | ex N397AE | | |
| ☐ | VH-ZRL | SAAB SF.340B | 340B-398 | ex N398AE | | |
| ☐ | VH-ZRM | SAAB SF.340B | 340B-400 | ex N400BR | | |
| ☐ | VH-ZRN | SAAB SF.340B | 340B-393 | ex N393AE | | |
| ☐ | VH-ZRY | SAAB SF.340B | 340B-401 | ex N901AE | | |
| ☐ | VH-ZRZ | SAAB SF.340B | 340B-388 | ex N388AE | | |

## ROYAL FLYING DOCTOR SERVICE

| | | | | | |
|---|---|---|---|---|---|
| ☐ | VH-AMQ | Beech B200 Super King Air | BL-166 | ex N80666 | South Eastern♦ |
| ☐ | VH-AMS | Beech B200C Super King Air | BL-168 | ex N81458 | South Easter♦ |
| ☐ | VH-FDA | Beech B200 Super King Air | BB-1986 | ex N986KA | Queensland |
| ☐ | VH-FDB | Beech B200 Super King Air | BB-1977 | ex N7317A | Queensland |
| ☐ | VH-FDC | Pilatus PC-12/45 | 426 | | Queensland |
| ☐ | VH-FDD | Beech B200 Super King Air | BB-1697 | ex N40483 | Queensland |
| ☐ | VH-FDE | Pilatus PC-12/45 | 332 | | Central Operations |
| ☐ | VH-FDF | Beech B200 Super King Air | BB-1696 | ex N40481 | Queensland |
| ☐ | VH-FDG | Beech B200 Super King Air | BB-2012 | ex N60312 | Queensland |
| ☐ | VH-FDI | Beech B200C Super King Air | BL-162 | ex N80562 | Queensland |
| ☐ | VH-FDJ | Pilatus PC-12/47 | 861 | ex HB-FST | Central Operations |
| ☐ | VH-FDK | Pilatus PC-12/47 | 466 | | Central Operations |
| ☐ | VH-FDM | Beech B200C Super King Air | BL-161 | ex N80761 | Queensland |
| ☐ | VH-FDO | Beech B200 Super King Air | BB-1056 | ex VH-RFX | Queensland |
| ☐ | VH-FDP | Pilatus PC-12/45 | 434 | | Queensland |
| ☐ | VH-FDR | Beech B200 Super King Air | BB-1881 | ex N36801 | Queensland |
| ☐ | VH-FDS | Beech B200C Super King Air | BL-158 | | Queensland♦ |
| ☐ | VH-FDT | Beech B200 Super King Air | BB-1990 | ex N990KA | Queensland |
| ☐ | VH-FDW | Beech B200 Super King Air | BB-1880 | ex N61800 | Queensland |
| ☐ | VH-FDZ | Beech B200 Super King Air | BB-1882 | ex N37082 | Queensland |
| ☐ | VH-FFI | Beech B200 Super King Air | BB-1037 | ex VH-FDI | Queensland |
| ☐ | VH-FGR | Pilatus PC-12/45 | 438 | ex HB-FRW | Central Operations |
| ☐ | VH-FGS | Pilatus PC-12/45 | 440 | ex HB-FRX | Central Operations |
| ☐ | VH-FGT | Pilatus PC-12/45 | 442 | ex HB-FRY | Central Operations |
| ☐ | VH-FMP | Pilatus PC-12/45 | 122 | | Central Operations |
| ☐ | VH-FMW | Pilatus PC-12/45 | 123 | | Central Operations |
| ☐ | VH-FMZ | Pilatus PC-12/45 | 138 | | Central Operations |
| ☐ | VH-FVA | Pilatus PC-12/47E | 1182 | | Central Operations♦ |
| ☐ | VH-FVB | Pilatus PC-12/47E | 1187 | ex HB-FTI | Central Operations |
| ☐ | VH-FVD | Pilatus PC-12/47E | 1206 | ex HB-FTT | Central Operations |
| ☐ | VH-FVE | Pilatus PC-12/47E | 1221 | ex HB-FQQ | Central Operations |
| ☐ | VH-FVF | Pilatus PC-12.47E | 1228 | ex HB-FQY | Central Operations♦ |
| ☐ | VH-KWO | Pilatus PC-12/45 | 363 | | Western Operations |
| ☐ | VH-MSH | Beech B200 Super King Air | BB-1787 | ex N44857 | South Eastern |
| ☐ | VH-MSM | Beech B200 Super King Air | BB-1464 | ex N133LC | South Eastern |
| ☐ | VH-MSU | Beech B200C Super King Air | BL-48 | ex N1860B | South Eastern |
| ☐ | VH-MSZ | Beech 200 Super King Air | BB-866 | ex ZK-PBG | South Eastern |
| ☐ | VH-MVJ | Beech B200 Super King Air | BB-1842 | ex N50152 | South Eastern |
| ☐ | VH-MVL | Beech B200 Super King Air | BB-1333 | ex N1101W | South Eastern |
| ☐ | VH-MVP | Beech B200 Super King Air | BB-1812 | ex VH-AMR | South Eastern |
| ☐ | VH-MVS | Beech B200 Super King Air | BB-1813 | ex VH-AMQ | South Eastern |
| ☐ | VH-MVW | Beech B200 Super King Air | BB-1980 | ex N980KA | South Eastern |
| ☐ | VH-MVX | Beech B200C Super King Air | BL-153 | ex N3203R | South Eastern |
| ☐ | VH-MVY | Beech B200 Super King Air | BB-1324 | ex N7087N | South Eastern |
| ☐ | VH-MWH | Beech B200 Super King Air | BB-2003 | ex N32030 | South Eastern |
| ☐ | VH-MWK | Beech B200C Super King Air | BL-152 | ex N3202W | South Eastern |
| ☐ | VH-MWO | Pilatus PC-12/45 | 379 | | Western Operations |
| ☐ | VH-MWQ | Beech B200 Super King Air | BB-1416 | ex N8254H | South Eastern |
| ☐ | VH-MWU | Beech B200 Super King Air | BB-1418 | ex N131GA | South Eastern |
| ☐ | VH-MWV | Beech B200 Super King Air | BB-1814 | ex VH-AMS | South Eastern |
| ☐ | VH-MWX | Beech B200 Super King Air | BB-1424 | ex N8236K | South Eastern |
| ☐ | VH-MWZ | Beech B200 Super King Air | BB-1430 | ex VH-MSM | South Eastern |
| ☐ | VH-NAJ | Beech B300C Super King Air | FM-47 | ex N81307 | South Eastern♦ |
| ☐ | VH-NAO | Beech B300C Super King Air | FM-49 | ex N81339 | South Eastern♦ |
| ☐ | VH-NQA | Beech B200C Super King Air | BL-68 | ex VH-FDS | Queensland |
| ☐ | VH-NQB | Pilatus PC-12/45 | 428 | ex VH-FDM | Queensland |
| ☐ | VH-NQC | Cessna 208B Grand Caravan | 208B2138 | ex N52645 | Queensland |
| ☐ | VH-NQD | Cessna 208B Grand Caravan | 208B2139 | ex N50756 | Queensland |
| ☐ | VH-NWO | Pilatus PC-12/45 | 396 | ex HB-FQQ | Western Operations |
| ☐ | VH-OWA | Pilatus PC-12/47E | 1115 | ex HB-FQR | Western Operations |
| ☐ | VH-OWB | Pilatus PC-12/47E | 1104 | ex HB-FQD | Western Operations |
| ☐ | VH-OWD | Pilatus PC-12/47E | 1140 | ex HB-FRN | Western Operations |
| ☐ | VH-OWG | Pilatus PC-12/47E | 1155 | ex HB-FSV | Western Operations |
| ☐ | VH-OWI | Pilatus PC-12/47E | 1232 | ex HB-FRD | Western Operations |
| ☐ | VH-OWP | Pilatus PC-12/47E | 1032 | ex HB-FQL | Western Operations |
| ☐ | VH-OWQ | Pilatus PC-12/47E | 1052 | ex HB-FRF | Western Operations |
| ☐ | VH-OWR | Pilatus PC-12/47E | 1082 | ex HB-FSK | Western Operations |
| ☐ | VH-VWO | Pilatus PC-12/45 | 400 | ex HB-FQR | Western Operations |
| ☐ | VH-YWO | Pilatus PC-12/45 | 725 | | Western Operations |
| ☐ | VH-ZWO | Pilatus PC-12/45 | 467 | ex HB-FQM | Western Operat+ions |
| ☐ | VH- | Beech B200 Super King Air | BL-167 | ex N80467 | South Eastern♦ |

## SEAIR PACIFIC GOLD COAST          Gold Coast, QLD (OOL)

| | | | | | |
|---|---|---|---|---|---|
| ☐ | VH-LMD | Cessna 208 Caravan I | 20800217 | ex 9M-FBA | FP |
| ☐ | VH-LMZ | Cessna 208 Caravan I | 20800173 | ex LN-SEA | FP |
| ☐ | VH-LYT | Cessna 208B Caravan I | 208B1208 | ex N1320B | |
| ☐ | VH-MBF | Britten-Norman BN-2A-8 Islander | 646 | ex P2-MBF | |
| ☐ | VH-MBK | Britten-Norman BN-2A Islander | 158 | ex P2-MBD | |

| | | | | | | |
|---|---|---|---|---|---|---|
| ☐ | VH-OZH | Cessna 208B Caravan I | 208B0464 | ex N13313 | | ♦ |
| ☐ | VH-SDU | Cessna 210M Centurion | 21062253 | ex VH-OUR | | ♦ |
| ☐ | VH-VCW | Cessna 208B Caravan I | 208B1102 | ex N678HC | | ♦ |

## SEAWING AIRWAYS                                    Sydney Rose Bay, NSW (RSE)

| | | | | | | |
|---|---|---|---|---|---|---|
| ☐ | VH-SWB | de Havilland DHC-2 Beaver | 1557 | ex ZK-CKD | | FP |

## SHARP AIRLINES                                          Hamilton, VIC (HML)

| | | | | | | |
|---|---|---|---|---|---|---|
| ☐ | VH-HWR | Swearingen SA.227DC Metro 23 | DC-851B | ex N3025T | | |
| ☐ | VH-LCE | Piper PA-31-350 Navajo Chieftain | 31-7305088 | ex N305SP | | |
| ☐ | VH-MYI | Swearingen SA.227DC Metro 23 | DC-869B | ex 9M-APB | | |
| ☐ | VH-OZV | Swearingen SA.227AC Metro III | AC-610B | ex VH-TGQ | | >FQ♦ |
| ☐ | VH-SEZ | Swearingen SA.227AC Metro III | AC-637 | ex ZK-RCA | | |
| ☐ | VH-SWK | Swearingen SA.227DC Metro 23 | DC-826B | ex N52ML | | ♦ |
| ☐ | VH-UUB | Swearingen SA.227DC Metro 23 | DC-894B | ex N3032F | | |
| ☐ | VH-UUN | Swearingen SA.227AC Metro III | AC-686 | ex N686AV | | |

## SHINE AIR SERVICES / SHINE AIR                          Geraldtown, WA (GET)

| | | | | | | |
|---|---|---|---|---|---|---|
| ☐ | VH-AFY | Piper PA-31 Navajo | 31-8012084 | ex ZK-CJO | | ♦ |
| ☐ | VH-EKG | Beech 1900D | UE-135 | ex ZS-SSY | | ♦ |
| ☐ | VH-PNS | Partenavia P.68B | 71 | | | ♦ |
| ☐ | VH-SXS | Beech Baron 58 | TH-81 | ex ZK-EJJ | | ♦ |

## SHOAL AIR                                              Kunanurra, WA (KNS)

| | | | | | | |
|---|---|---|---|---|---|---|
| ☐ | VH-ARN | Cessna 310R | 310R0611 | ex VH-ARS | | ♦ |
| ☐ | VH-BFL | GippsAero GA-8 Airvan | GA8-06-107 | | | ♦ |
| ☐ | VH-HJR | Piper PA-31-350 Chieftain | 31-8252016 | ex VH-MZX | | ♦ |
| ☐ | VH-HZR | Cessna 310Q | 310Q0468 | ex N8700Q | | ♦ |
| ☐ | VH-MNN | Cessna 210L Centurion | 21060746 | ex ZS-MNM | | ♦ |
| ☐ | VH-OTB | Cessna 210L Centurion | 21060067 | ex ZK-FMG | | ♦ |
| ☐ | VH-SMP | Cessna 210L Centurion | 210L61544 | ex N732JG | | ♦ |
| ☐ | VH-SUE | Cessna 310P | 310P0132 | ex N5832M | | ♦ |
| ☐ | VH-UJF | Cessna 310R | 310R1342 | ex N6215C | | ♦ |

## SHORTSTOP AIR CHARTER                              Melbourne-Essendon, VIC (MEB)

| | | | | | |
|---|---|---|---|---|---|
| ☐ | VH-OVC | Swearingen SA.226T Merlin II | T-318 | ex OE-FOW | |
| ☐ | VH-OVM | Douglas DC-3 | 16354/33102 | ex VH-JXD | Arthur Schutt MBE |

## SKIPPERS AVIATION                    (JW)            Perth-International, WA (PER)

| | | | | | | |
|---|---|---|---|---|---|---|
| ☐ | VH-FMQ | Cessna 441 Conquest II | 441-0109 | ex N26226 | | |
| ☐ | VH-LBX | Cessna 441 Conquest II | 441-0091 | ex VH-AZY | | |
| ☐ | VH-LBY | Cessna 441 Conquest II | 441-0023 | ex VH-TFW | | |
| ☐ | VH-LBZ | Cessna 441 Conquest II | 441-0038 | ex VH-HWD | | |
| ☐ | VH-SJQ | Cessna 441 Conquest II | 441-0173 | ex N2722Y | | ♦ |
| | | | | | | |
| ☐ | VH-XFP | de Havilland DHC-8-102A | 346 | ex VH-TQU | | |
| ☐ | VH-XFQ | de Havilland DHC-8-106 | 306 | ex VH-TQW | | |
| ☐ | VH-XFT | de Havilland DHC-8-102 | 52 | ex ZK-NEW | | |
| ☐ | VH-XFU | de Havilland DHC-8-102 | 151 | ex ZK-NEV | | |
| ☐ | VH-XFV | de Havilland DHC-8-314A | 350 | ex D-BMUC | | |
| ☐ | VH-XFW | de Havilland DHC-8-314A | 356 | ex D-BKIM | | |
| ☐ | VH-XFX | de Havilland DHC-8-314A | 313 | ex D-BHAM | | |
| ☐ | VH-XFZ | de Havilland DHC-8-314A | 365 | ex D-BACH | | |
| ☐ | VH-XKI | de Havilland DHC-8Q-315 | 587 | ex C-GKUX | | ♦ |
| ☐ | VH-XKJ | de Havilland DHC-8Q-315 | 588 | ex C-GLPG | | ♦ |
| | | | | | | |
| ☐ | VH-XUA | Embraer EMB.120ER Brasilia | 120045 | ex N272UE | | |
| ☐ | VH-XUB | Embraer EMB.120ER Brasilia | 120181 | ex VH-XFW | | |
| ☐ | VH-XUC | Embraer EMB.120ER Brasilia | 120208 | ex VH-XFV | Pelsaert Princess | |
| ☐ | VH-XUD | Embraer EMB.120ER Brasilia | 120140 | ex VH-XFZ | Monket Mia Flyer | |
| ☐ | VH-XUE | Embraer EMB.120ER Brasilia | 120115 | ex VH-XFQ | | |
| ☐ | VH-XUF | Embraer EMB.120ER Brasilia | 120207 | ex N268UE | | |
| | | | | | | |
| ☐ | VH-WAI | Swearingen SA.227DC Metro 23 | DC-874B | ex N3032L | | |
| ☐ | VH-WAJ | Swearingen SA.227DC Metro 23 | DC-876B | ex N3033U | | |
| ☐ | VH-WAX | Swearingen SA.227DC Metro 23 | DC-877B | ex N30337 | | |
| ☐ | VH-WBA | Swearingen SA.227DC Metro 23 | DC-883B | ex N30042 | | |
| ☐ | VH-WBQ | Swearingen SA.227DC Metro 23 | DC-884B | ex N30046 | Laverton | |

## SKYFORCE AVIATION                              Sydney-Bankstown, NSW (BWU)

| | | | | | | |
|---|---|---|---|---|---|---|
| ☐ | VH-PDL | Convair 580F | 137 | ex ZK-PNR | | ♦ |
| ☐ | VH-PDW | Convair 580F | 86 | ex C-GKFQ | | ♦ |

| | | | | | | |
|---|---|---|---|---|---|---|
| ☐ | VH-PDX | Convair 580F | 126 | ex C-FIWN | | ♦ |
| ☐ | VH- | HS.748 Srs.2A | 1687 | ex N687AP | | o/o [SEN]♦ |

## SKYTRACKERS
*Melbourne-Tullamarine, VIC (MEL)*

| | | | | | | |
|---|---|---|---|---|---|---|
| ☐ | VH-VHA | CASA C.212 Srs.400 | 474 | | Ginger | Wheels or skis |
| ☐ | VH-VHB | CASA C.212 Srs.400 | 475 | | Gadget | Wheels or skis |
| ☐ | VH-VHD | Airbus A319-115CJ | 1999 | ex F-GYAS | | |

## SKYTRANS REGIONAL
*(Q6/SKP)* — *Cairns, QLD (CNS)*

| | | | | | |
|---|---|---|---|---|---|
| ☐ | VH-QQA | de Havilland DHC-8-102 | 005 | ex P2-MCN | |
| ☐ | VH-QQB | de Havilland DHC-8-102 | 004 | ex VH-TQO | >Maroomba |
| ☐ | VH-QQC | de Havilland DHC-8-102 | 008 | ex VH-JSZ | |
| ☐ | VH-QQE | de Havilland DHC-8-102 | 173 | ex N821EX | |
| ☐ | VH-QQF | de Havilland DHC-8-102 | 014 | ex P2-MCO | |
| ☐ | VH-QQG | de Havilland DHC-8-102 | 036 | ex 5W-FAA | based DRW for Toll |
| ☐ | VH-QQH | de Havilland DHC-8-102 | 380 | ex N982HA | ♦ |
| ☐ | VH-QQI | de Havilland DHC-8-102 | 117 | ex N717AV | |
| ☐ | VH-QQJ | de havilland DHC-8-102 | 392 | ex N828EX | ♦ |
| ☐ | VH-QQK | de Havilland DHC-8-102 | 326 | ex N846EX | |
| ☐ | VH-QQL | de Havilland DHC-8-102A | 388 | ex N825EX | |
| ☐ | VH-QQP | de Havilland DHC-8-311A | 232 | ex V2-LGA | ♦ |
| ☐ | VH-QQM | de Havilland DHC-8-311 | 286 | ex G-WOWD | ♦ |
| ☐ | VH-QQN | de Havilland DHC-8-311 | 276 | ex C-GMOH | ♦ |

## SKYWEST AIRLINES
*(XR/OZW)* — *Perth-International, WA (PER)*

| | | | | | | |
|---|---|---|---|---|---|---|
| ☐ | VH-FVH | ATR 72-212A | 0954 | ex F-WWEG | | ♦ |
| ☐ | VH-FVI | ATR 72-212A | 0955 | ex F-WWEH | | ♦ |
| ☐ | VH-FVL | ATR 72-212A | 0974 | ex F-WWES | Virgin Australia c/s | ♦ |
| ☐ | VH-FVM | ATR 72-212A | 0979 | ex F-WWEX | woolamai beach | ♦ |
| ☐ | VH-FVU | ATR 72-212A | 978 | ex OY-CJU | Double Island Point | ♦ |
| ☐ | VH-FVZ | ATR 72-212A | 986 | ex OY-CJV | Kirra Beach | ♦ |
| ☐ | VH-FNA | Fokker 50 | 20106 | ex PH-EXG | City of Albany | |
| ☐ | VH-FNB | Fokker 50 | 20107 | ex PH-EXF | Shire of Esperance | |
| ☐ | VH-FND | Fokker 50 | 20129 | ex PH-EXB | | |
| ☐ | VH-FNE | Fokker 50 | 20212 | ex PH-PRJ | | |
| ☐ | VH-FNF | Fokker 50 | 20200 | ex PH-PRH | | |
| ☐ | VH-FNH | Fokker 50 | 20113 | ex PH-EXY | Shire of Carnarvon | |
| ☐ | VH-FNI | Fokker 50 | 20114 | ex PH-EXZ | City of Geraldton | |
| ☐ | VH-FSL | Fokker 50 | 20249 | ex PH-KXH | | ♦ |
| ☐ | VH-FNC | Fokker 100 | 11334 | ex D-AGPO | | |
| ☐ | VH-FNJ | Fokker 100 | 11489 | ex G-BVJA | | |
| ☐ | VH-FNN | Fokker 100 | 11326 | ex PH-CFD | | |
| ☐ | VH-FNR | Fokker 100 | 11488 | ex G-BVJB | | |
| ☐ | VH-FNT | Fokker 100 | 11461 | ex B-12297 | | |
| ☐ | VH-FNU | Fokker 100 | 11373 | ex OO-TUF | | |
| ☐ | VH-FNY | Fokker 100 | 11484 | ex N108ML | | |
| ☐ | VH-FSQ | Fokker 100 | 11450 | ex N450DR | | ♦ |
| ☐ | VH-FSW | Fokker 100 | 11391 | ex D-AGPR | | |
| ☐ | VH-FXF | Fokker 100 | 11494 | ex PH-ABX | | [PER]♦ |
| ☐ | VH-FZO | Fokker 100 | 11305 | ex PH-LMY | | [PER]♦ |
| ☐ | VH-FNP | Airbus A320-231 | 0429 | ex G-BYTH | | ♦ |
| ☐ | VH-FVX | ATR 72-600 | 986 | ex OY-CJV | | o/o♦ |

## SLINGAIR
*Kununurra, WA (KNX)*

| | | | | | |
|---|---|---|---|---|---|
| ☐ | VH-HAM | Cessna 208 Caravan I | 20800296 | ex N208MM | |
| ☐ | VH-KSA | Cessna 208B Caravan I | 208B0516 | ex N6302B | |
| ☐ | VH-LNH | Cessna 208B Caravan I | 208B0590 | ex N590TA | |
| ☐ | VH-LNN | Cessna 208B Caravan I | 208B0801 | ex 9M-PMB | |
| ☐ | VH-LNO | Cessna 208B Caravan I | 208B0925 | ex N125AR | |
| ☐ | VH-HOC | Cessna 210N Centurion II | 21064689 | ex N1360U | |
| ☐ | VH-NLV | Cessna 210N Centurion II | 21063093 | ex VH-APU | |
| ☐ | VH-NLZ | Cessna 210N Centurion II | 21063769 | ex VH-RZZ | |
| ☐ | VH-STB | Cessna 210M Centurion II | 21062771 | ex N6467B | |
| ☐ | VH-URX | Cessna 210N Centurion II | 21064449 | ex N6595Y | |
| ☐ | VH-AJZ | GippsAero GA-8 Airvan | GA8-05-096 | | ♦ |
| ☐ | VH-DER | Piper PA-31 Navajo C | 31-7912110 | ex N3539D | |
| ☐ | VH-FGH | GippsAero GA-8 Airvan | GA8-02-012 | ex VH-WOG | ♦ |
| ☐ | VH-IEU | Cessna 207 Skywagon | 20700231 | ex N69336 | |
| ☐ | VH-JVO | Cessna 310R | 310R0539 | ex N145FB | |
| ☐ | VH-LVA | GippsAero GA-8 Airvan | GA8-05-079 | | ♦ |
| ☐ | VH-NLG | Cessna U206G Stationair | U20603930 | ex ZS-JGH | |

| | | | | | | |
|---|---|---|---|---|---|---|
| ☐ | VH-NOQ | GippsAero GA-8 Airvan | GA8-07-127 | ex VH-WOQ | | ♦ |
| ☐ | VH-RKD | Piper PA-31-350 Chieftain | 31-8152048 | ex N4076Z | | |
| ☐ | VH-TWY | Cessna 310R | 310R0090 | ex N69336 | | |
| ☐ | VH-XMM | Piper PA-31-350 Chieftain | 31-8052020 | ex N3547D | | ♦ |

### SUNSTATE AIRLINES — Sunstate (QF/SSQ) — Brisbane, QLD (BNE)

Wholly owned by Qantas and ops scheduled services in full colours as QantasLink (qv)

### SYDNEY SEAPLANES — Sydney Rose Bay, NSW

| | | | | | | |
|---|---|---|---|---|---|---|
| ☐ | VH-AAM | de Havilland DHC-2 Beaver | 1492 | ex VH-IMR | Caledonia | FP |
| ☐ | VH-MBQ | Cessna 208 Caravan I | 20800278 | | | ♦ |
| ☐ | VH-NOO | de Havilland DHC-2 Beaver | 1535 | ex VH-IDI | Cambria | FP |
| ☐ | VH-SXF | Cessna 208 Caravan I | 20800405 | ex N1122Y | Corsair | FP |

### TASAIR — Hobart, TAS (HBT)

| | | | | | |
|---|---|---|---|---|---|
| ☐ | VH-SMQ | British Aerospace Jetstream 31 | 665 | ex VH-ESW | wfs |

### TIGER AIRWAYS — (TR/TGV) — Melbourne-Tullamarine, VIC (MEL)

| | | | | | |
|---|---|---|---|---|---|
| ☐ | VH-VNB | Airbus A320-232 | 2906 | ex 9V-TAG | |
| ☐ | VH-VNC | Airbus A320-232 | 3275 | ex F-WWDE | |
| ☐ | VH-VND | Airbus A320-232 | 3296 | ex F-WWDX | |
| ☐ | VH-VNF | Airbus A320-232 | 3332 | ex F-WWBI | |
| ☐ | VH-VNG | Airbus A320-232 | 3674 | ex 9V-TAJ | |
| ☐ | VH-VNH | Airbus A320-232 | 3734 | ex F-WWDN | ♦ |
| ☐ | VH-VNJ | Airbus A320-232 | 2982 | ex 9V-TAI | |
| ☐ | VH-VNK | Airbus A320-232 | 3986 | ex 9V-TAK | ♦ |
| ☐ | VH-VNO | Airbus A320-232 | 4053 | ex 9V-TAL | ♦ |
| ☐ | VH-VNP | Airbus A320-232 | 2952 | ex 9V-TAH | ♦ |

### TOLL PRIORITY — (JCC) — Brisbane, QLD

| | | | | | | |
|---|---|---|---|---|---|---|
| ☐ | VH-UUO | Swearingen SA.227AC Metro III | AC-530 | ex ZK-NST | | |
| ☐ | VH-UZD | Swearingen SA.227AC Metro III | AC-490 | ex N30693 | | |
| ☐ | VH-UZG | Swearingen SA.227AC Metro III | AC-553 | ex N220CT | | |
| ☐ | VH-UZP | Swearingen SA.227AC Metro III | AC-498 | ex OY-BPL | David Fell | |
| ☐ | VH-UZS | Swearingen SA.227AC Metro III | AC-517 | ex VH-UUG | | |
| ☐ | VH-UZW | Swearingen SA.227AC Metro III | AC-526 | ex OY-GAW | Toll c/s | |
| ☐ | VH-HPE | Swearingen SA.227DC Metro 23 | DC-823B | ex N823MM | Toll c/s | |
| ☐ | VH-TOQ | ATR 42-300F | 0079 | ex EI-SLB | Toll c/s | |
| ☐ | VH-TOX | ATR 42-300F | 0024 | ex EI-SLE | Toll c/s | |
| ☐ | VH-UZA | Swearingen SA.227AT Merlin IVC | AT-502 | ex VH-UUA | | |
| ☐ | VH-UZI | Swearingen SA.227AT Expediter | AT-570 | ex N570UP | | |
| ☐ | VH-UZN | Swearingen SA.227DC Metro 23 | DC-881B | ex N6BN | The Australian c/s | |
| ☐ | ZK-TLA | Boeing 737-3B7 (SF) | 23383/1425 | ex N508AU | | Op by AWK |
| ☐ | ZK-TLC | Boeing 737-3B7 (SF) | 23705/1497 | ex N519AU | | Op by AWK |
| ☐ | ZK-TLD | Boeing 737-3B7 (SF) | 23706/1499 | ex N520AU | | Op by AWK |
| ☐ | ZK-TLE | Boeing 737-3S1F | 24834/1896 | ex N919GF | | Op by AWK♦ |

### VINCENT AVIATION (AUSTRALIA) — (BF/VIN) — Darwin, NT (DAW)

| | | | | | |
|---|---|---|---|---|---|
| ☐ | VH-EMK | Beech 1900C-1 | UC-159 | ex N159GL | |
| ☐ | VH-FWA | Beech 1900C | UB-61 | ex N818BE | ♦ |
| ☐ | VH-VAQ | Beech 1900D | UE-302 | ex ZK-VAB | |
| ☐ | VH-VAZ | Beech 1900D | UE-115 | ex ZS-PMD | |
| ☐ | VH-VNT | Beech 1900D | UE-91 | ex (VH-ZOA) | |
| ☐ | VH-VNV | Beech 1900C-1 | UC-56 | ex ZK-VAE | |

### VIRGIN AUSTRALIA — Virgin Blue (DJ/VOZ) — Brisbane-International, QLD (BNE)

| | | | | | | |
|---|---|---|---|---|---|---|
| ☐ | VH-XFA | Airbus A330-243 | 365 | ex A6-EAB | | |
| ☐ | VH-XFB | Airbus A330-243 | 372 | ex A6-EAC | | ♦ |
| ☐ | VH-XFC | Airbus A330-243 | 1293 | ex F-WWYU | | |
| ☐ | VH-XFD | Airbus A330-243 | 1306 | ex F-WWYY | | o/o♦ |
| ☐ | VH-XFE | Airbus A330-243 | 1319 | ex F-WW | | o/o♦ |
| ☐ | VH-VBC | Boeing 737-7Q8 | 30638/858 | | | |
| ☐ | VH-VBJ | Boeing 737-7Q8/W | 30647/1159 | | Perth Princess | |
| ☐ | VH-VBK | Boeing 737-7Q8/W | 30648/1171 | | Lady Victoria | |
| ☐ | VH-VBL | Boeing 737-7Q8/W | 30633/1220 | | Victoria Vixen | |
| ☐ | VH-VBN | Boeing 737-76N/W | 33005/1134 | ex N330SF | | [KUL] |
| ☐ | VH-VBO | Boeing 737-76N/W | 33418/1226 | | Tropical Temptress | |
| ☐ | VH-VBP | Boeing 737-7BX/W | 30743/922 | ex N368ML | Deja Blue | |
| ☐ | VH-VBU | Boeing 737-7BK/W | 30288/1322 | | Darwin Diva | |
| ☐ | VH-VBV | Boeing 737-7BK/W | 33015/1384 | | Moulin Blue | |

| | | | | | | |
|---|---|---|---|---|---|---|
| ☐ | VH-VBY | Boeing 737-7FE/W | 34323/1751 | | Kingston Beach | |
| ☐ | VH-VBZ | Boeing 737-7FE/W | 34322/1777 | | Maliblue | |
| | | | | | | |
| ☐ | VH-BZG | Boeing 737-8FE/W | 37822/3355 | ex(VH-VUW) | Brett'sJet | |
| ☐ | VH-VOD | Boeing 737-8BK/W | 30624/1193 | ex N60656 | Blue Moon | |
| ☐ | VH-VOK | Boeing 737-8FE/W | 33758/1359 | | Johanna Beach | |
| ☐ | VH-VOL | Boeing 737-8FE/W | 33759/1364 | | Goldie Coast | |
| ☐ | VH-VOM | Boeing 737-8FE/W | 33794/1373 | | Little Blue Peep | |
| ☐ | VH-VON | Boeing 737-8FE/W | 33795/1375 | | Scarlett Blue | |
| ☐ | VH-VOQ | Boeing 737-8FE/W | 33798/1391 | | Margaret River | |
| ☐ | VH-VOS | Boeing 737-8FE/W | 33800/1483 | | Kimberley Cutie | |
| ☐ | VH-VOT | Boeing 737-8FE/W | 33801/1504 | | Butterfly Blue | |
| ☐ | VH-VOU | Boeing 737-8Q8/W | 30665/1436 | | Blue Billie | |
| ☐ | VH-VOV | Boeing 737-82R | 30658/1325 | | Alluring Alice | |
| ☐ | VH-VOW | Boeing 737-8Q8/W | 32798/1470 | | Jillaroo Blue | |
| ☐ | VH-VOX | Boeing 737-8BK/W | 33017/1446 | ex ZK-PBC | Missy Mainlander | |
| ☐ | VH-VUA | Boeing 737-8FE/W | 33997/1559 | | Bondi Baby | |
| ☐ | VH-VUC | Boeing 737-8FE/W | 34014/1582 | | Foxy Rock'sy | |
| ☐ | VH-VUE | Boeing 737-8FE/W | 34167/1676 | | Prue Blue | |
| ☐ | VH-VUF | Boeing 737-8FE/W | 34168/1697 | | | |
| ☐ | VH-VUG | Boeing 737-8FE/W | 34438/1948 | | | |
| ☐ | VH-VUI | Boeing 737-8FE/W | 34441/2015 | | Brandi Blue | |
| ☐ | VH-VUJ | Boeing 737-8FE/W | 34443/2056 | | Suzzie Blue | |
| ☐ | VH-VUK | Boeing 737-8FE/W | 36602/2353 | | Mackay-be Diva | |
| ☐ | VH-VUL | Boeing 737-8FE/W | 36603/2356 | ex N1782B | Ballina-rina Blue | |
| ☐ | VH-VUM | Boeing 737-8BK/W | 29675/2414 | ex N1786B | Brindabella Blue | |
| ☐ | VH-VUN | Boeing 737-8BK/W | 29676/2432 | | Madelaide | |
| ☐ | VH-VUR | Boeing 737-8FE/W | 36606/3059 | ex N1786B | Star City | |
| ☐ | VH-VUS | Boeing 737-8FE/W | 36607/3082 | | Chitty Chitty Broome Broome | |
| ☐ | VH-VUT | Boeing 737-8FE/W | 36608/3132 | | Yabba Dabba Blue | |
| ☐ | VH-VUU | Boeing 737-8FE/W | 36609/3232 | ex N1786B | Lady Blue-tiful | |
| ☐ | VH-VUV | Boeing 737-8FE/W | 37821/3288 | ex N1796B | Ruby Blue | |
| ☐ | VH-VUW | Boeing 737-8KG/W | 39449/3398 | | Sydney Siren | |
| ☐ | VH-VUX | Boeing 737-8FE/W | 37823/3415 | ex N1786B | Balina Ballerina | |
| ☐ | VH-VUY | Boeing 737-8KG/W | 39450/3494 | | Snapper Rocks | |
| ☐ | VH-VUZ | Boeing 737-8FE/W | 39921/3536 | | Mendil Beach | ♦ |
| ☐ | VH-YFC | Boeing 737-81D/W | 39413/3592 | | Bondi Beach | ♦ |
| ☐ | VH-YFE | Boeing 737-81D/W | 39414/3623 | | Sunshine Beach | ♦ |
| ☐ | VH-YFF | Boeing 737-8FE/W | 40994/3664 | | | ♦ |
| ☐ | VH-YFG | Boeing 737-8FE/W | 40999/3941 | | Hanson Bay | ♦ |
| ☐ | VH-YFH | Boeing 737-3FE/W | 40996/3801 | | Mindi Beach | |
| ☐ | VH-YFI | Boeing 737-8FE/W | 41000/3963 | | Porpoise Bay | ♦ |
| ☐ | VH-YFJ | Boeing 737-8FE/W | 41001 | | | o/o♦ |
| ☐ | VH-YFK | Boeing 737-8FE/W | 41004/3861 | | Long Beach | ♦ |
| ☐ | VH-YFL | Boeing 737-8FE/W | 41002 | | | o/o♦ |
| ☐ | VH-YIA | Boeing 737-8FE/W | 37824/3718 | | Henley Beach | ♦ |
| ☐ | VH-YIB | Boeing 737-8FE/W | 37825/3758 | | Trinity Beach | ♦ |
| ☐ | VH-YID | Boeing 737-8FE/W | 38709/3851 | | Rainbow Beach | ♦ |
| ☐ | VH-YIE | Boeing 737-8FE/W | 38708/3875 | | Fingal Beach | ♦ |
| ☐ | VH-YIF | Boeing 737-8FE/W | 38710/3904 | | Sorrento Beach | ♦ |
| ☐ | VH-YIG | Boeing 737-8FE/W | 38711/3921 | | Kings Beach | ♦ |
| ☐ | VH-YIH | Boeing 737-8FE/W | 38712 | | | o/o |
| ☐ | VH-YIJ | Boeing 737-8FE/W | 39924 | | | o/o |
| ☐ | VH-YIR | Boeing 737-8FE/W | 39925 | | | o/o |
| ☐ | VH-YIS | Boeing 737-8FE/W | 39926 | | | o/o |
| ☐ | VH-YLF | Boeing 737-8FE/W | 41002 | | | o/o |
| ☐ | VH-YVA | Boeing 737-8FE/W | 40995/3680 | | | |
| ☐ | VH-YVC | Boeing 737-8FE/W | 40997/3832 | | Jetty Beach | |
| ☐ | VH-YVD | Boeing 737-8FE/W | 40998/3848 | ex N1786D | Salmon Beach | |
| ☐ | VH- | Boeing 737-8FE/W | | | | o/o |
| | | | | | | |
| ☐ | VH-VOZ | Boeing 777-3ZGER | 35302/745 | | Didgeree Blue | |
| ☐ | VH-VPD | Boeing 777-3ZGER | 37938/756 | | | |
| ☐ | VH-VPE | Boeing 777-3ZGER | 37939/764 | | African Beauty | |
| ☐ | VH-VPF | Boeing 777-3ZGER | 37940/801 | | | |
| ☐ | VH-VPH | Boeing 777-3ZGER | 37943/898 | | | |
| | | | | | | |
| ☐ | VH-ZPA | Embraer ERJ-190AR | 19000148 | ex PT-SAB | Candid Canberra | |
| ☐ | VH-ZPB | Embraer ERJ-190AR | 19000162 | ex PT-SAR | Rio de Gold Coast | |
| ☐ | VH-ZPC | Embraer ERJ-190AR | 19000170 | ex PT-SDF | Jilla Blue | |
| ☐ | VH-ZPD | Embraer ERJ-190AR | 19000176 | ex PT-SDL | Tickled Blue | |
| ☐ | VH-ZPE | Embraer ERJ-190AR | 19000187 | ex PT-SDV | Bluephoria | |
| ☐ | VH-ZPF | Embraer ERJ-190AR | 19000193 | ex PT-SGB | Maiden Brazil | |
| ☐ | VH-ZPG | Embraer ERJ-190AR | 19000195 | ex PT-SGD | Ella E-Jet | |
| ☐ | VH-ZPH | Embraer ERJ-190AR | 19000199 | ex PT-SGD | Hastings Highness | |
| ☐ | VH-ZPI | Embraer ERJ-190AR | 19000202 | ex PT-SGK | Allie Albury | |
| ☐ | VH-ZPJ | Embraer ERJ-190AR | 19000209 | ex PT-SGS | Bambino Blue | |
| ☐ | VH-ZPK | Embraer ERJ-190AR | 19000218 | ex PT-SHB | Aussie Rob | |
| ☐ | VH-ZPL | Embraer ERJ-190AR | 19000220 | ex PT-SHD | Samba Blue | |
| ☐ | VH-ZPM | Embraer ERJ-190AR | 19000262 | ex PT-TLC | | |
| ☐ | VH-ZPN | Embraer ERJ-190AR | 19000312 | ex PT-TXA | Kanga Blue | |
| ☐ | VH-ZPO | Embraer ERJ-190AR | 19000321 | ex PT-TXJ | Portia Macquarie | |
| ☐ | VH-ZPQ | Embraer ERJ-190AR | 19000412 | ex PT-TBK | Main Beach | ♦ |

| | | | | | | |
|---|---|---|---|---|---|---|
| ☐ | VH-ZPR | Embraer ERJ-190AR | 19000424 | ex PT-TCG | Dundee Beach | ♦ |
| ☐ | VH-ZPT | Embraer ERJ-190AR | 19000451 | ex | | ♦ |
| ☐ | VH-ZHE | Embraer ERJ-170LR | 17000247 | ex PT-SFY | Bee bop a Blue | |

## WEST WING AVIATION
**Mount Isa, QLD (ISA)**

| | | | | | | |
|---|---|---|---|---|---|---|
| ☐ | VH-ABP | Beech Baron 58 | TH-709 | ex N6771S | | |
| ☐ | VH-BAM | Beech Baron 58 | TH-478 | ex VH-FDC | | |
| ☐ | VH-BWC | Beech Baron 58 | TH-478 | ex VH-BAM | | |
| ☐ | VH-EZN | Beech Baron 58 | TH-1222 | ex N3722P | | ♦ |
| ☐ | VH-LAP | Beech Baron 58 | TH-646 | ex 5N-ATC | | |
| ☐ | VH-LSB | Beecg Baron 58 | TH-819 | ex N206SB | | ♦ |
| ☐ | VH-SKJ | Cessna 404 Titan II | 404-0086 | ex VH-BPO | | ♦ |
| ☐ | VH-SKV | Cessna 404 Titan II | 404-0412 | ex VH-TLE | | ♦ |
| ☐ | VH-SKW | Cessna 404 Titan II | 404-0042 | ex VH-PNY | | ♦ |
| ☐ | VH-SKZ | Cessna 404 Titan II | 404-0080 | ex VH-JOH | | ♦ |
| ☐ | VH-XDA | Cessna 404 Titan II | 404-0408 | ex VH-HOA | | |
| ☐ | VH-XDP | Cessna 404 Titan II | 404-0845 | ex ZS-PNW | | |
| ☐ | VH-RDZ | Cessna 402A | 402A0125 | ex ZK-CSX | | |
| ☐ | VH-SBM | Beech B200 Super King Air | BB-964 | ex VH-HTU | | |
| ☐ | VH-TAN | Cessna 402C | 402C1008 | ex N1237D | | |
| ☐ | VH-TIV | Cessna 402B | 402B0623 | ex N3774C | | |
| ☐ | VH-TIY | Cessna 208B Caravan I | 208B0649 | ex P2-TWW | | ♦ |
| ☐ | VH-UZY | Cessna 208B Caravan I | 208B0937 | ex EC-IEX | | ♦ |
| ☐ | VH-VCB | Beech 200 Super King Air | BB-579 | ex P2-MML | | ♦ |
| ☐ | VH-WQA | Britten-Norman BN-2A-21 Islander | 494 | ex T3-JMR | | ♦ |
| ☐ | VH-WZD | Britten-Norman BN.2A-21 Islander | 450 | ex VH-USD | | ♦ |
| ☐ | VH-WZF | Britten-Norman BN-2A-21 Islander | 537 | ex 5Y-RAJ | | ♦ |
| ☐ | VH-WZJ | Cessna 208B Caravan I | 208B1108 | ex N208JJ | | |
| ☐ | VH-WZK | Britten-Norman BN-2A-20 Islander | 421 | ex VH-UBN | | |
| ☐ | VH-WZP | Britten-Norman BN-2B-20 Islander | 2284 | ex VH-ZZY | | |
| ☐ | VH-WZV | Aero Commander 500U | 1656-11 | ex N197K | | |
| ☐ | VH-WZY | Cessna 208B Caravan I | 208B1035 | ex VH-ZGS | | |
| ☐ | VH-XDV | Beech B200 Super King Air | BB-1100 | ex N63971 | | |
| ☐ | VH-XDW | Beech B200 Super King Air | BB-1258 | ex N2748X | | |
| ☐ | VH-XDY | Beech 1900D | UE-396 | ex N838CA | | |

## WETTENHALL AIR SERVICES
**Deniliguin, NSW (DNQ)**

| | | | | | |
|---|---|---|---|---|---|
| ☐ | VH-MAV | Rockwell 500S Shrike Commander | 3280 | ex N81512 | |
| ☐ | VH-SSL | Swearingen SA.226T Merlin | T-210 | ex N173SP | |

## WHITSUNDAY AIR SERVICES
**Hamilton Island, QLD (HTI)**

| | | | | | |
|---|---|---|---|---|---|
| ☐ | VH-WTY | Cessna 208 Caravan I | 20800522 | ex N1027V | ♦ |

## VN-   VIETNAM (Socialist Republic of Vietnam)

## AIR MEKONG
**(P8/MKG)**      **Ho Chi Minh City (SGN)**

| | | | | | |
|---|---|---|---|---|---|
| ☐ | VN-A801 | Canadair CRJ-900 | 15102 | ex EI-DUU | |
| ☐ | VN-A802 | Canadair CRJ-900 | 15103 | ex EI-DUM | |
| ☐ | VN-A803 | Canadair CRJ-900 | 15110 | ex EI-DUX | |
| ☐ | VN-A804 | Canadair CRJ-900 | 15112 | ex EI-DUY | |

## JETSTAR PACIFIC AIRLINES
**Pacific Airlines (BL/PIC)**      **Ho Chi Minh City (SGN)**

| | | | | | | |
|---|---|---|---|---|---|---|
| ☐ | VN-A189 | Boeing 737-43Q | 28490/2830 | ex PK-GWY | | |
| ☐ | VN-A190 | Boeing 737-4H6 | 27383/2657 | ex 9M-MQJ | | |
| ☐ | VN-A191 | Boeing 737-4H6 | 27306/2685 | ex 9M-MQM | | |
| ☐ | VN-A192 | Boeing 737-4Q8 | 26289/2486 | ex OK-YGU | all white | |
| ☐ | VN-A194 | Boeing 737-436 | 25850/2386 | ex N850BB | | ♦ |
| ☐ | VH-VFD | Airbus A320-232 | 4922 | ex F-WWIK | | ♦ |
| ☐ | VN-A195 | Airbus A320-232 | 0990 | ex CC-CZB | | |
| ☐ | VN-A198 | Airbus A320-232 | 4459 | ex D-AXAB | | |

## VASCO
**Vasco Air (0V/VFC)**      **Ho Chi Minh City (SGN)**

| | | | | | |
|---|---|---|---|---|---|
| ☐ | VN-B594 | Beech B200 Super King Air | BB-1329 | ex VH-SWC | |

## VIETJET
**(VJC)**

| | | | | | | |
|---|---|---|---|---|---|---|
| ☐ | VN-A666 | Airbus A320-214 | 3739 | ex 9K-EAA | Giá rẻ hơn, bay nhiều thêm | ♦ |
| ☐ | VN-A668 | Airbus A320-214 | 3791 | ex 9K-EAB | | ♦ |
| ☐ | VN-A669 | Airbus A320-214 | 4049 | ex 9K-EAD | | ♦ |

| VIETNAM AIRLINES | | Vietnam Airlines (VN/HVN) | | Hanoi-Noi Bal (HAN) |
|---|---|---|---|---|
| ☐ VN-A302 | Airbus A320-214 | 0594 | ex S7-ASB | |
| ☐ VN-A303 | Airbus A320-214 | 0601 | ex S7-ASC | |
| ☐ VN-A304 | Airbus A320-214 | 0605 | ex S7-ASD | |
| ☐ VN-A305 | Airbus A320-214 | 0607 | ex S7-ASE | |
| ☐ VN-A306 | Airbus A320-214 | 0611 | ex S7-ASF | |
| ☐ VN-A307 | Airbus A320-214 | 0617 | ex S7-ASG | |
| ☐ VN-A308 | Airbus A320-214 | 0619 | ex S7-ASH | |
| ☐ VN-A309 | Airbus A320-214 | 0648 | ex S7-ASI | ◆ |
| ☐ VN-A311 | Airbus A320-214 | 0650 | ex S7-ASJ | ◆ |
| ☐ VN-A322 | Airbus A321-231 | 4311 | ex D-AVZU | |
| ☐ VN-A323 | Airbus A321-231 | 4669 | ex D-AZAE | |
| ☐ VN-A324 | Airbus A321-231 | 4703 | ex D-AZAW | |
| ☐ VN-A325 | Airbus A321-231 | 4737 | ex D-AVZB | |
| ☐ VN-A326 | Airbus A321-231 | 4783 | ex D-AVZM | |
| ☐ VN-A327 | Airbus A321-231 | 4826 | ex D-AVXS | |
| ☐ VN-A329 | Airbus A321-231 | 4863 | ex D-AZAA | |
| ☐ VN-A331 | Airbus A321-231 | 4945 | ex D-AZAC | |
| ☐ VN-A332 | Airbus A321-231 | 4971 | ex D-AZAH | |
| ☐ VN-A344 | Airbus A321-231 | 2255 | ex D-AVZH | |
| ☐ VN-A345 | Airbus A321-231 | 2261 | ex D-AVZJ | |
| ☐ VN-A347 | Airbus A321-231 | 2267 | ex D-AVZL | |
| ☐ VN-A348 | Airbus A321-231 | 2303 | ex D-AVZC | |
| ☐ VN-A349 | Airbus A321-231 | 2480 | ex D-AVXC | |
| ☐ VN-A350 | Airbus A321-231 | 2974 | ex D-AVZN | |
| ☐ VN-A351 | Airbus A321-231 | 3005 | ex D-AVZI | |
| ☐ VN-A352 | Airbus A321-231 | 3013 | ex D-AVZW | |
| ☐ VN-A353 | Airbus A321-231 | 3022 | ex D-AVZY | |
| ☐ VN-A354 | Airbus A321-231 | 3198 | ex D-AVZX | |
| ☐ VN-A356 | Airbus A321-231 | 3315 | ex D-AVZA | |
| ☐ VN-A357 | Airbus A321-231 | 3355 | ex D-AVZB | |
| ☐ VN-A358 | Airbus A321-231 | 3600 | ex D-AZAC | |
| ☐ VN-A359 | Airbus A321-231 | 3737 | ex D-AZAJ | |
| ☐ VN-A360 | Airbus A321-231 | 3862 | ex D-AVZJ | |
| ☐ VN-A361 | Airbus A321-231 | 3964 | ex D-AZAW | |
| ☐ VN-A362 | Airbus A321-231 | 3966 | ex D-AVZC | |
| ☐ VN-A363 | Airbus A321-231 | 4136 | ex D-AZAT | |
| ☐ VN-A365 | Airbus A321-231 | 4213 | ex D-AVZG | |
| ☐ VN-A366 | Airbus A321-231 | 4277 | ex D-AZAO | |
| ☐ VN-A367 | Airbus A321-231 | 4315 | ex D-AVZV | |
| ☐ VN-A370 | Airbus A330-223 | 262 | ex 9M-MKT | |
| ☐ VN-A371 | Airbus A330-223 | 275 | ex HB-IQG | |
| ☐ VN-A372 | Airbus A330-223 | 294 | ex HB-IQJ | |
| ☐ VN-A374 | Airbus A330-223 | 299 | ex HB-IQK | |
| ☐ VN-A375 | Airbus A330-223 | 366 | ex HB-IQP | |
| ☐ VN-A376 | Airbus A330-223 | 943 | ex EI-ELI | |
| ☐ VN-A377 | Airbus A330-223 | 962 | ex EI-ELJ | |
| ☐ VN-A378 | Airbus A330-223 | 1019 | ex F-WJKM | |
| ☐ VN-A379 | Airbus A330-223 | 1256 | ex F-WWYO | ◆ |
| ☐ VN-A381 | Airbus A330-223 | 1266 | ex F-WWKR | ◆ |
| ☐ VN-B210 | ATR 72-212A | 0678 | ex F-WWET | |
| ☐ VN-B212 | ATR 72-212A | 0685 | ex F-WWEH | |
| ☐ VN-B214 | ATR 72-212A | 0688 | ex F-WWEK | |
| ☐ VN-B216 | ATR 72-212A | 0450 | ex F-WQNF | |
| ☐ VN-B218 | ATR 72-212A | 0877 | ex F-WWEE | |
| ☐ VN-B219 | ATR 72-212A | 0886 | ex F-WWEP | |
| ☐ VN-B220 | ATR 72-212A | 0890 | ex F-WWEV | |
| ☐ VN-B221 | ATR 72-212A | 0892 | ex F-WWEX | |
| ☐ VN-B223 | ATR 72-212A | 0896 | ex F-WWEG | |
| ☐ VN-B225 | ATR 72-212A | 0897 | ex F-WW | |
| ☐ VN-B233 | ATR 72-212A | 0912 | ex F-WWEG | |
| ☐ VN-B236 | ATR 72-212A | 0914 | ex F-WWEJ | |
| ☐ VN-B237 | ATR 72-212A | 0925 | ex F-WWEZ | |
| ☐ VN-B239 | ATR 72-212A | 0927 | ex F-WWEC | |
| ☐ VN-B240 | ATR 72-212A | 0939 | ex F-WWEO | |
| ☐ VN-A141 | Boeing 777-2Q8ER | 28688/436 | | |
| ☐ VN-A142 | Boeing 777-2Q8ER | 32701/443 | | |
| ☐ VN-A143 | Boeing 777-26KER | 33502/450 | | |
| ☐ VN-A144 | Boeing 777-26KER | 33503/453 | | |
| ☐ VN-A145 | Boeing 777-26KER | 33504/491 | | |
| ☐ VN-A146 | Boeing 777-26KER | 33505/486 | | |
| ☐ VN-A147 | Boeing 777-2Q8ER | 27607/135 | ex VP-BAS | |
| ☐ VN-A149 | Boeing 777-2Q8ER | 32716/518 | ex (VN-A147) | |
| ☐ VN-A150 | Boeing 777-2Q8ER | 32717/541 | | |
| ☐ VN-A151 | Boeing 777-2Q8ER | 27608/164 | ex VP-BAU | |
| ☐ VN-A502 | Fokker 70 | 11580 | ex PH-EZL | |
| ☐ VN-A504 | Fokker 70 | 11585 | ex PH-EZM | |

## VP-A  ANGUILLA (UK Dependency)

### ANGUILLA AIR SERVICES — Anguilla-Wallbake (AXA)

| | | | | |
|---|---|---|---|---|
| ☐ | VP-AAS | Britten-Norman BN-2A-26 Islander | 206 | ex G-ISLA |

### CARIBE AIR CHARTERS — Anguilla-Wallbake (AXA)

| | | | | | |
|---|---|---|---|---|---|
| ☐ | VP-AAJ | Britten-Norman BN-2A-26 Islander | 2006 | ex V4-AAC | ♦ |

### TRANS ANGUILLA AIRLINES — Anguilla-Wallbake/St Thomas-Cyril E King, VI (AXA/STT)

| | | | | |
|---|---|---|---|---|
| ☐ | VP-AAA | Britten-Norman BN-2A-21 Islander | 382 | ex N361RA |
| ☐ | VP-AAF | Britten-Norman BN-2B-21 Islander | 2024 | ex N21DA |

## VP-C  CAYMAN ISLANDS (UK Colony)

### CAYMAN AIRWAYS — Cayman (KX/CAY) — Georgetown, Grand Cayman (GCM)

| | | | | | | |
|---|---|---|---|---|---|---|
| ☐ | VP-CAY | Boeing 737-3Q8 | 26286/2424 | ex N241LF | Spirit of Recovery | |
| ☐ | VP-CKW | Boeing 737-36E | 26322/2769 | ex EI-CRZ | | |
| ☐ | VP-CKY | Boeing 737-3Q8 | 26282/2355 | ex N262KS | The Cayman Islands | |
| ☐ | VP-CKZ | Boeing 737-36E | 27626/2792 | ex EI-CSU | | o/o |

### CAYMAN AIRWAYS EXPRESS — Georgetown, Grand Cayman (GCM)

| | | | | |
|---|---|---|---|---|
| ☐ | VP-CXA | de Havilland DHC-6 Twin Otter 300 | 602 | ex N602DH |
| ☐ | VP-CXB | de Havilland DHC-6 Twin Otter 300 | 563 | ex N563DH |

### CHC HELICOPTERS

| | | | | | |
|---|---|---|---|---|---|
| ☐ | VP-CHB | Aérespatiale AS.332L | 2582 | ex LN-OHI | op in Falklands♦ |
| ☐ | VP-CHC | Aérospatiale AS.332L | 2393 | ex LN-OHC | op in Falklands♦ |

## VP-F  FALKLAND ISLANDS (UK Dependency)

### BRITISH ANTARCTIC SURVEY — Penguin (BAN) — Rothera Base, Antarctica

| | | | | | |
|---|---|---|---|---|---|
| ☐ | VP-FAZ | de Havilland DHC-6 Twin Otter 300 | 748 | ex C-GEOA | Wheels or skis |
| ☐ | VP-FBB | de Havilland DHC-6 Twin Otter 310 | 783 | ex C-GDKL | Wheels or skis |
| ☐ | VP-FBC | de Havilland DHC-6 Twin Otter 310 | 787 | ex C-GDIU | Wheels or skis |
| ☐ | VP-FBL | de Havilland DHC-6 Twin Otter 300 | 839 | ex C-GDCZ | Wheels or skis |
| ☐ | VP-FBQ | de Havilland DHC-7-110 | 111 | ex G-BOAX | |

### FIGAS - FALKLAND ISLANDS GOVERNMENT AIR SERVICES — Port Stanley (PSY)

| | | | | | |
|---|---|---|---|---|---|
| ☐ | VP-FBD | Britten-Norman BN-2B-26 Islander | 2160 | ex G-BKJK | |
| ☐ | VP-FBM | Britten-Norman BN-2B-26 Islander | 2200 | ex G-BLNZ | |
| ☐ | VP-FBN | Britten-Norman BN-2B-26 Islander | 2216 | ex G-BRFY | Fishery Patrol |
| ☐ | VP-FBO | Britten-Norman BN-2B-26 Islander | 2218 | ex G-BRGA | Fishery Patrol |
| ☐ | VP-FBR | Britten-Norman BN-2B-26 Islander | 2252 | ex G-BTLX | |

## VP-M  MONTSERRAT (UK Colony)

### AIR MONTSERRAT — Plymouth (MNI)

| | | | | |
|---|---|---|---|---|
| ☐ | VP-MNT | Britten-Norman BN-2B-26 Islander | 2186 | |
| ☐ | VP-MON | Britten-Norman BN-2A-26 Islander | 82 | ex C-GCTZ |

## VQ-T  TURKS & CAICOS ISLANDS (UK Colony)

### AIR TURKS & CAICOS — Islandways (IWY) — Providenciales (PLS)

| | | | | | |
|---|---|---|---|---|---|
| ☐ | VQ-TAQ | Embraer EMB.120RT Brasilia | 120036 | ex N232AS | ♦ |
| ☐ | VQ-TBC | Embraer EMB.120ER Brasilia | 120283 | ex N639AS | |
| ☐ | VQ-TCI | Beech B200C Super King Air | BL-125 | ex VH-BRF | ♦ |
| ☐ | VQ-TDA | Britten-Norman BN-2A-27 Islander | 504 | ex HI-704CT | |
| ☐ | VQ-TDG | Embraer EMB.120ER Brasilia | 120275 | ex N503AS | |
| ☐ | VQ-TMJ | Embraer EMB.120ER | 120274 | ex N502AS | ♦ |
| ☐ | VQ-TRJ | Cessna 401A | 401A0061 | ex N60EM | ♦ |

| | | | | |
|---|---|---|---|---|
| **CAICOS EXPRESS AIRWAYS** | | | | **Providenciales (PLS)** |
| ☐ VQ-TIN | Cessna 402C | 402C0227 | ex N68CT | ◆ |
| ☐ VQ-TRF | Cessna 402C | 402C0021 | ex N402RR | ◆ |

| | | | | |
|---|---|---|---|---|
| **GLOBAL AIRWAYS** | | | | **Providenciales (PLS)** |
| ☐ VQ-TBF | Piper PA-23 Aztec 250C | 27-2615 | ex N5517Y | ◆ |
| ☐ VQ-TGA | Cessna 401A | 401A0114 | ex N401DD | ◆ |
| ☐ VQ-TGS | Piper PA-23 Aztec 250E | 27-7554008 | ex C-GWVS | ◆ |

| | | |
|---|---|---|
| **SKYKING AIRLINES** | **Skyking (RU/SKI)** | **Providenciales (PLS)** |

Ceased ops

## VT-    INDIA (Republic of India)

| **AIR INDIA** | | **Airindia (AI/AIC)** | **Mumbai-Chhatrapatti Shivaji Intl (BOM)** |
|---|---|---|---|
| ☐ VT-SCA | Airbus A319-112 | 2593 | ex D-AVXL |
| ☐ VT-SCB | Airbus A319-112 | 2624 | ex D-AVYX |
| ☐ VT-SCC | Airbus A319-112 | 2629 | ex D-AVWC |
| ☐ VT-SCD | Airbus A319-112 | 1668 | ex C-GJTC |
| ☐ VT-SCE | Airbus A319-112 | 1718 | ex C-GJVS |
| ☐ VT-SCF | Airbus A319-112 | 2907 | ex D-AVWT |
| ☐ VT-SCG | Airbus A319-112 | 3271 | ex D-AVYH |
| ☐ VT-SCH | Airbus A319-112 | 3288 | ex D-AVWM |
| ☐ VT-SCI | Airbus A319-112 | 3300 | ex D-AVYN |
| ☐ VT-SCJ | Airbus A319-112 | 3305 | ex D-AVYO |
| ☐ VT-SCK | Airbus A319-112 | 3344 | ex D-AVYT |
| ☐ VT-SCL | Airbus A319-112 | 3551 | ex D-AVWO |
| ☐ VT-SCM | Airbus A319-112 | 3620 | ex D-AVYN |
| ☐ VT-SCN | Airbus A319-112 | 3687 | ex D-AVWE |
| ☐ VT-SCO | Airbus A319-112 | 3822 | ex D-AVYH |
| ☐ VT-SCP | Airbus A319-112 | 3874 | ex D-AVWF |
| ☐ VT-SCQ | Airbus A319-112 | 3918 | ex D-AVYY |
| ☐ VT-SCR | Airbus A319-112 | 3970 | ex D-AVYB |
| ☐ VT-SCS | Airbus A319-112 | 4020 | ex D-AVYH |
| ☐ VT-SCT | Airbus A319-112 | 4029 | ex D-AVYJ |
| ☐ VT-SCU | Airbus A319-112 | 4052 | ex D-AVYQ |
| ☐ VT-SCV | Airbus A319-112 | 4089 | ex D-AVYY |
| ☐ VT-SCW | Airbus A319-112 | 4121 | ex D-AVWB |
| ☐ VT-SCX | Airbus A319-112 | 4164 | ex D-AVYZ |
| ☐ VT-EDC | Airbus A320-214 | 4201 | ex F-WWBD |
| ☐ VT-EDD | Airbus A320-214 | 4212 | ex F-WWDJ |
| ☐ VT-EDE | Airbus A320-214 | 4236 | ex F-WWDE |
| ☐ VT-EDF | Airbus A320-214 | 4237 | ex F-WWDG |
| ☐ VT-EPB | Airbus A320-231 | 0045 | ex F-WWDY |
| ☐ VT-EPC | Airbus A320-231 | 0046 | ex F-WWDG |
| ☐ VT-EPD | Airbus A320-231 | 0047 | ex F-WWDP |
| ☐ VT-EPF | Airbus A320-231 | 0049 | ex F-WWIA |
| ☐ VT-EPG | Airbus A320-231 | 0050 | ex F-WWDR |
| ☐ VT-EPH | Airbus A320-231 | 0051 | ex F-WWIB |
| ☐ VT-EPI | Airbus A320-231 | 0056 | ex F-WWIC |
| ☐ VT-EPJ | Airbus A320-231 | 0057 | ex F-WWIF | 50 years titles |
| ☐ VT-EPL | Airbus A320-231 | 0074 | ex F-WWIQ |
| ☐ VT-EPM | Airbus A320-231 | 0075 | ex F-WWIR | 50 years titles |
| ☐ VT-EPO | Airbus A320-231 | 0080 | ex F-WWIX |
| ☐ VT-EPQ | Airbus A320-231 | 0090 | ex F-WWDX |
| ☐ VT-EPS | Airbus A320-231 | 0096 | ex F-WWDU |
| ☐ VT-ESA | Airbus A320-231 | 0396 | ex F-WWBK |
| ☐ VT-ESB | Airbus A320-231 | 0398 | ex F-WWDQ |
| ☐ VT-ESC | Airbus A320-231 | 0416 | ex F-WWBP |
| ☐ VT-ESD | Airbus A320-231 | 0423 | ex F-WWIT |
| ☐ VT-ESE | Airbus A320-231 | 0431 | ex F-WWBQ |
| ☐ VT-ESF | Airbus A320-231 | 0432 | ex F-WWBS |
| ☐ VT-ESG | Airbus A320-231 | 0451 | ex F-WWIN |
| ☐ VT-ESH | Airbus A320-231 | 0469 | ex F-WWBD |
| ☐ VT-ESI | Airbus A320-231 | 0486 | ex F-WWBH | 50 years titles |
| ☐ VT-ESJ | Airbus A320-231 | 0490 | ex F-WWDT | 50 years titles |
| ☐ VT-ESK | Airbus A320-231 | 0492 | ex F-WWBU | 50 years titles |
| ☐ VT-ESL | Airbus A320-231 | 0499 | ex F-WWDO |
| ☐ VT-EYL | Airbus A320-231 | 0480 | ex G-MEDA |
| ☐ VT-PPA | Airbus A321-211 | 3130 | ex D-AVZT |
| ☐ VT-PPB | Airbus A321-211 | 3146 | ex D-AVZU |
| ☐ VT-PPD | Airbus A321-211 | 3212 | ex D-AVZA |
| ☐ VT-PPE | Airbus A321-211 | 3326 | ex D-AVZW |

| | | | | | | |
|---|---|---|---|---|---|---|
| ☐ | VT-PPF | Airbus A321-211 | 3340 | ex D-AVZH | | |
| ☐ | VT-PPG | Airbus A321-211 | 3367 | ex D-AVZG | | |
| ☐ | VT-PPH | Airbus A321-211 | 3498 | ex D-AVZG | | |
| ☐ | VT-PPI | Airbus A321-211 | 3557 | ex D-AVZQ | | |
| ☐ | VT-PPJ | Airbus A321-211 | 3573 | ex D-AVZC | | |
| ☐ | VT-PPK | Airbus A321-211 | 3619 | ex D-AVZF | | |
| ☐ | VT-PPL | Airbus A321-211 | 3752 | ex D-AZAM | | |
| ☐ | VT-PPM | Airbus A321-211 | 3792 | ex D-AZAR | | |
| ☐ | VT-PPN | Airbus A321-211 | 3955 | ex D-AZAU | | |
| ☐ | VT-PPO | Airbus A321-211 | 4002 | ex D-AVZB | | |
| ☐ | VT-PPQ | Airbus A321-211 | 4009 | ex D-AVZE | | |
| ☐ | VT-PPT | Airbus A321-211 | 4078 | ex D-AVZU | | |
| ☐ | VT-PPU | Airbus A321-211 | 4096 | ex D-AVZY | | |
| ☐ | VT-PPV | Airbus A321-211 | 4138 | ex D-AZAU | | |
| ☐ | VT-PPW | Airbus A321-211 | 4155 | ex D-AVZZ | | |
| ☐ | VT-PPX | Airbus A321-211 | 4280 | ex D-AZAP | | |
| | | | | | | |
| ☐ | VT-ESN | Boeing 747-437 | 27164/1003 | | Tanjore | |
| ☐ | VT-ESO | Boeing 747-437 | 27165/1009 | | Khajurao | |
| ☐ | VT-ESP | Boeing 747-437 | 27214/1034 | | Ajanta | |
| ☐ | VT-EVA | Boeing 747-437 | 28094/1089 | | Agra | |
| ☐ | VT-EVB | Boeing 747-437 | 28095/1093 | | Velha Goa | |
| | | | | | | |
| ☐ | VT-ALA | Boeing 777-237LR | 36300/610 | ex N6018N | Andhra Pradesh | |
| ☐ | VT-ALB | Boeing 777-237LR | 36301/621 | ex N5028Y | Arunachal Pradesh | |
| ☐ | VT-ALC | Boeing 777-237LR | 36302/629 | ex N5020K | Assam | |
| ☐ | VT-ALD | Boeing 777-237LR | 36303/663 | ex N5016R | Gujarat | |
| ☐ | VT-ALE | Boeing 777-237LR | 36304/698 | | Haryana | |
| ☐ | VT-ALF | Boeing 777-237LR | 36305/793 | | Jhardkand | |
| ☐ | VT-ALG | Boeing 777-237LR | 36306/800 | | Kerala | |
| ☐ | VT-ALH | Boeing 777-237LR | 36307/805 | | Maharashtra | |
| | | | | | | |
| ☐ | VT-ALJ | Boeing 777-337ER | 36308/643 | | Bihar | |
| ☐ | VT-ALK | Boeing 777-337ER | 36309/652 | | Chattisgarh | |
| ☐ | VT-ALL | Boeing 777-337ER | 36310/656 | | Goa | |
| ☐ | VT-ALM | Boeing 777-337ER | 36311/713 | | Himachal Pradesh | |
| ☐ | VT-ALN | Boeing 777-337ER | 36312/719 | | Jammu and Kashmir | |
| ☐ | VT-ALO | Boeing 777-337ER | 36313/798 | | Karnataka | |
| ☐ | VT-ALP | Boeing 777-337ER | 36314/804 | | Madhya Pradesh | |
| ☐ | VT-ALQ | Boeing 777-337ER | 36315/809 | | Manipur | |
| ☐ | VT-ALR | Boeing 777-337ER | 36316/814 | | Meghalaya | |
| ☐ | VT-ALS | Boeing 777-337ER | 36317/864 | | Mizoram | |
| ☐ | VT-ALT | Boeing 777-337ER | 36318/871 | | Nagaland | |
| ☐ | VT-ALU | Boeing 777-337ER | 36319/880 | | Orissa | |
| ☐ | VT-ALV | Boeing 777-337ER | 36320 | | | o/o♦ |
| ☐ | VT-ALW | Boeing 777-337ER | 36321 | | | o/o♦ |
| ☐ | VT-ALX | Boeing 777-337ER | 36322 | | | o/o♦ |
| | | | | | | |
| ☐ | VT-ANA | Boeing 787-8 | 36273/25 | | | o/o |
| ☐ | VT-ANC | Boeing 787-8 | 36274/28 | | | o/o |
| ☐ | VT-AND | Boeing 787-8 | 36278/29 | | | o/o |
| ☐ | VT-ANE | Boeing 787-8 | 36280/30 | | | o/o |
| ☐ | VT-ANG | Boeing 787-8 | 36275/32 | | | o/o |
| ☐ | VT-ANH | Boeing 787-8 | 36276/35 | ex N1015B | | o/o |
| | | | | | | |
| ☐ | VT-EIO | Dornier 228-201 | 8037 | ex D-IDBG | | |
| ☐ | VT-EJH | Airbus A310-304F | 407 | ex F-WWCH | Teesta | wfs |
| ☐ | VT-EJK | Airbus A310-304 | 429 | ex F-WWCS | Gomati | wfs |
| ☐ | VT-EQT | Airbus A310-304F | 544 | ex F-WWCL | Narmada | wfs |
| ☐ | VT-IWA | Airbus A330-223 | 353 | ex F-WQVY | | |
| ☐ | VT-IWB | Airbus A330-223 | 362 | ex F-WQVZ | | |

## AIR INDIA EXPRESS  (AI/AXB)  Mumbai-Chhatrapatti Shivaji Intl (BOM)

| | | | | | |
|---|---|---|---|---|---|
| ☐ | VT-AXD | Boeing 737-8Q8/W | 30696/1892 | | |
| ☐ | VT-AXE | Boeing 737-8Q8/W | 29368/1910 | | |
| ☐ | VT-AXF | Boeing 737-8Q8/W | 29369/1939 | ex N1787B | |
| ☐ | VT-AXG | Boeing 737-8Q8/W | 30701/1946 | ex N1787B | |
| ☐ | VT-AXH | Boeing 737-8HG/W | 36323/2108 | | |
| ☐ | VT-AXI | Boeing 737-8HG/W | 36324/2132 | | |
| ☐ | VT-AXJ | Boeing 737-8HG/W | 36325/2142 | | |
| ☐ | VT-AXM | Boeing 737-8HG/W | 36326/2148 | | |
| ☐ | VT-AXN | Boeing 737-8HG/W | 36327/2154 | | |
| ☐ | VT-AXP | Boeing 737-8HG/W | 36328/2177 | | |
| ☐ | VT-AXQ | Boeing 737-8HG/W | 36329/2258 | | |
| ☐ | VT-AXR | Boeing 737-8HG/W | 36330/2317 | | |
| ☐ | VT-AXT | Boeing 737-8HG/W | 36331/2324 | | |
| ☐ | VT-AXU | Boeing 737-8HG/W | 36332/2381 | | |
| ☐ | VT-AXW | Boeing 737-8HG/W | 36334/2612 | | |
| ☐ | VT-AXX | Boeing 737-8HG/W | 36335/2672 | | |
| ☐ | VT-AXZ | Boeing 737-8HG/W | 36336/2782 | ex N1786B | |
| ☐ | VT-AYA | Boeing 737-8HG/W | 36337/2861 | ex N6065Y | |

| | | | | | |
|---|---|---|---|---|---|
| ☐ | VT-AYB | Boeing 737-8HG/W | 36338/2962 | | |
| ☐ | VT-AYC | Boeing 737-8HG/W | 36339/3039 | ex N1786B | |
| ☐ | VT-AYD | Boeing 737-8HG/W | 36320 | | o/o♦ |

## AIR INDIA REGIONAL

| | | | | |
|---|---|---|---|---|
| ☐ | VT-ABA | ATR 42-320 | 0390 | ex F-WQNK |
| ☐ | VT-ABB | ATR 42-320 | 0392 | ex F-WQNL |
| ☐ | VT-ABC | ATR 42-320 | 0315 | ex F-WQNB |
| ☐ | VT-ABD | ATR 42-320 | 0356 | ex F-WQNF |
| ☐ | VT-ABE | ATR 42-320 | 0333 | ex F-WQNF |
| ☐ | VT-ABF | ATR 42-320 | 0351 | ex F-WQNC |
| ☐ | VT-ABO | ATR 42-320 | 0406 | ex F-WQNE |

## ALLIANCE AIR      Allied (CD/LLR)      Delhi-Indira Gandhi Intl (DEL)

| | | | | | |
|---|---|---|---|---|---|
| ☐ | VT-EGF | Boeing 737-2A8F | 22282/681 | ex N8292V | [DEL] |
| ☐ | VT-EGG | Boeing 737-2A8F | 22283/689 | ex N8290V | [DEL] |
| ☐ | VT-EGH | Boeing 737-2A8 | 22284/739 | | [DEL] |
| ☐ | VT-EGI | Boeing 737-2A8F | 22285/798 | | [DEL] |
| ☐ | VT-EGJ | Boeing 737-2A8F | 22286/799 | | [DEL] |
| ☐ | VT-EHH | Boeing 737-2A8F | 22863/907 | | [DEL] |
| | | | | | |
| ☐ | VT-RJB | Canadair CRJ-700 | 10217 | ex D-ALTE | |
| ☐ | VT-RJC | Canadair CRJ-700 | 10052 | ex B-KBB | |
| ☐ | VT-RJD | Canadair CRJ-700 | 10048 | ex G-DUOD | |
| ☐ | VT-RJE | Canadair CRJ-700 | 10029 | ex N290RB | |

## BLUE DART AVIATION      Blue Dart (BZ/BDA)      Chennai (MAA)

| | | | | | |
|---|---|---|---|---|---|
| ☐ | VT-BDG | Boeing 737-2K9F | 22415/702 | ex VT-SIE | Vision III |
| ☐ | VT-BDH | Boeing 737-25C | 24236/1585 | ex B-2524 | Vision IV |
| ☐ | VT-BDI | Boeing 737-2T4F | 23272/1093 | ex B-2506 | Vision V |
| ☐ | VT-BDJ | Boeing 757-236 (SF) | 24102/179 | ex OO-DPI | |
| ☐ | VT-BDK | Boeing 757-236 (SF) | 24267/211 | ex OO-DPL | |
| ☐ | VT-BDM | Boeing 757-23N (SF) | 27598/692 | ex EI-LTA | |
| ☐ | VT-BDN | Boeing 757-25CF | 25898/475 | ex N7273 | |

## DECCAN CARGO      Mumbai-Chhatrapatti Shivaji Intl (BOM)

Ceased ops Jun11

## FUTURA TRAVELS

| | | | | |
|---|---|---|---|---|
| ☐ | VT-ASH | Beech 1900D | UE-361 | ex C-GSKQ |

## GOAIR      Goair (G8/GOW)      Mumbai-Chhatrapatti Shivaji Intl (BOM)

| | | | | | |
|---|---|---|---|---|---|
| ☐ | VT-GOI | Airbus A320-214 | 5016 | ex D-AXAF | ♦ |
| ☐ | VT-GOJ | Airbus A320-214 | 5112 | ex F-WWIK | o/o♦ |
| ☐ | VT-WAE | Airbus A320-214 | 3256 | ex F-WWDF | |
| ☐ | VT-WAF | Airbus A320-214 | 3306 | ex F-WWIM | |
| ☐ | VT-WAG | Airbus A320-214 | 3597 | ex D-AVVE | |
| ☐ | VT-WAH | Airbus A320-214 | 3616 | ex F-WWII | |
| ☐ | VT-WAI | Airbus A320-214 | 3798 | ex F-WWBP | |
| ☐ | VT-WAJ | Airbus A320-214 | 3827 | ex F-WWIX | |
| ☐ | VT-WAK | Airbus A320-214 | 3900 | ex F-WWDU | |
| ☐ | VT-WAL | Airbus A320-214 | 3915 | ex F-WWBC | |
| ☐ | VT-WAM | Airbus A320-214 | 4399 | ex F-WWBC | |
| ☐ | VT-WAN | Airbus A320-214 | 4438 | ex F-WWDF | |
| ☐ | VT-WAO | Airbus A320-214 | 3933 | ex EC-LAQ | <IWD |

## HELIGO CHARTERS      Mumbai

| | | | | | |
|---|---|---|---|---|---|
| ☐ | VT-HLB | Agusta AW139 | 31095 | ex A6-AWD | |
| ☐ | VT-HLC | Agusta AW139 | 31106 | ex A6-AWE | |
| ☐ | VT-HLD | Agusta AW139 | 31281 | | ♦ |
| ☐ | VT-HLE | Bell 412EP | 36443 | ex VT-HGK | ♦ |

## INDIGO AIRLINES      (6E/IGO)      Bangalore (BLR)

| | | | | | |
|---|---|---|---|---|---|
| ☐ | VT-IEA | Airbus A320-232 | 4603 | ex D-AXAR | ♦ |
| ☐ | VT-IEB | Airbus A320-232 | 4609 | ex D-AXAT | ♦ |
| ☐ | VT-IEC | Airbus A320-232 | 4614 | ex F-WWBF | ♦ |
| ☐ | VT-IED | Airbus A320-232 | 4630 | ex F-WWDJ | ♦ |
| ☐ | VT-IEE | Airbus A320-232 | 4637 | ex F-WWIB | ♦ |
| ☐ | VT-IEF | Airbus A320-232 | 4752 | ex F-WWBG | ♦ |
| ☐ | VT-IEG | Airbus A320-232 | 4762 | ex F-WWBQ | ♦ |

| | Reg | Type | | MSN | Ex reg | |
|---|---|---|---|---|---|---|
| ☐ | VT-IEH | Airbus A320-232 | | 4757 | ex F-WWBI | ◆ |
| ☐ | VT-IEI | Airbus A320-232 | | 4813 | ex D-AXAI | ◆ |
| ☐ | VT-IEJ | Airbus A320-232 | | 4818 | ex D-AXAK | ◆ |
| ☐ | VT-IEK | Airbus A320-232 | | 4868 | ex D-AUBQ | ◆ |
| ☐ | VT-IEL | Airbus A320-232 | | 4888 | ex D-AVVE | ◆ |
| ☐ | VT-IEM | Airbus A320-232 | | 4947 | ex D-AXAR | ◆ |
| ☐ | VT-IEN | Airbus A320-232 | | 4954 | ex D-AXAV | ◆ |
| ☐ | VT-IEO | Airbus A320-232 | | 4965 | ex F-WWBC | ◆ |
| ☐ | VT-IEP | Airbus A320-232 | | 5027 | ex D-AXAJ | ◆ |
| ☐ | VT-IEQ | Airbus A320-232 | | 5036 | ex D-AXAM | ◆ |
| ☐ | VT-IER | Airbus A320-232 | | 5076 | ex F-WWBY | ◆ |
| ☐ | VT-IES | Airbus A320-232 | | 5090 | ex F-WWDN | ◆ |
| ☐ | VT-IET | Airbus A320-232 | | 5094 | ex D-AUBM | ◆ |
| ☐ | VT-IEU | Airbus A320-232 | | 5092 | ex D-AUBL | ◆ |
| ☐ | VT-IEV | Airbus A320-232 | | 5080 | ex F-WWIF | ◆ |
| ☐ | VT-IGH | Airbus A320-232 | | 4008 | ex F-WWDZ | |
| ☐ | VT-IGI | Airbus A320-232 | | 4113 | ex F-WWDV | |
| ☐ | VT-IGJ | Airbus A320-232 | | 4156 | ex F-WWBM | |
| ☐ | VT-IGK | Airbus A320-232 | | 4216 | ex F-WWBE | |
| ☐ | VT-IGL | Airbus A320-232 | | 4312 | ex F-WWBD | |
| ☐ | VT-IGS | Airbus A320-232 | | 4328 | ex F-WWIB | |
| ☐ | VT-IGT | Airbus A320-232 | | 4384 | ex F-WWBN | |
| ☐ | VT-IGU | Airbus A320-232 | | 4488 | ex D-AUBH | |
| ☐ | VT-IGV | Airbus A320-232 | | 4481 | ex F-WWDL | |
| ☐ | VT-IGW | Airbus A320-232 | | 4506 | ex D-AUBN | |
| ☐ | VT-IGX | Airbus A320-232 | | 4518 | ex D-AXAH | |
| ☐ | VT-IGY | Airbus A320-232 | | 4535 | ex F-WWDX | |
| ☐ | VT-IGZ | Airbus A320-232 | | 4552 | ex D-AUBR | |
| ☐ | VT-INA | Airbus A320-232 | | 2844 | ex F-WWIH | |
| ☐ | VT-INB | Airbus A320-232 | | 2863 | ex F-WWIZ | |
| ☐ | VT-INC | Airbus A320-232 | | 2883 | ex F-WWBR | |
| ☐ | VT-IND | Airbus A320-232 | | 2911 | ex F-WWDG | |
| ☐ | VT-INE | Airbus A320-232 | | 2958 | ex F-WWBM | |
| ☐ | VT-INF | Airbus A320-232 | | 2990 | ex F-WWIO | |
| ☐ | VT-INI | Airbus A320-232 | | 3086 | ex F-WWBN | |
| ☐ | VT-INJ | Airbus A320-232 | | 3159 | ex F-WWDQ | |
| ☐ | VT-INK | Airbus A320-232 | | 3192 | ex F-WWIT | |
| ☐ | VT-INL | Airbus A320-232 | | 3227 | ex F-WWBC | |
| ☐ | VT-INO | Airbus A320-232 | | 3335 | ex F-WWBJ | |
| ☐ | VT-INP | Airbus A320-232 | | 3357 | ex F-WWIH | |
| ☐ | VT-INQ | Airbus A320-232 | | 3414 | ex F-WWIM | |
| ☐ | VT-INR | Airbus A320-232 | | 3453 | ex F-WWBF | |
| ☐ | VT-INS | Airbus A320-232 | | 3457 | ex F-WWBI | |
| ☐ | VT-INT | Airbus A320-232 | | 3497 | ex F-WWIM | |
| ☐ | VT-INU | Airbus A320-232 | | 3541 | ex F-WWIP | |
| ☐ | VT-INV | Airbus A320-232 | | 3618 | ex F-WWIJ | |
| ☐ | VT-INX | Airbus A320-232 | | 3782 | ex D-AVVK | |
| ☐ | VT-INY | Airbus A320-232 | | 3863 | ex F-WWDY | |
| ☐ | VT-INZ | Airbus A320-232 | | 3943 | ex F-WWDT | |
| ☐ | VT- | Airbus A320-232 | | | ex | o/o |
| ☐ | VT- | Airbus A320-232 | | | ex | o/o |
| ☐ | VT- | Airbus A320-232 | | | ex | o/o |

## JAGSON AIRLINES — Delhi-Indira Gandhi Intl (DEL)

| | Reg | Type | MSN | Ex reg |
|---|---|---|---|---|
| ☐ | VT-ESQ | Dornier 228-201 | 8006 | ex A5-RGB |
| ☐ | VT-ESS | Dornier 228-201 | 8017 | ex A5-RGC |
| ☐ | VT-EUM | Dornier 228-201 | 8096 | ex D-CAAL |
| ☐ | VT-JJA | Mil Mi-172 | 365C157 | |
| ☐ | VT-JJB | Mil Mi-172 | 365C158 | |

## JET AIRWAYS — Jet Airways (9W/JAI)  Mumbai-Chhatrapatti Shivaji Intl (BOM)

| | Reg | Type | MSN | Ex reg | |
|---|---|---|---|---|---|
| ☐ | VT-JWD | Airbus A330-243 | 751 | ex F-WWKB | |
| ☐ | VT-JWE | Airbus A330-243 | 807 | ex F-WWYU | |
| ☐ | VT-JWF | Airbus A330-202 | 825 | ex F-WWKE | |
| ☐ | VT-JWG | Airbus A330-202 | 831 | ex F-WWKL | |
| ☐ | VT-JWH | Airbus A330-202 | 882 | ex F-WWKJ | |
| ☐ | VT-JWJ | Airbus A330-202 | 885 | ex F-WWKS | |
| ☐ | VT-JWK | Airbus A330-202 | 888 | ex F-WWKL | |
| ☐ | VT-JWL | Airbus A330-202 | 901 | ex F-WWKQ | |
| ☐ | VT-JWM | Airbus A330-202 | 923 | ex F-WWYZ | |
| ☐ | VT-JWN | Airbus A330-202 | 932 | ex F-WWKV | |
| ☐ | VT-JWP | Airbus A330-202 | 947 | ex F-WWKM | |
| ☐ | VT-JWQ | Airbus A330-202 | 956 | ex F-WWYA | |
| ☐ | VT-JWR | Airbus A330-203 | 1056 | ex F-WW | o/o◆ |
| ☐ | VT-JCA | ATR 72-212A | 0572 | ex F-WQKD | |
| ☐ | VT-JCB | ATR 72-212A | 0575 | ex F-WQKE | |
| ☐ | VT-JCC | ATR 72-212A | 0593 | ex F-WQKP | |
| ☐ | VT-JCD | ATR 72-212A | 0636 | ex F-WQMC | |
| ☐ | VT-JCF | ATR 72-212A | 0674 | ex F-WQMK | |

| | | | | | | |
|---|---|---|---|---|---|---|
| ☐ | VT-JCG | ATR 72-212A | 0679 | ex F-WQML | | |
| ☐ | VT-JCH | ATR 72-212A | 0681 | ex F-WQMM | | |
| ☐ | VT-JCJ | ATR 72-212A | 0771 | ex F-WWEJ | | |
| ☐ | VT-JCK | ATR 72-212A | 0775 | ex F-WWEN | | |
| ☐ | VT-JCL | ATR 72-212A | 0791 | ex F-WWEK | | |
| ☐ | VT-JCM | ATR 72-212A | 0793 | ex F-WWEN | | |
| ☐ | VT-JCN | ATR 72-212A | 0825 | ex F-WWEN | | |
| ☐ | VT-JCP | ATR 72-212A | 0841 | ex F-WWES | | |
| ☐ | VT-JCQ | ATR 72-212A | 0843 | ex F-WWEJ | | |
| ☐ | VT-JCR | ATR 72-212A | 0919 | ex F-WWER | | |
| ☐ | VT-JCS | ATR 72-212A | 0920 | ex F-WWES | | |
| ☐ | VT-JCT | ATR 72-212A | 0924 | ex F-WWEX | | |
| ☐ | VT-JCU | ATR 72-212A | 0928 | ex F-WWED | | |
| ☐ | VT-JCV | ATR 72-212A | 0932 | ex F-WWEH | | |
| ☐ | VT-JCW | ATR 72-212A | 0933 | ex F-WWEi | | |
| | | | | | | |
| ☐ | VT-JGB | Boeing 737-75R/W | 30411/1282 | ex N1787B | | |
| ☐ | VT-JGL | Boeing 737-76N/W | 32738/1392 | ex EI-DMD | | |
| ☐ | VT-JGX | Boeing 737-75N/W | 34805/2360 | ex N1781B | | |
| ☐ | VT-JGY | Boeing 737-75R/W | 34806/2404 | | | |
| ☐ | VT-JGZ | Boeing 737-76N/W | 35218/2342 | ex N1781B | | |
| ☐ | VT-JNG | Boeing 737-71Q | 29045/169 | ex N29975 | | |
| ☐ | VT-JNH | Boeing 737-71Q | 29046/181 | ex N29976 | | |
| ☐ | VT-JNS | Boeing 737-73A | 28498/775 | ex N498AW | | |
| ☐ | VT-JNU | Boeing 737-75R | 30404/835 | ex N1787B | | |
| ☐ | VT-JNV | Boeing 737-75R | 30405/927 | | | |
| ☐ | VT-JNW | Boeing 737-75R | 30406/1016 | ex N1787B | | |
| ☐ | VT- | Boeing 737-75R | | | | o/o |
| ☐ | VT- | Boeing 737-75R | | | | o/o |
| | | | | | | |
| ☐ | VT-JBB | Boeing 737-8HX/W | 36846/2368 | ex N846AG | | |
| ☐ | VT-JBC | Boeing 737-8HX/W | 36847/2388 | ex N847AG | | |
| ☐ | VT-JBD | Boeing 737-85R/W | 35099/2439 | | | |
| ☐ | VT-JBE | Boeing 737-85R/W | 35106/2530 | ex N1786B | | |
| ☐ | VT-JBF | Boeing 737-85R/W | 35082/2550 | ex N1786B | | |
| ☐ | VT-JBG | Boeing 737-85R/W | 35083/2535 | ex N1786B | | |
| ☐ | VT-JBH | Boeing 737-85R/W | 35289/2811 | ex N1786B | | |
| ☐ | VT-JBJ | Boeing 737-85R/W | 36551/2974 | ex N1786B | | |
| ☐ | VT-JBK | Boeing 737-85R/W | 36553/3074 | ex N1786B | | |
| ☐ | VT-JBL | Boeing 737-85R/W | 35651/3000 | | | |
| ☐ | VT-JBM | Boeing 737-86N/W | 36817/3055 | ex N1786B | | |
| ☐ | VT-JBN | Boeing 737-86N/W | 36818/3087 | ex N1786B | | |
| ☐ | VT-JBP | Boeing 737-86N/W | 36819/3101 | | | |
| ☐ | VT-JBQ | Boeing 737-85R/W | 36694/3264 | ex N1787B | | |
| ☐ | VT-JBR | Boeing 737-85R/W | 36695/3281 | | | |
| ☐ | VT-JBS | Boeing 737-85R/W | 36698/3433 | | | |
| ☐ | VT-JBT | Boeing 737-8BK | 33024/1688 | ex VT-AXC | | ♦ |
| ☐ | VT-JBU | Boeing 737-86N/W | 36825/3765 | | | ♦ |
| ☐ | VT-JBV | Boeing 737-86N/W | 36827/3836 | | | ♦ |
| ☐ | VT-JBW | Boeing 737-8AL/W | 37960/3809 | | | ♦ |
| ☐ | VT-JBX | Boeing 737-8AL/W | 37961/3847 | | | ♦ |
| ☐ | VT-JGA | Boeing 737-85R | 30410/1228 | | | |
| ☐ | VT-JGE | Boeing 737-83N/W | 32663/1608 | ex EI-DIL | | |
| ☐ | VT-JGF | Boeing 737-8FH/W | 29639/1643 | ex EI-DIM | | |
| ☐ | VT-JGG | Boeing 737-8FH/W | 29668/1686 | ex EI-DIN | | |
| ☐ | VT-JGH | Boeing 737-83N/W | 32577/973 | ex EI-DKX | | |
| ☐ | VT-JGJ | Boeing 737-83N/W | 32578/998 | ex EI-DKP | | |
| ☐ | VT-JGK | Boeing 737-83N/W | 32579/1002 | ex EI-DKR | | |
| ☐ | VT-JGM | Boeing 737-83N/W | 32614/1201 | ex EI-DME | | |
| ☐ | VT-JGN | Boeing 737-83N/W | 32616/1212 | ex EI-DMF | | |
| ☐ | VT-JGP | Boeing 737-85R/W | 34798/1920 | | | |
| ☐ | VT-JGQ | Boeing 737-85R/W | 34797/2007 | | | |
| ☐ | VT-JGR | Boeing 737-85R/W | 34799/2044 | | | |
| ☐ | VT-JGS | Boeing 737-85R/W | 34800/2085 | | | |
| ☐ | VT-JGT | Boeing 737-85R/W | 34801/2125 | | | |
| ☐ | VT-JGU | Boeing 737-85R/W | 34802/2170 | | | |
| ☐ | VT-JGV | Boeing 737-85R/W | 34803/2209 | | | |
| ☐ | VT-JGW | Boeing 737-85R/W | 34804/2297 | | | |
| ☐ | VT-JNJ | Boeing 737-85R | 29038/297 | | | |
| ☐ | VT-JNL | Boeing 737-85R | 29039/326 | | | |
| ☐ | VT-JNM | Boeing 737-85R | 29040/465 | | | |
| ☐ | VT-JNN | Boeing 737-85R | 29041/489 | | | |
| ☐ | VT-JNR | Boeing 737-85R | 30403/749 | ex N1781B | | |
| ☐ | VT-JNX | Boeing 737-85R | 30407/1073 | | | |
| ☐ | VT-JNY | Boeing 737-85R | 30408/1146 | ex (VT-JGA) | | |
| ☐ | VT-JNZ | Boeing 737-85R | 30409/1185 | ex (VT-JGB) | | |
| ☐ | VT- | Boeing 737-8AL | | | | o/o |
| ☐ | VT- | Boeing 737-8AL | | | | o/o |
| | | | | | | |
| ☐ | VT-JED | Boeing 777-35RER | 35160/653 | ex N5016R | | >THA |
| ☐ | VT-JEG | Boeing 777-35RER | 35163/675 | ex N1785B | | |
| ☐ | VT-JEH | Boeing 777-35RER | 35166/678 | ex N5014K | | |
| ☐ | VT-JEK | Boeing 777-35RER | 35165/696 | | | |

| | | | | | |
|---|---|---|---|---|---|
| ☐ | VT-JEL | Boeing 777-35RER | 35164/660 | ex TC-JJC | ♦ |
| ☐ | VT-JEM | Boeing 777-35RER | 35162/666 | ex TC-JJB | ♦ |
| | | | | | |
| ☐ | VT-JBY | Boeing 737-96NER/W | 35227/2621 | ex M-ABEP | ♦ |
| ☐ | VT-JBZ | Boeing 737-96NER/W | 36539/2596 | ex N347MS | o/o♦ |
| ☐ | VT-JGC | Boeing 737-95R | 30412/1314 | | |
| ☐ | VT-JGD | Boeing 737-95R | 33740/1350 | | |

### JETLITE — Sahara (S2/JLL) — Delhi-Indira Gandhi Intl (DEL)

| | | | | | |
|---|---|---|---|---|---|
| ☐ | VT-JLA | Boeing 737-7Q8 | 30037/1449 | ex EI-DZC | |
| ☐ | VT-JLB | Boeing 737-7Q8 | 28250/1142 | ex A4O-BT | |
| ☐ | VT-JLC | Boeing 737-71Q | 29043/138 | ex VT-JNE | |
| ☐ | VT-JLD | Boeing 737-71Q | 29044/152 | ex VT-JNF | |
| ☐ | VT-JLG | Boeing 737-73V | 32426/1474 | ex G-EZKE | ♦ |
| ☐ | VT-SIU | Boeing 737-7K9 | 28090/205 | ex SX-BLT | ♦ |
| ☐ | VT-SIV | Boeing 737-7K9 | 28091/223 | ex SX-BLU | [DEL] |
| ☐ | VT-SIZ | Boeing 737-7BK | 33025/1707 | ex N325CT | |
| ☐ | VT-SJA | Boeing 737-7BK | 33026/1715 | ex N326CT | |
| | | | | | |
| ☐ | VT-JLE | Boeing 737-8AS/W | 33555/1426 | ex EI-DAV | ♦ |
| ☐ | VT-JLF | Boeing 737-8AS/W | 33556/1428 | ex EI-DAW | ♦ |
| ☐ | VT-SIJ | Boeing 737-81Q | 29049/424 | ex N8253J | |
| ☐ | VT-SJF | Boeing 737-86N | 28610/449 | ex EI-DIS | |
| ☐ | VT-SJG | Boeing 737-8Q8/W | 30694/1863 | ex N164LF | |
| ☐ | VT-SJH | Boeing 737-8Q8/W | 30695/1891 | ex (N201LF) | |
| ☐ | VT-SJI | Boeing 737-8K9/W | 34399/2030 | | |
| ☐ | VT-SJJ | Boeing 737-8K9/W | 34400/2053 | | |
| | | | | | |
| ☐ | VT-JBY | Boeing 737-96NER/W | 35227/2621 | ex M-ABEP | ♦ |
| ☐ | VT-JLH | Boeing 737-96NER/W | 35223/2559 | ex M-ABEN | ♦ |
| ☐ | VT-JLJ | Boeing 737-96NER/W | 35255/2590 | ex M-ABEO | ♦ |

### KINGFISHER AIRLINES — (IT/KFR) — Mumbai-Chhatrapatti Shivaji Intl/Bangalore (BOM/BLR)

| | | | | | |
|---|---|---|---|---|---|
| ☐ | VT-VJK | Airbus A330-223 | 874 | ex F-WWKA | |
| ☐ | VT-VJO | Airbus A330-223 | 939 | ex F-WWKK | |
| ☐ | VT-VJP | Airbus A330-223 | 946 | ex F-WWYX | |

### KINGFISHER RED — (IT/KFR) — Mumbai-Chhatrapatti Shivaji Intl/Bangalore (BOM/BLR)

| | | | | | |
|---|---|---|---|---|---|
| ☐ | VT-ADR | Airbus A320-232 | 2922 | ex F-WWDS | wfs |
| ☐ | VT-ADU | Airbus A320-232 | 2874 | ex F-WWBH | [DEL] |
| ☐ | VT-ADV | Airbus A320-232 | 2366 | ex F-WWDN | |
| ☐ | VT-ADW | Airbus A320-232 | 2376 | ex F-WWBF | |
| ☐ | VT-DKR | Airbus A320-232 | 2731 | ex F-WWBC | [HYD] |
| ☐ | VT-DKV | Airbus A320-232 | 2645 | ex F-WWIC | |
| ☐ | VT-DNZ | Airbus A320-232 | 3012 | ex F-WWBK | |
| ☐ | VT-KFB | Airbus A320-232 | 2443 | ex F-WWBR | |
| ☐ | VT-KFF | Airbus A320-232 | 2531 | ex F-WWIH | [BOM] |
| ☐ | VT-KFG | Airbus A320-232 | 2576 | ex F-WWBI | wfs |
| ☐ | VT-KFK | Airbus A320-232 | 2670 | ex F-WWDA | [IST] |
| ☐ | VT-KFL | Airbus A320-232 | 2817 | ex F-WWDJ | |
| ☐ | VT-KFM | Airbus A320-232 | 2856 | ex F-WWIT | [IST] |
| ☐ | VT-KFT | Airbus A320-232 | 3089 | ex F-WWBY | |
| ☐ | VT-KFV | Airbus A320-232 | 3105 | ex F-WWII | |
| ☐ | VT-KFX | Airbus A320-232 | 3270 | ex F-WWBX | |
| | | | | | |
| ☐ | VT-KFN | Airbus A321-232 | 2916 | ex D-AVZQ | [BOM] |
| ☐ | VT-KFP | Airbus A321-232 | 2919 | ex D-AVZR | |
| ☐ | VT-KFR | Airbus A321-232 | 2933 | ex D-AVZS | |
| ☐ | VT-KFW | Airbus A321-232 | 3120 | ex D-AVZR | [BLR] |
| ☐ | VT-KFY | Airbus A321-232 | 3302 | ex D-AVZS | |
| ☐ | VT-KFZ | Airbus A321-232 | 3322 | ex D-AVZU | |
| | | | | | |
| ☐ | VT-DKA | ATR 72-212A | 0718 | ex F-WWES | |
| ☐ | VT-DKB | ATR 72-212A | 0720 | ex F-WWEA | |
| ☐ | VT-DKH | ATR 72-212A | 0739 | ex F-WWET | |
| ☐ | VT-DKI | ATR 72-212A | 0732 | ex F-WWEM | |
| ☐ | VT-DKJ | ATR 72-212A | 0733 | ex F-WWEN | |
| ☐ | VT-DKK | ATR 72-212A | 0740 | ex F-WWEU | |
| ☐ | VT-KAA | ATR 72-212A | 0699 | ex F-WWEV | |
| ☐ | VT-KAB | ATR 72-212A | 0728 | ex F-WWEI | |
| ☐ | VT-KAD | ATR 72-212A | 0730 | ex F-WWEK | |
| ☐ | VT-KAE | ATR 72-212A | 0737 | ex F-WWER | |
| ☐ | VT-KAF | ATR 72-212A | 0738 | ex F-WWES | |
| ☐ | VT-KAG | ATR 72-212A | 0743 | ex F-WWED | |
| ☐ | VT-KAH | ATR 72-212A | 0746 | ex F-WWEG | |
| ☐ | VT-KAI | ATR 72-212A | 0750 | ex F-WWEK | |

| | | | | | | |
|---|---|---|---|---|---|---|
| ☐ | VT-KAJ | ATR 72-212A | 0754 | ex F-WWEO | | |
| ☐ | VT-KAK | ATR 72-212A | 0758 | ex F-WWES | | |
| ☐ | VT-KAL | ATR 72-212A | 0759 | ex F-WWEV | | |
| ☐ | VT-KAM | ATR 72-212A | 0762 | ex F-WWEZ | | |
| ☐ | VT-KAN | ATR 72-212A | 0767 | ex F-WWEF | | |
| ☐ | VT-KAO | ATR 72-212A | 0772 | ex F-WWEK | | |
| ☐ | VT-KAP | ATR 72-212A | 0776 | ex F-WWEO | | |
| ☐ | VT-KAQ | ATR 72-212A | 0777 | ex F-WWEP | | |
| ☐ | VT-KAR | ATR 72-212A | 0782 | ex F-WWEX | | |
| | | | | | | |
| ☐ | VT-ADJ | ATR 42-500 | 0612 | ex N612VX | | |
| ☐ | VT-ADK | ATR 42-500 | 0613 | ex N316VX | | |
| ☐ | VT-KFH | Airbus A319-131 | 2621 | ex D-AVYM | | [DEL] |
| ☐ | VT-KFI | Airbus A319-131 | 2634 | ex D-AVWG | | [IST] |
| ☐ | VT-KFJ | Airbus A319-131 | 2664 | ex D-AVWW | | |
| ☐ | VT-VJM | Airbus A319-133X | 2650 | ex D-AICY | Sidhartha-Leana-Tanya | VIP |

## MDLR AIRLINES (MDD) Mumbai-Chhatrapatti Shivaji Intl (BOM)

| | | | | | |
|---|---|---|---|---|---|
| ☐ | VT-MDM | Avro 146-RJ70 | E1230 | ex G-CDNB | [DEL] |
| ☐ | VT-MDN | Avro 146-RJ70 | E1252 | ex G-CDNC | [BCM] |

## ORIENT FLIGHTS Chennai (MAA)

| | | | | | |
|---|---|---|---|---|---|
| ☐ | VT-EJO | Dornier 228-201 | 8054 | ex D-CALI | ♦ |

## PINNACLE AIR Bangalore (BLR)

| | | | | |
|---|---|---|---|---|
| ☐ | VT-VTP | Cessna 208 Caravan I | 2308 | ♦ |

## QUIKJET CARGO Bangalore (BLR)

| | | | | | |
|---|---|---|---|---|---|
| ☐ | VT-FQA | ATR 72-202F | 0313 | ex HB-AFH | <FAT♦ |
| ☐ | VT- | ATR 72-201F | 0341 | ex HB-AFV | <FAT o/o |
| ☐ | VT- | ATR 72-201F | 0419 | ex HB-AFW | <FAT o/o |

## SPICEJET SpiceJet (SG/SEJ) Delhi-Indira Ghandi International (DEL)

| | | | | | | |
|---|---|---|---|---|---|---|
| ☐ | VT-SGE | Boeing 737-8K2/W | 32693/1951 | ex PH-HZR | Tamarind | |
| ☐ | VT-SGF | Boeing 737-8GJ/W | 36367/3218 | ex N1786B | | |
| ☐ | VT-SGG | Boeing 737-8GJ/W | 36368/3310 | | | |
| ☐ | VT-SGH | Boeing 737-8GJ/W | 36369/3363 | | | |
| ☐ | VT-SGI | Boeing 737-8GJ/W | 37361/3506 | ex N1786B | | |
| ☐ | VT-SGJ | Boeing 737-86J/W | 29641/1654 | ex G-CGPP | | |
| ☐ | VT-SGK | Boeing 737-8BK/W | 33019/1502 | ex YR-BIC | | |
| ☐ | VT-SGL | Boeing 737-8AS/W | 29925/588 | ex YR-BIA | | |
| ☐ | VT-SGO | Boeing 737-8AS/W | 29926/722 | ex YR-BIB | | |
| ☐ | VT-SGQ | Boeing 737-8GJ/W | 37365/3539 | | | |
| ☐ | VT-SGS | Boeing 737-8Q8/W | 33699/1309 | ex N371LF | | ♦ |
| ☐ | VT-SGU | Boeing 737-8GJ/W | 37366/3628 | | Juniper | ♦ |
| ☐ | VT-SGV | Boeing 737-8GJ/W | 37362/3830 | ex N1782B | Nigella | ♦ |
| ☐ | VT-SGW | Boeing 737-8GJ/W | 37363/3843 | | Paprika | ♦ |
| ☐ | VT-SGX | Boeing 737-86J/W | 37751/3932 | | | ♦ |
| ☐ | VT-SGY | Boeing 737-8GJ/W | 37765/3986 | | Cayenne | ♦ |
| ☐ | VT-SGZ | Boeing 737-8GJ/W | 39423/ | | | o/o♦ |
| ☐ | VT-SPE | Boeing 737-86N | 28621/570 | ex EI-DIT | Ginger | |
| ☐ | VT-SPF | Boeing 737-8GJ/W | 34896/1861 | | Coriander | |
| ☐ | VT-SPJ | Boeing 737-8GJ/W | 34897/2069 | | Mint | |
| ☐ | VT-SPK | Boeing 737-8GJ/W | 34898/2104 | | Fennel | |
| ☐ | VT-SPL | Boeing 737-8GJ/W | 34899/2128 | | Cardamom | |
| ☐ | VT-SPM | Boeing 737-8GJ/W | 34900/2167 | | Pepper | |
| ☐ | VT-SPO | Boeing 737-86N/W | 35216/2321 | | Dill | |
| ☐ | VT-SPP | Boeing 737-86N/W | 35217/2359 | | Rosemary | |
| ☐ | VT-SPQ | Boeing 737-8GJ/W | 34903/2335 | | Basil | |
| ☐ | VT-SPR | Boeing 737-8GJ/W | 34904/2347 | ex N1782B | Thyme | |
| ☐ | VT-SPS | Boeing 737-8GJ/W | 34905/2392 | | Mustard | |
| ☐ | VT-SPW | Boeing 737-86N/W | 32672/1932 | ex PH-HSY | Cinnamon | |
| | | | | | | |
| ☐ | VT-SGB | Boeing 737-9GJER/W | 34956/2608 | | Oregano | |
| ☐ | VT-SGC | Boeing 737-9GJER/W | 34957/2639 | | Fenugreek | |
| ☐ | VT-SGD | Boeing 737-9GJER/W | 34961/2744 | ex N1786B | Sesame | |
| ☐ | VT-SGW | Boeing 737-9GJER/W | 37363/3843 | | | ♦ |
| ☐ | VT-SPT | Boeing 737-9GJER/W | 34952/2426 | | Clove | |
| ☐ | VT-SPU | Boeing 737-9GJER/W | 34953/2466 | | Anise | |
| | | | | | | |
| ☐ | VT-SUA | de Havilland DHC-8-402Q | 4373 | | Saunf | ♦ |
| ☐ | VT-SUB | de Havilland DHC-8-402Q | 4374 | | Heeng | ♦ |
| ☐ | VT-SUC | de Havilland DHC-8-402Q | 4377 | ex C-GKLF | Tulsi | ♦ |
| ☐ | VT-SUD | de Havilland DHC-8-402Q | 4378 | ex C-GKLZ | Tejpatta | ♦ |
| ☐ | VT-SUE | de Havilland DHC-8-402Q | 4379 | | Elaichi | ♦ |

| | | | | | | | |
|---|---|---|---|---|---|---|---|
| ☐ | VT-SUF | de Havilland DHC-8-402Q | 4382 | ex C-GKOI | Kesar | | ♦ |
| ☐ | VT-SUG | de Havilland DHC-8-402Q | 4387 | ex C-GKVM | | | ♦ |
| ☐ | VT-SUH | de Havilland DHC-8-402Q | 4389 | ex C-GKVP | | | o/o♦ |
| ☐ | VT-SUI | de Havilland DHC-8-402Q | 4395 | ex C-GLEP | Haldi | | o/o♦ |
| ☐ | VT-SUJ | de Havilland DHC-8-402Q | 4397 | ex C-GLFS | Daichini | | o/o♦ |
| ☐ | VT-SUK | de Havilland DHC-8-402Q | 4398 | ex C-GLKU | Sarson | | o/o♦ |
| ☐ | VT-SUL | de Havilland DHC-8-402Q | 4400 | ex C-GLUM | Javitri | | o/o♦ |
| ☐ | VT-SUM | de Havilland DHC-8-402Q | 4402 | ex C-GLKV | Jaiphal | | o/o♦ |
| ☐ | VT-SUO | de Havilland DHC-8-402Q | 4404 | ex C-GMOU | Laung | | o/o♦ |

## SPIRIT AIR
Bangalore (BLR)

| | | | | | |
|---|---|---|---|---|---|
| ☐ | VT-VAT | Cessna 208B Caravan I | 208B2069 | ex D-FXAA | ♦ |

## VENTURA AIRCONNECT

| | | | | | |
|---|---|---|---|---|---|
| ☐ | VT-VAK | Cessna 208B Caravan I | 208B2281 | ex N90015 | ♦ |
| ☐ | VT-VAM | Cessna 208B Caravan I | 208B2269 | ex N9000F | ♦ |

## V2-   ANTIGUA (State of Antigua and Barbuda)

### LIAT - THE CARIBBEAN AIRLINE
LIAT (LI/LIA)
Antigua-VC Bird Intl (ANU)

| | | | | | | |
|---|---|---|---|---|---|---|
| ☐ | V2-LDQ | de Havilland DHC-8-102 | 113 | ex EI-BWX | | |
| ☐ | V2-LDU | de Havilland DHC-8-103 | 270 | ex EI-CBV | | |
| ☐ | V2-LEF | de Havilland DHC-8-103 | 144 | ex HS-SKH | | |
| ☐ | V2-LES | de Havilland DHC-8-311B | 412 | ex C-GETI | | |
| ☐ | V2-LET | de Havilland DHC-8-311B | 416 | ex C-GFOD | | |
| ☐ | V2-LEU | de Havilland DHC-8-311 | 408 | ex C-FWBB | Sir Frank de Lisle | |
| ☐ | V2-LFF | de Havilland DHC-8-314 | 410 | ex N285BC | | |
| ☐ | V2-LFM | de Havilland DHC-8-311A | 267 | ex C-GFPZ | | |
| ☐ | V2-LFU | de Havilland DHC-8-311 | 250 | ex N802SA | | |
| ☐ | V2-LFV | de Havilland DHC-8-311A | 283 | ex PH-SDR | | |
| ☐ | V2-LGB | de Havilland DHC-8-311A | 266 | ex C-GZTB | | |
| ☐ | V2-LGC | de Havilland DHC-8-311 | 298 | ex PH-SDM | | |
| ☐ | V2-LGD | de Havilland DHC-8-311 | 300 | ex PH-SDP | | |
| ☐ | V2-LGG | de Havilland DHC-8-311A | 404 | ex C-FHFY | | ♦ |
| ☐ | V2-LGH | de Havilland DHC-8-311 | 242 | ex PJ-DHE | | |
| ☐ | V2-LGI | de Havilland DHC-8-311A | 325 | ex C-FHXB | | |
| ☐ | V2-LGN | de Havilland DHC-8-311 | 230 | ex PJ-DHL | | |

## V3-   BELIZE

### MAYA ISLAND AIR
Myland (MW/MYD)
Belize City-Municipal/San Pedro (TZA/SPR)

| | | | | | |
|---|---|---|---|---|---|
| ☐ | V3-HGD | Cessna 208B Caravan I | 208B0910 | ex N12522 | |
| ☐ | V3-HGF | Cessna 208B Caravan I | 208B0927 | ex N52627 | |
| ☐ | V3-HGJ | Cessna 208B Caravan I | 208B0946 | ex N52639 | |
| ☐ | V3-HGO | Cessna 208B Caravan I | 208B0995 | ex N1241G | |
| ☐ | V3-HGP | Cessna 208B Caravan I | 208B0998 | exN12419 | |
| ☐ | V3-HGQ | Cessna 208B Caravan I | 208B0973 | ex N1248G | |
| ☐ | V3-HGW | Cessna 208B Caravan I | 208B1095 | ex N1273Z | |
| ☐ | V3-HHA | Cessna 208B Caravan I | 208B1292 | ex N4117D | |
| | | | | | |
| ☐ | V3-HGE | Britten-Norman BN-2A-26 Islander | 911 | ex N103NE | |
| ☐ | V3-HGI | Gippsland GA-8 Airvan | GA8-01-008 | ex VH-AUV | |
| ☐ | V3-HGK | Britten-Norman BN-2A-26 Islander | 853 | ex N271RS | |

### TROPIC AIR COMMUTER
Tropiser (PM/TOS)
San Pedro (SPR)

| | | | | | |
|---|---|---|---|---|---|
| ☐ | V3-HFV | Cessna 208B Caravan I | 208B0647 | ex N5268M | |
| ☐ | V3-HGV | Cessna 208B Caravan I | 208B1072 | ex N5185V | |
| ☐ | V3-HGX | Cessna 208B Caravan I | 208B1162 | ex N5108G | |
| ☐ | V3-HHC | Cessna 208B Caravan I | 208B2004 | | ♦ |
| ☐ | V3-HHE | Cessna 208B Caravan I | 208B2062 | ex N5270K | ♦ |
| ☐ | V3-HHG | Cessna 208B Caravan I | 208B2051 | | ♦ |
| ☐ | V3-HHI | Cessna 208B Caravan I | 208B2149 | ex N52234 | ♦ |
| ☐ | V3-HHK | Cessna 208B Caravan I | 208B2249 | ex N52038 | ♦ |
| ☐ | V3-HHL | Cessna 208B Caravan I | 208B | | ♦ |
| ☐ | V3-HHM | Cessna 208B Caravan I | 208B | | ♦ |
| ☐ | V3-HIK | Cessna 208B Caravan I | 208B0707 | ex N23681 | |
| | | | | | |
| ☐ | V3-HDT | Cessna 207A Stationair 8 | 20700716 | ex (N9696M) | |

## V4- ST KITTS & NEVIS (Federation of St Christopher and Nevis)

### AIR ST KITTS & NEVIS | Sea Breeze (BEZ) | Basseterre-Golden Rock (SKB)

| | | | | | |
|---|---|---|---|---|---|
| ☐ | N785PA | Cessna 208B Caravan I | 208B0994 | ex C6-NFS | |
| ☐ | N920HL | Cessna 208B Caravan I | 208B2232 | | ♦ |
| ☐ | N930HL | Cessna 208B Caravan I | 208B2238 | | ♦ |

## V5- NAMIBIA (Republic of Namibia)

### AIR NAMIBIA | Namibia (SW/NMB) Windhoek-Eros/Hosea Kutako Intl (ERS)

| | | | | | |
|---|---|---|---|---|---|
| ☐ | V5-ANF | Embraer ERJ-135ER | 145243 | ex F-GOHC | <RAE♦ |
| ☐ | V5-ANG | Embraer ERJ-135ER | 145335 | ex F-GOHE | <RAE♦ |
| ☐ | V5-ANH | Embraer ERJ-135ER | 145347 | ex F-GOHF | <RAE♦ |
| ☐ | V5-ANK | Airbus A319-112 | 3586 | ex D-ABGL | ♦ |
| ☐ | V5-ANL | Airbus A319-112 | 3346 | ex D-ABGI | ♦ |
| ☐ | V5-NDI | Boeing 737-528 | 25228/2170 | ex F-GJNC | |
| ☐ | V5-NME | Airbus A340-311 | 051 | ex D-AIMG | |
| ☐ | V5-NMF | Airbus A340-311 | 047 | ex D-AIMF | |
| ☐ | V5-OKN | Beech 1900D | UE-23 | ex ZS-OKN | ♦ |
| ☐ | V5-OUB | Beech 1900C | UB-20 | ex V5-MMN | ♦ |
| ☐ | V5-OWN | Beech 1900D | UE-4 | ex ZS-OWN | ♦ |
| ☐ | V5-PEF | Beech 1900D | UE-9 | ex ZS-PEF | ♦ |
| ☐ | V5-TNP | Boeing 737-528 | 25229/2180 | ex F-GJND | |

### BAY AIR AVIATION | Nomad Air (NMD) | Walvis Bay (WVB)

| | | | | | |
|---|---|---|---|---|---|
| ☐ | V5-FUR | Cessna 310Q | 310Q0456 | ex ZS-FUR | |

### CARAVAN AIR

| | | | | | |
|---|---|---|---|---|---|
| ☐ | V5-GPX | Cessna 208 Caravan I | 20800177 | ex ZS-MVY | ♦ |

### COMAV AVIATION | Compion (COX) | Windhoek-Eros (ERS)

| | | | | | |
|---|---|---|---|---|---|
| ☐ | V5-NPR | Cessna 310Q | 310Q0985 | ex ZS-NPR | |
| ☐ | V5-SOS | Cessna 402C | 402C0437 | ex V5-AAS | EMS International SOS titles |

### DESERT AIR | | Windhoek-Eros (ERS)

| | | | | | |
|---|---|---|---|---|---|
| ☐ | V5-MAC | Rockwell 690B Turbo Commander | 11557 | ex N75WA | |
| ☐ | V5-MAX | Cessna 208B Caravan I | 208B0706 | ex N910HE | ♦ |
| ☐ | V5-MKR | Cessna T210N Turbo Centurion II | 21063060 | ex ZS-LAS | |
| ☐ | V5-MKS | Cessna T310R II | 310R0583 | ex N410AS | |
| ☐ | V5-SKY | Cessna T210L Turbo Centurion II | 21059953 | ex ZS-SKY | Sossus Air Taxi titles |
| ☐ | V5-TEM | Beech Baron 58 | TH-812 | ex V5-LZG | |

### NAMIBIA COMMERCIAL AIRWAYS | Med Rescue (MRE) | Windhoek-Eros (ERS)

| | | | | | |
|---|---|---|---|---|---|
| ☐ | ZS-NAT | Britten-Norman BN-2T Turbine Islander | 2158 | ex 7Q-CAV | |
| ☐ | V5-NCG | Douglas DC-6B | 45564/1040 | ex GBM112 | Batuleur |

### SEFOFANE AIR | | Windhoek-Eros (ERS)

| | | | | | |
|---|---|---|---|---|---|
| ☐ | V5-BAT | Cessna T210N Turbo Centurion II | 21064543 | ex ZS-MUG | |
| ☐ | V5-BUZ | Cessna T210N Turbo Centurion II | 21063539 | ex ZS-OXI | |
| ☐ | V5-ELE | Cessna 208B Caravan I | 208B0818 | ex N1289Y | |
| ☐ | V5-KUD | Cessna 210N Centurion II | 21063834 | ex ZS-KUD | |
| ☐ | V5-MTB | Cessna T210N Turbo Centurion II | 21062933 | ex ZS-MTB | |
| ☐ | V5-RNO | Cessna 208B Caravan I | 208B1304 | ex N41138 | |
| ☐ | ZS-SUN | Cessna 208B Caravan I | 208B0307 | ex V5-SUN | ♦ |

### WESTAIR WINGS | Westair Wings (WAA) | Windhoek-Eros (ERS)

| | | | | | |
|---|---|---|---|---|---|
| ☐ | V5-AAG | Cessna 210M Centurion II | 21062077 | ex N9646M | tail magnetometer |
| ☐ | V5-DHL | Reims Cessna F406 Caravan II | F406-0062 | ex N744C | DHL titles |
| ☐ | V5-LWH | Cessna 310R | 310R0571 | ex ZS-LWH | |
| ☐ | V5-LXZ | Cessna 210M Centurion II | 21063931 | ex ZS-LXZ | |
| ☐ | V5-MDY | Cessna 402B | 402B1353 | ex D2-FFW | |
| ☐ | V5-SAC | Cessna 340A | 340A0945 | ex ZS-KUH | |
| ☐ | V5-WAA | Cessna 404 Titan II (RAM) | 404-0210 | ex N88668 | Ghost Rider |
| ☐ | V5-WAB | Cessna 310Q | 310Q0727 | ex N4541Q | |
| ☐ | V5-WAC | Cessna 404 Titan II | 404-0616 | ex ZS-KRJ | |
| ☐ | V5-WAD | Cessna 310R | 310R1340 | ex ZS-KEE | |
| ☐ | V5-WAE | Cessna 402C | 402C0430 | ex ZS-NPA | |

| | | | | | |
|---|---|---|---|---|---|
| ☐ | V5-WAG | Cessna 310R | 310R1668 | ex V5-KRK | |
| ☐ | V5-WAK | Reims Cessna F406 Caravan II | F406-0048 | ex G-FLYN | DHL titles |

## V6- MICRONESIA (Federated States of Micronesia)

### CAROLINE ISLAND AIR — Pohnpei (PNI)

| | | | | | |
|---|---|---|---|---|---|
| ☐ | V6-01FM | Britten-Norman BN-2A-27 Islander | 2014 | ex V6-SFM | |
| ☐ | V6-02FM | Beech 65-80 Queen Air | LC-84 | ex N349N | |
| ☐ | V6-03FM | Britten-Norman BN-2A-21 Islander | 660 | ex VH-AUN | |

## V7- MARSHALL ISLANDS (Republic of the Marshall Islands)

### AIRLINE OF THE MARSHALL ISLANDS — Marshall Islands (CW/MRS) — Majuro Intl (MAJ)

| | | | | | |
|---|---|---|---|---|---|
| ☐ | V7-0210 | de Havilland DHC-8-102 | 218 | ex ZK-NEU | |
| ☐ | V7-9206 | Dornier 228-212 | 8194 | ex D-CAHD | [MAJ] |
| ☐ | V7-9207 | Dornier 228-212 | 8201 | ex D-CAHE | [MAJ] |

## V8- BRUNEI (Negara Brunei Darussalam)

### ROYAL BRUNEI AIRLINES — Brunei (BI/RBA) — Bandar Seri Begawan (BWN)

| | | | | | |
|---|---|---|---|---|---|
| ☐ | V8-BLA | Boeing 777-212ER | 30871/378 | ex 9V-SVF | <SIA |
| ☐ | V8-BLB | Boeing 777-212ER | 30872/398 | ex 9V-SVG | <SIA |
| ☐ | V8-BLC | Boeing 777-212ER | 28524/350 | ex 9V-SVA | <SIA |
| ☐ | V8-BLD | Boeing 777-212ER | 28525/353 | ex 9V-SVB | <SIA |
| ☐ | V8-BLE | Boeing 777-212ER | 28526/355 | ex 9V-SVC | <SIA |
| ☐ | V8-BLF | Boeing 777-212ER | 30869/366 | ex 9V-SVD | <SIA |
| ☐ | V8-RBP | Airbus A319-132 | 2023 | ex D-AVWW | |
| ☐ | V8-RBR | Airbus A319-132 | 2032 | ex D-AVYK | |
| ☐ | V8-RBS | Airbus A320-232 | 2135 | ex F-WWIV | |
| ☐ | V8-RBT | Airbus A320-232 | 2139 | ex F-WWDO | |

## XA- MEXICO (United Mexican States)

### AEREO CALAFIA — Calafia (CFV) — Los Cabos

| | | | | | |
|---|---|---|---|---|---|
| ☐ | XA-AVT | Cessna 208B Caravan I | 208B0301 | ex XA-SFJ | |
| ☐ | XA-BTS | Cessna 208B Caravan i | 208B1093 | ex XA-UCT | |
| ☐ | XA-HVB | Cessna 208B Caravan i | 208B1104 | ex N4047W | ♦ |
| ☐ | XA-HVT | Cessna 208B Caravan i | 208B2121 | ex N5135K | ♦ |
| ☐ | XA-TQW | Cessna 206H Stationair | 20608072 | ex N4002B | |
| ☐ | XA-TWN | Cessna 208B Caravan I | 208B0931 | ex N5296M | ♦ |
| ☐ | XA-UGI | Cessna 208B Caravan i | 208B1211 | ex N5166U | ♦ |
| ☐ | XA-VVT | Cessna 208B Caravan I | 208B1269 | | ♦ |

### AERO BINIZA — Oaxaca (OAX)

| | | | | | |
|---|---|---|---|---|---|
| ☐ | XA-GIL | Cessna 208B Caravan I | 208B1088 | ex N817SB | ♦ |
| ☐ | XA-UAB | Cessna 208B Caravan I | 208B1017 | ex XA-TVS | |

### AERO CUAHONTE — Cuahonte (CUO) — Uruapan (UPN)

| | | | | | |
|---|---|---|---|---|---|
| ☐ | XA-GUU | Swearingen SA.226TC Metro II | TC-389 | ex XA-STV | ♦ |
| ☐ | XA-HUO | Swearingen SA.226AC Metro II | | | ♦ |
| ☐ | XA-KOC | Cessna 402C | 402C0301 | ex N3271M | |
| ☐ | XA-SER | Swearingen SA.226AT Metroo II | TC-413 | ex N139WW | ♦ |
| ☐ | XA-UNB | Dornier 228-202K | 8139 | ex F-OGOL | |
| ☐ | XA- | Dornier 228-212 | 8238 | ex F-OHQK | |

### AERO DAVINCI INTERNACIONAL — Reynosa (REX)

| | | | | | |
|---|---|---|---|---|---|
| ☐ | XA-AFL | Swearingen SA.226TC Metro II | | | |
| ☐ | XA-TGV | Swearingen SA.226TC Metro II | TC-350 | ex N4254Y | |

### AERO FERINCO — Playa del Carmen (PCM)

| | | | | | |
|---|---|---|---|---|---|
| ☐ | XA-TFG | LET L-410UVP | 851409 | ex YL-PAH | Frtr [PCM] |
| ☐ | XA-TQC | LET L-410UVP-E3 | 882030 | ex Russ AF 2030 | |

532

## AERO JBR

| | | | | | |
|---|---|---|---|---|---|
| ☐ | XA-UFJ | NAMC YS-11A-607 | 2071 | ex XA-TTY | ♦ |

## AERO PACIFICO — Aero Costa (TAA) — Colima (CLQ)

| | | | | | |
|---|---|---|---|---|---|
| ☐ | XA-AFT | Swearingen SA.227AC Metro III | AC-581 | ex C-FAFE | Frtr |
| ☐ | XA-UAJ | Swearingen SA.227AC Metro III | AC-586 | ex N911EJ | Frtr |

## AERO SUDPACIFICO

| | | | | | |
|---|---|---|---|---|---|
| ☐ | XA-SJY | Swearingen SA.226TC Metro II | TC-340 | ex N247AM | ♦ |
| ☐ | XA- | Swearingen SA.226TC Metro II | TC-386 | ex N32AG | ♦ |

## AEROCEDROS — Ensenada (ESE)

| | | | | |
|---|---|---|---|---|
| ☐ | XA-RYV | Convair 440-0 | 474 | ex XB-CSE |
| ☐ | XA-STJ | Cessna 402B | 402B0801 | ex N3792C |
| ☐ | XA-TFY | Convair 440-0 | 472 | ex N411GA |
| ☐ | XA-TFZ | Convair 440-94 | 439 | ex N44829 |

Ops Convair 440s for Soc Coop Prod Pesque Pescado

## AERODAN — Saltillo (SLW)

| | | | | | |
|---|---|---|---|---|---|
| ☐ | XA-YYS | NAMC YS-11A-205 | 2077 | ex N917AX | ♦ |

## AEROFUTURO — Mexico City-Toluca (TLC)

| | | | | |
|---|---|---|---|---|
| ☐ | XA-UGN | Swearingen SA.226TC Metro II | TC-353 | ex XA-SFS |

## AEROLAMSA — Playa del Carmen (PCM)

| | | | | |
|---|---|---|---|---|
| ☐ | XA-TYL | El Gavilan 358 | 003 | ex TG-TDA |
| ☐ | XA-UBD | Britten-Norman BN-2A Mk.III-2 Trislander | | |
| | | | 1044 | ex YV-2523P |

## AEROLINEAS CENTAURO — Centauro (CTR) — Durango (DGO)

| | | | | |
|---|---|---|---|---|
| ☐ | XA-JAD | Cessna U206G Stationair 6 II | U20605279 | |
| ☐ | XA-NAQ | Cessna U206G Stationair 6 | U20603880 | ex XB-CJQ |
| ☐ | XA-PIQ | Britten-Norman BN-2A-26 Islander | 892 | ex XC-DUJ |
| ☐ | XA-RNC | Cessna TU206G Stationair 6 II | U20605747 | ex XB-CGX |

## AEROMAR AIRLINES — Trans-Aeromar (VW/TAO) — Mexico City-Toluca (TLC)

| | | | | | |
|---|---|---|---|---|---|
| ☐ | XA-SJJ | ATR 42-320 | 0039 | ex N71296 | |
| ☐ | XA-SYH | ATR 42-320 | 0062 | ex XA-PEP | Presidente Aleman |
| ☐ | XA-TAH | ATR 42-500 | 0471 | ex F-WWLS | |
| ☐ | XA-TAI | ATR 42-500 | 0474 | ex F-WWLF | |
| ☐ | XA-TIC | ATR 42-320 | 0058 | ex F-OGNF | |
| ☐ | XA-TKJ | ATR 42-500 | 0561 | ex F-WWLW | |
| ☐ | XA-TLN | ATR 42-500 | 0564 | ex F-WWEC | |
| ☐ | XA-TPR | ATR 42-500 | 0586 | ex F-WWEA | |
| ☐ | XA-TPS | ATR 42-500 | 0594 | ex F-WWEX | |
| ☐ | XA-TRI | ATR 42-500 | 0607 | ex F-WWEA | |
| ☐ | XA-TRJ | ATR 42-500 | 0608 | ex F-WWEB | |
| ☐ | XA-UAU | ATR 42-500 | 0462 | ex I-ADLF | Edo de Veracruz |
| ☐ | XA-UAV | ATR 42-500 | 0476 | ex I-ADLG | |
| ☐ | XA-UFA | ATR 42-500 | 0412 | ex F-WQNH | |
| ☐ | XA-UOZ | Canadair CRJ-200ER | 7544 | ex N119MN | |
| ☐ | XA-UPA | Canadair CRJ-200ER | 7545 | ex N122MN | |

## AEROMEXICO — AeroMexico (AM/AMX) — Mexico City-Benito Juarez Intl (MEX)

Member of Skyteam

| | | | | | |
|---|---|---|---|---|---|
| ☐ | EI-DRD | Boeing 737-752/W | 35117/2122 | ex N1786B | |
| ☐ | EI-DRE | Boeing 737-752/W | 35787/2111 | | |
| ☐ | N126AM | Boeing 737-7BK/W | 30617/812 | ex EI-EOV | |
| ☐ | N423AM | Boeing 737-73V/W | 32423/1433 | ex G-EZKB | ♦ |
| ☐ | N784XE | Boeing 737-752/W | 33784/1393 | ex XA-BAM | ♦ |
| ☐ | N788XA | Boeing 737-752/W | 33788/1439 | ex XA-GAM | |
| ☐ | N842AM | Boeing 737-752/W | 32842/1814 | | |
| ☐ | N850AM | Boeing 737-752/W | 33786/1403 | ex XA-DAM | |
| ☐ | N851AM | Boeing 737-752/W | 29363/1417 | ex XA-EAM | |
| ☐ | N852AM | Boeing 737-752/W | 33787/1421 | ex XA-FAM | |

| | | | | | | |
|---|---|---|---|---|---|---|
| ☐ | N853AM | Boeing 737-752/W | 33791/1557 | ex XA-JAM | | |
| ☐ | N855AM | Boeing 737-752/W | 33792/1571 | ex XA-KAM | | |
| ☐ | N857AM | Boeing 737-752/W | 33793/1597 | ex XA-LAM | | |
| ☐ | N904AM | Boeing 737-752/W | 28262/1565 | ex N854AM | | |
| ☐ | N906AM | Boeing 737-752/W | 29356/1586 | | | |
| ☐ | N908AM | Boeing 737-752/W | 30038/1601 | | | |
| ☐ | N997AM | Boeing 737-76Q/W | 30283/1156 | ex G-OSLH | | |
| ☐ | XA-AAM | Boeing 737-752/W | 33783/1381 | | | |
| ☐ | XA-AGM | Boeing 737-752/W | 35786/2098 | | | |
| ☐ | XA-CAM | Boeing 737-752/W | 33785/1398 | | | |
| ☐ | XA-CTG | Boeing 737-752/W | 35123/2374 | | | |
| ☐ | XA-CYM | Boeing 737-752/W | 35124/2456 | ex N1779B | | |
| ☐ | XA-GMV | Boeing 737-752/W | 35118/2151 | | | |
| ☐ | XA-GOL | Boeing 737-752/W | 35785/2011 | | | |
| ☐ | XA-HAM | Boeing 737-752/W | 33789/1524 | | | |
| ☐ | XA-MAH | Boeing 737-752/W | 35122/2348 | | | |
| ☐ | XA-NAM | Boeing 737-752/W | 33790/1533 | ex (XA-IAM) | | |
| ☐ | XA-PAM | Boeing 737-752/W | 34293/1747 | | | |
| ☐ | XA-QAM | Boeing 737-752/W | 34294/1761 | ex N1786B | | |
| ☐ | XA-VAM | Boeing 737-752/W | 34295/1765 | | | |
| ☐ | XA- | Boeing 737-752/W | | | | o/o |
| ☐ | XA- | Boeing 737-752/W | | | | o/o |
| ☐ | XA- | Boeing 737-752/W | | | | o/o |
| | | | | | | |
| ☐ | EI-DRA | Boeing 737-852/W | 35114/2037 | ex N1779B | | |
| ☐ | EI-DRB | Boeing 737-852/W | 35115/2070 | | | |
| ☐ | EI-DRC | Boeing 737-852/W | 35116/2081 | | | |
| ☐ | N359AM | Boeing 737-8CX/W | 32359/1041 | ex PR-GOJ | | |
| ☐ | N520AM | Boeing 737-81Q/W | 29052/557 | ex VP-BMI | | ◆ |
| ☐ | N858AM | Boeing 737-8Q8/W | 30671/1307 | ex C-GLBW | | ◆ |
| ☐ | N859AM | Boeing 737-8Q8/W | 32796/1272 | ex N641LF | | ◆ |
| ☐ | N860AM | Boeing 737-83N/W | 28249/1123 | ex N151LF | | ◆ |
| ☐ | N861AM | Boeing 737-83N/W | 30706/929 | ex N161LF | | ◆ |
| ☐ | PH-HZE | Boeing 737-8K2/W | 28377/277 | ex N1786B | | <TRA◆ |
| ☐ | PH-HZO | Boeing 737-8K2/W | 34169/2243 | | | <TRA◆ |
| ☐ | XA-JOY | Boeing 737-852/W | 35121/2327 | ex N1782B | | |
| ☐ | XA-MIA | Boeing 737-852/W | 35119/2273 | | | |
| ☐ | XA-ZAM | Boeing 737-852/W | 35120/2290 | ex N1780B | | |
| | | | | | | |
| ☐ | XA-AMX | Boeing 767-25DER | 24733/261 | ex N473AG | | |
| ☐ | XA-EAP | Boeing 767-25DER | 24734/266 | ex N734AG | | |
| ☐ | XA-FRJ | Boeing 767-283ER | 24728/305 | ex N728CG | | ◆ |
| ☐ | XA-JBC | Boeing 767-284ER | 24762/307 | ex XA-RVY | | ◆ |
| ☐ | XA-OAM | Boeing 767-2B1ER | 26471/511 | ex C9-BAF | | |
| ☐ | XA-TOJ | Boeing 767-283ER | 24727/301 | ex PT-TAI | | |
| | | | | | | |
| ☐ | N745AM | Boeing 777-2Q8ER | 32718/554 | | | |
| ☐ | N746AM | Boeing 777-2Q8ER | 32719/562 | | | |
| ☐ | N774AM | Boeing 777-2Q8ER | 28689/365 | ex N301LF | | |
| ☐ | N776AM | Boeing 777-2Q8 | 28692/373 | ex N181LF | | |
| ☐ | XA-APB | Boeing 767-3Q8ER | 27618/727 | ex (XA-TMG) | | |
| ☐ | XA-MAT | Boeing 767-3Y0ER | 24947/351 | ex N942AC | | |
| ☐ | XA-TPM | McDonnell-Douglas MD-87 | 49671/1463 | ex PZ-TCG | District of Para | [MEX] |

| | | | | | |
|---|---|---|---|---|---|
| **AEROMEXICO CONNECT** | | **Costera (5D/SLI)** | **Monterrey-Escobedo Intl/Vera Cruz (MTY/VER)** | | |

| | | | | |
|---|---|---|---|---|
| ☐ | XA-ACA | Embraer ERJ-145LR | 145144 | ex N261SK |
| ☐ | XA-ACB | Embraer ERJ-145LR | 145221 | ex N264SK |
| ☐ | XA-ALI | Embraer ERJ-145LR | 145795 | ex PT-SMW |
| ☐ | XA-BLI | Embraer ERJ-145LR | 145798 | ex PT-SMY |
| ☐ | XA-CLI | Embraer ERJ-145LR | 14500803 | ex PT-SNG |
| ☐ | XA-ELI | Embraer ERJ-145LR | 14500861 | ex PT-SXB |
| ☐ | XA-FLI | Embraer ERJ-145MP | 145444 | ex N973RP |
| ☐ | XA-GAC | Embraer ERJ-145MP | 145406 | ex SP-LGL |
| ☐ | XA-GLI | Embraer ERJ-145MP | 145203 | ex N974RP |
| ☐ | XA-HLI | Embraer ERJ-145MP | 145337 | ex N975RP |
| ☐ | XA-ILI | Embraer ERJ-145LU | 145564 | ex D-ACIA |
| ☐ | XA-JLI | Embraer ERJ-145MP | 145426 | ex N971RP |
| ☐ | XA-KAC | Embraer ERJ-145MP | 145322 | ex N976RP |
| ☐ | XA-KLI | Embraer ERJ-145MP | 145440 | ex N972RP |
| ☐ | XA-LLI | Embraer ERJ-145ER | 145060 | ex PT-SPH |
| ☐ | XA-MLI | Embraer ERJ-145ER | 145065 | ex PT-SPI |
| ☐ | XA-NLI | Embraer ERJ-145ER | 145083 | ex PT-SPJ |
| ☐ | XA-OLI | Embraer ERJ-145ER | 145089 | ex PT-SPK |
| ☐ | XA-PAC | Embraer ERJ-145LR | 145498 | ex N824HK |
| ☐ | XA-PLI | Embraer ERJ-145ER | 145090 | ex PT-SPL |
| ☐ | XA-QAC | Embraer ERJ-145LR | 145510 | ex N825HK |
| ☐ | XA-QLI | Embraer ERJ-145LU | 145588 | ex HB-JAX |
| ☐ | XA-RAC | Embraer ERJ-145LR | 145313 | ex N830HK |
| ☐ | XA-RLI | Embraer ERJ-145LU | 145559 | ex HB-JAS |
| ☐ | XA-SLI | Embraer ERJ-145LU | 145580 | ex HB-JAW |
| ☐ | XA-TAC | Embraer ERJ-145LR | 145475 | ex N823HK |

| | | | | | |
|---|---|---|---|---|---|
| ☐ | XA-TLI | Embraer ERJ-145LU | 145601 | ex HB-JAY | |
| ☐ | XA-ULI | Embraer ERJ-145LU | 145570 | ex HB-JAU | |
| ☐ | XA-VAC | Embraer ERJ-145LR | 145232 | ex N831HK | |
| ☐ | XA-VLI | Embraer ERJ-145LU | 145574 | ex HB-JAV | |
| ☐ | XA-WAC | Embraer ERJ-145LR | 145255 | ex N837HK | |
| ☐ | XA-WLI | Embraer ERJ-145LU | 145434 | ex HB-JAN | |
| ☐ | XA-XAC | Embraer ERJ-145LR | 145128 | ex N260SK | |
| ☐ | XA-XLI | Embraer ERJ-145LU | 145456 | ex HB-JAO | |
| ☐ | XA-YAC | Embraer ERJ-145LR | 145168 | ex N262SK | |
| ☐ | XA-YLI | Embraer ERJ-145LU | 145400 | ex HB-JAL | |
| ☐ | XA-ZAC | Embraer ERJ-145LR | 145199 | ex N263SK | <CHQ |
| ☐ | XA-ZLI | Embraer ERJ-145LU | 145420 | ex HB-JAM | |
| | | | | | |
| ☐ | XA-AAC | Embraer ERJ-190LR | 19000121 | ex PT-SQP | |
| ☐ | XA-ACC | Embraer ERJ-190LR | 19000499 | ex PT-TRE | ♦ |
| ☐ | XA-ACE | Embraer ERJ-190LR | 19000518 | ex PT-TUF | ♦ |
| ☐ | XA-ACI | Embraer ERJ-190LR | 19000525 | ex PT-TUN | ♦ |
| ☐ | XA-BAC | Embraer ERJ-190LR | 19000129 | ex PT-SQP | |
| ☐ | XA-CAC | Embraer ERJ-190LR | 19000135 | ex PT-SYN | |
| ☐ | XA-DAC | Embraer ERJ-190LR | 19000455 | ex PT-TJZ | ♦ |
| ☐ | XA-EAC | Embraer ERJ-190LR | 19000145 | ex PT-SYX | |
| ☐ | XA-FAC | Embraer ERJ-190LR | 19000234 | ex PT-SIF | |
| ☐ | XA-HAC | Embraer ERJ-190LR | 19000466 | ex PT-TOJ | ♦ |
| ☐ | XA-IAC | Embraer ERJ-190LR | 19000238 | ex PT-SIL | |
| ☐ | XA-JAC | Embraer ERJ-190LR | 19000248 | ex PT-SIS | |
| ☐ | XA-MAC | Embraer ERJ-190LR | 19000408 | ex PT- | ♦ |
| ☐ | XA- | Embraer ERJ-190LR | 19000531 | ex PT-TUT | o/o♦ |
| ☐ | XA- | Embraer ERJ-190LR | 19000546 | ex PT- | o/o♦ |

### AEROMEXICO TRAVEL

| | | | | | |
|---|---|---|---|---|---|
| ☐ | N583MD | McDonnell-Douglas MD-83 | 49659/1438 | ex YV-39C | wfs |
| ☐ | N838AM | McDonnell-Douglas MD-83 | 49397/1331 | ex N830VV | wfs |

### AEROMEXPRESS CARGO    Aeromexpress (QO/MPX)    Mexico City-Benito Juarez Intl (MEX)

Subsidiary of AeroMexico, ops services with Boeing 767-200(SF)s leased from ABX Air as required.

### AERONAVES TSM    (VTM)    Saltilo (SLW)

| | | | | | |
|---|---|---|---|---|---|
| ☐ | XA-DCX | Swearingen SA.227AC Metro III | AC-497 | ex N98EB | |
| ☐ | XA-EEE | Swearingen SA.227AC Metro III | AC-503 | ex N102GS | |
| ☐ | XA-EGC | Swearingen SA.227AC Metro III | AC-724 | ex N106GS | |
| ☐ | XA-MIO | Swearingen SA.227AC Metro III | AC-693B | ex N446MA | |
| ☐ | XA-PNG | Swearingen SA.227AC Metro III | AC-687B | ex N445MA | |
| ☐ | XA-SLW | Swearingen SA.227AC Metro III | AC-628B | ex N280EM | |
| ☐ | XA-SUS | Swearingen SA.227AC Metro III | AC-430B | ex M430PF | ♦ |
| ☐ | XA-TYX | Swearingen SA.227AC Metro III | AC-627B | ex N799BW | |
| ☐ | XA-UKJ | Swearingen SA.227AC Metro III | AC-532 | ex N372PH | |
| ☐ | XA-UMW | Swearingen SA.227AC Metro III | AC-717 | ex N434MA | ♦ |
| ☐ | XA-UNQ | Swearingen SA.227AC Metro III | AC-565 | ex N163WA | ♦ |
| ☐ | XA-UOS | Swearingen SA.227AC Metro III | AC-760B | ex N760TR | ♦ |
| | | | | | |
| ☐ | XA-ADQ | Swearingen SA.226TC Metro II | TC-409 | ex C-FLNG | |
| ☐ | XA-ADS | Swearingen SA.226TC Metro II | TC-404 | ex C-FGPW | |
| ☐ | XA-TSM | Swearingen SA.226TC Metro IIA | TC-412 | ex XA-SXB | |
| ☐ | XA-UFO | Swearingen SA.226TC Metro II | TC-281 | ex N396RY | |
| ☐ | XA-UKP | Swearingen SA.226TC Metro II | TC-376 | ex N637PJ | |
| ☐ | XA- | Swearingen SA.226TC Metro II | TC-337 | ex N851LH | |
| | | | | | |
| ☐ | XA-DHL | Douglas DC-9-33F (ABS 3) | 47193/311 | ex N941F | ♦ |
| ☐ | XA-TYF | Convair 600F | 101 | ex N94279 | ♦ |
| ☐ | XA-UGH | Swearingen SA.226AT | AT-009 | ex N479VK | ♦ |
| ☐ | XA-UJI | Convair 640F | 88 | ex N73137 | ♦ |
| ☐ | XA-UMI | Convair 640F | 48 | ex N3417 | ♦ |
| ☐ | XA-UNH | Convair 640 | 332 | ex N640R | |
| ☐ | XA-UOG | Douglas DC-9-33RC (ABS 3) | 47194/324 | ex N944F | ♦ |
| ☐ | XA-UPS | Douglas DC-9-33RC (ABS 3) | 47462/564 | ex N934AX | ♦ |
| ☐ | XA- | Douglas DC-9-33RC | 47191/280 | ex NN933F | [SLW]♦ |

### AEROPACIFICO    Transportes Pacifico (TFO)    Los Mochis (LMM)

| | | | | | |
|---|---|---|---|---|---|
| ☐ | XA-AFE | LET L-410UVP-E | 902508 | ex N19RZ | |
| ☐ | XA-UEP | British Aerospace Jetstream 31 | 794 | ex N417UE | |

### AEROPOSTAL DE MEXICO    Postal Cargo (PCG)    Mexico City-Benito Juarez Intl (MEX)

| | | | | | |
|---|---|---|---|---|---|
| ☐ | XA-RSH | Lockheed C-130A Hercules | 3224 | ex HP-1162TLN | ♦ |
| ☐ | XA-RYZ | Lockheed C-130A Hercules | 3225 | ex N9691N | ♦ |
| ☐ | XA-TXS | Douglas DC-8-63CF (BAC 3) | 46054/453 | ex N796AL | [QRO] |

| | | | | | |
|---|---|---|---|---|---|
| **AEROTRON AIR ADVENTURE** | | *Aerotron (TRN)* | | | *Puerto Vallarta (PVR)* |
| ☐ XA-ADZ | Cessna 402 | 402-0113 | ex N772EA | | |
| ☐ XA-TNI | Cessna 208B Caravan I | 208B0728 | | | op for Air Adventure |

| | | | | | |
|---|---|---|---|---|---|
| **AEROTUCAN** | | | | | *Oaxaca (OAX)* |
| ☐ XA-TDS | Cessna 208B Caravan I | 208B0559 | ex N51396 | | |

| | | | | | |
|---|---|---|---|---|---|
| **AEROUNION** | | *AeroUnion (6R/TNO)* | | *Mexico City-Benito Juarez Intl (MEX)* | |
| ☐ XA-FPP | Airbus A300B4-203F | 227 | ex N227TN | | |
| ☐ XA-LRL | Airbus A300B4-203F | 210 | ex N2101R | | |
| ☐ XA-MRC | Airbus A300B4-203F | 247 | ex N247AX | | |
| ☐ XA-TWQ | Airbus A300B4-203F | 045 | ex G-HLAB | Tata | |

| | | | | | |
|---|---|---|---|---|---|
| **AIR TRIBE** | | | | | |
| ☐ XA-TRB | Convair 580 | 52 | ex N588X | | [OPF]♦ |
| ☐ XA-UPL | Convair 580 | 24 | ex N584E | | ♦ |

| | | | | | |
|---|---|---|---|---|---|
| **ALCON SERVICIOS AEREOS** | | | | | |
| ☐ XA-TND | NAMC YS-11A-306 | 2073 | ex N111PH | | ♦ |

| | | | | | |
|---|---|---|---|---|---|
| **ALTERNATIVE AIR** | | | | | |
| ☐ XA-UFT | British Aerospace Jetstream 32 | 862 | ex N862JX | | ♦ |
| ☐ XA- | British Aerospace Jetstream 32 | 866 | ex N866AE | | ♦ |

| | | | | | |
|---|---|---|---|---|---|
| **COMERCIAL AEREA** | | | | | |
| ☐ XA-ESV | Cessna 208B Caravan I | 208B0807 | ex N5261R | | ♦ |

| | | | | | |
|---|---|---|---|---|---|
| **ESTAFETA CARGA AEREA** | | *(E7/ESF)* | | *San Luis Potosi (SLP)* | |
| ☐ XA-AJA | Boeing 737-3Y0 (SF) | 23747/1363 | ex N331AW | | |
| ☐ XA-ECA | Boeing 737-3M8 (SF) | 24024/1689 | ex N784DC | | |
| ☐ XA-EMX | Boeing 737-375F | 23707/1388 | ex N336AW | | |
| ☐ XA-SPO | Canadair CRJ-100ER | 7085 | ex F-GRJD | | |
| ☐ XA-GGB | Boeing 737-3M8 (SF) | 24023/1675 | ex N783DC | | |
| ☐ XA-ESA | Canadair CRJ-100ER | 7088 | ex F-GRJC | | |

| | | | | | |
|---|---|---|---|---|---|
| **FLYMEX** | | *(NTG)* | | | |
| ☐ XA-AAS | Dornier 328-300 (328JET) | 3127 | ex N430Z | | UN/WPF titles |
| ☐ XA-ALA | Dorner 328-310 (328JET) | 3167 | ex N117LM | | ♦ |
| ☐ XA-ASF | Embraer ERJ-135LR | 145737 | ex N841RP | | ♦ |
| ☐ XA-FAS | Dornier 328-300 (328JET) | 3125 | ex N410Z | | UN/WFP titles |

| | | | | | |
|---|---|---|---|---|---|
| **GLOBAL AIR** | | *Damojh* | | *Mexico City-Benito Juarez Intl (MEX)* | |
| ☐ XA-TWR | Boeing 737-2H4 (AvAero 3) | 21812/611 | ex N60SW | no titles | >VCV |
| ☐ XA-UBB | Boeing 737-291 | 21750/574 | ex N988UA | | [MEX] |
| ☐ XA-UHY | Boeing 737-2C3 | 21016/406 | ex XA-MAB | | [MEX]♦ |
| ☐ XA-UHZ | Boeing 737-201 | 21816/592 | ex XA-MAK | | ♦ |
| ☐ XA-UKW | Boeing 737-205 | 21184/440 | ex YV206T | | ♦ |
| ☐ XA-UMP | Boeing 737-2A3 | 22738/834 | ex CX-BOO | | [OPF]♦ |
| ☐ XA-UMQ | Boeing 737-2Q3 | 24103/1565 | ex N243AG | | |

| | | | | | |
|---|---|---|---|---|---|
| **HAWK DE MEXICO / HELIVAN** | | *Hawk Mexico (HMX)* | | *Mexico City/Cancun (MEX/CUN)* | |
| ☐ XA-MVD | Beech 1900D | UE-398 | ex N44118 | | |

| | | | | | |
|---|---|---|---|---|---|
| **HELI CAMPECHE** | | *Helicampeche (HEC)* | | *Campeche/Mexico City (CPE/-)* | |
| ☐ XA-HSC | Bell 412EP | 36417 | ex N30423 | | ♦ |
| ☐ XA-HSD | Bell 412EP | 36446 | ex N31011 | | |
| ☐ XA-HSG | Bell 412EP | 36473 | ex N321FB | | |
| ☐ XA-HSH | Bell 412EP | 36479 | ex N142AW | | |
| ☐ XA-HSJ | Bell 412EP | 36337 | ex N45388 | | |
| ☐ XA-HSK | Bell 412EP | 36340 | ex N45389 | | |
| ☐ XA-HSL | Bell 412EP | 36334 | ex N45377 | | |
| ☐ XA-HSM | Bell 412EP | 36324 | ex N8067M | | |
| ☐ XA-HSN | Bell 412EP | 36488 | ex N332TB | | |
| ☐ XA-HSO | Bell 412EP | 36489 | ex N331AB | | |

536

| | | | | | |
|---|---|---|---|---|---|
| ☐ | XA-SMW | Bell 412HP | 36038 | ex SU-CAW | |
| ☐ | XA-SYL | Bell 412HP | 36101 | ex N87746 | |
| ☐ | XA-TRC | Bell 412HP | 36157 | ex N389AL | |
| ☐ | XA-TTL | Bell 412HP | 36065 | ex D-HHZZ | |
| ☐ | XA-TXP | Bell 412EP | 36311 | ex N24129 | |
| ☐ | XA-TXQ | Bell 412EP | 36268 | ex N61318 | |
| ☐ | XA-TXR | Bell 412EP | 36289 | ex N2029N | |
| ☐ | XA-TXV | Bell 412EP | 36317 | ex N7020C | |
| ☐ | XA-TXZ | Bell 412EP | 36314 | ex N7030B | |
| ☐ | XA-TYA | Bell 412EP | 36315 | ex N7007Q | |
| ☐ | XA-UAR | Bell 412 | 36051 | ex D-HHYY | |
| ☐ | XA-ADL | Bell 407 | 53447 | ex N61201 | |
| ☐ | XA-HSE | Eurocopter EC135P2+ | 0591 | ex N135TZ | |
| ☐ | XA-HSF | Eurocopter EC135P2+ | 0598 | ex N435AL | |
| ☐ | XA-JMB | Bell 407 | 53274 | ex XA-TLB | |
| ☐ | XA-JOL | Bell 206B JetRanger III | 786 | ex N31AL | <OLOG |
| ☐ | XA-LOC | Bell 206B JetRanger III | 3284 | | <OLOG |
| ☐ | XA-SMX | Bell 206L-4 LongRanger IV | 52005 | ex N2064W | |
| ☐ | XA-TPC | Bell 407 | 53313 | ex N60664 | |
| ☐ | XA-TRP | Bell 212 | 30869 | ex N71AL | <OLOG |
| ☐ | XA-UEB | Bell 407 | 53046 | ex N416AL | <OLOG |
| ☐ | XA- | Sikorsky S-75C+ | 760639 | ex N873AL | ♦ |
| ☐ | XA- | Eurocopter EC155R1 | 6765 | ex G-ISSW | ♦ |

**HELIVAN**

Fleet returned to CHC Helicopters International (C-) May11

**INTERJET** (4O/AIJ) *Toluca (TLC)*

| | | | | | |
|---|---|---|---|---|---|
| ☐ | XA-ABC | Airbus A320-214 | 3690 | ex F-WWBE | |
| ☐ | XA-ACO | Airbus A320-214 | 1322 | ex F-WQUX | |
| ☐ | XA-ALM | Airbus A320-214 | 1308 | ex F-WQUU | |
| ☐ | XA-BIC | Airbus A320-214 | 3374 | ex XA-MXL | ♦ |
| ☐ | XA-BIO | Airbus A320-214 | 4730 | ex F-WWIL | ♦ |
| ☐ | XA-DOS | Airbus A320-214 | 4235 | ex OE-IAX | ♦ |
| ☐ | XA-ECO | Airbus A320-214 | 4733 | ex F-WWIN | ♦ |
| ☐ | XA-FOG | Airbus A320-214 | 2048 | ex N141LF | ♦ |
| ☐ | XA-IJA | Airbus A320-214 | 1244 | ex F-WQUT | |
| ☐ | XA-IJT | Airbus A320-214 | 1132 | ex F-WQUR | |
| ☐ | XA-ILY | Airbus A320-214 | 3123 | ex N213MX | |
| ☐ | XA-ING | Airbus A320-214 | 4304 | ex OE-IAY | ♦ |
| ☐ | XA-INJ | Airbus A320-214 | 1162 | ex F-WQUV | |
| ☐ | XA-JCV | Airbus A320-214 | 3514 | ex F-WWDO | |
| ☐ | XA-KNG | Airbus A320-214 | 1747 | ex 6Y-JMI | ♦ |
| ☐ | XA-KNO | Airbus A320-214 | 2539 | ex D-ABDA | ♦ |
| ☐ | XA-MLR | Airbus A320-214 | 2227 | ex EC-JAB | |
| ☐ | XA-MTO | Airbus A320-214 | 4924 | ex D-AXAB | ♦ |
| ☐ | XA-MTY | Airbus A320-214 | 1179 | ex XA-AIJ | |
| ☐ | XA-MXM | Airbus A320-214 | 3286 | ex F-WWDR | |
| ☐ | XA-MYR | Airbus A320-214 | 3021 | ex HB-IOV | |
| ☐ | XA-ROA | Airbus A320-214 | 0707 | ex N707CG | ♦ |
| ☐ | XA-SOB | Airbus A320-214 | 2189 | ex 9H-AEI | |
| ☐ | XA-SUN | Airbus A320-214 | 4411 | ex EI-ERY | ♦ |
| ☐ | XA-TLC | Airbus A320-214 | 3312 | ex F-WWIP | |
| ☐ | XA-UHE | Airbus A320-214 | 3149 | ex F-WWBS | |
| ☐ | XA-VAI | Airbus A320-214 | 3160 | ex F-WWDR | |
| ☐ | XA-VFI | Airbus A320-214 | 1780 | ex N471LF | |
| ☐ | XA-VIP | Airbus A320-214 | 3304 | ex XA-MXK | |
| ☐ | XA-VTA | Airbus A320-214 | 1259 | ex XA-ITJ | |
| ☐ | XA-XII | Airbus A320-214 | 3508 | ex F-WWBU | |
| ☐ | XA-YES | Airbus A320-214 | 4933 | ex D-AXAE | ♦ |
| ☐ | XA-ZIH | Airbus A320-214 | 3667 | ex F-WWDZ | |
| ☐ | XA- | Airbus A320-214 | | ex | o/o |
| ☐ | XA- | Airbus A320-214 | | ex | o/o |

**LINEAS AEREAS COMERCIALES**

| | | | | | |
|---|---|---|---|---|---|
| ☐ | XA-MIC | Cessna 208B Caravan I | 208B0496 | ex N5165T | ♦ |

**MAGNICHARTERS** **Grupomonterrey (GMT)**
**Monterrey-General Mariano Ecobedo Intl (MTY)**

| | | | | | |
|---|---|---|---|---|---|
| ☐ | XA-MAA | Boeing 737-377 | 23655/1274 | ex N812AR | |
| ☐ | XA-MAB | Boeing 737-301 | 23232/1169 | ex N502UW | |
| ☐ | XA-MAI | Boeing 737-322 | 24537/1774 | ex N368UA | ♦ |
| ☐ | XA-UNL | Boeing 737-322 | 24532/1754 | ex N185AQ | ♦ |
| ☐ | XA-UNM | Boeing 737-322 | 24248/1636 | ex N187AQ | ♦ |

| | | | | | |
|---|---|---|---|---|---|
| ☐ | XA-UNY | Boeing 737-322 | 24455/1752 | ex N184AQ | ♦ |
| ☐ | XA-MAD | Boeing 737-277 (Nordam 3) | 22652/831 | ex N185AW Magni titles | |
| ☐ | XA-MAE | Boeing 737-277 (Nordam 3) | 22648/789 | ex N181AW | |

## MAS AIR CARGO — Mas Carga (MY/MAA) — Mexico City-Benito Juarez Intl (MEX)

| | | | | | |
|---|---|---|---|---|---|
| ☐ | N314LA | Boeing 767-316ERF/W | 32573/848 | | <LCO |
| ☐ | N420LA | Boeing 767-316ERF/W | 34627/948 | | <LCO |
| ☐ | N526LA | Boeing 767-346ERF/W | 35817/959 | ex JA632J | ♦ |

## MAYAIR — (MYI) — Mexico City-Benito Juarez Intl (MEX)

| | | | | | |
|---|---|---|---|---|---|
| ☐ | XA-MYI | Short SD.3-60 | SH3602 | ex YN-CGF | |

## NOVA AIR — (M4) — Mexico City-Benito Juarez Intl (MEX)

Ceased ops Aug09

## REPUBLICAIR — Republicair (RBC) — Mexico City-Benito Juarez Intl (MEX)

| | | | | | |
|---|---|---|---|---|---|
| ☐ | XA-RBC | Boeing 737-277 (Nordam 3) | 22647/785 | ex N180AW | [MEX] |
| ☐ | XA-RBD | Boeing 737-277 (Nordam 3) | 22649/801 | ex N182AW | [MEX] |

## SAINTEX CARGO

Aircraft sold

## VIGO JET — Mejets (MJT) — Mexico City-Benito Juarez Intl (MEX)

| | | | | | |
|---|---|---|---|---|---|
| ☐ | XA-MJE | North American NA-265 Sabre 40 | 282-65 | ex XA-GGR | Frtr |
| ☐ | XA-UIT | SAAB SF.340A | 340A-030 | ex XA-UGM | |

## VIVA AEROBUS — (VIV) — Monterrey-Escobedo Intl (MTY)

| | | | | | |
|---|---|---|---|---|---|
| ☐ | EI-EOZ | Boeing 737-3Q8 | 24962/2139 | ex SE-RHT | ♦ |
| ☐ | EI-ERD | Boeing 737-36N | 28563/2921 | ex N557MS | ♦ |
| ☐ | XA-TAR | Boeing 737-301 | 23259/1132 | ex HS-AEF | |
| ☐ | XA-UGL | Boeing 737-3B7 | 22958/1137 | ex N385US | |
| ☐ | XA-VIA | Boeing 737-3B7 | 23856/1501 | ex N521AU | |
| ☐ | XA-VIB | Boeing 737-3B7 | 23378/1339 | ex HS-AAU | |
| ☐ | XA-VIF | Boeing 737-301 | 23552/1382 | ex PK-AWV | |
| ☐ | XA-VIH | Boeing 737-301 | 23554/1408 | ex PK-AWW | |
| ☐ | XA-VIJ | Boeing 737-3Y0 | 24677/1837 | ex 9M-AEC | |
| ☐ | XA-VIK | Boeing 737-3L9 | 26442/2277 | ex PK-AWN | |
| ☐ | XA-VIL | Boeing 737-33A | 25010/2008 | ex TS-IEC | |
| ☐ | XA-VIM | Boeing 737-33A | 25032/2014 | ex TS-IED | |
| ☐ | XA-VIN | Boeing 737-33A | 27458/2959 | ex LN-KKZ | ♦ |
| ☐ | XA-VIR | Boeing 737-33A | 27285/2608 | ex LN-KKE | ♦ |
| ☐ | XA-VIS | Boeing 737-33A | 27457/2756 | ex LN-KKB | ♦ |
| ☐ | XA-VIT | Boeing 737-3K2 | 27635/2721 | ex ZK-SJE | ♦ |
| ☐ | XA-VIV | Boeing 737-301 | 23560/1463 | ex N573US | |
| ☐ | XA-VIX | Boeing 737-3B7 | 23312/1162 | ex N390US | |
| ☐ | XA-VIY | Boeing 737-3B7 | 22959/1140 | ex N158VA | |

## VOLARIS — (V4/VOI) — Toluca (TLC)

| | | | | | |
|---|---|---|---|---|---|
| ☐ | N473TA | Airbus A319-132 | 1140 | ex D-AVYP | Cynthia |
| ☐ | N474TA | Airbus A319-132 | 1159 | ex D-AVWD | Aline |
| ☐ | N501VL | Airbus A319-133 | 2979 | ex D-AVXF | Guadalupe |
| ☐ | N502VL | Airbus A319-132 | 3463 | ex D-AVWL | Mercedes |
| ☐ | N503VL | Airbus A319-132 | 3491 | ex D-AVYU | Audrey |
| ☐ | N504VL | Airbus A319-132 | 3590 | ex D-AVYK | Lourdes |
| ☐ | XA-VOA | Airbus A319-132 | 2771 | ex D-AVWP | Andrea |
| ☐ | XA-VOB | Airbus A319-133 | 2780 | ex D-AVYJ | Alberto |
| ☐ | XA-VOC | Airbus A319-132 | 2997 | ex D-AVXK | Christina |
| ☐ | XA-VOD | Airbus A319-133 | 3045 | ex D-AVWO | Dina |
| ☐ | XA-VOE | Airbus A319-133 | 3069 | ex D-AVWT | Erick |
| ☐ | XA-VOF | Airbus A319-133 | 3077 | ex D-AVWQ | Fidel |
| ☐ | XA-VOG | Airbus A319-133 | 3175 | ex D-AVXI | Gerardo |
| ☐ | XA-VOH | Airbus A319-133 | 3253 | ex D-AVWU | Hector |
| ☐ | XA-VOI | Airbus A319-132 | 2657 | ex D-AVYN | Luis Miguel |
| ☐ | XA-VOJ | Airbus A319-133 | 3279 | ex D-AVYM | |
| ☐ | XA-VOK | Airbus A319-133 | 3450 | ex D-AVYT | Veronica |
| ☐ | XA-VOL | Airbus A319-132 | 2666 | ex D-AVWX | Juan Pablo |
| ☐ | XA-VOO | Airbus A319-133 | 3705 | ex D-AVWK | Andres |
| ☐ | XA-VOP | Airbus A319-133 | 4403 | ex D-AVXI | Fernando |
| ☐ | XA-VOQ | Airbus A319-133 | 4422 | ex D-AVXK | Martin |

| | | | | | | |
|---|---|---|---|---|---|---|
| ☐ | XA-VOR | Airbus A319-132 | 2296 | ex F-GXAG | Narciso | |
| ☐ | XA-VOS | Airbus A319-132 | 3252 | ex SX-OAL | Helder | |
| ☐ | XA-VOT | Airbus A319-132 | 3317 | ex SX-OAK | | |
| ☐ | XA- | Airbus A319-112 | | | o/o | |
| ☐ | XA- | Airbus A319-132 | | ex | | o/o |
| ☐ | XA- | Airbus A319-132 | | ex | | o/o |
| | | | | | | |
| ☐ | N505VL | Airbus A320-233 | 4798 | ex D-AVVT | | ♦ |
| ☐ | N506VL | Airbus A320-233 | 4828 | ex F-WWIJ | | ♦ |
| ☐ | N507VL | Airbus A320-233 | 4832 | ex D-AXAM | | ♦ |
| ☐ | N508VL | Airbus A320-233 | 4950 | ex D-AXAS | | ♦ |
| ☐ | N509VL | Airbus A320-233 | 5062 | ex D-AUBC | | ♦ |
| ☐ | XA-VOM | Airbus A320-233 | 3624 | ex F-WWIM | Luiz | |
| ☐ | XA-VON | Airbus A320-232 | 3672 | ex F-WWIN | Isaac | |
| ☐ | XA-VOU | Airbus A320-232 | 2204 | ex CS-TQK | Ulises | |
| ☐ | XA-VOV | Airbus A320-232 | 3524 | ex EI-ERB | | ♦ |
| ☐ | XA-VOW | Airbus A320-232 | 3543 | ex EI-ERC | | ♦ |
| ☐ | XA-VOX | Airbus A320-232 | 4741 | ex F-WWIQ | | ♦ |

## WESTAIR DE MEXICO

| | | | | | | |
|---|---|---|---|---|---|---|
| ☐ | XA-TLA | Swearingen SA.227AC Metro III | AC-723 | ex N2725D | | ♦ |

# XT-   BURKINA FASO (People's Democratic Republic of Burkina Faso)

## AIR BURKINA | Burkina (2J/VBW) | Ouagadougou (OUA)

| | | | | | |
|---|---|---|---|---|---|
| ☐ | XT-ABC | McDonnell-Douglas MD-87 | 49834/1714 | ex I-AFRA | |
| ☐ | XT-ABD | McDonnell-Douglas MD-87 | 49839/1739 | ex EC-EYX | |
| ☐ | XT-ABF | McDonnell-Douglas MD-83 | 53464/2091 | ex N161BS | |
| ☐ | XT-ABG | Canadair CRJ-200ER | 7363 | ex N113MN | ♦ |

# XU-   CAMBODIA (Kingdom of Cambodia)

## CAMBODIA ANGKOR AIR | (K6/KHV) | Phnom Penh-Pochentong (PNH)

| | | | | | |
|---|---|---|---|---|---|
| ☐ | VN-B227 | ATR 72-212A | 0899 | ex F-WWEJ | |
| ☐ | VN-B231 | ATR 72-212A | 0906 | ex F-WWEW | |

## IMTREC AVIATION | Imtrec (IMT) | Phnom Penh-Pochentong (PNH)

| | | | | | |
|---|---|---|---|---|---|
| ☐ | RDPL-34155 | Ilyushin Il-76T | 073411338 | ex ER-IBD | |
| ☐ | RDPL-34158 | Antonov An-32 | 402437 | ex ER-LID | op for Laotian Army |
| ☐ | XU-315 | Antonov An-12BP | 2400702 | ex RA-11131 | |

## PMT AIR | Multitrade (U4/PMT) | Phnom Penh-Pochentong (PNH)

Ceased ops 2008

## PRESIDENT AIRLINES | (TO/PSD) | Phnom Penh-Pochentong (PNH)

Ceased ops 2007

## ROYAL KHMER AIRLINES | Khymer Air (RK/RKH) | Phnom Penh-Pochentong (PNH)

| | | | | | | |
|---|---|---|---|---|---|---|
| ☐ | XU-RKH | Boeing 737-232 (Nordam 3) | 23105/1068 | ex N334DL | | [PNH] |
| ☐ | XU-RKJ | Boeing 727-223 (Raisbeck 3) | 20989/1144 | ex PK-JGQ | Air Dream c/s | [HAN] |

Ceased ops

## ROYAL PHNOM PENH AIRWAYS | Phnom-Penh-Air (RL/PPW) | Phnom Penh-Pochentong (PNH)

| | | | | | |
|---|---|---|---|---|---|
| ☐ | XU-070 | AVIC 1 Y-7-100C | 09706 | ex B-3448 | wfs |
| ☐ | XU-071 | AVIC 1 Y-7-100C | 08708 | ex B-3449 | wfs |
| ☐ | XU-072 | AVIC 1 Y-7-100C | 08705 | ex B-3494 | |

## SIEM REAP AIR INTERNATIONAL | Siemreap Air (FT/SRH) | Siem Reap (REP)

A wholly owned subsidiary of Bangkok Air and leases aircraft from parent as required;  some wear joint titles

## SKY WINGS ASIA AIRLINES | (ZA/SWM)

| | | | | | |
|---|---|---|---|---|---|
| ☐ | XU-ZAA | McDonnell-Douglas MD-83 | 49390/1269 | ex UR-CEL | <KHO♦ |
| ☐ | XU-ZAB | Airbus A320-231 | 0476 | ex N476PB | ♦ |

| | | | | | |
|---|---|---|---|---|---|
| **TONLE SAP AIRLINES** | | | **(K9)** | | |
| ☐ | OM-BEX | Boeing 737-382 | 24365/1695 | ex Z3-AAN | <AXE♦ |
| ☐ | XU-TSB | Boeing 737-7L9/W | 28007/136 | ex (D-ALAD) | ♦ |
| ☐ | XU-TSC | Boeing 757-256/W | 26251/897 | ex YL-BDB | <BTI♦ |

## XY- MYANMAR (Union of Myanmar)

| | | | | | |
|---|---|---|---|---|---|
| **AIR BAGAN** | | | **(W9/JAB)** | | **Yangon (RGN)** |
| ☐ | XY-AGC | Fokker 100 | 11327 | ex G-BXWE | |
| ☐ | XY-AGE | Airbus A310-222 | 320 | ex B-2302 | [RGN] |
| ☐ | XY-AGF | Fokker 100 | 11282 | ex N854US | |
| ☐ | XY-AIC | ATR 42-320 | 0159 | ex N34820 | |
| ☐ | XY-AID | ATR 42-300 | 0152 | ex N34817 | |
| ☐ | XY-AIH | ATR 72-212 | 0469 | ex F-OHFZ | |
| ☐ | XY-AIK | ATR 72-212 | 0592 | ex I-ATSL | ♦ |

| | | | | | |
|---|---|---|---|---|---|
| **AIR KBZ** | | | **(K7/KBZ)** | | |
| ☐ | XY-AIT | ATR 72-212A | 0543 | ex OY-PCK | wfs♦ |
| ☐ | XY-AIW | ATR 42-212A | 0582 | ex EC-HEZ | ♦ |
| ☐ | XY-AIY | ATR 72-212A | 0547 | ex N547NA | ♦ |

| | | | | | |
|---|---|---|---|---|---|
| **AIR MANDALAY** | | | **(6T/LMT)** | | **Mandalay/Yangon (MDL/RGN)** |
| ☐ | XY-AEY | ATR 72-212 | 0393 | ex F-OHFS | |
| ☐ | XY-AIJ | ATR 42-320 | 0268 | ex F-OHRN | |
| ☐ | XY-AIR | ATR 72-212 | 0467 | ex EI-CMJ | |

| | | | | | |
|---|---|---|---|---|---|
| **ASIAN WINGS** | | | **(AW/AWM)** | | |
| ☐ | XY-AIM | ATR 72-212 | 0479 | ex F-OIYA | ♦ |
| ☐ | XY-AIN | ATR 72-212 | 0481 | ex F-OIYB | ♦ |
| ☐ | XY-AIS | ATR 72-212A | 0626 | ex I-ATPA | ♦ |
| ☐ | XY-AIU | ATR 72-212A | 0557 | ex I-ADLN | ♦ |

| | | | | | | |
|---|---|---|---|---|---|---|
| **MYANMA AIRWAYS** | | | **Unionair (UB/UBA)** | | | **Yangon (RGN)** |
| ☐ | XY-ADZ | Fokker F.27 Friendship 600 | 10574 | ex PH-EXF | | [RGN] |
| ☐ | XY-AEQ | Fokker F.27 Friendship 400 | 10294 | ex 5Y-BIP | | [RGN] |
| ☐ | XY-AEZ | ATR 72-212 | 0475 | ex F-OGUO | all-white | |
| ☐ | XY-AGA | Fokker F.28 Fellowship 4000 | 11232 | ex PH-EZG | | |
| ☐ | XY-AGB | Fokker F.28 Fellowship 4000 | 11184 | ex YU-AOH | | |
| ☐ | XY-AGH | Fokker F.28 Fellowship 4000 | 11161 | ex ZS-JAV | | |
| ☐ | XY-AIA | ATR 72-212 | 0422 | ex F-WQNQ | | ♦ |
| ☐ | XY-AIB | ATR 42-320 | 0178 | ex F-WQNM | | |
| ☐ | XY-AIF | ATR 72-212A | 0765 | ex F-W | | |
| ☐ | XY-AIG | ATR 72-212A | 0781 | ex F-WWET | | |
| ☐ | XY-AIO | AVIC MA60 | 0806 | | | |
| ☐ | XY-AIP | AVIC MA60 | 0807 | | | ♦ |
| ☐ | XY-AIQ | AVIC MA60 | 0808 | | | ♦ |

| | | | | | |
|---|---|---|---|---|---|
| **MYANMAR AIRWAYS INTERNATIONAL** | | | **Mtanmar (8M/MMA)** | | **Yangon (RGN)** |
| ☐ | F-GYAZ | Airbus A321-111 | 0519 | ex D-ANJA | <BIE♦ |
| ☐ | XY-AGG | Airbus A320-231 | 0114 | ex S5-AAC | |
| ☐ | XY-AGI | Airbus A320-231 | 0113 | ex S5-AAB | |
| ☐ | XY-AGL | Airbus A320-231 | 0316 | ex M-ABCW | ♦ |
| ☐ | XY-AGM | Airbus A320-231 | 0295 | ex 5B-DBC | ♦ |

| | | | | |
|---|---|---|---|---|
| **YANGON AIRLINES** | | **(HK)** | | **Yangon (RGN)** |

Forced to cease ops by Myanmar authorities 03Dec10

## YA- AFGHANISTAN (State of Afghanistan)

| | | | | | |
|---|---|---|---|---|---|
| **ARIANA AFGHAN AIRLINES** | | | **Ariana (FG/AFG)** | | **Kabul (KBL)** |
| ☐ | YA-FAM | Boeing 727-223 (Raisbeck 3) | 21088/1255 | ex N861AA | |
| ☐ | YA-FAN | Boeing 727-227F (FedEx 3) | 21245/1202 | ex 9L-LFD | [KBL] |
| ☐ | YA-FAS | Boeing 727-223 (Raisbeck 3) | 21388/1345 | ex N876AA | |
| ☐ | YA-FAT | Boeing 727-221/W (Duganair 3) | 22542/1799 | ex 5N-BFY | |
| ☐ | YA-FAY | Boeing 727-228 | 22289/1719 | ex F-GCDH | |

| | | | | | | |
|---|---|---|---|---|---|---|
| ☐ | TC-SGB | Airbus A310-304 | 562 | ex N351LF | Akçaabat | <SGX♦ |
| ☐ | YA-CAQ | Airbus A310-304 | 496 | ex TC-JDA | Kabul | |
| ☐ | YA-CAV | Airbus A310-304ER | 497 | ex TC-JDB | Kandahar | |
| ☐ | YA-DAL | Antonov An-24RV | 57310409 | ex UR-48097 | | |
| ☐ | YA-DAM | Antonov An-24RV | 57310404 | ex YR-BMF | | [KBL] |
| ☐ | YA-GAX | de Havilland DHC-6 Twin Otter 300 | 331 | | | ♦ |
| ☐ | YA-PIB | Boeing 737-4Y0 | 26077/2425 | ex TC-JET | | ♦ |
| ☐ | YA-PIR | Boeing 737-232 (Nordam 3) | 23077/996 | ex N305DL | | ♦ |

## EAST HORIZON AIRLINES — Kabul (KBL)

| | | | | | |
|---|---|---|---|---|---|
| ☐ | YA-EHA01 | CASA C.212-CB | 096 | ex T.12B-53 | ♦ |
| ☐ | YA-EHA02 | CASA C.212.CB | 096 | ex T.12B-18 | ♦ |
| ☐ | YA-EHA03 | CASA C.212.CB | 031 | ex T.12B-23 | ♦ |
| ☐ | YA-EHA04 | CASA C.212-CB | 099 | ex T.12B-48 | ♦ |
| ☐ | YA-PAD | Hawker-Siddeley HS.748 Srs.2B/426 | 1799 | ex 4R-SER | ♦ |

## FAZA AIR

| | | | | | |
|---|---|---|---|---|---|
| ☐ | YA-FZA | Mil Mi-8T | 4864 | | ♦ |
| ☐ | YZ-FZB | Mil Mi-8T | 9754360 | | ♦ |

## KABUL AIR — Kabul (KBL)

| | | | | | |
|---|---|---|---|---|---|
| ☐ | YA-KAB | Mil Mi-8T | 98628503 | ex RA-24460 | ♦ |
| ☐ | YA-KAJ | Mil Mi-8T | 43601 | ex RA-25551 | ♦ |
| ☐ | YA-KAL | Antonov An-26 | 7505 | ex RA-26171 | ♦ |
| ☐ | YA-KAO | Mil Mi-8T | 8162 | ex RA-06119 | ♦ |

## KAM AIR — Kamgar (RQ/KMF) — Kabul (KBL)

| | | | | | |
|---|---|---|---|---|---|
| ☐ | YA-KME | Mil Mi-8AMT | 00804092692U | ex EX-40004 | ♦ |
| ☐ | YA-KMH | Mil Mi-8AMT | 00804092601U | ex EX-40003 | ♦ |
| ☐ | YA-KMJ | Mil Mi-171 | | | ♦ |
| ☐ | YA-KMK | Mil Mi-8T | 94235 | | ♦ |
| ☐ | YA-KML | Mil Mi-8MTV-1 | 95219 | | ♦ |
| ☐ | YA-KMM | Mil Mi-8MTV-1 | 94385 | | ♦ |
| ☐ | YA-KMN | Mil Mi-8MTV-1 | 93295 | | ♦ |
| ☐ | YA-KMP | Mil Mi-8MTV-1 | 103M01 | ex Bulgarian AF 401 | ♦ |
| ☐ | YA-KMR | Mil Mi-8T | 4286 | | ♦ |
| ☐ | YA-KMS | Mil Mi-8T | 9743808 | | ♦ |
| ☐ | YA-KMT | Mil Mi-8T | 4285 | | ♦ |
| ☐ | YA-KMU | Mil Mi-8T | 9733102 | | ♦ |
| ☐ | YA-KMV | Mil Mi-8T | 4774 | | ♦ |
| ☐ | YA-KMW | Mil Mi-8T | 98308444 | ex ST-SHR | ♦ |
| ☐ | YA-KMX | Mil Mi-8T | | | ♦ |
| ☐ | YA-KMY | Mil Mi-8T | 10317 | ex LZ-CAL | ♦ |
| ☐ | YA-KMZ | Mil Mi-8T | 99150947 | | ♦ |
| ☐ | YA-WTA | Mil Mi-8AMT | | | ♦ |
| ☐ | YA-WTB | Mil Mi-8AMT | 000804092604u | ex EX-40006 | ♦ |
| ☐ | YA-WTC | Mil Mi-8MTV-1 | 108M33 | ex Czech AF 0833 | ♦ |
| ☐ | YA-WTF | Mil Mi-8MTV-1 | 95490 | ex EX-911 | ♦ |
| | | | | | |
| ☐ | YA-KAM | Boeing 767-222 | 21879/49 | ex N619UA | |
| ☐ | YA-KMA | Airbus A320-231 | 0362 | ex VT-EYC | ♦ |
| ☐ | YA-KMB | Antonov An-26B | 17311802 | ex EK-26199 | |
| ☐ | YA-KMC | Antonov An-24RV | 37309008 | ex Z3-AAI | |
| ☐ | YA-KMD | McDonnell-Douglas MD-83 | 49785/1628 | ex EI-CIW | |
| ☐ | YA-KMF | McDonnell-Douglas MD-82 | 49704/1490 | ex N959U | ♦ |
| ☐ | YA-KMG | McDonnell-Douglas MD-83 | 49567/1367 | ex N9306T | |
| ☐ | YA-VIA | Cessna 421B | 421B0312 | ex N241DR | ♦ |

## KHORSAN AIR

| | | | | | |
|---|---|---|---|---|---|
| ☐ | YA-KHA | Mil Mi-8T | 1447 | ex EX-801 | ♦ |
| ☐ | YA-KHB | Mil Mi-8T | 9744015 | ex EX-802 | ♦ |
| ☐ | YA-KHC | Mil Mi-8T | 3186 | ex EX-804 | ♦ |
| ☐ | YA-KHD | Mil Mi-8T | 9754943 | ex EX-803 | ♦ |
| ☐ | YA-KHE | Mil Mi-8T | 9744109 | ex EX-40001 | ♦ |

## PAMIR AIR — Pamir (NR/PIR) — Kabul (KBL)

| | | | | | |
|---|---|---|---|---|---|
| ☐ | YA-CAH | Antonov An-24RV | 37308605 | ex ER-AWR | ♦ |
| ☐ | YA-CAJ | Antonov An-24RV | 87310810B | ex ER-AFB | ♦ |
| ☐ | YA-PID | Boeing 737-4Y0 | 26085/2468 | ex TC-JEV | [KBL] |

Ceased ops Mar11

## SAFI AIRWAYS | (4Q/SFW) | Kabul (KBL)

| | Reg | Type | MSN | ex | Name | |
|---|---|---|---|---|---|---|
| ☐ | YA-AQS | Boeing 767-2J6ER | 23745/156 | ex B-2554 | City of Kabul | |
| ☐ | YA-HSB | Boeing 737-3J6 | 23303/1237 | ex B-2532 | City of Mazar | |
| ☐ | YA-SFL | Boeing 737-3J6 | 23302/1224 | ex B-2531 | City of Heart | |
| ☐ | YA-TTC | Airbus A320-212 | 0671 | ex 9A-CTM | | |
| ☐ | YA-TTD | Airbus A320-214 | 0994 | ex b-2416 | City of Kandahar | ♦ |

## YI- IRAQ (Republic of Iraq)

## ALNASER AIRLINES | (6N)

| | | | | | |
|---|---|---|---|---|---|
| ☐ | JY-SOP | Boeing 767-233 | 22526/92 | ex JY-JRF | ♦ |
| ☐ | YI-APY | Boeing 737-201 (Nordam 3) | 22274/682 | ex J2-KCM | |
| ☐ | YI-APZ | Boeing 737-201 (Nordam 3) | 22354/736 | ex JY-JRA | <RFJ♦ |
| ☐ | YI-AQS | Boeing 737-48E | 25765/2335 | ex N765TA | ♦ |

## AZMAR AIRLINES

Status uncertain

## IRAQI AIRWAYS | Iraqi (IA/IAW) | Baghdad-Al Muthana/Intl (BGW/SDA)

| | | | | | | |
|---|---|---|---|---|---|---|
| ☐ | YI-AQA | Canadair CRJ-900NG | 15189 | ex C-FULE | | ♦ |
| ☐ | YI-AQB | Canadair CRJ-900NG | 15202 | ex C-FWPF | | ♦ |
| ☐ | YI-AQC | Canadair CRJ-900NG | 15213 | ex C-FWZH | | ♦ |
| ☐ | YI-AQD | Canadair CRJ-900NG | 15220 | ex C-FYED | | ♦ |
| ☐ | YI-AQE | Canadair CRJ-900NG | 15265 | ex C-GZQU | | ♦ |
| ☐ | YI-AQF | Canadair CRJ-900NG | 15266 | ex C-GICN | | ♦ |
| ☐ | YI-APW | Boeing 737-2B7 (Nordam 3) | 22885/966 | ex 9L-LEG | Lsd fr/op by TBN | |
| ☐ | YI-AQK | Boeing 737-7BD/W | 33935/2315 | ex N331AT | | |
| ☐ | YI-AQL | Boeing 737-7BD/W | 35789/2201 | ex N317AT | | |
| ☐ | YI-AQM | Boeing 767-33P6ER | 26235/502 | ex N90GV | | ♦ |
| ☐ | YI-AQQ | Boeing 747-446 | 27099/1031 | ex JY- | | |

## KURDISTAN AIRWAYS | Erbil /Beirut (EBL/BEY)

Leases Boeing 737-200 aircraft from Dolphin Air as required

## YJ- VANUATU (Republic of Vanuatu)

## AIR SAFARIS

| | | | | | |
|---|---|---|---|---|---|
| ☐ | YJ-CCM | Cessna A.185F Skywagon | 18503403 | ex N18TK | ♦ |

## AIR VANUATU | Air Van (NF/AVN) | Port Vila (VLI)

| | | | | | |
|---|---|---|---|---|---|
| ☐ | YJ-AV1 | Boeing 737-8Q8/W | 30734/2477 | ex N1779B | Spirit of Vanuatu |
| ☐ | YJ-AV3 | Britten-Norman BN-2A-21 Islander | 483 | ex F-OCXP | |
| ☐ | YJ-AV4 | Harbin Y-12 IV | 028 | ex B-958L | |
| ☐ | YJ-AV5 | Harbin Y-12 IV | 029 | ex B-978L | |
| ☐ | YJ-AV6 | Harbin Y-12 IV | 032 | ex B-979L | |
| ☐ | YJ-AV72 | ATR 72-212A | 0876 | ex F-WNUG | |
| ☐ | YJ-RV10 | de Havilland DHC-6 Twin Otter 300 | 679 | ex OY-SLI | Melanesian Princess |
| ☐ | YJ-RV16 | Britten-Norman BN-2A-27 Islander | 104 | ex ZK-FLU | |
| ☐ | YJ- | Britten-Norman BN-2B-207 Islander | 2172 | ex JA5290 | |

## UNITY AIRLINES | Port Vila (VLI)

| | | | | | |
|---|---|---|---|---|---|
| ☐ | YJ-009 | Britten-Norman BN-2A-26 Islander | 65 | ex V7-0009 | |

## YK- SYRIA (Syrian Arab Republic)

## CHAM WINGS AIRLINES | Damascus (DAM)

Status uncertain

## SYRIANAIR | Syrianair (RB/SYR) | Damascus (DAM)

| | | | | | |
|---|---|---|---|---|---|
| ☐ | YK-AKA | Airbus A320-232 | 0886 | ex F-WWDH | Ugarit |
| ☐ | YK-AKB | Airbus A320-232 | 0918 | ex F-WWIJ | Ebla |
| ☐ | YK-AKC | Airbus A320-232 | 1032 | ex F-WWDV | Afamia |

542

| | | | | | | |
|---|---|---|---|---|---|---|
| ☐ | YK-AKD | Airbus A320-232 | 1076 | ex F-WWIK | Mari | |
| ☐ | YK-AKE | Airbus A320-232 | 1085 | ex F-WWIX | Bosra | |
| ☐ | YK-AKF | Airbus A320-232 | 1117 | ex F-WWBN | Amrit | |
| ☐ | YK-ANA | Antonov An-24B | 87304203 | | | |
| ☐ | YK-ANC | Antonov An-26 | 3007 | | | Govt operated |
| ☐ | YK-AND | Antonov An-26 | 3008 | | | Govt operated |
| ☐ | YK-ANE | Antonov An-26 | 3103 | | | Govt operated |
| ☐ | YK-ANF | Antonov An-26 | 3104 | | | Govt operated |
| ☐ | YK-ANG | Antonov An-26B | 10907 | | | Govt operated |
| ☐ | YK-ANH | Antonov An-26B | 11406 | | | Govt operated |
| ☐ | YK-AQA | Yakovlev Yak-40 | 9341932 | | | Govt operated |
| ☐ | YK-AQB | Yakovlev Yak-40 | 9530443 | | | Govt operated |
| ☐ | YK-AQD | Yakovlev Yak-40 | 9830158 | | | VIP Govt operated |
| ☐ | YK-AQE | Yakovlev Yak-40K | 9830258 | | | Govt operated |
| ☐ | YK-AQF | Yakovlev Yak-40 | 9931859 | | | Govt operated |
| ☐ | YK-AQG | Yakovlev Yak-40K | 9941959 | | | Govt operated |
| ☐ | YK-AGB | Boeing 727-294 | 21204/1194 | | Damascus | [DAM] |
| ☐ | YK-AGD | Boeing 727-269 | 22360/1670 | ex 9K-AFB | | [DAM] |
| ☐ | YK-AHA | Boeing 747SP-94 | 21174/284 | | 16 Novembre | [DAM] |
| ☐ | YK-AHB | Boeing 747SP-94 | 21175/290 | | Arab Solidarity | [DAM] |
| ☐ | YK-ATA | Ilyushin Il-76TD | 093421613 | | | Govt operated |
| ☐ | YK-ATB | Ilyushin Il-76T | 093421619 | | | Govt operated |
| ☐ | YK-ATC | Ilyushin Il-76T | 0013431911 | | | Govt operated |
| ☐ | YK-ATD | Ilyushin Il-76T | 0013431915 | | | Govt operated |
| ☐ | YK-AHA | Boeing 747SP-94 | 21174/284 | | 16 Novembre | [DAM] |
| ☐ | YK-AHB | Boeing 747SP-94 | 21175/290 | | Arab Solidarity | [DAM] |
| ☐ | YK-AYA | Tupolev Tu-134B-3 | 63992 | | | |
| ☐ | YK-AYB | Tupolev Tu-134B-3 | 63994 | | | |
| ☐ | YK-AYE | Tupolev Tu-134B-3 | 66187 | | | |
| ☐ | YK-AYF | Tupolev Tu-134B-3 | 63190 | | | [DAM] |

## YL-   LATVIA (Republic of Latvia)

### AIRBALTIC — AirBaltic (BT/BTI) — Riga-Spilve (RIX)

| | | | | | | |
|---|---|---|---|---|---|---|
| ☐ | YL-BBI | Boeing 737-33A/W | 27454/2703 | ex PT-SSQ | | |
| ☐ | YL-BBJ | Boeing 737-36Q/W | 30333/3117 | ex D-ADIA | | |
| ☐ | YL-BBK | Boeing 737-33V/W | 29332/3072 | ex HA-LKR | | |
| ☐ | YL-BBL | Boeing 737-33V/W | 29334/3089 | ex HA-LKS | | |
| ☐ | YL-BBR | Boeing 737-31S | 29266/3092 | ex G-OTDA | | |
| ☐ | YL-BBS | Boeing 737-31S | 29267/3093 | ex G-GSPN | | |
| ☐ | YL-BBX | Boeing 737-36Q/W | 30334/3120 | ex D-ADIB | | |
| ☐ | YL-BBY | Boeing 737-36Q/W | 30335/3129 | ex D-ADIC | | |
| ☐ | YL-BBD | Boeing 737-53S | 29075/3101 | ex F-GJNU | | |
| ☐ | YL-BBE | Boeing 737-53S | 29073/3083 | ex EI-DDT | | |
| ☐ | YL-BBM | Boeing 737-522 | 26680/2366 | ex N680MV | | |
| ☐ | YL-BBN | Boeing 737-522 | 26683/2368 | ex N683MV | | |
| ☐ | YL-BBP | Boeing 737-522 | 26688/2404 | ex N688MV | | |
| ☐ | YL-BBQ | Boeing 737-522 | 26691/2408 | ex N691MV | | |
| ☐ | YL-BAE | de Havilland DHC-8-402Q | 4289 | ex C-FZGL | | |
| ☐ | YL-BAF | de Havilland DHC-8-402Q | 4293 | ex C-GAUI | | |
| ☐ | YL-BAH | de Havilland DHC-8-402Q | 4296 | ex C-GBJA | | |
| ☐ | YL-BAI | de Havilland DHC-8-402Q | 4302 | ex C-GCKV | | |
| ☐ | YL-BAJ | de Havilland DHC-8-402Q | 4309 | ex C-GCQG | | |
| ☐ | YL-BAQ | de Havilland DHC-8-402Q | 4313 | ex C-GDDU | | |
| ☐ | YL-BAX | de Havilland DHC-8-402Q | 4324 | ex C-GLTI | | |
| ☐ | YL-BAY | de Havilland DHC-8-402Q | 4331 | ex C-GKLC | | |
| ☐ | YL-BAA | Fokker 50 | 20120 | ex SE-LEB | | |
| ☐ | YL-BAC | Fokker 50 | 20216 | ex SE-LFS | | |
| ☐ | YL-BAO | Fokker 50 | 20189 | ex YL-LAO | | |
| ☐ | YL-BAR | Fokker 50 | 20149 | ex PH-LVL | Cesis | |
| ☐ | YL-BAS | Fokker 50 | 20162 | ex OY-KAE | Zemgale | |
| ☐ | YL-BAT | Fokker 50 | 20163 | ex OY-KAF | Riga | |
| ☐ | YL-BAU | Fokker 50 | 20126 | ex PH-AAO | | |
| ☐ | YL-BAV | Fokker 50 | 20190 | ex YL-BAV | | ♦ |
| ☐ | YL-BAW | Fokker 50 | 20148 | ex OY-MMS | | |
| ☐ | YY-BAZ | Fokker 50 | 20153 | ex YL-BAZ | | ♦ |
| ☐ | YL-BDB | Boeing 757-256/W | 26251/897 | ex EC-HDR | | >K9 |
| ☐ | YL-BDC | Boeing 757-256/W | 26253/902 | ex EC-HDU | | |

### RAF-AVIA — Mitavia (MTL) — Riga-Spilve (RIX)

| | | | | | |
|---|---|---|---|---|---|
| ☐ | YL-RAA | Antonov An-26B | 97311206 | ex RA-26064 | |
| ☐ | YL-RAB | Antonov An-26B | 07310508 | ex RA-26032 | ACS logo |

Page 543

| | Reg | Type | c/n | ex | Notes |
|---|---|---|---|---|---|
| ☐ | YL-RAC | Antonov An-26 | 07309903 | ex CCCP-79169 | ACS logo |
| ☐ | YL-RAD | Antonov An-26B | 47313909 | ex RA-26589 | |
| ☐ | YL-RAE | Antonov An-26B | 57314004 | ex CCCP-26200 | |
| ☐ | YL-RAJ | Antonov An-26B | 47313905 | ex UR-DWA | ♦ |
| ☐ | YL-RAG | SAAB SF.340A | 340A-052 | ex SE-E52 | Frtr |
| ☐ | YL-RAH | SAAB SF.340A | 340A-081 | ex EC-IRD | Frtr |

**SMARTLYNX** — (6Y/ART) — Riga-Spilve (RIX)

| | Reg | Type | c/n | ex | Notes |
|---|---|---|---|---|---|
| ☐ | YL-BBC | Airbus A320-211 | 0142 | ex SX-BVD | |
| ☐ | YL-LCA | Airbus A320-211 | 0333 | ex 4X-ABC | [BUD] |
| ☐ | YL-LCC | Airbus A320-211 | 0310 | ex C-FKPS | |
| ☐ | YL-LCD | Airbus A320-211 | 0359 | ex C-FMSV | |
| ☐ | YL-LCE | Airbus A320-211 | 0311 | ex F-HDCE | >LLC |
| ☐ | YL-LCH | Airbus A320-212 | 0426 | ex | 4X-ABH |
| ☐ | YL-LCI | Airbus A320-214 | 0724 | ex F-WTAO | ♦ |
| ☐ | YL-LCY | Boeing 767-3Y0ER | 24952/357 | ex C-GGFJ | >BBR |
| ☐ | YL-LCZ | Boeing 767-3Y0ER | 25000/386 | ex C-GHPA | >BBR |

## YN- NICARAGUA (Republic of Nicaragua)

**ATLANTIC AIRWAYS** — Atlantic Nicaragua (AYN) — Managua (MGA)

| | Reg | Type | c/n | ex | Notes |
|---|---|---|---|---|---|
| ☐ | YN-CFL | LET L-410UVP-E3 | 871917 | ex OK-SDH | |
| ☐ | YN-CFM | LET L-410UVP-E20 | 571916 | ex OE-SDG | ♦ |
| ☐ | YN-CFR | LET L-410UVP-E | 861705 | ex TG-CFD | |

**LA COSTENA** — Lacostena — Managua (MGA)

| | Reg | Type | c/n | ex | Notes |
|---|---|---|---|---|---|
| ☐ | YN-CFO | Cessna 208B Caravan I | 208B0758 | ex N5264M | |
| ☐ | YN-CGB | Cessna 208B Caravan I | 208B0611 | ex HP-1407APP | |
| ☐ | YN-CGS | Cessna 208B Caravan I | 208B0871 | ex YV-184T | ♦ |
| ☐ | YN-CGU | Cessna 208B Caravan I | 208B0607 | ex HP-1400 | |
| ☐ | YN-CHA | Cessna 208B Caravan I | 208B0614 | ex TI-BBL | ♦ |
| ☐ | YN-CHG | ATR 42-320 | 0323 | ex F-OHGL | |

## YR- ROMANIA (Republic of Romania)

**AIR BUCHAREST** — (BUR)

| | Reg | Type | c/n | ex | Notes |
|---|---|---|---|---|---|
| ☐ | YR-TIB | BOEING 737-3L9 | 27924/2760 | ex OE-ITA | ♦ |

**ALFA AIR ROMANIA**

| | Reg | Type | c/n | ex | Notes |
|---|---|---|---|---|---|
| ☐ | YR-ANJ | BAe146 Srs.200 | E2079 | ex G-MIMA | ♦ |

**BLUE AIR** — Blue Transport (0B/JOR) — Bucharest-Baneasa (BBU)

| | Reg | Type | c/n | ex | Notes |
|---|---|---|---|---|---|
| ☐ | YR-BAE | Boeing 737-4Y0 | 28723/2886 | ex EI-CXL | |
| ☐ | YR-BAJ | Boeing 737-430 | 27002/2323 | ex EI-COI | |
| ☐ | YR-BAK | Boeing 737-430 | 27005/2359 | ex EI-COJ | |
| ☐ | YR-BAL | Boeing 737-484 | 25314/2124 | ex N134AS | ♦ |
| ☐ | YR-BAM | Boeing 737-4Q8 | 26302/2620 | ex SE-RJA | ♦ |
| ☐ | YR-BAN | Boeing 737-4Q8 | 26306/2653 | ex 4L-TGT | ♦ |
| ☐ | YR-BAC | Boeing 737-377 | 23653/1260 | ex ZK-SLA | <AWK |
| ☐ | YR-BAF | Boeing 737-322F | 24453/1730 | ex N360UA | |
| ☐ | YR-BAG | Boeing 737-5L9 | 24778/1816 | ex N494ST | |

**CARPATAIR** — Carpatair (V3/KRP) — Timisoara-Giarmata (TSR)

| | Reg | Type | c/n | ex | Notes |
|---|---|---|---|---|---|
| ☐ | YR-SBB | SAAB 2000 | 2000-026 | ex HB-IZN | |
| ☐ | YR-SBC | SAAB 2000 | 2000-039 | ex HB-IZW | |
| ☐ | YR-SBD | SAAB 2000 | 2000-004 | ex HB-IZA | |
| ☐ | YR-SBE | SAAB 2000 | 2000-041 | ex HB-IZX | |
| ☐ | YR-SBJ | SAAB 2000 | 2000-018 | ex HB-IZK | |
| ☐ | YR-SBK | SAAB 2000 | 2000-033 | ex HB-IZR | |
| ☐ | YR-SBN | SAAB 2000 | 2000-044 | ex SE-LSC | |
| ☐ | YR-SFB | SAAB 2000 | 2000-022 | ex ER-SFB | ♦ |
| ☐ | YR-FKA | Fokker 100 | 11340 | ex C-GKZC | |
| ☐ | YR-FKB | Fokker 100 | 11369 | ex C-GKZK | |
| ☐ | YR-FZA | Fokker 100 | 11395 | ex ER-FZA | ♦ |
| ☐ | YR-KMA | Fokker 70 | 11564 | ex HA-LMA | |
| ☐ | YR-KMB | Fokker 70 | 11565 | ex HA-LMB | |
| ☐ | YR-KMC | Fokker 70 | 11569 | ex HA-LMC | |

## DIRECT AERO SERVICES (DSV)

| | | | | | | |
|---|---|---|---|---|---|---|
| ☐ | YR-DAA | SAAB SF.340A | 340A-116 | ex SE-F16 | | ♦ |
| ☐ | YR-DAC | SAAB SF.340A | 340A-117 | ex SE-F17 | | ♦ |
| ☐ | YR-DAH | SAAB SF.340A | 340A-091 | ex SE-LJL | | ♦ |

## JETRAN INTERNATIONAL AIRWAYS — Air Romania (RRM) — Bucharest-Baneasa (BBU)

| | | | | | |
|---|---|---|---|---|---|
| ☐ | YR-OTN | McDonnell-Douglas MD-82 | 49119/1070 | ex YR-MDM | |

## MEDALLION AIR — Medals (MDP) — Bucharest-Baneasa (BBU)

| | | | | | |
|---|---|---|---|---|---|
| ☐ | YR-HBB | McDonnell-Douglas MD-83 | 53186/2092 | ex TC-AKN | [IST]♦ |
| ☐ | YR-HBD | McDonnell-Douglas MD-83 | 49808/1836 | ex I-SMEC | ♦ |
| ☐ | YR-HBE | McDonnell-Douglas MD-83 | 49396/1305 | ex EC-GNY | >RVL |
| ☐ | YR-HBY | McDonnell-Douglas MD-83 | 49950/1913 | ex N347BF | ♦ |

## MIA AIRLINES — Salline (JLA) — Bucharest-Baneasa (BBU)

| | | | | | |
|---|---|---|---|---|---|
| ☐ | YR-HRS | BAC One-Eleven 488GH (QTA 3) | 259 | ex G-MAAH | |
| ☐ | YR-MIA | BAC One-Eleven 492GM (QTA 3) | 260 | ex HR-ATS | Mirjane |

## ROMAVIA — Aeromavia (WQ/RMV) — Bucharest-Baneasa/Otopeni (BBU/OTP)

| | | | | | | |
|---|---|---|---|---|---|---|
| ☐ | YR-ABB | Boeing 707-3K1C (Comtran 2) | 20804/883 | | CarpatiRomania titles | VIP [OTP] |
| ☐ | YR-BEC | British Aerospace 146-200 | E2062 | ex G-CEVF | | ♦ |

## TAROM — Tarom (RO/ROT) — Bucharest-Otopeni (OTP)

| | | | | | | |
|---|---|---|---|---|---|---|
| ☐ | YR-ATA | ATR 42-500 | 0566 | ex F-WWLF | Dunarea | |
| ☐ | YR-ATB | ATR 42-500 | 0569 | ex F-WWLH | Bistrita | |
| ☐ | YR-ATC | ATR 42-500 | 0589 | ex F-WWLR | Mures | |
| ☐ | YR-ATD | ATR 42-500 | 0591 | ex F-WWLS | Cris | |
| ☐ | YR-ATE | ATR 42-500 | 0596 | ex F-WWLY | Olt | |
| ☐ | YR-ATF | ATR 42-500 | 0599 | ex F-WWEB | Arges | |
| ☐ | YR-ATG | ATR 42-500 | 0605 | ex F-WWLG | Dambovita | |
| ☐ | YR-ATH | ATR 72-212 | 0861 | ex F-WWEH | Somes | |
| ☐ | YR-ATI | ATR 72-212 | 0867 | ex F-WWER | Ialomita | |
| ☐ | YR-BGA | Boeing 737-38J | 27179/2524 | ex N5573K | Alba Iulia | |
| ☐ | YR-BGB | Boeing 737-38J | 27180/2529 | | Bucuresti | |
| ☐ | YR-BGD | Boeing 737-38J | 27182/2663 | | Devaspecial c/s | |
| ☐ | YR-BGE | Boeing 737-38J | 27395/2671 | | Timisoara | |
| ☐ | YR-BGF | Boeing 737-78J/W | 28440/795 | | Brâila | |
| ☐ | YR-BGG | Boeing 737-78J/W | 28442/827 | | Craiova | |
| ☐ | YR-BGH | Boeing 737-78J/W | 28438/1394 | | Hunedoara | |
| ☐ | YR-BGI | Boeing 737-78J/W | 28439/1419 | | Iasi | |
| ☐ | YR-BGS | Boeing 737-8GJ/W | 37360/2783 | ex N1787B | Sibiu | o/o |
| ☐ | YR-LCA | Airbus A310-325 | 636 | ex F-WQAV | Transilvania | |
| ☐ | YR-LCB | Airbus A310-325 | 644 | ex F-WQAX | Moldova | |
| ☐ | YR-ASA | Airbus A318-111 | 2931 | ex D-AUAC | Aurel Vlaicu - Aviation Pioneer | |
| ☐ | YR-ASB | Airbus A318-111 | 2955 | ex D-AUAE | Traian Vuia - Aviation Pioneer | |
| ☐ | YR-ASC | Airbus A318-111 | 3220 | ex D-AUAF | Henri Coanda - Aviation Pioneer | |
| ☐ | YR-ASD | Airbus A318-111 | 3225 | ex D-AUAG | | |

## TEND AIR (MDJ)

| | | | | | | |
|---|---|---|---|---|---|---|
| ☐ | YR-MDJ | McDonnell-Douglas MD-81 | 48053/986 | ex 3D-JET | all-white | wfs♦ |
| ☐ | YR-MDK | McDonnell-Douglas MD-82 | 49139/1090 | ex N822US | | Stage 4 demonstrator♦ |
| ☐ | YR-MDL | McDonnell-Douglas MD-82 | 48079/1016 | ex N991PG | | [BBU]♦ |
| ☐ | YR-MDR | McDonnell-Douglas MD-82 | 48097/1059 | ex TC-MNR | all-white | ♦ |
| ☐ | YR-MDS | McDonnell-Douglas MD-82 | 48098/1060 | ex TC-MNS | | ♦ |
| ☐ | YR-MDT | McDonnell-Douglas MD-82 | 49570/1440 | ex EC-GTO | | wfs♦ |

## TIRIAC AIR

| | | | | | |
|---|---|---|---|---|---|
| ☐ | YR-TAO | Agusta AW139 | 31122 | ex HB-ZJJ | |

## YS- EL SALVADOR (Republic of El Salvador)

## TACA INTERNATIONAL AIRLINES — Taca (TA/TAI) — San Salvador-Comalapa Intl (SAL)

| | | | | | |
|---|---|---|---|---|---|
| ☐ | N476TA | Airbus A319-132 | 1934 | ex D-AVWH | |
| ☐ | N477TA | Airbus A319-132 | 1952 | ex D-AVWK | |
| ☐ | N478TA | Airbus A319-132 | 2339 | ex D-AVWG | Aviateca titles |
| ☐ | N479TA | Airbus A319-132 | 2444 | ex D-AVWS | Aviateca titles |
| ☐ | N480TA | Airbus A319-132 | 3057 | ex D-AVYV | |

| | | | | |
|---|---|---|---|---|
| ☐ N520TA | Airbus A319-132 | 3248 | ex D-AVWH | |
| ☐ N990TA | Airbus A319-112 | 1958 | ex XA-UAQ | |
| ☐ N991TA | Airbus A319-112 | 1625 | ex N62TY | ♦ |
| ☐ N992TA | Airbus A319-112 | 2066 | ex N602CT | >AVA♦ |
| | | | | |
| ☐ EI-TAB | Airbus A320-233 | 1624 | ex N485TA  Mensajero de Esperanza | |
| ☐ EI-TAD | Airbus A320-233 | 1334 | ex N462TA | |
| ☐ EI-TAG | Airbus A320-233 | 2791 | ex (N495TA) | |
| ☐ N490TA | Airbus A320-232 | 2282 | ex F-WWBO | |
| ☐ N492TA | Airbus A320-233 | 2434 | ex F-WWDL | |
| ☐ N493TA | Airbus A320-233 | 2917 | ex F-WWDR | |
| ☐ N494TA | Airbus A320-233 | 3042 | ex F-WWDM | |
| ☐ N495TA | Airbus A320-233 | 3103 | ex F-WWIH | |
| ☐ N496TA | Airbus A320-233 | 3113 | ex F-WWIU | |
| ☐ N497TA | Airbus A320-233 | 3378 | ex F-WWDK | |
| ☐ N498TA | Airbus A320-233 | 3418 | ex F-WWIO | |
| ☐ N499TA | Airbus A320-233 | 3510 | ex F-WWBX | |
| ☐ N680TA | Airbus A320-233 | 3538 | ex F-WWIF | |
| ☐ N681TA | Airbus A320-233 | 3577 | ex F-WWBO | |
| ☐ N682TA | Airbus A320-233 | 3581 | ex F-WWDC | |
| ☐ N683TA | Airbus A320-233 | 4906 | ex F-WWDE | |
| ☐ N684TA | Airbus A320-233 | 4944 | ex F-WWBZ | ♦ |
| ☐ N685TA | Airbus A320-233 | 5068 | ex D-AUBF | ♦ |
| | | | | |
| ☐ N564TA | Airbus A321-231 | 2862 | ex D-AVZB | |
| ☐ N566TA | Airbus A321-231 | 2553 | ex D-AVZJ | |
| ☐ N567TA | Airbus A321-231 | 2610 | ex D-AVZM | |
| ☐ N568TA | Airbus A321-231 | 2687 | ex D-AVZE | |
| ☐ N570TA | Airbus A321-231 | 3869 | ex D-AVZO | |
| | | | | |
| ☐ N935TA | Embraer ERJ-190AR | 19000205 | ex TI-BCF | |
| ☐ N936TA | Embraer ERJ-190AR | 19000215 | ex TI-BCG | ♦ |
| ☐ N937TA | Embraer ERJ-190AR | 19000221 | ex TI-BCH | ♦ |
| ☐ N938TA | Embraer ERJ-190AR | 19000228 | ex TI-BCI | ♦ |
| ☐ N982TA | Embraer ERJ-190AR | 19000259 | ex PT-STH | ♦ |
| ☐ N983TA | Embraer ERJ-190AR | 19000265 | ex PT-TLF | |
| ☐ N984TA | Embraer ERJ-190AR | 19000273 | ex PT-TLN | |
| ☐ N985TA | Embraer ERJ-190AR | 19000287 | ex PT-TZB | |
| ☐ N986TA | Embraer ERJ-190AR | 19000360 | ex PT-XNB | |
| ☐ N987TA | Embraer ERJ-190AR | 19000393 | ex PT-XNZ | |
| ☐ N989TA | Embraer ERJ-190AR | 19000482 | ex PT-TPH | ♦ |

## YU-   SERBIA (Republic of Serbia)

### AVIOGENEX — Genex (AGX) — Belgrade (BEG)

| | | | | |
|---|---|---|---|---|
| ☐ YU-ANP | Boeing 737-2K3 (Nordam 3) | 23912/1401 | Zadar | |

### JAT AIRWAYS — JAT (JU/JAT) — Belgrade (BEG)

| | | | | |
|---|---|---|---|---|
| ☐ YU-AND | Boeing 737-3H9 | 23329/1134 | | City of Krusevac |
| ☐ YU-ANF | Boeing 737-3H9 | 23330/1136 | | |
| ☐ YU-ANH | Boeing 737-3H9 | 23415/1171 | ex TC-CYO | |
| ☐ YU-ANI | Boeing 737-3H9 | 23416/1175 | ex Z3-AAA | |
| ☐ YU-ANJ | Boeing 737-3H9 | 23714/1305 | ex TC-MIO | |
| ☐ YU-ANK | Boeing 737-3H9 | 23715/1310 | | |
| ☐ YU-ANL | Boeing 737-3H9 | 23716/1321 | ex Z3-ARF | |
| ☐ YU-ANV | Boeing 737-3H9 | 24140/1524 | | |
| ☐ YU-ANW | Boeing 737-3H9 | 24141/1526 | ex TS-IED | |
| ☐ YU-AON | Boeing 737-3Q4 | 24208/1490 | ex N181LF | |
| | | | | |
| ☐ YU-ALN | ATR 72-202 | 0180 | ex F-WWEP | |
| ☐ YU-ALO | ATR 72-202 | 0186 | ex F-WWEW | |
| ☐ YU-ALP | ATR 72-202 | 0189 | ex F-WWED  all-white | |
| ☐ YU-ALS | ATR 72-202 | 0140 | ex ES-KRB | |

## YV-   VENEZUELA (Bolivarian Republic of Venezuela)

### AECA

| | | | | |
|---|---|---|---|---|
| ☐ YV211T | Douglas DC-3 | 10201 | ex HK-2666X | |
| ☐ YV214T | Douglas DC-6 | 43708/347 | ex HK-4046X | |

### AERO CARIBE — Coro

| | | | | |
|---|---|---|---|---|
| ☐ YV1425 | Cessna 402B | 402B0896 | ex YV-617C | ♦ |
| ☐ YV1427 | LET L-410UVP | 841224 | ex YV-595C | |

## AERO EJECUTIVOS — Venejecutiv (VEJ) — Caracas-Simon Bolivar Intl (CCS)

| | | | | |
|---|---|---|---|---|
| ☐ | YV1434 | LET L-410UVP-E3 | 872014 | ex YV-1026CP |
| ☐ | YV1854 | Douglas DC-3 | 6135 | ex YV-500C |
| ☐ | YV201T | Douglas DC-3 | 11775 | ex YV-1179C |
| ☐ | YV-426C | Douglas DC-3 | 4093 | ex N10DC |
| ☐ | YV-440C | Douglas DC-3 | 2201 | ex N31PB   Caballo Viejostatus? |

## AEROBOL - AEROVIAS BOLIVAR — Ciudad Bolivar (CBL)

| | | | | |
|---|---|---|---|---|
| ☐ | YV-315C | Cessna U206G Stationair 6 | U20604323 | ex YV-1465P |
| ☐ | YV-387C | Cessna U206G Stationair 6 | U20605398 | ex YV-1310P |
| ☐ | YV-389C | Cessna U206G Stationair 6 | | |
| ☐ | YV-408C | Cessna U206G Stationair 6 | | |
| ☐ | YV-615C | Cessna U206G Stationair 6 | U20604759 | ex YV-1704P |
| ☐ | YV-849C | Cessna U206G Stationair 6 | | |
| ☐ | YV-946C | Cessna U206G Stationair 6 | | |
| ☐ | YV-270C | Britten-Norman BN-2A-20 Islander | 573 | ex YV-142CP |
| ☐ | YV-288C | Cessna 207A Stationair 8 | 20700708 | ex YV-2143P |
| ☐ | YV-380C | Cessna 207A Stationair 8 | | |

## AEROMED

| | | | | |
|---|---|---|---|---|
| ☐ | YV2027 | LET L-410UVP-E | 861713 | YV-1023CP |

## AEROPOSTAL — Aeropostal (VH/ALV) — Caracas-Simon Bolivar Intl (CCS)

| | | | | | |
|---|---|---|---|---|---|
| ☐ | YV135T | Douglas DC-9-51 | 47713/820 | ex YV-10C | |
| ☐ | YV137T | Douglas DC-9-51 (ABS 3) | 47771/883 | ex YV-15C | |
| ☐ | YV139T | Douglas DC-9-51 | 47695/806 | ex YV-43C | |
| ☐ | YV445T | McDonnell-Douglas MD-82 | 49969/1719 | ex N969AG | ♦ |
| ☐ | YV505T | McDonnell-Douglas MD-82 | 49794/1600 | ex N794AG | ♦ |
| ☐ | YV2793 | McDonnell-Douglas MD-82 | 49796/1713 | ex YV444T | ♦ |

## AEROSERVICIOS OK

| | | | | |
|---|---|---|---|---|
| ☐ | YV1752 | LET L-410UVP-E | 861719 | ex YV-1176C |

## AEROSERVICIOS RANGER — Caracas-La Carlota/Lagunillas/Tumeremo (-/LGY/TMO)

| | | | | |
|---|---|---|---|---|
| ☐ | YV-429C | Bell 206B JetRanger III | 1959 | ex N9910K |
| ☐ | YV-431C | Bell 206B JetRanger III | 2588 | |
| ☐ | YV-433C | Bell 206B JetRanger II | 2106 | ex YV-330CP |
| ☐ | YV-455C | Bell 206B JetRanger | 1481 | ex N218AL |
| ☐ | YV-457C | Bell 206B JetRanger III | 2470 | ex N50056 |
| ☐ | YV-571C | Bell 206B JetRanger | 273 | ex N59Q |
| ☐ | YV-572C | Bell 206B JetRanger | 644 | ex N7906J |
| ☐ | YV1204 | Britten-Norman BN-2A-26 Islander | 56 | ex YV-920C |
| ☐ | YV1241 | Britten-Norman BN-2A-26 Islander | 149 | ex YV-921C |

## AEROVIAS CARIBE EXPRESS

| | | | | | |
|---|---|---|---|---|---|
| ☐ | YV158T | Cessna 208B Caravan I | 208B0444 | ex YV-1088CP | ♦ |

## AIR VENEZUELA

| | | | | | |
|---|---|---|---|---|---|
| ☐ | YV-687CP | Beech 1900C | UB-57 | ex N816BE | ♦ |

## ALBATROS AIRLINES

| | | | | | |
|---|---|---|---|---|---|
| ☐ | YV2484 | Cessna 208B Caravan I | 208B2125 | ex N52691 | ♦ |
| ☐ | YV2489 | Cessna 208B Caravan I | 208B2132 | ex N5183U | ♦ |

## ASAP CHARTER

| | | | | | |
|---|---|---|---|---|---|
| ☐ | YV1404 | Yakovlev Yak-40 | 9441137 | ex YV-1100CP | VIP |

## ASERCA AIRLINES — Aserca (R7/OCA) — Caracas-Simon Bolivar Intl (CCS)

| | | | | | | |
|---|---|---|---|---|---|---|
| ☐ | YV367T | Douglas DC-9-32 | 47128/210 | ex N614NW | Nuestra Señora del Rosario | [CCS] |
| ☐ | YV368T | Douglas DC-9-32 | 47518/614 | ex N619NW | Madre Teresa de Calcuta | |
| ☐ | YV371T | Douglas DC-9-32 | 47235/436 | ex N617NW | San Augustin | |
| ☐ | YV372T | Douglas DC-9-32 | 47575/680 | ex N622NW | Santa Teresa de Jesus | |
| ☐ | YV1879 | Douglas DC-9-31 | 48139/1024 | ex YV114T | Virgen del Pilar | |
| ☐ | YV2220 | Douglas DC-9-31 | 48155/1050 | ex YV297T | Nuestra Señora de Lourdes | |
| ☐ | YV2259 | Douglas DC-9-31 | 48120/949 | ex YV243T | San Miguel Arcangel all green c/s [CCS] | |

| | | | | | | |
|---|---|---|---|---|---|---|
| ☐ | YV2431 | Douglas DC-9-31 | 48119/943 | ex YV242T | San Francisco de Asis | |
| ☐ | YV2433 | Douglas DC-9-31 | 48141/1030 | ex YV244T | San Cristobal | [CCS] |
| ☐ | YV2434 | Douglas DC-9-31 | 47473/598 | ex YV286T | San Judas Tadeo | |
| ☐ | YV2444 | Douglas DC-9-32 (ABS 3) | 47282/446 | ex YV248T | Espiritu Santo | white c/s [CCS] |
| ☐ | YV153T | McDonnell-Douglas MD-82 | 49486/1317 | ex YV388T | | [MIA]♦ |
| ☐ | YV453T | McDonnell-Douglas MD-82 | 49517/1633 | ex N537SH | | ♦ |
| ☐ | YV494T | McDonnell-Douglas MD-82 | 49521/1690 | ex N574SH | | ♦ |
| ☐ | YV2749 | McDonnell-Douglas MD-82 | 49258/1161 | ex N246AA | | ♦ |
| ☐ | YV2754 | McDonnell-Douglas MD-82 | 49259/1161 | ex N248AA | | ♦ |
| ☐ | YV | McDonnell-Douglas MD-82 | 49253/1155 | ex N237AA | | o/o♦ |
| ☐ | YV | McDonnell-Douglas MD-82 | 49257/1160 | ex N245AA | | o/o♦ |

## AVIOR AIRLINES / AVIOR EXPRESS — Avior (9V/ROI) — Barcelona (BLA)

| | | | | | |
|---|---|---|---|---|---|
| ☐ | YV1364 | Beech 1900D | UE-270 | ex YV-401C | |
| ☐ | YV1365 | Beech 1900D | UE-268 | ex YV-402C | |
| ☐ | YV1366 | Beech 1900D | UE-279 | ex YV-403C | |
| ☐ | YV1367 | Beech 1900D | UE-298 | ex YV-404C | |
| ☐ | YV1368 | Beech 1900D | UE-304 | ex YV-406C | |
| ☐ | YV1369 | Beech 1900D | UE-342 | ex YV-438C | >ATK |
| ☐ | YV1370 | Beech 1900D | UE-343 | ex YV-466C | |
| ☐ | YV1372 | Beech 1900D | UE-331 | ex YV-660C | |
| ☐ | YV1373 | Beech 1900D | UE-355 | ex YV-663C | |
| ☐ | YV1374 | Beech 1900D | UE-356 | ex YV-664C | |
| ☐ | YV187T | Boeing 737-2H4 (AvAero 3) | 22964/933 | ex N92SW | |
| ☐ | YV234T | Boeing 737-2H4 (AvAero 3) | 21970/613 | ex YV-643C | |
| ☐ | YV340T | Boeing 737-232 (Nordam 3) | 23079/1003 | ex N307DL | [PZO] |
| ☐ | YV342T | Boeing 737-232 (Nordam 3) | 23090/1020 | ex N318DL | |
| ☐ | YV343T | Boeing 737-232 (Nordam 3) | 23101/1041 | ex N329DL | |
| ☐ | YV488T | Boeing 737-2Y5 (Nordam 3) | 23848/1418 | ex HC-CEQ | |
| ☐ | YV491T | Boeing 737-2T5 (Nordam 3) | 22979/950 | ex HC-CFH | |
| ☐ | YV495T | Boeing 737-2Y5 (Nordam 3) | 23847/1414 | ex HC-CER | |
| ☐ | YV1360 | Boeing 737-201 (Nordam 3) | 21665/534 | ex YV-917C | |
| ☐ | YV1361 | Boeing 737-2H4 (AvAero 3) | 22826/878 | ex N85SW | |
| ☐ | YV2794 | Boeing 737-232 (Nordam 3) | 23089/1019 | ex YV341T | |
| ☐ | YV1766 | Cessna 208B Caravan I | 208B0793 | ex YV-925C | |

## CARIBBEAN FLIGHTS — Valencia Intl (VLN)

| | | | | | |
|---|---|---|---|---|---|
| ☐ | YV-912C | Douglas DC-3 | 14506/25951 | ex CP-2255 | Falcon |

## CHAPI AIR — Marquetia

| | | | | | |
|---|---|---|---|---|---|
| ☐ | YV1416 | Britten-Norman BN-2A Mk.III-2 Trislander | 1034 | ex YV-872C | ♦ |
| ☐ | YV1996 | Britten-Norman BN-2A-7 Islander | 242 | ex YV178T | |
| ☐ | YV2238 | Britten_norman BN-2A-8 Islander | 296 | | ♦ |

## CIACA AIRLINES — Ciudad Bolivar (CBL)

| | | | | | |
|---|---|---|---|---|---|
| ☐ | YV-866CP | LET L-410UVP-E | 861717 | ex HK-4159 | |
| ☐ | YV-978C | LET L-410UVP | 810702 | ex CCCP-67066 | wfs |
| ☐ | YV-1070CP | Yakovlev Yak-40 | 9412032 | ex RA-87388 | |

## COMERAVIA — (CVV) — Cuidad Bolivar (CBL)

| | | | | | |
|---|---|---|---|---|---|
| ☐ | YV396T | Short SD.3-60 | SH3713 | ex G-XPSS | |
| ☐ | YV1232 | LET L-410UVP | 810640 | ex UR-67064 | |
| ☐ | YV1233 | LET L-410UVP | 851427 | ex YV-1185C | |
| ☐ | YV1332 | LET L-410UVP | 831028 | ex YV-906C | |

## CONVIASA — Conviasa (V0/VCV) — Caracas-Simon Bolivar Intl (CCS)

| | | | | | |
|---|---|---|---|---|---|
| ☐ | YV1005 | ATR 42-320 | 0491 | ex F-WQNK | [CCS] |
| ☐ | YV1008 | ATR 42-320 | 0346 | ex F-WQNB | [CCS] |
| ☐ | YV1009 | ATR 42-320 | 0487 | ex F-WQNL | |
| ☐ | YV1850 | ATR 72-201 | 0276 | ex F-WQNE | [CCS] |
| ☐ | YV2421 | ATR 72-212 | 0482 | ex F-WQNB | |
| ☐ | YV2422 | ATR 72-212 | 0486 | ex F-WQNA | |
| ☐ | YV475T | Boeing 737-230 | 22124/727 | ex N214AG | ♦ |
| ☐ | YV476T | Boeing 737-230 | 22121/720 | ex N212AG | |
| ☐ | YV1003 | de Havilland DHC-7-102 | 103 | ex C-FEDO | |
| ☐ | YV1004 | Airbus A340-211 | 031 | ex F-WQTN | |
| ☐ | YV1007 | Boeing 737-322 | 23949/1493 | ex N317UA | |
| ☐ | YV1111 | Canadair CRJ-701ER | 10270 | ex N627CP | ♦ |
| ☐ | YV1115 | Canadair CRJ-702NG | 10271 | ex N628CP | |

| | | | | | |
|---|---|---|---|---|---|
| ☐ | YV2088 | Canadair CRJ-702NG | 10274 | ex N259CP | |
| ☐ | YV2115 | Canadair CRJ-702NG | 10275 | ex N230CP | |
| ☐ | YV2556 | Boeing 737-3G7 | 24712/1869 | ex N311AW | ♦ |
| ☐ | YV2557 | Boeing 737-3G7 | 24633/1809 | ex N306AW | ♦ |
| ☐ | YV2558 | Boeing 737-232 (Nordam 3) | 23096/1028 | ex XA-UIZ | |
| ☐ | YV2559 | Boeing 737-232 (Nordam 3) | 23097/1029 | ex XA-UIY | |

### EL SOL DE AMERICA                    (6S)

| | | | | | |
|---|---|---|---|---|---|
| ☐ | YV397T | Boeing 737-236 | 23225/1102 | ex YV3375 | ♦ |
| ☐ | (YV1415) | Douglas DC-3 | 16013/32761 | ex YV-911C | |
| ☐ | YV2117 | Dornier 28D-2 Skyservant | | | |
| ☐ | YV-1120C | LET L-410UVP | 841329 | ex YV-982C | |

### ESTELAR LATINOAMERICA              (ETR)

| | | | | | |
|---|---|---|---|---|---|
| ☐ | YV497T | Boeing 737-247 | 23603/1361 | ex N632CC | ♦ |
| ☐ | YV498T | Boeing 737-2E3 (AvAero 3) | 22703/811 | ex HC-FCO | ♦ |
| ☐ | YV2722 | Boeing 737-2Y5 (Nordam 3) | 24031/1523 | ex YV399T | ♦ |
| ☐ | YV | Boeing 737-2B7 | 22887/976 | ex N240CD | wfs♦ |

### HELITEC                                                    Maturin (MUN)

| | | | | | |
|---|---|---|---|---|---|
| ☐ | YV171T | Swearingen SA.227AC Metro III | AC-594 | ex YV-1000C | |
| ☐ | YV185T | Swearingen SA.227DC Metro 23 | DC-904B | ex N904NJ | ♦ |
| ☐ | YV221T | Swearingen SA.227DC Metro 23 | DC-878B | ex N6ER | ♦ |
| ☐ | YV1412 | Swearingen SA.227TT Merlin IIIC | TT-465 | ex YV-696CP | |
| ☐ | YV1574 | Swearingen SA.227TT Merlin 300 | TT-435 | ex YV-808CP | |

### KAVOK AIRLINES                      (KVA)

| | | | | | |
|---|---|---|---|---|---|
| ☐ | YV2456 | British Aerospace Jetstream 32 | 884 | ex N476UE | ♦ |
| ☐ | YV2472 | British Aerospace Jetstream 32EP | 973 | ex N973JX | |
| ☐ | YV2532 | British Aerospace Jetstream 32EP | 910 | ex N910AE | [CCS] |

### LAMIA

| | | | | | |
|---|---|---|---|---|---|
| ☐ | YV2787 | Avro 146-RJ85 | E2349 | ex EI-RJL | o/o♦ |
| ☐ | YV | Avro 146-RJ85 | E2348 | ex EI-RJK | o/o♦ |
| ☐ | YV | Avro 146-RJ85 | E2350 | ex EI-RJM | o/o♦ |
| ☐ | YV | Avro 146-RJ85 | E2370 | ex EI-RJV | o/o♦ |

### LASER                          Laser (QL/LER)          Caracas-Simon Bolivar Intl (CCS)

| | | | | | |
|---|---|---|---|---|---|
| ☐ | YV167T | Douglas DC-9-32 (ABS 3) | 47281/427 | ex YV-1121C | |
| ☐ | YV231T | Douglas DC-9-32 | 47133/230 | ex HK-4310X | |
| ☐ | YV331T | Douglas DC-9-31 | 48157/1054 | ex N934LK | |
| ☐ | YV332T | Douglas DC-9-31 | 48158/1056 | ex N935DS | |
| ☐ | YV469T | McDonnell-Douglas MD-81 | 53299/2075 | ex JA8554 | ♦ |
| ☐ | YV480T | McDonnell-Douglas MD-81 | 53043/1982 | ex N820AG | ♦ |
| ☐ | YV492T | McDonnell-Douglas MD-81 | 53301/2082 | ex N821AG | [CCS] |
| ☐ | YV1240 | McDonnell-Douglas MD-81 | 49907/1734 | ex N228RF | ♦ |
| ☐ | YV1243 | McDonnell-Douglas MD-81 | 49908/1749 | ex N908RF | ♦ |

### LINEA TURISTICA AEREOTUY         Aereotuy (LD/TUY)     Caracas-Simon Bolivar Intl (CCS)

| | | | | | |
|---|---|---|---|---|---|
| ☐ | YV1182 | Cessna 208B Caravan I | 208B0720 | ex YV-659C | |
| ☐ | YV1184 | de Havilland DHC-7-102 | 030 | ex YV-639C | |
| ☐ | YV1185 | de Havilland DHC-7-102 | 005 | ex YV-638C | wfs |
| ☐ | YV1188 | Cessna 208B Caravan I | 208B0955 | ex YV-863C | |
| ☐ | YV382T | ATR 42-320 | 0110 | ex LN-FAP | [CCS] |
| ☐ | YV2757 | ATR 42-320 | 0206 | ex LN-FAR    ex YV383T | |

### PERLA AIRLINES

| | | | | | |
|---|---|---|---|---|---|
| ☐ | YV335T | McDonnell-Douglas MD-83 | 49232/1178 | ex N931AS | |

### PROFLIGHT VENEZUELA

| | | | | | |
|---|---|---|---|---|---|
| ☐ | YV215T | British Aerospace Jetstream 31 | 784 | ex N430UE | |

### RAINBOW AIR                          (TZR)                              Porlomar

| | | | | | |
|---|---|---|---|---|---|
| ☐ | YV307T | LET L-410UVP | 800407 | ex CCCP-67141 | |
| ☐ | YV308T | LET L-410UVP | 790307 | ex CCCP-67111 | |
| ☐ | YV309T | LET L-410UVP | 800407 | ex RA-67142 | ♦ |
| ☐ | YV322T | LET L-410UVP | 800507 | ex LZ-MNO | |
| ☐ | YV398T | LET L-410UVP | 851420 | ex YV301T | ♦ |

| ☐ | EX-024 | Antonov An-26B | 11901 | ex RA-26096 | |

## RUTACA — Rutaca (RUC) — Ciudad Bolivar (CBL)

| ☐ | YV-209C | Cessna U206D Super Skywagon | U206-1338 | ex N72247 | |
| ☐ | YV-229C | Cessna U206G Stationair | U20603541 | ex YV-1153P | |
| ☐ | YV-785C | Cessna U206G Stationair | U20603889 | ex YV-1314P | |
| ☐ | YV-786C | Cessna U206G Stationair 6 | U20605125 | ex YV-1719P | |
| ☐ | YV1943 | Cessna U206G Stationair 6 | U20605354 | ex YV-210C | |
| ☐ | YV1946 | Cessna U206G Stationair 6 | U20604803 | ex YV-793C | |
| ☐ | YV1947 | Cessna U206F Stationair | U20603192 | ex YV-789C | |
| ☐ | YV1948 | Cessna U206G Stationair 6 | U20604150 | ex YV-379C | |
| ☐ | YV169T | Boeing 737-2S3 (Nordam 3) | 21776/577 | ex YV-1155C | |
| ☐ | YV369T | Boeing 737-230 (Nordam 3) | 22113/649 | ex OB-1837-P | |
| ☐ | YV379T | Boeing 737-230 (Nordam 3) | 22115/694 | ex N215AG | |
| ☐ | YV380T | Boeing 737-230 (Nordam 3) | 22127/745 | ex N227AG | |
| ☐ | YV390T | Boeing 737-230 (Nordam 3) | 22128/752 | ex N128AG | |
| ☐ | YV472T | Boeing 737-242 | 22074/619 | ex N131MS | [MAR]♦ |
| ☐ | YV1381 | Boeing 737-2S3 (Nordam 3) | 21774/563 | ex YV-216C Vinotinto c/s | ♦ |
| ☐ | YV | Boeing 737-244 | 22589/843 | ex HC-CFM | [CCS]♦ |
| ☐ | YV-794C | Cessna 208B Caravan I | 208B0795 | ex N5264U | |
| ☐ | YV1670 | Cessna 208B Caravan I | 208B0608 | ex YV-792C | |
| ☐ | YV1671 | Cessna U206F | U20602386 | ex YV-214C | ♦ |
| ☐ | YV1950 | Cessna 208B Caravan I | 208B0555 | ex YV-791C | |
| ☐ | YV1951 | Cessna 208B Caravan I | 208B0527 | ex YV-790C | |

## SASCA – SERVICIOS AEREOS SUCRE — Porlamar

| ☐ | YV186T | British Aerospace Jetstream 3103 | 616 | ex YV-1163C | |
| ☐ | YV263T | British Aerospace Jetstream 31 | 645 | ex YV2211 | |
| ☐ | YV314T | British Aerospace Jetstream 31 | 721 | ex YV176T | |

## SBA - SANTA BARBARA AIRLINES — Santa Barbara (S3/BBR) — Maracaibo (MAR)

| ☐ | YV1421 | ATR 42-320 | 0300 | ex YV-1017C | |
| ☐ | YV1422 | ATR 42-320 | 0340 | ex YV-1018C | |
| ☐ | YV1423 | ATR 42-320 | 0360 | ex YV-1015C Virgen del Carmen | |
| ☐ | YV1424 | ATR 42-320 | 0368 | ex YV-1014C Mi Chinita | |
| ☐ | YV2314 | ATR 42-300 | 0038 | ex PR-TTD | |
| ☐ | YV288T | Boeing 757-21B | 24402/233 | ex N742PA | [MIA] |
| ☐ | YV304T | Boeing 757-21B | 24714/262 | ex N816PG | |
| ☐ | YV450T | Boeing 757-236 | 24370/218 | ex N580SH | ♦ |
| ☐ | YV2242 | Boeing 757-236 | 24119/167 | ex N962PG | |
| ☐ | YV2243 | Boeing 757-236 | 24118/163 | ex N958PG | [MIA] |
| ☐ | YV153T | McDonnell-Douglas MD-82 | 49486/1317 | ex N486SH | o/o♦ |
| ☐ | YV348T | McDonnell-Douglas MD-82 | 49120/1071 | ex N993PG | |
| ☐ | YV485T | McDonnell-Douglas MD-83 | 49668/1467 | ex N668SH | |
| ☐ | YV-1038C | Cessna 208B Caravan I | 208B0889 | ex N52677 | |
| ☐ | YV-1039C | Cessna 208B Caravan I | 208B0901 | ex N5267K | |

## SERAMI — Cuidad Bolivar (CBL)

| ☐ | YV183T | Cessna 208B Caravan I | 208B0669 | ex YV-1149C | ♦ |
| ☐ | YV2355 | Cessna 208B Caravan I | 208B1242 | ex N52178 | ♦ |
| ☐ | YV2367 | Cessna 210 | | ex YV-1156C | ♦ |
| ☐ | YV2368 | Cessna 404 | 4040851 | ex YV-160T | ♦ |

## SERVIVENSA — Marquetia

| ☐ | YV2225 | Beech 65-E90 King Air | LW-322 | ex YV-516CP | ♦ |

## SOLAR CARGO — Solarcargo (OLC) — Valencia (VLN)

| ☐ | YV1402 | Antonov An-26 | 87307207 | ex CU-T1501 | |
| ☐ | YV1403 | Antonov An-26 | 17309810 | ex YV-1134C | |

## SUNDANCE AIR

| ☐ | YV310T | British Aerospace Jetstream 31 | 909 | ex N490UE | wfs |
| ☐ | YV-1029C | LET L-410UVP | 831027 | ex PZ-TGR | |
| ☐ | YV1544 | LET L-410UVP | 831032 | ex YV-1114C | |
| ☐ | YV2063 | LET L-410UVP | 831010 | ex YV-1025C | |
| ☐ | YV2362 | LET L-410UVP-E | 561703 | ex HK-4142 | ♦ |

## TRANSAVEN – TRANSPORTE AEREO VENEZUELA (VEN) — Caracas-Simon Bolivar Intl (CCS)

| | | | | | |
|---|---|---|---|---|---|
| ☐ | YV1417 | LET L-410UVP | 830939 | ex YV-980C | |
| ☐ | YV1446 | Cessna 402B | 402B1079 | ex YV- | ◆ |
| ☐ | YV2082 | LET L-410UVP-E | 902430 | ex YV-1175C | |
| ☐ | YV2083 | LET L-410UVP-E | 892314 | ex YV-1113C | |
| ☐ | YV2170 | Britten-Norman BN-2A Mk.III-1 Trislander | 1007 | ex YV-1117C | |
| ☐ | YV2283 | Britten-Norman BN-2A-8 Islander | 296 | ex YV-1115C | ◆ |

## TRANSCARGA INTERNATIONAL AIRWAYS    Tiaca (TIW) — Caracas-Simon Bolivar Intl (CCS)

| | | | | | |
|---|---|---|---|---|---|
| ☐ | N210AS | Embraer EMB.120RTF Brasilia | 120006 | ex PT-SIA | o/o◆ |
| ☐ | YV276T | Cessna 402B | 402B1234 | ex N4188G | ◆ |
| ☐ | YV277T | Cessna 402B | 402B1024 | ex N98635 | ◆ |
| ☐ | YV1114 | Cessna 402B | 402B0814 | ex N3826C | ◆ |
| ☐ | YV1149 | Aero Commander 500B | 500B-899 | ex YV-941C | ex c/n 500A-899-B |
| ☐ | YV2546 | Embraer EMB.120ER Brasilia | 120017 | ex N125AM | |
| ☐ | YV2494 | Embraer EMB.120RT Brasilia | 120021 | ex N223AS | ◆ |

## TRANSMANDU — Ciudad Bolivar (CBL)

| | | | | | |
|---|---|---|---|---|---|
| ☐ | YV1019 | British Aerospace Jetstream 32 | 911 | ex N491UE | |
| ☐ | YV1258 | Cessna U206F | U20602122 | ex YV-193C | ◆ |
| ☐ | YV2532 | British Aerospace Jetstream 32EP | 965 | ex N965AE | ◆ |

## TRANSPORTE AIR CHECO — Caracas-Simon Bolivan Intl (CCS)

| | | | | | |
|---|---|---|---|---|---|
| ☐ | YV1275 | Antonov An-26 | 07310607 | ex YV-965CP | ◆ |
| ☐ | YV2263 | LET L-410UVP | 872016 | ex YV-1003CP | ◆ |

## TRANSVALCASA

| | | | | |
|---|---|---|---|---|
| ☐ | YV128T | Swearingen SA.226T Merlin II | TT-507 | |

## TURISMO AEREO AMAZONAS

| | | | | |
|---|---|---|---|---|
| ☐ | YV1157 | LET L-410UVP | 851412 | ex HH-PRT |
| ☐ | YV1219 | LET L-410UVP | 851319 | ex YV-1147C |

## TURISMO AIR IGLESIAS

| | | | | |
|---|---|---|---|---|
| YV1844 | LET L-410UVP | 831115 | ex YV-053C | ◆ |

## VENESCAR INTERNACIONAL    Vecar (V4/VEC) — Caracas-Simon Bolivar Intl (CCS)

| | | | | | | |
|---|---|---|---|---|---|---|
| ☐ | YV155T | Boeing 727-223F (FedEx 3) | 20992/1187 | ex YV-905C | 408 | DHL c/s |
| ☐ | YV236T | Boeing 727-227F (FedEx 3) | 21996/1571 | ex N781DH | | |
| ☐ | YV478T | Boeing 727-2Q4F (FedEx 3) | 22424/1683 | ex HP-1710DAE | | ◆ |
| ☐ | YV2308 | ATR 42-300F | 0061 | ex YV157T | 302 | DHL c/s |
| ☐ | YV2309 | Boeing 727-31F (FedEx 3) | 20114/712 | ex YV156T | | DHL c/s |

## VENEZOLANA    Venezolana (VNE) — Caracas-Simon Bolivar Intl (CCS)

| | | | | | |
|---|---|---|---|---|---|
| ☐ | YV268T | Boeing 737-232 (AvAero 3) | 23099/1035 | ex N327DL | |
| ☐ | YV287T | Boeing 737-217 (AvAero 3) | 22728/911 | ex N168WP | |
| ☐ | YV295T | Boeing 737-217 (AvAero 3) | 21717/581 | ex N167WP | |
| ☐ | YV296T | Boeing 737-2T5 (AvAero 3) | 22024/641 | ex N166WP | |
| ☐ | YV302T | Boeing 737-2T5 (AvAero 3) | 23087/1013 | ex N315DL | |
| ☐ | YV502T | Boeing 737-2A1 | 21598/512 | ex N976UA | ◆ |
| ☐ | YV | Boeing 737-230 | 23158/1089 | ex N89DL | [MAR]◆ |
| ☐ | YV191T | McDonnell-Douglas MD-83 | 49392/1272 | ex N392AP | |
| ☐ | YV179T | British Aerospace Jetstream 31 | 759 | ex YV-1086C | |
| ☐ | YV180T | British Aerospace Jetstream 31 | 770 | ex YV-1093C | |
| ☐ | YV270T | British Aerospace Jetstream 41 | 41097 | ex N329UE | wfs |
| ☐ | YV283T | British Aerospace Jetstream 41 | 41033 | ex N315UE | wfs |
| ☐ | YV293T | British Aerospace Jetstream 41 | 41026 | ex N313UE | wfs |
| ☐ | YV | British Aerospace Jetstream 41 | 41020 | ex N306UE | wfs |
| ☐ | YV-1084C | British Aerospace Jetstream 31 | 734 | ex N402UE | |
| ☐ | YV-1085C | British Aerospace Jetstream 31 | 729 | ex N401UE | |
| ☐ | YV | McDonnell-Douglas MD-82 | 49511/1537 | ex N511JZ | [MAR]◆WYNGS AVIATION |
| ☐ | YV1106 | Beech 1900D | UE-241 | ex YV-1152CP | |

## Z-    ZIMBABWE (Republic of Zimbabwe)

### AIR ZIMBABWE

**Air Zimbabwe (UM/AZW)**     **Harare-International (HRE)**

| | Reg | Type | c/n | ex | Name | Notes |
|---|---|---|---|---|---|---|
| ☐ | Z-WPA | Boeing 737-2N0 | 23677/1313 | ex C9-BAG | Mbuya Nehanda | |
| ☐ | Z-WPB | Boeing 737-2N0 | 23678/1405 | | Great Zimbabwe | |
| ☐ | Z-WPC | Boeing 737-2N0 | 23679/1415 | | Matojeni | |
| ☐ | Z-WPD | British Aerospace 146 Srs.200 | E2065 | ex G-5-065 | | [HRE] |
| ☐ | Z-WPE | Boeing 767-2N0ER | 24713/287 | | Victoria Falls | |
| ☐ | Z-WPF | Boeing 767-2N0ER | 24867/333 | | Chimanimani | |
| ☐ | Z-WPJ | CAIC MA60 | 0301 | ex B-674L | Nyami-Nyami | |
| ☐ | Z-WPK | CAIC MA60 | 0302 | | A'sambeni | |
| ☐ | Z-WPL | CAIC MA60 | 0303 | | | |
| ☐ | Z- | Airbus A320-214 | 0630 | ex M-YWAT | | [HRE]♦ |

### AVIENT AVIATION

**Avavia (Z3/SMJ)**     **Harare-International (HRE)**

| | Reg | Type | c/n | ex | Name | Notes |
|---|---|---|---|---|---|---|
| ☐ | Z-ALT | Douglas DC-10-30F | 47818/305 | ex 5X-ROY | | |
| ☐ | Z-ARL | Douglas DC-10-30CF | 47907/157 | ex N10MB | | wfs |
| ☐ | Z-AVT | Douglas DC-10-30F | 46590/266 | ex N401JR | Victor Trimble | [CGK] |
| ☐ | Z-BVT | McDonnell-Douglas MD-11BCF | 48410/495 | ex N575SH | | |

Grounded by Zimbabwe Govt 07Feb12

### DHL AVIATION (ZIMBABWE)

**Harare-International (HRE)**

| | Reg | Type | c/n | ex |
|---|---|---|---|---|
| ☐ | Z-KPS | Cessna 208B Caravan I | 208B0303 | ex N31SE |

### UNITED AIR CHARTERS

**Unitair (UAC)**     **Harare-Charles Prince**

| | Reg | Type | c/n | ex |
|---|---|---|---|---|
| ☐ | Z-BWK | Cessna U206G Stationair | U20603546 | ex N8794Q |
| ☐ | Z-UAC | Beech 58 Baron | TH-211 | ex 9J-ADK |
| ☐ | Z-UTD | Britten-Norman BN-2A Mk.III-2 Trislander | 1055 | ex A2-AGY |
| ☐ | Z-WHG | Beech 95-D55 Baron | TE-761 | ex VP-WHG |
| ☐ | Z-WHH | Beech 65-80 Queen Air | LD-101 | ex VP-WHH |
| ☐ | Z-WHX | Britten-Norman BN-2A-7 Islander | 192 | ex VP-WHX |
| ☐ | Z-WKL | Cessna U206F Stationair | U20601707 | ex ZS-ILV |
| ☐ | Z-WTA | Cessna U206F Stationair | U20602547 | ex OO-SPX |
| ☐ | Z-WTF | Cessna 414A Chancellor | 414A0062 | ex G-METR |
| ☐ | Z-YHS | Cessna U206C Super Skywagon | U206-1029 | ex VP-YHS |

## ZA-    ALBANIA (Republic of Albania)

### ALBANIAN AIRLINES

**Albanian (LV/LBC)**     **Tirana (TIA)**

Ops suspended 10Nov11

### BELLE AIR

**(LZ/LBY)**     **Tirana (TIA)**

| | Reg | Type | c/n | ex | Notes |
|---|---|---|---|---|---|
| ☐ | F-ORAA | ATR 72-212A | 0879 | ex F-WWEH | |
| ☐ | F-ORAD | Airbus A320-233 | 0558 | ex F-HBAE | |
| ☐ | F-ORAE | Airbus A320-233 | 0561 | ex F-HBAD | |
| ☐ | F-ORAG | Airbus A319-132 | 1098 | ex M-YVOL | |
| ☐ | ZA-ARD | McDonnell-Douglas MD-82 | 49104/1085 | ex N804NK | wfs |

### STAR AIRWAYS

**Tirana (TIA)**

| | Reg | Type | c/n | ex | Name | Notes |
|---|---|---|---|---|---|---|
| ☐ | ZA-ADA | Embraer EMB.110P2 Bandeirante | 110303 | ex F-GCMQ | DHL titles | [TIA] |

## ZK-    NEW ZEALAND (Dominion of New Zealand)

### AIR CHATHAMS

**Chatham (CV/CVA)**     **Chatham Island (CHT)**

| | Reg | Type | c/n | ex | Notes |
|---|---|---|---|---|---|
| ☐ | ZK-CIA | Beech 65-B80 Queen Air | LD-430 | ex N640K | |
| ☐ | ZK-CIB | Convair 580 | 327A | ex C-FCIB | |
| ☐ | ZK-CIC | Swearingen SA.227AC Metro III | AC-623B | ex N623AV | Frtr >OGN |
| ☐ | ZK-CID | Convair 580F | 385 | ex HZ-SN11 | [PMR] |
| ☐ | ZK-CIE | Convair 580 | 399 | ex N565EA | |
| ☐ | ZK-CIF | Convair 580 | 381 | ex N566EA | |
| ☐ | ZK-KAI | Cessna U206G Stationair | U20603711 | | |

### AIR FREIGHT NZ

**(TFR)**     **Auckland-Intl (AKL)**

| | Reg | Type | c/n | ex | Notes |
|---|---|---|---|---|---|
| ☐ | ZK-FTA | Convair 580 | 168 | ex C-GKFP | Frtr op for Parceline |
| ☐ | ZK-KFH | Convair 580F | 42 | ex C-FKFL | |

| | | | | | | |
|---|---|---|---|---|---|---|
| ☐ | ZK-KFJ | Convair 580F | 114 | ex C-GKFJ | | |
| ☐ | ZK-KFL | Convair 580 | 372 | ex C-FKFL | | Frtr op for Parceline |
| ☐ | ZK-KFS | Convair 5800 | 277 | ex C-FKFS | | Frtr |

## AIR MILFORD 2000

| | | | | | |
|---|---|---|---|---|---|
| ☐ | ZK-SKB | Cessna 208 Caravan I | 20800244 | ex VH-BSX | ♦ |

## AIR NATIONAL                                                                                     Auckland-Intl (AKL)

| | | | | | |
|---|---|---|---|---|---|
| ☐ | ZK-ECP | British Aerospace Jetstream 32EP | 878 | ex VH-BAE | |

Ops suspended Mar11

## AIR NELSON                                         Link (RLK)                           Nelson (NSN)

Wholly owned by Air New Zealand; operates as part of Air New Zealand Link (qv)

## AIR NEW ZEALAND                          NewZealand (NZ/ANZ)
Auckland-Intl/Wellington-Intl (AKL/WLG)

Member of Star Alliance

| | | | | | | |
|---|---|---|---|---|---|---|
| ☐ | EI-EWD | Airbus A320-232 | 2445 | ex PR-MBJ | | ♦ |
| ☐ | ZK-OAB | Airbus A320-232 | 4553 | ex F-WWDF | All Blacks c/s | ♦ |
| ☐ | ZK-OJA | Airbus A320-232 | 2085 | ex F-WWIN | | |
| ☐ | ZK-OJB | Airbus A320-232 | 2090 | ex F-WWBM | | |
| ☐ | ZK-OJC | Airbus A320-232 | 2112 | ex F-WWDQ | | |
| ☐ | ZK-OJD | Airbus A320-232 | 2130 | ex F-WWDK | | |
| ☐ | ZK-OJE | Airbus A320-232 | 2148 | ex F-WWIH | | |
| ☐ | ZK-OJF | Airbus A320-232 | 2153 | ex F-WWIS | | |
| ☐ | ZK-OJG | Airbus A320-232 | 2173 | ex F-WWDJ | | |
| ☐ | ZK-OJH | Airbus A320-232 | 2257 | ex F-WWDE | Star Alliance c/s | |
| ☐ | ZK-OJI | Airbus A320-232 | 2297 | ex F-WWBU | | |
| ☐ | ZK-OJM | Airbus A320-232 | 2533 | ex F-WWIB | | |
| ☐ | ZK-OJN | Airbus A320-232 | 2594 | ex F-WWBC | | |
| ☐ | ZK-OJO | Airbus A320-232 | 2663 | ex F-WWBM | Warner special c/s | |
| ☐ | ZK-OJQ | Airbus A320-232 | 4584 | ex F-WWIO | | ♦ |
| ☐ | ZK-OJR | Airbus A320-232 | 4884 | ex F-WWIP | All Blacks c/s | ♦ |
| ☐ | ZK-OJS | Airbus A320-232 | 4926 | ex F-WWIT | | ♦ |
| ☐ | ZK-NGD | Boeing 737-3U3 | 28732/2966 | ex N930WA | | |
| ☐ | ZK-NGE | Boeing 737-3U3 | 28733/2969 | ex N931WA | | |
| ☐ | ZK-NGF | Boeing 737-3U3 | 28734/2974 | ex N309FL | | |
| ☐ | ZK-NGG | Boeing 737-319 | 25606/3123 | ex N1795B | | |
| ☐ | ZK-NGH | Boeing 737-319 | 25607/3126 | ex N1786B | | |
| ☐ | ZK-NGI | Boeing 737-319 | 25608/3128 | ex N1786B | | |
| ☐ | ZK-NGJ | Boeing 737-319 | 25609/3130 | ex N1786B | | last 737-300 built |
| ☐ | ZK-NGK | Boeing 737-3K2 | 26318/2731 | ex PH-TSX | | |
| ☐ | ZK-NGM | Boeing 737-3K2 | 28085/2722 | ex PH-TSY | | |
| ☐ | ZK-NGO | Boeing 737-37Q | 28548/2961 | ex G-OAMS | | |
| ☐ | ZK-NGP | Boeing 737-33A | 27459/3007 | ex 9H-ADH | | |
| ☐ | ZK-NGR | Boeing 737-33A | 27460/3021 | ex 9H-ADI | | |
| ☐ | ZK-SJB | Boeing 737-33R | 28868/2881 | ex PP-SFK | | |
| ☐ | ZK-SJC | Boeing 737-3U3 | 28738/2988 | ex N308FL | | |
| ☐ | ZK-NCG | Boeing 767-319ER/W | 26912/509 | | | |
| ☐ | ZK-NCI | Boeing 767-319ER/W | 26913/558 | ex N6009F | | |
| ☐ | ZK-NCJ | Boeing 767-319ER/W | 26915/574 | ex N6018N | | |
| ☐ | ZK-NCK | Boeing 767-319ER/W | 26971/663 | | | |
| ☐ | ZK-NCL | Boeing 767-319ER/W | 28745/677 | | | |
| ☐ | ZK-OKA | Boeing 777-219ER | 29404/534 | | | |
| ☐ | ZK-OKB | Boeing 777-219ER | 34376/537 | | | |
| ☐ | ZK-OKC | Boeing 777-219ER | 34377/546 | | | |
| ☐ | ZK-OKD | Boeing 777-219ER | 29401/550 | | | |
| ☐ | ZK-OKE | Boeing 777-219ER | 32712/564 | | | |
| ☐ | ZK-OKF | Boeing 777-219ER | 34378/575 | | | |
| ☐ | ZK-OKG | Boeing 777-219ER | 29403/591 | | | |
| ☐ | ZK-OKH | Boeing 777-219ER | 34379/605 | | | |
| ☐ | ZK-OKM | Boeing 777-319ER | 38405/902 | | | |
| ☐ | ZK-OKN | Boeing 777-319ER | 38406/911 | | | |
| ☐ | ZK-OKO | Boeing 777-319ER | 38407/921 | | | |
| ☐ | ZK-OKP | Boeing 777-319ER | 39041/972 | | | ♦ |
| ☐ | ZK-OKQ | Boeing 777-319ER | 40689/984 | | | ♦ |
| ☐ | ZK-NZC | Boeing 787-9 | | | | o/o♦ |
| ☐ | ZK-NZD | Boeing 787-9 | | | | o/o♦ |
| ☐ | ZK-NZE | Boeing 787-9 | | | | o/o♦ |
| ☐ | ZK-NZF | Boeing 787-9 | | | | o/o♦ |

| | | | | | | |
|---|---|---|---|---|---|---|
| ☐ | ZK-NZG | Boeing 787-9 | | | | o/o♦ |
| ☐ | ZK-NZH | Boeing 787-9 | | | | o/o♦ |
| ☐ | ZK-NZI | Boeing 787-9 | | | | o/o♦ |
| ☐ | ZK-NZJ | Boeing 787-9 | | | | o/o♦ |
| ☐ | ZK-NBT | Boeing 747-419 | 24855/815 | ex N6018N | Kaikoura | [AKL] |
| ☐ | ZK-NBU | Boeing 747-419 | 25605/933 | | Rotorua | |
| ☐ | ZK-NBV | Boeing 747-419 | 26910/1180 | | Christchurch | |
| ☐ | ZK-SUH | Boeing 747-475 | 24896/855 | ex N891LF | Dunedin | |

### AIR NEW ZEALAND LINK — New Zealand (NZ/NZA)
**Christchurch-Intl/Nelson/Hamilton (CHC/NSN/HLZ)**

| | | | | | |
|---|---|---|---|---|---|
| ☐ | ZK-MCA | ATR 72-212A | 0597 | ex F-WQKC | Mount Cook |
| ☐ | ZK-MCB | ATR 72-212A | 0598 | ex F-WQKG | Mount Cook |
| ☐ | ZK-MCC | ATR 72-212A | 0714 | ex F-WQMV | Mount Cook |
| ☐ | ZK-MCF | ATR 72-212A | 0600 | ex F-WQKH | Mount Cook |
| ☐ | ZK-MCJ | ATR 72-212A | 0624 | ex F-WQKI | Mount Cook |
| ☐ | ZK-MCO | ATR 72-212A | 0628 | ex F-WQKJ | Mount Cook |
| ☐ | ZK-MCP | ATR 72-212A | 0630 | ex F-WQKK | Mount Cook |
| ☐ | ZK-MCU | ATR 72-212A | 0632 | ex F-WQKL | Mount Cook |
| ☐ | ZK-MCW | ATR 72-212A | 0646 | ex F-WQMG | Mount Cook |
| ☐ | ZK-MCX | ATR 72-212A | 0687 | ex F-WQMN | Mount Cook |
| ☐ | ZK-MCY | ATR 72-212A | 0703 | ex F-WQMR | Mount Cook |
| ☐ | ZK-EAA | Beech 1900D | UE-424 | ex N2335Y | Eagle |
| ☐ | ZK-EAB | Beech 1900D | UE-425 | ex N2335Z | Eagle |
| ☐ | ZK-EAC | Beech 1900D | UE-426 | ex N51226 | Eagle |
| ☐ | ZK-EAD | Beech 1900D | UE-427 | ex N50127 | Eagle |
| ☐ | ZK-EAE | Beech 1900D | UE-428 | ex N3188L | Eagle |
| ☐ | ZK-EAF | Beech 1900D | UE-429 | ex N50069 | Eagle |
| ☐ | ZK-EAG | Beech 1900D | UE-430 | ex N50430 | Eagle |
| ☐ | ZK-EAH | Beech 1900D | UE-431 | ex N51321 | Eagle |
| ☐ | ZK-EAI | Beech 1900D | UE-432 | ex N5032L | Eagle |
| ☐ | ZK-EAJ | Beech 1900D | UE-433 | ex N4469Q | Eagle |
| ☐ | ZK-EAK | Beech 1900D | UE-434 | ex N4474P | Eagle |
| ☐ | ZK-EAL | Beech 1900D | UE-435 | ex N50815 | Eagle |
| ☐ | ZK-EAM | Beech 1900D | UE-436 | ex N5016C | Eagle |
| ☐ | ZK-EAN | Beech 1900D | UE-437 | ex N50307 | Eagle |
| ☐ | ZK-EAO | Beech 1900D | UE-438 | ex N4470D | Eagle |
| ☐ | ZK-EAP | Beech 1900D | UE-439 | ex N50899 | Eagle |
| ☐ | ZK-EAQ | Beech 1900D | UE-363 | ex N846CA | Eagle♦ |
| ☐ | ZK-EAR | Beech 1900D | UE-388 | ex VH-EAS | Eagle |
| ☐ | ZK-NEA | de Havilland DHC-8Q-311 | 611 | ex C-FCPO | Air Nelson |
| ☐ | ZK-NEB | de Havilland DHC-8Q-311 | 615 | ex C-FDRG | Air Nelson |
| ☐ | ZK-NEC | de Havilland DHC-8Q-311 | 616 | ex C-FEDG | Air Nelson |
| ☐ | ZK-NED | de Havilland DHC-8Q-311 | 617 | ex C-FERB | Air Nelson |
| ☐ | ZK-NEE | de Havilland DHC-8Q-311 | 618 | ex C-FFBY | Air Nelson |
| ☐ | ZK-NEF | de Havilland DHC-8Q-311 | 620 | ex C-FFCC | Air Nelson |
| ☐ | ZK-NEG | de Havilland DHC-8Q-311 | 621 | ex C-FFOZ | Air Nelson |
| ☐ | ZK-NEH | de Havilland DHC-8Q-311 | 623 | ex C-FGAI | Air Nelson |
| ☐ | ZK-NEJ | de Havilland DHC-8Q-311 | 625 | ex C-FFPA | Air Nelson |
| ☐ | ZK-NEK | de Havilland DHC-8Q-311 | 629 | ex C-FHPZ | Air Nelson |
| ☐ | ZK-NEM | de Havilland DHC-8Q-311 | 630 | ex C-FHQB | Air Nelson |
| ☐ | ZK-NEO | de Havilland DHC-8Q-311 | 633 | ex C-FIOS | Air Nelson |
| ☐ | ZK-NEP | de Havilland DHC-8Q-311 | 634 | ex C-FIOV | Air Nelson |
| ☐ | ZK-NEQ | de Havilland DHC-8Q-311 | 636 | ex C-FJKL | Air Nelson |
| ☐ | ZK-NER | de Havilland DHC-8Q-311 | 639 | ex C-FJKO | Air Nelson |
| ☐ | ZK-NES | de Havilland DHC-8Q-311 | 641 | ex C-FJKP | Air Nelson |
| ☐ | ZK-NET | de Havilland DHC-8Q-311 | 642 | ex C-FJKQ | Air Nelson |
| ☐ | ZK-NEU | de Havilland DHC-8Q-311 | 647 | ex C-FLTZ | Air Nelson |
| ☐ | ZK-NEW | de Havilland DHC-8Q-311 | 648 | ex C-FLUH | Air Nelson |
| ☐ | ZK-NEZ | de Havilland DHC-8Q-311 | 654 | ex C-FNPY | Air Nelson |
| ☐ | ZK-NFA | de Havilland DHC-8Q-311 | 659 | ex C-FPPN | Air Nelson |
| ☐ | ZK-NFB | de Havilland DHC-8Q-311 | 670 | ex C-FVUF | Air Nelson |
| ☐ | ZK-NFI | de Havilland DHC-8Q-311 | 671 | ex C-FWGQ | Air Nelson |

### AIR SAFARIS & SERVICES — Airsafari (SRI) — Lake Tekapo

| | | | | | |
|---|---|---|---|---|---|
| ☐ | ZK-FJH | Cessna P206E Super Skylane | P206-0634 | ex G-BKSI | |
| ☐ | ZK-NMD | GAF N24A Nomad | N24A-060 | ex VH-DHU | |
| ☐ | ZK-NME | GAF N24A Nomad | N24A-122 | ex 5W-FAT | |
| ☐ | ZK-SAE | Gippsland GA-8 Airvan | GA8-04-055 | ex VH-VFF | |
| ☐ | ZK-SAF | Gippsland GA-8 Airvan | GA8-02-017 | ex VH-AAP | |
| ☐ | ZK-SAZ | Gippsland GA-8 Airvan | GA8-05-078 | | |
| ☐ | ZK-SEY | Cessna T207A Stationair 8 | 20700661 | ex N76012 | |
| ☐ | ZK-SRI | Cessna 208B Caravan I | 208B0636 | ex N208PR | |

## AIR2THERE.COM          Paraparaumu (PPQ)

| | | | | | |
|---|---|---|---|---|---|
| ☐ | ZK-MYF | Partenavia P.68B | 123 | ex ZK-ERA | |
| ☐ | ZK-MYH | Cessna 208B Caravan I | 208B0604 | ex N64BP | |
| ☐ | ZK-MYS | Piper PA-31-350 Navajo Chieftain | 31-7652032 | ex ZK-MCM | |

## AIRWORK NEW ZEALAND       Airwork (AWK)
### Auckland-Ardmore/ Christchurch/ Wellington (AMZ/CHC/WLG)

| | | | | | | |
|---|---|---|---|---|---|---|
| ☐ | ZK-FXT | Boeing 737-3B7F | 23862/1586 | ex N527AU | | ♦ |
| ☐ | ZK-TLA | Boeing 737-3B7 (SF) | 23383/1425 | ex N508AU | | op for Toll Logistics |
| ☐ | ZK-TLC | Boeing 737-3B7 (SF) | 23705/1497 | ex N519AU | | op for Toll Logistics |
| ☐ | ZK-TLD | Boeing 737-3B7 (SF) | 23706/1499 | ex N520AU | | op for Toll Logistics |
| ☐ | ZK-TLE | Boeing 737-3S1 (SF) | 24834/1896 | ex N919GF | | |
| ☐ | ZK-LFT | Swearingen SA.227AC Metro III | AC-582 | ex ZK-PAA | | EMS op for Life Flight NZ |
| ☐ | ZK-NSS | Swearingen SA.227AC Metro III | AC-692B | ex N2707D | | EMS |
| ☐ | ZK-POB | Swearingen SA.227AC Metro III | AC-606B | ex D-CABG | | op for SkyLink |
| ☐ | ZK-POE | Swearingen SA.227CC Metro 23 | CC-843B | ex N30228 | | op for NZ Post |
| ☐ | ZK-POF | Swearingen SA.227CC Metro 23 | CC-844B | ex N30229 | | |
| ☐ | ZK-FOP | Piper PA-31-350 Navajo Chieftain | 31-7405227 | ex N888SG | | EMS |
| ☐ | ZK-JTQ | Boeing 737-476 | 24442/2371 | ex VH-JTQ | | .>FWQ♦ |
| ☐ | ZK-NAO | Fokker F.27 Friendship 500 | 10364 | ex 9V-BFK | all-white | op for NZ Post |
| ☐ | ZK-NQC | Boeing 737-219C (Nordam 3) | 22994/928 | | all-white | |
| ☐ | ZK-PAX | Fokker F.27 Friendship 500 | 10596 | ex HB-ILJ | all-white | |
| ☐ | ZK-POH | Fokker F.27 Friendship 500 | 10680 | ex VT-NEH | all-white | op for NZ Post |
| ☐ | ZK-TLF | Boeing 737-4Q8F | 24709/2115 | ex N709AG | | ♦ |

## ASPIRING AIR / ASPIRING HELICOPTERS     (OI)        Wanaka (WKA)

| | | | | | | |
|---|---|---|---|---|---|---|
| ☐ | ZK-EVO | Britten-Norman BN-2A-26 Islander | 785 | ex 5W-FAQ | | |
| ☐ | ZK-EVT | Britten-Norman BN-2A-26 Islander | 152 | ex YJ-RV19 | Lake Wanaka | |
| ☐ | ZK-HMM | Aérospatiale AS350B2 Ecureuil | 2436 | | | ♦ |

## EAGLE AIRWAYS        (EX)        Hamilton (HLZ)

50% owned by Air New Zealand; ops as part of Air New Zealand Link (q.v.)

## FLIGHT 2000        Ardmore (AMZ)

| | | | | | | |
|---|---|---|---|---|---|---|
| ☐ | ZK-DAK | Douglas DC-3 | 15035/26480 | ex VH-SBT | RNZAF colours | |

## GOLDEN WINGS

| | | | | | |
|---|---|---|---|---|---|
| ☐ | ZK-MMM | Beech B300 Super King Air | FL-727 | ex N80427 | ♦ |

## GREAT BARRIER AIRLINES     (AFW)       Auckland-Intl (AKL)

| | | | | | | |
|---|---|---|---|---|---|---|
| ☐ | ZK-CNS | Piper PA-32-260 Cherokee Six | 32-686 | ex N3766W | Stitchbird | |
| ☐ | ZK-ENZ | Piper PA-32-260 Cherokee Six | 32-1117 | ex ZK-DBP | Tomtit | |
| ☐ | ZK-FVD | Britten-Norman BN-2A-26 Islander | 316 | ex G-BJWN | Pigeon | |
| ☐ | ZK-KTR | Britten-Norman BN-2A Islander | 759 | ex PK-VAB | | |
| ☐ | ZK-LGC | Britten-Norman BN-2A Mk.III-1 Trislander | 1042 | ex G-RHOP | | |
| ☐ | ZK-LGF | Britten-Norman BN-2A Mk.III-1 Trislander | 1023 | ex YJ-LGF | | |
| ☐ | ZK-LGR | Britten-Norman BN-2A Mk.III-1 Trislander | 372 | ex VH-BSP | | |
| ☐ | ZK-LOU | Britten-Norman BN-2A Mk.III-1 Trislander | 322 | ex VH-MRJ | | |
| ☐ | ZK-NSN | Piper PA-31 Turbo Navajo | 31-687 | ex VH-CFP | Bellbird | |
| ☐ | ZK-PLA | Partenavia P.68B | 86 | ex A6-ALO | Tui | |
| ☐ | ZK-RDT | Embraer EMB.820C Navajo | 820127 | ex PT-RDT | | |
| ☐ | ZK-REA | Britten-Norman BN-2A-26 Islander | 43 | ex ZK-FWH | Brown Teal | >Soundsair |

## JETCONNECT     Qantas Jetconnect (QNZ)       Auckland-Intl (AKL)

| | | | | | | |
|---|---|---|---|---|---|---|
| ☐ | ZK-ZQA | Boeing 737-838/W | 34200/2989 | ex VH-VZF | | |
| ☐ | ZK-ZQB | Boeing 737-838/W | 34201/3006 | ex VH-VZG | | |
| ☐ | ZK-ZQC | Boeing 737-838/W | 34202/3048 | ex VH-VZH | | |
| ☐ | ZK-ZQD | Boeing 737-838/W | 34203/3515 | | | |
| ☐ | ZK-ZQE | Boeing 737-838/W | 34185/3542 | | | ♦ |
| ☐ | ZK-ZQF | Boeing 737-838/W | 34204/3552 | | | ♦ |
| ☐ | ZK-ZQG | Boeing 737-838/W | 34190/3683 | | | ♦ |
| ☐ | ZK-ZQH | Boeing 737-838/W | 39357/3743 | | Charles Upham | ♦ |

## MILFORD HELICOPTERS
*Te Anau*

| | | | | |
|---|---|---|---|---|
| ☐ | ZK-ITY | Aérospatiale AS350B3 Ecureuil 2 | 4949 | ♦ |

## MILFORD SOUND FLIGHTSEEING
*Queenstown (ZQN)*

| | | | | |
|---|---|---|---|---|
| ☐ | ZK-DBV | Britten-Norman BN-2A-26 Islander | 164 | ex VH-EQX |
| ☐ | ZK-MCD | Britten-Norman BN-2A-26 Islander | 719 | ex G-BCAG |
| ☐ | ZK-MCE | Britten-Norman BN-2A-26 Islander | 724 | ex G-BCHB |
| ☐ | ZK-MFN | Britten-Norman BN-2B-26 Islander | 2168 | ex N2407B |
| ☐ | ZK-MSF | Britten-Norman BN-2A-26 Islander | 2037 | ex OY-PPP |
| ☐ | ZK-TSS | Britten-Norman BN-2A-26 Islander | 2043 | ex RP-C693 |
| ☐ | ZK-ZQN | Britten-Norman BN-2B-26 Islander | 2197 | ex G-BLNW |

## MILFORD SOUND SCENIC FLIGHTS
*Queenstown (ZQN)*

| | | | | |
|---|---|---|---|---|
| ☐ | ZK-DEW | Cessna 207 Skywagon | 20700161 | ex VH-UBQ |
| ☐ | ZK-DRY | Cessna 207 Skywagon | 20700196 | ex 5W-FAL |
| ☐ | ZK-LAW | Cessna 207A Stationair 8 | 20700723 | ex N9750M |
| ☐ | ZK-SEW | Cessna T207A Stationair 6 | 20700584 | ex N73394 |
| ☐ | ZK-SEX | Cessna T207A Stationair 6 | 20700609 | ex N73622 |
| ☐ | ZK-WET | Cessna 207A Skywagon | 20700375 | ex VH-SLD |

## MOUNT COOK AIRLINE
*Mountcook (NM/NZM)*     *Christchurch-Intl (CHC)*

77% owned by Air New Zealand; ops scheduled services as Air New Zealand Link in full colours using NZ flight numbers

## MOUNTAIN AIR
*Taumarunui*

| | | | | | |
|---|---|---|---|---|---|
| ☐ | ZK-DLA | Britten-Norman BN-2B-26 Islander | 2131 | ex VH-ISL | |
| ☐ | ZK-DOV | Cessna 206 Super Skywagon | 206-0248 | ex N5248U | |
| ☐ | ZK-PIW | Piper PA-23-250 Aztec E | 27-7305089 | ex VH-RCI | |
| ☐ | ZK-PIX | Piper PA-23-250 Aztec E | 27-4738 | ex N14174 | |
| ☐ | ZK-PIY | Britten-Norman BN-2A-20 Islander | 344 | ex JA5218 | |
| ☐ | ZK-PIZ | Britten-Norman BN-2B-26 Islander | 2012 | ex N2132M | Great Barrier Xpress titles |
| ☐ | ZK-SFK | Britten-Norman BN-2A-6 Islander | 236 | ex VH-CPG | |

## PIONAIR ADVENTURES
*Queenstown (ZQN)*

| | | | | | |
|---|---|---|---|---|---|
| ☐ | ZK-AMY | Douglas DC-3 | 13506 | ex VH-CAN | Lady Jane |

## SOUNDSAIR TRAVEL & TOURISM
*Wellington (WLG)*

| | | | | | |
|---|---|---|---|---|---|
| ☐ | ZK-ENT | Cessna U206G Stationair | U20603667 | ex N7551N | |
| ☐ | ZK-KLC | Gippsland GA-8 Airvan | GA8-03-040 | ex VH-BQR | |
| ☐ | ZK-PDM | Cessna 208 Caravan I | 20800240 | ex N1289N | |
| ☐ | ZK-REA | Britten-Norman BN-2A-26 Islander | 43 | ex ZK-FWH | <AFW |
| ☐ | ZK-TZR | Cessna 208 Caravan I | 20800360 | ex N800RA | ♦ |

## SOUTH EAST AIR
*Invercargill (IVC)*

| | | | | |
|---|---|---|---|---|
| ☐ | ZK-DIV | Piper PA-32-260 Cherokee Six | 32-7400015 | ex N57306 |
| ☐ | ZK-FWZ | Britten-Norman BN-2A-26 Islander | 52 | ex T3-ATH |
| ☐ | ZK-FXE | Britten-Norman BN-2A-26 Islander | 110 | ex F-OCFR |
| ☐ | ZK-JEM | Cessna A185E Skywagon | 18501780 | ex VH-JBM |
| ☐ | ZK-RTS | Piper PA-32-300 Cherokee Six | 32-7340070 | |

## SWIFT FLITE

| | | | | |
|---|---|---|---|---|
| ☐ | ZK-NKE | Embraer EMB.120ER Brasilia | 120296 | ex N226SW | ♦ |

## THE HELICOPTER LINE   Queenstown/Franz Josef Glacier/Fox Glacier/Mount Cook (ZQN/WHO/FGL/MON)

| | | | | |
|---|---|---|---|---|
| ☐ | ZK-HKY | Aérospatiale AS355F1 Twin Star | 5123 | ex N909CH |
| ☐ | ZK-HMB | Aérospatiale AS355F1 Twin Star | 5016 | ex N57812 |
| ☐ | ZK-HML | Aérospatiale AS355F1 Twin Star | 5032 | ex N5776A |
| ☐ | ZK-HPE | Aérospatiale AS355F1 Twin Star | 5229 | ex N58021 |
| ☐ | ZK-HPI | Aérospatiale AS355F1 Twin Star | 5211 | ex N5802N |
| ☐ | ZK-HPZ | Aérospatiale AS355F1 Twin Star | 5107 | ex N87906 |
| | | | | |
| ☐ | ZK-HKF | Aérospatiale AS355F1 Ecureuil 2 | 5200 | ex VH-HJK |
| ☐ | ZK-HKR | Aérospatiale AS350D AStar III | 1234 | ex N3606X |
| ☐ | ZK-HLW | Aérospatiale AS350BA Ecureuil | 1524 | ex JA9307 |
| ☐ | ZK-HNG | Aérospatiale AS350BA Ecureuil | 2409 | ex JA6039 |
| ☐ | ZK-HSM | Aérospatiale AS350B2 Ecureuil | 3529 | é |

## VINCENT AVIATION (BF/VIN) Wellington (WLG)

| | | | | | | |
|---|---|---|---|---|---|---|
| ☐ | ZK-ECI | British Aerospace Jetstream 32EP | 946 | ex ZK-JSU | | ♦ |
| ☐ | ZK-ECJ | British Aerospace Jetstream 32EP | 969 | ex ZK-JSR | | ♦ |
| ☐ | ZK-ECO | British Aerospace 146 Srs.200 | E2130 | ex C-GRNX | | ♦ |
| ☐ | ZK-ECR | British Aerospace Jetstream 32EP | 968 | ex ZK-JSQ | | ♦ |
| ☐ | ZK-JSH | British Aerospace Jetstream 31 | 838 | ex G-IBLW | | |
| ☐ | ZK-VAA | SAAB SF.340B | 340B-301 | ex VH-UYN | | ♦ |
| ☐ | ZK-VAB | SAAB SF.340B | 340B-357 | ex VH-UYA | | ♦ |
| ☐ | ZK-VAD | Cessna 402C | 402C0076 | ex VH-COH | | |
| ☐ | ZK-VAF | Reims Cessna F406 Caravan II | F406-0057 | ex F-ODYZ | | |

## VIRGIN AUSTRALIA (NEW ZEALAND) Bluebird (DJ/PBN) Christchurch Intl (CHC)

| | | | | | | |
|---|---|---|---|---|---|---|
| ☐ | ZK-PBA | Boeing 737-8FE/W | 33796/1377 | ex VH-VOO | Bonnie Blue | ♦ |
| ☐ | ZK-PBB | Boeing 737-8FE/W | 33797/1389 | ex VH-VOP | Whitney Sundays | ♦ |
| ☐ | ZK-PBD | Boeing 737-8FE/W | 33996/1551 | ex (VH-VOY) | Pacific Pearl | ♦ |
| ☐ | ZK-PBG | Boeing 737-8FE/W | 34015/1594 | ex VH-VUD | | ♦ |
| ☐ | ZK-PBI | Boeing 737-8FE/W | 34440/2003 | ex VH-VUH | | ♦ |
| ☐ | ZK-PBJ | Boeing 737-8FE/W | 34013/1573 | ex VH-VUB | | ♦ |
| ☐ | ZK-PBK | Boeing 737-8FE/W | 36604/2650 | ex VH-VUP | | ♦ |
| ☐ | ZK-PBL | Boeing 737-8FE/W | 36605/2710 | ex VH-VUQ | | ♦ |
| ☐ | ZK-PBM | Boeing 737-8FE/W | 36601/2525 | ex VH-VUO | | ♦ |

## VIRGIN SAMOA (PBL)

| | | | | | | |
|---|---|---|---|---|---|---|
| ☐ | ZK-PBF | Boeing 737-8FE/W | 33799/1462 | ex VH-VOR | Tapu'itea | ♦ |

## ZP-    PARAGUAY (Republic of Paraguay)

### AEROLINEAS PARAGUAYAS

| | | | | | |
|---|---|---|---|---|---|
| ☐ | ZP-TAZ | Cessna 208B Caravan i | 208B0686 | | ♦ |

### REGIONAL PARAGUAYA Asuncion (ASU)

| | | | | | |
|---|---|---|---|---|---|
| ☐ | ZP-CAQ | Boeing 737-201 (Nordam 3) | 20211/141 | ex 3C-HAC | |

### SOL DEL PARAGUAY LINEAS AEREAS (SGU) Asuncion (ASU)

| | | | | | | |
|---|---|---|---|---|---|---|
| ☐ | ZP-CAL | Fokker 100 | 11341 | ex XA-TCP | | |
| ☐ | ZP-CFL | Fokker 100 | 11348 | ex N348MX | Itapúa Poty | ♦ |
| ☐ | ZP-CJK | Fokker 100 | 11304 | ex N304MX | Héroes del Chaco | ♦ |
| ☐ | ZP- | Fokker 100 | 11320 | ex PH-LND | | o/o♦ |

### TAM MERCOSUR Paraguaya (PZ/LAP) Asuncion (ASU)

Ops services with Fokker 100 aircraft leased from parent (80% owner), TAM Brasil, as required

## ZS-    SOUTH AFRICA (Republic of South Africa)

### AFRICAN CHARTER AIRLINE

| | | | | | |
|---|---|---|---|---|---|
| ☐ | ZS-SIT | Boeing 737-236 | 21790/599 | ex V5-AND | <SFR♦ |

### AIR-TEC AFRICA / AIRCRAFT SYSTEMS SA Bethlehem

| | | | | | |
|---|---|---|---|---|---|
| ☐ | ZS-ATD | LET L-410UVP-E | 902527 | ex ST-CAT | ♦ |
| ☐ | ZS-ATF | LET L-410UVP-E3 | 902403 | ex ST-DMR | ♦ |
| ☐ | ZS-MWM | LET L-410UVP-E20 | 912613 | ex 7Q-YKV | OP FOR icrc |
| ☐ | ZS-OOF | LET L-410UVP-E20 | 871920 | ex 5H-PAJ | Op for Air Express Algeria |
| ☐ | ZS-OSE | LET L-420 | 922729A | ex N420Y | Op for ICRC |
| ☐ | ZS-OUE | LET L-420 | 012735A | ex OK-GDM | Op for Air Express Algeria |
| ☐ | ZS-OXR | LET L-410UVP | 922730 | ex 5H-HSA | Op for UN |
| ☐ | ZS-PNI | LET L-410UVP-E20 | 871904 | ex 5Y-BSV | Op for UN |
| ☐ | 5Y-BRU | LET L-410UVP-E9 | 912539 | ex 5X-UAY | >Aero Kenya |
| ☐ | 9G-LET | LET L-410UVP-E20 | 871922 | ex ZS-OOH | >CTQ |

### AIRLINK Link (4Z/LNK) Johannesburg-OR Tambo (JNB)

| | | | | | |
|---|---|---|---|---|---|
| ☐ | ZS-ASW | Avro 146-RJ85 | E2313 | ex N505XJ | <SFR |
| ☐ | ZS-ASX | Avro 146-RJ85 | E2314 | ex N506XJ | <SFR |
| ☐ | ZS-ASY | Avro 146-RJ85 | E2316 | ex N507XJ | <SFR |
| ☐ | ZS-ASZ | Avro 146-RJ85 | E2318 | ex N508XJ | <SFR |
| ☐ | ZS-SSH | Avro 146-RJ85 | E2285 | ex G-CGMT | |

| | | | | | | |
|---|---|---|---|---|---|---|
| ☐ | ZS-SSI | Avro 146-RJ85 | E2383 | ex G-LCYB | | |
| ☐ | ZS-SSJ | Avro 146-RJ85 | E2385 | ex G-LCYC | | |
| ☐ | ZS-SSK | Avro 146-RJ85 | E2251 | ex G-CGSM | | |
| | | | | | | |
| ☐ | ZS-NRE | British Aerospace Jetstream 41 | 41048 | ex G-4-048 | | |
| ☐ | ZS-NRF | British Aerospace Jetstream 41 | 41050 | ex G-4-050 | | |
| ☐ | ZS-NRG | British Aerospace Jetstream 41 | 41051 | ex G-4-051 | | |
| ☐ | ZS-NRH | British Aerospace Jetstream 41 | 41054 | ex G-4-054 | | |
| ☐ | ZS-NRI | British Aerospace Jetstream 41 | 41061 | ex G-4-061 | | |
| ☐ | ZS-NRJ | British Aerospace Jetstream 41 | 41062 | ex G-4-062 | | |
| ☐ | ZS-NRK | British Aerospace Jetstream 41 | 41065 | ex G-4-065 | | >SZL |
| ☐ | ZS-NRL | British Aerospace Jetstream 41 | 41068 | ex G-4-068 | | |
| ☐ | ZS-OEX | British Aerospace Jetstream 41 | 41103 | ex G-4-103 | | |
| ☐ | ZS-OMS | British Aerospace Jetstream 41 | 41035 | ex VH-JSX | | |
| ☐ | ZS-OMY | British Aerospace Jetstream 41 | 41036 | ex VH-CCJ | | |
| ☐ | ZS-OMZ | British Aerospace Jetstream 41 | 41037 | ex VH-CCW | | >PFZ |
| | | | | | | |
| ☐ | ZS-OTM | Embraer ERJ-135LR | 145485 | ex PT-SXE | | |
| ☐ | ZS-OTN | Embraer ERJ-135LR | 145491 | ex PT-SXK | | |
| ☐ | ZS-OUV | Embraer ERJ-135LR | 145493 | ex PT-SXM | Op as Airlink Zimbabwe | |
| ☐ | ZS-SJX | Embraer ERJ-135LR | 145428 | ex PT-STZ | | |
| ☐ | ZS-SNV | Embraer ERJ-135LR | 145551 | ex N845RP | | |
| ☐ | ZS-SNW | Embraer ERJ-135LR | 145720 | ex N838RP | | |
| ☐ | ZS-SNX | Embraer ERJ-135LR | 145620 | ex N844RP | | |
| ☐ | ZS-SNZ | Embraer ERJ-135LR | 145725 | ex N840RP | | |
| ☐ | ZS-SUV | Embraer EJR-135LR | 145663 | ex PT-TJA | | ♦ |
| | | | | | | |
| ☐ | ZS- | Embraer ERJ-170LR | | ex | | o/o |
| ☐ | ZS- | Embraer ERJ-170LR | | ex | | o/o |

### AIRQUARIUS AVIATION — Quarius (AQU) — Lanseria (HLA)

| | | | | | | |
|---|---|---|---|---|---|---|
| ☐ | ZS-DRF | Fokker F.28 Fellowship 4000 | 11239 | ex 5Y-LLL | Lynne | wfs |
| ☐ | ZS-ERI | Fokker 100 | 11256 | ex N285AP | | wfs♦ |
| ☐ | ZS-GAV | Fokker 100 | 11254 | ex N284AP | | wfs♦ |
| ☐ | ZS-SKA | Fokker 70 | 11559 | ex PH-ZFT | | |
| ☐ | ZS-SOP | British Aerospace 146 Srs.300 | E3187 | ex G-BSYT | | ♦ |
| ☐ | ZS-JES | Fokker F.28 Fellowship 4000 | 11236 | ex 5H-MVK | Jessica | |
| ☐ | ZS-XGW | Fokker F.28 Fellowship 4000 | 11130 | ex SE-DGN | | [HLA] |

### ALLEGIANCE AIR — (ANJ) — Kruger Mpumalanga International

| | | | | | |
|---|---|---|---|---|---|
| ☐ | ZS-AAG | Embraer EMB.120ER Brasilia | 120252 | ex TN-AHV | ♦ |

### AVEX AIR TRANSPORT

| | | | | | |
|---|---|---|---|---|---|
| ☐ | ZS-AAK | Dornier 328-300 (328JET) | 3162 | ex OY-NCR | ♦ |

### AWESOME FLIGHT SERVICES — Awesome (ASM) — Lanseria (HLA)

| | | | | | |
|---|---|---|---|---|---|
| ☐ | ZS-JAZ | Beech 1900D | UE-6 | ex VT-AVJ | |
| ☐ | ZS-PRG | Beech 1900D | UE-90 | ex VH-VAU | |
| ☐ | ZS-SNO | Beech 1900D | UE-96 | ex ZS-PPK | |

### BIONIC AIR

| | | | | | |
|---|---|---|---|---|---|
| ☐ | ZS-PVU | Boeing 737-2Q8C | 21959/610 | ex N741AS | >PGV |

### BRANSON AIR

| | | | | | |
|---|---|---|---|---|---|
| ☐ | TR-DAL | Boeing 737-2L9 | 22735/825 | ex ZS-GAV | [HLA]♦ |
| ☐ | ZS-KIS | Boeing 737-291 | 22743/909 | ex CC-CVG | [HLA]♦ |
| ☐ | ZS-MAD | Fokker F.28 Fellowship 4000 | 11225 | ex 5H-ZAS | ♦ |

### CEM AIR — (KEM)

| | | | | | |
|---|---|---|---|---|---|
| ☐ | ZS-CRJ | Canadair CRJ-100LR | 7338 | ex N798CA | [HLA]♦ |

### CHC HELICOPTERS (AFRICA) — Cape Town-International (CPT)

| | | | | | |
|---|---|---|---|---|---|
| ☐ | D2-EVP | Aérospatiale AS.332L2 II | 2398 | ex F-WQEA | >SOR |
| ☐ | ZS-HVJ | Sikorsky S-61N | 61493 | ex N9119Z | wfs |
| ☐ | ZS-KEI | Convair 580 | 141 | ex N5822 | |
| ☐ | ZS-LYL | Convair 580 | 39 | ex N511GA | |
| ☐ | ZS-RDI | Bell 206L-3 LongRanger III | 51392 | ex N521EV | |
| ☐ | ZS-RDV | Sikorsky S-61N | 61716 | ex G-BIHH | based SSG |
| ☐ | ZS-RGV | Bell 212 | 30952 | ex C-FRUU | |
| ☐ | ZS-RKO | Sikorsky S-76A++ | 760135 | ex VH-LAX | |

| | | | | | |
|---|---|---|---|---|---|
| ☐ | ZS-RKP | Sikorsky S-76A++ | 760198 | ex VH-LAY | Marine 2 |
| ☐ | ZS-RLK | Sikorsky S-61N | 61772 | ex G-BEWM | |
| ☐ | ZS-RLL | Sikorsky S-61N | 61778 | ex G-BFFK | |
| ☐ | ZS-RNG | Sikorsky S-76A++ | 760036 | ex D2-EXJ | based BSG <CHC Scotia |
| ☐ | ZS-RNP | Bell 212 | 30893 | ex C-FPKW | based Malabo |
| ☐ | ZS-RNR | Bell 212 | 30829 | ex C-FRWL | based Malabo |
| ☐ | ZS-RPI | Sikorsky S-76A++ | 760049 | ex G-BHGK | based BSG <CHC Scotia |

A member of CHC Helicopter Corp; ops from bases in Equatorial Guinea, Namibia and Angola as well as South Africa

| COMAIR | | Commercial (MN/CAW) | | Johannesburg-OR Tambo (JNB) | |
|---|---|---|---|---|---|
| ☐ | ZS-OAH | Boeing 737-33A | 24460/1831 | ex N460TF | Kulula colours |
| ☐ | ZS-OAI | Boeing 737-33A | 24030/1654 | ex N240TF | Kulula colours |
| ☐ | ZS-OKB | Boeing 737-376 | 23477/1225 | ex VH-TAF | BAW colours |
| ☐ | ZS-OKC | Boeing 737-376 | 23484/1270 | ex VH-TAJ | BAW colours |
| ☐ | ZS-OKG | Boeing 737-376 | 23483/1264 | ex VH-TAI | BAW colours |
| ☐ | ZS-OKH | Boeing 737-376 | 23479/1259 | ex VH-TAH | BAW colours |
| ☐ | ZS-OKI | Boeing 737-376 | 23489/1356 | ex VH-TAX | BAW colours |
| ☐ | ZS-OKJ | Boeing 737-376 | 23487/1306 | ex VH-TAV | BAW colours |
| ☐ | ZS-OKK | Boeing 737-376 | 23485/1277 | ex VH-TAK | BAW colours |
| | | | | | |
| ☐ | ZS-OAA | Boeing 737-4L7 | 26960/2483 | ex VH-RON | |
| ☐ | ZS-OAF | Boeing 737-4S3 | 25116/2061 | ex PP-VTL | Kulula colours |
| ☐ | ZS-OAG | Boeing 737-4H6 | 27168/2435 | ex JA737D | Kulula colours |
| ☐ | ZS-OAM | Boeing 737-4S3 | 24164/1702 | ex EI-DFE | Kulula colours |
| ☐ | ZS-OAO | Boeing 737-4S3 | 24163/1700 | ex EI-DFD | Kulula colours |
| ☐ | ZS-OAP | Boeing 737-4S3 | 24167/1736 | ex EI-DFF | Kulula colours |
| ☐ | ZS-OAV | Boeing 737-4H6 | 27086/2426 | ex JA737C | |
| ☐ | ZS-OTF | Boeing 737-436 | 25305/2147 | ex G-DOCC | Kulula colours |
| ☐ | ZS-OTG | Boeing 737-436 | 25840/2197 | ex G-DOCJ | BAW colours <SFR |
| ☐ | ZS-OTH | Boeing 737-436 | 25841/2222 | ex G-DOCK | kulula special colours |
| | | | | | |
| ☐ | ZS-ZWA | Boeing 737-8LD/W | 40851 | | o/o♦ |
| ☐ | ZS-ZWB | Boeing 737-8LD/W | 40852 | | o/o♦ |
| ☐ | ZS-ZWC | Boeing 737-8LD/W | 40853 | | o/o♦ |
| ☐ | ZS-ZWD | Boeing 737-8LD/W | 40855 | | o/o♦ |
| ☐ | ZS-ZWO | Boeing 737-8K2/W | 28373/51 | ex PH-HZA | |
| ☐ | ZS-ZWP | Boeing 737-86N/W | 28612/455 | ex OK-PIK | |
| ☐ | ZS-ZWQ | Boeing 737-8K2/W | 28374/57 | ex PH-HZB | |
| ☐ | ZS-ZWR | Boeing 737-85P/W | 28382/256 | ex EC-HBM | ♦ |
| ☐ | ZS-ZWS | Boeing 737-86N/W | 32732/1056 | ex M-ABDO | ♦ |

| DHL AVIATION | Worldstar (DHV) | Lanseria (HLA) |
|---|---|---|

Utilises Cessna 208B Caravans and ATR 42 op by Solenta Aviation in full DHL colours

| DODSON INTERNATIONAL CHARTER | | | | Pretoria-Wonderboom (PRY) | |
|---|---|---|---|---|---|
| ☐ | ZS-OJJ | AMI Turbo DC-3TP | 16213/32961 | ex N8194Q | op for UN / Red Cross |
| ☐ | ZS-OJM | AMI Turbo DC-3TP | 14101/25546 | ex N330RD | white c/s |

| EGOLI AIR | | | | Johannesburg-Rand (QRA) | |
|---|---|---|---|---|---|
| ☐ | ZS-PSO | Antonov An-32B | 2808 | ex RA-48059 | |

| EXECUJET SOUTH AFRICA | | | | | |
|---|---|---|---|---|---|
| ☐ | ZS-PDP | SAAB SF.340B | 340B-289 | ex B-3651 | ♦ |

| EXECUTIVE AEROSPACE | | Aerospace (EAS) | | Johannesburg-OR Tambo (JNB) | |
|---|---|---|---|---|---|
| ☐ | ZS-LSO | Hawker Siddeley HS.748 Srs.2B/FAA | 1783 | ex G-BMJU | |
| ☐ | ZS-NWW | Hawker Siddeley HS.748 Srs.2B/378 | 1786 | ex G-HDBC | |
| ☐ | ZS-PLO | Hawker Siddeley HS.748 Srs.2B/378 | 1797 | ex G-EMRD | [JNB] |

Ceased ops Sep07

| EXECUTIVE TURBINE AIR CHARTER / AIRCRAFT CONTRACTS AFRICA | | | | | |
|---|---|---|---|---|---|
| | | | (TEA) | | Lanseria (HLA) |
| ☐ | ZS-OKU | Beech 1900C-1 | UC-50 | ex 7Q-NXA | |
| ☐ | ZS-OUG | Beech 1900D | UE-14 | ex (ZS-OPI) | all-white |
| ☐ | ZS-OYG | Beech 1900D | UE-230 | ex 5N-BCQ | all-white |
| ☐ | ZS-PHL | Beech 1900C-1 | UC-74 | ex N374UC | |
| ☐ | ZS-PKA | Beech 1900D | UE-228 | ex N228GL | ♦ |
| ☐ | ZS-PKB | Beech 1900D | UE-3 | ex N3YV | >TravelMax |
| ☐ | ZS-PPM | Beech 1900D | UE-150 | ex N150GL | UNHS |
| ☐ | ZS-PVN | Beech 1900D | UE-51 | ex N51YV | ♦ |
| ☐ | ZS-PVV | Beech 1900D | UE-59 | ex N59YV | ♦ |
| ☐ | ZS-PZE | Beech 1900D | UE-32 | ex N83611 | ♦ |

| | | | | | |
|---|---|---|---|---|---|
| ☐ | ZS-ETA | Embraer EMB.120ER Brasilia | 120277 | ex N213SW | wfs |
| ☐ | ZS-LFM | Beech 200 Super King Air | BB-954 | ex N1839S | |
| ☐ | ZS-MES | Beech B200 Super King Air | BB-1038 | ex N223MH | |
| ☐ | ZS-PRC | Beech B200 Super King Air | BB-1341 | ex OY-GEU | Beech 1300 conversion |

## FAIR AVIATION

| | | | | | |
|---|---|---|---|---|---|
| ☐ | ZS-BIL | Boeing 737-277 | 22650/1981 | ex UP-B3702 | <Jet 4 Now♦ |
| ☐ | ZS-SMO | British Aerospace 146 Srs.300 | E3169 | ex G-BSNS | ♦ |

## FEDERAL AIR — Fedair (FDR) — Durban-Virginia (VIR)

| | | | | | | |
|---|---|---|---|---|---|---|
| ☐ | ZS-OXN | Beech 1900D | UE-83 | ex N831SK | all-white | |
| ☐ | ZS-PJY | Beech 1900D | UE-204 | ex N204GL | | op for UN♦ |
| ☐ | ZS-PRH | Beech 1900D | UE-316 | ex N21716 | all-white | <SLE |
| ☐ | ZS-PUC | Beech 1900D | UE-84 | ex N841SK | all-white | |
| ☐ | ZS-PWY | Beech 1900D | UE-87 | ex N87SK | all-white | |
| | | | | | | |
| ☐ | ZS-DAT | Pilatus PC-12/45 | 242 | ex HB-FRM | | |
| ☐ | ZS-FDR | Beech 200 Super King Air | BB-1234 | ex N971LE | | |
| ☐ | ZS-FDL | Cessna 208B Caravan I | 208B0896 | ex 5Y-TWJ | | |
| ☐ | ZS-KNL | Cessna 402C II | 402C0646 | ex N6814D | | |
| ☐ | ZS-LXO | Beech Baron 58 | TH-886 | ex N23527 | | |
| ☐ | ZS-OJC | Cessna 208B Caravan I | 208B0593 | ex N1194F | | |
| ☐ | ZS-THR | Cessna 208B Caravan I | 208B0571 | ex N282FV | | ♦ |
| ☐ | 5H-FED | Cessna 208B Caravan I | 208B0571 | ex ZS-FED | | |

## FUGRO AIRBORNE SURVEYS — Lanseria (HLA)

| | | | | | |
|---|---|---|---|---|---|
| ☐ | PR-FAS | Cessna 208B Caravan I | 208B0462 | ex C-GRCK | ♦ |
| ☐ | VH-FAY | Cessna 208B Caravan I | 208B0884 | ex C-GJQV | ♦ |
| ☐ | ZS-FGQ | Cessna 208 Caravan I | 20800251 | ex C-GFAV | ♦ |
| ☐ | ZS-FSA | Cessna 208B Caravan I | 208B0877 | ex N208LW | ♦ |
| ☐ | ZS-FSB | Cessna 208B Caravan i | 208B0860 | ex PR-SSB | ♦ |
| ☐ | ZS-MSJ | Cessna 208 Caravan I | 20800030 | ex A2-AHJ | ♦ |
| | | | | | |
| ☐ | VH-TEM | CASA C.212-200 | CC37-1-138 | ex P2-CNP | ♦ |
| ☐ | ZS-AIU | Cessna 404 Titan II | 404-0082 | ex A2-AIU | |
| ☐ | ZS-FTA | Cessna 210N Centurion II | 21063562 | ex VH-JBH | |
| ☐ | ZS-KRG | Cessna 404 Titan II | 404-0676 | ex N6761Y | |

## GIDEON AIR

| | | | | | |
|---|---|---|---|---|---|
| ☐ | ZS-SIL | Boeing 737-244 | 22591/859 | | ♦ |

## GLOBAL AVIATION LEASING — (GBB)

| | | | | | |
|---|---|---|---|---|---|
| ☐ | S9-GAS | McDonnell-Douglas DC-10-10 | 47832/318 | ex ZS-GAS | [TIP]♦ |
| ☐ | ZS-GAB | McDonnell-Douglas MD-82 | 49165/1117 | ex 3D-GAA | |
| ☐ | ZS-GAG | Douglas DC-9-32 | 47190/240 | ex 5X-GLO | [TIP]♦ |
| ☐ | ZS-GAP | McDonnell-Douglas DC10-10 | 46646/285 | ex S9-GAP | [JNB]♦ |
| ☐ | ZS-GAR | Douglas DC-9-32 | 47132/229 | ex 3D-MRO | [JNB]♦ |
| ☐ | ZS-GAT | Douglas DC-9-32 | 47797/913 | ex 3D-MRT | [JNB]♦ |
| ☐ | ZS-GAU | Douglas DC-9-32 | 47798/914 | ex 3D-MRU | >VEL♦ |
| ☐ | ZS-SUH | McDonnell-Douglas MD-82 | 49325/1290 | ex N33414 | ♦ |
| ☐ | ZS-TOG | McDonnell-Douglas MD-82 | 49905/1767 | ex N905TA | ♦ |

## IMPERIAL AIR CARGO — Johannesburg-OR Tambo (JNB)

| | | | | | |
|---|---|---|---|---|---|
| ☐ | ZS-IAB | Boeing 737-210C | 20917/344 | ex N834AL | |
| ☐ | ZS-IAC | Boeing 727-227F (Raisbeck 3) | 21247/1217 | ex N73751 | <SFR |
| ☐ | ZS-IAD | Boeing 737-2X6C | 23292/1113 | ex N817AL | ♦ |

## INTER-AIR — Inline (D6/ILN) — Johannesburg-OR Tambo (JNB)

| | | | | | |
|---|---|---|---|---|---|
| ☐ | ZS-IJA | Boeing 737-201 | 22751/857 | ex N245US | ♦ |
| ☐ | ZS-IJB | Boeing 767-266ERM | 23180/99 | ex N573JW | |
| ☐ | ZS-SIH | Boeing 737-244 | 22587/835 | | |
| ☐ | ZS-SIM | Boeing 737-244 | 22828/881 | | |

## INTERLINK AIRLINES — Interlink (ID/ITK) — Johannesburg-OR Tambo (JNB)

Ceased ops Feb10

## JET 4 NOW

| | | | | | |
|---|---|---|---|---|---|
| ☐ | ZS-BIL | Boeing 737-277 | 22650/1981 | ex UP-B3702 | >Fair Avn♦ |

## KING AIR CHARTER (RXX) Lanseria (HLA)

| | Reg | Type | Serial | Notes | |
|---|---|---|---|---|---|
| ☐ | ZS-HFG | Bell 206B JetRanger | 1864 | | |
| ☐ | ZS-JSC | Beech B200 Super King Air | BB-1985 | ex N71850 | |
| ☐ | ZS-LFW | Beech B200 Super King Air | BB-999 | ex 9Q-CPV | |
| ☐ | ZS-LRS | Beech 200C Super King Air | BL-20 | ex 5Y-LRS | |
| ☐ | ZS-MPC | Cessna 402C II | 402C0426 | ex C9-MEB | |
| ☐ | ZS-NHW | Grumman G-159 Gulfstream I | 141 | ex N800PA | |
| ☐ | ZS-OED | Beech B200 Super King Air | BB-1149 | ex N200HF | |
| ☐ | ZS-RFS | Bell 206L-4 LongRanger IV | 52116 | ex N4252S | |
| ☐ | ZS-RXR | Bell 205A-1 | 30290 | ex D-HAFW | ♦ |
| ☐ | ZS-SHH | Beech 1900D | UE-36 | ex N136MJ | |

## KULULA.COM Johannesburg-OR Tambo (JNB)

Wholly owned low cost, no frills subsidiary of Comair who op the aircraft

## MANGO (JE) Johannesburg-OR Tambo (JNB)

| | Reg | Type | Serial | Notes | |
|---|---|---|---|---|---|
| ☐ | ZS-SJG | Boeing 737-8BG/W | 32353/711 | ex N1786B | |
| ☐ | ZS-SJH | Boeing 737-8BG/W | 32354/725 | ex PH-HZQ | |
| ☐ | ZS-SJK | Boeing 737-8BG/W | 32355/807 | ex PH-HZT | |
| ☐ | ZS-SJL | Boeing 737-8BG/W | 32356/819 | ex PH-HZZ | |
| ☐ | ZS-SJP | Boeing 737-8BG/W | 32358/955 | ex PH-HZU | ♦ |

## NAC CHARTER Slipstream (SLE) Lanseria (HLA)

| | Reg | Type | Serial | Notes | | |
|---|---|---|---|---|---|---|
| ☐ | ZS-NBJ | Beech B200 Super King Air | BB-1070 | ex SE-KND | | |
| ☐ | ZS-OCI | Beech 200 Super King Air | BB-121 | ex TR-LDX | | |
| ☐ | ZS-ODI | Beech 200 Super King Air | BB-1542 | ex N202JT | | |
| ☐ | ZS-OUI | Beech 200 Super King Air | BB-688 | ex 5R-MGH | Catpass 250 conversion | |
| ☐ | ZS-PLJ | Beech B200 Super King Air | BB-1401 | ex VH-YDH | | ♦ |
| ☐ | ZS-SMC | Beech B200 Super King Air | BB-1489 | ex N1563M | | |
| ☐ | ZS- | Beech B200 Super King Air | BB-884 | ex N49JG | | ♦ |
| ☐ | ZS-ONI | Beech 1900D | UE-312 | ex D2-EVL | | ♦ |
| ☐ | ZS-OOW | Beech 1900D | UE-57 | ex N57ZV | | ♦ |
| ☐ | ZS-ORV | Beech 1900D | UE-42 | ex N42YV | all-white | |
| ☐ | ZS-OSF | Beech 1900D | UE-35 | ex N35YV | | |
| ☐ | ZS-OYD | Beech 1900D | UE-191 | ex VH-IAR | <Air Express Algeria♦ | |
| ☐ | ZS-OYF | Beech 1900D | UE-214 | VH-IMS | <Air Express Algeria♦ | |
| ☐ | ZS-OYL | Beech 1900D | UE-324 | ex A6-YST | | ♦ |
| ☐ | ZS-OZZ | Beech 1900C-1 | UC-73 | ex n1570b | | ♦ |
| ☐ | ZS-PMF | Beech 1900C-1 | UC-37 | ex N32017 | | |
| ☐ | ZS-PPI | Beech 1900D | UE-179 | ex N179GL | | ♦ |
| ☐ | ZS-PPM | Beech 1900D | UE-150 | ex N150GL | | ♦ |
| ☐ | ZS-PRH | Beech 1900D | UE-316 | ex N21716 | >FDR♦ | |
| ☐ | ZS-SET | Beech 1900D | UE-265 | ex VT-AVR | | ♦ |
| ☐ | ZS-SGH | Beech 1900D | UE-263 | ex CN-RLB | | |
| ☐ | ZS-SNJ | Beech 1900D | UE-131 | ex N131YV | | |
| ☐ | ZS-SNK | Beech 1900D | UE-132 | ex N132YV | | |
| ☐ | ZS-SRZ | Beech 1900D | UE-133 | ex N133YV | | |
| ☐ | ZS-CFA | British Aerospace 125-1000A | 259024 | ex ZS-ABG | | ♦ |
| ☐ | ZS-EPV | Pacific Aerospace 750XL | 144 | | | ♦ |
| ☐ | ZS-HKV | Aérospatiale AS350B Ecureuil | 1528 | | | |
| ☐ | ZS-MJW | Piper PA-46-350P Malibu | 46-36519 | ex N2441L | | ♦ |
| ☐ | ZS-MKI | Beech 65-C90A King Air | LJ-1099 | ex Z-MKI | | |
| ☐ | ZS-PNN | Beech 95-B55 Baron | TC-1794 | ex A2-EAH | | |
| ☐ | ZS-RDR | Bell 206B JetRanger III | 4183 | ex Z-RDR | | |
| ☐ | ZS-RJO | Bell 407 | 53206 | | | |
| ☐ | ZS-RPC | Bell 407 | 53365 | ex C-GAHJ | | |
| ☐ | ZS-SHJ | Pacific Aerospace 750XL | 148 | ex ZK-JSU | | ♦ |
| ☐ | ZS-SRR | Pilatus PC-12/45 | 319 | | | ♦ |
| ☐ | ZS-SUW | Beech 330 | RB-66 | ex G-VONJ | | |
| ☐ | ZS-TVT | Beech Baron 58 | TH-1962 | ex N584j | | |

## NATIONAL AIRWAYS CORP (LFI)

| | Reg | Type | Serial | Notes | |
|---|---|---|---|---|---|
| ☐ | ZS-PGY | Embraer EMB.120RT Brasilia | 120194 | ex N269UE | ♦ |
| ☐ | ZS-POE | Embraer EMB.120RT Brasilia | 120137 | ex N137H | ♦ |
| ☐ | ZS-PUH | Embraer EMB.120RT Brasilia | 120151 | ex N196SW | ♦ |
| ☐ | ZS-PVF | Embraer EMB.120RT Brasilia | 120261 | ex EC-HFZ | ♦ |
| ☐ | ZS-SAU | Embraer EMB.120RT Brasilia | 120212 | ex N243CA | ♦ |
| ☐ | ZS-SRW | Embraer EMB.120RT Brasilia | 120018 | ex N95644 | ♦ |
| ☐ | ZS-ACS | Beech B200 Super King Air | BB-961 | ex A2-AHA | ♦ |
| ☐ | ZS-KGW | Beech 200 Super King Air | BB-381 | ex N4848M | ♦ |
| ☐ | ZS-KMN | Beech 58 Baron | TH-153 | ex F-ODMJ | ♦ |
| ☐ | ZS-OXV | Cessna 208B Caravan I | 208B0563 | ex N330AK | ♦ |

| | ZS-PCC | Beech 1900C-1 | UC-143 | ex 9J-AWS | all-white | <City Square 526♦ |
| | ZS-PLL | Beech B200 Super King Air | BB-1189 | ex VH-KBH | | based KBL♦ |
| | ZS-RWN | Aérospatiale AS350BA Ecureuil | 1866 | ex F-GJAM | | ♦ |

## NELAIR CHARTERS & TRAVEL  Nelair (NLC)  Nelspruit (NLP)

| | ZS-EDG | Cessna U206 Super Skywagon | U206-0382 | ex N2182F | |
| | ZS-EVB | Piper PA-30 Twin Comanche 160B | 30-1218 | ex N8134Y | |
| | ZS-IKZ | Piper PA-32-300 Cherokee Six E | 32-7240070 | ex ZS-XAS | |
| | ZS-JGW | Cessna 401B | 401B0106 | ex N7966Q | |
| | ZS-JTX | Piper PA-31-350 Navajo Chieftain | 31-7652059 | ex N59800 | |
| | ZS-JZX | Piper PA-34-200T Seneca II | 34-7770269 | ex N5911V | |
| | ZS-LTL | Cessna 310Q | 310Q0025 | ex N8925Z | |
| | ZS-LVR | Douglas DC-3 | 20475 | ex N5000E | |
| | ZS-MHE | Piper PA-31-350 Navajo Chieftain | 31-7305096 | ex N74950 | |
| | ZS-MSO | Piper PA-32-300 Cherokee Six | 32-7540083 | ex N33050 | |
| | ZS-NAO | Cessna T210L Centurion II | 21060092 | ex N59104 | |
| | ZS-NKG | Cessna 208 Caravan I | 20800178 | ex 5Y-NKG | |
| | ZS-PHI | Grumman G-159 Gulfstream I | 164 | ex N290AS | |
| | ZS-RAN | Cessna 402B | 402B0439 | ex ZS-XAV | |

## NORSE AIR  Norse Air (NRX)  Lanseria (HLA)

| | ZS-PDR | SAAB SF.340B | 340B-292 | ex 9N-AHK | wfs |
| | ZS-PKM | Beech 200 Super King Air | BB-382 | ex N92M | |
| | ZS-PMJ | SAAF SF.340A | 340A-044 | ex 9G-CTL | <CTQ [ACC] |

## 1TIME AIRLINE  Next Time (1T/RNX)  Johannesburg-OR Tambo (JNB)

| | ZS-OPX | McDonnell-Douglas MD-83 | 53012/1736 | ex N825NK | | <SFR♦ |
| | ZS-OPZ | McDonnell-Douglas MD-83 | 49617/1464 | ex N831NK | | <SFR |
| | ZS-SKB | McDonnell-Douglas MD-83 | 49966/2047 | ex G-FLTK | | <SFR |
| | ZS-TRI | McDonnell-Douglas MD-83 | 49707/1487 | ex N315FV | | |
| | ZS-TRL | McDonnell-Douglas MD-83 | 49968/1668 | ex N499AR | | ♦ |
| | ZS-OBK | McDonnell-Douglas MD-82 | 49115/1135 | ex F-GPZE | kulula colours | <SFR |
| | ZS-TRD | McDonnell-Douglas MD-82 | 48022/1079 | ex PK-LMS | Tjooning You Straight | |
| | ZS-TRE | McDonnell-Douglas MD-82 | 49387/1288 | ex N954AS | | |
| | ZS-TRG | McDonnell-Douglas MD-87 | 49830/1684 | ex EC-GRN | | |
| | ZS-TRH | McDonnell-Douglas MD-87 | 49831/1688 | ex EC-GRO | | |
| | ZS-TRJ | McDonnell-Douglas MD-87 | 49829/1678 | ex EC-GRM | | ♦ |

## PEGASE AVIATION

| | ZS-PVU | Boeing 737-2Q8C | 21959/610 | ex N741AS | <Bionic [JNB}♦ |

## PELICAN AIR SERVICES  Pelican Airways (7V/PDF)  Johannesburg-OR Tambo (JNB)

Also ops services with AMI Turbo DC-3TP and Grumman G-159 Gulfstream aircraft leased from Dodson International and Nelair as required. Assoc with Ryan Blake Air Charter.

## PHOEBUS APOLLO AVIATION  Phoebus (PHB)  Johannesburg-Rand (QRA)

| | ZS-DIW | Douglas DC-3 | 11991 | ex SAAF 6871 | | Pegasus |
| | ZS-PAI | Douglas C-54E | 27319 | ex N4989K | Atlas | |
| | ZS-PAK | Douglas DC-9-32 | 47368/505 | ex D6-CAW | | ♦ |
| | ZS-PAL | Douglas DC-9-32CF | 47704/819 | ex 5N-BHC | | ♦ |
| | S9-DAB | Douglas DC-9-32 | 47313/268 | ex LV-YAB | | ♦ |

## PROGRESS AIR  Lanseria (HLA)

Aircraft sold Apr11

## QWILA AIR  Q-Charter (QWL)  Lanseria (HLA)

| | ZS-NUF | Beech 200C Super King Air | BL-4 | ex V5-AAL | |
| | ZS-OKL | Beech 1900D | UE-48 | ex 5Y-OKL | |
| | ZS-OMC | Beech 1900D | UE-18 | ex N18YV | |
| | ZS-PRE | Beech 1900C | UB-15 | ex N715GL | all-white |
| | ZS-SLG | Cessna 208B Caravan I | 208B0772 | ex N208LT | |

## ROSSAIR

| | ZS-OLP | Beech 1900C | UB-18 | ex Z-DHS | ♦ |
| | ZS-OLW | Beech 1900D | UE-33 | ex N33YV | ♦ |
| | ZS-PIR | Beech 1900D | UE-29 | ex PH-RAG | ♦ |

## ROVOS AIR      Rovos (VOS)      Pretoria-Wonderboom (PRY)

| | | | | | |
|---|---|---|---|---|---|
| ☐ | ZS-ARV | Convair 340-67 | 228 | ex CP-2237 | [PRY] |
| ☐ | ZS-AUA | Douglas DC-4 | 42934 | ex PH-DDS | Flying Dutchman colours |
| ☐ | ZS-BRV | Convair 340-67 | 215 | ex CP-2236 | [PRY] |
| ☐ | ZS-CRV | Douglas DC-3 | 13331 | ex ZS-PTG | Delaney |

## RYAN BLAKE AIR CHARTER      Johannesburg-Rand (QRA)

Ceased ops

## SA EXPRESS      Expressways (XZ/EXY)      Johannesburg-OR Tambo (JNB)

| | | | | | | |
|---|---|---|---|---|---|---|
| ☐ | ZS-NBA | Canadair CRJ-200ER | 7702 | ex N484CA | | |
| ☐ | ZS-NMC | Canadair CRJ-200ER | 7225 | ex N626BR | | |
| ☐ | ZS-NMD | Canadair CRJ-200ER | 7233 | ex N627BR | | |
| ☐ | ZS-NME | Canadair CRJ-200ER | 7240 | ex N628BR | | |
| ☐ | ZS-NMF | Canadair CRJ-200ER | 7287 | ex N634BR | | |
| ☐ | ZS-NMG | Canadair CRJ-200ER | 7772 | ex 5N-BJI | | |
| ☐ | ZS-NMH | Canadair CRJ-200ER | 7787 | ex 5N-BJK | | |
| ☐ | ZS-NMI | Canadair CRJ-200ER | 7153 | ex C-FZAN | | |
| ☐ | ZS-NMJ | Canadair CRJ-200ER | 7161 | ex C-GAUG | | |
| ☐ | ZS-NMK | Canadair CRJ-200ER | 7198 | ex C-GBMF | | |
| ☐ | ZS-NML | Canadair CRJ-200ER | 7201 | ex C-GBLX | | |
| ☐ | ZS-NMM | Canadair CRJ-200ER | 7234 | ex C-FMMT | | |
| ☐ | ZS-NMN | Canadair CRJ-200ER | 7237 | ex C-FMMX | | |
| ☐ | ZS-NBD | Canadair CRJ-701 | 10033 | ex N610QX | | |
| ☐ | ZS-NBF | Canadair CRJ-701ER | 10028 | ex D-ACSB | | |
| ☐ | ZS-NBG | Canadair CRJ-701ER | 10039 | ex D-ACSC | | ♦ |
| ☐ | ZS-NLT | Canadair CRJ-701 | 10024 | ex N607QX | | ♦ |
| ☐ | ZS-NLV | Canadair CRJ-701 | 10010 | ex N602QX | | |
| ☐ | ZS-NMO | de Havilland DHC-8-402Q | 4122 | ex C-FFCU | | ♦ |
| ☐ | ZS-NMS | de Havilland DHC-8-402Q | 4127 | ex C-FFPH | | |
| ☐ | ZS-YBP | de Havilland DHC-8-402Q | 4142 | ex G-JECS | | ♦ |
| ☐ | ZS-YBR | de Havilland DHC-8-402Q | 4144 | ex G-JECT | | ♦ |
| ☐ | ZS-YBT | de Havilland DHC-8-402Q | 4146 | ex G-JECU | | ♦ |
| ☐ | ZS-YBU | de Havilland DHC-8-402Q | 4370 | ex G-FLBJ | | ♦ |
| ☐ | ZS-YBW | de Havilland DHC-8-402Q | 4350 | ex G-FLBG | | ♦ |
| ☐ | ZS-YBX | de Havilland DHC-8-402Q | 4366 | ex G-FLBH | | ♦ |
| ☐ | ZS-YBY | de Havilland DHC-8-402Q | 4344 | ex G-FLBF | | ♦ |
| ☐ | ZS-NMB | de Havilland DHC-8-315 | 368 | ex C-GGIU | 306 | |
| ☐ | ZS-NMP | de Havilland DHC-8-315B | 420 | ex ZS-NNJ | 307 | |

## SAFAIR      Cargo (FA/(SFR)      Johannesburg-OR Tambo (JNB)

| | | | | | | |
|---|---|---|---|---|---|---|
| ☐ | ZS-JIZ | Lockheed L-382G-35C Hercules | 4695 | ex F-GNMM | | op for UN/WFP |
| ☐ | ZS-ORA | Lockheed L-382G-7C Hercules | 4208 | ex S9-CAY | | |
| ☐ | ZS-ORB | Lockheed L-382G-14C Hercules | 4248 | ex PK-YRW | | |
| ☐ | ZS-ORC | Lockheed L-382G-23C Hercules | 4388 | ex S9-BOQ | | |
| ☐ | ZS-RSC | Lockheed L-382G-28C Hercules | 4475 | ex S9-NAD | | |
| ☐ | ZS-RSF | Lockheed L-382G-31C Hercules | 4562 | ex S9-CAI | | op for UN |
| ☐ | ZS-RSG | Lockheed L-382G-31C Hercules | 4565 | ex S9-CAJ | | |
| ☐ | ZS-RSI | Lockheed L-382G-31C Hercules | 4600 | ex F-GIMV | | >FAB |
| ☐ | ZS-ASL | Boeing 737-3B3 (QC) | 24387/1693 | ex F-GFUE | | ♦ |
| ☐ | ZS-JRC | Boeing 737-42JF | 27143/2457 | ex N143HF | | [JNB]♦ |
| ☐ | ZS-OBK | McDonnell-Douglas MD-82 | 49115/1135 | ex F-GPZE | | >RNX |
| ☐ | ZS-OPX | McDonnell-Douglas MD-83 | 53012/1736 | ex N825NK | | >RNX |
| ☐ | ZS-OPZ | McDonnell-Douglas MD-83 | 49617/1464 | ex N831NK | | >RNX |
| ☐ | ZS-OTG | Boeing 737-436 | 25840/2197 | ex G-DOCJ | | >CAW |
| ☐ | ZS-SID | Boeing 737-244F | 22583/809 | | all-white | |
| ☐ | ZS-SIF | Boeing 737-244F | 22585/828 | | Komati | |
| ☐ | ZS-SIK | Boeing 737-244 | 22590/854 | ex 5N-YMM | | [JNB] |
| ☐ | ZS-SIT | Boeing 737-236 | 21790/599 | ex V5-AND | | >African Charter |
| ☐ | ZS-SKB | McDonnell-Douglas MD-83 | 49966/2047 | ex G-FLTK | | >RNX♦ |
| ☐ | ZS-SMG | Boeing 737-3Y0F | 23499/1242 | ex VP-BCJ | | ♦ |
| ☐ | ZS-SMJ | Boeing 737-3Y0F | 23500/1243 | ex VP-BCN | | ♦ |
| ☐ | 5Y-BXL | Boeing 737-33A | 23634/1423 | ex N175AW | | ♦ |

## SAHARA AFRICAN AVIATION

| | | | | | | |
|---|---|---|---|---|---|---|
| ☐ | ZS-PBT | Embraer EMB.120ER Brasilia | 120260 | ex N223BD | | ♦ |

## SKY ONE AIR      Lanseria (HLA)

| | | | | | |
|---|---|---|---|---|---|
| ☐ | ZS-PWM | Fokker F.28 Fellowship 000 | 11045 | ex PK-RJW | [MFC] |

## SKYHAUL | Skyhaul (HAU) | Johannesburg-OR Tambo (JNB)

| | | | | | |
|---|---|---|---|---|---|
| ☐ | ZS-SKI | Convair 580 | 186 | ex EC-GHN | >LAC SkyCongo |
| ☐ | ZS-SKK | Convair 580 | 135 | ex EC-GKH | >LAC SkyCongo |
| ☐ | ZS-SKL | Convair 580F | 458 | ex EC-GBF | |

## SOLENTA AVIATION | (SL/SET) | Lanseria (HLA)

| | | | | | | |
|---|---|---|---|---|---|---|
| ☐ | ZS-ATR | ATR 42-300F | 0060 | ex PH-XLC | | op for DHL |
| ☐ | ZS-LUC | ATR 42-320 | 0032 | ex PH-RAK | | |
| ☐ | ZS-OVP | ATR 42-300F | 0088 | ex F-WQNG | | op for DHL |
| ☐ | ZS-OVR | ATR 42-300F | 0116 | ex F-WQNB | | op for DHL |
| ☐ | ZS-OVS | ATR 42-300F | 0075 | ex F-WQNU | | op for DHL |
| ☐ | ZS-XCC | ATR 42-500 | 0528 | ex F-WKVI | | |
| ☐ | ZS-XCD | ATR 42-300F | 0228 | ex N422WA | | ♦ |
| | | | | | | |
| ☐ | ZS-AEA | Beech 1900D | UE-385 | ex HB-AEL | | ♦ |
| ☐ | ZS-MKE | Beech 1900D | UE-44 | ex PH-ACY | | op for UN |
| ☐ | ZS-NAC | Beech 1900D | UE-28 | ex N28YV | | |
| ☐ | ZS-NPT | Beech 1900C-1 | UC-113 | ex 5Y-HAC | | op for DHL |
| ☐ | ZS-ODG | Beech 1900C-1 | UC-158 | ex N158YV | | op for DHL |
| ☐ | ZS-OHE | Beech 1900C-1 | UC-48 | ex 9J-AFJ | | |
| ☐ | ZS-OLY | Beech 1900D | UE-39 | ex N39ZV | | op for UN |
| ☐ | ZS-OYC | Beech 1900D | UE-117 | ex VH-NTL | | |
| ☐ | ZS-OYE | Beech 1900D | UE-200 | ex VH-IAV | | op by Tullow Air |
| ☐ | ZS-OYJ | Beech 1900D | UE-273 | ex 5Y-NAC | | |
| ☐ | ZS-OYK | Beech 1900D | UE-318 | ex VH-NBN | all-white | op by Tullow Air |
| ☐ | ZS-PJX | Beech 1900D | UE-102 | ex P2-MBX | | |
| ☐ | ZS-ZED | Beech 1900D | UE-260 | ex N260GL | | op for UN |
| | | | | | | |
| ☐ | ZS-NIZ | Cessna 208B Caravan I | 208B0353 | ex 5Y-NIZ | | op for DHL |
| ☐ | ZS-OTV | Cessna 208B Caravan I | 208B0545 | ex 5Y-OTV | | ♦ |
| ☐ | ZS-SLR | Cessna 208B Caravan I | 208B0497 | ex N497AC | | op for DHL |
| ☐ | ZS-TIN | Cessna 208B Caravan I | 208B0261 | ex 9J-DHL | | op for DHL |
| ☐ | 5Y-OBY | Cessna 208B Caravan I | 208B0345 | ex ZS-OBY | | op for DHL |
| ☐ | 5Y-TLC | Cessna 208B Caravan I | 208B0472 | ex ZS-TLC | | op for DHL |
| | | | | | | |
| ☐ | TR-LIE | Antonov An-26 | 7504? | | | ♦ |
| ☐ | TR-LIN | Antonov An-26 | 2209? | | | ♦ |
| ☐ | ZS-BBI | Embraer ERJ-145LR | 145223 | ex N18982 | | ♦ |
| ☐ | ZS-BBJ | Embraer ERJ-145LR | 145277 | ex N13990 | | ♦ |
| ☐ | ZS-PEA | Beech 200C Super King Air | BL-29 | ex N500PH | all-white | |
| ☐ | ZS-XCB | ATR 72-212 | 0460 | ex 5H-PAR | | >SGG♦ |

## SOUTH AFRICAN AIRWAYS | Springbok (SA/SAA) | Johannesburg-OR Tambo (JNB)

Member of Star Alliance

| | | | | | | |
|---|---|---|---|---|---|---|
| ☐ | ZS-SFD | Airbus A319-131 | 2268 | ex D-AVWW | | |
| ☐ | ZS-SFE | Airbus A319-131 | 2281 | ex D-AVYK | | |
| ☐ | ZS-SFF | Airbus A319-131 | 2308 | ex D-AVYE | | |
| ☐ | ZS-SFG | Airbus A319-131 | 2326 | ex D-AVYT | | |
| ☐ | ZS-SFH | Airbus A319-131 | 2355 | ex D-AVWC | | |
| ☐ | ZS-SFI | Airbus A319-131 | 2375 | ex D-AVWR | | |
| ☐ | ZS-SFJ | Airbus A319-131 | 2379 | ex D-AVWU | | |
| ☐ | ZS-SFK | Airbus A319-131 | 2418 | ex D-AVYI | | |
| ☐ | ZS-SFL | Airbus A319-131 | 2438 | ex D-AVWP | | |
| ☐ | ZS-SFM | Airbus A319-131 | 2469 | ex D-AVYH | | |
| ☐ | ZS-SFN | Airbus A319-131 | 2501 | ex D-AVWD | | |
| | | | | | | |
| ☐ | ZS-SXU | Airbus A330-243 | 1271 | ex F-WWYX | | ♦ |
| ☐ | ZS-SXV | Airbus A330-243 | 1249 | ex F-WWYH | | ♦ |
| ☐ | ZS-SXW | Airbus A330-243 | 1236 | ex F-WWKA | | ♦ |
| ☐ | ZS-SXX | Airbus A330-243 | 1223 | ex F-WWYL | | ♦ |
| ☐ | ZS-SXY | Airbus A330-243 | 1210 | ex F-WWYS | | ♦ |
| ☐ | ZS-SXZ | Airbus A330-243 | 1191 | ex F-WWKL | | ♦ |
| | | | | | | |
| ☐ | ZS-SLC | Airbus A340-212 | 018 | ex D-AIBD | | |
| ☐ | ZS-SLF | Airbus A340-212 | 006 | ex D-AIBF | | |
| ☐ | ZS-SNA | Airbus A340-642 | 410 | ex F-WWCE | | |
| ☐ | ZS-SNB | Airbus A340-642 | 417 | ex F-WWCG | | |
| ☐ | ZS-SNC | Airbus A340-642 | 426 | ex F-WWCH | Star Alliance colours | |
| ☐ | ZS-SND | Airbus A340-642 | 531 | ex F-WWCX | | |
| ☐ | ZS-SNE | Airbus A340-642 | 534 | ex F-WWCY | | |
| ☐ | ZS-SNF | Airbus A340-642 | 547 | ex F-WWCI | | |
| ☐ | ZS-SNG | Airbus A340-642 | 557 | ex F-WWCG | | |
| ☐ | ZS-SNH | Airbus A340-642 | 626 | ex F-WWCF | | |
| ☐ | ZS-SNI | Airbus A340-642 | 630 | ex F-WWCG | | |
| ☐ | ZS-SXA | Airbus A340-313E | 544 | ex F-WWJS | | |
| ☐ | ZS-SXB | Airbus A340-313E | 582 | ex F-WWJT | | |
| ☐ | ZS-SXC | Airbus A340-313E | 590 | ex F-WWJY | | |

| ☐ | ZS-SXD | Airbus A340-313E | 643 | ex VT-JWA | |
| ☐ | ZS-SXE | Airbus A340-313E | 646 | ex VT-JWB | |
| ☐ | ZS-SXF | Airbus A340-313E | 651 | ex VT-JWC | |
| ☐ | ZS-SXG | Airbus A340-313X | 378 | ex F-WJKF | |
| ☐ | ZS-SXH | Airbus A340-313X | 197 | ex F-WJKP | |
| | | | | | |
| ☐ | ZS-SJA | Boeing 737-8S3/W | 29248/561 | | |
| ☐ | ZS-SJB | Boeing 737-8S3/W | 29249/653 | ex N1786B | |
| ☐ | ZS-SJC | Boeing 737-85F/W | 28828/565 | ex N1786B | |
| ☐ | ZS-SJD | Boeing 737-85F/W | 28829/582 | | |
| ☐ | ZS-SJE | Boeing 737-85F/W | 28830/669 | ex N1786B | |
| ☐ | ZS-SJF | Boeing 737-85F/W | 30006/688 | ex N1787B | |
| ☐ | ZS-SJG | Boeing 737-8BG/W | 32353/711 | ex N1786B | |
| ☐ | ZS-SJH | Boeing 737-8BG/W | 32354/725 | ex PH-HZQ | |
| ☐ | ZS-SJK | Boeing 737-8BG/W | 32355/807 | ex PH-HZT | |
| ☐ | ZS-SJL | Boeing 737-8BG/W | 32356/819 | ex PH-HZZ | |
| ☐ | ZS-SJM | Boeing 737-85F/W | 30476/789 | ex N788BA | |
| ☐ | ZS-SJN | Boeing 737-85F/W | 30569/850 | ex N1786B | |
| ☐ | ZS-SJO | Boeing 737-8BG/W | 32357/918 | ex PH-HZS | |
| ☐ | ZS-SJR | Boeing 737-844/W | 32631/1176 | ex N6067U | |
| ☐ | ZS-SJS | Boeing 737-844/W | 32632/1205 | | |
| ☐ | ZS-SJT | Boeing 737-844/W | 32633/1225 | | |
| ☐ | ZS-SJU | Boeing 737-844/W | 32634/1383 | | |
| ☐ | ZS-SJV | Boeing 737-844/W | 32635/1407 | ex N1787B | Star Alliance c/s |
| | | | | | |
| ☐ | ZS-SBA | Boeing 737-3Y0F | 26070/2349 | ex N700JZ | |
| ☐ | ZS-SBB | Boeing 737-3Y0F | 26072/2369 | ex N701JZ | |
| ☐ | ZS-SZY | Airbus A320-232 | 5011 | ex F-WWIA | ◆ |
| ☐ | ZS-SZZ | Airbus A320-232 | 4990 | ex D-AVVU | ◆ |

### SPRINGBOK CLASSIC AIR — Spring Classic (SPB) — Johannesburg-Rand (QRA)

| ☐ | ZS-CFC | Beech E-18S | BA-216 | | |

### STAR AIR CARGO — (BRH) — Johannesburg-OR Tambo (JNB)

| ☐ | A2-FMX | Boeing 737-247 (Nordam 3) | 23520/1329 | ex ZS-SHL | ◆ |
| ☐ | ZS-PUI | Boeing 737-2B7 (Nordam 3) | 22890/986 | ex 5N-BFJ | |
| ☐ | ZS-SFX | Boeing 737-2B7 (Nordam 3) | 22889/983 | ex 5N-BFH | |
| ☐ | ZS-SKW | Boeing 737-219 (Nordam 3) | 23474/1199 | ex 9J-KDK | |
| ☐ | ZS-SMD | Boeing 737-219 (Nordam 3) | 23472/1194 | ex N472BC | |
| ☐ | ZS-SSZ | Boeing 737-219 | 23470/1186 | ex N470C | ◆ |
| ☐ | ZS-SVT | Boeing 737-2K9 | 23405/1178 | ex 7Q-YKX | ◆ |

### STARS AWAY AVIATION — (STX) — Cape Town-International (CPT)

| ☐ | ZS-DBH | Douglas DC-9-33F (ABS 3) | 47384/543 | ex N931AX | |
| ☐ | ZS-OSI | Douglas DC-8-62F | 46098/516 | ex 3D-AIA | ◆ |
| ☐ | ZS-OZV | Douglas DC-8-62F | 45986/379 | ex 3D-CDL | wfs◆ |
| ☐ | ZS-YBD | Douglas DC-8-62AF | 46162/555 | ex 9G-AED | ◆ |

### SUMMERSET CHARTERS

| ☐ | ZS-PSB | Embraer EMB.120RT Brasilia | 120196 | ex N196CA | based Comores >MBN◆ |

### TAB AIR CHARTER

| ☐ | ZS-TAA | Embraer EMB-120ER Brasilia | 120280 | ex PR-UHT | ◆ |

### TRAMON AIR — Tramon (TMX) — Lanseria (HLA)

| ☐ | ZS-ALX | Grumman G-159 Gulfstream I | 086 | ex N10TB | |

### UTAIR SOUTH AFRICA — (UTR) — Lanseria (HLA)

| ☐ | ZS-HFI | Mil Mi-8MTV-1 | 95907 | ex RA-27071 | ◆ |
| ☐ | ZS-HFL | Mil Mi-8MTV-1 | 95958 | ex RA-27131 | ◆ |
| ☐ | ZS-HFM | Mil Mi-8MTV-1 | 94622 | ex RA-25558 | ◆ |
| ☐ | ZS-RUB | Mil Mi-8MTV-1 | 95960 | ex RA-27133 | |
| ☐ | ZS-RUC | Mil Mi-8MTV-1 | 95907 | ex RA-27071 | |
| ☐ | ZS-RVE | Mil Mi-8MTV-1 | 96264 | ex RA-25809 | |
| ☐ | ZS-SCF | Mil Mi-8MTV-1 | 93442 | ex RA-25829 | ◆ |
| ☐ | ZS-SOG | Mil Mi-8MTV-1 | 95955 | ex RA-27128 | ◆ |
| ☐ | ZS-SUF | Mil Mi-8MTV-1 | 93345 | ex RA-22978 | ◆ |
| ☐ | ZS-TUT | Mil Mi-8MTV-1 | 95151 | ex RA-25413 | |

| | | | | | |
|---|---|---|---|---|---|
| **VALAN INTERNATIONAL CARGO** | | *Nalau (VLN)* | | *Johannesburg-Rand (QRA)* | |

| ☐ | ZS-OWX | Antonov An-32B | 2806 | ex ER-AWB | all-white, no titles |
|---|---|---|---|---|---|
| ☐ | ZS-PEL | Antonov An-32B | 3004 | ex ER-AFG | all-white, no titles |
| ☐ | ZS-PSO | Antonov An-32B | 2808 | ex RA-48059 | |
| Reported to have ceased ops late 2007 | | | | | |

| **VELVET SKY AIRLINE** | | *(VZ/VEL)* | | |
|---|---|---|---|---|

| ☐ | ZS-GAU | Douglas DC-9-32 | 47798/914 | ex 3D-MRU | <GBB♦ |
|---|---|---|---|---|---|
| ☐ | ZS-SPU | Boeing 737-3S3 | 24059/1517 | ex N240AG | ♦ |
| ☐ | ZS-VDB | Boeing 737-31L | 27345/2625 | ex N745TP | ♦ |
| ☐ | ZS-VDP | Boeing 737-31L | 27346/2636 | ex N346TP | ♦ |

## Z3-   MACEDONIA (Republic of Macedonia)

| **MAT MACEDONIAN AIRLINES** | *Makavio (IN/MAK)* | *Skopje (SKP)* |
|---|---|---|

Ops suspended 20Jun11

| **SKYWINGS INTERNATIONAL** | *(GSW)* |
|---|---|

Ops suspended late 2010

| **STAR AIRLINES** | *Skopje (SKP)* |
|---|---|

Ceased ops 2010

## 3A-   MONACO (Principality of Monaco)

| **HELI AIR MONACO** | | *Heli Air (YO/MCM)* | | *Monte Carlo Heliport (MCM)* |
|---|---|---|---|---|

| ☐ | 3A-MAC | Aérospatiale AS350B Ecureuil | 1673 | ex HB-XBC |
|---|---|---|---|---|
| ☐ | 3A-MAX | Aérospatiale AS350BA Ecureuil | 1794 | ex F-GMBN |
| ☐ | 3A-MFC | Eurocopter EC130B4 Ecureuil | 3768 | |
| ☐ | 3A-MIL | Aérospatiale AS350BA Ecureuil | 1709 | ex F-GMBV |
| ☐ | 3A-MJB | Aérospatiale AS350B2 Ecureuil | 1988 | ex F-GJCM |
| ☐ | 3A-MPJ | Eurocopter EC130B4 Ecureuil | 3662 | |
| ☐ | 3A-MTT | Aérospatiale AS350B2 Ecureuil | 1967 | ex I-LUPJ |
| | | | | |
| ☐ | 3A-MCM | Aérospatiale SA365N Dauphin 2 | 6076 | ex N9UW |
| ☐ | 3A-MJP | Aérospatiale SA365C3 Dauphin 2 | 5015 | ex N90049 |
| ☐ | 3A-MPG | Eurocopter EC155B1 Dauphin 2 | 6771 | |
| ☐ | 3A-MXL | Aérospatiale AS355N Ecureuil 2 | 5712 | |

## 3B-   MAURITIUS (Republic of Mauritius)

| **AIR MAURITIUS** | | *AirMauritius (MK/MAU)* | | | *Plaisance (MRU)* |
|---|---|---|---|---|---|

| ☐ | 3B-NAU | Airbus A340-312 | 076 | ex F-WWJG | Pink Pigeon |
|---|---|---|---|---|---|
| ☐ | 3B-NAY | Airbus A340-313X | 152 | ex F-WWJX | Cardinal |
| ☐ | 3B-NBD | Airbus A340-313X | 194 | ex F-WWJP | Parakeet |
| ☐ | 3B-NBE | Airbus A340-313X | 268 | ex F-WWJG | Paille en Queue |
| ☐ | 3B-NBI | Airbus A340-313E | 793 | ex F-WWJE | Le Flamboyant |
| ☐ | 3B-NBJ | Airbus A340-313E | 800 | ex F-WWJF | Le Chamarel |
| | | | | | |
| ☐ | 3B-NBF | Airbus A319-112 | 1592 | ex D-AVYX | Mon Choisy |
| ☐ | 3B-NBG | ATR 72-212A | 0690 | ex F-WWEM | Port Mathurin |
| ☐ | 3B-NBH | Airbus A319-112 | 1936 | ex D-AVWF | Blue Bay |
| ☐ | 3B-NBL | Airbus A330-202 | 1057 | ex F-WWYF | Nenuphar |
| ☐ | 3B-NBM | Airbus A330-202 | 883 | ex F-WWKK | Trochetia |
| ☐ | 3B-NBN | ATR 72-212A | 0921 | ex F-WWET | Ile Aux Aigrettes |
| ☐ | 3B-NZD | Bell 206B JetRanger III | 4464 | | |
| ☐ | 3B-NZE | Bell 206B JetRanger III | 4465 | | |
| ☐ | 3B-NZF | Bell 206B JetRanger III | 4496 | ex N8152H | |

## 3C-   EQUATORIAL GUINEA (Republic of Equatorial Guinea)

| **CEIBA INTERCONTINENTAL** | | *(C2/CEL)* | | *Malabo (SSG)* |
|---|---|---|---|---|

| ☐ | TC-MND | Airbus A300C4-203F | 212 | ex ZS-SDG | <MNB |
|---|---|---|---|---|---|
| ☐ | 3C-LLG | ATR 42-300 | 0335 | ex F-ODYE | |
| ☐ | 3C-LLH | ATR 42-300 | 0671 | ex F-WWYE | |
| ☐ | 3C-LLI | ATR 72-212A | 0790 | ex F-WWEJ | |

| | | | | | |
|---|---|---|---|---|---|
| ☐ | 3C-LLM | ATR 72-212A | 0810 | ex F-WWEX | |
| ☐ | 3C-LLS | Boeing 777-2FBLR | 40668/937 | Djibloho | ♦ |

### GEASA — Geasa (GEA) — Malabo (SSG)

| | | | | |
|---|---|---|---|---|
| ☐ | RA-87956 | Yakovlev Yak-40K | 9821757 | ex CCCP-87956 |

### GENERAL WORKS AVIACION — (GWK) — Malabo (SSG)

| | | | | |
|---|---|---|---|---|
| ☐ | 3C-GWA | Fokker F.28 Fellowship 4000 | 11240 | ex HC-CDG |
| ☐ | 3C-GWB | Fokker F.28 Fellowship 4000 | 11156 | ex 3C-LGP |
| ☐ | 3C-GWC | Fokker F.28 Fellowship 4000 | 11238 | ex TU-TIY |

### GETRA — (GET) — Malabo (SSG)

| | | | | | |
|---|---|---|---|---|---|
| ☐ | 3C-LLF | Fokker F.28 Fellowship 1000 | 11073 | ex N941TD | wfs |

### GUINEA EQUATORIAL AIRLINES — (RGE) — Malabo (SSG)

| | | | | | |
|---|---|---|---|---|---|
| ☐ | 3C-CGA | Yakovlev Yak-40 | 9411132 | | ♦ |
| ☐ | 3C-LLP | LET L-410UVP-E20 | 092713 | | ♦ |

### NATIONALE GABON — Malabo (SSG)

| | | | | | |
|---|---|---|---|---|---|
| ☐ | ZS-DOA | SAAB SF.340A | 340A-077 | ex C-GQXD | [HLA] |

### STAR EQUATORIAL AIRLINES

| | | | | |
|---|---|---|---|---|
| ☐ | 3C-LLN | Boeing 737-260 | 23915/1583 | ex ET-AJB |

### TANGO

| | | | | | |
|---|---|---|---|---|---|
| ☐ | 3C- | McDonnell-Douglas MD-82 | 49987/1760 | ex N7533A | ♦ |

## 3D- SWAZILAND (Kingdom of Swaziland)

### AERO AFRICA — Aero Africa (RFC) — Johannesburg (JNB)

Ceased ops 2009

### EASTERN AIRWAYS — Manzini-Matsapha (MTS)

| | | | | | |
|---|---|---|---|---|---|
| ☐ | 3D-PAT | LET L-410UVP-E | 871924 | ex HA-LAS | ♦ |

### TRANS AIR WAYS

See C9-

## 3X- GUINEA (Republic of Guinea)

### AIR GUINEE EXPRESS — Future Express (2U/GIP) — Conakry (CKY)

Ceased ops 2005

### AVION EXPRESS

| | | | | | |
|---|---|---|---|---|---|
| ☐ | 3X-GDK | LET L-410UVP | 800419 | ex RA-67153 | ♦ |
| ☐ | 3X-GDL | LET L-410UVP | 800420 | ex RA-67154 | ♦ |

### EXIM TRADING

| | | | | | |
|---|---|---|---|---|---|
| ☐ | 3X-GEM | Antonov An-12BK | 00347005 | ex ER-AXK | wfs |

### GUINEE AIR CARGO — Conakry (CKY)

Status unknown

## 4K- AZERBAIJAN (Republic of Azerbaijan)

### AZAL CARGO — Azalaviacargo (AHC) — Baku-Bina (BAK)

| | Reg | Type | C/n | ex | Notes |
|---|---|---|---|---|---|
| ☐ | 4K-AZ16 | Ilyushin Il-76TD | 1023412411 | ex UK 76410 | |
| ☐ | 4K-AZ26 | Ilyushin Il-76TD | 1033416525 | ex UK 76844 | |
| ☐ | 4K-26584 | Antonov An-26B | 13509 | ex 26584 | [BAK] |

### AZERBAIJAN AIRLINES — Azal (J2/AHY) — Baku-Bina (BAK)

| | Reg | Type | C/n | ex | | Notes |
|---|---|---|---|---|---|---|
| ☐ | 4K-AZ54 | Airbus A320-211 | 0331 | ex 9H-ADZ | | [MLA] |
| ☐ | 4K-AZ77 | Airbus A320-214 | 2846 | ex D-ABDH | | |
| ☐ | 4K-AZ78 | Airbus A320-214 | 2853 | ex D-ABDI | | |
| ☐ | 4K-AZ79 | Airbus A320-214 | 2865 | ex D-ABDJ | | ♦ |
| ☐ | 4K-AZ80 | Airbus A320-214 | 2991 | ex HB-IOT | | ♦ |
| ☐ | 4K-AZ83 | Airbus A320-214 | 2685 | ex D-ABDD | | ♦ |
| ☐ | 4K-AZ84 | Airbus A320-214 | 3006 | ex HB-IOU | | ♦ |
| ☐ | 4K-AI01 | Boeing 767-32LER | 40342/990 | ex 4K-BAKU-1 | | op for Govt♦ |
| ☐ | 4K-AZ81 | Boeing 767-33LER | 40343/1004 | | | ♦ |
| ☐ | 4K-AZ82 | Boeing 767-33LER | 41063 | | | o/o♦ |
| ☐ | 4K-SW808 | Boeing 767-32LERF | 41068 | | | o/o♦ |
| ☐ | 4K-SW880 | Boeing 767-32LERF | 41069 | | | o/o♦ |
| ☐ | VP-BBR | Boeing 757-22L | 29305/894 | ex N6046P | Garabagh | |
| ☐ | VP-BBS | Boeing 757-22L | 30834/947 | ex (4K-AZ13) | | |
| ☐ | 4K-AI02 | Airbus A319-115CJ | 2487 | ex 4K-AZ01 | Baku | Op for Govt |
| ☐ | 4K-AZ03 | Airbus A319-111 | 2516 | ex D-AVWS | Ganja | |
| ☐ | 4K-AZ04 | Airbus A319-111 | 2588 | ex D-AVXJ | | |
| ☐ | 4K-AZ05 | Airbus A319-111 | 2788 | ex D-AVYY | Gazakh | |
| ☐ | 4K-AZ10 | Tupolev Tu-154M | 98A1013 | | | |
| ☐ | 4K-AZ38 | Boeing 757-256 | 26246/620 | ex N262CT | | |
| ☐ | 4K-AZ43 | Boeing 757-2M6 | 23453/100 | ex V8-RBB | | |
| ☐ | 4K-AZ49 | Antonov An-140-100 | 36525307041 | | | stored |
| ☐ | 4K-AZ52 | ATR 42-500 | 0667 | ex F-WWLA | Zagatala | |
| ☐ | 4K-AZ53 | ATR 42-500 | 0689 | ex F-WWLK | | |
| ☐ | 4K-AZ64 | ATR 72-212A | 0761 | ex F-WWEX | Gabala | |
| ☐ | 4K-AZ65 | ATR 72-212A | 0789 | ex F-WWEH | Gusar | |
| ☐ | 4K-AZ66 | ATR 72-212A | 0799 | ex F-WWEP | | |
| ☐ | 4K-AZ67 | ATR 72-212A | 0818 | ex F-WWEH | Khankandi | |
| ☐ | 4K-AZ734 | Tupolev Tu-154M | 92A916 | ex 4K-85734 | Shusha | |
| ☐ | 4K-AZ738 | Tupolev Tu-154M | 92A921 | ex 4K-85738 | | |

### IMAIR — Improtex (IK/ITX) — Baku-Bina (BAK)

| | Reg | Type | C/n | ex | Notes |
|---|---|---|---|---|---|
| ☐ | 4K-85732 | Tupolev Tu-154M | 92A914 | ex CCCP-85732 | |
| ☐ | 4K-AZ17 | Tupolev Tu-154M | 85A718 | ex B-2603 | ♦ |

### SILK WAY AIRLINES — Silk Line (ZP/AZQ) — Baku-Bina (BAK)

| | Reg | Type | C/n | ex | Notes |
|---|---|---|---|---|---|
| ☐ | 4K-AZ19 | Ilyushin Il-76TD | 0053460820 | ex UR-76408 | |
| ☐ | 4K-AZ26 | Inlyushin Il-76TD | 1033416525 | | ♦ |
| ☐ | 4K-AZ31 | Ilyushin Il-76TD | 1013405184 | ex RA-76426 | |
| ☐ | 4K-AZ40 | Ilyushin Il-76TD | 1043419632 | | |
| ☐ | 4K-AZ41 | Ilyushin Il-76TD | 1093420673 | | |
| ☐ | 4K-AZ61 | Ilyushin Il-76TD | 1023412411 | | |
| ☐ | 4K-AZ70 | Ilyushin Il-76TD | 2093421717 | | ♦ |
| ☐ | 4K-AZ100 | Ilyushin Il-76TD-90VD | 2073421208 | | |
| ☐ | 4K-AZ101 | Ilyushin Il-76TD-90VD | 2083421716 | | |
| ☐ | UR-CAF | Antonov An-12B | 3341209 | | ♦ |
| ☐ | UR-CGX | Antonov An-12BP | 5343510 | | ♦ |
| ☐ | 4K-AZ23 | Antonov An-12BK | 8345605 | ex 11715 | |
| ☐ | 4K-AZ63 | Antonov An-12BP | 9346308 | | ♦ |
| ☐ | 4K-AZ808 | ATR 42-500 | 0673 | ex F-WWLG | |
| ☐ | 4K-SW800 | Boeing 747-4R7F | 29729/1189 | ex 4K-800 | |
| ☐ | 4K-SW888 | Boeing 747-4R7F | 29730/1203 | ex CX-NCV | ♦ |

### SKY WIND — Sky Wind (AZH) — Baku-Bina (BAK)

| | Reg | Type | C/n | ex | Notes |
|---|---|---|---|---|---|
| ☐ | S9-DBS | Antonov An-26B | 9504 | | ♦ |
| ☐ | 4K-78129 | Ilyushin Il-76MD | 0083489683 | ex ER-IBC | |

### TURANAIR — Turan (3T/URN) — Baku-Bina (BAK)

| | Reg | Type | C/n | ex | Notes |
|---|---|---|---|---|---|
| ☐ | 4K-727 | Tupolev Tu-154M | 86A727 | ex LZ-LCS | [BAK] |
| ☐ | 4K-733 | Tupolev Tu-154M | 86A733 | | ♦ |

## 4L-    GEORGIA (Republic of Georgia)

### AIR BATUMI

Aircraft sold Sep11

### AIR SIRIN

| | | | | | |
|---|---|---|---|---|---|
| ☐ | 3X-GHA | Antonov An-26 | 97308608 | | ♦ |
| ☐ | 4L-AFL | Antonov An-26B | 17310610 | ex UR-AUA | |

### AIR VICTORY

| | | | | | |
|---|---|---|---|---|---|
| ☐ | 4L-ELE | Antonov An-12BP | 5342802 | | [EBB]♦ |
| ☐ | 4L-HUS | Antonov An-12BP | 6343708 | ex LZ-CBE | |
| ☐ | 4L-IRA | Antonov An-12B | 9346510 | ex EX-025 | ♦ |
| ☐ | 4L-ROM | Antonov An-12BK | 8345809 | | [FJR]♦ |
| ☐ | 4L-VAL | Antonov An-12BP | 9346807 | ex LZ-CBH | [EBB] |
| ☐ | 4L-VPI | Antonov An-12B | 8345510 | ex ER-ADY | |

### AIRZENA – GEORGIAN AIRWAYS          Tamazi (A9/TGZ)          Tbilisi-Lochini (TBS)

| | | | | | |
|---|---|---|---|---|---|
| ☐ | 4L-GAA | Canadair CL-600-2B19 (Chal 850) | 8046 | ex 4L-GAF | Op for Government |
| ☐ | 4L-GAL | Canadair CRJ-200ER | 7076 | ex F-GRJB | |
| ☐ | 4L-TGA | Boeing 737-5Q8 | 28055/3024 | ex B-2110 | |
| ☐ | 4L-TGB | Canadair CRJ-200LR | 7442 | ex OY-MBJ | |
| ☐ | 4L-TGF | Boeing 737-31S | 29116/3005 | ex TS-IEG | >VSV♦ |
| ☐ | 4L-TGG | Canadair CRJ-200ER | 7386 | ex OY-MAV | |
| ☐ | 4L-TGI | Boeing 737-505 | 26336/2805 | ex B-2973 | |
| ☐ | 4L-TGN | Yakovlev Yak-40 | 9611246 | ex 4L-88158 | |
| ☐ | 4L-TGS | Canadair CRJ-200LR | 7373 | ex EK-20073 | |

### EUREX

Ceased ops Feb11

### EUROLINE

Renamed Georgian International

### GEORGIAN INTERNATIONAL          (4L/GIL)          Tbilisi-Lochini (TBS)

| | | | | | |
|---|---|---|---|---|---|
| ☐ | 4L-AJA | Boeing 737-5C9 | 26439/2444 | ex LX-LGP | ♦ |
| ☐ | 4L-EUR | Tupolev Tu-134A | 63860 | ex 4L-AAJ | ♦ |

### GEORGIAN STAR INTERNATIONAL          (GST)

| | | | | | |
|---|---|---|---|---|---|
| ☐ | 4L-NAL | Boeing 737-2T5 | 21960/642 | ex E3-NAS | ♦ |
| ☐ | 4L-NAM | Boeing 737-2T5 | 22632/847 | ex E3-NAM | >SKA Arabia♦ |

### SAKAVIASERVICE          Sakservice (AZG)          Tbilisi-Lochini (TBS)

| | | | | | |
|---|---|---|---|---|---|
| ☐ | 4L-GLM | Ilyushin Il-76T | 093418543 | ex EX-117 | |
| ☐ | 4L-GLN | Antonov An-12BK | 9346704 | ex EX-131 | ♦ |
| ☐ | 4L-GLR | Ilyushin Il-76T | 0013432955 | ex UP-I7608 | |

### SKY GEORGIA          National (QB/GFG)          Tbilisi-Lochini (TBS)

| | | | | | |
|---|---|---|---|---|---|
| ☐ | 4L-GNL | Douglas DC-9-51 (ABS 3) | 48134/980 | ex UR-CCK | wfs |
| ☐ | 4L-GNN | Douglas DC-9-51 | 47657/787 | ex UR-BYL | [TBS] |
| ☐ | 4L-SKD | Ilyushin Il-76TD | 1023410344 | ex UP-I7639 | |
| ☐ | 4L-SKG | Ilyushin Il-76TD | 0013430890 | | ♦ |
| ☐ | 4L-SKL | Ilyushin Il-76TD | 0003423699 | | ♦ |
| ☐ | 4L-SKY | Ilyushin Il-76TD | 0053464934 | ex UP-I7638 | |

### TBILAVIAMSHENI          Tbilavia (L6/VNZ)          Tbilisi-Lochini (TBS)

| | | | | | |
|---|---|---|---|---|---|
| ☐ | 4L-AAK | Yakovlev Yak-40 | 9531043 | ex 4L-87242  Georgia titles | |
| ☐ | 4L-BZG | Antonov An-24RV | 37309109 | | ♦ |

### TRANSAVIA SERVICE          Transavia Service (5I/FNV)          Kutaisi (KUT)

| | | | | |
|---|---|---|---|---|
| ☐ | 4L-FAS | Antonov An-72-100 | 36572020358 | ex RA-72901 |
| ☐ | 4L-NAS | Antonov An-72 | 36572020362 | ex EK-72902 |
| ☐ | 4L-VAS | Antonov An-12BK | 7345201 | ex EK-12221 |

## TRADE LINKS AVIATION

| | | | | |
|---|---|---|---|---|
| ☐ | 4L-TAS | Antonov An-24B | 89901506 | ex EX-004 all-white |

## VIP-AVIA

**VIP Avia (VPV)**

**Tbilisi-Lochini (TBS)**

| | | | | |
|---|---|---|---|---|
| ☐ | 4L-VIP | Yakovlev Yak-40 | 9320129 | ex 4L-MGC | VIPop for Government |

## VISTA GEORGIA

| | | | | | |
|---|---|---|---|---|---|
| ☐ | 4L-AJB | Boeing 737-5H6 | 27354/2637 | ex N495MS | ♦ |
| ☐ | 4L-AJE | Boeing 737-522 | 26687/2402 | ex LZ-BOQ | ♦ |
| ☐ | 4L-AJS | Boeing 737-3L9 | 25125/2059 | ex D-ADIF | ♦ |
| ☐ | 4L-AJY | Boeing 737-33A | 27452/2679 | ex N270AE | ♦ |

# 4O-    MONTENEGRO (Republic of Montenegro)

## MONTENEGRO AIRLINES

**Motairo (YM/MGX)**

**Podgorica/Tivat (TGD/TIV)**

| | | | | | |
|---|---|---|---|---|---|
| ☐ | 4O-AOK | Fokker 100 | 11272 | ex YU-AOK | Sveti Petar Cetinjski |
| ☐ | 4O-AOL | Fokker 100 | 11268 | ex ZA-ARC | Podgorica |
| ☐ | 4O-AOM | Fokker 100 | 11321 | ex YU-AOM | Bar |
| ☐ | 4O-AOP | Fokker 100 | 11332 | ex YU-AOP | Boka |
| ☐ | 4O-AOT | Fokker 100 | 11350 | ex YU-AOT | |
| | | | | | |
| ☐ | YU-AOJ | Fokker F28-4000 | 11187 | ex F-WQPL | >ONR♦ |
| ☐ | 4O-AOA | Embraer ERJ-195LR | 19000180 | ex PT-SDO | |
| ☐ | 4O-AOB | Embraer ERJ-195LR | 19000283 | ex PT-TLX | |
| ☐ | 4O-AOC | Embraer ERJ-195LR | 19000358 | ex PT-PVM | |

# 4R-    SRI LANKA (Democratic Socialist Republic of Sri Lanka)

## AERO LANKA AIRLINES

**AeroLanka (QL/RNL)**
**Colombo-Bandaranayike Intl/Ratmalana (CMB/RML)**

| | | | | |
|---|---|---|---|---|
| ☐ | 4R-SEA | Cessna 404 | 404-0833 | ex N404AM |

## EXPO AVIATION

**Expoavia (8D/EXV)**
**Colombo-Bandaranayike Intl/Colombo-Ratmalana (CMB/RML)**

| | | | | | |
|---|---|---|---|---|---|
| ☐ | 4R-EXD | Ilyushin Il-18GrM | 187009802 | ex YR-IMZ | <RMV |
| ☐ | 4R-EXJ | Douglas DC-8-63CF (BAC 3) | 46049/479 | ex N867BX | |
| ☐ | 4R-EXK | Fokker F.27 Friendship 500RF | 10631 | ex 4R-MRA | ♦ |
| ☐ | 4R-MLA | Fokker F.27 Friendship 500RF | 10642 | ex 4R-EXH | >MLR♦ |

## HELITOURS

**Ratmalana (RML)**

| | | | | | |
|---|---|---|---|---|---|
| ☐ | 4R-HTA | Bell 412 | 33096 | ex SUH-4201 | ♦ |
| ☐ | 4R-HTB | Bell 412 | 33095 | ex SUH-4204 | ♦ |
| ☐ | 4R-HTN | AVIC MA-60 | 0708 | | ♦ |
| ☐ | 4R-HTO | AVIC MA-60 | 0709 | | ♦ |

## MIHIN LANKA

**(MJ/MLR)**

**Colombo-Bandaranayike Intl (CMB)**

| | | | | | |
|---|---|---|---|---|---|
| ☐ | 4R-EXH | Fokker F-27 Friendship 500RF | 10642 | ex A4O-FG | ♦ |
| ☐ | 4R-MLA | Fokker F.27 Friendship 500RF | 10642 | ex 4R-EXH | <EXV |
| ☐ | 4R-MRB | Airbus A320-232 | 0977 | ex VT-ADZ | |
| ☐ | 4R-MRC | Airbus A321-231 | 3106 | ex G-TTIF | |

## SRILANKAN

**Srilankan (UL/ALK)**

**Colombo-Bandaranayike Intl (CMB)**

| | | | | | |
|---|---|---|---|---|---|
| ☐ | 4R-ABJ | Airbus A320-232 | 2564 | ex VT-DKY | |
| ☐ | 4R-ABK | Airbus A320-214 | 2584 | ex 9K-CAB | |
| ☐ | 4R-ABL | Airbus A320-232 | 2345 | ex B-2374 | |
| ☐ | 4R-ABM | Airbus A320-214 | 4694 | ex F-WWDK | ♦ |
| ☐ | 4R-ABN | Airbus A320-214 | 4869 | ex F-WWDO | ♦ |
| ☐ | 4R-ABO | Airbus A320-214 | 4915 | ex F-WWDC | ♦ |
| ☐ | 4R-ABP | Airbus A320-214 | 5086 | ex F-WWIJ | ♦ |
| | | | | | |
| ☐ | 4R-ALA | Airbus A330-243 | 303 | ex F-WWYH | |
| ☐ | 4R-ALB | Airbus A330-243 | 306 | ex F-WWYL | |
| ☐ | 4R-ALC | Airbus A330-243 | 311 | ex F-WWYN | |
| ☐ | 4R-ALD | Airbus A330-243 | 313 | ex F-WWYP | |
| ☐ | 4R-ALG | Airbus A330-243 | 404 | ex G-WWBB | |
| ☐ | 4R-ALH | Airbus A330-243 | 627 | ex EI-ECK | ♦ |

| | | | | |
|---|---|---|---|---|
| ☐ | 4R-ALJ | Airbus A330-243 | 456 | ex G-OJMC | ♦ |

| | | | | |
|---|---|---|---|---|
| ☐ | 4R-ADA | Airbus A340-311 | 032 | ex F-WWJT |
| ☐ | 4R-ADB | Airbus A340-311 | 033 | ex F-WWJU |
| ☐ | 4R-ADC | Airbus A340-311 | 034 | ex F-WWJY |
| ☐ | 4R-ADE | Airbus A340-313X | 367 | ex F-GTUA |
| ☐ | 4R-ADF | Airbus A340-313X | 374 | ex F-GTUB |
| ☐ | 4R-ADG | Airbus A340-313X | 381 | ex B-HXL | ♦ |

## SRILANKAN AIR TAXI

| | | | | |
|---|---|---|---|---|
| ☐ | 4R- | de Havilland DHC-6 Twin Otter 300 | 276 | ex C-FBBA | ♦ |
| ☐ | 4R- | de Havilland DHC-6 Twin Otter 300 | 321 | ex C-GLKB | ♦ |

# 4X-    ISRAEL (State of Israel)

## ARKIA ISRAEL AIRLINES    Arkia (IZ/AIZ)    Tel Aviv-Ben Gurion/Sde Dov (TLV/SDV)

| | | | | |
|---|---|---|---|---|
| ☐ | 4X-AVT | ATR 72-212A | 0894 | ex F-WWEN |
| ☐ | 4X-AVU | ATR 72-212A | 0587 | ex F-WWES |
| ☐ | 4X-AVW | ATR 72-212A | 0583 | ex F-WWER |
| ☐ | 4X-AVX | ATR 72-212A | 0656 | ex F-WWEJ |
| ☐ | 4X-AVZ | ATR 72-212A | 0577 | ex F-WWEN |
| ☐ | 4X-BAU | Boeing 757-3E7/W | 30178/906 | ex N1003M |
| ☐ | 4X-BAW | Boeing 757-3E7/W | 30179/912 | |
| ☐ | 4X-EMA | Embraer ERJ-195LR | 19000172 | ex EC-KOZ |

## AYEET AVIATION    Ayeet (AYT)    Beer-Sheba (BEV)

| | | | | |
|---|---|---|---|---|
| ☐ | 4X-AHP | de Havilland DHC-6 Twin Otter 100 | 75 | ex C-FCSF |
| ☐ | 4X-AYS | Britten-Norman BN-2A-8 Islander | 376 | ex (G-BJWL) |

## CARGO AIR LINES    CAL (5C/ICL)    Tel Aviv-Ben Gurion (TLV)

| | | | | | |
|---|---|---|---|---|---|
| ☐ | 4X-ICM | Boeing 747-271C | 21965/438 | ex N539MC | all-white |
| ☐ | 4X-ICO | Boeing 747-230F | 23348/625 | ex TF-ARP | |

## EL AL ISRAEL AIRLINES    ElAl (LY/ELY)    Tel Aviv-Ben Gurion (TLV)

| | | | | | | |
|---|---|---|---|---|---|---|
| ☐ | 4X-EKA | Boeing 737-858 | 29957/204 | | 801 Tiberias | |
| ☐ | 4X-EKB | Boeing 737-858 | 29958/249 | | 802 Eilat | |
| ☐ | 4X-EKC | Boeing 737-858 | 29959/314 | | 803 Beit Shean | |
| ☐ | 4X-EKF | Boeing 737-8HX | 29638/2766 | | 804 Kinneret | |
| ☐ | 4X-EKH | Boeing 737-85P/W | 35485/2871 | | 807 Yarden | |
| ☐ | 4X-EKI | Boeing 737-86N | 28587/192 | ex N802NA | 812 | |
| ☐ | 4X-EKJ | Boeing 737-85P/W | 35486/2908 | ex N1786B | | |
| ☐ | 4X-EKL | Boeing 737-85P/W | 35487/2941 | ex N1796B | | |
| ☐ | 4X-EKO | Boeing 737-86Q/W | 30287/1308 | ex D-ATUI | | |
| ☐ | 4X-EKP | Boeing 737-8Q8/W | 30639/935 | ex 5W-SAO | | |
| ☐ | 4X-EKS | Boeing 737-8Q8/W | 36433/2702 | ex N1796B | | |
| ☐ | 4X-EKT | Boeing 737-8BK/W | 33030/1968 | ex 5B-DBZ | | |
| ☐ | 4X-ELA | Boeing 747-458 | 26055/1027 | | 201 Tel Aviv-Jaffa | |
| ☐ | 4X-ELB | Boeing 747-458 | 26056/1032 | ex N60697 | 202 Haifa | |
| ☐ | 4X-ELC | Boeing 747-458 | 27915/1062 | ex N6009F | 203 Beer Sheva | |
| ☐ | 4X-ELD | Boeing 747-458 | 29328/1215 | | 204 Jerusalem | |
| ☐ | 4X-ELE | Boeing 747-412 | 26551/1045 | ex 9V-SPB | | |
| ☐ | 4X-ELF | Boeing 747-412F | 26563/1036 | ex 9V-SFA | | |
| ☐ | 4X-ELH | Boeing 747-412 | 26555/1075 | ex EC-LGL | | ♦ |
| ☐ | 4X-EAC | Boeing 767-258ER | 22974/86 | ex N6018N | 603 | |
| ☐ | 4X-EAD | Boeing 767-258ER | 22975/89 | ex N6046P | 604 | |
| ☐ | 4X-EAE | Boeing 767-27EER | 24832/316 | ex F-GHGD | 605 | |
| ☐ | 4X-EAF | Boeing 767-27EER | 24854/326 | ex F-GHGE | 606 | |
| ☐ | 4X-EAJ | Boeing 767-330ER | 25208/381 | ex N208LS | 635 | |
| ☐ | 4X-EAK | Boeing 767-3Q8ER | 27600/655 | ex N271LF | 612 | |
| ☐ | 4X-EAL | Boeing 767-33AER | 27477/337 | ex N477AN | | ♦ |
| ☐ | 4X-EAM | Boeing 767-3Q8ER | 28132/692 | ex UR-VVT | | ♦ |
| ☐ | 4X-EAP | Boeing 767-3Y0ER | 24953/405 | ex TF-FIA | | ♦ |
| ☐ | 4X-EAR | Boeing 767-352ER | 26262/583 | ex VN-A769 | | |
| ☐ | 4X-ECA | Boeing 777-258ER | 30831/319 | | 101 Galillee | |
| ☐ | 4X-ECB | Boeing 777-258ER | 30832/325 | | 102 Negev | |
| ☐ | 4X-ECC | Boeing 777-258ER | 30833/335 | | 103 Hasharon | |
| ☐ | 4X-ECD | Boeing 777-258ER | 33169/405 | | 104 Carmel | |
| ☐ | 4X-ECE | Boeing 777-258ER | 36083/648 | ex N5017Q | 105 Sderot | |
| ☐ | 4X-ECF | Boeing 777-258ER | 36084/655 | ex N5022E | 106 | |

571

| | Reg | Type | Serial | Notes | |
|---|---|---|---|---|---|
| ☐ | 4X-AXL | Boeing 747-245F | 22151/478 | ex 9V-SQU | wfs |
| ☐ | 4X-EBU | Boeing 757-258 | 26053/529 | 506 | |
| ☐ | 4X-EBV | Boeing 757-258 | 26054/547 | 507 | |
| ☐ | 4X-EKD | Boeing 737-758 | 29960/327 | 701 Ashkelon | |
| ☐ | 4X-EKE | Boeing 737-758 | 29961/442 | 702 Nazareth | |

## ISRAIR — Israir (6H/ISR) — Tel Aviv-Ben Gurion (TLV)

| | Reg | Type | Serial | Notes | |
|---|---|---|---|---|---|
| ☐ | 4X-ABF | Airbus A320-232 | 4354 | ex F-WWDC | |
| ☐ | 4X-ABG | Airbus A320-232 | 4413 | ex F-WWIR | |
| ☐ | 4X-ATH | ATR 72-212A | 0931 | ex F-WWEG | |
| ☐ | 4X-ATI | ATR 72-212A | 0962 | ex F-WWEO | ♦ |
| ☐ | 4X-ATN | ATR 42-320 | 0053 | ex F-WQGN | ♦ |

## MOONAIR AVIATION — (MOO) — Tel Aviv-Sde Dov (SDV)

| | Reg | Type | Serial | Notes |
|---|---|---|---|---|
| ☐ | 4X-CBY | Piper PA-23-250 Aztec E | 27-7304990 | ex N405PB |
| ☐ | 4X-CCJ | Piper PA-31-350 Navajo Chieftain | 31-7405140 | ex G-FOEL |

## 5A- LIBYA (Socialist People's Libyan Arab Jamahiriya)

### AFRIQIYAH AIRWAYS — Afriqiyah (8U/AAW) — Tripoli-Ben Gashir Intl (TIP)

| | Reg | Type | Serial | Notes | |
|---|---|---|---|---|---|
| ☐ | 5A-ONA | Airbus A320-214 | 3224 | ex F-WWBY | |
| ☐ | 5A-ONB | Airbus A320-214 | 3236 | ex F-WWBI | |
| ☐ | 5A-ONJ | Airbus A320-214 | 4203 | ex F-WWBF | |
| ☐ | 5A-ONK | Airbus A320-214 | 4330 | ex F-WWIJ | [KUL] |
| ☐ | 5A-ONL | Airbus A320-214 | 4489 | ex F-WWDV | [TIP] |
| ☐ | 5A-ONM | Airbus A320-214 | 4521 | ex F-WWDI | |
| ☐ | 5A-ONC | Airbus A319-111 | 3615 | ex D-AVYM | |
| ☐ | 5A-OND | Airbus A319-111 | 3657 | ex D-AVYS | |
| ☐ | 5A-ONE | Airbus A340-213 | 151 | ex HZ-WBT4 | VIP/op for Govt/wfs |
| ☐ | 5A-ONF | Airbus A330-202 | 999 | ex F-WWYV | [BOD] |
| ☐ | 5A-ONH | Airbus A330-202 | 1043 | ex F-WWKM | [BOD] |
| ☐ | 5A-ONI | Airbus A319-111 | 4004 | ex D-AVYC | ♦ |

### AIR KUFRA — (7F/KFV)

| | Reg | Type | Serial | Notes | |
|---|---|---|---|---|---|
| ☐ | 5A-DGR | British Aerospace Jetstream 32 | 945 | ex HL5214 | wfs♦ |

### AIR LIBYA — Air Libya (7Q/TLR) — Tripoli-Mitiga/Benghazi (MJI/BEN)

| | Reg | Type | Serial | Notes | |
|---|---|---|---|---|---|
| ☐ | 5A-DKH | Yakovlev Yak-40 | 9631149 | | ♦ |
| ☐ | 5A-DKI | Yakovlev Yak-40 | 9331229 | ex 9L-LDK | |
| ☐ | 5A-DKJ | Yakovlev Yak-40K | 9720853 | ex EX-88270 | |
| ☐ | 5A-DKK | Yakovlev Yak-40 | 9420235 | ex EX-87426 | |
| ☐ | 5A-DKP | Yakovlev Yak-40 | 9411333 | | ♦ |
| ☐ | 5A-DKQ | British Aerospace 146 Srs.300 | E3191 | ex G-JEBD | |
| ☐ | 5A-DKV | Boeing 727-2D6 | 22374/1711 | ex 7T-VEV | |
| ☐ | 5A-DKX | Boeing 727-2D6 | 22765/1801 | ex 7T-VEX | [BEN] |
| ☐ | 5A-DKY | Boeing 737-2D6 (Nordam 3) | 22766/853 | ex 7T-VEY | |

### AL-AJNIHAH AIRWAYS — (ANH) — Tripoli-Ben Gashir Intl (TIP)

Ops services with Ilyushin Il-76s leased from other operators as required

### ALDAWLYH AIR — Aldawlyh Air (IIG) — Tripoli-Ben Gashir Intl/Mitiga (TIP/MJI)

Ops cargo services with Antonov An-124 leased from Libyan Air Cargo as required

### ALLEBIA AIR CARGO — Tripoli-Ben Gashir Intl (TIP)

| | Reg | Type | Serial | Notes |
|---|---|---|---|---|
| ☐ | 5A-DSH | Antonov An-72 | 36572020337 | ex 9Q-... |

### BURAQ AIR — Buraqair (UZ/BRQ) — Tripoli-Mitiga/Benghazi (MJI/BEN)

| | Reg | Type | Serial | Notes | |
|---|---|---|---|---|---|
| ☐ | 5A-DMG | Boeing 737-8GK/W | 34948/2074 | ex N1787B | Tripoli |
| ☐ | 5A-DMH | Boeing 737-8GK/W | 34949/2106 | | Benghazi | [TIP] |
| ☐ | 5A-DNA | Ilyushin Il-76TD | 0023439140 | | |
| ☐ | 5A-MAB | Boeing 737-406 | 24857/1902 | ex PH-BDU | |

### GHADAMES AIR TRANSPORT — (OG/GHT) — Tripoli-Ben Gashir Intl (TIP)

| | Reg | Type | Serial | Notes | |
|---|---|---|---|---|---|
| ☐ | C5-AEB | Douglas DC-9-31 | 48146/1044 | ex N926VJ | ♦ |
| ☐ | C5-LIM | Douglas DC-9-31 | 48145/1042 | ex N925VJ | [JNB] |

## GLOBAL AIR (GAK)

| | | | | |
|---|---|---|---|---|
| ☐ | 5A-DNO | Ilyushin Il-76T | 0043451509 | ♦ |
| ☐ | 5A-DQB | Ilyushin Il-86 | 51483208069 | ex UN-86101 |

## KALLAT ELSAKER AIR (KES) Kishinev-Chisinau / Sharjah (KIV/SHJ)

Status uncertain

## LIBYAN AIR CARGO Libac (LCR) Tripoli-Mitiga (MJI)

| | | | | | |
|---|---|---|---|---|---|
| ☐ | 5A-DOA | Antonov An-26B | 12306 | ex LAAF 8207 | |
| ☐ | 5A-DOB | Antonov An-26B | 12307 | ex LAAF 8208 | |
| ☐ | 5A-DOC | Antonov An-26B | 12308 | ex LAAF 8209 | Waddan |
| ☐ | 5A-DOD | Antonov An-26B | 12406 | ex LAAF 8210 | |
| ☐ | 5A-DOE | Antonov An-26B | 13003 | | |
| ☐ | 5A-DOF | Antonov An-26B | 13007 | | |
| ☐ | 5A-DOG | Antonov An-26-100 | 13008 | no titles | |
| ☐ | 5A-DOH | Antonov An-26B | 13202 | | |
| ☐ | 5A-DON | Antonov An-26B | 13009 | ex LAAF 8304 | |
| ☐ | 5A-DOQ | Antonov An-26B | 13202 | | ♦ |
| ☐ | 5A-DOU | Antonov An-26B-100 | 13201T | also reported as c/n 13202T and ex LAAF 8315 | |
| ☐ | 5A-DOV | Antonov An-26B-100 | 13109T | ex LAAF | |
| ☐ | 5A-DOZ | Antonov An-26B-100 | | ex LAAF 8214 | dam 31Oct07 |
| ☐ | 5A-DKS | Ilyushin Il-76TD | 1033418584 | ex RA-76843 | |
| ☐ | 5A-DNC | Ilyushin Il-76TD | 0023437084 | | |
| ☐ | 5A-DND | Ilyushin Il-76TD | 0033445299 | | |
| ☐ | 5A-DNG | Ilyushin Il-76TD | 0013432961 | | |
| ☐ | 5A-DNH | Ilyushin Il-76TD | 0033446356 | | |
| ☐ | 5A-DNI | Ilyushin Il-76T | 0013430878 | | [RKT] |
| ☐ | 5A-DNJ | Ilyushin Il-76T | 0013430869 | | |
| ☐ | 5A-DNK | Ilyushin Il-76T | 0013430882 | | |
| ☐ | 5A-DNT | Ilyushin Il-76TD | 0023439141 | | |
| ☐ | 5A-DNU | Ilyushin Il-76TD | 0043454651 | all-white | |
| ☐ | 5A-DNV | Ilyushin Il-76TD | 0043454645 | | |
| ☐ | 5A-DNX | Ilyushin Il-76TD | 1033414480 | | ♦ |
| ☐ | 5A-DRR | Ilyushin Il-76M | 083415469 | | |
| ☐ | 5A-DRS | Ilyushin Il-76M | 1033414474 | ex RA-76367 | |
| ☐ | 5A-DRT | Ilyushin Il-76TD | 1003403063 | ex LAAF-110 | |
| ☐ | 5A-DZZ | Ilyushin Il-76M | 093416501 | | |
| ☐ | 5A-DJQ | Lockheed L-382G-40C Hercules | 4798 | ex N501AK | |
| ☐ | 5A-DJR | Lockheed L-382E-15C Hercules | 4302 | ex RP-C99 | |
| ☐ | 5A-DOM | Lockheed L-382G-62C Hercules | 4992 | ex N4268M | |
| ☐ | 5A-DOO | Lockheed L-382G-64C Hercules | 5000 | ex 119 | |
| ☐ | 5A-DRC | Antonov An-32P | 0703 | ex UR-48093 | jt ops with LAAF |
| ☐ | 5A-DRD | Antonov An-32P | 1306 | ex UR-48004 | jt ops with LAAF |
| ☐ | 5A-DRF | Antonov An-32P | 3602 | | jt ops with LAAF |
| ☐ | 5A-DKL | Antonov An-124-100 | 19530502761 | | ♦ |
| ☐ | 5A-DKN | Antonov An-124-100 | 19530503792 | | ♦ |

## LIBYAN AIRLINES Libair (LN/LAA) Tripoli-Ben Gashir Intl (TIP)

| | | | | | |
|---|---|---|---|---|---|
| ☐ | 5A-LAA | Canadair CRJ-900 | 15120 | ex C-FPQO | wfs |
| ☐ | 5A-LAB | Canadair CRJ-900 | 15121 | ex C-FPUM | wfs |
| ☐ | 5A-LAC | Canadair CRJ-900 | 15122 | ex C-FPUN | |
| ☐ | 5A-LAD | Canadair CRJ-900 | 15214 | ex C- | [CGN] |
| ☐ | 5A-LAE | Canadair CRJ-900 | 15216 | ex C- | wfs |
| ☐ | 5A-LAL | Canadair CRJ-900 | 15256 | ex C- | |
| ☐ | 5A-LAM | Canadair CRJ-900 | 15257 | ex C-GZQW | |
| ☐ | 5A-LAN | Canadair CRJ-900 | 15258 | ex C-GIBO | |
| ☐ | 5A-DCT | de Havilland DHC-6 Twin Otter 300 | 627 | | |
| ☐ | 5A-DCV | de Havilland DHC-6 Twin Otter 300 | 637 | | |
| ☐ | 5A-DCX | de Havilland DHC-6 Twin Otter 300 | 641 | | |
| ☐ | 5A-DCZ | de Havilland DHC-6 Twin Otter 300 | 645 | | |
| ☐ | 5A-DDE | de Havilland DHC-6 Twin Otter 300 | 677 | | |
| ☐ | 5A-DHN | de Havilland DHC-6 Twin Otter 300 | 705 | | ♦ |
| ☐ | 5A-DHY | de Havilland DHC-6 Twin Otter 300 | 661 | ex C-GELZ | |
| ☐ | 5A-DJG | de Havilland DHC-6 Twin Otter 300 | 744 | ex C-GFHQ | |
| ☐ | 5A-DJH | de Havilland DHC-6 Twin Otter 300 | 747 | ex C-GEOA | |
| ☐ | 5A-DJI | de Havilland DHC-6 Twin Otter 300 | 757 | ex C-GIRL | |
| ☐ | 5A-DJJ | de Havilland DHC-6 Twin Otter 300 | 769 | ex C-GETI | |
| ☐ | 5A-DGC | Cessna 402C II | 402C0045 | ex N5800C | |
| ☐ | 5A-DHG | Cessna 402C II | 402C0464 | ex N8737Q | |
| ☐ | 5A-DHH | Cessna 402C II | 402C0444 | ex N6790F | |
| ☐ | 5A-DHZ | Swearingen SA.226AT Merlin III | T-345 | ex OO-HSC | |
| ☐ | 5A-DJB | Swearingen SA.226AT Merlin III | T-388 | ex OO-XSC | |
| ☐ | 5A-LAF | ATR 42-500 | 691 | ex F-WWLM | |

| | | | | | | |
|---|---|---|---|---|---|---|
| ☐ | 5A-LAG | ATR 42-500 | 802 | ex F-WWLU | | |
| ☐ | 5A-LAH | Airbus A320-214 | 4405 | ex F-WWBX | | |
| ☐ | 5A-LAI | Airbus A320-214 | 4450 | ex F-WWIO | | |
| ☐ | 5A-LAJ | Airbus A320-214 | 4490 | ex D-AUBI | | |
| ☐ | 5A-LAK | Airbus A320-214 | 4526 | ex F-WWDO | | |
| ☐ | 5A-DLY | Airbus A300B4-622R | 601 | ex TS-IAX | Al-Gordabia | <NVJ [TIP] |

### *LIBYAVIA* — *Tripoli-Ben Gashir Intl (TIP)*

Ceased ops 2009

### *PETRO AIR* — *(PEO)*

| | | | | | |
|---|---|---|---|---|---|
| ☐ | 5A-DLX | de Havilland DHC-8-311 | 254 | ex PH-SKD | ♦ |
| ☐ | 5A-DSO | Fokker F-28 Fellowship 2000 | 11110 | ex HB-AAS | wfs♦ |
| ☐ | 5A-PAA | Embraer ERJ-170LR | 17000275 | ex PT-TQB | |
| ☐ | 5A-PAB | Embraer ERJ-170LR | 17000279 | ex PT-TQF | |
| ☐ | 5A-PIC | de havilland DHC-6 Twin Otter 400 | 854 | ex C-GUVA | ♦ |
| ☐ | 5A-SOC | Embraer ERJ-170LR | 17000162 | | ♦ |

### *TOBRUK AIR* — *Tobruk Air (7T/TQB)* — *Tripoli-Ben Gashir Intl (TIP)*

Ops cargo flights with Douglas DC-10-30F and Ilyushin Il-76 aircraft leased from other operators when required

## *5B- CYPRUS (Republic of Cyprus)*

### *CYPRUS AIRWAYS* — *Cyprus (CY/CYP)* — *Larnaca (LCA)*

| | | | | | | |
|---|---|---|---|---|---|---|
| ☐ | 5B-DBB | Airbus A320-231 | 0256 | ex F-WWBH | Akamas | |
| ☐ | 5B-DCG | Airbus A320-232 | 4197 | ex F-WWIU | Aphrodite | |
| ☐ | 5B-DCH | Airbus A320-232 | 2359 | ex N674AW | Lefkosia | |
| ☐ | 5B-DCJ | Airbus A320-232 | 2108 | ex LZ-MDT | Amathus | |
| ☐ | 5B-DCK | Airbus A320-232 | 2275 | ex M-ABDA | Paphos | |
| ☐ | 5B-DCL | Airbus A320-232 | 2334 | ex M-ABDB | Pentadaktylos | ♦ |
| ☐ | 5B-DCM | Airbus A320-232 | 2343 | ex M-ABDC | | ♦ |
| ☐ | 5B-DBO | Airbus A319-112 | 1729 | ex D-AVWR | Nikoklis | [LCA] |
| ☐ | 5B-DBP | Airbus A319-112 | 1768 | ex D-AVWB | Chalkanor | [LCA] |
| ☐ | 5B-DBS | Airbus A330-243 | 505 | ex F-WWKO | Ammochostos | [TLS] |
| ☐ | 5B-DCF | Airbus A319-132 | 2718 | ex N518NK | Larnaka | |
| ☐ | 5B-DCN | Airbus A319-132 | 2383 | ex D-ABGA | | ♦ |

## *5H- TANZANIA (United Republic of Tanzania)*

### *AIR EXCEL* — *Tinga-Tinga (XLL)* — *Arusha (ARK)*

| | | | | | |
|---|---|---|---|---|---|
| ☐ | 5H-AXL | Cessna 208B Caravan I | 208B0401 | ex D-FHEW | |
| ☐ | 5H-IKI | Cessna 208B Caravan I | 208B2005 | ex N421WF | ♦ |
| ☐ | 5H-MEK | Cessna 208B Caravan i | 208B2017 | ex N2293Y | ♦ |
| ☐ | 5H-SMK | Cessna 208B Caravan I | 208B0654 | ex VT-TAP | |
| ☐ | 5H-VAN | Cessna 208B Caravan I | 208B1214 | ex N13204 | ♦ |
| ☐ | 5H-XLL | Cessna 208B Caravan I | 208B1192 | ex 5H-FAC | ♦ |
| ☐ | 5H- | Cessna 208B Caravan I | 208B2284 | ex N9005N | ♦ |
| ☐ | 5H-AES | LET L-410UVP-E20 | 871811 | ex 5H-PAD | |
| ☐ | 5H-EMK | Cessna TU206G Turbo Stationair 8 II | U20604638 | ex 5H-SDA | |
| ☐ | 5H-WOW | Reims Cessna F406 Caravan II | F406-0060 | ex PH-GUG | |

### *AIR TANZANIA* — *Tanzania (TC/ATC)* — *Dar-es-Salaam (DAR)*

| | | | | |
|---|---|---|---|---|
| ☐ | 5H-MWF | de Havilland DHC-8-311 | 474 | ex G-BRYW |

### *AURIC AIR SERVICES* — *Mwanza (MWZ)*

| | | | | | |
|---|---|---|---|---|---|
| ☐ | 5H-DTS | Cessna 208B Caravan i | 208B2159 | ex 5H-DTA | ♦ |
| ☐ | 5H-NCS | Cessna 208B Caravan I | 208B1311 | ex N2123S | |
| ☐ | 5H-TMS | Cessna 208B Caravan I | 208B2055 | ex N2208Y | ♦ |
| ☐ | 5H-TWO | Piper PA-34-200T Seneca | 34-8170030 | ex ZS-KTK | |
| ☐ | 5H- | Cessna 208B Caravan I | 208B2207 | ex N60253 | ♦ |

### *COASTAL AVIATION* — *Coastal Travel (7I/CSV)* — *Dar-es-Salaam (DAR)*

| | | | | | |
|---|---|---|---|---|---|
| ☐ | 5H-BAD | Cessna 208B Caravan I | 208B0586 | ex N5QP | |
| ☐ | 5H-GUS | Cessna 208B Caravan I | 208B1317 | ex N21738 | ♦ |
| ☐ | 5H-HOT | Cessna 208B Caravan I | 208B0677 | ex N1256N | |
| ☐ | 5H-JOE | Cessna 208B Caravan I | 208B0570 | ex N9EU | |

| | | | | | | |
|---|---|---|---|---|---|---|
| ☐ | 5H-LXJ | Cessna 208B Caravan I | 208B1230 | ex N1084Y | | |
| ☐ | 5H-MAD | Cessna 208B Caravan I | 208B0872 | ex N1294K | | |
| ☐ | 5H-POA | Cessna 208B Caravan I | 208B0965 | ex N1129Y | | |
| ☐ | 5H-SUN | Cessna 208B Caravan I | 208B0754 | ex 5H-PAF | | |
| ☐ | 5H-VIP | Cessna 208B Caravan I | 208B0714 | ex N208FK | | |
| ☐ | 5H- | Cessna 208B Caravan I | 208B2264 | ex N3041Q | | ♦ |
| | | | | | | |
| ☐ | 5H-CCT | Cessna TU206G Stationair 6 | U20604597 | ex ZS-MXV | | |
| ☐ | 5H-CTL | Cessna TU206F Stationair | U20601988 | ex 5H-PBF | | |
| ☐ | 5H-GUN | Cessna U206G Stationair 6 | U20605223 | ex 5H-TGT | | |
| ☐ | 5H-TOY | Cessna 404 Titan II | 404-0668 | ex 5Y-MCK | | |

## FLY540 TANZANIA (FTZ)

| | | | | | | |
|---|---|---|---|---|---|---|
| ☐ | 5H-YAH | Canadair CRJ-100ER | 7011 | ex C-GKTX | | ♦ |

## FLY SAFARI AIR LINK

| | | | | | | |
|---|---|---|---|---|---|---|
| ☐ | 5H-FOX | Cessna 208B Caravan I | 208B0074 | ex 5Y-BTM | | ♦ |

## KILWA AIR

| | | | | | |
|---|---|---|---|---|---|
| ☐ | 5H-KLA | Britten-Norman BN-2B-21 Islander | 2002 | ex 5X-MHB | |
| ☐ | 5H-MLB | Cessna T210N Centurion II | 21064259 | ex ZS-LVC | |

## NOMAD AVIATION

| | | | | | | |
|---|---|---|---|---|---|---|
| ☐ | 5H-FED | Cessna 208B Caravan I | 208B0437 | ex ZS-FED | | ♦ |
| ☐ | 5H-OJF | Cessna 208B Caravan I | 208B0481 | ex ZS-OJF | | ♦ |

## NORTHERN AIR | Arusha (ARK)

| | | | | | | |
|---|---|---|---|---|---|---|
| ☐ | 5H-SJF | Cessna 208B Caravan I | 208B0950 | ex N1130T | | |
| ☐ | 5H-SUZ | Cessna 208B Caravan I | 208B1247 | ex 5H-TOM | | ♦ |

## PRECISIONAIR | Precisionair (PW/PRF) | Arusha (ARK)

| | | | | | | |
|---|---|---|---|---|---|---|
| ☐ | 5H-PWA | ATR 72-212A | 0780 | ex F-WWES | | |
| ☐ | 5H-PWB | ATR 72-212A | 0834 | ex F-WWEB | | |
| ☐ | 5H-PWC | ATR 72-212A | 0866 | ex F-WWEP | | |
| ☐ | 5H-PWD | ATR 72-212A | 0880 | ex F-WWEI | | |
| ☐ | 5H-PWG | ATR 72-212A | 0923 | ex F-WWEW | Kilimanjaro | |
| | | | | | | |
| ☐ | 5H-PAA | ATR 42-320 | 0308 | ex F-WQHB | City of Arusha | |
| ☐ | 5H-PAG | ATR 42-320 | 0384 | ex F-WQJO | | |
| ☐ | 5H-PAY | Reims Cessna 406 Caravan I | F406-0035 | ex ZS-OGY | | |
| ☐ | 5H-PAZ | Boeing 737-3Y0 | 24770/1941 | ex RP-C4011 | | ♦ |
| ☐ | 5H-PMS | Boeing 737-36N | 28596/3112 | ex G-THON | | ♦ |
| ☐ | 5H-PWE | ATR 42-500 | 0815 | ex F-WW | | ♦ |
| ☐ | 5H-PWF | ATR 42-500 | 0819 | ex F-WWLA | Bukoba | |

## REGIONAL AIR SERVICES | Regional Services (REG) | Arusha (ARK)

| | | | | | | |
|---|---|---|---|---|---|---|
| ☐ | A6-MAR | de Havilland DHC-6 Twin Otter 300 | 841 | ex N9045S | | |
| ☐ | 5H-MUA | Cessna 208B Caravan I | 208B0487 | ex 5Y-BLM | | ♦ |
| ☐ | 5H-MUR | Cessna 208 Caravan I | 20800004 | ex 5Y-MAK | | <SLE♦ |

## SAFARI EXPRESS AIRWAYS

| | | | | | | |
|---|---|---|---|---|---|---|
| ☐ | 5H-SGH | Beech 1900D | UE-263 | ex CN-RLB | | ♦ |
| ☐ | 5H-SPB | Beech 1900D | UE-300 | ex EC-IJO | | ♦ |
| ☐ | 5H-SPC | Been 190D | UE-319 | ex ZS-SHA | | ♦ |

## SKY AVIATION TANZANIA | Dar-es-Salaam (DAR)

| | | | | | | |
|---|---|---|---|---|---|---|
| ☐ | 5H-EWA | Cessna 208 Caravan I | 20800109 | ex 5H-TAC | | ♦ |
| ☐ | 5H-SKT | Piper PA-31-350 Chieftain | 31-8152058 | ex A2-AHP | | |
| ☐ | 5H-SKX | Cessna 402B | 402B-0829 | ex 5Y-EAL | | |
| ☐ | 5H-SKY | Piper PA-32-300 Six | 32-770061 | ex N3258Q | | dbr? |

## TANZANAIR - TANZANIAN AIR SERVICES | Dar-es-Salaam (DAR)

| | | | | | |
|---|---|---|---|---|---|
| ☐ | 5H-GHL | Cessna U206F Stationair II | U20602583 | ex 5H-JBJ | |
| ☐ | 5H-LDS | Cessna 310I | 310I0029 | ex 5Y-AJN | |
| ☐ | 5H-TZC | Reims Cessna F406 Caravan II | F406-0028 | ex N7037C | |
| ☐ | 5H-TZE | Reims Cessna F406 Caravan II | F406-0046 | ex OY-PED | |
| ☐ | 5H-TZT | Cessna 208B Caravan I | 208B0664 | ex ZS-PSR | |

| | | | | | |
|---|---|---|---|---|---|
| ☐ | 5H-TZU | Cessna 208B Caravan I | 208B0639 | ex ZS-PJJ | |
| ☐ | 5H-TZX | Beech B200 Super King Air | BB-1196 | ex Z-ZLT | |

## TROPICAL AIR (ZANZIBAR) — Zanzibar (ZNZ)

| | | | | | |
|---|---|---|---|---|---|
| ☐ | 5N-ALO | Cessna 208B Caravan i | 208B0668 | ex ZS-OFK | ♦ |
| ☐ | 5H-AMI | ATR 42-300 | 0151 | ex LZ-ATR | ♦ |
| ☐ | 5H-NOW | Cessna 208B Caravan I | 208B2209 | ex N6026F | ♦ |
| ☐ | 5H-OLA | Cessna 208B Caravan I | 208B0384 | ex 7T-VIH | |
| ☐ | 5H-TAR | Piper PA-34-200T Seneca II | 34-7970038 | ex 5H-MNF | |
| ☐ | 5H-TZO | Partenavia P.68B | 120 | ex 5H-AZO | |
| ☐ | 5H-TZY | Partenavia P.68B | 149 | ex 5H-AZY | |
| ☐ | 5H-YES | LET L-410UVP-E | | | ♦ |

## ZANAIR – ZANZIBAR AIRLINE COMPANY — Zanair (B4/TAN) — Zanzibar (ZNZ)

| | | | | | |
|---|---|---|---|---|---|
| ☐ | 5H-CAR | Cessna 208B Caravan I | 208B2035 | ex N2327X | ♦ |
| ☐ | 5H-LET | LET L-410UVP-E9 | 892226 | ex 9L-LBK | |
| ☐ | 5H-ZAA | LET L-410UVP-E20 | 982631 | ex 5H-PAE | |
| ☐ | 5H-ZAP | LET L-410UVPE-9 | 871824 | ex 9L-LBV | |
| ☐ | 5H-ZAR | Cessna 404 Titan II | 404-0835 | ex 5H-AEL | |
| ☐ | 5H-ZAY | Cessna 404 Titan II | 404-0207 | ex N798A | |
| ☐ | 5H-ZAZ | Cessna 402C | 402C0029 | ex 5Y-NNM | |
| ☐ | 5H- | Cessna 208B Caravan I | 208B2199 | ex N1009U | ♦ |

## ZANTAS AIR SERVICE — Dar-es-Salaam (DAR)

| | | | | | |
|---|---|---|---|---|---|
| ☐ | 5H-FAT | Cessna 206H Stationair | 20608168 | ex 5H-CWF | |
| ☐ | 5H-NBL | Cessna 208B Caravan I | 208B1293 | ex N4115B | ♦ |
| ☐ | 5H-TAK | Cessna 208B Caravan I | 208B0891 | ex N1239B | |
| ☐ | 5H-TAZ | Cessna 208B Caravan I | 208B1186 | ex N12998 | |
| ☐ | 5H-ZAI | Cessna 208B Caravan I | 208B2031 | ex N2326S | ♦ |

# 5N-   NIGERIA (Federal Republic of Nigeria)

## AERO CONTRACTORS — Aeroline (AJ/NIG) — Lagos (LOS)

| | | | | | |
|---|---|---|---|---|---|
| ☐ | 5N-AQK | Aérospatiale SA365N Dauphin 2 | 6108 | | op for NNPC |
| ☐ | 5N-AQL | Aérospatiale SA365N Dauphin 2 | 6109 | | op for NNPC |
| ☐ | 5N-BAF | Aérospatiale SA365N2 Dauphin 2 | 6430 | ex F-WYMC | op for NNPC |
| ☐ | 5N-BDA | Aérospatiale SA365N Dauphin 2 | 6077 | ex 8P-PHM | |
| ☐ | 5N-BET | Aérospatiale SA365N Dauphin 2 | 6087 | ex TJ-DEM | |
| ☐ | 5N-BIX | Aérospatiale AS365N3 Dauphin 2 | 6657 | ex PH-SHI | |
| ☐ | 5N-ESO | Aérospatiale SA365N Dauphin 2 | 6072 | ex PH-SSP | |
| ☐ | 5N-STO | Aérospatiale SA365N Dauphin 2 | 6106 | ex PH-SSV | |
| | | | | | |
| ☐ | 5N-BIZ | Boeing 737-4B7 | 24558/1845 | ex N436US | |
| ☐ | 5N-BJA | Boeing 737-4B7 | 24873/1931 | ex N446US | |
| ☐ | 5N-BOB | Boeing 737-42C | 24232/2060 | ex EI-CWE | [PSR]♦ |
| ☐ | 5N-BOC | Boeing 737-42C | 24814/2270 | ex EI-CWF | ♦ |
| ☐ | 5N-BOT | Boeing 737-4U3 | 25713/2531 | ex PK-GWT | o/o♦ |
| ☐ | 5N-BOU | Boeing 737-4U3 | 25715/2537 | ex PK-GWM | o/o♦ |
| ☐ | 5N-BOV | Boeing 737-4U3 | 25716/2540 | ex PK-GWN | o/o♦ |
| ☐ | 5N-BOW | Boeing 737-4U3 | 25718/2548 | ex PK-GWP | o/o♦ |
| | | | | | |
| ☐ | 5N-BKQ | Boeing 737-522 | 26695/2423 | ex VP-BSW | |
| ☐ | 5N-BKR | Boeing 737-522 | 26699/2485 | ex VP-BSX | |
| ☐ | 5N-BLC | Boeing 737-522 | 26692/2421 | ex VP-BSV | |
| ☐ | 5N-BLD | Boeing 737-522 | 26675/2345 | ex VP-BSU | |
| ☐ | 5N-BLE | Boeing 737-522 | 26672/2343 | ex VP-BSQ | |
| ☐ | 5N-BLG | Boeing 737-522 | 25387/2179 | ex VP-BTI | |
| | | | | | |
| ☐ | 5N-AOA | Aérospatiale AS355F Ecureuil 2 | 5277 | ex F-WZFB | op for NNPC |
| ☐ | 5N-AOB | Aérospatiale AS355F Ecureuil 2 | 5278 | ex F-WZFV | op for NNPC |
| ☐ | 5N-BKG | Eurocopter EC225LP | 2681 | | |
| ☐ | 5N-BJO | de Havilland DHC-8Q-311 | 534 | ex C-FLGJ | ♦ |
| ☐ | 5N-RSN | Agusta AW139 | 31060 | ex 5N-BJB | op for River States Govt |

## AFRIJET AIRLINES — Afrijet (6F/FRJ) — Lagos (LOS)

| | | | | | |
|---|---|---|---|---|---|
| ☐ | 5N-BKO | McDonnell-Douglas MD-83 | 49855/1728 | ex N311FV | [TUS] |

Ceased ops 2009

## AIR MIDWEST — Lagos (LOS)

Ceased ops 2010

| | | | | | |
|---|---|---|---|---|---|
| **AIR NIGERIA** | | *(VK/ANP)* | | *Lagos (LOS)* | |
| ☐ 5N-VNC | Boeing 737-33V | 29338/3114 | ex G-EZYN | | |
| ☐ 5N-VND | Boeing 737-33V | 29337/3113 | ex G-EZYM | | |
| ☐ 5N-VNE | Boeing 737-33V | 29340/3121 | ex G-EZYP | | |
| ☐ 5N-VNF | Boeing 737-33V | 29341/3125 | ex OE-IAF | | |
| ☐ 5N-VNG | Boeing 737-33V | 29342/3127 | ex OE-IAI | | |
| ☐ 5N-VNJ | Boeing 737-36N | 28558/2876 | ex N524MS | | |
| ☐ 5N-VNK | Boeing 737-33A | 27469/2864 | ex N901AS | | |
| ☐ 5N-VNL | Boeing 737-33A | 27910/2873 | ex N902AS | | |
| ☐ 5N-BOC | Boeing 737-42C | 24814/2270 | ex EI-CWF | | ♦ |
| ☐ 5N-VNH | Embraer ERJ-190AR | 19000210 | ex PT-SGT | | |
| ☐ 5N-VNI | Embraer ERJ-190AR | 19000226 | ex PT-SHM | | |
| ☐ 5N-VNM | Boeing 737-4Q8 | 25375/2598 | ex TC-TJD | | ♦ |

| | | | | |
|---|---|---|---|---|
| **AIR TARABA** | | | | |
| ☐ M-ABFA | Embraer ERJ-145EU | 145617 | ex G-EMBY | ♦ |

| | | | | | |
|---|---|---|---|---|---|
| **ALLIED AIR CARGO** | | *Bambi (AJK)* | | *Lagos (LOS)* | |
| ☐ 5N-BJN | Boeing 727-221F (FedEx 3) | 22540/1796 | ex 5X-TON | | |
| ☐ 5N-BMQ | Boeing 727-2Q6F (FedEx 3) | 21971/1540 | ex N727WF | | |
| ☐ 5N-JNR | Boeing 727-217F (FedEx 3) | 21056/1122 | ex C-FACK | | |
| ☐ 5N-RKY | Boeing 727-217F (Raisbeck 3) | 21055/1117 | ex C-FACR | | |

| | | | | |
|---|---|---|---|---|
| **AMBJEK AIR SERVICES** | | | | *Abuja (ABV)* |
| ☐ 5N-BEA | LET L-410UVP-E | 902435 | ex OK-VDT | |
| ☐ 5N-BEB | LET L-410UVP-E3 | 882103 | ex OK-TDS | |

| | | | | | |
|---|---|---|---|---|---|
| **ARIK AIR** | | *Arik Air (W3/ARA)* | | *Lagos (LOS)* | |
| ☐ 5N-MJC | Boeing 737-7BD/W | 33932/2234 | ex N320AT | Martin | |
| ☐ 5N-MJD | Boeing 737-7BD/W | 36073/2248 | ex N323AT | Michael | |
| ☐ 5N-MJE | Boeing 737-7GL/W | 34761/2401 | ex N737AV | McTighe | |
| ☐ 5N-MJF | Boeing 737-7GL/W | 34762/2427 | ex N737BV | Queen of Angles | |
| ☐ 5N-MJG | Boeing 737-7BD/W | 33944/2576 | ex N346AT | | |
| ☐ 5N-MJH | Boeing 737-7BD/W | 36719/2589 | ex N347AT | | |
| ☐ 5N-MJI | Boeing 737-76N/W | 28640/799 | ex N740AL | | |
| ☐ 5N-MJJ | Boeing 737-76N/W | 28641/809 | ex N741AL | City of Benin | |
| ☐ 5N-MJK | Boeing 737-76N/W | 30830/855 | ex N742AL | | |
| ☐ CS-TFW | Airbus A340-542 | 910 | ex F-WWTK | Our Lady of Perpetual Help | >HFY |
| ☐ CS-TFX | Airbus A340-542 | 912 | ex F-WJKI | Captin Bob Hayes, OON | >HFY |
| ☐ 5N-BKU | de Havilland DHC-8-402Q | 4207 | ex C-FPPU | | |
| ☐ 5N-BKV | de Havilland DHC-8-402Q | 4219 | ex C-FSRN | | |
| ☐ 5N-JEA | Canadair CRJ-900ER | 15058 | ex C-FHRH | Anthony | |
| ☐ 5N-JEB | Canadair CRJ-900ER | 15059 | ex C-FHRK | Patrick | |
| ☐ 5N-JEC | Canadair CRJ-900ER | 15054 | ex C-FGNB | | wfs |
| ☐ 5N-JED | Canadair CRJ-900ER | 15114 | ex C-FMEP | Abraham | |
| ☐ 5N-MJA | Boeing 737-322 | 24454/1750 | ex N361UA | Eddington | [SEN] |
| ☐ 5N-MJB | Boeing 737-322 | 24360/1692 | ex N354UA | Augustine | [NWI] |
| ☐ 5N-MJN | Boeing 737-86N/W | 35638/2789 | | Eddington | |
| ☐ 5N-MJO | Boeing 737-86N/W | 35640/2819 | ex N358MT | Augustine | |
| ☐ 5N-MJP | Boeing 737-8JE/W | 38970/3030 | | Sultan of Sokoto | |
| ☐ 5N-MJQ | Boeing 737-8JE/W | 38971/3065 | | City of Calabar | |

| | | | | | |
|---|---|---|---|---|---|
| **ASSOCIATED AVIATION** | | *Associated (SCD)* | | *Lagos (LOS)* | |
| ☐ 5N-BBL | Short SD.3-60 | SH3637 | ex G-LEGS | | |
| ☐ 5N-BHV | Boeing 727-227F (FedEx 3) | 21364/1261 | ex N86426 | | |
| ☐ 5N-BIT | Embraer EMB.120RT Brasilia | 120050 | ex N190SW | | ♦ |
| ☐ 5N-BIU | Embraer EMB.120RT Brasilia | 120048 | ex N189SW | | ♦ |
| ☐ 5N-BJY | Embraer EMB.120ER Brasilia | 120174 | ex N388JR | | |
| ☐ 5N-BJZ | Embraer EMB.120ER Brasilia | 120095 | ex N788JR | | |
| ☐ 5N-BNQ | Boeing 727-2B7 | 22162/1717 | ex N762AT | | ♦ |

| | | | | |
|---|---|---|---|---|
| **AXIOM AIR** | | | | |
| ☐ 5N-BMA | Boeing 737-3Q4 (SF) | 24209/1492 | ex ZK-TLB | |

| | | | | |
|---|---|---|---|---|
| **BELLVIEW AIRLINES** | | *Bellview Airlines (B3/BLV)* | | *Lagos (LOS)* |

Ceased ops 2009

## BRISTOW HELICOPTERS (NIGERIA)  Bristow Helicopters (BHN)
Lagos/Calabar/Eket/Port Harcourt/Warri (LOS/CBQ/-/PHC/-)

| | Reg | Type | c/n | ex | Notes |
|---|---|---|---|---|---|
| ☐ | 5N-BGO | Aérospatiale AS.332L | 2092 | ex G-BRXU | |
| ☐ | 5N-BGP | Aérospatiale AS.332L | 2046 | ex G-BWMG | |
| ☐ | 5N-BKJ | Aérospatiale AS.332L | 2170 | ex G-PUMI | |
| ☐ | 5N-BNC | Aérospatiale AS.332L2 | 2500 | ex LN-ONI | |
| ☐ | 5N-BNU | Aérospatiale AS.332L2 | 2488 | ex G-CGTJ | ♦ |
| ☐ | 5N-AMQ | Bell 206L-1 LongRanger II | 45746 | ex N31800 | |
| ☐ | 5N-AQP | Bell 206L-1 LongRanger II | 45604 | ex N3907E | |
| ☐ | 5N-BAS | Bell 206L-1 LongRanger II | 45367 | ex N1076K | |
| ☐ | 5N-BBN | Bell 206L-3 LongRanger III | 51005 | ex SU-CAD | |
| ☐ | 5N-BCW | Bell 206L-3 LongRanger III | 51053 | ex SU-CAK | |
| ☐ | 5N-BFE | Bell 206L-4 LongRanger IV | 52272 | ex N20796 | |
| ☐ | 5N-BFF | Bell 206L-4 LongRanger IV | 52273 | ex N2080C | |
| ☐ | 5N-BFG | Bell 206L-4 LongRanger IV | 52274 | ex N2080W | |
| ☐ | 5N-BFH | Bell 206L-4 LongRanger IV | 52275 | ex N2081K | |
| ☐ | 5N-BFV | Bell 206L-4 LongRanger IV | 52160 | ex 5N-ESC | |
| ☐ | 5N-BHH | Bell 206L-4 LongRanger IV | 52291 | ex N274AL | |
| ☐ | 5N-BJR | Bell 206L-4 LongRanger IV | 52191 | ex N178AL | |
| ☐ | 5N-PAA | Bell 206L-1 LongRanger II | 45659 | ex N39118 | |
| ☐ | 5N-BCZ | Bell 412SP | 33179 | ex B-55521 | |
| ☐ | 5N-BDZ | Bell 412EP | 36278 | ex 9Y-ALI | |
| ☐ | 5N-BFU | Bell 412EP | 36318 | ex N7022F | |
| ☐ | 5N-BGS | Bell 412SP | 33186 | ex N464AC | |
| ☐ | 5N-BHB | Bell 412EP | 36273 | ex XA-TTF | |
| ☐ | 5N-BHD | Bell 412EP | 36354 | ex N4202A | |
| ☐ | 5N-BIM | Bell 412EP | 36373 | ex N31195 | |
| ☐ | 5N-BIO | Bell 412EP | 36378 | ex N106AL | |
| ☐ | 5N-BIP | Bell 412EP | 36383 | ex N105AL | |
| ☐ | 5N-BIR | Bell 412EP | 36386 | ex N107AL | |
| ☐ | 5N-BIS | Bell 412EP | 36387 | ex N132AL | |
| ☐ | 5N-BML | Bell 412EP | 36433 | ex G-OIBU | |
| ☐ | 5N-BDH | Eurocopter EC155B | 6591 | ex F-WQDQ | op for Shell Nigeria |
| ☐ | 5N-BDI | Eurocopter EC155B | 6602 | | op for Shell Nigeria |
| ☐ | 5N-BDJ | Eurocopter EC155B | 6607 | | op for Shell Nigeria |
| ☐ | 5N-BDK | Eurocopter EC155B | 6608 | | op for Shell Nigeria |
| ☐ | 5N-BDL | Eurocopter EC155B | 6610 | ex F-WQDA | op for Shell Nigeria |
| ☐ | 5N-BDM | Eurocopter EC155B | 6611 | ex F-WQDH | op for Shell Nigeria |
| ☐ | 5N-BBO | Sikorsky S-76A++ | 760114 | ex G-BVKP | |
| ☐ | 5N-BCT | Sikorsky S-76A++ | 760109 | ex G-BZJT | |
| ☐ | 5N-BGC | Sikorsky S-76C+ | 760481 | ex LN-ONY | |
| ☐ | 5N-BGD | Sikorsky S-76C+ | 760540 | ex N864AL | |
| ☐ | 5N-BGE | Sikorsky S-76C+ | 760545 | ex N20509 | |
| ☐ | 5N-BIL | Sikorsky S-76C+ | 760591 | ex N869AL | |
| ☐ | 5N-BJT | Sikorsky S-76C+ | 760638 | ex N872AL | |
| ☐ | 5N-BJU | Sikorsky S-76C+ | 760640 | ex N876AL | |
| ☐ | 5N-BKM | Sikorsky S-76C+ | 760660 | ex N45083 | |
| ☐ | 5N-BMD | Sikorsky S-76C+ | 760456 | ex LN-ONZ | |
| ☐ | 5N-BMI | Sikorsky S-76C+ | 760732 | ex G-CFPU | |
| ☐ | 5N-BMX | Sikorsky S-76C+ | 760754 | ex G-CFRD | |
| ☐ | 5N-BMZ | Sikorsky S-76C | 760802 | ex G-CGUJ | ♦ |
| ☐ | 5N-BNZ | Sikorsky S-76C++ | 760802 | ex G-CGUJ | ♦ |
| ☐ | 5N- | Sikorsky S-76C+ | 760652 | ex N879AL | ♦ |
| ☐ | 5N-BEM | Bell 407 | 53246 | ex N567AL | |
| ☐ | 5N-BEO | Bell 407 | 53190 | ex N467AL | |
| ☐ | 5N-BEP | Bell 407 | 53107 | ex N427AL | |
| ☐ | 5N-BFI | Bell 407 | 53550 | ex N2531G | |
| ☐ | 5N-BDD | Bell 412 | 33046 | ex N395AL | |
| ☐ | 5N-BDY | Bell 412EP | 36267 | ex N506AL | |
| ☐ | 5N-BES | Bell 206B JetRanger III | 3216 | ex N139H | |
| ☐ | 5N-BIQ | Bell 412EP | 36385 | ex N115AL | |
| ☐ | 5N-BIW | Cessna 208 Caravan I | 20800403 | ex N1316N | FP |
| ☐ | 5N-BJE | Aérospatiale AS365N2 Dauphin 2 | 6446 | ex EP-HCK | |
| ☐ | 5N-BLX | Sikorsky S-92A | 920082 | ex G-CFCA | |
| ☐ | 5N-BMN | Sikorsky S-92A | 920103 | ex G-CGCI | |
| ☐ | 5N- | Sikorsky S-92A | 920075 | ex N92TZ | ♦ |

## CAPITAL AIRLINES  Capital Shuttle (NCP)  Lagos (LOS)

| | Reg | Type | c/n | ex | Notes |
|---|---|---|---|---|---|
| ☐ | 5N-BLB | Embraer EMB.120ER Brasilia | 120247 | ex N258CA | wfs |

## CAVERTON HELICOPTERS  (CJR)  Lagos (LOS)

| | Reg | Type | c/n | ex | Notes |
|---|---|---|---|---|---|
| ☐ | 5N-BHK | Aérospatiale SA365N Dauphin 2 | 6128 | ex CS-HFH | <HeliPortugal |
| ☐ | 5N-BHS | Aérospatiale AS350B2 Ecureuil | 1871 | ex CS-HDK | <HeliPortugal |

| | | | | | | |
|---|---|---|---|---|---|---|
| ☐ | 5N-BHT | Aérospatiale AS350B2 Ecureuil | 1222 | ex CS-HEO | | <HeliPortugal |
| ☐ | 5N-BIK | Aérospatiale AS365N Dauphin 2 | 6138 | ex F-GNVS | | <HeliPortugal |
| ☐ | 5N-BJV | de Havilland DHC-6 Twin Otter 300 | 816 | ex HB-LUB | | ♦ |
| ☐ | 5N-BLJ | de Havilland DHC-6 Twin Otter 300 | 831 | ex VH-VHM | | |
| ☐ | 5N-BOI | Agusta AW139 | 31380 | | | ♦ |
| ☐ | 5N-BOJ | Agusta AW139 | 31385 | | | ♦ |
| ☐ | 5N- | Agusta AW139 | 31386 | ex I-EASH | | ♦ |
| ☐ | 5N- | Agusta AW139 | 31389 | | | ♦ |

## CHANCHANGI AIRLINES

| | | | | | |
|---|---|---|---|---|---|
| ☐ | 5N-BEW | Boeing 737-317 | 22865/960 | ex C-GQCP | wfs♦ |
| ☐ | 5N-BIF | Boeing 737-282 | 23043/972 | ex N233TM | [KAD]♦ |
| ☐ | 5N-BIH | Boeing 737-282 | 23046/981 | ex N789TM | [TNN]♦ |
| ☐ | 5N-BMB | Boeing 737-3J6 | 25079/2016 | ex B-2536 | [JNB]♦ |
| ☐ | 5N-BMC | Boeing 737-3Z0 | 25089/2027 | ex B-2537 | [BEG♦ |

## DANA — Dana Air (DAV) — Kaduna (KAD)

| | | | | | |
|---|---|---|---|---|---|
| ☐ | 5N-ARP | Dornier 228-201 | 8013 | ex (5N-AOH) | |
| ☐ | 5N-BCA | Piper PA-23 Aztec 250D | 27-4220 | ex G-AYZN | |
| ☐ | 5N-DOB | Dornier 228-202 | 8026 | ex N232RP | |
| ☐ | 5N-DOL | Dornier 228-202 | 8145 | ex N241RP | wfs |
| ☐ | 5N-DOW | Dornier 328-110 | 3070 | ex OY-NCS | ♦ |
| ☐ | 5N-DOX | Dornier 328-110 | 3073 | ex OE-LKF | |
| ☐ | 5N-DOY | Dornier 328-110 | 3089 | ex OE-LKG | |

## DANA AIR — (9J/DAV)

| | | | | | |
|---|---|---|---|---|---|
| ☐ | 5N-JAI | McDonnell-Douglas MD-83 | 53016/1850 | ex N968AS | |
| ☐ | 5N-RAM | McDonnell-Douglas MD-83 | 53019/1784 | ex N944AS | |
| ☐ | 5N-SAI | McDonnell-Douglas MD-83 | 53018/1779 | ex N943AS | |
| ☐ | 5N-SRI | McDonnell-Douglas MD-83 | 53020/1789 | ex N947AS | |

## EAS AIR LINES — Echoline (EXW) — Lagos (LOS)

Aircraft sold May11

## EASY LINK

| | | | | | |
|---|---|---|---|---|---|
| ☐ | 5N-BCM | LET L-410UVP-E | 902502 | ex HI-692CT | ♦ |

## FIRST NATION AIRLINES — (FRN) — Lagos (LOS)

| | | | | | | |
|---|---|---|---|---|---|---|
| ☐ | 5N-FNA | Airbus A320-212 | 0409 | ex N409AG | Resilience | [LOS]♦ |
| ☐ | 5N-FNB | Airbus A320-212 | 0466 | ex N466AG | Fortitude | ♦ |
| ☐ | 5N-FNC | Airbus A320-212 | 0497 | ex N997AG | Endurance | [LOS]♦ |

## FREEDOM AIR SERVICES — Inter Freedom (FFF) — Lagos (LOS)

Ceased ops 2007

## IRS AIRLINES — Silverbird (LVB) — Lagos (LOS)

| | | | | | | |
|---|---|---|---|---|---|---|
| ☐ | 5N-HIR | Fokker 100 | 11498 | ex G-CFBU | | |
| ☐ | 5N-SAT | Fokker 100 | 11293 | ex PH-MJO | | ♦ |
| ☐ | 5N-SIK | Fokker 100 | 11286 | ex SE-DUU | | |
| ☐ | 5N-SMR | Fokker 100 | 11291 | ex PH-MJN | | |
| ☐ | 5N-SWZ | Fokker 100 | 11295 | exZS-GAV | Hajiya Babba | ♦ |
| ☐ | 5N-BJM | Embraer ERJ-145LR | 1450984 | ex PT-SKE | | ♦ |
| ☐ | 5N-NCZ | Fokker F.28 Fellowship 4000 | 11241 | ex ZS-OPS | | |
| ☐ | 5N-SSZ | Fokker F.28 Fellowship 4000 | 11190 | ex ZS-BAL | | |
| ☐ | 5N-SWZ | Fokker F.28 Fellowship 4000 | 11191 | ex ZS-GAV | | [ABV}♦ |

## KABO AIR — Kabo (N2/QNK) — Kano (KAN)

| | | | | | |
|---|---|---|---|---|---|
| ☐ | 5N-DKB | Boeing 747-251B | 23548/644 | ex N637US | |
| ☐ | 5N-JRM | Boeing 747-251B | 23549/651 | ex N638US | |
| ☐ | 5N-MAD | Boeing 747-251B | 23547/642 | ex N636US | |

## MAXAIR — (NGL)

| | | | | | |
|---|---|---|---|---|---|
| ☐ | 5N-BLY | Boeing 727-2F9 | 22773/893 | ex 5N-ANY | ♦ |
| ☐ | 5N-BMG | Boeing 747-346 | 23638/658 | ex JA8177 | |
| ☐ | 5N-DBM | Boeing 747-346 | 23968/693 | ex JA8184 | |
| ☐ | 5N-DDK | Boeing 747-346 | 23967/692 | ex JA8183 | |

| | | | | | |
|---|---|---|---|---|---|
| ☐ | 5N-HMB | Boeing 747-438 | 25067/857 | ex VH-OJK | |
| ☐ | 5N-MBB | Boeing 747-346 | 24018/694 | ex HS-UTS | ♦ |

## MED-VIEW AIRLINES

Status unknown

| OVERLAND AIRWAYS | | | Overland (OJ/OLA) | | Lagos / Abuja (LOS/ABV) |
|---|---|---|---|---|---|
| ☐ | N340SS | SAAB SF.340A | 340A-022 | ex SE-C22 | wfs♦ |
| ☐ | 5N-BCO | Beech 1900D | UE-225 | ex N225GL | [HLA] |
| ☐ | 5N-BCP | Beech 1900D | UE-116 | ex N116YV | |
| ☐ | 5N-BCR | ATR 42-300 | 0031 | ex F-WQNR | |
| ☐ | 5N-BCS | ATR 42-300 | 0025 | ex EC-IYE | |
| ☐ | 5N-BND | ATR 42-300 | 0363 | ex F-WKVD | |

| PAN AFRICAN AIRLINES | | | (PNF) | | |
|---|---|---|---|---|---|
| ☐ | 5Y-TAZ | Douglas DC-9-32 | 47198/302 | ex TR-LHG | <VXG♦ |

| SKYPOWER EXPRESS AIRWAYS | | | Nigeria Express (EAN) | | Lagos (LOS) |
|---|---|---|---|---|---|
| ☐ | 5N-AXR | Embraer EMB.110P1 Bandeirante | 110459 | ex PT-SHM | wfs |

## TRADECRAFT

| | | | | | |
|---|---|---|---|---|---|
| ☐ | 5N-ASG | Boeing 767-332 | 23436/163 | ex N122DL | [DMK]♦ |

| TRANSKY AIRLINES | | | | | Lagos (LOS) |
|---|---|---|---|---|---|

Status uncertain

| WINGS AVIATION | | | | | Lagos (LOS) |
|---|---|---|---|---|---|
| ☐ | 5N-PTL | Beech 1900D | UE-215 | ex N850CA | |

## 5R-    MADAGASCAR (Democratic Republic of Madagascar)

| AEROMARINE | | | | | Antananarivo ((TNR) |
|---|---|---|---|---|---|
| ☐ | F-ODQI | Piper PA-31-350 Navajo Chieftain | 31-7305065 | ex F-BUOI | |
| ☐ | 5R-MCJ | Piper PA-23-250 Aztec C | 27-3644 | ex N6449Y | |
| ☐ | 5R-MCR | Piper PA-31 Turbo Navajo | 31-162 | ex N9122Y | |
| ☐ | 5R-MIK | Piper PA-23-250 Aztec B | 27-2191 | ex TL-ABA | |
| ☐ | 5R-MKG | Beech 99 | U-21 | ex F-GFPE | |
| ☐ | 5R-MLI | Cessna 207A Stationair 7 II | 20700496 | ex 5R-MVR | |
| ☐ | 5R-MLJ | Cessna 310R II | 310R1372 | ex F-GBGB | |
| ☐ | 5R-MLK | Beech 95-C55 Baron | TE-101 | ex F-BOJG | |
| ☐ | 5R-MLT | Cessna 310R II | 310R0328 | ex F-BXLT | |

| AIR MADAGASCAR | | | Air Madagascar (MD/MDG) | | Antananarivo (TNR) |
|---|---|---|---|---|---|
| ☐ | 5R-MFH | Boeing 737-3Q8 | 26305/2651 | | |
| ☐ | 5R-MFI | Boeing 737-3Q8 | 26301/2623 | ex N319FL | |
| ☐ | 5R-MFJ | Boeing 767-3Y0ER | 26200/450 | ex N330DF | |
| ☐ | 5R-MGC | de Havilland DHC-6 Twin Otter 300 | 328 | | |
| ☐ | 5R-MGD | de Havilland DHC-6 Twin Otter 300 | 329 | | |
| ☐ | 5R-MGF | de Havilland DHC-6 Twin Otter 300 | 482 | | |
| ☐ | 5R-MJE | ATR 72-212A | 0694 | ex F-WWEQ | |
| ☐ | 5R-MJF | ATR 72-212A | 0698 | ex F-WWEU | |
| ☐ | 5R-MJG | ATR 42-500 | 0649 | ex F-WWLG | |
| ☐ | 5R-MVT | ATR 42-320 | 0044 | ex F-WQAD | |
| ☐ | 5R-MLA | Piper PA-31-350 Chieftain | 31-7952076 | | |
| ☐ | 5R- | Airbus A340-313X | 210 | ex F-GLZL | o/o♦ |

| MADAGASCAR TRANS AIR | | | | | Ivato |
|---|---|---|---|---|---|
| ☐ | 5R-MKK | Piper PA-34-200T Seneca | 34-7970480 | ex ZS-KIG | ♦ |

| MALAGASY AIRLINES | | | (MLG) | | Antananarivo (TNR) |
|---|---|---|---|---|---|
| ☐ | 5R-MDB | Cessna 402B | 402B0572 | ex ZS-RES | |
| ☐ | 5R-MHJ | Piper PA-23-250 Aztec | 27-409 | ex 5R-MVJ | |
| ☐ | 5R-MKS | Cessna 402B | 402B0014 | ex 5R-MVC | |
| ☐ | 5R-MLZ | Cessna TU206G Stationair 6 | U20604526 | ex F-BVQK | |

### TIKO AIR
### Antananarivo (TNR)

| | | | |
|---|---|---|---|
| ☐ 5R-MJT | ATR 42-320 | 0221 | ex (5R-TIK) |

## 5T-   MAURITANIA (Islamic Republic of Mauritania)

### COMPAGNIE MAURITANIENNE DE TRANSPORTES – CMT      (CPM)      Nouakchott (NKC)

Ops cargo flights with Antonov aircraft leased from Aerocom and Pskovia when required

### MAURITANIA AIRLINES      (YD/MTW)      Nouakchott (NKC)

| | | | | |
|---|---|---|---|---|
| ☐ 5T-CLA | Boeing 737-55S | 28469/2849 | ex OK-CGH | |
| ☐ 5T-CLB | Boeing 737-55S | 28470/2861 | ex OK-CGJ | |
| ☐ 5T-CLC | Boeing 737-7EE/W | 34263/1739 | ex N426HZ | ♦ |

## 5U-   NIGER (Republic of Niger)

### AIR NIAMEY      Niamey

| | | | | |
|---|---|---|---|---|
| ☐ 5U-ACK | Yakovlev Yak-40 | 9630450 | ex RA-88218 | ♦ |

## 5V-   TOGO (Togolese Republic)

### AFRICA WEST CARGO      (FK/WTA)      Lome (LFW)

| | | | | |
|---|---|---|---|---|
| ☐ 5Y-BXM | Douglas DC-9-33CF | 47409/497 | ex S9-PSG | ♦ |
| ☐ S9-BOZ | Antonov An-12A | 2340803 | | <GLE♦ |
| ☐ S9-DBA | Antonov An-12ap | 2400802 | | <GLE♦ |

### ASKY AIRLINES      (SKK)      Lome (LFW)

| | | | | |
|---|---|---|---|---|
| ☐ ET-ANW | de Havilland DHC-8-402Q | 4320 | ex C-GEUN | <ETH |

## 5W-   SAMOA (Independent State of Western Samoa)

### POLYNESIAN AIRLINES      Polynesian (PH/PAO)      Apia (APW)

| | | | | |
|---|---|---|---|---|
| ☐ 5W-FAW | de Havilland DHC-6 Twin Otter 300 | 827 | ex C-FTLQ | Gogo |
| ☐ 5W-FAY | de Havilland DHC-6 Twin Otter 300 | 690 | ex VH-UQW | Gillian |

## 5X-   UGANDA (Republic of Uganda)

### AIR UGANDA      (U7/UGB)      Entebbe (EBB)

| | | | | |
|---|---|---|---|---|
| ☐ 5X-UGA | McDonnell-Douglas MD-87 | 49840/1745 | ex EC-EYY | |
| ☐ 5X-UGB | McDonnell-Douglas MD-87 | 49838/1733 | ex EC-EYB | |
| ☐ 5X-UGC | McDonnell-Douglas MD-87 | 49839/1739 | ex EC-EYX | [OLB] |
| ☐ 5X-UGE | Canadair CRJ-200ER | 7356 | ex N642BR | |
| ☐ 5X-UGG | Canadair CRJ-200ER | 7379 | ex N115MN | ♦ |

### EAGLE AIR      African Eagle (H7/EGU)      Entebbe (EBB)

| | | | | |
|---|---|---|---|---|
| ☐ 5X-EBZ | Beech 1900C-1 | UC-174 | ex ZS-PIT | |
| ☐ 5X-EIV | LET L-410UVP-E9 | 962632 | ex 5Y-BPX | |
| ☐ 5X-GNF | LET L-410UVP-E8 | 892320 | ex OK-UDA | |

### RELIANCE AIR      Entebbe (EBB)

Status uncertain

### ROYAL DAISY AIRLINES      (6D/KDR)      Entebbe (EBB)

Status uncertain

### SKYJET      (UQ/SJA)      Entebbe (EBB)

| | | | | |
|---|---|---|---|---|
| ☐ 5X-SKA | Boeing 737-232 | 23098/1031 | ex N326DL | [EBB]♦ |
| ☐ 5X- | Boeing 737-247 (Nordam 3) | 23518/1265 | ex TL-ADU | [KRT]♦ |

## UGANDA AIR CARGO

| | | | | | |
|---|---|---|---|---|---|
| ☐ | 5X-UCF | Lockheed L-382G Hercules | 4610 | ex (PH-AID) | ♦ |
| ☐ | 5X-UYX | Harbin Y-12-IV | 026 | ex Uganda AF | ♦ |
| ☐ | 5X-UYZ | Harbin Y-12-IV | 021 | ex Uganda AF | ♦ |
| ☐ | 5X-UXZ | Harbin Y-12-IV | 027 | ex Uganda AF | ♦ |

## 5Y- KENYA

### ABERDAIR AVIATION (BDV)

| | | | | | |
|---|---|---|---|---|---|
| ☐ | 5Y-FWA | Embraer EMB.110P1 Bandeirante | 110195 | ex ZS-OUM | ♦ |
| ☐ | 9G-FWC | Embraer EMB.110P1 Bandeirante | 110381 | ex ZS-OUM | ♦ |
| ☐ | 9G-FWD | Embraer EMB.110P1 Bandeirante | 110347 | ex VH-KEG | ♦ |

### AFRICAN EXPRESS AIRWAYS — Express Jet (XU/AXK) — Nairobi-Jomo Kenyatta Intl (NBO)

| | | | | | |
|---|---|---|---|---|---|
| ☐ | 5X-TEZ | Embraer EMB.120ER Brasilia | 120078 | ex ZS-CAE | >KDR♦ |
| ☐ | 5Y-AXD | Douglas DC-9-32 | 47088/180 | ex 9L-LDF | [NBO] |
| ☐ | 5Y-AXE | Boeing 727-256 | 21611/1382 | ex 9L-LDV all-white | |
| ☐ | 5Y-AXF | Douglas DC-9-32 | 47093/237 | ex 9L-LDG | |
| ☐ | 5Y-AXL | McDonnell-Douglas MD-82 | 49204/1179 | ex I-DAWL | |
| ☐ | 5Y-AXN | McDonnell-Douglas MD-82 | 49207/1189 | ex N461LF | |

### AIR TRAFFIC

| | | | | | |
|---|---|---|---|---|---|
| ☐ | 5Y-BUV | Dornier 228-201 | 8050 | ex A6-ZYE | ♦ |
| ☐ | 5Y-BUX | Dornier 228-201 | 8080 | ex SX-BHI | ♦ |
| ☐ | 5Y-BYC | Dornier 228-200 | 8058 | ex D-IMIK | ♦ |

### AIRKENYA EXPRESS (P2/XAK) — Nairobi-Wilson (WIL)

| | | | | | |
|---|---|---|---|---|---|
| ☐ | 5Y-BGH | de Havilland DHC-6 Twin Otter 300 | 574 | ex N4226J | |
| ☐ | 5Y-BIO | de Havilland DHC-6 Twin Otter 300 | 579 | ex 5H-MRB | |
| ☐ | 5H-BMP | de Havilland DHC-7-102 | 080 | ex 5Y-BMP | |
| ☐ | 5Y-BRU | LET L-410UVP-E9 | 912539 | ex 5X-UAY | |
| ☐ | 5Y-BTZ | de Havilland DHC-8-102 | 203 | ex VH-TNU | ♦ |
| ☐ | 5Y-BXW | Cessna 208B Caravan i | 208B2189 | ex N1008P | ♦ |
| ☐ | 5Y-BYO | Cessna 208B Caravan I | 208B0443 | ex 5H-REG | |
| ☐ | 5Y-PJP | de Havilland DHC-6 Twin Otter 300 | 424 | ex ZS-LGN | |

### AIRWORKS KENYA (SAVANNAH AIR SERVICES)

| | | | | | |
|---|---|---|---|---|---|
| ☐ | 5Y-NFY | Cessna 208B Caravan I | 208B0294 | ex ZS-NFY | |
| ☐ | 5Y-NKV | Cessna 208B Caravan I | 208B0387 | ex ZS-NKV | |
| ☐ | 5Y-NLM | Cessna 208B Caravan I | 208B0375 | ex ZS-NLM | |
| ☐ | 5Y-SAV | Cessna 208B Caravan I | 208B0312 | ex N208PA | |
| ☐ | 5Y-TAV | Cessna 208B Caravan I | 208B0688 | ex ZS-OIH | ♦ |
| ☐ | 5Y-TLC | Cessna 208B Caravan I | 208B0472 | ex ZS-TLC DHL c/s | ♦ |

### ALS / COMPION AVIATION — Nairobi-Wilson (WIL)

| | | | | | |
|---|---|---|---|---|---|
| ☐ | 5Y-BVP | Beech 1900D | UE-136 | ex ZS-PHM | op for ICRC |
| ☐ | 5Y-BVT | Beech 1900D | UE-226 | ex 5H-SXY | ♦ |
| ☐ | 5Y-BVV | Beech 1900C | UB-29 | ex ZS-OUC | |
| ☐ | 5Y-BVX | Beech 1900D | UE-101 | ex ZS-PJG | |
| ☐ | 5Y-DHL | Beech 1900C-1 | UC-100 | ex N15305 | op for ICRC |
| ☐ | 5Y-LKG | Beech 1900C | UB-63 | ex C-FUCB | op for Kenya Airlink |
| ☐ | 5Y-SGL | Beech 1900C-1 | UC-114 | ex V5-SGL | of for UN Humanitarian Service |
| ☐ | 5Y-BVO | de Havilland DHC-8-102 | 007 | ex C-GFQI | |
| ☐ | 5Y-BXH | de Havilland DHC-8-102 | 205 | ex C-FLAD | |
| ☐ | 5Y-BXI | de Havilland DHC-8-102 | 376 | ex C-GRGQ | |
| ☐ | 5Y-BXU | de Havilland DHC-8-102 | 344 | ex C-GFKC | |
| ☐ | 5Y-BZI | de Havilland DHC-8-102 | 105 | ex 9Q-CWP | |
| ☐ | 5Y-PRV | de Havilland DHC-8-102 | 185 | ex C-FGQI | ♦ |
| ☐ | 5Y-STN | de Havilland DHC-8-102 | 179 | ex C-FCON | |
| ☐ | 5Y-BLA | Beech 200C Super King Air | BL-10 | ex C-FAMB | |
| ☐ | 5Y-BVY | Embraer ERJ-135LR | 145599 | ex N843RP | |
| ☐ | 5Y-BVZ | Embraer ERJ-135LR | 145661 | ex N842RP | |

### ASTRAL AVIATION — Astral Cargo (8V/ACP) — Nairobi-Jomo Kenyatta Intl (NBO)

| | | | | | |
|---|---|---|---|---|---|
| ☐ | 5Y-SAN | Douglas DC-9-34CF | 47706/821 | ex S9-PSR | ♦ |

## BATELEUR AIR CHARTER

| | | | | |
|---|---|---|---|---|
| ☐ | 5Y-EOE | Beech 1900C-1 | UC-90 | ex N90YV | ♦ |

## BLUE BIRD AVIATION     Cobra (BBZ)     *Nairobi -Wilson (WIL)*

| | | | | | |
|---|---|---|---|---|---|
| ☐ | 5Y-VVN | de Havilland DHC-8-102 | 62 | ex VH-TQN | |
| ☐ | 5Y-VVP | de Havilland DHC-8-106 | 339 | ex C-FLPP | |
| ☐ | 5Y-VVR | de Havilland DHC-8-102 | 204 | ex VH-TQQ | |
| ☐ | 5Y-VVS | de Havilland DHC-8-102A | 349 | ex VH-TQT | |
| ☐ | 5Y-VVT | de Havilland DHC-8-102A | 362 | ex VH-TQV | |
| ☐ | 5Y-VVU | de Havilland DHC-8-402PF | 4008 | ex SE-LSM | ♦ |
| ☐ | 5Y-VVW | de Havilland DHC-8-402Q | 4011 | ex LN-RDL | |
| ☐ | 5Y-VVX | de Havilland DHC-8-402Q | 4018 | ex LN-RDB | |
| ☐ | 5Y-VVY | de Havilland DHC-8-402Q | 4009 | ex LN-RDD | |
| ☐ | 5Y-VVZ | de Havilland DHC-8-402Q | 4024 | ex LN-RDI | ♦ |
| ☐ | 5Y-VVF | Fokker 50 | 20136 | ex N136NM | |
| ☐ | 5Y-VVG | Fokker 50 | 20137 | ex N137NM | |
| ☐ | 5Y-VVH | Fokker 50 | 20203 | ex N203NM | |
| ☐ | 5Y-VVJ | Fokker 50 | 20133 | ex D-AFFZ | |
| ☐ | 5Y-VVK | Fokker 50 | 20213 | ex D-AFKL | |
| ☐ | 5Y-BOD | LET L-410UVP | 982727 | | ♦ |
| ☐ | 5Y-BSA | LET L-410UVP-E | 892323 | | ♦ |
| ☐ | 5Y-HHC | LET L-410A | 720204 | ex OK-DDU | |
| ☐ | 5Y-HHF | LET L-410AB | 710002 | ex OK-ADR | |
| ☐ | 5Y-VVA | LET L-410UVP-E9 | 962633 | ex OK-BDL | |
| ☐ | 5Y-VVC | LET L-410UVP-E20 | 922728 | ex ZS-NIJ | |
| ☐ | 5Y-VVE | LET L-410UVP-E20 | 922726 | ex 5Y-YYY | |
| ☐ | 5Y-VVF | LET L-410UVP | | | ♦ |
| ☐ | 5Y-VVL | LET L-410UVP-E7 | 872018 | ex 5Y-HHL | ♦ |
| ☐ | ET-AKZ | de Havilland DHC-8-202 | 469 | ex C-GLOT | >TNW |
| ☐ | 5Y-HHE | Beech 200 Super King Air | BB-547 | ex ZS-NIP | |
| ☐ | 5Y-UVM | Beech 1900D | UE-175 | ex N61HA | ♦ |

## BLUE SKY AVIATION     *Nairobi-Wilson (WIL)*

| | | | | | |
|---|---|---|---|---|---|
| ☐ | 5Y-BOD | LET L-410UVP-E20 | 982727 | ex OK-DDF | |
| ☐ | 5Y-BPH | LET L-410UVP | | | ♦ |
| ☐ | 5Y-BSA | LET L-410UVP-E9 | 892323 | ex OK-UDC | |

## CAPITAL AIRLINES     Capital Delta (CPD)     *Nairobi Wilson (WIL)*

| | | | | | |
|---|---|---|---|---|---|
| ☐ | 5Y-JAI | Beech 200 Super King Air | BB-557 | ex OY-PAM | |
| ☐ | 5Y-SJB | Beech 200 Super King Air | BB-467 | ex 5H-MUN | CatPass 250 conversion |

## CMC AVIATION

| | | | | | |
|---|---|---|---|---|---|
| ☐ | 5Y-BWG | de Havilland DHC-8Q-311 | 406 | ex C-FTYU | <Trident Avn♦ |
| ☐ | 5Y-DAC | de Havilland DHC-8-102 | 251 | ex C-GZAN | <Trident Avn♦ |
| ☐ | 5Y-ENA | de Havilland DHC-8-102 | 297 | ex N836EX | <Trident Avn♦ |
| ☐ | 5Y-GRS | de Havilland DHC-8-102 | 355 | ex SX-BIS | .<Trident Avn♦ |
| ☐ | 5Y-WJF | de Havilland DHC-8-202Q | 456 | ex N456YV | ♦ |

## DAC AVIATION

| | | | | | |
|---|---|---|---|---|---|
| ☐ | 5Y-MOC | de Havilland DHC-8-311 | 374 | ex C-FDYW | ♦ |

## D-CONNECTION     (Z9/DCP)

| | | | | | |
|---|---|---|---|---|---|
| ☐ | 5Y-JAP | Boeing 737-229C | 20915/401 | ex 5Y-KQN | <EAF |

## EAST AFRICAN AIR CHARTERS     *Nairobi-Wilson (WIL)*

| | | | | | |
|---|---|---|---|---|---|
| ☐ | 5Y-ALY | Cessna U206F Stationair | U20602266 | ex N15588U | |
| ☐ | 5Y-ART | Cessna 210L Centurion II | 21059817 | | |
| ☐ | 5Y-BIX | Reims Cessna F406 Caravan II | F406-0055 | ex N65912 | |
| ☐ | 5Y-BLN | Cessna 208B Caravan I | 208B0558 | ex N50398 | |
| ☐ | 5Y-BMH | Cessna 310R | 310R0501 | ex N87216 | |
| ☐ | 5Y-EOC | Cessna 208B Caravan I | 208B0737 | ex N1266A | ♦ |

## EAST AFRICAN SAFARI AIR     (B5/EXZ)     *Nairobi-Jomo Kenyatta Intl (NBO)*

| | | | | | |
|---|---|---|---|---|---|
| ☐ | 5Y-EEE | Fokker F.28 Fellowship 4000 | 11229 | ex 5Y-MNT | |

## EXECUTIVE TURBINE KENYA — Nairobi-Wilson (WIL)

| | | | | |
|---|---|---|---|---|
| ☐ | 5Y-BTG | Beech 1900C-1 | UC-96 | ex ZS-PBY | [WIL] |
| ☐ | 5Y-BVC | Short SD.3-60 | SH3717 | ex ZS-PBB | |

## FALCON AIR CHARTERS

| | | | | |
|---|---|---|---|---|
| ☐ | 5Y-GSV | Cessna 208 Caravan I | 20800024 ex N9358F | ♦ |

## FLEX AIR CARGO — Nairobi-Wilson (WIL)

| | | | | |
|---|---|---|---|---|
| ☐ | 5Y-BSI | Beech 1900C-1 | UC-172 | ex 5Y-BBI | ♦ |
| ☐ | 5Y-BUC | Cessna 208B Caravan I | 208B0400 | ex ZS-NLO | ♦ |
| ☐ | 5Y-LEX | Cessna 208B Caravan I | 208B0738 | ex ZS-CAT | ♦ |
| ☐ | 5Y-MJI | Cessna 208B Caravan I | 208B0155 | ex V5-ODL | ♦ |

## FLY540 — Fly Orange (5H/FFV) — Nairobi-Jomo Kenyatta Intl (NBO)

| | | | | | |
|---|---|---|---|---|---|
| ☐ | 5X-FFN | Fokker F.27 Friendship 500CRF | 10531 | ex TC-MBD | ♦ |
| ☐ | 5Y-BSS | Beech 1900C-1 | UC-88 | ex ZS-PJA | |
| ☐ | 5Y-BTN | Beech 1900D | UE-118 | ex ZS-PPJ | |
| ☐ | 5Y-BTT | Beech 1900C-1 | UC-125 | ex ZS-POU | ♦ |
| ☐ | 5Y-BUN | ATR 42-320 | 0205 | ex ZS-OZX | |
| ☐ | 5Y-BUZ | de Havilland DHC-8-102 | 253 | ex C-FOBU | |
| ☐ | 5Y-BVG | Beech 1900D | UE-62 | ex N62ZV | |
| ☐ | 5Y-BXB | de Havilland DHC-8-102 | 213 | ex N825PH | |
| ☐ | 5Y-BXC | Canadair CRJ-100ER | 7184 | ex C-FOVP | ♦ |
| ☐ | 5Y-BYB | de Havilland DHC-8-102 | 114 | ex C-GRGZ | ♦ |
| ☐ | 5Y-BXD | Canadair CRJ-100ER | 7042 | ex C-GLGU | ♦ |
| ☐ | 5Y-NON | Cessna 208 Caravan I | 20800036 | ex ZS-NON | ♦ |
| ☐ | 5Y-XXA | Douglas DC-9-14 (ABS 3) | 45725/19 | ex N600ME | [NBO]♦ |
| ☐ | 5Y-XXB | Douglas DC-9-14 (ABS 3) | 45711/4 | ex N500ME | [NBO]♦ |
| ☐ | 5Y-YEP | Cessna 208B Caravan I | 208B0525 | ex ZS-ORI | ♦ |

## FREEDOM AIR EXPRESS — Nairobi-Wilson (WIL)

| | | | | |
|---|---|---|---|---|
| ☐ | ZS-SOV | British Aerospace 146-200 | E2077 | ex G-UKRH | ♦ |
| ☐ | 5Y-BWN | Dornier 228-202 | 8124 | ex VH-UJD | ♦ |
| ☐ | 5Y-FAE | Embraer EMB.120RT Brasilia | 120156 | ex ZS-PPF | ♦ |

## JETLINK EXPRESS — Ken Jet (J0/JLX) — Nairobi-Jomo Kenyatta Intl (NBO)

| | | | | |
|---|---|---|---|---|
| ☐ | 5Y-JLB | Canadair CRJ-100LR | 7006 | ex XA-UHB | |
| ☐ | 5Y-JLC | Canadair CRJ-100ER | 7183 | ex F-GPTE | |
| ☐ | 5Y-JLE | Canadair CRJ-100LR | 7016 | ex XA-UGW | |
| ☐ | 5Y-JLF | Canadair CRJ-100ER | 7182 | ex F-GTPC | ♦ |
| ☐ | 5Y-JLG | Canadair CRJ-100ER | 7126 | ex F-GPYP | |
| ☐ | 5Y-JLH | Canadair CRJ-100LR | 7113 | ex C-FZGN | |
| ☐ | 5Y-JLI | Canadair CRJ-100LR | 7025 | ex C-FZQN | ♦ |
| | | | | | |
| ☐ | 5Y-JLA | Fokker F.28 Fellowship 4000 | 11093 | ex 5T-CLG | |

## KASKAZI AVIATION — Malindi (MYD)

| | | | | |
|---|---|---|---|---|
| ☐ | 5Y-BRX | Dornier 228-100 | 7004 | ex SE-KKX | |

## KENYA AIRWAYS — Kenya (KQ/KQA) — Nairobi-Jomo Kenyatta Intl (NBO)

Associate member of Skyteam

| | | | | |
|---|---|---|---|---|
| ☐ | 5Y-KQA | Boeing 737-3U8 | 28746/2863 | | |
| ☐ | 5Y-KQB | Boeing 737-3U8 | 28747/2884 | | |
| ☐ | 5Y-KQC | Boeing 737-3U8 | 29088/3034 | | |
| ☐ | 5Y-KQD | Boeing 737-3U8 | 29750/3095 | ex N5573L | |
| ☐ | 5Y-KYM | Boeing 737-306 | 28719/2930 | ex PH-BTH | ♦ |
| ☐ | 5Y-KYN | Boeing 737-306 | 28720/2957 | ex PH-BTI | |
| | | | | | |
| ☐ | 5Y-KYB | Boeing 737-8AL/W | 35070/2115 | | |
| ☐ | 5Y-KYC | Boeing 737-8AL/W | 35071/2138 | | |
| ☐ | 5Y-KYD | Boeing 737-86N/W | 35632/2690 | | |
| ☐ | 5Y-KYE | Boeing 737-86N/W | 35286/2757 | ex N1796B | |
| ☐ | 5Y-KYF | Boeing 737-86N/W | 35637/2803 | | |
| | | | | | |
| ☐ | 5Y-KQX | Boeing 767-36NER | 30854/844 | | |
| ☐ | 5Y-KQY | Boeing 767-36NER | 30841/841 | | |
| ☐ | 5Y-KQZ | Boeing 767-36NER | 30853/837 | | |
| ☐ | 5Y-KYW | Boeing 767-319ER | 30586/808 | ex G-CEOD | |
| ☐ | 5Y-KYX | Boeing 767-3P6ER | 24484/260 | ex N244AV | |

| | | | | | | |
|---|---|---|---|---|---|---|
| ☐ | 5Y-KYG | Embraer ERJ-170STD | 17000141 | ex OH-LEM | | |
| ☐ | 5Y-KYH | Embraer ERJ-170LR | 17000230 | ex PT-SFG | | |
| ☐ | 5Y-KYJ | Embraer ERJ-170LR | 17000128 | ex B-KXD | | |
| ☐ | 5Y-KYK | Embraer ERJ-170LR | 17000111 | ex B-KXC | | |
| ☐ | 5Y-KYL | Embraer ERJ-170STD | 17000146 | ex OH-LEN | | |
| | | | | | | |
| ☐ | 5Y-KYP | Embraer ERJ-190AR | 19000398 | ex PT-TYG | | |
| ☐ | 5Y-KYQ | Embraer ERJ-190AR | 19000440 | ex PT- | | |
| ☐ | 5Y-KYR | Embraer ERJ-190AR | 19000468 | ex PT-TOK | | ♦ |
| ☐ | 5Y-KYS | Embraer ERJ-190AR | 19000478 | ex PT-TPA | | |
| ☐ | 5Y- | Embraer ERJ-190AR | 19000544 | ex PT- | | o/o♦ |
| | | | | | | |
| ☐ | 5Y-KQE | Boeing 737-76N/W | 30133/877 | | | |
| ☐ | 5Y-KQF | Boeing 737-76N/W | 30136/1145 | | | |
| ☐ | 5Y-KQG | Boeing 737-7U8/W | 32371/1242 | ex N715BA | | |
| ☐ | 5Y-KQH | Boeing 737-7U8/W | 32372/1327 | | | |
| ☐ | 5Y-KQS | Boeing 777-2U8ER | 33683/522 | | | |
| ☐ | 5Y-KQT | Boeing 777-2U8ER | 33682/514 | | | |
| ☐ | 5Y-KQU | Boeing 777-2U8ER | 33681/479 | | The Pride of Africa | |
| ☐ | 5Y-KYZ | Boeing 777-2U8ER | 36124/614 | | | |

## KNIGHT AVIATION     *Nairobi-Wilson (WIL)*

| | | | | | |
|---|---|---|---|---|---|
| ☐ | 5Y-SRJ | Fokker F.27 Friendship 500F | 10372 | ex N19XD | dam 15Apr12 |

## MOMBASA AIR SAFARI     *Skyrover (RRV)*     *Mombasa (MBA)*

| | | | | | |
|---|---|---|---|---|---|
| ☐ | 5Y-BSM | LET L-410UVP-E3 | 871939 | ex 3D-SIG | ♦ |
| ☐ | 5Y-NIK | LET L-410UVP-E19 | 912619 | ex OK-WDW | |
| ☐ | 5Y-UVP | LET L-410UVP-E9 | 912627 | ex OK-WDY | |
| ☐ | 5Y-VAN | Cessna 208B Caravan I | 208B0346 | ex ZS-OHC | ♦ |
| ☐ | 5Y-WOW | Douglas DC-3/65ARTP | 14165/25610 | ex ZS-OJK | ♦ |

## PHOENIX AVIATION     *(PHN)*     *Nairobi-Wilson (WIL)*

| | | | | | |
|---|---|---|---|---|---|
| ☐ | 5Y-BYN | McDonnell-Douglas MD-83 | 53014/1740 | ex F-GMLI | ♦ |
| ☐ | 5Y-MJA | Cessna 208B Caravan I | 208B2203 | ex N2059S | ♦ |

## QUEENSWAY AIR SERVICES     *Nairobi-Wilson (WIL)*

| | | | | | |
|---|---|---|---|---|---|
| ☐ | 5Y-BKT | Beech 200 Super King Air | BB-258 | ex ZS-NTM | |

## ROSSAIR KENYA

| | | | | | |
|---|---|---|---|---|---|
| ☐ | 5Y-RDS | Douglas DC-3T | 15640/27085 | ex N146JR | ♦ |

## SAFARILINKS AVIATION     *(F2/XLK)*     *Nairobi-Wilson (WIL)*

| | | | | | |
|---|---|---|---|---|---|
| ☐ | 5Y-BNS | Cessna 208B Caravan I | 208B0394 | ex N894MA | |
| ☐ | 5Y-BOP | Cessna 208B Caravan I | 208B0642 | ex N208GJ | |
| ☐ | 5Y-SLA | Cessna 208B Caravan I | 208B0574 | ex F-OGXY | |
| ☐ | 5Y-SLD | de Havilland DHC-8-102 | 331 | ex C-FLPQ | |
| ☐ | 5Y-SLE | Cessna 208B Caravan I | 208B2091 | ex (5Y-SLC) | ♦ |
| ☐ | 5Y-SLF | de Havilland DHC-6 Twin Otter 300 | 513 | ex ZS-SCJ | ♦ |
| ☐ | 5Y-SLC | Cessna 208B Caravan I | 208B2241 | ex N60259 | ♦ |

## SAFE AIR KENYA

| | | | | | |
|---|---|---|---|---|---|
| ☐ | 5Y-BYE | Fokker 50 | 20204 | ex 9M-MGJ | ♦ |
| ☐ | 5Y-CAN | Fokker 50 | 20175 | em 9M-MGI | ♦ |
| ☐ | 5Y-TCO | Hawker Siddeley HS.748 Srs.2B/360LFD | 1772 | ex VH-IPA | ♦ |

## 748 AIR SERVICES     *Sierra Services (SVT)*     *Nairobi-Wilson (WIL)*

| | | | | | |
|---|---|---|---|---|---|
| ☐ | 5Y-BSX | Hawker Siddeley HS.780 Andover C.1 | Set 20 | ex 9Q-COE | |
| ☐ | 3C-KKC | Hawker Siddeley HS.780 Andover C.1 | Set 18 | ex NZ7625 | wfs |
| ☐ | 5Y-HAJ | Hawker Siddeley HS.748 Srs.2B/371LFD | 1776 | ex SE-LIB | |
| ☐ | 5Y-BVQ | Hawker Siddeley HS.748 Srs.2B/399LFD | 1778 | ex SE-LIC | |
| ☐ | 5Y-EVG | Aérospatiale AS350B2 | 4439 | ex ZK-IHT | |
| ☐ | 5Y-JGM | de Havilland DHC-8-102A | 287 | ex N828PH | |
| ☐ | 5Y-IHO | de Havilland DHC-8-106 | 268 | ex C-FOEN | |
| ☐ | 5Y-ZBL | Cessna 208B Caravan I | 208B0338 | | ♦ |

## SEVERIN AIR SAFARIS

| ☐ | 5Y-SXS | Cessna 208B Caravan I | 208B2108 | ex N6130K | ♦ |

## SKYTRAIL

**Skytrail** — **Mombasa (MBA)**

| ☐ | 5Y-AFD | Cessna TU206B Skywagon | U206-0724 | ex N3424L | |

## SKYWAYS KENYA

**Nairobi-Wilson (WIL)**

| ☐ | 5Y-BMB | Douglas DC-3 | 17108/34375 | ex N2025A | wfs |

## SOLENTA AVIATION (KENYA)

**Nairobi-Jomo Kenyatta Intl (NBO)**

| ☐ | 5Y-OBY | Cessna 208B Caravan I | 208B0345 | ex ZS-OBY | DHL c/s |

## SUPERIOR AVIATION SERVICES

**Skycargo (M7/SUK)** — **Nairobi-Wilson (WIL)**

| ☐ | 5Y-ATH | Piper PA-23-250 Aztec E | 27-7305138 | | |
| ☐ | 5Y-PEA | Beech 58 Baron | TH-1067 | ex N60664 | |

## TRACKMARK CARGO

**Nairobi-Wilson (WIL)**

| ☐ | 5Y-BNH | Cessna 208B Caravan I | 208B0385 | ex ZS-NYS | ♦ |
| ☐ | 5Y-TVM | Cessna 208B Caravan I | 208B0355 | ex N9697C | ♦ |

## TRANSWORLD SAFARIS

**Nairobi-Wilson (WIL)**

| ☐ | 5Y-ROH | Piper PA-31-350 Chieftain | 31-8152038 | ex N217JP | |

## TRIDENT AVIATION / ENTERPRISES

**Nairobi-Wilson (WIL)**

| ☐ | 5Y-BWG | de Havilland DHC-8Q-311 | 406 | ex C-FTYU | >CMC Avn |
| ☐ | 5Y-DAC | de Havilland DHC-8-102 | 251 | ex C-GZAN | >CMC Avn |
| ☐ | 5Y-ENA | de Havilland DHC-8-102 | 297 | ex N836EX | >CMC Avn |
| ☐ | 5Y-GRS | de Havilland DHC-8-102 | 355 | ex SX-BIS | >CMC Avn |
| ☐ | 5Y-PTA | de Havilland DHC-8-315 | 397 | ex N788BC | |
| ☐ | 5Y-MEG | de Havilland DHC-5D Buffalo | 62 | ex 5V-MAG | Op for UN-WFP |
| ☐ | 5Y-TAJ | de Havilland DHC-5E Buffalo | 108 | ex C-GDOB | Op for UN-WFP |
| ☐ | 5Y-TEL | de Havilland DHC-5D Buffalo | 68 | ex AF-318 | Op for UN-WFP |
| ☐ | 5Y-XMZ | de Havilland DHC-5D Buffalo | 81 | ex PK-XNZ | ♦ |

## TROPIC AIR

**Nairobi-Wilson (WIL)**

| ☐ | 5Y-BRT | Cessna 208B Caravan I | 208B0682 | ex ZS-ELE | |
| ☐ | 5Y-BSY | Cessna 208B Caravan I | 208B0907 | ex N32211 | |
| ☐ | 5Y-BWV | Aérospatiale AS350B3 Ecureuil | 4482 | ex ZS-RBS | |
| ☐ | 5Y-BYG | Aérospatiale AS350B3 Ecureuil | 4296 | ex ZS-RDU | ♦ |

## YELLOW WINGS AIR SERVICES

| ☐ | 5Y-ELO | Cessna 208B Caravan i | 208B2201 | ex N1032L | ♦ |

## ZB AIR (Z BOSCOVIC AIR CHARTER)

**Bosky (ZBA)** — **Nairobi-Wilson (WIL)**

| ☐ | 5Y-OPM | Cessna 208B Caravan I | 208B0330 | ex N1034S | |
| ☐ | 5Y-ZBD | Cessna 208B Caravan I | 208B1109 | ex N1275Z | |
| ☐ | 5Y-ZBE | Cessna 208B Caravan I | 208B2072 | ex N2212X | ♦ |
| ☐ | 5Y-ZBI | Cessna 208B Caravan I | 208B0324 | ex N1029P | ♦ |
| ☐ | 5Y-ZBL | Cessna 208B Caravan I | 208B0338 | ex N1042Y | |
| ☐ | 5Y-ZBR | Cessna 208B Caravan I | 208B0446 | ex N12922 | |
| ☐ | 5Y-ZBT | Cessna 208B Caravan I | 208B1243 | ex N1226X | |
| ☐ | 5Y-ZBW | Cessna 208B Caravan I | 208B0409 | ex N1115W | |
| ☐ | 5Y-ZBX | Cessna 208B Caravan I | 208B1170 | ex N1308N | |
| ☐ | 5Y- | Cessna 208B Caravan I | 208B2318 | ex N60207 | ♦ |
| ☐ | 5Y-AIS | Beech 95-D55 Baron | TE-680 | | |
| ☐ | 5Y-AUN | Cessna U206F Stationair | U20602531 | ex N1244V | |
| ☐ | 5Y-AYZ | Cessna 310R | 310R0121 | ex N4940J | |
| ☐ | 5Y-AZS | Cessna 310R | 310R0524 | ex N87350 | |
| ☐ | 5Y-SAB | Cessna 404 Titan II | 404-0675 | ex N6761X | |
| ☐ | 5Y-ZBK | Beech B200 Super King Air | BB-1714 | ex N3214D | |
| ☐ | 5Y-ZBM | Cessna U206H Stationair 6 | U20608114 | ex N259ME | |
| ☐ | 5Y-ZBO | Cessna U206H Stationair | U20608131 | ex N373ME | |

## 6O-    SOMALIA (Democratic Republic of Somalia)

### JUBBA AIRWAYS | Jubba (3J/JBW) | Dubai/Sharjah (DXB/SHJ)

| | | | | | |
|---|---|---|---|---|---|
| ☐ | 5Y-BXG | Boeing 737-247 (Nordam 3) | 23519/1299 | ex YA-GAE | |
| ☐ | 5Y-BZL | Boeing 737-4B7 | 24550/1793 | ex EY-537 | <ETJ♦ |
| ☐ | 5Y-BXZ | Boeing 737-247 (Nordam 3) | 23516/1257 | ex EX-25004 | ♦ |

### STAR AFRICAN AIR | Starsom (STU) | Dubai/Sharjah (DXB/SHJ)

Ops flights with Antonov An-24 and Ilyushin Il-18 aircraft leased when required

## 6V-    SENEGAL (Republic of Senegal)

### AERO SERVICE ASF | Servo (RSG) | Dakar (DKR)

| | | | | | |
|---|---|---|---|---|---|
| ☐ | 6V-AHF | Cessna 208B Caravan I | 208B0634 | ex N12386 | |
| ☐ | 6V-AHI | Cessna 402C | 402C0120 | ex F-OHCM | |

### AIR SENEGAL INTERNATIONAL | Air Senegal (V7/SNG) | Dakar (DKR)

Ceased ops 24Apr09

### ASECNA | (XKX) | Dakar (DKR)

| | | | | | |
|---|---|---|---|---|---|
| ☐ | 6V-AFW | ATR 42-300 | 0117 | ex F-WWEN | Calibrator/Pax |

### SENEGAL AIRLINES | (SGG) | Dakar (DKR)

| | | | | | | |
|---|---|---|---|---|---|---|
| ☐ | ZS-XCB | ATR 72-212 | 0460 | ex 5H-PAR | | >SET♦ |
| ☐ | 6V-AIH | Airbus A320-214 | 0799 | ex M-ABCV | | |
| ☐ | 6V-AII | Airbus A320-214 | 0879 | ex B-6258 | | |
| ☐ | 6V-AIJ | Airbus A320-214 | 1390 | ex M-ABD | Podor | ♦ |

## 6Y-    JAMAICA

### AIR JAMAICA | Jamaica (JM/AJM) | Kingston-Norman Manley Intl (KIN)

| | | | | | |
|---|---|---|---|---|---|
| ☐ | 9Y-JMA | Boeing 737-8Q8/W | 30645/1129 | ex 7O-ADL | ♦ |
| ☐ | 9Y-JMB | Boeing 737-8Q8/W | 30661/1186 | ex 7O-ADN | ♦ |
| ☐ | 9Y-JMC | Boeing 737-8Q8/W | 28252/1195 | ex N341LF | ♦ |
| ☐ | 9Y-JMD | Boeing 737-8Q8/W | 30720/2235 | ex F-WTAC | ♦ |
| ☐ | 9Y-JME | Boeing 737-86J/W | 32919/1279 | ex D-ABBH | ♦ |
| ☐ | 9Y-JMF | Boeing 737-8Q8/W | 30730/2399 | ex n351lf | ♦ |

### AIRWAYS INTERNATIONAL / JAMAICA AIR SHUTTLE (J6/ARW)

| | | | | | |
|---|---|---|---|---|---|
| ☐ | 6Y-JSA | Beech 99 | U-58 | ex V2-ANU | ♦ |
| ☐ | 6Y-JSC | Beech 99 | U-92 | ex SP- | ♦ |
| ☐ | 6Y-JSI | Beech 99 | U-98 | ex V2-DOM | ♦ |

### EXEC DIRECT AVIATION

| | | | | |
|---|---|---|---|---|
| ☐ | 6Y-JXD | SAAB SF.340A | 340A-089 | ex SE-LJK |

### INTERNATIONAL AIRLINK | Kingston-Tinson Peninsula (KTP)

| | | | | |
|---|---|---|---|---|
| ☐ | 6Y-JRD | Cessna U206G Stationair 6 | U20604522 | ex N9019M |

### SKYLAN AIRWAYS

| | | | | |
|---|---|---|---|---|
| ☐ | 6Y-JIC | British Aerospace Jetstream 32EP | 920 | ex N920AE |

### TIMAIR | Montego Bay (MBJ)

| | | | | |
|---|---|---|---|---|
| ☐ | 6Y-JLU | Britten-Norman BN-2B-26 Islander | 2170 | ex 6Y-JLG |
| ☐ | 6Y-JNA | Cessna U206G Stationair | U20603837 | ex N4515C |
| ☐ | 6Y-JNB | Cessna U206G Stationair | U20603615 | ex N7332N |
| ☐ | 6Y-JNJ | Cessna U206G Stationair 6 | U20606359 | ex N2447N |
| ☐ | 6Y-JNL | Cessna U206G Stationair 6 | U20605620 | ex N712RS |

## 7O-    YEMEN (Republic of Yemen)

### FELIX AIRWAYS | (FO/FXX) | Sana'a (SAH)

| | | | | | |
|---|---|---|---|---|---|
| ☐ | 7O-FAA | Canadair CRJ-702NG | 10267 | ex C- | |
| ☐ | 7O-FAB | Canadair CRJ-702NG | 10268 | ex C- | |
| ☐ | 7O- | Canadair CRJ-702NG | | ex C- | o/o |
| ☐ | 7O- | Canadair CRJ-702NG | | ex C- | o/o |
| ☐ | 7O- | Canadair CRJ-702NG | | ex C- | o/o |
| ☐ | 7O- | Canadair CRJ-702NG | | ex C- | o/o |
| ☐ | 7O- | Canadair CRJ-702NG | | ex C- | o/o |
| ☐ | 7O- | Canadair CRJ-702NG | | ex C- | o/o |
| | | | | | |
| ☐ | 7O-FAI | Canadair CRJ-200LR | 7307 | ex N636BR | |
| ☐ | 7O-FAJ | Canadair CRJ-200LR | 7308 | ex N637BR | |

### YEMENIA / YEMEN AIRWAYS | Yemeni (IY/IYE) | Sana'a (SAH)

| | | | | | | |
|---|---|---|---|---|---|---|
| ☐ | 7O-ADA | Boeing 727-2N8 | 21842/1512 | ex 4W-ACJ | | op for Govt |
| ☐ | 7O-ADD | Lockheed L-382C-86D Hercules | 4827 | ex 1160 | | jt ops with Air Force |
| ☐ | 7O-ADE | Lockheed L-382C-86D Hercules | 4825 | ex 1150 | | jt ops with Air Force |
| ☐ | 7O-ADF | Ilyushin Il-76TD | 1033418578 | ex RA-76380 | | jt ops with Air Force |
| ☐ | 7O-ADG | Ilyushin Il-76TD | 1023412402 | ex RA-76405 | | jt ops with Air Force |
| ☐ | 7O-ADH | de Havilland DHC-6 Twin Otter 310 | 764 | ex (VQ-TAN) | | |
| ☐ | 7O-ADI | de Havilland DHC-6 Twin Otter 300 | 664 | ex HB-LRT | | <FAT |
| ☐ | 7O-ADP | Airbus A330-243 | 625 | ex F-WWYD | Sana'a | |
| ☐ | 7O-ADR | Airbus A310-324ET | 568 | ex F-OGYO | Socotra | |
| ☐ | 7O-ADS | de Havilland DHC-8-102 | 280 | ex C-FMCZ | | |
| ☐ | 7O-ADT | Airbus A330-243 | 632 | ex F-WWYH | Aden | |
| ☐ | 7O-ADU | de Havilland DHC-8-102A | 327 | ex C-FHLO | | |
| ☐ | 7O-ADV | Airbus A310-325 | 702 | ex F-OHPR | Seiyun | |
| ☐ | 7O-ADW | Airbus A310-325 | 704 | ex F-OHPS | Marib | |
| ☐ | 7O-ADY | de Havilland DHC-8-103 | 333 | ex C-FSID | | |
| ☐ | 7O-AFA | Airbus A320-233 | 4653 | ex F-WWIA | Mukalla | ◆ |
| ☐ | 7O-AFB | Airbus A320-233 | 4691 | ex F-WWBO | Mareb | ◆ |
| ☐ | 7O-YMN | Boeing 747SP-27 | 21786/413 | ex A7-AHM | | op for Govt |

## 7Q-    MALAWI (Republic of Malawi)

### AIR MALAWI | Malawi (QM/AML) | Blantyre (BLZ)

| | | | | | | |
|---|---|---|---|---|---|---|
| ☐ | 7Q-YKP | Boeing 737-33A | 25056/2045 | | Kwacha | [JNB] |
| ☐ | 7Q-YKQ | ATR 42-320 | 0236 | ex F-WWES | Shire | |
| ☐ | 7Q-YKW | Boeing 737-522 | 25384/2149 | ex N917UA | Sapitwa | [JNB] |

## 7T-    ALGERIA (Democratic & Popular Republic of Algeria)

### AIR ALGERIE | Air Algerie (AH/DAH) | Algiers (ALG)

| | | | | | | |
|---|---|---|---|---|---|---|
| ☐ | 7T-VJV | Airbus A330-202 | 644 | ex F-WWKD | Tinhinan | |
| ☐ | 7T-VJW | Airbus A330-202 | 647 | ex F-WWKF | Lalla Setti | |
| ☐ | 7T-VJX | Airbus A330-202 | 650 | ex F-WWKK | Mers el Kebir | |
| ☐ | 7T-VJY | Airbus A330-202 | 653 | ex F-WWYK | Monts des Beni Chougrane | |
| ☐ | 7T-VJZ | Airbus A330-202 | 667 | ex F-WWKR | Teddis | |
| | | | | | | |
| ☐ | 7T-VUI | ATR 72-212A | 0644 | ex F-OHGM | | |
| ☐ | 7T-VUJ | ATR 72-212A | 0648 | ex F-OHGN | | |
| ☐ | 7T-VUK | ATR 72-212A | 0652 | ex F-OHGO | | |
| ☐ | 7T-VUL | ATR 72-212A | 0672 | ex F-OHGP | | |
| ☐ | 7T-VUM | ATR 72-212A | 0677 | ex F-OHGQ | | |
| ☐ | 7T-VUN | ATR 72-212A | 0684 | ex F-OHGR | | |
| ☐ | 7T-VUO | ATR 72-212A | 0901 | ex F-WWEP | | |
| ☐ | 7T-VUP | ATR 72-212A | 0903 | ex F-WWES | | |
| ☐ | 7T-VUQ | ATR 72-212A | 0909 | ex F-WWEB | | |
| ☐ | 7T-VUS | ATR 72-212A | 0913 | ex F-WWEI | | |
| ☐ | 7T-VVQ | ATR 72-212A | 0676 | ex F-WWEA | | |
| ☐ | 7T-VVR | ATR 72-212A | 0683 | ex F-WWEF | | |
| | | | | | | |
| ☐ | TC-SKD | Boeing 737-4Q8 | 25372/2280 | ex TC-JDI | | <SHY |
| ☐ | 7T-VJQ | Boeing 737-6D6 | 30209/1115 | | Kasbah d'Alger | |
| ☐ | 7T-VJR | Boeing 737-6D6 | 30545/1131 | | | |
| ☐ | 7T-VJS | Boeing 737-6D6 | 30210/1150 | ex N60559 | | |
| ☐ | 7T-VJT | Boeing 737-6D6 | 30546/1152 | | | |
| ☐ | 7T-VJU | Boeing 737-6D6 | 30211/1164 | | | |
| | | | | | | |
| ☐ | 7T-VJJ | Boeing 737-8D6 | 30202/610 | | Jugurtha | |
| ☐ | 7T-VJK | Boeing 737-8D6 | 30203/640 | ex N1781B | Mansourah | |

| | | | | | |
|---|---|---|---|---|---|
| ☐ | 7T-VJL | Boeing 737-8D6 | 30204/652 | | Allizi | |
| ☐ | 7T-VJM | Boeing 737-8D6 | 30205/691 | | | |
| ☐ | 7T-VJN | Boeing 737-8D6 | 30206/751 | | Oued Tafna | |
| ☐ | 7T-VJO | Boeing 737-8D6 | 30207/868 | ex N1787B | Tinerkouk | |
| ☐ | 7T-VJP | Boeing 737-8D6 | 30208/896 | ex N1787B | Mont Tahat | |
| ☐ | 7T-VKA | Boeing 737-8D6/W | 34164/1748 | | Monts Chaboro | |
| ☐ | 7T-VKB | Boeing 737-8D6/W | 34165/1768 | ex N1784B | Mont de l'Assekhrem | |
| ☐ | 7T-VKC | Boeing 737-8D6/W | 34166/1773 | | | |
| ☐ | 7T-VKD | Boeing 737-8D6/W | 40858/3406 | ex N1786B | | |
| ☐ | 7T-VKE | Boeing 737-8D6/W | 40859/3446 | | | |
| ☐ | 7T-VKF | Boeing 737-8D6/W | 40860/3471 | ex N1787B | | |
| ☐ | 7T-VKG | Boeing 737-8D6/W | 40861//3596 | | | ♦ |
| ☐ | 7T-VKH | Boeing 737-8D6/W | 40862/3625 | | | ♦ |
| ☐ | 7T-VKI | Boeing 737-8D6/W | 40863/3658 | | | ♦ |
| ☐ | 7T-VKJ | Boeing 737-8D6/W | 40864/3691 | | | ♦ |
| | | | | | | |
| ☐ | 7T-VCV | Beech A100 King Air | B-93 | ex N9369Q | | |
| ☐ | 7T-VHL | Lockheed L-382-51D Hercules | 4886 | ex N4160M | | |
| ☐ | 7T-VIG | Cessna 208B Caravan I | 208B0391 | ex N1122N | | |
| ☐ | 7T-VII | Cessna 208B Caravan I | 208B0393 | ex N1123G | >DTH | |
| ☐ | 7T-VIL | Cessna 208B Caravan I | 208B0601 | ex N1247H | | |
| ☐ | 7T-VIM | Cessna 208B Caravan I | 208B0602 | ex N1247K | | |
| ☐ | 7T-VJG | Boeing 767-3D6ER | 24766/310 | | | |
| ☐ | 7T-VJH | Boeing 767-3D6ER | 24767/323 | | | |
| ☐ | 7T-VJI | Boeing 767-3D6ER | 24768/332 | ex N6009F | | |
| | | | | | | |
| ☐ | 7T-VRF | Beech A100 King Air | B-147 | ex N1828W | | |

## AIR EXPRESS ALGERIA      *Algiers (ALG)*

| | | | | | |
|---|---|---|---|---|---|
| ☐ | ZS-OOF | LET L-410UVP-E20 | 871920 | ex 5H-PAJ | |
| ☐ | ZS-ORV | Beech 1900D | UE-42 | ex (ZS-OPK) | Op for UN WFP>NAC♦ |
| ☐ | ZS-OUE | LET L-420 | 012735A | ex OK-GDM | <Air-Tec Africa |
| ☐ | ZS-OYD | Beech 1900D | UE-191 | ex VH-IAR | NAC♦ |
| ☐ | 7T-VAE | LET L-410UVP-E20 | 872011 | ex OK-SDT | |
| ☐ | 7T-VAF | LET L-410UVP-E20 | 082629 | ex CCCP-67698 | |

## STAR AVIATION      *Algiers (ALG)*

| | | | | | |
|---|---|---|---|---|---|
| ☐ | 7T-VNA | Pilatus PC-6/B2-H4 Turbo Porter | 817 | ex HB-FFV | |
| ☐ | 7T-VNB | Beech 1900D | UE-305 | ex 7T-WRF | |
| ☐ | 7T-VND | de Havilland DHC-6 Twin Otter 300 | 502 | ex HB-LRS | |
| ☐ | 7T-VNE | de Havilland DHC-6 Twin Otter 300 | 717 | ex HB-LTD | |
| ☐ | 7T-VNG | Beech 1900D | UE-296 | ex HB-AEK | ♦ |

## TASSILI AIRLINES     *Tassili Air (SF/DTH)*     *Hassi Messaoud (HME)*

| | | | | | | |
|---|---|---|---|---|---|---|
| ☐ | 7T-VCL | de Havilland DHC-8Q-402 | 4167 | ex C-FMIT | | |
| ☐ | 7T-VCM | de Havilland DHC-8Q-402 | 4169 | ex C-FMIV | | |
| ☐ | 7T-VCN | de Havilland DHC-8Q-402 | 4173 | ex C-FMKF | | |
| ☐ | 7T-VCO | de Havilland DHC-8Q-402 | 4178 | ex C-FMTN | | |
| ☐ | 7T-VCP | de Havilland DHC-8-202 | 661 | ex C-FRIZ | | |
| ☐ | 7T-VCQ | de Havilland DHC-8-202 | 664 | ex C-FTGX | | |
| ☐ | 7T-VCR | de Havilland DHC-8-202 | 665 | ex C-FTUE | | |
| ☐ | 7T-VCS | de Havilland DHC-8-202 | 666 | ex C-FUCF | | |
| | | | | | | |
| ☐ | 7T-VCG | Pilatus PC-6/B2-H4 Turbo Porter | 917 | ex HB-FLJ | | |
| ☐ | 7T-VCH | Pilatus PC-6/B2-H4 Turbo Porter | 929 | ex HB-FLX | | |
| ☐ | 7T-VCI | Pilatus PC-6/B2-H4 Turbo Porter | 933 | ex HB-FLY | | |
| ☐ | 7T-VCJ | Pilatus PC-6/B2-H4 Turbo Porter | 934 | ex HB-FLZ | | |
| ☐ | 7T-VCK | Pilatus PC-6/B2-H4 Turbo Porter | 930 | ex HB-FMA | | |
| | | | | | | |
| ☐ | 7T-VCA | Boeing 737-8ZQ/W | 40884/3575 | | | ♦ |
| ☐ | 7T-VCB | Boeing 737-8ZQ/W | 40885/3606 | | La Tanezrouft | ♦ |
| ☐ | 7T-VCC | Boeing 737-8ZQ/W | 40886/3747 | | Ahaggar | ♦ |
| ☐ | 7T-VCD | Boeing 737-8ZQ/W | 40887/3786 | | | ♦ |
| ☐ | 7T-VIO | Beech 1900D | UE-366 | ex N30511 | | ♦ |
| ☐ | 7T-VIP | Beech 1900D | UE-369 | ex N30538 | | ♦ |
| ☐ | 7T-VIQ | Beech 1900D | UE-381 | ex N31683 | | VIP |

## 8P-    BARBADOS

## REDJET      *(RDJ)*

| | | | | | | |
|---|---|---|---|---|---|---|
| ☐ | 8P-ARB | McDonnell-Douglas MD-82 | 49469/1410 | ex N443AA | | |
| ☐ | 8P-IGB | McDonnell-Douglas MD-82 | 49471/1418 | ex N445AA | Jacquelicious | [BGI] |
| ☐ | 8P-KEV | McDonnell-Douglas MD-83 | 49344/1370 | ex N562AA | | ♦ |

| *TRANS ISLAND AIR 2000* | *Trans Island (TRD)* | *Bridgetown-Grantley Adams (BGI)* |

Services performed by Twin Otters operated by SVG Air (J8-)

## 8Q- MALDIVES (Republic of Maldives)

### ISLAND AVIATION SERVICES (Q2/DQA) Male (MLE)

| | | | | | |
|---|---|---|---|---|---|
| ☐ | 8Q-AMD | de Havilland DHC-8-202 | 429 | ex C-GDKL | |
| ☐ | 8Q-IAO | de Havilland DHC-8Q-314 | 544 | ex D-BHOQ | |
| ☐ | 8Q-IAP | de Havilland DHC-8Q-315 | 491 | ex LN-WFE | |
| ☐ | 8Q-IAQ | de Havilland DHC-8-202 | 542 | ex C-FIKT | |
| ☐ | 8Q-IAR | Dornier 228-212 | 8244 | ex D-CBDX | |

### MALDIVIAN AIR TAXI Male (MLE)

| | | | | | |
|---|---|---|---|---|---|
| ☐ | 8Q-MAD | de Havilland DHC-6 Twin Otter 300 | 273 | ex C-FAKB | FP |
| ☐ | 8Q-MAF | de Havilland DHC-6 Twin Otter 300 | 449 | ex C-FWKQ | FP |
| ☐ | 8Q-MAH | de Havilland DHC-6 Twin Otter 300 | 374 | ex C-FMYV | FP |
| ☐ | 8Q-MAI | de Havilland DHC-6 Twin Otter 300 | 279 | ex C-GKBM | FP |
| ☐ | 8Q-MAJ | de Havilland DHC-6 Twin Otter 300 | 837 | ex C-GJDP | FP |
| ☐ | 8Q-MAN | de Havilland DHC-6 Twin Otter 300 | 435 | ex C-FWKZ | FP |
| ☐ | 8Q-MAO | de Havilland DHC-6 Twin Otter 300 | 259 | ex C-FKBI | FP |
| ☐ | 8Q-MAP | de Havilland DHC-6 Twin Otter 300 | 571 | ex C-FKBX | FP |
| ☐ | 8Q-MAT | de Havilland DHC-6 Twin Otter 200 | 146 | ex 8Q-NTA | FP |
| ☐ | 8Q-MAW | de Havilland DHC-6 Twin Otter 300 | 722 | ex C-FWKO | FP |
| ☐ | 8Q-MAX | de Havilland DHC-6 Twin Otter 300 | 755 | ex C-FWKX | FP |
| ☐ | 8Q-MAZ | de Havilland DHC-6 Twin Otter 300 | 774 | ex C-FWKU | FP |
| ☐ | 8Q-MBA | de Havilland DHC-6 Twin Otter 300 | 691 | ex D-IHAI | FP |
| ☐ | 8Q-MBB | de Havilland DHC-6 Twin Otter 300 | 659 | ex HB-LUG | FP |
| ☐ | 8Q-MBC | de Havilland DHC-6 Twin Otter 300 | 256 | ex H4-SIB | ♦ |
| ☐ | 8Q-MBD | de Havilland DHC-6 Twin Otter 300 | 283 | ex D-IBVP | ♦ |
| ☐ | 8Q-MBE | de Havilland DHC-6 Twin Otter 300 | 561 | ex OY-ATY | FP |
| ☐ | 8Q-MBF | de Havilland DHC-6 Twin Otter 300 | 375 | ex C-GIZQ | FP♦ |
| ☐ | 8Q-MBG | de Havilland DHC-6 Twin Otter 300 | 288 | ex N102SK | FP♦ |
| ☐ | 8Q-OEQ | de Havilland DHC-6 Twin Otter 100 | 044 | ex C-FOEQ | FP |
| | | | | | |
| ☐ | 8Q-IAS | de Havilland DHC-8Q-315 | 546 | ex OE-LIE | ♦ |

### MEGA GLOBAL AIR SERVICES (9M/MEG) Male (MLE)

| | | | | | |
|---|---|---|---|---|---|
| ☐ | 8Q-MEG | Boeing 767-3P6ER | 24496/270 | ex N183AQ | |
| ☐ | 8Q-MEH | Boeing 767-3Y0ER | 26206/487 | ex C-GHPF | ♦ |

### TRANS MALDIVIAN AIRWAYS Hum (TMW) Male (MLE)

| | | | | | |
|---|---|---|---|---|---|
| ☐ | 8Q-TAB | de Havilland DHC-6 Twin Otter 300 | 582 | ex ZS-SAI | FP |
| ☐ | 8Q-TAC | de Havilland DHC-6 Twin Otter 300 | 580 | ex ZS-PZO | FP |
| ☐ | 8Q-TMB | de Havilland DHC-6 Twin Otter 300 | 587 | ex C-GASV | FP |
| ☐ | 8Q-TME | de Havilland DHC-6 Twin Otter 300 | 798 | ex 8Q-HIH | FP |
| ☐ | 8Q-TMF | de Havilland DHC-6 Twin Otter 300 | 657 | ex 8Q-HII | FP |
| ☐ | 8Q-TMG | de Havilland DHC-6 Twin Otter 310 | 597 | ex 8Q-HIJ | FP |
| ☐ | 8Q-TMH | de Havilland DHC-6 Twin Otter 300 | 668 | ex HK-4194X | FP |
| ☐ | 8Q-TMI | de Havilland DHC-6 Twin Otter 300 | 754 | ex N107JM | FP |
| ☐ | 8Q-TMJ | de Havilland DHC-6 Twin Otter 300 | 781 | ex N781JM | FP |
| ☐ | 8Q-TMK | de Havilland DHC-6 Twin Otter 300 | 751 | ex N710PV | FP |
| ☐ | 8Q-TML | de Havilland DHC-6 Twin Otter 300 | 640 | ex N709PV | FP |
| ☐ | 8Q-TMN | de Havilland DHC-6 Twin Otter 300 | 700 | ex TJ-OHN | FP |
| ☐ | 8Q-TMO | de Havilland DHC-6 Twin Otter 300 | 234 | ex C-FBZN | FP |
| ☐ | 8Q-TMP | de Havilland DHC-6 Twin Otter 300 | 652 | ex VH-KZN | FP |
| ☐ | 8Q-TMQ | de Havilland DHC-6 Twin Otter 300 | 753 | ex N162AY | FP |
| ☐ | 8Q-TMR | de Havilland DHC-6 Twin Otter 300 | 270 | ex N270CM | FP |
| ☐ | 8Q-TMS | de Havilland DHC-6 Twin Otter 300 | 663 | ex PK-TWH | FP |
| ☐ | 8Q-TMT | de Havilland DHC-6 Twin Otter 300 | 454 | ex C-FNBI | FP |
| ☐ | 8Q-TMU | de Havilland DHC-6 Twin Otter 300 | 467 | ex C-FOIM | FP |
| ☐ | 8Q-TMV | de Havilland DHC-6 Twin Otter 300 | 625 | ex C-FNBL | FP |
| ☐ | 8Q-TMW | de Havilland DHC-6 Twin Otter 300 | 768 | ex C-GDQM | FP |
| | | | | | |
| ☐ | 8Q-TMX | de Havilland DHC-6 Twin Otter 400 | 848 | ex C-GUVA | FP♦ |
| ☐ | 8Q-TMY | de Havilland DHC-6 Twin Otter 400 | 849 | ex C-GLCU | FP♦ |
| ☐ | 8Q-TMZ | de Havilland DHC-6 Twin Otter 400 | 850 | ex C-GLTI | FP♦ |

### VILLA AIR (VQI) Male (MLE)

| | | | | | |
|---|---|---|---|---|---|
| ☐ | 8Q-VAQ | ATR 42-500 | 0606 | ex I-ADLQ | ♦ |
| ☐ | 8Q-VAR | ATR 42-500 | 0518 | ex I-ADLL | ♦ |

## 8R- GUYANA (Co-operative Republic of Guyana)

### AIR GUYANA
**Georgetown-Ogle (OGL)**

| | | | | | |
|---|---|---|---|---|---|
| ☐ | N524AT | Boeing 757-23NEM | 30233/895 | ex M-ABDF | ♦ |
| ☐ | 8R-WAL | Cessna 208B Caravan I | 208B0990 | ex N208KT | |

### AIR SERVICES
**Georgetown-Ogle (OGL)**

| | | | | | |
|---|---|---|---|---|---|
| ☐ | 8R-GAA | Piper PA-34-200T Seneca II | 34-7870451 | ex 8R-GGJ | |
| ☐ | 8R-GAS | Cessna 208B Caravan I | 208B0691 | ex YN-CFK | |
| ☐ | 8R-GER | Britten-Norman BN-2A-27 Islander | 478 | ex G-BDJX | |
| ☐ | 8R-GFI | Britten-Norman BN-2A-9 Islander | 677 | ex G-AZGU | |
| ☐ | 8R-GFM | Cessna U206F Stationair | U20601731 | ex N9531G | |
| ☐ | 8R-GHB | Cessna U206G Stationair 6 | U20604889 | ex 8R-GPF | |
| ☐ | 8R-GHE | Britten-Norman BN-2A-6 Islander | 269 | ex 8R-GHB | |
| ☐ | 8R-GYA | Cessna U206G Stationair | U20603654 | ex 8R-GGF | R/STOL conv |
| ☐ | 8R-GZR | Cessna 208B Caravan I | 208B0407 | ex V3-HSS | ♦ |

### RORAIMA AIRWAYS
**Roraima (ROR)**
**Georgetown-Ogle (OGL)**

| | | | | | |
|---|---|---|---|---|---|
| ☐ | 8R-GRA | Britten-Norman BN-2A-26 Islander | 3006 | ex N42540 | |
| ☐ | 8R-GRB | Britten-Norman BN-2B-26 Islander | 431 | ex N431V | |
| ☐ | 8R-GRC | Britten-Norman BN-2B-27 Islander | 2114 | ex SX-DKA | |

### TRANS GUYANA AIRWAYS
**Trans Guyana (TGY)**
**Georgetown-Ogle (OGL)**

| | | | | | |
|---|---|---|---|---|---|
| ☐ | 8R-GGY | Britten-Norman BN-2A-26 Islander | 470 | ex N81567 | |
| ☐ | 8R-GHM | Britten-Norman BN-2A-27 Islander | 216 | ex PT-IAS | |
| ☐ | 8R-GHR | Cessna 208B Caravan I | 208B0519 | ex PT-MEZ | |
| ☐ | 8R-GHS | Cessna 208B Caravan I | 208B0830 | ex N408MN | ♦ |
| ☐ | 8R-GHT | Cessna 208B Caravan I | 208B0572 | ex TI-BBG | |
| ☐ | 8R-GTG | Cessna 208B Caravan I | 208B0397 | ex N397TA | |
| ☐ | 8R- | Cessna 208B Caravan I | 208B1070 | ex N90HL | ♦ |

## 9A- CROATIA (Republic of Croatia)

### CROATIA AIRLINES
**Croatia (OU/CTN)**
**Zagreb (ZAG)**

Member of Star Alliance

| | | | | | |
|---|---|---|---|---|---|
| ☐ | 9A-CQA | de Havilland DHC-8-402Q | 4205 | ex C-FPEL | Slavonija |
| ☐ | 9A-CQB | de Havilland DHC-8-402Q | 4211 | ex C-FPQD | |
| ☐ | 9A-CQC | de Havilland DHC-8-402Q | 4258 | ex C-FWIJ | |
| ☐ | 9A-CQD | de Havilland DHC-8-402Q | 4260 | ex C-FWZU | Dalmacija |
| ☐ | 9A-CQE | de Havilland DHC-8-402Q | 4300 | ex C-GBKD | Zagorje |
| ☐ | 9A-CQF | de Havilland DHC-8-402Q | 4301 | ex C-GCKE | |
| ☐ | 9A-CTF | Airbus A320-212 | 0258 | ex F-OKAI | Rijeka |
| ☐ | 9A-CTG | Airbus A319-112 | 0767 | ex D-AVYA | Zadar |
| ☐ | 9A-CTH | Airbus A319-112 | 0833 | ex D-AVYJ | Zagreb |
| ☐ | 9A-CTI | Airbus A319-112 | 1029 | ex D-AVYC | Vukova |
| ☐ | 9A-CTJ | Airbus A320-214 | 1009 | ex F-WWDN | Dubrovnik |
| ☐ | 9A-CTK | Airbus A320-214 | 1237 | ex F-WWIK | Split |
| ☐ | 9A-CTL | Airbus A319-112 | 1252 | ex D-AVYS | Pula |

### DUBROVNIK AIRLINE
**(DBK)**
**Dubrovnik (DBV)**

Ceased ops Oct11

### NORTH ADRIA

| | | | | |
|---|---|---|---|---|
| ☐ | 9A-BNA | LET L-410UVP | 851518 | ♦ |

### TRADE AIR
**Tradeair (TDR)**
**Zagreb (ZAG)**

| | | | | | |
|---|---|---|---|---|---|
| ☐ | 9A-BTD | Fokker 100 | 11407 | ex N1424M | op in Sun Adria colours |
| ☐ | 9A-BTE | Fokker 100 | 11416 | ex N1431B | op in Sun Adria colours |
| ☐ | 9A-BTF | Fokker 100 | 11336 | ex N336MX | ♦ |

## 9G- GHANA (Republic of Ghana)

### AIR GHANA

| | | | | | |
|---|---|---|---|---|---|
| ☐ | ZS-OKM | Beech 1900D | UE-74 | ex N74YV | ♦ |

### AIRLIFT INTERNATIONAL — (ALE) — Accra (ACC)

| | | | | | |
|---|---|---|---|---|---|
| ☐ | 9G-FAB | Douglas DC-8-63F (BAC 3) | 46121/500 | ex N786AL | [RKT] |
| ☐ | 9G-RAC | Douglas DC-8-63PF (BAC 3) | 46093/496 | ex N816AX | ♦ |
| ☐ | 9G-SIM | Douglas DC-8-63CF (BAC 3) | 46061/480 | ex N826AX | [RKT] |

### ANTRAK AIR GHANA — Antrak (O4/ABV) — Accra (ACC)

| | | | | | |
|---|---|---|---|---|---|
| ☐ | LY-MCA | ATR 72-212A | 0212 | ex SE-MCA | <DNU |
| ☐ | 9G-AAB | ATR 42-300 | 0041 | ex F-WQCT | |
| ☐ | 9G-ANT | ATR 42-300 | 0086 | ex ZS-ORE | |
| ☐ | 9G-HNK | Beech 1900D | UE-229 | ex N10675 | ♦ |

### CITYLINK — CityLink (CTQ) — Accra (ACC)

| | | | | | |
|---|---|---|---|---|---|
| ☐ | 9G-CTL | SAAB SF.340A | 340A-044 | ex ZS-PMJ | <NRX |
| ☐ | 9G-CTQ | SAAB SF.340A | 340A-137 | ex YR-DAB | ♦ |
| ☐ | 9G-CTS | SAAB SF.340A | 340A-017 | ex SE-ISR | ♦ |
| ☐ | 9G-LET | LET L-410UVP-E20 | 871922 | ex ZS-OOH | |

### FLY540 GHANA

| | | | | | |
|---|---|---|---|---|---|
| ☐ | 9G-FLY | ATR 72-500 | 0949 | ex F-WWEB | ♦ |

### JOHNSONS AIR — Johnsonsair (JON) — Accra/Sharjah (ACC/SHJ)

Ceased ops

### MERIDIAN AIRWAYS — (MAG) — Accra (ACC)

| | | | | | |
|---|---|---|---|---|---|
| ☐ | 9G-AXA | Douglas DC-8-63F (BAC 3) | 46113/521 | ex N811AX | |
| ☐ | 9G-AXB | Douglas DC-8-63PF (BAC 3) | 46097/503 | ex N815AX | [OST] |
| ☐ | 9G-AXC | Douglas DC-8-63F (BAC 3) | 45999/377 | ex N828AX | |
| ☐ | 9G-AXD | Douglas DC-8-63F (BAC 3) | 45927/327 | ex N819AX | |
| ☐ | 9G-AXE | Douglas DC-8-63F (BAC 3) | 46041/439 | ex N814AX | [OST] |

### SOBEL AIR — (SBL) — Accra (ACC)

Ceased ops

### STARBOW — (S9/IKM)

| | | | | | |
|---|---|---|---|---|---|
| ☐ | 9G-SBA | British Aerospace 146 Srs.300 | E3125 | ex G-UKSG | ♦ |
| ☐ | 9G-SBB | British Aerospace 146 Srs.300 | E3123 | ex G-UKHP | ♦ |
| ☐ | 9G- | British Aerospace 146 Srs.200 | E2059 | ex ZS-PUM | [JNB]♦ |
| ☐ | 9G- | British Aerospace 146 Srs.300 | E3183 | ex G-BUHB | [BUC]♦ |

## 9H- MALTA (Republic of Malta)

### AIR MALTA — Air Malta (KM/AMC) — Luqa (MLA)

| | | | | | | |
|---|---|---|---|---|---|---|
| ☐ | 9H-AEG | Airbus A319-112 | 2113 | ex C-GAEG | Mdina | |
| ☐ | 9H-AEH | Airbus A319-112 | 2122 | ex D-AVWA | Floriana | |
| ☐ | 9H-AEJ | Airbus A319-112 | 2186 | ex D-AVWX | San Pawl il-Bahr | |
| ☐ | 9H-AEL | Airbus A319-112 | 2332 | ex D-AVYZ | Marsaxlokk | |
| ☐ | 9H-AEM | Airbus A319-112 | 2382 | ex D-AVWW | Birgu | |
| ☐ | 9H-AEF | Airbus A320-214 | 2142 | ex F-WWBZ | Valletta | >YAP |
| ☐ | 9H-AEK | Airbus A320-214 | 2291 | ex F-WWBT | San Gijan | |
| ☐ | 9H-AEN | Airbus A320-214 | 2665 | ex F-WWBN | Bormla | |
| ☐ | 9H-AEO | Airbus A320-214 | 2768 | ex F-WWDK | Isla-Cita'Invicta | |
| ☐ | 9H-AEP | Airbus A320-214 | 3056 | ex F-WWDV | Nadur | |
| ☐ | 9H-AEQ | Airbus A320-214 | 3068 | ex F-WWIJ | Tarxien | |

### EFLY — (LEF) — Luqa (MLA)

| | | | | | |
|---|---|---|---|---|---|
| ☐ | 9H-ELE | British Aerospace 146 Srs.300 | E3209 | ex G-JEBG | wfs |

| HARBOUR AIR MALTA | | (HES) | | | Grand Harbour |
|---|---|---|---|---|---|
| ☐ 9H-AFA | de Havilland DHC-3 Turbo Otter | 406 | ex C-FHAH | | FP |

| MEDAVIA | | Medavia (MDM) | | | Luqa (MLA) |
|---|---|---|---|---|---|
| ☐ 9H-AAP | CASA C.212-200 | TC15-1-9 | ex EC-CRV | | |
| ☐ 9H-AAR | CASA C.212-200 | CC15-1-161 | | | |
| ☐ 9H-AAS | CASA C.212-200 | CC15-2-162 | | | |
| ☐ 9H-AEW | de Havilland DHC-8-102 | 222 | ex PH-SDH | | |
| ☐ 9H-AEY | de Havilland DHC-8Q-315 | 508 | ex G-BRYX | | >RVL |
| ☐ 9H-AFD | de Havilland DHC-8Q-315 | 458 | ex G-BRYU | | >ATW |
| ☐ 9H-AFH | Beech 1900D | UE-372 | ex PH-RAR | | op for ICRC |
| ☐ 9H-AFI | Beech 1900D | UE-31 | ex PH-RAH | | |
| ☐ 9H-MET | Dornier 328-110 | 3117 | ex D-COMM | | |

| MINILINER MALTA | | | | | |
|---|---|---|---|---|---|
| ☐ 9H-MQT | Fokker F.27 Friendship 400 | 10295 | ex I-MLQT | | ♦ |

## 9J-    ZAMBIA (Republic of Zambia)

| AIRWAVES AIRLINK | | Airlimited (WLA) | | | Lusaka (LUN) |
|---|---|---|---|---|---|
| ☐ 9J-CGC | Cessna 208B Caravan I | 208B0742 | ex N878C | | |

| PROFLIGHT AIR SERVICES | | Proflight-Zambia (PFZ) | | | Lusaka (LUN) |
|---|---|---|---|---|---|
| ☐ ZS-JSL | British Aerospace Jetstream 31 | 691 | ex C6-ASL | | ♦ |
| ☐ ZS-NOM | British Aerospace Jetstream 41 | 41047 | ex G-MAJO | | ♦ |
| ☐ ZS-OMF | British Aerospace Jetstream 41 | 41034 | ex G-MSKJ | | ♦ |
| ☐ ZS-OMZ | British Aerospace Jetstream 41 | 41037 | ex VH-CCW | | <LNK♦ |
| ☐ 7Q-YMJ | Piper PA-23-250 Aztec D | 27-4104 | ex ZS-FTO | | |
| ☐ 9J-ABD | Cessna P206D Super Skylane | P206-0461 | ex ZS-FDA | | |
| ☐ 9J-KKN | Piper PA-31-350 Chieftain | 31-8052113 | ex ZS-KKN | | |
| ☐ 9J-PCR | Cessna 208B Caravan I | 208B1302 | ex N2047V | | ♦ |
| ☐ 9J-PCS | British Aerospace Jetstream 32 | 824 | ex N3108 | | ♦ |
| ☐ 9J-PCT | British Aerospace Jetstream 32EP | 903 | ex VP-CEX | | ♦ |
| ☐ 9J-PCU | British Aerospace Jetstream 32EP | 800 | ex N290MA | | ♦ |
| ☐ 9J-PLJ | Britten-Norman BN-2A-21 Islander | 799 | ex Botswana OA3 | | |
| ☐ 9J-UAS | Britten-Norman BN-2A Islander | 155 | ex Z-UAS | | |
| ☐ 9J-WEX | Britten-Norman BN-2A Islander | 619 | ex Z-WEX | | |

| ROYAL AIR CHARTERS | | | | | |
|---|---|---|---|---|---|
| ☐ 9J-CID | Cessna 208B Caravan I | 208B1307 | ex N20527 | | |

| ZAMBEZI AIRLINES | | (ZJ/ZMA) | | | |
|---|---|---|---|---|---|

Ops suspended 31Oct11

| ZAMBIAN AIRWAYS | | Zambian (Q3/MBN) | | | Lusaka (LUN) |
|---|---|---|---|---|---|

Ops suspended 10Jan09

## 9K-    KUWAIT (State of Kuwait)

| JAZEERA AIRWAYS | | Jazeera (J9/JZR) | | | Kuwait City (KWI) |
|---|---|---|---|---|---|
| ☐ 9K-CAA | Airbus A320-214 | 2569 | ex F-WWBF | | |
| ☐ 9K-CAC | Airbus A320-214 | 2792 | ex F-WWBM | | |
| ☐ 9K-CAD | Airbus A320-214 | 2822 | ex F-WWDC | | |
| ☐ 9K-CAI | Airbus A320-214 | 3919 | ex F-WWBH | | |
| ☐ 9K-CAJ | Airbus A320-214 | 3939 | ex F-WWDR | | |
| ☐ 9K-CAK | Airbus A320-214 | 4162 | ex F-WWBS | | |
| ☐ 9K-CAL | Airbus A320-214 | 5033 | ex D-AXAL | | ♦ |

| KUWAIT AIRWAYS | | Kuwaiti (KU/KAC) | | | Kuwait City (KWI) |
|---|---|---|---|---|---|
| ☐ 9K-AHI | Airbus A300C4-620 | 344 | ex PK-MAY | Al-Sabahiya | op for Govt |
| ☐ 9K-AMA | Airbus A300B4-605R | 673 | ex F-WWAQ | Failaka | |
| ☐ 9K-AMB | Airbus A300B4-605R | 694 | ex F-WWAV | Burghan | |
| ☐ 9K-AMC | Airbus A300B4-605R | 699 | ex F-WWAM | Wafra | |
| ☐ 9K-AMD | Airbus A300B4-605R | 719 | ex F-WWAB | Wara | |
| ☐ 9K-AME | Airbus A300B4-605R | 721 | ex F-WWAG | Al-Rawdhatain | |

| | | | | | | |
|---|---|---|---|---|---|---|
| ☐ | 9K-ADE | Boeing 747-469M | 27338/1046 | | Al-Jabariya | op for Govt |
| ☐ | 9K-AKA | Airbus A320-212 | 0181 | ex F-WWIU | Bubbyan | |
| ☐ | 9K-AKB | Airbus A320-212 | 0182 | ex F-WWIV | Kubber | |
| ☐ | 9K-AKC | Airbus A320-212 | 0195 | ex F-WWDP | Qurtoba | |
| ☐ | 9K-AKD | Airbus A320-212 | 2046 | ex F-WWBG | Al-Mubarakiya | op for Govt |
| ☐ | 9K-ALA | Airbus A310-308 | 647 | ex F-WWCQ | Al-Jahra | |
| ☐ | 9K-ALB | Airbus A310-308 | 649 | ex F-WWCV | Gharnada | |
| ☐ | 9K-ALC | Airbus A310-308 | 663 | ex JY-AGT | Kazma | |
| ☐ | 9K-ALD | Airbus A310-308 | 648 | ex F-WWCR | Al-Salmiya | op for Govt |
| ☐ | 9K-ANA | Airbus A340-313 | 089 | ex F-WWJX | Warba | |
| ☐ | 9K-ANB | Airbus A340-313 | 090 | ex F-WWJZ | Bayan | |
| ☐ | 9K-ANC | Airbus A340-313 | 101 | ex F-WWJE | Meskan | |
| ☐ | 9K-AND | Airbus A340-313 | 104 | ex F-WWJJ | Al-Riggah | |
| ☐ | 9K-AOA | Boeing 777-269ER | 28743/125 | | Al-Gurain | |
| ☐ | 9K-AOB | Boeing 777-269ER | 28744/145 | | Garouh | |

## WATANIYA AIRWAYS — *Kuwait City (KWI)*

Ceased ops 16Mar11

## 9L-    SIERRA LEONE (Republic of Sierra Leone)

### AFRICAN AIR CHARTER

| | | | | | |
|---|---|---|---|---|---|
| ☐ | 9L-LBI | LET L-410UVP | 851440 | ex RA-67533 | ♦ |

### AIR RUM — *Air Rum (RUM)* — *Amman (AMM)*

Ceased ops 2008

### BELLVIEW AIRLINES — O3/ORJ — *Freetown (FNA)*

Ops services with aircraft leased from Bellview Airlines (5N) as required

## 9M-    MALAYSIA (Federation of Malaysia)

### AIRASIA — *Asian express (AK/AXM)*
*Kuala Lumpur-Sultan Abdul Aziz Shah (KUL)*

| | | | | | |
|---|---|---|---|---|---|
| ☐ | 9M-AFA | Airbus A320-214 | 2612 | ex F-WWBV | |
| ☐ | 9M-AFB | Airbus A320-214 | 2633 | ex F-WWDY | |
| ☐ | 9M-AFC | Airbus A320-214 | 2656 | ex F-WWIO | Manchester United c/s |
| ☐ | 9M-AFD | Airbus A320-214 | 2683 | ex F-WWIT | |
| ☐ | 9M-AFE | Airbus A320-214 | 2699 | ex F-WWDN | |
| ☐ | 9M-AFF | Airbus A320-214 | 2760 | ex F-WWDT | |
| ☐ | 9M-AFG | Airbus A320-214 | 2816 | ex F-WWIX | |
| ☐ | 9M-AFH | Airbus A320-216 | 2826 | ex F-WWDI | |
| ☐ | 9M-AFI | Airbus A320-216 | 2842 | ex F-WWIG | |
| ☐ | 9M-AFL | Airbus A320-216 | 2926 | ex F-WWDX | |
| ☐ | 9M-AFM | Airbus A320-216 | 2944 | ex F-WWIN | |
| ☐ | 9M-AFN | Airbus A320-216 | 2956 | ex F-WWBY | |
| ☐ | 9M-AFO | Airbus A320-216 | 2989 | ex F-WWIK | |
| ☐ | 9M-AFP | Airbus A320-216 | 3000 | ex F-WWBL | Special 3000th c/s |
| ☐ | 9M-AFQ | Airbus A320-216 | 3018 | ex F-WWBR | Malaysia anniversary c/s |
| ☐ | 9M-AFR | Airbus A320-216 | 3064 | ex F-WWIC | |
| ☐ | 9M-AFS | Airbus A320-216 | 3117 | ex F-WWBB | |
| ☐ | 9M-AFT | Airbus A320-216 | 3140 | ex F-WWDN | |
| ☐ | 9M-AFU | Airbus A320-216 | 3154 | ex F-WWDE | |
| ☐ | 9M-AFV | Airbus A320-216 | 3173 | ex F-WWIO | |
| ☐ | 9M-AFW | Airbus A320-216 | 3404 | ex F-WWBX | ATT & Williams c/s |
| ☐ | 9M-AFX | Airbus A320-216 | 3182 | ex F-WWDU | |
| ☐ | 9M-AFY | Airbus A320-216 | 3194 | ex F-WWIV | |
| ☐ | 9M-AFZ | Airbus A320-216 | 3201 | ex F-WWID | |
| ☐ | 9M-AHA | Airbus A320-216 | 3223 | ex F-WWBV | |
| ☐ | 9M-AHB | Airbus A320-216 | 3232 | ex F-WWBF | |
| ☐ | 9M-AHC | Airbus A320-216 | 3261 | ex F-WWDN | |
| ☐ | 9M-AHD | Airbus A320-216 | 3291 | ex F-WWDT | |
| ☐ | 9M-AHE | Airbus A320-216 | 3327 | ex F-WWBH | |
| ☐ | 9M-AHF | Airbus A320-216 | 3353 | ex F-WWIE | |
| ☐ | 9M-AHG | Airbus A320-216 | 3370 | ex F-WWDF | Manchester United c/s |
| ☐ | 9M-AHH | Airbus A320-216 | 3427 | ex F-WWBB | |
| ☐ | 9M-AHI | Airbus A320-216 | 3448 | ex F-WWIX | |
| ☐ | 9M-AHJ | Airbus A320-216 | 3477 | ex F-WWDH | |
| ☐ | 9M-AHL | Airbus A320-216 | 3521 | ex F-WWDS | |
| ☐ | 9M-AHM | Airbus A320-216 | 3536 | ex F-WWID | |
| ☐ | 9M-AHO | Airbus A320-216 | 3568 | ex F-WWBV | |
| ☐ | 9M-AHP | Airbus A320-216 | 3582 | ex F-WWDE | |

| | | | | | | |
|---|---|---|---|---|---|---|
| ☐ | 9M-AHQ | Airbus A320-216 | 3628 | ex F-WWIU | | |
| ☐ | 9M-AHR | Airbus A320-216 | 3701 | ex F-WWBP | | |
| ☐ | 9M-AHS | Airbus A320-216 | 3776 | ex F-WWDX | | |
| ☐ | 9M-AHT | Airbus A320-216 | 3997 | ex F-WWDH | | |
| ☐ | 9M-AHU | Airbus A320-216 | 4070 | ex F-WWBK | | |
| ☐ | 9M-AHV | Airbus A320-216 | 4079 | ex F-WWBP | | |
| ☐ | 9M-AHW | Airbus A320-216 | 4098 | ex F-WWDJ | | |
| ☐ | 9M-AHX | Airbus A320-216 | 4263 | ex F-WWBG | | |
| ☐ | 9M-AHY | Airbus A320-216 | 4293 | ex F-WWIY | | |
| ☐ | 9M-AHZ | Airbus A320-216 | 4361 | ex F-WWDP | | |
| ☐ | 9M-AQA | Airbus A320-216 | 4404 | ex F-WWBG | | |
| ☐ | 9M-AQB | Airbus A320-216 | 4458 | ex F-WWBF | | |
| ☐ | 9M-AQC | Airbus A320-216 | 4793 | ex F-WWID | | ♦ |
| ☐ | 9M-AQD | Airbus A320-216 | 4882 | ex F-WWIO | | ♦ |
| ☐ | 9M-AQE | Airbus A320-216 | 4571 | ex PK-AXP | | ♦ |
| ☐ | 9M-AQF | Airbus A320-216 | 4582 | ex PK-AXQ | | ♦ |
| ☐ | 9M-AQG | Airbus A320-216 | 4477 | ex PK-AXN | | ♦ |
| ☐ | 9M-AQH | Airbus A320-216 | 4969 | ex D-AVVB | | ♦ |
| ☐ | 9M-AQI | Airbus A320-216 | 4486 | ex PK-AXO | | ♦ |

### AIRASIA X     (D7/XAX)     Kuala Lumpur-Sultan Abdul Aziz Shah (KUL)

| | | | | | |
|---|---|---|---|---|---|
| ☐ | 9M-XAA | Airbus A330-301 | 054 | ex N54AN | |
| ☐ | 9M-XXA | Airbus A330-343E | 952 | ex F-WWKR | |
| ☐ | 9M-XXB | Airbus A330-343E | 974 | ex F-WWKD | |
| ☐ | 9M-XXC | Airbus A330-343E | 1048 | ex F-WWKI | |
| ☐ | 9M-XXD | Airbus A330-343E | 1066 | ex F-WWYI | |
| ☐ | 9M-XXE | Airbus A330-343E | 1075 | ex F-WWKS | |
| ☐ | 9M-XXF | Airbus A330-343E | 1126 | ex F-WWYQ | Northern Xposure |
| ☐ | 9M-XXG | Airbus A330-343E | 1131 | ex F-WWYY | Southern Xross |
| ☐ | 9M-XXH | Airbus A330-343E | 1165 | ex F-WWYG | |
| | | | | | |
| ☐ | 9M-XAB | Airbus A340-313X | 273 | ex C-GDVW | |
| ☐ | 9M-XAC | Airbus A340-313X | 278 | ex C-GDVZ | |

### AWAN INSPIRASI

| | | | | | |
|---|---|---|---|---|---|
| ☐ | 9M-AIH | Sikorsky S-92A | 920024 | ex C-GOHA | |
| ☐ | 9M-AIK | Sikorsky S-76C+ | 760622 | ex C-GHRK | |
| ☐ | 9M-AIM | Eurocopter EC225LP | 2769 | ex F-WGYO | ♦ |
| ☐ | 9M-AIN | Eurocopter EC225LP | | | ♦ |
| ☐ | 9M-AIP | Sikorsky S-76C++ | 760693 | ex C-FRSE | |

### BERJAYA AIR     Berjaya (J8/BVT)
### Subang-Sultan Abdul Aziz Shah International (SZB)

| | | | | | |
|---|---|---|---|---|---|
| ☐ | 9M-TAG | ATR 72-212A | 0858 | ex F-WWEC | |
| ☐ | 9M-TAH | de Havilland DHC-7-110 | 109 | ex G-BRYD | |
| ☐ | 9M-TAK | de Havilland DHC-7-110 | 110 | ex G-BOAW | |
| ☐ | 9M-TAL | de Havilland DHC-7-110 | 112 | ex G-BOAY | |
| ☐ | 9M-TAQ | ATR 72-212A | 0875 | ex F-WWEB | |

### FIREFLY     (7E/FFM)     Penang (PEN)

| | | | | | |
|---|---|---|---|---|---|
| ☐ | 9M-FYA | ATR 72-212A | 0812 | ex F-WWEB | |
| ☐ | 9M-FYB | ATR 72-212A | 0814 | ex F-WWED | |
| ☐ | 9M-FYC | ATR 72-212A | 0821 | ex F-WWEK | |
| ☐ | 9M-FYD | ATR 72-212A | 0830 | ex F-WWEE | |
| ☐ | 9M-FYE | ATR 72-212A | 0840 | ex F-WWER | |
| ☐ | 9M-FYF | ATR 72-212A | 0860 | ex F-WWEF | |
| ☐ | 9M-FYG | ATR 72-212A | 0868 | ex F-WWES | |
| ☐ | 9M-FYH | ATR 72-212A | 0934 | ex F-WWEJ | |
| ☐ | 9M-FYI | ATR 72-212A | 0935 | ex | |
| ☐ | 9M-FYJ | ATR 72-212A | 0941 | ex | |
| ☐ | 9M-FYK | ATR 72-212A | 0947 | ex F-WW | ♦ |
| ☐ | 9M-FYL | ATR 72-212A | 0948 | ex F-WW | ♦ |

### LAYANG-LAYANG AEROSPACE     Layang (LAY)     Miri (MYY)

| | | | | | |
|---|---|---|---|---|---|
| ☐ | 9M-LLB | GAF N22C Nomad | N22C-95 | ex VH-SNL | |
| ☐ | 9M-LLH | Bell 206B JetRanger III | 2919 | ex VH-WNA | |
| ☐ | 9M-LLI | GAF N22C Nomad | N22B-69 | ex VH-MSF | |
| ☐ | 9M-LLM | Bell 206B JetRanger | | | ♦ |
| ☐ | 9M-LLR | MBB Bo105CBS | | ♦ | |
| ☐ | 9M-LLT | Bell 206B JetRanger | 969 | ex G-TUCH | |
| ☐ | 9M-LLU | Bolkow 105C | | | |
| ☐ | RA-41900 | Antonov An-38-120 | 4160381607003 | | <NPO |

**MALAYSIA AIRLINES**  Malaysian (MH/MAS)  *Kuala Lumpur-Sultan Abdul Aziz Shah (KUL)*

| | Registration | Type | MSN | Ex/Notes | |
|---|---|---|---|---|---|
| ☐ | 9M-MKV | Airbus A330-223 | 296 | ex EI-CZS | |
| ☐ | 9M-MKW | Airbus A330-223 | 300 | ex EI-CZT | |
| ☐ | 9M-MKX | Airbus A330-223 | 290 | ex EI-CZR | |
| ☐ | 9M-MUA | Airbus A330-223F | 1136 | ex F-WWYZ | |
| ☐ | 9M-MUB | Airbus A330-223F | 1148 | ex F-WWYH | ♦ |
| ☐ | 9M-MUC | Airbus A330-223F | 1164 | ex F-WWKG | ♦ |
| ☐ | 9M-MUD | Airbus A330-223F | 1180 | ex F-WW | o/o♦ |
| | | | | | |
| ☐ | 9M-MKA | Airbus A330-322 | 067 | ex F-WWKK | |
| ☐ | 9M-MKC | Airbus A330-322 | 069 | ex F-WWKM | |
| ☐ | 9M-MKD | Airbus A330-322 | 073 | ex F-WWKN | |
| ☐ | 9M-MKE | Airbus A330-322 | 077 | ex F-WWKO | |
| ☐ | 9M-MKF | Airbus A330-322 | 100 | ex F-WWKZ | |
| ☐ | 9M-MKG | Airbus A330-322 | 107 | ex F-WWKV | |
| ☐ | 9M-MKH | Airbus A330-322 | 110 | ex F-WWKE | |
| ☐ | 9M-MKI | Airbus A330-322 | 116 | ex F-WWKT | |
| ☐ | 9M-MKJ | Airbus A330-322 | 119 | ex F-WWKJ | |
| ☐ | 9M-MTA | Airbus A330-323 | 1209 | ex F-WWYG | |
| ☐ | 9M-MTB | Airbus A330-323 | 1219 | ex F-WWYX | ♦ |
| ☐ | 9M-MTC | Airbus A330-323 | 1229 | ex F-WWYJ | ♦ |
| ☐ | 9M-MTD | Airbus A330-323 | 1234 | ex F-WWYN | ♦ |
| ☐ | 9M-MTE | Airbus A330-323 | 1243 | ex F-WWYP | ♦ |
| ☐ | 9M-MTF | Airbus A330-323 | 1281 | ex F-WWKO | ♦ |
| | | | | | |
| ☐ | 9M-MNA | Airbus A380-841 | 078 | ex F-WWSU | o/o♦ |
| ☐ | 9M-MNB | Airbus A380-841 | 081 | ex F-WWAJ | o/o♦ |
| ☐ | 9M-MNC | Airbus A380-841 | 084 | ex F-WWAD | o/o♦ |
| ☐ | 9M-MND | Airbus A380-841 | 089 | ex F-WWAN | o/o♦ |
| ☐ | 9M-MNE | Airbus A380-841 | 094 | ex F-WW | o/o♦ |
| | | | | | |
| ☐ | 9M-FZA | Boeing 737-430 | 27001/2316 | ex EI-COH | [KUL]♦ |
| ☐ | 9M-FZB | Boeing 737-430 | 27003/2328 | ex EI-COK | [KUL]♦ |
| ☐ | 9M-MMA | Boeing 737-4H6 | 26443/2272 | | |
| ☐ | 9M-MMB | Boeing 737-4H6 | 26444/2308 | | |
| ☐ | 9M-MMC | Boeing 737-4H6 | 26453/2332 | | |
| ☐ | 9M-MMD | Boeing 737-4H6 | 26464/2340 | | |
| ☐ | 9M-MMF | Boeing 737-4H6 | 26466/2372 | | |
| ☐ | 9M-MMG | Boeing 737-4H6 | 26467/2378 | | |
| ☐ | 9M-MMH | Boeing 737-4H6 | 27084/2391 | | |
| ☐ | 9M-MMI | Boeing 737-4H6 | 27096/2395 | | |
| ☐ | 9M-MMJ | Boeing 737-4H6 | 27097/2399 | | |
| ☐ | 9M-MMK | Boeing 737-4H6 | 27083/2403 | | |
| ☐ | 9M-MML | Boeing 737-4H6 | 27085/2407 | | |
| ☐ | 9M-MMN | Boeing 737-4H6 | 27167/2419 | | |
| ☐ | 9M-MMQ | Boeing 737-4H6 | 27087/2441 | | |
| ☐ | 9M-MMR | Boeing 737-4H6 | 26468/2445 | | |
| ☐ | 9M-MMS | Boeing 737-4H6 | 27169/2450 | | |
| ☐ | 9M-MMT | Boeing 737-4H6 | 27170/2462 | | |
| ☐ | 9M-MMU | Boeing 737-4H6 | 26447/2479 | ex VT-JAV | |
| ☐ | 9M-MMV | Boeing 737-4H6 | 26449/2491 | | |
| ☐ | 9M-MMW | Boeing 737-4H6 | 26451/2496 | | |
| ☐ | 9M-MMX | Boeing 737-4H6 | 26452/2501 | | |
| ☐ | 9M-MMY | Boeing 737-4H6 | 26455/2507 | | |
| ☐ | 9M-MMZ | Boeing 737-4H6 | 26457/2521 | | |
| ☐ | 9M-MQA | Boeing 737-4H6 | 26458/2525 | | |
| ☐ | 9M-MQB | Boeing 737-4H6 | 26459/2530 | | |
| ☐ | 9M-MQD | Boeing 737-4H6 | 26461/2536 | | |
| ☐ | 9M-MQE | Boeing 737-4H6 | 26462/2542 | | |
| ☐ | 9M-MQF | Boeing 737-4H6 | 26463/2560 | | |
| ☐ | 9M-MQG | Boeing 737-4H6 | 27190/2568 | | |
| ☐ | 9M-MQI | Boeing 737-4H6 | 27353/2632 | ex 9H-ADJ | |
| ☐ | 9M-MQK | Boeing 737-4H6 | 27384/2673 | | |
| ☐ | 9M-MQN | Boeing 737-4H6 | 27673/2852 | ex 9H-ADK | |
| ☐ | 9M-MQO | Boeing 737-4H6 | 27674/2877 | ex 9H-ADL | |
| ☐ | 9M-MQP | Boeing 737-46J | 28038/2794 | ex N380BG | [KUL] |
| ☐ | 9M-MQQ | Boeing 737-4Y0 | 24915/2055 | ex SX-BKL | |
| | | | | | |
| ☐ | 9M-FFA | Boeing 737-8Q8/W | 30702/1953 | ex 9M-MLA | ♦ |
| ☐ | 9M-FFB | Boeing 737-8Q8/W | 30703/1964 | ex 9M-MLB | ♦ |
| ☐ | 9M-FFC | Boeing 737-8Q8/W | 32690/2250 | ex 9M-MLC | ♦ |
| ☐ | 9M-FFD | Boeing 737-85F/W | 30007/746 | ex ZS-SJI | ♦ |
| ☐ | 9M-FFE | Boeing 737-85F/W | 30567/761 | ex ZS-SJJ | ♦ |
| ☐ | 9M-FFF | Boeing 737-8FZ/W | 39320/3690 | | ♦ |
| ☐ | 9M-MLD | Boeing 737-8GQ/W | 35793/2428 | ex N793AW | |
| ☐ | 9M-MLE | Boeing 737-8FH/W | 35105/2501 | ex N126RB | |
| ☐ | 9M-MLF | Boeing 737-8FZ/W | 29657/3335 | ex N1786B | |
| ☐ | 9M-MLG | Boeing 737-8FZ/W | 31779/3395 | ex N1787B | |
| ☐ | 9M-MLH | Boeing 737-8FZ/W | 31723/3435 | ex N1788B | |
| ☐ | 9M-MLI | Boeing 737-8FZ/W | 31793/3503 | | |
| ☐ | 9M-MLJ | Boeing 737-8FZ/W | 39319 | | o/o |

| | Reg | Type | C/n | Notes | | |
|---|---|---|---|---|---|---|
| ☐ | 9M-MLK | Boeing 737-8FZ/W | 39321/3778 | | | |
| ☐ | 9M-MLL | Boeing 737-8FZ/W | 39322/3834 | | | ♦ |
| ☐ | 9M-MLM | Boeing 737-8H6/W | 39323/3885 | | | ♦ |
| ☐ | 9M-MLN | Boeing 737-8H6/W | 39324 | | | o/o♦ |
| ☐ | 9M-MLO | Boeing 737-3H6/W | 39325 | | | o/o♦ |
| ☐ | 9M-MXA | Boeing 737-8H6/W | 40128/3421 | ex N1786B | | |
| ☐ | 9M-MXB | Boeing 737-8H6/W | 40129/3458 | | | |
| ☐ | 9M-MXC | Boeing 737-8H6/W | 40130/3495 | ex N1786B | | |
| ☐ | 9M-MXD | Boeing 737-8H6/W | 40131/3577 | | | |
| ☐ | 9M-MXE | Boeing 737-8H6/W | 40132/3723 | | | ♦ |
| ☐ | 9M-MXF | Boeing 737-8H6/W | 40133/3806 | | | ♦ |
| ☐ | 9M-MXG | Boeing 737-8H6/W | 40134/3873 | | | ♦ |
| ☐ | 9M-MXH | Boeing 737-8H6/W | 40135/3911 | | | ♦ |
| ☐ | 9M-MXI | Boeing 737-6H6/W | 40136 | | | o/o♦ |
| ☐ | 9M-MXJ | Boeing 737-8H6/W | 40137 | | | o/o♦ |
| ☐ | 9M-MXK | Boeing 737-8H6/W | 40138 | | | o/o♦ |
| ☐ | 9M-MXL | Boeing 737-8H6/W | 40139 | | | o/o♦ |
| ☐ | 9M-MXM | Boeing 737-8H6/W | 40140 | | | o/o♦ |
| ☐ | 9M-MXN | Boeing 737-8H6/W | 40141 | | | o/o♦ |
| ☐ | 9M-MXO | Boeing 737-8H6/W | 40142 | | | ono♦ |
| | | | | | | |
| ☐ | 9M-MPB | Boeing 747-4H6 | 25699/965 | | Shah AlamHibiscus | |
| ☐ | 9M-MPD | Boeing 747-4H6 | 25701/997 | | SerembanHibiscus c/s | [KUL]♦ |
| ☐ | 9M-MPF | Boeing 747-4H6 | 27043/1017 | | Kota Bharu | |
| ☐ | 9M-MPK | Boeing 747-4H6 | 28427/1147 | | Johor Bahru | |
| ☐ | 9M-MPL | Boeing 747-4H6 | 28428/1150 | | Penang | |
| ☐ | 9M-MPM | Boeing 747-4H6 | 28435/1152 | | Melaka | |
| ☐ | 9M-MPN | Boeing 747-4H6 | 28432/1247 | | Pangkor | |
| ☐ | 9M-MPO | Boeing 747-4H6 | 28433/1290 | | Alor Setar | |
| ☐ | 9M-MPP | Boeing 747-4H6 | 29900/1296 | | Putrajaya | |
| ☐ | 9M-MPQ | Boeing 747-4H6 | 29901/1301 | | Kuala Lumpur | |
| ☐ | 9M-MPR | Boeing 747-4H6F | 28434/1371 | | | |
| ☐ | 9M-MPS | Boeing 747-4H6F | 29902/1374 | | | |
| | | | | | | |
| ☐ | 9M-MRA | Boeing 777-2H6ER | 28408/64 | ex N5017V | | |
| ☐ | 9M-MRB | Boeing 777-2H6ER | 28409/74 | ex N50217 | | |
| ☐ | 9M-MRC | Boeing 777-2H6ER | 28410/78 | | | |
| ☐ | 9M-MRD | Boeing 777-2H6ER | 28411/84 | | Freedom of Space c/s | |
| ☐ | 9M-MRE | Boeing 777-2H6ER | 28412/115 | | | |
| ☐ | 9M-MRF | Boeing 777-2H6ER | 28413/128 | | | |
| ☐ | 9M-MRG | Boeing 777-2H6ER | 28414/140 | | | |
| ☐ | 9M-MRH | Boeing 777-2H6ER | 28415/151 | | | |
| ☐ | 9M-MRI | Boeing 777-2H6ER | 28416/155 | | | |
| ☐ | 9M-MRJ | Boeing 777-2H6ER | 28417/222 | | | |
| ☐ | 9M-MRK | Boeing 777-2H6ER | 28418/231 | | | |
| ☐ | 9M-MRL | Boeing 777-2H6ER | 29065/329 | | | |
| ☐ | 9M-MRM | Boeing 777-2H6ER | 29066/336 | | | |
| ☐ | 9M-MRN | Boeing 777-2H6ER | 28419/394 | | | |
| ☐ | 9M-MRO | Boeing 777-2H6ER | 28420/404 | | | |
| ☐ | 9M-MRP | Boeing 777-2H6ER | 28421/496 | ex N5016R | | |
| ☐ | 9M-MRQ | Boeing 777-2H6ER | 28422/498 | | | |

## MASWINGS (MWG)

| | Reg | Type | C/n | Notes | |
|---|---|---|---|---|---|
| ☐ | 9M-MWA | ATR 72-212A | 0817 | ex F-WWEG | |
| ☐ | 9M-MWB | ATR 72-212A | 0856 | ex F-WWEX | |
| ☐ | 9M-MWC | ATR 72-212A | 0863 | ex F-WWEL | |
| ☐ | 9M-MWD | ATR 72-212A | 0873 | ex F-WWEX | |
| ☐ | 9M-MWE | ATR 72-212A | 0885 | ex F-WWEO | |
| ☐ | 9M-MWF | ATR 72-212A | 0889 | ex F-WWET | |
| ☐ | 9M-MWG | ATR 72-212A | 0895 | ex F-WWEE | |
| ☐ | 9M-MWH | ATR 72-212A | 0900 | ex F-WWEO | |
| ☐ | 9M-MWI | ATR 72-212A | 0904 | ex F-WWET | Bario |
| ☐ | 9M-MWJ | ATR 72-212A | 0910 | ex F-WWEH | |
| | | | | | |
| ☐ | 9M-MDK | de Havilland DHC-6 Twin Otter 300 | 792 | ex C-GESR | |
| ☐ | 9M-MDL | de Havilland DHC-6 Twin Otter 300 | 802 | ex C-GDFT | |
| ☐ | 9M-MDM | de Havilland DHC-6 Twin Otter 300 | 804 | ex C-GDKL | |
| ☐ | 9M-MDO | de Havilland DHC-6 Twin Otter 310 | 629 | ex ZK-KHA | |

## MHS AVIATION / MALAYSIAN HELICOPTER SERVICES — Kerteh/Miri (KTE/MYY)

| | Reg | Type | C/n | Notes | |
|---|---|---|---|---|---|
| ☐ | 9M-SPB | Aérospatiale AS.332L2 | 2636 | ex F-WWOO | |
| ☐ | 9M-SPC | Aérospatiale AS.332L2 | 2639 | ex F-WWOJ | |
| ☐ | 9M-SPD | Aérospatiale AS.332L2 | 2646 | ex F-WWOO | |
| ☐ | 9M-STH | Eurocopter EC225LP | 2790 | ex G-CGUB | <BHL♦ |
| ☐ | 9M-STI | Eurocopter EC225LP | 2792 | ex G-CGUC | <BHL♦ |
| ☐ | 9M-STJ | Eurocopter EC225LP | 2785 | ex G-CGUA | <BHL♦ |
| ☐ | 9M-STS | Aérospatiale AS.332L1 | 2387 | | |
| ☐ | 9M-STV | Aérospatiale AS.332L1 | 2408 | | |
| ☐ | 9M-STW | Aérospatiale AS.332L1 | 2312 | ex LN-OBQ | <CHC Helicopters Intl |
| ☐ | 9M-AIM | Eurocopter EC225LP | 2769 | | |

| | | | | | | |
|---|---|---|---|---|---|---|
| ☐ | 9M-SPP | Sikorsky S-76C+ | 760661 | ex N45067 | | |
| ☐ | 9M-SPQ | Sikorsky S-76C | 760662 | ex N4507G | | |
| ☐ | 9M-SPR | Sikorsky S-76C | 760663 | ex N4508G | | |
| ☐ | 9M-SPS | Sikorsky S-76C+ | 760641 | ex G-CEKP | | |
| ☐ | 9M-SPT | Sikorsky S-76C+ | 760645 | ex G-CEKR | | |
| ☐ | 9M-SPW | Sikorsky S-76C+ | 760664 | ex G-KAZD | | |
| ☐ | 9M-STA | Sikorsky S-76C | 760383 | | | |
| ☐ | 9M-STB | Sikorsky S-76C | 760384 | | | |
| ☐ | 9M-STC | Sikorsky S-76C | 760392 | | | |
| ☐ | 9M-STD | Sikorsky S-76C | 760397 | | | |
| ☐ | 9M-STE | Sikorsky S-76C | 760398 | | | |
| ☐ | 9M-STF | Sikorsky S-76C | 760400 | | | |
| ☐ | 9M-STG | Sikorsky S-76C | 760385 | ex ZS-RTC | | |
| | | | | | | |
| ☐ | 9M-AVP | Sikorsky S-61N | 61768 | ex G-BEKJ | | |
| ☐ | 9M-SNA | Aérospatiale AS365N2 Dauphin 2 | 6246 | ex N634LH | | |
| ☐ | 9M-SSN | de Havilland DHC-6 Twin Otter | | | | |
| ☐ | 9M-SSV | Aérospatiale AS355F2 Ecureuil 2 | 5476 | | | ♦ |
| ☐ | 9M-SSW | Aérospatiale AS355F2 Twin Star | 5467 | ex N467CL | | |
| ☐ | 9M-SSZ | Aérospatiale AS355F2 Ecureuil 2 | 5292 | ex 3A-MVV | | |
| ☐ | 9M-STH | Eurocopter EC225LP | 2790 | ex G-CGUB | | |
| ☐ | 9M-STI | Eurocopter EC225LP | 2792 | ex G-CGUC | | ♦ |
| ☐ | 9M-STJ | Eurocopter EC225LP | 2785 | ex G-CGUA | | ♦ |
| ☐ | 9M-STL | Beech 1900D | UE-373 | ex N31110 | | ♦ |
| ☐ | 9M-STM | Beech 1900D | UE-374 | ex N31419 | | |

## NEPTUNE AIR — (N7/NEP)

| | | | | | | |
|---|---|---|---|---|---|---|
| ☐ | 9M-NEF | Boeing 737-3S3F | 23811/1445 | ex EC-KDY | | ♦ |
| ☐ | 9M-NEP | Boeing 727-277F (FedEx 3) | 22641/1753 | ex VH-VLI | | |
| ☐ | 9M- | Boeing 737-3Z0F | 23448/1168 | ex N448AG | | o/o♦ |

## PAN-MALAYSIAN AIR TRANSPORT — Pan Malaysia (PMA) — Subang-Sultan Abdul Aziz Shah International (SZB)

| | | | | | |
|---|---|---|---|---|---|
| ☐ | 9M-PIH | Short SC.7 Skyvan 3 | SH1962 | ex G-BFUM | |

## PERFECT AVIATION

Status uncertain

## SABAH AIR — Sabah Air (SAX) — Kota Kinabalu-Intl (BKI)

| | | | | | | |
|---|---|---|---|---|---|---|
| ☐ | 9M-AUA | GAF N22B Nomad | N22B-7 | | | |
| ☐ | 9M-AWC | Bell 206B JetRanger III | 2336 | | | |
| ☐ | 9M-AYN | Bell 206B JetRanger III | 3022 | ex N5738M | | |
| ☐ | 9M-AZK | Bell 206L-3 LongRanger III | 51484 | ex N4196G | | |
| ☐ | 9M-CMD | MBB Bk117C-2 | | | | ♦ |
| ☐ | 9M-MOH | Aérospatiale AS355NP Ecureuil | | | | ♦ |
| ☐ | 9M-SAC | Bell 206B JetRanger III | 2510 | | | |

## TRANSMILE AIR SERVICES — Transmile (TH/TSE) — Subang-Sultan Abdul Aziz Shah Intl (SZB)

| | | | | | | |
|---|---|---|---|---|---|---|
| ☐ | 9M-TGB | Boeing 727-2F2F/W (Duganair 3) | 22998/1810 | ex VH-DHF | | |
| ☐ | 9M-TGE | Boeing 727-247F (FedEx 3) | 21697/1471 | ex PK-TMA | | |
| ☐ | 9M-TGF | Boeing 727-247F (FedEx 3) | 21698/1474 | ex N209UP | | |
| ☐ | 9M-TGG | Boeing 727-247F (FedEx 3) | 21699/1485 | ex N207UP | | |
| ☐ | 9M-TGH | Boeing 727-247F (FedEx 3) | 21701/1493 | ex N208UP | | |
| ☐ | 9M-TGM | Boeing 727-225F (FedEx 3) | 22549/1737 | ex N902RF | | |
| ☐ | 9M-TGN | Boeing 727-225F (FedEx 3) | 21856/1537 | ex N8887Z | | ♦ |
| | | | | | | |
| ☐ | 9M-PMA | Cessna 208B Caravan I | 208B0800 | ex N1278M | | |
| ☐ | 9M-PML | Boeing 737-275C | 21116/427 | ex C-GDPW | DHL colours | Frtr |
| ☐ | 9M-PMW | Boeing 737-209F (AvAero 3) | 24197/1581 | ex PK-TME | | |
| ☐ | 9M-PMZ | Boeing 737-209 | 23796/1420 | ex PK-KAR | | |

# 9N- NEPAL (Kingdom of Nepal)

## AGNI AIR — Kathmandu (KTM)

| | | | | | | |
|---|---|---|---|---|---|---|
| ☐ | 9N-AIE | Dornier 228-202K | 8165 | ex 9M-VAA | | |
| ☐ | 9N-AIG | Dornier 228-212 | 8216 | ex 9M-VAM | | [KTM] |
| ☐ | 9N-AIO | British Aerospace Jetstream 4101 | 41055 | ex N316UE | | |
| ☐ | 9N-AIP | British Aerospace Jetstream 4101 | 41058 | ex N322UE | | |
| ☐ | 9N-AIQ | British Aerospace Jetstream 4101 | 41064 | ex N326UE | | |
| ☐ | 9N-AJN | Dornier 228-212 | 8198 | ex VH-ATZ | | ♦ |

## AIR KASTHAMANDAP
Kathmandu (KTM)

| | | | | |
|---|---|---|---|---|
| ☐ | 9N-AIZ | Pacific Aerospace 750XL | 154 | ex ZK-JJH |
| ☐ | 9N-AJB | Pacific Aerospace 750XL | 160 | ex ZK-KAZ |
| ☐ | 9N-AJF | Pacific Aerospace 750XL | 162 | ex ZK-KAO |

## BUDDHA AIR
Buddha Air (BHA)
Kathmandu (KTM)

| | | | | | |
|---|---|---|---|---|---|
| ☐ | 9N-AEE | Beech 1900D | UE-286 | ex N11194 | |
| ☐ | 9N-AEW | Beech 1900D | UE-328 | ex N23179 | |
| ☐ | 9N-AGH | Beech 1900D | UE-409 | ex N4192N | |
| ☐ | 9N-AIM | ATR 42-320 | 0388 | ex F-WQNF | |
| ☐ | 9N-AIN | ATR 42-320 | 0403 | ex F-WQNA | |
| ☐ | 9N-AIT | ATR 42-320 | 0409 | ex F-WKVF | |
| ☐ | 9N-AJO | ATR 72-212A | 0535 | ex F-WNUF | |
| ☐ | 9N-AJS | ATR 72-212A | 0531 | ex B-3023 | ♦ |

## GOMA AIR
Kathmandu (KTM)

| | | | | | |
|---|---|---|---|---|---|
| ☐ | 9N-AJT | Cessna 208B Caravan I | 208B0694 | ex N694MA | dam 02May11♦ |
| ☐ | 9N-AJU | Cessna 208B Caravan I | 208B0770 | ex N74KA | FP♦ |

## GORKHA AIRLINES
(G1)
Pokhara (PKR)

Status uncertain

## GUNA AIRLINES

| | | | | | |
|---|---|---|---|---|---|
| ☐ | 9N-AGI | Beech 1900C-1 | UC-97 | ex N97YV | ♦ |
| ☐ | 9N-AGL | Beech 1900C-1 | UC-108 | ex N15656 | ♦ |
| ☐ | 9N-AHZ | Beech 1900D | UE-180 | ex N862CA | ♦ |

## MAKALU AIR
Kathmandu (KTM)

| | | | | | |
|---|---|---|---|---|---|
| ☐ | 9N-AJG | Cessna 208B Caravan I | 208B0746 | ex N998LA | ♦ |
| ☐ | 9N-AJM | Cessna 208B Caravan I | 208B0561 | ex C-FWAM | |

## MOUNTAIN HELICOPTERS

| | | | | | |
|---|---|---|---|---|---|
| ☐ | 9N-AJJ | Aérospatiale AS350B2 Ecureuil | 3568 | ex ZS-RXR | ♦ |
| ☐ | 9N-AJP | Aérospatiale AS350B3 Ecureuil | 4681 | ex EC-KZY | ♦ |

## NEPAL AIRLINES
Nepal (RA/RNA)
Kathmandu (KTM)

| | | | | | | |
|---|---|---|---|---|---|---|
| ☐ | 9N-ABB | de Havilland DHC-6 Twin Otter 300 | 302 | | | |
| ☐ | 9N-ABM | de Havilland DHC-6 Twin Otter 300 | 455 | ex N302EH | | [KTM] |
| ☐ | 9N-ABO | de Havilland DHC-6 Twin Otter 300 | 638 | | | |
| ☐ | 9N-ABQ | de Havilland DHC-6 Twin Otter 300 | 655 | | | [KTM] |
| ☐ | 9N-ABU | de Havilland DHC-6 Twin Otter 300 | 814 | ex C-GHHY | | |
| ☐ | 9N-ABX | de Havilland DHC-6 Twin Otter 300 | 830 | ex C-GIQS | | dam 19Apr10 |
| ☐ | 9N-ACA | Boeing 757-2F8 | 23850/142 | | Karnali | |
| ☐ | 9N-ACB | Boeing 757-2F8C | 23863/182 | ex N5573K | Gandaki | |

## SHREE AIRLINES
Pokhara/Surkhet (PKR/SKH)

| | | | | | |
|---|---|---|---|---|---|
| ☐ | 9N-ADD | Mil Mi-17-1 (Mi-8ATM) | 59489607385 | ex RA-22160 | |
| ☐ | 9N-ADL | Mil Mi-17-1 (Mi-8ATM) | 59489605283 | ex RA-27093 | [KTM] |
| ☐ | 9N-ADM | Mil Mi-8AMTV-1 | 95640 | ex CCCP-25495 | |
| ☐ | 9N-AJA | Mil Mi-17 | 95895 | ex 9N-ADN | ♦ |

## SITA AIRLINES
Kathmandu (KTM)

| | | | | | |
|---|---|---|---|---|---|
| ☐ | 9N-AHA | Dornier 228-202K | 8123 | ex F-ODZG | |
| ☐ | 9N-AHB | Dornier 228-202K | 8169 | ex F-OGPI | [LUA] |
| ☐ | 9N-AHR | Dornier 228-202 | 8154 | ex C-GSAU | |
| ☐ | 9N-AIJ | Dornier 228-212 | 8239 | ex 8Q-IAS | |
| ☐ | 9N-AJH | Dornier 212 | 8198 | ex VH-ATZ | ♦ |

## SHANGRI-LA AIR

| | | | | | |
|---|---|---|---|---|---|
| ☐ | 9N-AFA | de Havilland DHC-6 Twin Otter 300 | 665 | ex VT-ERV | ♦ |

## YETI AIRLINES (YA) *Kathmandu (KTM)*

| | | | | | |
|---|---|---|---|---|---|
| ☐ | 9N-AHU | British Aerospace Jetstream 41 | 41072 | ex N555HK | |
| ☐ | 9N-AHV | British Aerospace Jetstream 41 | 41077 | ex N561HK | |
| ☐ | 9N-AHW | British Aerospace Jetstream 41 | 41078 | ex N562HK | |
| ☐ | 9N-AHY | British Aerospace Jetstream 41 | 41066 | ex N553HK | |
| ☐ | 9N-AIB | British Aerospace Jetstream 41 | 41017 | ex G-CDYH | |
| ☐ | 9N-AIH | British Aerospace Jetstream 41 | 41085 | ex N567HK | |
| ☐ | 9N-AJC | British Aerospace Jetstream 41 | 41096 | ex G-MAJM | |
| | | | | | |
| ☐ | 9N-AET | de Havilland DHC-6 Twin Otter 300 | 619 | ex C-GBQA | ♦ |
| ☐ | 9N-AEV | de Havilland DHC-6 Twin Otter 300 | 729 | ex C-FWQF | ♦ |

## 9Q- CONGO KINSHASA (Democratic Republic of Congo)

### AIR KASAI *Kinshasa-Ndolo (NLO)*

| | | | | | |
|---|---|---|---|---|---|
| ☐ | 9Q-CFG | LET L-410UVP-E3 | 571911 | ex 5V-TTH | ♦ |
| ☐ | 9Q-CFM | Antonov An-26B | 07310405 | ex RA-26235 | |
| ☐ | 9Q-CFP | Antonov An-26 | 07310605 | ex RA-26237 | |
| ☐ | 9Q-CJA | Britten-Norman BN-2A-21 Islander | 898 | ex I-301 | |
| ☐ | 9Q-CTR | Douglas DC-3 | 9452 | ex ZS-EDX | [FIH] |
| ☐ | 9Q-CYC | Douglas DC-3 | 18977 | ex N9984Q | [FIH] |
| ☐ | 9Q-CYE | Douglas DC-3 | 19771 | ex 79004 | [FIH] |
| ☐ | 9Q-CYN | Antonov An-26 | 4001 | | ♦ |

### AIR KATANGA

| | | | | | |
|---|---|---|---|---|---|
| ☐ | 9Q-CYD | Beech 1900C | UB-40 | ex N495KL | ♦ |

### AIR TROPIQUES *Kinshasa-Ndolo (NLO)*

| | | | | | |
|---|---|---|---|---|---|
| ☐ | 9Q-CEJ | Beech 1900C | UB-74 | ex ZS-ODR | |
| ☐ | 9Q-CEO | LET L-410UVP | 820837 | ex 5R-MGZ | ♦ |
| ☐ | 9Q-CFA | LET L-410UVP-E3 | 871921 | ex 5V-TTF | ♦ |
| ☐ | 9Q-CLN | Fokker F.27 Friendship 100 | 10152 | ex ZS-OEH | wfs |
| ☐ | 9Q-CUZ | Cessna 402B II | 402B1358 | ex OO-HFC | |

### ALAJNIHAH AIR TRANSPORT

| | | | | | |
|---|---|---|---|---|---|
| ☐ | 9Q-CGV | Ilyushin Il-76TD | 0033449441 | ex UR-76574 Morning Star | |

### ATO - AIR TRANSPORT OFFICE *Kinshasa-N'djili (FIH)*

| | | | | | |
|---|---|---|---|---|---|
| ☐ | 9Q-CTO | Lockheed L-188A Electra | 1073 | ex 9Q-CRM | |
| ☐ | 9Q-CVK | Hawker Siddeley HS.780 Andover E.3 | Set 17 | ex P4-BLL | |

### BRAVO AIR CONGO (BRV)

| | | | | | |
|---|---|---|---|---|---|
| ☐ | TN-AHQ | Douglas DC-9-32 | 48126/951 | ex N481SG | |
| ☐ | 9Q-CDO | Douglas DC-9-32 | 48125/947 | ex N481SF | [FIH] |
| ☐ | 9Q-CDT | Douglas DC-9-32 | 48128/964 | ex N128GE | |
| ☐ | 9Q-CVT | Douglas DC-9-32 | 48127/961 | ex N127GE | [FIH] |
| Ops suspended Aug08 | | | | | |

### BUSINESS AVIATION OF CONGO (4P) *Kinshasa-Ndolo (NLO)*

| | | | | | |
|---|---|---|---|---|---|
| ☐ | 9Q-CBA | Nord 262A-42 | 57 | ex OY-IVA | |
| ☐ | 9Q-CYM | LET L-410UVP-E3 | 902402 | ex RA-67620 | ♦ |

### BUTEMBO *Butembo*

| | | | | | |
|---|---|---|---|---|---|
| ☐ | 9Q-CAX | WZK/PZL Antonov An-28 | 1AJ002-08 | ex EX-28810 | |

### CAA – COMPAGNIE AFRICAINE D'AVIATION

| | | | | | |
|---|---|---|---|---|---|
| ☐ | 9Q-CCA | Airbus A320-211 | 0112 | ex N101LF | ♦ |
| ☐ | 9Q-CCO | Airbus A320-211 | 0342 | ex N342DK | ♦ |
| ☐ | 9Q-CSB | Airbus A320-212 | 0438 | ex N190AT | |
| ☐ | 9Q- | Airbus A320-212 | 0189 | ex F-GTHL | wfs♦ |
| ☐ | 9Q- | Airbus A320-211 | 1973 | ex F-WTHL | [FIH]♦ |
| | | | | | |
| ☐ | 9Q-CAB | Fokker 50 | 20276 | ex PH-LXP | |
| ☐ | 9Q-CBD | Fokker 50 | 20270 | ex PH-LXJ | |
| ☐ | 9Q-CHO | Fokker 100 | 11493 | ex PH-ABW | ♦ |
| ☐ | 9Q-CIB | McDonnell-Douglas MD-82 | 49394/1285 | ex N94EV | wfs |
| ☐ | 9Q-CJB | Fokker 50 | 20196 | ex PH-LMS | |

## CETRACA AIR SERVICE

| | | | | |
|---|---|---|---|---|
| ☐ | 9Q-CAZ | LET L-410UVP | 790205 | ex UR-67169 |
| ☐ | 9Q-CKO | Antonov An-26 | 5210 | ex ER-AFW |
| ☐ | 9Q-CKT | Antonov An-26B | 12001 | ex ER-AES |
| ☐ | 9Q-CKX | LET L-410UVP | 790303 | ex ER-LIB |

## CO-ZA AIRWAYS                                                              Goma (GOM)

| | | | | | |
|---|---|---|---|---|---|
| ☐ | 9Q-CBF | Boeing 727-89 | 19139/255 | ex 3D-INM | [FIH]♦ |
| ☐ | 9Q-CML | Antonov An-26 | 7408 | ex ER-AWN   no titles | |

## DOREN AIR CONGO                                                           Goma (GOM)

| | | | | | |
|---|---|---|---|---|---|
| ☐ | 9Q-CQZ | LET L-410UVP | 851339 | ex 9L-LEM | |
| ☐ | 9Q-CXZ | LET L-410UVP | 841201 | ex 9L-LBL | |
| ☐ | 9Q-CZA | LET L-410UVP | 851524 | ex OK-PDC | ♦ |

## ESPACE AVIATION

Ceased ops 2009

## ETRAM AIR WING                                              Kinshasa-N'djili (FIH)

| | | | | |
|---|---|---|---|---|
| ☐ | 4K-48136 | Antonov An-32B | 3103 | ex CCCP-48126 |

## FILAIR                                                      Kinshasa-N'djili (FIH)

| | | | | | |
|---|---|---|---|---|---|
| ☐ | RA-48014 | Antonov An-32B | 3401 | | ♦ |
| ☐ | 9Q-CDN | LET L-410UVP-E | 902422 | ex YU-BXX | |
| ☐ | 9Q-CTR | Antonov An-24RV | 77310802 | ex 9L-LBQ | |

## FREE AIRLINES

| | | | | | |
|---|---|---|---|---|---|
| ☐ | 9Q-COT | LET L-410UVP | 831023 | ex 9Q-CET | ♦ |

## GALAXY KAVATSI AVIATION

| | | | | |
|---|---|---|---|---|
| ☐ | 9Q-CVE | Antonov An-26 | 77305301 | ex RA-26193  Odessa |

## GOMAIR

| | | | | | |
|---|---|---|---|---|---|
| ☐ | 9Q-CBX | Boeing 737-291 | 22089/632 | ex N2089 | ♦ |
| ☐ | 9Q-CDJ | Boeing 727-41 | 20424/817 | ex PP-VLH | [FIH]♦ |
| ☐ | 9Q-CGB | Boeing 727-22 | 19195/406 | ex 9T-TCL | ♦ |
| ☐ | 9Q-CGW | Boeing 737-210 | 19594/102 | ex C-GJLN | ♦ |
| ☐ | 9Q-CMP | Boeing 727-22C | 19892/640 | ex 3D-KMJ | wfs♦ |

## GTRA AIRWAYS

| | | | | | |
|---|---|---|---|---|---|
| ☐ | 9Q-CGJ | Boeing 737-248C | 20220/215 | ex PT-MTA | [FOR]♦ |
| ☐ | 9M- | Boeing 737-230C | 20254/230 | ex PT-MTB | wfs♦ |

## HEWA BORA AIRWAYS                    Allcongo (EO/ALX)              Kinshasa-N'djili (FIH)

Ops suspended Jly11

## ITAB – INTERNATIONAL TRANS AIR BUSINESS                    Lubumbashi-Luano (FBM)

| | | | | | |
|---|---|---|---|---|---|
| ☐ | 9Q-CAP | Nord 262A-32 | 35 | ex F-BPNT | |
| ☐ | 9Q-CDH | Nord 262C-50P | 36 | ex XT-OAG | |
| ☐ | 9Q-CDP | LET L-410UVP-E | 902519 | ex 9L-LCL | |
| ☐ | 9Q-CJJ | Douglas DC-3 | 10110 | ex ZS-NZA | |
| ☐ | 9Q-CMD | LET L-410UVP | 851514 | ex 3D-AVP | ♦ |
| ☐ | (9Q-CON) | BAC One-Eleven 537GF | 261 | ex 9Q-CDY | |
| ☐ | 9Q-CVC | Hawker Siddeley HS.780 Andover C Mk.1 | Set 29 | ex 3C-KKT | |
| ☐ | 9Q-CYA | Britten-Norman BN-2A Islander | 617 | ex G-AYBB | |
| ☐ | 9Q-CYB | Hawker Siddeley HS.780 Andover C Mk.1 | Set 22 | ex NZ7628 | |

## JETAIR SERVICES                                   Kinshasa-Ndolo /N'djili (NLO/FIH)

| | | | | |
|---|---|---|---|---|
| ☐ | 9Q-CCJ | Partenavia P.68B | 163 | ex 9Q-CEZ |
| ☐ | 9Q-CCK | Cessna 402B | 402B0304 | ex TN-ACJ |

## KIN AVIA

| | | | | | |
|---|---|---|---|---|---|
| ☐ | 9Q-CEG | LET L-410UVP-E | 912607 | ex 3D-WDR | ♦ |
| ☐ | 9Q-CEN | LET L-410UVP-E10 | 892325 | ex 3D-DEN | ♦ |
| ☐ | 9Q-CIN | LET L-410UVP-E10 | 902515 | ex 3D-FTN | ♦ |
| ☐ | 9Q-CKA | LET L-410UVP-E | 861722 | | ♦ |
| ☐ | 9Q-CMA | LET L-410UVP-E | 902515 | | ♦ |
| ☐ | 9Q-CRJ | LET L-410UVP-E | 872006 | ex 3D-MSC | ♦ |

## KORONGO                                        (ZC)

| | | | | | |
|---|---|---|---|---|---|
| ☐ | OO-DJJ | British Aerospace 146 Srs.200 | E2196 | ex SE-DRM | <BEL o/o♦ |
| ☐ | OO-LTM | Boeing 737-3M8 | 25070/2037 | ex F-GMTM | <BEL o/o♦ |
| ☐ | OO-MJE | British Aerospace 146 Srs.200 | E2192 | ex G-6-192 | <BEL♦ |

## LIGNES AERIENNES CONGOLAISES          Congolaise (LCG)          Kinshasa-Ndolo (NLO)

| | | | | | |
|---|---|---|---|---|---|
| ☐ | 9Q-CSV | Boeing 737-281 | 20276/231 | ex 4X-BAG | [FIH] |
| ☐ | 9Q-CLG | Boeing 737-2L9 | 22071/620 | ex ZS-PIV | [FIH]♦ |

Ceased ops 2005 but believed to have recommenced limited services Aug06. Attempted partnerships with AZW and RKM in 2008 were unsuccessful. Plans to resume ops.

## LUBUMBASHI AIR SERVICE

| | | | | | |
|---|---|---|---|---|---|
| ☐ | 9Q- | Fokker F.27 Friendship 500 | 10634 | ex N19XG | [JNB]♦ |

## MALIFT AIR                              Malila (MLC)          Kinshasa-N'djili/Khartoum (FIH/KRT)

| | | | | | |
|---|---|---|---|---|---|
| ☐ | EW-26127 | Antonov An-26A | 12701 | | <BRU♦ |

## MALU AVIATION                                              Kinshasa-Ndolo (NLO)

| | | | | | |
|---|---|---|---|---|---|
| ☐ | 9Q-CDV | Partenavia P.68B | 207 | | |
| ☐ | 9Q-CKN | Nord 262C-61 | 74 | ex (F-OHRB) | ♦ |
| ☐ | 9Q-CLD | Short SC.7 Skyvan 3 | SH1870 | ex SE-LDK | ♦ |
| ☐ | 9Q-CSP | WSK-PZL/Antonov An-28 | 1AJ008-09 | ex 9Q-CJF | |
| ☐ | 9Q-CSD | Short SC.7 Skyvan | SH1831 | ex ZS-ORN | |

## MANGO MAT AIRLINES                                          Goma (GOM)

| | | | | | |
|---|---|---|---|---|---|
| ☐ | 9Q-CGM | Antonov An-26B | 6401 | | |
| ☐ | 9Q-CXG | LET L-410UVP | | | ♦ |

## PROTOCOLE AVIATION CARGO

| | | | | | |
|---|---|---|---|---|---|
| ☐ | TN-AIE | Douglas DC-8-62F | 46027/437 | ex 9G-MKG | ♦ |
| ☐ | 9Q-CTA | Douglas DC-8-54F | 45802/247 | ex 3D-AFR | ♦ |

## SERVICES AIR

| | | | | | |
|---|---|---|---|---|---|
| ☐ | 5X-HJI | Airbus A310-304F | 413 | ex VT-EJI | ♦ |
| ☐ | 9Q-CFL | Antonov An-26B | 14003 | ex RA-26593 | |
| ☐ | 9Q-CHS | Boeing 727-2S2F | 22930/1824 | ex N361CW | ♦ |
| ☐ | 9Q-CNJ | Boeing 727-2S2F | 22934/1828 | ex N3588W | ♦ |
| ☐ | 9Q-CSS | Boeing 727-2S2F | 22924/1818 | ex N358PZ | ♦ |
| ☐ | 9Q-CVS | Boeing 727-2S2F | 22931/1825 | ex N252CY | ♦ |

## STAG

| | | | | | |
|---|---|---|---|---|---|
| ☐ | 9Q-CFB | Antonov An-26B | 56312909 | ex RA-26577 | |

## SWALA AIRLINES                                          Bukavu (BKY)

| | | | | | |
|---|---|---|---|---|---|
| ☐ | 9Q-CXF | Short SC.7 Skyvan | SH1915 | ex (5Y-  ) | |

## TMK AIR COMMUTER                                          Goma (GOM)

| | | | | | |
|---|---|---|---|---|---|
| ☐ | 9Q-CRE | de Havilland DHC-6 Twin Otter 300 | 612 | ex PH-STK | ♦ |

Suspended ops 31Aug11

## TRANSAIR CARGO                                          Kinshasa-N'djili (FIH)

| | | | | | |
|---|---|---|---|---|---|
| ☐ | 3X-GHH | Douglas DC-8-73CF | 46133/534 | ex EC-IGZ | [JNB]♦ |
| ☐ | 9Q-CJG | Douglas DC-8-62F | 46110/487 | ex ZS-POL | ♦ |
| ☐ | 9Q-CJH | Douglas DC-8-62F (BAC 3) | 46023/407 | ex 3X-GEN | |

| | | | | | |
|---|---|---|---|---|---|
| ☐ | 9Q-CJL | Douglas DC-8-62F (BAC 3) | 45909/307 | ex N802BN | |
| ☐ | 9Q-CYS | NAMC YS-11A-205 | 2051 | ex 3D-CYS | wfs |

## TRANS SERVICE AIRLIFT

| | | | | | |
|---|---|---|---|---|---|
| ☐ | 9Q-CCR | Nord 262B-11 | 4 | ex F-GBEI | ♦ |

## VIRUNGA AIR CHARTER     Goma (GOM)

| | | | | |
|---|---|---|---|---|
| ☐ | 9Q-CDD | Dornier 28D-1 Skyservant | 4025 | ex D-IFAQ |
| ☐ | 9Q-CTL | Partenavia P.68B | 145 | ex 5Y-BCG |
| ☐ | 9Q-CTN | Partenavia P.68C-TC | 238-04-TC | ex OO-TZT |
| ☐ | 9Q-CTX | Dornier 128-6 Turbo Skyservant | 6007 | ex D-IDOQ |

## WILL AIRLIFT     Kinshasa-N'djili (FIH)

| | | | | | |
|---|---|---|---|---|---|
| ☐ | 9Q-CNR | Douglas DC-9-32 | 47090/190 | ex ZS-NRC | ♦ |

## WIMBI DIRA AIRWAYS     Wimbi Dera (9C/WDA)     Kinshasa-N'djili (FIH)

| | | | | | |
|---|---|---|---|---|---|
| ☐ | 9Q-CWE | Douglas DC-9-32 (ABS 3) | 47701/822 | ex N212ME | wfs |
| ☐ | 9Q-CWH | Douglas DC-9-32 (ABS 3) | 47744/837 | ex N215ME | wfs |

## 9U-     BURUNDI (Republic of Burundi)

## AIR BURUNDI     Air Burundi (8Y/PBU)     Bujumbura (BJM)

| | | | | | |
|---|---|---|---|---|---|
| ☐ | 9U-BHG | Beech 1900C-1 | UC-147 | ex TN-AFK | |

## 9V-     SINGAPORE (Republic of Singapore)

## AIRMARK SINGAPORE     Singapore-Seletar (XSP)

Leases aircraft from other operators as required

## JETSTAR ASIA AIRWAYS     Jetstar (3K/JSA)     Singapore-Changi (SIN)

| | | | | | |
|---|---|---|---|---|---|
| ☐ | 9V-JSA | Airbus A320-232 | 2316 | ex F-WWDR | |
| ☐ | 9V-JSB | Airbus A320-232 | 2356 | ex F-WWIQ | |
| ☐ | 9V-JSC | Airbus A320-232 | 2395 | ex F-WWIS | |
| ☐ | 9V-JSD | Airbus A320-232 | 2401 | ex F-WWIB | |
| ☐ | 9V-JSE | Airbus A320-232 | 2423 | ex VH-JQW | ♦ |
| ☐ | 9V-JSF | Airbus A320-232 | 2453 | ex VH-JQH | |
| ☐ | 9V-JSG | Airbus A320-232 | 2457 | ex VH-JQE | |
| ☐ | 9V-JSH | Airbus A320-232 | 2604 | ex VH-VQA | |
| ☐ | 9V-JSI | Airbus A320-232 | 4443 | ex F-WWIC | |
| ☐ | 9V-JSJ | Airbus A320-232 | 4515 | ex F-WWBN | ♦ |
| ☐ | 9V-JSK | Airbus A320-232 | 4772 | ex F-WWDH | |
| ☐ | 9V-JSL | Airbus A320-232 | 4786 | ex F-WWDU | ♦ |
| ☐ | 9V-JSM | Airbus A320-232 | 4872 | ex F-WWDQ | ♦ |
| ☐ | 9V-JSN | Airbus A320-232 | 4914 | ex D-AVVO | ♦ |
| ☐ | 9V-VLE | Airbus A320-232 | 2156 | ex 9V-VLA | ♦ |
| ☐ | 9V-VLF | Airbus A320-232 | 2164 | ex 9V-VLB | ♦ |

## JETT 8 AIRLINES     (JEC)     Singapore-Changi (SIN)

| | | | | | | |
|---|---|---|---|---|---|---|
| ☐ | 9V-JEA | Boeing 747-2D3B (SF) | 22579/514 | ex JA8192 | Tai-Pan | [SIN] |

## SCOOT

| | | | | | |
|---|---|---|---|---|---|
| ☐ | 9V-OVA | Boeing 777-212ER | 28507/67 | ex 9V-SGA | wfs♦ |
| ☐ | 9V-OVC | Boeing 777-212ER | 28509/86 | ex 9V-SQC | wfs♦ |

## SILKAIR     Silkair (MI/SLK)     Singapore-Changi (SIN)

| | | | | | |
|---|---|---|---|---|---|
| ☐ | 9V-SBC | Airbus A319-132 | 1228 | ex D-AVYL | |
| ☐ | 9V-SBD | Airbus A319-132 | 1698 | ex D-AVYE | |
| ☐ | 9V-SBE | Airbus A319-132 | 2568 | ex D-AVXA | |
| ☐ | 9V-SBF | Airbus A319-132 | 3104 | ex D-AVYI | |
| ☐ | 9V-SBG | Airbus A319-132 | 4215 | ex D-AVYH | |
| ☐ | 9V-SBH | Airbus A319-132 | 4259 | ex D-AVWO | |
| ☐ | 9V-SLB | Airbus A320-232 | 0899 | ex F-WWDL | |
| ☐ | 9V-SLC | Airbus A320-232 | 0969 | ex F-WWBO | |
| ☐ | 9V-SLD | Airbus A320-232 | 1422 | ex F-WWBK | |

| | | | | | | |
|---|---|---|---|---|---|---|
| ☐ | 9V-SLE | Airbus A320-232 | 1561 | ex F-WWBC | | |
| ☐ | 9V-SLF | Airbus A320-232 | 2058 | ex F-WWBK | | |
| ☐ | 9V-SLG | Airbus A320-233 | 2252 | ex F-WWBB | | |
| ☐ | 9V-SLH | Airbus A320-233 | 2517 | ex F-WWIG | | |
| ☐ | 9V-SLI | Airbus A320-233 | 2775 | ex F-WWDS | | |
| ☐ | 9V-SLJ | Airbus A320-233 | 3570 | ex F-WWBD | | |
| ☐ | 9V-SLK | Airbus A320-233 | 3821 | ex F-WWIQ | | |
| ☐ | 9V-SLL | Airbus A320-233 | 4118 | ex D-AVVU | | |
| ☐ | 9V-SLM | Airbus A320-233 | 4457 | ex D-AXAA | | |
| ☐ | 9V-SLN | Airbus A320-233 | 4701 | ex D-AUBE | | ♦ |
| ☐ | 9V-SLO | Airbus A320-233 | 5050 | ex F-WWDY | | ♦ |
| ☐ | 9V-SLP | Airbus A320-233 | 5089 | ex F-WWIM | | o/o♦ |

## SINGAPORE AIRLINES — Singapore (SQ/SIA) — Singapore-Changi (SIN)

Member of Star Alliance

| | | | | | | |
|---|---|---|---|---|---|---|
| ☐ | 9V-STA | Airbus A330-343E | 978 | ex F-WWKZ | | |
| ☐ | 9V-STB | Airbus A330-343E | 983 | ex F-WWYZ | | |
| ☐ | 9V-STC | Airbus A330-343E | 986 | ex F-WWKG | | |
| ☐ | 9V-STD | Airbus A330-343E | 997 | ex F-WWYM | | |
| ☐ | 9V-STE | Airbus A330-343E | 1006 | ex F-WWYB | | |
| ☐ | 9V-STF | Airbus A330-343E | 1010 | ex F-WWYF | | |
| ☐ | 9V-STG | Airbus A330-343E | 1012 | ex F-WWKA | | |
| ☐ | 9V-STH | Airbus A330-343E | 1015 | ex F-WWKV | | |
| ☐ | 9V-STI | Airbus A330-343E | 1085 | ex F-WWKA | | |
| ☐ | 9V-STJ | Airbus A330-343E | 1098 | ex F-WWKQ | | |
| ☐ | 9V-STK | Airbus A330-343E | 1099 | ex F-WWYD | | |
| ☐ | 9V-STL | Airbus A330-343E | 1105 | ex F-WWKR | | |
| ☐ | 9V-STM | Airbus A330-343E | 1107 | ex F-WWKP | | |
| ☐ | 9V-STN | Airbus A330-343E | 1124 | ex F-WWYK | | |
| ☐ | 9V-STO | Airbus A330-343E | 1132 | ex F-WWYL | | |
| ☐ | 9V-STP | Airbus A330-343E | 1146 | ex F-WWYV | | |
| ☐ | 9V-STQ | Airbus A330-343E | 1149 | ex F-WWYH | | |
| ☐ | 9V-STR | Airbus A330-343E | 1156 | ex F-WWKK | | |
| ☐ | 9V-STS | Airbus A330-343E | 1157 | ex F-WWYX | | |
| ☐ | 9V-SGA | Airbus A340-541 | 492 | ex F-WWTP | | |
| ☐ | 9V-SGB | Airbus A340-541 | 499 | ex F-WWTR | | |
| ☐ | 9V-SGC | Airbus A340-541 | 478 | ex F-WWTG | | |
| ☐ | 9V-SGD | Airbus A340-541 | 560 | ex F-WWTM | | |
| ☐ | 9V-SGE | Airbus A340-541 | 563 | ex F-WWTU | | |
| ☐ | 9V-SKA | Airbus A380-841 | 003 | ex F-WWSA | | |
| ☐ | 9V-SKB | Airbus A380-841 | 005 | ex F-WWSB | | |
| ☐ | 9V-SKC | Airbus A380-841 | 006 | ex F-WWSC | | |
| ☐ | 9V-SKD | Airbus A380-841 | 008 | ex F-WWSE | | |
| ☐ | 9V-SKE | Airbus A380-841 | 010 | ex F-WWSG | | |
| ☐ | 9V-SKF | Airbus A380-841 | 012 | ex F-WWSI | | |
| ☐ | 9V-SKG | Airbus A380-841 | 019 | ex F-WWSP | | |
| ☐ | 9V-SKH | Airbus A380-841 | 021 | ex F-WWSQ | | |
| ☐ | 9V-SKI | Airbus A380-841 | 034 | ex F-WWSC | | |
| ☐ | 9V-SKJ | Airbus A380-841 | 045 | ex F-WWSG | | |
| ☐ | 9V-SKK | Airbus A380-841 | 051 | ex F-WWAH | | |
| ☐ | 9V-SKL | Airbus A380-841 | 058 | ex F-WWSI | | |
| ☐ | 9V-SKM | Airbus A380-841 | 065 | ex F-WWSM | | |
| ☐ | 9V-SKN | Airbus A380-841 | 071 | ex F-WWSX | | |
| ☐ | 9V-SKP | Airbus A380-841 | 076 | ex F-WWSC | | |
| ☐ | 9V-SKQ | Airbus A380-841 | 079 | ex F-WWST | | |
| ☐ | 9V-SKR | Airbus A380-841 | 082 | ex F-WWSH | | ♦ |
| ☐ | 9V-SKS | Airbus A380-841 | 085 | ex F-WWAH | | ♦ |
| ☐ | 9V-SKT | Airbus A380-841 | 092 | ex F-WWSA | | o/o♦ |
| ☐ | 9V-SQB | Boeing 777-212ER | 28508/83 | | | |
| ☐ | 9V-SQD | Boeing 777-212ER | 28510/90 | | | |
| ☐ | 9V-SQE | Boeing 777-212ER | 28511/122 | | | |
| ☐ | 9V-SQF | Boeing 777-212ER | 28512/126 | | | |
| ☐ | 9V-SQH | Boeing 777-212ER | 28519/237 | | | |
| ☐ | 9V-SQI | Boeing 777-212ER | 28530/390 | ex N5023Q | | |
| ☐ | 9V-SQJ | Boeing 777-212ER | 30875/406 | | | |
| ☐ | 9V-SQK | Boeing 777-212ER | 33368/428 | | | |
| ☐ | 9V-SQL | Boeing 777-212ER | 33370/451 | | | |
| ☐ | 9V-SQM | Boeing 777-212ER | 33372/485 | | | |
| ☐ | 9V-SQN | Boeing 777-212ER | 33373/487 | | | |
| ☐ | 9V-SRF | Boeing 777-212ER | 28521/330 | | | |
| ☐ | 9V-SRG | Boeing 777-212ER | 28522/337 | | | |
| ☐ | 9V-SRH | Boeing 777-212ER | 30866/343 | | | |
| ☐ | 9V-SRI | Boeing 777-212ER | 30867/348 | | | |
| ☐ | 9V-SRJ | Boeing 777-212ER | 28527/372 | | | |
| ☐ | 9V-SRK | Boeing 777-212ER | 28529/389 | ex N5022E | | |
| ☐ | 9V-SRL | Boeing 777-212ER | 32334/409 | | | |
| ☐ | 9V-SRM | Boeing 777-212ER | 32320/438 | | | |

| | | | | | |
|---|---|---|---|---|---|
| ☐ | 9V-SRN | Boeing 777-212ER | 32318/441 | | |
| ☐ | 9V-SRO | Boeing 777-212ER | 32321/447 | | |
| ☐ | 9V-SRP | Boeing 777-212ER | 33369/448 | | |
| ☐ | 9V-SRQ | Boeing 777-212ER | 33371/449 | | |
| ☐ | 9V-SVE | Boeing 777-212ER | 30870/374 | | |
| ☐ | 9V-SVH | Boeing 777-212ER | 28532/407 | ex N5022E | |
| ☐ | 9V-SVI | Boeing 777-212ER | 32316/412 | | |
| ☐ | 9V-SVJ | Boeing 777-212ER | 32335/415 | | |
| ☐ | 9V-SVK | Boeing 777-212ER | 28520/419 | | |
| ☐ | 9V-SVL | Boeing 777-212ER | 32336/422 | | |
| ☐ | 9V-SVM | Boeing 777-212ER | 30874/430 | | |
| ☐ | 9V-SVN | Boeing 777-212ER | 30873/431 | | |
| ☐ | 9V-SVO | Boeing 777-212ER | 28533/471 | | |
| ☐ | 9V-SWA | Boeing 777-312ER | 34568/586 | ex N6018N | |
| ☐ | 9V-SWB | Boeing 777-312ER | 33377/592 | | |
| ☐ | 9V-SWD | Boeing 777-312ER | 34569/600 | | |
| ☐ | 9V-SWE | Boeing 777-312ER | 34570/602 | | |
| ☐ | 9V-SWF | Boeing 777-312ER | 34571/603 | | |
| ☐ | 9V-SWG | Boeing 777-312ER | 34572/604 | | |
| ☐ | 9V-SWH | Boeing 777-312ER | 34573/615 | | |
| ☐ | 9V-SWI | Boeing 777-312ER | 34574/618 | | |
| ☐ | 9V-SWJ | Boeing 777-312ER | 34575/623 | | |
| ☐ | 9V-SWK | Boeing 777-312ER | 34576/644 | ex N6009F | |
| ☐ | 9V-SWL | Boeing 777-312ER | 34577/673 | | |
| ☐ | 9V-SWM | Boeing 777-312ER | 34578/701 | | |
| ☐ | 9V-SWN | Boeing 777-312ER | 34579/703 | | |
| ☐ | 9V-SWO | Boeing 777-312ER | 34580/708 | | |
| ☐ | 9V-SWP | Boeing 777-312ER | 34581/710 | | |
| ☐ | 9V-SWQ | Boeing 777-312ER | 34582/716 | | |
| ☐ | 9V-SWR | Boeing 777-312ER | 34583/722 | | |
| ☐ | 9V-SWS | Boeing 777-312ER | 34584/729 | | |
| ☐ | 9V-SWT | Boeing 777-312ER | 34585/759 | | |
| ☐ | 9V-SYE | Boeing 777-312 | 28531/244 | | Star Alliance c/s |
| ☐ | 9V-SYF | Boeing 777-312 | 30868/360 | | |
| ☐ | 9V-SYG | Boeing 777-312 | 28528/364 | | |
| ☐ | 9V-SYH | Boeing 777-312 | 32317/420 | ex N5020K | |
| ☐ | 9V-SYI | Boeing 777-312 | 32327/484 | ex N5028Y | |
| ☐ | 9V-SYJ | Boeing 777-312 | 33374/503 | ex N50217 | |
| ☐ | 9V-SYK | Boeing 777-312 | 33375/505 | | |
| ☐ | 9V-SYL | Boeing 777-312 | 33376/515 | | |
| ☐ | 9V-SPP | Boeing 747-412 | 28029/1276 | | Star Alliance c/s |
| ☐ | 9V-SPQ | Boeing 747-412 | 28025/1289 | | |

| SINGAPORE AIRLINES CARGO | | Singapore Cargo (SQ/SQC) | | | Singapore-Changi (SIN) |
|---|---|---|---|---|---|
| ☐ | 9V-SCA | Boeing 747-412BCF | 26550/1040 | ex 9V-SPA | ♦ |
| ☐ | 9V-SCB | Boeing 747-412F | 26554/1070 | ex 9V-SPE | ♦ |
| ☐ | 9V-SFC | Boeing 747-412F | 26560/1052 | | >CCA |
| ☐ | 9V-SFD | Boeing 747-412F | 26553/1069 | | |
| ☐ | 9V-SFF | Boeing 747-412F | 28026/1105 | | |
| ☐ | 9V-SFG | Boeing 747-412F | 26558/1173 | | |
| ☐ | 9V-SFJ | Boeing 747-412F | 26559/1285 | | |
| ☐ | 9V-SFK | Boeing 747-412F | 28030/1298 | | |
| ☐ | 9V-SFL | Boeing 747-412F | 32897/1322 | ex N5022E | [VCV] |
| ☐ | 9V-SFM | Boeing 747-412F | 32898/1333 | | |
| ☐ | 9V-SFN | Boeing 747-412F | 32899/1342 | | |
| ☐ | 9V-SFO | Boeing 747-412F | 32900/1349 | | |
| ☐ | 9V-SFP | Boeing 747-412F | 32902/1364 | | |
| ☐ | 9V-SFQ | Boeing 747-412F | 32901/1369 | | |

| TIGER AIRWAYS | | (TR/TGW) | | | Singapore-Changi (SIN) |
|---|---|---|---|---|---|
| ☐ | PK-RMP | Airbus A320-232 | 5073 | ex D-AUBH | >MDL♦ |
| ☐ | 9V-TAB | Airbus A320-232 | 2195 | ex F-WWIZ | |
| ☐ | 9V-TAC | Airbus A320-232 | 2331 | ex F-WWIF | |
| ☐ | 9V-TAD | Airbus A320-232 | 2340 | ex F-WWIY | |
| ☐ | 9V-TAE | Airbus A320-232 | 2724 | ex F-WWDO | |
| ☐ | 9V-TAF | Airbus A320-232 | 2728 | ex F-WWDU | |
| ☐ | 9V-TAM | Airbus A320-232 | 4181 | ex F-WWIA | |
| ☐ | 9V-TAN | Airbus A320-232 | 4210 | ex F-WWBR | |
| ☐ | 9V-TAO | Airbus A320-232 | 4421 | ex F-WWDZ | |
| ☐ | 9V-TAP | Airbus A320-232 | 4445 | ex F-WWIH | |
| ☐ | 9V-TAQ | Airbus A320-232 | 4469 | ex F-WWBV | |
| ☐ | 9V-TAR | Airbus A320-232 | 4491 | ex F-WWIB | |
| ☐ | 9V-TAS | Airbus A320-232 | 4493 | ex F-WWID | |
| ☐ | 9V-TAT | Airbus A320-232 | 4532 | ex F-WWDR | |
| ☐ | 9V-TAU | Airbus A320-232 | 4561 | ex F-WWBB | |
| ☐ | 9V-TAV | Airbus A320-232 | 4608 | ex F-WWIK | ♦ |
| ☐ | 9V-TAW | Airbus A320-232 | 4804 | ex D-AVVX | ♦ |

| | | | | | | |
|---|---|---|---|---|---|---|
| ☐ | 9V-TAX | Airbus A320-232 | 4812 | ex F-WWDL | | ♦ |
| ☐ | 9V-TAY | Airbus A320-232 | 4874 | ex F-WWDY | | ♦ |
| ☐ | 9V-TAZ | Airbus A320-232 | 4879 | ex F-WWIN | | ♦ |
| ☐ | 9V-TJR | Airbus A320-232 | 4645 | ex VH-FJR | | ♦ |
| ☐ | 9V-TRD | Airbus A320-232 | 4931 | ex D-AXAD | | ♦ |
| ☐ | 9V-TRE | Airbus A320-232 | 4973 | ex 9V-TRE | | >MDL♦ |
| ☐ | 9V-TRF | Airbus A320-232 | 5120 | ex F-WWBI | | o/o♦ |
| ☐ | 9V-TRA | Airbus A319-132 | 3757 | ex D-AVXC | | >SRQ |
| ☐ | 9V-TRB | Airbus A319-132 | 3801 | ex D-AVYA | | >SRQ |

## 9XR-   RWANDA (Rwanda Republic)

### RWANDAIR EXPRESS — Rwandair (WB/RWD) — Kigali (KGL)

| | | | | | | |
|---|---|---|---|---|---|---|
| ☐ | ET-ALX | de Havilland DHC-8-202 | 475 | ex ZK-ECR | | <TNW |
| ☐ | 7Q-YKW | Boeing 737-522 | 25384/2149 | ex N917UA | Sapitwa | <AML |
| ☐ | 9XR-WA | Canadair CRJ-200LR | 7439 | ex D-ACHG | | |
| ☐ | 9XR-WB | Canadair CRJ-200LR | 7449 | ex D-ACHH | | |
| ☐ | 9XR-WD | Boeing 737-55D | 27416/2389 | ex SP-LKA | | |
| ☐ | 9XR-WE | Boeing 737-55D | 27417/2392 | ex SP-LKB | | |
| ☐ | 9XR-WF | Boeing 737-84Y/W | 40892/3737 | | | ♦ |
| ☐ | 9XR-WG | Boeing 737-84Y/W | 40893/3817 | | | ♦ |

### SILVERBACK CARGOFREIGHTERS — Silverback (VRB) — Kigali (KGL)

| | | | | | | |
|---|---|---|---|---|---|---|
| ☐ | 9XR-SC | Douglas DC-8-62F | 46068/463 | ex N990CF | | wfs |
| ☐ | 9XR-SD | Douglas DC-8-62F | 45956/376 | ex N994CF | | wfs |

## 9Y-     TRINIDAD & TOBAGO (Republic of Trinidad & Tobago)

### BRIKO AIR SERVICES — (BKO)

| | | | | | |
|---|---|---|---|---|---|
| ☐ | 9Y-BKO | British Aerospace Jetstream 31 | 932 | ex N338TE | |
| ☐ | 9Y-DAS | Aérospatiale AS355F2 Twin Star | 5402 | ex N227NR | |
| ☐ | 9Y-JET | British Aerospace Jetstream 31 | 939 | ex N340TE | |
| ☐ | 9Y-TIY | Cessna 402C | 402C0265 | ex N3146M | |

### BRISTOW CARIBBEAN — Port of Spain (POS)

| | | | | | | |
|---|---|---|---|---|---|---|
| ☐ | 9Y-BCO | Bell 412EP | 36401 | ex N8087N | | |
| ☐ | 9Y-BHI | Bell 412 | 33032 | ex N418EH | | |
| ☐ | 9Y-BOB | Bell 412SP | 36256 | ex N368AL | | |
| ☐ | 9Y-BRS | Bell 412EP | 36396 | ex N10269 | | |
| ☐ | 9Y-EVS | Bell 412SP | 33212 | ex XA-SBJ | | <OLOG |
| ☐ | 9Y-ONE | Bell 412EP | 36421 | ex N387AL | | |
| ☐ | 9Y-SKY | Bell 412EP | 36420 | ex N8010C | | |
| ☐ | 9Y-TJM | Bell 412SP | 33169 | ex PT-HUO | | |
| ☐ | 9Y-TNT | Bell 412EP | 36414 | ex N386AL | | |
| ☐ | 9Y-TSP | Bell 412SP | 33169 | ex XA-TAM | | |
| ☐ | 9Y-HWO | Sikorsky S-76C | 760804 | ex N804L | | ♦ |
| ☐ | 9Y-TJT | Sikorsky S-76C++ | 760618 | ex N877AL | | ♦ |

### CARIBBEAN AIRLINES — West Indian (BW/BWA) — Port of Spain (POS)

| | | | | | | |
|---|---|---|---|---|---|---|
| ☐ | 9Y-TTA | ATR 72-600 | 0968 | ex F-WWLS | | ♦ |
| ☐ | 9Y-TTB | ATR 72-600 | 0973 | ex F-WWLX | | ♦ |
| ☐ | 9Y-TTC | ATR 72-600 | 989 | ex F-WWLP | | o/o♦ |
| ☐ | 9Y- | ATR 72-600 | 993 | ex F-WWLS | | o/o♦ |
| ☐ | 9Y- | ATR 72-600 | 997 | ex F-WW | | o/o♦ |
| ☐ | 9Y- | ATR 72-600 | 1021 | ex F-WW | | o/o♦ |
| ☐ | 9Y-ANU | Boeing 737-8Q8/W | 28235/697 | (ex 9Y-SLU) | | |
| ☐ | 9Y-BGI | Boeing 737-8Q8/W | 28232/547 | | | |
| ☐ | 9Y-GEO | Boeing 737-8Q8/W | 28225/433 | ex PH-HSX | | |
| ☐ | 9Y-KIN | Boeing 737-8Q8/W | 28234/680 | (ex 9Y-ANU) | | |
| ☐ | 9Y-MBJ | Boeing 737-85P/W | 33980/2245 | ex EC-KBV | | |
| ☐ | 9Y-POS | Boeing 737-8Q8/W | 28230/506 | | | |
| ☐ | 9Y-SLU | Boeing 737-83N/W | 28246/1081 | ex N317TZ | | |
| ☐ | 9Y-TAB | Boeing 737-8Q8/W | 28233/598 | | | |
| ☐ | 9Y-TJR | Boeing 737-8K2/W | 37160/2880 | ex PH-HSW | | <TRA♦ |
| ☐ | 9Y-TJS | Boeing 737-8K2/W | 34171/2950 | ex PH-HSA | | <TRA♦ |
| ☐ | 9Y-WIL | de Havilland DHC-8Q-311 | 489 | ex C-GFCW | | |
| ☐ | 9Y-WIN | de Havilland DHC-8Q-311 | 499 | ex C-GDSG | | |

| | | | | | |
|---|---|---|---|---|---|
| ☐ | 9Y-WIP | de Havilland DHC-8Q-311 | 538 | ex C-FDII | |
| ☐ | 9Y-WIT | de Havilland DHC-8Q-311 | 487 | ex OE-LSA | |
| ☐ | 9Y-WIZ | de Havilland DHC-8Q-311 | 557 | ex C-GEMU | |
| ☐ | EC-KUL | ATR 72-212A | 809 | ex F-WWET | <SWT♦ |

## EVERGREEN HELICOPTERS INTERNATIONAL (TRINIDAD)

Fleet disposed of by Sep11

# JET AND TURBOPROP AIRLINERS IN NON-AIRLINE SERVICE

| | | | | |
|---|---|---|---|---|
| ☐ | F-BUAD | Airbus A300B-B1-100 | 003 | Centre d'Essais en Vol - CEV |
| ☐ | YI-APX | Airbus A300B-B4-200 | 239 | Republic of Iraq |
| | | | | |
| ☐ | A7-AFE | Airbus A310-308 | 667 | Qatar Amiri Flight |
| ☐ | EC-HLA | Airbus A310-324ET | 489 | EADS Military Transport Aircraft Division |
| ☐ | HS-TYQ | Airbus A310-324 | 591 | Royal Thai Air Force (also 60202) |
| ☐ | HZ-NSA | Airbus A310-304 | 431 | Al-Atheer Establishment |
| ☐ | N461VA | Airbus A310-222 | 367 | Van Vliet International |
| ☐ | N461WA | Airbus A310-222 | 372 | Van Vliet International |
| ☐ | J-757 | Airbus A310-304 | 473 | Pakistan Air Force |
| ☐ | T.22-1 | Airbus A310-304 | 550 | Spanish Air Force |
| ☐ | 10+22 | Airbus A310-304 | 503 | German Air Force |
| ☐ | T.22+2 | Airbus A310-304 | 551 | Spanish Air Force |
| | | | | |
| ☐ | A6-AJC | Airbus A318 Elite | 3985 | AJA - Al Jaber Aviation |
| ☐ | B-6186 | Airbus A318 Elite | 3333 | Asia United Business Aviation |
| ☐ | B-6188 | Airbus A318 Elite | 3617 | Air China Business Jet |
| ☐ | B-6411 | Airbus A318 Elite | 3886 | BAA Jet Management Ltd |
| ☐ | HZ-A5 | Airbus A318 Elite | 2910 | Alpha Star Aviation |
| ☐ | LX-GJC | Airbus A318 Elite | 3100 | Silver Arrows |
| ☐ | OE-ICE | Airbus A318-112CJ | 4503 | Jet Alliance |
| ☐ | VP-CCH | Airbus A318 Elite | 4211 | Gama Aviation |
| ☐ | VP-CKH | Airbus A318 Elite | 3530 | National Air Services (NAS) |
| ☐ | VP-CKS | Airbus A318 Elite | 3238 | National Air Services (NAS) |
| ☐ | VQ-BDD | Airbus A318 Elite | 3751 | Royal Flight of Jordan |
| ☐ | 9H-AFL | Airbus A318 Elite | 3363 | Comlux Aviation Malta |
| | | | | |
| ☐ | A4O-AJ | Airbus A319CJ | 4992 | Oman Royal Flight |
| ☐ | A6-ESH | Airbus A319CJ | 0910 | Sharjah Ruler's Flight |
| ☐ | A7-HHJ | Airbus A319CJ | 1335 | Qatar Amiri Flight |
| ☐ | A7-MED | Airbus A319-133LR | 4114 | Qatar Amiri Flight |
| ☐ | A7-MHH | Airbus A319-115CJ | 3994 | Qatar Amiri Flight |
| ☐ | B-6178 | Airbus A319-132 | 3548 | Capital Airlines |
| ☐ | CS-TLU | Airbus A319CJ | 1256 | White |
| ☐ | CS-TQJ | Airbus A319CJ | 2675 | White |
| ☐ | D-ADNA | Airbus A319CJ | 1053 | DC Aviation |
| ☐ | D-AHAD | Airbus A319CJ | 3632 | DC Aviation |
| ☐ | D-ALEY | Airbus A319CJ | 3513 | DC Aviation |
| ☐ | EK-RA01 | Airbus A319-132 | 0913 | Government of Armenia |
| ☐ | F-WHUJ | Airbus A319CJ | 4679 | Russian State Transport |
| ☐ | G-NMAK | Airbus A319CJ | 2550 | Twinjet Aircraft |
| ☐ | G-NOAH | Airbus A319CJ | 3826 | Acropolis Aviation Ltd |
| ☐ | HS-TYR | Airbus A319CJ | 1908 | Royal Thai Air Force (Also 60221) |
| ☐ | HZ-A4 | Airbus A319-112 | 1494 | Alpha Star Aviation Services |
| ☐ | LZ-AOB | Airbus A319-112 | 3188 | Aviodetachment 28 |
| ☐ | N3618F | Airbus A319CJ | 2748 | Frost Administrative Service |
| ☐ | OE-LGS | Airbus A319CJ | 3046 | Triple Alpha |
| ☐ | P4-ARL | Airbus A319CJ | 2192 | System Capital Management |
| ☐ | P4-MIS | Airbus A319CJ | 3133 | Silver Arrows |
| ☐ | P4-RLA | Airbus A319CJ | 4319 | System Capital Management |
| ☐ | P4-VNL | Airbus A319CJ | 2921 | Silver Arrows |
| ☐ | TC-ANA | Airbus A319CJ | 1002 | Government of Turkey |
| ☐ | UR-ABA | Airbus A319CJ | 3260 | Ukraine Air Enterprise |
| ☐ | VH-VHD | Airbus A319CJ | 1999 | Government of Australia |
| ☐ | VP-BED | Airbus A319CJ | 3073 | Planair |
| ☐ | VP-BEX | Airbus A319CJ | 2706 | Planair |
| ☐ | VP-BVA | Airbus A319CJ | 3542 | Global Jet |
| ☐ | VP-CAN | Airbus A319-112 | 1886 | National Air Services (NAS) |
| ☐ | VP-CCJ | Airbus A319CJ | 2421 | Aravco Ltd |
| ☐ | VP-CGX | Airbus A319CJ | 4956 | Sany Group |
| ☐ | VP-CIE | Airbus A319CJ | 1589 | Mid East Jet |
| ☐ | VP-CMJ | Airbus A319CJ | 4228 | Aviation Link |
| ☐ | VP-CSN | Airbus A319CJ | 3356 | Maz Aviation |
| ☐ | VP-CVX | Airbus A319CJ | 1212 | VW Air Services |
| ☐ | VQ-BVQ | Airbus A319CJ | 4842 | Rizon Jet |
| ☐ | VT-IAH | Airbus A319CJ | 2837 | Reliance Commercial Dealers Ltd |
| ☐ | VT-VJM | Airbus A319CJ | 2650 | Kingfisher Airlines |
| ☐ | 4K-A102 | Airbus A319CJ | 2487 | Government of Azerbaijan |
| ☐ | 9H-AFK | Airbus A319CJ | 2592 | Comlux Aviation Malta |
| ☐ | 9H-ALX | Airbus A319CJ | 4470 | Comlux Aviation Malta |
| ☐ | 9K-GEA | Airbus A319CJ | 3957 | Government of Kuwait |
| ☐ | 9M-NAA | Airbus A319CJ | 2949 | Malaysian Government |
| ☐ | 0001 | Airbus A319CJ | 1468 | Venezuelan Air Force |
| ☐ | 2101 | Airbus A319CJ | 2263 | Brazilian Air Force |
| ☐ | 2801 | Airbus A319CJ | 2801 | Czech Air Force |
| ☐ | 3085 | Airbus A319CJ | 3085 | Czech Air Force |
| ☐ | 15+01 | Airbus A319CJ | 3897 | German Air Force |
| ☐ | 15+02 | Airbus A319CJ | 4060 | German Air Force |

| | | | | |
|---|---|---|---|---|
| ☐ | MM62174 | Airbus A319CJ | 1157 | Italian Air Force |
| ☐ | MM62209 | Airbus A319CJ | 1795 | Italian Air Force |
| ☐ | MM62243 | Airbus A319CJ | 2507 | Italian Air Force |
| | | | | |
| ☐ | A4O-AA | Airbus A320-232 | 2566 | Oman Royal Flight |
| ☐ | A6-DLM | Airbus A320-232 | 2403 | Presidential Flight |
| ☐ | A6-HMS | Airbus A320-232 | 3379 | Fujairah Amiri Flight |
| ☐ | A7-AAG | Airbus A320-232 | 0927 | Qatar Amiri Flight |
| ☐ | CS-TFY | Airbus A320-232 | 1868 | Masterjet |
| ☐ | D-ATRA | Airbus A320-232 | 0659 | DLR Flugbetriebe |
| ☐ | EP-AJC | Airbus A320-232 | 0530 | Meraj Air |
| ☐ | F-WWBA | Airbus A320-111 | 0001 | Airbus |
| ☐ | HZ-A2 | Airbus A320-214X | 3164 | Alpha Star Aviation Services |
| ☐ | HZ-XY7 | Airbus A320-214 | 2165 | National Air Services (NAS) |
| ☐ | N60FC | Airbus A320-232CJ | 4388 | Deer Jet |
| ☐ | UP-A2001 | Airbus A320-214CJ | 3199 | Government of Kazakhstan |
| ☐ | VP-CSS | Airbus A320-232CJ | 3402 | SAAD Air |
| ☐ | 9H-AWK | Airbus A320-232CJ | 4199 | Comlux Malta |
| ☐ | 554 | Airbus A320-214CJ | 3723 | Royal Air Force of Oman |
| ☐ | 555 | Airbus A320-214CJ | 4117 | Royal Air Force of Oman |
| ☐ | 556 | Airbus A320-214CJ | 4795 | Royal Air Force of Oman |
| | | | | |
| ☐ | EP-AGB | Airbus A321-231 | 1202 | Government of Iran |
| | | | | |
| ☐ | A7-HHM | Airbus A330-203 | 605 | Qatar Amiri Flight |
| ☐ | A7-HJJ | Airbus A330-202 | 487 | Qatar Amiri Flight |
| ☐ | EC-330 | Airbus A330-203MRTT | 747 | EADS Military Transport Aircraft Division |
| ☐ | F-RARF | Airbus A330-223 | 240 | French Air Force |
| ☐ | F-WWKB | Airbus A330-203 | 925 | Airbus |
| ☐ | TC-TUR | Airbus A330-243 | 1240 | Turkish Government |
| ☐ | UP-A3001 | Airbus A330-223 | 863 | Government of Kazakhstan |
| | | | | |
| ☐ | A7-AAH | Airbus A340-313X | 528 | Qatar Amiri Flight |
| ☐ | A7-HHH | Airbus A340-541 | 495 | Qatar Amiri Flight |
| ☐ | A7-HHK | Airbus A340-211 | 026 | Qatar Amiri Flight |
| ☐ | F-RAJA | Airbus A340-212 | 075 | French Air Force |
| ☐ | F-RAJB | Airbus A340-212 | 081 | French Air Force |
| ☐ | F-WWAI | Airbus A340-311 | 001 | Airbus |
| ☐ | F-WWCA | Airbus A340-642 | 360 | Airbus |
| ☐ | HZ-HMS2 | Airbus A340-213X | 204 | Saudi Ministry of Defense and Aviation |
| ☐ | SU-GGG | Airbus A340-212 | 061 | Government of Egypt |
| ☐ | V8-BKH | Airbus A340-212 | 046 | Government of Brunei |
| ☐ | 7T-VPP | Airbus A340-541 | 917 | Government of Algeria |
| ☐ | 16+01 | Airbus A340-313X | 274 | German Air Force |
| ☐ | 16+02 | Airbus A340-313X | 355 | German Air Force |
| | | | | |
| ☐ | F-WWDD | Airbus A380-861 | 004 | Airbus |
| ☐ | F-WWOW | Airbus A380-841 | 001 | Airbus |
| | | | | |
| ☐ | UR-30044 | Antonov An-30A-100 | 0906 | Kiev City Administration |
| | | | | |
| ☐ | 3C-CMN | Antonov An-72 | 36572092858 | Government of Equatorial Guinea |
| | | | | |
| ☐ | 5A-CAA | Antonov An-74TK-300 | 3654701211080 | Libyan DCA |
| ☐ | RDPL-34177 | Antonov An-74TK-100 | 365470991005 | Government of Laos |
| ☐ | RDPL-34020 | Antonov An-74TK-300 | 36547098982 | Government of Laos |
| ☐ | ST-PRK | Antonov An-74 | 36547098956 | Sudan Government |
| | | | | |
| ☐ | UR-NTN | Antonov An-158 | 0102 | Antonov |
| | | | | |
| ☐ | F-WWLY | ATR 42-600 | 0811 | ATR |
| ☐ | TR-KJD | ATR 42-200 | 0131 | Gabon Air Force |
| | | | | |
| ☐ | F-WWEY | ATR 72-600 | 0098 | ATR |
| ☐ | HS-GCA | ATR 72-500 | 0872 | Royal Thai Air Force (Also 60313) |
| ☐ | HS-GCB | ATR 72-500 | 0881 | Royal Thai Air Force (Also 60314) |
| ☐ | HS-GCC | ATR 72-500 | 0887 | Royal Thai Air Force (Also 60315) |
| ☐ | HS-GCD | ATR 72-500 | 0893 | Royal Thai Air Force (Also 60316) |
| ☐ | XY-AIF | ATR 72-500 | 0765 | Government of Myanmar |
| | | | | |
| ☐ | N162W | BAC One-Eleven 401AK | 087 | Northrop Grumman Systems |
| ☐ | N164W | BAC One-Eleven 401AK | 090 | Northrop Grumman Systems |
| ☐ | N999BW | BAC One-Eleven 419EP | 120 | Jet Place Inc |
| ☐ | TZ-BSA | BAC One-Eleven 492GM | 260 | Government of Mali |
| ☐ | TZ-BSB | BAC One-Eleven 401AK | 086 | Government of Mali |
| ☐ | TZ-BSC | BAC One-Eleven 488GH | 259 | Government of Mali |
| ☐ | ZH763 | BAC One-Eleven 539GL | 263 | QinetiQ |
| | | | | |
| ☐ | A6-AAB | Avro RJ100 | E3387 | Presidential Flight |
| ☐ | A6-LIW | Avro RJ70 | E1267 | Presidential Flight |
| ☐ | A6-RJ1 | Avro RJ85 | E2323 | Dubai Air Wing |
| ☐ | A6-RJ2 | Avro RJ85 | E2325 | Dubai Air Wing |
| ☐ | A6- | BAE 146-300 | E3207 | Palm Aviation |

| | | | | | |
|---|---|---|---|---|---|
| ☐ | A6- | BAE 146-300 | E3214 | Palm Aviation |
| ☐ | A6- | BAE 146-300 | E3218 | Palm Aviation |
| ☐ | A6- | BAE 146-300 | E3219 | Palm Aviation |
| ☐ | A6- | BAE 146-300 | E3222 | Palm Aviation |
| ☐ | A9C-AWL | Avro RJ100 | E3386 | Royal Bahrain Air Force |
| ☐ | A9C-BDF | Avro RJ85 | E2390 | Royal Bahrain Air Force |
| ☐ | A9C-HWR | Avro RJ85 | E2306 | Royal Bahrain Air Force |
| ☐ | CP-2634 | BAE 146-200 | E2096 | Minera San Cristobal |
| ☐ | EP-MOB | BAE 146-300 | E3212 | Palm Aviation |
| ☐ | G-BLRA | BAE 146-100 | E1017 | British Aerospace |
| ☐ | G-LUXE | BAE 146-300 | E3001 | FAAM |
| ☐ | G-OFOA | BAE 146-100 | E1006 | Formula 1 |
| ☐ | G-OFOM | BAE 146-100 | E1144 | Formula 1 |
| ☐ | G-RAJJ | BAE 146-200 | E2108 | Cello Aviation |
| ☐ | G-TBAE | BAE 146-200 | E2018 | BAE Systems Corporate Air Travel |
| ☐ | G-TYPH | BAE 146-200 | E2200 | BAE Systems Corporate Air Travel |
| ☐ | LZ-TIM | Avro RJ70 | E1258 | Hemus Air |
| ☐ | N114M | BAE 146-100 | E1068 | Moncrief Oil |
| ☐ | YR-ANJ | BAE 146-200 | E2079 | Alfa Air Services |
| ☐ | ZE700 | BAE 146-100 | E1021 | Royal Air Force |
| ☐ | ZE701 | BAE 146-100 | E1029 | Royal Air Force |
| | | | | |
| ☐ | XS646 | BAe Andover C.1 | SET 30 | QinetiQ |
| | | | | |
| ☐ | C-GKGM | BAe Jetstream 31 | 727 | Gordon Peariso |
| ☐ | C-GNGI | BAe Jetstream 31 | 739 | Infinity Flight Services |
| ☐ | G-BWWW | BAe Jetstream 31 | 614 | BAE Systems (Operations) Ltd |
| ☐ | G-LNKS | BAe Jetstream 31 | 772 | Links Air |
| ☐ | G-NFLA | BAe Jetstream 31 | 637 | Cranfield Institute of Technology |
| ☐ | G-OAKI | BAe Jetstream 31 | 718 | Jetstream Executive Travel |
| ☐ | G-PLAJ | BAe Jetstream 31 | 738 | Aviation Rentals |
| ☐ | HR-AXG | BAe Jetstream 31 | 791 | LANHSA |
| ☐ | HS-DCA | BAe Jetstream 31 Super | 960 | Thai Department of Aviation |
| ☐ | N127UM | BAe Jetstream 31 | 777 | EAL Leasing |
| ☐ | N618SC | BAe Jetstream 31 | 618 | KSC Enterprises |
| ☐ | N668MP | BAe Jetstream 31 | 668 | 668 MP Aviation |
| ☐ | N723CA | BAe Jetstream 31 | 723 | Con Air Charter |
| ☐ | N743PE | BAe Jetstream 31 | 755 | Vee Neal Aviation |
| ☐ | N831JS | BAe Jetstream 31 | 716 | Small Community Airlines |
| ☐ | N888CY | BAe Jetstream 31 Super EP | 888 | Vertical de Aviacion |
| ☐ | N903EH | BAe Jetstream 31 | 605 | Sky High Aircraft |
| ☐ | N904EH | BAe Jetstream 31 | 613 | EAL Leasing |
| ☐ | N22746 | BAe Jetstream 31 | 745 | Sky Research |
| | | | | |
| ☐ | N307UE | BAe Jetstream 41 | 41021 | Milon Air |
| ☐ | N602JF | BAe Jetstream 41 | 41038 | FABCO Equipment I |
| ☐ | N680AS | BAe Jetstream 41 | 41030 | Northstar Aviation |
| ☐ | ZS-JSM | BAe Jetstream 41 | 41052 | MCC Aviation (Pty) |
| | | | | |
| ☐ | 5N-MPA | Beech 1900D | UE-149 | Mobil Producing Nigeria |
| ☐ | 5N-MPN | Beech 1900D | UE-77 | Mobil Producing Nigeria |
| ☐ | C-FJDF | Beech 1900C | UB-68 | Courtesy Air |
| ☐ | C-FJTF | Beech 1900C | UB-39 | Courtesy Air |
| ☐ | N27NG | Beech 1900D | UE-382 | Northrop Grumman Systems |
| ☐ | N1883M | Beech 1900D | UE-354 | Meijer Stores Limited Partnership |
| ☐ | N1900R | Beech 1900D | UE-64 | Beech Corp |
| ☐ | N191CS | Beech 1900D | UE-392 | Freeport-McMoran |
| ☐ | N470MM | Beech 1900D | UE-394 | Schwan's Shared Services |
| ☐ | N640MW | Beech 1900C-1 | UC-1 | Marvin Lumber & Cedar |
| ☐ | N655MW | Beech 1900D | UE-377 | Marvin Lumber & Cedar |
| ☐ | N83413 | Beech 1900D | UE-25 | Beech |
| ☐ | TT-ABB | Beech 1900D | UE-406 | Government of Chad |
| ☐ | VH-EMI | Beech 1900C-1 | UC-109 | Defence Science & Technology Organisation |
| ☐ | VT-ASH | Beech 1900D | UE-361 | Futura Travels |
| ☐ | YV1106 | Beech 1900D | UE-241 | Wings Aviation (Venezuela) |
| ☐ | YV1894 | Beech 1900D | UE-157 | Toyota of Venezuela |
| ☐ | 1907 | Beech 1900C-1 | UC-7 | Republic of China Air Force |
| | | | | |
| ☐ | RA-21511 | Beriev Be-200 | 7682000002 | Beriev TANTK |
| | | | | |
| ☐ | D2-MAN | Boeing 707-321B | 20025 | Government of Angola |
| ☐ | D2-TPR | Boeing 707-3J6B | 20715 | Government of Angola |
| ☐ | EP-AJD/1002 | Boeing 707-3J9C | 20832 | Iranian Air Force |
| ☐ | EP-AJE/1001 | Boeing 707-3086C | 21396 | Iranian Air Force |
| ☐ | N707JT | Boeing 707-1038B | 18740 | John Travolta |
| ☐ | N88ZL | Boeing 707-330B | 18928 | Lowa Ltd |
| ☐ | TZ-TAC | Boeing 707-3L6B | 21049 | Government of Mali |
| ☐ | 9Q-CLK | Boeing 707-138B | 19252 | Government of DRC |
| | | | | |
| ☐ | A9C-BA | Boeing 727-2M7RE/W | 21824 | Bahrain Royal Flight |
| ☐ | FAC-1203 | Boeing 727-151C | 19868 | Colombian Air Force |
| ☐ | FAC-1204 | Boeing 727-2X3F | 22608 | Colombian Air Force |
| ☐ | FAE-620 | Boeing 727-230 | 21620 | Ecuadorian Air Force |

| | | | | |
|---|---|---|---|---|
| ☐ | FAE-691 | Boeing 727-134 | 19691 | Ecuadorian Air Force |
| ☐ | HZ-AB3 | Boeing 727-2U5RE | 22362 | Al Anwa Establishment |
| ☐ | HZ-RKR | Boeing 727-21 | 19006 | Alsalam Aircraft |
| ☐ | HZ-SKI | Boeing 727-212RE | 21460 | Precision International |
| ☐ | J2-KBA | Boeing 727-191 | 19394 | Government of Djibouti |
| ☐ | M-FAHD | Boeing 727-076RE | 19254 | Flightec International |
| ☐ | M-FTOH | Boeing 727-269 | 22359 | Strong Aviation |
| ☐ | M-STAR | Boeing 727-2X8 | 22687 | Starling Aviation |
| ☐ | N25AZ | Boeing 727-030 | 18370 | Inter Air South Africa |
| ☐ | N30MP | Boeing 727-021 | 18998 | MP Global Charter |
| ☐ | N289MT | Boeing 727-223 | 22467 | Raytheon Corp |
| ☐ | N311AG | Boeing 727-017RE | 20512 | Gordon P & Ann G Getty |
| ☐ | N502MG | Boeing 727-191 | 19391 | RD Aviation |
| ☐ | N606DH | Boeing 727-030 | 18365 | Clementine Aviation Services Inc |
| ☐ | N615PA | Boeing 727-243 | 21266 | Paradigm Air Operators |
| ☐ | N698SS | Boeing 727-223 | 21369 | Paradigm Air Operators |
| ☐ | N724CL | Boeing 727-051 | 19121 | Clay Lacy Aviation |
| ☐ | N724YS | Boeing 727-281 | 21474 | Fry's Electronics |
| ☐ | N727AH | Boeing 727-021 | 19261 | Paxson Communication Management |
| ☐ | N727NK | Boeing 727-212 | 21945 | FBA Airplane |
| ☐ | N727VJ | Boeing 727-044 | 19318 | United Breweries |
| ☐ | N727XL | Boeing 727-1H2RE/W | 20533 | Next Century Aviation |
| ☐ | N800AK | Boeing 727-023 | 20045 | Arabasco |
| ☐ | N908JE | Boeing 727-031RE | 20115 | JEGE Inc |
| ☐ | P4-FLY | Boeing 727-022 | 19148 | Aviation Connections |
| ☐ | TU-VAO | Boeing 727-2Y4 | 22968 | Government of Côte d'Ivoire |
| ☐ | TZ-MBA | Boeing 727-2K5 | 21853 | Government of Mali |
| ☐ | VP-BAJ | Boeing 727-030RE | 18936 | Spectrum Aerospace |
| ☐ | VP-BAP | Boeing 727-021 | 19260 | Malibu Consulting |
| ☐ | VP-BDJ | Boeing 727-023 | 20046 | Trump Air |
| ☐ | VP-BPZ | Boeing 727-017RE | 20327 | Enterprise Aviation Bermuda |
| ☐ | VP-CJN | Boeing 727-076 | 20371 | Starling Aviation |
| ☐ | VP-CZY | Boeing 727-2P1RE | 21595 | Jet Aviation Business Jets |
| ☐ | XC-FAD/3501 | Boeing 727-014 | 18912 | Mexican Air Force |
| ☐ | XT-BFA | Boeing 727-282RE | 22430 | Government of Burkina Faso |
| ☐ | ZS-PVX | Boeing 727-2N6RE | 22825 | Fortune Air |
| ☐ | 4K-8888 | Boeing 727-251 | 22543 | SW Business Aviation |
| ☐ | 6V-AEF | Boeing 727-2M1RE | 21091 | Government of Senegal |
| | | | | |
| ☐ | A9C-DAA | Boeing 737-268 | 22050 | Delmun Aviation Services |
| ☐ | C-GXNR | Boeing 737-2S2C | 21929 | Xstrata Canada |
| ☐ | EP-AGA | Boeing 737-286 | 21317 | Government of Iran |
| ☐ | FAE-620 | Boeing 727-230 | 21620 | Ecuadorian Air Force |
| ☐ | FAP-350 | Boeing 737-244 | 19707 | Peruvian Air Force |
| ☐ | FAP-352 | Boeing 737-244 | 23042 | Peruvian Air Force |
| ☐ | HZ-MIS | Boeing 737-2K5 | 22600 | Sheikh M Edress |
| ☐ | K2412 | Boeing 737-2A8 | 23036 | Indian Air Force |
| ☐ | K2413 | Boeing 737-2A8 | 23037 | Indian Air Force |
| ☐ | K3186 | Boeing 737-2A8 | 20484 | Indian Air Force |
| ☐ | K-3187 | Boeing 737-2A8 | 20483 | Indian Air Force |
| ☐ | N165W | Boeing 737-2 200 | 19605 | Northrop Grumman Systems |
| ☐ | N73HK | Boeing 737-2S9 | 21957 | Executive Jet Aviation (Cayman Islands) |
| ☐ | N370BC | Boeing 737-247 | 23468 | Basic Capital Management |
| ☐ | N413JG | Boeing 737-28Q | 23148 | Weststar Aviation |
| ☐ | N500VP | Boeing 737-2H4 | 22062 | Sky King |
| ☐ | N733PA | Boeing 737-205 | 23466 | Atlantic Richfield |
| ☐ | N736BP | Boeing 737-205 | 23465 | Atlantic BP Exploration (Alaska) |
| ☐ | N902WG | Boeing 737-2H6 | 22620 | Gary 737 |
| ☐ | VP-CBA | Boeing 737-2W8 | 22628 | Sky Aviation |
| ☐ | ZS-IJA | Boeing 737-201 | 22751 | Inter Air South Africa |
| ☐ | 5U-BAG | Boeing 737-2N9C | 21499 | Government of Niger |
| ☐ | 0207 | Boeing 737-2N1 | 21167 | Venezuelan Air Force |
| ☐ | 2116 | Boeing 737-2N3 | 21166 | Brazilian Air Force |
| ☐ | 3520 | Boeing 737-2B7 | 23133 | Mexican Air Force |
| | | | | |
| ☐ | C-FPHS | Boeing 737-53A | 24970 | Global Aerospace Logistics |
| ☐ | FAP356 | Boeing 737-528 | 27426 | Peruvian Air Force (also OB-1860) |
| ☐ | G-BVKD | Boeing 737-59D | 26421 | TAG Aviation |
| ☐ | HS-CMV | Boeing 737-4Z6 | 27906 | Royal Thai Air Force (also 11-111) |
| ☐ | N35LX | Boeing 737-330 | 23528 | Lockheed Martin Corp |
| ☐ | N37NY | Boeing 737-4YO | 23976 | Starwood Flight Operations Inc |
| ☐ | N444HE | Boeing 737-39A/W | 23800 | Mirage Aviation |
| ☐ | N731VA | Boeing 737-33A | 27456 | Premier Aircraft Management |
| ☐ | PK-GWL | Boeing 737-4U3 | 25714 | Indonesian Govt |
| ☐ | PK-GWQ | Boeing 737-4U3 | 25719 | Indonesian Govt |
| ☐ | SX-MTF | Boeing 737-3Z9 | 23774 | GainJet Aviation S.A. |
| ☐ | XC-LJG | Boeing 737-322 | 24361 | Mexican Air Force (also TP-03) |
| ☐ | XC-UJB | Boeing 737-33A | 24095 | Mexican Air Force (also TP-02) |
| ☐ | 5N-BMA | Boeing 737-3Q4F | 24209 | Axiom Air |
| ☐ | 921 | Boeing 737-58N | 28866 | Chilean Air Force |
| ☐ | 85101 | Boeing 737-3Z8 | 23152 | Republic of Korea Air Force |
| | | | | |
| ☐ | A36-001 | Boeing 737 BBJ1 | 30829 | Royal Australian Air Force |

| | Reg | Type | MSN | Operator |
|---|---|---|---|---|
| ☐ | A36-002 | Boeing 737 BBJ1 | 30790 | Royal Australian Air Force |
| ☐ | A6-AIN | Boeing 737 BBJ1 | 29268 | Royal Jet |
| ☐ | A6-AUH | Boeing 737 BBJ2 | 33473 | Presidential Flight |
| ☐ | A6-DAS | Boeing 737 BBJ1 | 29858 | Royal Jet |
| ☐ | A6-DFR | Boeing 737 BBJ1 | 30884 | Royal Jet |
| ☐ | A6-HEH | Boeing 737 BBJ2 | 32825 | Dubai Air Wing |
| ☐ | A6-HRS | Boeing 737 BBJ1 | 29251 | Dubai Air Wing |
| ☐ | A6-MRM | Boeing 737 BBJ2 | 32450 | Dubai Air Wing |
| ☐ | A6-MRS | Boeing 737 BBJ2 | 35238 | Dubai Air Wing |
| ☐ | A6-RJX | Boeing 737 BBJ1 | 29865 | Royal Jet |
| ☐ | A6-RJY | Boeing 737 BBJ1 | 29857 | Royal Jet |
| ☐ | A6-RJZ | Boeing 737 BBJ1 | 29269 | Royal Jet |
| ☐ | B-4081 | Boeing 737-86N/W | 36775 | Chinese Air Force |
| ☐ | B-5266 | Boeing 737 BBJ1 | 29866 | Deer Jet |
| ☐ | B-5273 | Boeing 737 BBJ1 | 38633 | Deer Jet |
| ☐ | B-LEX | Boeing 737 BBJ1 | 34683 | Silverblatt Ltd |
| ☐ | B-3999 | Boeing 737 BBJ1 | 41090 | Air China Business Jet |
| ☐ | CN-MVI | Boeing 737 BBJ2 | 37545 | Government of Morocco |
| ☐ | EW-001PA | Boeing 737 BBJ2 | 33079 | Government of Belarus |
| ☐ | FAC0001 | Boeing 737 BBJ1 | 29272 | Colombian Air Force |
| ☐ | HL7227 | Boeing 737 BBJ1 | 35977 | Hanwha Chemical Corp |
| ☐ | HL7759 | Boeing 737 BBJ1 | 35990 | Samsung Techwin Aviation |
| ☐ | HL7787 | Boeing 737 BBJ1 | 36852 | Hyundai |
| ☐ | HL8222 | Boeing 737 BBJ1 | 37660 | Korean Air |
| ☐ | HS-TYS | Boeing 737-8Z6/W | 35478 | Royal Thai Air Force (also 55-555) |
| ☐ | HZ-101 | Boeing 737 BBJ1 | 32805 | Royal Saudi Arabian Air Force |
| ☐ | HZ-102 | Boeing 737 BBJ2 | 32451 | Royal Saudi Arabian Air Force |
| ☐ | HZ-MF1 | Boeing 737 BBJ1 | 33405 | Saudi Ministry of Finance & Economy |
| ☐ | HZ-MF2 | Boeing 737 BBJ1 | 33499 | Saudi Ministry of Finance & Economy |
| ☐ | K-5012 | Boeing 737 BBJ1 | 36106 | Indian Air Force |
| ☐ | K-5013 | Boeing 737 BBJ1 | 36107 | Indian Air Force |
| ☐ | K-5014 | Boeing 737 BBJ1 | 36108 | Indian Air Force |
| ☐ | M53-01 | Boeing 737 BBJ1 | 29274 | Royal Malaysian Air Force |
| ☐ | M-URUS | Boeing 737 BBJ1 | 34622 | Silver Arrows |
| ☐ | M-YBBJ | Boeing 737 BBJ1 | 36027 | Silver Arrows |
| ☐ | N2TS | Boeing 737 BBJ1 | 29102 | First Virtual Aviation |
| ☐ | N43PR | Boeing 737 BBJ1 | 28581 | The Town & Country Food Markets |
| ☐ | N50TC | Boeing 737 BBJ1 | 29024 | Tracinda Corp |
| ☐ | N88WR | Boeing 737 BBJ1 | 29441 | Las Vegas Jet |
| ☐ | N90R | Boeing 737 BBJ1 | 32775 | Occidental Petroleum |
| ☐ | N92SR | Boeing 737 BBJ1 | 37111 | Essar Shipping & Logistics |
| ☐ | N108MS | Boeing 737 BBJ1 | 33102 | YONA Aviation II |
| ☐ | N111VM | Boeing 737 BBJ1 | 36090 | MWWMMWM Ltd (BVI) |
| ☐ | N162WC | Boeing 737 BBJ1 | 30329 | WCA Holdings III |
| ☐ | N164RJ | Boeing 737 BBJ1 | 30328 | Akira Investments |
| ☐ | N315TS | Boeing 737 BBJ1 | 30772 | Tudor-Saliba |
| ☐ | N371BC | Boeing 737 BBJ2 | 32971 | Mid East Jet |
| ☐ | N377CJ | Boeing 737 BBC1 | 30739 | PT Exspres Transport |
| ☐ | N449BJ | Boeing 737 BBJ1 | 40117 | Deer Jet |
| ☐ | N450BJ | Boeing 737 BBJ1 | 38854 | Essar Shipping & Logistics |
| ☐ | N500LS | Boeing 737 BBJ1 | 29054 | Limited Stores |
| ☐ | N647SR | Boeing 737-505 | 24648 | Prestige Jet |
| ☐ | N660CP | Boeing 737-78D/W | 36721 | ConocoPhillips Alaska |
| ☐ | N720MM | Boeing 737 BBJ1 | 33010 | MGM Mirage |
| ☐ | N721UF | Boeing 737 BBJ1 | 30327 | F&L Aviaton III |
| ☐ | N737AG | Boeing 737 BBJ1 | 30496 | Funair |
| ☐ | N737CC | Boeing 737 BBJ1 | 29135 | Mid East Jet |
| ☐ | N737ER | Boeing 737 BBJ1 | 30754 | Boetti Air Inc |
| ☐ | N737KA | Boeing 737-7BX | 30740 | Kaiserair |
| ☐ | N737KV | Boeing 737 BBJ1 | 30031 | BB Aviation |
| ☐ | N737L | Boeing 737 BBJ1 | 30751 | Legatum Aviation |
| ☐ | N737M | Boeing 737 BBJ2 | 33361 | EIE Eagle Inc Establishment |
| ☐ | N737WH | Boeing 737 BBJ1 | 29142 | Victory Aviation |
| ☐ | N742PB | Boeing 737 BBJ1 | 29200 | Chartwell Partners |
| ☐ | N743A | Boeing 737-7AXC/W | 30184 | Saudi Aramco Aviation |
| ☐ | N744A | Boeing 737-7AXC/W | 30185 | Saudi Aramco Aviation |
| ☐ | N800KS | Boeing 737 BBJ1 | 30782 | Clay Lacy Aviation |
| ☐ | N835BA | Boeing 737 BBJ1 | 30572 | ShareJet |
| ☐ | N836BA | Boeing 737 BBJ1 | 30756 | Boeing |
| ☐ | N888TY | Boeing 737 BBJ1 | 29749 | TY Corp |
| ☐ | N888YF | Boeing 737 BBJ1 | 33036 | Evergreen International |
| ☐ | N920DS | Boeing 737 BBJ1 | 28579 | Delaware Global Operations |
| ☐ | N7600K | Boeing 737 BBJ1 | 32628 | SAS Institute |
| ☐ | N8767 | Boeing 737 BBJ1 | 32807 | Avjet Corp |
| ☐ | N79711 | Boeing 737 BBJ1 | 30547 | Dallah Avco |
| ☐ | OE-ILX | Boeing 737 BBJ2 | 32777 | Global Jet Austria |
| ☐ | PR-BBS | Boeing 737 BBJ1 | 32575 | Banco Safra |
| ☐ | P4-AFK | Boeing 737 BBJ1 | 36493 | Premier Avia |
| ☐ | P4-ASL | Boeing 737 BBJ1 | 29791 | Arabasco |
| ☐ | P4-BBJ | Boeing 737 BBJ1 | 30070 | Carre Aviation |
| ☐ | P4-KAZ | Boeing 737 BBJ1 | 32774 | Prime Aviation |
| ☐ | P4-LIG | Boeing 737 BBJ1 | 37592 | Petroff Air |
| ☐ | P4-NGK | Boeing 737 BBJ1 | 37583 | Itera Holdings |

| | Registration | Type | Serial | Operator |
|---|---|---|---|---|
| ☐ | TS-IOO | Boeing 737 BBJ1 | 29149 | Government of Tunisia |
| ☐ | TT-ABD | Boeing 737 BBJ1 | 29136 | Government of Chad |
| ☐ | VP-BBJ | Boeing 737 BBJ1 | 29273 | Picton II |
| ☐ | VP-BBW | Boeing 737 BBJ1 | 30076 | GAMA Aviation |
| ☐ | VP-BEL | Boeing 737 BBJ1 | 29139 | Orient Global |
| ☐ | VP-BFT | Boeing 737 BBJ1 | 36714 | Jet Aviation Business Jets |
| ☐ | VP-BHN | Boeing 737 BBJ2 | 32438 | Saudi Oger |
| ☐ | VP-BIZ | Boeing 737 BBJ1 | 34477 | Siva Air |
| ☐ | VP-BJJ | Boeing 737 BBJ1 | 30330 | Avenair Worldwide (BBJ) |
| ☐ | VP-BNZ | Boeing 737 BBJ1 | 35959 | Gazpromavia |
| ☐ | VP-BRM | Boeing 737 BBJ1 | 28976 | Zeem Corp |
| ☐ | VP-BRT | Boeing 737 BBJ1 | 32970 | Jet Aviation Business Jets |
| ☐ | VP-BWR | Boeing 737 BBJ1 | 29317 | Usal |
| ☐ | VP-BYA | Boeing 737 BBJ1 | 29972 | Saudi Oger |
| ☐ | VP-BZL | Boeing 737 BBJ2 | 32915 | Lowa |
| ☐ | VP-CBB | Boeing 737 BBJ2 | 32806 | A S Bugshan & Bros |
| ☐ | VP-CLR | Boeing 737 BBJ1 | 34865 | Lukoil Avia |
| ☐ | VP-CSK | Boeing 737 BBJ2 | 34620 | Nafo Aviation |
| ☐ | VQ-BOS | Boeing 737-8GQ/W | 35792 | Bayham |
| ☐ | ZS-RSA | Boeing 737 BBJ1 | 32627 | South African Air Force |
| ☐ | 3C-EGE | Boeing 737 BBJ1 | 33367 | Government of Equatorial Guinea |
| ☐ | 5N-FGT | Boeing 737 BBJ1 | 34260 | Nigerian Air Force |
| ☐ | 5R-MRP | Boeing 737-74U/W | 29233 | Government of Madagascar |
| ☐ | 9H-BBJ | Boeing 737 BBJ1 | 30791 | Privajet |
| ☐ | 3701 | Boeing 737-8AR/W | 30139 | Republic of China Air Force |
| ☐ | 01-0015 | Boeing 737 BBJ1 | 32916 | US Air Force |
| ☐ | 01-0040 | Boeing 737 BBJ1 | 29971 | US Air Force |
| ☐ | 01-0041 | Boeing 737 BBJ1 | 33080 | US Air Force |
| ☐ | 02-0042 | Boeing 737 BBJ1 | 33500 | US Air Force |
| ☐ | 02-0201 | Boeing 737 BBJ1 | 30755 | US Air Force |
| ☐ | 02-0202 | Boeing 737 BBJ1 | 30753 | US Air Force |
| ☐ | 02-0203 | Boeing 737 BBJ1 | 33434 | US Air Force |
| ☐ | 05-0730 | Boeing 737 BBJ1 | 34807 | US Air Force |
| ☐ | 05-0932 | Boeing 737 BBJ1 | 34808 | US Air Force |
| ☐ | 05-4613 | Boeing 737 BBJ1 | 34809 | US Air Force |
| | | | | |
| ☐ | A4O-OMN | Boeing 747-430 | 32445 | Oman Royal Flight |
| ☐ | A4O-SO | Boeing 747-SP27 | 21785 | Oman Royal Flight |
| ☐ | A6-COM | Boeing 747-433 | 25074 | Dubai Air Wing |
| ☐ | A6-HRM | Boeing 747-422 | 26903 | Dubai Air Wing |
| ☐ | A6-MMM | Boeing 747-422 | 26906 | Dubai Air Wing |
| ☐ | A6-UAE | Boeing 747-48E | 28551 | Presidential Flight |
| ☐ | A6-YAS | Boeing 747-4F6 | 28961 | Presidential Flight |
| ☐ | A7-HHE | Boeing 747-8KB | 37075 | Qatar Amiri Flight |
| ☐ | A9C-HAK | Boeing 747-SPP6 | 23610 | Bahrain Royal Flight |
| ☐ | A9C-HMK | Boeing 747-4P8 | 33684 | Bahrain Royal Flight |
| ☐ | HL7465 | Boeing 747-4B5 | 26412 | Republic of Korea Air Force |
| ☐ | HZ-AIF | Boeing 747-SP68 | 22503 | Government of Saudi Arabia |
| ☐ | HZ-AIJ | Boeing 747-SP68 | 22750 | Government of Saudi Arabia |
| ☐ | HZ-HM1A | Boeing 747-3G1 | 23070 | Government of Saudi Arabia |
| ☐ | HZ-HM1B | Boeing 747-SP68 | 21652 | Government of Saudi Arabia |
| ☐ | HZ-WBT7 | Boeing 747-4J6 | 25880 | Kingdom Holding |
| ☐ | N747A | Boeing 747-SP27 | 21992 | Fry's Electronics |
| ☐ | N747GE | Boeing 747-121F | 19651 | General Electric |
| ☐ | N787RR | Boeing 747-267B | 21966 | Rolls-Royce North America |
| ☐ | N911NA | Boeing 747-SR46 | 20781 | NASA |
| ☐ | N5017Q | Boeing 747-8KZF | 36136 | Boeing |
| ☐ | P4-FSH | Boeing 747-SP31 | 21963 | Ernest Angley Ministries |
| ☐ | VP-BAT | Boeing 747-SP21 | 21648 | Worldwide Aircraft Holding Co (Bermuda) |
| ☐ | VP-BLK | Boeing 747-SP31 | 21961 | Interface Operations Bermuda |
| ☐ | VQ-BMS | Boeing 747-SP21 | 21649 | Interface Operations Bermuda |
| ☐ | V8-ALI | Boeing 747-430 | 26426 | Government of Brunei |
| ☐ | 7O-YMN | Boeing 747-SP27 | 21786 | Government of Yemen Arab Republic |
| ☐ | 00-0001 | Boeing 747-YAL-1 | 30201 | Boeing Integrated Defense Systems |
| ☐ | 20-1101 | Boeing 747-47C | 24730 | Japan Air Self Defence Force |
| ☐ | 20-1102 | Boeing 747-47C | 24731 | Japan Air Self Defence Force |
| ☐ | 82-8000 | Boeing 747 VC-25A | 23824 | US Air Force |
| ☐ | 92-9000 | Boeing 747 VC-25A | 23825 | US Air Force |
| | | | | |
| ☐ | N757A | Boeing 757-200 | 22212 | Boeing Logistics Spares |
| ☐ | N757AG | Boeing 757-256/W | 29306 | Funair |
| ☐ | N757HW | Boeing 757-225 | 22194 | Honeywell International |
| ☐ | N757LL | Boeing 757-23N/W | 27972 | Talos Aviation |
| ☐ | N757MA | Boeing 757-24Q | 28463 | Mid East Jet |
| ☐ | N757SS | Boeing 757-236 | 22176 | Juliet Romeo Aviation |
| ☐ | N770BB | Boeing 757-2J4/W | 25220 | The Yucaipa Companies |
| ☐ | N801DM | Boeing 757-256 | 26240 | North American Airlines |
| ☐ | N1757 | Boeing 757-23A/W | 24923 | Vulcan Inc |
| ☐ | SX-RFA | Boeing 757-23N/W | 30232 | GainJet Aviation |
| ☐ | UP-B5701 | Boeing 757-2M6 | 23454 | Government of Kazakhstan |
| ☐ | XC-UJM | Boeing 757-225/W | 22690 | Mexican Air Force (also TP-01) |
| ☐ | T-01 | Boeing 757-23A | 25487 | Argentine Air Force |
| ☐ | 98-0001 | Boeing 757 C32A | 29025 | US Air Force |

| | | | | |
|---|---|---|---|---|
| ☐ | 98-0002 | Boeing 757 C32A | 29026 | US Air Force |
| ☐ | 99-0003 | Boeing 757 C32A | 29027 | US Air Force |
| ☐ | 99-0004 | Boeing 757 C32A | 29028 | US Air Force |
| ☐ | N673BF | Boeing 767-238ER | 23402 | Polaris Aviation Solutions |
| ☐ | N767A | Boeing 767-2AXER | 33685 | ARAMCO Associated |
| ☐ | N767KS | Boeing 767-24QER | 28270 | Mid East Jet |
| ☐ | N767MW | Boeing 767-277 | 22694 | Swift Air |
| ☐ | N804MS | Boeing 767-3P6ER | 27255 | Las Vegas Sands |
| ☐ | N2767 | Boeing 767-238ER | 23896 | Google |
| ☐ | P4-CLA | Boeing 767-2DXER | 32954 | Government of Kazakhstan |
| ☐ | P4-MES | Boeing 767-33AER | 33425 | Silver Arrows |
| ☐ | UK-67000 | Boeing 767-33PER | 35796 | Government of Uzbekistan |
| ☐ | V8-MHB | Boeing 767-27GER | 25537 | Government of Brunei |
| ☐ | VP-BKS | Boeing 767-3P6ER | 27254 | Kalair |
| ☐ | VP-CME | Boeing 767-231 | 22567 | Sheikh M Edress |
| ☐ | ZS-DJI | Boeing 767-216ER | 23624 | Aeronexus |
| ☐ | 985 | Boeing 767-3YOER | 26205 | Chilean Air Force |
| ☐ | A6-ALN | Boeing 777-2ANER | 29953 | Presidential Flight |
| ☐ | N777AS | Boeing 777-24Q | 29271 | Mid East Jet |
| ☐ | N787BA | Boeing 787-881 | 40690 | Boeing |
| ☐ | N787BX | Boeing 787-800 | 40692 | Boeing |
| ☐ | N787EX | Boeing 787-83Q | 40691 | Boeing |
| ☐ | N787FT | Boeing 787-800 | 40694 | Boeing |
| ☐ | N787ZA | Boeing 787-800 | 40695 | Boeing |
| ☐ | N7874 | Boeing 787-800 | 40693 | Boeing |
| ☐ | B-1110L | CAIC ARJ21-700 | 104 | China Aviation Industry Corp |
| ☐ | B-970L | CAIC ARJ21-700 | 101 | China Aviation Industry Corp |
| ☐ | B-991L | CAIC ARJ21-700 | 102 | China Aviation Industry Corp |
| ☐ | B-992L | CAIC ARJ21-700 | 103 | China Aviation Industry Corp |
| ☐ | B-3570 | Canadair Challenger 850 | 8102 | Yalian Jet |
| ☐ | B-4005 | Canadair Challenger 800 | 7138 | People's Liberation Army Air Force |
| ☐ | B-4006 | Canadair Challenger 800 | 7149 | People's Liberation Army Air Force |
| ☐ | B-4007 | Canadair Challenger 800 | 7180 | People's Liberation Army Air Force |
| ☐ | B-4010 | Canadair Challenger 800 | 7189 | People's Liberation Army Air Force |
| ☐ | B-4011 | Canadair Challenger 800 | 7193 | People's Liberation Army Air Force |
| ☐ | B-4701 | Canadair Challenger 800 | 7639 | China Ocean Aviation Group |
| ☐ | B-4702 | Canadair Challenger 800 | 7455 | China Ocean Aviation Group |
| ☐ | B-7695 | Canadair CRJ-200ER | 7268 | ZYB Lily Jet Business Aviation |
| ☐ | B-7697 | Canadair Challenger 850 | 8089 | ZYB Lily Jet Business Aviation |
| ☐ | B-7795 | Canadair Challgner 850 | 8098 | Zyb Lily Jet |
| ☐ | C-FUQZ | Canadair Challenger 850 | 8096 | Bombardier |
| ☐ | C-GDTD | Canadair Challenger 850 | 8067 | Flightexec |
| ☐ | C-GSLL | Canadair Challenger 850 | 8103 | Image Air Charter |
| ☐ | C-GSUW | Canadair Challenger 850 | 8047 | Suncor Energy |
| ☐ | D-AAIJ | Canadair Challenger 850 | 8065 | Imperial Jet |
| ☐ | D-ACRN | Canadair CRJ-200LR | 7486 | FAI rent-a-jet |
| ☐ | EI-EEZ | Canadair Challenger 850 | 8085 | Airlink Airways |
| ☐ | EW-301PJ | Canadair Challenger 850 | 8057 | Belavia |
| ☐ | G-IGWT | Canadair Challenger 850 | 8078 | Ocean Sky Aviation |
| ☐ | G-SHAL | Canadair Challenger 850 | 8066 | TAG Aviation |
| ☐ | HB-IDJ | Canadair Challenger 800 | 7136 | TAG Aviation |
| ☐ | M-ANTA | Canadair Challenger 850 | 8094 | Miklos Services |
| ☐ | M-FZMH | Canadair Challenger 850 | 8068 | ExecuJet Middle East |
| ☐ | M-TAKE | Canadair Challenger 850 | 8079 | Prime Aviation |
| ☐ | N155MW | Canadair CRJ-200LR | 7021 | Dog Leg Transportation |
| ☐ | N500PR | Canadair Challenger 800 | 7846 | Penske Racing |
| ☐ | N501LS | Canadair Challenger 800 | 7584 | Boston Enterprises |
| ☐ | N529DB | Canadair Challenger 800 | 7152 | Solairus Aviation |
| ☐ | N601LS | Canadair Challenger 800 | 7008 | Limited Brands |
| ☐ | N629DD | Canadair CRJ-200LR | 7730 | DD Aviation |
| ☐ | N666RD | Canadair Challenger 800 | 7717 | IFG Properties |
| ☐ | N711WM | Canadair Challenger 800 | 7140 | Gaughan Flying |
| ☐ | N850PL | Canadair CRJ-200ER | 7489 | Peterborough 850 |
| ☐ | N888AU | Canadair CRJ200 Phoenix | 7211 | Jet Asia |
| ☐ | N888GY | Canadair CRJ200 ExecLiner | 7471 | Wumac |
| ☐ | N888WU | Canadair CRJ200 ExecLiner | 7481 | Wu Air Corp |
| ☐ | N999YG | Canadair Challenger 800 | 7075 | DJ Burrell & Burrell Professional Labs et al |
| ☐ | OD-AMR | Canadair CRJ-200ER | 7255 | Med Airways |
| ☐ | OD-TAL | Canadair CRJ200 ExecLiner | 7086 | Emerald Jets |
| ☐ | OE-IKG | Canadair Challenger 850 | 8063 | MAP Executive Flightservice |
| ☐ | OE-ILI | Canadair Challenger 850 | 8048 | VistaJet Luftfahrtunternehmen |
| ☐ | OE-ILV | Canadair Challenger 850 | 8082 | VistaJet Luftfahrtunternehmen |
| ☐ | OE-ILY | Canadair Challenger 850 | 8076 | VistaJet Luftfahrtunternehmen |
| ☐ | OE-ILZ | Canadair Challenger 850 | 8086 | VistaJet Luftfahrtunternehmen |
| ☐ | OE-ISA | Canadair Challenger 850 | 8043 | Avcon Jet |
| ☐ | OH-SPB | Canadair Challenger 850 | 8056 | Jetflite |
| ☐ | OY-VEG | Canadair Challenger 850 | 8075 | ExecuJet Europe |
| ☐ | OY-VGA | Canadair Challenger 850 | 8077 | ExecuJet Europe |

| | | | | |
|---|---|---|---|---|
| ☐ | PH-AAG | Canadair CRJ200 Hemisphere | 7763 | Solid Air |
| ☐ | P4-GAZ | Canadair CRJ-100ER | 7159 | Premier Avia |
| ☐ | P4-GJL | Canadair Challenger 850 | 8053 | Silver Arrows |
| ☐ | P4-VIP | Canadair CRJ200 Renaissance | 7158 | Flight Test Consultants |
| ☐ | RA-67218 | Canadair Challenger 850 | 8074 | Kolavia |
| ☐ | RA-67219 | Canadair Challenger 850 | 8090 | Kolavia |
| ☐ | RA-67220 | Canadair Challenger 850 | 8091 | Kolavia |
| ☐ | UP-C8501 | Canadair Challenger 850 | 8054 | Comlux KZ |
| ☐ | UP-C8502 | Canadair Challenger 850 | 8049 | Comlux KZ |
| ☐ | UP-C8503 | Canadair Challenger 850 | 8093 | Euro-Asia Air |
| ☐ | UR-ICD | Canadair Challenger 850 | 8072 | ISD Avia |
| ☐ | UR-OAM | Canadair Challenger 850 | 8084 | ISD Avia |
| ☐ | UR-RUS | Canadair CRJ-200LR | 7990 | ISD Avia |
| ☐ | VH-LEF | Canadair Challenger 850 | 8060 | Air National Australia Pty |
| ☐ | VP-BSD | Canadair Challenger 850 | 8051 | Arabian Support and Services Co Ltd (ASASCO) |
| ☐ | VP-BVJ | Canadair Challenger 850 | 8071 | Vacuna Jets |
| ☐ | VP-CON | Canadair Challenger 850 | 8083 | Lukoil Avia |
| ☐ | VT-ARE | Canadair CRJ200 ExecLiner | 7163 | Club One Air |
| ☐ | VT-IBP | Canadair Challenger 850 | 8070 | Airmid Aviation Services Private |
| ☐ | VT-KML | Canadair Challenger 800 | 7351 | Span Air (India) |
| ☐ | 5A-UAD | Canadair Challenger 850 | 8087 | United Aviation |
| ☐ | 9H-AFU | Canadair Challenger 800 | 7176 | Carre Aviation |
| | | | | |
| ☐ | B-4060 | Canadair Challenger 870 | 10164 | People's Liberation Army Air Force |
| ☐ | B-4061 | Canadair Challenger 870 | 10183 | People's Liberation Army Air Force |
| ☐ | B-4062 | Canadair Challenger 870 | 10187 | People's Liberation Army Air Force |
| ☐ | B-4063 | Canadair Challenger 870 | 10204 | People's Liberation Army Air Force |
| ☐ | B-4064 | Canadair Challenger 870 | 10206 | People's Liberation Army Air Force |
| ☐ | N1RL | Canadair Challenger 870 | 10004 | Indycar Aviation |
| ☐ | N804X | Canadair CRJ-701 | 10002 | Northrop Grumman Systems Corp (Delaware) |
| ☐ | N870DC | Canadair Challenger 870 NG | 10314 | Dow Chemical |
| ☐ | N872DC | Canadair Challenger 870 NG | 10322 | Dow Chemical |
| ☐ | UP-CL001 | Canadair Challenger 870 NG | 10289 | Euro-Asia Air |
| ☐ | VP-BCL | Canadair Challenger 870 | 10247 | S & K Bermuda |
| | | | | |
| ☐ | C-GSUA | Canadair Challenger 890 NG | 15182 | Suncor Energy Oil Sands |
| ☐ | C-GSUM | Canadair Challenger 890 | 15158 | Suncor Energy Oil Sands |
| | | | | |
| ☐ | C-FNXG | Canadair CRJ-1000 NextGen | 19001 | Bombardier |
| ☐ | C-FRJX | Canadair CRJ-1000ER NextGen | 19991 | Bombardier |
| | | | | |
| ☐ | C-FBCS | de Havilland DHC-8-202B | 413 | Bombardier |
| ☐ | C-FBLY | de Havilland DHC-8-315 | 574 | Skyservice Business Aviation |
| ☐ | C-FJJA | de Havilland DHC-8-401Q | 4001 | Bombardier |
| ☐ | C-GBOS | de Havilland DHC-8Q-314 | 565 | Cenovus Energy |
| ☐ | C-FXAW | de Havilland DHC-8-402Q | 4262 | Bombardier |
| ☐ | D2-EAA | de Havilland DHC-8-402Q | 4294 | Goverment of Angola |
| ☐ | D2-EEB | de Havilland DHC-8-402Q | 4305 | Goverment of Angola |
| ☐ | N308RD | de Havilland DHC-8-102A | 265 | Presidential Airways |
| ☐ | N637CC | de Havilland DHC-8-202 | 637 | Northrop Grumman Systems |
| ☐ | N646CC | de Havilland DHC-8-202 | 646 | Northrop Grumman Systems |
| ☐ | N649CC | de Havilland DHC-8-202 | 649 | Northrop Grumman Systems |
| ☐ | OY-RUW | de Havilland DHC-8-102 | 060 | Nuuk Aircraft 1 ApS |
| ☐ | P4-TCO | de Havilland DHC-8-202 | 484 | Prime Aviation |
| | | | | |
| ☐ | 5V-TGF | Douglas DC-8-62 | 46071 | Government of Togo |
| ☐ | N817NA | Douglas DC-8-72 | 46082 | NASA |
| ☐ | VP-BHM | Douglas DC-8-62 | 46111 | Brisair |
| ☐ | VP-BHS | Douglas DC-8-72 | 46067/455 | Brisair |
| ☐ | 9T-TCN | Douglas DC-8-55F | 45753 | Democratic Republic of Congo Air Force |
| | | | | |
| ☐ | F-GVTH | Douglas DC-9-21 | 47308 | Thales |
| ☐ | N45NA | Douglas DC-9-33RC | 47410 | National Nuclear Security Adminstration |
| ☐ | N697BJ | Douglas DC-9-32 | 47799 | Blue Jackets Air |
| ☐ | N880DF | Douglas DC-9-32 | 47635 | Detroit Pistons |
| ☐ | N8860 | Douglas DC-9-15 | 45797 | Scaife Flight Operations |
| ☐ | ZS-MNT | Douglas DC-9-15 | 45740 | Government of South Africa |
| | | | | |
| ☐ | N910SF | Douglas DC-10-10 | 46524 | US Air Force |
| ☐ | N330AU | Douglas MD-10-30CF | 46800/96 | Project Orbis International |
| | | | | |
| ☐ | N101WJ | Embraer EMB.110P1 Bandeirante | 110203 | Ruhe Sales |
| ☐ | N103VA | Embraer EMP.110P1 Banderante | 110204 | Marta Corp |
| ☐ | N316AF | Embraer EMB.110P1 Bandeirante | 110271 | Agape Flights |
| ☐ | PP-EIX | Embraer EMB.110P1 Bandeirante | 110468 | State Government of Amapa |
| ☐ | PP-EMG | Embraer EMB.110E Bandeirante | 110032 | State Government of Minas Gerais |
| ☐ | PP-ERN | Embraer EMB.110P1 Bandeirante | 110344 | State Government of Rio Grande do Norte |
| ☐ | PP-FFV | Embraer EMB.110B Bandeirante | 110284 | INPE - Instituto Nacide Pesquisas Espaciais |
| ☐ | PT-SGM | Embraer EMB.110P1 Bandeirante | 110420 | Triton Taxi Aereo |
| ☐ | PT-SHO | Embraer EMB.110P1 Bandeirante | 110461 | Furnas Centrais Electricas SA |
| ☐ | PT-SHP | Embraer EMB.110P1 Bandeirante | 110462 | Hidroelectrica Sao Francisco |
| ☐ | PT-SHR | Embraer EMB.110P1 Bandeirante | 110464 | Furnas Centrais Electricas SA |
| ☐ | PT-SHU | Embraer EMB.110P1 Bandeirante | 110466 | Amazonaves Taxi Aereo |

| | | | |
|---|---|---|---|
| VH-BQB | Embraer EMB.110P1 Bandeirante | 110298 | Robert Keys |
| ZS-NVB | Embraer EMB.110P1KC Bandeirante | 110479 | Batair Charters |
| N331CR | Embraer EMB.120ER Brasilia | 120121 | RCR Air |
| N405PA | Embraer EMB.120ER Brasilia | 120160 | Evernham Motorsports |
| N410PA | Embraer EMB-120 Brasilia | 120195 | Evernham Motorsports |
| N591M | Embraer EMB.120ER Brasilia | 120316 | Menard |
| N597M | Embraer EMB.120ER Brasilia | 120306 | Team Aero |
| N652CT | Embraer EMB.120ER Brasilia | 120289 | Business Aircraft Group |
| N653CT | Embraer EMB.120ER Brasilia | 120243 | Business Aircraft Group |
| N707TG | Embraer EMB.120 Brasilia | 120182 | Gordon Air |
| N16731 | Embraer EMB.120 Brasilia | 120190 | MWR Racing |
| PP-IAS | Embraer EMB.120 Brasilia | 120111 | Imetame Metalmechanica |
| PT-SOK | Embraer EMB.120ER Brasilia | 120358 | Vale SA |
| PT-SXP | Embraer EMB.120ER Brasilia | 120323 | Embraer |
| TT-DAG | Embraer EMB.120RT Brasilia | 120253 | RJM Aviation |
| 9J-RYL | Embraer EMB.120ER Brasilia | 120292 | Royal Air Charters |
| A6-AJA | Embraer Legacy 600 | 14501089 | AJA - Al Jaber Aviation |
| A6-AJB | Embraer Legacy 600 | 14501098 | AJA - Al Jaber Aviation |
| A6-DPW | Embraer Legacy 600 | 14500955 | Prestige Jet |
| A6-FLL | Embraer Legacy 600 | 14501051 | Falcon Aviation Services |
| A6-FLO | Embraer Legacy 600 | 14501096 | Falcon Aviation Services |
| A6-NKL | Embraer Legacy 600 | 14500944 | Empire Aviation Group |
| A6-NLA | Embraer Legacy 600 | 14501075 | Prestige Jet |
| A6-PJE | Embraer Legacy 600 | 14500972 | Prestige Jet |
| A6-SSV | Embraer Legacy 600 | 14501041 | Empire Aviation Group |
| A6-UGH | Embraer Legacy 600 | 14500993 | DAS Holding |
| A6-VVV | Embraer Legacy 600 | 14501057 | GAMA Aviation |
| A9C-MTC | Embraer Legacy 600 | 14500975 | MAE Aircraft Management |
| CE-01 | Embraer ERJ-135ER | 145449 | Belgian Air Force |
| CE-02 | Embraer ERJ-135LR | 145480 | Belgian Air Force |
| CN-MBP | Embraer Legacy 600 | 14501117 | Dalia Air |
| D-ADCP | Embraer Legacy 600 | 14501067 | Flugbereitschaft |
| D-AKAT | Embraer Legacy 600 | 14501038 | KamAvia Handels |
| D-ARTN | Embraer Legacy 600 | 14500941 | DC Aviation |
| D-AVIB | Embraer Legacy 600 | 14501109 | Vibro Air Flugservice |
| EC-IIR | Embraer Legacy 600 | 145540 | Audeli |
| EC-KHT | Embraer Legacy 600 | 14500863 | Aerodynamics Malaga |
| FAE-051 | Embraer Legacy 600 | 14501082 | Ecuadorian Air Force |
| G-CFJA | Embraer Legacy 600 | 14501045 | TAG Aviation |
| G-CGSE | Embraer Legacy 600 | 14500995 | GE Capital Corporation (Leasing) |
| G-CJMD | Embraer Legacy 600 | 14500994 | Corporate Jet Management |
| G-HUBY | Embraer Legacy 600 | 14500854 | London Executive Aviation |
| G-IRSH | Embraer Legacy 600 | 14501048 | London Executive Aviation |
| G-LALE | Embraer Legacy 600 | 14501017 | London Executive Aviation |
| G-LEGC | Embraer Legacy 600 | 14501025 | London Executive Aviation |
| G-OGSK | Embraer Legacy 600 | 14501074 | TAG Aviation |
| G-PGRP | Embraer Legacy 600 | 14501102 | GAMA Aviation |
| G-PLVN | Embraer Legacy 650 | 14501136 | |
| G-RBNS | Embraer Legacy 650 | 14501121 | London Executive Aviation |
| G-RHMS | Embraer Legacy 600 | 14501072 | International Jet Club |
| G-RUBE | Embraer Legacy 600 | 14501100 | London Executive Aviation |
| G-SHSI | Embraer Legacy 600 | 14501114 | TAG Aviation UK) |
| G-SUGA | Embraer Legacy 650 | 14501128 | Titan Airways |
| G-SYLJ | Embraer Legacy 600 | 14500937 | TAG Aviation |
| G-THFC | Embraer Legacy 600 | 14500954 | London Executive Aviation |
| G-WCCI | Embraer Legacy 600 | 145505 | London Executive Aviation |
| HB-JED | Embraer Legacy 600 | 145644 | Nomad Aviation |
| HB-JEL | Embraer Legacy 600 | 14500933 | G5 Executive |
| HP-1A | Embraer Legacy 600 | 14501066 | SENAN - Servicio Nacional Aeronaval |
| JY-CMC | Embraer Legacy 650 | 14501126 | Arab Wings |
| JY-KME | Embraer Legacy 600 | 14501055 | Arab Wings |
| K3601 | Embraer Legacy 600 | 14500867 | Indian Air Force |
| K3602 | Embraer Legacy 600 | 14500880 | Indian Air Force |
| K3603 | Embraer Legacy 600 | 14500910 | Indian Air Force |
| K3604 | Embraer Legacy 600 | 14500919 | Indian Air Force |
| LX-NVB | Embraer Legacy 600 | 14501002 | Silver Arrows |
| LX-RLG | Embraer Legacy 600 | 14500967 | Silver Arrows |
| M-AKAK | Embraer Legacy 600 | 14500970 | AA Kassar Sal |
| M-DSCL | Embraer Legacy 600 | 14500851 | Legacy Aviation |
| M-ESGR | Embraer Legacy 600 | 14501016 | Hermes Executive Aviation |
| M-IMAK | Embraer Legacy 600 | 14501140 | Donard Trading |
| M-KPCO | Embraer Legacy 600 | 14500973 | National Legacy for Aircraft Management |
| M-OLEG | Embraer Legacy 600 | 14500991 | Club 17 |
| M-RCCG | Embraer Legacy 600 | 14501113 | RMK Group |
| M-YCUP | Embraer Legacy 600 | 145555 | |
| M-YNJC | Embraer Legacy 600 | 14500961 | Hermes Executive Aviation |
| N6GD | Embraer Legacy 600 | 14500983 | Elite Air |
| N10SV | Embraer Legacy 600 | 14500974 | Siva Air |
| N53NA | Embraer Legacy 600 | 145770 | Aero Air |
| N63AG | Embraer Legacy 600 | 14501061 | ACM Aviation |
| N89FE | Embraer Legacy 600 | 14501058 | FirstEnergy Solutions |

| | | | | |
|---|---|---|---|---|
| ☐ | N89LD | Embraer ERJ-135SE | 145648 | McKee Foods Transportation |
| ☐ | N124LS | Embraer Legacy 600 | 14500948 | Executive Jet Management |
| ☐ | N135SK | Embraer Legacy 600 | 14500989 | United Aviation |
| ☐ | N135SL | Embraer Legacy 600 | 145711 | United Aviation |
| ☐ | N226HY | Embraer Legacy 600 | 14501014 | Executive Flightways |
| ☐ | N227WE | Embraer Legacy 600 | 14501018 | United States Aviation |
| ☐ | N325JF | Embraer ERJ-135SE | 145499 | Intel Air Shuttle Aircraft |
| ☐ | N357TE | Embraer Legacy 600 | 14501079 | BUA Delaware |
| ☐ | N359AD | Embraer ERJ-145LR | 145169 | Aerodynamics |
| ☐ | N373RB | Embraer Legacy 600 | 14500957 | RBGT |
| ☐ | N386CH | Embraer ERJ-135SE | 145467 | Intel Air Shuttle Aircraft |
| ☐ | N451DJ | Embraer Legacy 600 | 145789 | Universal Jet Aviation |
| ☐ | N486TM | Embraer ERJ-135SE | 145364 | Intel Air Shuttle Aircraft |
| ☐ | N494TG | Embraer Legacy 600 | 145678 | Sentient Flight Group |
| ☐ | N503JT | Embraer Legacy 600 | 14501032 | ExcelAire Service |
| ☐ | N515JT | Embraer Legacy 600 | 14500950 | Excelaire |
| ☐ | N580ML | Embraer Legacy 600 | 14500990 | Stone Tower Air |
| ☐ | N600YC | Embraer Legacy 600 | 14501069 | Rimbaka Forestry Corp |
| ☐ | N605WG | Embraer Legacy 600 | 14500980 | Wings West Aircraft |
| ☐ | N615PG | Embraer Legacy 600 | 14501004 | Pacific Gas & Electric |
| ☐ | N642AG | Embraer Legacy 600 | 145642 | Swift Air |
| ☐ | N676TC | Embraer Legacy 600 | 145699 | Alpine Cascade |
| ☐ | N678RC | Embraer Legacy 600 | 14501064 | Financial Business Concepts |
| ☐ | N728PH | Embraer Legacy 600 | 14500985 | ExcelAire Service |
| ☐ | N730BH | Embraer Legacy 600 | 145730 | Swift Air |
| ☐ | N742SP | Embraer Legacy 600 | 14500884 | Insperity |
| ☐ | N752SP | Embraer Legacy 600 | 14500903 | Insperity |
| ☐ | N806D | Embraer Legacy 600 | 14501095 | Dominion Resources Services |
| ☐ | N809TD | Embraer Legacy 600 | 14500809 | Swift Air |
| ☐ | N818HR | Embraer Legacy 600 | 14501105 | HR INV |
| ☐ | N827TV | Embraer Legacy 600 | 14500971 | Pinnacle Aviation |
| ☐ | N829RN | Embraer ERJ-135SE | 145361 | Intel Air Shuttle Aircraft |
| ☐ | N865LS | Embraer Legacy 600 | 14501080 | Leon Advertising and Public Relations |
| ☐ | N888ML | Embraer Legacy 600 | 14500818 | New Macau Landmark Management |
| ☐ | N898JS | Embraer Legacy 600 | 14501071 | The LaLit Hotels |
| ☐ | N900EM | Embraer Legacy 600 | 14500976 | Air By Jet |
| ☐ | N904FL | Embraer Legacy 600 | 145780 | Nextant Aircraft |
| ☐ | N905FL | Embraer Legacy 600 | 145775 | Nextant Aircraft |
| ☐ | N908FL | Embraer Legacy 600 | 14500942 | Flight Options |
| ☐ | N909TT | Embraer Legacy 600 | 14501044 | Transcon International |
| ☐ | N910FL | Embraer Legacy 600 | 14500952 | MACJ |
| ☐ | N912JC | Embraer Legacy 600 | 14501015 | Vitesse Aviation Services |
| ☐ | N914FL | Embraer Legacy 600 | 14501007 | Flight Options |
| ☐ | N924AK | Embraer Legacy 600 | 14501034 | Talon Air |
| ☐ | N925FL | Embraer Legacy 600 | 14500825 | Lndes Investments |
| ☐ | N926FM | Embraer ERJ-135SE | 145466 | Intel Air Shuttle Aircraft |
| ☐ | N939AJ | Embraer Legacy 600 | 14500939 | Orfro LLC & Ares Technical Administration |
| ☐ | N948AL | Embraer ERJ-135SE | 145450 | Intel Air Shuttle Aircraft |
| ☐ | N966JS | Embraer Legacy 600 | 14500966 | Pebuny |
| ☐ | N983JC | Embraer ERJ-135LR | 14500977 | Johnson Controls |
| ☐ | N1023C | Embraer ERJ-135SE | 145550 | ConocoPhillips |
| ☐ | OE-IBK | Embraer Legacy 600 | 14501110 | Avcon Jet |
| ☐ | OE-IBR | Embraer Legacy 600 | 14500960 | Global Jet Austria |
| ☐ | OE-IDB | Embraer Legacy 600 | 14500999 | Avcon Jet |
| ☐ | OE-IDH | Embraer Legacy 600 | 14501026 | EUROP STAR Aircraft |
| ☐ | OE-IRK | Embraer Legacy 600 | 14500916 | Avcon Jet |
| ☐ | OK-GGG | Embraer Legacy 600 | 14500986 | ABS Jets |
| ☐ | OK-JNT | Embraer Legacy 600 | 14501087 | ABS Jets |
| ☐ | OK-ROM | Embraer Legacy 600 | 14501039 | ABS Jets |
| ☐ | OK-SLN | Embraer Legacy 600 | 145796 | ABS Jets |
| ☐ | OK-SUN | Embraer Legacy 600 | 14500963 | ABS Jets |
| ☐ | PK-DHK | Embraer Legacy 600 | 14501046 | Premiair |
| ☐ | PK-OME | Embraer Legacy 600 | 145516 | Airfast Indonesia |
| ☐ | PK-RJG | Embraer Legacy 600 | 14500969 | Premiair |
| ☐ | PK-RJW | Embraer Legacy 600 | 14501106 | Premiair |
| ☐ | PK-RSS | Embraer Legacy 600 | 14501020 | Enggang Air Service |
| ☐ | PP-VVA | Embraer ERJ-135LR | 145702 | Companhia Vale do Rio Doce |
| ☐ | PP-VVV | Embraer Legacy 600 | 14501099 | JBS |
| ☐ | PR-AVX | Embraer Legacy 600 | 14501037 | Grupo EBX Participacoes |
| ☐ | PR-BEB | Embraer Legacy 600 | 14501035 | Dedalus Administracao e Participacoes |
| ☐ | PR-LTC | Embraer Legacy 600 | 14501091 | Macbens Patrimonial |
| ☐ | PR-NIO | Embraer Legacy 600 | 14501012 | CBMM-Compania Brasileira de Metalurgia e Mineracao |
| ☐ | PR-ODF | Embraer Legacy 600 | 14501054 | Global Taxi Aereo Ltda / Reali Taxi Aereo |
| ☐ | PR-ORE | Embraer Legacy 600 | 145625 | Companhia Vale do Rio Doce |
| ☐ | PR-RIO | Embraer Legacy 600 | 145717 | Unibanco Leasing |
| ☐ | PT-SCR | Embraer Legacy 600 | 14500946 | Sao Conrado Taxi Aereo |
| ☐ | PT-SKM | Embraer Legacy 600 | 14501090 | Embraer |
| ☐ | PT-SKW | Embraer Legacy 600 | 14501006 | Sao Conrado Taxi Aereo |
| ☐ | PT-TKI | Embraer Legacy 650 | 14501115 | Embraer |
| ☐ | PT-TKV | Embraer Legacy 650 | 14501119 | Embraer |
| ☐ | P4-AEG | Embraer Legacy 600 | 14501111 | AEG Air AVV |
| ☐ | P4-KUL | Embraer Legacy 600 | 14500978 | Premier Avia |
| ☐ | P4-MIV | Embraer Legacy 600 | 14501031 | RusJet |

| | Reg | Type | Serial | Operator |
|---|---|---|---|---|
| ☐ | P4-MSG | Embraer Legacy 600 | 14500913 | PremierAvia |
| ☐ | P4-PAM | Embraer Legacy 600 | 14500982 | Petroff Air |
| ☐ | P4-SIS | Embraer Legacy 600 | 145586 | Premier Avia |
| ☐ | P4-SMS | Embraer Legacy 650 | 14501123 | Petroff Air |
| ☐ | P4-SVM | Embraer Legacy 600 | 14501060 | Petroff Air |
| ☐ | P4-VVP | Embraer Legacy 600 | 145549 | Petroff Air |
| ☐ | S5-ABL | Embraer Legacy 600 | 14501008 | Linxair Business Airlines |
| ☐ | S5-ALA | Embraer Legacy 600 | 14501029 | Linxair Business Airlines |
| ☐ | SE-DJG | Embraer Legacy 600 | 14501042 | EFS European Flight Service |
| ☐ | SX-CDK | Embraer Legacy 600 | 14500998 | K2 SmartJets |
| ☐ | SX-DGM | Embraer Legacy 600 | 14501023 | Interjet |
| ☐ | T-501 | Embraer Legacy 600 | 14500981 | Angolan Peoples Air Force |
| ☐ | VH-VLT | Embraer Legacy 600 | 14501107 | Southern Cross Jets |
| ☐ | VP-CFA | Embraer Legacy 600 | 145637 | SAMCO Aviation |
| ☐ | VP-CHP | Embraer Legacy 600 | 14500802 | JBJE |
| ☐ | VP-CLL | Embraer Legacy 600 | 14501052 | Titan Aviation |
| ☐ | VP-CMK | Embraer Legacy 600 | 14501083 | Comoro Gulf Aviation |
| ☐ | VQ-BFP | Embraer Legacy 600 | 14501049 | Planair |
| ☐ | VQ-BFQ | Embraer Legacy 600 | 14501062 | Planair |
| ☐ | VT-BSF | Embraer Legacy 600 | 14500901 | Indian Border Security Force |
| ☐ | VT-CKP | Embraer Legacy 600 | 14501094 | Krishnapatnam Port Company |
| ☐ | 5N-RSG | Embraer Legacy 600 | 14500891 | Government of River State of Nigeria |
| ☐ | 7Q-WPB | Embraer ERJ-135LR | 145676 | Paladin Energy |
| ☐ | 209 | Embraer ERJ-135ER | 145209 | Greek Air Force |
| ☐ | 484 | Embraer Legacy 600 | 145484 | Greek Air Force |
| ☐ | 1124 | Embraer ERJ-135LR | 14501124 | Royal Thai Army |
| ☐ | 2560 | Embraer ERJ-135LR | 145600 | Brazilian Air Force |
| ☐ | 2561 | Embraer ERJ-135LR | 145608 | Brazilian Air Force |
| ☐ | 2580 | Embraer Legacy 600 | 145412 | Brazilian Air Force |
| ☐ | 2581 | Embraer Legacy 600 | 145462 | Brazilian Air Force |
| ☐ | 2582 | Embraer Legacy 600 | 145495 | Brazilian Air Force |
| ☐ | 2583 | Embraer Legacy 600 | 145528 | Brazilian Air Force |
| ☐ | 2584 | Embraer Legacy 600 | 14500997 | Brazilian Air Force |
| ☐ | 2585 | Embraer Legacy 600 | 14501078 | Brazilian Air Force |
| ☐ | 1084/HS-AMP | Embraer ERJ-135LR | 14501084 | Royal Thai Army |
| ☐ | 2112/HS-NVA | Embraer ERJ-135LR | 14501077 | Royal Thai Navy |
| ☐ | 2113/HS-NVB | Embraer ERJ-135LR | 14501125 | Royal Thai Navy |
| ☐ | N138DE | Embraer ERJ-145LR | 145129 | Champion Air |
| ☐ | N500DE | Embraer ERJ-145EP | 145084 | Champion Air |
| ☐ | N978RP | Embraer ERJ-145EP | 145169 | Aerodynamics |
| ☐ | PR-DPF | Embraer ERJ-145EP | 145127 | Brazilian Federal Police Force |
| ☐ | PR-PFN | Embraer ERJ-145LR | 145002 | Brazilian Federal Police Force |
| ☐ | PT-SPM | Embraer ERJ-145LR | 145114 | Companhia Vale do Rio Doce |
| ☐ | 3C-QQH | Embraer ERJ-145EP | 145076 | Government of Equatorial Guinea |
| ☐ | 2520 | Embraer ERJ-145EP | 145023 | Brazilian Air Force |
| ☐ | 2521 | Embraer ERJ-145EP | 145020 | Brazilian Air Force |
| ☐ | 2522 | Embraer ERJ-145EP | 145027 | Brazilian Air Force |
| ☐ | 2523 | Embraer ERJ-145EP | 145028 | Brazilian Air Force |
| ☐ | 2524 | Embraer ERJ-145EP | 145034 | Brazilian Air Force |
| ☐ | 2525 | Embraer ERJ-145EP | 145038 | Brazilian Air Force |
| ☐ | 2526 | Embraer ERJ-145EP | 145137 | Brazilian Air Force |
| ☐ | 2550 | Embraer ERJ-145LR | 145350 | Brazilian Air Force |
| ☐ | CE-03 | Embraer ERJ-145LR | 145526 | Belgian Air Force |
| ☐ | CE-04 | Embraer ERJ-145LR | 145548 | Belgian Air Force |
| ☐ | N735A | Embraer 170 | 17000319 | Aramco |
| ☐ | N736A | Embraer 170 | 17000320 | Aramco |
| ☐ | PP-XJB | Embraer 170 | 17000003 | Embraer |
| ☐ | PP-XJD | Embraer 175 | 17000014 | Embraer |
| ☐ | SP-LIG | Embraer 175LR | 17000283 | Polish Air Force |
| ☐ | SP-LIH | Embraer 175LR | 17000288 | Polish Air Force |
| ☐ | PP-XMA | Embraer 190 | 19000001 | Embraer |
| ☐ | PP-XMI | Embraer 190 | 19000003 | Embraer |
| ☐ | 2590 | Embraer 190LR | 19000214 | Brazilian Air Force |
| ☐ | 2591 | Embraer 190LR | 19000277 | Brazilian Air Force |
| ☐ | A6-AJH | Embraer Lineage 1000 | 19000140 | AJA - Al Jaber Aviation |
| ☐ | A6-AJI | Embraer Lineage 1000 | 19000261 | AJA - Al Jaber Aviation |
| ☐ | A6-ARK | Embraer Lineage 1000 | 19000109 | Prestige Jet |
| ☐ | A6-HHS | Embraer Lineage 1000 | 19000296 | Falcon Aviation Services |
| ☐ | A6-KAH | Embraer Lineage 1000 | 19000236 | Al Habtoor Group |
| ☐ | M-SBAH | Embraer Lineage 1000 | 19000225 | Flemming House |
| ☐ | PP-XTF | Embraer Lineage 1000 | 19000159 | Embraer |
| ☐ | XA-AYJ | Embraer Lineage 1000 | 19000243 | Grupo Omnilife |
| ☐ | 2592 | Embraer Lineage 1000 | 19000177 | Brazilian Air Force |
| ☐ | MT-216 | Fairchild FH-227D | 578 | Mexican Navy |
| ☐ | PH-NLZ | Fairchild (Swearingen) Metro II | TC-277 | Stichting Nationaal Lucht en Ruimtevaart Lab. |
| ☐ | D-CNEU | Fairchild/Dornier 228-200NG | 8206 | RUAG Aerospace |

| | Registration | Type | Serial | Operator |
|---|---|---|---|---|
| ☐ | C-FSCO | Fairchild/Dornier 328-130 | 3109 | Shell Canada |
| ☐ | N28CG | Fairchild/Dornier 328-100 | 3024 | Corning Inc |
| ☐ | N38CG | Fairchild/Dornier 328-100 | 3034 | Corning Inc |
| ☐ | N338PH | Fairchild/Dornier 328-120 | 3029 | Lima Delta |
| ☐ | N391EF | Fairchild/Dornier 328-110 | 3091 | Sierra Nevada |
| ☐ | N565EF | Fairchild/Dornier 328-110 | 3068 | Sierra Nevada |
| ☐ | N907EF | Fairchild/Dornier 328-120 | 3104 | Sierra Nevada |
| ☐ | N929EF | Fairchild/Dornier 328-110 | 3026 | Sierra Nevada |
| ☐ | N975EF | Fairchild/Dornier 328-110 | 3031 | Sierra Nevada |
| ☐ | OB2 | Fairchild/Dornier 328-100 | 3083 | Botswana Defence Force |
| ☐ | C-GCPW | Fairchild/Dornier 328JET | 3129 | Pratt & Whitney Canada |
| ☐ | D-BADC | Fairchild/Dornier 328JET | 3216 | Aero Dienst |
| ☐ | D-BGAS | Fairchild/Dornier 328JET | 3139 | DC Aviation |
| ☐ | HB-AEU | Fairchild/Dornier 328JET Envoy 3 | 3199 | Swiss Jet |
| ☐ | N57TT | Fairchild/Dornier 328JET | 3205 | Thompson Tractor |
| ☐ | N117LM | Fairchild/Dornier 328JET | 3167 | Livemercial Aviation Holding |
| ☐ | N131BC | Fairchild/Dornier 328JET | 3168 | International Bank of Commerce |
| ☐ | N328WW | Fairchild/Dornier 328JET Envoy 3 | 3116 | Ultimate Jetcharters |
| ☐ | N359SK | Fairchild/Dornier 328JET | 3202 | Ultimate Jetcharters |
| ☐ | N401FJ | Fairchild/Dornier 328JET | 3145 | Greentech de Venezuela |
| ☐ | N406FJ | Fairchild/Dornier 328JET | 3156 | Ultimate Jetcharters |
| ☐ | N407FJ | Fairchild/Dornier 328JET | 3157 | Ultimate Jetcharters |
| ☐ | N419FJ | Fairchild/Dornier 328JET | 3173 | Flightworks |
| ☐ | N425FJ | Fairchild/Dornier 328JET | 3189 | Ultimate Jetcharters |
| ☐ | N429FJ | Fairchild/Dornier 328JET | 3194 | Ultimate Jetcharters |
| ☐ | N430FJ | Fairchild/Dornier 328JET | 3209 | Aviando Services |
| ☐ | N804CE | Fairchild/Dornier 328JET | 3184 | Cummins |
| ☐ | N807LM | Fairchild/Dornier 328JET | 3099 | Air Force Research Laboratory |
| ☐ | N3220U | Fairchild/Dornier 328JET | 3220 | US Department of State |
| ☐ | OE-HRJ | Fairchild/Dornier 328JET | 3206 | ILC Aviation |
| ☐ | UR-AER | Fairchild/Dornier 328JET | 3176 | Aerostar |
| ☐ | UR-DAV | Fairchild/Dornier 328JET | 3169 | Aerostar |
| ☐ | UR-WOG | Fairchild/Dornier 328JET | 3118 | Aerostar |
| ☐ | VP-CJD | Fairchild/Dornier 328JET Envoy 3 | 3221 | Easy Aviation |
| ☐ | XC-LLS | Fairchild/Dornier 328JET | 3197 | Procuraduria General de la Republica Nacional |
| ☐ | ZS-AAK | Fairchild/Dornier 328JET | 3162 | Anglo Aircraft |
| ☐ | ZS-IOC | Fairchild/Dornier 328JET | 3219 | Sishen Iron Ore |
| ☐ | 5N-SPE | Fairchild.Dornier 328JET Envoy 3 | 3151 | Shell Nigeria |
| ☐ | 5N-SPM | Fairchild/Dornier 328JET Envoy 3 | 3141 | Shell Nigeria |
| ☐ | 5N-SPN | Fairchild/Dornier 328JET Envoy 3 | 3120 | Shell Nigeria |
| ☐ | AP-BHZ | Fokker F.27-500 | 10686 | Aircraft Sales & Services |
| ☐ | J5-JIA | Fokker F.27-300M | 10156 | Africa Air Assistance |
| ☐ | A-2701 | Fokker F.27-400M | 10536 | Indonesian Air Force |
| ☐ | G-525 | Fokker F.27-400M | 10520 | Ghana Air Force |
| ☐ | 10669 | Fokker F.27-500RF | 10669 | Philippine Air Force |
| ☐ | 59-0259 | Fokker F.27-200 | 10115 | Philippine Air Force |
| ☐ | TJ-ALG | Fokker F.28-4000 | 11227 | Air Leasing Cameroon |
| ☐ | 5A-DSO | Fokker F.28-2000 | 11110 | Petro Air |
| ☐ | 5H-CCM | Fokker F.28-3000 | 11137 | Government of Tanzania |
| ☐ | 5V-TAI | Fokker F.28-1000 | 11079 | Government of Togo |
| ☐ | A-2801 | Fokker F.28-1000 | 11042 | Indonesian Air Force |
| ☐ | FAC0002 | Fokker F.28-1000 | 11992 | Colombian Air Force |
| ☐ | FAC1041 | Fokker F.28-3000C | 11162 | Colombian Air Force |
| ☐ | G-530 | Fokker F.28-3000 | 11125 | Ghana Air Force |
| ☐ | M28-01 | Fokker F.28-1000 | 11088 | Royal Malaysian Air Force |
| ☐ | T-02 | Fokker F.28-4000 | 11203 | Argentine Air Force |
| ☐ | T-03 | Fokker F.28-1000 | 11028 | Argentine Air Force |
| ☐ | T-50 | Fokker F.28-1000 | 11048 | Argentine Air Force |
| ☐ | 5H-TGF | Fokker 50 | 20231 | Government of Tanzania |
| ☐ | 5001 | Fokker 50 | 20229 | Republic of China Air Force |
| ☐ | 5002 | Fokker 50 | 20238 | Republic of China Air Force |
| ☐ | 5003 | Fokker 50 | 20242 | Republic of China Air Force |
| ☐ | 27228 | Fokker 50 | 20228 | Royal Thai Border Police |
| ☐ | KAF308 | Fokker 70 | 11557 | Government of Kenya |
| ☐ | PH-KBX | Fokker 70 | 11547 | Dutch Royal Flight |
| ☐ | OE-IIB | Fokker 100 | 11403 | Moscow Sky |
| ☐ | OE-IIC | Fokker 100 | 11406 | Moscow Sky |
| ☐ | OE-IID | Fokker 100 | 11368 | Moscow Sky |
| ☐ | PK-RJI | Fokker 100 | 11328 | Premiair |
| ☐ | N49 | General Dynamics (Convair) 580 | 479 | FAA / US DoT |
| ☐ | N580HW | General Dynamics (Convair) 580 | 2 | Honeywell |
| ☐ | N730RS | Gulfstream Aerospace Mallard | J-50 | Richard Sugden |
| ☐ | VP-CLK | Gulfstream Aerospace Mallard | J-34 | Mallard Aviation Corporation |
| ☐ | B-3826 | Harbin Y-12 IV | H5005 | Harbin Aircraft Manufacturing Corporation |

| | Reg | Type | Serial | Operator |
|---|---|---|---|---|
| ☐ | B-610L | Harbin Y-12 E | YUN12E001 | Harbin Aircraft Manufacturing Corporation |
| ☐ | VT-XSD | Hindustan Aeronautics Saras | PT-1 | National Aerospace Laboratories |
| ☐ | RA-75454 | Ilyushin Il-18D | 187010104 | Rossiya Special Flight Detachment |
| ☐ | RA-75900 | Ilyushin Il-18 (Il-22) | 0393609681 | Russian Air Force |
| ☐ | RA-75903 | Ilyushin Il-18 (Il-22) | 0393610235 | Russian Air Force |
| ☐ | RA-86495(2) | Ilyushin Il-62M | 2726628 | 223rd State Airline Flight Unit |
| ☐ | RA-86539 | Ilyushin Il-62M | 2344615 | 223rd State Airline Flight Unit |
| ☐ | RA-86555 | Ilyushin Il-62M | 4547315 | 223rd State Airline Flight Unit |
| ☐ | ST-PRA | Ilyushin Il-62M | 2357711 | Government of Sudan |
| ☐ | D2-MBJ | Ilyushin Il-76TD | 1023409280 | Angolan Air Force |
| ☐ | EW-76783 | Ilyushin Il-76TD | 0093498974 | Operator unknown |
| ☐ | TN-AES | Ilyushin Il-76TD | 1033415504 | Conga (Brazzaville) Government |
| ☐ | 4K-AZ60 | Ilyushin Il-76MD | 0093499982 | Operator unknown |
| ☐ | 76492 | Ilyushin Il-76LL | 30043452549 | Flight Research Institute 'GTRE-DRDO' |
| ☐ | RA-91003 | Ilyushin Il-114 | 2053800109 | Russian Navy |
| ☐ | TJ-AAS | Israel Aerospace Industries Arava | 081 | Government of Cameroon |
| ☐ | 5501 | Kawasaki Heavy Industries P-1 | PROTO001 | Japan Maritime SDF |
| ☐ | 5502 | Kawasaki Heavy Industries P-1 | PROTO002 | Japan Maritime SDF |
| ☐ | 08-1201 | Kawasaki Heavy Industries XC-2 (C-X) | 001 | Japan Air Self Defence Force |
| ☐ | HR-ADQ | LET L-410 | | Operator unknown |
| ☐ | J2-MBE | LET L-410UVP-E20 | 2732 | Djibouti Air Force |
| ☐ | PR-IBB | LET L-410UVP-E | 882024 | Operator unknown |
| ☐ | PR-IBD | LET L-410UVP-E | 861615 | Operator unknown |
| ☐ | RF-00195 | LET L-410UVP-E3 | 871819 | DOSAAF |
| ☐ | RF-67571 | LET L-410UVP-E19A | 912614 | Tartarstan Police |
| ☐ | RF-94658 | LET L-410UVP-E3 | 892240 | VVS Rossii |
| ☐ | RF-94667 | LET L-410UVP-E3 | 892330 | VVS Rossii |
| ☐ | ZS-ATD | LET L-410UVP-E | 902527 | Orsmond Aerial Spray |
| ☐ | ZS-ATE | LET L-410UVP-E20 | 932731 | Aircraft Systems South Africa |
| ☐ | 3D-AFH | LET L-410UVP-E3 | 892335 | Operator unknown |
| ☐ | 3X-GEK | LET L-410UVP | 800524 | Operator unknown |
| ☐ | 9Q-CMD | LET L-410 | | Operator unknown |
| ☐ | N168CF | McDonnell-Douglas MD-87 | 49670 | Sunrider International |
| ☐ | N287KB | McDonnell-Douglas MD-87 | 49768 | KEB Aircraft Sales |
| ☐ | N682RW | McDonnell-Douglas MD-81 | 48006 | Olympia Aviation |
| ☐ | N880DP | McDonnell-Douglas MD-83 | 49504 | Detroit Pistons |
| ☐ | P4-AIR | McDonnell-Douglas MD-87ER | 49412 | Sistema |
| ☐ | SX-IFA | McDonnell-Douglas MD-83 | 49809 | Amjet Executive |
| ☐ | TT-ABC | McDonnell-Douglas MD-87 | 49888 | Government of Chad |
| ☐ | VP-CBH | McDonnell-Douglas MD-82 | 53577 | Mineralogy Pty |
| ☐ | VP-CKN | McDonnell-Douglas MD-83 | 49458 | FC Mazembe |
| ☐ | VP-CNI | McDonnell-Douglas MD-87 | 49767 | Corporate Aviation Holdings |
| ☐ | VP-CTF | McDonnell-Douglas MD-87 | 49777 | AMAC Aerospace |
| ☐ | N44KS | SAAB SF.340A | 340A-050 | JMJ Flight Services |
| ☐ | N632RF | SAAB SF.340A | 340A-042 | Pegasus Air |
| ☐ | N702RS | SAAB SF.340B | 340B-233 | SST Aero Services |
| ☐ | N703RS | SAAB SF.340B | 340B-252 | SST Aero Services |
| ☐ | N727DL | SAAB SF.340A | 340A-036 | Club SAAB 340 |
| ☐ | UR-APM | SAAB SF.340B | 340B-230 | Business Airlines |
| ☐ | N508RH | SAAB SF.2000 | 2000-027 | Hendrick Motorsports |
| ☐ | N509RH | SAAB SF.2000 | 2000-030 | Hendrick Motorsports |
| ☐ | N511RH | SAAB SF.2000 | 2000-020 | Hendrick Motorsports |
| ☐ | N519JG | SAAB SF.2000 | 2000-017 | Joe Gibbs Racing |
| ☐ | SE-045 | SAAB SF.2000AEW | 2000-045 | SAAB Aircraft |
| ☐ | 82911 | Sukhoi SU-80GP | 0102 | Sukhoi Design Bureau |
| ☐ | 97003 | Sukhoi Superjet 100-95LR | 95003 | Sukhoi Design Bureau |
| ☐ | 97004 | Sukhoi Superjet 100-95LR | 95004 | Sukhoi Design Bureau |
| ☐ | 97005 | Sukhoi Superjet 100-95LR | 95005 | Sukhoi Design Bureau |
| ☐ | 63957 | Tupolev Tu-134A | 63957 | Ukrainian Air Force |
| ☐ | 65098 | Tupolev Tu-134Sh | 73550815 | MIR Scientific Industrial Enterprise |
| ☐ | 65606 | Tupolev Tu-134A | 46300 | Tupolev Design Bureau |
| ☐ | RA-63757 | Tupolev Tu-134A | 1363757 | Russian Navy |
| ☐ | RA-63769 | Tupolev Tu-134A | 63769 | SpetsTrans Servis |
| ☐ | RA-64454 | Tupolev Tu-134A | 66140 | Gromov Flight Research Institute ( LII ) |
| ☐ | RA-65550 | Tupolev Tu-134A | 66200 | Meridian Air |
| ☐ | RA-65559 | Tupolev Tu-134A | 49909 | JetAlliance East |
| ☐ | RA-65721 | Tupolev Tu-134A | 66130 | JetAlliance East |
| ☐ | RA-65723 | Tupolev Tu-134A | 66440 | Jetair Group |
| ☐ | RA-65724 | Tupolev Tu-134A | 66445 | Meridian Air |

| | Registration | Type | Serial | Operator |
|---|---|---|---|---|
| ☐ | RA-65733 | Tupolev Tu-134B | 64425 | 223rd State Airline Flight Unit |
| ☐ | RA-65798 | Tupolev Tu-134A | 63179 | Meridian Air |
| ☐ | RA-65830 | Tupolev Tu-134A | 12093 | Unconfirmed Russian operator |
| ☐ | RA-65917 | Tupolev Tu-134A | 63991 | Meridian Air |
| ☐ | RA-65921 | Tupolev Tu-134A | 63997 | Rossiya Special Flight Detachment |
| ☐ | RA-65926 | Tupolev Tu-134A | 66101 | Meridian Air |
| ☐ | RA-65927 | Tupolev Tu-134A | 66198 | Russian Air Force |
| ☐ | RA-65930 | Tupolev Tu-134A | 66500 | Jetair Group |
| ☐ | RA-65945 | Tupolev Tu-134B | 64010 | Unconfirmed Russian airline |
| ☐ | RA-65965 | Tupolev Tu-134A | 2351803 | Russian Air Force |
| ☐ | RA-65979 | Tupolev Tu-134A | 63158 | Russian Air Force |
| ☐ | RA-65984 | Tupolev Tu-134A | 63400 | Russian Air Force |
| ☐ | RA-65996 | Tupolev Tu-134A | 63825 | 236th State Airline Flight Unit |
| ☐ | RF-65150 | Tupolev Tu-134A-3 | | Yuri Gagarin Space Centre 01 BLUE |
| ☐ | UN-65683 | Tupolev Tu-134A | 62199 | Kazakhstan Ministry of Defence |
| ☐ | YK-AYA | Tupolev Tu-134B | 63992 | Syrianair |
| ☐ | YK-AYB | Tupolev Tu-134B | 63994 | Syrianair |
| ☐ | 4K-65496 | Tupolev Tu-134A | 63468 | Azerbaijan Defence Ministry |
| ☐ | 03 RED | Tupolev Tu-134Sh | ZR105 | Russian Air Force |
| ☐ | 100 BLUE | Tupolev Tu-134A | 63780 | Russian Navy |
| ☐ | 34 BLUE | Tupolev Tu-134Sh | 83550970 | Russian Air Force |
| | | | | |
| ☐ | 4K-85729 | Tupolev Tu-154M | 911 | Government of Azerbaijan |
| ☐ | B-4028 | Tupolev Tu-154M | 967 | People's Liberation Army Air Force |
| ☐ | B-4138 | Tupolev Tu-154M | 712 | People's Liberation Army Air Force |
| ☐ | EW-85815 | Tupolev Tu-154M | 1010 | Government of Belarus |
| ☐ | RA-85001 | Tupolev Tu-154M | 820 | Rossiya Special Flight Detachment |
| ☐ | RA-85019 | Tupolev Tu-154M | 1019 | Federal Security Service |
| ☐ | RA-85084 | Tupolev Tu-154M | 1004 | Federal Security Service |
| ☐ | RA-85135 | Tupolev Tu-154M | 92A922 | Russian Ministry of the Interior |
| ☐ | RA-85155 | Tupolev Tu-154M | 1000 | Russian Air Force |
| ☐ | RA-85360 | Tupolev Tu-154B | 360 | Russian Air Force |
| ☐ | RA-85510 | Tupolev Tu-154B | 510 | Russian Air Force |
| ☐ | RA-85563 | Tupolev Tu-154B-2 | 82A563 | Russian Air Force |
| ☐ | RA-85565 | Tupolev Tu-154B | 565 | Russian Ministry of the Interior |
| ☐ | RA-85614 | Tupolev Tu-154M | 723 | Russian Navy |
| ☐ | RA-85735 | Tupolev Tu-154M | 92A917 | Russian Ministry of the Interior |
| ☐ | RA-85754 | Tupolev Tu-154M | 92A936 | Avianergo |
| ☐ | UN-85464 | Tupolev Tu-154B | 80A464 | Government of Kazakhstan |
| ☐ | UP-T5401 | Tupolev Tu-154M | 91A889 | Government of Kazakhstan |
| ☐ | 102 | Tupolev Tu-154M | 862 | Polish Air Force |
| | | | | |
| ☐ | RA-64010 | Tupolev Tu-204-300A (Tu-234) | 1450743164010 | Biznes Aero VIP |
| ☐ | RA-64014 | Tupolev Tu-204 | 1450744364014 | Rossiya Special Flight Detachment |
| ☐ | RA-64015 | Tupolev Tu-204 | 1450741464015 | Rossiya Special Flight Detachment |
| ☐ | RA-64150 | Tupolev Tu-204-100SM | 145074##64150 | Aviastar-SP |
| | | | | |
| ☐ | 94005 | Tupolev Tu-334-100 | 01005 | Tupolev Design Bureau |
| ☐ | RA-94001 | Tupolev Tu-334-100 | 01001 | Tupolev Design Bureau |
| | | | | |
| ☐ | D-ADAM | VFW614 | G17 | DLR Flugbetriebe |
| | | | | |
| ☐ | J2-MAT | WSK/PZL Antonov An-28 | 1AJ009-14 | Djibouti Air Force |
| ☐ | UP-AN2801 | WSK/PZL Antonov An-28 | 1AJ009-04 | Unknown Operator |
| | | | | |
| ☐ | N319TW | WSK-PZL Mielec M28-05 Skytruck | AJE003-19 | USAF Special Operations |
| ☐ | N322PW | WSK-PZL Mielec M28-05 Skytruck | AJE003-22 | USAF Special Operations |
| ☐ | N323FG | WSK-PZL Mielec M28-05 Skytruck | AJE003-23 | USAF Special Operations |
| ☐ | N324HA | WSK-PZL Mielec M28-05 Skytruck | AJE003-24 | USAF Special Operations |
| ☐ | SP-DDF | WSK-PZL Mielec M28 Skytruck (P&W) | 1ANJP10-03 | WSK-PZL MIELEC |
| | | | | |
| ☐ | B-3489 | Xian Y-7-100 | 07708 | Peoples Republic of China Navy |
| ☐ | B-3493 | Xian Y-7-100 | 08704 | Peoples Republic of China Navy |
| | | | | |
| ☐ | EW-88187 | Yakovlev Yak-40 | 9620748 | Government of Belarus |
| ☐ | RA-21500 | Yakovlev Yak-40K | 9741356 | Rosneft Baltika |
| ☐ | RA-21504 | Yakovlev Yak-40K | 9831758 | Jetair Group |
| ☐ | RA-21506 | Yakovlev Yak-40K | 9840259 | Unconfirmed Russian operator |
| ☐ | RA-87216 | Yakovlev Yak-40 | 9510440 | Jet 2000 |
| ☐ | RA-87496 | Yakovlev Yak-40 | 9541945 | Aerolimousine |
| ☐ | RA-87499 | Yakovlev Yak-40 | 9610246 | Saratov Aviation Plant |
| ☐ | RA-87535 | Yakovlev Yak-40 | 9521941 | Jet Express |
| ☐ | RA-87569 | Yakovlev Yak-40D | 9220222 | Alliance Avia |
| ☐ | RA-87669 | Yakovlev Yak-40 | 9021760 | Unconfirmed Russian operator |
| ☐ | RA-87908 | Yakovlev Yak-40 | 9721354 | Aerolimousine |
| ☐ | RA-87938 | Yakovlev Yak-40K | 9710153 | Amur Regional Government |
| ☐ | RA-87953 | Yakovlev Yak-40K | 9811157 | AIST M Airclub |
| ☐ | RA-87983 | Yakovlev Yak-40 | 9540644 | AIST M Airclub |
| ☐ | RA-88227 | Yakovlev Yak-40K | 9641550 | Khanty-Mansi Autonomous District |
| ☐ | RA-88293 | Yakovlev Yak-40 | 9510138 | TGK-9 - Territorial Generating Company No 9 |
| ☐ | RA-88294 | Yakovlev Yak-40 | 9331029 | Unconfirmed Russian operator |
| ☐ | RA-88297 | Yakovlev Yak-40 | 9530142 | Lukoil Avia |
| ☐ | RA-88298 | Yakovlev Yak-40K | 9930160 | Vostotsnaya Neftyanaya Kompaniya |

| | | | | | |
|---|---|---|---|---|---|
| ☐ | RA-88306 | Yakovlev Yak-40K | 9640651 | Aviakompaniya SKOL | |
| ☐ | RF-88301 | Yakovlev Yak-40K | 9641251 | Russian Ministry of the Interior | |
| ☐ | UN-87213 | Yakovlev Yak-40K | 9641050 | Unconfirmed Kazakhstan operator | |
| ☐ | UN-87488 | Yakovlev Yak-40 | 9441638 | Government of Kazakhstan | |
| ☐ | UN-87816 | Yakovlev Yak-40 | 9230724 | Government of Kazakhstan | |
| ☐ | UN-87850 | Yakovlev Yak-40 | 9441738 | Kazakhstan Border Guards | |
| ☐ | UP-Y4007 | Yakovlev Yak-40 | 9431435 | Operator unknown | |
| ☐ | UP-Y4008 | Yakovlev Yak-40 | 9541741 | Rusline | |
| ☐ | UP-Y4015 | Yakovlev Yak-40 | 9530842 | TOO Gamma | |
| ☐ | UR-87964 | Yakovlev Yak-40 | 9820758 | Ukraine Air Enterprise | |
| ☐ | UR-88310 | Yakovlev Yak-40 | 9940760 | Challenge Aero | |
| ☐ | UR-BWF | Yakovlev Yak-40 | 9711352 | Privatbank | |
| ☐ | UR-CLH | Yakovlev Yak-40 | 9530642 | Challenge Aero | |
| ☐ | UR-ECL | Yakovlev Yak-40K | 9932059 | Challenge Aero | |
| ☐ | UR-PVS | Yakovlev Yak-40 | 9331430 | Mostobud | |
| ☐ | YK-AQB | Yakovlev Yak-40 | 9530443 | Government of Syria | |
| ☐ | YV-1070CP | Yakovlev Yak-40 | 9412032 | CAICA | |
| | | | | | |
| ☐ | B-4012 | Yakovlev Yak-42D | 4520424914375 | Peoples Republic of China Navy | |
| ☐ | B-4013 | Yakovlev Yak-42D | 45204249144## | Peoples Republic of China Navy | |
| ☐ | RA-42365 | Yakovlev Yak-42D | 4520424811447 | JetAlliance East | |
| ☐ | RA-42412 | Yakovlev Yak-42D | 4520422219055 | United Aircraft Corporation | |
| | | | | 'Russia 2018/2022 Ready to Inspire' | |
| ☐ | RA-42424 | Yakovlev Yak-42D-100 (Yak-142) | 4520421502016 | Lukoil Avia | |
| ☐ | RA-42427 | Yakovlev Yak-42D | 4520422305016 | JetAlliance East | |
| ☐ | UP-42721 | Yakovlev Yak-42D | 4520423310017 | Kazakhstan Air Force | |
| ☐ | UP-Y4201 | Yakovlev Yak-42D | 4520423302017 | Fly Jet | |
| ☐ | UP-Y4202 | Yakovlev Yak-42D | 4520423402116 | Avia Jaynar | |

# ADDITIONAL NOTES

# ICAO TWO-LETTER DESIGNATORS

| Code | Airline | |
|------|---------|---|
| 0B | Blue Air | YR |
| 0D | Darwin Airline | HB |
| 0V | Vasco | VN |
| 1I | Novair | SE |
| 1I | Pegasus Airlines | TC |
| 1T | 1Time Airline | ZS |
| 2B | Bahrain Air | A9C |
| 2D | Alania Airline | RA |
| 2E | AVE.com | A6 |
| 2E | Smokey Bay Air | N |
| 2F | Payim Intl Air | EP |
| 2F | Frontier Flying Service | N |
| 2G | Cargoitalia | I |
| 2G | Northwest Seaplanes | N |
| 2G | San Juan Airlines | N |
| 2I | Star peru | OB |
| 2J | Air Burkina | XT |
| 2K | Aerogal | HC |
| 2L | Helvetic Airways | HB |
| 2M | Moldavian Airlines | ER |
| 2N | NAS Air | HZ |
| 2N | Nextjet | SE |
| 2N | Yuzmashavia | UR |
| 2O | Island Air Service | N |
| 2P | Puerto Rico Air Management Services | N |
| 2P | AirPhil Express | RP |
| 2Q | Air Cargo Carriers | N |
| 2Q | Avitrans Nordic | SE |
| 2R | Sud D'Or Intl Airlines | 4X |
| 2T | Tulpar Air Service | UP |
| 2U | Air Guinee Express | 3X |
| 2W | Welcome Air | OE |
| 30 | Peau Vava'u Air | A3 |
| 3B | Central Connect Airlines | OK |
| 3F | Pacific Airways | N |
| 3G | Moskva Air Company | RA |
| 3H | Air Inuit | C |
| 3K | Everts Air Cargo | N |
| 3K | Jetstar Asia Airways | 9V |
| 3L | Intersky | OE |
| 3M | Gulfstream Intl | N |
| 3N | Air Urga | UR |
| 3O | Air Arabia Maroc | CN |
| 3P | Tiara Air | P4 |
| 3R | Moskoviya | RA |
| 3S | Air Antilles Express | F |
| 3S | Air Guyane Express | F |
| 3S | Aeroland Airways | SX |
| 3T | Turanair | 4K |
| 3U | Sichuan Airlines | B |
| 3V | TNT Airways | OO |
| 3X | Japan Air Commuter | JA |
| 3Y | Kartika Airlines | PK |
| 3Z | Everts Air Alaska | N |
| 3Z | Zoom Airways | S2 |
| 4A | Air Kiribati | T3 |
| 4B | Perimeter Aviation | C |
| 4B | Aviastar - Tupolev | RA |
| 4C | Click Airways | EX |
| 4C | Aires | HK |
| 4C | Tapo-Avia | UK |
| 4D | Air Sinai | SU |
| 4E | Tanana Air Service | N |
| 4G | Gazpromavia | RA |
| 4H | United Airways | S2 |
| 4I | Izmir Airlines | TC |
| 4K | Kenn Borek Air | C |
| 4M | LAN Argentina | LV |
| 4N | Air North | C |
| 4O | Interjet | XA |
| 4P | Business Aviation of Congo | 9Q |
| 4T | Belair Airlines | HB |
| 4U | Germanwings | D |
| 4U | Tavaj Linhas Aereas | PP |
| 4W | Warbelow's Air | N |
| 4Y | Airbus Transport Intl | F |

| Code | Airline | |
|------|---------|---|
| 4Y | Flight Alaska | N |
| 4Z | Airlink | ZS |
| 5A | Alpine Air Express | N |
| 5B | Euro Asia Intl | UP |
| 5C | Air Tahoma | N |
| 5C | Natureair | TI |
| 5C | Cargo Air Lines | 4X |
| 5D | Aeromexico Connect | XA |
| 5E | SGA Airlines | HS |
| 5F | Arctic Circle Air Service | N |
| 5F | Best Air | TC |
| 5H | Fly540 | 5Y |
| 5I | Transavia Service | 4L |
| 5J | Cebu Pacific Air | RP |
| 5K | Hi Fly | CS |
| 5K | Odessa Airlines | UR |
| 5L | Aerosur | CP |
| 5M | National Airlines | N |
| 5M | Sibaviatrans | RA |
| 5N | Arkhangelsk 2nd Aviation Enterprise | RA |
| 5N | Nordavia Regional Airlines | RA |
| 5O | Europe Airpost | F |
| 5P | PENTA - Pena Transportes Aereos | PP |
| 5Q | Best Air | S2 |
| 5R | Custom Air Transport | N |
| 5R | Karthago Airlines | TS |
| 5S | Sapair | HI |
| 5T | Canadian North | C |
| 5U | LADE | LV |
| 5U | Challenge Aero | UR |
| 5V | Lviv Airlines | UR |
| 5W | Astraeus | G |
| 5X | UPS Airlines | N |
| 5Y | Isles of Scilly Skybus | G |
| 5Y | Atlas Air | N |
| 5Z | Bismillah Airlines | S2 |
| 6B | Tuifly Nordic | SE |
| 6D | Pelita Air | PK |
| 6E | Indigo Airlines | VT |
| 6F | Ufly Airways | N |
| 6F | Afrijet Airlines | 5N |
| 6H | Israir | 4X |
| 6I | Aviast Air | RA |
| 6I | Euroair | SX |
| 6J | Skynet Asia Airways | JA |
| 6J | Jubba Airways | 6O |
| 6K | Zest Airways | RP |
| 6M | Air Minas | PP |
| 6N | Aerosucre | HK |
| 6O | Air Satellite | C |
| 6R | Alrosa Aviation | RA |
| 6R | Aerounion | XA |
| 6S | Star Air Intl | AP |
| 6T | Air Mandalay | XY |
| 6U | Air Cargo Germany | D |
| 6V | MRK Airlines | UR |
| 6W | Saratov Airlines | RA |
| 6Y | Smartlynx | YL |
| 6Z | Panavia Cargo Airlines | HP |
| 6Z | Van Air Europe | OK |
| 6Z | Ukrainian Cargo Airways | UR |
| 7A | Air Next | JA |
| 7C | Jeju Air | HL |
| 7D | Donbassaero | UR |
| 7E | Aeroline | D |
| 7E | Evergreen Helicopters | N |
| 7E | Firefly | 9M |
| 7F | First Air | C |
| 7G | Starflyer | JA |
| 7H | Era Aviation | N |
| 7H | Corendon Air | TC |
| 7I | Insel Air Intl | PJ |
| 7I | Coastal Aviation | 5H |
| 7J | Tajik Air | EY |
| 7K | Kolavia | RA |
| 7L | Aerocaribbean | CU |
| 7M | Air Atlantique | G |
| 7N | Inland Aviation Services | N |
| 7P | Batavia Air | PK |
| 7Q | Pan Am Dominica | HI |

| | | | | | | |
|---|---|---|---|---|---|
| 7Q | Air Libya | 5A | AW | CHC Airways | PH |
| 7S | Arctic Transportation Services | N | AW | Dirgantara Air Service | PK |
| 7T | Air Glaciers | HB | AX | American Connection | N |
| 7T | Trans Am | HC | AY | Finnair | OH |
| 7T | Wind Rose | UR | AZ | Alitalia | I |
| 7T | Tobruk Air | 5A | | | |
| 7U | Aviaenergo | RA | B2 | Belavia Belarussian Airlines | EW |
| 7V | Pelican Air Services | ZS | B3 | Bellview Airlines | 5N |
| 7Y | Flying Carpet Air Transport Services | OD | B4 | Bankair | N |
| 7Y | Mid Airlines | ST | B4 | Zanair | 5H |
| | | | B5 | East African Express | 5Y |
| 8A | Atlas Blue | CN | B6 | Jetblue Airways | N |
| 8A | Arrow Panama | HP | B7 | Uni Air | B |
| 8C | ATI - Air Transport Intl | N | B8 | Botir-Avia | EX |
| 8D | Interavia Airlines | RA | B8 | Eritrean Airlines | E3 |
| 8D | Expo Air | 4R | B9 | Iran Air Tour Airline | EP |
| 8E | Bering Air | N | BA | British Airways | G |
| 8J | Jet4You | CN | BB | Seaborne Airlines | N |
| 8K | K-Mile Air | HS | BC | Skymark Airlines | JA |
| 8L | Lucky Airlines | B | BD | BMI | G |
| 8M | Myanmar Airways Intl | XY | BD | BMI Regional | G |
| 8N | Barents Skylink | SE | BD | Servant Air | N |
| 8O | West Coast Air | C | BE | FlyBe | G |
| 8P | Pacific Coastal Airlines | C | BF | Bluebird Cargo | TF |
| 8Q | Baker Aviation | N | BF | Aeroservice | TN |
| 8Q | Onur Air | TC | BF | Vincent Aviation (Australia) | VH |
| 8R | SOL Lineas Aereas | LV | BG | Biman Bangladesh Airlines | S2 |
| 8R | Trip Linhas Aereas | PP | BH | Hawkair Aviation Service | C |
| 8T | Air Tindi | C | BI | Royal Brunei Airlines | V8 |
| 8U | Afriqiyah Airways | 5A | BJ | Nouvelair | TS |
| 8V | Wright Air Service | N | BK | OK Airways | B |
| 8V | Astral Aviation | 5Y | BL | Jetstar Pacific Airlines | VN |
| 8W | Private Wings | D | BP | Air Botswana | A2 |
| 8Y | China Postal Airlines | B | BR | EVA Airways | B |
| 8Y | Air Burundi | 9U | BS | British Intl | G |
| 8Z | Wizz Air Bulgaria | LZ | BT | Air Baltic | YL |
| | | | BV | Blu Express.com | I |
| 9D | Toumai Air Chad | TT | BV | Blue Panorama Airlines | I |
| 9H | Dutch Antilles Express | PJ | BW | Caribbean Airlines | 9Y |
| 9K | Cape Air | N | BX | Air Busan | HL |
| 9L | Colgan Air | N | BY | Thomsonfly.com | G |
| 9M | Central Mountain Air | C | BZ | Keystone Air Service | C |
| 9N | Satena | HK | BZ | Blue Dart Aviation | VT |
| 9N | JP Express | JA | | | |
| 9O | Inter - transportes Aereos Inter | TG | C4 | Zimex Aviation | HB |
| 9O | National Airways Cameroon | TJ | C6 | Canjet | C |
| 9S | Spring Airlines | B | C7 | Rico Linhas Aereas | PP |
| 9S | Southern Air | N | C7 | Samarkand Airways | UK |
| 9T | Transwest Air | C | C8 | Cargolux Italia | I |
| 9T | ACT Airlines | TC | C9 | Cirrus Airlines | D |
| 9U | Air Moldova | ER | CA | Air China | B |
| 9V | Avior Airlines | YV | CA | Air China Cargo | B |
| 9W | Jet Airways | VT | CB | Scotairways | G |
| 9X | Itali Airlines | I | CC | Air Atlanta | TF |
| | | | CD | Alliance Air | VT |
| A2 | Cielos Airlines | OB | CF | City Airline | SE |
| A2 | Astra Airlines | SX | CG | Airlines of Papua New Guinea | P2 |
| A3 | Aegean Airlines | SX | CH | Bemidji Airlines | N |
| A5 | Airlinair | F | CI | China Airlines | B |
| A6 | Air Alps Aviation | OE | CJ | BA Cityflyer | G |
| A8 | Benin Golf Air | TY | CK | China Cargo Airlines | B |
| A9 | Airzena - Georgian Airlines | 4L | CL | Lufthansa Cityline | D |
| AA | American Airlines | N | CM | Copa Airlines | HP |
| AB | AirBerlin | D | CN | Grand China Airlines | B |
| AC | Air Canada | C | CN | Islands Nationair | P2 |
| AE | Mandarin Airlines | B | CO | Expressjet Airlines | N |
| AF | Air France | F | CU | Cubana de Aviacion | CU |
| AG | Air Contractors | EI | CV | Cargolux Airlines Intl | LX |
| AH | Air Algerie | 7T | CV | Air Chathams | ZK |
| AI | Air India | VT | CW | Airline of the Marshall Islands | V7 |
| AI | Air India Express | VT | CX | Cathay Pacific Airways | B |
| AJ | Aero Contactors | 5N | CY | Cyprus Airways | 5B |
| AK | Airasia | 9M | CZ | China Southern Airlines | B |
| AL | Trans Avia Export Cargo Airlines | EW | | | |
| AL | Alsair | F | D0 | DHL Air | G |
| AI | Midwest Connect | N | D2 | Severstal Aircompany | RA |
| AM | Aeromexico | XA | D3 | Daalo Airlines | J2 |
| AO | Avianova | RA | D4 | Alidaunia | I |
| AR | Aerolineas Argentinas | LV | D5 | DHL Aero Expresso | HP |
| AS | Alaska Airlines | N | D6 | Inter-Air | ZS |
| AT | Royal Air Maroc | CN | D9 | Donavia | RA |
| AU | Austral Lineas Aereas | LV | DB | Brit'Air | F |
| AV | Avianca | HK | DC | Golden Air | SE |

| | | | | | | |
|---|---|---|---|---|---|
| DD | Nok Air | HS | | GA | Garuda Indonesia | PK |
| DE | Condor | D | | GB | ABX Air | N |
| DG | South East Asian Airlines | RP | | GD | Granstar Cargo Airlines | B |
| DJ | Virgin Blue Airlines | VH | | GD | Air Alpha Greenland | OY |
| DJ | Pacific Blue | ZK | | GE | Transasia Airways | B |
| DK | Thomas Cook Scandinavia | OY | | GF | Gulf Air | A9C |
| DL | Delta Airlines | N | | GI | Itek Air | EX |
| DL | Delta Connection | N | | GL | Air Greenland | OY |
| DO | Air Vallée | I | | GR | Aurigny Air Services | G |
| DQ | Coastal Air Transport | N | | GS | Tianjin Airlines | B |
| DS | Easyjet Switzerland | HB | | GV | XL Airways Germany | D |
| DT | TAAG Angola Airlines | D2 | | GV | Grant Aviation | N |
| DU | Hemus Air | LZ | | GW | Kuban Airlines | RA |
| DV | Scat Aircompany | UP | | GX | Pacificair | RP |
| DW | Aero-Charter Ukraine | UR | | GY | Tri-MG Intra-Asia Airlines | PK |
| DX | Danish Air Transport | OY | | GY | Gabon Airlines | TR |
| DY | Norwegian | LN | | GZ | Air Rarotonga | E5 |
| | | | | | | |
| E3 | Eagle Airlines | I | | H2 | Sky Airline | CC |
| E3 | Domodedovo Airlines | RA | | H3 | Harbour Air Seaplanes | C |
| E5 | Samara Airlines | RA | | H6 | Hageland Aviation Services | N |
| E7 | Estafeta Carga Aerea | XA | | H7 | Eagle Air | 5X |
| E9 | Boston-Maine Airways | N | | H8 | Dalavia | RA |
| EC | Avialeasing | UK | | HA | Hawaiian Airlines | N |
| ED | AirBlue | AP | | HD | Air Do | JA |
| EF | Strategic Airlines | VH | | HE | LGW - Luftfahrtgesellschaft Walter | D |
| EH | Air Nippon Network | JA | | HG | NikiOE | |
| EI | Aer Lingus | EI | | HI | Papillon Grand Canyon Airways | N |
| EJ | New England Airlines | N | | HJ | Hellas jet | SX |
| EK | Emirates | A6 | | HJ | Tasman Cargo Airlines | VH |
| EL | Air Nippon | JA | | HK | Four Star Air Cargo | N |
| EM | Aero Benin | TY | | HK | Yangon Airlines | XY |
| EN | Air Dolomiti | I | | HM | Air Seychelles | S7 |
| EO | Hewa Bora Airways | 9Q | | HN | Heavylift Cargo Airlines | VH |
| EP | Iran Aseman Airlines | EP | | HO | Juneyao Airlines | B |
| EQ | TAME | HC | | HS | Direktflyg | SE |
| ER | Astar Air Cargo | N | | HT | Aeromost Kharkov | UR |
| ES | DHL Intl Aviation | A9C | | HU | Chang An Airlines | B |
| ET | Ethiopian Airlines | ET | | HU | China Xinhua Airlines | B |
| EU | Chengdu Airlines | B | | HU | Hainan Airlines | B |
| EW | Eurowings | D | | HV | Transavia Airlines | PH |
| EX | Air Santo Domingo | HI | | HW | North Wright Airways | C |
| EY | Etihad Airways | A6 | | HW | Hello | HB |
| EZ | Evergreen Intl Airlines | N | | HX | Hong Kong Airlines | B |
| EZ | Sun-Air of Scandinavia | OY | | HX | Trans North Aviation | N |
| | | | | HY | Uzbekistan Airways | UK |
| F3 | Sky King | N | | HZ | SAT Airlines | RA |
| F4 | Shanghai Cargo | B | | | | |
| F5 | Cosmic Air | 9N | | I6 | Sky Eyes Aviation | HS |
| F7 | Baboo | HB | | I9 | Air Italy | I |
| F9 | Frontier Airlines | N | | IA | Iraqi Airways | YI |
| FA | Safair | ZS | | IB | Iberia | EC |
| FB | Bulgaria Air | LZ | | ID | Interlink Airlines | ZS |
| FC | Falcon Express Cargo Airlines | A6 | | IE | Solomons | H4 |
| FC | Finncomm Airlines | OH | | IF | Islas Airways | EC |
| FD | Thai Airasia | HS | | IG | Meridiana Fly | I |
| FG | Ariana Afghan Airlines | YA | | II | IBC Airways | N |
| FI | Icelandair | TF | | IJ | Great Wall Airlines | B |
| FJ | Air Pacific | DQ | | IK | Imair | 4K |
| FK | Keewatin Air | C | | IN | MAT Macedonian Air Transport | Z3 |
| FK | Kivalliq Air | C | | IP | Atyrau Air Ways | UP |
| FL | Airtran Airways | N | | IQ | Augsburg Airways | D |
| FM | Shanghai Airlines | B | | IR | Iran Air | EP |
| FN | Regional Air Lines | CN | | IS | Island Airlines | N |
| FO | Airlines of Tasmania | VH | | IT | Kingfisher Airlines | VT |
| FP | Freedom Air | N | | IT | Kingfisher Red | VT |
| FQ | Thomas Cook Airlines Belgium | OO | | IU | Hevi-Lift | P2 |
| FQ | Brindabella Airlines | VH | | IV | Windjet | I |
| FR | Ryanair | EI | | IW | Wings Air | PK |
| FV | Rossiya Russian Airlines | RA | | IY | Yemenia | 7O |
| FW | Ibex Airlines | JA | | IZ | Arkia Israeli Airlines | 4X |
| FX | Federal Express | N | | | | |
| FZ | FlyDubai | A6 | | J0 | Jetlink Express | 5Y |
| | | | | J2 | Azerbaijan Airlines | 4K |
| G1 | Gorkha Airlines | 9N | | J3 | Northwestern Air | C |
| G2 | Avirex | TR | | J4 | Buffalo Airways | C |
| G3 | Gol Transportes Aereos | PP | | J4 | Jordan Intl Air Cargo | JY |
| G3 | Sky Express | SX | | J5 | Donghai Airlines | B |
| G4 | Allegiant Air | N | | J5 | Alaska Seaplane Service | N |
| G5 | China Express Airlines | B | | J6 | Cruiser Taxi Aero Brasil | PP |
| G5 | Island Air | VP-C | | J7 | Centre-Avia Airlines | RA |
| G8 | Go Air | VT | | J8 | Berjaya Air Charter | 9M |
| G9 | Air Arabia | A6 | | J9 | Jazeera Airways | 9K |

| Code | Airline | Country |
|------|---------|---------|
| JA | BH Airlines | E9 |
| JB | HeliJet Intl | C |
| JC | JAL Express | JA |
| JD | Capital Airlines | B |
| JE | Mango | ZS |
| JF | LAB Flying Service | N |
| JH | Fuji Dream Airlines | JA |
| JI | Jade Cargo Intl | B |
| JI | Eastern Caribbean Air | N |
| JJ | TAM Linhas Aereas | PP |
| JK | Spanair | EC |
| JL | J-Air | JA |
| JL | Japan Airlines | JA |
| JM | Air Jamaica | 6Y |
| JP | Adria Airways | S5 |
| JQ | Jetstar Airways | VH |
| JS | Air Koryo | P |
| JT | Lion Airlines | PK |
| JU | JAT Airways | YU |
| JV | Bearskin Airlines | C |
| JY | Air Turks & Caicos | VQ-T |
| JZ | Skyways Express | SE |
| K2 | EuroLot | SP |
| K3 | Taquan Air Service | N |
| K4 | Kalitta Air | N |
| K5 | Wings of Alaska | N |
| K6 | Cambodia Angkor Air | XU |
| K7 | Yakutia Airlines | RA |
| KA | Dragonair | B |
| KB | Druk Air | A5 |
| KC | Air Astana | UP |
| KE | Korean Air | HL |
| KF | Blue1 | OH |
| KG | Aerogaviota | CU |
| KG | Linea Aerea Iaaca | YV |
| KK | Atlasjet Intl | TC |
| KL | KLM Royal Dutch Airlines | PH |
| KM | Air Malta | 9H |
| KN | China United Airlines | B |
| KN | Maroomba Airlines | VH |
| KO | Alaska Central Express | N |
| KQ | Kenya Airways | 5Y |
| KR | Comores Aviation | D6 |
| KR | Kitty Hawk Aircargo | N |
| KS | Penair | N |
| KU | Kuwait Airways | 9K |
| KV | KMV Mineralnye Vody Airlines | RA |
| KW | Kelowna Flightcraft Air Charter | C |
| KX | Cayman Airways | VP-C |
| KY | Kunming Airlines | B |
| KZ | Nippon Cargo Airlines | JA |
| L2 | Lynden Air Cargo | N |
| L3 | DHL de Guatemala | TG |
| L5 | CHC Helikopter Service | LN |
| L5 | Lufttransport | LN |
| L6 | Tbilaviamsheni | 4L |
| LA | LAN Airlines | CC |
| LB | LAB Airlines | CP |
| LB | Lobaye Airways | TL |
| LC | Varig Log | PP |
| LD | Air Hong Kong | B |
| LD | Linea Turistica Aereotuy | YV |
| LG | Luxair | LX |
| LH | Lufthansa | D |
| LH | Lufthansa Cargo | D |
| LI | LIAT - The Caribbean Airline | V2 |
| LJ | Jin Air | HL |
| LL | Miami Air Intl | N |
| LN | Libyan Airlines | 5A |
| LO | LOT - Polish Airlines | SP |
| LP | LAN Peru | OB |
| LS | Jet2 | G |
| LU | LAN Express | CC |
| LV | Albanian Airlines | ZA |
| LW | Pacific Wings | N |
| LX | Swiss Intl Airlines | HB |
| LY | El Al Israel Airlines | 4X |
| LZ | Belle Air | ZA |
| M3 | North Flying | OY |
| M3 | ABSA Cargo | PP |
| M4 | Nova Air | XA |
| M5 | Kenmore Air | N |
| M6 | Amerijet Intl | N |
| M7 | Marsland Aviation | ST |
| M7 | Superior Aviation Services | 5Y |
| M9 | Motor Sich Airlines | UR |
| MA | Malev | HA |
| MB | MNG Cargo Airlines | TC |
| ME | Middle East Airlines | OD |
| MF | Xiamen Airlines | B |
| MG | Midex Airlines | A6 |
| MH | Malaysia Airlines | 9M |
| MI | Silkair | 9V |
| MJ | Mihin Lanka | 4R |
| MK | Air Mauritius | 3B |
| ML | Trans Attico | ST |
| MM | Euro Atlantic Airways | CS |
| MM | SAM Colombia | HK |
| MN | Comair | ZS |
| MO | Calm Air | C |
| MP | Martinair | PH |
| MQ | American Eagle | N |
| MS | Egyptair | SU |
| MT | Thomas Cook Airlines | G |
| MU | China Eastern Airlines | B |
| MW | Maya Island Air | V3 |
| MX | Manx2 Airlines | G |
| MY | Midwest Airlines Egypt | SU |
| MY | MAS Air Cargo | XA |
| MZ | Merpati Nusantara Airlines | PK |
| N2 | Daghestan Airlines | RA |
| N2 | Kabo Air | 5N |
| N4 | Trans Air Benin | TY |
| N5 | Skagway Air Service | N |
| N6 | Air One Nine | 5A |
| N9 | Nordic Solutions Air Services | LY |
| N9 | North Coast Aviation | P2 |
| NA | North American Airlines | N |
| NC | Northern Air Cargo | N |
| NC | Cobham Aviation Services Australia | VH |
| NF | Air Vanuatu | YJ |
| NH | ANA - All Nippon Network | JA |
| NI | Portugalia Airlines | CS |
| NK | Spirit Airlines | N |
| NL | Sheheen Air Intl | AP |
| NN | Vim Airlines | RA |
| NO | Neos | I |
| NP | Skytrans Regional | VH |
| NQ | Air Japan | JA |
| NR | Pamir Air | YA |
| NS | Hebei Airlines | B |
| NT | Binter Canarias | EC |
| NU | Japan Transocean Air | JA |
| NV | Air Central | JA |
| NX | Air Macau | B |
| NY | Air Iceland | TF |
| NZ | Air New Zealand | ZK |
| NZ | Air New Zealand Link | ZK |
| O2 | Jet Air | SP |
| O3 | Bellview Airlines | 9L |
| O4 | Antrak Air Ghana | 9G |
| OA | Olympic Airways | SX |
| OB | Boliviana de Aviacion | CP |
| OC | Omni - Aviacao e Tecnologia | CS |
| OF | Air Finland | OH |
| OG | One-Two Go | HS |
| OG | Ghadames Air Transport | 5A |
| OI | Aspiring Air | ZK |
| OJ | Overland Airways | 5N |
| OK | CSA Czech Airlines | OK |
| OL | OLT - Ostfriesische Lufttransport | D |
| OM | MIAT - Mongolian Airlines | JU |
| ON | Our Airline | C2 |
| OO | Skywest Airlines | N |
| OQ | Chongqing Airlines | B |
| OR | Arkefly | PH |
| OS | Austrian Airlines | OE |
| OT | Aeropelican Air Services | VH |
| OU | Croatia Airlines | 9A |
| OV | Estonian Air | ES |
| OV | Estonian Air Regional | ES |

| | | |
|---|---|---|
| OX | Orient Thai Airlines | HS |
| OY | Omni Air Intl | N |
| OZ | Asiana Airlines | HL |
| P2 | Airkenya | 5Y |
| P4 | Aerolineas Sosa | HR |
| P5 | Aerorepublica Colombia | HK |
| P6 | Transair | N |
| P7 | Russian Sky Airlines | RA |
| P8 | Pantanal | PP |
| P9 | Perm Airlines | RA |
| PA | Florida Coastal Airlines | N |
| PB | Provincial Airlines | C |
| PC | Air Fiji | DQ |
| PC | Continental Airways | RA |
| PD | Porter Airlines | C |
| PF | Primera Air Scandinavia | OY |
| PG | Bangkok Airways | HS |
| PH | Transavia Denmark | OY |
| PH | Polynesian Airlines | 5W |
| PI | Pacific Sun | DQ |
| PI | Pacificflyer | T8A |
| PJ | Air St Pierre | F |
| PK | Pakistan Intl Airlines | AP |
| PL | Southern Air Charter | C6 |
| PL | Airstars Airways | RA |
| PM | Tropic Air Commuter | V3 |
| PN | West Air | B |
| PO | Polar Air Cargo | N |
| PR | Philippine Airlines | RP |
| PS | Ukraine Intl Airlines | UR |
| PT | Capital Cargo Intl Airlines | N |
| PT | West Air Europe | SE |
| PU | Pluna Lineas Aereas Uruguayas | CX |
| PV | Panair Lineas Aereas | EC |
| PV | St Barth Commuter | F |
| PW | Precisionair | 5H |
| PX | Air Niugini | P2 |
| PY | Surinam Airways | PZ |
| PZ | TAM Mercosur | ZP |
| Q2 | Island Aviation Services | 8Q |
| Q3 | Zambian Airways | 9J |
| Q5 | 40 Mile Air | N |
| Q6 | Aerocondor | OB |
| Q8 | Pacific East Asia Cargo Airlines | RP |
| Q8 | Transair Congo | TN |
| QB | Sky Georgia | 4L |
| QD | Air Class | CX |
| QE | Air Moorea | F |
| QF | QANTAS Airways | VH |
| QF | Qantaslink | VH |
| QH | Kyrgyzstan | EX |
| QI | Cimber Air | OY |
| QK | Air Canada Jazz | C |
| QL | Laser | YV |
| QL | Aero Lanka Airlines | 4R |
| QM | Air Malawi | 7Q |
| QN | Air Armenia | EK |
| QQ | Alliance Airlines | VH |
| QR | Qatar Airways | A7 |
| QS | Smartwings | OK |
| QS | Travel Service Airlines | OK |
| QT | Tampa Airlines | HK |
| QT | Regional Air | P2 |
| QU | East African Airlines | 5X |
| QV | Lao Airlines | RDPL |
| QX | Horizon Air | N |
| QZ | Indonesia Airasia | PK |
| R0 | Royal Airlines | AP |
| R2 | Orenair | RA |
| R5 | Jordan Aviation | JY |
| R6 | Danu Oro Transportas | LY |
| R6 | RACSA | TG |
| R7 | Aserca Airlines | YV |
| R8 | Kyrghyzstan Airlines | EX |
| RA | Nepal Airlines | 9N |
| RB | Syrianair | YK |
| RC | Atlantic Airways | OY |
| RD | Ryan Intl Airlines | N |
| RE | Aer Arann | EI |
| RF | Florida West Intl Airlines | N |

| | | |
|---|---|---|
| RG | Varig | PP |
| RH | Robin Hood Aviation | OE |
| RH | RPX Airlines | PK |
| RI | Mandala Airlines | PK |
| RJ | Royal Jordanian | JY |
| RK | Royal Khmer Airlines | XU |
| RL | Royal Phnom Penh Airways | XU |
| RO | Tarom | YR |
| RQ | Kam Air | YA |
| RT | Rak Airlines | A6 |
| RU | Airbridge Cargo | RA |
| RU | Skyking Airlines | VQ-T |
| RV | Caspian Airlines | EP |
| RX | Regent Airways | S2 |
| RY | Royal Wings Airlines | JY |
| RZ | Sansa Regional | TI |
| S0 | Slok Air Intl | C5 |
| S2 | Jetlite | VT |
| S3 | Santa Barbara Airlines | YV |
| S4 | SATA Internacional | CS |
| S5 | Trast Aero | EX |
| S5 | Shuttle America | N |
| S6 | Salmon Air | N |
| S6 | Star Air | OY |
| S7 | S7 Airlines | RA |
| S8 | Shovkovly Shlyah | UR |
| SA | South African Airways | ZS |
| SB | Aircalin | F |
| SC | Shandong Airlines | B |
| SD | Sudan Airways | ST |
| SE | XL Airways France | F |
| SF | Tassili Airlines | 7T |
| SG | Spicejet | VT |
| SI | Sierra Pacific Airlines | N |
| SJ | Sriwijaya Air | PK |
| SK | Scandinavian Airline System | SE |
| SO | Superior Aviation | N |
| SP | SATA Air Acores | CS |
| SQ | Singapore Airlines | 9V |
| SQ | Singapore Airlines Cargo | 9V |
| SS | Corsair | F |
| ST | Germania | D |
| SU | Aeroflot Russian Airlines | RA |
| SV | Saudi Arabian Airlines | HZ |
| SW | Air Namibia | V5 |
| SY | Sun Country Airlines | N |
| SY | Skippers Aviation | VH |
| T0 | TACA Peru | OB |
| T2 | Nakina Outpost Camps and Air | C |
| T3 | Eastern Airways | G |
| T5 | Turkmenistan Airlines | EZ |
| T6 | Tavrey Aircompany | UR |
| T7 | Twin Jet | F |
| TA | TACA Intl Airlines | YS |
| TB | Jetairfly | OO |
| TC | Air Tanzania | 5H |
| TF | Malmo Aviation | SE |
| TG | Thai Airways | HS |
| TH | Transmile Air Services | 9M |
| TI | Tolair Services | N |
| TI | TACA Costa Rica | TI |
| TK | Turkish Airlines | TC |
| TL | Airnorth Regional | VH |
| TL | Chartair | VH |
| TM | LAM - Linhas Aereas de Mocambique | C9 |
| TN | Air Tahiti Nui | F |
| TO | Transavia France | F |
| TO | President Airlines | XU |
| TP | TAP Air Portugal | CS |
| TR | Tiger Airways | 9V |
| TS | Air Transat | C |
| TT | Tiger Airways | VH |
| TU | Tunisair | TS |
| TV | Brussels Airlines | OO |
| TX | Air Caraibes | F |
| TX | Air Caraibes Atlantique | F |
| TY | Iberworld Airlines | EC |
| TY | Air Caledonie | F |
| U2 | Easyjet Airlines | G |
| U3 | Avies Air Company | ES |

| | | | | | | |
|---|---|---|---|---|---|---|
| U4 | PMT Air | XU | | WQ | Romavia | YR |
| U5 | USA 3000 Airlines | N | | WS | Westjet | C |
| U6 | Ural Airlines | RA | | WT | Wasaya Airways | C |
| U7 | Air Uganda | 5X | | WU | Wizz Air Ukraine | UR |
| U8 | Armavia | EK | | WW | BMIBaby | G |
| U9 | Tatarstan Air | RA | | WX | City Jet | EI |
| UA | United Air Lines | N | | WY | Oman Air | A4O |
| UA | United Express | N | | | | |
| UB | Myanma Airways | XY | | X3 | Tuifly | D |
| UC | LAN Cargo | CC | | X7 | Air Service Gabon | TR |
| UD | Hex'Air | F | | X8 | Icaro Express | HC |
| UF | Um Air | UR | | X9 | Khors Air | UR |
| UG | Sevenair | TS | | XA | Blue Islands | G |
| UJ | Almasria Universal Airlines | SU | | XC | KD Air | C |
| UL | Srilankan | 4R | | XF | Vladivostok Air | RA |
| UM | Air Zimbabwe | Z | | XK | Air Corsica | F |
| UN | Transaero Airlines | RA | | XL | LAN Ecuador | HC |
| UO | Hong Kong Express Airways | B | | XM | Alitalia Express | I |
| UO | Sky Shuttle Helicopters | B | | XM | Australian Air Express | VH |
| UP | Bahamasair | C6 | | XN | Xpress Air | PK |
| UR | Utair Express | RA | | XP | Xtra Airways | N |
| US | US Airways | N | | XQ | Sunexpress | TC |
| UT | Utair Airlines | RA | | XR | Skywest Airlines | VH |
| UU | Air Austral | F | | XT | Skystar Airways | HS |
| UV | Helisuretse | EC | | XU | African Express Airways | 5Y |
| UW | Uni-Top Airlines | B | | XW | Skyexpress | RA |
| UX | Air Europa | EC | | XZ | South African Express Airways | ZS |
| UY | Cameroon Airlines | TJ | | | | |
| UZ | Buraq Air | 5A | | Y5 | Pace Airlines | N |
| | | | | Y8 | Yangtze River Express | B |
| V0 | Conviasa | YV | | Y9 | Kish Air | EP |
| V3 | Carpatair | YR | | YA | Yeti Airlines | 9N |
| V4 | Volaris | XA | | YD | Gomelavia | EW |
| V4 | Venescar Intl | YV | | YD | Mauritania Airways | 5T |
| V5 | Danube Wings | OM | | YE | Eram Air | EP |
| V6 | VIP - Vuelos Internos Privados | HC | | YG | South Airlines | UR |
| V6 | Voyager Airlines | S2 | | YI | Air Sunshine | N |
| V7 | Air Senegal Intl | 6V | | YJ | AMC Airlines | SU |
| V8 | Air Mikisew | C | | YL | Yamal Airlines | RA |
| V8 | Iliamna Air Taxi | N | | YM | Montenegro Airlines | 4O |
| V8 | Atran - Aviatrans Cargo Airlines | RA | | YN | Air Creebec | C |
| VC | Voyageur Airways | C | | YO | Heli Air Monaco | 3A |
| VD | Henan Airlines | B | | YQ | Polet Aviakompania | RA |
| VF | Valuair | 9V | | YR | Scenic Airlines | N |
| VG | VLM Airlines | OO | | YS | Régional | F |
| VH | Aeropostal | YV | | YV | Mesa Airlines | N |
| VI | Volga-Dnepr Airlines | RA | | YW | Air Nostrum | EC |
| VJ | Jatayu Air | PK | | YX | Midwest Airlines | N |
| VK | Air Nigeria | 5N | | | | |
| VL | VIA - Air Via | LZ | | Z3 | Promech Air | N |
| VN | Vietnam Airlines | VN | | Z3 | Avient Aviation | Z |
| VQ | Vintage Prop and Jets | N | | Z5 | GMG Airlines | S2 |
| VR | TACV – Transp. Aer. de Cabo Verde | D4 | | Z6 | Dnepr-Air | UR |
| VS | Virgin Atlantic Airways | G | | Z8 | Amaszonas Transportes Aereos | CP |
| VT | Air Tahiti | F | | Z9 | Delta Connection | 5Y |
| VU | Air Ivoire | TU | | ZB | Monarch Airlines | G |
| VV | Aerosvit Airlines | UR | | ZD | Dolphin Air | A6 |
| VW | Aeromar Airlines | XA | | ZE | Arcus Air | D |
| VX | Virgin America | N | | ZF | Atlantic Airlines | HR |
| VY | Vueling Airlines | EC | | ZH | Shenzhen Airlines | B |
| | | | | ZI | Aigle Azur | F |
| W3 | Arik Air | 5N | | ZK | Great Lakes Airlines | N |
| W4 | M & N Aviation | N | | ZL | Air Link | VH |
| W5 | Mahan Air | EP | | ZL | REX - Regional Express | VH |
| W6 | Wizz Air | HA | | ZM | Cityline Hungary | HA |
| W7 | Sayakhat | UP | | ZN | Naysa Aerotaxis | EC |
| W8 | Cargojet Airways | C | | ZP | Air St Thomas | N |
| W9 | Air Bagan | XY | | ZP | Silk Way Airlines | 4K |
| WA | KLM Cityhopper | PH | | ZR | Aviacon Zitotrans | RA |
| WB | Rwandair Express | 9XR | | ZR | Alexandria Airlines | SU |
| WC | Islena Airlines | HR | | ZT | Titan Airways | G |
| WE | WDL Aviation | D | | ZV | Air Midwest | N |
| WE | Centurion II Air Cargo | N | | ZX | Air Georgian | C |
| WF | Wideroe's Flyveselskap | LN | | ZY | Ada Air | ZA |
| WG | Sunwing Airlines | C | | | | |
| WI | Skylease Air Cargo | N | | | | |
| WJ | Air Labrador | C | | | | |
| WK | Edelweiss Air | HB | | | | |
| WL | Aeroperlas | HP | | | | |
| WM | Winair | PJ | | | | |
| WN | Southwest Airlines | N | | | | |
| WO | World Airways | N | | | | |
| WP | Island Air | N | | | | |

# ICAO THREE-LETTER DESIGNATORS

| | | |
|---|---|---|
| AAF | Aigle Azur | F |
| AAG | Air Atlantique | G |
| AAG | Atlantic Reconnaissance | G |
| AAL | American Airlines | N |
| AAP | Aerovista Airlines | EX |
| AAQ | Copterline | OH |
| AAR | Asiana Airlines | HL |
| AAW | Afriqiyah Airways | 5A |
| AAY | Allegiant Air | N |
| ABA | Artem Avia | UR |
| ABD | Air Atlanta | TF |
| ABF | Scanwings | OH |
| ABG | Abakan-Avia | RA |
| ABJ | Abaete Linhas Aereas | PP |
| ABK | Alberta Citylink | C |
| ABL | Air Busan | HL |
| ABO | APSA - Aeroexpreso Bogota | HK |
| ABQ | AirBlue | AP |
| ABR | Air Contractors | EI |
| ABS | Transwest Air | C |
| ABV | Antrak Air Ghana | 9G |
| ABW | Airbridge Cargo | RA |
| ABX | ABX Air | N |
| ABY | Air Arabia | A6 |
| ABZ | ATA Brasil | PP |
| ACA | Air Canada | C |
| ACD | Academy Airlines | N |
| ACE | Meridian Airways | 9G |
| ACI | Aircalin | F |
| ACL | Itali Airlines | I |
| ACP | Astral Aviation | 5Y |
| ACT | Flight Line | N |
| ACX | Air Cargo Germany | D |
| ADB | Antonov Airlines | UR |
| ADE | Ada Air | ZA |
| ADI | Audeli | EC |
| ADO | Air Do | JA |
| ADR | Adria Airways | S5 |
| ADS | Aviones de Sonora | XA |
| AEA | Air Europa | EC |
| AEB | Aero Benin | TY |
| AEE | Aegean Airlines | SX |
| AEK | Aerocon | CP |
| AEN | Aeroland Airways | SX |
| AER | Alaska Central Express | N |
| AEU | Astraeus | G |
| AEW | Aerosvit Airlines | UR |
| AEY | Air Italy | I |
| AFE | Airfast Indonesia | PK |
| AFG | Ariana Afghan Airlines | YA |
| AFL | Aeroflot Russian Airlines | RA |
| AFR | Air France | F |
| AFW | Great Barrier Airlines | ZK |
| AGB | Air Service Gabon | TR |
| AGO | Angola Air Charter | D2 |
| AGU | Angara Airlines | RA |
| AGV | Air Glaciers | HB |
| AGX | Aviogenex | YU |
| AHA | Air Alpha Greenland | OY |
| AHC | Azal Cargo | 4K |
| AHF | Aspen Helicopters | N |
| AHK | Air Hong Kong | B |
| AHT | HTA Helicopters | CS |
| AHU | ABC Air Hungary | HA |
| AHW | Aeromost Kharkov | UR |
| AHX | Amakusa Airlines | JA |
| AHY | Azerbaijan Airlines | 4K |
| AIA | Avies Air Company | ES |
| AIC | Air India | VT |
| AIE | Air Inuit | C |
| AIP | Alpine Air Express | N |
| AIQ | Thai Airasia | HS |
| AIT | Airest | ES |
| AIZ | Arkia Israeli Airlines | 4X |
| AJI | Ameristar Air Charter | N |
| AJK | Allied Air Cargo | 5N |
| AJM | Air Jamaica | 6Y |
| AJT | Amerijet Intl | N |
| AJV | JP Express | JA |
| AJX | Air Japan | JA |
| AKF | Anikay Air | EX |
| AKM | Mak Air | UP |
| AKN | Alkan Air | C |
| AKY | Yak Service | RA |
| ALG | Bristows US | N |
| ALK | Srilankan | 4R |
| ALX | Hewa Bora Airways | 9Q |
| ALZ | Alta Flights | C |
| AMA | ATMA | UP |
| AMC | Air Malta | 9H |
| AMF | Ameriflight | N |
| AMK | Amerer Air | OE |
| AML | Air Malawi | 7Q |
| AMP | Aero Transporte | OB |
| AMU | Air Macau | B |
| AMV | AMC Airlines | SU |
| AMW | Air Midwest | N |
| AMX | Aeromexico | XA |
| ANA | Air Nippon Network | JA |
| ANA | ANA - All Nippon Network | JA |
| ANE | Air Nostrum | EC |
| ANG | Air Niugini | P2 |
| ANH | Al-Ajnihah Aiways | 5A |
| ANK | Air Nippon | JA |
| ANO | Airnorth Regional | VH |
| ANQ | ADA - Aerolineas de Antioquia | HK |
| ANS | Andes Lineas Aereas | LV |
| ANT | Air North | C |
| ANU | Starlink Aviation | C |
| ANX | Canadian North | C |
| ANZ | Air New Zealand | ZK |
| AOG | Aero VIP | LV |
| AOH | North Coast Aviation | P2 |
| APC | Airpac Airlines | N |
| APF | Amapola Flyg | SE |
| APP | Aeroperlas | HP |
| APT | LAP - Lineas Aéreas Petroleras | HK |
| AQU | Airquarius Aviation | ZS |
| ARA | Arik Air | 5N |
| ARE | Aires | HK |
| ARG | Aerolineas Argentinas | LV |
| ARL | Airlec Air Espace | F |
| ARR | Air Armenia | EK |
| ART | Smartlynx | YL |
| ASA | Alaska Airlines | N |
| ASB | Air-Spray | C |
| ASD | Air Sinai | SU |
| ASE | Airstars Airways | RA |
| ASH | Mesa Airlines | N |
| ASJ | Air Satellite | C |
| ASM | Awesome Flight Services | ZS |
| ATC | Air Tanzania | 5H |
| ATG | Aerotrans | UP |
| ATM | Airlines of Tasmania | VH |
| ATN | ATI - Air Transport Intl | N |
| ATU | Atlant Hungary | HA |
| AUA | Austrian Airlines | OE |
| AUB | Augsburg Airways | D |
| AUI | Ukraine Intl Airlines | UR |
| AUL | Nordavia Regional Airlines | RA |
| AUR | Aurigny Air Services | G |
| AUT | Austral Lineas Aereas | LV |
| AVA | Avianca | HK |
| AVJ | Avia Traffic Company | EX |
| AVN | Air Vanuatu | YJ |
| AVW | Aviator Airways | SX |
| AVX | Avirex | TR |
| AWC | Titan Airways | G |
| AWK | Airwork New Zealand | ZK |
| AWQ | Indonesia Airasia | PK |
| AWU | Aeroline | D |
| AWZ | Air West Cargo | ST |
| AWZ | Sun Air | ST |
| AXB | Air India Express | VT |
| AXF | Tasman Cargo Airlines | VH |
| AXK | African Express Airways | 5Y |
| AXM | Airasia | 9M |
| AXQ | Action Airlines | N |
| AYN | Atlantic Airways | YN |
| AYT | Ayeet Aviation | 4X |
| AYZ | Moskva Air Company | RA |

| | | | | | | |
|---|---|---|---|---|---|---|
| AZA | Alitalia | I | | BRQ | Buraq Air | 5A |
| AZE | Arcus Air | D | | BRU | Belavia Belarussian Airlines | EW |
| AZF | Air Zermatt | HB | | BRV | Bravo Air Congo | 9Q |
| AZG | Sakaviaservice | 4L | | BRZ | Samara Airlines | RA |
| AZH | Sky Wind | 4K | | BSK | Miami Air Intl | N |
| AZQ | Silk Way Airlines | 4K | | BSL | Air Brasil Cargo | PP |
| AZS | Aviacon Zitotrans | RA | | BST | Best Air | TC |
| AZU | Azul | PP | | BTA | Expressjet Airlines | N |
| AZV | Azov-Avia | UR | | BTI | Air Baltic | YL |
| AZW | Air Zimbabwe | Z | | BTL | Baltia Airlines | N |
| AZZ | Azza Air Transport | ST | | BTR | Botir-Avia | EX |
| | | | | BTV | Batavia Air | PK |
| BAB | Bahrain Air | A9C | | BUC | Bulgarian Air Charter | LZ |
| BAJ | Baker Aviation | N | | BUE | Orebro Aviation | SE |
| BAN | British Antarctic Survey | VP-F | | BUN | Bural | RA |
| BAW | British Airways | G | | BVT | Berjaya Air Charter | 9M |
| BBC | Biman Bangladesh Airlines | S2 | | BWA | Caribbean Airlines | 9Y |
| BBD | Bluebird Cargo | TF | | BXH | Bar XH Air | C |
| BBO | Baboo | HB | | BXR | Redding Aero Enterprises | N |
| BBR | Santa Barbara Airlines | YV | | BYA | Berry Aviation | N |
| BBT | Air Bashkortostan | RA | | BYL | Bylina | RA |
| BBZ | Bluebird Aviation | 5Y | | BZH | Brit'Air | F |
| BCI | Blue Islands | G | | | | |
| BCS | EAT Leipzig | D | | CAI | Corendon Air | TC |
| BCY | City Jet | EI | | CAJ | Air Caraibes Atlantique | F |
| BDA | Blue Dart Aviation | VT | | CAL | China Airlines | B |
| BDI | Benair Air Service | OY | | CAO | Air China Cargo | B |
| BDR | Badr Airlines | ST | | CAT | Copenhagen Airtaxi | OY |
| BEA | Best Air | S2 | | CAV | Calm Air | C |
| BEC | Berkut State Air Company | UP | | CAW | Comair | ZS |
| BEE | FlyBe | G | | CAY | Cayman Airways | VP-C |
| BEK | Berkut Air | UP | | CBC | Caribair | HI |
| BER | AirBerlin | D | | CBT | Catalina Flying Boats | N |
| BET | Beta Cargo Air | PP | | CCA | Air China | B |
| BEZ | Air St Kitts & Nevis | V4 | | CCE | Cairo Aviation | SU |
| BFC | Basler Airlines | N | | CCG | Central Connect Airlines | OK |
| BFF | Air Nunavut | C | | CCI | Capital Cargo Intl Airlines | N |
| BFL | Buffalo Airways | C | | CCM | Air Corsica | F |
| BGA | Airbus Transport Intl | F | | CCQ | Capital City Air Carrier | N |
| BGH | BH Air | LZ | | CCY | Cherry-Air | N |
| BGK | British Gulf Airlines | EX | | CDG | Shandong Airlines | B |
| BGL | Benin Golf Air | TY | | CDN | Canadian Helicopters | C |
| BGM | AK Bars Aero | RA | | CDP | Aerocondor | OB |
| BGT | Bergen Air Transport | LN | | CDV | Skol Aviakompania | RA |
| BHA | Buddha Air | 9N | | CEB | Cebu Pacific Air | RP |
| BHL | Bristow Helicopters | G | | CEM | Central Mongolian Airlines | JU |
| BHN | Bristow Helicopters (Nigeria) | 5N | | CES | China Eastern Airlines | B |
| BHP | Belair Airlines | HB | | CFA | China Flying Dragon Co | B |
| BHR | Bighorn Airways | N | | CFE | BA Cityflyer | G |
| BHS | Bahamasair | C6 | | CFG | Condor | D |
| BID | Binair | D | | CFV | Aero Calafia | XA |
| BIE | Air Mediterrannée | F | | CFZ | Zhongfei Airlines | B |
| BIG | Big Island Air | N | | CGI | Rusair | RA |
| BKA | Bankair | N | | CGK | Click Airways | EX |
| BKP | Bangkok Airways | HS | | CGN | Chang An Airlines | B |
| BLE | Blue Line | F | | CGS | Geodynamica Centre | RA |
| BLF | Blue1 | OH | | CHB | West Air | B |
| BLM | Blue Sky | EK | | CHC | CITIC Offshore Helicopters | B |
| BLS | Bearskin Airlines | C | | CHG | Challenge Aero | UR |
| BLV | Bellview Airlines | 5N | | CHH | Hainan Airlines | B |
| BLX | Tuifly Nordic | SE | | CHI | Cougar Helicopters | C |
| BMI | BMI | G | | CHN | Channel Island Aviation | N |
| BMI | BMIBaby | G | | CIB | Condor Berlin | D |
| BMJ | Bemidji Airlines | N | | CID | Asia Continental Airlines | UP |
| BML | Bismillah Airlines | S2 | | CIG | Sirius Aero | RA |
| BMM | Atlas Blue | CN | | CII | Cityfly | I |
| BMR | BMI Regional | G | | CIM | Cimber Air | OY |
| BMY | Bimini Island Air | N | | CIR | Arctic Circle Air Service | N |
| BND | Bond Offshore Helicopters | G | | CIU | Cielos Airlines | OB |
| BNT | Bentiu Air Transport | ST | | CIW | Civair | ZS |
| BNX | Linea Aerea Iaaca | YV | | CJA | Canjet | C |
| BOI | 2Go | RP | | CJC | Colgan Air | N |
| BOL | TAB Cargo | CP | | CJR | Caverton Helicopters | 5N |
| BON | BH Airlines | E9 | | CJT | Cargojet Airways | C |
| BOS | Open skies | F | | CKK | China Cargo Airlines | B |
| BOT | Air Botswana | A2 | | CKM | BKS Air | EC |
| BOV | Boliviana de Aviacion | CP | | CKS | Kalitta Air | N |
| BOX | Aerologic | D | | CLG | Chalair Aviation | F |
| BPA | Blu Express.com | I | | CLH | Lufthansa Cityline | D |
| BPA | Blue Panorama Airlines | I | | CLL | Aerovias Castillo | XA |
| BPS | Budapest Air Services | HA | | CLX | Cargolux Airlines Intl | LX |
| BRG | Bering Air | N | | CME | Prince Edward Air | C |
| BRP | Aerobratsk | RA | | CMN | Cimarron Aire | N |

| | | |
|---|---|---|
| CMP | Copa Airlines | HP |
| CMS | Aviation Commercial Aviation | C |
| CMV | Calima Aviacion | EC |
| CNB | Cityline Hungary | HA |
| CNI | Aerotaxi | CU |
| CNK | Sunwest Aviation | C |
| COX | Comav Aviation | V5 |
| COZ | Cosmic Air | 9N |
| CPA | Cathay Pacific Airways | B |
| CPB | Corporate Express Airline | C |
| CPD | Capital Airlines | 5Y |
| CPJ | Corpjet | N |
| CPM | Comp. Mauritanienne de Transportes | 5T |
| CPN | Caspian Airlines | EP |
| CPT | Corporate Air | N |
| CQH | Spring Airlines | B |
| CQN | Chongqing Airlines | B |
| CRC | Conair Aviation | C |
| CRF | Air Central | JA |
| CRG | Cargoitalia | I |
| CRK | Hong Kong Airlines | B |
| CRL | Corsair | F |
| CRN | Aerocaribbean | CU |
| CRQ | Air Creebec | C |
| CRT | Caribintair | HH |
| CSA | CSA Czech Airlines | OK |
| CSC | Sichuan Airlines | B |
| CSH | Shanghai Airlines | B |
| CSJ | Castle Aviation | N |
| CSN | China Southern Airlines | B |
| CSQ | IBC Airways | N |
| CSV | Coastal Aviation | 5H |
| CSY | Shuangyang Aviation | B |
| CSZ | Shenzhen Airlines | B |
| CTA | Aero Charter | N |
| CTL | Central Air Southwest | N |
| CTN | Croatia Airlines | 9A |
| CTP | Tapo-Avia | UK |
| CTQ | Citylink | 9G |
| CTR | Aerolineas Centauro | XA |
| CTS | Center-South Airlines | RA |
| CTT | Custom Air Transport | N |
| CUA | China United Airlines | B |
| CUB | Cubana de Aviacion | CU |
| CUO | Aero Cuahonte | XA |
| CVA | Air Chathams | ZK |
| CVC | Centre-Avia Airlines | RA |
| CVE | Cabo Verde Express | D4 |
| CVU | Grand Canyon Airlines | N |
| CVV | Comeravia | YV |
| CWC | Centurion II Air Cargo | N |
| CWY | Woodgate Executive Air Services | G |
| CXA | Xiamen Airlines | B |
| CXH | China Xinhua Airlines | B |
| CXI | Shan Xi Airlines | B |
| CXP | Xtra Airways | N |
| CXS | Boston-Maine Airways | N |
| CXT | Coastal Air Transport | N |
| CYP | Cyprus Airways | 5B |
| CYZ | China Postal Airlines | B |
| | | |
| DAE | DHL Aero Expresso | HP |
| DAG | Daghestan Airlines | RA |
| DAH | Air Algerie | 7T |
| DAL | Delta Airlines | N |
| DAL | Delta Connection | N |
| DAO | Daalo Airlines | J2 |
| DAP | Aerovias DAP | CC |
| DAT | Brussels Airlines | OO |
| DAV | Dana | 5N |
| DBH | Hebei Airlines | B |
| DBK | Dubrovnik Airlines | 9A |
| DCD | Air 26 | D2 |
| DCL | Transportes Aereos Don Carlos | CC |
| DCP | Delta Connection | 5Y |
| DCT | Direct Flight | G |
| DES | CC Helicopters | C |
| DHE | DAP Helicopteros | CC |
| DHK | DHL Air | G |
| DHL | Astar Air Cargo | N |
| DHX | DHL Intl Aviation | A9C |
| DIR | Dirgantara Air Service | PK |
| DKH | Juneyao Airlines | B |

| | | |
|---|---|---|
| DKT | Business Aviation Courier | N |
| DLA | Air Dolomiti | I |
| DLH | Lufthansa | D |
| DMJ | Global Air | XA |
| DMO | Domodedovo Airlines | RA |
| DNL | Dutch Antilles Express | PJ |
| DNU | Danu Oro Transportas | LY |
| DNV | Donavia | RA |
| DOC | Norsk Luftambulance | LN |
| DRA | Capital Airlines | B |
| DRK | Druk Air | A5 |
| DRU | Alrosa Aviation | RA |
| DRY | Deraya Air Taxi | PK |
| DSM | LAN Argentina | LV |
| DST | Aex Air | N |
| DTA | TAAG Angola Airlines | D2 |
| DTH | Tassili Airlines | 7T |
| DTR | Danish Air Transport | OY |
| DVR | Divi Divi Air | PJ |
| DWT | Darwin Airline | HB |
| DYL | Seair Airways | C6 |
| | | |
| EAA | Eastok Avia | A6 |
| EAI | Elite Air | 5V |
| EAK | Euro Asia Intl | UP |
| EAN | Skypower Express Airways | 5N |
| EAS | Executive Aerospace | ZS |
| EAV | Kyrghyz Airways | EX |
| ECN | Euro Continental Air | EC |
| ECT | East Coast Airways | ZS |
| EDJ | Edwards Jet Centre of Montana | N |
| EDO | Elidolomiti | I |
| EDW | Edelweiss Air | HB |
| EEX | Avanti Air | D |
| EEZ | Meridiana Fly | I |
| EFA | Express Freighters Australia | VH |
| EFG | Elifriula | I |
| EGS | Eagle Airlines | I |
| EGU | Eagle Air | 5X |
| EIA | Evergreen Intl Airlines | N |
| EIN | Aer Lingus | EI |
| ELH | Elilario Italia | I |
| ELL | Estonian Air | ES |
| ELL | Estonian Air Regional | ES |
| ELO | EuroLot | SP |
| ELR | El-Rom Airlines | 4X |
| ELY | El Al Israel Airlines | 4X |
| EMT | Emetebe Taxi Aero | HC |
| ENI | Enimex | ES |
| ENJ | Enerjet | C |
| EPA | Donghai Airlines | B |
| EPS | Epps Aviation Charter | N |
| EQA | Elilombarda | I |
| EQF | American Eagle | N |
| ERG | Aviaenergo | RA |
| ERH | Era Aviation | N |
| ERO | Sud D'Or Intl Airlines | 4X |
| ERT | Eritrean Airlines | E3 |
| ESC | Sol America | YV |
| ESD | Essen Air | EX |
| ESF | Estafeta Carga Aerea | XA |
| ESJ | Eastern Skyjets | A6 |
| ESL | Russian Sky Airlines | RA |
| ETC | Trans Attico | ST |
| ETD | Etihad Airways | A6 |
| ETH | Ethiopian Airlines | ET |
| ETS | Avitrans Nordic | SE |
| EUP | Euroair | SX |
| EVA | EVA Airways | B |
| EWG | Eurowings | D |
| EWZ | East Wing | UP |
| EXN | Exin | SP |
| EXS | Jet2 | G |
| EXT | Nightexpress | D |
| EXV | Expo Air | 4R |
| EXW | EAS Air Lines | 5N |
| EXY | South African Express Airways | ZS |
| EXZ | East African Express | 5Y |
| EZA | Enzis Airways | JU |
| EZE | Eastern Airways | G |
| EZS | Easyjet Switzerland | HB |
| EZY | Easyjet Airlines | G |

| | | | | | | |
|---|---|---|---|---|---|---|
| FAB | First Air | C | | GOA | Province of Alberta | C |
| FAH | Farnair Hungary | HA | | GOM | Gomelavia | EW |
| FAJ | Air Fiji | DQ | | GOR | Gorlitsa Airlines | UR |
| FAM | FAASA Aviacion | EC | | GOS | Goldfields Air Services | VH |
| FAO | Ufly Airways | N | | GOT | Waltair Europe | SE |
| FAT | Farnair Switzerland | HB | | GOW | Go Air | VT |
| FCL | Florida Coastal Airlines | N | | GRL | Air Greenland | OY |
| FCP | Flight Corporation | ZK | | GRV | Epsilon Aviation | SX |
| FCR | Flying Carpet Air Transport Services | OD | | GSC | Granstar Cargo Airlines | B |
| FDA | Fuji Dream Airlines | JA | | GSS | Global Supply Systems | G |
| FDD | Feeder Airlines | ST | | GSW | Sky Wings | SX |
| FDE | Federico Helicopters | N | | GSW | Skywings Intl | Z3 |
| FDN | Dolphin Air | A6 | | GTI | Atlas Air | N |
| FDR | Federal Air | ZS | | GTV | Aerogaviota | CU |
| FDX | Federal Express | N | | GUM | Gum Air | PZ |
| FEI | Ernir Air | TF | | GUM | Transportes Aereos Guatemaltecos | TG |
| FFA | Avialesookhrana Vladimir Air Enterprise | RA | | GUN | Grant Aviation | N |
| FFF | Freedom Air Services | 5N | | GUY | Air Guyane Express | F |
| FFG | Flugdienst Fehlhaber | D | | GWI | Germanwings | D |
| FFM | Firefly | 9M | | GWL | Great Wall Airlines | B |
| FFT | Frontier Airlines | N | | GWY | USA 3000 Airlines | N |
| FFV | Fly540 | 5Y | | GXL | XL Airways Germany | D |
| FHE | Hello | HB | | GZA | Excellent Air | D |
| FHY | Freebird Airlines | TC | | GZP | Gazpromavia | RA |
| FIF | Air Finland | OH | | | | |
| FIN | Finnair | OH | | HAD | Dragonair | B |
| FJI | Air Pacific | DQ | | HAG | Hageland Aviation Services | N |
| FKI | FLM Aviation | D | | HAL | Hawaiian Airlines | N |
| FLE | Flair Airlines | C | | HAX | Benair | LN |
| FLI | Atlantic Airways | OY | | HBI | CHC Denmark | OY |
| FLX | Flight Express | N | | HCW | Star1 Airlines | LY |
| FNT | Flight Intl Aviation | N | | HEC | Heli Campeche | XA |
| FNV | Transavia Service | 4L | | HEJ | Hellas jet | SX |
| FPO | Europe Airpost | F | | HEL | Helicol | HK |
| FRE | Freedom Air | N | | HEM | CHC Helicopters (Australia) | VH |
| FRG | Freight Runners Express | N | | HER | Hex'Air | F |
| FRJ | Afrijet Airlines | 5N | | HES | Harbourair | 9H |
| FSC | Four Star Air Cargo | N | | HET | TAF Helicopters | EC |
| FTA | Frontier Flying Service | N | | HFY | Hi Fly | CS |
| FTL | Flightline | EC | | HHA | Atlantic Airlines | HR |
| FTR | Finist'Air | F | | HHH | Helicsa Helicopteros | EC |
| FVS | Falcon Express Cargo Airlines | A6 | | HHK | Sky Shuttle Helicopters | B |
| FWI | Air Caraibes | F | | HIB | Helibravo Aviacao | CS |
| FWL | Florida West Intl Airlines | N | | HIS | Heliswiss | HB |
| FXI | Air Iceland | TF | | HIT | Heli-Italia | I |
| FYA | Saicus Air | EC | | HKA | Superior Aviation | N |
| FZB | FlyDubai | A6 | | HKE | Hong Kong Express Airways | B |
| | | | | HKN | Jim Hankins Air Service | N |
| GAE | Tricoastal Air | N | | HKR | Hawk Air | LV |
| GAI | Moskoviya | RA | | HKS | CHC Helikopter Service | LN |
| GAK | Global Air | 5A | | HLF | Tuifly | D |
| GAL | Galaxy Airlines | EX | | HLG | Helog | HB |
| GAO | Golden Air | SE | | HLR | Heli Air | LZ |
| GAP | AirPhil Express | RP | | HLU | Heli-Union | F |
| GBK | Gabon Airlines | TR | | HLW | Heliworks | CC |
| GBX | GB Airlink | N | | HMA | Air Tahoma | N |
| GCK | Aerogem Airlines | 9G | | HMF | Norrlandsflyg | SE |
| GCR | Tianjin Airlines | B | | HMS | Hemus Air | LZ |
| GDC | Grand China Airlines | B | | HMX | Hawk de Mexico | XA |
| GEA | Geasa | 3C | | HPL | Heliportugal | CS |
| GEC | Lufthansa Cargo | D | | HPR | Helipro | ZK |
| GEN | Gensa | PP | | HSE | Helisuretse | EC |
| GET | Getra | 3C | | HSS | Transportes Aereos del Sur | EC |
| GFA | Gulf Air | A9C | | HSU | Helisul | CS |
| GFG | Sky Georgia | 4L | | HSV | Direktflyg | SE |
| GFT | Gulfstream Intl | N | | HSW | Heliswiss Iberica | EC |
| GGL | Gira Globo | D2 | | HTA | Helitrans | LN |
| GGN | Air Georgian | C | | HTG | Grossmann Air Transport | OE |
| GGZ | Global Georgian Airways | 4L | | HVL | Heavylift Intl | A6 |
| GHS | Gatari Air Service | PK | | HVN | Vietnam Airlines | VN |
| GHT | Ghadames Air Transport | 5A | | HVY | Heavylift Cargo Airlines | VH |
| GHY | German SkyAirlines | D | | HXA | China Express Airlines | B |
| GIA | Garuda Indonesia | PK | | HYD | Hydro-Quebec | C |
| GIP | Air Guinee Express | 3X | | | | |
| GLA | Great Lakes Airlines | N | | IAR | Iliamna Air Taxi | N |
| GLE | Goliaf Air | S9 | | IAW | Iraqi Airways | YI |
| GLG | Aerogal | HC | | IBB | Binter Canarias | EC |
| GLL | Air Gemini | D2 | | IBE | Iberia | EC |
| GLO | Gol Transportes Aereos | PP | | IBX | Ibex Airlines | JA |
| GLP | Globus | RA | | ICD | Icaro Express | HC |
| GLR | Central Mountain Air | C | | ICE | Icelandair | TF |
| GMI | Germania | D | | ICJ | Icejet | TF |
| GMT | Magnicharters | XA | | ICL | Cargo Air Lines | 4X |

| | | | | | | |
|---|---|---|---|---|---|
| ICV | Cargolux Italia | I | JZR | Jazeera Airways | 9K |
| IDA | Indonesia Air Transport | PK | | | |
| IGA | Sky Taxi | SP | KAC | Kuwait Airways | 9K |
| IGO | Indigo Airlines | VT | KAD | Kirovohradavia | UR |
| IIG | Aldawlyh Air | 5A | KAE | Kartika Airlines | PK |
| IKA | Itek Air | EX | KAJ | Karthago Airlines | TS |
| ILF | Island Air Charters | N | KAL | Korean Air | HL |
| ILN | Inter-Air | ZS | KAO | Kapo | RA |
| IMP | Hellenic Imperial Airways | SX | KAP | Cape Air | N |
| IMT | Imtrec Aviation | XU | KAW | Kazair West | UP |
| IMX | Zimex Aviation | HB | KBA | Kenn Borek Air | C |
| INC | Insel Air Intl | PJ | KBR | Koral Blue | SU |
| INJ | Interjet | XA | KDC | KD Air | C |
| INL | Intal Air | EX | KEE | Keystone Air Service | C |
| INV | Inversija | YL | KEN | Kenmore Air | N |
| IOS | Isles of Scilly Skybus | G | KES | Kallat el Saker Air | 5A |
| IRA | Iran Air | EP | KFA | Kelowna Flightcraft Air Charter | C |
| IRB | Iran Air Tour Airline | EP | KFR | Kingfisher Airlines | VT |
| IRC | Iran Aseman Airlines | EP | KFR | Kingfisher Red | VT |
| IRG | Naft Air | EP | KFS | Kalitta Charters II | N |
| IRI | Navid Air | EP | KFS | Kalitta Flying Services | N |
| IRK | Kish Air | EP | KGA | Kyrghyzstan Airlines | EX |
| IRM | Mahan Air | EP | KGL | Kolavia | RA |
| IRP | Payim Intl Air | EP | KHA | Kitty Hawk Aircargo | N |
| IRQ | Qeshm Air | EP | KHB | Dalavia | RA |
| IRR | Tara Airlines | EP | KHH | Alexandria Airlines | SU |
| IRU | Chabahar Air | EP | KHO | Khors Air | UR |
| IRX | Aria Air | EP | KIL | Kuban Airlines | RA |
| IRY | Eram Air | EP | KIS | Contact Air | D |
| IRZ | Saha Airline | EP | KKK | Atlasjet Intl | TC |
| ISA | Island Airlines | N | KLC | KLM Cityhopper | PH |
| ISD | ISD Avia | UR | KLM | KLM Royal Dutch Airlines | PH |
| ISK | Intersky | OE | KMF | Kam Air | YA |
| ISN | Interisland Airways | RP | KMG | Kosmas Air Cargo | YU |
| ISR | Israir | 4X | KMI | K-Mile Air | HS |
| ISV | Islena Airlines | HR | KMV | Utair Express | RA |
| ISW | Islas Airways | EC | KMZ | Comores Aviation | D6 |
| ITK | Interlink Airlines | ZS | KNA | Kunming Airlines | B |
| ITX | Imair | 4K | KNE | NAS Air | HZ |
| IWD | Iberworld Airlines | EC | KNM | Knaapo | RA |
| IYE | Yemenia | 7O | KOP | Copters | CC |
| IZA | Izhavia | RA | KOR | Air Koryo | P |
| IZG | Zagros Airlines | EP | KPA | Henan Airlines | B |
| IZM | Izmir Airlines | TC | KQA | Kenya Airways | 5Y |
| | | | KRE | Aerosucre | HK |
| JAB | Air Bagan | XY | KRP | Carpatair | YR |
| JAC | Japan Air Commuter | JA | KRT | Kokshetau Airlines | UP |
| JAE | Jade Cargo Intl | B | KSA | KS Avia | YL |
| JAF | Jetairfly | OO | KSM | Kosmos Airlines | RA |
| JAI | Jet Airways | VT | KSP | SAEP | HK |
| JAL | J-Air | JA | KST | PTL Luftfahrtunternehmen | D |
| JAL | Japan Airlines | JA | KTA | Kirov Avia Enterprise | RA |
| JAT | JAT Airways | YU | KTC | Kyrgyz Trans Air | EX |
| JAV | Jordan Aviation | JY | KTK | Katekavia | RA |
| JBA | HeliJet Intl | C | KVA | Kavok Airlines | YV |
| JBU | Jetblue Airways | N | KYM | Krym | UR |
| JCI | Jordan Intl Air Cargo | JY | KZH | Zhezhair | UP |
| JCK | Jackson Air Services | C | KZR | Air Astana | UP |
| JEA | Jet Air | SP | | | |
| JEC | Jett 8 Airlines Cargo | 9V | LAA | Libyan Airlines | 5A |
| JET | Windjet | I | LAB | LAB Flying Service | N |
| JEX | JAL Express | JA | LAL | Air Labrador | C |
| JFU | Jet4You | CN | LAM | LAM - Linhas Aereas de Mocambique | C9 |
| JJA | Jeju Air | HL | LAN | LAN Airlines | CC |
| JKK | Spanair | EC | LAO | Lao Airlines | RDPL |
| JLA | Mia Airlines | YR | LAP | TAM Mercosur | ZP |
| JLX | Jetlink Express | 5Y | LAU | Lineas Aéreas Sudamericanas | |
| JNA | Jin Air | HL | | Colombia | HK |
| JOL | Atyrau Air Ways | UP | LAV | Aeropostal | YV |
| JON | Johnsons Air | 9G | LAV | Alba Star | EC |
| JOR | Blue Air | YR | LAY | Layang-layang Aerospace | 9M |
| JOS | DHL de Guatemala | TG | LBC | Albanian Airlines | ZA |
| JSA | Jetstar Asia Airways | 9V | LBT | Nouvelair | TS |
| JSI | Jet Air Group | RA | LBY | Belle Air | ZA |
| JSJ | JS Focus Air | AP | LCB | LC Burse | OB |
| JST | Jetstar Airways | VH | LCG | Lignes Aeriennes Congolaises | 9Q |
| JTA | Japan Transocean Air | JA | LCN | Lineas Aereas Canedo | CP |
| JTG | Jettime | OY | LCO | LAN Cargo | CC |
| JTU | Zhetysu Avia | UP | LCR | Libyan Air Cargo | 5A |
| JTY | Jatayu Air | PK | LDE | LADE | LV |
| JUB | Jubba Airways | 6O | LER | Laser | YV |
| JUS | USA Jet Airlines | N | LFL | Exec-Air | Z |
| JZA | Air Canada Jazz | C | LGL | Luxair | LX |

| | | | | | |
|---|---|---|---|---|---|
| LGW | LGW - Luftfahrtgesellschaft Walter | D | MJT | Vigo Jet | XA |
| LIA | LIAT - The Caribbean Airline | V2 | MKU | Island Air | N |
| LID | Alidaunia | I | MLA | 40 Mile Air | N |
| LIQ | Flygcentrum | SE | MLC | Malift Air | 9Q |
| LKE | Lucky Airlines | B | MLD | Air Moldova | ER |
| LLB | LAB Airlines | CP | MLG | Malagasy Airlines | 5R |
| LLC | Small Planet Airlines | LY | MLR | Mihin Lanka | 4R |
| LLL | Lao Aviation | RDPL | MMA | Myanmar Airways Intl | XY |
| LLM | Yamal Airlines | RA | MMZ | Euro Atlantic Airways | CS |
| LLR | Alliance Air | VT | MNA | Merpati Nusantara Airlines | PK |
| LMU | Almasria Universal Airlines | SU | MNB | MNG Cargo Airlines | TC |
| LMY | Air Almaty | UP | MNG | Aero Mongolia | JU |
| LNE | LAN Ecuador | HC | MNL | Miniliner | I |
| LNI | Lion Airlines | PK | MON | Monarch Airlines | G |
| LNK | Airlink | ZS | MOO | Moonair Aviation | 4X |
| LOD | Fly Logic Sweden | SE | MOV | Vim Airlines | RA |
| LOF | American Connection | N | MPH | Martinair | PH |
| LOG | Loganair | G | MPJ | Mapjet | OE |
| LOT | LOT - Polish Airlines | SP | MPT | Miapet Avia | EK |
| LOU | Air Saint Louis | 6V | MRA | Martinaire | N |
| LPE | LAN Peru | OB | MRE | Namibia Commercial Airways | V5 |
| LPV | Air Alps Aviation | OE | MRR | Northwest Seaplanes | N |
| LRA | Little Red Air Service | C | MRR | San Juan Airlines | N |
| LRB | LR Airlines | OK | MRS | Airline of the Marshall Islands | V7 |
| LRO | Alrosa Avia | RA | MSA | Mistral Air | I |
| LRS | Sansa Regional | TI | MSC | Air Cairo | SU |
| LSE | Lassa - Lineas de Aeroservicios | CC | MSE | Egyptair Express | SU |
| LSK | Aurela | LY | MSI | Motor Sich Airlines | UR |
| LSR | Alsair | F | MSL | Marsland Aviation | ST |
| LSY | Lindsay Aviation | N | MSM | Aeromas | CX |
| LTR | Lufttransport | LN | MSQ | META - Mesquita Transportes Aero | PP |
| LTS | Flight Inspections & Systems | RA | MSR | Egyptair | SU |
| LUZ | Luzair | CS | MST | MTA Cargo | PP |
| LVB | IRS Airlines | 5N | MSV | Aero-Kamov | RA |
| LVR | Aviavilsa | LY | MTL | RAF-Avia | YL |
| LXF | Lynx Air Intl | N | MTN | Mountain Air Cargo | N |
| LXP | LAN Express | CC | MTW | Mauritania Airways | 5T |
| LYC | Lynden Air Cargo | N | MUA | National Airlines | N |
| LYD | Lydd Air | G | MUI | Transair | N |
| LYM | Key Lime Air | N | MVD | KMV Mineralnye Vody Airlines | RA |
| LYN | Kyrgyzstan | EX | MWA | Midwest Airlines Egypt | SU |
| LYT | Apatas | LY | MWT | Midwest Aviation | N |
| LZB | Bulgaria Air | LZ | MXE | Mocambique Expresso | C9 |
| LZT | Lanzarote Aircargo | EC | MXU | Maximus Air Cargo | A6 |
| | | | MYA | Myflug | TF |
| MAA | MAS Air Cargo | XA | MYD | Maya Island Air | V3 |
| MAC | Air Arabia Maroc | CN | MYI | Mayair | XA |
| MAH | Malev | HA | MZL | Aerovias Montes Azules | XA |
| MAK | MAT Macedonian Air Transport | Z3 | | | |
| MAL | Morningstar Air Express | C | NAC | Northern Air Cargo | N |
| MAS | Malaysia Airlines | 9M | NAL | Northway Aviation | C |
| MAU | Air Mauritius | 3B | NAO | North American Airlines | N |
| MAW | Mustique Airways | J8 | NAX | Norwegian | LN |
| MAX | Max Aviation | C | NAY | Naysa Aerotaxis | EC |
| MBB | Air Manas | EX | NBE | Novosibirsk Air Enterprise | RA |
| MBC | Aerojet | D2 | NCA | Nippon Cargo Airlines | JA |
| MBI | Salmon Air | N | NCB | North Cariboo Air | C |
| MBM | Starjet | JY | NCH | Phillips Air Charter | N |
| MBN | Zambian Airways | 9J | NCP | Capital Airlines | 5N |
| MBV | Aeriantur-M Airlines | ER | NCS | Simpson Air Commuter Canada | C |
| MCM | Heli Air Monaco | 3A | NDN | Transportes Aereos Cielos Andinos | OB |
| MCW | AMW Tchad | TT | NEA | New England Airlines | N |
| MDA | Mandarin Airlines | B | NFA | North Flying | OY |
| MDC | Mid-Atlantic Freight | N | NFS | Afrique Cargo Services | 6V |
| MDF | Swiftair Hellas | SX | NGK | Oriental Air Bridge | JA |
| MDJ | Jetran Intl Airways | YR | NHG | NHT Linhas Aereas | PP |
| MDL | Mandala Airlines | PK | NIG | Aero Contactors | 5N |
| MDM | Medavia | 9H | NJS | Cobham Aviation Services Australia | VH |
| MDN | Mudan Airlines | 6O | NKF | Barents Skylink | SE |
| MDS | McNeely Charter Service | N | NKS | Spirit Airlines | N |
| MDV | Moldavian Airlines | ER | NKZ | Aerokuzbass | RA |
| MEA | Middle East Airlines | OD | NLC | Nelair Charters & Travel | ZS |
| MEM | Meridian | UR | NLF | Westair Aviation | C |
| MEP | Midwest Airlines | N | NLK | Elbrus Avia | RA |
| MGE | Asia Pacific Airlines | N | NLY | Niki | OE |
| MGG | El Magal Aviation | ST | NMB | Air Namibia | V5 |
| MGK | Mega Aircompany | UP | NMD | Bay Air Aviation | V5 |
| MGL | MIAT - Mongolian Airlines | JU | NMI | Pacific Wings | N |
| MGX | Montenegro Airlines | 4O | NOF | Fonnafly | LN |
| MHS | Air Memphis | SU | NOK | Nok Air | HS |
| MIF | Miras Air | UP | NOR | Bristow Norway | LN |
| MIX | Midex Airlines | A6 | NOS | Neos | I |
| MJA | Almajara Aviation | ST | NOT | Linea Aerea Costa Norte | CC |

| | | |
|---|---|---|
| NPO | Napo Aviatrans | RA |
| NPR | Air Napier | ZK |
| NPT | West Atlantic | G |
| NRG | Ross Aviation | N |
| NRK | Naturelink Charter | ZS |
| NRL | Nolinor Aviation | C |
| NRO | Aero Rent | RA |
| NRR | Natureair | TI |
| NRX | Norse Air Charter | ZS |
| NSE | Satena | HK |
| NTA | NT Air | C |
| NTC | Heartland Aviation | N |
| NTH | Hokkaido Air System | JA |
| NTJ | Nextjet | SE |
| NTV | Air Inter Ivoire | TU |
| NVD | Nordic Solutions Air Services | LY |
| NVI | Avial Aviation Co | RA |
| NVR | Novair | SE |
| NVS | Nouvelles Air Affaires Gabon | TR |
| NWL | North Wright Airways | C |
| NXA | Air Next | JA |
| NYL | Mid Airlines | ST |
| NZA | Air New Zealand Link | ZK |
| | | |
| OAE | Omni Air Intl | N |
| OAL | Olympic Airways | SX |
| OAO | Arkhangelsk 2nd Aviation Enterprise | RA |
| OAV | Omni - Aviacao e Tecnoligia | CS |
| OAW | Helvetic Airways | HB |
| OBS | Orbest | CS |
| OCA | Aserca Airlines | YV |
| ODS | Odessa Airlines | UR |
| OEA | Orient Thai Airlines | HS |
| OHY | Onur Air | TC |
| OKA | OK Airways | B |
| OKS | Slok Air Intl | C5 |
| OLA | Overland Airways | 5N |
| OLC | Solar Cargo | YV |
| OLS | SOL Lineas Aereas | LV |
| OLT | OLT - Ostfriesische Lufttransport | D |
| OMA | Oman Air | A4O |
| OMR | Minair | TL |
| ONE | Avianca Brazil | PP |
| ONR | Air One Nine | 5A |
| ORB | Orenair | RA |
| ORJ | Bellview Airlines | 9L |
| ORZ | Zorex | EC |
| OST | Alania Airline | RA |
| OTL | South Airlines | UR |
| OVA | Aeronova | EC |
| OZU | Khozu Avia | UP |
| OZW | Skywest Airlines | VH |
| | | |
| PAC | Polar Air Cargo | N |
| PAG | Perimeter Aviation | C |
| PAL | Philippine Airlines | RP |
| PAO | Polynesian Airlines | 5W |
| PAS | Pelita Air | PK |
| PBN | Pacific Blue | ZK |
| PBU | Air Burundi | 9U |
| PCE | Pace Airlines | N |
| PCG | Aeropostal | XA |
| PCO | Pacific Coastal Airlines | C |
| PCP | Aerolinea Principal Chile | CC |
| PDA | Podilia Avia | UR |
| PDF | Pelican Air Services | ZS |
| PDG | PDG Helicopters | G |
| PEA | Pan Européenne Air Service | F |
| PEC | Pacific East Asia Cargo Airlines | RP |
| PEL | Aeropelican Air Services | VH |
| PEN | Penair | N |
| PEP | PENTA - Pena Transportes Aereos | PP |
| PFL | Pacificflyer | T8A |
| PFR | Pacificair | RP |
| PFZ | Profilight Air Services | 9J |
| PGA | Portugalia Airlines | CS |
| PGL | Premiair Aviation Services | G |
| PGP | Perm Airlines | RA |
| PGT | Pegasus Airlines | TC |
| PGX | Paragon Air Express | N |
| PHA | Phoenix Air | N |
| PHB | Phoebus Apollo Aviation | ZS |
| PHE | Pawan Hans Helicopters | VT |
| PHM | PHI - Petroleum Helicopters | N |
| PHW | AVE.com | A6 |
| PHY | Phoenix Avia | EK |
| PIA | Pakistan Intl Airlines | AP |
| PIC | Jetstar Pacific Airlines | VN |
| PIR | Pamir Air | YA |
| PIV | Sokol | RA |
| PKW | Sierra West Airlines | N |
| PLC | Police Aviation Services | G |
| PLJ | Platinum Air Linhas Aereas | PP |
| PLM | Pullmantur Air | EC |
| PLR | Northwestern Air | C |
| PLS | Aeroflot Plus | RA |
| PLY | Puma Air Linhas Aereas | PP |
| PMA | Pan-Malaysian Air Transport | 9M |
| PMS | Planemasters | N |
| PMT | PMT Air | XU |
| PNA | Universal Airlines | N |
| PNP | Pineapple Air | C6 |
| PNR | Panair Lineas Aereas | EC |
| PNS | Penas | PK |
| POE | Porter Airlines | C |
| POT | Polet Aviakompania | RA |
| PPG | Phoenix Airtransport | N |
| PPK | Ramp 66 | N |
| PPW | Royal Phnom Penh Airways | XU |
| PRF | Precisionair | 5H |
| PRG | Empressa Aero - Servicios Parrague | CC |
| PRN | Pirinair Express | EC |
| PRO | Propair | C |
| PRY | Priority Air Charter | N |
| PSC | Pascan Aviation | C |
| PSD | President Airlines | XU |
| PSS | Progress Aviakompania | RA |
| PST | Air Panama | HP |
| PSV | Sapair | HI |
| PSW | Pskovavia | RA |
| PTG | Privatair | D |
| PTI | Privatair | HB |
| PTK | Petropavlovsk-Kamchatsky Air Enterprise | RA |
| PTN | Pantanal | PP |
| PUA | Pluna Lineas Aereas Uruguayas | CX |
| PVG | Privalege Style | EC |
| PVI | Panavia Cargo Airlines | HP |
| PVU | Peau Vava'u Air | A3 |
| PVV | Continental Airways | RA |
| PWF | Private Wings | D |
| PYZ | Players Air | N |
| | | |
| QAT | Air Quasar | C |
| QCL | Air Class | CX |
| QFA | QANTAS Airways | VH |
| QFA | Qantaslink | VH |
| QNK | Kabo Air | 5N |
| QNT | Qanot Sharq | UK |
| QNZ | Jetconnect | ZK |
| QTG | One-Two Go | HS |
| QTR | Qatar Airways | A7 |
| QUE | Government of Quebec | C |
| QWA | Pel-Air | VH |
| QWL | Qwila Air | ZS |
| QXE | Horizon Air | N |
| | | |
| RAC | Ryukyu Air Commuter | JA |
| RAD | Alada | D2 |
| RAE | Régional | F |
| RAG | Regio-Air | D |
| RAI | Aerotur Air | UP |
| RAM | Royal Air Maroc | CN |
| RAX | Royal Air Freight | N |
| RBA | Royal Brunei Airlines | V8 |
| RBC | Republicair | XA |
| RBW | Rainbow Jet | B |
| RCQ | Aerolineas Regionales | XA |
| RCT | Arctic Transportation Services | N |
| RDS | Rhoades Intl | N |
| REA | Aer Arann | EI |
| REG | Regional Air Services | 5H |
| REU | Air Austral | F |
| REX | RAM Air Freight | N |
| RFC | Aero Africa | 3D |
| RFS | Rossair Charter | VH |

| Code | Airline | Country |
|---|---|---|
| RGE | Guinea Equatorial Airlines | 3C |
| RGE | Star Equatorial Airlines | 3C |
| RGL | Regional Air Lines | CN |
| RGN | Gestair Cargo | EC |
| RHA | Robin Hood Aviation | OE |
| RHD | Bond Air Services | G |
| RHL | Air Archipels | F |
| RIT | Zest Airways | RP |
| RIU | Riau Airlines | PK |
| RJA | Royal Jordanian | JY |
| RKH | Royal Khmer Airlines | XU |
| RKM | Rak Airlines | A6 |
| RLA | Airlinair | F |
| RLE | Rico Linhas Aereas | PP |
| RLR | Airnow | N |
| RLS | S-Air | RA |
| RLU | Rusline Air | RA |
| RMO | Saturn Aviakompania | RA |
| RMV | Romavia | YR |
| RMX | Air Max | LZ |
| RNA | Nepal Airlines | 9N |
| RNB | Rosneft-Baltika | RA |
| RNG | Orange Aircraft Leasing | PH |
| RNL | Aero Lanka Airlines | 4R |
| RNV | Armavia | EK |
| RNX | 1Time Airline | ZS |
| ROE | Aeroeste | CP |
| ROI | Avior Airlines | YV |
| RON | Our Airline | C2 |
| ROR | Roraima Airways | 8R |
| ROT | Tarom | YR |
| ROX | Roblex Aviation | N |
| RPB | Aerorepublica Colombia | HK |
| RPC | Aeropacsa | HC |
| RPH | RPX Airlines | PK |
| RPK | Royal Airlines | AP |
| RPX | HD Air | G |
| RRV | Mombasa Air Safari | 5Y |
| RSB | Rubystar | EW |
| RSE | SNAS Aviation | HZ |
| RSG | Aero Service ASF | 6V |
| RSH | Jetlite | VT |
| RSI | Air Sunshine | N |
| RSR | Aeroservice | TN |
| RSU | Aerosur | CP |
| RTM | Trans Am | HC |
| RUC | Rutaca | YV |
| RUM | Air Rum | 9L |
| RUN | ACT Airlines | TC |
| RUS | Cirrus Airlines | D |
| RVE | Airventure | OO |
| RVL | Air Vallée | I |
| RVT | Veteran Airline | EK |
| RWD | Rwandair Express | 9XR |
| RWG | C&M Airways | N |
| RWS | Air Whitsunday Seaplanes | VH |
| RXA | REX - Regional Express | VH |
| RYN | Ryan Intl Airlines | N |
| RYR | Ryanair | EI |
| RYW | Royal Wings Airlines | JY |
| RYZ | Ryazanavia Trans | RA |
| RZO | SATA Internacional | CS |
| RZZ | Anoka Air Charter | N |
| SAA | South African Airways | ZS |
| SAB | Sky Way Air | EX |
| SAH | Sayakhat | UP |
| SAI | Sheheen Air Intl | AP |
| SAM | SAM Colombia | HK |
| SAP | Avia Jaynar | UP |
| SAS | Scandinavian Airline System | SE |
| SAT | SATA Air Acores | CS |
| SAV | Samal Air | UP |
| SAX | Sabah Air | 9M |
| SAY | Scotairways | G |
| SBF | SB Air | N |
| SBI | S7 Airlines | RA |
| SBM | Sky Bahamas | C6 |
| SBU | St Barth Commuter | F |
| SBX | North Star Air Cargo | N |
| SCD | Associated Air Cargo | 5N |
| SCE | Scenic Airlines | N |
| SCH | CHC Airways | PH |
| SCU | Air Scorpio | LZ |
| SCW | Malmo Aviation | SE |
| SCX | Sun Country Airlines | N |
| SDK | SADELCA | HK |
| SDL | Skysouth | G |
| SDM | Rossiya Russian Airlines | RA |
| SDO | Air Santo Domingo | HI |
| SDR | City Airline | SE |
| SE H | Sky Express | SX |
| SEE | Sheheen Air Cargo | AP |
| SEJ | Spicejet | VT |
| SEQ | Sky Eyes Aviation | HS |
| SEV | Serair | EC |
| SEY | Air Seychelles | S7 |
| SFF | Safewing Aviation | N |
| SFJ | Starflyer | JA |
| SFN | Safiran Airlines | EP |
| SFR | Safair | ZS |
| SGB | Sky King | N |
| SGD | Skygate Intl | JY |
| SGG | Senegal Airlines | 6V |
| SGS | Saskatchewan Government Northern Air Operations | C |
| SGX | Saga Airlines | TC |
| SGY | Skagway Air Service | N |
| SHQ | Shanghai Cargo | B |
| SHU | SAT Airlines | RA |
| SHY | Sky Airlines | TC |
| SHZ | CHC Scotia Helicopters | G |
| SIA | Singapore Airlines | 9V |
| SIB | Sibaviatrans | RA |
| SJY | Sriwijaya Air | PK |
| SKC | Skymaster Airlines | PP |
| SKI | Skyking Airlines | VQ-T |
| SKK | Asky Airlines | 5V |
| SKS | Sky Service | OO |
| SKT | Skystar Airways | HS |
| SKU | Sky Airline | CC |
| SKW | Skywest Airlines | N |
| SKX | Skyways Express | SE |
| SKY | Skymark Airlines | JA |
| SKZ | Skyway Enterprises | N |
| SLD | Silver Air | OK |
| SLE | NAC Charter | ZS |
| SLI | Aeromexico Connect | XA |
| SLK | Silkair | 9V |
| SLM | Surinam Airways | PZ |
| SMC | Sabang Merauke Raya Air Charter | PK |
| SMH | Smithair | N |
| SMJ | Avient Aviation | Z |
| SMK | Semeyavia | UP |
| SMX | Alitalia Express | I |
| SNC | Air Cargo Carriers | N |
| SNG | Air Senegal Intl | 6V |
| SNJ | Skynet Asia Airways | JA |
| SOA | Southern Air Charter | C6 |
| SOL | Solomons | H4 |
| SOO | Southern Air | N |
| SOP | Solinair | S5 |
| SOR | Sonair | D2 |
| SOV | Saratov Airlines | RA |
| SOY | Island Aviation | RP |
| SOZ | SAT Airlines | UP |
| SPA | Sierra Pacific Airlines | N |
| SPB | Springbok Classic Air | ZS |
| SPM | Air St Pierre | F |
| SPP | Sapphire Aviation | N |
| SPR | Provincial Airlines | C |
| SQC | Singapore Airlines Cargo | 9V |
| SRC | Searca Colombia | HK |
| SRF | Transportes Aereos San Rafael | CC |
| SRI | Air Safaris & Services | ZK |
| SRK | Skywork Airlines | HB |
| SRO | SAEREO | HC |
| SRQ | South East Asian Airlines | RP |
| SRR | Star Air | OY |
| SRU | Star peru | OB |
| SSC | Southern Seaplane | N |
| SSF | Severstal Aircompany | RA |
| SSG | Slovak Government Flying Service | OM |
| SSS | SAESA | EC |
| STH | South Airlines | EK |
| STI | Sontair | C |

| | | | | | | |
|---|---|---|---|---|---|---|
| STT | Air St Thomas | N | TIM | TEAM Airlines – Team | | |
| STU | Star African Air | 6O | | Transportes Aereos | PP | |
| STX | Stars Away Aviation | ZS | TIW | Transcarga Intl Airways | YV | |
| SUB | Suburban Air Freight | N | TJK | Tajik Air | EY | |
| SUD | Sudan Airways | ST | TJS | Tyrolean Jet Service | OE | |
| SUF | Pacific Sun | DQ | TJT | Trast Aero | EX | |
| SUK | Superior Aviation Services | 5Y | TJT | Twin Jet | F | |
| SUM | MCHS Rossii | RA | TLB | Atlantique Air Assistance | F | |
| SUS | Sun-Air of Scandinavia | OY | TLG | Investavia | UP | |
| SUW | Interavia Airlines | RA | TLR | Air Libya | 5A | |
| SVA | Saudi Arabian Airlines | HZ | TLT | Turtle Airways | DQ | |
| SVD | SVG Air | J8 | TLX | Telesis Transair | N | |
| SVE | Asesa | XA | TLY | Top-Fly | EC | |
| SVH | Sterling Aviation | G | TMG | Tri-MG Intra-Asia Airlines | PK | |
| SVJ | Silver Air | J2 | TMI | Tamir Aviation | 4X | |
| SVL | Sevastopol Avia | UR | TMS | Temsco Helicopters | N | |
| SVM | Aeroservicios Monterrey | XA | TMW | Trans Maldivian Airways | 8Q | |
| SVR | Ural Airlines | RA | TMX | Tramon Air | ZS | |
| SVT | 748 Air Services | 5Y | TNA | Transasia Airways | B | |
| SWA | Southwest Airlines | N | TNB | Trans Air Benin | TY | |
| SWG | Sunwing Airlines | C | TNL | Sky Horse Aviation | JU | |
| SWH | Adler Aviation | C | TNM | Tiara Air | P4 | |
| SWN | West Air Europe | SE | TNO | Aerounion | XA | |
| SWR | Swiss Intl Airlines | HB | TNR | Tanana Air Service | N | |
| SWT | Swiftair | EC | TNT | Trans North Helicopters | C | |
| SWU | Swiss European Air Lines | HB | TNV | Transnorthern Aviation | N | |
| SWW | Shovkovly Shlyah | UR | TNW | Trans Nation Airways | ET | |
| SXM | Saemsa | XA | TOK | Airlines of Papua New Guinea | P2 | |
| SXN | Air Sweden | SE | TOL | Tolair Services | N | |
| SXP | Sprint Air | SP | TOM | Thomsonfly.com | G | |
| SXR | Skyexpress | RA | TOS | Tropic Air Commuter | V3 | |
| SXS | Sunexpress | TC | TPA | Tampa Airlines | HK | |
| SYJ | Slate Falls Airways | C | TPC | Air Caledonie | F | |
| SYL | Yakutia Airlines | RA | TPG | Transportes Aereos Pegaso | XA | |
| SYM | Sayat Air | UP | TPK | Air Horizon Afrique | TT | |
| SYR | Syrianair | YK | TPS | Tapsa Aviacion | LV | |
| SYX | Midwest Connect | N | TPU | TACA Peru | OB | |
| | | | TRA | Transavia Airlines | PH | |
| TAA | Aeropacifico | XA | TRD | Trans Island Air 2000 | 8P | |
| TAC | Turbot Air Cargo | 6V | TRG | Tragsa Medios Aereos | EC | |
| TAE | TAME | HC | TRI | Ontario Ministry of Natural Resources | | |
| TAH | Air Moorea | F | | Aviation Services | C | |
| TAI | TACA Intl Airlines | YS | TRN | Aerotron | XA | |
| TAJ | Tunisavia | TS | TRS | Airtran Airways | N | |
| TAK | Tatarstan Air | RA | TSC | Air Transat | C | |
| TAM | TAM Linhas Aereas | PP | TSD | TAF Linhas Aereas | PP | |
| TAN | Zanair | 5H | TSE | Transmile Air Services | 9M | |
| TAO | Aeromar Airlines | XA | TSG | Transair Congo | TN | |
| TAP | TAP Air Portugal | CS | TSH | Regional 1 Airlines | C | |
| TAR | Tunisair | TS | TSK | Tomskavia | RA | |
| TAS | Lotus Air | SU | TSO | Transaero Airlines | RA | |
| TAT | TACA Costa Rica | TI | TSP | Inter - transportes Aereos Inter | TG | |
| TAY | TNT Airways | OO | TSU | Gulf and Caribbean Air | N | |
| TBM | Taban Air | EP | TSY | Tristar Air | SU | |
| TBN | Teebah Airlines | J2 | TTA | TTA - Sociedade de Transportes e | | |
| TBQ | Tobruk Air | 5A | | Trabalho Aereo | C9 | |
| TCF | Shuttle America | N | TTC | Transteco | D2 | |
| TCI | Air Turks & Caicos | VQ-T | TTH | Tarhan Air | TC | |
| TCV | TACV - Transportes Aereos de | | TTL | Total Linhas Aereas | PP | |
| | Cabo Verde | D4 | TUA | Turkmenistan Airlines | EZ | |
| TCW | Thomas Cook Airlines Belgium | OO | TUI | Sevenair | TS | |
| TCX | Thomas Cook Airlines | G | TUL | Tulpar Air | RA | |
| TCY | Twin Cities Air Service | N | TUM | Tyumenspecavia | RA | |
| TDK | Transavia Denmark | OY | TUP | Aviastar - Tupolev | RA | |
| TDR | Trade Air | 9A | TUR | Atur | HC | |
| TDX | Skylease Air Cargo | N | TUS | ABSA Cargo | PP | |
| TEB | Tenir Airlines | EX | TUX | Tulpar Air Service | UP | |
| TET | Tepavia Trans Airline | ER | TUY | Linea Turistica Aereotuy | YV | |
| TFK | Transafrik Intl | S9 | TVF | Transavia France | F | |
| TFL | Arkefly | PH | TVH | Tavasa | EC | |
| TFO | Aeropacifico | XA | TVJ | Tavaj Linhas Aereas | PP | |
| TFR | Toll Priority | VH | TVL | Travel Service Hungary | HA | |
| TFT | Thai Flying Service | HS | TVR | Tavrey Aircompany | UR | |
| TGN | Trigana Air Service | PK | TVS | Smartwings | OK | |
| TGW | Tiger Airways | 9V | TVS | Travel Service Airlines | OK | |
| TGY | Trans Guyana Airways | 8R | TWM | Transairways | C9 | |
| TGZ | Airzena - Georgian Airlines | 4L | TWN | Avialeasing | UK | |
| THA | Thai Airways | HS | TXC | Trans Avia Export Cargo Airlines | EW | |
| THE | Toumai Air Chad | TT | TXU | Atesa | HC | |
| THK | THK - Turk Hava Kurumu | TC | TZR | Rainbow Air | YV | |
| THT | Air Tahiti Nui | F | | | | |
| THU | Thunder Airlines | C | UAC | United Air Charters | Z | |
| THY | Turkish Airlines | TC | UAE | Emirates | A6 | |

| Code | Airline | Country |
|---|---|---|
| UAK | Aviant | UR |
| UAL | United Air Lines | N |
| UAR | Aerostar | UR |
| UBA | Myanma Airways | XY |
| UCR | Aero-Charter Ukraine | UR |
| UDC | Donbassaero | UR |
| UDN | Dnepr-Air | UR |
| UFA | Ukraine Flight State Academy | UR |
| UGB | Air Uganda | 5X |
| UGN | Yuzhnaya Aircompany | UP |
| UGP | Shar Ink | RA |
| UGX | East African Airlines | 5X |
| UHS | Uvuaga | RA |
| UIA | Uni Air | B |
| UIL | United Intl Airlines | YU |
| UKL | Ukraine Air Alliance | UR |
| UKM | Um Air | UR |
| UKN | Ukraine Air Enterprise | UR |
| UKS | Ukrainian Cargo Airways | UR |
| UKU | Sverdlovsk 2nd Air Enterprise | RA |
| UKW | Lviv Airlines | UR |
| UMK | Yuzmashavia | UR |
| UNF | Union Flights | N |
| UNR | Rivne Universal Avia | UR |
| UNS | Uensped Paket Servisi / UPS | TC |
| UPL | Ukrainian Pilot School | UR |
| UPX | UPS Airlines | N |
| URG | Air Urga | UR |
| URJ | Star Air Intl | AP |
| URN | Turanair | 4K |
| URP | ARP 410 Airlines | UR |
| URR | Aurora Airlines | S5 |
| USA | US Airways | N |
| USC | Airnet Systems | N |
| USX | US Airways Express | N |
| UTA | Utair Airlines | RA |
| UTG | Utage | 3C |
| UTR | Utair South Africa | ZS |
| UTY | Alliance Airlines | VH |
| UYA | Flight Alaska | N |
| UYC | Cameroon Airlines | TJ |
| UZA | Constanta Airlines | UR |
| UZB | Uzbekistan Airways | UK |
| UZS | Samarkand Airways | UK |
| | | |
| VAA | Van Air Europe | OK |
| VAL | Voyageur Airways | C |
| VAS | Atran - Aviatrans Cargo Airlines | RA |
| VAT | Vision Air | EI |
| VAZ | Red Wings | RA |
| VBG | Vyborg Airlines | RA |
| VBW | Air Burkina | XT |
| VCV | Conviasa | YV |
| VDA | Volga-Dnepr Airlines | RA |
| VEA | Cargo Air | LZ |
| VEC | Venescar Intl | YV |
| VEJ | Aero Ejectivos | YV |
| VEN | Transaven | YV |
| VES | Vieques Air Link | N |
| VFC | Vasco | VN |
| VGN | Air Nigeria | 5N |
| VGV | Vologda Air Enterprise | RA |
| VIM | VIA - Air Via | LZ |
| VIN | Vincent Aviation (Australia) | VH |
| VIR | Virgin Atlantic Airways | G |
| VIS | Vision Air Intl | AP |
| VIV | Viva Aerobus | XA |
| VIZ | Aerovis Airlines | UR |
| VKG | Thomas Cook Scandinavia | OY |
| VLA | Valan Intl Cargo | ZS |
| VLG | Vueling Airlines | EC |
| VLK | Vladivostok Air | RA |
| VLM | VLM Airlines | OO |
| VLO | Varig Log | PP |
| VLU | Valuair | 9V |
| VMM | Vuelos Mediterrano | EC |
| VNE | Venezolana | YV |
| VNZ | Tbilaviamsheni | 4L |
| VOG | Voyager Airlines | S2 |
| VOI | Volaris | XA |
| VOS | Rovos Air | ZS |
| VOZ | Virgin Blue Airlines | VH |
| VPB | Veteran Airlines | UR |
| VPV | Vip-Avia | 4L |
| VRA | British Intl | G |
| VRB | Silverback Cargo Freighters | 9XR |
| VRD | Virgin America | N |
| VRE | Volare Aviation Enterprise | UR |
| VRN | Varig | PP |
| VSO | Aerolineas Sosa | HR |
| VSV | Scat Aircompany | UP |
| VTA | Air Tahiti | F |
| VTE | Corporate Flight Management | N |
| VTK | Vostok Airlines | RA |
| VTS | Everts Air Cargo | N |
| VTS | Everts Air Alaska | N |
| VUN | Air Ivoire | TU |
| VUR | VIP - Vuelos Internos Privados | HC |
| VVA | Aviast Air | RA |
| VXP | Mali Air Express | TZ |
| VXX | Aviaexpress Aircompany | UR |
| VZR | Air Loyauté | F |
| | | |
| WAA | Westair Wings | V5 |
| WAB | Aero Industries | N |
| WAE | Western Air Express | N |
| WAK | Wings of Alaska | N |
| WAM | Air Taxi & Cargo | ST |
| WAP | Arrow Panama | HP |
| WAV | Warbelow's Air | N |
| WBA | Finncomm Airlines | OH |
| WBR | Air Choice One | N |
| WCO | Columbia Helicopters | N |
| WDL | WDL Aviation | D |
| WEA | White Eagle General Aviation | SP |
| WEB | Webjet Linhas Aereas | PP |
| WEW | Express Air | C |
| WEW | West Wind Aviation | C |
| WFR | Alwafeer Air | HZ |
| WHT | White | CS |
| WIA | Winair | PJ |
| WIF | Wideroe's Flyveselskap | LN |
| WIG | Wiggins Airways | N |
| WJA | Westjet | C |
| WKH | Kharkov Aviation Production Association | UR |
| WLA | Airwaves Airlink | 9J |
| WLB | Wings Of Lebanon Aviation | OD |
| WLC | Welcome Air | OE |
| WLG | Volga Aviaexpress | RA |
| WLX | West Air Europe | LX |
| WOA | World Airways | N |
| WON | Wings Air | PK |
| WOW | Air Southwest | G |
| WRC | Wind Rose | UR |
| WRT | Wright Air Service | N |
| WSG | Wasaya Airways | C |
| WST | Western Air | C6 |
| WTV | Western Aviators | N |
| WUA | Wizz Air Ukraine | UR |
| WVL | Wizz Air Bulgaria | LZ |
| WZZ | Wizz Air | HA |
| | | |
| XAK | Airkenya | 5Y |
| XAR | Xpress Air | PK |
| XKX | Asecna | 6V |
| XLF | XL Airways France | F |
| XLL | Air Excel | 5H |
| XME | Australian Air Express | VH |
| | | |
| YZR | Yangtze River Express | B |
| | | |
| ZAQ | Zoom Airways | S2 |
| ZBA | ZB Air | 5Y |

# AIRPORT THREE-LETTER CODES

| | |
|---|---|
| AAC | Al-Arish, SU |
| AAH | Aachen-Merzbrück, D |
| AAL | Aalborg, OY |
| AAN | Al Ain (A6) |
| AAR | Aarhus-Tirstrup, OY |
| ABA | Abakan,RA |
| ABD | Abadan- Boigny Intl, EP |
| ABI | Abilene Regional, TX |
| ABJ | Abidjan-Felix Houphouet Boigirly, TU |
| ABQ | Albuquerque Intl, NM |
| ABS | Abu Simbel, SU |
| ABV | Abuja-Intl, 5N |
| ABX | Albury, NSW |
| ABZ | Aberdeen-Dyce, G |
| ACA | Acapulco-Gen.Alvarez Intl, XA |
| ACC | Accra-Kotoka Intl, 9G |
| ACE | Arrecife, Lanzarote, EC |
| ACH | Altenrhein, HB |
| ACI | Alderney-The Blaye, G |
| ACK | Nantucket Memorial, MA |
| ACO | Ascona, HB |
| ACS | Achinsk, RA |
| ACT | Waco Regional, TX |
| ACY | Atlantic City Intl, NJ |
| ADA | Adana-Sakirpasa, TC |
| ADB | Izmir-Adnan Menderes, TC |
| ADD | Addis Ababa-Bole Intl, ET |
| ADE | Aden Intl, 7O |
| ADL | Adelaide, SA |
| ADM | Ardmore Municipal, OK |
| ADQ | Kodiak, AK |
| ADS | Dallas-Addison, TX |
| ADZ | San Andres-Sesquicentenario, HK |
| AEH | Abecher, TT |
| AEP | Buenos Aires Aeroparque Jorge Newbery, LV |
| AER | Sochi-Adler, RA |
| AES | Aalesund-Vigra, LN |
| AET | Allakaiket, AK |
| AEX | Alexandria-Intl, LA |
| AEY | Akureyri, TF |
| AFW | Fort Worth Alliance, TX |
| AGA | Agadir-Inezgane, CN |
| AGB | Augsburg-Mühlhausen, D |
| AGC | Pittsburgh-Allegheny Co, PA |
| AGF | Agen-La Gareenne, F |
| AGP | Malaga, EC |
| AGR | Agra-Kheria, VT |
| AGV | Acarigua Oswaldo Guevara Mujica, YV |
| AID | Anderson Municipal, IN |
| AJA | Ajaccio-Campo Dell'Oro, F |
| AKC | Akron-Fulton Intl, OH |
| AKL | Auckland Intl, ZK |
| AKN | King Salmon, AK |
| AKT | Akrotiri, 5B |
| AKX | Aktobe/Aktyubinsk, UN |
| ALA | Almaty, UN |
| ALB | Albany-County, NY |
| ALC | Alicante, EC |
| ALF | Alta, LN |
| ALG | Algiers-Houari Boumediene, 7T |
| ALW | Walla Walla Regional, WA |
| ALY | Alexandria, SU |
| AMA | Amarillo Intl, TX |
| AMD | Ahmedabad, VT |
| AMM | Amman-Queen Alia Intl, JY |
| AMS | Amsterdam-Schiphol, PH |
| AMZ | Auckland-Ardmore, NZ |
| ANC | Anchorage Intl, AK |

| | |
|---|---|
| ANE | Angers-Marce, F |
| ANF | Antofagasta-Cerro Moreno Intl, CC |
| ANG | Angouleme / Brie-Champniers, F |
| ANI | Aniak, AK |
| ANK | Ankara-Etimesgut, TC |
| ANR | Antwerp-Deurne, OO |
| ANU | Saint Johns/VC Bird, V2 |
| AOC | Altenburg-Nobitz, D |
| AOG | Anshun, B |
| AOI | Ancona-Falconara, I |
| AOR | Alor Setar, 9M |
| AOT | Aosta-Corrado Gex, I |
| APA | Denver-Centennial, CO |
| APF | Naples-Municipal, FL |
| APS | Anapolis, PP |
| APV | Apple Valley, CA |
| APW | Apia-Faleolo, 5W |
| AQJ | Aqaba, JY |
| ARA | New Iberia-Acadiana, LA |
| ARG | Walnut Ridge, AR |
| ARH | Arkhangelsk-Talagi, RA |
| ARK | Arusha, 5H |
| ARN | Stockholm-Arlanda, SE |
| ASB | Ashgabat/Ashkhabad, EZ |
| ASF | Astrakhan-Narimanovo, RA |
| ASH | Nashua-Boise Field, NH |
| ASJ | Amami O Shima, JA |
| ASM | Asmara Intl, E3 |
| ASP | Alice Springs, NWT |
| ASU | Asuncion-Silvio Pettirossi, ZP |
| ASW | Aswan, SU |
| ATH | Athens-Eleftherios Venizelos Intl, SX |
| ATL | Atlanta-William B Hartsfield Intl, GA |
| ATW | Appleton-Outagamie Co, WI |
| AUA | Oranjestad-Reina Beatrix, P4 |
| AUF | Auxerre-Branches, F |
| AUH | Abu Dhabi Intl, A6 |
| AUR | Aurillac, F |
| AUS | Austin-Bergstrom Intl, TX |
| AUZ | Aurora-Municipal, IL |
| AVB | Aviano, I |
| AVN | Avignon-Caumont, F |
| AVP | Scranton-Wilkes Barre Intl, PA |
| AVV | Avalon, VIC |
| AVW | Marana-Regional, AZ |
| AWK | Wake Island, V6 |
| AWM | West Memphis-Municipal, AR |
| AWZ | Ahwaz,EP |
| AXA | Anguilla-Wallblake, VP-A |
| AYK | Arkalyk, UN |
| AYT | Antalya, TC |
| AYU | Aiyura, P2 |
| AZI | Abu Dhabi-Bateen, A6 |
| AZP | Mexico City-Atizapan, XA |
| BAH | Bahrain Intl, A9C |
| BAK | Baku-Geidar Aliev Intl, 4K |
| BAQ | Barranquilla-Ernisto Cortissoz, HK |
| BAX | Barnaul-Mikhailovka, RA |
| BBF | Burlington, MA |
| BBJ | Bitburg, D |
| BBP | Bembridge, G |
| BBU | Bucharest-Baneasa, YR |
| BBX | Blue Bell-Wing Field, PA |
| BBZ | Zambezi, 9J |
| BCN | Barcelona-le Prat, EC |

| | |
|---|---|
| BCS | Belle Chase, LA |
| BCT | Boca Raton, FL |
| BDA | Bermuda Intl Hamilton, VP-B |
| BDB | Bundaberg, Qld |
| BDG | Blanding-Municipal, UT |
| BDJ | Banjarmasin-Syamsuddin Noor, PK |
| BDL | Windsor Locks-Bradley Intl, CT |
| BDO | Bandung-Husein Sastranegara, PK |
| BDQ | Vadodora, VT |
| BDR | Bridgeport-Sikorsky Memorial, CT |
| BDS | Brindisi-Papola Casale, I |
| BDU | Bardufoss, LN |
| BEB | Benbecula, G |
| BEC | Wichita-Beech Field, KS |
| BED | Bedford-Hanscom Field, MA |
| BEG | Belgrade Intl, YU |
| BEL | Belem-Val de Caes, PP |
| BEN | Benghazi-Benina, 5A |
| BEO | Newcastle-Belmont, NSW |
| BES | Brest-Guipavas, F |
| BET | Bethel, AK |
| BEV | Beer-Sheba-Teyman, 4X |
| BEW | Beira, C9 |
| BEY | Beirut Intl, OD |
| BFE | Bielefeld, D |
| BFF | Scottsbluff-Western Nebraska Regional, NE |
| BFI | Seattle-Boeing Field, WA |
| BFM | Mobile Downtown, AL |
| BFN | Bloemfontein-JBM Hertzog, ZS |
| BFP | Beaver Falls, PA |
| BFS | Belfast-Intl, G |
| BGA | Bucaramanga, HK |
| BGF | Bangui-M'Poko, TL |
| BGI | Bridgetown-Grantley Adams Intl, VP-B |
| BGO | Bergen-Flesland, LN |
| BGR | Bangor, ME |
| BGW | Baghdad-Al Muthana, YI |
| BGY | Bergamo-Orio al Serio, I |
| BHB | Bar Harbor-Hancock Co, ME |
| BHD | Belfast-City, G |
| BHE | Blenheim, ZK |
| BHM | Birmingham ,AL |
| BHQ | Broken Hill, SA |
| BHX | Birmingham Intl, G |
| BIA | Bastia-Poretta, F |
| BIK | Biak-Frans Kaiieppo, PK |
| BIL | Billings-Logan Intl, MT |
| BIM | Bimini Intl, C6 |
| BIO | Bilbao, EC |
| BIQ | Biarritz-Parme,F |
| BIR | Biratnagar, 9N |
| BJI | Bemidji, MN |
| BJL | Banjul-Yundum Intl, C5 |
| BJM | Bujumbura Intl, 9U |
| BJS | Beijing-Metropolitan, B |
| BJY | Belgrade-Batajnica, YU |
| BKA | Moscow-Bykovo, RA |
| BKI | Kota Kinabalu Intl, 9M |
| BKK | Bangkok Suvarnabhumi, HS |
| BKO | Bamako-Senou, TZ |
| BKV | Brooksville-Pilot Co, FL |
| BKY | Bukavu-Kavumu, 9Q |
| BLA | Barcelona-Gen Anzoategui Intl, YV |
| BLD | Boulder City, NV |
| BLI | Bellingham-Intl, WA |

| | | | | | | |
|---|---|---|---|---|---|
| BLK | Blackpool, G | BZV | Brazzaville Maya-Maya, TN | CMN | Casablanca-Mohammed V, CN |
| BLL | Billund, OY | BZZ | Brize Norton, G | CMR | Colmar-Houssen, F |
| BLQ | Bologna-Guglielmo Marconi, I | CAE | Columbia Metropolitan, SC | CMU | Kundiawa-Chimbu, P2 |
| BLR | Bangalore-Hindustan, VT | CAG | Cagliari-Elmas, I | CMV | Coromandel, ZK |
| BLX | Belluno, I | CAI | Cairo Intl, SU | CND | Constanta-Kogalniceanu, YR |
| BLZ | Blantyre-Chileka, 7Q | CAK | Akron-Canton Regional, OH | CNF | Belo Horizonte-Neves Intl, PP |
| BMA | Stockholm-Bromma, SE | CAN | Guangzhou-Baiyun, B | CNI | Shanghai, B |
| BME | Broome, WA | CAP | Cap Haitien Intl, HH | CNL | Sindal, OY |
| BNA | Nashville Intl, TN | CAS | Casablanca-Anfa, CN | CNS | Cairns, Qld |
| BND | Bandar Abbas, EP | CAY | Cayenne-Rochambeau, F-O | CNW | Waco-James Connolly, TX |
| BNE | Brisbane Intl, Qld | CBB | Cochabamba-Jorge Wilsterman, CP | COA | Columbia, CA |
| BNI | Benin City, TY | | | COE | Coeur d'Alene, ID |
| BNK | Ballina, NSW | CBG | Cambridge, G | CON | Concord-Municipal, NH |
| BNS | Barinas, YV | CBL | Cuidad Bolivar, YV | COO | Cotonou-Cadjehoun, TY |
| BNX | Banja Luka, T9 | CBQ | Calabar, 5N | COR | Cordoba-Pajas Blancas, LV |
| BOD | Bordeaux-Merignac, F | CBR | Canberra, ACT | COS | Colorado Springs Memorial, CO |
| BOG | Bogota-Eldorado, HK | CCL | Chinchilla, Qld | | |
| BOH | Bournemouth Intl, G | CCP | Concepcion-Carriel Sur, CC | COU | Columbia Regional, MO |
| BOI | Boise Air Terminal (Gowen Field), ID | CCS | Caracas-Simon Bolivar Intl, YV | CPE | Campeche-Intl, XA |
| | | CCU | Calcutta-Chadra Bose Intl, VT | CPH | Copenhagen-Kastrup, OY |
| BOM | Mumbai Intl, VT | CDB | Cold Bay, AK | CPQ | Campinhas-Viracopos Intl, PP |
| BON | Kralendijk-Flamingo Int, Bonaire, PJ | CDC | Cedar City-Municipal, UT | CPR | Casper-Natrona County Intl, WY |
| | | CDG | Paris-Charles de Gaulle, F | CPT | Cape Town-DF Malan Intl, ZS |
| BOO | Bodo, LN | CDU | Camden, NSW | CRD | Comodoro Rivadavia / Gen Mosconi, LV |
| BOS | Boston-Logan Intl, MA | CDW | Caldwell-Essex Co, NJ | | |
| BPN | Balikpapan-Sepinggan, PK | CEB | Cebu-Lahug, RP | CRE | Myrtle Beach-Grand Strand, SC |
| BQH | Biggin Hill, UK | CEE | Cherepovets, RA | CRK | Diosdado Macapagal Intl, RP |
| BQK | Brunswick-Glynco Jetport, GA | CEJ | Chernigov-Shestovitsa, UR | CRL | Brussels-Charleroi, OO |
| BQN | Aguadilla-Rafael Hernandez, PR | CEK | Chelyabinsk-Balandino, RA | CRU | Carriacou Island, J3 |
| | | CEQ | Cannes-Mandelieu, F | CRZ | Chardzhev, EZ |
| BQS | Blagoveschensk-Ignatyevo, RA | CER | Cherbourg-Maupertun, F | CSE | Crested Butte, CO |
| BRE | Bremen, D | CEW | Crestview-Bob Sikes, FL | CSL | San Luis Obispo-O'Sullivan, CA |
| BRN | Bern-Belp, HB | CFE | Clermont-Ferrand, F | CSM | Clinton, OK |
| BRO | Brownsville, TX | CFN | Donegal-Carrickfin, EI | CSN | Carson City, NV |
| BRQ | Brno-Turany, OK | CFR | Caen-Carpiquet, F | CSY | Cheboksary, RA |
| BRS | Bristol-Lulsgate, G | CFS | Coffs Harbour, NSW | CTA | Catania-Fontanarossa, I |
| BRU | Brussels-National, OO | CFU | Corfu: Kerkira-Ioannis Kapodidtrias, SX | CTC | Catamarca, LV |
| BRV | Bremerhaven, D | | | CTG | Cartagena-Rafael Nunez, HK |
| BRW | Barrow-Wiley Post / Will Rogers Memorial, AK | CGH | Sao Paulo-Congonhas, PP | CTM | Chetumal, XA |
| | | CGK | Jakarta-Soekarno Hatta Intl, PK | CTN | Cooktown, Qld |
| BSB | Brasilia Intl, PP | | | CTS | Sapporo-New Chitose, JA |
| BSG | Bata, 3C | CGN | Cologne-Bonn, D | CTU | Chengdu-Shuangliu, B |
| BSL | Basle-Mulhouse EuroAirport, HB | CGO | Zhengzhou, B | CUB | Columbus-Owens Field, SC |
| | | CGP | Chittagong Intl, S2 | CUD | Caloundra, Qld |
| BSR | Basrah Intl, YI | CGQ | Changchun, B | CUE | Cuenca, EC |
| BTK | Bratsk, RA | CGR | Campo Grande Intl, PP | CUG | Cudal, NSW |
| BTR | Baton Rouge, LA | CHA | Chattanooga, TN | CUH | Cushing-Municipal, OK |
| BTS | Bratislava-MR Stefanik, OM | CHC | Christchurch Intl, ZK | CUM | Cumana-Antonio Jose de Sucre, YV |
| BTV | Burlington Intl, VT | CHD | Chandler-Williams AFB, AZ | | |
| BTZ | Bursa, TC | CHR | Chateauroux-Deols, F | CUN | Cancun Intl, XA |
| BUD | Budapest-Ferihegy, HA | CHS | Charleston Intl, SC | CUR | Curacao-Willemstadt, YV |
| BUF | Buffalo-Greater Buffalo Intl, NY | CHT | Chathams Island-Karewa, ZK | CUU | Chihuahua / Gen Villalobos Intl, XA |
| BUG | Benguela, D2 | CIA | Rome-Ciampino, I | | |
| BUQ | Bulawayo, Z | CIC | Chico, CA | CUZ | Cuzco-Velaazco Astete, OB |
| BUR | Burbank-Glendale Pasadena, CA | CIH | Changzhi, B | CVF | Courchevel, F |
| | | CIX | Chiclayo-Cornel Ruiz, OB | CVG | Cincinnati-Covington Intl, OH |
| BUS | Batumi-Chorokh, 4L | CJB | Coimbatore-Peelamedu, VT | | |
| BVA | Beauvais-Tille, F | CJJ | Cheongju City, HL | CVJ | Cuernavaca, XA |
| BVB | Boa Vista Intl, PP | CJN | El Cajun, CA | CVN | Clovis-Municipal, NM |
| BVO | Bartlesville, OK | CJU | Cheju Intl, HL | CVQ | Carnarvon, G |
| BVX | Batesville-Municipal, AR | CKC | Cherkassy, UR | CVR | Culver City, CA |
| BWB | Barrow Island, WA | CKG | Chongqing, B | CVT | Coventry-Baginton, G |
| BWE | Braunschweig, D | CKY | Conakry-Gbessia, 3X | CWA | Mosinee Central, WI |
| BWI | Baltimore-Washington Intl, MD | CLD | Carlsbad, CA | CWB | Curitiba-Alfonso Pena, PP |
| BWN | Bandar Seri Begawan / Brunei Intl, V8 | CLE | Cleveland-Hopkins Intl, OH | CWC | Chernovtsy, UR |
| | | CLO | Cali-Alfonso Bonilla Aragon, HK | CWF | Chenault Airpark, AK |
| BWO | Balakovo, RA | CLQ | Colima, XA | CWL | Cardiff-Wales, G |
| BWS | Blaine, WA | CLT | Charlotte-Douglas Intl, NC | CXH | Vancouver-Coal Harbour, BC |
| BWU | Sydney-Bankstown, NSW | CLU | Columbus-Municipal, IN | CYM | Chatham SPB, AK |
| BXJ | Burundai, UN | CMB | Colombo-Bandaranaike Intl, 4R | CYS | Cheyenne, WY |
| BYG | Buffalo-Municipal, WY | | | CZM | Cozumel Intl, XA |
| BZE | Belize City-Philip SW Goldson Intl, V3 | CMD | Cootamundra, NSW | CZS | Cruzeiro do Sul-Campo Intl, PP |
| | | CME | Cuidad del Carmen, XA | | |
| BZG | Bydgoszcz, SP | CMF | Chambery/Aix les Bains, F | CZX | Changzhou, B |
| BZK | Bryansk, RA | CMH | Columbus-Port Intl, OH | | |

| | | |
|---|---|---|
| GOA | Genoa-Cristoforo Colombo, I | |
| GOH | Godthaab-Nuuk, OY | |
| GOI | Goa-Dabolim, VT | |
| GOJ | Nizhny Novogorod-Streigino, RA | |
| GOM | Goma, 9Q | |
| GON | Groton-New London, CT | |
| GOT | Gothenburg-Landvetter, SE | |
| GOV | Gove-Nhulunbuy, NWT | |
| GPT | Gulfport-Biloxi Regional, MS | |
| GRO | Gerona-Costa Brava, EC | |
| GRQ | Groningen-Eelde, OY | |
| GRR | Grand Rapids-Kent County, MI | |
| GRU | Sao Paulo-Guarulhos, PP | |
| GRV | Grozny, RA | |
| GRZ | Graz-Thalerhof, OE | |
| GSE | Gothenburg-Save, SE | |
| GSO | Greensboro-Piedmont Triad Intl, SC | |
| GTR | Columbus-Golden Triangle Regional, GA | |
| GUA | Guatemala City-La Aurora, TG | |
| GUB | Guerrero Negro, XA | |
| GUM | Guam-Ab Won Pat Intl, N | |
| GUP | Gallup-Sen Clark Municipal, NM | |
| GUW | Akyrau, UN | |
| GVA | Geneva-Cointrin, HB | |
| GVL | Gainsville, GA | |
| GVQ | Coyhaique-Teniente Vidal, CC | |
| GVT | Greenville-Majors Field, TX | |
| GWO | Greenwood-le Floor, MS | |
| GWT | Westerland-Sylt, D | |
| GWY | Galway-Carnmore, EI | |
| GXQ | Coyhaique-Teniente Vidal, CC | |
| GYE | Guayaquil-Simon Bolivar, HK | |
| GYN | Goiania-Santa Genoveva, PP | |
| GYR | Goodyear-Litchfield, AZ | |
| GZA | Gaza-Yasser Arafat Intl, SU-Y | |
| GZM | Gozo, 9H | |
| | | |
| HAH | Moroni-Prince Said Ibrahim, D6 | |
| HAJ | Hannover, D | |
| HAK | Haikou-Dayingshan, B | |
| HAM | Hamburg-Fuhlsbüttel; D | |
| HAN | Hanoi-Gialam, VN | |
| HAO | Hamilton, OH | |
| HAU | Haugesund, LN | |
| HAV | Havana-Jose Marti Intl, CU | |
| HBA | Hobart, TAS | |
| HDD | Hyderabad, VT | |
| HEL | Helsinki-Vantaa, OH | |
| HEM | Helsinki-Malmi, OH | |
| HER | Heraklion, SX | |
| HEX | Santo Domingo-la Herrara, HI | |
| HFA | Haifa U Michaeli, 4X | |
| HGH | Hangzhou-Jianqio, B | |
| HGL | Helgoland-Dune, D | |
| HGR | Hagerstown, MD | |
| HGU | Mount Hagen-Kagamuga, P2 | |
| HHN | Hahn, D | |
| HHR | Hawthorne, CA | |
| HID | Horn Island, Qld | |
| HIG | Highbury, Qld | |
| HII | Lake Havasu City-Honolulu-Oahu Island, HI | |
| HIK | Honolulu-Oahu Island, HI | |
| HIR | Honiara-Henderson, H4 | |
| HKD | Hakodate, JA | |
| HKG | Hong Kong Intl, B-H | |
| HKT | Phuket Intl, HS | |
| HLA | Lanseria, ZS | |
| HLF | Hultsfred, SE | |
| HLP | Jakarta-Halim Perdanakusuma, PK | |

| | | |
|---|---|---|
| HLT | Hamilton, VIC | |
| HLZ | Hamilton, ZK | |
| HME | Hassi Messaoud, 7T | |
| HMJ | Khmelnitsky-Ruzichnaya, UR | |
| HMO | Hermosillo-Gen Garcia Intl, XA | |
| HMT | Hemet-Ryan Field, CA | |
| HND | Tokyo-Haneda Intl, JA | |
| HNL | Honolulu Intl, HI | |
| HNS | Haines Municipal, AK | |
| HOH | Hohenems-Dornbirn, OE | |
| HOM | Homer, AK | |
| HOT | East Hampton, NY | |
| HOU | Houston-Hobby, TX | |
| HRB | Harbin-Yanjiagang, B | |
| HRE | Harare Intl, Z | |
| HRG | Hurghada, SU | |
| HRK | Kharkiv-Osnova, UR | |
| HSH | Las Vegas-Henderson, NV | |
| HSM | Horsham, VIC | |
| HST | Homestead, FL | |
| HTA | Chita-Kadala, RA | |
| HTI | Hamilton Island, Qld | |
| HTO | East Hampton, NY | |
| HUF | Terre Haute-Hulman Regional, IN | |
| HUM | Houma-Terrebonne, LA | |
| HUV | Hudiksvall, SE | |
| HUY | Humberside, G | |
| HVB | Hervey Bay, Qld | |
| HVN | New Haven-Tweed, CT | |
| HWO | Hollywood-North Perry, FL | |
| HYA | Hyannis-Barnstable Municipal, MA | |
| HZB | Mervilel-Calonnel, F | |
| | | |
| IAB | Wichita-McConnell AFB, KS | |
| IAD | Washington-Dulles Intl, DC | |
| IAG | Niagara Falls-Intl, NY | |
| IAH | Houston-George Bush Intl, TX | |
| IBA | Ibadan, 5N | |
| IBE | Ibague-Perales, HK | |
| IBZ | Ibiza, EC | |
| ICN | Seoul-Incheon, HL | |
| ICT | Wichita-Mid Continent, KS | |
| IEV | Kiev-Zhulyany, UR | |
| IFJ | Isafjordur, TF | |
| IFN | Isfahan, EP | |
| IFO | Ivano-Frankivsk, UR | |
| IFP | Laughlin-Bullhead Intl, AZ | |
| IGM | Kingman, AZ | |
| IJK | Izhevsk, RA | |
| IKI | Iki, JA | |
| IKT | Irkutsk, RA | |
| ILG | Wilmington-Newcastle, DE | |
| ILI | Iliamna, AK | |
| ILN | Wilmington-Airborne Airpark, OH | |
| ILR | Ilorin, 5N | |
| IMT | Iron Mountain-Ford, MI | |
| IND | Indianapolis Intl, IN | |
| INI | Nis, YU | |
| INN | Innsbruck-Kranebitten, OE | |
| INT | Winston-Salem-Smith Reynolds, NC Municipal | |
| INU | Nauru Island Intl, C2 | |
| INV | Inverness-Dalcross, G | |
| IOM | Ronaldsway, M | |
| IQQ | Iquique-Diego Aracena, CC | |
| IQT | Iquitos-Coronel Vignetta, OB | |
| IRK | Kirksville-Regional, MO | |
| ISA | Mount Isa, Qld | |
| ISB | Islamabad-Chaklala, AP | |
| ISM | Kissimmee Municipal, FL | |

| | | |
|---|---|---|
| ISO | Kinston-Stalling Field, NC | |
| IST | Istanbul-Ataturk, TC | |
| ITB | Itaituba, PP | |
| ITM | Osaka-Itami Intl, JA | |
| ITO | Hilo Intl, HI | |
| IVC | Invercargill, ZK | |
| IWA | Ivanovo-Zhukovka, RA | |
| | | |
| JAA | Jalalabad, YA | |
| JAB | Jabiru, NT | |
| JAN | Jackson Intl, MS | |
| JAV | Ilulissat-Jakobshavn, OY | |
| JAX | Jacksonville Intl, FL | |
| JDP | Paris-Heliport, F | |
| JED | Jeddah-King Abdul Aziz Intl, HZ | |
| JER | Jersey, G | |
| JFK | New York-JFK Intl, NY | |
| JGC | Grand Canyon Heliport, AZ | |
| JHB | Johor Bahru-Sultan Ismail Intl, 9M | |
| JHE | Helsingborg Heliport, SE | |
| JHW | Jamestown-Chautauqua Co, NY | |
| JIB | Djibouti-Ambouli, J2 | |
| JIL | Jilin, B | |
| JJN | Jinjiang, B | |
| JKG | Jonkoping-Axamo, SE | |
| JNB | Johannesburg-OR Tambo Intl, ZS | |
| JNU | Juneau Intl, AK | |
| JST | Johnstown-Cambria County, PA | |
| JUB | Juba, ST | |
| JVL | Janesville-Rock County, WI | |
| | | |
| KAD | Kaduna, 5N | |
| KAN | Kano Mallam Aminu Intl, 5N | |
| KBL | Kabul-Khwaja Rawash, YA | |
| KBP | Kiev-Borispol, UR | |
| KCH | Koching, 9M | |
| KDH | Kandahar, YA | |
| KDK | Kodiak Municipal, AK | |
| KEF | Keflavik Intl, TF | |
| KEH | Kenmore Air Harbor, WA | |
| KEJ | Kemorovo, RA | |
| KEP | Nepalgunj, 9N | |
| KER | Kerman, EP | |
| KGC | Kingscote, SA | |
| KGD | Kaliningrad-Khrabovo, RA | |
| KGF | Qaragandy-Sary Arka, UN | |
| KGI | Kalgoorlie, WA | |
| KGL | Kigali-Gregoire Kayibanda, 9XR | |
| KGO | Kirovograd-Khmelyovoye, UR | |
| KGP | Kogalym, RA | |
| KHH | Kaoshiung Intl, B | |
| KHI | Karachi Jinnah Intl, AP | |
| KHV | Khabarovsk-Novy, ra | |
| KIH | Kish Island, EP | |
| KIN | Kingston-Norman Manley Internatonal, 6Y | |
| KIV | Kishinev-Chisinau, ER | |
| KIW | Kitwe-Southdowns, 9J | |
| KIX | Osaka-Kansai Intl, JA | |
| KJA | Krasnoyarsk-Yemelyanovo, RA | |
| KJK | Kortrijk-Wevelgem, OO | |
| KKZ | Kitakyushu-Kokura, JA | |
| KLF | Kaluga, RA | |
| KLU | Klagenfurt, OE | |
| KMG | Kunming-Wujiaba, B | |
| KMI | Miyazaki, JA | |
| KMJ | Kumamoto, JA | |
| KMW | Kostroma, RA | |
| KNX | Kununurra, WA | |
| KOA | Kailua Kona, HI | |
| KOV | Kokhshetan, UN | |

| | |
|---|---|
| KOW | Ganzhou, B |
| KRB | Karumba, Qld |
| KRH | Redhill, G |
| KRK | Krakow Intl, SP |
| KRN | Kiruna, SE |
| KRO | Kurgan, RA |
| KRP | Karup, OY |
| KRR | Krasnodar-Pashkovskaya, RA |
| KRS | Kristiansand-Kjevik, LN |
| KRT | Khartoum-Civil, ST |
| KSC | Kosice-Barca, OM |
| KSD | Karlstad, SE |
| KSF | Kassel-Calden, D |
| KSK | Karlskoga, SE |
| KSM | St Mary's Bethel, AK |
| KSN | Kustanay, UN |
| KSZ | Kotlas, RA |
| KTA | Karratha, WA |
| KTE | Kerteh-Petronas, 9M |
| KTM | Kathmandu-Tribhuvan Intl, 9N |
| KTN | Ketchikan Intl, AK |
| KTP | Kingston-Tinson Peninsula, 6Y |
| KTR | Katherine-Tindal, NWT |
| KTW | Katowice-Pyrzowice, SP |
| KUF | Samara-Kurumoch, RA |
| KUL | Kuala Lumpur Intl, 9M |
| KUN | Kaunus-Karlelava Intl, LY |
| KUT | Kutaisi, 4L |
| KVB | Skovde, SE |
| KVX | Kirov, RA |
| KWE | Guiyang, B |
| KWI | Kuwait Intl, 9K |
| KXK | Komsomolsk, RA |
| KYZ | Kyzyi, RA |
| KZN | Kazan-Bonsoglebskow, RA |
| KZO | Kzyl-Orda, UN |
| | |
| LAD | Luanda-4 de Fevereiro, D2 |
| LAE | Lae-Nadzab, P2 |
| LAF | Lafayette-Purdue University, IN |
| LAJ | Lages, PP |
| LAL | Lakeland Regional, FL |
| LAO | Laoag Intl, RP |
| LAP | La Paz Gen Leon Intl, XA |
| LAS | Las Vegas-McCarran Intl, NV |
| LAW | Lawton, OK |
| LAX | Los Angeles Intl, CA |
| LBA | Leeds-Bradford, G |
| LBB | Lubbock, TX |
| LBD | Khudzhand, EY |
| LBE | Latrobe-Westmoreland Co, PA |
| LBG | Paris-le Bourget, F |
| LBH | Sydney-Palm Beach SPB, NSW |
| LBV | Libreville-Leon M'Ba, TR |
| LCA | Larnaca Intl, 5B |
| LCE | La Ceibe-Goloson Intl, TG |
| LCH | Lake Charles-Regional, LA |
| LCK | Columbus-Rickenbacker, OH |
| LCY | London-City, G |
| LDB | Londrina, PP |
| LDE | Tarbes-Ossun-Lourdes, F |
| LDH | Lord Howe Island, NSW |
| LDK | Lidkoping-Hovby, SE |
| LED | St Petersburg-Pulkovo, RA |
| LEH | le Havre-Octeville, F |
| LEJ | Leipzig-Halle, D |
| LEN | Leon, EC |
| LEQ | Lands End-St Just, G |
| LEW | Lewiston-Auburn Municipal, ME |
| LEY | Lelystad, PH |
| LFT | Lafayette-Regional, AL |

| | |
|---|---|
| LFW | Lome-Tokoin, 5V |
| LGA | New York-La Guardia, NY |
| LGB | Long Beach-Daugherty Field, CA |
| LGG | Liege-Bierset, OO |
| LGW | London Gatwick, G |
| LGY | Lagunillas, YV |
| LHD | Anchorage-Lake Hood SPB, AK |
| LHE | Lahore Allama Iqbal Intl, AP |
| LHR | London-Heathrow, G |
| LHW | Lanzhou, B |
| LIG | Limoges-Bellegarde, F |
| LIL | Lille-Lesquin, F |
| LIM | Lima-Jorge Chavez Intl, OB |
| LIN | Milan-Linate, I |
| LIS | Lisbon, CS |
| LIT | Little Rock-Adams Field, AR |
| LJU | Ljubljana-Brnik, S5 |
| LKE | Seattle-Lake Union, WA |
| LKO | Lucknow-Amausi, VT |
| LKP | Lake Placid, NY |
| LLA | Lulea-Kallax, SE |
| LLC | Valdez, AK |
| LLW | Lilongwe-Tilange Intl, 7Q |
| LME | Le Mans-Arnage, F |
| LMM | Los Mochis, XA |
| LNA | West Palm Beach-Lantana Co Park, FL |
| LNX | Smolensk, RA |
| LNZ | Linz-Hoersching, OE |
| LOS | Lagos-Murtala Mohammed, 5N |
| LPA | Las Palmas-Gran Canaria, EC |
| LPB | La Paz-El Alto, CP |
| LPI | Linkoping-Malmen, SE |
| LPK | Lipetsk, RA |
| LPL | Liverpool-John Lennon Intl, G |
| LPP | Lappeenranta, OH |
| LPY | Le Puy-Loudes, F |
| LRD | Laredo Intl, TX |
| LRE | Longreach, Qld |
| LRH | La Rochelle-Laleu, F |
| LRR | Lar, EP |
| LSI | Sumburgh, G |
| LST | Launceston, TAS |
| LTN | London-Luton, G |
| LTX | Latacunga, HC |
| LUG | Lugano, I |
| LUK | Cincinatti Municipal, OH |
| LUN | Lusaka Intl, 9J |
| LUX | Luxembourg, LX |
| LWB | Lewisburg-Greenbrier Valley, WV |
| LWO | Lviv-Snilow, UR |
| LWR | Leeuwarden, PH |
| LXA | Lhasa, B |
| LXR | Luxor, SU |
| LXT | Latacunga, HC |
| LYN | Lyon-Bron, F |
| LYP | Faisalabad, AP |
| LYS | Lyon-Satolas, F |
| LYT | Lady Elliott Island, Qld |
| LYX | Lydd Intl, G |
| | |
| MAA | Chennai, VT |
| MAC | Macon-Smart, GA |
| MAD | Madrid-Barajas, EC |
| MAG | Madang, P2 |
| MAH | Menorca-Mahon, EC |
| MAJ | Majuro-Amata Kabua Intl, V7 |
| MAN | Manchester Intl, G |
| MAO | Manaus-Eduardo Gomes, PP |

| | |
|---|---|
| MAR | Maracaibo-La Chinita Internatonal, YV |
| MAW | Malden, MO |
| MBA | Mombasa-Moi Intl, 5Y |
| MBD | Mmbatho Intl, ZS |
| MBH | Maryborough, Qld |
| MBJ | Montego Bay-Sangster Internatonal, 6Y |
| MBW | Melbourne-Moorabin, VIC |
| MBX | Maribor, S5 |
| MCI | Kansas City Intl, MO |
| MCM | Monte Carlo Heliport, 3A |
| MCO | Orlando Intl, FL |
| MCP | Macapa-Intl, PP |
| MCT | Muscat-Seeb Intl, A4O |
| MCW | Mason City-Municipal, IA |
| MCX | Makhachkala-Uytash, RA |
| MCY | Sunshine Coast, Qld |
| MDE | Medellin-Olaya Herrera, HK |
| MDL | Mandalay, XY |
| MDT | Harrisburg Intl, PA |
| MDU | Mendi, P2 |
| MDW | Chicago-Midway, IL |
| MEA | Macae & Sao Tome, PP |
| MEB | Melbourne-Essendon, VIC |
| MEL | Melbourne-Tullamarine, VIC |
| MEM | Memphis Intl, TN |
| MER | Merced-Castle AFB, CA |
| MES | Medan-Polonia, PK |
| MEV | Minden-Douglas Co, NV |
| MEX | Mexico City-Juarez Intl, XA |
| MFE | McAllen-Miller, TX |
| MFM | Macau Intl, B-M |
| MFN | Milford Sound, ZK |
| MGA | Managua-Sandino, YN |
| MGB | Mount Gambier, VIC |
| MGL | Mönchengladbach, D |
| MGQ | Mogadishu Intl, 6O |
| MHB | Auckland-Mechanics Bay, ZK |
| MHD | Mashad-Shahid Hashemi Nejad Intl, EP |
| MHG | Mannheim-Neu Ostheim, D |
| MHH | Marsh Harnour, C6 |
| MHP | Minsk 1 Intl, EW |
| MHQ | Mariehamn, OH |
| MHR | Sacramento-Mather, CA |
| MHV | Mojave-Kern Co, CA |
| MIA | Miami Intl, FL |
| MID | Merida, XA |
| MIE | Newcastle, IN |
| MIR | Monastir-Habib Bourguiba Intl, TS |
| MIU | Maiduguri, 5N |
| MJI | Mitiga, 5A |
| MJM | Mbuji Mayi, 9Q |
| MJZ | Mirny, RA |
| MKC | Kansas City Downtown, MO |
| MKE | Milwaukee-Mitchell Field, WI |
| MKY | MacKay, Qld |
| MLA | Malta-Luqa, 9H |
| MLB | Melbourne-Cape Kennedy, FL |
| MLC | McAlester-Regional, OK |
| MLE | Male Intl, 8Q |
| MLH | Basle-Mulhouse EuroAirport, F |
| MLU | Monroe-Regional, LA |
| MLW | Monrovia-Spriggs Payne. A8 |
| MMK | Murmansk, RA |
| MML | Marshall-Ryan Field, MN |
| MMX | Malmo-Sturup, SE |
| MNI | Plymouth-WH Bramble (VP-M) |
| MNL | Manila-Nino Aquino Intl, RP |
| MNZ | Manassas, VA |
| MOB | Mobile-Regional, AL |
| MOL | Molde, LN |

| | |
|---|---|
| MON | Mount Cook, ZK |
| MOR | Morristown, TN |
| MPB | Miami-Watson Island SPB, FL |
| MPL | Montpellier-Mediterranean, F |
| MPM | Maputo, C9 |
| MPR | McPherson, KS |
| MPW | Marlupol, UR |
| MQF | Magnitogorsk, RA |
| MQL | Mildura, VIC |
| MQS | Mustique Intl, J8 |
| MQT | Marquette-Sawyer, MI |
| MQY | Smyrna, TN |
| MRI | Anchorage-Merrill Field, AK |
| MRO | Masterton, ZK |
| MRS | Marseille-Marignane, F |
| MRU | Plaisance Intl, 3B |
| MRV | Mineralnye Vody, RA |
| MRX | Morristown Nexrad, TN |
| MSC | Mesa-Falcon Field, AZ |
| MSE | Manston-Kent Intl, G |
| MSO | Missoula Johnson-Bell Field, MT |
| MSP | Minneapolis-St Paul Intl, MN |
| MSQ | Minsk 2 Intl, , EW |
| MST | Maastricht-Aachen, PH |
| MSU | Maseru-Moshoeshoe, 7P |
| MSY | New Orleans Intl, LA |
| MTM | Metlakatla, AK |
| MTN | Baltimore-Glenn L Martin, MD |
| MTS | Manzini-Matsapha, 3D |
| MTY | Monterey-Gen Escobedo Intl, XA |
| MUB | Maun, A2 |
| MUC | Munich-Franz Joseph Straus, D |
| MUN | Maturin, YV |
| MVA | Myvatn-Rykiahlid, TF |
| MVD | Montevideo-Carrasco Intl, CX |
| MVQ | Mogilev, EW |
| MVY | Martha's Vineyard, MA |
| MWO | Middletown-Hook Field Memorial, OH |
| MWZ | Mwanza, 5H |
| MXE | Maxton, NC |
| MXN | Morlaix-Ploujean, F |
| MXP | Milan-Malpensa, I |
| MXX | Mora-Siljan, SE |
| MYD | Malindi, 5Y |
| MYL | McCall, ID |
| MYR | Myrtle Beach, SC |
| MYV | Marysville-Yuba Co, CA |
| MYY | Miri, 9M |
| MZJ | Marana-Pinal Airpark, AZ |
| | |
| NAG | Nagpur-Sonegaon, VT |
| NAL | Nalchik, RA |
| NAN | Nadi Intl, DQ |
| NAP | Naples-Capodichino, I |
| NAS | Nassau Intl, C6 |
| NAY | Beijing-Nan Yuan, B |
| NBO | Nairobi-Jomo Kenyatta Intl, 5Y |
| NCE | Nice-Cote d'Azur, F |
| NCL | Newcastle, G |
| NDJ | N'djamena, TT |
| NEV | Nevis-Newcastle, V4 |
| NEW | New Orleans-Lakefront, LA |
| NFG | Nefteyugansk, RA |
| NGO | Nagoya-Chubu, JA |
| NGS | Nagasaki, JA |
| NHT | RAF Northolt, G |
| NIC | Nicosia, 5B |
| NIM | Niamey-Diori Hamani, 5U |
| NKC | Nouakchott, 5T |
| NKG | Nanjing, B |
| NKM | Nagoya-Komaki AFB, JA |
| NLK | Norfolk Island, NSW |

| | |
|---|---|
| NLO | Kinshasa-N'dolo, 9Q |
| NLP | Nelspruit, ZS |
| NNK | Naknek, AK |
| NNR | Connemara, EI |
| NOA | Nowra, NSW |
| NOE | Norden-Norddeich, D |
| NOU | Noumea-La Tontouta, F-O |
| NOZ | Novokuznetsk, RA |
| NPE | Napier, ZK |
| NQA | Millington, TN |
| NQN | Neuquen, LV |
| NQY | Newquay-St Mawgan, G |
| NRK | Norrkoping, SE |
| NRT | Tokyo-Narita Intl, JA |
| NSI | Yaounde, TJ |
| NSK | Norilsk, RA |
| NSN | Nelson, ZK |
| NSO | Scone, NSW |
| NTB | Notodden, LN |
| NTE | Nantes-Atlantique, F |
| NTL | Newcastle-Williamstown, NSW |
| NTY | Sun City-Pilansberg, ZS |
| NUE | Nurenburg, D |
| NVA | Neiva-La Marquita, HK |
| NVR | Novgorod, RA |
| NWI | Norwich, G |
| NYM | Nadym, RA |
| NYO | Nykoping-Skavsta, SE |
| NZC | Jackonsville Cecil Field, FL |
| | |
| OAG | Orange, NSW |
| OAJ | Jacksonville, NC |
| OAK | Oakland Intl, CA |
| OAX | Oaxaca-Xoxocotlan, XA |
| OBF | Oberpfaffenhofen, D |
| OBN | Oban, G |
| OBO | Obihiro, JA |
| OCF | Ocala-Taylor Field, FL |
| ODB | Cordoba-Palma del Rio, EC |
| ODE | Odense-Beldringe, OY |
| ODS | Odessa-Tsentralny, UR |
| ODW | Oak Harbor, WA |
| OEL | Orel, RA |
| OGG | Kahului-Intl, HI |
| OGL | Georgetown-Ogle, 8R |
| OGZ | Vladivkavkaz-Beslan, RA |
| OKA | Okinawa-Naha, JA |
| OKC | Oklahoma City-Will Roger, OK |
| OKD | Sapporo-Okadama, JA |
| OLB | Olbia-Costa Smeralda, I |
| OLM | Olympia, WA |
| OMA | Omaha-Eppley Field, NE |
| OME | Nome, AK |
| OMS | Omsk-Severny, RA |
| ONT | Ontario Intl, CA |
| OOL | Coolangatta, Qld |
| OPF | Opa Locka, FL |
| OPO | Porto, CS |
| ORB | Orebro-Bofors, SE |
| ORD | Chicago-O'Hare Intl, IL |
| ORG | Paramaribo-Zorg en Hoop, PZ |
| ORK | Cork, EI |
| ORL | Orlando-Executive, FL |
| ORY | Paris-Orly, F |
| OSC | Oscoda-Wurtsmith AFB, MI |
| OSH | Oshkosh-Wittman Field, WI |
| OSL | Oslo Intl, LN |
| OSR | Ostrava-Mosnov, OK |
| OSS | Osh, EX |
| OST | Ostend, OO |
| OTP | Bucharest-Otopeni Intl, YR |
| OTS | Anacortes, WA |
| OTZ | Kotzebue-Wien Memorial, AK |
| OUA | Ouagadougou, XT |
| OUL | Oulu, OH |
| OVB | Novosibirsk-Tolmachevo, RA |

| | |
|---|---|
| OVD | Castrillón-Asturias (EC) |
| OWD | Norwood Memorial, MA |
| OXB | Bissau Vierira Intl, J5 |
| OXC | Oxford-Waterbury, CT |
| OXR | Oxnard, CA |
| OYS | Mariposa-Yosemite, CA |
| OZH | Zaporozhye-Mokraya, UR |
| | |
| PAC | Albrook-Marcos A Gelabert Panama City, HP |
| PAD | Paderborn-Lippstadt, D |
| PAE | Everett-Paine Field, WA |
| PAP | Port-au-Prince Intl, HH |
| PAQ | Palmer Municipal, AK |
| PAZ | Poza Rica, XA |
| PBG | Plattsburgh, NY |
| PBH | Paro, A5 |
| PBI | Palm Beach Intl, FL |
| PBM | Paramaribo-Pengel Interntional, PZ |
| PCB | Pondok Cabe, PK |
| PCL | Pucalipa-Rolden, OB |
| PCM | Playa del Carmen, XA |
| PDC | La Verne-Bracketts Field, CA |
| PDK | Atlanta-Peachtree, GA |
| PDL | Ponta Delgada, CS |
| PDV | Plovdiv, LZ |
| PDX | Portland Intl, OR |
| PEE | Perm-Bolshoe-Savino, RA |
| PEK | Beijing-Capital, B |
| PEN | Penang-Intl, 9M |
| PER | Perth Intl, WA |
| PEZ | Penza, RA |
| PFO | Paphos Intl, 5B |
| PGA | Page, AZ |
| PGD | Punta Gorda-Charlotte Co, FL |
| PGF | Perpignan-Rivesaltes, F |
| PGX | Periguex-Brassillac, F |
| PHC | Port Harcourt, 5N |
| PHE | Port Hedland, WA |
| PHF | Newport News, VA |
| PHL | Philadelphia Intl, PA |
| PHS | Phitsanulok-Sarit Sena, HS |
| PHX | Phoenix-Sky Harbor Intl, AZ |
| PHY | Phetchabun, HS |
| PIE | St Petersburg-Clearwater Intl, FL |
| PIK | Prestwick, G |
| PIR | Pierre-Regional, SD |
| PIT | Pittsburgh Intl, PA |
| PKC | Petropavlovsk Kamchatsky-Yelizovo, RA |
| PKR | Pokhara, 9N |
| PKU | Pekanbaru-Simpang Tiga, PK |
| PKV | Pskov, RA |
| PLB | Plattsburg-Clinton Co, NY |
| PLH | Plymouth, G |
| PLL | Manaus-Ponta Pelada, PP |
| PLS | Providenciales Intl, VQ-T |
| PLU | Belo Horizonte-Pampulha, PP |
| PLV | Poltava, UR |
| PLX | Semipalatisnk, UN |
| PMB | Pembina, ND |
| PMC | Puerto Montt, CC |
| PMD | Palmdale, CA |
| PMF | Parma, I |
| PMI | Palma de Mallorca, EC |
| PMO | Palermo-Punta Raisi, I |
| PMR | Palmerston-North, ZK |
| PNA | Pamplona, EC |
| PNE | Philadelphia-Northern, PA |
| PNH | Phnom Penh-Pochentong, XU |
| PNI | Pohnpei-Caroline Islands, V6 |
| PNK | Pontianak-Supadio, PK |
| PNR | Pointe Noire, TN |
| PNS | Pensacola-Regional, FL |

PNX Sherman-Denison, TX
POA Porto Alegre-Canoas, PP
POC La Verne-Brackett Field, CA
POG Port Gentil, TR
POM Port Moresby, P2
POP Puerto Plata Intl, HI
POS Port of Spain-Piarco, 9Y
POW Portoroz, S5
POX Pontoise-Cormeilles, F
PPB Presidente Prudente, PP
PPG Pago Pago Intl, N
PPK Petropavlovsk, UN
PPQ Paraparaumu, ZK
PPT Papeete-Faaa, , F-O
PQQ Port Macquarie, NSW
PRA Parana, LV
PRC Prescott-
Ernest A Love Field, AZ
PRG Prague-Ruzyne, OK
PRN Pristina, YU
PRV Prerov, OK
PRY Pretoria-Wonderboom, ZS
PSA Pisa-Galileo, I
PSM Portsmouth-Pease Intl, NH
PSR Pescara, I
PSY Port Stanley, VP-F
PTA Port Alsworth, AK
PTG Pietersburg-Gateway, ZS
PTI Port Douglas, Qld
PTK Pontiac-Oakland, MI
PTN Ptterson-HPW Memorial, LA
PTP Pointe a Pitre-Le Raizet, F-O
PTY Panama City-Tocumen Intl, HP
PUF Pau-Pyrenees, F
PUG Port Agusta, SA
PUQ Punta Arenas, CC
PUU Puerto Asi, HK
PUY Pula, 9A
PVG Shanghai-Pu Dong Intl, B
PVH Porto Velho, PP
PVR Puerto Vallarta-Lic Gustavo
Dias Ordaz Intl, XA
PVU Provo-Municipal. UT
PWK Chicago-Pal Waukee, IL
PWM Portland Intl Jetport, ME
PWQ Pavlodar, UN
PYL Perry Island SPB, AK
PZE Penzance, G

QKC Karaj-Payam, EP
QLA Lasham, G
QPG Paya Lebar, 9V
QPI Palmira, CP
QRA Johannesburg-Rand, ZS
QRC Rancagua-
de la Independence, CC
QSC San Carlos, PP
QSM Utersen, D
QTK Rothenburg, D

RAB Rabaul, P2
RAI Praia-Mendes, D4
RAK Marrakesh-Menara, CN
RAO Ribeirao Preto, PP
RAR Rarotonga, E5
RAS Rasht, EP
RBA Rabat-Sale, CN
RBR Rio Branco-Medici, PP
RBY Ruby-Municipal, AK
RCM Richmond, Qld
RDD Redding-Municipal, CA
RDG Reading-Gen Spaatz Field, PA
RDM Redmond-Roberts Field, OR
RDU Raleigh-Durham Intl, NC
REC Recife-Guararapes, PP
REK Reykjavik, TF

REN Orenburg-Tsentralny, RA
REP Siem Reap, XU
REX Reynosa-Gen Lucio Blanco
Intl, XA
RFD Rockford, IL
RGN Yangon Intl, XY
RHE Reims Champagne, F
RHI Rhinelander-Oneida Co, WI
RHO Rhodes-Diagoras, SX
RIC Richmond-Byrd Intl, VA
RIX Riga-Skulte Intl, YL
RJK Rijeka, 9A
RKD Rockland-Knox County, ME
RKE Roskilde, OY
RKT Ras al Khaimah Intl, A6
RLG Rostock-Laage, D
RMA Roma, Qld
RMI Rimini, I
RML Colombo-Ratmalana, 4R
RNC McMinnville-Warren Co, OR
RNO Reno-Cannon Intl, NV
RNS Rennes-St Jacques, F
RNT Seattle-Renton, WA
ROB Monrovia Roberts Intl, A8
ROK Rockhampton, IL
ROM Rome Urbe, I
ROR Koror-Airai, T8A
ROS Rosario-Fisherton, LV
ROT Rotorua, ZK
ROV Rostov-on-Don, RA
ROW Roswell-
Industrial Air Center, NM
RPM Ngukurr, NT
RSE Sydney-Au Rose, Qld
RTM Rotterdam, PH
RTW Saratov-Tsentrainy, RA
RUH Riyadh-
King Khalid Intl, HZ
RUN St Denis-Gilot, F-O
RVH St Petersburg-Rzhevka, RA
RWN Rivnu, UR
RYB Rybinsk-Staroselye, RA
RZN Ryazan, RA

SAH Sana'a Intl, 7O
SAL San Salvador-
Comalapa Intl, YS
SAN San Diego-Lindbergh Intl, CA
SAT San Antonio Intl, TX
SAW Instanbul-Sabiha Gokcen
Intl, TC
SBA Santa Barbara Municipal, CA
SBD San Bernadino-Norton AFB, CA
SBH St Barthelemy, F-O
SBP San Luis Obispo, CA
SBY Salisbury-Wicomico, MD
SCC Prudhoe Bay, AK
SCH Schenectady County, NY
SCI San Cristobal-Paramilio, YV
SCK Stockton Metropolitan, CA
SCL Santiago-Merino Benitez
Intl, CC
SCN Saarbrucken-Ensheim, D
SCU Santiago de Cuba, CU
SCW Syktyvkov, RA
SDA Damascus- Intl, YK
SDF Louisville-Standiford Field, KY
SDJ Sendai, JA
SDQ Santo Domingo Intl, HI
SDU Rio de Janeiro-
Santos Dumont, PP
SDV Tel Aviv-Sde Dov, 4X
SEA Seattle-Tacoma Intl, WA
SEL Seoul-Kimpo Intl, HL
SEN Southend, G
SEZ Mahe-Seychelles Intl, S7

SFB Sanford Regional, FL
SFC St Francois, F-O
SFD San Fernando de Apure, YV
SFG St Martin-Esperance, F-O
SFJ Kangerlussuaq-
Sondre Stromfjord, OY
SFO San Francisco Intl, CA
SFS Subic Bay Intl, PR
SFT Skelleftea, SE
SGC Surgut, RA
SGD Sondeberg, OY
SGF Springfield-
Branson Regional, MO
SGH Springfield-Beckley, OH
SGL Manila-Sangley Point, RP
SGN Ho Chi Minh City-
Tansonnhat, VN
SGU St George Municipal UT
SGW Saginaw Bay, AK
SGY Skagway Municipal, AK
SGZ Songkhla, HS
SHA Shanghai-Hongqiao, B
SHE Shenyang, B
SHJ Sharjah Intl, A6
SHR Sheridan County, WY
SIA Xi'an-Xiguan, B
SID Sal-Amilcar Cabral Intl, D4
SIG San Juan-Isla Grande, PR
SIN Singapore-Changi, 9V
SIP Simferopol, UR
SIR Sion, HB
SIT Sitka, AK
SIX Singleton, NSW
SJC San Jose Intl, CA
SJJ Sarajevo-Butmir, T9
SJK Sao Jose dos Campos, PP
SJO San Jose-Juan Santamaria
Intl, YS
SJU San Juan-Luis Munoz
Marin Intl, PR
SJY Deinajoki-Ilmajoki, OH
SKB Basseterre-Golden Rock, V4
SKD Samarkand, UK
SKE Skien-Geiteryggen, LN
SKF San Antonio-Kelly AFB, TX
SKH Surkhet, 9N
SKP Skopje, Z3
SKX Saransk, RA
SKY Sandusky, OH
SLA Salta Intl, LV
SLC Salt Lake City Intl, UT
SLM Salamanca Matacan, EC
SLU Castries, J6
SLW Saltillo, XA
SLY Salekhard, RA
SMA Santa Maria-Vila do Porto, CS
SMF Sacramento-Metropolitan, CA
SML Stella Maris, C6
SMN Salmon, ID
SMO Santa Monica, CA
SMX Santa Maria-Public, CA
SNA John Wayne-Orange Co, CA
SNN Shannon, EI
SNR St Nazaire-Montoir, F
SOD Sorocaba, PP
SOF Sofia-Vrazhdebna Intl, LZ
SOU Southampton Intl, G
SOW Show Low-Municipal, AZ
SPB St Thomas Seaplane, VI
SPI Springfield Capital, IL
SPN Saipan Island Intl, N
SPR San Pedro, V3
SPU Split, 9A
SPW Spencer Municipal, IA
SPZ Springdale, AR
SRG Senerang, PK

| | | | | | | | |
|---|---|---|---|---|---|---|---|
| SRN | Strahan, Tas | | TIA | Tirana-Rinas, ZA | | UNU | Juneau-Dodge Co, AK |
| SRQ | Sarasota-Bradenton Intl, FL | | TIF | Taif, HZ | | UPG | Ujang Pendang, PK |
| SRZ | Santa Cruz-El Trompillo, CP | | TIJ | Tijuana-Rodriguez Intl, XA | | UPN | Uruapan, XA |
| SSA | Salvador-Dois de Julho, PP | | TIP | Tripoli Intl, 5A | | URA | Uratsk, UN |
| SSG | Malabo, 3C | | TIS | Thursday Island, Qld | | URC | Urumqi-Diwopou, B |
| SSH | Sharm el Sheikh, SU | | TIV | Tivat, YU | | URS | Kursk, RA |
| SSQ | La Sarre, QU | | TJM | Tyumen-Roschino, RA | | UTN | Upington, ZS |
| STA | Stauning, OY | | TKA | Talkeetna, AK | | UTP | Utapao, HS |
| STI | Santiago Intl, HI | | TKJ | Tok, AK | | UTT | Umtata, ZS |
| STL | St Louis-Lambert Intl, MO | | TKU | Turku, OH | | UUA | Bugulma, RA |
| STM | Santarem-Gomez Intl, PP | | TLC | Toluca-Alfonso Lopez, XA | | UUD | Ulan Ude-Mukhino, RA |
| STN | London-Stansted, G | | TLL | Tallinn-Ylemiste, ES | | UUS | Yuzhno-Sakhalinsk, RA |
| STR | Stuttgart, D | | TLR | Tulare-Mefford Field, CA | | | |
| STS | Santa Rosa-Sonoma, CA | | TLS | Toulouse-Blagnac, F | | VAI | Vanimo, P2 |
| STT | St Thomas-Cyril E King, VI | | TLV | Tel Aviv-Ben Gurion Intl, 4X | | VAR | Varna Intl, LZ |
| STU | Santa Cruz, V3 | | TMB | Miami-New Tamiami, FL | | VBS | Brescia, I |
| STW | Stavropol-Shpakovskoye, RA | | TML | Tamale, 9G | | VCE | Venice-Marco Polo, I |
| STX | St Croix -Hamilton Airport, VI | | TMO | Tumeremo, YV | | VCP | Sao Paulo-Viracopos, PP |
| SUA | Stuart-Witham Field, FL | | TMP | Tampere-Pirkkala, OH | | VCT | Victoria-Regional, TX |
| SUB | Surabaya-Juanda, PK | | TMS | Sao Tome Intl, 9L | | VCV | Victorville, CA |
| SUI | Sukhumi, 4L | | TMW | Tamworth-Westdale, NSW | | VDM | Viedma-Castello, LV |
| SUS | St Louis-Spirit of St Louis, MO | | TNA | Jinan, B | | VDZ | Valdez-Municipal, AK |
| SUV | Suva-Nausori, DQ | | TNF | Toussus-le-Noble, F | | VER | Vera Cruz-Jara Intl, XA |
| SVD | Kingstown-ET Joshua , V8 | | TNN | Tainan, B | | VFA | Victoria Falls, Z |
| SVG | Stavanger-Sola, LN | | TNR | Antananarivo, 5R | | VGD | Vologda, RA |
| SVH | Statesville Municipal, NC | | TOA | Torrance, CA | | VGT | Las Vegas-North, NV |
| SVO | Moscow-Sheremetyevo, RA | | TOE | Tozeur-Nefta, TS | | VIE | Vienna-Schwechat, OE |
| SVQ | Seville-San Pablo, EC | | TOF | Tomsk, RA | | VIH | Vichy-Rolla National, MO |
| SVU | SavuSavu, DQ | | TOL | Toledo-Express, OH | | VIR | Durban-Virginia, ZS |
| SVX | Yekaterinburg-Koltsovo, RA | | TOM | Tombouctu, TZ | | VIS | Visalia-Municipal, CA |
| SWA | Shantou, B | | TPA | Tampa Intl, FL | | VKO | Moscow-Vnukovo, RA |
| SWF | Newburgh-Steward-Hudson | | TPE | Taipei-Chiang Kai Shek Intl, B | | VLC | Valencia, EC |
| | Valley Intl, NY | | TPQ | Tepic, XA | | VLE | Valle-J Robidoux , AZ |
| SWH | Swan Hill, Vic | | TPS | Trapani, I | | VLI | Port Vila-Bauerfield, YJ |
| SXF | Berlin-Schönefeld, D | | TRD | Trondheim-Vaernes, LN | | VLK | Volgodonsk, RA |
| SXM | St Maarten-Philipsburg, PJ | | TRG | Tauranga, ZK | | VLL | Volladolid, EC |
| SXQ | Soldotna, AK | | TRN | Turin-Caselle, I | | VLN | Valencia Intl, YV |
| SYD | Sydney-Kingsford Smith | | TRS | Trieste, I | | VLU | Velikie Linki, RA |
| | Intl, NSW | | TRW | Tarawa, T3 | | VNC | Venice, FL |
| SYR | Syracuse-Hancock Intl, NY | | TSA | Taipei-Sung Shan, B | | VNE | Vannes-Meucon, F |
| SYQ | San Jose-Tobias Bolanos | | TSE | Astana, UN | | VNO | Vilnius Intl, LY |
| | Intl, YS | | TSM | Taos-Municipal, NM | | VNY | Van Nuys, CA |
| SYX | Sanya-Fenghuang, B | | TSN | Tianjin, B | | VOG | Volgograd-Gumrak, RA |
| SYY | Stornoway, G | | TSR | Timisoara-Giarmata, YR | | VOZ | Voronezh-Chertovtskye, RA |
| SYZ | Shiraz Intl, EP | | TSV | Townsville, Qld | | VPC | Cartersville, GA |
| SZB | Subang-Sultan Abdul | | TTD | Portland-Troutdale, OR | | VQS | Vieques, PR |
| | Aziz Shah Intl, 9M | | TTN | Mercer-County, Trenton, NJ | | VRN | Verona-Villafranca, I |
| SZG | Salzburg, OE | | TUL | Tulsa Intl, OK | | VSG | Lugansk, UR |
| SZO | Shanzhou, B | | TUN | Tunis-Carthage, TS | | VTE | Vientiane-Wattay, RDPL |
| SZX | Shenzhen-Huangtian, B | | TUO | Taupo, ZK | | VTG | Vung Tau, VN |
| SZZ | Szczecin-Goleniow, SP | | TUS | Tucson Intl, AZ | | VVC | Villavicencio- |
| | | | TWB | Toowomba, Qld | | | La Vanguardia, HK |
| TAB | Scarborough-Crown Point, 9Y | | TWF | Twin Falls, Joslin Field- | | VVI | Santa Cruz-Viru Viru Intl, CP |
| TAM | Tampico-Gen Francisco | | | Sun Valley Regional, ID | | VVO | Vladivostock-Knevichi, RA |
| | Javier Mina Intl, XA | | TXK | Texarkana Municipal, AR | | | |
| TAR | Taranto-Grottaglie, I | | TXL | Berlin-Tegel, D | | WAG | Wanganui, ZK |
| TAS | Tashkent-Yuzhny, UK | | TYA | Tula, RA | | WAT | Waterford, EI |
| TAT | Tatry-Poprad, OM | | TYF | Torsby-Frylanda, SE | | WAW | Warsaw-Okecie, SP |
| TBG | Tabubil, P2 | | TYN | Taiyuan-Wusu, B | | WDH | Windhoek-Hosea Kutako |
| TBS | Tbilisi-Novo Alexeyevka, 4L | | TYS | Knoxville-McGhee Tyson, TN | | | Intl, V5 |
| TBU | Tongatapu-Fua'Amotu Intl, A3 | | TYZ | Taylor, AZ | | WDR | Winder-Barrow Co, GA |
| TBZ | Tabriz, EP | | TZA | Belize-Municipal, V3 | | WFB | Ketchikan Waterfront SPB, AK |
| TBW | Tambov, RA | | | | | WGA | Wagga Wagga, NSW |
| TEB | Teterboro, NJ | | UAO | Aurora-State, OR | | WHO | Franz Josef Glacier, ZK |
| TED | Thisted, OY | | UBS | Columbus-Lowndes Co, MS | | WHP | Los Angeles- |
| TER | Lajes-Terceira Island, CS | | UCT | Ukhta, RA | | | Whiteman Field, CA |
| TFN | Tenerife-Norte los Rodeos, EC | | UES | Waukesha, WI | | WIL | Nairobi-Wilson, 5Y |
| TFS | Tenerife-Sur Reine Sofia, EC | | UFA | Ufa, RA | | WIR | Wairoa, ZK |
| TGD | Podgorica, YU | | UIK | Ust-Ilimsk, RA | | WKA | Wanaka, ZK |
| TGR | Touggourt, 7T | | UIO | Quito-Mariscal Sucre, HC | | WLG | Wellington Intl, ZK |
| TGU | Tegucigalpa-Toncontin Intl, HR | | UKK | Ust-Kamenogorsk, UN | | WMX | Wamena, PK |
| TGZ | Tuxtla-Gutierrez, XA | | UKX | Ust-Kut, RA | | WOE | Woensdrecht, PH |
| THE | Terresina, PP | | ULN | Ulan Bator, JU | | WOW | Willow, AK |
| THF | Berlin-Tempelhof, D | | ULY | Ulyanovsk, RA | | WRO | Wroclaw-Strachowice, SP |
| THN | Trolhattan-Vanersborg, SE | | UME | Umea, SE | | WST | Westerly State, RI |
| THR | Teheran-Mehrabad Intl, EP | | UNK | Unalakleet Municipal, AK | | WSY | Airlie Beach-Whitsunday, Qld |

| | |
|---|---|
| WUH | Wuhan, B |
| WVB | Walvis Bay, V5 |
| WVL | Waterville-Lafleur, ME |
| WVN | Wilhelmshaven-Mariensiel, D |
| WWA | Wasilla, AK |
| WYA | Whyalla, SA |
| WYN | Wyndham, WA |
| | |
| XBE | Bearskin Lake, ON |
| XCM | Chatham, ON |
| XCR | Vatry, F |
| XFW | Hamburg-Finkenwerder, D |
| XIY | Xi'an Xianyang, B |
| XLS | Saint Louis, 6V |
| XLW | Lemwerder, D |
| XMN | Xiamen-Gaoqi, B |
| XPK | Pukatawagan, MB |
| XSP | Singapore-Seletar, 9V |
| | |
| YAG | Fort Frances Municipal, QC |
| YAM | Sault Ste Marie, ON |
| YAO | Yaounde, TJ |
| YAW | Halifax-Shearwater CFB, NS |
| YBC | Baie Comeau, QC |
| YBL | Campbell River, BC |
| YBW | Calgary Springbank, AL |
| YBX | Lourdes-de-Blanc Sablon, QC |
| YCA | Courtenay, BC |
| YCB | Cambridge Bay, NT |
| YCD | Nanaimo-Cassidy, BC |
| YCE | Centralia, ON |
| YCH | Miramichi, NB |
| YCL | Charlo, NB |
| YCN | Cochrane-Lillabelle Lake, ON |
| YCR | Cross Lake-Sinclair Memorial, MB |
| YCW | Chilliwack, BC |
| YDF | Deer Lake, NL |
| YDL | Dease Lake, BC |
| YDQ | Dawson Creek, BC |
| YDT | Vancouver-Boundary Bay, BC |
| YDU | Kasba Lake, NT |
| YEG | Edmonton-Intl, AB |
| YEL | Elliott Lake-Municipal, ON |
| YEV | Inuvik-Mike Zubko, NT |
| YFB | Iqaluit, NT |
| YFC | Fredericton, NB |
| YFO | Flin Flon, MB |
| YFS | Fort Simpson, NT |
| YGG | Ganges Harbour, AK |
| YGH | Fort Good Hope, NT |
| YGL | La Grande Riviere, QC |
| YGM | Gimli, MB |
| YGR | Iles de la Madelaine, QC |
| YGV | Havre St Pierre, QC |
| YGX | Gillam, MB |
| YHF | Hearst, ON |
| YHM | Hamilton, ON |
| YHN | Homepayne, ON |
| YHR | Chevery, QC |
| YHS | Sechelt-Gibson, BC |
| YHT | Haines Junction, YK |
| YHU | Montreal-St Hubert, QC |
| YHY | Hay River, NT |
| YHZ | Halifax Intl, NS |
| YIB | Atikokan Municipal, ON |
| YIP | Detroit-Willow Run, MI |
| YJF | Fort Liard, NT |
| YJN | St Jean, QC |
| YKA | Kamloops, BC |
| YKE | Knee Lake, MB |
| YKF | Kitchener-Waterloo, ON |
| YKL | Schefferville, QC |
| YKS | Yakutsk, RA |
| YKZ | Toronto-Buttonville, ON |
| YLB | Lac la Biche, AB |

| | |
|---|---|
| YLJ | Meadow Lake, SK |
| YLL | Lloydminster, AB |
| YLP | Mingan, QC |
| YLQ | La Tuque, QC |
| YLT | Alert, NT |
| YLW | Kelowna, BC |
| YMM | Fort McMurray, AB |
| YMO | Moosonee, ON |
| YMP | Port McNeil, BC |
| YMT | Chibougamau-Chapais, QC |
| YMX | Montreal-Mirabel Intl, QC |
| YNA | Natashquan, QC |
| YNC | Wemindji, QC |
| YND | Ottawa-Gatineau, QC |
| YNF | Corner Brook, NL |
| YNR | Arnes, MB |
| YOJ | High Level/Footner Lake, AB |
| YOO | Oshawa, ON |
| YOW | Ottawa-McDonald Cartier Intl, QC |
| YPA | Prince Albert, SK |
| YPB | Port Alberni-Sproat Lake, BC |
| YPD | Parry Sound, ON |
| YPE | Peace River, AB |
| YPL | Pickle Lake, ON |
| YPQ | Peterborough |
| YPR | Prince Rupert-Digby Island, BC |
| YPZ | Burns Lake, BC |
| YQA | Muskoka, ON |
| YQB | Quebec-Jean Lesage Intl, QC |
| YQD | The Pas, MB |
| YQF | Red Deer, AB |
| YQH | Watson Lake, YT |
| YQK | Kenora, ON |
| YQN | Nakina, ON |
| YQR | Regina, SK |
| YQS | St Thomas, ON |
| YQT | Thunder Bay, ON |
| YQU | Grande Prairie, AB |
| YQV | Yorkton, SK |
| YQX | Gander Intl, NL |
| YRB | Resolute Bay, NT |
| YRJ | Roberval, QC |
| YRL | Red Lake, ON |
| YRO | Ottawa-Rockcliffe, ON |
| YRP | Carp, ON |
| YRT | Rankin Inket, NU |
| YSB | Sudbury, ON |
| YSE | Squamish, BC |
| YSF | Stony Rapids, SK |
| YSJ | Saint John, NB |
| YSM | Fort Smith, NT |
| YSN | Salmon Arm, BC |
| YSQ | Atlin-Spring Island, BC |
| YTA | Pembroke, ON |
| YTF | Alma, QC |
| YTH | Thompson, MB |
| YTP | Tofino SPB, BC |
| YTZ | Toronto-City Centre, ON |
| YUL | Montreal-Pierre Elliot Trudeau, QC |
| YUY | Rouyn-Noranda, QC |
| YVA | Moroni-Iconi, D6 |
| YVC | La Ronge, SK |
| YVG | Vermillion Bay, AB |
| YVO | Val d'Or/La Grande, QC |
| YVP | Kuujjuaq, QC |
| YVQ | Norman Wells, NT |
| YVR | Vancouver Intl, BC |
| YVT | Buffalo Narrows, SK |
| YVV | Wiarton, ON |
| YWF | Halifax-Waterfront Heliport, NS |
| YWG | Winnipeg Intl, MB |
| YWH | Victoria-Inner Harbour, BC |
| YWJ | Deline, NT |
| YWK | Wabush, NL |

| | |
|---|---|
| YWR | White River, ON |
| YWS | Whistler, BC |
| YXD | Edmonton Municipal, AB |
| YXE | Saskatoon-John D Diefenbacker, SK |
| YXH | Medicine Hat, AB |
| YXJ | Fort St John, BC |
| YXK | Rimouski, QC |
| YXL | Sioux Lookout, ON |
| YXS | Prince George, BC |
| YXT | Terrace, BC |
| YXU | London, ON |
| YXX | Abbotsford, BC |
| YXY | Whitehorse, YT |
| YXZ | Wawa-Hawk Junction, ON |
| YYB | North Bay, ON |
| YYC | Calgary-Intl, AB |
| YYD | Smithers, BC |
| YYE | Fort Nelson, BC |
| YYF | Penticton, BC |
| YYG | Charlottetown, PE |
| YYJ | Victoria-Intl, BC |
| YYL | Lynn Lake, MB |
| YYQ | Churchill, MB |
| YYR | Goose Bay, NL |
| YYT | St Johns, NL |
| YYW | Armstrong, ON |
| YYZ | Toronto-Lester B Pearson Intl, ON |
| YZF | Yellowknife, NT |
| YZH | Slave Lake, AB |
| YZT | Port Hardy, BC |
| YZU | Whitecourt, AB |
| YZV | Sept-Iles, QC |
| | |
| ZAG | Zagreb-Pleso, 9A |
| ZAM | Zamboanga Intl, RP |
| ZAZ | Zaragoza, EC |
| ZFD | Fond du Lac, SK |
| ZFM | Fort McPherson, NT |
| ZIH | Ixtapa-Zihuatenejo Intl, XA |
| ZJN | Swan River, MB |
| ZNQ | Ingolstadt, D |
| ZNZ | Zanzibar-Kisuani, 5H |
| ZPB | Sachigo Lake , ON |
| ZQN | Queenstown-Frankston, NZ |
| ZQS | Queen Charlotte, BC |
| ZRH | Zurich-Kloten, HB |
| ZRJ | Weagqmow-Round Lake, ON |
| ZSJ | Sandy Lake, ON |
| ZSW | Price Rupert-Seal Cove, BC |
| ZTH | Zante-Zakinthos, SX |
| ZTR | Zhitomyr, UR |
| ZUC | Ignace, ON |
| ZUH | Zhuhai-Jiuzhou, B |

# NATIONALITY INDEX

This index lists the world's current registration prefixes and is a guide to their location in the main part of this book.

| | | | | | | |
|---|---|---|---|---|---|---|
| LN- | Norway | 232 | | EC- | Spain | 134 |
| | | | | 4R- | Sri Lanka | 569 |
| A4O- | Oman | 10 | | ST- | Sudan | 466 |
| | | | | PZ- | Suriname | 425 |
| AP- | Pakistan | 7 | | 3D- | Swaziland | 566 |
| T8A | Palau | 490 | | SE- | Sweden | 460 |
| SU-Y | Palestine | 471 | | HB- | Switzerland & Liechtenstein | 189 |
| HP- | Panama | 205 | | YK- | Syria | 541 |
| P2- | Papua New Guinea | 426 | | | | |
| ZP- | Paraguay | 556 | | EY- | Tajikistan | 159 |
| OB- | Peru | 383 | | 5H- | Tanzania | 573 |
| RP- | Philippines | 456 | | TT- | Tchad | 488 |
| SP- | Poland | 464 | | HS- | Thailand | 207 |
| CS- | Portugal | 111 | | 5V- | Togo | 580 |
| | | | | A3- | Tonga | 9 |
| A7- | Qatar | 17 | | 9Y- | Trinidad & Tobago | 605 |
| | | | | TS- | Tunisia | 487 |
| YR- | Romania | 543 | | TC- | Turkey | 476 |
| RA- | Russia | 428 | | EZ- | Turkmenistan | 160 |
| 9XR- | Rwanda | 605 | | VQ-T | Turks & Caicos Islands | 521 |
| | | | | T2- | Tuvalu | - |
| VQ-H | St Helena | - | | | | |
| V4- | St Kitts Nevis | 530 | | 5X- | Uganda | 580 |
| J6- | St Lucia | - | | UR- | Ukraine | 495 |
| J8- | St Vincent & Grenadines | 231 | | A6- | United Arab Emirates | 10 |
| 5W- | Samoa | 580 | | G- | United Kingdom | 171 |
| T7- | San Marino | - | | N | United States of America | 241 |
| S9- | Sao Tome | 475 | | CX- | Uruguay | 114 |
| HZ- | Saudi Arabia | 211 | | UK- | Uzbekistan | 490 |
| 6V- | Senegal | 586 | | | | |
| YU- | Serbia | 545 | | YJ- | Vanuatu | 541 |
| S7- | Seychelles | 475 | | YV- | Venezuela | 545 |
| 9L- | Sierra Leone | 593 | | VN- | Vietnam | 519 |
| 9V- | Singapore | 602 | | | | |
| OM- | Slovak Republic | 392 | | 7O- | Yemen | 587 |
| S5- | Slovenia | 474 | | | | |
| H4- | Solomon Islands | 214 | | 9J- | Zambia | 592 |
| 6O- | Somalia | 586 | | Z- | Zimbabwe | 551 |
| ZS- | South Africa | 556 | | | | |

# OPERATOR INDEX

| | | | |
|---|---|---|---|
| Air America | N | Air Ivoire | TU |
| Air Antilles Express | F | Air Jamaica | 6Y |
| Air Arabia | A6 | Air Japan | JA |
| Air Arabia Egypt | SU | Air Kaibu | DQ |
| Air Arabia Maroc | CN | Air Kasai | 9Q |
| Air Archipels | F | Air Kasthamandap | 9N |
| Air Arctic | N | Air Katanga | 9Q |
| Air Armenia | EK | Air KBZ | XY |
| Air Armenia Cargo | EK | Air Kiribati | T3 |
| Air Asia X | EK | Air Korea | HL |
| Air Astana | UP | Air Koryo | P |
| Air Atlanta | TF | Air Kufra | 5A |
| Air Atlantique | G | Air Labrador | C |
| Air Austral | F | Air Leasing Cameroon | TJ |
| Air Australia | VH | Air Libya | 5A |
| Air Bagan | XY | Air Link | VH |
| Air Bashkortostan | RA | Air Link International Airways | RP |
| Air Batumi | 4L | Air Loyauté | F |
| Air Bellevue | VH | Air Macatina | C |
| Air Botswana | A2 | Air Macau | B |
| Air Boyoma | 9Q | Air Madagascar | 5R |
| Air Bravo | C | Air Majoro | OB |
| Air Bright | LZ | Air Malawi | 7Q |
| Air Bucharest | YR | Air Maleo | PK |
| Air Burkina | XT | Air Mali | TZ |
| Air Burundi | 9U | Air Malta | 9H |
| Air Busan | HL | Air Manas | EX |
| Air Cab | C | Air Mandalay | XY |
| Air Cairo | SU | Air Mark | UP |
| Air Caledonie International | F | Air Mark Indonesia Aviation | PK |
| Air Canada | C | Air Mauritius | 3B |
| Air Canada Express | C | Air Max | LZ |
| Air Caraibes | F | Air Mediterrannée | F |
| Air Caraibes Atlantique | F | Air Mekong | VN |
| Air Cargo Carriers | N | Air Melancon | C |
| Air Cargo Germany | D | Air Memphis | SU |
| Air Charter Botswana | A2 | Air Midwest | 5N |
| Air Chathams | ZK | Air Mikisew | C |
| Air China | B | Air Milford 2000 | ZK |
| Air China Cargo | B | Air Minas | PP |
| Air Class | CX | Air Moldova | ER |
| Air Colombia | HK | Air Mont-Laurier | C |
| Air Congo International | TN | Air Montmagny | C |
| Air Contractors | EI | Air Montserrat | VP-M |
| Air Contracts Africa | ZS | Air Moorea | F |
| Air Corsica | F | Air Namibia | V5 |
| Air Creebec | C | Air National | ZK |
| Air Cuahonte | XA | Air New Zealand | ZK |
| Air Direct | N | Air New Zealand Link | ZK |
| Air Dolomiti | I | Air Niamey | 5U |
| Air Dolphin | JA | Air Nigeria | 5N |
| Air Europa | EC | Air Nippon | JA |
| Air Excel | 5H | Air Niugini | P2 |
| Air Express Algeria | 7T | Air North | C |
| Air Fiji | DQ | Air Nostrum | EC |
| Air Finland | OH | Air Nunavut | C |
| Air Flamenco | N | Air Pacific | DQ |
| Air France | F | Air Pack Express | D |
| Air Freight NZ | ZK | Air Panama | HP |
| Air Gemini | D2 | Air Rarotonga | E5 |
| Air Georgian | C | Air Roberval | C |
| Air Ghana | 9G | Air Rum | 9L |
| Air Glaciers | HB | Air Safaris | YJ |
| Air Grand Canyon | N | Air Safaris & Services | ZK |
| Air Greenland | OY | Air Saguenay | C |
| Air Guinee Express | 3X | Air Sanga | P2 |
| Air Guyana | 8R | Air Santo Domingo | HI |
| Air Guyane Express | F | Air Scorpio | LZ |
| Air Hamburg | D | Air Senegal International | 6V |
| Air Highnesses | EK | Air Service Berlin | D |
| Air Hong Kong | B | Air Service Gabon | TR |
| Air Horizon Afrique | TT | Air Service Liege | OO |
| Air Iceland | TF | Air Service Wildgruber | D |
| Air India | VT | Air Services | 8R |
| Air India Express | VT | Air Seychelles | S7 |
| Air India Regional | VT | Air Sinai | SU |
| Air Intr Island | HI | Air Sirin | 4L |
| Air Inter Ivoire | TU | Air South Regional | VH |
| Air Inuit | C | Air Southwest | G |
| Air Italy | I | Air St Kitts & Nevis | V4 |
| Air Italy Polska | SP | Air St Pierre | F |
| Air Ivanhoe | C | Air Sunshine | N |

| Airline | Code | Airline | Code |
|---|---|---|---|
| Air Sweden | SE | Al-Ajnihah Aiways | 5A |
| Air Tahiti | F | Alania Airline | RA |
| Air Tahiti Nui | F | Alaska Airlines | N |
| Air Tahoma | N | Alaska Central Express | N |
| Air Tango | LV | Alaska Seaplane Service | N |
| Air Tanzania | 5H | Alaska West Air | N |
| Air Taraba | 5N | Alba Star | EC |
| Air Taxi & Cargo | ST | Albanian Airlines | ZA |
| Air Tindi | C | Albatros Airlines | YV |
| Air Traffic | 5Y | Alberta Central Airways | C |
| Air Transat | C | Alcon Servicios Aereos | XA |
| Air Tranzit | RA | Aldawlyh Air | 5A |
| Air Tribe | XA | Alexandria Airlines | SU |
| Air Tropiques | 9Q | Alfa Air Romania | YR |
| Air Tunilik | C | Alfa Airlines | ST |
| Air Turks & Caicos | VQ-T | Aliansa | HK |
| Air Uganda | 5X | Alidaunia | I |
| Air Urga | UR | Alitalia | I |
| Air Vallée | I | Alitalia Cityliner | I |
| Air Vanuatu | YJ | Alitalia Express | I |
| Air Venezuela | YV | Alkan Air | C |
| Air Victory | 4L | Allebia Air Cargo | 5A |
| Air Wakaya | DQ | Allegiance Air | ZS |
| Air Wemindji | C | Allegiant Air | N |
| Air West Cargo | ST | Allen Airways | C |
| Air Whitsunday Seaplanes | VH | Alliance Air | VT |
| Air Zermatt | HB | Alliance Airlines | VH |
| Air Zimbabwe | Z | Allied Air Cargo | 5N |
| Air2there.com | ZK | Alligator Airways | VH |
| Airasia | 9M | Allwest Freight | N |
| Airasia Philippines | RP | Almajara Aviation | ST |
| Airawak | F | Almasria Universal Airlines | SU |
| Airbaltic | YL | Alnaser Airlines | YI |
| AirBerlin | D | Aloha Air Cargo | N |
| AirBerlin Turkey | TC | Alok Air | ST |
| AirBlue | AP | Alpine Air Express | N |
| Airborne Support | N | Alpine Aviation | C |
| Airbridge Cargo | RA | Alpine Helicopters | C |
| Airbus Transport International | F | Alpine Lakes Air | C |
| Aircalin | F | Alrosa Avia | RA |
| Airco Aircraft Charters | C | Alrosa Aviation | RA |
| Aircraft Contracts Africa | ZS | ALS | 5Y |
| Aircraft Systems | ZS | Alsair | F |
| Air-Dale Flying Service | C | Alta Flights | C |
| Airexplore | OM | Alternative Air | XA |
| Airexpress Ontario | C | Alwafeer Air | HZ |
| Airfast Indonesia | PK | Amakusa Airlines | JA |
| Airfreight Aviation | HK | Amapola Flyg | SE |
| Airjet Angola | D2 | Amaszonas Transportes Aereos | CP |
| Airkenya Express | 5Y | Amazon Sky | OB |
| Airlec Air Espace | F | Amazonaves Taxi Aero | PP |
| Airlift International | 9G | Ambjek Air Service | 5N |
| Airlinair | F | AMC Airlines | SU |
| Airlinair Portugal | CS | Amerer Air | OE |
| Airline of the Marshall Islands | V7 | America do Sul Taxi Aereo - ATSA | PP |
| Airlines of Papua New Guinea | P2 | American Airlines | N |
| Airlines of Tasmania | VH | American Connection | N |
| Airlines Tonga | A3 | American Eagle | N |
| Airlink | ZS | American Jet | LV |
| Airlink Arabia | ER | Ameriflight | N |
| Airnet Systems | N | Amerijet International | N |
| Airnorth Regional | VH | Ameristar Air Charter | N |
| Airnow | N | Amsterdam Airlines | PH |
| Airpac Airlines | N | Amur Artel Staratelei Aviakompania | RA |
| AirPhil Express | RP | AMW Tchad | TT |
| Airquarius Aviation | ZS | ANA - All Nippon Network | JA |
| Airserv International | N | ANA Wings | JA |
| Air-Spray | C | Anadolu Jet | TC |
| Airstars Airways | RA | Andes Lineas Aereas | LV |
| Air-Tec Africa | ZS | Andrew Airways | N |
| Airtran Airways | N | Angara Airlines | RA |
| Airventure | OO | Angola Air Charter | D2 |
| Airwaves Airlink | 9J | Angolan Airservices | D2 |
| Airways International | 6Y | Anguilla Air Services | VP-A |
| Airwing | LN | Anikay Air | EX |
| Airwork New Zealand | ZK | Antonov Airlines | UR |
| Airworks Kenya | 5Y | Antrak Air Ghana | 9G |
| Airzena - Georgian Airlines | 4L | AP Airlines | LY |
| AK Bars Aero | RA | Apatas | LY |
| Al Khayala | HZ | Apui Taxi Aero | PP |
| Alada | D2 | Aqua Airlines | I |
| Alajnihah Air Transport | 9Q | Aqualata Air | EC |

| | |
|---|---|
| Ararat International Airlines | EK |
| Arctic Circle Air Service | N |
| Arctic Sunwest Charters | C |
| Arctic Transportation Services | N |
| Arcus Air | D |
| Aria Air | EP |
| Ariana Afghan Airlines | YA |
| Arik Air | 5N |
| Arizona Taxi Aerea | PR |
| Ark Airways | EK |
| Arkas | HK |
| Arkefly | PH |
| Arkhangelsk 2nd Aviation Enterprise | RA |
| Arkhangelsk Airlines | RA |
| Arkia Israeli Airlines | 4X |
| Armavia | EK |
| ARP 410 Airlines | UR |
| ASAP Charter | YV |
| Asecna | 6V |
| Aserca Airlines | YV |
| Asi Pudjiastuti Aviation | PK |
| Asia Pacific Airlines | N |
| Asia Pacific Airlines | P2 |
| Asialink Cargo Airlines | PK |
| Asian Spirit | RP |
| Asian Wings | XY |
| Asiana Airlines | HL |
| Askari Aviation | TZ |
| Asky Airlines | 5V |
| Aspen Helicopters | N |
| Aspiring Air/Helicopters | ZK |
| Associated Aviation | 5N |
| Astair | RA |
| Astar Air Cargo | N |
| Astra Airlines | SX |
| Astraeus | G |
| Astral Aviation | 5Y |
| Ata Air | EP |
| ATA Airlines | UR |
| ATA Brasil | PP |
| ATI - Air Transport International | N |
| Atikokan Aero Service | C |
| Atlant Hungary | HA |
| Atlantic Aero | N |
| Atlantic Air Cargo | N |
| Atlantic Airlines | G |
| Atlantic Airlines | HR |
| Atlantic Airways | OY |
| Atlantic Airways | YN |
| Atlantic Reconnaissance | G |
| Atlantico Transporte Aereo | PR |
| Atlantique Air Assistance | F |
| Atlas Air | N |
| Atlasjet International | TC |
| Atleo River Air Service | C |
| Atlin Air Charters | C |
| ATMA | UP |
| ATO - Air Transport Office | 9Q |
| Atran - Aviatrans Cargo Airlines | RA |
| Atyrau Air Ways | UP |
| Augsburg Airways | D |
| Aurela | LY |
| Auric Air Services | 5H |
| Aurigny Air Services | G |
| Aurora Airlines | S5 |
| Austral Lineas Aereas | LV |
| Austrian Airlines | OE |
| Avanti Air | D |
| Avcom | TG |
| AVE.com | A6 |
| Avex Air Transport | ZS |
| AVFL Logistics | UR |
| Avia Jaynar | UP |
| Avia Express Sweden | SE |
| Avia Traffic Company | EX |
| Aviacon Zitotrans | RA |
| Aviaenergo | RA |
| Avial Aviation Co | RA |
| Avialeasing | UK |
| Avialesookhrana Vladimir Air Enterprise | RA |
| Avianca | HK |
| Avianca Brazil | PP |

| | |
|---|---|
| Aviant | UR |
| Aviaprad | RA |
| Aviast Air | RA |
| Aviastar - Tupolev | RA |
| Aviastar Mandiri | PK |
| Aviateca | TG |
| Aviation Commercial Aviation | C |
| Aviation Maurice | C |
| Aviator Airways | SX |
| Aviatrans | UR |
| Aviavilsa | LY |
| Avient Aviation | Z |
| Avies Air Company | ES |
| Aviheco Colombia | HK |
| Aviogenex | YU |
| Avion Express | LY |
| Avion Express | 3C |
| Aviones Taxi Aereo | TI |
| Avior Airlines | YV |
| Avior Express | YV |
| Avirex | TR |
| Avitrans Nordic | SE |
| Awan Inspirasi | 9M |
| Awesome Flight Services | ZS |
| Axe Taxi Aereo | PT |
| Axiom Air | 5N |
| Ayeet Aviation | 4X |
| Ayk Avia | EK |
| Ayr Aviation | ST |
| Azal Cargo | 4K |
| Azerbaijan Airlines | 4K |
| Azmar Airlines | YI |
| Azul Linhas Aereas Brasileiras | PP |
| Azza Air Transport | ST |
| | |
| BA Cityflyer | G |
| Badr Airlines | ST |
| Bahamasair | C6 |
| Bahrain Air | A9C |
| Bailey Helicopters | C |
| Baires Fly | LV |
| Baker Aviation | N |
| Bakers Narrows Air Service | C |
| Baltia Airlines | N |
| Bamaji Air | C |
| Bangkok Airways | HS |
| Bankair | N |
| Bar XH Air | C |
| Barents Skylink | SE |
| Barkol Aviakompania | RA |
| Barq Aviation | JY |
| Barrier Aviation | VH |
| Basler Airlines | N |
| Batavia Air | PK |
| Bateleur Air Charter | 5Y |
| Bay Air Aviation | V5 |
| Bayview Air Service | C |
| Bearskin Airlines | C |
| Bearskin Lake Air Service | C |
| Beaver Air Services | C |
| Beibars | UP |
| Beijing Capital Airlines | B |
| Belair Airlines | HB |
| Belavia Belarussian Airlines | EW |
| Belle Air | ZA |
| Belle Air Europe | I |
| Bellview Airlines | 9L |
| Bemidji Airlines | N |
| Benair | LN |
| Benair Air Service | OY |
| Benin Golf Air | TY |
| Bentiu Air Transport | ST |
| Bergen Air Transport | LN |
| Bering Air | N |
| Berjaya Air Charter | 9M |
| Berkut Air | UP |
| Berkut State Air Company | UP |
| Berry Aviation | N |
| Best Air | TC |
| Best Air | S2 |
| Beta Cargo Air | PP |
| BH Air | E7 |

| | |
|---|---|
| BH Airlines | E9 |
| BHS - Brazilian Helicopter Services Taxi Aero | PP |
| Big Island Air | N |
| Bighorn Airways | N |
| Biman Bangladesh Airlines | S2 |
| Bimini Island Air | N |
| Binair Aero Service | D |
| Binter Canarias | EC |
| Bionic Air | ZS |
| Bismillah Airlines | S2 |
| BKS Air | EC |
| Black Sheep Aviation | C |
| Blu Express.com | I |
| Blue Air | YR |
| Blue Bird Airlines | ST |
| Blue Dart Aviation | VT |
| Blue Islands | G |
| Blue Panorama Airlines | I |
| Blue Sky | EK |
| Blue Sky Airways | A2 |
| Blue Sky Aviation | JU |
| Blue Sky Aviation | 5Y |
| Blue Water Aviation Services | C |
| Blue Wings Airlines | PZ |
| Blue1 | OH |
| Bluebird Airways | SX |
| Bluebird Aviation | 5Y |
| Bluebird Cargo | TF |
| BMI | G |
| BMI Regional | G |
| BMIBaby | G |
| Boliviana de Aviacion | CP |
| Bond Air Services | G |
| Bond Air Services (Ireland) | EI |
| Bond Offshore Helicopters | G |
| Borajet | TC |
| Botir-Avia | EX |
| BQB Lineas Aereas | CX |
| Bradley AirServices | C |
| Branson Air | ZS |
| Bravo Air Congo | 9Q |
| Bravo Airlines | N |
| BremenFly | D |
| Briko Air Services | 9Y |
| Brindabella Airlines | VH |
| Bristow Caribbean | 9Y |
| Bristow Helicopters | G |
| Bristow Helicopters (Australia) | VH |
| Bristow Helicopters (Nigeria) | 5N |
| Bristow Norway | LN |
| Bristows US | N |
| Brit'Air | F |
| British Airways | G |
| British Antarctic Survey | VP-F |
| British Gulf Airlines | EX |
| British International | G |
| Brooks Aviation | N |
| Broome Aviation | VH |
| Brroks Fuel | N |
| Brussels Airlines | OO |
| Budapest Air Services | HA |
| Buddha Air | 9N |
| Buffalo Airways | C |
| Bukovyna Airlines | UR |
| Bulgaria Air | LZ |
| Bulgarian Air Charter | LZ |
| Buraq Air | 5A |
| Buryat Avia | RA |
| Buryat Avia | UR |
| Business Air | HS |
| Business Air | N |
| Business Aviation Centre | UR |
| Business Aviation Courier | N |
| Business Aviation of Congo | 9Q |
| Businesswings | D |
| Butembo | 9Q |
| Butler Aircraft | N |
| Bylina | RA |
| | |
| C&M Airways | N |
| CAA - Compagnie Africane D'Aviation | 9Q |
| Cabo Verde Express | D4 |
| Caicos Express Airways | VQ-T |
| Cairns Seaplanes | VH |
| Cairo Aviation | SU |
| Calima Aviacion | EC |
| Calm Air | C |
| Cambodia Angkor Air | XU |
| Cameron Air Service | C |
| Cameroon Airlines | TJ |
| Canadian Helicopters | C |
| Canadian North | C |
| Canjet | C |
| Can-West Corporate Air Charter | C |
| Cape Air | N |
| Capital Airlines | 5Y |
| Capital Airlines | 5N |
| Capital Cargo International Airlines | N |
| Caravan Air | V5 |
| Cardig Air | PK |
| Cargo Air | LZ |
| Cargo Air Lines | 4X |
| Cargoitalia | I |
| Cargojet Airways | C |
| Cargolux International Airlines | LX |
| Cargolux Italia | I |
| Caribair | HI |
| Caribbean Airlines | 9Y |
| Caribbean Flights | YV |
| Caribintair | HH |
| Caroline Island Air | V6 |
| Carpatair | YR |
| Carson Air | C |
| Carson Helicopters | N |
| Casair | VH |
| Cascade Air | N |
| Caspian Airlines | EP |
| Castle Aviation | N |
| Cat Island Air | C6 |
| Catalina Flying Boats | N |
| Cathay Pacific Airways | B |
| Caverton Helicopters | 5N |
| Cayman Airways | VP-C |
| Cayman Airways Express | VP-C |
| CDF Aviation | N |
| Cebu Pacific Air | RP |
| Cegisa | EC |
| Ceiba Intercontinental GE | 3C |
| Center-South Airlines | RA |
| Central Air Transport | P2 |
| Central Airways | EK |
| Central Connect Airlines | OK |
| Central Mongolian Airlines | JU |
| Central Mountain Air | C |
| Centralafrique Air Express | TL |
| Centre-Avia Airlines | RA |
| Centurion Cargo | N |
| Cetraca Air Service | 9Q |
| Chabahar Air | EP |
| Chalair Aviation | F |
| Cham Wings Air | YK |
| Champlain Air | N |
| Chanchangi Airlines | 5N |
| Chang An Airlines | B |
| Channel Island Aviation | N |
| Chapi Air | YV |
| Chartair | VH |
| Chathams Pacific | A3 |
| CHC Airways | PH |
| CHC Cameroon | TJ |
| CHC Denmark | OY |
| CHC Helicopters (Africa) | ZS |
| CHC Helicopters (Australia) | VH |
| CHC Helicopters (Cayman Islands) | VP-C |
| CHC Helicopters International | C |
| CHC Helicopters Netherlands | PH |
| CHC Helikopter Service | LN |
| CHC Ireland | EI |
| CHC Scotia Helicopters | G |
| Chemtrad Aviation | RP |
| Chengdu Airlines | B |
| Cherokee Air | C6 |
| Cherry-Air | N |
| Chimo Air Service | C |

| | | | |
|---|---|---|---|
| China Airlines | B | Daalo Airlines | J2 |
| China Cargo Airlines | B | DAC Aviation | 5Y |
| China Eastern Airlines | B | Daghestan Airlines | RA |
| China Eastern Yunnan Airlines | B | Daily Air | B |
| China Express Airlines | B | Dalavia | RA |
| China Flying Dragon Co | B | Dalian Airlines | B |
| China Postal Airlines | B | Dana | 5N |
| China Southern Airlines | B | Dana Air | 5N |
| China United Airlines | B | Dancopter | OY |
| China Xinhua Airlines | B | Danish Air Transport | OY |
| Chongqing Airlines | B | Danu Oro Transportas | LY |
| Chukotavia | RA | Danube Wings | OM |
| Ciaca Airlines | YV | DAP Helicopteros | CC |
| Cielos Airlines | OB | Darwin Airline | HB |
| Cimber Air | OY | Dauria | RA |
| Cimber Sterling | OY | D-Connection | 5Y |
| Cirrus Airlines | D | De Bruin Air | VH |
| CITIC Offshore Helicopters | B | Deccan Cargo | VT |
| Citilink | PK | Delbitur | CX |
| City Airline | SE | Delta Air | A2 |
| City Jet | EI | Delta Airlines | N |
| Cityfly | I | Delta Connection | N |
| Cityline Hungary | HA | Denim Air ACMI | PH |
| Citylink | 9G | Denis Beahan Aviation | VH |
| Click Airways | EX | Deraya Air Taxi | PK |
| CM Airlines | HR | Desert Air | N |
| CMC Aviation | 5Y | Desert Air | V5 |
| Coastal Air Transport | N | Destination Air | HS |
| Coastal Aviation | 5H | Deta Air | UP |
| Cobham Aviation Services Australia | VH | DHL Aero Expresso | HP |
| Cochrane Air Services | C | DHL Air | G |
| Colgan Air | N | DHL Aviation (Zimbabwe) | Z |
| Columbia Helicopters | N | DHL de Guatemala | TG |
| Columbia Helicopters | P2 | DHL International Aviation | A9C |
| Comair | ZS | Diexim Expresso | D2 |
| Comav Aviation | V5 | Direct Aero Services | YR |
| Comeravia | YV | Direct Flight | G |
| Comercial Aerea | XA | Direktflyg | SE |
| Comercial Aerea | XA | Dirgantara Air Service | PK |
| Comores Air Service | D6 | Divi Divi Air | PJ |
| Comores Aviation | D6 | Djibouti Air | J2 |
| Comores Island Airways | D6 | Djibouti Airlines | J2 |
| Compagnie Mauritanienne de Transportes | 5T | Dnepr-Air | UR |
| Compion Aviation | 5Y | Dodita Air Cargo | N |
| Conair Aviation | C | Dodson International Charter | ZS |
| Concors | YL | Dolphin Air | A6 |
| Condor | D | Dolphin Airlines | N |
| Condor Berlin | D | Domodedovo Airlines | RA |
| Constanta Airlines | UR | Donavia | RA |
| Contact Air | D | Donbassaero | UR |
| Continental Airways | RA | Donghai Airlines | B |
| Conviasa | YV | Donghua Airlines | B |
| COPA Airlines | HP | Doren Air Cargo | 9Q |
| COPA Airlines Colombia | HK | Dove Air | ST |
| Copenhagen Airtaxi | OY | Dragonair | B |
| Coral Sun Airways | T3 | Druk Air | A5 |
| Corendon Air | TC | Dubnica Air | OM |
| Corendon Dutch Airlines | PH | Dubrovnik Airlines | 9A |
| Corilar Charters | C | Dutch Antilles Express | PJ |
| Corpjet | N | Dynamic Airways | N |
| Corpo Forestale Dello Stato | I | | |
| Corporate Air | N | Eagle Air | 5X |
| Corporate Air | VH | Eagle Air Transport | N |
| Corporate Express Airline | C | Eagle Copters | C |
| Corporate Flight Management | N | Eagle Copters | CC |
| Corsair | F | EAS Air Lines | 5N |
| Cotair | TU | East African Air Charters | 5Y |
| Cougar Helicopters | C | East African Safari Air | 5Y |
| Coulson Aircrane | C | East Air | EY |
| Courtesy Air | C | East Asia Airlines | HL |
| Coyotair | OB | East Horizon Airlines | YA |
| Co-Za Airways | 9Q | East Kazakhstan Avia | UP |
| Croatia Airlines | 9A | East Wing | UP |
| Cruiser Taxi Aero Brasil | PP | Eastarjet | HL |
| CSA Czech Airlines | OK | Eastern Airways | G |
| CTA | PT | Eastern Airways | 3D |
| Cubana de Aviacion | CU | Eastern Express | UP |
| Custom Helicopters | C | Eastern Skyjets | A6 |
| CV Cargo | HK | Eastindo | PK |
| Cybrair | LN | Easy Fly Express | S2 |
| Cyprus Airways | 5B | Easy Link | 5N |
| Czech Connect Airlines | OK | Easyfly | HK |

| | |
|---|---|
| Easyjet Airline | G |
| Easyjet Switzerland | HB |
| EAT Leipzig | D |
| Eco Express | CP |
| Edelweiss Air | HB |
| Efly | 9H |
| EG & G | N |
| Egoli Air | ZS |
| Egyptair | SU |
| Egyptair Express | SU |
| El Al Israel Airlines | 4X |
| El Magal Aviation | ST |
| El Sol de America | YV |
| Elbafly | I |
| Elbow River Helicopters | C |
| Elidolomiti | I |
| Elifriula | I |
| Elilario Italia | I |
| Elitaliana | I |
| Emerald Air | P2 |
| Emerald Coast Air | N |
| Emetebe Taxi Aero | HC |
| Emirates | A6 |
| Empire Airlines | N |
| Empressa Aero - Servicios Parrague | CC |
| Enerjet | C |
| Enimex | ES |
| Enter Air | SP |
| Enterlake Air Services | C |
| Enzis Airways | JU |
| EP Aviation | N |
| Epps Aviation Charter | N |
| Epsilon Aviation | SX |
| Equaflight Service | TN |
| Era Aviation | N |
| Era Helicopters | N |
| Erickson Air Crane | N |
| Eritrean Airlines | E3 |
| Ernir Air | TF |
| Espace Aviation | 9Q |
| Essen Air | EX |
| Estafeta Carga Aerea | XA |
| Estonian Air | ES |
| Estonian Air Regional | ES |
| Ethiopian Airlines | ET |
| Etihad Airways | A6 |
| Etram Air Wing | 9Q |
| Eurex | 4L |
| Euro Asia International | UP |
| Euro Atlantic Airways | CS |
| Euro Continental Air | EC |
| Euroair | SX |
| Euroline | 4L |
| EuroLot | SP |
| Europe Airpost | F |
| Eurowings | D |
| EVA Airways | B |
| Evenkia Avia | RA |
| Evergreen Helicopters | N |
| Evergreen Helicopters Intl (Trinidad) | 9Y |
| Evergreen International Airlines | N |
| Everts Air Alaska | N |
| Everts Air Cargo | N |
| Everts Air Fuel | N |
| Excellent Air | D |
| Excellent Glide | UP |
| Exec Direct Aviation | 6Y |
| Execujet South Africa | ZS |
| Executive Aerospace | ZS |
| Executive Turbine Air Charter | ZS |
| Executive Turbine Kenya | 5Y |
| Exim Trading | 3X |
| Exin | SP |
| Exploits Valley Air Service | C |
| Expo Aviation | 4R |
| Express Air | C |
| Express Freighters Australia | VH |
| Expressair | PK |
| Expressjet Airlines | N |
| | |
| Fair Aviation | ZS |
| Falcon Air Charters | 5Y |

| | |
|---|---|
| Falcon Air Express | N |
| Falcon Air Service | N |
| Falcon Express Cargo Airlines | A6 |
| Far Eastern Air Transport | B |
| Farnair Hungary | HA |
| Farnair Switzerland | HB |
| Fars Air | EP |
| Fast Air | C |
| Faza Air | YA |
| Federal Air | ZS |
| Federal Express | N |
| Feeder Airlines | ST |
| Felix Airways | 7O |
| FIGAS | VP-F |
| Filair | 9Q |
| Finist'Air | F |
| Finnair | OH |
| Firefly | 9M |
| First Air | C |
| First Nation Airlines | 5N |
| Flair Airlines | C |
| Fleet Air International | HA |
| Fleet Management Airways | F |
| Flex Air Cargo | 5Y |
| Flight 2000 | ZK |
| Flight Alaska | N |
| Flight Inspections & Systems | RA |
| Flight International Aviation | N |
| Flightline | EC |
| FLM Aviation | D |
| Florida Air Cargo | N |
| Florida Air Transport | N |
| Florida Coastal Airlines | N |
| Florida Gulf Airlines | N |
| Florida West International Airlines | N |
| Flugdienst Fehlhaber | D |
| Fly Air Ethiopia | ET |
| Fly Aruba | P4 |
| Fly Express | D |
| Fly Hellas | SX |
| Fly Logic Sweden | SE |
| Fly Safari Air Link | 5H |
| Fly Wales | G |
| Fly540 | 5Y |
| Fly540 Angola | D2 |
| Fly540 Tanzania | 5H |
| FlyBe | G |
| FlyBe Nordic | OH |
| FlyDubai | A6 |
| Flying America | LV |
| Flying Bulls | OE |
| Flymex | XA |
| Fort Francis Sportsmen Airways | C |
| Four Star Air Cargo | N |
| Free Airlines | 9Q |
| Freebird Airlines | TC |
| Freedom Air | N |
| Freedom Air Services | 5N |
| Freedom Express | 5Y |
| Freight Runners Express | N |
| Fretax Taxi Aereo | PP |
| Frisia Luftverkehr | D |
| Frontier Airlines | N |
| Fugro Airborne Surveys | ZS |
| Fugro Aviation Canada | C |
| Fuji Dream Airlines | JA |
| Futura Travels | VT |
| | |
| Gabon Airlines | TR |
| Gading Sari Aviation Services | PK |
| Gainjet | SX |
| Galaxy Airlines | EX |
| Galaxy Kavatsi Aviation | 9Q |
| Gallup Flying Service | N |
| GAM Services | VH |
| Garinco Airways | EX |
| Garuda Indonesia | PK |
| Gatari Air Service | PK |
| Gazpromavia | RA |
| GB Airlink | N |
| Geasa | 3C |
| General Works Aviacon | 3C |

| | |
|---|---|
| Genex | EW |
| Gensa | PP |
| Geo Air | N |
| Georgian International | 4L |
| Georgian Star Interntional | 4L |
| German SkyAirlines | D |
| Germania | D |
| Germanwings | D |
| Gestair Cargo | EC |
| Getra | 3C |
| Ghadames Air Transport | 5A |
| Gideon Air | ZS |
| Gillam Air Services | C |
| Gira Globo | D2 |
| Global Air | XA |
| Global Air | 5A |
| Global Airways | VQ-T |
| Global Aviation Leasing | ZS |
| Global Supply Systems | G |
| Globus | RA |
| GMG Airlines | S2 |
| Go Air | VT |
| Go! | N |
| Gogal Air Services | C |
| Gol Transportes Aereos | PP |
| Gold Coast Seaplanes | VH |
| Goldak Airborne Surveys | C |
| Golden Air | SE |
| Golden Eagle Airlines | VH |
| Golden Wings | ZK |
| Goldfields Air Services | VH |
| Golfo International | S9 |
| Goliaf Air | S9 |
| Goma Air | 9N |
| Gomair | 9Q |
| Gomelavia | EW |
| Gorkha Airlines | 9N |
| Government of Quebec | C |
| Grand Canyon Airlines | N |
| Grand China Airlines | B |
| Granstar Cargo Airlines | B |
| Grant Aviation | N |
| Great Barrier Airlines | ZK |
| Great Lakes Airlines | N |
| Great Wing Airlines | B |
| Green Airways | C |
| Green Flag Aviation | ST |
| Grenadine Airways | J8 |
| Griffin Flying Service | N |
| Grixona | ER |
| Grondair | C |
| Grondin Transport | C |
| Groznyavia | RA |
| GST Aero | UP |
| GT Air | PK |
| GTRA Airways | 9Q |
| Guam Marianas Air | N |
| Guardian Air Transport | N |
| Guinea Equatorial Airlines | 3C |
| Guinee Air Cargo | 3X |
| Guizhou Airlines | B |
| Gulf Air | A9C |
| Gulf and Caribbean Air | N |
| Gulf Atlantic Airways | N |
| Gulf Helicopters | A7 |
| Gum Air | PZ |
| Guna Airlines | 9N |
| | |
| Hageland Aviation Services | N |
| Hainan Airlines | B |
| Halcyon Air | D4 |
| Hamburg Airways | D |
| Hanair | HH |
| Hangar Uno | LV |
| Hankyu Airlines | JA |
| Happy Air | HS |
| Happy Airlines | B |
| Harbour Air Seaplanes | C |
| Harbour Air Malta | 9H |
| Hardy Aviation | VH |
| Hawaiian Airlines | N |
| Hawk Air | LV |

| | |
|---|---|
| Hawk Air | C |
| Hawk Airlines | AP |
| Hawk de Mexico | XA |
| Hawkair Aviation Service | C |
| HD Air | G |
| Hearst Air Service | C |
| Heavylift Cargo Airlines | VH |
| Heavylift International | A6 |
| Hebei Airlines | B |
| Hebridean Air Services | G |
| Hegedus | HA |
| Heli Air Monaco | 3A |
| Heli Air Services | LZ |
| Heli Express | C |
| Heliand | C3 |
| Helicopter Line | ZK |
| Helicopter Seychelles | S7 |
| Helicopteros del Sur | OB |
| Helicsa Helicopteros | EC |
| Heliduero | CC |
| Helifor Industries | C |
| Heligo Charters | VT |
| Heli-Italia | I |
| HeliJet International | C |
| Heli-Lift International | C |
| Helimalongo | D2 |
| Heliportugal | CS |
| Helistara Colombia | HK |
| Helisul Taxi Aereo | PP |
| Helisur | OB |
| Helisuretse | EC |
| Heliswiss | HB |
| Heliswiss Iberica | EC |
| Helitaxi | HK |
| Helitours | 4R |
| Helitec | YV |
| Helitrans | LN |
| Helitrans | C3 |
| Heli-Union | F |
| Helivan | XA |
| Heliwest | VH |
| Heliworks | CC |
| Hellenic Imperial Airways | SX |
| Hellitt Lineas Aereas | EC |
| Hello | HB |
| Helog | HB |
| Helog Lufttransport | D |
| Helvetic Airways | HB |
| Hemus Air | LZ |
| Henan Airlines | B |
| Heritage Aviation | D6 |
| Hermes Airlines | SX |
| Hesa Airlines | EP |
| Hewa Bora Airways | 9Q |
| Hex'Air | F |
| Heyes Helicopter Services | C |
| Hi Fly | CS |
| Highland Helicopters | C |
| Hinterland Aviation | VH |
| HM Airways | D2 |
| Hokkaido Air System | JA |
| Hokkaido International Airlines | JA |
| Holidays Czech Airlines | OK |
| Homer Air | N |
| Hong Kong Airlines | B |
| Hong Kong Express Airways | B |
| Horizon Air | N |
| Horne Air | C |
| Huron Air and Outfitters | C |
| Hyannis Air Service | N |
| Hydro-Quebec | C |
| | |
| IBC Airways | N |
| Iberia | EC |
| Ibex Airlines | JA |
| ICAR Airlines | E7 |
| Icaro Express | HC |
| Icarus Flying Service | C |
| Icejet | TF |
| Iceland Express | TF |
| Icelandair | TF |
| IDC Aircraft | S7 |

| | |
|---|---|
| Ifly | RA |
| Ignace Airways | C |
| Ikar | RA |
| Iliamna Air Taxi | N |
| Ilin Aviakompania | RA |
| Ilyich Avia | UR |
| Imair | 4K |
| IMD Airways | EC |
| Imperial Air Cargo | ZS |
| Imperial Jet | OD |
| Imtrec Aviation | XU |
| INAER Helicopter Chile | CC |
| Indicator Airlines | TL |
| Indigo Airlines | VT |
| Indonesia Air Transport | PK |
| Indonesia Airasia | PK |
| Infinity Flight Services | C |
| Inland Air Charters | C |
| Inland Aviation Services | N |
| Insel Air Aruba | P4 |
| Insel Air International | PJ |
| Intal Air | EX |
| Integra Air | C |
| Inter Coastal Air | N |
| Inter Island Airways | N |
| Inter-Air | ZS |
| Inter-Archipelago Airways | N |
| Inter-Island Airways | RP |
| Inter-Transportes Aereos Inter | TG |
| Interandes | HK |
| Interavia Airlines | RA |
| Interavia Taxi Aero | PP |
| Interisland Airways | RP |
| Interjet | XA |
| Interlink Airlines | ZS |
| International Air Link | 6Y |
| International Air Response | N |
| Intersky | OE |
| Investavia | UP |
| Iraero | RA |
| Iran Air | EP |
| Iran Air Tour Airline | EP |
| Iran Aseman Airlines | EP |
| Iranian Air Transport | EP |
| Iraqi Airways | YI |
| Irish Helicopters | EI |
| IRS Airlines | 5N |
| ISD Avia | UR |
| Island Air | VP-C |
| Island Air | N |
| Island Air Charters | N |
| Island Air Service | N |
| Island Airlines | N |
| Island Airways | N |
| Island Aviation | RP |
| Island Aviation Services | 8Q |
| Island Hoppers | DQ |
| Island Seaplane Service | N |
| Island Transvoyager | RP |
| Island Valley Airways | C |
| Island Wings Air Service | N |
| Islas Airways | EC |
| Islena Airlines | HR |
| Isles of Scilly Skybus | G |
| Israir | 4X |
| ITAB - International Trans Air Business | 9Q |
| Itali Airlines | I |
| Italiatour | I |
| Itek Air | EX |
| Ivoirienne de Transports Aeriens | TU |
| Izhavia | RA |
| | |
| Jackson Air Services | C |
| Jade Cargo International | B |
| Jagson Airlines | VT |
| J-Air | JA |
| JAL Express | JA |
| Jamaica Air Shuttle | 6Y |
| Japan Air Commuter | JA |
| Japan Airlines International | JA |
| Japan Transocean Air | JA |
| JAT Airways | YU |
| Jatayu Air | PK |
| Jazeera Airways | 9K |
| Jeju Air | HL |
| Jet 2000 | RA |
| Jet Air Group | RA |
| Jet Airways | VT |
| Jet Asia | B-M |
| Jet Eagle Internaional | RP |
| Jet Netherlands | PH |
| Jet2 | G |
| Jet4Now | ZS |
| Jet4You | CN |
| Jetair Services | 9Q |
| Jetairfly | OO |
| Jetblue Airways | N |
| Jetconnect | ZK |
| Jetexpress | TR |
| Jetfly Aviation | TJ |
| Jetgo Australia | VH |
| Jetisfaction | D |
| Jetisfaction | PH |
| Jetlink Express | 5Y |
| Jetlite | VT |
| Jetran International Airways | YR |
| Jetstar Airways | VH |
| Jetstar Asia Airways | 9V |
| Jetstar Japan | JA |
| Jetstar Pacific Airlines | VN |
| Jett 8 Airlines | 9V |
| Jettime | OY |
| Jiangnan Universal Aviation | B |
| Jim Hankins Air Service | N |
| Jin Air | HL |
| Johnny May's Air Charters | C |
| Johnsons Air | 9G |
| Jordan Aviation | JY |
| Jordan International Air Cargo | JY |
| Joy Air | B |
| JP Air Cargo | ES |
| JS Focus Air | AP |
| Jubba Airways | 6O |
| Juneyao Airlines | B |
| Jungle Flying | TG |
| | |
| Kabeelo Airways | C |
| Kabo Air | 5N |
| Kabul Air | YA |
| Kakadu Air Services | VH |
| Kalahari Air Services & Charter | A2 |
| Kalitta Air | N |
| Kalitta Charters II | N |
| Kalitta Flying Services | N |
| Kallat el Saker Air | 5A |
| Kalstar | PK |
| Kam Air | YA |
| Kamaka Air | N |
| Kan Air | HS |
| Kapa Air | SX |
| Kapo | RA |
| Karratha Flying Services | VH |
| Karthago Airlines | TS |
| Kartika Airlines | PK |
| Kasba Air Service | C |
| Kaskazi Aviation | 5Y |
| Kata Transport Company | ST |
| Katekavia | RA |
| Katmai Air | N |
| Kato Airlines | LN |
| Kavango Air | A2 |
| Kavok Airlines | YV |
| Kaya Airlines | C9 |
| Kayair | C |
| Kazair West | UP |
| Kazakhmys | UP |
| Kazan Air Enterprises | RA |
| Kazaviaspas | UP |
| K.D. Air | C |
| Keewatin Air | C |
| Kelowna Flightcraft Air Charter | C |
| Kenai River Express | N |
| Kenmore Air | N |
| Kenn Borek Air | C |

| | |
|---|---|
| Kenora Air Service | C |
| Kenya Airways | 5Y |
| Key Lime Air | N |
| Keystone Air Service | C |
| Khabarovsk Airlines | RA |
| Khors Air | UR |
| Khorsan Air | YA |
| Kilwa Air | 5H |
| Kin Avia | 9Q |
| King Air Charter | ZS |
| King Airelines | N |
| King Island Airways | VH |
| Kingfisher Airlines | VT |
| Kingfisher Red | VT |
| Kirov Avia Enterprise | RA |
| Kish Air | EP |
| Kississing Air | C |
| Kississing Lake Lodge | C |
| Kivalliq Air | C |
| KLM Cityhopper | PH |
| KLM Royal Dutch Airlines | PH |
| Kluane Airways | C |
| K-Mile Air | HS |
| KMV Mineralnye Vody Airlines | RA |
| Knaapo | RA |
| Knight Aviation | 5Y |
| Kokshetau Airlines | UP |
| Kolavia | RA |
| Kolob Canyon Air Service | N |
| Koral Blue | SU |
| Korean Air | HL |
| Korean Air Express | HL |
| Korongo | 9Q |
| Koryakavia | RA |
| Kosmos Airlines | RA |
| Kostroma Air | UR |
| Kostroma Air Enterprise | RA |
| KS Avia | YL |
| Kuban Airlines | RA |
| Kunming Airlines | B |
| Kuwait Airways | 9K |
| Kyrgyz Airways | EX |
| Kyrgyz Trans Air | EX |
| Kyrgyzstan | EX |
| Kyrgyzstan Airlines | EX |
| | |
| L and A Aviation | C |
| La Costena | YN |
| La Nationale | TR |
| LAB Flying Service | N |
| Labrador Air Safari | C |
| Labrador Airways | C |
| Lac la Croix Quetico Air Service | C |
| Lac Seul Airways | C |
| LADE | LV |
| Lake & Peninsula Airlines | N |
| Lake Clark Air | N |
| Lakeland Airways | C |
| Lakelse Air | C |
| Lakes District Air Services | C |
| LAM - Linhas Aereas de Mocambique | C9 |
| LAMIA | YV |
| LAN Airlines | CC |
| LAN Airlines Colombia | HK |
| LAN Argentina | LV |
| LAN Cargo | CC |
| LAN Cargo Colombia | HK |
| LAN Ecuador | HC |
| LAN Express | CC |
| LAN Peru | OB |
| LANHSA | HR |
| Lao Airlines | RDPL |
| Lao Aviation | RDPL |
| Lao Capricorn Air | RDPL |
| Lao Central Airlines | RDPL |
| Laser | YV |
| Lassa - Lineas de Aeroservicios | CC |
| Latina de Aviacon | HK |
| Lauzon Aviation | C |
| Layang-layang Aerospace | 9M |
| LC Busre | OB |
| Leair Charter Services | C6 |

| | |
|---|---|
| Lets Fly | EC |
| Leuenberger Air Service | C |
| LGW - Luftfahrtgesellschaft Walter | D |
| LIAT - The Caribbean Airline | V2 |
| Libyan Air Cargo | 5A |
| Libyan Airlines | 5A |
| Libyavia | 5A |
| Lignes Aeriennes Congolaises | 9Q |
| Linea Aerea Costa Norte | CC |
| Linea Turistica Aereotuy | YV |
| Lineas Aereas Canedo | CP |
| Lineas Aereas Commerciales | XA |
| Lineas Aereas de Argentina | LV |
| Lineas Aéreas Sudamericanas Colombia | HK |
| Links Air | G |
| Linxair Business Airlines | S5 |
| Lion Airlines | PK |
| Lionair | RP |
| Lipetsk Avia | RA |
| Little Red Air Service | C |
| Lloyd Helicopters | VH |
| Loch Lomand Seaplanes | G |
| Loganair | G |
| Logistic Air | N |
| LOT - Polish Airlines | SP |
| LOT Charters | SP |
| Lotus Air | SU |
| LR Airlines | OK |
| Lubumbashi Air Service | 9Q |
| Lucky Airlines | B |
| Lufthansa | D |
| Lufthansa Cargo | D |
| Lufthansa Cityline | D |
| Lufttransport | LN |
| Luftverkehr Friesland Harle | D |
| Lugansk Aviation Enterprise | RA |
| Lukiaviatrans | RA |
| Luxair | LX |
| Luzair | CS |
| Lviv Airlines | UR |
| Lynden Air Cargo | N |
| Lynden Air Cargo Niuguini | P2 |
| Lynx Air International | N |
| | |
| M & N Aviation | N |
| Macair Jet | LV |
| Mack Air | A2 |
| Madagascar Trans Air | 5R |
| Magnicharters | XA |
| Mahan Air | EP |
| Mais Linhas Aereas | PR |
| Majestic Air Cargo | N |
| Major Blue Air | A2 |
| Major's Air Services | C6 |
| Mak Air | UP |
| Makalu Air | 9N |
| Malagasy Airlines | 5R |
| Malaysia Airlines | 9M |
| Malaysian Helicopter Services | 9M |
| Maldivian Air Taxi | 8Q |
| Malev | HA |
| Mali Air Express | TZ |
| Mali Air Transport | TZ |
| Malift Air | 9Q |
| Malmo Aviation | SE |
| Malu Aviation | 9Q |
| Mandala Airlines | PK |
| Mandarin Airlines | B |
| Mango | ZS |
| Mango Mat Airlines | 9Q |
| Manitoba Government Air Services | C |
| Manunggal Air Service | PK |
| Manx2 Airlines | G |
| MAP Linhas Aereas | PR |
| Mapjet | OE |
| Marin Air | TC |
| Maritime Air Charter | C |
| Maroomba Airlines | VH |
| Mars RK Airlines | UR |
| Marsland Aviation | ST |
| Martinair | PH |
| Martinaire | N |

| | | | |
|---|---|---|---|
| Martini Aviation | C | Motor Sich Airlines | UR |
| MAS Air Cargo | XA | Mountain Air | ZK |
| Maswings | 9M | Mountain Air Cargo | N |
| MAT Macedonian Air Transport | Z3 | Mountain Helicopters | 9N |
| Mauritania Airlines | 5T | MRK Airlines | UR |
| Maverick Helicopters | N | MTA Cargo | PP |
| Max Aviation | C | Mustang Helicopters | C |
| Maxair | 5N | Mustique Airways | J8 |
| Maxfly Aviation | N | Myanma Airways | XY |
| Maximus Air Cargo | A6 | Myanmar Airways International | XY |
| Maya Island Air | V3 | Mycargo Airlines | TC |
| Mayair | XA | Myflug | TF |
| MCHS Rossii | RA | | |
| McMurray Aviation | C | NAC Charter | ZS |
| McNeely Charter Service | N | NAC Executive Charter | A2 |
| MDLR Airlines | VT | Nacional de Aviacion Colombia | HK |
| Meadow Air | C | Nadeau Air Service | C |
| Med Airlines | CN | Naft Air | EP |
| Med Airways | OD | Nakina Outpost Camps and Air | C |
| Medallion Air | YR | Namibia Commercial Airways | V5 |
| Medavia | 9H | Napo Aviatrans | RA |
| Med-View Airlines | 5N | NAS Air | HZ |
| Meelad Air | JY | Nas Air | E3 |
| Mega Aircompany | UP | Nation Air | HH |
| Mega Global Air Services | 8Q | National Airlines | N |
| Melaire | C | National Airways Cameroon | TJ |
| Mena Aerospace Cargo | A9C | National Airways Corporation | ZS |
| Meridian Airways | 9G | National Aviation Services | P2 |
| Meridiana Fly | I | National Helicopters | C |
| Meridien | UR | Nationale Gabon | 3C |
| Merlin Airways | N | Native American Air Service | N |
| Merpati Nusantara Airlines | PK | Natureair | TI |
| Mesa Airlines | N | Navair | N |
| Mesoamerica Air Service | TR | Navigator Airlines | EK |
| META - Mesquita Transportes Aero | PP | Naysa Aerotaxis | EC |
| MHS Aviation | 9M | Nelair Charters & Travel | ZS |
| Mia Airlines | YR | Neos | I |
| Miami Air International | N | Nepal Airlines | 9N |
| Miami Air Lease | N | Neptune Air | 9M |
| Miapet Avia | EK | Neptune Aviation Services | N |
| MIAT Mongolian Airlines | JU | Nesma Airlines | SU |
| Mid Airlines | ST | Nestor Falls Fly-in Outposts | C |
| Mid Express Tchad | TT | Network Aviation Australia | VH |
| Mid-Atlantic Freight | N | New Central Aviation | JA |
| Mid-Sea Express | RP | New England Airlines | N |
| Midline Air Freight | N | New Mexico Airlines | N |
| Middle East Airlines | OD | Newfoundland & Labrador Air Services | C |
| Midex Airlines | A6 | Nextime Jet | SE |
| Midwest Airlines | N | NHR Taxi Aereo | PP |
| Midwest Airlines Egypt | SU | NHT Linhas Aereas | PP |
| Mihin Lanka | 4R | Nightexpress | D |
| Milford Helicopters | ZK | Niki | OE |
| Milford Sound Flightseeing | ZK | Nile Air | SU |
| Milford Sound Scenic Flights | ZK | Nippon Cargo Airlines | JA |
| Military Support Services | VH | Nok Air | HS |
| Millenium Aviation Transportes | TG | Nolinor Aviation | C |
| Minair | TL | Nomad Aviation | 5H |
| Minden Air | N | Noordzee Helikopters Vlaanderen | OO |
| Miniliner | I | Nord Aviation | N |
| Miniliner Malta | 9H | Nordavia Regional Airlines | RA |
| Minipi Aviation | C | Nordeste Linhas Aereas Regionais | PR |
| Mint Airways | EC | Nordic Global Airlines | OH |
| Miras Cargo | UP | Nordplus | C |
| Missinippi Airways | C | Nordstar | RA |
| Mistral Air | I | Nordwind | RA |
| MNG Cargo Airlines | TC | Norfolk Air | VH |
| Mocambique Expresso | C9 | Norlandair | TF |
| Mokulele Airlines | N | Norrlandsflyg | SE |
| Moldavian Airlines | ER | Norse Air | ZS |
| Molson Air | C | Norsk Luftambulance | LN |
| Mombasa Air Safari | 5Y | North Adria | 9A |
| Monarch Airlines | G | North American Airlines | N |
| Mongolian Airlines | JU | North Cariboo Air | C |
| Montenegro Airlines | 4O | North Coast Aviation | P2 |
| Montmagny Air Service | C | North Flying | OY |
| Moonair Aviation | 4X | North Pacific Seaplanes | C |
| Mordovia Air | RA | North South Airlines | RP |
| Moremi Air Services | A2 | North Star Air | C |
| Morningstar Air Express | C | North Star Air Cargo | N |
| Morokuru Air | ZS | North Star Aviation | N |
| Moskoviya | RA | North-Wright Airways | C |
| Moskva Air Company | RA | Northern Air Charter | A2 |

| | | | |
|---|---|---|---|
| Northern Air | 5H | Payim International Air | EP |
| Northern Air Cargo | N | PC Air | HS |
| Northern Air Charter | C | PDG Helicopters | G |
| Northern Air Charter Services | DQ | Peach | JA |
| Northern Air Solutions | C | Pearl Aviation | VH |
| Northern Thunderbird Air | C | Peau Vava'u Air | A3 |
| Northward Air | C | Pegase Aviation | ZS |
| Northway Aviation | C | Pegasus Airlines | TC |
| Northwest Flying | C | Pel-Air | VH |
| Northwest Seaplanes | N | Pelican Air Services | ZS |
| Northwestern Air | C | Pelican Narrows Air Services | C |
| Norwegian | LN | Pelita Air | PK |
| Nouvelair | TS | Penair | N |
| Nouvelles Air Affaires Gabon | TR | Peninsular Airways | N |
| Nova Air | XA | PENTA - Pena Transportes Aereos | PP |
| Nova Airlines | ST | Perfect Aviation | 9M |
| Novair | SE | Perimeter Aviation | C |
| Novosibirsk Air Enterprise | RA | Perla Air | YV |
| NT Air | C | Perm Airlines | RA |
| Nueltin Lake Air Service | C | Peruvian Air Line | OB |
| Nusantara Air Charter | PK | Petra Airlines | JY |
| Nusantara Buana Air | PK | Petro Air | 5A |
| | | Petroleum Air Service | HK |
| Ocean Pacific Air Services | C | Petroleum Air Services | SU |
| Okay Airways | B | Petropavlovsk-Kamchatsky Air Enterprise | RA |
| OLT - Ostfriesische Lufttransport | D | PGA Express | CS |
| OLT Express | SP | PHI - Petroleum Helicopters | N |
| OLT Jetair | SP | Philippine Airlines | RP |
| Olympic Air | SX | Phillips Air Charter | N |
| Oman Air | A4O | Phoebus Apollo Aviation | ZS |
| Omni - Aviacao e Tecnologia | CS | Phoenix Air | N |
| Omni Air International | N | Phoenix Airtransport | N |
| Omniflight Helicopters | N | Phoenix Avia | EK |
| Ontario Ministry of Natural Resources | | Phoenix Aviation | 5Y |
| Aviation Services | C | Phuket Airlines | HS |
| Onur Air | TC | Pinnacle Air | VT |
| Open skies | F | Pineapple Air | C6 |
| Orbest | CS | Pionair Adventures | ZK |
| Orbest Orizonia | EC | Piper East | N |
| Orca Air | C | Pirinair Express | EC |
| Orenair | RA | Planemasters | N |
| Orient Flights | VT | Players Air | N |
| Orient Thai Airlines | HS | Pluna Lineas Aereas Uruguayas | CX |
| Oriental Air Bridge | JA | PMT Air | XU |
| Ornge Air | C | Podilia Avia | UR |
| Osnaburgh Airways | C | Points North Air | C |
| Osprey Wings | C | Polar Air Cargo | N |
| Ostseeflug | D | Polar Airlines | RA |
| Our Airline | C2 | Polet Aviakompania | RA |
| Overland Airways | 5N | Police Aviation Services | G |
| Oyonnair | F | Polyarnya Avia | RA |
| | | Polynesian Airlines | 5W |
| Pace Airlines | N | Porter Airlines | C |
| Pacific Air Express | N | Portugalia Airlines | CS |
| Pacific Airways | N | Precisionair | 5H |
| Pacific Coastal Airlines | C | Premiair | PK |
| Pacific East Asia Cargo Airlines | RP | Premiair Aviation Services | G |
| Pacific Island Air | DQ | President Airlines | XU |
| Pacific Royale Airways | PK | Presidential Airways | N |
| Pacific Sky Aviation | C | Primera Air Scandinavia | OY |
| Pacific Sun | DQ | Priority Air | N |
| Pacific Wings | N | Priority Air Charter | N |
| Pacificair | RP | Privalege Style | EC |
| Pacificflyer | T8A | Privatair | D |
| Pakistan International Airlines | AP | Privatair | HB |
| Palestinian Airways | SU-Y | Private Wings | D |
| Pamir Airways | YA | Profilght Air Services | 9J |
| Pan African Airways | 5N | Proflight Venezuela | YV |
| Pan Am Clipper Connection | N | Progress Air | ZS |
| Pan Am Dominica | HI | Progress Aviakompania | RA |
| Pan Européenne Air Service | F | Promech Air | N |
| Panair Cargo | HP | Pronto Airways | C |
| Panair Lineas Aereas | EC | Propair | C |
| Pan-Malaysian Air Transport | 9M | Protezione Civile | I |
| Pantanal | PP | Protocole Aviation Cargo | 9Q |
| Papillon Grand Canyon Airways | N | Province of Alberta | C |
| Paradise Air | TI | Provincial Airlines | C |
| Paragon Air Express | N | Pskovavia | RA |
| Paramount Jet | N | PTL Luftfahrtunturnehmen | D |
| Pascan Aviation | C | Pullmantur Air | EC |
| Passaredo Transportes Aereos | PP | Puma Air Linhas Aereas | PP |
| Patagonia Airlines | CC | | |

| Airline | Code | | Airline | Code |
|---|---|---|---|---|
| Qanot Sharq | UK | | Rusline Air | RA |
| QANTAS Airways | VH | | Russian Sky Airlines | RA |
| Qantaslink | VH | | Russian State Transport | RA |
| Qatar Airways | A7 | | Rusts Flying Service | N |
| Quantum Helicopters | C | | Rusty Myers Flying Service | C |
| Queensway Air Services | 5Y | | Rutaca | YV |
| Qwikjet Cargo Airlines | VT | | Rwandair Express | 9XR |
| Qwila Air | ZS | | Ryan Air | N |
| | | | Ryan Blake Air Charter | ZS |
| RACSA | TG | | Ryan International Airlines | N |
| RAF-Avia | YL | | Ryanair | EI |
| Rainbow Air | YV | | Ryazanavia Trans | RA |
| Rainbow Airways | C | | Ryjet | EC |
| Rainbow Jet | B | | Ryukyu Air Commuter | JA |
| Rak Airlines | A6 | | | |
| Ram Air Services | N | | S7 Airlines | RA |
| Rayyan Air | AP | | SA Express | ZS |
| RCMP | C | | Sabah Air | 9M |
| Red Line Air | N | | Sabang Merauke Raya Air Charter | PK |
| Red Sea Air | E3 | | Sabourin Lake Lodge | C |
| Red Sucker Lake Air Services | C | | Sacso Airlines | ST |
| Red Wings | RA | | SADELCA | HK |
| Redding Aero Enterprises | N | | SAEP | HK |
| RedJet | 8P | | SAEREO | HC |
| Redstar Aviation | TC | | Safair | ZS |
| Reeve Air Alaska | N | | Safari Air | A2 |
| Regent Airways | S2 | | Safari Express Airways | 5H |
| Regio-Air | D | | Safarilinks Aviation | 5Y |
| Region Avia | RA | | Safat Airlines | EP |
| Régional | F | | Safe Air Kenya | 5Y |
| Regional 1 Airlines | C | | Safi Airways | YA |
| Regional Air | P2 | | Safiran Airlines | EP |
| Regional Air | C6 | | Saga Airlines | TC |
| Regional Air Lines | CN | | Saha Airlines | EP |
| | 5H | | Sahara African Aviation | ZS |
| Regional Paraguaya | ZP | | Saicus Air | EC |
| Regourd Aviation | F | | Saintex Cargo | XA |
| Reliance Air | 5X | | S-Air | RA |
| Rent Air | HK | | Sakaviaservice | 4L |
| Republic Air | XA | | SAL - Sociedade de Aviacao Ligeira | D2 |
| REX - Regional Express | VH | | Salamis Aviation | C6 |
| Rhoades International | N | | Salmon Air | N |
| Rico Linhas Aereas | PP | | Salsa d'Haiti | HH |
| Rico Taxi Aereo | PP | | Salt Spring Air | C |
| Rio Branco Taxi Aereo | PR | | SAM Colombia | HK |
| Rio Linhas Aereas | PP | | SAM Intercontinental | TZ |
| River Air | C | | Samair | OM |
| Robin Hood Aviation | OE | | Samal Air | UP |
| Roblex Aviation | N | | Samara Airlines | RA |
| Roc Aviation | B | | Samarkand Airways | UK |
| Rollins Air | HR | | Sandbar Air | N |
| Romavia | YR | | Sandy Lake Seaplane Service | C |
| Roraima Airways | 8R | | Sansa Regional | TI |
| Rosneft-Baltika | RA | | Santa Barbara Airlines - SBA | YV |
| Ross Air | C | | Santa Barbara Taxi Aereo | PT |
| Ross Air Service | C | | Sapair | HI |
| Ross Aviation | N | | Sapawe Air | C |
| Rossair | ZS | | Saravia | RA |
| Rossair Kenya | 5Y | | Sarpa | HK |
| Rossiya Russian Airlines | RA | | SASCA - Servicios Aereos Sucre | YV |
| Rotkopf Aviation Italy | I | | Saskatchewan Government Northern | |
| Rovos Air | ZS | | Air Operations | C |
| Royal Air | TY | | SAT Airlines | RA |
| Royal Air Charters | 9J | | SAT Airlines | UP |
| Royal Air Freight | N | | SATA Air Acores | CS |
| Royal Air Maroc | CN | | SATA Internacional | CS |
| Royal Bengal Airlines | S2 | | Satena | HK |
| Royal Brunei Airlines | V8 | | Saturn Aviakompania | RA |
| Royal Canadian Mounted Police | C | | Saudi Arabian Airlines | HZ |
| Royal Daisy Airlines | 5X | | Savannah Air Services | 5Y |
| Royal Falcon | JY | | Sayakhat | UP |
| Royal Flying Doctor Service | VH | | Sayat Air | UP |
| Royal Jordanian | JY | | Scandinavian Airline System | SE |
| Royal Khmer Airlines | XU | | Scanwings | OH |
| Royal Phnom Penh Airways | XU | | Scat Aircompany | UP |
| Royal Star Airlines | RP | | SCD Aviation | TR |
| Royal Wings Airlines | JY | | Scenic Airlines | N |
| RPX Airlines | PK | | Scoot | 9V |
| Rubystar | EW | | Scotairways | G |
| Rus Aviation | EY | | SEAA | D2 |
| Rusair | RA | | Sea Bird Airlines | TC |
| Rusjet | RA | | Seaborne Virgin Islands | N |

| | | | |
|---|---|---|---|
| Seair | RP | Sky Bahamas | C6 |
| Seair Airways | C6 | Sky Bosnia | E7 |
| Seair Pacific Gold Coast | VH | Sky Castle Aviation | N |
| Seair Seaplanes | C | Sky Express | SX |
| Seaport Airlines | N | Sky Gabon SA | TR |
| Searca Colombia | HK | Sky Georgia | 4L |
| Seawing Airways | VH | Sky Horse Aviation | JU |
| Seawings | A6 | Sky King | N |
| Seawings Europe | LZ | Sky Lease Cargo | N |
| Securité Civile | F | Sky One Air | ZS |
| Sefofane Air | V5 | Sky Pearl Aviation | TZ |
| Sefofane Air Charter | A2 | Sky Regional Airlines | C |
| Selkirk Air | C | Sky Shuttle Helicopters | B |
| Selva | HK | Sky Taxi | SP |
| Semeyavia | UP | Sky Way Air | EX |
| Senegal Airlines | 6V | Sky Wind | 4K |
| Serair | EC | Sky Wings | SX |
| Serami - Servicios Aeromineiros | YV | Sky Wings Asia Airlines | XU |
| Services Air | 9Q | Skybridge Airops | I |
| Servicio Aereo Regional | HC | Skyexpress | RA |
| Servicios Aereos de Los Andes | OB | Skyforce Aviation | VH |
| Servicios Aereos Patagonicos | LV | Skyhaul | ZS |
| Servis Air | D2 | Skyjet | 5X |
| Setco | HR | Skyking Airlines | VQ-T |
| Sete Taxi Aereo | PP | Skylan Airways | 6Y |
| Severin Air Safaris | 5Y | Skylift Taxi Aereo | PP |
| Severstal Aircompany | RA | Skyline FZE | A6 |
| SF Airlines | B | Skylink Arabia | A6 |
| SGA Airlines | HS | Skylink Express | C |
| Shan Xi Airlines | B | Skymark Airlines | JA |
| Shandong Airlines | B | Skynorth Air | C |
| Shanghai Airlines | B | Skypower Express Airways | 5N |
| Shanghai Airlines Cargo | B | Skysouth | G |
| Shangri-La Air | 9N | Skytrackers | VH |
| Shar Ink | RA | Skytrail | 5Y |
| Sharp Airlines | VH | Skytrans Regional | VH |
| Sharp Wings | C | Skyway Enterprises | N |
| Sheheen Air Cargo | AP | Skyways Express | SE |
| Sheheen Air International | AP | Skyways Kenya | 5Y |
| Shenzhen Airlines | B | Skywest Airlines | N |
| Shenzhen Grand Sea Aviation | B | Skywest Airlines | VH |
| Shin Chuo Koku | JA | Skywings International | Z3 |
| Shine Air Services | VH | Skywork Airlines | HB |
| Shoal Air | VH | Slate Falls Airways | C |
| Shortstop Air Charter | VH | Slingair | VH |
| Shovkovly Shlyah | UR | Slok Air International | C5 |
| Showalter's Fly-In Service | C | Slovak Government Flying Service | OM |
| Shree Airlines | 9N | Slovakian Airlines | OM |
| Shuangyang Aviation | B | Small Planet Airlines | LY |
| Shuttle America | N | Small Planet Airlines Estonia | ES |
| Shuttle Bird | TU | Small Planet Airlines Poland | SP |
| Siam General Aviation | HS | Smart Aviation | SU |
| Sibaviatrans | RA | Smartlynx | YL |
| Sichuan Airlines | B | Smartwings | OK |
| Sichuan Aolin General Aviation | B | Smokey Bay Air | N |
| Sideral Air Cargo | PP | SNAS Aviation | HZ |
| Sierra Pacific Airlines | N | Sobel Air | 9G |
| Sierra West Airlines | N | Sol de Paraguay Lineas Aereas | ZP |
| Sifton Air Yukon | C | SOL Lineas Aereas | LV |
| Sil Aviation | P2 | Sol Linhas Aereas | PR |
| Silk Road Cargo | UK | Solar Air | HS |
| Silk Way Airlines | 4K | Solar Aviation | HS |
| Silkair | 9V | Solar Cargo | YV |
| Silver Air | OK | Solaseed Air | JA |
| Silver Air | J2 | Solenta Aviation | ZS |
| Silver Air | A6 | Solenta Aviation Gabon | TR |
| Silver Airways | N | Solenta Aviation Kenya | 5Y |
| Silverback Cargo Freighters | 9XR | Solid Air | PH |
| Simpson Air Commuter Canada | C | Solinair | S5 |
| Singapore Airlines | 9V | Solomons | H4 |
| Singapore Airlines Cargo | 9V | Somon Air | EY |
| Sioux Narrows Airways | C | Sonair | D2 |
| Sirius Aero | RA | Sophia Airlines | TU |
| Sita Airlines | 9N | Sorem | I |
| Ska Arabia | A6 | Soundsair Travel & Tourism | ZK |
| Skagway Air Service | N | South Aero | N |
| Skippers Aviation | VH | South African Airways | ZS |
| Skol Aviakompania | RA | South Airlines | UR |
| Sky Airline | CC | South Airlines | EK |
| Sky Airlines | TC | South China Sea Rescue Aviation | B |
| Sky Aviation | PK | South East Air | ZK |
| Sky Aviation Tanzania | 5H | South East Airlines | RA |

| | | | |
|---|---|---|---|
| South Nahanni Airways | C | Syphax Airlines | TS |
| South Pacific Express | N | Syrianair | YK |
| Southern Air | N | | |
| Southern Air Charter | C6 | TAAG Angola Airlines | D2 |
| Southern Seaplane | N | Tab Air Charter | ZS |
| Southern Sudan Airways | ST | TAB Cargo | CP |
| Southwest Air | P2 | Taban Air | EP |
| Southwest Airlines | N | TACA Costa Rica | TI |
| Spanair | EC | TACA International Airlines | YS |
| Spectrum Air Service | N | TACA Peru | OB |
| Speedstar Express | N | TACV - Transportes Aereos de Cabo Verde | D4 |
| Spernak Airways | N | TAF Helicopters | EC |
| Spicejet | VT | TAF Linhas Aereas | PP |
| Spirit Air | VT | Taftan Air | EP |
| Spirit Airlines | N | Tailwind Airlines | TC |
| Spirit of Manila Airlines | RP | Tajik Air | EY |
| Spring Airlines | B | Take Air Lines | F |
| Springbok Classic Air | ZS | Talkeetna Air Taxi | N |
| Sprint Air | SP | TAM - Taxi Aereo Marilia | PP |
| Srilankan | 4R | TAM - Transportes Aereo Militar | CP |
| Srilankan Air Taxi | 4R | TAM Bolivia | CP |
| Sriwijaya Air | PK | TAM Linhas Aereas | PP |
| SRX Transcontinental | N | TAM Mercosur | ZP |
| St Barth Commuter | F | TAME | HC |
| STA - Sociedade de Transport Aereos | C9 | Tampa Airlines | HK |
| STA Mali | TZ | Tanana Air Service | N |
| Stag | 9Q | Tango | 3C |
| Star African Air | 6O | Tanzanair - Tanzanian Air Services | 5H |
| Star Air | OY | TAP Air Portugal | CS |
| Star Air Cargo | ZS | Tapo-Avia | UK |
| Star Air International | AP | Tapsa Aviacion | LV |
| Star Airlines | Z3 | Taquan Air Service | N |
| Star Airways | ZA | Tara Airlines | EP |
| Star Aviation | 7T | Tarco Air | ST |
| Star Equatorial Airlines | 3C | Tarhan Air | TC |
| Star Flyer | JA | Tarom | YR |
| Star Peru | OB | Taron Avia | EK |
| Star1 Airlines | LY | TAS - Transporte Aereo de Santander | HK |
| Starbow | 9G | TAS - Transportes Aereos del Sur | EC |
| Starlink Aviation | C | Tasair | VH |
| Stars and Stripes Air Tours | N | Tassili Airlines | 7T |
| Stars Away Aviation | ZS | Tatarstan Air | RA |
| Stenberg Aviation | OY | Tavaj Linhas Aereas | PP |
| Strait Air | C | Tavasa | EC |
| Strategic Airlines | VH | Taxi Aerea de Caldas | HK |
| Suburban Air Freight | N | Taxi Aereo de Ibague | HK |
| Sud D'Or International Airlines | 4X | Taxi Aereo Cusiana | HK |
| Sudan Airways | ST | Taxi Aereo Itaituba | PP |
| Sudanese States Aviation | ST | Taxi Aereo Weiss | PP |
| Sudbury Aviation | C | Tbilaviamsheni | 4L |
| Summerset Charters | ZS | TBM | N |
| Summit Air Charters | C | TEAM Airlines - Team Transportes Aereos | PP |
| Sun Air | ST | Teebah Airlines | J2 |
| Sun Country Airlines | N | Temsco Helicopters | N |
| Sun-Air of Scandinavia | OY | Tend Air | YR |
| Sunbird Aviation | P2 | Tengerin Elch | JU |
| Sundance Air | YV | Tenir Airlines | EX |
| Sunexpress | TC | Tepavia Trans Airline | ER |
| Sunexpress Germany | D | Tepper Aviation | N |
| Sunny Airways | HS | Tessel Air | PH |
| Sunrise Airways | HH | Thai Airasia | HS |
| Sunshine Helicopters | N | Thai Airways | HS |
| Sunwest Aviation | C | Thai Aviation Services | HS |
| Sunwing Airlines | C | Thai Flying Service | HS |
| Superior Aviation | N | The Helicopter Line | ZK |
| Superior Aviation Services | 5Y | THK - Turk Hava Kurumu | TC |
| Sur Lineas Aereas | LV | Thomas Air | JU |
| Surinam Airways | PZ | Thomas Cook Airlines | G |
| Susi Air | PK | Thomas Cook Airlines Belgium | OO |
| Sustut Air | C | Thomas Cook Scandinavia | OY |
| Sverdlovsk 2nd Air Enterprise | RA | Thomsonfly.com | G |
| SVG Air | J8 | Thunder Airlines | C |
| Swala Airlines | 9Q | Thunderbird Aviation | C |
| Swanberg Air | C | Tianjin Airlines | B |
| Sweden Airways | SE | Tiara Air | P4 |
| Swift Air | N | Tibet Airlines | B |
| Swift Lite | ZK | Tiger Airways | 9V |
| Swiftair | EC | Tiger Airways | VH |
| Swiftair Hellas | SX | Tiko Air | 5R |
| Swiss European Air Lines | HB | Timair | 6Y |
| Swiss International Airlines | HB | Tiriac Air | YR |
| Sydney Seaplanes | VH | Titan Airways | G |

| | |
|---|---|
| TMK Air Commuter | 9Q |
| TNT Airways | OO |
| Tobruk Air | 5A |
| Tofino Airlines | C |
| Tolair Services | N |
| Toll Priority | VH |
| Tombouctou Aviation | TZ |
| Tomskavia | RA |
| Tonle Sap Airlines | XU |
| Top-Fly | EC |
| Tor-Air | SE |
| Tortug Air | HH |
| Total Linhas Aereas | PP |
| Toumai Air Chad | TT |
| Trade Air | 9A |
| Trade Links Aviation | 4L |
| Tradecraft | 5N |
| Tragsa | EC |
| Tramon Air | ZS |
| Transaca | YV |
| Trans Air | EX |
| Trans Air | N |
| Trans Air Benin | TY |
| Trans Air Ways | 3D |
| Trans Am | HC |
| Trans Anguilla Airlines | VP-A |
| Trans Attico | ST |
| Trans Avia Export Cargo Airlines | EW |
| Trans Capital Air | C |
| Trans Guyana Airways | 8R |
| Trans Island Air 2000 | 8P |
| Trans Maldivian Airways | 8Q |
| Trans Nation Airways | ET |
| Trans North Helicopters | C |
| Trans North Turbo Air | C |
| Trans Oriente | HK |
| Trans Service Airlift | 9Q |
| Transaero Airlines | RA |
| Transafrik International | S9 |
| Transair | N |
| Transair Cargo | 9Q |
| Transair Congo | TN |
| Transasia Airways | B |
| Transaven - Transporte Aero Venezuela | YV |
| Transavia Airlines | PH |
| Transavia France | F |
| Transavia Garantia | RA |
| Transavia Service | 4L |
| Transcarga International Airways | YV |
| Transglobal Airlways | RP |
| Transky Airlines | 5N |
| Transliz Aviation | S9 |
| Transmandu | YV |
| Transmark cargo | 5Y |
| Transmile Air Services | 9M |
| Transniugini Airways | P2 |
| Transnorthern Aviation | N |
| Transnusa Air Services | PK |
| Transporte Air Chaco | YV |
| Transport Canada | C |
| Transporte Aereo de Colombia | HK |
| Transportes Aereos Bolivianos | CP |
| Transportes Aereos Cielos Andinos | OB |
| Transportes Aereos Corporativos | CC |
| Transportes Aereos del Sur | EC |
| Transportes Aereos Don Carlos | CC |
| Transportes Aereos Guatemaltecos | TG |
| Transportes Aereos San Rafael | CC |
| Transportes Bragado | LV |
| Transportes San Francisco | CC |
| Transvalcasa | YV |
| Transwest Air | C |
| Transwisata Air | PK |
| Transworld Safaris | 5Y |
| Trast Aero | EX |
| Travel Air | P2 |
| Travel Service Airlines | OK |
| Travel Service Hungary | HA |
| Travel Service Slovakia | OM |
| Travira Air | PK |
| Trident Aviation/Enterprises | 5Y |
| Trigana Air Service | PK |
| Tri-MG Intra-Asia Airlines | PK |
| Trip Linhas Aereas | PP |
| Tristar Air | SU |
| Triumph Airways | C |
| Tropic Air | F |
| Tropic Air | 5Y |
| Tropic Air Charters | N |
| Tropic Air Commuter | V3 |
| Tropicair | P2 |
| Tropical Air (Zanzibar) | 5H |
| Tropical Airways | HH |
| Tropicana | D2 |
| Tsayta Aviation | C |
| TTA - Sociedade de Transportes e Trabalho Aereo | C9 |
| Tudhope Airways | C |
| Tui Netherlands | PH |
| Tuifly | D |
| Tuifly Nordic | SE |
| Tulpar Air | RA |
| Tulpar Air Service | UP |
| Tunisair | TS |
| Tunisair Express | TS |
| Tunisavia | TS |
| Turanair | 4K |
| Turismo Aereo Amazonas | YV |
| Turismo Air Iglesias | YV |
| Turkish Airlines | TC |
| Turkmenistan Airlines | EZ |
| Turkuaz Air | TC |
| Turtle Airways | DQ |
| Tuva Airlines | RA |
| Tway Air | HL |
| Tweedsmuir Air Services | C |
| Twin Cities Air Service | N |
| Twin Jet | F |
| Two Taxi Aereo | PR |
| Tyax Air Service | C |
| Tyrolean Jet Service | OE |
| Tyumenspecavia | RA |
| Uensped Paket Servisi / UPS | TC |
| Ufly Airways | N |
| Uganda Air Cargo | 5X |
| Ukraine Air Alliance | UR |
| Ukraine International Airlines | UR |
| Ukrainian Cargo Airways | UR |
| ULS Cargo | TC |
| Um Air | UR |
| Uni Air | B |
| Union Air | LV |
| Union Flights | N |
| United Air Charters | Z |
| United Air Lines | N |
| United Airways | S2 |
| United Express | N |
| Uni-Top Airlines | B |
| Unity Airlines | YJ |
| Universal Airlines | B |
| Universal Airlines | N |
| Universal Avia | UR |
| Universal Helicopters | C |
| UPS Airlines | N |
| Ural Airlines | RA |
| US Airways | N |
| US Airways Express | N |
| USDA Forest Service | N |
| US Helicopters | N |
| USA 3000 Airlines | N |
| USA Jet Airlines | N |
| Utair Airlines | RA |
| Utain Cargo | RA |
| Utair Express | RA |
| Utair South Africa | ZS |
| UTAir Ukraine | UR |
| Utin Lento | OH |
| Uvuaga | RA |
| Uzbekistan Airways | UK |
| Valan International Cargo | ZS |
| Van Air | P2 |
| Van Air Europe | OK |
| Vancouver Island Air | C |

| | |
|---|---|
| Vancouver Island Helicopters | C |
| Varig | PP |
| Varig Log | PP |
| Vasco | VN |
| Vee Neal Aviation | N |
| Velvet Sky Airline | ZS |
| Venescar International | YV |
| Venezolana | YV |
| Vent Airlines | N |
| Ventura Airconnect | VH |
| Ver-Avia | SX |
| Vera Cruz Taxi Aereo | PR |
| Vertical de Aviacion | HK |
| Vertir | EK |
| Veteran Airline | EK |
| Veteran Airlines | UR |
| VIA - Air Via | LZ |
| Viarco | HK |
| Vias Aereas Nacionales | HK |
| Victoria Air | RP |
| Vieques Air Link | N |
| Vietjet | VN |
| Vietnam Airlines | VN |
| Vigo Jet | XA |
| VIH Helicopters | C |
| Villa Air | 8Q |
| Villiers Air Services | C |
| Vim Airlines | RA |
| Vincent Aviation | ZK |
| Vincent Aviation (Australia) | VH |
| Vintage Prop and Jets | N |
| VIP - Vuelos Internos Privados | HC |
| Vip-Avia | 4L |
| Virgin America | N |
| Virgin Atlantic Airways | G |
| Virgin Australia | VH |
| Virgin Australia (NZ) | ZK |
| Virgin Samoa | ZK |
| Virunga Air Charter | 9Q |
| Vision Air | C6 |
| Vision Air | HH |
| Vision Air | N |
| Vision Air International | AP |
| Vista Georgia | 4L |
| Vista Jet | OE |
| Viva Aerobus | XA |
| Vladivostok Air | RA |
| VLM Airlines | OO |
| Vol Air | HI |
| Volaris | XA |
| Volga Aviaexpress | RA |
| Volga-Dnepr Airlines | RA |
| Vologda Air Enterprise | RA |
| Volotea Airlines | EC |
| Vostok Airlines | RA |
| Voyage Air | C |
| Voyager Airlines | S2 |
| Voyageur Airways | C |
| Vueling Airlines | EC |
| Vuelos Mediterrano | EC |
| Vyborg Airlines | RA |
| | |
| Waasheshkun Airways | C |
| Wabakimi Air | C |
| Wahkash Contracting | C |
| Wamair Service & Outfitting | C |
| Warbelow's Air | N |
| Ward Air | N |
| Wasaya Airways | C |
| Watson's Skyways | C |
| Waweig Air | C |
| WDL Aviation | D |
| Weagamow Air | C |
| Webjet Linhas Aereas | PP |
| Welcome Air | OE |
| West Air | B |
| West Air Luxembourg | LX |
| West Air Sweden | SE |
| West Caribbean Airways | HK |
| West Caribou Air Service | C |
| Westair Cargo Airlines | TU |
| Westair de Mexico | XA |

| | |
|---|---|
| West Atlantic | G |
| West Coast Air | C |
| West Wind Aviation | C |
| West Wing Aviation | VH |
| Westair Wings | V5 |
| Western Air | C6 |
| Western Air Express | N |
| Western Aviators | N |
| Westjet | C |
| Westmann Islands Airlines | TF |
| Westwind Aviation | N |
| Wettenhall Air Services | VH |
| Whistler Air Services | C |
| White Airways | CS |
| White River Air Services | C |
| Whitejets | PP |
| Whitsunday Air Services | VH |
| Wideroe's Flyveselskap | LN |
| Wiggins Airways | N |
| Wilderness Air | C |
| Will Airlift | 9Q |
| Williams Air Service | N |
| Wimbi Dira Airways | 9Q |
| Winair | PJ |
| Wind Rose | UR |
| Windjet | I |
| Windward Express Airways | PJ |
| Windward Islands Airwys International | PJ |
| Wings Abadi Air | PK |
| Wings Aviation | 5N |
| Wings of Alaska | N |
| Wings Of Lebanon Aviation | OD |
| Wings Over Kississing | C |
| Wizz Air | HA |
| Wizz Air Ukraine | UR |
| Wolverine Air | C |
| Woodgate Executive Air Services | G |
| World Airways | N |
| World Atlantic Airlines | N |
| Wright Air Service | N |
| | |
| Xiamen Airlines | B |
| Xinjiang General Aviation | B |
| XL Airways France | F |
| XL Airways Germany | D |
| XP Taxi Aereo | PR |
| Xtra Airways | N |
| Xunaga Air | A2 |
| | |
| Yak Service | RA |
| Yakutia Airlines | RA |
| Yamal Airlines | RA |
| Yangon Airlines | XY |
| Yangtze River Express | B |
| Yas Air | EP |
| Yellow Wings Air Services | 5Y |
| Yemenia/Yemen Airways | 7O |
| Yeti Airlines | 9N |
| Ying'An Airlines | B |
| Youngone | S2 |
| Yukon Aviation | N |
| Yuzmashavia | UR |
| | |
| Z Boscovic Air | 5Y |
| Zagros Airlines | EP |
| Zambezi Airlines | 9J |
| Zambian Airways | 9J |
| Zanair - Zanzibar Airline Company | 5H |
| Zantas Air Service | 5H |
| Zapolyarye Aviakompania | RA |
| ZB Air | 5Y |
| Zest Airways | RP |
| Zetavia | UR |
| Zhetysu Avia | UP |
| Zhezhair | UP |
| Zhezkazgan Air | UP |
| Zhongfei General Aviation | B |
| Zhongshan Eagle | B |
| Zhuhai General Aviation | B |
| Zimex Aviation | HB |
| Zoom Airways | S2 |
| Zorex | EC |

NOTES

NOTES

NOTES

NOTES

# AIR-BRITAIN MEMBERSHIP
## Join on-line at www.air-britain.co.uk

If you are not currently a member of Air-Britain, the publishers of this book, you may be interested in what we have on offer to provide for your interest in aviation.

### About Air-Britain
Formed 64 years ago, we are the world's most progressive aviation society, and exist to bring together aviation enthusiasts with every type of interest. Our members include aircraft historians, aviation writers, spotters and pilots - and those who just have a fascination with aircraft and aviation. Air-Britain is a non-profit organisation, which is independently audited, and any financial surpluses are used to provide services to the world-wide membership which currently stands at around 4,000, some 700 of whom live overseas.

### Membership of Air-Britain
Membership is open to all. A basic membership fee is charged and every member receives a copy of the quarterly house magazine, Air-Britain Aviation World, and is entitled to use all the Air-Britain specialist services and buy **Air-Britain publications at discounted prices**. A membership subscription includes the choice to add any or all of our other three magazines, News &/or Archive &/or Aeromilitaria. Air-Britain also publishes 10-20 books per annum (around 70 titles in stock at any one time). Membership runs January - December each year, but new members have a choice of options periods to get their initial subscription started.

**Air-Britain Aviation World** is the quarterly 52-page house magazine containing not only news of Air-Britain activities, but also a wealth of features, illustrated substantially in colour, on many different aviation subjects, contemporary and historical, contributed by our members. Extra colour Photo News pages are now included.

**Air-Britain News** is the world aviation news monthly, containing data on aircraft registrations worldwide and news of Airlines and Airliners, Business Jets, Local Airfield News, Civil and Military Air Show Reports, and International Military Aviation News. An average 160 pages of lavishly-illustrated information for the dedicated enthusiast.

**Air-Britain Archive** is the quarterly 48-page specialist journal of civil aviation history. Packed with the results of historical research by Air-Britain specialists into aircraft types, overseas registers and previously unpublished facts about the rich heritage of civil aviation. Up to 100 photographs per issue, some in colour.

**Air-Britain Aeromilitaria** is the quarterly 48-page unique source for meticulously researched details of military aviation history edited by the acclaimed authors of Air-Britain's military monographs featuring British, Commonwealth, European and U.S. Military aviation articles. Illustrated in colour and black & white.

### Other Benefits
Additional to the above, members have exclusive access to the Air-Britain e-mail Information Exchange Service (ab-ix) where they can exchange information and solve each other's queries, and to an on-line UK airfield residents database. Other benefits include numerous Branches, use of the Specialists Information Service; Air-Britain trips; and access to black & white and colour photograph libraries. During the summer we also host our own popular FLY-IN. Each autumn, we host an Aircraft Recognition Contest.

### Membership Subscription Rates - from £20 per annum.
Membership subscription rates start from as little as £20 per annum (2012), and this amount provides a copy of 'Air-Britain Aviation World' quarterly as well as all the other benefits covered above. Subscriptions to include any or all of our other three magazines vary between £25 and £57 per annum (slightly higher to overseas).
*Join in 2012 for two years (2012-2013) and save money off the total subscription at all levels*

**Join on-line at www.air-britain.co.uk or write to 'Air-Britain' at 1 Rose Cottages, 179 Penn Road, Hazlemere, High Wycombe, Bucks HP15 7NE, UK. Alternatively telephone/fax on 01394 450767 (+44 1394 450767 from outside UK) or e-mail membenquiry@air-britain.co.uk and ask for a membership pack containing the full details of subscription rates, samples of our magazines and a book list.**

# AIR-BRITAIN SALES

Companion publications to this AIRLINE FLEETS 2012 are also available by post-free mail order from:

**Air-Britain Sales Department (Dept AF12)**
**41 Penshurst Road, Leigh,**
**Tonbridge, Kent TN11 8HL**

Orders may also be placed by Answerphone/Fax 01732 835637 or by e-mail to
sales@air-britain.co.uk

For a full list of current titles and details of how to order, visit our e-commerce site at www.air-britain.co.uk  Visa credit / Visa debit / Mastercard / Solo / Maestro accepted - please give full details of card number and expiry date.

## AIRLINE FLEETS QUICK   REFERENCE - AFQR 2012

Contains 256 pages of airline fleet lists of all the major national and international carriers likely to be seen in Western Europe and in major airports world wide. The companion A5 size volume to Airline Fleets, AFQR includes types, c/ns, fleet numbers, lease data, corporate airliners and easy-to-use tick boxes.

*Price £8-95 (or £6-95 to Air-Britain members)*

## BUSINESS   JETS &   TURBOPROPS QUICK   REFERENCE– BizQR 2012

Contains 168 A5-pages listing all currently active civil or military business jets and corporate airliners by country in registration/serial order. Now expanded to include Business Turboprops. Correct to January 6th 2012 and also includes US reserved registrations. *Price £8-95 (or £6-95 to Air-Britain members)*

## UK/IRELAND CIVIL/MILITARY REGISTERS QUICK REFERENCE– UKQR 2012

Now 168 A5-size pages giving the regns and types of all current UK, Irish, Manx and foreign-registered aircraft based in the UK, serials and types of all current military aircraft, and lists of which aircraft are based at all of the major and many of the minor UK/Ireland civil airfields and microlight strips.

*Price £8-95 (or £6-95 to Air-Britain members)*

## UK/IRELAND CIVIL REGISTERS 2012

The 48th annual edition of our longest-running title lists all current G-, M- and EI- allocations, plus overseas-registered aircraft based in the UK, alphabetical index by type, military-civil marks de-code, full BGA and microlight details, museum aircraft etc. Now at 640 pages this is the UK civil aircraft register bible.

*Price £26.00 (or £19.95 to Air-Britain members)  Publication scheduled for May 2012*

## BUSINESS JETS INTERNATIONAL 2012

The only publication that gives full production lists for all biz-jets in c/n order with details of all regns/serials carried, model numbers and fates, plus a 65,000+ index of biz-jet regns, now in its 27th edition at around 600 pages. *Publication scheduled for June 2012*

## EUROPEAN REGISTERS HANDBOOK 2012

Now in combined book/CD format for the 27th edition, ERH contains the current civil aircraft registers of all 45 European countries lying to the west of Russia except the UK. The book is in A5 quick-reference format while the searchable CD contains all the c/ns with full previous identities and additional data including balloons, gliders and microlights. Many colour images of selected 2011 European civil flying events are also featured.

*Publication scheduled for Summer 2012*

*IMPORTANT NOTE -  Members receive substantial discounts on prices of all the above Air-Britain publications, as shown, together with many other direct benefits. Remember to quote your Membership number when ordering.*

**For details of membership see previous page or visit our website at**
**http://www.air-britain.co.uk**